Get connected to the power of the Internet

McDougal Littell's online resources for teachers provide time-saving planning, instruction, and assessment support.

classzone.com

- Links correlated to the text
- Web Research Guide
- Self-scoring quizzes
- Interactive games and activities
- Links to current events
- Test practice
- Teacher Center

You have immediate access to *ClassZone's* teacher resources.

MCD3P9T4LV47R

Use this code to create your own username and password.

Visit classzone.com for purchasing information and free demos

easyPlanner Plus ONLINE

- Customizable lesson plans
- Trackable standards correlated to each lesson

eEdition Plus ONLINE

- Online version of the text
- Interactive features to explore world history

eTest Plus ONLINE

- Customizable assessment tool
- Automatically grades tests
- Generates reports correlated to standards

Now it all clicks!™

McDougal Littell

CALIFORNIA TEACHER'S EDITION

McDougal Littell

MODERN WORLD HISTORY

PATTERNS OF INTERACTION

California Advisers and Reviewers

The following educators participated in planning, reviewed prototypes, reviewed content outlines, reviewed manuscript, or wrote classroom activities.

Anna Bolla
Lincoln High School
San Francisco, California

Wendell Brooks
Berkeley High School
Berkeley, California

Kevin Burgo
Banning High School
Wilmington, California

Ernest Cervantes
East Bakersfield High School
Bakersfield, California

Mike Cuckovich
Johnson High School
Sacramento, California

Michael Denman
Grant High School
Van Nuys, California

Nick Garcia
Salinas High School
Salinas, California

Jim Fletcher
Clairemont High School
San Diego, California

Roger Gold
Banning High School
Wilmington, California

Dennis Gregg
Washington High School
San Francisco, California

Dr. Bill Hanna
Social Science Department
Director, History-Social Science Project
San Jose State University
San Jose, California

Brian Irvine
Silver Creek High School
San Jose, California

Carolyn Keller
Fremont Senior High School
Oakland, California

Jim Lloyd
Bullard High School
Fresno, California

Judith Mahnke
Wallenberg High School
San Francisco, California

Sharlynn Mar
Westmont High School
Campbell, California

Douglas E. Miller
Stanford Teaching Education Program
Palo Alto, California

Karl Ochi
Washington High School
San Francisco, California

Ellen Oicles
Piedmont Hills High School
San Jose, California

Tim Paulson
Cerritos High School
Cerritos, California

Bob Piercy
Wilson High School
Long Beach, California

Greg Raby
Bonita Vista High School
Chula Vista, California

Stefanie Raczka
Norco High School
Norco, California

Lauren Ream
Henry Gunn High School
Palo Alto, California

Steve Rosenberg
Whitney High School
Artesia, California

Ingrid Seyer
Washington High School
San Francisco, California

Bill Smiley
Leigh High School
San Jose, California

Claudia Udd
Del Mar High School
San Jose, California

Ysidro Valenzuela
Fresno High School
Fresno, California

Danny Villa
James Logan High School
Union City, California

Ruben Zepeda
Compliance Advisor, Language Acquisition and Curriculum Development
Los Angeles Unified School District
Los Angeles, California

California Reviewers of *Strategies for Taking Tests*

The following educators reviewed the Pupil's Edition section entitled Strategies for Taking Tests, which was customized for California.

Mark Aguirre
Scripps Ranch High School
San Diego, California

Ysidro Valenzuelo
Fresno High School
Fresno, California

Sue Verne
Florin High School
Sacramento, California

John Seeley
Westminster High School
Westminster, California

History-Social Science Content Standards for California Public Schools reproduced by permission, California Department of Education, CDE Press, 1430 N Street, Suite 3207, Sacramento, Ca 95814.

ISBN 0-618-55716-4
Printed in the United States of America.
X 2 3 4 5 6 7 8 9–DWO–10 09 08 07 06 05

Contents

MODERN
WORLD
HISTORY

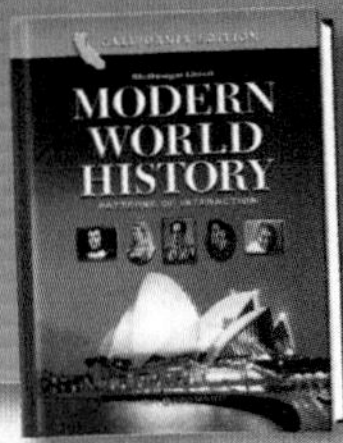

An Emphasis on the Big Picture

Chapter Openers
give students a preview of key concepts supported by visuals that put the ideas into context.

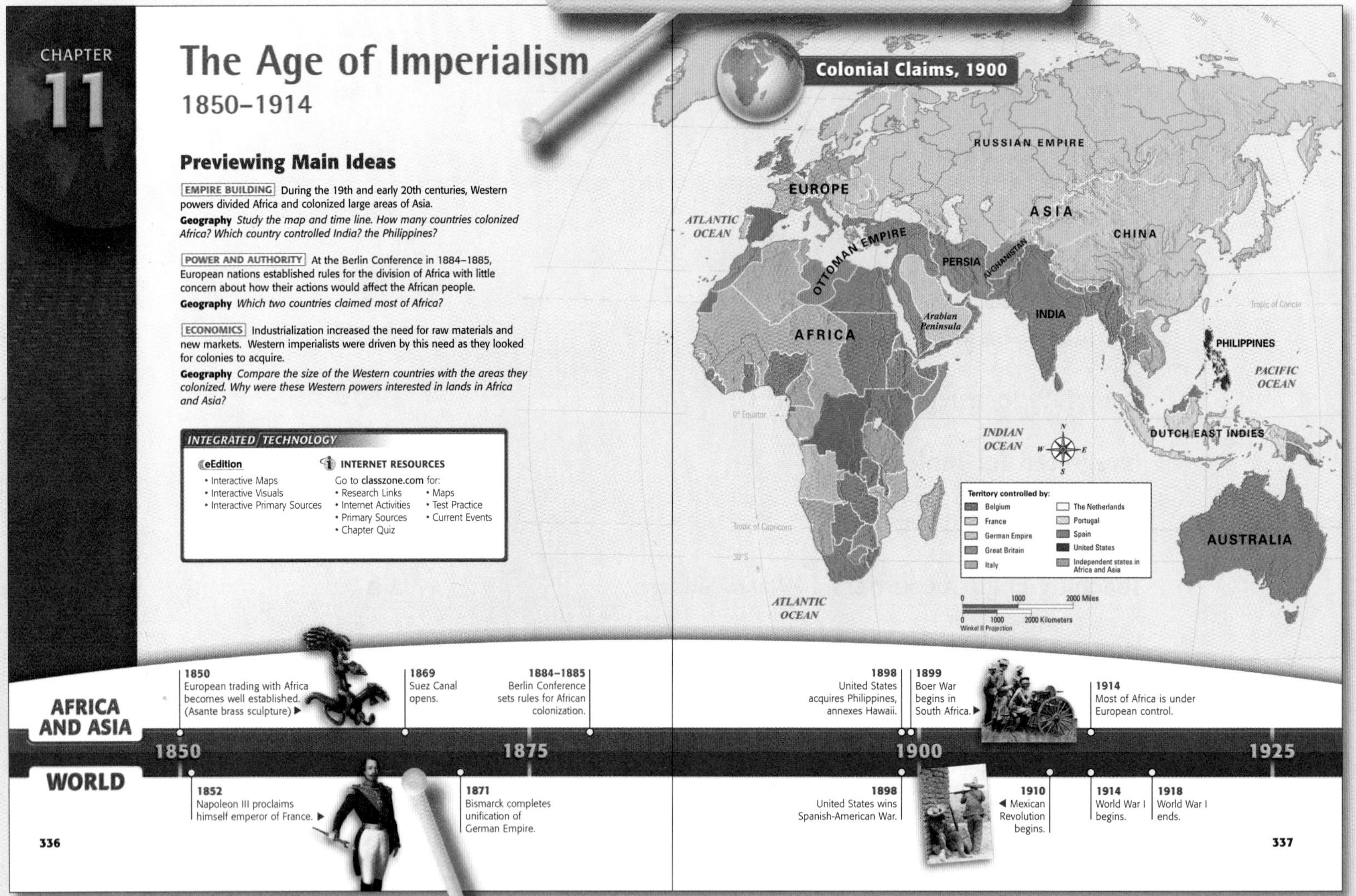

CHAPTER 11

The Age of Imperialism
1850–1914

Previewing Main Ideas

EMPIRE BUILDING During the 19th and early 20th centuries, Western powers divided Africa and colonized large areas of Asia.
Geography *Study the map and time line. How many countries colonized Africa? Which country controlled India? the Philippines?*

POWER AND AUTHORITY At the Berlin Conference in 1884–1885, European nations established rules for the division of Africa with little concern about how their actions would affect the African people.
Geography *Which two countries claimed most of Africa?*

ECONOMICS Industrialization increased the need for raw materials and new markets. Western imperialists were driven by this need as they looked for colonies to acquire.
Geography *Compare the size of the Western countries with the areas they colonized. Why were these Western powers interested in lands in Africa and Asia?*

INTEGRATED TECHNOLOGY

eEdition
- Interactive Maps
- Interactive Visuals
- Interactive Primary Sources

INTERNET RESOURCES
Go to classzone.com for:
- Research Links
- Internet Activities
- Primary Sources
- Chapter Quiz
- Maps
- Test Practice
- Current Events

Colonial Claims, 1900
RUSSIAN EMPIRE
EUROPE
ASIA
CHINA
ATLANTIC OCEAN
OTTOMAN EMPIRE
PERSIA
AFGHANISTAN
Arabian Peninsula
INDIA
AFRICA
PHILIPPINES
PACIFIC OCEAN
Tropic of Cancer
0° Equator
INDIAN OCEAN
DUTCH EAST INDIES
Tropic of Capricorn
30°S
ATLANTIC OCEAN
AUSTRALIA
Territory controlled by:
Belgium
France
German Empire
Great Britain
Italy
The Netherlands
Portugal
Spain
United States
Independent states in Africa and Asia
0 1000 2000 Miles
0 1000 2000 Kilometers
Winkel II Projection

AFRICA AND ASIA

1850 European trading with Africa becomes well established. (Asante brass sculpture) ▶

1869 Suez Canal opens.

1884–1885 Berlin Conference sets rules for African colonization.

1898 United States acquires Philippines, annexes Hawaii.

1899 Boer War begins in South Africa. ▶

1914 Most of Africa is under European control.

1850 — 1875 — 1900 — 1925

WORLD

1852 Napoleon III proclaims himself emperor of France. ▶

1871 Bismarck completes unification of German Empire.

1898 United States wins Spanish-American War.

1910 ◀ Mexican Revolution begins.

1914 World War I begins.

1918 World War I ends.

336 337

Time Lines
give a world historical context to events from the chapter.

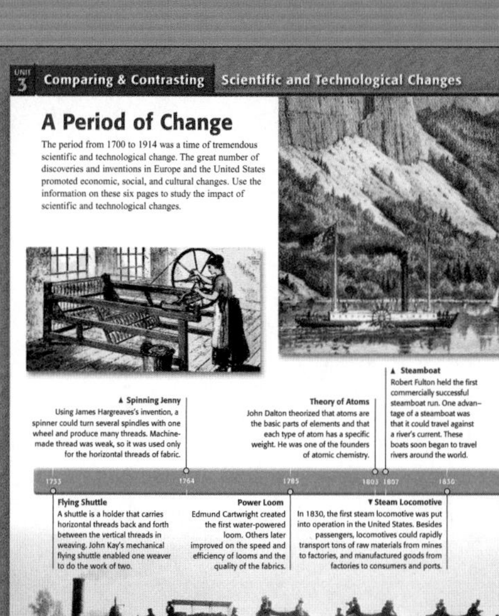

Comparing and Contrasting

The Comparing and Contrasting feature found at the end of each unit helps students see the impact of historical events on today's world.

UNIT 3 Comparing & Contrasting: Scientific and Technological Changes

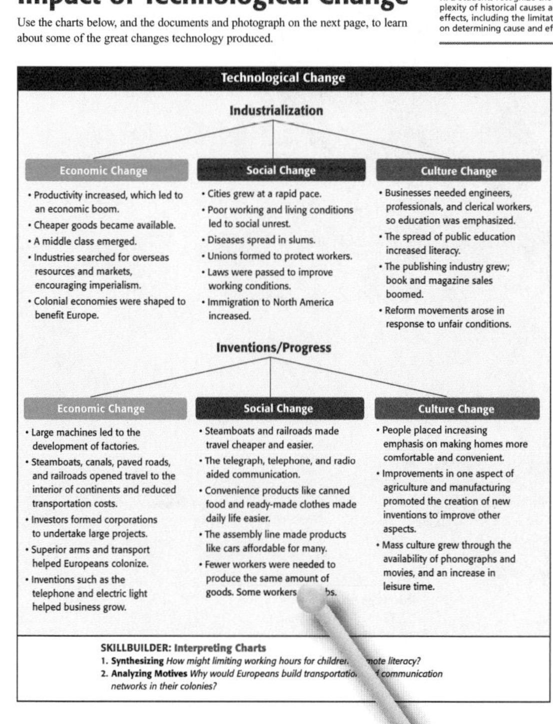

Impact of Technological Change

Use the charts below, and the documents and photograph on the next page, to learn about some of the great changes technology produced.

CALIFORNIA STANDARDS

HI 2 Students recognize the complexity of historical causes and effects, including the limitations on determining cause and effect.

Technological Change

Industrialization

Economic Change	Social Change	Culture Change
• Productivity increased, which led to an economic boom. • Cheaper goods became available. • A middle class emerged. • Industries searched for overseas resources and markets, encouraging imperialism. • Colonial economies were shaped to benefit Europe.	• Cities grew at a rapid pace. • Poor working and living conditions led to social unrest. • Diseases spread in slums. • Unions formed to protect workers. • Laws were passed to improve working conditions. • Immigration to North America increased.	• Businesses needed engineers, professionals, and clerical workers, so education was emphasized. • The spread of public education increased literacy. • The publishing industry grew; book and magazine sales boomed. • Reform movements arose in response to unfair conditions.

Inventions/Progress

Economic Change	Social Change	Culture Change
• Large machines led to the development of factories. • Steamboats, canals, paved roads, and railroads opened travel to the interior of continents and reduced transportation costs. • Investors formed corporations to undertake large projects. • Superior arms and transport helped Europeans colonize. • Inventions such as the telephone and electric light helped business grow.	• Steamboats and railroads made travel cheaper and easier. • The telegraph, telephone, and radio aided communication. • Convenience products like canned food and ready-made clothes made daily life easier. • The assembly line made products like cars affordable for many. • Fewer workers were needed to produce the same amount of goods. Some workers ... bs.	• People placed increasing emphasis on making homes more comfortable and convenient. • Improvements in one aspect of agriculture and manufacturing promoted the creation of new inventions to improve other aspects. • Mass culture grew through the availability of phonographs and movies, and an increase in leisure time.

SKILLBUILDER: Interpreting Charts

1. **Synthesizing** *How might limiting working hours for childre... ...mote literacy?*
2. **Analyzing Motives** *Why would Europeans build transportatio... ...f communication networks in their colonies?*

398 Unit 3 Comparing & Contrasting

PRIMARY SOURCE

Child Workers in Textile Factory

Many jobs did not require skilled workers, so children were hired to do them because they could be paid lower wages than adults. Some industries also hired children because their small fingers could fit between the machinery or handle fine parts more easily than adult fingers could.

DOCUMENT-BASED QUESTION

Judging by the children's appearance, how generous were the wages they received? Explain your answer.

PRIMARY SOURCE

INTERACTIVE

Impact of the Telephone

In this excerpt from "Thirty Years of the Telephone," published in September 1906, John Vaughn discussed how Bell's invention affected life in the United States.

Various industries, unknown thirty years ago, but now sources of employment to many thousands of workers, depend entirely on the telephone for support. . . . The Bell Companies employ over 87,000 persons, and it may be added, pay them well. . . . These figures may be supplemented by the number of telephones in use (5,698,000), by the number of miles of wire (6,043,000) in the Bell lines, and by the number of conversations (4,479,500,000) electrically conveyed in 1905. The network of wire connects more than 33,000 cities, towns, villages, and hamlets.

DOCUMENT-BASED QUESTION

What were some of the effects of the invention of the telephone?

SECONDARY SOURCE

INTERACTIVE

How Technology Aided Imperialism

In this excerpt from the book *Guns, Germs, and Steel,* Jared Diamond related an incident to show how technology helped Europeans conquer other lands.

In 1808 a British sailor named Charlie Savage equipped with muskets and excellent aim arrived in the Fiji Islands. [He] proceeded single-handedly to upset Fiji's balance of power. Among his many exploits, he paddled his canoe up a river to the Fijian village of Kasavu, halted less than a pistol shot's length from the village fence, and fired away at the undefended inhabitants. His victims were so numerous that . . . the stream beside the village was red with blood. Such examples of the power of guns against native peoples lacking guns could be multiplied indefinitely.

DOCUMENT-BASED QUESTION

How did guns give Europeans an advantage over native peoples?

Comparing & Contrasting

1. Reread the passage by John Vaughn and then compare it with the information on the chart. What could you add to the chart based on this passage?
2. Does the photograph of factory workers confirm or contradict the information on the chart? Explain.

399

Graphic Organizers

summarize content from the narrative, encouraging students to look at events from a broader perspective.

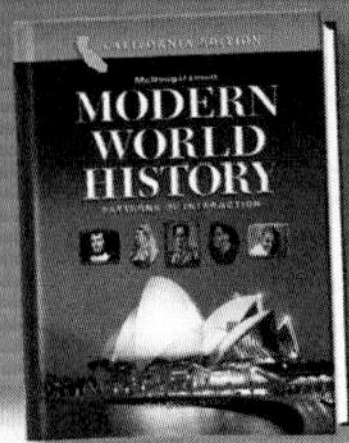

Support for All Learners

Colorful maps
An abundance of colorful maps motivate and engage students.

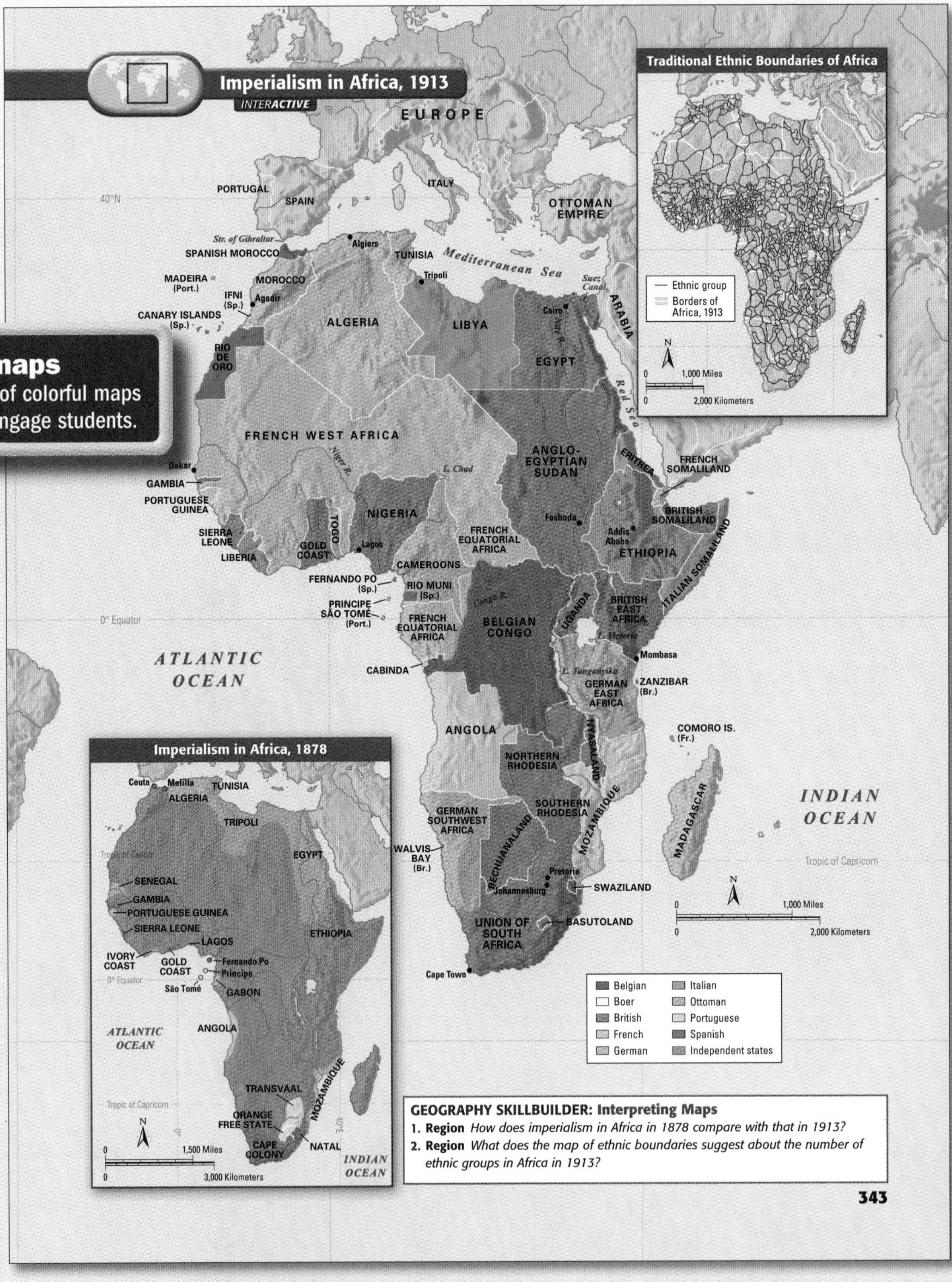

GEOGRAPHY SKILLBUILDER: Interpreting Maps

1. **Region** *How does imperialism in Africa in 1878 compare with that in 1913?*
2. **Region** *What does the map of ethnic boundaries suggest about the number of ethnic groups in Africa in 1913?*

343

Global Impact: Food Exchange

The Columbian Exchange

Few events transformed the world like the Columbian Exchange. This global transfer of plants, animals, disease, and especially food brought together the Eastern and Western hemispheres and touched, in some way, nearly all the peoples of the world.

Frightening Foods

Several foods from the Americas that we now take for granted at first amazed and terrified Europeans. Early on, people thought the tomato was harmful to eat. One German official warned that the tomato "should not be taken internally." In 1619, officials in Burgundy, France, banned potatoes, explaining that "too frequent use of them caused the leprosy." In 1774, starving peasants in Prussia refused to eat the spud.

CALIFORNIA STANDARDS

10.4.1 Describe the rise of industrial economies and their link to imperialism and colonialism (e.g., the role played by national security and strategic advantage; moral issues raised by the search for national hegemony, Social Darwinism, and the missionary impulse; material issues such as land, resources, and technology).

HI 2 Students recognize the complexity of historical causes and effects, including the limitations on determining cause and effect.

High-Interest Visuals
Graphic organizers and high-interest visuals make world history content more accessible.

The Columbian Exchange

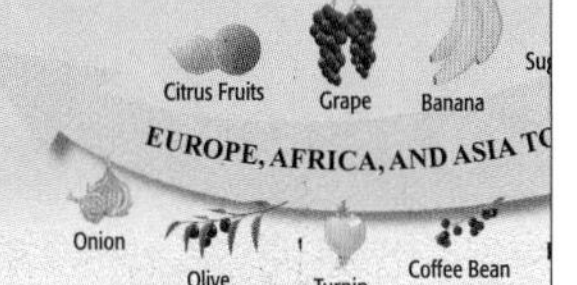

Patterns of Interaction
The Geography of Food: The Impact of Potatoes and Sugar

Think about your favorite foods. Chances are that at least one originated in a distant land. Throughout history, the introduction of new foods into a region has dramatically changed lives—for better and worse. Dependence on the potato, for example, led to a famine in Ireland. This prompted a massive migration of Irish people to other countries. In the Americas, the introduction of sugar led to riches for some and enslavement for many others.

138 Chapter 4

> Analyzing Key Concepts

Imperialism

Imperialism is a policy in which one country seeks to extend its authority by conquering other countries or by establishing economic and political dominance over other countries. The first chart below discusses the four forms of imperialist authority. The second chart shows the two management methods that can be used to control an area.

CALIFORNIA STANDARDS
10.4.1, REP 4

Forms of Imperialism

Form	Definition	Example
Colony	A country or a territory governed internally by a foreign power	Somaliland in East Africa was a French colony.
Protectorate	A country or a territory with its own internal government but under the control of an outside power	Britain established a protectorate over the Niger River delta.
Sphere of Influence	An area in which an outside power claims exclusive investment or trading privileges	Liberia was under the sphere of influence of the United States.
Economic Imperialism	An independent but less-developed country controlled by private business interests rather than other governments	The Dole Fruit company controlled pineapple trade in Hawaii.

Imperial Management Methods

Indirect Control	Direct Control
• Local government officials used	• Foreign officials brought in to rule
• Limited self-rule	• No self-rule
• Goal: to develop future leaders	• Goal: assimilation
• Government institutions are based on European styles but may have local rules	• Government institutions are based only on European styles.
	...ples:
	...ch colonies such as Somaliland, ...tnam
	...man colonies such as German ... Africa
	...tuguese colonies such as Angola

Analyzing Key Concepts
Analyzing Key Concepts features focus on the impact of important ideas in world history.

INTEGRATED TECHNOLOGY
RESEARCH LINKS For more on imperialism, go to **classzone.com**

> DATA FILE

In 1905, the British Empire
- was the largest and most powerful in the world's history.
- covered about 11 million square miles.
- had about 400 million inhabitants.

Today, the United Kingdom has 13 small dependent territories and is the head of a voluntary association of 54 independent states.

African Colonization and Independence
- In 1884, Western leaders met to divide Africa into colonial holdings.
- By 1914, nearly all of Africa had been distributed among European powers.
- European imperial powers set national borders in Africa without regard for local ethnic or political divisions. This continues to be a problem for African nations today.

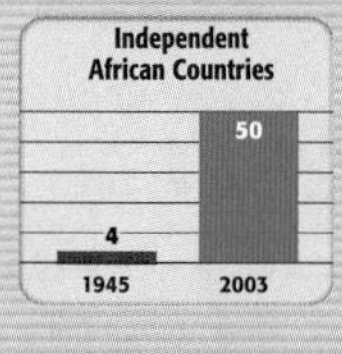

Connect *to* Today

1. **Forming and Supporting Opinions** Which form of managing imperial interests do you think would be most effective and why?
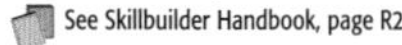
See Skillbuilder Handbook, page R20.
2. **Recognizing Effects** Use the Internet or library resources to research the problems many African nations are facing today as a result of imperialism. Report your findings to the class.

346 Chapter 11

A Focus on Critical Thinking

Primary Source Handbook

The Primary Source Handbook appears in the reference section of the text and includes key primary sources with related document-based questions.

Primary Source Handbook

CONTENTS

from the Memoirs of Madame Vigée-Lebrun

by Élisabeth Vigée-Lebrun

SETTING THE STAGE Élisabeth Vigée-Lebrun was a gifted artist who painted portraits of the French nobility. In her memoirs she recalls events of her own life amidst the turmoil of the French Revolution, which began in 1789. She frequently painted Marie Antoinette, queen of France. Vigée-Lebrun became frightened by the increasingly aggressive harassment of the nobility by the revolutionaries and resolved to leave France. She and her daughter escaped at night by stagecoach.

PRIMARY SOURCE

I had my carriage loaded, and my passport ready, so that I might leave next day with my daughter and her governess, when a crowd of national guardsmen burst into my room with their muskets. Most of them were drunk and shabby, and had terrible faces. A few of them came up to me and told me in the coarsest language that I must not go, but that I must remain. I answered that since everybody had been called upon to enjoy his liberty, I intended to make use of mine. They would barely listen to me, and kept on repeating, "You will not go, citizeness; you will not go!" Finally they went away. I was plunged into a state of cruel anxiety when I saw two of them return. But they did not frighten me, although they belonged to the gang, so quickly did I recognize that they wished me no harm. "Madame," said one of them, "we are your neighbors, and we have come to advise you to leave, and as soon as possible. You cannot live here; you are changed so much that we feel sorry for you. But do not go in your carriage: go in the stage-coach; it is much safer." . . .

Opposite me in the coach was a very filthy man, who stunk like the plague, and told me quite simply that he had stolen watches and other things. . . . Not satisfied with relating his fine exploits to us, the thief talked incessantly of

▲ *Self-Portrait in a Straw Hat* by Élisabeth Vigée-Lebrun

... read, how did you feel about the ... Vigée-Lebrun finds herself in?
... seem to be Vigée-Lebrun's feelings about ... French Revolution?
... find Vigée-Lebrun a sympathetic person? ... why not?

Primary Sources

Selected primary sources are supported by document-based questions and visuals to promote critical thinking.

> Analyzing Primary Sources

Starvation in Ireland

A traveler described what he saw on a journey through Ireland in 1847:

PRIMARY SOURCE

We entered a cabin. Stretched in one dark corner, scarcely visible, from the smoke and rags that covered them, were three children huddled together, lying there because they were too weak to rise, pale and ghastly, their little limbs—on removing a portion of the filthy covering—perfectly emaciated, eyes sunk, voice gone, and evidently in the last stage of actual starvation.

WILLIAM BENNETT, quoted in *Narrative of a Recent Journey of Six Weeks in Ireland*

DOCUMENT-BASED QUESTIONS

1. **Determining Main Ideas** *What was the effect of the destruction of Ireland's potato crop on the population of Ireland?*
2. **Clarifying** *How did 18 percent of the population deal with the famine?*
3. **Comparing** *Which country received the most Irish emigrants?*

The Great Famine, 1845–1851

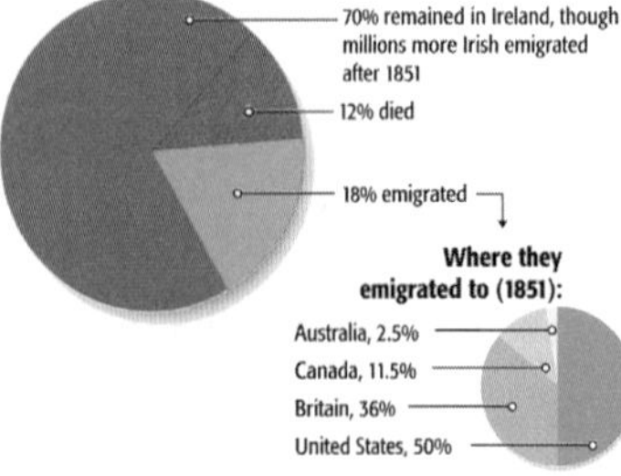

Sources: R. F. Foster, *Modern Ireland, 1600–1972;* D. Fitzpatrick, *Irish Emigration, 1804–1921*

INTERACTIVE

Views of Imperialism

CALIFORNIA STANDARDS

10.4.3 Explain imperialism from the perspective of the colonizers and the colonized and the varied immediate and long-term responses by the people under colonial rule.

European imperialism extended to the continents beyond Africa. As imperialism spread, the colonizer and the colonized viewed the experience of imperialism in very different ways. Some Europeans were outspoken about the superiority they felt toward the peoples they conquered. Others thought imperialism was very wrong. Even the conquered had mixed feelings about their encounter with the Europeans.

Different Perspectives

Different Perspectives presents alternative views of key world events through primary sources and secondary sources.

A) PRIMARY SOURCE

J. A. Hobson

Hobson's 1902 book, *Imperialism,* made a great impression on his fellow Britons.

For Europe to rule Asia by force for

Asia has to give, her priceless stores of wisdom garnered from her experience of ages, we refuse to take; the much or little which we could give we spoil by the brutal manner of our giving. This is what Imperialism has done, and is doing, for Asia.

B) PRIMARY SOURCE

Dadabhai Naoroji

Dadabhai Naoroji was the first Indian elected to the British Parliament. In 1871, he delivered a speech about the impact of Great Britain on India.

whole, the British rule rally, a great blessing; e and order on one s on the other, materially, ent. . . . The natives call the British system "Sakar ki Churi," the knife of sugar. That is to say there is no oppression, it is all smooth and sweet, but it is the knife, notwithstanding. I mention this that you should know these feelings. Our great misfortune is that you do not know our wants. When you will know our real wishes, I have not the least doubt that you would do justice. The genius and spirit of the British people is fair play and justice.

C) PRIMARY SOURCE

Jules Ferry

The following is from a speech Ferry delivered before the French National Assembly on July 28,1883.

Nations are great in our times only by means of the activities which they develop; it is not simply 'by the peaceful shining forth of institutions . . .' that they are great at this hour. . . . Something else is needed for France: . . . that she must also be a great country exercising all of her rightful influence over the destiny of Europe, that she ought to propagate this influence throughout the world and carry everywhere that she can her language, her customs, her flag, her arms, and her genius.

D) PRIMARY SOURCE

This 1882 American political cartoon, titled "The Devilfish in Egyptian Waters," depicts England as an octopus. Notice that Egypt is not yet one of the areas controlled by the British.

THE DEVILFISH IN EGYPTIAN WATERS.

Document-Based QUESTIONS

1. According to Hobson (Source A), what mistake did European imperialists make in Asia?
2. What position on imperialism does Jules Ferry take in Source C?
3. In Source D, what does the representation of England suggest about the cartoonist's view of British imperialism?
4. In what way does the view of imperialism in Source B contrast with that in Source D?

Standards-Based Pupil's Edition

Modern World History: Patterns of Interaction is designed to meet the needs of California students and teachers. The Pupil's Edition provides comprehensive coverage of the California History–Social Science Content Standards and Analysis Skills. In addition, the text presents historical events in an engaging narrative with special features that extend and enhance the instruction.

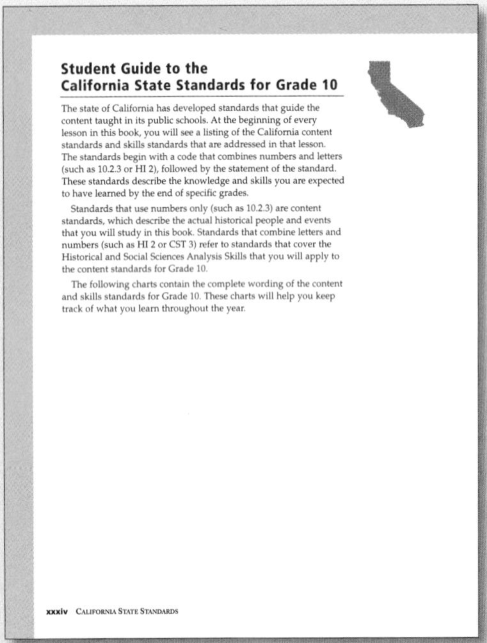

Student Guide to the California State Standards for Grade 10

The state of California has developed standards that guide the content taught in its public schools. At the beginning of every lesson in this book, you will see a listing of the California content standards and skills standards that are addressed in that lesson. The standards begin with a code that combines numbers and letters (such as 10.2.3 or HI 2), followed by the statement of the standard. These standards describe the knowledge and skills you are expected to have learned by the end of specific grades.

Standards that use numbers only (such as 10.2.3) are content standards, which describe the actual historical people and events that you will study in this book. Standards that combine letters and numbers (such as HI 2 or CST 3) refer to standards that cover the Historical and Social Sciences Analysis Skills that you will apply to the content standards for Grade 10.

The following charts contain the complete wording of the content and skills standards for Grade 10. These charts will help you keep track of what you learn throughout the year.

xxxiv California State Standards

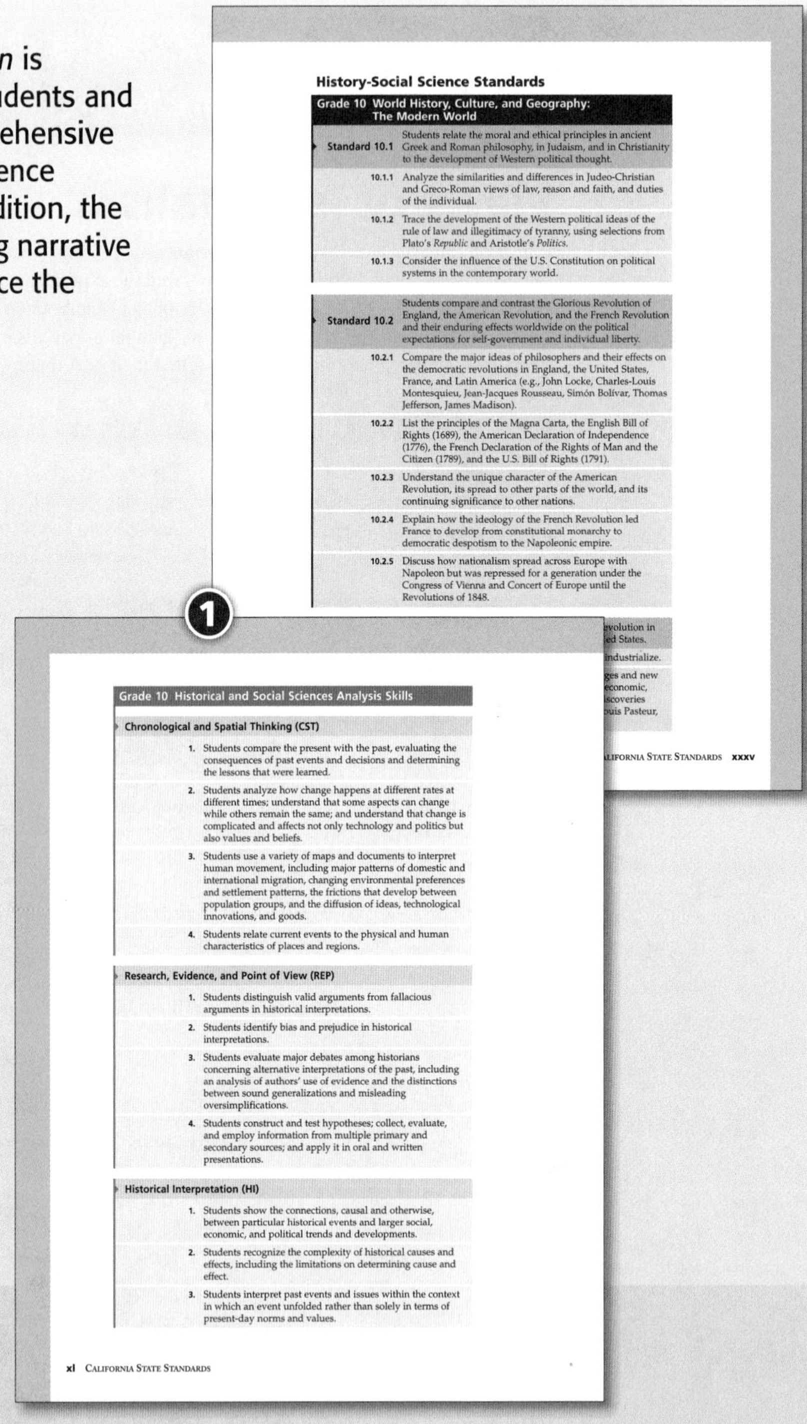

History-Social Science Standards

Grade 10 World History, Culture, and Geography: The Modern World	
Standard 10.1	Students relate the moral and ethical principles in ancient Greek and Roman philosophy, in Judaism, and in Christianity to the development of Western political thought.
10.1.1	Analyze the similarities and differences in Judeo-Christian and Greco-Roman views of law, reason and faith, and duties of the individual.
10.1.2	Trace the development of the Western political ideas of the rule of law and illegitimacy of tyranny, using selections from Plato's *Republic* and Aristotle's *Politics*.
10.1.3	Consider the influence of the U.S. Constitution on political systems in the contemporary world.
Standard 10.2	Students compare and contrast the Glorious Revolution of England, the American Revolution, and the French Revolution and their enduring effects worldwide on the political expectations for self-government and individual liberty.
10.2.1	Compare the major ideas of philosophers and their effects on the democratic revolutions in England, the United States, France, and Latin America (e.g., John Locke, Charles-Louis Montesquieu, Jean-Jacques Rousseau, Simón Bolívar, Thomas Jefferson, James Madison).
10.2.2	List the principles of the Magna Carta, the English Bill of Rights (1689), the American Declaration of Independence (1776), the French Declaration of the Rights of Man and the Citizen (1789), and the U.S. Bill of Rights (1791).
10.2.3	Understand the unique character of the American Revolution, its spread to other parts of the world, and its continuing significance to other nations.
10.2.4	Explain how the ideology of the French Revolution led France to develop from constitutional monarchy to democratic despotism to the Napoleonic empire.
10.2.5	Discuss how nationalism spread across Europe with Napoleon but was repressed for a generation under the Congress of Vienna and Concert of Europe until the Revolutions of 1848.

...volution in ...ed States. ...ndustrialize. ...ges and new ...conomic, ...scoveries ...uis Pasteur,

...lifornia State Standards xxxv

Grade 10 Historical and Social Sciences Analysis Skills

Chronological and Spatial Thinking (CST)

1. Students compare the present with the past, evaluating the consequences of past events and decisions and determining the lessons that were learned.
2. Students analyze how change happens at different rates at different times; understand that some aspects can change while others remain the same; and understand that change is complicated and affects not only technology and politics but also values and beliefs.
3. Students use a variety of maps and documents to interpret human movement, including major patterns of domestic and international migration, changing environmental preferences and settlement patterns, the frictions that develop between population groups, and the diffusion of ideas, technological innovations, and goods.
4. Students relate current events to the physical and human characteristics of places and regions.

Research, Evidence, and Point of View (REP)

1. Students distinguish valid arguments from fallacious arguments in historical interpretations.
2. Students identify bias and prejudice in historical interpretations.
3. Students evaluate major debates among historians concerning alternative interpretations of the past, including an analysis of authors' use of evidence and the distinctions between sound generalizations and misleading oversimplifications.
4. Students construct and test hypotheses; collect, evaluate, and employ information from multiple primary and secondary sources; and apply it in oral and written presentations.

Historical Interpretation (HI)

1. Students show the connections, causal and otherwise, between particular historical events and larger social, economic, and political trends and developments.
2. Students recognize the complexity of historical causes and effects, including the limitations on determining cause and effect.
3. Students interpret past events and issues within the context in which an event unfolded rather than solely in terms of present-day norms and values.

xl California State Standards

① California Standards

A complete list of the California History–Social Science Content Standards for Grade 10 and Analysis Skills standards is provided in the early pages of the Pupil's Edition. Students and their parents can become familiar with the standards that guide the content in the textbook.

Strategies for Taking Tests

Modern World History: Patterns of Interaction includes a special section titled Strategies for Taking Tests. It offers students information on study skills and test-taking strategies that will help them to improve their performance on standards-based assessments.

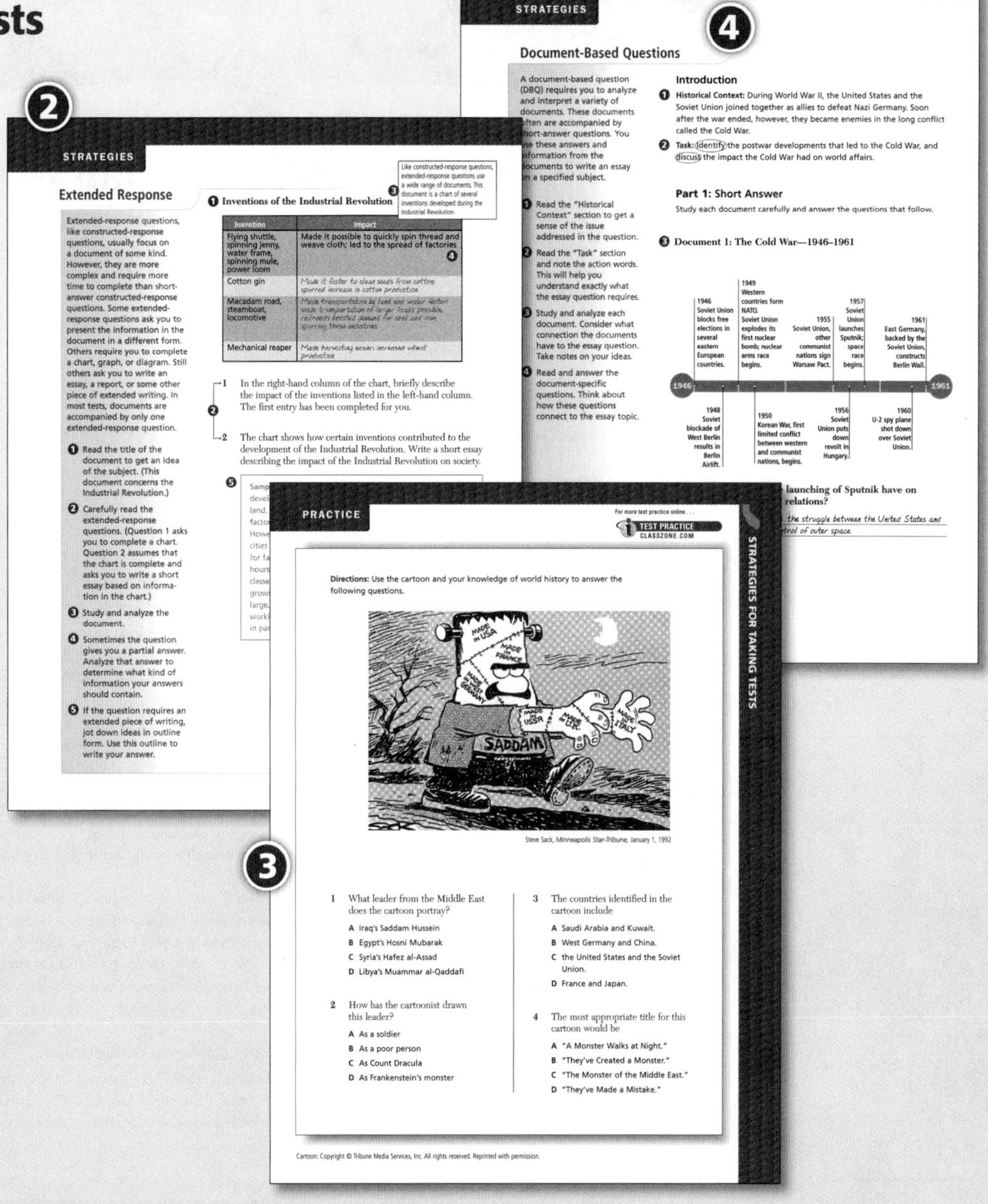

❷ Strategies

These pages offer students strategies for handling the various items they will find in tests that they take. For every type of item, strategies are presented in step-by-step format. Items types include multiple-choice, constructed-response, extended-response, primary and secondary sources, political cartoons, charts and graphs, maps, and time lines.

❸ Practice

Each strategy page is followed by a practice page, where students can apply the strategies they have learned to a set of practice items.

❹ Document-Based Questions

This section ends with strategies and practice for document-based questions. In these items, students analyze a variety of historical documents, including primary and secondary sources, charts and graphs, political cartoons, posters, and maps. They then write an essay.

Standards-Based Pupil's Edition

Modernization in Japan

MAIN IDEA	WHY IT MATTERS NOW	TERMS & NAMES
CULTURAL INTERACTION Japan followed the model of Western powers by industrializing and expanding its foreign influence.	Japan's continued development of its own way of life has made it a leading world power.	• Treaty of Kanagawa • Meiji era • Russo-Japanese War • annexation

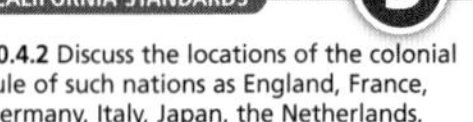

CALIFORNIA STANDARDS

10.4.2 Discuss the locations of the colonial rule of such nations as England, France, Germany, Italy, Japan, the Netherlands, Russia, Spain, Portugal, and the United States.

CST 2 Students analyze how change happens at different rates at different times; understand that some aspects can change while others remain the same; and understand that change is complicated and affects not only technology and politics but also values and beliefs.

REP 4 Students construct and test hypotheses; collect, evaluate, and employ information from multiple primary and secondary sources; and apply it in oral and written presentations.

HI 1 Students show the connections, causal and otherwise, between particular historical events and larger social, economic, and political trends and developments.

TAKING NOTES

Analyzing Causes List the steps that Japan took toward modernization and the events that contributed to its growth as an imperialistic power.

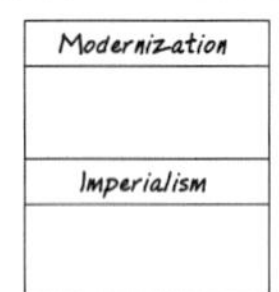

Modernization
Imperialism

SETTING THE STAGE In the early 17th century, Japan had shut itself off from almost all contact with other nations. Under the rule of the Tokugawa shoguns, Japanese society was very tightly ordered. The shogun parceled out land to the daimyo, or lords. The peasants worked for and lived under the protection of their daimyo and his small army of samurai, or warriors. This rigid feudal system managed to keep the country free of civil war. Peace and relative prosperity reigned in Japan for two centuries.

Japan Ends Its Isolation

The Japanese had almost no contact with the industrialized world during this time of isolation. They continued, however, to trade with China and with Dutch merchants from Indonesia. They also had diplomatic contact with Korea. However, trade was growing in importance, both inside and outside Japan.

The Demand for Foreign Trade Beginning in the early 19th century, Westerners tried to convince the Japanese to open their ports to trade. British, French, Russian, and American officials occasionally anchored off the Japanese coast. Like China, however, Japan repeatedly refused to receive them. Then, in 1853, U.S. Commodore Matthew Perry took four ships into what is now Tokyo Harbor. These massive black wooden ships powered by steam astounded the Japanese. The ships' cannons also shocked them. The Tokugawa shogun realized he had no choice but to receive Perry and the letter Perry had brought from U.S. president Millard Fillmore.

Fillmore's letter politely asked the shogun to allow free trade between the United States and Japan. Perry delivered it with a threat, however. He would come back with a larger fleet in a year to receive Japan's reply. That reply was the **Treaty of Kanagawa** of 1854. Under its terms, Japan opened two ports at which U.S. ships could take on supplies. After the United States had pushed open the door, other Western powers soon followed. By 1860, Japan, like China, had granted foreigners permission to trade at several treaty ports. It had also extended extraterritorial rights to many foreign nations.

Meiji Reform and Modernization The Japanese were angry that the shogun had given in to the foreigners' demands. They turned to Japan's young emperor, Mutsuhito (moot•soo•HEE•toh), who seemed to symbolize the country's sense of

376 Chapter 12

1 Main Idea and Why It Matters Now

Main Idea and Why It Matters Now at the beginning of every section build critical reading skills by telling students why the information they are about to read is important.

2 Taking Notes

Students use a variety of reading skills to take notes as they read. These skills include comparing and contrasting, cause and effect, sequencing, and categorizing.

3 California Standards

Each section opener includes the full text of the content and skills standards covered in that section. These standards are covered in the narrative for the section, in special features that accompany the section, and in the Section Assessment questions.

4

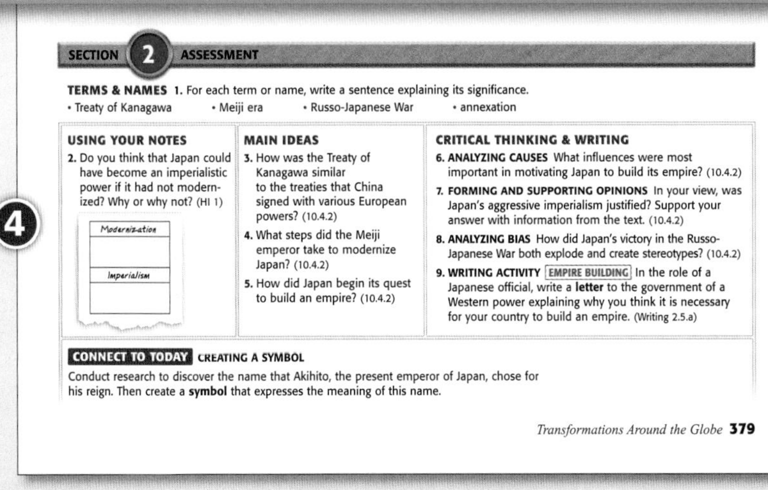
SECTION 2 ASSESSMENT

TERMS & NAMES 1. For each term or name, write a sentence explaining its significance.
• Treaty of Kanagawa • Meiji era • Russo-Japanese War • annexation

USING YOUR NOTES
2. Do you think that Japan could have become an imperialistic power if it had not modernized? Why or why not? (HI 1)

MAIN IDEAS
3. How was the Treaty of Kanagawa similar to the treaties that China signed with various European powers? (10.4.2)
4. What steps did the Meiji emperor take to modernize Japan? (10.4.2)
5. How did Japan begin its quest to build an empire? (10.4.2)

CRITICAL THINKING & WRITING
6. **ANALYZING CAUSES** What influences were most important in motivating Japan to build its empire? (10.4.2)
7. **FORMING AND SUPPORTING OPINIONS** In your view, was Japan's aggressive imperialism justified? Support your answer with information from the text. (10.4.2)
8. **ANALYZING BIAS** How did Japan's victory in the Russo-Japanese War both explode and create stereotypes? (10.4.2)
9. **WRITING ACTIVITY** EMPIRE BUILDING In the role of a Japanese official, write a **letter** to the government of a Western power explaining why you think it is necessary for your country to build an empire. (Writing 2.5.a)

CONNECT TO TODAY CREATING A SYMBOL
Conduct research to discover the name that Akihito, the present emperor of Japan, chose for his reign. Then create a **symbol** that expresses the meaning of this name.

Transformations Around the Globe **379**

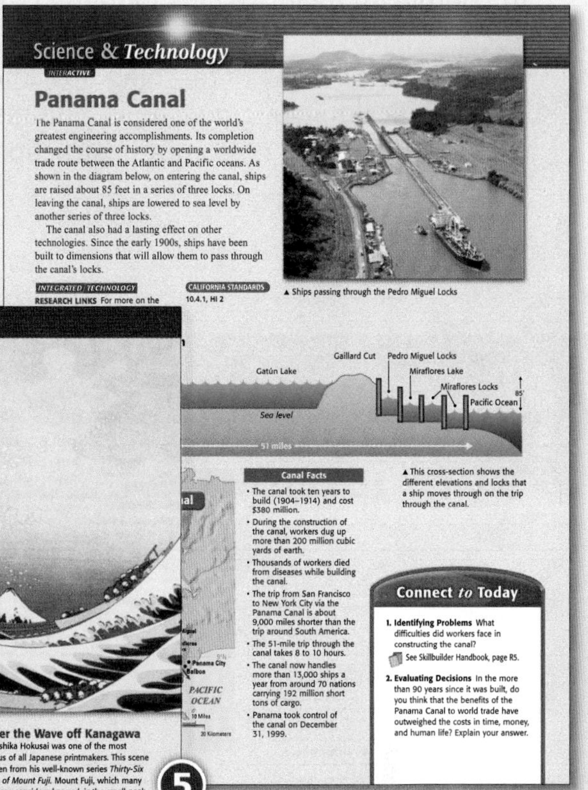

Science & Technology
INTERACTIVE

Panama Canal

The Panama Canal is considered one of the world's greatest engineering accomplishments. Its completion changed the course of history by opening a worldwide trade route between the Atlantic and Pacific oceans. As shown in the diagram below, on entering the canal, ships are raised about 85 feet in a series of three locks. On leaving the canal, ships are lowered to sea level by another series of three locks.

The canal also had a lasting effect on other technologies. Since the early 1900s, ships have been built to dimensions that will allow them to pass through the canal's locks.

CALIFORNIA STANDARDS 10.4.1, HI 2

▲ Ships passing through the Pedro Miguel Locks

Gatún Lake · Gaillard Cut · Pedro Miguel Locks · Miraflores Lake · Miraflores Locks · Pacific Ocean · Sea level · 85' · 51 miles

▲ This cross-section shows the different elevations and locks that a ship moves through on the trip through the canal.

Canal Facts
- The canal took ten years to build (1904–1914) and cost $380 million.
- During the construction of the canal, workers dug up more than 200 million cubic yards of earth.
- Thousands of workers died from diseases while building the canal.
- The trip from San Francisco to New York City via the Panama Canal is about 9,000 miles shorter than the trip around South America.
- The 51-mile trip through the canal takes 8 to 10 hours.
- The canal now handles more than 13,000 ships a year from around 70 nations carrying 192 million short tons of cargo.
- Panama took control of the canal on December 31, 1999.

Connect to Today
1. **Identifying Problems** What difficulties did workers face in constructing the canal?
See Skillbuilder Handbook, page R5.
2. **Evaluating Decisions** In the more than 90 years since it was built, do you think that the benefits of the Panama Canal to world trade have outweighed the costs in time, money, and human life? Explain your answer.

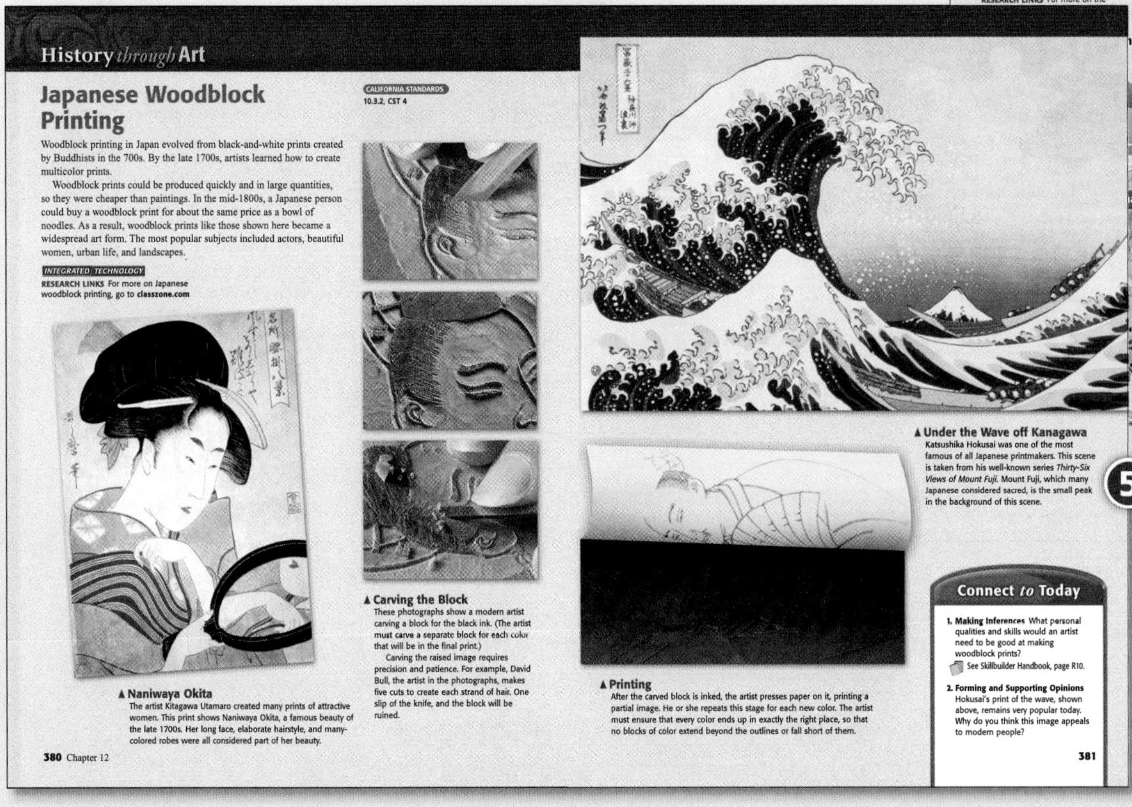

History through Art

Japanese Woodblock Printing

CALIFORNIA STANDARDS 10.3.2, CST 4

Woodblock printing in Japan evolved from black-and-white prints created by Buddhists in the 700s. By the late 1700s, artists learned how to create multicolor prints.

Woodblock prints could be produced quickly and in large quantities, so they were cheaper than paintings. In the mid-1800s, a Japanese person could buy a woodblock print for about the same price as a bowl of noodles. As a result, woodblock prints like those shown here became a widespread art form. The most popular subjects included actors, beautiful women, urban life, and landscapes.

INTEGRATED TECHNOLOGY
RESEARCH LINKS For more on Japanese woodblock printing, go to **classzone.com**

▲ **Naniwaya Okita**
The artist Kitagawa Utamaro created many prints of attractive women. This print shows Naniwaya Okita, a famous beauty of the late 1700s. Her long face, elaborate hairstyle, and many-colored robes were all considered part of her beauty.

▲ **Carving the Block**
These photographs show a modern artist carving a block for the black ink. (The artist must carve a separate block for each color that will be in the final print.)
Carving the raised image requires precision and patience. For example, David Bull, the artist in the photographs, makes five cuts to create each strand of hair. One slip of the knife, and the block will be ruined.

▲ **Under the Wave off Kanagawa**
Katsushika Hokusai was one of the most famous of all Japanese printmakers. This scene is taken from his well-known series *Thirty-Six Views of Mount Fuji.* Mount Fuji, which many Japanese considered sacred, is the small peak in the background of this scene.

5

▲ **Printing**
After the carved block is inked, the artist presses paper on it, printing a partial image. He or she repeats this stage for each new color. The artist must ensure that every color ends up in exactly the right place, so that no blocks of color extend beyond the outlines or fall short of them.

Connect to Today
1. **Making Inferences** What personal qualities and skills would an artist need to be good at making woodblock prints?
See Skillbuilder Handbook, page R10.
2. **Forming and Supporting Opinions** Hokusai's print of the wave, shown above, remains very popular today. Why do you think this image appeals to modern people?

380 Chapter 12 **381**

4 Section and Chapter Assessment

A range of questions, including Main Idea and Critical Thinking questions, are provided in the Section Assessment and Chapter Assessment. Each question addresses a California content or skills standard, which is identified in parentheses after the question.

5 Special Features

A collection of special features that accompany the sections extend the instruction in the text. Longer features—including Social History, Analyzing Key Concepts, and History through Art—display the California standard addressed in the feature.

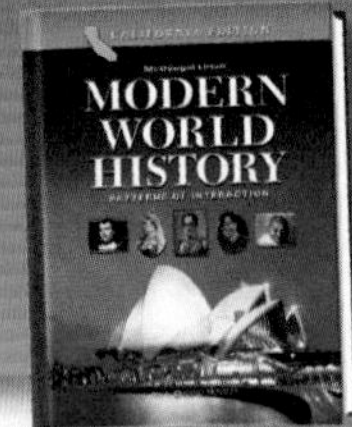

Standards-Based Teacher's Edition

The Teacher's Edition of *Modern World History: Patterns of Interaction* provides the information teachers need to coordinate their teaching with the California History–Social Science Content Standards and Analysis Skills. In addition, a variety of teaching tips, informational notes, critical thinking questions, and resource listings make it possible to customize instruction for all student populations.

1

Correlations to California History–Social Science Content Standards and Analysis Skills

Students in grade ten study major turning points that shaped the modern world, from the late eighteenth century through the present, including the cause and course of the two world wars. They trace the rise of democratic ideas and develop an understanding of the historical roots of current world issues, especially as they pertain to international relations. They extrapolate from the American experience that democratic ideals are often achieved at a high price, remain vulnerable, and are not practiced everywhere in the world. Students develop an understanding of current world issues and relate them to their historical, geographic, political, economic, and cultural contexts. Students consider multiple accounts of events in order to understand international relations from a variety of perspectives.

Standard		Primary Citations	Supporting Citations
10.1	Students relate the moral and ethical principles in ancient Greek and Roman philosophy, in Judaism, and in Christianity to the development of Western political thought.	**Pupil & Teacher & eEdition** Common Pages: 2, 3, 5–11, 12–17, 18–23, 26–27, 29–30, 54–60, 61–66, 67–68, 127–131, 141, 144–149, 155–161, 174–179, 181–182, 183, 184, 191, 194, 209–212, 700–701, 704–705, 710–711, 714–715 Add'l Teacher Edition: 5–7, 12–16, 54–56, 58–61, 61–65, 67, 127–130, 144, 146–148, 155–160, 174–176, 181–182, 191, 209–210, 704–705, 710–711 **PRINT COMPONENT(S)** CA Standards Enrichment Wrkbk: 17–18, 19–20, 21–22	**PRINT COMPONENT(S)** In-Depth Resources Unit 1: 1, 2, 5, 6, 18, 20, 21, 23, 26–30, 33–36, 82, 86, 100; Unit 2: 1, 4, 5, 7, 11–13, 18–20, 23–25, 28, 30, 31, 33, 37, 38, 41, 44, 47 In-Depth Resources in Spanish Unit 1: 11, 12, 15, 16, 18, 20–22, 38, 41; Unit 2: 44, 47–49, 52, 55, 56, 57 History Makers Unit 1: 15, 34, Unit 2: 18 CA Reading Toolkit: L11, L12, 20, 23, 26, 27, 28, 31 CA Modified Lesson Plans for English Learners: Prol.1, Prol.2, 19.2, 20.3 CA Standards Planner & Lesson Plans: L1, L3, L5, L13, L15, L31, L37, L43, L45, L47, L53 **TRANSPARENCIES/TECHNOLOGY** World Art & Cultures Transparencies: AT12, AT36, AT37, AT45, AT46, AT47, AT48 Geography Transparencies: GT17, GT21, GT22 Critical Thinking Transparencies: CT17, CT21, CT53, CT57, CT58 Benchmark Tests: Prol.1, Prol.2, 1.1, 1.3, 1.4, 4.2, 5.1, 5.4, 5.5, 6.1, 6.4 Power Presentations: Prol.1, Prol.2, 1.1, 1.3, 1.4, 4.2, 5.1, 5.4, 5.5, 6.1, 6.4
			OMPONENT(S) Resources Unit 1: 20, 21, 23, 28, 29; Unit 2: 5, 12–13, 18, 19, 24, 25, 3, 38, 41, 44 Resources in Spanish Unit 1: 11, 12, 15, 16, 20–22; Unit 2: 48, 52, Makers Unit 1: 15, 34; Unit 2: 18, 41 ing Toolkit: L11, L12, 27, 28 fied Lesson Plans for English Learners: Prol.1, Prol.2 dards Planner & Lesson Plans: L3, L5, L13, L15, L45, L47 ARENCIES/TECHNOLOGY t & Cultures Transparencies: AT12, AT48 hy Transparencies: GT17, GT22 hinking Transparencies: CT17, CT53, CT57 rk Tests: Prol.1, Prol.2, 1.3, 1.4, 5.5, 6.1 esentations: Prol.1, Prol.2, 1.3, 1.4, 5.5, 6.1

Teacher's Edition • **CA33**

2

CHAPTER 7 PLANNING GUIDE

The French Revolution and Napoleon, 1789–1815

CHAPTER RESOURCES	COPYMASTERS	ASSESSMENT	INTEGRATED TECHNOLOGY
CHAPTER OVERVIEW The French Revolution established a new political order, Napoleon Bonaparte forged and lost an empire, and the Congress of Vienna created a balance of power in Europe.	**In-Depth Resources: Unit 2** • Building Vocabulary, p. 53 **Chapters in Brief** (in English and Spanish) **Block Schedule Pacing Guide**	**Chapter Assessment,** pp. 242–243 **Formal Assessment** • Chapter Tests, Forms A, B, and C, pp. 124–135 **Test Generator** **Online Test Practice**	• eEdition Plus Online • EasyPlanner Plus Online • eTest Plus Online **Audio CDs** • Voices from the Past • Reading Study Guides **CD-ROMs** • eEdition • Power Presentations • EasyPlanner • Electronic Library of Primary Sources • Test Generator
SECTION 1 **The French Revolution Begins** pp. 217–221 **OBJECTIVE** Describe the factors that led to the French Revolution.	**In-Depth Resources: Unit 2** • Guided Reading, p. 48 • History Makers: Marie Antoinette, p. 64 • Reteaching Activity, p. 68 **Reading Study Guide,** p. 73	**Section 1 Assessment,** p. 221 **Formal Assessment** • Section Quiz, p. 119 **California Daily Standards Practice Transparencies,** TT84	**eEdition CD-ROM** **Geography Transparencies** • GT23 Early Sites of the French Revolution **World Art and Cultures Transparencies** • AT50 *Portrait of Marie Antoinette* **Electronic Library of Primary Sources** **classzone.com** • NetExplorations: The French Revolution
SECTION 2 **Revolution Brings Reform and Terror** pp. 222–228 **OBJECTIVE** Summarize the political reforms in France and describe the Reign of Terror.	**In-Depth Resources: Unit 2** • Guided Reading, p. 49 • Geography Application, p. 55 • Primary Sources, pp. 57, 58, 59 • Literature: from *A Tale of Two Cities,* p. 61 • History Makers: Robespierre, p. 65 • Connections Across Time/Cultures, p. 66 • Science & Technology, p. 67 **Reading Study Guide,** p. 75	**Section 2 Assessment,** p. 227 **Formal Assessment** • Section Quiz, p. 120 **California Daily Standards Practice Transparencies,** TT85	**eEdition CD-ROM** **Electronic Library of Primary Sources** • from "Execution by Guillotine" • from "Frenchmen, Is This What You Want?" **classzone.com**
SECTION 3 **Napoleon Forges an Empire** pp. 229–233 **OBJECTIVE** Trace Napoleon's rise to power.	**In-Depth Resources: Unit 2** • Guided Reading, p. 50 • Primary Source, p. 60 • Reteaching Activity, p. 70 **Reading Study Guide,** p. 77	**Section 3 Assessment,** p. 233 **Formal Assessment** • Section Quiz, p. 121 **California Daily Standards Practice Transparencies,** TT86	**eEdition CD-ROM** **World Art and Cultures Transparencies** • AT51 *Napoleon* **Electronic Library of Primary Sources** **classzone.com**
SECTION 4 **Napoleon's Empire Collapses** pp. 234–237 **OBJECTIVE** Explain the collapse of Napoleon's empire.	**In-Depth Resources: Unit 2** • Guided Reading, p. 51 • Skillbuilder Practice, p. 54 • Reteaching Activity, p. 71 **Reading Study Guide,** p. 79	**Section 4 Assessment,** p. 237 **Formal Assessment** • Section Quiz, p. 122 **California Daily Standards Practice Transparencies,** TT87	**eEdition CD-ROM** **Electronic Library of Primary Sources** • "The Battle of Waterloo: The Finale" **classzone.com**
SECTION 5 **The Congress of Vienna** pp. 238–241 **OBJECTIVE** Describe the influence of the Congress of Vienna.	**In-Depth Resources: Unit 2** • Guided Reading, p. 52 • Reteaching Activity, p. 72 **Reading Study Guide,** p. 81	**Section 5 Assessment,** p. 241 **Formal Assessment** • Section Quiz, p. 123 **California Daily Standards Practice Transparencies,** TT88	**eEdition CD-ROM** **Critical Thinking Transparencies** • CT23 The French Revolution • CT59 Chapter 7 Visual Summary **Electronic Library of Primary Sources** **classzone.com** • NetExplorations: The French Revolution

3

OVERVIEW OF CALIFORNIA RESOURCES

	Section 1	Section 2	Section 3	Section 4	Section 5
California Reading Toolkit	p. L32	p. L33	p. L34	p. L35	p. L36
California Modified Lesson Plans for English Learners	p. 59	p. 61	p. 63	p. 65	p. 67
California Daily Standards Practice Transparencies	TT24	TT25	TT26	TT27	TT28
California Standards Enrichment Workbook	pp. 23–24	pp. 25–26, 29–30, 45–46	pp. 29–30 31–32,	pp. 29–30	pp. 31–32, 105–106
California Standards Planner and Lesson Plans	p. L55	p. L57	p. L59	p. L61	p. L63
California Online Test Practice	classzone.com	classzone.com	classzone.com	classzone.com	classzone.com
California Test Generator CD-ROM	⦿	⦿	⦿	⦿	⦿
California Easy Planner CD-ROM	⦿	⦿	⦿	⦿	⦿
California eEdition CD-ROM	⦿	⦿	⦿	⦿	⦿

Chart Key: Pupil's Edition; Teacher's Edition; Overhead Transparency; Block Scheduling; Copymaster; Audio Library; CD-ROM; Internet; Video

NO TIME? If you do not have time to teach this chapter in full, assign the **Chapter in Brief** (also available in Spanish).

213A Chapter 7

Teacher's Edition **213B**

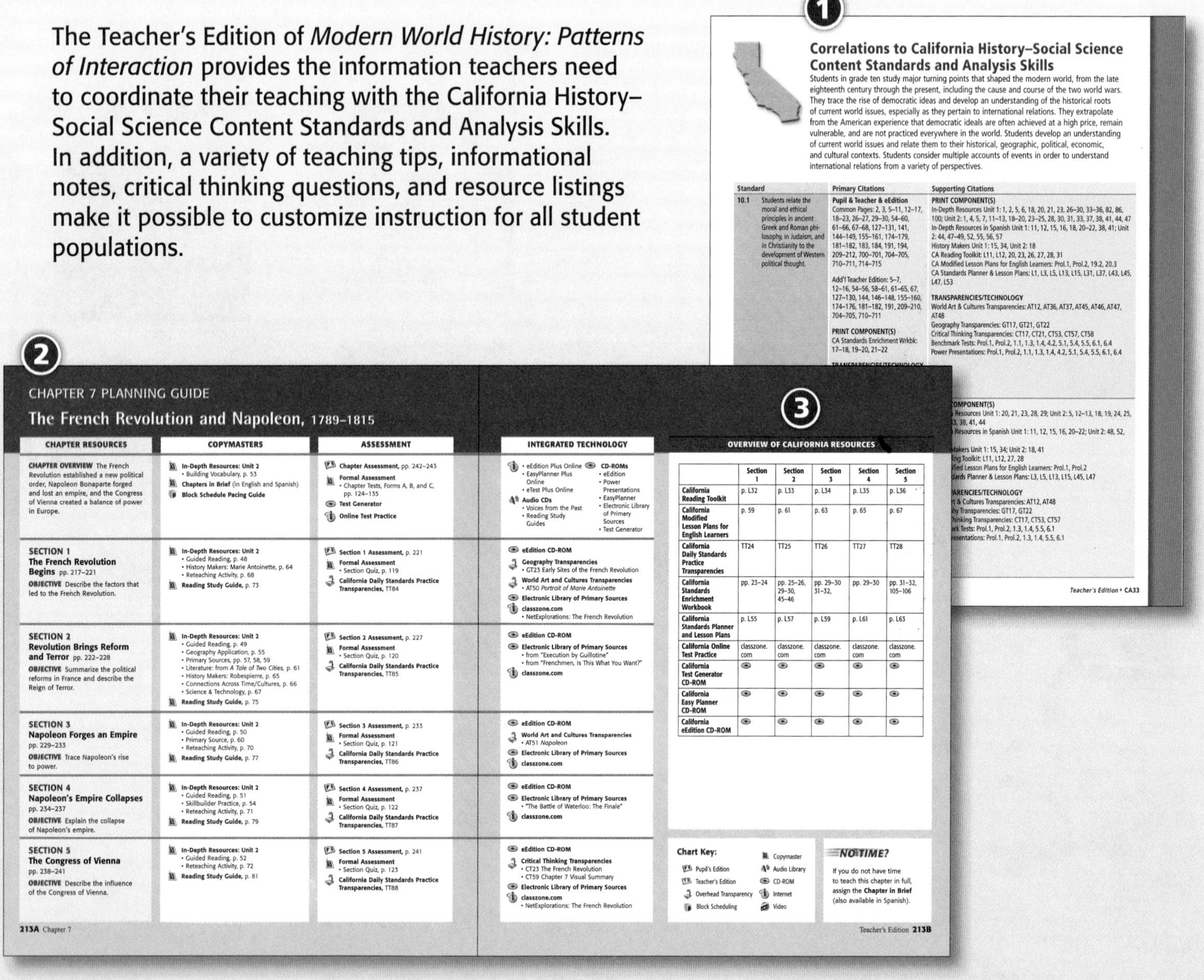

1 Correlation to California Standards

An easy-to-read chart correlates the text with the California content and skills standards for Grade 10. This correlation provides specific page references to the Pupil's Edition, Teacher's Edition, and selected ancillaries, with the strongest references shown in boldfaced type.

2 Chapter Planning Guide

The Chapter Planning Guide gives complete listings of reproducible materials for the chapter as a whole and for each lesson. The listings reveal the depth of available resource materials.

3 California Chapter Resources

The Chapter Planning Guide provides a chart of California resources for each section. These resources include the *California Standards Enrichment Workbook*, the *California Standards Planner and Lesson Plans,* and *the California EasyPlanner CD-ROM.* This information is also provided at the section level.

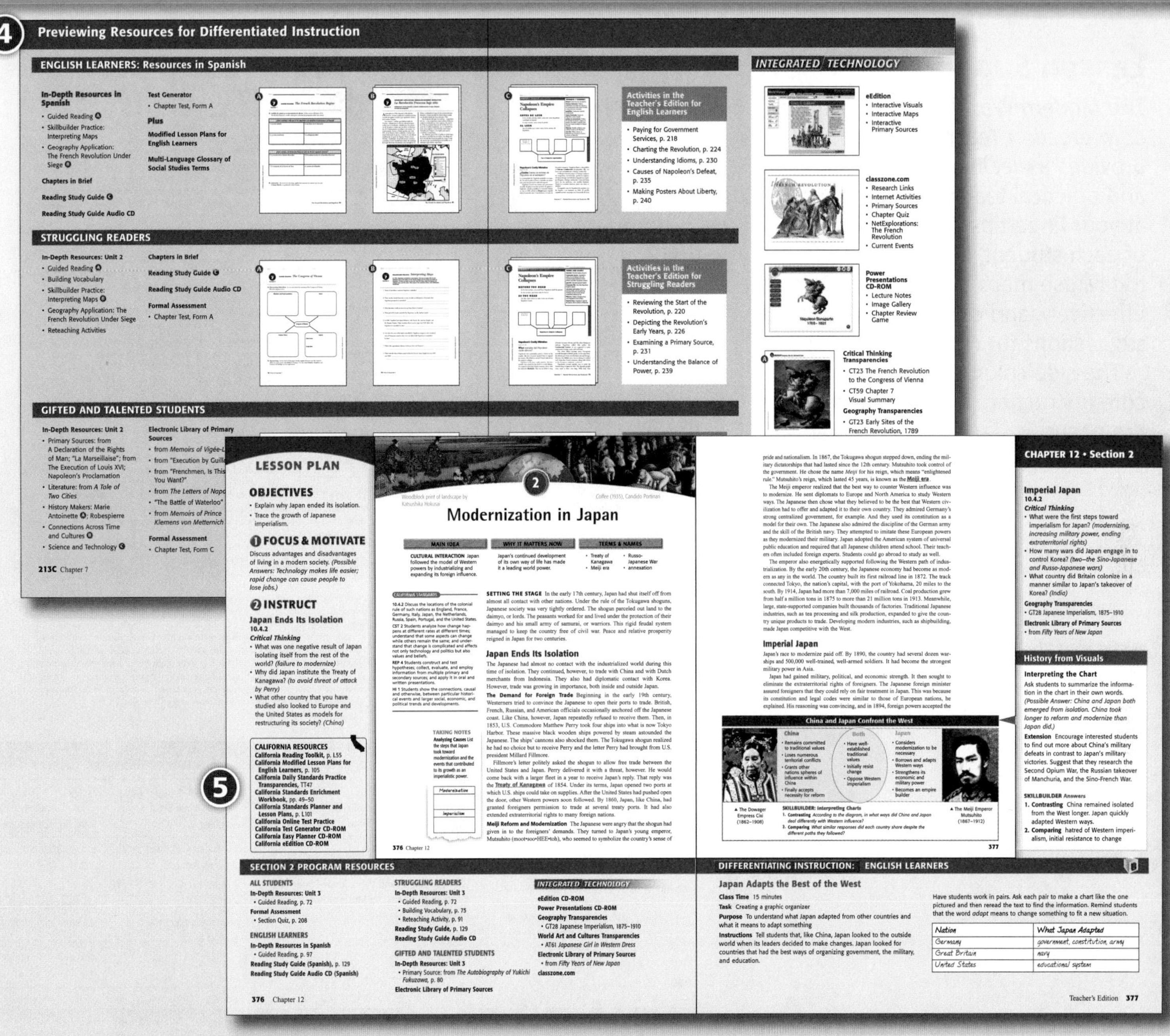

④ Resources for Differentiated Instruction

Each planning guide includes a listing of resources for teaching various student populations: English learners, struggling readers, and gifted and talented students. "Thumbnails" preview materials that support differentiation. Teacher's Edition activities for differentiation are also highlighted.

⑤ California Section Resources

A list of California resources available for each section is provided in the side column of the section openers in the Teacher's Edition.

Standards-Based Teacher's Edition

Lesson Support

The *Modern World History: Patterns of Interaction* Teacher's Edition provides a wealth of information and practical teaching suggestions at your fingertips. Meet the needs of each student, link history to today, use maps and other visuals effectively, and draw from abundant suggestions for classroom activities.

The side columns focus on core instruction. At the bottom of the pages, you will find optional suggestions and teaching activities.

CHAPTER 7 • Section 3

Napoleon Rules France

Critical Thinking

- In general, did Napoleon make the French government stronger or weaker? *(He strengthened it by improving the tax collection system, starting lycées and a national banking system, and restricting freedoms of speech and the press.)*
- What made the admissions policies of the lycées significant? *(provided opportunity to males of all classes)*
- What caused Napoleon to reach an agreement with the pope? *(Many clergy and peasants disliked the restrictions on the church started during the Revolution.)*

1 **History Makers**

Napoleon Bonaparte

Which traits of Napoleon are emphasized in the portrait of him? *(Possible Answer: his pride)*

Discuss whether students think any contemporary rulers share traits of Napoleon's.

2 **World Art and Cultures Transparencies**

- AT51 *Napoleon Crossing the St. Bernard Pass*

History Makers

Napoleon Bonaparte
1769–1821

Because of his small stature and thick Corsican accent, Napoleon was mocked by his fellow students at military school. Haughty and proud, Napoleon refused to grace his tormentors' behavior with any kind of response. He simply ignored them, preferring to lose himself in his studies. He showed a particular passion for three subjects—classical history, geography, and mathematics.

In 1784, Napoleon was recommended for a career in the army and he transferred to the Ecole Militaire (the French equivalent of West Point) in Paris. There, he proved to be a fairly poor soldier, except when it came to artillery. His artillery instructor quickly noticed Napoleon's abilities: "He is most proud, ambitious, aspiring to everything. This young man merits our attention."

dissolve the Directory. In its place, they established a group of three consuls, one of whom was Napoleon. Napoleon quickly took the title of first consul and assumed the powers of a dictator. A sudden seizure of power like Napoleon's is known as a *coup*—from the French phrase **coup d'état** (KOO day•TAH), or "blow to the state." A

At the time of Napoleon's coup, France was still at war. In 1799, Britain, Austria, and Russia joined forces with one goal in mind, to drive Napoleon from power. Once again, Napoleon rode from Paris at the head of his troops. Eventually, as a result of war and diplomacy, all three nations signed peace agreements with France. By 1802, Europe was at peace for the first time in ten years. Napoleon was free to focus his energies on restoring order in France.

MAIN IDEA
Analyzing Causes
A How was Napoleon able to become a dictator?
A. Answer General political chaos created a need for a strong leader, and Napoleon had control of the army.

Napoleon Rules France

At first, Napoleon pretended to be the constitutionally chosen leader of a free republic. In 1800, a **plebiscite** (PLEHB•ih•SYT), or vote of the people, was held to approve a new constitution. Desperate for strong leadership, the people voted overwhelmingly in favor of the constitution. This gave all real power to Napoleon as first consul.

Restoring Order at Home Napoleon did not try to return the nation to the days of Louis XVI. Rather, he kept many of the changes that had come with the Revolution. In general, he supported laws that would both strengthen the central government and achieve some of the goals of the Revolution.

His first task was to get the economy on a solid footing. Napoleon set up an efficient method of tax collection and established a national banking system. In addition to ensuring the government a steady supply of tax money, these actions promoted sound financial management and better control of the economy. Napoleon also took steps to end corruption and inefficiency in government. He dismissed corrupt officials and, in order to provide the government with trained officials, set up **lycées**, or government-run public schools. These lycées were open to male students of all backgrounds. Graduates were appointed to public office on the basis of merit rather than family connections.

One area where Napoleon disregarded changes introduced by the Revolution was religion. Both the clergy and many peasants wanted to restore the position of the Church in France. Responding to their wishes, Napoleon signed a **concordat**, or agreement, with Pope Pius VII. This established a new relationship between church and state. The government recognized the influence of the Church, but rejected Church control in national affairs. The concordat gained Napoleon the support of the organized Church as well as the majority of the French people.

Napoleon thought that his greatest work was his comprehensive system of laws, known as the **Napoleonic Code**. This gave the country a uniform set of laws and eliminated many injustices. However, it actually limited liberty and promoted order and authority over individual rights. For example, freedom of speech and of the press, established during the Revolution, were restricted under the code. The code also restored slavery in the French colonies of the Caribbean.

230 Chapter 7

3 **DIFFERENTIATING INSTRUCTION: ENGLISH LEARNERS**

Understanding Idioms

Class Time 25 minutes

Task Identifying and understanding idioms in the text

Purpose To improve text comprehension

Instructions Explain that an idiom is a commonly used expression that has an intended meaning that is different from its literal meaning. For example, people often say "It's a piece of cake" when they mean "It's easy," or "She's a hothead" rather than "She is bad-tempered."

Challenge students to find three idioms on pages 230 and 231. Write these idioms on the board and explain what they mean in the context of the passage. An example is shown at right.

For more help with this section, refer students to the Reading Study Guide, available in English and Spanish.

Napoleon had to get the economy **on a solid footing.**	He had to make sure the economy was stable and would not fail.
Napoleon decided to **cut his losses** and sell the Louisiana Territory.	He wanted to end a losing situation.
Napoleon set up a **puppet government** in Switzerland.	He created a foreign government that pretended to be independent but did whatever he wanted it to do.

230 Chapter 7

1 History Makers

Short features in the Pupil's Edition are supplemented with additional information and suggested activities.

2 Resource References at Point of Use

Throughout the Teacher's Edition, references to the program resources at their point of use will help you plan and teach every section.

3 Differentiating Instruction

The *World History: Patterns of Interaction* Teacher's Edition provides several options at the bottom of pages. These options include activities for teaching struggling readers, English learners, and gifted and talented students.

MAIN IDEA

Analyzing Motives

B Why do you think Napoleon crowned himself emperor?

B. Answer to show that he was not under the control of anyone

Napoleon Crowned as Emperor In 1804, Napoleon decided to make himself emperor, and the French voters supported him. On December 2, 1804, dressed in a splendid robe of purple velvet, Napoleon walked down the long aisle of Notre Dame Cathedral in Paris. The pope waited for him with a glittering crown. As thousands watched, the new emperor took the crown from the pope and placed it on his own head. With this gesture, Napoleon signaled that he was more powerful than the Church, which had traditionally crowned the rulers of France. B

Napoleon Creates an Empire

Napoleon was not content simply to be master of France. He wanted to control the rest of Europe and to reassert French power in the Americas. He envisioned his western empire including Louisiana, Florida, French Guiana, and the French West Indies. He knew that the key to this area was the sugar-producing colony of Saint Domingue (now called Haiti) on the island of Hispaniola.

Loss of American Territories In 1789, when the ideas of the Revolution reached the planters in Saint Domingue, they demanded that the National Assembly give them the same privileges as the people of France. Eventually, enslaved Africans in the colony demanded their rights too—in other words, their freedom. A civil war erupted, and enslaved Africans under the leadership of Toussaint L'Ouverture seized control of the colony. In 1801, Napoleon decided to take back the colony and restore its productive sugar industry. However, the French forces were devastated by disease. And the rebels proved to be fierce fighters.

After the failure of the expedition to Saint Domingue, Napoleon decided to cut his losses in the Americas. He offered to sell all of the Louisiana Territory to the United States, and in 1803 President Jefferson's administration agreed to purchase the land for $15 million. Napoleon saw a twofold benefit to the sale. First, he would gain money to finance operations in Europe. Second, he would punish the British. "The sale assures forever the power of the United States," he observed, "and I have given England a rival who, sooner or later, will humble her pride." C

MAIN IDEA

Recognizing Effects

C What effects did Napoleon intend the sale of Louisiana to have on France? on the United States? on Britain?

C. Answer Napoleon hoped to obtain the money he needed to continue his conquest of Europe and to increase the power of the United States in order to punish Britain.

▼ This painting by Jacques Louis David shows Napoleon in a heroic pose.

Conquering Europe Having abandoned his imperial ambitions in the New World, Napoleon turned his attention to Europe. He had already annexed the Austrian Netherlands and parts of Italy to France and set up a puppet government in Switzerland. Now he looked to expand his influence further. Fearful of his ambitions, the British persuaded Russia, Austria, and Sweden to join them against France.

Napoleon met this challenge with his usual boldness. In a series of brilliant battles, he crushed the opposition. (See the map on page 232.) The commanders of the enemy armies could never predict his next move and often took heavy losses. After the Battle of Austerlitz in 1805, Napoleon issued a proclamation expressing his pride in his troops:

PRIMARY SOURCE

> Soldiers! I am pleased with you. On the day of Austerlitz, you justified everything that I was expecting of [you]. . . . In less than four hours, an army of 100,000 men, commanded by the emperors of Russia and Austria, was cut up and dispersed. . . . 120 pieces of artillery, 20 generals, and more than 30,000 men taken prisoner—such are the results of this day which will forever be famous. . . . And it will be enough for you to say, "I was at Austerlitz," to hear the reply: "There is a brave man!"
>
> **NAPOLEON**, quoted in *Napoleon* by André Castelot

CHAPTER 7 • Section 3

Napoleon Creates an Empire

Critical Thinking 4

- How did L'Ouverture's revolution benefit the United States? *(It prompted Napoleon to sell the Louisiana Territory to the United States.)*
- How does the Battle of Trafalgar show the importance of naval power? *(Britain's victory protected it from invasion.)*
- How long did Napoleon's empire remain at its peak? *(five years)*
- How did Napoleon's belief in equal opportunity conflict with his method of selecting leaders for puppet governments? *(He often chose family members.)*

In-Depth Resources: Unit 2

- Primary Source: Napoleon's Proclamation at Austerlitz, p. 60

More About . . . 5

Empires Face Disease

Napoleon's imperial aspirations were limited by a tiny foe: germs. The French expedition to Saint Domingue suffered heavy losses from yellow fever. During the campaign in Russia in 1812, typhus fever infected over 80,000 soldiers. Disease has had an impact on other empires as well. Malaria weakened the Roman Empire. Smallpox and other diseases killed millions of native people in the Americas, Siberia, and Australia, weakening them in the face of European expansion. Until yellow fever was controlled, building a canal through Panama was nearly impossible.

DIFFERENTIATING INSTRUCTION: STRUGGLING READERS

Examining a Primary Source

Class Time 25 minutes

Task Summarizing and analyzing part of a proclamation by Napoleon

Purpose To improve understanding of a primary source and discuss motivations of an important leader

Instructions Have pairs of students reread the primary source on this page and write a summary of it in their own words. *(Possible Answer: I am proud of you, soldiers. You won an important battle. Your performance was so outstanding that everyone will remember you.)* Share summaries to be sure that students understand the primary source. Then create a chart on the chalkboard and have the class answer the questions. A sample is shown here.

Who?	Napoleon Bonaparte
What?	proclamation to soldiers about the Battle of Austerlitz
Where?	Austerlitz was in the Austrian Empire.
When?	1805
Why?	to tell the soldiers of his pride; to brag about the victory; to motivate the troops to keep fighting

Teacher's Edition **231**

Teacher's Edition notes also include:

- Assessment Suggestions
- Time Line Discussions
- Recommendations for books, videos, and software
- Motivation Activities

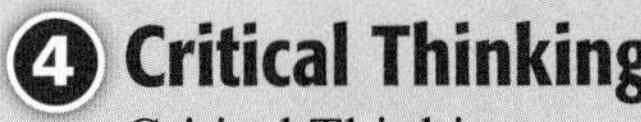

4 Critical Thinking

Critical Thinking questions focus on the main points students need to understand in order to meet specific section objectives.

5 More About . . .

These terrific nuggets of information occur often to supplement the text.

Connections to Other Disciplines

In addition to suggestions for differentiating instruction, the bottom section of the Teacher's Edition offers activities that link to other disciplines, including math, science, and language arts.

Standards-Based Assessment

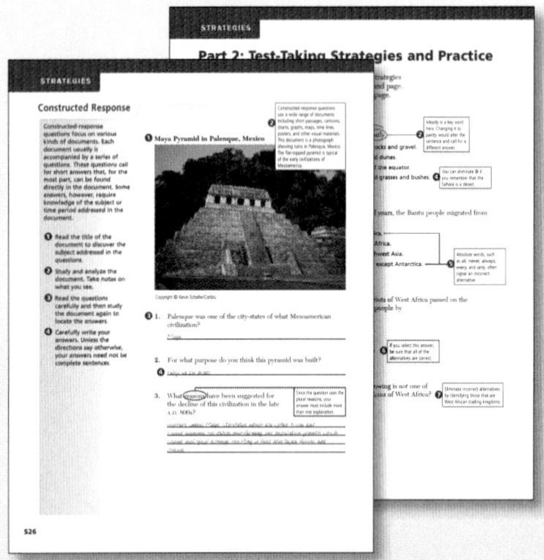

Strategies for Taking Tests
This innovative section of the *Pupil's Edition* includes strategies for answering multiple-choice, constructed-response, extended-response, and document-based questions, and guidelines for analyzing primary and secondary sources.

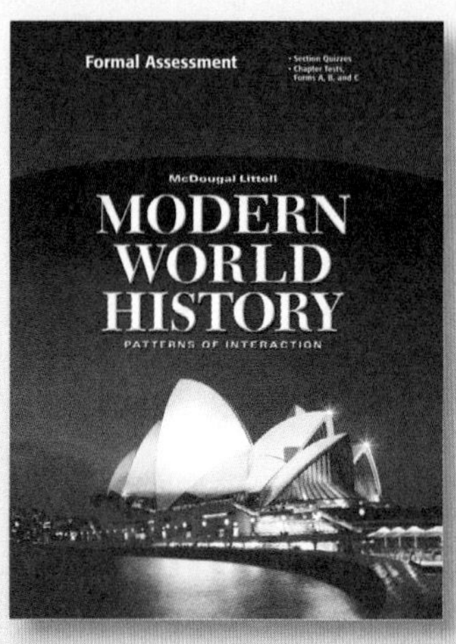

Formal Assessment
The formal assessment book includes section quizzes and three levels of chapter tests.

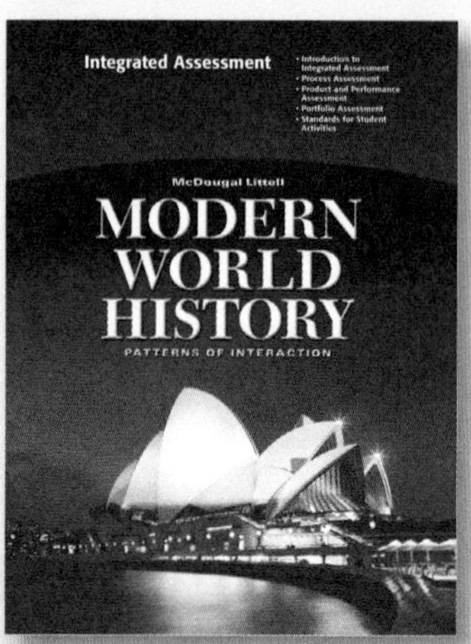

Integrated Assessment
This booklet includes rubrics for grading alternative assessments and portfolios.

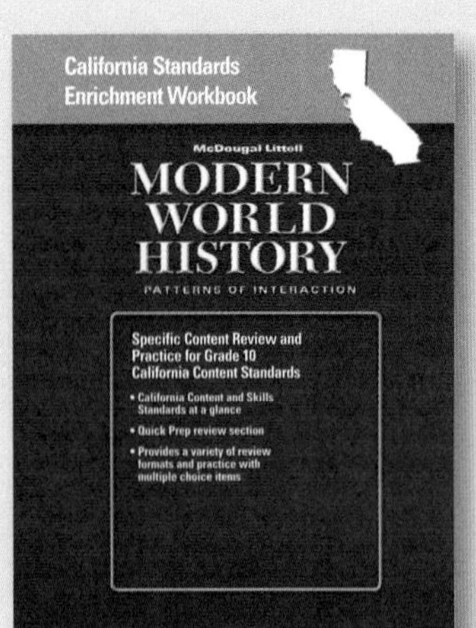

California Standards Enrichment Workbook
This ancillary provides a content review of the California History–Social Science standards. The book includes a pre-test, content review and practice items, and a post-test to measure student improvement.

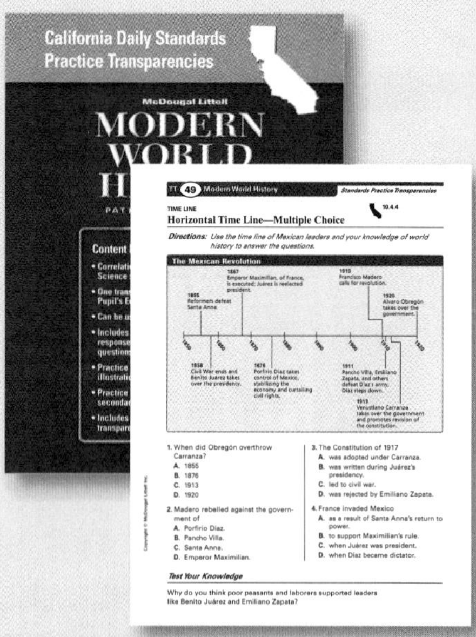

California Daily Standards Practice Transparencies
This booklet includes one transparency for each section of the textbook that covers the content and familiarizes students with a variety of testing items. Each transparency is correlated to the California standards.

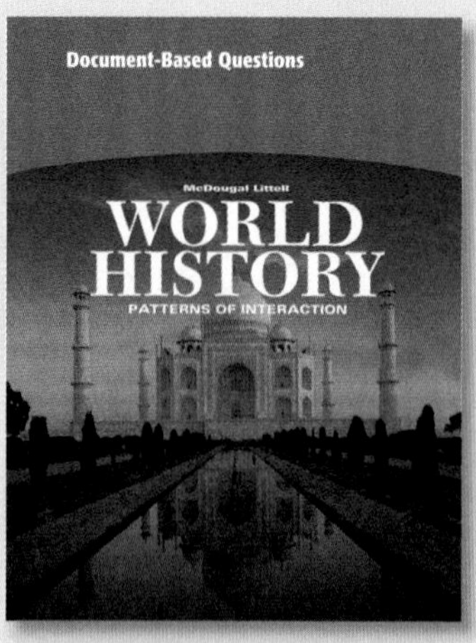

Document-Based Questions
This set of document-based, constructed-response, and essay questions allows students to practice test-taking strategies.

Edusoft®
easyGrader

With this high-speed, low-cost testing system, teachers can

- print social studies tests correlated to the California standards
- build answer sheets that avoid the use of scan cards
- score tests automatically using a standard, inexpensive scanner
- generate individual or group reports to help identify each student's needs
- customize results by state standard and identify at-risk students and standards immediately
- use McDougal Littell resources to reteach concepts
- develop individual student instructional plans

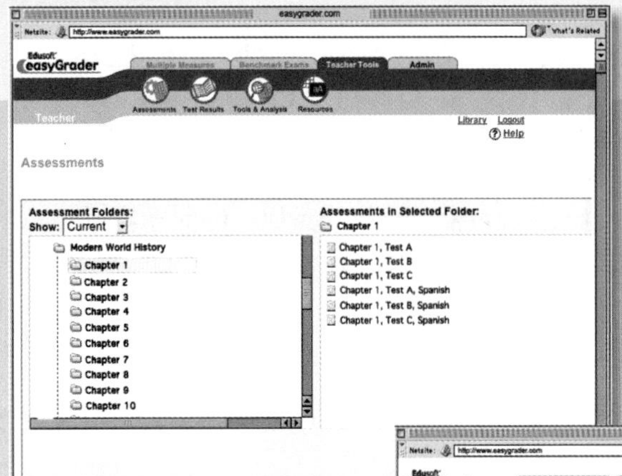

Choose a preloaded social studies test. Print the test and answer sheet on plain paper. After students take the test, use Edusoft's plain paper scanning technology to score 20 tests per minute.

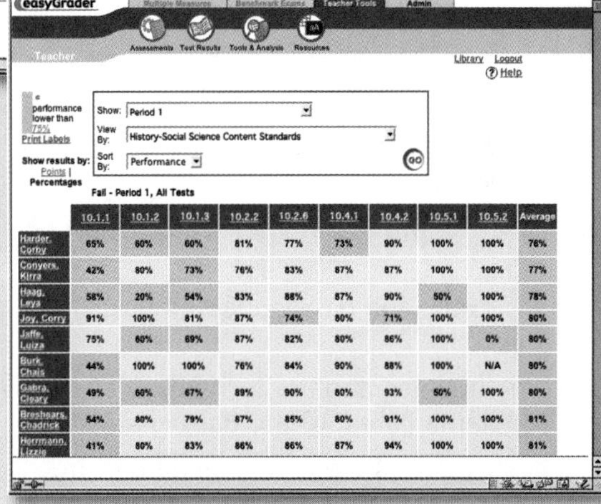

	10.1.1	10.1.2	10.1.3	10.2.2	10.2.6	10.4.1	10.4.2	10.5.1	10.5.2	Average
Harder, Corby	65%	60%	60%	81%	77%	73%	90%	100%	100%	76%
Conyers, Kirra	42%	80%	73%	76%	83%	87%	87%	100%	100%	77%
Haag, Leya	58%	20%	54%	83%	88%	87%	90%	50%	100%	78%
Joy, Corry	91%	100%	81%	87%	74%	80%	71%	100%	100%	80%
Jaffe, Luiza	75%	60%	69%	87%	82%	80%	86%	100%	0%	80%
Burk, Chais	44%	100%	100%	76%	84%	90%	88%	100%	N/A	80%
Gabra, Cleary	49%	60%	67%	89%	90%	80%	93%	50%	100%	80%
Breshears, Chadrick	54%	80%	79%	87%	85%	80%	91%	100%	100%	81%
Herrmann, Lizzie	41%	80%	83%	86%	86%	87%	94%	100%	100%	81%

Test results appear within minutes on the EasyGrader Web site and show how well students performed within each state standard. Access the Instructional Tool to create a reteaching package of worksheets and activities.

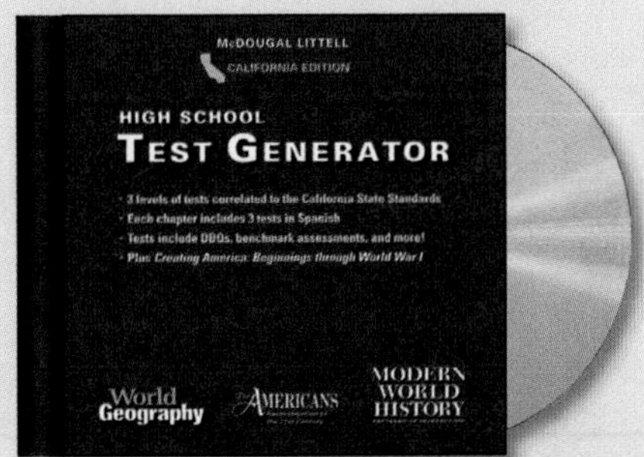

California Test Generator CD-ROM
Pre-made, customizable tests with three levels of questions (including document-based questions) are correlated to California state standards. Chapter tests are also available in Spanish. **Standards-Based Benchmark Tests** assess each subpoint in the California History-Social Science Standards for Grade 10.

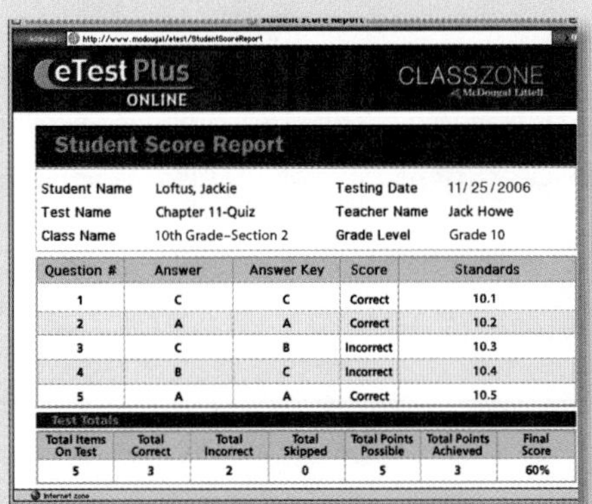

Question #	Answer	Answer Key	Score	Standards
1	C	C	Correct	10.1
2	A	A	Correct	10.2
3	C	B	Incorrect	10.3
4	B	C	Incorrect	10.4
5	A	A	Correct	10.5

Test Totals

Total Items On Test	Total Correct	Total Incorrect	Total Skipped	Total Points Possible	Total Points Achieved	Final Score
5	3	2	0	5	3	60%

eTest Plus Online
This customizable assessment tool allows teachers to publish tests from the *Test Generator*. Tests are administered and graded online. Individual and group score reports can be viewed, printed, and correlated to national and state standards.

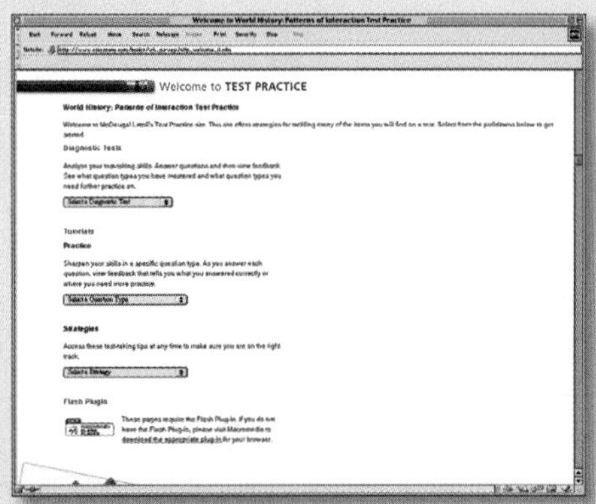

California Online Test Practice
Online student test practice can be accessed through the *ClassZone* Web site. The test practice includes test-taking tips, diagnostic tests, skill-based tutorials, and skills and strategies help.

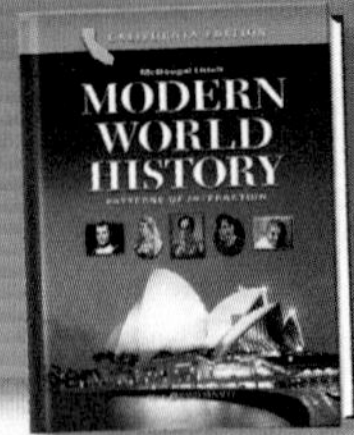

Complete Instructional Support

The Teacher's Resource Package for *Modern World History: Patterns of Interaction* gives California teachers resource materials developed especially for them—correlated to the California standards. The five products described below make it possible to plan each day's lesson around coverage of the social studies standards, and to teach and reteach those standards in the classroom every day.

Plan

California Standards Planner and Lesson Plans

- Provides correlations to California History–Social Science Standards
- Gives a Day-by-Day Planner for teaching all state standards
- Features flexible and detailed lesson plans for every unit
- Facilitates the integration of technology and other supplemental tools into daily lessons
- Enhances teaching, reteaching, tailored instruction, and assessment

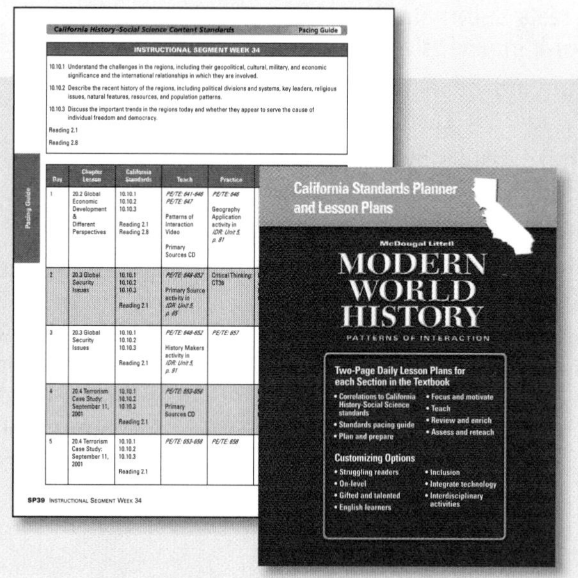

Teach/Reteach

California Standards Enrichment Workbook

- Reinforces learning of the California History–Social Science Standards
- Includes a unit-by-unit listing of the standards covered
- Provides a Pre-Test in standardized test format on standards covered
- Offers content review with graphic organizers and practice items for reteaching
- Ends with a Post-Test of the standards that provides a measure of student improvement

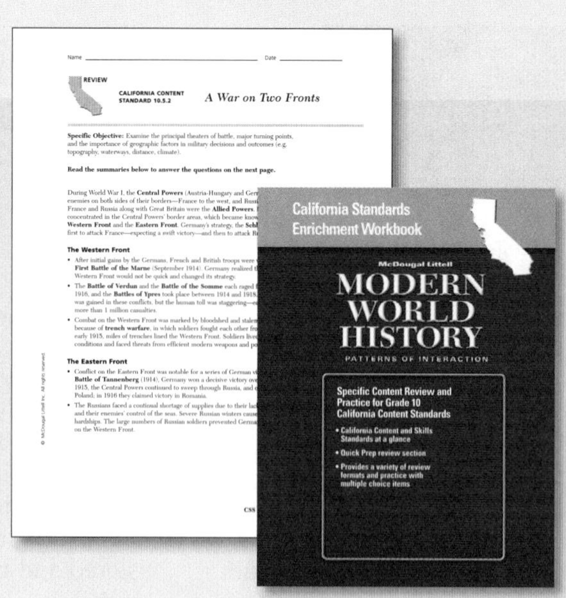

Teach/Reteach

California Daily Standards Practice Transparencies

- Provides one transparency per section
- Correlates transparencies with California standards
- Includes multiple choice and other item formats
- Uses maps, charts, graphs, and time lines
- Uses primary sources and secondary sources

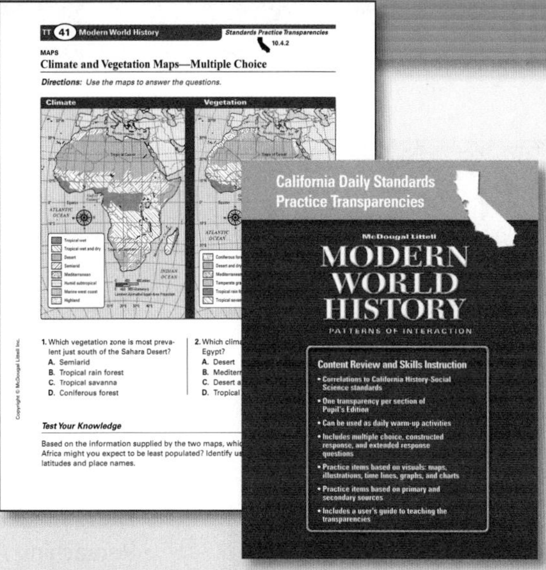

California Reading Toolkit for Social Studies

- Explains how to teach 30 reading strategies
- Correlates section-level lesson plans to California standards
- Includes overhead transparencies for each strategy
- Includes articles by experts on teaching reading skills and building vocabulary in the social studies classroom

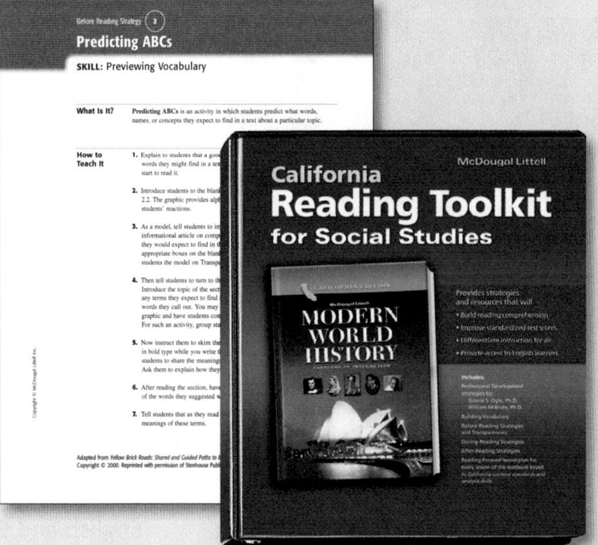

California Modified Lesson Plans for English Learners

- Provides 41 strategies to help students learning English
- Correlates section-level lesson plans to California standards
- Provides research support for teaching English learners in the social studies classroom

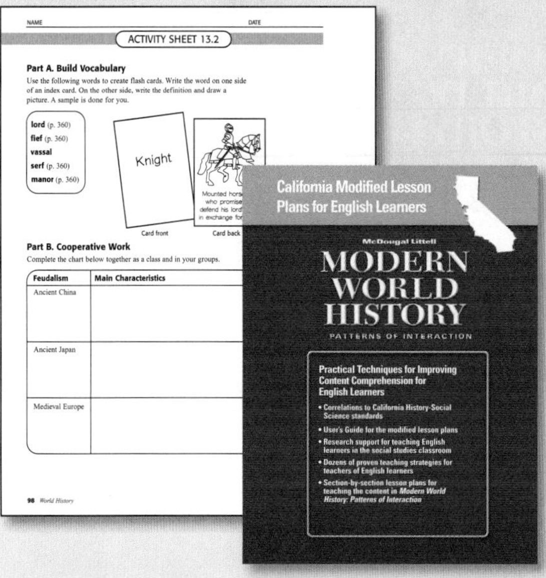

Complete Instructional Support

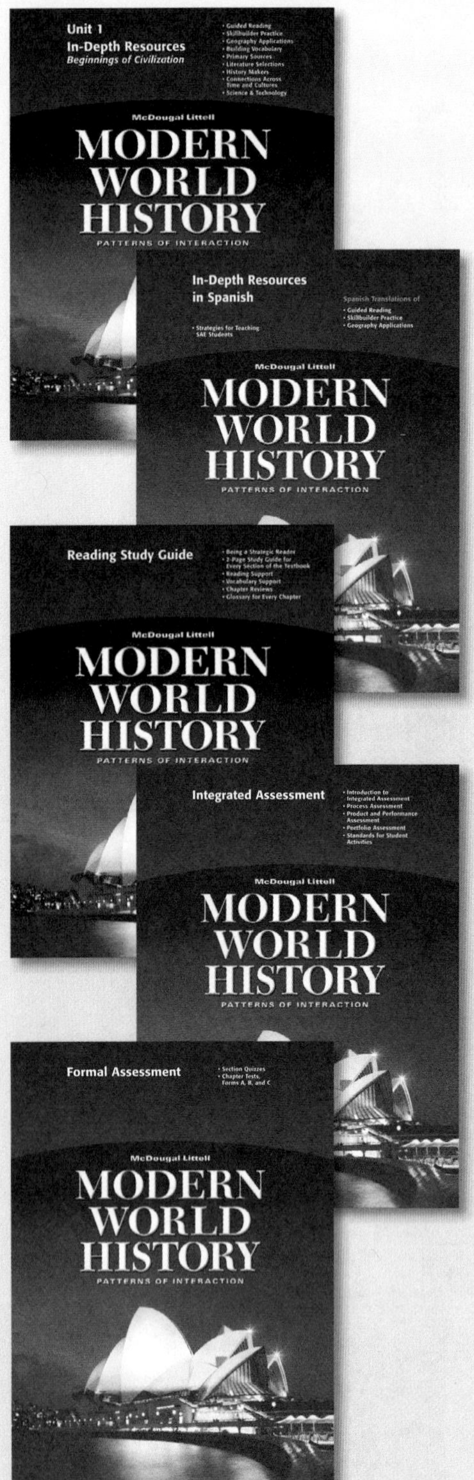

In-Depth Unit Resources
Includes one booklet for each unit, organized by chapter and section, featuring:

- Guided Reading
- Skillbuilder Practice
- Geography Applications
- Building Vocabulary
- Primary Sources
- Literature Selections
- History Makers
- Reteaching Activities
- Connections Across Time and Cultures
- Science & Technology

In-Depth Resources in Spanish
Provides Spanish translations of selected *In-Depth Resources* and strategies for teaching EL students.

Block Schedule Pacing Guide
Includes a pacing guide, chapter teaching models, organization charts, and suggestions for addressing multiple learning styles.

Reading Study Guide Workbook
Provides chapter summaries and reading comprehension questions to support struggling readers. (English and Spanish)

Chapters in Brief: Chapter Summaries
Offers teaching flexibility and opportunities for students to focus their reading and review key ideas from each chapter. (English and Spanish)

Geography Skills and Outline Maps
Provides blackline masters for skills development.

Multi-Language Glossary of Social Studies Terms
Includes key terms from the text and other commonly-used social studies terms defined in English with Spanish, Chinese, Vietnamese, Khmer, Laotian, Portuguese, Russian, Arabic, and Haitian Creole translations.

Document-Based Questions
Provides a set of document-based, constructed-response, and multiple-choice questions for each chapter, allowing students to practice test-taking strategies.

Formal Assessment
Includes section quizzes and three levels of tests, with maps.

Integrated Assessment
Includes cooperative learning, role-playing, and rubrics for alternative lesson support.

Case Studies
Provides in-depth explorations of contemporary issues.

Early African History: To 1500
Provides additional perspective on the history of Africa and Africans in the premodern era.

World History Workbook
Features note-taking strategies for enhancing reading comprehension.

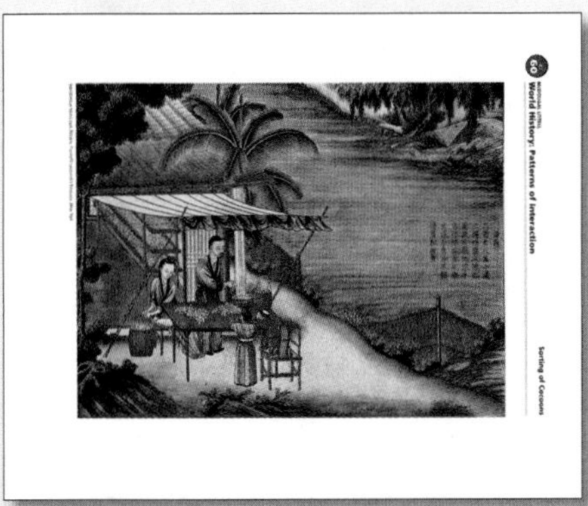

World Art and Cultures Transparencies
Integrates fine art, photographs, and other historical artifacts from each chapter.

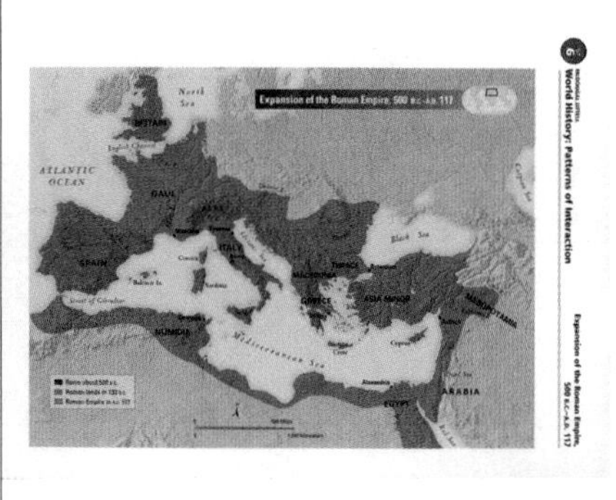

Geography Transparencies
Includes maps to provide additional background and support.

Critical Thinking Transparencies
Provides charts, graphic organizers, and visual summaries for each chapter.

Martin Luther King Jr.: His Life & Contributions
Provides a biography of civil rights leader Martin Luther King, Jr., with historical, cultural, and economic contexts for his life and work. Includes an illustrated time line, as well as five detailed lesson plans for each grade, from Grade Six through Grade Eleven. Each lesson plan explicitly connects King to historical topics required by California History-Social Science Content Standards.

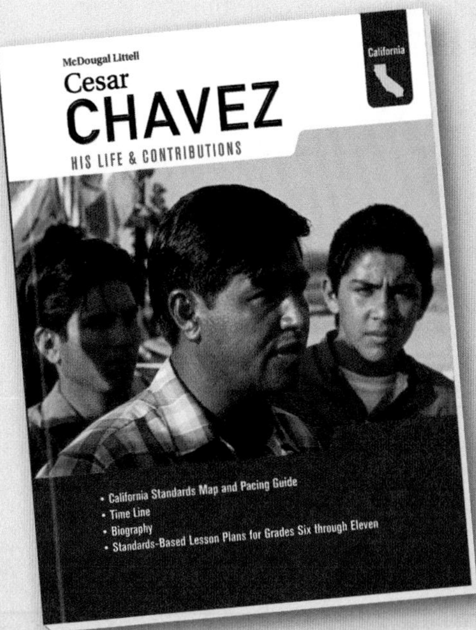

Cesar Chavez: His Life & Contributions
Provi des a biography of the labor leader Cesar Chavez, with historical, cultural, and economic contexts for his life and work. Includes an illustrated time line, as well as five lesson plans for each grade, from Grade Six through Grade Eleven. Each lesson plan explicitly connects Chavez's contributions to historical topics required by California History-Social Science Content Standards.

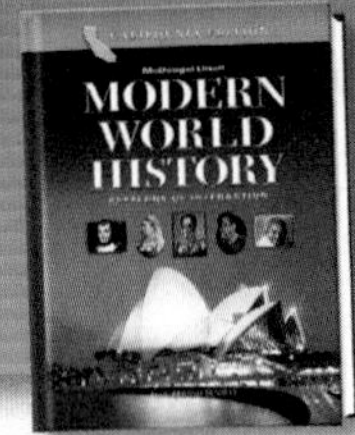

Integrated Technology

The technology resources that accompany *Modern World History* enhance and extend the content beyond the Pupil's Edition. Each of the products shown here supports the teaching of the California standards, from the standards references in the *eEdition CD-ROM* to the Standards-Based Benchmark Tests on the *California Test Generator CD-ROM.* And the new EasyGrader conveniently scores standards-based tests and generates score reports—a great tool to help teachers monitor student peformance.

Plan

California EasyPlanner CD-ROM

- Customize lesson plans using all teacher resources.
- Plan a lesson, or plan the whole year.
- Access, view, and print all teacher resources.
- Print plans in daily, weekly, or monthly views.
- Track state standards correlated to each lesson.

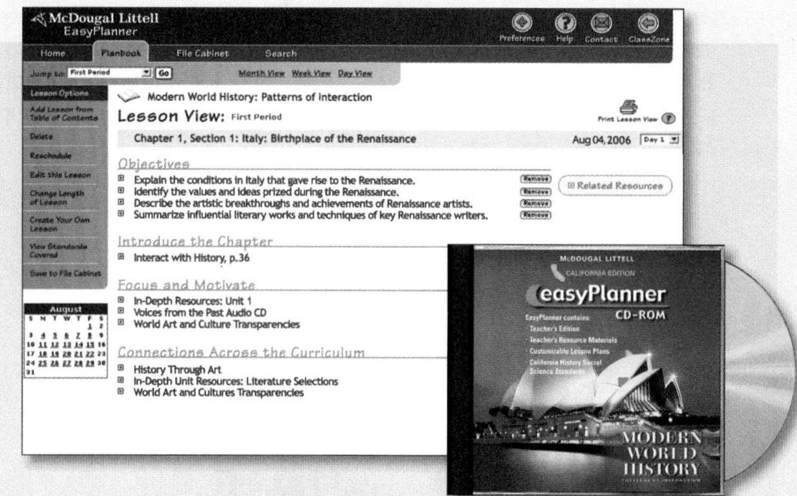

Teach

California eEdition CD-ROM

- Access all features of the student textbook.
- Engage learning with animated maps and infographics.
- Access activities, research links, and current events through ClassZone.
- Listen to the audio stories, *Voices From the Past.*

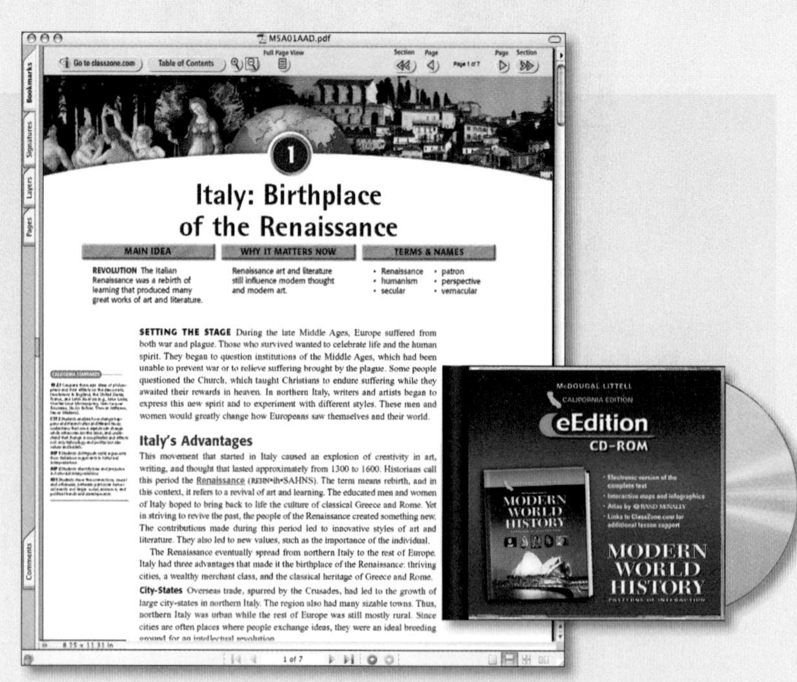

Assess

Edusoft EasyGrader

- Access tests that have been aligned to California State Standards.
- Print tests and answer keys on plain paper.
- Score tests quickly using a standard scanner.
- Read test results within minutes by individual test or by standards.
- Identify at-risk students and standards.
- Generate a customized package of reteaching materials that are aligned to test results.
- Track performance over time to measure and monitor improvement.

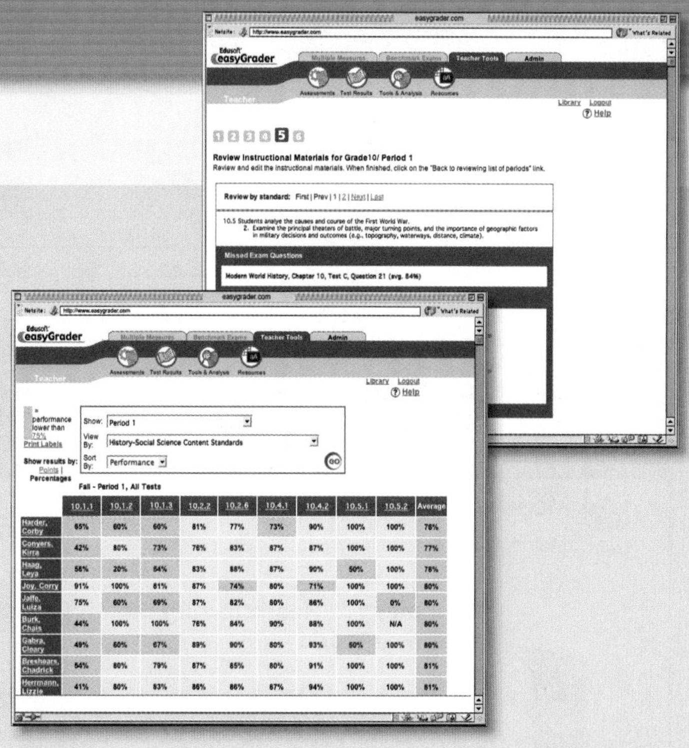

California Test Generator CD-ROM
with Standards-Based Benchmark Tests

- Three levels of tests are correlated to the California State Standards.
- Each chapter includes three tests in Spanish.
- Tests include DBQs, constructed-response, and extended-response questions.
- Each unit has Standards-Based Benchmark Tests to assess each subpoint in the California History–Social Science Standards for Grade 10.

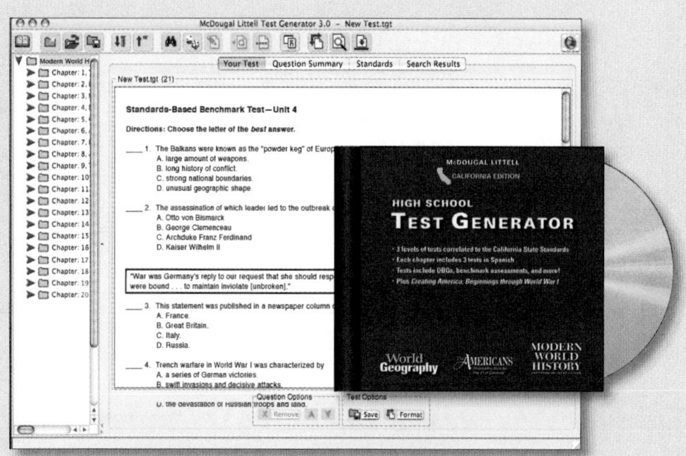

California Online Test Practice

- Take diagnostic tests.
- Get skill-based tutorials.
- Learn test-taking strategies.
- Tailored to California state standards.
- Easy access through ClassZone.com.

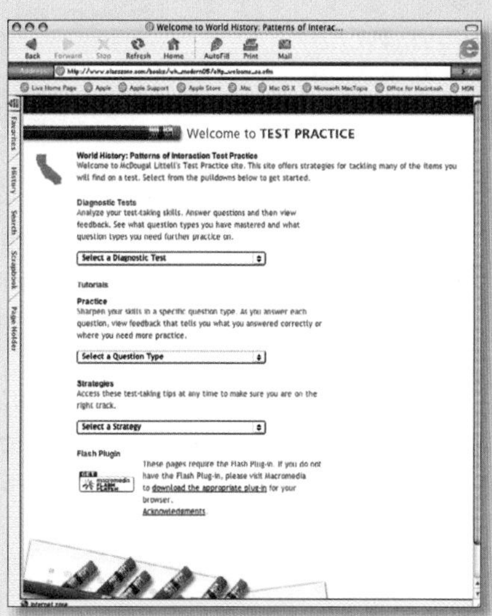

CLASSZONE.COM

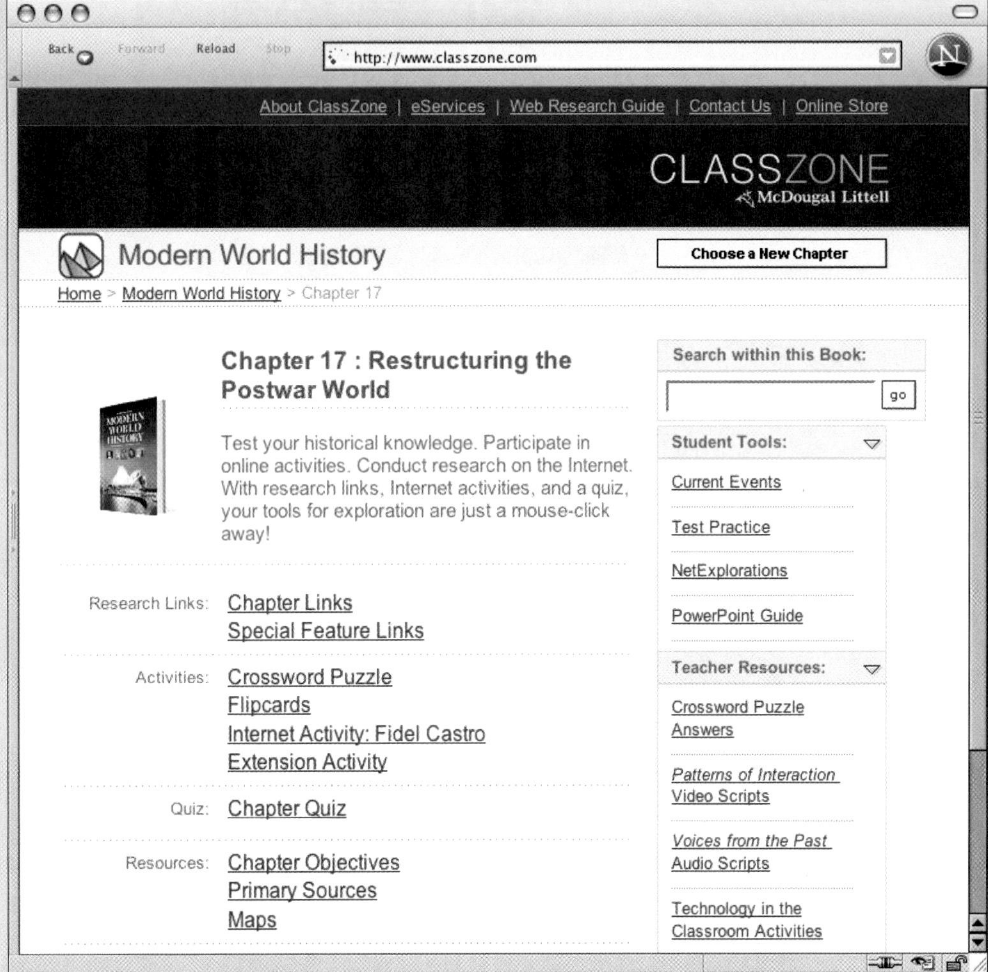

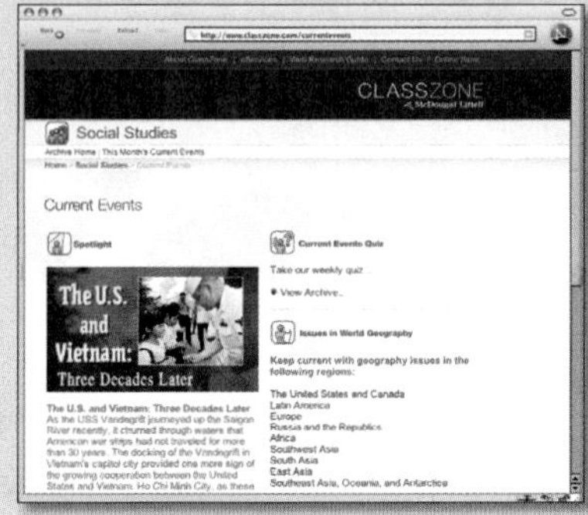

Current Events
Create real-world connections with links to current events.

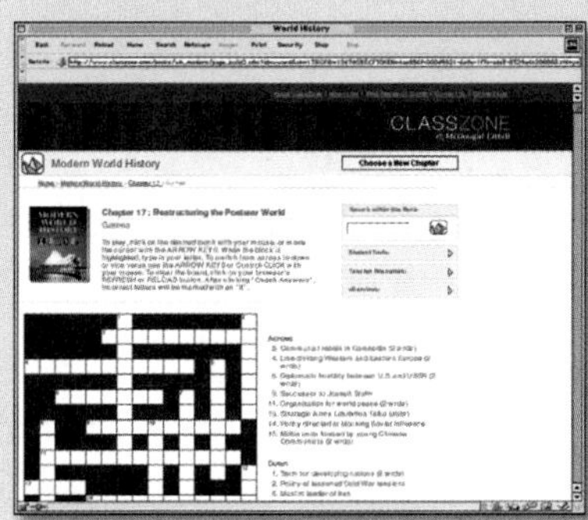

Activities
Encourage student interactivity through online activities.

ClassZone

Your online guide to *Modern World History: Patterns of Interaction* offers

- Research Links
- Internet Activities
- Current Events
- Crossword Puzzles
- Flipcards
- Quizzes
- Primary Sources
- Maps
- Test Practice

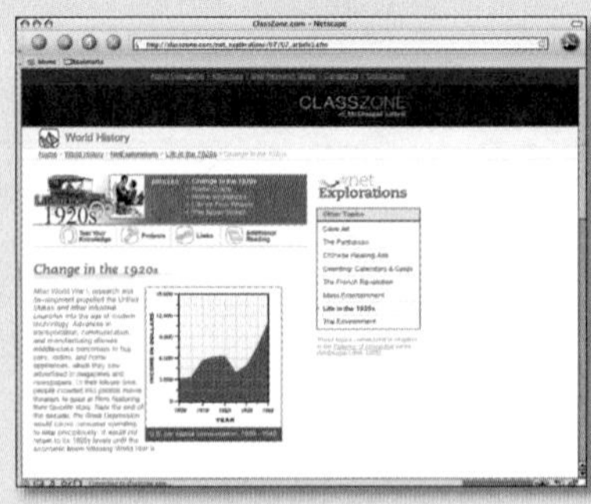

Net Explorations
Take an in-depth look at world history topics and expand research opportunities.

Quizzes
Check students' history knowledge with interactive quizzes.

eEdition Plus Online
The online edition of the textbook features animated maps and infographics, and the capability to post assignments and announcements through an online message center.

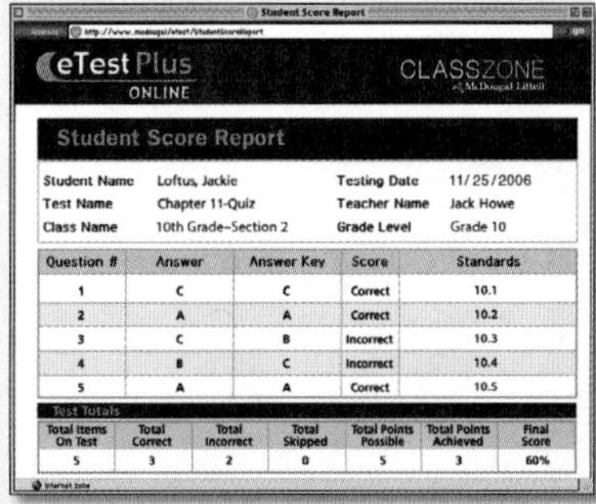

Student Score Report

Student Name	Loftus, Jackie	Testing Date	11/25/2006
Test Name	Chapter 11-Quiz	Teacher Name	Jack Howe
Class Name	10th Grade–Section 2	Grade Level	Grade 10

Question #	Answer	Answer Key	Score	Standards
1	C	C	Correct	10.1
2	A	A	Correct	10.2
3	C	B	Incorrect	10.3
4	B	C	Incorrect	10.4
5	A	A	Correct	10.5

Test Totals

Total Items On Test	Total Correct	Total Incorrect	Total Skipped	Total Points Possible	Total Points Achieved	Final Score
5	3	2	0	5	3	60%

eTest Plus Online
Customizable assessment tool allows teachers to publish tests from the *Test Generator*. Students take the tests online, with results graded automatically. Individual and group score reports can be viewed, printed, and correlated to state and national standards.

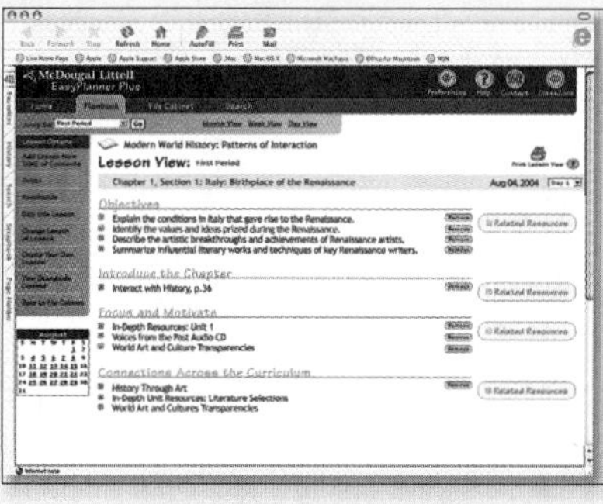

EasyPlanner Plus Online
This online planning tool allows teachers to customize lesson plans and track state standards correlated to each lesson. All teacher resources, plus PDF files of the Teacher's Edition pages, are available to view and print.

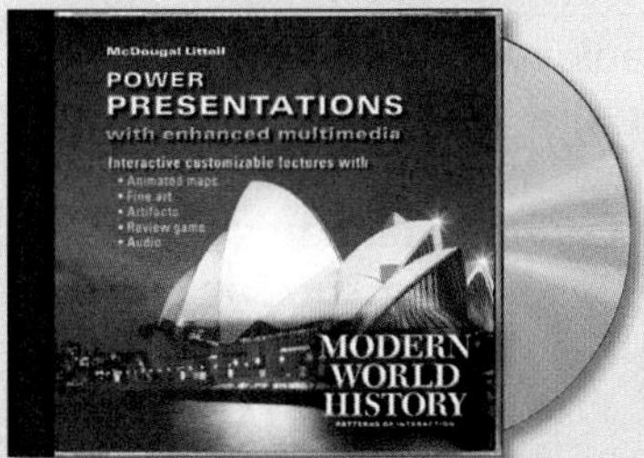

Power Presentations CD-ROM
This multimedia presentation tool augments lectures and allows teachers to create presentations. Detailed lecture notes are enhanced by maps, charts, fine art, artifacts, and an interactive review game.

The World's Music Audio CD
A variety of recordings gives students the opportunity to hear music from different cultures.

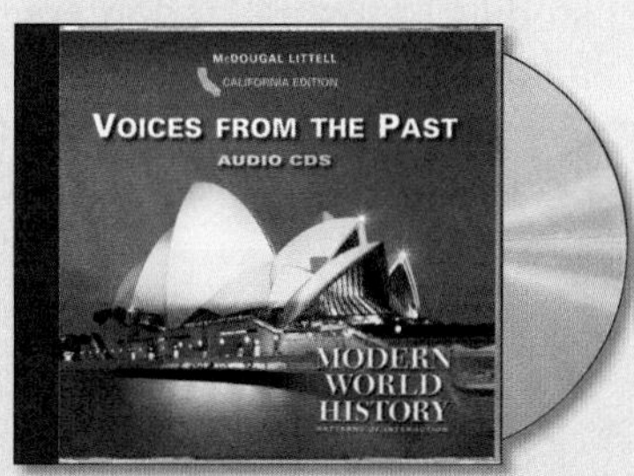

Voices From the Past Audio CDs
Engaging, high-interest stories on audio CD introduce each chapter of the Pupil's Edition.

Patterns of Interaction Video Series
These videos relate to the Global Impact features in the text and show students how cultural interactions have shaped our world.

Volume 1

Building Empires:
The Rise of the Persians and the Inca
Trade Connects the World:
Silk Roads and the Pacific Rim

Volume 2

The Spread of Epidemic Disease:
Bubonic Plague and Smallpox
The Geography of Food:
The Impact of Potatoes and Sugar

Volume 3

Struggling Toward Democracy:
Revolutions in Latin America and South Africa
Technology Transforms an Age:
The Industrial and Electronic Revolutions

Volume 4

Arming for War:
Modern and Medieval Weapons
Cultural Crossroads:
The United States and the World

Differentiated Instruction

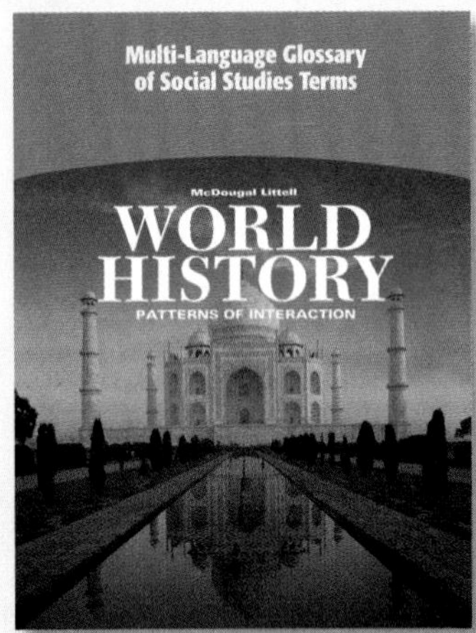

Multi-Language Glossary of Social Studies Terms
This valuable glossary includes key terms from the text and other commonly-used social studies terms defined in English with Spanish, Chinese, Vietnamese, Khmer, Laotian, Portuguese, Russian, Arabic, and Haitian Creole translations.

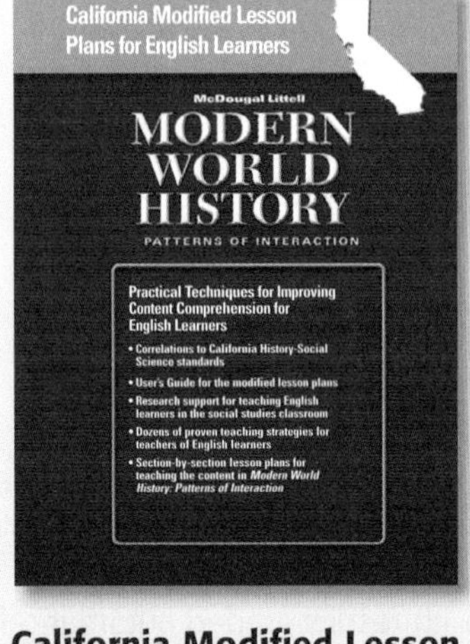

California Modified Lesson Plans for English Learners
Resourceful tips on adapting lessons and activities accompany lesson-by-lesson plans for teaching the content of *Modern World History*. Proven strategies for teaching English learners are included with clear explanations of how they should be applied. Correlated to California History–Social Science Content Standards and English Language Development/English Language Arts Standards.

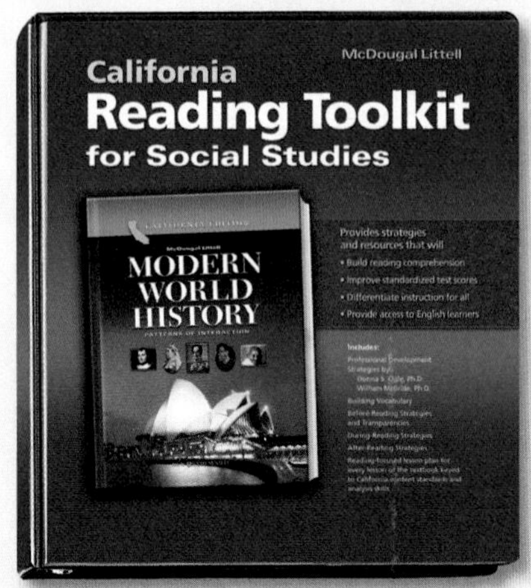

California Reading Toolkit for Social Studies
This classroom-tested reading support guide provides specific lesson plans correlated to before-, during-, and after-reading strategies, overhead transparencies, and vocabulary practice. Correlated to California History–Social Science Content Standards and English Language Development/English Language Arts Standards.

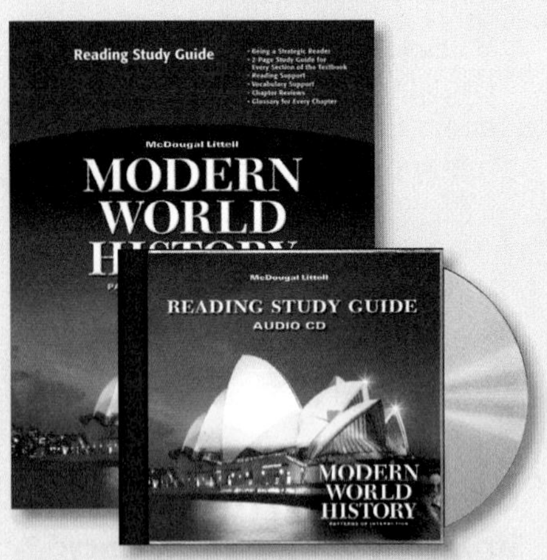

Reading Study Guide
Main idea questions, vocabulary activities, and section summaries written below grade level provide support for less-proficient readers. Also available in Spanish.

Reading Study Guide Audio CDs
Reading Study Guide section summaries on audio CD support struggling readers. Also available in Spanish.

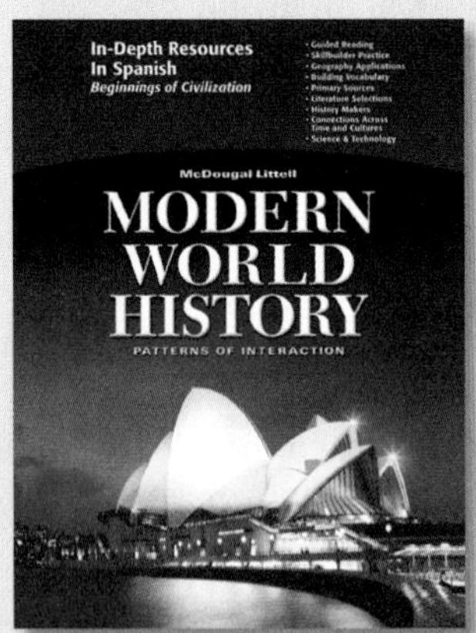

In-Depth Resources in Spanish
Spanish translations of selected *In-Depth Resources* are augmented with focused strategies for teaching English learners.

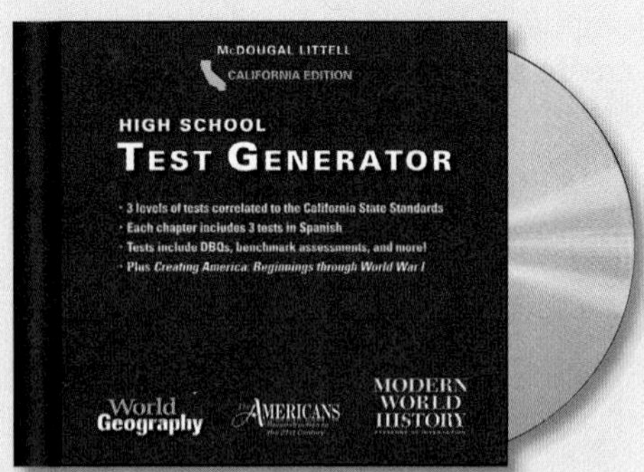

California Test Generator CD-ROM
Pre-made, customizable tests with three levels of questions translated into Spanish.

Teaching English Learners

NANCY SIDDENS

Consulting Editor, English for Speakers of Other Languages
McDougal Littell

McDougal Littell recognizes the challenges that English learners and their teachers face in the mainstream classroom. The trend to use English instruction in content classes (with less support in students' primary languages) and the federal legislation (No Child Left Behind) requiring instruction in content simultaneously with instruction in English, have driven the need for comprehensive, flexible support materials for teaching in English to English learners.

McDougal Littell *Modern World History: Patterns of Interaction* provides a wide range of support for these students and their teachers. This support gives teachers the tools needed to employ research-based principles for teaching standards-based curriculum to English learners while they learn the English language in meaningful historical contexts.

Research on facilitating the learning of content by students acquiring English has determined that effective instruction is built on these three principles:

- **Increase comprehension**
- **Enhance student interaction**
- **Improve thinking and study skills**

These principles, identified as effective through research by the Center for Applied Linguistics (Jameson), have guided McDougal Littell's approach to developing materials for teaching social studies and language to English learners.

Principle 1: Increase comprehension

Providing understandable information to the English learner is crucial for accessing both language and content. *Modern World History: Patterns of Interaction* provides materials that enable teachers to employ practical strategies for increasing student comprehension. Verbal as well as nonverbal support is provided to make history more accessible to the English learner. The role of visual and experiential clues is especially important to beginning and intermediate language learners. Examples of nonverbal instruction include:

- A strong visual component in the Pupil's Edition, including vivid images, large maps, a variety of graphic organizers, charts, graphs, and timelines.
- Complete audiovisual support through a Patterns of Interaction video for each unit, audio chapter summaries, and extensive online services.
- A transparency program that includes *Geography Transparencies, Critical Thinking Transparencies,* and *World Art and Cultures Transparencies.*

Examples of verbal and print support include:

- The *Reading Study Guide* in both English and Spanish, chapter summaries written below grade level, accompanied by comprehension questions.
- The *Multi-Language Glossary of Social Studies Terms*, a compilation of translations of the key terms from the Pupil's Edition in nine languages.
- *In-Depth Resources in Spanish*, Spanish translations of selected ancillary support pages.

Principle 2: Enhance student interaction

Research shows that language is learned through communication with others—negotiating meaning to accomplish real purposes (Long and Porter). Participants in a discussion restate, question, explain, and clarify in order to come to a common understanding. This process helps students learn social studies as well as language. *Modern World History: Patterns of Interaction*—and *Modified Lesson Plans for English Learners,* which accompanies it—provide opportunities to increase interaction in the classroom in a variety of ways, including:

- Pair activities, in which students work in pairs to compare their own experiences relating to a particular lesson or topic
- Group work such as "jigsaw" reading, in which each student takes on responsibility for presenting one part of a lesson to a small group
- Class activities such as debates, unit projects, or games
- Opportunities for family involvement

Principle 3: Improve thinking and study skills

Explicit teaching of academic skills helps develop thinking skills and "thinking language" for English learners (Chamot and O'Malley). *Modern World History: Patterns of Interaction* provides materials that focus instruction on performing higher-order thinking tasks, asking critical-thinking questions, assessing learning in a manner and language consistent with instruction, and reinforcing study and test-taking skills.

In the Pupil's Edition of *Modern World History: Patterns of Interaction*, support for developing thinking and study skills includes:

- An emphasis on the main idea of each section before reading begins.
- Graphic organizers for notetaking practice in each section.
- Highlighted vocabulary terms.
- Main Idea comprehension questions that reinforce important content.
- Skillbuilder questions accompanying large visuals such as maps and charts.
- Section and chapter assessments that provide leveled questions from Main Idea to Critical Thinking.
- A skills strand woven throughout the section and chapter assessments and reinforced in the Skillbuilder Handbook.
- Test practice opportunities such as the 32-page "Strategies for Taking Tests" in the front of the book and Standards-Based Assessment practice in the chapter assessments.

The Teacher's Edition and ancillaries for *Modern World History: Patterns of Interaction* provide additional support for developing students' skills through activities for differentiated instruction and Guided Reading and Skillbuilder Practice pages.

Modern World History: Patterns of Interaction provides teachers with the comprehensive support they need for teaching English learners. The program provides verbal and nonverbal support to increase understanding, promotes increased interaction and opportunities for communication, and encourages the development of academic thinking and study skills. Each of these areas has been identified, through research, as crucial for promoting the success of the English learner in acquiring content knowledge as well as language.

For more information:

Chamot, A.U. and O'Malley, J.M. (1994). *The CALLA Handbook: Implementing the Cognitive Academic Language Learning Approach.* Addison-Wesley: Reading, MA.

Jameson, J. (1998). "Three Principles for Success: English Language Learners in Mainstream Content Classes," *From Theory to Practice* 6, Center for Applied Linguistics: Region XIV Comprehensive Center.

Long, M. and Porter, P.A. (1985). "Group Work, Interlanguage Talk, and Second Language Acquisition," in *TESOL Quarterly* 19: 207–227.

Helping Students Read History

DONNA M. OGLE

Professor, Reading and Language, National-Louis University, Evanston, Illinois; Past-President, International Reading Association

Supporting Readers

World History: Patterns of Interaction uses many strategies to help students become active and engaged readers.

Various Learning Styles *Modern World History* addresses various learning styles by posing problems, providing graphic organizers to help students take notes, asking thought-provoking questions for discussion, and including a variety of activities.

Visual Information In *Modern World History,* photos and artifacts create a context for new ideas; maps help readers associate ideas. In addition, charts of ideas and events summarize and clarify information. A visual summary at the end of each chapter provides another way of remembering ideas and events.

Inner-Column Notes Inner-column notes in *Modern World History* help students read the text. Vocabulary notes explain and define words.

Personal Connections Personal stories and human connections can help to bring a subject such as history alive. *Modern World History* uses personal voices throughout to support student learning.

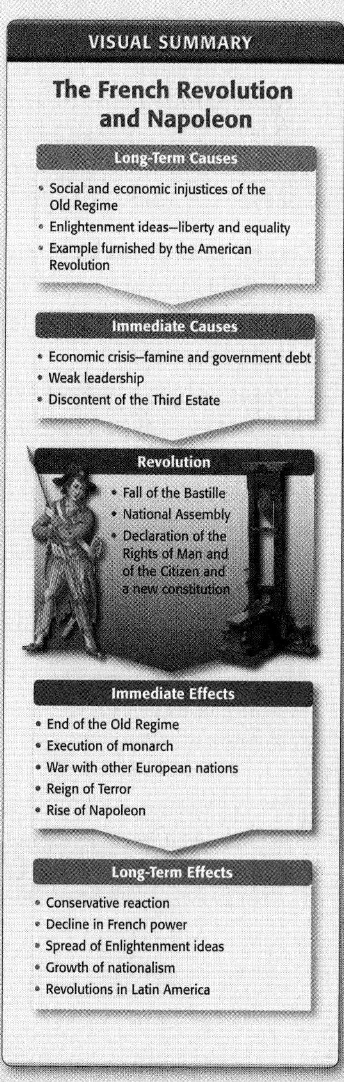

VISUAL SUMMARY
The French Revolution and Napoleon
Long-Term Causes
• Social and economic injustices of the Old Regime
• Enlightenment ideas—liberty and equality
• Example furnished by the American Revolution
Immediate Causes
• Economic crisis—famine and government debt
• Weak leadership
• Discontent of the Third Estate
Revolution
• Fall of the Bastille
• National Assembly
• Declaration of the Rights of Man and of the Citizen and a new constitution
Immediate Effects
• End of the Old Regime
• Execution of monarch
• War with other European nations
• Reign of Terror
• Rise of Napoleon
Long-Term Effects
• Conservative reaction
• Decline in French power
• Spread of Enlightenment ideas
• Growth of nationalism
• Revolutions in Latin America

PRIMARY SOURCE

The first maxim of our politics ought to be to lead the people by means of reason and the enemies of the people by terror. If the basis of popular government in time of peace is virtue, the basis of popular government in time of revolution is both virtue and terror: virtue without which terror is murderous, terror without which virtue is powerless. Terror is nothing else than swift, severe, indomitable justice; it flows, then, from virtue.

MAXIMILIEN ROBESPIERRE, quoted in *Problems of Western Civilization: The Challenge of History*

English Learners Second-language learners need to have information and ideas presented to them in multiple ways. Being able to "see" history helps make it real for them. *Modern World History* uses illustrations and visuals to present information to students in a variety of ways.

Evolving Forms of Reading

Students today need to be able to read in new ways.

Nonlinear Materials Today's students must

- gather ideas from multiple sources—resource books, magazines, computerized databases, CD-ROMs, the Internet.
- find their way through nonlinear materials, such as by deciding which area of a computer screen contains the information they want.

Several components of *Modern World History* will give students experience in accessing historical materials in these new formats. They include the Electronic Library of Primary Sources and ClassZone—the Web site for the program.

Graphic Layouts Today's readers must deal with informational materials that come in various formats, including:

- multiple columns of text with many pictures, graphs, and maps
- single-column texts with large marginal areas used for illustrations, highlighted information, and thought-provoking ideas

Modern World History familiarizes students with these multiple text formats and teaches students strategies for effectively obtaining information from each format.

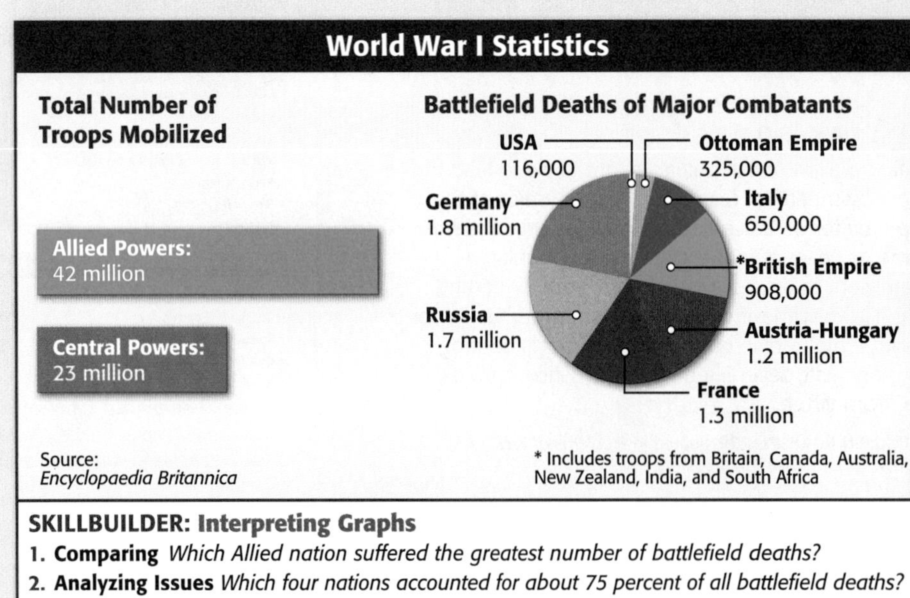

SKILLBUILDER: Interpreting Graphs

1. **Comparing** *Which Allied nation suffered the greatest number of battlefield deaths?*
2. **Analyzing Issues** *Which four nations accounted for about 75 percent of all battlefield deaths?*

Correlations to California History–Social Science Content Standards and Analysis Skills

Students in grade ten study major turning points that shaped the modern world, from the late eighteenth century through the present, including the cause and course of the two world wars. They trace the rise of democratic ideas and develop an understanding of the historical roots of current world issues, especially as they pertain to international relations. They extrapolate from the American experience that democratic ideals are often achieved at a high price, remain vulnerable, and are not practiced everywhere in the world. Students develop an understanding of current world issues and relate them to their historical, geographic, political, economic, and cultural contexts. Students consider multiple accounts of events in order to understand international relations from a variety of perspectives.

Standard		Primary Citations	Supporting Citations
10.1	Students relate the moral and ethical principles in ancient Greek and Roman philosophy, in Judaism, and in Christianity to the development of Western political thought.	**Pupil & Teacher & eEdition** Common Pages: 2, 3, 5–11, 12–17, 18–23, 26–27, 29–30, 54–60, 61–66, 67–68, 127–131, 141, 144–149, 155–161, 174–179, 181–182, 183, 184, 191, 194, 209–212, 700–701, 704–705, 710–711, 714–715 Add'l Teacher Edition: 5–7, 12–16, 54–56, 58–61, 61–65, 67, 127–130, 144, 146–148, 155–160, 174–176, 181–182, 191, 209–210, 704–705, 710–711 **PRINT COMPONENT(S)** CA Standards Enrichment Wrkbk: 17–18, 19–20, 21–22 **TRANSPARENCIES/TECHNOLOGY** CA Daily Standards Practice Transparencies: TTA, TTB, TT1, TT18	**PRINT COMPONENT(S)** In-Depth Resources Unit 1: 1, 2, 5, 6, 9, 15, 18, 20, 21, 23, 26–30, 33–36, 82, 86, 100; Unit 2: 1, 4, 5, 7, 11–13, 18–20, 23–25, 28, 30, 31, 33, 37, 38, 41, 44, 47 In-Depth Resources in Spanish Unit 1: 11, 12, 15, 16, 18, 20–22, 38, 41; Unit 2: 44, 47–49, 52, 55, 56, 57 History Makers Unit 1: 15, 34, Unit 2: 18 CA Reading Toolkit: L11, L12, 20, 23, 26, 27, 28, 31 CA Modified Lesson Plans for English Learners: Prol.1, Prol.2, 19.2, 20.3 CA Standards Planner & Lesson Plans: L1, L3, L5, L13, L15, L31, L37, L43, L45, L47, L53 **TRANSPARENCIES/TECHNOLOGY** World Art & Cultures Transparencies: AT12, AT36, AT37, AT45, AT46, AT47, AT48 Geography Transparencies: GT17, GT21, GT22 Critical Thinking Transparencies: CT5, CT6, CT17, CT21, CT53, CT57, CT58 Benchmark Tests: Prol.1, Prol.2, 1.1, 1.3, 1.4, 4.2, 5.1, 5.4, 5.5, 6.1, 6.4 Power Presentations: Prol.1, Prol.2, 1.1, 1.3, 1.4, 4.2, 5.1, 5.4, 5.5, 6.1, 6.4
10.1.1	Analyze the similarities and differences in Judeo-Christian and Greco-Roman views of law, reason and faith, and duties of the individual.	**Pupil & Teacher & eEdition** Common Pages: **5–11, 12–17,** 30, 54–60, 61–66, 67, 68, **181–182,** 183, 191, 194, 700–701, 704–705, 710–711, **714–715** Add'l Teacher Edition: 5–7, 12–16, 54–56, 58–61, 61–65, 67, 181–182, 191, 704–705, 710–711 **PRINT COMPONENT(S)** CA Standards Enrichment Wrkbk: 17–18 **TRANSPARENCIES/TECHNOLOGY** CA Daily Standards Practice Transparencies: TTB	**PRINT COMPONENT(S)** In-Depth Resources Unit 1: 9, 15, 20, 21, 23, 28, 29; Unit 2: 5, 12–13, 18, 19, 24, 25, 30, 31, 33, 38, 41, 44 In-Depth Resources in Spanish Unit 1: 11, 12, 15, 16, 20–22; Unit 2: 48, 52, 56, 57 History Makers Unit 1: 15, 34; Unit 2: 18, 41 CA Reading Toolkit: L11, L12, 27, 28 CA Modified Lesson Plans for English Learners: Prol.1, Prol.2 CA Standards Planner & Lesson Plans: L3, L5, L13, L15, L45, L47 **TRANSPARENCIES/TECHNOLOGY** World Art & Cultures Transparencies: AT12, AT48 Geography Transparencies: GT17, GT22 Critical Thinking Transparencies: CT5, CT6, CT17, CT53, CT57 Benchmark Tests: Prol.1, Prol.2, 1.3, 1.4, 5.5, 6.1 Power Presentations: Prol.1, Prol.2, 1.3, 1.4, 5.5, 6.1

Correlations to California History–Social Science Content Standards and Analysis Skills

Standard		Primary Citations	Supporting Citations
10.1.2	Trace the development of the Western political ideas of the rule of law and illegitimacy of tyranny, using selections from Plato's *Republic* and Aristotle's *Politics.*	**Pupil & Teacher & eEdition** Common Pages: **5–11, 18–23, 30,** 127–131, 141, 144–149, 155–161, 174–179, 184 Add'l Teacher Edition: 5–7, 127–130, 144, 146–148, 155–160, 174–176 **PRINT COMPONENT(S)** CA Standards Enrichment Wrkbk: 19–20 **TRANSPARENCIES/TECHNOLOGY** CA Daily Standards Practice Transparencies: TTA, TT18	**PRINT COMPONENT(S)** In-Depth Resources Unit 1: 8, 82, 86, 100, Unit 2: 1, 20 In-Depth Resources in Spanish Unit 1: 11, 15, 16, 38, 41, Unit 2: 47, 49 History Makers Unit 1: 15 CA Reading Toolkit: 20, 23, 26 CA Modified Lesson Plans for English Learners: Prol.1 CA Standards Planner & Lesson Plans: L1, L31, L37, L43 **TRANSPARENCIES/TECHNOLOGY** World Art & Cultures Transparencies: AT12, AT45, AT48 Geography Transparencies: GT21 Critical Thinking Transparencies: CT57 Benchmark Tests: Prol.1, 4.2, 5.1, 5.4 Power Presentations: Prol.1, 4.2, 5.1, 5.4
10.1.3	Consider the influence of the U.S. Constitution on political systems in the contemporary world.	**Pupil & Teacher & eEdition** Common Pages: 2, 3, **26–27,** 29, 30, **209–211, 212** Add'l Teacher Edition: 209–210 **PRINT COMPONENT(S)** CA Standards Enrichment Wrkbk: 21–22	**PRINT COMPONENT(S)** In-Depth Resources Unit 2: 28, 37, 47 In-Depth Resources in Spanish Unit 2: 55 CA Reading Toolkit: 31 CA Modified Lesson Plans for English Learners: 19.2, 20.3 CA Standards Planner & Lesson Plans: L53 **TRANSPARENCIES/TECHNOLOGY** Critical Thinking Transparencies: CT58 Benchmark Tests: 6.4 Power Presentations: 6.4

Standard		Primary Citations	Supporting Citations
10.2	Students compare and contrast the Glorious Revolution of England, the American Revolution, and the French Revolution and their enduring effects worldwide on the political expectations for self-government and individual liberty.	**Pupil & Teacher & eEdition** Common Pages: 18, 19–23, 24–25, 27–28, 29–30, 37–53, 67, 68, 162–168, 180–183, 184, 185, 186, 189–194, 196–200, 204, 206–211, 212, 216, 217–221, 222–223, 227, 228, 229–233, 234–237, 238–241, 242, 243, 244–245, 247–252, 253–257, 258–263, 264–267, 270–271, 272–273, 274–275, 276–277, 315–316, 334, 438 Add'l Teacher Edition: 18–22, 24–28, 37–42, 46–50, 53, 67, 162–167, 180–182, 186, 189–193, 196–199, 206–216, 217–220, 222–226, 228, 229–232, 232, 234–236, 238–240, 244, 247–251, 253–256, 258–262, 264–266, 272–273, 274–275, 276–277, 315 **PRINT COMPONENT(S)** CA Standards Enrichment Wrkbk: 23–24, 25–26, 27–28, 29–30, 31–32 **TRANSPARENCIES/TECHNOLOGY** CA Daily Standards Practice Transparencies: TTC, TTD, TT16, TT19, TT21, TT22, TT23, TT24, TT25, TT26, TT27, TT28, TT30a–TT30b, TT31	**PRINT COMPONENT(S)** In-Depth Resources Unit 1: 14, 16; Unit 2: 9, 27, 28, 30, 35, 37, 43, 46–53, 55, 57–59, 60, 61, 63–68, 70–72, 74–76, 79, 82–84, 89, 90, 92, 94; Unit 3: 23, 31, 40, 43; Unit 4: 24, 29, 32, 40, 43 In-Depth Resources in Spanish Unit 1: 13, 14, 18, 19, 21, 23; Unit 2: 45, 48, 52–57, 59, 61–64, 67, 68–72; Unit 3: 81; Unit 4: 110, 114 History Makers Unit 1: 16, 33; Unit 2: 18, 41, 42, 64, 65, 88, 89; Unit 3: 40 CA Reading Toolkit: L9, L10, L12, 24, 27, 28, 29, 30, 31, 32, 33, 34, 35, 36, 37, 38, 39, 40, 45, 62 CA Modified Lesson Plans for English Learners: Prol.3, Prol.4, 5.5, 6.2, 6.3, 6.4, 7.1, 7.2, 7.3, 7.4, 7.5, 8.2, 8.3 CA Standards Planner & Lesson Plans: L5, L7, L9, L11, L15, L39, L45, L47, L49, L51, L53, L55, L57, L61, L65, L67, L71, L81 **TRANSPARENCIES/TECHNOLOGY** World Art & Cultures Transparencies: AT36, AT37, AT38, AT48, AT50, AT51, AT52, AT53, AT65 Geography Transparencies: GT17, GT22, GT23 Critical Thinking Transparencies: CT17, CT22, CT23, CT53, CT57, CT58, CT59, CT60 Videos: "Revolutions in Latin America and South Africa" Benchmark Tests: Prol.3, 1.1, 1.2, 1.4, 5.2, 5.5, 6.1, 6.2, 6.3, 6.4, 7.1, 7.2, 7.3, 7.4, 7.5, 8.1, 8.2, 8.3, 8.4, 10.1, 14.1 Power Presentations: Prol.3, 1.1, 1.2, 1.4, 5.2, 5.5, 6.1, 6.2, 6.3, 6.4, 7.1, 7.2, 7.3, 7.4, 7.5, 8.1, 8.2, 8.3, 8.4, 10.1, 14.1

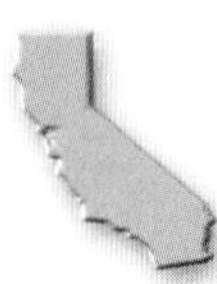

Correlations to California History–Social Science Content Standards and Analysis Skills

Standard		Primary Citations	Supporting Citations
10.2.1	Compare the major ideas of philosophers and their effects on the democratic revolutions in England, the United States, France, and Latin America (e.g., John Locke, Charles-Louis Montesquieu, Jean-Jacques Rousseau, Simón Bolívar, Thomas Jefferson, James Madison).	**Pupil & Teacher & eEdition** Common Pages: **24–25, 27–28,** 29, 30, 37–53, 67, 68, 163–164, 186, 189–194, 196–200, 204, **207–208,** 209, 212, 216, **217–221,** 243, **247–252,** 270, 274–275, 276–277, 316 Add'l Teacher Edition: 24–25, 27, 37–42, 46–50, 53, 67, 163–164, 186, 189–193, 196–199, 207–208, 209, 216, 217–220, 247–251, 274–275, 276–277 **PRINT COMPONENT(S)** CA Standards Enrichment Wrkbk: 23–24 **TRANSPARENCIES/TECHNOLOGY** CA Daily Standards Practice Transparencies: TT21, TT22	**PRINT COMPONENT(S)** In-Depth Resources Unit 1: 16; Unit 2: 27, 28, 30, 35, 63, 70 In-Depth Resources in Spanish Unit 1: 13, 18, 19, 21, 23, Unit 2: 45, 52–57, 59, 67, 71 History Makers Unit 1: 33; Unit 2: 41, 42, 64, 88 CA Reading Toolkit: L9, L10, L12, 24, 28, 29, 30, 31, 32, 37 CA Modified Lesson Plans for English Learners: Prol.3, Prol.4, 5.5, 6.2, 6.3, 6.4 CA Standards Planner & Lesson Plans: L7, L9, L11, L15, L39, L47, L49, L51, L53, L55, L65 **TRANSPARENCIES/TECHNOLOGY** World Art & Cultures Transparencies: AT36, AT37, AT38, AT48, AT50, AT52 Geography Transparencies: GT17, GT22, GT23 Critical Thinking Transparencies: CT17, CT22, CT53, CT58 Video: "Revolutions in Latin America and South Africa" Benchmark Tests: Prol.3, 1.1, 1.2, 1.4, 5.2, 6.1, 6.2, 6.3, 6.4, 7.1, 8.1 Power Presentations: Prol.3, 1.1, 1.2, 1.4, 5.2, 6.1, 6.2, 6.3, 6.4, 7.1, 8.1
10.2.2	List the principles of the Magna Carta, the English Bill of Rights (1689), the American Declaration of Independence (1776), the French Declaration of the Rights of Man and the Citizen (1789), and the U.S. Bill of Rights (1791).	**Pupil & Teacher & eEdition** Common Pages: 18, **19–23,** 25, 28–30, 180–183, 184, 185, **207–208,** 211, 212, **222–223,** 227, 242, 267, **274–275, 276–277,** R48 Add'l Teacher Edition: 18–22, 25, 28, 180–182, 207–208, 222–223, 274–275, 276–277 **PRINT COMPONENT(S)** CA Standards Enrichment Wrkbk: 25–26 **TRANSPARENCIES/TECHNOLOGY** CA Daily Standards Practice Transparencies: TT19, TT23, TT25	**PRINT COMPONENT(S)** In-Depth Resources Unit 1: 10; Unit 2: 12, 30, 45, 49, 55, 57–59, 61, 65–67, 76, 89, 94 In-Depth Resources in Spanish Unit 1: 13; Unit 2: 48, 55, 70 History Makers Unit 2: 18, 65, 89 CA Reading Toolkit: 27, 31, 33, 40 CA Modified Lesson Plans for English Learners: Prol.3, 5.5, 6.4, 7.2 CA Standards Planner & Lesson Plans: L5, L45, L53, L57, L71 **TRANSPARENCIES/TECHNOLOGY** World Art & Cultures Transparencies: AT53 Critical Thinking Transparencies: CT57, CT58, CT60 Benchmark Tests: Prol.3, 5.5, 6.4, 7.2, 8.4 Power Presentations: Prol.3, 5.5, 6.4, 7.2, 8.4

Standard		Primary Citations	Supporting Citations
10.2.3	Understand the unique character of the American Revolution, its spread to other parts of the world, and its continuing significance to other nations.	**Pupil & Teacher & eEdition** Common Pages: 25–27, 29, 30, **206–211, 212, 272–273,** 274, **276–277, 438** Add'l Teacher Edition: 25–27, 206–211, 272–273, 274, 276–277 **PRINT COMPONENT(S)** CA Standards Enrichment Wrkbk: 27–28	**PRINT COMPONENT(S)** In-Depth Resources Unit 1: 4, 10, 13; Unit 2: 28, 37, 47, Unit 4: 24, 29, 32, 40, 43 In-Depth Resources in Spanish Unit 1: 13, Unit 2: 55, Unit 4: 110, 114 CA Reading Toolkit: 31, 62 CA Modified Lesson Plans for English Learners: Prol.3, Prol.4, 6.4 CA Standards Planner & Lesson Plans: L53 **TRANSPARENCIES/TECHNOLOGY** World Art & Cultures Transparencies: AT65 Critical Thinking Transparencies: CT58 Benchmark Tests: Prol.3, 6.4, 14.1 Power Presentations: Prol.3, 6.4, 14.1
10.2.4	Explain how the ideology of the French Revolution led France to develop from constitutional monarchy to democratic despotism to the Napoleonic empire.	**Pupil & Teacher & eEdition** Common Pages: 27–28, 29, 162–168, 184, **216–227, 228, 229–233, 234–237, 242,** 256, 272–273, 274–275, 276–277, 315–316, 334 Add'l Teacher Edition: 27–28, 162–167, 216–220, 222–226, 228, 229–232, 234–236, 256, 272–273, 274, 276–277, 315 **PRINT COMPONENT(S)** CA Standards Enrichment Wrkbk: 29–30 **TRANSPARENCIES/TECHNOLOGY** CA Daily Standards Practice Transparencies: TTD, TT16, TT24, TT25, TT26, TT27	**PRINT COMPONENT(S)** In-Depth Resources Unit 2: 9, 43, 46–53, 55, 57, 58, 59, 61, 64, 65, 66, 67, 68, 70, 71, 72, 74, 82, 92; Unit 3: 23, 31, 40, 43 In-Depth Resources in Spanish Unit 1: 14; Unit 2: 45, 59, 61, 62, 63, 64, 68; Unit 3: 81 History Makers Unit 1: 16; Unit 2: 64, 65; Unit 3: 40 CA Reading Toolkit: 24, 33, 34, 35, 38, 45 CA Modified Lesson Plans for English Learners: Prol.4, 7.1, 7.2, 7.3 CA Standards Planner & Lesson Plans: L7, L39, L57, L59, L61, L67, L81 **TRANSPARENCIES/TECHNOLOGY** World Art & Cultures Transparencies: AT50, AT51 Geography Transparencies: GT23 Critical Thinking Transparencies: CT59 Benchmark Tests: Prol.4, 5.2, 7.1, 7.2, 7.3, 7.4, 8.2, 10.1 Power Presentations: Prol.4, 5.2, 7.1, 7.2, 7.3, 7.4, 8.2, 10.1

Correlations to California History–Social Science Content Standards and Analysis Skills

<table>
<tr><th colspan="2">Standard</th><th>Primary Citations</th><th>Supporting Citations</th></tr>
<tr><td>10.2.5</td><td>Discuss how nationalism spread across Europe with Napoleon but was repressed for a generation under the Congress of Vienna and Concert of Europe until the Revolutions of 1848.</td><td>Pupil & Teacher & eEdition
Common Pages: 232, 238–241, 242, 244–245, 253–257, 258–263, 264–267, 270–271

Add'l Teacher Edition: 232, 238–240, 244, 253–256, 258–262, 264–266

PRINT COMPONENT(S)
CA Standards Enrichment Wrkbk: 31–32

TRANSPARENCIES/TECHNOLOGY
CA Daily Standards Practice Transparencies: TT26, TT28, TT30a–TT30b, TT31</td><td>PRINT COMPONENT(S)
In-Depth Resources Unit 2: 50, 52, 60, 70, 72, 74–76, 79, 82–84, 89, 90, 92–94; Unit 5: 61, 64–65
In-Depth Resources in Spanish Unit 2: 61, 63, 68–70, 72
History Makers Unit 2: 89
CA Reading Toolkit: 34, 36, 38, 39, 40
CA Modified Lesson Plans for English Learners: 7.3, 7.4, 7.5, 8.2, 8.3
CA Standards Planner & Lesson Plans: L59, L63, L67, L69, L71

TRANSPARENCIES/TECHNOLOGY
World Art & Cultures Transparencies: AT51, AT53
Geography Transparencies: GT24
Critical Thinking Transparencies: CT23, CT24, CT59, CT60
Benchmark Tests: 7.3, 7.5, 8.2, 8.3, 8.4
Power Presentations: 7.3, 7.5, 8.2, 8.3, 8.4</td></tr>
<tr><td>10.3</td><td>Students analyze the effects of the Industrial Revolution in England, France, Germany, Japan, and the United States.</td><td>Pupil & Teacher & eEdition
Common Pages: 139, 228, 264–265, 267–270, 282, 283–288, 289–294, 295–299, 300–301, 304–306, 307, 308, 309, 313–315, 324–327, 328–333, 334, 396–397, 398–399, 400–401, 438

Add'l Teacher Edition: 228, 264–265, 268–269, 282, 283–287, 289–293, 295–298, 300–305, 307, 313–315, 324–236, 328–332, 396–397, 398–399, 400–401, 438

PRINT COMPONENT(S)
CA Standards Enrichment Wrkbk: 33–34, 35–36, 37–38, 39–40, 41–42, 43–44, 45–46

TRANSPARENCIES/TECHNOLOGY
CA Daily Standards Practice Transparencies: TT32, TT33a–TT33b, TT35, TT36, TT39, TT40, TT54</td><td>PRINT COMPONENT(S)
In-Depth Resources Unit 1: 84, 87, 98, 102; Unit 2: 49, 55, 57–59, 61, 65–67, 70, 76, 89, 94; Unit 3: 1–22, 25, 26, 28, 31, 33, 34, 37, 40–43, 45, 46; Unit 4: 24, 29, 32, 40, 43
In-Depth Resources in Spanish Unit 1: 40, 42; Unit 2: 70; Unit 3: 74–79, 83, 84, 85; Unit 4: 110, 114
History Makers Unit 2: 65, 89; Unit 3: 16, 17, 40, 41; Unit 4: 40
CA Reading Toolkit: 22, 33, 40, 41, 42, 43, 44, 45, 47, 48, 62
CA Modified Lesson Plans for English Learners: 8.4, 9.1, 9.2, 9.3, 9.4, 10.1
CA Standards Planner & Lesson Plans: L35, L57, L73, L75, L77, L79, L81, L85,L87, L115

TRANSPARENCIES/TECHNOLOGY
World Art & Cultures Transparencies: AT53, AT54, AT55, AT65
Geography Transparencies: GT20, GT25
Critical Thinking Transparencies: CT25, CT26, CT56, CT60, CT61, CT62
Videos: "The Industrial and Electronic Revolutions," "The Impact of Potatoes and Sugar"
Benchmark Tests: 4.4, 7.2, 8.4, 9.1, 9.2, 9.3, 9.4, 10.1, 10.3, 10.4, 14.1
Power Presentations: 4.4, 7.2, 8.4, 9.1, 9.2, 9.3, 9.4, 10.1, 10.3, 10.4, 14.1</td></tr>
</table>

Standard		Primary Citations	Supporting Citations
10.3.1	Analyze why England was the first country to industrialize.	**Pupil & Teacher & eEdition** Common Pages: **283–288, 308** Add'l Teacher Edition: 283–287 **PRINT COMPONENT(S)** CA Standards Enrichment Wrkbk: 33–34	**PRINT COMPONENT(S)** In-Depth Resources Unit 3: 1, 8 In-Depth Resources in Spanish Unit 3: 74 History Makers Unit 3: 16 CA Reading Toolkit: 41 CA Modified Lesson Plans for English Learners: 9.1, 9.2 CA Standards Planner & Lesson Plans: L73 **TRANSPARENCIES/TECHNOLOGY** Geography Transparencies: GT25 Videos: "The Industrial and Electronic Revolutions" Benchmark Tests: 9.1 Power Presentations: 9.1
10.3.2	Examine how scientific and technological changes and new forms of energy brought about massive social, economic, and cultural change (e.g., the inventions and discoveries of James Watt, Eli Whitney, Henry Bessemer, Louis Pasteur, Thomas Edison).	**Pupil & Teacher & eEdition** Common Pages: **284–288, 289–294, 295–299,** 305–306, 308, **328–333,** 334, **396–397, 398–399,** 400–401 Add'l Teacher Edition: 284–287, 289–293, 295–298, 305, 328–332, 396–397, 398–399, 400–401 **PRINT COMPONENT(S)** CA Standards Enrichment Wrkbk: 35–36 **TRANSPARENCIES/TECHNOLOGY** CA Daily Standards Practice Transparencies: TT33a–TT33b, TT34a–TT34b, TT35, TT36, TT40	**PRINT COMPONENT(S)** In-Depth Resources Unit 3: 1–14, 15, 16–22, 26, 28, 34, 37, 41, 42, 46 In-Depth Resources in Spanish Unit 3: 74–79, 84, 85 History Makers Unit 3: 16, 17, 41 CA Reading Toolkit: 41, 42, 43, 44, 48 CA Modified Lesson Plans for English Learners: 9.1, 9.3 CA Standards Planner & Lesson Plans: L73, L75, L77, L79, L87 **TRANSPARENCIES/TECHNOLOGY** World Art & Cultures Transparencies: AT54, AT55 Geography Transparencies: GT25 Critical Thinking Transparencies: CT25, CT26, CT61, CT62 Videos: "The Industrial and Electronic Revolutions" Benchmark Tests: 9.1, 9.2, 9.3, 9.4, 10.4 Power Presentations: 9.1, 9.2, 9.3, 9.4, 10.4
10.3.3	Describe the growth of population, rural to urban migration, and growth of cities associated with the Industrial Revolution.	**Pupil & Teacher & eEdition** Common Pages: **289–290, 292–293, 299, 308, 327** Add'l Teacher Edition: 289–290, 292–293 **PRINT COMPONENT(S)** CA Standards Enrichment Wrkbk: 37–38 **TRANSPARENCIES/TECHNOLOGY** CA Daily Standards Practice Transparencies: TT34a–TT34b, TT35, TT36	**PRINT COMPONENT(S)** In-Depth Resources Unit 3: 2–4, 6, 7, 10–13, 17, 18, 20–22, 25, 33, 45 In-Depth Resources in Spanish Unit 3: 75–79, 83 History Makers Unit 3: 17, 40, 41 CA Reading Toolkit: 42, 43, 47 CA Modified Lesson Plans for English Learners: 9.2 CA Standards Planner & Lesson Plans: L75, L77, L85 **TRANSPARENCIES/TECHNOLOGY** World Art & Cultures Transparencies: AT54, AT55 Geography Transparencies: GT25 Critical Thinking Transparencies: CT25, CT61, CT62 Benchmark Tests: 9.2, 9.3, 9.4, 10.3 Power Presentations: 9.2, 9.3, 9.4, 10.3

Correlations to California History–Social Science Content Standards and Analysis Skills

Standard		Primary Citations	Supporting Citations
10.3.4	Trace the evolution of work and labor, including the demise of the slave trade and the effects of immigration, mining and manufacturing, division of labor, and the union movement.	**Pupil & Teacher & eEdition** Common Pages: **282,** 291–294, **304–306,** 307, 308, 313–315, **324–327, 334, 398–399** Add'l Teacher Edition: 282, 291–293, 304–305, 307, 313–315, 324–236, 398–399 **PRINT COMPONENT(S)** CA Standards Enrichment Wrkbk: 39–40 **TRANSPARENCIES/TECHNOLOGY** CA Daily Standards Practice Transparencies: TT39	**PRINT COMPONENT(S)** In-Depth Resources Unit 3: 2–3, 6–7, 10, 11, 23, 25, 31, 33, 40, 43, 45 In-Depth Resources in Spanish Unit 3: 75, 77, 78, 79, 81, 83 History Makers Unit 3: 17, 40 CA Reading Toolkit: 42, 44, 45, 47 CA Modified Lesson Plans for English Learners: 9.2, 9.4 CA Standards Planner & Lesson Plans: L75, L79, L81, L85 **TRANSPARENCIES/TECHNOLOGY** World Art & Cultures Transparencies: AT54 Geography Transparencies: GT25 Critical Thinking Transparencies: CT20, CT25, CT61 Benchmark Tests: 9.2, 9.4, 10.1, 10.3 Power Presentations: 9.2, 9.4, 10.1, 10.3
10.3.5	Understand the connections among natural resources, entrepreneurship, labor, and capital in an industrial economy.	**Pupil & Teacher & eEdition** Common Pages: **283–284, 287, 288,** 298, **300–301, 308** Add'l Teacher Edition: 283–284, 287, 298, 300–301 **PRINT COMPONENT(S)** CA Standards Enrichment Wrkbk: 41–42 **TRANSPARENCIES/TECHNOLOGY** CA Daily Standards Practice Transparencies: TT33a–TT33b	**PRINT COMPONENT(S)** In-Depth Resources Unit 3: 1, 3, 4, 6, 9, 11, 12, 16–19, 21, 22 In-Depth Resources in Spanish Unit 3: 74, 76, 77, 78 History Makers Unit 3: 16, 17 CA Reading Toolkit: 41, 43, 44 CA Modified Lesson Plans for English Learners: 9.1, 9.2 CA Standards Planner & Lesson Plans: L73, L77, L79 **TRANSPARENCIES/TECHNOLOGY** World Art & Cultures Transparencies: AT55 Critical Thinking Transparencies: CT25, CT61 Benchmark Tests: 9.1, 9.3, 9.4 Power Presentations: 9.1, 9.3, 9.4
10.3.6	Analyze the emergence of capitalism as a dominant economic pattern and the responses to it, including Utopianism, Social Democracy, Socialism, and Communism.	**Pupil & Teacher & eEdition** Common Pages: **139, 300–306, 307, 308, 438** Add'l Teacher Edition: 300–305, 307, 438 **PRINT COMPONENT(S)** CA Standards Enrichment Wrkbk: 43–44 **TRANSPARENCIES/TECHNOLOGY** CA Daily Standards Practice Transparencies: TT54	**PRINT COMPONENT(S)** In-Depth Resources Unit 1: 84, 87, 98, 102; Unit 3: 4, 6, 12, 16, 17, 18, 22; Unit 4: 24, 29, 32, 40, 43 In-Depth Resources in Spanish Unit 1: 40, 42; Unit 3: 77, 78, Unit 4: 110, 114 History Makers Unit 3: 17; Unit 4: 40 CA Reading Toolkit: 22, 44, 62 CA Modified Lesson Plans for English Learners: 9.3, 9.4, 10.1 CA Standards Planner & Lesson Plans: L35, L79, L115 **TRANSPARENCIES/TECHNOLOGY** World Art & Cultures Transparencies: AT65 Geography Transparencies: GT20 Critical Thinking Transparencies: CT25, CT56, CT61 Videos: "The Impact of Potatoes and Sugar" Benchmark Tests: 4.4, 9.4, 14.1 Power Presentations: 4.4, 9.4, 14.1

Standard		Primary Citations	Supporting Citations
10.3.7	Describe the emergence of Romanticism in art and literature (e.g., the poetry of William Blake and William Wordsworth), social criticism (e.g., the novels of Charles Dickens), and the move away from Classicism in Europe.	**Pupil & Teacher & eEdition** Common Pages: **228, 264–265, 267, 268–269, 270, 309** Add'l Teacher Edition: 228, 264–265, 268–269 **PRINT COMPONENT(S)** CA Standards Enrichment Wrkbk: 45–46 **TRANSPARENCIES/TECHNOLOGY** CA Daily Standards Practice Transparencies: TT32	**PRINT COMPONENT(S)** In-Depth Resources Unit 2: 49, 55, 57–59, 61, 65–67, 70, 76, 89, 94 In-Depth Resources in Spanish Unit 2: 70 History Makers Unit 2: 65, 89 CA Reading Toolkit: 33, 40 CA Modified Lesson Plans for English Learners: 8.4 CA Standards Planner & Lesson Plans: L57, L71 **TRANSPARENCIES/TECHNOLOGY** World Art & Cultures Transparencies: AT53 Critical Thinking Transparencies: CT60 Benchmark Tests: 7.2, 8.4 Power Presentations: 7.2, 8.4
10.4	Students analyze patterns of global change in the era of New Imperialism in at least two of the following regions or countries: Africa, Southeast Asia, China, India, Latin America, and the Philippines.	**Pupil & Teacher & eEdition** Common Pages: 82–89, 90, 94–113, 114, 115, 118, 119–125, 132–136, 137–141, 142, 143, 247–252, 270, 299, 317–323, 332, 334, 336–347, 348–350, 351, 352–356, 357–361, 362–365, 366, 371–375, 376–379, 382–387, 388–393, 394–395, 432, 448–452, 453–457, 458, 544–547, 558, 563–569, 570–575, 578–582, 594, 667–673, 698 Add'l Teacher Edition: 82–88, 94–100, 102–206, 108–112, 118, 119–124, 132–135, 137–140, 247–251, 317–322, 336–343, 345–349, 352–355, 357–360, 362–364, 371–374, 376–378, 382–386, 388–392, 448–451, 453–456, 544–546, 463–468, 570–574, 578–581, 667–672 **PRINT COMPONENT(S)** CA Standards Enrichment Wrkbk: 47–48, 49–50, 51–52, 53–54 **TRANSPARENCIES/TECHNOLOGY** CA Daily Standards Practice Transparencies: TT8a–TT8b, TT29, TT38a–TT38b, TT41, TT42, TT43, TT44, TT45a–TT45b, TT46a–TT46b, TT47, TT48, TT49, TT72a–TT72b, TT74a–TT74b	**PRINT COMPONENT(S)** In-Depth Resources Unit 1: 42, 45, 49, 50, 55, 56, 59, 60–80, 81, 83, 89, 91–93, 96–99, 101, 102; Unit 2: 73, 78, 81, 85, 88, 91; Unit 3: 3, 11, 21, 23, 24, 26, 28, 29, 31, 32, 34, 35, 37, 38, 40–43, 46, 47–65, 71–74, 76, 77, 79, 82, 83, 86–93; Unit 4: 27, 35, 42, 46; Unit 5: 2, 7, 10, 22, 26, 27, 28, 32, 33, 35, 36, 37, 39, 40, 42, 44 In-Depth Resources in Spanish Unit 1: 27, 29, 31–35, 40, 42; Unit 2: 67, 71; Unit 3: 76, 81, 82, 84, 85, 86, 88–94, 96–99, 101; Unit 4: 113: ; Unit 5: 134, 140–142, 144, 145 History Makers Unit 1: 55, 74, 75; Unit 2: 88; Unit 3: 40, 41, 63, 64; Unit 5: 17, 42 CA Reading Toolkit: L15, 16, 17, 18, 19, 21, 22, 37, 43, 46, 48, 49, 50, 51, 52, 53, 54, 55, 56, 57, 65, 77, 80, 81 CA Modified Lesson Plans for English Learners: 8.1, 10.3, 11.1, 11.2, 11.3, 11.4, 11.5, 12.1, 12.2, 12.3, 12.4, 14.4 CA Standards Planner & Lesson Plans: L21, L23, L25, L27, L29, L33, L35, L65, L77, L83, L87, L89, L91, L93, L95, L97, L99, L101, L103, L105, L121, L145, L151, L153, L155 **TRANSPARENCIES/TECHNOLOGY** World Art & Cultures Transparencies: AT40, AT41, AT42, AT44, AT52, AT55, AT58, AT59, AT61, AT62, AT66, AT73, AT74 Geography Transparencies: GT19, GT20, GT27, GT28, GT34 Critical Thinking Transparencies: CT18, CT19, CT20, CT27, CT37, CT55, CT56, CT26, CT27, CT28, CT30, CT62, CT63, CT64, CT66 Videos: "The Impact of Potatoes and Sugar," "The Spread of Epidemic Disease," "Revolutions in Latin America and South Africa," "The Geography of Food" Benchmark Tests: 2.3, 3.1, 3.2, 3.3, 4.1, 4.3, 4.4, 8.1, 9.3, 10.2, 10.4, 11.1, 11.2, 11.3, 11.4, 11.5, 12.1, 12.2, 12.3, 12.4, 14.4, 17.3, 18.1, 18.2, 18.3 Power Presentations: 2.3, 3.1, 3.2, 3.3, 4.1, 4.3, 4.4, 8.1, 9.3, 10.2, 10.4, 11.1, 11.2, 11.3, 11.4, 11.5, 12.1, 12.2, 12.3, 12.4, 14.4, 17.3, 18.1, 18.2, 18.3

Correlations to California History–Social Science Content Standards and Analysis Skills

Standard		Primary Citations	Supporting Citations
10.4.1	Describe the rise of industrial economies and their link to imperialism and colonialism (e.g., the role played by national security and strategic advantage; moral issues raised by the search for national hegemony, Social Darwinism, and the missionary impulse; material issues such as land, resources, and technology).	**Pupil & Teacher & eEdition** Common Pages: 96, 112, 132, **137–141,** 142, 299, 332, **337–344, 345–350,** 351, **357–361, 362–365,** 366, 382–387, 394 Add'l Teacher Edition: 96, 112, 132, 137–140, 337–343, 345–349, 357–360, 362–364, 382–386 **PRINT COMPONENT(S)** CA Standards Enrichment Wrkbk: 47–48 **TRANSPARENCIES/TECHNOLOGY** CA Daily Standards Practice Transparencies: TT43, TT44, TT45a–TT45b, TT47, TT48	**PRINT COMPONENT(S)** In-Depth Resources Unit 1: 60, 62, 67, 68, 73–78, 80, 84, 87, 98, 102, Unit 3: 3, 11, 21, 26, 28, 34, 37–38, 42, 46, 47, 48, 49–53, 54, 55, 56, 57, 58–65, 72, 73, 76, 80, 81, 88, 89, 91, 92 In-Depth Resources in Spanish Unit 1: 31, 33, 40, 42; Unit 3: 76, 84, 85, 88–94, 97, 98 History Makers Unit 1: 74, 75; Unit 3: 41, 63, 64 CA Reading Toolkit: 16, 18, 21, 22, 43, 48, 49, 50, 52, 53, 56 CA Modified Lesson Plans for English Learners: 10.3, 11.1, 11.2, 11.3, 11.4, 11.5 CA Standards Planner & Lesson Plans: L23, L27, L33, L35, L77, L87, L89, L91, L95, L97, L103 **TRANSPARENCIES/TECHNOLOGY** World Art & Cultures Transparencies: AT41, AT42, AT55, AT58, AT59, AT61 Geography Transparencies: GT19, GT20, GT27, GT28 Critical Thinking Transparencies: CT19, CT55, CT56, CT26, CT27, CT28, CT62, CT63 Videos: "The Impact of Potatoes and Sugar" Benchmark Tests: 3.1, 3.3, 4.3, 4.4, 9.3, 10.4, 11.1, 11.2, 11.3, 11.4, 11.5, 12.2, 12.3 Power Presentations: 3.1, 3.3, 4.3, 4.4, 9.3, 10.4, 11.1, 11.2, 11.3, 11.4, 11.5, 12.2, 12.3
10.4.2	Discuss the locations of the colonial rule of such nations as England, France, Germany, Italy, Japan, the Netherlands, Russia, Spain, Portugal, and the United States.	**Pupil & Teacher & eEdition** Common Pages: 82–89, 90, **94–113,** 114, 115, 118, **119–125,** 132–136, 142, **247–252,** 270, **317–323,** 334, **339–344,** 345–350, 352–356, 357–361, 362–365, 366, 376–379, 394 Add'l Teacher Edition: 82–88, 94–100, 102–206, 108–112, 118, 119–124, 132–135, 247–251, 317–322, 339–343, 345–349, 357–360, 362–364, 376–378 **PRINT COMPONENT(S)** CA Standards Enrichment Wrkbk: 49–50 **TRANSPARENCIES/TECHNOLOGY** CA Daily Standards Practice Transparencies: TT8a–TT8b, TT38a–TT38b, TT41	**PRINT COMPONENT(S)** In-Depth Resources Unit 1: 42, 45, 49, 50, 55, 56, 59, 60–80, 81, 83, 89, 91–93, 96, 97, 99, 101; Unit 2: 73, 78, 81, 85, 88, 91; Unit 3: 23, 31, 37, 40, 41, 43, 47–56, 57, 58–65, 72, 76, 80, 91 In-Depth Resources in Spanish Unit 1: 27, 29, 31–35; Unit 2: 67, 71: Unit 3: 81; 88–94, 97 History Makers Unit 1: 55, 75; Unit 2: 88; Unit 3: 40, 63, 64 CA Reading Toolkit: L15, 16, 17, 18, 19, 21, 37, 46, 49, 50, 51, 52, 53, 55 CA Modified Lesson Plans for English Learners: 8.1, 10.3, 11.1, 11.2, 11.3, 11.4, 11.5, 12.1, 12.3 CA Standards Planner & Lesson Plans: L21, L23, L25, L27, L29, L33, L65, L83, L89, L91, L93, L97, L101 **TRANSPARENCIES/TECHNOLOGY** World Art & Cultures Transparencies: AT40, AT41, AT42, AT44, AT52, AT58, AT59, AT61 Geography Transparencies: GT19, GT26, GT27, GT28 Critical Thinking Transparencies: CT18, CT19, CT20, CT27, CT37, CT55, CT63 Videos: "The Spread of Epidemic Disease," "Revolutions in Latin America and South Africa" Benchmark Tests: 2.3, 3.1, 3.2, 3.3, 4.1, 4.3, 8.1, 10.2, 11.1, 11.2, 11.3, 11.4, 11.5, 12.2 Power Presentations: 2.3, 3.1, 3.2, 3.3, 4.1, 4.3, 8.1, 10.2, 11.1, 11.2, 11.3, 11.4, 11.5, 12.2

Standard	Primary Citations	Supporting Citations
10.4.3 Explain imperialism from the perspective of the colonizers and the colonized and the varied immediate and long-term responses by the people under colonial rule.	**Pupil & Teacher & eEdition** Common Pages: **95–101,** 114, **132–136,** 142, 143, **247–252,** 270, **336–344,** 345–350, **352–356,** 357–361, 362–265, 366 Add'l Teacher Edition: 95–100, 132–135, 247–251, 336–343, 345–349, 352–355, 357–360, 362–364 **PRINT COMPONENT(S)** CA Standards Enrichment Wrkbk: 51–52 **TRANSPARENCIES/TECHNOLOGY** CA Daily Standards Practice Transparencies: TT29, TT38a–TT38b, TT42, TT44, TT45a–TT45b	**PRINT COMPONENT(S)** In-Depth Resources Unit 2: 73, 78, 81, 85, 88, 91; Unit 3: 24, 29, 32, 35, 38, 40, 44, 45, 46, 47–49, 50–53, 54, 55, 56, 57, 58–65, 71; Unit 4: 29 In-Depth Resources in Spanish Unit 1: 31, 39; Unit 2: 67, 71; Unit 3: 82, 86, 88–94 History Makers Unit 1: 74; Unit 2: 88, Unit 3: 63, 64 CA Reading Toolkit: 16, 21, 37, 49, 50, 51, 52, 53 CA Modified Lesson Plans for English Learners: 8.1, 10.3, 11.1, 11.2, 11.3, 11.4, 11.5, 12.2, 12.3, 12.4, 14.4 CA Standards Planner & Lesson Plans: L23, L33, L65, L89, L91, L93, L95, L97 **TRANSPARENCIES/TECHNOLOGY** World Art & Cultures Transparencies: AT41, AT44, AT52, AT57, AT58, AT59 Geography Transparencies: GT20, GT26, GT27 Critical Thinking Transparencies: CT20, CT27, CT28, CT63, CT64 Videos: "Revolutions in Latin America and South Africa," "The Geography of Food" Benchmark Tests: 3.1, 4.3, 8.1, 10.2, 11.1, 11.2, 11.3, 11.4, 11.5 Power Presentations: 3.1, 4.3, 8.1, 10.2, 11.1, 11.2, 11.3, 11.4, 11.5
10.4.4 Describe the independence struggles of the colonized regions of the world, including the roles of leaders, such as Sun Yat-sen in China, and the roles of ideology and religion.	**Pupil & Teacher & eEdition** Common Pages: 247–252, 270, 348–350, 359–361, 366, 371–375, **388–393,** 394–395, 432, **448–452, 453–457,** 458, 544–547, 558, **563–569,** 570–575, **578–582,** 594, 667–673, 698 Add'l Teacher Edition: 247–251, 348–349, 359–360, 371–374, 388–392, 448–451, 453–456, 544–546, 463–468, 570–574, 578–581, 667–672 **PRINT COMPONENT(S)** CA Standards Enrichment Wrkbk: 53–54 **TRANSPARENCIES/TECHNOLOGY** CA Daily Standards Practice Transparencies: TT46a–TT46b, TT49, TT72a–TT72b, TT74a–TT74b	**PRINT COMPONENT(S)** In-Depth Resources Unit 2: 73, 78, 81, 85, 88, 91; Unit 3: 47, 54, 56, 58–59, 60, 71, 74, 77, 79, 82, 83, 86, 87, 90, 93, Unit 4: 27, 29, 35, 42, 46; Unit 5: 2, 7, 10, 22, 26, 27, 28, 32, 33, 35, 36, 37, 39, 40, 42, 44 In-Depth Resources in Spanish Unit 2: 67, 71; Unit 3: 88, 94, 96, 99, 101; Unit 4: 113: Unit 5: 134, 140–142, 144, 145 History Makers Unit 2: 88: Unit 5: 17, 42 CA Reading Toolkit: 37, 50, 52, 54, 57, 65, 77, 80, 81 CA Modified Lesson Plans for English Learners: 8.1, 11.2, 11.4, 11.5, 12.2, 12.4, 14.4 CA Standards Planner & Lesson Plans: L65, L95, L99, L105, L121, L145, L151, L153, L155 **TRANSPARENCIES/TECHNOLOGY** World Art & Cultures Transparencies: AT52, AT61, AT62, AT66, AT73, AT74 Geography Transparencies: GT28, GT34 Critical Thinking Transparencies: CT28, CT30, CT64, CT66 Videos: "Revolutions in Latin America and South Africa" Benchmark Tests: 8.1, 11.4, 12.1, 12.4, 14.4, 17.3, 18.1, 18.2, 18.3 Power Presentations: 8.1, 11.4, 12.1, 12.4, 14.4, 17.3, 18.1, 18.2, 18.3

Correlations to California History–Social Science Content Standards and Analysis Skills

Standard		Primary Citations	Supporting Citations
10.5	Students analyze the causes and course of the First World War.	**Pupil & Teacher & eEdition** Common Pages: 407–410, 411–416, 417–418, 419–420, 421–422, 423, 428, 429, 433–436, 439, 458, 523 Add'l Teacher Edition: 407–409, 411–415, 417–420, 421, 423, 433–436, 523 **PRINT COMPONENT(S)** CA Standards Enrichment Wrkbk: 55–56, 57–58, 59–60, 61–62, 63–64 **TRANSPARENCIES/TECHNOLOGY** CA Daily Standards Practice Transparencies: TT50, TT51, TT52a–TT52b	**PRINT COMPONENT(S)** In-Depth Resources Unit 2: 3, 8, 17, 22; Unit 4: 1, 2, 3, 6, 7, 9–11, 13, 15, 16, 19, 20–22, 24, 29, 32, 40, 43 In-Depth Resources in Spanish Unit 2: 46, 50; Unit 4: 103, 104, 105, 107, 108, 110, 114 History Makers Unit 2: 17; Unit 4: 16, 40 CA Reading Toolkit: 25, 58, 59, 60, 62 CA Modified Lesson Plans for English Learners: 13.1, 13.2, 13.3, 14.1 CA Standards Planner & Lesson Plans: L41, L107, L109, L111, L115 **TRANSPARENCIES/TECHNOLOGY** World Art & Cultures Transparencies: AT63, AT64, AT65 Geography Transparencies: GT29 Critical Thinking Transparencies: CT29, CT65 Benchmark Tests: 5.3, 13.1, 13.2, 13.3, 14.1 Power Presentations: 5.3, 13.1, 13.2, 13.3, 14.1
10.5.1	Analyze the arguments for entering into war presented by leaders from all sides of the Great War and the role of political and economic rivalries, ethnic and ideological conflicts, domestic discontent and disorder, and propaganda and nationalism in mobilizing the civilian population in support of "total war."	**Pupil & Teacher & eEdition** Common Pages: **407–410, 418–420,** 422, 423, 428–429 Add'l Teacher Edition: 407–409, 418–420, 423 **PRINT COMPONENT(S)** CA Standards Enrichment Wrkbk: 55–56 **TRANSPARENCIES/TECHNOLOGY** CA Daily Standards Practice Transparencies: TT50, TT52a–TT52b	**PRINT COMPONENT(S)** In-Depth Resources Unit 2: 3, 8, 17, 22; Unit 4: 1, 3, 5, 6, 8, 9, 11, 15, 16, 20, 22 In-Depth Resources in Spanish Unit 2: 46, 50; Unit 4: 103, 105, 107 History Makers Unit 2: 17, Unit 4: 16 CA Reading Toolkit: 25, 58, 60 CA Modified Lesson Plans for English Learners: 13.1, 13.2, 13.3 CA Standards Planner & Lesson Plans: L41, L107, L111 **TRANSPARENCIES/TECHNOLOGY** World Art & Cultures Transparencies: AT63, AT64 Geography Transparencies: GT29 Critical Thinking Transparencies: CT29, CT65 Benchmark Tests: 5.3, 13.1, 13.3 Power Presentations: 5.3, 13.1, 13.3
10.5.2	Examine the principal theaters of battle, major turning points, and the importance of geographic factors in military decisions and outcomes (e.g., topography, waterways, distance, climate).	**Pupil & Teacher & eEdition** Common Pages: **411–416, 428** Add'l Teacher Edition: 411–415 **PRINT COMPONENT(S)** CA Standards Enrichment Wrkbk: 57–58	**PRINT COMPONENT(S)** In-Depth Resources Unit 4: 2, 3, 6 In-Depth Resources in Spanish Unit 4: 104, 108 CA Reading Toolkit: 59 CA Modified Lesson Plans for English Learners: 13.2, 13.3 CA Standards Planner & Lesson Plans: L109 **TRANSPARENCIES/TECHNOLOGY** World Art & Cultures Transparencies: AT63, AT64 Benchmark Tests: 13.2 Power Presentations: 13.2

Standard		Primary Citations	Supporting Citations
10.5.3	Explain how the Russian Revolution and the entry of the United States affected the course and outcome of the war.	**Pupil & Teacher & eEdition** Common Pages: **418–420, 422, 433–436, 439, 458** Add'l Teacher Edition: 418–420, 433–436 **PRINT COMPONENT(S)** CA Standards Enrichment Wrkbk: 59–60	**PRINT COMPONENT(S)** In-Depth Resources Unit 4: 3, 11, 19, 22, 24, 29, 32, 40, 43 In-Depth Resources in Spanish Unit 4: 105, 110, 114 History Makers Unit 4: 40 CA Reading Toolkit: 60, 62 CA Modified Lesson Plans for English Learners: 13.3, 14.1 CA Standards Planner & Lesson Plans: L111, L115 **TRANSPARENCIES/TECHNOLOGY** World Art & Cultures Transparencies: AT65 Critical Thinking Transparencies: CT29, CT66 Benchmark Tests: 13.3, 14.1 Power Presentations: 13.3, 14.1
10.5.4	Understand the nature of the war and its human costs (military and civilian) on all sides of the conflict, including how colonial peoples contributed to the war effort.	**Pupil & Teacher & eEdition** Common Pages: **417–418, 419–420, 421–422, 428, 429** Add'l Teacher Edition: 417–418, 418–420, 421 **PRINT COMPONENT(S)** CA Standards Enrichment Wrkbk: 61–62 **TRANSPARENCIES/TECHNOLOGY** CA Daily Standards Practice Transparencies: TT51	**PRINT COMPONENT(S)** In-Depth Resources Unit 4: 2, 3, 7, 10, 11, 13, 15, 18, 19, 21, 22 In-Depth Resources in Spanish Unit 4: 103, 104, 107, 108 CA Reading Toolkit: 60 CA Modified Lesson Plans for English Learners: 13.3 CA Standards Planner & Lesson Plans: L111 **TRANSPARENCIES/TECHNOLOGY** World Art & Cultures Transparencies: AT63, AT64 Critical Thinking Transparencies: CT29 Benchmark Tests: 13.2, 13.3 Power Presentations: 13.2, 13.3
10.5.5	Discuss human rights violations and genocide, including the Ottoman government's actions against Armenian citizens.	**Pupil & Teacher & eEdition** Common Pages: **410, 523** Add'l Teacher Edition: 523 **PRINT COMPONENT(S)** CA Standards Enrichment Wrkbk: 63–64	**PRINT COMPONENT(S)** In-Depth Resources Unit 4: 1, 6, 9, 16, 20 In-Depth Resources in Spanish Unit 4: 103, 107 History Makers Unit 4: 16 CA Reading Toolkit: 58 CA Modified Lesson Plans for English Learners: 13.1 CA Standards Planner & Lesson Plans: L107 **TRANSPARENCIES/TECHNOLOGY** Benchmark Tests: 13.1 Power Presentations: 13.1

Correlations to California History–Social Science Content Standards and Analysis Skills

Standard		Primary Citations	Supporting Citations
10.6	Students analyze the effects of the First World War.	**Pupil & Teacher & eEdition** Common Pages: 420–422, 423, 424–427, 428, 436–435, 436–445, 446–447, 448–452, 458–459, 464–465, 467, 470–475, 484, 486, R58 Add'l Teacher Edition: 423, 420–421, 424–426, 436–348, 440–444, 446–447, 448–451, 464–465, 470–474 **PRINT COMPONENT(S)** CA Standards Enrichment Wrkbk: 65–66, 67–68, 69–70, 71–72 **TRANSPARENCIES/TECHNOLOGY** CA Daily Standards Practice Transparencies: TT53a–TT53b, TT58	**PRINT COMPONENT(S)** In-Depth Resources Unit 4: 3, 4, 11, 12, 17, 18, 22–26, 29, 30, 32–34, 36, 38, 40, 41, 43–45, 47, 48, 52, 55, 56, 59, 62, 63, 65, 66, 68 In-Depth Resources in Spanish Unit 4: 105, 106, 110, 112, 114, 115, 117, 118, 120–122 History Makers Unit 4: 17, 40, 41, 62, 63 CA Reading Toolkit: 60, 61, 62, 63, 64, 66, 67, 69 CA Modified Lesson Plans for English Learners: 13.4, 15.1, 15.2, 15.3 CA Standards Planner & Lesson Plans: L111, L113, L115, L119, L123, L125, L129 **TRANSPARENCIES/TECHNOLOGY** World Art & Cultures Transparencies: AT66, AT67, AT68 Geography Transparencies: GT29, GT30, GT31, GT35 Critical Thinking Transparencies: CT29, CT30, CT65, CT67 Benchmark Tests: 13.3, 13.4, 14.1, 14.2, 14.3, 15.1, 15.2, 15.4 Power Presentations: 13.3, 13.4, 14.1, 14.2, 14.3, 15.1, 15.2, 15.4
10.6.1	Analyze the aims and negotiating roles of world leaders, the terms and influence of the Treaty of Versailles and Woodrow Wilson's Fourteen Points, and the causes and effects of the United States's rejection of the League of Nations on world politics.	**Pupil & Teacher & eEdition** Common Pages: **424–427, 428, 449, 472, R58** Add'l Teacher Edition: 424–426 **PRINT COMPONENT(S)** CA Standards Enrichment Wrkbk: 65–66	**PRINT COMPONENT(S)** In-Depth Resources Unit 4: 4, 11, 17, 26, 30, 34, 41, 45, 48, 52, 56, 66 In-Depth Resources in Spanish Unit 4: 105, 112, 115, 118, 121 History Makers Unit 4: 41 CA Reading Toolkit: 61, 64, 67 CA Modified Lesson Plans for English Learners: 13.4 CA Standards Planner & Lesson Plans: L113, L119 **TRANSPARENCIES/TECHNOLOGY** Critical Thinking Transparencies: CT29 Benchmark Tests: 13.4, 14.3, 15.2 Power Presentations: 13.4, 14.3, 15.2
10.6.2	Describe the effects of the war and resulting peace treaties on population movement, the international economy, and shifts in the geographic and political borders of Europe and the Middle East.	**Pupil & Teacher & eEdition** Common Pages: **420–422, 424–427, 428,** 435, **470–475, 486** Add'l Teacher Edition: 420–421, 424–426, 470–474 **PRINT COMPONENT(S)** CA Standards Enrichment Wrkbk: 67–68 **TRANSPARENCIES/TECHNOLOGY** CA Daily Standards Practice Transparencies: TT53a–TT53b	**PRINT COMPONENT(S)** In-Depth Resources Unit 4: 3, 4, 11, 12, 17, 18, 22, 23, 24, 29, 32, 40, 43, 45, 48, 52, 56, 66 In-Depth Resources in Spanish Unit 4: 105, 106, 110, 114, 118, 121 History Makers Unit 4: 17, 40 CA Reading Toolkit: 60, 61, 62, 67 CA Modified Lesson Plans for English Learners: 13.4, 15.2, 15.3 CA Standards Planner & Lesson Plans: L111 L113, L125 **TRANSPARENCIES/TECHNOLOGY** Geography Transparencies: GT29, GT30, GT35 Critical Thinking Transparencies: CT29, CT65 Benchmark Tests: 13.3, 13.4, 14.1, 15.2 Power Presentations: 13.3, 13.4, 14.1, 15.2

Standard		Primary Citations	Supporting Citations
10.6.3	Understand the widespread disillusionment with prewar institutions, authorities, and values that resulted in a void that was later filled by totalitarians.	**Pupil & Teacher & eEdition** Common Pages: 421, 422, **436–445, 446–447, 448–452, 458–459, 470** Add'l Teacher Edition: 436–348, 440–444, 446–447, 448–451, 470 **PRINT COMPONENT(S)** CA Standards Enrichment Wrkbk: 69–70	**PRINT COMPONENT(S)** In-Depth Resources Unit 4: 3, 11, 22, 24–26, 29, 30, 32–34, 36, 38, 40, 41, 43–45, 47, 55, 59, 62, 65 In-Depth Resources in Spanish Unit 4: 105, 112, 115, 117 History Makers Unit 4: 41, 62 CA Reading Toolkit: 60, 62, 63, 64, 67 CA Modified Lesson Plans for English Learners: 15.1, 15.2, 15.3 CA Standards Planner & Lesson Plans: L111, L115, L125 **TRANSPARENCIES/TECHNOLOGY** World Art & Cultures Transparencies: AT66, AT67, AT68 Geography Transparencies: GT30 Critical Thinking Transparencies: CT29, CT30 Benchmark Tests: 13.3, 14.1, 14.2, 14.3, 15.2 Power Presentations: 13.3, 14.1, 14.2, 14.3, 15.2
10.6.4	Discuss the influence of World War I on literature, art, and intellectual life in the West (e.g., Pablo Picasso, the "lost generation" of Gertrude Stein, Ernest Hemingway).	**Pupil & Teacher & eEdition** Common Pages: **421–422, 423,** 428, **464–465, 467, 484** Add'l Teacher Edition: 423, 464–465 **PRINT COMPONENT(S)** CA Standards Enrichment Wrkbk: 71–72 **TRANSPARENCIES/TECHNOLOGY** CA Daily Standards Practice Transparencies: TT58	**PRINT COMPONENT(S)** In-Depth Resources Unit 4: 3, 11, 12, 14, 22, 47, 50, 53, 55, 58, 59, 62, 63, 65, 68 In-Depth Resources in Spanish Unit 4: 105, 117, 120, 122 History Makers Unit 4: 62, 63 CA Reading Toolkit: 60, 66, 69 CA Modified Lesson Plans for English Learners: 15.1 CA Standards Planner & Lesson Plans: L123, L129 **TRANSPARENCIES/TECHNOLOGY** World Art & Cultures Transparencies: AT67, AT68 Geography Transparencies: GT31 Critical Thinking Transparencies: CT29, CT67 Benchmark Tests: 13.3, 15.1, 15.4 Power Presentations: 13.3, 15.1, 15.4
10.7	Students analyze the rise of totalitarian governments after World War I.	**Pupil & Teacher & eEdition** Common Pages: 433–439, 440–445, 446–447, 458, 462, 476–480, 482–485, 486, 491–492 Add'l Teacher Edition: 433–438, 440–444, 446–447, 462, 476–479, 482–484, 491–492 **PRINT COMPONENT(S)** CA Standards Enrichment Wrkbk: 73–74, 75–76, 77–78 **TRANSPARENCIES/TECHNOLOGY** CA Daily Standards Practice Transparencies: TT55	**PRINT COMPONENT(S)** In-Depth Resources Unit 4: 19, 20, 23, 24, 25, 26, 27, 29, 30, 32, 33, 34, 36, 38, 40, 43, 44, 49, 50, 53, 57, 58, 60, 63, 64, 67, 68, 69, 78, 85, 86, 88 In-Depth Resources in Spanish Unit 4: 110, 111, 114, 119, 120, 122 History Makers Unit 4: 40, 63 CA Reading Toolkit: 62, 63, 68, 69, 70 CA Modified Lesson Plans for English Learners: 14.1, 14.2 CA Standards Planner & Lesson Plans: L115, L117, L127, L129, L131 **TRANSPARENCIES/TECHNOLOGY** World Art & Cultures Transparencies: AT65, AT69 Geography Transparencies: GT30, GT32 Critical Thinking Transparencies: CT30, CT31, CT66, CT67 Benchmark Tests: 14.1, 14.2, 15.3, 15.4, 16.1 Power Presentations: 14.1, 14.2, 15.3, 15.4, 16.1

Correlations to California History–Social Science Content Standards and Analysis Skills

Standard		Primary Citations	Supporting Citations
10.7.1	Understand the causes and consequences of the Russian Revolution, including Lenin's use of totalitarian means to seize and maintain control (e.g., the Gulag).	**Pupil & Teacher & eEdition** Common Pages: **433–439, 441, 458** Add'l Teacher Edition: 433–438, 441 **PRINT COMPONENT(S)** CA Standards Enrichment Wrkbk: 73–74	**PRINT COMPONENT(S)** In-Depth Resources Unit 4: 19, 23, 24, 25, 26, 29, 32, 33, 34, 36, 38, 40, 43, 44 In-Depth Resources in Spanish Unit 4: 110, 111, 114 History Makers Unit 4: 40 CA Reading Toolkit: 62, 63 CA Modified Lesson Plans for English Learners: 14.1 CA Standards Planner & Lesson Plans: L115, L117 **TRANSPARENCIES/TECHNOLOGY** World Art & Cultures Transparencies: AT65 Geography Transparencies: GT30 Critical Thinking Transparencies: CT30, CT66 Benchmark Tests: 14.1, 14.2 Power Presentations: 14.1, 14.2
10.7.2	Trace Stalin's rise to power in the Soviet Union and the connection between economic policies, political policies, the absence of a free press, and systematic violations of human rights (e.g., the Terror Famine in Ukraine).	**Pupil & Teacher & eEdition** Common Pages: **439, 440–445, 446–447, 458** Add'l Teacher Edition: 440–444, 446–447 **PRINT COMPONENT(S)** CA Standards Enrichment Wrkbk: 75–76 **TRANSPARENCIES/TECHNOLOGY** CA Daily Standards Practice Transparencies: TT55	**PRINT COMPONENT(S)** In-Depth Resources Unit 4: 20, 24, 25, 27, 29, 30, 32, 33, 36, 38, 40, 43, 44 In-Depth Resources in Spanish Unit 4: 110, 111, 114 History Makers Unit 4: 40 CA Reading Toolkit: 62, 63 CA Modified Lesson Plans for English Learners: 14.2 CA Standards Planner & Lesson Plans: L115, L117 **TRANSPARENCIES/TECHNOLOGY** World Art & Cultures Transparencies: AT65 Geography Transparencies: GT30 Benchmark Tests: 14.1, 14.2 Power Presentations: 14.1, 14.2
10.7.3	Analyze the rise, aggression, and human costs of totalitarian regimes (Fascist and Communist) in Germany, Italy, and the Soviet Union, noting especially their common and dissimilar traits.	**Pupil & Teacher & eEdition** Common Pages: 438, 439, **440–445**, 458, 462, **476–480, 482–485, 486, 491–492** Add'l Teacher Edition: 440–444, 462, 476–479, 482–484, 491–492 **PRINT COMPONENT(S)** CA Standards Enrichment Wrkbk: 77–78	**PRINT COMPONENT(S)** In-Depth Resources Unit 4: 24, 25, 29, 32, 33, 36, 38, 39, 40, 42, 43, 44, 49, 50, 53, 57, 58, 60, 63, 64, 67, 68, 69, 78, 85, 86, 88 In-Depth Resources in Spanish Unit 4: 110, 111, 114, 119, 120, 122 History Makers Unit 4: 40, 63 CA Reading Toolkit: 62, 63, 68, 69, 70 CA Modified Lesson Plans for English Learners: 14.2 CA Standards Planner & Lesson Plans: L115, L117, L127, L129, L131 **TRANSPARENCIES/TECHNOLOGY** World Art & Cultures Transparencies: AT65, AT69 Geography Transparencies: GT30, GT31, GT32 Critical Thinking Transparencies: CT31, CT67 Benchmark Tests: 14.1, 14.2, 15.3, 15.4, 16.1 Power Presentations: 14.1, 14.2, 15.3, 15.4, 16.1

Standard		Primary Citations	Supporting Citations
10.8	Students analyze the causes and consequences of World War II.	**Pupil & Teacher & eEdition** Common Pages: 427, 439, 442–445, 447, 450–452, 456, 458, 470–475, 476–480, 481–485, 486–487, 491–496, 497–501, 502–505, 506–513, 514–517, 518–519, 522–523, 524–527 Add'l Teacher Edition: 405–512, 442–444, 446–447, 450–451, 470–474, 476–479, 481–484, 491–495, 497–500, 501, 502–504, 510, 514–516, 522–523, 524–525 **PRINT COMPONENT(S)** CA Standards Enrichment Wrkbk: 78–79, 81–82, 83–84, 85–86, 87–88, 89–90 **TRANSPARENCIES/TECHNOLOGY** CA Daily Standards Practice Transparencies: TT59, TT60, TT61, TT62, TT63, TT64, TT65, TT66	**PRINT COMPONENT(S)** In-Depth Resources Unit 4: 12, 17, 18, 23, 25, 26, 30, 33, 34, 36, 38, 40, 41, 44, 45, 48–50, 52–60, 63, 64, 66–92 In-Depth Resources in Spanish Unit 4: 106, 111, 112, 115, 118–122, 124–130 History Makers Unit 4: 17, 41, 63, 85, 86 CA Reading Toolkit: 61, 62, 63, 64, 67, 68, 69, 70, 71, 72, 73, 74 CA Modified Lesson Plans for English Learners: 15.2, 15.3, 15.4, 16.1, 16.2, 16.3, 16.4, 16.5 CA Standards Planner & Lesson Plans: L113, L117, L119, L125, L127, L129, L131, L133, L135, L137, L139 **TRANSPARENCIES/TECHNOLOGY** World Art & Cultures Transparencies: AT69, AT70, AT71 Geography Transparencies: GT29, GT30, GT31, GT32 Critical Thinking Transparencies: CT31, CT32, CT65, CT67, CT68 Videos: "Modern and Medieval Weapons" Benchmark Tests: 13.4, 14.2, 14.3, 15.2, 15.3, 15.4, 16.1, 16.2, 16.3, 16.4, 16.5 Power Presentations: 13.4, 14.2, 14.3, 15.2, 15.3, 15.4, 16.1, 16.2, 16.3, 16.4, 16.5
10.8.1	Compare the German, Italian, and Japanese drives for empire in the 1930s, including the 1937 Rape of Nanking, other atrocities in China, and the Stalin-Hitler Pact of 1939.	**Pupil & Teacher & eEdition** Common Pages: **450–452, 458, 476–480, 481–485, 486–487** Add'l Teacher Edition: 450–451, 476–479, 481–484 **PRINT COMPONENT(S)** CA Standards Enrichment Wrkbk: 78–79 **TRANSPARENCIES/TECHNOLOGY** CA Daily Standards Practice Transparencies: TT61	**PRINT COMPONENT(S)** In-Depth Resources Unit 4: 26, 30, 34, 41, 45, 49, 40, 53, 57, 58, 60, 63, 64, 67, 68 In-Depth Resources in Spanish Unit 4: 112, 115, 120, 122 History Makers Unit 4: 41, 63 CA Reading Toolkit: 64, 68, 69 CA Modified Lesson Plans for English Learners: 15.4, 16.1, 16.2 CA Standards Planner & Lesson Plans: L119, L127 **TRANSPARENCIES/TECHNOLOGY** World Art & Cultures Transparencies: AT69 Geography Transparencies: GT31 Critical Thinking Transparencies: CT31, CT32, CT67 Benchmark Tests: 14.3, 15.3, 15.4 Power Presentations: 14.3, 15.3, 15.4

Correlations to California History–Social Science Content Standards and Analysis Skills

Standard		Primary Citations	Supporting Citations
10.8.2	Understand the role of appeasement, nonintervention (isolationism), and the domestic distractions in Europe and the United States prior to the outbreak of World War II.	**Pupil & Teacher & eEdition** Common Pages: **427, 470–475, 481–485, 486–487** Add'l Teacher Edition: 470–474, 481–484 **PRINT COMPONENT(S)** CA Standards Enrichment Wrkbk: 81–82 **TRANSPARENCIES/TECHNOLOGY** CA Daily Standards Practice Transparencies: TT59	**PRINT COMPONENT(S)** In-Depth Resources Unit 4: 12, 17, 18, 23, 41, 48, 50, 52, 53, 56, 58, 63, 66, 68 In-Depth Resources in Spanish Unit 4: 106, 118, 120–122 History Makers Unit 4: 17, 63 CA Reading Toolkit: 61, 67, 69 CA Modified Lesson Plans for English Learners: 15.2, 15.3, 15.4, 16.1 CA Standards Planner & Lesson Plans: L113, L125, L129 **TRANSPARENCIES/TECHNOLOGY** Geography Transparencies: GT29, GT31 Critical Thinking Transparencies: CT31, CT32, CT65, CT67 Benchmark Tests: 13.4, 15.2, 15.4 Power Presentations: 13.4, 15.2, 15.4
10.8.3	Identify and locate the Allied and Axis powers on a map and discuss the major turning points of the war, the principal theaters of conflict, key strategic decisions, and the resulting war conferences and political resolutions, with emphasis on the importance of geographic factors.	**Pupil & Teacher & eEdition** Common Pages: **491–496, 497–501, 506–513, 518–519** Add'l Teacher Edition: 491–495, 497–500, 405–512 **PRINT COMPONENT(S)** CA Standards Enrichment Wrkbk: 83–84 **TRANSPARENCIES/TECHNOLOGY** CA Daily Standards Practice Transparencies: TT63, TT65	**PRINT COMPONENT(S)** In-Depth Resources Unit 4: 54, 55, 59, 60, 65, 69, 70, 72, 75, 76, 78, 79, 81, 85, 86, 88, 89, 91 In-Depth Resources in Spanish Unit 4: 124, 125, 127, 129, 130 History Makers Unit 4: 86 CA Reading Toolkit: 70, 71, 73 CA Modified Lesson Plans for English Learners: 16.1, 16.2, 16.4, 16.5 CA Standards Planner & Lesson Plans: L131, L133, L137 **TRANSPARENCIES/TECHNOLOGY** Videos: "Modern and Medieval Weapons" Geography Transparencies: GT32 Critical Thinking Transparencies: CT32, CT38 Benchmark Tests: 16.1, 16.2, 16.4 Power Presentations: 16.1, 16.2, 16.4
10.8.4	Describe the political, diplomatic, and military leaders during the war (e.g., Winston Churchill, Franklin Delano Roosevelt, Emperor Hirohito, Adolf Hitler, Benito Mussolini, Joseph Stalin, Douglas MacArthur, Dwight Eisenhower).	**Pupil & Teacher & eEdition** Common Pages: 439, **442–445,** 446–447, 456, 458, **475, 476–479,** 481, 485, 486–487, **493,** 496, 497, **500–501,** 503, 505, 506–507, 509–511, 513, 516–517, 518–519 Add'l Teacher Edition: 442–444, 446–447, 476–478, 493, 501, 503, 510, 516 **PRINT COMPONENT(S)** CA Standards Enrichment Wrkbk: 85–86 **TRANSPARENCIES/TECHNOLOGY** CA Daily Standards Practice Transparencies: TT62	**PRINT COMPONENT(S)** In-Depth Resources Unit 4: 25, 33, 36, 38, 44, 48, 52, 56, 66, 69, 70, 71–92 In-Depth Resources in Spanish Unit 4: 111, 118, 121, 124–130 History Makers Unit 4: 85, 86 CA Reading Toolkit: 62, 63, 67, 68, 69, 70, 71, 72, 73, 74 CA Modified Lesson Plans for English Learners: 16.2, 16.4 CA Standards Planner & Lesson Plans: L117, L125, L129, L131, L133, L135, L137, L139 **TRANSPARENCIES/TECHNOLOGY** World Art & Cultures Transparencies: AT70, AT71 Geography Transparencies: GT30, GT32 Critical Thinking Transparencies: CT32, CT68 Videos: "Modern and Medieval Weapons" Benchmark Tests: 14.2, 15.2, 15.4, 16.1, 16.2, 16.3, 16.4, 16.5 Power Presentations: 14.2, 15.2, 15.4, 16.1, 16.2, 16.3, 16.4, 16.5

Standard		Primary Citations	Supporting Citations
10.8.5	Analyze the Nazi policy of pursuing racial purity, especially against the European Jews; its transformation into the Final Solution; and the Holocaust that resulted in the murder of six million Jewish civilians.	**Pupil & Teacher & eEdition** Common Pages: **479–480, 502–505, 518–519, 523** Add'l Teacher Edition: 502–504, 523 **PRINT COMPONENT(S)** CA Standards Enrichment Wrkbk: 87–88 **TRANSPARENCIES/TECHNOLOGY** CA Daily Standards Practice Transparencies: TT60, TT64	**PRINT COMPONENT(S)** In-Depth Resources Unit 4: 46, 49, 56, 57, 60, 64, 66, 67, 71, 80, 82, 90 In-Depth Resources in Spanish Unit 4: 119, 126 CA Reading Toolkit: 68, 72 CA Modified Lesson Plans for English Learners: 16.3 CA Standards Planner & Lesson Plans: L127, L135 **TRANSPARENCIES/TECHNOLOGY** World Art & Cultures Transparencies: AT69, AT70 Critical Thinking Transparencies: CT31 Benchmark Tests: 15.3, 16.3 Power Presentations: 15.3, 16.3
10.8.6	Discuss the human costs of the war, with particular attention to the civilian and military losses in Russia, Germany, Britain, the United States, China, and Japan.	**Pupil & Teacher & eEdition** Common Pages: **491–496, 497–501,** 502–505, **514–517,** 518–519, **522–523, 524–525** Add'l Teacher Edition: 491–495, 497–500, 502–504, 514–516, 522–523, 524–525 **PRINT COMPONENT(S)** CA Standards Enrichment Wrkbk: 89–90 **TRANSPARENCIES/TECHNOLOGY** CA Daily Standards Practice Transparencies: TT63, TT66	**PRINT COMPONENT(S)** In-Depth Resources Unit 4: 63, 65, 69, 70, 71, 72–92 In-Depth Resources in Spanish Unit 4: 124–130 History Makers Unit 4: 85, 86 CA Reading Toolkit: 70, 71, 72, 74 CA Modified Lesson Plans for English Learners: 16.3, 16.4, 16.5 CA Standards Planner & Lesson Plans: L131, L133, L135, L139 **TRANSPARENCIES/TECHNOLOGY** World Art & Cultures Transparencies: AT70, AT71 Geography Transparencies: GT32 Critical Thinking Transparencies: CT32, CT68 Videos: "Modern and Medieval Weapons" Benchmark Tests: 16.1, 16.2, 16.3, 16.4, 16.5 Power Presentations: 16.1, 16.2, 16.3, 16.4, 16.5

Correlations to California History–Social Science Content Standards and Analysis Skills

Standard		Primary Citations	Supporting Citations
10.9	Students analyze the international developments in the post-World War II world.	**Pupil & Teacher & eEdition** Common Pages: 28–29, 78–80, 89, 241, 254, 432, 448–452, 458, 512, 521, 531–532, 533–536, 538–541, 542–547, 550–551, 552–553, 554–556, 557, 558, 581–582, 583–589, 590–593, 594–595, 612–617, 618–624, 625–628, 630, 632–633, 648, 649, 650, 652, 666–671, 691–692, 693, 694, 696, 697 Add'l Teacher Edition: 28, 78–80, 254, 241, 432, 448–451, 512, 520–521, 531–535, 537–540, 542–546, 548–552, 554–556, 581–588, 590–592, 612–616, 618–623, 625–627, 648, 650, 666–670, 691–692, 694, 696 **PRINT COMPONENT(S)** CA Standards Enrichment Wrkbk: 91–92, 93–94, 95–96, 97–98, 99–100, 101–102, 103–104, 105–106 **TRANSPARENCIES/TECHNOLOGY** CA Daily Standards Practice Transparencies: TT56, TT67, TT68a–TT68b, TT69, TT70, TT71, TT75, TT75.5, TT78, TT79	**PRINT COMPONENT(S)** In-Depth Resources Unit 1: 41, 58; Unit 2: 52, 72, 74, 82, 92; Unit 4: 26, 30, 34, 41, 45, 72, 75, 79, 81, 91, 53, 62, 68, 72, 76, 85, 91, 95; Unit 5: 1–25, 28–30, 32, 33, 37, 38, 40, 42- 44, 52–55, 61, 62, 68, 71, 72, 73, 76, 85, 91, 95 In-Depth Resources in Spanish ; Unit 1: 26; Unit 2: 62–64, 68; Unit 4: 112, 115, 127, 129; Unit 5: 132–138, 142–145, 149–152, 157 History Makers Unit 4: 41; Unit 5: 17, 18, 42, 43, 91 CA Reading Toolkit: L14, 36, 38, 64, 73, 75, 76, 77, 78, 79, 83, 84, 88, 89, 92 CA Modified Lesson Plans for English Learners: 14.3, 17.1, 17.2, 17.3, 17.4, 17.5, 18.4, 19.3, 19.4, 19.5, 20.3 CA Standards Planner & Lesson Plans: L7, L19, L63, L67, L119, L137, L141, L143, L147, L149, L155, L157, L159, L165, L167, L169, L175 **TRANSPARENCIES/TECHNOLOGY** World Art & Cultures Transparencies: AT35, AT72, AT73, AT75, AT78 Geography Transparencies: GT33, GT35 Critical Thinking Transparencies: CT23, CT32, CT33, CT34, CT36, CT59, CT71 Videos: "Modern and Medieval Weapons" Benchmark Tests: 2.2, 7.5, 8.2, 14.3, 16.4, 17.1, 17.2, 17.3, 17.4, 17.5, 18.3, 18.4, 18.5, 19.3, 19.4, 19.5, 20.3 Power Presentations: 2.2, 7.5, 8.2, 14.3, 16.4, 17.1, 17.2, 17.3, 17.4, 17.5, 18.3, 18.4, 18.5, 19.3, 19.4, 19.5, 20.3

Standard		Primary Citations	Supporting Citations
10.9.1	Compare the economic and military power shifts caused by the war, including the Yalta Pact, the development of nuclear weapons, Soviet control over Eastern European nations, and the economic recoveries of Germany and Japan.	**Pupil & Teacher & eEdition** Common Pages: **512,** 520–521, **531–532, 533–536, 554–556, 558,** 618–624, 632, 649, 691–692, 693 Add'l Teacher Edition: 512, 520–521, 531–532, 533–535, 554–556, 618–623, 691–692 **PRINT COMPONENT(S)** CA Standards Enrichment Wrkbk: 91–92 **TRANSPARENCIES/TECHNOLOGY** CA Daily Standards Practice Transparencies: TT79	**PRINT COMPONENT(S)** In-Depth Resources Unit 4: 72, 75, 79, 81, 91, 53, 62, 68, 72, 76, 85, 91, 95; Unit 5: 1, 4, 8, 12, 14, 18–21, 24, 53, 62, 68, 72 In-Depth Resources in Spanish Unit 4: 127, 129, Unit 5: 132, 135, 138, 150, 157 History Makers Unit 5: 18, 91 CA Reading Toolkit: 73, 75, 79, 88, 92 CA Modified Lesson Plans for English Learners: 17.1, 17.5 CA Standards Planner & Lesson Plans: L137, L149, L167, L175 **TRANSPARENCIES/TECHNOLOGY** World Art & Cultures Transparencies: AT35, AT78 Geography Transparencies: GT33, GT35 Critical Thinking Transparencies: CT32, CT33, CT36 Videos: "Modern and Medieval Weapons" Benchmark Tests: 16.4, 17.1, 17.5, 19.4, 20.3 Power Presentations: 16.4, 17.1, 17.5, 19.4, 20.3
10.9.2	Analyze the causes of the Cold War, with the free world on one side and Soviet client states on the other, including competition for influence in such places as Egypt, the Congo, Vietnam, and Chile.	**Pupil & Teacher & eEdition** Common Pages: **531–557, 558, 581–582, 594–595** Add'l Teacher Edition: 531–535, 537, 538–540, 542–546, 548–552, 554–556, 581 **PRINT COMPONENT(S)** CA Standards Enrichment Wrkbk: 93–94 **TRANSPARENCIES/TECHNOLOGY** CA Daily Standards Practice Transparencies: TT69, TT70	**PRINT COMPONENT(S)** In-Depth Resources Unit 5: 1–3, 4, 5–10, 11, 12, 13, 25, 28, 32, 33, 37, 40, 42, 44, 76, 85, 91, 95 In-Depth Resources in Spanish Unit 5: 132–138, 142, 144, 145, 157 History Makers Unit 5: 17, 18, 42, 91 CA Reading Toolkit: 75, 76, 77, 78, 79, 82 CA Modified Lesson Plans for English Learners: 17.1, 17.2, 17.3, 17.4 CA Standards Planner & Lesson Plans: L143, L147, L149, L155 **TRANSPARENCIES/TECHNOLOGY** World Art & Cultures Transparencies: AT72, AT73 Geography Transparencies: GT33 Critical Thinking Transparencies: CT33, CT36, CT69 Benchmark Tests: 17.1, 17.2, 17.3, 17.4, 17.5, 18.3, 20.3 Power Presentations: 17.1, 17.2, 17.3, 17.4, 17.5, 18.3, 20.3

Correlations to California History–Social Science Content Standards and Analysis Skills

Standard		Primary Citations	Supporting Citations
10.9.3	Understand the importance of the Truman Doctrine and the Marshall Plan, which established the pattern for America's postwar policy of supplying economic and military aid to prevent the spread of Communism and the resulting economic and political competition in arenas such as Southeast Asia (i.e., the Korean War, Vietnam War), Cuba, and Africa.	**Pupil & Teacher & eEdition** Common Pages: **534, 536, 542–547, 550–553, 557,** 558 Add'l Teacher Edition: 534, 542–546, 550–552 **PRINT COMPONENT(S)** CA Standards Enrichment Wrkbk: 95–96 **TRANSPARENCIES/TECHNOLOGY** CA Daily Standards Practice Transparencies: TT70	**PRINT COMPONENT(S)** In-Depth Resources Unit 5: 1, 2, 3, 4, 5, 6, 7, 8, 9, 10, 11, 12–25 In-Depth Resources in Spanish Unit 5: 132–138 History Makers Unit 5: 17, 18 CA Reading Toolkit: 75, 77, 78, 79 CA Modified Lesson Plans for English Learners: 17.1, 17.2, 17.3, 17.4, 17.5 CA Standards Planner & Lesson Plans: L141, L147 **TRANSPARENCIES/TECHNOLOGY** World Art & Cultures Transparencies: AT72, AT73 Geography Transparencies: GT33 Critical Thinking Transparencies: CT33, CT69 Benchmark Tests: 17.1, 17.3, 17.4, 17.5 Power Presentations: 17.1, 17.3, 17.4, 17.5
10.9.4	Analyze the Chinese Civil War, the rise of Mao Tse-tung, and the subsequent political and economic upheavals in China (e.g., the Great Leap Forward, the Cultural Revolution, and the Tiananmen Square uprising).	**Pupil & Teacher & eEdition** Common Pages: 432, **448–452,** 458, **538–553,** 558, **625–628, 630, 632–633** Add'l Teacher Edition: 432, 448–451, 538–540, 542–546, 548–552, 625–627 **PRINT COMPONENT(S)** CA Standards Enrichment Wrkbk: 97–98 **TRANSPARENCIES/TECHNOLOGY** CA Daily Standards Practice Transparencies: TT56, TT68a–TT68b	**PRINT COMPONENT(S)** In-Depth Resources Unit 4: 26, 30, 34, 41, 45; Unit 5: 2, 7, 9, 10, 22, 41, 53, 54, 56, 62, 68, 72, 73 In-Depth Resources in Spanish Unit 4: 112, 115; Unit 5: 133, 137, 150, 151, 152 History Makers Unit 4: 41 CA Reading Toolkit: 64, 76, 89 CA Modified Lesson Plans for English Learners: 14.3, 17.2, 19.5 CA Standards Planner & Lesson Plans: L119, L143, L169 **TRANSPARENCIES/TECHNOLOGY** World Art & Cultures Transparencies: AT72, AT78 Geography Transparencies: GT35 Critical Thinking Transparencies: CT35, CT71 Benchmark Tests: 14.3, 17.2, 19.4, 19.5 Power Presentations: 14.3, 17.2, 19.4, 19.5

Standard	Primary Citations	Supporting Citations
10.9.5 Describe the uprisings in Poland (1952), Hungary (1956), and Czechoslovakia (1968) and those countries' resurgence in the 1970s and 1980s as people in Soviet satellites sought freedom from Soviet control.	**Pupil & Teacher & eEdition** Common Pages: **552–553, 554–555, 556, 618–624, 632** Add'l Teacher Edition: 552, 554, 556, 618–623 **PRINT COMPONENT(S)** CA Standards Enrichment Wrkbk: 99–100 **TRANSPARENCIES/TECHNOLOGY** CA Daily Standards Practice Transparencies: TT71	**PRINT COMPONENT(S)** In-Depth Resources Unit 5: 4, 5, 8, 12, 13, 18, 24, 25, 53, 54, 56, 62, 68, 72, 73 In-Depth Resources in Spanish Unit 5: 134–136, 138, 150–152 History Makers Unit 5: 17, 18 CA Reading Toolkit: 78, 79, 88 CA Modified Lesson Plans for English Learners: 17.4, 17.5, 19.3 CA Standards Planner & Lesson Plans: L147, L149, L167 **TRANSPARENCIES/TECHNOLOGY** World Art & Cultures Transparencies: AT73, AT78 Geography Transparencies: GT35 Critical Thinking Transparencies: CT33, CT35, CT69, CT71 Benchmark Tests: 17.4, 17.5, 19.4, 19.5 Power Presentations: 17.4, 17.5, 19.4, 19.5
10.9.6 Understand how the forces of nationalism developed in the Middle East, how the Holocaust affected world opinion regarding the need for a Jewish state, and the significance and effects of the location and establishment of Israel on world affairs.	**Pupil & Teacher & eEdition** Common Pages: **78–80**, 89, **254, 583–589, 594–595, 666–671** Add'l Teacher Edition: 78–80, 254, 582–588, 666–670 **PRINT COMPONENT(S)** CA Standards Enrichment Wrkbk: 101–102 **TRANSPARENCIES/TECHNOLOGY** CA Daily Standards Practice Transparencies: TT75	**PRINT COMPONENT(S)** In-Depth Resources Unit 1: 41, 58; Unit 2: 74, 82, 92; Unit 5: 23, 29, 30, 35, 38, 43 In-Depth Resources in Spanish Unit 1: 26; Unit 2: 68; Unit 5: 143 History Makers Unit 5: 43 CA Reading Toolkit: L14, 38, 83 CA Modified Lesson Plans for English Learners: 17.4, 17.5, 18.4, 19.3 CA Standards Planner & Lesson Plans: L19, L67, L157 **TRANSPARENCIES/TECHNOLOGY** World Art & Cultures Transparencies: AT75 Critical Thinking Transparencies: CT34 Benchmark Tests: 2.2, 8.2, 18.4 Power Presentations: 2.2, 8.2, 18.4
10.9.7 Analyze the reasons for the collapse of the Soviet Union, including the weakness of the command economy, burdens of military commitments, and growing resistance to Soviet rule by dissidents in satellite states and the non-Russian Soviet republics.	**Pupil & Teacher & eEdition** Common Pages: **556–557, 590–593, 594, 612–617, 618–624,** 632 Add'l Teacher Edition: 556, 590–592, 612–616, 618–623 **PRINT COMPONENT(S)** CA Standards Enrichment Wrkbk: 103–104 **TRANSPARENCIES/TECHNOLOGY** CA Daily Standards Practice Transparencies: TT71, TT75.5, TT78	**PRINT COMPONENT(S)** In-Depth Resources Unit 5: 5, 13, 25, 30, 39, 52, 53, 61, 62, 68, 71, 72 In-Depth Resources in Spanish Unit 5: 136, 144, 149, 150 CA Reading Toolkit: 79, 84, 87, 88, 89 CA Modified Lesson Plans for English Learners: 19.4 CA Standards Planner & Lesson Plans: L149, L159, L165, L167 **TRANSPARENCIES/TECHNOLOGY** World Art & Cultures Transparencies: AT78 Geography Transparencies: GT35 Critical Thinking Transparencies: CT35, CT69, CT70 Benchmark Tests: 17.5, 18.5, 19.3, 19.4 Power Presentations: 17.5, 18.5, 19.3, 19.4

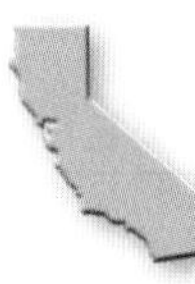

Correlations to California History–Social Science Content Standards and Analysis Skills

Standard		Primary Citations	Supporting Citations
10.9.8	Discuss the establishment and work of the United Nations and the purposes and functions of the Warsaw Pact, SEATO, NATO, and the Organization of American States.	**Pupil & Teacher & eEdition** Common Pages: **28–29,** 241, **532, 535, 536, 648,** 650, 652, 692, 693, 694, 696, 697 Add'l Teacher Edition: 28, 241, 532, 648, 650, 692, 694, 696 **PRINT COMPONENT(S)** CA Standards Enrichment Wrkbk: 105–106 **TRANSPARENCIES/TECHNOLOGY** CA Daily Standards Practice Transparencies: TT67	**PRINT COMPONENT(S)** In-Depth Resources Unit 2: 52, 72; Unit 5: 1, 14, 19, 20, 21, 76, 85, 91, 95; Unit 2: 52, 72 In-Depth Resources in Spanish Unit 2: 62–64; Unit 5: 132, 157 History Makers Unit 5: 91 CA Reading Toolkit: 36, 75, 92 CA Modified Lesson Plans for English Learners: 17.1, 20.3 CA Standards Planner & Lesson Plans: L7, L63, L175 **TRANSPARENCIES/TECHNOLOGY** Geography Transparencies: GT33 Critical Thinking Transparencies: CT23, CT36, CT59 Benchmark Tests: 7.5, 17.1, 20.3 Power Presentations: 7.5, 17.1, 20.3
10.10	Students analyze instances of nation-building in the contemporary world in at least two of the following regions or countries: the Middle East, Africa, Mexico and other parts of Latin America, and China.	**Pupil & Teacher & eEdition** Common Pages: 72–77, 78–81, 90, 599–605, 608–609, 610–611, 625–638, 641–647, 648–652, 653–658, 659–663, 664, 670–671, 675–678, 679–682, 683–686, 687–689, 698, 699, 606–611, 626–629, 632, 648–652, 664, 666–667, 668–669, 694–697, 698 Add'l Teacher Edition: 72–76, 78–80, 599–604, 606–610, 624–638, 641–646, 648–651, 653–657, 659–662, 666–667, 668–669, 670–671, 675–677, 679–681, 683–685, 687–688, 694–696 **PRINT COMPONENT(S)** CA Standards Enrichment Wrkbk: 107–108, 109–110, 111–112 **TRANSPARENCIES/TECHNOLOGY** CA Daily Standards Practice Transparencies: TT68a–TT68b, TT74a–TT74b, TT76, TT77a–TT77b, TT80, TT83.5, TT83a–TT83b	**PRINT COMPONENT(S)** In-Depth Resources Unit 1: 40, 41, 44, 47, 51, 54, 57, 58; Unit 5: 2, 7, 10, 22, 23, 28, 32, 33, 37, 40, 42, 44, 50, 51, 53–60, 62–70, 72, 73, 75–77, 78, 80, 81, 84–86, 87, 91, 92, 94–97 In-Depth Resources in Spanish Unit 1: 25, 26, 28; Unit 5: 133, 137, 142, 144, 145, 147, 148, 150–153, 156–160 History Makers Unit 1: 54; Unit 5: 42, 66, 67, 91 CA Reading Toolkit: L13, L14, 85, 86, 89, 91, 92, 93, 94 CA Modified Lesson Plans for English Learners: 18.1, 18.2, 18.3, 18.4, 18.5, 19.1, 19.5, 19.5, 20.2, 20.3, 20.4, 20.5, Epil.1, Epil.3, Epil.4 CA Standards Planner & Lesson Plans: L17, L19, L161, L163, L169, L173, L175, L177, L179 **TRANSPARENCIES/TECHNOLOGY** World Art & Cultures Transparencies: AT39, AT72, AT75, AT76, AT77, AT78 Geography Transparencies: GT18, GT35, GT36 Critical Thinking Transparencies: CT35, CT36, CT71, CT72 Videos: "Revolutions in Latin America and South Africa," "Trade Connects the World," "The United States and The World" Benchmark Tests: 2.1, 2.2, 19.1, 19.2, 19.4, 19.5, 20.2, 20.3, 20.4, 20.5 Power Presentations: 2.1, 2.2, 19.1, 19.2, 19.4, 19.5, 20.2, 20.3, 20.4, 20.5

Standard	Primary Citations	Supporting Citations
10.10.1 Understand the challenges in the regions, including their geopolitical, cultural, military, and economic significance and the international relationships in which they are involved.	**Pupil & Teacher & eEdition** Common Pages: 72–77, 78–81, 90, **599–605, 606–611, 625–632, 641–647, 659–663,** 664, 694–697, 698 Add'l Teacher Edition: 72–76, 78–80, 599–604, 606–610, 624–638, 630–631, 641–646, 659–662, 694–696 **PRINT COMPONENT(S)** CA Standards Enrichment Wrkbk: 107–108 **TRANSPARENCIES/TECHNOLOGY** CA Daily Standards Practice Transparencies: TT74a–TT74b, TT76, TT83.5	**PRINT COMPONENT(S)** In-Depth Resources Unit 1: 40, 41, 44, 47, 51, 54, 57, 58; Unit 5: 22, 23, 24, 25, 28, 32, 33, 37, 38, 40, 42, 44, 50, 51, 53–60, 62–70, 72, 73, 75, 77, 78, 80, 81, 84, 86, 87, 92, 94, 96, 97 In-Depth Resources in Spanish Unit 1: 25, 26, 28, Unit 5: 142, 144, 145, 147, 148, 150–153, 156, 158–160 History Makers Unit 1: 54; Unit 5: 42, 66, 67 CA Reading Toolkit: L13, L14, 85, 86, 89, 91, 94 CA Modified Lesson Plans for English Learners: 18.1, 18.2, 18.3, 18.4, 18.5, 19.1, 19.5, 20.2, 20.3, 20.4, Epil.1, Epil.4 CA Standards Planner & Lesson Plans: L17, L19, L161, L163, L169, L173, L179 **TRANSPARENCIES/TECHNOLOGY** World Art & Cultures Transparencies: AT39, AT75, AT76, AT77, AT78 Geography Transparencies: GT18, GT35, GT36 Critical Thinking Transparencies: CT35, CT71, CT72 Videos: "Revolutions in Latin America and South Africa," "Trade Connects the World," "The United States and The World" Benchmark Tests: 2.1, 2.2, 18.3, 19.1, 19.2, 19.4, 19.5, 20.2, 20.4, 20.5 Power Presentations: 2.1, 2.2, 18.3, 19.1, 19.2, 19.4, 19.5, 20.2, 20.4, 20.5
10.10.2 Describe the recent history of the regions, including political divisions and systems, key leaders, religious issues, natural features, resources, and population patterns.	**Pupil & Teacher & eEdition** Common Pages: **599–605, 606–611, 626–629,** 632, 648–652, 664, **666–667, 668–669** Add'l Teacher Edition: 599–604, 606–610, 626–628, 648–651, 666–667, 668–669 **PRINT COMPONENT(S)** CA Standards Enrichment Wrkbk: 109–110 **TRANSPARENCIES/TECHNOLOGY** CA Daily Standards Practice Transparencies: TT68a–TT68b, TT77a–TT77b, TT80, TT83a–TT83b, TT83.5	**PRINT COMPONENT(S)** In-Depth Resources Unit 5: 2, 7, 10, 22, 23, 34, 35, 41, 50, 51, 53–57, 59, 60, 62, 63, 66–70, 72, 73, 76, 77, 85, 91, 95, 96 In-Depth Resources in Spanish Unit 5: 133, 137, 147, 148, 150–152, 157, 158 History Makers Unit 5: 66, 67, 91 CA Reading Toolkit: 85, 86, 89, 92 CA Modified Lesson Plans for English Learners: 18.1, 18.2, 18.3, 18.4, 18.5, 19.5, 20.2, 20.3, Epil.3 CA Standards Planner & Lesson Plans: L161, L163, L169, L175 **TRANSPARENCIES/TECHNOLOGY** World Art & Cultures Transparencies: AT72, AT76, AT77, AT78 Geography Transparencies: GT35 Critical Thinking Transparencies: CT35, CT36, CT71 Videos: "Revolutions in Latin America and South Africa" Benchmark Tests: 17.2, 19.1, 19.2, 19.4, 19.5, 20.3, 20.4 Power Presentations: 17.2, 19.1, 19.2, 19.4, 19.5, 20.3, 20.4

Correlations to California History–Social Science Content Standards and Analysis Skills

Standard	Primary Citations	Supporting Citations
10.10.3 Discuss the important trends in the regions today and whether they appear to serve the cause of individual freedom and democracy.	**Pupil & Teacher & eEdition** Common Pages: 602–605, 608–611, 628–629, 632, **641–647, 648–652,** 653–658, 664, **670–671,** 675–678, 679–682, **683–686, 687–689,** 698, 699 Add'l Teacher Edition: 602–604, 608–610, 628, 641–646, 648–651, 653–657, 670–671, 675–677, 679–681, 683–685, 687–688 **PRINT COMPONENT(S)** CA Standards Enrichment Wrkbk: 111–112 **TRANSPARENCIES/TECHNOLOGY** CA Daily Standards Practice Transparencies: TT77a–TT77b	**PRINT COMPONENT(S)** In-Depth Resources Unit 5: 37, 38, 41, 43, 50, 51, 53–60, 62–70, 72, 73, 75–77, 80, 81, 84, 85, 87, 91, 94–96 In-Depth Resources in Spanish Unit 5: 147, 148, 149–152, 156–160 History Makers Unit 5: 66, 67, 91 CA Reading Toolkit: 85, 86, 89, 91, 92, 93 CA Modified Lesson Plans for English Learners: 18.1, 18.2, 18.3, 19.5, 20.2, 20.3, 20.5 CA Standards Planner & Lesson Plans: L161, L163, L169, L173, L175, L177 **TRANSPARENCIES/TECHNOLOGY** World Art & Cultures Transparencies: AT76, AT77, AT78 Geography Transparencies: GT35, GT36 Critical Thinking Transparencies: CT35, CT36, CT71 Videos: "Revolutions in Latin America and South Africa," "Trade Connects the World" Benchmark Tests: 19.1, 19.2, 19.4, 19.5, 20.2, 20.3, 20.4 Power Presentations: 19.1, 19.2, 19.4, 19.5, 20.2, 20.3, 20.4
10.11 Students analyze the integration of countries into the world economy and the information, technological, and communications revolutions (e.g., television, satellites, computers).	**Pupil & Teacher & eEdition** Common Pages: **637–640, 641–647, 648–652, 659–663, 675–678** Add'l Teacher Edition: 637–639, 641–646, 648–651, 659–662, 675–677 **PRINT COMPONENT(S)** CA Standards Enrichment Wrkbk: 113–114 **TRANSPARENCIES/TECHNOLOGY** CA Daily Standards Practice Transparencies: TT73, TT81, TT82, TT84a–TT84b	**PRINT COMPONENT(S)** In-Depth Resources Unit 1: 1, 2, 5, 6, 8, 9, 11, 15, 16, 18, 19, 21, 23, 24, 33, 42, 45, 49, 50, 55, 56, 59, 60, 62, 67, 68, 73–75, 76, 77, 78, 80, 84; Unit 2: 4, 5, 7, 11, 12, 13, 18, 19, 23, 24, 25, 27, 30, 31, 33, 38, 41–44, 46, 49–52, 54, 55, 57–59, 61, 65–69, 71, 72; Unit 3: 1, 2, 4, 6, 7, 9–11, 13, 16–20, 22, 24, 29, 32, 35, 44, 71, 77, 79, 86, 90; Unit 4: 17, 23, 26, 30, 34, 41, 45, 72, 73, 75, 79, 81, 87, 91, 92; Unit 5: 3, 4, 8, 11, 12, 17, 18, 23, 24, 26, 35, 36, 54 In-Depth Resources in Spanish Unit 1: 11, 12, 15, 16, 19, 21, 23, 25–28, 29, 31, 33; Unit 2: 46–50, 52, 54, 56, 57, 62–64, 68, 69, 72; Unit 3: 74, 75–79, 81, 82, 86, 96, 97, 101, 104, 108; Unit 4: 112, 115, 117, 127–129; Unit 5: 134, 135, 138, 141, 150, 156, 159, 160 History Makers Unit 1: 5, 15, 33, 55, 74, 75; Unit 2: 17, 18, 41, 65; Unit 3: 16, 17, 40, 86; Unit 4: 41, 62; Unit 5: 17, 18 CA Reading Toolkit: 90, 91, 92, 94 CA Modified Lesson Plans for English Learners: 20.1, 20.3, 20.4, 20.5, Epil.1, Epil.3, Epil.4 CA Standards Planner & Lesson Plans: L171, L173, L175, L179 **TRANSPARENCIES/TECHNOLOGY** World Art & Cultures Transparencies: AT12, AT36, AT37, AT38, AT40, AT41, AT42, AT46, AT47, AT48, AT54, AT55, AT57, AT60, AT61, AT63, AT64, AT67, AT68, AT70, AT71, AT73, AT74, AT78 Geography Transparencies: GT19, GT22, GT24, GT25, GT26, GT37, GT25, GT28, GT34, GT35, GT36 Critical Thinking Transparencies: CT17, CT18, CT19, CT21, CT22, CT23, CT24, CT25, CT32, CT33, CT34, CT37, CT53, CT55, CT57, CT59, CT61, CT68, CT72 Videos: "The Industrial and Electronic Revolutions," "The Geography of Food," "Modern and Medieval Weapons," "Trade Connects the World" Benchmark Tests: 18.2, 20.1, 20.2, 20.3, 20.5 Power Presentations: 18.2, 20.1, 20.2, 20.3, 20.5

Standard		Primary Citations	Supporting Citations
CHRONOLOGICAL AND SPATIAL THINKING			
CST(1)	Students compare the present with the past, evaluating the consequences of past events and decisions and determining the lessons that were learned.	**Pupil & Teacher & eEdition** Common Pages: 8, **9**, 49, **52–53,** 85, 98, 101, 111, 178–179, **183,** 203, 223, 241, **285,** 294, 304, 321, **322–323,** 372, 449, 516, 547, **553,** 565, 631 Add'l Teacher Edition: 8, 9, 49, 52–53, 85, 98, 101, 111, 178–179, 203, 223, 285, 322–323, 372, 449, 516, 565, 631 **PRINT COMPONENT(S)** CA Standards Enrichment Wrkbk: 1–16 **TRANSPARENCIES/TECHNOLOGY** CA Daily Standards Practice Transparencies: TT20	**PRINT COMPONENT(S)** In-Depth Resources Unit 1: 1, 2, 5, 6, 8, 9, 15, 19, 24, 42, 45, 49, 50, 55, 56, 59, 60, 62, 67, 68, 73–75, 76, 77, 78, 80, 84; Unit 2: 4, 5, 7, 11, 12, 13, 18, 19, 23, 24, 25, 27, 30, 31, 33, 38, 41, 43, 44, 46, 49, 51, 52, 54, 55, 57–59, 61, 65, 66, 67, 71, 72; Unit 3: 1, 2, 4, 6, 7, 9–11, 13, 16–20, 22, 24, 29, 32, 35, 44, 71, 77, 79, 86, 90; Unit 4: 17, 23, 26, 30, 34, 41, 45, 72, 73, 75, 79, 81, 87, 91, 92; Unit 5: 3, 4, 8, 11, 12, 17, 18, 23, 24, 26, 35, 36, 54 In-Depth Resources in Spanish Unit 1: 11, 12, 15, 16, 19, 23, 27, 29, 31, 33, 47–49, 52, 54, 56, 57, 62–64; Unit 3: 74, 75, 77–79, 82, 86, 96, 101: Unit 4: 112, 115, 127–129; Unit 5: 134, 135, 138 History Makers Unit 1: 15, 55, 74, 75; Unit 2: 18, 41, 65; Unit 3: 16, 17, 86; Unit 4: 41; Unit 5: 17, 18 CA Reading Toolkit: L10, L15, 16, 18, 26, 27, 30, 33, 36, 41, 42, 44, 46, 54, 64, 74, 77, 78, 80 CA Modified Lesson Plans for English Learners: Prol.1, Prol.2, Prol.3, Prol.4, 1.2, 1.4, 2.1, 2.3, 3.1, 5.2, 5.3, 5.4, 5.5, 6.2, 6.3, 7.1, 7.2, 7.5, 8.1, 8.3, 9.1, 9.3, 9.4, 10.1, 10.2, 10.4, 13.3, 14.2, 15.1, 15.4, 16.3, 16.4, 16.5, 18.3, 18.4, 18.5 **TRANSPARENCIES/TECHNOLOGY** World Art & Cultures Transparencies: AT12, AT38, AT40, AT41, AT42, AT46, AT47, AT48, AT54, AT57, AT60, AT70, AT71, AT73, AT74 Geography Transparencies: GT19, GT22, GT25, GT26 Critical Thinking Transparencies: CT18, CT19, CT21, CT22, CT23, CT25, CT32, CT33, CT34, CT37, CT55, CT57, CT59, CT61, CT68 Videos: "The Industrial and Electronic Revolutions," "The Geography of Food," "Modern and Medieval Weapons" Benchmark Tests: Prol.1, Prol.2, 1.2, 2.3, 3.1, 3.3, 5.4, 5.5, 6.1, 6.3, 7.2, 7.4, 7.5, 9.1, 9.2, 9.4, 10.2, 12.1, 14.3, 16.4, 16.5, 17.3, 17.4, 18.1 Power Presentations: Prol.1, Prol.2, 1.2, 2.3, 3.1, 3.3, 5.4, 5.5, 6.1, 6.3, 7.2, 7.4, 7.5, 9.1, 9.2, 9.4, 10.2, 12.1, 14.3, 16.4, 16.5, 17.3, 17.4, 18.1

Correlations to California History–Social Science Content Standards and Analysis Skills

Standard		Primary Citations	Supporting Citations
CST(2)	Students analyze how change happens at different rates at different times; understand that some aspects can change while others remain the same; and understand that change is complicated and affects not only technology and politics but also values and beliefs.	**Pupil & Teacher & eEdition** Common Pages: 34, 43, 50, **254, 293,** 298, 303, 315, 379, 414, **468–469, 577,** 596–597, 621, **644** Add'l Teacher Edition: 34, 50, 254, 293, 298, 303, 315, 414, 468–469, 577, 596–597, 621, 644 **PRINT COMPONENT(S)** CA Standards Enrichment Wrkbk: 1–16 **TRANSPARENCIES/TECHNOLOGY** CA Daily Standards Practice Transparencies: TT2a–TT2b, TT4, TT10a–TT10b, TT17a–TT17b, TT30a–TT30b, TT37, TTA	**PRINT COMPONENT(S)** In-Depth Resources Unit 1: 4, 38, 68; Unit 2: 5, 54; Unit 3: 21, 35; Unit 4: 3, 17, 36, 40, 53, 58, 71; Unit 5: 4, 20, 55 In-Depth Resources in Spanish Unit 1: 11, 15, 16, 18, 19, 21, 23, 33; Unit 2: 46, 50, 68, 69, 72; Unit 3: 75–79, 81, 97, 104, 108; Unit 4: 117; Unit 5: 141, 150, 156, 159, 160 History Makers Unit 1: 5, 33, 75; Unit 2: 17; Unit 3: 17, 40; Unit 4: 62 CA Reading Toolkit: L9, L10, 38, 42, 43, 44, 45, 55, 59, 66, 81, 88, 91 CA Modified Lesson Plans for English Learners: 1.3, 2.2, 2.3, 3.1, 4.2, 4.4, 5.1, 5.2, 5.3, 5.4, 5.5, 6.1, 6.2, 6.4, 8.1, 8.2, 8.3, 8.4, 9.1, 9.2, 9.4, 11.4, 13.1, 13.2, 13.3, 14.1, 14.3, 14.4, 15.1, 15.2, 15.3, 15.4, 16.1, 16.4, 16.5, 18.1, Epil.1 **TRANSPARENCIES/TECHNOLOGY** World Art & Cultures Transparencies: AT12, AT36, AT37, AT38, AT42, AT54, AT55, AT61, AT63, AT64, AT67, AT68, AT78 Geography Transparencies: GT19, GT24, GT37, GT25, GT28, GT34, GT35, GT36 Critical Thinking Transparencies: CT17, CT19, CT23, CT24, CT25, CT30, CT53, CT55, CT60, CT61, CT64 Videos: "Trade Connects the World" Benchmark Tests: Prol.1, 1.1, 1.2, 1.4, 3.3, 5.3, 8.2, 8.3, 9.2, 9.3, 9.4, 10.1, 12.2, 13.2, 15.1, 18.2, 19.4, 20.2 Power Presentations: Prol.1, 1.1, 1.2, 1.4, 3.3, 5.3, 8.2, 8.3, 9.2, 9.3, 9.4, 10.1, 12.2, 13.2, 15.1, 18.2, 19.4, 20.2

Standard		Primary Citations	Supporting Citations
CST(3)	Students use a variety of maps and documents to interpret human movement, including major patterns of domestic and international migration, changing environmental preferences and settlement patterns, the frictions that develop between population groups, and the diffusion of ideas, technological innovations, and goods.	**Pupil & Teacher & eEdition** Common Pages: **63,** 83, 97, 106, 117, 121, 122, 134, **138,** 158, 170, 176, 177, 178–179, 208, 215, 218, 221–223, 225, 240, 250, 258, 293, **296,** 309, 318, 320, 323, 325, 329, 337, 355, 359, 369, **386,** 398, 400, 416, 461, 535, 537, 561, 604, 615, **623,** 637–640, 660, 665 Add'l Teacher Edition: 63, 83, 97, 106, 117, 121, 122, 134, 138, 158, 170, 176, 177, 178–179, 208, 215, 218, 221–223, 225, 240, 250, 258, 293, 296, 309, 318, 320, 323, 325, 329, 337, 355, 359, 369, 386, 398, 400, 416, 461, 535, 537, 561, 604, 615, 623, 637–640, 660, 665 **PRINT COMPONENT(S)** CA Standards Enrichment Wrkbk: 1–16 **TRANSPARENCIES/TECHNOLOGY** CA Daily Standards Practice Transparencies: TT5, TT6a–TT6b, TT7, TT9, TT13, TT57, TT76, TTA	**PRINT COMPONENT(S)** In-Depth Resources Unit 1: 6, 10, 11, 23, 39, 55, 73; Unit 2: 7, 42, 43, 61; Unit 3: 6, 23, 43, 60; Unit 4: 6, 24, 42, 60; Unit 5: 25, 43, 46, 60, 62, 64 In-Depth Resources in Spanish Unit 1: 11, 15, 16, 21, 25–28, 31, 32, 34, 35, 37–42, Unit 2: 44, 46, 47, 49, 50, 55, 59–64, 67, 69, 71, 72; Unit 3: 75, 76, 79, 82–86, 91, 93, 98; Unit 4: 104, 108, 113, 132; Unit 5: 147, 149, 150, 153, 155, 158 History Makers Unit 1: 15, 54, 55, 74, 97; Unit 2: 17, 64, 65, 88; Unit 3: 41; Unit 5: 66, 67 CA Reading Toolkit: L12, L15, 16, 17, 19, 21, 22, 23, 25, 26, 31, 32, 33, 36, 37, 39, 42, 43, 46, 47, 48, 51, 52, 56, 59, 75, 85, 87, 88 CA Modified Lesson Plans for English Learners: 1.4, 2.1, 2.2, 2.3, 3.1, 3.2, 4.2, 4.3, 4.4, 5.1, 5.3, 5.4, 5.5, 7.2, 7.3, 7.4, 7.5, 8.1, 8.3, 9.2, 9.3, 10.2, 10.3, 11.1, 11.2, 11.3, 11.4, 12.1, 12.2, 12.3, 13.1, 13.2, 13.3, 13.4, 14.1, 14.2, 14.3, 14.4, 15.4, 16.1, 16.2, 16.4, 17.1, 17.2, 17.3, 17.4, 17.5, 18.1, 18.2, 18.3, 18.4, 19.1, 19.2, 19.4, 19.5, 20.1, 20.2, Epil.1, Epil.2, Epil.3, Epil.4 **TRANSPARENCIES/TECHNOLOGY** World Art & Cultures Transparencies: AT12, AT39, AT40, AT41, AT43, AT44, AT45, AT46, AT47, AT48, AT50, AT52, AT54, AT55, AT57, AT59, AT63, AT64, AT66, AT76, AT78 Geography Transparencies: GT17, GT18, GT20, GT21, GT23, GT24, GT25, GT26, GT27, GT33, GT35 Critical Thinking Transparencies: CT17, CT18, CT20, CT21, CT23, CT24, CT26, CT28, CT30, CT37, CT53, CT56, CT58, CT59, CT62, CT66 Videos: "The Spread of Epidemic Disease," "The Impact of Potatoes and Sugar," "Revolutions in Latin America and South Africa," "the Geography of Food," "The Industrial And Electronic Revolutions" Benchmark Tests: Prol.1, 1.4, 2.1, 2.2, 2.3, 3.1, 3.2, 4.1, 4.2, 4.3, 4.4, 5.1, 5.3, 5.4, 6.4, 7.1, 7.2, 7.4, 7.5, 8.1, 8.3, 9.2, 9.3, 10.2, 10.3, 10.4, 11.3, 11.4, 12.3, 13.2, 14.4, 17.1, 19.1, 19.3, 19.4, 20.1, 20.5 Power Presentations: Prol.1, 1.4, 2.1, 2.2, 2.3, 3.1, 3.2, 4.1, 4.2, 4.3, 4.4, 5.1, 5.3, 5.4, 6.4, 7.1, 7.2, 7.4, 7.5, 8.1, 8.3, 9.2, 9.3, 10.2, 10.3, 10.4, 11.3, 11.4, 12.3, 13.2, 14.4, 17.1, 19.1, 19.3, 19.4, 20.1, 20.5

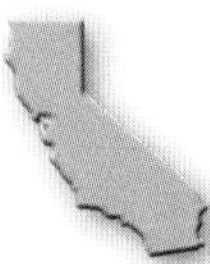

Correlations to California History–Social Science Content Standards and Analysis Skills

Standard	Primary Citations	Supporting Citations
CST(4) Students relate current events to the physical and human characteristics of places and regions.	**Pupil & Teacher & eEdition** Common Pages: 49, **85,** 101, 111, 183, 203, **225,** 241, 294, **304, 321,** 372, 449, 516, 547, 553, 565, **672–699** Add'l Teacher Edition: 49, 85, 101, 111, 183, 203, 225, 241, 294, 304, 321, 372, 449, 516, 547, 553, 565, 672–699 **PRINT COMPONENT(S)** CA Standards Enrichment Wrkbk: 1–16	**PRINT COMPONENT(S)** In-Depth Resources Unit 1: 18, 26, 27, 30, 33, 35, 36, 42, 45, 49, 50, 55, 56, 59, 60, 67, 68, 74, 77, 78, Unit 2: 5, 12–13, 18, 19, 24, 27, 43, 46, 49, 51, 52, 54, 55, 57–59, 61, 65–67, 71, 72; Unit 3: 2, 4, 6, 7, 10, 12, 13, 17, 18, 20, 22, 71, 77, 79, 86, 90; Unit 4: 26, 30, 34, 41, 45, 72, 73, 75, 79, 81, 87, 91, 92; Unit 5: 3, 4, 11, 12, 17, 18, 23, 24, 26, 35, 60 In-Depth Resources in Spanish Unit 1: 18, 27, 29, 31; Unit 2: 48, 54, 62–64; Unit 3: 75, 77, 78, 79, 96, 101; Unit 4: 112, 115, 127–129; Unit 5: 134, 135, 138, 140 History Makers Unit 1: 33, 55, 74; Unit 3: 17, 86; Unit 4: 41; Unit 5: 17, 18 CA Reading Toolkit: L10, L15, 16, 27, 30, 33, 36, 42, 44, 46, 54, 64, 74, 77, 78, 80 CA Modified Lesson Plans for English Learners: 5.1, 5.4, 5.5, 17.1, 18.1, Epil.2, Epil.3 **TRANSPARENCIES/TECHNOLOGY** World Art & Cultures Transparencies: AT37, AT38, AT40, AT41, AT54, AT60, AT71, AT73, AT74 Geography Transparencies: Gt25 Critical Thinking Transparencies: CT18, CT23, CT25, CT32, CT33, CT37, CT57, CT59, CT61, CT68 Videos: "Modern and Medieval Weapons" Benchmark Tests: 1.2, 2.3, 3.1, 5.5, 6.3, 7.2, 7.4, 7.5, 9.2, 9.4, 10.2, 12.1, 14.3, 16.4, 16.5, 17.3, 17.4, 18.1 Power Presentations: 1.2, 2.3, 3.1, 5.5, 6.3, 7.2, 7.4, 7.5, 9.2, 9.4, 10.2, 12.1, 14.3, 16.4, 16.5, 17.3, 17.4, 18.1

Standard		Primary Citations	Supporting Citations
RESEARCH, EVIDENCE, AND POINT OF VIEW			
REP(1)	Students distinguish valid arguments from fallacious arguments in historical interpretations.	**Pupil & Teacher & eEdition** Common Pages: 39, **75,** 135, 197, **320,** 431, 454, 464, **586, 608, 627** Add'l Teacher Edition: 39, 75, 135, 197, 320, 431, 454, 464, 586, 608, 627 **PRINT COMPONENT(S)** CA Standards Enrichment Wrkbk: 1–16	**PRINT COMPONENT(S)** In-Depth Resources Unit 1: 18, 26, 27, 30, 33, 35, 36, 40, 44, 47, 51, 54, 57, 83, 92, 101; Unit 2: 26, 34, 35, 36, 42, 45; Unit 3: 24, 29, 32, 35, 44; Unit 4: 27, 35, 42, 46, 47, 55, 59, 62, 65; Unit 5: 29, 38, 43, 51, 53, 59, 60, 62, 67, 68, 70, 72 In-Depth Resources in Spanish Unit 1: 18, 25, 28, 39; Unit 2: 53; Unit 3: 82, 86; Unit 4: 113, 117; Unit 5: 143, 148, 150 History Makers Unit 1: 33, 54; Unit 2: 42; Unit 4: 62; Unit 5: 67 CA Reading Toolkit: L9, L13, 21, 29, 46, 65, 66, 83, 86, 89 CA Modified Lesson Plans for English Learners: 1.4, 4.1, 6.2, 7.5, 9.4, 10.1, 10.3, 11.1, 11.2, 14.3, 19.1, 19.5, 20.1, 20.2, Epil.2, Epil.3 **TRANSPARENCIES/TECHNOLOGY** World Art & Cultures Transparencies: AT36, AT37, AT39, AT44, AT57, AT66, AT67, AT68, AT75, AT77, AT78 Geography Transparencies: GT18, GT26, GT35 Critical Thinking Transparencies: CT20, CT22, CT30, CT34, CT66, CT79 Videos: "The Geography of Food," "Revolutions in Latin America and South Africa" Benchmark Tests: 1.1, 2.1, 4.3, 6.2, 10.2, 14.4, 15.1, 18.4, 19.2, 19.4 Power Presentations: 1.1, 2.1, 4.3, 6.2, 10.2, 14.4, 15.1, 18.4, 19.2, 19.4
REP(2)	Students identify bias and prejudice in historical interpretations.	**Pupil & Teacher & eEdition** Common Pages: 39, 75, 135, **197, 320,** 431, 454, **464, 586,** 608, **627,** R18 Add'l Teacher Edition: 39, 75, 135, 197, 320, 431, 454, 464, 586, 608, 627 **PRINT COMPONENT(S)** CA Standards Enrichment Wrkbk: 1–16 **TRANSPARENCIES/TECHNOLOGY** CA Daily Standards Practice Transparencies: TTD	**PRINT COMPONENT(S)** In-Depth Resources Unit 1: 18, 26, 27, 30, 33, 35, 36, 40, 44, 47, 51, 54, 57, 61, 64, 65, 69, 71, 79; Unit 2: 26, 34, 35, 36, 42, 45; Unit 3: 24, 29, 32, 35, 42, 44; Unit 4: 27, 35, 42, 46, 47, 55, 59, 62, 65; Unit 5: 29, 38, 43, 51, 53, 59, 60, 62, 67, 68, 70, 72 In-Depth Resources in Spanish Unit 1: 18, 25, 28, 32, 34, 35; Unit 2: 53; Unit 3: 82, 86; Unit 4: 113, 117; Unit 5: 143, 148, 150 History Makers Unit 1: 33, 54; Unit 2: 42; Unit 4: 62; Unit 5: 43, 67 CA Reading Toolkit: L9, L13, 17, 29, 46, 65, 66, 83, 86, 89 CA Modified Lesson Plans for English Learners: Prol.1, 1.4, 4.1, 6.2, 7.5, 9.2, 9.3, 9.4, 10.3, 11.1, 17.4, 17.5, 18.3, 19.5, 20.2, Epil.2 **TRANSPARENCIES/TECHNOLOGY** World Art & Cultures Transparencies: AT36, AT37, AT39, AT57, AT66, AT67, AT68, AT75, AT77, AT78 Geography Transparencies: GT18, GT26, GT35 Critical Thinking Transparencies: CT22, CT30, CT34, CT66 Videos: "The Geography of Food," "Revolutions in Latin America and South Africa" Benchmark Tests: Prol.1, 1.1, 2.1, 3.2, 6.2, 10.2, 14.4, 15.1, 18.4, 19.2, 19.4 Power Presentations: Prol.1, 1.1, 2.1, 3.2, 6.2, 10.2, 14.4, 15.1, 18.4, 19.2, 19.4

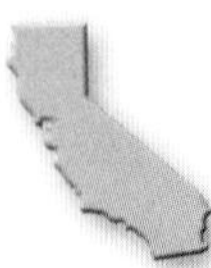

Correlations to California History–Social Science Content Standards and Analysis Skills

Standard		Primary Citations	Supporting Citations
REP(3)	Students evaluate major debates among historians concerning alternative interpretations of the past, including an analysis of authors' use of evidence and the distinctions between sound generalizations and misleading oversimplifications.	**Pupil & Teacher & eEdition** Common Pages: 39, **67**, 75, 126, 135, 197, 201, **228**, **307**, 320, **351**, 423, 431, 454, 464, 586, 608, 627, 647, R7–R8 Add'l Teacher Edition: 39, 67, 75, 126, 135, 197, 201, 228, 307, 320, 351, 423, 431, 454, 464, 586, 608, 627, 647 **PRINT COMPONENT(S)** CA Standards Enrichment Wrkbk: 1–16	**PRINT COMPONENT(S)** In-Depth Resources Unit 1: 18, 26, 27, 30, 33, 35, 36, 21, 40, 44, 47, 51, 54, 57, 81, 83, 89, 91, 93, 92, 96, 97, 99, 101; Unit 2: 26, 34, 35, 36, 42, 45, 49, 55, 57–59, 61, 655, 66, 67; Unit 3: 4, 6, 12, 17, 18, 22, 24, 29, 32, 35, 44, 48, 577, 61, 63, 65; Unit 4: 3, 11, 22, 27, 35, 42, 46, 47, 55, 59, 62, 65; Unit 5: 29, 38, 43, 51, 53, 59, 60, 62, 67, 68, 70, 72 In-Depth Resources in Spanish Unit 1: 18, 25, 28, 37, 39, Unit 2: 53, 65; Unit 3: 77, 78, 82, 86, 89: Unit 4: 105, 113, 117; Unit 5: 143, 148, 150 History Makers Unit 1: 33, 54, 96, 97, Unit 2: 42; Unit 3: 17, 63; Unit 4: 62; Unit 5: 43, 67 CA Reading Toolkit: L12, L13, 19, 21, 29, 44, 46, 50, 60, 65, 66, 83, 86, 89, 91 CA Modified Lesson Plans for English Learners: Prol.1, 1.4, 4.1, 7.5, 9.2, 9.3, 9.4 **TRANSPARENCIES/TECHNOLOGY** World Art & Cultures Transparencies: AT36, AT37, AT39, AT43, AT44, AT57, AT66, AT67, AT68, AT75, AT77, AT78 Geography Transparencies: GT17, GT26, GT35 Critical Thinking Transparencies: CT17, CT20, CT22, CT25, CT29, CT30, CT34, CT53, CT61, CT66 Videos: "The Spread of Epidemic Disease," "The Geography of Food," "Revolutions in Latin America and South Africa" Benchmark Tests: 1.1, 1.4, 2.1, 4.1, 4.3, 6.2, 7.2, 9.4, 10.2, 11.2, 13.3, 14.4, 15.1, 18.4, 19.2, 19.4 Power Presentations: 1.1, 1.4, 2.1, 4.1, 4.3, 6.2, 7.2, 9.4, 10.2, 11.2, 13.3, 14.4, 15.1, 18.4, 19.2, 19.4
REP(4)	Students construct and test hypotheses; collect, evaluate, and employ information from multiple primary and secondary sources; and apply it in oral and written presentations.	**Pupil & Teacher & eEdition** Common Pages: 39, 40, 47, 67, **98**, 75, 104, 135, 145, **188**, 197, 261, 266, 320, 332, 378, **390**, 431, 454, 464, **484**, 586, 603, 608, **613**, 627, R6 Add'l Teacher Edition: 39, 40, 47, 67, 98, 75, 104, 135, 145, 188, 197, 261, 266, 320, 332, 378, 390, 431, 454, 464, 484, 586, 603, 608, 613, 627, R6 **PRINT COMPONENT(S)** CA Standards Enrichment Wrkbk: 1–16	**PRINT COMPONENT(S)** In-Depth Resources Unit 1: 2, 5, 36, 53, 70; Unit 2: 22, 56, 59; Unit 3: 8, 11, 25, 27, 28, 45–48, 62–68; Unit 4: 5, 41; Unit 5: 9–15, 27–33, 42, 45–51, 62–69 In-Depth Resources in Spanish Unit 1: 18, 19, 21, 23, 25, 28, 31, 32, 34, 35, 38, 41; Unit 2: 69, 70, 72; Unit 3: 82, 84–86, 97, 99; Unit 4: 113, 117, 120, 122; Unit 5: 143, 147–150, 153 History Makers Unit 1: 33, 54; Unit 2: 89; Unit 3: 41, 87; Unit 4: 62, 63; Unit 5: 43, 66, 67 CA Reading Toolkit: L9, L10, L12, L13 CA Modified Lesson Plans for English Learners: Prol.1, Prol.2, Prol.3, Prol.4, 1.1, 1.2, 1.3, 1.4, 2.1, 2.2, 2.3, 3.1, 3.2, 3.3, 4.1, 4.2, 4.3, 5.1, 5.2, 5.3, 5.4, 5.5, 6.1, 6.2, 6.3, 6.4, 7.2, 7.3, 7.4, 7.5, 8.1, 8.2, 8.3, 8.4, 9.2, 9.3, 9.4, 11.1, 12.3, 13.1, 13.2, 13.3, 13.4, 14.1, 14.2, 14.3, 14.4, 15.1, 15.2, 15.3, 15.4, 16.1, 16.2, 16.3, 16.4, 16.5, 17.1, 17.3, 18.1, 18.2, 18.4, 18.5, 20.1, 20.2, 20.3, 20.4, 20.5, Epil.4, Epil.5, Epil.6 **TRANSPARENCIES/TECHNOLOGY** World Art & Cultures Transparencies: AT36, AT37, AT38, AT39, AT41, AT53, AT67, AT68, AT57, AT61, AT62, AT66, AT75, AT76, AT77, AT78 Geography Transparencies: GT17, GT18, GT26, GT28, GT31 Critical Thinking Transparencies: CT17, CT26, CT30, CT34, CT35, CT53, CT60, CT62, CT64, CT66, CT67 Videos: "The Geography of Food," "Revolutions in Latin America" Benchmark Tests: 1.1, 1.2, 1.4, 2.1, 3.1, 3.2, 4.2, 8.3, 8.4, 10.2, 10.4, 12.2, 12.4, 14.4, 15.1, 15.4, 18.4, 19.1, 19.2, 19.3, 19.4 Power Presentations: 1.1, 1.2, 1.4, 2.1, 3.1, 3.2, 4.2, 8.3, 8.4, 10.2, 10.4, 12.2, 12.4, 14.4, 15.1, 15.4, 18.4, 19.1, 19.2, 19.3, 19.4

Standard		Primary Citations	Supporting Citations
HISTORICAL INTERPRETATION			
HI(1)	Students show the connections, causal and otherwise, between particular historical events and larger social, economic, and political trends and developments.	**Pupil & Teacher & eEdition** Common Pages: 44–45, 54, 57, 88–89, 132–136, 140, 144–145, 160, **209,** 210, 221, 250, 254, 257, 268–269, 272–273, 285, 293, 303, **346,** 380–381, 396–397, 410, 438, 441, 446–447, 477, **480,** 520–521, 630–631, **644, 666–667** Add'l Teacher Edition: 44–45, 54, 57, 88–89, 132–135, 140, 144–145, 160, 209, 210, 221, 250, 254, 257, 268–269, 272–273, 285, 293, 303, 346, 380–381, 396–397, 410, 438, 441, 446–447, 477, 480, 520–521, 630–631, 644, 666–667 **PRINT COMPONENT(S)** CA Standards Enrichment Wrkbk: 1–16 **TRANSPARENCIES/TECHNOLOGY** CA Daily Standards Practice Transparencies: TTC, TT3, TT12, TT14, TT15, TT17a–TT17b	**PRINT COMPONENT(S)** In-Depth Resources Unit 1: 1, 3, 10, 12, 17, 18, 19, 20, 22, 23, 26, 27, 28, 29, 30, 33, 34, 35, 36, 42, 45, 49, 50, 52, 55, 56, 59, 71, 82, 102; Unit 2: 1, 3, 8, 17, 20, 22, 28, 37, 40, 47, 48, 51, 54, 64, 68, 71, 73, 74, 76–78, 80–83, 85–89, 91, 92, 94; Unit 3: 1, 2, 4–10, 12–16, 17, 18–20, 22, 47, 54, 56, 60, 72, 76, 80, 91; Unit 4: 1, 6, 9, 16, 20, 24, 25, 29, 32, 33, 36, 38, 40, 43, 44, 49, 57, 60, 64, 67; Unit 5: 20–22, 36, 53, 57–58, 62, 68, 72, 75, 80, 81, 84, 87, 94 In-Depth Resources in Spanish Unit 1: 13, 18, 20, 22, 27, 29, 38–42; Unit 2: 44, 46, 50, 55, 59, 63, 67, 68, 70, 71; Unit 3: 74, 75, 77–79, 88, 94, 97; Unit 4: 103, 107, 110, 111, 114, 119; Unit 5: 150, 156, 159, 160 History Makers Unit 1: 33, 34, 55; Unit 2: 17, 64, 88, 89; Unit 3: 16, 17; Unit 4: 16, 40 CA Reading Toolkit: L9, L11, L15, 21, 22, 23, 31, 32, 37, 38, 40, 41, 42, 44, 50, 55, 58, 62, 63, 68, 89 CA Modified Lesson Plans for English Learners: Prol.1, Prol.2, Prol.3, Prol.4, 1.1, 1.2, 1.3, 1.4, 2.1, 2.2, 2.3, 3.1, 3.2, 3.3, 4.1, 4.2, 4.3, 4.4, 5.1, 5.2, 5.4, 5.5, 6.1, 6.2, 6.3, 6.4, 7.1, 7.2, 7.3, 7.4, 7.5, 8.1, 8.3, 8.4, 9.4, 10.1, 11.1, 11.2, 11.3, 12.2, 12.3, 13.1, 13.2, 13.4, 14.1, 14.2, 14.3, 14.4, 15.1, 15.2, 15.3, 16.1, 16.3, 16.5, 17.1, 18.2, 19.1, 19.3, 20.3, 20.4, 20.5, Epil.1, Epil.2, Epil.3, Epil.5, Epil.6 **TRANSPARENCIES/TECHNOLOGY** World Art & Cultures Transparencies: AT40, AT44, AT45, AT48, AT50, AT52, AT53, AT54, AT61, AT65, AT69, AT78 Geography Transparencies: GT20, GT21, GT23, GT25, GT28, GT30, GT35, GT36 Critical Thinking Transparencies: CT18, CT20, CT25, CT31, CT33, CT37, CT56, CT58, CT60, CT61, CT72 Videos: "The Impact of Potatoes and Sugar," "Revolutions in Latin America and South Africa," "The Industrial and Electronic Revolutions," "Trade Connects the World" Benchmark Tests: Prol.3, 1.1, 1.3, 2.3, 4.2, 4.3, 4.4, 5.1, 5.3, 6.4, 7.1, 7.4, 8.1, 8.2, 8.4, 9.1, 9.2, 9.4, 11.2, 12.2, 13.1, 14.1, 14.2, 15.3, 19.4, 20.2 Power Presentations: Prol.3, 1.1, 1.3, 2.3, 4.2, 4.3, 4.4, 5.1, 5.3, 6.4, 7.1, 7.4, 8.1, 8.2, 8.4, 9.1, 9.2, 9.4, 11.2, 12.2, 13.1, 14.1, 14.2, 15.3, 19.4, 20.2

Correlations to California History–Social Science Content Standards and Analysis Skills

Standard		Primary Citations	Supporting Citations
HI(2)	Students recognize the complexity of historical causes and effects, including the limitations on determining cause and effect.	**Pupil & Teacher & eEdition** Common Pages: 4, 67, **126**, 166, 201, 228, 272–273, **307**, 344, 351, 359, 396–397, 423, 445, 451, 473, 512, 520–521, 541, **549**, 592, **647**, 666–667, R6, R16 Add'l Teacher Edition: 4, 67, 126, 166, 201, 228, 272–273, 307, 344, 351, 359, 396–397, 423, 445, 451, 473, 512, 520–521, 541, 549, 592, 647, 666–667 **PRINT COMPONENT(S)** CA Standards Enrichment Wrkbk: 1–16	**PRINT COMPONENT(S)** In-Depth Resources Unit 1: 3, 10, 12, 17, 20, 21, 81, 89, 91, 93, 96, 97, 99; Unit 2: 2, 10, 14, 21, 26, 34–36, 42, 45; Unit 3: 1–2, 4, 6, 12, 17, 18, 19, 22, 39, 40, 47–49, 51, 52, 54–57, 59–65; Unit 4: 3, 11, 22, 23, 25, 26, 30, 33, 34, 36, 38, 41, 44, 45, 48, 52, 56, 57, 66, 72, 75, 79, 81, 91; Unit 5: 1, 2, 3, 4, 7, 8, 10, 12, 18, 22, 23, 24, 30, 38–39, 41, 75, 80, 81, 84, 87, 94 In-Depth Resources in Spanish Unit 1: 13, 21, 37; Unit 2: 45, 53; Unit 3: 77, 78, 88–90, 92, 94; Unit 4: 105, 111, 112, 115, 118, 121, 127, 129; Unit 5: 135, 138, 144, 156, 159, 160 History Makers Unit 1: 96, 97; Unit 2: 42; Unit 3: 17, 63, 64; Unit 4: 41; Unit 5: 18 CA Reading Toolkit: L12, 19, 24, 29, 44, 49, 50, 52, 60, 63, 64, 67, 73, 76, 78, 84, 91 CA Modified Lesson Plans for English Learners: Prol.2, Prol.3, Prol.4, 1.1, 1.2, 1.3, 1.4, 2.1, 2.3, 3.1, 3.2, 4.1, 4.3, 4.4, 5.1, 5.2, 5.3, 5.4, 6.1, 6.2, 6.3, 6.4, 7.1, 7.2, 7.3, 7.5, 8.1, 8.2, 8.3, 8.4, 9.1, 9.3, 9.4, 10.2, 11.1, 11.2, 11.3, 11.4, 12.1, 12.2, 12.4, 13.1, 14.1, 14.2, 14.3, 14.4, 15.2, 15.3, 15.4, 16.1, 16.2, 16.3, 16.4, 16.5, 17.1, 17.3, 18.2, 18.3, 18.4, 18.5, 19.1, 19.2, 19.3, 19.4, 19.5, 20.1, 20.2, 20.3, 20.4, Epil.1, Epil.2, Epil.3, Epil.4, Epil.5, Epil.6 **TRANSPARENCIES/TECHNOLOGY** World Art & Cultures Transparencies: AT43, AT59, AT63, AT64, AT72 Geography Transparencies: GT17, GT27, GT30, GT36 Critical Thinking Transparencies: CT6, CT17, CT22, CT25, CT26, CT32, CT33, CT53, CT59, CT61, CT63, CT65, CT70 Videos: "The Spread of Epidemic Disease," "Modern and Medieval Weapons," "Trade Connects the World" Benchmark Tests: Prol.3, 1.4, 4.1, 5.2, 6.2, 9.4, 11.1, 11.2, 11.4, 13.3, 14.2, 14.3, 15.2, 16.4, 17.2, 17.4, 18.5, 20.2 Power Presentations: Prol.3, 1.4, 4.1, 5.2, 6.2, 9.4, 11.1, 11.2, 11.4, 13.3, 14.2, 14.3, 15.2, 16.4, 17.2, 17.4, 18.5, 20.2

Standard		Primary Citations	Supporting Citations
HI(3)	Students interpret past events and issues within the context in which an event unfolded rather than solely in terms of present-day norms and values.	**Pupil & Teacher & eEdition** Common Pages: 57, 140, **160,** 166, 209, **254,** 272–273, 359, **396–397,** 438, 441, 445, 451, 473, 477, 512, **520–521,** 541, 549, 592, 644, **666–667,** R12–13 Add'l Teacher Edition: 57, 140, 160, 166, 209, 254, 272–273, 359, 396–397, 438, 441, 445, 451, 473, 477, 512, 520–521, 541, 549, 592, 644, 666–667 **PRINT COMPONENT(S)** CA Standards Enrichment Wrkbk: 1–16 **TRANSPARENCIES/TECHNOLOGY** CA Daily Standards Practice Transparencies: TTB, TT11	**PRINT COMPONENT(S)** In-Depth Resources Unit 1: 2, 9, 20, 23, 28, 29, 34, 51, 68, 81, 84, 87, 89, 91, 93, 96, 97, 98, 99, 102; Unit 2: 1, 2, 4, 10, 14, 20, 21, 38, 74, 82, 92; Unit 3: 3, 4, 5, 21, 50, 53, 54, 58, 59; Unit 4: 24, 25, 29, 32, 33, 36, 38, 39, 40, 43, 44, 48, 49, 52, 54, 56, 57, 59, 60, 64, 66, 67, 72, 75, 81, 91; Unit 5: 1, 4, 8, 12, 14, 18–21, 24, 30, 75, 80, 81, 84, 87, 94 In-Depth Resources in Spanish Unit 1: 13, 20, 22, 37, 40, 42; Unit 2: 44, 45, 65; Unit 3: 91, 93; Unit 4: 111, 118, 119, 121, 127, 129; Unit 5: 135, 138, 144, 156, 159, 160 History Makers Unit 1: 34, 96, 97; Unit 4: 40; Unit 5: 18 CA Reading Toolkit: L11, 22, 23, 24, 38, 52, 62, 63, 64, 67, 68, 73, 76, 78, 84, 91 CA Modified Lesson Plans for English Learners: Prol.2, Prol.3, Prol.4, 1.1, 1.2, 1.3, 1.4, 2.1, 2.3, 3.2, 3.3, 4.2, 4.3, 5.2, 5.4, 6.1, 6.2, 6.3, 6.4, 7.1, 7.2, 7.3, 9.1, 9.2, 9.3, 9.4, 10.1, 10.2, 10.3, 11.5, 12.1, 12.2, 12.4, 13.2, 13.4, 14.1, 14.2, 14.3, 15.1, 15.4, 16.2, 16.3, 16.4, 17.1, 17.2, 17.3, 17.4, 17.5, 18.2, 18.3, 18.4, 18.5, 19.1, 19.2, 19.4, 19.5, 20.1, 20.2, 20.3, 20.4, Epil.2, Epil.4, Epil.5, Epil.6 **TRANSPARENCIES/TECHNOLOGY** World Art & Cultures Transparencies: AT43, AT45, AT48, AT59, AT65, AT69, AT70 Geography Transparencies: GT20, GT21, GT27, GT30, GT36 Critical Thinking Transparencies: CT31, CT33, CT56, CT70 Videos: "The Spread of Epidemic Disease," "The Impact of Potatoes and Sugar," "Modern and Medieval Weapons," "Trade Connects the World" Benchmark Tests: Prol.2, 1.3, 4.1, 4.4, 5.1, 5.2, 8.2, 11.4, 14.1, 14.2, 15.2, 15.3, 16.4, 17.2, 17.4, 18.5, 20.2 Power Presentations: Prol.2, 1.3, 4.1, 4.4, 5.1, 5.2, 8.2, 11.4, 14.1, 14.2, 15.2, 15.3, 16.4, 17.2, 17.4, 18.5, 20.2

Correlations to California History–Social Science Content Standards and Analysis Skills

Standard		Primary Citations	Supporting Citations
HI(4)	Students understand the meaning, implication, and impact of historical events and recognize that events could have taken other directions.	**Pupil & Teacher & eEdition** Common Pages: 4, 57, 67, **126,** 140, **160,** 201, **209,** 228, 254, 256, 307, 351, 415, 423, 438, **441, 477,** 504, 588, 644, 647, R19 Add'l Teacher Edition: 4, 57, 67, 126, 140, 160, 201, 209, 228, 254, 256, 307, 351, 415, 423, 438, 441, 477, 504, 588, 644, 647 **PRINT COMPONENT(S)** CA Standards Enrichment Wrkbk: 1–16 **TRANSPARENCIES/TECHNOLOGY** CA Daily Standards Practice Transparencies: TTC	**PRINT COMPONENT(S)** In-Depth Resources Unit 1: 21, 37, 52, 72; Unit 2: 39, 41, 57, 58; Unit 3: 4, 38, 41, 55; Unit 4: 4, 38, 44; Unit 5: 37 In-Depth Resources in Spanish Unit 1: 1–17, 10–22, 37, 40, 42; Unit 2: 44, 45, 54, 55, 68, 77, 78; Unit 3: 89, 104, 105, 108; Unit 4: 110, 111, 114, 119, 126; Unit 5: 133, 137, 142–145, 148 History Makers Unit 1: 16, 37; Unit 2: 17; Unit 3: 63; Unit 4: 40; Unit 5: 67 CA Reading Toolkit: L11, L12, 19, 22, 23, 29, 31, 38, 44, 50, 59, 60, 62, 63, 68, 72, 83, 91 CA Modified Lesson Plans for English Learners: Prol.1, Prol.2, Prol.3, Prol.4, 2.1, 2.2, 3.1, 3.2, 3.3, 4.1, 4.2, 4.3, 5.1, 5.2, 5.3, 5.4, 5.5, 6.1, 6.2, 6.3, 6.4, 7.1, 7.2, 7.3, 7.4, 7.5, 8.1, 8.3, 9.4, 10.4, 11.2, 12.2, 12.3, 13.3, 13.4, 14.1, 14.2, 14.3, 15.4, 16.1, 16.2, 16.4, 16.5, 17.2, 17.3, 17.4, 17.5, 18.2, 18.3, 18.4, 18.5, 19.1, 19.3, 20.1, 20.2, 20.3, Epil.2, Epil.4 **TRANSPARENCIES/TECHNOLOGY** World Art & Cultures Transparencies: AT12, AT43, AT45, AT48, AT50, AT63, AT64, AT65, AT69, AT70, AT72, AT75, AT77 Geography Transparencies: GT17, GT20, GT21, GT30 Critical Thinking Transparencies: CT17, CT22, CT25, CT29, CT31, CT34, CT53, CT56, CT58, CT61, CT77, CT78 Videos: "The Spread of Epidemic Disease," "The Impact of Potatoes and Sugar," "Revolutions in Latin America and South Africa" Benchmark Tests: 1.3, 1.4, 4.1, 4.4, 5.1, 5.2, 6.2, 6.4, 8.2, 9.4, 11.2, 13.2, 13.3, 14.1, 14.2, 15.3, 16.3, 17.2, 18.4, 18.5, 20.2, Prol.1–4 Power Presentations: Prol.1, Prol.2, Prol.3, Prol.4, 1.3, 5.1, 5.2, 17.2, 18.5
HI(5)	Students analyze human modifications of land-scapes and examine the resulting environmental policy issues.	**Pupil & Teacher & eEdition** Common Pages: **355, 386, 646, 647** Add'l Teacher Edition: 355, 386, 646, 647 **PRINT COMPONENT(S)** CA Standards Enrichment Wrkbk: 1–16 **TRANSPARENCIES/TECHNOLOGY** CA Daily Standards Practice Transparencies: TT82	**PRINT COMPONENT(S)** In-Depth Resources Unit 3: 6–7, 20, 49, 73, 81, 88, 89, 92; Unit 5: 60–61, 74, 80, 81, 84, 87, 94 In-Depth Resources in Spanish Unit 3: 90, 98; Unit 5: 156, 159, 160 CA Reading Toolkit: 51, 56, 91 CA Modified Lesson Plans for English Learners: 4.2, 4.4, 13.2, 14.2, 20.2, Epil.2 **TRANSPARENCIES/TECHNOLOGY** World Art & Cultures Transparencies: AT58 Geography Transparencies: GT36 Critical Thinking Transparencies: CT28 Videos: "Trade Connects the World" Benchmark Tests: 11.3, 12.3, 20.2 Power Presentations: 11.3, 12.3, 20.2

Standard		Primary Citations	Supporting Citations
HI(6)	Students conduct cost-benefit analyses and apply basic economic indicators to analyze the aggregate economic behavior of the U.S. economy.	**Pupil & Teacher & eEdition** Common Pages: 218, **303,** 395, 459, **472, 474, 534, 641–647** Add'l Teacher Edition: 218, 303, 395, 459, 472, 474, 534, 641–647 **PRINT COMPONENT(S)** CA Standards Enrichment Wrkbk: 1–16	**PRINT COMPONENT(S)** In-Depth Resources Unit 2: 48, 64, 68; Unit 3: 4, 6, 12, 17, 18, 22; Unit 4: 48, 52, 56, 66; Unit 5: 1, 14, 19, 20, 21, 75, 80, 81, 84, 87, 94 In-Depth Resources in Spanish Unit 2: 59; Unit 3: 77, 78; Unit 4: 118, 121; Unit 5: 132, 156, 159, 160 History Makers Unit 2: 64; Unit 3: 17 CA Reading Toolkit: 32, 44, 67, 75, 91 CA Modified Lesson Plans for English Learners: 9.3, 10.3, 20.2, Epil.4 **TRANSPARENCIES/TECHNOLOGY** World Art & Cultures Transparencies: AT50 Geography Transparencies: GT23, GT33, GT36 Critical Thinking Transparencies: CT25, CT61 Videos: "Trade Connects the World" Benchmark Tests: 7.1, 9.4, 15.2, 17.1, 20.2 Power Presentations: 7.1, 9.4, 15.2, 17.1, 20.2

McDougal Littell

MODERN WORLD HISTORY

PATTERNS OF INTERACTION

Napoleon,
Portrait, 1810

Queen Victoria,
Portrait, 1861

Bolivar,
Portrait, 1820

Aung San,
Portrait, 2001

MODERN WORLD HISTORY

PATTERNS OF INTERACTION

Roger B. Beck

Linda Black

Larry S. Krieger

Phillip C. Naylor

Dahia Ibo Shabaka

Ghandi,
Portrait, 1948

McDougal Littell
A DIVISION OF HOUGHTON MIFFLIN COMPANY

Senior Consultants

Roger B. Beck, Ph.D.

Roger B. Beck is a professor of African History, World History, History of the Third World, and Social Studies Methods at Eastern Illinois University. He is also a social studies student teacher supervisor at that university. Dr. Beck recently served as associate dean of the Graduate School and International Programs at Eastern Illinois University. In addition to his distinguished teaching career at high school, college, and graduate school levels, Dr. Beck is a contributing author to several books and has written numerous articles, reviews, and papers. He is also an active member of the National Council for the Social Studies, the World History Association, and the African Studies Association. Dr. Beck was a key contributor to the National Standards for World History.

Linda Black, B.A., M.Ed.

Linda Black teaches World History at Cypress Falls High School in Houston, Texas, and has had a distinguished career in education as a teacher of world history, American history, and Texas history. In 1993–1994, Mrs. Black was named an Outstanding Secondary Social Studies Teacher in the United States by the National Council for the Social Studies. In 1996, she was elected to the Board of Directors of the National Council for the Social Studies. She is an active member of that council, the Texas Council for the Social Studies, and the World History Association. She served on the College Board Test Development for Advanced Placement World History from 1995 to 2003.

Larry S. Krieger, B.A., M.A., M.A.T.

Larry S. Krieger is the social studies supervisor for grades K-12 in Montgomery Township Public Schools in New Jersey. For 26 years he has taught world history in public schools. He has also introduced many innovative in-service programs, such as "Putting the Story Back in History," and has co-authored several successful history textbooks. Mr. Krieger earned his B.A. and M.A.T. from the University of North Carolina and his M.A. from Wake Forest University.

Phillip C. Naylor, Ph.D.

Phillip C. Naylor is an associate professor of history at Marquette University and teaches European, North African, and West Asian undergraduate and graduate courses. He was the director of the Western Civilization program for nine years where he inaugurated a "transcultural approach" to the teaching of the traditional survey. He has authored *France and Algeria: A History of Decolonization and Transformation*, coauthored *The Historical Dictionary of Algeria*, and coedited *State and Society in Algeria*. He has published numerous articles, papers, and reviews, and produced CD-ROM projects. In 1996, Dr. Naylor received the Reverend John P. Raynor, S.J., Faculty Award for Teaching Excellence at Marquette University. In 1992, he received the Edward G. Roddy Teaching Award at Merrimack College.

Dahia Ibo Shabaka, B.A., M.A., Ed.S.

Dahia Ibo Shabaka is the director of Social Studies and African-Centered Education in the Detroit Public Schools system. She has an extensive educational and scholarly background in the disciplines of history, political science, economics, law, and reading, and in secondary education, curriculum development, and school administration and supervision. Ms. Shabaka has been a teacher, a curriculum coordinator, and a supervisor of social studies in the Detroit Secondary Schools. In 1991 she was named Social Studies Educator of the Year by the Michigan Council for the Social Studies. Ms. Shabaka is the recipient of a Fulbright Fellowship at the Hebrew University in Israel and has served as an executive board member of the National Social Studies Supervisors Association.

Acknowledgments begin on page R117.
ISBN 0-618-55716-4
Printed in the United States of America.
X 2 3 4 5 6 7 8 9–DWO–09 08 07 06 05
This text contains material that appeared originally in *World History: Perspectives on the Past* (D.C. Heath and Company) by Larry S. Krieger, Kenneth Neill, and Dr. Edward Reynolds.

iv

Consultants and Reviewers

Content Consultants

The content consultants reviewed the content for historical depth and accuracy and for clarity of presentation.

Jerry Bentley
Department of History
University of Hawaii
Honolulu, Hawaii

Marc Brettler
Department of Near Eastern and Judaic Studies
Brandeis University
Waltham, Massachusetts

Steve Gosch
Department of History
University of Wisconsin at Eau Claire
Eau Claire, Wisconsin

Don Holsinger
Department of History
Seattle Pacific University
Seattle, Washington

Patrick Manning
World History Center
Department of History
Northeastern University
Boston, Massachusetts

Richard Saller
Department of History
University of Chicago
Chicago, Illinois

Wolfgang Schlauch
Department of History
Eastern Illinois University
Charleston, Illinois

Susan Schroeder
Department of History
Loyola University of Chicago
Chicago, Illinois

Scott Waugh
Department of History
University of California, Los Angeles
Los Angeles, California

Multicultural Advisory Board Consultants

The multicultural advisers reviewed the manuscript for appropriate historical content.

Pat A. Brown
Director of the Indianapolis Public Schools Office of African Centered Multicultural Education
Indianapolis Public Schools
Indianapolis, Indiana

Ogle B. Duff
Associate Professor of English
University of Pittsburgh
Pittsburgh, Pennsylvania

Mary Ellen Maddox
Black Education Commission Director
Los Angeles Unified School District
Los Angeles, California

Jon Reyhner
Associate Professor and Coordinator of the Bilingual Multicultural Education Program
Northern Arizona University
Flagstaff, Arizona

Ysidro Valenzuela
Fresno High School
Fresno, California

Teacher Review Panels

The following educators provided ongoing review during the development of prototypes, the table of contents, and key components of the program.

Patrick Adams
Pasadena High School
Pasadena, Texas

Bruce Bekemeyer
Marquette High School
Chesterfield, Missouri

Ellen Bell
Bellaire High School
Bellaire, Texas

Margaret Campbell
Central High School
St. Louis, Missouri

Nancy Coates
Belleville East High School
Belleville, Illinois

Kim Coil
Francis Howell North High School
St. Charles, Missouri

Craig T. Grace
Lanier High School
West Austin, Texas

Katie Ivey
Dimmitt High School
Dimmitt, Texas

Gary Kasprovich
Granite City High School
Granite City, Illinois

Pat Knapp
Burgess High School
El Paso, Texas

Eric R. Larson
Clark High School
Plano, Texas

Linda Marrs
Naaman Forest High School
Garland, Texas

Harry McCown
Hazelwood West High School
Hazelwood, Missouri

Terry McRae
Robert E. Lee High School
Tyler, Texas

Joseph Naumann (retired)
McCluer North High School
Florissant, Missouri

Sherrie Prahl
The Woodlands High School
The Woodlands, Texas

Dorothy Schulze
Health Careers High School
San Antonio, Texas

Liz Silva
Townview Magnet Center
Dallas, Texas

Linda Stevens
Central High School
San Angelo, Texas

Leonard Sullivan
Pattonville High School
Maryland Hts., Missouri

Carole Weeden
Fort Zumwalt South High School
St. Peters, Missouri

Rita Wylie
Parkway West Sr. High School
Ballwin, Missouri

v

Reviewers (continued)

Teacher Consultants

Glenn Bird
Springville High School
Springville, Utah

Michael Cady
North High School
Phoenix, Arizona

William Canter
Guilford High School
Rockford, Illinois

Nancy Coates
Belleville East High School
Belleville, Illinois

Paul Fitzgerald
Estancia High School
Costa Mesa, California

Craig T. Grace
Lanier High School
West Austin, Texas

Tom McDonald
Phoenix Union HSD
Phoenix, Arizona

Joy McKee
Lamar High School
Arlington, Texas

Terry McRae
Robert E. Lee High School
Tyler, Texas

Myra Osman
Homewood Flossmoor High School
Flossmoor, Illinois

Dorothy Schulze
Health Careers High School
Dallas, Texas

Linda Stevens
Central High School
San Angelo, Texas

The following educators wrote activities for the program.

Charlotte Albaugh
Grand Prairie High School
Grand Prairie, Texas

Mark Aguirre
Scripps Ranch High School
San Diego, California

Sharon Ballard
L.D. Bell High School
Hurst, Texas

Bryon Borgelt
St. John's Jesuit High School
Toledo, Ohio

William Brown (retired)
Northeast High School
Philadelphia, Pennsylvania

Haley Brice Clark
DeBakey Health Prof. High School
Houston, Texas

John Devine
Elgin High School
Elgin, Illinois

Karen Dingeldein
Cudahy High School
Cudahy, Wisconsin

Joanne Dodd
Scarborough High School
Houston, Texas

Jan Ellersieck
Ft. Zummalt South High School
St. Peters, Missouri

Craig T. Grace
Lanier High School
West Austin, Texas

Korri Kinney
Meridian High School
Meridian, Idaho

Jerome Love
Beaumont High School
St. Louis, Missouri

Melissa Mack
St. Margaret's High School
San Juan Capistrano, California

Harry McCown
Hazelwood West High School
Hazelwood, Missouri

Terry McRae
Robert E. Lee High School
Tyler, Texas

Joseph Naumann (retired)
McCluer North High School
Florissant, Missouri

Theresa C. Noonan
West Irondequoit High School
Rochester, New York

Robert Parker
St. Margaret's High School
San Juan Capistrano, California

Janet Rogolsky
Sylvania Southview High School
Sylvania, Ohio

Dorothy Schulze
Health Careers High School
San Antonio, Texas

Evelyn Sims
Skyline Center High School
Dallas, Texas

Brenda Smith
Colorado Springs School District 11
Colorado Springs, Colorado

Linda Stevens
Central High School
San Angelo, Texas

Leonard Sullivan
Pattonville High School
Maryland Heights, Missouri

Linda Tillis
South Oak Cliff High School
Dallas, Texas

Andrew White
Morrow High School
Clayton, Georgia

vi

Student Board

The following students reviewed prototype materials for the textbook.

LaShaunda Allen
Weston High School
Greenville, MS

Brandy Andreas
Rayburn High School
Pasadena, TX

Adam Bishop
Jordan High School
Sandy, UT

Jennifer Bragg
Midlothian High School
Midlothian, VA

Nicole Fevry
Midwood High School
Brooklyn, NY

Phillip Gallegos
Hilltop High School
Chula Vista, CA

Matt Gave
Stevenson Senior High School
Sterling Heights, MI

Blair Hogan
Leesville Road High School
Raleigh, NC

Ngoc Hong
Watkins Mill Senior High School
Gaithersburg, MD

Iman Jalali
Glenbrook North High School
Northbrook, IL

Vivek Makhijani
Durfee High School
Fall River, MA

Todd McDavitt
Derby High School
Derby, KS

Teniqua Mitchell
Linden-McKinley High School
Columbus, OH

Cicely Nash
Edmond Memorial High School
Edmond, OK

Brian Nebrensky
Hillsboro High School
Hillsboro, OR

Jesse Neumyer
Cumberland Valley High School
Mechanicsburg, PA

Nora Patronas
Alba High School
Bayou La Batre, LA

Lindsey Petersen
Stoughton High School
Stoughton, WI

Nicholas Price
Central Lafourche Senior High School
Mathews, LA

Ben Richey
Fort Vancouver High School
Vancouver, WA

Karen Ryan
Silver Creek High School
San Jose, CA

Matt Shaver
Weatherford High School
Weatherford, TX

Richie Spitler
Atlantic High School
Port Orange, FL

Jessie Stoneberg
Burnsville High School
Burnsville, MN

Kelly Swick
Ocean Township High School
Oakhurst, NJ

Jason Utzig
Kenmore East High School
Tonawanda, NY

Justin Woodly
North Cobb High School
Kennesaw, GA

vii

Introduction

Juries in Athens (page 9)

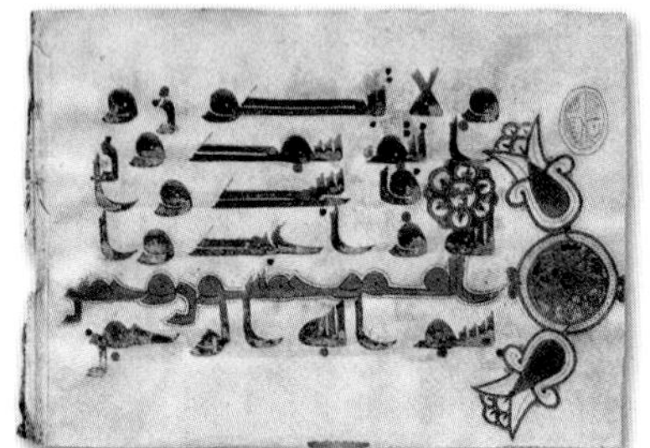

The Qur'an (page 15)

Constitutional Convention, 1787 (page 26)

viii

UNIT 1

1300–1800
Beginnings of the Modern World

Elizabeth I of England (page 59)

Safavid shah (page 72)

Early globe (page 95)

ix

UNIT 2

1500–1900

Absolutism to Revolution

Louis XIV of France (page 154)

Early telescope (page 192)

Riots in Paris (page 256)

UNIT 3

1700–1914

Industrialism and the Race for Empire

Singer sewing machine (page 286)

Marie Curie (page 331)

England as an octopus in an American political cartoon (page 351)

xi

1900–1945
The World at War

Machine gun (page 414)

Mohandas K. Gandhi (page 432)

Japanese attack on Pearl Harbor (page 498)

xii

UNIT 5

1945–Present

Perspectives on the Present

Winston Churchill, Franklin D. Roosevelt, and Joseph Stalin (page 531)

Nelson Mandela (page 610)

ISS satellite (page 638)

xiii

EPILOGUE

Unresolved Problems of the Modern World

Human Transporter (page 676)

Families of the missing in Chile march for justice (page 695)

xiv

REFERENCE

Skillbuilder Handbook R1

Primary Source Handbook R39

xv

Patterns of Interaction Video Series

Each video in the series *Patterns of Interaction* relates to a *Global Impact* feature in the text. These eight exciting videos show how cultural interactions have shaped our world and how patterns in history continue to the present day.

Volume 1

Building Empires
The Rise of the Persians and the Inca

Watch the Persian and Incan empires expand and rule other peoples, with unexpected results for both conquered and conquering cultures.

Trade Connects the World
Silk Roads and the Pacific Rim

Explore the legendary trade routes of the Silk Roads and the modern trade in the Pacific Rim, and notice how both affect much more than economics.

Volume 2

The Spread of Epidemic Disease
Bubonic Plague and Smallpox

Look for sweeping calamities and incredible consequences when interacting peoples bring devastating diseases to one another.

The Geography of Food
The Impact of Potatoes and Sugar

Notice how the introduction of new foods to a region provides security to some and spells disaster for others.

Volume 3

Struggling Toward Democracy
Revolutions in Latin America and South Africa

Examine the impact of democratic ideas that incite people to join revolutions in 19th-century Latin America and 20th-century South Africa.

Technology Transforms an Age
The Industrial and Electronic Revolutions

See how another kind of revolution, caused by innovations in industry and communication, brings change to the modern world.

Volume 4

Arming for War
Modern and Medieval Weapons

Watch how warring peoples' competition in military technology has resulted in a dangerous game of developing bigger, better, and faster weaponry throughout the ages.

Cultural Crossroads
The United States and the World

Observe how universal enjoyments like music, sports, and fashion become instruments of cultural blending worldwide.

Global Impact: Arming for War

The Atomic Bomb

On the eve of World War II, scientists in Germany succeeded in splitting the nucleus of a uranium atom, releasing a huge amount of energy. Albert Einstein wrote to President Franklin Roosevelt and warned him that Nazi Germany might be working to develop atomic weapons. Roosevelt responded by giving his approval for an American program, later code-named the Manhattan Project, to develop an atomic bomb. Roosevelt's decision set off a race to ensure that the United States would be the first to develop the bomb.

▼ On the morning of August 6, 1945, the B-29 bomber *Enola Gay*, flown by Colonel Paul W. Tibbets, Jr., took off from Tinian Island in the Mariana Islands.

▶ At precisely 8:16 A.M., the atomic bomb exploded above Hiroshima, a city on the Japanese island of Honshu.

Hiroshima: Day of Fire

Impact of the Bombing	
Ground temperatures	7,000°F
Hurricane force winds	980 miles per hour
Energy released	20,000 tons of TNT
Buildings destroyed	62,000 buildings
Killed immediately	70,000 people
Dead by the end of 1945	140,000 people
Total deaths related to A-bomb	200,000 people

The overwhelming destructive power of the Hiroshima bomb, and of the bomb dropped on Nagasaki three days later, changed the nature of war forever. Nuclear destruction also led to questions about the ethics of scientists and politicians who chose to develop and use the bomb.

Patterns of Interaction
Arming for War: Modern and Medieval Weapons

Just as in World War I, the conflicts of World War II spurred the development of ever more powerful weapons. Mightier tanks, more elusive submarines, faster fighter planes—all emerged from this period. From ancient times to the present day, the pattern remains the same: Every new weapon causes other countries to develop weapons of similar or greater force. This pattern results in a deadly race for an ultimate weapon: for example, the atomic bomb.

▼ Nagasaki citizens trudge through the still smoldering ruins of their city in this photograph by Yosuke Yamahata.

Connect *to* Today

1. **Making Inferences** What advantages did the United States have over Germany in the race to develop the atomic bomb?
   See Skillbuilder Handbook, page R10.
2. **Comparing and Contrasting** If you were to design a memorial to the victims of the Hiroshima and Nagasaki bombings, what symbol would you use? Make a sketch of your memorial.

512

The video icon in the *Global Impact* feature provides you with a link to the *Patterns of Interaction* video series.

xvi

Features

Analyzing Key Concepts

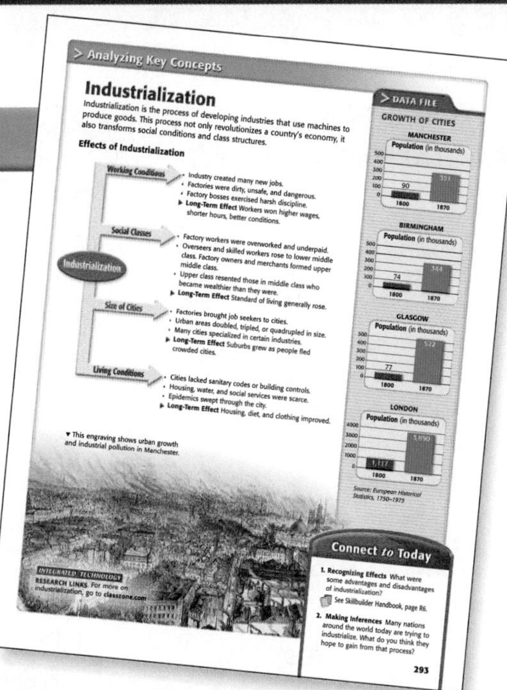

> Analyzing Key Concepts

Industrialization

Industrialization is the process of developing industries that use machines to produce goods. This process not only revolutionizes a country's economy, it also transforms social conditions and class structures.

Effects of Industrialization

Industrialization

Working Conditions
- Industry created many new jobs.
- Factories were dirty, unsafe, and dangerous.
- Factory bosses exercised harsh discipline.
- ▶ **Long-Term Effect** Workers won higher wages, shorter hours, better conditions.

Social Classes
- Factory workers were overworked and underpaid.
- Overseers and skilled workers rose to lower middle class. Factory owners and merchants formed upper middle class.
- Upper class resented those in middle class who became wealthier than they were.
- ▶ **Long-Term Effect** Standard of living generally rose.

Size of Cities
- Factories brought job seekers to cities.
- Urban areas doubled, tripled, or quadrupled in size.
- Many cities specialized in certain industries.
- ▶ **Long-Term Effect** Suburbs grew as people fled crowded cities.

Living Conditions
- Cities lacked sanitary codes or building controls.
- Housing, water, and social services were scarce.
- Epidemics swept through the city.
- ▶ **Long-Term Effect** Housing, diet, and clothing improved.

▼ This engraving shows urban growth and industrial pollution in Manchester.

INTEGRATED TECHNOLOGY
RESEARCH LINKS For more on industrialization, go to classzone.com

> DATA FILE

GROWTH OF CITIES

MANCHESTER
Population (in thousands)
90
1800 1870

BIRMINGHAM
Population (in thousands)
74 344
1800 1870

GLASGOW
Population (in thousands)
77 522
1800 1870

LONDON
Population (in thousands)
1,117 3,890
1800 1870

Source: European Historical Statistics, 1750–1975

Connect *to* Today

1. **Recognizing Effects** What were some advantages and disadvantages of industrialization?
   See Skillbuilder Handbook, page R6.
2. **Making Inferences** Many nations around the world today are trying to industrialize. What do you think they hope to gain from that process?

293

Analyzing Primary Sources

Analyzing Art, Artifacts, Architecture, Political Cartoons, Photographs

Different Perspectives: Using Primary and Secondary Sources

xvii

Features

Social History

Science & *Technology*

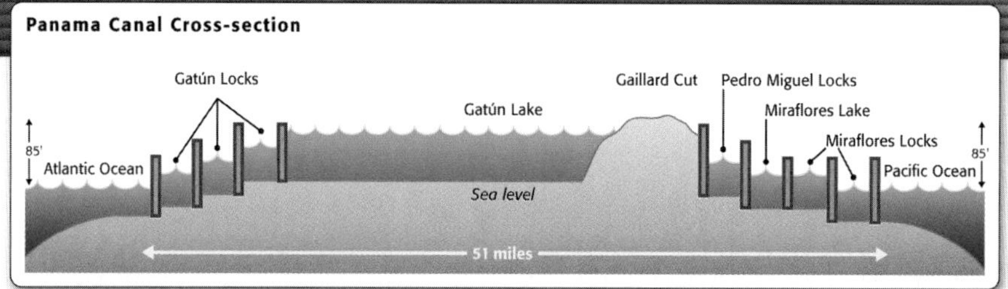

History *in* Depth

History *in* Depth

Ethnic Groups in the Former Yugoslavia

Many ethnic and religious groups lived within Yugoslavia, which was a federation of six republics. The map shows how the ethnic groups were distributed. Some of those groups held ancient grudges against one another. The chart summarizes some of the cultural differences among the groups.

Ethnic Groups in the Former Yugoslavia, 1992

Differences Among the Ethnic Groups

Group	Language (slavic unless noted)	Religion
Albanians	Albanian (not Slavic)	mostly Muslim
Croats	dialect of Serbo-Croatian*	mostly Roman Catholic
Hungarians	Magyar (not Slavic)	many types of Christians
Macedonians	Macedonian	mostly Eastern Orthodox
Montenegrins	dialect of Serbo-Croatian*	mostly Eastern Orthodox
Muslims	dialect of Serbo-Croatian*	Muslim (converted under Ottoman rule)
Serbs	dialect of Serbo-Croatian*	mostly Eastern Orthodox
Slovenes	Slovenian	mostly Roman Catholic

* Since Yugoslavia broke apart, many residents of the former republics have started to refer to their dialects as separate languages: Croatian for Croats, Bosnian for Muslims, Serbian for Serbs and Montenegrins.

SKILLBUILDER: Interpreting Visuals

1. **Analyzing Issues** *Use the chart to find out information about the various groups that lived in Bosnia and Herzegovina (as shown on the map). What were some of the differences among those groups?*
2. **Contrasting** *Kosovo was a province within Serbia. What group was in the majority there, and how did it differ from Serbs?*

Struggles for Democracy **623**

History *in* Depth

Building the Taj Mahal

Some 20,000 workers labored for 22 years to build the famous tomb. It is made of white marble brought from 250 miles away. The minaret towers are about 130 feet high. The building itself is 186 feet square.

The design of the building is a blend of Hindu and Muslim styles. The pointed arches are of Muslim design, and the perforated marble windows and doors are typical of a style found in Hindu temples.

The inside of the building is a glittering garden of thousands of carved marble flowers inlaid with tiny precious stones. One tiny flower, one inch square, had 60 different inlays.

INTEGRATED TECHNOLOGY

INTERNET ACTIVITY Use the Internet to take a virtual trip to the Taj Mahal. Create a brochure about the building. Go to **classzone.com** for your research.

History *through* Art

History *through* Art

Renaissance Ideas Influence Renaissance Art

The Renaissance in Italy produced extraordinary achievements in many different forms of art, including painting, architecture, sculpture, and drawing. These art forms were used by talented artists to express important ideas and attitudes of the age.

The value of humanism is shown in Raphael's *School of Athens,* a depiction of the greatest Greek philosophers. The realism of Renaissance art is seen in a portrait such as the *Mona Lisa,* which is an expression of the subject's unique features and personality. And Michelangelo's *David* shares stylistic qualities with ancient Greek and Roman sculpture.

INTEGRATED TECHNOLOGY
RESEARCH LINKS For more on Renaissance art, go to **classzone.com**

▼ **Classical and Renaissance Sculpture**
Michelangelo Influenced by classical statues, Michelangelo sculpted *David* from 1501 to 1504. Michelangelo portrayed the biblical hero in the moments just before battle. David's posture is graceful, yet his figure also displays strength. The statue, which is 18 feet tall, towers over the viewer.

▲ **Portraying Individuals**
Da Vinci The *Mona Lisa* (c. 1504–1506) is thought to be a portrait of Lisa Gherardini, who, at 16, married Francesco del Giocondo, a wealthy merchant of Florence who commissioned the portrait. Mona Lisa is a shortened form of Madonna Lisa (Madam, or My Lady, Lisa). Renaissance artists showed individuals as they really looked.

44 Chapter 1

Connect *to* Today

Global Impact

Global Patterns

xix

Features (continued)

History Makers

Comparing & Contrasting

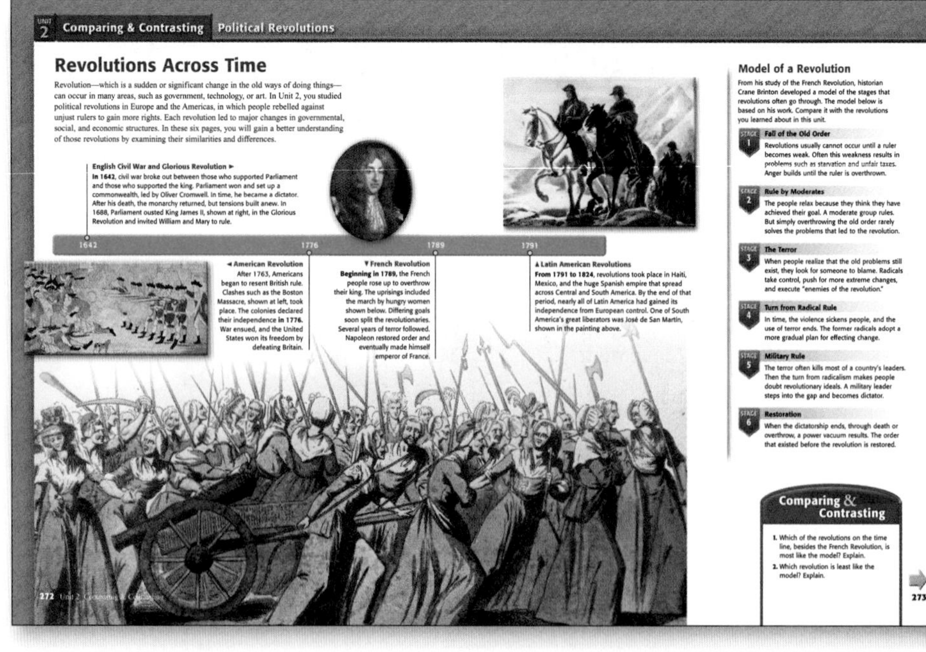

UNIT 2 Comparing & Contrasting Political Revolutions

Revolutions Across Time

Revolution—which is a sudden or significant change in the old ways of doing things—can occur in many areas, such as government, technology, or art. In Unit 2, you studied political revolutions in Europe and the Americas, in which people rebelled against unjust rulers to gain more rights. Each revolution led to major changes in governmental, social, and economic structures. In these six pages, you will gain a better understanding of those revolutions by examining their similarities and differences.

English Civil War and Glorious Revolution ►
In 1642, civil war broke out between those who supported Parliament and those who supported the king. Parliament won and set up a commonwealth, led by Oliver Cromwell. In time, he became a dictator. After his death, the monarchy returned, but tensions built anew. In 1688, Parliament ousted King James II, shown at right, in the Glorious Revolution and invited William and Mary to rule.

1642 1776 1789 1791

◄ American Revolution
After 1763, Americans began to resent British rule. Clashes such as the Boston Massacre, shown at left, took place. The colonies declared their independence in 1776. War ensued, and the United States won its freedom by defeating Britain.

▼ French Revolution
Beginning in 1789, the French people rose up to overthrow their king. The uprisings included the march by hungry women shown below. Differing goals soon split the revolutionaries. Several years of terror followed. Napoleon restored order and eventually made himself emperor of France.

▲ Latin American Revolutions
From 1791 to 1824, revolutions took place in Haiti, Mexico, and the huge Spanish empire that spread across Central and South America. By the end of that period, nearly all of Latin America had gained its independence from European control. One of South America's great liberators was José de San Martín, shown in the painting above.

Model of a Revolution

From his study of the French Revolution, historian Crane Brinton developed a model of the stages that revolutions often go through. The model below is based on his work. Compare it with the revolutions you learned about in this unit.

STAGE 1 Fall of the Old Order
Revolutions usually cannot occur until a ruler becomes weak. Often this weakness results in problems such as starvation and unfair taxes. Anger builds until the ruler is overthrown.

STAGE 2 Rule by Moderates
The people relax because they think they have achieved their goal. A moderate group rules. But simply overthrowing the old order rarely solves the problems that led to the revolution.

STAGE 3 The Terror
When people realize that the old problems still exist, they look for someone to blame. Radicals take control, push for more extreme changes, and execute "enemies of the revolution."

STAGE 4 Turn from Radical Rule
In time, the violence sickens people, and the use of terror ends. The former radicals adopt a more gradual plan for effecting change.

STAGE 5 Military Rule
The terror often kills most of a country's leaders. Then the turn from radicalism makes people doubt revolutionary ideals. A military leader steps into the gap and becomes dictator.

STAGE 6 Restoration
When the dictatorship ends, through death or overthrow, a power vacuum results. The order that existed before the revolution is restored.

Comparing & Contrasting

1. Which of the revolutions on the time line, besides the French Revolution, is most like the model? Explain.
2. Which revolution is least like the model? Explain.

272 Unit 2 Comparing & Contrasting

273

xx

Historical and Political Maps

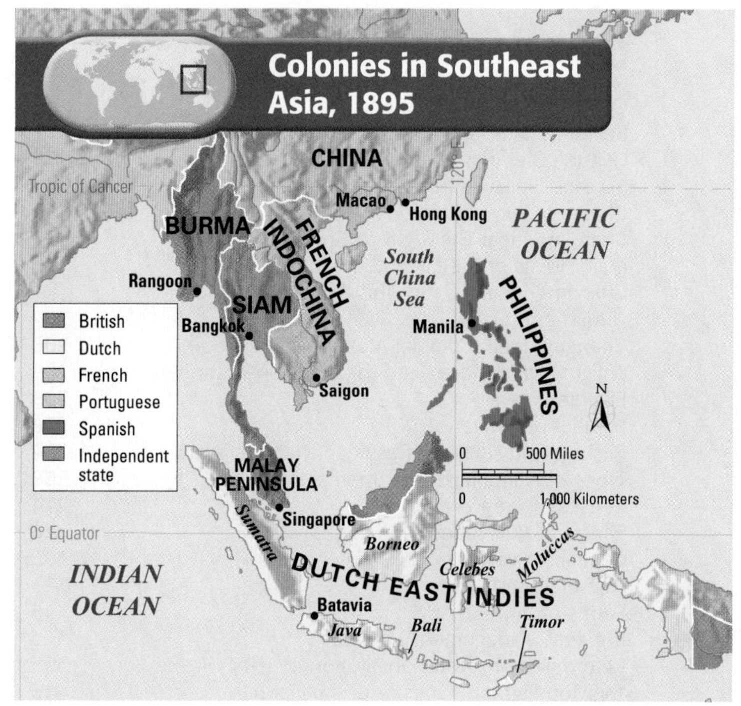

Colonies in Southeast Asia, 1895
CHINA
Tropic of Cancer
Macao
Hong Kong
PACIFIC OCEAN
BURMA
FRENCH INDOCHINA
South China Sea
Rangoon
SIAM
PHILIPPINES
British
Dutch
French
Portuguese
Spanish
Independent state
Bangkok
Manila
Saigon
N
MALAY PENINSULA
0 500 Miles
0 1,000 Kilometers
Singapore
0° Equator
Sumatra
Borneo
Celebes
Moluccas
INDIAN OCEAN
DUTCH EAST INDIES
Batavia
Java
Bali
Timor

xxi

Charts and Graphs

Charts

Graphs

xxii

Time Lines, Infographics, and Political Cartoons

Time Lines

Infographics

Political Cartoons

JEFF STAHLER
Courtesy Cincinnati Post

xxiii

Primary and Secondary Sources

PRIMARY SOURCE

Soldiers! I am pleased with you. On the day of Austerlitz, you justified everything that I was expecting of [you]... In less than four hours, an army of 100,000 men, commanded by the emperors of Russia and Austria, was cut up and dispersed... 120 pieces of artillery, 20 generals, and more than 30,000 men taken prisoner—such are the results of this day which will forever be famous... And it will be enough for you to say, "I was at Austerlitz," to hear the reply: "There is a brave man!"

NAPOLEON, quoted in *Napoleon* by André Castelot

xxiv

Primary and Secondary Sources (continued)

xxv

World History Themes

While historical events are unique, they often are driven by similar, repeated forces. In telling the history of our world, this book pays special attention to eight significant and recurring themes. These themes are presented to show that from America, to Africa, to Asia, people are more alike than they realize. Throughout history humans have confronted similar obstacles, have struggled to achieve similar goals, and continually have strived to better themselves and the world around them.

Power and Authority

History is often made by the people and institutions in power. As you read about the world's powerful people and governments, try to answer several key questions.

- Who holds the power?
- How did that person or group get power?
- What system of government provides order in this society?
- How does the group or person in power keep or lose power?

Religious and Ethical Systems

Throughout history, humans around the world have been guided by, as much as anything else, their religious and ethical beliefs. As you examine the world's religious and ethical systems, pay attention to several important issues.

- What beliefs are held by a majority of people in a region?
- How do these major religious beliefs differ from one another?
- How do the various religious groups interact with one another?
- How do religious groups react toward nonmembers?

Revolution

Often in history, great change has been achieved only through force. As you read about the continuous overthrow of governments, institutions, and even ideas throughout history, examine several key questions.

- What long-term ideas or institutions are being overthrown?
- What caused people to make this radical change?
- What are the results of the change?

Interaction with Environment

Since the earliest of times, humans have had to deal with their surroundings in order to survive. As you read about our continuous interaction with the environment, keep in mind several important issues.

- How do humans adjust to the climate and terrain where they live?
- How have changes in the natural world forced people to change?
- What positive and negative changes have people made to their environment?

xxvi

Economics

Economics has proven to be a powerful force in human history. From early times to the present, human cultures have been concerned with how to use their scarce resources to satisfy their needs. As you read about different groups, note several key issues regarding the role of economics in world history.

- What goods and services does a society produce?
- Who controls the wealth and resources of a society?
- How does a society obtain more goods and services?

Cultural Interaction

Today, people around the world share many things, from music, to food, to ideas. Human cultures actually have interacted with each other since ancient times. As you read about how different cultures have interacted, note several significant issues.

- How have cultures interacted (trade, migration, or conquest)?
- What items have cultures passed on to each other?
- What political, economic, and religious ideas have cultures shared?
- What positive and negative effects have resulted from cultural interaction?

Empire Building

Since the beginning of time, human cultures have shared a similar desire to grow more powerful—often by dominating other groups. As you read about empire building through the ages, keep in mind several key issues.

- What motivates groups to conquer other lands and people?
- How does one society gain control of others?
- How does a dominating society control and rule its subjects?

Science and Technology

All humans share an endless desire to know more about their world and to solve whatever problems they encounter. The development of science and technology has played a key role in these quests. As you read about the role of science and technology in world history, try to answer several key questions.

- What tools and methods do people use to solve the various problems they face?
- How do people gain knowledge about their world? How do they use that knowledge?
- How do new discoveries and inventions change the way people live?

Geography Themes

Geography is the study of the earth and its features. It is also an important part of human history. Since the beginning of time, all civilizations have had to control their surroundings in order to survive. In addition, geography has played a vital role in many historical events. Like history itself, geography reflects several key themes. These themes help us to understand the different ways in which geography has helped shape the story of world history.

Location

Location tells us where in the world a certain area is. Geographers describe location in two ways: absolute location and relative location. An area's absolute location is its point of latitude and longitude. Latitude is the distance in degrees north or south of the equator. Longitude is the degree distance east or west of an imaginary vertical line that runs through Greenwich, England, called the prime meridian. An area's relative location describes where it is in terms of other areas.

In absolute terms, the middle of Singapore lies at 1°20' north latitude and 103°50' east longitude. This information allows you to pinpoint Singapore on a map. In relative terms, Singapore is an island country on the southern tip of the Malay Peninsula near where the South China Sea and the Indian Ocean meet. How might Singapore's location on the sea have helped it develop into an economic power?

Human/Environment Interaction

Throughout history, humans have changed and have been changed by their environment. Because they live on an island, the people of Singapore have built a bridge in order to travel more easily to mainland Malaysia. In addition, Singapore residents have carved an inviting harbor out of parts of its coastline in order to accommodate the island's busy ocean traffic.

Singapore is one of the most densely populated countries in the world. Many of its over four million citizens live in the capital city, Singapore. The country's population density is almost 18,000 persons per square mile. In contrast, the United States has a population density of 82 persons per square mile. What environmental challenges does this situation pose?

xxviii

Region

A region is any area that has common characteristics. These characteristics may include physical factors, such as landforms or climate. They also may include cultural aspects, such as language or religion. Singapore is part of a region known as Southeast Asia. The countries of this region share such characteristics as rich, fertile soil, as well as a strong influence of Buddhism and Islam.

Because regions share similar characteristics, they often share similar concerns. In 1967, Singapore joined with the other countries of Southeast Asia to form the Association of Southeast Asian Nations. This body was created to address the region's concerns. What concerns might Singapore have that are unique?

Place

Place, in geography, indicates what an area looks like in both physical and human terms. The physical setting of an area—its landforms, soil, climate, and resources—are aspects of place. So are the different cultures which inhabit an area.

The physical characteristics of Singapore include a hot, moist climate with numerous rain forests. In human terms, Singapore's population is mostly Chinese. How does Singapore's human characteristic tie it to other countries?

Movement

In geography, movement is the transfer of people, goods, and ideas from one place to another. In many ways, history is the story of movement. Since early times, people have migrated in search of better places to live. They have traded with distant peoples to obtain new goods. And they have spread a wealth of ideas from culture to culture.

Singapore, which is a prosperous center of trade and finance, attracts numerous people in search of greater wealth and new goods. What about Singapore's geography makes it the ideal place for the trading of goods?

xxix

Time

While history is the story of people, it is also the examination of when events occurred. Keeping track of the order of historical events will help you to better retain and understand the material. To help you remember the order and dates of important events in history, this book contains numerous time lines. Below is some instruction on how to read a time line, as well as a look at some terms associated with tracking time in history.

How to Read a Time Line

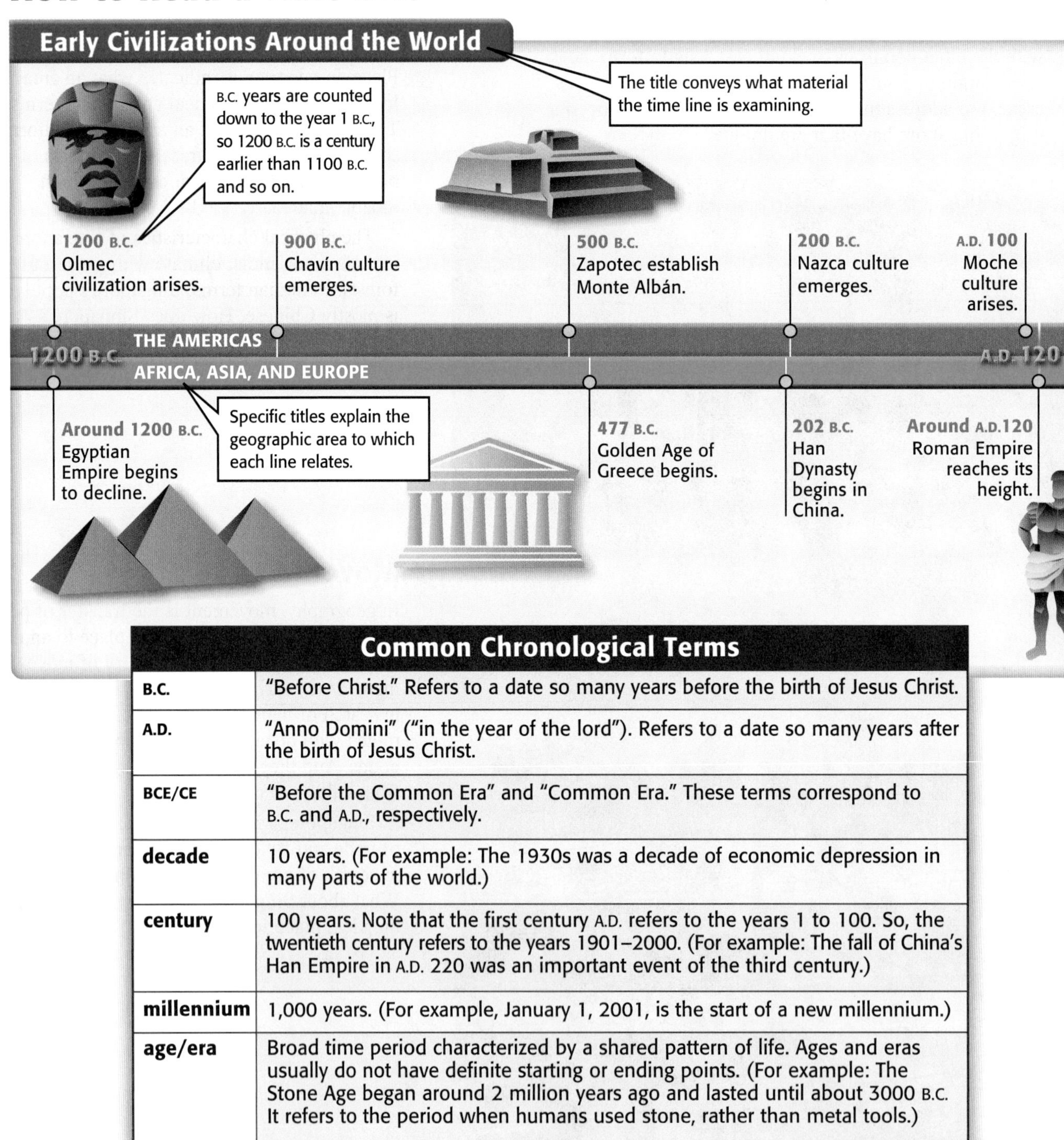
Early Civilizations Around the World
The title conveys what material the time line is examining.
B.C. years are counted down to the year 1 B.C., so 1200 B.C. is a century earlier than 1100 B.C. and so on.
1200 B.C. Olmec civilization arises.
900 B.C. Chavín culture emerges.
500 B.C. Zapotec establish Monte Albán.
200 B.C. Nazca culture emerges.
A.D. 100 Moche culture arises.
1200 B.C.
THE AMERICAS
AFRICA, ASIA, AND EUROPE
A.D. 120
Around 1200 B.C. Egyptian Empire begins to decline.
Specific titles explain the geographic area to which each line relates.
477 B.C. Golden Age of Greece begins.
202 B.C. Han Dynasty begins in China.
Around A.D.120 Roman Empire reaches its height.

Common Chronological Terms	
B.C.	"Before Christ." Refers to a date so many years before the birth of Jesus Christ.
A.D.	"Anno Domini" ("in the year of the lord"). Refers to a date so many years after the birth of Jesus Christ.
BCE/CE	"Before the Common Era" and "Common Era." These terms correspond to B.C. and A.D., respectively.
decade	10 years. (For example: The 1930s was a decade of economic depression in many parts of the world.)
century	100 years. Note that the first century A.D. refers to the years 1 to 100. So, the twentieth century refers to the years 1901–2000. (For example: The fall of China's Han Empire in A.D. 220 was an important event of the third century.)
millennium	1,000 years. (For example, January 1, 2001, is the start of a new millennium.)
age/era	Broad time period characterized by a shared pattern of life. Ages and eras usually do not have definite starting or ending points. (For example: The Stone Age began around 2 million years ago and lasted until about 3000 B.C. It refers to the period when humans used stone, rather than metal tools.)

xxx

Place

You are about to examine not only thousands of years of history, but nearly every region of the globe. To help you visualize the faraway places you read about, this book contains numerous maps. Many of these maps contain several layers of information that provide a better understanding of how and why events in history occurred. Below is a look at how to read a map in order to obtain all of the rich information it offers.

How to Read a Map

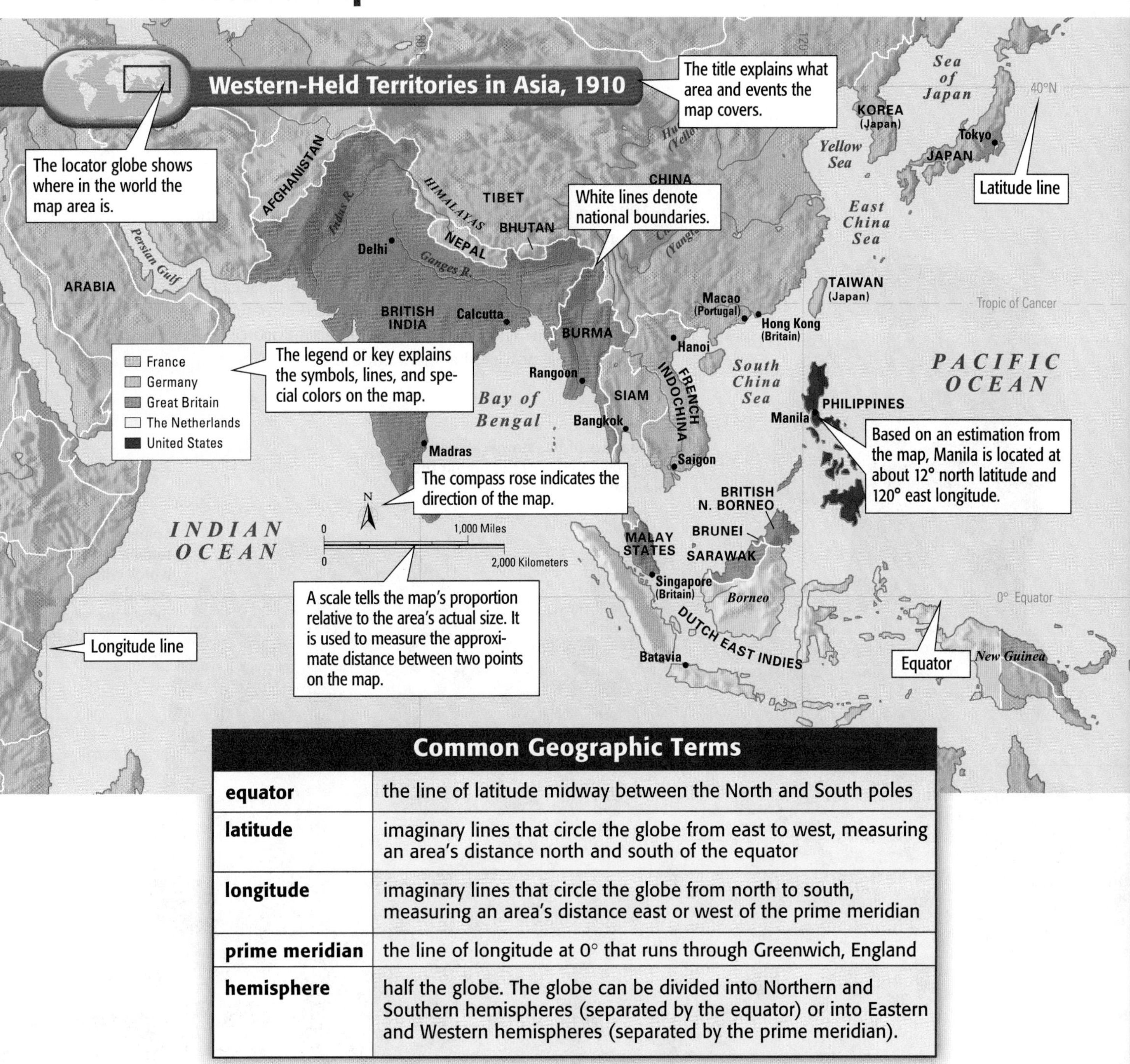

Western-Held Territories in Asia, 1910
The title explains what area and events the map covers.
The locator globe shows where in the world the map area is.
White lines denote national boundaries.
Latitude line
The legend or key explains the symbols, lines, and special colors on the map.
France
Germany
Great Britain
The Netherlands
United States
Based on an estimation from the map, Manila is located at about 12° north latitude and 120° east longitude.
The compass rose indicates the direction of the map.
A scale tells the map's proportion relative to the area's actual size. It is used to measure the approximate distance between two points on the map.
Longitude line
Equator
0 1,000 Miles
0 2,000 Kilometers
N
40°N
Tropic of Cancer
0° Equator
Sea of Japan
KOREA (Japan)
Tokyo
JAPAN
Yellow Sea
East China Sea
TAIWAN (Japan)
CHINA
TIBET
BHUTAN
NEPAL
HIMALAYAS
AFGHANISTAN
Indus R.
Delhi
Ganges R.
Persian Gulf
ARABIA
BRITISH INDIA
Calcutta
BURMA
Macao (Portugal)
Hong Kong (Britain)
Hanoi
South China Sea
PACIFIC OCEAN
Rangoon
SIAM
FRENCH INDOCHINA
Bay of Bengal
Bangkok
Madras
Manila
PHILIPPINES
Saigon
BRITISH N. BORNEO
BRUNEI
SARAWAK
MALAY STATES
Singapore (Britain)
Borneo
DUTCH EAST INDIES
Batavia
New Guinea
INDIAN OCEAN

Common Geographic Terms	
equator	the line of latitude midway between the North and South poles
latitude	imaginary lines that circle the globe from east to west, measuring an area's distance north and south of the equator
longitude	imaginary lines that circle the globe from north to south, measuring an area's distance east or west of the prime meridian
prime meridian	the line of longitude at 0° that runs through Greenwich, England
hemisphere	half the globe. The globe can be divided into Northern and Southern hemispheres (separated by the equator) or into Eastern and Western hemispheres (separated by the prime meridian).

xxxi

How Do We Know?

Do you like puzzles? If so, you are in luck. You are about to encounter the greatest puzzle there is: history. The study of history is much more than the recollection of dates and names. It is an attempt to answer a continuous and puzzling question: what really happened?

In their effort to solve this puzzle, historians and researchers use a variety of methods. From digging up artifacts, to uncovering eyewitness accounts, experts collect and analyze mountains of data in numerous ways. As a result, the history books you read more accurately depict what life was like in a culture 5,000 years ago, or what caused the outbreak of a devastating war. The following two pages examine some of the pieces used to solve the puzzle of history.

Clues from an Ancient Girl

In 1995, an anthropologist discovered the mummified and frozen remains of a teenage girl in the Andes Mountains of South America. Scientists believe that she is about 500 years old and was a member of the Inca Empire. Because much of her remains are well preserved, scientists hope she will provide them with new information about one of the Americas' most powerful ancient cultures.

An analysis of her stomach content may provide information about the Inca diet.

Some of her DNA remains intact, which will help scientists determine whether she has any living descendants.

Her clothing, believed to belong to the upper class, should shed new light on how noble Inca women dressed.

xxxii

Modern Science

The ever-improving field of science has lent its hand in the search to learn more about the past. Using everything from microscopes to computers, researchers have shed new light on many historical mysteries. Here, a researcher uses computer technology to determine what the owner of a prehistoric human skull may have looked like.

Written Sources

Historians often look to written documents for insight into the past. There are various types of written sources. Documents written during the same time period as an event are known as *primary* sources. They include such things as diaries and newspapers. They also include drawings, such as the one shown here by Italian painter and inventor, Leonardo da Vinci. His rough sketch of a helicopter-type machine tells us that as early as the late 1400s, humans considered mechanical flight. Material written about an event later, such as books, are known as *secondary* sources. Some written sources began as oral tradition—legends, myths, and beliefs passed on by spoken word from generation to generation.

Digging Up History

Researchers have learned much about the past by discovering the remains of ancient societies. Spearheads like these, which date back to around 9,500 B.C., were found throughout North America. They tell us among other things that the early Americans were hunters. These spearheads were once considered to be the earliest evidence of humankind in the Americas. However, as an example of how history continues to change, scientists recently found evidence of human life in South America as early as 10,500 B.C.

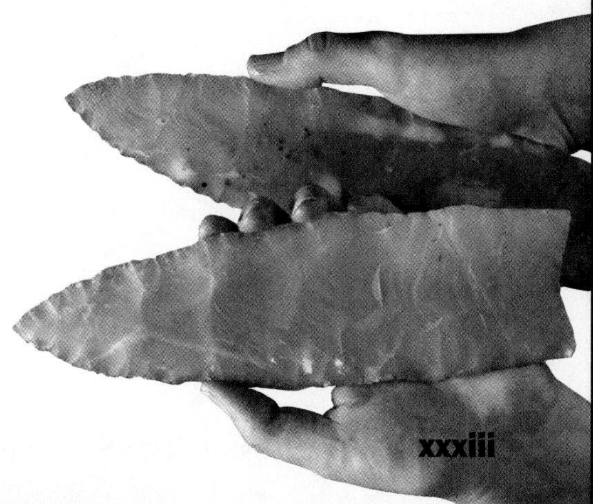

xxxiii

Student Guide to the California State Standards for Grade 10

The state of California has developed standards that guide the content taught in its public schools. At the beginning of every lesson in this book, you will see a listing of the California content standards and skills standards that are addressed in that lesson. The standards begin with a code that combines numbers and letters (such as 10.2.3 or HI 2), followed by the statement of the standard. These standards describe the knowledge and skills you are expected to have learned by the end of specific grades.

Standards that use numbers only (such as 10.2.3) are content standards, which describe the actual historical people and events that you will study in this book. Standards that combine letters and numbers (such as HI 2 or CST 3) refer to standards that cover the Historical and Social Sciences Analysis Skills that you will apply to the content standards for Grade 10.

The following charts contain the complete wording of the content and skills standards for Grade 10. These charts will help you keep track of what you learn throughout the year.

xxxiv

History-Social Science Standards

Grade 10	World History, Culture, and Geography: The Modern World
Standard 10.1	Students relate the moral and ethical principles in ancient Greek and Roman philosophy, in Judaism, and in Christianity to the development of Western political thought.
10.1.1	Analyze the similarities and differences in Judeo-Christian and Greco-Roman views of law, reason and faith, and duties of the individual.
10.1.2	Trace the development of the Western political ideas of the rule of law and illegitimacy of tyranny, using selections from Plato's *Republic* and Aristotle's *Politics*.
10.1.3	Consider the influence of the U.S. Constitution on political systems in the contemporary world.
Standard 10.2	Students compare and contrast the Glorious Revolution of England, the American Revolution, and the French Revolution and their enduring effects worldwide on the political expectations for self-government and individual liberty.
10.2.1	Compare the major ideas of philosophers and their effects on the democratic revolutions in England, the United States, France, and Latin America (e.g., John Locke, Charles-Louis Montesquieu, Jean-Jacques Rousseau, Simón Bolívar, Thomas Jefferson, James Madison).
10.2.2	List the principles of the Magna Carta, the English Bill of Rights (1689), the American Declaration of Independence (1776), the French Declaration of the Rights of Man and the Citizen (1789), and the U.S. Bill of Rights (1791).
10.2.3	Understand the unique character of the American Revolution, its spread to other parts of the world, and its continuing significance to other nations.
10.2.4	Explain how the ideology of the French Revolution led France to develop from constitutional monarchy to democratic despotism to the Napoleonic empire.
10.2.5	Discuss how nationalism spread across Europe with Napoleon but was repressed for a generation under the Congress of Vienna and Concert of Europe until the Revolutions of 1848.
Standard 10.3	Students analyze the effects of the Industrial Revolution in England, France, Germany, Japan, and the United States.
10.3.1	Analyze why England was the first country to industrialize.
10.3.2	Examine how scientific and technological changes and new forms of energy brought about massive social, economic, and cultural change (e.g., the inventions and discoveries of James Watt, Eli Whitney, Henry Bessemer, Louis Pasteur, Thomas Edison).

xxxv

10.3.3 Describe the growth of population, rural to urban migration, and growth of cities associated with the Industrial Revolution.

10.3.4 Trace the evolution of work and labor, including the demise of the slave trade and the effects of immigration, mining and manufacturing, division of labor, and the union movement.

10.3.5 Understand the connections among natural resources, entrepreneurship, labor, and capital in an industrial economy.

10.3.6 Analyze the emergence of capitalism as a dominant economic pattern and the responses to it, including Utopianism, Social Democracy, Socialism, and Communism.

10.3.7 Describe the emergence of Romanticism in art and literature (e.g., the poetry of William Blake and William Wordsworth), social criticism (e.g., the novels of Charles Dickens), and the move away from Classicism in Europe.

Standard 10.4

Students analyze patterns of global change in the era of New Imperialism in at least two of the following regions or countries: Africa, Southeast Asia, China, India, Latin America, and the Philippines.

10.4.1 Describe the rise of industrial economies and their link to imperialism and colonialism (e.g., the role played by national security and strategic advantage; moral issues raised by the search for national hegemony, Social Darwinism, and the missionary impulse; material issues such as land, resources, and technology).

10.4.2 Discuss the locations of the colonial rule of such nations as England, France, Germany, Italy, Japan, the Netherlands, Russia, Spain, Portugal, and the United States.

10.4.3 Explain imperialism from the perspective of the colonizers and the colonized and the varied immediate and long-term responses by the people under colonial rule.

10.4.4 Describe the independence struggles of the colonized regions of the world, including the roles of leaders, such as Sun Yat-sen in China, and the roles of ideology and religion.

Standard 10.5

Students analyze the causes and course of the First World War.

10.5.1 Analyze the arguments for entering into war presented by leaders from all sides of the Great War and the role of political and economic rivalries, ethnic and ideological conflicts, domestic discontent and disorder, and propaganda and nationalism in mobilizing the civilian population in support of "total war."

10.5.2 Examine the principal theaters of battle, major turning points, and the importance of geographic factors in military decisions and outcomes (e.g., topography, waterways, distance, climate).

xxxvi

10.5.3	Explain how the Russian Revolution and the entry of the United States affected the course and outcome of the war.
10.5.4	Understand the nature of the war and its human costs (military and civilian) on all sides of the conflict, including how colonial peoples contributed to the war effort.
10.5.5	Discuss human rights violations and genocide, including the Ottoman government's actions against Armenian citizens.

Standard 10.6	Students analyze the effects of the First World War.
10.6.1	Analyze the aims and negotiating roles of world leaders, the terms and influence of the Treaty of Versailles and Woodrow Wilson's Fourteen Points, and the causes and effects of the United States's rejection of the League of Nations on world politics.
10.6.2	Describe the effects of the war and resulting peace treaties on population movement, the international economy, and shifts in the geographic and political borders of Europe and the Middle East.
10.6.3	Understand the widespread disillusionment with prewar institutions, authorities, and values that resulted in a void that was later filled by totalitarians.
10.6.4	Discuss the influence of World War I on literature, art, and intellectual life in the West (e.g., Pablo Picasso, the "lost generation" of Gertrude Stein, Ernest Hemingway).

Standard 10.7	Students analyze the rise of totalitarian governments after World War I.
10.7.1	Understand the causes and consequences of the Russian Revolution, including Lenin's use of totalitarian means to seize and maintain control (e.g., the Gulag).
10.7.2	Trace Stalin's rise to power in the Soviet Union and the connection between economic policies, political policies, the absence of a free press, and systematic violations of human rights (e.g., the Terror Famine in Ukraine).
10.7.3	Analyze the rise, aggression, and human costs of totalitarian regimes (Fascist and Communist) in Germany, Italy, and the Soviet Union, noting especially their common and dissimilar traits.

Standard 10.8	Students analyze the causes and consequences of World War II.
10.8.1	Compare the German, Italian, and Japanese drives for empire in the 1930s, including the 1937 Rape of Nanking, other atrocities in China, and the Stalin-Hitler Pact of 1939.
10.8.2	Understand the role of appeasement, nonintervention (isolationism), and the domestic distractions in Europe and the United States prior to the outbreak of World War II.

xxxvii

10.8.3	Identify and locate the Allied and Axis powers on a map and discuss the major turning points of the war, the principal theaters of conflict, key strategic decisions, and the resulting war conferences and political resolutions, with emphasis on the importance of geographic factors.
10.8.4	Describe the political, diplomatic, and military leaders during the war (e.g., Winston Churchill, Franklin Delano Roosevelt, Emperor Hirohito, Adolf Hitler, Benito Mussolini, Joseph Stalin, Douglas MacArthur, Dwight Eisenhower).
10.8.5	Analyze the Nazi policy of pursuing racial purity, especially against the European Jews; its transformation into the Final Solution; and the Holocaust that resulted in the murder of six million Jewish civilians.
10.8.6	Discuss the human costs of the war, with particular attention to the civilian and military losses in Russia, Germany, Britain, the United States, China, and Japan.

Standard 10.9	Students analyze the international developments in the post-World War II world.
10.9.1	Compare the economic and military power shifts caused by the war, including the Yalta Pact, the development of nuclear weapons, Soviet control over Eastern European nations, and the economic recoveries of Germany and Japan.
10.9.2	Analyze the causes of the Cold War, with the free world on one side and Soviet client states on the other, including competition for influence in such places as Egypt, the Congo, Vietnam, and Chile.
10.9.3	Understand the importance of the Truman Doctrine and the Marshall Plan, which established the pattern for America's postwar policy of supplying economic and military aid to prevent the spread of Communism and the resulting economic and political competition in arenas such as Southeast Asia (i.e., the Korean War, Vietnam War), Cuba, and Africa.
10.9.4	Analyze the Chinese Civil War, the rise of Mao Tse-tung, and the subsequent political and economic upheavals in China (e.g., the Great Leap Forward, the Cultural Revolution, and the Tiananmen Square uprising).
10.9.5	Describe the uprisings in Poland (1952), Hungary (1956), and Czechoslovakia (1968) and those countries' resurgence in the 1970s and 1980s as people in Soviet satellites sought freedom from Soviet control.
10.9.6	Understand how the forces of nationalism developed in the Middle East, how the Holocaust affected world opinion regarding the need for a Jewish state, and the significance and effects of the location and establishment of Israel on world affairs.

10.9.7	Analyze the reasons for the collapse of the Soviet Union, including the weakness of the command economy, burdens of military commitments, and growing resistance to Soviet rule by dissidents in satellite states and the non-Russian Soviet republics.
10.9.8	Discuss the establishment and work of the United Nations and the purposes and functions of the Warsaw Pact, SEATO, NATO, and the Organization of American States.

Standard 10.10	Students analyze instances of nation-building in the contemporary world in at least two of the following regions or countries: the Middle East, Africa, Mexico and other parts of Latin America, and China.
10.10.1	Understand the challenges in the regions, including their geopolitical, cultural, military, and economic significance and the international relationships in which they are involved.
10.10.2	Describe the recent history of the regions, including political divisions and systems, key leaders, religious issues, natural features, resources, and population patterns.
10.10.3	Discuss the important trends in the regions today and whether they appear to serve the cause of individual freedom and democracy.

Standard 10.11	Students analyze the integration of countries into the world economy and the information, technological, and communications revolutions (e.g., television, satellites, computers).

xxxix

Grade 10 Historical and Social Sciences Analysis Skills

Chronological and Spatial Thinking (CST)

1. Students compare the present with the past, evaluating the consequences of past events and decisions and determining the lessons that were learned.
2. Students analyze how change happens at different rates at different times; understand that some aspects can change while others remain the same; and understand that change is complicated and affects not only technology and politics but also values and beliefs.
3. Students use a variety of maps and documents to interpret human movement, including major patterns of domestic and international migration, changing environmental preferences and settlement patterns, the frictions that develop between population groups, and the diffusion of ideas, technological innovations, and goods.
4. Students relate current events to the physical and human characteristics of places and regions.

Research, Evidence, and Point of View (REP)

1. Students distinguish valid arguments from fallacious arguments in historical interpretations.
2. Students identify bias and prejudice in historical interpretations.
3. Students evaluate major debates among historians concerning alternative interpretations of the past, including an analysis of authors' use of evidence and the distinctions between sound generalizations and misleading oversimplifications.
4. Students construct and test hypotheses; collect, evaluate, and employ information from multiple primary and secondary sources; and apply it in oral and written presentations.

Historical Interpretation (HI)

1. Students show the connections, causal and otherwise, between particular historical events and larger social, economic, and political trends and developments.
2. Students recognize the complexity of historical causes and effects, including the limitations on determining cause and effect.
3. Students interpret past events and issues within the context in which an event unfolded rather than solely in terms of present-day norms and values.

4. Students understand the meaning, implication, and impact of historical events and recognize that events could have taken other directions.
5. Students analyze human modifications of landscapes and examine the resulting environmental policy issues.
6. Students conduct cost-benefit analyses and apply basic economic indicators to analyze the aggregate economic behavior of the U.S. economy.

xli

Strategies for Taking Tests

This section of the textbook helps you develop and practice the skills you need to study history and to take tests. Part 1, **Strategies for Studying History,** takes you through the features of the textbook and offers suggestions on how to use these features to improve your reading and study skills.

Part 2, **Test-Taking Strategies and Practice,** offers specific strategies for tackling many of the items you will find on tests that you take. It gives tips for answering multiple-choice, constructed-response, extended-response, and document-based questions. In addition, it offers guidelines for analyzing primary and secondary sources, maps, political cartoons, charts, graphs, and time lines. Each strategy is followed by a set of questions you can use for practice.

CONTENTS

S1

Part 1: Strategies for Studying History

Reading is the central skill in the effective study of history or any other subject. You can improve your reading skills by using helpful techniques and by practicing. The better your reading skills, the more you will remember what you read. Below you will find several strategies that involve built-in features of *Modern World History: Patterns of Interaction.* Careful use of these strategies will help you learn and understand history more effectively.

Preview Chapters Before You Read

Each chapter begins with a two-page chapter opener and a one-page Interact with History feature. Study these materials to help you get ready to read.

1. Read the chapter title for clues to what will be covered in the chapter.
2. Study the **Previewing Main Ideas** feature and the map. Gain more background information on chapter content by answering the questions in the feature.
3. Preview the time line and note the years covered in the chapter. Consider the important events that took place during this time period.
4. Read the **Interact with History** feature (see page S3). Study **Examining the Issues** to gain insight on a major theme addressed in the chapter.

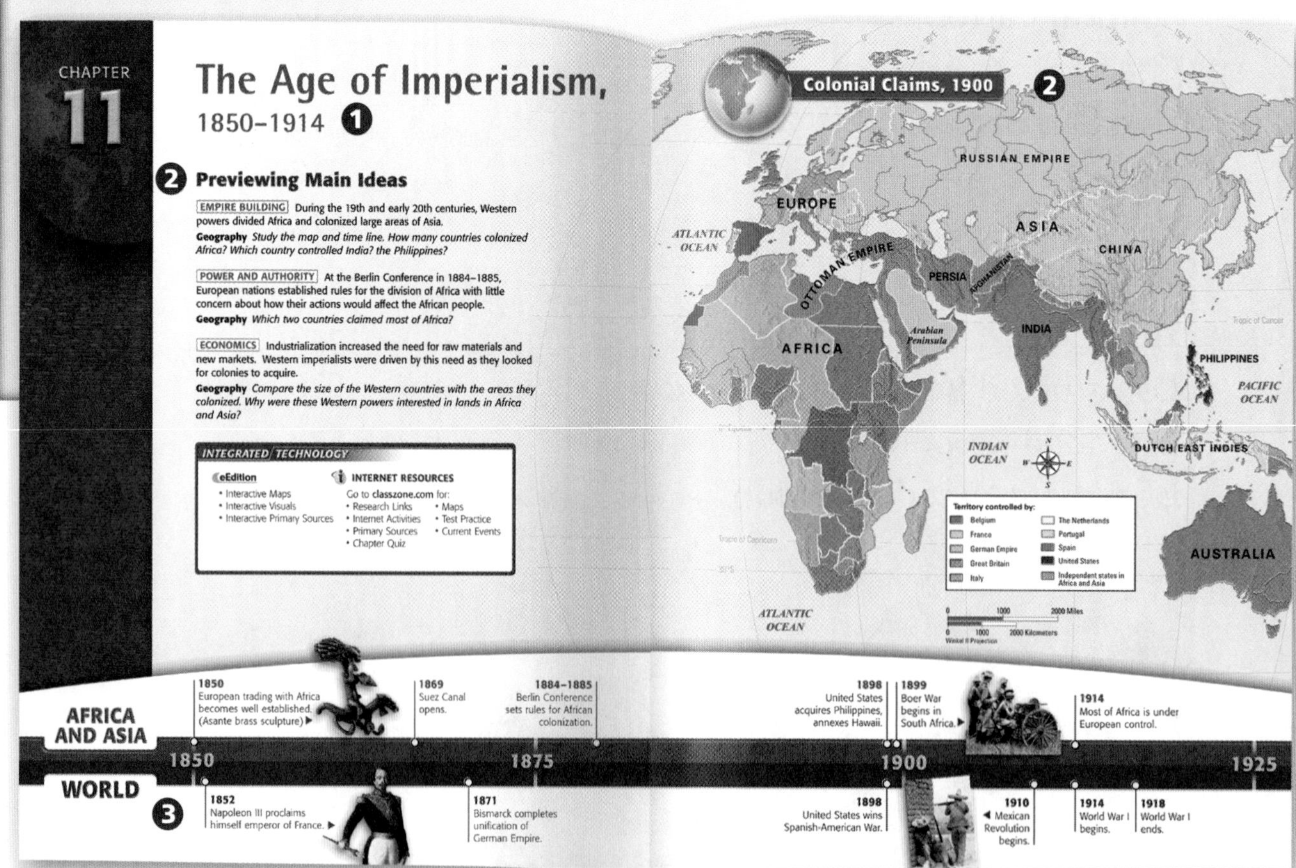

CHAPTER 11

The Age of Imperialism, 1850–1914 ❶

❷ **Previewing Main Ideas**

EMPIRE BUILDING During the 19th and early 20th centuries, Western powers divided Africa and colonized large areas of Asia.
Geography *Study the map and time line. How many countries colonized Africa? Which country controlled India? the Philippines?*

POWER AND AUTHORITY At the Berlin Conference in 1884–1885, European nations established rules for the division of Africa with little concern about how their actions would affect the African people.
Geography *Which two countries claimed most of Africa?*

ECONOMICS Industrialization increased the need for raw materials and new markets. Western imperialists were driven by this need as they looked for colonies to acquire.
Geography *Compare the size of the Western countries with the areas they colonized. Why were these Western powers interested in lands in Africa and Asia?*

INTEGRATED TECHNOLOGY
eEdition
• Interactive Maps
• Interactive Visuals
• Interactive Primary Sources
INTERNET RESOURCES
Go to classzone.com for:
• Research Links
• Internet Activities
• Primary Sources
• Chapter Quiz
• Maps
• Test Practice
• Current Events

AFRICA AND ASIA
1850 European trading with Africa becomes well established. (Asante brass sculpture) ▶
1869 Suez Canal opens.
1884–1885 Berlin Conference sets rules for African colonization.
1898 United States acquires Philippines, annexes Hawaii.
1899 Boer War begins in South Africa. ▶
1914 Most of Africa is under European control.

1850 — 1875 — 1900 — 1925

WORLD ❸
1852 Napoleon III proclaims himself emperor of France. ▶
1871 Bismarck completes unification of German Empire.
1898 United States wins Spanish-American War.
1910 ◀ Mexican Revolution begins.
1914 World War I begins.
1918 World War I ends.

S2

Preview Sections Before You Read

Each chapter consists of three, four, or five sections. Use the section openers to help you prepare to read.

5. Study the information under the headings **Main Idea** and **Why It Matters Now.** These features tell you what is important in the material you are about to read.
6. Preview the **Terms & Names** list. This will give you an idea of the issues and people you will read about in the section.
7. Read the paragraph under the heading **Setting the Stage.** This links the content of the section to previous sections or chapters.
8. **Red** heads label the major topics; **black** subheads signal smaller topics within major topics. Together, these heads provide you with a quick outline of the section.
9. Each section opener lists the California standards that are covered in the section.

TERMS & NAMES
- paternalism
- assimilation
- Menelik II

How would you react to the colonizers?

You are a young South African living in the 1880s. Gold and diamonds have recently been discovered in your country. The European colonizers need laborers to work the mines, such as the one shown below in an 1888 photograph. Along with thousands of other South Africans, you've left your farm and rural village to work for the colonizers. Separated from your family and living in a city for the first time, you don't know what to expect.

Many Africans, such as these in a South African gold mine, left their farms and families behind to work in the mining centers. As a result, new towns developed and existing ones greatly expanded.
The migrant labor system that developed as a result of the mines would have a great impact on South African society and culture.
The European owners built railways and roads to connect the mining centers, bridging the huge distances between villages and towns in South Africa.

EXAMINING *the* ISSUES 4

- What advantages and disadvantages might colonizers bring?
- What does the photograph suggest about colonization?

Discuss these questions with your classmates. In your discussion, remember what you have already learned about conquests and cultural interaction. As you read about imperialism in this chapter, look for its effects on both the colonizers and the colonized.

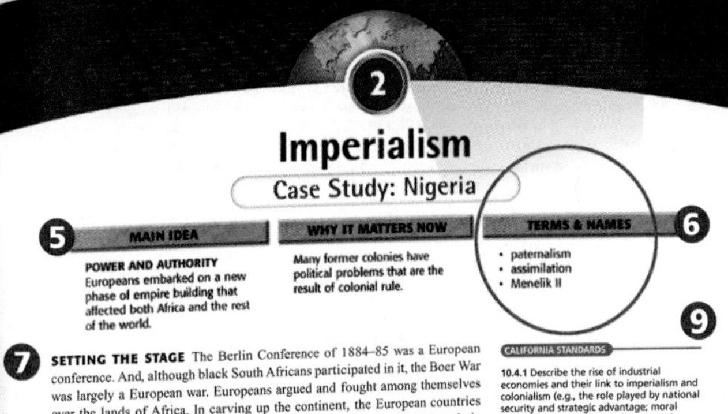

2
Imperialism
Case Study: Nigeria
5 MAIN IDEA
POWER AND AUTHORITY Europeans embarked on a new phase of empire building that affected both Africa and the rest of the world.
WHY IT MATTERS NOW
Many former colonies have political problems that are the result of colonial rule.
TERMS & NAMES 6
• paternalism
• assimilation
• Menelik II

9

CALIFORNIA STANDARDS

10.4.1 Describe the rise of industrial economies and their link to imperialism and colonialism (e.g., the role played by national security and strategic advantage; moral issues raised by the search for national hegemony, Social Darwinism, and the missionary impulse; material issues such as land, resources, and technology).

10.4.2 Discuss the locations of the colonial rule of such nations as England, France, Germany, Italy, Japan, the Netherlands, Russia, Spain, Portugal, and the United States.

10.4.3 Explain imperialism from the perspective of the colonizers and the colonized and the varied immediate and long-term responses by the people under colonial rule.

7 **SETTING THE STAGE** The Berlin Conference of 1884–85 was a European conference. And, although black South Africans participated in it, the Boer War was largely a European war. Europeans argued and fought among themselves over the lands of Africa. In carving up the continent, the European countries paid little or no attention to historical political divisions or to the many ethnic and language groupings in Africa. Uppermost in the minds of the Europeans was the ability to control Africa's land, its people, and its resources.

8 A New Period of Imperialism

The imperialism of the 18th and 19th centuries was conducted differently from the explorations of the 15th and 16th centuries. In the earlier period, imperial powers often did not penetrate far into the conquered areas in Asia and Africa. Nor did they always have a substantial influence on the lives of the people. During this new period of imperialism, the Europeans demanded more influence over the economic, political, and social lives of the people. They were determined to shape the economies of the lands to benefit European economies. They also wanted the people to adopt European customs.

Forms of Control Each European nation had certain policies and goals for establishing colonies. To establish control of an area, Europeans used different techniques. Over time, four forms of colonial control emerged: colony, protectorate, sphere of influence, and economic imperialism. These terms are defined and discussed in the chart on page 346. In practice, gaining control of an area might involve the use of several of these forms.

Methods of Management European rulers also developed methods of day-to-day management of the colony. Two basic methods emerged. Britain and other nations—such as the United States in its Pacific Island colonies—preferred indirect control. France and most other European nations wielded a more direct control. Later, when colonies gained independence, the management method used had an influence on the type of government chosen in the new nation.

Indirect Control Indirect control relied on existing political rulers. In some areas, the British asked a local ruler to accept British authority to rule. These local officials handled much of the daily management of the colony. In addition,

TAKING NOTES

Summarizing Use a web to record the forms and methods of European imperialism in Africa, the resistance it met with, and its impact.

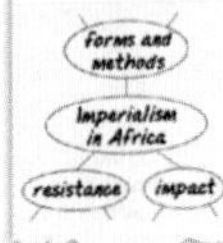

Discuss these questions with your classmates. In your discussion, remember what you have already learned about conquests and cultural interaction. As you read about imperialism in this chapter, look for its effects on both the colonizers and the colonized.

Use Active Reading Strategies As You Read

Now you are ready to read the chapter. Read one section at a time, from beginning to end.

1. Ask and answer questions as you read. Look for the **Main Idea** questions in the margin. Answering these questions will show whether you understand what you have just read.
2. Try to visualize the people, places, and events you read about. Studying the pictures, maps, and other illustrations will help you do this.
3. Read to build your vocabulary. Use the marginal **Vocabulary** notes to find the meaning of unfamiliar words.
4. Look for the story behind the events. Study the boxed features for additional information and interesting sidelights on the section content.

MAIN IDEA

Summarizing

A On which continents were Indian goods being traded?

British Transport Trade Goods India became increasingly valuable to the British after they established a railroad network there. Railroads transported raw products from the interior to the ports and manufactured goods back again. Most of the raw materials were agricultural products produced on plantations. Plantation crops included tea, indigo, coffee, cotton, and jute. Another crop was opium. The British shipped opium to China and exchanged it for tea, which they then sold in England. 3

Trade in these crops was closely tied to international events. For example, the Crimean War in the 1850s cut off the supply of Russian jute to Scottish jute mills. This boosted the export of raw jute from Bengal, a province in India. Likewise, cotton production in India increased when the Civil War in the United States cut off supplies of cotton for British textile mills. A 1

Vocabulary
jute: a fiber used for sacks and cord

MAIN IDEA

Summarizing

A On which continents were Indian goods being traded?

Impact of Colonialism India both benefited from and was harmed by British colonialism. On the negative side, the British held much of the political and economic power. The British restricted Indian-owned industries such as cotton textiles. The emphasis on cash crops resulted in a loss of self-sufficiency for many villagers. The conversion to cash crops reduced food production, causing famines in the late 1800s. The British officially adopted a hands-off policy regarding Indian religious and social customs. Even so, the increased presence of missionaries and the racist attitude of most British officials threatened traditional Indian life.

On the positive side, the laying of the world's third largest railroad network was a major British achievement. When completed, the railroads enabled India to develop a modern economy and brought unity to the connected regions. Along with the railroads, a modern road network, telephone and telegraph lines, dams, bridges, and irrigation canals enabled India to modernize. Sanitation and public health improved. Schools and colleges were founded, and literacy increased. Also, British troops cleared central India of bandits and put an end to local warfare among competing local rulers.

Western-Held Territories in Asia, 1910 2

France
Germany
Great Britain
The Netherlands
United States

GEOGRAPHY SKILLBUILDER: Interpreting Maps
1. **Region** *Which nation in 1910 held the most land in colonies?*
2. **Location** *How is the location of India a great advantage for trade?*

4 **Social History**

Social Class in India
In the photograph at right, a British officer is waited on by Indian servants. This reflects the class system in India.

British Army
Social class determined the way of life for the British Army in India. Upper-class men served as officers. Lower-class British served at lesser rank and did not advance past the rank of sergeant. Only men with the rank of sergeant and above were allowed to bring their wives to India.

Each English officer's wife attempted to re-create England in the home setting. Like a general, she directed an army of 20 to 30 servants.

Indian Servants
Caste determined Indian occupations. Castes were divided into four broad categories called varna. Indian civil servants were of the third varna. House and personal servants were of the fourth varna.

Even within the varna, jobs were strictly regulated, which is why such large servant staffs were required. For example, in the picture here, both servants were of the same varna. However, the person washing the British officer's feet was of a different caste than the person doing the fanning.

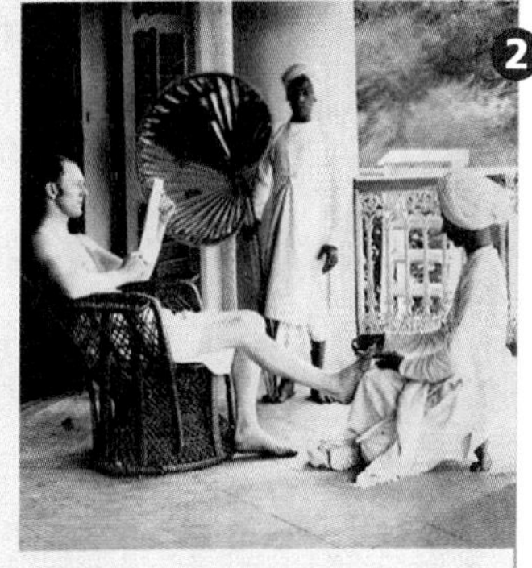
2

The Sepoy Mutiny

By 1850, the British controlled most of the Indian subcontinent. However, there were many pockets of discontent. Many Indians believed that in addition to controlling their land, the British were trying to convert them to Christianity. The Indian people also resented the constant racism that the British expressed toward them.

Indians Rebel As economic problems increased for Indians, so did their feelings of resentment and nationalism. In 1857, gossip spread among the sepoys, the Indian soldiers, that the cartridges of their new Enfield rifles were greased with beef and pork fat. To use the cartridges, soldiers had to bite off the ends. Both Hindus, who consider the cow sacred, and Muslims, who do not eat pork, were outraged by the news.

A garrison commander was shocked when 85 of the 90 sepoys refused to accept the cartridges. The British handled the crisis badly. The soldiers who had disobeyed were jailed. The next day, on May 10, 1857, the sepoys rebelled. They marched to Delhi, where they were joined by Indian soldiers stationed there. They captured the city of Delhi. From Delhi, the rebellion spread to northern and central India.

Some historians have called this outbreak the **Sepoy Mutiny**. The uprising spread over much of northern India. Fierce fighting took place. Both British and sepoys tried to slaughter each other's armies. The East India Company took more than a year to regain control of the country. The British government sent troops to help them. B

MAIN IDEA

Recognizing Effects

B Look back at Elphinstone's comment on page 791. Did the Sepoy Mutiny prove him correct?

The Indians could not unite against the British due to weak leadership and serious splits between Hindus and Muslims. Hindus did not want the Muslim Mughal Empire restored. Indeed, many Hindus preferred British rule to Muslim rule. Most of the princes and maharajahs who had made alliances with the East India

S4

Review and Summarize What You Have Read

When you finish reading a section, review and summarize what you have read. If necessary, go back and reread information that was not clear the first time through.

5 Reread the red heads and black subheads for a quick summary of the major points covered in the section

6 Study any charts, graphs, or maps in the section. These visual materials usually provide a condensed version of information in the section.

7 Review the visuals—photographs, charts, graphs, maps, and time lines—and any illustrated boxed features and note how they relate to the section content.

8 Complete all the questions in the **Section Assessment.** This will help you think critically about what you have just read.

British Take the Malayan Peninsula To compete with the Dutch, the British sought a trading base that would serve as a stop for their ships that traveled the India-China sea routes. They found a large, sheltered harbor on Singapore, an island just off the tip of the Malay Peninsula. The opening of the Suez Canal and the increased demand for tin and rubber combined to make Singapore one of the world's busiest ports.

Britain also gained colonies in Malaysia and in Burma (modern Myanmar). Malaysia had large deposits of tin and became the world's leading rubber exporter. Needing workers to mine the tin and tap the rubber trees, Britain encouraged Chinese to immigrate to Malaysia. Chinese flocked to the area. As a result of such immigration, the Malays soon became a minority in their own country. Conflict between the resident Chinese and the native Malays remains unresolved today. A

MAIN IDEA
Analyzing Motives
A Why do you think so many Chinese moved to Malaysia?

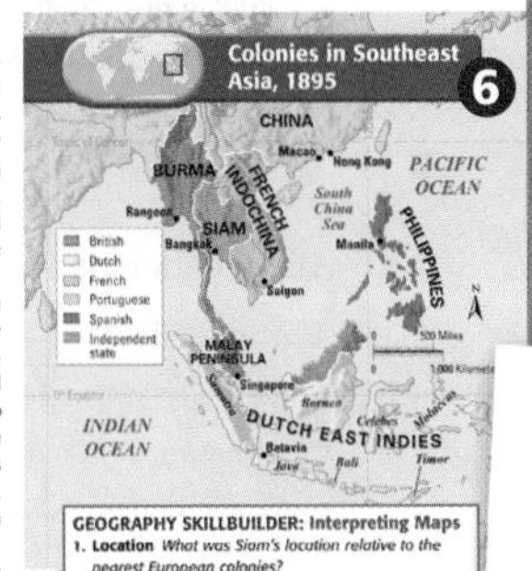

GEOGRAPHY SKILLBUILDER: Interpreting Maps
1. **Location** *What was Siam's location relative to the nearest European colonies?*
2. **Region** *Which European country could access both the Indian and the Pacific oceans from its colony?*

French Control Indochina The French had been active in Southeast Asia since the 17th century. They even helped the Nguyen (nuh•WIN) dynasty rise to power in Vietnam. In the 1840s, during the rule of an anti-Christian Vietnamese emperor, seven French missionaries were killed. Church leaders and capitalists who wanted a larger share of the overseas market demanded military intervention. Emperor Napoleon III ordered the French army to invade southern Vietnam. Later, the French added Laos, Cambodia, and northern Vietnam to the territory. The combined states would eventually be called French Indochina.

Using direct colonial management, the French themselves filled all important positions in the government bureaucracy. They did not encourage local industry. Four times as much land was devoted to rice production. However, the peasants' consumption of rice decreased because much of the rice was exported. Anger over this reduction set the stage for Vietnamese resistance against the French.

Colonial Impact In Southeast Asia, colonization brought mixed results. Economies grew based on cash crops or goods that could be sold on the world market. Roads, harbors, and rail systems improved communication and transportation but mostly benefited European business. However, education, health, and sanitation did improve.

Unlike other colonial areas, millions of people from other areas of Asia and the world migrated to work on plantations and in the mines in Southeast Asia. The region became a melting pot of Hindus, Muslims, Christians, and Buddhists. The resulting cultural changes often led to racial and religious clashes that are still seen today.

5 Siam Remains Independent

While its neighbors on all sides fell under the control of imperialists, Siam (present-day Thailand) maintained its independence throughout the colonial period. Siam lay between British-controlled Burma and French Indochina. (See map above.) France and Britain each aimed to prevent the other from gaining control of Siam. Knowing this, Siamese kings skillfully promoted Siam as a neutral zone between the two powers.

Then in 1890, the McKinley Tariff Act passed by the U.S. government set off a crisis in the islands. The act eliminated the tariffs on all sugar entering the United States. Now, sugar from Hawaii was no longer cheaper than sugar produced elsewhere. That change cut into the sugar producers' profits. Some U.S. business leaders pushed for **annexation** of Hawaii, or the adding of the territory to the United States. Making Hawaii a part of the United States meant that Hawaiian sugar could be sold for greater profits because American producers got an extra two cents a pound from the U.S. government.

About the same time, the new Hawaiian ruler, **Queen Liliuokalani** (luh•LEE•uh•oh•kuh•LAH•nee), took the throne. In 1893, she called for a new constitution that would increase her power. It would also restore the political power of Hawaiians at the expense of wealthy planters. To prevent this from happening, a group of American businessmen hatched a plot to overthrow the Hawaiian monarchy. In 1893, Queen Liliuokalani was removed from power.

In 1894, Sanford B. Dole, a wealthy plantation owner and politician, was named president of the new Republic of Hawaii. The president of the new republic asked the United States to annex it. At first, President Cleveland refused. In 1898, however, the Republic of Hawaii was annexed by the United States.

The period of imperialism was a time of great power and domination of others by mostly European powers. As the 19th century closed, the lands of the world were all claimed. The European powers now faced each other with competing claims. Their battles would become the focus of the 20th century.

History Makers

7

Queen Liliuokalani
1838–1917
Liliuokalani was Hawaii's only queen and the last monarch of Hawaii. She bitterly regretted her brother's loss of power to American planters and worked to regain power for the Hawaiian monarchy. As queen, she refused to renew a treaty signed by her brother that would have given commercial privileges to foreign businessmen. It was a decision that would cost her the crown.

INTEGRATED TECHNOLOGY
RESEARCH LINKS For more on Queen Liliuokalani, go to **classzone.com**

SECTION 5 ASSESSMENT 8

TERMS & NAMES 1. For each term or name, write a sentence explaining its significance.
• Pacific Rim • King Mongkut • Emilio Aguinaldo • annexation • Queen Liliuokalani

USING YOUR NOTES
2. Which Western power do you think had the most negative impact on its colonies? (10.4.1)

Western powers in Southeast Asia

MAIN IDEAS
3. How were the Dutch East India Trading Company and the British East India Company similar? (10.4.2)
4. What changes took place in Southeast Asia as a result of colonial control? (10.4.3)
5. Why did some groups believe that the United States should colonize like the Europeans? (10.4.3)

CRITICAL THINKING & WRITING
6. **DRAWING CONCLUSIONS** How did the reforms of the Siamese kings help Siam remain independent? (10.4.3)
7. **ANALYZING BIAS** What does President McKinley's desire to "uplift and Christianize" the Filipinos suggest about his perception of the people? (10.4.3)
8. **ANALYZING MOTIVES** Why do you think Sanford Dole wanted the United States to annex Hawaii? (10.4.3)
9. **WRITING ACTIVITY** ECONOMICS Compose a **letter to the editor** expressing a Hawaiian's view on the U.S. businessmen who pushed for the annexation of Hawaii for economic gain. (Writing 2.5.d)

CONNECT TO TODAY DRAWING A BAR GRAPH
Research to find out about the economic situation of Southeast Asian countries today. Rank the economies and present your findings in a **bar graph.** (10.4.3)

S5

Part 2: Test-Taking Strategies and Practice

You can improve your test-taking skills by practicing the strategies discussed in this section. First, read the tips on the left-hand page. Then apply them to the practice items on the right-hand page.

Using Strategies For . . .

Multiple Choice

Explain to students that they will do best on test questions by thinking them through carefully and by applying test-taking strategies, such as the following.

1. *Negative* is a key word. Look for the alternative describing a negative impact of European colonialism in Africa. (A), (B), and (C) describe positive impacts, so (D) is the correct answer.
2. This is an example of an *all of the above* question. In order for (D) to be correct, each other choice must be true. You can eliminate (A) as the strategy hint suggests, as well as (D). Now, you can choose between (B) and (C). If you know that Ethiopia and Liberia were the only countries south of the Sahara not colonized by Europeans, you will choose the correct answer, (B).
3. Look for modifiers to help you rule out alternatives. (B), (C), and (D) have absolute modifiers, signaling incorrect answers. The correct answer is (A).
4. Be careful when reading questions that contain *except.* First find the three motives that drove Europeans to colonize Africa, (A), (B), and (D). The one that remains, (C), is the correct answer.

General Test-Taking Tips

Share these tips with your students.

- The night before a test, make sure you get at least eight hours of sleep.
- Have a healthy breakfast or lunch before taking your test.
- Wear comfortable clothes.
- Relax and enjoy the challenge!

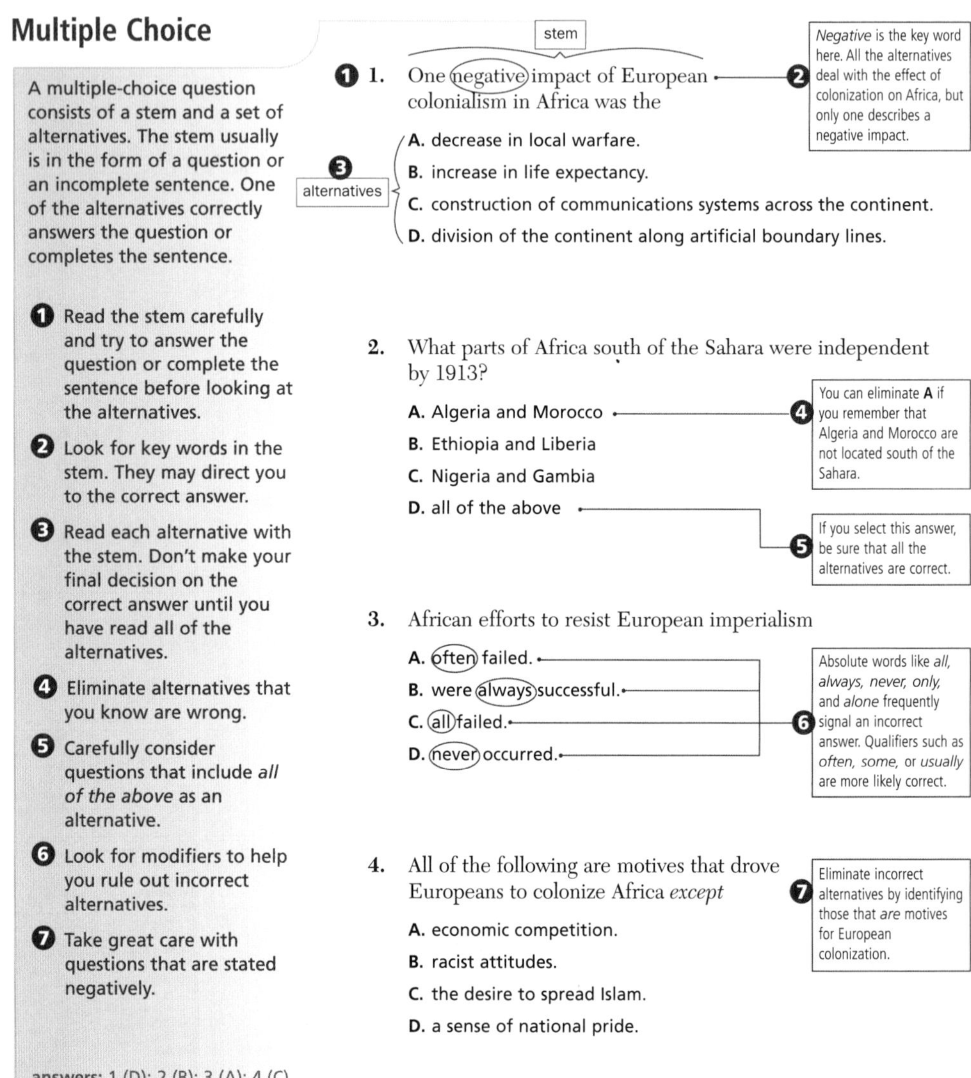

Multiple Choice

A multiple-choice question consists of a stem and a set of alternatives. The stem usually is in the form of a question or an incomplete sentence. One of the alternatives correctly answers the question or completes the sentence.

1. Read the stem carefully and try to answer the question or complete the sentence before looking at the alternatives.
2. Look for key words in the stem. They may direct you to the correct answer.
3. Read each alternative with the stem. Don't make your final decision on the correct answer until you have read all of the alternatives.
4. Eliminate alternatives that you know are wrong.
5. Carefully consider questions that include *all of the above* as an alternative.
6. Look for modifiers to help you rule out incorrect alternatives.
7. Take great care with questions that are stated negatively.

answers: 1 (D); 2 (B); 3 (A); 4 (C)

1. One negative impact of European colonialism in Africa was the
   - A. decrease in local warfare.
   - B. increase in life expectancy.
   - C. construction of communications systems across the continent.
   - D. division of the continent along artificial boundary lines.

(2) *Negative* is the key word here. All the alternatives deal with the effect of colonization on Africa, but only one describes a negative impact.

2. What parts of Africa south of the Sahara were independent by 1913?
   - A. Algeria and Morocco
   - B. Ethiopia and Liberia
   - C. Nigeria and Gambia
   - D. all of the above

(4) You can eliminate **A** if you remember that Algeria and Morocco are not located south of the Sahara.

(5) If you select this answer, be sure that all the alternatives are correct.

3. African efforts to resist European imperialism
   - A. often failed.
   - B. were always successful.
   - C. all failed.
   - D. never occurred.

(6) Absolute words like *all, always, never, only,* and *alone* frequently signal an incorrect answer. Qualifiers such as *often, some,* or *usually* are more likely correct.

4. All of the following are motives that drove Europeans to colonize Africa *except*
   - A. economic competition.
   - B. racist attitudes.
   - C. the desire to spread Islam.
   - D. a sense of national pride.

(7) Eliminate incorrect alternatives by identifying those that *are* motives for European colonization.

S6

TEACHING OPTIONS: CUSTOMIZING FOR SPECIAL NEEDS

STUDENTS ACQUIRING ENGLISH

Vocabulary Make sure students understand the following terms and concepts in the sample questions on these pages.

Strategy Page

Question 1 *artificial:* unnatural
Question 3 *imperialism:* a policy in which a strong nation seeks to dominate other countries politically, economically, or socially
Question 4 *racist attitudes:* the belief that one race is superior to others
Islam: the religion followed by Muslims that developed in Arabia in the seventh century

Practice Page

Be sure that students have studied the following topics:

Renaissance
Reformation
Mughal Empire
Atlantic slave trade

For more test practice online . . .
TEST PRACTICE
CLASSZONE.COM

Directions: Read each question carefully and choose the *best* answer from the four alternatives.

1. The Greek philosopher Plato believed that in a perfect society, people would be governed by
   A. the state's wealthiest citizens.
   B. a single ruler or tyrant.
   C. a group of democratically elected officials.
   D. the state's philosophers or wisest men.

2. The rise of democratic ideas can be traced back to which of the following Judeo-Christian beliefs?
   A. eternal life
   B. worth of individuals
   C. submission to authority
   D. complete freedom to do as one wishes

3. President Woodrow Wilson's plan for achieving a lasting peace after World War I was known as the
   A. Atlantic Charter.
   B. Paris Pact.
   C. Fourteen Points.
   D. Wilson Doctrine.

4. All of the following are examples of the communications revolution of the latter part of the twentieth century *except*
   A. cellular phones and fax machines.
   B. the Internet and electronic mail.
   C. the typewriter and Dictaphone.
   D. satellite communication systems.

Practice Questions

Thinking It Through

Share the following explanations with students as they discuss the strategies they used to answer the practice questions.

1. Read the stem carefully and try to complete the sentence before looking at the alternatives. Eliminate (A), (B), and (C) since Plato believed that in a perfect society the thinkers or wise people should govern the people. The correct answer is (D).

2. Eliminate obviously incorrect answers. Democratic ideas have nothing to do with eternal life, so eliminate (A). Eliminate alternatives (C) and (D) since these ideas go against Judeo-Christian beliefs and democratic ideas. The correct answer is (B), since this is a basic Judeo-Christian belief and democratic idea.

3. Eliminate (A) since the Atlantic Charter was issued in 1941, during World War II. Eliminate (B) since the Paris Pact was a peace plan arranged by the U.S. Secretary of State Frank Kellogg and France's foreign minister Aristide Briand. The correct answer is (C), since this was the name given to Wilson's series of proposals outlining his plan for a lasting peace after World War I.

4. Take care with questions that contain *except.* Eliminate incorrect alternatives (A), (B), and (D) by identifying those as examples of the communications revolution of the latter part of the twentieth century. The correct answer is (C), since the typewriter and the Dictaphone were invented long before the latter part of the twentieth century.

CALIFORNIA CONTENT STANDARDS AND SKILLS

	Item	Standard/Skill Tested
STRATEGY	4. 1.	**CST 2:** understand that change affects values and beliefs **HI 2:** recognize historical causes and effects
	1. 2. 3. 4.	**10.4.1:** describe European colonialism in Africa
	2. 3.	**10.4.4:** describe independence struggles of colonized regions
	4.	**10.4.3:** explain imperialism from perspective of colonizers

	Item	Standard/Skill Tested
PRACTICE	4. 2. 3.	**CST 1:** compare present with past **CST 2:** analyze how change happens **HI 1:** show connections between historical events and political developments
	1. 2.	**10.1.1:** analyze Judeo-Christian and Greco Roman views of society
	1. 2. 3.	**10.1.2:** trace development of Western political ideas
	3.	**10.6.1:** analyze Woodrow Wilson's Fourteen Points
	4.	**10.11:** analyze communications revolutions

CST=Chronological and Spatial Thinking, **HI**=Historical Interpretation, **REP**=Research, Evidence, and Point of View

Using Strategies For . . .

Primary Sources

Explain to students that they will do best on test questions by thinking them through carefully and by applying test-taking strategies, such as the following.

1. Refer back to the primary source when answering the questions. In question 1, *most important* are key words. You should skim the passage to find information that would help identify the part of the economy that Mao suggests is most important. The correct answer is (A).
2. Read the title and skim the document to find the main idea. The document expresses Mao Zedong's economic and social goals for China under communism. Under communism, China's government will make the economic decisions, so (B) is the correct answer.

General Test-Taking Tips

Share these tips with your students.

- Read the directions carefully before you begin to answer the questions.
- Plan the time you are given to take the test.
- Check your answers.
- Believe in yourself.

Primary Sources

Primary sources are written or made by people who were at historical events, either as observers or participants. Primary sources include journals, diaries, letters, speeches, newspaper articles, autobiographies, wills, deeds, and financial records.

1. Look at the source line to learn about the document and its author. Consider the reliability of the information in the document.
2. Skim the document to get an idea of what it is about. (This source expresses Mao Zedong's economic and social goals for China under communism.)
3. Note any special punctuation. Ellipses, for example, indicate that words or sentences have been removed from the original text.
4. Use active reading strategies. For instance, ask and answer questions on the content as you read.
5. Use context clues to help you understand difficult or unfamiliar words. (From the context, you realize that *confiscate* means "take control of.")
6. Before rereading the document, skim the questions. This will help you focus your reading and more easily locate answers.

answers: 1 (A); 2 (B)

New Policies in China

We must establish in China a republic that is politically new-democratic as well as economically new-democratic.

Big banks and big industrial and commercial enterprises shall be owned by this republic. . . . ❸

The state-operated enterprises of the new-democratic republic are socialist in character and constitute the leading force in the national economy. . . .

This republic will . . . confiscate the land of landlords and ❺ distribute it to those peasants having no land or only a little land. . . .

China's economy . . . must never be "monopolist by a few"; we must never let . . . capitalists and landlords "dominate the livelihood of the people"; we must never establish a capitalist society of the European-American type, nor allow the old semi-feudal society to remain.

—Mao Zedong, *On New Democracy* (1940)

Mao Zedong was the leader of the Communists who began fighting to gain control of China's government in the late 1920s. ❶

1. Which part of the economy does Mao suggest is the most important?
   - **A.** State-run large enterprises
   - **B.** Retail stores
   - **C.** Farms
   - **D.** Small private businesses

2. Which sentence expresses the main idea shared by these paragraphs?
   - **A.** Private property will be respected.
   - **B.** China's government will make economic decisions.
   - **C.** China will follow the examples of Europe and the United States.
   - **D.** China's economy will depend on farming.

S8

TEACHING OPTIONS: CUSTOMIZING FOR SPECIAL NEEDS

STUDENTS ACQUIRING ENGLISH

Vocabulary Make sure students understand the following terms and concepts in the primary sources and questions on these pages.

Strategy Page

enterprises: business operations
socialist: economic system in which the factors of production are owned by the public through the government
monopolist: exclusive, uncompetitive
capitalist: describing an economic system based on private ownership

Practice Page

temporal: secular, or not related to the church
parliament: law-making body
levying: collecting
petition: to make a request to
Question 4 *United States Bill of Rights:* first ten amendments to the Constitution

For more test practice online . . .
TEST PRACTICE
CLASSZONE.COM

Directions: Use this passage taken from the English Bill of Rights to answer the questions below.

A Declaration of English Rights

The . . . lords spiritual and temporal, and commons, . . . being now assembled in a full and free representative of this nation, . . . declare:

1. That the pretended power of suspending of laws, or the execution of laws, by regal authority, without consent of parliament, is illegal. . . .

4. That levying money for or to the use of the crown . . . , without grant of parliament, . . . is illegal.

5. That it is the right of the subjects to petition the King, and all commitments and prosecutions for such petitioning are illegal.

6. That the raising or keeping a standing army within the kingdom in time of peace, unless it be with consent of parliament, is against the law. . . .

9. That the freedom of speech, and debates or proceedings in parliament, ought not to be impeached or questioned in any court or place out of parliament.

10. That excessive bail ought not to be required, nor excessive fines imposed; nor cruel and unusual punishments inflicted.

—*Declaration of Rights,* 1689 (English Bill of Rights)

1. Article 4 of the Bill of Rights says that the King cannot
   - A. raise and keep a standing army.
   - B. impose a tax without Parliament's consent.
   - C. spend money without Parliament's consent.
   - D. prosecute a person for petitioning the crown.

2. The Declaration of Rights was aimed at limiting the power of the
   - A. Parliament.
   - B. nobles and clergy.
   - C. rising middle class.
   - D. King.

3. In the "Glorious Revolution," the English issued the Declaration of Rights and
   - A. replaced James II with William and Mary.
   - B. unseated James II and declared a republic.
   - C. won their independence.
   - D. approved the Constitution.

4. Which of the rights mentioned in this passage also appears in the United States Bill of Rights?
   - A. freedom of religion
   - B. right to bear arms
   - C. right to a speedy trial
   - D. limits on fines and punishments

Practice Questions

Thinking It Through

Share the following explanations with students as they discuss the strategies they used to answer the practice questions.

1. *Article 4* is a key phrase. You need to skim Article 4 to answer this question. The correct answer is (B).
2. Reread the passage to find out whose power was limited by the Declaration of Rights. Note that the articles refer to limiting the power of "regal authority," "the crown," and "the King." These all refer to the king, so the correct answer is (D).
3. Use your knowledge of world history to answer this question. The correct answer is (A).
4. Reread the passage to answer this question. The only rights listed in the choices are in Article 10—no "excessive fines imposed; nor cruel and unusual punishment inflicted." The correct answer is (D).

CALIFORNIA CONTENT STANDARDS AND SKILLS

	Item	Standard/Skill Tested		Item	Standard/Skill Tested
STRATEGY	1. 2. 1. 2.	**REP 4:** evaluate information from primary sources **HI 1:** interpret past events and issues	PRACTICE	1. 2. 3. 4. 1. 2. 3. 4. 1. 2. 3. 4. 3. 4.	**CST 2:** understand how change affects values and beliefs **CST 3:** use documents to interpret the diffusion of ideas **REP 4:** evaluate primary sources **HI 1:** show connections between events and political trends faith, and duties
	1. 2.	**10.9.4:** analyze the rise of Mao Zedong and political and economic upheavals in China		1. 2. 3. 4.	**10.2.2:** list principles of the English Bill of Rights (1689) and U.S. Bill of Rights

CST=Chronological and Spatial Thinking, **HI**=Historical Interpretation, **REP**=Research, Evidence, and Point of View

Using Strategies For . . .

Secondary Sources

Explain to students that they will do best on test questions by thinking them through carefully and by applying test-taking strategies, such as the following.

1. Question 1 asks you to identify a statement that is verifiable. (B) is the correct answer, since the author states that Nanjing fell on December 12 [1937] after heavy shelling and bombing by the Japanese. (A), (C), and (D) express estimates or opinions, which cannot be proven.
2. Remember that the words "Based on this account," signal that you have to make inferences from information in the passage. Skim the passage to find information about the "rural pacification" campaigns by the Japanese. You can infer from the information that (A) is the correct answer, since the passage describes the pacification campaign as being anti-Communist and that the campaign reduced by millions the population of the areas made up mostly of Chinese Communists.

General Test-Taking Tips

Share these tips with your students.

- Glance over the test to determine the types and numbers of questions.
- Estimate the amount of time you have to spend on each type of question.

Secondary Sources

Secondary sources are written or made by people who were not at the original events. They often combine information from several primary sources. The most common types of written secondary sources are biographies and history books.

1. Read the title to preview the content of the passage. (The title here signals that the passage is about some extremely unpleasant events that took place in Nanjing.)
2. Skim the passage to locate the main idea—the central point that is supported by other details.
3. Notice words and phrases that clarify the sequence of events.
4. Read actively by asking and answering questions about what you read. (You might ask yourself: What was the goal of the Japanese rural pacification campaigns?)
5. Before rereading the passage, review the questions to identify the information you need to find.

answers: 1 (B); 2 (A)

1 **The Nanjing Atrocities**

[Nanjing] fell on December 12 [1937] after heavy shelling and 2 bombing, and for the next six weeks Japanese troops engaged in the widespread execution . . . and random murder of Chinese . . . in the captured city and outlying communities. The total number of Chinese killed is controversial, but a middle-range estimate puts the combined deaths from both the shelling and subsequent atrocities at two hundred thousand. Much smaller killings occurred in other Chinese cities that fell into Japanese hands. . . . In attempting to consolidate their control over northern China, the Japanese subsequently turned to "rural pacification" campaigns that 4 amounted to indiscriminate terror against the peasantry. 3 And by 1941-42, this fundamentally anti-Communist "pacification" campaign had evolved into the devastating "three-all" policy (*sanko seisaku:* "kill all, burn all, destroy all"), during which it is estimated that the population in the areas dominated by the Chinese Communists was reduced, through flight and death, from 44 million to 25 million persons.

—John Dower, *War Without Mercy* (1986)

5

1. Which of the following statements is a fact?
   - **A.** 200,000 Chinese were killed in Nanjing.
   - **B.** Nanjing fell to the Japanese in 1937.
   - **C.** The Chinese offered no resistance.
   - **D.** The Japanese hated the Chinese Communists.

Remember that a fact is a verifiable statement. An opinion is a statement of someone's belief about something.

2. Based on this account, in their rural pacification campaigns the Japanese were most likely to direct their vengeance on which of the following?
   - **A.** Communists led by Mao Zedong
   - **B.** Nationalists led by Jiang Jieshi
   - **C.** Chinese laborers in large cities
   - **D.** Foreign nationals living in China

These words signal that you have to make inferences from information in the passage.

TEACHING OPTIONS: CUSTOMIZING FOR SPECIAL NEEDS

STUDENTS ACQUIRING ENGLISH

Vocabulary Make sure students understand the following terms and concepts on these pages.

Strategy Page

atrocities: brutalities
consolidate: combine; strengthen
dominated: made up mostly of
Question 2 *vengeance:* rage; extreme anger

Practice Page

alliances: formal agreements among groups of countries designed to further common interests
neutral: taking no side in a conflict

For more test practice online . . .
TEST PRACTICE
CLASSZONE.COM

Directions: Using your knowledge of history answer questions 1 through 4.

Entangling Alliances

[England's] Lord Palmerston . . . secured an international treaty guaranteeing Belgium as an "independent and perpetually neutral state." The treaty was signed . . . by England, France, Russia, [Germany], and Austria.

Ever since 1892, when France and Russia had joined in military alliance, it was clear that four of the five signatories of the Belgian treaty would be automatically engaged—two against two—in the war for which [the German military commanders] had to plan. . . . Under the terms of the Austro-German alliance, Germany was obliged to support Austria in any conflict with Russia. Under the terms of the alliance between France and Russia, both parties were obliged to move against Germany if either became involved in a "defensive war" with Germany. These arrangements made it inevitable that in any war in which she engaged, Germany would have to fight on two fronts against both Russia and France.

What part England would play was uncertain; she might remain neutral; she might, if given cause, come in against Germany.

— Barbara Tuchman, *The Guns of August* (1962)

1. The system of tangled alliances described here helped lead to
   - **A.** the French Revolution.
   - **B.** the Napoleonic Wars.
   - **C.** World War I.
   - **D.** World War II.

2. The small country of Belgium was in danger if war broke out in Europe because it was located between
   - **A.** England and France.
   - **B.** France and Germany.
   - **C.** Germany and Austria.
   - **D.** Austria and Russia.

3. If Austria went to war, which country could it depend on for support?
   - **A.** Germany
   - **B.** France
   - **C.** Russia
   - **D.** England

4. What event set off a chain reaction within this alliance system that led to World War I?
   - **A.** Germany's invasion of Belgium
   - **B.** Germany's invasion of Poland
   - **C.** the Communist revolution in Russia
   - **D.** the assassination of Archduke Franz Ferdinand

STRATEGIES FOR TAKING TESTS

Practice Questions

Thinking It Through

Share the following explanations with students as they discuss the strategies they used to answer the practice questions.

1. Skim the passage to find the time period that the passage describes. The phrase "ever since 1892" in paragraph 2 of the passage indicates that the passage describes the time period after 1892. Next, look at the events listed in the answer choices. Eliminate (A) and (B) since both of these events happened before 1892. The correct answer is (C).
2. Use your knowledge of world geography to answer question 2. The correct answer is (B).
3. Skim the passage to find which country had an alliance with Austria. The correct answer is (A).
4. Use your knowledge of world history to answer this question. The correct answer is (D).

CALIFORNIA CONTENT STANDARDS AND SKILLS

	Item	Standard/Skill Tested		Item	Standard/Skill Tested
STRATEGY	1. 2. 1. 2.	**REP 4:** evaluate information from secondary sources **HI 1:** interpret past events and issues	PRACTICE	1. 2. 3. 4. 1. 2. 3. 4. 1. 2. 3. 4. 1. 2. 3. 4.	**CST 3:** use documents to interpret frictions that develop between groups **REP 4:** evaluate secondary sources **HI 1:** show connections between events and political developments **HI 2:** recognize complexity of causes and effects
	1. 2.	**10.8.1:** compare Japanese drive for empire in Nanking and other atrocities in China		1. 2. 3. 4.	**10.5.1:** analyze arguments for entering into First World War

CST=Chronological and Spatial Thinking, **HI**=Historical Interpretation, **REP**=Research, Evidence, and Point of View

Using Strategies For . . .

Political Cartoons

Political cartoons are one kind of primary source. Remind students to analyze the political cartoon before reading the questions. They should identify the subject, note important symbols and details, interpret the message, and analyze the point of view. Then they should read the questions to identify the information they need to find.

Explain to students that they will do best on test questions by thinking them through carefully and by applying test-taking strategies, such as the following.

1. Since the swastika was the symbol of the Nazi Party in Germany, the correct answer for question 1 is (A).
2. To answer question 2, analyze the cartoonist's point of view. Look at how the cartoonist uses caricature in the cartoon. The swastika, which represents Nazi Germany, is huge and appears to be turning like a wheel, about to roll down onto Poland and crush it. Therefore, (D) is the correct answer.

General Test-Taking Tips

Share these tips with your students.

- Ask questions before the test begins.
- Know how to fill in the answer form.
- Read and listen to directions carefully.

Political Cartoons

Political cartoons use a combination of words and images to express a point of view on political issues. They are useful primary sources, because they reflect the opinions of the time.

1. Identify the subject of the cartoon. Titles and captions often provide clues to the subject matter.
2. Use labels to help identify the people, places, and events represented in the cartoon.
3. Note where and when the cartoon was published for more information on people, places, and events.
4. Identify any important symbols—ideas or images that stand for something else—in the cartoon.
5. Analyze the point of view presented in the cartoon. The use of caricature—the exaggeration of physical features—often signals how the cartoonist feels.
6. Interpret the cartoonist's message.

answers: 1 (A); 2 (D)

❶ "NEXT!"

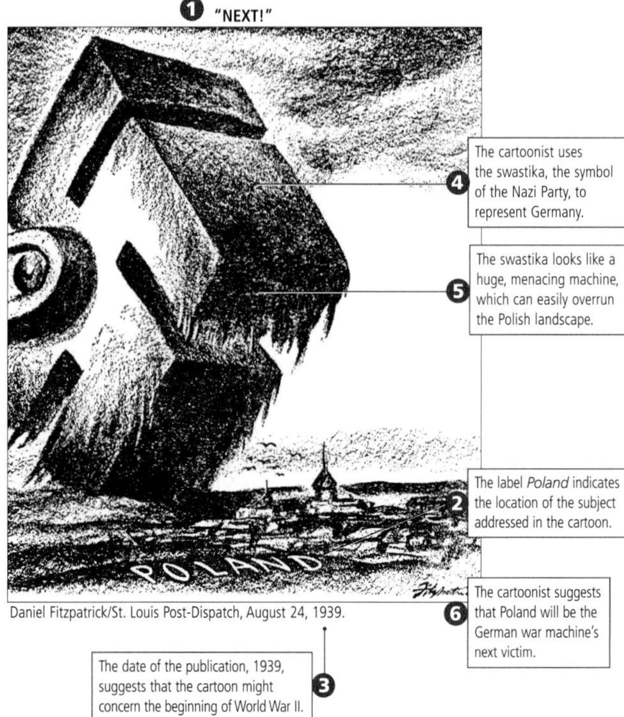

POLAND
❹ The cartoonist uses the swastika, the symbol of the Nazi Party, to represent Germany.
❺ The swastika looks like a huge, menacing machine, which can easily overrun the Polish landscape.
❷ The label *Poland* indicates the location of the subject addressed in the cartoon.
❻ The cartoonist suggests that Poland will be the German war machine's next victim.
❸ The date of the publication, 1939, suggests that the cartoon might concern the beginning of World War II.

Daniel Fitzpatrick/St. Louis Post-Dispatch, August 24, 1939.

1. The machine-like swastika in the cartoon represents
   A. Nazi Germany.
   B. the Soviet Union.
   C. Napoleon's empire.
   D. the Polish military.

2. Which sentence *best* summarizes the cartoonist's message?
   A. Germany must beware of Poland.
   B. Poland is in danger of civil war.
   C. Germany and Poland are military giants.
   D. Poland will be Germany's next victim.

TEACHING OPTIONS: CUSTOMIZING FOR SPECIAL NEEDS

STUDENTS ACQUIRING ENGLISH

Vocabulary Make sure students understand the following terms and concepts on these pages.

Strategy Page

Question 2 *military giants:* idiom meaning nations with large, powerful militaries

Practice Page

Question 2 *Count Dracula:* a fictional monster in literature, said to be a vampire who lives off the blood of others

Frankenstein: the fictional creator of a monster made out of body parts from different people

For more test practice online . . .
TEST PRACTICE
CLASSZONE.COM

Directions: Use the cartoon to answer the questions below.

Steve Sack, *Minneapolis Star-Tribune,* January 1, 1992

1. What leader from the Middle East does the cartoon portray?
   - **A.** Iraq's Saddam Hussein
   - **B.** Egypt's Hosni Mubarak
   - **C.** Syria's Hafez al-Assad
   - **D.** Libya's Muammar al-Qaddafi

2. How has the cartoonist drawn this leader?
   - **A.** as a soldier
   - **B.** as a poor person
   - **C.** as Count Dracula
   - **D.** as Frankenstein's monster

3. The countries identified in the cartoon include
   - **A.** Saudi Arabia and Kuwait.
   - **B.** West Germany and China.
   - **C.** the United States and the Soviet Union.
   - **D.** France and Japan.

4. The most appropriate title for this cartoon would be
   - **A.** "A Monster Walks at Night."
   - **B.** "They've Created a Monster."
   - **C.** "The Monster of the Middle East."
   - **D.** "They've Made a Mistake."

STRATEGIES FOR TAKING TESTS

STRATEGIES FOR TAKING TESTS

Practice Questions

Thinking It Through

Share the following explanations with students as they discuss the strategies they used to answer the practice questions.

1. This question is asking you to identify the main character in the cartoon. The monster is labeled Saddam, which is the first name of Iraq's former leader, Saddam Hussein. The correct answer is (A).
2. To correctly answer this question, you must use your own knowledge that the character in the cartoon is a caricature of Frankenstein's monster. The correct answer is (D).
3. To answer this question, you need to look for labels that identify which countries are included in the cartoon. The correct answer is (C).
4. To answer this question, you need to analyze the cartoon to interpret its main idea. All the parts of the monster are labeled "made in (a country)." This indicates that all those countries created this monster, so the correct answer is (B).

CALIFORNIA CONTENT STANDARDS AND SKILLS

	Item	Standard/Skill Tested
STRATEGY	1. 2.	**REP 4:** evaluate information from primary sources
	1. 2.	**HI 3:** interpret past events and issues
	1. 2.	**10.7.3:** analyze totalitarian regime in Germany
	1. 2.	**10.7.2:** understand role of appeasement prior to World War II

	Item	Standard/Skill Tested
PRACTICE	1. 2. 3. 4.	**CST 3:** use documents to interpret frictions that develop between population groups
	1. 2. 3. 4.	**HI 1:** show connections between events and political developments
	1. 2. 3. 4.	**10.10.1:** understand challenges in Middle East
	1. 2. 3. 4.	**10.10.2:** describe recent key leaders in Middle East

CST=Chronological and Spatial Thinking, **HI**=Historical Interpretation, **REP**=Research, Evidence, and Point of View

Using Strategies For . . .

Charts

Explain to students that they will do best on test questions that they think through carefully by applying test-taking strategies, such as the following.

1. Question 1 asks you to compare and contrast the number of immigrants from row to row for the countries shown in the chart. The correct answer is (D) because the United States had the greatest number of immigrants.
2. To answer question 2, you should look at the first and third columns of the chart and figure out which Latin American country received the most immigrants. The correct answer is (A), Argentina.

General Test-Taking Tips

Share these tips with your students.

- Use practice tests, such as the one you are taking now, to learn about your test-taking habits and weaknesses.
- Use this information to practice strategies that will help you be a successful test-taker.

Charts

Charts present information in a visual form. History textbooks use several types of charts, including tables, flow charts, Venn diagrams, and infographics. The chart most commonly found in standardized tests is the table. This organizes information in columns and rows for easy viewing.

1. Read the title and identify the broad subject of the chart.
2. Read the column and row headings and any other labels. These will provide more details about the subject of the chart.
3. Note how the information in the chart is organized.
4. Compare and contrast the information from column to column and row to row.
5. Try to draw conclusions from the information in the chart.
6. Read the questions and then study the chart again.

answers: 1 (D); 2 (A)

1 This chart is about the number of people who immigrated to different countries.

4 Notice that the years covered in the table are not the same for all countries.

Immigration to Selected Countries

Country	Period	Number of Immigrants
Argentina	1856–1932	6,405,000
Australia	1861–1932	2,913,000
Brazil	1821–1932	4,431,000
British West Indies	1836–1932	1,587,000
Canada	1821–1932	5,206,000
Cuba	1901–1932	857,000
Mexico	1911–1931	226,000
New Zealand	1851–1932	594,000
South Africa	1881–1932	852,000
United States	1821–1932	34,244,000
Uruguay	1836–1932	713,000

Source: Alfred W. Crosby, Jr., *The Columbian Exchange: Biological and Cultural Consequences of 1492*

3 This chart organizes the countries alphabetically. In some charts, information is organized according to years or the value of the numbers displayed.

5 Think about what the countries with the highest number of immigrants have in common.

1. The country that received the vast majority of immigrants was

A. Argentina.
B. Brazil.
C. Canada.
D. the United States.

2. The Latin American country that received the most immigrants was

A. Argentina.
B. Brazil.
C. Cuba.
D. Uruguay.

TEACHING OPTIONS: CUSTOMIZING FOR SPECIAL NEEDS

STUDENTS ACQUIRING ENGLISH

Vocabulary Make sure students understand the following terms and concepts on these pages.

Strategy Page

Chart

immigrants: people who move to another country to live

Practice Page

Chart

United Kingdom: Great Britain or Britain; includes England, Scotland, Wales, and Northern Ireland

For more test practice online . . .
TEST PRACTICE
CLASSZONE.COM

Directions: Use the chart to answer the questions below.

Crude Steel Production for Selected Countries (in Thousands of Metric Tons)							
Year	China	Germany*	Japan	Korea	Russia/ USSR	United Kingdom	United States
1900	—	6,646	1	—	2,214	4,979	10,351
1910	—	13,699	250	—	3,444	6,476	26,512
1920	—	8,538	845	—	162	9,212	42,807
1930	—	11,511	2,289	—	5,761	7,443	41,351
1940	—	19,141	7,528	—	19,000	13,183	60,765
1950	61	12,121	4,839	—	27,300	16,553	87,848
1960	1,866	34,100	22,138	—	65,292	24,695	91,920
1970	1,779	45,041	93,322	—	115,886	28,314	119,310
1980	3,712	43,838	111,935	8,558	148,000	11,278	101,457
1990	6,535	44,022	110,339	23,125	154,414	17,896	89,276
2000	127,200	46,400	106,400	43,100	59,100	15,200	101,500

* Figures from 1950 through 1990 are West Germany only.

Source: International Iron and Steel Institute; Japan Iron and Steel Federation

1. Which country produced the most crude steel in 1900?
   - **A.** Germany
   - **B.** Russia/USSR
   - **C.** United Kingdom
   - **D.** United States

2. Japanese crude steel production most likely dropped from 1940 to 1950 due to
   - **A.** growing competition from Korea and the USSR.
   - **B.** rising production in China.
   - **C.** damage to the industry suffered in World War II.
   - **D.** mergers with American companies.

3. By 2000, the largest share of crude steel was being produced by countries in
   - **A.** Africa.
   - **B.** Asia.
   - **C.** Europe.
   - **D.** North America.

4. What country rose from no crude steel production to be the world's largest producer in 50 years?
   - **A.** China
   - **B.** Germany
   - **C.** Korea
   - **D.** United Kingdom

Practice Questions

Thinking It Through

Share the following explanations with students as they discuss the strategies they used to answer the practice questions.

1. The key word in this question is *1900.* Read the row headed "1900" to find the country that produced the most crude steel in that year. The correct answer is (D).
2. This question requires you to use the chart and your knowledge of world history to answer the question. You can eliminate choice (A) because according to the chart, Korea did not produce crude steel during this time period. Eliminate (B) because China's rise in production was minimal. The correct answer is (C).
3. Read the row headed "2000" to find the countries producing the largest share of crude steel. Then determine in which continent these countries are located. The correct answer is (B).
4. You need to compare and contrast information from column to column and row to row to answer this question. Check each choice to find the correct answer. The correct answer is (A).

CALIFORNIA CONTENT STANDARDS AND SKILLS

	Item	Standard/Skill Tested
STRATEGY	1. 2.	**CST 3:** use charts to interpret human movement

	Item	Standard/Skill Tested
PRACTICE	1. 2. 3. 4.	**CST 1:** compare present with past
	1. 2. 3. 4.	**CST 2:** analyze how change happens at different rates at different times
	1. 2. 3. 4.	**CST 3:** use charts to interpret the diffusion of goods
	1.	**10.6.2:** describe effects of First World War on international economy
	2.	**10.9.1:** compare economic power shifts after World War 2, including Japanese recovery
	1. 2. 3. 4.	**10.11:** analyze the integration of countries into world economy

CST=Chronological and Spatial Thinking, **HI**=Historical Interpretation, **REP**=Research, Evidence, and Point of View

Using Strategies For . . .

Line and Bar Graphs

Remind students that in line and bar graphs, the vertical axis goes up and down and is normally shown on the left side of the graph. The horizontal axis runs from left to right across the bottom of the graph.

Explain to students that they will do best on test questions by thinking them through carefully and by applying test-taking strategies, such as the following.

1. To answer question 1, you need to study the information in the graph and note any trends over time. Notice that the trend of both total and Atlantic exports is to grow over time. The correct answer is (C).
2. To answer question 2, you need to study the information in the bar graph to find the country with the tallest bar, which represents more debt than the other countries' bars. The correct answer is (B).

General Test-Taking Tips

Share these tips with your students.

- Do not spend too much time on one question.
- Skip a question you are having problems with. Go back to it later, if you have time.
- If you skip a question, be sure to skip the answer space for the same number on your answer sheet.

Line and Bar Graphs

Graphs show statistics in a visual form. Line graphs are particularly useful for showing changes over time. Bar graphs make it easy to compare numbers or sets of numbers.

1. Read the title and identify the broad subject of the graph.
2. Study the labels on the vertical and horizontal axes to see the kinds of information presented in the graph. Note the intervals between amounts and between dates. This will help you read the graph more efficiently.
3. Look at the source line and evaluate the reliability of the information in the graph.
4. If the graph presents information over time, look for trends—generalizations you can make about changes over time.
5. Draw conclusions and make inferences based on information in the graph.
6. Read the questions carefully and then study the graph again.

answers: 1 (C); 2 (B)

1 Exports of English Manufactured Goods, 1699–1774

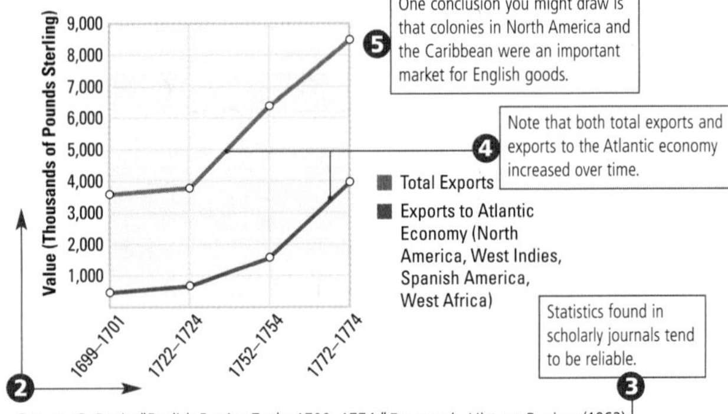

Source: R. Davis, "English Foreign Trade, 1700–1774," *Economic History Review* (1962)

6 1. Which statement *best* describes the change in proportion of Atlantic economy exports to total exports?

A. It started small and remained small.
B. It started large and remained large.
C. It grew over time.
D. It decreased over time.

1 Nations with High Foreign Debt, 2000

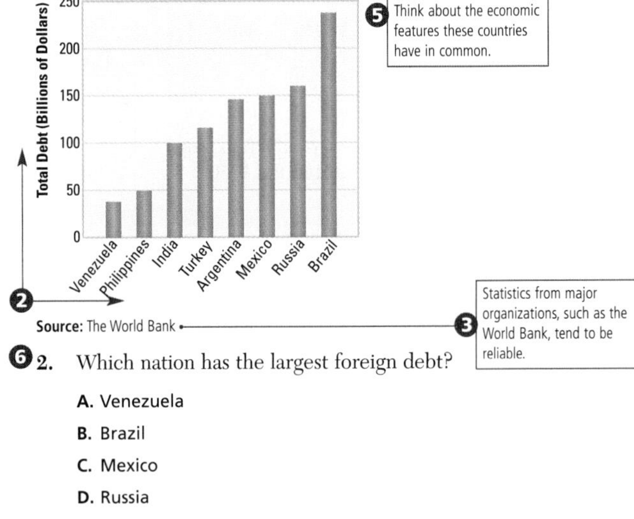

Source: The World Bank

6 2. Which nation has the largest foreign debt?

A. Venezuela
B. Brazil
C. Mexico
D. Russia

TEACHING OPTIONS: CUSTOMIZING FOR SPECIAL NEEDS

STUDENTS ACQUIRING ENGLISH

Vocabulary Make sure students understand the following terms and concepts on these pages.

Strategy Page

Line Graph

Point out that the line graph covers years of discovery and exploration (1699–1774), which explains why one land is called "Spanish America," a phrase not used now.

Practice Page

Question 1 *decline:* downward movement

For more test practice online . . .
TEST PRACTICE
CLASSZONE.COM

Directions: Use the graphs to answer the questions below.

Japan: Gross Domestic Product, 1984–2000

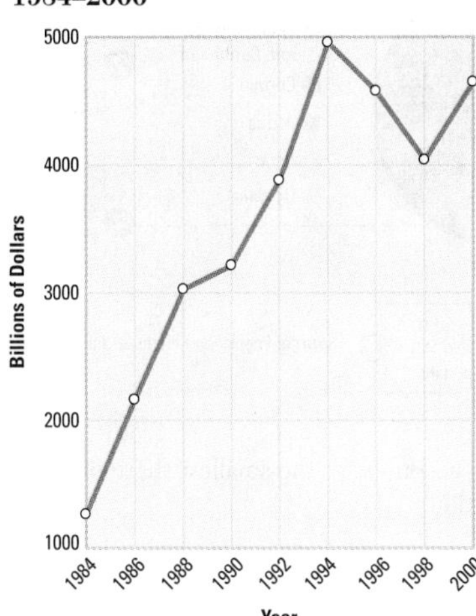

Source: *Annual Report on National Accounts 2002,* Cabinet Office of the Government of Japan

Unemployment Rates for Selected Countries, 2002

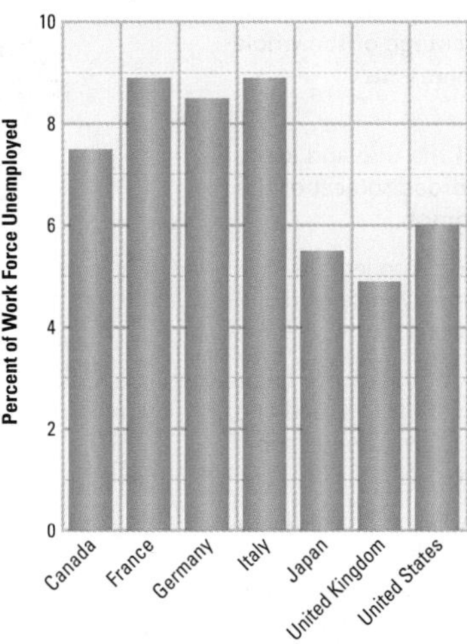

Source: Organization for Economic Cooperation and Development

1. Which of the following periods saw a decline in the gross domestic product of Japan?
   - **A.** 1984 to 1988
   - **B.** 1988 to 1992
   - **C.** 1990 to 1994
   - **D.** 1994 to 1998

2. From 1986 to 1994, Japan's gross domestic product
   - **A.** more than doubled.
   - **B.** more than tripled.
   - **C.** grew by about five times.
   - **D.** grew nearly ten times.

3. Which of these countries had the lowest unemployment rate in 2002?
   - **A.** Italy
   - **B.** Japan
   - **C.** United Kingdom
   - **D.** United States

4. In 2002, France's unemployment rate stood at
   - **A.** about 9 percent
   - **B.** well over 9 percent.
   - **C.** about 7 percent.
   - **D.** less than 7 percent.

Practice Questions

Thinking It Through

Share the following explanations with students as they discuss the strategies they used to answer the practice questions.

1. This is an example of a question in which you need to note the intervals between amounts and between dates. Since the gross domestic product of Japan declined from 1994 to 1998, the correct answer is (D).
2. In this question, you need to find Japan's gross domestic product in 1986 and in 1994, then calculate the increase. It was less than $2,500 billion in 1986 and about $5,000 billion in 1994. Since 2 times 2,500 is 5,000, the correct answer is (A), more than doubled.
3. To answer this question, you need to study the information in the bar graph to find the country with the shortest bar, or lowest unemployment rate. The correct answer is (C).
4. To answer this question, you need to find the bar that represents France and read how high it is. Since the bar reaches 9 percent on the vertical axis, the correct answer is (A).

CALIFORNIA CONTENT STANDARDS AND SKILLS

	Item	Standard/Skill Tested
STRATEGY	1. 2.	**CST 2:** analyze how change happens at different rates and times
	1.	**CST 3:** use graphs to interpret human movement
	1.	**HI 2:** recognize causes and effects
	1. 2.	**10.10.1:** understand the challenges in regions

	Item	Standard/Skill Tested
PRACTICE	1. 2.	**CST 1:** compare present with past
	1. 2.	**CST 2:** analyze how change happens at different rates at different times
	1. 2.	**CST 3:** use graphs to interpret the diffusion of goods
	1. 2. 3. 4.	**REP 4:** evaluate secondary sources
	1. 2. 3. 4.	**10.10.1:** understand economic challenges in contemporary world

CST=Chronological and Spatial Thinking, **HI**=Historical Interpretation, **REP**=Research, Evidence, and Point of View

Using Strategies For . . .

Pie Graphs

Explain to students that they will do best on test questions by thinking them through carefully and by applying test-taking strategies, such as the following.

1. The key word is *smallest.* To answer question 1, you should compare the slices of the pie graph and read their percentages to find the smallest slice. Then read the legend to see which region is represented by that slice. The correct answer is (D).
2. Use the pie graph and legend to find the answer to this question. Compare the population percentage for each region in each answer choice to find the region that has a smaller share of the world's population than Latin America and the Caribbean. Of the four alternatives, only North America has a smaller share. The correct answer, therefore, is (C).

General Test-Taking Tips

Share these tips with your students.

- Read the question and each answer choice before answering.
- Many items include choices that may seem right at first glance, but are actually wrong.

STRATEGIES

Pie Graphs

A pie, or circle, graph shows relationships among the parts of a whole. These parts look like slices of a pie. The size of each slice is proportional to the percentage of the whole that it represents.

1. Read the title and identify the broad subject of the pie graph.
2. Look at the legend to see what each slice of the pie represents.
3. Look at the source line and evaluate the reliability of the information in the graph.
4. Compare the slices of the pie and try to make generalizations and draw conclusions from your comparisons.
5. Read the questions carefully.
6. Eliminate choices that you know are wrong and then select the best answer from the remaining choices.

2 A greater share of the world's population lives in Latin America and the Caribbean than lives in

A. Africa.
B. Europe.
C. North America.
D. Asia.

answers: 1 (D); 2 (C)

1 World Population by Region, 2002

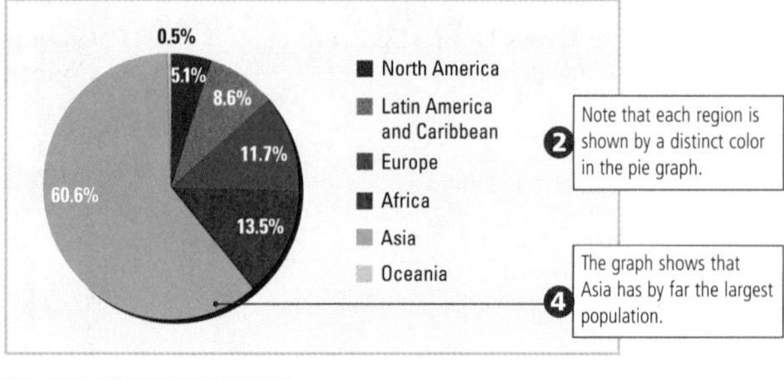

2 Note that each region is shown by a distinct color in the pie graph.

4 The graph shows that Asia has by far the largest population.

3 The Population Reference Bureau specializes in studies of United States and international population data.

Source: Population Reference Bureau

5

1. Which region accounts for the smallest share of the world population?

A. Africa
B. North America
C. Latin America and the Caribbean
D. Oceania

2. A greater share of the world's population lives in Latin America and the Caribbean than lives in

A. Africa.
B. Europe.
C. North America.
D. Asia.

6 For this question, find the "pie slices" for each of the regions listed in the alternatives. Compare each one to the "pie slice" for Latin America and the Caribbean.

S18

TEACHING OPTIONS: CUSTOMIZING FOR SPECIAL NEEDS

STUDENTS ACQUIRING ENGLISH

Vocabulary Make sure students understand the following concepts and terms on these pages.

Strategy Page

Question 1 *accounts for:* has

Practice Page

Pie Graph

energy consumption: energy use

For more test practice online . . .
TEST PRACTICE
CLASSZONE.COM

Directions: Use the pie graph to answer the questions below.

World Energy Consumption by Region

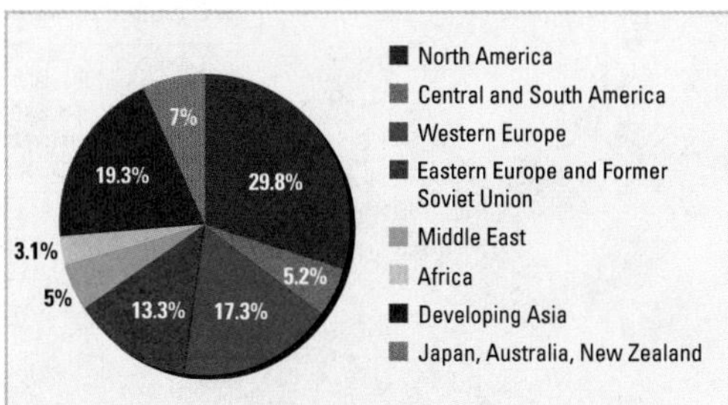

Source: "Earth Pulse," *National Geographic* (March 2001)

1. Energy consumption statistics for Russia are included in the region called
   - **A.** North America.
   - **B.** Western Europe.
   - **C.** Eastern Europe and former Soviet Union.
   - **D.** Developing Asia.

2. Which region uses the highest proportion of energy?
   - **A.** North America
   - **B.** Western Europe
   - **C.** Eastern Europe and former Soviet Union
   - **D.** Developing Asia

3. The word *Developing* in the legend refers to countries that are
   - **A.** growing in population.
   - **B.** adopting new methods of agriculture.
   - **C.** developing nuclear weapons.
   - **D.** moving toward industrial economies.

4. Japan, Australia, and New Zealand are grouped together because they are in the same part of the world and
   - **A.** have roughly equal populations.
   - **B.** have advanced industrial economies.
   - **C.** rely on fishing for food.
   - **D.** rely on other countries for economic aid.

S19

STRATEGIES FOR TAKING TESTS

Practice Questions

Thinking It Through

Share the following explanations with students as they discuss the strategies they used to answer the practice questions.

1. You should use your knowledge of world history to know that the former Soviet Union included Russia. The correct answer is (C).
2. The key word is *highest.* Compare the slices of the pie. At 29.8 percent, North America has the highest percentage of world energy use. The correct answer is (A).
3. You should use your knowledge of world history to know that *developing* refers to a country's movement toward an industrial economy. The correct answer is (D).
4. To answer this question, you need to use your knowledge of world history to know that a country's energy use is most closely related to its degree of industrialization, not the other factors cited in choices (A), (C), and (D). The correct answer is (B).

CALIFORNIA CONTENT STANDARDS AND SKILLS

	Item	Standard/Skill Tested		Item	Standard/Skill Tested
STRATEGY	1. 2.	**CST 3:** use charts to interpret settlement patterns	PRACTICE	1. 2. 3. 4.	**CST 4:** relate current events to physical and human characteristics of regions
	1. 2.	**CST 2:** relate current events to human characteristics of regions		1. 2. 3. 4.	**HI 5:** analyze human modification and environmental policy issues
	1. 2.	**REP 4:** evaluate information from secondary sources			
	1. 2.	**10.10.2:** discuss recent population patterns of regions		1. 2. 3. 4.	**10.10.1:** understand challenges in regions

CST=Chronological and Spatial Thinking, **HI**=Historical Interpretation, **REP**=Research, Evidence, and Point of View

Using Strategies For . . .

Political Maps

Explain to students that they will do best on test questions by thinking them through carefully and by applying test-taking strategies, such as the following.

1. Take care with questions that contain *except*. To answer question 1, read the labels on the map. Check each answer choice to see which province was *not* part of Canada in 1867. The correct answer is (B).
2. To answer question 2, use the scale to estimate the distance of the United States-Canada border from western Lake Superior to the Pacific Ocean. If you are allowed to use scratch paper during your test, place the paper next to the United States-Canada border. Mark the length of the border from western Lake Superior to the Pacific Ocean on your paper. Then mark off how many times the map scale fits on the border length on your paper. Since the scale fits about one and a half times, the correct answer is (C).

General Test-Taking Tips

Share these tips with your students.

- Try to answer every question on the test.
- If you are not sure of an answer, make an educated guess.
- First eliminate the choices you are sure are *not* correct. Then choose from the choices that remain.

Political Maps

Political maps show countries and the political divisions within them—states or provinces, for example. They also show the location of major cities. In addition, political maps often show some physical features, such as mountain ranges, oceans, seas, lakes, and rivers.

1. Read the title of the map to identify the subject and purpose of the map.
2. Review the labels on the map. They also will reveal information about the map's subject and purpose.
3. Study the legend to find the meaning of the symbols used on the map.
4. Use the scale to estimate distances between places shown on the map.
5. Use the compass rose to determine the direction on the map.
6. Read the questions, and then carefully study the map to determine the answers.

answers: 1 (B); 2 (C)

1 Canada in 1871

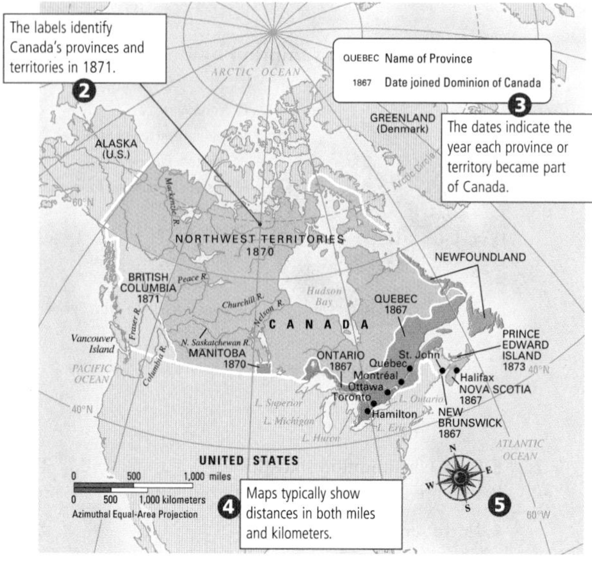

6

1. All of the following provinces were part of Canada in 1867 *except*
   A. New Brunswick.
   B. Manitoba.
   C. Ontario.
   D. Quebec.

2. About how long is the United States-Canada border from western Lake Superior to the Pacific Ocean?
   A. 900 miles
   B. 1,200 miles
   C. 1,500 miles
   D. 1,800 miles

Use the scale to answer questions like this.

TEACHING OPTIONS: CUSTOMIZING FOR SPECIAL NEEDS

STUDENTS ACQUIRING ENGLISH

Vocabulary Make sure students understand the following terms and concepts on these pages.

Strategy Page

political maps: maps not referring to politics, but showing borders of countries, states, and the like
N, S, E, W: the directions north, south, east, and west
province: a political division of a country
territory: a geographical area belonging to a government

Practice Page

Question 3 dominant: main

For more test practice online . . .
TEST PRACTICE
CLASSZONE.COM

Directions: Use the map to answer the questions below.

Empires in South and Southwest Asia, 1500–1660

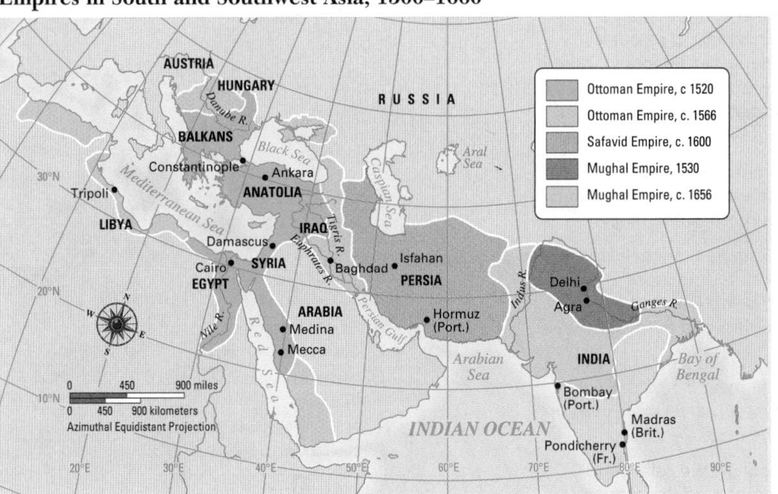

1. All of the following cities were within the Ottoman Empire *except*
   A. Cairo.
   B. Damascus.
   C. Isfahan.
   D. Constantinople.

2. Which empire controlled part of Europe?
   A. Ottoman
   B. Safavid
   C. Mughal
   D. All of the above

3. In all of these empires, the dominant religion was
   A. Buddhism.
   B. Christianity.
   C. Islam.
   D. Hinduism.

4. Which city was within the Mughal Empire by 1530?
   A. Bombay
   B. Delhi
   C. Madras
   D. Pondicherry

Practice Questions

Thinking It Through

Share the following explanations with students as they discuss the strategies they used to answer the practice questions.

1. Be careful with questions that contain *except.* This question asks you to find the city that was not within the Ottoman Empire. First, study the legend to find the color that stands for the Ottoman Empire. In this case, the Ottoman Empire is light and dark green. Next, eliminate the cities that are within the Ottoman Empire. The city that remains, Isfahan, is not within the Ottoman Empire, so the correct answer is (C).
2. This is an example of a question with *All of the above.* Make sure that all the choices are correct if you choose (D). To answer this question, you need to use your knowledge of world geography to know where Europe is located. Since only the Ottoman Empire occupied part of Europe, the correct answer is (A).
3. Use your knowledge of world history to answer this question. The correct answer is (C) since these were Muslim empires. Muslims follow Islam.
4. Use the legend to find the color that stands for the Mughal Empire by 1530. Locate this region on the map. Next, find the city in the answer choices that was located in this region. The correct answer is (B).

CALIFORNIA CONTENT STANDARDS AND SKILLS

	Item	Standard/Skill Tested		Item	Standard/Skill Tested
STRATEGY	1. 2.	**CST 3:** use maps to interpret settlement patterns	PRACTICE	1. 2. 3. 4.	**CST 3:** use maps to interpret human movement **HI 1:** show connections between events and social developments

CST=Chronological and Spatial Thinking, **HI**=Historical Interpretation, **REP**=Research, Evidence, and Point of View

Using Strategies For . . .

Thematic Maps

Explain to students that they will do best on test questions by thinking them through carefully and by applying test-taking strategies, such as the following.

1. To answer question 1, use the map legend and labels to find the symbols used on the map to stand for the Sino-Japanese War and the Russo-Japanese War. Next, find the city that shows symbols of both wars. The correct answer is (B).
2. To answer question 2, use the map legend to find the symbol used to show industrial centers. Next, find the industrial centers and the labels of the cities in which they were located on the map. The correct answer is (C).

General Test-Taking Tips

Share these tips with your students.

- Think positively.
- Tell yourself that you can do it!
- If you have studied for the test, you are prepared to succeed.

Thematic Maps

A thematic map, or special-purpose map, focuses on a particular topic. The movements of peoples, a country's natural resources, and major battles in a war are all topics you might see illustrated on a thematic map.

❶ Read the title to determine the subject and purpose of the map.

❷ Examine the labels on the map to find more information on the map's subject and purpose.

❸ Study the legend to find the meaning of the symbols and colors used on the map.

❹ Look at the colors and symbols on the map to try to identify patterns.

❺ Read the questions, and then carefully study the map to determine the answers.

answers: 1 (B); 2 (C)

❶ **Japan, 1850–1914**

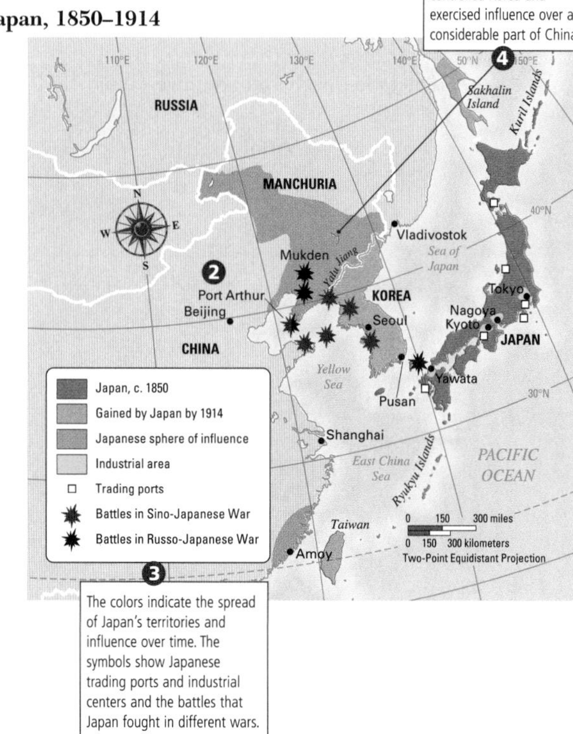

❺

1. Which city was the site of battles in both the Sino-Japanese War and the Russo-Japanese War?
   A. Mukden
   B. Port Arthur
   C. Pusan
   D. Tokyo

2. Which of the following was a major Japanese industrial center?
   A. Shanghai
   B. Seoul
   C. Nagoya
   D. Amoy

TEACHING OPTIONS: CUSTOMIZING FOR SPECIAL NEEDS

STUDENTS ACQUIRING ENGLISH

Vocabulary Make sure students understand the following terms and concepts on these pages.

Strategy Page

Thematic Map

The letter *c.* that appears in the legend before 1850 is an abbreviation for the Latin word *circa,* which means "about" or "around."

sphere of influence: a foreign region in which a nation has control over trade and other economic activities

For more test practice online . . .
TEST PRACTICE
CLASSZONE.COM

Directions: Use the map to answer the questions below.

European Empires in North America, 1700

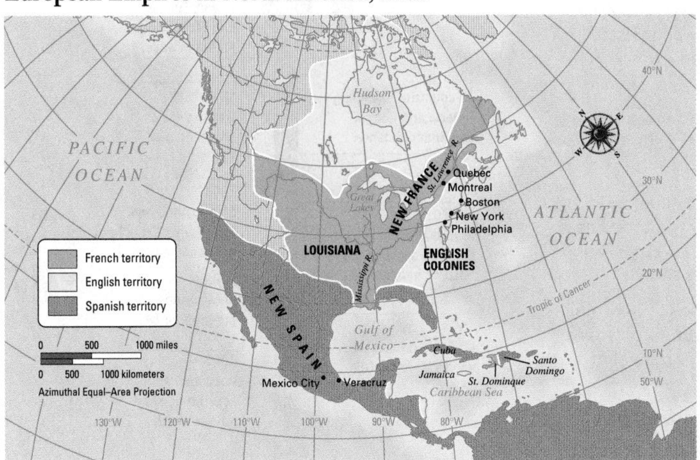

1. Which European power held lands along the shores of Hudson Bay?
   - **A.** England
   - **B.** France
   - **C.** Spain
   - **D.** All of the above

2. The land around the Great Lakes was controlled by
   - **A.** England.
   - **B.** France.
   - **C.** Spain.
   - **D.** all of the above

3. Which of the following statements about the English colonial empire in North America is *not* true?
   - **A.** English lands shared borders with both French and Spanish lands.
   - **B.** English lands did not stretch as far west as those held by Spain.
   - **C.** England held no land on the Pacific Coast of North America.
   - **D.** England held no lands east of 60° W longitude.

4. All of the following could be considered ports *except*
   - **A.** Boston.
   - **B.** Mexico City.
   - **C.** Quebec.
   - **D.** Veracruz.

Practice Questions

Thinking It Through

Share the following explanations with students as they discuss the strategies they used to answer the practice questions.

1. If you select (D) *All of the above,* be sure all the choices are correct. First, use the map labels to find Hudson Bay. Then use the map legend to find the meaning of the color along the shores of Hudson Bay. The correct answer is (A).

2. Use the map labels to find the Great Lakes. Then use the map legend to find the meaning of the color around the Great Lakes. The correct answer is (B).

3. Be careful with questions that contain *not.* This question asks you to find the statement that is *not* true. To do this, check each answer choice with the infor-mation shown on the map and eliminate true statements. Since (A), (B), and (C) are all true statements, the correct answer is (D) because this statement is not true.

4. Be careful with questions that contain *except.* This question is asking you to find the city that could *not* be consid-ered a port. Use the map labels to find each city in the answer choices and eliminate those that can be considered ports. Since choices (A), (C), and (D) are located along major waterways, they can be considered ports. The cor-rect answer is (B) because Mexico City is not located along a major waterway.

CALIFORNIA CONTENT STANDARDS AND SKILLS

	Item	Standard/Skill Tested
STRATEGY	1. 2.	**CST 3:** use maps to interpret human movement
	1. 2.	**10.4.1:** describe the rise of industrial economies and their link to imperialism
	1. 2.	**10.4.4:** describe independence struggles of colonized regions
	1. 2.	**10.3.1:** analyze effects of Industrial Revolution in Japan

	Item	Standard/Skill Tested
PRACTICE	1. 2. 3. 4.	**CST 3:** use maps to interpret settlement patterns
	1. 2. 3. 4.	**REP 4:** evaluate secondary sources
	1. 2. 3. 4.	**10.4.2:** discuss locations of colonial rule of England, Spain, and France

CST=Chronological and Spatial Thinking, **HI**=Historical Interpretation, **REP**=Research, Evidence, and Point of View

Using Strategies For . . .

Time Lines

Explain to students that they will do best on test questions by thinking them through carefully and by applying test-taking strategies, such as the following.

1. *First* is a key word. To answer question 1, you need to read the time line and use your knowledge of world geography to know that these countries are located in North Africa. The correct answer is (A).
2. To answer question 2, note how the events on the time line are related to one another. Look for a theme. The correct answer is (C).

General Test-Taking Tips

Share these tips with your students.

- Relax during the test.
- Several times during the test, take a few seconds to relax and breathe deeply.
- Occasional deep breaths will help relieve anxiety and keep you focused.

Time Lines

A time line is a type of chart that lists events in the order in which they occurred. In other words, time lines are a visual method of showing what happened when.

1. Read the title to discover the subject of the time line.
2. Identify the time period covered by the time line by noting the earliest and latest dates shown.
3. Read the events and their dates in sequence. Notice the intervals between events.
4. Use your knowledge of history to develop a fuller picture of the events listed in the time line. For example, place the events in a broader context by considering what was happening elsewhere in the world.
5. Use the information you have gathered from these strategies to answer the questions.

answers: 1 (A); 2 (C)

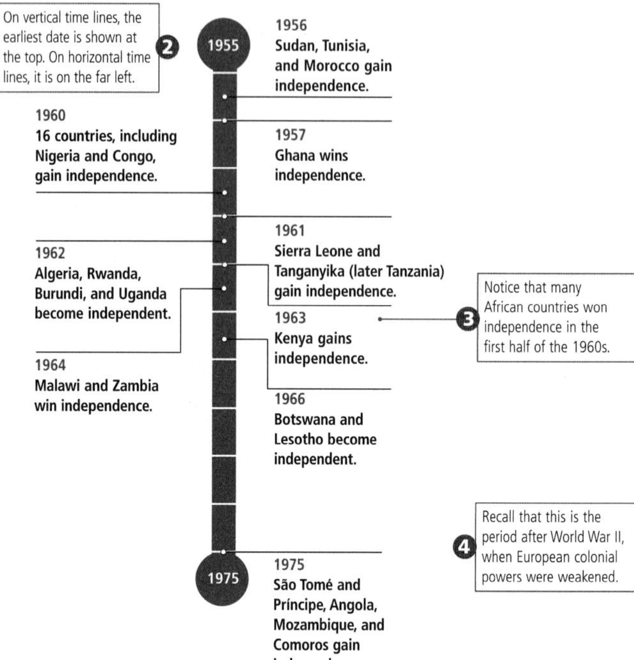

1 The End of Colonialism in Africa
On vertical time lines, the earliest date is shown at the top. On horizontal time lines, it is on the far left. 2
1955
1956 Sudan, Tunisia, and Morocco gain independence.
1957 Ghana wins independence.
1960 16 countries, including Nigeria and Congo, gain independence.
1961 Sierra Leone and Tanganyika (later Tanzania) gain independence.
1962 Algeria, Rwanda, Burundi, and Uganda become independent.
1963 Kenya gains independence.
3 Notice that many African countries won independence in the first half of the 1960s.
1964 Malawi and Zambia win independence.
1966 Botswana and Lesotho become independent.
4 Recall that this is the period after World War II, when European colonial powers were weakened.
1975
1975 São Tomé and Príncipe, Angola, Mozambique, and Comoros gain independence.

5

1. The first countries to win independence were all located in
   - **A.** North Africa.
   - **B.** West Africa.
   - **C.** East Africa.
   - **D.** Southern Africa.

2. Which of the following titles *best* describes events in the 1960s?
   - **A.** The Rise of Communism
   - **B.** The Rise of Colonialism
   - **C.** The Decade of Independence
   - **D.** The Decade of Suffering

TEACHING OPTIONS: CUSTOMIZING FOR SPECIAL NEEDS

STUDENTS ACQUIRING ENGLISH

Vocabulary Make sure students understand the following terms and concepts on the Practice page.

Practice Page

Time Line

glasnost: official policy of openness about social problems and shortcomings in the former Soviet Union
perestroika: restructuring of the Soviet bureaucracy and economy
hardliners: uncompromising communists

For more test practice online . . .

TEST PRACTICE
CLASSZONE.COM

Directions: Use the time line to answer the questions below.

The Breakup of the Soviet Union

1985 – 1991

- 1985 Mikhail Gorbachev becomes leader of Soviet Union.
- 1986 Gorbachev launches glasnost and perestroika reforms.
- 1988 New Soviet constitution allows for open elections.
- 1989 Soviet elections result in defeat of many Communist candidates.
- 1990 Lithuania declares independence; over the next several months 13 other republics follow suit.
- 1991 Boris Yeltsin elected president of Russia. Communist and army hardliners seize power; Yeltsin leads resistance that defeats them. Soviet Union ceases to exist.

1. What event was a direct result of the new constitution that took effect in 1988?
   - **A.** Gorbachev launched glasnost and perestroika reforms.
   - **B.** Many communist candidates lost elections.
   - **C.** Communist hardliners seized power.
   - **D.** Several Soviet republics declared independence.

2. When did Lithuania declare its independence from the Soviet Union?
   - **A.** 1988
   - **B.** 1989
   - **C.** 1990
   - **D.** 1991

3. What was the result of the hardliners' attempt to seize power in 1991?
   - **A.** They prevented the collapse of the Soviet Union.
   - **B.** Leaders in other communist countries joined their cause.
   - **C.** Gorbachev defeated Yeltsin in a struggle for power.
   - **D.** They failed to gain control, and the country rapidly fell apart.

4. For much of the time it existed, the Soviet Union was engaged with the United States in a long conflict called
   - **A.** World War I.
   - **B.** World War II.
   - **C.** the Gulf War.
   - **D.** the Cold War.

S25

Practice Questions

Thinking It Through

Share the following explanations with students as they discuss the strategies they used to answer the practice questions.

1. *Direct result* are key words. Read the time line for cause-and-effect relationships. Find the 1988 entry on the time line. The next event on the time line says almost the same thing as (B), many Communist candidates lost elections. The correct answer is (B).
2. Find the name *Lithuania* on the time line to find the answer to this question. The correct answer is (C).
3. First find 1991 on the time line and the entry for when the hardliners seized power—look for the word *hardliners.* Read the entry for that same date, just below the hardliners entry. You will find that the entry tells what happened after the hardliners seized power. The correct answer is (D).
4. Use your knowledge of world history to develop a fuller picture of the events listed in the time line. The correct answer is (D).

CALIFORNIA CONTENT STANDARDS AND SKILLS

	Item	Standard/Skill Tested
STRATEGY	1. 2.	**CST 2:** analyze how change happens at different rates at different times
	1. 2.	**CST 3:** use documents to interpret frictions between population groups
	1. 2.	**HI 1:** show connections between historical events and political trends
	1. 2.	**10.4.4:** describe independence struggles of colonized regions

	Item	Standard/Skill Tested
PRACTICE	1. 2. 3. 4.	**CST 2:** understand that change affects politics
	1. 2. 3. 4.	**CST 3:** use time lines to interpret frictions that develop between population groups
	1. 2. 3. 4.	**HI 1:** show connections between historical events and political trends
	1. 2. 3. 4.	**10.9.7:** analyze reasons for collapse of Soviet Union

CST=Chronological and Spatial Thinking, **HI**=Historical Interpretation, **REP**=Research, Evidence, and Point of View

Using Strategies For . . .

Constructed Response

Remind students of the following test-taking strategies.

- To answer the constructed-response questions on this page, you need to use the document and your knowledge of world history.
- Some constructed-response questions do not include a document. Instead, all the questions may require you to use only your knowledge of world history to answer the questions.
- Sometimes constructed-response questions start with short answer questions and build up to a short essay. The short answers may help you write the short essay, so try to answer the questions in the order they are asked. When your responses are scored, each part will be worth some points, but the short essay will probably be worth more than the short-answer questions.
- Useful information may be found in a title, a caption, or a source line as well as in the document itself.

General Test-Taking Tips

Share these tips with your students.

- Be sure to answer all parts of constructed-response questions or as many parts as you can. Each part is worth points.
- As you answer each question, make sure that the number of the answer and the number of the question are the same.

Constructed Response

Constructed-response questions focus on various kinds of documents. Each document usually is accompanied by a series of questions. These questions call for short answers that, for the most part, can be found directly in the document. Some answers, however, require knowledge of the subject or time period addressed in the document.

1. Read the title of the document to discover the subject addressed in the questions.
2. Study and analyze the document. Take notes on what you see.
3. Read the questions carefully, and then study the document again to locate the answers.
4. Carefully write your answers. Unless the directions say otherwise, your answers need not be complete sentences.

(1) Mohandas Gandhi Leads the Salt March, 1930

(2) Constructed-response questions use a wide range of documents including short passages, cartoons, charts, graphs, maps, time lines, posters, and other visual materials. This document is a photograph of Mohandas K. Gandhi leading a demonstration.

Mohandas K. Gandhi, accompanied by the poet Sarojini Naidu, leads a protest march against the Salt Acts.

(3) **1.** What demonstration is Mohandas Gandhi shown leading in the photograph?

(4) *the Salt March of 1930*

2. What was this demonstration about?

It was a demonstration against the Salt Acts, which required Indians to buy salt only from the British government and to pay sales taxes on their salt purchases.

3. What principle did Gandhi follow in his campaign to win Indian independence? Describe the tactics he used to put this principle into action.

Passive resistance, civil disobedience, or nonviolence. He led peaceful demonstrations against unjust laws, organized boycotts of British goods, and encouraged people not to cooperate with the British government.

S26

TEACHING OPTIONS: CUSTOMIZING FOR SPECIAL NEEDS

STUDENTS ACQUIRING ENGLISH

Vocabulary Make sure students understand the following terms and concepts on these pages.

Strategy Page

Salt Acts: sales tax imposed by the British government on salt purchased by Indians

Question 3 *principle:* a rule or code of conduct

Practice Page

Nelson Mandela: Make sure students know who Nelson Mandela is and how the South African government treated him in the past.

Students may not understand every word in the document or the questions, but they should get the gist of what is being said. If they do not, help them understand some key words:

spurned
isolated
ideology
racism
oppression
political emancipation
covenant
government policy
significant

For more test practice online . . .
TEST PRACTICE
CLASSZONE.COM

Directions: Use the passage to answer the questions below. Your answers need not be in complete sentences.

A New South Africa

. . . [W]e all carried [pain] in our hearts as we saw our country tear itself apart in terrible conflict, and as we saw it spurned, outlawed and isolated by the peoples of the world, precisely because it has become the universal base of the [destructive] ideology and practice of racism and racial oppression. . . .

We have, at last, achieved our political emancipation. We pledge ourselves to liberate all our people from the continuing bondage of poverty, deprivation, suffering, gender, and other discrimination. . . . We enter into a covenant that we shall build the society in which all South Africans, both black and white, will be able to walk tall, without any fear in their hearts, assured of their inalienable right to human dignity—a rainbow nation at peace with itself and the world. . . .

Never, never and never again shall it be that this beautiful land will again experience the oppression of one by another and suffer the indignity of being the skunk of the world.

—Nelson Mandela, Inaugural Address as President of South Africa (1994)

1. What was the name of the government policy that Nelson Mandela called the "[destructive ideology] and practice of racism and racial oppression"?

2. How did other nations outlaw and isolate South Africa?

3. Why was Mandela's election as president significant?

Practice Questions

Thinking It Through

Share the following explanations with students as they discuss the strategies they used to answer the practice questions.

1. Study and analyze the passage. Next, read the question. Use your knowledge of world history to answer the question. The government policy was apartheid.
2. You need to use your knowledge of world history to answer the question. The answer is that other nations boycotted South African goods and banned South Africa from world activities, such as the Olympics.
3. You need to use the passage and your knowledge of the history of the time period. Mandela's election was significant because he was a black South African who had been jailed for resisting apartheid. His victory in open elections showed that South Africa had ended the policy of apartheid.

Scoring Constructed-Response Questions

Constructed-response questions usually are scored using a rubric, or scoring guide. The questions on this page might be scored by giving 1 point for each question—a total score of 3 points. Another way of scoring these questions might be to give 1 point for each correct answer for questions 1 and 2, and 2 points for question 3 (1 point for knowing that Mandela was a black South African who had been jailed for resisting apartheid and 1 point for knowing that his election showed that South Africa had ended the policy of apartheid)—a total score of 4 points.

CALIFORNIA CONTENT STANDARDS AND SKILLS

	Item	Standard/Skill Tested
STRATEGY	1. 2. 3. 1. 2. 3.	**REP 4:** evaluate primary sources **HI 3:** interpret past events and issues
STRATEGY	1. 2. 3.	**10.4.3:** explain imperialism from perspective of colonized and responses by people under colonial rule
STRATEGY	1. 2. 3.	**10.4.4:** describe independence struggles of colonized regions, including roles of leaders
PRACTICE	1. 2. 3. 1. 2. 3.	**CST 2:** understand that change affects values and beliefs **CST 3:** use primary sources to interpret frictions that develop between population groups
PRACTICE	1. 2. 3.	**10.10.1:** understand challenges in regions
PRACTICE	1. 2. 3.	**10.10.2:** describe recent history of regions

CST=Chronological and Spatial Thinking, **HI**=Historical Interpretation, **REP**=Research, Evidence, and Point of View

Using Strategies For . . .

Extended Response

Remind students of the following test-taking strategies.

- Read the extended-response questions that go with one document before beginning to answer any questions. Look for words that tell you how to organize your answer.
- In question 1, you are asked to complete a chart. You need to apply your knowledge of history to complete the chart.
- In question 2, you need to apply your knowledge of the Industrial Revolution to write the essay. Key words are impact and society. Jot down your ideas and create an outline on a separate piece of paper. Use this outline to write a short essay to answer the question. Support your main ideas with details and examples.

General Test-Taking Tips

Share these tips with your students.

- Write in complete sentences whenever appropriate. Extended-response essays require complete sentences.
- Remember, neatness counts! If the scorer cannot read your answer, you will not get credit for it.
- Use correct grammar, punctuation, and spelling to help the scorer understand your answer.

STRATEGIES

Extended Response

Extended-response questions, like constructed-response questions, usually focus on a document of some kind. However, they are more complex and require more time to complete than short-answer constructed-response questions. Some extended-response questions ask you to present the information in the document in a different form. Others require you to complete a chart, graph, or diagram. Still others ask you to write an essay, a report, or some other piece of extended writing. In most standardized tests, documents are accompanied by only one extended-response question.

1. Read the title of the document to get an idea of the subject. (This document concerns the Industrial Revolution.)
2. Carefully read the extended-response questions. (Question 1 asks you to complete a chart. Question 2 assumes that the chart is complete and asks you to write a short essay based on information in the chart.)
3. Study and analyze the document.
4. Sometimes the question gives you a partial answer. Analyze that answer to determine what kind of information your answers should contain.
5. If the question requires an extended piece of writing, jot down ideas in outline form. Use this outline to write your answer.

❶ Inventions of the Industrial Revolution

❸ Like constructed-response questions, extended-response questions use a wide range of documents. This document is a chart of several inventions developed during the Industrial Revolution.

Invention	Impact
Flying shuttle, spinning jenny, water frame, spinning mule, power loom	Made it possible to quickly spin thread and weave cloth; led to the spread of factories ❹
Cotton gin	*Made it faster to clean seeds from cotton; spurred increase in cotton production*
Macadam road, steamboat, locomotive	*Made transportation by land and water faster; made transportation of larger loads possible; railroads boosted demand for coal and iron, spurring those industries*
Mechanical reaper	*Made harvesting easier; increased wheat production*

❷

1. In the right-hand column of the chart, briefly describe the impact of the inventions listed in the left-hand column. The first entry has been completed for you.

2. The chart shows how certain inventions contributed to the development of the Industrial Revolution. Write a short essay describing the impact of the Industrial Revolution on society.

❺ **Sample Response** The best essays will point out that developments in agriculture reduced the need for labor on the land. Many farm workers left the country seeking work in factories in the cities. As a result, cities grew much larger. However, lack of sanitation and poor quality buildings made cities unhealthy, and sometimes dangerous, places to live. Life for factory workers was made worse because they worked long hours under dreadful conditions. Society split into clear social classes, with an upper class of landowners and aristocrats, a growing middle class of merchants and factory owners, and a large, generally poor lower class. Over the long term, though, working and living conditions improved for the working class, in part because factory-produced goods were cheaper.

S28

TEACHING OPTIONS: CUSTOMIZING FOR SPECIAL NEEDS

STUDENTS ACQUIRING ENGLISH

Vocabulary Make sure students understand the following terms and concepts on this page.

Strategy Page

Explain that the Industrial Revolution was not a war like the American Revolution, but rather, the term describes the radical changes toward mechanization in making products and in farming in this country.

Question 1; 2 *impact:* effect

Question 2 *society:* all the people in one country, who generally share certain characteristics, interests, and a common culture

Practice Page

saluted; salutation: greeted; greeting

loathsomeness: great dislike

stench: stink; bad odor

Essay Question *Atlantic slave trade:* the buying and selling of Africans for work in the Americas

For more test practice online . . .
TEST PRACTICE
CLASSZONE.COM

Directions: Use the passage to answer the question below.

Josef Stalin

Stalin originated the concept "enemy of the people." This term . . . made possible the usage of the most cruel repression . . . against anyone who in any way disagreed with Stalin, against those who were only suspected of hostile intent. . . .

Lenin used severe methods only in the most necessary cases, when the exploiting classes were still in existence and were vigorously opposing the revolution, when the struggle for survival was decidedly assuming the sharpest forms, even including a civil war.

Stalin, on the other hand, used extreme methods and mass repressions at a time when the revolution was already victorious, when the Soviet state was strengthened, when the exploiting classes were already liquidated. . . . It is clear that here Stalin showed in a whole series of cases his intolerance, his brutality and his abuse of power. Instead of proving his political correctness and mobilizing the masses, he often chose the path of repression and physical annihilation, not only against actual enemies, but also against individuals who had not committed any crimes against the Party and the Soviet government. Here we see no wisdom but only a demonstration of the brutal force which had once so alarmed . . . Lenin.

Nikita Khrushchev, *Khrushchev Remembers* (1970)

1. Write a short essay explaining how Josef Stalin gained and retained power in the Soviet Union.

Practice Questions

Thinking It Through

Share the following explanations with students as they discuss the strategies they used to answer the practice question.

- Study the passage and the extended-response question. This question requires you to explain how Joseph Stalin: (1) gained power in the Soviet Union, and: (2) how he retained that power.
- Use the information in the document and your knowledge of history to answer the question.

The best essays should include the following information:

How Joseph Stalin gained power

- Joseph Stalin worked his way up through the Communist Party. In 1922 he became general secretary of the Communist Party where he gave his followers strategic positions. By 1928 he controlled the Communists. In 1929 he became dictator of the Soviet Union.

How Joseph Stalin retained power

- Stalin built a totalitarian state which controlled every aspect of public and private life. Stalin repressed anyone who was an "enemy of the people." This included anyone who in any way disagreed with Stalin, as well as anyone just suspected of disagreeing. Secret police arrested and executed millions of Russians, including Communist Party members. Stalin used the Great Purge—a campaign of terror, indoctrination, propaganda, censorship, and religious persecution—to help retain power.

Scoring Extended-Response Questions

Extended-response questions usually are scored using a rubric, or scoring guide. The question on this page might be scored by giving each part 3 points, for a total score of 6 points.

CALIFORNIA CONTENT STANDARDS AND SKILLS

	Item	Standard/Skill Tested		Item	Standard/Skill Tested
STRATEGY	1. 2.	**CST 2:** analyze how change happens **HI 2:** recognize cause and effects **HI 4:** understand impact of historical events **10.3.2:** examine how technological changes brought social, economic, and cultural change **10.3.3:** describe rural to urban migration and growth of cities	PRACTICE	Essay	**CST 2:** analyze how change happens **REP 4:** evaluate and employ information from secondary sources in written presentations **HI 3:** interpret past events and issues **10.7.2:** trace Stalin's rise to power in Soviet Union **10.7.3:** analyze rise, aggression, and human costs of totalitarian regime in Soviet Union

CST=Chronological and Spatial Thinking, **HI**=Historical Interpretation, **REP**=Research, Evidence, and Point of View

Using Strategies For . . .

Document-Based Questions

Remind students of the following:

- Document-based questions are designed to help you work like a historian. You are given several documents from a variety of sources that you must analyze, evaluate, and synthesize in order to write an essay, much the way a historian would proceed.
- Use the information in the "Introduction" to help you organize your essay. The "Historical Context" gives you the focus of the document-based question. This question focuses on the Cold War between the United States and the Soviet Union after World War II.
- Use the information in the "Task" section to help you make a graphic organizer such as an outline, chart, or concept web to organize the information for your essay. This "Task" section explains that the essay must discuss two things: (1) the postwar developments that led to the Cold War; (2) what impact the Cold War had on world affairs. Make a two-column chart on a piece of scratch paper. Label the columns "Postwar Developments Leading to the Cold War" and "Impact of the Cold War on World Affairs."
- As you answer the "Part 1: Short Answer" questions, also complete the chart.
- To answer the "Part 2: Essay" question, use the documents, the answers to the short-answer questions, the notes in your graphic organizer, and your knowledge of history to help you write the essay.

General Test-Taking Tips

Share these tips with your students.

- Write legibly.
- Write dark enough for electronic scanners to read.

Document-Based Questions

A document-based question (DBQ) requires you to analyze and interpret a variety of documents. These documents often are accompanied by short-answer questions. You use these answers and information from the documents to write an essay on a specified subject.

1. Read the "Historical Context" section to get a sense of the issue addressed in the question.
2. Read the "Task" section and note the action words. This will help you understand exactly what the essay question requires.
3. Study and analyze each document. Consider what connection the documents have to the essay question. Take notes on your ideas.
4. Read and answer the document-specific questions. Think about how these questions connect to the essay topic.

Introduction

1 **Historical Context:** During World War II, the United States and the Soviet Union joined together as allies to defeat Nazi Germany. Soon after the war ended, however, they became enemies in the long conflict called the Cold War.

2 **Task:** Identify the postwar developments that led to the Cold War, and discuss the impact the Cold War had on world affairs.

Part 1: Short Answer

Study each document carefully and answer the questions that follow.

3 **Document 1: The Cold War—1946–1961**

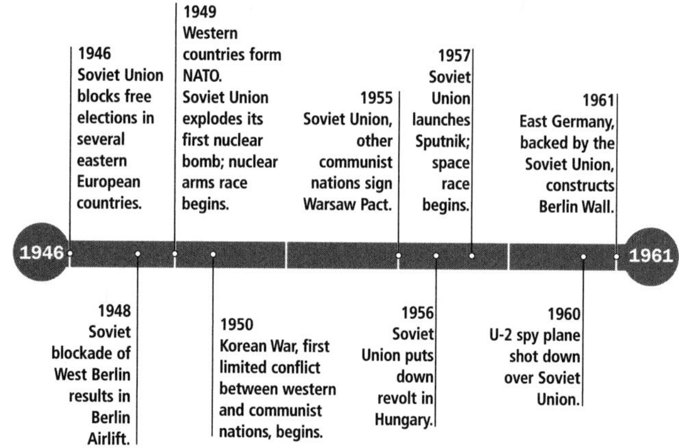
1946
1961
1946 Soviet Union blocks free elections in several eastern European countries.
1948 Soviet blockade of West Berlin results in Berlin Airlift.
1949 Western countries form NATO. Soviet Union explodes its first nuclear bomb; nuclear arms race begins.
1950 Korean War, first limited conflict between western and communist nations, begins.
1955 Soviet Union, other communist nations sign Warsaw Pact.
1956 Soviet Union puts down revolt in Hungary.
1957 Soviet Union launches Sputnik; space race begins.
1960 U-2 spy plane shot down over Soviet Union.
1961 East Germany, backed by the Soviet Union, constructs Berlin Wall.

4 **What impact did the launching of Sputnik have on United States-Soviet relations?**

It led to the space race the struggle between the United States and the Soviet Union for control of outer space.

S30

TEACHING OPTIONS: CUSTOMIZING FOR SPECIAL NEEDS

STUDENTS ACQUIRING ENGLISH

Vocabulary Make sure students understand the following terms and concepts on these pages.

Strategy Pages

Document 1 *NATO:* North Atlantic Treaty Organization, a defensive military alliance formed in 1949 by ten Western European nations, the U.S., and Canada

Warsaw Pact: a defensive military alliance formed in 1955 by the Soviet Union and seven eastern European countries

Sputnik: the first unmanned satellite above the earth's atmosphere

Document 2 *iron curtain:* phrase first used by Winston Churchill to represent Europe's division between mostly democratic Western Europe and a Communist Eastern Europe

the Continent: refers to Europe

totalitarian control: government control over every aspect of public and private life

Document 2: The Iron Curtain

From Stettin in the Baltic to Trieste in the Adriatic, an iron curtain has descended across the Continent. Behind that line lie all the capitals of the ancient states of Central and Eastern Europe. . . . All these famous cities and the populations around them lie in what I must call the Soviet sphere and all are subject in one form or another, not only to Soviet influence but to a very high, and in many cases, increasing measure of control from Moscow. . . . The Communist parties, which were very small in all these Eastern States of Europe, have been raised to pre-eminence and power far beyond their numbers and are seeking everywhere to obtain totalitarian control.

—Winston Churchill, Speech at Westminster College, Fulton, Missouri 1946

What did the Iron Curtain represent to Winston Churchill?

The barrier that separated Soviet-dominated Eastern Europe from free, democratic Western Europe.

Document 3: United States Military Spending, 1946–1959

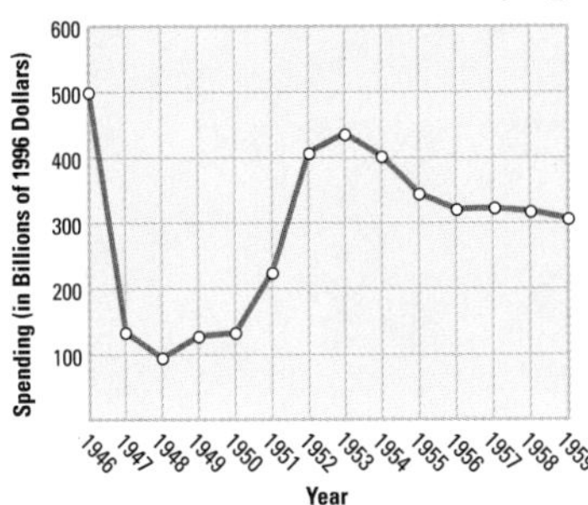

Source: Center for Defense Information

What trend in United States military spending is shown in the graph?

United States military spending fell dramatically in the immediate postwar years. However, it rose markedly in the early 1950s, then leveled off, but remained considerably higher than in the immediate postwar years.

❺ Part 2: Essay

Using information from the documents, your answers to the questions in Part 1, and your knowledge of world history, write an essay that identifies the postwar developments that led to the Cold War and discusses the impact the Cold War had on world affairs. ❻

❺ Carefully read the essay question. Then write an outline for your essay.

❻ Write your essay. Be sure that it has an introductory paragraph that introduces your argument, main body paragraphs that explain it, and a concluding paragraph that restates your position. In your essay, include quotations or details from specific documents to support your ideas. Add other supporting facts or details that you know from your study of world history.

Sample Response The best essays will point out such developments as the imposition of Soviet control in Eastern Europe (Documents 1 and 2), the blockade of Berlin and the Berlin Airlift (Document 1), and the formation of eastern and western military alliances (Document 1). Essays also will point out that the Cold War led to a division of Europe and much of the rest of the world between countries that sided with the United States and those that allied with the Soviet Union. Increased military spending (Document 3) related to the nuclear arms race (Document 1) made this division potentially dangerous.

Rubric for DBQ Essay

This sample rubric might be used to score a document-based question essay.

To score a 5, the DBQ essay:
- thoroughly answers all parts of the Task.
- uses data from all documents.
- is supported with relevant facts.
- has relevant outside knowledge.
- is well developed and organized.
- has a strong intro and conclusion.

To score a 4, the DBQ essay:
- answers all parts of the Task.
- uses data from most documents.
- is supported with relevant facts.
- has relevant outside knowledge.
- is well developed and organized.
- has a good intro and conclusion.

To score a 3, the DBQ essay:
- answers most parts of the Task.
- uses data from some documents.
- is supported by some relevant facts.
- has little relevant outside knowledge.
- is satisfactorily developed and organized.
- restates the essay theme.

To score a 2, the DBQ essay:
- answers some parts of the Task or all parts in a limited way.
- uses limited data from documents.
- uses few facts to support essay.
- has little or no relevant outside knowledge.
- is poorly organized.
- has limited intro or conclusion.

To score a 1, the DBQ essay:
- shows limited understanding of the Task.
- uses limited data from documents.
- uses few or no supporting facts.
- has no relevant outside knowledge.
- is poorly organized.
- has no intro or conclusion.

To score a 0, the DBQ essay:
- does not answer the Task.
- is illegible.
- is blank or missing.

CALIFORNIA CONTENT STANDARDS AND SKILLS

	Item	Standard/Skill Tested
STRATEGY	1. 2. 3.	**CST 2:** analyze how change happens **CST 3:** use documents to interpret frictions between groups **HI 1:** show connections between events and political developments **HI 3:** interpret past events and issues **10.9.1:** compare economic and military power shifts after World War II **10.9.2:** analyze causes of Cold War
STRATEGY	Essay	**CST 2:** analyze how change happens at different rates and times **REP 4:** evaluate and employ information from primary and secondary sources and apply to written presentations **HI 1:** show connections between events and political developments **HI 3:** interpret past events and issues **10.9.1:** compare economic and military power shifts after World War II **10.9.2:** analyze causes of Cold War

CST=Chronological and Spatial Thinking, **HI**=Historical Interpretation, **REP**=Research, Evidence, and Point of View

Practice Questions

Thinking It Through

Share the following explanations with students as they discuss the strategies they used to answer the practice questions.

Part 1: Short Answer

Document 1. Analyze the picture and the caption (*abus:* "injustice"). The peasant woman represents the Third Estate. The noblewoman represents the Second Estate, or nobility. The nun represents the clergy, the First Estate. The Third Estate paid most of the taxes, and so "carried" the other estates.

Document 2. Skim the source: Such ideas as natural rights, equality, and the rights of all citizens to take part in government reflect Enlightenment ideas.

Document 3. Read the time line: Except for the Bastille, early events were fairly moderate. Nobles lost feudal rights and priests lost land. Later, the king's power was limited. Events became more violent after a mob captured the king and arrested the royal family.

Part 2: Essay: Share the sample rubric on page S31 with students so they know the criteria they must meet to earn the maximum points for this essay. Tell students the following:

- Use the "Introduction" to help you organize your essay. Jot down things you know about the time period or question theme. Use the "Task" to help you make a graphic organizer, such as an outline. As you answer the questions, complete this outline.
- Use the documents, the answers to the short-answer questions, the notes in your graphic organizer, and your knowledge of history to help you write the essay.

Introduction

Historical Context: For many centuries, kings and queens ruled the countries of Europe. Their power was supported by nobles and armies. European society began to change, however, and in the late 1700s, those changes produced a violent upheaval in France.

Task: Discuss how social conflict and intellectual movements contributed to the French Revolution and why the Revolution turned radical.

Part 1: Short Answer

Study each document carefully and answer the questions that follow.

Document 1: Social Classes in Pre-Revolutionary France

LE GRAND ABUS

What do the peasant woman, the noblewoman, and the nun represent? Why is the peasant woman shown carrying the noblewoman and the nun?

S32

Engraving: *Le Grand Abus.* Engraving of a cartoon held in the collection of M. de baron de Vinck d'Orp of Brussels/Mary Evans Picture Library, London.

TEACHING OPTIONS: CUSTOMIZING FOR SPECIAL NEEDS

STUDENTS ACQUIRING ENGLISH

Vocabulary Make sure students understand the following terms and concepts on these pages.

Practice Pages

Document 1 *classes:* social levels
peasants: people in the lowest social levels 200 years ago in France

Document 2 *the general good:* the benefit of everyone
the general will: what most people want

Document 3 Make sure students understand the difference between *moderate* and *radical.*

For more test practice online . . .
TEST PRACTICE
CLASSZONE.COM

Document 2: A Declaration of Rights

1. Men are born and remain free and equal in rights. Social distinctions may be founded only upon the general good.
2. The aim of all political association is the preservation of the natural . . . rights of man. These rights are liberty, property, security, and resistance to oppression. . . .
6. Law is the expression of the general will. Every citizen has a right to participate personally, or through his representative, in its foundation. It must be the same for all, whether it protects or punishes. All citizens, being equal in the eyes of the law, are equally eligible to all dignities and to all public positions and occupations, according to their abilities, and without distinction except that of their virtues and talents.

—*Declaration of the Rights of Man and of the Citizen* (1789)

How do these statements reflect the ideals of the Enlightenment?

Document 3: The French Revolution—Major Events

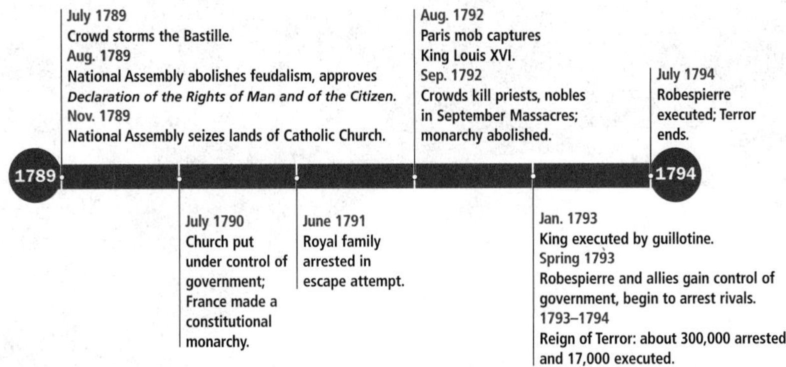

1789
July 1789
Crowd storms the Bastille.
Aug. 1789
National Assembly abolishes feudalism, approves *Declaration of the Rights of Man and of the Citizen.*
Nov. 1789
National Assembly seizes lands of Catholic Church.
July 1790
Church put under control of government; France made a constitutional monarchy.
June 1791
Royal family arrested in escape attempt.
Aug. 1792
Paris mob captures King Louis XVI.
Sep. 1792
Crowds kill priests, nobles in September Massacres; monarchy abolished.
Jan. 1793
King executed by guillotine.
Spring 1793
Robespierre and allies gain control of government, begin to arrest rivals.
1793–1794
Reign of Terror: about 300,000 arrested and 17,000 executed.
July 1794
Robespierre executed; Terror ends.
1794

The French Revolution was moderate at first but quickly became radical. How does the information in the time line illustrate this?

Part 2: Essay

Using information from the documents, your answers to the questions in Part 1, and your knowledge of world history, write an essay discussing how social conflict and intellectual movements contributed to the French Revolution and why the Revolution turned radical.

S33

STRATEGIES FOR TAKING TESTS

Practice Questions

Rubric for Essay

The best essays will address all three parts of the question—how social conflict contributed to the French Revolution, how intellectual movements contributed to the French Revolution, and why the Revolution turned radical.

Social Conflict

- Food shortages
- Resentment felt by the peasants and other members of the Third Estate
  - —toward the high taxes they paid
  - —toward the privileges enjoyed by the nobles, the clergy, and the king

(Documents 1 and 3)

Intellectual Movements

The spread of the Enlightenment ideas promoted values that the Third Estate embraced, such as

- Natural rights
- Liberty
- Equality

(Document 2)

Radicalization of the Revolution

- Rumors of conservative reaction against revolutionary advances
- France's war with Austria and Prussia
- The radicalism of the Paris *sansculottes*
- Internal struggles among the revolutionaries

(outside knowledge)

CALIFORNIA CONTENT STANDARDS AND SKILLS

	Item	Standard/Skill Tested
PRACTICE	1. 2. 3.	**CST 2:** analyze how change happens **CST 3:** use documents to interpret frictions that develop between population groups **HI 1:** show connections between events and political developments **HI 3:** interpret past events and issues **10.2.2:** list principles of Declaration of Rights of Man and Citizen **10.2.4:** explain ideology of French Revolution
PRACTICE	Essay	**CST 2:** analyze how change happens **CST 3:** use documents to interpret frictions between groups **REP 4:** evaluate and employ information from primary and secondary sources and apply to written presentations **HI 1:** show connections between events and political developments **10.2.2:** list principles of Declaration of Rights of Man and Citizen **10.2.4:** explain ideology of French Revolution

CST=Chronological and Spatial Thinking, **HI**=Historical Interpretation, **REP**=Research, Evidence, and Point of View

RAND McNALLY
World Atlas

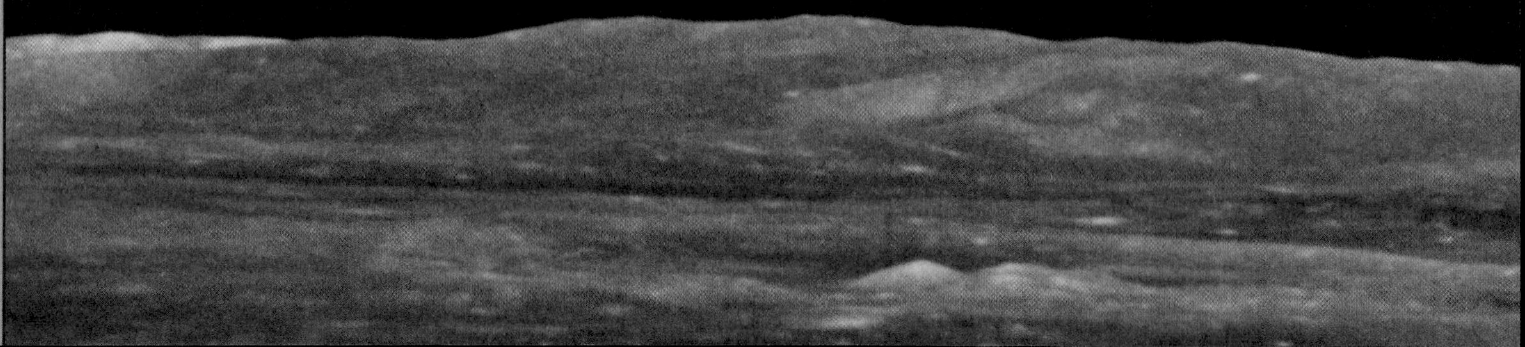

Contents

Complete Legend for Physical and Political Maps

Symbols

Lake

Salt Lake

Seasonal Lake

River

Waterfall

Canal

Mountain Peak

Highest Mountain Peak

Cities

■ Los Angeles — City over 1,000,000 population

▣ Calgary — City of 250,000 to 1,000,000 population

• Haifa — City under 250,000 population

⊛ *Paris* — National Capital

★ Vancouver — Secondary Capital (State, Province, or Territory)

Type Styles Used to Name Features

CHINA	Country
ONTARIO	State, Province, or Territory
PUERTO RICO (U.S.)	Possession
ATLANTIC OCEAN	Ocean or Sea
Alps	Physical Feature
Borneo	Island

Boundaries

International Boundary

Secondary Boundary

Land Elevation and Water Depths

Land Elevation

Meters	Feet
3,000 and over	9,840 and over
2,000 - 3,000	6,560 - 9,840
500 - 2,000	1,640 - 6,560
200 - 500	656 - 1,640
0 - 200	0 - 656

Water Depth

Meters	Feet
Less than 200	Less than 656
200 - 2,000	656 - 6,560
Over 2,000	Over 6,560

A1

ARCTIC OCEAN
GREENLAND
(Den.)
Baffin Bay
Arctic Circle
ICELAND
FAROE IS. (Den.)
RUSSIA
ALASKA
Yukon
(U.S.)
Anchorage
Hudson Bay
CANADA
Aleutian Islands
IRELAND
Vancouver
Newfoundland
Missouri
Montréal
Ottawa
Chicago
New York
Washington D.C.
UNITED STATES
Colorado
Mississippi
Azores (Port.)
PORTUGAL
Los Angeles
Casablanca
Houston
MIDWAY IS. (U.S.)
Gulf of Mexico
ATLANTIC
Canary Islands (Sp.)
Tropic of Cancer
MEXICO
BAHAMAS
Hawaiian Islands (U.S)
CUBA
Mexico City
HAITI
DOM. REP.
PUERTO RICO (U.S.)
CAPE VERDE
MAURITANIA
BELIZE
JAMAICA
Caribbean Sea
SENEGAL
GUAT.
HOND.
GAMBIA
EL SAL.
NIC.
GUINEA-BISSAU
GUINEA
PACIFIC
Caracas
TRINIDAD AND TOBAGO
COSTA RICA
PANAMA
VENEZUELA
GUYANA
SIERRA LEONE
SURINAME
FRENCH GUIANA
LIBERIA
COLOMBIA
Galapagos Islands (Ecuador)
ECUADOR
Amazon
KIRIBATI
BRAZIL
PERU
Lima
OCEAN
OCEAN
SAMOA
AMERICAN SAMOA
COOK ISLANDS (N.Z.)
TONGA
ST. HELENA (U.K.)
BOLIVIA
FRENCH POLYNESIA
Tropic of Capricorn
PARAGUAY
Rio de Janeiro
Easter Island (Chile)
ARGENTINA
Santiago
URUGUAY
Buenos Aires
CHILE
N
0
1000
2000 Miles
0
1000
2000
3000 Kilometers
Copyright by Rand McNally & Co.
Robinson Projection
FALKLAND IS. (U.K.)
South Georgia (U.K.)
South Orkney Is. (U.K.)
South Shetland Is. (U.K.)
Antarctic Circle
Weddell Sea
180°
165°
150°
135°
120°
105°
90°
75°
60°
45°
30°
15°

RAND McNALLY

A3

ARCTIC OCEAN
Baffin Bay
Baffin Island
Greenland
Jan Ma
Arctic Cir
Iceland
Faroe Is.
Mt. McKinley △ 20,320 Ft. 6,194m
Yukon
Mackenzie
Hudson Bay
Canadian Shield
NORTH AMERICA
Rocky Mountains
Great Plains
Aleutian Islands
Vancouver
Newfoundland
St. Lawrence
Appalachian Mts.
Washington D.C.
Cape Hatteras
Azores
Colorado
Mississippi
Los Angeles
Midway Is.
Baja California
Gulf of Mexico
ATLANTIC
Canary Islands
Tropic of Cancer
Hawaiian Islands
Yucatan Peninsula
Cuba
Hispaniola
Puerto Rico
Jamaica
Caribbean Sea
Cape Verde Islands
Cape Verde
Niger
PACIFIC
Trinidad
Orinoco
OCEAN
Palmyra
Equator
Galapagos Islands
Kiribati
OCEAN
Amazon
Amazon
SOUTH AMERICA
Basin
Andes
Marquesas Is.
Samoa Islands
Mato Grosso Plateau
St. Helena
Cook Islands
Tonga Is.
Tahiti
Tropic of Capricorn
Rio de Janeiro
Easter Island
Paraná
Andes
△ Mt. Aconcagua 22,831 Ft. 6,959m
Buenos Aires
Archipiélago Juan Fernández
N
Chatham Is.
Patagonia
0 1000 2000 Miles
0 1000 2000 3000 Kilometers
Copyright by Rand McNally & Co.
Robinson Projection
Falkland Is.
South Georgia
Tierra del Fuego
Cape Horn
South Sandwich Is.
South Orkney Is.
South Shetland Is.
Antarctic Circle
Antarctic Peninsula
Weddell Sea
Ross Sea
Marie Byrd Land
△ Vinson Massif 16,066 Ft. 4,897m

ARCTIC OCEAN
Spitsbergen
Franz Josef Land
Novaya Zemlya
North Cape
Scandinavian Peninsula
Yenisey
Lena
Ob'
Ural Mts.
Siberia
EUROPE
Volga
Moscow
Don
Alps
Balkan Peninsula
Black Sea
Caucasus
Mt. Elbrus 18,510 Ft. 5,642m
Caspian Sea
Aral Sea
ASIA
Altai Mts.
Amur
Sea of Okhotsk
Bering Sea
Kamchatka Peninsula
Sakhalin
Gobi Desert
Beijing
Huang
Sea of Japan
Hokkaidō
Honshū
Kyūshū
East China Sea
Yangtze
Pamir
Plateau of Tibet
Himalayas
Mt. Everest 29,035 Ft. 8,850m
Indus
Ganges
Sardinia
Mediterranean Sea
Sicily
Crete
Cyprus
Cairo
Zagros Mts.
Sahara Desert
Arabian Peninsula
Red Sea
AFRICA
Nile
Sahel
Mumbai (Bombay)
Arabian Sea
Deccan Plateau
Bay of Bengal
Socotra
Lakshadweep
Sri Lanka
Mekong
Hainan Island
Taiwan
South China Sea
Luzon
Mindanao
PACIFIC
OCEAN
Tropic of Cancer
Mariana Islands
Wake Island
Guam
Palau Islands
Caroline Islands
Marshall Islands
Equator
Ethiopian Plateau
Congo
Congo Basin
Rift Valley
Kilimanjaro 19,340 Ft. 5,895m
Maldive Islands
Malay Peninsula
Borneo
Celebes
New Guinea
Solomon Islands
Sumatra
Java
Timor
Seychelles
INDIAN
Cocos Island
Zambezi
Madagascar
Mauritius
Reunion
Kalahari Desert
Coral Sea
New Hebrides
New Caledonia
Fiji Is.
Great Sandy Desert
Tropic of Capricorn
AUSTRALIA
Great Dividing Range
Darling
Sydney
OCEAN
Cape Town
Cape of Good Hope
Cape Leeuwin
North Island
Aoraki (Mt. Cook) 12,316 Ft. 3,754m
Tasmania
South Island
Kerguelen Islands
Antarctic Circle
Queen Maud Land
Enderby Land
Wilkes Land
Victoria Land
ANTARCTICA
15° 30° 45° 60° 75° 90° 105° 120° 135° 150° 165° 180°
75° 60° 45° 30° 15° 0° 15° 30° 45° 60° 75°
Land Elevation
Meters
Feet
3,000
9,840
2,000
6,560
500
1,640
200
656
0
0
Water Depth
0
0
200
656
2,000
6,560

A5

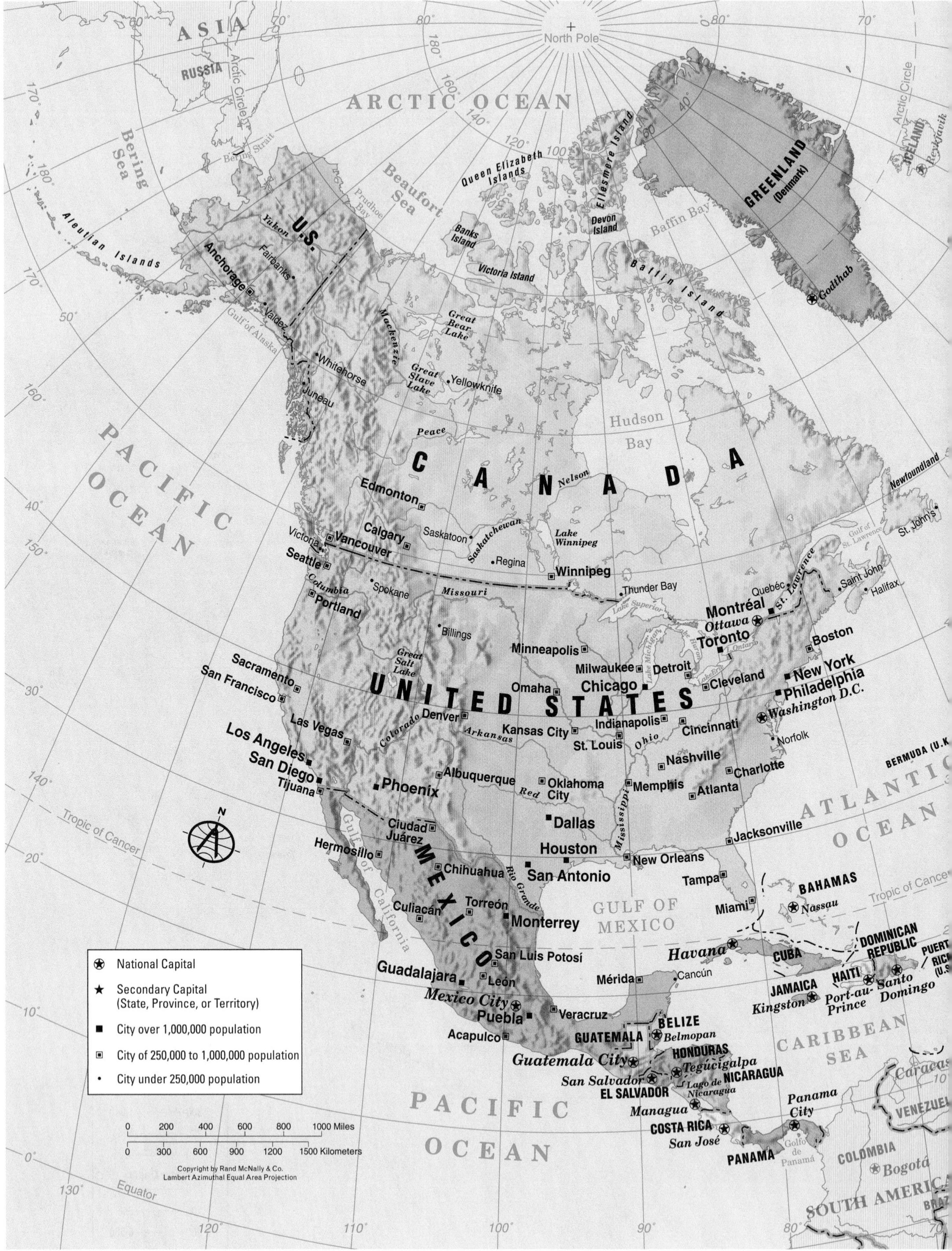
North Pole
ASIA
RUSSIA
Arctic Circle
ARCTIC OCEAN
Bering Sea
Bering Strait
Beaufort Sea
Prudhoe Bay
Queen Elizabeth Islands
Ellesmere Island
Devon Island
Banks Island
Victoria Island
Baffin Bay
Baffin Island
GREENLAND (Denmark)
Godthab
ICELAND
Reykjavik
Aleutian Islands
U.S.
Yukon
Fairbanks
Anchorage
Valdez
Gulf of Alaska
Mackenzie
Great Bear Lake
Whitehorse
Juneau
Great Slave Lake
Yellowknife
Hudson Bay
Peace
PACIFIC OCEAN
CANADA
Nelson
Edmonton
Calgary
Saskatoon
Saskatchewan
Lake Winnipeg
Regina
Winnipeg
Victoria
Vancouver
Seattle
Columbia
Spokane
Missouri
Thunder Bay
Lake Superior
Portland
Newfoundland
St. John's
Gulf of St. Lawrence
St. Lawrence
Québec
Saint John
Halifax
Montréal
Ottawa
Toronto
Boston
Billings
Minneapolis
Great Salt Lake
Milwaukee
Detroit
Lake Michigan
Lake Huron
Lake Ontario
Lake Erie
Sacramento
San Francisco
Omaha
Chicago
Cleveland
New York
Philadelphia
Washington D.C.
UNITED STATES
Denver
Colorado
Las Vegas
Arkansas
Kansas City
Indianapolis
Cincinnati
St. Louis
Ohio
Norfolk
Los Angeles
San Diego
Tijuana
Nashville
Charlotte
Albuquerque
Oklahoma City
Memphis
Atlanta
Phoenix
Red
BERMUDA (U.K.)
ATLANTIC OCEAN
Tropic of Cancer
Ciudad Juárez
Dallas
Mississippi
Jacksonville
Hermosillo
Houston
New Orleans
Gulf of California
Chihuahua
Rio Grande
San Antonio
Tampa
BAHAMAS
Nassau
MEXICO
Torreón
Culiacán
GULF OF MEXICO
Miami
Monterrey
San Luis Potosí
Havana
CUBA
DOMINICAN REPUBLIC
PUERTO RICO (U.S.)
Guadalajara
León
Mérida
Cancún
JAMAICA
HAITI
Kingston
Port-au-Prince
Santo Domingo
Mexico City
Puebla
Veracruz
BELIZE
Belmopan
Acapulco
GUATEMALA
CARIBBEAN SEA
Guatemala City
HONDURAS
Tegucigalpa
San Salvador
Lago de Nicaragua
NICARAGUA
EL SALVADOR
Caracas
Managua
Panama City
VENEZUELA
COSTA RICA
San José
PANAMA
Golfo de Panamá
COLOMBIA
Bogotá
SOUTH AMERICA
Equator
National Capital
Secondary Capital (State, Province, or Territory)
City over 1,000,000 population
City of 250,000 to 1,000,000 population
City under 250,000 population
0 200 400 600 800 1000 Miles
0 300 600 900 1200 1500 Kilometers
Copyright by Rand McNally & Co.
Lambert Azimuthal Equal Area Projection

A6

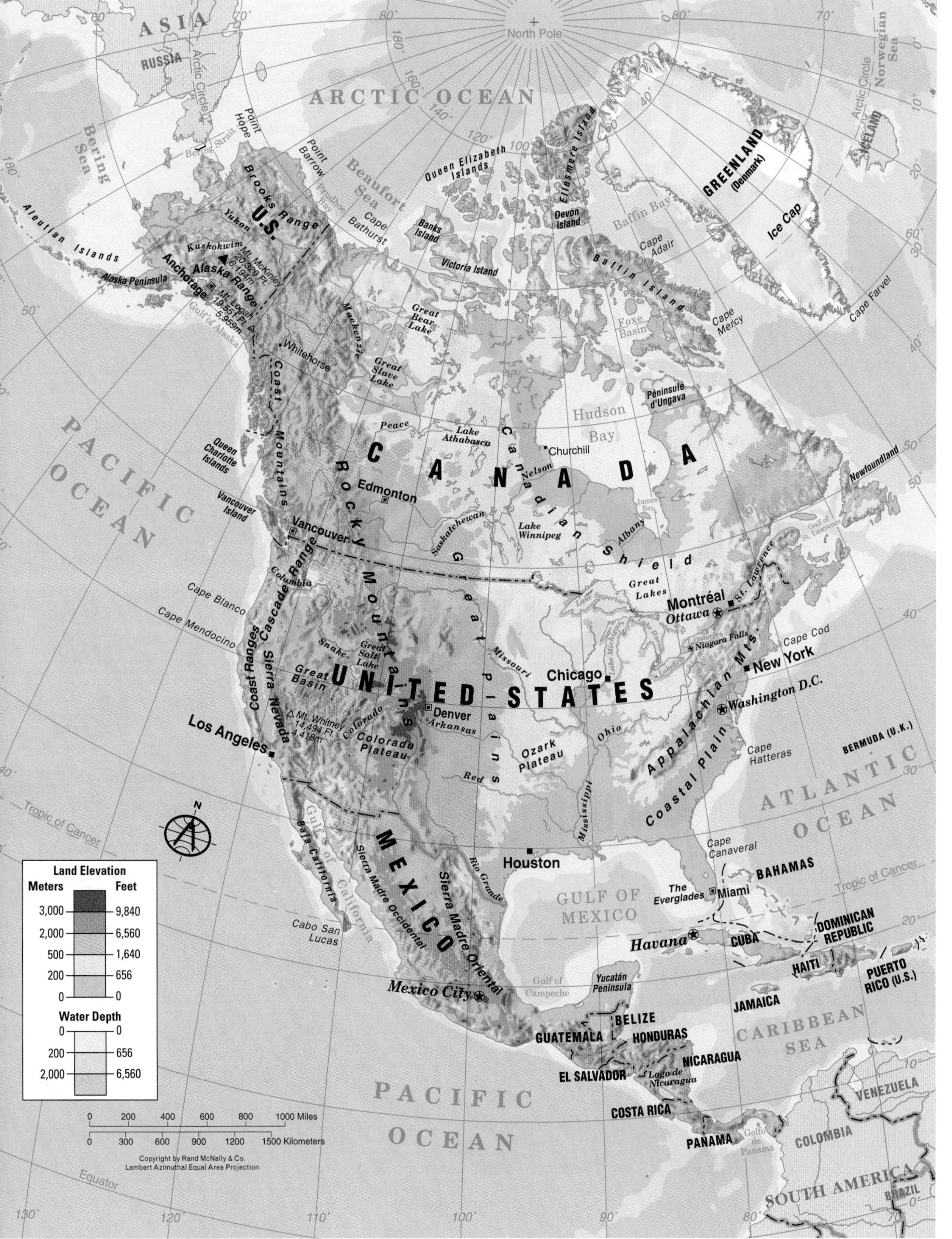
ARCTIC OCEAN
North Pole
ASIA
RUSSIA
Bering Sea
Bering Strait
Arctic Circle
Point Hope
Point Barrow
Beaufort Sea
Prudhoe Bay
Cape Bathurst
Aleutian Islands
Alaska Peninsula
Brooks Range
Yukon
U.S.
Kuskokwim
Mt. McKinley 20,320 Ft. 6,194m
Alaska Range
Anchorage
Mt. Logan 19,551 Ft. 5,959m
Gulf of Alaska
Whitehorse
Queen Elizabeth Islands
Banks Island
Victoria Island
Ellesmere Island
Devon Island
GREENLAND (Denmark)
Ice Cap
ICELAND
Norwegian Sea
Baffin Bay
Cape Adair
Baffin Island
Foxe Basin
Cape Mercy
Cape Farvel
Mackenzie
Great Bear Lake
Great Slave Lake
Péninsule d'Ungava
Hudson Bay
Churchill
Peace
Lake Athabasca
CANADA
Canadian Shield
Nelson
Edmonton
Rocky Mountains
Coast Mountains
Queen Charlotte Islands
Vancouver Island
Vancouver
Saskatchewan
Lake Winnipeg
James Bay
Albany
Gulf of St. Lawrence
Newfoundland
PACIFIC OCEAN
Columbia
Cape Blanco
Cape Mendocino
Cascade Range
Great Plains
Great Lakes
Lake Superior
Montréal
Ottawa
St. Lawrence
Niagara Falls
Cape Cod
New York
Snake
Great Salt Lake
Great Basin
Missouri
Chicago
UNITED STATES
Coast Ranges
Sierra Nevada
Mt. Whitney 14,494 Ft. 4,418m
Colorado
Denver
Arkansas
Washington D.C.
Los Angeles
Colorado Plateau
Ozark Plateau
Ohio
Appalachian Mts.
Coastal Plain
Cape Hatteras
BERMUDA (U.K.)
ATLANTIC OCEAN
Red
Mississippi
Tropic of Cancer
Baja California
Gulf of California
MEXICO
Sierra Madre Occidental
Sierra Madre Oriental
Rio Grande
Houston
Cape Canaveral
BAHAMAS
The Everglades
Miami
GULF OF MEXICO
Cabo San Lucas
Havana
CUBA
DOMINICAN REPUBLIC
HAITI
PUERTO RICO (U.S.)
Gulf of Campeche
Yucatán Peninsula
Mexico City
JAMAICA
BELIZE
GUATEMALA
HONDURAS
CARIBBEAN SEA
EL SALVADOR
NICARAGUA
Lago de Nicaragua
COSTA RICA
PANAMA
Golfo de Panamá
VENEZUELA
COLOMBIA
SOUTH AMERICA
BRAZIL
Equator
Land Elevation
Meters
Feet
3,000
9,840
2,000
6,560
500
1,640
200
656
0
0
Water Depth
0
0
200
656
2,000
6,560
0 200 400 600 800 1000 Miles
0 300 600 900 1200 1500 Kilometers
Lambert Azimuthal Equal Area Projection

A7

Principal status quo powers
Principal Revisionist powers
1914 Boundaries
1922 Boundaries
UNION OF SOVIET SOCIALIST REPUBLICS
Moscow
Leningrad (Petrograd)
BLACK SEA
CASPIAN SEA
TURKEY
SYRIA
IRAQ
PERSIA
ARABIA
PALESTINE
TRANSJORDAN
KUWAIT
ALEXANDRETTA
TURKESTAN
Aral Sea
Persian Gulf

Africa About A.D. 1400

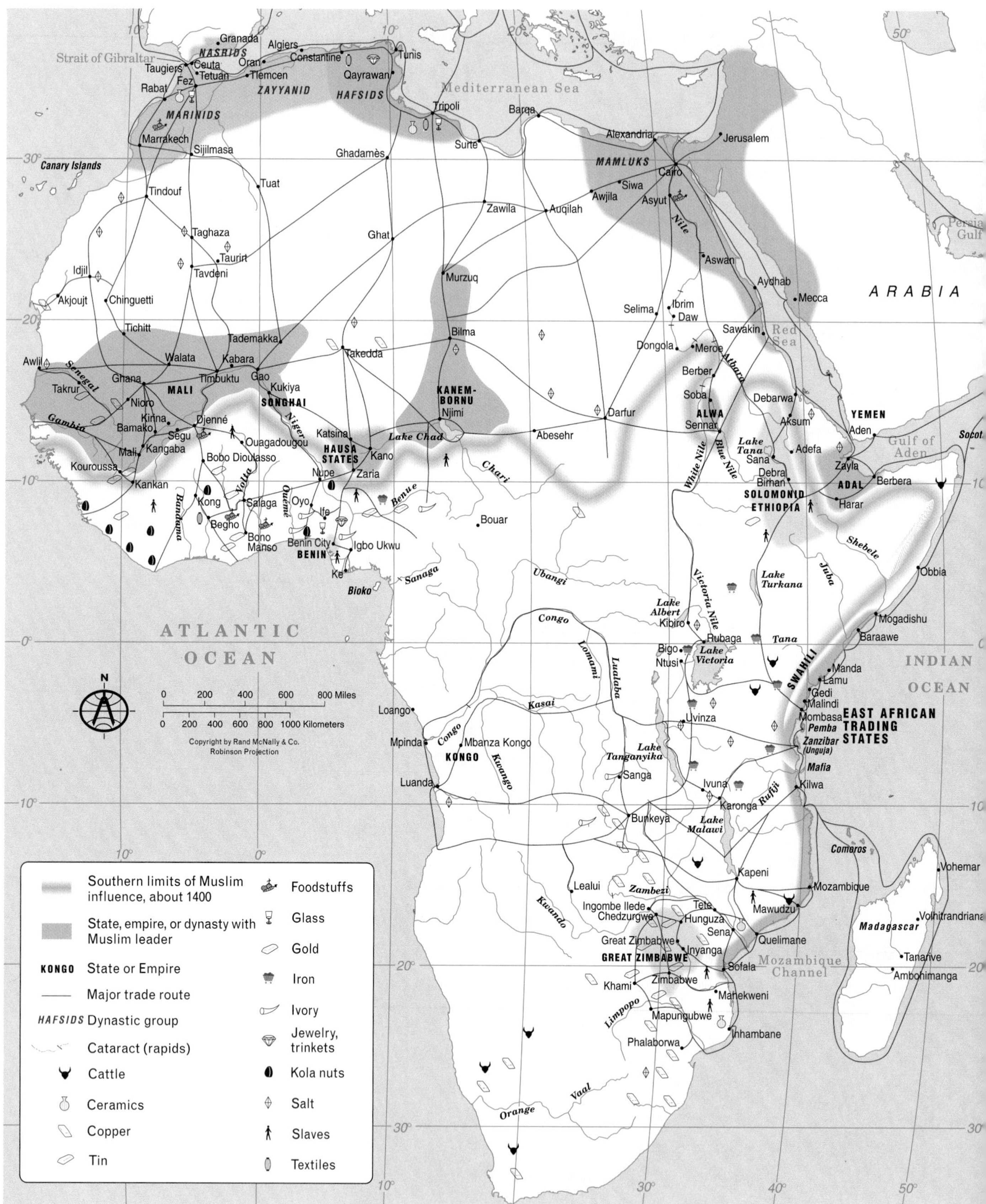

A36

European Partition of Africa: 19th Century

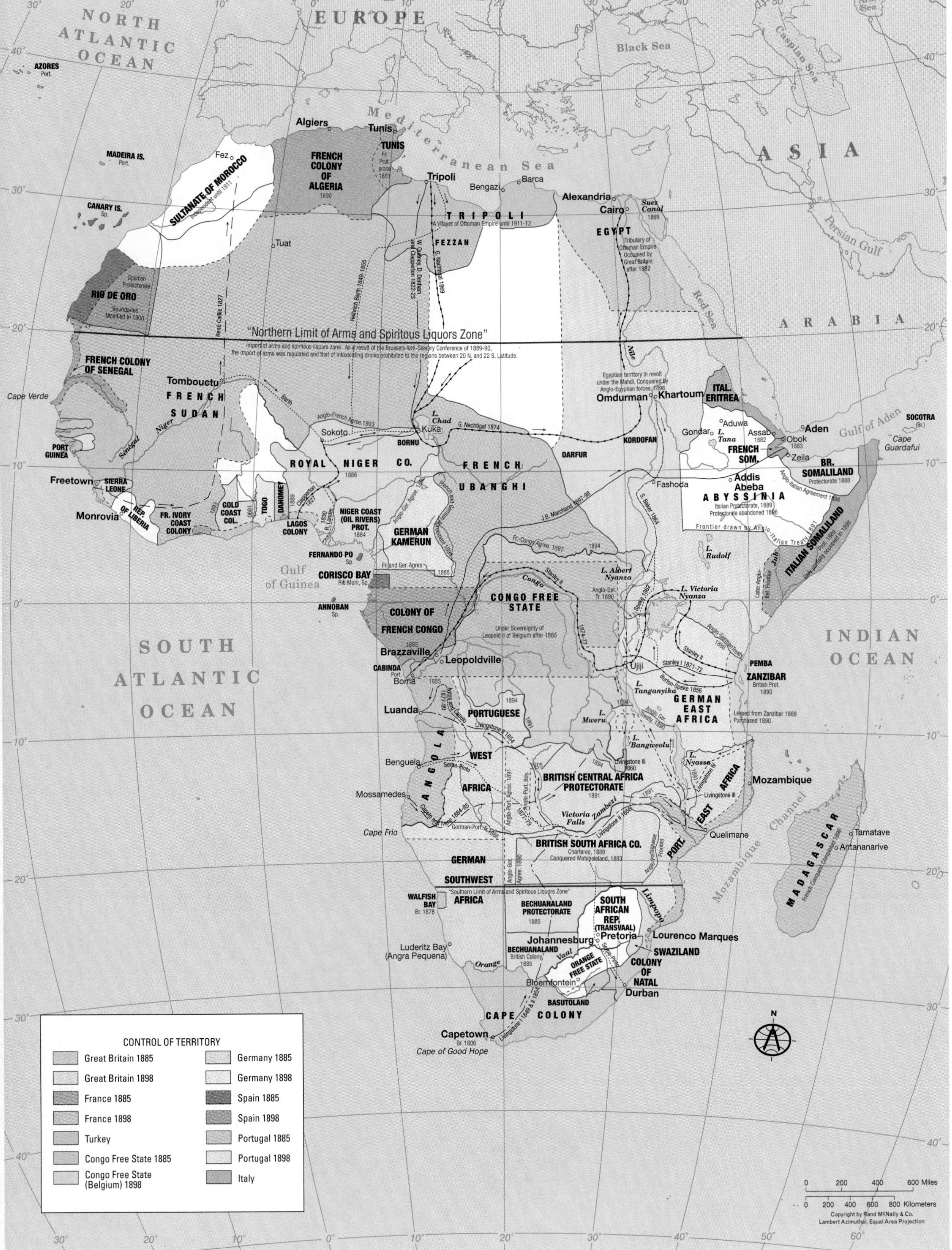

NORTH ATLANTIC OCEAN
EUROPE
AZORES
Port.
Black Sea
Caspian Sea
Aral Sea
ASIA
Mediterranean Sea
Algiers
Tunis
TUNIS
Fr. Prot. since 1881
MADEIRA IS.
Port.
Fez
SULTANATE OF MOROCCO
Independent until 1911
FRENCH COLONY OF ALGERIA
1830
Tripoli
Bengazi
Barca
Alexandria
Cairo
Suez Canal
1869
Persian Gulf
CANARY IS.
Sp.
TRIPOLI
A Vilayet of Ottoman Empire until 1911-12
FEZZAN
EGYPT
Tributary of Ottoman Empire Occupied by Great Britain after 1882
Tuat
Spanish Protectorate
RIO DE ORO
Boundaries Modified in 1900
René Caillié 1827
Heinrich Barth 1849-1855
W. Oudney, D. Denham and Clapperton 1822-23
G. Nachtigal 1869
Red Sea
ARABIA
"Northern Limit of Arms and Spiritous Liquors Zone"
Import of arms and spiritous liquors zone. As a result of the Brussels Anti-Slavery Conference of 1889-90, the import of arms was regulated and that of intoxicating drinks prohibited to the regions between 20 N. and 22 S. Latitude.
Nile
FRENCH COLONY OF SENEGAL
Tombouctu
FRENCH SUDAN
Cape Verde
Barth
Niger
Senegal
Egyptian territory in revolt under the Mahdi. Conquered by Anglo-Egyptian forces, 1898
Omdurman
Khartoum
ITAL. ERITREA
Anglo-French Agree. 1893
Sokoto
L. Chad
Kuka
G. Nachtigal 1874
BORNU
KORDOFAN
Gondar
Aduwa
L. Tana
Assab
1882
Aden
Gulf of Aden
SOCOTRA
(Br.)
Cape Guardafui
Obok
1883
FRENCH SOM.
Zeila
PORT. GUINEA
ROYAL NIGER CO.
1886
FRENCH UBANGHI
DARFUR
BR. SOMALILAND
Protectorate 1888
Freetown
SIERRA LEONE
Fashoda
Addis Abeba
ABYSSINIA
Italian Protectorate, 1889 Protectorate abandoned 1896
Anglo-Italian Agreement 1894
Monrovia
REP. OF LIBERIA
FR. IVORY COAST COLONY
GOLD COAST COL.
TOGO
DAHOMEY
LAGOS COLONY
NIGER COAST (OIL RIVERS) PROT.
1884
GERMAN KAMERUN
J.B. Marchand 1897-98
S. Baker 1864
Frontier drawn by Anglo-Italian Treaty 1891
ITALIAN SOMALILAND
L. Rudolf
FERNANDO PO
Sp.
Gulf of Guinea
CORISCO BAY
Rio Muni, Sp.
Fr. and Ger. Agree.
1885
Fr.-Congo Agree. 1887
1894
Congo
Stanley II
L. Albert Nyanza
Anglo-Ger. Tr. 1890
L. Victoria Nyanza
Speke 1862
Jub
ANNOBAN
Sp.
COLONY OF FRENCH CONGO
CONGO FREE STATE
Under Sovereignty of Leopold II of Belgium after 1885
Anglo-German Treaty 1890
SOUTH ATLANTIC OCEAN
INDIAN OCEAN
Brazzaville
1865
Leopoldville
CABINDA
Port.
Boma
Ujiji
Stanley I 1871-72
PEMBA
ZANZIBAR
British Prot. 1890
L. Tanganyika
Burton-Speke 1856
GERMAN EAST AFRICA
Leased from Zanzibar 1888 Purchased 1890
Luanda
PORTUGUESE
1894
1891
L. Mweru
L. Bangweolu
Livingstone II 1854
Benguela
ANGOLA
WEST AFRICA
Serpa Pinto
Mossamedes
BRITISH CENTRAL AFRICA PROTECTORATE
1891
L. Nyassa
EAST AFRICA
Mozambique
Livingstone III
Victoria Falls
Zambezi
Capelo and Ivens 1884-85
Cape Frio
German-Port. Tr. 1886
Anglo-Port. Agree. 1891
PORT.
Quelimane
Mozambique Channel
Tamatave
Antananarive
MADAGASCAR
French Conquest Completed 1896
BRITISH SOUTH AFRICA CO.
Chartered, 1889
Conquered Matabeleland, 1893
GERMAN SOUTHWEST AFRICA
WALFISH BAY
Br. 1878
"Southern Limit of Arms and Spiritous Liquors Zone"
BECHUANALAND PROTECTORATE
1885
SOUTH AFRICAN REP. (TRANSVAAL)
Limpopo
Johannesburg
Pretoria
Lourenco Marques
Luderitz Bay
(Angra Pequena)
BECHUANALAND
British Colony, 1885
Vaal
Orange
ORANGE FREE STATE
SWAZILAND
COLONY OF NATAL
Bloemfontein
Durban
BASUTOLAND
CAPE COLONY
Capetown
Br. 1806
Cape of Good Hope
Livingstone I 1840 & II 1854
N
CONTROL OF TERRITORY
Great Britain 1885
Great Britain 1898
France 1885
France 1898
Turkey
Congo Free State 1885
Congo Free State (Belgium) 1898
Germany 1885
Germany 1898
Spain 1885
Spain 1898
Portugal 1885
Portugal 1898
Italy
0 200 400 600 Miles
0 200 400 600 800 Kilometers
Copyright by Rand McNally & Co.
Lambert Azimuthal, Equal Area Projection

RAND McNALLY

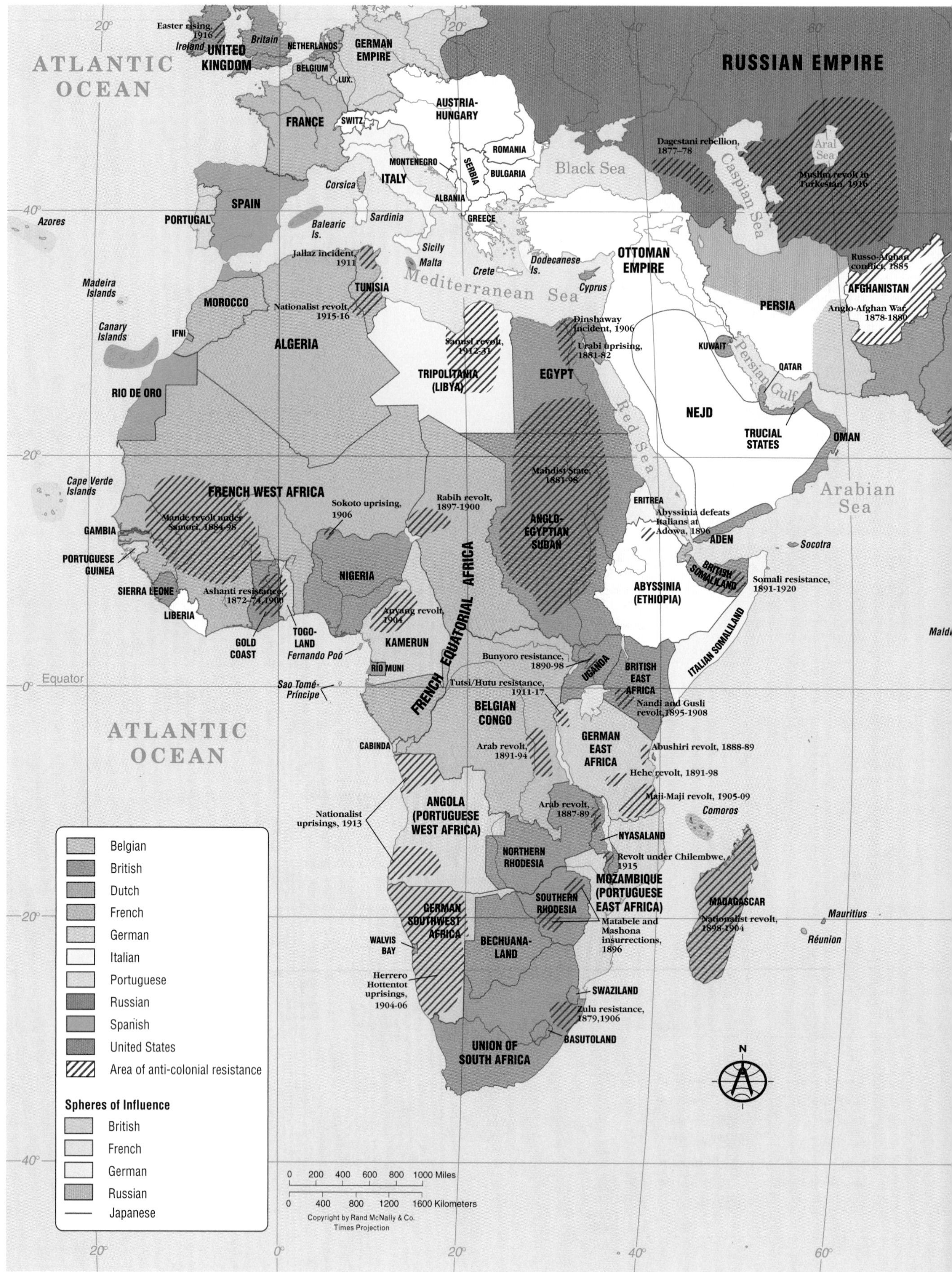
ATLANTIC OCEAN
Easter rising, 1916
Ireland
UNITED KINGDOM
Britain
NETHERLANDS
BELGIUM
LUX.
GERMAN EMPIRE
RUSSIAN EMPIRE
AUSTRIA-HUNGARY
FRANCE
SWITZ.
ROMANIA
MONTENEGRO
SERBIA
BULGARIA
Black Sea
Dagestani rebellion, 1877–78
Caspian Sea
Aral Sea
Muslim revolt in Turkestan, 1916
Corsica
ITALY
ALBANIA
SPAIN
PORTUGAL
Azores
Balearic Is.
Sardinia
GREECE
Sicily
Malta
Crete
Dodecanese Is.
Jallaz incident, 1911
OTTOMAN EMPIRE
Russo-Afghan conflict, 1885
AFGHANISTAN
Madeira Islands
TUNISIA
Mediterranean Sea
Cyprus
PERSIA
Anglo-Afghan War, 1878-1880
MOROCCO
Nationalist revolt, 1915-16
Canary Islands
IFNI
ALGERIA
Sanusi revolt, 1912-31
Dinshaway incident, 1906
Urabi uprising, 1881-82
KUWAIT
Persian Gulf
QATAR
RIO DE ORO
TRIPOLITANIA (LIBYA)
EGYPT
NEJD
TRUCIAL STATES
OMAN
Red Sea
Mahdist State, 1881-98
Arabian Sea
Cape Verde Islands
FRENCH WEST AFRICA
Sokoto uprising, 1906
Rabih revolt, 1897-1900
ERITREA
Abyssinia defeats Italians at Adowa, 1896
GAMBIA
Mande revolt under Samori, 1884-98
ANGLO-EGYPTIAN SUDAN
ADEN
Socotra
PORTUGUESE GUINEA
BRITISH SOMALILAND
NIGERIA
SIERRA LEONE
Ashanti resistance, 1872-74,1900
ABYSSINIA (ETHIOPIA)
Somali resistance, 1891-1920
LIBERIA
Anyang revolt, 1904
FRENCH EQUATORIAL AFRICA
ITALIAN SOMALILAND
GOLD COAST
TOGO-LAND
Fernando Poó
KAMERUN
Bunyoro resistance, 1890-98
UGANDA
BRITISH EAST AFRICA
RÍO MUNI
Equator
Sao Tomé-Príncipe
Tutsi/Hutu resistance, 1911-17
BELGIAN CONGO
Nandi and Gusli revolt,1895-1908
ATLANTIC OCEAN
CABINDA
Arab revolt, 1891-94
GERMAN EAST AFRICA
Abushiri revolt, 1888-89
Hehe revolt, 1891-98
Maji-Maji revolt, 1905-09
Nationalist uprisings, 1913
ANGOLA (PORTUGUESE WEST AFRICA)
Arab revolt, 1887-89
Comoros
NYASALAND
NORTHERN RHODESIA
Revolt under Chilembwe, 1915
MOZAMBIQUE (PORTUGUESE EAST AFRICA)
SOUTHERN RHODESIA
GERMAN SOUTHWEST AFRICA
MADAGASCAR
Nationalist revolt, 1898-1904
Mauritius
Réunion
Matabele and Mashona insurrections, 1896
WALVIS BAY
BECHUANA-LAND
Herrero Hottentot uprisings, 1904-06
SWAZILAND
Zulu resistance, 1879,1906
BASUTOLAND
UNION OF SOUTH AFRICA
N
Belgian
British
Dutch
French
German
Italian
Portuguese
Russian
Spanish
United States
Area of anti-colonial resistance
Spheres of Influence
British
French
German
Russian
Japanese
0 200 400 600 800 1000 Miles
0 400 800 1200 1600 Kilometers
Copyright by Rand McNally & Co.
Times Projection
20°
0°
20°
40°
60°
40°
20°
0°
20°
40°

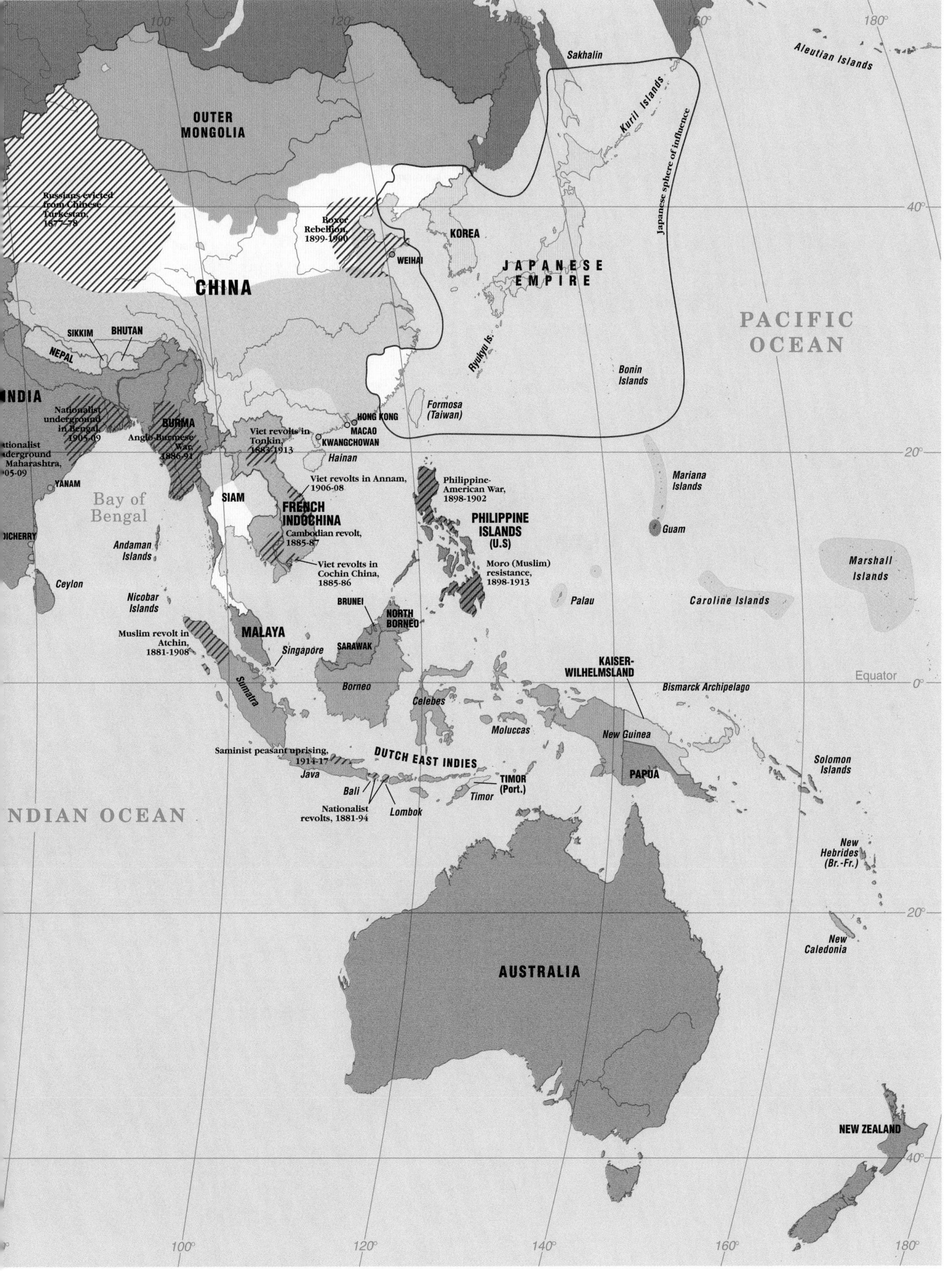

OUTER MONGOLIA
Russians evicted from Chinese Turkestan, 1877–78
Boxer Rebellion, 1899-1900
WEIHAI
CHINA
KOREA
JAPANESE EMPIRE
Sakhalin
Kuril Islands
Japanese sphere of influence
Aleutian Islands
PACIFIC OCEAN
Ryukyu Is.
Bonin Islands
Formosa (Taiwan)
SIKKIM
BHUTAN
NEPAL
INDIA
Nationalist underground in Bengal, 1905-09
BURMA
Anglo-Burmese War, 1886-91
Nationalist underground in Maharashtra, 1905-09
YANAM
Viet revolts in Tonkin, 1883-1913
HONG KONG
MACAO
KWANGCHOWAN
Hainan
Viet revolts in Annam, 1906-08
Philippine-American War, 1898-1902
Mariana Islands
Guam
Bay of Bengal
SIAM
FRENCH INDOCHINA
Cambodian revolt, 1885-87
Viet revolts in Cochin China, 1885-86
PHILIPPINE ISLANDS (U.S)
Moro (Muslim) resistance, 1898-1913
Marshall Islands
Andaman Islands
Ceylon
Nicobar Islands
BRUNEI
NORTH BORNEO
Palau
Caroline Islands
Muslim revolt in Atchin, 1881-1908
MALAYA
Singapore
SARAWAK
KAISER-WILHELMSLAND
Equator
Bismarck Archipelago
Sumatra
Borneo
Celebes
Moluccas
New Guinea
Saminist peasant uprising, 1914-17
DUTCH EAST INDIES
Java
Bali
Lombok
Nationalist revolts, 1881-94
TIMOR (Port.)
Timor
PAPUA
Solomon Islands
INDIAN OCEAN
New Hebrides (Br.-Fr.)
New Caledonia
AUSTRALIA
NEW ZEALAND
100°
120°
140°
160°
180°
40°
20°
0°

Resistance to Colonialism 1870–1930

RAND McNALLY

Middle East/Israel: Political

RAND McNALLY

A40

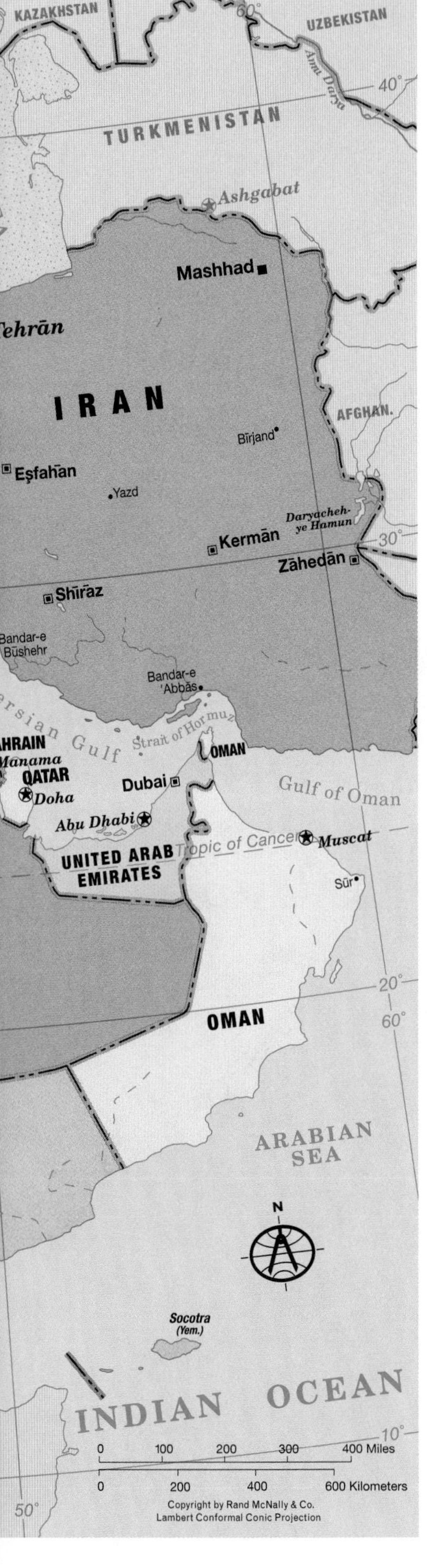
KAZAKHSTAN
UZBEKISTAN
Amu Darya
TURKMENISTAN
Ashgabat
Mashhad
Tehrān
IRAN
Bīrjand
AFGHAN.
Eşfahān
Yazd
Daryācheh-ye Hamun
Kermān
Zāhedān
Shīrāz
Bandar-e Būshehr
Bandar-e 'Abbās
Persian Gulf
Strait of Hormuz
BAHRAIN
Manama
QATAR
Doha
OMAN
Dubai
Gulf of Oman
Abu Dhabi
Tropic of Cancer
Muscat
UNITED ARAB EMIRATES
Şūr
OMAN
ARABIAN SEA
N
Socotra (Yem.)
INDIAN OCEAN
0 100 200 300 400 Miles
0 200 400 600 Kilometers
Copyright by Rand McNally & Co.
Lambert Conformal Conic Projection

0 10 20 30 40 50 Miles
0 20 40 60 80 Kilometers
Copyright by Rand McNally & Co.
Lambert Conformal Conic Projection
Beirut
Sidon
LEBANON
Litani
Tyre
MEDITERRANEAN SEA
Golan Heights
Acre
Haifa
Sea of Galilee
Tiberias
Nazareth
N
Ⓐ Golan Heights. Occupied and unilaterally annexed by Israel.
Ⓑ West Bank. Controlled by Israel, parts administered by the Palestinian Authority. Permanent status to be determined.
Ⓒ Gaza Strip. Controlled by Israel, parts administered by the Palestinian Authority. Permanent status to be determined.
Hadera
Janīn
Irbid
Netanya
Nābulus
Jordan
Tel Aviv-Yafo
West Bank
As Salt
Rehovot
Ammān
Ashdod
Jericho
Jerusalem
Ashqelon
Bethlehem
Gaza
Gaza Strip
Hebron
Dead Sea
Khan Yunus
Port Said
Pelusium Bay
Beersheba
Al Karak
El Arish
Suez Canal
Dimona
El Qantara el-Sharqîya
Aţ Ţafīlah
ISRAEL
Ismailia
Negev Desert
JORDAN
Great Bitter Lake
Ma'ān
EGYPT
Suez
Gulf of Suez
Sinai Peninsula
Elat
Aqaba
Gulf of Aqaba

A41

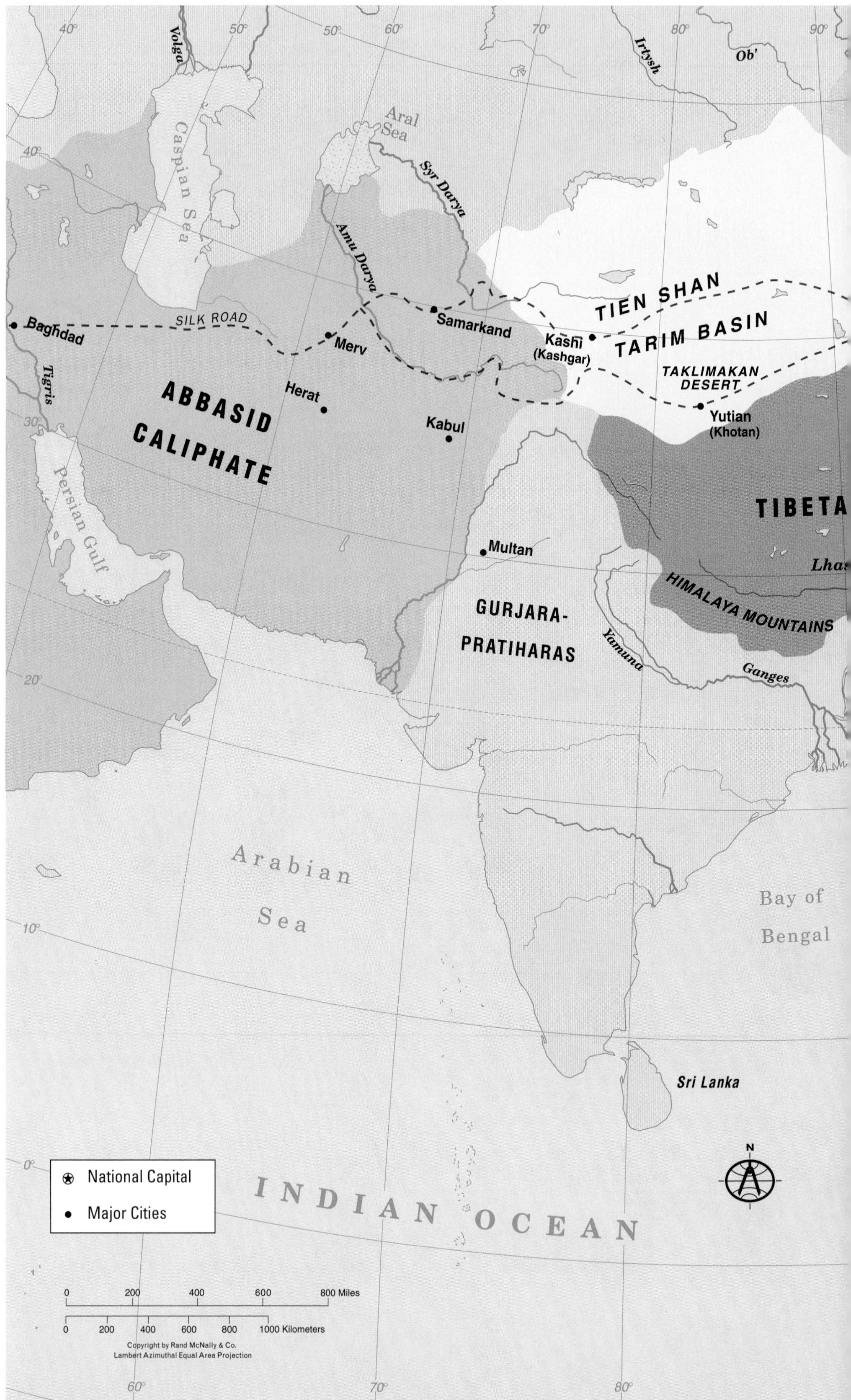
Volga
Irtysh
Ob'
Aral Sea
Caspian Sea
Syr Darya
Amu Darya
TIEN SHAN
TARIM BASIN
TAKLIMAKAN DESERT
SILK ROAD
Baghdad
Samarkand
Merv
Kashi (Kashgar)
Yutian (Khotan)
Herat
Kabul
Tigris
ABBASID CALIPHATE
Persian Gulf
TIBETA
Lhas
Multan
HIMALAYA MOUNTAINS
GURJARA-PRATIHARAS
Yamuna
Ganges
Arabian Sea
Bay of Bengal
Sri Lanka
INDIAN OCEAN
National Capital
Major Cities
N
0 200 400 600 800 Miles
0 200 400 600 800 1000 Kilometers
Copyright by Rand McNally & Co.
Lambert Azimuthal Equal Area Projection
40° 50° 60° 70° 80° 90°
40° 30° 20° 10° 0°

A42

UIGHUR EMPIRE
GOBI DESERT
PARHAE
SILLA
JAPAN
Sea of Japan
Heian-kyo (Kyoto)
Nara
GREAT WALL
Dunhuang
SILK ROAD
Huang (Yellow)
Yellow Sea
Grand Canal
Yangzhou
Luoyang
Chang-an (Xi'an)
Hangzhou
East China Sea
Chang (Yangtze)
T'ANG EMPIRE (CHINA)
MPIRE
PACIFIC OCEAN
Taiwan
ahmaputra
NAN-CHAO
Xi (West)
Guangzhou (Canton)
Philippine Islands
South China Sea
Mekong
CHAMPA
CHEN-LA
SRIVIJAYA
Sumatra
Srivijaya (Palembang)
Borneo
Celebes
Java
100°
110°
120°
130°
140°
50°
40°
30°
20°
10°
0°

A43

AUSTRIA-HUNGARY
MONT.
SERB.
ROMANIA
BULGARIA
OTTOMAN EMPIRE
GREECE
Constantinople
Black Sea
Moscow
Dnieper
Volga
Samara
RUSSIAN
Omsk
Ob'
Irtysh
Cyprus (Br.)
Mediterranean Sea
Suez Canal
Cairo
Jerusalem
EGYPT
Euphrates
Tigris
Baghdad
Caspian Sea
Aral Sea
Lake Balkhash
TURKESTAN
Tashkent
Bukhara
Samarkand
TIEN SHAN
TARIM BA
TAKLIMAKAN DESERT
Tehran
PERSIA
KUWAIT
Persian Gulf
Kabul
AFGHANISTAN
KASHMIR
PUNJAB
ARABIA
BAHRAIN
QATAR
TRUCIAL OMAN
Red Sea
Mecca
BALUCHISTAN
Indus
SIND
RAJPUTANA
Delhi
Yamuna
HIMALAYA M
NEPAL
Gang
BEN
OMAN
ERITREA
HADRAMAUT
Aden (Br.)
FR. SOM.
BRITISH
ORISS
Bombay
HYDERABAD
Hyderabad
ABYSSINIA
BRITISH SOMALILAND
Arabian Sea
Goa (Port.)
MYSORE
MADRAS
Madras
ITALIAN SOMALILAND
Ceylon
Colombo
N
INDIAN OCEAN
British
French
Dutch
Italian
Portuguese
United States
0 200 400 600 800 Miles
0 200 400 600 800 1000 Kilometers
Copyright by Rand McNally & Co.
Lambert Azimuthal Equal Area Projection

A44

EMPIRE
Lena
Angara
Lake Baikal
Chita
Irkutsk
Amur
MANCHURIA
Vladivostok
Sakhalin
Hokkaido
Sea of Japan
Honshu
Tokyo
JAPANESE EMPIRE
MONGOLIA
INNER MONGOLIA
KOREA
Seoul
GOBI DESERT
Beijing
Lushun (Rus.)
Tianjin
Weihai (Br.)
Qingdao (Ger.)
Shikoku
Kyushu
Huang (Yellow)
Shanghai
Hangzhou
CHINESE EMPIRE
Wuhan
Ryukyu Islands (Japan)
PACIFIC OCEAN
(Yangtze)
Chang
Chongqing
BET
Fuzhou
Taiwan (Japan)
BHUTAN
ASSAM
Xi (West)
Canton (Guangzhou)
Hong Kong (Br.)
Macao (Port.)
Kwangchowan (Fr.)
Luzon
PHILIPPINE ISLANDS (U.S.)
Manila
NDIA
BURMA
ANNAM
Mekong
South China Sea
Rangoon
SIAM
FRENCH INDOCHINA
Bangkok
Saigon
Mindanao
Andaman Islands (Br.)
BRITISH NORTH BORNEO
BRUNEI
Nicobar Islands (Br.)
SARAWAK
Moluccas
MALAYA
Singapore
Borneo
Celebes
Sumatra
DUTCH EAST INDIES
TIMOR (Port.)
Batavia
Java

RAND McNALLY

A45

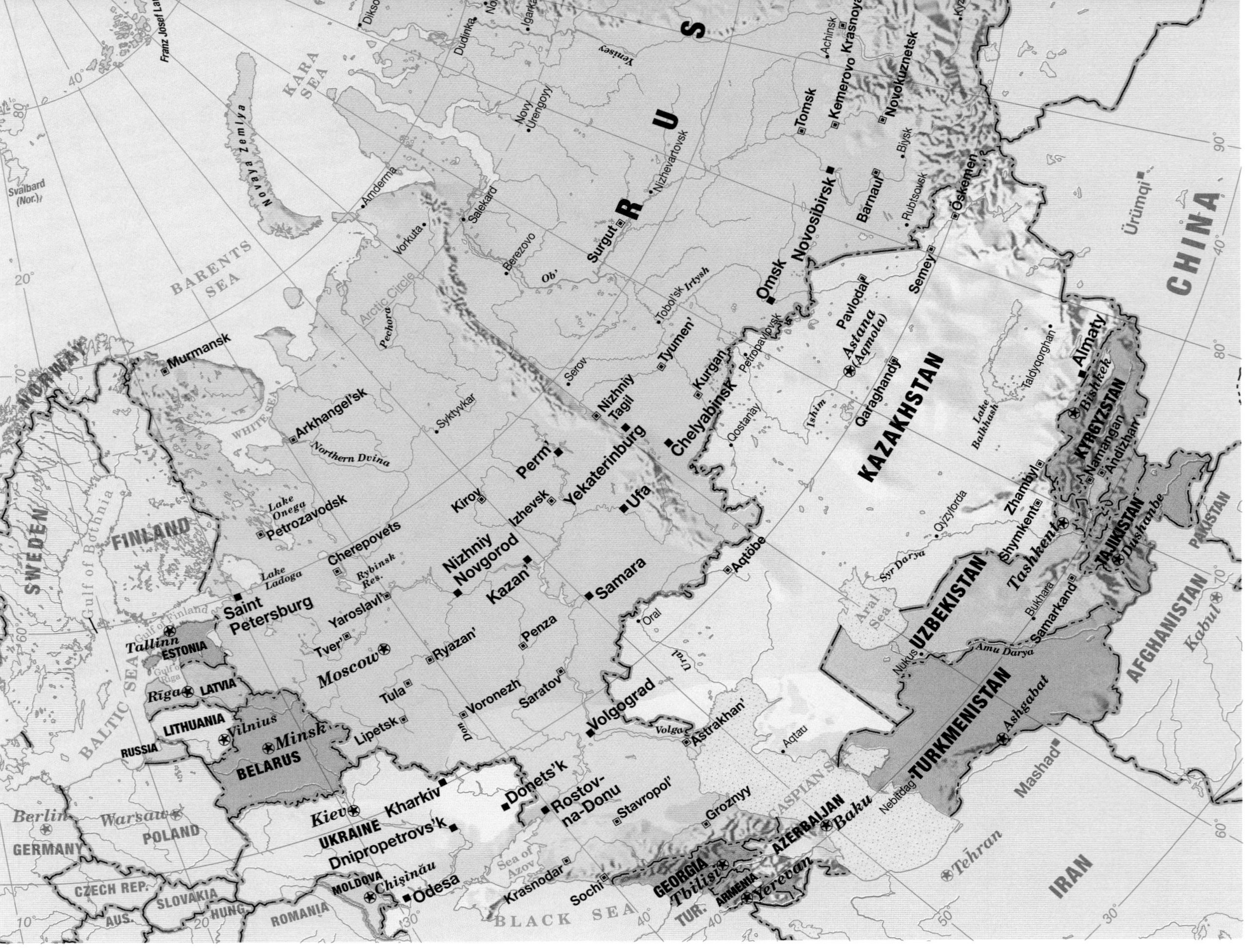
SWEDEN
NORWAY
FINLAND
Gulf of Bothnia
BALTIC SEA
Gulf of Finland
ESTONIA
Tallinn
LATVIA
Riga
LITHUANIA
Vilnius
RUSSIA
BELARUS
Minsk
POLAND
Warsaw
GERMANY
Berlin
CZECH REP.
SLOVAKIA
AUS.
HUNG.
ROMANIA
MOLDOVA
Chişinău
UKRAINE
Kiev
Kharkiv
Dnipropetrovs'k
Odesa
Donets'k
Sea of Azov
BLACK SEA
Krasnodar
Sochi
GEORGIA
Tbilisi
ARMENIA
Yerevan
TUR.
AZERBAIJAN
Baku
CASPIAN SEA
Saint Petersburg
Lake Ladoga
Lake Onega
Petrozavodsk
Murmansk
BARENTS SEA
WHITE SEA
Arkhangel'sk
Northern Dvina
Cherepovets
Rybinsk Res.
Yaroslavl'
Tver'
Moscow
Tula
Lipetsk
Ryazan'
Voronezh
Don
Nizhniy Novgorod
Kazan'
Kirov
Syktyvkar
Penza
Saratov
Samara
Volgograd
Rostov-na-Donu
Stavropol'
Groznyy
Astrakhan'
Volga
Ural
Oral
Aqtöbe
Izhevsk
Perm'
Ufa
Yekaterinburg
Chelyabinsk
Nizhniy Tagil
Serov
Tyumen'
Kurgan
Tobol'sk
Irtysh
Pechora
Arctic Circle
Vorkuta
Amderma
Novaya Zemlya
KARA SEA
Franz Josef Land
Svalbard (Nor.)
Salekhard
Berezovo
Ob'
Surgut
Nizhnevartovsk
Novy Urengoy
Dudinka
Igarka
Dikson
Yenisey
RUS
Qostanay
Petropavlovsk
Omsk
Novosibirsk
Tomsk
Kemerovo
Achinsk
Krasnoyarsk
Barnaul
Novokuznetsk
Biysk
Rubtsovsk
Pavlodar
Ishim
Astana (Aqmola)
Qaraghandy
Semey
Öskemen
KAZAKHSTAN
Lake Balkhash
Taldyqorghan
Almaty
Aral Sea
Syr Darya
Qyzylorda
Aqtau
Nebitdag
Nukus
UZBEKISTAN
TURKMENISTAN
Ashgabat
Amu Darya
Bukhara
Samarkand
Tashkent
Shymkent
Zhambyl
KYRGYZSTAN
Bishkek
Namangan
Andizhan
TAJIKISTAN
Dushanbe
IRAN
Tehran
Mashad
AFGHANISTAN
Kabul
PAKISTAN
CHINA
Ürümqi

A46

UNITED STATES
Bering Strait
Saint Lawrence Island
Wrangell Island
ARCTIC OCEAN
EAST SIBERIAN SEA
BERING SEA
New Siberian Islands
Novaya Sibir Island
Kotelny Island
LAPTEV SEA
Anadyr'
Srednekolymsk
Indigirka
Tiksi
Kolyma
Seymchan
Verkhoyansk
Komandorskiye Islands
Ust'-Kamchatsk
Kamchatka Peninsula
Petropavlovsk-Kamchatskiy
Zhigansk
Lena
Magadan
Vilyuysk
Yakutsk
Tura
Lower Tunguska
Aldan
SEA OF OKHOTSK
S I A
Olëkminsk
Okha
Angara
Bodaybo
Nikolayevsk-na-Amure
Sakhalin
Ust'-Kut
Bratsk
Kuril Islands
Zeya
Amur
Komsomol'sk-na-Amure
Yuzhno-Sakhalinsk
Svobodnyy
Blagoveshchensk
Cheremkhovo
Lake Baikal
Khabarovsk
La Perouse Strait
Angarsk
Irkutsk
Chita
Ulan-Ude
Birobidzhan
Hokkaidō
JAPAN
PACIFIC OCEAN
Ulan Bator
Harbin
Vladivostok
Nakhodka
MONGOLIA
N
Shenyang
NORTH KOREA
P'yŏngyang
SEA OF JAPAN
National Capital
City over 1,000,000 population
City of 250,000 to 1,000,000 population
City under 250,000 population
0 100 200 300 400 500 Miles
0 200 400 600 800 Kilometers
Copyright by Rand McNally & Co.
Lambert Azimuthal Equal Area Projection
80° 180° 170° 70° 160° 60° 140° 120° 100° 50° 40° 150° 110° 120° 130° 140°

A47

"Everyone has the right to take part in the government of his [or her] country."

Universal Declaration of Human Rights
United Nations, 1948

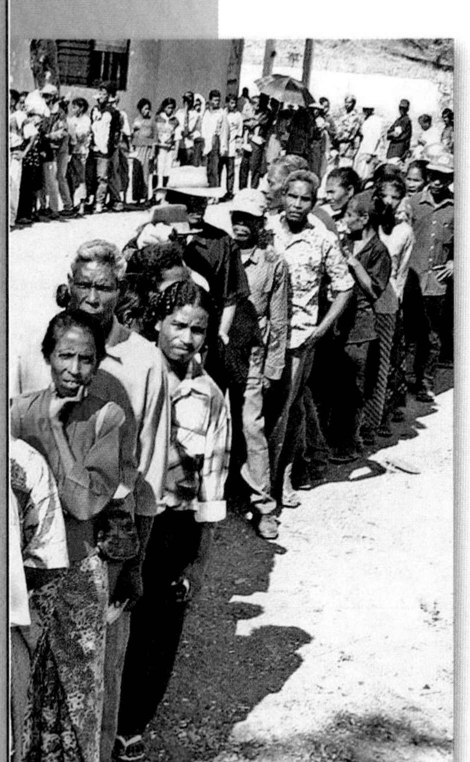

In 2001, citizens of one of the newest nations in the world—East Timor in Southeast Asia—cast ballots to establish a democratic government. The East Timorese had been waiting a long time for that day. After more than 400 years of Portuguese domination, and 25 years under military occupation by Indonesia, they finally had a free land.

As Americans, we applaud as other countries embrace democracy. Our nation's political ideals as expressed in our most treasured political documents—the Declaration of Independence and the Constitution—have inspired people around the world to adopt democratic forms of government. In the last two decades, democratic revolutions have transformed many countries. Additional millions of people now live under democratic rule.

As you read this book, you will learn about the people and events that have shaped our modern world. You will also follow the centuries-long struggle for individual freedom. To help understand today's world, we need to understand why democracy matters. We need to know how the idea of democracy has become a reality for so many people in the world, and a goal for others.

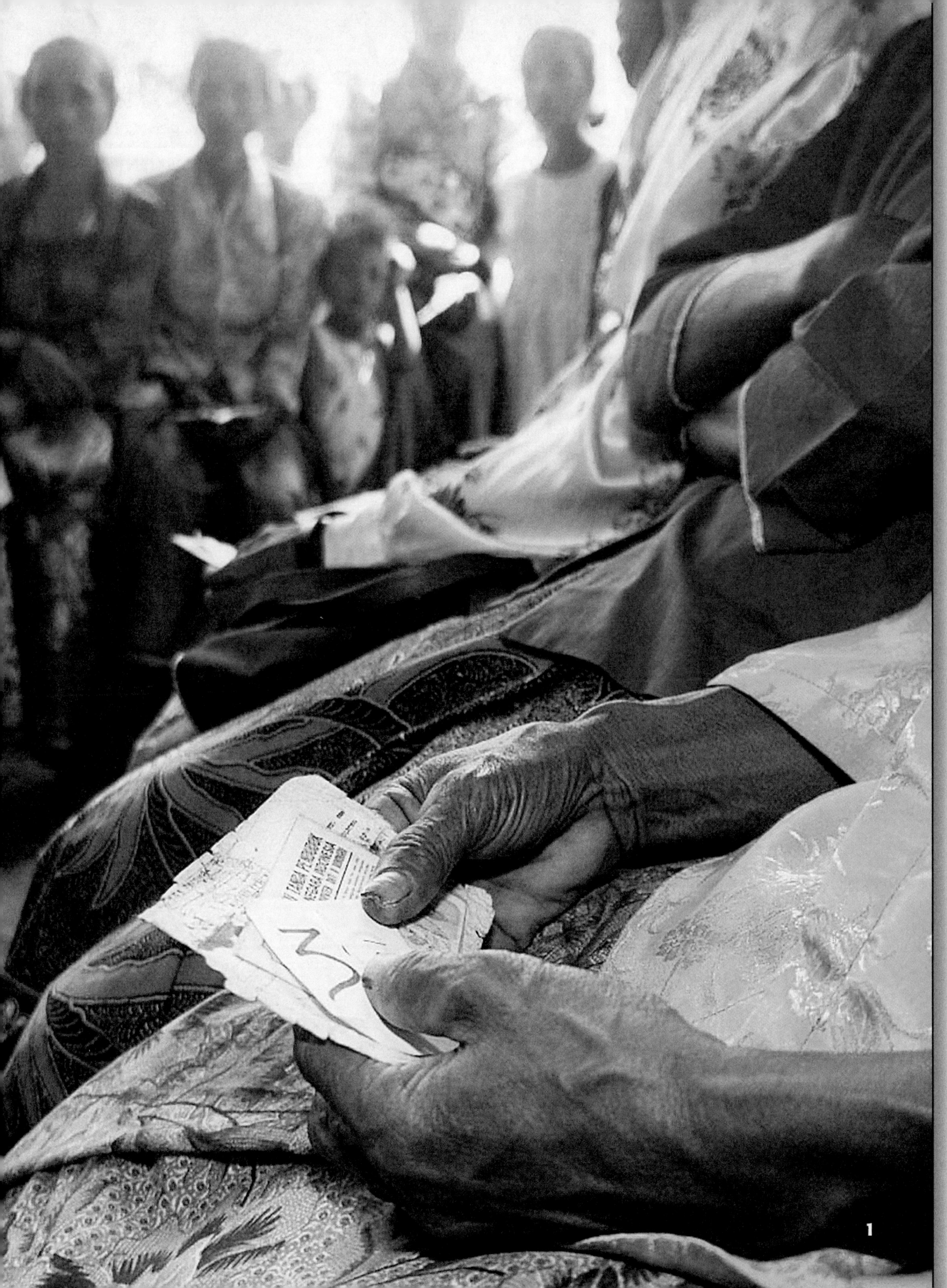

PROLOGUE PLANNING GUIDE

The Rise of Democratic Ideas

CHAPTER RESOURCES	COPYMASTERS	ASSESSMENT
CHAPTER OVERVIEW From ancient Greece to modern East Timor, governments have struggled over issues of power, fairness, balance, and representation.	**Chapters in Brief** (in English and Spanish) **Block Schedule Pacing Guide**	**Prologue Assessment,** pp. 30–31 **Formal Assessment** • Chapter Tests, Forms A, B, and C, pp. 9–20 **Test Generator** **Integrated Assessment Book** **Online Test Practice**
SECTION 1 **The Legacy of Ancient Greece and Rome** pp. 5–11 **OBJECTIVE** Compare and contrast the direct democracy of Athens with the republican government of Rome.	**In-Depth Resources: Unit 1** • Guided Reading, p. 1 • Skillbuilder Practice: Drawing Conclusions, p. 5 • Geography Application: The Roads of the Roman Empire, p. 6 • Primary Source: from *Politics,* p. 8 • History Makers: Justinian I, p. 15 **Reading Study Guide,** p. 5	**Section 1 Assessment,** p. 11 **Formal Assessment** • Section Quiz, p. 5
SECTION 2 **Judeo-Christian Tradition** pp. 12–17 **OBJECTIVE** Summarize how ideas from Judaism, Christianity, and Islam helped shape democratic traditions.	**In-Depth Resources: Unit 1** • Guided Reading, p. 2 • Primary Source: The Ten Commandments, p. 9 **Reading Study Guide,** p. 7	**Section 2 Assessment,** p. 17 **Formal Assessment** • Section Quiz, p. 6
SECTION 3 **Democracy Develops in England** pp. 18–23 **OBJECTIVE** Trace the development of democratic institutions that limited the power of the English monarchy.	**In-Depth Resources: Unit 1** • Guided Reading, p. 3 • Primary Source: from the Magna Carta, p. 10 • Literature: from *Here Be Dragons,* p. 12 • Connections Across Time and Cultures: New Beginnings for Democracy, p. 17 **Reading Study Guide,** p. 9	**Section 3 Assessment,** p. 23 **Formal Assessment** • Section Quiz, p. 7
SECTION 4 **The Enlightenment and Democratic Revolutions** pp. 24–29 **OBJECTIVE** Explain how Enlightenment ideas helped to bring about the American and French revolutions.	**In-Depth Resources: Unit 1** • Guided Reading, p. 4 • Primary Source: from the Iroquois Constitution, p. 11 • Literature: from *1776,* p. 13 • History Makers: John Locke, p. 16 • Connections Across Time and Cultures: New Beginnings for Democracy, p. 17 **Reading Study Guide,** p. 11	**Section 4 Assessment,** p. 29 **Formal Assessment** • Section Quiz, p. 8

INTEGRATED TECHNOLOGY

- eEdition Plus Online
- EasyPlanner Plus Online
- eTest Plus Online

 **Audio CDs**
- Reading Study Guides

 **CD-ROMs**
- eEdition
- Power Presentations
- EasyPlanner
- Electronic Library of Primary Sources
- Test Generator

 **eEdition CD-ROM**

 **World Art and Cultures Transparencies**
- AT12 *The Forum*

Electronic Library of Primary Sources
- Wall Inscriptions from Pompeii, A.D. 79

 **classzone.com**

eEdition CD-ROM

 **Electronic Library of Primary Sources**
- from the Book of Exodus in the Bible, about 900 B.C.

 **classzone.com**

 **eEdition CD-ROM**

 **Electronic Library of Primary Sources**
- "The Restoration of Charles II"

 **classzone.com**

 **eEdition CD-ROM**

 **World Art and Cultures Transparencies**
- AT50 *Portrait of Marie Antoinette and Her Children*

Electronic Library of Primary Sources
- Destruction of the Berlin Wall

 **classzone.com**

OVERVIEW OF CALIFORNIA RESOURCES

	Section 1	Section 2	Section 3	Section 4
California Reading Toolkit	p. L5	p. L6	p. L7	p. L8
California Modified Lesson Plans for English Learners	p. 3	p. 7	p. 9	p. 11
California Daily Standards Practice Transparencies	TTA	TTB	TTC	TTD
California Standards Enrichment Workbook	pp. 19–20	pp. 17–18	pp. 17–18, 25–26	pp. 23–24, 29–30, 105–106
California Standards Planner and Lesson Plans	p. L1	p. L3	p. L5	p. L7
California Online Test Practice	classzone.com	classzone.com	classzone.com	classzone.com
California Test Generator CD-ROM				
California Easy Planner CD-ROM				
California eEdition CD-ROM				

Chart Key:

 Pupil's Edition

 Teacher's Edition

 Overhead Transparency

Block Scheduling

 Copymaster

 Audio Library

 CD-ROM

 Internet

Video

NO TIME?

If you do not have time to teach this chapter in full, assign the **Chapter in Brief** (also available in Spanish).

Previewing Resources for Differentiated Instruction

ENGLISH LEARNERS: Resources in Spanish

In-Depth Resources in Spanish

- Guided Reading **A**
- Skillbuilder Practice: Drawing Conclusions
- Geography Application: The Roads of the Roman Empire **B**

Chapters in Brief

Reading Study Guide C

Reading Study Guide Audio CD

Test Generator CD-ROM

- Chapter Test, Forms A, B, and C

Plus

Modified Lesson Plans for English Learners

Multi-Language Glossary of Social Studies Terms

A

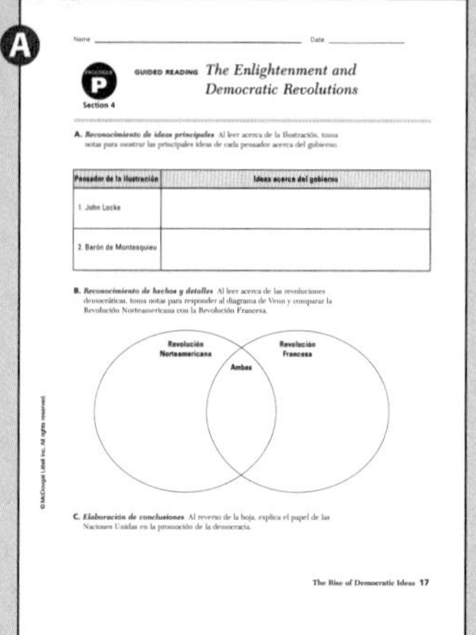

GUIDED READING The Enlightenment and Democratic Revolutions
Section 4
Revolución Norteamericana
Ambas
Revolución Francesa
The Rise of Democratic Ideas 17

B

STRUGGLING READERS

In-Depth Resources: Unit 1

- Guided Reading **A**
- Skillbuilder Practice: Drawing Conclusions **B**
- Geography Application: The Roads of the Roman Empire

Chapters in Brief

Reading Study Guide C

Reading Study Guide Audio CD

Formal Assessment

- Chapter Test, Form A

Plus

Reading Toolkit

A

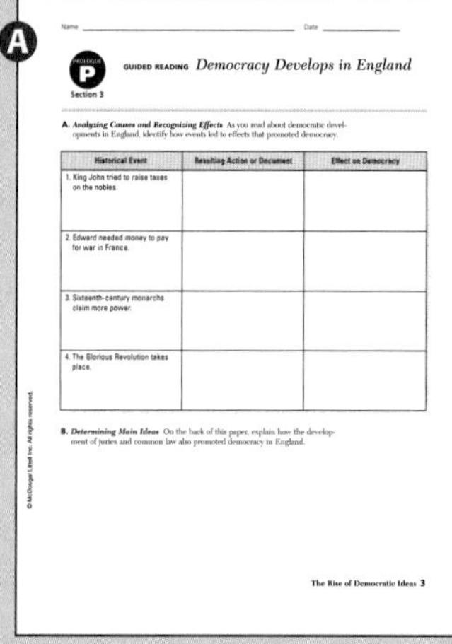

GUIDED READING Democracy Develops in England
Section 3
Historical Event
Resulting Action or Document
Effect on Democracy
1. King John tried to raise taxes on the nobles.
2. Edward needed money to pay for war in France.
3. Sixteenth-century monarchs claim more power.
4. The Glorious Revolution takes place.
The Rise of Democratic Ideas 3

B

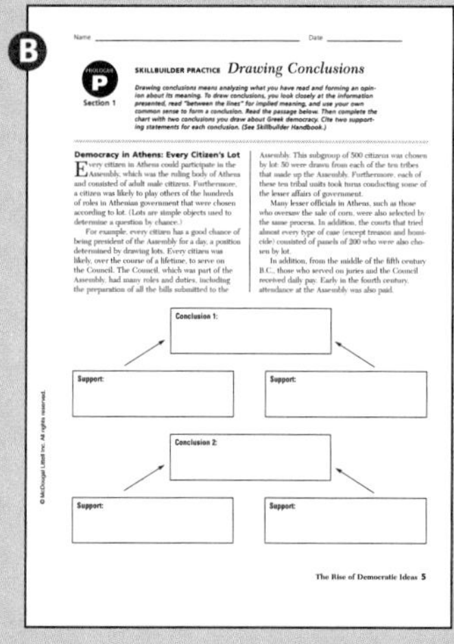

GIFTED AND TALENTED STUDENTS

In-Depth Resources: Unit 1

- Primary Sources: from *Politics;* from The Ten Commandments **A**; from the Magna Carta; from the Iroquois Constitution
- History Makers: Justinian I; John Locke
- Literature: from *Here Be Dragons;* from *1776* **B**
- Connections Across Time and Cultures: New Beginnings for Democracy

Electronic Library of Primary Sources

- Wall Inscriptions from Pompeii, A.D. 79 **C**
- from the Book of Exodus in the Bible, about 900 B.C.
- "The Restoration of Charles II"
- Destruction of the Berlin Wall

Formal Assessment

- Chapter Test, Form C

A

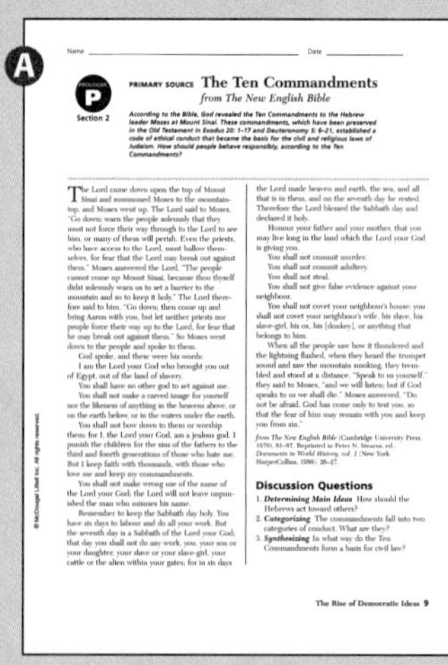

B

INTEGRATED TECHNOLOGY

C

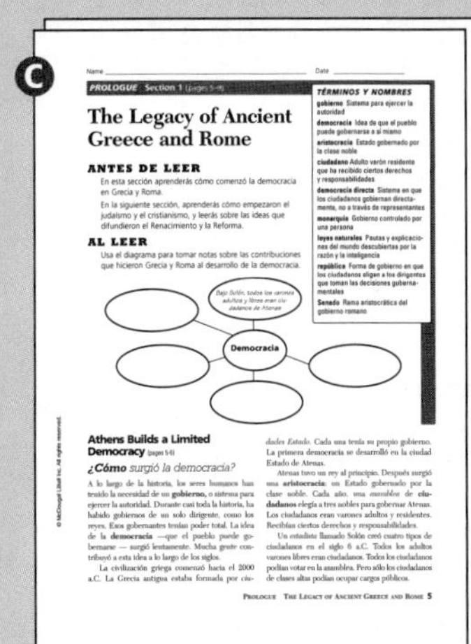

PROLOGUE Section 1

The Legacy of Ancient Greece and Rome

ANTES DE LEER

AL LEER

Democracia

Athens Builds a Limited Democracy

¿Cómo surgió la democracia?

TÉRMINOS Y NOMBRES

PROLOGUE THE LEGACY OF ANCIENT GREECE AND ROME 5

Activities in the Teacher's Edition for English Learners

- Summarizing the Evolution of Greek Democracy, p. 7
- Judaism, Christianity, and Islam, p. 15
- Paraphrasing a Passage, p. 20
- Debating British Control of the American Colonies, p. 26

C

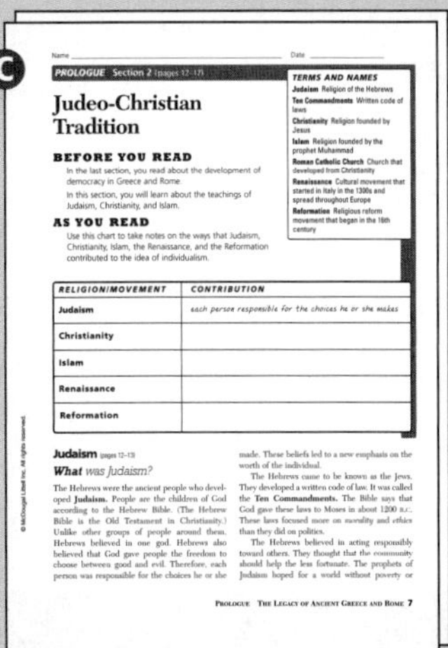

PROLOGUE Section 2

Judeo-Christian Tradition

BEFORE YOU READ

AS YOU READ

TERMS AND NAMES

RELIGION/MOVEMENT	CONTRIBUTION
Judaism	each person responsible for the choices he or she makes
Christianity	
Islam	
Renaissance	
Reformation	

Judaism

What was Judaism?

PROLOGUE THE LEGACY OF ANCIENT GREECE AND ROME 7

Activities in the Teacher's Edition for Struggling Readers

- Using Headers to Understand the Text, p. 8
- Key Ideas of the Renaissance and Reformation, p. 16
- "Who Am I?", p. 22
- Designing a French Revolution Trivia Game, p. 27

C

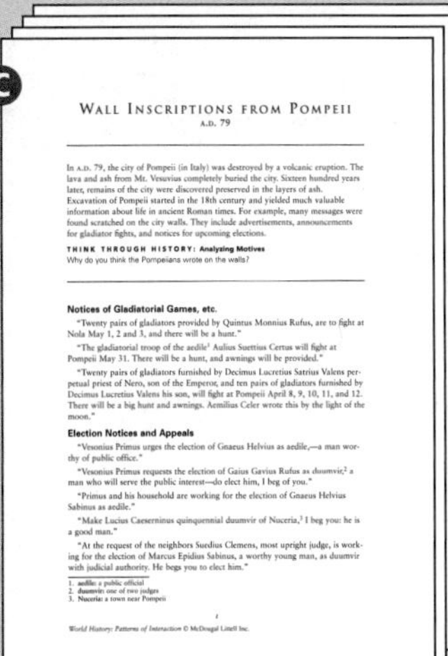

WALL INSCRIPTIONS FROM POMPEII

A.D. 79

THINK THROUGH HISTORY: Analyzing Motives

Notices of Gladiatorial Games, etc.

Election Notices and Appeals

Activities in the Teacher's Edition for Gifted and Talented Students

- Patricians and Plebeians, p. 10
- Mapping Paul's Travels, p. 14
- Creating a Skit About the Magna Carta, p. 19
- Designing a Travel Brochure for a World Heritage Site, p. 28

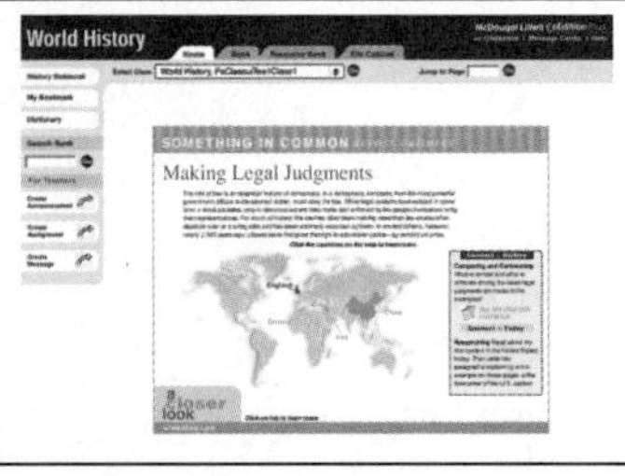

eEdition

- Interactive Visuals
- Interactive Maps
- Interactive Primary Sources

classzone.com

- Research Links
- Internet Activities
- Primary Sources
- Chapter Quiz
- Current Events

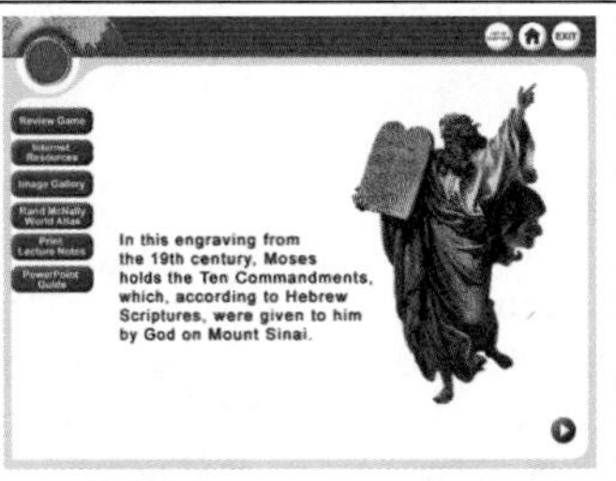

Power Presentations CD-ROM

- Lecture Notes
- Image Gallery
- Chapter Review Game

A

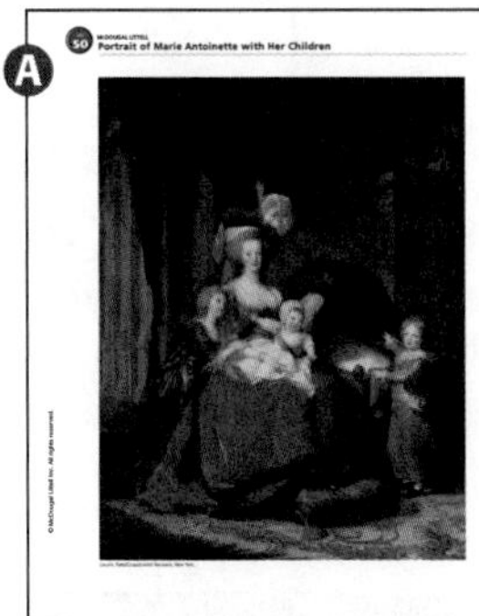

World Art and Cultures Transparencies

- AT12 The Forum
- AT50 *Portrait of Marie Antoinette and Her Children* A

Test Generator CD-ROM

EasyPlanner CD-ROM

Voices from the Past Audio CD

Online Test Practice

Electronic Library of Primary Sources

PROLOGUE • OBJECTIVE

Study the evolution of democracy, analyzing how it has changed since it began in ancient Greece.

Previewing Main Ideas

Ask students to express their opinions about why democracy did not become more pervasive earlier in history and why there are still countries today that have not adopted democratic systems of government. Encourage students to consider a variety of factors—for example, a society's economic practices, religious beliefs, or educational values.

Accessing Prior Knowledge

Discuss what students already know about the rise of democratic ideas. Have them look at the map, and ask how democratic ideas originating in the Mediterranean region in the sixth century B.C. could possibly have an influence today. *(Possible Answer: People of all times and places have wanted freedom and fair treatment.)*

Geography *Answers*

POWER AND AUTHORITY *Possible Answers:* 509 B.C., Romans choose representative government; 1215, the Magna Carta limits English monarchy; 1690, John Locke proposes government by the consent of the governed; 1787, the U.S. Constitution is written.

REVOLUTION One hundred years separate the two events.

CULTURAL INTERACTION Athens and Rome were very small compared with later sites.

PROLOGUE P

The Rise of Democratic Ideas

Previewing Main Ideas

POWER AND AUTHORITY People living in groups recognize the need for government, or a system for exercising authority. For much of history, people lived under authoritarian rulers, such as kings. With the rise of democratic ideas, people came to demand a role in governing themselves.

Geography *Study the time line. Identify two events that illustrate a move toward democratic rule.*

REVOLUTION In the Glorious Revolution, the English established the right to limit a ruler's power. This Revolution and Enlightenment ideas sparked a rebellion of the American colonies against British rule. In turn, the American Revolution helped spur the French Revolution.

Geography *Study the map key. How many years separate the English Bill of Rights from the establishment of democracy in the United States?*

CULTURAL INTERACTION Democratic ideas developed first in ancient Athens and later in Rome. They then spread to England and England's American colonies. Eventually, democratic movements sprang up throughout the world, inspired by the U.S. Constitution.

Geography *What can be said about the size of the early areas where democracy developed as compared to later sites?*

INTEGRATED TECHNOLOGY

eEdition
- Interactive Maps
- Interactive Visuals
- Interactive Primary Sources

VIDEO *Patterns of Interaction: The Rise of the Persians and the Inca*

INTERNET RESOURCES
Go to classzone.com for:
- Research Links
- Internet Activities
- Primary Sources
- Chapter Quiz
- Maps
- Test Practice
- Current Events

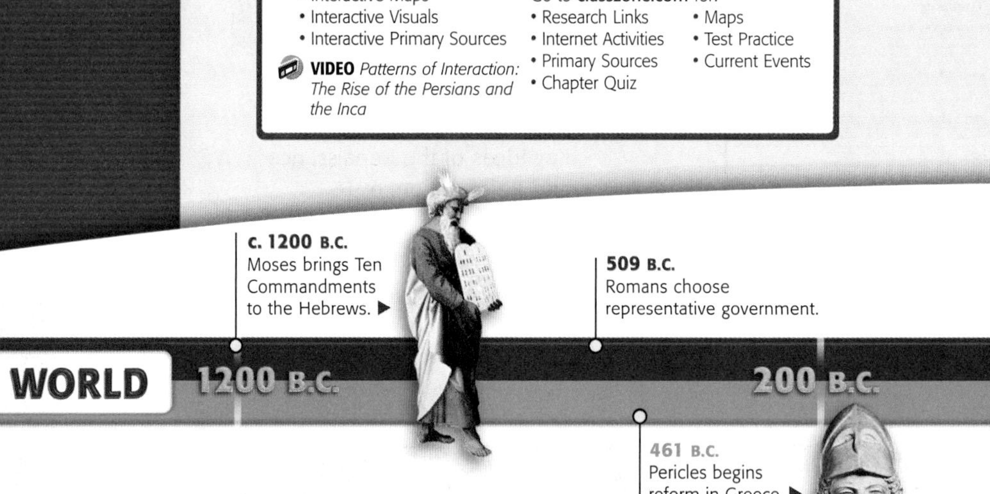

c. 1200 B.C.
Moses brings Ten Commandments to the Hebrews.
509 B.C.
Romans choose representative government.
WORLD
1200 B.C.
200 B.C.
461 B.C.
Pericles begins reform in Greece.

TIME LINE DISCUSSION

Point out that the time line highlights some of the major achievements in creating democratic forms of government.

1. To what group was the Ten Commandments originally given? *(the Hebrews)*
2. How much time passed between the adoption of a representative form of government in Rome and Pericles' initiation of reforms in ancient Greece? *(48 years)*
3. What document placed limits on English monarchs? *(the Magna Carta)*
4. Which is the more likely influence on the U.S. Constitution: John Locke's theory of government or the Declaration of the Rights of Man? *(John Locke's theory of government; the Declaration of the Rights of Man came later)*
5. How much time separates the Ten Commandments and the Justinian Code? *(more than 1,700 years)*
6. In which century did the United States adopt its Constitution? *(the 18th century)*

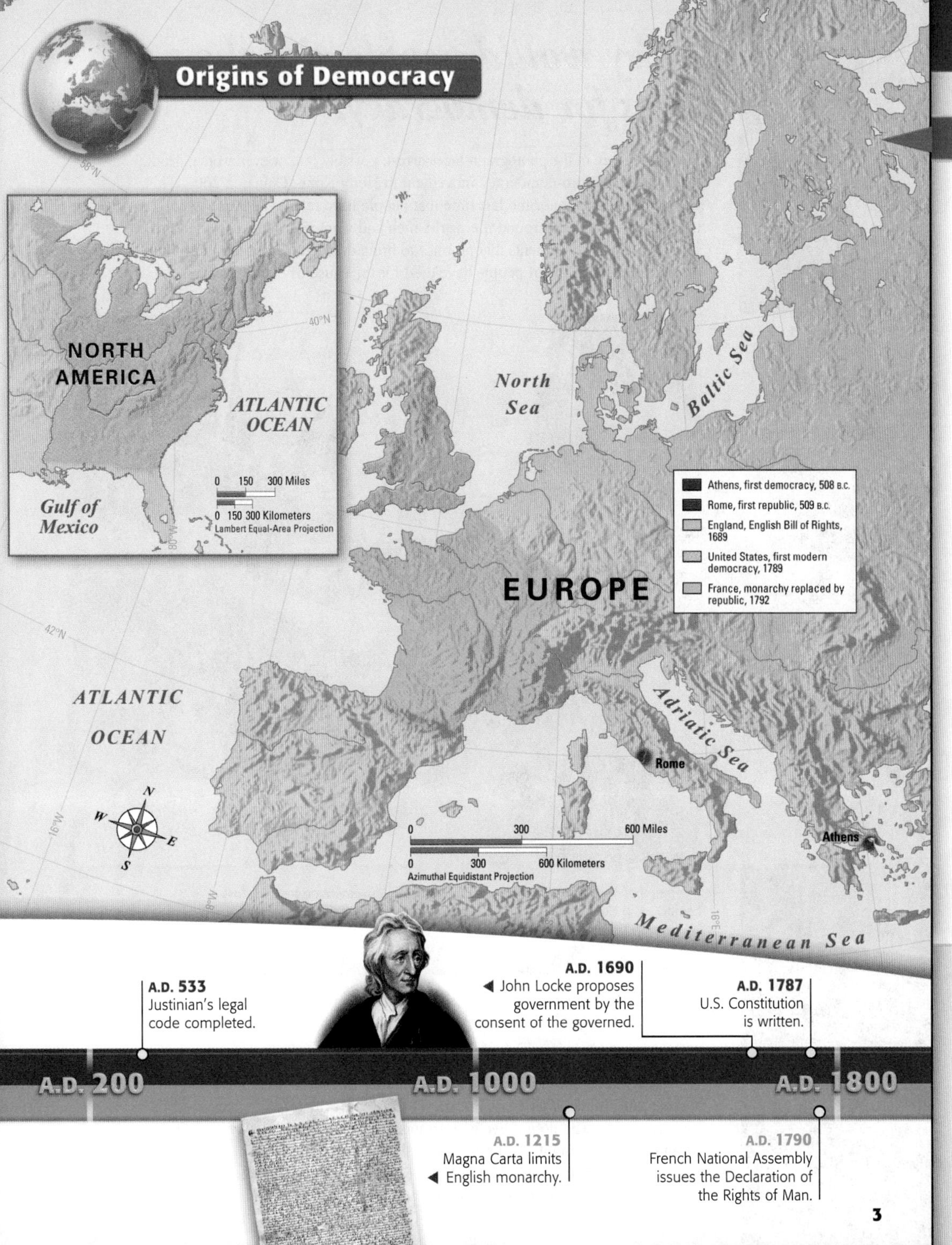

History from Visuals

Interpreting the Map

Democratic ideas first arose in Greece. Greece is a mountainous country that, in ancient times, was divided into city-states. Each city-state was independent and had a fairly small population—about 20,000 people. Discuss how these factors might have helped contribute to the rise of democracy in ancient Greece. *(Possible Answer: Small size, isolation, and independence of political units might have made it easy for people to know and trust one another, which might spur democratic ideas.)*

Extension Ask students to further explore the relationship of population size to democracy by studying the ratio of population to representation in the U.S. House of Representatives. Provide students with a copy of *Federalist Paper* No. 55, and ask what ratio is discussed by James Madison. Then ask students to follow up by using the library or the Internet to find out what the ratio is today. *(Madison discussed a ratio of one representative for 30,000 people. In September 2003, the ratio was one representative for approximately 670,000.)*

RECOMMENDED RESOURCES

Books for the Teacher

Almond, Mark. ***Revolution: 500 Years of Struggle for Change.*** New York: De Agostini, 1996. Account of 27 revolutions.

Aston, Margaret, ed. ***The Panorama of the Renaissance.*** New York: Abrams, 1996.

Barber, James David. ***The Book of Democracy.*** Englewood Cliffs, NJ: Prentice Hall, 1995.

Books for the Student

Hardy, W. G. ***The Greek and Roman World.*** Cambridge, MA: Schenkman, 1970.

Buranelli, Nan. ***The Renaissance.*** Trans. Michel Pierre. Morristown, NJ: Silver Burdett, 1987.

Swisher, Clarice. ***The Glorious Revolution.*** San Diego: Lucent, 1996. Explains how the English Parliament gained supremacy over the monarchy.

Videos and Software

Athenian Democracy. VHS. Britannica, 1993. 800-554-9862. Fifteen-minute running time.

The Age of Enlightenment. VHS. Cambridge Social Studies, 1991. 800-468-4227.

French Revolution. CD-ROM. Educational Software Institute, 800-955-5570.

Renaissance and Reformation. CD-ROM. Queue, 1994. 800-232-2224.

Interact *with* History

Objectives

- Help students understand the sacrifices people have made for democracy.
- Ask students to consider what benefits might merit such sacrifices.

EXAMINING *the* ISSUES

Possible Answers

- Students may mention freedom of speech, freedom of religion, and the right to privacy as freedoms associated with democracy. These freedoms allow people to express themselves and to live in harmony with their ideals, even if those ideals differ from others'.
- Voting, holding or attending protests, and contacting newspapers or members of government are all ways to bring democracy into a person's life. Students who want to learn more about the struggle for democracy may wish to research organizations such as Amnesty International or Human Rights Watch, which work to protect and defend human rights.

Discussion

Discuss the USA Patriot Act, passed by Congress after the attacks of September 11, 2001. Encourage students to learn more about the act's provisions and to form an opinion about how the act might affect their civil liberties. *(Some students may decide that the act is necessary to protect the lives and liberty of the American people from a global terrorist network, as the government has argued. Other students may decide that the act goes too far and may even violate the Constitution, as some civil liberties organizations have contended.)*

Interact *with* History

Why would people risk their lives for democracy?

The young man in the photograph faces arrest, possibly jail, or even worse, death for supporting a pro-democracy movement in Hong Kong, China, in 2002. This was neither the first nor the last time that people have rebelled against tyranny. In countless incidents around the world, men and women have taken a stand to support political movements that promise to bring democracy to their lands. Over the centuries, millions of people have died for the cause of democracy.

▲ A member of a political group called the April 5th Movement protests the loss of democracy in Hong Kong.

EXAMINING *the* ISSUES

- **How do the personal freedoms associated with democracy affect the quality of a person's life?**
- **How can people bring democracy into their lives?**

Discuss these questions with your classmates. In your discussion, first think about what you value most in life, and why. Then imagine what people who do not live in a democratic country might value and what they might do to protect or gain those things they value.

As you read about the rise of democratic ideas in this prologue, think about how these ideas are expressed today.

WHY STUDY THE RISE OF DEMOCRATIC IDEAS?

- Understanding what conditions must be present for a democracy to thrive is vital now that the United States has undertaken to bring democratic practices and institutions to other nations, such as Afghanistan and Iraq.
- A familiarity with the contributions that religions have made to the democratic tradition may help in the search for a solution to problems in the Middle East.
- An understanding of democracy is important for U.S. citizens. Without the active participation of a democracy's citizenry, the future of that democracy becomes uncertain. As Thomas Jefferson warned, "Lethargy [is] the forerunner of death to the public liberty."
- The nations of the world are becoming more interconnected. An increasing number of international institutions—such as the United Nations, the World Trade Organization, and the International Criminal Court—oversee these new relationships. A knowledge of the democratic tradition is crucial for those who want to ensure that these institutions are operated democratically.

Young girl winning chariot race. Engraving from red-figure Greek vase.

The Propylaea and the Parthenon, Athens, Greece

1

The Legacy of Ancient Greece and Rome

MAIN IDEA	WHY IT MATTERS NOW	TERMS & NAMES
POWER AND AUTHORITY The Greeks developed democracy, and the Romans added representative government.	Representation and citizen participation are important features of democratic governments around the world.	• government • monarchy • aristocracy • oligarchy • democracy • direct democracy • republic • senate

SETTING THE STAGE Throughout history, people have recognized the need for a system for exercising authority and control in their society. Small bands of people often did not need a formal organization. Councils of elders, for example, worked together to control a group. However, most people in larger groups lived under rulers, such as chieftains, kings, or pharaohs, who often had total power. Over the course of thousands of years, people began to believe that even in large groups they could govern themselves without a powerful ruler.

CALIFORNIA STANDARDS

10.1.2 Trace the development of the Western political ideas of the rule of law and illegitimacy of tyranny, using selections from Plato's *Republic* and Aristotle's *Politics*.

CST 1 Students compare the present with the past, evaluating the consequences of past events and decisions and determining the lessons that were learned.

Athens Builds a Limited Democracy

About 2000 B.C., the Greeks established cities in the small fertile valleys along Greece's rocky coast. Each city-state had its own **government**, a system for controlling the society.

The Greek city-states adopted many styles of government. In some, a single person called a king or monarch ruled in a government called a **monarchy**. Others adopted an **aristocracy** (AR•uh•STAHK• ruh•see), a government ruled by a small group of noble, land-owning families. Later, as trade expanded, a new class of wealthy merchants emerged in some cities. Sometimes these groups took power or shared it with the nobility. They formed an **oligarchy**, a government ruled by a few powerful people.

Ancient Greek civilization claims the distinction of developing the first democracy in a country. In fact, the word **democracy**, meaning "rule of the people," comes from the Greek words *demos,* meaning "people," and *kratos,* meaning "power."

Building Democracy Athens was the largest and most powerful city-state to emerge in Greece. In Athens, citizens participated in governmental decision making. Citizens were adult male residents who enjoyed certain rights and responsibilities. Each year, an assembly of citizens elected three nobles to rule the city-state. After a year of service, the nobles became part of a larger council of advisers.

Around 600 B.C., Athens suffered severe economic problems. In order to pay their debts, poor farmers pledged part of their crops to wealthy landowners. They later pledged their land. Then, they sold themselves into slavery and were not able to leave the land. Eventually, a strong leader stepped in to deal with the political and economic crisis.

TAKING NOTES

Determining Main Ideas
Use a web diagram to record the contributions of Greece and Rome to democracy.

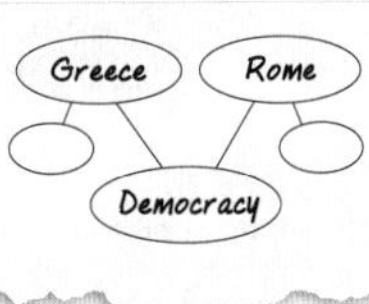

LESSON PLAN

OBJECTIVES

- Identify political systems of Athens.
- Trace changes in Greek democracy and the flowering of Greek philosophy.
- Compare democracy in Athens with that under the Roman Republic.
- Describe the influence of Roman law.

1 FOCUS & MOTIVATE

Ask students if they can think of English words that reflect the influence of ancient Greece or Rome on U.S. democracy. *(Possible Answer: U.S. Senate named after legislative body of Roman Republic)*

2 INSTRUCT

Athens Builds a Limited Democracy

10.1.2

Critical Thinking

- Why was the situation in 600 B.C. a crisis? *(Farmers didn't want to sell themselves into slavery; they probably would have supported a revolution or a civil war.)*

CALIFORNIA RESOURCES
California Reading Toolkit, p. L5
California Modified Lesson Plans for English Learners, p. 3
California Daily Standards Practice Transparencies, TTA
California Standards Enrichment Workbook, pp. 19–20
California Standards Planner and Lesson Plans, p. L1
California Online Test Practice
California Test Generator CD-ROM
California Easy Planner CD-ROM
California eEdition CD-ROM

SECTION 1 PROGRAM RESOURCES

ALL STUDENTS

In-Depth Resources: Unit 1
- Guided Reading, p. 1
- Skillbuilder Practice: Drawing Conclusions, p. 5
- History Makers: Justinian I, p. 15
- Geography Application, p. 6

Formal Assessment
- Section Quiz, p. 5

ENGLISH LEARNERS

In-Depth Resources in Spanish
- Guided Reading, p. 11
- Skillbuilder Practice: Drawing Conclusions, p. 15
- Geography Application, p. 16

Reading Study Guide (Spanish), p. 5
Reading Study Guide Audio CD (Spanish)

STRUGGLING READERS

In-Depth Resources: Unit 1
- Guided Reading, p. 1
- Skillbuilder Practice: Drawing Conclusions, p. 5
- Geography Application, p. 6

Reading Study Guide, p. 5
Reading Study Guide Audio CD

GIFTED AND TALENTED STUDENTS

In-Depth Resources: Unit 1
- Primary Source: from *Politics,* p. 8

INTEGRATED TECHNOLOGY

eEdition CD-ROM
Voices from the Past Audio CD
Power Presentations CD-ROM
World Art and Cultures Transparencies
- AT12 *The Forum*

Electronic Library of Primary Sources
- "Wall Inscriptions from Pompeii," A.D. 79

classzone.com

Analyzing Key Concepts

OBJECTIVE

- Identify the major functions and forms of government.

INSTRUCT

Explain that the name of a country's government is not always a reliable indicator of social conditions. For example, the United Kingdom has a constitutional monarchy. The popular connotations of monarchy may mislead people into thinking that the United Kingdom is undemocratic. Communist East Germany was officially known as the German Democratic Republic (GDR), yet the GDR's citizens were denied many of the freedoms one normally associates with democratic forms of government.

More About . . .

"Natural Aristocracy"

The American statesman Thomas Jefferson wrote that the best government will be made up of a "natural aristocracy," based on virtue and talent, rather than a "tinsel aristocracy," based on wealth and birth.

More About . . .

The Igbo People

Older people were accorded great respect in Igbo villages. The village council was traditionally made up of all men between ages 65 and 83. Men between the ages of 30 and 50 were considered "small boys"; only rarely were they involved in important decisions for the village. Men did not retire from the village council until they were in their eighties. Even then, they served as advisers to the council.

> Analyzing Key Concepts

Government

CALIFORNIA STANDARDS
10.1.1, REP 4

Every society must create ways to regulate the behaviors of its members. Government consists of the people and institutions with the authority to establish and enforce rules for society. The rules are designed to keep order within the society, to promote the behaviors that the society approves of, and to protect the society from outside dangers. The government has the authority to administer punishments if the rules are broken. Different societies have forms of government that may feature different types of leaders, lawmakers, and enforcers, such as police or the military.

Major Forms of Government

Monarchy	Aristocracy
• State ruled by a king • Rule is hereditary • Some rulers claim divine right	• State ruled by nobility • Rule is hereditary and based on family ties, social rank, wealth • Social status and wealth support rulers' authority
Oligarchy	**Direct Democracy**
• State ruled by a small group of citizens • Rule is based on wealth or ability • Ruling group controls military	• State ruled by its citizens • Rule is based on citizenship • Majority rule decides vote

One Early Democracy: The Igbo People

The Igbo (IHG•boh) people—also called Ibo—of southern Nigeria in Africa practiced a form of democracy as early as the ninth century. Igbo village government was made up of a council of elders and a village assembly. In the council, any adult male could take part in discussion, although the elders made the final decisions. In the assembly, everyone—young or old, rich or poor—had the right to speak. This practice encouraged a spirit of equality among the Igbo.

INTEGRATED TECHNOLOGY
RESEARCH LINKS For more on forms of government, go to **classzone.com**

> DATA FILE

CURRENT WORLD GOVERNMENTS

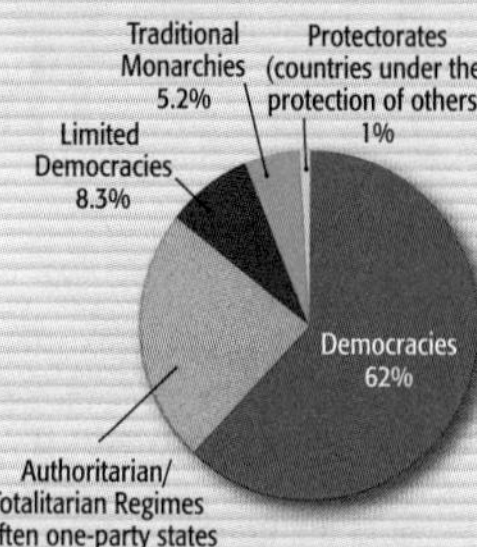

Democracy Facts

- Theoretically, 40,000 people could attend the Greek Assembly. In practice, about 6,000 people attended.
- In 1215, King John of England granted the Magna Carta, which largely influenced subsequent democratic thought.
- In the 1970s, there were 40 democratic governments worldwide.
- In 2002, over 120 established and emerging democracies met to discuss their common issues.

Source: adapted from *Democracy's Century*, Freedom House online (2003)

Connect *to* Today

1. **Categorizing** In which forms of government is rule based on wealth or property ownership?
See Skillbuilder Handbook, page R9.
2. **Hypothesizing** How might the mass media in modern life help make democracy an achievable form of government?

CONNECT TO TODAY: ANSWERS

1. **Categorizing** aristocracy, oligarchy
2. **Hypothesizing** *Possible Answer:* Mass media allows access to information and positions on issues.

Reforms of Solon In 594 B.C., Solon (SO•luhn), a respected statesman, passed a law outlawing slavery based on debt and canceled the farmers' debts. This simple act enabled Athens to avoid revolution or civil war.

Solon continued his policies of political reform. He established four classes of citizenship based on wealth rather than heredity. Only citizens of the three higher classes were able to hold public office. Yet, even the lowest class of citizens could vote in the assembly. All free adult males were citizens. Solon also created a new Council of Four Hundred. This body prepared business for the already existing council. Solon also introduced the legal concept that any citizen could bring charges against wrongdoers.

Although these acts increased participation in government, Athens was still limited as a democracy. Only citizens could participate in government, and only about one-tenth of the population were citizens at the time. Athenian law denied citizenship to women, slaves, and foreign residents. Slaves formed about one-third of the Athenian population.

Cleisthenes Enacts More Reforms Beginning in 508 B.C., the Athenian leader Cleisthenes (KLYS•thuh•neez) introduced further reforms. Because of his reforms, Cleisthenes is generally regarded as the founder of democracy in Athens. He worked to make Athens a full democracy by reorganizing the assembly to balance the power of the rich and poor. He also increased the power of the assembly by allowing all citizens to submit laws for debate and passage. Cleisthenes then created the Council of Five Hundred.

The Council proposed laws and counseled the assembly. Council members were chosen at random from among the citizens. These reforms allowed Athenian citizens to participate in a limited democracy. However, still only one-fifth of Athenian residents were actual citizens. (A)

A. Possible Answer because his political reforms allowed Athenian citizens to participate in a limited democracy

MAIN IDEA

Summarizing

(A) Why is Cleisthenes generally considered the founder of Athenian democracy?

History Makers

Solon
630?–560? B.C.

Solon is known as one of the Seven Wise Men of Greece. Solon began a series of political reforms that greatly increased citizen participation in Athenian government. He said that he "stood with a strong shield before both parties [the common people and the powerful] and allowed neither to win an unfair victory." His reforms, unfortunately, did not please either the wealthy or the poor.

Solon left Athens for ten years to travel. He spent that period warning people wherever he traveled against rulers who would not uphold his reforms.

INTEGRATED TECHNOLOGY

RESEARCH LINKS For more on Solon, go to **classzone.com**

Greek Democracy Changes

From 490 to 479 B.C., the Greeks fought Persian invaders who were attempting to conquer Greece. The Greek city-states fought side by side as allies and defeated the Persian forces.

The Athenians maintained democracy during the Persian Wars by holding public debates about how to defend their city. After Persia's defeat, Athens continued to develop democracy. A wise and able statesman named Pericles led Athens for 32 years, from 461 to 429 B.C.

Pericles Strengthens Democracy Pericles strengthened Greek democracy by increasing the number of paid public officials and by paying jurors. This enabled poorer citizens to participate in the government. Through greater citizen participation, Athens evolved into a **direct democracy**. This is a form of government in which citizens rule and make laws directly rather than through representatives. In Athens, more citizens were actively involved in government than in any other city-state. In a speech, Pericles expressed his great pride in Athenian democracy when

History Makers

Solon

Why might the poor have been dissatisfied with Solon's reforms? *(Possible Answer: They may have believed that his reforms did not go far enough.)*
A marble figure of Solon on the eastern pediment of the U.S. Supreme Court building testifies to his significance to U.S. history.

Greek Democracy Changes

10.1.2

Critical Thinking

- How might the size of Athens have made it suitable for a *direct* democracy? *(A relatively small number of people participated in government, so representatives were unnecessary.)*
- How might the Greek view of the universe be related to Greek political systems? *(Possible Answers: Greeks tried to create orderly, logical, lasting laws.)*
- Why might the Greeks have divided their government into three branches? *(Possible Answer: They may have hoped to prevent the concentration of power.)*

DIFFERENTIATING INSTRUCTION: ENGLISH LEARNERS

Summarizing the Evolution of Greek Democracy

Class Time 20 minutes

Task Creating a chart showing how Greek democracy changed over time

Purpose To practice identifying essential information

Instructions Ask students to create a chart using the main headings from "Athens Builds a Limited Democracy." Then have them reread the passage. As they read, have students fill in the chart with a summary of each subsection. Students who need more help should use the Reading Study Guide.

Athens Builds a Limited Democracy	
Introduction	The ancient Greeks developed the first democracy in a country. Democracy is rule of the people.
Building Democracy	Around 600 B.C., there were problems in Athens because rich landowners forced poor farmers into slavery.
Reforms of Solon	Solon made reforms so that people could not be made slaves for owing money. About 10 percent of people could take part in government.
Cleisthenes Enacts More Reforms	Cleisthenes made more reforms. About 20 percent of people could take part in government.

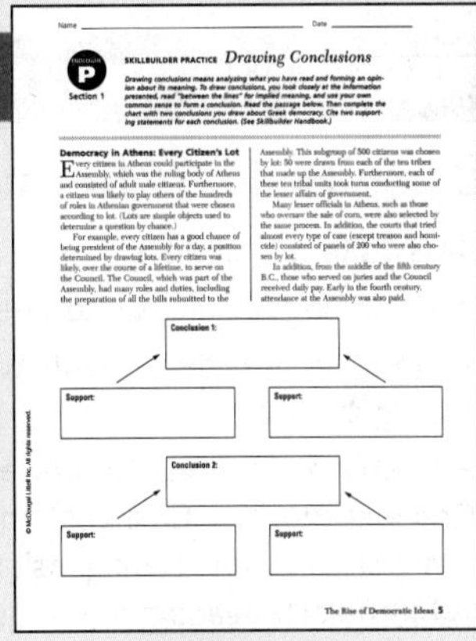

Reading Study Guide: Spanish Translation

Tip for Gifted and Talented Students

Explain that the demise of Greek democracy furnished an important lesson to Americans. In the *Federalist Papers*, James Madison compared the weakness of the United States under the Articles of Confederation to the fragility of the ancient Greek confederacy: "Had Greece . . . been united by a stricter confederation, and preserved in her Union, she would never have worn the chains of Macedon; and might have proved a barrier to the vast projects of Rome."

More About . . .

Socrates, Plato, and Aristotle

These philosophers laid some of the firmest foundations for Western education. The Socratic method is still used commonly in education. In the fields of law and medicine, for example, it is used to train students in analytical thinking. Plato opened an academy that lasted for about 900 years. Aristotle opened a rival school called the Lyceum, which served as a model for a later educational movement of the same name that began in New England in the early 1800s. The lyceums there were voluntary associations that brought speakers to lecture and debate on current topics. The lyceums helped to broaden school curricula and fostered the development of local museums and libraries.

In-Depth Resources: Unit 1

- Primary Source: from *Politics,* p. 8

he said, "Our constitution is called a democracy because power is in the hands not of a minority but of the whole people."

Democracy ended in Greece after a war between the two strongest city-states, Athens and Sparta. Macedonia, a nearby state, invaded Greece and defeated the weakened city-states.

Greek Philosophers Use Reason During the fourth century B.C. in Athens, several great thinkers appeared. They used logic and reason to investigate the nature of the universe, human society, and morality. These Greek thinkers based their philosophy on the following assumptions: (1) The universe (land, sky, and sea) is put together in an orderly way and is subject to absolute and unchanging laws; and (2) people can understand these laws through logic and reason. The Greeks' respect for human intelligence and the power of reason had allowed the ideas of democracy to flourish.

The first of these great philosophers was Socrates (SAHK•ruh•TEEZ). He encouraged his students to examine their most closely held beliefs. He used a question-and-answer approach that became known as the Socratic method. Socrates' greatest pupil was Plato (PLAY•toh). In his famous work *The Republic,* Plato set forth his vision of a perfectly governed society. He wanted society governed not by the richest and most powerful but by the wisest, whom he called philosopher-kings.

PRIMARY SOURCE (B)

Until philosophers are kings, or the kings and princes of this world have the spirit and power of philosophy, and political greatness and wisdom meet in one, and those commoner natures who pursue either to the exclusion of the other are compelled to stand aside, cities will never have rest from their evils, no, nor the human race.

PLATO, *The Republic*

MAIN IDEA

Analyzing Primary Sources

(B) What does Plato believe needs to happen to bring peace and harmony to cities and to the human race?

B. Answer rule by philosopher-kings who would have the wisdom to rule fairly

Plato's student Aristotle (AR•ih•STAHT•uhl) examined the nature of the world and of human belief, thought, and knowledge. In *Politics,* he wrote, "Man is by nature a political animal; it is his nature to live in a state."

Legacy of Greece Greece set lasting standards in government and philosophy. The Greeks used reason and intelligence to discover patterns and explanations of the world that they called natural laws. The Greeks did not wish to be subject to authoritarian rulers. So they developed direct democracy in order that citizens could actively participate in political decisions. They also were the first to develop three branches of government—a legislative branch to pass laws, an executive branch to carry out the laws, and a judicial branch to settle disputes about the laws. (The chart below compares democracy in ancient Athens and in the United States.)

Athenian and United States Democracy

Athenian Democracy	Both	U.S. Democracy
• Citizens: male; at least 18 years old; with citizen parents • Laws voted on and proposed directly by assembly of all citizens • Leader chosen by lot • Executive branch: a council of 500 men • Juries varied in size • No attorneys; no appeals; one-day trials	• Political power exercised by citizens • Three branches of government • Legislative branch passes laws • Executive branch carries out laws • Judicial branch conducts trials with paid jurors	• Citizens: born in United States or completed citizenship process • Representatives elected to propose and vote on laws • Elected president • Executive branch made up of elected and appointed officials • Juries composed of 12 jurors • Defendants and plaintiffs have attorneys; long appeals process

DIFFERENTIATING INSTRUCTION: STRUGGLING READERS

Using Headers to Understand the Text

Class Time 15 minutes

Task Turning headings into questions

Purpose To provide students with a useful reading strategy

Instructions As a way to preview the material in "Greek Democracy Changes" and to provide students with a strategy for reading, ask them to read the headings and turn each heading into a question. For example, students may formulate such questions as:

- How did Pericles strengthen Greek democracy?
- Who were some of the major philosophers in ancient Greece, and what were their most important and lasting ideas?
- What impact did ancient Greece have on later civilizations? Did ancient Greek civilization influence the United States?

Encourage students to look for answers to their questions as they read each section.

Students who need more help may use the Guided Reading activity for this section, available in English and Spanish.

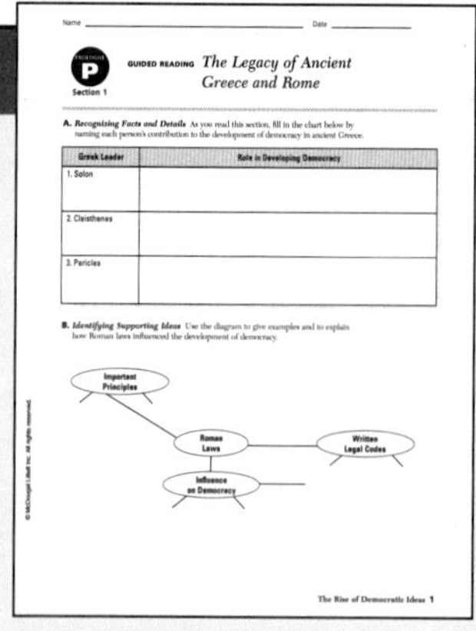

In-Depth Resources: Unit 1

History *in* Depth

Juries in Athens

Jury duty was one of the most important civic functions of a citizen of Athens. Juries ranged in size from at least 201 to as many as 2,500 men. (Athenian women were not allowed to serve as jurors.) The jurors would hear both sides of a legal case. Then they would render their verdict by casting bronze ballots in a large ballot box.

▲ Selecting a Jury

Each potential juror was given a bronze ticket inscribed with his name. After the tickets had been placed in a basket, jurors were randomly selected.

CALIFORNIA STANDARDS

10.1.1 Analyze the similarities and differences in Judeo-Christian and Greco-Roman views of law, reason and faith, and duties of the individual.

CST 1 Students compare the present with the past, evaluating the consequences of past events and decisions and determining the lessons that were learned.

solid ballot

hollow ballot

ballot box

◄ Making a Decision

These round disks are ballots. A hollow ballot was cast for a guilty vote, while a solid ballot indicated a vote in favor of the defendant. (The detail from a Greek drinking cup pictured above shows ballots being cast in a ballot box.)

► Deciding on a Punishment

Citizens could vote to ostracize, or banish, a leader from Athens for ten years to prevent a person from gaining too much power. The person's name was inscribed on a pottery fragment called an ostrakon. This one bears the name of Pericles.

SKILLBUILDER: Interpreting Visual Sources

1. **Comparing and Contrasting** *In what ways are the jury practices of Athens similar to those of the United States? How are they different?*
2. **Forming and Supporting Opinions** *What advantages or disadvantages do you see in the number of jurors on an Athenian jury?*

History *in* Depth

OBJECTIVES

- Identify the different features of the Athenian jury system.
- Explain the practice of ostracism.

INSTRUCT

Explain that jury trials are an important part of the U.S. legal system. The right to a trial by jury is guaranteed by the Bill of Rights. The Sixth Amendment guarantees the right of a jury trial in all criminal proceedings. The Seventh Amendment guarantees the right to a jury trial in all civil cases in which the amount of the judgment might exceed $20. In contrast to the large juries of ancient Greece, trial juries in the United States usually consist of 12 persons.

SKILLBUILDER: Answers

1. **Comparing and Contrasting** *Possible Answers:* In the United States, a jury pool is randomly selected, but lawyers interview potential jurors; jurors do not use disks; U.S. juries are smaller.
2. **Forming and Supporting Opinions** Advantage—Many people were involved in the decision. Disadvantage—It might be difficult to come to a clear decision with that many jurors.

SKILLBUILDER PRACTICE: DRAWING CONCLUSIONS

Understanding Implied Meanings

Class Time 25 minutes

Task Examining the History in Depth feature and drawing conclusions from it

Purpose To practice the skill of drawing conclusions and better understand the text

Instructions Explain that drawing a conclusion is more than just making a guess. To draw an effective conclusion, you must consider the various facts that are available to you and form an opinion about their meaning.

Have small groups students read the History in Depth feature on this page. Ask them to write down a conclusion they can draw from the passage, with at least two facts from the feature or from their own knowledge to support it. *(Possible Answer: Conclusion—Jurors in Athens were powerful. Support—could vote on the guilt or innocence of their fellow citizens; could banish a leader for ten years.)* Discuss groups' conclusions as a class. To practice this skill, students can complete the Skillbuilder Practice activity for this chapter.

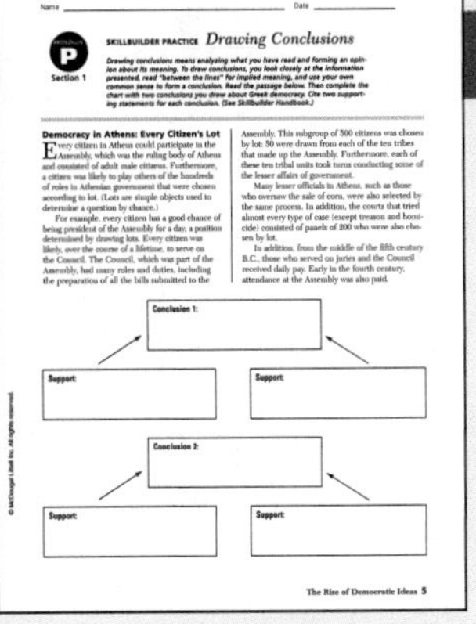

Name ______________________ Date ____________

P Section 1

SKILLBUILDER PRACTICE *Drawing Conclusions*

Drawing conclusions means analyzing what you have read and forming an opinion about its meaning. To draw conclusions, you look closely at the information presented, read "between the lines" for implied meaning, and use your own common sense to form a conclusion. Read the passage below. Then complete the chart with two conclusions you draw about Greek democracy. Cite two supporting statements for each conclusion. (See Skillbuilder Handbook.)

Democracy in Athens: Every Citizen's Lot

Every citizen in Athens could participate in the Assembly, which was the ruling body of Athens and consisted of adult male citizens. Furthermore, a citizen was likely to play others of the hundreds of roles in Athenian government that were chosen according to lot. (Lots are simple objects used to determine a question by chance.)

For example, every citizen has a good chance of being president of the Assembly for a day, a position determined by drawing lots. Every citizen was likely, over the course of a lifetime, to serve on the Council. The Council, which was part of the Assembly, had many roles and duties, including the preparation of all the bills submitted to the Assembly. This subgroup of 500 citizens was chosen by lot: 50 were drawn from each of the ten tribes that made up the Assembly. Furthermore, each of these ten tribal units took turns conducting some of the lesser affairs of government.

Many lesser officials in Athens, such as those who oversaw the sale of corn, were also selected by the same process. In addition, the courts that tried almost every type of case (except treason and homicide) consisted of panels of 200 who were also chosen by lot.

In addition, from the middle of the fifth century B.C., those who served on juries and the Council received daily pay. Early in the fourth century, attendance at the Assembly was also paid.

Conclusion 1:

Support:

Support:

Conclusion 2:

Support:

Support:

The Rise of Democratic Ideas 5

In-Depth Resources: Unit 1

Rome Develops a Republic
10.1.2

Critical Thinking

- Why did patricians eventually grant plebeians more political power? *(Possible Answer: may have been concessions given because of the plebeians' growing numbers or economic power)*
- Why would the Roman Republic provide for dictatorial rule in times of crisis? *(Possible Answer: legislative processes too slow in wartime)*

History Makers

Justinian

Ask students how the Justinian Code and the Twelve Tables differed. *(Possible Answer: The Justinian Code was compiled at the behest of an emperor, while the Twelve Tables were the result of plebeian demands.)*

In his official writings about Justinian, court historian Procopius described the emperor as a serious, even-tempered ruler who worked from dawn to midnight. But in *The Secret History* (a book published after both had died), Procopius portrayed Justinian as "deceitful, devious, false, hypocritical, two-faced, and cruel."

INTEGRATED TECHNOLOGY

Rubric Tables should

- be logical and well organized.
- cite key similarities and differences.

In-Depth Resources: Unit 1

- History Makers: Justinian I, p. 15

Rome Develops a Republic

While Greece was in decline, a new civilization to the west was developing. From about 1000 to 500 B.C., the earliest Romans—the Latins—battled with Greeks and Etruscans for control of the Italian peninsula. The Romans were the victors.

From Kingdom to Republic Beginning about 600 B.C., a series of kings ruled Rome. Then, in 509 B.C., a group of Roman aristocrats overthrew a harsh king. They set up a new government, calling it a **republic**. A republic is a form of government in which power rests with citizens who have the right to elect the leaders who make governmental decisions. It is an indirect democracy, in contrast to the direct democracy in which all citizens participate directly in the government. In Rome, as in Greece, citizenship with voting rights was granted only to free-born males. C

In the early republic, two groups struggled for power. The patricians were aristocratic landowners who held most of the power. The plebeians were common farmers, artisans, and merchants. The patricians inherited their power and social status. They claimed that their ancestry gave them the authority to make laws for Rome and its people. The plebeians were citizens of Rome with the right to vote. But they were barred by law from holding most important government positions. In time, plebeian pressure on the patricians gained them political power.

MAIN IDEA

Contrasting

C How does an indirect democracy differ from a direct democracy?

C. Possible Answer In an indirect democracy, citizens select leaders who make decisions for them rather than participating directly in the decision-making.

History Makers

Justinian
482–565

Justinian believed that "imperial majesty should not only be adorned with military might but also graced with laws, so that in times of peace and war alike the state may be governed aright."

To regulate the Byzantine Empire, Justinian set up a panel of legal experts to comb through hundreds of years of Roman law and opinion. The panel's task was to create a single, uniform legal code for Justinian's "New Rome."

The Justinian Code has had a profound impact on the law of most Western countries.

INTEGRATED TECHNOLOGY

INTERNET ACTIVITY Create a table comparing some of Justinian's laws with similar ones in the United States. Go to **classzone.com** for your research.

Twelve Tables An important victory for the plebeians was forcing creation of a written law code. With laws unwritten, patrician officials often interpreted the law to suit themselves. In 451 B.C., a group of ten officials began writing down Rome's laws. They had the laws carved on 12 tables, or tablets, and publicly displayed. The Twelve Tables established the idea that all free citizens had the right to protection of the law and that laws would be fairly administered.

Republican Government Like the Athenians, the Romans had established a government with separate branches. Two officials called consuls commanded the army and directed the government. Their term of office was only one year. The legislative branch was made up of a **senate** and two assemblies. Patricians made up the senate. It controlled foreign and financial policies and advised the consuls. The two assemblies included other classes of citizens. In times of crisis, the republic also provided for a dictator, a leader who had absolute power to make laws and command the army. The dictator was limited to a six-month term.

For hundreds of years after the founding of the republic, Rome expanded its territories through conquest and trade. But expansion created problems. For decades, Rome alternated between the chaos of civil war and the authoritarian rule of a series of dictators. Eventually, the republic collapsed. In 27 B.C., Rome came under the rule of an emperor.

Roman Law

Rome had become a great power not only by conquering other lands but also by bringing the conquered peoples into its system. The Romans tried to create a system of laws that could be applied throughout the Roman Empire. Like the

DIFFERENTIATING INSTRUCTION: GIFTED AND TALENTED STUDENTS

Patricians and Plebeians

Class Time 35 minutes

Task Writing a mock interview

Purpose To understand class tensions within the Roman Republic

Instructions Ask students to imagine how a patrician might justify that group's wanting most or all of the power in Rome. How might a plebeian respond, and what arguments could be made to justify that group's ascending to power? Have students write a transcript of a talk-show interview in which a Roman patrician and a plebeian debate this issue. Students may work individually or in pairs. Encourage additional research on the topic.

Points to consider include the following:

- the differences between plebeians and patricians
- social and political restrictions placed on plebeians, such as their exclusion from public offices or the prohibition against intermarriage with patricians
- the plebeian campaign, known as the "Conflict of the Orders," to win greater social and political freedom

If time permits, ask for volunteers to act out the interviews.

Greeks, they believed that laws should be based on principles of reason and justice and should protect citizens and their property. This idea applied to all people regardless of their nationality. It had a great influence on the development of democracy throughout the Western world.

Some important principles of Roman law were

- All citizens had the right to equal treatment under the law.
- A person was considered innocent until proven guilty.
- The burden of proof rested with the accuser rather than the accused.
- Any law that seemed unreasonable or grossly unfair could be set aside.

▲ A coin from 137 B.C. shows a Roman citizen taking part in the democratic process by voting.

A Written Legal Code Another major characteristic of Roman government was its regard for written law as exemplified by the creation of the Twelve Tables in 451 B.C. Nearly 1,000 years later, in A.D. 528, Emperor Justinian ordered the compilation of all Roman laws since the earlier code. After its completion, this new code consisted of four works. *The Code* contained nearly 5,000 Roman laws. *The Digest* was a summary of legal opinions. *The Institutes* served as a textbook for law students. *The Novellae* contained laws passed after 534. The Code of Justinian later became a guide on legal matters throughout Western Europe. Written laws helped establish the idea of "a government of laws, not of men," in which even rulers and other powerful persons could be held accountable for their actions.

D. Possible Answers Rome gave the world the idea of a republic; contributed a written legal code and the idea it should be applied impartially; and passed on democratic traditions to civilizations that followed.

MAIN IDEA

Recognizing Effects

D How did Rome influence the development of democracy in the Western world?

Legacy of Rome Rome gave the world the idea of a republic. Rome also adopted from the Greeks the notion that an individual is a citizen in a state rather than the subject of a ruler. Perhaps Rome's greatest and most lasting legacy was its written legal code and the idea that this code should be applied equally and impartially to all citizens. Rome preserved and added to Greece's idea of democracy and passed on the early democratic tradition to civilizations that followed. D

SECTION 1 ASSESSMENT

TERMS & NAMES 1. For each term or name, write a sentence explaining its significance.

• government • monarchy • aristocracy • oligarchy • democracy • direct democracy • republic • senate

USING YOUR NOTES

2. Which contribution, shown on your web diagram, do you think had the greatest impact on the modern world? (CST 1)

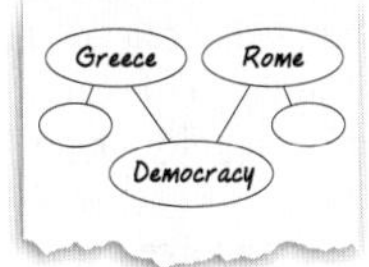

MAIN IDEAS

3. How does an aristocracy differ from an oligarchy? (10.1.2)
4. What steps did Cleisthenes take to strengthen democracy in Athens? (10.1.2)
5. What are the four basic principles of Roman law? (10.1.2)

CRITICAL THINKING & WRITING

6. **DRAWING CONCLUSIONS** How do the steps taken by leaders of Athens reflect a turn toward democracy? (10.1.2)
7. **FORMING AND SUPPORTING OPINIONS** Was Athenian democracy under Pericles truly a democracy? Explain. (10.1.2)
8. **SYNTHESIZING** Which characteristic of the government under the Roman Republic had the greatest impact on the democratic tradition? (CST 1)
9. **WRITING ACTIVITY** POWER AND AUTHORITY Write a **dialogue** between a Roman citizen and a Greek citizen each arguing that their style of democracy is a better form of government. (Writing 2.4.a)

CONNECT TO TODAY CREATING AN ORAL REPORT

New England town meetings are similar to the kind of democracy practiced in Ancient Greece. Research New England town meetings and prepare an **oral report** on your findings. (Writing 2.3.b)

Roman Law

Critical Thinking

- How might Rome's legal system have contributed to its expansion? *(Possible Answer: Protection under Roman laws may have minimized discontent in conquered territories.)*
- Why is it important to publish legal opinions in addition to laws? *(Possible Answer: explains reasoning behind the laws)*

In-Depth Resources: Unit 1

- Geography Application: The Roads of the Roman Empire, p. 6

World Art and Cultures Transparencies

- AT12 *The Forum*

Electronic Library of Primary Sources

- "Wall Inscriptions from Pompeii," A.D. 79

3 ASSESS

SECTION 1 ASSESSMENT

Have pairs of students answer the questions. Then have partners compare answers with another pair.

Formal Assessment

- Section Quiz, p. 5

4 RETEACH

Draw a Venn diagram on the board. Label one side *Greek Democracy* and the other *Roman Republic.* Work with the class to add similarities and differences to the diagram.

ANSWERS

1. government, p. 5 • monarchy, p. 5 • aristocracy, p. 5 • oligarchy, p. 5 • democracy, p. 5 • direct democracy, p. 7 • republic, p. 10 • senate, p. 10
2. **Sample Answer:** Greece—Direct democracy, trial by jury, three branches of government. Rome—Republic, written law code, equal treatment under law. Greatest impact—Republic; used by most democracies today.
3. Aristocracies are governed by wealthy landowners and are hereditary, while oligarchies are ruled by a small group of citizens with great wealth or ability.
4. balanced power of rich and poor in assembly, allowed all citizens to submit laws to the assembly
5. right to equal treatment under law; innocent until proven guilty; burden of proof rests with accuser; unreasonable or unfair laws could be set aside
6. more people given political power and direct voice in the government
7. **Possible Answer:** No—It applied to only a small part of the population.
8. **Possible Answer:** regard for written laws, because laws are less likely to be arbitrary or to change
9. **Rubric** Dialogues should
   - explain Greek and Roman democracy.
   - identify reasons one style is superior.

CONNECT TO TODAY

Rubric Oral reports should

- explain New England town meetings.
- show how a town meeting is similar to Greek direct democracy.

LESSON PLAN

OBJECTIVES

- Explain the importance of Judaism's values.
- Describe how Christianity spread and helped further democratic ideas.
- Analyze the impact of the Renaissance and Reformation on democratic thinking.

1 FOCUS & MOTIVATE

Ask students what they know about the history of Judaism, Christianity, and Islam. *(Possible Answer: All three believe in one god, but each has a different sacred text.)*

2 INSTRUCT

Judaism

10.1.1

Critical Thinking

- How could belief in individual worth help shape a democratic tradition? *(Possible Answer: If individuals have worth, then they can choose their leaders and political systems.)*

CALIFORNIA RESOURCES
California Reading Toolkit, p. L6
California Modified Lesson Plans for English Learners, p. 7
California Daily Standards Practice Transparencies, TTB
California Standards Enrichment Workbook, pp. 17–18
California Standards Planner and Lesson Plans, p. L3
California Online Test Practice
California Test Generator CD-ROM
California Easy Planner CD-ROM
California eEdition CD-ROM

A pointer in the shape of a hand is used to help read a Torah scroll

Detail from fourth-century mosaic, Pisces Synagogue, Tiberias, Israel

2

Judeo-Christian Tradition

MAIN IDEA

CULTURAL INTERACTION Judaism and Christianity taught individual worth, ethical values, and the need to fight injustice.

WHY IT MATTERS NOW

These ideals continue to be important to democracy today.

TERMS & NAMES

- Judaism
- Ten Commandments
- Christianity
- Islam
- Roman Catholic Church
- Renaissance
- Reformation

CALIFORNIA STANDARDS

10.1.1 Analyze the similarities and differences in Judeo-Christian and Greco-Roman views of law, reason and faith, and duties of the individual.

HI 2 Students recognize the complexity of historical causes and effects, including the limitations on determining cause and effect.

HI 4 Students understand the meaning, implication, and impact of historical events and recognize that events could have taken other directions.

SETTING THE STAGE Ideas from three monotheistic religions helped shape democratic traditions. Judaism, Christianity, and Islam all began in a small corner of southwest Asia, and later spread across the world. Their ideas about the worth of individuals and the responsibility of individuals to the community had a strong impact on the development of democracy. More ideas about the value of the individual and the questioning of authority emerged during the periods of the Renaissance and the Reformation.

Judaism

Much of what we know about the early history of the Hebrews, later called the Jews, is contained in the first five books of the Hebrew Bible, the Torah. In the Torah, God chose Abraham to be the "father," or ancestor, of the Hebrew people. God commanded Abraham to move his people to Canaan, an area of ancient Palestine. This occurred around 1800 B.C.

Created in God's Image Other groups around the Hebrews were polytheists, people who believed in more than one God. The Hebrews, however, were monotheists. They believed in one God. This God was perfect, all-knowing, all-powerful, and eternal. Earlier, people had generally thought that what the gods wanted from human beings was the performance of rituals and sacrifices in their honor. The Hebrews believed that it was God's wish for people to live moral lives. The religion of the Hebrews was called **Judaism**.

The Hebrew Bible (the Old Testament, to Christians) states that human beings are created in God's image. The Hebrews interpreted this to mean that each human being has a divine spark that gives him or her a dignity that can never be taken away. For the Greeks and Romans, the individual had dignity because of his or her ability to reason. For the Hebrews, each person had dignity simply by being a child of God.

The Hebrews believed that God had given human beings moral freedom—the capacity to choose between good and evil. Therefore, each person was responsible for the choices he or she made. These beliefs led to a new emphasis on the worth of the individual.

Jewish Law Teaches Morality Like the Greeks, the Romans, and other ancient peoples, the Jews had a written code of laws. The Bible states that God gave this

TAKING NOTES

Clarifying Use a chart to list one contribution to democracy with each item on the list.

Category	Contribution
Judaism	
Islam	
Renaissance	
Reformation	

SECTION 2 PROGRAM RESOURCES

ALL STUDENTS
In-Depth Resources: Unit 1
- Guided Reading, p. 2

Formal Assessment
- Section Quiz, p. 6

ENGLISH LEARNERS
In-Depth Resources in Spanish
- Guided Reading, p. 12

Reading Study Guide (Spanish), p. 7
Reading Study Guide Audio CD

STRUGGLING READERS
In-Depth Resources: Unit 1
- Guided Reading, p. 2

Reading Study Guide, p. 7
Reading Study Guide Audio CD

GIFTED AND TALENTED STUDENTS
In-Depth Resources: Unit 1
- Primary Source: The Ten Commandments, p. 9

Electronic Library of Primary Sources
- from the Book of Exodus in the Bible, about 900 B.C.

INTEGRATED TECHNOLOGY
eEdition CD-ROM
Power Presentations CD-ROM
Electronic Library of Primary Sources
- from the Book of Exodus in the Bible, about 900s B.C.

classzone.com

code to their leader Moses in the form of the **Ten Commandments** and other laws. This event occurred sometime between 1300 and 1200 B.C. Unlike the laws of other peoples, the Hebrews' code focused more on morality and ethics and less on politics. The code included rules of social and religious behavior to which even rulers were subject. While the Hebrew code of justice was strict, it was softened by expressions of God's mercy.

An expansion of the religious thought of the Jews occurred with the emergence of prophets in the eighth century B.C. The prophets were leaders and teachers who were believed by the Jews to be messengers from God. The prophets attacked war, oppression, and greed in statements such as these from the Old Testament:

PRIMARY SOURCE

He has told you, O mortal, what is good; and what does the Lord require of you but to do justice, and to love kindness, and to walk humbly with your God?

MICAH 6:8

The prophets strengthened the Jews' social conscience, which has become part of the Western tradition. The Jews believed that it is the responsibility of every person to oppose injustice and oppression and that the community should assist the unfortunate. The prophets held out the hope that life on earth could be improved, that poverty and injustice need not exist, and that individuals are capable of living according to high moral standards. (A)

A. Answer They taught that each person has a responsibility to oppose injustice and oppression.

MAIN IDEA

Clarifying

(A) What did the prophets teach about injustice and oppression?

Analyzing Primary Sources

The Ten Commandments

The Ten Commandments are the ten orders or laws given by God to Moses on Mount Sinai. These orders serve as the basis for Jewish laws.

PRIMARY SOURCE

1. I am the Lord thy God. . . Thou shalt have no other gods before me.
2. Thou shalt not make unto thee any graven image. . .
3. Thou shalt not take the name of the Lord thy God in vain. . .
4. Remember the Sabbath day to keep it holy.
5. Honor thy father and thy mother. . .
6. Thou shalt not kill.
7. Thou shalt not commit adultery.
8. Thou shalt not steal.
9. Thou shalt not bear false witness against thy neighbor.
10. Thou shalt not covet. . . anything that is thy neighbor's.

Deuteronomy 5:6–22

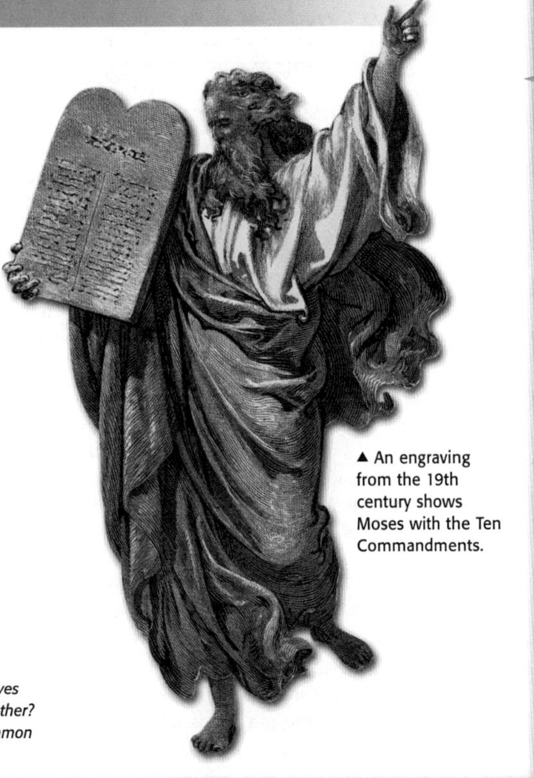

▲ An engraving from the 19th century shows Moses with the Ten Commandments.

DOCUMENT-BASED QUESTIONS

1. **Comparing** *Do the first four commandments concern themselves more with the Hebrews' relationship with God or with one another?*
2. **Contrasting** *What do the last six commandments have in common that distinguish them from the first four?*

More About . . .

Moses

Moses is considered by many to be the greatest figure in Jewish history. He is believed to have been a diplomat, lawmaker, political organizer, and a military leader, as well as a judge and religious leader. The Hebrew scriptures record that Moses led the Exodus—the liberation of the Hebrews from slavery in Egypt. Through Moses, the Hebrews formed a *covenant,* an agreement with their God. In exchange for God's love and protection, they agreed to be ruled by God and to obey God's laws.

Analyzing Primary Sources

The Ten Commandments

Have students read the primary source from Deuteronomy. Ask them if any of the Mosaic laws appear to contradict the laws of the United States. *(Possible Answer: The First, Second, and Third Commandments appear to violate the First Amendment to the U.S. Constitution, which states that "Congress shall make no law respecting the establishment of religion, or prohibiting the free exercise thereof; or abridging the freedom of speech . . . ")*

Answers to Document-Based Questions

1. **Comparing** with God
2. **Contrasting** They concern the relationship of people with one another.

CONNECTIONS ACROSS TIME AND CULTURES

Analyzing the Ten Commandments

Class Time 30 minutes

Task Comparing the Ten Commandments with federal and state laws in the United States

Purpose To see connections between an ancient text and life today

Instructions Give students the primary source translation of the Ten Commandments from In-Depth Resources: Unit 1. Have students take turns reading portions of the text aloud. Ask students to identify the commandments that have to do with religion and personal practices and the ones that might be reflected in public laws. They may say the commandments against killing, stealing, and bearing false witness are related to laws prohibiting such behavior. Make sure students understand that bearing false witness means to give false evidence against another person. In other words, it is a crime to lie in court about the actions of another.

Tell students that the commandment about keeping the Sabbath day holy was reflected in some states by laws prohibiting work on Sundays and preventing stores from being open then. The laws were known as "blue laws." The other commandments are not related to public laws in the United States because of the constitutional provisions that essentially separate church and state.

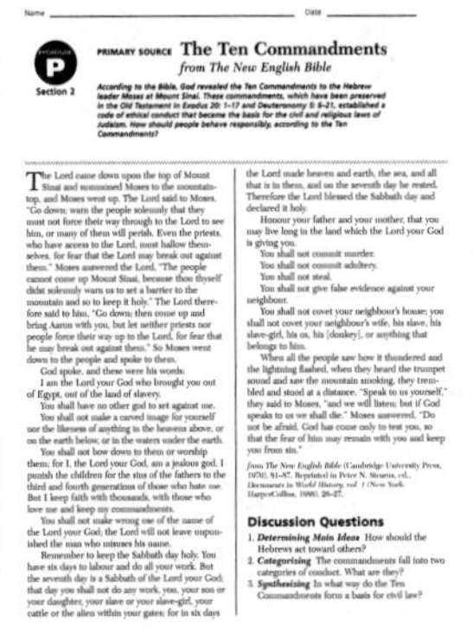

PRIMARY SOURCE The Ten Commandments *from The New English Bible*

In-Depth Resources: Unit 1

History from Visuals

Interpreting the Map

Ask students to discuss why the spread of Christianity might have paralleled the boundaries of the Roman Empire so closely. *(Possible Answer: Missionaries used the roads and trade routes of the empire to travel to distant places.)*

Extension Ask students to write one sentence that summarizes the information the map presents. *(From 325 to 500, Christianity developed first in the major cities and then spread outward, reaching every province of the Roman Empire.)*

SKILLBUILDER: Answers

1. **Location** Anatolia
2. **Region** Britain to the north, Egypt to the south, Spain and western Britain to the west, and Armenia to the east

Christianity

10.1.1

Critical Thinking

- Why might the belief in life after death be important to Christianity and other religions? *(Possible Answer: It may provide believers with the courage needed to follow the principles of their faith.)*
- Why might Roman leaders consider Paul's missionary work politically threatening? *(Possible Answer: Paul's preaching about the essential equality of all human beings probably appeared dangerous to those in power.)*

In-Depth Resources: Unit 1

- Primary Source: The Ten Commandments, p. 9

Electronic Library of Primary Sources

- from the Book of Exodus in the Bible

Spread of Christianity in the Roman World to A.D. 500

GEOGRAPHY SKILLBUILDER: Interpreting Maps

1. **Location** *Where was Christianity most widespread in A.D. 325?*
2. **Region** *What was the extent (north to south, east to west) of Christianity's spread by A.D. 500?*

Christianity

As Rome expanded, its power spread throughout the Mediterranean. It took control of Judea, homeland of the Jews, around 63 B.C. By 6 B.C., the Romans ruled Judea directly as a part of their empire.

According to the New Testament, Jesus of Nazareth was born around 6 to 4 B.C. He was both a Jew and a Roman subject. He began his public ministry at the age of 30. His preaching contained many ideas from Jewish tradition, such as monotheism and the principles of the Ten Commandments. Jesus emphasized God's personal relationship to each human being.

The Teachings of Christianity Jesus' ideas went beyond traditional morality. He stressed the importance of people's love for God, their neighbors, their enemies, and themselves. In the Sermon on the Mount, Jesus told the people, "I say unto you, Love your enemies, bless them that curse you, do good to them that hate you, and pray for them which despitefully use you, and persecute you." He also taught that God would eventually end wickedness in the world and would establish an eternal kingdom in which he would reign. People who sincerely repented their sins would find life after death in this kingdom.

About A.D. 29, Jesus visited Jerusalem. Because some referred to him as the "king of the Jews," the Roman governor considered him a political threat. Jesus was put to death by crucifixion. According to Jesus' followers, he rose from the dead three days later and ascended into heaven. His followers believed he was the Messiah, or savior. Jesus came to be referred to as Jesus Christ. *Christos* is a Greek word meaning "messiah" or "savior." The word **Christianity**, the name of the religion founded by Jesus, was derived from the name Christ.

DIFFERENTIATING INSTRUCTION: GIFTED AND TALENTED STUDENTS

Mapping Paul's Travels

Class Time 30 minutes

Task Researching and mapping the travels of Paul

Purpose To help students understand the spread of Christianity

Instructions Tell students that Paul made three separate voyages in his missionary work. The voyages occurred in about A.D. 46–48, A.D. 49–51, and A.D. 53–57. Some of the places overlapped from voyage to voyage. Divide students into three groups and assign each group one of the voyages to research. Each group will briefly describe the cities that Paul visited, summarize his missionary activities in each city during a particular voyage, and draw a map showing his route among the cities. Each group will present its findings to the class beginning with the first voyage.

In addition to mapping the voyages, students should describe Paul's traveling companions and explain the dangers and difficulties Paul encountered on his travels. Remind students that Christianity was not widely accepted in Paul's time and that he faced many challenges in his missionary work.

Vocabulary
An *apostle* is one of the followers of Jesus who preached and spread his teaching.

The Spread of Christianity In the first century after Jesus' death, his followers began to teach this new religion based on his message. Christianity spread slowly but steadily across the Roman Empire. One man, the apostle Paul, had enormous influence on Christianity's development.

Paul preached in cities around the eastern Mediterranean. He stressed that Jesus was the son of God and that he had died for people's sins. Paul declared that Christianity was a universal religion. It should welcome all converts, Jew and non-Jew. He said, "There is neither Jew nor Greek, there is neither slave nor free, there is neither male nor female; for you are all one in Christ Jesus." He stressed the essential equality of all human beings, a belief central to democracy.

B. Answer They were spread by the Jews who shared their beliefs while in exile and by the Christians who wanted to convert others to their faith.

Rome Spreads Judeo-Christian Ideas In the beginning, the Roman Empire was hostile to the beliefs of Judaism and Christianity. Yet it was the empire that helped spread the ideas of these religions in two ways. The first way was indirect. After the Jews began to rebel against the Romans in the first century, they were exiled from their homeland in A.D. 70. This dispersal was called the Diaspora. The Jews then fled to many parts of the world, where they shared their beliefs that all people had the right to be treated with justice and dignity.

MAIN IDEA
Summarizing
B How were Judeo-Christian ideas spread throughout the Roman Empire?

The second way the empire spread Judeo-Christian ideas was more direct. Despite Roman persecution of Christians, Christianity became a powerful religion throughout the empire and beyond. By 380, it had become the official religion of the empire. Eventually it took root in Europe, the Near East, and northern Africa. B

Islam

Another monotheistic religion that taught equality of all persons and individual worth also developed in southwest Asia in the early 600s. **Islam** was based on the teachings of the prophet Muhammad. Muhammad's teachings, which are the revealed word of God (Allah in Arabic), are found in the holy book called the Qur'an. He emphasized the dignity of all human beings and the brotherhood of all people. A belief in the bond of community and the unity of all people led to a tolerance of different groups within the community.

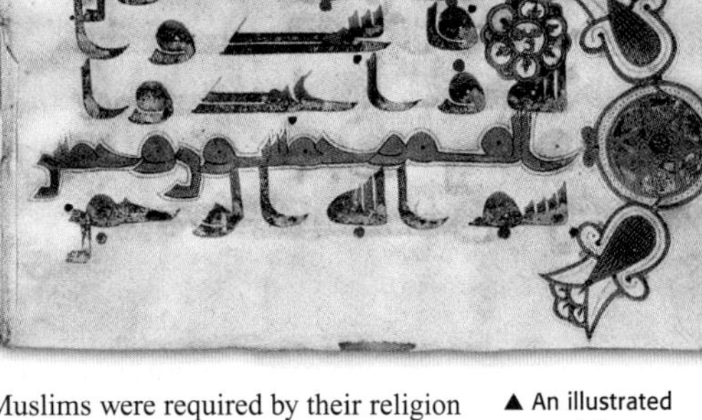

▲ An illustrated page of the Qur'an from the Ninth century

Followers of Islam are called Muslims. Muslims were required by their religion to offer charity and help to those in need. Under Muslim law, rulers had to obey the same laws as those they ruled. In lands controlled by Muslims, the Muslims were required to show tolerance for the religious practices of Jews and Christians.

The Legacy of Monotheistic Religions Several ideals crucial to the shaping of a democratic outlook emerged from the early monotheistic religions of southwest Asia. They include the following:

- the duty of the individual and the community to combat oppression
- the worth of the individual
- the equality of people before God

These ideas would form part of the basis of democratic thinking. More ideas about the value of the individual and about the questioning of authority would surface during the Renaissance and Reformation.

More About . . .

Constantine and the Spread of Christianity

Christianity spread quickly through the Roman Empire after the emperor Constantine I took a favorable view toward the religion. In A.D. 312, he was fighting his rivals for the imperial throne and prayed for divine help before going into battle. Constantine reported that he then saw a cross of light in the heavens bearing the inscription, "In this sign, conquer." He ordered artisans to put the Christian symbol of the cross on his soldiers' shields, and his troops were victorious. Constantine gave credit for his success to the Christian god and put an end to the Roman persecution of Christians. By 380, Christianity was the empire's official religion.

Islam
10.1.1

Critical Thinking

- Why might Islamic leaders have required Muslims to show tolerance for the religious practices of Jews and Christians? *(Possible Answer: because their values and beliefs were so similar)*
- Why might three different monotheistic religions develop so near to one another? *(Possible Answer: Changing social, economic, cultural, and political circumstances may have created environments with different spiritual needs.)*

DIFFERENTIATING INSTRUCTION: ENGLISH LEARNERS

Judaism, Christianity, and Islam

Class Time 45 minutes
Task Answering questions about religions
Purpose To improve understanding of the text
Instructions Have students work in pairs to reread the text on pages 12–15. Tell them that beliefs from each of the three religions contributed to the idea of *individualism,* the belief in the inherent dignity and worth of each person. Remind students that the ideas of individualism are strongly related to the basic ideas of democracy. Have the pairs of students answer these questions.

1. What are two beliefs of Judaism? *(a belief in one god, each person responsible for choices he or she makes)*
2. Why do Jews believe that people are responsible for their own choices? *(because God gave people the freedom to choose between good and evil)*
3. What is the key difference between Christian and Jewish beliefs? *(belief in Jesus as the savior)*
4. What are two teachings of Muhammad? *(All people are brothers. Muslims must help those in need.)*
5. How did all three religions shape democratic ideas? *(All believe in the worth of each individual.)*

Reading Study Guide: Spanish Translation

Global Impact

Printing Spreads Ideas

Printing played an important part in the Protestant Reformation as well as in the Renaissance. Protestants believed that the Catholic Church had distorted the Bible's message and encouraged Protestants to read and interpret the Bible for themselves in order to return to the scriptural truths. Ask students how the development of movable type and the printing press might have advanced the Reformation. *(Possible Answer: by making relatively inexpensive Bibles widely available)*

Renaissance and Reformation

10.1.1

Critical Thinking

- How did a religion that insisted on the essential equality of all human beings develop into an authoritarian structure? *(Possible Answer: Once Christianity became institutionalized, religious leaders became more interested in power and less interested in the spiritual aspects of their faith.)*
- How did Martin Luther respond to the power and abuses of the Church? *(He argued that salvation came through faith, thereby undermining the authority of the clergy, who insisted that salvation came only through the Church.)*

Global Impact

Printing Spreads Ideas

The development of a movable type printing press around 1440, shown above in a 16th-century French woodcut, revolutionized the sharing of ideas. The press made it possible to print books quickly and cheaply. This fueled Renaissance learning because scholars could read each other's works soon after they were written. The ideas of the Renaissance and, later, of the Enlightenment were spread through the printed word.

The spread of reading matter made literacy for large numbers of people suddenly possible. And an informed citizenry contributed to the rise of democracy. These informed citizens began to question authority. This ultimately spurred democratic revolutions in America and France in the late 1700s.

Renaissance and Reformation

The **Roman Catholic Church** developed from Roman Christianity. By the Middle Ages, it had become the most powerful institution in Europe. It influenced all aspects of life—religious, social, and political. It was strongly authoritarian in structure, that is, it expected unquestioned obedience to its authority.

Renaissance Revives Classical Ideas In the 1300s, a brilliant cultural movement arose in Italy. Over the next 300 years, it spread to the rest of Europe, helped by the development of the printing press. This movement was called the **Renaissance**, from the French word for "rebirth." The Renaissance was marked by renewed interest in classical culture. This included the restoration of old monuments and works of art and the rediscovery of forgotten Greek and Latin manuscripts. Renaissance thinkers were interested in earthly life for its own sake. They rejected the medieval view that life was only a preparation for the afterlife.

Renaissance education was intended to prepare some men for public service rather than just for service to the Church. Scholars placed increasing value on subjects concerned with humankind and culture. The study of classical texts led to an intellectual movement that encouraged ideas about human potential and achievement. Some Christian writers were critical of the failure of the Church to encourage people to live a life that was moral and ethical. They also discussed ways in which the lives of all in society could improve.

Renaissance thinkers and writers began to explore ideas about political power and the role of government in the lives of ordinary people. The Greek and Roman ideas about democracy were quite different from the oligarchic governments they were experiencing.

During the Renaissance, individualism became deeply rooted in Western culture. Artists expressed it by seeking to capture individual character. Explorers and conquerors demonstrated it by venturing into uncharted seas and by carving out vast empires in the Americas. It also was shown by merchant-capitalists, who amassed huge fortunes by taking great economic risks.

Vocabulary
Individualism is the belief in the importance of the individual and in the virtues of self-reliance and personal independence.

The Reformation Challenges Church Power Although Christianity remained a strong force in Europe during the Renaissance, people began to be more critical of the Church. The spirit of questioning that started during the Renaissance came to full bloom in the **Reformation**. The Reformation was a religious reform movement that began in the 16th century. Those who wanted to reform the Catholic Church were called Protestants, because they protested against the power and abuses of the Church. Reformers stressed the importance of a direct relationship with God.

The Reformation started in Germany. In 1517, a monk and teacher named Martin Luther criticized the Church's practice of selling pardons for sins. Soon, Luther went further. He contradicted the Church's position that salvation came through faith and good works. He said people could be saved only through faith in God. What began as a reform movement ended up as a new division of Christianity—Protestantism.

Vocabulary
A *pardon* is a cancellation of punishment still due for a sin that has been forgiven.

DIFFERENTIATING INSTRUCTION: STRUGGLING READERS

Key Ideas of the Renaissance and Reformation

Class Time 30 minutes

Task Creating a chart of key ideas

Purpose To familiarize students with important ideas of the Renaissance and Reformation

Instructions Ask students to review the text on the Renaissance and Reformation on pages 16 and 17. Draw a chart on the chalkboard containing key terms from the text. Lead a discussion to help students fill in the meanings of the terms. Then ask students to show how these key ideas contributed to the rise of democracy. Point out that new beliefs in the importance of the individual, the value of self-reliance, and the focus on earthly life led to the development of democratic ideas.

Key Term	Meaning
Renaissance	Cultural movement marked by interest in Greek and Roman art and learning with its focus on the value of earthly life for its own sake
Individualism	The belief in the importance of the individual and the value of self-reliance and independence
Reformation	A religious movement to reform the Catholic Church that led to a new division of Christianity—Protestantism

Because Protestantism encouraged people to make their own religious judgments, Protestants began to have differences of belief. They then established new churches in addition to the already-formed Lutheran Church. These included the Anglican, Presbyterian, and Calvinist churches.

Catholics and Protestants differed on many issues. The Catholic Church claimed the right to interpret the Bible for all Christians. Protestants called on believers to interpret the Bible for themselves. The Catholic Church said the only way to salvation was through the Church. Protestants said that the clergy had no special powers; people could find individual paths to God. The Protestant emphasis on private judgment in religious matters—on a sense of conviction rather than a reliance on authority—strengthened the importance of the individual even more. It also led to a questioning of political authority. (See History in Depth on this page.)

C. Answer Both emphasized the importance of the individual and challenged the rule of authoritarian leaders.

MAIN IDEA

Synthesizing

C How did the Renaissance and the Reformation shape ideas about democracy?

Legacy of the Renaissance and Reformation The Reformation and the other changes that swept Europe during and after the Middle Ages greatly influenced the shaping of the modern world. By challenging the authority of monarchs and popes, the Reformation indirectly contributed to the growth of democracy. Also, by calling on believers to read and interpret the Bible for themselves, it introduced individuals to reading and exposed them to more than just religious ideas.

Both the Renaissance and the Reformation placed emphasis on the importance of the individual. This was an important idea in the democratic revolutions that followed and in the growth of political liberty in modern times. C

History *in* Depth

The Peasants' Revolt

Luther questioned Church authority. But peasants in southern Germany took Luther's example further. In 1524, they questioned political and social authority. They wanted an end to serfdom, or being forced to serve a master. They stormed the castles of the nobles, forcing them, at least initially, to give in to their demands.

It was the largest mass uprising in the history of Germany. The peasants looked to Luther to support their rights, but Luther supported the nobles instead. As many as 100,000 peasants were killed during the rebellion.

SECTION 2 ASSESSMENT

TERMS & NAMES 1. For each term or name, write a sentence explaining its significance.

• Judaism • Ten Commandments • Christianity • Islam • Roman Catholic Church • Renaissance • Reformation

USING YOUR NOTES

2. How do the contributions listed on your chart support the ideals of democracy? (10.1.1)

Category	Contribution
Christianity	
Judaism	
Islam	
Renaissance	
Reformation	

MAIN IDEAS

3. How are the Ten Commandments different from the laws of other groups? (10.1.1)
4. Which of the Christian teachings supports the central idea of democracy? (10.1.1)
5. How did the Reformation indirectly contribute to the growth of democracy? (10.1.1)

CRITICAL THINKING & WRITING

6. **COMPARING** What ideas crucial to the shaping of democracy did Judaism and Christianity share? (10.1.1)
7. **DRAWING CONCLUSIONS** How did the Reformation promote the idea of individualism? (10.1.1)
8. **SYNTHESIZING** How did the printing press help promote the ideas of democracy? (HI 4)
9. **WRITING ACTIVITY** CULTURAL INTERACTION Write a **summary paragraph** that illustrates how the Judeo-Christian view of reason and faith, and the duties of the individual and community contributed to the development of democratic thought. (Writing 2.3.c)

CONNECT TO TODAY **CREATING A COLLAGE**

Using newspapers or magazines, create a **collage** showing modern nations practicing ideas of democracy. You might include headlines, pictures, or articles about equality of all people and community efforts to combat oppression. (HI 4)

History *in* Depth

The Peasants' Revolt

German peasants had revolted several times in the 1400s before Luther's teachings incited them to rebel. Crops failed in 1523 and 1524, and peasants complained of new fees imposed by their lords. Luther's words, taken out of context, justified their uprisings: "A Christian man is the most free lord of all, and subject to none."

3 ASSESS

SECTION 2 ASSESSMENT

Have groups of three students take turns quizzing each other on the terms and names in question 1 and work together in making the chart in question 2.

Formal Assessment

• Section Quiz, p. 6

4 RETEACH

To help students review the main ideas of this section, pair students and ask each pair to write a brief summary of the content of one heading. Let students post their summaries on a bulletin board.

In-Depth Resources: Unit 1

• Guided Reading, p. 2

ANSWERS

1. Judaism, p. 12 • Ten Commandments, p. 13 • Christianity, p. 14 • Islam, p. 15 • Roman Catholic Church, p. 16 • Renaissance, p. 16 • Reformation, p. 16

2. **Sample Answer:** Judaism—emphasis on individual morality; Christianity—equality of believers; Islam—dignity of all human beings; Renaissance—growth of individualism; Reformation—challenging of traditional authority. These traits all support the democratic idea that people are capable of governing themselves.
3. They focus on morality and ethics.
4. the equality of all human beings
5. by challenging the authority of monarchs and popes
6. They respected the worth of the individual and emphasized morality and each person's responsibility to make moral choices.
7. by asserting that people could have a direct relationship with God and read and interpret the Bible for themselves
8. by helping to create a literate and informed citizenry
9. **Rubric** Summary paragraphs should
   • discuss reason, faith, and the duties of the individual and community.
   • show logical connections between Judeo-Christian and democratic views.

CONNECT TO TODAY

Rubric Collages should
• include examples of democratic ideas.
• cover several nations.

LESSON PLAN

OBJECTIVES

- List medieval legal reforms in England.
- Explain how Parliament gained power between 1300 and 1650.
- Trace events that led to establishment of a constitutional monarchy.

1 FOCUS & MOTIVATE

In this section, students will learn about England's famous Magna Carta, considered to be a cornerstone of democratic government. Ask students to name some of the United States' most important documents. *(Possible Answers: Constitution, Emancipation Proclamation)*

2 INSTRUCT

Reforms in Medieval England
10.2.2

Critical Thinking

- What are advantages or disadvantages of a common law system? *(Advantage–Laws may be fairer and more practical. Disadvantage–"Bad" precedents may be difficult to overturn.)*

CALIFORNIA RESOURCES

California Reading Toolkit, p. L7
California Modified Lesson Plans for English Learners, p. 9
California Daily Standards Practice Transparencies, TTC
California Standards Enrichment Workbook, pp. 17–18, 25–26
California Standards Planner and Lesson Plans, p. L5
California Online Test Practice
California Test Generator CD-ROM
California Easy Planner CD-ROM
California eEdition CD-ROM

3

Windows and ceiling of Bath Cathedral, Bath, England

Illuminated manuscript with knight traveling to the Holy Land

Democracy Develops in England

MAIN IDEA	WHY IT MATTERS NOW	TERMS & NAMES
POWER AND AUTHORITY England began to develop democratic institutions that limited the power of the monarchy.	Democratic traditions developed in England have influenced many countries, including the United States.	• common law • Magna Carta • due process of law • Parliament • divine right • Glorious Revolution • constitutional monarchy • bill of rights

CALIFORNIA STANDARDS

10.1.1 Analyze the similarities and differences in Judeo-Christian and Greco-Roman views of law, reason and faith, and duties of the individual.

10.2.2 List the principles of the Magna Carta, the English Bill of Rights (1689), the American Declaration of Independence (1776), the French Declaration of the Rights of Man and the Citizen (1789), and the U.S. Bill of Rights (1791).

CST 1 Students compare the present with the past, evaluating the consequences of past events and decisions and determining the lessons that were learned.

SETTING THE STAGE The idea of democracy developed gradually over the centuries, as you read in previous sections. From its beginnings in the city-states of ancient Greece, democracy moved to Rome. There, the Romans adapted democratic ideas to establish a republican form of government. Judaism and Christianity spread the ideas of individual worth and responsibility to community. Democracy finally took root and found permanence in England in the late Middle Ages.

Reforms in Medieval England

In 1066, William, duke of Normandy in France, invaded England and defeated the Anglo-Saxons at the Battle of Hastings. William then claimed the English throne. This set in motion events that led to: (1) the end of feudalism—the political and economic system of the Middle Ages, (2) the beginnings of centralized government in England, and (3) the development of democracy there. One of William's descendants was Henry II, who ruled from 1154 to 1189. He controlled most of the western half of France, as well as all of England. A man of great wisdom and vigor, Henry is considered one of the most gifted statesmen of the 12th century.

Juries and Common Law One of Henry's greatest achievements was the development of the jury trial as a means of administering royal justice. Before then, people were tried in courts of feudal lords. In such courts, the accused would usually have to survive a duel or some physically painful or dangerous ordeal to be set free.

With Henry's innovation, a royal judge would visit each shire, or county, at least once a year. First, the judge would review the crime that had been committed. Then he would ask 12 men, often neighbors of the accused, to answer questions about the facts of the case. These people were known as a jury. Unlike modern juries, they did not decide guilt or innocence. People came to prefer the jury trial to the feudal-court trial because they found it more just.

TAKING NOTES
Following Chronological Order Use a time line to show the main events in the development of democracy in England.

1215 Magna Carta

King John of England ▸

SECTION 3 PROGRAM RESOURCES

ALL STUDENTS

In-Depth Resources: Unit 1
- Guided Reading, p. 3

Formal Assessment
- Section Quiz, p. 7

ENGLISH LEARNERS

In-Depth Resources in Spanish
- Guided Reading, p. 13

Reading Study Guide (Spanish), p. 9
Reading Study Guide Audio CD (Spanish)

STRUGGLING READERS

In-Depth Resources: Unit 1
- Guided Reading, p. 3

Reading Study Guide, p. 9
Reading Study Guide Audio CD

GIFTED AND TALENTED STUDENTS

In-Depth Resources: Unit 8
- Primary Source: from the Magna Carta, p. 10
- Literature: from *Here Be Dragons,* p. 12
- Connections Across Time and Cultures: New Beginnings for Democracy, p. 17

Electronic Library of Primary Sources
- "The Restoration of Charles II"

INTEGRATED TECHNOLOGY

eEdition CD-ROM
Power Presentations CD-ROM
Electronic Library of Primary Sources
- "The Restoration of Charles II"

classzone.com

Legal decisions made by royal justices were used as precedents in new cases. Gradually, England was unified under a single legal system. This was called "common law" because it was common to the whole kingdom. Unlike Roman law, which expressed the will of a ruler or a lawmaker, **common law** reflected customs and principles established over time. Common law became the basis of the legal systems in many English-speaking countries, including the United States.

The Magna Carta When Henry II died, his son Richard the Lion-Hearted assumed the throne. Richard's brother John, an unpopular king, followed him. King John fought a costly and unsuccessful war with France. Not only did England lose many of its land holdings in France, but John also tried to raise taxes to pay for the war. This led to conflict between the English nobles and the king. In 1215 the angry nobles rebelled and forced John to grant guarantees of certain traditional political rights. They presented their demands to him in written form as the **Magna Carta** (Great Charter).

Vocabulary
A *contract* is an agreement between two or more parties, especially one that is written and enforceable by law.

The Magna Carta is the major source of traditional English respect for individual rights and liberties. Basically, it was a contract between the king and nobles of England. However, the Magna Carta contained certain important principles that limited the power of the English monarch over all his English subjects. It implied the idea that monarchs had no right to rule in any way they pleased. They had to govern according to law.

Analyzing Primary Sources

The Magna Carta

The Magna Carta is considered one of the cornerstones of democratic government. The underlying principle of the document is the idea that all must obey the law, even the king. Its guaranteed rights are an important part of modern liberties and justice.

PRIMARY SOURCE

38. No bailiff [officer of the court] for the future shall, upon his own unsupported complaint, put anyone to his "law," without credible witnesses brought for this purpose.

39. No freeman shall be taken or imprisoned . . . or exiled or in any way destroyed, nor will we [the king] go upon him nor send upon him, except by the lawful judgement of his peers or by the law of the land.

40. To no one will we sell, to no one will we refuse or delay, right or justice.

45. We will appoint as justices, constables, sheriffs, or bailiffs only such as know the law of the realm and mean to observe it well.

DOCUMENT-BASED QUESTIONS

1. **Analyzing Motives** *Why might the English nobles have insisted on the right listed in number 45?*
2. **Making Inferences** *Which of the statements is a forerunner to the right to a speedy public trial guaranteed in the Sixth Amendment of the U.S. Constitution?*

Tip for English Learners

Explain that *precedent* is related to the word *precede* and, in law, refers to a judicial decision that can serve as a rule to be applied under similar circumstances in future cases.

More About . . .

Limits on Monarchy

The Magna Carta was only the first step in the ongoing struggle between the English monarchy and nobility. In 1258, English barons forced King Henry III to sign the Provisions of Oxford. The Provisions gave the barons the right to rule with the king in exchange for financial aid. Although soon discarded, the Provisions are regarded as the first written constitution in English history. Had the Provisions been enforced, they would have effectively established a constitutional monarchy 400 years earlier than its establishment under William and Mary.

Analyzing Primary Sources

The Magna Carta

Ask students to restate law 38.
(Possible Answer: Government officials cannot arrest anyone without believable witnesses.)

Answers to Document-Based Questions

1. **Analyzing Motives** to prevent the king from appointing men who would do anything he told them to
2. **Making Inferences** number 40

DIFFERENTIATING INSTRUCTION: GIFTED AND TALENTED STUDENTS

Creating a Skit About the Magna Carta

Class Time 45 minutes
Task Researching and writing a short skit
Purpose To demonstrate understanding of the Magna Carta's contents and importance
Instructions Divide students into groups. Have each group research the Magna Carta, the events that led to its signing, and the scene of its signing at Runnymeade. Then ask them to write a brief skit in which a news reporter on the scene describes the events leading up to the signing, interviews a group of nobles presenting their demands to King John, reads excerpts from the document, and interviews the king before he signs it. Skits should mention what grievances the nobles have and how the king feels about signing. If time permits, ask for volunteers to perform one or more skits.

Students may wish to use the primary source excerpt from the Magna Carta or the literature excerpt from *Here Be Dragons.* Both are available in In-Depth Resources: Unit 1.

In-Depth Resources: Unit 1

The Magna Carta had 63 clauses. Two established basic legal rights for individuals. Clause 12 declared that taxes "shall be levied in our kingdom only by the common consent of our kingdom." This meant that the king had to ask for popular consent before he could tax. Clause 39 declared, "No man shall be arrested or imprisoned . . . except by the lawful judgment of his peers or by the law of the land." This meant that a person had the right to a jury trial and to the protection of the law. This right—to have the law work in known, orderly ways—is called **due process of law**. In other words, the king could not willfully, or arbitrarily, punish his subjects. (A)

Over the centuries, the principles of the Magna Carta were extended to protect the liberties of all the English people. Clause 12, for example, was later interpreted to mean that the king could not levy taxes without the consent of **Parliament**, England's national legislature. The principle of "no taxation without representation" was a rallying cry, over five centuries later, of the American Revolution.

MAIN IDEA

Drawing Conclusions

(A) How did the principle of rule by law, as implied in the Magna Carta, limit the power of the king?

A. Possible Answer It implied that monarchs could not rule as they pleased; they had to govern according to the law.

Model Parliament Even before the Norman Conquest, Anglo-Saxon kings had discussed important issues with members of the nobility who acted as a council of advisers. This practice continued through the centuries. In 1295, King John's grandson, Edward I, needed money to pay for yet another war in France. He wanted wide support for the war. So he called together not only the lords but also lesser knights and some burgesses, or leading citizens of the towns. Edward explained his action by saying, "What affects all, by all should be approved." Historians refer to this famous gathering as the Model Parliament, because it established a standard for later parliaments. The Model Parliament voted on taxes and helped Edward make reforms and consolidate laws.

By the mid-1300s, the knights and burgesses had gained an official role in the government. They had formed an assembly of their own—the House of Commons, which was the lower house of Parliament. Nobles and bishops met separately in the upper house, the House of Lords. Because the great majority of English people had no part in Parliament, it was not truly a democratic body. Even so, its existence limited the power of the monarch and established the principle of representation.

▼ The House of Commons meeting in its chamber

Parliament Grows Stronger

Over the next few centuries, Parliament's "power of the purse," or its right to approve certain expenses, gave it strong influence in governing. The House of Commons, which controlled those purse strings, was gradually becoming the equal of the House of Lords. Parliament increasingly viewed itself as a partner with the monarch in governing. It voted on taxes, passed laws, and advised on royal policies.

Conflict With the Monarch The struggle to limit the power of the monarchy continued over the centuries. In the 1600s, monarchs on the European continent were asserting greater authority over lords than they had during the Middle Ages. These kings claimed not just the right to rule but the right to rule with absolute power. They claimed that a king's power came from God. This assertion was known as the theory of the **divine right** of kings. Advocates of divine right said that monarchs were chosen by God and responsible only to God.

Parliament Grows Stronger
10.1.1

Critical Thinking

- Why might English kings have resorted to the Star Chamber? *(They could more successfully prosecute their opponents there than in the parliamentary courts.)*
- What impact might the execution of Charles I have had on English government? *(Possible Answers: signaled the ascendancy of Parliament, weakened the notion of divine-right monarchy)*

More About . . .

Power of the Purse

Struggles between Parliament and monarchy over the issue of money must seem familiar to U.S. presidents and to Congress. The president proposes a yearly budget, which Congress either approves or amends. The tension between the two branches of government over the budget can reach a crisis level.

At the end of 1995, President Clinton vetoed a budget amended by the House of Representatives. The House then refused to vote for emergency funding to operate the government, which shut down for several weeks. Both sides eventually agreed to a compromise.

DIFFERENTIATING INSTRUCTION: ENGLISH LEARNERS

Paraphrasing a Passage

Class Time 20 minutes

Task Rewriting a textbook passage in informal language

Purpose To better understand the text by paraphrasing it

Instructions Tell students to pick two paragraphs from "Parliament Grows Stronger" and rewrite them in their own words. Make the activity more enjoyable for students by encouraging them to use informal language. A sample paragraph follows.

A woman named Elizabeth came from a family called the Tudors. At some point, she became England's queen and went by the name of Elizabeth I. She died in 1603. Usually, when an English monarch died, one of the monarch's children became the new monarch. Since Elizabeth didn't have any children, a relative from Scotland was put in charge. He was called James I and was from a family called the Stuarts. The Stuarts said monarchs get their power straight from God. This belief that James I had about divine rights, along with his ignorance about how they did things in England, soon got him into trouble with the English Parliament.

Elizabeth I, the last Tudor monarch of England, died in 1603, without a child. She was succeeded by a new line of monarchs, the Stuarts, who were relatives from Scotland. The Stuarts were strong believers in divine right. King James VI of Scotland became James I, the first Stuart king of England. Because he came from Scotland and knew little of English laws and institutions, he clashed with Parliament over the rights of the people.

Three issues caused conflict. First, religious reformers known as Puritans were trying to change the Church of England, or Anglican Church, through legislation. They wanted to simplify, or purify, Church doctrines and ceremonies. They felt the Church of England was still too much like the Roman Catholic Church, from which it had separated. The Puritans entered an ongoing battle with James, the official head of the Church.

Second, James used the Star Chamber, a royal court of law, to administer justice. He ignored parliamentary courts, which used common law. The people began to accuse the king of tyranny. Third, and most important, was the issue of money. Elizabeth had left James a large debt. In addition, he wanted more money in order to have an extravagant court and to wage war. Parliament declined to grant him any additional funds. James then ignored Parliament and tried to raise money by other means. B

Vocabulary
Tyranny is absolute power, especially when exercised harshly or unjustly.

MAIN IDEA
Analyzing Issues
B Explain the controversy between James I and Parliament.
B. Possible Answer James believed in divine right–that he was responsible only to God. Parliament felt that this clashed with the traditional rights of the English people.

Parliament Overthrows the King The troubles under James became explosions under his son, Charles I, who became king in 1625. Like James, Charles needed funds. He asked Parliament for money in 1628. In return for granting revenue from taxes, Parliament tried to limit royal power further. It sought to force Charles to accept the Petition of Right.

The Petition of Right went against theories of absolute monarchy. It is viewed as a landmark in constitutional history. It demanded an end to

- taxing without Parliament's consent
- imprisoning citizens illegally
- housing troops in citizens' homes
- maintaining military government in peacetime

Charles agreed to sign the petition in order to get the funds he wanted. Later, he ignored the commitments secured in the document.

Charles dismissed Parliament in 1629 and refused to convene it again. When the Scots invaded England in 1640, Charles was forced to call Parliament to get funds to defend the country. In a show of independence, Parliament refused to discuss money until Charles considered how he had wronged Parliament. Parliament passed laws to reduce the power of the monarchy, angering the king. Grievances continued to grow. Eventually, in 1642, the English Civil War broke out. Royalists, who upheld the monarchy, were opposed by antiroyalists, who supported Parliament.

After years of conflict, antiroyalist forces, commanded by Puritan leader Oliver Cromwell, won control of the government. Charles was condemned as a "tyrant, murderer, and public enemy" and, in 1649, was executed.

History Makers

James I
1566–1625

As king, James believed he had absolute authority to govern England as he saw fit. Royal authority came directly from God, and kings were answerable only to God, not to the people or Parliament.

In a speech to Parliament in 1609, James declared:

> *The state of monarchy is the supremest thing upon earth . . . Kings are justly called Gods, for that they exercise a manner or resemblance of divine power upon earth . . . [T]o dispute what God may do, is blasphemy . . . so is it sedition in subjects, to dispute what a king may do.*

James had passed down these views to a son a decade earlier in *Basilicon Doron*, a book of instructions he wrote on the ways of kingship.

More About . . .

James's Conflict with the Puritans

Among the demands for reform that the Puritans made of King James I was the request to set up a group of elders to help each bishop decide religious questions. James refused to make this change because he had control over the bishops and did not want to give up his power to a more democratic body.

History Makers

James I

Do you think James I used religion cynically to gain greater power, or was he genuinely faithful and a believer in his divine right to rule? *(Possible Answer: Based on the quoted passage, it appears that he truly believed in such rights.)*

James was very interested in religion and scholarship. He agreed with Church reformers that, although there were many English translations of the Bible, none was well written enough to be an official version. Therefore, he sponsored a committee of Bible scholars to create a new translation.

The new version of the Bible was first printed in 1611. The King James Bible is noted for the elegance and power of its language. It is still read by millions of English-speaking Protestants throughout the world.

COOPERATIVE LEARNING

English Civil War Trading Cards

Class Time 40 minutes

Task Creating a set of trading cards featuring major figures from the English Civil War

Purpose To learn more about the English Civil War

Instructions Divide the class into groups. Explain that each group will make a set of English Civil War trading cards. Tell them to begin their project by rereading "Parliament Grows Stronger." Then have students use the library or the Internet to do further research on the war. Next, students should work as a group to design a format for their cards. Information might include date and place of birth and death, role in the war, interesting biographical information, and quotations about or by the individual.

Students should also work as a team to put together a pamphlet that will be included in the card set. The pamphlet will put the trading cards in context by providing a brief general history of the war. After they have agreed on a design, each team member should make a trading card for a different individual. As a class, discuss what people and information students chose to include.

Establishment of Constitutional Monarchy
10.2.2

Critical Thinking

- Why might Charles II have accepted the limitations Parliament imposed? *(Possible Answer: The memory of his father's execution probably made him more cooperative.)*
- Why wouldn't Parliament simply pick a suitable leader from outside the royal family? *(Possible Answers: They may have believed that such a move would appear illegitimate and cause renewed unrest.)*

In-Depth Resources: Unit 1

- Connections Across Time and Cultures: New Beginnings for Democracy, p. 17

Electronic Library of Primary Sources

- "The Restoration of Charles II"

Global Impact

Prelude to the American Revolution

On April 18, 1689, New Englanders in the English North American colonies captured the hated royal governor, Sir Edmund Andros, and put him in jail. Although Andros was overthrown, England retained power over the New England colonies. The king chose the governor of the colony, who could refuse to seat specific elected representatives in the colony's government.

Establishment of Constitutional Monarchy

After Charles's execution, Cromwell established a republic called the Commonwealth of England. He spent several years crushing a series of uprisings against his rule. He was opposed both by supporters of monarchy and by more extreme Puritans. Cromwell became unhappy with Parliament's failure to enact his religious, social, and economic reforms. In 1653 he dissolved Parliament and created a government called the Protectorate. He named himself Lord Protector, in effect becoming a military dictator.

Cromwell's rule was increasingly authoritarian, and he became extremely unpopular. Most of the English were not unhappy at his death in 1658.

The Restoration Cromwell's son Richard succeeded him as Lord Protector. He was not a strong ruler, and the military dictatorship continued to be unpopular. Cromwell resigned in 1659. In 1660, a new Parliament restored the monarchy and invited Charles Stuart, the son of Charles I, to take the throne. This period was called the Restoration, because the monarchy was restored to the throne. Yet Parliament retained the powers it had gained during the struggles of the previous two decades. For example, the monarch could not tax without Parliament's consent. C

MAIN IDEA
Analyzing Causes
C What caused Parliament to restore the monarchy?
C. Possible Answer The military dictatorship was extremely unpopular because it was authoritarian.

In addition, Parliament continued to try to limit the monarchy and to expand rights. In 1679 it passed the Habeas Corpus Amendment Act. *Habeas corpus* is a Latin term meaning "you are ordered to have the body." When someone is arrested, the police must produce the person in court. That person must be informed of what he or she is accused of having done. The court then decides if there is reason to hold the accused. Habeas corpus prevents authorities from detaining a person wrongfully or unjustly. (This right is still important in democracies today. It is mentioned in the U.S. Constitution.)

Glorious Revolution When Charles II died in 1685, his younger brother became King James II. James was a Roman Catholic and a believer in the divine right of kings. English Protestants were afraid that he wanted to make Catholicism the official religion. They hoped that when James died, his Protestant daughter, Mary, would become queen. But James's wife gave birth to a son in 1688. Because a male heir to the throne took precedence, or came before, a female, it appeared that rule by Catholic monarchs would continue. This was unacceptable to most of the English people.

Parliament withdrew its support from James and offered the English throne to his daughter, Mary, and her husband, William of Orange, ruler of the Netherlands, both Protestants. William invaded England, and James fled to France. In 1689 William and Mary were crowned co-rulers of England. The **Glorious Revolution**, as it came to be called, was a turning point in English constitutional history. Parliament had established its right to limit the English monarch's power and to control succession to the throne. England was now a **constitutional monarchy**, in which the powers of the ruler are restricted by the constitution and the laws of the country.

Global Impact

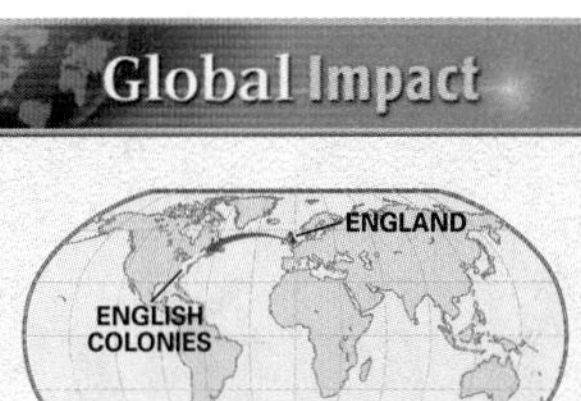

Prelude to the American Revolution

James II's unpopularity extended across the Atlantic Ocean to England's American colonies.

In 1684, a royal court took away the charter of the Massachusetts Bay Colony. James had decided to create a union of all colonies from New Jersey to New Hampshire. He appointed Sir Edmund Andros as royal governor of the Dominion of New England. Andros abolished elective assemblies, declared town meetings illegal, and collected taxes the people had never voted on.

When word of the Glorious Revolution reached America, the colonists overthrew Andros in their own version of the revolt. This action may have contributed to the colonists' belief that it was their right to overthrow an unjust king.

DIFFERENTIATING INSTRUCTION: STRUGGLING READERS

"Who Am I?"

Class Time 20 minutes

Task Defining or describing people and events in history

Purpose To help students understand complex material

Instructions Explain that the text under "Establishment of Constitutional Monarchy" is especially challenging because it includes many names, dates, and concepts that are new to students. Pair students and assign each pair a term or name from the following list:

- Parliament
- Oliver Cromwell
- Richard Cromwell
- Charles II
- habeas corpus
- James II
- Glorious Revolution
- constitutional monarchy
- bill of rights

Each pair should write a few sentences that answer the question "Who am I?" or "What am I?" about their term or name. For example, the answer to "Oliver Cromwell" might be, "I ruled England as Lord Protector in the mid-1600s. I was a strong ruler but very unpopular." Have pairs share their answers, emphasizing how the different terms and names are connected.

English Bill of Rights In 1689, William and Mary accepted from Parliament a **bill of rights**, or formal summary of the rights and liberties believed essential to the people. The English Bill of Rights limited the monarchy's power and protected free speech in Parliament.

The Bill of Rights did not allow the monarch to suspend laws, to tax without Parliament's consent, or to raise an army in peacetime without approval from Parliament. It assured the people the right to petition the king to seek remedies for grievances against government. Excessive bail and cruel and unusual punishment were forbidden. And foremost, the Bill of Rights declared:

▲ William and Mary became rulers of England in 1689.

PRIMARY SOURCE

. . . that for redress of all grievances, and for the amending, strengthening, and preserving of the laws, parliament ought to be held frequently.

English Bill of Rights

D. Possible Answers England gave the world the guarantee of the rule of law, parliamentary government, individual liberties, and constitutional monarchy.

MAIN IDEA

Summarizing

D What was England's legacy to democracy?

England's Legacy England's Glorious Revolution and the bill of rights that it produced had a great impact. English citizens were guaranteed the rule of law, parliamentary government, individual liberties, and a constitutional monarchy. This completed a process begun with the Magna Carta. The Bill of Rights also set an example for England's American colonists when they considered grievances against Britain nearly 100 years later. These legal and political developments, along with the ideas of the Enlightenment, would give rise to democratic revolutions in America and France in the late 18th century. D

More About . . .

The English Bill of Rights

The United States adopted many of the government reforms and institutions that the English developed in this period, including

- the right to habeas corpus—a document that stops authorities from holding a person in jail without being charged
- a Bill of Rights guaranteeing freedom of speech and freedom of worship
- a strong legislature and strong executive, which act as checks on each other

SECTION 3 ASSESSMENT

TERMS & NAMES 1. For each term or name, write a sentence explaining its significance.

• common law • Magna Carta • due process of law • Parliament • divine right • Glorious Revolution • constitutional monarchy • bill of rights

USING YOUR NOTES

2. Which of the events listed do you think was the most important? Explain. (10.2.2)

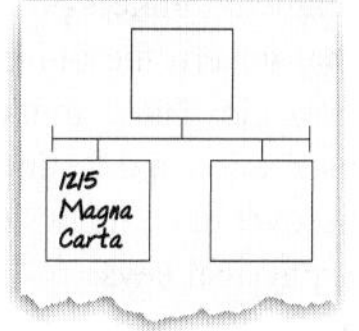

MAIN IDEAS

3. What were three eventual consequences of William the Conqueror's victory at Hastings? (10.2.2)
4. What important legal practice dates back to Henry II? (10.2.2)
5. Why did Parliament invite William and Mary to rule England in 1689? (10.1.1)

CRITICAL THINKING & WRITING

6. **RECOGNIZING EFFECTS** What impact did the English common law have on the United States? (CST 1)
7. **COMPARING** Why was Oliver Cromwell's rule like that of an absolute monarch? (10.1.1)
8. **SUMMARIZING** What were the main achievements of the Glorious Revolution? (10.2.2)
9. **WRITING ACTIVITY** POWER AND AUTHORITY Think of yourself as an adviser to King John. Write him a **letter** in which you argue for or against accepting the Magna Carta. Tell the king the advantages and disadvantages of agreeing to the demands of the nobles. (Writing 2.4.d)

CONNECT TO TODAY **COMPARING HISTORICAL DOCUMENTS**

Locate a copy of the Magna Carta and a copy of the Bill of Rights of the U.S. Constitution. Study both documents and create a **table** showing where the U.S. Bill of Rights reflects the ideas of the Magna Carta. (CST 1)

3 ASSESS

SECTION 3 ASSESSMENT

After students have worked on the first five questions independently, have them work in pairs to check their answers and to complete the remainder of the questions.

Formal Assessment

- Section Quiz, p. 7

4 RETEACH

Use question 2 to review the section. Hold a class discussion about the event students think was most important and why.

ANSWERS

1. common law, p. 19 • Magna Carta, p. 19 • due process of law, p. 20 • Parliament, p. 20 • divine right, p. 20 • Glorious Revolution, p. 22 • constitutional monarchy, p. 22 • bill of rights, p. 23
2. **Sample Answer:** 1295—Model Parliament, 1679—habeas corpus, 1689—Bill of Rights. Most important—Magna Carta, as it was the foundation for further progress.
3. Feudalism ended; centralized government began in England; democracy developed there
4. trial by jury
5. to keep England Protestant
6. Principles of English common law are the basis for law in the United States.
7. Cromwell dissolved Parliament and became increasingly authoritarian.
8. Parliament's right to limit the power of monarchs; guarantee of citizens' rights and liberties
9. **Rubric** Letters should
   - list advantages and disadvantages of signing.
   - take a position on the monarch's signing.

CONNECT TO TODAY

Rubric Tables should

- identify elements of the Magna Carta reflected in the U.S. Bill of Rights.
- link the Magna Carta elements to the correct locations in the U.S. Bill of Rights.

LESSON PLAN

OBJECTIVES

- Compare ideas of the Enlightenment and discuss their influence.
- Trace democracy in North America.
- Outline changes in government that occurred during the French Revolution.
- Describe modern struggles for democracy.

1 FOCUS & MOTIVATE

Ask students what are the foundations of U.S. democracy. *(Possible Answers: Constitution, Bill of Rights, rule of law)*

2 INSTRUCT

Enlightenment Thinkers and Ideas

10.2.1

Critical Thinking

- Where does the belief in equal rights come from? *(from the Christian belief in the equality of all human beings)*

CALIFORNIA RESOURCES

California Reading Toolkit, p. L8
California Modified Lesson Plans for English Learners, p. 11
California Daily Standards Practice Transparencies, TTD
California Standards Enrichment Workbook, pp. 23–24, 29–30, 105–106
California Standards Planner and Lesson Plans, p. L7
California Online Test Practice
California Test Generator CD-ROM
California Easy Planner CD-ROM
California eEdition CD-ROM

Andreæ Cellarius, Copernican Solar System, From *Harmonia Macrocosmica*

Stearns, *The Signing of the Constitution in 1787*

4

The Enlightenment and Democratic Revolutions

MAIN IDEA	WHY IT MATTERS NOW	TERMS & NAMES
REVOLUTION Enlightenment ideas helped bring about the American and French revolutions.	These revolutions and the documents they produced have inspired other democratic movements.	• Enlightenment • social contract • natural rights • separation of powers • representative government • federal system • United Nations

CALIFORNIA STANDARDS

10.2.1 Compare the major ideas of philosophers and their effects on the democratic revolutions in England, the United States, France, and Latin America (e.g., John Locke, Charles-Louis Montesquieu, Jean-Jacques Rousseau, Simón Bolívar, Thomas Jefferson, James Madison).

10.2.4 Explain how the ideology of the French Revolution led France to develop from constitutional monarchy to democratic despotism to the Napoleonic empire.

10.9.8 Discuss the establishment and work of the United Nations and the purposes and functions of the Warsaw Pact, SEATO, NATO, and the Organization of American States.

SETTING THE STAGE The Renaissance continued to affect European thinking throughout the 17th century. The Renaissance emphasis on the individual and on expanding human potential were especially influential. At the same time, Europeans began to explore their physical world. They extended the boundaries of the known world in what came to be called the Age of Exploration. New ideas and discoveries had a great impact on Europeans' understanding of themselves and the world.

Enlightenment Thinkers and Ideas

During the 17th and 18th centuries, an intellectual movement called the **Enlightenment** developed. Enlightenment thinkers tried to apply the principles of reason and the methods of science to all aspects of society. They built upon the long history of Western thought.

The philosophers of ancient Greece had established the idea of natural laws that could be discovered by careful observation and reasoned inquiry. Christianity contributed the belief in the equality of all human beings. (This belief would later lead to the principle of equal rights in society.) During the Renaissance, thinkers had focused on worldly concerns. They criticized medieval philosophy for concentrating on questions that seemed unrelated to human conditions.

The Scientific Revolution of the 1500s and 1600s was an even more immediate source of Enlightenment thought. It stimulated new ideas about society and government. The Scientific Revolution caused thinkers to rely on rational thought rather than just accept traditional beliefs. Enlightenment thinkers praised both Isaac Newton's discovery of the mechanical laws that govern the universe and the scientific method that made such a discovery possible. These thinkers wanted to apply the scientific method, which relied on observation and testing of theories, to human affairs. They hoped to use reason to discover natural laws that governed society just as scientists had used it to discover physical laws.

TAKING NOTES

Outlining Use an outline to organize the main ideas and details.

I. Enlightenment Thinkers and Ideas
  A.
  B.
II. The Beginnings of Democracy in America
  A.
  B.
III. The French Revolution

Hobbes and Locke The English philosophers Thomas Hobbes and John Locke were important Enlightenment thinkers. Both considered human nature and the role of government. In his masterpiece of political theory, *Leviathan* (1651), Hobbes stated that people were by nature selfish and ambitious. He thought the type of government needed to control selfish ambitions was absolute monarchy.

SECTION 4 PROGRAM RESOURCES

ALL STUDENTS

In-Depth Resources: Unit 1
- Guided Reading, p. 4
- History Makers: John Locke, p. 16

Formal Assessment
- Section Quiz, p. 8

ENGLISH LEARNERS

In-Depth Resources in Spanish
- Guided Reading, p. 14

Reading Study Guide (Spanish), p. 11
Reading Study Guide Audio CD (Spanish)

STRUGGLING READERS

In-Depth Resources: Unit 1
- Guided Reading, p. 4

Reading Study Guide, p. 11
Reading Study Guide Audio CD

GIFTED AND TALENTED STUDENTS

In-Depth Resources: Unit 1
- Primary Source: from the Iroquois Constitution, p. 11
- Literature: from *1776,* p. 13

Electronic Library of Primary Sources
- Destruction of the Berlin Wall

INTEGRATED TECHNOLOGY

eEdition CD-ROM
Power Presentations CD-ROM
World Art and Cultures Transparencies
- AT50 *Portrait of Marie Antoinette and Her Children*

Electronic Library of Primary Sources
- Destruction of the Berlin Wall

classzone.com

In a kind of **social contract**, or agreement among members of society, people submitted to an authoritarian ruler to prevent disorder. Although Hobbes was a monarchist, his idea of a social contract was important for the development of democracy.

Locke held a more positive view of human nature. His book *Two Treatises of Government* was published in 1690, the year after the Glorious Revolution. Locke argued that the English people had been justified in overthrowing James II. The government had failed under James to perform its most fundamental duty—protecting the rights of the people. Locke said that all human beings had, by nature, the right to life, liberty, and property. In order to protect these **natural rights**, they formed governments. The people had an absolute right, he said, to rebel against a government that violated or failed to protect their rights.

Locke believed that a government's power comes from the people, not from God. Thus, Locke provided a strong argument against the divine right of kings. Locke's ideas about self-government inspired people and became cornerstones of modern democratic thought. (A)

A. Possible Answer Locke believed that a government's power comes from the people, not from God.

MAIN IDEA

Summarizing

(A) What was John Locke's argument against the divine right of kings?

Voltaire and Rousseau Other thinkers of the Enlightenment admired the democratic nature of English institutions. They themselves, however, lived under absolute monarchs. Voltaire was a brilliant 18th-century French historian. He argued in favor of tolerance, freedom of religion, and free speech. The French government and Christianity were often targets of his criticism.

Vocabulary

A *freethinker* is one who rejects dogma and authority.

Perhaps the most freethinking of all Enlightenment philosophers was Jean-Jacques Rousseau. His most famous work was *The Social Contract* (1762). In it, Rousseau advocated democracy. Unlike Hobbes, he called the social contract an agreement among free individuals to create a government that would respond to the people's will:

PRIMARY SOURCE

The problem is to find a form of association which will defend and protect with the whole common force the person and goods of each associate, and in which each, while uniting himself with all, may still obey himself alone, and remain as free as before.

JEAN-JACQUES ROUSSEAU, *The Social Contract*

For Rousseau, the only legitimate, or authentic, government came from the consent of the governed. The people, he hoped, would follow their consciences to vote for, or choose, what was best for the community as a whole.

Montesquieu Another French philosopher, Baron de Montesquieu, also recognized liberty as a natural right. In *The Spirit of the Laws* (1748), Montesquieu pointed out that any person or group in power will try to increase its power. Like Aristotle, Montesquieu searched for a way to control government. He concluded that liberty could best be safeguarded by a **separation of powers**, that is, by dividing government into three separate branches. These branches were (1) a legislature to make laws, (2) an executive to enforce them, and (3) courts to interpret them. The United States and many other democratic countries use this basic plan.

The Beginnings of Democracy in America

The ideas of the Enlightenment had a strong impact on Britain's North American colonies. By the mid-1700s, 13 British colonies had been established in North America. They were administered by the British government. To the north and west of Britain's colonies was New France, a French colony. In 1754, Britain and France went to war for control of North America. The war was called the French and Indian War. France and England also fought in Europe. There the conflict was known as the Seven Years' War.

More About . . .

John Locke

During Charles II's reign, John Locke fell under suspicion of treason. He fled England for the Netherlands. There he was befriended by Prince William of Orange and his wife, Mary. When they became the ruling monarchs of England, Locke also returned and became a court favorite.

In addition to his political writings, Locke published *An Essay Concerning Human Understanding* (1690). It describes how the mind learns about the world. Locke believed that at birth, the mind is a clean slate, a *tabula rasa*. As a person grows, he or she is affected by many experiences. People used reason, Locke asserted, to make sense of their experiences and to discover order in the universe.

In-Depth Resources: Unit 1

• History Makers: John Locke, p. 16

The Beginnings of Democracy in America

10.2.1

Critical Thinking

- Do you think the colonists were justified in protesting the Stamp Act? *(Yes—Taxation without representation is wrong. No—The colonists should have helped to pay for the war.)*
- Why did the founders opt for an indirect rather than a direct democracy? *(Possible Answer: They probably believed a direct democracy would be too unwieldy in a large nation.)*

COOPERATIVE LEARNING

Depicting Enlightenment Thinkers and Ideas

Class Time 45 minutes

Task Creating posters

Purpose To learn about people and ideas of the Enlightenment

Instructions Divide students into pairs and tell them that they will be making posters that feature major Enlightenment thinkers. Have students begin the project by reviewing the material under "Enlightenment Thinkers and Ideas." Pairs should each choose one figure from the text as the subject of their poster. (You may expand the list to include others, such as Denis Diderot, David Hume, Immanuel Kant, and Blaise Pascal.) Once students have chosen their subject, ask them to carry out further research using the library or the Internet. The aim of their research should be images of or related to their subjects, biographical information, discussions of their subject's major works and ideas, and interesting or representative quotations and anecdotes. Encourage students to be creative. When students have completed their projects, plan a "gallery opening" to show and discuss their work.

More About . . .

Thomas Jefferson

The author of the Declaration of Independence, Thomas Jefferson of Virginia was a true figure of the Enlightenment. Of his many achievements, Jefferson wanted to be remembered for three: author of the Declaration of Independence, author of the Statute of Virginia for Religious Freedom, and founder of the University of Virginia.

More About . . .

Other North American Governments

The Iroquois Confederacy was a loose organization of Native American groups from what is now New York state. It was formed in the late 1500s and lasted more than 200 years. The federation impressed the colonists with its efficient organization, and it may even have influenced the federal structure of the United States government.

In-Depth Resources: Unit 1

- Primary Source: from the Iroquois Constitution, p. 11

Americans Protest British Policies The American colonists helped Britain defeat France in the French and Indian War, which ended in 1763. The war had been very costly, however, and further expenses lay ahead. Britain believed its colonies should pay some of the cost because they shared some of the benefits. To protect the newly acquired territory, the British needed to keep even more soldiers in America. To raise money, Britain sought to tax the colonists. The British Parliament passed the Stamp Act in 1765. It was the first in a series of such tax measures.

The colonists, who were not represented in Parliament, protested what they viewed as a violation of their rights as British citizens—there should be no taxation without representation. The colonists also resented the British for preventing them from settling on land west of the Appalachian Mountains. They felt that the French and Indian War had been fought to allow westward expansion.

Americans Win Independence The colonists opposed each tax measure Parliament imposed. Eventually, to protect their economic and political rights, the colonists united and began to arm themselves against what they called British oppression. The colonists' fight for independence from Great Britain, the American Revolution, began with the Battle of Lexington and Concord on April 19, 1775. The Americans issued a Declaration of Independence on July 4, 1776. In it, they declared to King George III of England and to the world why they should be free of British rule. The ideas of the Enlightenment—especially Locke's ideas that governments are created by the people to protect their rights—strongly influenced the writers of the Declaration. After five more years of war, the British army surrendered in 1781. The Americans had won their independence.

For several years, the new nation existed as a loose federation, or union, of states under a plan of government called the Articles of Confederation. Americans had wanted a weak central government. They feared that a strong government would lead to the kind of tyranny they had rebelled against. The Articles established one body, the Congress. But it was too weak. It did not have the power to collect taxes to pay war debt or to finance the government.

Enlightenment Ideas Shape the Constitution In the summer of 1787, a group of American leaders met in Philadelphia. They had been chosen by their state legislatures to frame, or work out, a better plan of government. The result of their efforts was the Constitution of the United States. This document has served as an inspiration and a model for new democracies around the world for more than 200

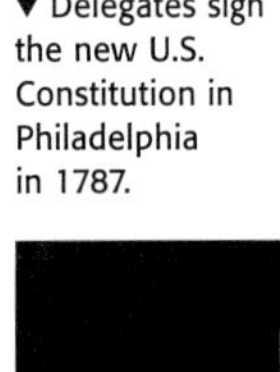

▼ Delegates sign the new U.S. Constitution in Philadelphia in 1787.

DIFFERENTIATING INSTRUCTION: ENGLISH LEARNERS

Debating British Control of the American Colonies

Class Time 35 minutes

Task Summarizing information and conducting a debate

Purpose To understand the conflict between Britain and the colonies

Instructions Pair students. Have pairs read "The Beginnings of Democracy in America" on pages 25–27, helping each other with difficult words and concepts. Then have one member of each pair list reasons that the colonies should be loyal to Britain and the other list reasons that the colonies should break away. When pairs have finished, debate as a class whether Britain was right to tax its colonists.

British Point of View

- *British protected colonists from French soldiers.*
- *Colonists were kept safe, so they should help pay for British soldiers.*
- *Colonists should be loyal to "mother country."*

Colonists' Point of View

- *No taxes unless colonists can vote in Parliament.*
- *Colonists should be allowed to settle on conquered land.*
- *Government is to protect people, not to make them do what they don't want to do.*

years. Creating the Constitution was not an easy task, however. There was great debate over a very basic question: Is it possible to establish a government that is strong and stable but not tyrannical? The answer that the framers reached was yes—such a government was possible if they created a system in which power and responsibility were shared in a balanced way.

First, the framers agreed to set up a **representative government**, one in which citizens elect representatives to make laws and policies for them. This was to ensure that the power to govern ultimately rested with the people, as advocated by Rousseau. Yet, unlike Rousseau, they selected an indirect form of government over direct democracy. The Romans, too, had chosen an indirect democracy when they established a republic.

B. Possible Answers The power to govern rested with the people; power and responsibility should be shared in a balanced way.

MAIN IDEA

Recognizing Effects

B What Enlightenment ideas influenced the U.S. Constitution?

Second, the framers created a **federal system**. The powers of government were to be divided between the federal, or central, government and the states, or local, governments.

Third, within the federal government, the framers set up a separation of powers based on the writings of Montesquieu. Power was divided among the executive, legislative, and judicial branches. This provided a system of checks and balances to prevent any branch from having too much power. James Madison played an important role in the constitutional debates. (See History Makers on this page.) B

History Makers

James Madison
1751–1836

As a young man, James Madison was strongly influenced by the Enlightenment. When the Constitutional Convention was called, he spent a year preparing by reading the works of Locke, Montesquieu, Voltaire, and other Enlightenment philosophers.

Madison is known as the Father of the Constitution. He designed the plan that included the three branches of government. He also helped to create the federal system. Madison kept careful records of the debates at the convention so that future Americans could know how the delegates made their decisions. Later, he served as the fourth president of the United States.

The French Revolution

During the 1700s, the impulse toward democracy had also been stirring in France. Under Louis XIV, who ruled from 1643 to 1715, France experienced the excesses of absolute monarchy. He left unresolved problems, massive debts, and growing unrest for his heirs—Louis XV and Louis XVI.

Causes of the Revolution Louis XVI came to the throne at the age of 19 in 1774. He was a well-intentioned but weak leader often dominated by his wife, Marie Antoinette. She was Austrian by birth and unpopular with the French people. France's problems, however, went deeper than the monarchy. The clergy and the nobility enjoyed many privileges. Even though the monarchy was deeply in debt, only commoners paid taxes. Many historians say that the French Revolution was fought to balance the inequalities in French society.

During the 18th century, Enlightenment ideas caused people to rethink the structure of society. The French middle class and some nobles were strongly impressed with ideas such as the social contract and freedom of speech. They were also inspired by the example of the American people throwing off an oppressive government in the 1770s. French peasants, too, were dissatisfied and restless. There had been poor harvests in the late 1780s. The people were hungry and felt that neither the king nor the nobility cared about their plight.

Early Reforms of the Revolution In 1789, Louis XVI's government was about to go bankrupt. In desperation, Louis sought to raise taxes. He called the Estates-General into session. This representative assembly had not been called to meet since 1614. The commoners in the Estates-General, however, felt their class was not fairly represented. They left in protest and formed the National Assembly.

History Makers

James Madison

Why do you think Madison spent a year reading the works of Enlightenment philosophers? *(Possible Answer: to find out what great thinkers of the times believed was the best form of government)*

In-Depth Resources: Unit 1
- Literature: from *1776,* p. 13

The French Revolution
10.2.4

Critical Thinking
- Which of the causes of the French Revolution discussed in this passage seems most important? *(Possible Answer: economic issues, such as the unequal tax burden and peasant hardship)*
- Why would the National Assembly retain its monarch instead of creating an executive similar to the U.S. president? *(Possible Answer: The United States was very young, and the success of its government was far from certain.)*

World Art and Cultures Transparencies
- AT50 *Portrait of Marie Antoinette with Her Children*

DIFFERENTIATING INSTRUCTION: STRUGGLING READERS

Designing a French Revolution Trivia Game

Class Time 45 minutes

Task Making a trivia board game

Purpose To help students become more knowledgeable about the French Revolution

Instructions Divide students into groups and ask them to read "The French Revolution" on pages 27–28. After they finish, explain to students that they will be making a board game that uses cards with multiple-choice trivia questions. Groups should consider the rules of the game and how accessories–such as the game board, pieces, and trivia cards–will look.

After working out these details, students should use the information from the text and other sources to create their trivia cards. Help students create answers so that questions are not too easy. A sample question and answer might be phrased as follows: The Bastille was: A. the hall where meetings of the Estates-General were held; B. a Parisian prison that was a symbol of the king's rule; C. the public square where executions took place; D. the name of Napoleon's headquarters. *(Answer: B)* After the students complete their projects, have groups exchange and play the games.

The Struggle for Democracy Continues
10.9.8

Critical Thinking

- Why might autocratic rulers voice agreement with the idea of democracy yet fail to follow through with democratic actions? *(Possible Answer: may believe they can prevent their people from taking matters into their own hands)*
- Why might some UN member nations who are party to the Universal Declaration of Human Rights violate its standards? *(Possible Answer: difficult or impossible to enforce the declaration's standards)*

In-Depth Resources: Unit 1

- Connections Across Time and Cultures: New Beginnings for Democracy, p. 17

Case Study 3—Russia and Germany, p. 30

Case Study 8—Argentina and South Africa, p. 100

Case Study 9—Mexico and Japan, p. 114

More About . . .

The United Nations

The United Nations has a number of programs to maintain international peace, foster economic cooperation and social equality, and develop and institute international law. The United Nations Children's Fund (UNICEF) works to improve the education, nutrition, and health of children around the world. The International Court of Justice rules on issues brought by member nations.

▲ During the Reign of Terror, thousands of people suspected of not supporting the French Revolution were beheaded.

Eventually, members of other classes joined them. In the meantime, on July 14, 1789, the people of Paris stormed the Bastille, a much-hated prison in Paris that symbolized autocratic rule. Peasant uprisings then spread from Paris throughout the country. The fight to win democratic freedoms for the people, the French Revolution, had begun.

The National Assembly made many reforms. It adopted the Declaration of the Rights of Man and of the Citizen. This document was influenced by Enlightenment ideas and the American Declaration of Independence. It guaranteed the rights of "liberty, property, security, and resistance to oppression" to all people. The National Assembly also drafted a constitution that made France a limited monarchy. It reorganized the Catholic Church in France and redistributed its land. It reformed the court system. Believing its work done, it disbanded in 1791 so that a newly elected Legislative Assembly could take over.

Democratic Reforms Undone The new French assembly was not accepted by the king, the aristocracy, or many Catholics. Also, European countries that had absolute monarchs feared the spread of democratic ideas. They went to war with France, hoping to undo the new French republic. The country was in a state of crisis. In 1792, the royal family was imprisoned. A new legislature, even more radical, took charge. A period called the Reign of Terror followed. People thought to be opponents of the revolution were killed for their beliefs. Included among them were the king and queen. Finally, in 1799, a military leader, Napoleon Bonaparte, took control of France and created a dictatorship. C

C. Possible Answers The Assembly was not accepted by the king; other European countries went to war with France; a more radical legislature led to a military ruler.

MAIN IDEA

Recognizing Effects

C What factors brought an end to the French Republic?

Not until the mid-1800s did democracy develop in France. The French Revolution illustrates why democracy is hard to achieve. It is not enough to promise equality and freedom or to have representative government. For democracy to work, a society must have rule by law, protections for both civil rights and civil liberties, tolerance of dissent, and acceptance of majority decisions by the minority.

The Struggle for Democracy Continues

It took centuries for the ideas of democracy to develop and take hold in the world. Today, most people view democracy as the preferred form of government. Even some authoritarian governments voice agreement with the idea of democracy. Generally, however, they do not follow through with democratic actions.

The United Nations Promotes Democracy Before the end of World War II in 1945, a new international organization called the **United Nations** was established. Its goal was to work for world peace and the betterment of humanity. One branch of the UN, the General Assembly, is a kind of democracy. There, nations discuss problems, hoping to settle conflicts peacefully. Each nation has equal representation. The UN's charter is based on the traditions of democracy. The UN's authority comes from the nations of the world. The charter reaffirms basic human rights, the need for justice and the rule of law, and the desire for social progress.

DIFFERENTIATING INSTRUCTION: GIFTED AND TALENTED STUDENTS

Designing a Travel Brochure for a World Heritage Site

Class Time 45 minutes

Task Creating a travel brochure

Purpose To familiarize students with other activities of the United Nations

Instructions Divide students into pairs and tell them that they will be assembling a travel brochure for a United Nations World Heritage Site. Explain that, in 1972, the United Nations Educational, Scientific, and Cultural Organization (UNESCO) created a committee to establish a list of World Heritage Sites and work for their preservation. In 2003, the World Heritage List included 754 sites (582 cultural, 149 natural, and 23 mixed). Tell students to use the library or the Internet to find a current list of sites and to choose one as the subject of their brochure. Ask each group to carry out preliminary research to decide on the kind of information their brochure will contain and what sort of layout will best convey the information. They should then allocate responsibility for individual sections of their booklet and do further in-depth research before creating the brochure. Encourage students to be creative in designing their guides. Display the finished brochures in class.

One of the UN's most important contributions is the Universal Declaration of Human Rights. The General Assembly adopted the Declaration in 1948. This document draws on democratic ideas. It sets a worldwide standard for basic social, political, and economic rights. Included are the right to life, liberty, and security. Also stated are the rights to equal protection under the law, free movement, and free association and assembly with other people. To these rights were added social and economic rights: the rights to work, to rest and leisure, and to education. The declaration's purpose is to serve as an international code of conduct.

New Movements Toward Democracy In many places in the world, the ideals of the UN's Universal Declaration of Human Rights have yet to be wholly achieved. Nations are struggling to move toward more democratic government. But it is not easy to establish democratic policies where, for example, dictatorship has been the rule. Still, beginnings have been made in a number of countries.

In the early 1990s, the breakup of the Soviet Union enabled 15 new republics to assert their people's national identity and interests. In South Africa, after many years of apartheid, or racial segregation, a democratic, all-race government was established. In 2002, East Timor regained its independence following a UN-sponsored referendum. It had been seized nearly 30 years earlier by Indonesia.

There is no guarantee democracy can be achieved in any particular time and place. Nor is it guaranteed that once achieved, democracy will not be lost if people are not constantly watchful. Yet, as you read the history that follows, you will see that the idea of democracy has survived wars and oppression. It is an idea whose strength comes from the people. D

D. Possible Answer The idea of having a say in government has been a force in history for 2,000 years. People want political freedom. The American Revolution and the democracy it created have been a continuing example in modern times. The UN also has promoted political rights.

MAIN IDEA

Forming and Supporting Opinions

D Why do you think people and nations continue to struggle toward more democratic government? Explain.

Global Impact

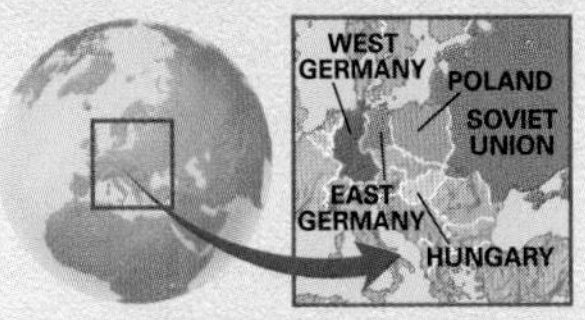

Revolutions of 1989

Democratic revolutions swept Eastern Europe in 1989. Reforms in the Soviet Union opened the door for more freedoms throughout Communist-controlled Eastern Europe. In April 1989, Poland held its first free election since the Communists seized control during World War II.

Hungary also launched a sweeping reform program. It then began to admit East Germans who claimed to be tourists but actually planned to escape to freedom. Soon, demonstrations began in East Germany, leading to the tearing down of the Berlin Wall. Eventually, the Communists fell from power, and East and West Germany voted to reunite.

SECTION 4 ASSESSMENT

TERMS & NAMES 1. For each term or name, write a sentence explaining its significance.

• Enlightenment • social contract • natural rights • separation of powers • representative government • federal system • United Nations

USING YOUR NOTES

2. Which Enlightenment idea contributed most to the democratic revolutions in America and France? Why? (10.2.1)

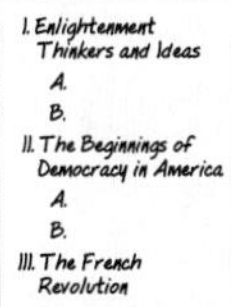

I. Enlightenment Thinkers and Ideas
A.
B.
II. The Beginnings of Democracy in America
A.
B.
III. The French Revolution

MAIN IDEAS

3. What were natural rights? (10.2.1)
4. What was Rousseau's idea of government? (10.2.1)
5. What political rights are set forth in the Universal Declaration of Human Rights? (10.9.8)

CRITICAL THINKING & WRITING

6. **RECOGNIZING EFFECTS** How did the writers of the U.S. Constitution adapt the political theories of the Enlightenment? (10.2.1)
7. **COMPARING AND CONTRASTING** In what ways was the French Revolution similar to and different from the American Revolution? (10.2.4)
8. **DEVELOPING HISTORICAL PERSPECTIVE** Why has the idea of democracy survived wars and oppression? (10.2.1)
9. **WRITING ACTIVITY** REVOLUTION Prepare a series of **slogans** for display at a pro-democracy rally during either the American or the French revolutions. (Writing 2.4.b)

INTEGRATED TECHNOLOGY **INTERNET ACTIVITY**

Use the Internet to research new members of the United Nations since 1990. Prepare a **chart** showing the name of the nation, the date of its admission into the UN, and its form of government. (10.9.8)

INTERNET KEYWORD
United Nations members

Global Impact

Revolutions of 1989

In 2003, a wave of nostalgia for everyday life in the former East Germany swept over Germany. The controversial phenomenon was dubbed *Ostalgie*, after *Ost*, the German word for east. Many have expressed alarm at the sentimentality about a regime that shot people who tried to escape. Ask students why such a phenomenon might have occurred. *(Possible Answer: Economic insecurity and the fading memory of East Germany's abuses may have moved some to reminisce about the less negative features of the regime, such as the security of people's jobs and their futures.)*

3 ASSESS

SECTION 4 ASSESSMENT

Divide the class into small groups. Have each work on question 2. Then discuss each group's conclusions.

Formal Assessment

• Section Quiz, p. 8

4 RETEACH

On the board, draw a concept web with the word *democracy* in the center. Work with the class to complete the web with facts and concepts from this section.

ANSWERS

1. Enlightenment, p. 24 • social contract, p. 25 • natural rights, p. 25 • separation of powers, p. 25 • representative government, p. 27 • federal system, p. 27 • United Nations, p. 28

2. **Sample Answer:** I A. People agree to a social contract to prevent disorder. B. People have natural rights to life, liberty, and property. C. Government should have separation of powers so no one part dominates. II A. Americans protested British taxation. B. Americans won independence. C. Enlightenment ideas shaped the government. Most important idea—Natural rights, because they made "the common people" important.

3. rights to life, liberty, and property that John Locke said all human beings had
4. Legitimate government ruled with the consent of the governed.
5. life, liberty, security, equal protection under law, free movement, free association and assembly, work, rest and leisure, education
6. representative government, balance of powers
7. Similar—Wanted freedom, responsive government. Different—French democracy collapsed.
8. **Possible Answer:** All humans want freedom.
9. **Rubric** Slogans should
• show an understanding of the topic.
• be short and to the point.

INTEGRATED TECHNOLOGY

Rubric Charts should
• include accurate information.
• list all new members from 1990 to present.
• cite at least one source.

TERMS & NAMES

1. aristocracy, p. 5
2. monarchy, p. 5
3. direct democracy, p. 7
4. republic, p. 10
5. due process of law, p. 20
6. divine right, p. 20
7. social contract, p. 25
8. representative government, p. 27

MAIN IDEAS

Answers will vary.

9. He increased the number of paid public officials, which allowed more poor people to participate in government, and he introduced direct democracy.
10. In a direct democracy, all citizens participate directly in the decision-making of the government. In a republic, citizens elect leaders to make the decisions on their behalf.
11. All persons, even rulers, are accountable before the law.
12. Both the individual and the community were supposed to work to decrease oppression and injustice.
13. The emphasis on the importance of the individual and the support for questioning authority played a part in the growth of political liberty.
14. Common law reflects the customs and principles of a country. Roman law represents the will of a ruler or lawmaker.
15. the right to a jury trial, the protection of the law
16. The monarch was forbidden to suspend laws, tax without consent of Parliament, or raise an army during peacetime without Parliament's approval.
17. "Is it possible to establish a government that is strong and stable but not tyrannical?" Yes—It was possible if they created a system in which power and responsibility were shared in a balanced way.
18. rule by law, protections for civil rights, tolerance of dissent, acceptance of majority decisions by the minority

Prologue Assessment

TERMS & NAMES

Briefly explain the importance of each of the following to the rise of democratic ideas.

1. aristocracy
2. monarchy
3. direct democracy
4. republic
5. due process of law
6. divine right
7. social contract
8. representative government

MAIN IDEAS

The Legacy of Ancient Greece and Rome Section 1 (pages 5–11)

9. What changes did Pericles introduce into Greek government to make it more democratic? (10.1.2)
10. How is a republic different from direct democracy? (10.1.2)
11. What does the phrase "government of laws, not of men" mean? (10.1.2)

Judeo-Christian Tradition Section 2 (pages 12–17)

12. What did the Hebrew tradition teach about the responsibilities of the individual and community to combat injustice? (10.1.1)
13. How did the Reformation contribute to the growth of democracy? (10.1.1)

Democracy Develops in England Section 3 (pages 18–23)

14. How does common law differ from Roman law? (10.2.2)
15. Name two basic individual rights guaranteed in the Magna Carta. (10.2.2)
16. In what three ways was the power of the English monarch limited by the English Bill of Rights? (10.2.2)

The Enlightenment and Democratic Revolutions Section 4 (pages 24–29)

17. What question did the framers of the American Constitution have to deal with, and what was the answer? (10.2.1)
18. What is required in a society for democracy to work? (10.2.1)

CRITICAL THINKING

1. **USING YOUR NOTES**
In a chart, show the Enlightenment ideas about government with which each philosopher is connected. (10.2.1)

Philosopher	Idea

2. **EVALUATING COURSES OF ACTION**
POWER AND AUTHORITY For what reasons would a nation in today's world choose representative democracy rather than direct democracy? (CST 1)

3. **SYNTHESIZING**
What do the basic ideals of monotheistic religions and the ideals of democracy have in common? (10.1.1)

4. **DRAWING CONCLUSIONS**
How did the Magna Carta, the Petition of Right, and the English Bill of Rights advance the ideals of democracy? (CST 1)

5. **ANALYZING CAUSES AND RECOGNIZING EFFECTS**
CULTURAL INTERACTION What impact did Enlightenment ideas have on the spread of democracy in the 18th century? (HI 2)

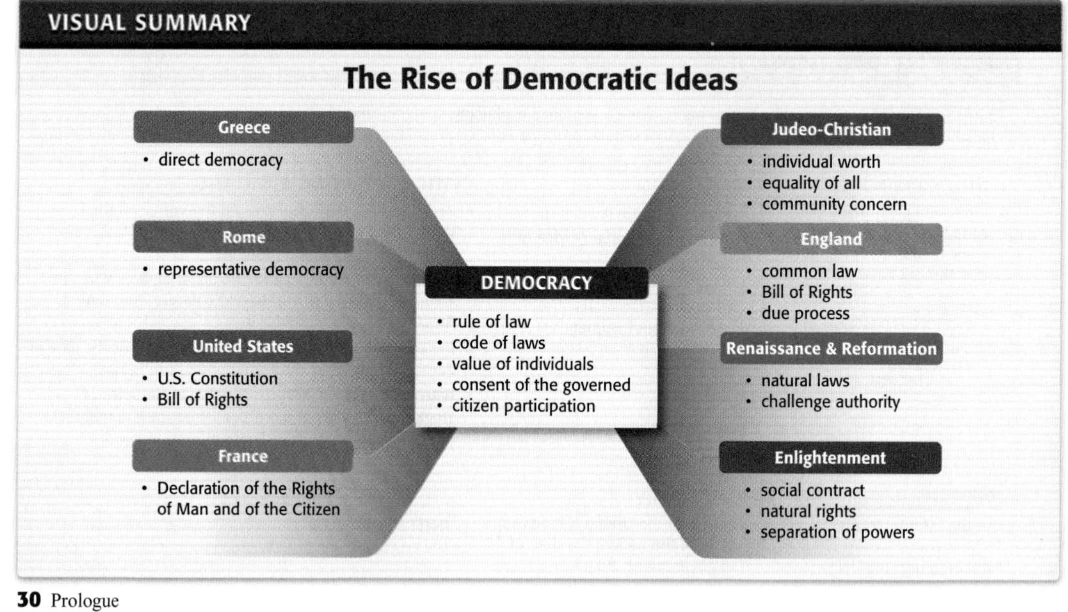

VISUAL SUMMARY
The Rise of Democratic Ideas
Greece
• direct democracy
Rome
• representative democracy
United States
• U.S. Constitution
• Bill of Rights
France
• Declaration of the Rights of Man and of the Citizen
DEMOCRACY
• rule of law
• code of laws
• value of individuals
• consent of the governed
• citizen participation
Judeo-Christian
• individual worth
• equality of all
• community concern
England
• common law
• Bill of Rights
• due process
Renaissance & Reformation
• natural laws
• challenge authority
Enlightenment
• social contract
• natural rights
• separation of powers

CRITICAL THINKING

Answers will vary.

1. Hobbes, social contract; Locke, people's right to rebel; Voltaire, freedom of religion and free speech; Rousseau, consent of the governed; Montesquieu, separation of powers
2. The physical size of a country and the inclusion of all the legal voters makes direct democracy impossible. Choosing representatives is the only logical way to handle day-to-day decisions.
3. Monotheistic religions support the worth of the individual and the equality of all people—ideals that are also fundamental for democracy.
4. Each of these documents increased the rights and protections of individual citizens. The Magna Carta promoted due process of law, the Petition of Right prohibited illegal imprisonment and illegal taxation, and the English Bill of Rights assured the right to petition the king and forbade excessive bail and cruel and unusual punishment.
5. Enlightenment ideas from England and France influenced revolutions in the American colonies and in France.

In the following selection from *Politics,* Aristotle presents his views on where the power of the state should reside. Use the quotation and your knowledge of world history to answer questions 1 and 2.
Additional Test Practice pp. S1–S33

PRIMARY SOURCE

Where ought the sovereign power of the state to reside? . . . The state aims to consist as far as possible of those who are alike and equal, a condition found chiefly among the middle section. . . . The middle class is also the steadiest element, the least eager for change. They neither covet, like the poor the possessions of others, nor do others covet theirs, as the poor covet those of the rich. . . . Tyranny often emerges from an over-enthusiastic democracy or from an oligarchy, but much more rarely from middle class constitutions

ARISTOTLE, *Politics*

1. With which group does Aristotle say political power is best located? (10.1.2)
   A. the rich
   B. the middle class
   C. the poor
   D. the oligarchy

2. According to Aristotle what causes tyranny? (10.1.2)
   A. the middle class
   B. the rich
   C. the poor
   D. over-enthusiastic democracy

Use the graph and your knowledge of world history to answer question 3.

3. How does the percentage of voters participating in United States elections compare to that of other nations? (HI 2)
   A. It is slightly higher than all but two nations.
   B. It is slightly lower than all but two nations.
   C. It is much lower than most nations.
   D. It is not possible to tell from the graph.

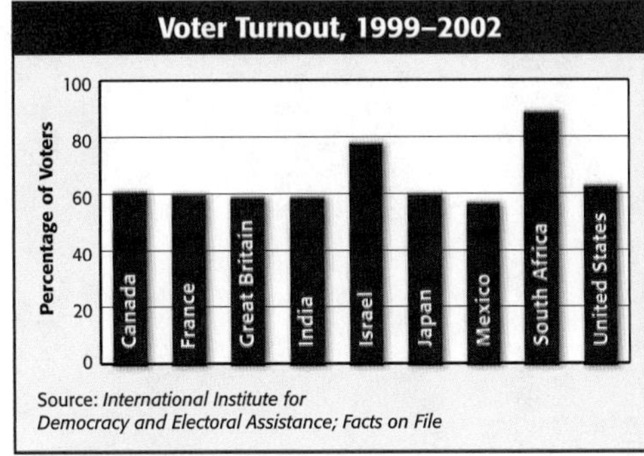

INTEGRATED TECHNOLOGY
TEST PRACTICE Go to **classzone.com**
- Diagnostic tests
- Tutorials
- Strategies
- Additional practice

ALTERNATIVE ASSESSMENT

1. **Interact *with* History** (Writing 2.5.b)
   On page 4, you were asked to think about why people would risk arrest, jail, or even death to have or preserve democracy. Imagine yourself as a television news reporter. Write at least five questions that you would ask the young man in the photograph on that page. Compare your questions with those of at least one other person in your class.

2. 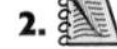 **WRITING ABOUT HISTORY** (Writing 2.4.a)
   REVOLUTION Write an **editorial** supporting or rejecting the idea that the only way to gain democracy in a country that does not have a democratic government is to wage a revolution.

   Consider the following:
   - No established government willingly gives up power.
   - Complete change of government will only occur with the support of the people.
   - Rule of law is basic to any democratic government.

INTEGRATED TECHNOLOGY

Creating a Database (Writing 2.3.d)
Democratic ideas continue to have enormous appeal throughout the world. During recent decades, democratic institutions were adopted in Brazil, Mexico, South Africa, and some countries of the former Soviet Union. Working with a team, use the Internet or your library to research changes that have taken place in the countries listed above. Then create a database comparing steps toward democracy in each country. The database might include the following:
- adoption of democratic election practices
- enforcement of laws regarding freedom of speech and the press
- peaceful transfer of power to democratically elected leaders
- the military's retreat from politics

PROLOGUE ASSESSMENT

STANDARDS-BASED ASSESSMENT

1. The correct answer is letter **B**. Letters **A**, **C**, and **D** are incorrect because Aristotle specifically identifies the middle class as the steadiest element of a state.
2. The correct answer is letter **D**. Letters **A**, **B**, and **C** are incorrect because they are not identified with tyranny in the quotation.
3. The correct answer is letter **A**. Letters **B** and **C** are incorrect because the United States figure is higher than most nations. Letter **D** is not correct because the graph shows the necessary information to answer the question.

Formal Assessment
- Chapter Test, Forms A, B, and C, pp. 9–20

California Test Generator CD-ROM
- Chapter Tests, Forms A, B, and C (English and Spanish)

ALTERNATIVE ASSESSMENT

1. **Possible Answers:** Students' questions may focus on the cause the young man supports; why he feels he must respond this way; the possible harm to him, his friends, or his family; the risks to his future life; whether he believes violence is justified in the struggle for democracy; or what he believes constitutes a democratic society.
2. **Rubric** Editorials should
   - clearly state a position on the issue.
   - present arguments supporting the position.
   - refute points of view opposing the position.

INTEGRATED TECHNOLOGY
Rubric Databases should
- include all countries listed in the assignment.
- clearly and accurately compare steps toward democracy in the different countries.
- be easy to read and to understand.
- cite sources.

Connecting Hemispheres 1300–1800

***La Salle's 1684 Expedition to Louisiana* (1844), Theodore Gudin (1802–1880)**

In 1682, the French explorer Rene Robert Cavelier, Sieur de La Salle (1643–1687) made a successful voyage down the Mississippi to the Gulf of Mexico. There, on April 9, 1682, he claimed for France the entire Mississippi basin, naming the territory Louisiana in honor of King Louis XIV.

France was one of several European nations that participated in the great era of exploration that began in the 1400s. Competing with the French were explorers from Portugal, Spain, the Netherlands, and Britain. Like La Salle, these explorers sought land and wealth that would enrich themselves and their countries. They were also motivated by the wish to spread Christianity and a longing for adventure and fame. The Age of Exploration is often summed up as a mission for "God, glory, and gold."

In 1684, La Salle persuaded Louis XIV to provide men, ships, and money for another expedition to the Gulf. This expedition was beset by misfortunes, including La Salle's failure to find the mouth of the Mississippi River. In March 1687, three of La Salle's men murdered him.

Nevertheless, La Salle's efforts gave France claim to a vast, fertile territory in the Americas. In 1803, the French government sold the land to the U.S. government for $15 million—about three cents per acre.

Seeking new land and new markets, European explorers sailed around the world. This painting by Theodore Gudin depicts French explorer La Salle's Louisiana expedition of 1684.

Comparing & Contrasting

Methods of Government
In Unit 1, you will learn about different methods of ruling a nation or empire. At the end of the unit, you will have a chance to compare and contrast the governments you have studied. (See pages 144–149.)

33

Previewing the Unit

This unit covers developments in the Eastern and Western hemispheres that result in connections through exploration and trade beginning in the late 1400s.

Interaction with Environment In the Americas, many diverse civilizations, including the Maya, Aztec, and Inca, flourish prior to the arrival of Europeans.

Revolution Europe is transformed from 1300 to 1650 by two powerful movements: the Renaissance and the Reformation.

Empire Building In the area stretching from the Balkans to India, three Islamic empires emerge between the 1300s and the 1500s: the Ottomans of Turkey, the Safavids of Persia, and the Mughals of India.

Cultural Interaction The desire for profit and the hope of spreading Christianity lead European explorers to Asia. Traders and missionaries exchange goods and ideas with the peoples of Asia. The Chinese and the Japanese, however, eventually limit European influence.

European exploration of the Americas begins with the voyages of Columbus. Interactions between Americans and Europeans lead to a global exchange of foods, animals, and ideas; the enrichment of Europe; and the devastation of Native American cultures.

Comparing & Contrasting

The unit feature on pages 144–149 uses charts, diagrams, maps, and primary sources to explore different methods of government. Explain to students that these resources will help them understand how different cultures organized and governed themselves.

CHAPTER 1 PLANNING GUIDE

European Renaissance and Reformation, 1300–1600

CHAPTER RESOURCES	COPYMASTERS	ASSESSMENT
CHAPTER OVERVIEW Two great European movements, the Renaissance and the Reformation, ushered in dramatic cultural and social changes.	**In-Depth Resources: Unit 1** • Building Vocabulary, p. 22 **Chapters in Brief** (in English and Spanish) **Block Schedule Pacing Guide**	**Chapter Assessment,** pp. 68–69 **Formal Assessment** • Chapter Tests, Forms A, B, and C, pp. 25–39 **Test Generator** **Integrated Assessment Book** **Online Test Practice**
SECTION 1 **Italy: Birthplace of the Renaissance** pp. 37–45 **OBJECTIVE** Explain the origins and innovations of the early Renaissance.	**In-Depth Resources: Unit 1** • Guided Reading, p. 18 • Primary Sources: from *The Courtier,* p. 26; from *The Prince,* p. 27 • Literature: from *The Agony and the Ecstasy,* p. 30 • History Makers: Machiavelli, p. 33 • Connections Across Time, p. 35 • Reteaching Activity, p. 36 **Reading Study Guide,** p. 15	**Section 1 Assessment,** p. 43 **Formal Assessment** • Section Quiz, p. 21 **California Daily Standards Practice Transparencies,** TT61
SECTION 2 **The Northern Renaissance** pp. 46–53 **OBJECTIVE** Trace the spread of Renaissance ideas to Germany, Flanders, Holland, and England.	**In-Depth Resources: Unit 1** • Guided Reading, p. 19 • Geography Application: Trade in Renaissance Europe, p. 24 **Reading Study Guide,** p. 17	**Section 2 Assessment,** p. 51 **Formal Assessment** • Section Quiz, p. 22 **California Daily Standards Practice Transparencies,** TT62
SECTION 3 **Luther Leads the Reformation** pp. 54–60 **OBJECTIVE** Analyze causes and effects of the Protestant Reformation.	**In-Depth Resources: Unit 1** • Guided Reading, p. 20 • Skillbuilder Practice: Synthesizing, p. 23 • Primary Sources: A Conference with Elizabeth I, p. 28; Report on the English Reformation, p. 29 • History Makers: Elizabeth I, p. 34 **Reading Study Guide,** p. 19	**Section 3 Assessment,** p. 60 **Formal Assessment** • Section Quiz, p. 23 **California Daily Standards Practice Transparencies,** TT63
SECTION 4 **The Reformation Continues** pp. 61–67 **OBJECTIVE** Describe further changes in Protestantism and the Catholic Reformation.	**In-Depth Resources: Unit 1** • Guided Reading, p. 21 **Reading Study Guide,** p. 19	**Section 4 Assessment,** p. 66 **Formal Assessment** • Section Quiz, p. 24 **California Daily Standards Practice Transparencies,** TT64

INTEGRATED TECHNOLOGY

- eEdition Plus Online
- EasyPlanner Plus Online
- eTest Plus Online

Audio CDs
- Voices from the Past
- Reading Study Guides

CD-ROMs
- eEdition
- Power Presentations
- EasyPlanner
- Electronic Library of Primary Sources
- Test Generator

eEdition CD-ROM

World Art and Cultures Transparencies
- AT36 *The Last Supper*
- AT37 *Mona Lisa*

Electronic Library of Primary Sources
- "The Art of Painting," from *Notebooks*

classzone.com

eEdition CD-ROM

World Art and Cultures Transparencies
- AT38 Van Eyck's *Wedding Portrait*

classzone.com

eEdition CD-ROM

Electronic Library of Primary Sources

- from the Ninety-Five Theses

classzone.com

Geography Transparencies

- GT17 Reformation

Critical Thinking Transparencies
- CT17 The Protestant and Catholic Reformations
- CT53 Chapter 1 Visual Summary

Electronic Library of Primary Sources
- "The St. Bartholomew's Day Massacre"
- "Luther: Giant of His Time and Ours"

classzone.com

OVERVIEW OF CALIFORNIA RESOURCES

	Section 1	Section 2	Section 3	Section 4
California Reading Toolkit	p. L9	p. L10	p. L11	p. L12
California Modified Lesson Plans for English Learners	p. 13	p. 15	p. 17	p. 19
California Daily Standards Practice Transparencies	TT1	TT2	TT3	TT4
California Standards Enrichment Workbook	pp. 23–24	pp. 23–24	pp. 17–18	pp. 17–18, 23–24
California Standards Planner and Lesson Plans	p. L9	p. L11	p. L13	p. L15
California Online Test Practice	classzone.com	classzone.com	classzone.com	classzone.com
California Test Generator CD-ROM				
California Easy Planner CD-ROM				
California eEdition CD-ROM				

Chart Key:

 Pupil's Edition

Teacher's Edition

 Overhead Transparency

 Block Scheduling

 Copymaster

Audio Library

 CD-ROM

 Internet

 Video

NO TIME?

If you do not have time to teach this chapter in full, assign the **Chapter in Brief** (also available in Spanish).

Previewing Resources for Differentiated Instruction

ENGLISH LEARNERS: Resources in Spanish

In-Depth Resources in Spanish

- Guided Reading (A)
- Skillbuilder Practice: Synthesizing
- Geography Application: Trade in Renaissance Europe (B)

Chapters in Brief

Reading Study Guide (C)

Reading Study Guide Audio CD

Test Generator CD-ROM

- Chapter Test, Forms A, B, and C

Plus

Modified Lesson Plans for English Learners

Multi-Language Glossary of Social Studies Terms

(A)

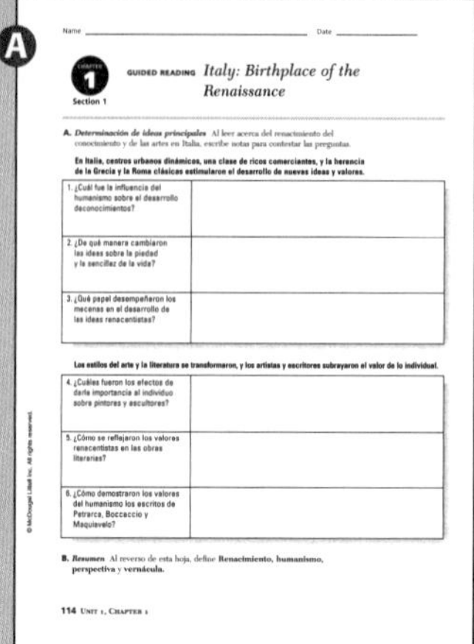

GUIDED READING *Italy: Birthplace of the Renaissance*

(B)

GEOGRAPHY APPLICATION: MOVEMENT *El comercio en la Europa renacentista*

STRUGGLING READERS

In-Depth Resources: Unit 1

- Guided Reading (A)
- Building Vocabulary
- Skillbuilder Practice: Synthesizing (B)
- Geography Application: Trade in Renaissance Europe
- Reteaching Activities

Chapters in Brief

Reading Study Guide

Reading Study Guide Audio CD

Formal Assessment

- Chapter Test, Form A (C)

Plus

Reading Toolkit

(A)

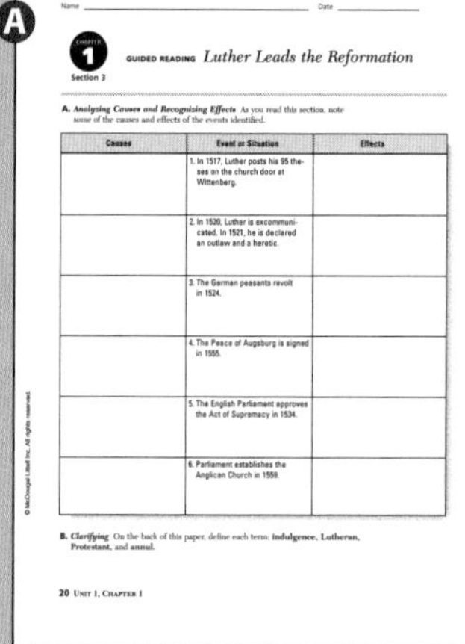

GUIDED READING *Luther Leads the Reformation*

(B)

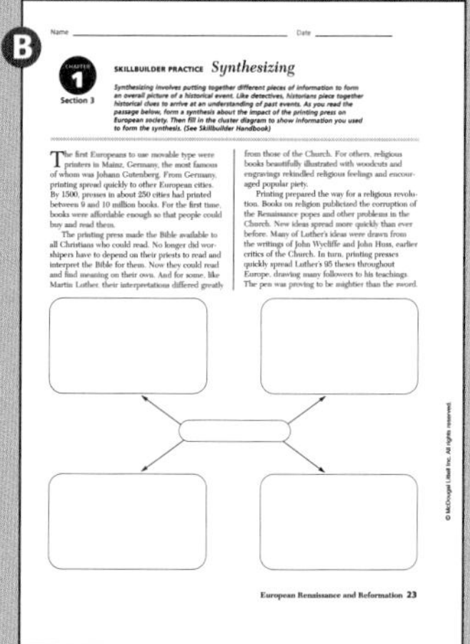

SKILLBUILDER PRACTICE *Synthesizing*

GIFTED AND TALENTED STUDENTS

In-Depth Resources: Unit 1

- Primary Sources: from *The Courtier;* from *The Prince;* A Conference with Elizabeth I (A); Report on the English Reformation
- Literature: from *The Agony and the Ecstasy* (B)
- History Makers: Niccolò Machiavelli; Elizabeth I
- Connections Across Time and Cultures: A Flowering of Creativity and Knowledge (C)

Electronic Library of Primary Sources CD-ROM

- "The Art of Painting," from *Notebooks*
- from the Ninety-Five Theses
- "The St. Bartholomew's Day Massacre"
- "Luther: Giant of His Time and Ours"

Formal Assessment

- Chapter Test, Form C

(A)

PRIMARY SOURCE A Conference with Elizabeth I by André Hurault

(B)

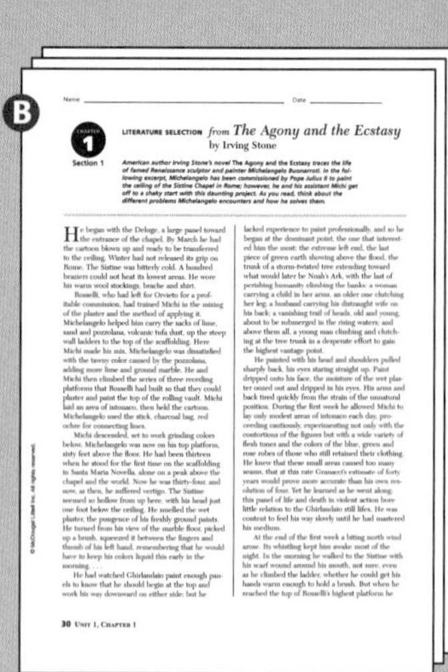

LITERATURE SELECTION *from The Agony and the Ecstasy* by Irving Stone

Luther Leads the Reformation

Activities in the Teacher's Edition for English Learners

- Focus on Vocabulary, p. 38
- Question Words Used as Intensifiers, p. 49
- Tracing Religious Change in England, p. 58
- The Catholic Church and the Reformation, p. 65

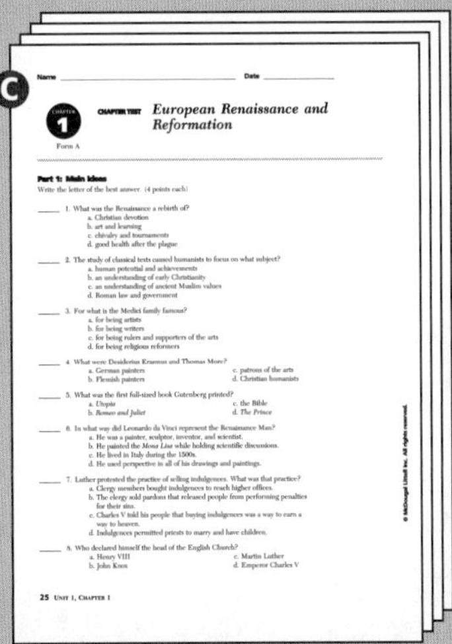

European Renaissance and Reformation

Activities in the Teacher's Edition for Struggling Readers

- Analyzing a Primary Source, p. 42
- Planning a Utopian Community, p. 48
- Understanding the Response to Luther, p. 56
- Persuading People to Come to Geneva, p. 62

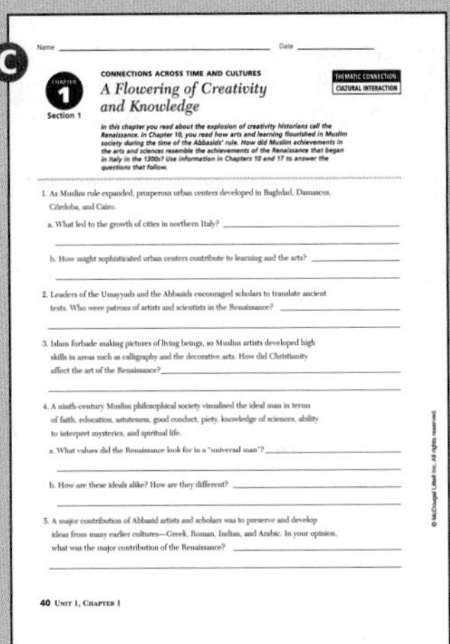

A Flowering of Creativity and Knowledge

Activities in the Teacher's Edition for Gifted and Talented Students

- Leonardo's Inventions, p. 41
- The Poetry of William Carlos Williams, p. 47
- Forming and Supporting Opinions, p. 59
- Making Inferences, p. 64

INTEGRATED TECHNOLOGY

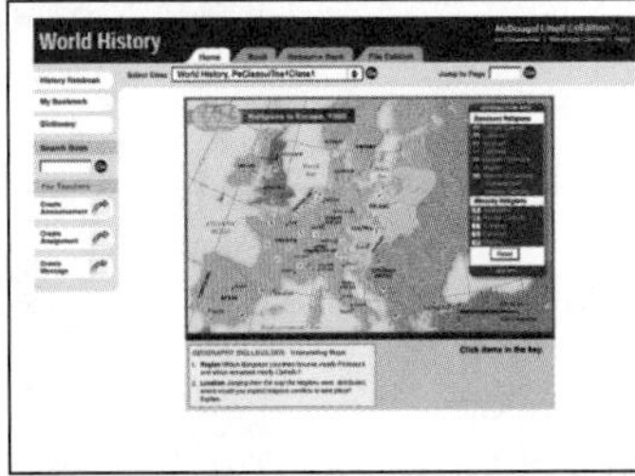

eEdition
- Interactive Visuals
- Interactive Maps
- Interactive Primary Sources

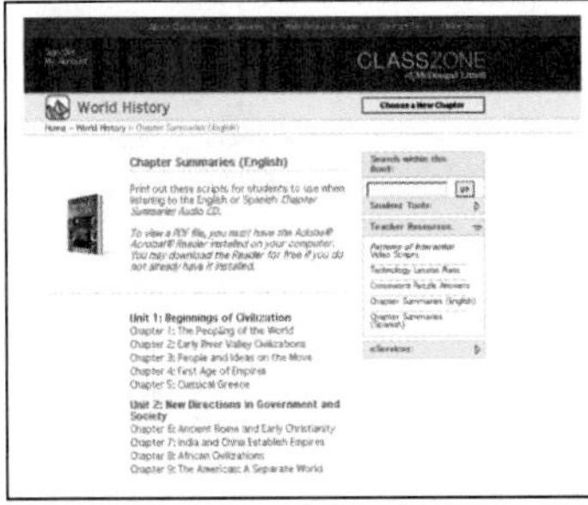

classzone.com
- Research Links
- Internet Activities
- Chapter Quiz
- Current Events

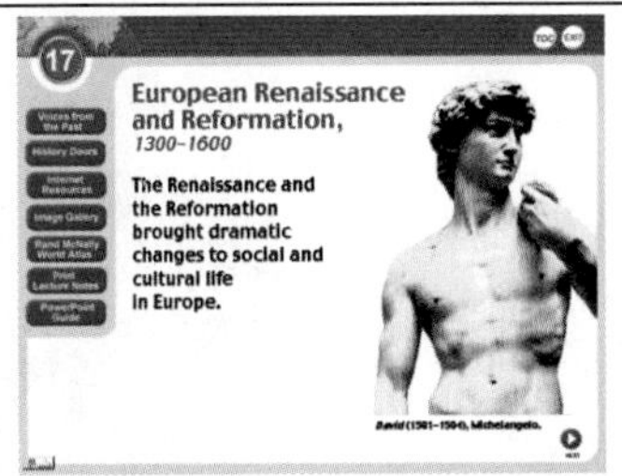

Power Presentations CD-ROM
- Lecture Notes
- Image Gallery
- Chapter Review Game

Critical Thinking Transparencies

CT17 The Protestant and Catholic Reformations

- CT53 Chapter 1 Visual Summary

Geography Transparencies
- GT17 Reformation

World Art and Cultures Transparencies
- AT36 *The Last Supper*
- AT37 *Mona Lisa* (A)
- AT38 Van Eyck's *Wedding Portrait*

Test Practice Transparencies TT61–TT64

Test Generator CD-ROM

EasyPlanner CD-ROM

Voices from the Past Audio CD

Online Test Practice

Electronic Library of Primary Sources

CHAPTER 1 • OBJECTIVE

Analyze the new ideas and values that led to the Renaissance and the Reformation.

Previewing Main Ideas

Note that the three main ideas presented here are also among the significant world history themes outlined on pages xxvi and xxvii. These universal ideas apply not only to the European Renaissance and Reformation but to many other historical times and events.

Accessing Prior Knowledge

Ask students to discuss what they already know about the Renaissance and Reformation. Have they heard those words before? What do they think they mean? Have them think about the words *reform* and *protest.* Tell them that Reformation and Protestant come from those words. Have them talk about the concepts of rebirth, reform, and protest and how they relate to this period in history.

Geography *Answers*

CULTURAL INTERACTION The Renaissance began in Italy in city-states such as Florence, Milan, and Mantua.

RELIGIOUS AND ETHICAL SYSTEMS Wittenberg is near the center of Europe, and it is on a river. Travelers and traders could have easily spread the ideas of the Reformation to other parts of Europe.

REVOLUTION Like Wittenberg, Mainz is near the center of Europe, and it is on a river.

CHAPTER 1

European Renaissance and Reformation, 1300–1600

Previewing Main Ideas

CULTURAL INTERACTION Trade with the East and the rediscovery of ancient manuscripts caused Europeans to develop new ideas about culture and art. This period was called the "Renaissance," which means rebirth.

Geography *Study the time line and the map. In which countries did the Renaissance begin?*

RELIGIOUS AND ETHICAL SYSTEMS Martin Luther began a movement to reform practices in the Catholic Church that he believed were wrong. That movement, the Reformation, led to the founding of non-Catholic churches.

Geography *Locate Wittenberg, the city where the Reformation began. What geographical features helped the Reformation spread from there?*

REVOLUTION The invention of the printing press allowed books and pamphlets to be made faster and more cheaply. This new technology helped spread the revolutionary ideas of the Renaissance and Reformation.

Geography *Printing spread from Mainz to other parts of Europe. How might the location of Mainz have helped the spread of printing?*

INTEGRATED TECHNOLOGY

eEdition
- Interactive Maps
- Interactive Visuals
- Interactive Primary Sources

INTERNET RESOURCES
Go to classzone.com for:
- Research Links
- Internet Activities
- Primary Sources
- Chapter Quiz
- Maps
- Test Practice
- Current Events

EUROPE

1300 In the 1300s the Renaissance begins in Italian city-states such as Florence, Milan, and Mantua.

1434 ◀ Medici family takes control of Florence. (bust of Lorenzo Medici)

1300 — 1400

WORLD

1324 Mali king Mansa Musa makes a pilgrimage to Mecca.

1368 ◀ Hongwu founds Ming Dynasty in China. (vase from that period)

1405 Chinese explorer Zheng He begins exploration of Asia and Africa.

34

TIME LINE DISCUSSION

Explain that the period 1300–1600 was a time of important and far-reaching changes, many of which affect us today.

1. Point out that the Gutenberg Bible, the first book printed from movable type, was printed in 1455. Ask what effect this printing technology might have had on the development of new ideas. *(The printing press made books more available. As a result, ideas could have spread more quickly and easily.)*
2. What world event happened a few years before Martin Luther began the Reformation? *(Columbus reached the Americas.)*
3. After the Reformation began, what happened in England? *(King Henry VIII started the Church of England.)*
4. How many years passed between the beginning of the Reformation and the reforms in the Catholic Church made at the Council of Trent? *(46)* What can be inferred about the strength of the Reformation from that span of time? *(The Catholic Church responded quickly to the Reformation. If students feel that nearly 50 years is not a quick response, remind them that the Catholic Church was the only official church of all people in Western Europe for centuries. The Reformation was strong enough to cause reforms in the huge and wealthy Catholic Church.)*

Europe, 1500

— Boundary of the Holy Roman Empire

1453 Ottoman Turks capture Constantinople.

1455 Gutenberg Bible printed in Mainz. ▶

1492 Columbus reaches the Americas.

1517 Martin Luther begins the Reformation in Wittenberg.

1526 Babur establishes Mughal Empire in India. (Mughal noble) ▶

1534 English king Henry VIII starts the Church of England.

1563 Council of Trent mandates reforms in Catholic Church.

1500 — 1600

35

CHAPTER 1

History from Visuals

Interpreting the Map

Have students look for the cities on the map and note which ones are on a river or near a coastline.

What role would their location have played in the growth of the cities? *(Rivers and the sea allowed trade to develop. The jobs and prosperity connected to trade led to growth.)*

Ask students to discuss why cities that are centers of trade are more likely to be exposed to new cultural ideas. *(Such cities are full of traders and travelers who bring new ideas and inventions.)*

Extension Have students note the boundaries of the Holy Roman Empire and the Papal States. Then have them turn to the textbook atlas to examine modern European nations that now fall at least partly within these borders.

Ask students to name the European countries that eventually arose from this vast region. *(Italy, Germany, the Netherlands, Belgium, Liechtenstein, the Czech Republic, Slovenia, Poland, Switzerland, Austria)*

RECOMMENDED RESOURCES

Books for the Teacher

Ozment, Steven E. ***Protestants: The Birth of a Revolution.*** New York: Doubleday, 1992. Shows the significance of becoming a Protestant during the Reformation.

Norman J. Wilson, ed. ***World Eras: The European Renaissance and Reformation, 1350–1600.*** Farmington Hills: Gale Group, 2001.

Books for the Student

McDougal Littell Nextext. ***Reformation and Enlightenment.*** High-interest fiction, narratives, historical background, and visuals.

Videos and Software

Printing Transforms Knowledge. Video. Society for Visual Education. 800-829-1900. Presents the impact of the printing press on education and the Reformation.

The Renaissance. Video. BBC Films. Distributed by 20th Century Fox. A journey through art and history. Filmed on location.

The Renaissance of Florence. CD-ROM. Films for the Humanities & Sciences. 800-257-5126.

Interact *with* History

Objectives

- Set the stage for studying the Renaissance by using a painting as a primary source.
- Help students understand how to gain insights into historical periods through art.

INTEGRATED TECHNOLOGY

Interactive This image is available in an interactive format on the eEdition. Students can examine parts of the painting in greater detail and will have the opportunity to think about the painting's significance.

EXAMINING *the* ISSUES

Answers

- The setting is rich and elegant. The chancellor is wearing a fur-trimmed robe, Mary's cloak is full and beautiful, and the floor design and the walls of the room are ornate.
- Mary presents the child to the kneeling Chancellor Rolin, who is clearly powerful and wealthy. The chancellor's hands are clasped in prayer, showing his respect. A hovering angel holds a crown over Mary's head. These details show that religion was a central part of the society.

Discussion

Ask students what they remember about the function of art in Egypt and India. *(In Egypt, much of the art was created to honor the ruler, who was considered a god. In India, many pieces of art depicted religious figures.)*

Interact *with* History

What can you learn from art?

You work at a museum that is considering buying this painting by Jan van Eyck. It is a portrait of Chancellor Rolin, a powerful government official in Burgundy (later part of France). Before deciding, the museum director wants to know what this painting can teach the public about the Renaissance.

INTER*ACTIVE*

1 **Classical Art** Renaissance artists admired classical art. The columns show classical style.

2 **Perspective** Van Eyck used the technique of perspective, which shows distant objects as smaller than close ones. He also used oil paints, a new invention.

3 **Religion** This painting portrays the infant Jesus and his mother Mary in 15th-century Europe. Such a depiction shows the continuing importance of religion during the Renaissance.

4 **The Individual** Renaissance artists portrayed the importance of individuals. Chancellor Rolin is wearing a fur-trimmed robe that shows his high status.

5 **Beauty** Van Eyck included many details simply to add beauty. These include the design on the floor, the folds of Mary's cloak, and the scenery outside.

▲ *The Madonna of Chancellor Rolin* (about 1435), Jan van Eyck

EXAMINING *the* ISSUES

- **What can you infer about the setting of the painting?**
- **What details in the painting give you an idea of the role of religion in society?**

As a class, discuss these questions to see what you can learn about this art. Also recall what you know about art in such places as Egypt and India. As you read about the Renaissance, notice what the art of that time reveals about European society.

WHY STUDY THE RENAISSANCE AND REFORMATION?

- Paintings, sculpture, and architecture of the Renaissance are still admired and copied today.
- People still argue about the best way to attain and keep power, a topic Niccolò Machiavelli covered in his book *The Prince.*
- People still debate how to create the perfect society, a subject Thomas More wrote about in *Utopia.*
- Shakespeare's plays and poems continue to be popular (see the Connect to Today feature on page 49).
- Mass production of books, such as this textbook, began with the printing press invented by Johann Gutenberg (see the Global Impact feature on page 50).
- The Protestant and Catholic Reformations dramatically changed Christianity. Tensions between Catholics and Protestants still exist in many parts of the world.

Bottecelli *Allegory of Spring*

Italian hill town

Italy: Birthplace of the Renaissance

MAIN IDEA

REVOLUTION The Italian Renaissance was a rebirth of learning that produced many great works of art and literature.

WHY IT MATTERS NOW

Renaissance art and literature still influence modern thought and modern art.

TERMS & NAMES

- Renaissance
- humanism
- secular
- patron
- perspective
- vernacular

SETTING THE STAGE During the late Middle Ages, Europe suffered from both war and plague. Those who survived wanted to celebrate life and the human spirit. They began to question institutions of the Middle Ages, which had been unable to prevent war or to relieve suffering brought by the plague. Some people questioned the Church, which taught Christians to endure suffering while they awaited their rewards in heaven. In northern Italy, writers and artists began to express this new spirit and to experiment with different styles. These men and women would greatly change how Europeans saw themselves and their world.

Italy's Advantages

This movement that started in Italy caused an explosion of creativity in art, writing, and thought that lasted approximately from 1300 to 1600. Historians call this period the **Renaissance** (REHN•ih•SAHNS). The term means rebirth, and in this context, it refers to a revival of art and learning. The educated men and women of Italy hoped to bring back to life the culture of classical Greece and Rome. Yet in striving to revive the past, the people of the Renaissance created something new. The contributions made during this period led to innovative styles of art and literature. They also led to new values, such as the importance of the individual.

The Renaissance eventually spread from northern Italy to the rest of Europe. Italy had three advantages that made it the birthplace of the Renaissance: thriving cities, a wealthy merchant class, and the classical heritage of Greece and Rome.

City-States Overseas trade, spurred by the Crusades, had led to the growth of large city-states in northern Italy. The region also had many sizable towns. Thus, northern Italy was urban while the rest of Europe was still mostly rural. Since cities are often places where people exchange ideas, they were an ideal breeding ground for an intellectual revolution.

In the 1300s, the bubonic plague struck these cities hard, killing up to 60 percent of the population. This brought economic changes. Because there were fewer laborers, survivors could demand higher wages. With few opportunities to expand business, merchants began to pursue other interests, such as art.

Merchants and the Medici A wealthy merchant class developed in each Italian city-state. Because city-states like Milan and Florence were relatively small, a high percentage of citizens could be intensely involved in political life.

CALIFORNIA STANDARDS

10.2.1 Compare the major ideas of philosophers and their effects on the democratic revolutions in England, the United States, France, and Latin America (e.g., John Locke, Charles-Louis Montesquieu, Jean-Jacques Rousseau, Simón Bolívar, Thomas Jefferson, James Madison).

CST 2 Students analyze how change happens at different rates at different times; understand that some aspects can change while others remain the same; and understand that change is complicated and affects not only technology and politics but also values and beliefs.

REP 1 Students distinguish valid arguments from fallacious arguments in historical interpretations.

REP 2 Students identify bias and prejudice in historical interpretations.

HI 1 Students show the connections, causal and otherwise, between particular historical events and larger social, economic, and political trends and developments.

TAKING NOTES

Outlining Use an outline to organize main ideas and details.

Italian Renaissance
I. Italy's advantages
A.
B.
II. Classical and worldly values

LESSON PLAN

OBJECTIVES

- Explain the conditions in Italy that gave rise to the Renaissance.
- Identify the values and ideas prized during the Renaissance.
- Describe the artistic breakthroughs and achievements of Renaissance artists.
- Summarize influential literary works and techniques of key Renaissance writers.

1 FOCUS & MOTIVATE

Explain that the Renaissance was a time of great creativity. Ask students to describe ways that they show their own creativity. *(Possible Answers: art, music, writing, type of clothing worn)*

2 INSTRUCT

Italy's Advantages

10.2.1

Critical Thinking

- What is your opinion of the Medici family? *(Positive–Supported arts and culture. Negative–Publicly executed enemies, ruled as dictators.)*

CALIFORNIA RESOURCES

California Reading Toolkit, p. L9
California Modified Lesson Plans for English Learners, p. 13
California Daily Standards Practice Transparencies, TT1
California Standards Enrichment Workbook, pp. 23–24
California Standards Planner and Lesson Plans, p. L9
California Online Test Practice
California Test Generator CD-ROM
California Easy Planner CD-ROM
California eEdition CD-ROM

SECTION 1 PROGRAM RESOURCES

ALL STUDENTS

In-Depth Resources: Unit 1
- Guided Reading, p. 18
- History Makers: Niccolò Machiavelli, p. 33

Formal Assessment
- Section Quiz, p. 21

ENGLISH LEARNERS

In-Depth Resources in Spanish
- Guided Reading, p. 18

Reading Study Guide (Spanish), p. 15
Reading Study Guide Audio CD (Spanish)

STRUGGLING READERS

In-Depth Resources: Unit 1
- Guided Reading, p. 18
- Building Vocabulary, p. 22
- Reteaching Activity, p. 36

Reading Study Guide, p. 15
Reading Study Guide Audio CD

GIFTED AND TALENTED STUDENTS

In-Depth Resources: Unit 1
- Primary Sources: from *The Courtier,* p. 26; from *The Prince,* p. 27
- Literature: from *The Agony and the Ecstasy,* p. 30
- Connections Across Time and Cultures, p. 35

Electronic Library of Primary Sources

INTEGRATED TECHNOLOGY

eEdition CD-ROM
Voices from the Past Audio CD
Power Presentations CD-ROM
Electronic Library of Primary Sources
- "The Art of Painting," from *Notebooks*

World Art and Cultures Transparencies
- AT36 *The Last Supper*
- AT37 *Mona Lisa*

classzone.com

History Makers

Medici Family

Ask students to identify the personality traits revealed by Lorenzo's actions. *(bravery, vengefulness, generosity)*

Medici power and influence eventually spread far beyond the city of Florence. The family produced several popes and two queens of France. Ask students to use an encyclopedia to find out more about the Medici. Interesting family members include Giuliano, Catherine, Marie, and Piero.

Classical and Worldly Values

10.2.1

Critical Thinking

- How did humanism influence Renaissance ideas? *(focused on people and their achievements, so art and thought became more concerned with the here and now)*
- Why did church leaders and wealthy merchants support the arts? *(showed their importance by having portraits painted and decorating churches and other public places)*
- What were the differences and similarities between upper-class Renaissance men and women? *(Both were expected to know the classics, but most women lacked political power.)*

History Makers

Medici Family

A rival family grew so jealous of the Medici that they plotted to kill Lorenzo (above) and his brother Giuliano. As the Medici attended Mass, assassins murdered Giuliano at the altar. Drawing his sword, Lorenzo escaped to a small room and held off his attackers until help arrived. Later, he had the killers brutally, publicly executed.

More positively, Lorenzo was a generous patron of the arts who collected many rare manuscripts. Eventually the Medici family made their library available to the public.

Merchants dominated politics. Unlike nobles, merchants did not inherit social rank. To succeed in business, they used their wits. As a result, many successful merchants believed they deserved power and wealth because of their individual merit. This belief in individual achievement became important during the Renaissance.

Since the late 1200s, the city-state of Florence had a republican form of government. But during the Renaissance, Florence came under the rule of one powerful banking family, the Medici (MEHD•ih•chee). The Medici family bank had branch offices throughout Italy and in the major cities of Europe. Cosimo de Medici was the wealthiest European of his time. In 1434, he won control of Florence's government. He did not seek political office for himself, but influenced members of the ruling council by giving them loans. For 30 years, he was dictator of Florence.

Cosimo de Medici died in 1464, but his family continued to control Florence. His grandson, Lorenzo de Medici, came to power in 1469. Known as Lorenzo the Magnificent, he ruled as a dictator yet kept up the appearance of having an elected government.

Looking to Greece and Rome Renaissance scholars looked down on the art and literature of the Middle Ages. Instead, they wanted to return to the learning of the Greeks and Romans. They achieved this in several ways. First, the artists and scholars of Italy drew inspiration from the ruins of Rome that surrounded them. Second, Western scholars studied ancient Latin manuscripts that had been preserved in monasteries. Third, Christian scholars in Constantinople fled to Rome with Greek manuscripts when the Turks conquered Constantinople in 1453. (A)

A. Answer thriving cities, a wealthy merchant class, and the heritage of Greece and Rome

MAIN IDEA

Analyzing Causes

(A) What three advantages fostered the Renaissance in Italy?

Classical and Worldly Values

As scholars studied these manuscripts, they became more influenced by classical ideas. These ideas helped them to develop a new outlook on life and art.

Classics Lead to Humanism The study of classical texts led to **humanism**, an intellectual movement that focused on human potential and achievements. Instead of trying to make classical texts agree with Christian teaching as medieval scholars had, humanists studied them to understand ancient Greek values. Humanists influenced artists and architects to carry on classical traditions. Also, humanists popularized the study of subjects common to classical education, such as history, literature, and philosophy. These subjects are called the humanities.

Vocabulary

The words *humanist* and *humanities* come from the Latin word *humanitas,* which refers to the literary culture that every educated person should possess.

Worldly Pleasures In the Middle Ages, some people had demonstrated their piety by wearing rough clothing and eating plain foods. However, humanists suggested that a person might enjoy life without offending God. In Renaissance Italy, the wealthy enjoyed material luxuries, good music, and fine foods.

Most people remained devout Catholics. However, the basic spirit of Renaissance society was **secular**—worldly rather than spiritual and concerned with the here and now. Even church leaders became more worldly. Some lived in beautiful mansions, threw lavish banquets, and wore expensive clothes.

Patrons of the Arts Church leaders during the Renaissance beautified Rome and other cities by spending huge amounts of money for art. They became **patrons** of the

---

DIFFERENTIATING INSTRUCTION: ENGLISH LEARNERS

Focus on Vocabulary

Class Time 30 minutes

Task Creating a chart showing the meaning of four key terms

Purpose To better understand the Renaissance

Instructions Have students create a chart in which they define the key terms in their own words. An example is at right.

For help, have students use the Reading Study Guide for Section 1, available in English and Spanish.

Term	Meaning	Examples
Renaissance	Rebirth	New interest in classical Greece and Rome
humanism	Focus on people and their achievements	Art and literature were valued and encouraged.
secular	Concerned with the here and now	Some church leaders lived in mansions and wore expensive clothes.
patron	A person who supports artists	The Medici family in Italy

Italy: Birthplace of the Renaissance

Reading Study Guide: Spanish Translation

arts by financially supporting artists. Renaissance merchants and wealthy families also were patrons of the arts. By having their portraits painted or by donating art to the city to place in public squares, the wealthy demonstrated their own importance.

The Renaissance Man Renaissance writers introduced the idea that all educated people were expected to create art. In fact, the ideal individual strove to master almost every area of study. A man who excelled in many fields was praised as a "universal man." Later ages called such people "Renaissance men."

Baldassare Castiglione (KAHS•teel•YOH•nay) wrote a book called *The Courtier* (1528) that taught how to become such a person. A young man should be charming, witty, and well educated in the classics. He should dance, sing, play music, and write poetry. In addition, he should be a skilled rider, wrestler, and swordsman.

B. Possible Answer Both were expected to be educated and knowledgeable of art and culture.

MAIN IDEA

Comparing
B How were expectations for Renaissance men and Renaissance women similar?

The Renaissance Woman According to *The Courtier,* upper-class women also should know the classics and be charming. Yet they were not expected to seek fame. They were expected to inspire art but rarely to create it. Upper-class Renaissance women were better educated than medieval women. However, most Renaissance women had little influence in politics.

A few women, such as Isabella d'Este, did exercise power. Born into the ruling family of the city-state of Ferrara, she married the ruler of another city-state, Mantua. She brought many Renaissance artists to her court and built a famous art collection. She was also skilled in politics. When her husband was taken captive in war, she defended Mantua and won his release. B

Analyzing Primary Sources

The Renaissance Man

In *The Courtier,* Baldassare Castiglione described the type of accomplished person who later came to be called the Renaissance man.

PRIMARY SOURCE

Let the man we are seeking be very bold, stern, and always among the first, where the enemy are to be seen; and in every other place, gentle, modest, reserved, above all things avoiding ostentation [showiness] and that impudent [bold] self-praise by which men ever excite hatred and disgust in all who hear them. . . .

I would have him more than passably accomplished in letters, at least in those studies that are called the humanities, and conversant not only with the Latin language but with Greek, for the sake of the many different things that have been admirably written therein. Let him be well versed in the poets, and not less in the orators and historians, and also proficient in writing verse and prose.

BALDASSARE CASTIGLIONE, *The Courtier*

The Renaissance Woman

Although Renaissance women were not expected to create art, wealthy women often were patrons of artists, as this letter by Isabella d'Este demonstrates.

PRIMARY SOURCE

To Master Leonardo da Vinci, the painter: Hearing that you are settled at Florence, we have begun to hope that our cherished desire to obtain a work by your hand might be at length realized. When you were in this city and drew our portrait in carbon, you promised us that you would some day paint it in colors. But because this would be almost impossible, since you are unable to come here, we beg you to keep your promise by converting our portrait into another figure, which would be still more acceptable to us; that is to say, a youthful Christ of about twelve years . . . executed with all that sweetness and charm of atmosphere which is the peculiar excellence of your art.
Mantua, May 14, 1504

ISABELLA D'ESTE, *Letters*

DOCUMENT-BASED QUESTIONS

1. **Drawing Conclusions** *Do the qualities called for in the ideal Renaissance man and woman seem to emphasize the individual or the group?*
2. **Making Inferences** *Isabella d'Este's portrait was painted by Titian, and Castiglione's by Raphael, two famous painters. What does this tell you about the subjects' social status?*

More About . . .

Isabella d'Este

Isabella d'Este had a privileged upbringing. She could speak Greek and Latin and was an accomplished musician and dancer. An avid collector of art and antiques, she turned her home into an art museum. She had several children but remained involved in politics, governing Mantua while her husband was away and for a short period after he died.

Analyzing Primary Sources

The Renaissance Man and Woman

Ask students to read the primary source from Baldassare Castiglione. Then ask them why he suggests that men should avoid ostentation and self-praise. *(Perhaps because in social settings, ostentation and self-praise would be considered impolite.)*

Answers to Document-Based Questions

1. **Drawing Conclusions** The qualities called for seem to emphasize individual achievement rather than group identity. In other words, the qualities require the individual to stand out from the crowd.
2. **Making Inferences** The fact that both had their portraits painted by famous painters suggests that Isabella d'Este and Castiglione were both important people of their time.

In-Depth Resources: Unit 1

• from *The Courtier,* p. 26

CONNECTIONS ACROSS TIME AND CULTURES

Government Support of the Arts

Class Time 20 minutes

Task Researching government support of the arts

Purpose To understand modern connections to Renaissance patrons of art

Instructions Tell students that President Franklin Roosevelt formed the Works Progress Administration (WPA) to help lift the country out of the Great Depression. Between 1935 and 1938 the WPA became the largest public arts program in the world. At one point, it employed 40,000 people. The program ended in 1943.

In 1965, Congress created the National Endowment for the Arts (NEA). Its goal was to fund art projects around the United States. The NEA's budget grew from $16 million in 1970 to $180 million in 1979. Congress supported strong funding for the NEA throughout the 1980s but reduced its funding in later years.

Have students research current government funding for the arts. Why would a government provide funding for art? Do students think arts funding is a good use of taxpayer money? Ask students to name some people who are art patrons. *(Bill Gates—purchased a manuscript by Leonardo da Vinci; the Rockefellers; Peggy Guggenheim; people whose names are on local museums or libraries)*

The Renaissance Revolutionizes Art
10.2.1

Critical Thinking

- In what ways was Renaissance art revolutionary? *(use of perspective; revealed the subject's personality)*
- How do you think Leonardo's scientific studies helped his art? *(would allow him to make his art even more realistic)*

The Renaissance Revolutionizes Art

Supported by patrons like Isabella d'Este, dozens of artists worked in northern Italy. As the Renaissance advanced, artistic styles changed. Medieval artists had used religious subjects to convey a spiritual ideal. Renaissance artists often portrayed religious subjects, but they used a realistic style copied from classical models. Greek and Roman subjects also became popular. Renaissance painters used the technique of **perspective**, which shows three dimensions on a flat surface.

Realistic Painting and Sculpture Following the new emphasis on individuals, painters began to paint prominent citizens. These realistic portraits revealed what was distinctive about each person. In addition, artists such as the sculptor, poet, architect, and painter Michelangelo (MY•kuhl•AN•juh•LOH) Buonarroti used a realistic style when depicting the human body. C

C. Possible Answer a focus on revealing the uniqueness of each person

MAIN IDEA

Synthesizing

C What major change did a belief in individual merit bring about in art?

Donatello (DAHN•uh•TEHL•oh) also made sculpture more realistic by carving natural postures and expressions that reveal personality. He revived a classical form in his statue of David, a boy who, according to the Bible, became a great king. Donatello's statue was created in the late 1460s. It was the first European sculpture of a large, free-standing nude since ancient times. For sculptors of the period, including Michelangelo, David (page 44) was a favorite subject.

Analyzing Art

Perspective

Point out to students that the location of the vanishing point in Raphael's painting is the opened door of the church. Explain that some Renaissance artists used grids and devices with peepholes to help calculate perspective.

SKILLBUILDER Answer

Contrasting The figures in the background are smaller; the figures in the foreground are larger. This makes the figures in the background seem farther away and the figures in the foreground seem closer to the viewer.

> Analyzing Art

Perspective

Perspective creates the appearance of three dimensions. Classical artists had used perspective, but medieval artists abandoned the technique. In the 1400s, Italian artists rediscovered it.

Perspective is based on an optical illusion. As parallel lines stretch away from a viewer, they seem to draw together, until they meet at a spot on the horizon called the vanishing point. The use of perspective was a feature of most Western painting for the next 450 years.

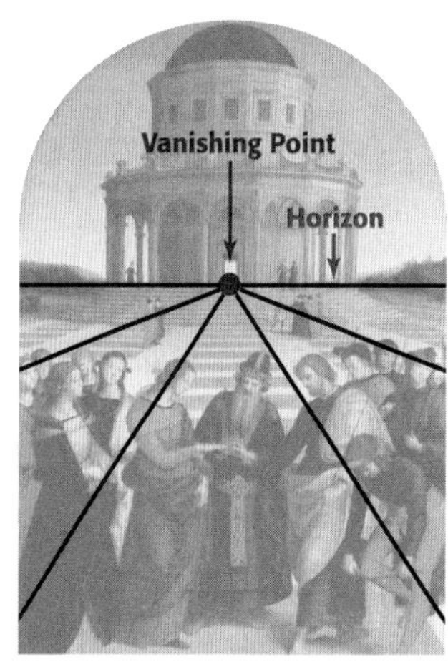

Marriage of the Virgin (1504), Raphael

SKILLBUILDER: Interpreting Visual Sources

Contrasting *What is the major difference between the figures in the background of the painting and the figures in the foreground? What is the effect of this difference?*

COOPERATIVE LEARNING

Comparing and Contrasting Art

Class Time 20 minutes

Task Comparing and contrasting medieval and Renaissance art

Purpose To better understand the art of the Renaissance

Instructions Divide students into groups of two or three. Display World Art and Cultures Transparency AT37, the *Mona Lisa*. Then have students use classroom or library resources to find an example of medieval portraiture. Ask groups to list similarities and differences for these two works of art. Suggest that groups focus on the following:

- facial expressions
- use of color
- amount of detail
- background
- use of light and shadow

As a class, discuss groups' results. Ask students, Based on this analysis and information in the text, what can you conclude about Renaissance art? *(Possible Answer: more realistic than medieval art, especially in use of light, shadow, and perspective)*

World Art and Cultures Transparencies

Leonardo, Renaissance Man Leonardo da Vinci (LAY•uh•NAHR•doh duh•VIHN•chee) was a painter, sculptor, inventor, and scientist. A true "Renaissance man," he was interested in how things worked. He studied how a muscle moves and how veins are arranged in a leaf. He filled his notebooks with observations and sketches. Then he incorporated his findings in his art.

Among his many masterpieces, Leonardo painted one of the best-known portraits in the world, the *Mona Lisa* (page 44). The woman in the portrait seems so real that many writers have tried to explain the thoughts behind her smile. Leonardo also produced a famous religious painting, *The Last Supper.* It shows the personalities of Jesus' disciples through facial expressions.

Raphael Advances Realism Raphael (RAHF•ee•uhl) Sanzio was younger than Michelangelo and Leonardo. He learned from studying their works. One of Raphael's favorite subjects was the Madonna and child. Raphael often portrayed their expressions as gentle and calm. He was famous for his use of perspective.

In his greatest achievement, Raphael filled the walls of Pope Julius II's library with paintings. One of these, *School of Athens* (page 45), conveys the classical influence on the Renaissance. Raphael painted famous Renaissance figures, such as Michelangelo, Leonardo, and himself, as classical philosophers and their students.

Anguissola and Gentileschi Renaissance society generally restricted women's roles. However, a few Italian women became notable painters. Sofonisba Anguissola (ahng•GWEES•soh•lah) was the first woman artist to gain an international reputation. She is known for her portraits of her sisters and of prominent people such as King Philip II of Spain. Artemisia Gentileschi (JAYN•tee•LEHS•kee) was another accomplished artist. She trained with her painter father and helped with his work. In her own paintings, Gentileschi painted pictures of strong, heroic women.

History Makers

Leonardo da Vinci
1452–1519

Leonardo da Vinci's notebooks—and life—are mysterious. Some 3,500 pages closely covered with writings and drawings survive. His writing is clear and easy to read, but only if you look at it in a mirror. No one knows why he wrote backwards.

Leonardo planned scholarly works and great feats of engineering that were never completed. Only 17 of his paintings survive. And yet the work that Leonardo did produce is so amazing that it confirms his genius.

Michelangelo Buonarroti
1475–1564

Like Leonardo, Michelangelo was a Renaissance man. He excelled as a painter, sculptor, architect, and poet.

Michelangelo is most famous for the way he portrayed the human body in painting and sculpture. Influenced by classical art, he created figures that are forceful and show heroic grandeur.

Among his achievements are the dome of St. Peter's, the paintings on the ceiling of the Sistine Chapel, and the statue of David.

INTEGRATED TECHNOLOGY

INTERNET ACTIVITY Plan a Web site on Renaissance leaders that showcases these two artists. Go to **classzone.com** for your research.

Renaissance Writers Change Literature

Renaissance writers produced works that reflected their time, but they also used techniques that writers rely on today. Some followed the example of the medieval writer Dante. He wrote in the **vernacular**, his native language, instead of Latin. Dante's native language was Italian. In addition, Renaissance writers wrote either for self-expression or to portray the individuality of their subjects. In these ways, writers of the Renaissance began trends that modern writers still follow.

Petrarch and Boccaccio Francesco Petrarch (PEE•trahrk) was one of the earliest and most influential humanists. Some have called him the father of Renaissance humanism. He was also a great poet. Petrarch wrote both in Italian and in Latin. In

History Makers

Leonardo da Vinci and Michelangelo Buonarroti

Why do you think that both artists are considered Renaissance men? *(Both were creative geniuses who excelled as painters, sculptors, and designers.)* Both Michelangelo and Leonardo were commissioned by the city of Florence to paint frescoes on the walls of a new city hall—in honor of the city's many military victories.

INTEGRATED TECHNOLOGY

Rubric Web sites should
- give examples of the artist's work.
- explain why the artist's work was important.
- present information clearly and concisely.

Electronic Library of Primary Sources
- "The Art of Painting" from *Notebooks*

Renaissance Writers Change Literature
10.2.1

Critical Thinking
- Why was it important that writers began writing in the vernacular? *(more accessible to everyday people; possible to read literature without learning to speak Latin)*
- Why do you think Machiavelli's writings remain popular? *(people still interested in getting and keeping power)*

DIFFERENTIATING INSTRUCTION: GIFTED AND TALENTED STUDENTS

Leonardo's Inventions

Class Time 45 minutes

Task Researching Leonardo da Vinci's inventions

Purpose To show how Leonardo anticipated many modern scientific inventions

Instructions Like many other Renaissance humanists, Leonardo da Vinci believed in the limitless possibilities of human achievement. Leonardo's faith in human creativity found expression in his notebooks, which were filled with drawings and descriptions of an astonishing range of inventions. Many of these inventions, such as a flying machine and an alarm clock, have a somewhat modern look and purpose. Here are some other examples of Leonardo's inventions:

- parachute
- power loom
- armored tank
- diving suit
- submarine
- construction crane

Have each student research one of Leonardo da Vinci's inventions and find illustrations and descriptions of some of his drawings. Ask students to compare Leonardo's invention with its modern version. Students should share their findings with the class.

More About . . .

Bubonic Plague

Within five years of its appearance in western Europe, the bubonic plague—so called because it causes a swelling of the lymph nodes, or buboes—killed about one-third of the population. Feudalism itself was threatened, as the value of labor rose and peasants began moving into towns in search of employment.

More About . . .

Machiavelli

"The end justifies the means" is one of the most widely known phrases from *The Prince.* Machiavelli is also probably best remembered for his defense of lies and trickery. "A prince never lacks legitimate reasons to break his promise," he wrote, and "The fact is that a man who wants to act virtuously in every way necessarily comes to grief among so many who are not virtuous." The word *Machiavellian* describes any crafty or deceitful action used for one's own advantage.

In-Depth Resources: Unit 1

- Primary Source: from *The Prince,* p. 27
- History Makers: Niccolò Machiavelli, p. 33

Italian, he wrote sonnets—14-line poems. They were about a mysterious woman named Laura, who was his ideal. (Little is known of Laura except that she died of the plague in 1348.) In classical Latin, he wrote letters to many important friends.

The Italian writer Giovanni Boccaccio (boh•KAH•chee•oh) is best known for the *Decameron,* a series of realistic, sometimes off-color stories. The stories are supposedly told by a group of worldly young people waiting in a rural villa to avoid the plague sweeping through Florence:

PRIMARY SOURCE

In the year of Our Lord 1348 the deadly plague broke out in the great city of Florence, most beautiful of Italian cities. Whether through the operation of the heavenly bodies or because of our own iniquities [sins] which the just wrath of God sought to correct, the plague had arisen in the East some years before, causing the death of countless human beings. It spread without stop from one place to another, until, unfortunately, it swept over the West. Neither knowledge nor human foresight availed against it, though the city was cleansed of much filth by chosen officers in charge and sick persons were forbidden to enter it, while advice was broadcast for the preservation of health.

GIOVANNI BOCCACCIO, Preface, *Decameron*

The *Decameron* presents both tragic and comic views of life. In its stories, the author uses cutting humor to illustrate the human condition. Boccaccio presents his characters in all of their individuality and all their folly.

Machiavelli Advises Rulers *The Prince* (1513) by Niccolò Machiavelli (MAK•ee•uh•VEHL•ee) also examines the imperfect conduct of human beings. It does so by taking the form of a political guidebook. In *The Prince,* Machiavelli examines how a ruler can gain power and keep it in spite of his enemies. In answering this question, he began with the idea that most people are selfish, fickle, and corrupt.

To succeed in such a wicked world, Machiavelli said, a prince must be strong as a lion and shrewd as a fox. He might have to trick his enemies and even his own people for the good of the state. In *The Prince,* Machiavelli was not concerned with what was morally right, but with what was politically effective.

He pointed out that most people think it is praiseworthy in a prince to keep his word and live with integrity. Nevertheless, Machiavelli argued that in the real world of power and politics a prince must sometimes mislead the people and lie to his opponents. As a historian and political thinker, Machiavelli suggested that in order for a prince to accomplish great things, he must be crafty enough to not only overcome the suspicions but also gain the trust of others:

PRIMARY SOURCE D

From this arises the question whether it is better to be loved more than feared, or feared more than loved. The reply is, that one ought to be both feared and loved, but as it is difficult for the two to go together, it is much safer to be feared than loved, if one of the two has to be wanting. For it may be said of men in general that they are ungrateful, voluble [changeable], dissemblers [liars], anxious to avoid danger, and covetous of gain; as long as you benefit them, they are entirely yours; they offer you their blood, their goods, their life, and their children, as I have before said, when the necessity is remote; but when it approaches, they revolt. And the prince who has relied solely on their words, without making preparations, is ruined.

NICCOLÒ MACHIAVELLI, *The Prince*

MAIN IDEA

Analyzing Primary Sources

D Does Machiavelli think that a prince should prefer to be loved or feared? Why?

D. Answer feared; people are more likely to respond to someone they fear

DIFFERENTIATING INSTRUCTION: STRUGGLING READERS

Analyzing a Primary Source

Class Time 30 minutes

Task Expressing the ideas of Machiavelli in everyday language

Purpose To better understand a primary source

Instructions Pair students and have them read the excerpt from *The Prince* by Machiavelli. Have them write down in their own words what they think each sentence means. For example, the first sentence might be rewritten as follows:

People wonder whether a leader should try to be loved or feared.

Have students discuss what they think of the ideas. Can they think of any rulers who are feared or loved? *(Students may mention current local, national, or international leaders, or they may cite retired leaders such as Nelson Mandela.)* Do they see any instances in the world today where leaders have misled the people? *(Students may mention wrongdoing in office or broken campaign promises.)*

For students who may need additional help, use the Guided Reading activity for this section.

In-Depth Resources: Unit 1

Vittoria Colonna The women writers who gained fame during the Renaissance usually wrote about personal subjects, not politics. Yet, some of them had great influence. Vittoria Colonna (1492–1547) was born of a noble family. In 1509, she married the Marquis of Pescara. He spent most of his life away from home on military campaigns.

Vittoria Colonna exchanged sonnets with Michelangelo and helped Castiglione publish *The Courtier.* Her own poems express personal emotions. When her husband was away at the Battle of Ravenna in 1512, she wrote to him:

PRIMARY SOURCE

But now in this perilous assault,
in this horrible, pitiless battle
that has so hardened my mind and heart,
your great valor has shown you an equal
to Hector and Achilles. But what good is
this to me, sorrowful, abandoned? . . .
Your uncertain enterprises do not hurt you;
but we who wait, mournfully grieving,
are wounded by doubt and fear.
You men, driven by rage, considering nothing
but your honor, commonly go off, shouting,
with great fury, to confront danger.
We remain, with fear in our heart and
grief on our brow for you; sister longs for
brother, wife for husband, mother for son.

VITTORIA COLONNA, *Poems*

Toward the end of the 15th century, Renaissance ideas began to spread north from Italy. As you will read in Section 2, northern artists and thinkers adapted Renaissance ideals in their own ways.

Global Patterns

Other Renaissances

In addition to the Italian Renaissance, there have been rebirths and revivals in other places around the world. For example, the Tang (618–907) and Song (960–1279) dynasties in China saw periods of great artistic and technological advances.

Like the Italian Renaissance, the achievements of the Tang and the Song had roots in an earlier time, the Han Dynasty (202 B.C. to A.D. 220). After the Han collapsed, China experienced turmoil.

When order was restored, Chinese culture flourished. The Chinese invented gunpowder and printing. Chinese poets wrote literary masterpieces. Breakthroughs were made in architecture, painting, and pottery. The Song painting above, *Waiting for Guests by Lamplight,* was done with ink and color on silk.

SECTION 1 ASSESSMENT

TERMS & NAMES 1. For each term or name, write a sentence explaining its significance.
• Renaissance • humanism • secular • patron • perspective • vernacular

USING YOUR NOTES

2. What was Italy's most important advantage? Why? (10.2.1)

Italian Renaissance
I. Italy's advantages
A.
B.
II. Classical and worldly values

MAIN IDEAS

3. What are some of the characteristics of the "Renaissance man" and "Renaissance woman"? (10.2.1)
4. How did Italy's cities help to make it the birthplace of the Renaissance? (10.2.1)
5. What was the attitude of Church leaders and the wealthy toward the arts? Why? (10.2.1)

CRITICAL THINKING & WRITING

6. **DRAWING CONCLUSIONS** How did study of the classics influence branches of learning such as history, literature, and philosophy? (10.2.1)
7. **MAKING INFERENCES** How is humanism reflected in Renaissance art? Explain with examples. (10.2.1)
8. **COMPARING** What were the differences between the Middle Ages and the Renaissance in the attitude toward worldly pleasures? (10.2.1)
9. **WRITING ACTIVITY** REVOLUTION How did the Renaissance revolutionize European art and thought? Support your opinions in a three-paragraph **essay.** (Writing 2.3.a)

CONNECT TO TODAY **WRITING A DESCRIPTION**
In a book on modern art, find an artist who worked in more than one medium, such as painting and sculpture. Write a **description** of one of the artist's works in each medium. (Writing 2.3.b)

Global Patterns

Other Renaissances

Since the days of the Italian Renaissance, the word *renaissance* has been used to describe a period of great achievements in art, literature, and culture. During the Harlem Renaissance, which took place in the 1920s in New York City, African-American creativity flowered. Writers, painters, and musicians created works of art celebrating African-American culture. Some of the best-known artists of the Harlem Renaissance include Langston Hughes, Zora Neale Hurston, Paul Robeson, Duke Ellington, and Bessie Smith.

In-Depth Resources: Unit 1
• Connections Across Time and Cultures, p. 35

3 ASSESS

SECTION 1 ASSESSMENT

Have students work in pairs to answer the questions and to note the location of the answers in the text.

Formal Assessment
• Section Quiz, p. 21

4 RETEACH

Use the Guided Reading worksheet for Section 1 to review the main ideas of the section.

In-Depth Resources, Unit 1
• Guided Reading, p. 18
• Reteaching Activity, p. 36

ANSWERS

1. Renaissance, p. 37 • humanism, p. 38 • secular, p. 38 • patron, p. 38 • perspective, p. 40 • vernacular, p. 41
2. **Sample Answer:** I. Advantages: A. thriving cities, B. wealthy merchants, C. classical heritage (most important). II. Values: A. citizens involved in politics, B. merchants dominated politics.
3. Man—Excelled in many fields, charming, witty, educated, politically powerful. Woman—Well educated in classics, charming, modest, knowledgeable in arts.
4. Cities offered wealth, talent, and new ideas.
5. They supported the arts because they wanted to beautify their communities and show their own importance.
6. Study of classical texts led to a different outlook on life, one emphasizing human potential and achievements.
7. Renaissance art such as *David* celebrates the human body and individual achievement.
8. In the Middle Ages, some people believed that denial of worldly pleasures would please God. During the Renaissance, many believed that God intended them to enjoy those things.
9. **Rubric** Essays should
• discuss how Renaissance scholars looked to classical writers for inspiration.
• note the ways Renaissance artists revolutionized art by using perspective, a more realistic style, and glorifying individuals.

CONNECT TO TODAY

Rubric Descriptions should
• include artists such as Picasso or Matisse, who were both painters and sculptors.
• identify examples of the artist's work.

History *through* Art

OBJECTIVES

- Explain how Renaissance ideas were expressed in the art of the time.
- Identify some of the important Renaissance artists and their achievements.

FOCUS & MOTIVATE

Ask students how they respond to Leonardo's *Mona Lisa* or Michelangelo's *David*. What do they think the artists were trying to achieve? Ask students if they know anything about any of the artists in this feature.

INSTRUCT

Critical Thinking

- Why do you think the *Mona Lisa* has become such a famous work of art? *(Possible Answers: realistic yet mysterious style, painted with a high degree of skill, people wonder about her half-smile)*
- What characteristics of *David* and *School of Athens* indicate that Renaissance artists admired classical works? *(*David *resembles Greek and Roman sculptures;* School of Athens *portrays Greek scholars and shows Greek architecture.)*

History *through* Art

Renaissance Ideas Influence Renaissance Art

CALIFORNIA STANDARDS

CST 1 Students compare the present with the past, evaluating the consequences of past events and decisions and determining the lessons that were learned.

The Renaissance in Italy produced extraordinary achievements in many different forms of art, including painting, architecture, sculpture, and drawing. These art forms were used by talented artists to express important ideas and attitudes of the age.

The value of humanism is shown in Raphael's *School of Athens,* a depiction of the greatest Greek philosophers. The realism of Renaissance art is seen in a portrait such as the *Mona Lisa,* which is an expression of the subject's unique features and personality. And Michelangelo's *David* shares stylistic qualities with ancient Greek and Roman sculpture.

INTEGRATED TECHNOLOGY

RESEARCH LINKS For more on Renaissance art, go to **classzone.com**

▲ **Portraying Individuals**

Da Vinci The *Mona Lisa* (c. 1504–1506) is thought to be a portrait of Lisa Gherardini, who, at 16, married Francesco del Giocondo, a wealthy merchant of Florence who commissioned the portrait. Mona Lisa is a shortened form of Madonna Lisa (Madam, or My Lady, Lisa). Renaissance artists showed individuals as they really looked.

44 Chapter 1

RECOMMENDED RESOURCES

Books

Hibbard, Howard. ***Michelangelo.*** New York: Harper, 1985. A fine and readable introduction to the artist.

Brown, David Alan. ***Leonardo da Vinci: Origins of a Genius.*** New Haven: Yale University Press, 1998.

Labella, Vincenzo. ***A Season of Giants: Michaelangelo, Leonardo, Raphael, 1492–1508.*** Boston: Little, Brown, 1990.

Videos and Software

Renaissance Art and Music. Clearvue. 800-253-2788. Explores how Renaissance artists and composers developed new forms and techniques.

History Through Art: The Renaissance. DVD. Clearvue. 800-253-2788. Interactive format with high-quality images.

The Renaissance of Florence. CD-ROM for Windows. Social Studies School Service. 800-421-4246. A collection of narrated slide shows augmented by video clips, period music, and a hypertext dictionary of names and terms.

◄ **Classical and Renaissance Sculpture**
Michelangelo Influenced by classical statues, Michelangelo sculpted *David* from 1501 to 1504. Michelangelo portrayed the biblical hero in the moments just before battle. David's posture is graceful, yet his figure also displays strength. The statue, which is 18 feet tall, towers over the viewer.

▲ **The Importance of Ancient Greece**
Raphael The painting *School of Athens* (1508) for the pope's apartments in the Vatican shows that the scholars of ancient Greece were highly honored. Under the center arch stand Plato and Aristotle. To their right, Socrates argues with several young men. Toward the front, Pythagoras draws a lesson on a slate and Ptolemy holds a globe.

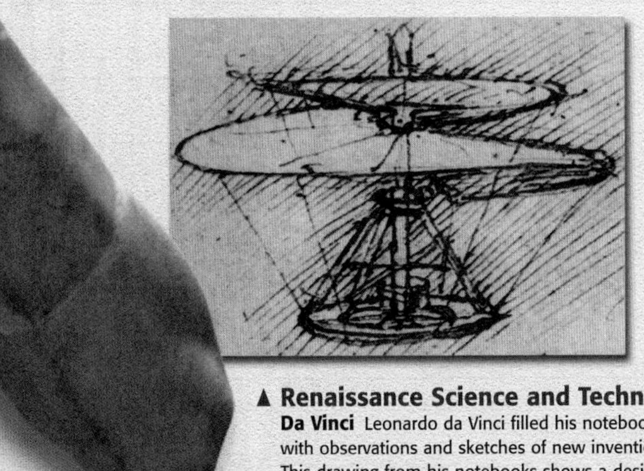

▲ **Renaissance Science and Technology**
Da Vinci Leonardo da Vinci filled his notebooks with observations and sketches of new inventions. This drawing from his notebooks shows a design for a spiral screw to achieve vertical flight. Leonardo's drawing anticipated the helicopter.

Connect *to* Today

1. **Clarifying** How do the works of Renaissance artists and architects reflect Renaissance ideas? Explain.
   See Skillbuilder Handbook, page R4.
2. **Synthesizing** Look through books on architecture to find examples of American architects who were influenced by the architects and buildings of the Italian Renaissance. Share your findings with the class.

45

More About . . .

School of Athens

Raphael was only 27 when he painted this magnificent fresco in which great scholars of different ages are shown in a timeless academy. The figure of Plato at the center holds *Timaeus,* his writings about the origin of the world, while pointing his finger to the heavens. Aristotle holds a copy of *Ethics,* his moral teachings, while he gestures toward the earth in a sweeping horizontal movement.

More About . . .

Mona Lisa

Many viewers comment on how much Lisa del Giocondo seems to be alive, unlike the more wooden figures in paintings before this time. Leonardo invented a technique called *sfumato* to achieve his effect. In this technique, outlines are slightly blurred, colors are mellow, and forms merge with one another, always leaving something to the imagination. Notice how the corners of the mouth and the corners of the eyes are left deliberately indistinct as they merge into a soft shadow.

CONNECT TO TODAY: ANSWERS

1. Clarifying

The ideas of humanism, realism, and classicism are reflected in Renaissance art. Humanists, who focused on human potential and achievements, were interested in Greek values. Raphael even depicted Greek philosophers in *School of Athens.* Renaissance artworks glorify the individual and the human body and reflect classical influence. Classical art and architecture influenced Renaissance artists and architects.

2. Synthesizing

Rubric Students should

- provide examples of American architects and buildings that were influenced by the Italian Renaissance. One notable example is Monticello, the home designed by Thomas Jefferson. He was influenced by Andrea Palladio, a Renaissance architect.
- explain how the influence can be seen in the American buildings.

LESSON PLAN

OBJECTIVES

- Explain the origins and characteristics of the Northern Renaissance.
- Trace the impact of the Renaissance on German and Flemish painters.
- Profile key Northern Renaissance writers.
- Describe the origins of the Elizabethan Age and Elizabethan drama.
- Explain how printing spread ideas.

1 FOCUS & MOTIVATE

Have students read the Connect to Today feature on page 49. What do the posters indicate about why Shakespeare's plays are still performed today? *(adaptable to modern themes and settings)*

2 INSTRUCT

The Northern Renaissance Begins

10.2.1

Critical Thinking

- Why and how did an increase in wealth affect the spread of the Renaissance? *(Merchants and rulers could sponsor artists and writers.)*

CALIFORNIA RESOURCES

California Reading Toolkit, p. L10
California Modified Lesson Plans for English Learners, p. 15
California Daily Standards Practice Transparencies, TT2
California Standards Enrichment Workbook, pp. 23–24
California Standards Planner and Lesson Plans, p. L11
California Online Test Practice
California Test Generator CD-ROM
California Easy Planner CD-ROM
California eEdition CD-ROM

Bottecelli *Allegory of Spring*

2

Italian hill town

The Northern Renaissance

MAIN IDEA	WHY IT MATTERS NOW	TERMS & NAMES
CULTURAL INTERACTION In the 1400s, the ideas of the Italian Renaissance began to spread to Northern Europe.	Renaissance ideas such as the importance of the individual are a strong part of modern thought.	• utopia • William Shakespeare • Johann Gutenberg

CALIFORNIA STANDARDS

10.2.1 Compare the major ideas of philosophers and their effects on the democratic revolutions in England, the United States, France, and Latin America (e.g., John Locke, Charles-Louis Montesquieu, Jean-Jacques Rousseau, Simón Bolívar, Thomas Jefferson, James Madison).

CST 2 Students analyze how change happens at different rates at different times; understand that some aspects can change while others remain the same; and understand that change is complicated and affects not only technology and politics but also values and beliefs.

CST 4 Students relate current events to the physical and human characteristics of places and regions.

REP 4 Students construct and test hypotheses; collect, evaluate, and employ information from multiple primary and secondary sources; and apply it in oral and written presentations.

TAKING NOTES

Following Chronological Order
On a time line, note important events of the Northern Renaissance.

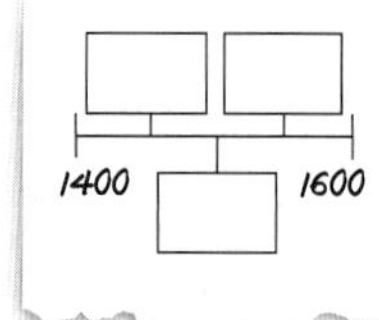

SETTING THE STAGE The work of such artists as Leonardo da Vinci, Michelangelo, and Raphael showed the Renaissance spirit. All three artists demonstrated an interest in classical culture, a curiosity about the world, and a belief in human potential. Humanist writers expanded ideas about individuality. These ideas impressed scholars, students, and merchants who visited Italy. By the late 1400s, Renaissance ideas had spread to Northern Europe—especially England, France, Germany, and Flanders (now part of France and the Netherlands).

The Northern Renaissance Begins

By 1450 the population of northern Europe, which had declined due to bubonic plague, was beginning to grow again. When the destructive Hundred Years' War between France and England ended in 1453, many cities grew rapidly. Urban merchants became wealthy enough to sponsor artists. This happened first in Flanders, which was rich from long-distance trade and the cloth industry. Then, as wealth increased in other parts of Northern Europe, patronage of artists increased as well.

As Section 1 explained, Italy was divided into city-states. In contrast, England and France were unified under strong monarchs. These rulers often sponsored the arts by purchasing paintings and by supporting artists and writers. For example, Francis I of France invited Leonardo da Vinci to retire in France, and hired Italian artists and architects to rebuild and decorate his castle at Fontainebleau (FAHN•tihn•BLOH). The castle became a showcase for Renaissance art.

As Renaissance ideas spread out of Italy, they mingled with northern traditions. As a result, the northern Renaissance developed its own character. For example, the artists were especially interested in realism. The Renaissance ideal of human dignity inspired some northern humanists to develop plans for social reform based on Judeo-Christian values.

Artistic Ideas Spread

In 1494, a French king claimed the throne of Naples in southern Italy and launched an invasion through northern Italy. As the war dragged on, many Italian artists and writers left for a safer life in Northern Europe. They brought with them the styles and techniques of the Italian Renaissance. In addition, Northern European artists who studied in Italy carried Renaissance ideas back to their homelands.

SECTION 2 PROGRAM RESOURCES

ALL STUDENTS

In-Depth Resources: Unit 1
- Guided Reading, p. 19
- Geography Application, p. 24

Formal Assessment
- Section Quiz, p. 22

Integrated Assessment Book

ENGLISH LEARNERS

In-Depth Resources in Spanish
- Guided Reading, p. 19
- Geography Application, p. 23

Reading Study Guide (Spanish), p. 17
Reading Study Guide Audio CD (Spanish)

STRUGGLING READERS

In-Depth Resources: Unit 1
- Guided Reading, p. 19
- Building Vocabulary, p. 22
- Geography Application, p. 24

Reading Study Guide, p. 17
Reading Study Guide Audio CD

INTEGRATED TECHNOLOGY

eEdition CD-ROM
Power Presentations CD-ROM
World Art and Cultures Transparencies
- AT38 Van Eyck's *Wedding Portrait*

classzone.com

German Painters Perhaps the most famous person to do this was the German artist Albrecht Dürer (DYUR•uhr). He traveled to Italy to study in 1494. After returning to Germany, Dürer produced woodcuts and engravings. Many of his prints portray religious subjects. Others portray classical myths or realistic landscapes. The popularity of Dürer's work helped to spread Renaissance styles.

Dürer's emphasis upon realism influenced the work of another German artist, Hans Holbein (HOHL•byn) the Younger. Holbein specialized in painting portraits that are almost photographic in detail. He emigrated to England where he painted portraits of King Henry VIII and other members of the English royal family.

Flemish Painters The support of wealthy merchant families in Flanders helped to make Flanders the artistic center of northern Europe. The first great Flemish Renaissance painter was Jan van Eyck (yahn van YK). Van Eyck used recently developed oil-based paints to develop techniques that painters still use. By applying layer upon layer of paint, van Eyck was able to create a variety of subtle colors in clothing and jewels. Oil painting became popular and spread to Italy.

A. Answer rich colors, vivid details, balanced use of space

In addition to new techniques, van Eyck's paintings display unusually realistic details and reveal the personality of their subjects. His work influenced later artists in Northern Europe.

MAIN IDEA

Summarizing

A What techniques does Bruegel use to give life to his paintings?

Flemish painting reached its peak after 1550 with the work of Pieter Bruegel (BROY•guhl) the Elder. Bruegel was also interested in realistic details and individual people. He was very skillful in portraying large numbers of people. He captured scenes from everyday peasant life such as weddings, dances, and harvests. Bruegel's rich colors, vivid details, and balanced use of space give a sense of life and feeling. A

Artistic Ideas Spread

10.2.1

Critical Thinking

- What factors might have influenced the trend toward a more realistic style of art? *(Artists could travel and thereby learn better techniques; oil paints made more realistic, subtle paintings possible.)*
- What can be learned about people's daily lives from examining the painting *Peasant Wedding? (Possible Answers: where ordinary people lived, what they ate, how they dressed, how they celebrated)*

World Art and Cultures Transparencies

- AT38 Van Eyck's *Wedding Portrait*

> Analyzing Art

Peasant Life

The Flemish painter Pieter Bruegel's paintings provide information about peasant life in the 1500s. *Peasant Wedding* (1568) portrays a wedding feast.

- **The Bride** The bride sits under the paper crown hanging on the green cloth.
- **The Servers** Men who may be her brothers are passing out plates.
- **The Guests** Several children have come to the party.
- **The Musicians** They are carrying bagpipes. One glances hungrily at the food.

SKILLBUILDER:
Interpreting Visual Sources
Forming Generalizations
In what ways does this painting present a snapshot of peasant life?

47

Analyzing Art

Peasant Life

A comparison between this painting and Raphael's *Marriage of the Virgin* (shown in section 1) reveals differences between the northern and the southern versions of the Renaissance. While Raphael's painting is formal, solemn, and filled with idealized figures, Bruegel's *Wedding* is relaxed, humorous, and focused on ordinary people. Both painters, however, have used perspective and fully modeled human forms.

SKILLBUILDER Answer
Forming Generalizations People are shown in conversation or in mid-movement; the setting and objects are carefully observed and realistic.

DIFFERENTIATING INSTRUCTION: GIFTED AND TALENTED STUDENTS

The Poetry of William Carlos Williams

Class Time 45 minutes

Task Comparing Renaissance paintings and poetry

Purpose To deepen understanding of the relationship between painting and literature

Instructions The American poet William Carlos Williams (1883–1963) found the paintings of Bruegel (also spelled Brueghel) a source of inspiration for his own work. Williams won the 1963 Pulitzer Prize in poetry for *Pictures from Brueghel, and other Poems.* In his book, Williams wrote a series of poems—"word pictures"—that captured the images and mood of several of Bruegel's paintings.

Bring a copy of Williams's book to class. Then ask students to find two or three of the following paintings on the Internet, in art history books, or in other reference materials: *The Wedding Dance in the Open Air, Kermess, Haymaking, The Harvesters, The Parable of the Blind, The Fall of Icarus, Children's Games.*

Have students analyze the paintings and read aloud the corresponding poems by Williams. Challenge students to write their own poems based on Bruegel's paintings.

Northern Writers Try to Reform Society
10.2.1

Critical Thinking

- What similarities were there in the works of Desiderius Erasmus and Thomas More? *(Both wanted to improve society; both believed that greed caused problems.)*
- What qualities made Christine de Pizan unusual for her time and place? *(few highly educated, outspoken women authors in Europe during the Renaissance)*

More About . . .

Utopia

The Republic by Plato (427–347 B.C.) provided Thomas More with many of his ideas for his own "utopia." In Plato's ideal society, the person with the greatest insight and intellect from the ruling class would be chosen philosopher-king. The goal of More's *Utopia* was social and political equality for all.

Tip for Gifted and Talented Students

Encourage students to compare the Christian humanists' view of society with that of Niccolò Machiavelli. Ask, Is it more effective to focus on how society could or should be or to concentrate on how life really is? *(Answers will vary, but students should support their opinions with examples from the text or other sources.)*

Northern Writers Try to Reform Society

Italian humanists were very interested in reviving classical languages and classical texts. When the Italian humanist ideas reached the north, people used them to examine the traditional teachings of the Church. The northern humanists were critical of the failure of the Christian Church to inspire people to live a Christian life. This criticism produced a new movement known as Christian humanism. The focus of Christian humanism was the reform of society. Of particular importance to humanists was education. The humanists promoted the education of women and founded schools attended by both boys and girls.

Christian Humanists The best known of the Christian humanists were Desiderius Erasmus (DEHZ•ih•DEER•ee•uhs ih•RAZ•muhs) of Holland and Thomas More of England. The two were close friends.

In 1509, Erasmus wrote his most famous work, *The Praise of Folly.* This book poked fun at greedy merchants, heartsick lovers, quarrelsome scholars, and pompous priests. Erasmus believed in a Christianity of the heart, not one of ceremonies or rules. He thought that in order to improve society, all people should study the Bible.

Thomas More tried to show a better model of society. In 1516, he wrote the book *Utopia.* In Greek, **utopia** means "no place." In English it has come to mean an ideal place as depicted in More's book. The book is about an imaginary land where greed, corruption, and war have been weeded out. In Utopia, because there was little greed, Utopians had little use for money:

▼ Christian humanist Thomas More

PRIMARY SOURCE

Gold and silver, of which money is made, are so treated . . . that no one values them more highly than their true nature deserves. Who does not see that they are far inferior to iron in usefulness since without iron mortals cannot live any more than without fire and water?

THOMAS MORE, *Utopia*

More wrote in Latin. As his work became popular, More's works were translated into a variety of languages including French, German, English, Spanish, and Italian.

Women's Reforms During this period the vast majority of Europeans were unable to read or write. Those families who could afford formal schooling usually sent only their sons. One woman spoke out against this practice. Christine de Pizan was highly educated for the time and was one of the first women to earn a living as a writer. Writing in French, she produced many books, including short stories, biographies, novels, and manuals on military techniques. She frequently wrote about the objections men had to educating women. In one book, *The Book of The City of Ladies,* she wrote:

▼ Christine de Pizan is best known for her works defending women.

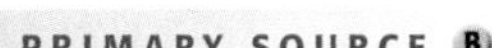

PRIMARY SOURCE B

I am amazed by the opinion of some men who claim that they do not want their daughters, wives, or kinswomen to be educated because their mores [morals] would be ruined as a result. . . . Here you can clearly see that not all opinions of men are based on reason and that these men are wrong.

CHRISTINE DE PIZAN, *The Book of The City of Ladies*

MAIN IDEA

Analyzing Primary Sources

B What does de Pizan argue for in this passage?

B. Answer education for women

Christine de Pizan was one of the first European writers to question different treatment of boys and girls. However, her goal of formal education for children of both sexes would not be achieved for several centuries.

DIFFERENTIATING INSTRUCTION: STRUGGLING READERS

Planning a Utopian Community

Class Time 45 minutes

Task Describing and discussing a utopian community

Purpose To understand the problems involved in creating an ideal community

Instructions To be sure that students understand the meaning of the word *Utopia,* write the word on the chalkboard and ask students to brainstorm other ways to describe the same idea. *(Utopia = perfect place, ideal society, city with no problems)* Using the spider map provided in the Critical Thinking Transparencies (CT79), brainstorm different features of a perfect community. The following questions can help you guide the discussion:

- What is special about the society More imagined? *(peaceful, no cheating or stealing, people don't want more than they need)*
- What ideas of More's should be added to the class's utopian community? *(Possible Answers: no war, no greed, no corruption)*
- What new ideas should be added? *(Possible Answers: equality for all races, equality for men and women, free schooling for all)*
- What makes a utopian community difficult or impossible to create? *(People are selfish and imperfect.)*

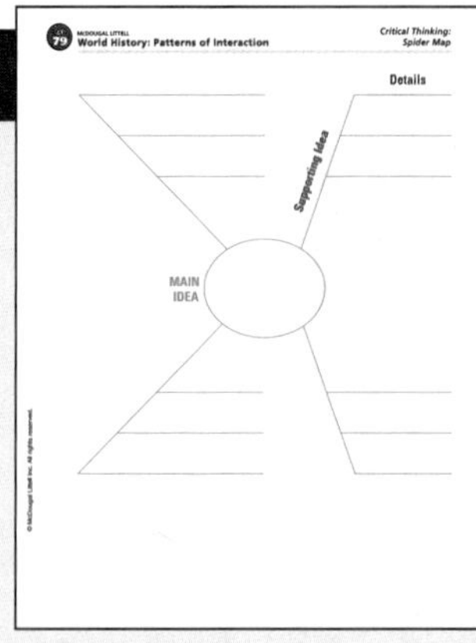

Critical Thinking Transparencies

The Elizabethan Age

The Renaissance spread to England in the mid-1500s. The period was known as the Elizabethan Age, after Queen Elizabeth I. Elizabeth reigned from 1558 to 1603. She was well educated and spoke French, Italian, Latin, and Greek. She also wrote poetry and music. As queen she did much to support the development of English art and literature.

William Shakespeare The most famous writer of the Elizabethan Age was **William Shakespeare**. Many people regard him as the greatest playwright of all time. Shakespeare was born in 1564 in Stratford-upon-Avon, a small town about 90 miles northwest of London. By 1592 he was living in London and writing poems and plays, and soon he would be performing at the Globe Theater.

Like many Renaissance writers, Shakespeare revered the classics and drew on them for inspiration and plots. His works display a masterful command of the English language and a deep understanding of human beings. He revealed the souls of men and women through scenes of dramatic conflict. Many of these plays examine human flaws. However, Shakespeare also had one of his characters deliver a speech that expresses the Renaissance's high view of human nature:

C. Answer They drew from classic works and displayed a deep understanding of human beings.

MAIN IDEA

Summarizing

C What are two ways in which Shakespeare's work showed Renaissance influences?

PRIMARY SOURCE

What a piece of work is a man, how noble in reason, how infinite in faculties, in form and moving, how express and admirable; in action how like an angel, in apprehension [understanding] how like a god: the beauty of the world, the paragon of animals.

WILLIAM SHAKESPEARE, *Hamlet (Act 2, Scene 2)*

Shakespeare's most famous plays include the tragedies *Macbeth, Hamlet, Othello, Romeo and Juliet,* and *King Lear,* and the comedies *A Midsummer Night's Dream* and *The Taming of the Shrew.* C

Connect *to* Today

Shakespeare's Popularity

Even though he has been dead for about 400 years, Shakespeare is one of the favorite writers of filmmakers. His works are produced both in period costumes and in modern attire. The themes or dialogue have been adapted for many films, including some in foreign languages. The posters at the right illustrate *Othello* (done in period costume); *Romeo and Juliet* in a modern setting; a Japanese film, *Ran,* an adaptation of *King Lear;.* and *10 Things I Hate About You,* an adaptation of *The Taming of the Shrew.*

The Elizabethan Age

10.2.1

Critical Thinking

- How did Elizabeth I contribute to the Renaissance? *(She was well educated and supported writers and artists.)*
- How did the Elizabethan Age reflect the values of the Italian Renaissance? *(focus on art and literature, positive view of humans and human nature)*

Connect *to* Today

Shakespeare's Popularity

Today, almost 400 years after his death, the language of Shakespeare is all around us. Whether we know it or not, we hear and use quotations from Shakespeare every day of our lives. Here are some of the phrases from Shakespeare's plays that have become part of modern English: "at one fell swoop," "foul play," "good riddance," "high time," "lie low," "mum's the word," "vanish into thin air," "neither here nor there," and "the game is up."

DIFFERENTIATING INSTRUCTION: ENGLISH LEARNERS

Question Words Used as Intensifiers

Class Time 30 minutes

Task Examining and rephrasing sentences in the primary source

Purpose To improve student understanding of the primary source

Instructions Students acquiring English may have trouble understanding the use of the words *what* and *how* in the Shakespeare quotation. Explain that the words what and how are usually found in questions. However, sometimes *what* and *how* are used in exclamations to emphasize something. For example, "What a piece of work is a man. . ." could be rewritten as "Man is an extraordinary piece of work!" without changing the meaning of the sentence.

Divide students into groups of three or four. Assign each group part of the primary-source quotation. Direct them to rewrite the excerpt so that *what* or *how* does not begin the phrase. Then have them explain its meaning in their own words. When groups are finished, combine their work into a chart:

Shakespeare	Restatement	Explanation
"how noble in reason"	Man is noble in reason.	Human beings are intelligent.
"in action how like an angel"	Man is like an angel in action.	Humans move beautifully and perfectly.

Printing Spreads Renaissance Ideas
10.2.1

Critical Thinking
- Why do you think the Bible was the first book printed with movable type? *(Many Europeans were religious.)*
- How would you compare and contrast the impact of the printing press with the impact of the Internet? *(information easier to access, changes affect society, more ways to access information today, Internet spreads information faster)*

Global Impact

The Printing Press
The history of book making is outlined below:
- 2700 B.C. Egyptians write books on papyrus scrolls.
- 1000 B.C. Chinese make books by writing on strips of bamboo.
- A.D. 300 Romans write on sheets of parchment (treated animal skin).
- A.D. 800 Irish monks hand-write and hand-illustrate *The Book of Kells.*
- About 1455 Gutenberg prints the first complete book on a printing press.

SKILLBUILDER Answers
1. **Drawing Conclusions** About 100
2. **Making Inferences** Europe and Asia

Printing Spreads Renaissance Ideas
The Chinese invented block printing, in which a printer carved words or letters on a wooden block, inked the block, and then used it to print on paper. Around 1045, Bi Sheng invented movable type, or a separate piece of type for each character in the language. The Chinese writing system contains thousands of different characters, so most Chinese printers found movable type impractical. However, the method would prove practical for Europeans because their languages have a very small number of letters in their alphabets.

Gutenberg Improves the Printing Process During the 13th century, block-printed items reached Europe from China. European printers began to use block printing to create whole pages to bind into books. However, this process was too slow to satisfy the Renaissance demand for knowledge, information, and books.

Around 1440 **Johann Gutenberg**, a craftsman from Mainz, Germany, developed a printing press that incorporated a number of technologies in a new way. The process made it possible to produce books quickly and cheaply. Using this improved process, Gutenberg printed a complete Bible, the Gutenberg Bible, in about 1455. It was the first full-sized book printed with movable type. **D**

The printing press enabled a printer to produce hundreds of copies of a single work. For the first time, books were cheap enough that many people could buy them. At first printers produced mainly religious works. Soon they began to provide books on other subjects such as travel guides and medical manuals.

D. Possible Answer It made books readily available and cheap enough for people to afford.

MAIN IDEA
Recognizing Effects
D What were the major effects of the invention of the printing press?

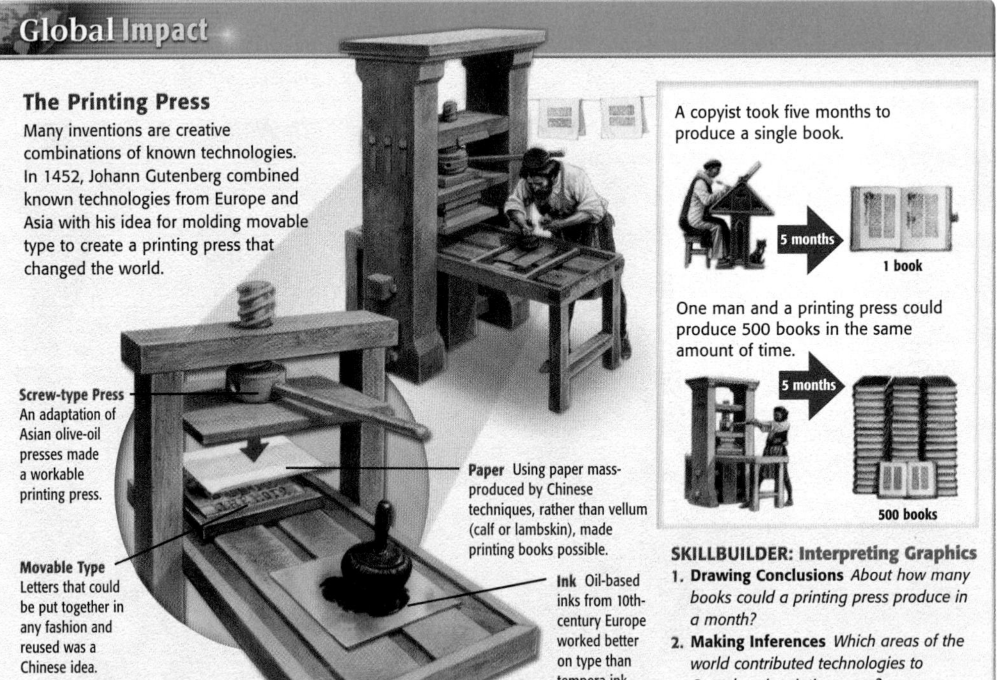

Global Impact
The Printing Press
Many inventions are creative combinations of known technologies. In 1452, Johann Gutenberg combined known technologies from Europe and Asia with his idea for molding movable type to create a printing press that changed the world.
A copyist took five months to produce a single book.
5 months
1 book
One man and a printing press could produce 500 books in the same amount of time.
5 months
500 books
Screw-type Press An adaptation of Asian olive-oil presses made a workable printing press.
Paper Using paper mass-produced by Chinese techniques, rather than vellum (calf or lambskin), made printing books possible.
Movable Type Letters that could be put together in any fashion and reused was a Chinese idea.
Ink Oil-based inks from 10th-century Europe worked better on type than tempera ink.
SKILLBUILDER: Interpreting Graphics
1. Drawing Conclusions About how many books could a printing press produce in a month?
2. Making Inferences Which areas of the world contributed technologies to Gutenberg's printing press?

CONNECTIONS TO MATHEMATICS

Comparing Book Production Methods
Class Time 45 minutes

Task Comparing methods of book production

Purpose To understand the revolutionary impact of the printing press

Have student pairs copy a paragraph from a book by hand and record how long it takes. Next, ask them to estimate the amount of time it would take to copy the entire page. Tell them to multiply this amount by the total number of book pages. Their answer represents the estimated number of hours required to create a handwritten version of the book. Challenge student pairs to estimate how long it would take to reproduce a set of these books for the entire class.

Point out the part of the Global Impact feature that explains how a person with a printing press could do 500 times as much work as a copyist in the same amount of time. Ask students, What would be the effects of such an invention? *(Information could spread more widely and more quickly.)*

To relate the spread of information to geography, have students complete the Geography Application for this chapter.

In-Depth Resources: Unit 1

The Legacy of the Renaissance

The European Renaissance was a period of great artistic and social change. It marked a break with the medieval-period ideals focused around the Church. The Renaissance belief in the dignity of the individual played a key role in the gradual rise of democratic ideas. Furthermore, the impact of the movable-type printing press was tremendous. Some historians have suggested that its effects were even more dramatic than the arrival of personal computers in the 20th century. Below is a summary of the changes that resulted from the Renaissance.

Changes in the Arts

- Art drew on techniques and styles of classical Greece and Rome.
- Paintings and sculptures portrayed individuals and nature in more realistic and lifelike ways.
- Artists created works that were secular as well as those that were religious.
- Writers began to use vernacular languages to express their ideas.
- The arts praised individual achievement.

Changes in Society

- Printing changed society by making more information available and inexpensive enough for society at large.
- A greater availability of books prompted an increased desire for learning and a rise in literacy throughout Europe.
- Published accounts of new discoveries, maps, and charts led to further discoveries in a variety of fields.
- Published legal proceedings made the laws clear so that people were more likely to understand their rights.
- Christian humanists' attempts to reform society changed views about how life should be lived.
- People began to question political structures and religious practices.

Renaissance ideas continued to influence European thought—including religious thought—as you will see in Section 3.

SECTION 2 ASSESSMENT

TERMS & NAMES 1. For each term or name, write a sentence explaining its significance.
- utopia
- William Shakespeare
- Johann Gutenberg

USING YOUR NOTES

2. Which of the events listed do you think was most important? Explain. (10.2.1)

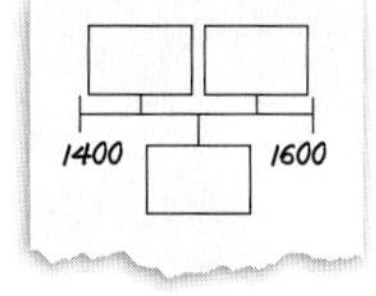

MAIN IDEAS

3. How did Albrecht Dürer's work reflect the influence of the Italian Renaissance? (10.2.1)
4. What was one way the Renaissance changed society? (10.2.1)
5. Why was the invention of the printing press so important? (10.2.1)

CRITICAL THINKING & WRITING

6. **COMPARING** How were the works of German painters different from those of the Flemish painters? Give examples. (10.2.1)
7. **ANALYZING MOTIVES** What reasons did humanists give for wanting to reform society? Explain. (10.2.1)
8. **RECOGNIZING EFFECTS** How did the availability of cheap books spread learning? (10.2.1)
9. **WRITING ACTIVITY** CULTURAL INTERACTION Reread the primary source quotation from Christine de Pizan on page 48. Write a one paragraph **opinion piece** about the ideas expressed there. (Writing 2.4.c)

INTEGRATED TECHNOLOGY **INTERNET ACTIVITY**

Use the Internet to find information on the number of books published in print and those published electronically last year. Create a **pie graph** showing the results of your research. (Writing 2.3.d)

INTERNET KEYWORD
book publishing statistics

The Legacy of the Renaissance
10.2.1

Critical Thinking

- In what ways did Renaissance art connect to the past? *(copied Greek and Roman styles, created religious works)* In what ways did it break with the past? *(increase in secular art, more realistic style, use of vernacular, emphasis on the individual)*
- How did printing and publishing affect social reforms? *(made social reforms more widespread because information, including Christian humanist works, was distributed more widely and freely)*

3 ASSESS

SECTION 2 ASSESSMENT

Have students work individually to answer the questions. Then have them share with the class their answers for item 2.

Formal Assessment
- Section Quiz, p. 22

4 RETEACH

Use the Reading Study Guide for Section 2 to review the main ideas of the section.

Reading Study Guide, pp. 17–18

In-Depth Resources: Unit 1
- Reteaching Activity, p. 37

ANSWERS

1. utopia, p. 48 • Willliam Shakespeare, p. 49 • Johann Gutenberg, p. 50
2. **Sample Answer:** about 1440–Gutenberg invents printing press (most important); 1450s–Northern Renaissance begins; 1509–Erasmus writes *The Praise of Folly;* 1516–More writes *Utopia;* mid-1500s–Elizabethan Age begins; late 1500s–Shakespeare writes plays and poems.
3. He portrayed classical myths, religious subjects, and realistic landscapes.
4. **Possible Answer:** More people were exposed to ideas because they could read the information in their own language.
5. It made more information available not only to scholars but also to ordinary people.
6. German painters such as Dürer used classic myths and religious subjects. Flemish painters such as Bruegel focused on ordinary subjects and used a great amount of detail.
7. They wanted people to live a Christian life. To do so they had to give up greed, corruption, and war and provide education for women and children.
8. More people could afford books and the ideas could be shared with those who could not read. More information led to more discoveries. Literacy increased.
9. **Rubric** Paragraphs should
   - clearly state an opinion about de Pizan.
   - support the opinion with facts and details.

INTEGRATED TECHNOLOGY

Rubric Pie charts should
- have a title.
- clearly label data for print and electronic books.
- cite at least two sources.

Social History

OBJECTIVES

- Describe what city life in Renaissance Europe was like.
- Understand the cost of living in Renaissance London.

FOCUS & MOTIVATE

Ask students to discuss the similarities and differences between city life in Renaissance London and cities in the United States today. *(Possible Answers: Crime, sanitation, food, transportation, and entertainment are still important. Garbage is picked up. Theatergoers do not throw things at the stage.)*

INSTRUCT

Critical Thinking

- How do the problems in London during the Renaissance compare to problems in cities today? *(Crime, pollution, and crowding still exist in many places.)*
- Consider the cost of living. What was the price of a chicken in today's dollars? *(about $1.66)* a place to stay for a week? *(about $7–$14)* the wages of a skilled worker for a week? *($100)*

Social History

City Life in Renaissance Europe

CALIFORNIA STANDARDS
CST 1

Throughout the 1500s, the vast majority of Europeans—more than 75 percent—lived in rural areas. However, the capital and port cities of most European countries experienced remarkable growth during this time. The population of London, for example, stood at about 200,000 in 1600, making it perhaps the largest city in Europe. In London, and in other large European cities, a distinctively urban way of life developed in the Renaissance era.

INTEGRATED TECHNOLOGY
RESEARCH LINKS For more on life in Renaissance Europe, go to **classzone.com**

▲ Entertainment
Performances at playhouses like the Globe often were wild affairs. If audiences did not like the play, they booed loudly, pelted the stage with garbage, and sometimes attacked the actors.

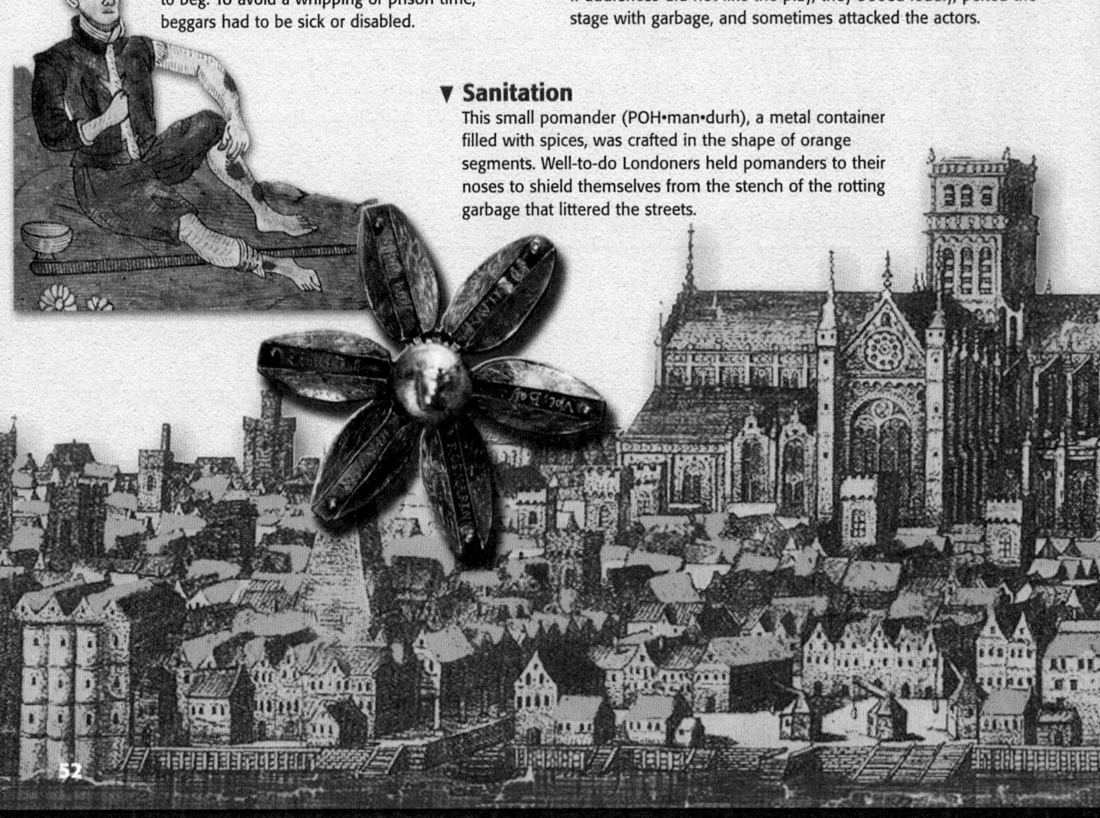

▼ Joblessness
Many newcomers to London struggled to find jobs and shelter. Some turned to crime to make a living. Others became beggars. However, it was illegal for able-bodied people to beg. To avoid a whipping or prison time, beggars had to be sick or disabled.

▼ Sanitation
This small pomander (POH•man•durh), a metal container filled with spices, was crafted in the shape of orange segments. Well-to-do Londoners held pomanders to their noses to shield themselves from the stench of the rotting garbage that littered the streets.

52

RECOMMENDED RESOURCES

Books

What Life Was Like in the Realm of Elizabeth: England, A.D. 1533–1603. Alexandria, VA: Time-Life Books, 1998.

Elizabeth S. Cohen and Thomas V. Cohen. ***Daily Life in Renaissance Italy.*** Westport: Greenwood Press, 2001.

Patricia Fumerton and Simon Hunt, eds. ***Renaissance Culture and the Everyday.*** Philadelphia: University of Pennsylvania Press, 1999.

Videos

The Elizabethan Age. Video. Clearvue. 800-253-2788. The political and social life of the Elizabethan age.

▼ Food

A typical meal for wealthy Londoners might include fish, several kinds of meat, bread, and a variety of vegetables, served on silver or pewter tableware. The diet of the poor was simpler. They rarely ate fish, meat, or cheese. Usually, their meals consisted of a pottage—a kind of soup—of vegetables. And the poor ate their meals from a trencher, a hollowed-out slab of stale bread or wood.

▼ Transportation

Many of London's streets were so narrow that walking was the only practical means of transportation. Often, however, the quickest way to get from here to there in the city was to take the river. Boat traffic was especially heavy when the playhouses were open. On those days, as many as 4,000 people crossed the Thames from the city to Southwark, where most of the theaters were located.

> DATA FILE

COST OF LIVING IN RENAISSANCE LONDON

These tables show what typical Londoners earned and spent in the late 1500s. The basic denominations in English currency at the time were the pound (£), the shilling, and the penny (12 pence equaled 1 shilling, and 20 shillings equaled 1 pound). The pound of the late 1500s is roughly equivalent to $400 in today's U.S. currency.

Typical Earnings

Merchant	£100 per year
Skilled Worker	£13 per year (about 5 shillings/week)
Unskilled Worker	£5 per year (about 4 pence/day)
Servant	£1 to £2 per year (plus food and lodging)

Typical Prices

Lodging	4 to 8 pence a week
Beef	3 pence per lb
Chickens	1 penny each
Eggs	2 pence per dozen
Apples	1 penny per dozen
Onions	1/2 penny a sack
Various Spices	10 to 11 shillings per lb

Connect *to* Today

1. **Making Inferences** Study the images and captions as well as the information in the Data File. What inferences about the standard of living of London's wealthy citizens can you make from this information? How did it compare to the standard of living of London's common people?

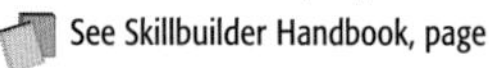

See Skillbuilder Handbook, page R9.

2. **Comparing** How does diet in the United States today compare to the diet of Renaissance Europeans? Cite specific examples in your answer.

53

More About . . .

Entertainment

A full house at the Globe probably meant around 3,000 paying customers, all expecting to interact with the performers and the play. The crowd might hurl oranges, nuts, apples, and gingerbread at the actors and sometimes got involved in scenes from the play. The noise from the audience was tremendous. Few props were used. Shakespeare asked audiences to "Think when we talk of horses that you see them, Printing their proud hoofs I' the receiving earth."

More About . . .

The Cost of Living

If a pound was worth $400 in today's currency, then a shilling was worth $20 and a penny was worth about $1.66. This means, for example, that a skilled worker earned $5,200 per year. A merchant would earn about $40,000. The cost of a theater performance was 1 shilling ($20) for the lords' room, 6 pence ($10) for the gentlemen's rooms, 2 pence ($3.30) for the galleries, and 1 penny ($1.66) for the pit. Owning a theater could be profitable because Londoners were passionate theatergoers. One in every 10 people in London went to the theater at least once a week.

CONNECT TO TODAY: ANSWERS

1. Making Inferences

Merchants and other wealthy citizens had a very high standard of living because their yearly income put even luxuries, such as rare spices, easily within their reach. In comparison, it was a struggle for the common people to maintain a decent standard of living because even basic necessities like food took a huge share of their income.

2. Comparing

Rubric Comparisons should
- describe the diet of Renaissance Europeans.
- describe the diet of modern Americans.
- point out what the two diets have in common.

LESSON PLAN

OBJECTIVES

- Analyze historical forces and religious issues that sparked the Reformation.
- Trace Martin Luther's role in the movement to reform the Catholic Church.
- Analyze the impact of Luther's religious revolt.
- Explain the spread of the Protestant faith to England.

1 FOCUS & MOTIVATE

Ask students how people protest today. *(Possible Answers: picketing, marching, writing to representatives in government)*

2 INSTRUCT

Causes of the Reformation
10.1.1

Critical Thinking

- Why did German rulers want to challenge the political power of the Church? *(resented distant control; new ideas were weakening the Church)*

CALIFORNIA RESOURCES
California Reading Toolkit, p. L11
California Modified Lesson Plans for English Learners, p. 17
California Daily Standards Practice Transparencies, TT3
California Standards Enrichment Workbook, pp. 17–18
California Standards Planner and Lesson Plans, p. L13
California Online Test Practice
California Test Generator CD-ROM
California Easy Planner CD-ROM
California eEdition CD-ROM

Bottecelli *Allegory of Spring*

3

Italian hill town

Luther Leads the Reformation

MAIN IDEA

REVOLUTION Martin Luther's protest over abuses in the Catholic Church led to the founding of Protestant churches.

WHY IT MATTERS NOW

Nearly one-fifth of the Christians in today's world are Protestants.

TERMS & NAMES

- indulgence
- Reformation
- Lutheran
- Protestant
- Peace of Augsburg
- annul
- Anglican

CALIFORNIA STANDARDS

10.1.1 Analyze the similarities and differences in Judeo-Christian and Greco-Roman views of law, reason and faith, and duties of the individual.

HI 1 Students show the connections, causal and otherwise, between particular historical events and larger social, economic, and political trends and developments.

HI 3 Students interpret past events and issues within the context in which an event unfolded rather than solely in terms of present-day norms and values.

HI 4 Students understand the meaning, implication, and impact of historical events and recognize that events could have taken other directions.

SETTING THE STAGE By the tenth century, the Roman Catholic Church had come to dominate religious life in Northern and Western Europe. However, the Church had not won universal approval. Over the centuries, many people criticized its practices. They felt that Church leaders were too interested in worldly pursuits, such as gaining wealth and political power. Even though the Church made some reforms during the Middle Ages, people continued to criticize it. Prompted by the actions of one man, that criticism would lead to rebellion.

Causes of the Reformation

By 1500, additional forces weakened the Church. The Renaissance emphasis on the secular and the individual challenged Church authority. The printing press spread these secular ideas. In addition, some rulers began to challenge the Church's political power. In Germany, which was divided into many competing states, it was difficult for the pope or the emperor to impose central authority. Finally, northern merchants resented paying church taxes to Rome. Spurred by these social, political, and economic forces, a new movement for religious reform began in Germany. It then swept much of Europe.

Criticisms of the Catholic Church Critics of the Church claimed that its leaders were corrupt. The popes who ruled during the Renaissance patronized the arts, spent extravagantly on personal pleasure, and fought wars. Pope Alexander VI,

TAKING NOTES
Recognizing Effects Use a chart to identify the effects of Martin Luther's protests.

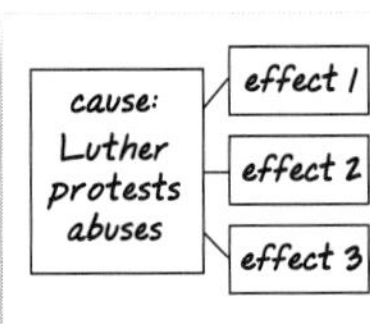

Causes of the Reformation

Social	Political	Economic	Religious
• The Renaissance values of humanism and secularism led people to question the Church. • The printing press helped to spread ideas critical of the Church.	• Powerful monarchs challenged the Church as the supreme power in Europe. • Many leaders viewed the pope as a foreign ruler and challenged his authority.	• European princes and kings were jealous of the Church's wealth. • Merchants and others resented having to pay taxes to the Church.	• Some Church leaders had become worldly and corrupt. • Many people found Church practices such as the sale of indulgences unacceptable.

SECTION 3 PROGRAM RESOURCES

ALL STUDENTS
In-Depth Resources: Unit 1
- Guided Reading, p. 20
- Skillbuilder Practice: Synthesizing, p. 23
- History Makers: Elizabeth I, p. 34

Formal Assessment
- Section Quiz, p. 23

ENGLISH LEARNERS
In-Depth Resources in Spanish
- Guided Reading, p. 20
- Skillbuilder Practice, p. 22

Reading Study Guide (Spanish), p. 19
Reading Study Guide Audio CD (Spanish)

STRUGGLING READERS
In-Depth Resources: Unit 1
- Guided Reading, p. 20
- Building Vocabulary, p. 22
- Skillbuilder Practice: Synthesizing, p. 23
- Reteaching Activity, p. 38

Reading Study Guide, p. 19
Reading Study Guide Audio CD

GIFTED AND TALENTED STUDENTS
In-Depth Resources: Unit 1
- Primary Sources: Elizabeth I, p. 28; Reformation, p. 29

Electronic Library of Primary Sources
- from the Ninety-Five Theses

INTEGRATED TECHNOLOGY

eEdition Plus Online
eEdition CD-ROM
Electronic Library of Primary Sources
- from the Ninety-Five Theses

classzone.com

for example, admitted that he had fathered several children. Many popes were too busy pursuing worldly affairs to have much time for spiritual duties.

The lower clergy had problems as well. Many priests and monks were so poorly educated that they could scarcely read, let alone teach people. Others broke their priestly vows by marrying, and some drank to excess or gambled.

Early Calls for Reform Influenced by reformers, people had come to expect higher standards of conduct from priests and church leaders. In the late 1300s and early 1400s, John Wycliffe of England and Jan Hus of Bohemia had advocated Church reform. They denied that the pope had the right to worldly power. They also taught that the Bible had more authority than Church leaders did. In the 1500s, Christian humanists like Desiderius Erasmus and Thomas More added their voices to the chorus of criticism. In addition, many Europeans were reading religious works and forming their own opinions about the Church. The atmosphere in Europe was ripe for reform by the early 1500s.

Luther Challenges the Church

Martin Luther's parents wanted him to be a lawyer. Instead, he became a monk and a teacher. From 1512 until his death, he taught scripture at the University of Wittenberg in the German state of Saxony. All he wanted was to be a good Christian, not to lead a religious revolution.

The 95 Theses In 1517, Luther decided to take a public stand against the actions of a friar named Johann Tetzel. Tetzel was raising money to rebuild St. Peter's Cathedral in Rome. He did this by selling indulgences. An **indulgence** was a pardon. It released a sinner from performing the penalty that a priest imposed for sins. Indulgences were not supposed to affect God's right to judge. Unfortunately, Tetzel gave people the impression that by buying indulgences, they could buy their way into heaven.

Luther was troubled by Tetzel's tactics. In response, he wrote 95 Theses, or formal statements, attacking the "pardon-merchants." On October 31, 1517, he posted these statements on the door of the castle church in Wittenberg and invited other scholars to debate him. Someone copied Luther's words and took them to a printer. Quickly, Luther's name became known all over Germany. His actions began the **Reformation**, a movement for religious reform. It led to the founding of Christian churches that did not accept the pope's authority.

Luther's Teachings Soon Luther went beyond criticizing indulgences. He wanted full reform of the Church. His teachings rested on three main ideas:

- People could win salvation only by faith in God's gift of forgiveness. The Church taught that faith and "good works" were needed for salvation.
- All Church teachings should be clearly based on the words of the Bible. Both the pope and Church traditions were false authorities.
- All people with faith were equal. Therefore, people did not need priests to interpret the Bible for them. (A)

A. Answer belief in God's forgiveness; authority of the Bible; equality among all with faith

MAIN IDEA

Summarizing

(A) What were the main points of Luther's teachings?

History Makers

Martin Luther
1483–1546

In one way, fear led Luther to become a monk. At the age of 21, Luther was caught in a terrible thunderstorm. Convinced he would die, he cried out, "Saint Anne, help me! I will become a monk."

Even after entering the monastery, Luther felt fearful, lost, sinful, and rejected by God. He confessed his sins regularly, fasted, and did penance. However, by studying the Bible, Luther came to the conclusion that faith alone was the key to salvation. Only then did he experience peace.

INTEGRATED TECHNOLOGY

RESEARCH LINKS For more on Martin Luther, go to **classzone.com**

History Makers

Martin Luther

How did Luther's fears change him? *(motivated him to become a monk and study the Bible, which in turn caused him to question Church practices)*

Remind students that Luther's goal was to become a good Christian, not to stage a religious revolt. Have students use reference books, the Internet, and **classzone.com** to research Luther as a revolutionary. In a class discussion, have students give examples of Luther's break with tradition, his defiance of authority, and his role in launching a new era.

Electronic Library of Primary Sources
- from the Ninety-Five Theses

Luther Challenges the Church

10.1.1

Critical Thinking

- Why was Martin Luther unhappy with the sale of indulgences? *(People thought that buying an indulgence would get them into heaven.)*
- What caused Luther's ideas to spread throughout Germany? *(Someone had Luther's words printed; his ideas allowed people to think about and express their own dissatisfaction with the Church.)*

SKILLBUILDER PRACTICE: SYNTHESIZING

Learning to Form an Overall Picture

Class Time 30 minutes

Task Putting together information to support an overall understanding

Purpose To practice the skill of synthesizing

Instructions Like detective work, synthesizing involves putting together clues, facts, and ideas to form an overall picture of a historical event. To answer the question, "Why did Luther think it was all right to defy the Pope?" (a synthesis), suggest that students use the following strategy: Have them reread the bulleted list of Luther's teachings and look for information to support the synthesis. Then ask students to create a cluster diagram showing how the synthesis was formed. Have students use the Skillbuilder Practice activity for more examples and practice.

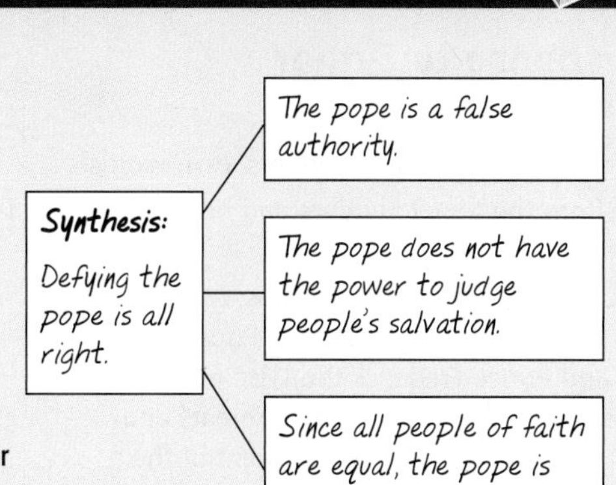
Synthesis:
Defying the pope is all right.
The pope is a false authority.
The pope does not have the power to judge people's salvation.
Since all people of faith are equal, the pope is not a supreme authority.

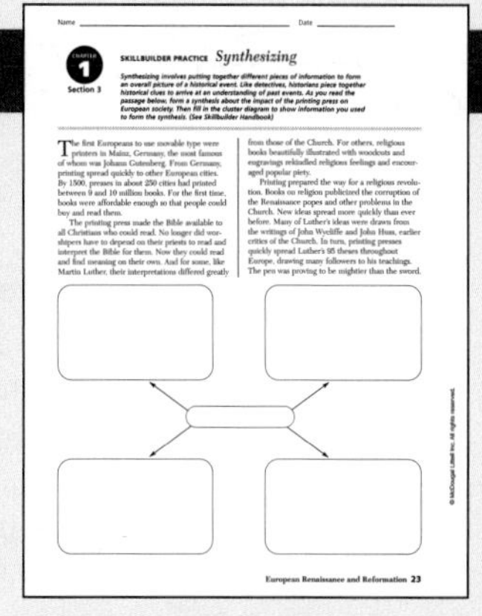

In-Depth Resources: Unit 1

The Response to Luther
10.1.1

Critical Thinking
- What in Luther's teachings inspired the peasants to revolt? *(Luther taught that people were free to make their own decisions about religion. The peasants wanted more freedom.)*
- Why do you think Charles V could not force the Protestant princes back into the Catholic Church even after defeating them in war? *(Possible Answers: Luther's ideas were too strong; the abuses in the Catholic Church caused people to lose faith.)*

Vocabulary Note: Roots and Affixes
Point out that the word *excommunication* can be broken into parts. The prefix *ex-* often means "outside" or "away from," and the suffix *-tion* usually means "state of being." The root comes from the Latin *communis,* which means "common, public, or general." Challenge students to think of other words with the same root. *(community, Communion, Communist)*

Tip for English Learners
Remind students that a peasant is a farm laborer. Most peasants farmed land that belonged to the local lord. They had to provide goods and services in exchange for working the land. The lord had a great deal of control over their lives.

The Response to Luther
Luther was astonished at how rapidly his ideas spread and attracted followers. Many people had been unhappy with the Church for political and economic reasons. They saw Luther's protests as a way to challenge Church control.

The Pope's Threat Initially, Church officials in Rome viewed Luther simply as a rebellious monk who needed to be punished by his superiors. However, as Luther's ideas became more popular, the pope realized that this monk was a serious threat. In one angry reply to Church criticism, Luther actually suggested that Christians drive the pope from the Church by force.

In 1520, Pope Leo X issued a decree threatening Luther with excommunication unless he took back his statements. Luther did not take back a word. Instead, his students at Wittenberg gathered around a bonfire and cheered as he threw the pope's decree into the flames. Leo excommunicated Luther.

Vocabulary
Excommunication is the taking away of a person's right to membership in the Church.

The Emperor's Opposition Holy Roman Emperor Charles V, a devout Catholic, also opposed Luther's teaching. Charles controlled a vast empire, including the German states. He summoned Luther to the town of Worms (vawrmz) in 1521 to stand trial. Told to recant, or take back his statements, Luther refused:

PRIMARY SOURCE
I am bound by the Scriptures I have quoted and my conscience is captive to the Word of God. I cannot and I will not retract anything, since it is neither safe nor right to go against conscience. I cannot do otherwise, here I stand, may God help me. Amen.
MARTIN LUTHER, quoted in *The Protestant Reformation* by Lewis W. Spitz

A month after Luther made that speech, Charles issued an imperial order, the Edict of Worms. It declared Luther an outlaw and a heretic. According to this edict, no one in the empire was to give Luther food or shelter. All his books were to be burned. However, Prince Frederick the Wise of Saxony disobeyed the emperor. For almost a year after the trial, he sheltered Luther in one of his castles. While there, Luther translated the New Testament into German.

Vocabulary
A *heretic* is a person who holds beliefs that differ from official Church teachings.

Luther returned to Wittenberg in 1522. There he discovered that many of his ideas were already being put into practice. Instead of continuing to seek reforms in the Catholic Church, Luther and his followers had become a separate religious group, called **Lutherans**.

The Peasants' Revolt Some people began to apply Luther's revolutionary ideas to society. In 1524, German peasants, excited by reformers' talk of Christian freedom, demanded an end to serfdom. Bands of angry peasants went about the countryside raiding monasteries, pillaging, and burning. The revolt horrified Luther. He wrote a pamphlet urging the German princes to show the peasants no mercy. The princes' armies crushed the revolt, killing as many as 100,000 people. Feeling betrayed, many peasants rejected Luther's religious leadership. **B**

MAIN IDEA
Analyzing Causes
B Why did Luther's ideas encourage the German peasants to revolt?
B. Possible Answer Luther's ideas were revolutionary and reform-minded, which the peasants applied to their own demands.

Germany at War In contrast to the bitter peasants, many northern German princes supported Lutheranism. While some princes genuinely shared Luther's beliefs, others liked Luther's ideas for selfish reasons. They saw his teachings as a good excuse to seize Church property and to assert their independence from Charles V.

In 1529, German princes who remained loyal to the pope agreed to join forces against Luther's ideas. Those princes who supported Luther signed a protest against that agreement. These protesting princes came to be known as Protestants. Eventually, the term **Protestant** was applied to Christians who belonged to non-Catholic churches.

DIFFERENTIATING INSTRUCTION: STRUGGLING READERS

Understanding the Response to Luther
Class Time 30 minutes

Task Explaining the positions of historical figures in students' own words

Purpose To summarize material from the text; to understand how different historical figures reacted to Luther's teachings

Instructions Divide students into four heterogeneous groups. Assign each group one of the following roles to research: Martin Luther, Pope Leo X, Holy Roman Emperor Charles V, and Prince Frederick the Wise of Saxony. Have each group reread the subsections titled "The Pope's Threat" and "The Emperor's Opposition" and then summarize the viewpoint of their assigned historical figure. Examples of summaries are at right.

Luther:	The pope should not be part of the Church any more.
Pope Leo X:	If you don't change your mind, I will take away your right to membership in the Church.
Charles V:	Luther, take back what you have said.
Luther:	No. I have to do what I believe is right.
Charles V:	You are an outlaw. Nobody in my lands is allowed to help you. All the books you have written will be burned.
Prince Frederick:	I will protect you, Luther.

> Analyzing Key Concepts

Protestantism

Protestantism is a branch of Christianity. It developed out of the Reformation, the 16th-century protest in Europe against beliefs and practices of the Catholic Church. Three distinct branches of Protestantism emerged at first. They were Lutheranism, based on the teachings of Martin Luther in Germany; Calvinism, based on the teachings of John Calvin in Switzerland; and Anglicanism, which was established by King Henry VIII in England. Protestantism spread throughout Europe in the 16th century, and later, the world. As differences in beliefs developed, new denominations formed.

The Division of Christianity

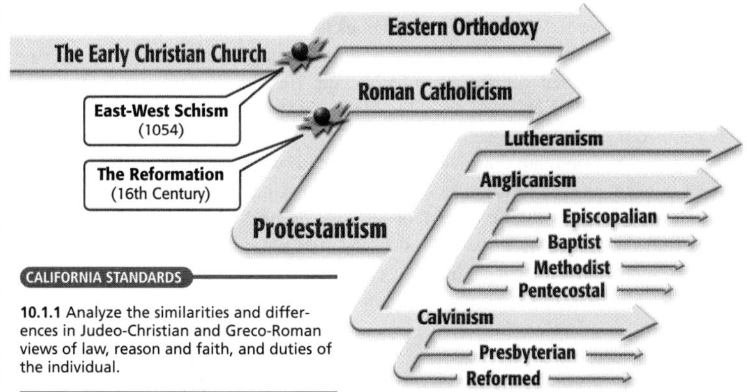

CALIFORNIA STANDARDS

10.1.1 Analyze the similarities and differences in Judeo-Christian and Greco-Roman views of law, reason and faith, and duties of the individual.

Religious Beliefs and Practices in the 16th Century

	Roman Catholicism	Lutheranism	Calvinism	Anglicanism
Leadership	Pope is head of the Church	Ministers lead congregations	Council of elders govern each church	English monarch is head of the Church
Salvation	Salvation by faith and good works	Salvation by faith alone	God has predetermined who will be saved	Salvation by faith alone
Bible	Church and Bible tradition are sources of revealed truth	Bible is sole source of revealed truth	Bible is sole source of revealed truth	Bible is sole source of revealed truth
Worship Service	Worship service based on ritual	Worship service focused on preaching and ritual	Worship service focused on preaching	Worship service based on ritual and preaching
Interpretation of Beliefs	Priests interpret Bible and Church teachings for believers	Believers interpret the Bible for themselves	Believers interpret the Bible for themselves	Believers interpret the Bible using tradition and reason

INTEGRATED TECHNOLOGY

RESEARCH LINKS For more on Protestantism, go to **classzone.com**

> DATA FILE

PROTESTANTISM TODAY

Membership:
- Nearly 400 million Protestants worldwide
- About 65 million Protestants in the United States

Branches:
- More than 465 major Protestant denominations worldwide
- Major denominational families worldwide: Anglican, Assemblies of God, Baptist, Methodist, Lutheran, and Presbyterian
- More than 250 denominations in the United States
- About 40 denominations with more than 400,000 members each in the United States

Religious Adherents in the United States:

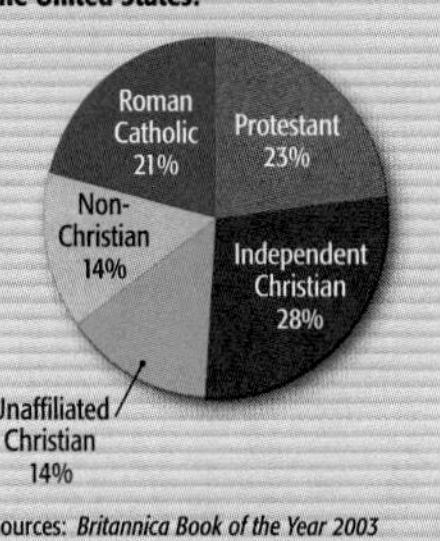

Sources: *Britannica Book of the Year 2003*

Connect *to* Today

1. **Comparing** Which of the branches on the chart at left are most different and which are most similar?
   See Skillbuilder Handbook, page R7.
2. **Developing Historical Perspective** Do research on Protestantism. Select a denomination not shown on this page and write a paragraph tracing its roots to Reformation Protestantism.

57

Analyzing Key Concepts

OBJECTIVES

- Compare and contrast religious beliefs and practices in the 16th century.
- Trace the development of Protestantism.

INSTRUCT

Introduce Protestantism to students as a key to understanding European history after the 16th century. The Reformation had an enduring impact on the religious, social, and political life of Europe. As students finish this chapter, have them list the impacts of the Reformation on the lives of the people of Europe.

More About . . .

Data on Religions

Although statistics on religious membership tend to be estimates, it is generally thought that the three largest religions are Christianity, Islam, and Hinduism. The two largest religious bodies, Catholics and Sunni Muslims, account for 33% of the world's population.

CONNECT TO TODAY: ANSWERS

1. Comparing

Of the three branches of Protestantism, the most different are Anglicanism and Calvinism. For example, Calvinists believe that God has predetermined who will be saved, and church leadership differs greatly among the branches. The most similar are Lutheranism and Anglicanism.

2. Researching

Rubric Paragraphs should
- clearly identify the denomination and explain its beliefs.
- trace the denomination's roots in the Protestant Reformation and provide facts and examples to support the explanation.

England Becomes Protestant
10.1.1

Critical Thinking

- Why did Henry VIII need either a divorce or an annulment? *(to marry a woman who could give him a son)*
- Elizabeth I came to power at a time of religious turmoil. How did she deal with the question of religion? *(She returned England to Protestantism and established a state church.)*

Still determined that his subjects should remain Catholic, Charles V went to war against the Protestant princes. Even though he defeated them in 1547, he failed to force them back into the Catholic Church. In 1555, Charles, weary of fighting, ordered all German princes, both Protestant and Catholic, to assemble in the city of Augsburg. There the princes agreed that each ruler would decide the religion of his state. This famous religious settlement was known as the **Peace of Augsburg**.

England Becomes Protestant

The Catholic Church soon faced another great challenge to its authority, this time in England. Unlike Luther, the man who broke England's ties to the Roman Catholic Church did so for political and personal, not religious, reasons.

Henry VIII Wants a Son When Henry VIII became king of England in 1509, he was a devout Catholic. Indeed, in 1521, Henry wrote a stinging attack on Luther's ideas. In recognition of Henry's support, the pope gave him the title "Defender of the Faith." Political needs, however, soon tested his religious loyalty. He needed a male heir. Henry's father had become king after a long civil war. Henry feared that a similar war would start if he died without a son as his heir. He and his wife, Catherine of Aragon, had one living child—a daughter, Mary—but no woman had ever successfully claimed the English throne.

By 1527, Henry was convinced that the 42-year-old Catherine would have no more children. He wanted to divorce her and take a younger queen. Church law did not allow divorce. However, the pope could **annul**, or set aside, Henry's marriage if proof could be found that it had never been legal in the first place. In 1527, Henry asked the pope to annul his marriage, but the pope turned him down. The pope did not want to offend Catherine's powerful nephew, the Holy Roman Emperor Charles V.

The Reformation Parliament Henry took steps to solve his marriage problem himself. In 1529, he called Parliament into session and asked it to pass a set of laws

History from Visuals

Analyzing the Time Line

Ask students to notice how many years are represented on the time line. *(51)* How many rulers of England are shown on the time line? *(4)* How many years did Mary reign as queen? *(5)*

Henry VIII Causes Religious Turmoil

Henry's many marriages led to conflict with the Catholic Church and the founding of the Church of England.

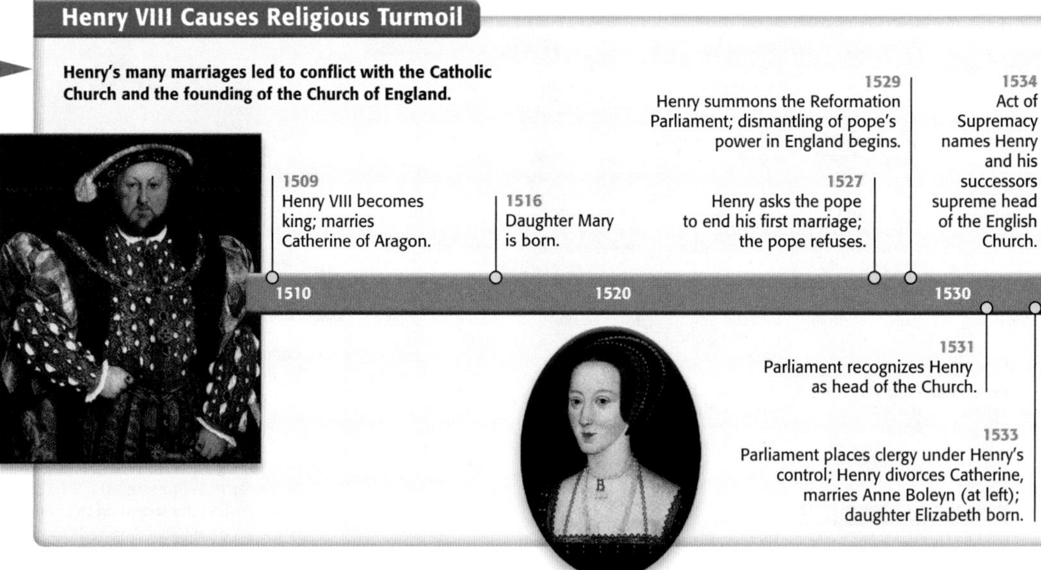

1509 Henry VIII becomes king; marries Catherine of Aragon.
1516 Daughter Mary is born.
1527 Henry asks the pope to end his first marriage; the pope refuses.
1529 Henry summons the Reformation Parliament; dismantling of pope's power in England begins.
1534 Act of Supremacy names Henry and his successors supreme head of the English Church.
1510
1520
1530
1531 Parliament recognizes Henry as head of the Church.
1533 Parliament places clergy under Henry's control; Henry divorces Catherine, marries Anne Boleyn (at left); daughter Elizabeth born.
B

DIFFERENTIATING INSTRUCTION: ENGLISH LEARNERS

Tracing Religious Changes in England

Class Time 30 minutes

Task Creating a chart of English monarchs and their religious beliefs

Purpose To clarify the connection between Church and State

Instructions Have pairs of students read the "England Becomes Protestant" section and analyze the time line. Encourage students to look up difficult words in a glossary or dictionary. You may want to list challenging terms on the board. *(heir—someone who will be the next king or queen; oath—a very serious promise to take a certain action)* When students are finished, create a chart on the chalkboard that shows the rulers of England and their religions. An example is shown at right.

Ask students, What was the effect of all these changes? *(Possible Answers: Some people executed; religious confusion; government was becoming unstable.)*

King or Queen	Religion	Reasons for Religious Beliefs
Henry VIII	Catholic, became Protestant	Political reasons; needed an heir
Edward VI	Protestant	Too young to rule by himself; advisers were Protestant
Mary I	Catholic	Very religious
Elizabeth	Protestant	Religious; wanted an end to extremes

that ended the pope's power in England. This Parliament is known as the Reformation Parliament.

In 1533, Henry secretly married Anne Boleyn (BUL•ihn), who was in her twenties. Shortly after, Parliament legalized Henry's divorce from Catherine. In 1534, Henry's break with the pope was completed when Parliament voted to approve the Act of Supremacy. This called on people to take an oath recognizing the divorce and accepting Henry, not the pope, as the official head of England's Church.

The Act of Supremacy met some opposition. Thomas More, even though he had strongly criticized the Church, remained a devout Catholic. His faith, he said, would not allow him to accept the terms of the act and he refused to take the oath. In response, Henry had him arrested and imprisoned in the Tower of London. In 1535, More was found guilty of high treason and executed.

Consequences of Henry's Changes Henry did not immediately get the male heir he sought. After Anne Boleyn gave birth to a daughter, Elizabeth, she fell out of Henry's favor. Eventually, she was charged with treason. Like Thomas More, she was imprisoned in the Tower of London. She was found guilty and beheaded in 1536. Almost at once, Henry took a third wife, Jane Seymour. In 1537, she gave him a son named Edward. Henry's happiness was tempered by his wife's death just two weeks later. Henry married three more times. None of these marriages, however, produced children.

After Henry's death in 1547, each of his three children ruled England in turn. This created religious turmoil. Henry's son, Edward, became king when he was just nine years old. Too young to rule alone, Edward VI was guided by adult advisers. These men were devout Protestants, and they introduced Protestant reforms to the English Church. Almost constantly in ill health, Edward reigned for just six years. Mary, the daughter of Catherine of Aragon, took the throne in 1553. She was a Catholic who returned the English Church to the rule of the pope. Her efforts met with considerable resistance, and she had many Protestants executed. When Mary died in 1558, Elizabeth, Anne Boleyn's daughter, inherited the throne.

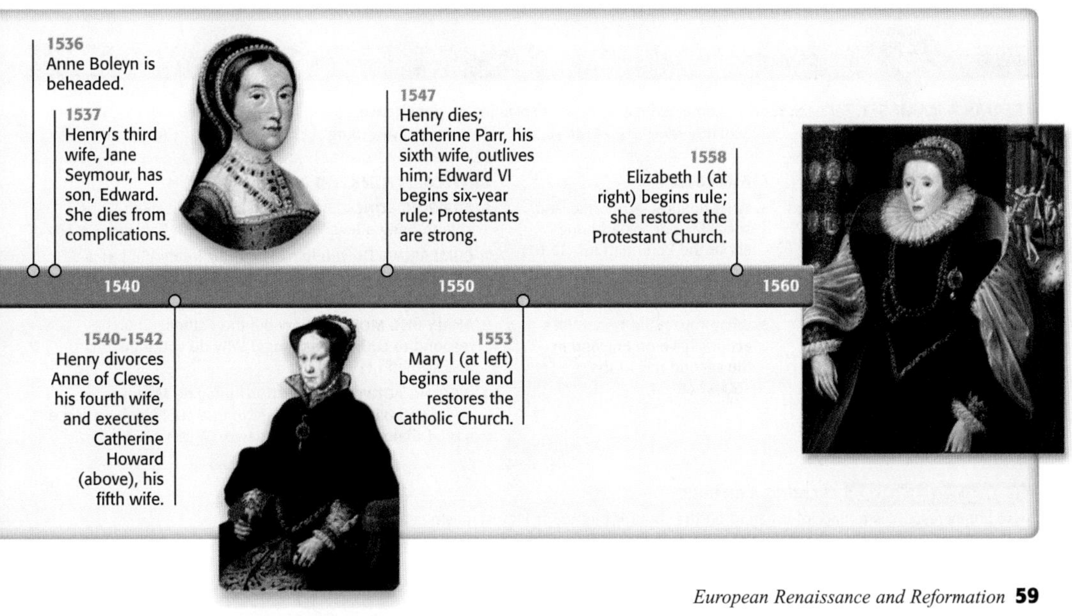

1536
Anne Boleyn is beheaded.
1537
Henry's third wife, Jane Seymour, has son, Edward. She dies from complications.
1547
Henry dies; Catherine Parr, his sixth wife, outlives him; Edward VI begins six-year rule; Protestants are strong.
1558
Elizabeth I (at right) begins rule; she restores the Protestant Church.
1540
1550
1560
1540-1542
Henry divorces Anne of Cleves, his fourth wife, and executes Catherine Howard (above), his fifth wife.
1553
Mary I (at left) begins rule and restores the Catholic Church.

More About . . .

Henry VIII

Most English people followed Roman Catholicism at the time of Henry's break with Rome. There was a small minority of English dissenters—people who wanted to reform the church. However, Henry was careful to change nothing about the way people worshiped. This explains why there was not greater outcry from his subjects about his actions.

Vocabulary Note: Words in Context
Students may be unfamiliar with the meaning of the word *oath* in this context. Explain that oath can refer to cursing, but in this case it refers to a serious, formal promise that calls on God to witness what has been said.

DIFFERENTIATING INSTRUCTION: GIFTED AND TALENTED STUDENTS

Forming and Supporting Opinions

Class Time 40 minutes

Task Investigating the character of Henry VIII

Purpose To learn more about this historical figure

Instructions Henry VIII is a well-known figure in history, but opinions of his character, actions, and personality still differ. For example, in 1515 the Venetian ambassador to Henry's court wrote, "Believe me, he is in every respect a most accomplished Prince . . . ." Other sources state that Henry openly celebrated the death of his first wife, Catherine of Aragon.

Have students use the Research Links at **classzone.com,** other Internet sources, or books to find primary and secondary sources that express opinions about Henry. Once students have formed an opinion about him, they should write a paragraph expressing their opinion and supporting it with at least two sources.

When students have finished, distribute the Self-Assessment form from the Integrated Assessment book and ask them to evaluate their results.

Integrated Assessment Book

History Makers

Elizabeth I

Ask students to make a list of Elizabeth's strengths as a ruler. *(Possible Answers: courage, intelligence, determination)*

In-Depth Resources: Unit 1
- Primary Source: A Conference with Elizabeth I, p. 28
- History Makers: Elizabeth I, p. 34

History Makers

Elizabeth I
1533–1603

Elizabeth I, like her father, had a robust nature and loved physical activity. She had a particular passion for dancing. Her fondness for exercise diminished little with age, and she showed amazing energy and strength well into her sixties.

Elizabeth also resembled her father in character and temperament. She was stubborn, strong-willed, and arrogant, and she expected to be obeyed without question. And Elizabeth had a fierce and unpredictable temper. To her subjects, Elizabeth was an object of both fear and love. She was their "most dread sovereign lady."

Elizabeth Restores Protestantism Elizabeth I was determined to return her kingdom to Protestantism. In 1559, Parliament followed Elizabeth's wishes and set up the Church of England, or **Anglican** Church, with Elizabeth as its head. This was to be the only legal church in England.

Elizabeth decided to establish a state church that moderate Catholics and moderate Protestants might both accept. To please Protestants, priests in the Church of England were allowed to marry. They could deliver sermons in English, not Latin. To please Catholics, the Church of England kept some of the trappings of the Catholic service such as rich robes. In addition, church services were revised to be somewhat more acceptable to Catholics. C

MAIN IDEA
Recognizing Effects
C How did Henry VIII's marriages and divorces cause religious turmoil in England?
C. Answer They led to the general abandonment of Catholicism in England and the creation of the Anglican Church..

Elizabeth Faces Other Challenges By taking this moderate approach, Elizabeth brought a level of religious peace to England. Religion, however, remained a problem. Some Protestants pushed for Elizabeth to make more far-reaching church reforms. At the same time, some Catholics tried to overthrow Elizabeth and replace her with her cousin, the Catholic Mary Queen of Scots. Elizabeth also faced threats from Philip II, the Catholic king of Spain.

Elizabeth faced other difficulties. Money was one problem. In the late 1500s, the English began to think about building an American empire as a new source of income. While colonies strengthened England economically, they did not enrich the queen directly. Elizabeth's constant need for money would carry over into the next reign and lead to bitter conflict between the monarch and Parliament. You will read more about Elizabeth's reign in Chapter 5. In the meantime, the Reformation gained ground in other European countries.

3 ASSESS

SECTION 1 ASSESSMENT

Have pairs of students take turns quizzing each other on the questions.

Formal Assessment
- Section Quiz, p. 23

4 RETEACH

Use the chart on page 57 to review the Reformation and the religious beliefs and practices in the 16th century.

In-Depth Resources, Unit 1
- Guided Reading, p. 22
- Reteaching Activity, p. 38

SECTION 3 ASSESSMENT

TERMS & NAMES 1. For each term or name, write a sentence explaining its significance.
• indulgence • Reformation • Lutheran • Protestant • Peace of Augsburg • annul • Anglican

USING YOUR NOTES

2. Which effect do you think had the most permanent impact? Explain. (10.1.1)

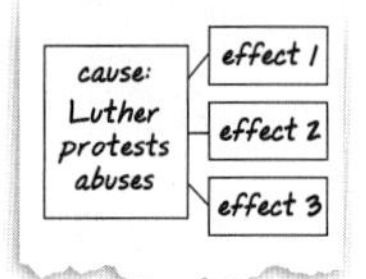

MAIN IDEAS

3. What political, economic, and social factors helped bring about the Reformation? (10.1.1)
4. From where did the term *Protestantism* originate? (10.1.1)
5. What impact did Henry VIII's actions have on England in the second half of the 1500s? (10.1.1)

CRITICAL THINKING & WRITING

6. **DRAWING CONCLUSIONS** Explain how Elizabeth I was able to bring a level of religious peace to England. (10.1.1)
7. **COMPARING** Do you think Luther or Henry VIII had a better reason to break with the Church? Provide details to support your answer. (10.1.1)
8. **ANALYZING MOTIVES** How did the Catholic Church respond to Luther's teachings? Why do you think this was so? (10.1.1)
9. **WRITING ACTIVITY** REVOLUTION Imagine Martin Luther and a Catholic Church leader are in a public debate. Write a brief **dialogue** between the two. (Writing 2.1.c)

CONNECT TO TODAY CREATING A GRAPHIC
Use library resources to find information on the countries in which Protestantism is a major religion. Use your findings to create a **graphic** that makes a comparison among those countries. (HI 1)

ANSWERS

1. indulgence, p. 55 • Reformation, p. 55 • Protestant, p. 56 • Lutheran, p. 56 • Peace of Augsburg, p. 58 • annul, p. 58 • Anglican, p. 60
2. **Sample Answer:** 1. Luther excommunicated. 2. Peasants revolt. 3. Lutheran Church founded (most permanent effect).
3. Political–Rise of competing states; rulers resented pope's control. Economic– Rulers jealous of Church's wealth; merchants resented paying Church taxes. Social–People question Church; printing presses spread ideas critical of Church.
4. from German princes who protested
5. His children brought religious turmoil by switching from Protestant to Catholic and back.
6. Her church was acceptable to moderate Catholics and moderate Protestants. The church kept some elements of Catholic service.
7. **Possible Answers:** Luther had legitimate complaints about indulgences and other Church problems; Henry's annulment denied; he needed an heir to prevent another civil war.
8. excommunicated him; viewed his teachings as a threat
9. **Rubric** Dialogues should
   - explain the views of both sides.
   - cite facts and details from the text.

CONNECT TO TODAY
Rubric Graphics should
- have a title and be clearly labeled.
- cite source material.

For help with pie charts, see the Skillbuilder Handbook.

Bottecelli *Allegory of Spring*

Italian hill town

4

The Reformation Continues

MAIN IDEA

RELIGIOUS AND ETHICAL SYSTEMS As Protestant reformers divided over beliefs, the Catholic Church made reforms.

WHY IT MATTERS NOW

Many Protestant churches began during this period, and many Catholic schools are the result of reforms in the Church.

TERMS & NAMES

- predestination
- Calvinism
- theocracy
- Presbyterian
- Anabaptist
- Catholic Reformation
- Jesuits
- Council of Trent

SETTING THE STAGE Under the leadership of Queen Elizabeth I, the Anglican Church, though Protestant, remained similar to the Catholic Church in many of its doctrines and ceremonies. Meanwhile, other forms of Protestantism were developing elsewhere in Europe. Martin Luther had launched the Reformation in northern Germany, but reformers were at work in other countries. In Switzerland, another major branch of Protestantism emerged. Based mainly on the teachings of John Calvin, a French follower of Luther, it promoted unique ideas about the relationship between people and God.

CALIFORNIA STANDARDS

10.1.1 Analyze the similarities and differences in Judeo-Christian and Greco-Roman views of law, reason and faith, and duties of the individual.

10.2.1 Compare the major ideas of philosophers and their effects on the democratic revolutions in England, the United States, France, and Latin America (e.g., John Locke, Charles-Louis Montesquieu, Jean-Jacques Rousseau, Simón Bolívar, Thomas Jefferson, James Madison).

REP 3 Students evaluate major debates among historians concerning alternative interpretations of the past, including an analysis of authors' use of evidence and the distinctions between sound generalizations and misleading oversimplifications.

HI 4 Students understand the meaning, implication, and impact of historical events and recognize that events could have taken other directions.

Calvin Continues the Reformation

Religious reform in Switzerland was begun by Huldrych Zwingli (HUL•drykh ZWIHNG•lee), a Catholic priest in Zurich. He was influenced both by the Christian humanism of Erasmus and by the reforms of Luther. In 1520, Zwingli openly attacked abuses in the Catholic Church. He called for a return to the more personal faith of early Christianity. He also wanted believers to have more control over the Church.

Zwingli's reforms were adopted in Zurich and other cities. In 1531, a bitter war between Swiss Protestants and Catholics broke out. During the fighting, Zwingli met his death. Meanwhile, John Calvin, then a young law student in France with a growing interest in Church doctrine, was beginning to clarify his religious beliefs.

Calvin Formalizes Protestant Ideas When Martin Luther posted his 95 Theses in 1517, John Calvin had been only eight years old. But Calvin grew up to have as much influence in the spread of Protestantism as Luther did. He would give order to the faith Luther had begun.

In 1536, Calvin published *Institutes of the Christian Religion.* This book expressed ideas about God, salvation, and human nature. It was a summary of Protestant theology, or religious beliefs. Calvin wrote that men and women are sinful by nature. Taking Luther's idea that humans cannot earn salvation, Calvin went on to say that God chooses a very few people to save. Calvin called these few the "elect." He believed that God has known since the beginning of time who will be saved. This doctrine is called **predestination**. The religion based on Calvin's teachings is called **Calvinism**.

TAKING NOTES

Comparing Use a chart to compare the ideas of the reformers who came after Luther.

Reformers	Ideas
Zwingli	
Calvin	
Anabaptists	
Catholic Reformers	

LESSON PLAN

OBJECTIVES

- Explain Calvin's Protestant teachings
- Describe the beliefs of other reformers and the roles of women in the Reformation.
- Trace reforms in the Catholic Church.
- Summarize the legacy of the Reformation.

1 FOCUS & MOTIVATE

Have students turn to page 62 and skim the first two paragraphs. Ask, How would your life be different if you lived in a theocracy like Geneva? *(no colorful clothing, no card games, perhaps no computer games, stricter punishments)*

2 INSTRUCT

Calvin Continues the Reformation

10.1.1

Critical Thinking

- Why is John Calvin important today? *(His ideas influenced the development of many different Protestant churches.)*

CALIFORNIA RESOURCES

California Reading Toolkit, p. L12
California Modified Lesson Plans for English Learners, p. 19
California Daily Standards Practice Transparencies, TT4
California Standards Enrichment Workbook, pp. 17–18, 23–24
California Standards Planner and Lesson Plans, p. L15
California Online Test Practice
California Test Generator CD-ROM
California Easy Planner CD-ROM
California eEdition CD-ROM

SECTION 4 PROGRAM RESOURCES

ALL STUDENTS

In-Depth Resources: Unit 1
- Guided Reading, p. 21

Formal Assessment
- Section Quiz, p. 24

ENGLISH LEARNERS

In-Depth Resources in Spanish
- Guided Reading, p. 21

Reading Study Guide (Spanish), p. 21
Reading Study Guide Audio CD (Spanish)

STRUGGLING READERS

In-Depth Resources: Unit 1
- Guided Reading, p. 21
- Building Vocabulary, p. 22
- Reteaching Activity, p. 39

Reading Study Guide, p. 21
Reading Study Guide Audio CD

GIFTED AND TALENTED STUDENTS

Electronic Library of Primary Sources
- "The St. Bartholomew's Day Massacre"
- "Luther: Giant of His Time and Ours"

INTEGRATED TECHNOLOGY

eEdition Plus Online
eEdition CD-ROM
Power Presentations CD-ROM
Geography Transparencies
- GT17 Reformation: Lutheranism and Calvinism

Critical Thinking Transparencies
- CT17 The Protestant and Catholic Reformations
- CT53 Chapter 1 Visual Summary

Electronic Library of Primary Sources
classzone.com

History Makers

John Calvin

Why did Calvin and his followers want to regulate morality? *(They believed that people were naturally sinful and could not regulate themselves.)*

Calvinist ritual, or religious ceremony, differed from that of Catholics and Lutherans. Calvin forbade the clergy to wear rich, colorful religious garments. Many traditional religious objects, such as statues, incense, altars, candles, chants, organ music, and stained-glass windows, were not allowed in Calvinist churches.

Electronic Library of Primary Sources

- "The St. Bartholomew's Day Massacre"

History Makers

John Calvin
1509–1564

A quiet boy, Calvin grew up to study law and philosophy at the University of Paris. In the 1530s, he was influenced by French followers of Luther. When King Francis I ordered Protestants arrested, Calvin fled. Eventually, he moved to Geneva.

Because Calvin and his followers rigidly regulated morality in Geneva, Calvinism is often described as strict and grim. But Calvin taught that people should enjoy God's gifts. He wrote that it should not be "forbidden to laugh, or to enjoy food, or to add new possessions to old."

Calvin Leads the Reformation in Switzerland Calvin believed that the ideal government was a **theocracy**, a government controlled by religious leaders. In 1541, Protestants in Geneva, Switzerland, asked Calvin to lead their city.

When Calvin arrived there in the 1540s, Geneva was a self-governing city of about 20,000 people. He and his followers ran the city according to strict rules. Everyone attended religion class. No one wore bright clothing or played card games. Authorities would imprison, excommunicate, or banish those who broke such rules. Anyone who preached different doctrines might be burned at the stake. Yet, to many Protestants, Calvin's Geneva was a model city of highly moral citizens.

Calvinism Spreads One admiring visitor to Geneva was a Scottish preacher named John Knox. When he returned to Scotland in 1559, Knox put Calvin's ideas to work. Each community church was governed by a group of laymen called elders or presbyters (PREHZ•buh•tuhrs). Followers of Knox became known as **Presbyterians**. In the 1560s, Protestant nobles led by Knox made Calvinism Scotland's official religion. They also deposed their Catholic ruler, Mary Queen of Scots, in favor of her infant son, James.

Elsewhere, Swiss, Dutch, and French reformers adopted the Calvinist form of church organization. One reason Calvin is considered so influential is that many Protestant churches today trace their roots to Calvin. Over the years, however, many of them have softened Calvin's strict teachings.

In France, Calvin's followers were called Huguenots. Hatred between Catholics and Huguenots frequently led to violence. The most violent clash occurred in Paris on August 24, 1572—the Catholic feast of St. Bartholomew's Day. At dawn, Catholic mobs began hunting for Protestants and murdering them. The massacres spread to other cities and lasted six months. Scholars believe that as many as 12,000 Huguenots were killed.

Other Protestant Reformers

10.1.1

Critical Thinking

- What lasting influence did the Anabaptists have? *(Anabaptist beliefs influenced the Amish, Mennonites, Quakers, and Baptists of today.)*
- How did women influence the Reformation? *(protected reformers, managed households, performed good works)*

Other Protestant Reformers

Protestants taught that the Bible is the source of all religious truth and that people should read it to discover those truths. As Christians interpreted the Bible for themselves, new Protestant groups formed over differences in belief. **A**

MAIN IDEA
Analyzing Causes
A How did Protestant teaching lead to the forming of new groups?
A. Possible Answer It encouraged people to discover their own truths in the Bible.

The Anabaptists One such group baptized only those persons who were old enough to decide to be Christian. They said that persons who had been baptized as children should be rebaptized as adults. These believers were called **Anabaptists**, from a Greek word meaning "baptize again." The Anabaptists also taught that church and state should be separate, and they refused to fight in wars. They shared their possessions.

Viewing Anabaptists as radicals who threatened society, both Catholics and Protestants persecuted them. But the Anabaptists survived and became the forerunners of the Mennonites and the Amish. Their teaching influenced the later Quakers and Baptists, groups who split from the Anglican Church.

Women's Role in the Reformation Many women played prominent roles in the Reformation, especially during the early years. For example, the sister of King

DIFFERENTIATING INSTRUCTION: STRUGGLING READERS

Persuading People to Come to Geneva

Class Time 40 minutes

Task Creating and performing a radio commercial for the city of Geneva

Purpose To explain what made Geneva different and important; to hone persuasive writing skills

Instructions Divide students into small groups. Have groups reread the subsection "Calvin Leads the Reformation in Switzerland." Remind students that many people of the time admired the way Calvin ran the theocracy (religious government) of Geneva. Ask students to imagine that they have been hired by John Calvin to write a radio advertisement encouraging people to visit Geneva. Each group should write a script for a radio commercial lasting 30 to 90 seconds. Groups should consider the following questions when writing:

- What makes Geneva different from other cities?
- What activities might you find its citizens doing?
- What activities are not allowed in Geneva? Why?
- What happens to people who break the rules?

Encourage students to be persuasive–using vivid, descriptive language and perhaps even sound effects. When groups are finished, have each one perform its commercial for the class.

GEOGRAPHY SKILLBUILDER: Interpreting Maps

1. **Region** *Which European countries became mostly Protestant and which remained mostly Roman Catholic?*
2. **Location** *Judging from the way the religions were distributed, where would you expect religious conflicts to take place? Explain.*

History from Visuals

Interpreting the Map

Point out the complex color code in the legend. Have students find an example of each religion on the map that is explained in the legend. Ask, Why was Elizabeth I constantly on guard against a Catholic invasion? *(Most of the nations bordering England were Catholic.)*

SKILLBUILDER Answers

1. **Region** Mostly Protestant—England, Scotland, Denmark-Norway, Sweden. Mostly Roman Catholic—Ireland, Spain, France, Italy.
2. **Location** *Possible Answer:* in the German states, and the Swiss Confederation, where there was a mixture of faiths

Geography Transparencies

- G17 The Protestant and Catholic Reformations

INTEGRATED TECHNOLOGY

Interactive This map is available in an interactive format on the eEdition. Students can view the locations of the dominant and minority religions one at a time or all at once.

COOPERATIVE LEARNING

Data on Religious Groups

Class Time 20 minutes

Task Surveying community religious groups

Purpose To explore the impact the Reformation had on the United States

Instructions Divide the class into groups of 3 to 4 students. Have them use the local Yellow Pages to count the houses of worship in their community. Then have them create a chart listing 8 to 10 of the religious groups. For each group, have them note its religious affiliation. You may want to refer to the section on World Religions, pp. 700–715, for help. An example is shown at right.

House of Worship	Religious Affiliation
United Methodist Church	Protestant
Trinity Lutheran Church	Protestant
St. Nicholas Roman Catholic Church	Catholic
Calvary Baptist Church	Protestant
Congregation Beth Shalom	Jewish
Zen Buddhist Temple	Buddhist

Have students note the Protestant churches in the community and remind them of the direct connection to the Reformation.

The Catholic Reformation

10.1.1

Critical Thinking

- How did Jesuit reforms help the Catholic Church keep its members from becoming Protestant? *(Their schools helped educate priests to do better work; students learned more about Catholic theology; missionaries did good works and made converts.)*
- Why did the Catholic Church feel the need for reforms, and what did church leaders do? *(Protestantism was reducing Catholic membership; Church investigated corruption; supported Jesuits; used Inquisition; called Council of Trent; created Index of Forbidden Books)*

Tip for English Learners

"Counter" in this context means "to go against." So the Counter Reformation was a movement against the Reformation. Tell students to think of the related word, "counterclockwise."

▲ Although Catholic, Marguerite of Navarre supported the call for reform in the Church.

Francis I, Marguerite of Navarre, protected John Calvin from being executed for his beliefs while he lived in France. Other noblewomen also protected reformers. The wives of some reformers, too, had influence. Katherina Zell, married to Matthew Zell of Strasbourg, once scolded a minister for speaking harshly of another reformer. The minister responded by saying that she had "disturbed the peace." She answered his criticism sharply:

> **PRIMARY SOURCE**
> Do you call this disturbing the peace that instead of spending my time in frivolous amusements I have visited the plague-infested and carried out the dead? I have visited those in prison and under sentence of death. Often for three days and three nights I have neither eaten nor slept. I have never mounted the pulpit, but I have done more than any minister in visiting those in misery.
>
> **KATHERINA ZELL,** quoted in *Women of the Reformation*

Katherina von Bora played a more typical, behind-the-scenes role as Luther's wife. Katherina was sent to a convent at about age ten, and had become a nun. Inspired by Luther's teaching, she fled the convent. After marrying Luther, Katherina had six children. She also managed the family finances, fed all who visited their house, and supported her husband's work. She respected Luther's position but argued with him about woman's equal role in marriage.

As Protestant religions became more firmly established, their organization became more formal. Male religious leaders narrowly limited women's activities to the home and discouraged them from being leaders in the church. In fact, it was Luther who said, "God's highest gift on earth is a pious, cheerful, God-fearing, home-keeping wife." (B)

MAIN IDEA

Making Inferences

(B) Why was it easier for women to take part in the earlier stages of the Reformation than in the later stages?

B. Possible Answer In the earlier stages, most churches did not have formal leaders who could tell women what to do.

The Catholic Reformation

While Protestant churches won many followers, millions remained true to Catholicism. Helping Catholics to remain loyal was a movement within the Catholic Church to reform itself. This movement is now known as the **Catholic Reformation**. Historians once referred to it as the Counter Reformation. Important leaders in this movement were reformers, such as Ignatius (ihg•NAY•shuhs) of Loyola, who founded new religious orders, and two popes—Paul III and Paul IV—who took actions to reform and renew the Church from within.

Ignatius of Loyola Ignatius grew up in his father's castle in Loyola, Spain. The great turning point in his life came in 1521 when he was injured in a war. While recovering, he thought about his past sins and about the life of Jesus. His daily devotions, he believed, cleansed his soul. In 1522, Ignatius began writing a book called *Spiritual Exercises* that laid out a day-by-day plan of meditation, prayer, and study. In it, he compared spiritual and physical exercise:

> **PRIMARY SOURCE**
> Just as walking, traveling, and running are bodily exercises, preparing the soul to remove ill-ordered affections, and after their removal seeking and finding the will of God with respect to the ordering of one's own life and the salvation of one's soul, are Spiritual Exercises.
>
> **IGNATIUS OF LOYOLA,** *Spiritual Exercises*

DIFFERENTIATING INSTRUCTION: GIFTED AND TALENTED STUDENTS

Making Inferences

Class Time 10 minutes

Task Discussing a primary source

Purpose To make inferences about a person based on her writings

Instructions In a letter to the minister Ludwig Rabus, Katherina Zell wrote, "Ever since I was ten years old I have been a student and a sort of church mother, much given to attending sermons. I have loved and frequented the company of learned men, and I conversed much with them, not about dancing, masquerades and worldly pleasures but about the kingdom of God . . ."

Based on this excerpt and the primary source quotation on this page, have students make inferences about how Katherina Zell views her religious role and her relationship to men. Use the Standards for Evaluating a Group Discussion chart once the class has finished the discussion.

Integrated Assessment Book

▲ Church leaders consult on reforms at the Council of Trent in this 16th-century painting.

For the next 18 years, Ignatius gathered followers. In 1540, the pope created a religious order for his followers called the Society of Jesus. Members were called **Jesuits** (JEHZH•oo•ihts). The Jesuits focused on three activities. First, they founded schools throughout Europe. Jesuit teachers were well-trained in both classical studies and theology. The Jesuits' second mission was to convert non-Christians to Catholicism. So they sent out missionaries around the world. Their third goal was to stop the spread of Protestantism. The zeal of the Jesuits overcame the drift toward Protestantism in Poland and southern Germany.

Reforming Popes Two popes took the lead in reforming the Catholic Church. Paul III, pope from 1534 to 1549, took four important steps. First, he directed a council of cardinals to investigate indulgence selling and other abuses in the Church. Second, he approved the Jesuit order. Third, he used the Inquisition to seek out heresy in papal territory. Fourth, and most important, he called a council of Church leaders to meet in Trent, in northern Italy.

Vocabulary
The *Inquisition* was a papal judicial process established to try and punish those thought to be heretics.

From 1545 to 1563, at the **Council of Trent**, Catholic bishops and cardinals agreed on several doctrines:

- The Church's interpretation of the Bible was final. Any Christian who substituted his or her own interpretation was a heretic.
- Christians needed faith and good works for salvation. They were not saved by faith alone, as Luther argued.
- The Bible and Church tradition were equally powerful authorities for guiding Christian life.
- Indulgences were valid expressions of faith. But the false selling of indulgences was banned.

The next pope, Paul IV, vigorously carried out the council's decrees. In 1559, he had officials draw up a list of books considered dangerous to the Catholic faith. This list was known as the Index of Forbidden Books. Catholic bishops throughout Europe were ordered to gather up the offensive books (including Protestant Bibles) and burn them in bonfires. In Venice alone, followers burned 10,000 books in one day.

More About . . .

The Inquisition

In Catholic countries, the Inquisition stepped up its activities, threatening Protestants and heretics with imprisonment or death. Even the most faithful believers might be reported to the Inquisition by their enemies. Ignatius of Loyola himself was brought before the Inquisition several times. However, he was always found innocent.

More About . . .

The Council of Trent

The Catholic hierarchy called the Council of Trent to counter the Protestant Reformation and protect the Church. Some significant results of the Council of Trent were:

- disregard for Christian humanism and liberal movements within the church
- better educated Catholic bishops and clergy
- clearly defined Catholic doctrine

DIFFERENTIATING INSTRUCTION: ENGLISH LEARNERS

The Catholic Church and the Reformation

Class Time 45 minutes

Task Identifying reforms made by the Catholic Church

Purpose To learn more about how the Catholic Church responded to the Reformation

Instructions Remind students that many Catholics were leaving the church and becoming Protestant. The Catholic Church needed to do something to keep its members. Review with your students the steps the Church took to respond to the Reformation. Have students make a chart like the one here to identify the responses.

To get more help, have students work through the Reading Study Guide in Spanish, p. 21.

Actions by the Catholic Church	Reason
Set up a meeting of Cardinals (called a council)	To investigate the selling of indulgences and other abuses
Set up a meeting of church leaders (the Council of Trent, which met for more than 10 years)	To state Catholic beliefs clearly
Approved the order of Jesuits	To support this new religious order which established schools and did missionary work
Started the Inquisition	To punish people who broke the rules of the Church

The Legacy of the Reformation
10.2.1

Critical Thinking

- How did education benefit from the Reformation? *(schools established, clergy better educated)*
- What political changes started by the Reformation are present today? *(Nations developed that exist today; wars to expand territory began; church political power declined.)*

Global Impact

Jesuit Missionaries

The Jesuits were like a spiritual army, willing to go anywhere in the world in the service of the pope. Jesuit missionaries in Asia adapted their religious teachings to fit the culture of each country. Church officials criticized the missionaries for this approach. Matteo Ricci, for instance, was accused of allowing idolatry when he permitted the Chinese to conduct traditional rituals of reverence for their ancestors.

3 ASSESS

SECTION 4 ASSESSMENT

Assign pairs of students to answer the questions and find supporting information in the text.

Formal Assessment
- Section Quiz, p. 24

4 RETEACH

Use the Visual Summary to review this section and chapter.

Critical Thinking Transparencies
- CT53 Chapter 1 Visual Summary

Global Impact

Jesuit Missionaries

The work of Jesuit missionaries has had a lasting impact around the globe. By the time Ignatius died in 1556, about a thousand Jesuits had brought his ministry to Europe, Africa, Asia, and the Americas. Two of the most famous Jesuit missionaries of the 1500s were Francis Xavier, who worked in India and Japan, and Matteo Ricci, who worked in China.

One reason the Jesuits had such an impact is that they founded schools throughout the world. For example, the Jesuits today run about 45 high schools and 28 colleges and universities in the United States. Four of these are Georgetown University (shown above), Boston College, Marquette University, and Loyola University of Chicago.

The Legacy of the Reformation

The Reformation had an enduring impact. Through its religious, social, and political effects, the Reformation set the stage for the modern world. It also ended the Christian unity of Europe and left it culturally divided.

Religious and Social Effects of the Reformation Despite religious wars and persecutions, Protestant churches flourished and new denominations developed. The Roman Catholic Church itself became more unified as a result of the reforms started at the Council of Trent. Both Catholics and Protestants gave more emphasis to the role of education in promoting their beliefs. This led to the founding of parish schools and new colleges and universities throughout Europe.

Some women reformers had hoped to see the status of women in the church and society improve as a result of the Reformation. But it remained much the same both under Protestantism and Roman Catholicism. Women were still mainly limited to the concerns of home and family.

Political Effects of the Reformation As the Catholic Church's moral and political authority declined, individual monarchs and states gained power. This led to the development of modern nation-states. In the 1600s, rulers of nation-states would seek more power for themselves and their countries through warfare, exploration, and expansion.

The Reformation's questioning of beliefs and authority also laid the groundwork for the Enlightenment. As you will read in Chapter 6, this intellectual movement would sweep Europe in the late 18th century. It led some to reject all religions and others to call for the overthrow of existing governments.

SECTION 4 ASSESSMENT

TERMS & NAMES 1. For each term or name, write a sentence explaining its significance.
• predestination • Calvinism • theocracy • Presbyterian • Anabaptist • Catholic Reformation • Jesuits • Council of Trent

USING YOUR NOTES

2. Which Catholic reform do you think had the most impact? (10.1.1)

Reformers	Ideas
Zwingli	
Calvin	
Anabaptists	
Catholic Reformers	

MAIN IDEAS

3. What was Calvin's idea of the "elect" and their place in society? (10.1.1)
4. What role did noblewomen play in the Reformation? (10.1.1)
5. What were the goals of the Jesuits? (10.1.1)

CRITICAL THINKING & WRITING

6. **DRAWING CONCLUSIONS** How did the Reformation set the stage for the modern world? Give examples. (10.1.1)
7. **MAKING INFERENCES** Why do you think the Church wanted to forbid people to read certain books? (10.1.1)
8. **COMPARING** How did steps taken by Paul III and Paul IV to reform the Catholic Church differ from Protestant reforms? Support your answer with details from the text. (10.1.1)
9. **WRITING ACTIVITY** RELIGIOUS AND ETHICAL SYSTEMS Write a two-paragraph **essay** on whether church leaders should be political rulers. (Writing 2.4.a)

CONNECT TO TODAY **PRESENTING AN ORAL REPORT**
Research the religious origins of a university in the United States. Then present your findings to the class in an **oral report.** (HI 4)

ANSWERS

1. predestination, p. 61 • Calvinism, p. 61 • theocracy, p. 62 • Presbyterian, p. 62 • Anabaptist, p. 62 • Catholic Reformation, p. 64 • Jesuits, p. 65 • Council of Trent, p. 65
2. **Sample Answer:** Zwingli attacked abuses in Church; Calvin built on Luther's ideas, developed idea of predestination, and led a theocracy; Catholic reformers improved unity within Catholic Church and established high-quality education (most impact).
3. "Elect" were the few God chose to be saved. They had a high position in society.
4. Noblewomen, such as Marguerite of Navarre, protected reformers.
5. improve Catholic education, convert non-Christians, stop spread of Protestantism
6. **Possible Answers:** Protestant churches grew; Catholic Church became more unified and established schools and universities; strong nation-states developed.
7. If certain books were read, people might question authority and teachings of the Church.
8. Protestant reformers attacked abuses and developed new religious beliefs; reformers in Catholic Church stayed within the Church to correct abuses
9. **Rubric** Essays should
   - include a thesis.
   - support the student's evaluation with reasons.
   - have a clearly drawn conclusion.

CONNECT TO TODAY

Rubric Oral reports should
- mention three universities such as Harvard (1636), Yale (1701), U of PA (1740), Princeton (1746), or Columbia (1754).
- explain how the founding of those schools related to religion.

INTERACTIVE

The Reformation

Martin Luther's criticisms of the Catholic Church grew sharper over time. Some Catholics, in turn, responded with personal attacks on Luther. In recent times, historians have focused less on the theological and personal issues connected with the Reformation. Instead, many modern scholars analyze the political, social, and economic conditions that contributed to the Reformation.

CALIFORNIA STANDARDS

10.1.1 Analyze the similarities and differences in Judeo-Christian and Greco-Roman views of law, reason and faith, and duties of the individual.

REP 1 Students distinguish valid arguments from fallacious arguments in historical interpretations.

A PRIMARY SOURCE

Martin Luther

In 1520, Martin Luther attacked the whole system of Church government and sent the pope the following criticism of the Church leaders who served under him in Rome.

The Roman Church has become the most licentious [sinful] den of thieves. . . . They err who ascribe to thee the right of interpreting Scripture, for under cover of thy name they seek to set up their own wickedness in the Church, and, alas, through them Satan has already made much headway under thy predecessors. In short, believe none who exalt thee, believe those who humble thee.

B SECONDARY SOURCE

Steven Ozment

In 1992, historian Steven Ozment published *Protestants: The Birth of a Revolution.* Here, he comments on some of the political aspects of the Reformation.

Beginning as a protest against arbitrary, self-aggrandizing, hierarchical authority in the person of the pope, the Reformation came to be closely identified in the minds of contemporaries with what we today might call states' rights or local control. To many townspeople and villagers, Luther seemed a godsend for their struggle to remain politically free and independent; they embraced his Reformation as a conserving political force, even though they knew it threatened to undo traditional religious beliefs and practices.

C SECONDARY SOURCE

G. R. Elton

In *Reformation Europe,* published in 1963, historian G. R. Elton notes the role of geography and trade in the spread of Reformation ideas.

Could the Reformation have spread so far and so fast if it had started anywhere but in Germany? The fact that it had its beginnings in the middle of Europe made possible a very rapid radiation in all directions. . . . Germany's position at the center of European trade also helped greatly. German merchants carried not only goods but Lutheran ideas and books to Venice and France; the north German Hanse [a trade league] transported the Reformation to the Scandinavian countries.

D PRIMARY SOURCE

Hans Brosamer

"Seven-Headed Martin Luther" (1529) The invention of the printing press enabled both Protestants and Catholics to engage in a war of words and images. This anti-Luther illustration by German painter Hans Brosamer depicted Martin Luther as a seven-headed monster—doctor, monk, infidel, preacher, fanatic swarmed by bees, self-appointed pope, and thief Barabbas from the Bible.

Document-Based
QUESTIONS

1. In what way does Luther's letter (Source A) support the point of view of the historian in Source B?
2. Based on Source C, why was Germany's location important to the spread of Reformation ideas?
3. Why might Hans Brosamer's woodcut (Source D) be an effective propaganda weapon against Martin Luther?

67

Different Perspectives

OBJECTIVE

- Understand that the Reformation can be examined from more than one perspective.

INSTRUCT

Help students see that each primary source on this page takes a different approach to the Reformation. Luther focuses on the excesses of the priests. Ozment examines people's desire to be independent of Church control. Elton understands how trade spread new ideas, and Brosamer draws a powerful picture, a bit like present-day advertising.

More About . . .

Attacks on Luther

Henry VIII of England also had unkind words for Martin Luther: "What serpent so venomous as he who calls the pope's authority tyrannous?" Though Henry later rejected the pope's authority, he never changed his opinion of Luther.

Electronic Library of Primary Sources

- "Luther: Giant of His Time and Ours"

INTEGRATED TECHNOLOGY

Interactive This feature is available in an interactive format on the eEdition.

Inclusion Tip

Students who are visually impaired may benefit from the larger version of the Brosamer illustration, available on the eEdition at **classzone.com**

DOCUMENT-BASED QUESTIONS: ANSWERS

1. Luther's letter denies the pope's right to interpret Scripture for others and states that the pope should not be exalted above other men. Steven Ozment focuses on the desire of people to have more local control of their affairs.
2. Germany's geographic location at the center of Europe and its position at the center of European trade made the spread of Reformation ideas quick and thorough. Merchants carried ideas and books all over Europe.
3. Many people in the 1500s could not read. The woodcut is a powerful visual statement against Luther.

CHAPTER 1 ASSESSMENT

TERMS & NAMES

1. Renaissance, p. 37
2. vernacular, p. 41
3. utopia, p. 48
4. Reformation, p. 55
5. Protestant, p. 56
6. Peace of Augsburg, p. 58
7. Catholic Reformation, p. 64
8. Council of Trent, p. 65

MAIN IDEAS

Answers will vary.

9. Merchants' belief in individual merit would become a recurring theme in the Renaissance; merchants also were patrons of the arts.
10. Artists and writers chose secular and classical subjects as well as Christian subjects. Writers began using the vernacular instead of Latin and started writing for self-expression. Artists painted prominent individuals, glorified the human body, and used new artistic techniques and a more realistic style.
11. They purchased Renaissance art and supported Italian and northern artists.
12. Christian humanists adopted humanist ideals but gave them a religious slant and interpreted the ideals based on Christian principles.
13. People could win salvation only through faith, not good works. Church teachings should be based on the Bible only, not on a combination of the Bible and Church tradition. People did not need priests to interpret the Bible for them.
14. He wanted to force the Protestant German princes to rejoin the Catholic Church.
15. Henry's desire for a male heir pushed him to split with the Church and create the Church of England.
16. believed in predestination, followed strict rules, promoted theocracy
17. The goal was for the Catholic Church to reform itself so that it could retain loyal Catholics.
18. **Possible Answers:** Religion no longer united Europe; paved the way for the modern nation-states; laid the groundwork for later rejection of Christian beliefs; Catholic Church became more unified; new schools founded

Chapter 1 Assessment

VISUAL SUMMARY

European Renaissance and Reformation

The Renaissance and the Reformation bring dramatic changes to social and cultural life in Europe.

1. Italy: Birthplace of the Renaissance

- A period of intellectual and artistic creativity begins in Italy around the 1300s.
- Artists and writers revive techniques, styles, and subjects from classical Greece and Rome and celebrate human achievements.

2. The Northern Renaissance

- Renaissance ideas spread to Northern Europe, where German and Flemish artists create distinctive works of art.
- Thousands of books and pamphlets created on printing presses spread political, social, and artistic ideas.

3. Luther Leads the Reformation

- Martin Luther starts a movement for religious reform and challenges the authority of the Catholic Church.
- King Henry VIII breaks ties with the Catholic Church and starts the Church of England.

4. The Reformation Continues

- Protestant groups divide into several denominations, including the Calvinists and the Anabaptists.
- The Catholic Church introduces its own reforms.

TERMS & NAMES

For each term or name below, briefly explain its connection to European history from 1300 to 1600.

1. Renaissance
2. vernacular
3. utopia
4. Reformation
5. Protestant
6. Peace of Augsburg
7. Catholic Reformation
8. Council of Trent

MAIN IDEAS

Italy: Birthplace of the Renaissance Section 1 (pages 37–45)

9. How did the merchant class in northern Italy influence the Renaissance? (HI 1)
10. How did literature and the arts change during the Renaissance? (CST 2)

The Northern Renaissance Section 2 (pages 46–53)

11. What did northern European rulers do to encourage the spread of Renaissance ideas? (HI 1)
12. How were the Christian humanists different from the humanists of the Italian Renaissance? (10.1.1)

Luther Leads the Reformation Section 3 (pages 54–60)

13. On what three teachings did Martin Luther rest his Reformation movement? (10.1.1)
14. Why did the Holy Roman emperor go to war against Protestant German princes? (HI 4)
15. Why did Henry VIII create his own church? Refer to the time line on pages 58–59. (10.1.1)

The Reformation Continues Section 4 (pages 61–67)

16. In what ways was John Calvin's church different from the Lutheran Church? (10.1.1)
17. What was the goal of the Catholic Reformation? (10.1.1)
18. What are three legacies of the Reformation? (10.1.1)

CRITICAL THINKING

1. USING YOUR NOTES
In a diagram, show how the Reformation led to great changes in European ideas and institutions. (HI 1)

Effects of the Reformation
Religious | Political | Social

2. ANALYZING ISSUES
REVOLUTION What role did the printing press play in the spread of the Reformation and the spread of democracy? (HI 1)

3. RECOGNIZING EFFECTS
CULTURAL INTERACTION How did the Renaissance and Reformation expand cultural interaction both within Europe and outside of it? (HI 3)

4. DEVELOPING HISTORICAL PERSPECTIVE
What conditions needed to exist before the Renaissance could occur? (HI 2)

5. SYNTHESIZING
How did views of women's roles of change in the Renaissance period? (HI 3)

CRITICAL THINKING

Answers will vary.

1. Religious—Split the church; divided Protestants into many groups, established Church of England. Political—Monarchs and states gained power; modern nation-states developed. Social—Peasant revolts, demands to end serfdom.
2. The printing press enabled more people to read the Bible. This created less dependence on the Church and a greater awareness of its faults. Ideas about democracy and government structure circulated among scholars and ordinary people.
3. Italian ideas inspired northern artists and writers. The classics that inspired the Renaissance had been preserved in Muslim libraries.
4. Europe needed to be at peace. Scholars and writers had to be supported. Access to classical works had to be available.
5. Attitudes changed a bit, but not dramatically. Christian humanists viewed women as worthy of education. Some women were writers and painters, while others were patrons of the arts.

Use the quotation and your knowledge of world history to answer questions 1 and 2.
Additional Test Practice, pp. S1–S33

PRIMARY SOURCE

A prince must also show himself a lover of merit [excellence], give preferment [promotion] to the able, and honour those who excel in every art. Moreover he must encourage his citizens to follow their callings [professions] quietly, whether in commerce, or agriculture, or any other trade that men follow. . . . [The prince] should offer rewards to whoever does these things, and to whoever seeks in any way to improve his city or state.

NICCOLÒ MACHIAVELLI, *The Prince*

1. Which phrase best describes the advice given by Machiavelli? (HI 3)
   - **A.** Rule with an iron hand in a velvet glove.
   - **B.** Do not give your subjects any freedoms.
   - **C.** Reward hard work and patriotism.
   - **D.** To retain your rule, you must interfere in the lives of your subjects.
2. In his book *The Prince,* the writer of this advice also suggested (HI 3)
   - **A.** the pope should listen to the calls for reform of the Church.
   - **B.** a prince might have to trick his people for the good of the state.
   - **C.** merchants should try to take control of the cities away from the prince.
   - **D.** the prince should reform society by establishing a utopia.

Use this drawing of a machine from the notebooks of Leonardo da Vinci and your knowledge of world history to answer question 3.

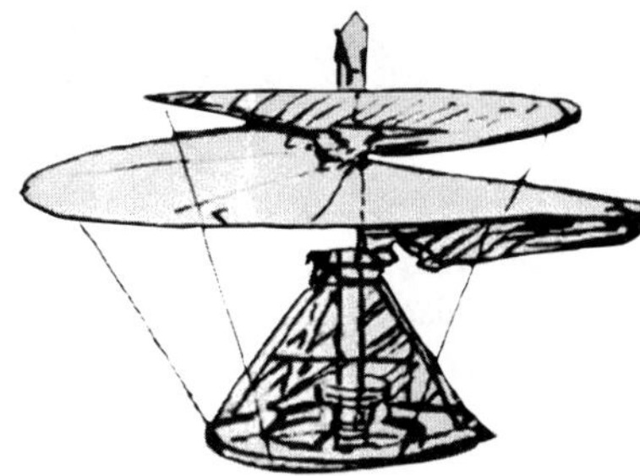

3. The principles upon which this machine is based evolved into what modern machine? (CST 2)
   - **A.** food blender
   - **B.** a fan
   - **C.** a well-digging machine
   - **D.** helicopter

INTEGRATED TECHNOLOGY

TEST PRACTICE Go to **classzone.com**
- Diagnostic tests
- Tutorials
- Strategies
- Additional practice

ALTERNATIVE ASSESSMENT

1. **Interact *with* History** (REP 4)
   On page 36, you looked at a painting and discussed what you learned about Renaissance society from that painting. Now choose one other piece of art from the chapter. Explain what you can learn about Renaissance or Reformation society from that piece of art.
2. **WRITING ABOUT HISTORY** (Writing 2.3.b, 2.3.c)
   RELIGIOUS AND ETHICAL SYSTEMS Study the information about Protestantism in the Analyzing Key Concepts on page 57. Write a three-paragraph **essay** analyzing the effects Protestantism had on the Christian Church.
   - Examine its impact on the number of denominations.
   - Explain the different beliefs and practices it promoted.

INTEGRATED TECHNOLOGY

Writing an Internet-based Research Paper

(Writing 2.3.b)

Go to the *Web Research Guide* at **classzone.com** to learn about conducting research on the Internet. Then, working with a partner, use the Internet to research major religious reforms of the 20th century. You might search for information on changes in the Catholic Church as a result of Vatican II, or major shifts in the practices or doctrines of a branch of Hinduism, Islam, Judaism, or Protestantism. Compare the 20th-century reforms with those of the Protestant Reformation. Present the results of your research in a well-organized paper. Be sure to

- apply a search strategy when using directories and search engines to locate Web resources.
- judge the usefulness and reliability of each Web site.
- correctly cite your Web sources.
- peer-edit for organization and correct use of language.

STANDARDS-BASED ASSESSMENT

1. The correct answer is letter **C**. In this excerpt Machiavelli recommends rewards for hard work and patriotism as a way to gain a good reputation with citizens. Letter **A** is incorrect because there is no mention of harsh treatment. Letter **B** is incorrect because the subject of freedoms is not mentioned. Letter **D** is incorrect because the passage refers to rewards, not interference.
2. Letter **B** is correct. Elsewhere in *The Prince,* Machiavelli suggests the prince must work for the good of the state at all costs. Letter **A** is not correct because the book is not about religion. Letter **C** is not correct because the book focuses on how to retain power and prevent merchants from gaining it. Letter **D** is not correct. Machiavelli does not discuss a utopia.
3. Letter **D** is correct. This is a design for a flying machine.

Formal Assessment
- Chapter Test, Forms A, B, and C, pp. 25–39

California Test Generator CD-ROM
- Chapter Tests, Forms A, B, and C (English and Spanish)

ALTERNATIVE ASSESSMENT

1. Students may cite some of these features: more concern for human rather than spiritual matters; emphasis on ordinary people in everyday situations; pride in individuality and creativity; admiration for classical culture; interest in realism; enjoyment of worldly pleasures; uniqueness of each individual, including biblical figures.
2. **Rubric** Essays should
   - identify effects of Protestantism on the Christian Church.
   - analyze the cited effects on the Church.
   - have a concluding statement.
   - use correct grammar and punctuation.

INTEGRATED TECHNOLOGY

Rubric Research papers should
- identify and analyze religious reforms.
- compare those reforms with the Protestant Reformation.
- cite at least three Internet sources.
- be well organized and logical.

CHAPTER 2 PLANNING GUIDE

The Muslim World Expands, 1300–1700

CHAPTER RESOURCES	COPYMASTERS	ASSESSMENT
CHAPTER OVERVIEW Three great Muslim empires rose and fell between 1300 and 1700.	**In-Depth Resources: Unit 1** • Building Vocabulary, p. 43 **Chapters in Brief** (in English and Spanish) **Block Schedule Pacing Guide**	**Chapter Assessment,** pp. 90–91 **Formal Assessment** • Chapter Tests, Forms A, B, and C, pp. 43–54 **Test Generator** **Integrated Assessment Book** **Online Test Practice**
SECTION 1 **The Ottomans Build a Vast Empire** pp. 73–77 **OBJECTIVE** Trace the origins, growth, and decline of the Ottoman Empire.	**In-Depth Resources: Unit 1** • Guided Reading, p. 40 • Skillbuilder Practice: Categorizing, p. 44 • Primary Source: *Suleyman the Magnificent,* p. 47 • Literature: from *The Bride of Suleiman,* p. 51 • History Makers: Suleiman, p. 54 • Reteaching Activity, p. 57 **Reading Study Guide,** p. 25	**Section 1 Assessment,** p. 77 **Formal Assessment** • Section Quiz, p. 40 **California Daily Standards Practice Transparencies,** TT65
SECTION 2 **Case Study: Cultural Blending—The Safavid Empire** pp. 78–81 **OBJECTIVE** Analyze how cultural blending resulted in new cultures and how the Safavid Empire developed.	**In-Depth Resources: Unit 1** • Guided Reading, p. 41 • Reteaching Activity, p. 58 **Reading Study Guide,** p. 27	**Section 2 Assessment,** p. 81 **Formal Assessment** • Section Quiz, p. 41 **California Daily Standards Practice Transparencies,** TT66
SECTION 3 **The Mughal Empire in India** pp. 82–89 **OBJECTIVE** Analyze the rise and decline of the Mughal Empire and the achievements of Akbar.	**In-Depth Resources: Unit 1** • Guided Reading, p. 42 • Geography Application: Europe Discovers the Riches of India, p. 45 • Primary Sources: Akbar, p. 49; Jahangir's Birthday, p. 50 • History Makers: Shah Jahan, p. 55 • Connections Across Time and Cultures: How to Treat the Conquered, p. 56 • Reteaching Activity, p. 59 **Reading Study Guide,** p. 29	**Section 3 Assessment,** p. 87 **Formal Assessment** • Section Quiz, p. 42 **California Daily Standards Practice Transparencies,** TT67

INTEGRATED TECHNOLOGY

- eEdition Plus Online
- EasyPlanner Plus Online
- eTest Plus Online

 **Audio CDs**
- Voices from the Past
- Reading Study Guides

CD-ROMs
- eEdition
- Power Presentations
- EasyPlanner
- Electronic Library of Primary Sources
- Test Generator

eEdition CD-ROM

 **Geography Transparencies**
- GT18, The Fall of Constantinople, 1453

 **World Art and Cultures Transparencies**
- AT39 Military Campaigns of Suleiman

 **Electronic Library of Primary Sources**
- "Descriptions of the Turks and the Christians"
- "The Fall of Constantinople"

 **classzone.com**

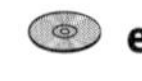 **eEdition CD-ROM**

 **Electronic Library of Primary Sources**
- "Report on Persia, Persians, and 'Abbas I"

 **classzone.com**

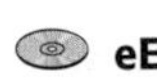 **eEdition CD-ROM**

 **Critical Thinking Transparencies**
- CT18 Muslim Empires in Anatolia and India
- CT37 Chapter 2 Visual Summary

 **World Art and Cultures Transparencies**
- AT40 Mughal miniature painting

 **classzone.com**

OVERVIEW OF CALIFORNIA RESOURCES

	Section 1	Section 2	Section 3
California Reading Toolkit	p. L13	p. L14	p. L15
California Modified Lesson Plans for English Learners	p. 21	p. 23	p. 25
California Daily Standards Practice Transparencies	TT5	TT6	TT7
California Standards Enrichment Workbook	pp. 107–108	pp. 101–102, 107–108	pp. 49–50
California Standards Planner and Lesson Plans	p. L17	p. L19	p. L21
California Online Test Practice	classzone.com	classzone.com	classzone.com
California Test Generator CD-ROM			
California Easy Planner CD-ROM			
California eEdition CD-ROM			

Chart Key:

 Pupil's Edition

 Teacher's Edition

Overhead Transparency

 Block Scheduling

 Copymaster

 Audio Library

 CD-ROM

 Internet

Video

NO TIME?

If you do not have time to teach this chapter in full, assign the **Chapter in Brief** (also available in Spanish).

Previewing Resources for Differentiated Instruction

ENGLISH LEARNERS: Resources in Spanish

In-Depth Resources in Spanish
- Guided Reading Ⓐ
- Skillbuilder Practice: Categorizing
- Geography Application: Europe Discovers the Riches of India Ⓑ

Chapters in Brief

Reading Study Guide Ⓒ

Reading Study Guide Audio CD

Test Generator CD-ROM
- Chapter Test, Forms A, B, and C

Plus

Modified Lesson Plans for English Learners

Multi-Language Glossary of Social Studies Terms

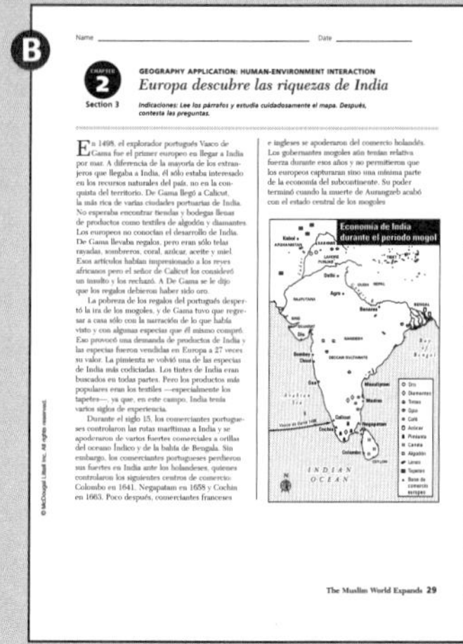

STRUGGLING READERS

In-Depth Resources: Unit 1
- Guided Reading Ⓐ
- Skillbuilder Practice: Categorizing
- Geography Application: Europe Discovers the Riches of India Ⓑ
- Reteaching Activities

Chapters in Brief

Reading Study Guide Ⓒ

Reading Study Guide Audio CD

Formal Assessment
- Chapter Test, Form A

Plus

Reading Toolkit

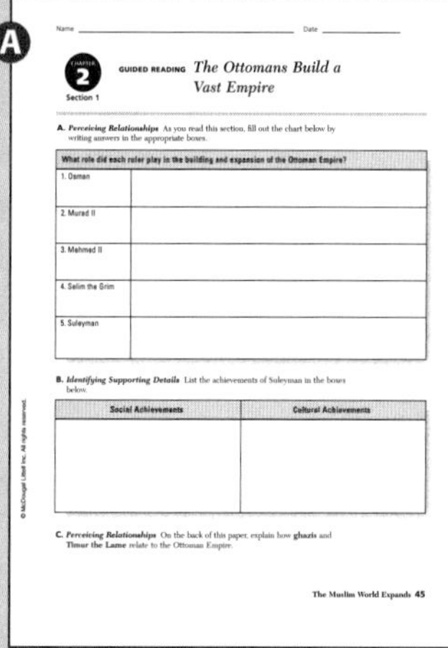

GIFTED AND TALENTED STUDENTS

In-Depth Resources: Unit 1
- Primary Source: *Suleyman the Magnificent* Ⓐ; Akbar; Jahangir's Birthday
- Literature: from *The Bride of Suleiman*
- History Makers: Sulieman; Shah Jahan
- Connections Across Time and Cultures: How to Treat the Conquered Ⓑ

Electronic Library of Primary Sources CD-ROM
- "Descriptions of the Turks and the Christians"
- "The Fall of Constantinople"
- "Report on Persia, Persians, and 'Abbas I"

Formal Assessment
- Chapter Test, Form C Ⓒ

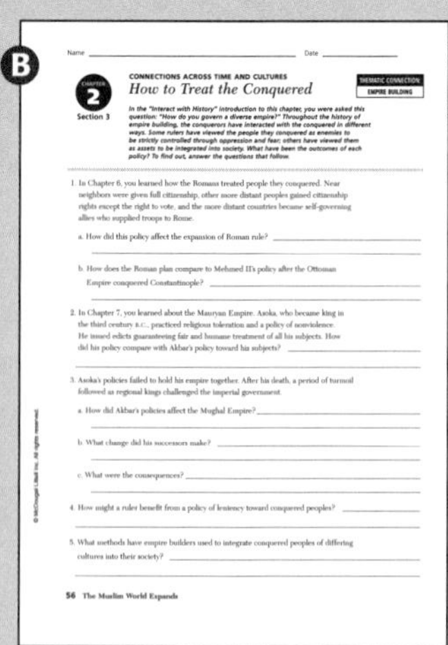

Activities in the Teacher's Edition for English Learners

- Taking Notes and Understanding Challenging Vocabulary, p. 74
- Writing Historical Dialogues, p. 79
- Understanding Idioms, p. 85

Activities in the Teacher's Edition for Struggling Readers

- Reporting on the Conquest of Constantinople, p. 75
- Creating a Commercial for the Safavid Empire, p. 80
- Investigating Mughal Art, p. 84

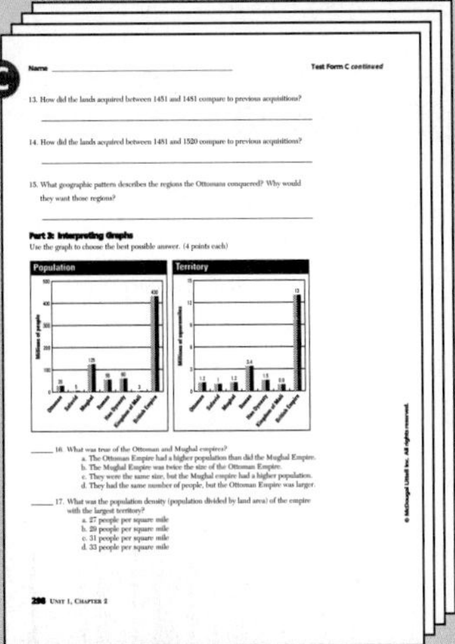

Name ________ Test Form C *continued*

13. How did the lands acquired between 1451 and 1481 compare to previous acquisitions?

14. How did the lands acquired between 1481 and 1520 compare to previous acquisitions?

15. What geographic pattern describes the regions the Ottomans conquered? Why would they want those regions?

Part 3: Interpreting Graphs

Use the graph to choose the best possible answer. (4 points each)

____ 16. What was true of the Ottoman and Mughal empires?
a. The Ottoman Empire had a higher population than did the Mughal Empire.
b. The Mughal Empire was twice the size of the Ottoman Empire.
c. They were the same size, but the Mughal empire had a higher population.
d. They had the same number of people, but the Ottoman Empire was larger.

____ 17. What was the population density (population divided by land area) of the empire with the largest territory?
a. 27 people per square mile
b. 29 people per square mile
c. 31 people per square mile
d. 33 people per square mile

© McDougal Littell Inc. All rights reserved.

298 Unit 1, Chapter 2

Activities in the Teacher's Edition for Gifted and Talented Students

- Evaluating Taxation, p. 83

INTEGRATED TECHNOLOGY

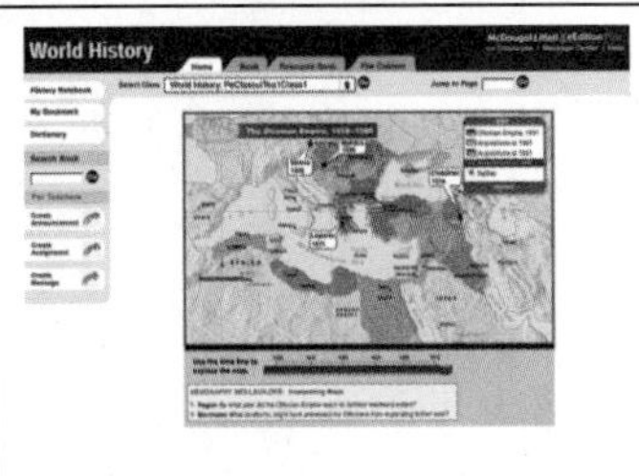

eEdition
- Interactive Visuals
- Interactive Maps
- Interactive Primary Sources

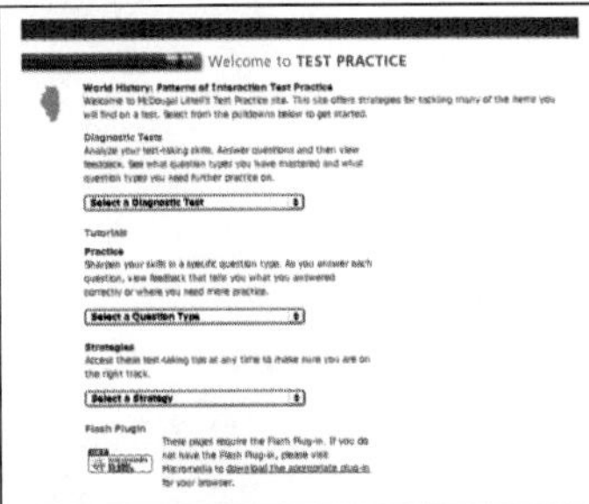

classzone.com
- Research Links
- Internet Activities
- Primary Sources
- Chapter Quiz
- Current Events

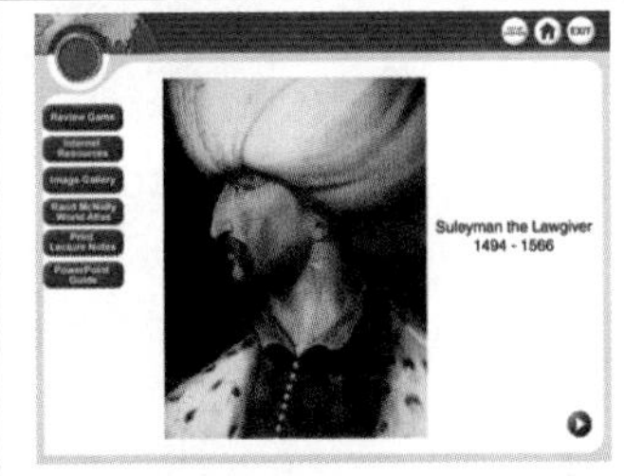

Power Presentations CD-ROM
- Lecture Notes
- Image Gallery
- Chapter Review Game

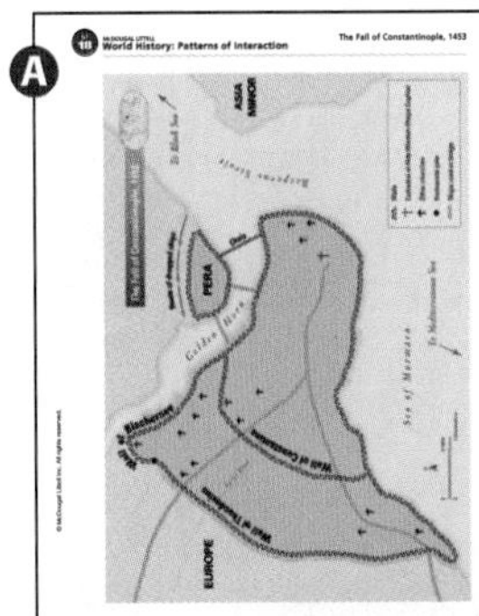

Critical Thinking Transparencies
- CT18 Muslim Empires in Anatolia and India
- CT37 Chapter 2 Visual Summary

Geography Transparencies
- GT18, The Fall of Constantinople, 1453 A

World Art and Cultures Transparencies
- AT39 Military Campaigns of Suleiman
- AT40 Mughal miniature painting

Test Practice Transparencies TT65–TT67

Test Generator CD-ROM

EasyPlanner CD-ROM

Voices from the Past Audio CD

Online Test Practice

Electronic Library of Primary Sources

CHAPTER 2 • OBJECTIVE

Analyze the causes of the rise and decline of Muslim empires between 1300 and 1700.

Previewing Main Ideas

Three great Muslim empires were based in today's Turkey, Iran, and India. Their success demonstrates how cultural exchange promotes growth and prosperity. However, problems in transferring power from one generation to the next contributed to the decline of each empire.

Accessing Prior Knowledge

Ask students to list examples of how power passes from one leader to another. *(Possible Answers: elections, selection by a small group of leaders, legal succession after a death, violent overthrow)*

Point out that when people do not agree on a legitimate process for choosing a new leader, violence is common. Discuss succession battles that have taken place in recent years. *(Possible Answers: replacement of President Daniel arap Moi in Kenya; other local, national, or international struggles)*

Geography *Answers*

EMPIRE BUILDING The Ottoman Empire was largest. It was located in southwest Asia, on the northern coast of Africa, and in southeastern Europe.

CULTURAL INTERACTION It included parts of Asia, Africa, and Europe.

POWER AND AUTHORITY The Mughal Empire was founded in 1526. Most of it was located in what is now India and Pakistan.

CHAPTER 2

The Muslim World Expands, 1300–1700

Previewing Main Ideas

EMPIRE BUILDING Three of the great empires of history—the Ottomans in Turkey, the Safavids in Persia, and the Mughals in India—emerged in the Muslim world between the 14th and the 18th centuries.

Geography *Locate the empires on the map. Which of the empires was the largest? Where was it located?*

CULTURAL INTERACTION As powerful societies moved to expand their empires, Turkish, Persian, Mongol, and Arab ways of life blended. The result was a flowering of Islamic culture that peaked in the 16th century.

Geography *The Ottoman Empire included cultures from which continents?*

POWER AND AUTHORITY The rulers of all three great Muslim empires of this era based their authority on Islam. They based their power on strong armies, advanced technology, and loyal administrative officers.

Geography *Study the time line and the map. When was the Mughal Empire founded? Where was Babur's empire located?*

INTEGRATED TECHNOLOGY

eEdition
- Interactive Maps
- Interactive Visuals
- Interactive Primary Sources

INTERNET RESOURCES
Go to classzone.com for:
- Research Links
- Internet Activities
- Primary Sources
- Chapter Quiz
- Maps
- Test Practice
- Current Events

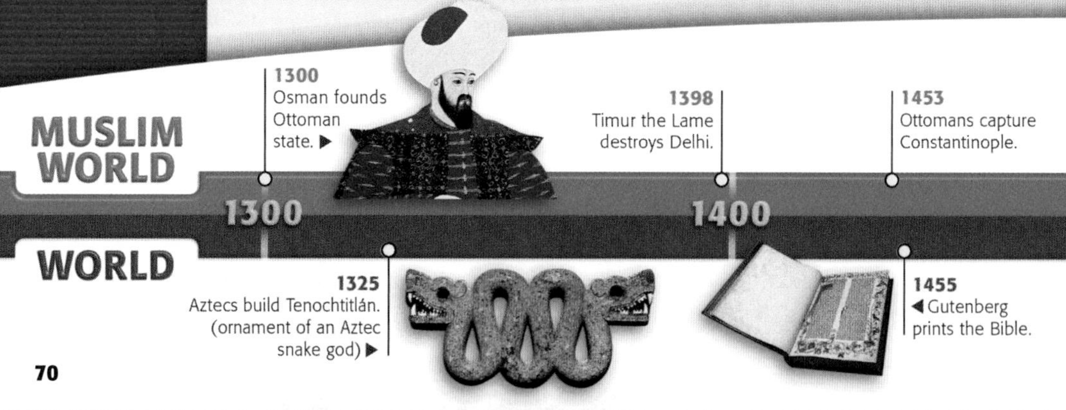

1300 Osman founds Ottoman state. ▶

1398 Timur the Lame destroys Delhi.

1453 Ottomans capture Constantinople.

1325 Aztecs build Tenochtitlán. (ornament of an Aztec snake god) ▶

1455 ◀ Gutenberg prints the Bible.

70

TIME LINE DISCUSSION

Tell students that as Mongol power receded in Eurasia, large new empires took its place. Three of these were led by Muslims.

1. How long after the founding of the Ottoman Empire did the Ottomans capture Constantinople? *(153 years)*
2. In what order were the three Muslim empires founded? *(Ottoman, Safavid, Mughal)* How does their development chronologically correspond to their location? *(Each new empire was based farther east.)* Why might this be important? *(might indicate spread of an idea or technology that was aiding builders of new empires)*
3. Which two events show the growing interaction between different parts of the globe? *(1522–Magellan's crew sails around the world; 1607–British settle in North America at Jamestown)*
4. Which two entries show creativity? *(Possible Answers: 1455–Gutenberg prints the Bible; 1632–Shah Jahan orders construction of Taj Mahal)*
5. What event is listed for 1603? *(Tokugawa regime begins in Japan)* How is it similar to the events listed for the Muslim world? *(It marked the political unification of another part of Asia.)*

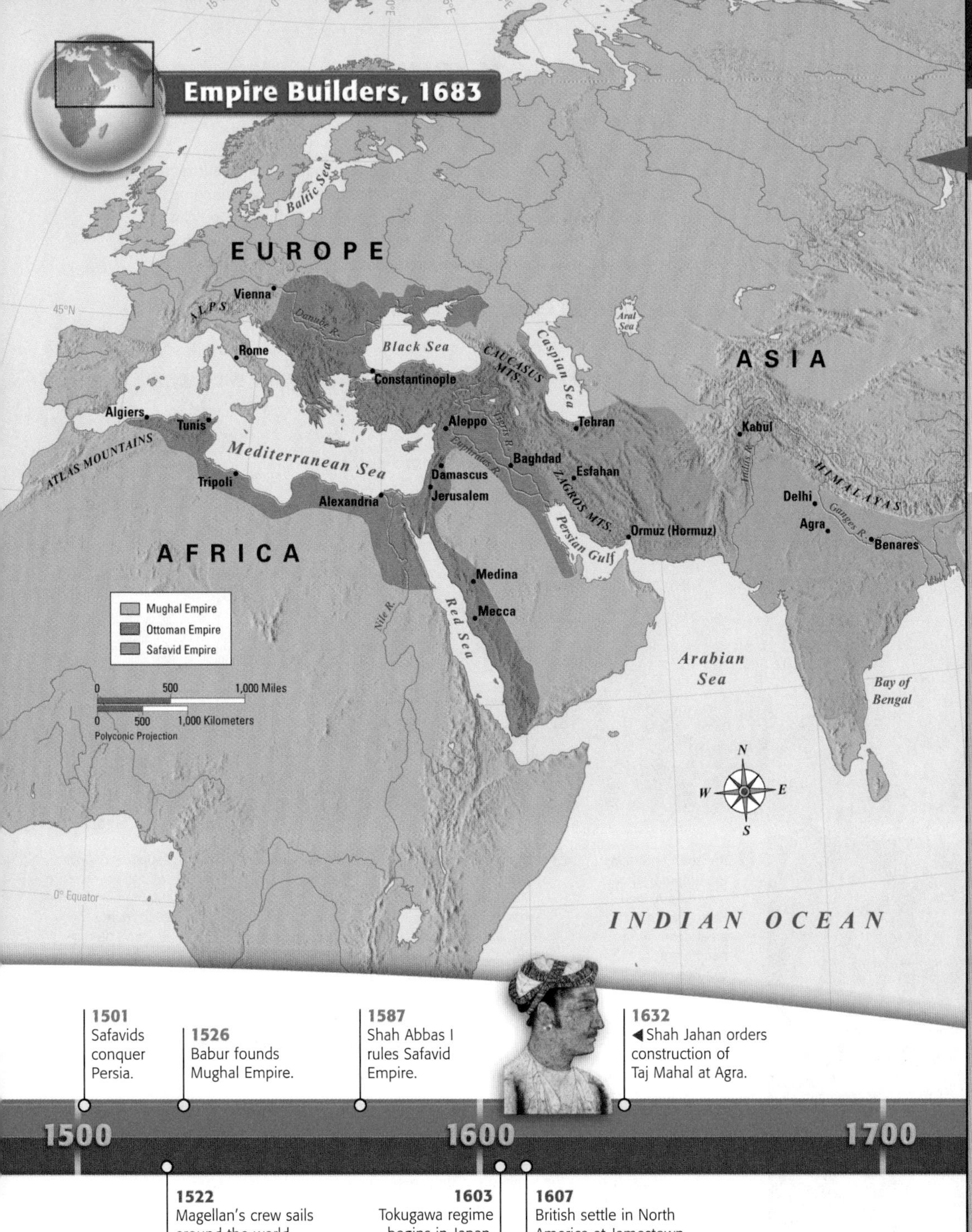

CHAPTER 2

History from Visuals

Interpreting the Map

Have students compare the geography of the three empires. Which included the most coastline? *(Ottoman)* Which was most mountainous? *(Safavid)*

Discuss which empire's geographic features might have made it easier to rule. *(Possible Answer: The compactness of the Safavid Empire might have made ruling easier.)*

RECOMMENDED RESOURCES

Books for the Teacher

Mansel, Philip. ***Constantinople: City of the World's Desire, 1453–1924.*** New York: St. Martin's, 1996.

Inalcik, Halil. ***An Economic and Social History of the Ottoman Empire: Vol. 1, 1300–1600.*** Repr. ed. Cambridge, England: Cambridge UP, 1997. Covers the Ottoman Empire from an economic perspective.

Books for the Student

Ghose, Sudhin N. ***Folk Tales and Fairy Stories from India.*** Mineola, NY: Dover, 1996.

Rothfarb, Ed. ***In the Land of the Taj Mahal: The World of the Fabled Mughals.*** New York: Henry Holt, 1998. Focuses on the Mughals' triumphs in art, architecture, and literature.

Videos

The Siege of Constantinople. VHS. Library Video Company, 1995. 800-843-3620. Explores the invasion of Constantinople through dramatic re-creations, on-location footage, and computer graphics.

The Taj Mahal: A Love Story. VHS and DVD. Films for the Humanities & Sciences, 1986. Studies Mughal history during the reign of Shah Jahan, which many experts believe marked the culture's peak of refinement.

Interact *with* History

Objectives

- Understand the diversity among people and cultures of the Muslim empires.
- Consider the role of tolerance in ruling an empire.

EXAMINING *the* ISSUES

Possible Answers

- They might rebel against rule by their new conquerors, reject new religious ideas or customs, or have destabilizing conflicts within their community. Some might support a rival ruler.
- A conqueror might integrate new people by offering jobs and positions in the military. A ruler could also encourage respect for the conquered culture and cross-cultural marriage.

Discussion

Ask students to recall how earlier empires treated conquered peoples. *(The Romans and the Persians often treated them with respect. The Assyrians were harsh rulers.)*

INTEGRATED TECHNOLOGY

Interactive This image is available in an interactive format on the eEdition. Students can examine parts of the painting in greater detail and will have the opportunity to learn about the painting's significance.

Interact *with* History

How do you govern a diverse empire?

Your father is a Safavid shah, the ruler of a growing empire. With a well-trained army and modern weapons, he has easily conquered most of the surrounding area. Because you are likely to become the next ruler, you are learning all you can about how to rule. You wonder what is best for the empire. Should conquered people be given the freedom to practice a religion that is different from your own and to follow their own traditions? Or would it be better to try and force them to accept your beliefs and way of life—or even to enslave them?

INTERACTIVE

1. The shah entertains the emperor of a neighboring land. Both lands have great diversity of people and cultures.
2. Distinctive headgear marks the status of military leaders and scholars gathered from all parts of the empire.
3. Clothing, music, dancing, and food reflect the customs of several groups within the empire.
4. People in the court, from the servants to the members of the court, mirror the empire's diversity.

EXAMINING *the* ISSUES

- **What problems might conquered people present for their conqueror?**
- **In what ways might a conqueror integrate conquered people into the society?**

As a class, discuss the ways other empires—such as those of Rome, Assyria, and Persia—treated their conquered peoples. As you read about the three empires featured in this chapter, notice how the rulers dealt with empires made up of different cultures.

WHY STUDY THE MUSLIM WORLD?

- The great leaders of these empires, such as Suleyman I, Shah Abbas, and Akbar, are often viewed as heroic figures whose examples of wisdom and tolerance remain inspiring.
- The religious patterns of the region—Sunni in Turkey, Shi'a in Iran, and a mix of Muslims and Hindus in India—continue today. These patterns help explain ongoing tensions.
- The success of these empires' religious diversity and cultural blending are regarded as models for countries aspiring to greater power and influence.
- The history of this period provides a backdrop to territorial divisions that occurred during the 20th century.
- Works of art created in these empires, such as the Mosque of Suleyman, Persian miniature paintings, and the Taj Mahal, are still appreciated for their beauty.
- Islam is a prominent religion in parts of Europe as a result of the Ottoman conquest of Istanbul and the empire's expansion in southeastern Europe.
- Hindi and Urdu evolved under the Mughals and are still among the most widely spoken languages in south-central Asia.

Hagia Sophia, Istanbul, Turkey

Wall mural, Ladakh, India

1 The Ottomans Build a Vast Empire

MAIN IDEA	WHY IT MATTERS NOW	TERMS & NAMES
EMPIRE BUILDING The Ottomans established a Muslim empire that combined many cultures and lasted for more than 600 years.	Many modern societies, from Algeria to Turkey, had their origins under Ottoman rule.	• ghazi • Ottoman • sultan • Timur the Lame • Mehmed II • Suleyman the Lawgiver • *devshirme* • janissary

SETTING THE STAGE By 1300, the Byzantine Empire was declining, and the Mongols had destroyed the Turkish Seljuk kingdom of Rum. Anatolia was inhabited mostly by the descendants of nomadic Turks. These militaristic people had a long history of invading other countries. Loyal to their own groups, they were not united by a strong central power. A small Turkish state occupied land between the Byzantine Empire and that of the Muslims. From this place, a strong leader would emerge to unite the Turks into what eventually would become an immense empire stretching across three continents.

Turks Move into Byzantium

Many Anatolian Turks saw themselves as **ghazis** (GAH•zees), or warriors for Islam. They formed military societies under the leadership of an emir, a chief commander, and followed a strict Islamic code of conduct. They raided the territories of the "infidels," or people who didn't believe in Islam. These infidels lived on the frontiers of the Byzantine Empire.

Osman Establishes a State The most successful ghazi was Osman. People in the West called him Othman and named his followers **Ottomans**. Osman built a small Muslim state in Anatolia between 1300 and 1326. His successors expanded it by buying land, forming alliances with some emirs, and conquering others.

The Ottomans' military success was largely based on the use of gunpowder. They replaced their archers on horseback with musket-carrying foot soldiers. They also were among the first people to use cannons as weapons of attack. Even heavily walled cities fell to an all-out attack by the Turks.

The second Ottoman leader, Orkhan I, was Osman's son. He felt strong enough to declare himself **sultan**, meaning "overlord" or "one with power." And in 1361, the Ottomans captured Adrianople (ay•dree•uh•NOH•puhl), the second most important city in the Byzantine Empire. A new Turkish empire was on the rise.

The Ottomans acted kindly toward the people they conquered. They ruled through local officials appointed by the sultan and often improved the lives of the peasants. Most Muslims were required to serve in Turkish armies but did not have to pay a personal tax to the state. Non-Muslims did not have to serve in the army but had to pay the tax.

CALIFORNIA STANDARDS

10.10.1 Understand the challenges in the regions, including their geopolitical, cultural, military, and economic significance and the international relationships in which they are involved.

REP 1 Students distinguish valid arguments from fallacious arguments in historical interpretations.

REP 2 Students identify bias and prejudice in historical interpretations.

REP 3 Students evaluate major debates among historians concerning alternative interpretations of the past, including an analysis of authors' use of evidence and the distinctions between sound generalizations and misleading oversimplifications.

REP 4 Students construct and test hypotheses; collect, evaluate, and employ information from multiple primary and secondary sources; and apply it in oral and written presentations.

TAKING NOTES

Comparing List the main rulers of the Ottoman Empire and their successes.

Rulers	Successes

LESSON PLAN

OBJECTIVES

- Describe the Ottoman Empire's origins.
- Trace the expansion of Ottoman power.
- Identify achievements under Suleyman the Lawgiver.
- Explain the empire's slow decline.

1 FOCUS & MOTIVATE

Discuss why leaders today rarely get nicknames such as "the Wise." *(use of family names reduces need for distinguishing labels)*

2 INSTRUCT

Turks Move into Byzantium
10.10.1

Critical Thinking

- How did new technology help the Ottomans? *(They used muskets and cannons in their conquests.)*
- Do you think the actions of Timur the Lame were justified? Why? *(Yes—He opposed imperialism. No—He destroyed Baghdad.)*

CALIFORNIA RESOURCES

California Reading Toolkit, p. L13
California Modified Lesson Plans for English Learners, p. 21
California Daily Standards Practice Transparencies, TT5
California Standards Enrichment Workbook, pp. 107–108
California Standards Planner and Lesson Plans, p. L17
California Online Test Practice
California Test Generator CD-ROM
California Easy Planner CD-ROM
California eEdition CD-ROM

SECTION 1 PROGRAM RESOURCES

ALL STUDENTS

In-Depth Resources: Unit 1
- Guided Reading, p. 45
- Skillbuilder Practice: Categorizing, p. 44
- History Makers: Suleyman, p. 54

Formal Assessment
- Section Quiz, p. 40

ENGLISH LEARNERS

In-Depth Resources in Spanish
- Guided Reading, p. 25
- Skillbuilder Practice: Categorizing, p. 28

Reading Study Guide (Spanish), p. 25
Reading Study Guide Audio CD (Spanish)

STRUGGLING READERS

In-Depth Resources: Unit 1
- Guided Reading, p. 40
- Building Vocabulary, p. 43
- Skillbuilder Practice: Categorizing, p. 44
- Reteaching Activity, p. 57

Reading Study Guide, p. 25
Reading Study Guide Audio CD

GIFTED AND TALENTED STUDENTS

In-Depth Resources: Unit 1
- Primary Source: *Suleyman the Magnificent*, p. 47
- Literature: from *The Bride of Suleiman,* p. 51

INTEGRATED TECHNOLOGY

eEdition CD-ROM
Voices from the Past Audio CD
Geography Transparencies
- GT18 The Fall of Constantinople, 1453

World Art and Cultures Transparencies
- AT39 Military Campaigns of Suleyman

Powerful Sultans Spur Dramatic Expansion

10.10.1

Critical Thinking

- How did the conquest of Constantinople help unite the empire? *(made trade between territories in Asia and the Balkans easier)*
- Why were the conquests of Selim the Grim culturally significant? *(included religious centers, Mecca and Medina, and an intellectual center, Cairo)*

History from Visuals

Interpreting the Map

What is the status of Crete and Cyprus? *(not part of the empire)* Does this indicate that the Ottoman Empire was a land-based or a sea-based empire? *(land-based: a sea-based empire would have conquered the islands)* Considering events in England, Spain, and Portugal, why is this important? *(Their sea-based empires were colonizing the world.)*

Extension Compare the Ottoman and Byzantine empires. *(They faced similar geographic and political barriers.)*

SKILLBUILDER Answers

1. **Location** Mediterranean Sea, Red Sea, Black Sea, Adriatic Sea, Persian Gulf
2. **Movement** between 1521 and 1566

INTEGRATED TECHNOLOGY

Interactive This map is available in an interactive format on the eEdition.

Timur the Lame Halts Expansion The rise of the Ottoman Empire was briefly interrupted in the early 1400s by a rebellious warrior and conqueror from Samarkand in Central Asia. Permanently injured by an arrow in the leg, he was called Timur-i-Lang, or **Timur the Lame**. Europeans called him Tamerlane. Timur burned the powerful city of Baghdad in present-day Iraq to the ground. He crushed the Ottoman forces at the Battle of Ankara in 1402. This defeat halted the expansion of their empire.

Powerful Sultans Spur Dramatic Expansion

Soon Timur turned his attention to China. When he did, war broke out among the four sons of the Ottoman sultan. Mehmed I defeated his brothers and took the throne. His son, Murad II, defeated the Venetians, invaded Hungary, and overcame an army of Italian crusaders in the Balkans. He was the first of four powerful sultans who led the expansion of the Ottoman Empire through 1566.

Mehmed II Conquers Constantinople Murad's son **Mehmed II**, or Mehmed the Conqueror, achieved the most dramatic feat in Ottoman history. By the time Mehmed took power in 1451, the ancient city of Constantinople had shrunk from a population of a million to a mere 50,000. Although it controlled no territory outside its walls, it still dominated the Bosporus Strait. Controlling this waterway meant that it could choke off traffic between the Ottomans' territories in Asia and in the Balkans.

Mehmed II decided to face this situation head-on. "Give me Constantinople!" he thundered, shortly after taking power at age 21. Then, in 1453, he launched his attack.

GEOGRAPHY SKILLBUILDER: Interpreting Maps
1. **Location** *To which waterways did the Ottoman Empire have access?*
2. **Movement** *In which time period did the Ottoman Empire gain the most land?*

74 Chapter 2

DIFFERENTIATING INSTRUCTION: ENGLISH LEARNERS

Taking Notes and Understanding Challenging Vocabulary

Class Time 30 minutes

Task Taking notes using a graphic organizer; understanding vocabulary words in the main text

Purpose To improve understanding of content

Instructions Provide each student with a copy of the Reading Study Guide for this section, in English or Spanish, as appropriate. Then divide students into pairs. Have each pair use the graphic organizer and the questions in the study guide to take notes on the Ottoman Empire.

As students take notes, have them keep a list of unfamiliar words that appear in the text. As a class, review the lists. Have students look up words in a dictionary or glossary. Discuss the definitions of each and the context in which each is used. Students may want to draw pictures or symbols to help them remember the words.

- *Rebellious* is related to *belligerent;* both refer to warlike behavior.
- *Head-on* means to confront directly.
- A *tactic* is a way of completing a goal.
- *Thundered* means spoke loudly, similar to the noise associated with lightning.

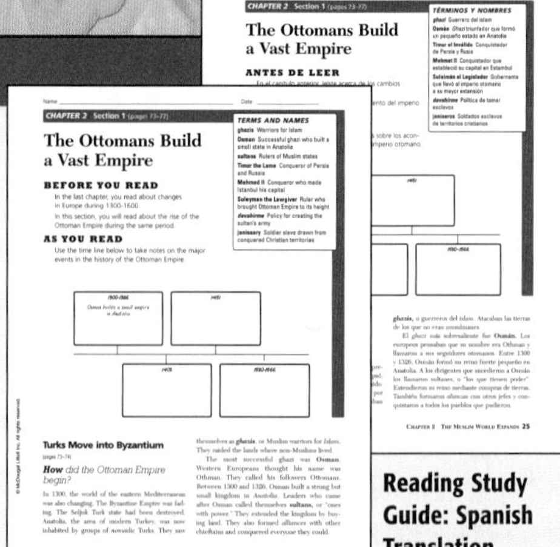

Reading Study Guide

Reading Study Guide: Spanish Translation

Analyzing Primary Sources

The Conquest of Constantinople

Kritovoulos, a Greek who served in the Ottoman administration, recorded the following about the Ottoman takeover of Constantinople. The second source, the French miniature at the right, shows a view of the siege of Constantinople.

PRIMARY SOURCE

After this the Sultan entered the City and looked about to see its great size, its situation, its grandeur and beauty, its teeming population, its loveliness, and the costliness of its churches and public buildings and of the private houses and community houses and those of the officials. . . .

When he saw what a large number had been killed and the ruin of the buildings, and the wholesale ruin and destruction of the City, he was filled with compassion and repented not a little at the destruction and plundering. Tears fell from his eyes as he groaned deeply and passionately: "What a city we have given over to plunder and destruction."

KRITOVOULOS, *History of Mehmed the Conqueror*

DOCUMENT-BASED QUESTIONS

1. **Comparing and Contrasting** *In what details do the two sources agree? disagree?*
2. **Making Inferences** *Why do you think the sultan wept over the destruction?*

Mehmed's Turkish forces began firing on the city walls with mighty cannons. One of these was a 26-foot gun that fired 1,200-pound boulders. A chain across the Golden Horn between the Bosporus Strait and the Sea of Marmara kept the Turkish fleet out of the city's harbor. Finally, one night Mehmed's army tried a daring tactic. They dragged 70 ships over a hill on greased runners from the Bosporus to the harbor. Now Mehmed's army was attacking Constantinople from two sides. The city held out for over seven weeks, but the Turks finally found a break in the wall and entered the city.

Mehmed the Conqueror, as he was now called, proved to be an able ruler as well as a magnificent warrior. He opened Constantinople to new citizens of many religions and backgrounds. Jews, Christians, and Muslims, Turks and non-Turks all flowed in. They helped rebuild the city, which was now called Istanbul. (A)

MAIN IDEA
Analyzing Motives
(A) Why was taking Constantinople so important to Mehmed II?
A. Answer The city controlled many waterways that kept the Ottoman Empire divided.

Ottomans Take Islam's Holy Cities Mehmed's grandson, Selim the Grim, came to power in 1512. He was an effective sultan and a great general. In 1514, he defeated the Safavids (suh•FAH•vihdz) of Persia at the Battle of Chaldiran. Then he swept south through Syria and Palestine and into North Africa. At the same time that Cortez was toppling the Aztec Empire in the Americas, Selim captured Mecca and Medina, the holiest cities of Islam. Finally he took Cairo, the intellectual center of the Muslim world. The once-great civilization of Egypt had become just another province in the growing Ottoman Empire.

Analyzing Primary Sources

The Conquest of Constantinople

Ask students to compare the comments by Kritovoulos with the information in the text on page 74 about Constantinople in 1451. How do they differ? *(Kritovoulos discusses the size and grandeur of the city. The text on page 74 explains that the city's population was quite small.)*

Answers to Document-Based Questions

1. **Comparing and Contrasting** Agree—Both depict a grand city filled with churches and other public buildings. Disagree—The painting does not show the destruction of the city.
2. **Making Inferences** *Possible Answer:* He was sad to see the loss of wealth and beauty, particularly when it might bring trade and prestige to the Ottoman Empire.

Geography Transparencies

- GT18 The Fall of Constantinople, 1453

More About . . .

Selim the Grim

Like many tyrants of his age, Selim was fond of literature and the arts and wrote poetry in three languages. But his troops knew him as *Yavuz*—"the Inflexible." He went through officers called viziers so quickly that the phrase "May you become the Sultan's vizier" came to be understood as a curse.

DIFFERENTIATING INSTRUCTION: STRUGGLING READERS

Reporting on the Conquest of Constantinople

Class Time 30 minutes

Task Preparing a newscast on the Ottoman capture of Constantinople

Purpose To understand the drama and significance of this historical event

Instructions Divide the class into three groups. Each group should plan and present a newscast on the Ottoman conquest of Constantinople. Students should use their textbooks as sources of facts, details, and quotations. Newscasts might include:

- a summary of the week's events
- updates on breaking developments
- analysis of military strategy
- reports on reactions from Mecca, Baghdad, or other cities
- stories on human-interest topics
- interviews with people on the scene
- commentaries expressing opinions on the situation
- biographies of key leaders

After each group presents its newscast, have students compare the newscasts for depth, interest, and balance.

History Makers

Suleyman the Lawgiver

How well does the United States government follow the policies of Suleyman? *(It follows most, except it often does not balance its budget.)*

Suleyman's income of $10 million a year far outstripped that of his European contemporaries.

World Art and Cultures Transparencies

- AT39 Military Campaigns of Suleyman the Magnificent: 1529 Siege of Vienna

In-Depth Resources: Unit 1

- History Makers: Suleyman, p. 76

Suleyman the Lawgiver

10.10.1

Critical Thinking

- What does the third paragraph under this headline imply about the influence of the Ottoman Empire in northern Africa? *(Besides controlling the coastal cities, they had influence inland.)*
- How did the *devshirme* system strengthen the Ottoman Empire? *(by providing an efficient bureaucracy and by including Christians)*
- What can you infer about the relationship of religion to other activities from the description of the Mosque of Suleyman? *(was connected to education and health care)*

History Makers

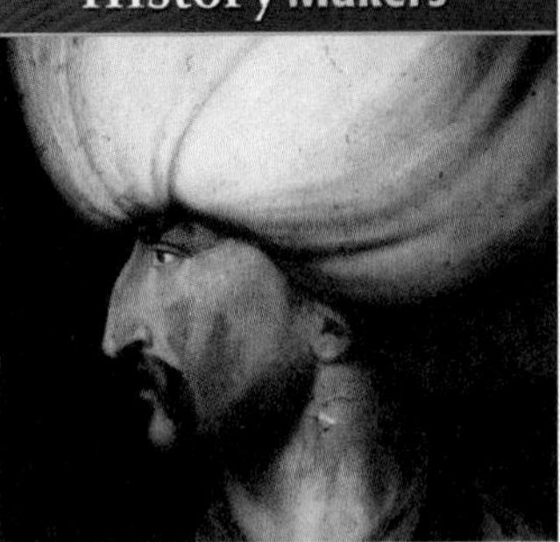

Suleyman the Lawgiver
1494–1566

In the halls of the U.S. Congress are images of some of the greatest lawgivers of all time. Included in that group are such persons as Thomas Jefferson, Moses, and Suleyman.

Suleyman's law code prescribed penalties for various criminal acts and for bureaucratic and financial corruption. He also sought to reduce bribes, did not allow imprisonment without a trial, and rejected promotions that were not based on merit. He also introduced the idea of a balanced budget for governments.

INTEGRATED TECHNOLOGY

RESEARCH LINKS For more on Suleyman, go to **classzone.com**

Suleyman the Lawgiver

The Ottoman Empire didn't reach its peak size and grandeur until the reign of Selim's son, Suleyman I (SOO•lay•mahn). Suleyman came to the throne in 1520 and ruled for 46 years. His own people called him **Suleyman the Lawgiver**. He was known in the West, though, as Suleyman the Magnificent. This title was a tribute to the splendor of his court and to his cultural achievements.

The Empire Reaches Its Limits Suleyman was a superb military leader. He conquered the important European city of Belgrade in 1521. The next year, Turkish forces captured the island of Rhodes in the Mediterranean and now dominated the whole eastern Mediterranean.

Applying their immense naval power, the Ottomans captured Tripoli on the coast of North Africa. They continued conquering peoples along the North African coastline. Although the Ottomans occupied only the coastal cities of North Africa, they managed to control trade routes to the interior of the continent.

In 1526, Suleyman advanced into Hungary and Austria, throwing central Europe into a panic. Suleyman's armies then pushed to the outskirts of Vienna, Austria. Reigning from Istanbul, Suleyman had waged war with central Europeans, North Africans, and Central Asians. He had become the most powerful monarch on earth. Only Charles V, head of the Hapsburg Empire in Europe, came close to rivaling his power.

Highly Structured Social Organization Binding the Ottoman Empire together in a workable social structure was Suleyman's crowning achievement. The massive empire required an efficient government structure and social organization. Suleyman created a law code to handle both criminal and civil actions. He also simplified the system of taxation and reduced government bureaucracy. These changes bettered the daily life of almost every citizen and helped earn Suleyman the title of Lawgiver.

The sultan's 20,000 personal slaves staffed the palace bureaucracy. The slaves were acquired as part of a policy called *devshirme* (dehv•SHEER•meh). Under the ***devshirme*** system, the sultan's army drafted boys from the peoples of conquered Christian territories. The army educated them, converted them to Islam, and trained them as soldiers. An elite force of 30,000 soldiers known as **janissaries** was trained to be loyal to the sultan only. Their superb discipline made them the heart of the Ottoman war machine. In fact, Christian families sometimes bribed officials to take their children into the sultan's service, because the brightest ones could rise to high government posts or military positions. B

As a Muslim, Suleyman was required to follow Islamic law. In accordance with Islamic law, the Ottomans granted freedom of worship to other religious communities, particularly to Christians and Jews. They treated these communities as *millets,* or nations. They allowed each *millet* to follow its own religious laws and practices. The head of the *millets* reported to the sultan and his staff. This system kept conflict among people of the various religions to a minimum.

B. Answer The sultan had a loyal force that was highly trained and able to run and defend his empire.

MAIN IDEA

Making Inferences

B What were the advantages of the *devshirme* system to the sultan?

SKILLBUILDER PRACTICE: CATEGORIZING

Organizing Information About Suleyman

Class Time 45 minutes

Task Grouping facts about Suleyman's accomplishments

Purpose To improve skill at organizing information

Instructions Explain that grouping information into categories is a valuable skill. Historians categorize data so they can identify patterns more easily.

Ask students to study the table of contents and determine how this textbook organizes information into chapters. *(It uses a mixture of chronology and geography.)* Discuss how material would be covered if the book were organized only by chronology. *(Organized only by chronology, each chapter would cover the entire world for one time period.)*

As a class, make a list of Suleyman's accomplishments. Then divide students into small groups. Have each group organize the accomplishments into categories. Compare the categories the groups chose and which facts they placed in each. *(Possible Answer: Political—Law code, balanced budgets. Military—Controlled eastern Mediterranean and North Africa, invaded Europe, was most powerful ruler of his time. Culture—Religious tolerance; studied many subjects; art, literature, and architecture flourished under his rule.)*

For more practice, have students complete the Skillbuilder Practice activity for this section, found in In Depth Resources: Unit 1.

C. Possible Answer flowering of architecture, art, and literature

MAIN IDEA

Comparing

Ⓒ Which cultural achievements of Suleyman's reign were similar to the European Renaissance?

Cultural Flowering Suleyman had broad interests, which contributed to the cultural achievements of the empire. He found time to study poetry, history, geography, astronomy, mathematics, and architecture. He employed one of the world's finest architects, Sinan, who was probably from Albania. Sinan's masterpiece, the Mosque of Suleyman, is an immense complex topped with domes and half domes. It includes four schools, a library, a bath, and a hospital.

Art and literature also flourished under Suleyman's rule. This creative period was similar to the European Renaissance. Painters and poets looked to Persia and Arabia for models. The works that they produced used these foreign influences to express original Ottoman ideas in the Turkish style. They are excellent examples of cultural blending. Ⓒ

▲ Sinan's Mosque of Suleyman in Istanbul is the largest mosque in the Ottoman Empire.

The Empire Declines Slowly

Despite Suleyman's magnificent social and cultural achievements, the Ottoman Empire was losing ground. Suleyman killed his ablest son and drove another into exile. His third son, the incompetent Selim II, inherited the throne.

Suleyman set the pattern for later sultans to gain and hold power. It became customary for each new sultan to have his brothers strangled. The sultan would then keep his sons prisoner in the harem, cutting them off from education or contact with the world. This practice produced a long line of weak sultans who eventually brought ruin on the empire. However, the Ottoman Empire continued to influence the world into the early 20th century.

SECTION 1 ASSESSMENT

TERMS & NAMES 1. For each term or name, write a sentence explaining its significance.

• ghazi • Ottoman • sultan • Timur the Lame • Mehmed II • Suleyman the Lawgiver • *devshirme* • janissary

USING YOUR NOTES

2. Which were more significant to the Ottoman Empire, the accomplishments of Mehmed II or those of Selim the Grim? Explain. (10.1.1)

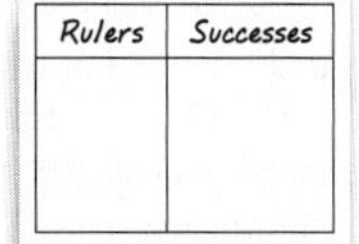

Rulers	Successes

MAIN IDEAS

3. By what means did the early Ottomans expand their empire? (10.1.1)
4. Why was Suleyman called the Lawgiver? (10.1.1)
5. How powerful was the Ottoman Empire compared to other empires of the time? (10.1.1)

CRITICAL THINKING & WRITING

6. **EVALUATING DECISIONS** Do you think that the Ottomans were wise in staffing their military and government with slaves? Explain. (10.1.1)
7. **EVALUATING COURSES OF ACTION** How did Suleyman's selection of a successor eventually spell disaster for the Ottoman Empire? (10.1.1)
8. **ANALYZING MOTIVES** Do you think Suleyman's religious tolerance helped or hurt the Ottoman Empire? (10.1.1)
9. **WRITING ACTIVITY** EMPIRE BUILDING Using the description of Mehmed II's forces taking Constantinople, write a **newspaper article** describing the action. (Writing 2.6.a)

CONNECT TO TODAY CREATING A TIME LINE

Create a **time line** showing events in the decline of the Ottoman Empire and the creation of the modern nation of Turkey. (REP 4)

The Empire Declines Slowly
10.10.1

Critical Thinking

- What methods could the Ottomans have used to produce better rulers? *(Possible Answers: hold elections, have oldest child inherit the throne, use a lottery)*
- Do you think Suleyman was a wise ruler? *(Yes—He led expansion and cultural flowering. No—He set a pattern for succession that destroyed the empire.)*
- In general, what factor caused the decline of the Ottoman Empire? *(weak leadership)*

In-Depth Resources: Unit 1

- Primary Source: Suleyman the Magnificent, p. 47
- Literature Selection: from *The Bride of Suleiman,* p. 51

❸ ASSESS

SECTION 1 ASSESSMENT

Have students work in pairs to answer the questions.

Formal Assessment

- Section Quiz, p. 40

❹ RETEACH

Have pairs of students create charts that answer the questions *who, what, where, when, why,* and *how* about the Ottoman Empire.

In-Depth Resources: Unit 1

- Reteaching Activity, p. 57

ANSWERS

1. ghazi, p. 73 • Ottoman, p. 73 • sultan, p. 73 • Timur the Lame, p. 74 • Mehmed II, p. 74 • Suleyman the Lawgiver, p. 76 • *devshirme*, p. 76 • janissary, p. 76
2. **Sample Answer:** Osman—Established Muslim state in Anatolia. Orkhan I—Captured Adrianople. Mehmed I—Defeated his brothers. Murad II—Invaded Europe. Mehmed II more important because he conquered Constantinople. Selim the Grim—Captured Mecca, Medina, and Cairo. Suleyman I—Was most powerful ruler of his time.
3. buying land, forming alliances, using new technology
4. He created a law code, simplified taxation, and reduced bureaucracy.
5. It was the most powerful.
6. Yes—The slaves received excellent education and had opportunities, so they were loyal. No—They would be alert for opportunities to rebel or escape.
7. set a pattern of killing able rulers
8. Helped—It kept people content. Hurt—It did not promote unity.
9. **Rubric** Newspaper articles should
   - present the basic facts clearly.
   - include significant details.
   - use a newspaper style.

CONNECT TO TODAY

Rubric Time lines should
- list historically significant events.
- cover the period 1566 to 1923.
- use parallel language for all entries.

LESSON PLAN

OBJECTIVES

- Explain how cultural blending results in new cultures.
- Summarize the rise of the Safavid Empire.

1 FOCUS & MOTIVATE

Discuss current examples of cultural blending that students see in fashion, food, and other parts of their lives. Ask whether changes in transportation and communication have accelerated the process of cultural blending.

2 INSTRUCT

Patterns of Cultural Blending

10.10.1

Critical Thinking

- What trait of a society can prevent cultural blending? *(resistance to new ideas)*
- What results of cultural blending do you see in the United States today? *(Possible Answers: interracial or interfaith marriages, words such as* judo *and* salsa*)*

CALIFORNIA RESOURCES

California Reading Toolkit, p. L14
California Modified Lesson Plans for English Learners, p. 23
California Daily Standards Practice Transparencies, TT6
California Standards Enrichment Workbook, pp. 101–102, 107–108
California Standards Planner and Lesson Plans, p. L19
California Online Test Practice
California Test Generator CD-ROM
California Easy Planner CD-ROM
California eEdition CD-ROM

2

Cultural Blending

CASE STUDY: The Safavid Empire

MAIN IDEA	WHY IT MATTERS NOW	TERMS & NAMES
CULTURAL INTERACTION The Safavid Empire produced a rich and complex blended culture in Persia.	Modern Iran, which plays a key role in global politics, descended from the culturally diverse Safavid Empire.	• Safavid • Isma'il • shah • Shah Abbas • Esfahan

CALIFORNIA STANDARDS

10.9.6 Understand how the forces of nationalism developed in the Middle East, how the Holocaust affected world opinion regarding the need for a Jewish state, and the significance and effects of the location and establishment of Israel on world affairs.

10.10.1 Understand the challenges in the regions, including their geopolitical, cultural, military, and economic significance and the international relationships in which they are involved.

SETTING THE STAGE Throughout the course of world history, cultures have interacted with each other. Often such interaction has resulted in the mixing of different cultures in new and exciting ways. This process is referred to as cultural blending. The **Safavid** Empire, a Shi'ite Muslim dynasty that ruled in Persia between the 16th and 18th centuries, provides a striking example of how interaction among peoples can produce a blending of cultures. This culturally diverse empire drew from the traditions of Persians, Ottomans, and Arabs.

TAKING NOTES

Drawing Conclusions Identify examples of cultural blending in the Safavid Empire.

Cultural Blending

Patterns of Cultural Blending

Each time a culture interacts with another, it is exposed to ideas, technologies, foods, and ways of life not exactly like its own. Continental crossroads, trade routes, ports, and the borders of countries are places where cultural blending commonly begins. Societies that are able to benefit from cultural blending are those that are open to new ways and are willing to adapt and change. The blended ideas spread throughout the culture and produce a new pattern of behavior. Cultural blending has several basic causes.

Causes of Cultural Blending Cultural change is most often prompted by one or more of the following four activities:

- migration
- pursuit of religious freedom or conversion
- trade
- conquest

The blending that contributed to the culture of the Ottomans, which you just read about in Section 1, depended on all of these activities. Surrounded by the peoples of Christian Byzantium, the Turks were motivated to win both territory for their empire and converts to their Muslim religion. The Ottoman Empire's location on a major trading route created many opportunities for contact with different cultures. Suleyman's interest in learning and culture prompted him to bring the best foreign artists and scholars to his court. They brought new ideas about art, literature, and learning to the empire.

Results of Cultural Blending Cultural blending may lead to changes in language, religion, styles of government, the use of technology, and military tactics.

SECTION 2 PROGRAM RESOURCES

ALL STUDENTS

In-Depth Resources: Unit 1
- Guided Reading, p. 41

Formal Assessment
- Section Quiz, p. 41

ENGLISH LEARNERS

In-Depth Resources in Spanish
- Guided Reading, p. 26

Reading Study Guide (Spanish), p. 27
Reading Study Guide Audio CD (Spanish)

STRUGGLING READERS

In-Depth Resources: Unit 1
- Guided Reading, p. 41
- Building Vocabulary, p. 43
- Reteaching Activity, p. 58

Reading Study Guide, p. 27
Reading Study Guide Audio CD

GIFTED AND TALENTED STUDENTS

Electronic Library of Primary Sources
- "Report on Persia, Persians, and 'Abbas I"

INTEGRATED TECHNOLOGY

eEdition CD-ROM
Power Presentations CD-ROM
Electronic Library of Primary Sources
- "Report on Persia, Persians, and 'Abbas I"

classzone.com

Cultural Blending			
Location	**Interacting Cultures**	**Reason for Interaction**	**Some Results of Interaction**
India—1000 B.C.	Aryan and Dravidian Indian Arab, African, Indian	Migration	Vedic culture, forerunner of Hinduism
East Africa—A.D. 700	Islamic, Christian	Trade, religious conversion	New trade language, Swahili
Russia—A.D. 1000	Christian and Slavic	Religious conversion	Eastern Christianity, Russian identity
Mexico—A.D. 1500	Spanish and Aztec	Conquest	Mestizo culture, Mexican Catholicism
United States—A.D. 1900	European, Asian, Caribbean	Migration, religious freedom	Cultural diversity

SKILLBUILDER: Interpreting Charts
1. **Determining Main Ideas** *What are the reasons for interaction in the Americas?*
2. **Hypothesizing** *What are some aspects of cultural diversity?*

These changes often reflect unique aspects of several cultures. For example:

- **Language** Sometimes the written characters of one language are used in another, as in the case of written Chinese characters used in the Japanese language. In the Safavid Empire, the language spoken was Persian. But after the area converted to Islam, a significant number of Arabic words appeared in the Persian language.
- **Religion and ethical systems** Buddhism spread throughout Asia. Yet the Buddhism practiced by Tibetans is different from Japanese Zen Buddhism.
- **Styles of government** The concept of a democratic government spread to many areas of the globe. Although the basic principles are similar, it is not practiced exactly the same way in each country.
- **Racial or ethnic blending** One example is the mestizo, people of mixed European and Indian ancestry who live in Mexico.
- **Arts and architecture** Cultural styles may be incorporated or adapted into art or architecture. For example, Chinese artistic elements are found in Safavid Empire tiles and carpets as well as in European paintings.

The chart above shows other examples of cultural blending that have occurred over time in various areas of the world. (A)

A. Possible Answer language, religious systems, or government, because they are a direct part of everyday life

MAIN IDEA

Recognizing Effects

(A) Which of the effects of cultural blending do you think is the most significant? Explain.

CASE STUDY: The Safavid Empire

The Safavids Build an Empire

Conquest and ongoing cultural interaction fueled the development of the Safavid Empire. Originally, the Safavids were members of an Islamic religious brotherhood named after their founder, Safi al-Din. In the 15th century, the Safavids aligned themselves with the Shi'a branch of Islam.

The Safavids were also squeezed geographically between the Ottomans and Uzbek tribespeople and the Mughal Empire. (See the map on page 80.) To protect themselves from these potential enemies, the Safavids concentrated on building a powerful army.

Isma'il Conquers Persia The Safavid military became a force to reckon with. In 1499, a 12-year-old named **Isma'il** (ihs•MAH•eel) began to seize most of what is now Iran. Two years later he completed the task.

▼ Grandson of Isma'il, Shah Abbas led the Safavid Empire during its Golden Age.

History from Visuals

Interpreting the Chart

Make sure that students understand that they should read across each row of the chart to learn about cultural blending in each of the five regions listed. Where on this chart would students insert a row for the Ottoman Empire? *(just below the entry on Mexico)*

Extension Have students discuss how they would fill in a row of the chart for the Ottoman Empire.

SKILLBUILDER Answers
1. **Determining Main Ideas** conquest, migration, religious freedom
2. **Hypothesizing** intermixing of customs, religions, languages, races

The Safavids Build an Empire
10.10.1

Critical Thinking

- How did religion both unite and divide the Safavids and the Ottomans? *(Both were Muslim cultures. Safavids were Shi'a; Ottomans were Sunni.)*
- How would you compare the policies on religious toleration of Isma'il and Suleyman? *(Isma'il became a tyrant; Suleyman practiced toleration.)*
- How did the motive for the development of a strong military change between the time of the early Safavids and of Tahmasp? *(It changed from defense to conquest.)*

DIFFERENTIATING INSTRUCTION: ENGLISH LEARNERS

Writing Historical Dialogues

Class Time 45 minutes

Task Writing imaginary conversations between foreigners and officials of the Safavid Empire

Purpose To understand the culture of the Safavids and their relationship with other cultures

Instructions Divide the class into pairs, with one student in each pair taking the role of a Safavid official and the other student representing the Ottoman Empire, Spain, England, or another country. Each pair should discuss an issue that leaders might have addressed in the 1500s, such as:

- the rivalry between the Ottomans and the Safavids
- geographic and political pressures on the Safavid Empire
- the relationship between Christians and Muslims
- the news about the voyage of Christopher Columbus

Students should identify the title of the individual they represent and how that individual would have felt about the topic selected. Have students use their textbooks to find facts and details. Each pair should write an outline of their dialogue and practice it before presenting it to the class.

History from Visuals

Interpreting the Map

How does the distance between Tehran and Esfahan compare to the distance between Mosul and Baghdad? *(similar)* Based on features shown on the map, which pair of cities probably had better communication? *(Mosul and Baghdad—separated by flat land and a major river)*

SKILLBUILDER Answers

1. **Movement** Persian Gulf, Caspian Sea
2. **Location** squeezed between Ottoman and Mughal empires

A Safavid Golden Age

10.9.6

Critical Thinking

- What does the third paragraph imply about the promotion policies of other rulers? *(sometimes promoted disloyal or incompetent people)*
- How did the military and art policies of Shah Abbas differ? *(He divided military units by religion, but he supported blending in art.)*
- What action implies that Shah Abbas thought Europeans had knowledge that his people should learn? *(sent artists to Italy to study under Raphael)*

Electronic Library of Primary Sources

- "Report on Persia, Persians, and 'Abbas I"

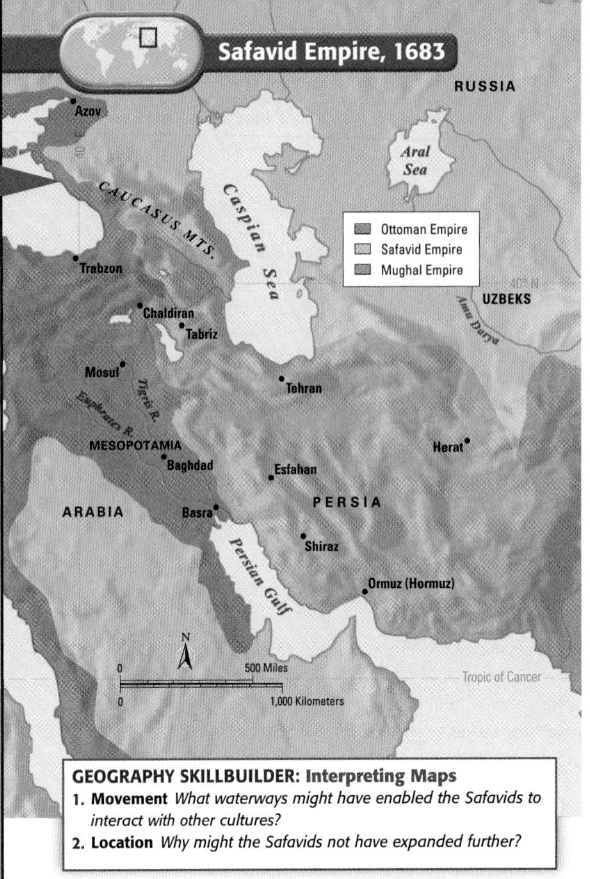

GEOGRAPHY SKILLBUILDER: Interpreting Maps
1. **Movement** *What waterways might have enabled the Safavids to interact with other cultures?*
2. **Location** *Why might the Safavids not have expanded further?*

To celebrate his achievement, he took the ancient Persian title of **shah**, or king. He also established Shi'a Islam as the state religion.

Isma'il became a religious tyrant. Any citizen who did not convert to Shi'ism was put to death. Isma'il destroyed the Sunni population of Baghdad in his confrontation with the Ottomans. Their leader, Selim the Grim, later ordered the execution of all Shi'a in the Ottoman Empire. As many as 40,000 died. Their final face-off took place at the Battle of Chaldiran in 1514. Using artillery, the Ottomans pounded the Safavids into defeat. Another outcome of the battle was to set the border between the two empires. It remains the border today between Iran and Iraq.

Isma'il's son Tahmasp learned from the Safavids' defeat at Chaldiran. He adopted the use of artillery with his military forces. He expanded the Safavid Empire up to the Caucasus Mountains, northeast of Turkey, and brought Christians under Safavid rule. Tahmasp laid the groundwork for the golden age of the Safavids. B

MAIN IDEA
Drawing Conclusions
B How did Tahmasp's cultural borrowing lead to the expansion of the Safavid Empire?
B. Answer By adopting artillery from the Ottomans he was able to conquer more lands for the empire.

A Safavid Golden Age

Shah Abbas, or Abbas the Great, took the throne in 1587. He helped create a Safavid culture and golden age that drew from the best of the Ottoman, Persian, and Arab worlds.

Reforms Shah Abbas reformed aspects of both military and civilian life. He limited the power of the military and created two new armies that would be loyal to him alone. One of these was an army of Persians. The other was a force that Abbas recruited from the Christian north and modeled after the Ottoman janissaries. He equipped both of these armies with modern artillery.

Abbas also reformed his government. He punished corruption severely and promoted only officials who proved their competence and loyalty. He hired foreigners from neighboring countries to fill positions in the government.

To convince European merchants that his empire was tolerant of other religions, Abbas brought members of Christian religious orders into the empire. As a result, Europeans moved into the land. Then industry, trade, and art exchanges grew between the empire and European nations.

A New Capital The Shah built a new capital at **Esfahan**. With a design that covered four and a half miles, the city was considered one of the most beautiful in the world. It was a showplace for the many artisans, both foreign and Safavid, who worked on the buildings and the objects in them. For example, 300 Chinese potters produced

DIFFERENTIATING INSTRUCTION: STRUGGLING READERS

Creating a Commercial for the Safavid Empire

Class Time 35 minutes

Task Writing a script for a radio or television advertisement

Purpose To express main ideas and details in students' own words; to hone persuasive writing skills

Instructions Divide students into groups. Have each group imagine that it has been hired by Shah Abbas to create a commercial that will encourage people to visit Esfahan. The commercial should take between 30 and 90 seconds to perform and should answer at least one of these questions:

- What makes Esfahan special?
- What kind of art, crafts, and architecture can a visitor find there?
- What cultural influences might a visitor from another country recognize?

Groups should designate different tasks for each member, such as finding relevant details in their textbooks, brainstorming ideas, looking up difficult words in a dictionary or glossary, and reading the script aloud for the group. Scripts may include notations for sound effects, music, or images. Encourage students to be persuasive and to use richly descriptive language. Each group should then nominate a member to perform the script for the class.

glazed building tiles for the buildings in the city, and Armenians wove carpets.

Art Works Shah Abbas brought hundreds of Chinese artisans to Esfahan. Working with Safavid artists, they produced intricate metalwork, miniature paintings, calligraphy, glasswork, tile work, and pottery. This collaboration gave rise to artwork that blended Chinese and Persian ideas. These decorations beautified the many mosques, palaces, and marketplaces.

Carpets The most important result of Western influence on the Safavids, however, may have been the demand for Persian carpets. This demand helped change carpet weaving from a local craft to a national industry. In the beginning, the carpets reflected traditional Persian themes. As the empire became more culturally blended, the designs incorporated new themes. In the 16th century, Shah Abbas sent artists to Italy to study under the Renaissance artist Raphael. Rugs then began to reflect European designs. C

MAIN IDEA
Comparing
C In what ways were Shah Abbas and Suleyman the Lawgiver similar?
C. Possible Answer They both reformed civilian life and brought culture to their empires, adapting the best from around the world.

▲ The Masjid-e-Imam mosque in Esfahan is a beautiful example of the flowering of the arts in the Safavid Empire.

The Dynasty Declines Quickly

In finding a successor, Shah Abbas made the same mistake the Ottoman monarch Suleyman made. He killed or blinded his ablest sons. His incompetent grandson, Safi, succeeded Abbas. This pampered young prince led the Safavids down the same road to decline that the Ottomans had taken, only more quickly.

In 1736, however, Nadir Shah Afshar conquered land all the way to India and created an expanded empire. But Nadir Shah was so cruel that one of his own troops assassinated him. With Nadir Shah's death in 1747, the Safavid Empire fell apart.

At the same time that the Safavids flourished, cultural blending and conquest led to the growth of a new empire in India, as you will learn in Section 3.

SECTION 2 ASSESSMENT

TERMS & NAMES 1. For each term or name, write a sentence explaining its significance.
• Safavid • Isma'il • shah • Shah Abbas • Esfahan

USING YOUR NOTES
2. What are some examples of cultural blending in the Safavid Empire? (10.10.1)

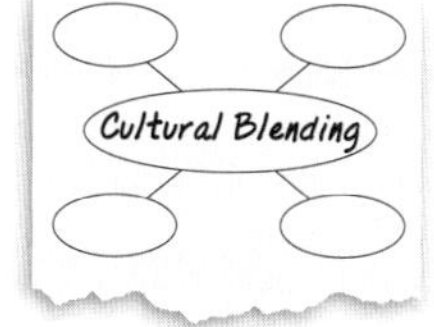

MAIN IDEAS
3. What are the four causes of cultural blending? (10.10.1)
4. What reforms took place in the Safavid Empire under Shah Abbas? (10.10.1)
5. Why did the Safavid Empire decline so quickly? (10.10.1)

CRITICAL THINKING & WRITING
6. **FORMING OPINIONS** Which of the results of cultural blending do you think has the most lasting effect on a country? Explain. (10.10.1)
7. **DRAWING CONCLUSIONS** How did the location of the Safavid Empire contribute to the cultural blending in the empire? (10.10.1)
8. **ANALYZING MOTIVES** Why might Isma'il have become so intolerant of the Sunni Muslims? (10.10.1)
9. **WRITING ACTIVITY** CULTURAL INTERACTION Write a **letter** from Shah Abbas to persuade a Chinese artist to come teach and work in the Safavid Empire. (Writing 2.2.a)

INTEGRATED TECHNOLOGY **INTERNET ACTIVITY**
Use the Internet to research the charge that Persian rugs are largely made by children under the age of 14. Write a television documentary **script** detailing your research results. (10.10.1)

INTERNET KEYWORD
child labor rug making

More About . . .

Shah Abbas

Shah Abbas was a Shi'a Muslim but far more mild in his views than his predecessors. He welcomed Christians and foreigners at his court, and he ate and drank with the Spanish ambassador during the Muslim month of fasting. To promote an alliance with Europeans against the Ottomans, he even hinted that he might convert to Christianity.

The Dynasty Declines Quickly
10.10.1

Critical Thinking
• What factors contributed to the decline of the Safavids? *(incompetence, cruelty)*
• How was Nadir Shah Afshar unlike Shah Abbas? *(He was cruel.)*

3 ASSESS

SECTION 2 ASSESSMENT

Have students work individually to answer the questions, noting where they find the answers.

Formal Assessment
• Section Quiz, p. 41

4 RETEACH

Have students create a new row for the Safavid Empire in the chart on page 79.

In-Depth Resources: Unit 1
• Reteaching Activity, p. 58

ANSWERS

1. Safavid, p. 78 • Isma'il, p. 79 • shah, p. 80 • Shah Abbas, p. 80 • Esfahan, p. 80
2. **Sample Answer:** copied the Ottoman style of military, used Chinese artisans' work in buildings, blended designs into carpets
3. migration, trade, conquest, pursuit of religious conversion or religious freedom
4. limited the power of the military, created armies loyal to him, began using artillery, punished corruption, brought Christians into the land
5. All the capable heirs were killed.
6. **Possible Answer:** new languages, because people use them every day
7. It had powerful empires on two sides and the Chinese nearby.
8. out of fear that they might prove disloyal
9. **Rubric** Letters should
• emphasize the tolerance and respect for foreigners in the Safavid Empire.
• discuss Shah Abbas's interest in other cultures.
• point out cosmopolitan aspects of Esfahan.

INTEGRATED TECHNOLOGY
Rubric Scripts should
• present facts regarding child labor.
• include images to support information.
• draw conclusions based on presented facts.
• identify sources consulted.

LESSON PLAN

OBJECTIVES

- Describe the rise of the Mughal Empire.
- Analyze the achievements of Akbar.
- List triumphs and failures of Akbar's successors.
- Explain why the empire declined.

1 FOCUS & MOTIVATE

Note that Hindu-Muslim relations are a key issue in this section. Discuss the tension between India and Pakistan. *(India is mostly Hindu; Pakistan is mostly Muslim. Both want to control Kashmir.)* Have students check maps to see how the disputed border of Kashmir is shown.

2 INSTRUCT

Early History of the Mughals

10.4.2

Critical Thinking

- What can you infer about the military balance between Muslims and Hindus between 700 and 1000? *(It was roughly even.)*
- Do you think the comment on Delhi's ruin is truthful? *(may be exaggerated)*

CALIFORNIA RESOURCES

California Reading Toolkit, p. L15
California Modified Lesson Plans for English Learners, p. 25
California Daily Standards Practice Transparencies, TT7
California Standards Enrichment Workbook, pp. 49–50
California Standards Planner and Lesson Plans, p. L21
California Online Test Practice
California Test Generator CD-ROM
California Easy Planner CD-ROM
California eEdition CD-ROM

Hagia Sophia, Istanbul, Turkey — Wall mural, Ladakh, India

3

The Mughal Empire in India

MAIN IDEA	WHY IT MATTERS NOW	TERMS & NAMES
POWER AND AUTHORITY The Mughal Empire brought Turks, Persians, and Indians together in a vast empire.	The legacy of great art and deep social division left by the Mughal Empire still influences southern Asia.	• Mughal • Babur • Akbar • Sikh • Shah Jahan • Taj Mahal • Aurangzeb

CALIFORNIA STANDARDS

10.4.2 Discuss the locations of the colonial rule of such nations as England, France, Germany, Italy, Japan, the Netherlands, Russia, Spain, Portugal, and the United States.

CST 1 Students compare the present with the past, evaluating the consequences of past events and decisions and determining the lessons that were learned.

CST 3 Students use a variety of maps and documents to interpret human movement, including major patterns of domestic and international migration, changing environmental preferences and settlement patterns, the frictions that develop between population groups, and the diffusion of ideas, technological innovations, and goods.

CST 4 Students relate current events to the physical and human characteristics of places and regions.

HI 1 Students show the connections, causal and otherwise, between particular historical events and larger social, economic, and political trends and developments.

SETTING THE STAGE The Gupta Empire crumbled in the late 400s. First, Arabs invaded. Then, warlike Muslim tribes from Central Asia carved northwestern India into many small kingdoms. Leaders called *rajputs*, or "sons of kings," ruled those kingdoms. The people who invaded descended from Muslim Turks and Afghans. Their leader was a descendant of Timur the Lame and of the Mongol conqueror Genghis Khan. They called themselves **Mughals**, which means "Mongols." The land they invaded had been through a long period of turmoil.

Early History of the Mughals

The 8th century began with a long, bloody clash between Hindus and Muslims in this fragmented land. For almost 300 years, the Muslims were able to advance only as far as the Indus River valley. Starting around the year 1000, however, well-trained Turkish armies swept into India. Led by Sultan Mahmud (muh•MOOD) of Ghazni, they devastated Indian cities and temples in 17 brutal campaigns. These attacks left the region weakened and vulnerable to other conquerors. Delhi eventually became the capital of a loose empire of Turkish warlords called the Delhi Sultanate. These sultans treated the Hindus as conquered people.

Delhi Sultanate Between the 13th and 16th centuries, 33 different sultans ruled this divided territory from their seat in Delhi. In 1398, Timur the Lame destroyed Delhi. The city was so completely devastated that according to one witness, "for months, not a bird moved in the city." Delhi eventually was rebuilt. But it was not until the 16th century that a leader arose who would unify the empire.

TAKING NOTES

Following Chronological Order Create a time line of the Mughal emperors and their successes.

1494
Babur

Babur Founds an Empire In 1494, an 11-year-old boy named **Babur** inherited a kingdom in the area that is now Uzbekistan and Tajikistan. It was only a tiny kingdom, and his elders soon took it away and drove him south. But Babur built up an army. In the years that followed, he swept down into India and laid the foundation for the vast Mughal Empire.

Babur was a brilliant general. In 1526, for example, he led 12,000 troops to victory against an army of 100,000 commanded by a sultan of Delhi. A year later, Babur also defeated a massive rajput army. After Babur's death, his incompetent son, Humayun, lost most of the territory Babur had gained. Babur's 13-year-old grandson took over the throne after Humayun's death.

SECTION 3 PROGRAM RESOURCES

ALL STUDENTS

In-Depth Resources: Unit 1
- Guided Reading, p. 42
- Geography Application, p. 45
- History Makers: Shah Jahan, p. 55

Formal Assessment
- Section Quiz, p. 42

ENGLISH LEARNERS

In-Depth Resources in Spanish
- Guided Reading, p. 27
- Geography Application, p. 29

Reading Study Guide (Spanish), p. 29
Reading Study Guide Audio CD (Spanish)

STRUGGLING READERS

In-Depth Resources: Unit 1
- Guided Reading, p. 42
- Building Vocabulary, p. 43
- Geography Application, p. 45
- Reteaching Activity, p. 59

Reading Study Guide, p. 29
Reading Study Guide Audio CD

GIFTED AND TALENTED STUDENTS

In-Depth Resources: Unit 1
- Primary Sources: Akbar, p. 49; Jahangir's Birthday, p. 50
- Connections Across Time and Cultures, p. 56

INTEGRATED TECHNOLOGY

eEdition CD-ROM
Power Presentations CD-ROM
Critical Thinking Transparencies
- CT18 Muslim Empires in Anatolia and India
- CT54 Chapter 2 Visual Summary

World Art and Cultures Transparencies
- AT40 Mughal miniature painting

classzone.com

Akbar's Golden Age

Babur's grandson was called **Akbar**, which means "Greatest One." Akbar certainly lived up to his name, ruling India with wisdom and tolerance from 1556 to 1605.

A Military Conqueror Akbar recognized military power as the root of his strength. In his opinion, "A monarch should ever be intent on conquest, otherwise his neighbors rise in arms against him."

Like the Safavids and the Ottomans, Akbar equipped his armies with heavy artillery. Cannons enabled him to break into walled cities and extend his rule into much of the Deccan plateau. In a brilliant move, he appointed some rajputs as officers. In this way he turned potential enemies into allies. This combination of military power and political wisdom enabled Akbar to unify a land of at least 100 million people—more than in all of Europe put together.

A Liberal Ruler Akbar was a genius at cultural blending. He was a Muslim, and he firmly defended religious freedom. He permitted people of other religions to practice their faiths. He proved his tolerance by marrying, among others, two Hindus, a Christian, and a Muslim. He allowed his wives to practice their religious rituals in the palace. He proved his tolerance again by abolishing both the tax on Hindu pilgrims and the hated *jizya*, or tax on non-Muslims. He even appointed a Spanish Jesuit to tutor his second son.

Akbar governed through a bureaucracy of officials. Natives and foreigners, Hindus and Muslims, could all rise to high office. This approach contributed to the quality of his government. Akbar's chief finance minister, Todar Mal, a Hindu, created a clever—and effective—taxation policy. He levied a tax similar to the present-day U.S. graduated income tax, calculating it as a percentage of the value of the peasants' crops. Because this tax was fair and affordable, the number of peasants who paid it increased. This payment brought in much needed money for the empire. (A)

Akbar's land policies had more mixed results. He gave generous land grants to his bureaucrats. After they died, however, he reclaimed the lands and distributed them as he saw fit. On the positive side, this policy prevented the growth of feudal aristocracies. On the other hand, it did not encourage dedication and hard work by the Mughal officials. Their children would not inherit the land or benefit from their parents' work. So the officials apparently saw no point in devoting themselves to their property.

A. Possible Answer Both men were extremely tolerant–Akbar in both his personal life and government policies, and Suleyman through the millet system.

MAIN IDEA
Comparing
(A) In what ways were Akbar's attitudes toward religion similar to those of Suleyman the Lawgiver?

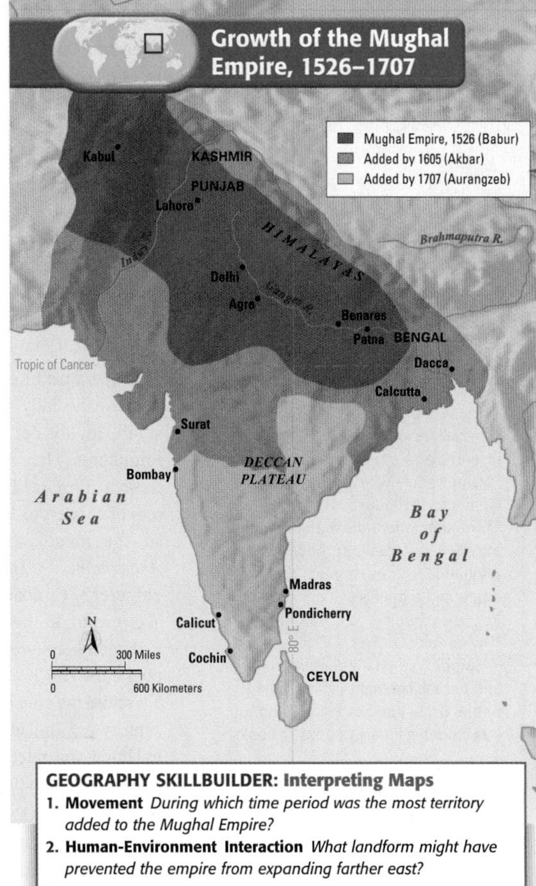

GEOGRAPHY SKILLBUILDER: Interpreting Maps
1. **Movement** *During which time period was the most territory added to the Mughal Empire?*
2. **Human-Environment Interaction** *What landform might have prevented the empire from expanding farther east?*

History from Visuals

Interpreting the Map

Have students identify the Indus River, which was as far as the Arab conquests penetrated into India.

Extension Compare the sizes of the Mughal Empire in 1707 and the United States today, excluding Alaska and Hawaii. *(The United States is slightly larger.)*

SKILLBUILDER Answers
1. **Movement** before 1605
2. **Human-Environment Interaction** the Himalaya Mountains

Akbar's Golden Age
10.4.2

Critical Thinking
- Do you think Akbar's taxes were fair? Why? *(Yes—Payments increased with wealth. No—Some paid more than others.)*
- How might Akbar have appealed to bureaucrats to work hard? *(Possible Answer: permanent land grants)*
- How did the stonework created under Akbar reflect his religious toleration? *(Akbar was a Muslim; stonework often portrayed Hindu themes.)*

In-Depth Resources: Unit 1
- Primary Source: Akbar, p. 49
- Connections Across Time and Cultures: How to Treat the Conquered, p. 56

DIFFERENTIATING INSTRUCTION: GIFTED AND TALENTED STUDENTS

Evaluating Taxation

Class Time 40 minutes

Task Debating the merits of increasing the percentage of tax as income increases

Purpose To understand the reasons for and against a graduated income tax; to improve persuasive speaking skills

Instructions Divide the class into four or six groups. Half of the groups should develop arguments in favor of graduated income taxes. The other half should oppose them.

Each group should consider issues such as the following:
- the functions of government
- the economic impact of a graduated tax
- the fairness of a graduated tax
- alternative methods of funding government

Groups should prepare notes or outlines that address these issues.

When groups are ready, select one group from each side and have them debate the issue. Students in the other groups should vote on which side presented its arguments most convincingly.

History Makers

Akbar

Sensitive to public opinion, Akbar stood at an open palace window each morning so that his people could see him. He wanted them to feel a connection with their emperor.

Akbar's Successors

10.4.2

Critical Thinking

- What evidence shows Nur Jahan's ability to exert power? *(Jahangir's family members took orders from her.)*
- What caused Shah Jahan to build the Taj Mahal? *(in memory of his wife)*
- How did Aurangzeb's use of tax money weaken the empire? *(He used it for war and repression.)*

In-Depth Resources: Unit 1

- Geography Application, p. 45
- Primary Source: Jahangir's Birthday, p. 50

More About . . .

Nur Jahan

According to legend, Nur Jahan was born while her parents were fleeing Persia. They abandoned her under a tree, but a cobra protected her from the hot sun with its hood until her remorseful parents returned. At age 30, Nur Jahan was called to serve at court, where the emperor noticed her. Four years later, he married her.

History Makers

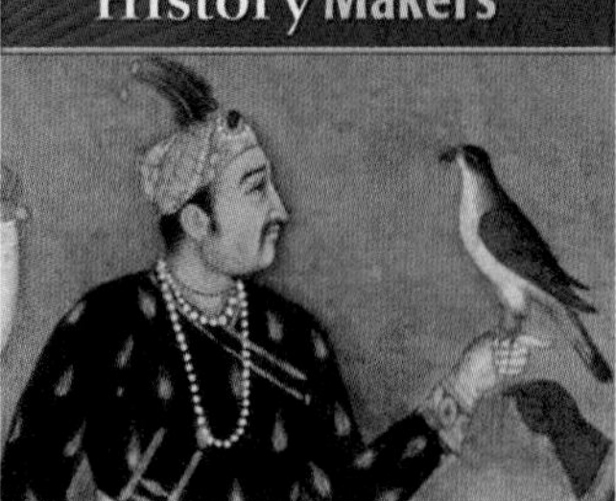

Akbar
1542–1605

Akbar was brilliant and curious, especially about religion. He even invented a religion of his own—the "Divine Faith"—which combined elements of Hinduism, Jainism, Christianity, and Sufism. The religion attracted few followers, however, and offended Muslims so much that they attempted a brief revolt against Akbar in 1581. When he died, so did the "Divine Faith."

Surprisingly, despite his wisdom and his achievements, Akbar could not read. He hired others to read to him from his library of 24,000 books.

INTEGRATED TECHNOLOGY

RESEARCH LINKS For more on Akbar, go to **classzone.com**

Blended Cultures As Akbar extended the Mughal Empire, he welcomed influences from the many cultures in the empire. This cultural blending affected art, education, politics, and language. Persian was the language of Akbar's court and of high culture. The common people, however, spoke Hindi, a mixture of Persian and a local language. Hindi remains one of the most widely spoken languages in India today. Out of the Mughal armies, where soldiers of many backgrounds rubbed shoulders, came yet another new language. This language was Urdu, which means "from the soldier's camp." A blend of Arabic, Persian, and Hindi, Urdu is today the official language of Pakistan.

The Arts and Literature The arts flourished at the Mughal court, especially in the form of book illustrations. These small, highly detailed, and colorful paintings were called miniatures. They were brought to a peak of perfection in the Safavid Empire. Babur's son, Humayun, brought two masters of this art to his court to teach it to the Mughals. Some of the most famous Mughal miniatures adorned the *Akbarnamah* ("Book of Akbar"), the story of the great emperor's campaigns and deeds. Indian art drew from Western traditions as well.

Hindu literature also enjoyed a revival in Akbar's time. The poet Tulsi Das, for example, was a contemporary of Akbar's. He retold the epic love story of Rama and Sita from the fourth century B.C. Indian poem the *Ramayana* (rah•MAH•yuh•nuh) in Hindi. This retelling, the *Ramcaritmanas,* is now even more popular than the original.

Architecture Akbar devoted himself to architecture too. The style developed under his reign is still known as Akbar period architecture. Its massive but graceful structures are decorated with intricate stonework that portrays Hindu themes. The capital city of Fatehpur Sikri is one of the most important examples of this type of architecture. Akbar had this red-sandstone city built to thank a holy man who had predicted the birth of his first son. (B)

B. Answer His combination of military might and political wisdom enabled him to get rid of enemies and build allies.

MAIN IDEA

Drawing Conclusions

(B) How was Akbar able to build such an immense empire?

Akbar's Successors

With Akbar's death in 1605, the Mughal court changed to deal with the changing times. The next three emperors each left his mark on the Mughal Empire.

Jahangir and Nur Jahan Akbar's son called himself Jahangir (juh•hahn•GEER), or "Grasper of the World." And he certainly did hold India in a powerful grasp. It was not his hand in the iron glove, however. For most of his reign, he left the affairs of state to his wife.

Jahangir's wife was the Persian princess Nur Jahan. She was a brilliant politician who perfectly understood the use of power. As the real ruler of India, she installed her father as prime minister in the Mughal court. She saw Jahangir's son Khusrau as her ticket to future power. But when Khusrau rebelled against his father, Nur Jahan removed him. She then shifted her favor to another son.

This rejection of Khusrau affected more than the political future of the empire. It was also the basis of a long and bitter religious conflict. Jahangir tried to promote Islam in the Mughal state, but was tolerant of other religions. When Khusrau

DIFFERENTIATING INSTRUCTION: STRUGGLING READERS

Investigating Mughal Art

Class Time 15 minutes

Task Studying and noting features of a Mughal painting

Purpose To understand how art can function as a primary source

Instructions Display World Art and Cultures Transparency AT40, Festivities During the Occasion of the Coronation of Jahangir. Refer to the User's Guide at the back of the transparency book for background information about this miniature painting. Use the following questions to spark a discussion:

- Based on this painting, what do you think a coronation is? *(a ceremony in which a ruler comes to power)*
- What similarities do you see between this miniature and the other examples of art in this chapter? *(Possible Answers: rich colors, lots of detail, intricate designs)*
- How does this painting show evidence of cultural blending? *(People of many different skin colors are pictured, and they are wearing a variety of costumes.)*

World Art and Cultures Transparencies

Connect to Today

Women Leaders of the Indian Subcontinent

Since World War II, the subcontinent of India has seen the rise of several powerful women. Unlike Nur Jahan, however, they achieved power on their own—not through their husbands.

Indira Gandhi headed the Congress Party and dominated Indian politics for almost 30 years. She was elected prime minister in 1966 and again in 1980. Gandhi was assassinated in 1984 by Sikh separatists.

Benazir Bhutto took charge of the Pakistan People's Party after her father was executed by his political enemies. She won election as her country's prime minister in 1988, the first woman to run a modern Muslim state. She was reelected in 1993.

Khaleda Zia became Bangladesh's first woman prime minister in 1991. She was reelected several times, the last time in 2001. She has made progress in empowering women and girls in her nation.

Chandrika Bandaranaike Kumaratunga is the president of Sri Lanka. She was elected in 1994 with 62 percent of the votes cast. She survived an assassination attempt in 1999 and was reelected.

Indira Gandhi

Benazir Bhutto

Khaleda Zia

Chandrika Bandaranaike Kumaratunga

rebelled, he turned to the **Sikhs**. This was a nonviolent religious group whose doctrines blended Buddhism, Hinduism, and Sufism (Islamic mysticism). Their leader, Guru Arjun, sheltered Khusrau and defended him. In response, the Mughal rulers had Arjun arrested and tortured to death. The Sikhs became the target of the Mughals' particular hatred. C

MAIN IDEA
Analyzing Causes
C How did the Mughals' dislike of the Sikhs develop?
C. Answer Sikhs sheltered and defended Jahangir's son, who had rebelled against his father.

Shah Jahan Jahangir's son and successor, **Shah Jahan**, could not tolerate competition and secured his throne by assassinating all his possible rivals. He had a great passion for two things: beautiful buildings and his wife Mumtaz Mahal (moom•TAHZ mah•HAHL). Nur Jahan had arranged this marriage between Jahangir's son and her niece for political reasons. Shah Jahan, however, fell genuinely in love with his Persian princess.

In 1631, Mumtaz Mahal died at age 39 while giving birth to her 14th child. To enshrine his wife's memory, he ordered that a tomb be built "as beautiful as she was beautiful." Fine white marble and fabulous jewels were gathered from many parts of Asia. This memorial, the **Taj Mahal**, has been called one of the most beautiful buildings in the world. Its towering marble dome and slender minaret towers look like lace and seem to change color as the sun moves across the sky.

The People Suffer But while Shah Jahan was building lovely things, his country was suffering. There was famine in the land. Furthermore, farmers needed tools, roads, and ways of irrigating their crops and dealing with India's harsh environment. What they got instead were taxes and more taxes to support the building of monuments, their rulers' extravagant living, and war.

Connect to Today

Women Leaders of the Indian Subcontinent

South Asia has given the world six women prime ministers. Sirimavo Bandaranaike of Ceylon—an island off the southern tip of India that is now called Sri Lanka—was the world's first woman prime minister. She initially took office in 1960. Ask students to speculate on why women have often held political power in this region. *(Possible Answer: tradition of powerful women dating back to Nur Jahan)*

More About . . .

Mumtaz Mahal

According to popular stories, it was love at first sight between Mumtaz Mahal and Prince Khurram, who later became Shah Jahan. On seeing her, the prince reportedly said, "Oh, that I were a glove upon that hand." Mumtaz traveled everywhere with her husband, even on military campaigns. She gave birth on the battlefield to four sons, including the next emperor, Aurangzeb.

In-Depth Resources: Unit 1
- History Makers: Shah Jahan, p. 55

Tip for English Learners

Have students create a collage of images and comments about the Taj Mahal. Ask, Why do people find the Taj Mahal so beautiful? *(Possible Answer: its color, detail, and symmetry)*

DIFFERENTIATING INSTRUCTION: ENGLISH LEARNERS

Understanding Idioms

Class Time 15 minutes

Task Learning to recognize and understand idioms

Purpose To improve understanding of challenging texts

Instructions Explain that an idiom is a commonly used expression whose intended meaning is different from its literal meaning. For example, if you complain about having a frog in your throat, it means that your voice is hoarse or scratchy. It does not mean that you have swallowed an animal! Challenge students to find the three idioms on page 84 and determine their meanings.

- Soldiers of many backgrounds "rubbed shoulders," which means they lived and worked together. The context of the paragraph can help readers understand this idiom—the soldiers spoke a language that was a blend of their different languages.
- Each of the next three emperors "left his mark" on the Mughal Empire, which means he made important and lasting changes to it.
- Nur Jahan had a hand in an "iron glove," which means that she had power over people.

Invite students to share idioms from other languages. *(Possible Answer: in Spanish,* estar a un grito*—literally, "to be on a scream"—means to be in pain.)*

More About . . .

Aurangzeb's Harshness

Shah Jahan preferred his mystical, humane son, Dara Shikoh, over his younger, fiercer son, Aurangzeb. Aurangzeb never forgot this. One legend claims that Aurangzeb jailed his father and had Dara Shikoh's severed head delivered to Shah Jahan with the message: "Your son sends this [gift] to your majesty to let him see that he does not forget him."

Aurangzeb was strict in less violent ways as well. For example, he forbade parties that involved drinking, singing, and dancing, and he tore down all large-scale pre-Mughal monuments built by Hindus. As a result, the only pre-Mughal architecture remaining in India is in the southern sections that Aurangzeb never conquered.

History *in* Depth

Building the Taj Mahal

The Taj Mahal was designed by a team of architects that included Indians, Persians, and others. Claims that it was designed by an Italian or by fourth-century Hindus have little support.

INTEGRATED TECHNOLOGY

Rubric Brochures should
- include relevant facts and details.
- use inviting, persuasive language.
- include attractive visuals.

▲ Mirrored in a reflecting pool is the Taj Mahal, a monument to love and the Mughal Empire.

History *in* Depth

Building the Taj Mahal

Some 20,000 workers labored for 22 years to build the famous tomb. It is made of white marble brought from 250 miles away. The minaret towers are about 130 feet high. The building itself is 186 feet square.

The design of the building is a blend of Hindu and Muslim styles. The pointed arches are of Muslim design, and the perforated marble windows and doors are typical of a style found in Hindu temples.

The inside of the building is a glittering garden of thousands of carved marble flowers inlaid with tiny precious stones. One tiny flower, one inch square, had 60 different inlays.

INTEGRATED TECHNOLOGY

INTERNET ACTIVITY Use the Internet to take a virtual trip to the Taj Mahal. Create a brochure about the building. Go to **classzone.com** for your research.

All was not well in the royal court either. When Shah Jahan became ill in 1657, his four sons scrambled for the throne. The third son, **Aurangzeb** (AWR•uhng•zehb), moved first and most decisively. In a bitter civil war, he executed his older brother, who was his most serious rival. Then he arrested his father and put him in prison, where he died several years later. After Shah Jahan's death, a mirror was found in his room, angled so that he could look out at the reflection of the Taj Mahal.

Aurangzeb's Reign A master at military strategy and an aggressive empire builder, Aurangzeb ruled from 1658 to 1707. He expanded the Mughal holdings to their greatest size. However, the power of the empire weakened during his reign.

This loss of power was due largely to Aurangzeb's oppression of the people. He rigidly enforced Islamic laws, outlawing drinking, gambling, and other activities viewed as vices. He appointed censors to police his subjects' morals and make sure they prayed at the appointed times. He also tried to erase all the gains Hindus had made under Akbar. For example, he brought back the hated tax on non-Muslims and dismissed Hindus from high positions in his government. He banned the construction of new temples and had Hindu monuments destroyed. Not surprisingly, these actions outraged the Hindus.

COOPERATIVE LEARNING

Evaluating Aurangzeb

Class Time 30 minutes

Task Collecting historical accounts of Aurangzeb and analyzing how they portray him

Purpose To recognize the disagreements among historians

Instructions Divide students into heterogeneous groups. Explain that Aurangzeb is a controversial figure in Indian history. Historians differ widely on how to evaluate his reign.

Have each group find three or more sources describing Aurangzeb. Groups might check general encyclopedias, encyclopedias of history, books on the history of India, biographical dictionaries, and the Internet. Groups should write one-paragraph descriptions of the sources, evaluating how critical or sympathetic each is toward Aurangzeb. Then, as a class, make a list of the sources found by students and rank them from most critical to most sympathetic. Discuss why historians disagree on Aurangzeb. *(Possible Answer: Aurangzeb was intelligent, serious-minded, and a skilled military strategist. Under his rule, the Mughal Empire reached its largest size. However, his ruthlessness and violence caused great turmoil and contributed to the collapse of the empire.)*

D. Answer He depleted the empire's resources and began the weakening of central power that led to its ruin.

MAIN IDEA

Recognizing Effects

D How did Aurangzeb's personal qualities and political policies affect the Mughal Empire?

The Hindu rajputs, whom Akbar had converted from potential enemies to allies, rebelled. Aurangzeb defeated them repeatedly, but never completely. In the southwest, militant Hindus called Marathas founded their own state. Aurangzeb captured their leader but could never conquer them. Meanwhile, the Sikhs transformed themselves into a militant brotherhood. They began building a state in the Punjab, an area in northwest India.

Aurangzeb levied oppressive taxes to pay for the wars against the increasing numbers of enemies. He had done away with all taxes not authorized by Islamic law, so he doubled the taxes on Hindu merchants. This increased tax burden deepened the Hindus' bitterness and led to further rebellion. As a result, Aurangzeb needed to raise more money to increase his army. The more territory he conquered, the more desperate his situation became. D

The Empire's Decline and Decay

By the end of Aurangzeb's reign, he had drained the empire of its resources. Over 2 million people died in a famine while Aurangzeb was away waging war. Most of his subjects felt little or no loyalty to him.

As the power of the central state weakened, the power of local lords grew. After Aurangzeb's death, his sons fought a war of succession. In fact, three emperors reigned in the first 12 years after Aurangzeb died. By the end of this period, the Mughal emperor was nothing but a wealthy figurehead. He ruled not a united empire but a patchwork of independent states.

As the Mughal Empire rose and fell, Western traders slowly built their own power in the region. The Portuguese were the first Europeans to reach India. In fact, they arrived just before Babur did. Next came the Dutch, who in turn gave way to the French and the English. However, the great Mughal emperors did not feel threatened by the European traders. Shah Jahan let the English build a fortified trading post at Madras. In 1661, Aurangzeb casually handed them the port of Bombay. Aurangzeb had no idea that he had given India's next conquerors their first foothold in a future empire.

SECTION 3 ASSESSMENT

TERMS & NAMES 1. For each term or name, write a sentence explaining its significance.

- Mughal • Babur • Akbar • Sikh • Shah Jahan • Taj Mahal • Aurangzeb

USING YOUR NOTES

2. Which of the Mughal emperors on your time line had a positive effect on the empire? Which had negative effects? (10.4.2)

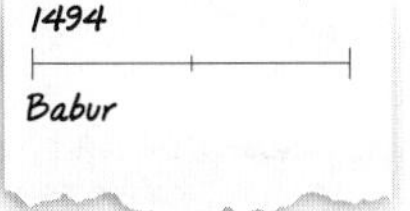

MAIN IDEAS

3. How did Akbar demonstrate tolerance in his empire? (10.4.2)
4. What pattern is seen in the ways individuals came to power in the Mughal Empire? (10.4.2)
5. Why did the empire weaken under the rule of Aurangzeb? (10.4.2)

CRITICAL THINKING & WRITING

6. **CLARIFYING** Why were Akbar's tax policies so successful? (10.4.2)
7. **MAKING INFERENCES** Why was Nur Jahan able to hold so much power in Jahangir's court? (10.4.2)
8. **EVALUATING COURSES OF ACTION** Why were the policies of Aurangzeb so destructive to the Mughal Empire? (10.4.2)
9. **WRITING ACTIVITY** POWER AND AUTHORITY Write a **compare-and-contrast essay** on the policies of Akbar and Aurangzeb. Use references from the text in your response. (Writing 2.2.b)

CONNECT TO TODAY **CREATING A BIOGRAPHY**

Select one of the women leaders in Connect to Today on page 85. Research her life and write a short **biography** of her. (Writing 2.1.a)

The Empire's Decline and Decay

10.4.2

Critical Thinking

- How large an impact did the famine have on Aurangzeb's empire? *(Possible Answer: substantial, as the number of deaths equaled the present population of a large city, such as Houston)*
- What is a one-sentence summary of the impact of the reign of Aurangzeb? *(Possible Answer: His aggressive and oppressive policies led to ruin for the Mughal Empire.)*

3 ASSESS

SECTION 3 ASSESSMENT

Using students' answers to question 2, create a time line on the board. Discuss which emperors had positive or negative effects.

Formal Assessment

- Section Quiz, p. 42

4 RETEACH

Use the following transparencies or the Reteaching Activity to review this section and chapter.

Critical Thinking Transparencies

- CT18 Muslim Empires in Anatolia and India
- CT54 Chapter 2 Visual Summary

In-Depth Resources: Unit 1

- Reteaching Activity, p. 59

ANSWERS

1. Mughal, p. 82 • Babur, p. 82 • Akbar, p. 83 • Sikh, p. 85 • Shah Jahan, p. 85 • Taj Mahal, p. 85 • Aurangzeb, p. 86
2. **Sample Answer:** 1494, Babur; early 1500s, Humayun; 1556, Akbar; 1605, Jahangir (and Nur Jahan); early 1600s, Shah Jahan; 1658, Aurangzeb. Positive—Babur expanded the empire; Akbar oversaw a flowering of culture. Negative—Jahangir, Nur Jahan, and Shah Jahan sparked religious conflict; Aurangzeb waged costly wars.
3. He married women from different ethnic groups and abolished the taxes on Hindu pilgrims and non-Muslims.
4. new leader killed all opponents
5. He oppressed people, provoked Hindus and Sikhs, and increased taxes to pay for wars.
6. They were fair and affordable, so more people paid.
7. She knew how to use power, and he apparently lacked interest in ruling.
8. He ended policies of toleration, which led to bitterness and rebellion.
9. **Rubric** Compare-and-contrast essays should
   - identify similarities between the men.
   - explain differences in policies.
   - draw conclusions about each reign.

CONNECT TO TODAY

Rubric Biographies should

- present biographical data.
- explain how the leader came to power.
- identify actions or policies of the leader.

History *through* Art

OBJECTIVES

- Identify examples of cultural blending in Mughal art.
- Recognize traits in Mughal art that give it lasting significance.

FOCUS & MOTIVATE

Have students look at the images on this page and the next. Ask, Which looks most like your impression of art from India or southwest Asia? *(Possible Answer: the building, because of its dome)*

INSTRUCT

Critical Thinking

- How is Humayun's Tomb similar to the Taj Mahal shown on page 86? *(in their domes, arches, and symmetry)*
- What details make the horse on the dagger handle realistic? *(Possible Answer: the eye and the harness)*
- Do you think of the painting as dramatic? *(Possible Answers: Yes—It is filled with action and bright color. No—It does not focus on a single drama.)*
- What is your reaction to the fabric as a work of art? *(Possible Answer: Its balanced design, soft colors, and intricate work make it warm and attractive.)*

History *through* Art

Cultural Blending in Mughal India

As you have read, Mughal India enjoyed a golden age under Akbar. Part of Akbar's success—indeed, the success of the Mughals—came from his religious tolerance. India's population was largely Hindu, and the incoming Mughal rulers were Muslim. The Mughal emperors encouraged the blending of cultures to create a united India.

This cultural integration can be seen in the art of Mughal India. Muslim artists focused heavily on art with ornate patterns of flowers and leaves, called arabesque or geometric patterns. Hindu artists created naturalistic and often extravagant artworks. These two artistic traditions came together and created a style unique to Mughal India. As you can see, the artistic collaboration covered a wide range of art forms.

INTEGRATED TECHNOLOGY

RESEARCH LINKS For more on art in Mughal India, go to **classzone.com**

CALIFORNIA STANDARDS

10.4.3 Explain imperialism from the perspective of the colonizers and the colonized and the varied immediate and long-term responses by the people under colonial rule.

REP 4 Students construct and test hypotheses; collect, evaluate, and employ information from multiple primary and secondary sources; and apply it in oral and written presentations.

▼ Decorative Arts

Decorative work on items from dagger handles to pottery exhibits the same cultural blending as other Mughal art forms. This dagger handle shows some of the floral and geometric elements common in Muslim art, but the realistic depiction of the horse comes out of the Hindu tradition.

▼ Architecture

Mughal emperors brought to India a strong Muslim architectural tradition. Indian artisans were extremely talented with local building materials–specifically, marble and sandstone. Together, they created some of the most striking and enduring architecture in the world, like Humayun's Tomb shown here.

RECOMMENDED RESOURCES

Books

Keene, Manuel. ***Treasury of the World: Jeweled Arts of India in the Age of the Mughals.*** New York: Thames and Hudson, 2001. Examines the jewelry art of Mughal India.

Stronge, Susan. ***Painting for the Mughal Emperor: The Art of the Book 1560–1660.*** London: Victoria & Albert Museum, 2002. Covers 100 years of the Mughal Golden Age of painting.

Video

The Splendors of the Mogul Dynasty. VHS. Films for the Humanities & Sciences, 1986. 800-257-5126. Explores how Mughal (also called Mogul) architecture and sculpture express their legacy.

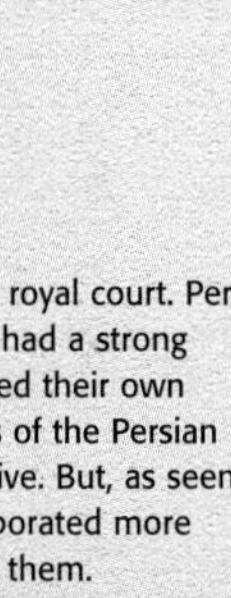

▼ Painting
Mughal painting was largely a product of the royal court. Persian artists brought to court by Mughal emperors had a strong influence, but Mughal artists quickly developed their own characteristics. The Mughal style kept aspects of the Persian influence—particularly the flat aerial perspective. But, as seen in this colorful painting, the Indian artists incorporated more naturalism and detail from the world around them.

▲ Fabrics
Mughal fabrics included geometric patterns found in Persian designs, but Mughal weavers, like other Mughal artisans, also produced original designs. Themes that were common in Mughal fabrics were landscapes, animal chases, floral latticeworks, and central flowering plants like the one on this tent hanging.

Connect *to* Today

1. **Clarifying** What does the art suggest about the culture of Mughal India?
   See Skillbuilder Handbook, page R4.
2. **Forming and Supporting Opinions** What are some modern examples of cultural blending in art? What elements of each culture are represented in the artwork? Consider other art forms, such as music and literature, as well.

Vocabulary Note: Technical Terms
Encourage students to read more about fabric arts and to keep track of unfamiliar words. Some common terms that students might see are:

- *atelier:* a workroom used by an artist
- *dye:* a substance used to give color to cloth or other material
- *motif:* a color or pattern repeated as a theme
- *palmette:* a common fabric element that resembles a palm leaf
- *warp:* the strands of thread or yarn that go lengthwise in a woven fabric
- *weft:* the strands of thread or yarn that go across a woven fabric

More About . . .

Indian Painting

Artists in regions of India outside of the Mughal Empire developed their own distinctive style of painting. While Mughal artists portrayed contemporary and political themes in their paintings, these other artists used more traditional and spiritual themes. And unlike the naturalism favored by Mughal artists, these artists used a more romantic style.

CONNECT TO TODAY: ANSWERS

1. Clarifying
The religious tolerance of the early Mughal emperors and the adaptability of the local Hindu population allowed two distinct cultures to produce unusual and innovative pieces of art while forming a united empire.

2. Forming and Supporting Opinions
Possible Answers: Jazz is a musical form that developed using African-American musical styles, American band instruments, and European harmonies and structure. Rap blends poetry and slang with beats, samples, and live music. Modern tragic and comedic theater can be traced to the ancient Greeks, but modern theater has also absorbed modern cultural influences. Japanese animated film has had an influence on animated features in the United States.

TERMS & NAMES

1. Suleyman the Lawgiver, p. 76
2. *devshirme*, p. 76
3. janissary, p. 76
4. shah, p. 80
5. Shah Abbas, p. 80
6. Akbar, p. 83
7. Sikh, p. 85
8. Taj Mahal, p. 85

MAIN IDEAS

Answers will vary.

9. They used modern military technology—muskets and cannons—and treated conquered peoples humanely.
10. He opened Constantinople to Jews and Christians, and to non-Turks.
11. Mecca and Medina were the holiest cities of Islam, and Cairo was its intellectual center. Capturing these cities gave the Ottomans great influence in the Muslim world.
12. influence of Ottoman, Persian, and Arab cultures, conquest of Christian regions
13. The Safavids borrowed Ottoman ideas of government and military strategy, Persian art and literary ideas, and Chinese artistic ideas.
14. married two Hindus, a Christian, and a Muslim; abolished taxes on non-Muslims; appointed a Spanish Jesuit to tutor his son; allowed people of all faiths to compete for high office
15. Nur Jahan and Jahangir persecuted Sikhs. Aurangzeb reversed Akbar's tolerant policies and levied oppressive taxes on Hindus.

Chapter 2 Assessment

TERMS & NAMES

Briefly explain the importance of each of the following to the Ottoman, Safavid, or Mughal empires.

1. Suleyman the Lawgiver
2. *devshirme*
3. janissary
4. shah
5. Shah Abbas
6. Akbar
7. Sikh
8. Taj Mahal

MAIN IDEAS

The Ottomans Build a Vast Empire Section 1 (pages 73–77)

9. Why were the Ottomans successful conquerors? (10.10.1)
10. How did Mehmed the Conqueror show his tolerance of other cultures? (10.10.1)
11. Why was Selim's capture of Mecca, Medina, and Cairo so significant? (10.10.1)

Case Study: Cultural Blending Section 2 (pages 78–81)

12. What are some of the causes of cultural blending in the Safavid Empire? (10.10.1)
13. In what ways did the Safavids weave foreign ideas into their culture? (10.10.1)

The Mughal Empire in India Section 3 (pages 82–89)

14. In what ways did Akbar defend religious freedom during his reign? (10.4.2)
15. How did Akbar's successors promote religious conflict in the empire? (10.4.2)

CRITICAL THINKING

1. **USING YOUR NOTES**
In a chart, compare and contrast the Mughal Empire under Akbar, the Safavid Empire under Shah Abbas, and the Ottoman Empire under Suleyman I. (HI 1)

	Government Reforms	Cultural Blending
Akbar		
Abbas		
Suleyman		

2. **EVALUATING COURSES OF ACTION**
POWER AND AUTHORITY How did the use of artillery change the way empires in this chapter and lands that bordered them reacted to each other? (HI 1)
3. **RECOGNIZING EFFECTS**
CULTURAL INTERACTION What impact did religion have on governing each of the three empires in this chapter? (HI 1)
4. **EVALUATING DECISIONS**
EMPIRE BUILDING What was the value of treating conquered peoples in a way that did not oppress them? (HI 1)
5. **MAKING INFERENCES**
Why do you think the three empires in this chapter did not unite into one huge empire? Give reasons for your answer. (REP 4)
6. **MAKING INFERENCES**
Conquest of new territories contributed to the growth of the Muslim empires you read about in this chapter. How might it have also hindered this growth? (REP 4)

VISUAL SUMMARY

The Muslim World Expands

Muslims control Middle East, India, North Africa, and parts of Europe.

Ottoman Empire
- Move into Byzantium
- Take Constantinople
- Add Syria and Palestine
- Use janissaries and *devshirme* to control the empire

Safavid Empire
- Take old Persian Empire
- Expand to Caucasus Mountains
- Build a new capital
- Use janissary-style army to control the empire

Mughal Empire
- Delhi Sultanate loosely controls Indian subcontinent
- Babur lays groundwork for an empire
- Akbar controls most of subcontinent in empire
- Aurangzeb expands empire to its largest size

CRITICAL THINKING

Answers will vary.

1. Akbar—Government Reforms: fair taxes; Cultural Blending: architecture, arts, literature. Abbas—Government Reforms: limited power of the military, reduced corruption; Cultural Blending: architecture, arts. Suleyman—Government Reforms: simplified taxation, created a law code; Cultural Blending: architecture, arts, literature.
2. Artillery allowed an army to be successful with fewer soldiers. If a neighboring power did not have artillery, that power would lose land.
3. Each empire had to deal with religious issues. Taxes imposed on specific religious groups caused resentment. In some cases, persecution of certain groups created permanent resentment.
4. It discouraged rebellion, encouraged payment of taxes, and freed armies to focus on more conquest.
5. All were Muslim, but cultural backgrounds and rivalries kept them apart.
6. Overaggressive empire building may have led to overspending, rebellion, and eventually the decline of the empire.

Use the graphs and your knowledge of world history to answer questions 1 and 2.
Additional Test Practice, pp. S1–S33

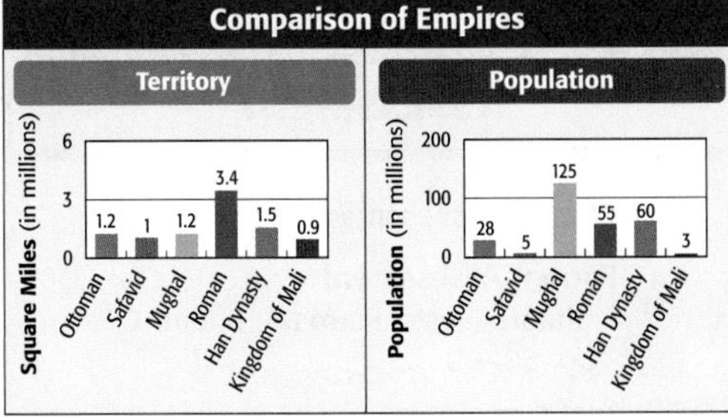

Source: Atlas of World Population History

1. Which empire was most densely populated? (CST 3)
   - **A.** Han
   - **B.** Roman
   - **C.** Mughal
   - **D.** Mali

2. Of the three Asian Muslim empires shown on the graph, which one had the smallest territory? (CST 3)
   - **A.** Ottoman
   - **B.** Safavid
   - **C.** Mughal
   - **D.** Mali

Use the quotation from Kritovoulos, a Greek historian and a governor in the court of Mehmed II, and your knowledge of world history to answer question 3.

PRIMARY SOURCE

When the Sultan [Mehmed] had captured the City of Constantinople, almost his very first care was to have the City repopulated. He also undertook the further care and repairs of it. He sent an order in the form of an imperial command to every part of his realm, that as many inhabitants as possible be transferred to the City, not only Christians but also his own people and many of the Hebrews.

KRITOVOULOS, *History of Mehmed the Conqueror*

3. What groups of people were to be sent to Constantinople? (HI 1)
   - **A.** Hebrews and Christians
   - **B.** Christians and Turks
   - **C.** Christians, Hebrews, and Turkish Muslims
   - **D.** Imperial armies

INTEGRATED TECHNOLOGY

TEST PRACTICE Go to **classzone.com**
- Diagnostic tests
- Strategies
- Tutorials
- Additional practice

ALTERNATIVE ASSESSMENT

1. **Interact *with* History** (HI 1)
   On page 72, you considered how you might treat the people you conquered. Now that you have learned more about three Muslim empires, in what ways do you think you would change your policies? Discuss your thoughts with a small group of classmates.

2.  **WRITING ABOUT HISTORY** (Writing 2.1.e)
   Think about the experience of being a janissary in the court of Suleyman the Lawgiver. Write a **journal entry** about your daily activities. Consider the following:
   - how a janissary was recruited
   - what jobs or activities a janissary may have done
   - the grandeur of the court of Suleyman

INTEGRATED TECHNOLOGY

Creating a Database (Writing 2.3.d)

The three empires discussed in this chapter governed many religious and ethnic groups. Gather information on the religious and ethnic makeup of the modern nations of the former Ottoman, Safavid, and Mughal empires. Organize the information in a population database.
- Create one table for each empire.
- Make row headings for each modern nation occupying the lands of that empire.
- Make column headings for each ethnic group and each religious group.
- Insert the most recent population figures or percentages for each group.
- Use the final column to record the population total for each modern nation.

CHAPTER 2 ASSESSMENT

STANDARDS-BASED ASSESSMENT

1. Letter **C** is correct. The Mughal Empire had 104.17 persons per square mile. Letter **A** is incorrect. The Han Empire had 40 persons per square mile. Letter **B** is incorrect. The Roman Empire had 16.17 persons per square mile. Letter **D** is incorrect. Mali had 3.33 persons per square mile.
2. The correct answer is letter **B**, the Safavid Empire, with 1 million square miles of territory. Letters **A** and **C** are incorrect because each of those empires had more territory than the Safavid Empire. Letter **D** is incorrect because Mali was located in Africa.
3. The correct answer is letter **C**. Members of all three groups were sent to Constantinople. Letter **A** is not correct because it does not include Turkish Muslims. Letter **B** is not correct because it does not include Hebrews. Letter **D** is not correct because armies were not sent in to rebuild the city.

Formal Assessment
- Chapter Test, Forms A, B, and C, pp. 43–54

California Test Generator CD-ROM
- Chapter Tests, Forms A, B, and C (English and Spanish)

ALTERNATIVE ASSESSMENT

1. **Possible Answers:** Tolerance and cultural blending are the best way to accommodate the people of a diverse empire. Ruling forcefully will keep various groups under control and demonstrate power.

2. **Rubric** Journal entries should
   - explain how the individual became a janissary.
   - list a janissary's daily tasks.
   - describe the court of Suleyman.

INTEGRATED TECHNOLOGY

Rubric Databases should
- contain up-to-date information on nations found in the three empires.
- present information in a clear, easy-to-read format.
- list the sources of information used in building the database.

For help creating databases, refer students to the Skillbuilder Handbook.

An Age of Explorations and Isolation, 1400–1800

CHAPTER RESOURCES	COPYMASTERS	ASSESSMENT
CHAPTER OVERVIEW Europeans explored faraway lands and the Japanese and Chinese isolated themselves from Europeans.	**In-Depth Resources: Unit 1** • Building Vocabulary, p. 53 **Chapters in Brief** (in English and Spanish) **Block Schedule Pacing Guide**	**Chapter Assessment,** pp. 114–115 **Formal Assessment** • Chapter Tests, Forms A, B, and C, pp. 58–69 **Test Generator** **Integrated Assessment Book** **Online Test Practice**
SECTION 1 **Europeans Explore the East** pp. 95–101 **OBJECTIVE** Analyze European exploration of the East, the rivalry between Spain and Portugal, and the trading empires in the Indian Ocean.	**In-Depth Resources: Unit 1** • Guided Reading, p. 60 • Primary Sources: Exploration of Cape Verde, p. 67; The Treaty of Tordesillas, p. 68 • History Makers: Vasco da Gama, p. 74 • Science & Technology: A Revolution in Cartography, p. 77 • Reteaching Activity, p. 78 **Reading Study Guide,** p. 33	**Section 1 Assessment,** p. 101 **Formal Assessment** • Section Quiz, p. 55 **California Daily Standards Practice Transparencies,** TT68
SECTION 2 **China Limits European Contacts** pp. 102–107 **OBJECTIVE** Describe the Ming and Qing dynasties, their effect on foreign countries, and what life was like in China during this time.	**In-Depth Resources: Unit 1** • Guided Reading, p. 61 • Skillbuilder Practice: Interpreting Graphs, p. 64 • Geography Application: The Voyages of Zheng He, p. 65 • Primary Source: from *The Journals of Matteo Ricci,* p. 69 • Literature: from *The Dream of the Red Chamber,* p. 71 • Reteaching Activity, p. 79 **Reading Study Guide,** p. 35	**Section 2 Assessment,** p. 107 **Formal Assessment** • Section Quiz, p. 56 **California Daily Standards Practice Transparencies,** TT69
SECTION 3 **Japan Returns to Isolation** pp. 108–113 **OBJECTIVE** Describe feudalism in Japan, life in Tokugawa Japan, and contact between Europe and Japan in the 16th century.	**In-Depth Resources: Unit 1** • Guided Reading, p. 62 • Literature: Haiku, p. 73 • History Makers: Tokugawa Ieyasu, p. 75 • Connections Across Time and Cultures: Breakdown of Feudal Societies, p. 76 • Reteaching Activity, p. 80 **Reading Study Guide,** p. 37	**Section 3 Assessment,** p. 113 **Formal Assessment** • Section Quiz, p. 57 **California Daily Standards Practice Transparencies,** TT70

INTEGRATED TECHNOLOGY

- eEdition Plus Online
- EasyPlanner Plus Online
- eTest Plus Online

 **Audio CDs**
- Voices from the Past
- Reading Study Guides

CD-ROMs
- eEdition
- Power Presentations
- EasyPlanner
- Electronic Library of Primary Sources
- Test Generator

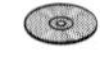 **eEdition CD-ROM**

 **World Art and Cultures Transparencies**
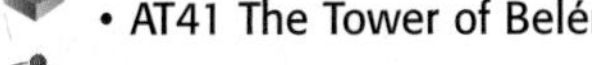
- AT41 The Tower of Belém

 **classzone.com**

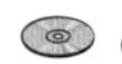 **eEdition CD-ROM**

 **Electronic Library of Primary Sources**
- Letter to King George III

 **classzone.com**

 **eEdition CD-ROM**

 **Geography Transparencies**
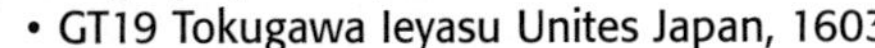
- GT19 Tokugawa Ieyasu Unites Japan, 1603

 **World Art and Cultures Transparencies**
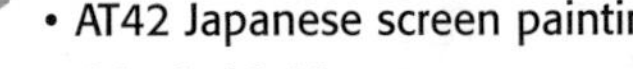
- AT42 Japanese screen painting

 **Critical Thinking Transparencies**
- CT19 The Impact of Exploration on East Asia
- CT55 Chapter 3 Visual Summary

Electronic Library of Primary Sources
- from *The Life and Letters of St. Francis Xavier*
- from the Act of Seclusion

 **classzone.com**

OVERVIEW OF CALIFORNIA RESOURCES

	Section 1	Section 2	Section 3
California Reading Toolkit	p. L16	p. L17	p. L18
California Modified Lesson Plans for English Learners	p. 27	p. 29	p. 31
California Daily Standards Practice Transparencies	TT8	TT9	TT10
California Standards Enrichment Workbook	pp. 47–48, 49–50, 51–52	pp. 49–50	pp. 47–48, 49–50
California Standards Planner and Lesson Plans	p. L23	p. L25	p. L27
California Online Test Practice	classzone.com	classzone.com	classzone.com
California Test Generator CD-ROM	CD-ROM	CD-ROM	CD-ROM
California Easy Planner CD-ROM	CD-ROM	CD-ROM	CD-ROM
California eEdition CD-ROM	CD-ROM	CD-ROM	CD-ROM

Chart Key:

  Pupil's Edition

 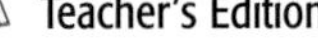 Teacher's Edition

Overhead Transparency

 Block Scheduling

 Copymaster

 Audio Library

 CD-ROM

Internet

 Video

NO TIME?

If you do not have time to teach this chapter in full, assign the **Chapter in Brief** (also available in Spanish).

ENGLISH LEARNERS: Resources in Spanish

In-Depth Resources in Spanish
- Guided Reading **A**
- Skillbuilder Practice: Interpreting Graphs
- Geography Application: The Voyages of Zheng He **B**

Chapters in Brief

Reading Study Guide C

Reading Study Guide Audio CD

Test Generator CD-ROM
- Chapter Test, Forms A, B, and C

Plus

Modified Lesson Plans for English Learners

Multi-Language Glossary of Social Studies Terms

A

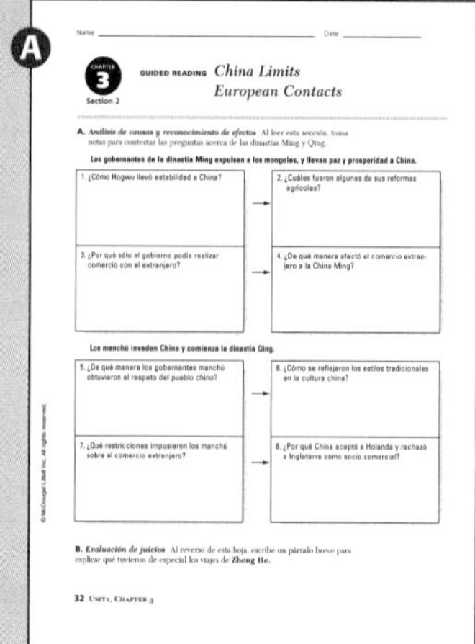
CHAPTER 3 Section 2 GUIDED READING China Limits European Contacts

B

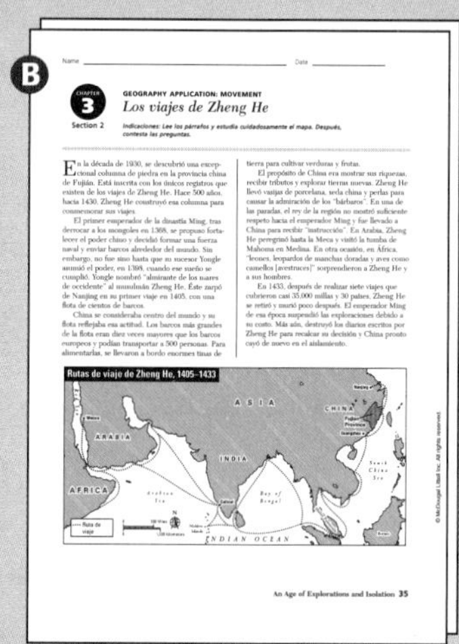
CHAPTER 3 Section 2 GEOGRAPHY APPLICATION: MOVEMENT Los viajes de Zheng He

STRUGGLING READERS

In-Depth Resources: Unit 1
- Guided Reading **A**
- Building Vocabulary
- Skillbuilder Practice: Interpreting Graphs **B**
- Geography Application: The Voyages of Zheng He
- Reteaching Activities

Chapters in Brief

Reading Study Guide C

Reading Study Guide Audio CD

Formal Assessment
- Chapter Test, Form A

Plus

Reading Toolkit

A

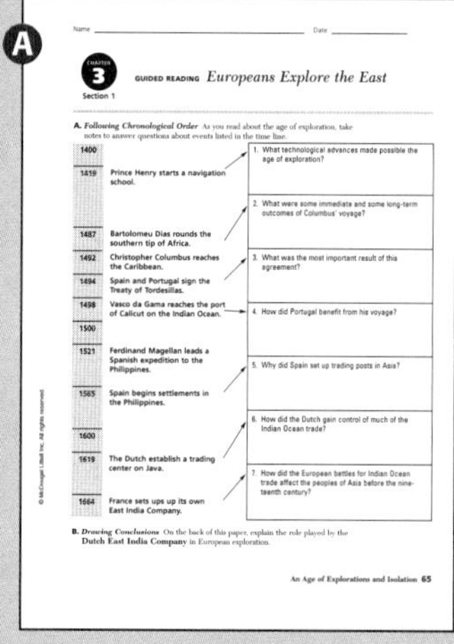
CHAPTER 3 Section 1 GUIDED READING Europeans Explore the East

B

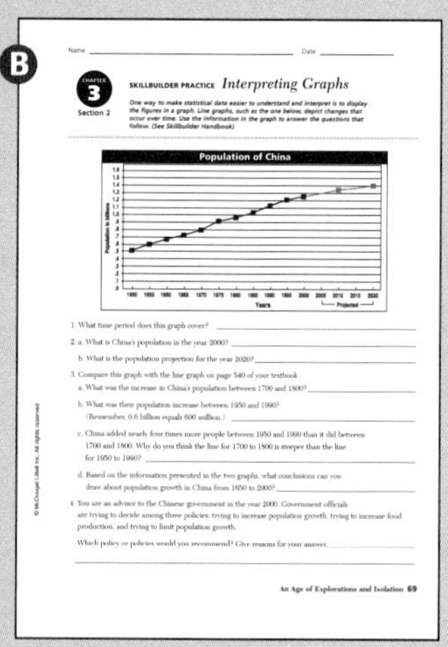
CHAPTER 3 Section 2 SKILLBUILDER PRACTICE Interpreting Graphs

GIFTED AND TALENTED STUDENTS

In-Depth Resources: Unit 1
- Primary Sources: Exploration of Cape Verde; The Treaty of Tordesillas; from *The Journals of Matteo Ricci*
- Literature: from *The Dream of the Red Chamber;* Haiku **A**
- History Makers: Vasco da Gama; Tokugawa Ieyasu
- Connections Across Time and Cultures: Breakdown of Feudal Societies **B**
- Science and Technology: A Revolution in Cartography **C**

Electronic Library of Primary Sources
- Letter to King George III
- from *The Life and Letters of St. Francis Xavier*
- from the Act of Seclusion

Formal Assessment
- Chapter Test, Form C

A

CHAPTER 3 Section 3 LITERATURE SELECTION Haiku by Matsuo Basho

B

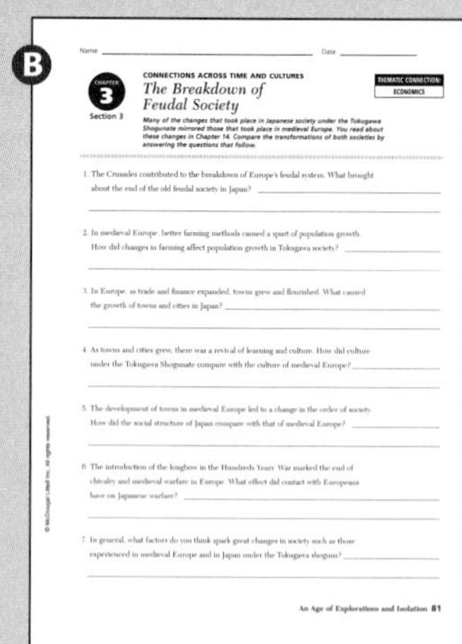
CHAPTER 3 Section 3 CONNECTIONS ACROSS TIME AND CULTURES The Breakdown of Feudal Society

C

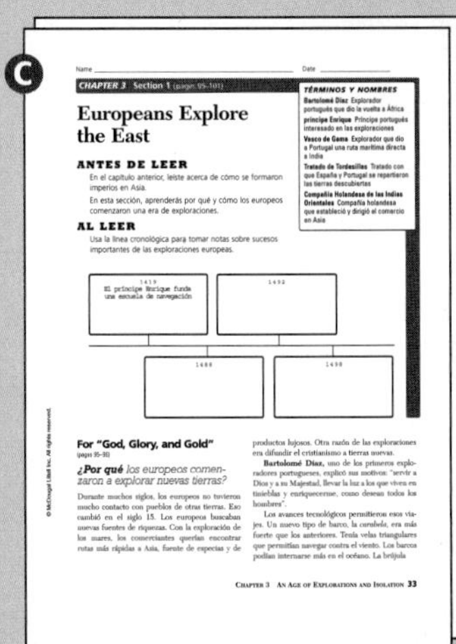

CHAPTER 3 Section 1

Europeans Explore the East

ANTES DE LEER

AL LEER

TÉRMINOS Y NOMBRES

For "God, Glory, and Gold"

¿Por qué los europeos comenzaron a explorar nuevas tierras?

CHAPTER 3 AN AGE OF EXPLORATIONS AND ISOLATION 33

Activities in the Teacher's Edition for English Learners

- Using Nouns as Adjectives, p. 98
- Understanding Professional Titles, p. 103
- Political Terms, p. 109

C

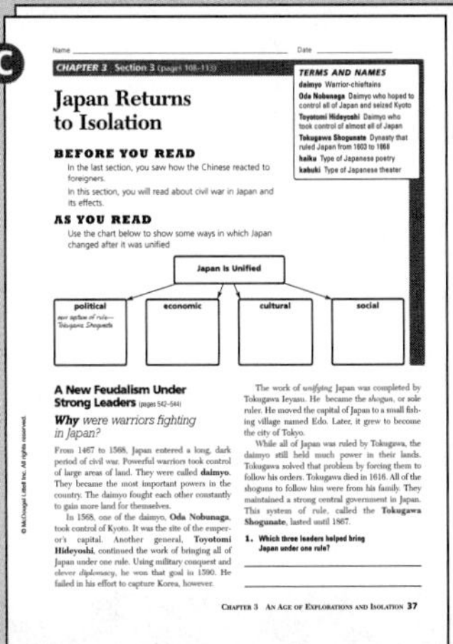

CHAPTER 3 Section 3

Japan Returns to Isolation

BEFORE YOU READ

AS YOU READ

TERMS AND NAMES

Japan Is Unified

political | economic | cultural | social

A New Feudalism Under Strong Leaders

Why were warriors fighting in Japan?

CHAPTER 3 AN AGE OF EXPLORATIONS AND ISOLATION 37

Activities in the Teacher's Edition for Struggling Readers

- Understanding Sequence of Events, p. 96
- Comparing the Ming and Qing Dynasties, p. 105
- The Rise and Fall of Christianity in Japan, p. 112

C

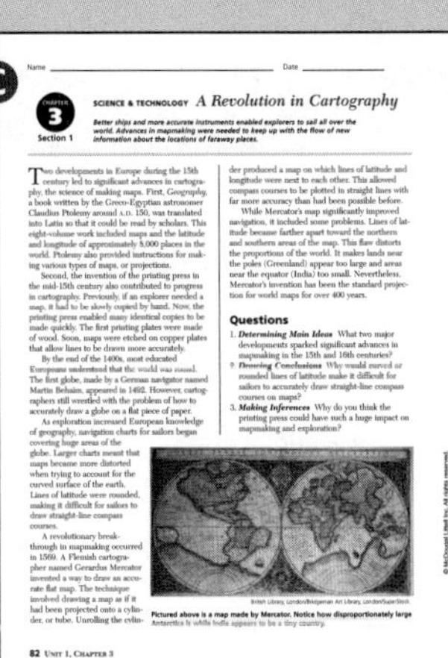

3 Section 1

SCIENCE & TECHNOLOGY A Revolution in Cartography

Questions

82 UNIT 1, CHAPTER 3

Activities in the Teacher's Edition for Gifted and Talented Students

- Understanding the Treaty of Tordesillas, p. 99
- Haiku, p. 110

INTEGRATED TECHNOLOGY

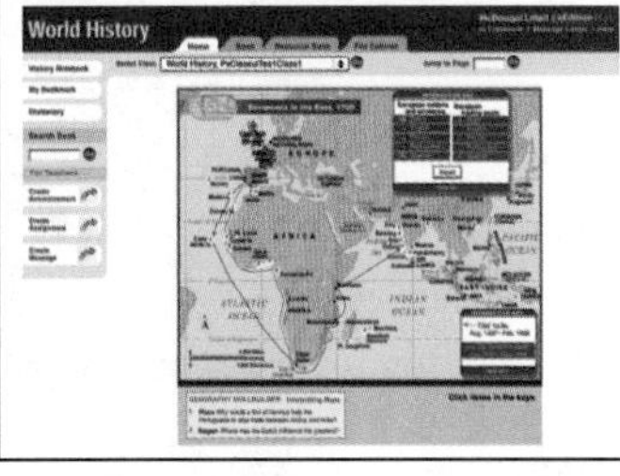

eEdition

- Interactive Visuals
- Interactive Maps
- Interactive Primary Sources

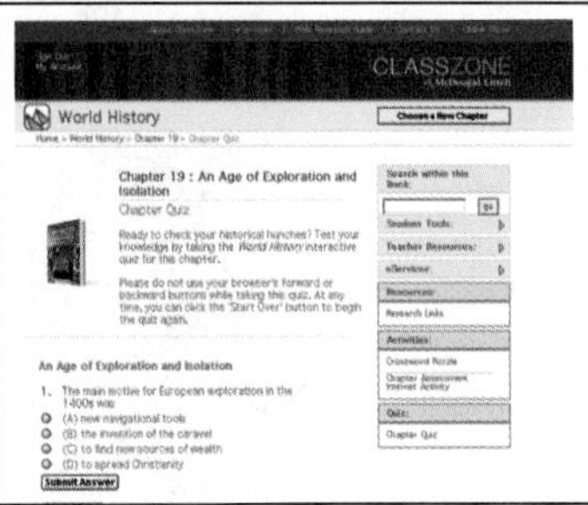

classzone.com

- Research Links
- Internet Activities
- Primary Sources
- Chapter Quiz
- Current Events

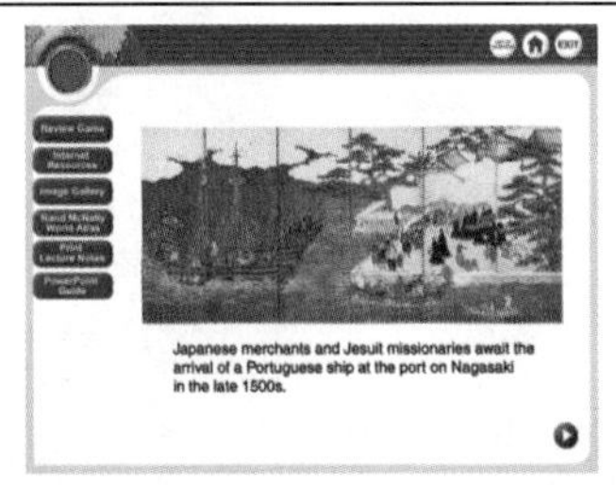

Power Presentations CD-ROM

- Lecture Notes
- Image Gallery
- Chapter Review Game

A

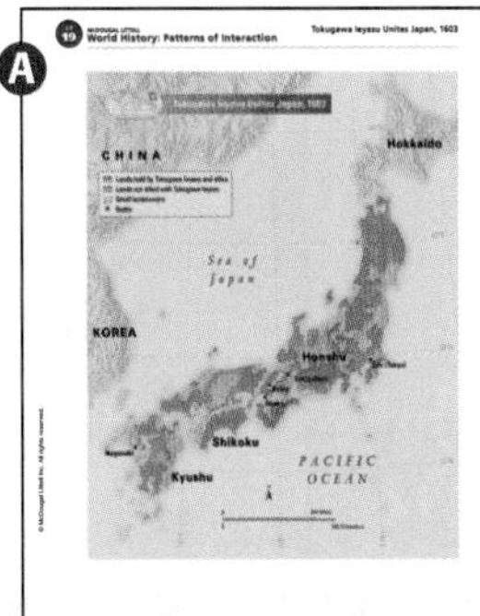

Critical Thinking Transparencies

- CT19 The Impact of Exploration on East Asia
- CT55 Chapter 3 Visual Summary

Geography Transparencies

- GT19 Tokugawa Ieyasu Unites Japan, 1603 A

World Art and Cultures Transparencies

- AT41 The Tower of Belém
- AT42 Japanese screen painting

Test Practice Transparencies TT68–TT70

Test Generator CD-ROM

EasyPlanner CD-ROM

Voices from the Past Audio CD

Online Test Practice

Electronic Library of Primary Sources

CHAPTER 3 • OBJECTIVE

Examine the era of European and Chinese exploration and the events that caused Japan and China to withdraw into isolation.

Previewing Main Ideas

Point out that economics fueled the age of exploration, and the consequences included worldwide interaction among people of many cultures. The isolation of China and Japan was an effort to preserve their cultures from being overwhelmed by the outside world.

Accessing Prior Knowledge

Ask students to look through their personal items and identify where the objects were made. List the different countries. Ask students how international trade affects their lives. Is this interaction a good thing, or a bad thing? Point out that exploration and trade between 1400 and 1800 had far-reaching effects.

Geography *Answers*

CULTURAL INTERACTION Portugal first sent explorers to India.

ECONOMICS Da Gama's voyage was about twice as long.

SCIENCE AND TECHNOLOGY China sent the first expedition to explore the Indian Ocean in the 15th century.

CHAPTER 3

An Age of Explorations and Isolation, 1400–1800

Previewing Main Ideas

CULTURAL INTERACTION Asians resisted European influence, but this cultural interaction did produce an exchange of goods and ideas.

Geography *Study the map. What European power first sent explorers into the Indian Ocean?*

ECONOMICS The desire for wealth was a driving force behind the European exploration of the East. Europeans wanted to control trade with Asian countries.

Geography *How did the voyages of Bartolomeu Dias and Vasco da Gama compare in length?*

SCIENCE AND TECHNOLOGY Europeans were able to explore faraway lands after they improved their sailing technology.

Geography *Look at the map and time line. What country sent the first expedition to explore the Indian Ocean in the 15th century?*

INTEGRATED TECHNOLOGY

eEdition
- Interactive Maps
- Interactive Visuals
- Interactive Primary Sources

INTERNET RESOURCES

Go to **classzone.com** for:
- Research Links
- Internet Activities
- Primary Sources
- Chapter Quiz
- Maps
- Test Practice
- Current Events

EUROPE AND ASIA

1405 Zheng He takes first voyage.

1419 Prince Henry ▶ founds navigation school.

1494 Spain and Portugal sign Treaty of Tordesillas.

1400 — 1500

WORLD

1453 ◀ Ottomans capture Constantinople.

1464 Songhai Empire begins in West Africa.

1511 First enslaved Africans arrive in the Americas.

92

TIME LINE DISCUSSION

Call students' attention to the time line. Point out that civilization was spreading throughout the world during this time period, and major events were happening everywhere.

1. In what year did Prince Henry found a school for navigation? *(1419)* Why was the founding of this school so important? *(The ability to cross oceans was essential for exploration and trade.)*
2. What events occurred in North America during this period? *(First slaves arrived; Champlain founded Quebec; American colonies became independent.)*
3. What event occurred in Europe and Asia at about the same time that the American colonies were declaring their independence? *(Britain tried to open trade with China.)*
4. What can you conclude from this time line about relations among nations of the world? *(Many countries, even those in distant parts of the world, were making contact.)*
5. What countries signed the Treaty of Tordesillas? *(Spain and Portugal)*

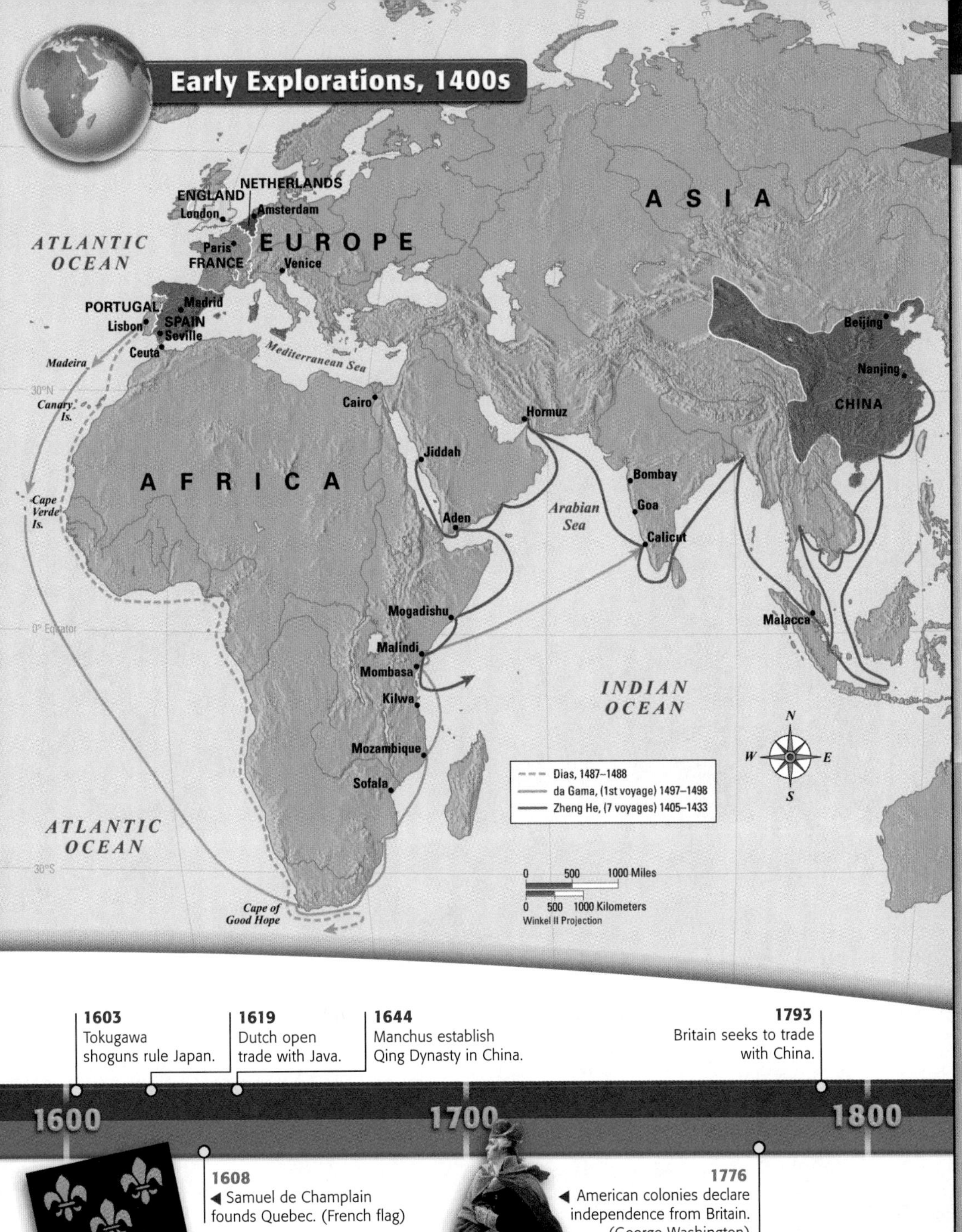

93

History from Visuals

Interpreting the Map

Point out to students that the most direct water route from western Europe to eastern Asia led around the tip of southern Africa. Have students use the distance scale to estimate the sailing distance from the port of Lisbon to the coasts of India and China. *(about 14,000 miles; 19,000 miles)* Then have students estimate the distance by land from Lisbon to India. *(about 5,000 miles)*

Extension Have students turn to the world map in the atlas and trace the route followed by da Gama. In what present-day countries did da Gama stop? *(South Africa, Mozambique, Kenya, India)* Have students identify the modern countries visited by Zheng He. *(Vietnam, Thailand, Indonesia, Malaysia, India, Sri Lanka, United Arab Emirates, Yemen, Iran, Saudi Arabia, Somalia, Kenya)*

RECOMMENDED RESOURCES

Books for the Teacher

Berry, Mary Elizabeth. ***The Culture of Civil War in Kyoto***. Berkeley: U of California P, 1994.

Levathes, Louise. ***When China Ruled the Seas: The Treasure Fleet of the Dragon Throne, 1405–1433***. New York: Oxford UP, 1996.

Wood, Francis. ***Did Marco Polo Go to China***? Boulder, CO: Westview, 1997. A presentation of the passionate debate concerning the authenticity of Marco Polo's travels.

Books for the Student

Reid, Struan. ***Exploration by Sea***. New York: New Discovery, 1994. European trade empires.

Vollmer, John M. ***Clothed to Rule the Universe: Ming to Qing Dynasty Textiles at the Art Institute of Chicago***. Seattle: U of Washington P, 2000. Richly illustrated with full-color reproductions, this book showcases approximately eighty Chinese luxury textiles, which served as both works of art and as instruments of society.

Videos and Software

Asia: 1600–1800. VHS. Social Studies School Service, 1985. Asians respond to Western intrusions.

Forbidden City: The Great Within. VHS. Cambridge Social Studies, 1995. 800-468-4227.

The Golden Age of Exploration. VHS. Knowledge Unlimited, 1997. 800-356-2303.

Exploration. CD-ROM. Queue, 1997. 800-232-2224. Describes the voyages of the Portuguese, Columbus, and other explorers.

Interact *with* History

Objectives

- Set the stage for European exploration of the East.
- Help students understand some of the reasons for exploration.

EXAMINING *the* ISSUES

Possible Answers

- new, different, or cheaper trade goods; profits from trade; expansion of empire; adventure; sources of raw materials; strategic bases for trade and naval power
- loss of lives and ships; conflict with other peoples and with competing national powers

Discussion

Guide a review discussion of the civilizations and economies of China, Japan, and the other empires of Southeast Asia. Have students compare the accomplishments of these civilizations with those of Western Europe. Ask them how the countries might benefit from an exchange of ideas or goods.

Interact *with* History

Would you sail into the unknown?

It is a gray morning in 1430. You are standing on a dock in the European country of Portugal, staring out at the mysterious Atlantic Ocean. You have been asked to go on a voyage of exploration. Yet, like most people at the time, you have no idea what lies beyond the horizon. The maps that have been drawn show some of the dangers you might face. And you've heard the terrifying stories of sea monsters and shipwrecks (see map below). You also have heard that riches await those who help explore and claim new lands. Now, you must decide whether to go.

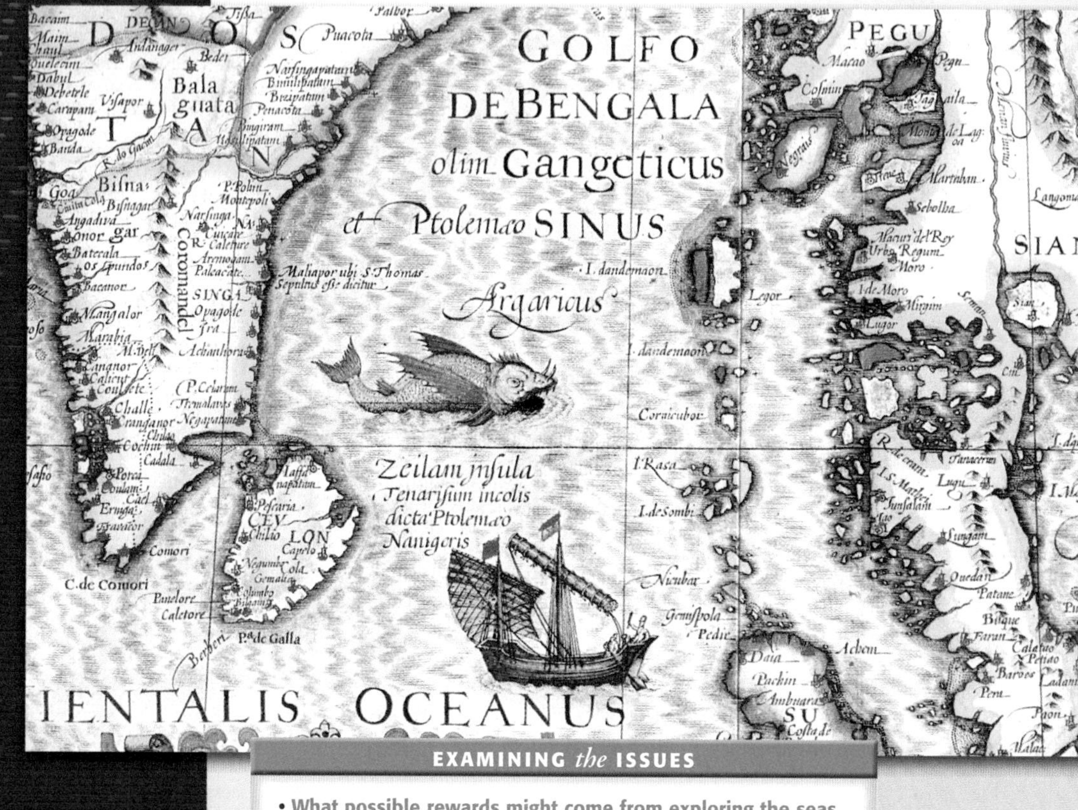

EXAMINING *the* ISSUES

- What possible rewards might come from exploring the seas for new lands?
- What are the risks involved in embarking on a voyage into the unknown?

Discuss these questions with your classmates. In your discussion, recall what you have learned about the lands beyond Europe and what they have to offer. As you read about the age of explorations and isolation, see why Europeans explored and what they achieved.

94 Chapter 3

WHY STUDY THE AGE OF EXPLORATIONS AND ISOLATION?

- The desire to obtain more and different goods at better prices influences our relations with other countries, just as it influenced the actions of nations in the period from 1400 to 1800.
- Peoples of many nations continue to act to preserve their culture against that of outsiders.
- Languages and culture carried by explorers to new lands still influence those places. Portuguese is the official language of Brazil; Spanish is spoken in much of the rest of Latin America; English is widely spoken in India.
- Today's explorers still face the unknown when journeying to new places.
- Advances in technology allow present-day explorers to travel faster, farther, and safer and to visit new places, just as advances in technology expanded the range of explorers during the age of exploration.

Station 37 by Ando Tokitaro Hiroshige

Silk tapestry, China c1600

1

Europeans Explore the East

MAIN IDEA

SCIENCE AND TECHNOLOGY Advances in sailing technology enabled Europeans to explore other parts of the world.

WHY IT MATTERS NOW

European exploration was an important step toward the global interaction existing in the world today.

TERMS & NAMES

- Bartolomeu Dias
- Prince Henry
- Vasco da Gama
- Treaty of Tordesillas
- Dutch East India Company

SETTING THE STAGE By the early 1400s, Europeans were ready to venture beyond their borders. The Renaissance encouraged a spirit of adventure and curiosity. This spirit of adventure, along with several other important reasons, prompted Europeans to explore the world around them. This chapter and the next one describe how these explorations began a long process that would bring together the peoples of many different lands and permanently change the world.

CALIFORNIA STANDARDS

10.4.1 Describe the rise of industrial economies and their link to imperialism and colonialism (e.g., the role played by national security and strategic advantage; moral issues raised by the search for national hegemony, Social Darwinism, and the missionary impulse; material issues such as land, resources, and technology).

10.4.2 Discuss the locations of the colonial rule of such nations as England, France, Germany, Italy, Japan, the Netherlands, Russia, Spain, Portugal, and the United States.

10.4.3 Explain imperialism from the perspective of the colonizers and the colonized and the varied immediate and long-term responses by the people under colonial rule.

CST 1 Students compare the present with the past, evaluating the consequences of past events and decisions and determining the lessons that were learned.

REP 4 Students construct and test hypotheses; collect, evaluate, and employ information from multiple primary and secondary sources; and apply it in oral and written presentations.

For "God, Glory, and Gold"

Europeans had not been completely isolated from the rest of the world before the 1400s. Beginning around 1100, European crusaders battled Muslims for control of the Holy Lands in Southwest Asia. In 1275, the Italian trader Marco Polo reached the court of Kublai Khan in China. For the most part, however, Europeans had neither the interest nor the ability to explore foreign lands. That changed by the early 1400s. The desire to grow rich and to spread Christianity, coupled with advances in sailing technology, spurred an age of European exploration.

Europeans Seek New Trade Routes The desire for new sources of wealth was the main reason for European exploration. Through overseas exploration, merchants and traders hoped ultimately to benefit from what had become a profitable business in Europe: the trade of spices and other luxury goods from Asia. The people of Europe had been introduced to these items during the Crusades, the wars fought between Christians and Muslims from 1096 to 1270. After the Crusades ended, Europeans continued to demand such spices as nutmeg, ginger, cinnamon, and pepper, all of which added flavor to the bland foods of Europe. Because demand for these goods was greater than the supply, merchants could charge high prices and thus make great profits.

The Muslims and the Italians controlled the trade of goods from East to West. Muslims sold Asian goods to Italian merchants, who controlled trade across the land routes of the Mediterranean region. The Italian merchants resold the items at increased prices to merchants

▲ This early globe depicts the Europeans' view of Europe and Africa around 1492.

TAKING NOTES

Following Chronological Order On a time line, note the important events in the European exploration of the East.

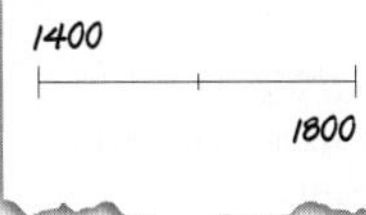

LESSON PLAN

OBJECTIVES

- Explain what led to European exploration.
- Describe steps in Portugal's discovery of a sea route to Asia.
- Explain the rivalry between Spain and Portugal and how the pope resolved it.
- Identify nations that set up trading empires in eastern Asia.

1 FOCUS & MOTIVATE

Explain that a spirit of adventure motivated Europeans to cross oceans and face danger. Ask students what they do to satisfy their sense of adventure. *(Possible Answers: travel to new places, join in sports, learn new skills)*

2 INSTRUCT

For "God, Glory, and Gold"

10.4.1

Critical Thinking

- Why were merchants able to sell spices at a high price? *(Many people wanted spices but supplies were limited, which drove up prices.)*

CALIFORNIA RESOURCES

California Reading Toolkit, p. L16
California Modified Lesson Plans for English Learners, p. 27
California Daily Standards Practice Transparencies, TT8
California Standards Enrichment Workbook, pp. 47–48, 49–50, 51–52
California Standards Planner and Lesson Plans, p. L23
California Online Test Practice
California Test Generator CD-ROM
California Easy Planner CD-ROM
California eEdition CD-ROM

SECTION 1 PROGRAM RESOURCES

ALL STUDENTS

In-Depth Resources: Unit 1
- Guided Reading, p. 60
- History Makers: Vasco da Gama, p. 74

Formal Assessment
- Section Quiz, p. 55

ENGLISH LEARNERS

In-Depth Resources in Spanish
- Guided Reading, p. 31

Reading Study Guide (Spanish), p. 33
Reading Study Guide Audio CD (Spanish)

STRUGGLING READERS

In-Depth Resources: Unit 1
- Guided Reading, p. 60
- Building Vocabulary, p. 63
- Reteaching Activity, p. 78

Reading Study Guide, p. 33
Reading Study Guide Audio CD

GIFTED AND TALENTED STUDENTS

In-Depth Resources: Unit 1
- Primary Sources: Exploration of Cape Verde, p. 67; The Treaty of Tordesillas, p. 68
- Science and Technology: A Revolution in Cartography, p. 77

INTEGRATED TECHNOLOGY

eEdition CD-ROM
Voices from the Past Audio CD
Power Presentations CD-ROM
World Art and Cultures Transparencies
- AT41 The Tower of Belém

classzone.com

History Makers

Prince Henry

Why do you think Prince Henry never went on a voyage of exploration himself? *(Possible Answers: He was the head of state. His skills were in organizing and financing expeditions, not leading them. He did not want to experience the hardships of a long voyage.)*

In 1415, Prince Henry led the invasion of Ceuta in North Africa. One of the prizes from the victory were maps that were more accurate than any in Europe. Four years later, Henry established his navigation school at Sagres. It included libraries, an observatory, and a shipbuilding facility. It was there that the first caravel was developed.

In-Depth Resources: Unit 1

- Primary Source: Exploration of Cape Verde, p. 67

throughout Europe. Other European traders did not like this arrangement. Paying such high prices to the Italians severely cut into their own profits. By the 1400s, European merchants—as well as the new monarchs of England, Spain, Portugal, and France—sought to bypass the Italian merchants. This meant finding a sea route directly to Asia.

The Spread of Christianity The desire to spread Christianity also motivated Europeans to explore. The Crusades had left Europeans with a taste for spices, but more significantly with feelings of hostility between Christians and Muslims. European countries believed that they had a sacred duty not only to continue fighting Muslims, but also to convert non-Christians throughout the world.

Europeans hoped to obtain popular goods directly from the peoples of Asia. They also hoped to Christianize them. **Bartolomeu Dias**, an early Portuguese explorer, explained his motives: "To serve God and His Majesty, to give light to those who were in darkness and to grow rich as all men desire to do." (A)

MAIN IDEA

Summarizing

(A) How might the phrase "God, glory, and gold" summarize the Europeans' motives for exploration?

A. Possible Answer European explorers wanted to spread Christianity, bring fame to themselves and their country, and become rich.

Technology Makes Exploration Possible While "God, glory, and gold" were the primary motives for exploration, advances in technology made the voyages of discovery possible. During the 1200s, it would have been nearly impossible for a European sea captain to cross 3,000 miles of ocean and return again. The main problem was that European ships could not sail against the wind. In the 1400s, shipbuilders designed a new vessel, the caravel. The caravel was sturdier than earlier vessels. In addition, triangular sails adopted from the Arabs allowed it to sail effectively against the wind.

Europeans also improved their navigational techniques. To better determine their location at sea, sailors used the astrolabe, which the Muslims had perfected. The astrolabe was a brass circle with carefully adjusted rings marked off in degrees. Using the rings to sight the stars, a sea captain could calculate latitude, or how far north or south of the equator the ship was. Explorers were also able to more accurately track direction by using a magnetic compass, a Chinese invention.

History Makers

Prince Henry
1394–1460

For his role in promoting Portuguese exploration, historians call Prince Henry "the Navigator." Although he never went on voyages of discovery, Henry was consumed by the quest to find new lands and to spread Christianity. A devout Catholic, he wanted "to make increase in the faith of our lord Jesus Christ and bring to him all the souls that should be saved."

To that end, Henry used his own fortune to organize more than 14 voyages along the western coast of Africa, which was previously unexplored by Europeans. As a result, Henry died in debt. The Portuguese crown spent more than 60 years paying off his debts.

INTEGRATED TECHNOLOGY

RESEARCH LINKS For more on Prince Henry, go to **classzone.com**

Portugal Leads the Way

The leader in developing and applying these sailing innovations was Portugal. Located on the Atlantic Ocean at the southwest corner of Europe, Portugal was the first European country to establish trading outposts along the west coast of Africa. Eventually, Portuguese explorers pushed farther east into the Indian Ocean.

The Portuguese Explore Africa Portugal took the lead in overseas exploration in part due to strong government support. The nation's most enthusiastic supporter of exploration was **Prince Henry**, the son of Portugal's king. Henry's dreams of overseas exploration began in 1415 when he helped conquer the Muslim city of Ceuta in North Africa. There, he had his first glimpse of the dazzling wealth that lay beyond Europe. In Ceuta, the Portuguese invaders found exotic stores filled with pepper, cinnamon, cloves, and other spices. In addition, they encountered large supplies of gold, silver, and jewels.

Portugal Leads the Way

10.4.2

Critical Thinking

- Why did Henry found a navigation school as a means to gain access to the riches of East Asia? *(Europeans had to learn how to sail great distances to reach East Asia and its wealth.)*
- Why did the Portuguese have to explore the coast of Africa so many times before finally sailing around the tip into the Indian Ocean? *(They didn't know where the tip of Africa was or how far they had to travel to reach it.)*

DIFFERENTIATING INSTRUCTION: STRUGGLING READERS

Understanding Sequence of Events

Class Time 45 minutes

Task Creating a time line

Purpose To help students remember the order of events

Instructions Draw a time line on the chalkboard for the period 1400 to 1800. Ask students to identify the first event in this section that should be added to the time line. *(Prince Henry conquers Ceuta in North Africa.)* Add the event to the time line. Then ask, Why was this event important? *(It inspired Prince Henry to become active in exploration.)* Now ask students to work in pairs and to complete their own time lines. Have them continue to add important events to the time line as they read the section. Tell them to answer the question "Why is it important?" as they add each event to their diagram. When students reach the end of the section, have them meet in a group to compare their time lines and discuss the significance of each event. Encourage students to add additional dates that they may have missed. For more ideas and practice, have students use Guided Reading, In-Depth Resources: Unit 1, p. 60.

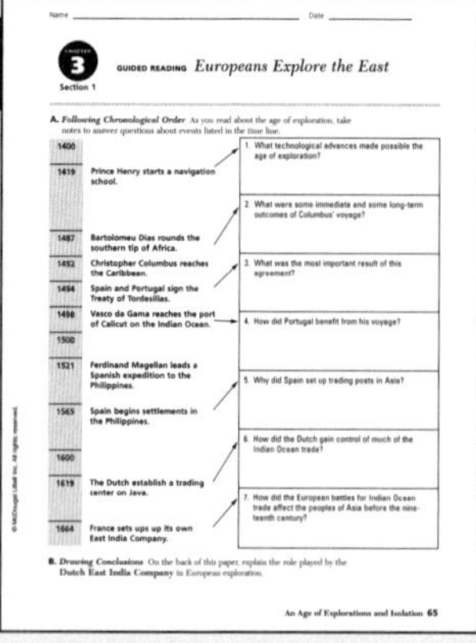

Name ______ Date ______

CHAPTER 3 Section 1 GUIDED READING *Europeans Explore the East*

A. *Following Chronological Order* As you read about the age of exploration, take notes to answer questions about events listed in the time line.

1400

1419 Prince Henry starts a navigation school.

1487 Bartolomeu Dias rounds the southern tip of Africa.

1492 Christopher Columbus reaches the Caribbean.

1494 Spain and Portugal sign the Treaty of Tordesillas.

1498 Vasco da Gama reaches the port of Calicut on the Indian Ocean.

1500

1521 Ferdinand Magellan leads a Spanish expedition to the Philippines.

1565 Spain begins settlements in the Philippines.

1600

1619 The Dutch establish a trading center on Java.

1664 France sets ups up its own East India Company.

1. What technological advances made possible the age of exploration?
2. What were some immediate and some long-term outcomes of Columbus' voyage?
3. What was the most important result of this agreement?
4. How did Portugal benefit from his voyage?
5. Why did Spain set up trading posts in Asia?
6. How did the Dutch gain control of much of the Indian Ocean trade?
7. How did the European battles for Indian Ocean trade affect the peoples of Asia before the nineteenth century?

B. *Drawing Conclusions* On the back of this paper, explain the role played by the **Dutch East India Company** in European exploration.

An Age of Explorations and Isolation 65

In-Depth Resources: Unit 1

Science & *Technology*

INTERACTIVE

The Tools of Exploration

Out on the open seas, winds easily blew ships off course. With only the sun, moon, and stars to guide them, few sailors willingly ventured beyond the sight of land. In order to travel to distant places, European inventors and sailors experimented with new tools for navigation and new designs for sailing ships, often borrowing from other cultures.

INTEGRATED TECHNOLOGY

RESEARCH LINKS For more on the tools of exploration, go to **classzone.com**

▲ Here, a French mariner uses an early navigation instrument that he has brought ashore to fix his ship's position. It was difficult to make accurate calculations aboard wave-tossed vessels.

1. The average caravel was 65 feet long. This versatile ship had triangular sails for maneuverability and square sails for power.

2. The large cargo area could hold the numerous supplies needed for long voyages.

3. Its shallow draft (depth of the ship's keel below the water) allowed it to explore close to the shore.

CALIFORNIA STANDARDS

10.3.2 Examine how scientific and technological changes and new forms of energy brought about massive social, economic, and cultural change (e.g., the inventions and discoveries of James Watt, Eli Whitney, Henry Bessemer, Louis Pasteur, Thomas Edison).

◀ The sextant replaced the astrolabe in the mid-1700s as the instrument for measuring the height of the stars above the horizon—to determine latitude and longitude.

▲ This 17th-century compass is typical of those taken by navigators on voyages of exploration. The compass was invented by the Chinese.

Connect *to* Today

1. **Analyzing Motives** Why did inventors and sailors develop better tools for navigation?
   See Skillbuilder Handbook, page R16.
2. **Summarizing** What types of navigational or other tools do sailors use today? Choose one type of tool and write a brief explanation of what it does.

97

Science & *Technology*

OBJECTIVE

- Explain technology breakthroughs that allowed early sailors to travel long distances across the ocean.

INSTRUCT

Point out that early sailors never willingly sailed out of sight of land. However, following the coast added many miles to a long journey. Have students look at the map on page 100. Ask why da Gama's route was more efficient than Dias's route. Then discuss the inventions on this page. Have students tell how each invention helped sailors follow da Gama's route.

In-Depth Resources: Unit 1

- Science and Technology: A Revolution in Cartography, p. 77

INTEGRATED TECHNOLOGY

Interactive This feature is available in an interactive format on the eEdition.

More About . . .

The Sextant

The sextant incorporated a telescope, mirrors, and an arc of a circle calibrated in degrees. With this device, a mariner could read the angle of elevation above the horizon of the moon, the sun, or another star. With this information, plus the exact time of day and published tables, the ship's latitude could be determined.

CONNECT TO TODAY: ANSWERS

1. Analyzing Motives

Possible Answer: They wanted to sail into the wind and to cross large bodies of water more efficiently. Often, this meant sailing far out of sight of land, so better navigation tools were needed.

2. Summarizing

Rubric Summaries should

- be clear and concise.
- list the specific functions of the tool.
- explain the benefits of the tool.

History *in* Depth

Sailors were often at sea for six months or more. Meat was salted to preserve it. Biscuits, also called hardtack, were a hard bread baked to remove all moisture. Water went bad in a few weeks, but beer and wine lasted much longer. Sailors received daily rations of each.

INTEGRATED TECHNOLOGY

Rubric Successful menus should
- include foods typical on warships.
- be balanced among different food groups.

More About . . .

Vasco da Gama

In July 1497, da Gama sailed from Lisbon with four ships. Ten months later, he arrived in Calicut. Da Gama announced that he came seeking "Christians and spices." He found spices but no Christians. Instead, he found an ancient seagoing commerce run mainly by Muslims.

In-Depth Resources: Unit 1
- History Maker: Vasco da Gama, p. 74

Spain Also Makes Claims

10.4.2

Critical Thinking
- How did Columbus expect to get to Asia by sailing west? *(He believed the world was round. By sailing west, he would eventually reach Asia.)*
- How might Columbus have mistaken the Caribbean for the East Indies? *(He didn't know another continent blocked the route to Asia.)*

History *in* Depth

A Ship's Rations

The captain of a 17th-century sailing vessel, with a crew of 190 sailors, would normally order the following food items for a three-month trip:
- 8,000 pounds of salt beef; 2,800 pounds of salt pork; 600 pounds of salt cod; a few beef tongues
- 15,000 brown biscuits; 5,000 white biscuits
- 30 bushels of oatmeal; 40 bushels of dried peas; 1 1/2 bushels of mustard seed
- 1 barrel of salt; 1 barrel of flour
- 11 small wooden casks of butter; 1 large cask of vinegar
- 10,500 gallons of beer; 3,500 gallons of water; 2 large casks of cider

INTEGRATED TECHNOLOGY

INTERNET ACTIVITY Research food services aboard a modern U.S. warship and prepare a menu for a typical meal. Go to **classzone.com** for your research.

Henry returned to Portugal determined to reach the source of these treasures in the East. The prince also wished to spread the Christian faith. In 1419, Henry founded a navigation school on the southwestern coast of Portugal. Mapmakers, instrument makers, shipbuilders, scientists, and sea captains gathered there to perfect their trade.

Within several years, Portuguese ships began sailing down the western coast of Africa. By the time Henry died in 1460, the Portuguese had established a series of trading posts along western Africa's shores. There, they traded with Africans for such profitable items as gold and ivory. Eventually, they traded for African captives to be used as slaves. Having established their presence along the African coast, Portuguese explorers plotted their next move. They would attempt to find a sea route to Asia.

Portuguese Sailors Reach Asia The Portuguese believed that to reach Asia by sea, they would have to sail around the southern tip of Africa. In 1488, Portuguese captain Bartolomeu Dias ventured far down the coast of Africa until he and his crew reached the tip. As they arrived, a huge storm rose and battered the fleet for days. When the storm ended, Dias realized his ships had been blown around the tip to the other side. Dias explored the southeast coast of Africa and then considered sailing to India. However, his crew was exhausted and food supplies were low. As a result, the captain returned home.

With the tip of Africa finally rounded, the Portuguese continued pushing east. In 1497, Portuguese explorer **Vasco da Gama** began exploring the east African coast. In 1498, he reached the port of Calicut, on the southwestern coast of India. Da Gama and his crew were amazed by the spices, rare silks, and precious gems that filled Calicut's shops. The Portuguese sailors filled their ships with such spices as pepper and cinnamon and returned to Portugal in 1499. Their cargo was worth 60 times the cost of the voyage. Da Gama's remarkable voyage of 27,000 miles had given Portugal a direct sea route to India.

Spain Also Makes Claims

As the Portuguese were establishing trading posts along the west coast of Africa, Spain watched with increasing envy. The Spanish monarchs also desired a direct sea route to Asia.

In 1492, an Italian sea captain, Christopher Columbus, convinced Spain to finance a bold plan: finding a route to Asia by sailing west across the Atlantic Ocean. In October of that year, Columbus reached an island in the Caribbean. He was mistaken in his thought that he had reached the East Indies. But his voyage would open the way for European colonization of the Americas—a process that would forever change the world. The immediate impact of Columbus's voyage, however, was to increase tensions between Spain and Portugal.

The Portuguese believed that Columbus had indeed reached Asia. Portugal suspected that Columbus had claimed for Spain lands that Portuguese sailors might

DIFFERENTIATING INSTRUCTION: ENGLISH LEARNERS

Using Nouns as Adjectives

Class Time 25 minutes

Task Identifying and using nouns as adjectives

Purpose To understand the use of nouns as adjectives

Instructions Write the following sentence on the chalkboard: "The Portuguese believed that to reach Asia by *sea,* they would have to sail around the southern tip of Africa." Underline the word *sea,* and tell students that the word is a noun. Then write this sentence on the board: "They would attempt to find a *sea* route to Asia." Ask, What part of speech is *sea* in this sentence? *(adjective)* Explain that nouns are sometimes used as adjectives. Often, nouns are used without a change in form, as in this example. At other times, nouns are changed to the possessive form, as in the sentence "Da Gama and his crew were amazed by the spices, . . . that filled Calicut's shops." Now refer students to the first two paragraphs on this page, and have them identify nouns used as adjectives. Use the horizontal chart on Critical Thinking Transparency CT80 and record students' answers in the first column. Have students provide sentences using the noun as a noun. Write their sentences in the second column. Have students work on their own and create a similar chart for the remainder of the page.

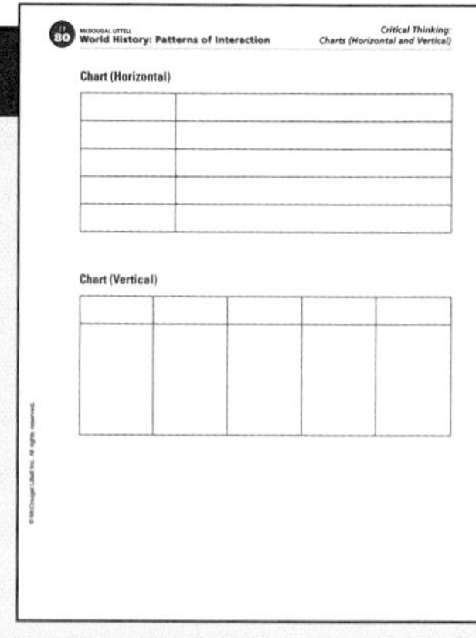

Critical Thinking Transparencies

B. Possible Answer It appeased both nations by granting them their own territories to colonize.

MAIN IDEA

Analyzing Issues

B How did the Treaty of Tordesillas ease tensions between Spain and Portugal?

have reached first. The rivalry between Spain and Portugal grew more tense. In 1493, Pope Alexander VI stepped in to keep peace between the two nations. He suggested an imaginary dividing line, drawn north to south, through the Atlantic Ocean. All lands to the west of the line, known as the Line of Demarcation, would be Spain's. These lands included most of the Americas. All lands to the east of the line would belong to Portugal.

Portugal complained that the line gave too much to Spain. So it was moved farther west to include parts of modern-day Brazil for the Portuguese. In 1494, Spain and Portugal signed the **Treaty of Tordesillas**, in which they agreed to honor the line. The era of exploration and colonization was about to begin in earnest. B

Trading Empires in the Indian Ocean

With da Gama's voyage, Europeans had finally opened direct sea trade with Asia. They also opened an era of violent conflict in the East. European nations scrambled to establish profitable trading outposts along the shores of South and Southeast Asia. And all the while they battled the region's inhabitants, as well as each other.

Portugal's Trading Empire In the years following da Gama's voyage, Portugal built a bustling trading empire throughout the Indian Ocean. As the Portuguese moved into the region, they took control of the spice trade from Muslim merchants. In 1509, Portugal extended its control over the area when it defeated a Muslim fleet off the coast of India, a victory made possible by the cannons they had added aboard their ships.

Portugal strengthened its hold on the region by building a fort at Hormuz in 1514. It established control of the Straits of Hormuz, connecting the Persian Gulf and Arabian Sea, and helped stop Muslim traders from reaching India.

In 1510, the Portuguese captured Goa, a port city on India's west coast. They made it the capital of their trading empire. They then sailed farther east to Indonesia, also known as the East Indies. In 1511, a Portuguese fleet attacked the city of Malacca on the west coast of the Malay Peninsula. In capturing the town, the Portuguese seized control of the Strait of Malacca. Seizing this waterway gave them control of the Moluccas. These were islands so rich in spices that they became known as the Spice Islands.

In convincing his crew to attack Malacca, Portuguese sea captain Afonso de Albuquerque stressed his country's intense desire to crush the Muslim-Italian domination over Asian trade:

MAIN IDEA

Analyzing Primary Sources

C What did de Albuquerque see as the outcome of a Portuguese victory at Malacca?

C. Answer the end to Muslim domination of the Indian Ocean trade

PRIMARY SOURCE C

If we deprive them [Muslims] of this their ancient market there, there does not remain for them a single port in the whole of these parts, where they can carry on their trade in these things. . . . I hold it as very certain that if we take this trade of Malacca away out of their hands, Cairo and Mecca are entirely ruined, and to Venice will no spiceries . . . [be] . . . conveyed except that which her merchants go and buy in Portugal.

AFONSO DE ALBUQUERQUE, from *The Commentaries of the Great Afonso Dalbuquerque*

Portugal did break the old Muslim-Italian domination on trade from the East, much to the delight of European consumers. Portuguese merchants brought back goods from Asia at about one-fifth of what they cost when purchased through the Arabs and Italians. As a result, more Europeans could afford these items.

Trading Empires in the Indian Ocean

10.4.3

Critical Thinking

- Why were the Portuguese determined to prevent Muslim traders from continuing their spice trade? *(The Portuguese would make higher profits if they didn't have any competitors.)*
- How was the Dutch East India Company able to drive out the English and Portuguese? *(It had ships, money, and armies.)*
- Why didn't the Europeans have more influence on the countries of southeast Asia? *(They controlled only port cities, not inland areas.)*

More About . . .

Afonso de Albuquerque

Afonso de Albuquerque was more than just a sea captain. He gained fame as "the Portuguese Mars" (Mars was the Roman god of war) for his leadership of the armed fleets that took Goa and the Strait of Malacca. Albuquerque also served as the viceroy of India, governing the Portuguese holdings there for six years. He died at sea in 1515 while returning to Portugal after the new king had replaced him and ordered him home.

DIFFERENTIATING INSTRUCTION: GIFTED AND TALENTED STUDENTS

Understanding the Treaty of Tordesillas

Class Time 45 minutes

Task Using primary sources and maps

Purpose To compare historic treaties with present-day maps

Instructions Have students work in a small group to study the Treaty of Tordesillas and to explain it to their class.

- Give students a copy of the primary source, The Treaty of Tordesillas, in In-Depth Resources, Unit 1, page 68.
- Using a world map or globe, have students locate the Cape Verde Islands off the coast of west Africa and decide where the Line of Demarcation would be drawn. (Explain that a *league* is approximately 3 statute miles.)
- Tell the group to discuss the significance of the treaty to Spain and Portugal. Was the Line of Demarcation fairly drawn?
- Next, have the group explain the Treaty of Tordesillas to the class. The group should explain the agreement and show where the Line of Demarcation would be drawn on a modern map. Have students reach conclusions about the fairness of the division to Portugal and to Spain.

In-Depth Resources: Unit 1

History from Visuals

Interpreting the Map

Have students trace da Gama's route on the map from Lisbon to Calicut. Using the distance scale, ask them how far da Gama traveled. *(about 15,000 miles)*

Extension Ask students to speculate about why so many European nations established trading posts in India. *(Possible Answers: India had spices and other goods for trade; India was a good central location for the Indian Ocean trade.)*

INTEGRATED TECHNOLOGY

Interactive This map is available in an interactive format on the eEdition. Students can view each route and follow it step by step.

SKILLBUILDER Answers

1. **Place** Hormuz is on the strait connecting the Persian Gulf and the Arabian Sea. Any ship carrying goods to or from the gulf would have to pass by Hormuz.
2. **Region** East Indies

Tip for Gifted and Talented Students

The Spice Islands (now named Moluccas) are a small group of islands in Indonesia that played a major role in the European exploration of Asia. Have students learn about the spices grown there and the colonial rule of the islands.

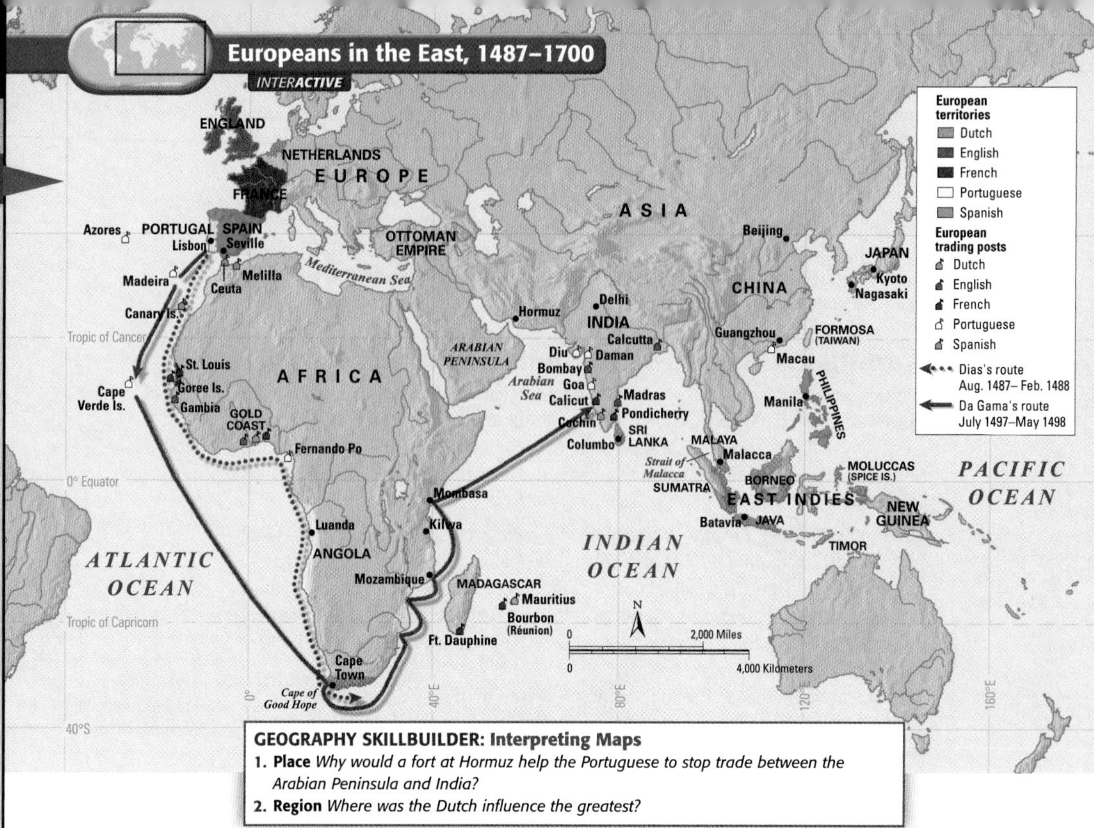

GEOGRAPHY SKILLBUILDER: Interpreting Maps

1. **Place** *Why would a fort at Hormuz help the Portuguese to stop trade between the Arabian Peninsula and India?*
2. **Region** *Where was the Dutch influence the greatest?*

In time, Portugal's success in Asia attracted the attention of other European nations. As early as 1521, a Spanish expedition led by Ferdinand Magellan arrived in the Philippines. Spain claimed the islands and began settling them in 1565. By the early 1600s, the rest of Europe had begun to descend upon Asia. They wanted to establish their own trade empires in the East.

Other Nations Challenge the Portuguese Beginning around 1600, the English and Dutch began to challenge Portugal's dominance over the Indian Ocean trade. The Dutch Republic, also known as the Netherlands, was a small country situated along the North Sea in northwestern Europe. Since the early 1500s, Spain had ruled the area. In 1581, the people of the region declared their independence from Spain and established the Dutch Republic.

In a short time, the Netherlands became a leading sea power. By 1600, the Dutch owned the largest fleet of ships in the world—20,000 vessels. Pressure from Dutch and also English fleets eroded Portuguese control of the Asian region. The Dutch and English then battled one another for dominance of the area.

Both countries had formed an East India Company to establish and direct trade throughout Asia. These companies had the power to mint money, make treaties, and even raise their own armies. The **Dutch East India Company** was richer and more powerful than England's company. As a result, the Dutch eventually drove out the English and established their dominance over the region. D

Dutch Trade Outposts In 1619, the Dutch established their trading headquarters at Batavia on the island of Java. From there, they expanded west to

D. Answer The Dutch were a great naval power; also, the Dutch East India Company was richer and more powerful than England's company.

MAIN IDEA

Analyzing Issues

D How were the Dutch able to dominate the Indian Ocean trade?

CONNECTIONS ACROSS TIME AND CULTURES

Understanding the Effect of Competition

Class Time 20 minutes

Task Comparing prices of goods and analyzing the effects

Purpose To appreciate the effect of the Portuguese trading empire

Instructions Remind students that as a result of Portugal's success in establishing a trading empire in Southeast Asia, the cost to consumers of Asian goods fell to about a fifth of their former price. Have students make a chart listing a variety of consumer goods that come from Southeast Asia today. Examples might include automobiles, televisions, cameras, and computer games. Students should show the regular retail price of these items and 20 percent of the retail price. (They might find prices for such goods in newspaper advertisements or department store fliers.) Have students meet in a group to compare their charts and discuss the following questions:

- How would such a drop in prices affect what you bought?
- How would it affect U.S. companies?
- How would it affect the people of Southeast Asia?
- What would be the effects on the economies of countries in Southeast Asia?

conquer several nearby islands. In addition, the Dutch seized both the port of Malacca and the valuable Spice Islands from Portugal. Throughout the 1600s, the Netherlands increased its control over the Indian Ocean trade. With so many goods from the East traveling to the Netherlands, the nation's capital, Amsterdam, became a leading commercial center. By 1700, the Dutch ruled much of Indonesia and had trading posts in several Asian countries. They also controlled the Cape of Good Hope on the southern tip of Africa, which was used as a resupply stop.

British and French Traders By 1700 also, Britain and France had gained a foothold in the region. Having failed to win control of the larger area, the English East India Company focused much of its energy on establishing outposts in India. There, the English developed a successful business trading Indian cloth in Europe. In 1664, France also entered the Asia trade with its own East India Company. It struggled at first, as it faced continual attacks by the Dutch. Eventually, the French company established an outpost in India in the 1720s. However, it never showed much of a profit.

As the Europeans battled for a share of the profitable Indian Ocean trade, their influence inland in Southeast Asia remained limited. European traders did take control of many port cities in the region. But their impact rarely spread beyond the ports. From 1500 to about 1800, when Europeans began to conquer much of the region, the peoples of Asia remained largely unaffected by European contact. As the next two sections explain, European traders who sailed farther east to seek riches in China and Japan had even less success in spreading Western culture. (E)

E. Answer It did not greatly affect them, for European influence did not spread much beyond port cities of the East.

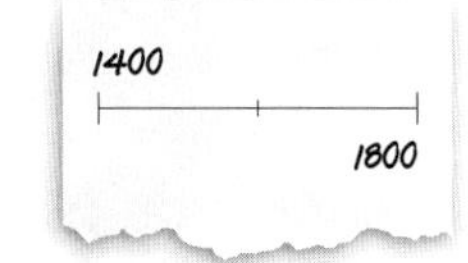

MAIN IDEA

Recognizing Effects

(E) How did the arrival of Europeans affect the peoples of the East in general?

Connect *to* Today

Trading Partners

Global trade is important to the economies of Asian countries now just as it was when the region first began to export spices, silks, and gems centuries ago. Today, a variety of products, including automobiles and electronic goods, as well as tea and textiles, are shipped around the world. (Hong Kong harbor is pictured.)

Regional trade organizations help to strengthen economic cooperation among Asian nations and promote international trade. They include the Association of Southeast Asian Nations (ASEAN) and the South Asian Association of Regional Co-operation (SAARC).

SECTION 1 ASSESSMENT

TERMS & NAMES 1. For each term or name, write a sentence explaining its significance.

• Bartolomeu Dias • Prince Henry • Vasco da Gama • Treaty of Tordesillas • Dutch East India Company

USING YOUR NOTES

2. Which event in the European exploration of the East is the most significant? Explain with references from the text. (10.4.3)

1400 — 1800

MAIN IDEAS

3. What role did the Renaissance play in launching an age of exploration? (REP 4)
4. What was Prince Henry's goal and who actually achieved it? (10.4.2)
5. What European countries were competing for Asian trade during the age of exploration? (10.4.2)

CRITICAL THINKING & WRITING

6. **MAKING INFERENCES** What did the Treaty of Tordesillas reveal about Europeans' attitudes toward non-European lands and peoples? (10.4.3)
7. **ANALYZING MOTIVES** What were the motives behind European exploration in the 1400s? Explain. (10.4.3)
8. **RECOGNIZING EFFECTS** In what ways did Europeans owe some of their sailing technology to other peoples? (10.4.2)
9. **WRITING ACTIVITY** SCIENCE AND TECHNOLOGY Review "The Tools of Exploration" on page 97. Write a one-paragraph **opinion piece** on which technological advancement was the most important for European exploration. (Writing 2.4.b)

CONNECT TO TODAY **WRITING A DESCRIPTION**

Research the Global Positioning System (GPS). Then write a brief **description** of this modern navigation system. (Writing 2.3.b)

Connect *to* Today

Trading Partners

Trade with Asia is currently the fastest growing segment of U.S. foreign trade. It has been growing by an average of 9.7 percent per year since 1988. The United States is by far the world's biggest exporter of goods. In 2001, the United States exported $731 billion in goods. However, Asian economies are expanding. In 2001, Japan exported $403 billion in goods, China, $266 billion, and six other leading East Asian countries exported a combined $568 billion in goods.

3 ASSESS

SECTION 1 ASSESSMENT

Instruct students to work in pairs to answer the questions. Have them find details in the text to support their answers.

Formal Assessment

• Section Quiz, p. 55

4 RETEACH

Use the Reteaching Activity for Section 1 to review the main ideas of the section.

In-Depth Resources: Unit 1

• Reteaching Activity, p. 78

ANSWERS

1. Bartolomeu Dias, p. 96 • Prince Henry, p. 96 • Vasco da Gama, p. 98 • Treaty of Tordesillas, p. 99 • Dutch East India Company, p. 100
2. **Sample Answer:** 1419—Prince Henry founds navigation school; 1487—Dias sails around tip of Africa; 1498—Da Gama reaches Calicut; 1511—Portuguese gain control of Strait of Malacca. **Possible Answer:** navigation school because it made explorations possible
3. The Renaissance encouraged a new spirit of adventure and curiosity.
4. Prince Henry wanted to explore new lands, find treasures, and spread the Christian faith; Vasco da Gama.
5. Portugal, Spain, the Netherlands, England, France
6. Europeans believed that non-European lands and peoples were fair game for conquest and exploitation.
7. **Possible Answer:** Europeans wanted to explore new lands to increase their wealth and to spread the Christian faith.
8. **Possible Answer:** Europeans adopted some technology from other peoples: triangular sails of the Arabs, magnetic compass of the Chinese, and astrolabe of the Muslims.
9. **Rubric** Opinion pieces should
   • show an understanding of the connection between sailing technology and voyages of exploration.
   • clearly state the reasons for the technological advancement chosen.
   • present supporting data for the selection.

CONNECT TO TODAY

Rubric Descriptions should

• show evidence of adequate research.
• demonstrate an understanding of the GPS.
• present the information in a logical and concise manner.

LESSON PLAN

OBJECTIVES

- Identify the successes of the early Ming emperors.
- Describe China and Korea under the Qing dynasty.
- Describe life in Ming and Qing China.

1 FOCUS & MOTIVATE

Point out that the Chinese of the 1400s and 1500s resisted interaction with outsiders because they wanted to preserve their culture. Ask students if they share these feelings. Why? *(Possible Answer: Yes; they don't like change.)*

2 INSTRUCT

China Under the Powerful Ming Dynasty

10.4.2

Critical Thinking

- Why might Hongwu have become a tyrant when problems developed? *(When people resisted change, he used forceful methods.)*

CALIFORNIA RESOURCES
California Reading Toolkit, p. L17
California Modified Lesson Plans for English Learners, p. 29
California Daily Standards Practice Transparencies, TT9
California Standards Enrichment Workbook, pp. 49–50
California Standards Planner and Lesson Plans, p. L25
California Online Test Practice
California Test Generator CD-ROM
California Easy Planner CD-ROM
California eEdition CD-ROM

Station 37 by Ando Tokitaro Hiroshige

Silk tapestry, China c1600

2

China Limits European Contacts

MAIN IDEA

CULTURAL INTERACTION Advances under the Ming and Qing dynasties left China uninterested in European contact.

WHY IT MATTERS NOW

China's independence from the West continues today, even as it forges new economic ties with the outside world.

TERMS & NAMES

- Ming Dynasty
- Hongwu
- Yonglo
- Zheng He
- Manchus
- Qing Dynasty
- Kangxi

CALIFORNIA STANDARDS

10.4.2 Discuss the locations of the colonial rule of such nations as England, France, Germany, Italy, Japan, the Netherlands, Russia, Spain, Portugal, and the United States.

CST 3 Students use a variety of maps and documents to interpret human movement, including major patterns of domestic and international migration, changing environmental preferences and settlement patterns, the frictions that develop between population groups, and the diffusion of ideas, technological innovations, and goods.

REP 2 Students identify bias and prejudice in historical interpretations.

REP 4 Students construct and test hypotheses; collect, evaluate, and employ information from multiple primary and secondary sources; and apply it in oral and written presentations.

SETTING THE STAGE The European voyages of exploration had led to opportunities for trade. Europeans made healthy profits from trade in the Indian Ocean region. They began looking for additional sources of wealth. Soon, European countries were seeking trade relationships in East Asia, first with China and later with Japan. By the time Portuguese ships moored in China in 1514, the Chinese had driven out their Mongol rulers and had united under a new dynasty.

China Under the Powerful Ming Dynasty

China had become the dominant power in Asia under the **Ming Dynasty** (1368–1644). In recognition of China's power, vassal states from Korea to Southeast Asia paid their Ming overlords regular tribute, which is a payment by one country to another to acknowledge its submission. China expected Europeans to do the same. Ming rulers were not going to allow them to threaten the peace and prosperity the Ming had brought to China when they ended Mongol rule.

The Rise of the Ming A peasant's son, **Hongwu**, commanded the rebel army that drove the Mongols out of China in 1368. That year, he became the first Ming emperor. Hongwu continued to rule from the former Yuan capital of Nanjing. (See the map on page 93.) He began reforms designed to restore agricultural lands devastated by war, erase all traces of the Mongol past, and promote China's power and prosperity. His agricultural reforms increased rice production and improved irrigation. He also encouraged fish farming and growing commercial crops.

TAKING NOTES

Summarizing Use a chart to summarize relevant facts about each emperor.

Emperor	Facts
1.	1.
2.	2.
3.	3.

Hongwu used respected traditions and institutions to bring stability to China. For example, he encouraged a return to Confucian moral standards. He improved imperial administration by restoring the merit-based civil service examination system. Later in his rule, however, when problems developed, Hongwu became a ruthless tyrant. Suspecting plots against his rule everywhere, he conducted purges of the government, killing thousands of officials.

Hongwu's death in 1398 led to a power struggle. His son **Yonglo** (yung•lu) emerged victorious. Yonglo continued many of his father's policies, although he moved the royal court to Beijing. (See the Forbidden City feature on page 104.)

▲ Ming Dynasty Porcelain vase

SECTION 2 PROGRAM RESOURCES

ALL STUDENTS

In-Depth Resources: Unit 1
- Guided Reading, p. 61
- Skillbuilder Practice: Interpreting Graphs, p. 64
- Geography Application: The Voyages of Zheng He, p. 65

Formal Assessment
- Section Quiz, p. 56

ENGLISH LEARNERS

In-Depth Resources in Spanish
- Guided Reading, p. 32
- Skillbuilder Practice, p. 34
- Geography Application, p. 35

Reading Study Guide (Spanish), p. 35
Reading Study Guide Audio CD (Spanish)

STRUGGLING READERS

In-Depth Resources: Unit 1
- Guided Reading, p. 61
- Building Vocabulary, p. 63
- Reteaching Activity, p. 79

Reading Study Guide, p. 35
Reading Study Guide Audio CD

GIFTED AND TALENTED STUDENTS

In-Depth Resources: Unit 1
- Primary Source: from *Matteo Ricci,* p. 69
- Literature: from *Red Chamber,* p. 71

Electronic Library of Primary Sources

INTEGRATED TECHNOLOGY

eEdition CD-ROM
Power Presentations CD-ROM
Electronic Library of Primary Sources
- Letter to King George III

classzone.com

◀ Zheng He's treasure ship compared with Christopher Columbus's *Santa Maria*

Yonglo also had a far-ranging curiosity about the outside world. In 1405, before Europeans began to sail beyond their borders, he launched the first of seven voyages of exploration. He hoped they would impress the world with the power and splendor of Ming China. He also wanted to expand China's tribute system.

The Voyages of Zheng He A Chinese Muslim admiral named **Zheng He** (jung huh) led all of the seven voyages. His expeditions were remarkable for their size. Everything about them was large—distances traveled, fleet size, and ship measurements. The voyages ranged from Southeast Asia to eastern Africa. From 40 to 300 ships sailed in each expedition. Among them were fighting ships, storage vessels, and huge "treasure" ships measuring more than 400 feet long. The fleet's crews numbered over 27,000 on some voyages. They included sailors, soldiers, carpenters, interpreters, accountants, doctors, and religious leaders. Like a huge floating city, the fleet sailed from port to port along the Indian Ocean.

Everywhere Zheng He went, he distributed gifts including silver and silk to show Chinese superiority. As a result, more than 16 countries sent tribute to the Ming court. Even so, Chinese scholar-officials complained that the voyages wasted valuable resources that could be used to defend against barbarians' attacks on the northern frontier. After the seventh voyage, in 1433, China withdrew into isolation. (A)

MAIN IDEA
Making Inferences
(A) What do you think the people of other countries thought about China after one of Zheng He's visits?

A. Possible Answer that China must be very powerful to send so many ships, men, and goods on such a voyage and, therefore, they should pay tribute

Ming Relations with Foreign Countries China's official trade policies in the 1500s reflected its isolation. To keep the influence of outsiders to a minimum, only the government was to conduct foreign trade, and only through three coastal ports, Canton, Macao, and Ningbo. In reality, trade flourished up and down the coast. Profit-minded merchants smuggled cargoes of silk, porcelain, and other valuable goods out of the country into the eager hands of European merchants. Usually, Europeans paid for purchases with silver, much of it from mines in the Americas.

Demand for Chinese goods had a ripple effect on the economy. Industries such as silk-making and ceramics grew rapidly. Manufacturing and commerce increased. But China did not become highly industrialized for two main reasons. First, the idea of commerce offended China's Confucian beliefs. Merchants, it was said, made their money "supporting foreigners and robbery." Second, Chinese economic policies traditionally favored agriculture. Taxes on agriculture stayed low. Taxes on manufacturing and trade skyrocketed.

Christian missionaries accompanied European traders into China. They brought Christianity and knowledge of European science and technology, such as the clock. The first missionary to have an impact was an Italian Jesuit named Matteo Ricci. He

More About . . .

Zheng He

Zheng He's (1371–1433?) parents were Muslims of Mongol and Arab descent. As a young man, he was drafted into the army. When his commander usurped the Chinese throne and became Yonglo Emperor, Zheng He was promoted. A few years later, in 1405, he led the first of his explorations. Zheng He's ships were among the largest wooden vessels ever built. The rudderpost of a treasure ship was found in 1962. Scientists calculate that the ship might have been 500 feet long.

In-Depth Resources: Unit 1
- Geography Application: The Voyages of Zheng He, p. 65

More About . . .

Matteo Ricci

Matteo Ricci (1552–1610) had an immense impact on Chinese thought. He introduced trigonometry and astronomical instruments to China. He also wrote and translated several books into Chinese, including Euclid's *Elements.* Ricci is still well known in China. In 1983, the four hundredth anniversary of his arrival in China was celebrated by official radio programs and magazine articles.

In-Depth Resources: Unit 1
- Primary Source: From *The Journals of Matteo Ricci,* p. 69

DIFFERENTIATING INSTRUCTION: ENGLISH LEARNERS

Understanding Professional Titles

Class Time 20 minutes

Task Finding the meaning of professional titles

Purpose To clarify understanding of kinds of workers

Instructions Write the following words on the chalkboard: *admiral, sailor, soldier, carpenter, interpreter, accountant, doctor, religious leader, envoy, scholar-official, merchant.* Explain that each of these words describes the specific work or profession that a person follows. Have students find the words in the text above. Then display Critical Thinking Transparency CT80, and write *admiral* in the first column of the horizontal chart. Ask students to explain the meaning *(commander or highest officer in a navy or fleet).* If students need help, encourage them to use context clues. If needed, allow them to use a dictionary. Write the definition in the second column. Point out that two of these titles–*religious leader* and *scholar-official*–are compound nouns. Students will have to find the meaning by putting together the meaning of each word that makes up the compound. Help students figure out the meaning of *religious leader.* Now divide students into pairs and have them create their own charts and complete them for each of the words listed on the board.

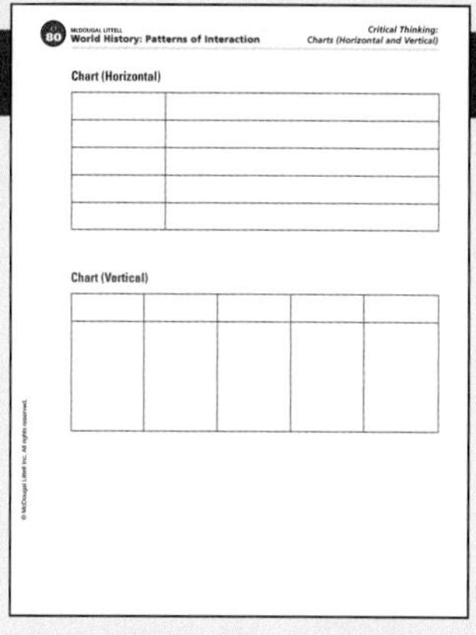

Critical Thinking Transparencies

History *in* Depth

OBJECTIVES

- Understand the significance of the architecture of the Forbidden City.

INSTRUCT

Point out that the Forbidden City was the seat of government as well as the home of the Chinese emperor. The buildings and walkways of the complex were created to evoke awe at the power of the emperor and the wealth of China. Invite students to compare it with modern seats of government, such as Washington, D.C.

More About . . .

The Forbidden City

The Forbidden City is a huge complex of buildings, walkways, and gardens. At its peak, it consisted of 9,000 rooms and included living quarters, libraries, galleries, and audience halls for ceremonies. Maintaining such a splendid palace city was expensive. For example, every day some 6,000 cooks made meals for 10,000 to 15,000 people. The palace served as the home of the Chinese emperor until 1912. In 1949, the palace complex was converted into a museum and opened to the public.

History *in* Depth

The Forbidden City

CALIFORNIA STANDARDS HI 3

When Yonglo moved the Chinese capital to Beijing, he ordered the building of a great palace complex to symbolize his power and might. Construction took 14 years, from 1406 to 1420. Red walls 35 feet in height surrounded the complex, which had dozens of buildings, including palaces and temples. The complex became known as the Forbidden City because commoners and foreigners were not allowed to enter.

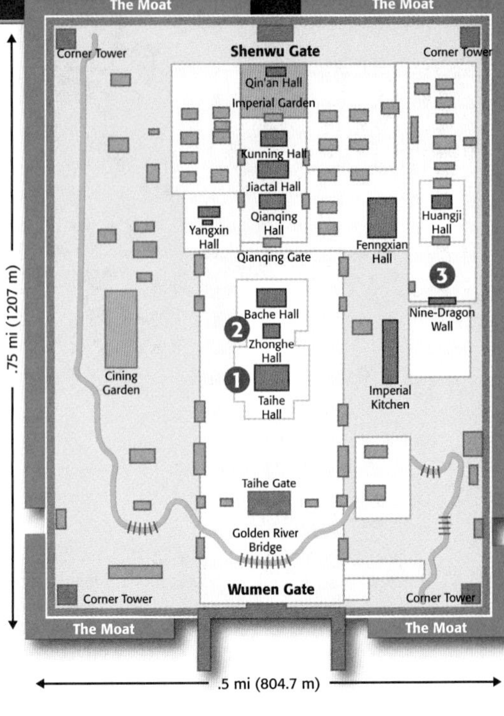

1

▲ **Hall of Supreme Harmony**
Taihe Hall, or the Hall of Supreme Harmony, is the largest building in the compound. It measures 201 by 122 feet and stands about 125 feet high. This hall was used for important ceremonies, such as those marking the emperor's birthday or the day the crown prince took the throne.

2

▲ **Hall of Central Harmony**
Zhonge Hall, or the Hall of Central Harmony, was a smaller square building between the two main halls. It was a sort of private office where the emperor could stop to rest on his way to ceremonies.

▼ **Nine-Dragon Wall**
This wall, or screen, of glazed tiles shows nine dragons playing with pearls against a background of sea and sky. From ancient times, the dragon was the symbol of the imperial family. This is the largest of three famous nine-dragon screens that exist in China.

3

SKILLBUILDER: Interpreting Visuals

1. **Analyzing Motives** *Why do you think the emperor wanted to keep common people out of the Forbidden City?*
2. **Drawing Conclusions** *What aspects of the Forbidden City helped to convey the power of the emperor?*

SKILLBUILDER: ANSWERS

1. **Analyzing Motives** *Possible Answers:* He thought that commoners were not worthy to be near him. He feared for his safety. He thought he would seem more like a divine being if he was inaccessible.
2. **Drawing Conclusions** *Possible Answer:* The immense size of the complex, the ornate thrones and elaborate art, and the mystery surrounding a forbidden zone all helped convey his power.

104 Chapter 3

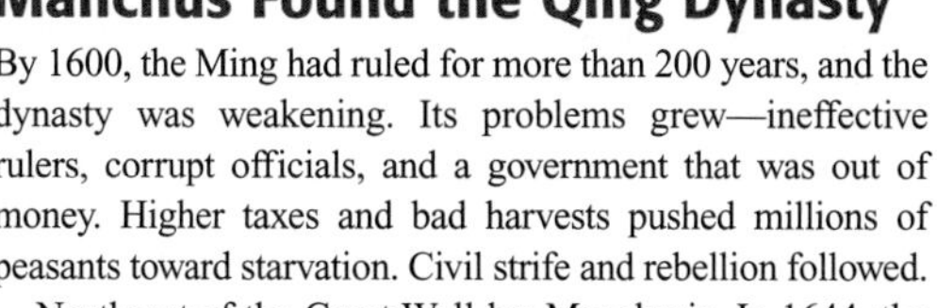

gained special favor at the Ming court through his intelligence and fluency in Chinese. Still, many educated Chinese opposed the European and Christian presence.

Manchus Found the Qing Dynasty

By 1600, the Ming had ruled for more than 200 years, and the dynasty was weakening. Its problems grew—ineffective rulers, corrupt officials, and a government that was out of money. Higher taxes and bad harvests pushed millions of peasants toward starvation. Civil strife and rebellion followed.

Northeast of the Great Wall lay Manchuria. In 1644, the **Manchus** (MAN•chooz), the people of that region, invaded China and the Ming Dynasty collapsed. The Manchus seized Beijing, and their leader became China's new emperor. As the Mongols had done in the 1300s, the Manchus took a Chinese name for their dynasty, the **Qing** (chihng) **Dynasty**. They would rule for more than 260 years and expand China's borders to include Taiwan, Chinese Central Asia, Mongolia, and Tibet.

China Under the Qing Many Chinese resisted rule by the non-Chinese Manchus. Rebellions flared up periodically for decades. The Manchus, however, slowly earned the people's respect. They upheld China's traditional Confucian beliefs and social structures. They made the country's frontiers safe and restored China's prosperity. Two powerful Manchu rulers contributed greatly to the acceptance of the new dynasty.

The first, **Kangxi** (kahng•shee), became emperor in 1661 and ruled for some 60 years. He reduced government expenses and lowered taxes. A scholar and patron of the arts, Kangxi gained the support of intellectuals by offering them government positions. He also enjoyed the company of the Jesuits at court. They told him about developments in science, medicine, and mathematics in Europe. Under his grandson Qian-long (chyahn•lung), who ruled from 1736 to 1795, China reached its greatest size and prosperity. An industrious emperor like his grandfather, Qian-long often rose at dawn to work on the empire's problems. These included armed nomads on its borders and the expanding presence of European missionaries and merchants in China.

History Makers

Kangxi
1654–1722

The emperor Kangxi had too much curiosity to remain isolated in the Forbidden City. To calm the Chinese in areas devastated by the Manchu conquest, Kangxi set out on a series of "tours."

> *On tours I learned about the common people's grievances by talking with them. . . . I asked peasants about their officials, looked at their houses, and discussed their crops.*

In 1696, with Mongols threatening the northern border, Kangxi exhibited leadership unheard of in later Ming times. Instead of waiting in the palace for reports, he personally led 80,000 troops to victory over the Mongols.

Manchus Continue Chinese Isolation To the Chinese, their country—called the Middle Kingdom—had been the cultural center of the universe for 2,000 years. If foreign states wished to trade with China, they would have to follow Chinese rules. These rules included trading only at special ports and paying tribute.

The Dutch were masters of the Indian Ocean trade by the time of Qian-long. They accepted China's restrictions. Their diplomats paid tribute to the emperor through gifts and by performing the required "kowtow" ritual. This ritual involved kneeling in front of the emperor and touching one's head to the ground nine times. As a result, the Chinese accepted the Dutch as trading partners. The Dutch returned home with traditional porcelains and silk, as well as a new trade item, tea. By 1800, tea would make up 80 percent of shipments to Europe. (B)

Great Britain also wanted to increase trade with China. But the British did not like China's trade restrictions. In 1793, Lord George Macartney delivered a letter from King George III to Qian-long. It asked for a better trade arrangement,

B. Possible Answer It reaffirmed for him the Chinese belief that their culture was vastly superior to others.

MAIN IDEA

Making Inferences

(B) Why do you think the kowtow ritual was so important to the Chinese emperor?

Manchus Found the Qing Dynasty

10.4.2

Critical Thinking

- Why did the Manchu emperors take a Chinese name for their dynasty and uphold Chinese traditions? *(to earn the people's loyalty)*
- Why did the British resent China's trade restrictions? *(Possible Answer: They were eager to make profits from trade with China.)*
- Why did the Korean attitude toward China change after the Manchu invasion? *(Possible Answer: They developed strong feelings of nationalism.)*

History Makers

Kangxi

What qualities made Kangxi a strong leader? *(respect for Chinese traditions; interest in learning; courage in making decisions and leading his army)*

The people in southern China had fought fiercely against the Manchu invaders. When Kangxi toured their region, many Chinese resented the Manchu emperor. Kangxi wanted to improve the Manchus' image. His ability to speak and write Chinese and his admiration of Chinese culture helped him in this effort.

Vocabulary Note: **kowtow**

Point out the word *kowtow* and explain that the word comes from Mandarin, the principal language spoken in China. It means, literally, "to bump, or knock, one's head."

DIFFERENTIATING INSTRUCTION: STRUGGLING READERS

Comparing the Ming and Qing Dynasties

Class Time 45 minutes

Task Comparing and contrasting the Ming and Qing dynasties

Purpose To understand similarities and differences between the Ming and Qing dynasties

Instructions Point out to students that both the Ming and Qing dynasties ruled China for hundreds of years. There were many similarities between the two dynasties as well as some important differences. Project Critical Thinking Transparency CT81, the Venn diagram. Label one circle Ming Dynasty and the other Qing Dynasty. Then ask the following questions:

- When did the Ming dynasty rule China? *(1368–1644)*
- When did the Qing dynasty rule China? *(1644–about 1911)*
- Which dynasty followed an isolationist policy? *(both)*

Write the answers in the correct circles on the diagram. Then tell students to copy the diagram and continue finding facts from the text and entering them in the correct portion of the diagram. For help, you may wish to have students use the Reading Study Guide for Section 2. When students have completed their diagram, meet with them as a group to review their diagrams. Have students correct and add to their diagrams during the discussion.

Reading Study Guide

Tip for English Learners

Point out the phrase *existed in China's shadow* in the paragraph titled Korea Under the Manchus. Explain that the phrase means "to follow after" or "be under the influence of" something else. Here, the meaning is that Korea existed under the influence of China.

including Chinese acceptance of British manufactured goods. Macartney refused to kowtow, and Qian-long denied Britain's request. As the emperor made clear in a letter to the king, China was self-sufficient and did not need the British:

> **PRIMARY SOURCE**
>
> There is nothing we lack, as your principal envoy and others have themselves observed. We have never set much store on strange or ingenious objects, nor do we need any more of your country's manufactures.
>
> **QIAN-LONG**, from a letter to King George III of Great Britain

In the 1800s, the British, Dutch, and others would attempt to chip away at China's trade restrictions until the empire itself began to crack, as Chapter 12 will describe.

Korea Under the Manchus In 1636, even before they came to power in China, the Manchus conquered nearby Korea and made it a vassal state. As a member of the Chinese tribute system, Korea had long existed in China's shadow. Koreans organized their government according to Confucian principles. They also adopted China's technology, its culture, and especially its policy of isolation.

When the Manchus established the Qing Dynasty, Korea's political relationship with China did not change. But Korea's attitude did. The Manchu invasion, combined with a Japanese attack in the 1590s, provoked strong feelings of nationalism in the Korean people. This sentiment was most evident in their art. Instead of traditional Chinese subjects, many artists chose to show popular Korean scenes.

Social History

China's Population Boom

Prior to 1700, China had an essentially feudal society. The lives of China's peasants were hard. People wanted large families to help work the fields and support the family. However, poor health care, epidemics, and natural disasters stunted population growth. Wars and rebellions, moreover, periodically erupted and huge losses of life occurred. Overall, population growth was limited during this extended period.

SKILLBUILDER Answer
Comparing by about 250 percent

Social History

China's Population Boom

China's population grew dramatically from 1650 to 1900. General peace and increased agricultural productivity were the causes.

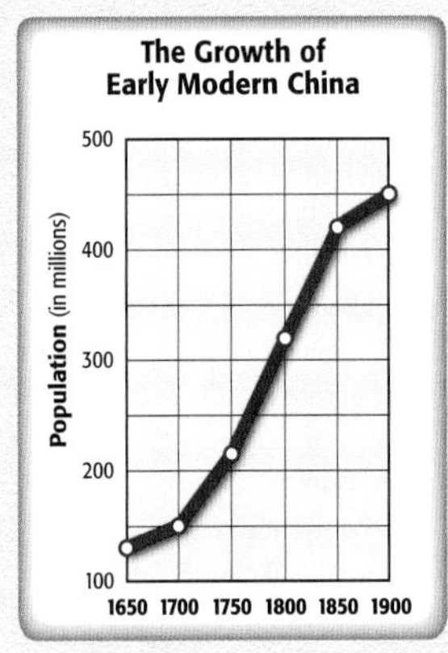

▲ A Chinese family prepares for a wedding in the 1800s.

SKILLBUILDER: Interpreting Graphs
Comparing *By what percentage did China's population increase between 1650 and 1900?*

SKILLBUILDER PRACTICE: INTERPRETING GRAPHS

Learning to Combine Information

Class Time 40 minutes

Task Getting information from a graph and picture

Purpose To develop skill in understanding graphs

Instructions Explain to students that graphs are used to make numerical information and relationships among various data easier to understand. Visual features such as color, size, labels, and measurements are used to clarify the information. Point out that the information in the graph is reinforced by the inclusion of pictorial material. Have students study the line graph on this page, noting how the lines and dots are used to communicate information. Then ask,

1. What was the increase in population between 1650 and 1900? *(more than 300 million)*
2. During what 100-year period did the greatest growth occur? What was the increase during that period? *(1750–1850; about 200 million)*
3. About what year did the growth spurt begin to taper off? *(about 1850)*
4. What does the painting tell about China during this period? *(Possible Answers: Families were large; marriage and family life were important in the society.)*

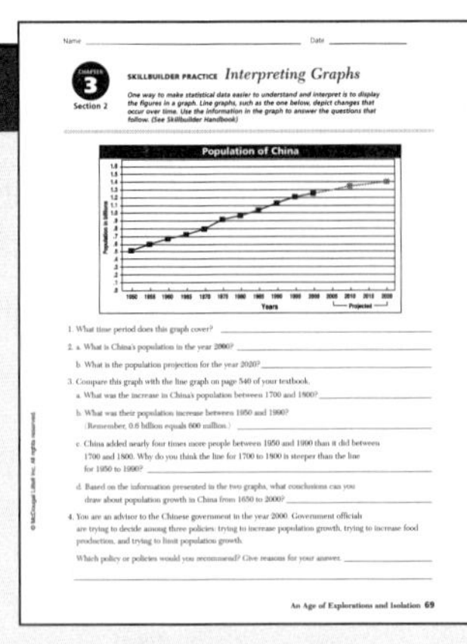

In-Depth Resources: Unit 1

Life in Ming and Qing China

In the 1600s and 1700s, there was general peace and prosperity in China. Life improved for most Chinese.

Families and the Role of Women Most Chinese families had farmed the land the same way their ancestors had. However, during the Qing Dynasty, irrigation and fertilizer use increased. Farmers grew rice and new crops, such as corn and sweet potatoes, brought by Europeans from the Americas. As food production increased, nutrition improved and families expanded. A population explosion followed.

These expanded Chinese families favored sons over daughters. Only a son was allowed to perform vital religious rituals. A son also would raise his own family under his parents' roof, assuring aging parents of help with the farming. As a result, females were not valued, and many female infants were killed. Although men dominated the household and their wives, women had significant responsibilities. Besides working in the fields, they supervised the children's education and managed the family's finances. While most women were forced to remain secluded in their homes, some found outside jobs such as working as midwives or textile workers.

▲ These 12th-century Chinese women work outside the home making silk.

Vocabulary
A *midwife* is a woman trained to assist women in childbirth.

Cultural Developments The culture of early modern China was based mainly on traditional forms. The great masterpiece of traditional Chinese fiction was written during this period. *Dream of the Red Chamber* by Cao Zhan examines upper class Manchu society in the 1700s. Most artists of the time painted in traditional styles, which valued technique over creativity. In pottery, technical skill as well as experimentation led to the production of high-quality ceramics, including porcelain. Drama was a popular entertainment, especially in rural China where literacy rates were low. Plays that presented Chinese history and cultural heroes entertained and also helped unify Chinese society by creating a national culture. C

While China preserved its traditions in isolation, another civilization that developed in seclusion—the Japanese—was in conflict, as you will read in Section 3.

MAIN IDEA
Making Inferences
C What was the effect of the emphasis on tradition in early modern China?

C. Possible Answer produced little creativity but provided stability in time of change and helped unify Chinese society

SECTION 2 ASSESSMENT

TERMS & NAMES 1. For each term or name, write a sentence explaining its significance.
• Ming Dynasty • Hongwu • Yonglo • Zheng He • Manchus • Qing Dynasty • Kangxi

USING YOUR NOTES

2. Which of these emperors was most influential? Explain with text references. (10.4.2)

Emperor	Facts
1.	1.
2.	2.
3.	3.

MAIN IDEAS

3. How did Beijing become the capital of China? (10.4.2)
4. What evidence indicates that China lost interest in contacts abroad after 1433? (10.4.2)
5. What did Christian missionaries bring to China? (10.4.2)

CRITICAL THINKING & WRITING

6. **MAKING DECISIONS** Do you think Lord Macartney should have kowtowed to Emperor Qian-long? Why? (10.4.2)
7. **ANALYZING CAUSES** What factors, both within China and outside its borders, contributed to the downfall of the Ming Dynasty? (10.4.2)
8. **DRAWING CONCLUSIONS** What was Korea's relationship with China under the Qing Dynasty? (10.4.2)
9. **WRITING ACTIVITY** CULTURAL INTERACTION Choose one emperor of China and write a one-paragraph **biography** using the information you listed in your Taking Notes chart and from the text. (Writing 2.1.a)

CONNECT TO TODAY **WRITING AN ESSAY**

Learn more about popular culture in China today. Then write a two-paragraph **expository essay** on some form of popular entertainment in the arts or sports. (Writing 2.3.b)

Life in Ming and Qing China
10.4.2

Critical Thinking

- How were women's responsibilities important in Chinese society? *(Educating children affected future generations; handling the family finances affected the economy)*
- What was one negative effect of the emphasis on tradition in Chinese art? *(Creativity was not encouraged.)*

More About . . .

Cao Zhan

Cao Zhan (1717–1763) is believed to have written the first 80 chapters of *The Dream of the Red Chamber.* The novel is autobiographical, telling of the fall of a wealthy family and of a scandalous love affair.

In-Depth Resources: Unit 1
- Literature: from *The Dream of the Red Chamber,* p. 71

3 ASSESS

SECTION 2 ASSESSMENT

Have students work in small groups to answer the questions.

Formal Assessment
- Section Quiz, p. 56

4 RETEACH

Use the Reteaching Activity to review the section.

In-Depth Resources: Unit 1
- Reteaching Activity, p. 79

ANSWERS

1. Ming dynasty, p. 102 • Hongwu, p. 102 • Yonglo, p. 102 • Zheng He, p. 103 • Manchus, p. 105 • Qing dynasty, p. 105 • Kangxi, p. 105

2. **Sample Answer:** Hongwu–defeated Mongols; ruled 1368–1398; first Ming emperor; encouraged agriculture, Confucian standards, administrative reforms; became brutal.
Yonglo–1398, assumed throne; moved capital to Beijing; built Forbidden City; sponsored first Zheng He voyage; increased tributaries.
Kangxi–ruled 1661–1722; first Manchu emperor; lowered taxes; defeated Mongols; patronized arts. Qian-long–1736–1795; hard-working; dealt with border unrest and Europeans. **Possible Answer:** Hongwu because of long-term reforms
3. Yonglo moved the royal court to Beijing.
4. The voyages of Zheng He were stopped.
5. Christianity and European inventions
6. **Possible Answers:** Yes–to get the right to trade. No–to show equality.
7. **Possible Answer:** ineffective rulers, corrupt officials, money problems
8. **Possible Answer:** under China's domination, but Korean nationalism began to assert itself
9. **Rubric** Biographies should
   - give facts about emperor and time period.
   - accurately convey the information in text.
   - be logically organized.

CONNECT TO TODAY

Rubric Expository essays should
- show evidence of research.
- show understanding of the emperor.
- include enough detail to enable the reader to understand the topic.

LESSON PLAN

OBJECTIVES

- Summarize how three powerful daimyo succeeded in unifying feudal Japan.
- Describe Japanese society and culture during the Tokugawa Shogunate.
- Explain how Japan's policies toward Europeans changed.
- Explain the purpose and effect of Japan's closed country policy.

1 FOCUS & MOTIVATE

A Japanese daimyo had the motto "Rule the empire by force." Ask, What do you think of the motto? Have you seen it put into practice? *(Possible Answer: Most will dislike the motto. Possible examples: dictators, neighborhood gangs)*

2 INSTRUCT

A New Feudalism Under Strong Leaders

10.4.1

Critical Thinking

- Why might people have opposed Nobunaga's effort to unify Japan? *(They feared his rule would be ruthless.)*

CALIFORNIA RESOURCES

California Reading Toolkit, p. L18
California Modified Lesson Plans for English Learners, p. 31
California Daily Standards Practice Transparencies, TT10
California Standards Enrichment Workbook, pp. 47–48, 49–50
California Standards Planner and Lesson Plans, p. L27
California Online Test Practice
California Test Generator CD-ROM
California Easy Planner CD-ROM
California eEdition CD-ROM

Station 37 by Ando Tokitaro Hiroshige

Silk tapestry, China c1600

3

Japan Returns to Isolation

MAIN IDEA	WHY IT MATTERS NOW	TERMS & NAMES
ECONOMICS The Tokugawa regime unified Japan and began 250 years of isolation, autocracy, and economic growth.	Even now, Japan continues to limit and control dealings with foreigners, especially in the area of trade.	• daimyo • Oda Nobunaga • Toyotomi Hideyoshi • Tokugawa Shogunate • haiku • kabuki

CALIFORNIA STANDARDS

10.4.1 Describe the rise of industrial economies and their link to imperialism and colonialism (e.g., the role played by national security and strategic advantage; moral issues raised by the search for national hegemony, Social Darwinism, and the missionary impulse; material issues such as land, resources, and technology).

10.4.2 Discuss the locations of the colonial rule of such nations as England, France, Germany, Italy, Japan, the Netherlands, Russia, Spain, Portugal, and the United States.

CST 1 Students compare the present with the past, evaluating the consequences of past events and decisions and determining the lessons that were learned.

SETTING THE STAGE In the 1300s, the unity that had been achieved in Japan in the previous century broke down. Shoguns, or military leaders, in the north and south fiercely fought one another for power. Although these two rival courts later came back together at the end of the century, a series of politically weak shoguns let control of the country slip from their grasp. Japan was torn by factional strife and economic unrest. It would be centuries before Japan would again be unified.

A New Feudalism Under Strong Leaders

In 1467, civil war shattered Japan's old feudal system. The country collapsed into chaos. Centralized rule ended. Power drained away from the shogun to territorial lords in hundreds of separate domains.

Local Lords Rule A violent era of disorder followed. This time in Japanese history, which lasted from 1467 to 1568, is known as the Sengoku, or "Warring States," period. Powerful samurai seized control of old feudal estates. They offered peasants and others protection in return for their loyalty. These warrior-chieftains, called **daimyo** (DY•mee•OH), became lords in a new kind of Japanese feudalism. Daimyo meant "great name." Under this system, security came from this group of powerful warlords. The emperor at Kyoto became a figurehead, having a leadership title but no actual power.

The new Japanese feudalism resembled European feudalism in many ways. The daimyo built fortified castles and created small armies of samurai on horses. Later they added foot soldiers with muskets (guns). Rival daimyo often fought for territory. This led to disorder throughout the land.

New Leaders Restore Order A number of ambitious daimyo hoped to take control of the entire country. One, the brutal and ambitious **Oda Nobunaga** (oh•dah noh•boo•nah•gah), defeated his rivals and seized the imperial capital Kyoto in 1568.

Following his own motto "Rule the empire by force," Nobunaga sought to eliminate his remaining enemies. These included rival daimyo as well as wealthy Buddhist monasteries aligned with them. In 1575, Nobunaga's 3,000 soldiers armed with muskets crushed an enemy force of samurai cavalry. This was the first time firearms had been used effectively in battle in Japan. However,

TAKING NOTES

Comparing Use a chart to compare the achievements of the daimyos who unified Japan.

Daimyo	Achievements

SECTION 3 PROGRAM RESOURCES

ALL STUDENTS

In-Depth Resources: Unit 1
- Guided Reading, p. 62
- History Makers: Tokugawa Ieyasu, p. 75

Formal Assessment
- Section Quiz, p. 57

ENGLISH LEARNERS

In-Depth Resources in Spanish
- Guided Reading, p. 33

Reading Study Guide (Spanish), p. 37
Reading Study Guide Audio CD (Spanish)

STRUGGLING READERS

In-Depth Resources: Unit 1
- Guided Reading, p. 62
- Building Vocabulary, p. 63
- Reteaching Activity, p. 80

Reading Study Guide, p. 37
Reading Study Guide Audio CD

GIFTED AND TALENTED STUDENTS

In-Depth Resources: Unit 1
- Literature: Haiku, p. 73
- Connections Across Time and Cultures, p. 76

Electronic Library of Primary Sources

INTEGRATED TECHNOLOGY

eEdition CD-ROM
Power Presentations CD-ROM
Geography Transparencies
- GT19 Tokugawa Ieyasu Unites Japan, 1603

World Art and Cultures Transparencies
- AT42 Japanese screen painting

Critical Thinking Transparencies
- CT19 The Impact of Exploration on East Asia
- CT55 Chapter 3 Visual Summary

Electronic Library of Primary Sources
classzone.com

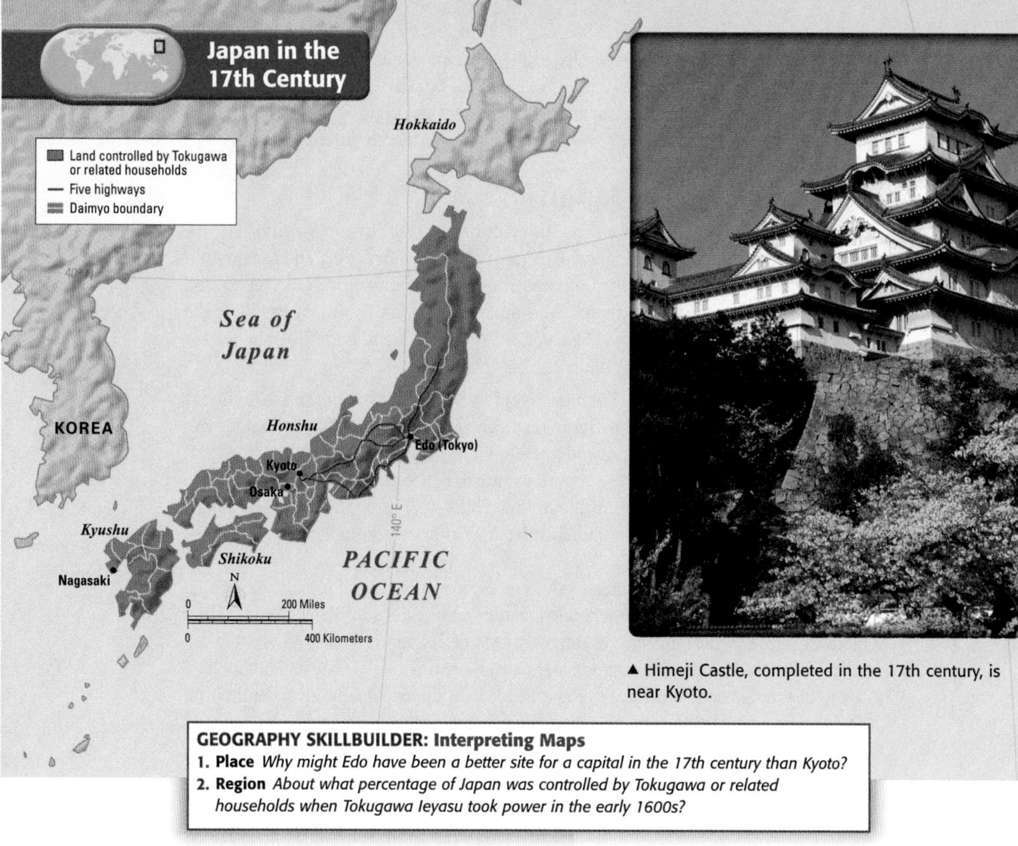

▲ Himeji Castle, completed in the 17th century, is near Kyoto.

GEOGRAPHY SKILLBUILDER: Interpreting Maps
1. **Place** *Why might Edo have been a better site for a capital in the 17th century than Kyoto?*
2. **Region** *About what percentage of Japan was controlled by Tokugawa or related households when Tokugawa Ieyasu took power in the early 1600s?*

Nobunaga was not able to unify Japan. He committed *seppuku,* the ritual suicide of a samurai, in 1582, when one of his own generals turned on him.

Nobunaga's best general, **Toyotomi Hideyoshi** (toh•you•toh•mee hee•deh•yoh•shee), continued his fallen leader's mission. Hideyoshi set out to destroy the daimyo that remained hostile. By 1590, by combining brute force with shrewd political alliances, he controlled most of the country. Hideyoshi did not stop with Japan. With the idea of eventually conquering China, he invaded Korea in 1592 and began a long campaign against the Koreans and their Ming Chinese allies. When Hideyoshi died in 1598, his troops withdrew from Korea.

A. Answer families held hostage, financial burden maintaining two residences, time wasted moving back and forth

Tokugawa Shogunate Unites Japan One of Hideyoshi's strongest daimyo allies, Tokugawa Ieyasu (toh•koo•gah•wah ee•yeh•yah•soo), completed the unification of Japan. In 1600, Ieyasu defeated his rivals at the Battle of Sekigahara. His victory earned him the loyalty of daimyo throughout Japan. Three years later, Ieyasu became the sole ruler, or shogun. He then moved Japan's capital to his power base at Edo, a small fishing village that would later become the city of Tokyo.

MAIN IDEA
Drawing Conclusions
A How would the "alternate attendance policy" restrict the daimyo?

Japan was unified, but the daimyo still governed at the local level. To keep them from rebelling, Ieyasu required that they spend every other year in the capital. Even when they returned to their lands, they had to leave their families behind as hostages in Edo. Through this "alternate attendance policy" and other restrictions, Ieyasu tamed the daimyo. This was a major step toward restoring centralized government to Japan. As a result, the rule of law overcame the rule of the sword. A

History from Visuals

Interpreting the Map

Have students look at the legend and note the land controlled by the Tokugawa Shogunate and that controlled by the daimyo. Ask, Which of the major cities was controlled by the Tokugawa? *(Edo)*

SKILLBUILDER Answers
1. **Place** It was accessible by water.
2. **Region** about 20 percent

More About . . .

Tokugawa Ieyasu

One of Ieyasu's goals was to keep his rival daimyo disorganized and weak. He not only forced them to live in Edo, he also kept them busy. In 1604, Ieyasu put the daimyo to work enlarging the castle at Edo. Thousands of ships carried logs and stones to Edo. Thousands of workers turned those materials into the world's largest castle, with tall stone walls, massive gatehouses, and moats. Ieyasu forced the daimyo to help pay for this project.

In-Depth Resources: Unit 1
• History Makers: Tokugawa Ieyasu, p. 75

Tip for Struggling Readers

Point out the final sentence, "the rule of law overcame the rule of the sword." Ask students to paraphrase it. *(A centralized government established order in Japan.)*

DIFFERENTIATING INSTRUCTION: ENGLISH LEARNERS

Political Terms

Class Time 20 minutes
Task Completing a chart of political terms
Purpose To develop understanding of political terms
Instructions Have students find the term *political alliances* in the text. Ask students what *political* means *(having to do with affairs of government).* Then ask what an *alliance* is *(a union of people with the same purpose).* Now help students develop a definition for the combined term *(a union of people in government who have the same purpose).* Have students work in pairs and complete charts with additional political terms. Urge them to use dictionaries as necessary.

Term	Meaning
political alliance	a union of people in government who have the same purpose
unification	a joining of independent states into a state with one government
power base	place where a leader has political allies or other advantages
centralized government	a single government that has all of the power

Life in Tokugawa Japan
10.4.1

Critical Thinking

- Why did merchants have such low status in Tokugawa society? *(Possible Answer: Society valued warriors and farmers more highly. Merchants didn't produce anything.)*
- What can you infer about Japanese society from the development of realistic stories and the kabuki theater? *(Possible Answer: People of the lower classes—the peasants, artisans, and merchants—were beginning to enjoy art.)*

World Art and Cultures Transparencies

- AT42 Japanese Screen Painting

More About . . .

Basho

As a youth, Matsuo Basho loved haiku. In this type of poetry, simple descriptions of nature evoke a powerful emotional response. At twenty-two, Basho put down his samurai sword and devoted himself to poetry. He refined the traditional haiku, turning what was considered a trifle into a respected literary form. Basho is known for his simple, evocative descriptions and his ability to bring together unrelated images in a style that suggests Zen Buddhism.

In-Depth Resources: Unit 1

- Literature: Haiku by Matsuo Basho, p. 73

Ieyasu founded the **Tokugawa Shogunate**, which would hold power until 1867. On his deathbed in 1616, Ieyasu advised his son, Hidetada, "Take care of the people. Strive to be virtuous. Never neglect to protect the country." Most Tokugawa shoguns followed that advice. Their rule brought a welcome order to Japan.

Vocabulary
A *shogunate* is the administration or rule of a shogun.

Life in Tokugawa Japan

Japan enjoyed more than two and a half centuries of stability, prosperity, and isolation under the Tokugawa shoguns. Farmers produced more food, and the population rose. Still, the vast majority of peasants, weighed down by heavy taxes, led lives filled with misery. The people who prospered in Tokugawa society were the merchant class and the wealthy. However, everyone, rich and poor alike, benefited from a flowering of Japanese culture during this era.

Society in Tokugawa Japan Tokugawa society was very structured. The emperor had the top rank but was just a figurehead. The actual ruler was the shogun, who was the supreme military commander. Below him were the daimyo, the powerful landholding samurai. Samurai warriors came next. The peasants and artisans followed them. Peasants made up about four-fifths of the population. Merchants were at the bottom, but they gradually became more important as the Japanese economy expanded.

In Japan, as in China, Confucian values influenced ideas about society. According to Confucius, the ideal society depended on agriculture, not commerce. Farmers, not merchants, made ideal citizens. In the real world of Tokugawa Japan, however, peasant farmers bore the main tax burden and faced more difficulties than any other class. Many of them abandoned farm life and headed for the expanding towns and cities. There, they mixed with samurai, artisans, and merchants.

By the mid-1700s, Japan began to shift from a rural to an urban society. Edo had grown from a small village in 1600 to perhaps the largest city in the world. Its population was more than 1 million. The rise of large commercial centers also increased employment opportunities for women. Women found jobs in entertainment, textile manufacturing, and publishing. Still, the majority of Japanese women led sheltered and restricted lives as peasant wives. They worked in the fields, managed the household, cared for the children, and each woman obeyed her husband without question.

Culture Under the Tokugawa Shogunate Traditional culture continued to thrive. Samurai attended ceremonial *noh* dramas, which were based on tragic themes. They read tales of ancient warriors and their courage in battle. In their homes, they hung paintings that showed scenes from classical literature. But traditional entertainment faced competition in the cities from new styles of literature, drama, and art.

Townspeople read a new type of fiction, realistic stories about self-made merchants or the hardships of life. The people also read **haiku** (HY•koo), 5-7-5-syllable, 3-line verse poetry. This poetry presents images rather than ideas. For example, Matsuo Basho, the greatest haiku poet, wrote before his death in 1694:

B. Possible Answer Basho writes about being ill and on a journey perhaps toward death.

PRIMARY SOURCE B

On a journey, ailing—
My dreams roam about
Over a withered moor.

MATSUO BASHO, from *Matsuo Basho*

Tabi ni yande
Yume wa Kareno o
Kakemeguru

MATSUO BASHO, in Japanese

MAIN IDEA

Analyzing Primary Sources

B How is Matsuo Basho's haiku a poem about death?

Townspeople also attended **kabuki** theater. Actors in elaborate costumes, using music, dance, and mime, performed skits about modern life. The paintings the people enjoyed were often woodblock prints showing city life.

DIFFERENTIATING INSTRUCTION: GIFTED AND TALENTED STUDENTS

Haiku

Class Time 45 minutes

Task Writing haiku

Purpose To learn about the traditional Japanese haiku

Instructions Give students copies of Basho's haiku on page 73 of In-Depth Resources: Unit 1. Discuss the poems. Then explain that haiku follow very strict rules:

- constructed of 3 lines with 5 syllables in the first line, 7 in the second, and 5 in the last line
- refer to or imply a season or month of the year
- use images from nature

Additionally, haiku are written in two parts, which are divided by what is called the "cutting word." In the first example in the text, the cutting word (or phrase) is "My dreams." Everything that comes before (the first line) is one thought. Everything that follows the cutting word (the last two lines) is a separate thought. The cutting word may fall in different places in a haiku. The purpose of the cutting word is to enable the reader to respond personally to the poem by filling in the gap created by the cutting word. Help students identify these elements in the example haiku. Then challenge students to write their own haiku.

Name ______ Date ______

CHAPTER 3 Section 3 LITERATURE SELECTION **Haiku**
by Matsuo Basho

Matsuo Basho (1644–1694) was one of the greatest Japanese haiku poets. What natural objects or scenes does Basho describe in the following haiku?

On the Road to Nara
Oh, these spring days!
A nameless little mountain,
wrapped in morning haze!

The Autumn Storm
Wild boars and all
are blown along with it—
storm-wind of fall!

The Cuckoo
Little gray cuckoo:
sing and sing; and fly and fly—
Oh, so much to do!

from Harold G. Henderson, ed., *An Introduction to Haiku* (Garden City, New York: Doubleday & Company, Inc., 1958) 33–44.

The Chestnut Burr
The winds of fall
are blowing, yet how green
the chestnut burr.

Beauty
The usually hateful crow:
he, too—this morning,
on the snow!

The Mushroom
The mushroom:
from an unknown tree, a leaf
sticks to it.

Research Options

1. ***Writing Expository Paragraphs*** Find out about the form of Japanese poetry known as *haiku*. Then write a brief explanation and share it with classmates.
2. ***Creating an Oral Presentation*** Find one or two examples of *haiku* by other Japanese poets and read them aloud to the class. Then work with your classmates to assemble an illustrated anthology of your favorite *haiku*.

78 Unit 1, Chapter 3

In-Depth Resources: Unit 1

Connect *to* Today

Kabuki Theater

Kabuki is a traditional form of Japanese theater. It makes use of extravagant costumes, masklike makeup, and exaggerated postures and gestures. The illustrations to the right show a contemporary actor and a 19th-century performer playing warriors.

Although kabuki was created by a woman, all roles, both male and female, are performed by men. Kabuki plays are about grand historical events or the everyday life of people in Tokugawa Japan.

For 400 years, kabuki has provided entertainment for the Japanese people. And more recently, kabuki has been performed for audiences around the world, including the United States. Major centers for kabuki theater in Japan are Tokyo, Kyoto, and Osaka.

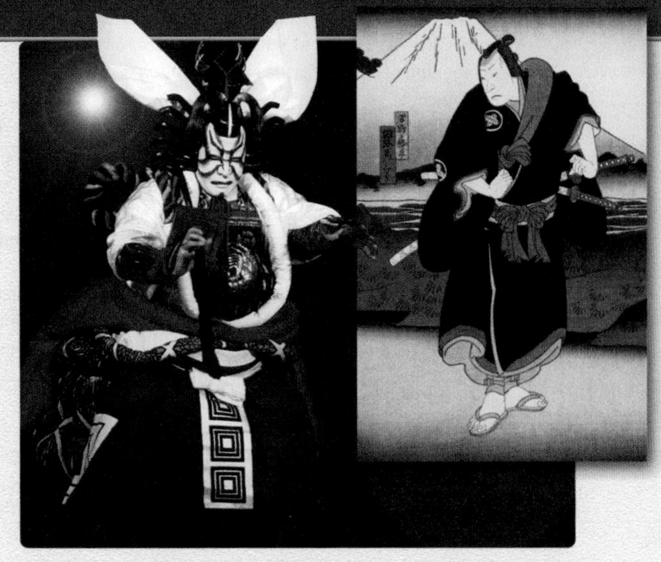

Contact Between Europe and Japan

Europeans began coming to Japan in the 16th century, during the Warring States period. Despite the severe disorder in the country, the Japanese welcomed traders and missionaries, from Portugal and, later, other European countries. These newcomers introduced fascinating new technologies and ideas. Within a century, however, the aggressive Europeans had worn out their welcome.

Portugal Sends Ships, Merchants, and Technology to Japan The Japanese first encountered Europeans in 1543, when shipwrecked Portuguese sailors washed up on the shores of southern Japan. Portuguese merchants soon followed. They hoped to involve themselves in Japan's trade with China and Southeast Asia. The Portuguese brought clocks, eyeglasses, tobacco, firearms, and other unfamiliar items from Europe. Japanese merchants, eager to expand their markets, were happy to receive the newcomers and their goods. (C)

MAIN IDEA
Analyzing Motives
(C) Why did Europeans want to open trade with Japan?
C. Answer They hoped to involve themselves in Japan's trade network.

The daimyo, too, welcomed the strangers. They were particularly interested in the Portuguese muskets and cannons, because every daimyo sought an advantage over his rivals. One of these warlords listened intently to a Japanese observer's description of a musket:

PRIMARY SOURCE

> In their hands they carried something two or three feet long, straight on the outside with a passage inside, and made of a heavy substance. . . . This thing with one blow can smash a mountain of silver and a wall of iron. If one sought to do mischief in another man's domain and he was touched by it, he would lose his life instantly.
>
> **ANONYMOUS JAPANESE WRITER**, quoted in *Sources of Japanese Tradition* (1958)

The Japanese purchased weapons from the Portuguese and soon began their own production. Firearms forever changed the time-honored tradition of the Japanese warrior, whose principal weapon had been the sword. Some daimyo recruited and trained corps of peasants to use muskets. Many samurai, who retained the sword as their principal weapon, would lose their lives to musket fire in future combat.

Connect *to* Today

Kabuki Theater

Originally women played female roles in kabuki drama. In 1629, however, authorities noticed that men were taking too much interest in the female actors, so they banned women from acting. Male actors immediately took over the female roles. The ban on women was lifted in the nineteenth century, but the tradition of men playing the female roles was so strong that women still have not taken back their parts.

Contact Between Europe and Japan

10.4.2

Critical Thinking

- How did the building of castles attract merchants, artisans, and others? *(People came to the castles to help build them; others came to feed and support the workers and their families.)*
- How did the Japanese response to missionaries differ from the Chinese response? *(Both initially accepted the missionaries, but Japan later banned Christianity altogether.)*

Critical Thinking Transparencies

- CT19 The Impact of Exploration on East Asia

Electronic Library of Primary Sources

- from The Act of Seclusion

CONNECTIONS ACROSS TIME AND CULTURES

Meeting Between Cultures

Class Time 35 minutes

Task Writing a dialogue

Purpose To help students see similarities between Japanese and European feudal society

Instructions Have students work in pairs and review aspects of feudalism in Europe so they can compare it to life in Japan during the Tokugawa Shogunate. Tell them to imagine that they are living during the period when the first Europeans visited Japan. Then have them each take a role, such as that of a European noble and a Japanese samurai. Instruct them to discuss their roles and decide how each of the characters would see his or her place in society. Have students use In-Depth Resources, Unit 1, Connections Across Time and Cultures, p. 76 to develop ideas. Students should then write a dialogue in which the two characters discuss events from the perspective of their different cultures. Topics might include

- the introduction of firearms into Japan
- the building of castles and the growth of towns
- the power of the daimyo and shoguns

Have students practice and present their dialogue to the class.

In-Depth Resources: Unit 1

More About . . .

Francis Xavier

Francis Xavier epitomized the missionary spirit of the Jesuits. Through selfless devotion, he helped establish Christianity in India, Malacca, and the Spice Islands. His strong beliefs and aura of goodness attracted many converts. In 1549, he sought a new challenge among the more culturally advanced Japanese, whom he called "the best people yet discovered."

Electronic Library of Primary Sources

- from *The Life and Letters of St. Francis Xavier*

The cannon also had a huge impact on warfare and life in Japan. Daimyo had to build fortified castles to withstand the destructive force of cannonballs. (See the photograph of Himeji Castle on page 109.) The castles attracted merchants, artisans, and others to surrounding lands. Many of these lands were to grow into the towns and cities of modern Japan, including Edo (Tokyo), Osaka, Himeji, and Nagoya.

Christian Missionaries in Japan In 1549, Christian missionaries began arriving in Japan. The Japanese accepted the missionaries in part because they associated them with the muskets and other European goods that they wanted to purchase. However, the religious orders of Jesuits, Franciscans, and Dominicans came to convert the Japanese.

Francis Xavier, a Jesuit, led the first mission to Japan. He wrote that the Japanese were "very sociable. . . and much concerned with their honor, which they prize above everything else." Francis Xavier baptized about a hundred converts before he left Japan. By the year 1600, other European missionaries had converted about 300,000 Japanese to Christianity.

The success of the missionaries upset Tokugawa Ieyasu. He found aspects of the Christian invasion troublesome. Missionaries, actively seeking converts, scorned traditional Japanese beliefs and sometimes involved themselves in local politics. At first, Ieyasu did not take any action. He feared driving off the Portuguese, English, Spanish, and Dutch traders who spurred Japan's economy. By 1612, however, the shogun had come to fear religious uprisings more. He banned Christianity and focused on ridding his country of all Christians.

Ieyasu died in 1616, but repression of Christianity continued off and on for the next two decades under his successors. In 1637, the issue came to a head. An uprising in southern Japan of some 30,000 peasants, led by dissatisfied samurai, shook the Tokugawa shogunate. Because so many of the rebels were Christian, the shogun decided that Christianity was at the root of the rebellion. After that, the shoguns ruthlessly persecuted Christians. European missionaries were killed or driven out of Japan. All Japanese were forced to demonstrate faithfulness to some branch of Buddhism. These policies eventually eliminated Christianity in Japan and led to the formation of an exclusion policy. D

D. Possible Answer The Japanese were more receptive at first to European contact than the Chinese were; however, both countries eventually rebuffed European influences and entered an age of isolation.

MAIN IDEA

Comparing

D How was the treatment of Europeans different in Japan and China? How was it similar?

▼ Japanese merchants and Jesuit missionaries await the arrival of a Portuguese ship at Nagasaki in the 1500s in this painting on wood panels.

DIFFERENTIATING INSTRUCTION: STRUGGLING READERS

The Rise and Fall of Christianity in Japan

Class Time 15 minutes

Task Clarifying sequence of events

Purpose To understand events leading to the banning of Christianity and the closing of the country to Europeans

Instructions Remind students that Christianity was introduced into Japan in 1549 by missionaries. Following a series of events, the Tokugawa shoguns banned Christianity and closed the country to Europeans. Help students understand the sequence of events by displaying Critical Thinking Transparency CT73. Have students copy the chart. Write "Missionaries arrive in Japan, 1549" in the first box. Then elicit the following sequence of events that led to the closing of Japan to Europeans.

- 300,000 Japanese converted by 1600
- shogun fears religious uprisings
- shogun bans Christianity
- 1637, uprising by 30,000 peasants
- shogun forces all Japanese to accept Buddhism
- Christianity eliminated in Japan
- closed country policy adopted

Write the events on the chart and have students copy them into their own charts.

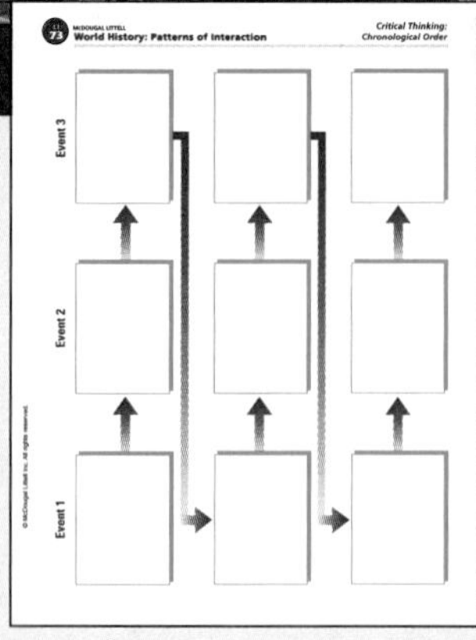

Critical Thinking Transparencies

The Closed Country Policy

The persecution of Christians was part of an attempt to control foreign ideas. When Europeans first arrived, no central authority existed to contain them. The strong leaders who later took power did not like the introduction of European ideas and ways, but they valued European trade. As time passed, the Tokugawa shoguns realized that they could safely exclude both the missionaries and the merchants. By 1639, they had sealed Japan's borders and instituted a "closed country policy."

Japan in Isolation Most commercial contacts with Europeans ended. One port, Nagasaki, remained open to foreign traders. But only Dutch and Chinese merchants were allowed into the port. Earlier, the English had left Japan voluntarily; the Spanish and the Portuguese had been expelled. Since the Tokugawa shoguns controlled Nagasaki, they now had a monopoly on foreign trade, which continued to be profitable.

For more than 200 years, Japan remained basically closed to Europeans. In addition, the Japanese were forbidden to leave, so as not to bring back foreign ideas. Japan would continue to develop, but as a self-sufficient country, free from European attempts to colonize or to establish their presence.

Europeans had met with much resistance in their efforts to open the East to trade. But expansion to the West, in the Americas, as you will learn in Chapter 4, would prove much more successful for European traders, missionaries, and colonizers.

History *in* Depth

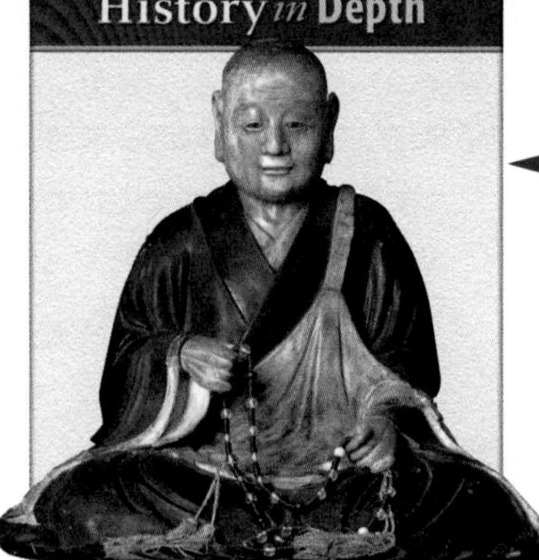

Zen Buddhism

The form of Buddhism that had the greatest impact on Japanese culture was Zen Buddhism. It especially influenced the samurai.

Zen Buddhists sought spiritual enlightenment through meditation. Strict discipline of mind and body was the Zen path to wisdom. Zen monks would sit in meditation for hours, as shown in the sculpture above. If they showed signs of losing concentration, a Zen master might shout at them or hit them with a stick.

SECTION 3 ASSESSMENT

TERMS & NAMES 1. For each term or name, write a sentence explaining its significance.
• daimyo • Oda Nobunaga • Toyotomi Hideyoshi • Tokugawa Shogunate • haiku • kabuki

USING YOUR NOTES

2. Which contribution by a daimyo was the most significant? Why? (10.4.1)

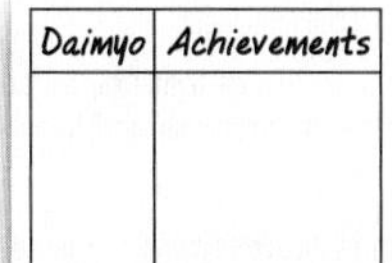

MAIN IDEAS

3. What happened during the period of the "Warring States"? (10.4.1)
4. What was the structure of society in Tokugawa Japan? (10.4.1)
5. What were the new styles of drama, art, and literature in Tokugawa Japan? (10.4.1)

CRITICAL THINKING & WRITING

6. **DRAWING CONCLUSIONS** Why do you think that the emperor had less power than a shogun? (10.4.1)
7. **ANALYZING CAUSES** Why did the Japanese policy toward Christians change from acceptance to repression? (10.4.2)
8. **FORMING OPINIONS** Do you think Japan's closed country policy effectively kept Western ideas and customs out of Japan? (10.4.2)
9. **WRITING ACTIVITY** CULTURAL INTERACTION Write a two-paragraph **comparison** of the similarities and differences between the roles of women in China (discussed on page 107) and in Japan (page 110). (Writing 2.2.b)

INTEGRATED TECHNOLOGY **INTERNET ACTIVITY**
Use the Internet to find information on the Japanese government today. Then create an **organizational chart** showing the structure of the government. (Writing 2.6.a)

INTERNET KEYWORD
country profiles

History *in* Depth

Tell students that characteristics of an enlightened master of Zen Buddhism include serenity, fearlessness, and spontaneity. Ask students how these characteristics might be reflected in Japanese arts, sports, or garden design.

The Closed Country Policy
10.4.2

Critical Thinking

- How did the closed country policy strengthen the Tokugawa shoguns? *(Possible Answers: eliminated European ideas that undermined Tokugawa authority; limiting trade produced monopoly and high profits)*
- What might have been the long-term effect of Japan's closed country policy? *(Possible Answers: missed technological advances; stagnation of ideas)*

3 ASSESS

SECTION 3 ASSESSMENT

Tell students to meet in small groups and discuss answers to the questions.

Formal Assessment
Section Quiz, p. 57

4 RETEACH

Have students use the Visual Summary to review the main ideas of the section and the chapter.

Critical Thinking Transparencies
CT57 Chapter 3 Visual Summary

In-Depth Resources: Unit 1
• Reteaching Activity, p. 80

ANSWERS

1. daimyo, p. 108 • Oda Nobunaga, p. 108 • Toyotomi Hideyoshi, p. 109 • Tokugawa Shogunate, p. 110 • haiku, p. 110 • kabuki, p. 110
2. **Sample Answer:** Oda Nobunaga—1568, took Kyoto; defeated enemy daimyo; 1575, used firearms in battle. Hideyoshi—1590, claimed most of Japan; 1592, invaded Korea. Ieyasu—1600, defeated rivals; 1603, took shogun title; moved capital to Edo; restricted daimyo power, rule of law. **Possible Answer:** Ieyasu because he established rule of law.
3. Samurai seized control of feudal estates.
4. emperor at the top; next, the shogun; large landowners, the daimyo, followed; next, the samurai warriors; peasants and artisans, next; merchants at the bottom
5. kabuki theater, woodblock printing, urban fiction, and haiku poetry
6. **Possible Answers:** The emperor had no army, no control of land; shogun was supreme military commander.
7. **Possible Answer:** Tokugawa leaders believed Christians scorned traditional beliefs, and this might have led to rebellion.
8. **Possible Answers:** Yes—European influence confined to Nagasaki; shoguns censored information. No—European ideas as well as trade entered Nagasaki.
9. **Rubric** Comparisons should
   - reflect an understanding of the roles of women in Chinese and Japanese society.
   - present similarities and differences.
   - be clear, focused, and logical.

INTEGRATED TECHNOLOGY

Rubric Charts should
- include accurate information on the Japanese government.
- be clearly labeled.

TERMS & NAMES

1. Bartolomeu Dias, p. 96
2. Vasco da Gama, p. 98
3. Treaty of Tordesillas, p. 99
4. Dutch East India Company, p. 100
5. Ming dynasty, p. 102
6. Manchus, p. 105
7. Qing dynasty, p. 105
8. Oda Nobunaga, p. 108
9. Toyotomi Hideyoshi, p. 109
10. Tokugawa Shogunate, p. 110

MAIN IDEAS

Answers will vary.

11. desire for new sources of wealth; desire to spread Christianity; technological advancements in sailing and navigation
12. He encouraged exploration by establishing a navigation school for sailors to perfect their trade and financed voyages of discovery.
13. Dias showed that the southern tip of Africa could be circumnavigated; da Gama established a sea route from Europe to India.
14. The Dutch owned the largest fleet of ships in the world, and the Dutch East India Company was more powerful and better financed than other nations' trading companies.
15. Idea of commerce offended China's Confucian beliefs; economic policy gave priority to agriculture.
16. the clock and the prism
17. ineffective rulers, corrupt officials, bankrupt government, high taxes, bad harvests
18. It was an era of disorder when powerful warrior-chieftains, called daimyo, seized control of old feudal estates, set up a new type of feudalism, and often fought each other for territory.
19. Ideal—Japan was an agricultural society and the farmer was the ideal citizen. Reality—farmers were overburdened and over-taxed and often moved to the city for a better life.
20. kabuki plays, popular stories, haiku poetry, and woodblock prints

Chapter 3 Assessment

VISUAL SUMMARY

An Age of Explorations and Isolation

Explorations

1405 **Zheng He of China** launches voyages of exploration to Southeast Asia, India, Arabia, and eastern Africa.

1500s **The Portuguese** establish trading outposts throughout Asia and gain control of the spice trade.

1600s **The Dutch** drive out the Portuguese and establish their own trading empire in the East. (Below, a Dutch ship is pictured on a plate made in China for European trade.)

Europeans sail farther east to China and Japan in search of more trade; both nations ultimately reject European advances.

Isolation

1433 **China** abandons its voyages of exploration.

1500s **The Chinese** severely restrict trade with foreigners.

1612 **Japan** outlaws Christianity and drives out Christian missionaries.

1630s **The Japanese** institute a "closed country policy" and remain isolated from Europe for 200 years.

TERMS & NAMES

For each term or name below, briefly explain its importance to European exploration and the development of China and Japan.

1. Bartolomeu Dias
2. Vasco da Gama
3. Treaty of Tordesillas
4. Dutch East India Company
5. Ming dynasty
6. Manchus
7. Qing dynasty
8. Oda Nobunaga
9. Toyotomi Hideyoshi
10. Tokugawa Shogunate

MAIN IDEAS

Europeans Explore the East Section 1 (pages 95–101)

11. What factors helped spur European exploration? (10.4.2)
12. What role did Portugal's Prince Henry play in overseas exploration? (10.4.3)
13. What was the significance of Dias's voyage? da Gama's voyage? (10.4.3)
14. Why were the Dutch so successful in establishing a trading empire in the Indian Ocean? (10.4.2)

China Limits European Contacts Section 2 (pages 102–107)

15. Why did China not undergo widespread industrialization? (10.4.1)
16. What did Christian missionaries bring to China? (10.4.1)
17. What are five reasons the Ming Dynasty fell to civil disorder? (10.4.1)

Japan Returns to Isolation Section 3 (pages 108–113)

18. Why was the time between 1467 and 1568 called the period of the "Warring States"? (10.4.1)
19. What was the difference between the Confucian ideal of society and the real society of Japan? (10.4.1)
20. How did the Japanese express themselves culturally under the Tokugawa shoguns? (10.4.1)

CRITICAL THINKING

1. USING YOUR NOTES
In a time line, trace the events that led to Japan's expulsion of European Christians. (CST 3)

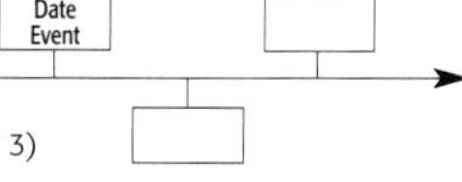

2. RECOGNIZING EFFECTS
How might a Chinese emperor's leadership be affected by living in the Forbidden City? Explain and support your opinion. (REP 2)

3. ANALYZING ISSUES
SCIENCE AND TECHNOLOGY Of the technological advances that helped spur European exploration, which do you think was the most important? Why? (REP 4)

4. ANALYZING CAUSES
CULTURAL INTERACTION What caused Japan to institute a policy of isolation? Defend your viewpoint with text references. (REP 2)

5. SUMMARIZING
ECONOMICS How did the Manchus earn the respect of the Chinese? Support your answer with details from the chapter. (REP 4)

CRITICAL THINKING

Answers will vary.

1. 1549—Missionaries welcomed; 1600—Some 300,000 Japanese converted; 1612—Christianity prohibited; 1637—About 30,000 peasants, mostly Christian, revolt; Christianity suppressed
2. emperors out of touch; may develop a lack of compassion; heightened contempt for foreigners; pleasure, greed, and court intrigue distract from leadership; corrupt officials may assume power
3. Answers should show an understanding of the impact of the technological advance selected.
4. The Japanese feared the influence of European ideas and the threat of European colonization of Japan.
5. They upheld China's traditional Confucian beliefs and social structures, secured the country's frontiers and, most importantly, restored China's prosperity.

Use the quotation and your knowledge of world history to answer questions 1 and 2.
Additional Test Practice, pp. S1–S33

PRIMARY SOURCE

But I was careful not to refer to these Westerners as "Great Officials," and corrected Governor Liu Yin-shu when he referred to the Jesuits Regis and Fridelli . . . as if they were honored imperial commissioners. For even though some of the Western methods are different from our own, and may even be an improvement, there is little about them that is new. The principles of mathematics all derive from the Book of Changes, and the Western methods are Chinese in origin: this algebra—"A-erh-chu-pa-erh"—springs from an Eastern word. And though it was indeed the Westerners who showed us something our ancient calendar experts did not know—namely how to calculate the angles of the northern pole—this but shows the truth of what Chu Hsi arrived at through his investigation of things: the earth is like the yolk within an egg.

KANGXI, quoted in *Emperor of China: Self-Portrait of K'Ang-Hsi*

1. Which phrase best describes Kangxi's thoughts about Europeans, or "Westerners"? (REP 4)
   - **A.** Westerners use methods that are inferior to Chinese methods.
   - **B.** Westerners would make good trading partners.
   - **C.** Westerners use methods that are based on Chinese methods.
   - **D.** There are too many Westerners in China.

2. What can be inferred about Kangxi's beliefs about China? (REP 2)
   - **A.** China needs the assistance of Westerners.
   - **B.** China is superior to countries of the West.
   - **C.** China has many problems.
   - **D.** China is destined to rule the world.

Use this map produced by German cartographer Henricus Martellus in about 1490 and your knowledge of world history to answer question 3.

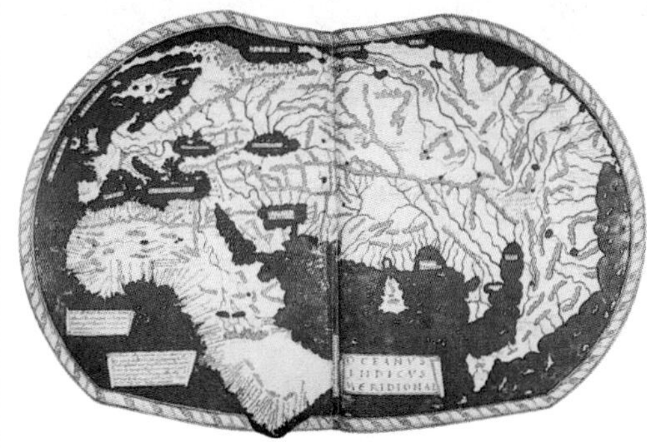

3. Which of these statements about Martellus's map is not accurate? (REP 2)
   - **A.** Martellus shows Europe, Africa, and Asia.
   - **B.** Martellus's map includes the oceans.
   - **C.** Martellus shows North America.
   - **D.** Martellus's map has many ports marked on the western coast of Africa.

INTEGRATED TECHNOLOGY

TEST PRACTICE Go to **classzone.com**
- Diagnostic tests
- Tutorials
- Strategies
- Additional practice

ALTERNATIVE ASSESSMENT

1. **Interact *with* History** (REP 4)
   On page 94, you decided whether or not you would sail into the unknown. Now that you have read the chapter, reevaluate your decision. If you decided to go, did what you read reaffirm your decision? Why or why not? If you chose not to go, explain what your feelings are now. Discuss your answers within a small group.

2. **WRITING ABOUT HISTORY** (Writing 2.3.a)
   Imagine you are the Jesuit missionary Matteo Ricci. Write an **expository essay** describing your impressions of Chinese rule and culture. Consider the following in the essay:
   - Matteo Ricci's values
   - Chinese culture as compared with Western Christian culture

INTEGRATED TECHNOLOGY

Planning a Television Special (Writing 2.1.c)
Use the Internet, books, and other reference materials to create a script for a television special "The Voyages of Zheng He." The script should address the historical context of Zheng He's voyages and their impact on China and the lands visited. The script should include narration, sound, re-creations, and locations. In researching, consider the following:
- biographical data on Zheng He
- information on the ships, crews, and cargo
- descriptions of the voyages
- music and visuals

STANDARDS-BASED ASSESSMENT

1. Letter **C** is correct. Letter **A** is not correct because Kangxi says that some of the Western methods may be improvements. Letter **B** is not correct because there is no reference to trade. Letter **D** is incorrect because the quotation does not mention numbers of Westerners in China.
2. Letter **B** is correct. Letter **A** is incorrect because Kangxi does not believe that China needs help from Westerners. Letter **C** is incorrect because there is no mention of problems in China. Letter **D** is incorrect because Kangxi makes no mention of any desire by the Chinese to rule the world.
3. Letter **C** is correct because North America is not shown. Letter **A** is not correct because the Martellus map does picture Europe, Africa, and Asia. Letter **B** is incorrect because the map does include the oceans. Letter **D** is incorrect because the map does show many ports on the west coast of Africa.

Formal Assessment
- Chapter Test, Forms A, B, and C, pp. 58–69

California Test Generator CD-ROM
- Chapter Tests, Forms A, B, and C (English and Spanish)

ALTERNATIVE ASSESSMENT

1. Students who originally wanted to sail may now say that the rewards were not great enough to go through all the hardship and give up that much time from their lives. Others may say that the opportunity to bring glory and prestige to their country and make some financial gain would be worth the sacrifice.
2. **Rubric** Expository essays should
   - reflect the values of Matteo Ricci.
   - present information about the Chinese culture.
   - compare Chinese culture with Western culture.

INTEGRATED TECHNOLOGY

Rubric Scripts should
- portray the voyages accurately and in a dramatic style.
- cover the topic adequately.
- clearly demonstrate an understanding of the material.
- include some historical evaluation of the voyages.

CHAPTER 4 PLANNING GUIDE

The Atlantic World, 1492–1800

CHAPTER RESOURCES	COPYMASTERS	ASSESSMENT
CHAPTER OVERVIEW Europeans explored and colonized the Americas, which strongly affected both the Eastern and Western hemispheres.	**In-Depth Resources: Unit 1** • Building Vocabulary, p. 85 **Chapters in Brief** (in English and Spanish) **Block Schedule Pacing Guide**	**Chapter Assessment,** pp. 142–143 **Formal Assessment** • Chapter Tests, Forms A, B, and C, pp. 74–85 **Test Generator** **Integrated Assessment Book** **Online Test Practice**
SECTION 1 **Spain Builds an American Empire** pp. 119–126 **OBJECTIVE** Analyze the voyages of Columbus and other Spanish explorers and the Spanish colonization of the Americas.	**In-Depth Resources: Unit 1** • Guided Reading, p. 81 • Primary Sources: from *The Journal of Christopher Columbus,* p. 89; from *The Broken Spears,* p. 91 • Literature: from *The Feathered Serpent,* p. 93 • History Makers: Ferdinand Magellan, p. 96; Hernando Cortés, p. 97 • Reteaching Activity, p. 99 **Reading Study Guide,** p. 41	**Section 1 Assessment,** p. 125 **Formal Assessment** • Section Quiz, p. 70 **California Daily Standards Practice Transparencies,** TT71
SECTION 2 **European Nations Settle North America** pp. 127–131 **OBJECTIVE** Describe the colonial activities of Europeans in North America.	**In-Depth Resources: Unit 1** • Guided Reading, p. 82 • Skillbuilder Practice: Comparing and Contrasting, p. 86 • Reteaching Activity, p. 100 **Reading Study Guide,** p. 43	**Section 2 Assessment,** p. 131 **Formal Assessment** • Section Quiz, p. 71 **California Daily Standards Practice Transparencies,** TT72
SECTION 3 **The Atlantic Slave Trade** pp. 132–136 **OBJECTIVE** Explain the Atlantic slave trade and the life of enslaved Africans in the colonies.	**In-Depth Resources: Unit 1** • Guided Reading, p. 83 • Primary Source: from *The Life of Olaudah Equiano,* p. 92 • Reteaching Activity, p. 101 **Reading Study Guide,** p. 45	**Section 3 Assessment,** p. 136 **Formal Assessment** • Section Quiz, p. 72 **California Daily Standards Practice Transparencies,** TT73
SECTION 4 **The Columbian Exchange and Global Trade** pp. 137–141 **OBJECTIVE** Describe the Columbian Exchange, global trade, and mercantilism.	**In-Depth Resources: Unit 1** • Guided Reading, p. 84 • Geography Application: The Potato Impacts the World, p. 87 • Connections Across Time and Cultures: Impact of the Columbian Exchange, p. 98 • Reteaching Activity, p. 102 **Reading Study Guide,** p. 47	**Section 4 Assessment,** p. 141 **Formal Assessment** • Section Quiz, p. 73 **California Daily Standards Practice Transparencies,** TT74

- eEdition Plus Online
- EasyPlanner Plus Online
- eTest Plus Online

Audio CDs
- Voices from the Past
- Reading Study Guides

CD-ROMs
- eEdition
- Power Presentations
- EasyPlanner
- Electronic Library of Primary Sources
- Test Generator

eEdition CD-ROM

World Art and Cultures Transparencies
- AT43 *Meeting of Cortés and Montezuma*

Electronic Library of Primary Sources
- "On the Destruction of the Indies"
- from Letter to King Charles V of Spain

Patterns of Interaction Video Series
- The Spread of Epidemic Disease

classzone.com

eEdition CD-ROM

Electronic Library of Primary Sources
- "The French Lose Quebec"

classzone.com

eEdition CD-ROM

World Art and Cultures Transparencies
- AT44 Meynell's *Slaves Below the Deck*

Critical Thinking Transparencies
- CT20 The Atlantic Slave Trade, 1451–1870

Electronic Library of Primary Sources
- Letter to the King of Portugal

classzone.com

eEdition CD-ROM

Geography Transparencies
- GT20 Spain's Colonies

Critical Thinking Transparencies
- CT56 Chapter 4 Visual Summary

Electronic Library of Primary Sources
- "Concerning the Dearness of All Things"

Patterns of Interaction Video Series
- The Impact of Potatoes and Sugar

classzone.com

	Section 1	Section 2	Section 3	Section 4
California Reading Toolkit	p. L19	p. L20	p. L21	p. L22
California Modified Lesson Plans for English Learners	p. 33	p. 35	p. 37	p. 39
California Daily Standards Practice Transparencies	TT11	TT12	TT13	TT14
California Standards Enrichment Workbook	pp. 49–50	pp. 19–20	pp. 47–48, 49–50, 51–52	pp. 43–44, 47–48
California Standards Planner and Lesson Plans	p. L29	p. L31	p. L33	p. L35
California Online Test Practice	classzone.com	classzone.com	classzone.com	classzone.com
California Test Generator CD-ROM				
California Easy Planner CD-ROM				
California eEdition CD-ROM				

Chart Key:

Copymaster

Pupil's Edition

Audio Library

Teacher's Edition

CD-ROM

Overhead Transparency

Internet

Block Scheduling

Video

NO TIME?

If you do not have time to teach this chapter in full, assign the **Chapter in Brief** (also available in Spanish).

Previewing Resources for Differentiated Instruction

ENGLISH LEARNERS: Resources in Spanish

In-Depth Resources in Spanish
- Guided Reading Ⓐ
- Skillbuilder Practice: Comparing and Contrasting
- Geography Application: The Potato Impacts the World Ⓑ

Chapters in Brief

Reading Study Guide Ⓒ

Reading Study Guide Audio CD

Test Generator CD-ROM
- Chapter Test, Forms A, B, and C

Plus

Modified Lesson Plans for English Learners

Multi-Language Glossary of Social Studies Terms

Ⓐ

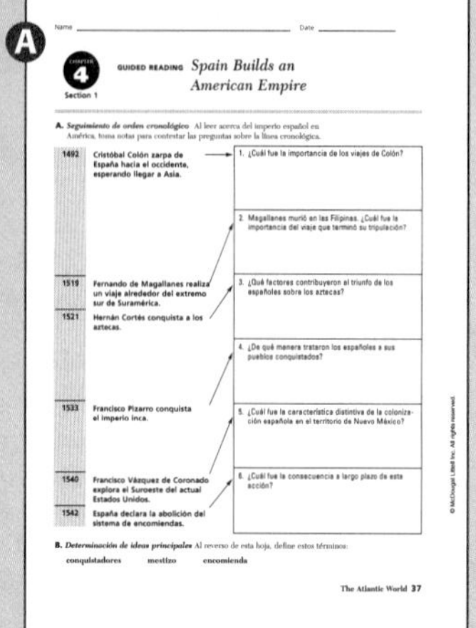

CHAPTER 4 Section 1 GUIDED READING *Spain Builds an American Empire*

Ⓑ

CHAPTER 4 Section 4 GEOGRAPHY APPLICATION: MOVEMENT *El efecto de la papa sobre el mundo*

The Spread of the Potato to Europe and North America

STRUGGLING READERS

In-Depth Resources: Unit 0
- Guided Reading Ⓐ
- Building Vocabulary
- Skillbuilder Practice: Comparing and Contrasting Ⓑ
- Geography Application: The Potato Impacts the World
- Reteaching Activities

Chapters in Brief

Reading Study Guide

Reading Study Guide Audio CD

Formal Assessment
- Chapter Test, Form A Ⓒ

Plus

Reading Toolkit

Ⓐ

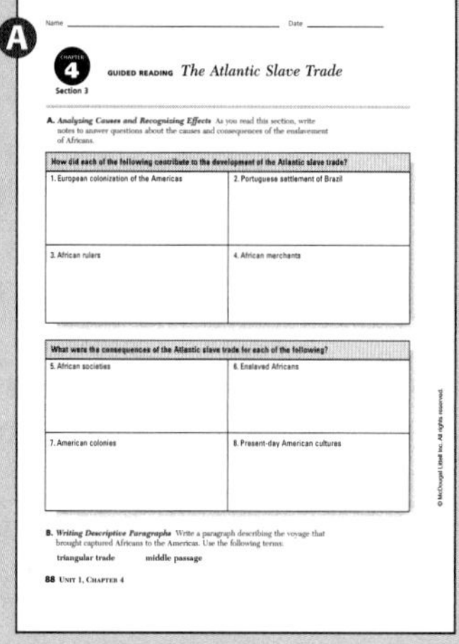

CHAPTER 4 Section 3 GUIDED READING *The Atlantic Slave Trade*

Ⓑ

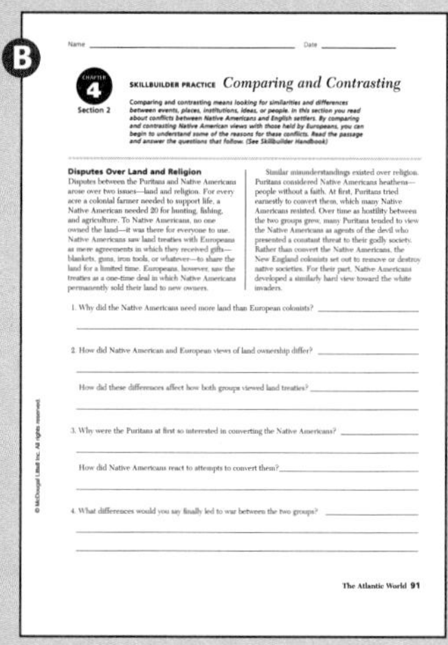

CHAPTER 4 Section 2 SKILLBUILDER PRACTICE *Comparing and Contrasting*

GIFTED AND TALENTED STUDENTS

In-Depth Resources: Unit 1
- Primary Sources: from *The Journal of Christopher Columbus* Ⓐ; from *The Broken Spears;* from *The Life of Olaudah Equiano*
- Literature: from *The Feathered Serpent*
- History Makers: Ferdinand Magellan; Hernando Cortés
- Connections Across Time and Cultures: Impact of the Columbian Exchange Ⓑ

Electronic Library of Primary Sources
- "On the Destruction of the Indies"
- from Letter to King Charles V of Spain
- "The French Lose Quebec"
- Letter to the King of Portugal
- "Concerning the Dearness of All Things and the Remedy Thereof"

Formal Assessment
- Chapter Test, Form C Ⓒ, Formal Assessment, p. 84

Ⓐ

CHAPTER 4 Section 1 PRIMARY SOURCE *from The Journal of Christopher Columbus*

Ⓑ

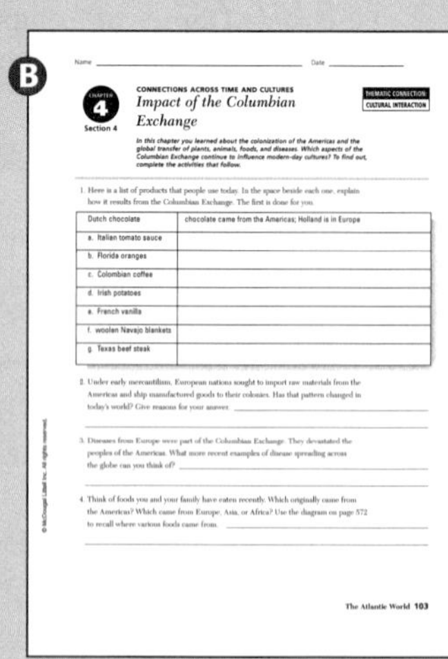

CHAPTER 4 Section 4 CONNECTIONS ACROSS TIME AND CULTURES *Impact of the Columbian Exchange*

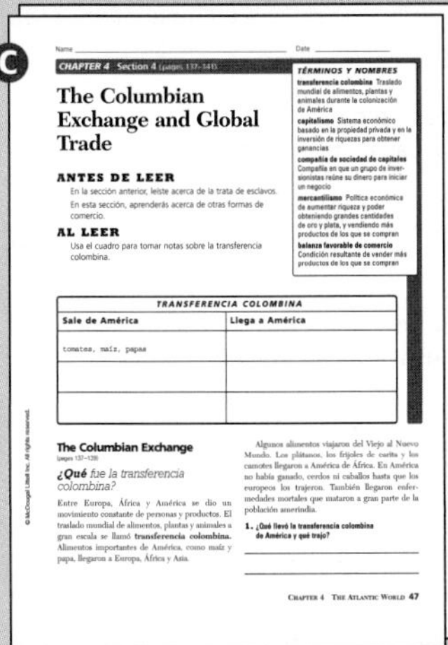

CHAPTER 4 Section 4

The Columbian Exchange and Global Trade

ANTES DE LEER

AL LEER

TRANSFERENCIA COLOMBINA

Sale de América	Llega a América
tomates, maíz, papas	

The Columbian Exchange

¿Qué fue la transferencia colombina?

CHAPTER 4 THE ATLANTIC WORLD 47

Activities in the Teacher's Edition for English Learners

- Understanding English Words that Have Spanish Origins, p. 123
- Interpreting Charts and Graphs, p. 134

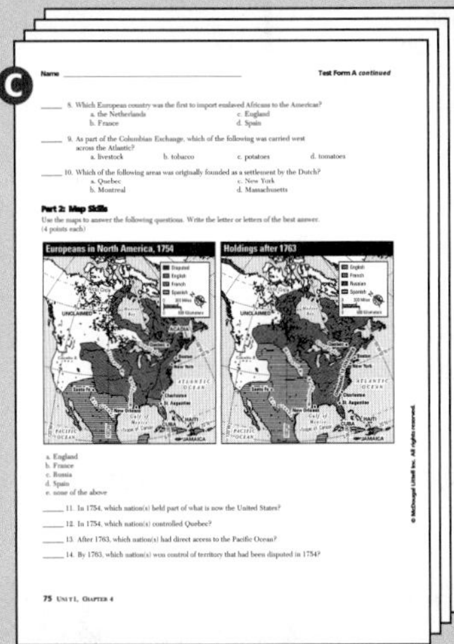

Test Form A *continued*

Part 2: Map Skills

Europeans in North America, 1754

Holdings after 1763

Activities in the Teacher's Edition for Struggling Readers

- Expressing Opinions Visually, p. 122
- European Colonies in the 17th Century, p. 129
- Understanding the African Slave Trade, p. 133
- Vocabulary Activity: "Interviewing" Words, p. 139

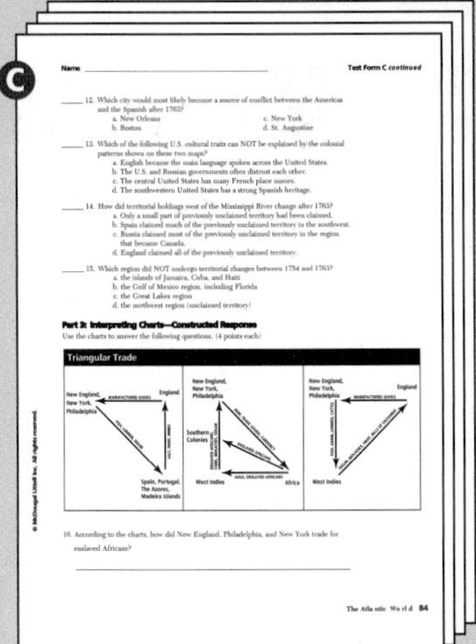

Test Form C *continued*

Triangular Trade

Activities in the Teacher's Edition for Gifted and Talented Students

- Eyewitness to History, p. 120
- Researching the French and Indian War, p. 130
- Understanding Primary Sources, p. 135
- Principles of Mercantilism, p. 140

INTEGRATED TECHNOLOGY

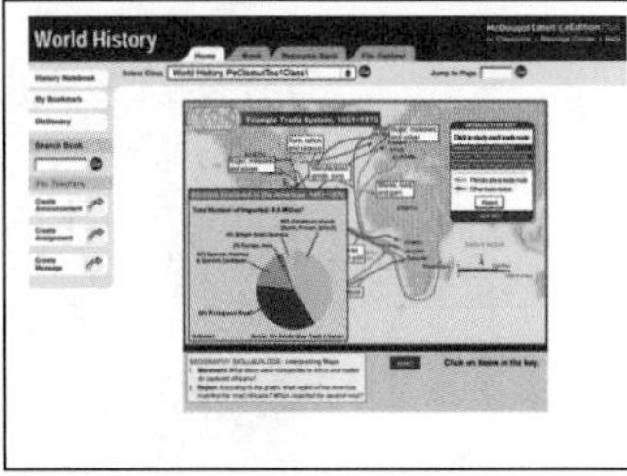

eEdition
- Interactive Visuals
- Interactive Maps
- Interactive Primary Sources

classzone.com
- Research Links
- Internet Activities
- Primary Sources
- Chapter Quiz
- Current Events

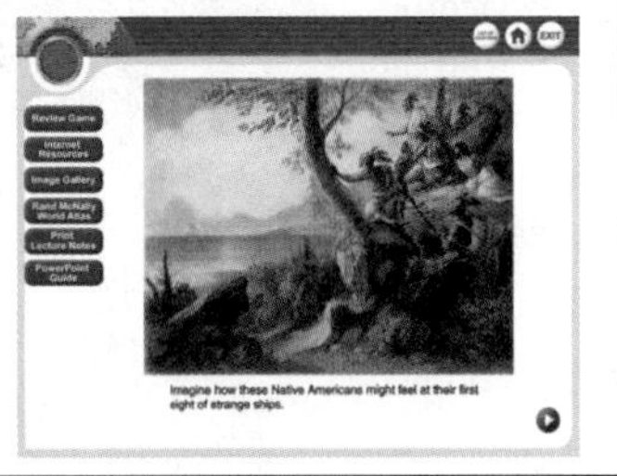

Power Presentations CD-ROM
- Lecture Notes
- Image Gallery
- Chapter Review Game

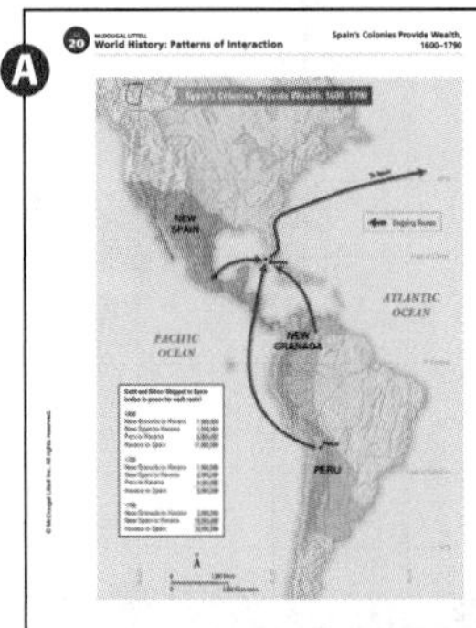

Critical Thinking Transparencies
- CT20 The Atlantic Slave Trade, 1451–1870
- CT56 Chapter 4 Visual Summary

Geography Transparencies
- GT20 Spain's Colonies Provide Wealth, 1600–1790

World Art and Cultures Transparencies
- AT43 *Meeting of Cortés and Montezuma*
- AT44 Meynell's *Slaves Below the Deck of the* Albanez

Test Practice Transparencies TT71–TT74

Test Generator CD-ROM

EasyPlanner CD-ROM

Voices from the Past Audio CD

Online Test Practice

Electronic Library of Primary Sources

Patterns of Interaction Video Series

CHAPTER 4 • OBJECTIVE

Analyze the impact of European exploration and colonization of the Americas.

Previewing Main Ideas

Note that the main ideas focus on the variety of ways that the Europeans interacted with the native inhabitants of the Americas. While there was some mutual exchange, generally the Europeans exploited the native people and natural resources for economic and political gain.

Accessing Prior Knowledge

Ask students what they know about Columbus. Then ask them if they know about controversies over the impact of Columbus's voyages to the Americas. Why is it inaccurate to say that Columbus discovered America? (*Many indigenous people already lived here.*)

Geography *Answers*

CULTURAL INTERACTION The viceroyalty of New Spain included Mexican lands stretching into the current American Southwest and into Central America, modern Florida, most of the West Indies, and a small section of South America.

ECONOMICS Enslaved Africans arrived on the eastern coast.

EMPIRE BUILDING The Spanish conquered the Aztec and Incan empires.

CHAPTER 4

The Atlantic World, 1492–1800

Previewing Main Ideas

CULTURAL INTERACTION The voyages of Columbus prompted a worldwide exchange of everything from religious and political ideas to new foods and plants.

Geography *According to the map, what lands were included in the viceroyalty of New Spain in 1700?*

ECONOMICS The vast wealth to be had from colonizing the Americas sealed the fate of millions of Native Americans and Africans who were forced to work in mines and on plantations.

Geography *On which coast of the Americas would enslaved persons from Africa have arrived?*

EMPIRE BUILDING Over the span of several centuries, Europeans conquered the Americas' native inhabitants and built powerful American empires.

Geography *What two major Native American empires did the Spanish conquer in the sixteenth century?*

INTEGRATED TECHNOLOGY

eEdition
- Interactive Maps
- Interactive Visuals
- Interactive Primary Sources

VIDEO *Patterns of Interaction: The Impact of Potatoes and Sugar*

INTERNET RESOURCES
Go to classzone.com for:
- Research Links
- Internet Activities
- Primary Sources
- Chapter Quiz
- Maps
- Test Practice
- Current Events

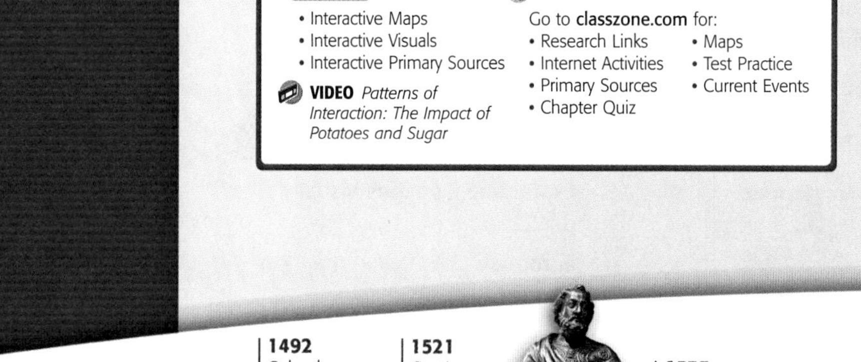

AMERICAS

1492 Columbus makes first voyage.

1521 Cortés conquers Aztec Empire. ▶

1533 Pizarro conquers Incan Empire.

1607 English found Jamestown.

1500 — 1600

WORLD

1494 Spain and Portugal sign Treaty of Tordesillas.

1547 Ivan the Terrible assumes throne of Russia.

1603 ◀ Tokugawa shoguns rule Japan.

116

TIME LINE DISCUSSION

The time line reflects the competition among Spain, France, and Britain to claim the Americas. Spain was the first to establish permanent settlements, but Britain and France quickly followed.

1. When did Columbus make his first voyage and what other important event happened at about that time? (*1492; Spain and Portugal signed the Treaty of Tordesillas in 1494*)
2. What was the first Spanish conquest in the Americas? (*Cortés conquered the Aztecs in 1521.*)
3. When and where did Britain and France establish their first colonies in the Americas? (*Britain–1607, Jamestown; France–1608, Quebec*) Approximately how long was this after Spain conquered the Aztecs? (*86 years*)
4. About how long after they had established colonies were the British and French engaged in a major war for control of much of eastern North America? (*147 years between Jamestown's founding and the beginning of the French and Indian War*)

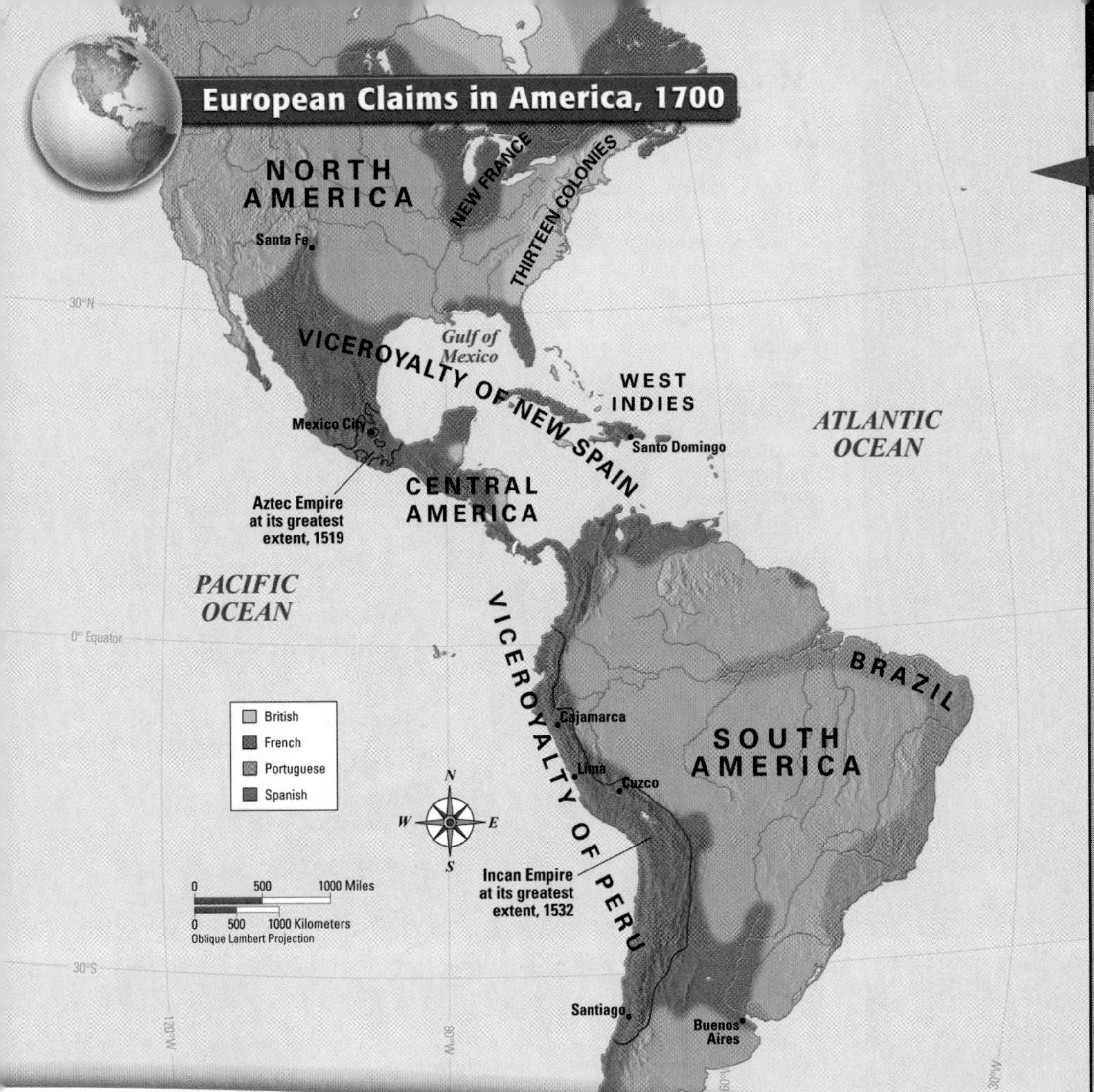

European Claims in America, 1700

NORTH AMERICA
NEW FRANCE
THIRTEEN COLONIES
Santa Fe
30°N
Gulf of Mexico
VICEROYALTY OF NEW SPAIN
WEST INDIES
Mexico City
Santo Domingo
ATLANTIC OCEAN
Aztec Empire at its greatest extent, 1519
CENTRAL AMERICA
PACIFIC OCEAN
0° Equator
VICEROYALTY OF PERU
BRAZIL
Cajamarca
SOUTH AMERICA
Lima
Cuzco
Incan Empire at its greatest extent, 1532
Santiago
Buenos Aires
30°S
120°W
90°W
60°W
30°W

British
French
Portuguese
Spanish

N S E W

0 500 1000 Miles
0 500 1000 Kilometers
Oblique Lambert Projection

1608 Champlain claims Quebec for France. ▶

1649 King Charles I of England is executed.

1700

1754 French and Indian War begins.

1789 ◀ Storming of Bastille ignites French Revolution.

1800

117

History from Visuals

Interpreting the Map

Have students name and identify the two major continents and the two regions labeled on the map. *(North and South America; Central America, the West Indies)* Point out that the Spanish conquered Central America after establishing settlements in the West Indies. Besides the wealth the Spanish found in Central America, what else made this region a highly strategic location for the conquerors? *(Possible Answers: It was close to West Indies' supply routes to Spain; it gave the Spanish a base for striking into North and South America by land or sea; it offered relatively easy access to the Pacific and Atlantic Oceans.)*

Extension Ask students to name the modern countries where the cities shown on the map are located. Students can use the atlas maps of North and South America to check their answers. *(Santa Fe–United States; Mexico City–Mexico; Santo Domingo–Dominican Republic; Cajamarca, Lima, Cuzco–Peru; Santiago–Chile; Buenos Aires–Argentina)*

RECOMMENDED RESOURCES

Books for the Teacher

Dor-Ner, Zvi, and William Scheller. ***Columbus and the Age of Discovery.*** New York: William Morrow, 1991.

Marks, Richard Lee. ***Cortés: The Great Adventurer and the Fate of Aztec Mexico.*** New York: Knopf, 1993.

Walvin, James. ***Making the Black Atlantic: Britain and the African Diaspora.*** London and New York: Cassell Academic, 2000. An excellent summary of Britain's role in the African slave trade.

Books for the Student

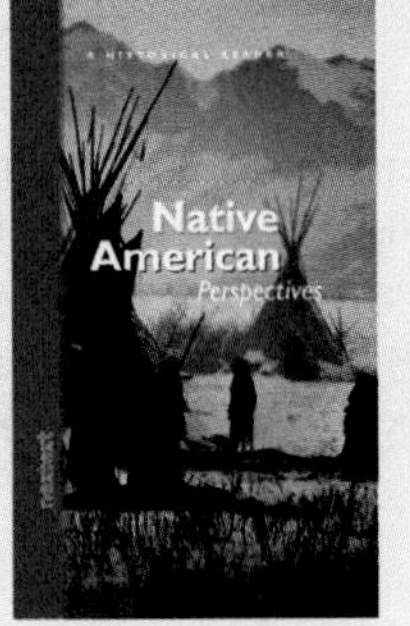

McDougal Littell Nextext. ***Native American Perspectives.*** The Age of Exploration from the Native American viewpoint.

Dodge, Stephen C. ***Christopher Columbus and the First Voyages to the New World.*** Broomall, PA: Chelsea, 1991. A well-researched chronicle of the life and times of Christopher Columbus.

Millar, Heather. ***Spain in the Age of Exploration (Cultures of the Past).*** Tarrytown, NY: Marshall Cavendish, 1999. Written for the young adult, this book covers Spanish culture, literature, theater, and the role of religion in society.

Video

Christopher Columbus: Explorer of the New World. VHS. Library Video Company, 1995. 800-843-3620. Examines why Columbus was nearly forgotten in his own time.

Interact *with* History

Objectives

- Set the stage for the Spanish conquest of the Americas.
- Help students understand some of the reasons for exploration and conquest.
- Help students connect with the people and events they will study in this chapter.

EXAMINING *the* ISSUES

Answers

- Advantages—not picking the losing side; possibly avoiding the conflict. Disadvantages—being considered the enemy by both sides; failing to receive any benefits of victory.
- Students might think about whether they would join a group of people like themselves, or one whose members were different.

Discussion

Ask students to discuss the issue of choosing sides in situations involving conquest. Conquered peoples often do not have much choice in how they respond. Ask students to discuss situations they recall from their study of history.

Interact *with* History

What might you gain or lose by joining the fight?

You are a Native American living in central Mexico in 1520. Suddenly you are faced with a decision that may change your life forever. Invaders, known as the Spanish, are engaged in a fierce battle with the nearby Aztecs, who are cruel and harsh rulers. Like many of your people, you hate the powerful Aztecs and hope for their defeat. The newcomers, however, are equally frightening. They ride on large beasts and fire loud, deadly weapons. You wonder whether you should follow the example of your friends and join the fight, or not fight at all.

▲ This 16th-century painting by an Indian artist depicts a battle on the left between the Aztecs and Spanish. The right side shows the Spanish with their main Indian allies, the Tlaxcalans.

EXAMINING *the* ISSUES

- **What are the advantages and disadvantages of not fighting?**
- **Which might be the lesser of two evils—supporting the Aztecs, whom you know as oppressors, or the fierce invaders, about whom you know almost nothing?**

Discuss these questions with your classmates. In your discussion, examine whether invading armies throughout history have made life better or worse for people in the areas they conquer. As you read about colonization in the Americas, learn the outcome of the battle between the Aztecs and the Spanish.

WHY STUDY THE ATLANTIC WORLD?

- People are still debating the legacy of Columbus's voyages to the Americas (see the Different Perspectives feature on page 126).
- Throughout the Americas, Spanish culture, language, and descendants are legacies of this period.
- English settlers left a legacy of law and government that guides the United States today.
- Today Native American peoples are revitalizing their cultures.
- Enslaved Africans contributed culture and labor to the Americas. Their descendants are a significant part of the population of the Americas today.
- The Columbian Exchange permanently changed diets, economies, and lives in Europe, Asia, Africa, and the Americas (see the Global Impact feature on page 138).

Colored engraving of colonists landing at Jamestown, Virginia

Letter from Christopher Columbus to his son Diego, discussing Amerigo Vespucci

1 Spain Builds an American Empire

MAIN IDEA

EMPIRE BUILDING The voyages of Columbus prompted the Spanish to establish colonies in the Americas.

WHY IT MATTERS NOW

Throughout the Americas, Spanish culture, language, and descendants are the legacy of this period.

TERMS & NAMES

- Christopher Columbus
- colony
- Hernando Cortés
- conquistador
- Francisco Pizarro
- Atahualpa
- mestizo
- *encomienda*

SETTING THE STAGE Competition for wealth in Asia among European nations was fierce. This competition prompted a Genoese sea captain named Christopher Columbus to make a daring voyage from Spain in 1492. Instead of sailing south around Africa and then east, Columbus sailed west across the Atlantic in search of an alternate trade route to Asia and its riches. Columbus never reached Asia. Instead, he stepped onto an island in the Caribbean. That event would bring together the peoples of Europe, Africa, and the Americas.

The Voyages of Columbus

The *Niña, Pinta,* and *Santa María* sailed out of a Spanish port around dawn on August 3, 1492. In a matter of months, Columbus's fleet would reach the shores of what Europeans saw as an astonishing new world.

First Encounters In the early hours of October 12, 1492, the long-awaited cry came. A lookout aboard the *Pinta* caught sight of a shoreline in the distance. *"Tierra! Tierra!"* he shouted. "Land! Land!" By dawn, Columbus and his crew were ashore. Thinking he had successfully reached the East Indies, Columbus called the surprised inhabitants who greeted him, *los indios.* The term translated into "Indian," a word mistakenly applied to all the native peoples of the Americas. In his journal, Columbus recounted his first meeting with the native peoples:

PRIMARY SOURCE

I presented them with some red caps, and strings of glass beads to wear upon the neck, and many other trifles of small value, wherewith they were much delighted, and became wonderfully attached to us. Afterwards they came swimming to the boats where we were, bringing parrots, balls of cotton thread, javelins, and many other things which they exchanged for articles we gave them . . . in fact they accepted anything and gave what they had with the utmost good will.

CHRISTOPHER COLUMBUS, *Journal of Columbus*

Columbus had miscalculated where he was. He had not reached the East Indies. Scholars believe he landed instead on an island in the Bahamas in the Caribbean Sea. The natives there were not Indians, but a group who called themselves the Taino. Nonetheless, Columbus claimed the island for Spain. He named it San Salvador, or "Holy Savior."

CALIFORNIA STANDARDS

10.4.2 Discuss the locations of the colonial rule of such nations as England, France, Germany, Italy, Japan, the Netherlands, Russia, Spain, Portugal, and the United States.

CST 3 Students use a variety of maps and documents to interpret human movement, including major patterns of domestic and international migration, changing environmental preferences and settlement patterns, the frictions that develop between population groups, and the diffusion of ideas, technological innovations, and goods.

REP 3 Students evaluate major debates among historians concerning alternative interpretations of the past, including an analysis of authors' use of evidence and the distinctions between sound generalizations and misleading oversimplifications.

TAKING NOTES

Following Chronological Order Use a diagram to trace the major events in the establishment of Spain's empire in the Americas.

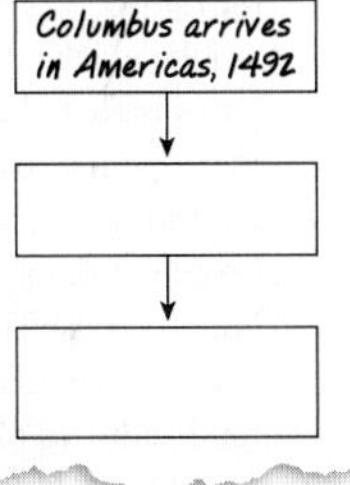

LESSON PLAN

OBJECTIVES

- Describe the voyages of Columbus and his contemporaries.
- Describe the Spanish conquests of the Aztecs and the Inca.
- Identify the effects of Spanish colonization on the Americas.
- Trace the level of resistance to Spanish rule by indigenous people.

1 FOCUS & MOTIVATE

Ask students how they have experienced Spanish influence in the Americas. *(Possible Answers: Mexican food, salsa music, language, architecture)*

2 INSTRUCT

The Voyages of Columbus

10.4.2

Critical Thinking

- What actions showed that Columbus had an interest in empire even on his first voyage? *(He wanted to take possession of every island he passed and claim it for Spain.)*

CALIFORNIA RESOURCES

California Reading Toolkit, p. L19
California Modified Lesson Plans for English Learners, p. 33
California Daily Standards Practice Transparencies, TT11
California Standards Enrichment Workbook, pp. 49–50
California Standards Planner and Lesson Plans, p. L29
California Online Test Practice
California Test Generator CD-ROM
California Easy Planner CD-ROM
California eEdition CD-ROM

SECTION 1 PROGRAM RESOURCES

ALL STUDENTS

In-Depth Resources: Unit 1
- Guided Reading, p. 81
- History Makers: Ferdinand Magellan, p. 96; Hernando Cortés, p. 97

Formal Assessment
- Section Quiz, p. 70

ENGLISH LEARNERS

In-Depth Resources in Spanish
- Guided Reading, p. 37

Reading Study Guide (Spanish), p. 41
Reading Study Guide Audio CD (Spanish)

STRUGGLING READERS

In-Depth Resources: Unit 1
- Guided Reading, p. 81
- Building Vocabulary, p. 85
- Reteaching Activity, p. 99

Reading Study Guide, p. 41
Reading Study Guide Audio CD

GIFTED AND TALENTED STUDENTS

In-Depth Resources: Unit 1
- Primary Sources: from *The Journal of Christopher Columbus,* p. 89; from *The Broken Spears,* p. 91
- Literature: from *The Feathered Serpent,* p. 93

Electronic Library of Primary Sources
- "On the Destruction of the Indies"
- from Letter to King Charles V of Spain

INTEGRATED TECHNOLOGY

eEdition CD-ROM
Voices from the Past Audio CD
Power Presentations CD-ROM
World Art and Cultures Transparencies
- AT43 *Meeting of Cortés and Montezuma*

Patterns of Interaction Video Series
- The Spread of Epidemic Disease

classzone.com

More About . . .

Magellan

Although Balboa was the first European to see the Pacific Ocean, Magellan named it. After sailing through the stormy Atlantic, Magellan rounded the tip of South America and sailed into a quiet sea, which he named Pacific, meaning "peaceful."

In-Depth Resources: Unit 1

- History Makers: Ferdinand Magellan, p. 96

▲ *Portrait of a Man Called Christopher Columbus* (1519) by Sebastiano del Piombo

Columbus, like other explorers, was interested in gold. Finding none on San Salvador, he explored other islands, staking his claim to each one. "It was my wish to bypass no island without taking possession," he wrote.

In early 1493, Columbus returned to Spain. The reports he relayed about his journey delighted the Spanish monarchs. Spain's rulers, who had funded his first voyage, agreed to finance three more trips. Columbus embarked on his second voyage to the Americas in September of 1493. He journeyed no longer as an explorer, but as an empire builder. He commanded a fleet of some 17 ships that carried over 1,000 soldiers, crewmen, and colonists. The Spanish intended to transform the islands of the Caribbean into **colonies**, or lands that are controlled by another nation. Over the next two centuries, other European explorers began sailing across the Atlantic in search of new lands to claim.

Other Explorers Take to the Seas In 1500, the Portuguese explorer Pedro Álvares Cabral reached the shores of modern-day Brazil and claimed the land for his country. A year later, Amerigo Vespucci (vehs•POO•chee), an Italian in the service of Portugal, also traveled along the eastern coast of South America. Upon his return to Europe, he claimed that the land was not part of Asia, but a "new" world. In 1507, a German mapmaker named the new continent "America" in honor of Amerigo Vespucci.

In 1519, Portuguese explorer Ferdinand Magellan led the boldest exploration yet. Several years earlier, Spanish explorer Vasco Núñez de Balboa had marched through modern-day Panama and had become the first European to gaze upon the Pacific Ocean. Soon after, Magellan convinced the king of Spain to fund his voyage into the newly discovered ocean.

With about 250 men and five ships, Magellan sailed around the southern end of South America and into the waters of the Pacific. The fleet sailed for months without seeing land, except for some small islands. Food supplies soon ran out.

After exploring the island of Guam, Magellan and his crew eventually reached the Philippines. Unfortunately, Magellan became involved in a local war there and was killed. His crew, greatly reduced by disease and starvation, continued sailing west toward home. Out of Magellan's original crew, only 18 men and one ship arrived back in Spain in 1522, nearly three years after they had left. They were the first persons to circumnavigate, or sail around, the world. (A)

A. Answer It was the first voyage around the globe.

MAIN IDEA

Making Inferences

(A) What was the significance of Magellan's voyage?

Spanish Conquests in Mexico

In 1519, as Magellan embarked on his historic voyage, a Spaniard named **Hernando Cortés** landed on the shores of Mexico. After colonizing several Caribbean islands, the Spanish had turned their attention to the American mainland. Cortés marched inland, looking to claim new lands for Spain. Cortés and the many other Spanish explorers who followed him were known as **conquistadors** (conquerors). Lured by rumors of vast lands filled with gold and silver, conquistadors carved out colonies in regions that would become Mexico, South America, and the United States. The Spanish were the first European settlers in the Americas. As a result of their colonization, the Spanish greatly enriched their empire and left a mark on the cultures of North and South America that exists today.

Spanish Conquests in Mexico
10.4.2

Critical Thinking

- What fate was shared by the Aztecs and the natives who fought with the Spanish against them? *(Both died from European diseases.)*
- Why might Montezuma have thought Cortés was a god? *(Possible Answers: His white skin made him seem otherworldly. European weapons seemed to work by magic.)*

In-Depth Resources: Unit 1

- Primary Source: from *The Broken Spears,* p. 91
- Literature: from *The Feathered Serpent,* p. 93
- History Makers: Hernando Cortés, p. 97

DIFFERENTIATING INSTRUCTION: GIFTED AND TALENTED STUDENTS

Eyewitness to History

Class Time 45 minutes

Task Researching and reporting the news of a historical event from primary sources

Purpose To deepen understanding of the age of exploration

Instructions Have students read the excerpt from Columbus's journal contained in In-Depth Resources: Unit 1 to get a feel for Columbus's writing. Then have them use the Internet or books to find other primary sources, such as Columbus's letters.

Have students create a short news report on this breaking story. Students may write for any medium they choose—print, radio, or television. Have them think about how to include quotations from their sources and visuals such as illustrations or maps. They could write a straight factual report; an investigative report on some aspect of the story, such as who is profiting from the discovery of gold; or an editorial expressing an opinion about the consequences of this event. Another angle is to write about how news of Columbus's discoveries was spreading across Europe and the impact the story was having. Have students present their reports to the class.

In-Depth Resources: Unit 1

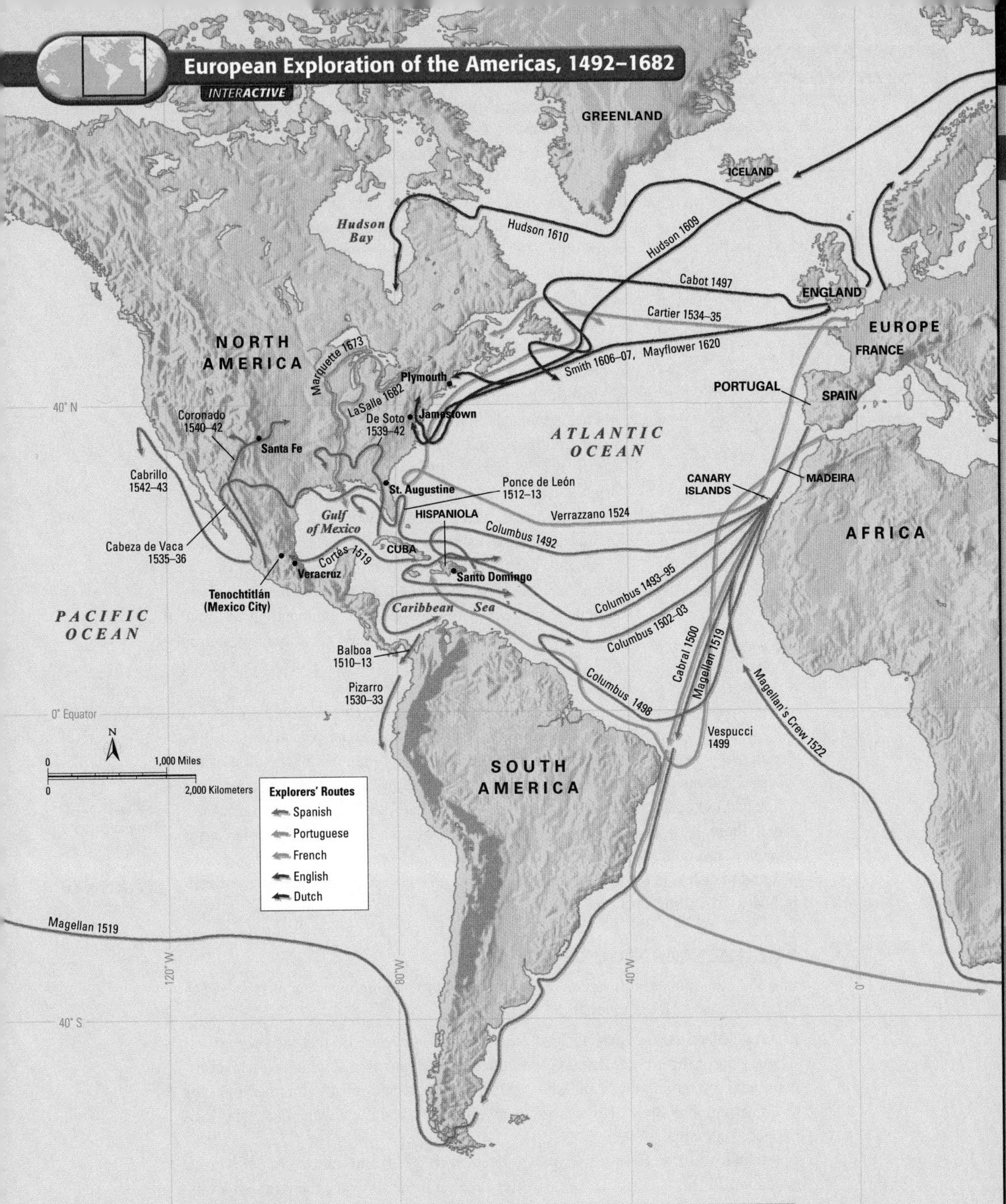

European Exploration of the Americas, 1492–1682

INTERACTIVE

GREENLAND
ICELAND
Hudson Bay
Hudson 1610
Hudson 1609
Cabot 1497
ENGLAND
Cartier 1534–35
EUROPE
FRANCE
NORTH AMERICA
Marquette 1673
Smith 1606–07, Mayflower 1620
Plymouth
PORTUGAL
SPAIN
40° N
Coronado 1540–42
LaSalle 1682
De Soto 1539–42
Jamestown
Santa Fe
ATLANTIC OCEAN
Cabrillo 1542–43
St. Augustine
Ponce de León 1512–13
CANARY ISLANDS
MADEIRA
HISPANIOLA
Verrazzano 1524
Gulf of Mexico
Columbus 1492
AFRICA
Cabeza de Vaca 1535–36
CUBA
Cortés 1519
Veracruz
Santo Domingo
Tenochtitlán (Mexico City)
Columbus 1493–95
PACIFIC OCEAN
Caribbean Sea
Columbus 1502–03
Balboa 1510–13
Cabral 1500
Magellan 1519
Magellan's Crew 1522
Columbus 1498
Pizarro 1530–33
0° Equator
Vespucci 1499
N
0 1,000 Miles
0 2,000 Kilometers
SOUTH AMERICA

Explorers' Routes
- Spanish
- Portuguese
- French
- English
- Dutch

Magellan 1519
120° W
80° W
40° W
0°
40° S

GEOGRAPHY SKILLBUILDER: Interpreting Maps
1. **Movement** *How many different voyages did Columbus make to the Americas?*
2. **Region** *Which general region did the Spanish and Portuguese explore? Where did the English, Dutch, and French explore?*

History from Visuals

Interpreting the Map

Have students trace with a finger the route of one explorer at a time.

Extension Have students speculate on why the English and French explorers stayed so much farther north than the Spanish. *(Possible Answer: The Spanish had already laid claim to parts of South America and the Caribbean.)*

SKILLBUILDER Answers

1. **Movement** four
2. **Region** The Spanish and Portuguese explored South and Central America; the English, Dutch, French, and Spanish explored North America.

INTEGRATED TECHNOLOGY

Interactive An interactive version of this map is available on the eEdition. Students may trace the routes of each explorer separately, see all the voyages for individual countries simultaneously, or see all the voyages together.

COOPERATIVE LEARNING

Displaying Explorers' Sailing Ships

Class Time 30 minutes

Task Researching and creating a classroom display

Purpose To learn what life was like for explorers 500 years ago

Instructions Divide students into groups. Have them use the Internet, encyclopedias, or library resources to find out about the design of ships and conditions on board during the time period shown on the map. Then have them draw pictures or make mockups of the ships. Ask them to think about why there were frequent mutinies on the ships. *(terrible conditions—tight quarters, bad food, lack of fresh water, harsh work, stormy weather—and uncertainty about where they were going)*

Help students design a space in the classroom for the mockups or graphics of these ships as well as the accompanying information. Some students may want to share photos of re-creations of the *Niña* and the *Pinta* on display in Corpus Christi, Texas.

To evaluate this activity, use the Standards for Evaluating a Cooperative Activity chart in the Integrated Assessment book.

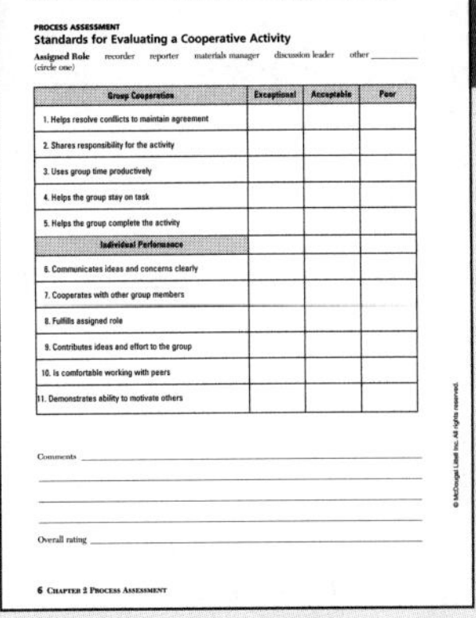
Name ______ Group ______

PROCESS ASSESSMENT
Standards for Evaluating a Cooperative Activity

Assigned Role (circle one) recorder reporter materials manager discussion leader other ______

Group Cooperation	Exceptional	Acceptable	Poor
1. Helps resolve conflicts to maintain agreement			
2. Shares responsibility for the activity			
3. Uses group time productively			
4. Helps the group stay on task			
5. Helps the group complete the activity			
Individual Performance			
6. Communicates ideas and concerns clearly			
7. Cooperates with other group members			
8. Fulfills assigned role			
9. Contributes ideas and effort to the group			
10. Is comfortable working with peers			
11. Demonstrates ability to motivate others			

Comments ______

Overall rating ______

6 CHAPTER 2 PROCESS ASSESSMENT

© McDougal Littell Inc. All rights reserved.

Integrated Assessment

History from Visuals

Interpreting the Graph

Help students read the graph by explaining the horizontal axis, showing periods of time in 20-year increments, and the vertical axis, showing population in millions.

Extension Ask why the rate of population loss might have started out very high and then slowed somewhat over time. *(Possible Answer: death from disease highest at first encounter, declined as natives developed immunity)*

SKILLBUILDER Answers

1. **Drawing Conclusions** 96 percent
2. **Making Inferences** The natives offered little resistance.

More About . . .

Smallpox

The video explains the effect smallpox had in the Americas.

Patterns of Interaction Video Series

- The Spread of Epidemic Disease: Bubonic Plague and Smallpox

Spanish Conquests in Peru

10.4.2

Critical Thinking

- What might the Inca have thought of the Spaniards' character? *(Possible Answers: brutal, untrustworthy)*
- What comparisons and contrasts can you make between the Spanish and the Portuguese? *(Possible Answer: Both established colonies and exploited people to gain wealth—Spanish from gold, Portuguese from sugar.)*

Native Population of Central Mexico, 1500–1620

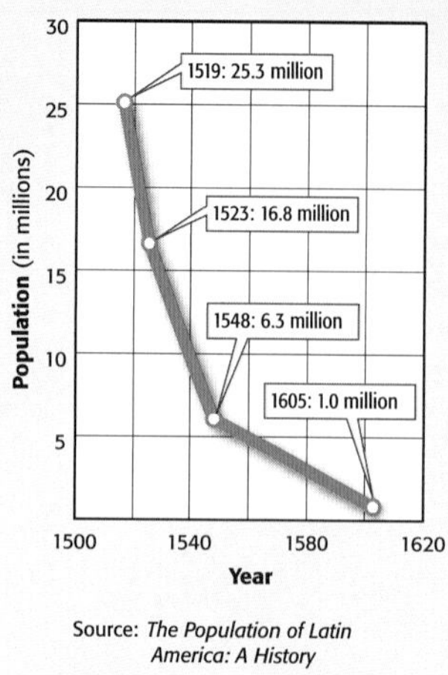

Source: *The Population of Latin America: A History*

SKILLBUILDER: Interpreting Graphs

1. **Drawing Conclusions** *By what percentage did the native population decrease between 1519 and 1605?*
2. **Making Inferences** *How did the sharp decline in the native population, due greatly to disease, affect the Spaniards' attempts to conquer the region?*

Cortés Conquers the Aztecs Soon after landing in Mexico, Cortés learned of the vast and wealthy Aztec Empire in the region's interior. After marching for weeks through difficult mountain passes, Cortés and his force of roughly 600 men finally reached the magnificent Aztec capital of Tenochtitlán (teh•NAWCH•tee•TLAHN). The Aztec emperor, Montezuma II, was convinced at first that Cortés was a god wearing armor. He agreed to give the Spanish explorer a share of the empire's existing gold supply. The conquistador was not satisfied. Cortés admitted that he and his comrades had a "disease of the heart that only gold can cure."

In the late spring of 1520, some of Cortés's men killed many Aztec warriors and chiefs while they were celebrating a religious festival. In June of 1520, the Aztecs rebelled against the Spanish intruders and drove out Cortés's forces.

The Spaniards, however, struck back. Despite being greatly outnumbered, Cortés and his men conquered the Aztecs in 1521. Several factors played a key role in the stunning victory. First, the Spanish had the advantage of superior weaponry. Aztec arrows were no match for the Spaniards' muskets and cannons.

Second, Cortés was able to enlist the help of various native groups. With the aid of a native woman translator named Malinche, Cortés learned that some natives resented the Aztecs. They hated their harsh practices, including human sacrifice. Through Malinche, Cortés convinced these natives to fight on his side.

Finally, and most important, the natives could do little to stop the invisible warrior that marched alongside the Spaniards—disease. Measles, mumps, smallpox, and typhus were just some of the diseases Europeans were to bring with them to the Americas. Native Americans had never been exposed to these diseases. Thus, they had developed no natural immunity to them. As a result, they died by the hundreds of thousands. By the time Cortés launched his counterattack, the Aztec population had been greatly reduced by smallpox and measles. In time, European disease would truly devastate the natives of central Mexico, killing millions of them. **B**

B. Answer superior weaponry, help from other natives, and the spread of European diseases

MAIN IDEA

Summarizing

B What factors enabled the Spanish to defeat the Aztecs?

Spanish Conquests in Peru

In 1532, another conquistador, **Francisco Pizarro**, marched a small force into South America. He conquered the Incan Empire.

Pizarro Subdues the Inca Pizarro and his army of about 200 met the Incan ruler, **Atahualpa** (AH•tuh•WAHL•puh), near the city of Cajamarca. Atahualpa, who commanded a force of about 30,000, brought several thousand mostly unarmed men for the meeting. The Spaniards waited in ambush, crushed the Incan force, and kidnapped Atahualpa.

Atahualpa offered to fill a room once with gold and twice with silver in exchange for his release. However, after receiving the ransom, the Spanish strangled the Incan king. Demoralized by their leader's death, the remaining Incan force retreated from Cajamarca. Pizarro then marched on the Incan capital, Cuzco. He captured it without a struggle in 1533.

DIFFERENTIATING INSTRUCTION: STRUGGLING READERS

Expressing Opinions Visually

Class Time 20 minutes

Task Analyzing a painting and creating an editorial cartoon

Purpose To understand the conquest of the Americas from the Aztec and Incan points of view

Instructions Show students *Meeting of Cortés and Montezuma,* a European painting found in World Art and Cultures Transparencies AT43. Ask them if they think there is any bias in the painting. *(The painter favored the Spanish because he showed the Aztecs as submissive, with Montezuma kneeling in front of Cortés.)* Discuss some of the ways the natives might have seen things differently. *(The Aztec and Incan civilizations were advanced, with great cities and much wealth. They saw their offers of friendship met with betrayal. They saw their people dying.)*

Then ask students to imagine they are Aztec and Incan artists at the time of the conquest of the Americas. Ask students to draw editorial cartoons that depict the explorers and their actions from the point of view of the people already living in the Americas. The cartoons may be funny or angry, as long as each one expresses an opinion. Display the cartoons in the classroom.

World Art and Cultures Transparencies

As Cortés and Pizarro conquered the civilizations of the Americas, fellow conquistadors defeated other native peoples. Spanish explorers also conquered the Maya in Yucatan and Guatemala. By the middle of the 16th century, Spain had created an American empire. It included New Spain (Mexico and parts of Guatemala), as well as other lands in Central and South America and the Caribbean.

Spain's Pattern of Conquest In building their new American empire, the Spaniards drew from techniques used during the *reconquista* of Spain. When conquering the Muslims, the Spanish lived among them and imposed their Spanish culture upon them. The Spanish settlers to the Americas, known as *peninsulares,* were mostly men. As a result, relationships between Spanish settlers and native women were common. These relationships created a large **mestizo**—or mixed Spanish and Native American—population.

Although the Spanish conquerors lived among the native people, they also oppressed them. In their effort to exploit the land for its precious resources, the Spanish forced Native Americans to work within a system known as ***encomienda***. Under this system, natives farmed, ranched, or mined for Spanish landlords. These landlords had received the rights to the natives' labor from Spanish authorities. The holders of *encomiendas* promised the Spanish rulers that they would act fairly and respect the workers. However, many abused the natives and worked many laborers to death, especially inside dangerous mines.

The Portuguese in Brazil One area of South America that remained outside of Spanish control was Brazil. In 1500, Cabral claimed the land for Portugal. During the 1530s, colonists began settling Brazil's coastal region. Finding little gold or silver, the settlers began growing sugar. Clearing out huge swaths of forest land, the Portuguese built giant sugar plantations. The demand for sugar in Europe was great, and the colony soon enriched Portugal. In time, the colonists pushed farther west into Brazil. They settled even more land for the production of sugar.

History Makers

Francisco Pizarro
1475?–1541

Pizarro was the son of an infantry captain and a young peasant woman. His parents never married. Raised by his mother's poor family, he never learned to read. Ambitious, brave, and ruthless, he determined to make his fortune as an explorer and conqueror.

Embarked on a voyage of conquest down the west coast of South America, Pizarro was ordered by the governor of Panama to abandon the expedition to prevent the loss of lives. Pizarro took his sword and drew a line in the dust, inviting those of his followers who desired wealth and fame to cross the line and follow him. Thus began the conquest of Peru.

Pizarro founded the city of Lima, Peru's capital, in 1535. He became governor of Peru and encouraged settlers from Spain.

Atahualpa
1502?–1533

Atahualpa was the last ruler of the Incan empire in Peru. After Atahualpa was captured and held for ransom by the Spanish, the Incan people throughout the empire brought gold and silver that the Spanish then had melted down into bullion and ingots. They accumulated 24 tons of gold and silver, the richest ransom in history.

The Spanish executed Atahualpa despite the ransom paid by his people. As he was about to be burned at the stake, the Spanish offered him a more merciful death by strangulation if he agreed to convert to Christianity, which he did. Thus died the last emperor of the Inca.

INTEGRATED TECHNOLOGY

INTERNET ACTIVITY Create a poster about the ransom paid by the Incan people to rescue Atahualpa. Go to **classzone.com** for your research.

More About . . .

The *Reconquista*

Literally meaning "reconquest," the *reconquista* began in the eighth century shortly after the Muslims conquered most of the Iberian Peninsula. The movement peaked in the 11th to 13th centuries. The last state to fall was Granada, defeated under Ferdinand and Isabella in 1492.

Tip for Gifted and Talented Students

Peninsulares were Spanish colonists born in Spain, so called because they came from the Iberian Peninsula. In the colonies they occupied the highest rank on the social scale and discriminated against those of Spanish descent born in the Americas.

History Makers

Pizarro and Atahualpa

What character qualities did Pizarro exhibit in his treatment of Atahualpa? *(ambition and ruthlessness)* Atahualpa also had these characteristics. He had shared the throne with his half-brother until Atahualpa went to war against him and had him murdered shortly before Pizarro came to Peru.

INTEGRATED TECHNOLOGY

Rubric Posters should

- describe the size and contents of the ransom.
- reflect the results of research.

DIFFERENTIATING INSTRUCTION: ENGLISH LEARNERS

Understanding English Words That Have Spanish Origins

Class Time 30 minutes

Task Tracing the origins of certain English words

Purpose To discover the etymology of English words that come from Spanish

Instructions Use the Spanish words on this page as a springboard to consider the many English words that come from Spanish. Beginning with the words *mestizo* and *encomienda,* students can use a Spanish-English dictionary to find the meaning of each and then write each on a word chart like the one shown to the right. Then suggest that they consider words that are identified with the American Southwest—*corral, mesa, lariat, mustang, canyon, arroyo, machete, tortilla, patio, fiesta, stampede, burro, adobe, padre, plaza,* and others. Have them look up each word in a dictionary to see if the original Spanish word is the same as or different from the form used today and what the word originally meant. Have them also enter this information on the chart. Ask students to identify the kinds of words that came into English from Spanish.

English Word/Definition	Spanish Word	Meaning
Mustang: half-wild horse	mestengo	untamed

More About . . .

Coronado

Coronado came to New Spain in 1535. He was lured to explore the north in 1540 by reports of the fabled wealth of the Seven Golden Cities of Cibola. Instead, he found the Zuni Pueblo. One of the members of Coronado's expedition was the first European to see the Grand Canyon in Arizona.

Spain's Influence Expands
10.4.2

Critical Thinking

- How were conquistadors and Spanish missionaries similar? *(Both wanted to convert native peoples to Christianity.)*
- In what way was Coronado's journey pivotal in Spain's settlement of the southwestern United States? *(His failure to find gold caused the Spanish to assign more priests than soldiers there.)*

More About . . .

Spanish Missions

Most of the Spanish missions were located in the area between Texas and California. The priests tried to persuade local Indians from miles around to move to these agricultural settlements and adopt Spanish ways, including Christianity. As was true elsewhere, most natives died from European diseases. The more well-known and successful California missions were established in the 18th century. Several became the basis for later cities, including Los Angeles.

This U.S. postage stamp was issued in 1940 to celebrate the 400th anniversary of the Coronado expedition. ▶

Spain's Influence Expands

Spain's American colonies helped make it the richest, most powerful nation in the world during much of the 16th century. Ships filled with treasures from the Americas continually sailed into Spanish harbors. This newfound wealth helped usher in a golden age of art and culture in Spain. (See Chapter 5.)

Throughout the 16th century, Spain also increased its military might. To protect its treasure-filled ships, Spain built a powerful navy. The Spanish also strengthened their other military forces, creating a skillful and determined army. For a century and a half, Spain's army seldom lost a battle. Meanwhile, Spain enlarged its American empire by settling in parts of what is now the United States.

Conquistadors Push North Dreams of new conquests prompted Spain to back a series of expeditions into the southwestern United States. The Spanish actually had settled in parts of the United States before they even dreamed of building an empire on the American mainland. In 1513, Spanish explorer Juan Ponce de León landed on the coast of modern-day Florida and claimed it for Spain.

By 1540, after building an empire that stretched from Mexico to Peru, the Spanish once again looked to the land that is now the United States. In 1540–1541, Francisco Vásquez de Coronado led an expedition throughout much of present-day Arizona, New Mexico, Texas, Oklahoma, and Kansas. He was searching for another wealthy empire to conquer. Coronado found little gold amidst the dry deserts of the Southwest. As a result, the Spanish monarchy assigned mostly priests to explore and colonize the future United States.

Catholic priests had accompanied conquistadors from the very beginning of American colonization. The conquistadors had come in search of wealth. The priests who accompanied them had come in search of converts. In the winter of 1609–1610, Pedro de Peralta, governor of Spain's northern holdings, called New Mexico, led settlers to a tributary on the upper Rio Grande. They built a capital called Santa Fe, or "Holy Faith." In the next two decades, a string of Christian missions arose among the Pueblo, the native inhabitants of the region. Scattered missions, forts, and small ranches dotted the lands of New Mexico. These became the headquarters for advancing the Catholic religion. C

C. Possible Answer New Mexico offered little in the way of wealth, so the Spanish were more concerned there with spreading the Catholic religion.

MAIN IDEA

Contrasting

C How did Spain's colony in New Mexico differ from its colonies in New Spain?

CONNECTIONS TO SCIENCE

Gold Deposits and Plate Tectonics

Class Time 40 minutes

Task Conducting research and drawing a map

Purpose To learn more about geology and its relation to the 16th-century search for gold in North America

Instructions Explain to students that if Coronado and his men had had a modern understanding of plate tectonics, they might have found gold in the United States. Geologists have learned that many gold deposits are at the present or former boundaries of the earth's slowly moving plates. The reason for this is not fully known. But a look at a gold distribution map shows that major sources of gold lie along the Sierra Nevada in the western United States and along the Sierra Madre and Andes ranges in Mexico and South America, just where the Aztecs and Inca lived.

Have students work in pairs to research the geology of the Sierra Nevada. Ask them to locate gold mines in this region. *(It was the center of the 19th-century gold rush.)* Then have them research the route of Coronado's expedition. Have them use the physical map of North America in the Geography Skills and Outline Maps book to compare Coronado's route and the location of gold.

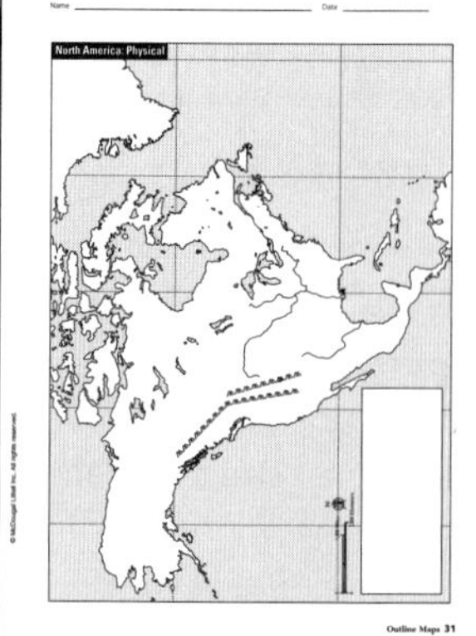

Geography Skills and Outline Maps

Opposition to Spanish Rule

Spanish priests worked to spread Christianity in the Americas. They also pushed for better treatment of Native Americans. Priests spoke out against the cruel treatment of natives. In particular, they criticized the harsh pattern of labor that emerged under the *encomienda* system. "There is nothing more detestable or more cruel," Dominican monk Bartolomé de Las Casas wrote, "than the tyranny which the Spaniards use toward the Indians for the getting of pearl [riches]."

African Slavery and Native Resistance The Spanish government abolished the *encomienda* system in 1542. To meet the colonies' need for labor, Las Casas suggested Africans. "The labor of one . . . [African] . . . [is] more valuable than that of four Indians," he said. The priest later changed his view and denounced African slavery. However, others promoted it.

Opposition to the Spanish method of colonization came not only from Spanish priests, but also from the natives themselves. Resistance to Spain's attempt at domination began shortly after the Spanish arrived in the Caribbean. In November of 1493, Columbus encountered resistance in his attempt to conquer the present-day island of St. Croix. Before finally surrendering, the inhabitants defended themselves by firing poison arrows.

As late as the end of the 17th century, natives in New Mexico fought Spanish rule. Although they were not risking their lives in silver mines, the natives still felt the weight of Spanish force. In converting the natives, Spanish priests and soldiers burned their sacred objects and prohibited native rituals. The Spanish also forced natives to work for them and sometimes abused them physically.

In 1680, Popé, a Pueblo ruler, led a well-organized rebellion against the Spanish. The rebellion involved more than 8,000 warriors from villages all over New Mexico. The native fighters drove the Spanish back into New Spain. For the next 12 years, until the Spanish regained control of the area, the southwest region of the future United States once again belonged to its original inhabitants. D

By this time, however, the rulers of Spain had far greater concerns. The other nations of Europe had begun to establish their own colonies in the Americas.

D. Possible Answer Spanish attempts to destroy their culture and repressive measures, including beatings

MAIN IDEA

Analyzing Causes

D Why did the natives of New Mexico revolt against Spanish settlers?

SECTION 1 ASSESSMENT

TERMS & NAMES 1. For each term or name, write a sentence explaining its significance.

• Christopher Columbus • colony • Hernando Cortés • conquistador • Francisco Pizarro • Atahualpa • mestizo • *encomienda*

USING YOUR NOTES

2. Which event do you think had the greatest impact? (10.4.2)

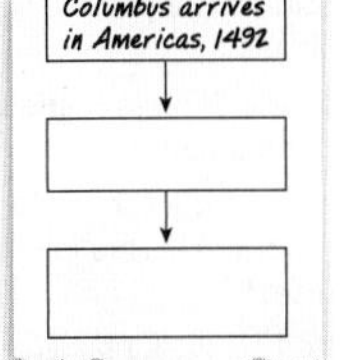

MAIN IDEAS

3. What process did Columbus and his followers begin? (10.4.2)
4. Why were most of the Spanish explorers drawn to the Americas? (10.4.2)
5. Which country was the richest and most powerful in the 16th century, and why? (10.4.2)

CRITICAL THINKING & WRITING

6. **ANALYZING PRIMARY SOURCES** Reread the primary source on page 119. How might Columbus's view of the Taino have led the Spanish to think they could take advantage of and impose their will on the natives? (10.4.2)
7. **COMPARING** What might have been some similarities in character between Cortés and Pizarro? (10.4.2)
8. **CLARIFYING** Through what modern-day states did Coronado lead his expedition? (10.4.2)
9. **WRITING ACTIVITY** EMPIRE BUILDING Write a **dialogue** in which a Native American and a conquistador debate the merits of Spain's colonization of the Americas. (Writing 2.1.c)

CONNECT TO TODAY MAKING A DATABASE

Use library resources to compile a **database** of places and geographical features in the Americas named after Columbus. Display your list in the classroom. (Writing 2.6.a)

Opposition to Spanish Rule
10.4.2

Critical Thinking

- How did the end of the *encomienda* system lead to the use of enslaved Africans? *(Indians could not be forced to work, so the Spaniards imported Africans.)*
- Why was the Pueblo victory over the Spaniards in 1680 significant? *(showed that Spain was not invincible and that even after 70 years the Spanish had not subdued the natives)*

More About . . .

Pueblo Resistance

The Pueblo Indians sought to wipe out all traces of Spanish religion and culture. Popé had his followers burn Christian images, churches, rosaries, and crosses. He did not allow the teaching of the Spanish language, and he destroyed Spanish agriculture.

3 ASSESS

SECTION 1 ASSESSMENT

Have students work in pairs, asking each other the questions.

Formal Assessment

- Section Quiz, p. 70

4 RETEACH

Review the main ideas of the section using the Reteaching Activity.

In-Depth Resources: Unit 1

- Reteaching Activity, p. 99

ANSWERS

1. Christopher Columbus, p. 119 • colony, p. 120 • Hernando Cortés, p. 120 • conquistador, p. 120 • Francisco Pizarro, p. 122 • Atahualpa, p. 122 • mestizo, p. 123 • *encomienda*, p. 123

2. **Sample Answer:** Most important—Columbus's arrival. Other events—Cortés defeats the Aztecs; Pizarro conquers the Inca; conquistadors colonize the southwest United States.
3. bringing together the peoples of Europe, Africa, and the Americas
4. lured by gold, silver, and land
5. Spain, because of its colonies and the wealth they provided
6. **Possible Answer:** the Taino's generosity and peacefulness perhaps seen as gullibility and docility
7. ambitious, adventurous, ruthless
8. Arizona, New Mexico, Texas, Oklahoma, Kansas
9. **Rubric** Dialogues should
   - present both points of view.
   - use specific examples.
   - be clear and concise.

CONNECT TO TODAY

Rubric Databases should

- list a variety of locations.
- include such places as Colombia; Columbus, Ohio; the Columbia River; and the District of Columbia.

See Skillbuilder Handbook page R33 for help creating a database.

Different Perspectives

OBJECTIVE

- Explore the legacy of Columbus's voyages from different points of view.

INSTRUCT

Encourage students to look at the sources to understand their points of view. Notice how the creators of each piece reflect their own cultures. Ask students to summarize each of the written sources in their own words. *(Possible Answers: Morison believes Columbus is a hero. De las Casas strongly criticizes his fellow Spaniards' massacre of Native Americans. Harjo finds it hard to celebrate Columbus Day because of the suffering Native Americans have endured.)*

Electronic Library of Primary Sources
- "On the Destruction of the Indies"

INTEGRATED TECHNOLOGY

Interactive This feature is available in an expanded interactive format on the eEdition. The primary source image is enlarged, and hyperlinks provide more information.

Inclusion Tip

Students who have difficulty reading may benefit from the dramatic reading of the de las Casas excerpt, available on the eEdition.

INTERACTIVE

The Legacy of Columbus

In the years and centuries since Christopher Columbus's historic journeys, people still debate the legacy of his voyages. Some argue they were the heroic first steps in the creation of great and democratic societies. Others claim they were the beginnings of an era of widespread cruelty, bloodshed, and epidemic disease.

CALIFORNIA STANDARDS

10.4.2 Discuss the locations of the colonial rule of such nations as England, France, Germany, Italy, Japan, the Netherlands, Russia, Spain, Portugal, and the United States.

REP 3 Students evaluate major debates among historians concerning alternative interpretations of the past, including an analysis of authors' use of evidence and the distinctions between sound generalizations and misleading oversimplifications.

A SECONDARY SOURCE

Samuel Eliot Morison

Morison, a strong supporter of Columbus, laments that the sea captain died without realizing the true greatness of his deeds.

One only wishes that the Admiral might have been afforded the sense of fulfillment that would have come from foreseeing all that flowed from his discoveries; that would have turned all the sorrows of his last years to joy. The whole history of the Americas stems from the Four Voyages of Columbus; and as the Greek city-states looked back to the deathless gods as their founders, so today a score of independent nations and dominions unite in homage to Christopher, the stout-hearted son of Genoa, who carried Christian civilization across the Ocean Sea.

B PRIMARY SOURCE

Bartolomé de Las Casas

Las Casas was an early Spanish missionary who watched fellow Spaniards unleash attack dogs on Native Americans.

Their other frightening weapon after the horses: twenty hunting greyhounds. They were unleashed and fell on the Indians at the cry of *Tómalo!* ["Get them!"]. Within an hour they had preyed on one hundred of them. As the Indians were used to going completely naked, it is easy to imagine what the fierce greyhounds did, urged to bite naked bodies and skin much more delicate than that of the wild boars they were used to. . . . This tactic, begun here and invented by the devil, spread throughout these Indies and will end when there is no more land nor people to subjugate and destroy in this part of the world.

C SECONDARY SOURCE

Suzan Shown Harjo

Harjo, a Native American, disputes the benefits that resulted from Columbus's voyages and the European colonization of the Americas that followed.

Columbus Day, never on Native America's list of favorite holidays, became somewhat tolerable as its significance diminished to little more than a good shopping day. But this next long year [1992] of Columbus hoopla will be tough to take amid the spending sprees and horn blowing to tout a five-century feeding frenzy that has left Native people and this red quarter of Mother Earth in a state of emergency. For Native people, this half millennium of land grabs and one-cent treaty sales has been no bargain.

D PRIMARY SOURCE

Anonymous

Contemporary with the Spanish conquest of the Americas, this illustration depicts a medicine man tending to an Aztec suffering from smallpox, which killed millions of Native Americans.

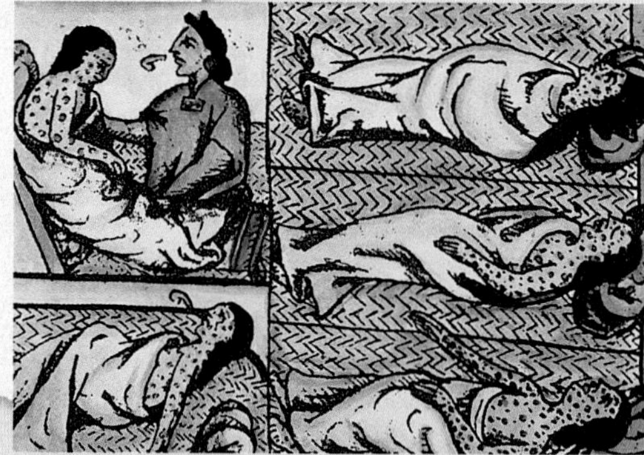

Document-Based QUESTIONS

1. Based on Source A, was the legacy of Columbus a positive or negative thing?
2. In what ways do Sources B and C agree about Columbus?
3. Which aspect of the legacy of Columbus does the illustration in Source D show?
4. If you had to construct a balance sheet on Columbus, would you come up with a positive or negative balance? On a poster board, make up a list of positive and negative elements, and display your chart in the classroom.

DOCUMENT-BASED QUESTIONS: ANSWERS

1. According to Samuel Eliot Morison, the legacy of Columbus was unreservedly positive.
2. Both of these sources see the legacy of Columbus as disastrous for Native Americans.
3. The illustration shows the effect of smallpox—a disease brought by Europeans to the Americas—upon Native Americans.
4. **Rubric** Lists should
   - include positive elements such as new ideas, new food sources, new livestock, and contact with the wider world.
   - include negative elements such as loss of population, loss of land, and loss of many aspects of culture.
   - be based on factual information.
   - show understanding of both sides of the issue.

Colored engraving of colonists landing at Jamestown, Virginia

Letter from Christopher Columbus to his son Diego, discussing Amerigo Vespucci

2

European Nations Settle North America

MAIN IDEA

EMPIRE BUILDING Several European nations fought for control of North America, and England emerged victorious.

WHY IT MATTERS NOW

The English settlers in North America left a legacy of law and government that guides the United States today.

TERMS & NAMES

- New France
- Jamestown
- Pilgrims
- Puritans
- New Netherland
- French and Indian War
- Metacom

SETTING THE STAGE Spain's successful colonization efforts in the Americas did not go unnoticed. Other European nations, such as England, France, and the Netherlands, soon became interested in obtaining their own valuable colonies. The Treaty of Tordesillas, signed in 1494, had divided the newly discovered lands between Spain and Portugal. However, other European countries ignored the treaty. They set out to build their own empires in the Americas. This resulted in a struggle for North America.

CALIFORNIA STANDARDS

10.1.2 Trace the development of the Western political ideas of the rule of law and illegitimacy of tyranny, using selections from Plato's *Republic* and Aristotle's *Politics*.

CST 3 Students use a variety of maps and documents to interpret human movement, including major patterns of domestic and international migration, changing environmental preferences and settlement patterns, the frictions that develop between population groups, and the diffusion of ideas, technological innovations, and goods.

REP 4 Students construct and test hypotheses; collect, evaluate, and employ information from multiple primary and secondary sources; and apply it in oral and written presentations.

HI 1 Students show the connections, causal and otherwise, between particular historical events and larger social, economic, and political trends and developments.

Competing Claims in North America

Magellan's voyage showed that ships could reach Asia by way of the Pacific Ocean. Spain claimed the route around the southern tip of South America. Other European countries hoped to find an easier and more direct route to the Pacific. If it existed, a northwest trade route through North America to Asia would become highly profitable. Not finding the route, the French, English, and Dutch instead established colonies in North America.

Explorers Establish New France The early French explorers sailed west with dreams of reaching the East Indies. One explorer was Giovanni da Verrazzano (VEHR•uh•ZAHN•noh), an Italian in the service of France. In 1524, he sailed to North America in search of a sea route to the Pacific. While he did not find the route, Verrazzano did discover what is today New York harbor. Ten years later, the Frenchman Jacques Cartier (kahr•TYAY) reached a gulf off the eastern coast of Canada that led to a broad river. Cartier named it the St. Lawrence. He followed it inward until he reached a large island dominated by a mountain. He named the island Mont Real (Mount Royal), which later became known as Montreal. In 1608, another French explorer, Samuel de Champlain, sailed up the St. Lawrence with about 32 colonists. They founded Quebec, which became the base of France's colonial empire in North America, known as **New France**.

Then the French penetrated the North American continent. In 1673, French Jesuit priest Jacques Marquette and trader Louis Joliet explored the Great Lakes and the upper Mississippi River. Nearly 10 years later, Sieur de La Salle explored the lower Mississippi. He claimed the entire river valley for France. He named it Louisiana in honor of the French king, Louis XIV. By the early 1700s, New France covered much of what is now the midwestern United States and eastern Canada.

TAKING NOTES

Clarifying Use a chart to record information about early settlements.

Name of Settlement	General Location
New France	
New Netherland	
Massachusetts Bay	

LESSON PLAN

OBJECTIVES

- Summarize competing claims in North America.
- Identify English colonial activities in North America.
- Describe the Native American response to land claims made by Europeans.

1 FOCUS & MOTIVATE

Ask students to list some of the ways they know that the English once controlled much of North America. *(Possible Answers: English language, place names, system of law and government)*

2 INSTRUCT

Competing Claims in North America

10.1.2

Critical Thinking

- How would you compare and contrast New France and New Spain? *(both found wealth, converted natives—New Spain: south, gold, cities; New France: north, furs, scattered)*

CALIFORNIA RESOURCES

California Reading Toolkit, p. L20
California Modified Lesson Plans for English Learners, p. 35
California Daily Standards Practice Transparencies, TT12
California Standards Enrichment Workbook, pp. 19–20
California Standards Planner and Lesson Plans, p. L31
California Online Test Practice
California Test Generator CD-ROM
California Easy Planner CD-ROM
California eEdition CD-ROM

SECTION 2 PROGRAM RESOURCES

ALL STUDENTS

In-Depth Resources: Unit 1
- Guided Reading, p. 82
- Skillbuilder Practice: Comparing and Contrasting, p. 86

Formal Assessment
- Section Quiz, p. 71

ENGLISH LEARNERS

In-Depth Resources in Spanish
- Guided Reading, p. 38
- Skillbuilder Practice: Comparing and Contrasting, p. 41

Reading Study Guide (Spanish), p. 43
Reading Study Guide Audio CD (Spanish)

STRUGGLING READERS

In-Depth Resources: Unit 1
- Guided Reading, p. 82
- Building Vocabulary, p. 85
- Skillbuilder Practice: Comparing and Contrasting, p. 86
- Reteaching Activity, p. 100

Reading Study Guide, p. 43
Reading Study Guide Audio CD

GIFTED AND TALENTED STUDENTS

Electronic Library of Primary Sources
- "The French Lose Quebec"

INTEGRATED TECHNOLOGY

eEdition CD-ROM
Power Presentations CD-ROM
Electronic Library of Primary Sources
- "The French Lose Quebec"

classzone.com

A Trading Empire France's North American empire was immense. But it was sparsely populated. By 1760, the European population of New France had grown to only about 65,000. A large number of French colonists had no desire to build towns or raise families. These settlers included Catholic priests who sought to convert Native Americans. They also included young, single men engaged in what had become New France's main economic activity, the fur trade. Unlike the English, the French were less interested in occupying territories than they were in making money off the land. (A)

MAIN IDEA
Summarizing
(A) Why were France's North American holdings so sparsely populated?

A. Answer because most of the settlers were priests or fur trappers who had no desire to build towns or start families

The English Arrive in North America

The explorations of the Spanish and French inspired the English. In 1606, a company of London investors received from King James a charter to found a colony in North America. In late 1606, the company's three ships, and more than 100 settlers, pushed out of an English harbor. About four months later, in 1607, they reached the coast of Virginia. The colonists claimed the land as theirs. They named the settlement **Jamestown** in honor of their king.

The Settlement at Jamestown The colony's start was disastrous. The settlers were more interested in finding gold than in planting crops. During the first few years, seven out of every ten people died of hunger, disease, or battles with the Native Americans.

Despite their nightmarish start, the colonists eventually gained a foothold in their new land. Jamestown became England's first permanent settlement in North America. The colony's outlook improved greatly after farmers there discovered tobacco. High demand in England for tobacco turned it into a profitable cash crop.

Puritans Create a "New England" In 1620, a group known as **Pilgrims** founded a second English colony, Plymouth, in Massachusetts. Persecuted for their religious beliefs in England, these colonists sought religious freedom. Ten years later, a group known as **Puritans** also sought religious freedom from England's Anglican Church. They established a larger colony at nearby Massachusetts Bay.

▼ Henry Hudson's ship arrives in the bay of New York on September 12, 1609.

More About . . .

The Fur Trade

From the 1600s to the 1800s, the beaver was hunted until the species was almost extinct. In the late 1600s, one beaver pelt could buy a cooking kettle or a pound of tobacco, and 12 pelts could buy a rifle. Both Canada and the United States have passed laws regulating the hunting season for beavers.

The English Arrive in North America

Critical Thinking

- Why was the presence of families such a crucial factor in the success of a settlement? *(larger population, more stable lifestyle)*
- How would you compare and contrast French and Dutch colonies? *(Both—settled along waterways, fur trade; vast French territory, smaller Dutch area)*

More About . . .

Jamestown

Captain John Smith, one of the original Jamestown colonists, wrote about the lust for gold among the settlers: "No talke, no hope, no worke, but dig gold, wash gold, refine gold, load gold." This was unfortunate, for the colonists found no gold in Virginia.

Tip for Struggling Readers

Explain that the Puritans took their name from their desire to "purify" the English church.

SKILLBUILDER PRACTICE: COMPARING AND CONTRASTING

Comparing and Contrasting English Colonies

Class Time 35 minutes

Task Reading to discover similarities and differences

Purpose To understand historical readings using the skills of comparing and contrasting

Instructions Explain that finding the differences among ideas, institutions, behaviors, and events helps us understand historical events more clearly. Often one concept is easier to grasp if its features can be contrasted with similar features of something else. Have students review the text and answer this question: How did the colonies at Jamestown and Massachusetts Bay differ?

Then ask the following questions:

1. Who settled Jamestown, why did they come, and what was their experience? *(mostly single males; to make money; hard times)*
2. Who founded New England, why did they settle there, and what kind of community did they seek? *(Puritans, many families; religious freedom; to build a model community)*

Then have students answer the Main Idea question on page 129. For more comparing and contrasting, use the Skillbuilder Practice activity in In-Depth Resources: Unit 1 (also available in Spanish).

In-Depth Resources: Unit 1

The Puritans wanted to build a model community that would set an example for other Christians to follow. Although the colony experienced early difficulties, it gradually took hold. This was due in large part to the numerous families in the colony, unlike the mostly single, male population in Jamestown.

The Dutch Found New Netherland Following the English and French into North America were the Dutch. In 1609, Henry Hudson, an Englishman in the service of the Netherlands, sailed west. He was searching for a northwest sea route to Asia. Hudson did not find a route. He did, however, explore three waterways that were later named for him—the Hudson River, Hudson Bay, and Hudson Strait.

B. Answer The English colonies were more populated and begun for religious reasons. Dutch and French Colonies were begun mainly for commerce.

The Dutch claimed the region along these waterways. They established a fur trade with the Iroquois Indians. They built trading posts along the Hudson River at Fort Orange (now Albany) and on Manhattan Island. Dutch merchants formed the Dutch West India Company. In 1621, the Dutch government granted the company permission to colonize the region and expand the fur trade. The Dutch holdings in North America became known as **New Netherland**.

Although the Dutch company profited from its fur trade, it was slow to attract Dutch colonists. To encourage settlers, the colony opened its doors to a variety of peoples. Gradually more Dutch, as well as Germans, French, Scandinavians, and other Europeans, settled the area. (B)

MAIN IDEA

Contrasting

(B) How were the Dutch and French colonies different from the English colonies in North America?

Colonizing the Caribbean During the 1600s, the nations of Europe also colonized the Caribbean. The French seized control of present-day Haiti, Guadeloupe, and Martinique. The English settled Barbados and Jamaica. In 1634, the Dutch captured what are now the Netherlands Antilles and Aruba from Spain.

On these islands, the Europeans built huge cotton and sugar plantations. These products, although profitable, demanded a large and steady supply of labor. Enslaved Africans eventually would supply this labor.

The Struggle for North America

As they expanded their settlements in North America, the nations of France, England, and the Netherlands battled each other for colonial supremacy.

The English Oust the Dutch To the English, New Netherland separated their northern and southern colonies. In 1664, the English king, Charles II, granted his brother, the Duke of York, permission to drive out the Dutch. When the duke's fleet arrived at New Netherland, the Dutch surrendered without firing a shot. The Duke of York claimed the colony for England and renamed it New York.

With the Dutch gone, the English colonized the Atlantic coast of North America. By 1750, about 1.2 million English settlers lived in 13 colonies from Maine to Georgia.

England Battles France The English soon became hungry for more land for their colonial population. So they pushed farther west into the continent. By doing so, they collided with France's North American holdings. As their colonies expanded, France and England began to interfere with each other. It seemed that a major conflict was on the horizon.

In 1754 a dispute over land claims in the Ohio Valley led to a war between the British and French on the North

History *in* Depth

Pirates

The battle for colonial supremacy occurred not only on land, but also on the sea. Acting on behalf of their government, privately owned armed ships, known as privateers, attacked merchant ships of enemy nations and sank or robbed them.

Also patrolling the high seas were pirates. They attacked ships for their valuables and did not care what nation the vessels represented. One of the best-known pirates was Edward B. Teach, whose prominent beard earned him the nickname Blackbeard. According to one account, Blackbeard attempted to frighten his victims by sticking "lighted matches under his hat, which appeared on both sides of his face and eyes, naturally fierce and wild."

More About . . .

The Dutch

When the English took over New Netherland, the English language quickly outpaced the Dutch. However, many familiar English words are borrowed from Dutch, including *cookie, boss,* and *crib.*

The Struggle for North America

10.1.2

Critical Thinking

- How did the Netherlands and France react differently to English expansion? *(Dutch colony was smaller, caught between English colonies and chose to surrender; France fought Britain fiercely, realizing that its vast American empire was at stake.)*

History *in* Depth

Pirates

A British navy crew finally trapped Blackbeard in 1718 in an inlet of Okracoke Island, off North Carolina. It is said of Blackbeard's last battle that he fought with a pistol in one hand and a sword in the other, before dying with more than 25 wounds. Ask students to find more information about Blackbeard's last battle and to bring copies of the accounts they find to class.

DIFFERENTIATING INSTRUCTION: STRUGGLING READERS

European Colonies in the 17th Century

Class Time 20 minutes

Task Locating information on a map

Purpose To strengthen understanding of colonization patterns

Instructions Pair a struggling reader with a more proficient reader. Have them read this page together, listing all the place names that are mentioned. Then have them use the maps on page 130 and in the textbook atlas to find where they are located.

Then ask the following questions:

1. How were the Dutch situated relative to the English colonies? *(between Virginia and New England)*
2. In what modern country is Hudson Bay located? *(Canada)*
3. What country controlled Jamaica in the 17th century? *(Britain)*
4. The Ohio Valley was located along the Ohio River. What French-controlled river did the Ohio flow into? *(Mississippi)*

Ask students to share what they learned from this exercise. Encourage them to consult an atlas when reading information that has geographical references.

History from Visuals

Interpreting the Map

Have students examine the map legend to see which colors are used for the various European claims and how these colored areas shift, grow, or shrink from the first map to the second.

Extension Ask students to read the map to see which national group had claims in 1754 but had lost most of them by 1763 *(the French)* and which national group had no claims in 1754 but had entered the picture by 1763 *(the Russians).*

SKILLBUILDER Answers

1. **Region** France
2. **Place** It increased greatly as the British seized most of the French territory and took control of nearly the entire eastern half of the continent.

Electronic Library of Primary Sources

• "The French Lose Quebec"

Native Americans Respond

10.1.2

Critical Thinking

- Why did many Native Americans ally with the French against the British? *(history of better relations between them, wanted to limit settlers on their land)*
- What was the overriding attitude of the British toward the Native Americans? *(that British civilization was superior, and that they were therefore entitled to take and use native land as they saw fit)*

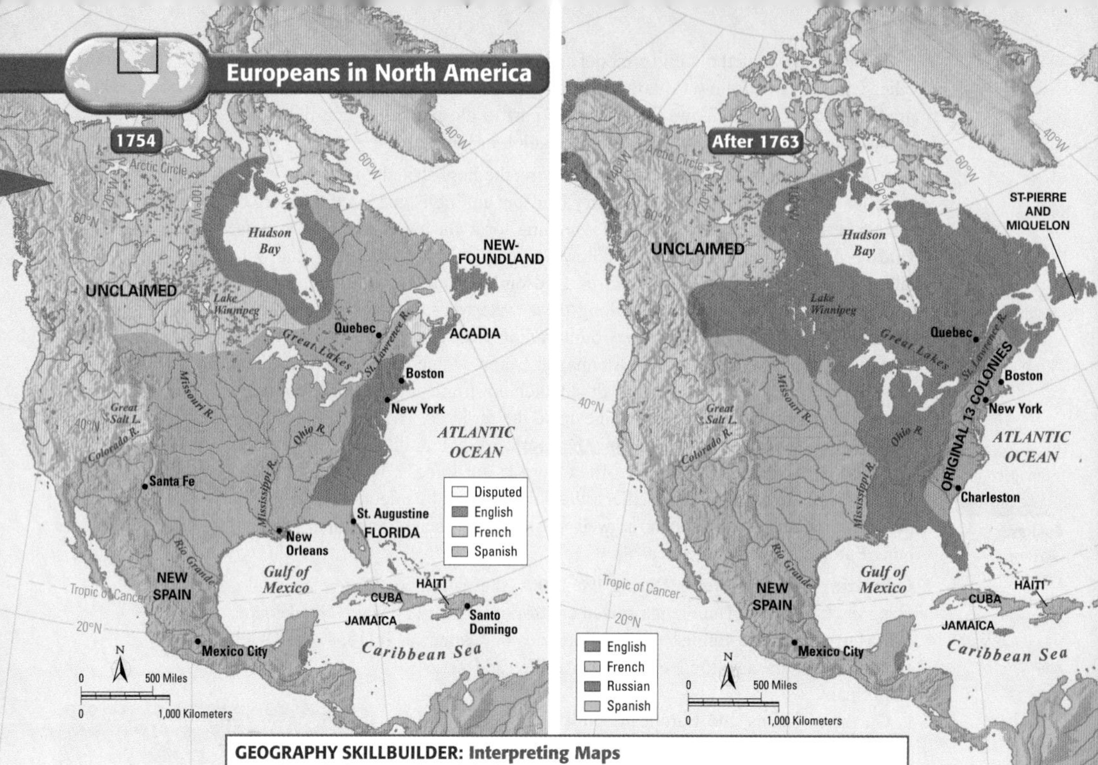

GEOGRAPHY SKILLBUILDER: Interpreting Maps

1. **Region** *Which nation claimed the largest area of the present-day United States in 1754?*
2. **Place** *How did Britain's North American empire change by 1763?*

American continent. The conflict became known as the **French and Indian War**. The war became part of a larger conflict known as the Seven Years' War. Britain and France, along with their European allies, also battled for supremacy in Europe, the West Indies, and India.

In North America, the British colonists, with the help of the British Army, defeated the French in 1763. The French surrendered their North American holdings. As a result of the war, the British seized control of the eastern half of North America.

Native Americans Respond

As in Mexico and South America, the arrival of Europeans in the present-day United States had a great impact on Native Americans. European colonization brought mostly disaster for the lands' original inhabitants.

A Strained Relationship French and Dutch settlers developed a mostly cooperative relationship with the Native Americans. This was due mainly to the mutual benefits of the fur trade. Native Americans did most of the trapping and then traded the furs to the French for such items as guns, hatchets, mirrors, and beads. The Dutch also cooperated with Native Americans in an effort to establish a fur-trading enterprise.

The groups did not live together in complete harmony. Dutch settlers fought with various Native American groups over land claims and trading rights. For the most part, however, the French and Dutch colonists lived together peacefully with their North American hosts. C

C. Possible Answer Both groups benefited from the fur trade: the Indians did the trapping and then traded the furs to the French and Dutch for goods.

MAIN IDEA

Analyzing Issues

C Why were the Dutch and French able to coexist in relative peace with the Native Americans?

DIFFERENTIATING INSTRUCTION: GIFTED AND TALENTED STUDENTS

Researching the French and Indian War

Class Time 45 minutes

Task Researching and preparing a presentation

Purpose To expand knowledge of this important historical event

Instructions Ask individual students to do research on the Internet, in an encyclopedia, or in books to learn more about the French and Indian War. Have each student choose a particular aspect of the war to present to the class. Topics can depend on the student's interest. Presentations might be in the form of an oral report, a graphic organizer, a display board, a skit or dialogue, or any other form appropriate to the topic. Students may collaborate on presentations of compatible topics.

Possible topics include:

- graphic organizer of causes and effects
- terms of the Treaty of Paris of 1763
- overview of the phases of the war
- significance of the fall of Quebec
- why most Native Americans chose to ally with France
- what the Iroquois Confederacy was and why it allied with Britain

The same could not be said of the English. Early relations between English settlers and Native Americans were cooperative. However, they quickly worsened over the issues of land and religion. Unlike the French and Dutch, the English sought to populate their colonies in North America. This meant pushing the natives off their land. The English colonists seized more land for their population—and to grow tobacco.

Religious differences also heightened tensions. The English settlers considered Native Americans heathens, people without a faith. Over time, many Puritans viewed Native Americans as agents of the devil and as a threat to their godly society. Native Americans developed a similarly harsh view of the European invaders. D

MAIN IDEA
Identifying Problems
D Why did the issues of land and religion cause strife between Native Americans and settlers?
D. Answer Settlers wanted more land for growing population and crops; they also viewed natives as godless devils.

Settlers and Native Americans Battle The hostility between the English settlers and Native Americans led to warfare. As early as 1622, the Powhatan tribe attacked colonial villages around Jamestown and killed about 350 settlers. During the next few years, the colonists struck back and massacred hundreds of Powhatan.

One of the bloodiest conflicts between colonists and Native Americans was known as King Philip's War. It began in 1675 when the Native American ruler **Metacom** (also known as King Philip) led an attack on colonial villages throughout Massachusetts. In the months that followed, both sides massacred hundreds of victims. After a year of fierce fighting, the colonists defeated the natives. During the 17th century, many skirmishes erupted throughout North America.

Natives Fall to Disease More destructive than the Europeans' weapons were their diseases. Like the Spanish in Central and South America, the Europeans who settled North America brought with them several diseases. The diseases devastated the native population in North America.

In 1616, for example, an epidemic of smallpox ravaged Native Americans living along the New England coast. The population of one tribe, the Massachusett, dropped from 24,000 to 750 by 1631. From South Carolina to Missouri, nearly whole tribes fell to smallpox, measles, and other diseases.

One of the effects of this loss was a severe shortage of labor in the colonies. In order to meet their growing labor needs, European colonists soon turned to another group: Africans, whom they would enslave by the million.

SECTION 2 ASSESSMENT

TERMS & NAMES 1. For each term or name, write a sentence explaining its significance.
• New France • Jamestown • Pilgrims • Puritans • New Netherland • French and Indian War • Metacom

USING YOUR NOTES

2. What did these settlements have in common? (10.1.2)

Name of Settlement	General Location	Reasons Settled
New France		
New Netherland		
Massachusetts Bay		

MAIN IDEAS

3. What was a basic difference between French and English attitudes about the land they acquired in North America? (10.1.2)
4. What was the main result of the French and Indian War? (10.1.2)
5. What were some of the results for Native Americans of European colonization of North America? (10.1.2)

CRITICAL THINKING & WRITING

6. **MAKING INFERENCES** What may have been one reason the English eventually beat the French in North America? (10.1.2)
7. **DRAWING CONCLUSIONS** What need drove the English farther west into the North American continent? (10.1.2)
8. **COMPARING** In what ways did the colonies at Jamestown and Massachusetts Bay differ? (10.1.2)
9. **WRITING ACTIVITY** EMPIRE BUILDING What were some of the grievances of Native Americans toward English colonists? Make a bulleted **list** of Native American complaints to display in the classroom. (Writing 2.6.b)

INTEGRATED TECHNOLOGY **INTERNET ACTIVITY**

Use the Internet to research French Cajun culture in Louisiana. Make a **poster** displaying your findings. (Writing 2.3.d)

INTERNET KEYWORD
Cajun

More About . . .

Metacom

Like his father, Metacom wanted to maintain peace with the Europeans, but he found it difficult when he saw native land being sold. The uneasy truce of 13 years was shattered when the government of Plymouth executed three natives for killing a man who had informed on the tribe. Metacom led a coalition of tribes for more than a year before he died in battle. To celebrate their victory over Metacom, the Puritans cut off his head and displayed it at Plymouth for many years.

3 ASSESS

SECTION 2 ASSESSMENT

Have students answer the questions and write down the page number(s) for each answer.

Formal Assessment
• Section Quiz, p. 71

4 RETEACH

Review students' charts for question 2 in the section assessment. Based on the information, ask them to write a letter encouraging someone to settle in one of the colonies.

In-Depth Resources: Unit 1
• Reteaching Activity, p. 100

ANSWERS

1. New France, p. 127 • Jamestown, p. 128 • Pilgrims, p. 128 • Puritans, p. 128 • New Netherland, p. 129 • French and Indian War, p. 130 • Metacom, p. 131

2. **Sample Answer:** New France—St. Lawrence and Mississippi Rivers, fur trade. New Netherland—Hudson River and Hudson Bay, fur trade. Massachusetts Bay—Coastal Massachusetts, religious freedom. Similarities—New France and New Netherland had fur-trading posts; New France had missionaries, and Massachusetts Bay had religious refuge.

3. English wanted to farm; French wanted to take part in fur trade.
4. The British controlled most of the eastern half of North America.
5. Native Americans lost their land and their lives from disease and warfare.
6. **Possible Answer:** English had more settlers.
7. more land for growing population
8. Jamestown—Mostly single males, seeking financial gain. Massachusetts Bay—Numerous families, fleeing religious persecution.

9. **Rubric** Lists should mention
• colonists seizing land.
• diseases brought by colonists.
• missionary activities of colonists.

INTEGRATED TECHNOLOGY

Rubric Posters should feature
• Cajun food.
• Cajun words.
• Cajun music.

LESSON PLAN

OBJECTIVES

- Identify the causes of African slavery.
- Trace the spread of slavery throughout the Americas.
- Explain the triangular trade.
- Describe the life of enslaved Africans in the colonies.
- Identify the consequences of the Atlantic slave trade.

1 FOCUS & MOTIVATE

Ask students to name some well-known African Americans. *(Possible Answers: Dr. Martin Luther King, Jr., Malcolm X, Jesse Jackson, Michael Jordan)*

2 INSTRUCT

The Causes of African Slavery
10.4.2

Critical Thinking

- Why were Spain and Portugal the early leaders in the slave trade? *(Possible Answer: They were the first colonizers and needed labor to work mines and plantations in the Caribbean and in South America.)*

CALIFORNIA RESOURCES
California Reading Toolkit, p. L21
California Modified Lesson Plans for English Learners, p. 37
California Daily Standards Practice Transparencies, TT13
California Standards Enrichment Workbook, pp. 47–48, 49–50, 51–52
California Standards Planner and Lesson Plans, p. L33
California Online Test Practice
California Test Generator CD-ROM
California Easy Planner CD-ROM
California eEdition CD-ROM

3

Colored engraving of colonists landing at Jamestown, Virginia

Letter from Christopher Columbus to his son Diego, discussing Amerigo Vespucci

The Atlantic Slave Trade

MAIN IDEA

CULTURAL INTERACTION To meet their growing labor needs, Europeans enslaved millions of Africans in the Americas.

WHY IT MATTERS NOW

Descendants of enslaved Africans represent a significant part of the Americas' population today.

TERMS & NAMES

- Atlantic slave trade
- triangular trade
- middle passage

CALIFORNIA STANDARDS

10.4.1 Describe the rise of industrial economies and their link to imperialism and colonialism (e.g., the role played by national security and strategic advantage; moral issues raised by the search for national hegemony, Social Darwinism, and the missionary impulse; material issues such as land, resources, and technology).

10.4.2 Discuss the locations of the colonial rule of such nations as England, France, Germany, Italy, Japan, the Netherlands, Russia, Spain, Portugal, and the United States.

10.4.3 Explain imperialism from the perspective of the colonizers and the colonized and the varied immediate and long-term responses by the people under colonial rule.

REP 1 Students distinguish valid arguments from fallacious arguments in historical interpretations.

TAKING NOTES
Recognizing Effects Use a diagram like the one below to list effects of the Atlantic slave trade.

Consequences of the slave trade
I. in Africa
A.
B.
II. in the Americas
A.
B.

SETTING THE STAGE Sugar plantations and tobacco farms required a large supply of workers to make them profitable for their owners. European owners had planned to use Native Americans as a source of cheap labor. But millions of Native Americans died from disease, warfare, and brutal treatment. Therefore, the Europeans in Brazil, the Caribbean, and the southern colonies of North America soon turned to Africa for workers. This demand for cheap labor resulted in the brutalities of the slave trade.

The Causes of African Slavery

Beginning around 1500, European colonists in the Americas who needed cheap labor began using enslaved Africans on plantations and farms.

Slavery in Africa Slavery had existed in Africa for centuries. In most regions, it was a relatively minor institution. The spread of Islam into Africa during the seventh century, however, ushered in an increase in slavery and the slave trade. Muslim rulers in Africa justified enslavement with the Muslim belief that non-Muslim prisoners of war could be bought and sold as slaves. As a result, between 650 and 1600, Muslims transported about 17 million Africans to the Muslim lands of North Africa and Southwest Asia.

In most African and Muslim societies, slaves had some legal rights and an opportunity for social mobility. In the Muslim world, a few slaves even occupied positions of influence and power. Some served as generals in the army. In African societies, slaves could escape their bondage in numerous ways, including marrying into the family they served.

The Demand for Africans The first Europeans to explore Africa were the Portuguese during the 1400s. Initially, Portuguese traders were more interested in trading for gold than for captured Africans. That changed with the colonization of the Americas, as natives began dying by the millions.

Europeans saw advantages in using Africans in the Americas. First, many Africans had been exposed to European diseases and had built up some immunity. Second, many Africans had experience in farming and could be taught plantation work. Third, Africans were less likely to escape because they did not know their way around the new land. Fourth, their skin color made it easier to catch them if they escaped and tried to live among others.

SECTION 3 PROGRAM RESOURCES

ALL STUDENTS
In-Depth Resources: Unit 1
- Guided Reading, p. 83

Formal Assessment
- Section Quiz, p. 72

ENGLISH LEARNERS
In-Depth Resources in Spanish
- Guided Reading, p. 39

Reading Study Guide (Spanish), p. 45
Reading Study Guide Audio CD (Spanish)

STRUGGLING READERS
In-Depth Resources: Unit 1
- Guided Reading, p. 83
- Building Vocabulary, p. 85
- Reteaching Activity, p. 101

Reading Study Guide, p. 45
Reading Study Guide Audio CD

GIFTED AND TALENTED STUDENTS
In-Depth Resources: Unit 1
- Primary Source: from *The Life of Olaudah Equiano,* p. 92

Electronic Library of Primary Sources
- Letter to the King of Portugal

INTEGRATED TECHNOLOGY
eEdition CD-ROM
Power Presentations CD-ROM
World Art and Cultures Transparencies
- AT44 Meynell's *Slaves Below the Deck of the* Albanez

Critical Thinking Transparencies
- CT20 The Atlantic Slave Trade, 1451–1870

Electronic Library of Primary Sources
- Letter to the King of Portugal

classzone.com

In time, the buying and selling of Africans for work in the Americas—known as the **Atlantic slave trade**—became a massive enterprise. Between 1500 and 1600, nearly 300,000 Africans were transported to the Americas. During the next century, that number climbed to almost 1.3 million. By the time the Atlantic slave trade ended around 1870, Europeans had imported about 9.5 million Africans to the Americas. (A)

MAIN IDEA
Analyzing Motives
(A) What advantages did Europeans see in enslaving Africans?

A. Answer Slaves had built up immunity to many diseases, they were experienced in farming, they were in an alien environment that made them less likely to escape.

Spain and Portugal Lead the Way The Spanish took an early lead in importing Africans to the Americas. Spain moved on from the Caribbean and began to colonize the American mainland. As a result, the Spanish imported and enslaved thousands more Africans. By 1650, nearly 300,000 Africans labored throughout Spanish America on plantations and in gold and silver mines.

By this time, however, the Portuguese had surpassed the Spanish in the importation of Africans to the Americas. During the 1600s, Brazil dominated the European sugar market. As the colony's sugar industry grew, so too did European colonists' demand for cheap labor. During the 17th century, more than 40 percent of all Africans brought to the Americas went to Brazil.

Slavery Spreads Throughout the Americas

As the other European nations established colonies in the Americas, their demand for cheap labor grew. Thus, they also began to import large numbers of Africans.

England Dominates the Slave Trade As England's presence in the Americas grew, it came to dominate the Atlantic slave trade. From 1690 until England abolished the slave trade in 1807, it was the leading carrier of enslaved Africans. By the time the slave trade ended, the English had transported nearly 1.7 million Africans to their colonies in the West Indies.

African slaves were also brought to what is now the United States. In all, nearly 400,000 Africans were sold to Britain's North American colonies. Once in North America, however, the slave population steadily grew. By 1830, roughly 2 million slaves toiled in the United States.

History *in* Depth

Slavery

Slavery probably began with the development of farming about 10,000 years ago. Farmers used prisoners of war to work for them.

Slavery has existed in societies around the world. People were enslaved in civilizations from Egypt to China to India. The picture at the right shows slaves working in a Roman coal mine.

Race was not always a factor in slavery. Often, slaves were captured prisoners of war, or people of a different nationality or religion.

However, the slavery that developed in the Americas was based largely on race. Europeans viewed black people as naturally inferior. Because of this, slavery in the Americas was hereditary.

More About . . .

Slavery on Plantations

Plantation owners in the British Caribbean colony of Barbados determined that it was more profitable to buy new slaves to replace those who died from disease and overwork than to institute measures to provide for a more humane life for slaves.

Slavery Spreads Throughout the Americas
10.4.1

Critical Thinking

- Why does the number of slaves transported by the British to the United States understate the scope of slavery there? *(number transported was only about 20 percent of the total)*
- How was British involvement in the slave trade similar to that of the Spanish? *(Both transported huge numbers of Africans.)*

History *in* Depth

Slavery

The slave trade was as old as the institution of slavery. Prisoners of war were often sent far away to keep them separate from their families. In addition to Africans, large populations that were sources of slaves included the Slavs of eastern Europe and farmers in what is now Iran. The Vikings raided for slaves throughout northern Europe during the Middle Ages. While some Europeans opposed slavery in the 16th century, most did not begin to think of it as immoral until the mid-1700s.

DIFFERENTIATING INSTRUCTION: STRUGGLING READERS

Understanding the African Slave Trade

Class Time 20 minutes

Task Creating a time line

Purpose To understand the growth of the slave trade over time

Instructions Pair a struggling reader with a more proficient reader. Explain to students that historians have various ways of expressing time periods. For example, "the 15th century" is another way of saying "the 1400s." Point out that sometimes students need to infer dates by looking at a comparison that an author uses, such as "during the next century" or "with the colonization of the Americas." Have them reread pages 132 and 133, noting all chronological references. Then have them make a time line using the earliest and latest dates mentioned (650 and 1870) as the range. Their time lines might look like this:

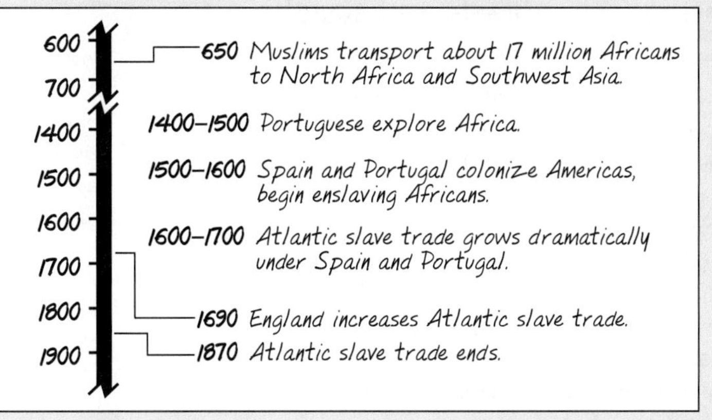

600
700
1400
1500
1600
1700
1800
1900
650 Muslims transport about 17 million Africans to North Africa and Southwest Asia.
1400–1500 Portuguese explore Africa.
1500–1600 Spain and Portugal colonize Americas, begin enslaving Africans.
1600–1700 Atlantic slave trade grows dramatically under Spain and Portugal.
1690 England increases Atlantic slave trade.
1870 Atlantic slave trade ends.

A Forced Journey
10.4.3

Critical Thinking

- What pivotal role did the West Indies play in the triangular trade? *(principal market for slaves who worked on the plantations, producing sugar and molasses used in making rum that was traded for slaves)*
- In what ways did the conditions of the middle passage work against the interests of the European merchants? *(contributed to an increased death rate, lowering profits)*

African Cooperation and Resistance Many African rulers and merchants played a willing role in the Atlantic slave trade. Most European traders, rather than travel inland, waited in ports along the coasts of Africa. African merchants, with the help of local rulers, captured Africans to be enslaved. They then delivered them to the Europeans in exchange for gold, guns, and other goods. **B**

As the slave trade grew, some African rulers voiced their opposition to the practice. Nonetheless, the slave trade steadily grew. Lured by its profits, many African rulers continued to participate. African merchants developed new trade routes to avoid rulers who refused to cooperate.

MAIN IDEA
Analyzing Issues
B Why did many African rulers participate in the Atlantic slave trade?
B. Answer It was profitable, and they received valuable goods in return.

A Forced Journey

After being captured, African men and women were shipped to the Americas as part of a profitable trade network. Along the way, millions of Africans died.

The Triangular Trade Africans transported to the Americas were part of a transatlantic trading network known as the **triangular trade**. Over one trade route, Europeans transported manufactured goods to the west coast of Africa. There, traders exchanged these goods for captured Africans. The Africans were then transported across the Atlantic and sold in the West Indies. Merchants bought sugar, coffee, and tobacco in the West Indies and sailed to Europe with these products.

On another triangular route, merchants carried rum and other goods from the New England colonies to Africa. There they exchanged their merchandise for Africans. The traders transported the Africans to the West Indies and sold them for sugar and molasses. They then sold these goods to rum producers in New England.

History from Visuals

Interpreting the Map

Have students read the map and the circle graph and compare and contrast the information presented in each. *(The map shows the routes and the products and human cargo of the triangular trade. The graph shows the percentage of slaves taken to each area of the world.)*

Extension Have students trace the routes on the map that show the middle passage. Note that the routes are different depending on the destination.

SKILLBUILDER Answers

1. **Movement** tobacco, rum, manufactured goods, guns
2. **Region** Caribbean islands; Brazil

INTEGRATED TECHNOLOGY

Interactive An interactive version of this map is available on the eEdition.

Triangle Trade System, 1451–1870
INTERACTIVE

GREAT BRITAIN, London, Paris, EUROPE, NORTH AMERICA, New York, Charleston, MEXICO, CARIBBEAN, JAMAICA, PACIFIC OCEAN, SOUTH AMERICA, Rio de Janeiro, ATLANTIC OCEAN, AFRICA, KONGO, Luanda, Benguela, Mozambique, INDIAN OCEAN

Manufactures; Cotton, Tobacco; Rum; Sugar, Molasses, Slaves; Sugar, Molasses, Cotton; Manufactures, Guns; Slaves, Ivory, Gum; Rum; Slaves, Gold; Tobacco; Slaves

40°N; Tropic of Cancer; 0° Equator; Tropic of Capricorn; 40°W

Primary slave trade routes
Other trade routes

0 — 2,000 Miles
0 — 4,000 Kilometers

Africans Enslaved in the Americas, 1451–1870

Total Number Imported: 9.5 Million*

- 40% Caribbean Islands (Dutch, French, British)
- 4% British North America
- 2% Europe, Asia
- 16% Spanish America and Spanish Caribbean
- 38% Portuguese Brazil

*Estimated
Source: *The Atlantic Slave Trade: A Census*

GEOGRAPHY SKILLBUILDER: Interpreting Maps

1. **Movement** *What items were transported to Africa and traded for captured Africans?*
2. **Region** *According to the graph, which region of the Americas imported the most Africans? Which imported the second most?*

DIFFERENTIATING INSTRUCTION: ENGLISH LEARNERS

Interpreting Charts and Graphs

Class Time 20 minutes

Task Interpreting a chart and a graph

Purpose To understand the impact of the Atlantic slave trade

Instructions Show students Critical Thinking Transparency CT20. Point out that the graph shows the percentage of slaves arriving in a given region over the whole period. Tell students that each row shows the number of slaves for each region. The totals shown at the end of each row relate to the percentages shown in the circle graph. For example, the 399,000 slaves transported to British North America is the number represented by 4 percent of the total slaves transported. Then point out that each column represents a particular time period. By reading down the column, students can see the numbers going to each region as well as the total for the time period. Ask students when the largest number of slaves was transported. *(1701–1810)* What are the reasons for the growth in this period compared with the previous and following periods? *(Possible Answer: England's colonial presence grew in the 18th century, but Great Britain abolished its slave trade in 1807.)*

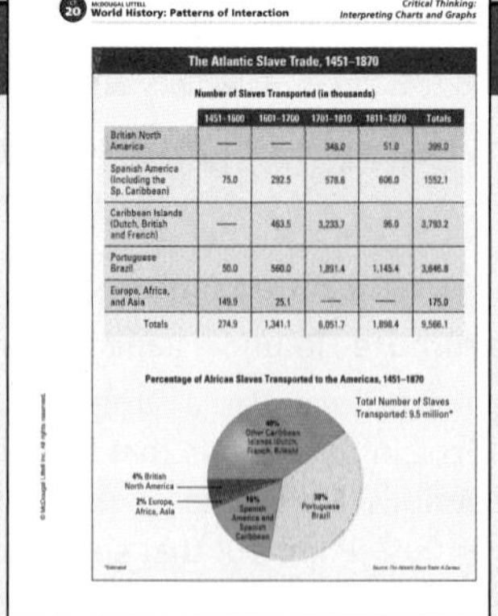
CT20 McDougal Littell World History: Patterns of Interaction — *Critical Thinking: Interpreting Charts and Graphs*

The Atlantic Slave Trade, 1451–1870

Number of Slaves Transported (in thousands)

	1451–1600	1601–1700	1701–1810	1811–1870	Totals
British North America	—	—	348.0	51.0	399.0
Spanish America (including the Sp. Caribbean)	75.0	292.5	578.6	606.0	1552.1
Caribbean Islands (Dutch, British and French)	—	463.5	3,233.7	96.0	3,793.2
Portuguese Brazil	50.0	560.0	1,891.4	1,145.4	3,646.8
Europe, Africa, and Asia	149.9	25.1	—	—	175.0
Totals	274.9	1,341.1	6,051.7	1,898.4	9,566.1

Percentage of African Slaves Transported to the Americas, 1451–1870

Critical Thinking Transparencies

Analyzing Primary Sources

The Horrors of the Middle Passage

One African, Olaudah Equiano, recalled the inhumane conditions on his trip from West Africa to the West Indies at age 12 in 1762.

PRIMARY SOURCE

I was soon put down under the decks, and there I received such a salutation [greeting] in my nostrils as I never experienced in my life; so that, with the loathsomeness of the stench, and crying together, I became so sick and low that I was not able to eat . . . but soon, to my grief, two of the white men offered me eatables; and on my refusing to eat, one of them held me fast by the hands, and laid me across . . . the windlass, while the other flogged me severely.

OLAUDAH EQUIANO, quoted in *Eyewitness: The Negro in American History*

This diagram of a British slave ship shows how slave traders packed Africans onto slave ships in the hold below decks for the brutal middle passage.

DOCUMENT-BASED QUESTIONS

1. **Making Inferences** *Why might the white men have forced Equiano to eat?*
2. **Drawing Conclusions** *What does the diagram of the slave ship suggest about conditions on board?*

Various other transatlantic routes existed. The "triangular" trade encompassed a network of trade routes crisscrossing the northern and southern colonies, the West Indies, England, Europe, and Africa. The network carried a variety of traded goods.

The Middle Passage The voyage that brought captured Africans to the West Indies and later to North and South America was known as the **middle passage**. It was considered the middle leg of the transatlantic trade triangle. Sickening cruelty characterized this journey. In African ports, European traders packed Africans into the dark holds of large ships. On board, Africans endured whippings and beatings from merchants, as well as diseases that swept through the vessel. Numerous Africans died from disease or physical abuse aboard the slave ships. Many others committed suicide by drowning. Scholars estimate that roughly 20 percent of the Africans aboard each slave ship perished during the brutal trip.

Slavery in the Americas

Africans who survived their ocean voyage faced a difficult life in the Americas. Forced to work in a strange land, enslaved Africans coped in a variety of ways.

A Harsh Life Upon arriving in the Americas, captured Africans usually were auctioned off to the highest bidder. After being sold, slaves worked in mines or fields or as domestic servants. Slaves lived a grueling existence. Many lived on little food in small, dreary huts. They worked long days and suffered beatings. In much of the Americas, slavery was a lifelong condition, as well as a hereditary one.

Resistance and Rebellion To cope with the horrors of slavery, Africans developed a way of life based on their cultural heritage. They kept alive such things as their musical traditions as well as the stories of their ancestors.

Analyzing Primary Sources

The Horrors of the Middle Passage

Have students read the primary source by Olaudah Equiano. Ask them why he did not feel like eating. (*terrible smells and feelings of sadness*)

Answers to Document-Based Questions

1. **Making Inferences** He was valuable property that they wished to keep alive.
2. **Drawing Conclusions** Conditions were intolerably crowded and likely to spread disease.

More About . . .

The Middle Passage

The captain of a slave ship was either a "tight packer" or a "loose packer," referring to the number of slaves he jammed into the ship's hold. Tight packers arranged people in spoon style, lying on top of one another.

World Art and Cultures Transparencies

- AT44 *Slaves Below the Deck of the* Albanez

Slavery in the Americas

10.4.3

Critical Thinking

- In what ways were enslaved Africans treated as property? *(They were bought and sold and owned for life; their children were slaves.)*
- How did the preservation of their cultures help people cope with slavery? *(Possible Answer: It reminded them of their life as humans apart from their current condition.)*

DIFFERENTIATING INSTRUCTION: GIFTED AND TALENTED STUDENTS

Understanding Primary Sources

Class Time 45 minutes

Task Reading and paraphrasing a primary source

Purpose To gain greater knowledge of slavery

Instructions Explain to students that Olaudah Equiano told his story in his autobiography, *The Interesting Narrative of the Life of Olaudah Equiano,* which was published in 1789 and soon became a bestseller. It is the first of a genre of world literature written by African slaves, former slaves, and postslavery African Americans who have described their struggles for freedom. Equiano wrote his story for several reasons. Many white people tried to defend slavery by saying that black people were well suited for heavy work. They said slaves were well treated and that since they could not read or write, they did not need to be free. Equiano wanted to show these arguments for the lies that they were. He also wanted to provide a model for other black people. Ask students to read the additional primary source excerpt in the In-Depth Resources book. Then ask them to find additional excerpts from his autobiography using the Internet or library resources. If time permits, have students prepare a presentation for the class, with each student reading and explaining a short excerpt.

PRIMARY SOURCE *from The Life of Olaudah Equiano*

In-Depth Resources: Unit 1

More About . . .

Slave Resistance

Slave resistance also included ways to supplement a slave's meager food rations. Some took their masters' pigs, buried the hides, and pretended they were eating opossum, which was available to slaves.

Consequences of the Slave Trade

10.4.3

Critical Thinking

- In what ways were slaves a source of profit for Europeans? *(slave trade–wealth for merchants; slave labor–wealth for owners)*
- What made enslaved Africans more attractive than Native Americans to plantation owners? *(agricultural expertise versus many Native Americans' hunting-gathering expertise)*

3 ASSESS

SECTION 3 ASSESSMENT

Have students work in pairs and use a quiz-show format to ask each other the questions and then check each other's answers.

Formal Assessment

- Section Quiz, p. 72

4 RETEACH

Go over the key terms to help students understand the main concepts in this section.

In-Depth Resources: Unit 1

- Reteaching Activity, p. 101

Slaves also found ways to resist. They made themselves less productive by breaking tools, uprooting plants, and working slowly. Thousands also ran away.

Some slaves pushed their resistance to open revolt. As early as 1522, about 20 slaves on Hispaniola attacked and killed several Spanish colonists. Larger revolts occurred throughout Spanish settlements during the 16th century.

Occasional uprisings also occurred in Brazil, the West Indies, and North America. In 1739, a group of slaves in South Carolina led an uprising known as the Stono Rebellion. Uprisings continued into the 1800s.

Consequences of the Slave Trade

The Atlantic slave trade had a profound impact on both Africa and the Americas. In Africa, numerous cultures lost generations of their fittest members—their young and able—to European traders and plantation owners. In addition, countless African families were torn apart. Many of them were never reunited. The slave trade devastated African societies in another way: by introducing guns into the continent.

While they were unwilling participants in the growth of the colonies, African slaves contributed greatly to the economic and cultural development of the Americas. Their greatest contribution was their labor. Without their back-breaking work, colonies such as those on Haiti and Barbados may not have survived. In addition to their muscle, enslaved Africans brought their expertise, especially in agriculture. They also brought their culture. Their art, music, religion, and food continue to influence American societies.

The influx of so many Africans to the Americas also has left its mark on the very population itself. From the United States to Brazil, many of the nations of the Western Hemisphere today have substantial African-American populations. Many Latin American countries have sizable mixed-race populations.

As the next section explains, Africans were not the only cargo transported across the Atlantic during the colonization of the Americas. The settlement of the Americas brought many different items from Europe, Asia, and Africa to North and South America. It also introduced items from the Americas to the rest of the world.

SECTION 3 ASSESSMENT

TERMS & NAMES 1. For each term or name, write a sentence explaining its significance.
• Atlantic slave trade • triangular trade • middle passage

USING YOUR NOTES

2. What seems to have been the most important consequence? Explain. (10.4.2)

Consequences of the slave trade
I. in Africa
A.
B.
II. in the Americas
A.
B.

MAIN IDEAS

3. What effect did the spread of Islam have on the slave trade? (10.4.3)
4. How did enslaved Africans resist their bondage? (10.4.3)
5. How did African slaves contribute to the development of the Americas? (10.4.3)

CRITICAL THINKING & WRITING

6. **COMPARING AND CONTRASTING** How was slavery in the Americas different from slavery in Africa? (10.4.3)
7. **SYNTHESIZING** What does the percentage of enslaved Africans imported to the Caribbean Islands and Brazil suggest about the racial makeup of these areas? (10.4.2)
8. **MAKING INFERENCES** Why do you think the slave trade flourished for so long? (10.4.3)
9. **WRITING ACTIVITY** CULTURAL INTERACTION Imagine you are an African ruler. Write a **letter** to a European leader in which you try to convince him or her to stop participating in the slave trade. (Writing 2.6.a)

CONNECT TO TODAY MAKING A MAP

Research which of the original 13 colonies had the greatest numbers of slaves in the late 18th century. Then make a **map** of the colonies in which you show the numbers for each state. (CST 3)

ANSWERS

1. Atlantic slave trade, p. 133 • triangular trade, p. 134 • middle passage, p. 135
2. **Sample Answer:** In Africa–Loss of population, families torn apart, and cultures lost. In the Americas–Slave traders benefited, slave owners benefited, enslaved Africans forced to adapt to brutal conditions, African cultures spread. Most important consequence–Loss of cultures, because they are difficult or impossible to reconstruct today.
3. increase in the slave trade
4. broke tools, uprooted plants, worked slowly, escaped, revolted
5. through labor, knowledge of agriculture, culture
6. Africa–Slaves could escape their bondage. Americas–Most slaves worked for life; slavery was hereditary.
7. great racial diversity
8. Slaves and slavery were sources of wealth.
9. **Rubric** Letters should
- present a thoughtful, logical argument.
- be supported by facts.
- show an understanding of the injustices of the slave trade.
- be well written and engaging.

CONNECT TO TODAY

Rubric Maps should show
- the original 13 colonies.
- the number of enslaved persons in each colony.

4 The Columbian Exchange and Global Trade

Colored engraving of colonists landing at Jamestown, Virginia

Letter from Christopher Columbus to his son Diego, discussing Amerigo Vespucci

MAIN IDEA

ECONOMICS The colonization of the Americas introduced new items into the Eastern and Western hemispheres.

WHY IT MATTERS NOW

This global exchange of goods permanently changed Europe, Asia, Africa, and the Americas.

TERMS & NAMES

- Columbian Exchange
- capitalism
- joint-stock company
- mercantilism
- favorable balance of trade

SETTING THE STAGE The colonization of the Americas dramatically changed the world. It prompted both voluntary and forced migration of millions of people. It led to the establishment of new and powerful societies. Other effects of European settlement of the Americas were less noticeable but equally important. Colonization resulted in the exchange of new items that greatly influenced the lives of people throughout the world. The new wealth from the Americas resulted in new business and trade practices in Europe.

CALIFORNIA STANDARDS

10.3.6 Analyze the emergence of capitalism as a dominant economic pattern and the responses to it, including Utopianism, Social Democracy, Socialism, and Communism.

10.4.1 Describe the rise of industrial economies and their link to imperialism and colonialism (e.g., the role played by national security and strategic advantage; moral issues raised by the search for national hegemony, Social Darwinism, and the missionary impulse; material issues such as land, resources, and technology).

HI 1 Students show the connections, causal and otherwise, between particular historical events and larger social, economic, and political trends and developments.

HI 4 Students understand the meaning, implication, and impact of historical events and recognize that events could have taken other directions.

The Columbian Exchange

The global transfer of foods, plants, and animals during the colonization of the Americas is known as the **Columbian Exchange**. Ships from the Americas brought back a wide array of items that Europeans, Asians, and Africans had never before seen. They included such plants as tomatoes, squash, pineapples, tobacco, and cacao beans (for chocolate). And they included animals such as the turkey, which became a source of food in the Eastern Hemisphere.

Perhaps the most important items to travel from the Americas to the rest of the world were corn and potatoes. Both were inexpensive to grow and nutritious. Potatoes, especially, supplied many essential vitamins and minerals. Over time, both crops became an important and steady part of diets throughout the world. These foods helped people live longer. Thus they played a significant role in boosting the world's population. The planting of the first white potato in Ireland and the first sweet potato in China probably changed more lives than the deeds of 100 kings.

Traffic across the Atlantic did not flow in just one direction, however. Europeans introduced various livestock animals into the Americas. These included horses, cattle, sheep, and pigs. Foods from Africa (including some that originated in Asia) migrated west in European ships. They included bananas, black-eyed peas, and yams. Grains introduced to the Americas included wheat, rice, barley, and oats.

Some aspects of the Columbian Exchange had a tragic impact on many Native Americans. Disease was just as much a part of the Columbian Exchange as goods and food. The diseases Europeans brought with them, which included smallpox and measles, led to the deaths of millions of Native Americans.

TAKING NOTES

Recognizing Effects Use a chart to record information about the Columbian Exchange.

Food/ Livestock/ Disease	Place of Origin	Effect
Potato		
Horse		
Smallpox		

LESSON PLAN

OBJECTIVES

- Explain the Columbian Exchange.
- Identify factors that led to the development of global trade.
- Describe the effects of new economic policies on European society.

1 FOCUS & MOTIVATE

Ask students to think about things they own that come from other countries. *(Possible Answers: consumer electronics, clothes)*

2 INSTRUCT

The Columbian Exchange
10.4.1

Critical Thinking

- Why is the Columbian Exchange so called? *(because it resulted from Christopher Columbus's initial contact with the Americas)*
- How did the introduction of European livestock change the lives of Native Americans? *(Possible Answer: Horses allowed them to travel farther and faster and were valuable property.)*

CALIFORNIA RESOURCES

California Reading Toolkit, p. L22
California Modified Lesson Plans for English Learners, p. 39
California Daily Standards Practice Transparencies, TT14
California Standards Enrichment Workbook, pp. 43–44, 47–48
California Standards Planner and Lesson Plans, p. L35
California Online Test Practice
California Test Generator CD-ROM
California Easy Planner CD-ROM
California eEdition CD-ROM

SECTION 4 PROGRAM RESOURCES

ALL STUDENTS

In-Depth Resources: Unit 1
- Guided Reading, p. 84
- Geography Application: The Potato Impacts the World, p. 87

Formal Assessment
- Section Quiz, p. 73

ENGLISH LEARNERS

In-Depth Resources in Spanish
- Guided Reading, p. 40
- Geography Application, p. 42

Reading Study Guide (Spanish), p. 47
Reading Study Guide Audio CD (Spanish)

STRUGGLING READERS

In-Depth Resources: Unit 1
- Guided Reading, p. 84
- Building Vocabulary, p. 85
- Geography Application, p. 87
- Reteaching Activity, p. 102

Reading Study Guide, p. 47
Reading Study Guide Audio CD

GIFTED AND TALENTED STUDENTS

In-Depth Resources: Unit 1
- Connections Across Time and Cultures, p. 98

INTEGRATED TECHNOLOGY

eEdition CD-ROM
Power Presentations CD-ROM
Electronic Library of Primary Sources
- "Concerning the Dearness of All Things"

Geography Transparencies
- GT20 Spain's Colonies Provide Wealth, 1600–1790

Critical Thinking Transparencies
- CT56 Chapter 4 Visual Summary

Patterns of Interaction Video Series
- The Impact of Potatoes and Sugar

classzone.com

Global Impact

OBJECTIVES

- Describe the scope and impact of the Columbian food exchange.
- Describe the specific items that moved in each direction as a result of the Columbian Exchange.

INSTRUCT

Tell students that in the United States today, about one-third of the annual harvest is of food crops that had been cultivated by Native Americans prior to the arrival of European settlers. The following six crops each have yearly sales totaling more than $1 billion: corn, cotton, tobacco, potatoes, tomatoes, and peanuts. Have students create a class cookbook of their favorite meals that contain one or more of the four food items in this group.

Viewing the Video

Show the video to examine how people have brought foods from one part of the globe to another with positive and negative effects.

Patterns of Interaction Video Series

- The Geography of Food: The Impact of Potatoes and Sugar

In-Depth Resources: Unit 1

- Geography Application: The Potato Impacts the World, p. 87
- Connections Across Time and Cultures: Impact of the Columbian Exchange, p. 98

The Columbian Exchange

Few events transformed the world like the Columbian Exchange. This global transfer of plants, animals, disease, and especially food brought together the Eastern and Western hemispheres and touched, in some way, nearly all the peoples of the world.

Frightening Foods

Several foods from the Americas that we now take for granted at first amazed and terrified Europeans. Early on, people thought the tomato was harmful to eat. One German official warned that the tomato "should not be taken internally." In 1619, officials in Burgundy, France, banned potatoes, explaining that "too frequent use of them caused the leprosy." In 1774, starving peasants in Prussia refused to eat the spud.

CALIFORNIA STANDARDS

10.4.1 Describe the rise of industrial economies and their link to imperialism and colonialism (e.g., the role played by national security and strategic advantage; moral issues raised by the search for national hegemony, Social Darwinism, and the missionary impulse; material issues such as land, resources, and technology).

HI 2 Students recognize the complexity of historical causes and effects, including the limitations on determining cause and effect.

The Columbian Exchange

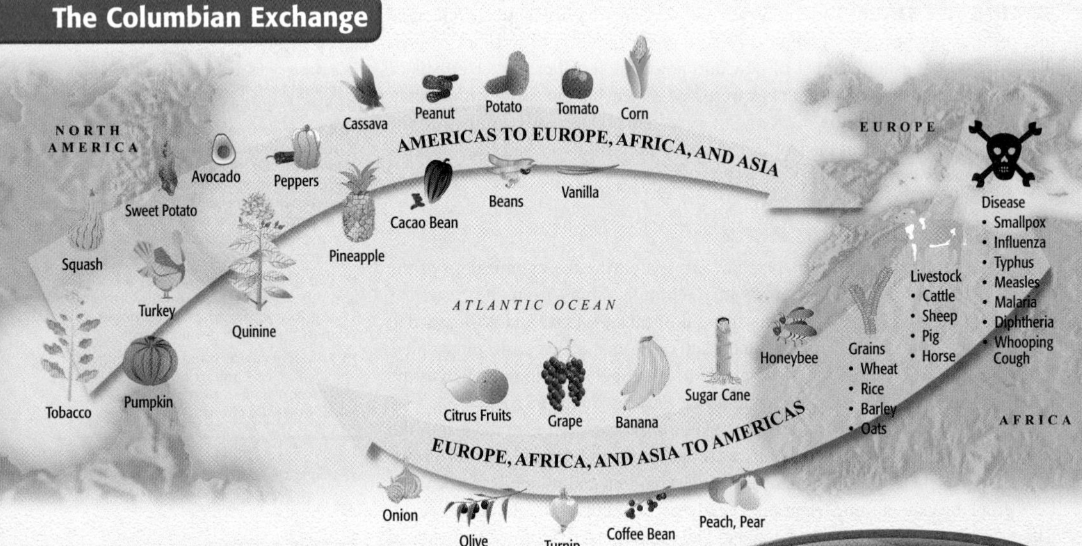

Patterns of Interaction

The Geography of Food: The Impact of Potatoes and Sugar

Think about your favorite foods. Chances are that at least one originated in a distant land. Throughout history, the introduction of new foods into a region has dramatically changed lives—for better and worse. Dependence on the potato, for example, led to a famine in Ireland. This prompted a massive migration of Irish people to other countries. In the Americas, the introduction of sugar led to riches for some and enslavement for many others.

Connect *to* Today

1. **Forming Opinions** Have students work in small groups to pose and answer questions about the beneficial and harmful aspects of the Columbian Exchange.
   See Skillbuilder Handbook, page R20.
2. **Comparing and Contrasting** Find out what major items are exchanged or traded between the United States and either Asia, Africa, or Europe. How do the items compare with those of the Columbian Exchange? Report your findings to the class.

CONNECT TO TODAY: ANSWERS

1. Forming Opinions

Possible Answers: What was beneficial about the Columbian Exchange? Both sides received many new foods. What was harmful? European diseases killed millions of Native Americans. Who benefited the most? Europeans.

2. Comparing and Contrasting

Suggest that students use various resources to find information about trade between the United States and Asia, Africa, or Europe. For example, students might consult magazines (by means of the *Readers' Guide to Periodical Literature*), newspapers, current encyclopedias (in book, CD-ROM, and online form), almanacs (such as *Information Please*), and the *Statistical Abstract of the United States*, as well as the Internet.

A Spanish missionary in Mexico described the effects of smallpox on the Aztecs:

PRIMARY SOURCE
There was a great havoc. Very many died of it. They could not walk. . . . They could not move; they could not stir; they could not change position, nor lie on one side; nor face down, nor on their backs. And if they stirred, much did they cry out. Great was its destruction.

BERNARDINO DE SAHAGUN, quoted in *Seeds of Change*

MAIN IDEA
Making Inferences
A Why is the Columbian Exchange considered a significant event?
A. Possible Answer It greatly improved diets and lifestyles in Europe and Asia and helped prompt an increase in the world's population; it also led to the death of millions of Native Americans from disease.

Other diseases Europeans brought with them included influenza, typhus, malaria, and diphtheria. A

Global Trade

The establishment of colonial empires in the Americas influenced the nations of Europe in still other ways. New wealth from the Americas was coupled with a dramatic growth in overseas trade. The two factors together prompted a wave of new business and trade practices in Europe during the 16th and 17th centuries. These practices, many of which served as the root of today's financial dealings, dramatically changed the economic atmosphere of Europe.

The Rise of Capitalism One aspect of the European economic revolution was the growth of **capitalism**. Capitalism is an economic system based on private ownership and the investment of resources, such as money, for profit. No longer were governments the sole owners of great wealth. Due to overseas colonization and trade, numerous merchants had obtained great wealth. These merchants continued to invest their money in trade and overseas exploration. Profits from these investments enabled merchants and traders to reinvest even more money in other enterprises. As a result, businesses across Europe grew and flourished.

The increase in economic activity in Europe led to an overall increase in many nations' money supply. This in turn brought on inflation, or the steady rise in the price of goods. Inflation occurs when people have more money to spend and thus demand more goods and services. Because the supply of goods is less than the demand for them, the goods become both scarce and more valuable. Prices then rise. At this time in Europe, the costs of many goods rose. Spain, for example, endured a crushing bout of inflation during the 1600s, as boatloads of gold and silver from the Americas greatly increased the nation's money supply.

Joint-Stock Companies Another business venture that developed during this period was known as the **joint-stock company**. The joint-stock company worked much like the modern-day corporation, with investors buying shares of stock in a company. It involved a number of people combining their wealth for a common purpose.

Three Worlds Meet, 1492–1700

1500 · 1550 · 1600 · 1650 · 1700

1492 (Europeans)
Columbus embarks on voyage.

1511 (Africans)
Africans begin working as slaves in the Americas.

1521 (Americans)
The Aztec Empire in Mexico is conquered by Hernando Cortés.

1533 (Americans)
The Inca Empire in South America falls to Francisco Pizarro.

1630 (Europeans)
Puritans establish the Massachusetts Bay Colony in North America.

1650 (Africans)
The number of Africans toiling in Spanish America reaches 300,000.

1675 (Americans)
Native Americans battle colonists in King Philip's War.

CHAPTER 4 • Section 4

History from Visuals

Interpreting the Time Line
Help students understand the time line by pointing out that each event includes the name of the affected group.

Extension Ask students to make a list of additional events from the chapter that affected each of the three groups.

Global Trade
10.3.6

Critical Thinking
- How did capitalism change the balance of power in European countries? *(Some individuals and some governments had great wealth.)*
- How did joint-stock companies reflect the capitalist system? *(individuals invested their wealth, shared risk and reward)*

More About . . .

Spanish Gold
Spain may have been too rich for its own good. Other nations and individuals began to attack Spanish ships and holdings to get some of the gold for themselves and to limit Spain's power. In Spain the desire for gold meant that fewer people invested in skilled work, farming, and trade.

Electronic Library of Primary Sources
- "Concerning the Dearness of All Things and the Remedy Therefor"

Geography Transparencies
- GT20 Spain's Colonies Provide Wealth, 1600–1790

DIFFERENTIATING INSTRUCTION: STRUGGLING READERS

Vocabulary Activity: "Interviewing" Words

Class Time 20 minutes

Task Developing strategies for remembering definitions

Purpose To learn the meaning of key terms

Instructions Pair a struggling reader with a more proficient reader and ask them to help each other learn the key terms in Section 4. One strategy they might use to remember a term's meaning is to "interview" the term, playing the part of journalists investigating the who, what, where, when, how, and why of a situation.

An example interview question is, "Who are you?" For *capitalism,* the answer might be, "I am an economic system based on private ownership and the investment of wealth for profit." For *joint-stock company,* students might ask, "What do you want?" The answer might be, "I want to pool the wealth of a number of different people for a common purpose, such as colonization of the Americas." By asking, "When did you begin?" or "When were you popular?" students can discover a term's historical context.

Have students apply this strategy to other key terms in the section: *Columbian Exchange, mercantilism,* and *favorable balance of trade.*

Analyzing Key Concepts

Mercantilism

Under the mercantilist system, the economy was strictly regulated by the government. This regulation extended to a country's colonies. For instance, Britain forbade American colonies to manufacture certain items. Later it required that all American ships pass through British ports on the way to their final destinations. This practice allowed Britain to collect a duty on American shipping.

SKILLBUILDER Answer
Identifying Problems and Solutions
by establishing a colony that could provide gold or a raw material that France could turn into a manufactured item and sell to other countries

Tip for Struggling Readers

Mercantilism comes from the word *mercantile,* which refers to anything having to do with merchants.

The Growth of Mercantilism
10.3.6

Critical Thinking

- Why were strong navies important to European mercantilism? *(Possible Answer: They protected ships engaged in trade or the transporting of wealth from colonies.)*
- Why was self-sufficiency so important to a country practicing mercantilism? *(It minimized the amount a country had to import, contributing to a favorable balance of trade.)*

> Analyzing Key Concepts

Mercantilism

As you have read, mercantilism was an economic theory practiced in Europe from the 16th to the 18th centuries. Economists of the period believed that a country's power came from its wealth. Thus, a country would do everything possible to acquire more gold, preferably at the expense of its rivals. A mercantilist country primarily sought gold in two ways: establishing and exploiting colonies, and establishing a favorable balance of trade with a rival country. In the example to the right, England is the home country, America is England's colony, and France is England's rival.

1 **England** wants gold.
2 **England** establishes a colony: **America.**
3 **America** does not have gold, but can produce cotton.
4 **England** buys cotton cheap and does not allow **America** to produce cloth.
5 **England** sells finished cloth to **America,** and to England's rival, France.
6 **England** gets gold and depletes **France's** gold reserves.

SKILLBUILDER: Interpreting Charts
Identifying Problems and Solutions Under the mercantilism model, how might France try to acquire gold and become more powerful than England?

In Europe during the 1500s and 1600s, that common purpose was American colonization. It took large amounts of money to establish overseas colonies. Moreover, while profits may have been great, so were risks. Many ships, for instance, never completed the long and dangerous ocean voyage. Because joint-stock companies involved numerous investors, the individual members paid only a fraction of the total colonization cost. If the colony failed, investors lost only their small share. If the colony thrived, the investors shared in the profits. It was a joint-stock company that was responsible for establishing Jamestown, England's first North American colony. (B)

MAIN IDEA
Making Inferences
(B) Why would a joint-stock company be popular with investors in overseas colonies?

B. Answer because they paid only a fraction of the total colonization cost

The Growth of Mercantilism

During this time, the nations of Europe adopted a new economic policy known as **mercantilism**. The theory of mercantilism (shown above) held that a country's power depended mainly on its wealth. Wealth, after all, allowed nations to build strong navies and purchase vital goods. As a result, the goal of every nation became the attainment of as much wealth as possible.

DIFFERENTIATING INSTRUCTION: GIFTED AND TALENTED STUDENTS

Principles of Mercantilism

Class Time 30 minutes

Task Researching and writing a newspaper op-ed piece

Purpose To understand the thinking of 17th-century mercantilists

Instructions Tell students that in addition to Thomas Mun, the British mercantilist quoted on page 141, other leading economic thinkers of the time included the Frenchman Jean-Baptiste Colbert and the Italian Antonio Serra. Ask individual students to research one of these three thinkers on the Internet or in encyclopedias or books. Ask the students to learn enough about their chosen person to be able to write a newspaper editorial in that person's voice outlining the reasons mercantilism is good for their country.

Editorials should reflect an understanding of the basic principles of mercantilism, incorporate the ideas and style of that historical figure, and be well organized and persuasive.

Have students compare the ideas of the three thinkers to see how they all express a similar theory. Ask students if they see any significant differences.

Balance of Trade According to the theory of mercantilism, a nation could increase its wealth and power in two ways. First, it could obtain as much gold and silver as possible. Second, it could establish a **favorable balance of trade**, in which it sold more goods than it bought. A nation's ultimate goal under mercantilism was to become self-sufficient, not dependent on other countries for goods. An English author of the time wrote about the new economic idea of mercantilism:

PRIMARY SOURCE

Although a Kingdom may be enriched by gifts received, or by purchases taken from some other Nations . . . these are things uncertain and of small consideration when they happen. The ordinary means therefore to increase our wealth and treasure is by Foreign Trade, wherein we must ever observe this rule: to sell more to strangers yearly than we consume of theirs in value.

THOMAS MUN, quoted in *World Civilizations*

Mercantilism went hand in hand with colonization, for colonies played a vital role in this new economic practice. Aside from providing silver and gold, colonies provided raw materials that could not be found in the home country, such as wood or furs. In addition to playing the role of supplier, the colonies also provided a market. The home country could sell its goods to its colonies. C

MAIN IDEA

Summarizing

C What role did colonies play in mercantilism?

C. Answer They provided gold and silver, as well as raw materials, and were a market for the home country to sell its goods.

Economic Revolution Changes European Society The economic changes that swept through much of Europe during the age of American colonization also led to changes in European society. The economic revolution spurred the growth of towns and the rise of a class of merchants who controlled great wealth.

The changes in European society, however, only went so far. While towns and cities grew in size, much of Europe's population continued to live in rural areas. And although merchants and traders enjoyed social mobility, the majority of Europeans remained poor. More than anything else, the economic revolution increased the wealth of European nations. In addition, mercantilism contributed to the creation of a national identity. Also, as Chapter 5 will describe, the new economic practices helped expand the power of European monarchs, who became powerful rulers.

SECTION 4 ASSESSMENT

TERMS & NAMES 1. For each term or name, write a sentence explaining its significance.

• Columbian Exchange • capitalism • joint-stock company • mercantilism • favorable balance of trade

USING YOUR NOTES

2. Which effect do you think had the most impact on history? (10.3.6)

Food/ Livestock/ Disease	Place of Origin	Effect
Potato		
Horse		
Smallpox		

MAIN IDEAS

3. What were some of the food items that traveled from the Americas to the rest of the world? (10.4.1)
4. What food and livestock from the rest of the world traveled to the Americas? (10.4.1)
5. What were some of the effects on European society of the economic revolution that took place in the 16th and 17th centuries? (10.4.1)

CRITICAL THINKING & WRITING

6. **MAKING INFERENCES** Why were colonies considered so important to the nations of Europe? (10.4.1)
7. **DRAWING CONCLUSIONS** Why might establishing overseas colonies have justified high profits for those who financed the colonies? (10.3.6)
8. **COMPARING** What were some positive and negative consequences of the Columbian Exchange? (10.3.6)
9. **WRITING ACTIVITY** ECONOMICS Do you think the economic changes in Europe during the American colonization era qualify as a revolution? Why or why not? Support your opinions in a two-paragraph **essay.** (Writing 2.4.a)

CONNECT TO TODAY **MAKING A POSTER**

Research one crop that developed in the Americas (such as corn or potatoes) and its impact on the world today. Show your findings in a **poster.** (Writing 2.3.d)

More About . . .

Colonies

Colonies were considered, in part, a dumping ground for Europeans who did not fit in at home. The British poet John Donne told the Virginia Company, a joint-stock company, in 1622, "[Jamestown] shall redeem many a wretch from the jaws of death, from the hands of the executioner . . . It shall sweep your streets and wash your doors from idle persons and the children of idle persons, and employ them."

3 ASSESS

SECTION 4 ASSESSMENT

Have students take turns leading the class. They can ask individual classmates to answer the questions in the Assessment and have other students determine whether the answers are correct.

Formal Assessment

• Section Quiz, p. 73

4 RETEACH

Have students make a two-column chart listing the various items that passed from west to east and from east to west in the Columbian Exchange. Then use the Visual Summary to review this section and chapter.

Critical Thinking Transparencies

• CT56 Chapter 4 Visual Summary

In-Depth Resources: Unit 1

• Reteaching Activity, p. 102

ANSWERS

1. Columbian Exchange, p. 137 • capitalism, p. 139 • joint-stock company, p. 139 • mercantilism, p. 140 • favorable balance of trade, p. 141
2. **Sample Answer:** Potato, Americas, nourished millions; Horse, Europe, transformed transportation; Smallpox, Europe, killed millions. Greatest impact—Potatoes, because people still eat them.
3. **Possible Answers:** potatoes, corn, tomatoes, peppers
4. **Possible Answers:** bananas, coffee, onions, cattle, sheep, pigs, horses
5. growth of towns and rise of the merchant class; more social mobility; European nations wealthier
6. **Possible Answer:** provided precious metals, raw materials, and markets for European goods, promoting favorable balance of trade for European nations
7. Investors took on many risks.
8. Positive—different foods, both plant and animal, that increased variety of diet and improved nutrition. Negative—warfare, disease.
9. **Rubric** Essays should
   • include examples of economic changes.
   • provide facts to support opinions.

CONNECT TO TODAY

Rubric Posters should provide
• relevant illustrations.
• supporting captions and text.
• statistics about the crop's impact.

TERMS & NAMES

1. conquistador, p. 120
2. *encomienda*, p. 123
3. Jamestown, p. 128
4. French and Indian War, p. 130
5. Atlantic slave trade, p. 133
6. triangular trade, p. 134
7. Columbian Exchange, p. 137
8. mercantilism, p. 140

MAIN IDEAS

Answers will vary.

9. to seek an alternative trade route to Asia
10. to enrich Spain, to colonize the land, to convert Native Americans to Christianity
11. The Spanish abused the natives and tried to destroy their culture.
12. sugar and tobacco
13. The English took control of the eastern half of the United States.
14. Native Americans dying; Africans experienced at farming, had built up some immunity to disease, were unfamiliar with the land and could not blend in with the white population, so were less likely to escape
15. Slaves were crammed into the bottom of the boat, where they lived amid their own waste and suffered from disease, beatings, and poor food.
16. African slaves resisted by preserving their cultural heritage, sabotaging work efforts, running away, and forming armed rebellions.
17. inexpensive and nutritious and thus improved diets throughout Europe and Asia
18. Mercantilism held that a country's true power was measured by its wealth, which it acquired by obtaining as much gold and silver as possible and by establishing a favorable balance of trade.

Chapter 4 Assessment

TERMS & NAMES

For each term or name below, briefly explain its connection to the Atlantic world from 1492 to 1800.

1. conquistador
2. *encomienda*
3. Jamestown
4. French and Indian War
5. Atlantic slave trade
6. triangular trade
7. Columbian Exchange
8. mercantilism

MAIN IDEAS

Spain Builds an American Empire Section 1 (pages 119–126)

9. Why did Columbus set sail westward? (10.4.2)
10. What were three goals of the Spanish in the Americas? (10.4.3)
11. Why did Popé lead a rebellion against the Spanish? (10.4.3)

European Nations Settle North America Section 2 (pages 127–131)

12. What did the Europeans mostly grow in their Caribbean colonies? (10.4.1)
13. What was the result of the French and Indian War? (10.1.2)

The Atlantic Slave Trade Section 3 (pages 132–136)

14. What factors led European colonists to use Africans to resupply their labor force? (10.4.3)
15. What were the conditions on board a slave ship? (10.1.2)
16. What were several ways in which enslaved Africans resisted their treatment in the Americas? (10.1.2)

The Columbian Exchange and Global Trade Section 4 (pages 137–141)

17. Why was the introduction of corn and potatoes to Europe and Asia so significant? (HI 1)
18. What was the economic policy of mercantilism? (10.4.1)

CRITICAL THINKING

1. **USING YOUR NOTES**
Use the chart to identify which nation sponsored each explorer and the regions he explored. (10.4.2)

Explorer	Nation	Regions
Cabral		
Magellan		
Cartier		

2. **DRAWING CONCLUSIONS**
EMPIRE BUILDING What factors helped the Europeans conquer the Americas? Which was the most important? Why? (10.4.3)

3. **RECOGNIZING EFFECTS**
ECONOMICS Explain the statement, "Columbus's voyage began a process that changed the world forever." Consider all the peoples and places American colonization affected economically. (HI 1)

4. **COMPARING AND CONTRASTING**
CULTURAL INTERACTION What might have been some of the differences in the Europeans' and Native Americans' views of colonization? (10.4.3)

5. **SYNTHESIZING**
How did enslaved Africans help create the societies in the New World? (REP 4)

VISUAL SUMMARY

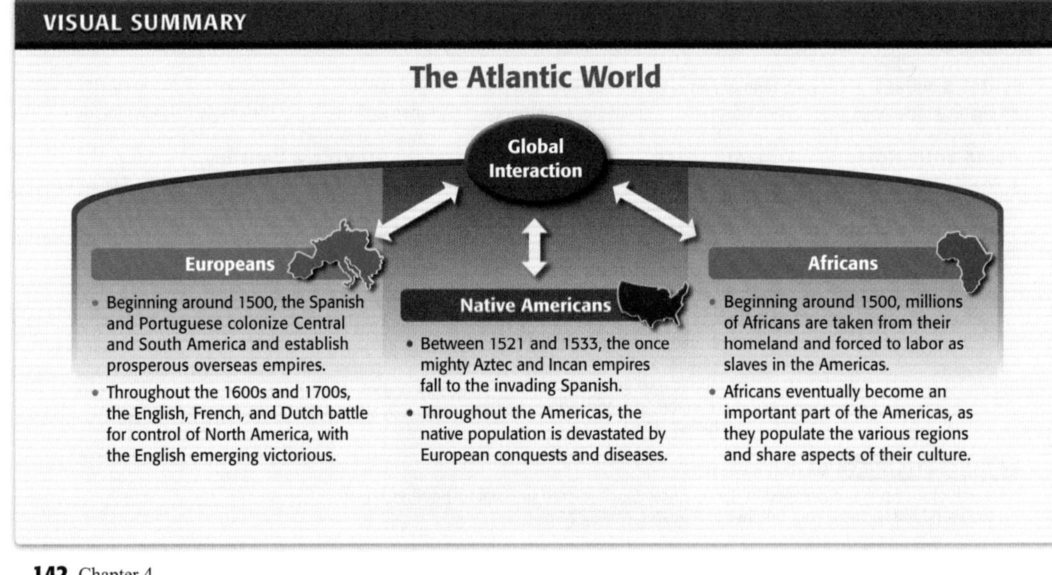

The Atlantic World
Global Interaction
Europeans
• Beginning around 1500, the Spanish and Portuguese colonize Central and South America and establish prosperous overseas empires.
• Throughout the 1600s and 1700s, the English, French, and Dutch battle for control of North America, with the English emerging victorious.
Native Americans
• Between 1521 and 1533, the once mighty Aztec and Incan empires fall to the invading Spanish.
• Throughout the Americas, the native population is devastated by European conquests and diseases.
Africans
• Beginning around 1500, millions of Africans are taken from their homeland and forced to labor as slaves in the Americas.
• Africans eventually become an important part of the Americas, as they populate the various regions and share aspects of their culture.

CRITICAL THINKING

Answers will vary.

1. Cabral—Portugal/Brazil. Magellan—Spain/Pacific Ocean, Philippines, crew circled the globe. Cartier—France/St. Lawrence River, Montreal.
2. Factors—disease, superior weaponry, aid from native allies. Most important—Disease, because it wiped out much of the native population of the Americas.
3. After Columbus, Native American civilizations declined while Europeans prospered. New foods, plants, animals, and diseases spread to peoples of both hemispheres.
4. Europeans probably positive—they gained land and property and the opportunity to start a new life with more than they had in Europe. Native Americans probably negative—it deprived them of their property, freedom, and even, in some cases, health and life.
5. Enslaved Africans made economic, political, cultural, and religious contributions to American societies.

Use the quotation and your knowledge of world history to answer questions 1 and 2.
Additional Test Practice, pp. S1–S33

PRIMARY SOURCE

Where there is a vacant place, there is liberty for . . . [Christians] to come and inhabit, though they neither buy it nor ask their leaves. . . . Indeed, no nation is to drive out another without special commission from Heaven . . . unless the natives do unjustly wrong them, and will not recompense the wrongs done in a peaceable fort [way]. And then they may right themselves by lawful war and subdue the country unto themselves.

JOHN COTTON, from *"God's Promise to His Plantation"*

1. What do you think Native Americans might have said about Cotton's statement that America was a "vacant place"? (10.4.3)
   A. agreed that the continent was largely empty
   B. discussed development plans with him
   C. pointed out that they inhabited the land
   D. offered to sell the land to him

2. How might the last part of Cotton's statement have helped the Puritans justify taking land from the Native Americans? (10.4.3)
   A. Puritans could claim natives had wronged them.
   B. Natives could claim Puritans had wronged them.
   C. Puritans believed war was wrong in all circumstances.
   D. Native Americans were willing to negotiate their grievances.

Use the Aztec drawing below and your knowledge of world history to answer question 3.

3. How does the artist depict the clash of Aztec and Spanish cultures? (CST 3)
   A. meeting to negotiate peace
   B. meeting as warriors
   C. engaging in a sports competition
   D. meeting as friends

INTEGRATED TECHNOLOGY
TEST PRACTICE Go to **classzone.com**
- Diagnostic tests
- Strategies
- Tutorials
- Additional practice

ALTERNATIVE ASSESSMENT

1. **Interact *with* History** (10.4.3)
   On page 118 you examined the choices some Native Americans faced during the invasion by Spanish conquistadors. Now that you have read the chapter, rethink the choice you made. If you chose to side with the Spaniards, would you now change your mind? Why? If you decided to fight with the Aztecs, what are your feelings now? Discuss your thoughts and opinions with a small group.

2.  **WRITING ABOUT HISTORY** (Writing 2.1.e)
   An English colony would have looked strange and different to a Native American of the time. Write a **paragraph** describing an English colony of the 17th century. In your paragraph, provide details about the following:
   - clothes
   - food
   - shelter
   - weapons

INTEGRATED TECHNOLOGY

Participating in a WebQuest (Writing 2.3.b)

Introduction The Columbian Exchange marked the beginning of worldwide trade. Imagine that you are an exporter of a product and want to know how tariffs will affect your sales in various countries.

Task Collect and organize data about a particular product, including how much of the product various countries import and the tariff each country imposes.

Process and Resources With a team of four other students, use the Internet to research your product. Internet keyword: *customs tariffs various countries.* Identify at least five countries that import the product. Organize your findings in a spreadsheet.

Evaluation and Conclusion How did this project contribute to your understanding of global trade? How do you think tariffs will affect demand for your product in each country?

STANDARDS-BASED ASSESSMENT

1. Letter **C** is correct. Letter **A** is incorrect because millions of Native Americans inhabited the land. Letter **B** is incorrect because neither side was inclined to cooperate. Letter **D** is incorrect because Native Americans did not believe that land could be privately owned.
2. Letter **A** is correct. Letter **B** is incorrect because if the Native Americans had been wronged, this would hardly justify Puritans seizing their land. Letter **C** is incorrect because there is nothing in the passage that suggests Puritans believed war could never be justified. Letter **D** is incorrect because if Native Americans had been willing to negotiate their grievances, then the Puritans would not have been justified.
3. Letter **B** is correct. Letter **A** is incorrect because both sides are armed. Letter **C** is incorrect because both sides are clearly about to fight. Letter **D** is incorrect because friends don't use weapons against each other.

Formal Assessment
- Chapter Test, Forms A, B, and C, pp. 74–85

California Test Generator CD-ROM
- Chapter Tests, Forms A, B, and C (English and Spanish)

ALTERNATIVE ASSESSMENT

1. **Possible Answers:** Students who originally chose to side with the Spaniards may now say that the Spaniards were cruel and unjust in their treatment of Native Americans. Others may say their decision to fight for the Aztecs was unwise, because they were doomed, in any event, by European diseases.
2. **Rubric** Paragraphs should
   - provide details about clothes, food, shelter, and weapons.
   - use standard grammar and punctuation.

INTEGRATED TECHNOLOGY

Rubric Spreadsheets should
- clearly mark the journey of the product around the world.
- note which countries export and which import the product.
- note the tariffs imposed on the product.

LESSON PLAN

OBJECTIVES

- Explain how different types of government function.
- Compare the characteristics of four governments.

1 FOCUS & MOTIVATE

Ask the class to think of ways in which the United States might be different if it were governed in a totally different way. What if our country was ruled by a monarch who inherited his or her power? What if the military ruled the country? Spend five to ten minutes writing some of the class's ideas on the board.

2 INSTRUCT

Critical Thinking

- Which government's people might have been most likely to be devoted to their ruler? Why? *(Possible Answer: The Inca people may have been more devoted to their ruler because his basis of authority was an extension of their religion.)*

SKILLBUILDER Answer

Drawing Conclusions *Possible Answer*: Most rulers stayed in power through military might. Military power allowed them to control other aspects of society. Only in Italy was financial power the source of political power.

Four Governments

In Unit 1, you studied how cultures around the world organized and governed themselves. The next six pages focus on four of those governments—the Incan Empire, Italian city-states, Tokugawa Japan, and the Ottoman Empire. How they functioned and the physical symbols they used to communicate their power are important themes. The chart below identifies some key characteristics of the four different governments, and the map locates them in time and place. Take notes on the similarities and differences between the four governments.

CALIFORNIA STANDARDS

10.1.2 Trace the development of the Western political ideas of the rule of law and illegitimacy of tyranny, using selections from Plato's *Republic* and Aristotle's *Politics*.

HI 1 Students show the connections, causal and otherwise, between particular historical events and larger social, economic, and political trends and developments.

Key Characteristics

	Incan Empire	Italian City-States	Tokugawa Japan	Ottoman Empire
Title of Ruler	• Inca	• varied by city: some had title of nobility, others of an elected position	• Shogun; emperor was a figurehead only	• Sultan
Ruling Structure	• monarchical	• oligarchic	• militaristic	• bureaucratic
Basis of Authority	• ruler believed to be descendant of the Sun god	• inheritance or social status supported by financial influence	• absolute loyalty and devoted service of samurai to their daimyo	• military power
Distinctive Feature of Government	• Officials reported from the village level up to the king. • Members of an ethnic group, or *mitimas,* were moved from their homes to other areas to increase agricultural output or put down rebellions. • Children of Inca, local officials, and some others were taken to Cuzco for training.	• Power was in the hands of the ruling family or of a few wealthy families of bankers and merchants. • Many cities had constitutions and elected assemblies with little power.	• Daimyo were the shogun's vassals and local administrators. • Shogun controlled daimyo's marriage alliances and the number of samurai each had. • To ensure cooperation, daimyo's families were held hostage at court while daimyos administered their home regions.	• Sultan owned everything of value (such as land and labor); his bureaucracy was in charge of managing and protecting it. • Members of the bureaucracy derived status from the sultan but were his slaves along with their families. • Heads of *millets* governed locally.

SKILLBUILDER: Interpreting Charts
Drawing Conclusions *How did the rulers of most of these governments keep themselves in power?*

Monarchy in the Incan Empire, 1438–1535

The Incan monarchy was different from European monarchies. In the Incan Empire, all people worked for the state, either as farmers, or artisans making cloth, for example. Men also served as road builders, as messengers, or as soldiers. The state provided clothing, food, and any necessities in short supply. Every year, the amount of land every family had was reviewed to make sure it could produce enough food to live on.

SOUTH AMERICA

DIFFERENTIATING INSTRUCTION: GIFTED AND TALENTED STUDENTS

Methods of Governing

Class Time 30 minutes

Task Applying different ruling structures

Purpose To understand how ruling structures affect how governments operate

Divide students into four groups. Assign each group one of the four governments from the chart on this page. Then ask each group to imagine what their school would be like if the student government had the same ruling structure as their assigned government. For instance, what if the student government was made up only of students from wealthy families? What programs might be affected, and how? Who would gain in that type of environment and who would lose? Or, what if the student government was ruled by just one student and only his or her decisions mattered?

If there are any students in the class who are members of student government, ask them to explain to others how the current student government works.

After the groups have had a chance to discuss their ruling structures, have each group present their ideas to the class.

Oligarchy in the Italian City-States, 1000–1870

Oligarchy is government by a small group of people. In Venice, citizens elected a great council, but real power was held by the senate, which made all decisions. Only members of 125 to 150 wealthy and cultured families were eligible for membership.

Militarism in Tokugawa Japan, 1603–1867

A militaristic government is run by the military. All those in power under the Tokugawa shoguns were samurai. As the samurais' work became more administrative than military, the Tokugawa rulers encouraged cultural pursuits such as poetry, calligraphy, and the tea ceremony to keep warlike tendencies in check.

ASIA

Sea of Japan

PACIFIC OCEAN

Bureaucracy in the Ottoman Empire, 1451–1922

A bureaucratic government is organized into departments and offices staffed by workers who perform limited tasks. Because of the size of the empire, the Ottoman bureaucracy required tens of thousands of civil servants. The empire also supported and encouraged the arts.

INDIAN OCEAN

Comparing & Contrasting

1. In what ways did the Incan government resemble the Ottoman bureaucracy?
2. What similarities and differences were there in the way the sultans and shoguns controlled government officials?
3. What characteristic did the ruling class of the Italian city-states and Tokugawa Japan have in common?

145

Comparing & Contrasting

1. *Possible Answer:* Both had a hierarchy of government officials from the local to the palace level who ran the government.
2. *Possible Answers:* Both demanded absolute loyalty. In the Ottoman Empire, all government officials and janissaries were the sultan's personal slaves. In Tokugawa Japan, daimyo were tied to the shogun by the samurai code of loyalty. In Japan, however, the shogun also held the daimyo's families hostage while the daimyo returned home to administer their region.
3. *Possible Answer:* Both took a strong interest in the arts as part of their superior position.

RECOMMENDED RESOURCES

Books for the Teacher

Quataert, Donald. ***The Ottoman Empire, 1700–1922.*** New York: Cambridge UP, 2000.

Gordon, Andrew. ***A Modern History of Japan: From Tokugawa Times to the Present.*** New York: Oxford UP, 2003.

Books for the Student

Malpass, Michael A. ***Daily Life in the Inca Empire.*** Westport, CT: Greenwood, 1996.

McDougal Littell *Nextext.* ***The Renaissance.*** Presents fifteen stories that cover all aspects of the Renaissance.

Videos and Software

The Age of the Shoguns (1600–1868). VHS and DVD. Films for the Humanities and Sciences. 800-257-5126. Examines political structure and classes in the age of the Tokugawa family.

The Renaissance. CD-ROM. Social Studies School Service. 800-421-4246.

Structures of Government

Critical Thinking

- Why might the influence of merchants have grown over time in the Tokugawa government? *(Possible Answer: Merchants may have gained influence as they brought money to the empire.)*
- Why might landowners have had a higher place in the governmental structure of Tokugawa Japan than in the Ottoman government? *(Possible Answer: In the Ottoman Empire, the sultan owned everything, so landowners didn't exist.)*

More About . . .

Shogun

The word *shogun,* loosely translated, means "commander in chief." According to tradition, the first shoguns in Japanese history served under Emperor Sujin in the third century A.D. In order to put down a rebellion, Emperor Sujin sent four armies into the far corners of Japan. The four generals appointed to lead these armies were given the title shogun.

SKILLBUILDER Answers

1. **Clarifying** All *millets* were answerable to the Imperial Council.
2. **Drawing Conclusions** The samurai might be asked to defend opposing interests.

Structures of Government

All of the governments have officials at different levels with varying degrees of power and responsibility. Compare the governmental structure of the Ottoman bureaucracy with that of Tokugawa Shogunate's militaristic government using the charts below.

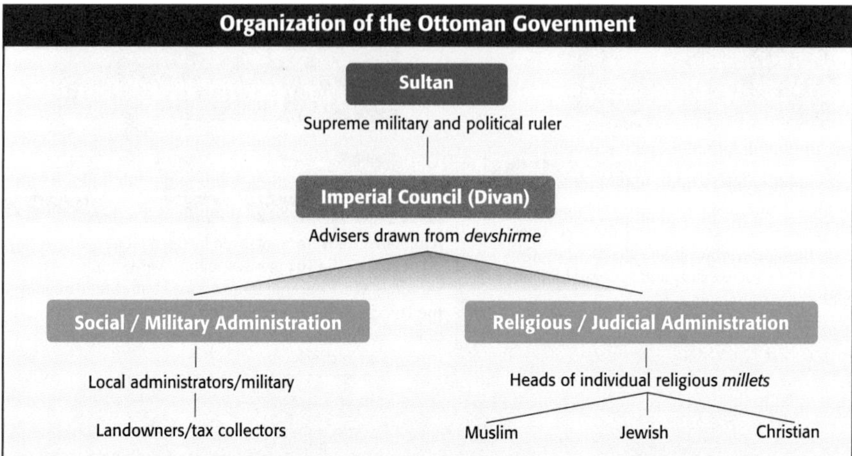

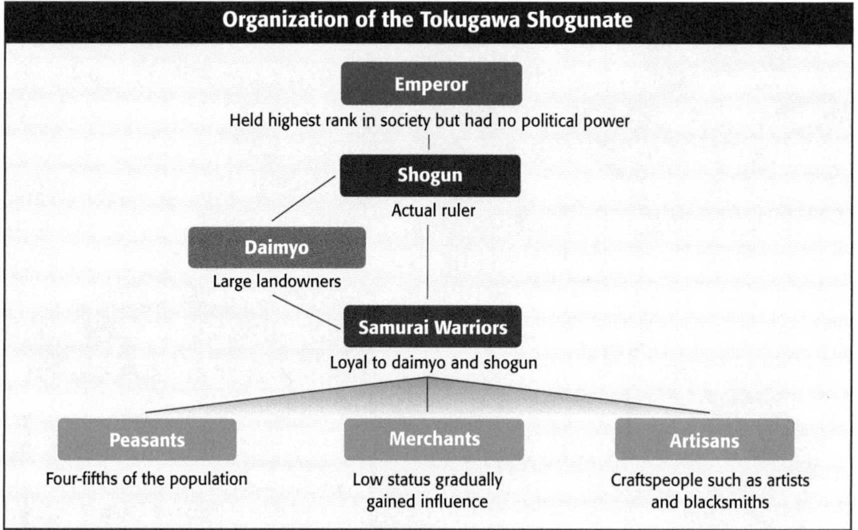

SKILLBUILDER: Interpreting Charts

1. **Clarifying** *To whom were the heads of the millets answerable?*
2. **Drawing Conclusions** *How might the samurai's loyalty to his daimyo conflict with his loyalty to the shogun?*

DIFFERENTIATING INSTRUCTION: STRUGGLING READERS

Analyzing the Structures of Government

Class Time 30 minutes

Task Defining terms

Purpose To increase understanding of the structures of government

Group students into teams of three or four. Have the groups read pages 144–146 of this feature and answer the following questions:

1. In the Ottoman government, who were the advisers drawn from *devshirme*? (*The* devshirme *(p. 76) were males drafted from conquered peoples who were educated, converted to Islam, and trained as soldiers.)*
2. What were religious *millets*? *(religious communities, treated as nations (or* millets, *p. 76). Each* millet *could follow its own religious practices.)*
3. How do we know that the Samurai Warriors were more than just soldiers? *(peasants, merchants, and artisans, all reported to the Samurai.)*

Have the groups share their answers and then create two new questions about the structures of government shown on the chart.

Artifacts of Power

The everyday objects used by members of government often serve a symbolic purpose. Note how the objects below communicated the rank and importance of the person who used them. Examine them and consider the effect they probably had on the people who saw them.

CALIFORNIA STANDARDS

10.1.2 Trace the development of the Western political ideas of the rule of law and illegitimacy of tyranny, using selections from Plato's *Republic* and Aristotle's *Politics*.

HI 1 Students show the connections, causal and otherwise, between particular historical events and larger social, economic, and political trends and developments.

◄ Japanese Sword
Beautiful weapons and armor were symbols of status and power in Tokugawa Japan. Swords were the special weapons of the samurai, who were the only people allowed to carry arms. Daimyo had artisans make fine swords with expensively decorated hilts and scabbards for ceremonial occasions.

◄ Incan Headdress
All of the people in the Incan Empire were required to wear the clothing of their particular ethnic group. The patterns on clothes and headdresses immediately identified a person's place of birth and social rank.

Italian Medici Pitcher ▲
As well as being great patrons of the fine arts, wealthy Italians surrounded themselves with luxurious practical objects. Even ordinary items, like a pitcher, were elaborately made of expensive materials.

Comparing & Contrasting

1. How did the role of the sultan compare with the role of the Japanese emperor?
2. What message were expensive personal items meant to convey?
3. How does a household item like the pitcher differ from a sword or headdress as a symbol of power?

Artifacts of Power

Critical Thinking

- Which of these items reflect the type of government they represent? *(Possible Answer: The Japanese sword is militaristic.)*
- Which items were particularly useful to rulers? Why? *(Possible Answer: Japanese sword used as military weapon. Incan headdress used for identification of population.)*

Comparing & Contrasting

1. *Possible Answer:* Both the Japanese emperor and the sultan had the highest rank in society, but the sultan had supreme control in the Ottoman Empire, whereas the shogun had the power in Tokugawa Japan.
2. *Possible Answer:* The message was that their owners were superior to most people, perhaps deserving of greater respect or privileges.
3. *Possible Answer:* An article like the pitcher would be seen only by those who entered someone's home or office. An article that is worn would be seen by anyone the wearer passed on the street.

DIFFERENTIATING INSTRUCTION: ENGLISH LEARNERS

Analyzing Text

Class Time 30 minutes

Task Understanding artifacts of power

Purpose To understand descriptions of symbolic artifacts

Pair English learners with more proficient readers. Have the pairs of students carefully review the descriptions on this page, paying particular attention to any words or phrases that are unfamiliar to the English learners. Students should spend extra time going over special vocabulary from Unit 1, such as *samurai* and *daimyo*. Some other vocabulary words they should pay attention to are as follows:

- *communicated,* here meaning "conveyed information about."
- *patrons,* which means "people who support something."
- *elaborate,* meaning "intricate and rich in detail."

Have students rewrite the main idea of the descriptions in their own words.

Here is an example for the Incan headdress:

Everyone in the Incan Empire had to wear clothes that showed where they were born and what their social rank was.

Architecture of Government

Critical Thinking

- How might these palaces have been inspiring to the common people of these empires? *(Possible Answer: People may have been inspired to see the grandeur and beauty that their culture could produce.)*
- In what ways might these palaces have had a negative effect on the common population? *(Possible Answer: For the most part, common people could never have attained the degree of wealth displayed by such palaces, so some people may have felt bitterness or resentment toward their rulers.)*

More About . . .

Osaka

Osaka, with a population of more than 2.5 million people, is the third largest city in Japan after Tokyo and Yokohama. With its many canals and rivers, it was called the "Venice of the East." Because of the shortage of land, many of Osaka's shopping centers have been built underground. Today, Osaka Castle houses a museum.

Architecture of Government

A ruler's castle or palace was a luxurious and safe home where he was surrounded by vassals who protected him. It was also a center of government where his administrators carried on their work under his supervision. Castles and palaces are a show of greatness. Large rooms that accommodate many guests demonstrate the ruler's authority over many people. Rich decorations display the ruler's wealth, refinement, and superior rank.

Japanese Palace ►
Osaka Castle was originally built by Toyotami Hideyoshi and has been rebuilt twice since then due to fire. It is surrounded by gardens, and the interior was known for its wall paintings and painted screens. During the Tokugawa period, the city of Osaka was a center of trade for agricultural and manufactured goods. The city was governed directly by the shoguns who owned the castle.

◄ Ottoman Palace
Topkapi Palace in modern Istanbul, Turkey, was the home of the Ottoman sultans. The buildings were built around several courtyards. Within the outer walls were gardens, a school for future officials, the treasury, and an arsenal. Elaborate paintings, woodwork, and tile designs decorated the walls and ceilings of rooms used by the sultan and his high officials.

CONNECTIONS ACROSS TIME AND CULTURES

American Palace

Class Time 45 minutes

Task Analyzing the architecture of government

Purpose To apply knowledge of palaces to United States architecture

Divide the class into small groups and ask them to think about how the White House and the Capitol building in Washington, D.C., serve as centers of government in the United States. Students can use the library or the Internet to research the history of the White House, from its design and decoration to its daily operation. When the groups have gathered enough information, have them create webs that display some key features of the White House and the Capitol building. How do these buildings achieve some of the same purposes as the palaces shown on this page? How do these buildings differ from those palaces? A student web about the White House should mention the Oval Office where the president works, the large grounds, the historic decorations, and the relative simplicity of the house.

Descriptions of Government

The following passages were written by writers who were reflecting not only on the past, but also on places and events they had personally witnessed.

PRIMARY SOURCE

INTERACTIVE

Machiavelli

In this excerpt from *The Discourses,* Italian writer Niccolò Machiavelli discusses six types of government—three good and three bad.

[T]he three bad ones result from the degradation of the other three. . . . Thus monarchy becomes tyranny; aristocracy degenerates into oligarchy; and the popular government lapses readily into licentiousness [lack of restraint].

[S]agacious legislators . . . have chosen one that should partake of all of them, judging that to be the most stable and solid. In fact, when there is combined under the same constitution a prince, a nobility, and the power of the people, then these three powers will watch and keep each other reciprocally in check.

DOCUMENT-BASED QUESTION

Why does Machiavelli think a combined government is the best type of government?

PRIMARY SOURCE

INTERACTIVE

Garcilaso de la Vega

This description of government administration comes from Garcilaso's history of the Inca.

[Local administrators] were obliged each lunar month to furnish their superiors . . . with a record of the births and deaths that had occurred in the territory administered by them. . . .

[E]very two years . . . the wool from the royal herds was distributed in every village, in order that each person should be decently clothed during his entire life. It should be recalled that . . . the people . . . possessed only very few cattle, whereas the Inca's and the Sun's herds were . . . numerous. . . . Thus everyone was always provided with clothing, shoes, food, and all that is necessary in life.

DOCUMENT-BASED QUESTION

What and how did the Incan authorities provide for the common people's needs?

CALIFORNIA STANDARDS

10.1.2 Trace the development of the Western political ideas of the rule of law and illegitimacy of tyranny, using selections from Plato's *Republic* and Aristotle's *Politics.*

REP 4 Students construct and test hypotheses; collect, evaluate, and employ information from multiple primary and secondary sources; and apply it in oral and written presentations.

Comparing & Contrasting

1. How do Osaka Castle and Topkapi Palace project the importance of their owners? Explain.
2. Does Machiavelli favor a system of government that would provide directly for people's needs? Explain.

EXTENSION ACTIVITY

Use the library to get some additional information about the government structure of the Incan Empire and Renaissance Venice. Then draw an organizational chart for each of those governments like the charts on page 146.

149

Descriptions of Government

Critical Thinking

- What do you think Machiavelli's opinion was of the Italian city-states' government? *(Possible Answer: He may have been critical of it, since he lists oligarchy as one of the bad types of government.)*
- Would Italy's government be likely to provide people with common necessities, as the Incan government did? Why or why not? *(Possible Answer: Italy's wealthy ruling class might have been too concerned with its own wealth to share that wealth with the common people.)*

PRIMARY SOURCE

Machiavelli

Answer to Document-Based Question

By having a prince, a nobility, and the people involved, each group prevented the others from taking over and allowing the government to degenerate.

PRIMARY SOURCE

Garcilaso de la Vega

Answer to Document-Based Question

The Incan authorities took an ongoing census that let them know how many people to provide for. The people received food and clothing as needed.

Comparing & Contrasting

1. *Possible Answer:* They are both very large with many architectural details. Only someone wealthy and important could cause them to be built.
2. No, Machiavelli's idea of a good government is one that would give rights to as many people as possible and avoid committing abuses. He does not consider having a welfare state.

EXTENSION ACTIVITY

Rubric Student charts should

- show the structure of the governments of the Incan Empire and of Renaissance Venice.
- display all information clearly.
- use a structure similar to the charts on page 580.

INTEGRATED TECHNOLOGY

Interactive The primary sources on this page are available in an interactive format on the eEdition. Students can hear the sources read aloud and can get help with vocabulary and background information.

Absolutism to Revolution 1500–1900

Storming of the Bastille, July 14, 1789

The French Revolution began less than six years after the end of the United States War of Independence. The beginning of the Revolution is usually associated with the storming of the Bastille on July 14, 1789.

The Bastille was a medieval fortress in eastern Paris, with 100-foot-high towers and walls and an 80-foot moat. In the 17th and 18th centuries, French kings began using the fortress as a state prison. The enormous fortress soon came to symbolize the despotism of France's Bourbon monarchy.

The painting at right, by an unknown artist, depicts the conclusion of the events of July 14. Trouble began when a mob approached the Bastille to demand the arms and ammunition stored there. When troops guarding the Bastille resisted, the attackers captured the prison and liberated the seven prisoners held there.

In the bottom right of the painting, French soldiers are arresting the Bastille's governor. (Many soldiers had deserted to join in the attack.) Later, a mob beheaded the governor and marched around Paris with his head mounted on a pike.

Shortly after the Bastille's fall, the revolutionary government ordered its demolition. Today, in the Place de la Bastille, the "July Column" (which actually celebrates a different revolution) marks the site of the former prison.

UNIT 2

On July 14, 1789, an angry French mob attacked the Bastille, a state prison in Paris, because they were looking for arms and gunpowder. The capture of this prison is considered the beginning of the French Revolution.

Comparing & Contrasting

Political Revolutions

In Unit 2, you will learn that new ideas about human rights and government led to political revolutions in many countries during the late 1700s and the 1800s. At the end of the unit, you will have a chance to compare and contrast those revolutions. (See pages 272–277.)

151

Previewing the Unit

This unit examines the struggles of people in Europe and the Americas who seek to build their own nations and create new forms of government.

Power and Authority The years 1500 to 1800 mark the era of absolute monarchs in Europe. Although in some countries monarchs have vast power and wealth, constitutional law is already limiting royal power in England and the Netherlands toward the end of the 1500s.

Science and Technology The Enlightenment ushers in a new age of discovery and inquiry. This movement influences the American Revolution and the resulting creation of a democratic federal government.

Revolution Revolution sweeps through France, overthrowing the monarchy. Instead of creating a democracy, however, France embraces Napoleon, who tries to conquer most of Europe. After Napoleon's downfall, Europe enjoys a brief period of peace and stability.

Nationalism spurs Germany, Italy, and several Latin American nations to forge their own political identities in the 1800s.

Comparing & Contrasting

Tell students that the unit feature on pages 272–277 will help them compare revolutions through time lines, charts, and primary source documents. Studying the causes, characteristics, and effects of revolutions will help students synthesize the information in Unit 2.

CHAPTER 5 PLANNING GUIDE

Absolute Monarchs in Europe, 1500–1800

CHAPTER RESOURCES	COPYMASTERS	ASSESSMENT
CHAPTER OVERVIEW Several countries in Europe came under the control of absolute monarchs, and Parliament challenged the monarch's authority in Great Britain.	**In-Depth Resources: Unit 2** • Building Vocabulary, p. 6 **Chapters in Brief** (in English and Spanish) **Block Schedule Pacing Guide**	**Chapter Assessment,** pp. 184–185 **Formal Assessment** • Chapter Tests, Forms A, B, and C, pp. 91–102 **Test Generator** **Integrated Assessment Book** **Online Test Practice**
SECTION 1 **Spain's Empire and European Absolutism** pp. 155–161 **OBJECTIVE** Describe Spain's empire and the growth of absolute monarchy in Europe.	**In-Depth Resources: Unit 2** • Guided Reading, p. 1 • Reteaching Activity, p. 20 **Reading Study Guide,** p. 51	**Section 1 Assessment,** p. 161 **Formal Assessment** • Section Quiz, p. 86 **California Daily Standards Practice Transparencies,** TT75
SECTION 2 **The Reign of Louis XIV** pp. 162–168 **OBJECTIVE** Describe the reign of Louis XIV and the power struggles in Europe.	**In-Depth Resources: Unit 2** • Guided Reading, p. 2 • Primary Source, p. 10 • Literature: from *The Cat and King,* p. 14 • Reteaching Activity, p. 21 **Reading Study Guide,** p. 53	**Section 2 Assessment,** p. 168 **Formal Assessment** • Section Quiz, p. 87 **California Daily Standards Practice Transparencies,** TT76
SECTION 3 **Central European Monarchs Clash** pp. 169–173 **OBJECTIVE** Summarize the Thirty Years' War, and the formation of central European states.	**In-Depth Resources: Unit 2** • Guided Reading, p. 3 • Geography Application, p. 8 • History Makers: Maria Theresa, p. 17 • Reteaching Activity, p. 22 **Reading Study Guide,** p. 55	**Section 3 Assessment,** p. 173 **Formal Assessment** • Section Quiz, p. 88 **California Daily Standards Practice Transparencies,** TT77
SECTION 4 **Absolute Rulers of Russia** pp. 174–179 **OBJECTIVE** Describe the Russian state and the rule of Peter the Great.	**In-Depth Resources: Unit 2** • Guided Reading, p. 4 • Skillbuilder Practice, p. 7 • Primary Source: Peter the Great, p. 11 • Reteaching Activity, p. 23 **Reading Study Guide,** p. 57	**Section 4 Assessment,** p. 177 **Formal Assessment** • Section Quiz, p. 89 **California Daily Standards Practice Transparencies,** TT78
SECTION 5 **Parliament Limits the English Monarchy** pp. 180–183 **OBJECTIVE** Explain the conflicts that led to changes to the English political system.	**In-Depth Resources: Unit 2** • Guided Reading, p. 5 • Primary Sources, pp. 12–13 • History Makers: William of Orange, p. 18 • Connections Across Time/Cultures, p. 19 • Reteaching Activity, p. 24 **Reading Study Guide,** p. 59	**Section 5 Assessment,** p. 183 **Formal Assessment** • Section Quiz, p. 90 **California Daily Standards Practice Transparencies,** TT79

INTEGRATED TECHNOLOGY

- eEdition Plus Online
- EasyPlanner Plus Online
- eTest Plus Online

 **Audio CDs**
- Voices from the Past
- Reading Study Guides

CD-ROMs
- eEdition
- Power Presentations
- EasyPlanner
- Electronic Library of Primary Sources
- Test Generator

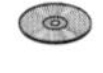 **eEdition CD-ROM**

Geography Transparencies

- GT21 Hapsburg Europe, 1560

World Art and Cultures Transparencies
- AT45 Banquet of Haarlem's Civil Guard
- AT48 *The Astronomer,* Vermeer

 **classzone.com**

eEdition CD-ROM

Electronic Library of Primary Sources
- Two Views of Versailles

 **classzone.com**

eEdition CD-ROM

Electronic Library of Primary Sources
- from *Essay on Forms of Government*

 **classzone.com**

 **eEdition CD-ROM**

 **World Art and Cultures Transparencies**
- AT46 Peter the Great Interrogating Alexei
- AT47 Saint Basil's Cathedral

 **Critical Thinking Transparencies**
- CT21 The Age of Absolute Monarchs

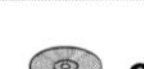 **eEdition CD-ROM**

 **Critical Thinking Transparencies**
- CT57 Chapter 5 Visual Summary

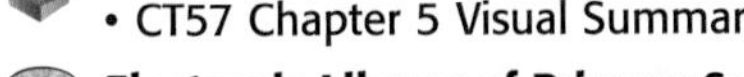
Electronic Library of Primary Sources
- "The Restoration of Charles II"

classzone.com

OVERVIEW OF CALIFORNIA RESOURCES

	Section 1	Section 2	Section 3	Section 4	Section 5
California Reading Toolkit	p. L23	p. L24	p. L25	p. L26	p. L27
California Modified Lesson Plans for English Learners	p. 41	p. 43	p. 45	p. 47	p. 49
California Daily Standards Practice Transparencies	TT15	TT16	TT17	TT18	TT19
California Standards Enrichment Workbook	pp. 19–20	pp. 23–24, 29–30	pp. 55–56	pp. 19–20	pp. 17–18, 23–24
California Standards Planner and Lesson Plans	p. L37	p. L39	p. L41	p. L43	p. L45
California Online Test Practice	classzone.com	classzone.com	classzone.com	classzone.com	classzone.com
California Test Generator CD-ROM					
California Easy Planner CD-ROM					
California eEdition CD-ROM					

Chart Key:

 Copymaster

 Pupil's Edition

 Audio Library

Teacher's Edition

CD-ROM

 Overhead Transparency

 Internet

Block Scheduling

Video

NO TIME?

If you do not have time to teach this chapter in full, assign the **Chapter in Brief** (also available in Spanish).

Previewing Resources for Differentiated Instruction

ENGLISH LEARNERS: Resources in Spanish

In-Depth Resources in Spanish
- Guided Reading (A)
- Skillbuilder Practice: Evaluating Decisions and Courses of Action
- Geography Application: Old Empires and New Powers (B)

Chapters in Brief

Reading Study Guide (C)

Reading Study Guide Audio CD

Test Generator CD-ROM
- Chapter Test, Forms A, B, and C

Plus

Modified Lesson Plans for English Learners

Multi-Language Glossary of Social Studies Terms

(A)
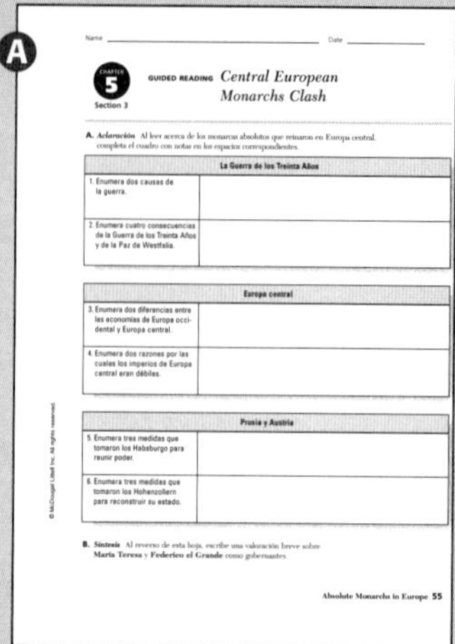
Chapter 5 Section 3 GUIDED READING *Central European Monarchs Clash*

La Guerra de los Treinta Años

Europa central

Prusia y Austria

Absolute Monarchs in Europe 55

(B)
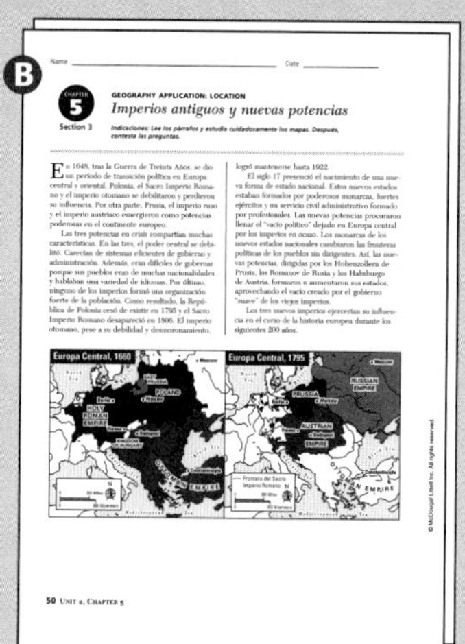
Chapter 5 Section 3 GEOGRAPHY APPLICATION: LOCATION *Imperios antiguos y nuevas potencias*

Europa Central, 1648

Europa Central, 1795

STRUGGLING READERS

In-Depth Resources: Unit 2
- Guided Reading (A)
- Building Vocabulary
- Skillbuilder Practice: Evaluating Decisions and Courses of Action (B)
- Geography Application: Old Empires and New Powers
- Reteaching Activities

Chapters in Brief

Reading Study Guide

Reading Study Guide Audio CD

Formal Assessment
- Chapter Test, Form A (C)

Plus

Reading Toolkit

(A)
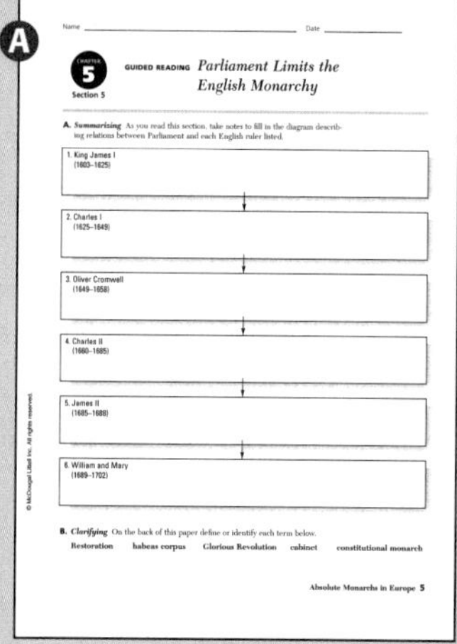
Chapter 5 Section 5 GUIDED READING *Parliament Limits the English Monarchy*

1. King James I (1603–1625)

2. Charles I (1625–1649)

3. Oliver Cromwell (1649–1658)

4. Charles II (1660–1685)

5. James II (1685–1688)

6. William and Mary (1689–1702)

Restoration habeas corpus Glorious Revolution cabinet constitutional monarch

Absolute Monarchs in Europe 5

(B)
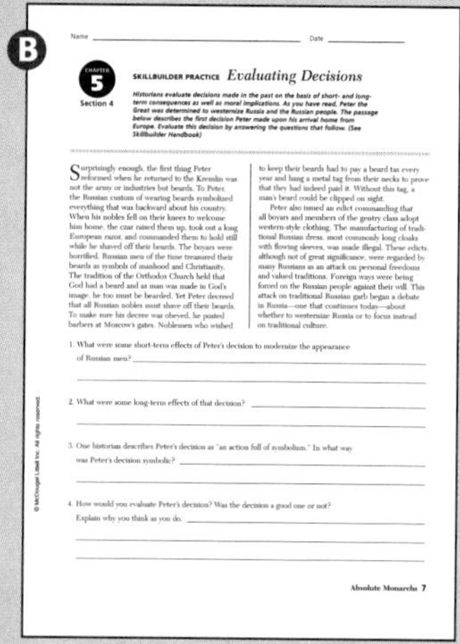
Chapter 5 Section 4 SKILLBUILDER PRACTICE *Evaluating Decisions*

Absolute Monarchs 7

GIFTED AND TALENTED STUDENTS

In-Depth Resources: Unit 2
- Primary Source: Louis XIV's Advice to His Son; Peter the Great's Reforms; from *Diary of Samuel Pepys;* from the English Bill of Rights (A)
- Literature: from *The Cat and the King*
- History Makers: Maria Theresa; William of Orange
- Connections Across Time and Cultures: The Absolute Power of Rulers

Electronic Library of Primary Sources
- "Defeat of the Spanish Armada"
- Two Views of Versailles
- from *Essay on Forms of Government*
- from Letters of Peter the Great (B)
- "The Restoration of Charles II"

Formal Assessment
- Chapter Test, Form C (C)

(A)

Chapter 5 Section 5 PRIMARY SOURCE *from* the English Bill of Rights

The English Bill of Rights, 1689

Research Option

Absolute Monarchs in Europe 13

(B)
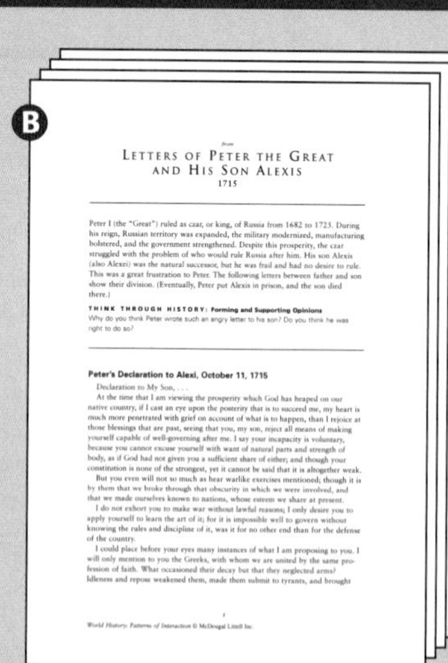
from LETTERS OF PETER THE GREAT AND HIS SON ALEXIS 1715

Peter's Declaration to Alexi, October 11, 1715

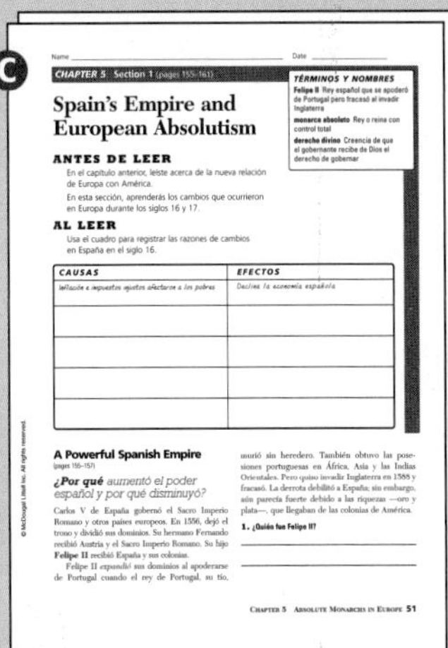

CHAPTER 5 Section 1

Spain's Empire and European Absolutism

ANTES DE LEER

AL LEER

CAUSAS	EFECTOS

A Powerful Spanish Empire

¿Por qué aumentó el poder español y por qué disminuyó?

Activities in the Teacher's Edition for English Learners

- Causes and Effects of Absolutism, p. 160
- Understanding How Louis XIV Came to Power, p. 164
- Political Transition in Central and Eastern Europe, p. 172
- Contrasting Russia and Western Europe, p. 175

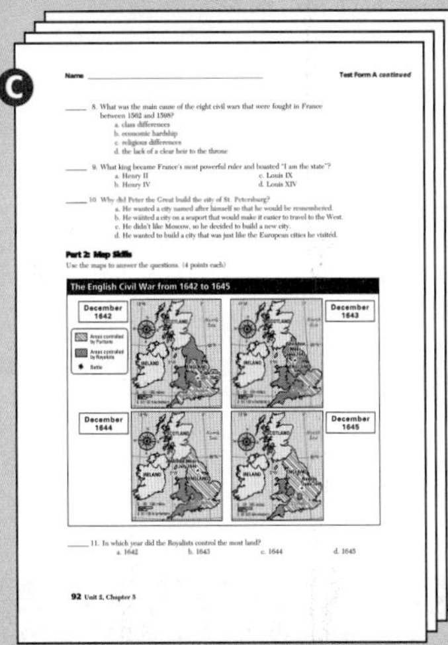

Part 2: Map Skills

The English Civil War from 1642 to 1645

Activities in the Teacher's Edition for Struggling Readers

- Causes of the Spanish Empire's Decline, p. 158
- Montaigne and Descartes, p. 163
- Understanding How States Formed, p. 171
- Creating a Board Game, p. 181

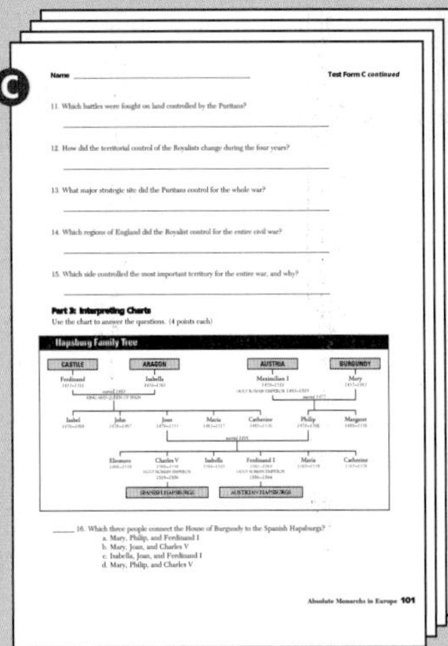

Part 2: Interpreting Charts

Hapsburg Family Tree

Activities in the Teacher's Edition for Gifted and Talented Students

- Comparing the Spanish and English Navies, p. 156
- The War of the Spanish Succession, p. 167
- Researching The Thirty Years' War, p. 170
- The Life and Death of William of Orange, p. 182

INTEGRATED TECHNOLOGY

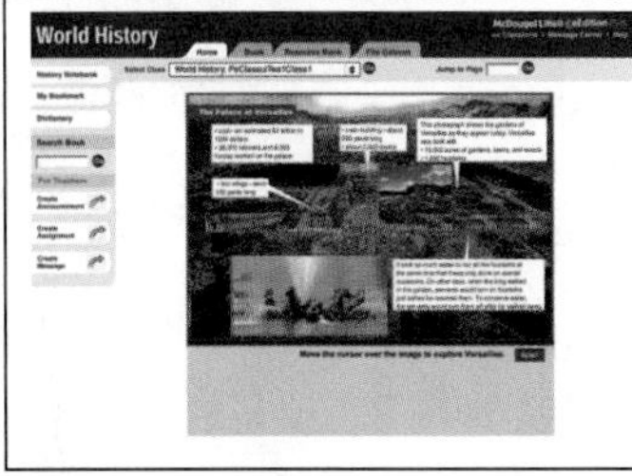

eEdition
- Interactive Visuals
- Interactive Maps
- Interactive Primary Sources

classzone.com
- Research Links
- Internet Activities
- Primary Sources
- Chapter Quiz
- Current Events

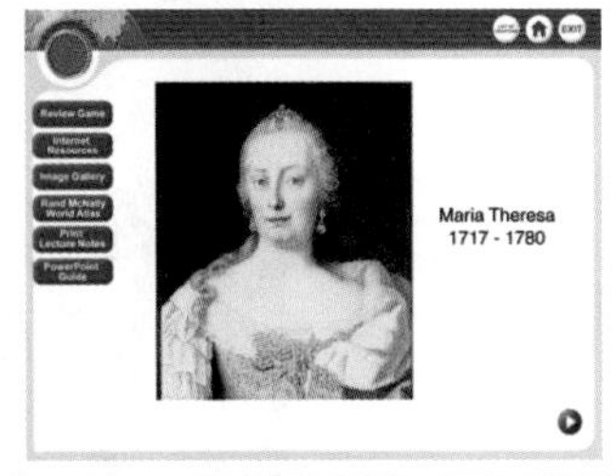

Power Presentations CD-ROM
- Lecture Notes
- Image Gallery
- Chapter Review Game

Critical Thinking Transparencies
- CT21 The Age of Absolute Monarchs
- CT57 Chapter 5 Visual Summary

Geography Transparencies
- GT21 Hapsburg Europe, 1560

World Art and Cultures Transparencies
- AT45 Banquet of the Officers of Haarlem's Civil Guard
- AT46 Peter the Great Interrogating Alexei
- AT47 Saint Basil's Cathedral (A)

Test Practice Transparencies TT75–TT79

Test Generator CD-ROM

EasyPlanner CD-ROM

Voices from the Past Audio CD

Online Test Practice

Electronic Library of Primary Sources

CHAPTER 5 • OBJECTIVE

Study the development of absolute and constitutional monarchies in Europe from 1500 until 1800.

Previewing Main Ideas

Ask students to think about well-known national and world leaders. Then conduct a discussion that explores the scope of and limits to these leaders' power. Ask students to consider both formal and informal checks on these leaders' authority.

Accessing Prior Knowledge

Have students discuss what they already know about absolute monarchs, such as Louis XIV and Peter the Great. Ask how absolute monarchy might differ from other forms of government, such as dictatorship, that also concentrate authority in a single person or group.

Geography *Answers*

POWER AND AUTHORITY Many of these kingdoms surrounded the Holy Roman Empire.

ECONOMICS *Possible Answer:* Frederick the Great begins a war against Austria.

REVOLUTION England and Scotland were most affected.

CHAPTER 5

Absolute Monarchs in Europe, 1500–1800

Previewing Main Ideas

POWER AND AUTHORITY As feudalism declined, stronger national kingdoms in Spain, France, Austria, Prussia, and Russia emerged under the control of absolute rulers.

Geography *Study the map. What large empire was surrounded by many of these national kingdoms?*

ECONOMICS Absolute rulers wanted to control their countries' economies so that they could free themselves from limitations imposed by the nobility. In France, Louis XIV's unrestrained spending left his country with huge debts.

Geography *What other evidence of unrestrained spending by an absolute ruler does the time line suggest?*

REVOLUTION In Great Britain, Parliament and the British people challenged the monarch's authority. The overthrow of the king led to important political changes.

Geography *Study the map and the time line. Which British Stuart lands were most affected by the event occurring in 1649?*

INTEGRATED TECHNOLOGY

eEdition
- Interactive Maps
- Interactive Visuals
- Interactive Primary Sources

INTERNET RESOURCES
Go to classzone.com for:
- Research Links
- Internet Activities
- Primary Sources
- Chapter Quiz
- Maps
- Test Practice
- Current Events

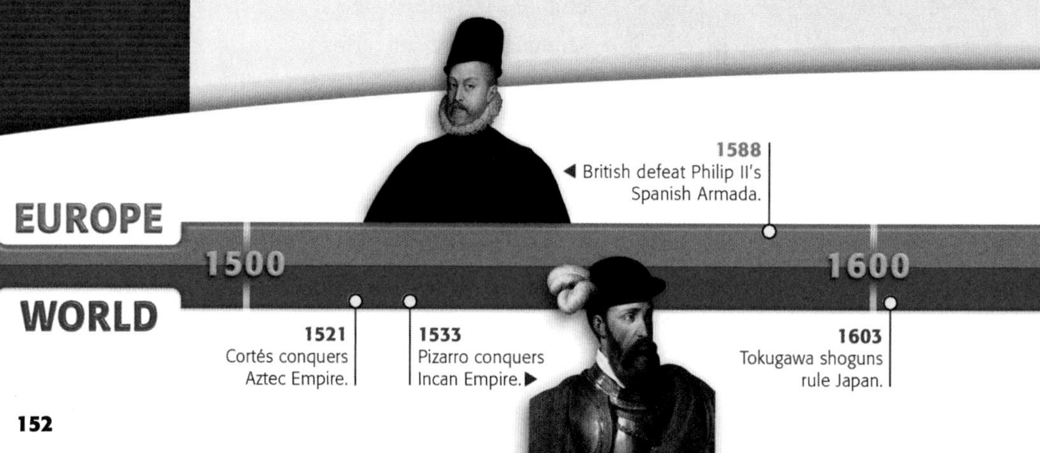

EUROPE
1588
◀ British defeat Philip II's Spanish Armada.
1500
1600
WORLD
1521
Cortés conquers Aztec Empire.
1533
Pizarro conquers Incan Empire.▶
1603
Tokugawa shoguns rule Japan.

152

TIME LINE DISCUSSION

This time line highlights some of Europe's most influential monarchs, including Peter of Russia and Frederick of Prussia.

1. What country conquered the Incan and Aztec empires and saw its Armada defeated in 1588? *(Spain)*
2. While other countries were being ruled by monarchs, which country lost its king? *(England, in 1649)*
3. How long after the beginning of the construction of the Taj Mahal did Louis XIV take power in France? *(about 12 years)*
4. How many decades separate the rise to power of Louis XIV in France and Peter the Great in Russia? *(about five)*
5. How much time passed between the beginning of the Seven Years' War and the American colonies' declaration of independence? *(about 20 years)*

Europe, 1650

0 250 500 Miles
0 250 500 Kilometers
Conic Projection

- Austrian Hapsburg lands
- British Stuart lands
- French Bourbon lands
- Prussian lands
- Russian lands
- Spanish Hapsburg lands
- Boundary of Holy Roman Empire

1631 Shah Jahan orders construction of Taj Mahal. ▶

1643 Louis XIV begins to rule France.

1649 Puritans under Oliver Cromwell (at right) execute English king. ▶

1696 Peter the Great becomes sole czar of Russia.

1700

1756 Prussian king Frederick the Great begins Seven Years' War against Austria.

1776 American colonists declare their independence from England.

1800

153

CHAPTER 5

History from Visuals

Interpreting the Map

Tell students that the idea of region is important to the events covered in this chapter. Ask which European powers are represented in the key. *(Austria, Britain, France, Prussia, Russia, Spain, and the Holy Roman Empire)*

Why might Europe have been a likely center of conflict between powers with territorial ambitions? *(No single power dominated it.)*

Extension Ask students to locate Russia on the map. Discuss the possible benefits and drawbacks of Russia's location in relation to western Europe. How might Russia's location affect its development? *(Possible Answers: Benefits—Russia might be less likely to go to war with, or be invaded by, western European countries. Drawbacks—Russia might be less able to exchange goods and ideas with western European countries. Distance could slow Russia's development.)*

RECOMMENDED RESOURCES

Books for the Teacher

Duffy, James P. and Vincent L. Ricci. ***Czars: Russia's Rulers for More Than One Thousand Years***. New York: Facts on File, 1995.

Massie, Robert K. ***Peter the Great: His Life and World***. New York: Ballantine, 1992. The Pulitzer Prize-winning biography.

Books for the Student

Swisher, Clarice. ***The Glorious Revolution.*** San Diego: Lucent, 1996. How the English Parliament gained supremacy over the monarchy.

De Cervantes, Miguel. ***Don Quixote de la Mancha.*** Trans. Charles Jarvis. Oxford, England: Oxford UP, 1998. Considered the first modern European novel, this classic was published in 1605 and tells the tale of a poor Spanish nobleman.

Videos and Software

The Baroque. VHS. Society for Visual Education, 1992. 800-829-1900.

The Spanish Armada. VHS. Ambrose Video, 1997. 800-526-4663.

The Baroque. CD-ROM. Society for Visual Education. 800-829-1900.

Interact *with* History

Objectives

- Help students imagine what life would be like for people who lived in France during the reign of Louis XIV.
- Consider whether opinions about Louis XIV among his subjects might have been determined in part by their class and economic status.

INTEGRATED TECHNOLOGY

Interactive An interactive version of this feature is available on the eEdition. Students will learn how rulers of different times and cultures have used clothing to express status and authority.

EXAMINING *the* ISSUES

Possible Answers

- People might gain protection and take pride in their country's prestige.
- The rise of powerful foreign enemies, a weak economy, or minority groups in society that identify with foreign powers could weaken an absolute monarch's power.

Discussion

Ask students what they remember about the governments of the Roman, Ottoman, and Carolingian empires. *(The early Romans founded a republic based in what is now Italy that later became a vast empire. The Ottomans established a Muslim empire based in what is now Turkey, and the Carolingians created a Christian empire based in central Europe.)*

In-Depth Resources: Unit 2

- Connections Across Time and Cultures: The Absolute Power of Rulers, p. 19

Interact *with* History

What are the benefits and drawbacks of having an absolute ruler?

You live under the most powerful monarch in 17th-century Europe, Louis XIV of France, shown below. As Louis's subject, you feel proud and well protected because the French army is the strongest in Europe. But Louis's desire to gain lands for France and battle enemies has resulted in costly wars. And he expects you and his other subjects to pay for them.

INTERACTIVE

1 Louis XIV uses his clothing to demonstrate his power and status, as his portrait shows. The gold flower on his robe is the symbol of French kings.

2 Louis's love of finery is apparent not only in his clothing but also in the ornate setting for this painting. As absolute ruler, Louis imposes taxes to pay for the construction of a magnificent new palace and to finance wars.

3 The government of Louis XIV enforces laws and provides security. His sword, scepter, and crown symbolize the power he wields. Yet the French people have no say in what laws are passed or how they are enforced.

EXAMINING *the* ISSUES

- **What might people gain from having a ruler whose power is total, or absolute?**
- **What factors might weaken the power of an absolute monarch?**

As a class, discuss these questions. You may want to refer to earlier rulers, such as those of the Roman, Ottoman, and Carolingian empires. As you read about absolute monarchs in Europe, notice what strengthened and weakened their power.

WHY STUDY THE ABSOLUTE MONARCHS OF EUROPE?

- The experiences of the British under a monarchical system greatly influenced the framers of the U.S. Constitution.
- To this day, the United Kingdom is governed by a constitutional monarchy.
- Absolutism formed the backdrop to some of the key events of later European history, including the French Revolution, Napoleon's rise to power, and the revolutions of 1848.
- Knowledge of European history is key to understanding pivotal events of the 20th century, such as the two world wars, the reemergence of independent republics following the collapse of the Soviet Union in 1991, and the conflicts in the Balkans in the 1990s.
- Many historians consider the Soviet dictatorship to be a continuation of the style of rule in Russia under the tsars.

Marriage of Louis XIV to Marie Thérèse of Austria. Artist unknown

Statue of Louis XIV, Lyon, France

1

Spain's Empire and European Absolutism

MAIN IDEA	WHY IT MATTERS NOW	TERMS & NAMES
ECONOMICS During a time of religious and economic instability, Philip II ruled Spain with a strong hand.	When faced with crises, many heads of government take on additional economic or political powers.	• Philip II • absolute monarch • divine right

SETTING THE STAGE As you learned in Chapter 2, from 1520 to 1566, Suleyman I exercised great power as sultan of the Ottoman Empire. A European monarch of the same period, Charles V, came close to matching Suleyman's power. As the Hapsburg king, Charles inherited Spain, Spain's American colonies, parts of Italy, and lands in Austria and the Netherlands. As the elected Holy Roman emperor, he ruled much of Germany. It was the first time since Charlemagne that a European ruler controlled so much territory.

A Powerful Spanish Empire

A devout Catholic, Charles not only fought Muslims but also opposed Lutherans. In 1555, he unwillingly agreed to the Peace of Augsburg, which allowed German princes to choose the religion for their territory. The following year, Charles V divided his immense empire and retired to a monastery. To his brother Ferdinand, he left Austria and the Holy Roman Empire. His son, **Philip II**, inherited Spain, the Spanish Netherlands, and the American colonies.

Philip II's Empire Philip was shy, serious, and—like his father—deeply religious. He was also very hard working. Yet Philip would not allow anyone to help him. Deeply suspicious, he trusted no one for long. As his own court historian wrote, "His smile and his dagger were very close."

Perhaps above all, Philip could be aggressive for the sake of his empire. In 1580, the king of Portugal died without an heir. Because Philip was the king's nephew, he seized the Portuguese kingdom. Counting Portuguese strongholds in Africa, India, and the East Indies, he now had an empire that circled the globe.

Philip's empire provided him with incredible wealth. By 1600, American mines had supplied Spain with an estimated 339,000 pounds of gold. Between 1550 and 1650, roughly 16,000 tons of silver bullion were unloaded from Spanish galleons, or ships. The king of Spain claimed between a fourth and a fifth of every shipload of treasure as his royal share. With this wealth, Spain was able to support a large standing army of about 50,000 soldiers.

Defender of Catholicism When Philip assumed the throne, Europe was experiencing religious wars caused by the Reformation. However, religious conflict was not new to Spain. The Reconquista, the campaign to drive Muslims from Spain, had been completed only 64 years before. In addition, Philip's great-grandparents

CALIFORNIA STANDARDS

10.1.2 Trace the development of the Western political ideas of the rule of law and illegitimacy of tyranny, using selections from Plato's *Republic* and Aristotle's *Politics*.

CST 3 Students use a variety of maps and documents to interpret human movement, including major patterns of domestic and international migration, changing environmental preferences and settlement patterns, the frictions that develop between population groups, and the diffusion of ideas, technological innovations, and goods.

HI 1 Students show the connections, causal and otherwise, between particular historical events and larger social, economic, and political trends and developments.

HI 3 Students interpret past events and issues within the context in which an event unfolded rather than solely in terms of present-day norms and values.

HI 4 Students understand the meaning, implication, and impact of historical events and recognize that events could have taken other directions.

TAKING NOTES

Clarifying Use a chart to list the conditions that allowed European monarchs to gain power.

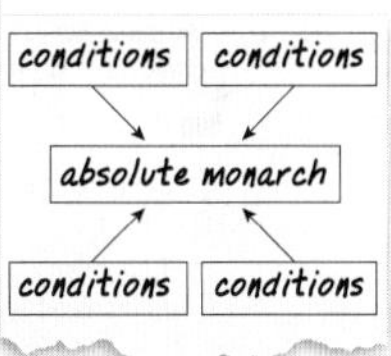

LESSON PLAN

OBJECTIVES

- Describe Spanish power under Philip II.
- Identify major figures from the Golden Age of Spanish art and literature.
- Describe the birth of the Netherlands.
- Explain the origins of absolute monarchy.

1 FOCUS & MOTIVATE

Ask students to think of ways in which the legacy of imperial Spain is felt in the United States today. *(Possible Answer: Spanish is widely spoken here.)*

2 INSTRUCT

A Powerful Spanish Empire
10.1.2

Critical Thinking

- What non-religious factors might have provoked Philip II to send the Armada against England? *(England was a major maritime rival.)*

In-Depth Resources: Unit 2

- Guided Reading, p. 1 (also in Spanish)

CALIFORNIA RESOURCES

California Reading Toolkit, p. L23
California Modified Lesson Plans for English Learners, p. 41
California Daily Standards Practice Transparencies, TT15
California Standards Enrichment Workbook, pp. 19–20
California Standards Planner and Lesson Plans, p. L37
California Online Test Practice
California Test Generator CD-ROM
California Easy Planner CD-ROM
California eEdition CD-ROM

SECTION 1 PROGRAM RESOURCES

ALL STUDENTS

In-Depth Resources: Unit 2
- Guided Reading, p. 1

Formal Assessment
- Section Quiz, p. 86

ENGLISH LEARNERS

In-Depth Resources in Spanish
- Guided Reading, p. 44

Reading Study Guide (Spanish), p. 51
Reading Study Guide Audio CD (Spanish)

STRUGGLING READERS

In-Depth Resources: Unit 2
- Guided Reading, p. 1
- Building Vocabulary, p. 6
- Reteaching Activity, p. 20

Reading Study Guide, p. 51
Reading Study Guide Audio CD

GIFTED AND TALENTED STUDENTS

Electronic Library of Primary Sources
- "Defeat of the Spanish Armada"

INTEGRATED TECHNOLOGY

eEdition CD-ROM
Voices from the Past Audio CD
Power Presentations CD-ROM
Geography Transparencies
- GT21 Hapsburg Europe, 1560

World Art and Cultures Transparencies
- AT45 Banquet of the Officers of Haarlem's Civil Guard
- AT48 *The Astronomer*, Vermeer

classzone.com

History from Visuals

Interpreting the Map

What advantages did the English navy have over the Spanish Armada? *(Possible Answers: English ships did not have to travel as far, replenishing supplies was easier, more familiar with the English Channel)*

Extension Ask students to speculate about the causes of the shipwrecks suffered by the Spanish Armada off the west coast of Ireland. *(Winds may have driven their heavy ships into the coast.)*

SKILLBUILDER Answers

1. **Location** Plymouth
2. **Movement** They wanted to avoid another battle with English warships.

More About . . .

The Defeat of the Spanish Armada

English artillery made an important difference in the sea battle with Spain. More efficient guns and better gunners enabled the English to fire ten rounds for every one fired by the Spanish. The English also used unconventional tactics, such as setting alight explosive-laden ships with no crew and using the wind and currents to send them careering into the tight formations of slow-moving Spanish ships.

Geography Transparencies

- GT21 Hapsburg Europe, 1560

Electronic Library of Primary Sources

- "Defeat of the Spanish Armada"

Defeat of the Spanish Armada, 1588

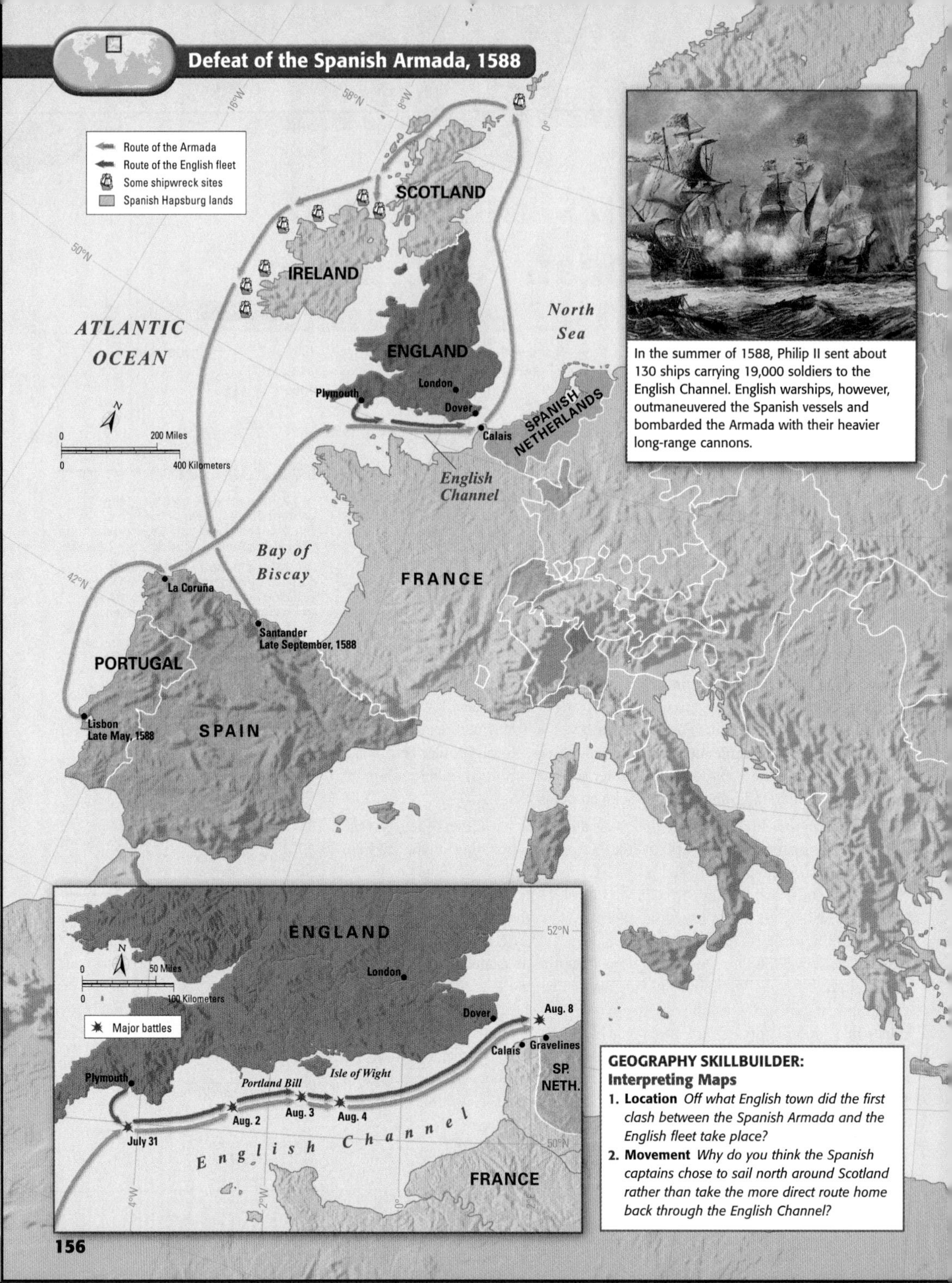

In the summer of 1588, Philip II sent about 130 ships carrying 19,000 soldiers to the English Channel. English warships, however, outmaneuvered the Spanish vessels and bombarded the Armada with their heavier long-range cannons.

GEOGRAPHY SKILLBUILDER: Interpreting Maps

1. **Location** *Off what English town did the first clash between the Spanish Armada and the English fleet take place?*
2. **Movement** *Why do you think the Spanish captains chose to sail north around Scotland rather than take the more direct route home back through the English Channel?*

DIFFERENTIATING INSTRUCTION: GIFTED AND TALENTED STUDENTS

Comparing the Spanish and English Navies

Class Time 35 minutes

Task Making a table of the strengths and weaknesses of the Spanish Armada and the English naval fleet in their battles in the English Channel

Purpose To help students understand why the Spanish were unable to invade England

Instructions Have students use the library or the Internet to gather information on the number of ships, guns, and troops the Spanish and the English had, and the number of casualties and shipwrecks each side suffered when the Spanish entered the English Channel. Have students organize the information in a table as in the example below. The figures students use in the table will be approximate, since historical accounts differ on the precise figures.

	Ships	Guns	Sailors and soldiers	Ships destroyed	Casualties
Spain	125–150	1,100	27,000	60–70	15,000–20,000
England	150–200	2,000	16,000	0	Several thousand (mostly from disease)

Isabella and Ferdinand had used the Inquisition to investigate suspected heretics, or nonbelievers in Christianity.

Philip believed it was his duty to defend Catholicism against the Muslims of the Ottoman Empire and the Protestants of Europe. In 1571, the pope called on all Catholic princes to take up arms against the mounting power of the Ottoman Empire. Philip responded like a true crusader. More than 200 Spanish and Venetian ships defeated a large Ottoman fleet in a fierce battle near Lepanto. In 1588, Philip launched the Spanish Armada in an attempt to punish Protestant England and its queen, Elizabeth I. Elizabeth had supported Protestant subjects who had rebelled against Philip. However, his fleet was defeated. (See map opposite.)

Although this setback seriously weakened Spain, its wealth gave it the appearance of strength for a while longer. Philip's gray granite palace, the Escorial, had massive walls and huge gates that demonstrated his power. The Escorial also reflected Philip's faith. Within its walls stood a monastery as well as a palace. (A)

A. Answer that he was a strong and religious king

MAIN IDEA

Making Inferences

(A) What did Philip want his palace to demonstrate about his monarchy?

Golden Age of Spanish Art and Literature

Spain's great wealth did more than support navies and build palaces. It also allowed monarchs and nobles to become patrons of artists. During the 16th and 17th centuries, Spain experienced a golden age in the arts. The works of two great painters show both the faith and the pride of Spain during this period.

El Greco and Velázquez Born in Crete, El Greco (GREHK•oh) spent much of his adult life in Spain. His real name was Domenikos Theotokopoulos, but Spaniards called him El Greco, meaning "the Greek." El Greco's art often puzzled the people of his time. He chose brilliant, sometimes clashing colors, distorted the human figure, and expressed emotion symbolically in his paintings. Although unusual, El Greco's techniques showed the deep Catholic faith of Spain. He painted saints and martyrs as huge, long-limbed figures that have a supernatural air.

The paintings of Diego Velázquez (vuh•LAHS•kehs), on the other hand, reflected the pride of the Spanish monarchy. Velázquez, who painted 50 years after El Greco, was the court painter to Philip IV of Spain. He is best known for his portraits of the royal family and scenes of court life. Like El Greco, he was noted for using rich colors.

Don Quixote The publication of *Don Quixote de la Mancha* in 1605 is often called the birth of the modern European novel. In this book, Miguel de Cervantes (suhr•VAN•teez) wrote about a poor Spanish nobleman who went a little crazy after reading too many books about heroic knights.

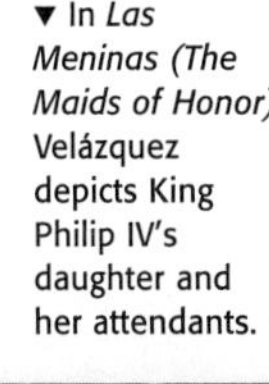

▼ In *Las Meninas (The Maids of Honor),* Velázquez depicts King Philip IV's daughter and her attendants.

Golden Age of Spanish Art and Literature

10.1.2

Critical Thinking

- Why might an artist like El Greco distort human figures rather than paint them realistically? *(Possible Answer: He distorted the figures purposefully to express some idea or emotion.)*
- What artistic limits might an artist such as Velázquez have faced? *(Possible Answer: Velázquez was probably not permitted to paint anything critical of his patron, Philip IV.)*
- Why might readers still take an interest in the 400-year-old novel *Don Quixote? (Possible Answers: The book's style and humor still appeal to readers. Cervantes's themes, such as idealism and materialism, are still relevant.)*

Tip for English Learners

Tell students that the word *air*, in the phrase ". . . long-limbed figures that have a supernatural air," describes the look or appearance of a person, especially as expressive of some personal quality or emotion.

More About . . .

Las Meninas

Point out to students that *Las Meninas* shows Velázquez standing with brush and palette in front of his canvas. Presumably, he is painting a portrait of the king and queen, whose images can be seen in the mirror above their daughter.

CONNECTIONS TO ART

Exploring *Las Meninas*

Class Time 45 minutes

Task Making a poster

Purpose To help students explore the richness and complexity of a great work of art

Instructions Explain to students that there is a large body of writing devoted to explaining Velázquez's *Las Meninas*. Have students use the library or the Internet to explore these analyses and to use the information they find to create a poster. Students should place a reproduction of *Las Meninas* in the center of their posters. They should then use the margins to write short captions that explain the painting's features. Aspects of the painting that students might explore include: the identities of the figures in the painting; the historical significance of specific elements, such as the dwarves; and technical details, such as the painting's composition or Velázquez's use of color and texture. Students might also choose to include background information, such as details of the relationship between Velázquez and Philip IV.

The Spanish Empire Weakens
10.1.2

Critical Thinking

- What measures might Spain have taken to restore its economy? *(Possible Answers: restrict the amount of money in circulation; impose taxes on the rich; rescind expulsion orders to bring back businesspeople; impose price controls)*
- Could Philip II have pursued other policies in the Netherlands that would have resulted in a better outcome? *(Possible Answers: Yes—Rather than forcing Protestants to abandon their faith, he might have respected the practice of Protestantism in the Netherlands. No—Philip believed Protestantism was an abomination; nothing short of its defeat would have satisfied him.)*

Global Impact

Tulip Mania

During the tulip craze, people paid the equivalent of hundreds of dollars for some individual bulbs. Speculation was so rampant that bulbs might be sold and resold several times while still in the ground. The Netherlands is still one of the world's biggest exporters of tulip bulbs.

Hoping to "right every manner of wrong," Don Quixote rode forth in a rusty suit of armor, mounted on a feeble horse. At one point, he mistook some windmills for giants:

PRIMARY SOURCE

He rushed with [his horse's] utmost speed upon the first windmill he could come at, and, running his lance into the sail, the wind whirled about with such swiftness, that the rapidity of the motion presently broke the lance into shivers, and hurled away both knight and horse along with it, till down he fell, rolling a good way off in the field.

MIGUEL DE CERVANTES, *Don Quixote de la Mancha*

Some critics believe that Cervantes was mocking chivalry, the knightly code of the Middle Ages. Others maintain that the book is about an idealistic person who longs for the romantic past because he is frustrated with his materialistic world.

The Spanish Empire Weakens

Certainly, the age in which Cervantes wrote was a materialistic one. The gold and silver coming from the Americas made Spain temporarily wealthy. However, such treasure helped to cause long-term economic problems.

Inflation and Taxes One of these problems was severe inflation, which is a decline in the value of money, accompanied by a rise in the prices of goods and services. Inflation in Spain had two main causes. First, Spain's population had been growing. As more people demanded food and other goods, merchants were able to raise prices. Second, as silver bullion flooded the market, its value dropped. People needed more and more amounts of silver to buy things.

Spain's economic decline also had other causes. When Spain expelled the Jews and Moors (Muslims) around 1500, it lost many valuable artisans and businesspeople. In addition, Spain's nobles did not have to pay taxes. The tax burden fell on the lower classes. That burden prevented them from accumulating enough wealth to start their own businesses. As a result, Spain never developed a middle class.

Global Impact

Tulip Mania

Tulips came to Europe from Turkey around 1550. People went wild over the flowers and began to buy rare varieties. However, the supply of tulips could not meet the demand, and prices began to rise. Soon people were spending all their savings on bulbs and taking out loans so that they could buy more.

Tulip mania reached a peak between 1633 and 1637. Soon after, tulip prices sank rapidly. Many Dutch families lost property and were left with bulbs that were nearly worthless.

Making Spain's Enemies Rich Guilds that had emerged in the Middle Ages still dominated business in Spain. Such guilds used old-fashioned methods. This made Spanish cloth and manufactured goods more expensive than those made elsewhere. As a result, Spaniards bought much of what they needed from France, England, and the Netherlands. Spain's great wealth flowed into the pockets of foreigners, who were mostly Spain's enemies.

To finance their wars, Spanish kings borrowed money from German and Italian bankers. When shiploads of silver came in, the money was sent abroad to repay debts. The economy was so feeble that Philip had to declare the Spanish state bankrupt three times. **B**

The Dutch Revolt In the Spanish Netherlands, Philip had to maintain an army to keep his subjects under control. The Dutch had little in common with their Spanish rulers. While Spain was Catholic, the Netherlands had many Calvinist congregations. Also, Spain had a sluggish economy, while the Dutch had a prosperous middle class.

Philip raised taxes in the Netherlands and took steps to crush Protestantism. In response, in 1566, angry Protestant mobs swept through Catholic churches. Philip then sent an

B. Possible Answers Silver flooded the market, causing its value to drop; gold and silver were not used to buy Spanish goods but to buy foreign goods or to pay off foreign loans.

MAIN IDEA

Identifying Problems

B Why didn't Spain's economy benefit from the gold and silver from the Americas?

158 Chapter 5

DIFFERENTIATING INSTRUCTION: STRUGGLING READERS

Causes of the Spanish Empire's Decline

Class Time 30 minutes

Task Creating a flow chart

Purpose To help students think about the causes of the Spanish Empire's decline

Instructions Have students make a list of factors that contributed to the weakening of the Spanish Empire. Then have them choose one factor from their list that they think may have given rise to the others. *(Example: Major cause—Gold and silver mining operations in Latin America; Effects—Inflation in Spain, little investment in new types of business, no development of a middle class, Spanish manufacturing products cannot compete with those from other parts of Europe, ruler relies increasingly on imperial holdings for wealth.)* Have students organize the factors in a graphic organizer with the major cause at the top and its factors stemming from it. For help with the section, have students complete the chart in the Guided Reading activity.

In-Depth Resources: Unit 2

army under the Spanish duke of Alva to punish the rebels. On a single day in 1568, the duke executed 1,500 Protestants and suspected rebels.

The Dutch continued to fight the Spanish for another 11 years. Finally, in 1579, the seven northern provinces of the Netherlands, which were largely Protestant, united and declared their independence from Spain. They became the United Provinces of the Netherlands. The ten southern provinces (present-day Belgium) were Catholic and remained under Spanish control.

The Independent Dutch Prosper

The United Provinces of the Netherlands was different from other European states of the time. For one thing, the people there practiced religious toleration. In addition, the United Provinces was not a kingdom but a republic. Each province had an elected governor, whose power depended on the support of merchants and landholders.

Dutch Art During the 1600s, the Netherlands became what Florence had been during the 1400s. It boasted not only the best banks but also many of the best artists in Europe. As in Florence, wealthy merchants sponsored many of these artists.

Rembrandt van Rijn (REHM•BRANT vahn RYN) was the greatest Dutch artist of the period. Rembrandt painted portraits of wealthy middle-class merchants. He also produced group portraits. In *The Night Watch* (shown below), he portrayed a group of city guards. Rembrandt used sharp contrasts of light and shadow to draw attention to his focus.

Another artist fascinated with the effects of light and dark was Jan Vermeer (YAHN vuhr•MEER). Like many other Dutch artists, he chose domestic, indoor settings for his portraits. He often painted women doing such familiar activities as pouring milk from a jug or reading a letter. The work of both Rembrandt and Vermeer reveals how important merchants, civic leaders, and the middle class in general were in 17th-century Netherlands.

◄In *The Night Watch,* Rembrandt showed the individuality of each man by capturing distinctive facial expressions and postures.

The Independent Dutch Prosper
10.1.2

Critical Thinking

- Do you think a wealthy society is necessary for the production of great art. *(Yes—Wealth allows the leisure to appreciate art and to be a patron of art. No—Wealth does not guarantee that a person will demand, or even appreciate, fine art.)*
- Ask students whether Dutch sales of Polish grain to southern Europe were an economic success. *(Possible Answer: The sales were a success, but the high prices may have caused hardship in southern Europe.)*

World Art and Cultural Transparencies

- AT45 Banquet of the Officers of Haarlem's Civil Guard

More About . . .

Jan Vermeer

Vermeer's work was barely recognized during his life, and he struggled with financial difficulties. A number of his paintings were given to local bakers and grocers in exchange for food. Images of some of that food, such as loaves of bread and jugs of milk, made their way into Vermeer's paintings.

World Art and Cultures Transparencies

- AT48 *The Astronomer*, Vermeer

COOPERATIVE LEARNING

Famous Dutch Artists

Class Time 40 minutes

Task Create artist trading cards

Purpose To familiarize students with important Dutch artists

Instructions Divide students into groups of five, and explain that they will be making Dutch artist trading cards. Tell them to begin their project by rereading the passage on Dutch art on page 159. Then have students research other Dutch artists from this period. After completing their research, students should work as a group to design a format for the cards, deciding what image to feature on the front of the card and what "stats" to include on the back. Students might include dates of birth and death, famous work(s), typical subject matter, style, and a biographical profile on the cards. After a group has agreed on a design, each group member should make a trading card for a different Dutch artist. Possible choices include:

- Rembrandt
- Vermeer
- Frans Hals
- Jan Steen
- Jacob van Ruisdael

When each has finished his or her cards, students should reconvene as a group to design packaging for the set.

Absolutism in Europe
10.1.2

Critical Thinking
- Why might an absolute monarch view a republic, such as the Netherlands, as a political threat? *(Possible Answer: A republic might spread the idea that legitimacy is conferred on rulers by the people, not by God.)*
- How might limitations demanded by parliaments and nobility have differed? *(Possible Answer: The nobility wanted to limit monarchs' influence over land. If controlled by merchants, a parliament might seek to limit a monarch's authority to levy taxes on trade.)*

Analyzing Key Concepts

Absolutism

Ask students which effect would contribute most to the durability of an absolute monarch's reign. *(Possible Answer: bureaucracies, because monarchs could use them to extend their power over large territories)*

SKILLBUILDER Answers
1. **Making Inferences** *Possible Answer:* Social gatherings are places where ideas are shared. Some of these ideas might question absolutism.
2. **Hypothesizing** *Possible Answers:* Absolute rulers can reduce political turmoil. In states with a wide gap between rich and poor, the rich sometimes support an absolute ruler who will protect their wealth.

Dutch Trading Empire The stability of the government allowed the Dutch people to concentrate on economic growth. The merchants of Amsterdam bought surplus grain in Poland and crammed it into their warehouses. When they heard about poor harvests in southern Europe, they shipped the grain south while prices were highest. The Dutch had the largest fleet of ships in the world—perhaps 4,800 ships in 1636. This fleet helped the Dutch East India Company (a trading company controlled by the Dutch government) to dominate the Asian spice trade and the Indian Ocean trade. Gradually, the Dutch replaced the Italians as the bankers of Europe.

C. Answer He involved himself in every aspect of government, trusted no one, built an imposing palace, tried to force his subjects to accept his religion, and raised taxes.

Absolutism in Europe

Even though Philip II lost his Dutch possessions, he was a forceful ruler in many ways. He tried to control every aspect of his empire's affairs. During the next few centuries, many European monarchs would also claim the authority to rule without limits on their power.

The Theory of Absolutism These rulers wanted to be **absolute monarchs**, kings or queens who held all of the power within their states' boundaries. Their goal was to control every aspect of society. Absolute monarchs believed in **divine right**, the idea that God created the monarchy and that the monarch acted as God's representative on Earth. An absolute monarch answered only to God, not to his or her subjects. C

MAIN IDEA

Drawing Conclusions

C How was Philip II typical of an absolute monarch?

Analyzing Key Concepts

Absolutism

Absolutism was the political belief that one ruler should hold all of the power within the boundaries of a country. Although practiced by several monarchs in Europe during the 16th through 18th centuries, absolutism has been used in many regions throughout history. In ancient times, Shi Huangdi in China, Darius in Persia, and the Roman caesars were all absolute rulers. (See Chapters 4, 5, and 6.)

Causes
- Religious and territorial conflicts created fear and uncertainty.
- The growth of armies to deal with conflicts caused rulers to raise taxes to pay troops.
- Heavy taxes led to additional unrest and peasant revolts.

ABSOLUTISM

Effects
- Rulers regulated religious worship and social gatherings to control the spread of ideas.
- Rulers increased the size of their courts to appear more powerful.
- Rulers created bureaucracies to control their countries' economies.

SKILLBUILDER: Interpreting Charts
1. **Making Inferences** *Why do you think absolute rulers controlled social gatherings?* See Skillbuilder Handbook, page R10.
2. **Hypothesizing** *Today several nations of the world (such as Saudi Arabia) have absolute rulers. Judging from what you know of past causes of absolutism, why do you think absolute rulers still exist today?*

DIFFERENTIATING INSTRUCTION: ENGLISH LEARNERS

Causes and Effects of Absolutism

Class Time 20 minutes

Task Rephrasing sentences

Purpose To make students better readers

Instructions Ask students to examine the cause and effect boxes in the "Analyzing Key Concepts" chart on this page. Ask them to explain each of the points in their own words. Examples follow.

Causes
- Religious and territorial conflicts created fear and uncertainty. *(People fought over religion and land. The fighting made people afraid and uncertain about their future.)*
- Heavy taxes led to additional unrest and peasant revolts. *(People were unhappy about paying high taxes. Some protested, and some even used violence. Peasants got together to fight the government.)*

Effects
- Rulers regulated religious worship and social gatherings to control the spread of ideas. *(To stop people from spreading new ideas, rulers made laws about how people would practice their religion and where and when people could gather.)*

Growing Power of Europe's Monarchs As Europe emerged from the Middle Ages, monarchs grew increasingly powerful. The decline of feudalism, the rise of cities, and the growth of national kingdoms all helped to centralize authority. In addition, the growing middle class usually backed monarchs, because they promised a peaceful, supportive climate for business. Monarchs used the wealth of colonies to pay for their ambitions. Church authority also broke down during the late Middle Ages and the Reformation. That opened the way for monarchs to assume even greater control. In 1576, Jean Bodin, an influential French writer, defined absolute rule:

PRIMARY SOURCE

The first characteristic of the sovereign prince is the power to make general and special laws, but—and this qualification is important—without the consent of superiors, equals, or inferiors. If the prince requires the consent of superiors, then he is a subject himself; if that of equals, he shares his authority with others; if that of his subjects, senate or people, he is not sovereign.

JEAN BODIN, *Six Books on the State*

Crises Lead to Absolutism The 17th century was a period of great upheaval in Europe. Religious and territorial conflicts between states led to almost continuous warfare. This caused governments to build huge armies and to levy even heavier taxes on an already suffering population. These pressures in turn brought about widespread unrest. Sometimes peasants revolted.

In response to these crises, monarchs tried to impose order by increasing their own power. As absolute rulers, they regulated everything from religious worship to social gatherings. They created new government bureaucracies to control their countries' economic life. Their goal was to free themselves from the limitations imposed by the nobility and by representative bodies such as Parliament. Only with such freedom could they rule absolutely, as did the most famous monarch of his time, Louis XIV of France. You'll learn more about him in the next section.

More About . . .

Jean Bodin

The political philosopher Jean Bodin was among the first to explain how the concept of sovereignty affects politics and law. Bodin identified three types of political systems—monarchy, aristocracy, and democracy. Bodin preferred a combination of monarchy and representative assembly.

SECTION 1 ASSESSMENT

TERMS & NAMES 1. For each term or name, write a sentence explaining its significance.
• Philip II • absolute monarch • divine right

USING YOUR NOTES

2. Which condition is probably most necessary for a monarch to gain power? Why? (10.1.2)

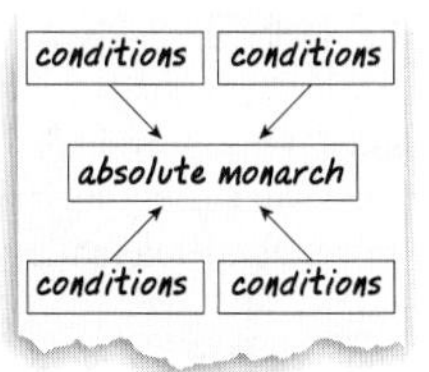

MAIN IDEAS

3. What is the significance of England's defeat of the Spanish Armada? (10.1.2)
4. Why did the Dutch revolt against Spain? (HI 3)
5. Why did absolute monarchs believe that they were justified in exercising absolute power? (10.1.2)

CRITICAL THINKING & WRITING

6. **DRAWING CONCLUSIONS** What does the art described in this section reveal about the cultures of Spain and the Netherlands? (HI 1)
7. **ANALYZING CAUSES** What role did religion play in the struggle between the Spanish and the Dutch? (HI 4)
8. **MAKING INFERENCES** How did the lack of a middle class contribute to the decline of Spain's economy? (HI 1)
9. **WRITING ACTIVITY** ECONOMICS Write a **comparison-contrast paragraph** on the economies of Spain and the Netherlands around 1600. (Writing 2.6.a)

INTEGRATED TECHNOLOGY **INTERNET ACTIVITY**

Use the Internet to identify the religious affiliations of people in Spain and in the Netherlands today. Create a **graph** for each country showing the results of your research. (Writing 2.3.d)

INTERNET KEYWORD
religion in Spain; religion in the Netherlands

3 ASSESS

SECTION 1 ASSESSMENT

Have students work in pairs or small groups to answer the questions. As they share answers, have them refer to information in the text that supports their responses.

Formal Assessment
• Section Quiz, p. 86

4 RETEACH

Use the Guided Reading activity to review the main ideas of the section.

In-Depth Resources: Unit 2
• Guided Reading, p. 1
• Reteaching Activity, p. 20

ANSWERS

1. Philip II, p. 155 • absolute monarch, p. 160 • divine right, p. 160

2. **Sample Answer:** Conditions—Decline of feudalism, colonial wealth, religious conflicts, territorial conflicts. Most necessary condition—Decline of feudalism, because local rulers had to become weak for a single figure to become monarch and centralize power.
3. It weakened Spain and opened the way for more European ventures in the Americas.
4. because Philip II raised taxes and tried to crush Protestantism
5. because they believed their power was God-given
6. **Possible Answer:** Religion and the monarchy were central to Spanish culture. Merchants, civic leaders, and the middle class were prominent in the culture of the Netherlands.
7. Philip II thought it his duty to defend Catholicism and tried to crush Protestantism in the Netherlands.
8. There were few businesspeople to stimulate economic growth at home or to promote trade abroad.
9. **Rubric** Paragraphs should
• use specific details to support ideas.
• draw a conclusion about which country had the stronger economy.

INTEGRATED TECHNOLOGY

Rubric Graphs should
• follow standard graphing conventions.
• cite sources.

LESSON PLAN

OBJECTIVES

- Describe conflicts in Europe.
- Analyze ideas of important French thinkers.
- Explain Louis XIV's policies and characterize the style of his court.
- Describe France's disastrous wars.

1 FOCUS & MOTIVATE

In this section, students will learn about Louis XIV's patronage of the arts. Ask students if the U.S. government supports the arts. *(Students might mention the National Endowment for the Arts.)*

2 INSTRUCT

Religious Wars and Power Struggles

10.2.1

Critical Thinking

- How did the religious attitudes of Henry IV and Philip II differ? *(Possible Answer: Philip II was hostile toward non-Catholics. Henry IV tolerated religious differences and converted for political reasons.)*

CALIFORNIA RESOURCES

California Reading Toolkit, p. L24
California Modified Lesson Plans for English Learners, p. 43
California Daily Standards Practice Transparencies, TT16
California Standards Enrichment Workbook, pp. 23–24, 29–30
California Standards Planner and Lesson Plans, p. L39
California Online Test Practice
California Test Generator CD-ROM
California Easy Planner CD-ROM
California eEdition CD-ROM

Marriage of Louis XIV to Marie Thérèse of Austria. Artist unknown

Statue of Louis XIV, Lyon, France

2

The Reign of Louis XIV

MAIN IDEA

POWER AND AUTHORITY After a century of war and riots, France was ruled by Louis XIV, the most powerful monarch of his time.

WHY IT MATTERS NOW

Louis's abuse of power led to revolution that would inspire the call for democratic government throughout the world.

TERMS & NAMES

- Edict of Nantes
- Cardinal Richelieu
- skepticism
- Louis XIV
- intendant
- Jean Baptiste Colbert
- War of the Spanish Succession

CALIFORNIA STANDARDS

10.2.1 Compare the major ideas of philosophers and their effects on the democratic revolutions in England, the United States, France, and Latin America (e.g., John Locke, Charles-Louis Montesquieu, Jean-Jacques Rousseau, Simón Bolívar, Thomas Jefferson, James Madison).

10.2.4 Explain how the ideology of the French Revolution led France to develop from constitutional monarchy to democratic despotism to the Napoleonic empire.

HI 2 Students recognize the complexity of historical causes and effects, including the limitations on determining cause and effect.

HI 3 Students interpret past events and issues within the context in which an event unfolded rather than solely in terms of present-day norms and values.

SETTING THE STAGE In 1559, King Henry II of France died, leaving four young sons. Three of them ruled, one after the other, but all proved incompetent. The real power behind the throne during this period was their mother, Catherine de Médicis. Catherine tried to preserve royal authority, but growing conflicts between Catholics and Huguenots—French Protestants—rocked the country. Between 1562 and 1598, Huguenots and Catholics fought eight religious wars. Chaos spread through France.

Religious Wars and Power Struggles

In 1572, the St. Bartholomew's Day Massacre in Paris sparked a six-week, nationwide slaughter of Huguenots. The massacre occurred when many Huguenot nobles were in Paris. They were attending the marriage of Catherine's daughter to a Huguenot prince, Henry of Navarre. Most of these nobles died, but Henry survived.

Henry of Navarre Descended from the popular medieval king Louis IX, Henry was robust, athletic, and handsome. In 1589, when both Catherine and her last son died, Prince Henry inherited the throne. He became Henry IV, the first king of the Bourbon dynasty in France. As king, he showed himself to be decisive, fearless in battle, and a clever politician.

Many Catholics, including the people of Paris, opposed Henry. For the sake of his war-weary country, Henry chose to give up Protestantism and become a Catholic. Explaining his conversion, Henry reportedly declared, "Paris is well worth a mass."

In 1598, Henry took another step toward healing France's wounds. He declared that the Huguenots could live in peace in France and set up their own houses of worship in some cities. This declaration of religious toleration was called the **Edict of Nantes**.

Aided by an adviser who enacted wise financial policies, Henry devoted his reign to rebuilding France and its prosperity. He restored the French monarchy to a strong position. After a generation of war, most French people welcomed peace. Some people, however, hated Henry for his religious compromises. In 1610, a fanatic leaped into the royal carriage and stabbed Henry to death.

TAKING NOTES

Following Chronological Order Use a time line to list the major events of Louis XIV's reign.

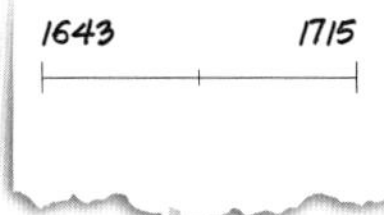

SECTION 2 PROGRAM RESOURCES

ALL STUDENTS

In-Depth Resources: Unit 2
- Guided Reading, p. 2

Formal Assessment
- Section Quiz, p. 87

ENGLISH LEARNERS

In-Depth Resources in Spanish
- Guided Reading, p. 45

Reading Study Guide (Spanish), p. 53
Reading Study Guide Audio CD (Spanish)

STRUGGLING READERS

In-Depth Resources: Unit 2
- Guided Reading, p. 2
- Building Vocabulary, p. 6
- Reteaching Activity, p. 21

Reading Study Guide, p. 53
Reading Study Guide Audio CD

GIFTED AND TALENTED STUDENTS

In-Depth Resources: Unit 2
- Primary Source: Louis XIV's Advice to His Son, p. 10
- Literature: from *The Cat and the King,* p. 14

Electronic Library of Primary Sources
- Two Views of Versailles

INTEGRATED TECHNOLOGY

eEdition CD-ROM
Power Presentations CD-ROM
Electronic Library of Primary Sources
- Two Views of Versailles

classzone.com

Louis XIII and Cardinal Richelieu After Henry IV's death, his son Louis XIII reigned. Louis was a weak king, but in 1624, he appointed a strong minister who made up for all of Louis's weaknesses.

Cardinal Richelieu (RIHSH•uh•LOO) became, in effect, the ruler of France. For several years, he had been a hard-working leader of the Catholic church in France. Although he tried sincerely to lead according to moral principles, he was also ambitious and enjoyed exercising authority. As Louis XIII's minister, he was able to pursue his ambitions in the political arena.

Richelieu took two steps to increase the power of the Bourbon monarchy. First, he moved against Huguenots. He believed that Protestantism often served as an excuse for political conspiracies against the Catholic king. Although Richelieu did not take away the Huguenots' right to worship, he forbade Protestant cities to have walls. He did not want them to be able to defy the king and then withdraw behind strong defenses.

Second, he sought to weaken the nobles' power. Richelieu ordered nobles to take down their fortified castles. He increased the power of government agents who came from the middle class. The king relied on these agents, so there was less need to use noble officials.

Richelieu also wanted to make France the strongest state in Europe. The greatest obstacle to this, he believed, was the Hapsburg rulers, whose lands surrounded France. The Hapsburgs ruled Spain, Austria, the Netherlands, and parts of the Holy Roman Empire. To limit Hapsburg power, Richelieu involved France in the Thirty Years' War. (A)

A. Answer By taking away their fortifications, he lessened the chance they could defy the king; by relying on middle-class officials, he made the king more independent of nobles.

MAIN IDEA

Making Inferences

(A) How did Richelieu's actions toward Huguenots and the nobility strengthen the monarchy?

▲ Cardinal Richelieu probably had himself portrayed in a standing position in this painting to underscore his role as ruler.

Writers Turn Toward Skepticism

As France regained political power, a new French intellectual movement developed. French thinkers had witnessed the religious wars with horror. What they saw turned them toward **skepticism**, the idea that nothing can ever be known for certain. These thinkers expressed an attitude of doubt toward churches that claimed to have the only correct set of doctrines. To doubt old ideas, skeptics thought, was the first step toward finding truth.

Montaigne and Descartes Michel de Montaigne lived during the worst years of the French religious wars. After the death of a dear friend, Montaigne thought deeply about life's meaning. To communicate his ideas, Montaigne developed a new form of literature, the essay. An essay is a brief work that expresses a person's thoughts and opinions.

In one essay, Montaigne pointed out that whenever a new belief arose, it replaced an old belief that people once accepted as truth. In the same way, he went on, the new belief would also probably be replaced by some different idea in the future. For these reasons, Montaigne believed that humans could never have absolute knowledge of what is true.

Another French writer of the time, René Descartes, was a brilliant thinker. In his *Meditations on First Philosophy,* Descartes examined the skeptical argument that one could never be certain of anything. Descartes used his observations and his reason to answer such arguments. In doing so, he created a philosophy that influenced modern thinkers and helped to develop the scientific method. Because of

More About . . .

The Bourbons

The Bourbons are one of the most famous ruling dynasties in Europe. Beginning with Henry IV, a number of French kings came from this family. Bourbons also held royal titles in Spain, Sicily, and other parts of Europe. The current king of Spain, Juan Carlos I, is a Bourbon.

Writers Turn Toward Skepticism

10.2.1

Critical Thinking

- How might political and religious leaders have reacted to the work of Montaigne? *(Possible Answer: Both groups would likely have felt threatened by Montaigne's notion that humans could never know the truth for certain.)*
- Ask students whether Descartes's response to the challenges of skeptics such as Montaigne put an end to the skeptics' arguments. *(Possible Answer: No—Philosophers still debate the nature of truth.)*

DIFFERENTIATING INSTRUCTION: STRUGGLING READERS

Montaigne and Descartes

Class Time 15 minutes

Task Answering questions about the text

Purpose To help students focus on what they are reading

Instructions Ask students the following questions after reading "Writers Turn Toward Skepticism" on pp. 163–164.

1. How did religious wars between Huguenots (Protestants) and Catholics affect French thinkers? *(Many turned to skepticism.)*
2. What is skepticism? *(the idea that nothing is known for certain)*
3. What would churches have said about the ideas of skepticism? *(Churches would claim that their beliefs are certain and true.)*
4. What is an essay? *(a short work that tells a person's thoughts and opinions)*
5. According to Montaigne, what evidence is there that humans can never know the truth absolutely? *(Ideas that were once accepted as true are constantly replaced by new ones.)*
6. Was Descartes a skeptic? *(No—He challenged their arguments.)*

For help with the section, have students complete the chart in in the Guided Reading activity.

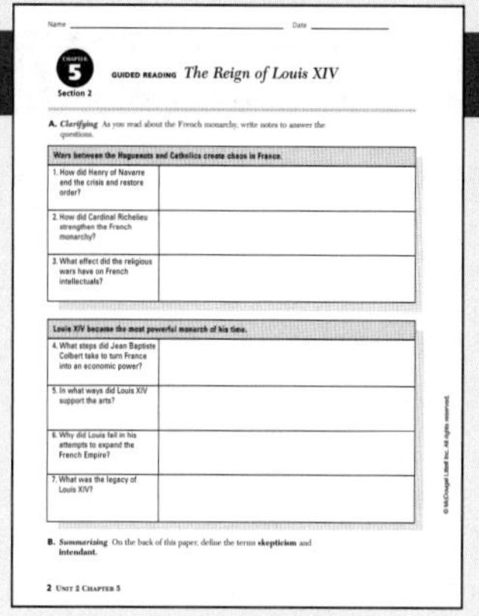

Name ______________ Date ______________

CHAPTER 5 Section 2 GUIDED READING *The Reign of Louis XIV*

A. ***Clarifying*** As you read about the French monarchy, write notes to answer the questions.

Wars between the Huguenots and Catholics create chaos in France.	
1. How did Henry of Navarre end the crisis and restore order?	
2. How did Cardinal Richelieu strengthen the French monarchy?	
3. What effect did the religious wars have on French intellectuals?	

Louis XIV became the most powerful monarch of his time.	
4. What steps did Jean Baptiste Colbert take to turn France into an economic power?	
5. In what ways did Louis XIV support the arts?	
6. Why did Louis fail in his attempts to expand the French Empire?	
7. What was the legacy of Louis XIV?	

B. ***Summarizing*** On the back of this paper, define the terms **skepticism** and **intendant**.

2 Unit 2 Chapter 5

In-Depth Resources: Unit 2

History Makers

Louis XIV

Why might a leader's height be important? *(Possible Answer: Tall leaders who appear physically powerful might inspire more confidence.)*

As king, Louis XIV worked hard and paid great attention to the smallest details of government. He explained to his son the secrets of his success: "Two things without doubt were absolutely necessary; very hard work on my part; and a wise choice of persons capable of seconding it."

In-Depth Resources: Unit 2

- Primary Sources: Louis XIV's Advice to His Son, p. 10

Louis XIV Comes to Power

10.2.4

Critical Thinking

- What should a government consider in crafting policies toward different religious or ethnic groups? *(Possible Answers: potential economic, social, and political effects; fairness)*
- What does Louis XIV's use of intendants suggest about his approach to controlling the nobility? *(Possible Answer: He wanted to offset the nobles' power by granting more powers to government agents.)*
- Ask students to name drawbacks to Colbert's mercantilism. *(Possible Answer: It prohibited foreign trade, even when such trade might have been economically beneficial.)*

History Makers

Louis XIV
1638–1715

Although Louis XIV stood only 5 feet 5 inches tall, his erect and dignified posture made him appear much taller. (It also helped that he wore high-heeled shoes.)

Louis had very strong likes and dislikes. He hated cities and loved to travel through France's countryside. The people who traveled with him were at his mercy, however, for he allowed no stopping except for his own comfort.

It is small wonder that the vain Louis XIV liked to be called the Sun King. He believed that, as with the sun, all power radiated from him.

INTEGRATED TECHNOLOGY

RESEARCH LINKS For more on Louis XIV, go to **classzone.com**

this, he became an important figure in the Enlightenment, which you will read about in Chapter 6.

Louis XIV Comes to Power

The efforts of Henry IV and Richelieu to strengthen the French monarchy paved the way for the most powerful ruler in French history—**Louis XIV**. In Louis's view, he and the state were one and the same. He reportedly boasted, *"L'état, c'est moi,"* meaning "I am the state." Although Louis XIV became the strongest king of his time, he was only a four-year-old boy when he began his reign.

Louis, the Boy King When Louis became king in 1643 after the death of his father, Louis XIII, the true ruler of France was Richelieu's successor, Cardinal Mazarin (MAZ•uh•RAN). Mazarin's greatest triumph came in 1648, with the ending of the Thirty Years' War.

Many people in France, particularly the nobles, hated Mazarin because he increased taxes and strengthened the central government. From 1648 to 1653, violent anti-Mazarin riots tore France apart. At times, the nobles who led the riots threatened the young king's life. Even after the violence was over, Louis never forgot his fear or his anger at the nobility. He determined to become so strong that they could never threaten him again.

In the end, the nobles' rebellion failed for three reasons. Its leaders distrusted one another even more than they distrusted Mazarin. In addition, the government used violent repression. Finally, peasants and townspeople grew weary of disorder and fighting. For many years afterward, the people of France accepted the oppressive laws of an absolute king. They were convinced that the alternative—rebellion—was even worse. **B**

B. Answer Louis increased his power so no one could ever threaten him again; the subjects hoped a strong leader would prevent future turmoil.

MAIN IDEA

Recognizing Effects

B What effects did the years of riots have on Louis XIV? on his subjects?

Louis Weakens the Nobles' Authority When Cardinal Mazarin died in 1661, the 22-year-old Louis took control of the government himself. He weakened the power of the nobles by excluding them from his councils. In contrast, he increased the power of the government agents called **intendants**, who collected taxes and administered justice. To keep power under central control, he made sure that local officials communicated regularly with him.

Economic Growth Louis devoted himself to helping France attain economic, political, and cultural brilliance. No one assisted him more in achieving these goals than his minister of finance, **Jean Baptiste Colbert** (kawl•BEHR). Colbert believed in the theory of mercantilism. To prevent wealth from leaving the country, Colbert tried to make France self-sufficient. He wanted it to be able to manufacture everything it needed instead of relying on imports.

Vocabulary
mercantilism: the economic theory that nations should protect their home industries and export more than they import

To expand manufacturing, Colbert gave government funds and tax benefits to French companies. To protect France's industries, he placed a high tariff on goods from other countries. Colbert also recognized the importance of colonies, which provided raw materials and a market for manufactured goods. The French government encouraged people to migrate to France's colony in Canada. There the fur trade added to French trade and wealth.

DIFFERENTIATING INSTRUCTION: ENGLISH LEARNERS

Understanding How Louis XIV Came to Power

Class Time 30 minutes

Task Creating a chart

Purpose To understand the text on Louis XIV better

Instructions Have students create a chart in which they define challenging words and phrases from the section in their own words and provide an example of each. A sample chart is at right. For help, have students use the Reading Study Guide in Spanish for Section 2.

Term	Meaning	Examples
paved the way	made things easy and smooth	Richelieu set policies that later helped Louis XIV.
repression	a government's harsh treatment of a society or group	restrictions on the lives of Huguenots
oppressive laws	laws that allowed little personal freedom	As absolute monarch, Louis XIV made laws that kept people quiet and obedient.
successor	a person who takes over the leadership	Cardinal Mazarin was Richelieu's successor.

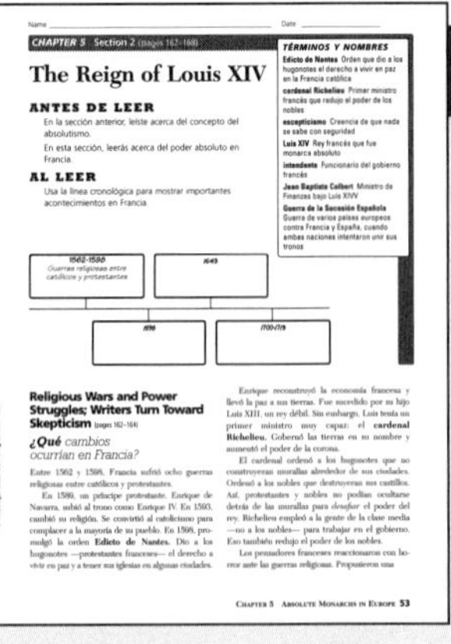

The Reign of Louis XIV

ANTES DE LEER

AL LEER

Reading Study Guide: Spanish Translation

After Colbert's death, Louis announced a policy that slowed France's economic progress. In 1685, he canceled the Edict of Nantes, which protected the religious freedom of Huguenots. In response, thousands of Huguenot artisans and business people fled the country. Louis's policy thus robbed France of many skilled workers.

The Sun King's Grand Style

In his personal finances, Louis spent a fortune to surround himself with luxury. For example, each meal was a feast. An observer claimed that the king once devoured four plates of soup, a whole pheasant, a partridge in garlic sauce, two slices of ham, a salad, a plate of pastries, fruit, and hard-boiled eggs in a single sitting! Nearly 500 cooks, waiters, and other servants worked to satisfy his tastes.

Louis Controls the Nobility Every morning, the chief valet woke Louis at 8:30. Outside the curtains of Louis's canopy bed stood at least 100 of the most privileged nobles at court. They were waiting to help the great king dress. Only four would be allowed the honor of handing Louis his slippers or holding his sleeves for him.

Meanwhile, outside the bedchamber, lesser nobles waited in the palace halls and hoped Louis would notice them. A kingly nod, a glance of approval, a kind word—these marks of royal attention determined whether a noble succeeded or failed. A duke recorded how Louis turned against nobles who did not come to court to flatter him:

▼ Though full of errors, Saint-Simon's memoirs provide valuable insight into Louis XIV's character and life at Versailles.

MAIN IDEA
Analyzing Primary Sources
C How did Louis's treatment of the nobles reflect his belief in his absolute authority?

C. Possible Answer He wanted to control the nobles' lives, so he made them live at court, where he could watch them.

PRIMARY SOURCE C

He looked to the right and to the left, not only upon rising but upon going to bed, at his meals, in passing through his apartments, or his gardens. . . . He marked well all absentees from the Court, found out the reason of their absence, and never lost an opportunity of acting toward them as the occasion might seem to justify. . . . When their names were in any way mentioned, "I do not know them," the King would reply haughtily.

DUKE OF SAINT-SIMON, *Memoirs of Louis XIV and the Regency*

Having the nobles at the palace increased royal authority in two ways. It made the nobility totally dependent on Louis. It also took them from their homes, thereby giving more power to the intendants. Louis required hundreds of nobles to live with him at the splendid palace he built at Versailles, about 11 miles southwest of Paris.

As you can see from the pictures on the following page, everything about the Versailles palace was immense. It faced a huge royal courtyard dominated by a statue of Louis XIV. The palace itself stretched for a distance of about 500 yards. Because of its great size, Versailles was like a small royal city. Its rich decoration and furnishings clearly showed Louis's wealth and power to everyone who came to the palace.

Patronage of the Arts Versailles was a center of the arts during Louis's reign. Louis made opera and ballet more popular. He even danced the title role in the ballet *The Sun King*. One of his favorite writers was Molière (mohl•YAIR), who wrote some of the funniest plays in French literature. Molière's comedies include *Tartuffe,* which mocks religious hypocrisy.

Not since Augustus of Rome had there been a European monarch who supported the arts as much as Louis. Under Louis, the chief purpose of art was no longer to glorify God, as it had been in the Middle Ages. Nor was its purpose to glorify human potential, as it had been in the Renaissance. Now the purpose of art was to glorify the king and promote values that supported Louis's absolute rule.

The Sun King's Grand Style
10.2.4

Critical Thinking

- Why might nobles tolerate Louis XIV's high expectations? *(Louis had power over their incomes and their social status.)*
- How might different classes of French people have reacted to the opulence of Versailles? *(Possible Answers: Merchants did not object as long as Louis provided economic stability. The poor might have been either awed or resentful. The nobility probably enjoyed Versailles's luxury, while it is likely that the clergy disapproved of its decadence.)*

More About . . .

Molière

Molière's comedies ridicule human folly, poking fun at misers, hypocrites, and snobs. Those he targeted with his humor sometimes took offense. His greatest play, *Tartuffe*, so angered some Parisians that they called for him to be burned at the stake. Louis XIV protected him, however, and supported his work.

COOPERATIVE LEARNING

Dramatizing the Court of Louis XIV

Class Time 35 minutes

Task Making a recording for a radio play

Purpose To familiarize students with life in Louis XIV's court

Instructions Divide students into groups of four. Have them read the Literature Selection from *The Cat and the King,* by Louis Auchincloss, in In-Depth Resources: Unit 2. After they read the selection, tell students that they are going to make a recording of the piece as a mock radio broadcast. Each member of the group should portray one of the story's characters: Louis de Rouvroy, the second duc de Saint-Simon; the duchesse Gabrielle, wife of Louis de Rouvroy; the duc de Beauvillier; or Louis XIV. Before making their recordings, students should spend time rehearsing to identify potential problems. For example, the person playing Louis de Rouvroy will need to perform both dialogue and interior monologue. Students should decide how to differentiate these two voices. Because most of the speaking is done by Louis de Rouvroy, the other members of the group can operate the tape recorder, make observations, and offer suggestions about how to improve the recording.

LITERATURE SELECTION *from The Cat and the King* by Louis Auchincloss

In-Depth Resources: Unit 2

History *in* Depth

OBJECTIVES

- Explain how the palace at Versailles reflects the political system of 17th-century France.
- Identify some of the palace's major features.

INSTRUCT

As students read about and study photographs of Versailles, ask them to think about what they have learned about absolutism. Encourage them to consider how different features of Versailles might have both reflected and strengthened the power of Louis XIV.

More About . . .

Building the Palace

A small, unfashionable hunting lodge built on a sandy, shifting hill by Louis XIV's father stood on the site chosen for Versailles. Louis insisted, over his architect's objections, on leaving the lodge and building around it.

Versailles was the love of Louis's life. Whenever he was away from it, he required daily reports on the progress of the building. He continued to add to and improve the palace until he died, and he probably never saw it completely free of scaffolding.

Electronic Library of Primary Sources

- Two Views of Versailles

INTEGRATED TECHNOLOGY

Interactive Students can learn more about Versailles by exploring the interactive version of this feature on the eEdition.

History *in* Depth

INTERACTIVE

The Palace at Versailles

CALIFORNIA STANDARDS
10.2.4, HI 3

Louis XIV's palace at Versailles was proof of his absolute power. Only a ruler with total control over his country's economy could afford such a lavish palace. It cost an estimated $2.5 billion in 2003 dollars. Louis XIV was also able to force 36,000 laborers and 6,000 horses to work on the project.

Many people consider the Hall of Mirrors the most beautiful room in the palace. Along one wall are 17 tall mirrors. The opposite wall has 17 windows that open onto the gardens. The hall has gilded statues, crystal chandeliers, and a painted ceiling.

It took so much water to run all the fountains at once that it was done only for special events. On other days, when the king walked in the garden, servants would turn on fountains just before he reached them. The fountains were turned off after he walked away.

The gardens at Versailles remain beautiful today. Originally, Versailles was built with:
- 5,000 acres of gardens, lawns, and woods
- 1,400 fountains

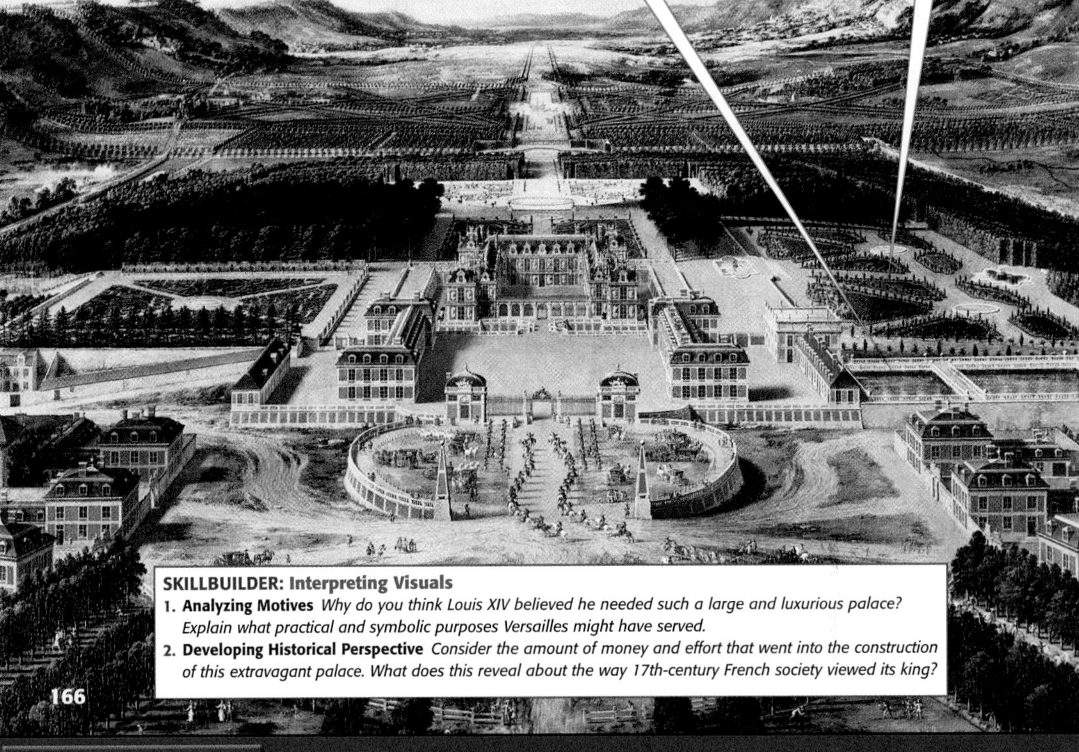

SKILLBUILDER: Interpreting Visuals

1. **Analyzing Motives** *Why do you think Louis XIV believed he needed such a large and luxurious palace? Explain what practical and symbolic purposes Versailles might have served.*
2. **Developing Historical Perspective** *Consider the amount of money and effort that went into the construction of this extravagant palace. What does this reveal about the way 17th-century French society viewed its king?*

166

SKILLBUILDER: ANSWERS

1. Analyzing Motives

Possible Answer: Practically, it was a place to house the court and to entertain foreign visitors. Symbolically, it made Louis XIV seem almost like a god.

2. Developing Historical Perspective

Possible Answer: It shows that French society accepted the idea that the king was far above everyone else and that he deserved whatever luxuries he desired.

Louis Fights Disastrous Wars

Under Louis, France was the most powerful country in Europe. In 1660, France had about 20 million people. This was four times as many as England and ten times as many as the Dutch republic. The French army was far ahead of other states' armies in size, training, and weaponry.

Attempts to Expand France's Boundaries In 1667, just six years after Mazarin's death, Louis invaded the Spanish Netherlands in an effort to expand France's boundaries. Through this campaign, he gained 12 towns. Encouraged by his success, he personally led an army into the Dutch Netherlands in 1672. The Dutch saved their country by opening the dikes and flooding the countryside. This was the same tactic they had used in their revolt against Spain a century earlier. The war ended in 1678 with the Treaty of Nijmegen. France gained several towns and a region called Franche-Comté.

Louis decided to fight additional wars, but his luck had run out. By the end of the 1680s, a Europeanwide alliance had formed to stop France. By banding together, weaker countries could match France's strength. This defensive strategy was meant to achieve a balance of power, in which no single country or group of countries could dominate others.

In 1689, the Dutch prince William of Orange became the king of England. He joined the League of Augsburg, which consisted of the Austrian Hapsburg emperor, the kings of Sweden and Spain, and the leaders of several smaller European states. Together, these countries equaled France's strength.

France at this time had been weakened by a series of poor harvests. That, added to the constant warfare, brought great suffering to the French people. So, too, did new taxes, which Louis imposed to finance his wars. D

MAIN IDEA

Recognizing Effects

D How did Louis's wars against weaker countries backfire?

D. Answer He motivated his enemies to band together and thereby become strong enough to rival France.

War of the Spanish Succession Tired of hardship, the French people longed for peace. What they got was another war. In 1700, the childless king of Spain, Charles II, died after promising his throne to Louis XIV's 16-year-old grandson, Philip of Anjou. The two greatest powers in Europe, enemies for so long, were now both ruled by the French Bourbons.

Other countries felt threatened by this increase in the Bourbon dynasty's power. In 1701, England, Austria, the Dutch Republic, Portugal, and several German and Italian states joined together to prevent the union of the French and Spanish thrones. The long struggle that followed is known as the **War of the Spanish Succession**.

The costly war dragged on until 1714. The Treaty of Utrecht was signed in that year. Under its terms, Louis's grandson was allowed to remain king of Spain so long as the thrones of France and Spain were not united.

The big winner in the war was Great Britain. From Spain, Britain took Gibraltar, a fortress that controlled the entrance to the Mediterranean. Spain also granted a British company an *asiento*, permission to send enslaved Africans to Spain's American colonies. This increased Britain's involvement in trading enslaved Africans.

▼ The painting below shows the Battle of Denain, one of the last battles fought during the War of the Spanish Succession.

Louis Fights Disastrous Wars

10.2.4

Critical Thinking

- Ask students what factors, besides the threat of another power, might be needed to establish a "balance of power." *(Possible Answer: Skillful diplomacy would be needed to overcome the competing interests of the different states.)*
- Why might Britain be considered the big winner during the War of the Spanish Succession? *(Possible Answer: Britain came out of the war with new, strategic territory and trade.)*

More About . . .

Gibraltar

After nearly 300 years of British rule, Gibraltar remains a dependent territory of the United Kingdom. Recently, officials from both countries have struggled to work out a plan for joint sovereignty. However, these negotiations were complicated in November 2002 when 99 percent of Gibraltar's people voted in a referendum to remain British.

DIFFERENTIATING INSTRUCTION: GIFTED AND TALENTED STUDENTS

The War of the Spanish Succession

Class Time 35 minutes

Task Creating a design for an interactive time line

Purpose To provide students with an in-depth knowledge of the War of the Spanish Succession

Instructions Divide students into small groups. Tell students that they will be creating a design for an interactive time line of the War of the Spanish Succession. Students should begin by making a list of elements that they want users to access, such as: images of individuals, battles, and artifacts; animated maps; graphs; charts; primary and secondary sources; and links to related sites. After they have developed a preliminary design students should use the library or the Internet to find images and information. As they refine their designs, they should begin to consider more detailed questions, such as how they will show the relative importance of events, and how much detail is appropriate.

History from Visuals

Interpreting the Graph

Point out that the graph gives the numbers of livres in millions. So 1,200 means 1.2 billion livres.

Extension Have students determine the equivalent in 1992 U.S. dollars of the royal debt in 1708. *(about $12.6 billion)*

SKILLBUILDER Answers

1. **Comparing** about five times greater
2. **Synthesizing** about $21 billion

Debt of the Royal Family, 1643–1715

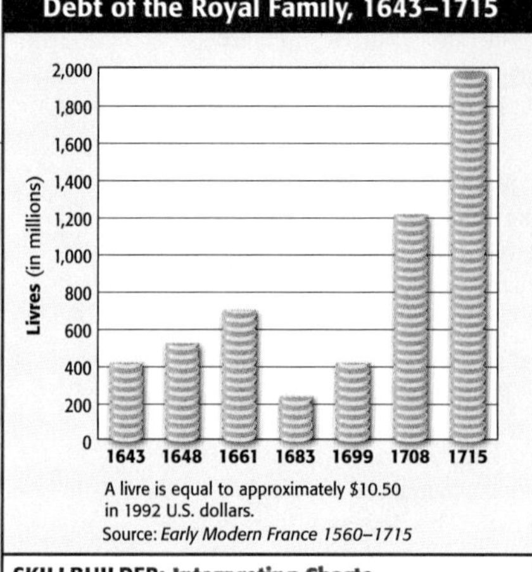

A livre is equal to approximately $10.50 in 1992 U.S. dollars.
Source: *Early Modern France 1560–1715*

SKILLBUILDER: Interpreting Charts

1. **Comparing** *How many times greater was the royal debt in 1715 than in 1643?*
2. **Synthesizing** *What was the royal debt of 1715 equal to in 1992 dollars?*

In addition, France gave Britain the North American territories of Nova Scotia and Newfoundland, and abandoned claims to the Hudson Bay region. The Austrian Hapsburgs took the Spanish Netherlands and other Spanish lands in Italy. Prussia and Savoy were recognized as kingdoms.

Louis's Death and Legacy Louis's last years were more sad than glorious. Realizing that his wars had ruined France, he regretted the suffering he had brought to his people. He died in bed in 1715. News of his death prompted rejoicing throughout France. The people had had enough of the Sun King.

Louis left a mixed legacy to his country. On the positive side, France was certainly a power to be reckoned with in Europe. France ranked above all other European nations in art, literature, and statesmanship during Louis's reign. In addition, France was considered the military leader of Europe. This military might allowed France to develop a strong empire of colonies, which provided resources and goods for trade.

On the negative side, constant warfare and the construction of the Palace of Versailles plunged France into staggering debt. Also, resentment over the tax burden imposed on the poor and Louis's abuse of power would plague his heirs—and eventually lead to revolution.

Absolute rule didn't die with Louis XIV. His enemies in Prussia and Austria had been experimenting with their own forms of absolute monarchy, as you will learn in Section 3.

3 ASSESS

SECTION 2 ASSESSMENT

Have pairs of students work together to quiz each other on terms and names.

Formal Assessment

• Section Quiz, p. 87

4 RETEACH

To help students review the section, have them make a time line of key events.

In-Depth Resources: Unit 2

• Reteaching Activity, p. 21

SECTION 2 ASSESSMENT

TERMS & NAMES 1. For each term or name, write a sentence explaining its significance.

• Edict of Nantes • Cardinal Richelieu • skepticism • Louis XIV • intendant • Jean Baptiste Colbert • War of the Spanish Succession

USING YOUR NOTES

2. Which events on your time line strengthened the French monarchy? Which weakened it? (10.2.4)

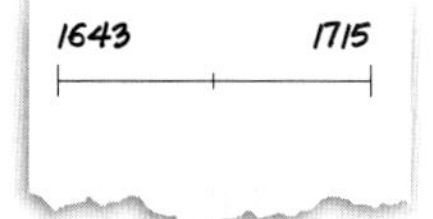

MAIN IDEAS

3. What impact did the French religious wars have on French thinkers? (10.2.1)
4. How did Jean Baptiste Colbert intend to stimulate economic growth in France? (10.2.4)
5. What was the result of the War of the Spanish Succession? (10.2.4)

CRITICAL THINKING & WRITING

6. **SUPPORTING OPINIONS** Many historians think of Louis XIV as the perfect example of an absolute monarch. Do you agree? Explain why or why not. (10.2.4)
7. **RECOGNIZING EFFECTS** How did the policies of Colbert and Louis XIV affect the French economy? Explain both positive and negative effects. (10.2.4)
8. **SYNTHESIZING** To what extent did anti-Protestantism contribute to Louis's downfall? (10.2.1)
9. **WRITING ACTIVITY** POWER AND AUTHORITY Write a **character sketch** of Louis XIV. Discuss his experiences and character traits. (Writing 2.1.c)

CONNECT TO TODAY **CREATING AN ORAL PRESENTATION**

Research to find out what happened to Versailles after Louis's death and what its function is today. Then present your findings in an **oral presentation.** (HI 2)

ANSWERS

1. Edict of Nantes, p. 162 • Cardinal Richelieu, p. 163 • skepticism, p. 163 • Louis XIV, p. 164 • intendant, p. 164 • Jean Baptiste Colbert, p. 164 • War of the Spanish Succession, p. 167
2. **Sample Answer:** Strengthened—1643, Louis XIV becomes king; 1661, Louis takes control of government; Weakened—1701–1713, War of Spanish Succession.
3. It turned them toward skepticism.
4. with mercantilist policies to make France self-sufficient
5. France and Spain were not allowed to unite; Britain gained Gibraltar; Austrian Hapsburgs took Spanish Netherlands.
6. **Possible Answer:** Agree—He controlled the economy, regulated worship, weakened the nobility, built a magnificent palace to show his power.
7. Helped—Built up and protected French industries; Hurt—Drove out Huguenots and overspent on buildings and wars.
8. Canceling the Edict of Nantes cost France many skilled workers, and wars against Protestant countries damaged the French economy.
9. **Rubric** Character sketches should
   • describe Louis's behavior at court.
   • give examples of his interests.
   • draw conclusions about his character.

CONNECT TO TODAY

Rubric Oral presentations should

• mention the destruction of Versailles during the French Revolution.
• explain that the treaty ending World War I was signed at Versailles.
• refer to the restoration of Versailles in the 1900s and its use today as a museum.

Marriage of Louis XIV to Marie Thérèse of Austria. Artist unknown

Statue of Louis XIV, Lyon, France

3

Central European Monarchs Clash

MAIN IDEA	WHY IT MATTERS NOW	TERMS & NAMES
POWER AND AUTHORITY After a period of turmoil, absolute monarchs ruled Austria and the Germanic state of Prussia.	Prussia built a strong military tradition in Germany that contributed in part to world wars in the 20th century.	• Thirty Years' War • Maria Theresa • Frederick the Great • Seven Years' War

SETTING THE STAGE For a brief while, the German rulers appeared to have settled their religious differences through the Peace of Augsburg (1555). They had agreed that the faith of each prince would determine the religion of his subjects. Churches in Germany could be either Lutheran or Catholic, but not Calvinist. The peace was short-lived—soon to be replaced by a long war. After the Peace of Augsburg, the Catholic and Lutheran princes of Germany watched each other suspiciously.

CALIFORNIA STANDARDS

10.5.1 Analyze the arguments for entering into war presented by leaders from all sides of the Great War and the role of political and economic rivalries, ethnic and ideological conflicts, domestic discontent and disorder, and propaganda and nationalism in mobilizing the civilian population in support of "total war."

CST 3 Students use a variety of maps and documents to interpret human movement, including major patterns of domestic and international migration, changing environmental preferences and settlement patterns, the frictions that develop between population groups, and the diffusion of ideas, technological innovations, and goods.

The Thirty Years' War

Both the Lutheran and the Catholic princes tried to gain followers. In addition, both sides felt threatened by Calvinism, which was spreading in Germany and gaining many followers. As tension mounted, the Lutherans joined together in the Protestant Union in 1608. The following year, the Catholic princes formed the Catholic League. Now, it would take only a spark to set off a war.

Bohemian Protestants Revolt That spark came in 1618. The future Holy Roman emperor, Ferdinand II, was head of the Hapsburg family. As such, he ruled the Czech kingdom of Bohemia. The Protestants in Bohemia did not trust Ferdinand, who was a foreigner and a Catholic. When he closed some Protestant churches, the Protestants revolted. Ferdinand sent an army into Bohemia to crush the revolt. Several German Protestant princes took this chance to challenge their Catholic emperor.

Thus began the **Thirty Years' War**, a conflict over religion and territory and for power among European ruling families. The war can be divided into two main phases: the phase of Hapsburg triumphs and the phase of Hapsburg defeats.

Hapsburg Triumphs The Thirty Years' War lasted from 1618 to 1648. During the first 12 years, Hapsburg armies from Austria and Spain crushed the troops hired by the Protestant princes. They succeeded in putting down the Czech uprising. They also defeated the German Protestants who had supported the Czechs.

Ferdinand II paid his army of 125,000 men by allowing them to plunder, or rob, German villages. This huge army destroyed everything in its path.

Hapsburg Defeats The Protestant Gustavus Adolphus of Sweden and his disciplined army of 23,000 shifted the tide of war in 1630. They drove the Hapsburg

TAKING NOTES

Comparing Use a chart to compare Maria Theresa with Frederick the Great. Compare their years of reign, foreign policy, and success in war.

Maria Theresa	Frederick the Great

LESSON PLAN

OBJECTIVES

- Describe the Thirty Years' War.
- Explain the growth of central European states.
- Identify conflicts between Prussia and Austria.

1 FOCUS & MOTIVATE

Ask students if they are familiar with the Seven Years' War. *(Some students may recall from their study of American history that the French and Indian War was the American phase of this conflict.)*

2 INSTRUCT

The Thirty Years' War

10.5.1

Critical Thinking

- How might Catholic Church officials have reacted to Richelieu's and Mazarin's actions during the Thirty Years' War? *(Possible Answer: might have worried over French troops fighting on the side of Protestants)*

In-Depth Resources: Unit 2

- Guided Reading, p. 3 (also in Spanish)

CALIFORNIA RESOURCES

California Reading Toolkit, p. L25
California Modified Lesson Plans for English Learners, p. 45
California Daily Standards Practice Transparencies, TT17
California Standards Enrichment Workbook, pp. 55–56
California Standards Planner and Lesson Plans, p. L41
California Online Test Practice
California Test Generator CD-ROM
California Easy Planner CD-ROM
California eEdition CD-ROM

SECTION 3 PROGRAM RESOURCES

ALL STUDENTS

In-Depth Resources: Unit 2
- Guided Reading, p. 3
- Geography Application: Old Empires and New Powers, p. 8
- History Makers: Maria Theresa, p. 17

Formal Assessment
- Section Quiz, p. 88

ENGLISH LEARNERS

In-Depth Resources in Spanish
- Guided Reading, p. 46
- Geography Application: Old Empires and New Powers, p. 50

Reading Study Guide (Spanish), p. 55
Reading Study Guide Audio CD (Spanish)

STRUGGLING READERS

In-Depth Resources: Unit 2
- Guided Reading, p. 3
- Building Vocabulary, p. 6
- Geography Application: Old Empires and New Powers, p. 8
- Reteaching Activity, p. 22

Reading Study Guide, p. 55
Reading Study Guide Audio CD

GIFTED AND TALENTED STUDENTS

Electronic Library of Primary Sources
- from *Essay on Forms of Government*

INTEGRATED TECHNOLOGY

eEdition CD-ROM
Power Presentations CD-ROM
Electronic Library of Primary Sources
- from *Essay on Forms of Government*

classzone.com

More About . . .

Gustavus Adolphus

Gustavus entered the Thirty Years' War at a time when Catholic forces threatened to cross the Baltic Sea and attack Protestant Sweden. His brilliant military tactics saved Sweden and helped preserve Protestant religion in Germany. Gustavus was also a skilled administrator and is considered the founder of the modern Swedish state.

History from Visuals

Interpreting the Map

Have students examine the main map and inset map. Ask what the two maps show. *(Europe after the war; population losses in the Holy Roman Empire)* Have students explain how population data are shown.

Extension Have students look at the political map of Europe in the atlas. Ask them to identify ways that the borders in Europe today differ from those in 1648.

SKILLBUILDER Answers

1. **Place** Austria, Denmark, England, France, Hungary, Ireland, the Netherlands, Poland, Portugal, Spain, Switzerland, Sweden
2. **Region** Pomerania, Brandenburg, Silesia, the Palatinate

INTEGRATED TECHNOLOGY

Interactive Students can access an interactive version of this map on the eEdition.

armies out of northern Germany. However, Gustavus Adolphus was killed in battle in 1632.

Cardinal Richelieu and Cardinal Mazarin of France dominated the remaining years of the war. Although Catholic, these two cardinals feared the Hapsburgs more than the Protestants. They did not want other European rulers to have as much power as the French king. Therefore, in 1635, Richelieu sent French troops to join the German and Swedish Protestants in their struggle against the Hapsburg armies.

Peace of Westphalia The war did great damage to Germany. Its population dropped from 20 million to about 16 million. Both trade and agriculture were disrupted, and Germany's economy was ruined. Germany had a long, difficult recovery from this devastation. That is a major reason it did not become a unified state until the 1800s.

The Peace of Westphalia (1648) ended the war. The treaty had these important consequences:

- weakened the Hapsburg states of Spain and Austria;
- strengthened France by awarding it German territory;
- made German princes independent of the Holy Roman emperor;
- ended religious wars in Europe;
- introduced a new method of peace negotiation whereby all participants meet to settle the problems of a war and decide the terms of peace. This method is still used today. (A)

Beginning of Modern States The treaty thus abandoned the idea of a Catholic empire that would rule most of Europe. It recognized Europe as a group of equal, independent states. This marked the beginning of the modern state system and was the most important result of the Thirty Years' War.

A. Possible Answer politics, because they put the needs of their king ahead of the fight against Protestantism

MAIN IDEA

Drawing Conclusions

(A) Judging from their actions, do you think the two French cardinals were motivated more by religion or politics? Why?

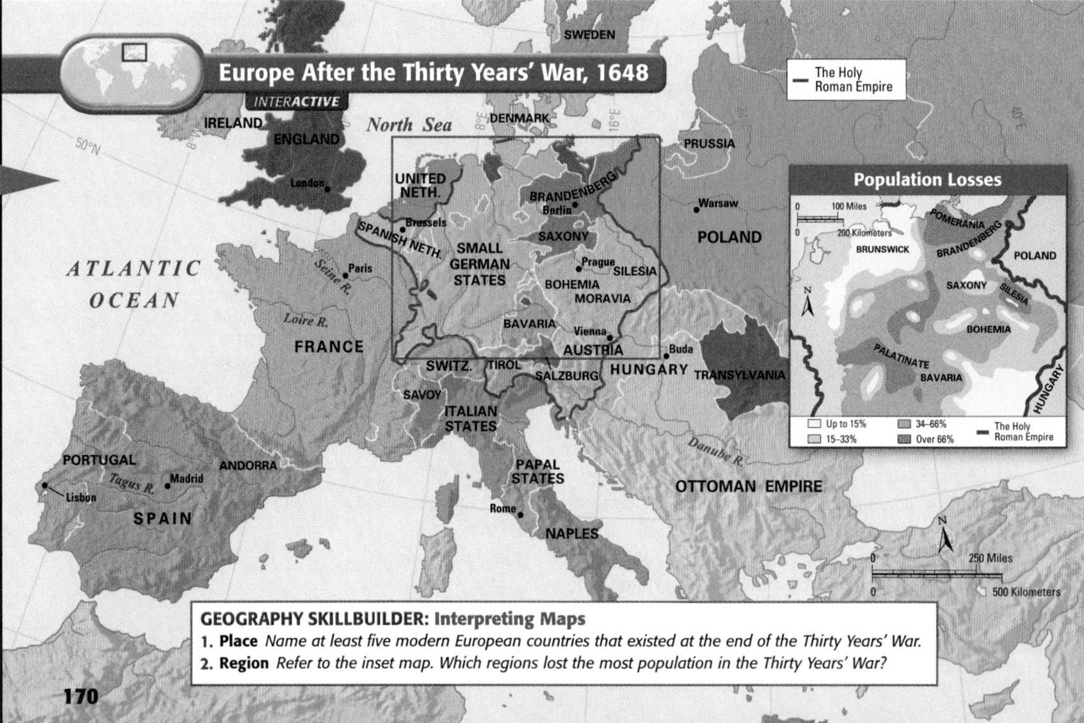

GEOGRAPHY SKILLBUILDER: Interpreting Maps

1. **Place** *Name at least five modern European countries that existed at the end of the Thirty Years' War.*
2. **Region** *Refer to the inset map. Which regions lost the most population in the Thirty Years' War?*

170

DIFFERENTIATING INSTRUCTION: GIFTED AND TALENTED STUDENTS

Researching the Thirty Years' War

Class Time 40 minutes

Task Examining a primary source and writing an e-mail

Purpose To deepen students' understanding of historical events with firsthand accounts and interpretations

Instructions Have students examine the material about the Thirty Years' War on pages 169–170. Then have them study one of the following primary sources, which are all based on their creators' firsthand experience of the war. Students might choose to read part or all of Grimmelhausen's *Simplicius Simplicissimus* (1669), a biting satire recounting the vagabond adventures of a simpleton during the war. Or they might examine the work of French engraver Jacques Callot, who created a series of engravings called *The Miseries of War* (1632–1633) that show the life of a typical soldier. A final option is Hugo Grotius's *On the Law of War and Peace* (1625). Grotius was a Swedish diplomat who responded to the war by writing a treatise that became a foundation of modern international law. After they have examined one of these accounts, have students write an e-mail that recommends it to a friend. E-mails should be at least 300 words long.

States Form in Central Europe

Strong states formed more slowly in central Europe than in western Europe. The major powers of this region were the kingdom of Poland, the Holy Roman Empire, and the Ottoman Empire. None of them was very strong in the mid-1600s.

Economic Contrasts with the West One reason for this is that the economy of central Europe developed differently from that of western Europe. During the late Middle Ages, serfs in western Europe slowly won freedom and moved to towns. There, they joined middle-class townspeople, who gained economic power because of the commercial revolution and the development of capitalism.

By contrast, the landowning aristocracy in central Europe passed laws restricting the ability of serfs to gain freedom and move to cities. These nobles wanted to keep the serfs on the land, where they could produce large harvests. The nobles could then sell the surplus crops to western European cities at great profit.

Several Weak Empires The landowning nobles in central Europe not only held down the serfs but also blocked the development of strong kings. For example, the Polish nobility elected the Polish king and sharply limited his power. They allowed the king little income, no law courts, and no standing army. As a result, there was not a strong ruler who could form a unified state.

The two empires of central Europe were also weak. Although Suleyman the Magnificent had conquered Hungary and threatened Vienna in 1529, the Ottoman Empire could not take its European conquest any farther. From then on, the Ottoman Empire declined from its peak of power.

In addition, the Holy Roman Empire was seriously weakened by the Thirty Years' War. No longer able to command the obedience of the German states, the Holy Roman Empire had no real power. These old, weakened empires and kingdoms left a power vacuum in central Europe. In the late 1600s, two German-speaking families decided to try to fill this vacuum by becoming absolute rulers themselves.

Austria Grows Stronger One of these families was the Hapsburgs of Austria. The Austrian Hapsburgs took several steps to become absolute monarchs. First, during the Thirty Years' War, they reconquered Bohemia. The Hapsburgs wiped out Protestantism there and created a new Czech nobility that pledged loyalty to them. Second, after the war, the Hapsburg ruler centralized the government and created a standing army. Third, by 1699, the Hapsburgs had retaken Hungary from the Ottoman Empire.

In 1711, Charles VI became the Hapsburg ruler. Charles's empire was a difficult one to rule. Within its borders lived a diverse assortment of people—Czechs, Hungarians, Italians, Croatians, and Germans. Only the fact that one Hapsburg ruler wore the Austrian, Hungarian, and Bohemian crowns kept the empire together.

▼ The imperial crest of the Hapsburgs shows a double-headed eagle with a crown.

Maria Theresa Inherits the Austrian Throne How could the Hapsburgs make sure that they continued to rule all those lands? Charles VI spent his entire reign working out an answer to this problem. With endless arm-twisting, he persuaded other leaders of Europe to sign an agreement that declared they would recognize Charles's eldest daughter as the heir to all his Hapsburg territories. That heir was a young woman named **Maria Theresa**. In theory, this agreement guaranteed Maria Theresa a peaceful reign. Instead, she faced years of war. Her main enemy was Prussia, a state to the north of Austria. (See map opposite.)

States Form in Central Europe
10.5.1

Critical Thinking

- Which step taken by the Austrian Hapsburgs to become absolute rulers was most important? *(Possible Answer: creation of a standing army to control the nobility and hold on to territories)*
- What tactics might a ruler use to establish stability in a territory with an extremely diverse population? *(Possible Answers: Use the threat of force to preserve order. Maintain the legal equality of the different groups. Prevent the economic status of the groups from becoming too uneven.)*

Tip for Struggling Readers

Tell students that standing armies—permanent armies of paid soldiers—are usually contrasted with militias, which are called on only in emergencies. In modern usage, army usually means "standing army."

More About . . .

The Hapsburgs

The Hapsburgs, a royal German family, were one of the chief ruling dynasties of Europe from the 15th century to the 20th. Hapsburgs ruled Austria continuously from 1282 to 1918. They also ruled Hungary, Bohemia, Spain, and other lands. The Holy Roman Empire was under Hapsburg control from the mid-1400s until its disintegration in 1806.

DIFFERENTIATING INSTRUCTION: STRUGGLING READERS

Understanding How States Formed

Class Time 25 minutes

Task Making an informal outline

Purpose To help students study the text

Instructions Explain that condensing information may help them to understand the text better. Have students read "States Form in Central Europe" on this page. After they have read the selection, have them outline the material. For each subsection, ask students to write one or more sentences that express that subsection's main idea. A partially completed example follows.

States Form in Central Europe

Introduction

- *States formed more slowly in central Europe than in western Europe.*

Economic Contrasts with the West

- *Serfs in western Europe moved to towns and got jobs. The middle class got strong. Serfs in central Europe were forced to stay on the farms. A strong middle class couldn't develop.*

History Makers

Maria Theresa and Frederick the Great

Ask students how individuals as different as Maria Theresa and Frederick the Great could both become powerful rulers. *(Possible Answer: Both inherited their authority from ruling families with firmly established power bases.)*

Electronic Library of Primary Sources
- from *Essay on Forms of Government*

In-Depth Resources: Unit 2
- History Makers: Maria Theresa, p. 17

INTEGRATED TECHNOLOGY

Rubric Family trees should
- clearly label family relationships.
- show dates of birth and death.

Prussia Challenges Austria
10.5.1

Critical Thinking
- What precedent suggests that Frederick II's assumption about the weakness of women leaders was misguided? *(Queen Elizabeth's routing of the Spanish Armada in 1588.)*
- Why would Frederick II's attack on Saxony result in conflicts in North America and India? *(Possible Answer: Allies of the two countries probably used the attack as an excuse to seize enemy territory overseas.)*

History Makers

Maria Theresa
1717–1780

An able ruler, Maria Theresa also devoted herself to her children, whom she continued to advise even after they were grown. Perhaps her most famous child was Marie Antoinette, wife of Louis XVI of France.

As the Austrian empress, Maria Theresa decreased the power of the nobility. She also limited the amount of labor that nobles could force peasants to do. She argued: "The peasantry must be able to sustain itself."

Frederick the Great
1712–1786

Although they reigned during the same time, Frederick the Great and Maria Theresa were very different. Where Maria was religious, Frederick was practical and atheistic. Maria Theresa had a happy home life and a huge family, while Frederick died without a son to succeed him.

An aggressor in foreign affairs, Frederick once wrote that "the fundamental role of governments is the principle of extending their territories." Frederick earned the title "the Great" by achieving his goals for Prussia.

INTEGRATED TECHNOLOGY

INTERNET ACTIVITY Create a family tree showing Maria Theresa's parents and children. Go to **classzone.com** for your research.

Prussia Challenges Austria

Like Austria, Prussia rose to power in the late 1600s. Like the Hapsburgs of Austria, Prussia's ruling family, the Hohenzollerns, also had ambitions. Those ambitions threatened to upset central Europe's delicate balance of power.

The Rise of Prussia The Hohenzollerns built up their state from a number of small holdings, beginning with the German states of Brandenburg and Prussia. In 1640, a 20-year-old Hohenzollern named Frederick William inherited the title of elector of Brandenburg. After seeing the destruction of the Thirty Years' War, Frederick William, later known as the Great Elector, decided that having a strong army was the only way to ensure safety.

To protect their lands, the Great Elector and his descendants moved toward absolute monarchy. They created a standing army, the best in Europe. They built it to a force of 80,000 men. To pay for the army, they introduced permanent taxation. Beginning with the Great Elector's son, they called themselves kings. They also weakened the representative assemblies of their territories.

Prussia's landowning nobility, the Junkers (YUNG•kuhrz), resisted the king's growing power. However, in the early 1700s, King Frederick William I bought their cooperation. He gave the Junkers the exclusive right to be officers in his army. As a result, Prussia became a rigidly controlled, highly militarized society. **B**

MAIN IDEA
Clarifying
B What steps did the Prussian monarchs take to become absolute monarchs?

B. Answer They created a standing army, limited the power of the nobles, and made military conquests.

Frederick the Great Frederick William worried that his son, Frederick, was not military enough to rule. The prince loved music, philosophy, and poetry. In 1730, when he and a friend tried to run away, they were caught. To punish Frederick, the king ordered him to witness his friend's beheading. Despite such bitter memories, Frederick II, known as **Frederick the Great**, followed his father's military policies when he came to power. However, he also softened some of his father's laws. With regard to domestic affairs, he encouraged religious toleration and legal reform. According to his theory of government, Frederick believed that a ruler should be like a father to his people:

PRIMARY SOURCE

A prince . . . is only the first servant of the state, who is obliged to act with probity [honesty] and prudence. . . . As the sovereign is properly the head of a family of citizens, the father of his people, he ought on all occasions to be the last refuge of the unfortunate.

FREDERICK II, *Essay on Forms of Government*

DIFFERENTIATING INSTRUCTION: ENGLISH LEARNERS

Political Transition in Central and Eastern Europe

Class Time 30 minutes

Task Studying geographic changes

Purpose To help students understand the power changes in Europe

Instructions Divide students into small groups that include both proficient readers and English learners. Have each group read the Geography Application for this section in In-Depth Resources: Unit 2. Students should take turns reading the selection aloud. When they have finished reading the selection, ask students to look at the maps and identify changes that occurred in the political geography of central Europe between 1660 and 1795. What is the most striking difference in the two maps? *(The Holy Roman Empire has disappeared.)* By 1795 what three new powers have emerged? *(Prussia, Russian Empire, Austrian Empire)* Students should then work again in their groups to answer the questions that follow the selection.

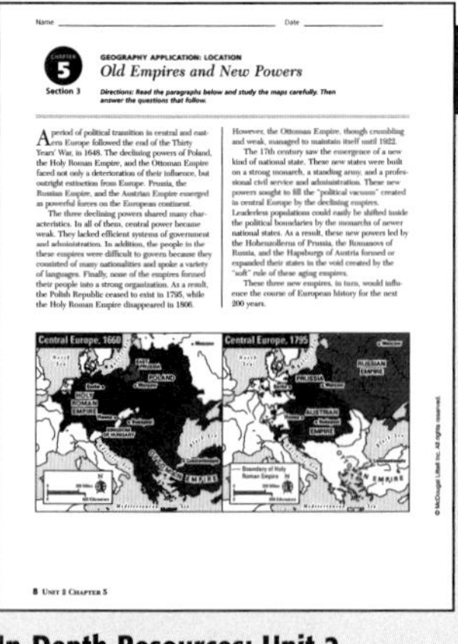
GEOGRAPHY APPLICATION: LOCATION
Old Empires and New Powers

In-Depth Resources: Unit 2

172 Chapter 5

War of the Austrian Succession In 1740, Maria Theresa succeeded her father, just five months after Frederick II became king of Prussia. Frederick wanted the Austrian land of Silesia, which bordered Prussia. Silesia produced iron ore, textiles, and food products. Frederick underestimated Maria Theresa's strength. He assumed that because she was a woman, she would not be forceful enough to defend her lands. In 1740, he sent his army to occupy Silesia, beginning the War of the Austrian Succession. C

MAIN IDEA

Clarifying

C Why would iron ore, agricultural lands, and textiles be helpful acquisitions for Frederick the Great?

C. Possible Answer Frederick needed to feed and clothe his troops and supply them with weapons.

Even though Maria Theresa had recently given birth, she journeyed to Hungary. There she held her infant in her arms as she asked the Hungarian nobles for aid. Even though the nobles resented their Hapsburg rulers, they pledged to give Maria Theresa an army. Great Britain also joined Austria to fight its longtime enemy France, which was Prussia's ally. Although Maria Theresa did stop Prussia's aggression, she lost Silesia in the Treaty of Aix-la-Chapelle in 1748. With the acquisition of Silesia, Prussia became a major European power.

The Seven Years' War Maria Theresa decided that the French kings were no longer Austria's chief enemies. She made an alliance with them. The result was a diplomatic revolution. When Frederick heard of her actions, he signed a treaty with Britain—Austria's former ally. Now, Austria, France, Russia, and others were allied against Britain and Prussia. Not only had Austria and Prussia switched allies, but for the first time, Russia was playing a role in European affairs.

In 1756, Frederick attacked Saxony, an Austrian ally. Soon every great European power was involved in the war. Fought in Europe, India, and North America, the war lasted until 1763. It was called the **Seven Years' War**. The war did not change the territorial situation in Europe.

It was a different story on other continents. Both France and Britain had colonies in North America and the West Indies. Both were competing economically in India. The British emerged as the real victors in the Seven Years' War. France lost its colonies in North America, and Britain gained sole economic domination of India. This set the stage for further British expansion in India in the 1800s, as you will see in Chapter 11.

SECTION 3 ASSESSMENT

TERMS & NAMES 1. For each term or name, write a sentence explaining its significance.
• Thirty Years' War • Maria Theresa • Frederick the Great • Seven Years' War

USING YOUR NOTES

2. In what ways were the rulers similar? (CST 3)

Maria Theresa	Frederick the Great

MAIN IDEAS

3. What were the major conflicts in the Thirty Years' War? (10.5.1)
4. What steps did the Austrian Hapsburgs take toward becoming absolute monarchs? (10.5.1)
5. What countries were allies during the Seven Years' War? (10.5.1)

CRITICAL THINKING & WRITING

6. **RECOGNIZING EFFECTS** How did the Peace of Westphalia lay the foundations of modern Europe? (10.5.1)
7. **ANALYZING MOTIVES** Why did Maria Theresa make an alliance with the French kings, Austria's enemies? (10.5.1)
8. **DRAWING CONCLUSIONS** Based on Frederick's assumption about Maria Theresa at the outset of the War of the Austrian Succession, what are your conclusions about how men viewed women in 1700s Europe? (10.5.1)
9. **WRITING ACTIVITY** POWER AND AUTHORITY Write an **outline** for a lecture on "How to Increase Royal Power and Become an Absolute Monarch." (Writing 2.6.a)

CONNECT TO TODAY **CREATING A POSTER**

Today much of western Europe belongs to an organization called the European Union (EU). Find out which countries belong to the EU and how they are linked economically and politically. Present your findings—including maps, charts, and pictures—in a **poster.** (CST 3)

More About . . .

Monarchs and Baroque Art

The absolute monarchs of central Europe used the artistic style known as baroque in their palaces to overwhelm people and to symbolize the grandeur and power of the centralized state. The art was monumental in scale and emphasized elaborate decoration and bold curving forms.

3 ASSESS

SECTION 3 ASSESSMENT

Ask pairs of students to share their responses to questions 6 and 9 and to revise their answers based on any new insights or information.

Formal Assessment
• Section Quiz, p. 88

4 RETEACH

Use the compare-and-contrast graphic organizer transparency to extend the Using Your Notes question in the assessment.

Critical Thinking Transparencies
• CT74 Compare and Contrast

In-Depth Resources: Unit 2
• Reteaching Activity, p. 22

ANSWERS

1. Thirty Years' War, p. 169 • Maria Theresa, p. 171 • Frederick the Great, p. 172 • Seven Years' War, p. 173
2. **Sample Answer:** Maria Theresa—Decreased power of nobility; fought Prussia; allied with France; limited forced labor of peasants. Frederick—Fought Austria; allied with Britain; encouraged religious toleration and legal reform. Both reigned for decades and were ambitious, shrewd, and more tolerant than other rulers.
3. religious and territorial disputes; competition among ruling families for power
4. reconquered Bohemia; centralized government; created standing army; retook Hungary from the Ottomans
5. Austria, France, and Russia were allies against Prussia and Britain.
6. by ending religious wars, recognizing Europe as collection of independent states, and establishing a modern way of negotiating
7. to thwart Prussia and steal its powerful ally
8. as weak and only interested in family
9. **Rubric** Outlines should
• be organized logically.
• include examples from Hapsburg and Hohenzollern history.

CONNECT TO TODAY

Rubric Posters should
• provide the names of the member nations.
• mention the euro, the EU's currency.
• list trade agreements and political organizations.
• use relevant visuals.

LESSON PLAN

OBJECTIVES

- Explain how Russian rulers began to build a stronger Russian state.
- Characterize the differences between Russia and western Europe.
- Describe Peter the Great's reforms and their impact on Russia.

1 FOCUS & MOTIVATE

Ask students whether they consider Russia to be part of Europe. *(Some students will argue that Russia is part of both Europe and Asia.)*

2 INSTRUCT

The First Czar
10.1.2

Critical Thinking

- Why might boyars have wanted to elect another czar? *(Possible Answers: a central authority could help mediate conflicts among the boyars; to present a unified front against their enemies)*

In-Depth Resources: Unit 2
- Guided Reading, p. 4 (also in Spanish)

CALIFORNIA RESOURCES
California Reading Toolkit, p. L26
California Modified Lesson Plans for English Learners, p. 47
California Daily Standards Practice Transparencies, TT18
California Standards Enrichment Workbook, pp. 19–20
California Standards Planner and Lesson Plans, p. L43
California Online Test Practice
California Test Generator CD-ROM
California Easy Planner CD-ROM
California eEdition CD-ROM

Marriage of Louis XIV to Marie Thérèse of Austria. Artist unknown

4

Statue of Louis XIV, Lyon, France

Absolute Rulers of Russia

MAIN IDEA	WHY IT MATTERS NOW	TERMS & NAMES
POWER AND AUTHORITY Peter the Great made many changes in Russia to try to make it more like western Europe.	Many Russians today debate whether to model themselves on the West or to focus on traditional Russian culture.	• Ivan the Terrible • boyar • Peter the Great • westernization

CALIFORNIA STANDARDS

10.1.2 Trace the development of the Western political ideas of the rule of law and illegitimacy of tyranny, using selections from Plato's *Republic* and Aristotle's *Politics*.

CST 1 Students compare the present with the past, evaluating the consequences of past events and decisions and determining the lessons that were learned.

CST 3 Students use a variety of maps and documents to interpret human movement, including major patterns of domestic and international migration, changing environmental preferences and settlement patterns, the frictions that develop between population groups, and the diffusion of ideas, technological innovations, and goods.

SETTING THE STAGE Ivan III of Moscow, who ruled Russia from 1462 to 1505, accomplished several things. First, he conquered much of the territory around Moscow. Second, he liberated Russia from the Mongols. Third, he began to centralize the Russian government. Ivan III was succeeded by his son, Vasily, who ruled for 28 years. Vasily continued his father's work of adding territory to the growing Russian state. He also increased the power of the central government. This trend continued under his son, Ivan IV, who would become an absolute ruler.

The First Czar

Ivan IV, called **Ivan the Terrible**, came to the throne in 1533 when he was only three years old. His young life was disrupted by struggles for power among Russia's landowning nobles, known as **boyars**. The boyars fought to control young Ivan. When he was 16, Ivan seized power and had himself crowned czar. This title meant "caesar," and Ivan was the first Russian ruler to use it officially. He also married the beautiful Anastasia, related to an old boyar family, the Romanovs.

The years from 1547 to 1560 are often called Ivan's "good period." He won great victories, added lands to Russia, gave Russia a code of laws, and ruled justly.

TAKING NOTES
Summarizing Use a cluster diagram to list the important events of Peter the Great's reign.

Rule by Terror Ivan's "bad period" began in 1560 after Anastasia died. Accusing the boyars of poisoning his wife, Ivan turned against them. He organized his own police force, whose chief duty was to hunt down and murder people Ivan considered traitors. The members of this police force dressed in black and rode black horses.

Using these secret police, Ivan executed many boyars, their families, and the peasants who worked their lands. Thousands of people died. Ivan seized the boyars' estates and gave them to a new class of nobles, who had to remain loyal to him or lose their land.

Eventually, Ivan committed an act that was both a personal tragedy and a national disaster. In 1581, during a violent quarrel, he killed his oldest son and heir. When Ivan died three years later, only his weak second son was left to rule.

Rise of the Romanovs Ivan's son proved to be physically and mentally incapable of ruling. After he died without an heir, Russia experienced a period of

SECTION 4 PROGRAM RESOURCES

ALL STUDENTS
In-Depth Resources: Unit 2
- Guided Reading, p. 4
- Skillbuilder Practice, p. 7

Formal Assessment
- Section Quiz, p. 89

ENGLISH LEARNERS
In-Depth Resources in Spanish
- Guided Reading, p. 47
- Skillbuilder Practice, p. 49

Reading Study Guide (Spanish), p. 57
Reading Study Guide Audio CD (Spanish)

STRUGGLING READERS
In-Depth Resources: Unit 2
- Guided Reading, p. 4
- Building Vocabulary, p. 6
- Reteaching Activity, p. 23

Reading Study Guide, p. 57
Reading Study Guide Audio CD

GIFTED AND TALENTED STUDENTS
In-Depth Resources: Unit 2
- Primary Source: Peter the Great's Reforms, p. 11

Electronic Library of Primary Sources
- from Letters of Peter the Great

INTEGRATED TECHNOLOGY
eEdition CD-ROM
Power Presentations CD-ROM
Critical Thinking Transparencies
- CT21 The Age of Absolute Monarchs

World Art and Cultures Transparencies
- AT46 Peter the Great Interrogating Alexei
- AT47 Saint Basil's Cathedral

classzone.com

MAIN IDEA
Recognizing Effects
(A) What were the long-term effects of Ivan's murder of his oldest son?

A. Answer First, Russia was ruled by a weak czar, then it experienced turmoil as several struggled to gain power, and finally the Romanov dynasty was established.

turmoil known as the Time of Troubles. Boyars struggled for power, and heirs of czars died under mysterious conditions. Several impostors tried to claim the throne.

Finally, in 1613, representatives from many Russian cities met to choose the next czar. Their choice was Michael Romanov, grandnephew of Ivan the Terrible's wife, Anastasia. Thus began the Romanov dynasty, which ruled Russia for 300 years (1613–1917). (A)

Peter the Great Comes to Power

Over time, the Romanovs restored order to Russia. They strengthened government by passing a law code and putting down a revolt. This paved the way for the absolute rule of Czar Peter I. At first, Peter shared the throne with his half-brother. However, in 1696, Peter became sole ruler of Russia. He is known to history as **Peter the Great**, because he was one of Russia's greatest reformers. He also continued the trend of increasing the czar's power.

Russia Contrasts with Europe When Peter I came to power, Russia was still a land of boyars and serfs. Serfdom in Russia lasted into the mid-1800s, much longer than it did in western Europe. Russian landowners wanted serfs to stay on the land and produce large harvests. The landowners treated the serfs like property. When a Russian landowner sold a piece of land, he sold the serfs with it. Landowners could give away serfs as presents or to pay debts. It was also against the law for serfs to run away from their owners.

Most boyars knew little of western Europe. In the Middle Ages, Russia had looked to Constantinople, not to Rome, for leadership. Then Mongol rule had cut Russia off from the Renaissance and the Age of Exploration. Geographic barriers also isolated Russia. Its only seaport, Archangel in northern Russia, was choked with ice much of the year. The few travelers who reached Moscow were usually Dutch or German, and they had to stay in a separate part of the city.

Religious differences widened the gap between western Europe and Russia. The Russians had adopted the Eastern Orthodox branch of Christianity. Western Europeans were mostly Catholics or Protestants, and the Russians viewed them as heretics and avoided them. (B)

MAIN IDEA
Summarizing
(B) Why was Russia culturally different from western Europe?

B. Answers It had a feudal rather than a commercial economy; it had been influenced by Constantinople and the Mongols; it followed a different form of Christianity.

Peter Visits the West In the 1680s, people in the German quarter of Moscow were accustomed to seeing the young Peter striding through their neighborhood on his long legs. (Peter was more than six and a half feet tall.) He was fascinated by the modern tools and machines in the foreigners' shops. Above all, he had a passion for ships and the sea. The young czar believed that Russia's future depended on having a warm-water port. Only then could Russia compete with the more modern states of western Europe.

Peter was 24 years old when he became the sole ruler of Russia. In 1697, just one year later, he embarked on the "Grand Embassy," a long visit to western Europe. One of Peter's goals was to learn about European customs and manufacturing techniques. Never before had a czar traveled among Western "heretics."

History Makers

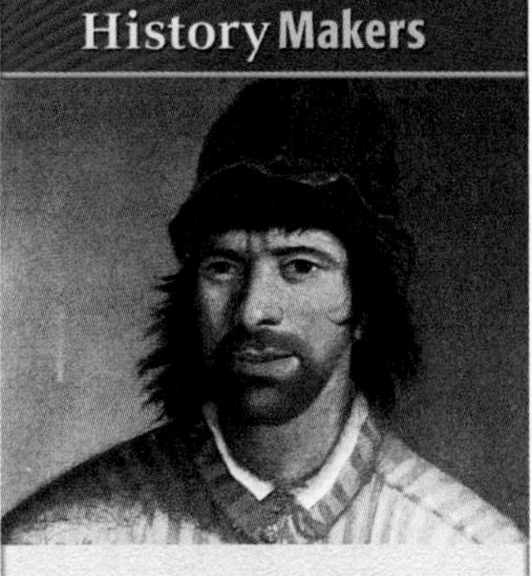

Peter the Great
1672–1725

Peter the Great had the mind of a genius, the body of a giant, and the ferocious temper of a bear. He was so strong that he was known to take a heavy silver plate and roll it up as if it were a piece of paper. If someone annoyed him, he would knock the offender unconscious.

The painting above represents Peter as he looked when he traveled through western Europe. He dressed in the plain clothes of an ordinary worker to keep his identity a secret.

INTEGRATED TECHNOLOGY
RESEARCH LINKS For more on Peter the Great, go to **classzone.com**

Peter the Great Comes to Power
10.1.2

Critical Thinking

- Why might travelers to Russia have had to stay in a separate part of the city? *(Possible Answers: Russians were suspicious of strangers.)*
- Were geographical or cultural factors more important in isolating Russia from the rest of Europe? *(Possible Answer: Cultural factors, such as religion and language, and geography kept Russia isolated.)*

History Makers

Peter the Great

Why might Peter have traveled through Europe incognito? *(He may have felt that he could learn more about the economic and cultural life of Europe if he did not attract attention to himself.)*

Peter's son, Alexei, was sentenced to death for opposing his father's reforms. He died in prison, presumably by violence, before the formal execution of the sentence.

In-Depth Resources: Unit 2
- Primary Sources: Peter the Great's Reforms, p. 11

World Art and Cultures Transparencies
- AT46: Peter the Great Interrogating Alexei
- AT47 St. Basil's Cathedral

Electronic Library of Primary Sources
- from Letters of Peter the Great

DIFFERENTIATING INSTRUCTION: ENGLISH LEARNERS

Contrasting Russia and Western Europe

Class Time 20 minutes

Task Using a table to contrast two regions

Purpose To help students identify the differences between Russia and western Europe

Instructions Ask students to draw a table in their notebooks with three columns and four rows. Tell them to label the columns as shown. Then ask students to read "Russia Contrasts with Europe" on this page. Have them fill in their tables using information from the selection and from previous sections.

Category	Russia	Western Europe
Labor	Russian landowners treated serfs like property. Serfdom lasted until the mid-1800s.	In western Europe, many serfs won their freedom and moved to cities.
Religion	Russians were Orthodox Christians.	Western Europeans were mostly Catholics and Protestants.
Geography	Russia was geographically isolated and had few seaports.	The geography of western Europe helped trade and made political connections possible.

Peter Rules Absolutely

10.1.2

Critical Thinking

- Why did Peter want to bring the Orthodox Church under state control? *(The Church might be a potential obstacle to his reforms.)*
- Why might Peter have believed that education was key to progress? *(Possible Answers: help new values take root; advances required knowledge of science and mathematics.)*

Critical Thinking Transparencies

- CT21 The Age of Absolute Monarchs, 1500–1800

History from Visuals

Interpreting the Map

By what year had Russia gained land on the Arctic Ocean? *(1505)*

Extension Have students compare this map with the political map of Europe in the atlas. What modern European nations are completely engulfed by the territory covered by Russia in 1800? *(Russia, Estonia, Latvia, Lithuania, Belarus)*

SKILLBUILDER Answers

1. **Location** Baltic Sea, Sea of Okhotsk, Pacific Ocean
2. **Region** Peter the Great

INTEGRATED TECHNOLOGY

Interactive This map is available in an interactive format on the eEdition.

Peter Rules Absolutely

Inspired by his trip to the West, Peter resolved that Russia would compete with Europe on both military and commercial terms. Peter's goal of **westernization**, of using western Europe as a model for change, was not an end in itself. Peter saw it as a way to make Russia stronger.

Peter's Reforms Although Peter believed Russia needed to change, he knew that many of his people disagreed. As he said to one official, "For you know yourself that, though a thing be good and necessary, our people will not do it unless forced to." To force change upon his state, Peter increased his powers as an absolute ruler. C

Peter brought the Russian Orthodox Church under state control. He abolished the office of patriarch, head of the Church. He set up a group called the Holy Synod to run the Church under his direction.

Like Ivan the Terrible, Peter reduced the power of the great landowners. He recruited men from lower-ranking families. He then promoted them to positions of authority and rewarded them with grants of land.

To modernize his army, Peter hired European officers, who drilled his soldiers in European tactics with European weapons. Being a soldier became a lifetime job. By the time of Peter's death, the Russian army numbered 200,000 men. To pay for this huge army, Peter imposed heavy taxes.

Westernizing Russia As part of his attempts to westernize Russia, Peter undertook the following:

- introduced potatoes, which became a staple of the Russian diet
- started Russia's first newspaper and edited its first issue himself
- raised women's status by having them attend social gatherings
- ordered the nobles to give up their traditional clothes for Western fashions
- advanced education by opening a school of navigation and introducing schools for the arts and sciences

MAIN IDEA

Analyzing Bias

C Judging from this remark, what was Peter's view of his people?

C. Possible Answers that they were backward and stubborn; that they were wrong and he was right

GEOGRAPHY SKILLBUILDER: Interpreting Maps

1. **Location** *Locate the territories that Peter added to Russia during his reign, from 1682 to 1725. What bodies of water did Russia gain access to because of these acquisitions?*
2. **Region** *Who added a larger amount of territory to Russia—Ivan III, who ruled from 1462 to 1505, or Peter the Great?*

176

SKILLBUILDER PRACTICE: EVALUATING DECISIONS AND COURSES OF ACTION

Judging Peter's Decision to Westernize Russia

Class Time 20 minutes

Task Answering questions about Peter the Great

Purpose To help students learn to evaluate the decisions of important historical figures

Instructions Historians evaluate the decisions of the past partly by looking at the short-term and long-term consequences of those decisions. Have students read about Peter's steps to westernize Russia on pages 176–177. Then ask these questions:

1. What were some key short-term effects of the decision to westernize Russia? *(The Russian army was trained in western tactics; St. Petersburg was built.)*
2. What was a key long-term effect? *(Russia could compete militarily and commercially with western Europe.)*
3. Was the decision to westernize a good one? Why or why not? *(Yes—It helped make Russia a great European power. No—Westernizing the military required imposing heavy taxes, and building St. Petersburg cost many lives.)*

Have students complete the Skillbuilder Practice activity in In-Depth Resources: Unit 2.

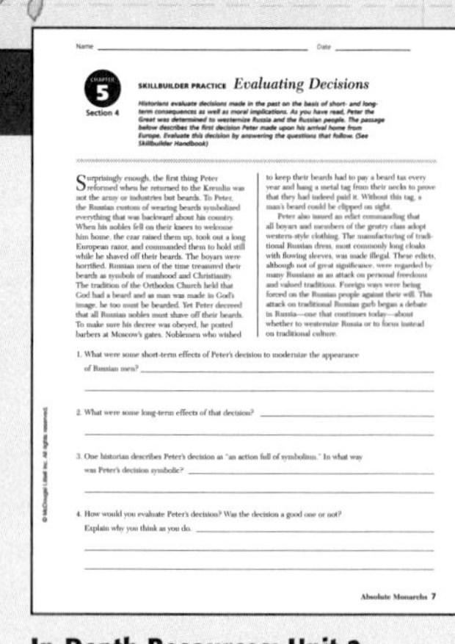

In-Depth Resources: Unit 2

Peter believed that education was a key to Russia's progress. In former times, subjects were forbidden under pain of death to study the sciences in foreign lands. Now subjects were not only permitted to leave the country, many were forced to do it.

Establishing St. Petersburg To promote education and growth, Peter wanted a seaport that would make it easier to travel to the West. Therefore, Peter fought Sweden to gain a piece of the Baltic coast. After 21 long years of war, Russia finally won the "window on Europe" that Peter had so desperately wanted.

Actually, Peter had secured that window many years before Sweden officially surrendered it. In 1703, he began building a new city on Swedish lands occupied by Russian troops. Although the swampy site was unhealthful, it seemed ideal to Peter. Ships could sail down the Neva River into the Baltic Sea and on to western Europe. Peter called the city St. Petersburg, after his patron saint.

To build a city on a desolate swamp was no easy matter. Every summer, the army forced thousands of luckless serfs to leave home and work in St. Petersburg. An estimated 25,000 to 100,000 people died from the terrible working conditions and widespread diseases. When St. Petersburg was finished, Peter ordered many Russian nobles to leave the comforts of Moscow and settle in his new capital. In time, St. Petersburg became a busy port. D

For better or for worse, Peter the Great had tried to westernize and reform the culture and government of Russia. To an amazing extent he had succeeded. By the time of his death in 1725, Russia was a power to be reckoned with in Europe. Meanwhile, another great European power, England, had been developing a form of government that limited the power of absolute monarchs, as you will see in Section 5.

D. Answer He ordered peasants to work there, and he ordered nobles to move there.

MAIN IDEA
Synthesizing
D Which of Peter's actions in building St. Petersburg show his power as an absolute monarch?

Global Patterns

East Meets West

In the East, Western influence would affect not only Russia. Other eastern nations would give way—not always willingly—to the West and Western culture. In 1854, Japan was forced to open its doors to the United States. By 1867, however, Japan had decided to embrace Western civilization. The Japanese modernized their military based on the German and British models. They also adopted the American system of public education. China and Korea, on the other hand, would resist foreign intervention well into the 1900s.

Global Patterns

East Meets West

Cultural influence also flows from east to west. For example, in the second half of the 19th century, Japanese art was an important influence on European painters such as Édouard Manet and Vincent Van Gogh. Since the 1960s, the United States has seen an explosion of interest in Eastern religions, such as Buddhism. The Indian practice of yoga, a system of exercises for attaining bodily and mental control, has become extremely popular in the United States. Ask students if they can think of other examples of "West meeting East."

SECTION 4 ASSESSMENT

TERMS & NAMES 1. For each term or name, write a sentence explaining its significance.
• Ivan the Terrible • boyar • Peter the Great • westernization

USING YOUR NOTES

2. Which event had the most impact on modern Russia? Why? (CST 1)

MAIN IDEAS

3. How did Ivan the Terrible deal with his enemies during his "bad period"? (10.1.2)
4. Why did Peter the Great believe that Russia's future depended on having a warm-water port? (10.1.2)
5. What were some of the ways Peter tried to westernize Russia? (10.1.2)

CRITICAL THINKING & WRITING

6. **SUPPORTING OPINIONS** Who was more of an absolute monarch: Ivan the Terrible or Peter the Great? (10.1.2)
7. **DRAWING CONCLUSIONS** Which class of Russian society probably didn't benefit from Peter's reforms? Why? (10.1.2)
8. **HYPOTHESIZING** How might Peter's attempts at westernization have affected his people's opinion of Christians in western Europe? (10.1.2)
9. **WRITING ACTIVITY** POWER AND AUTHORITY Write a one-paragraph **expository essay** explaining which of Peter the Great's actions reveal that he saw himself as the highest authority in Russia. (Writing 2.3.a)

CONNECT TO TODAY STAGING A DEBATE

Peter the Great's reforms were a first step toward Russia's westernization. Today the country continues the process by experimenting with democratization. Research to find out how Russia has fared as a democracy. Then stage a **debate** to argue whether the experiment is working. (CST 1)

③ ASSESS

SECTION 4 ASSESSMENT

Suggest that students jot down important points that they want to include in each response before they write their final responses.

Formal Assessment
• Section Quiz, p. 89

④ RETEACH

Have pairs of students work together to answer question 6. Each partner should search for information about one ruler. Then partners should pool their information to write a final answer.

In-Depth Resources: Unit 2
• Reteaching Activity, p. 23

ANSWERS

1. Ivan the Terrible, p. 174 • boyar, p. 174 • Peter the Great, p. 175 • westernization, p. 176
2. **Sample Answer:** visited western Europe, built St. Petersburg, brought the Orthodox Church under state control, reduced power of the nobles, promoted men from lower ranks, modernized the army, opened schools, promoted western ideas. Most impact—Westernization, as it laid groundwork for Russia's economic and political power.
3. He had his police force hunt them down and murder them.
4. because only then could Russia compete economically with western Europe
5. started Russia's first newspaper; raised women's status; ordered nobles to wear western fashions; promoted education
6. **Possible Answer:** Peter, because he took control of the church, reduced the power of landowners, strengthened the army, imposed taxes, and forced his reforms on the Russian people
7. **Possible Answer:** serfs, because most of the reforms improved the lives of the nobles and wealthy only
8. They may have been less likely to view Catholics and Protestants as heretics.
9. **Rubric** Expository essays should
• explain how Peter used his power.
• cite specific details to support ideas.

CONNECT TO TODAY
Rubric Debates should
• rely on facts and examples to support opinions.
• allow both sides equal time to present their arguments.

Social History

OBJECTIVES

- Explain important climatic features of Russia.
- Identify Russian methods for coping with their environment.

FOCUS & MOTIVATE

Ask students to identify ways in which climatic factors have influenced the culture of their region. Encourage students to consider local diets, entertainment, dress, transportation, and architecture. *(Answers will vary, but students should be prepared to explain how their examples reflect the influence of climatic factors.)*

INSTRUCT

Critical Thinking

- Ask students if climatic factors have become less significant with technological progress. *(Yes—New heating and cooling technologies mean people can pay less attention to the effects of their climate. No—New technologies have made climatic issues, such as global warming, even more significant.)*
- Ask students if they can think of any U.S. festivals or holidays that are related to climatic factors. *(Some students may note that the origin of summer vacations from school was established at a time when the U.S. still had an agricultural economy. Families wanted a three-month vacation so that their children could help plant crops in the spring and harvest them during late summer.)*

Social History

Surviving the Russian Winter

Much of Russia has severe winters. In Moscow, snow usually begins to fall in mid-October and lasts until mid-April. Siberia has been known to have temperatures as low as -90°F. Back in the 18th century, Russians did not have down parkas or high-tech insulation for their homes. But they had other ways to cope with the climate.

For example, in the 18th century, Russian peasants added potatoes and corn to their diet. During the winter, these nutritious foods were used in soups and stews. Such dishes were warming and provided plenty of calories to help fight off the cold.

INTEGRATED TECHNOLOGY

RESEARCH LINKS For more on Russian winters, go to **classzone.com**

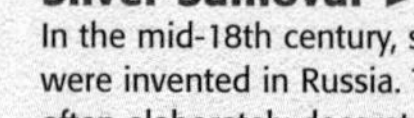

Silver Samovar ►
In the mid-18th century, samovars were invented in Russia. These large, often elaborately decorated urns were used to boil water for tea. Fire was kept burning in a tube running up the middle of the urn—keeping the water piping hot.

◄ Crimean Dress
These people are wearing the traditional dress of tribes from the Crimean Peninsula, a region that Russia took over in the 1700s. Notice the heavy hats, the fur trim on some of the robes, and the leggings worn by those with shorter robes. All these features help to conserve body heat.

▼ Troika
To travel in winter, the wealthy often used sleighs called troikas. *Troika* means "group of three"; the name comes from the three horses that draw this kind of sleigh. The middle horse trotted while the two outside horses galloped.

RECOMMENDED RESOURCES

Books

Bushkovitch, Paul, and Donald T. Critchlow. ***Peter the Great***. Lanham, MD: Rowman & Littlefield, 2001. A modern view of Peter the Great.

Hughes, Lindsey. ***Russia in the Age of Peter the Great***. New Haven and London: Yale UP, 2000. A history of Peter the Great and the society and culture of the Russia he ruled.

Video

Peter the Great. VHS and DVD. Films for the Humanities & Sciences, 1996. 800-257-5126. Describes cultural and social reforms enacted by Peter the Great.

Peter the Great: The Tyrant Reformer. VHS. Library Video Company, 2000. 800-843-3620. Uses archival material to examine both the public and private lives of Peter the Great.

CALIFORNIA STANDARDS

CST 1 Students compare the present with the past, evaluating the consequences of past events and decisions and determining the lessons that were learned.

Winter Festival ►

Russians have never let their climate stop them from having fun outdoors. Here, they are shown enjoying a Shrovetide festival, which occurs near the end of winter. Vendors sold food such as blinis (pancakes with sour cream). Entertainments included ice skating, dancing bears, and magic shows.

The people in the foreground are wearing heavy fur coats. Otter fur was often used for winter clothing. This fur is extremely thick and has about one million hairs per square inch.

▼ Wooden House

Wooden houses, made of logs, were common in Russia during Peter the Great's time. To insulate the house from the wind, people stuffed moss between the logs. Russians used double panes of glass in their windows. For extra protection, many houses had shutters to cover the windows. The roofs were steep so snow would slide off.

> DATA FILE

FROSTY FACTS

- According to a 2001 estimate, Russian women spend about $500 million a year on fur coats and caps.
- The record low temperature in Asia of -90°F was reached twice, first in Verkhoyansk, Russia, in 1892 and then in Oimekon, Russia, in 1933.
- The record low temperature in Europe of -67°F was recorded in Ust'Shchugor, Russia.
- One reason for Russia's cold climate is that most of the country lies north of the 45° latitude line, closer to the North Pole than to the Equator.

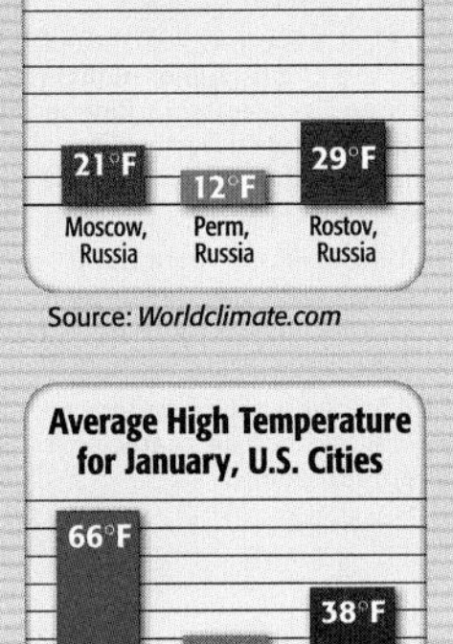

Source: *Worldclimate.com*

Average High Temperature for January, U.S. Cities

Los Angeles, California	Minneapolis, Minnesota	New York, New York
66°F	21°F	38°F

Source: *Worldclimate.com*

Connect *to* Today

1. **Making Inferences** In the 18th century, how did Russians use their natural resources to help them cope with the climate?

   See Skillbuilder Handbook, page R10.

2. **Comparing and Contrasting** How has coping with winter weather changed from 18th-century Russia to today's world? How has it stayed the same?

179

More About . . .

Gaits of the Troika

Most horses have four different gaits—sequences of foot movements by which a horse moves forward. They are the walk, trot, canter, and gallop. In a walk, the slowest gait, the horse always has two or three hooves on the ground. The trot, canter, and gallop are faster movements that involve periods of suspension, in which all of the horse's hooves are simultaneously in the air. Many writers have described the picturesque movement produced by the troika's combination of trot and gallop.

More About . . .

Samovars

The city of Tula in western Russia became famous as the center of samovar manufacturing. The Russian equivalent of the proverb "to carry water to a river"—meaning to do what is superfluous—is "to go to Tula with a samovar."

More About . . .

Shrovetide

Shrovetide, known in many places as Carnival, is a short period of merrymaking. It precedes Lent—the 40 weekdays from Ash Wednesday to Easter observed by the Roman Catholic, Eastern, and some Protestant churches as a period of penitence and fasting.

CONNECT TO TODAY: ANSWERS

1. Making Inferences

Russians used furs to make warm clothing. They used lumber from extensive forests for buildings and abundant moss as an insulating material. They cooked soups and stews using potatoes and corn to provide needed nutrition to fight off the cold.

2. Comparing and Contrasting

Many of today's homes and workplaces have central heating and cooling. Transportation today is not open to the weather, and most vehicles are heated. In some ways coping with winter weather has remained the same because people continue to wear warm clothing and to eat soups and stews. Winter sports and festivals remain popular.

LESSON PLAN

OBJECTIVES

- Identify conflicts between English rulers and Parliament.
- Explain the causes and results of the English Civil War.
- Describe the Restoration and the Glorious Revolution.
- Explain changes under William and Mary.

1 FOCUS & MOTIVATE

In this section students will study the English monarchy. Ask students if they know the name of the current British monarch. *(Elizabeth II has been queen since 1952.)*

2 INSTRUCT

Monarchs Defy Parliament

10.1.1

Critical Thinking

- Why was the Petition of Right important even if King Charles simply ignored it? *(It signaled a change in the way the English viewed government.)*

CALIFORNIA RESOURCES

California Reading Toolkit, p. L27
California Modified Lesson Plans for English Learners, p. 49
California Daily Standards Practice Transparencies, TT19
California Standards Enrichment Workbook, pp. 17–18, 23–24
California Standards Planner and Lesson Plans, p. L45
California Online Test Practice
California Test Generator CD-ROM
California Easy Planner CD-ROM
California eEdition CD-ROM

Marriage of Louis XIV to Marie Thérèse of Austria. Artist unknown

Statue of Louis XIV, Lyon, France

5

Parliament Limits the English Monarchy

MAIN IDEA

REVOLUTION Absolute rulers in England were overthrown, and Parliament gained power.

WHY IT MATTERS NOW

Many of the government reforms of this period contributed to the democratic tradition of the United States.

TERMS & NAMES

- Charles I
- English Civil War
- Oliver Cromwell
- Restoration
- *habeas corpus*
- Glorious Revolution
- constitutional monarchy
- cabinet

CALIFORNIA STANDARDS

10.1.1 Analyze the similarities and differences in Judeo-Christian and Greco-Roman views of law, reason and faith, and duties of the individual.

10.2.2 List the principles of the Magna Carta, the English Bill of Rights (1689), the American Declaration of Independence (1776), the French Declaration of the Rights of Man and the Citizen (1789), and the U.S. Bill of Rights (1791).

CST 1 Students compare the present with the past, evaluating the consequences of past events and decisions and determining the lessons that were learned.

CST 4 Students relate current events to the physical and human characteristics of places and regions.

SETTING THE STAGE During her reign, Queen Elizabeth I of England had had frequent conflicts with Parliament. Many of the arguments were over money, because the treasury did not have enough funds to pay the queen's expenses. By the time Elizabeth died in 1603, she had left a huge debt for her successor to deal with. Parliament's financial power was one obstacle to English rulers' becoming absolute monarchs. The resulting struggle between Parliament and the monarchy would have serious consequences for England.

Monarchs Defy Parliament

Elizabeth had no child, and her nearest relative was her cousin, James Stuart. Already king of Scotland, James Stuart became King James I of England in 1603. Although England and Scotland were not united until 1707, they now shared a ruler.

James's Problems James inherited the unsettled issues of Elizabeth's reign. His worst struggles with Parliament were over money. In addition, James offended the Puritan members of Parliament. The Puritans hoped he would enact reforms to purify the English church of Catholic practices. Except for agreeing to a new translation of the Bible, however, he refused to make Puritan reforms.

TAKING NOTES

Analyzing Causes Use a chart to list the causes of each monarch's conflicts with Parliament.

Monarch	Conflicts with Parliament
James I	
Charles I	
James II	

Charles I Fights Parliament In 1625, James I died. **Charles I**, his son, took the throne. Charles always needed money, in part because he was at war with both Spain and France. Several times when Parliament refused to give him funds, he dissolved it.

By 1628, Charles was forced to call Parliament again. This time it refused to grant him any money until he signed a document that is known as the Petition of Right. In this petition, the king agreed to four points:

- He would not imprison subjects without due cause.
- He would not levy taxes without Parliament's consent.
- He would not house soldiers in private homes.
- He would not impose martial law in peacetime.

After agreeing to the petition, Charles ignored it. Even so, the petition was important. It set forth the idea that the law was higher than the king. This idea contradicted theories of absolute monarchy. In 1629, Charles dissolved Parliament and refused to call it back into session. To get money, he imposed all kinds of fees and fines on the English people. His popularity decreased year by year.

SECTION 5 PROGRAM RESOURCES

ALL STUDENTS

In-Depth Resources: Unit 2
- Guided Reading, p. 5
- History Makers: William of Orange, p. 18

Formal Assessment
- Section Quiz, p. 90

ENGLISH LEARNERS

In-Depth Resources in Spanish
- Guided Reading, p. 48

Reading Study Guide (Spanish), p. 59
Reading Study Guide Audio CD (Spanish)

STRUGGLING READERS

In-Depth Resources: Unit 2
- Guided Reading, p. 5
- Building Vocabulary, p. 6
- Reteaching Activity, p. 24

Reading Study Guide, p. 59
Reading Study Guide Audio CD

GIFTED AND TALENTED STUDENTS

In-Depth Resources: Unit 2
- Primary Sources: from *Diary of Samuel Pepys,* p. 12; from the English Bill of Rights, p. 13
- Connections Across Time and Cultures, p. 19

Electronic Library of Primary Sources
- "The Restoration of Charles II"

INTEGRATED TECHNOLOGY

eEdition CD-ROM
Power Presentations CD-ROM
Critical Thinking Transparencies
- CT57 Chapter 5 Visual Summary

Electronic Library of Primary Sources
- "The Restoration of Charles II"

classzone.com

English Civil War

Charles offended Puritans by upholding the rituals of the Anglican Church. In addition, in 1637, Charles tried to force the Presbyterian Scots to accept a version of the Anglican prayer book. He wanted both his kingdoms to follow one religion. The Scots rebelled, assembled a huge army, and threatened to invade England. To meet this danger, Charles needed money—money he could get only by calling Parliament into session. This gave Parliament a chance to oppose him.

War Topples a King During the autumn of 1641, Parliament passed laws to limit royal power. Furious, Charles tried to arrest Parliament's leaders in January 1642, but they escaped. Equally furious, a mob of Londoners raged outside the palace. Charles fled London and raised an army in the north of England, where people were loyal to him.

From 1642 to 1649, supporters and opponents of King Charles fought the **English Civil War**. Those who remained loyal to Charles were called Royalists or Cavaliers. On the other side were Puritan supporters of Parliament. Because these men wore their hair short over their ears, Cavaliers called them Roundheads.

At first neither side could gain a lasting advantage. However, by 1644 the Puritans found a general who could win—**Oliver Cromwell**. In 1645, Cromwell's New Model Army began defeating the Cavaliers, and the tide turned toward the Puritans. In 1647, they held the king prisoner.

In 1649, Cromwell and the Puritans brought Charles to trial for treason against Parliament. They found him guilty and sentenced him to death. The execution of Charles was revolutionary. Kings had often been overthrown, killed in battle, or put to death in secret. Never before, however, had a reigning monarch faced a public trial and execution.

Cromwell's Rule Cromwell now held the reins of power. In 1649, he abolished the monarchy and the House of Lords. He established a commonwealth, a republican form of government. In 1653, Cromwell sent home the remaining members of Parliament. Cromwell's associate John Lambert drafted a constitution, the first written constitution of any modern European state. However, Cromwell eventually tore up the document and became a military dictator. (A)

MAIN IDEA
Comparing
(A) What did Cromwell's rule have in common with an absolute monarchy?
A. Possible Answer He abolished the legislative body and set himself above the law.

Cromwell almost immediately had to put down a rebellion in Ireland. English colonization of Ireland had begun in the 1100s under Henry II. Henry VIII and his children had brought the country firmly under English rule in the 1500s. In 1649, Cromwell landed on Irish shores with an army and crushed the uprising. He seized the lands and homes of the Irish and gave them to English soldiers. Fighting, plague, and famine killed hundreds of thousands.

▼ This engraving depicts the beheading of Charles I.

Puritan Morality In England, Cromwell and the Puritans sought to reform society. They made laws that promoted Puritan morality and abolished activities they found sinful, such as the theater, sporting events, and dancing. Although he was a strict

Tip for Struggling Readers

Some students may have difficulty remembering the differences among religious groups. Remind students that, in this section, the main distinction is between Catholics and Protestants and that Puritans, Anglicans, and Presbyterians are all Protestant groups.

English Civil War
10.1.1

Critical Thinking

- Why might Charles have had more loyalty from the north of England than from London? *(Possible Answer: The new ideas that had taken hold in the city had not yet spread to the north.)*
- Why might it be difficult to form a new government after overthrowing the previous regime—even if the population supported the overthrow? *(Possible Answer: It can take a long time to replace institutions and officials of the old regime.)*
- How might the English have reacted to Cromwell's social reforms? *(Possible Answer: Puritans liked the strict rules; others would have disliked the rules.)*

In-Depth Resources: Unit 2

- Connections Across Time and Cultures: The Absolute Power of Rulers, p. 19

DIFFERENTIATING INSTRUCTION: STRUGGLING READERS

Creating a Board Game

Class Time 45 minutes

Task Making a trivia board game

Purpose To help readers learn about the English Civil War

Instructions Divide students into small groups and ask them to read "Monarchs Defy Parliament" and "English Civil War" on pages 180–181. Then explain to students that they will be making a trivia board game that uses cards with multiple-choice questions. Ask students to work as a group to design their game. Students should use the information in the text to create the questions.

For example:

- The _____ remained loyal to Charles I during the English Civil War: A. Cavaliers; B. Roundheads; C. Royalists; D. Both A and C *(Answer: D)*
- Royalists in the English Civil War never controlled: A. London; B. the north of England; C. western England; D. none of the above *(Answer: A)*

After groups complete the project, have them exchange and play the games. For overall help with the section, have students complete the Reading Study Guide activity for this section.

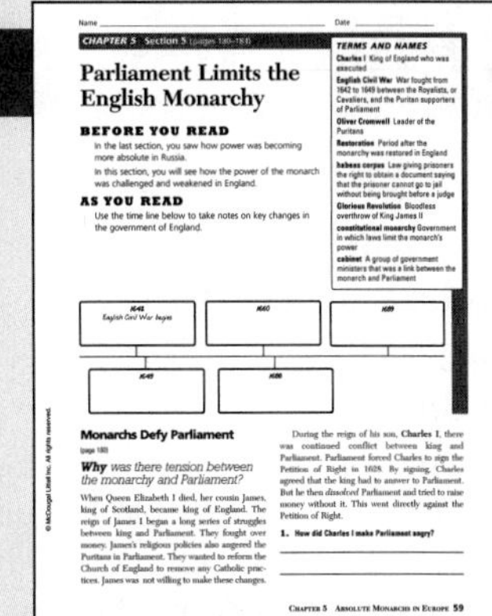

Reading Study Guide

History from Visuals

Interpreting the Map

Point out the colors showing the areas controlled by each side. Which part of England did the Puritans control during all four years? *(the southeast part)*

Extension Have groups of students create a time line of key events in the civil war from 1646 through 1649.

SKILLBUILDER Answers

1. **Movement** 1643—Royalists gained; 1644, 1645—Puritans gained
2. **Place** Puritans; Control of London was important because it was the country's political and economic center of power.

Restoration and Revolution

10.1.1

Critical Thinking

- What factors might have contributed to the success of laws passed by Parliament during the Restoration? *(Possible Answers: People welcomed the restoration of Parliament's legislative powers, and Charles II, as the first monarch of the Restoration, recognized the need to respect Parliament.)*
- Why would Parliament, after so many reforms, continue to support the monarchy? *(Possible Answer: They may have viewed the monarchy as a symbolic institution that promoted unity and order.)*

Electronic Library of Primary Sources

- "The Restoration of Charles II"

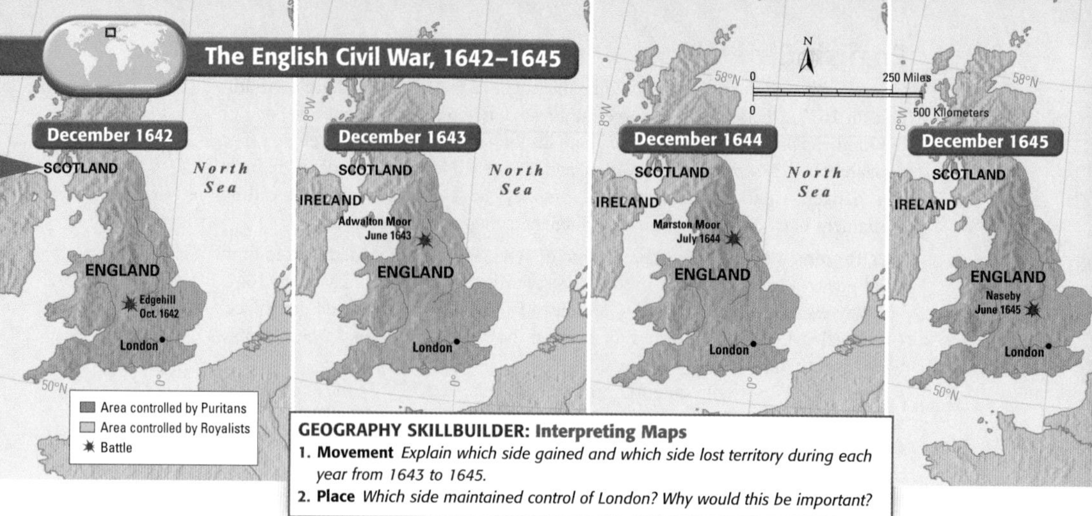

GEOGRAPHY SKILLBUILDER: Interpreting Maps

1. **Movement** *Explain which side gained and which side lost territory during each year from 1643 to 1645.*
2. **Place** *Which side maintained control of London? Why would this be important?*

Puritan, Cromwell favored religious toleration for all Christians except Catholics. He even allowed Jews to return; they had been expelled from England in 1290.

Restoration and Revolution

Oliver Cromwell ruled until his death in 1658. Shortly afterward, the government he had established collapsed, and a new Parliament was selected. The English people were sick of military rule. In 1659, Parliament voted to ask the older son of Charles I to rule England.

Charles II Reigns When Prince Charles entered London in 1660, crowds shouted joyfully and bells rang. On this note of celebration, the reign of Charles II began. Because he restored the monarchy, the period of his rule is called the **Restoration**.

During Charles II's reign, Parliament passed an important guarantee of freedom, ***habeas corpus***. *Habeas corpus* is Latin meaning "to have the body." This 1679 law gave every prisoner the right to obtain a writ or document ordering that the prisoner be brought before a judge to specify the charges against the prisoner. The judge would decide whether the prisoner should be tried or set free. Because of the Habeas Corpus Act, a monarch could not put someone in jail simply for opposing the ruler. Also, prisoners could not be held indefinitely without trials.

In addition, Parliament debated who should inherit Charles's throne. Because Charles had no legitimate child, his heir was his brother James, who was Catholic. A group called the Whigs opposed James, and a group called the Tories supported him. These two groups were the ancestors of England's first political parties.

James II and the Glorious Revolution In 1685, Charles II died, and James II became king. James soon offended his subjects by displaying his Catholicism. Violating English law, he appointed several Catholics to high office. When Parliament protested, James dissolved it. In 1688, James's second wife gave birth to a son. English Protestants became terrified at the prospect of a line of Catholic kings.

James had an older daughter, Mary, who was Protestant. She was also the wife of William of Orange, a prince of the Netherlands. Seven members of Parliament invited William and Mary to overthrow James for the sake of Protestantism. When William led his army to London in 1688, James fled to France. This bloodless overthrow of King James II is called the **Glorious Revolution**. **B**

B. Answer There was no execution of the king; the monarchy was not abolished.

MAIN IDEA

Contrasting

B How was the overthrow of James II different from the overthrow of Charles I?

DIFFERENTIATING INSTRUCTION: GIFTED AND TALENTED STUDENTS

The Life and Death of William of Orange

Class Time 20 minutes

Task Writing an obituary

Purpose To have students learn more about William of Orange

Instructions Have students complete the History Maker activity in In-Depth Resources: Unit 2. Tell students to use what they learned from the History Maker to write an obituary for William of Orange. Students might choose to write the obituary from the perspective of a newspaper based in England, Scotland, Ireland, France, or the Netherlands. Students can use local or national newspaper obituaries as models. Tell students to think carefully about what information is appropriate for their obituaries before they begin. Explain that the tone should be respectful—although it may reflect an English or anti-English bias—and that the obituary should be up to 250 words long. Students should include William's family history, his military activities, his marriage, and his religious beliefs.

HISTORYMAKERS William of Orange
Protestant Champion

In-Depth Resources: Unit 2

Limits on Monarch's Power

At their coronation, William and Mary vowed to recognize Parliament as their partner in governing. England had become not an absolute monarchy but a **constitutional monarchy**, where laws limited the ruler's power.

Bill of Rights To make clear the limits of royal power, Parliament drafted a Bill of Rights in 1689. This document listed many things that a ruler could not do:

- no suspending of Parliament's laws
- no levying of taxes without a specific grant from Parliament
- no interfering with freedom of speech in Parliament
- no penalty for a citizen who petitions the king about grievances

William and Mary consented to these and other limits on their royal power.

Cabinet System Develops After 1688, no British monarch could rule without the consent of Parliament. At the same time, Parliament could not rule without the consent of the monarch. If the two disagreed, government came to a standstill.

During the 1700s, this potential problem was remedied by the development of a group of government ministers, or officials, called the **cabinet**. These ministers acted in the ruler's name but in reality represented the major party of Parliament. Therefore, they became the link between the monarch and the majority party in Parliament.

Over time, the cabinet became the center of power and policymaking. Under the cabinet system, the leader of the majority party in Parliament heads the cabinet and is called the prime minister. This system of English government continues today.

Connect *to* Today

U.S. Democracy

Today, the United States still relies on many of the government reforms and institutions that the English developed during this period. These include the following:

- the right to obtain *habeas corpus*, a document that prevents authorities from holding a person in jail without being charged
- a Bill of Rights, guaranteeing such rights as freedom of speech and freedom of worship
- a strong legislature and strong executive, which act as checks on each other
- a cabinet, made up of heads of executive departments, such as the Department of State
- two dominant political parties

SECTION 5 ASSESSMENT

TERMS & NAMES 1. For each term or name, write a sentence explaining its significance.

• Charles I • English Civil War • Oliver Cromwell • Restoration • *habeas corpus* • Glorious Revolution • constitutional monarchy • cabinet

USING YOUR NOTES

2. What patterns do you see in the conflicts' causes? (10.1.1)

Monarch	Conflicts with Parliament
James I	
Charles I	
James II	

MAIN IDEAS

3. Why was the death of Charles I revolutionary? (10.1.1)
4. What rights were guaranteed by the Habeas Corpus Act? (10.2.2)
5. How does a constitutional monarchy differ from an absolute monarchy? (10.1.1)

CRITICAL THINKING & WRITING

6. **EVALUATING DECISIONS** In your opinion, which decisions by Charles I made his conflict with Parliament worse? Explain. (10.1.1)
7. **MAKING INFERENCES** Why do you think James II fled when William of Orange led his army to London? (10.1.1)
8. **SYNTHESIZING** What conditions in England made the execution of one king and the overthrow of another possible? (10.1.1)
9. **WRITING ACTIVITY** REVOLUTION Write a **persuasive essay** for an underground newspaper designed to incite the British people to overthrow Charles I. (Writing 2.4.d)

CONNECT TO TODAY **DRAWING A POLITICAL CARTOON**

Yet another revolution threatens the monarchy today in Great Britain. Some people would like to see the monarchy ended altogether. Find out what you can about the issue and choose a side. Represent your position on the issue in an original **political cartoon.** (CST 4)

Limits on Monarch's Power

10.2.2

Critical Thinking

- Why might William and Mary have been willing to accept the limits placed on their power? *(Possible Answer: because their position was not powerful enough to demand more)*
- What factors might have determined whether a cabinet was loyal to the monarchy or to the Parliament? *(Possible Answers: who appointed the cabinet members; the political beliefs of the cabinet members)*

In-Depth Resources: Unit 2

- Primary Sources: from *Diary of Samuel Pepys,* p. 12
- Primary Sources: from the English Bill of Rights, p. 13

3 ASSESS

SECTION 5 ASSESSMENT

Have pairs of students help each other with key terms by making word cards with definitions on the back. Students can take turns quizzing one another.

Formal Assessment

- Section Quiz, p. 90

4 RETEACH

Use the Visual Summary to review this section and chapter.

Critical Thinking Transparencies

- CT57 Chapter 5 Visual Summary

In-Depth Resources: Unit 2

- Reteaching Activity, p. 24

ANSWERS

1. Charles I, p. 180 • English Civil War, p. 181 • Oliver Cromwell, p. 181 • Restoration, p. 182 • *habeas corpus,* p. 182 • Glorious Revolution, p. 182 • constitutional monarchy, p. 183 • cabinet, p. 183
2. **Sample Answers:** James I—Money and reform of the English church; Charles I—Money, rule of law, and Anglican ritual; James II—Appointment of Catholic officials. Pattern—Religious conflict.
3. Never before had a reigning monarch faced a public trial and execution.
4. the right to have a judge decide whether a prisoner should be tried or set free
5. Under a constitutional monarchy, laws written by a legislative body limit the ruler's power.
6. **Possible Answers:** dissolving Parliament, ignoring Petition of Right
7. He may have feared being arrested and executed.
8. **Possible Answer:** the power of Parliament
9. **Rubric** Persuasive essays should
   - clearly call for removal of Charles I.
   - offer supporting facts and examples.
   - conclude with a call to action.

CONNECT TO TODAY

Rubric Political cartoons should

- take a clear position on whether the British monarchy should be retained.
- identify the people represented.

TERMS & NAMES

1. absolute monarch, p. 160
2. divine right, p. 160
3. Louis XIV, p. 164
4. War of the Spanish Succession, p. 167
5. Thirty Years' War, p. 169
6. Seven Years' War, p. 173
7. Peter the Great, p. 175
8. English Civil War, p. 181
9. Glorious Revolution, p. 182
10. constitutional monarchy, p. 183

MAIN IDEAS

Answers will vary.

11. fought Muslim Ottoman Empire; sent Armada against Protestant England; fought Protestantism in the Netherlands
12. no, because if he does, he becomes that person's subject
13. He used intendants and forced nobles to live at Versailles.
14. He ran up huge debts, fought unpopular wars, and imposed heavy taxes.
15. weakened Spain and Austria; strengthened France; made German princes independent of Holy Roman emperor; ended religious wars in Europe; introduced new method of negotiating peace; established modern state system
16. They were battling over territory.
17. Russian serfdom was firmly implanted; Russian people knew little of the Renaissance; Russians were Eastern Orthodox
18. to westernize Russia so that the country could compete militarily and commercially with western Europe
19. Royalists (also called Cavaliers) and Roundheads (also called Puritans) fought over religion, money, and the extent of the king's power. The Roundheads won and beheaded Charles I.
20. By refusing to grant funds; it forced Charles I to sign the Petition of Right. Parliament leaders invited William and Mary to rule as partners of Parliament. Parliament drafted a Bill of Rights.

Chapter 5 Assessment

VISUAL SUMMARY

Absolute Monarchs in Europe

Long-Term Causes

- decline of feudalism
- rise of cities and support of middle class
- growth of national kingdoms
- loss of Church authority

Immediate Causes

- religious and territorial conflicts
- buildup of armies
- need for increased taxes
- revolts by peasants or nobles

European Monarchs Claim Divine Right to Rule Absolutely

Immediate Effects

- regulation of religion and society
- larger courts
- huge building projects
- new government bureaucracies appointed by the government
- loss of power by nobility and legislatures

Long-Term Effects

- revolution in France
- western European influence on Russia
- English political reforms that influence U.S. democracy

TERMS & NAMES

For each term or name below, briefly explain its connection to European history from 1500 to 1800.

1. absolute monarch
2. divine right
3. Louis XIV
4. War of the Spanish Succession
5. Thirty Years' War
6. Seven Years' War
7. Peter the Great
8. English Civil War
9. Glorious Revolution
10. constitutional monarchy

MAIN IDEAS

Spain's Empire and European Absolutism Section 1 (pages 155–161)

11. What three actions demonstrated that Philip II of Spain saw himself as a defender of Catholicism? (10.1.2)
12. According to French writer Jean Bodin, should a prince share power with anyone else? Explain why or why not. (10.1.2)

The Reign of Louis XIV Section 2 (pages 162–168)

13. What strategies did Louis XIV use to control the French nobility? (10.2.4)
14. In what ways did Louis XIV cause suffering to the French people? (10.2.4)

Central European Monarchs Clash Section 3 (pages 169–173)

15. What were six results of the Peace of Westphalia? (10.5.1)
16. Why did Maria Theresa and Frederick the Great fight two wars against each other? (10.5.1)

Absolute Rulers of Russia Section 4 (pages 174–179)

17. What were three differences between Russia and western Europe? (10.1.2)
18. What was Peter the Great's primary goal for Russia? (10.1.2)

Parliament Limits the English Monarchy Section 5 (pages 180–183)

19. List the causes, participants, and outcome of the English Civil War. (10.2.1)
20. How did Parliament try to limit the power of the English monarchy? (10.1.1)

CRITICAL THINKING

1. **USING YOUR NOTES**
POWER AND AUTHORITY In a chart, list actions that absolute monarchs took to increase their power. Then identify the monarchs who took these actions. (10.2.1)

Actions of Absolute Rulers	Monarchs Who Took Them

2. **DRAWING CONCLUSIONS**
ECONOMICS What benefits might absolute monarchs hope to gain by increasing their countries' territory? (10.2.1)

3. **DEVELOPING HISTORICAL PERSPECTIVE**
What conditions fostered the rise of absolute monarchs in Europe? (HI 1)

4. **COMPARING AND CONTRASTING**
Compare the reign of Louis XIV with that of Peter the Great. Which absolute ruler had a more lasting impact on his country? Explain why. (HI 1)

5. **HYPOTHESIZING**
Would Charles I have had a different fate if he had been king of another country in western or central Europe? Why or why not? (HI 3)

CRITICAL THINKING

Answers will vary.

1. Controlled religious life—Philip II, Louis XIV, Peter I; Controlled society—Ivan IV, Louis XIV, Frederick II, Peter I; Controlled economy—Louis XIV, Peter I; Reduced power of nobles—Louis XIV, Maria Theresa, Ivan IV, Peter I.
2. more power, resources, and prestige
3. Power became centralized with the decline of feudalism and growth of cities. The decline of Church authority gave monarchs greater control.
4. Peter the Great—His westernization of Russia continues to have an impact on Russia today. Louis XIV—Literature and arts flourished during his reign and the debt he left was a direct cause of the French Revolution.
5. yes, because his power would not have been contested by a legislative body such as Parliament or by his own people

Use the excerpt from the English Bill of Rights passed in 1689 and your knowledge of world history to answer questions 1 and 2.
Additional Test Practice, pp. S1–S33.

PRIMARY SOURCE

That the pretended power of suspending [canceling] of laws or the execution [carrying out] of laws by regal authority without consent of Parliament is illegal; . . .

That it is the right of the subjects to petition [make requests of] the king, and all commitments [imprisonments] and prosecutions for such petitioning are illegal;

That the raising or keeping a standing army within the kingdom in time of peace, unless it be with consent of Parliament, is against the law; . . .

That election of members of Parliament ought to be free [not restricted].

English Bill of Rights

1. According to the excerpt, which of the following is illegal? (10.2.2)
   - **A.** the enactment of laws without Parliament's permission
   - **B.** the unrestricted election of members of Parliament
   - **C.** the right of subjects to make requests of the king
   - **D.** keeping a standing army in time of peace with Parliament's consent

2. The English Bill of Rights was passed as a means to (10.2.2)
   - **A.** limit Parliament's power.
   - **B.** increase Parliament's power.
   - **C.** overthrow the monarch.
   - **D.** increase the monarch's power.

Use the map and your knowledge of world history to answer question 3.

Modern European Monarchs, 2003

3. Of the countries that you studied in this chapter, which have monarchs today? (10.1.2)
   - **A.** Spain, Great Britain, the Netherlands
   - **B.** Liechtenstein, Monaco
   - **C.** Luxembourg, Andorra
   - **D.** Great Britain, Norway, Sweden

INTEGRATED TECHNOLOGY

TEST PRACTICE Go to **classzone.com**
- Diagnostic tests
- Tutorials
- Strategies
- Additional practice

ALTERNATIVE ASSESSMENT

1. **Interact *with* History** (HI 3)
   On page 154, you thought about the advantages and disadvantages of absolute power. Now that you have read the chapter, what do you consider to be the main advantage and the main disadvantage of being an absolute ruler?

2. **WRITING ABOUT HISTORY** (Writing 2.1.a)
   REVOLUTION Reread the information on Oliver Cromwell. Then write a **History Maker,** like the ones you've seen throughout this textbook, on Cromwell as a leader of a successful revolution. Be sure to
   - include biographical information about Cromwell.
   - discuss his effectiveness as a leader.
   - use vivid language to hold your reader's attention.

INTEGRATED TECHNOLOGY

Creating a Television News Report (Writing 2.1.a)

Use a video recorder to tape a television news report on the trial of Charles I. Role-play an announcer reporting a breaking news story. Relate the facts of the trial and interview key participants, including:
- a member of Parliament
- a Puritan
- a Royalist
- Charles I

STANDARDS-BASED ASSESSMENT

1. The correct answer is letter **A**. This excerpt states that "the execution of laws by regal authority without consent of Parliament is illegal." Letter **B** is incorrect because the excerpt calls for the unrestricted election of members of Parliament. Letter **C** is incorrect because the excerpt states that subjects have the right to petition the king. Letter **D** is incorrect because the excerpt states that keeping a standing army in time of peace without Parliament's consent is illegal.
2. The correct answer is letter **B**. The regulations proposed in the Bill of Rights resulted in an increase in Parliament's power. Letters **A**, **C**, and **D** are incorrect.
3. The correct answer is letter **A**. Spain, Great Britain, and the Netherlands were covered in the textbook and still have monarchs today. Letters **B**, **C**, and **D** are incorrect because either the countries are not ruled by monarchs today or were not the subject of the chapter.

Formal Assessment
- Chapter Test, Forms A, B, and C, pp. 91–102

California Test Generator CD-ROM
- Chapter Tests, Forms A, B, and C (English and Spanish)

ALTERNATIVE ASSESSMENT

1. *Possible Answers*: Main advantage—Unlimited money, power, and authority. Main disadvantage—Resentment of government and people may result in rebellion.

2. **Rubric** History Makers should
   - accurately convey biographical information about Oliver Cromwell.
   - focus on Cromwell's leadership.
   - be written in a lively style.

INTEGRATED TECHNOLOGY

Rubric News reports should
- convey the facts of the trial.
- contain interviews with key participants.
- hold the viewer's attention.
- be written and read in a journalistic style.

CHAPTER 6 PLANNING GUIDE

Enlightenment and Revolution, 1550–1789

CHAPTER RESOURCES	COPYMASTERS	ASSESSMENT
CHAPTER OVERVIEW Enlightenment scientists and thinkers challenge old ideas and revolutionize science, the arts, government, and religion.	**In-Depth Resources: Unit 2** • Building Vocabulary, p. 29 **Chapters in Brief** (in English and Spanish) **Block Schedule Pacing Guide**	**Chapter Assessment,** pp. 212–213 **Formal Assessment** • Chapter Tests, Forms A, B, and C, pp. 107–118 **Test Generator** **Integrated Assessment Book** **Online Test Practice**
SECTION 1 **The Scientific Revolution** pp. 189–194 **OBJECTIVE** Explain the development of the Scientific Revolution and the impact of the scientific method on different fields of study.	**In-Depth Resources: Unit 2** • Guided Reading, p. 25 • Skillbuilder Practice: Clarifying, p. 30 • Geography Application: Three Theories of the Solar System, p. 31 • Primary Source: *Starry Messenger,* p. 33 • Literature: from *The Recantation of Galileo Galilei,* p. 38 • History Makers: Nicolaus Copernicus, p. 41 • Reteaching Activity, p. 44 **Reading Study Guide,** p. 63	**Section 1 Assessment,** p. 194 **Formal Assessment** • Section Quiz, p. 103 **California Daily Standards Practice Transparencies,** TT80
SECTION 2 **The Enlightenment in Europe** pp. 195–201 **OBJECTIVE** Analyze the ideas of Enlightenment philosophers and the impact of these ideas.	**In-Depth Resources: Unit 2** • Guided Reading, p. 26 • Primary Sources: from *The Social Contract,* p. 34; from *Two Treatises on Government,* p. 35; from *A Vindication of the Rights of Woman,* p. 36 • History Makers: Baron de Montesquieu, p. 42 • Reteaching Activity, p. 45 **Reading Study Guide,** p. 65	**Section 2 Assessment,** p. 200 **Formal Assessment** • Section Quiz, p. 104 **California Daily Standards Practice Transparencies,** TT81
SECTION 3 **The Enlightenment Spreads** pp. 202–205 **OBJECTIVE** Trace the spread and impact of Enlightenment ideas throughout Europe.	**In-Depth Resources: Unit 2** • Guided Reading, p. 27 • Connections Across Time and Cultures: The Search for Truth and Reason, p. 43 • Reteaching Activity, p. 46 **Reading Study Guide,** p. 67	**Section 3 Assessment,** p. 205 **Formal Assessment** • Section Quiz, p. 105 **California Daily Standards Practice Transparencies,** TT82
SECTION 4 **American Revolution** pp. 206–211 **OBJECTIVE** Describe the events that led to the American Revolution and the influence of Enlightenment ideas on American government.	**In-Depth Resources: Unit 2** • Guided Reading, p. 28 • Primary Source: from The Declaration of Independence, p. 37 • Reteaching Activity, p. 47 **Reading Study Guide,** p. 69	**Section 4 Assessment,** p. 211 **Formal Assessment** • Section Quiz, p. 106 **California Daily Standards Practice Transparencies,** TT83

INTEGRATED TECHNOLOGY

- eEdition Plus Online
- EasyPlanner Plus Online
- eTest Plus Online

Audio CDs
- Voices from the Past
- Reading Study Guides

CD-ROMs
- eEdition
- Power Presentations
- EasyPlanner
- Electronic Library of Primary Sources
- Test Generator

eEdition CD-ROM

Geography Transparencies
- GT22 Maps of the World, 1492–1761

World Art and Cultures Transparencies
- AT48 Vermeer's *The Astronomer*

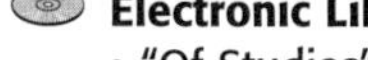

Electronic Library of Primary Sources
- "Of Studies"

classzone.com

eEdition CD-ROM

Critical Thinking Transparencies
- CT22 The Spread of Enlightenment Ideas

Electronic Library of Primary Sources
- from *The Persian Letters*
- from *Gulliver's Travels*

classzone.com

eEdition CD-ROM

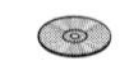

Electronic Library of Primary Sources
- Letter to Catherine the Great

classzone.com

eEdition CD-ROM

Critical Thinking Transparencies
- CT58 Chapter 6 Visual Summary

Electronic Library of Primary Sources
- Conflicting Accounts of the Battles of Lexington and Concord

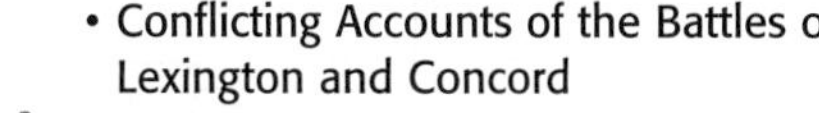

classzone.com

OVERVIEW OF CALIFORNIA RESOURCES

	Section 1	Section 2	Section 3	Section 4
California Reading Toolkit	p. L28	p. L29	p. L30	p. L31
California Modified Lesson Plans for English Learners	p. 51	p. 53	p. 55	p. 57
California Daily Standards Practice Transparencies	TT20	TT21	TT22	TT23
California Standards Enrichment Workbook	pp. 17–18, 23–24	pp. 23–24	pp. 23–24	pp. 21–22, 23–24, 25–26, 27–28
California Standards Planner and Lesson Plans	p. L47	p. L49	p. L51	p. L53
California Online Test Practice	classzone.com	classzone.com	classzone.com	classzone.com
California Test Generator CD-ROM				
California Easy Planner CD-ROM				
California eEdition CD-ROM				

Chart Key:

 Pupil's Edition

 Teacher's Edition

 Overhead Transparency

Block Scheduling

 Copymaster

 Audio Library

 CD-ROM

 Internet

Video

NO TIME?

If you do not have time to teach this chapter in full, assign the **Chapter in Brief** (also available in Spanish).

Previewing Resources for Differentiated Instruction

ENGLISH LEARNERS: Resources in Spanish

In-Depth Resources in Spanish

- Guided Reading (A)
- Skillbuilder Practice: Clarifying (B)
- Geography Application: Three Theories of the Solar System

Chapters in Brief

Reading Study Guide (C)

Reading Study Guide Audio CD

Test Generator CD-ROM

- Chapter Test, Forms A, B, and C

Plus

Modified Lesson Plans for English Learners

Multi-Language Glossary of Social Studies Terms

(A)

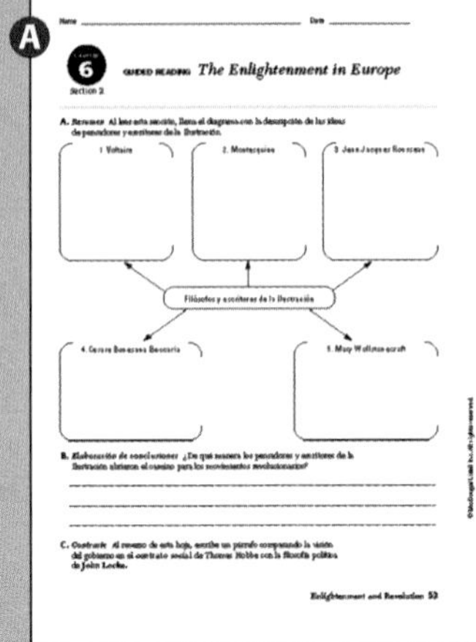

(B)

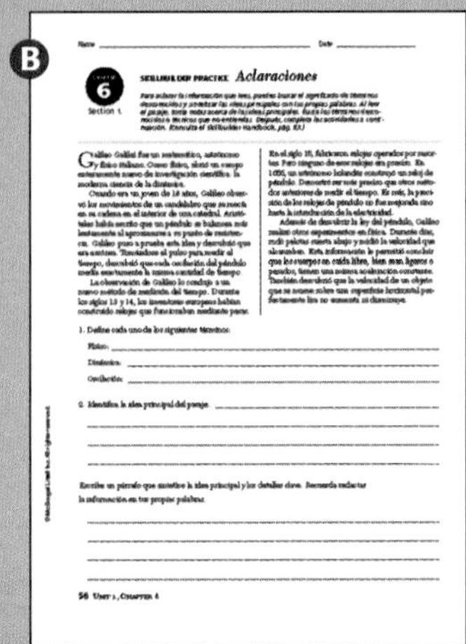

STRUGGLING READERS

In-Depth Resources: Unit 2

- Guided Reading (A)
- Building Vocabulary
- Skillbuilder Practice: Clarifying
- Geography Application: Three Theories of the Solar System (B)
- Reteaching Activities

Chapters in Brief

Reading Study Guide (C)

Reading Study Guide Audio CD

Formal Assessment

- Chapter Test, Form A

Plus

Reading Toolkit

(A)

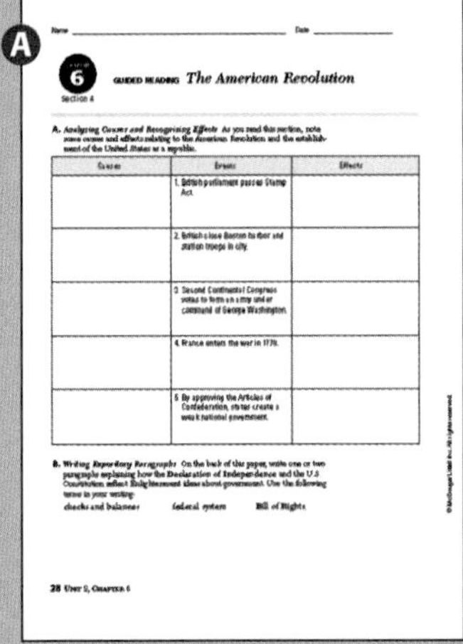

(B)

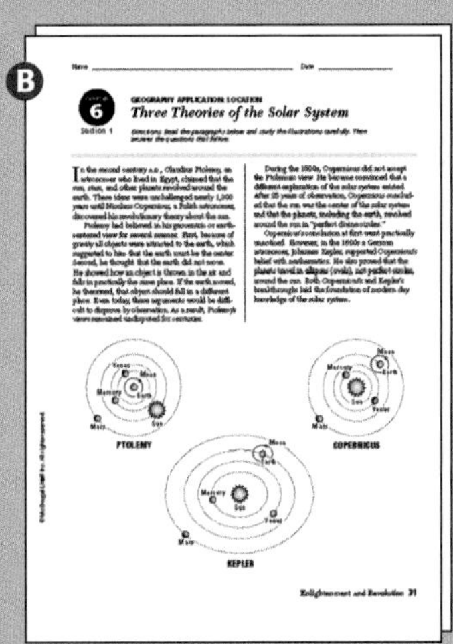

GIFTED AND TALENTED STUDENTS

In-Depth Resources: Unit 2

- Primary Source: from *Starry Messenger;* from *The Social Contract* (A); from *Two Treatises on Government;* from *A Vindication of the Rights of Woman;* from The Declaration of Independence
- Literature: from *The Recantation of Galileo Galilei*
- History Makers: Nicolaus Copernicus; Baron de Montesquieu
- Connections Across Time and Cultures: The Search for Truth and Reason (B)

Electronic Library of Primary Sources

- "Of Studies"
- from *The Persian Letters*
- from *Gulliver's Travels*
- Letter to Catherine the Great
- Conflicting Accounts of the Battles of Lexington and Concord

Formal Assessment

- Chapter Test, Form C (C)

(A)

(B)

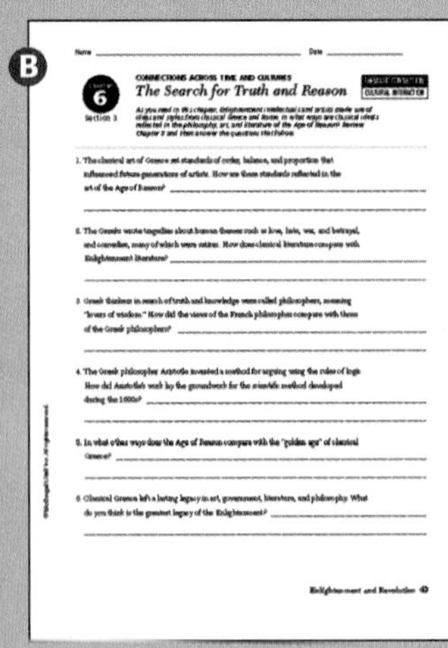

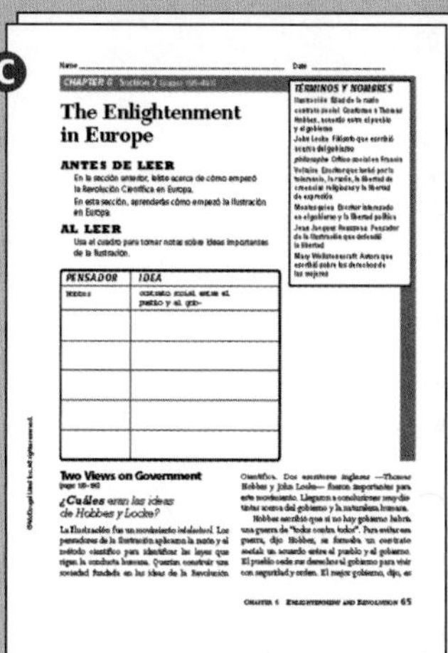

Activities in the Teacher's Edition for English Learners

- The Scientific Revolution, p. 192
- Illustrating Enlightenment Ideas, p. 198
- Connecting Enlightenment Ideas and Democracy, p. 210

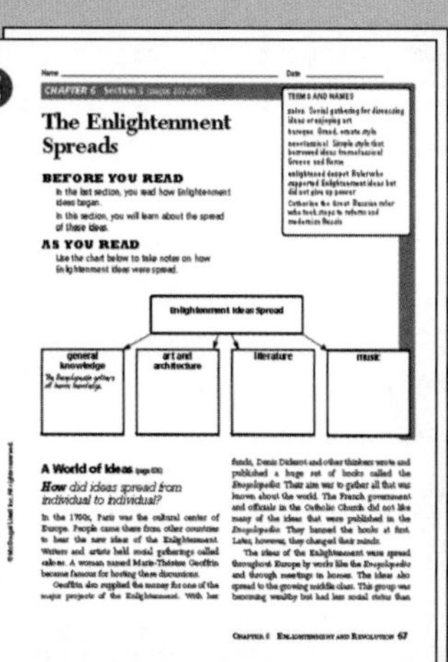

Activities in the Teacher's Edition for Struggling Readers

- Summarizing Scientific Advances, p. 193
- Enlightenment Beliefs, p. 196
- Creating Flash Cards, p. 204
- Causes of the American Revolution, p. 207

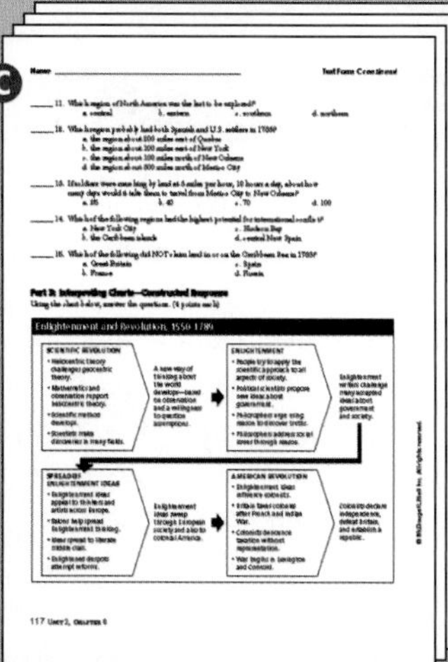

Activities in the Teacher's Edition for Gifted and Talented Students

- Exploring Galileo's Recantation, p. 191
- Exploring Mary Wollstonecraft's Ideas, p. 199
- Researching Enlightenment Arts, p. 203
- Reporting on the Enlightenment, p, 208

INTEGRATED TECHNOLOGY

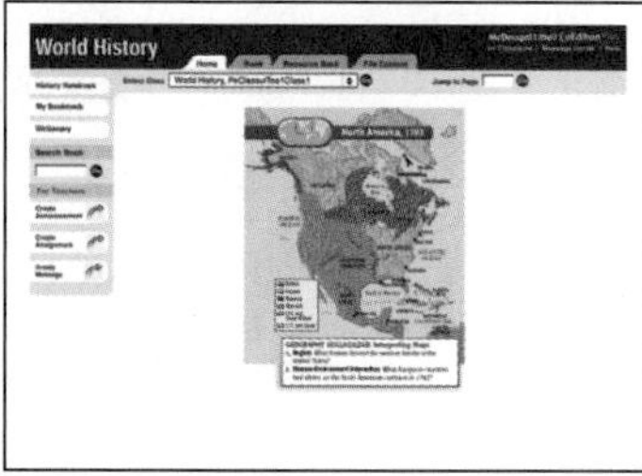

eEdition
- Interactive Visuals
- Interactive Maps
- Interactive Primary Sources

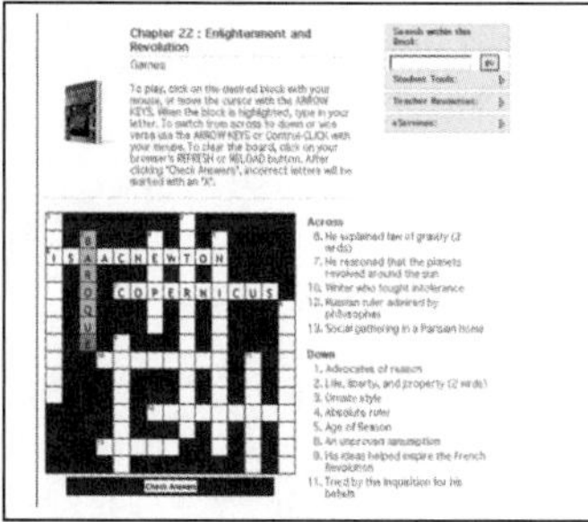

classzone.com
- Research Links
- Internet Activities
- Primary Sources
- Chapter Quiz
- Current Events

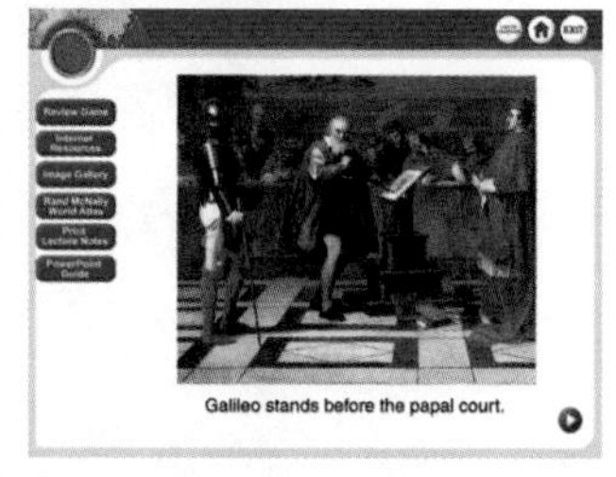
Galileo stands before the papal court.

Power Presentations CD-ROM
- Lecture Notes
- Image Gallery
- Chapter Review Game

Critical Thinking Transparencies
- CT22 The Spread of Enlightenment Ideas
- CT58 Chapter 6 Visual Summary

Geography Transparencies
- GT22 Maps of the World, 1492–1761

World Art and Cultures Transparencies
- AT48 Vermeer's *The Astronomer* (A)

Test Practice Transparencies TT80–TT83

Test Generator CD-ROM

EasyPlanner CD-ROM

Voices from the Past Audio CD

Online Test Practice

Electronic Library of Primary Sources

CHAPTER 6 • OBJECTIVE

Analyze events that led Enlightenment scientists and thinkers to question old ideas and to revolutionize the arts, religion, government, and society.

Previewing Main Ideas

Tell students that revolutions—of thought or action—begin with questions. Enlightenment thinkers asked questions about religion, about science, about authority. Once they began asking questions, each question led to another until their world was turned upside down. Challenge students to look for these questions as they read.

Accessing Prior Knowledge

Post the words *Enlightenment* and *Revolution* on the board. Write *light* and *revolve* below them, explaining that these are the root words. Discuss how enlightenment and revolution could be applied to people's ways of thinking as well as their actions.

Geography *Answers*

SCIENCE AND TECHNOLOGY

Berlin was an Enlightenment center in Brandenburg-Prussia.

POWER AND AUTHORITY

St. Petersburg was an Enlightenment center in Russia.

REVOLUTION They had spread to England's North American colonies.

CHAPTER 6

Enlightenment and Revolution, 1550–1789

Previewing Main Ideas

SCIENCE AND TECHNOLOGY The Scientific Revolution began when astronomers questioned how the universe operates. By shattering long-held views, these astronomers opened a new world of discovery.

Geography *In what Russian city did Enlightenment ideas bloom?*

POWER AND AUTHORITY The thinkers of the Enlightenment challenged old ideas about power and authority. Such new ways of thinking led to, among other things, the American Revolution.

Geography *Where had Enlightenment ideas spread outside Europe?*

REVOLUTION Between the 16th and 18th centuries, a series of revolutions helped to usher in the modern era in Western history. Revolutions in both thought and action forever changed European and American society.

Geography *What city in Brandenburg-Prussia was an Enlightenment center?*

INTEGRATED TECHNOLOGY

eEdition
- Interactive Maps
- Interactive Visuals
- Interactive Primary Sources

INTERNET RESOURCES

Go to **classzone.com** for:
- Research Links
- Internet Activities
- Primary Sources
- Chapter Quiz
- Maps
- Test Practice
- Current Events

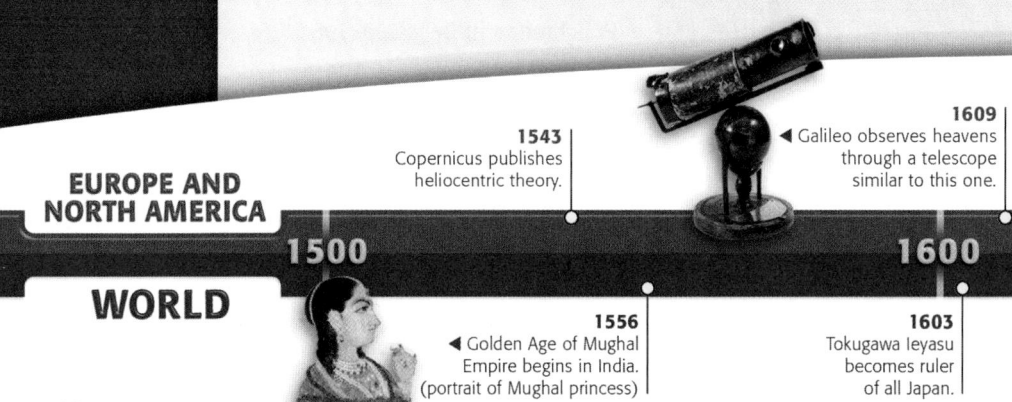

EUROPE AND NORTH AMERICA

1543 Copernicus publishes heliocentric theory.

1609 Galileo observes heavens through a telescope similar to this one.

1500

1600

WORLD

1556 Golden Age of Mughal Empire begins in India. (portrait of Mughal princess)

1603 Tokugawa Ieyasu becomes ruler of all Japan.

TIME LINE DISCUSSION

Explain that this time line focuses on some of the major achievements in science and political thought during the Enlightenment.

1. Ask students to name three milestones in math and astronomy. *(1543—Copernicus's heliocentric theory; 1609—Galileo's use of a telescope to view the heavens; 1687—Newton's law of gravity)*
2. How many years passed between each of the math and astronomy discoveries? *(66, 78)* What does this suggest about the scientific communities of the times? *(They were active over time.)*
3. Which Chinese emperor reigned for 61 years? *(Kangxi)*
4. What events occurred in America and France in the late 1700s? *(The American colonies declared independence; revolution erupted in France.)* What can be inferred about these events following 200 years of new scientific and political thought? *(Revolutionary thought led to revolutionary action.)*
5. Summarize the events elsewhere in the world between 1500–1800. *(Many new rulers were taking power and changing governments.)*

Centers of Enlightenment, c. 1740

British North American Colonies

0 150 300 Miles
0 150 300 Kilometers
Conic Projection

◆ Enlightenment Centers

0 250 500 Miles
0 250 500 Kilometers
Conic Projection

1687
Newton publishes treatise on law of gravity.

1776
◀ With Liberty Bell symbolizing their freedom, American colonies declare independence.

1789
Revolution erupts in France.

1700 **1800**

1644
Manchus invade China and establish Qing Dynasty. (Qing ruler Lohan) ▶

1722
Chinese emperor Kangxi dies after a 61-year reign.

1776
Tukolor Kingdom arises in the former Songhai region of West Africa.

187

CHAPTER 6

History from Visuals

Interpreting the Map

Ask students to note the centers of Enlightenment in Europe. Then ask how students can tell that most of the Enlightenment ideas came from western Europe and not from Russia or Poland. *(Most of the centers are in this area.)* Next, have students use the scale to calculate distances between Paris and Berlin *(about 1,200 miles)*; and London and Vienna *(about 775 miles)*. Point out that most of the Enlightenment centers are close together in western Europe.
Ask how this might have affected the spread of ideas.

Extension Have students look at the inset map and the map of North America on page 208. Ask them to identify the countries with colonies in North America. How might Enlightenment ideas have spread to North America? *(colonization)* Have students predict whether the spread of these ideas will strengthen or weaken ties between Europe and the colonies. Urge students to confirm their predictions as they read the chapter.

RECOMMENDED RESOURCES

Books for the Teacher

Almond, Mark. ***Revolution: 500 Years of Struggle for Change.*** London: De Agostini, 1996. Account of 27 revolutions and movements.

Beaglehole, J. C., Philip Edwards, and James Cook. ***The Journals of Captain Cook.*** Abr. ed. New York: Penguin, 2000. The exciting adventures of the English navigator and mapmaker James Cook as he charts the South Pacific.

Shapin, Steven. ***The Scientific Revolution.*** Chicago: U of Chicago P, 1996.

Books for the Student

McDougal Littell Nextext. ***Reformation and Enlightenment.*** Contains many tales that give insight into the remarkable changes in human thought and behavior that occurred during the "Age of Reason."

Videos

The Enlightenment: Keeping the Fire Burning. VHS and DVD. Films for the Humanities & Sciences, 2003. 800-257-5126. Focuses on the literature of the "Age of Reason."

Galileo's Dialogue. VHS and DVD. Films for the Humanities & Sciences, 1997. Examines Galileo's controversial books and the events surrounding his scientific achievements.

Interact *with* History

Objectives

- Set the stage for studying the Scientific Revolution and the Enlightenment, and the intellectual climate in which they began.
- Connect the events and historical figures of the chapter with students' lives.

EXAMINING *the* ISSUES

Possible Answers

- People often become set in their ways of thinking and thus are reluctant to try new methods.
- not knowing if new ideas will work; missing out on progress and possibly better solutions

Discussion

Ask students to remember other revolutionary times they have studied, such as the Reformation or the spread of Islam. In general, expressing new ideas meets with resistance; revolution creates upheaval and reorganization.

Interact *with* History

How would you react to a revolutionary idea?

You are a university student during the late 1600s, and it seems that the world as you know it has turned upside down. An English scientist named Isaac Newton has just theorized that the universe is not a dark mystery but a system whose parts work together in ways that can be expressed mathematically. This is just the latest in a series of arguments that have challenged old ways of thinking in fields from astronomy to medicine. Many of these ideas promise to open the way for improving society. And yet they are such radical ideas that many people refuse to accept them.

▲ This painting by English artist Joseph Wright depicts adults and children gazing at a miniature planetarium and its new ideas about the universe.

EXAMINING *the* ISSUES

- **Why might people have difficulty accepting new ideas or ways of thinking?**
- **What are the risks of embracing a different idea? What are some risks of always refusing to do so?**

Meet in small groups and discuss these questions. As you discuss these and other issues, recall other times in history when people expressed ideas that were different from accepted ones. As you read this chapter, watch for the effects of revolutionary ideas, beliefs, and discoveries.

WHY STUDY ENLIGHTENMENT AND REVOLUTION?

- The scientific method developed during this time is still in use today.
- Democratic governments, such as those in North America, Europe, and other regions, trace their foundations to Enlightenment ideas.
- Scientific advances discovered in the Scientific Revolution continue to impact our lives today, for example, through ongoing vaccine research that uses microscopes.
- Enlightenment arts, such as the novel and classical music, continue to offer entertainment and the opportunity for artistic expression.
- Understanding American revolutionary history and the ideas behind the nation's government helps today's Americans participate as full citizens.
- Tension between scientific and religious communities continues in modern society, for example, over the issue of evolution.

Copernican Solar System, from Andreae Cellarius, *Harmonia Macrocosmica*, 1661

Signing of the U.S. Constitution

1

The Scientific Revolution

MAIN IDEA

SCIENCE AND TECHNOLOGY In the mid-1500s, scientists began to question accepted beliefs and make new theories based on experimentation.

WHY IT MATTERS NOW

Such questioning led to the development of the scientific method still in use today.

TERMS & NAMES

- geocentric theory
- Scientific Revolution
- heliocentric theory
- Galileo Galilei
- scientific method
- Isaac Newton

SETTING THE STAGE As you recall, the period between 1300 and 1600 was a time of great change in Europe. The Renaissance, a rebirth of learning and the arts, inspired a spirit of curiosity in many fields. Scholars began to question ideas that had been accepted for hundreds of years. Meanwhile, the religious movement known as the Reformation prompted followers to challenge accepted ways of thinking about God and salvation. While the Reformation was taking place, another revolution in European thought had begun, one that would permanently change how people viewed the physical world.

CALIFORNIA STANDARDS

10.1.1 Analyze the similarities and differences in Judeo-Christian and Greco-Roman views of law, reason and faith, and duties of the individual.

10.2.1 Compare the major ideas of philosophers and their effects on the democratic revolutions in England, the United States, France, and Latin America (e.g., John Locke, Charles-Louis Montesquieu, Jean-Jacques Rousseau, Simón Bolívar, Thomas Jefferson, James Madison).

The Roots of Modern Science

Before 1500, scholars generally decided what was true or false by referring to an ancient Greek or Roman author or to the Bible. Few European scholars challenged the scientific ideas of the ancient thinkers or the church by carefully observing nature for themselves.

The Medieval View During the Middle Ages, most scholars believed that the earth was an immovable object located at the center of the universe. According to that belief, the moon, the sun, and the planets all moved in perfectly circular paths around the earth. Common sense seemed to support this view. After all, the sun appeared to be moving around the earth as it rose in the morning and set in the evening.

This earth-centered view of the universe was called the **geocentric theory**. The idea came from Aristotle, the Greek philosopher of the fourth century B.C. The Greek astronomer Ptolemy (TOL•a•mee) expanded the theory in the second century A.D. In addition, Christianity taught that God had deliberately placed the earth at the center of the universe. Earth was thus a special place on which the great drama of life unfolded.

TAKING NOTES

Analyzing Causes Use a diagram to list the events and circumstances that led to the Scientific Revolution.

A New Way of Thinking Beginning in the mid-1500s, a few scholars published works that challenged the ideas of the ancient thinkers and the church. As these scholars replaced old assumptions with new theories, they launched a change in European thought that historians call the **Scientific Revolution**. The Scientific Revolution was a new way of thinking about the natural world. That way was based upon careful observation and a willingness to question accepted beliefs.

LESSON PLAN

OBJECTIVES

- List circumstances that led to the Scientific Revolution.
- Summarize the development of the heliocentric theory.
- Describe the scientific method and explain Newton's law of gravity.
- Describe the importance of the scientific method in different fields.

1 FOCUS & MOTIVATE

Note that the Scientific Revolution began with questions about accepted beliefs. What are some ways that people today question accepted beliefs? *(Possible Answers: voting, editorials, letters to the editor)*

2 INSTRUCT

The Roots of Modern Science
10.1.1

Critical Thinking

- Why would the peoples and animals of Africa open Europeans to new ideas? *(They realized they didn't know everything.)*

CALIFORNIA RESOURCES
California Reading Toolkit, p. L28
California Modified Lesson Plans for English Learners, p. 51
California Daily Standards Practice Transparencies, TT20
California Standards Enrichment Workbook, pp. 17–18, 23–24
California Standards Planner and Lesson Plans, p. L47
California Online Test Practice
California Test Generator CD-ROM
California Easy Planner CD-ROM
California eEdition CD-ROM

SECTION 1 PROGRAM RESOURCES

ALL STUDENTS

In-Depth Resources: Unit 2
- Guided Reading, p. 25
- Skillbuilder Practice, p. 30
- Geography Application, p. 31
- History Makers: Nicolaus Copernicus, p. 41

ENGLISH LEARNERS

In-Depth Resources in Spanish
- Guided Reading, p. 52
- Skillbuilder Practice, p. 56
- Geography Application, p. 57

Reading Study Guide (Spanish), p. 63
Reading Study Guide Audio CD (Spanish)

STRUGGLING READERS

In-Depth Resources: Unit 2
- Guided Reading, p. 25
- Building Vocabulary, p. 29
- Reteaching Activity, p. 44

Reading Study Guide, p. 63
Reading Study Guide Audio CD

GIFTED AND TALENTED STUDENTS

In-Depth Resources: Unit 2
- Primary Source: from *Starry Messenger,* p. 33
- Literature: from *The Recantation,* p. 38

INTEGRATED TECHNOLOGY

eEdition CD-ROM
Voices from the Past Audio CD
Power Presentations CD-ROM
Geography Transparencies
- GT22 Maps of the World, 1492–1761

World Art and Cultures Transparencies
- AT48 Vermeer's *The Astronomer*

Electronic Library of Primary Sources
- "Of Studies"

classzone.com

A Revolutionary Model of the Universe

10.1.1

Critical Thinking

- In what way did Copernicus's theory contradict religious views? *(Christianity taught that Earth was the center of the universe, not the sun.)*
- Why do you think that Galileo chose to recant? *(Possible Answers: fear of torture; valued the Church, accepted its authority)*

In-Depth Resources: Unit 2

- Geography Application: Theories of the Solar System, p. 31
- History Makers: Copernicus, p. 41

Tip for English Learners

The word *heliocentric* is a combination of the prefix *helio* and the suffix *centric* meaning "center." *Helio* comes from the Greek *helios* meaning "sun," so *heliocentric* means "sun-centered."

A combination of discoveries and circumstances led to the Scientific Revolution and helped spread its impact. During the Renaissance, European explorers traveled to Africa, Asia, and the Americas. Such lands were inhabited by peoples and animals previously unknown in Europe. These discoveries opened Europeans to the possibility that there were new truths to be found. The invention of the printing press during this period helped spread challenging ideas—both old and new—more widely among Europe's thinkers.

The age of European exploration also fueled a great deal of scientific research, especially in astronomy and mathematics. Navigators needed better instruments and geographic measurements, for example, to determine their location in the open sea. As scientists began to look more closely at the world around them, they made observations that did not match the ancient beliefs. They found they had reached the limit of the classical world's knowledge. Yet, they still needed to know more.

A Revolutionary Model of the Universe

An early challenge to accepted scientific thinking came in the field of astronomy. It started when a small group of scholars began to question the geocentric theory.

The Heliocentric Theory Although backed by authority and common sense, the geocentric theory did not accurately explain the movements of the sun, moon, and planets. This problem troubled a Polish cleric and astronomer named Nicolaus Copernicus (koh•PUR•nuh•kuhs). In the early 1500s, Copernicus became interested in an old Greek idea that the sun stood at the center of the universe. After studying planetary movements for more than 25 years, Copernicus reasoned that indeed, the stars, the earth, and the other planets revolved around the sun.

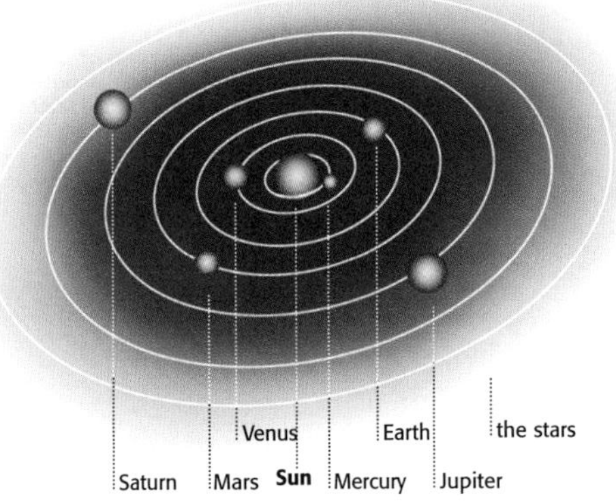

▲ This model shows how Copernicus saw the planets revolving around the sun.

Copernicus's **heliocentric**, or sun-centered, **theory** still did not completely explain why the planets orbited the way they did. He also knew that most scholars and clergy would reject his theory because it contradicted their religious views. Fearing ridicule or persecution, Copernicus did not publish his findings until 1543, the last year of his life. He received a copy of his book, *On the Revolutions of the Heavenly Bodies,* on his deathbed.

While revolutionary, Copernicus's book caused little stir at first. Over the next century and a half, other scientists built on the foundations he had laid. A Danish astronomer, Tycho Brahe (TEE•koh brah), carefully recorded the movements of the planets for many years. Brahe produced mountains of accurate data based on his observations. However, it was left to his followers to make mathematical sense of them.

After Brahe's death in 1601, his assistant, a brilliant mathematician named Johannes Kepler, continued his work. After studying Brahe's data, Kepler concluded that certain mathematical laws govern planetary motion. One of these laws showed that the planets revolve around the sun in elliptical orbits instead of circles, as was previously thought. Kepler's laws showed that Copernicus's basic ideas were true. They demonstrated mathematically that the planets revolve around the sun. **A**

A. Answer They supported the theory mathematically.

MAIN IDEA

Recognizing Effects

A How did Kepler's findings support the heliocentric theory?

SKILLBUILDER PRACTICE: CLARIFYING; SUMMARIZING

Clarifying Scientific Terms

Class Time 30 minutes

Task Defining and restating unfamiliar terms

Purpose To better understand the heliocentric model

Instructions Explain that clarifying means defining unfamiliar terms in the material and restating content in the students' own words. This process can help reinforce students' understanding of concepts. Have students use a dictionary and the glossary to define the following terms: *geocentric theory, heliocentric theory, revolved, orbited, elliptical orbit.*

Then have students reread "The Heliocentric Theory" on page 190. Have students work in pairs to write questions about the main ideas of the passage. Questions might include "How did the heliocentric theory develop?" or "Why was the heliocentric theory revolutionary?" Students should write other questions about the passage. Have partners answer the questions in their own words and use their answers to write a summary.

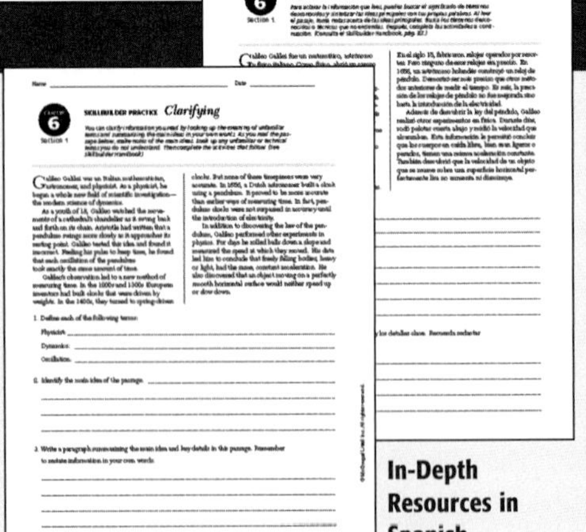

In-Depth Resources in Spanish

In-Depth Resources: Unit 2

Galileo's Discoveries An Italian scientist named **Galileo Galilei** built on the new theories about astronomy. As a young man, Galileo learned that a Dutch lens maker had built an instrument that could enlarge far-off objects. Galileo built his own telescope and used it to study the heavens in 1609.

Then, in 1610, he published a small book called *Starry Messenger,* which described his astonishing observations. Galileo announced that Jupiter had four moons and that the sun had dark spots. He also noted that the earth's moon had a rough, uneven surface. This shattered Aristotle's theory that the moon and stars were made of a pure, perfect substance. Galileo's observations, as well as his laws of motion, also clearly supported the theories of Copernicus.

Conflict with the Church Galileo's findings frightened both Catholic and Protestant leaders because they went against church teaching and authority. If people believed the church could be wrong about this, they could question other church teachings as well.

In 1616, the Catholic Church warned Galileo not to defend the ideas of Copernicus. Although Galileo remained publicly silent, he continued his studies. Then, in 1632, he published *Dialogue Concerning the Two Chief World Systems.* This book presented the ideas of both Copernicus and Ptolemy, but it clearly showed that Galileo supported the Copernican theory. The pope angrily summoned Galileo to Rome to stand trial before the Inquisition.

Galileo stood before the court in 1633. Under the threat of torture, he knelt before the cardinals and read aloud a signed confession. In it, he agreed that the ideas of Copernicus were false.

MAIN IDEA

Analyzing Primary Sources

B In what two ways does Galileo seek to appease the Church?

B. Answer He declares his former beliefs to be false and swears not to contradict Church doctrine again.

PRIMARY SOURCE B

With sincere heart and unpretended faith I abjure, curse, and detest the aforesaid errors and heresies [of Copernicus] and also every other error . . . contrary to the Holy Church, and I swear that in the future I will never again say or assert . . . anything that might cause a similar suspicion toward me.

GALILEO GALILEI, quoted in *The Discoverers*

▲ Galileo stands before the papal court.

Galileo was never again a free man. He lived under house arrest and died in 1642 at his villa near Florence. However, his books and ideas still spread all over Europe. (In 1992, the Catholic Church officially acknowledged that Galileo had been right.)

The Scientific Method

The revolution in scientific thinking that Copernicus, Kepler, and Galileo began eventually developed into a new approach to science called the **scientific method**. The scientific method is a logical procedure for gathering and testing ideas. It begins with a problem or question arising from an observation. Scientists next form a hypothesis, or unproved assumption. The hypothesis is then tested in an experiment or on the basis of data. In the final step, scientists analyze and interpret their data to reach a new conclusion. That conclusion either confirms or disproves the hypothesis.

More About . . .

Galileo's Trial

In front of the pope, Galileo retracted his support of the theory that the earth moved around the sun. A popular legend reports that as Galileo was being led away from the pope, he muttered, "And yet it moves." Although most historians reject this account, the statement was discovered inscribed on a portrait of Galileo painted around 1640.

In-Depth Resources: Unit 2

- Primary Source: from *Starry Messenger,* p. 33
- Literature: *The Recantation of Galileo Galilei,* p. 38

World Art and Cultures Transparencies

- AT48 Vermeer's *The Astronomer*

The Scientific Method

10.2.1

Critical Thinking

- How was the scientific method of exploring ideas different from looking to history for answers? *(It was based on observation and experimentation.)*
- Why might the Church dislike the ideas of Bacon and Descartes? *(Both questioned old ideas and urged experimentation and logic rather than faith.)*

Electronic Library of Primary Sources

- "Of Studies"

DIFFERENTIATING INSTRUCTION: GIFTED AND TALENTED STUDENTS

Exploring Galileo's Recantation

Class Time 25 minutes

Task Studying primary sources within historical context

Purpose To understand actions of Galileo and the pope

Instructions Tell students that Pope Urban VIII was elected in 1623. He loved art, music, and architecture, even writing a sonnet complimenting Galileo on his scientific work. Galileo hoped that a man open to new ideas in the arts would be equally enthusiastic about new scientific theories. Instead, Pope Urban VIII in effect handed Galileo over to the Inquisition. At the trial, instruments of torture were displayed as a threatening promise of what Galileo could expect if he did not cooperate. Not surprisingly, Galileo retracted his support for heliocentric theory—at least in front of the pope. Suggest that students read the excerpt from the play *The Recantation of Galileo Galilei* in In-Depth Resources: Unit 2. Have students read the play aloud, taking the various parts. Discuss with students why the pope might have abandoned his support for Galileo's work and why Galileo might have chosen to sign the confession. Ask students if they agree with Galileo's decision.

LITERATURE SELECTION *from The Recantation of Galileo Galilei* by Eric Bentley

In-Depth Resources: Unit 2

CHAPTER 6 • Section 1

History from Visuals

Interpreting the Chart

Have students tell how the time line suggests that the scientific revolution was spreading by the 1600s. *(Important scientific events are more frequent after 1600.)*

Extension Tell students to connect early events on the time line with later scientific developments. For example, the invention of the microscope in 1590 probably led to the observation of bacteria in 1674.

More About . . .

Newton's Law of Gravity

What does an apple have to do with gravity? Supposedly, Newton was sitting under an apple tree when an apple fell nearby. Newton began to wonder why apples always fall to the ground, but never sideways or up. He reasoned that the earth must have a power that draws objects to it. Thus began observation and study of the force of gravity.

Newton Explains the Law of Gravity

10.2.1

Critical Thinking

- Why were the new scientific views so revolutionary? *(Possible Answer: They didn't simply accept answers from the Church or classical scholars but based conclusions on logic and experimentation.)*
- What was the universe like, according to Newton? *(a giant clock)*

Major Steps in the Scientific Revolution

▲ Nicolaus Copernicus began the Scientific Revolution with his heliocentric theory.

1520 — 1570 — 1620

1543 Copernicus publishes heliocentric theory. Vesalius publishes human anatomy textbook.

1566 Marie de Coste Blanche publishes *The Nature of the Sun and Earth.*

1590 Janssen invents microscope.

1609 Kepler publishes first two laws of planetary motion.

1610 Galileo publishes *Starry Messenger.*

1620 Bacon's book *Novum Organum* (New Instrument) encourages experimental method.

Bacon and Descartes The scientific method did not develop overnight. The work of two important thinkers of the 1600s, Francis Bacon and René Descartes (day•KAHRT), helped to advance the new approach.

Francis Bacon, an English statesman and writer, had a passionate interest in science. He believed that by better understanding the world, scientists would generate practical knowledge that would improve people's lives. In his writings, Bacon attacked medieval scholars for relying too heavily on the conclusions of Aristotle and other ancient thinkers. Instead of reasoning from abstract theories, he urged scientists to experiment and then draw conclusions. This approach is called empiricism, or the experimental method.

In France, René Descartes also took a keen interest in science. He developed analytical geometry, which linked algebra and geometry. This provided an important new tool for scientific research.

Like Bacon, Descartes believed that scientists needed to reject old assumptions and teachings. As a mathematician, however, he approached gaining knowledge differently than Bacon. Rather than using experimentation, Descartes relied on mathematics and logic. He believed that everything should be doubted until proved by reason. The only thing he knew for certain was that he existed—because, as he wrote, "I think, therefore I am." From this starting point, he followed a train of strict reasoning to arrive at other basic truths. C

Modern scientific methods are based on the ideas of Bacon and Descartes. Scientists have shown that observation and experimentation, together with general laws that can be expressed mathematically, can lead people to a better understanding of the natural world.

MAIN IDEA

Contrasting

C How did Descartes's approach to science differ from Bacon's?

C. Answer Descartes emphasized mathematical reasoning; Bacon, experimentation.

Newton Explains the Law of Gravity

By the mid-1600s, the accomplishments of Copernicus, Kepler, and Galileo had shattered the old views of astronomy and physics. Later, the great English scientist **Isaac Newton** helped to bring together their breakthroughs under a single theory of motion.

Changing Idea: Scientific Method

Old Science	New Science
Scholars generally relied on ancient authorities, church teachings, common sense, and reasoning to explain the physical world.	In time, scholars began to use observation, experimentation, and scientific reasoning to gather knowledge and draw conclusions about the physical world.

DIFFERENTIATING INSTRUCTION: ENGLISH LEARNERS

The Scientific Revolution

Class Time 20 minutes

Task Examining scientific discoveries

Purpose To better understand the scientific revolution

Instructions Tell students to look at the time line at the top of pages 192 and 193. They should notice the increasing frequency of scientific discoveries beginning in the early 1600s. Have pairs of students answer the following questions.

1. What are the four steps of the scientific method? *(1. Stating a problem or question 2. Stating a hypothesis or idea about the problem 3. Testing the idea in an experiment 4. Looking at the results of the test and stating whether the idea in no. 3 is correct or incorrect.)*
2. Before the 1500s, looking inside a human body had rarely been done. Why was it important to dissect a human body? *(It showed doctors how the body functions and helped them treat diseases.)*
3. Why would a microscope help doctors treat disease? *(With a microscope, it is possible to identify different types of bacteria and thus identify the disease.)*

Students can use the Reading Study Guide in Spanish for additional help with Section 1.

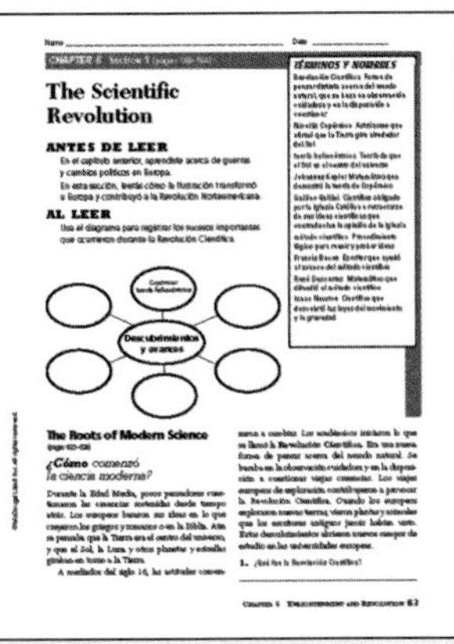

Reading Study Guide: Spanish Translation

1628 Harvey reveals how human heart functions.

1633 Galileo faces Inquisition for support of Copernicus's theory.

1637 Descartes's book *Discourse on Method* sets forth his scientific method of reasoning from the basis of doubt.

1643 Torricelli invents barometer.

1660 England establishes Royal Society to support scientific study.

1662 Boyle discovers mathematical relationship between the pressure and volume of gases, known as Boyle's law.

1666 France establishes Academy of Sciences.

1674 Leeuwenhoek observes bacteria through microscope.

1687 Newton publishes law of gravity.

1714 Fahrenheit invents mercury thermometer.

1620 — 1670 — 1720

▲ Isaac Newton's law of gravity explained how the same physical laws governed motion both on earth and in the heavens.

Newton studied mathematics and physics at Cambridge University. By the time he was 26, Newton was certain that all physical objects were affected equally by the same forces. Newton's great discovery was that the same force ruled motion of the planets and all matter on earth and in space. The key idea that linked motion in the heavens with motion on the earth was the law of universal gravitation. According to this law, every object in the universe attracts every other object. The degree of attraction depends on the mass of the objects and the distance between them.

In 1687, Newton published his ideas in a work called *The Mathematical Principles of Natural Philosophy*. It was one of the most important scientific books ever written. The universe he described was like a giant clock. Its parts all worked together perfectly in ways that could be expressed mathematically. Newton believed that God was the creator of this orderly universe, the clockmaker who had set everything in motion. D

MAIN IDEA

Clarifying

D Why was the law of gravitation important?

D. Answer It explained motion both on the earth and in the heavens and helped prove that the same physical laws govern both.

The Scientific Revolution Spreads

As astronomers explored the secrets of the universe, other scientists began to study the secrets of nature on earth. Careful observation and the use of the scientific method eventually became important in many different fields.

Scientific Instruments Scientists developed new tools and instruments to make the precise observations that the scientific method demanded. The first microscope was invented by a Dutch maker of eyeglasses, Zacharias Janssen (YAHN•suhn), in 1590. In the 1670s, a Dutch drapery merchant and amateur scientist named Anton van Leeuwenhoek (LAY•vuhn•HUK) used a microscope to observe bacteria swimming in tooth scrapings. He also examined red blood cells for the first time.

In 1643, one of Galileo's students, Evangelista Torricelli (TAWR•uh•CHEHL•ee), developed the first mercury barometer, a tool for measuring atmospheric pressure and predicting weather. In 1714, the German physicist Gabriel Fahrenheit (FAR•uhn•HYT) made the first thermometer to use mercury in glass. Fahrenheit's thermometer showed water freezing at 32°. A Swedish astronomer, Anders Celsius (SEHL•see•uhs), created another scale for the mercury thermometer in 1742. Celsius's scale showed freezing at 0°.

Medicine and the Human Body During the Middle Ages, European doctors had accepted as fact the writings of an ancient Greek physician named Galen. However, Galen had never dissected the body of a human being. Instead, he had studied the anatomy of pigs and other animals. Galen assumed that human anatomy was much the same. A Flemish physician named Andreas Vesalius proved Galen's assumptions wrong. Vesalius dissected human corpses and published his observations. His

The Scientific Revolution Spreads

10.2.1

Critical Thinking

- How does the Scientific Revolution support the saying "Necessity is the mother of invention"? *(Possible Answer: Scientists developed tools in order to continue their studies.)*
- What was the likely danger of using live germs to inoculate? Why were the risks lower if the germs were for a mild disease? *(Possible Answers: getting the disease; The disease was less serious.)*

More About . . .

Scientific Expeditions

In 1768, the English navigator and mapmaker James Cook set out on the first of three voyages to explore and chart the South Pacific. These scientific expeditions were sponsored by the Royal Society of London, a group founded in the mid-1600s to encourage the growth of scientific knowledge. Astronomers, artists, and a botanist went with Cook to gather information about distant parts of the world. Captain Cook became one of the first to chart the east coast of Australia and the islands of Tahiti, New Zealand, and Hawaii.

Geography Transparencies

- GT22 Maps of the World, 1492–1761

DIFFERENTIATING INSTRUCTION: STRUGGLING READERS

Summarizing Scientific Advances

Class Time 20 minutes

Task Charting advances in scientific thought and discovery

Purpose To understand the impact of the Scientific Revolution

Instructions Have students work in pairs to complete a chart describing the new ideas and discoveries that were happening in different areas of science. Post the following list of discoveries for reference:

- Zacharias Janssen invents microscope
- Anton van Leeuwenhoek views bacteria and blood cells
- Evangelista Torricellis develops mercury barometer
- Gabriel Fahrenheit and Anders Celsius invent mercury thermometers
- Andreas Vesalius creates accurate anatomical drawings of human body
- William Harvey shows function of the heart and blood vessels
- Edward Jenner introduces inoculation for smallpox

Tell partners to use a chart like the one here and to write two to three items in each column.

Scientific Ideas and Discoveries		
Scientific Instruments	Biology and Medicine	Chemistry

More About . . .

Smallpox Inoculations

In the 1600s and 1700s, smallpox killed or horribly scarred many infants and young children. In the early 1700s, English writer Lady Mary Wortley Montague saw women in Turkey deliberately infecting their young children with smallpox. They did this by breaking the skin and applying some liquid from a victim's sore. These children caught a mild case of the disease and gained protection from ever having it again. Lady Montague had her own son inoculated, then brought the procedure back to Britain, from which it spread all over Europe.

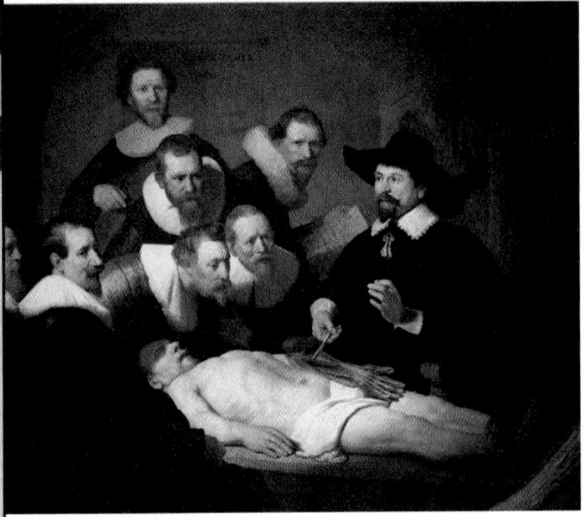

▲ The famous Dutch painter Rembrandt painted *Anatomy Lesson of Dr. Tulp* in 1632 from an actual anatomy lesson. The corpse was that of a criminal.

book, *On the Structure of the Human Body* (1543), was filled with detailed drawings of human organs, bones, and muscle.

In the late 1700s, British physician Edward Jenner introduced a vaccine to prevent smallpox. Inoculation using live smallpox germs had been practiced in Asia for centuries. While beneficial, this technique could also be dangerous. Jenner discovered that inoculation with germs from a cattle disease called cowpox gave permanent protection from smallpox for humans. Because cowpox was a much milder disease, the risks for this form of inoculation were much lower. Jenner used cowpox to produce the world's first vaccination.

Vocabulary
Inoculation is the act of injecting a germ into a person's body so as to create an immunity to the disease.

Discoveries in Chemistry Robert Boyle pioneered the use of the scientific method in chemistry. He is considered the founder of modern chemistry. In a book called *The Sceptical Chymist* (1661), Boyle challenged Aristotle's idea that the physical world consisted of four elements—earth, air, fire, and water. Instead, Boyle proposed that matter was made up of smaller primary particles that joined together in different ways. Boyle's most famous contribution to chemistry is Boyle's law. This law explains how the volume, temperature, and pressure of gas affect each other.

The notions of reason and order, which spurred so many breakthroughs in science, soon moved into other fields of life. Philosophers and scholars across Europe began to rethink long-held beliefs about the human condition, most notably the rights and liberties of ordinary citizens. These thinkers helped to usher in a movement that challenged the age-old relationship between a government and its people, and eventually changed forever the political landscape in numerous societies.

3 ASSESS

SECTION 1 ASSESSMENT

Group students to complete the web organizer in question 2. Invite groups to share their completed webs.

Formal Assessment
- Section Quiz, p. 103

4 RETEACH

Use the Guided Reading worksheet to reteach the information in the section. Have student pairs answer the questions with information from the text.

In-Depth Resources, Unit 2
- Guided Reading, p. 25
- Reteaching Activity, p. 44

SECTION 1 ASSESSMENT

TERMS & NAMES 1. For each term or name, write a sentence explaining its significance.
- geocentric theory
- Scientific Revolution
- heliocentric theory
- Galileo Galilei
- scientific method
- Isaac Newton

USING YOUR NOTES

2. Which event or circumstance do you consider to be the most significant? Why? (10.2.1)

MAIN IDEAS

3. Before the 1500s, who and what were the final authorities with regard to most knowledge? (10.1.1)
4. How did the heliocentric theory of the universe differ from the geocentric theory? (10.2.1)
5. What are the main steps of the scientific method? (10.2.1)

CRITICAL THINKING & WRITING

6. **DRAWING CONCLUSIONS** "If I have seen farther than others," said Newton, "it is because I have stood on the shoulders of giants." Could this be said of most scientific accomplishments? Explain. (10.2.1)
7. **ANALYZING MOTIVES** Why might institutions of authority tend to reject new ideas? (10.1.1)
8. **FORMING AND SUPPORTING OPINIONS** Do you agree with Galileo's actions during his Inquisition? Explain. (10.1.1)
9. **WRITING ACTIVITY** SCIENCE AND TECHNOLOGY Create a television **script** for a discovery of the Scientific Revolution. Include key people, ideas, and achievements. (Writing 2.5.b)

CONNECT TO TODAY CREATING A GRAPHIC

Research a modern-day invention or new way of thinking and then describe it and its impact on society to the class in a **poster** or **annotated diagram.** (Writing 2.3.d)

ANSWERS

1. geocentric theory, p. 189 • Scientific Revolution, p. 189 • heliocentric theory, p. 190 • Galileo Galilei, p. 191 • scientific method, p. 191 • Isaac Newton, p. 192
2. **Sample Answer:** A. Renaissance inspires new curiosity. B. Exploration broadens European horizons. C. Scientific discoveries challenge accepted thinking. Printing press spreads ideas. Most significant—the work of astronomers or of Newton, or advances in medicine
3. ancient Greek or Roman thinkers and the Bible
4. Heliocentric—Planets revolved around the sun. Geocentric—Planets moved around the earth.
5. observation; hypothesis; experimentation to test; data analysis and interpretation; conclusion
6. **Possible Answer:** Yes—Most scientific accomplishments are based on earlier discoveries.
7. **Possible Answer:** They upset the status quo and threaten authority.
8. Agree—Galileo faced torture and had to appease the Church. Disagree—Galileo hurt the Scientific Revolution by publicly renouncing the truth.
9. **Rubric** Television scripts should
   - be well organized and easy to follow.
   - tell a well-rounded story of the discovery.

CONNECT TO TODAY

Rubric Graphics should
- clearly illustrate the invention.
- explain the invention's impact.

Copernican Solar System, from Andreae Cellarius, *Harmonia Macrocosmica*, 1661

Signing of the U.S. Constitution

2

The Enlightenment in Europe

MAIN IDEA

POWER AND AUTHORITY A revolution in intellectual activity changed Europeans' view of government and society.

WHY IT MATTERS NOW

The various freedoms enjoyed in many countries today are a result of Enlightenment thinking.

TERMS & NAMES

- Enlightenment
- social contract
- John Locke
- philosophe
- Voltaire
- Montesquieu
- Rousseau
- Mary Wollstonecraft

SETTING THE STAGE In the wake of the Scientific Revolution, and the new ways of thinking it prompted, scholars and philosophers began to reevaluate old notions about other aspects of society. They sought new insight into the underlying beliefs regarding government, religion, economics, and education. Their efforts spurred the **Enlightenment**, a new intellectual movement that stressed reason and thought and the power of individuals to solve problems. Known also as the Age of Reason, the movement reached its height in the mid-1700s and brought great change to many aspects of Western civilization.

Two Views on Government

The Enlightenment started from some key ideas put forth by two English political thinkers of the 1600s, Thomas Hobbes and John Locke. Both men experienced the political turmoil of England early in that century. However, they came to very different conclusions about government and human nature.

Hobbes's Social Contract Thomas Hobbes expressed his views in a work called *Leviathan* (1651). The horrors of the English Civil War convinced him that all humans were naturally selfish and wicked. Without governments to keep order, Hobbes said, there would be "war . . . of every man against every man," and life would be "solitary, poor, nasty, brutish, and short."

Hobbes argued that to escape such a bleak life, people had to hand over their rights to a strong ruler. In exchange, they gained law and order. Hobbes called this agreement by which people created a government the **social contract**. Because people acted in their own self-interest, Hobbes said, the ruler needed total power to keep citizens under control. The best government was one that had the awesome power of a leviathan (sea monster). In Hobbes's view, such a government was an absolute monarchy, which could impose order and demand obedience.

Changing Idea: The Right to Govern	
Old Idea	**New Idea**
A monarch's rule is justified by divine right.	A government's power comes from the consent of the governed.

CALIFORNIA STANDARDS

10.2.1 Compare the major ideas of philosophers and their effects on the democratic revolutions in England, the United States, France, and Latin America (e.g., John Locke, Charles-Louis Montesquieu, Jean-Jacques Rousseau, Simón Bolívar, Thomas Jefferson, James Madison).

REP 3 Students evaluate major debates among historians concerning alternative interpretations of the past, including an analysis of authors' use of evidence and the distinctions between sound generalizations and misleading oversimplifications.

HI 2 Students recognize the complexity of historical causes and effects, including the limitations on determining cause and effect.

TAKING NOTES

Outlining Use an outline to organize main ideas and details.

Enlightenment in Europe
I. Two Views on Government
A.
B.
II. The Philosophes Advocate Reason
A.
B.

LESSON PLAN

OBJECTIVES

- Explain the ideas of Hobbes and Locke and other Enlightenment philosophers.
- Describe women and the Enlightenment.
- Explain the legacy of the Enlightenment.

1 FOCUS & MOTIVATE

Tell students that Enlightenment philosophers thought a lot about the responsibilities of individuals and governments toward each other. Ask students what responsibilities they have as citizens. *(Possible Answer: follow laws, respect others' rights, be informed)*

2 INSTRUCT

Two Views on Government
10.2.1

Critical Thinking

- What are some arguments for and against an absolute monarchy as proposed by Hobbes? *(For–creates law and order. Against–abuse of power.)*

CALIFORNIA RESOURCES

California Reading Toolkit, p. L29
California Modified Lesson Plans for English Learners, p. 53
California Daily Standards Practice Transparencies, TT21
California Standards Enrichment Workbook, pp. 23–24
California Standards Planner and Lesson Plans, p. L49
California Online Test Practice
California Test Generator CD-ROM
California Easy Planner CD-ROM
California eEdition CD-ROM

SECTION 2 PROGRAM RESOURCES

ALL STUDENTS

In-Depth Resources: Unit 2
- Guided Reading, p. 26
- History Makers: Baron de Montesquieu, p. 42

Formal Assessment
- Section Quiz, p. 104

ENGLISH LEARNERS

In-Depth Resources in Spanish
- Guided Reading, p. 53

Reading Study Guide (Spanish), p. 65
Reading Study Guide Audio CD (Spanish)

STRUGGLING READERS

In-Depth Resources: Unit 2
- Guided Reading, p. 26
- Building Vocabulary, p. 29
- Reteaching Activity, p. 45

Reading Study Guide, p. 65
Reading Study Guide Audio CD

GIFTED AND TALENTED STUDENTS

In-Depth Resources: Unit 2
- Primary Sources: from *The Social Contract,* p. 34; from *Two Treatises on Government,* p. 35; from *A Vindication of the Rights of Woman,* p. 36

Electronic Library of Primary Sources

INTEGRATED TECHNOLOGY

eEdition CD-ROM
Power Presentations CD-ROM
Critical Thinking Transparencies
- CT22 The Spread of Enlightenment Ideas

Electronic Library of Primary Sources
- from *The Persian Letters*
- from *Gulliver's Travels*

classzone.com

The Philosophes Advocate Reason

10.2.1

Critical Thinking

- What is the meaning of Voltaire's famous quotation "I do not agree with a word you say but will defend to the death your right to say it"? *(Possible Answers: You have a right to say what you think, even if others disagree.)*
- How does power check power in today's U.S. government? *(three government branches, each with limited powers)*

Electronic Library of Primary Sources

- from *The Persian Letters*

History Makers

Voltaire

Why would a monarch be interested in Voltaire? *(Voltaire was brilliant and witty.)* Voltaire left his studies at age 16 to focus on literary pursuits. He joined a group of irreverent young aristocrats and began to write witty political verses. While his writing sometimes got him into trouble, it also introduced him to like-minded people. His acquaintance with these philosophers, artists, and thinkers helped Voltaire become a great thinker.

Tip for English Learners

Explain that writers sometimes use names other than their own when they publish. This is a *pen name,* or the name used for the writings of one's pen.

Locke's Natural Rights The philosopher **John Locke** held a different, more positive, view of human nature. He believed that people could learn from experience and improve themselves. As reasonable beings, they had the natural ability to govern their own affairs and to look after the welfare of society. Locke criticized absolute monarchy and favored the idea of self-government.

According to Locke, all people are born free and equal, with three natural rights—life, liberty, and property. The purpose of government, said Locke, is to protect these rights. If a government fails to do so, citizens have a right to overthrow it. Locke's theory had a deep influence on modern political thinking. His belief that a government's power comes from the consent of the people is the foundation of modern democracy. The ideas of government by popular consent and the right to rebel against unjust rulers helped inspire struggles for liberty in Europe and the Americas. (A)

MAIN IDEA

Contrasting

(A) How does Locke's view of human nature differ from that of Hobbes?

A. Answer Hobbes believed that humans were naturally selfish and wicked; Locke's view was more positive—humans were reasonable, could learn and grow, and had natural rights.

The Philosophes Advocate Reason

The Enlightenment reached its height in France in the mid-1700s. Paris became the meeting place for people who wanted to discuss politics and ideas. The social critics of this period in France were known as **philosophes** (FIHL•uh•SAHFS), the French word for philosophers. The philosophes believed that people could apply reason to all aspects of life, just as Isaac Newton had applied reason to science. Five concepts formed the core of their beliefs:

1. **Reason** Enlightened thinkers believed truth could be discovered through reason or logical thinking.
2. **Nature** The philosophes believed that what was natural was also good and reasonable.
3. **Happiness** The philosophes rejected the medieval notion that people should find joy in the hereafter and urged people to seek well-being on earth.
4. **Progress** The philosophes stressed that society and humankind could improve.
5. **Liberty** The philosophes called for the liberties that the English people had won in their Glorious Revolution and Bill of Rights.

History Makers

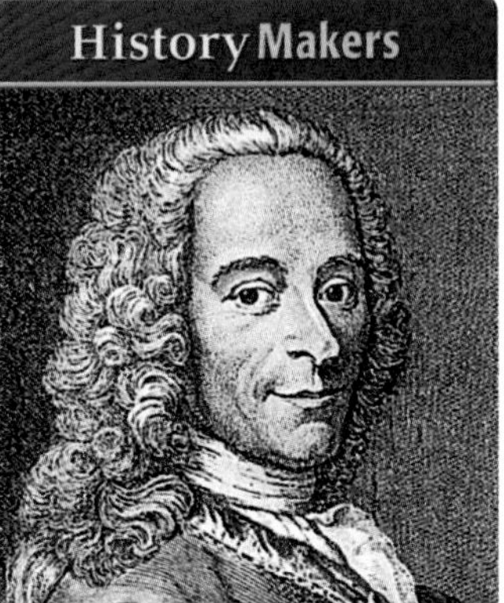

Voltaire
1694–1778

Voltaire befriended several European monarchs and nobles. Among them was the Prussian king Frederick II. The two men seemed like ideal companions. Both were witty and preferred to dress in shabby, rumpled clothes.

Their relationship eventually soured, however. Voltaire disliked editing Frederick's mediocre poetry, while Frederick suspected Voltaire of shady business dealings. Voltaire eventually described the Prussian king as "a nasty monkey, perfidious friend, [and] wretched poet." Frederick in turn called Voltaire a "miser, dirty rogue, [and] coward."

INTEGRATED TECHNOLOGY

RESEARCH LINKS For more on Voltaire, go to **classzone.com**

Voltaire Combats Intolerance Probably the most brilliant and influential of the philosophes was François Marie Arouet. Using the pen name **Voltaire**, he published more than 70 books of political essays, philosophy, and drama.

Voltaire often used satire against his opponents. He made frequent targets of the clergy, the aristocracy, and the government. His sharp tongue made him enemies at the French court, and twice he was sent to prison. After his second jail term, Voltaire was exiled to England for more than two years.

Vocabulary

Satire is the use of irony, sarcasm, or wit to attack folly, vice, or stupidity.

Although he made powerful enemies, Voltaire never stopped fighting for tolerance, reason, freedom of religious belief, and freedom of speech. He used his quill pen as if it were a deadly weapon in a thinker's war against humanity's worst enemies—intolerance, prejudice, and superstition. He summed up his staunch defense of liberty in one of his most famous quotes: "I do not agree with a word you say but will defend to the death your right to say it."

DIFFERENTIATING INSTRUCTION: STRUGGLING READERS

Enlightenment Beliefs

Class Time 20 minutes

Task Analyzing the core beliefs of the philosophes

Purpose To understand views of different Enlightenment philosophes

Instructions To help students understand the five core beliefs of the philosophes, have them attach each belief to a concrete example. Students will fill out a chart, giving an example for each belief. First, have them create a chart like the one here. Give them the text under Beliefs. With a series of questions, help them come up with examples. Some possibilities are shown here.

Beliefs	Example
1. Truth can be found through reason.	1. People can reason about right and wrong. Not necessary to look only to the Bible for answers.
2. The natural is also good and reasonable.	2. Children's natural desire to run and play is good and does not need to be stopped.
3. People can find happiness in this life.	3. Happiness can be found in the here and now, not only in the afterlife.
4. People and society can improve.	4. Our local government can get better.
5. People should have the protection of the law.	5. Laws protecting freedom of speech can work.

Montesquieu and the Separation of Powers Another influential French writer, the Baron de **Montesquieu** (MAHN•tuh•SKYOO), devoted himself to the study of political liberty. Montesquieu believed that Britain was the best-governed and most politically balanced country of his own day. The British king and his ministers held executive power. They carried out the laws of the state. The members of Parliament held legislative power. They made the laws. The judges of the English courts held judicial power. They interpreted the laws to see how each applied to a specific case. Montesquieu called this division of power among different branches separation of powers.

B. Answer It would keep any individual or group from gaining total power; each branch would check the power of the other branches.

Montesquieu oversimplified the British system. It did not actually separate powers this way. His idea, however, became a part of his most famous book, *On the Spirit of Laws* (1748). In his book, Montesquieu proposed that separation of powers would keep any individual or group from gaining total control of the government. "Power," he wrote, "should be a check to power." This idea later would be called checks and balances.

MAIN IDEA

Analyzing Issues
B What advantages did Montesquieu see in the separation of powers?

Montesquieu's book was admired by political leaders in the British colonies of North America. His ideas about separation of powers and checks and balances became the basis for the United States Constitution. B

Rousseau: Champion of Freedom A third great philosophe, Jean Jacques **Rousseau** (roo•SOH), was passionately committed to individual freedom. The son of a poor Swiss watchmaker, Rousseau won recognition as a writer of essays. A strange, brilliant, and controversial figure, Rousseau strongly disagreed with other

Analyzing Primary Sources

Laws Protect Freedom

Both Montesquieu and Rousseau believed firmly that fair and just laws—not monarchs or unrestrained mobs—should govern society. Here, Rousseau argues that laws established by and for the people are the hallmark of a free society.

PRIMARY SOURCE

I . . . therefore give the name "Republic" to every state that is governed by laws, no matter what the form of its administration may be: for only in such a case does the public interest govern, and the *res republica* rank as a *reality*. . . . Laws are, properly speaking, only the conditions of civil association. The people, being subject to the laws, ought to be their author: the conditions of the society ought to be regulated . . . by those who come together to form it.

JEAN JACQUES ROUSSEAU, *The Social Contract*

Laws Ensure Security

While laws work to protect citizens from abusive rulers, Montesquieu argues that they also guard against anarchy and mob rule.

PRIMARY SOURCE

It is true that in democracies the people seem to act as they please; but political liberty does not consist in an unlimited freedom. . . . We must have continually present to our minds the difference between independence and liberty. Liberty is a right of doing whatever the laws permit, and if a citizen could do what they [the laws] forbid he would be no longer possessed of liberty, because all his fellow-citizens would have the same power.

BARON DE MONTESQUIEU, *The Spirit of Laws*

DOCUMENT-BASED QUESTIONS

1. **Analyzing Issues** *Why should citizens be the authors of society's laws, according to Rousseau?*
2. **Making Inferences** *Why does Montesquieu believe that disobeying laws leads to a loss of liberty?*

More About . . .

Jean Jacques Rousseau

All through his life, Rousseau was plagued by feelings of guilt, depression, and inferiority. His attempts to form friendships often failed, and he spent his life as an outsider. These difficulties may have been the result of a very unhappy childhood. Rousseau's mother died giving birth to him. His father made him feel guilty for this and was either warm and affectionate or very cold and rejecting. When Rousseau was ten, his father abandoned him. As an adult, Rousseau realized he was more comfortable opposing society than trying to fit into it.

Analyzing Primary Sources

Laws Protect Freedom and Ensure Security

Ask students to read the primary source from Rousseau. Then ask them what Rousseau says about people's responsibility to laws. Challenge them to think of responsibilities U.S. citizens have to the nation's laws. *(Possible Answers: to create them and abide by them)*

Answers to Document-Based Questions

1. **Analyzing Issues** They are the ones who will be subject to the laws.
2. **Making Inferences** Without a sense of justice, people would do whatever they wanted.

In-Depth Resources: Unit 2

- History Makers: Montesquieu, p. 42
- Primary Source: *Social Contract,* p. 34

COOPERATIVE LEARNING

Analyzing Enlightenment Philosophers

Class Time 45 minutes

Task Writing reports about Enlightenment philosophers

Purpose To understand the ideas of the Enlightenment philosophers

Instructions Divide the class into five groups and assign each group one of the following philosophers:

- Hobbes
- Locke
- Voltaire
- Montesquieu
- Rousseau

Group members should work together to research and write reports about their philosopher. Each report should explain who the man was, what his ideas about government were, and how he agreed or disagreed with the ideas of one of the other philosophers. Each group should choose one member to present its report to the class.

Refer students to Primary Sources and History Makers for more information. Use the Standards for Evaluating a Cooperative Activity once the class has finished the activity.

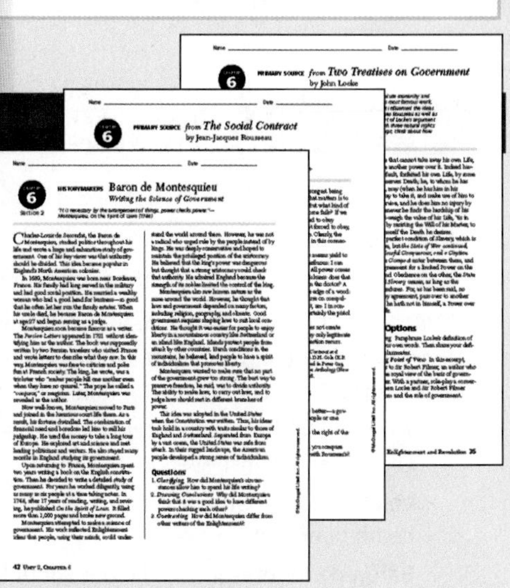

In-Depth Resources: Unit 2

More About . . .

The State of Nature

Hobbes, Locke, and Rousseau all discussed the state of nature, or human nature, in their philosophies. This referred to the way humans behaved before the structures of society existed. Hobbes thought this state of nature was self-centered and brutish. Locke believed humans were naturally reasonable and able to make decisions. Rousseau thought they were happiest when solitary.

History from Visuals

Interpreting the Chart

Ask students how Voltaire's and Beccaria's views impacted the U.S. *(Possible Answer: freedom of speech; religion guaranteed; no torture)*

Extension Have pairs prompt each other with items from the chart, for example the first item in the "Idea" column. Partners then make up a question that the item answers, such as "How did Locke's ideas affect the United States?"

SKILLBUILDER Answers

1. **Analyzing Issues** U.S. Declaration of Independence and Bill of Rights, various constitutions, French Declaration of Rights of Man/Citizens
2. **Forming Opinions** *Possible Answers:* freedom of expression: allows individuality; no torture: forbids inhumane treatment

Critical Thinking Transparencies

- CT22 The Spread of Enlightenment Ideas

Enlightenment thinkers on many matters. Most philosophes believed that reason, science, and art would improve life for all people. Rousseau, however, argued that civilization corrupted people's natural goodness. "Man is born free, and everywhere he is in chains," he wrote.

Rousseau believed that the only good government was one that was freely formed by the people and guided by the "general will" of society—a direct democracy. Under such a government, people agree to give up some of their freedom in favor of the common good. In 1762, he explained his political philosophy in a book called *The Social Contract.*

Rousseau's view of the social contract differed greatly from that of Hobbes. For Hobbes, the social contract was an agreement between a society and its government. For Rousseau, it was an agreement among free individuals to create a society and a government.

Like Locke, Rousseau argued that legitimate government came from the consent of the governed. However, Rousseau believed in a much broader democracy than Locke had promoted. He argued that all people were equal and that titles of nobility should be abolished. Rousseau's ideas inspired many of the leaders of the French Revolution who overthrew the monarchy in 1789.

Beccaria Promotes Criminal Justice An Italian philosophe named Cesare Bonesana Beccaria (BAYK•uh•REE•ah) turned his thoughts to the justice system. He believed that laws existed to preserve social order, not to avenge crimes. Beccaria regularly criticized common abuses of justice. They included torturing of witnesses and suspects, irregular proceedings in trials, and punishments that were arbitrary or cruel. He argued that a person accused of a crime should receive a speedy trial, and that torture should never be used. Moreover, he said, the degree of punishment should be based on the seriousness of the crime. He also believed that capital punishment should be abolished.

Beccaria based his ideas about justice on the principle that governments should seek the greatest good for the greatest number of people. His ideas influenced criminal law reformers in Europe and North America.

Major Ideas of the Enlightenment

Idea	Thinker	Impact
Natural rights—life, liberty, property	Locke	Fundamental to U.S. Declaration of Independence
Separation of powers	Montesquieu	France, United States, and Latin American nations use separation of powers in new constitutions
Freedom of thought and expression	Voltaire	Guaranteed in U.S. Bill of Rights and French Declaration of the Rights of Man and Citizen; European monarchs reduce or eliminate censorship
Abolishment of torture	Beccaria	Guaranteed in U.S. Bill of Rights; torture outlawed or reduced in nations of Europe and the Americas
Religious freedom	Voltaire	Guaranteed in U.S. Bill of Rights and French Declaration of the Rights of Man and Citizen; European monarchs reduce persecution
Women's equality	Wollstonecraft	Women's rights groups form in Europe and North America

SKILLBUILDER: Interpreting Charts

1. **Analyzing Issues** *What important documents reflect the influence of Enlightenment ideas?*
2. **Forming Opinions** *Which are the two most important Enlightenment ideas? Support your answer with reasons.*

DIFFERENTIATING INSTRUCTION: ENGLISH LEARNERS

Illustrating Enlightenment Ideas

Class Time 30 minutes

Task Creating posters to illustrate quotations from the section

Purpose To improve students' understanding of Enlightenment ideas

Instructions Organize students in small groups and assign each group a quote from the section. Use the following quotes:

- Thomas Hobbes: Without governments, there would be "war . . . of every man against every man."
- Voltaire: "I do not agree with a word you say but will defend to the death your right to say it."
- Baron de Montesquieu: "Power should be a check to power."
- Jean Jacques Rousseau: "Man is born free, and everywhere he is in chains."
- Mary Astell: "If absolute sovereignty be not necessary in a state, how comes it to be so in a family? . . . If all men are born free, how is it that all women are born slaves?"

Discuss all the quotes, helping students paraphrase and build meaning. Clarify terms and phrases such as *check to power, absolute sovereignty,* and *in chains.* Then have each group copy its quote onto poster paper and create an image to illustrate it. Ask groups to present their posters to the class.

Women and the Enlightenment

The philosophes challenged many assumptions about government and society. But they often took a traditional view toward women. Rousseau, for example, developed many progressive ideas about education. However, he believed that a girl's education should mainly teach her how to be a helpful wife and mother. Other male social critics scolded women for reading novels because they thought it encouraged idleness and wickedness. Still, some male writers argued for more education for women and for women's equality in marriage.

Women writers also tried to improve the status of women. In 1694, the English writer Mary Astell published *A Serious Proposal to the Ladies.* Her book addressed the lack of educational opportunities for women. In later writings, she used Enlightenment arguments about government to criticize the unequal relationship between men and women in marriage. She wrote, "If absolute sovereignty be not necessary in a state, how comes it to be so in a family? . . . If all men are born free, how is it that all women are born slaves?"

During the 1700s, other women picked up these themes. Among the most persuasive was **Mary Wollstonecraft**, who published an essay called *A Vindication of the Rights of Woman* in 1792. In the essay, she disagreed with Rousseau that women's education should be secondary to men's. Rather, she argued that women, like men, need education to become virtuous and useful. Wollstonecraft also urged women to enter the male-dominated fields of medicine and politics. C

MAIN IDEA

Drawing Conclusions

C Why do you think the issue of education was important to both Astell and Wollstonecraft?

C. Answer Education was closed to women; it could help women improve themselves and was key to exercising the same rights as men

Women made important contributions to the Enlightenment in other ways. In Paris and other European cities, wealthy women helped spread Enlightenment ideas through social gatherings called salons, which you will read about later in this chapter.

One woman fortunate enough to receive an education in the sciences was Emilie du Châtelet (shah•tlay). Du Châtelet was an aristocrat trained as a mathematician and physicist. By translating Newton's work from Latin into French, she helped stimulate interest in science in France.

History Makers

Mary Wollstonecraft
1759–1797

A strong advocate of education for women, Wollstonecraft herself received little formal schooling. She and her two sisters taught themselves by studying books at home. With her sisters, she briefly ran a school. These experiences shaped much of her thoughts about education.

Wollstonecraft eventually took a job with a London publisher. There, she met many leading radicals of the day. One of them was her future husband, the writer William Godwin. Wollstonecraft died at age 38, after giving birth to their daughter, Mary. This child, whose married name was Mary Wollstonecraft Shelley, went on to write the classic novel *Frankenstein.*

INTEGRATED TECHNOLOGY

RESEARCH LINKS For more on Mary Wollstonecraft, go to **classzone.com**

Legacy of the Enlightenment

Over a span of a few decades, Enlightenment writers challenged long-held ideas about society. They examined such principles as the divine right of monarchs, the union of church and state, and the existence of unequal social classes. They held these beliefs up to the light of reason and found them in need of reform.

The philosophes mainly lived in the world of ideas. They formed and popularized new theories. Although they encouraged reform, they were not active revolutionaries. However, their theories eventually inspired the American and French revolutions and other revolutionary movements in the 1800s. Enlightenment thinking produced three other long-term effects that helped shape Western civilization.

Belief in Progress The first effect was a belief in progress. Pioneers such as Galileo and Newton had discovered the key for unlocking the mysteries of nature in the 1500s and 1600s. With the door thus opened, the growth of scientific knowledge

Women and the Enlightenment
10.2.1

Critical Thinking

- Why might men hesitate to give women education and equality under the law? *(Possible Answer: to avoid losing power)*
- What does Mary Astell mean that women are "born slaves"? *(They are not free to make their own decisions.)*

History Makers

Mary Wollstonecraft

Read aloud the following quote from Mary Wollstonecraft's *A Vindication of the Rights of Woman*. Then ask students what ideas about women and education the quote expresses.

"...[women] spend many of the first years of their lives acquiring a smattering of accomplishments; meanwhile strength of body and mind are sacrificed to [indulgent] notions of beauty, to the desire of establishing themselves—the only way women can rise in the world—by marriage."

Legacy of the Enlightenment
10.2.1

Critical Thinking

- How can you link the belief in reason to the desire to end slavery and promote social equality? *(Possible Answer: If everyone has reason, everyone is equal.)*
- How would explaining mysteries by math change one's view of God? *(Possible Answer: One might question if God was behind the mysteries.)*

DIFFERENTIATING INSTRUCTION: GIFTED AND TALENTED STUDENTS

Exploring Mary Wollstonecraft's Ideas

Class Time 30 minutes

Task Connecting background information to a primary source

Purpose To extend understanding of Mary Wollstonecraft's views and their impact

Instructions Make sure that students have read the text on this page titled "Women and the Enlightenment." Then give students the excerpt from *A Vindication of the Rights of Woman* from In-Depth Resources: Unit 2. Have them read the excerpt and then work in small groups to answer the questions. After all groups have finished, discuss their answers as a whole. Challenge students to link Mary Wollstonecraft's ideas to the women's liberation efforts of the late 1900s. Explain that these efforts sought equal social, political, and economic rights for women. Peaking in the 1960s and 1970s, many women in the U.S. protested unequal treatment of women and demanded the right to earn and spend money, and to receive equal pay for doing equal work. Encourage students to share what they learned about Mary Wollstonecraft's ideas with the rest of the class.

PRIMARY SOURCE from *A Vindication of the Rights of Woman* by Mary Wollstonecraft

Discussion Questions

In-Depth Resources: Unit 2

More About . . .

Attitudes Toward Children

The Enlightenment changed people's views about children, too. People had believed that children were naturally sinful small adults and thus needed a harsh hand. During the Enlightenment, people came to believe that children should be better educated and could be allowed to mature into adulthood. Slowly, use of corporal punishment lessened and playtime increased.

seemed to quicken in the 1700s. Scientists made key new discoveries in chemistry, physics, biology, and mechanics. The successes of the Scientific Revolution gave people the confidence that human reason could solve social problems. Philosophes and reformers urged an end to the practice of slavery and argued for greater social equality, as well as a more democratic style of government.

A More Secular Outlook A second outcome was the rise of a more secular, or non-religious, outlook. During the Enlightenment, people began to question openly their religious beliefs and the teachings of the church. Before the Scientific Revolution, people accepted the mysteries of the universe as the workings of God. One by one, scientists discovered that these mysteries could be explained mathematically. Newton himself was a deeply religious man, and he sought to reveal God's majesty through his work. However, his findings often caused people to change the way they thought about God.

Meanwhile, Voltaire and other critics attacked some of the beliefs and practices of organized Christianity. They wanted to rid religious faith of superstition and fear and promote tolerance of all religions.

Importance of the Individual Faith in science and in progress produced a third outcome, the rise of individualism. As people began to turn away from the church and royalty for guidance, they looked to themselves instead.

The philosophes encouraged people to use their own ability to reason in order to judge what was right or wrong. They also emphasized the importance of the individual in society. Government, they argued, was formed by individuals to promote their welfare. The British thinker Adam Smith extended the emphasis on the individual to economic thinking. He believed that individuals acting in their own self-interest created economic progress. Smith's theory is discussed in detail in Chapter 9.

During the Enlightenment, reason took center stage. The greatest minds of Europe followed each other's work with interest and often met to discuss their ideas. Some of the kings and queens of Europe were also very interested. As you will learn in Section 3, they sought to apply some of the philosophes' ideas to create progress in their countries.

3 ASSESS

SECTION 2 ASSESSMENT

Group students of different reading proficiencies to answer the questions. Then have groups share their answers with the whole class.

Formal Assessment
- Section Quiz, p. 104

4 RETEACH

Have students complete the Guided Reading worksheet for Section 2. Then draw the organizer on the board and review students' answers as a class.

In-Depth Resources: Unit 2
- Guided Reading, p. 26
- Reteaching Activity, p. 45

SECTION 2 ASSESSMENT

TERMS & NAMES 1. For each term or name, write a sentence explaining its significance.
• Enlightenment • social contract • John Locke • philosophe • Voltaire • Montesquieu • Rousseau • Mary Wollstonecraft

USING YOUR NOTES

2. Which impact of the Enlightenment do you consider most important? Why? (10.2.1)

Enlightenment in Europe
I. Two Views on Government
A.
B.
II. The Philosophes Advocate Reason
A.
B.

MAIN IDEAS

3. What are the natural rights with which people are born, according to John Locke? (10.2.1)
4. Who were the philosophes and what did they advocate? (10.2.1)
5. What was the legacy of the Enlightenment? (10.2.1)

CRITICAL THINKING & WRITING

6. **SYNTHESIZING** Explain how the following statement reflects Enlightenment ideas: "Power should be a check to power." (10.2.1)
7. **ANALYZING ISSUES** Why might some women have been critical of the Enlightenment? (10.2.1)
8. **DRAWING CONCLUSIONS** Were the philosophes optimistic about the future of humankind? Explain. (10.2.1)
9. **WRITING ACTIVITY** POWER AND AUTHORITY Compare the views of Hobbes, Locke, and Rousseau on government. Then write one **paragraph** about how their ideas reflect their understanding of human behavior. (Writing 2.2.b)

CONNECT TO TODAY PRESENTING AN ORAL REPORT

Identify someone considered a modern-day social critic. Explore the person's beliefs and methods and present your findings to the class in a brief **oral report.** (Writing 2.3.b)

ANSWERS

1. Enlightenment, p. 195 • social contract, p. 195 • John Locke, p. 196 • philosophe, p. 196 • Voltaire, p. 196 • Montesquieu, p. 197 • Rousseau, p. 197 • Mary Wollstonecraft, p. 199

2. **Sample Answer:** I. A. Hobbes's social contract, B. Locke's natural rights. II. A. Reason supports all, B. Philosophes support tolerance, separation of powers, freedoms, humanity. III. A. Women want education and equality, B. Women spread Enlightenment ideas. IV. A. Belief in progress, B. More secular outlook, C. Importance of individual. **Possible Answer:** Belief in progress–Spurred efforts to improve society. Importance of individual–Promoted growth of democratic ideas.

3. life, liberty, and property
4. French thinkers and social critics; applying reason to many aspects of life
5. greater belief in progress, rise of secularism, the rise of individualism
6. No one powerful group should be in charge, but various groups should check the influence of others, thus forcing compromise.
7. Many of its thinkers had little interest in improving women's rights.

8. **Possible Answer:** Yes, they believed in progress and urged people to find joy and well-being on earth.
9. **Rubric** Paragraphs should
- identify and compare the three views.
- link each view to human behavior.

CONNECT TO TODAY

Rubric Oral reports should
- explain the person's beliefs and methods.
- provide examples of the critic's philosophy.
- be delivered in a concise manner.

INTERACTIVE

European Values During the Enlightenment

CALIFORNIA STANDARDS

10.3.7 Describe the emergence of Romanticism in art and literature (e.g., the poetry of William Blake and William Wordsworth), social criticism (e.g., the novels of Charles Dickens), and the move away from Classicism in Europe.

Writers and artists of the Enlightenment often used satire to comment on European values. Using wit and humor, they ridiculed various ideas and customs. Satire allowed artists to explore human faults in a way that is powerful but not preachy. In the two literary excerpts and the painting below, notice how the writer or artist makes his point.

A PRIMARY SOURCE

Voltaire

Voltaire wrote *Candide* (1759) to attack a philosophy called Optimism, which held that all is right with the world. The hero of the story, a young man named Candide, encounters the most awful disasters and human evils. In this passage, Candide meets a slave in South America, who explains why he is missing a leg and a hand.

"When we're working at the sugar mill and catch our finger in the grinding-wheel, they cut off our hand. When we try to run away, they cut off a leg. I have been in both of these situations. This is the price you pay for the sugar you eat in Europe. . . .

"The Dutch fetishes [i.e., missionaries] who converted me [to Christianity] tell me every Sunday that we are all the sons of Adam, Whites and Blacks alike. I'm no genealogist, but if these preachers are right, we are all cousins born of first cousins. Well, you will grant me that you can't treat a relative much worse than this."

B PRIMARY SOURCE

Jonathan Swift

The narrator of *Gulliver's Travels* (1726), an English doctor named Lemuel Gulliver, takes four disastrous voyages that leave him stranded in strange lands. In the following passage, Gulliver tries to win points with the king of Brobdingnag—a land of giants—by offering to show him how to make guns and cannons.

The king was struck with horror at the description I had given of those terrible engines. . . . He was amazed how so impotent and grovelling an insect as I (these were his expressions) could entertain such inhuman ideas, and in so familiar a manner as to appear wholly unmoved at all the scenes of blood and desolation, which I had painted as the common effects of those destructive machines; whereof, he said, some evil genius, enemy to mankind, must have been the first contriver [inventor].

C PRIMARY SOURCE

William Hogarth

The English artist William Hogarth often used satire in his paintings. In this painting, *Canvassing for Votes,* he comments on political corruption. While the candidate flirts with the ladies on the balcony, his supporters offer a man money for his vote.

Document-Based QUESTIONS

1. What is the main point that Voltaire is making in Source A? What technique does he use to reinforce his message?
2. What does the king's reaction in Source B say about Swift's view of Europe's military technology?
3. Why might Hogarth's painting in Source C be difficult for modern audiences to understand? Does this take away from his message?

201

Different Perspectives

OBJECTIVE

- Understand that European Enlightenment values can be examined from more than one perspective.

INSTRUCT

Discuss how the three primary sources explore Enlightenment values in different ways. Voltaire undercuts optimism. Swift criticizes the inhumanity of which humans are capable. Hogarth comments on political corruption.

INTEGRATED TECHNOLOGY

Interactive This feature is available in an interactive format on the eEdition. Students can view a large version of the Hogarth painting, follow hyperlinks for vocabulary help, and listen to audio excerpts.

More About . . .

Satire

Satire is an artistic style that uses humor to ridicule the practices of a society or institution through art instead of open criticism. For example, Voltaire's main characters maintain optimism despite constant evidence of stupidity and evil, implying that optimism and its followers lack reason.

Electronic Library of Primary Sources

- from *Gulliver's Travels*

DOCUMENT-BASED QUESTIONS: ANSWERS

1. Christian missionaries are hypocritical in their treatment of slaves. Voltaire shows this by contrasting the brutality of slavery with the missionaries' empty words about all men being the sons of Adam. Voltaire uses satire to reinforce the message of hypocrisy.
2. He saw such technology as cruel and wasteful.
3. Hogarth's painting requires knowledge of the unfamiliar elements in the scene that most modern audiences will lack. However, once the elements are understood, observers can more easily empathize with Hogarth's message about political corruption.

LESSON PLAN

OBJECTIVES

- Explain how Enlightenment ideas spread throughout Europe.
- Describe changes in art, music, and literature during the Enlightenment.
- Show how Enlightenment ideas reformed monarchies in Prussia, Austria, and Russia.

1 FOCUS & MOTIVATE

Explain that Enlightenment ideas spread through discussion, printed materials, songs, and visual arts, as well as laws and governmental decisions. Ask students how *they* learn about new ideas. *(Possible Answers: television, Internet, print media, at the mall, from friends)*

2 INSTRUCT

A World of Ideas

10.2.1

Critical Thinking

- Why do you think Enlightenment ideas spread so readily? What does this suggest about their appeal? *(improved communication; widespread appeal)*

CALIFORNIA RESOURCES

California Reading Toolkit, p. L30
California Modified Lesson Plans for English Learners, p. 55
California Daily Standards Practice Transparencies, TT22
California Standards Enrichment Workbook, pp. 23–24
California Standards Planner and Lesson Plans, p. L51
California Online Test Practice
California Test Generator CD-ROM
California Easy Planner CD-ROM
California eEdition CD-ROM

Copernican Solar System, from Andreae Cellarius, *Harmonia Macrocosmica*, 1661

Signing of the U.S. Constitution

3

The Enlightenment Spreads

MAIN IDEA	WHY IT MATTERS NOW	TERMS & NAMES
POWER AND AUTHORITY Enlightenment ideas spread through the Western world and profoundly influenced the arts and government.	An "enlightened" problem-solving approach to government and society prevails in modern civilization today.	• salon • baroque • neoclassical • enlightened despot • Catherine the Great

CALIFORNIA STANDARDS

10.2.1 Compare the major ideas of philosophers and their effects on the democratic revolutions in England, the United States, France, and Latin America (e.g., John Locke, Charles-Louis Montesquieu, Jean-Jacques Rousseau, Simón Bolívar, Thomas Jefferson, James Madison).

CST 1 Students compare the present with the past, evaluating the consequences of past events and decisions and determining the lessons that were learned.

CST 4 Students relate current events to the physical and human characteristics of places and regions.

SETTING THE STAGE The philosophes' views about society often got them in trouble. In France it was illegal to criticize either the Catholic Church or the government. Many philosophes landed in jail or were exiled. Voltaire, for example, experienced both punishments. Nevertheless, the Enlightenment spread throughout Europe with the help of books, magazines, and word of mouth. In time, Enlightenment ideas influenced everything from the artistic world to the royal courts across the continent.

A World of Ideas

In the 1700s, Paris was the cultural and intellectual capital of Europe. Young people from around Europe—and also from the Americas—came to study, philosophize, and enjoy the culture of the bustling city. The brightest minds of the age gathered there. From their circles radiated the ideas of the Enlightenment.

The buzz of Enlightenment ideas was most intense in the mansions of several wealthy women of Paris. There, in their large drawing rooms, these hostesses held regular social gatherings called **salons**. At these events, philosophers, writers, artists, scientists, and other great intellects met to discuss ideas.

TAKING NOTES
Summarizing Use a web diagram to list examples of each concept related to the spread of ideas.

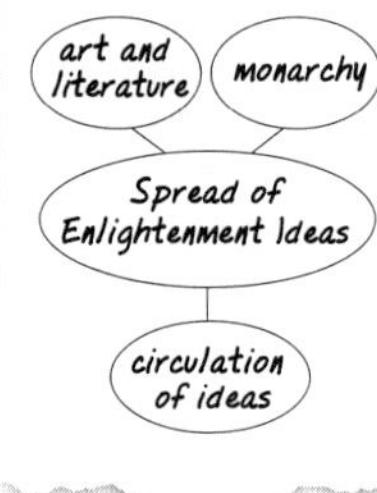

Diderot's *Encyclopedia* The most influential of the salon hostesses in Voltaire's time was Marie-Thérèse Geoffrin (zhuh•frehn). She helped finance the project of a leading philosophe named Denis Diderot (DEE•duh•ROH). Diderot created a large set of books to which many leading scholars of Europe contributed articles and essays. He called it *Encyclopedia* and began publishing the first volumes in 1751.

The Enlightenment views expressed in the articles soon angered both the French government and the Catholic Church. Their censors banned the work. They said it undermined royal authority, encouraged a spirit of revolt, and fostered "moral corruption, irreligion, and unbelief." Nonetheless, Diderot continued publishing his *Encyclopedia.*

The salons and the *Encyclopedia* helped spread Enlightenment ideas to educated people all over Europe. Enlightenment ideas also eventually spread through newspapers, pamphlets, and even political songs. Enlightenment ideas about government and equality attracted the attention of a growing literate middle class, which could afford to buy many books and support the work of artists.

SECTION 3 PROGRAM RESOURCES

ALL STUDENTS

In-Depth Resources: Unit 2
- Guided Reading, p. 27

Formal Assessment
- Section Quiz, p. 105

ENGLISH LEARNERS

In-Depth Resources in Spanish
- Guided Reading, p. 54

Reading Study Guide (Spanish), p. 67
Reading Study Guide Audio CD (Spanish)

STRUGGLING READERS

In-Depth Resources: Unit 2
- Guided Reading, p. 27
- Building Vocabulary, p. 29
- Reteaching Activity, p. 46

Reading Study Guide, p. 67
Reading Study Guide Audio CD

GIFTED AND TALENTED STUDENTS

In-Depth Resources: Unit 2
- Connections Across Time and Cultures: The Search for Truth and Reason, p. 43

Electronic Library of Primary Sources
- Letter to Catherine the Great

INTEGRATED TECHNOLOGY

eEdition CD-ROM
Power Presentations CD-ROM
Electronic Library of Primary Sources
- Letter to Catherine the Great

classzone.com

Connect *to* Today

Cybercafés

These days, when people around the world gather to explore new ideas and discuss current events, many do so at Internet cafés. These are coffee shops or restaurants that also provide access to computers for a small fee.

While Internet cafés originated in the United States, they are thought to be on the decline in America as more people become able to afford their own computers.

Overseas, however, Internet cafés continue to boom. Observers estimate that some 200,000 operate in China. Most of them are illegal. China's Communist government has little desire to give so many of its citizens access to the kind of uncensored information that the Internet provides. As was the case with the Enlightenment, however, the spread of new ideas is often too powerful to stop.

New Artistic Styles

The Enlightenment ideals of order and reason were reflected in the arts—music, literature, painting, and architecture.

Neoclassical Style Emerges European art of the 1600s and early 1700s had been dominated by the style called **baroque**, which was characterized by a grand, ornate design. Baroque styles could be seen in elaborate palaces such as Versailles (see page 166) and in numerous paintings.

Under the influence of the Enlightenment, styles began to change. Artists and architects worked in a simple and elegant style that borrowed ideas and themes from classical Greece and Rome. The artistic style of the late 1700s is therefore called **neoclassical** ("new classical").

Changes in Music and Literature Music styles also changed to reflect Enlightenment ideals. The music scene in Europe had been dominated by such composers as Johann Sebastian Bach of Germany and George Friedrich Handel of England. These artists wrote dramatic organ and choral music. During the Enlightenment, a new, lighter, and more elegant style of music known as *classical* emerged. Three composers in Vienna, Austria, rank among the greatest figures of the classical period in music. They were Franz Joseph Haydn, Wolfgang Amadeus Mozart, and Ludwig van Beethoven.

Writers in the 18th century also developed new styles and forms of literature. A number of European authors began writing novels, which are lengthy works of prose fiction. Their works had carefully crafted plots, used suspense, and explored characters' thoughts and feelings. These books were popular with a wide middle-class audience, who liked the entertaining stories written in everyday language. Writers, including many women, turned out a flood of popular novels in the 1700s.

Samuel Richardson's *Pamela* is often considered the first true English novel. It tells the story of a young servant girl who refuses the advances of her master. Another English masterpiece, *Tom Jones,* by Henry Fielding, tells the story of an orphan who travels all over England to win the hand of his lady.

Connect *to* Today

Cybercafés

By late 2002, China's government had either permanently or temporarily closed about 12,000 Internet cafés, officially for safety code violations. Still, many accused the government of simply trying to limit Internet access. Certainly, China's laws—cafés off-limits to those under 16, cafés list users' names—do much to control access. In addition, the government blocks many sites.

New Artistic Styles
10.2.1

Critical Thinking

- How does neoclassicism reflect the ideas of order and reason? *(Possible Answer: Simple structures with limited decoration suggest order and reason.)*
- Why did novels become popular in the 18th century? *(Possible Answers: The middle class had more leisure time; more people knew how to read; they wanted entertainment.)*

More About . . .

The Literate Middle Class

The middle class, eager for news, ideas, and entertainment, readily purchased popular magazines that began to circulate in the 18th century. One of the most famous, *The Spectator,* offered essays about social behavior, love, marriage, and literature. Another, *The Ladies Diary,* was aimed at middle-class women. By the 1780s, over 150 magazines were available in England.

DIFFERENTIATING INSTRUCTION: GIFTED AND TALENTED STUDENTS

Researching Enlightenment Arts

Class Time 40 minutes

Task Developing oral reports about architecture and the arts during the Enlightenment

Purpose To help students recognize the Enlightenment's impact on culture

Instructions Organize students into five groups and assign each group one of the following topics: painting and sculpture, architecture, music, literature, and drama. Groups should conduct research to learn how their art form changed during the Enlightenment and who were the most important persons associated with it. Students can begin their research with the textbook and then extend to general and topic encyclopedias and other books. Each group will develop and present an oral report that includes examples of the art form. These can include pictures, books, audio recordings, videos, and other items. The literature and drama groups may wish to read aloud a short excerpt from a novel or play.

After students present their reports, have them complete the Connections Across Time and Cultures activity. Use the Standards for Evaluating an Oral Presentation to assess students' work.

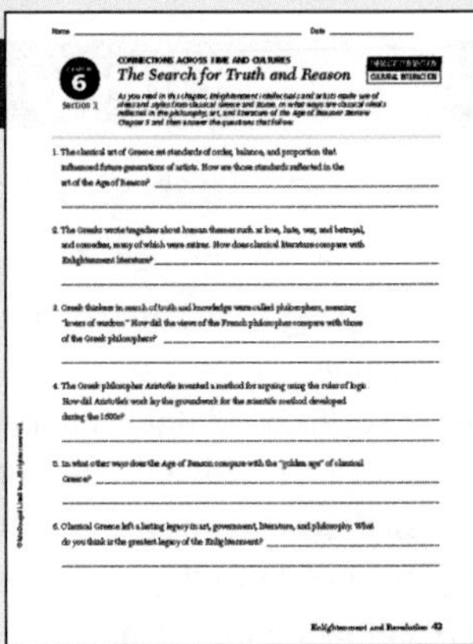
CONNECTIONS ACROSS TIME AND CULTURES
The Search for Truth and Reason

In-Depth Resources: Unit 2

Enlightenment and Monarchy
10.2.1

Critical Thinking

- Why must all rulers balance their philosophical goals with practical concerns about support? *(Without support, they cannot stay in power or make any changes.)*
- Why were most of the reforms applied to middle and upper classes? How did rulers view the peasants? *(Reformers came from the middle classes. Peasants had little power and were viewed as unimportant.)*

More About . . .

Joseph II

In 1765, Joseph was appointed co-regent by his mother, Maria Theresa. He had little power and could do almost nothing without his mother's approval. He proposed many radical reforms, such as mandatory military service for young nobles, religious toleration, an end to government spying on private affairs, limiting nobles' power, and using the army for public works projects. Joseph was unable to implement any of these reforms until Maria Theresa's death in 1780.

Vocabulary Note

Explain that the suffix *-dom* creates a noun that describes state or condition, position or rank, office or character. Examples include *freedom, serfdom, stardom,* and *kingdom*.

Enlightenment and Monarchy

From the salons, artists' studios, and concert halls of Europe, the Enlightenment spirit also swept through Europe's royal courts. Many philosophes, including Voltaire, believed that the best form of government was a monarchy in which the ruler respected the people's rights. The philosophes tried to convince monarchs to rule justly. Some monarchs embraced the new ideas and made reforms that reflected the Enlightenment spirit. They became known as **enlightened despots**. Despot means "absolute ruler."

The enlightened despots supported the philosophes' ideas. But they also had no intention of giving up any power. The changes they made were motivated by two desires: they wanted to make their countries stronger and their own rule more effective. The foremost of Europe's enlightened despots were Frederick II of Prussia, Holy Roman Emperor Joseph II of Austria, and Catherine the Great of Russia. (A)

A. Answer Intrigued by Enlightenment ideas and convinced by philosophes, they wanted to make their countries stronger and their own rule more effective.

MAIN IDEA

Analyzing Motives

(A) Why did the enlightened despots undertake reforms?

Frederick the Great Frederick II, the king of Prussia from 1740 to 1786, committed himself to reforming Prussia. He granted many religious freedoms, reduced censorship, and improved education. He also reformed the justice system and abolished the use of torture. However, Frederick's changes only went so far. For example, he believed that serfdom was wrong, but he did nothing to end it since he needed the support of wealthy landowners. As a result, he never tried to change the existing social order.

Vocabulary

Serfdom was a system in which peasants were forced to live and work on a landowner's estate.

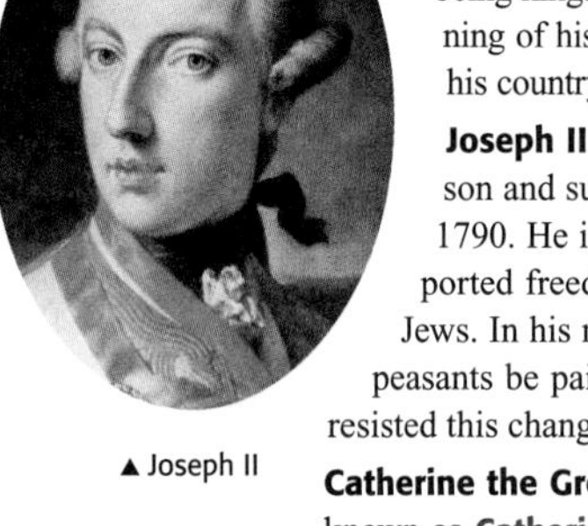

▲ Joseph II

Perhaps Frederick's most important contribution was his attitude toward being king. He called himself "the first servant of the state." From the beginning of his reign, he made it clear that his goal was to serve and strengthen his country. This attitude was clearly one that appealed to the philosophes.

Joseph II The most radical royal reformer was Joseph II of Austria. The son and successor of Maria Theresa, Joseph II ruled Austria from 1780 to 1790. He introduced legal reforms and freedom of the press. He also supported freedom of worship, even for Protestants, Orthodox Christians, and Jews. In his most radical reform, Joseph abolished serfdom and ordered that peasants be paid for their labor with cash. Not surprisingly, the nobles firmly resisted this change. Like many of Joseph's reforms, it was undone after his death.

Catherine the Great The ruler most admired by the philosophes was Catherine II, known as **Catherine the Great**. She ruled Russia from 1762 to 1796. The well-educated empress read the works of philosophes, and she exchanged many letters with Voltaire. She ruled with absolute authority but also sought to reform Russia.

In 1767, Catherine formed a commission to review Russia's laws. She presented it with a brilliant proposal for reforms based on the ideas of Montesquieu and Beccaria. Among other changes, she recommended allowing religious toleration and abolishing torture and capital punishment. Her commission, however, accomplished none of these lofty goals.

Catherine eventually put in place limited reforms, but she did little to improve the life of the Russian peasants. Her views about enlightened ideas changed after a massive uprising of serfs in 1773. With great brutality, Catherine's army crushed the

Changing Idea: Relationship Between Ruler and State

Old Idea	New Idea
The state and its citizens exist to serve the monarch. As Louis XIV reportedly said, "I am the state."	The monarch exists to serve the state and support citizens' welfare. As Frederick the Great said, a ruler is only "the first servant of the state."

DIFFERENTIATING INSTRUCTION: STRUGGLING READERS

Creating Flash Cards

Class Time 45 minutes

Task Making flash cards of important persons in the section

Purpose To build understanding of key persons and reinforce knowledge of their significance

Instructions Organize students in small groups. Review key persons from the section, such as the following:

- Catherine the Great
- Joseph II
- Frederick the Great
- Denis Diderot
- Marie-Therése Geoffrin
- Samuel Richardson
- Wolfgang Amadeus Mozart
- Franz Haydn
- Ludwig van Beethoven
- Henry Fielding

Have group members work together to make flash cards for each person. Each flash card should include the name of the person, a drawing of the person or something associated with the person and, on the back, facts about the person, and a sentence linking the person to Enlightenment ideas. After group members have finished, have them use the cards to quiz each other.

For students who need help, provide the Guided Reading worksheet for Section 3.

In-Depth Resources: Unit 2

MAIN IDEA
Synthesizing
B How accurately does the term enlightened despot describe Catherine the Great? Explain.

B. Possible Answer It accurately describes two sides of her rule–she tried to make reforms, but she also ruled with absolute authority; it's not very accurate, since she was ultimately more despotic than enlightened.

rebellion. Catherine had previously favored an end to serfdom. However, the revolt convinced her that she needed the nobles' support to keep her throne. Therefore, she gave the nobles absolute power over the serfs. As a result, Russian serfs lost their last traces of freedom. **B**

Catherine Expands Russia Peter the Great, who ruled Russia in the early 1700s, had fought for years to win a port on the Baltic Sea. Likewise, Catherine sought access to the Black Sea. In two wars with the Ottoman Turks, her armies finally won control of the northern shore of the Black Sea. Russia also gained the right to send ships through Ottoman-controlled straits leading from the Black Sea to the Mediterranean Sea.

Catherine also expanded her empire westward into Poland. In Poland, the king was relatively weak, and independent nobles held the most power. The three neighboring powers—Russia, Prussia, and Austria—each tried to assert their influence over the country. In 1772, these land-hungry neighbors each took a piece of Poland in what is called the First Partition of Poland. In further partitions in 1793 and 1795, they grabbed up the rest of Poland's territory. With these partitions, Poland disappeared as an independent country for more than a century.

By the end of her remarkable reign, Catherine had vastly enlarged the Russian empire. Meanwhile, as Russia was becoming an international power, another great power, Britain, faced a challenge from its North American colonies. Inspired by Enlightenment ideas, colonial leaders decided to do the unthinkable: break away from their ruling country and found an independent republic.

History Makers

Catherine the Great
1729–1796

The daughter of a minor German prince, Catherine was 15 when she was handed over to marry the Grand Duke Peter, heir to the Russian throne.

Peter was mentally unstable. Catherine viewed her husband's weakness as her chance for power. She made important friends among Russia's army officers and became known as the most intelligent and best-informed person at court. In 1762, only months after her husband became czar, Catherine had him arrested and confined. Soon afterward, Peter conveniently died, probably by murder.

History Makers

Catherine the Great

Ask students, With which of Catherine the Great's decisions might Voltaire have disagreed? *(Possible Answer: crushing the peasant rebellion)* In fact, Catherine the Great wrote letters to Voltaire and claimed to rule by enlightened principles. Voltaire, in turn, flattered Catherine, calling her "the star of the north," "benefactress of Europe," and "the first person in the universe." What might have been his motivation for praising her? *(Possible Answer: to gain her favor)*

Electronic Library of Primary Sources
- Letter to Catherine the Great

SECTION 3 ASSESSMENT

TERMS & NAMES 1. For each term or name, write a sentence explaining its significance.
- salon • baroque • neoclassical • enlightened despot • Catherine the Great

USING YOUR NOTES

2. What are two generalizations you can make about the spread of Enlightenment ideas? (10.2.1)

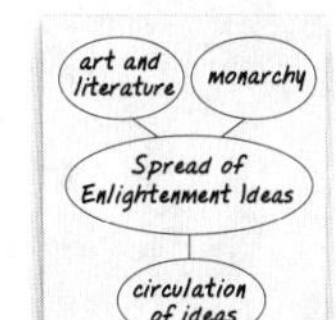

MAIN IDEAS

3. What were the defining aspects of neoclassical art? (10.2.1)
4. What new form of literature emerged during the 18th century and what were its main characteristics? (10.2.1)
5. Why were several rulers in 18th century Europe known as enlightened despots? (10.2.1)

CRITICAL THINKING & WRITING

6. **DRAWING CONCLUSIONS** What advantages did salons have over earlier ways of spreading ideas? (10.2.1)
7. **ANALYZING ISSUES** In what way were the enlightened despots less than true reformers? Cite specific examples from the text. (10.2.1)
8. **MAKING INFERENCES** How did the *Encyclopedia* project reflect the age of Enlightenment? (10.2.1)
9. **WRITING ACTIVITY** POWER AND AUTHORITY Imagine you are a public relations consultant for an enlightened despot. Write a **press release** explaining why your client is "Most Enlightened Despot of the 1700s." (Writing 2.6.a)

INTEGRATED TECHNOLOGY **INTERNET ACTIVITY**

Use the Internet to find out more about a composer or writer mentioned in this section. Then write a brief **character sketch** on that artist, focusing on interesting pieces of information about his or her life. (Writing 2.1.a)

INTERNET KEYWORDS
biography European Enlightenment

3 ASSESS

SECTION 3 ASSESSMENT

Ask students to complete the questions independently. Then pair students to discuss their answers in peer conferences.

Formal Assessment
- Section Quiz, p. 105

4 RETEACH

Use the Reteaching Activity to review the ideas of the section.

In-Depth Resources: Unit 2
- Reteaching Activity, p. 46

ANSWERS

1. salon, p. 202 • baroque, p. 203 • neoclassical, p. 203 • enlightened despot, p. 204 • Catherine the Great, p. 204
2. **Sample Answer:** Ideas–Encyclopedia, salon. Literature/art–Neoclassicism, novels, classical music. Monarchy–Frederick II, "servant of state"; Joseph II, abolished serfdom. **Possible Answer:** Ideas spread via written materials and salons; enlightened despots instituted limited reforms.
3. **Possible Answer:** a simple and elegant style that borrowed ideas and themes from classical Greece and Rome
4. the novel; long prose fiction, suspense, carefully crafted plots, revealed characters' thoughts and feelings
5. They were absolute rulers who attempted reforms in the Enlightenment spirit.
6. access to many great artists and educated people; held in private homes so guests could speak freely without threat of jail
7. wouldn't give up real power or complete reforms such as abolishing serfdom
8. **Possible Answer:** collected, examined, and spread new ideas; urged people to learn and reason
9. **Rubric** Press releases should
   - discuss reforms and their effects.
   - include specific details.
   - use effective persuasive language.

INTEGRATED TECHNOLOGY

Rubric Sketches should
- include key facts about the subject.
- depict the subject's personality.

Go to **classzone.com** for a Web research guide.

LESSON PLAN

OBJECTIVES

- Describe America's colonies in the late 1700s.
- List events that led to the American Revolution.
- Explain the Enlightenment's influence on American government.

1 FOCUS & MOTIVATE

Explain that Enlightenment ideas inspired the American Revolution and the new government that followed it. Ask students what they like/dislike, about America's system of government *(Possible Answers: freedom of speech, religious tolerance; power goes with money)*

2 INSTRUCT

Britain and Its American Colonies
10.2.1

Critical Thinking

- Why might Parliament want to restrict American colonial trade? *(increased British control and income)*

CALIFORNIA RESOURCES
California Reading Toolkit, p. L31
California Modified Lesson Plans for English Learners, p. 57
California Daily Standards Practice Transparencies, TT23
California Standards Enrichment Workbook, pp. 21–22, 23–24, 25–26, 27–28
California Standards Planner and Lesson Plans, p. L53
California Online Test Practice
California Test Generator CD-ROM
California Easy Planner CD-ROM
California eEdition CD-ROM

Copernican Solar System, from Andreae Cellarius, *Harmonia Macrocosmica*, 1661

Signing of the U.S. Constitution

4

The American Revolution

MAIN IDEA	WHY IT MATTERS NOW	TERMS & NAMES
REVOLUTION Enlightenment ideas helped spur the American colonies to shed British rule and create a new nation.	The revolution created a republic, the United States of America, that became a model for many nations of the world.	• Declaration of Independence • Thomas Jefferson • checks and balances • federal system • Bill of Rights

CALIFORNIA STANDARDS

10.1.3 Consider the influence of the U.S. Constitution on political systems in the contemporary world.

10.2.1 Compare the major ideas of philosophers and their effects on the democratic revolutions in England, the United States, France, and Latin America (e.g., John Locke, Charles-Louis Montesquieu, Jean-Jacques Rousseau, Simón Bolívar, Thomas Jefferson, James Madison).

10.2.2 List the principles of the Magna Carta, the English Bill of Rights (1689), the American Declaration of Independence (1776), the French Declaration of the Rights of Man and the Citizen (1789), and the U.S. Bill of Rights (1791).

10.2.3 Understand the unique character of the American Revolution, its spread to other parts of the world, and its continuing significance to other nations.

HI 4 Students understand the meaning, implication, and impact of historical events and recognize that events could have taken other directions.

TAKING NOTES
Identifying Problems and Solutions Use a chart to list the problems American colonists faced in shaping their republic and solutions they found.

Problem	Solution
1.	1.
2.	2.
3.	3.

SETTING THE STAGE Philosophes such as Voltaire considered England's government the most progressive in Europe. The Glorious Revolution of 1688 had given England a constitutional monarchy. In essence, this meant that various laws limited the power of the English king. Despite the view of the philosophes, however, a growing number of England's colonists in North America accused England of tyrannical rule. Emboldened by Enlightenment ideas, they would attempt to overthrow what was then the mightiest power on earth and create their own nation.

Britain and Its American Colonies

Throughout the 1600s and 1700s, British colonists had formed a large and thriving settlement along the eastern shore of North America. When George III became king of Great Britain in 1760, his North American colonies were growing by leaps and bounds. Their combined population soared from about 250,000 in 1700 to 2,150,000 in 1770, a nearly ninefold increase. Economically, the colonies thrived on trade with the nations of Europe.

Along with increasing population and prosperity, a new sense of identity was growing in the colonists' minds. By the mid-1700s, colonists had been living in America for nearly 150 years. Each of the 13 colonies had its own government, and people were used to a great degree of independence. Colonists saw themselves less as British and more as Virginians or Pennsylvanians. However, they were still British subjects and were expected to obey British law.

In 1651, the British Parliament passed a trade law called the Navigation Act. This and subsequent trade laws prevented colonists from selling their most valuable products to any country except Britain. In addition, colonists had to pay high taxes on imported French and Dutch goods. Nonetheless, Britain's policies benefited both the colonies and the motherland. Britain bought American raw materials for low prices and sold manufactured goods to the colonists. And despite various British trade restrictions, colonial merchants also thrived. Such a spirit of relative harmony, however, soon would change.

▲ This French snuffbox pictures (left to right) Voltaire, Rousseau, and colonial statesman Benjamin Franklin.

SECTION 4 PROGRAM RESOURCES

ALL STUDENTS
In-Depth Resources: Unit 2
- Guided Reading, p. 28

Formal Assessment
- Section Quiz, p. 106

ENGLISH LEARNERS
In-Depth Resources in Spanish
- Guided Reading, p. 55

Reading Study Guide (Spanish), p. 69
Reading Study Guide Audio CD (Spanish)

STRUGGLING READERS
In-Depth Resources: Unit 2
- Guided Reading, p. 28
- Building Vocabulary, p. 29
- Reteaching Activity, p. 47

Reading Study Guide, p. 69
Reading Study Guide Audio CD

GIFTED AND TALENTED STUDENTS
In-Depth Resources: Unit 2
- Primary Source: from The Declaration of Independence, p. 37

Electronic Library of Primary Sources
- Conflicting Accounts of the Battles of Lexington and Concord

INTEGRATED TECHNOLOGY
eEdition CD-ROM
Power Presentations CD-ROM
Critical Thinking Transparencies
- CT58 Chapter 6 Visual Summary

Electronic Library of Primary Sources
- Conflicting Accounts of the Battles of Lexington and Concord

classzone.com

Americans Win Independence

In 1754, war erupted on the North American continent between the English and the French. As you recall, the French had also colonized parts of North America throughout the 1600s and 1700s. The conflict was known as the French and Indian War. (The name stems from the fact that the French enlisted numerous Native American tribes to fight on their side.) The fighting lasted until 1763, when Britain and her colonists emerged victorious—and seized nearly all French land in North America.

The victory, however, only led to growing tensions between Britain and its colonists. In order to fight the war, Great Britain had run up a huge debt. Because American colonists benefited from Britain's victory, Britain expected the colonists to help pay the costs of the war. In 1765, Parliament passed the Stamp Act. According to this law, colonists had to pay a tax to have an official stamp put on wills, deeds, newspapers, and other printed material. (A)

MAIN IDEA

Analyzing Causes
(A) How did the French and Indian War lead to the Stamp Act?
A. Answer Britain passed the act to help pay the costs of the war.

American colonists were outraged. They had never paid taxes directly to the British government before. Colonial lawyers argued that the stamp tax violated colonists' natural rights, and they accused the government of "taxation without representation." In Britain, citizens consented to taxes through their representatives in Parliament. The colonists, however, had no representation in Parliament. Thus, they argued they could not be taxed.

Growing Hostility Leads to War Over the next decade, hostilities between the two sides increased. Some colonial leaders favored independence from Britain. In 1773, to protest an import tax on tea, a group of colonists dumped a large load of British tea into Boston Harbor. George III, infuriated by the "Boston Tea Party," as it was called, ordered the British navy to close the port of Boston.

Such harsh tactics by the British made enemies of many moderate colonists. In September 1774, representatives from every colony except Georgia gathered in Philadelphia to form the First Continental Congress. This group protested the treatment of Boston. When the king paid little attention to their complaints, the colonies decided to form the Second Continental Congress to debate their next move.

On April 19, 1775, British soldiers and American militiamen exchanged gunfire on the village green in Lexington, Massachusetts. The fighting spread to nearby Concord. The Second Continental Congress voted to raise an army and organize for battle under the command of a Virginian named George Washington. The American Revolution had begun.

The Influence of the Enlightenment Colonial leaders used Enlightenment ideas to justify independence. The colonists had asked for the same political rights as people in Britain, they said, but the king had stubbornly refused. Therefore, the colonists were justified in rebelling against a tyrant who had broken the social contract.

In July 1776, the Second Continental Congress issued the **Declaration of Independence**. This document, written by political leader **Thomas Jefferson**,

History Makers

Thomas Jefferson
1743–1826

The author of the Declaration of Independence, Thomas Jefferson of Virginia, was a true figure of the Enlightenment. As a writer and statesman, he supported free speech, religious freedom, and other civil liberties. At the same time, he was also a slave owner.

Jefferson was a man of many talents. He was an inventor as well as one of the great architects of early America. He designed the Virginia state capitol building in Richmond and many buildings for the University of Virginia. Of all his achievements, Jefferson wanted to be most remembered for three: author of the Declaration of Independence, author of the Statute of Virginia for Religious Freedom, and founder of the University of Virginia.

INTEGRATED TECHNOLOGY

INTERNET ACTIVITY Create a time line of Jefferson's major achievements. Go to **classzone.com** for your research.

Americans Win Independence
10.2.1; 10.2.2

Critical Thinking

- Why would taxation without representation seem unfair to Enlightenment thinkers? *(Possible Answer: no chance to present reasons, to think and discuss, to vote)*
- Was the Declaration of Independence justified or was it treason? Explain. *(Possible Answer: Enlightenment ideas justified it, but it was a rebellion.)*

Electronic Library of Primary Sources

- Battles of Lexington and Concord

History Makers

Thomas Jefferson

How do you think Jefferson's ideas, interests, and career reflect the spirit of the Enlightenment? *(Possible Answer: They demonstrate belief in progress, in reason, in individual liberties.)* Tell students that in his lifetime, Jefferson held many different positions, including governor, congressman, minister to France, secretary of state, vice-president, and president. In retirement, he pursued his interests in music, architecture, and scientific exploration.

In-Depth Resources: Unit 2

- Primary Source: from the Declaration of Independence, p. 37

INTEGRATED TECHNOLOGY

Rubric Time lines should

- include Jefferson's major achievements.
- reflect accurate historical data.
- present clear and concise information.

DIFFERENTIATING INSTRUCTION: STRUGGLING READERS

Causes of the American Revolution

Class Time 30 minutes

Task Retelling events leading to the American Revolution and identifying its causes

Purpose To help students understand events and trace their effect

Instructions To help students understand the events that led to the American Revolution, have them complete a chart like the one at the right. As preparation, pair students to read the first part of the section titled "Americans Win Independence." After both have finished, one partner should retell the information as the other listens. After the retelling, partners can then list causes in the chart, before continuing to read the subsection. For help, refer students to the Guided Reading worksheet for Section 4.

Cause: Colonists protest the Stamp Act
↓
Cause:
↓
Cause:
↓
Effect: The American Revolution begins.

Tip for English Learners

Explain that the phrase *go down in quick defeat* means "lose quickly." The adjective *ragtag* means "messy, wearing dirty, torn clothing."

History from Visuals

Interpreting the Map

Have students use the map key to identify which European country claimed the largest area of land in North America and which claimed the smallest. *(Largest–Spain. Smallest–France.)*

Extension Assign pairs a territory from the map and have them use an encyclopedia to learn more about the territory in 1783. Pairs can share their findings with the class.

SKILLBUILDER Answers

1. **Region** Mississippi River
2. **Human-Environment Interaction** Spain, Russia, Britain, France

Changing Idea: Colonial Attachment to Britain	
Old Idea	**New Idea**
American colonists considered themselves to be subjects of the British king.	After a long train of perceived abuses by the king, the colonists asserted their right to declare independence.

was firmly based on the ideas of John Locke and the Enlightenment. The Declaration reflected these ideas in its eloquent argument for natural rights. "We hold these truths to be self-evident," states the beginning of the Declaration, "that all men are created equal, that they are endowed by their Creator with certain unalienable rights, that among these are life, liberty, and the pursuit of happiness."

Since Locke had asserted that people had the right to rebel against an unjust ruler, the Declaration of Independence included a long list of George III's abuses. The document ended by declaring the colonies' separation from Britain. The colonies, the Declaration said, "are absolved from all allegiance to the British crown."

Success for the Colonists The British were not about to let their colonies leave without a fight. Shortly after the publication of the Declaration of Independence, the two sides went to war. At first glance, the colonists seemed destined to go down in quick defeat. Washington's ragtag, poorly trained army faced the well-trained forces of the most powerful country in the world. In the end, however, the Americans won their war for independence.

Several reasons explain the colonists' success. First, the Americans' motivation for fighting was much stronger than that of the British, since their army was defending their homeland. Second, the overconfident British generals made several mistakes. Third, time itself was on the side of the Americans. The British could win battle after battle, as they did, and still lose the war. Fighting an overseas war, 3,000 miles from London, was terribly expensive. After a few years, tax-weary British citizens called for peace.

Finally, the Americans did not fight alone. Louis XVI of France had little sympathy for the ideals of the American Revolution. However, he was eager to weaken France's rival, Britain. French entry into the war in 1778 was decisive. In 1781, combined forces of about 9,500 Americans and 7,800 French trapped a British army commanded by Lord Cornwallis near Yorktown, Virginia. Unable to escape, Cornwallis eventually surrendered. The Americans had shocked the world and won their independence.

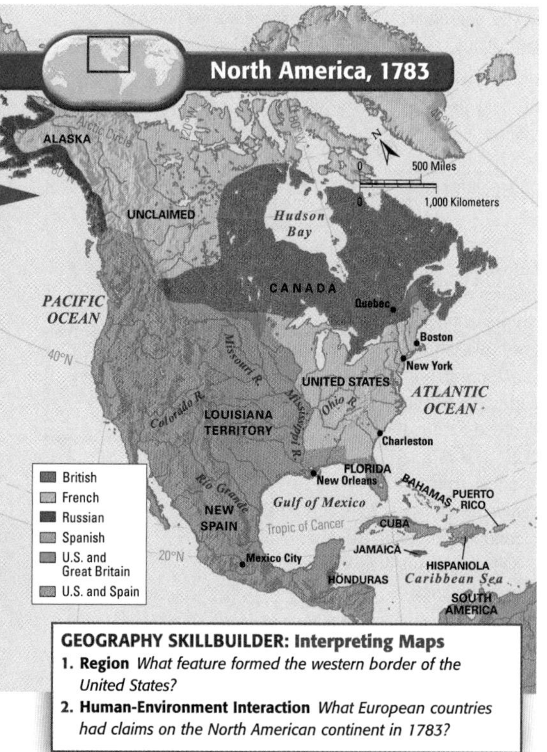

GEOGRAPHY SKILLBUILDER: Interpreting Maps

1. **Region** *What feature formed the western border of the United States?*
2. **Human-Environment Interaction** *What European countries had claims on the North American continent in 1783?*

DIFFERENTIATING INSTRUCTION: GIFTED AND TALENTED STUDENTS

Reporting on the Enlightenment

Class Time 30 minutes

Task Finding evidence of Enlightenment ideas

Purpose To recognize the influence of Enlightenment ideas today

Instructions Brainstorm with students a list of Enlightenment thinkers' ideas. These should include

- separation of powers
- election and direct democracy
- freedom of speech and religion
- protection of the accused
- prohibition of torture
- importance of reason and scientific inquiry
- government power from the consent of the governed

Have students work in pairs. Tell each pair to find an article in a newspaper or magazine that reflects Enlightenment ideas. For example, partners might find an article about a local election or about the courts' ruling on the constitutionality of a law. Students will then develop an oral report that describes what the article is about, tells which Englightenment ideas and thinkers the article reflects, and explains how it does this.

Analyzing Key Concepts

Democracy

CALIFORNIA STANDARDS
10.2.1, REP 4

Ancient Greece and Rome were strong influences on the framers of the U.S. system of government. Democracy as it is practiced today, however, is different from the Greek and Roman models.

The most famous democracy today is the United States. The type of government the United States uses is called a federal republic. "Federal" means power is divided between the national and state governments. In a republic, the people vote for their representatives. Two key components of democracy in the United States are the Constitution and voting.

Enlightenment Ideas and the U.S. Constitution

Many of the ideas contained in the Constitution are built on the ideas of Enlightenment thinkers.

Enlightenment Idea	U.S. Constitution
Locke A government's power comes from the consent of the people.	• Preamble begins "We the people of the United States" to establish legitimacy. • Creates representative government • Limits government powers
Montesquieu Separation of powers	• Federal system of government • Powers divided among three branches • System of checks and balances
Rousseau Direct democracy	• Public election of president and Congress
Voltaire Free speech, religious toleration	• Bill of Rights provides for freedom of speech and religion.
Beccaria Accused have rights, no torture	• Bill of Rights protects rights of accused and prohibits cruel and unusual punishment.

Who Votes?

Voting is an essential part of democracy. Universal suffrage means that all adult citizens can vote. Universal suffrage is part of democracy in the United States today, but that was not always the case. This chart shows how the United States gradually moved toward giving all citizens the right to vote.

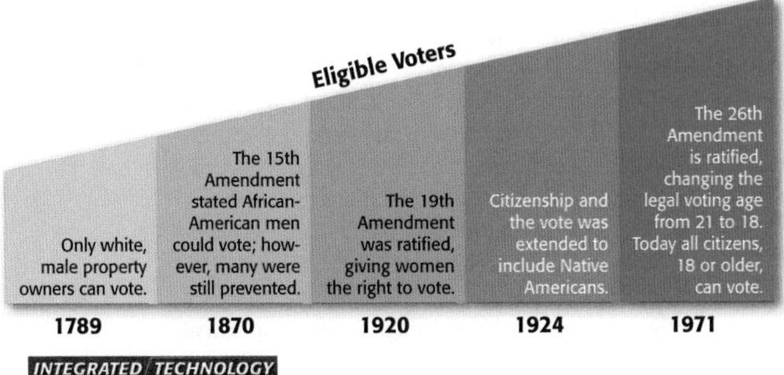
Eligible Voters
Only white, male property owners can vote.
The 15th Amendment stated African-American men could vote; however, many were still prevented.
The 19th Amendment was ratified, giving women the right to vote.
Citizenship and the vote was extended to include Native Americans.
The 26th Amendment is ratified, changing the legal voting age from 21 to 18. Today all citizens, 18 or older, can vote.
1789
1870
1920
1924
1971

INTEGRATED TECHNOLOGY
RESEARCH LINKS For more on democracy, go to **classzone.com**

DATA FILE

U.S. Constitution

- There have been 27 amendments to the Constitution since its creation.
- The U.S. Constitution has been used by many other countries as a model for their constitutions.
- In 2002, over 120 established and emerging democracies met to discuss their common issues.

Voting

- In the 2000 U.S. presidential election, only 36.1 percent of people between 18 and 24 years old voted.
- Some countries, such as Australia, fine citizens for not voting. Australia's voter turnout has been over 90 percent since 1925.

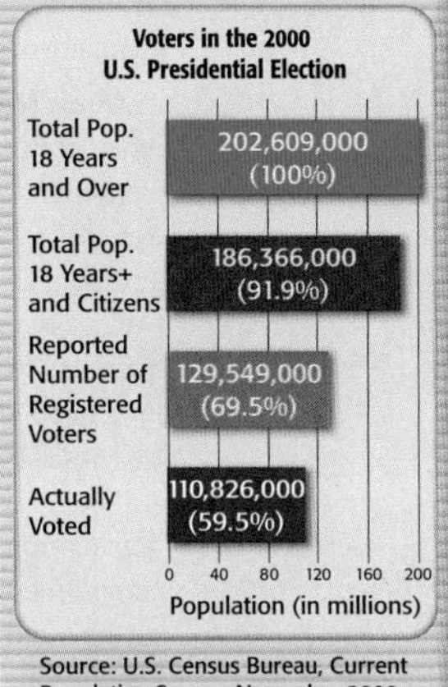
Voters in the 2000 U.S. Presidential Election
Total Pop. 18 Years and Over
202,609,000 (100%)
Total Pop. 18 Years+ and Citizens
186,366,000 (91.9%)
Reported Number of Registered Voters
129,549,000 (69.5%)
Actually Voted
110,826,000 (59.5%)
0 40 80 120 160 200
Population (in millions)

Source: U.S. Census Bureau, Current Population Survey, November 2000.

Connect *to* Today

1. **Synthesizing** If so much of the U.S. Constitution can be found in European ideas, why were the framers of the U.S. Constitution so important?
   See Skillbuilder Handbook, Page R21.
2. **Hypothesizing** Why is it important that every citizen has, and exercises, his or her right to vote?

Analyzing Key Concepts

OBJECTIVE

• Trace the development of democracy in the United States.

INSTRUCT

Explain to students that American democracy was a logical outgrowth of Enlightenment ideas. Emphasize that these ideas formed the basic foundation of the fledgling American government.

More About . . .

The Division of Power

In America, states retain many powers. For example, states have their own constitutions. Those of the original 13 states predate the U.S. Constitution. In addition, states have their own elections. These contest local and state representation, as well as many tax and social policies.

More About . . .

The Electoral College

Americans elect their president through the electoral college. In this system, each state has the number of electors that it has congressional representatives. The candidate receiving the most citizen votes on election day earns all the votes of that state's electors (except in Maine and Nebraska). Thus, as George W. Bush did in 2000, one can win the presidency without winning the popular vote.

CONNECT TO TODAY: ANSWERS

1. Synthesizing

Possible Answer: The framers of the Constitution took the ideas of different thinkers in different times and combined them into a new and unique way of thinking about government, which the U.S. Constitution represents.

2. Hypothesizing

Possible Answer: It is important that everyone has the right to vote so that not just one part of the population is represented. It is important that everyone exercises his or her right to vote because it is the only way to ensure that every voice gets heard and the only way representative government can be truly effective.

Global Impact

The French Revolution

In 1789, a French writer made this comment about the newly formed United States: "This vast continent which the seas surround will soon change Europe and the universe." What does this writer believe about the United States? What kind of change might the writer be predicting? Would kings and commoners have viewed this change in the same way? Explain. *(Possible Answers: U.S. democracy will inspire Europeans to want a similar government; Commoners would like this change, while kings would not.)*

Americans Create a Republic

10.1.3; 10.2.3

Critical Thinking

- Why would the states want to avoid a strong national government? *(Possible Answer: to avoid problems of monarchies)* Which Enlightenment thinkers does this recall? *(Montesquieu and Locke)*
- The delegates argued for four months to create the U.S. Constitution. What united and motivated them for so long? *(Possible Answer: dedication to new country; passion for its ideas)*

Global Impact

The French Revolution

The American Revolution inspired the growing number of French people who sought reform in their own country. They saw the new government of the United States as the fulfillment of Enlightenment ideals, and longed for such a government in France.

The Declaration of Independence was widely circulated and admired in France. French officers like the Marquis de Lafayette (shown here), who fought for American independence, captivated his fellow citizens with accounts of the war. One Frenchman remarked about this time period, "We talked of nothing but America." Less than a decade after the American Revolution ended, an armed struggle to topple the government would begin in France.

Americans Create a Republic

Shortly after declaring their independence, the 13 individual states recognized the need for a national government. As victory became certain, all 13 states ratified a constitution in 1781. This plan of government was known as the Articles of Confederation. The Articles established the United States as a republic, a government in which citizens rule through elected representatives.

A Weak National Government To protect their authority, the 13 states created a loose confederation in which they held most of the power. Thus, the Articles of Confederation deliberately created a weak national government. There were no executive or judicial branches. Instead, the Articles established only one body of government, the Congress. Each state, regardless of size, had one vote in Congress. Congress could declare war, enter into treaties, and coin money. It had no power, however, to collect taxes or regulate trade. Passing new laws was difficult because laws needed the approval of 9 of the 13 states.

These limits on the national government soon produced many problems. Although the new national government needed money to operate, it could only request contributions from the states. Angry Revolutionary War veterans bitterly complained that Congress still owed them back pay for their services. Meanwhile, several states issued their own money. Some states even put tariffs on goods from neighboring states. **B**

> **MAIN IDEA**
> **Making Inferences**
> **B** What was the main cause of the nation's problems under the Articles?
> B. Answer a weak federal government

A New Constitution Colonial leaders eventually recognized the need for a strong national government. In February 1787, Congress approved a Constitutional Convention to revise the Articles of Confederation. The Constitutional Convention held its first session on May 25, 1787. The 55 delegates were experienced statesmen who were familiar with the political theories of Locke, Montesquieu, and Rousseau.

Although the delegates shared basic ideas on government, they sometimes disagreed on how to put them into practice. For almost four months the delegates argued over important questions. Who should be represented in Congress? How many representatives should each state have? The delegates' deliberations produced not only compromises but also new approaches to governing. Using the political ideas of the Enlightenment, the delegates created a new system of government.

The Federal System Like Montesquieu, the delegates distrusted a powerful central government controlled by one person or group. They therefore established

DIFFERENTIATING INSTRUCTION: ENGLISH LEARNERS

Connecting Enlightenment Ideas and Democracy

Class Time 20 minutes

Task Reviewing Enlightenment ideas and the U.S. Constitution

Purpose To clarify the connection of Enlightenment ideas and U.S. democracy

Instructions Put students into small groups with a range of reading levels in each group. Have each group review the Analyzing Key Concepts feature on page 209. Each group will paraphrase the text of the chart in their own words and give an example of how the idea works. For example, for the first row, students might write "People must agree to give government certain powers."

Make sure that students, especially English learners, know what the following words and phrases mean:

- establish legitimacy *(to set up legally)*
- representative government *(government speaks for and acts for the people)*
- limits government powers *(sets up restrictions on what a government can do)*
- Federal system *(has both national and state governments)*
- three branches *(courts, Congress, the presidency)*
- checks and balances *(Each branch can stop or slow down the actions of other branches.)*
- cruel and unusual punishment *(Punishments must be just and reasonable.)*

After students have finished paraphrasing the ideas and giving examples, have them share their work. Use the Reading Study Guide in Spanish for additional help.

three separate branches—legislative, executive, and judicial. This setup provided a built-in system of **checks and balances**, with each branch checking the actions of the other two. For example, the president received the power to veto legislation passed by Congress. However, the Congress could override a presidential veto with the approval of two-thirds of its members.

Although the Constitution created a strong central government, it did not eliminate local governments. Instead, the Constitution set up a **federal system** in which power was divided between national and state governments.

The Bill of Rights The delegates signed the new Constitution on September 17, 1787. In order to become law, however, the Constitution required approval by conventions in at least 9 of the 13 states. These conventions were marked by sharp debate. Supporters of the Constitution were called Federalists. They argued in their famous work, the *Federalist Papers*, that the new government would provide a better balance between national and state powers. Their opponents, the Antifederalists, feared that the Constitution gave the central government too much power. They also wanted a bill of rights to protect the rights of individual citizens. C

C. Possible Answer Federalists believed the Constitution reflected balance between federal and state powers; Antifederalists thought federal government too powerful, wanted bill of rights to protect individual freedoms.

MAIN IDEA

Analyzing Issues

C What were the opposing views regarding ratification of the Constitution?

In order to gain support, the Federalists promised to add a bill of rights to the Constitution. This promise cleared the way for approval. Congress formally added to the Constitution the ten amendments known as the **Bill of Rights**. These amendments protected such basic rights as freedom of speech, press, assembly, and religion. Many of these rights had been advocated by Voltaire, Rousseau, and Locke.

The Constitution and Bill of Rights marked a turning point in people's ideas about government. Both documents put Enlightenment ideas into practice. They expressed an optimistic view that reason and reform could prevail and that progress was inevitable. Such optimism swept across the Atlantic. However, the monarchies and the privileged classes didn't give up power and position easily. As Chapter 7 explains, the struggle to attain the principles of the Enlightenment led to violent revolution in France.

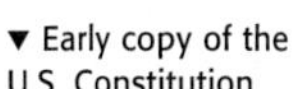

▼ Early copy of the U.S. Constitution

More About . . .

The Colonies

Enlightenment ideas spread through the American colonies in books and pamphlets. Literacy rates in the colonies were high among white males. While only one-third of the males in England could read, in some colonies, over 50% of the white males could read. Literacy rates in New England were particularly high because the Puritans who settled there advocated public education so that everyone, women included, could read the Bible.

SECTION 4 ASSESSMENT

TERMS & NAMES 1. For each term or name, write a sentence explaining its significance.
• Declaration of Independence • Thomas Jefferson • checks and balances • federal system • Bill of Rights

USING YOUR NOTES

2. Which of the solutions that you recorded represented a compromise? (10.2.1)

Problem	Solution
1.	1.
2.	2.
3.	3.

MAIN IDEAS

3. Why did the colonists criticize the Stamp Act as "taxation without representation"? (10.2.3)
4. How did John Locke's notion of the social contract influence the American colonists? (10.2.1)
5. Why were the colonists able to achieve victory in the American Revolution? (10.2.3)

CRITICAL THINKING & WRITING

6. **MAKING INFERENCES** Why might it be important to have a Bill of Rights that guarantees basic rights? (10.2.2)
7. **FORMING AND SUPPORTING OPINIONS** Do you think the American Revolution would have happened if there had not been an Age of Enlightenment? (10.2.3)
8. **ANALYZING CAUSES** Why do you think the colonists at first created such a weak central government? (10.2.3)
9. **WRITING ACTIVITY** REVOLUTION Summarize in several **paragraphs** the ideas from the American Revolution concerning separation of powers, basic rights of freedom, and popular sovereignty. (Writing 2.3.b)

CONNECT TO TODAY CELEBRATING AMERICA'S BIRTHDAY

Create a **birthday poster** to present to the United States this July 4th. The poster should include images or quotes that demonstrate the ideals upon which the nation was founded. (10.2.2)

3 ASSESS

SECTION 4 ASSESSMENT

Have partners prompt each other with the list of terms and names. Then encourage discussion of the questions before students answer them individually.

Formal Assessment
• Section Quiz, p. 106

4 RETEACH

Use the Visual Summary to review the chapter as a whole.

Critical Thinking Transparencies
• CT58 Chapter 6 Visual Summary

In-Depth Resources: Unit 2
• Reteaching Activity, p. 47

ANSWERS

1. Declaration of Independence, p. 207 • Thomas Jefferson, p. 207 • checks and balances, p. 211 • federal system, p. 211 • Bill of Rights, p. 211
2. **Sample Answer:** Stamp Act/Protest; Tea tax/Boston Tea Party; Weak Articles of Confederation/Constitutional Convention; Mistrust of central government/Federal system; **Possible Answer:** federal system, which divided the power
3. The colonists felt they should not have to pay taxes on which they had no vote.
4. It suggested that citizens had a right to overthrow an unjust government that did not promote their rights.
5. stronger motivation; British mistakes of overconfidence; British weary of taxes; help from European allies
6. **Possible Answer:** prevents government from suppressing rights whenever it wishes
7. **Possible Answer:** No—Need belief in human progress and supremacy of reason; ideas of natural rights and need for consent of the governed. Yes—The colonists felt so oppressed that they eventually would have acted.
8. **Possible Answer:** to avoid tyranny as under King George II
9. **Rubric** Paragraphs should
• discuss checks and balances.
• summarize Bill of Rights guarantees.
• explain consent of the governed.

CONNECT TO TODAY

Rubric Posters should
• convey the nation's founding ideals.
• be visually clear and appealing.

TERMS & NAMES

1. heliocentric theory, p. 190
2. Isaac Newton, p. 192
3. social contract, p. 195
4. philosophe, p. 196
5. salon, p. 202
6. enlightened despot, p. 204
7. Declaration of Independence, p. 207
8. federal system, p. 211

MAIN IDEAS

Answers will vary.

9. Center; Copernicus's theory was that Earth revolved around the sun.
10. identify problem based on hypothesis; form hypothesis; test hypothesis; analyze and interpret results and form conclusion
11. Telescope—Enlarge distant objects. Microscope—Enlarge tiny objects. Thermometer—Measure temperature. Barometer—Measure atmospheric pressure.
12. Hobbes—People are naturally selfish; need governments of absolute monarchy to protect society from this selfishness. Locke—People have natural ability to reason and to govern their own affairs; governments should protect natural rights.
13. separation of powers
14. offered new explanations for mysteries of nature, prompted people to question authority and religious teaching
15. neoclassicism; classical music; novel
16. increased religious toleration, reduced censorship and torture, improved education, abolished serfdom, allowed freedom of press
17. no executive or judicial branches; Congress lacked power to collect taxes or regulate trade; new laws hard to pass, needed approval of 9 of 13 states
18. created separate executive, legislative, and judicial branches of government; gave each branch controls on the others

Chapter 6 Assessment

TERMS & NAMES

For each term or name below, briefly explain its connection to European history from 1550–1789.

1. heliocentric theory
2. Isaac Newton
3. social contract
4. philosophe
5. salon
6. enlightened despot
7. Declaration of Independence
8. federal system

MAIN IDEAS

The Scientific Revolution Section 1 (pages 189–194)

9. According to Ptolemy, what was the earth's position in the universe? How did Copernicus's view differ? (10.1.1)
10. What are the four steps in the scientific method? (10.1.1)
11. What four new instruments emerged in the Scientific Revolution? What was the purpose of each? (10.1.1)

The Enlightenment in Europe Section 2 (pages 195–201)

12. How did the ideas of Hobbes and Locke differ? (10.2.1)
13. What did Montesquieu admire about the government of Britain? (10.2.1)
14. How did the Enlightenment lead to a more secular outlook? (10.2.1)

The Enlightenment Spreads Section 3 (pages 202–205)

15. What were three developments in the arts during the Enlightenment? (10.2.1)
16. What reforms did the enlightened despots make? (10.2.1)

The American Revolution Section 4 (pages 206–211)

17. Why did the Articles of Confederation result in a weak national government? (10.2.3)
18. How did the writers of the U.S. Constitution put into practice the idea of separation of powers? A system of checks and balances? (10.2.3)

CRITICAL THINKING

1. USING YOUR NOTES

List in a table important new ideas that arose during the Scientific Revolution and Enlightenment. In the right column, briefly explain why each idea was revolutionary. (10.2.1)

New Idea	Why Revolutionary

2. RECOGNIZING EFFECTS

SCIENCE AND TECHNOLOGY What role did technology play in the Scientific Revolution? (10.1.1)

3. ANALYZING ISSUES

POWER AND AUTHORITY How did the U.S. Constitution reflect the ideas of the Enlightenment? Refer to specific Enlightenment thinkers to support your answer. (10.2.3)

4. CLARIFYING

How did the statement by Prussian ruler Frederick the Great that a ruler is only "the first servant of the state" highlight Enlightenment ideas about government? (10.2.1)

VISUAL SUMMARY

Enlightenment and Revolution, 1550–1789

Scientific Revolution
- Heliocentric theory challenges geocentric theory.
- Mathematics and observation support heliocentric theory.
- Scientific method develops.
- Scientists make discoveries in many fields.

A new way of thinking about the world develops, based on observation and a willingness to question assumptions.

Enlightenment
- People try to apply the scientific approach to aspects of society.
- Political scientists propose new ideas about government.
- Philosophes advocate the use of reason to discover truths.
- Philosophes address social issues through reason.

Enlightenment writers challenge many accepted ideas about government and society.

Spread of Ideas
- Enlightenment ideas appeal to thinkers and artists across Europe.
- Salons help spread Enlightenment thinking.
- Ideas spread to literate middle class.
- Enlightened despots attempt reforms.

Enlightenment ideas sweep through European society and to colonial America.

American Revolution
- Enlightenment ideas influence colonists.
- Britain taxes colonists after French and Indian War.
- Colonists denounce taxation without representation.
- War begins in Lexington and Concord.

Colonists declare independence, defeat Britain, and establish republic.

CRITICAL THINKING

Answers will vary.

1. Heliocentric theory—Contradicted earlier theories and Church teaching. Scientific method—Permanently changed approach to science. Consent of the governed—Challenged divine right. Separation of powers—Challenged absolutism.
2. Telescope and microscope—Greatly improved methods of observation and experimentation. Printing press—Helped spread ideas.
3. checks and balances reflected Montesquieu; Bill of Rights secured liberties urged by Voltaire, Rousseau, and Locke
4. highlighted Enlightenment ideas that government existed for the people's benefit and that rulers should serve their subjects

Use the quotation and your knowledge of world history to answer questions 1 and 2.
Additional Test Practice, pp. S1–S33

PRIMARY SOURCE

We the People of the United States, in order to form a more perfect Union, establish Justice, insure domestic Tranquility, provide for the common defense, promote the general Welfare, and secure the Blessings of Liberty to ourselves and our Posterity, do ordain and establish this Constitution of the United States of America.

Preamble, *Constitution of the United States of America*

1. All of the following are stated objectives of the Constitution except (10.2.3)

A. justice.
B. liberty.
C. defense.
D. prosperity.

2. With whom does the ultimate power in society lie, according to the Constitution? (10.2.3)

A. the church
B. the military
C. the citizens
D. the monarchy

Use this engraving, entitled *The Sleep of Reason Produces Monsters,* and your knowledge of world history to answer question 3.

3. Which of the following statements best summarizes the main idea of this Enlightenment engraving? (10.2.1)

A. Nothing good comes from relaxation or laziness.
B. A lack of reason fosters superstition and irrational fears.
C. Dreams are not restricted by the boundaries of reason.
D. Rulers that let down their guard risk rebellion and overthrow.

INTEGRATED TECHNOLOGY
TEST PRACTICE Go to **classzone.com**
- Diagnostic tests
- Strategies
- Tutorials
- Additional practice

STANDARD-BASED ASSESSMENT

1. Letter **D** is correct. Attaining prosperity was not among the objectives of the Constitution. Letter **A** is incorrect because the authors explicitly state that establishing justice is a goal of the Constitution. Letter **B** is incorrect because the authors state as an objective securing "the Blessings of Liberty." Letter **C** is incorrect because the authors cite providing "for the common defense" as a key objective of the Constitution.

2. Letter **C** is correct. The passage states up front that it is the "people" who are in charge of creating the Constitution, and thus the laws of society. Letter **A** is incorrect because it doesn't mention religion or the Church. Letter **B** is incorrect because it talks about the "people," not the military, insuring domestic tranquility and providing for a common defense. Letter **D** is incorrect because the American colonists rejected monarchy in their revolution.

3. Letter **B** is correct because it reflects the idea that irrational fears take over if reason "goes to sleep." Letter **A** is incorrect because the statement is not very pertinent to the Enlightenment. Letter **C** is incorrect because dreams are not discussed in the question. Letter **D** is incorrect because the image is not of a king or ruler.

Formal Assessment
- Chapter Tests, Forms A, B, and C, pp. 107–118

California Test Generator CD-ROM
- Chapter Tests, Forms A, B, and C (English and Spanish)

ALTERNATIVE ASSESSMENT

1. Interact *with* History (10.2.1)

On page 188, you examined how you would react to a different or revolutionary idea or way of doing things. Now that you have read the chapter, consider how such breakthroughs impacted society. Discuss in a small group what you feel were the most significant new ideas or procedures and explain why.

2. WRITING ABOUT HISTORY (Writing 2.3.c)

REVOLUTION Re-examine the material on the Scientific Revolution. Then write a three paragraph **essay** summarizing the difference in scientific understanding before and after the various scientific breakthroughs. Focus on

- the ultimate authority on many matters before the Scientific Revolution.
- how and why that changed after the Revolution.

INTEGRATED TECHNOLOGY

Writing an Internet-based Research Paper
(Writing 2.3.b)

Go to the *Web Research Guide* at **classzone.com** to learn about conducting research on the Internet. Use the Internet to explore a recent breakthrough in science or medicine. Look for information that will help you explain why the discovery is significant and how the new knowledge changes what scientists had thought about the topic.

In a well-organized paper, compare the significance of the discovery you are writing about with major scientific or medical discoveries of the Scientific Revolution. Be sure to

- apply a search strategy when using directories and search engines to locate Web resources.
- judge the usefulness of each Web site.
- correctly cite your Web resources.
- revise and edit for correct use of language.

ALTERNATIVE ASSESSMENT

1. *Possible Answers:* the Scientific Revolution, because it encouraged people to question their beliefs; the idea that all people are created equal, because it eventually let to drastic changes in government and society.

2. Rubric Essays should
- identify key scientific discoveries.
- explain changes caused by discoveries.
- be well organized with a clear structure and supporting facts.

INTEGRATED TECHNOLOGY

Rubric Research papers should
- identify and summarize the discovery.
- compare the discovery to those of the Scientific Revolution.
- reflect thorough Internet research.

CHAPTER 7 PLANNING GUIDE

The French Revolution and Napoleon, 1789–1815

CHAPTER RESOURCES	COPYMASTERS	ASSESSMENT
CHAPTER OVERVIEW The French Revolution established a new political order, Napoleon Bonaparte forged and lost an empire, and the Congress of Vienna created a balance of power in Europe.	**In-Depth Resources: Unit 2** • Building Vocabulary, p. 53 **Chapters in Brief** (in English and Spanish) **Block Schedule Pacing Guide**	**Chapter Assessment,** pp. 242–243 **Formal Assessment** • Chapter Tests, Forms A, B, and C, pp. 124–135 **Test Generator** **Online Test Practice**
SECTION 1 **The French Revolution Begins** pp. 217–221 **OBJECTIVE** Describe the factors that led to the French Revolution.	**In-Depth Resources: Unit 2** • Guided Reading, p. 48 • History Makers: Marie Antoinette, p. 64 • Reteaching Activity, p. 68 **Reading Study Guide,** p. 73	**Section 1 Assessment,** p. 221 **Formal Assessment** • Section Quiz, p. 119 **California Daily Standards Practice Transparencies,** TT84
SECTION 2 **Revolution Brings Reform and Terror** pp. 222–228 **OBJECTIVE** Summarize the political reforms in France and describe the Reign of Terror.	**In-Depth Resources: Unit 2** • Guided Reading, p. 49 • Geography Application, p. 55 • Primary Sources, pp. 57, 58, 59 • Literature: from *A Tale of Two Cities,* p. 61 • History Makers: Robespierre, p. 65 • Connections Across Time/Cultures, p. 66 • Science & Technology, p. 67 **Reading Study Guide,** p. 75	**Section 2 Assessment,** p. 227 **Formal Assessment** • Section Quiz, p. 120 **California Daily Standards Practice Transparencies,** TT85
SECTION 3 **Napoleon Forges an Empire** pp. 229–233 **OBJECTIVE** Trace Napoleon's rise to power.	**In-Depth Resources: Unit 2** • Guided Reading, p. 50 • Primary Source, p. 60 • Reteaching Activity, p. 70 **Reading Study Guide,** p. 77	**Section 3 Assessment,** p. 233 **Formal Assessment** • Section Quiz, p. 121 **California Daily Standards Practice Transparencies,** TT86
SECTION 4 **Napoleon's Empire Collapses** pp. 234–237 **OBJECTIVE** Explain the collapse of Napoleon's empire.	**In-Depth Resources: Unit 2** • Guided Reading, p. 51 • Skillbuilder Practice, p. 54 • Reteaching Activity, p. 71 **Reading Study Guide,** p. 79	**Section 4 Assessment,** p. 237 **Formal Assessment** • Section Quiz, p. 122 **California Daily Standards Practice Transparencies,** TT87
SECTION 5 **The Congress of Vienna** pp. 238–241 **OBJECTIVE** Describe the influence of the Congress of Vienna.	**In-Depth Resources: Unit 2** • Guided Reading, p. 52 • Reteaching Activity, p. 72 **Reading Study Guide,** p. 81	**Section 5 Assessment,** p. 241 **Formal Assessment** • Section Quiz, p. 123 **California Daily Standards Practice Transparencies,** TT88

INTEGRATED TECHNOLOGY

- eEdition Plus Online
- EasyPlanner Plus Online
- eTest Plus Online

 **Audio CDs**
- Voices from the Past
- Reading Study Guides

 **CD-ROMs**
- eEdition
- Power Presentations
- EasyPlanner
- Electronic Library of Primary Sources
- Test Generator

---

eEdition CD-ROM

 **Geography Transparencies**
- GT23 Early Sites of the French Revolution

 **World Art and Cultures Transparencies**
- AT50 *Portrait of Marie Antoinette*

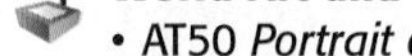

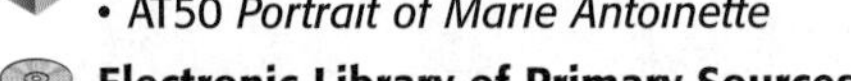 **Electronic Library of Primary Sources**

 **classzone.com**
- NetExplorations: The French Revolution

 **eEdition CD-ROM**

 **Electronic Library of Primary Sources**
- from "Execution by Guillotine"
- from "Frenchmen, Is This What You Want?"

 **classzone.com**

 **eEdition CD-ROM**

 **World Art and Cultures Transparencies**
- AT51 *Napoleon*

 **Electronic Library of Primary Sources**

 **classzone.com**

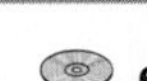 **eEdition CD-ROM**

 **Electronic Library of Primary Sources**
- "The Battle of Waterloo: The Finale"

 **classzone.com**

 **eEdition CD-ROM**

 **Critical Thinking Transparencies**
- CT23 The French Revolution
- CT59 Chapter 7 Visual Summary

 **Electronic Library of Primary Sources**

 **classzone.com**
- NetExplorations: The French Revolution

OVERVIEW OF CALIFORNIA RESOURCES

	Section 1	Section 2	Section 3	Section 4	Section 5
California Reading Toolkit	p. L32	p. L33	p. L34	p. L35	p. L36
California Modified Lesson Plans for English Learners	p. 59	p. 61	p. 63	p. 65	p. 67
California Daily Standards Practice Transparencies	TT24	TT25	TT26	TT27	TT28
California Standards Enrichment Workbook	pp. 23–24	pp. 25–26, 29–30, 45–46	pp. 29–30 31–32,	pp. 29–30	pp. 31–32, 105–106
California Standards Planner and Lesson Plans	p. L55	p. L57	p. L59	p. L61	p. L63
California Online Test Practice	classzone.com	classzone.com	classzone.com	classzone.com	classzone.com
California Test Generator CD-ROM					
California Easy Planner CD-ROM					
California eEdition CD-ROM					

Chart Key:

 Pupil's Edition

 Teacher's Edition

Overhead Transparency

Block Scheduling

 Copymaster

Audio Library

 CD-ROM

 Internet

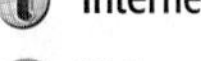

 Video

NO TIME?

If you do not have time to teach this chapter in full, assign the **Chapter in Brief** (also available in Spanish).

Previewing Resources for Differentiated Instruction

ENGLISH LEARNERS: Resources in Spanish

In-Depth Resources in Spanish

- Guided Reading Ⓐ
- Skillbuilder Practice: Interpreting Maps
- Geography Application: The French Revolution Under Siege Ⓑ

Chapters in Brief

Reading Study Guide Ⓒ

Reading Study Guide Audio CD

Test Generator CD-ROM

- Chapter Test, Forms A, B, and C

Plus

Modified Lesson Plans for English Learners

Multi-Language Glossary of Social Studies Terms

Ⓐ

The French Revolution Begins

Ⓑ

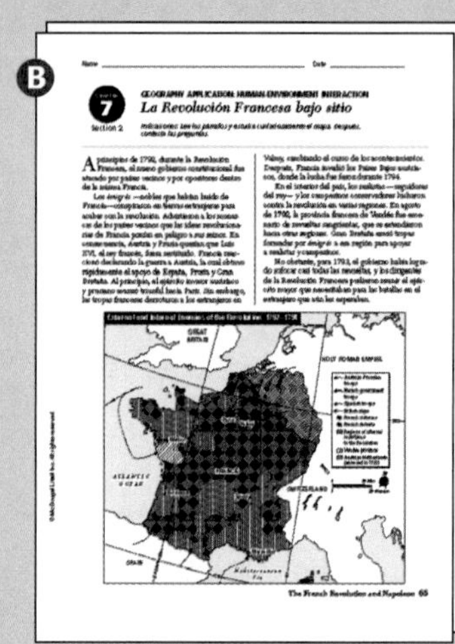

La Revolución Francesa bajo sitio

STRUGGLING READERS

In-Depth Resources: Unit 2

- Guided Reading Ⓐ
- Building Vocabulary
- Skillbuilder Practice: Interpreting Maps Ⓑ
- Geography Application: The French Revolution Under Siege
- Reteaching Activities

Chapters in Brief

Reading Study Guide Ⓒ

Reading Study Guide Audio CD

Formal Assessment

- Chapter Test, Form A

Plus

Reading Toolkit

Ⓐ

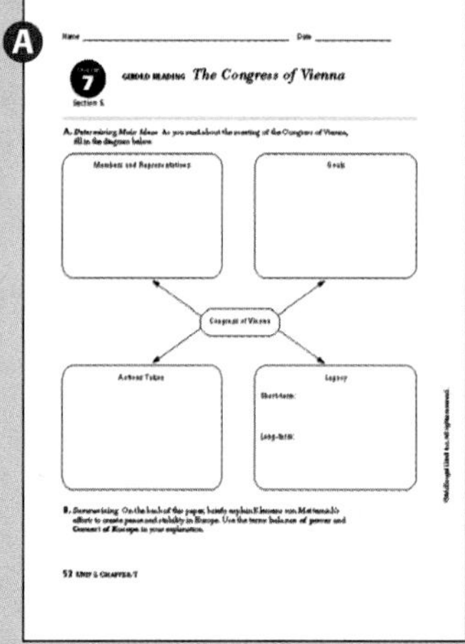

The Congress of Vienna

Ⓑ

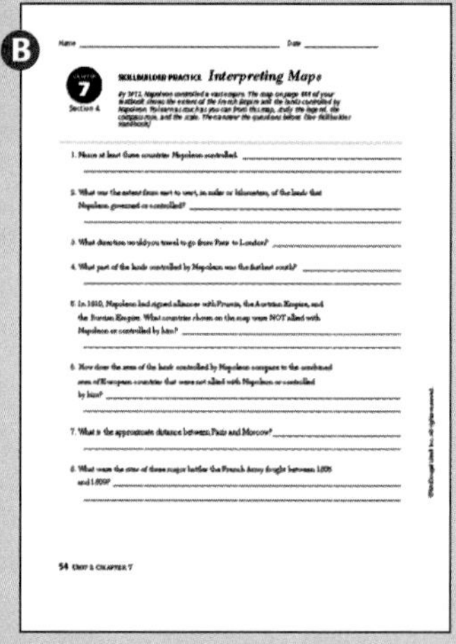

Interpreting Maps

GIFTED AND TALENTED STUDENTS

In-Depth Resources: Unit 2

- Primary Sources: from A Declaration of the Rights of Man; “La Marseillaise”; from The Execution of Louis XVI; Napoleon’s Proclamation
- Literature: from *A Tale of Two Cities*
- History Makers: Marie Antoinette Ⓐ; Robespierre
- Connections Across Time and Cultures Ⓑ
- Science and Technology Ⓒ

Electronic Library of Primary Sources

- from *Memoirs of Vigée-Lebrun*
- from “Execution by Guillotine”
- from “Frenchmen, Is This What You Want?”
- from *The Letters of Napoleon I*
- “The Battle of Waterloo”
- from *Memoirs of Prince Klemens von Metternich*

Formal Assessment

- Chapter Test, Form C

Ⓐ

Marie Antoinette

Tragic Queen

Ⓑ

Comparing Revolutions in America and France

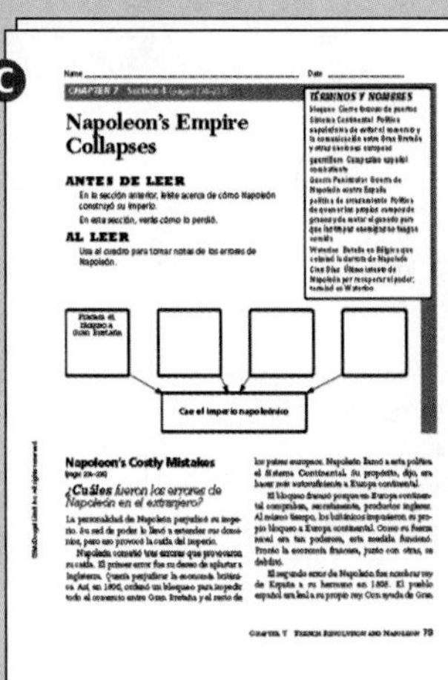
CHAPTER 7 Section 4

Napoleon's Empire Collapses

ANTES DE LEER

AL LEER

TÉRMINOS Y NOMBRES

Napoleon's Costly Mistakes

¿Cuáles fueron los errores de Napoleón en el extranjero?

Activities in the Teacher's Edition for English Learners

- Paying for Government Services, p. 218
- Charting the Revolution, p. 224
- Understanding Idioms, p. 230
- Causes of Napoleon's Defeat, p. 235
- Making Posters About Liberty, p. 240

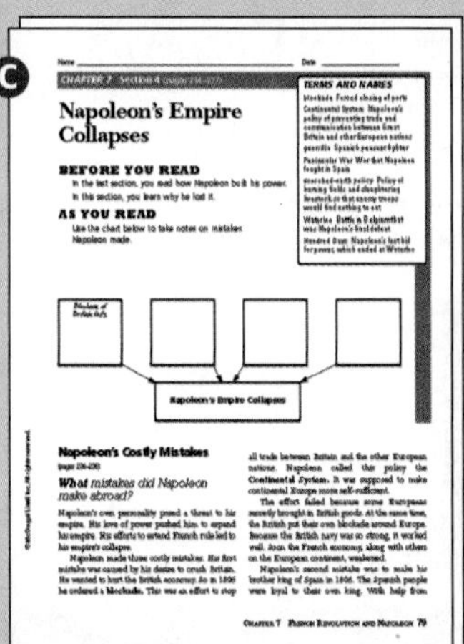
CHAPTER 7 Section 4

Napoleon's Empire Collapses

BEFORE YOU READ

AS YOU READ

TERMS AND NAMES

Napoleon's Empire Collapses

Napoleon's Costly Mistakes

What mistakes did Napoleon make abroad?

Activities in the Teacher's Edition for Struggling Readers

- Reviewing the Start of the Revolution, p. 220
- Depicting the Revolution's Early Years, p. 226
- Examining a Primary Source, p. 231
- Understanding the Balance of Power, p. 239

7

Science Helps Create the Metric System

Questions

Activities in the Teacher's Edition for Gifted and Talented Students

- Marie Antoinette and Élisabeth Vigée-Lebrun, p. 219
- Comparing Sources on the French Revolution, p. 223
- Analyzing Napoleon's Control of the Media, p. 232

INTEGRATED TECHNOLOGY

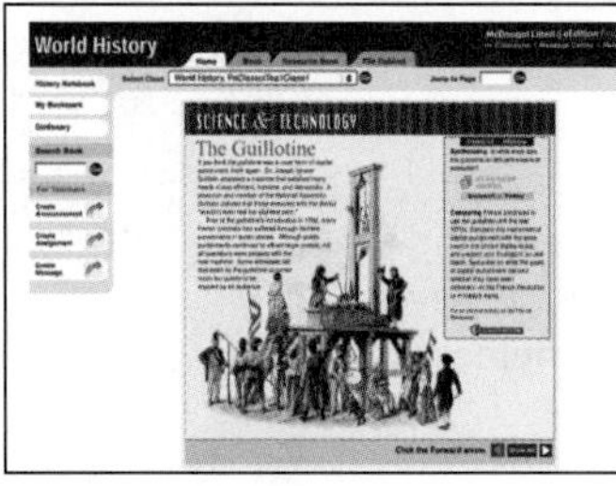

eEdition
- Interactive Visuals
- Interactive Maps
- Interactive Primary Sources

classzone.com
- Research Links
- Internet Activities
- Primary Sources
- Chapter Quiz
- NetExplorations: The French Revolution
- Current Events

Power Presentations CD-ROM
- Lecture Notes
- Image Gallery
- Chapter Review Game

Critical Thinking Transparencies
- CT23 The French Revolution to the Congress of Vienna
- CT59 Chapter 7 Visual Summary

Geography Transparencies
- GT23 Early Sites of the French Revolution, 1789

World Art and Cultures Transparencies
- AT50 *Portrait of Marie Antoinette*
- AT51 *Napoleon Crossing the St. Bernard Pass* A

Test Practice Transparencies TT84–TT88

Test Generator CD-ROM

EasyPlanner CD-ROM

Voices from the Past Audio CD

Online Test Practice

Electronic Library of Primary Sources

CHAPTER 7 • OBJECTIVE

Analyze the French Revolution, the rise and fall of Napoleon, and the Congress of Vienna.

Previewing Main Ideas

Discuss how the themes of economic inequality, political revolution, and imperial expansion remain topics in the news today. Explore which of these themes is most influential.

Accessing Prior Knowledge

Ask students to discuss what they know about the Enlightenment values of liberty, equality, and democracy. Ask them why they think many people in France opposed these values as dangerous. Consider why people might want to control individual behavior, to grant special privileges to a few individuals, and to allow only the wealthy to rule.

Geography *Answers*

ECONOMICS It symbolized the decadence of the monarchy.

REVOLUTION The example of the American Revolution convinced many French people that political liberty was a realistic goal.

POWER AND AUTHORITY The Russian Empire was far from France and much larger.

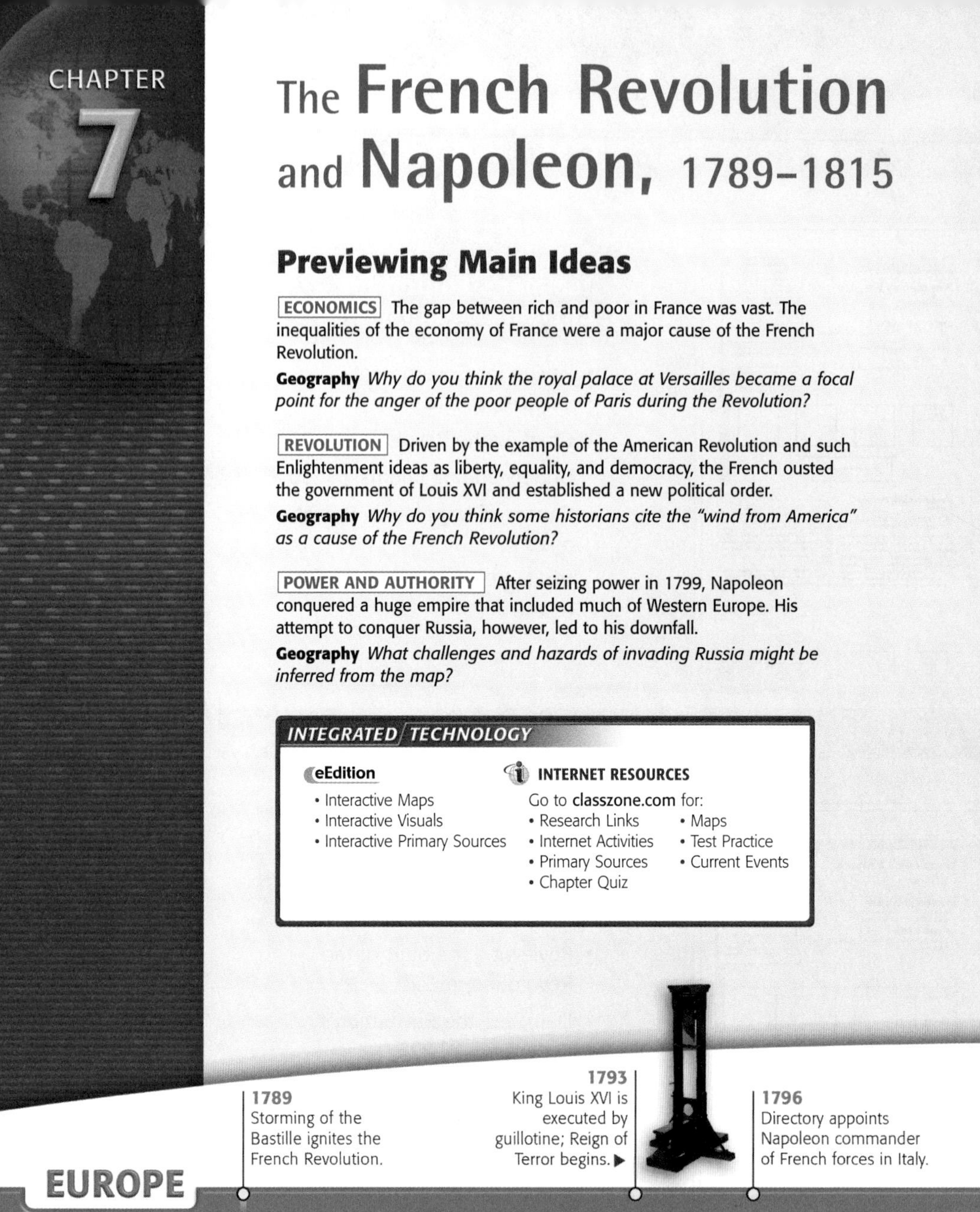

CHAPTER 7

The French Revolution and Napoleon, 1789–1815

Previewing Main Ideas

ECONOMICS The gap between rich and poor in France was vast. The inequalities of the economy of France were a major cause of the French Revolution.

Geography *Why do you think the royal palace at Versailles became a focal point for the anger of the poor people of Paris during the Revolution?*

REVOLUTION Driven by the example of the American Revolution and such Enlightenment ideas as liberty, equality, and democracy, the French ousted the government of Louis XVI and established a new political order.

Geography *Why do you think some historians cite the "wind from America" as a cause of the French Revolution?*

POWER AND AUTHORITY After seizing power in 1799, Napoleon conquered a huge empire that included much of Western Europe. His attempt to conquer Russia, however, led to his downfall.

Geography *What challenges and hazards of invading Russia might be inferred from the map?*

INTEGRATED TECHNOLOGY

eEdition
- Interactive Maps
- Interactive Visuals
- Interactive Primary Sources

INTERNET RESOURCES
Go to **classzone.com** for:
- Research Links
- Internet Activities
- Primary Sources
- Chapter Quiz
- Maps
- Test Practice
- Current Events

EUROPE

1789 Storming of the Bastille ignites the French Revolution.

1793 King Louis XVI is executed by guillotine; Reign of Terror begins. ▶

1796 Directory appoints Napoleon commander of French forces in Italy.

1789

WORLD

1789 George Washington is inaugurated as first U.S. president. ▶

1795 Great Britain seizes the Cape Colony in South Africa from the Dutch.

214

TIME LINE DISCUSSION

Discuss how democracy and nationalism were revolutionary ideas in Europe before 1815.

1. How long after the French Revolution began did Napoleon carry out a coup d'état? *(10 years)*
2. Napoleon was at the peak of his power while emperor. How long was he emperor before he was defeated at Waterloo? *(11 years)*
3. Entries for which three dates show the spread of anticolonialism and the creation of new countries? *(1789, 1804, 1810)*
4. According to the map, what was the status of Spain when Mexicans began calling for independence? *(Napoleon controlled Spain.)*
5. Write a one-sentence summary of the career of Napoleon. *(Possible Answer: Napoleon rose from French military officer to emperor before being defeated at Waterloo.)*
6. The opium trade in China was run by foreigners. When did it begin? *(1800)* What does this imply about China? *(It was too weak to halt the trade.)*

Napoleon's Empire, 1810

- French Empire
- Countries allied with Napoleon
- Countries controlled by Napoleon
- Countries at war with Napoleon

1799	Napoleon overthrows the Directory through a coup d'état.
1800	Opium trade begins in China.
1804	Napoleon crowns himself emperor, begins to create a vast European empire. ▶
1804	Saint Domingue gains independence. (Toussaint L'Ouverture) ▶
1810	Padre Hidalgo calls for Mexican independence.
1814	War of 1812 between Great Britain and the United States ends.
1815	Napoleon is defeated at the Battle of Waterloo.

History from Visuals

Interpreting the Map

What geographic features challenged French efforts to conquer new territory? *(Mountains separated France from Spain and Italy. Water separated France from Britain. A river separated France from eastern Europe. Great distance separated France from Russia.)*

Point out that part of Napoleon's success as a military leader was his ability to figure out ways to overcome geographic barriers.

Extension Compare this map with the political map of Europe in the textbook atlas. Which countries have the same names they had in 1810? *(Portugal and Spain)*

RECOMMENDED RESOURCES

Books for the Teacher

Hibbert, Christopher. ***The Days of the French Revolution***. New York: Quill, 1999. An excellent introduction to the Revolution.

Johnson, Paul. ***Napoleon***. New York: Viking, 2002. Examines Napoleon and his legacy.

Schama, Simon. ***Citizens: A Chronicle of the French Revolution***. Reprint ed. New York: Vintage, 1990. *Citizens* is a detailed and fascinating account of the years leading up to the French Revolution and of the Revolution itself.

Books for the Student

McDougal Littell Literature Connections. Dickens, Charles. ***A Tale of Two Cities (and related readings)***. 1997. A classic tale of the French Revolution, with themes of love and self-sacrifice, heroes and quests. Also available in Spanish.

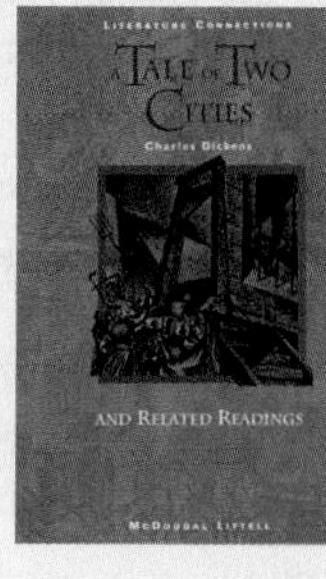

Shenkman, Richard. ***Legends, Lies, and Cherished Myths of World History***. New York: Harper, 1993.

Videos

Conquerors: Napoleon. VHS and DVD. Films for the Humanities & Sciences, 1996. 800-257-5126.

Marie Antoinette: The Tragic Queen. VHS. Arts and Entertainment, 1996. 888-423-1212.

Interact *with* History

Objectives
- Set the stage for studying the French Revolution.
- Help students understand some of the forces that can fuel a revolution.

EXAMINING *the* ISSUES

Possible Answers
- An unjust government is one that favors one group of citizens over another, that refuses to recognize basic human rights, or that is harsh and repressive.
- Students might say that they would take part in a violent revolution against a government that threatened their families' safety.

Discussion
Ask students what they recall about the start of the American Revolution and the beginning of the English Civil War. *(Each started when groups thought that the government was trampling their fundamental rights and abusing its power to tax.)*

Tip for English Learners
Have students make a list of words that describe protests against a government. *(revolution, rebellion, coup, demonstration, uprising, upheaval, mutiny, insurrection, overthrow)* Discuss the context in which each might be used.

Interact *with* History

How would you change an unjust government?

You are living in France in the late 1700s. Your parents are merchants who earn a good living. However, after taxes they have hardly any money left. You know that other people, especially the peasants in the countryside, are even worse off than you. At the same time, the nobility lives in luxury and pays practically no taxes.

Many people in France are desperate for change. But they are uncertain how to bring about that change. Some think that representatives of the people should demand fair taxes and just laws. Others support violent revolution. In Paris, that revolution seems to have begun. An angry mob has attacked and taken over the Bastille, a royal prison. You wonder what will happen next.

1. One of the mob leaders triumphantly displays the keys to the Bastille.
2. Although they were in search of gunpowder and firearms, the conquerors of the Bastille took whatever they could find.
3. One man drags the royal standard behind him.

▲ The conquerors of the Bastille parade outside City Hall in Paris.

EXAMINING *the* ISSUES

- **How would you define an unjust government?**
- **What, if anything, would lead you to take part in a violent revolution?**

Discuss these questions with your classmates. In your discussion, remember what you've learned about the causes of revolutionary conflicts such as the American Revolution and the English Civil War. As you read about the French Revolution in this chapter, see what changes take place and how these changes came about.

WHY STUDY THE FRENCH REVOLUTION AND NAPOLEON?

- The Enlightenment ideals expressed in the slogan of the French Revolution, "Liberty, Equality, Fraternity," continue to shape aspirations of people today.
- The Declaration of the Rights of Man and of the Citizen still inspires people to work for human rights.
- The Reign of Terror in 1793 and 1794 has become a warning to democratic societies of the dangers of resorting to violence to enforce values.
- The storming of the Bastille is a symbol of popular resistance to oppression.
- The French Revolution spread the ideas of democracy and nationalism around the globe.
- Guerrilla warfare, which has become common around the world, received its name from the resistance efforts by the Spanish against French invaders.
- The set of laws known as the Napoleonic Code shaped the legal systems of most of Europe and Latin America.
- Napoleon's decision to sell the Louisiana Territory resulted in a major expansion of the United States.

French Revolution: Assault on the Bastille, Jean-Baptiste Lallemand

1

Napoleon and His General Staff in Egypt, Jean-Léon Gérome

The French Revolution Begins

MAIN IDEA

ECONOMICS Economic and social inequalities in the Old Regime helped cause the French Revolution.

WHY IT MATTERS NOW

Throughout history, economic and social inequalities have at times led peoples to revolt against their governments.

TERMS & NAMES

- Old Regime
- estate
- Louis XVI
- Marie Antoinette
- Estates-General
- National Assembly
- Tennis Court Oath
- Great Fear

SETTING THE STAGE In the 1700s, France was considered the most advanced country of Europe. It had a large population and a prosperous foreign trade. It was the center of the Enlightenment, and France's culture was widely praised and imitated by the rest of the world. However, the appearance of success was deceiving. There was great unrest in France, caused by bad harvests, high prices, high taxes, and disturbing questions raised by the Enlightenment ideas of Locke, Rousseau, and Voltaire.

The Old Order

In the 1770s, the social and political system of France—the **Old Regime**—remained in place. Under this system, the people of France were divided into three large social classes, or **estates**.

The Privileged Estates Two of the estates had privileges, including access to high offices and exemptions from paying taxes, that were not granted to the members of the third. The Roman Catholic Church, whose clergy formed the First Estate, owned 10 percent of the land in France. It provided education and relief services to the poor and contributed about 2 percent of its income to the government. The Second Estate was made up of rich nobles. Although they accounted for just 2 percent of the population, the nobles owned 20 percent of the land and paid almost no taxes. The majority of the clergy and the nobility scorned Enlightenment ideas as radical notions that threatened their status and power as privileged persons.

The Third Estate About 97 percent of the people belonged to the Third Estate. The three groups that made up this estate differed greatly in their economic conditions. The first group—the bourgeoisie (BUR•zhwah•ZEE), or middle class—were bankers, factory owners, merchants, professionals, and skilled artisans. Often, they were well educated and believed strongly in the Enlightenment ideals of liberty and equality. Although some of the bourgeoisie were as rich as nobles, they paid high taxes and, like the rest of the Third Estate, lacked privileges. Many felt that their wealth entitled them to a greater degree of social status and political power.

The workers of France's cities formed the second, and poorest, group within the Third Estate. These urban workers included tradespeople, apprentices, laborers, and domestic servants. Paid low wages and frequently out of work, they often

CALIFORNIA STANDARDS

10.2.1 Compare the major ideas of philosophers and their effects on the democratic revolutions in England, the United States, France, and Latin America (e.g., John Locke, Charles-Louis Montesquieu, Jean-Jacques Rousseau, Simón Bolívar, Thomas Jefferson, James Madison).

CST 3 Students use a variety of maps and documents to interpret human movement, including major patterns of domestic and international migration, changing environmental preferences and settlement patterns, the frictions that develop between population groups, and the diffusion of ideas, technological innovations, and goods.

HI 1 Students show the connections, causal and otherwise, between particular historical events and larger social, economic, and political trends and developments.

HI 6 Students conduct cost-benefit analyses and apply basic economic indicators to analyze the aggregate economic behavior of the U.S. economy.

TAKING NOTES

Analyzing Causes
Use a web diagram to identify the causes of the French Revolution.

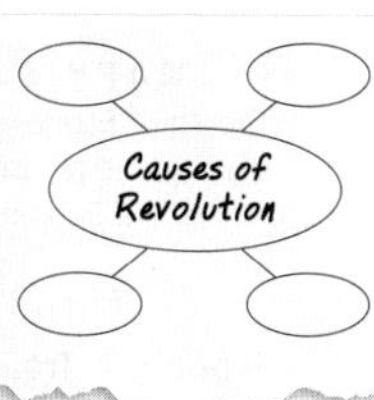

LESSON PLAN

OBJECTIVES

- List the three estates of the Old Regime.
- Summarize the factors that led to the French Revolution.
- Describe the creation of the National Assembly and the storming of the Bastille.
- Explain the importance of the Great Fear and the women's march on Versailles.

1 FOCUS & MOTIVATE

Discuss what determines a person's class in the United States today. *(Possible Answers: type of job, income, wealth)* Estimate the percentages of the population by economic class today.

2 INSTRUCT

The Old Order

10.2.1

Critical Thinking

- What did the clergy do for society that might justify their low tax rate? *(provided education and relief to the poor)*

CALIFORNIA RESOURCES

California Reading Toolkit, p. L32
California Modified Lesson Plans for English Learners, p. 59
California Daily Standards Practice Transparencies, TT24
California Standards Enrichment Workbook, pp. 23–24
California Standards Planner and Lesson Plans, p. L55
California Online Test Practice
California Test Generator CD-ROM
California Easy Planner CD-ROM
California eEdition CD-ROM

SECTION 1 PROGRAM RESOURCES

ALL STUDENTS

In-Depth Resources: Unit 2
- Guided Reading, p. 48
- History Makers: Marie Antoinette, p. 64

Formal Assessment
- Section Quiz, p. 119

ENGLISH LEARNERS

In-Depth Resources in Spanish
- Guided Reading, p. 59

Reading Study Guide (Spanish), p. 73
Reading Study Guide Audio CD (Spanish)

STRUGGLING READERS

In-Depth Resources: Unit 2
- Guided Reading, p. 48
- Building Vocabulary, p. 53
- Reteaching Activity, p. 68

Reading Study Guide, p. 73
Reading Study Guide Audio CD

GIFTED AND TALENTED STUDENTS

Electronic Library of Primary Sources
- from *Memoirs of Élisabeth Vigée-Lebrun*

INTEGRATED TECHNOLOGY

eEdition CD-ROM
Voices from the Past Audio CD
Power Presentations CD-ROM
Geography Transparencies
- GT23 Early Sites of the French Revolution, 1789

World Art and Cultures Transparencies
- AT50 *Portrait of Marie Antoinette*

Electronic Library of Primary Sources
- from *Memoirs of Élisabeth Vigée-Lebrun*

classzone.com
- NetExplorations: The French Revolution

History from Visuals

Interpreting the Graphics

Look at the bar graph. Would the gap between the Second and Third estates become larger or smaller over time? *(larger—low taxes meant that Second Estate could pass fortunes from generation to generation)*

SKILLBUILDER Answers

1. **Drawing Conclusions** The privileged 3 percent were supported by the Third Estate, who were paying high taxes.
2. **Making Inferences** They already had privilege and wealth; they probably had little desire for change.

The Forces of Change

10.2.1

Critical Thinking

- Did France's system of estates violate the principle of equality? *(Yes, because the Third Estate had no power in government.)*
- Which group within the Third Estate would suffer most from the increase in the price of bread? *(urban workers, since peasants could raise grain and the bourgeoisie had more money)*
- Why do you think Louis chose to raise taxes on the nobility? *(They had more wealth than the clergy and lower taxes than the Third Estate.)*

The Three Estates

A First Estate
- made up of clergy of Roman Catholic Church
- scorned Enlightenment ideas

B Second Estate
- made up of rich nobles
- held highest offices in government
- disagreed about Enlightenment ideas

C Third Estate
- included bourgeoisie, urban lower class, and peasant farmers
- had no power to influence government
- embraced Enlightenment ideas
- resented the wealthy First and Second Estates.

Population of France, 1787

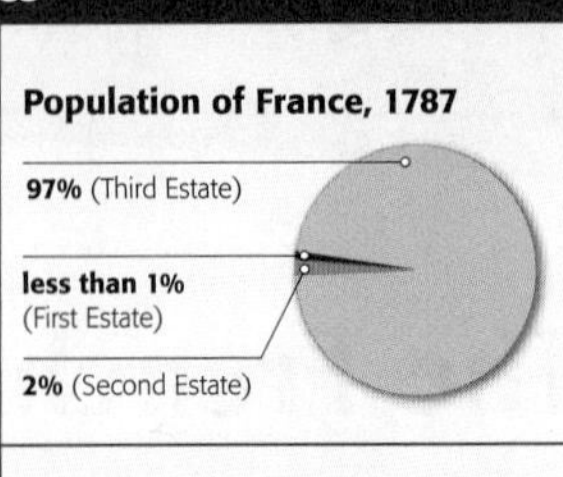

Percent of Income Paid in Taxes

2% (First Estate)
0% (Second Estate)
50% (Third Estate)
0% 20% 40% 60% 80% 100%

SKILLBUILDER: Interpreting Charts and Political Cartoons

1. **Drawing Conclusions** *How do the chart and the graphs help explain the political cartoon?*
2. **Making Inferences** *Why might the First and Second Estates be opposed to change?*

went hungry. If the cost of bread rose, mobs of these workers might attack grain carts and bread shops to steal what they needed.

Peasants formed the largest group within the Third Estate, more than 80 percent of France's 26 million people. Peasants paid about half their income in dues to nobles, tithes to the Church, and taxes to the king's agents. They even paid taxes on such basic staples as salt. Peasants and the urban poor resented the clergy and the nobles for their privileges and special treatment. The heavily taxed and discontented Third Estate was eager for change.

Vocabulary
tithe: a church tax, normally about one-tenth of a family's income

The Forces of Change

In addition to the growing resentment among the lower classes, other factors contributed to the revolutionary mood in France. New ideas about government, serious economic problems, and weak and indecisive leadership all helped to generate a desire for change.

Enlightenment Ideas New views about power and authority in government were spreading among the Third Estate. Members of the Third Estate were inspired by the success of the American Revolution. They began questioning long-standing notions about the structure of society. Quoting Rousseau and Voltaire, they began to demand equality, liberty, and democracy. The Comte D'Antraigues, a friend of Rousseau, best summed up their ideas on what government should be:

PRIMARY SOURCE

The Third Estate is the People and the People is the foundation of the State; it is in fact the State itself; the . . . People is everything. Everything should be subordinated to it. . . . It is in the People that all national power resides and for the People that all states exist.

COMTE D'ANTRAIGUES, quoted in *Citizens: A Chronicle of the French Revolution*

Economic Troubles By the 1780s, France's once prosperous economy was in decline. This caused alarm, particularly among the merchants, factory owners, and

DIFFERENTIATING INSTRUCTION: ENGLISH LEARNERS

Paying for Government Services

Class Time 30 minutes

Task Collecting opinions on how much people pay for government services

Purpose To provide a context for understanding the issues of public finance for France under Louis XVI

Instructions As a class, make a list of all the ways the government gets revenue. Some of these are taxes on income, property, and sales; fees for cars and licenses; and tolls for roads. Then have each student survey two to five adults to find out what percentage of their total income they think goes to the government, and how much they think they should contribute. Compile the data in class to determine

- the percentage of income that people think they pay to the government
- the percentage of income that people think they should pay to the government
- whether there is a relationship between what people think they pay and how much they think they should pay for government services

Use the Reading Study Guide in Spanish for more help with this section.

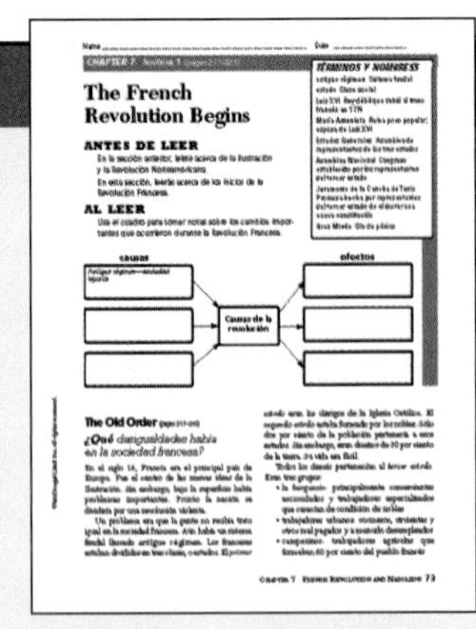

Reading Study Guide: Spanish Translation

bankers of the Third Estate. On the surface, the economy appeared to be sound, because both production and trade were expanding rapidly. However, the heavy burden of taxes made it almost impossible to conduct business profitably within France. Further, the cost of living was rising sharply. In addition, bad weather in the 1780s caused widespread crop failures, resulting in a severe shortage of grain. The price of bread doubled in 1789, and many people faced starvation.

During the 1770s and 1780s, France's government sank deeply into debt. Part of the problem was the extravagant spending of **Louis XVI** and his queen, **Marie Antoinette**. Louis also inherited a considerable debt from previous kings. And he borrowed heavily in order to help the American revolutionaries in their war against Great Britain, France's chief rival. This nearly doubled the government's debt. In 1786, when bankers refused to lend the government any more money, Louis faced serious problems.

A Weak Leader Strong leadership might have solved these and other problems. Louis XVI, however, was indecisive and allowed matters to drift. He paid little attention to his government advisers, and had little patience for the details of governing. The queen only added to Louis's problems. She often interfered in the government, and frequently offered Louis poor advice. Further, since she was a member of the royal family of Austria, France's long-time enemy, Marie Antoinette had been unpopular from the moment she set foot in France. Her behavior only made the situation worse. As queen, she spent so much money on gowns, jewels, gambling, and gifts that she became known as "Madame Deficit."

Vocabulary
deficit: debt

Rather than cutting expenses, Louis put off dealing with the emergency until he practically had no money left. His solution was to impose taxes on the nobility. However, the Second Estate forced him to call a meeting of the **Estates-General**—an assembly of representatives from all three estates—to approve this new tax. The meeting, the first in 175 years, was held on May 5, 1789, at Versailles.

History Makers

Louis XVI
1754–1793

Louis XVI's tutors made little effort to prepare him for his role as king—and it showed. He was easily bored with affairs of state, and much preferred to spend his time in physical activities, particularly hunting. He also loved to work with his hands, and was skilled in several trades, including lock-making, metalworking, and bricklaying.

Despite these shortcomings, Louis was well intentioned and sincerely wanted to improve the lives of the common people. However, he lacked the ability to make decisions and the determination to see policies through. When he did take action, it often was based on poor advice from ill-informed members of his court. As one politician of the time noted, "His reign was a succession of feeble attempts at doing good, shows of weakness, and clear evidence of his inadequacy as a leader."

Marie Antoinette
1755–1793

Marie Antoinette was a pretty, lighthearted, charming woman. However, she was unpopular with the French because of her spending and her involvement in controversial court affairs. She referred to Louis as "the poor man" and sometimes set the clock forward an hour to be rid of his presence.

Marie Antoinette refused to wear the tight-fitting clothing styles of the day and introduced a loose cotton dress for women. The elderly, who viewed the dress as an undergarment, thought that her clothing was scandalous. The French silk industry was equally angry.

In constant need of entertainment, Marie Antoinette often spent hours playing cards. One year she lost the equivalent of $1.5 million by gambling in card games.

INTEGRATED TECHNOLOGY
RESEARCH LINKS For more on Louis XVI and Marie Antoinette, go to **classzone.com**

Tip for Gifted and Talented Students

Explain that people are still debating what equality, liberty, and democracy mean. Issues such as affirmative action, environmental regulation, and restrictions on campaign contributions reflect conflicting interpretations of these ideals.

History Makers

Louis XVI and Marie Antoinette

Louis XVI was known to be a lethargic and rather dull man. On the day the Bastille fell in Paris, the king wrote only, "*Rien*," or "Nothing," in his diary—a reference to his lack of success at hunting.

Marie Antoinette was only a teenager when she came to France. Although she made many enemies, she did have redeeming qualities. Ask students to investigate Marie Antoinette's life and to list actions or behaviors of hers that might be considered either foolish or admirable.

In-Depth Resources: Unit 2
- History Makers: Marie Antoinette, p. 64

World Art and Cultures Transparencies
- AT50 *Portrait of Marie Antoinette with Her Children*

DIFFERENTIATING INSTRUCTION: GIFTED AND TALENTED STUDENTS

Marie Antoinette and Élisabeth Vigée-Lebrun

Class Time 40 minutes

Task Researching two historical figures

Purpose To understand their life and times

Instructions Have students research the character of Marie Antoinette. Most accounts give a negative picture of her. Ask students to research her life to give a more balanced portrait. Have them list some of her actions that might be considered foolish and some that might be seen as admirable. Students might begin their research by reading the History Maker activity in In-Depth Resources: Unit 2.

Some students may also wish to research the life and work of Élisabeth Vigée-Lebrun, portrait painter and friend of Marie Antoinette. Vigée-Lebrun later wrote about life at court. The Electronic Library of Primary Sources includes an excerpt from *Memoirs of Élisabeth Vigée-Lebrun.*

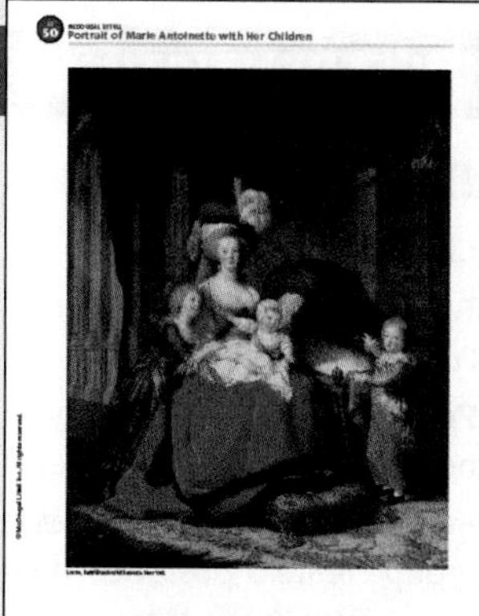

World Art and Cultures Transparencies

Dawn of the Revolution
10.2.1
Critical Thinking
- Why did nobles expect each estate to have one vote? *(That system protected their privileges.)*
- What results would show that the National Assembly was a legitimate government? *(Possible Answer: if people followed its laws)*

More About . . .
The Bastille

The Bastille was built in the 1300s. In the 1700s, it held people imprisoned by order of the king. It came to be known as a symbol of the royal abuse of power. Many of those imprisoned stood accused of political agitation or were unruly children of aristocrats. On July 14, 1789, the prison held only seven people.

About 100 people died in the storming of the Bastille. Later, the government tore it down. The bricks were used to build a bridge.

Dawn of the Revolution

The clergy and the nobles had dominated the Estates-General throughout the Middle Ages and expected to do so in the 1789 meeting. Under the assembly's medieval rules, each estate's delegates met in a separate hall to vote, and each estate had one vote. The two privileged estates could always outvote the Third Estate.

The National Assembly The Third Estate delegates, mostly members of the bourgeoisie whose views had been shaped by the Enlightenment, were eager to make changes in the government. They insisted that all three estates meet together and that each delegate have a vote. This would give the advantage to the Third Estate, which had as many delegates as the other two estates combined. Ⓐ

MAIN IDEA
Analyzing Motives
Ⓐ Why did the Third Estate propose a change in the Estates-General's voting rules?
A. Answer to gain control of, and exercise more power in, the meeting of the Estates-General

Siding with the nobles, the king ordered the Estates-General to follow the medieval rules. The delegates of the Third Estate, however, became more and more determined to wield power. A leading spokesperson for their viewpoint was a clergyman sympathetic to their cause, Emmanuel-Joseph Sieyès (syay•YEHS). In a dramatic speech, Sieyès suggested that the Third Estate delegates name themselves the **National Assembly** and pass laws and reforms in the name of the French people.

After a long night of excited debate, the delegates of the Third Estate agreed to Sieyès's idea by an overwhelming majority. On June 17, 1789, they voted to establish the National Assembly, in effect proclaiming the end of absolute monarchy and the beginning of representative government. This vote was the first deliberate act of revolution.

Three days later, the Third Estate delegates found themselves locked out of their meeting room. They broke down a door to an indoor tennis court, pledging to stay until they had drawn up a new constitution. This pledge became known as the **Tennis Court Oath**. Soon after, nobles and members of the clergy who favored reform joined the Third Estate delegates. In response to these events, Louis stationed his mercenary army of Swiss guards around Versailles.

Vocabulary
mercenary army: a group of soldiers who will work for any country or employer that will pay them

Storming the Bastille In Paris, rumors flew. Some people suggested that Louis was intent on using military force to dismiss the National Assembly. Others charged that the foreign troops were coming to Paris to massacre French citizens.

▼ The attack on the Bastille claimed the lives of about 100 people.

DIFFERENTIATING INSTRUCTION: STRUGGLING READERS

Reviewing the Start of the Revolution

Class Time 40 minutes

Task Creating a poster about the first phase of the French Revolution

Purpose To understand the main events that marked the beginning of the French Revolution

Instructions Divide the class into small groups. Have each group create a poster covering the period from the start of the Revolution through the storming of the Bastille. Writers should assume that the audience for the poster is learning about the French Revolution for the first time.

The poster should address
- conditions in France in the 1780s
- conflicts between the estates
- the formation of the National Assembly
- the Tennis Court Oath
- the storming of the Bastille

Each group should draw or find pictures to illustrate the events. Have students write descriptive captions for each picture and present their posters to the class. For more help, have students complete the Guided Reading activity for this section.

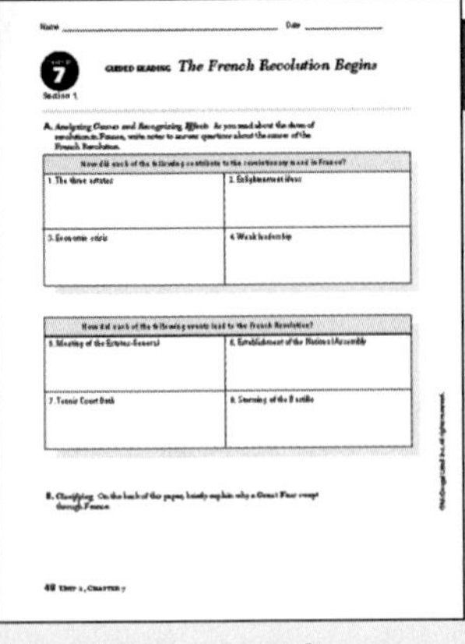

In-Depth Resources: Unit 2

People began to gather weapons in order to defend the city against attack. On July 14, a mob searching for gunpowder and arms stormed the Bastille, a Paris prison. The mob overwhelmed the guard and seized control of the building. The angry attackers hacked the prison commander and several guards to death, and then paraded around the streets with the dead men's heads on pikes.

The fall of the Bastille became a great symbolic act of revolution to the French people. Ever since, July 14—Bastille Day—has been a French national holiday, similar to the Fourth of July in the United States.

Social History

Bread

Bread was a staple of the diet of the common people of France. Most families consumed three or four 4-pound loaves a day. And the purchase of bread took about half of a worker's wages—when times were good. So, when the price of bread jumped dramatically, as it did in the fall of 1789, people faced a real threat of starvation.

On their march back from Versailles, the women of Paris happily sang that they were bringing "the baker, the baker's wife, and the baker's lad" with them. They expected the "baker"—Louis—to provide the cheap bread that they needed to live.

Social History

Bread

According to legend, when Marie Antoinette was told that the poor had no bread to eat, she coldly replied, "Let them eat cake." Actually, this comment was probably made years earlier by another noble and attributed to Marie Antoinette in order to make her appear hardhearted.

A Great Fear Sweeps France

Before long, rebellion spread from Paris into the countryside. From one village to the next, wild rumors circulated that the nobles were hiring outlaws to terrorize the peasants. A wave of senseless panic called the **Great Fear** rolled through France. The peasants soon became outlaws themselves. Armed with pitchforks and other farm tools, they broke into nobles' manor houses and destroyed the old legal papers that bound them to pay feudal dues. In some cases, the peasants simply burned down the manor houses.

In October 1789, thousands of Parisian women rioted over the rising price of bread. Brandishing knives, axes, and other weapons, the women marched on Versailles. First, they demanded that the National Assembly take action to provide bread. Then they turned their anger on the king and queen. They broke into the palace, killing some of the guards. The women demanded that Louis and Marie Antoinette return to Paris. After some time, Louis agreed.

A few hours later the king, his family, and servants left Versailles, never again to see the magnificent palace. Their exit signaled the change of power and radical reforms about to overtake France. (B)

B. Answer The king had to bow to the will of the people.

MAIN IDEA

Recognizing Effects

(B) How did the women's march mark a turning point in the relationship between the king and the people?

SECTION 1 ASSESSMENT

TERMS & NAMES 1. For each term or name, write a sentence explaining its significance.

• Old Regime • estates • Louis XVI • Marie Antoinette • Estates-General • National Assembly • Tennis Court Oath • Great Fear

USING YOUR NOTES

2. Select one of the causes you listed and explain how it contributed to the French Revolution. (10.2.1)

MAIN IDEAS

3. Why were members of the Third Estate dissatisfied with life under the Old Regime? (10.2.1)
4. How did Louis XVI's weak leadership contribute to the growing crisis in France? (10.2.1)
5. How did the purpose of the meeting of the Estates-General in 1789 change? (10.2.1)

CRITICAL THINKING & WRITING

6. **FORMING AND SUPPORTING OPINIONS** Were changes in the French government inevitable? Explain. (10.2.1)
7. **ANALYZING MOTIVES** Why do you think some members of the First and Second Estates joined the National Assembly and worked to reform the government? (10.2.1)
8. **COMPARING AND CONTRASTING** How were the storming of the Bastille and the women's march on Versailles similar? How were they different? (10.2.1)
9. **WRITING ACTIVITY** POWER AND AUTHORITY In the role of a Third Estate member, write a brief **speech** explaining why the French political system needs to change. (Writing 2.5.a)

CONNECT TO TODAY CREATING A COLLAGE

Conduct research on how Bastille Day is celebrated in France today. Use your findings to create an **annotated collage** titled "Celebrating the Revolution." (Writing 2.3.b)

A Great Fear Sweeps France

10.2.1

Critical Thinking

- After years of oppression, what finally caused the French people to revolt? *(the threat of starvation)*
- Do you think the riots were justified? *(Yes—People needed food. No—Violence is never justified.)*

Geography Transparencies

- GT23 Early Sites of the French Revolution, 1789

3 ASSESS

SECTION 1 ASSESSMENT

Have pairs of students help each other answer the questions.

Formal Assessment

- Section Quiz, p. 119

4 RETEACH

Use the Reteaching Activity for Section 1 to review the section.

In-Depth Resources: Unit 2

- Reteaching Activity, p. 68

ANSWERS

1. Old Regime, p. 217 • estates, p. 217 • Louis XVI, p. 219 • Marie Antoinette, p. 219 • Estates-General, p. 219 • National Assembly, p. 220 • Tennis Court Oath, p. 220 • Great Fear, p. 221
2. **Sample Answer:** rising debt, new taxes, weak leadership, rise in bread prices. The rise in bread prices helped spark the Revolution because it weighed heavily on the poor.
3. They had little political power.
4. He let political problems and mounting debt get out of hand.
5. from a debate on new taxes to an effort to reform the entire political system of France
6. Yes—Economic conditions were bad and Enlightenment ideas were powerful. No—Better leadership and sharing of power could have kept the peace.
7. **Possible Answers:** They hoped to avoid more radical steps; they genuinely sympathized with the problems of the Third Estate.
8. Both were spontaneous acts: one to get arms, the other to demand bread.
9. **Rubric** Speeches should
   - identify existing inequalities.
   - list proposed reforms.
   - be precise and persuasive.

CONNECT TO TODAY

Rubric Annotated collages should

- explain the origins of Bastille Day.
- show how Bastille Day is celebrated today.
- integrate visuals and text.

LESSON PLAN

OBJECTIVES

- Explain how the National Assembly changed France's government.
- Summarize the positions of the three factions that tried to govern France.
- Explain how war and the king's execution affected the Revolution.
- Describe the events and the aftermath of the Reign of Terror.

1 FOCUS & MOTIVATE

Why do people obey government? *(Possible Answers: respect, self-interest, fear)* Discuss which motive produces the most stability.

2 INSTRUCT

The Assembly Reforms France

10.2.2

Critical Thinking

- Would a U.S. legislature treat religion as the National Assembly did? *(No—That would violate the separation of church and state.)*

CALIFORNIA RESOURCES

California Reading Toolkit, p. L33
California Modified Lesson Plans for English Learners, p. 61
California Daily Standards Practice Transparencies, TT25
California Standards Enrichment Workbook, pp. 25–26, 29–30, 45–46
California Standards Planner and Lesson Plans, p. L57
California Online Test Practice
California Test Generator CD-ROM
California Easy Planner CD-ROM
California eEdition CD-ROM

French Revolution: Assault on the Bastille, Jean-Baptiste Lallemand

Napoleon and His General Staff in Egypt, Jean-Léon Gérome

2

Revolution Brings Reform and Terror

MAIN IDEA	WHY IT MATTERS NOW	TERMS & NAMES
REVOLUTION The revolutionary government of France made reforms but also used terror and violence to retain power.	Some governments that lack the support of a majority of their people still use fear to control their citizens.	• Legislative Assembly • émigré • sans-culotte • Jacobin • guillotine • Maximilien Robespierre • Reign of Terror

CALIFORNIA STANDARDS

10.2.2 List the principles of the Magna Carta, the English Bill of Rights (1689), the American Declaration of Independence (1776), the French Declaration of the Rights of Man and the Citizen (1789), and the U.S. Bill of Rights (1791).

10.2.4 Explain how the ideology of the French Revolution led France to develop from constitutional monarchy to democratic despotism to the Napoleonic empire.

10.3.7 Describe the emergence of Romanticism in art and literature (e.g., the poetry of William Blake and William Wordsworth), social criticism (e.g., the novels of Charles Dickens), and the move away from Classicism in Europe.

REP 3 Students evaluate major debates among historians concerning alternative interpretations of the past, including an analysis of authors' use of evidence and the distinctions between sound generalizations and misleading oversimplifications.

SETTING THE STAGE Peasants were not the only members of French society to feel the Great Fear. Nobles and officers of the Church were equally afraid. Throughout France, bands of angry peasants struck out against members of the upper classes, attacking and destroying many manor houses. In the summer of 1789, a few months before the women's march to Versailles, some nobles and members of clergy in the National Assembly responded to the uprisings in an emotional late-night meeting.

The Assembly Reforms France

Throughout the night of August 4, 1789, noblemen made grand speeches, declaring their love of liberty and equality. Motivated more by fear than by idealism, they joined other members of the National Assembly in sweeping away the feudal privileges of the First and Second Estates, thus making commoners equal to the nobles and the clergy. By morning, the Old Regime was dead.

The Rights of Man Three weeks later, the National Assembly adopted a statement of revolutionary ideals, the Declaration of the Rights of Man and of the Citizen. Reflecting the influence of the Declaration of Independence, the document stated that "men are born and remain free and equal in rights." These rights included "liberty, property, security, and resistance to oppression." The document also guaranteed citizens equal justice, freedom of speech, and freedom of religion.

In keeping with these principles, revolutionary leaders adopted the expression "Liberty, Equality, Fraternity" as their slogan. Such sentiments, however, did not apply to everyone. When writer Olympe de Gouges (aw•LIMP duh GOOZH) published a declaration of the rights of women, her ideas were rejected. Later, in 1793, she was declared an enemy of the Revolution and executed.

TAKING NOTES

Recognizing Effects Use a flow chart to identify the major events that followed the creation of the Constitution of 1791.

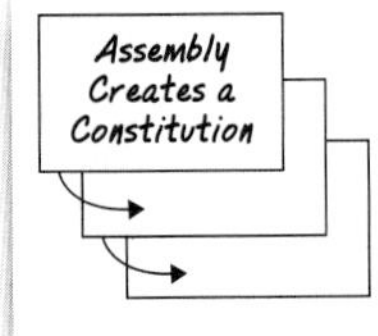

A State-Controlled Church Many of the National Assembly's early reforms focused on the Church. The assembly took over Church lands and declared that Church officials and priests were to be elected and paid as state officials. Thus, the Catholic Church lost both its lands and its political independence. The reasons for the assembly's actions were largely economic. Proceeds from the sale of Church lands helped pay off France's huge debt.

The assembly's actions alarmed millions of French peasants, who were devout Catholics. The effort to make the Church a part of the state offended them, even

SECTION 2 PROGRAM RESOURCES

ALL STUDENTS

In-Depth Resources: Unit 2
- Guided Reading, p. 49
- Geography Application, p. 55
- History Makers: Robespierre, p. 65

Formal Assessment
- Section Quiz, p. 120

ENGLISH LEARNERS

In-Depth Resources: Unit 2
- Guided Reading, p. 161
- Geography Application, p. 166

Reading Study Guide (Spanish), p. 75

Reading Study Guide Audio CD (Spanish)

STRUGGLING READERS

In-Depth Resources: Unit 2
- Guided Reading, p. 49
- Building Vocabulary, p. 53
- Geography Application, p. 55
- Reteaching Activity, p. 69

Reading Study Guide, p. 75

Reading Study Guide Audio CD

GIFTED AND TALENTED STUDENTS

In-Depth Resources: Unit 2
- Primary Sources: from A Declaration, p. 57; "La Marseillaise," p. 58; from The Execution of Louis XVI, p. 59
- Literature: from *A Tale of Two Cities,* p. 61
- Connections Across Time and Cultures, p. 66
- Science & Technology, p. 67

INTEGRATED TECHNOLOGY

eEdition CD-ROM

Power Presentations CD-ROM

Electronic Library of Primary Sources
- from "Execution by Guillotine"
- from "Frenchmen, Is This What You Want?"

classzone.com

◀ One of the people who stopped Louis from escaping said that he recognized the king from his portrait on a French bank note.

though it was in accord with Enlightenment philosophy. They believed that the pope should rule over a church independent of the state. From this time on, many peasants opposed the assembly's reforms.

Louis Tries to Escape As the National Assembly restructured the relationship between church and state, Louis XVI pondered his fate as a monarch. Some of his advisers warned him that he and his family were in danger. Many supporters of the monarchy thought France unsafe and left the country. Then, in June 1791, the royal family tried to escape from France to the Austrian Netherlands. As they neared the border, however, they were apprehended and returned to Paris under guard. Louis's attempted escape increased the influence of his radical enemies in the government and sealed his fate.

Divisions Develop

For two years, the National Assembly argued over a new constitution for France. By 1791, the delegates had made significant changes in France's government and society.

A Limited Monarchy In September 1791, the National Assembly completed the new constitution, which Louis reluctantly approved. The constitution created a limited constitutional monarchy. It stripped the king of much of his authority. It also created a new legislative body—the **Legislative Assembly**. This body had the power to create laws and to approve or reject declarations of war. However, the king still held the executive power to enforce laws.

Factions Split France Despite the new government, old problems, such as food shortages and government debt, remained. The question of how to handle these problems caused the Legislative Assembly to split into three general groups, each of which sat in a different part of the meeting hall. Radicals, who sat on the left side of the hall, opposed the idea of a monarchy and wanted sweeping changes in the way the government was run. Moderates sat in the center of the hall and wanted some changes in government, but not as many as the radicals. Conservatives sat on the right side of the hall. They upheld the idea of a limited monarchy and wanted few changes in government. A

A. Answer These differences caused the Assembly to split into three factions: radicals, moderates, and conservatives.

MAIN IDEA

Recognizing Effects

A How did differences of opinion on how to handle such issues as food shortages and debt affect the Legislative Assembly?

Connect *to* Today

Left, Right, and Center

The terms we use today to describe where people stand politically derive from the factions that developed in the Legislative Assembly in 1791.

- People who want to radically change government are called left wing or are said to be on the left.
- People with moderate views often are called centrist or are said to be in the center.
- People who want few or no changes in government often are called right wing or are said to be on the right.

More About . . .

The French Catholic Church

The French Catholic Church, inspired by nationalism, often rebelled against the power of the papacy. The set of ideas that they expressed in these rebellions became known as Gallicanism. They were expressed most clearly in a statement by the clergy of France in 1682. In this statement, French church leaders declared that the pope's power was strictly spiritual: the pope had no power over the French monarch in political affairs.

Divisions Develop

10.2.4

Critical Thinking

- What can you infer about the power of Louis from his signing of the 1791 constitution? *(that he was weak)*
- What evidence supports the view that the 1791 constitution was moderate rather than radical? *(The king retained power to enforce laws.)*

Electronic Library of Primary Sources

- from "Frenchmen, Is This What You Want?"

Connect *to* Today

Left, Right, and Center

Have students make a list of political leaders that they consider liberal, moderate, or conservative. Share the lists with the class and discuss whether students categorized well-known leaders the same way.

DIFFERENTIATING INSTRUCTION: GIFTED AND TALENTED STUDENTS

Comparing Sources on the French Revolution

Class Time 45 minutes

Task Comparing and contrasting two important primary sources from the French Revolution

Purpose To see similarities and differences between different types of political statements

Instructions Provide students with copies of the lyrics to "La Marseillaise" and the excerpt from the Declaration on the Rights of Man and of the Citizen. Both can be found in In-Depth Resources: Unit 2. Divide the class into small groups. Have each group make a table like the one shown to help them compare the two documents. Compare the completed tables in class.

	Purpose	Tone	Philosophy
A Declaration of the Rights of Man and of the Citizen	to protect civil rights and limit government power	legalistic	Government should infringe as little as possible on personal liberty.
"La Marseillaise"	to rouse French people to the cause of the Revolution	emotional	People should use force to defend themselves against tyranny.

War and Execution

10.2.4; 10.3.7

Critical Thinking

- What caused Prussia to invade France? *(fear that the revolt in France would spread to Prussia)*
- Why do you think the revolutionaries did not give women the right to vote? *(Possible Answer: The idea of the will of the people had become popular, while women's rights had not.)*
- In what way was the National Convention that took office in September 1792 more radical than the National Assembly of September 1791? *(It abolished the monarchy.)*

In-Depth Resources: Unit 2

- Geography Application: The French Revolution Under Siege, p. 55
- Primary Source: from The Execution of Louis XVI, p. 59

History Makers

Jean-Paul Marat

Marat had a talent for self-dramatization, once even pressing a pistol to his head during a speech. Ask students to find out more about Marat's ideas and about Charlotte Corday's reasons for assassinating him.

In addition, factions outside the Legislative Assembly wanted to influence the direction of the government too. **Émigrés** (EHM•ih•GRAYZ), nobles and others who had fled France, hoped to undo the Revolution and restore the Old Regime. In contrast, some Parisian workers and small shopkeepers wanted the Revolution to bring even greater changes to France. They were called **sans-culottes** (SANZ kyoo•LAHTS), or "those without knee breeches." Unlike the upper classes, who wore fancy knee-length pants, sans-culottes wore regular trousers. Although they did not have a role in the assembly, they soon discovered ways to exert their power on the streets of Paris.

War and Execution

Monarchs and nobles in many European countries watched the changes taking place in France with alarm. They feared that similar revolts might break out in their own countries. In fact, some radicals were keen to spread their revolutionary ideas across Europe. As a result, some countries took action. Austria and Prussia, for example, urged the French to restore Louis to his position as an absolute monarch. The Legislative Assembly responded by declaring war in April 1792.

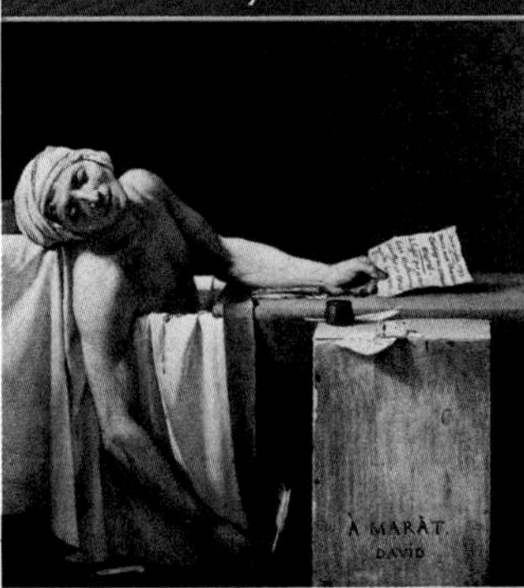
A MARAT
DAVID

Jean-Paul Marat
1743–1793

Marat was a thin, high-strung, sickly man whose revolutionary writings stirred up the violent mood in Paris. Because he suffered from a painful skin disease, he often found comfort by relaxing in a cold bath—even arranging things so that he could work in his bathtub!

During the summer of 1793, Charlotte Corday, a supporter of a rival faction whose members had been jailed, gained an audience with Marat by pretending to have information about traitors. Once inside Marat's private chambers, she fatally stabbed him as he bathed. For her crime, Corday went to the guillotine.

France at War The war began badly for the French. By the summer of 1792, Prussian forces were advancing on Paris. The Prussian commander threatened to destroy Paris if the revolutionaries harmed any member of the royal family. This enraged the Parisians. On August 10, about 20,000 men and women invaded the Tuileries, the palace where the royal family was staying. The mob massacred the royal guards and imprisoned Louis, Marie Antoinette, and their children.

Shortly after, the French troops defending Paris were sent to reinforce the French army in the field. Rumors began to spread that supporters of the king held in Paris prisons planned to break out and seize control of the city. Angry and fearful citizens responded by taking the law into their own hands. For several days in early September, they raided the prisons and murdered over 1,000 prisoners. Many nobles, priests, and royalist sympathizers fell victim to the angry mobs in these September Massacres. (B)

MAIN IDEA
Analyzing Causes
(B) What did the September Massacres show about the mood of the people?
B. Answer The people were impatient and fearful. They were willing to act violently.

Under pressure from radicals in the streets and among its members, the Legislative Assembly set aside the Constitution of 1791. It declared the king deposed, dissolved the assembly, and called for the election of a new legislature. This new governing body, the National Convention, took office on September 21. It quickly abolished the monarchy and declared France a republic. Adult male citizens were granted the right to vote and hold office. Despite the important part they had already played in the Revolution, women were not given the vote.

Jacobins Take Control Most of the people involved in the governmental changes in September 1792 were members of a radical political organization, the Jacobin (JAK•uh•bihn) Club. One of the most prominent **Jacobins**, as club members were called, was Jean-Paul Marat (mah•RAH). During the Revolution, he edited a newspaper called *L'Ami du Peuple* (Friend of the People). In his fiery editorials, Marat called for

DIFFERENTIATING INSTRUCTION: ENGLISH LEARNERS

Charting the Revolution

Class Time 45 minutes

Task Making a flow chart of events in the Revolution through September 1792

Purpose To identify the cause-and-effect relationships between key events

Instructions Divide the class into small groups and have each group make a flow chart of the major events in the Revolution from August 1789 through September 1792. Explain to students that a flow chart is different from a time line in that each event in a flow chart must follow both chronologically and logically from the one that precedes it. Once all the flow charts have been completed, have each group compare flow charts with another group and discuss the different choices they made.

Noblemen agree to end Old Regime privileges.

National Assembly adopts the Declaration of the Rights of Man and of the Citizen.

Louis XVI tries to flee France.

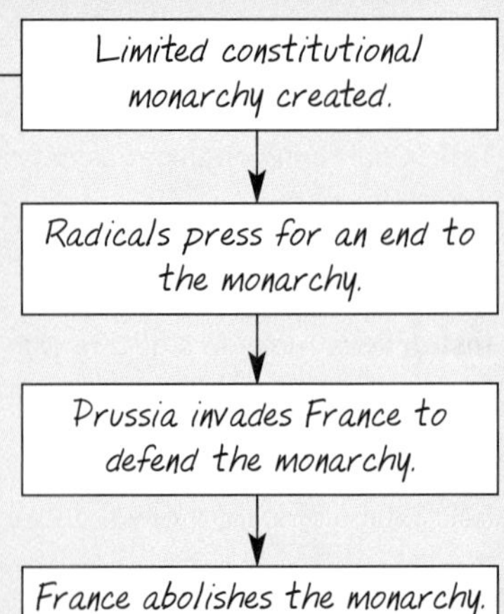
Limited constitutional monarchy created.
Radicals press for an end to the monarchy.
Prussia invades France to defend the monarchy.
France abolishes the monarchy.

INTERACTIVE

The Guillotine

CALIFORNIA STANDARDS

10.2.4 Explain how the ideology of the French Revolution led France to develop from constitutional monarchy to democratic despotism to the Napoleonic empire.

CST 2 Students analyze how change happens at different rates at different times; understand that some aspects can change while others remain the same; and understand that change is complicated and affects not only technology and politics but also values and beliefs.

If you think the guillotine was a cruel form of capital punishment, think again. Dr. Joseph Ignace Guillotin proposed a machine that satisfied many needs—it was efficient, humane, and democratic. A physician and member of the National Assembly, Guillotin claimed that those executed with the device "wouldn't even feel the slightest pain."

Prior to the guillotine's introduction in 1792, many French criminals had suffered through horrible punishments in public places. Although public punishments continued to attract large crowds, not all spectators were pleased with the new machine. Some witnesses felt that death by the guillotine occurred much too quickly to be enjoyed by an audience.

INTEGRATED TECHNOLOGY

RESEARCH LINKS For more on the guillotine, go to **classzone.com**

Once the executioner cranked the blade to the top, a mechanism released it. The sharp weighted blade fell, severing the victim's head from his or her body.

Some doctors believed that a victim's head retained its hearing and eyesight for up to 15 minutes after the blade's deadly blow. All remains were eventually gathered and buried in simple graves.

Tricoteuses, or "woman knitters," were regular spectators at executions and knitted stockings for soldiers as they sat near the base of the scaffold.

Before each execution, bound victims traveled from the prison to the scaffold in horse-drawn carts during a one and one-half hour procession through city streets.

Beheading by Class

More than 2,100 people were executed during the last 132 days of the Reign of Terror. The pie graph below displays the breakdown of beheadings by class.

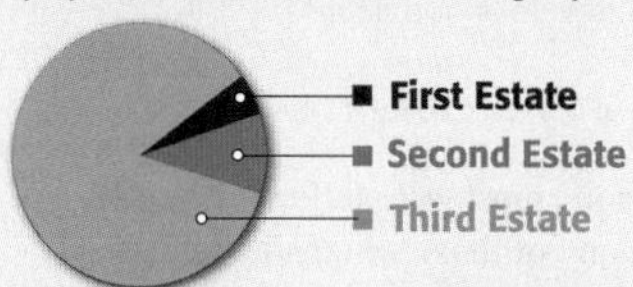

Connect *to* Today

1. **Synthesizing** In what ways was the guillotine an efficient means of execution?

   See Skillbuilder Handbook, page R21.

2. **Comparing** France continued to use the guillotine until 1977. Four years later, France abolished capital punishment. Conduct research to identify countries where capital punishment is still used. Use your findings to create a map titled "Countries Using Capital Punishment."

225

Science & Technology

OBJECTIVES

- Explain how the guillotine worked.
- Analyze the attitudes that made people support the use of the guillotine.

INSTRUCT

Explain to students that the guillotine expressed Enlightenment ideals. It reflected a desire to apply capital punishment equally to all social classes. The guillotine gave common prisoners a dignified execution, something previously reserved for nobles.

Electronic Library of Primary Sources
- from "Execution by Guillotine"

INTEGRATED TECHNOLOGY

Interactive This image is available in an interactive format on the eEdition. Students can examine parts of the diagram in detail.

Vocabulary Note: Word Origins
The word *guillotine* is one of many terms from this era that were based on a person's name. Sacher tortes, named for an Austrian hotelier, were first served at the Congress of Vienna. A napoleon is a type of pastry. Beef Wellington is a dish that was favored by the Duke of Wellington.

CONNECT TO TODAY: ANSWERS

1. Synthesizing
It was simple to operate and fast, allowing many executions in a short time.

2. Comparing
Rubric Maps should
- distinguish between countries that use capital punishment and those that do not.
- include a title and a key.
- be neat and accurate.
- cite sources.

More About . . .

Long-Term Changes in France

More than a century before the adoption of the metric system, Gabriel Mouton, a vicar at a church in Lyon, France, proposed a measurement system that shared the metric system's main features. Mouton, a remarkably skilled amateur mathematician and astronomer, recommended a system of linear measurement using the length of the arc of a line of longitude on the earth's surface as its fundamental unit. He suggested that this unit be divided by ten repeatedly to get smaller units of measure. The idea was debated for 120 years before Talleyrand, one of the foremost members of the National Assembly, reintroduced it in 1790. Louis XVI gave the proposed system his formal approval on June 19, 1791, one day before he attempted to flee France.

In-Depth Resources: Unit 2

- Science & Technology: Science Helps Create the Metric System, p. 67

The Terror Grips France

10.2.4

Critical Thinking

- How would you summarize the quotation from Robespierre? *(Virtue and terror are necessary parts of government.)*
- What does the large number of executions among the urban poor and middle class suggest about support for the revolution? *(Many in these groups apparently opposed it.)*

the death of all those who continued to support the king. Georges Danton (zhawrzh dahn•TAWN), a lawyer, was among the club's most talented and passionate speakers. He also was known for his devotion to the rights of Paris's poor people.

The National Convention had reduced Louis XVI's role from that of a king to that of a common citizen and prisoner. Now, guided by radical Jacobins, it tried Louis for treason. The Convention found him guilty, and, by a very close vote, sentenced him to death. On January 21, 1793, the former king walked with calm dignity up the steps of the scaffold to be beheaded by a machine called the **guillotine** (GIHL•uh•TEEN). (See the Science & Technology feature on page 225.)

The War Continues The National Convention also had to contend with the continuing war with Austria and Prussia. At about the time the Convention took office, the French army won a stunning victory against the Austrians and Prussians at the Battle of Valmy. Early in 1793, however, Great Britain, Holland, and Spain joined Prussia and Austria against France. Forced to contend with so many enemies, the French suffered a string of defeats. To reinforce the French army, Jacobin leaders in the Convention took an extreme step. At their urging, in February 1793 the Convention ordered a draft of 300,000 French citizens between the ages of 18 and 40. By 1794, the army had grown to 800,000 and included women.

The Terror Grips France

Foreign armies were not the only enemies of the French republic. The Jacobins had thousands of enemies within France itself. These included peasants who were horrified by the king's execution, priests who would not accept government control, and rival leaders who were stirring up rebellion in the provinces. How to contain and control these enemies became a central issue.

Robespierre Assumes Control In the early months of 1793, one Jacobin leader, **Maximilien Robespierre** (ROHBZ•peer), slowly gained power. Robespierre and his supporters set out to build a "republic of virtue" by wiping out every trace of France's past. Firm believers in reason, they changed the calendar, dividing the year into 12 months of 30 days and renaming each month. This calendar had no Sundays because the radicals considered religion old-fashioned and dangerous. They even closed all churches in Paris, and cities and towns all over France soon did the same.

In July 1793, Robespierre became leader of the Committee of Public Safety. For the next year, Robespierre governed France virtually as a dictator, and the period of his rule became known as the **Reign of Terror**. The Committee of Public Safety's chief task was to protect the Revolution from its enemies. Under Robespierre's leadership, the committee often had these "enemies" tried in the morning and guillotined in the afternoon. Robespierre justified his use of terror by suggesting that it enabled French citizens to remain true to the ideals of the Revolution. He also saw a connection between virtue and terror:

PRIMARY SOURCE C

The first maxim of our politics ought to be to lead the people by means of reason and the enemies of the people by terror. If the basis of popular government in time of peace is virtue, the basis of popular government in time of revolution is both virtue and terror: virtue without which terror is murderous, terror without which virtue is powerless. Terror is nothing else than swift, severe, indomitable justice; it flows, then, from virtue.

MAXIMILIEN ROBESPIERRE, "On the Morals and Political Principles of Domestic Policy" (1794)

MAIN IDEA

Analyzing Primary Sources

C How did Robespierre justify the use of terror?

C. Possible Answer by saying that terror was the same thing as justice

The "enemies of the Revolution" who troubled Robespierre the most were fellow radicals who challenged his leadership. In 1793 and 1794, many of those who had led the Revolution received death sentences. Their only crime was that they were

DIFFERENTIATING INSTRUCTION: STRUGGLING READERS

Depicting the Revolution's Early Years

Class Time 30 minutes

Task Creating a poster about the early French Revolution

Purpose To understand the significance of key events

Instructions Divide the class into groups and have each group create a poster depicting—literally or figuratively—five important events in the early years of the French Revolution. Have students use the time line in the Guided Reading activity, available in In-Depth Resources: Unit 2, for help in selecting events. Each poster should include

- at least one image for each event, including the date and location
- names of key individuals and groups involved in each event

Students can use this textbook, reference books, and the Internet to find images. They should write captions and callouts to explain what the images represent.

Display the posters in class and have students discuss the different methods used to depict events.

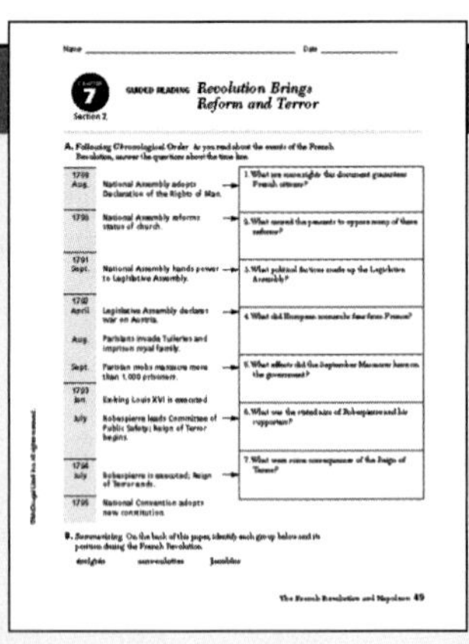

Revolution Brings Reform and Terror

In-Depth Resources: Unit 2

considered less radical than Robespierre. By early 1794, even Georges Danton found himself in danger. Danton's friends in the National Convention, afraid to defend him, joined in condemning him. On the scaffold, he told the executioner, "Don't forget to show my head to the people. It's well worth seeing."

The Terror claimed not only the famous, such as Danton and Marie Antoinette, the widowed queen. Thousands of unknown people also were sent to their deaths, often on the flimsiest of charges. For example, an 18-year-old youth was sentenced to die for cutting down a tree that had been planted as a symbol of liberty. Perhaps as many as 40,000 were executed during the Terror. About 85 percent were peasants or members of the urban poor or middle class—for whose benefit the Revolution had been launched.

▲ At his trial, Georges Danton defended himself so skillfully that the authorities eventually denied him the right to speak.

End of the Terror

In July 1794, fearing for their own safety, some members of the National Convention turned on Robespierre. They demanded his arrest and execution. The Reign of Terror, the radical phase of the French Revolution, ended on July 28, 1794, when Robespierre went to the guillotine.

French public opinion shifted dramatically after Robespierre's death. People of all classes had grown weary of the Terror. They were also tired of the skyrocketing prices for bread, salt, and other necessities of life. In 1795, moderate leaders in the National Convention drafted a new plan of government, the third since 1789. It placed power firmly in the hands of the upper middle class and called for a two-house legislature and an executive body of five men, known as the Directory. These five were moderates, not revolutionary idealists. Some of them were corrupt and made themselves rich at the country's expense. Even so, they gave their troubled country a period of order. They also found the right general to command France's armies—Napoleon Bonaparte.

SECTION 2 ASSESSMENT

TERMS & NAMES 1. For each term or name, write a sentence explaining its significance.
• Legislative Assembly • émigré • sans-culotte • Jacobin • guillotine • Maximilien Robespierre • Reign of Terror

USING YOUR NOTES

2. Do you think this chain of events could have been changed in any way? Explain. (10.2.4)

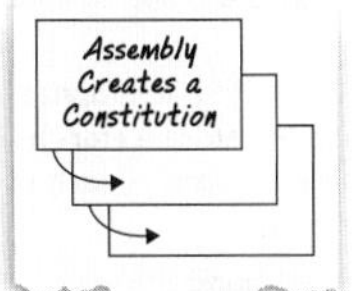

MAIN IDEAS

3. What major reforms did the National Assembly introduce? (10.2.4)
4. What did the divisions in the Legislative Assembly say about the differences in French society? (10.2.4)
5. How did the Reign of Terror come to an end? (10.2.4)

CRITICAL THINKING & WRITING

6. **SYNTHESIZING** How did the slogan "Liberty, Equality, Fraternity" sum up the goals of the Revolution? (10.2.2)
7. **COMPARING AND CONTRASTING** What similarities and differences do you see between the political factions in the Legislative Assembly and those in the U.S. government today? (10.2.4)
8. **ANALYZING CAUSES** What factors led to Robespierre becoming a dictator? (10.2.4)
9. **WRITING ACTIVITY** REVOLUTION Working in small teams, write short **biographies** of three revolutionary figures mentioned in this section. (Writing 2.1.e)

INTEGRATED TECHNOLOGY **INTERNET ACTIVITY**

Use the Internet to conduct research on governments that use terrorism against their own people. Prepare an **oral report** on the methods these countries use. (Writing 2.3.b)

INTERNET KEYWORD
human rights

More About . . .

Robespierre

Robespierre was a ruthless leader, yet he had some progressive ideas. He opposed slavery and fought discrimination against Jews.

In-Depth Resources: Unit 2
• History Makers: Robespierre, p. 65

End of the Terror
10.2.4

Critical Thinking

• Compare reasons that members of the National Convention and the general public opposed the Terror. *(Possible Answer: Weariness motivated most people, but fear motivated Convention members.)*
• How was the Directory similar to the king before the Revolution? *(Both were the executives of the government.)*

In-Depth Resources: Unit 2
• Connections Across Time and Cultures: Comparing Revolutions in America and France, p. 66

3 ASSESS

SECTION 2 ASSESSMENT

Discuss question 7 as a class.

Formal Assessment
• Section Quiz, p. 120

4 RETEACH

Have students work with a partner to make an outline of this section.

In-Depth Resources: Unit 2
• Reteaching Activity, p. 69

ANSWERS

1. Legislative Assembly, p. 223 • émigré, p. 224 • sans-culotte, p. 224 • Jacobin, p. 224 • guillotine, p. 226 • Maximilien Robespierre, p. 226 • Reign of Terror, p. 226
2. **Sample Answer:** War with Prussia and Austria; monarchy abolished; Reign of Terror; Directory governs. Events changed: Yes—If conservatives had been willing to compromise and if moderates had spoken out more strongly.
3. issued the Declaration of the Rights of Man and of the Citizen and reformed the Church
4. The political changes did not wipe out the deep divisions of the Old Regime.
5. Fearing for their safety, leaders turned on Robespierre.
6. desire for freedom from old class structures, equal rights for all citizens, and unity among the French people
7. **Possible Answer:** both divided by ideology, but fewer extremes in Congress
8. **Possible Answer:** war, economic problems, struggling political factions, and Robespierre's strong personality
9. **Rubric** Biographies should
   • present biographical data about each subject.
   • explain each subject's role in the Revolution.
   • compare and contrast the three figures.

INTEGRATED TECHNOLOGY

Rubric Oral reports should
• identify modern countries that use terrorism against their inhabitants.
• include a definition of terrorism.

Different Perspectives

OBJECTIVE

- Understand why people have conflicting views on the French Revolution.
- Compare interpretations of the French Revolution.

INSTRUCT

Explain that the French Revolution was an enormously influential event that set the course for much of European history in the nineteenth century. While it may have contributed to revolutionary fervor elsewhere, it also provided a cautionary tale of what could follow when people rose up in the name of democracy and liberty. While the American Revolution mainly tried to restore rights under attack, the French Revolution is one of the clearest examples in history of people trying to create a new society.

In-Depth Resources: Unit 2

- Literature Selection: from *A Tale of Two Cities,* p. 61

INTEGRATED TECHNOLOGY

Interactive This feature is available in an interactive format on the eEdition that includes background information, definitions of selected words and concepts, and dramatic readings.

Inclusion Tip

Students who have difficulty reading can listen to primary sources read aloud.

Different Perspectives: Using Primary and Secondary Sources

INTERACTIVE

The French Revolution

Over time, people have expressed a wide variety of opinions about the causes and outcomes of the French Revolution. The following excerpts, dating from the 1790s to 1859, illustrate this diversity of opinion.

CALIFORNIA STANDARDS

10.2.3 Understand the unique character of the American Revolution, its spread to other parts of the world, and its continuing significance to other nations.

REP 2 Students identify bias and prejudice in historical interpretations.

A) SECONDARY SOURCE

Charles Dickens

In 1859, the English writer Dickens wrote *A Tale of Two Cities,* a novel about the French Revolution for which he did much research. In the following scene, Charles Darnay—an aristocrat who gave up his title because he hated the injustices done to the people—has returned to France and been put on trial.

His judges sat upon the bench in feathered hats; but the rough red cap and tricolored cockade was the headdress otherwise prevailing. Looking at the jury and the turbulent audience, he might have thought that the usual order of things was reversed, and that the felons were trying the honest men. The lowest, cruelest, and worst populace of a city, never without its quantity of low, cruel, and bad, were the directing spirits of the scene. . . .

Charles Evrémonde, called Darnay, was accused by the public prosecutor as an emigrant, whose life was forfeit to the Republic, under the decree which banished all emigrants on pain of Death. It was nothing that the decree bore date since his return to France. There he was, and there was the decree; he had been taken in France, and his head was demanded.

"Take off his head!" cried the audience. "An enemy to the Republic!"

▶ In this illustration from *A Tale of Two Cities,* Sidney Carton goes to the guillotine in Darnay's place.

B) PRIMARY SOURCE

Edmund Burke

Burke, a British politician, was one of the earliest and most severe critics of the French Revolution. In 1790, he expressed this opinion.

[The French have rebelled] against a mild and lawful monarch, with more fury, outrage, and insult, than ever any people has been known to rise against the most illegal usurper, or the most [bloodthirsty] tyrant. . . .

They have found their punishment in their success. Laws overturned; tribunals subverted; . . . the people impoverished; a church pillaged, and . . . civil and military anarchy made the constitution of the kingdom. . . .

Were all these dreadful things necessary?

C) PRIMARY SOURCE

Thomas Paine

In 1790, Paine—a strong supporter of the American Revolution—defended the French Revolution against Burke and other critics.

It is no longer the paltry cause of kings or of this or of that individual, that calls France and her armies into action. It is the great cause of all. It is the establishment of a new era, that shall blot despotism from the earth, and fix, on the lasting principles of peace and citizenship, the great Republic of Man.

The scene that now opens itself to France extends far beyond the boundaries of her own dominions. Every nation is becoming her ally, and every court has become her enemy. It is now the cause of all nations, against the cause of all courts.

Document-Based **QUESTIONS**

1. In your own words, summarize the attitude toward the French Revolution expressed in each of these excerpts.
2. Why might Edmund Burke (Source B) be so against the French Revolution?
3. In Source C, what is the distinction Thomas Paine is making between nations and courts?

DOCUMENT-BASED QUESTIONS: ANSWERS

1. *Possible Answer:* Dickens—The Revolution gave power to the lowest and cruelest members of the populace, leading to rampant injustice and mob rule. Burke—The French rebelled with great ferocity against a lawful king and left the country worse off than before. Paine—The great cause of eliminating despotism justifies revolution.
2. *Possible Answer:* As a member of the British government, Burke may have feared doctrines that called for equality, rapid change, or overthrow of established leaders.
3. *Possible Answer:* Thomas Paine is saying that courts are small ruling groups that put their self-interest before what is best for the country, and that nations are countries that govern with the consent and participation of the people.

French Revolution: Assault on the Bastille, Jean-Baptiste Lallemand

Napoleon and His General Staff in Egypt, Jean-Léon Gérome

3

Napoleon Forges an Empire

MAIN IDEA	WHY IT MATTERS NOW	TERMS & NAMES
POWER AND AUTHORITY Napoleon Bonaparte, a military genius, seized power in France and made himself emperor.	In times of political turmoil, military dictators often seize control of nations.	• Napoleon Bonaparte • coup d'état • plebiscite • lycée • concordat • Napoleonic Code • Battle of Trafalgar

SETTING THE STAGE Napoleon Bonaparte was quite a short man—just five feet three inches tall. However, he cast a long shadow over the history of modern times. He would come to be recognized as one of the world's greatest military geniuses, along with Alexander the Great of Macedonia, Hannibal of Carthage, and Julius Caesar of Rome. In only four years, from 1795 to 1799, Napoleon rose from a relatively obscure position as an officer in the French army to become master of France.

CALIFORNIA STANDARDS

10.2.4 Explain how the ideology of the French Revolution led France to develop from constitutional monarchy to democratic despotism to the Napoleonic empire.

10.2.5 Discuss how nationalism spread across Europe with Napoleon but was repressed for a generation under the Congress of Vienna and Concert of Europe until the Revolutions of 1848.

Napoleon Seizes Power

Napoleon Bonaparte was born in 1769 on the Mediterranean island of Corsica. When he was nine years old, his parents sent him to a military school. In 1785, at the age of 16, he finished school and became a lieutenant in the artillery. When the Revolution broke out, Napoleon joined the army of the new government.

Hero of the Hour In October 1795, fate handed the young officer a chance for glory. When royalist rebels marched on the National Convention, a government official told Napoleon to defend the delegates. Napoleon and his gunners greeted the thousands of royalists with a cannonade. Within minutes, the attackers fled in panic and confusion. Napoleon Bonaparte became the hero of the hour and was hailed throughout Paris as the savior of the French republic.

In 1796, the Directory appointed Napoleon to lead a French army against the forces of Austria and the Kingdom of Sardinia. Crossing the Alps, the young general swept into Italy and won a series of remarkable victories. Next, in an attempt to protect French trade interests and to disrupt British trade with India, Napoleon led an expedition to Egypt. But he was unable to repeat the successes he had achieved in Europe. His army was pinned down in Egypt, and the British admiral Horatio Nelson defeated his naval forces. However, Napoleon managed to keep stories about his setbacks out of the newspapers and thereby remained a great hero to the people of France.

Coup d'État By 1799, the Directory had lost control of the political situation and the confidence of the French people. When Napoleon returned from Egypt, his friends urged him to seize political power. Napoleon took action in early November 1799. Troops under his command surrounded the national legislature and drove out most of its members. The lawmakers who remained then voted to

TAKING NOTES

Following Chronological Order On a time line, note the events that led to Napoleon's crowning as emperor of France.

1789 — French Revolution breaks out.
1804 — Napoleon crowned emperor.

LESSON PLAN

OBJECTIVES

- Explain how Napoleon Bonaparte came to power.
- Summarize how Napoleon restored order in France.
- Describe the extent and weaknesses of Napoleon's empire.

1 FOCUS & MOTIVATE

Discuss what makes an empire and whether empires exist today. *(Possible Answer: An empire exists when one ruler or country controls several countries. Some people contend that the breadth of U.S. power is making it an empire.)*

2 INSTRUCT

Napoleon Seizes Power
HI 3

Critical Thinking

- How would you compare Napoleon's actions in October 1795 and November 1799? *(protected stability of France both times, first by defending government, then by overturning it)*

CALIFORNIA RESOURCES

California Reading Toolkit, p. L34
California Modified Lesson Plans for English Learners, p. 63
California Daily Standards Practice Transparencies, TT26
California Standards Enrichment Workbook, pp. 29–30, 31–32
California Standards Planner and Lesson Plans, p. L59
California Online Test Practice
California Test Generator CD-ROM
California Easy Planner CD-ROM
California eEdition CD-ROM

SECTION 3 PROGRAM RESOURCES

ALL STUDENTS

In-Depth Resources: Unit 2
- Guided Reading, p. 50

Formal Assessment
- Section Quiz, p. 121

ENGLISH LEARNERS

In-Depth Resources in Spanish
- Guided Reading, p. 61

Reading Study Guide (Spanish), p. 77
Reading Study Guide Audio CD (Spanish)

STRUGGLING READERS

In-Depth Resources: Unit 2
- Guided Reading, p. 50
- Building Vocabulary, p. 53
- Reteaching Activity, p. 70

Reading Study Guide, p. 77
Reading Study Guide Audio CD

GIFTED AND TALENTED STUDENTS

In-Depth Resources: Unit 2
- Primary Source: Napoleon's Proclamation at Austerlitz, p. 60

Electronic Library of Primary Sources
- from *The Letters of Napoleon I*

INTEGRATED TECHNOLOGY

eEdition CD-ROM
Power Presentations CD-ROM
World Art and Cultures Transparencies
- AT51 *Napoleon Crossing the St. Bernard Pass*

Electronic Library of Primary Sources
- from *The Letters of Napoleon I*

classzone.com

Napoleon Rules France
10.2.4

Critical Thinking

- In general, did Napoleon make the French government stronger or weaker? *(He strengthened it by improving the tax collection system, starting lycées and a national banking system, and restricting freedoms of speech and the press.)*
- What made the admissions policies of the lycées significant? *(provided opportunity to males of all classes)*
- What caused Napoleon to reach an agreement with the pope? *(Many clergy and peasants disliked the restrictions on the church started during the Revolution.)*

History Makers

Napoleon Bonaparte

Which traits of Napoleon are emphasized in the portrait of him? *(Possible Answer: his pride)*

Discuss whether students think any contemporary rulers share traits of Napoleon's.

World Art and Cultures Transparencies

- AT51 *Napoleon Crossing the St. Bernard Pass*

History Makers

Napoleon Bonaparte
1769–1821

Because of his small stature and thick Corsican accent, Napoleon was mocked by his fellow students at military school. Haughty and proud, Napoleon refused to grace his tormentors' behavior with any kind of response. He simply ignored them, preferring to lose himself in his studies. He showed a particular passion for three subjects—classical history, geography, and mathematics.

In 1784, Napoleon was recommended for a career in the army and he transferred to the Ecole Militaire (the French equivalent of West Point) in Paris. There, he proved to be a fairly poor soldier, except when it came to artillery. His artillery instructor quickly noticed Napoleon's abilities: "He is most proud, ambitious, aspiring to everything. This young man merits our attention."

dissolve the Directory. In its place, they established a group of three consuls, one of whom was Napoleon. Napoleon quickly took the title of first consul and assumed the powers of a dictator. A sudden seizure of power like Napoleon's is known as a *coup*—from the French phrase **coup d'état** (KOO day•TAH), or "blow to the state." Ⓐ

At the time of Napoleon's coup, France was still at war. In 1799, Britain, Austria, and Russia joined forces with one goal in mind, to drive Napoleon from power. Once again, Napoleon rode from Paris at the head of his troops. Eventually, as a result of war and diplomacy, all three nations signed peace agreements with France. By 1802, Europe was at peace for the first time in ten years. Napoleon was free to focus his energies on restoring order in France.

MAIN IDEA

Analyzing Causes

Ⓐ How was Napoleon able to become a dictator?

A. Answer General political chaos created a need for a strong leader, and Napoleon had control of the army.

Napoleon Rules France

At first, Napoleon pretended to be the constitutionally chosen leader of a free republic. In 1800, a **plebiscite** (PLEHB•ih•SYT), or vote of the people, was held to approve a new constitution. Desperate for strong leadership, the people voted overwhelmingly in favor of the constitution. This gave all real power to Napoleon as first consul.

Restoring Order at Home Napoleon did not try to return the nation to the days of Louis XVI. Rather, he kept many of the changes that had come with the Revolution. In general, he supported laws that would both strengthen the central government and achieve some of the goals of the Revolution.

His first task was to get the economy on a solid footing. Napoleon set up an efficient method of tax collection and established a national banking system. In addition to ensuring the government a steady supply of tax money, these actions promoted sound financial management and better control of the economy. Napoleon also took steps to end corruption and inefficiency in government. He dismissed corrupt officials and, in order to provide the government with trained officials, set up **lycées**, or government-run public schools. These lycées were open to male students of all backgrounds. Graduates were appointed to public office on the basis of merit rather than family connections.

One area where Napoleon disregarded changes introduced by the Revolution was religion. Both the clergy and many peasants wanted to restore the position of the Church in France. Responding to their wishes, Napoleon signed a **concordat**, or agreement, with Pope Pius VII. This established a new relationship between church and state. The government recognized the influence of the Church, but rejected Church control in national affairs. The concordat gained Napoleon the support of the organized Church as well as the majority of the French people.

Napoleon thought that his greatest work was his comprehensive system of laws, known as the **Napoleonic Code**. This gave the country a uniform set of laws and eliminated many injustices. However, it actually limited liberty and promoted order and authority over individual rights. For example, freedom of speech and of the press, established during the Revolution, were restricted under the code. The code also restored slavery in the French colonies of the Caribbean.

DIFFERENTIATING INSTRUCTION: ENGLISH LEARNERS

Understanding Idioms

Class Time 25 minutes

Task Identifying and understanding idioms in the text

Purpose To improve text comprehension

Instructions Explain that an idiom is a commonly used expression that has an intended meaning that is different from its literal meaning. For example, people often say "It's a piece of cake" when they mean "It's easy," or "She's a hothead" rather than "She is bad-tempered."

Challenge students to find three idioms on pages 230 and 231. Write these idioms on the board and explain what they mean in the context of the passage. An example is shown at right.

For more help with this section, refer students to the Reading Study Guide, available in English and Spanish.

Napoleon had to get the economy **on a solid footing.**	He had to make sure the economy was stable and would not fail.
Napoleon decided to **cut his losses** and sell the Louisiana Territory.	He wanted to end a losing situation.
Napoleon set up a **puppet government** in Switzerland.	He created a foreign government that pretended to be independent but did whatever he wanted it to do.

MAIN IDEA
Analyzing Motives
B Why do you think Napoleon crowned himself emperor?

B. Answer to show that he was not under the control of anyone

Napoleon Crowned as Emperor In 1804, Napoleon decided to make himself emperor, and the French voters supported him. On December 2, 1804, dressed in a splendid robe of purple velvet, Napoleon walked down the long aisle of Notre Dame Cathedral in Paris. The pope waited for him with a glittering crown. As thousands watched, the new emperor took the crown from the pope and placed it on his own head. With this gesture, Napoleon signaled that he was more powerful than the Church, which had traditionally crowned the rulers of France. **B**

Napoleon Creates an Empire

Napoleon was not content simply to be master of France. He wanted to control the rest of Europe and to reassert French power in the Americas. He envisioned his western empire including Louisiana, Florida, French Guiana, and the French West Indies. He knew that the key to this area was the sugar-producing colony of Saint Domingue (now called Haiti) on the island of Hispaniola.

Loss of American Territories In 1789, when the ideas of the Revolution reached the planters in Saint Domingue, they demanded that the National Assembly give them the same privileges as the people of France. Eventually, enslaved Africans in the colony demanded their rights too—in other words, their freedom. A civil war erupted, and enslaved Africans under the leadership of Toussaint L'Ouverture seized control of the colony. In 1801, Napoleon decided to take back the colony and restore its productive sugar industry. However, the French forces were devastated by disease. And the rebels proved to be fierce fighters.

After the failure of the expedition to Saint Domingue, Napoleon decided to cut his losses in the Americas. He offered to sell all of the Louisiana Territory to the United States, and in 1803 President Jefferson's administration agreed to purchase the land for $15 million. Napoleon saw a twofold benefit to the sale. First, he would gain money to finance operations in Europe. Second, he would punish the British. "The sale assures forever the power of the United States," he observed, "and I have given England a rival who, sooner or later, will humble her pride." **C**

MAIN IDEA
Recognizing Effects
C What effects did Napoleon intend the sale of Louisiana to have on France? on the United States? on Britain?

C. Answer Napoleon hoped to obtain the money he needed to continue his conquest of Europe and to increase the power of the United States in order to punish Britain.

Conquering Europe Having abandoned his imperial ambitions in the New World, Napoleon turned his attention to Europe. He had already annexed the Austrian Netherlands and parts of Italy to France and set up a puppet government in Switzerland. Now he looked to expand his influence further. Fearful of his ambitions, the British persuaded Russia, Austria, and Sweden to join them against France.

Napoleon met this challenge with his usual boldness. In a series of brilliant battles, he crushed the opposition. (See the map on page 232.) The commanders of the enemy armies could never predict his next move and often took heavy losses. After the Battle of Austerlitz in 1805, Napoleon issued a proclamation expressing his pride in his troops:

PRIMARY SOURCE

Soldiers! I am pleased with you. On the day of Austerlitz, you justified everything that I was expecting of [you]. . . . In less than four hours, an army of 100,000 men, commanded by the emperors of Russia and Austria, was cut up and dispersed. . . . 120 pieces of artillery, 20 generals, and more than 30,000 men taken prisoner—such are the results of this day which will forever be famous. . . . And it will be enough for you to say, "I was at Austerlitz," to hear the reply: "There is a brave man!"

NAPOLEON, quoted in *Napoleon* by André Castelot

▼ This painting by Jacques Louis David shows Napoleon in a heroic pose.

Napoleon Creates an Empire
10.2.4

Critical Thinking

- How did L'Ouverture's revolution benefit the United States? *(It prompted Napoleon to sell the Louisiana Territory to the United States.)*
- How does the Battle of Trafalgar show the importance of naval power? *(Britain's victory protected it from invasion.)*
- How long did Napoleon's empire remain at its peak? *(five years)*
- How did Napoleon's belief in equal opportunity conflict with his method of selecting leaders for puppet governments? *(He often chose family members.)*

In-Depth Resources: Unit 2

- Primary Source: Napoleon's Proclamation at Austerlitz, p. 60

More About . . .

Empires Face Disease

Napoleon's imperial aspirations were limited by a tiny foe: germs. The French expedition to Saint Domingue suffered heavy losses from yellow fever. During the campaign in Russia in 1812, typhus fever infected over 80,000 soldiers. Disease has had an impact on other empires as well. Malaria weakened the Roman Empire. Smallpox and other diseases killed millions of native people in the Americas, Siberia, and Australia, weakening them in the face of European expansion. Until yellow fever was controlled, building a canal through Panama was nearly impossible.

DIFFERENTIATING INSTRUCTION: STRUGGLING READERS

Examining a Primary Source

Class Time 25 minutes

Task Summarizing and analyzing part of a proclamation by Napoleon

Purpose To improve understanding of a primary source and discuss motivations of an important leader

Instructions Have pairs of students reread the primary source on this page and write a summary of it in their own words. *(Possible Answer: I am proud of you, soldiers. You won an important battle. Your performance was so outstanding that everyone will remember you.)*

Share summaries to be sure that students understand the primary source. Then create a chart on the chalkboard and have the class answer the questions. A sample is shown here.

Who?	Napoleon Bonaparte
What?	proclamation to soldiers about the Battle of Austerlitz
Where?	Austerlitz was in the Austrian Empire.
When?	1805
Why?	to tell the soldiers of his pride; to brag about the victory; to motivate the troops to keep fighting

History from Visuals

Interpreting the Map

Compare this map with the political map of Europe in the textbook atlas. How are the borders of France different today? *(Today, France is smaller. Spain, Italy, Germany, Belgium, and the Netherlands all contain land that Napoleon ruled.)*

SKILLBUILDER Answers

1. **Region** from the North Sea in the north to Italy in the south, and from the Illyrian Provinces in the east to the Atlantic in the west
2. **Location** In the Atlantic, just west of Gibraltar; Nelson split French fleet, enabling his forces to attack smaller groups of ships

INTEGRATED TECHNOLOGY

Interactive This map is available in an interactive format on the eEdition.

War in Europe, 1805–1813

INTERACTIVE

French Empire
Controlled by Napoleon
French victory
French defeat
British blockade

Battle of Trafalgar, Oct. 21, 1805

By dividing Villeneuve's formation, Admiral Nelson captured nearly two-thirds of the enemy fleet.

Battle of Austerlitz, Dec. 2, 1805

By drawing an Allied attack on his right flank, Napoleon was able to split the Allied line at its center.

GEOGRAPHY SKILLBUILDER: Interpreting Maps

1. **Region** *What was the extent of the lands under Napoleon's control?*
2. **Location** *Where was the Battle of Trafalgar fought? What tactic did Nelson use in the battle, and why was it successful?*

232 Chapter 7

DIFFERENTIATING INSTRUCTION: GIFTED AND TALENTED STUDENTS

Analyzing Napoleon's Control of the Media

Class Time 40 minutes

Task Reading and responding to a primary source

Purpose To better understand the control rulers can exercise

Instructions Distribute the excerpts from the letters of Napoleon Bonaparte, available in the Electronic Library of Primary Sources. Use these questions to spark a discussion:

- How far did Napoleon's control of the media reach? *(newspapers, books, pamphlets, plays, advertisements, trial transcripts, and sermons)*
- Why do you think Napoleon told his aide, "Don't make your intervention public"? *(Possible Answer: Napoleon might have become unpopular if the extent of his media control had become public knowledge.)*
- Would it be possible for a present-day ruler to exercise such a degree of control over the media? Why or why not? *(Probably not—Today there are many more publications than in Napoleon's time, and the existence of the Internet, telephones, radios, and television make it more difficult to suppress opinions.)*

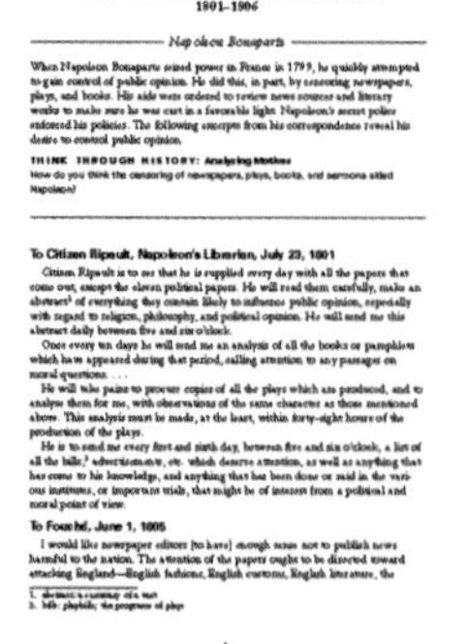
from The Letters of Napoleon I 1801–1806

Napoleon Bonaparte

Electronic Library of Primary Sources

In time, Napoleon's battlefield successes forced the rulers of Austria, Prussia, and Russia to sign peace treaties. These successes also enabled him to build the largest European empire since that of the Romans. France's only major enemy left undefeated was the great naval power, Britain.

The Battle of Trafalgar In his drive for a European empire, Napoleon lost only one major battle, the **Battle of Trafalgar** (truh•FAL•guhr). This naval defeat, however, was more important than all of his victories on land. The battle took place in 1805 off the southwest coast of Spain. The British commander, Horatio Nelson, was as brilliant in warfare at sea as Napoleon was in warfare on land. In a bold maneuver, he split the larger French fleet, capturing many ships. (See the map inset on the opposite page.)

The destruction of the French fleet had two major results. First, it ensured the supremacy of the British navy for the next 100 years. Second, it forced Napoleon to give up his plans of invading Britain. He had to look for another way to control his powerful enemy across the English Channel. Eventually, Napoleon's extravagant efforts to crush Britain would lead to his own undoing.

The French Empire During the first decade of the 1800s, Napoleon's victories had given him mastery over most of Europe. By 1812, the only areas of Europe free from Napoleon's control were Britain, Portugal, Sweden, and the Ottoman Empire. In addition to the lands of the French Empire, Napoleon also controlled numerous supposedly independent countries. (See the map on the opposite page.) These included Spain, the Grand Duchy of Warsaw, and a number of German kingdoms in Central Europe. The rulers of these countries were Napoleon's puppets; some, in fact, were members of his family. Furthermore, the powerful countries of Russia, Prussia, and Austria were loosely attached to Napoleon's empire through alliances. Although not totally under Napoleon's control, they were easily manipulated by threats of military action. D

D. Possible Answer Napoleon had been quite successful, since by 1805 he controlled most of Europe except Britain.

MAIN IDEA

Drawing Conclusions

D By 1805, how successful had Napoleon been in his efforts to build an empire?

The French Empire was huge but unstable. Napoleon was able to maintain it at its greatest extent for only five years—from 1807 to 1812. Then it quickly fell to pieces. Its sudden collapse was caused in part by Napoleon's actions.

SECTION 3 ASSESSMENT

TERMS & NAMES 1. For each term or name, write a sentence explaining its significance.
• Napoleon Bonaparte • coup d'état • plebiscite • lycée • concordat • Napoleonic Code • Battle of Trafalgar

USING YOUR NOTES

2. Which of these events do you think had the greatest impact on Napoleon's rise to power? (10.2.4)

1789 French Revolution breaks out. — [ ] — 1804 Napoleon crowned emperor.

MAIN IDEAS

3. How did Napoleon become a hero in France? (10.2.4)
4. What did Napoleon consider his greatest triumph in domestic policy? (10.2.4)
5. How was Napoleon able to control the countries neighboring the French Empire? (10.2.4)

CRITICAL THINKING & WRITING

6. **FORMING OPINIONS** In your opinion, was Napoleon the creator or the creation of his times? (10.2.5)
7. **ANALYZING ISSUES** Napoleon had to deal with forces both inside and outside the French Empire. Which area do you think was more important to control? (10.2.5)
8. **MAKING INFERENCES** If you had been a member of the bourgeoisie, would you have been satisfied with the results of Napoleon's actions? Explain. (10.2.4)
9. **WRITING ACTIVITY** POWER AND AUTHORITY Look at the painting on page 231. Write a **paragraph** discussing why the painter portrayed Napoleon in this way. (Writing 2.2.b)

CONNECT TO TODAY CREATING A VENN DIAGRAM

Identify and conduct research on a present-day world leader who has used dictatorial powers to rule his or her country. Use your findings to create a **Venn diagram** comparing this leader's use of power to Napoleon's use of power. (Writing 2.3.d)

More About . . .

The Battle of Trafalgar

Highly motivated British sailors under Admiral Nelson formed two squadrons and attacked the line of French ships, splitting them into smaller groups (see map on page 232). Nelson's sailors were better trained and more accurate shots than the sailors in the French fleet. In the end, the British captured the French commander and the French surrendered 19 or 20 ships out of their total of 33. Although Nelson was killed, no British ships were lost. Nelson is commemorated with a huge statue in Trafalgar Square in the heart of London. The 17-foot-high statue stands atop a column 185 feet tall.

3 ASSESS

SECTION 3 ASSESSMENT

Go over the section assessment as a class, identifying the location in the text of the answers to each item.

Formal Assessment
• Section Quiz, p. 121

Reading Study Guide, p. 77

4 RETEACH

Write two column heads on the board, *Successes* and *Failures.* Ask students to list actions of Napoleon that fit under each heading.

In-Depth Resources: Unit 2
• Reteaching Activity, p. 70

ANSWERS

1. Napoleon Bonaparte, p. 229 • coup d'état, p. 230 • plebiscite, p. 230 • lycée, p. 230 • concordat, p. 230 • Napoleonic Code, p. 230 • Battle of Trafalgar, p. 233
2. **Sample Answer:** 1795—Napoleon defends against royalists; 1796—Victories in Italy; 1799—Coup brings him to power; 1800—Plebiscite gives him total power. Most important—1799 coup.
3. He drove off the royalists who attacked the National Assembly, and he led the army to great victories in Italy.
4. the Napoleonic Code
5. puppet rulers and threat of force
6. Creation—He was able to seize power due to a political crisis. Creator—His genius and personality helped him dominate his era.
7. Inside—Chaos at home would have made military success abroad impossible. Outside—Victory abroad increased support for him.
8. Yes—Napoleon brought stability to France. No—Napoleon did not grant special privileges.
9. **Rubric** Paragraphs should
   • describe the picture accurately.
   • list the qualities it portrays.

CONNECT TO TODAY

Rubric Venn diagrams should
• identify dictatorial powers.
• list similarities and differences between Napoleon and a present-day leader.

LESSON PLAN

OBJECTIVES

- Explain Napoleon's tactical and political mistakes.
- Summarize Napoleon's defeat, comeback, and final downfall.

1 FOCUS & MOTIVATE

Ask students to rate how emotionally attached they feel toward their city, state, or nation or to various groups such as a school or a political party. Note that the concept of nationalism is relatively new. It has emerged only in recent centuries.

2 INSTRUCT

Napoleon's Costly Mistakes

10.2.4; 10.2.5

Critical Thinking

- What would Napoleon have needed to make his Continental System work? *(a stronger navy and more cooperative allies)*
- How did nationalism affect Napoleon's empire? *(It helped forge opposition to French rule.)*

CALIFORNIA RESOURCES

California Reading Toolkit, p. L35
California Modified Lesson Plans for English Learners, p. 65
California Daily Standards Practice Transparencies, TT27
California Standards Enrichment Workbook, pp. 29–30
California Standards Planner and Lesson Plans, p. L61
California Online Test Practice
California Test Generator CD-ROM
California Easy Planner CD-ROM
California eEdition CD-ROM

French Revolution: Assault on the Bastille, Jean-Baptiste Lallemand

Napoleon and His General Staff in Egypt, Jean-Léon Gérome

4

Napoleon's Empire Collapses

MAIN IDEA

POWER AND AUTHORITY Napoleon's conquests aroused nationalistic feelings across Europe and contributed to his downfall.

WHY IT MATTERS NOW

In the 1990s, nationalistic feelings contributed to the breakup of nations such as Yugoslavia.

TERMS & NAMES

- blockade
- Continental System
- guerrilla
- Peninsular War
- scorched-earth policy
- Waterloo
- Hundred Days

CALIFORNIA STANDARDS

10.2.4 Explain how the ideology of the French Revolution led France to develop from constitutional monarchy to democratic despotism to the Napoleonic empire.

CST 1 Students compare the present with the past, evaluating the consequences of past events and decisions and determining the lessons that were learned.

CST 3 Students use a variety of maps and documents to interpret human movement, including major patterns of domestic and international migration, changing environmental preferences and settlement patterns, the frictions that develop between population groups, and the diffusion of ideas, technological innovations, and goods.

CST 4 Students relate current events to the physical and human characteristics of places and regions.

HI 1 Students show the connections, causal and otherwise, between particular historical events and larger social, economic, and political trends and developments.

TAKING NOTES

Recognizing Effects Use a chart to identify Napoleon's three mistakes and the impact they had on the French Empire.

Napoleon's Mistakes	Effect on Empire

SETTING THE STAGE Napoleon worried about what would happen to his vast empire after his death. He feared it would fall apart unless he had an undisputed heir. His wife, Josephine, had failed to bear him a child. He, therefore, divorced her and formed an alliance with the Austrian royal family by marrying Marie Louise, the grandniece of Marie Antoinette. In 1811, Marie Louise gave birth to a son, Napoleon II, whom Napoleon named king of Rome.

Napoleon's Costly Mistakes

Napoleon's own personality proved to be the greatest danger to the future of his empire. His desire for power had raised him to great heights, and the same love of power led him to his doom. In his efforts to extend the French Empire and crush Great Britain, Napoleon made three disastrous mistakes.

The Continental System In November 1806, Napoleon set up a **blockade**—a forcible closing of ports—to prevent all trade and communication between Great Britain and other European nations. Napoleon called this policy the **Continental System** as it would make continental Europe more self-sufficient. He also intended it to destroy Great Britain's commercial and industrial economy.

Napoleon's blockade, however, was not nearly tight enough. Aided by the British, smugglers managed to bring cargo from Britain into Europe. At times, Napoleon's allies also disregarded the blockade. Even members of his family defied the policy, including his brother, Louis, whom he had made king of Holland. While the blockade weakened British trade, it did not destroy it. In addition, Britain responded with its own blockade. The stronger British navy was better able to make their blockade work.

To enforce the blockade, the British navy stopped neutral ships bound for the continent and forced them to sail to a British port to be searched and taxed. American ships were among those stopped by the British navy. Angered, the U.S.

▲ "Little Johnny Bull"—Great Britain—waves a sword at Napoleon as the emperor straddles the globe.

SECTION 4 PROGRAM RESOURCES

ALL STUDENTS

In-Depth Resources: Unit 2
- Guided Reading, p. 51
- Skillbuilder Practice: Interpreting Maps, p. 54

Formal Assessment
- Section Quiz, p. 122

ENGLISH LEARNERS

In-Depth Resources in Spanish
- Guided Reading, p. 62
- Skillbuilder Practice: Interpreting Maps, p. 64

Reading Study Guide (Spanish), p. 79
Reading Study Guide Audio CD (Spanish)

STRUGGLING READERS

In-Depth Resources: Unit 2
- Guided Reading, p. 51
- Building Vocabulary, p. 53
- Skillbuilder Practice: Interpreting Maps, p. 54
- Reteaching Activity, p. 71

Reading Study Guide, p. 79
Reading Study Guide Audio CD

GIFTED AND TALENTED STUDENTS

Electronic Library of Primary Sources
- "The Battle of Waterloo: The Finale"

INTEGRATED TECHNOLOGY

eEdition CD-ROM
Power Presentations CD-ROM
Electronic Library of Primary Sources
- "The Battle of Waterloo: The Finale"

classzone.com

Congress declared war on Britain in 1812. Even though the War of 1812 lasted two years, it was only a minor inconvenience to Britain in its struggle with Napoleon.

The Peninsular War In 1808, Napoleon made a second costly mistake. In an effort to get Portugal to accept the Continental System, he sent an invasion force through Spain. The Spanish people protested this action. In response, Napoleon removed the Spanish king and put his own brother, Joseph, on the throne. This outraged the Spanish people and inflamed their nationalistic feelings. The Spanish, who were devoutly Catholic, also worried that Napoleon would attack the Church. They had seen how the French Revolution had weakened the Catholic Church in France, and they feared that the same thing would happen to the Church in Spain.

For six years, bands of Spanish peasant fighters, known as **guerrillas**, struck at French armies in Spain. The guerrillas were not an army that Napoleon could defeat in open battle. Rather, they worked in small groups that ambushed French troops and then fled into hiding. The British added to the French troubles by sending troops to aid the Spanish. Napoleon lost about 300,000 men during this **Peninsular War**—so called because Spain lies on the Iberian Peninsula. These losses weakened the French Empire.

In Spain and elsewhere, nationalism, or loyalty to one's own country, was becoming a powerful weapon against Napoleon. People who had at first welcomed the French as their liberators now felt abused by a foreign conqueror. Like the Spanish guerrillas, Germans and Italians and other conquered peoples turned against the French. (A)

MAIN IDEA

Recognizing Effects

(A) How could the growing feelings of nationalism in European countries hurt Napoleon?

A. Possible Answer Feelings of nationalism inspired fierce, persistent resistance to Napoleon's rule.

The Invasion of Russia Napoleon's most disastrous mistake of all came in 1812. Even though Alexander I had become Napoleon's ally, the Russian czar refused to stop selling grain to Britain. In addition, the French and Russian rulers suspected each other of having competing designs on Poland. Because of this breakdown in their alliance, Napoleon decided to invade Russia.

In June 1812, Napoleon and his Grand Army of more than 420,000 soldiers marched into Russia. As Napoleon advanced, Alexander pulled back his troops, refusing to be lured into an unequal battle. On this retreat, the Russians practiced a **scorched-earth policy**. This involved burning grain fields and slaughtering livestock so as to leave nothing for the enemy to eat.

▼ Francisco Goya's painting *The Third of May, 1808* shows a French firing squad executing Spanish peasants suspected of being guerrillas.

235

More About . . .

Scorched-Earth Policies

Scorched-earth policies were well suited to a large country such as Russia where an army could retreat for hundreds of miles, drawing an invader farther from home. Russia had used the tactic a century earlier during a Swedish invasion. Even smaller countries employed it effectively: the Parthians slowed a Roman advance in the 3rd century, the Vietnamese stopped the Mongols in the 13th century, and the French used it against the Holy Roman Empire in the 1530s. Russians would use it again in the 1940s to stop the German army.

More About . . .

Francisco Goya

Goya's painting *The Third of May, 1808: The Execution of the Defenders of Madrid* was a scathing attack on French wartime brutality. Goya painted it to honor those who had defended Madrid against a French invasion. During the invasion, Goya produced a set of etchings, *The Disasters of War,* that would be even more influential among artists. Although not published until 1863, these etchings inspired others, long after Goya's death, to create art in opposition to the cruelty of war. Among the most famous was another Spaniard, Pablo Picasso, whose 1937 painting *Guernica* is shown on page 484.

DIFFERENTIATING INSTRUCTION: ENGLISH LEARNERS

Causes of Napoleon's Defeat

Class Time 30 minutes

Task Making a chart showing the causes of Napoleon's defeat

Purpose To understand how Napoleon was defeated

Instructions Tell students that Napoleon's action in making his brother king of Spain had an effect not only on the people of Spain but on people in South America as well. People of Spanish ancestry in Mexico, for example, did not want a French king. That led to unrest, as students will learn in Chapter 8.

Have students list Napoleon's three mistakes: the blockade, the invasion of Spain, and the invasion of Russia. Then have them note how each mistake contributed to Napoleon's final defeat. Have students use the Guided Reading activity for Section 4 for help.

Mistakes	Results
Blockade	Hurt European economy, also caused War of 1812
Invasion of Spain	Spanish resistance weakened the French
Invasion of Russia	French were defeated

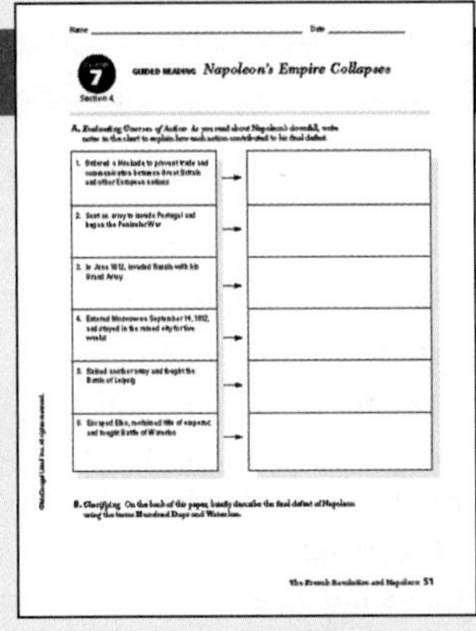

In-Depth Resources: Unit 2

History from Visuals

Interpreting the Map

Have students begin by examining the map key. Then they should read the blue boxes from left to right followed by the red boxes from right to left. Ask them, approximately how far did Napoleon's troops travel? *(more than 1,000 miles)*

Extension Ask students to calculate the length of the Russian campaign. *(six months)* How was Napoleon's army traveling? *(on foot)*

SKILLBUILDER Answers

1. **Movement** about 3 months, from June to September
2. **Place** His army got caught in the bitter cold of the Russian winter.

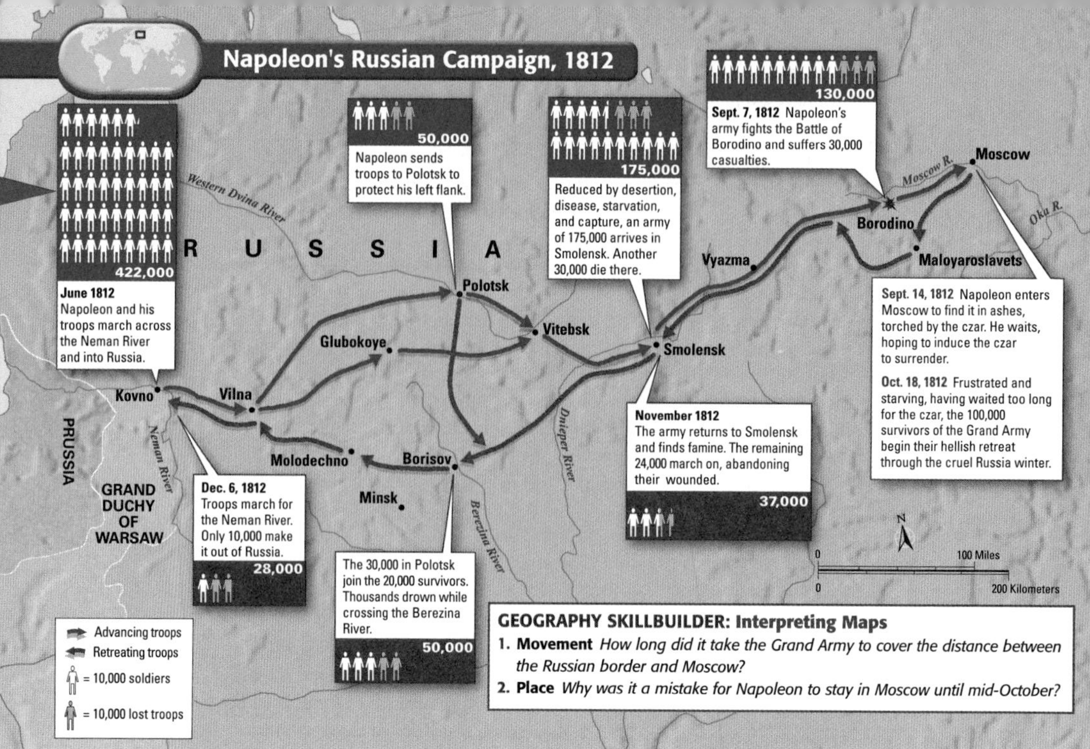

Napoleon's Russian Campaign, 1812
422,000
June 1812 Napoleon and his troops march across the Neman River and into Russia.
50,000
Napoleon sends troops to Polotsk to protect his left flank.
175,000
Reduced by desertion, disease, starvation, and capture, an army of 175,000 arrives in Smolensk. Another 30,000 die there.
130,000
Sept. 7, 1812 Napoleon's army fights the Battle of Borodino and suffers 30,000 casualties.
Sept. 14, 1812 Napoleon enters Moscow to find it in ashes, torched by the czar. He waits, hoping to induce the czar to surrender.
Oct. 18, 1812 Frustrated and starving, having waited too long for the czar, the 100,000 survivors of the Grand Army begin their hellish retreat through the cruel Russia winter.
November 1812 The army returns to Smolensk and finds famine. The remaining 24,000 march on, abandoning their wounded.
37,000
The 30,000 in Polotsk join the 20,000 survivors. Thousands drown while crossing the Berezina River.
50,000
Dec. 6, 1812 Troops march for the Neman River. Only 10,000 make it out of Russia.
28,000
RUSSIA
PRUSSIA
GRAND DUCHY OF WARSAW
Western Dvina River
Neman River
Dnieper River
Berezina River
Moscow R.
Oka R.
Kovno
Vilna
Glubokoye
Polotsk
Vitebsk
Smolensk
Vyazma
Borodino
Moscow
Maloyaroslavets
Molodechno
Borisov
Minsk
Advancing troops
Retreating troops
= 10,000 soldiers
= 10,000 lost troops
0 100 Miles
0 200 Kilometers
N

GEOGRAPHY SKILLBUILDER: Interpreting Maps

1. **Movement** *How long did it take the Grand Army to cover the distance between the Russian border and Moscow?*
2. **Place** *Why was it a mistake for Napoleon to stay in Moscow until mid-October?*

On September 7, 1812, the two armies finally clashed in the Battle of Borodino. (See the map on this page.) After several hours of indecisive fighting, the Russians fell back, allowing Napoleon to move on Moscow. When Napoleon entered Moscow seven days later, the city was in flames. Rather than surrender Russia's "holy city" to the French, Alexander had destroyed it. Napoleon stayed in the ruined city until the middle of October, when he decided to turn back toward France.

As the snows—and the temperature—began to fall in early November, Russian raiders mercilessly attacked Napoleon's ragged, retreating army. Many soldiers were killed in these clashes or died of their wounds. Still more dropped in their tracks from exhaustion, hunger, and cold. Finally, in the middle of December, the last survivors straggled out of Russia. The retreat from Moscow had devastated the Grand Army—only 10,000 soldiers were left to fight.

Napoleon's Downfall

Napoleon's enemies were quick to take advantage of his weakness. Britain, Russia, Prussia, and Sweden joined forces against him. Austria also declared war on Napoleon, despite his marriage to Marie Louise. All of the main powers of Europe were now at war with France.

Napoleon Suffers Defeat In only a few months, Napoleon managed to raise another army. However, most of his troops were untrained and ill prepared for battle. He faced the allied armies of the European powers outside the German city of Leipzig (LYP•sihg) in October 1813. The allied forces easily defeated his inexperienced army and French resistance crumbled quickly. By January of 1814, the allied armies were pushing steadily toward Paris. Some two months later, King

Napoleon's Downfall

10.2.4

Critical Thinking

- What evidence suggests that Napoleon was not a military genius? *(His decisions led to defeats in Spain and Russia.)*
- Why would the French want Napoleon to return? *(Possible Answers: He had led them to greatness before; they didn't want another king.)*

Electronic Library of Primary Sources

- "The Battle of Waterloo: The Finale"

SKILLBUILDER PRACTICE: INTERPRETING MAPS

Understanding Napoleon's Russian Campaign

Class Time 20 minutes

Task Answering questions based on a map

Purpose To understand events of the Russian campaign

Instructions Tell students that three useful tools for understanding maps are the legend, the compass rose, and the scale. The legend shows what each color or symbol represents. For example, in the map on this page, red arrows indicate the path of Napoleon's retreat. The compass rose shows the map's orientation by pointing to the north, and the scale indicates distances. Ask students the following questions:

1. What is the distance between Napoleon's starting point and Moscow? *(about 650 miles)*
2. What direction were the troops marching as they advanced? *(east)*
3. How many troops had been lost by September 7? *(about 292,000)*

For more help, use the Skillbuilder Practice for this chapter.

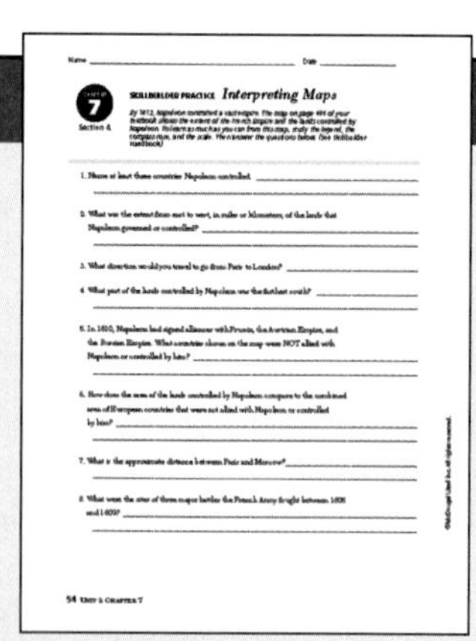

In-Depth Resources: Unit 2

Frederick William III of Prussia and Czar Alexander I of Russia led their troops in a triumphant parade through the French capital.

Napoleon wanted to fight on, but his generals refused. In April 1814, he accepted the terms of surrender and gave up his throne. The victors gave Napoleon a small pension and exiled, or banished, him to Elba, a tiny island off the Italian coast. The allies expected no further trouble from Napoleon, but they were wrong.

The Hundred Days Louis XVI's brother assumed the throne as Louis XVIII. (The executed king's son, Louis XVII, had died in prison in 1795.) However, the new king quickly became unpopular among his subjects, especially the peasants. They suspected him of wanting to undo the Revolution's land reforms.

The news of Louis's troubles was all the incentive Napoleon needed to try to regain power. He escaped from Elba and, on March 1, 1815, landed in France. Joyous crowds welcomed him on the march to Paris. And thousands of volunteers swelled the ranks of his army. Within days, Napoleon was again emperor of France. B

MAIN IDEA

Analyzing Motives

B Why do you think the French people welcomed back Napoleon so eagerly?

B. Possible Answers They expected Napoleon to protect the gains they had made under the Revolution. They thought he could return France to the great power it was early in his reign.

In response, the European allies quickly marshaled their armies. The British army, led by the Duke of Wellington, prepared for battle near the village of **Waterloo** in Belgium. On June 18, 1815, Napoleon attacked. The British army defended its ground all day. Late in the afternoon, the Prussian army arrived. Together, the British and the Prussian forces attacked the French. Two days later, Napoleon's exhausted troops gave way, and the British and Prussian forces chased them from the field.

▲ British soldiers who fought at the battle of Waterloo received this medal.

This defeat ended Napoleon's last bid for power, called the **Hundred Days**. Taking no chances this time, the British shipped Napoleon to St. Helena, a remote island in the South Atlantic. There, he lived in lonely exile for six years, writing his memoirs. He died in 1821 of a stomach ailment, perhaps cancer.

Without doubt, Napoleon was a military genius and a brilliant administrator. Yet all his victories and other achievements must be measured against the millions of lives that were lost in his wars. The French writer Alexis de Tocqueville summed up Napoleon's character by saying, "He was as great as a man can be without virtue." Napoleon's defeat opened the door for the freed European countries to establish a new order.

SECTION 4 ASSESSMENT

TERMS & NAMES 1. For each term or name, write a sentence explaining its significance.

- blockade
- Continental System
- guerrilla
- Peninsular War
- scorched-earth policy
- Waterloo
- Hundred Days

USING YOUR NOTES

2. Which of Napoleon's mistakes was the most serious? Why? (10.2.4)

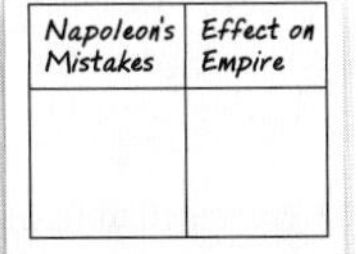

MAIN IDEAS

3. How did Great Britain combat Napoleon's naval blockade? (10.2.4)
4. Why did Napoleon have trouble fighting the enemy forces in the Peninsular War? (10.2.4)
5. Why was Napoleon's delay of the retreat from Moscow such a great blunder? (10.2.4)

CRITICAL THINKING & WRITING

6. **ANALYZING MOTIVES** Why did some people resist Napoleon's efforts to build an empire? (10.2.4)
7. **EVALUATING COURSES OF ACTION** Napoleon had no choice but to invade Russia. Do you agree with this statement? Why or why not? (10.2.4)
8. **FORMING AND SUPPORTING OPINIONS** Do you think that Napoleon was a great leader? Explain. (10.2.4)
9. **WRITING ACTIVITY** POWER AND AUTHORITY In the role of a volunteer in Napoleon's army during the Hundred Days, write a **letter** to a friend explaining why you are willing to fight for the emperor. (Writing 2.4.d)

CONNECT TO TODAY CREATING A MAP

Conduct research on how nationalist feelings affect world affairs today. Create a **map** showing the areas of the world where nationalist movements are active. Annotate the map with explanations of the situation in each area. (CST 3)

More About . . .

Napoleon's Family

When Napoleon was exiled to Elba, his second wife (Marie-Louise) and their son were sent to live with his wife's father, the emperor of Austria. Napoleon never saw his wife or son again. While Napoleon was in exile for the second time, on St. Helena, Marie-Louise became romantically involved with the Austrian officer appointed to watch over her. She married him secretly while Napoleon was still alive. The son of Napoleon and Marie-Louise, Napoleon II, grew up in Austria, but died of tuberculosis at age 21.

3 ASSESS

SECTION 4 ASSESSMENT

Have students list the numbers of the pages on which the answers to the questions can be found.

Formal Assessment

- Section Quiz, p. 122

4 RETEACH

Have students share the charts they made for item 2 in the Section Assessment.

In-Depth Resources: Unit 2

- Reteaching Activity, p. 71

ANSWERS

1. blockade, p. 234 • Continental System, p. 234 • guerrilla, p. 235 • Peninsular War, p. 235 • scorched-earth policy, p. 235 • Waterloo, p. 237 • Hundred Days, p. 237
2. **Sample Answer:** Blockade—British blockade hurt the French; Invasion of Spain—Guerrillas weakened the French; Invasion of Russia—French defeated. Most serious—The invasion of Russia; it ruined his army.
3. Great Britain supported smugglers who broke the blockade and established a blockade of its own—more effective than that of the French.
4. The Spanish used guerrilla tactics, ambushing the French and disappearing.
5. If the retreat had begun in September, the Grand Army might have exited Russia by early winter.
6. nationalism; people wanted their own leaders, not French rulers
7. Yes—To maintain his empire, he had to punish the Russians for violating the Continental System. No—He could have stopped his imperialism.
8. Yes—Initially he restored stability to France. No—He caused turmoil in Europe.
9. **Rubric** Letters should
   - explain the situation in France during the Hundred Days.
   - state why people wanted Napoleon back.

CONNECT TO TODAY

Rubric Maps should

- identify the major areas in the world affected by nationalist movements.
- briefly explain the impact of nationalism on these areas.

LESSON PLAN

OBJECTIVES

- List the results of the Congress of Vienna.
- Show how the ideas of the French Revolution continued to influence people.

1 FOCUS & MOTIVATE

List in order of importance the main functions of government. *(Possible Answer: protect property, protect liberty, provide safety, promote prosperity)* Discuss how rankings reflect one's values or social position.

2 INSTRUCT

Metternich's Plan for Europe
10.2.5

Critical Thinking

- How could Napoleon's behavior be the result of experiments with democracy? *(Possible Answer: Napoleon gained power because France's democracy was unstable.)*

In-Depth Resources: Unit 2
- Guided Reading, p. 52 (also in Spanish)

CALIFORNIA RESOURCES
California Reading Toolkit, p. L36
California Modified Lesson Plans for English Learners, p. 67
California Daily Standards Practice Transparencies, TT28
California Standards Enrichment Workbook, pp. 31–32, 105–106
California Standards Planner and Lesson Plans, p. L63
California Online Test Practice
California Test Generator CD-ROM
California Easy Planner CD-ROM
California eEdition CD-ROM

French Revolution: Assault on the Bastille, Jean-Baptiste Lallemand

Napoleon and His General Staff in Egypt, Jean-Léon Gérome

5

The Congress of Vienna

MAIN IDEA

POWER AND AUTHORITY After exiling Napoleon, European leaders at the Congress of Vienna tried to restore order and reestablish peace.

WHY IT MATTERS NOW

International bodies such as the United Nations play an active role in trying to maintain world peace and stability today.

TERMS & NAMES

- Congress of Vienna
- Klemens von Metternich
- balance of power
- legitimacy
- Holy Alliance
- Concert of Europe

CALIFORNIA STANDARDS

10.2.5 Discuss how nationalism spread across Europe with Napoleon but was repressed for a generation under the Congress of Vienna and Concert of Europe until the Revolutions of 1848.

10.9.8 Discuss the establishment and work of the United Nations and the purposes and functions of the Warsaw Pact, SEATO, NATO, and the Organization of American States.

CST 1 Students compare the present with the past, evaluating the consequences of past events and decisions and determining the lessons that were learned.

CST 3 Students use a variety of maps and documents to interpret human movement, including major patterns of domestic and international migration, changing environmental preferences and settlement patterns, the frictions that develop between population groups, and the diffusion of ideas, technological innovations, and goods.

SETTING THE STAGE European heads of government were looking to establish long-lasting peace and stability on the continent after the defeat of Napoleon. They had a goal of the new European order—one of collective security and stability for the entire continent. A series of meetings in Vienna, known as the **Congress of Vienna**, were called to set up policies to achieve this goal. Originally, the Congress of Vienna was scheduled to last for four weeks. Instead, it went on for eight months.

TAKING NOTES

Recognizing Effects Use a chart to show how the three goals of Metternich's plan at the Congress of Vienna solved a political problem.

Metternich's Plan	
Problem	Solution

Metternich's Plan for Europe

Most of the decisions made in Vienna during the winter of 1814–1815 were made in secret among representatives of the five "great powers"—Russia, Prussia, Austria, Great Britain, and France. By far the most influential of these representatives was the foreign minister of Austria, Prince **Klemens von Metternich** (MEHT•uhr•nihk).

Metternich distrusted the democratic ideals of the French Revolution. Like most other European aristocrats, he felt that Napoleon's behavior had been a natural outcome of experiments with democracy. Metternich wanted to keep things as they were and remarked, "The first and greatest concern for the immense majority of every nation is the stability of laws—never their change." Metternich had three goals at the Congress of Vienna. First, he wanted to prevent future French aggression by surrounding France with strong countries. Second, he wanted to restore a **balance of power**, so that no country would be a threat to others. Third, he wanted to restore Europe's royal families to the thrones they had held before Napoleon's conquests.

The Containment of France The Congress took the following steps to make the weak countries around France stronger:

- The former Austrian Netherlands and Dutch Republic were united to form the Kingdom of the Netherlands.
- A group of 39 German states were loosely joined as the newly created German Confederation, dominated by Austria.
- Switzerland was recognized as an independent nation.
- The Kingdom of Sardinia in Italy was strengthened by the addition of Genoa.

SECTION 5 PROGRAM RESOURCES

ALL STUDENTS

In-Depth Resources: Unit 2
- Guided Reading, p. 52

Formal Assessment
- Section Quiz, p. 123

ENGLISH LEARNERS

In-Depth Resources in Spanish
- Guided Reading, p. 63

Reading Study Guide (Spanish), p. 81
Reading Study Guide Audio CD (Spanish)

STRUGGLING READERS

In-Depth Resources: Unit 2
- Guided Reading, p. 52
- Building Vocabulary, p. 53
- Reteaching Activity, p. 72

Reading Study Guide, p. 81
Reading Study Guide Audio CD

GIFTED AND TALENTED STUDENTS

Electronic Library of Primary Sources
- from *Memoirs of Prince Klemens von Metternich*

INTEGRATED TECHNOLOGY

eEdition CD-ROM
Power Presentations CD-ROM
Critical Thinking Transparencies
- CT23 The French Revolution to the Congress of Vienna
- CT59 Chapter 7 Visual Summary

Electronic Library of Primary Sources
- from *Memoirs of Prince Klemens von Metternich*

classzone.com
- NetExplorations: The French Revolution

▲ Delegates at the Congress of Vienna study a map of Europe.

These changes enabled the countries of Europe to contain France and prevent it from overpowering weaker nations. (See the map on page 240.)

Balance of Power Although the leaders of Europe wanted to weaken France, they did not want to leave it powerless. If they severely punished France, they might encourage the French to take revenge. If they broke up France, then another country might become so strong that it would threaten them all. Thus, the victorious powers did not exact a great price from the defeated nation. As a result, France remained a major but diminished European power. Also, no country in Europe could easily overpower another.

Legitimacy The great powers affirmed the principle of **legitimacy**—agreeing that as many as possible of the rulers whom Napoleon had driven from their thrones be restored to power. The ruling families of France, Spain, and several states in Italy and Central Europe regained their thrones. The participants in the Congress of Vienna believed that the return of the former monarchs would stabilize political relations among the nations.

The Congress of Vienna was a political triumph in many ways. For the first time, the nations of an entire continent had cooperated to control political affairs. The settlements they agreed upon were fair enough that no country was left bearing a grudge. Therefore, the Congress did not sow the seeds of future wars. In that sense, it was more successful than many other peace meetings in history.

By agreeing to come to one another's aid in case of threats to peace, the European nations had temporarily ensured that there would be a balance of power on the continent. The Congress of Vienna, then, created a time of peace in Europe. It was a lasting peace. None of the five great powers waged war on one another for nearly 40 years, when Britain and France fought Russia in the Crimean War. (A)

MAIN IDEA

Drawing Conclusions

(A) In what ways was the Congress of Vienna a success?

A. Answer involved cooperation of nations of entire continent; created a new balance of power; created a time of peace

Political Changes Beyond Vienna

The Congress of Vienna was a victory for conservatives. Kings and princes resumed power in country after country, in keeping with Metternich's goals. Nevertheless, there were important differences from one country to another. Britain and France now had constitutional monarchies. Generally speaking, however, the governments in Eastern and Central Europe were more conservative. The rulers of Russia, Prussia, and Austria were absolute monarchs.

More About . . .

Metternich

Klemens von Metternich was more flexible with other countries than with internal dissent. He led a 30-year crusade to stamp out liberal and revolutionary ideas in the German states. In a set of decrees issued in 1819, he required the states to root out subversive ideas in their universities and newspapers. He established a permanent committee, with spies and informers, to punish liberal or radical organizations. Metternich advocated the ruthless suppression of any ideas promoting liberty and equality.

Critical Thinking Transparencies

- CT23 The French Revolution to the Congress of Vienna

Electronic Library of Primary Sources

- from *Memoirs of Prince Klemens von Metternich*

Political Changes Beyond Vienna

10.9.8

Critical Thinking

- Was the Congress of Vienna good for stability in the long run? *(Possible Answer: It discouraged wars but angered the lower classes.)*
- Explain whether you agree with the Congress of Vienna diplomats that stability was more important than liberty. *(Possible Answers: Agree–Stability allows people to plan. Disagree–Liberty is the basis of lasting stability.)*

DIFFERENTIATING INSTRUCTION: STRUGGLING READERS

Understanding the Balance of Power

Class Time 30 minutes

Task Analyzing the results of the Congress of Vienna

Purpose To understand the balance of power in Europe in the early 1800s

Instructions Have students use a physical outline map of Europe to visualize how the Congress of Vienna attempted to create a balance of power. Using colored pencils or crayons, students should show on the map the territory of France in 1817 and the territories of the countries that surrounded it. Have students answer the following questions:

1. Why would joining the Austrian Netherlands and the Dutch Republic help to contain France? *(It removed the temptation for France to overpower small, weak neighbors.)*
2. How did joining the 39 German states into a confederation help keep France in check? *(For the same reason: to prevent taking small, weak states.)*
3. Why didn't the Congress of Vienna take more land from France? *(Victorious countries might fight over the spoils, upsetting the balance of power.)*

Have students use the Guided Reading activity for more help.

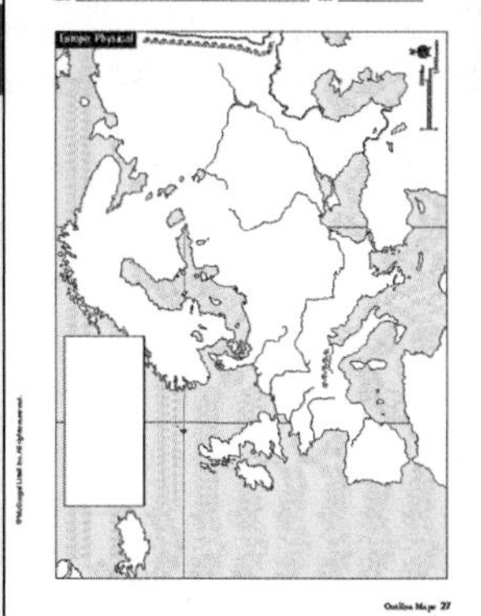

Geography Skills and Outline Maps

History from Visuals

Interpreting the Map

Ask students to compare the maps to see how the Congress of Vienna changed borders in Europe. In which part of Europe did the borders change the most? *(central)*

Extension Have students research disputes over borders between countries in the past ten years. Discuss how these disputes have been handled.

SKILLBUILDER Answers

1. **Region** all territory outside its pre-revolutionary boundaries
2. **Region** Countries that Napoleon had controlled or allied with became independent states.

INTEGRATED TECHNOLOGY

Interactive This map is available in an interactive format on the eEdition.

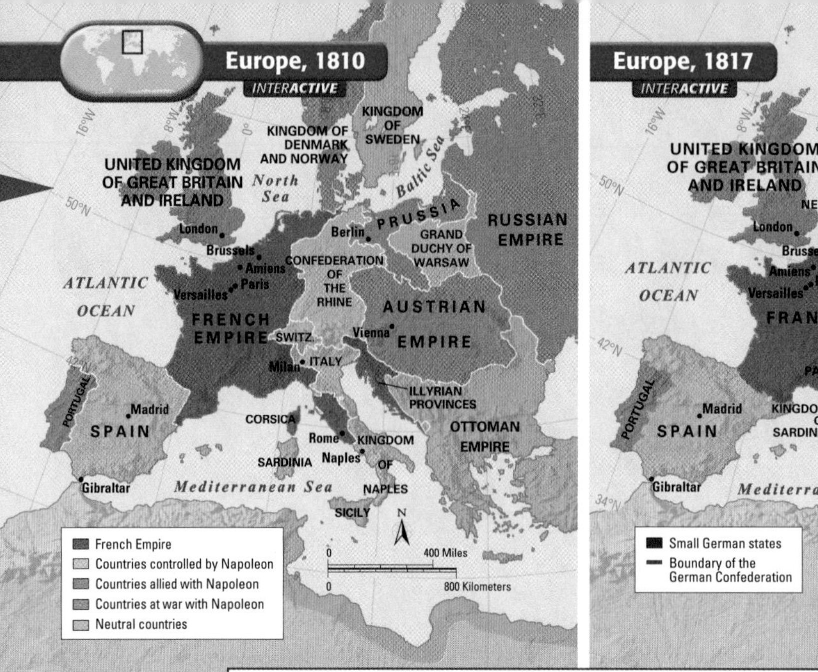

GEOGRAPHY SKILLBUILDER: Interpreting Maps

1. **Region** *What parts of Napoleon's French Empire did France lose as a result of the Congress of Vienna?*
2. **Region** *In what sense did the territorial changes of 1815 reflect a restoration of order and balance?*

Conservative Europe The rulers of Europe were very nervous about the legacy of the French Revolution. They worried that the ideals of liberty, equality, and fraternity might encourage revolutions elsewhere. Late in 1815, Czar Alexander I, Emperor Francis I of Austria, and King Frederick William III of Prussia signed an agreement called the **Holy Alliance**. In it, they pledged to base their relations with other nations on Christian principles in order to combat the forces of revolution. Finally, a series of alliances devised by Metternich, called the **Concert of Europe**, ensured that nations would help one another if any revolutions broke out.

Across Europe, conservatives held firm control of the governments, but they could not contain the ideas that had emerged during the French Revolution. France after 1815 was deeply divided politically. Conservatives were happy with the monarchy of Louis XVIII and were determined to make it last. Liberals, however, wanted the king to share more power with the legislature. And many people in the lower classes remained committed to the ideals of liberty, equality, and fraternity. Similarly, in other countries there was an explosive mixture of ideas and factions that would contribute directly to revolutions in 1830 and 1848. **B**

B. Possible Answers sharing of power, social equality, freedom of speech and religion, fair taxation, voting rights

MAIN IDEA

Making Inferences

B What seeds of democracy had been sown by the French Revolution?

Despite their efforts to undo the French Revolution, the leaders at the Congress of Vienna could not turn back the clock. The Revolution had given Europe its first experiment in democratic government. Although the experiment had failed, it had set new political ideas in motion. The major political upheavals of the early 1800s had their roots in the French Revolution.

Revolution in Latin America The actions of the Congress of Vienna had consequences far beyond events in Europe. When Napoleon deposed the king of Spain during the Peninsular War, liberal Creoles (colonists born in Spanish America)

DIFFERENTIATING INSTRUCTION: ENGLISH LEARNERS

Making Posters About Liberty

Class Time 30 minutes

Task Creating political posters that illustrate the ideals of liberty, equality, and fraternity

Purpose To understand why rulers were afraid of these ideals

Instructions Review with students the meanings of the words *liberty, equality, fraternity*. Create a chart on the chalkboard with the words and lead a discussion of their meanings:

Liberty	Freedom to own property, to speak freely, to worship freely
Equality	All persons equal under the law
Fraternity	People with a shared purpose and culture

Now have students create posters that illustrate these ideals. On their posters, students might use original drawings or photocopies of images or political cartoons. Students should also include captions, callouts, or other short sections of text. Students should present their posters to the class and explain how the poster represents the ideals so feared by the rulers of Europe.

seized control of many colonies in the Americas. When the Congress of Vienna restored the king to the Spanish throne, royalist *peninsulares* (colonists born in Spain) tried to regain control of these colonial governments. The Creoles, however, attempted to retain and expand their power. In response, the Spanish king took steps to tighten control over the American colonies.

This action angered the Mexicans, who rose in revolt and successfully threw off Spain's control. Other Spanish colonies in Latin America also claimed independence. At about the same time, Brazil declared independence from Portugal. (See Chapter 8.)

Long-Term Legacy The Congress of Vienna left a legacy that would influence world politics for the next 100 years. The continent-wide efforts to establish and maintain a balance of power diminished the size and the power of France. At the same time, the power of Britain and Prussia increased.

Nationalism began to spread in Italy, Germany, Greece, and to other areas that the Congress had put under foreign control. Eventually, the nationalistic feelings would explode into revolutions, and new nations would be formed. European colonies also responded to the power shift. Spanish colonies took advantage of the events in Europe to declare their independence and break away from Spain.

At the same time, ideas about the basis of power and authority had changed permanently as a result of the French Revolution. More and more, people saw democracy as the best way to ensure equality and justice for all. The French Revolution, then, changed the social attitudes and assumptions that had dominated Europe for centuries. A new era had begun. C

C. Answer Colonies wanted independence, and ideas about power and authority changed forever.

MAIN IDEA

Recognizing Effects

C How did the French Revolution affect not only Europe but also other areas of the world?

Connect *to* Today

Congress of Vienna and the United Nations

The Congress of Vienna and the Concert of Europe tried to keep the world safe from war. The modern equivalent of these agreements is the United Nations (UN), an international organization established in 1945 and continuing today, whose purpose is to promote world peace.

Like the Congress of Vienna, the United Nations was formed by major powers after a war—World War II. These powers agreed to cooperate to reduce tensions and bring greater harmony to international relations. Throughout its history, the United Nations has used diplomacy as its chief method of keeping the peace.

INTEGRATED TECHNOLOGY

INTERNET ACTIVITY Create a graphic organizer to show the major agencies and functions of the United Nations. Go to **classzone.com** for your research.

SECTION 5 ASSESSMENT

TERMS & NAMES 1. For each term or name, write a sentence explaining its significance.

• Congress of Vienna • Klemens von Metternich • balance of power • legitimacy • Holy Alliance • Concert of Europe

USING YOUR NOTES

2. What was the overall effect of Metternich's plan on France? (10.2.5)

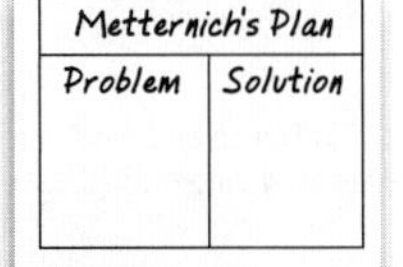

MAIN IDEAS

3. What were the three points of Metternich's plan for Europe? (10.2.5)
4. Why was the Congress of Vienna considered a success? (10.2.5)
5. What was the long-term legacy of the Congress of Vienna? (10.2.5)

CRITICAL THINKING & WRITING

6. **DRAWING CONCLUSIONS** From France's point of view, were Congress of Vienna's decisions fair? (10.2.5)
7. **ANALYZING ISSUES** Why did liberals and conservatives differ over who should have power? (10.2.5)
8. **MAKING INFERENCES** What do you think is meant by the statement that the French Revolution let the "genie out of the bottle"? (10.2.5)
9. **WRITING ACTIVITY** POWER AND AUTHORITY In the role of a newspaper editor in the early 1800s, write an **editorial**—pro or con—on the Congress of Vienna and its impact on politics in Europe. (Writing 2.6.b)

CONNECT TO TODAY **CREATING A SCRAPBOOK**

Work in pairs to locate recent articles in newspapers and magazines on the peacekeeping efforts of the UN. Photocopy or clip the articles and use them to create a **scrapbook** titled "The UN as Peacekeeper." (10.9.8)

Connect *to* Today

Congress of Vienna and the United Nations

Ask one group of students to check national newspapers for one week and to clip all articles referring to the United Nations. Assign another group to take notes about coverage of the UN on television news shows. As a class, make a list of current UN activities.

INTEGRATED TECHNOLOGY

Rubric Graphic organizers should

- include the most important UN agencies.
- identify functions of agencies.
- show clear lines of connection between agencies.

3 ASSESS

SECTION 5 ASSESSMENT

Have students work in pairs to answer the questions, then share their answers with another pair of students.

Formal Assessment

- Section Quiz, p. 123

4 RETEACH

Have students propose up to twenty questions for a quiz on this section. Then select the ten questions that students think are most important. Discuss the answers to the questions in class.

Critical Thinking Transparencies

- CT59 Chapter 7 Visual Summary

In-Depth Resources: Unit 2

- Reteaching Activity, p. 72

ANSWERS

1. Congress of Vienna, p. 238 • Klemens von Metternich, p. 238 • balance of power, p. 238 • legitimacy, p. 239 • Holy Alliance, p. 240 • Concert of Europe, p. 240

2. **Sample Answer:** Problems—1. Contain France. 2. Establish a government for France. Solutions—1. Surround France with stronger countries. 2. Restore the French monarchy. Effect—France remained intact; peace lasted for 40 years.
3. strengthen France's neighbors, restore the balance of power in Europe, restore Europe's monarchs to their thrones
4. because it lasted for 40 years
5. Foreign control led to calls for revolution.
6. Yes—France remained intact. No—France lost all it had won.
7. **Possible Answer:** Liberals shared ideas with the lower classes.
8. **Possible Answer:** Once the French Revolution exposed the people to liberty, equality, and democracy, these ideas could not be ignored.
9. **Rubric** Editorials should
   - describe clearly agreements made at the Congress of Vienna.
   - use facts and details to support the main point.

CONNECT TO TODAY

Rubric Scrapbooks should

- illustrate the peacekeeping role of the UN.
- include at least four articles on the UN as peacekeeper.

TERMS & NAMES

1. estate, p. 217
2. Great Fear, p. 221
3. guillotine, p. 226
4. Maximilien Robespierre, p. 226
5. coup d'état, p. 230
6. Napoleonic Code, p. 230
7. Waterloo, p. 237
8. Congress of Vienna, p. 238

MAIN IDEAS

Answers will vary.

9. They were heavily taxed and lacked political power.
10. The Bastille symbolized repression under the Old Regime.
11. creation of a limited constitutional monarchy with power to create laws and approve or reject declarations of war
12. an effort to rid France of "enemies of the Revolution"; ended when members of the National Convention turned against Robespierre and executed him
13. a code of laws; a fairer tax code; took steps to end government corruption; public schools open to all; merit-based bureaucracy; Church power reduced, religious tolerance supported
14. He conquered much of Europe and put members of his family on the thrones of several nations.
15. scorched-earth policy by Russians, bitterly cold Russian winter
16. Napoleon's army had been greatly weakened by Russian and peninsular campaigns; enemy forces were too numerous.
17. prevent further French aggression, restore balance of power, restore royal families to thrones held before Napoleon's conquests
18. balance of power worked; mutual-aid agreements among nations helped ensure stability

Chapter 7 Assessment

VISUAL SUMMARY

The French Revolution and Napoleon

Long-Term Causes
- Social and economic injustices of the Old Regime
- Enlightenment ideas—liberty and equality
- Example furnished by the American Revolution

Immediate Causes
- Economic crisis—famine and government debt
- Weak leadership
- Discontent of the Third Estate

Revolution
- Fall of the Bastille
- National Assembly
- Declaration of the Rights of Man and of the Citizen and a new constitution

Immediate Effects
- End of the Old Regime
- Execution of monarch
- War with other European nations
- Reign of Terror
- Rise of Napoleon

Long-Term Effects
- Conservative reaction
- Decline in French power
- Spread of Enlightenment ideas
- Growth of nationalism
- Revolutions in Latin America

TERMS & NAMES

For each term or name below, briefly explain its connection to the French Revolution or the rise and fall of Napoleon.

1. estate
2. Great Fear
3. guillotine
4. Maximilien Robespierre
5. coup d'état
6. Napoleonic Code
7. Waterloo
8. Congress of Vienna

MAIN IDEAS

The French Revolution Begins Section 1 (pages 217–221)

9. Why were the members of the Third Estate dissatisfied with their way of life under the Old Regime? (10.2.4)
10. Why was the fall of the Bastille important to the French people? (10.2.4)

Revolution Brings Reform and Terror Section 2 (pages 222–228)

11. What political reforms resulted from the French Revolution? (10.2.4)
12. What was the Reign of Terror, and how did it end? (10.2.4)

Napoleon Forges an Empire Section 3 (pages 229–233)

13. What reforms did Napoleon introduce? (10.2.5)
14. What steps did Napoleon take to create an empire in Europe? (10.2.4)

Napoleon's Empire Collapses Section 4 (pages 234–237)

15. What factors led to Napoleon's defeat in Russia? (10.2.4)
16. Why were the European allies able to defeat Napoleon in 1814 and again in 1815? (10.2.4)

The Congress of Vienna Section 5 (pages 238–241)

17. What were Metternich's three goals at the Congress of Vienna? (10.2.5)
18. How did the Congress of Vienna ensure peace in Europe? (10.2.5)

CRITICAL THINKING

1. **USING YOUR NOTES**
Copy the chart of dates and events in Napoleon's career into your notebook. For each event, draw an arrow up or down to show whether Napoleon gained or lost power because of the event. (10.2.5)

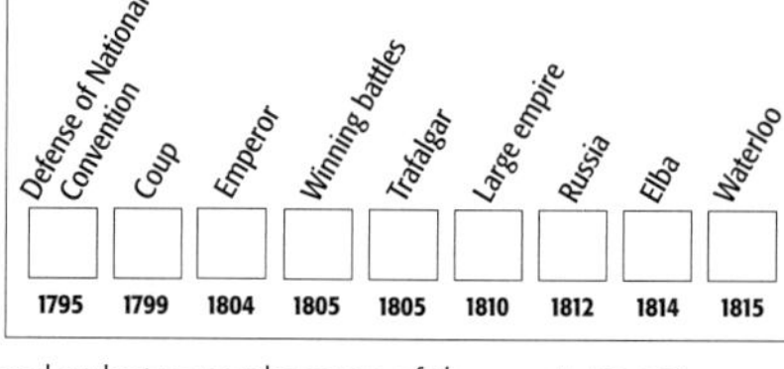

2. **COMPARING AND CONTRASTING**
ECONOMICS How were the economic conditions in France and the American colonies before their revolutions similar? How were they different? (10.2.4)

3. **ANALYZING ISSUES**
REVOLUTION There is a saying: "Revolutions devour their own children." What evidence from this chapter supports that statement? (10.2.4)

4. **RECOGNIZING EFFECTS**
POWER AND AUTHORITY How did the Congress of Vienna affect power and authority in European countries after Napoleon's defeat? Consider who held power in the countries and the power of the countries themselves. (10.2.5)

CRITICAL THINKING

Answers will vary.

1. Defense of National Convention—Gained; Coup—Gained; Emperor—Gained; Winning battles—Gained; Trafalgar—Lost; Large empire—Gained; Russia—Lost; Elba—Lost; Waterloo—Lost.
2. **Sample Answer:** Similarities—Unfair taxes, resentment of the monarchy; Differences—Colonies had slavery, France had a rigid class system.
3. **Possible Answer:** Revolution degenerated into mob rule and a bloody dictatorship. Many revolutionary leaders were executed during the Reign of Terror.
4. **Possible Answer:** It restored the royalty and aristocracy to power and established a balance of power among the European nations.

STANDARDS-BASED ASSESSMENT

Use the excerpt—from the South American liberator Simón Bolívar, whose country considered giving refuge to Napoleon after Waterloo—and your knowledge of world history to answer questions 1 and 2.
Additional Test Practice, pp. S1–S33

PRIMARY SOURCE

If South America is struck by the thunderbolt of Bonaparte's arrival, misfortune will ever be ours if our country accords him a friendly reception. His thirst for conquest is insatiable [cannot be satisfied]; he has mowed down the flower of European youth . . . in order to carry out his ambitious projects. The same designs will bring him to the New World.

SIMÓN BOLÍVAR

1. In Bolívar's opinion, if his country gave Napoleon a friendly reception, it would (10.2.4)
   - **A.** be beset by misfortune.
   - **B.** become a great power in South America.
   - **C.** become a part of the French Empire.
   - **D.** be attacked by the United States.
2. Which of the following gives Bolívar's view of Napoleon? (10.2.4)
   - **A.** His desire for power cannot be satisfied.
   - **B.** He is not ambitious.
   - **C.** He cares for the lives of others.
   - **D.** He does not want to come to the New World.

Use the map, which shows Great Britain and the French Empire in 1810, and your knowledge of world history to answer question 3.

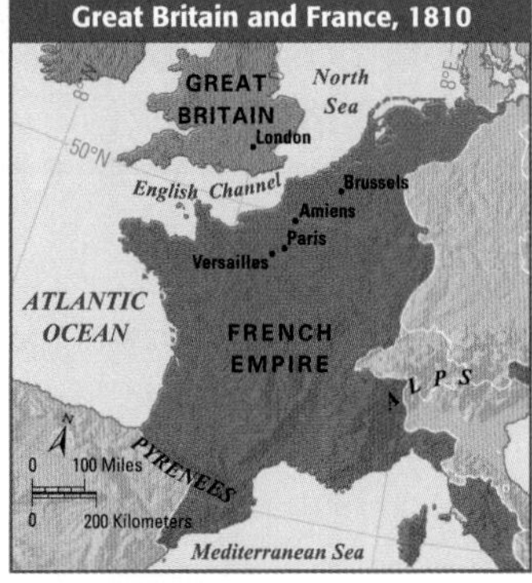

3. What geographical barrier helped to protect Britain from an invasion by Napoleon? (10.2.4)
   - **A.** Mediterranean Sea
   - **B.** English Channel
   - **C.** Alps
   - **D.** Pyrenees

INTEGRATED TECHNOLOGY

TEST PRACTICE Go to **classzone.com**
- Diagnostic tests
- Tutorials
- Strategies
- Additional practice

ALTERNATIVE ASSESSMENT

1. **Interact *with* History** (10.2.4)
   On page 216, you considered how to bring about change in the French government in the late 1700s. Now that you have read the chapter, reevaluate your thoughts on how to change an unjust government. Was violent revolution justified? effective? Would you have advised different actions? Discuss your opinions with a small group.
2. **WRITING ABOUT HISTORY** (Writing 2.1.c)
   Imagine that you lived in Paris throughout the French Revolution. Write **journal entries** on several of the major events of the Revolution. Include the following events:
   - the storming of the Bastille
   - the women's march on Versailles
   - the trial of Louis XVI
   - the Reign of Terror
   - the rise of Napoleon

INTEGRATED TECHNOLOGY

NetExplorations: The French Revolution (Writing 2.6.b)

Go to *NetExplorations* at **classzone.com** to learn more about the French Revolution. Then plan a virtual field trip to sites in France related to the revolution. Be sure to include sites outside Paris. Begin your research by exploring the Web sites recommended at *NetExplorations*. Include the following in your field trip plan:
- a one-paragraph description of each site and the events that happened there
- specific buildings, statues, or other items to view at each site
- documents and other readings to help visitors prepare for each stop on the field trip
- topics to discuss at each site
- a list of Web sites used to create your virtual field trip

STANDARDS-BASED ASSESSMENT

1. Letter **A** is the correct answer, since Bolívar states that "misfortune will ever be ours" if the country welcomes Napoleon warmly. Letter **B** is incorrect, since Bolívar does not discuss the power situation in South America. Letter **C** is incorrect, because the French Empire was dismantled after Waterloo. Letter **D** is incorrect; the United States is not mentioned in the excerpt.
2. Letter **A** is correct, since Bolívar refers to Napoleon's "insatiable" ambition. Letter **B** is incorrect, since Bolívar clearly states that Napoleon is motivated by ambition. Letters **C** and **D** are incorrect. Bolívar does not say whether Napoleon is motivated by a concern for people or whether he wants to come to South America.
3. Letter **B** is correct. The English Channel provided Great Britain with some protection from a direct attack by Napoleon. Letter **A** is incorrect, since the Mediterranean Sea lies to the south of France, while Great Britain lies to the north. Letter **C** is incorrect, since the Alps mark the southeast border of France. Similarly, letter **D** is incorrect because the Pyrenees mark France's southwest border.

Formal Assessment
- Chapter Test, Forms A, B, and C, pp. 124–135

California Test Generator CD-ROM
- Chapter Tests, Forms A, B, and C (English and Spanish)

ALTERNATIVE ASSESSMENT

1. Students might be more skeptical of violence, fearing that it would lead to terror, military dictatorship, or war. Others might argue that violence was necessary because of the reluctance of the Old Regime to compromise and the lack of alternatives in the face of dire conditions.
2. **Rubric** Journal entries should
   - provide a vivid picture of events of the French Revolution.
   - be written as if the writer were an eyewitness to these events.
   - use standard grammar, spelling, and punctuation.

INTEGRATED TECHNOLOGY

Rubric Virtual field trips should
- include sites inside and outside Paris.
- have detailed, accurate, relevant information.
- feature documents and discussion topics.
- cite sources.

CHAPTER 8 PLANNING GUIDE

Nationalist Revolutions Sweep the West, 1789–1900

CHAPTER RESOURCES	COPYMASTERS	ASSESSMENT
CHAPTER OVERVIEW Inspired by Enlightenment ideas, nationalist revolutions swept through Latin America and Europe.	**In-Depth Resources: Unit 2** • Building Vocabulary, p. 77 **Chapters in Brief** (in English and Spanish) **Block Schedule Pacing Guide**	**Chapter Assessment,** pp. 270–271 **Formal Assessment** • Chapter Tests, Forms A, B, and C, pp. 140-154 **Test Generator** **Integrated Assessment Book** **Online Test Practice**
SECTION 1 **Latin American Peoples Win Independence** pp. 247–252 **OBJECTIVE** Describe colonial society in Latin America and explain how the peoples of Latin America won their independence.	**In-Depth Resources: Unit 2** • Guided Reading, p. 73 • Skillbuilder Practice: Hypothesizing, p. 78 • Primary Source: from Proclamation of 1813, p. 81 • Literature: from *All Souls' Rising,* p. 85 • History Makers: Simón Bolívar, p. 88 • Reteaching Activity, p. 91 **Reading Study Guide,** p. 85	**Section 1 Assessment,** p. 252 **Formal Assessment** • Section Quiz, p. 136 **California Daily Standards Practice Transparencies,** TT89
SECTION 2 **Europe Faces Revolutions** pp. 253–257 **OBJECTIVE** Explain the three schools of political thought and trace the spread of nationalist movements throughout Europe.	**In-Depth Resources: Unit 2** • Guided Reading, p. 74 • Primary Source: *Letter to Thomas Moore,* p. 82 • Reteaching Activity, p. 92 **Reading Study Guide,** p. 87	**Section 2 Assessment,** p. 257 **Formal Assessment** • Section Quiz, p. 137 **California Daily Standards Practice Transparencies,** TT90
SECTION 3 **Case Study: Nationalism—Italy and Germany** pp. 258–263 **OBJECTIVE** Summarize how nationalism led to the weakening of several empires and the unification of Italy and Germany.	**In-Depth Resources: Unit 2** • Guided Reading, p. 75 • Geography Application, p. 79 • Primary Sources: Proclamation of 1860, p. 83; Nationalist Speech, p. 84 • Connections Across Time and Cultures: Bonds That Create a Nation-State, p. 90 • Reteaching Activity, p. 93 **Reading Study Guide,** p. 89	**Section 3 Assessment,** p. 263 **Formal Assessment** • Section Quiz, p. 138 **California Daily Standards Practice Transparencies,** TT91
SECTION 4 **Revolutions in the Arts** pp. 264–269 **OBJECTIVE** Analyze romanticism, realism, and impressionism in the arts.	**In-Depth Resources: Unit 2** • Guided Reading, p. 76 • History Makers: Beethoven, p. 89 • Reteaching Activity, p. 94 **Reading Study Guide,** p. 91	**Section 4 Assessment,** p. 267 **Formal Assessment** • Section Quiz, p. 139 **California Daily Standards Practice Transparencies,** TT92

INTEGRATED TECHNOLOGY

- eEdition Plus Online
- EasyPlanner Plus Online
- eTest Plus Online

Audio CDs
- Voices from the Past
- Reading Study Guides

 **CD-ROMs**
- eEdition
- Power Presentations
- EasyPlanner
- Electronic Library of Primary Sources
- Test Generator

 **eEdition CD-ROM**

World Art and Cultures Transparencies
- AT52 *Father Miguel Hidalgo Crowns Mexico*

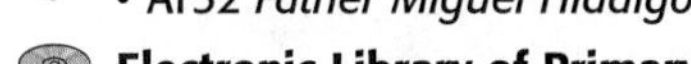
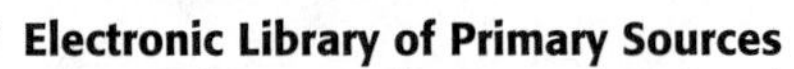
Electronic Library of Primary Sources
- from Address to the Second National Congress of Venezuela, 1819

Patterns of Interaction Video Series
- *Revolutions in Latin America and South Africa*

classzone.com

 **eEdition CD-ROM**

 **classzone.com**

 **eEdition CD-ROM**

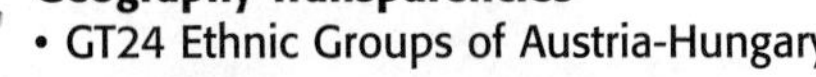
Geography Transparencies
- GT24 Ethnic Groups of Austria-Hungary

 **Critical Thinking Transparencies**
- CT24 The Unification of Germany and Italy

Electronic Library of Primary Sources
- from "Duties of Country"

 **classzone.com**

 **eEdition CD-ROM**

 **World Art and Cultures Transparencies**
- AT53 *Couturiere*

Critical Thinking Transparencies
- CT60 Chapter 8 Visual Summary

Electronic Library of Primary Sources
- "Kubla Khan"
- from *Frankenstein*

 **classzone.com**

OVERVIEW OF CALIFORNIA RESOURCES

	Section 1	Section 2	Section 3	Section 4
California Reading Toolkit	p. L37	p. L38	p. L39	p. L40
California Modified Lesson Plans for English Learners	p. 69	p. 71	p. 73	p. 75
California Daily Standards Practice Transparencies	TT29	TT30	TT31	TT32
California Standards Enrichment Workbook	pp. 23–24, 49–50, 51–52, 53–54	pp. 29–30, 31–32, 101–102	pp. 31–32	pp. 25–26, 31–32, 45–46
California Standards Planner and Lesson Plans	p. L65	p. L67	p. L69	p. L71
California Online Test Practice	classzone.com	classzone.com	classzone.com	classzone.com
California Test Generator CD-ROM				
California Easy Planner CD-ROM				
California eEdition CD-ROM				

Chart Key:

 Copymaster

 Pupil's Edition

Audio Library

Teacher's Edition

 CD-ROM

 Overhead Transparency

 Internet

 Block Scheduling

 Video

NO TIME?

If you do not have time to teach this chapter in full, assign the **Chapter in Brief** (also available in Spanish).

Previewing Resources for Differentiated Instruction

ENGLISH LEARNERS: Resources in Spanish

In-Depth Resources in Spanish
- Guided Reading Ⓐ
- Skillbuilder Practice: Hypothesizing Ⓑ
- Geography Application: Languages Fuel Nationalism

Chapters in Brief

Reading Study Guide Ⓒ

Reading Study Guide Audio CD

Test Generator CD-ROM
- Chapter Test, Forms A, B, and C

Plus

Modified Lesson Plans for English Learners

Multi-Language Glossary of Social Studies Terms

Ⓐ
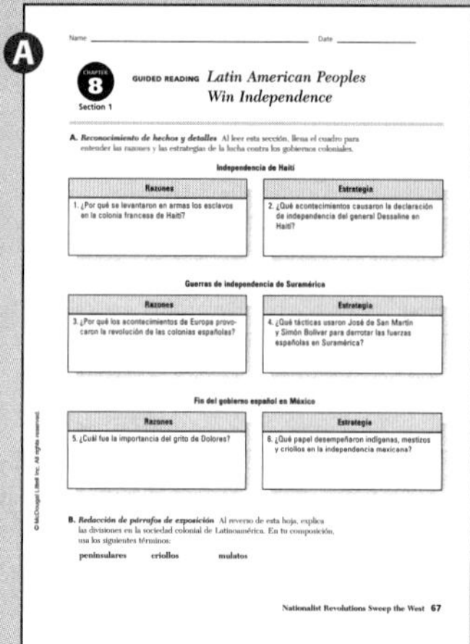
CHAPTER 8 Section 1 GUIDED READING *Latin American Peoples Win Independence*

Independencia de Haití

Guerras de independencia de Suramérica

Fin del gobierno español en México

peninsulares criollos mulatos

Nationalist Revolutions Sweep the West 67

Ⓑ
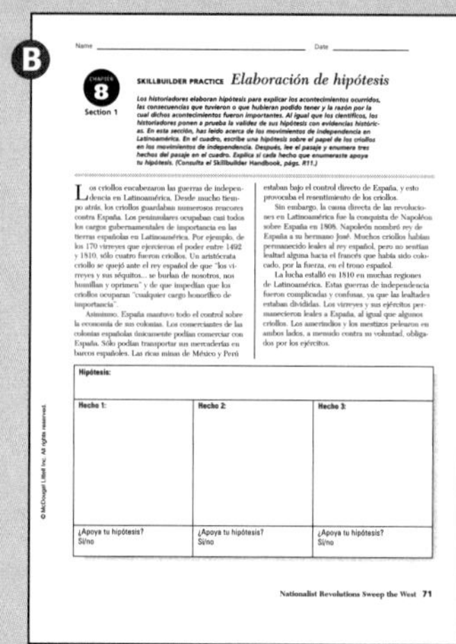
CHAPTER 8 Section 1 SKILLBUILDER PRACTICE *Elaboración de hipótesis*

Hipótesis:

Hecho 1: Hecho 2: Hecho 3:

Nationalist Revolutions Sweep the West 71

STRUGGLING READERS

In-Depth Resources: Unit 2
- Guided Reading Ⓐ
- Building Vocabulary
- Skillbuilder Practice: Hypothesizing
- Geography Application: Languages Fuel Nationalism Ⓑ
- Reteaching Activities

Chapters in Brief

Reading Study Guide Ⓒ

Reading Study Guide Audio CD

Formal Assessment
- Chapter Test, Form A

Plus

Reading Toolkit

Ⓐ
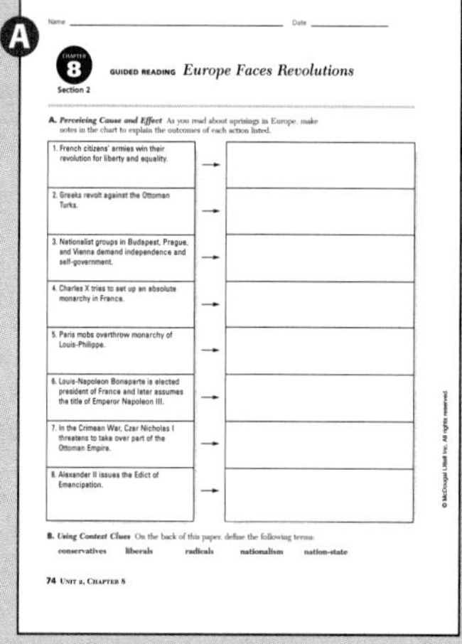
CHAPTER 8 Section 2 GUIDED READING *Europe Faces Revolutions*

A. *Perceiving Cause and Effect* As you read about uprisings in Europe, make notes in the chart to explain the outcomes of each action listed.

1. French citizens' armies win their revolution for liberty and equality.
2. Greeks revolt against the Ottoman Turks.
3. Nationalist groups in Budapest, Prague, and Vienna demand independence and self-government.
4. Charles X tries to set up an absolute monarchy in France.
5. Paris mobs overthrow monarchy of Louis-Philippe.
6. Louis-Napoleon Bonaparte is elected president of France and later assumes the title of Emperor Napoleon III.
7. In the Crimean War, Czar Nicholas I threatens to take over part of the Ottoman Empire.
8. Alexander II issues the Edict of Emancipation.

B. *Using Context Clues* On the back of this paper, define the following terms.

conservatives liberals radicals nationalism nation-state

74 Unit 2, Chapter 8

Ⓑ
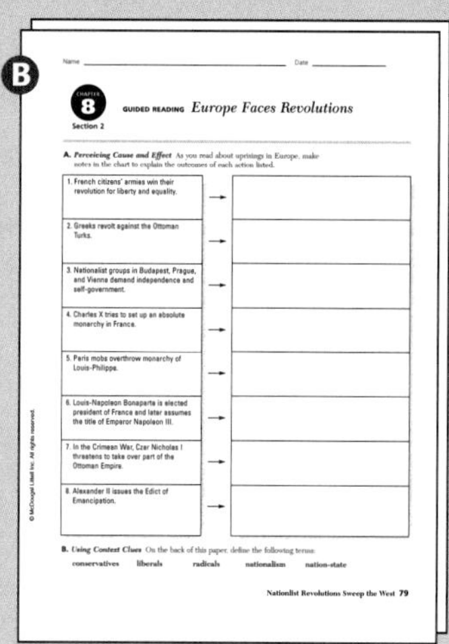
CHAPTER 8 Section 2 GUIDED READING *Europe Faces Revolutions*

Nationalist Revolutions Sweep the West 79

GIFTED AND TALENTED STUDENTS

In-Depth Resources: Unit 2
- Primary Source: from Proclamation of 1813; *Letter to Thomas Moore;* Proclamation of 1860 Ⓐ; Nationalist Speech by Otto von Bismarck
- Literature: from *All Souls' Rising*
- History Makers: Simón Bolívar; Beethoven
- Connections Across Time and Cultures: Bonds that Create a Nation-State Ⓑ

Electronic Library of Primary Sources
- from Address to the Second National Congress of Venezuela, 1819
- from "Duties of Country"
- "Kubla Khan"
- from *Frankenstein*

Formal Assessment
- Chapter Test, Form C Ⓒ

Ⓐ
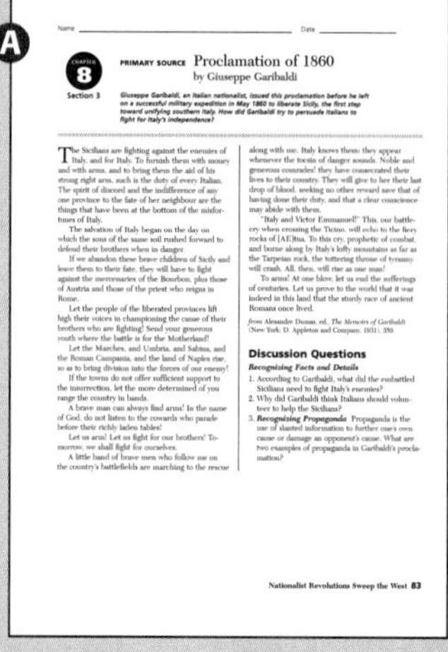
CHAPTER 8 Section 3 PRIMARY SOURCE Proclamation of 1860 by Giuseppe Garibaldi

Discussion Questions

Nationalist Revolutions Sweep the West 83

Ⓑ

CHAPTER 8 Section 3 CONNECTIONS ACROSS TIME AND CULTURES *Bonds That Create a Nation-State*

Common Bonds That Link the People of the United States Today

1. Nationality
2. Territory/Land
3. Government
4. Language
5. Religion
6. Culture
7. Economy
8. Other

90 Unit 2, Chapter 8

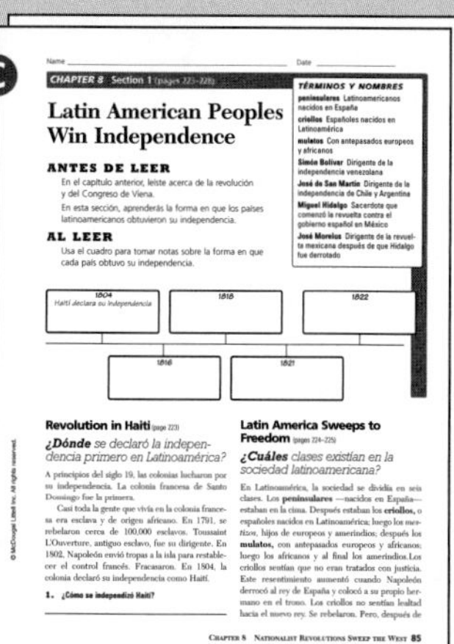
CHAPTER 8 Section 1

Latin American Peoples Win Independence

ANTES DE LEER

AL LEER

Revolution in Haiti

Latin America Sweeps to Freedom

Activities in the Teacher's Edition for English Learners

- Independence Day Celebrations, p. 251
- Nationalist Revolutions: Key Terms, p. 255
- Understanding Italian and German Unification, p. 261
- Words Related to the Arts, p. 265

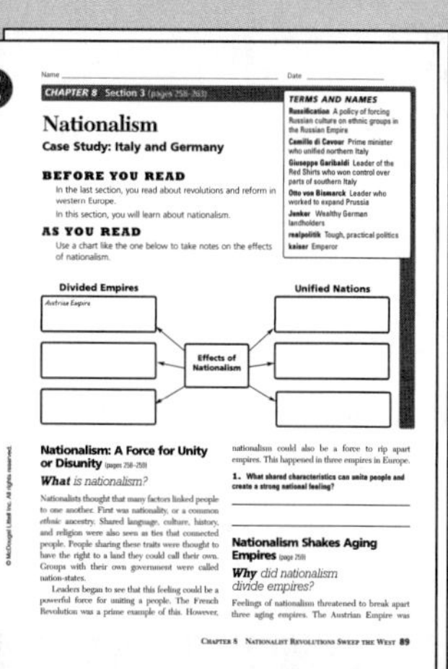
CHAPTER 8 Section 3

Nationalism

Case Study: Italy and Germany

BEFORE YOU READ

AS YOU READ

Divided Empires

Unified Nations

Nationalism: A Force for Unity or Disunity

Nationalism Shakes Aging Empires

Activities in the Teacher's Edition for Struggling Readers

- Understanding Class Structure, p. 248
- Role Playing Political Positions, p. 256
- Images Related to Nationalism, p. 262
- Understanding Art Movements, p. 266

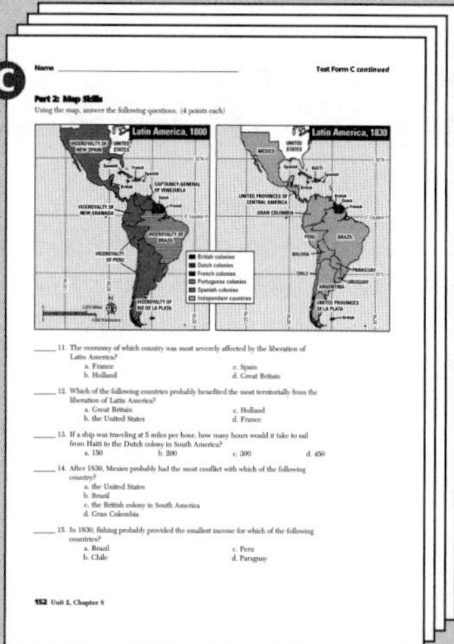
Part 2: Map Skills

Latin America, 1800

Latin America, 1830

Activities in the Teacher's Edition for Gifted and Talented Students

- Creating a News Report about Garibaldi, p. 260

INTEGRATED TECHNOLOGY

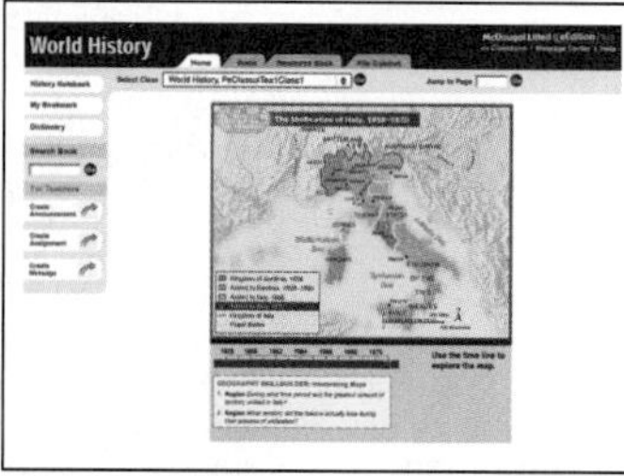

eEdition
- Interactive Visuals
- Interactive Maps
- Interactive Primary Sources

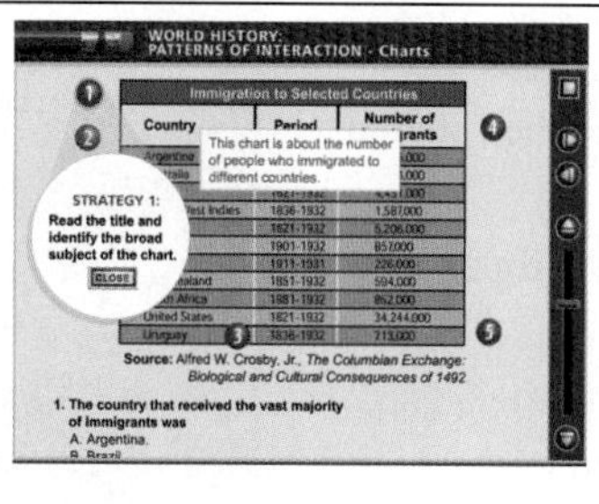

classzone.com
- Research Links
- Internet Activities
- Primary Sources
- Chapter Quiz
- Current Events

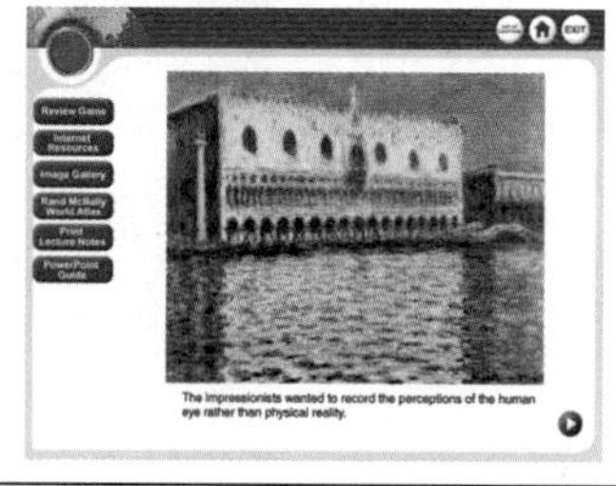

Power Presentations CD-ROM
- Lecture Notes
- Image Gallery
- Chapter Review Game

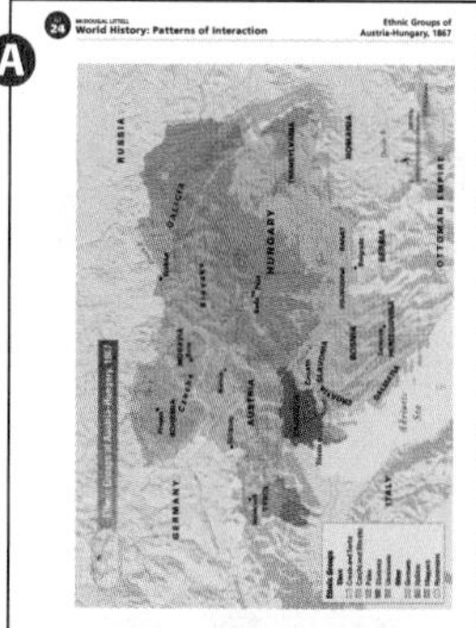

Critical Thinking Transparencies
- CT24 The Unification of Germany and Italy
- CT60 Chapter 8 Visual Summary

Geography Transparencies
- GT24 Ethnic Groups of Austria-Hungary, 1867 Ⓐ

World Art and Cultures Transparencies
- AT52 *Father Miguel Hidalgo Crowns Mexico*
- AT53 *Couturiere*

Test Practice Transparencies TT89–TT92

Test Generator CD-ROM

EasyPlanner CD-ROM

Voices from the Past Audio CD

Online Test Practice

Electronic Library of Primary Sources

Patterns of Interaction Video Series

CHAPTER 8 • OBJECTIVE

Examine the great shifts in thinking that altered politics and the arts during the period 1789–1900.

Previewing Main Ideas

Emphasize that between 1789 and 1900 great changes occurred in Western thinking. These new ideas sparked rebellions and wars throughout Europe and Latin America as adherents of democracy, nationalism, and monarchy clashed. These same changes affected the arts as classicism gave way to the exuberance of romanticism, which in turn faded into realism and then shifted to impressionism.

Accessing Prior Knowledge

Ask students to recall the last Olympic competition and the excitement it stirred up as U.S. teams competed for gold medals. Ask students which teams they rooted for. Point out that their loyalty to American teams is a form of nationalism. This same feeling of loyalty to one's own culture and people propelled many of the events of 1789–1900.

Geography *Answers*

REVOLUTION Haiti and Mexico worked toward independence.

POWER AND AUTHORITY The greatest number of revolts occurred in the Austrian Empire.

CULTURAL INTERACTION In 1837, Louis Daguerre perfected a method for photography.

CHAPTER 8

Nationalist Revolutions Sweep the West, 1789–1900

Previewing Main Ideas

REVOLUTION Inspired by Enlightenment ideas, the people of Latin America rebelled against European rule in the early 19th century. Rebels in Europe responded to nationalistic calls for independence.

Geography *Study the time line. What were the first two countries in Latin America and the Caribbean to work toward independence?*

POWER AND AUTHORITY Challenges by nationalist groups created unrest in Europe. Strong leaders united Italian lands and German-speaking lands.

Geography *Based on the map, in which area of Europe did the greatest number of revolts occur?*

CULTURAL INTERACTION Artists and intellectuals created new schools of thought. Romanticism and realism changed the way the world was viewed.

Geography *Which event shown on the time line involves a realistic way to view the world?*

INTEGRATED TECHNOLOGY

eEdition
- Interactive Maps
- Interactive Visuals
- Interactive Primary Sources

VIDEO *Patterns of Interaction: Revolutions in Latin America and South Africa*

INTERNET RESOURCES

Go to **classzone.com** for:
- Research Links
- Internet Activities
- Primary Sources
- Chapter Quiz
- Maps
- Test Practice
- Current Events

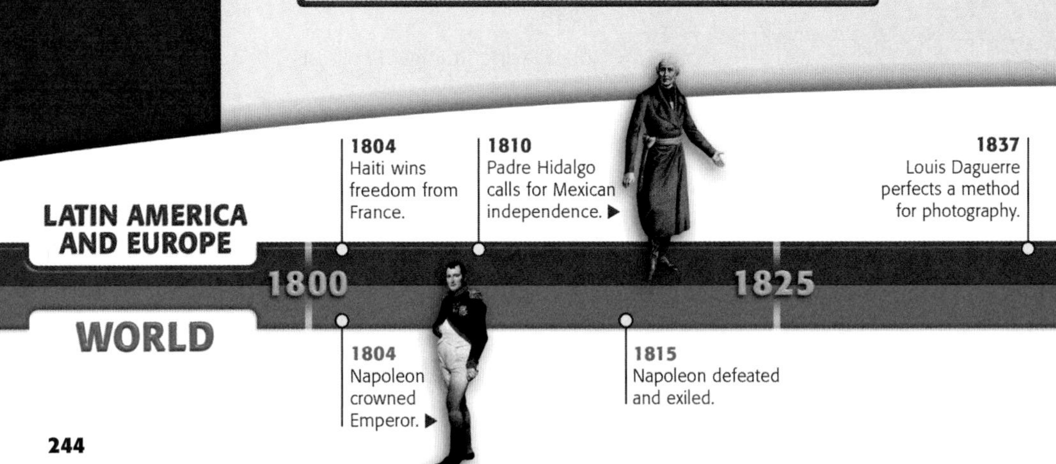
LATIN AMERICA AND EUROPE
WORLD
1800
1825
1804
Haiti wins freedom from France.
1810
Padre Hidalgo calls for Mexican independence. ▶
1837
Louis Daguerre perfects a method for photography.
1804
Napoleon crowned Emperor. ▶
1815
Napoleon defeated and exiled.

244

TIME LINE DISCUSSION

Point out that Western civilization underwent radical changes during the period 1789–1900. Many of these changes continue to affect us today.

1. In what year did Padre Hidalgo call for Mexican independence? Why is this event still important? *(1810; Mexico continues as a free, democratic country.)*
2. For how many years did Napoleon rule France as emperor? *(11 years)*
3. What two major events occurred during the 1860s? How were they similar? *(Russia freed the serfs in 1861; Lincoln freed slaves in the Confederate states in 1863. Both events brought freedom to a large class of people who'd never known freedom before.)*
4. How did the final event shown on the time line close out the century on the exact opposite tone than that with which it began? *(Haiti won its independence at the beginning of the century; the Berlin Conference took place at the end. The Haitian victory ended colonial rule of that nation, whereas the Berlin Conference divided Africa into colonies.)*

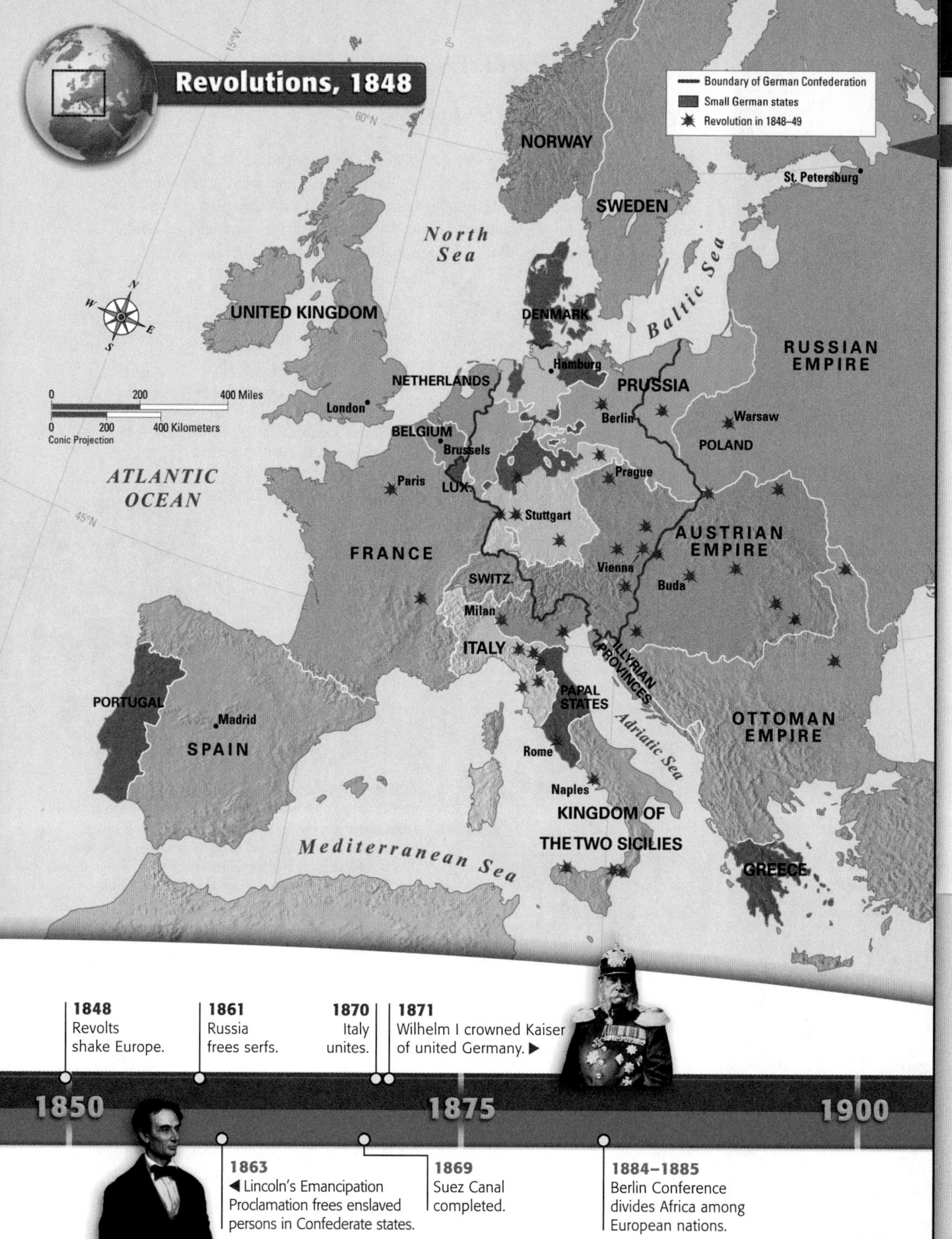

CHAPTER 8

History from Visuals

Interpreting the Map

Remind students that places within a region share certain similarities. Tell students that Spain and Portugal are part of a region. Ask, What similarities do they share? *(They share the same [Iberian] peninsula.)*

Ask students to identify other regions shown on the map and to name a common characteristic of each. *(Possible Answers: Italy, Papal States, Kingdom of the Two Sicilies share the same peninsula; Norway and Sweden share a peninsula and, along with Denmark, border the North Sea; the Ottoman Empire and Russia border the Black Sea.)*

Extension The events of the 1800s resulted in many changes to the boundaries of European countries. Have students examine the Political Atlas of Europe. Ask students which modern countries have been formed in part from the Austrian Empire? *(Germany, Austria, Hungary, Slovenia, Slovakia, Poland, Czech Republic, Italy, Romania, Croatia, Serbia, and Montenegro)*

RECOMMENDED RESOURCES

Books for the Teacher

Friedrich, Otto. ***Blood and Iron: From Bismarck to Hitler, the Von Moltke Family's Impact on German History.*** New York: HarperCollins, 1995.

Tenenbaum, Barbara A., ed. ***Encyclopedia of Latin American History and Culture.*** New York: Scribner's, 1996.

Books for the Student

Stefoff, Rebecca. ***Independence and the Revolution in Mexico, 1810–1940.*** New York: Facts on File, 1993.

Time-Life Books, eds. ***What Life Was Like: At Empire's End: Austro-Hungarian Empire A.D. 1848–1918.*** New York: Time-Life Books, 2000. A chance to connect to the people and the times during the end of a great empire. A close examination of the forces that led to World War I.

Videos and Software

Nineteenth-Century Nationalism. CD-ROM. Society for Visual Education, 1989. 800-829-1900.

Simón Bolívar: The Liberator. VHS and DVD. Films for the Humanities & Sciences, 2000. 800-257-5126.

Interact *with* History

Objectives

- Set the stage for studying the spread of revolutions throughout the West during the 19th century by analyzing national symbols.
- Guide students in creating a symbol for an imaginary country.

EXAMINING *the* ISSUES

Answers

- Each of the elements of the symbol should have a clear and consistent meaning.
- The symbols should be positive and represent values and ideals that the people of the country would take pride in.

Discussion

Have students look again at the symbol of the United States. Ask, How does this symbol make you feel? Are you proud of the ideas expressed in this symbol?

Interact *with* History

What symbolizes your country's values?

You are an artist in a nation that has just freed itself from foreign rule. The new government is asking you to design a symbol that will show what your country stands for. It's up to you to design the symbol that best suits the spirit and values of your people. Look at the symbols below. Will your symbol be peaceful or warlike, dignified or joyful? Or will it be a combination of these and other qualities?

Botswana
Industry and livestock are connected by water, the key to the country's prosperity. *Pula* in the Setswana language means "rain." But to a Setswana speaker, it is also a common greeting meaning luck, life, and prosperity.

Austria
The eagle was the symbol of the old Austrian Empire. The shield goes back to medieval times. The hammer and sickle symbolize agriculture and industry. The broken chains celebrate Austria's liberation from Germany at the end of World War II.

United States
The 13 original colonies are symbolized in the stars, stripes, leaves, and arrows. The Latin phrase *E pluribus unum* means "Out of many, one," expressing unity of the states. The American bald eagle holds an olive branch and arrows to symbolize a desire for peace but a readiness for war.

EXAMINING *the* ISSUES

- **What values and goals of your new country do you want to show?**
- **Will your symbols represent your country's past or future?**

As a class, discuss these questions. During the discussion, think of the role played by symbols in expressing a country's view of itself and the world. As you read about the rise of new nations in Latin America and Europe, think of how artists encourage national pride.

WHY STUDY NATIONALIST REVOLUTIONS THAT SWEPT THE WEST?

- The revolutions that occurred in the Western Hemisphere and Europe during the 19th century helped form the modern nations that we know today. Many of these nations are our allies and trading partners.
- The spirit of nationalism that led to the revolutions of the 19th century continues to drive people in the world today. The Palestinians, the Kurds, the people of Quebec, and the Basques are a few of the peoples still clamoring for their own national governments.
- Neighboring nations still do not always get along. Knowing the history of their relationships can help us better understand why and how conflicts have developed.
- The revolutions of the past occurred because people had differing ideas on how a nation should be governed and the rights that individuals should have. These issues are still being debated today.

Arc de Triomphe, Paris, France

Claude Monet, *Poppies*

1

Latin American Peoples Win Independence

MAIN IDEA

REVOLUTION Spurred by discontent and Enlightenment ideas, peoples in Latin America fought colonial rule.

WHY IT MATTERS NOW

Sixteen of today's Latin American nations gained their independence at this time.

TERMS & NAMES

- *peninsulare*
- creole
- mulatto
- Simón Bolívar
- José de San Martín
- Miguel Hidalgo
- José María Morelos

SETTING THE STAGE The successful American Revolution, the French Revolution, and the Enlightenment changed ideas about who should control government. Ideas of liberty, equality, and democratic rule found their way across the seas to European colonies. In Latin America, most of the population resented the domination of European colonial powers. The time seemed right for the people who lived there to sweep away old colonial masters and gain control of the land.

Colonial Society Divided

In Latin American colonial society, class dictated people's place in society and jobs. At the top of Spanish-American society were the ***peninsulares*** (peh•neen•soo•LAH•rehs), people who had been born in Spain, which is on the Iberian peninsula. They formed a tiny percentage of the population. Only *peninsulares* could hold high office in Spanish colonial government. **Creoles**, Spaniards born in Latin America, were below the *peninsulares* in rank. Creoles could not hold high-level political office, but they could rise as officers in

The Divisions in Spanish Colonial Society, 1789

Source: *Colonial Spanish America*, by Leslie Bethell

SKILLBUILDER: Interpreting Graphs

1. **Clarifying** *Which two groups made up the vast majority of the population in Spanish America?*
2. **Making Inferences** *Of the Europeans, which group—peninsulares or creoles—probably made up a larger percentage?*

CALIFORNIA STANDARDS

10.2.1 Compare the major ideas of philosophers and their effects on the democratic revolutions in England, the United States, France, and Latin America (e.g., John Locke, Charles-Louis Montesquieu, Jean-Jacques Rousseau, Simón Bolívar, Thomas Jefferson, James Madison).

10.4.2 Discuss the locations of the colonial rule of such nations as England, France, Germany, Italy, Japan, the Netherlands, Russia, Spain, Portugal, and the United States.

10.4.3 Explain imperialism from the perspective of the colonizers and the colonized and the varied immediate and long-term responses by the people under colonial rule.

10.4.4 Describe the independence struggles of the colonized regions of the world, including the roles of leaders, such as Sun Yat-sen in China, and the roles of ideology and religion.

HI 1 Students show the connections, causal and otherwise, between particular historical events and larger social, economic, and political trends and developments.

TAKING NOTES

Clarifying Identify details about Latin American independence movements.

Who	Where
When	Why

LESSON PLAN

OBJECTIVES

- Identify the elements of colonial society that caused unrest in Latin America.
- Explain how Haiti won independence.
- Describe the activities of Bolívar, San Martín, Native Americans, and mestizos in liberation events.
- Describe Brazil's peaceful liberation.

1 FOCUS & MOTIVATE

During the colonial period, most people had few rights or opportunities. Ask students, Have you ever felt that way? Describe your feelings. *(Possible Answers: Yes; anger, humiliation, determination)*

2 INSTRUCT

Colonial Society Divided

10.4.3

Critical Thinking

- How did the Spanish feel about Indians? *(least important people)*

SKILLBUILDER Answers

1. **Clarifying** Indians and Europeans
2. **Making Inferences** creoles

CALIFORNIA RESOURCES

California Reading Toolkit, p. L37
California Modified Lesson Plans for English Learners, p. 69
California Daily Standards Practice Transparencies, TT29
California Standards Enrichment Workbook, pp. 23–24, 49–50, 51–52, 53–54
California Standards Planner and Lesson Plans, p. L65
California Online Test Practice
California Test Generator CD-ROM
California Easy Planner CD-ROM
California eEdition CD-ROM

SECTION 1 PROGRAM RESOURCES

ALL STUDENTS

In-Depth Resources: Unit 2
- Guided Reading, p. 73
- Skillbuilder Practice: Hypothesizing, p. 78
- History Makers: Simón Bolívar, p. 88

Formal Assessment
- Section Quiz, p. 136

ENGLISH LEARNERS

In-Depth Resources in Spanish
- Guided Reading, p. 67
- Skillbuilder Practice: Hypothesizing, p. 71

Reading Study Guide (Spanish), p. 85
Reading Study Guide Audio CD (Spanish)

STRUGGLING READERS

In-Depth Resources: Unit 2
- Guided Reading, p. 73
- Building Vocabulary, p. 77
- Reteaching Activity, p. 91

Reading Study Guide, p. 85
Reading Study Guide Audio CD

GIFTED AND TALENTED STUDENTS

In-Depth Resources: Unit 2
- Primary Source: from *Proclamation of 1813,* p. 81
- Literature: from *All Souls' Rising,* p. 85

Electronic Library of Primary Sources

INTEGRATED TECHNOLOGY

eEdition CD-ROM
Voices from the Past Audio CD
Power Presentations CD-ROM
World Art and Cultures Transparencies
- AT52 Father Miguel Hidalgo Crowns Mexico

Electronic Library of Primary Sources
Patterns of Interaction Video Series
- Revolutions in Latin America and South Africa

classzone.com

Revolutions in the Americas
10.2.1

Critical Thinking

- How did the American Revolution inspire the slaves of Saint Domingue to revolt? *(Possible Answer: The slaves thought if the American colonists could win freedom, then they could also.)*
- How could just 30,000 French troops force Toussaint and his army of 100,000 to halt the revolution? *(Possible Answer: They were better equipped and trained.)*

Creoles Lead Independence
10.2.1

Critical Thinking

- From the view of the colonial powers, why were the creoles the most dangerous part of the population? *(well-educated, trained as soldiers, wealthy)*
- What factors caused the revolution in Latin America? *(Possible Answer: Creole discontent over privileges of the* peninsulares*; Enlightenment ideas; Napoleon's takeover)*

Tip for Gifted and Talented Students

Toussaint L'Ouverture was one of the most fascinating leaders of a liberation movement. A complex, mysterious man, he was also a brilliant general. Ask students to read the excerpt from *All Souls' Rising,* a novel about Haiti's liberation.

In-Depth Resources: Unit 2

- Literature: from *All Souls' Rising,* p. 85

Spanish colonial armies. Together these two groups controlled land, wealth, and power in the Spanish colonies.

Below the *peninsulares* and creoles came the mestizos, persons of mixed European and Indian ancestry. Next were the **mulattos**, persons of mixed European and African ancestry, and enslaved Africans. Indians were at the bottom of the social ladder.

Revolutions in the Americas

By the late 1700s, colonists in Latin America, already aware of Enlightenment ideas, were electrified by the news of the American and French Revolutions. The success of the American Revolution encouraged them to try to gain freedom from their European masters.

Revolution in Haiti The French colony called Saint Domingue was the first Latin American territory to free itself from European rule. The colony, now known as Haiti, occupied the western third of the island of Hispaniola in the Caribbean Sea.

Nearly 500,000 enslaved Africans worked on French plantations, and they outnumbered their masters dramatically. White masters used brutal methods to terrorize them and keep them powerless.

While the French Revolution was taking place, oppressed people in the French colony of Haiti rose up against their French masters. In August 1791, 100,000 enslaved Africans rose in revolt. A leader soon emerged, Toussaint L'Ouverture (too•SAN loo•vair•TOOR). Formerly enslaved, Toussaint was unfamiliar with military and diplomatic matters. Even so, he rose to become a skilled general and diplomat. By 1801, Toussaint had taken control of the entire island and freed all the enslaved Africans.

▼ Toussaint L'Ouverture led enslaved Africans in a revolt against the French that ended slavery and resulted in the new nation of Haiti.

In January 1802, 30,000 French troops landed in Saint Domingue to remove Toussaint from power. In May, Toussaint agreed to halt the revolution if the French would end slavery. Despite the agreement, the French soon accused him of planning another uprising. They seized him and sent him to a prison in the French Alps, where he died in April 1803.

Haiti's Independence Toussaint's lieutenant, Jean-Jacques Dessalines (zhahn•ZHAHK day•sah•LEEN), took up the fight for freedom. On January 1, 1804, General Dessalines declared the colony an independent country. It was the first black colony to free itself from European control. Dessalines called the country Haiti, which in the language of the Arawak natives meant "mountainous land."

Creoles Lead Independence

Even though they could not hold high public office, creoles were the least oppressed of those born in Latin America. They were also the best educated. In fact, many wealthy young creoles traveled to Europe for their education. In Europe, they read about and adopted Enlightenment ideas. When they returned to Latin America, they brought ideas of revolution with them.

Napoleon's conquest of Spain in 1808 triggered revolts in the Spanish colonies. Removing Spain's King Ferdinand VII, Napoleon made his brother Joseph king of Spain. Many creoles might have supported a Spanish king. However, they felt no loyalty to a king imposed by the French. Creoles, recalling Locke's idea of the consent of the governed, argued that when the real king was removed, power shifted to the people. In 1810, rebellion broke out in several parts of Latin America. The drive toward independence had begun. (A)

A. Possible Answer The French Revolution inspired Latin Americans; the Haitians rebelled against the French when they were least able to respond.

MAIN IDEA

Recognizing Effects

(A) How did the French Revolution affect the colonists in the Americas?

DIFFERENTIATING INSTRUCTION: STRUGGLING READERS

Understanding Class Structure

Class Time 15 minutes

Task Creating a graphic representation of class structure

Purpose To clarify understanding of class structure in colonial Latin America

Instructions Draw a blank diagram on the chalkboard like the one shown. Then guide a discussion of the hierarchy of social classes in Latin America during the colonial period. Have students create their own diagrams and complete them by writing the names of each class in the correct box. You might extend the activity by having students add the percentages of the population that make up each group. If students need additional help, use Reading Study Guide, p. 85.

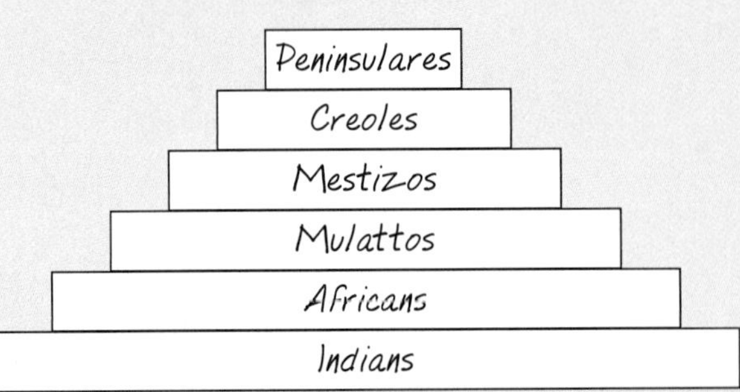

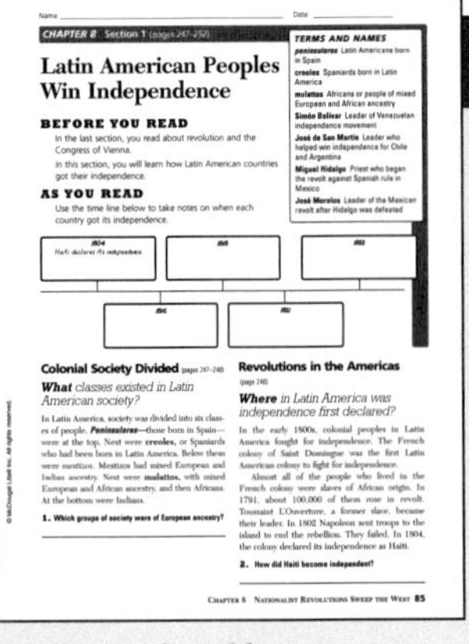

Name ______ Date ______

CHAPTER 8 Section 1 (pages 247–252)

Latin American Peoples Win Independence

BEFORE YOU READ

In the last section, you read about revolution and the Congress of Vienna.

In this section, you will learn how Latin American countries got their independence.

AS YOU READ

Use the time line below to take notes on when each country got its independence.

TERMS AND NAMES

peninsulares Latin Americans born in Spain

creoles Spaniards born in Latin America

mulattos Africans or people of mixed European and African ancestry

Simón Bolívar Leader of Venezuelan independence movement

José de San Martín Leader who helped win independence for Chile and Argentina

Miguel Hidalgo Priest who began the revolt against Spanish rule in Mexico

José Morelos Leader of the Mexican revolt after Hidalgo was defeated

1804 Haiti declares its independence

Colonial Society Divided (pages 247–248)

***What** classes existed in Latin American society?*

In Latin America, society was divided into six classes of people. ***Peninsulares***—those born in Spain—were at the top. Next were **creoles,** or Spaniards who had been born in Latin America. Below them were mestizos. Mestizos had mixed European and Indian ancestry. Next were **mulattos,** with mixed European and African ancestry, and then Africans. At the bottom were Indians.

1. Which groups of society were of European ancestry?

Revolutions in the Americas (page 248)

***Where** in Latin America was independence first declared?*

In the early 1800s, colonial peoples in Latin America fought for independence. The French colony of Saint Domingue was the first Latin American colony to fight for independence.

Almost all of the people who lived in the French colony were slaves of African origin. In 1791, about 100,000 of them rose in revolt. Toussaint L'Ouverture, a former slave, became their leader. In 1802 Napoleon sent troops to the island to end the rebellion. They failed. In 1804, the colony declared its independence as Haiti.

2. How did Haiti become independent?

CHAPTER 8 NATIONALIST REVOLUTIONS SWEEP THE WEST 85

Reading Study Guide

History Makers

Simón Bolívar
1783–1830

Called *Libertador* (Liberator), Bolívar was a brilliant general, a visionary, a writer, and a fighter. He is called the "George Washington of South America." Bolívar planned to unite the Spanish colonies of South America into a single country called Gran Colombia. The area of upper Peru was renamed Bolivia in his honor.

Discouraged by political disputes that tore the new Latin American nations apart, he is reported to have said, "America is ungovernable. Those who have served the revolution have ploughed the sea."

José de San Martín
1778–1850

Unlike the dashing Bolívar, San Martín was a modest man. Though born in Argentina, he spent much of his youth in Spain as a career military officer. He fought with Spanish forces against Napoleon. He returned to Latin America to be a part of its liberation from Spain. Fighting for 10 years, he became the liberator of Argentina, Chile, and Peru.

Discouraged by political infighting, San Martín sailed for Europe. He died, almost forgotten, on French soil in 1850.

The South American wars of independence rested on the achievements of two brilliant creole generals. One was **Simón Bolívar** (see•MAWN boh•LEE•vahr), a wealthy Venezuelan creole. The other great liberator was **José de San Martín** (hoh•SAY day san mahr•TEEN), an Argentinian.

Bolívar's Route to Victory Simón Bolívar's native Venezuela declared its independence from Spain in 1811. But the struggle for independence had only begun. Bolívar's volunteer army of revolutionaries suffered numerous defeats. Twice Bolívar had to go into exile. A turning point came in August 1819. Bolívar led over 2,000 soldiers on a daring march through the Andes into what is now Colombia. (See the 1830 map on page 251.) Coming from this direction, he took the Spanish army in Bogotá completely by surprise and won a decisive victory.

By 1821, Bolívar had won Venezuela's independence. He then marched south into Ecuador. In Ecuador, Bolívar finally met José de San Martín. Together they would decide the future of the Latin American revolutionary movement.

San Martín Leads Southern Liberation Forces San Martín's Argentina had declared its independence in 1816. However, Spanish forces in nearby Chile and Peru still posed a threat. In 1817, San Martín led an army on a grueling march across the Andes to Chile. He was joined there by forces led by Bernardo O'Higgins, son of a former viceroy of Peru. With O'Higgins's help, San Martín finally freed Chile.

In 1821, San Martín planned to drive the remaining Spanish forces out of Lima, Peru. But to do so, he needed a much larger force. San Martín and Bolívar discussed this problem when they met at Guayaquil, Ecuador, in 1822.

No one knows how the two men reached an agreement. But San Martín left his army for Bolívar to command. With unified revolutionary forces, Bolívar's army went on to defeat the Spanish at the Battle of Ayacucho (Peru) on December 9, 1824. In this last major battle of the war for independence, the Spanish colonies in Latin America won their freedom. The future countries of Venezuela, Colombia, Panama, and Ecuador were united into a country called Gran Colombia.

History Makers

Simón Bolívar and José de San Martín

How were Bolívar and San Martín alike? *(brilliant generals, liberated nations of South America, discouraged by political infighting that followed liberation)*

One of the most important events in the liberation of South America occurred at Guayaquil (now in Ecuador) in 1822 when Bolívar and San Martín met. No records exist of the meeting. What is known is that Bolívar took charge of the combined armies and completed the liberation of Peru. San Martín returned to Lima in disappointment. He resigned his protectorship of Peru a few months later and went into exile in Europe, where he lived the rest of his life.

In-Depth Resources: Unit 2

- Primary Source: from *Proclamation of 1813,* p. 81
- History Makers: Simón Bolívar, p. 88

Electronic Library of Primary Sources

- from Address to the Second National Congress of Venezuela, 1819

SKILLBUILDER PRACTICE: HYPOTHESIZING

Examining Bolívar and San Martín

Class Time 15 minutes

Task Asking questions about history

Purpose To develop in-depth knowledge of a historical topic

Instructions Explain to students that historians develop hypotheses, or possible explanations, about events in order to better understand why the events happened, what the consequences were or might be, and why the events are significant. Then they test their hypotheses against historical evidence to check their validity. Ask students to hypothesize about what happened at the meeting in Guayaquil and why San Martín turned over his army to Bolívar. *(Some historians think that San Martín left in anger after a quarrel with Bolívar. Others think San Martín deliberately stepped aside in favor of Bolívar so that the independence movement could unite behind a single leader).* Have students reread the text that describes the character and actions of Bolívar and San Martín. You might also encourage them to do additional research. Then have them write a hypothesis about events at Guayaquil and support it with reasons and facts.

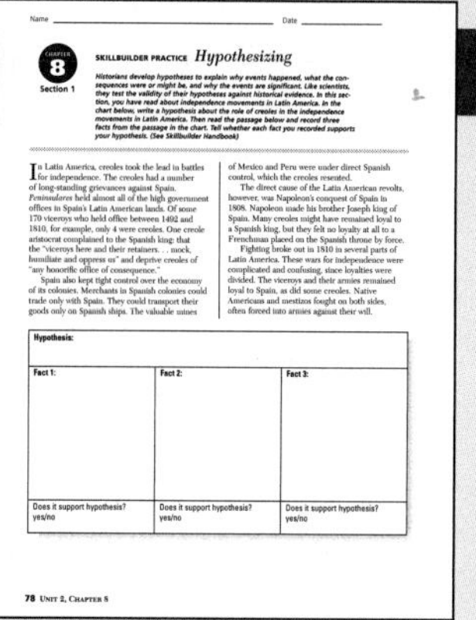

SKILLBUILDER PRACTICE *Hypothesizing*

Hypothesis:		
Fact 1:	Fact 2:	Fact 3:
Does it support hypothesis? yes/no	Does it support hypothesis? yes/no	Does it support hypothesis? yes/no

In-Depth Resources: Unit 2

Global Impact

OBJECTIVE

- Understand the impact of Enlightenment ideas on democracy in South America.

INSTRUCT

Explain to students that Bolívar was an inspiration to later revolutionaries throughout Latin America. For example, he inspired the Cubans who rose up against Spain in the struggle for independence in 1895, as well as a later revolution in Cuba led by Fidel Castro in the 1950s. Often these revolutions were influenced by a variety of sources, such as Marxist doctrine, as well as Bolívar's example.

INTEGRATED TECHNOLOGY

Interactive This image is available in an interactive format on the eEdition. Students can view the locations that Bolívar visited and trace the sources of his ideas.

Struggling Toward Democracy

CALIFORNIA STANDARDS
10.2.3, HI 1

Revolutions are as much a matter of ideas as they are of weapons. Simón Bolívar, the hero of Latin American independence, was both a thinker and a fighter. By 1800, Enlightenment ideas spread widely across the Latin American colonies. Bolívar combined Enlightenment political ideas, ideas from Greece and Rome, and his own original thinking. The result was a system of democratic ideas that would help spark revolutions throughout Latin America.

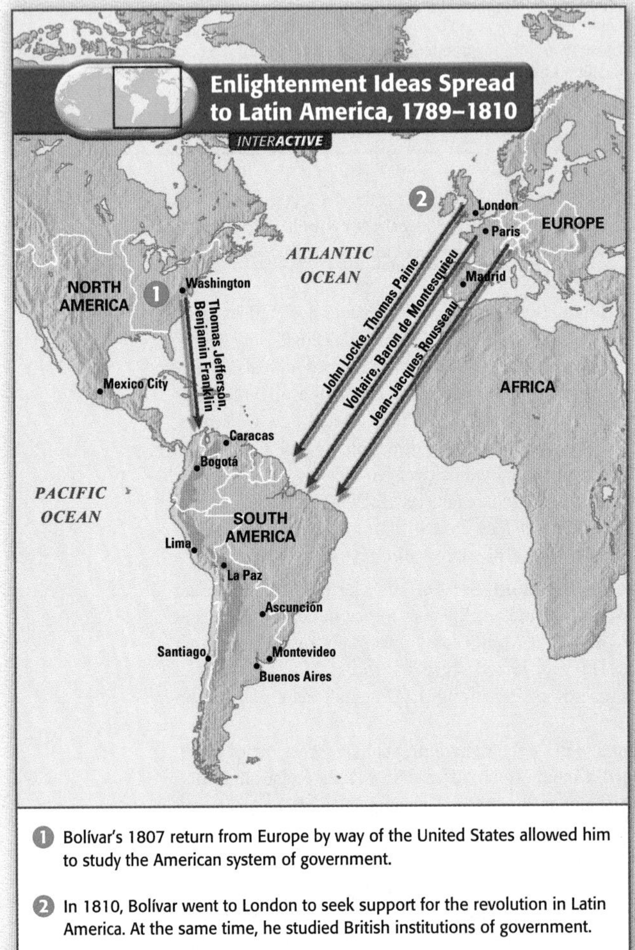

1. Bolívar's 1807 return from Europe by way of the United States allowed him to study the American system of government.
2. In 1810, Bolívar went to London to seek support for the revolution in Latin America. At the same time, he studied British institutions of government.

After winning South American independence, Simón Bolívar realized his dream of Gran Colombia, a sort of United States of South America.

Patterns of Interaction

Struggling Toward Democracy: Revolutions in Latin America and South Africa

The Latin American independence movement is one example of how the Enlightenment spread democratic ideals throughout the world. Democratic ideals continue to inspire people to struggle for political independence and to overthrow oppressive governments.

Connect *to* Today

1. **Making Inferences** How are Enlightenment thought and the successes of the American and French Revolutions reflected in Bolívar's thinking?
   See Skillbuilder Handbook, page R10.
2. **Comparing** What recent events in today's world are similar to Simón Bolívar's movement for Latin American independence?

CONNECT TO TODAY: ANSWERS

1. Making Inferences
Possible Answer: Bolívar promoted the idea of government by consent of the governed, he believed in the ideal of democracy, and he wanted to unite all of the people.

2. Comparing
Possible Answers: Students might mention the struggles in eastern European nations, the Basques in Spain, East Timor, and Afghanistan.

Mexico Ends Spanish Rule

In most Latin American countries, creoles led the revolutionary movements. But in Mexico, ethnic and racial groups mixed more freely. There, Indians and mestizos played the leading role.

A Cry for Freedom In 1810, Padre **Miguel Hidalgo** (mee•GEHL ee•THAHL•goh), a priest in the small village of Dolores, took the first step toward independence. Hidalgo was a poor but well-educated man. He firmly believed in Enlightenment ideals. On September 16, 1810, he rang the bells of his village church. When the peasants gathered in the church, he issued a call for rebellion against the Spanish. Today, that call is known as the *grito de Dolores* (the cry of Dolores).

The very next day, Hidalgo's Indian and mestizo followers began a march toward Mexico City. This unruly army soon numbered 80,000 men. The uprising of the lower classes alarmed the Spanish army and creoles, who feared the loss of their property, control of the land, and their lives. The army defeated Hidalgo in 1811. The rebels then rallied around another strong leader, Padre **José María Morelos** (moh•RAY•lohs). Morelos led the revolution for four years. However, in 1815, a creole officer, Agustín de Iturbide (ah•goos•TEEN day ee•toor•BEE•day), defeated him.

Mexico's Independence Events in Mexico took yet another turn in 1820 when a revolution in Spain put a liberal group in power there. Mexico's creoles feared the loss of their privileges in the Spanish-controlled colony. So they united in support of Mexico's independence from Spain. Ironically, Agustín de Iturbide—the man who had defeated the rebel Padre Morelos—proclaimed independence in 1821.

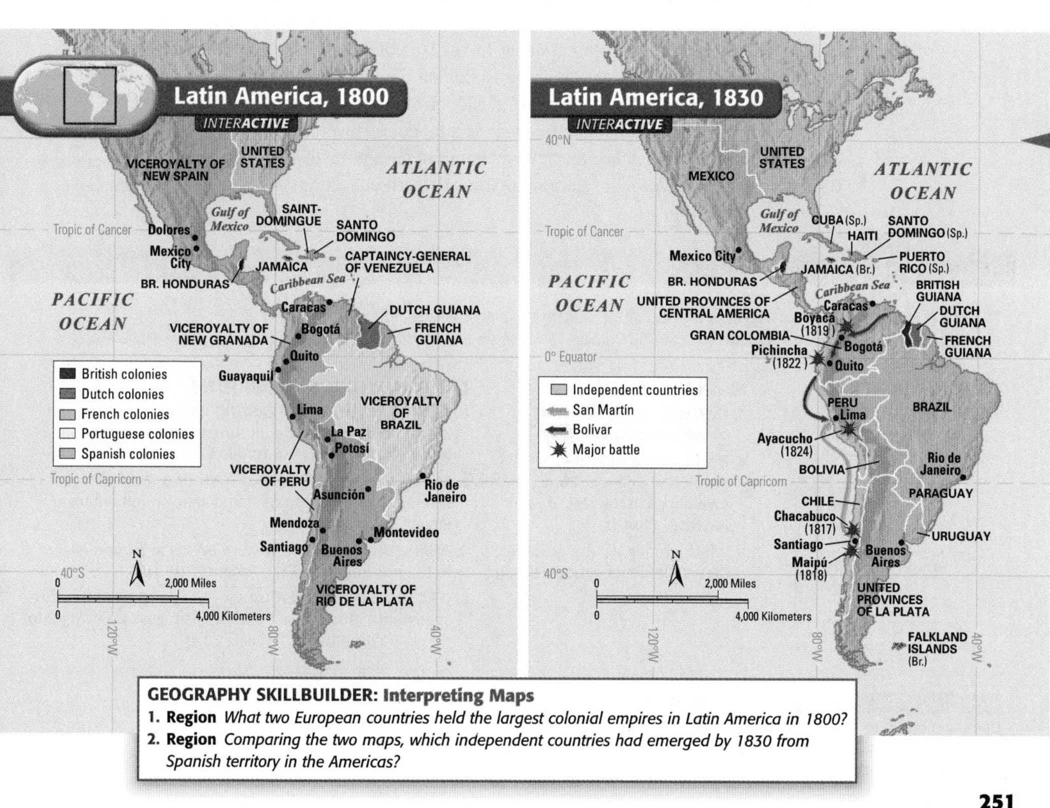

GEOGRAPHY SKILLBUILDER: Interpreting Maps
1. **Region** *What two European countries held the largest colonial empires in Latin America in 1800?*
2. **Region** *Comparing the two maps, which independent countries had emerged by 1830 from Spanish territory in the Americas?*

Mexico Ends Spanish Rule
10.4.2

Critical Thinking
- What was there about Padre Miguel Hidalgo that inspired people to follow him in rebellion? *(He was poor like his followers but well educated. They felt they could trust him.)*
- Why did Iturbide first defeat a revolution and then lead one? *(He wanted to keep power for the creoles.)*

History from Visuals

Interpreting the Map

Point out to students that the best way to understand the differences between the two maps is to look at the different elements in each key.

Extension Have students compare the map of 1830 with the map of South America in the atlas to see what countries have remained the same and what political boundaries and names have changed since 1830.

SKILLBUILDER Answers
1. **Region** Spain and Portugal
2. **Region** Mexico, United Provinces of Central America, Gran Colombia, Bolivia, Peru, Chile, Paraguay, Uruguay, United Provinces of La Plata

INTEGRATED TECHNOLOGY

Interactive These images are available in an interactive format on the eEdition. Students can view the colonies ruled by each European nation, the routes of Bolívar and San Martín, and the sites of the battles.

DIFFERENTIATING INSTRUCTION: ENGLISH LEARNERS

Independence Day Celebrations

Class Time 45 minutes

Task Creating a multimedia presentation

Purpose To learn more about independence day celebrations

Instructions Project Transparency AT52 and discuss the significance of the painting. Point out that it was created to celebrate Mexican Independence Day, which is September 16—the day Padre Hidalgo rallied the people of Dolores to fight for independence. By tradition, each year on this day, the president of Mexico shouts the "el Grito" from the National Palace in Mexico City: *Viva Mexico! Viva la Independencia! Vivan los Heroes!* Mexicans have other traditions for celebrating their liberation as well, and so do many other countries. Have students work together to prepare a multimedia presentation about the independence day celebrations of different countries. They should divide into groups. One group should investigate Mexico's Independence Day traditions. Other groups should investigate the traditions of other countries. Have students combine their work into a class presentation.

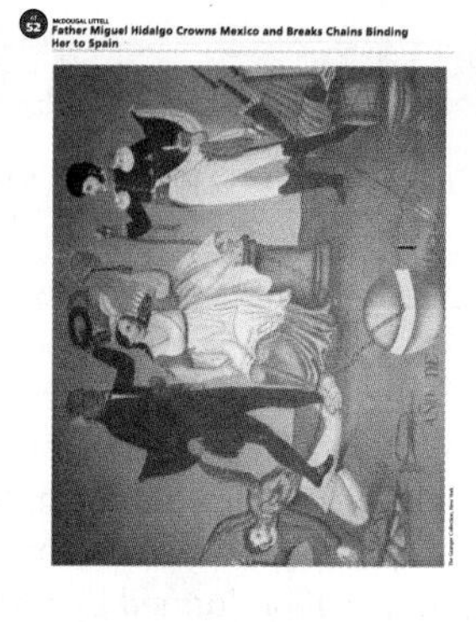

World Art and Cultures Transparencies

Brazil's Royal Liberator
10.4.4

Critical Thinking

- Why did the Brazilians like having the Portuguese capital in Rio de Janiero? *(The king was more concerned about their welfare than when he was across the ocean.)*
- Why didn't King John VI object to giving Brazil its freedom? *(Possible Answers: It had been his refuge for 14 years; his son would be the new leader.)*

3 ASSESS

SECTION 1 ASSESSMENT

Have students answer the questions individually. Then have them meet in small groups to compare their answers.

Formal Assessment

- Section Quiz, p. 136

4 RETEACH

Have students work in pairs and use the Reading Study Guide for Section 1 to review the section.

Reading Study Guide, p. 85 (also in Spanish)

In-Depth Resources: Unit 2

- Reteaching Activity, p. 91

Before the Mexican revolution, Central America was part of the viceroyalty of New Spain. It had been governed by the Spanish from the seat of colonial government in Mexico. In 1821, several Central American states declared their independence from Spain—and from Mexico as well. However, Iturbide (who had declared himself emperor), refused to recognize the declarations of independence. Iturbide was finally overthrown in 1823. Central America then declared its absolute independence from Mexico. It took the name the United Provinces of Central America. The future countries of Nicaragua, Guatemala, Honduras, El Salvador, and Costa Rica would develop in this region.

Brazil's Royal Liberator

Brazil's quest for independence was unique in this period of Latin American history because it occurred without violent upheavals or widespread bloodshed. In fact, a member of the Portuguese royal family actually played a key role in freeing Brazil from Portugal.

In 1807, Napoleon's armies invaded both Spain and Portugal. Napoleon's aim was to close the ports of these countries to British shipping. As French troops approached Lisbon, the Portuguese capital, Prince John (later King John VI) and the royal family boarded ships to escape capture. They took their court and royal treasury to Portugal's largest colony, Brazil. Rio de Janiero became the capital of the Portuguese empire. For 14 years, the Portuguese ran their empire from Brazil. After Napoleon's defeat in 1815, King John and the Portuguese government returned to Portugal six years later. Dom Pedro, King John's son, stayed behind in Brazil.

King John planned to make Brazil a colony again. However, many Brazilians could not accept a return to colonial status. In 1822, creoles demanded Brazil's independence from Portugal. Eight thousand Brazilians signed a petition asking Dom Pedro to rule. He agreed. On September 7, 1822, he officially declared Brazil's independence. Brazil had won its independence in a bloodless revolution. (B)

Meanwhile, the ideas of the French Revolution and the aftermath of the Napoleonic Wars were causing upheaval in Europe, as you will learn in Section 2.

B. Possible Answer Dom Pedro lived in Brazil and agreed with the creoles' demands to become independent.

MAIN IDEA

Making Inferences

(B) In what way did the presence of the royal family in Brazil help Portugal's largest colony?

SECTION 1 ASSESSMENT

TERMS & NAMES 1. For each term or name, write a sentence explaining its significance.

• *peninsulare* • creole • mulatto • Simón Bolívar • José de San Martín • Miguel Hidalgo • José María Morelos

USING YOUR NOTES

2. Which independence movement was led by Toussaint L'Ouverture? (10.2.1)

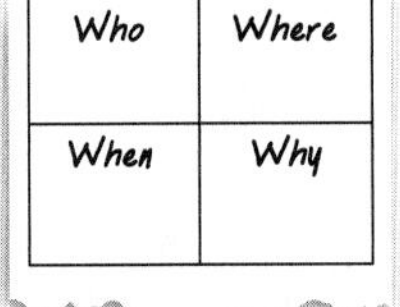

MAIN IDEAS

3. How was Spanish colonial society structured? (10.4.2)
4. How was the Haitian Revolution different from revolutions in the rest of Latin America? (10.4.4)
5. Which groups led the quest for Mexican independence? (10.4.4)

CRITICAL THINKING & WRITING

6. **COMPARING AND CONTRASTING** Compare and contrast the leadership of the South American revolutions to the leadership of Mexico's revolution. (10.4.4)
7. **FORMING AND SUPPORTING OPINIONS** Would creole revolutionaries tend to be democratic or authoritarian leaders? Explain. (10.4.3)
8. **ANALYZING CAUSES** How were events in Europe related to the revolutions in Latin America? (HI 1)
9. **WRITING ACTIVITY** REVOLUTION Write a **response** to this statement: "Through its policies, Spain gave up its right to rule in South America." (Writing 2.2.d)

INTEGRATED TECHNOLOGY **INTERNET ACTIVITY**

Use the Internet to find information on the Mexican Indian rebel group, the *Zapatistas*. Create a **multimedia presentation** describing the group and its goals. (10.4.4)

INTERNET KEYWORD
Zapatistas

ANSWERS

1. *peninsulares*, p. 247 • creoles, p. 247 • mulattos, p. 248 • Simón Bolívar, p. 249 • José de San Martín, p. 249 • Miguel Hidalgo, p. 251 • José María Morelos, p. 251
2. **Sample Answer:** Haiti—Slaves; fought France; new nation. Spanish South America—Creoles, fought Spain; new nations. Mexico—Indians, mestizos, creoles; fought Spain; new nation. Brazil—Creoles, royal family; end colonial rule; royal declaration; new nation. **Answer:** Brazil only nation formed by royal decree.
3. *peninsulares* at the top, then creoles, mestizos, mulattos, slaves, and Indians
4. This revolt was accomplished by slaves.
5. Indians and mestizos
6. **Possible Answers:** Similar—Fought Spain, led by creoles. Different—South America, two liberation groups; Mexico, led by Indians and mestizos, then creoles, Central American countries split away.
7. **Possible Answers:** Democratic—Creoles educated, knew Enlightenment, economic interests. Authoritarian—military background; felt superior to lower classes; economic interests to protect.
8. French Revolution set off events linked to Haiti and the Spanish-held colonies.
9. **Rubric** The response should
   - take a position either pro or con.
   - support the position with logic.
   - contain a summary and support of the position.

INTEGRATED TECHNOLOGY

Rubric The multimedia presentation should

- present up-to-date information.
- use facts from several media sources.
- use appropriate software.

Arc de Triomphe, Paris, France

Claude Monet, *Poppies*

Europe Faces Revolutions

MAIN IDEA

REVOLUTION Liberal and nationalist uprisings challenged the old conservative order of Europe.

WHY IT MATTERS NOW

The system of nation-states established in Europe during this period continues today.

TERMS & NAMES

- conservative
- liberal
- radical
- nationalism
- nation-state
- the Balkans
- Louis-Napoleon
- Alexander II

SETTING THE STAGE As revolutions shook the colonies in Latin America, Europe was also undergoing dramatic changes. Under the leadership of Prince Metternich of Austria, the Congress of Vienna had tried to restore the old monarchies and territorial divisions that had existed before the French Revolution. (See Chapter 7.) Internationally, it was met with success. For the next century, European countries seldom turned to war to solve their differences. Within countries, however, the effort failed. Revolutions erupted across Europe between 1815 and 1848.

CALIFORNIA STANDARDS

10.2.4 Explain how the ideology of the French Revolution led France to develop from constitutional monarchy to democratic despotism to the Napoleonic empire.

10.2.5 Discuss how nationalism spread across Europe with Napoleon but was repressed for a generation under the Congress of Vienna and Concert of Europe until the Revolutions of 1848.

10.9.6 Understand how the forces of nationalism developed in the Middle East, how the Holocaust affected world opinion regarding the need for a Jewish state, and the significance and effects of the location and establishment of Israel on world affairs.

CST 2 Students analyze how change happens at different rates at different times; understand that some aspects can change while others remain the same; and understand that change is complicated and affects not only technology and politics but also values and beliefs.

Clash of Philosophies

In the first half of the 1800s, three schools of political thought struggled for supremacy in European societies. Each believed that its style of government would best serve the people. Each attracted a different set of followers. The list below identifies the philosophies, goals, and followers.

- **Conservative**: usually wealthy property owners and nobility. They argued for protecting the traditional monarchies of Europe.
- **Liberal**: mostly middle-class business leaders and merchants. They wanted to give more power to elected parliaments, but only the educated and the landowners would vote.
- **Radical**: favored drastic change to extend democracy to all people. They believed that governments should practice the ideals of the French Revolution—liberty, equality, and brotherhood.

Nationalism Develops

As the three schools debated issues of government, a new movement called nationalism emerged. **Nationalism** is the belief that people's greatest loyalty should not be to a king or an empire but to a nation of people who share a common culture and history. The nationalist movement would blur the lines that separated the three political theories.

When a nation had its own independent government, it became a **nation-state** that defended its territory and way of life. It represents the nation to the rest of the world. In Europe in 1815, only

TAKING NOTES

Summarizing Identify major revolutions in Europe.

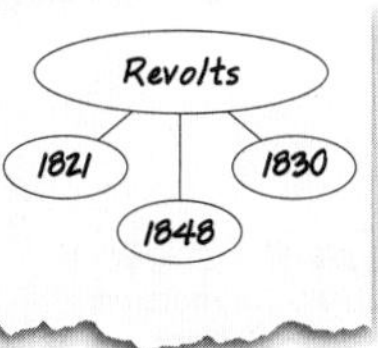

◂ Prince Clemens von Metternich shaped conservative control of Europe for almost 40 years.

LESSON PLAN

OBJECTIVES

- Identify three schools of political thought.
- Trace the development of nationalism.
- Describe nationalism in the Balkans.
- Analyze reform in France and Russia.

1 FOCUS & MOTIVATE

Ask students how one can voice their opinion. *(Possible Answers: letters to editors, marches, demonstrations, speeches)*

2 INSTRUCT

Clash of Philosophies

10.2.4

Critical Thinking

- How can people have such different philosophies? *(Possible Answers: personal experiences, education)*

Nationalism Develops

10.2.5

Critical Thinking

- How did nationalism blur the line between philosophies? *(attracted people from all schools)*

CALIFORNIA RESOURCES

California Reading Toolkit, p. L38
California Modified Lesson Plans for English Learners, p. 71
California Daily Standards Practice Transparencies, TT30
California Standards Enrichment Workbook, pp. 29–30, 31–32, 101–102
California Standards Planner and Lesson Plans, p. L67
California Online Test Practice
California Test Generator CD-ROM
California Easy Planner CD-ROM
California eEdition CD-ROM

SECTION 2 PROGRAM RESOURCES

ALL STUDENTS

In-Depth Resources: Unit 2
- Guided Reading, p. 74

Formal Assessment
- Section Quiz, p. 137

ENGLISH LEARNERS

In-Depth Resources in Spanish
- Guided Reading, p. 68

Reading Study Guide (Spanish), p. 87
Reading Study Guide Audio CD (Spanish)

STRUGGLING READERS

In-Depth Resources: Unit 2
- Guided Reading, p. 74
- Building Vocabulary, p. 77
- Reteaching Activity, p. 92

Reading Study Guide, p. 87
Reading Study Guide Audio CD

GIFTED AND TALENTED STUDENTS

In-Depth Resources: Unit 2
- Primary Source: *Letter to Thomas Moore,* p. 82

INTEGRATED TECHNOLOGY

eEdition CD-ROM
Power Presentations CD-ROM
Test Generator CD-ROM
Strategies for Test Preparation
Test Practice Transparencies, TT90
Online Test Practice
classzone.com

Analyzing Key Concepts

OBJECTIVE

- Analyze the characteristics and effects of nationalism.

INSTRUCT

Emphasize to students that nationalism arose in the early 1800s as a relatively new and vital point of view, and it drove many of the events that occurred during the 1800s and 1900s. Tell students to look for evidence of nationalism as a leading cause of the events they will read about in the remaining pages of this chapter.

More About . . .

Nationalism

Prior to the American and French Revolutions, nationalism wasn't a common consideration in establishing a government or defining a civilization. People gave their loyalty to a religion, a dynasty, an empire, a feudal fief, or a city-state. The Roman Empire is an example. People were loyal to the empire, even though it included people of many different cultures, languages, and lands. Only with the rise of an educated middle class did values shift to nationalism with its emphasis on nationality—a common language, culture, and ethnicity.

> Analyzing Key Concepts

Nationalism

Nationalism—the belief that people should be loyal to their nation—was not widespread until the 1800s. The rise of modern nationalism is tied to the spread of democratic ideas and the growth of an educated middle class. People wanted to decide how they were governed, instead of having monarchs impose government on them.

Bonds That Create a Nation-State

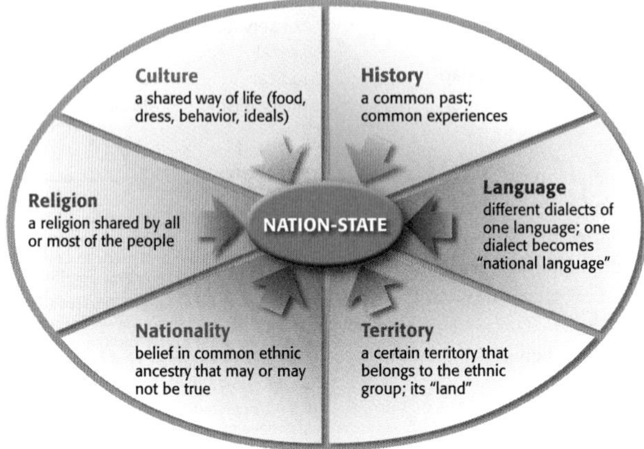

Culture
a shared way of life (food, dress, behavior, ideals)
History
a common past; common experiences
Religion
a religion shared by all or most of the people
NATION-STATE
Language
different dialects of one language; one dialect becomes "national language"
Nationality
belief in common ethnic ancestry that may or may not be true
Territory
a certain territory that belongs to the ethnic group; its "land"

Positive and Negative Results of Nationalism

Nationalism has not always been a positive influence. For example, extremely strong nationalistic feelings sometimes lead a group to turn against outsiders. The chart below lists some positive and negative results of nationalism. Note how some results, such as competition, can be both positive and negative.

Positive Results	Negative Results
• People within a nation overcoming their differences for the common good	• Forced assimilation of minority cultures into a nation's majority culture
• The overthrow of colonial rule	• Ethnic cleansing, such as in Bosnia and Herzegovina in the 1990s
• Democratic governments in nations throughout the world	• The rise of extreme nationalistic movements, such as Nazism
• Competition among nations spurring scientific and technological advances	• Competition between nations leading to warfare

CALIFORNIA STANDARDS

10.2.5 Discuss how nationalism spread across Europe with Napoleon but was repressed for a generation under the Congress of Vienna and Concert of Europe until the Revolutions of 1848.

INTEGRATED TECHNOLOGY

RESEARCH LINKS For more on nationalism, go to **classzone.com**

> DATA FILE

IMPACT OF NATIONALISM

- Between 1950 and 1980, 47 African countries overthrew colonial rulers and became independent nations.
- In the 1990s, the republics of Bosnia and Herzegovina, Croatia, Slovenia, and Macedonia broke away from Yugoslavia.
- In 2003, Yugoslavia changed its name to Serbia and Montenegro.
- Europe has 47 countries. (Some of those lie partially in Europe, partially in Asia.) About 50 languages are spoken in the region.
- In most of Latin America, Spanish or Portuguese is the official language. However, many native languages are still spoken. For example, Bolivia has three official languages: Spanish and the Indian languages of Aymara and Quechua.

Connect *to* Today

1. **Forming and Supporting Opinions** Do you think nationalism has had more of a positive or negative impact on the world? Support your opinion with evidence.

 See Skillbuilder Handbook, page R20.

2. **Comparing and Contrasting** Which of the bonds used to create nation-states are found in the United States?

CONNECT TO TODAY: ANSWERS

1. Forming and Supporting Opinions

Possible Answers: Positive—Even though nationalism resulted in Nazism, it has given rise to many more democracies. It also led to the end of colonialism. It spurred scientific and technological advances, which have made life better for millions of people. Negative—It may force a group to assimilate an unwanted culture. It may promote persecution or ethnic cleansing as in Bosnia and Herzegovina. It could promote extremist groups such as the Nazis. It may encourage nationalistic competition between nations leading to war.

2. Comparing and Contrasting

Possible Answers: national language, shared way of life, certain territory or land, shared national institutions

France, England, and Spain could be called nation-states. But soon that would change as nationalist movements achieved success.

Most of the people who believed in nationalism were either liberals or radicals. In most cases, the liberal middle class—teachers, lawyers, and businesspeople—led the struggle for constitutional government and the formation of nation-states. In Germany, for example, liberals wanted to gather the many different German states into a single nation-state. Other liberals in large empires, such as the Hungarians in the Austrian Empire, wanted to split away and establish self-rule.

Nationalists Challenge Conservative Power

The first people to win self-rule during this period were the Greeks. For centuries, Greece had been part of the Ottoman Empire. The Ottomans controlled most of **the Balkans**. That region includes all or part of present-day Greece, Albania, Bulgaria, Romania, Turkey, and the former Yugoslavia. Greeks, however, had kept alive the memory of their ancient history and culture. Spurred on by the nationalist spirit, they demanded independence and rebelled against the Ottoman Turks in 1821.

Greeks Gain Independence The most powerful European governments opposed revolution. However, the cause of Greek independence was popular with people around the world. Russians, for example, felt a connection to Greek Orthodox Christians, who were ruled by the Muslim Ottomans. Educated Europeans and Americans loved and respected ancient Greek culture.

Eventually, as popular support for Greece grew, the powerful nations of Europe took the side of the Greeks. In 1827, a combined British, French, and Russian fleet destroyed the Ottoman fleet at the Battle of Navarino. In 1830, Britain, France, and Russia signed a treaty guaranteeing an independent kingdom of Greece. A

MAIN IDEA

Analyzing Motives

A Why would Europeans and Americans support the Greek revolutionary movement?

A. Possible Answers They appreciated the culture; they wanted the area to be free of Ottoman control; they felt connected with Greek Orthodox Christians.

1830s Uprisings Crushed By the 1830s, the old order, carefully arranged at the Congress of Vienna, was breaking down. Revolutionary zeal swept across Europe. Liberals and nationalists throughout Europe were openly revolting against conservative governments.

Nationalist riots broke out against Dutch rule in the Belgian city of Brussels. In October 1830, the Belgians declared their independence from Dutch control. In Italy, nationalists worked to unite the many separate states on the Italian peninsula. Some were independent. Others were ruled by Austria, or by the pope. Eventually, Prince Metternich sent Austrian troops to restore order in Italy. The Poles living under the rule of Russia staged a revolt in Warsaw late in 1830. Russian armies took nearly an entire year to crush the Polish uprising. By the mid-1830s, the old order seemed to have reestablished itself. But the appearance of stability did not last long.

1848 Revolutions Fail to Unite In 1848, ethnic uprisings erupted throughout Europe. (See the map on page 245.) After an unruly mob in Vienna clashed with police, Metternich resigned and liberal uprisings broke out throughout the Austrian empire. In Budapest, nationalist leader Louis Kossuth called for a parliament and self-government

Social History

Nationalistic Music

As the force of nationalism began to rise in Europe, ethnic groups recognized their music as a unique element of their culture. Composers used folk melodies in their works. For example, Czech composer Antonin Dvořák (DVAWR•zhahk), pictured above, and the Norwegian composer Edvard Grieg incorporated popular melodies and legends into their works. These works became a source of pride and further encouraged the sense of nationalism. Richard Wagner created a cycle of four musical dramas called *Der Ring des Nibelungen*. His operas are considered the pinnacle of German nationalism.

Nationalists Challenge Conservative Power

10.2.5; 10.3.7

Critical Thinking

- Why did leaders of powerful countries oppose revolution even when not directed against them? *(They knew revolutions could spread and bring down their own government.)*
- How were the revolutions in Italy different from the revolutions in Greece, Belgium, and Poland? *(Italian revolution sought to combine smaller states; the other revolutions sought to split up a larger nation.)*

In-Depth Resouces: Unit 2

- Primary Source: *Letter to Thomas Moore*, p. 82

Tip for Struggling Readers

Remind students that many Russians belonged to the Greek Orthodox Church and had other close ties to Greek culture.

Social History

Nationalistic Music

Nationalistic music developed out of the romantic tradition. As such it is rich in color and sound. It also grew out of the 19th century interest in exoticism. People wanted to experience faraway places and cultures. So the music that made people proud of their German or Italian or Bohemian culture was also popular in other parts of Europe and America for its romantic and exotic qualities.

DIFFERENTIATING INSTRUCTION: ENGLISH LEARNERS

Nationalist Revolutions: Key Terms

Class Time 20 minutes

Task Developing a concept web for key terms

Purpose To develop deeper understanding of key terms

Instructions Write the key terms for this section on the chalkboard. Then project Critical Thinking Transparency CT78 and write *The Balkans* in the center circle. Guide students in providing details about the term.

Then have students work in pairs. Tell them to create a concept web for each of the other key terms in the section. When students finish, review the terms with the group. Use the Reading Study Guide in Spanish for additional help.

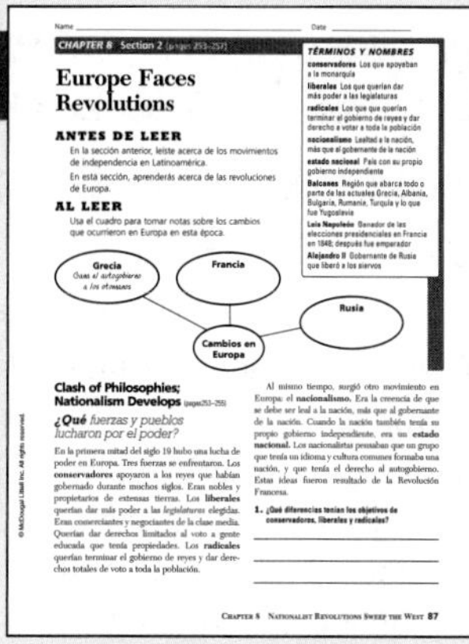
CHAPTER 8 Section 2

Europe Faces Revolutions

ANTES DE LEER

AL LEER

TÉRMINOS Y NOMBRES

Clash of Philosophies: Nationalism Develops

Reading Study Guide: Spanish Translation

Tip for English Learners

Call students' attention to the word *seesaw.* Explain that in this context the word does not refer to the familiar piece of playground equipment. Here, the word means that politics went up and down.

Radicals Change France
10.2.4

Critical Thinking

- How were the actions of the radicals contrary to their philosophy? *(They advocated rule by democracy but tried to get their way through violence.)*
- Was the election of Louis-Napoleon a victory for the radicals? Explain. *(Possible Answers: No, because he later declared himself emperor. Yes, because he was elected by the people.)*

Reform in Russia
10.2.5

Critical Thinking

- How did Russia's defeat in the Crimean War push it toward political reform? *(It proved that Russia's political system must be reformed for Russia to compete with western Europe.)*
- Were the peasants better off after the serfs were freed? Explain. *(Possible Answers: Yes, because they were free. No, because they were poor and still tied to the land by debt.)*

▲ In *Combat Before the Hotel de Ville, July 28th, 1830,* Victor Schnetz portrays the riots in Paris that forced Charles X to flee to Great Britain.

for Hungary. Meanwhile in Prague, Czech liberals demanded Bohemian independence.

European politics continued to seesaw. Many liberal gains were lost to conservatives within a year. In one country after another, the revolutionaries failed to unite themselves or their nations. Conservatives regained their nerve and their power. By 1849, Europe had practically returned to the conservatism that had controlled governments before 1848. **B**

MAIN IDEA

Hypothesizing

B Why weren't the revolutions of 1830 and 1848 successful?

B. Possible Answers The conservatives held far more power; the uprisings were ethnic in nature and may not have attracted enough people to be successful.

Radicals Change France

Radicals participated in many of the 1848 revolts. Only in France, however, was the radical demand for democratic government the main goal of revolution. In 1830, France's King Charles X tried to stage a return to absolute monarchy. The attempt sparked riots that forced Charles to flee to Great Britain. He was replaced by Louis-Philippe, who had long supported liberal reforms in France.

The Third Republic However, in 1848, after a reign of almost 18 years, Louis-Philippe fell from popular favor. Once again, a Paris mob overturned a monarchy and established a republic. The new republican government began to fall apart almost immediately. The radicals split into factions. One side wanted only political reform. The other side also wanted social and economic reform. The differences set off bloody battles in Parisian streets. The violence turned French citizens away from the radicals. As a result, a moderate constitution was drawn up later in 1848. It called for a parliament and a strong president to be elected by the people.

France Accepts a Strong Ruler In December 1848, **Louis-Napoleon**, the nephew of Napoleon Bonaparte, won the presidential election. Four years later, Louis-Napoleon Bonaparte took the title of Emperor Napoleon III. A majority of French voters accepted this action without complaint. The French were weary of instability. They welcomed a strong ruler who would bring peace to France. **C**

C. Answer Absolute monarchy (Charles X) to liberal monarchy (Louis-Philippe) to radical republic (1848 revolution) to constitutional government (Louis-Napoleon Bonaparte) to monarchy (Emperor Napoleon III)

MAIN IDEA

Summarizing

C How would you describe the political swings occurring in France between 1830 and 1852?

As France's emperor, Louis-Napoleon built railroads, encouraged industrialization, and promoted an ambitious program of public works. Gradually, because of Louis-Napoleon's policies, unemployment decreased in France, and the country experienced real prosperity.

Reform in Russia

Unlike France, Russia in the 1800s had yet to leap into the modern industrialized world. Under Russia's feudal system, serfs were bound to the nobles whose land they worked. Nobles enjoyed almost unlimited power over them. By the 1820s, many Russians believed that serfdom must end. In their eyes, the system was morally wrong. It also prevented the empire from advancing economically. The czars, however, were reluctant to free the serfs. Freeing them would anger the landowners, whose support the czars needed to stay in power.

DIFFERENTIATING INSTRUCTION: STRUGGLING READERS

Role Playing Political Positions

Class Time 45 minutes

Task Role playing conservatives, liberals, radicals

Purpose To identify causes of events

Instructions Group students into pairs. Assign each pair a role as a conservative, liberal, or radical. Then have them choose one of the revolutions or situations discussed in this chapter as the subject for a position statement. For example, they might choose the subject of Louis-Napoleon's decision to make himself emperor. Tell them to review the text and notes they've taken from class discussion. You might encourage them to talk about the situation with other students who have chosen the same topic. The Guided Reading worksheet for Section 2 will help them choose a revolution or situation. Then ask them to state their position on the revolution or situation. Their statement should

- reflect their point of view as conservative, liberal, or radical.
- give reasons for their point of view.
- tell what has happened and why.
- suggest a solution.

Have students make their statements to the group.

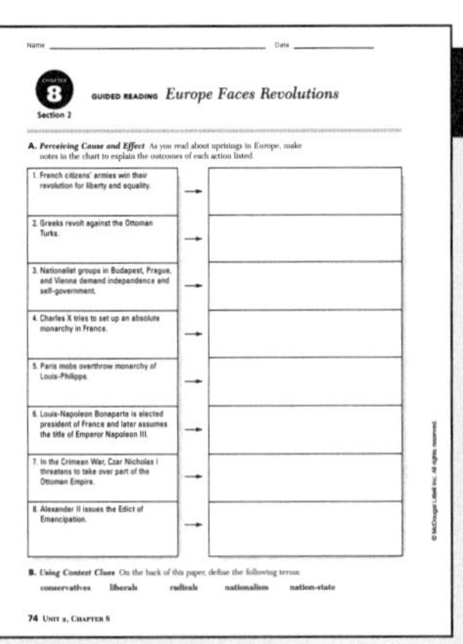

In-Depth Resouces: Unit 2

Defeat Brings Change Eventually, Russia's lack of development became obvious to Russians and to the whole world. In 1853, Czar Nicholas I threatened to take over part of the Ottoman Empire in the Crimean War. However, Russia's industries and transportation system failed to provide adequate supplies for the country's troops. As a result, in 1856, Russia lost the war against the combined forces of France, Great Britain, Sardinia, and the Ottoman Empire.

After the war, Nicholas's son, **Alexander II**, decided to move Russia toward modernization and social change. Alexander and his advisers believed that his reforms would allow Russia to compete with western Europe for world power.

Reform and Reaction The first and boldest of Alexander's reforms was a decree freeing the serfs in 1861. The abolition of serfdom, however, went only halfway. Peasant communities—rather than individual peasants—received about half the farmland in the country. Nobles kept the other half. The government paid the nobles for their land. Each peasant community, on the other hand, had 49 years to pay the government for the land it had received. So, while the serfs were legally free, the debt still tied them to the land.

Political and social reforms ground to a halt when terrorists assassinated Alexander II in 1881. His successor, Alexander III, tightened czarist control over the country. Alexander III and his ministers, however, encouraged industrial development to expand Russia's power. A major force behind Russia's drive toward industrial expansion was nationalism. Nationalism also stirred other ethnic groups. During the 1800s, such groups were uniting into nations and building industries to survive among other nation-states. D

D. Possible Answer The czars needed to reform Russia to bring its power up to the level of western European powers.

MAIN IDEA
Analyzing Issues
D Why did czars push for industrialization?

History *in* Depth

Emancipation

In 1861, on the day before Abraham Lincoln became president of the United States, Czar Alexander II issued the Edict of Emancipation, freeing 20 million serfs. Less than two years later, President Lincoln issued the Emancipation Proclamation, freeing enslaved peoples living under the Confederacy.

The emancipation edicts did not entirely fulfill the hopes of Russian serfs or former slaves in the United States. Russian peasant communities, like the one pictured above, were still tied to the land. And Lincoln did not free enslaved people in the border states.

History *in* Depth

Emancipation

How were the serfs and slaves alike? *(Neither had many rights; neither could move without the master's or noble's approval.)*

An important difference between serfs and slaves was that serfs were tied to the land, which they didn't own, whereas slaves in the United States were owned by white masters. Serfs could own property, including cattle and tools, although not the land, and they had some rights in choosing who to marry. Slaves owned nothing and had no rights in choosing spouses. Serfs could also be made to pay taxes and serve in the military; slaves did not have these obligations.

SECTION 2 ASSESSMENT

TERMS & NAMES 1. For each term or name, write a sentence explaining its significance.
• conservative • liberal • radical • nationalism • nation-state • the Balkans • Louis-Napoleon • Alexander II

USING YOUR NOTES

2. Why did most of the revolts fail? (10.2.5)

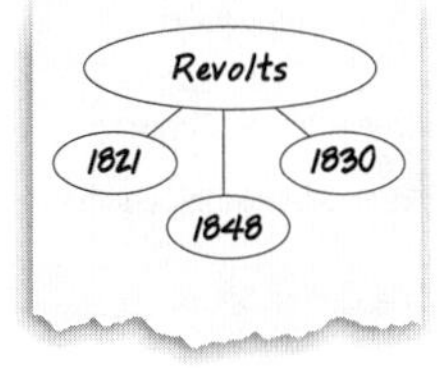

MAIN IDEAS

3. How were radicals different from liberals? (10.2.5)
4. Why did France's Third Republic fail? (10.2.4)
5. What was the driving force behind Russia's industrial expansion? (10.2.5)

CRITICAL THINKING & WRITING

6. **MAKING INFERENCES** Why might liberals and radicals join together in a nationalist cause? (10.2.5)
7. **DRAWING CONCLUSIONS** Why did some liberals disapprove of the way Louis-Napoleon ruled France after the uprisings of 1848? (10.2.4)
8. **EVALUATING DECISIONS** What consequences did Alexander's reforms have on Russia? (10.2.5)
9. **WRITING ACTIVITY** REVOLUTION Imagine you live in Europe in 1848. Write a **letter** to a friend, stating your political position—conservative, liberal, or radical. Relate your feelings about the uprisings and Europe's future. (Writing 2.4.d)

CONNECT TO TODAY WRITING A TV NEWS SCRIPT

Early in the 21st century, hostility between Greeks and Turks on the island of Cyprus was reduced. Prepare a **TV news script** about the current status of governing the island. (CST 2)

❸ ASSESS

SECTION 2 ASSESSMENT

Have students work in pairs to complete the assessment. Ask volunteers to share their answers with the class.

Formal Assessment
• Section Quiz, p. 137

❹ RETEACH

Have students use the Reteaching Activity to review Section 2.

In-Depth Resources: Unit 2
• Reteaching Activity, p. 92

ANSWERS

1. conservative, p. 253 • liberal, p. 253 • radical, p. 253 • nationalism, p. 253 • nation-state, p. 253 • the Balkans, p. 255 • Louis-Napoleon, p. 256 • Alexander II, p. 257
2. **Sample Answer:** 1821—Greece rebels against Ottomans. 1830—Belgians rebel against Dutch; Poles rebel against Russia; French depose Charles X. 1848—Hungarians demand self-government; Czechs demand Bohemian independence; liberal revolt in German states; French demand democratic government.
Answer: Conservatives still held enough power to put down the revolts.
3. Radicals wanted to extend democratic government to all people. Liberals would limit power to elected parliaments of the educated or landholders.
4. There were sharp divides between the goals of radicals, which led to fights between factions. Moderates took over.
5. nationalism
6. **Possible Answer:** They might cooperate to get rid of the conservative control of the country.
7. Liberals wanted a strong parliament, but Louis-Napoleon made himself sole ruler.
8. **Possible Answer:** Terrorists assassinated Alexander II. However, eventually some industrialization and modernization did take place.
9. **Rubric** The letter should
• clearly state your position.
• express an opinion about the uprisings.
• predict a future course for Europe.

CONNECT TO TODAY

Rubric The news script should
• give a brief history of past disputes.
• identify the current status.
• include suggestions for visuals.

LESSON PLAN

OBJECTIVES

- Identify the links that create nation-states and explain how nationalism weakened empires.
- Summarize how Cavour unified Italy.
- Describe the unification of Germany and explain shifts in power.

1 FOCUS & MOTIVATE

Ask students if nationalism still provokes rebellions and violence. What are some examples? *(Yes. Examples include Palestine, Bosnia and Herzegovina, Taiwan, Korea, some areas of Africa.)*

2 INSTRUCT

Nationalism: A Force for Unity or Disunity

10.2.5

Critical Thinking

- How was the revolt in the Balkans an example of nationalism? *(Greeks broke away from an empire of many cultures.)*

CALIFORNIA RESOURCES

California Reading Toolkit, p. L39
California Modified Lesson Plans for English Learners, p. 73
California Daily Standards Practice Transparencies, TT31
California Standards Enrichment Workbook, pp. 31–32
California Standards Planner and Lesson Plans, p. L69
California Online Test Practice
California Test Generator CD-ROM
California Easy Planner CD-ROM
California eEdition CD-ROM

3

Nationalism

CASE STUDY: Italy and Germany

MAIN IDEA

POWER AND AUTHORITY Nationalism contributed to the formation of two new nations and a new political order in Europe.

WHY IT MATTERS NOW

Nationalism is the basis of world politics today and has often caused conflicts and wars.

TERMS & NAMES

- Russification
- Camillo di Cavour
- Giuseppe Garibaldi
- Junker
- Otto von Bismarck
- realpolitik
- kaiser

CALIFORNIA STANDARDS

10.2.5 Discuss how nationalism spread across Europe with Napoleon but was repressed for a generation under the Congress of Vienna and Concert of Europe until the Revolutions of 1848.

CST 3 Students use a variety of maps and documents to interpret human movement, including major patterns of domestic and international migration, changing environmental preferences and settlement patterns, the frictions that develop between population groups, and the diffusion of ideas, technological innovations, and goods.

REP 4 Students construct and test hypotheses; collect, evaluate, and employ information from multiple primary and secondary sources; and apply it in oral and written presentations.

SETTING THE STAGE Nationalism was the most powerful idea of the 1800s. Its influence stretched throughout Europe and the Americas. It shaped countries by creating new ones or breaking up old ones. In Europe, it also upset the balance of power set up at the Congress of Vienna in 1815, affecting the lives of millions. Empires in Europe were made up of many different groups of people. Nationalism fed the desire of most of those groups to be free of the rule of empires and govern themselves in their traditional lands.

Nationalism: A Force for Unity or Disunity

During the 1800s, nationalism fueled efforts to build nation-states. Nationalists were not loyal to kings, but to their people—to those who shared common bonds. Nationalists believed that people of a single "nationality," or ancestry, should unite under a single government. However, people who wanted to restore the old order from before the French Revolution saw nationalism as a force for disunity.

Gradually, authoritarian rulers began to see that nationalism could also unify masses of people. They soon began to use nationalist feelings for their own purposes. They built nation-states in areas where they remained firmly in control.

TAKING NOTES

Following Chronological Order List major events in the unification of Italy and of Germany.

Types of Nationalist Movements

Type	Characteristics	Examples
Unification	• Mergers of politically divided but culturally similar lands	• 19th century Germany • 19th century Italy
Separation	• Culturally distinct group resists being added to a state or tries to break away	• Greeks in the Ottoman Empire • French-speaking Canadians
State-building	• Culturally distinct groups form into a new state by accepting a single culture	• The United States • Turkey

SKILLBUILDER: Interpreting Charts

1. **Categorizing** *What types of nationalist movements can evolve in lands with culturally distinct groups?*
2. **Drawing Conclusions** *What must be present for state-building to take place?*

SECTION 3 PROGRAM RESOURCES

ALL STUDENTS

In-Depth Resources: Unit 2
- Guided Reading, p. 75
- Geography Application, p. 79

Formal Assessment
- Section Quiz, p. 138

ENGLISH LEARNERS

In-Depth Resources in Spanish
- Guided Reading, p. 69
- Geography Application, p. 72

Reading Study Guide (Spanish), p. 89
Reading Study Guide Audio CD (Spanish)

STRUGGLING READERS

In-Depth Resources: Unit 2
- Guided Reading, p. 75
- Building Vocabulary, p. 77
- Geography Application, p. 79
- Reteaching Activity, p. 93

Reading Study Guide, p. 89
Reading Study Guide Audio CD

GIFTED AND TALENTED STUDENTS

In-Depth Resources: Unit 2
- Primary Sources: *Proclamation of 1860,* p. 83; Nationalist Speech, p. 84
- Connections Across Time and Cultures, p. 90

Electronic Library of Primary Sources

INTEGRATED TECHNOLOGY

eEdition CD-ROM
Power Presentations CD-ROM
Geography Transparencies
- GT24 Ethnic Groups of Austria-Hungary, 1867

Critical Thinking Transparencies
- CT24 The Unification of Germany and Italy

Electronic Library of Primary Sources
- from "Duties of Country"

classzone.com

In the chart on page 258, you can see the characteristics and examples of three types of nationalist movements. In today's world, groups still use the spirit of nationalism to unify, separate, or build up nation-states.

Nationalism Shakes Aging Empires

Three aging empires—the Austrian Empire of the Hapsburgs, the Russian Empire of the Romanovs, and the Ottoman Empire of the Turks—contained a mixture of ethnic groups. Control of land and ethnic groups moved back and forth between these empires, depending on victories or defeats in war and on royal marriages. When nationalism emerged in the 19th century, ethnic unrest threatened and eventually toppled these empires.

The Breakup of the Austrian Empire The Austrian Empire brought together Slovenes, Hungarians, Germans, Czechs, Slovaks, Croats, Poles, Serbs, and Italians. In 1866, Prussia defeated Austria in the Austro-Prussian War. With its victory, Prussia gained control of the newly organized North German Confederation, a union of Prussia and 21 smaller German political units. Then, pressured by the Hungarians, Emperor Francis Joseph of Austria split his empire in half, declaring Austria and Hungary independent states, with himself as ruler of both. The empire was now called Austria-Hungary or the Austro-Hungarian Empire. Nationalist disputes continued to weaken the empire for more than 40 years. Finally, after World War I, Austria-Hungary broke into several separate nation-states.

The Russian Empire Crumbles Nationalism also helped break up the 370-year-old empire of the czars in Russia. In addition to the Russians themselves, the czar ruled over 22 million Ukrainians, 8 million Poles, and smaller numbers of Lithuanians, Latvians, Estonians, Finns, Jews, Romanians, Georgians, Armenians, Turks, and others. Each group had its own culture.

The ruling Romanov dynasty of Russia was determined to maintain iron control over this diversity. They instituted a policy of **Russification**, forcing Russian culture on all the ethnic groups in the empire. This policy actually strengthened ethnic nationalist feelings and helped to disunify Russia. The weakened czarist empire finally could not withstand the double shock of World War I and the communist revolution. The last Romanov czar gave up his power in 1917. (A)

A. Possible Answer Trying to force a culture or language on a group of people will probably create resentment. As a reaction, the group may take even greater pride in its own language and culture.

MAIN IDEA

Making Inferences

(A) Why might a policy like Russification produce results that are opposite those intended?

The Ottoman Empire Weakens The ruling Turks of the Ottoman Empire controlled Greeks, Slavs, Arabs, Bulgarians, and Armenians. In 1856, under pressure from the British and French, the Ottomans granted equal citizenship to all the people under their rule. That measure angered conservative Turks, who wanted no change in the situation, and caused tensions in the empire. For example, in response to nationalism in

◄ Driven from their homes, Armenians beg for bread at a refugee center.

CHAPTER 8 • Section 3

SKILLBUILDER Answers

1. **Categorizing** separation, state-building
2. **Drawing Conclusions** acceptance of a single culture for the nation

Nationalism Shakes Aging Empires
10.2.5

Critical Thinking

- What did Francis Joseph hope to achieve by breaking his empire into two states? *(satisfy nationalist spirit while keeping control of both states)*
- How was Russification supposed to strengthen the empire? *(If people shared the same culture they would identify with the empire.)*

Geography Transparencies

- GT24 Ethnic Groups of Austria-Hungary, 1867

More About . . .

Russification

Russification, which began in the 1860s, had various elements. In many places, a strong effort was made to make Russian the principal language. In Poland, for example, school instruction was entirely in Russian, even in the primary grades. And in the Baltic provinces, the German university was closed. Conversion to the Orthodox Church was also encouraged, and people who converted were not allowed to return to their old religions.

In-Depth Resources: Unit 2

- Geography Application: Languages Fuel Nationalism, p. 79

CONNECTIONS ACROSS TIME AND CULTURES

The United States as a Nation-State

Class Time 15 minutes

Task Identifying characteristics of the nation-state

Purpose To identify ways in which the United States is a nation-state

Instructions Remind students that nationalist movements can occur in one of three ways: by unification, separation, or state-building. People of the United States have very strong feelings of nationalism, yet it is a highly diverse country made up of immigrants from many different countries. In coming to this country, however, people have adopted a common culture that unites them. For example, beginning with the first colonies, immigrants have brought different languages with them. Many languages are still spoken, and yet English has developed as the common language of the land and acts as one of the unifying elements of the national spirit. Give students a copy of Connections Across Time and Cultures from In-Depth Resources: Unit 2, p. 90. Then break them into small groups and have them complete the chart. Encourage them to use encyclopedias, almanacs, or other resource materials. After 15 minutes, bring the groups together, and discuss students' ideas.

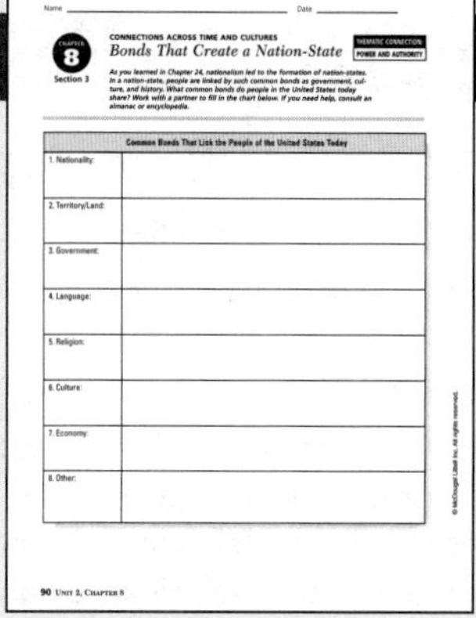

In-Depth Resources: Unit 2

Cavour Unites Italy
10.2.5

Critical Thinking

- Why would Napoleon III agree to help Sardinia drive out Austria? *(It would weaken Austria, a rival of France.)*
- Why was Rome made the capital of Italy? *(Possible Answers: largest city; as the capital of ancient Rome, it had symbolic importance)*

Electronic Library of Primary Sources

- from "Duties of Country"

History from Visuals

Interpreting the Map

Have students identify areas that were added to Sardinia and areas that were later added to Italy.

Extension Ask students to read about one or more regions shown on this map, and write a brief report describing its history and any other distinguishing characteristics.

INTEGRATED TECHNOLOGY

Interactive This image is available in an interactive format on the eEdition. A time line shows which areas were added to Italy at different times during unification.

SKILLBUILDER Answers

1. **Movement** 1859–1860
2. **Region** the provinces of Savoy and Nice

Armenia, the Ottomans massacred and deported Armenians from 1894 to 1896 and again in 1915. Like Austria-Hungary, the Ottoman Empire broke apart soon after World War I.

CASE STUDY: ITALY

Cavour Unites Italy

While nationalism destroyed empires, it also built nations. Italy was one of the countries to form from the territory of crumbling empires. Between 1815 and 1848, fewer and fewer Italians were content to live under foreign rulers.

Cavour Leads Italian Unification Italian nationalists looked for leadership from the kingdom of Piedmont-Sardinia, the largest and most powerful of the Italian states. The kingdom had adopted a liberal constitution in 1848. So, to the liberal Italian middle classes, unification under Piedmont-Sardinia seemed a good plan.

In 1852, Sardinia's king, Victor Emmanuel II, named Count **Camillo di Cavour** (kuh•VOOR) as his prime minister. Cavour was a cunning statesman who worked tirelessly to expand Piedmont-Sardinia's power. Using skillful diplomacy and well-chosen alliances he set about gaining control of northern Italy for Sardinia.

Cavour realized that the greatest roadblock to annexing northern Italy was Austria. In 1858, the French emperor Napoleon III agreed to help drive Austria out of the northern Italian provinces. Cavour then provoked a war with the Austrians. A combined French-Sardinian army won two quick victories. Sardinia succeeded in taking all of northern Italy, except Venetia.

GEOGRAPHY SKILLBUILDER: Interpreting Maps
1. **Movement** *During what time period was the greatest share of territory unified in Italy?*
2. **Region** *Which territories did the Italians lose to France during their process of unification?*

Garibaldi Brings Unity As Cavour was uniting northern Italy, he secretly started helping nationalist rebels in southern Italy. In May 1860, a small army of Italian nationalists led by a bold and visionary soldier, **Giuseppe Garibaldi** (GAR•uh• BAWL•dee), captured Sicily. In battle, Garibaldi always wore a bright red shirt, as did his followers. As a result, they became known as the Red Shirts.

From Sicily, Garibaldi and his forces crossed to the Italian mainland and marched north. Eventually, Garibaldi agreed to unite the southern areas he had conquered with the kingdom of Piedmont-Sardinia. Cavour arranged for King Victor Emmanuel II to meet Garibaldi in Naples. "The Red One" willingly agreed to step aside and let the Sardinian king rule. **B**

In 1866, the Austrian province of Venetia, which included the city of Venice, became part of Italy. In 1870,

B. Possible Answer He may have felt the king had more supporters than he did, or that he trusted the king to rule well.

MAIN IDEA

Hypothesizing

B What reasons might Garibaldi have had to step aside and let the Sardinian king rule?

DIFFERENTIATING INSTRUCTION: GIFTED AND TALENTED STUDENTS

Creating a News Report about Garibaldi

Class Time 45 minutes

Task Presenting a news report featuring Giuseppe Garibaldi

Purpose To learn more about Garibaldi and his times

Instructions Tell students that Garibaldi was one of the most fascinating figures of the 19th century. He was a fisherman, trader, naval commander, guerrilla fighter, poet, teacher, and idealistic revolutionary who fought in Latin America as well as in Italy. He was even offered a command in the Union Army by President Abraham Lincoln. The French writer Alexandre Dumas wrote of him: "Once mention the word independence, or that of Italy, and he becomes a volcano in eruption." Have students work as a group and do research to learn more about Garibaldi. Then have them imagine that they can bring him into the 21st century for a TV news feature. Have them share responsibilities and write a script and present the news feature for the class. They should take different roles as Garibaldi, news reporters, a news anchor, Lincoln, Dumas, and other key historic figures. Tell them to try to present the character as well as the facts about Garibaldi.

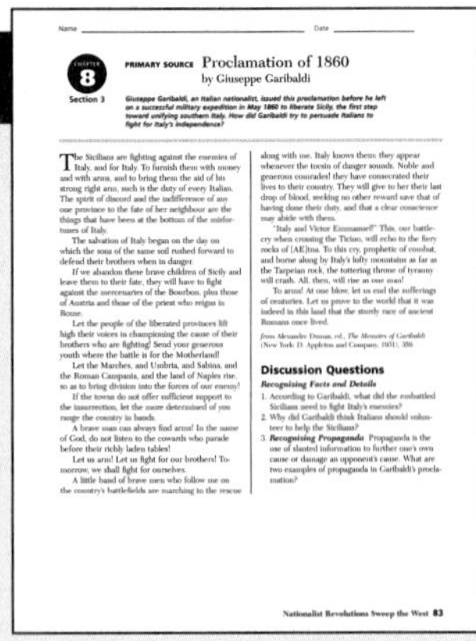
Proclamation of 1860
by Giuseppe Garibaldi

In-Depth Resources: Unit 2

> Analyzing Political Cartoons

"Right Leg in the Boot at Last"

In this 1860 British cartoon, the king of Sardinia is receiving control of lands taken by the nationalist Garibaldi. The act was one of the final steps in the unification of Italy.

SKILLBUILDER: Analyzing Political Cartoons

1. **Clarifying** *What symbol does the cartoonist use for the soon-to-be nation of Italy?*
2. **Making Inferences** *How is Garibaldi portrayed?*
3. **Analyzing Bias** *What does the title of the cartoon say about the cartoonist's view of Italian unification?*

 See Skillbuilder Handbook, page R29

Italian forces took over the last part of a territory known as the Papal States. With this victory, the city of Rome came under Italian control. Soon after, Rome became the capital of the united kingdom of Italy. The pope, however, would continue to govern a section of Rome known as Vatican City.

CASE STUDY: GERMANY

Bismarck Unites Germany

Like Italy, Germany also achieved national unity in the mid-1800s. Beginning in 1815, 39 German states formed a loose grouping called the German Confederation. The Austrian Empire dominated the confederation. However, Prussia was ready to unify all the German states.

Prussia Leads German Unification Prussia enjoyed several advantages that would eventually help it forge a strong German state. First of all, unlike the Austro-Hungarian Empire, Prussia had a mainly German population. As a result, nationalism actually unified Prussia. In contrast, ethnic groups in Austria-Hungary tore the empire apart. Moreover, Prussia's army was by far the most powerful in central Europe. In 1848, Berlin rioters forced a constitutional convention to write up a liberal constitution for the kingdom, paving the way for unification.

Bismarck Takes Control In 1861, Wilhelm I succeeded Frederick William to the throne. The liberal parliament refused him money for reforms that would double the strength of the army. Wilhelm saw the parliament's refusal as a major challenge to his authority. He was supported in his view by the **Junkers** (YUNG•kuhrz), strongly conservative members of Prussia's wealthy landowning class. In 1862, Wilhelm chose a conservative Junker named **Otto von Bismarck** as his prime minister. Bismarck was a master of what came to be known as **realpolitik**. This

Analyzing Political Cartoons

Remind students that the unification of Italy took place through the efforts of Garibaldi and the king of Sardinia. Point out that this is a British cartoon. Ask students what tone the cartoonist uses. What is his opinion of unification? *(Tone is respectful. Opinion—Unification of Italy is a good development and probably overdue.)*

SKILLBUILDER Answers

1. **Clarifying** a boot
2. **Making Inferences** in his trademark red shirt acting as a servant to the king
3. **Analyzing Bias** *Possible Answer:* The cartoonist believes that Italian unification will finally take place with the cooperation of Garibaldi and the king of Sardinia.

Bismarck Unites Germany
10.2.5

Critical Thinking

- What can you infer from the liberal parliament's refusal to provide money for Wilhelm I's reforms? *(Possible Answer: Parliament wanted to undermine the monarchy so it could be replaced with a democratic government.)*
- How did Bismarck's provocation of war with Austria demonstrate realpolitik? *(He unethically provoked a war he knew Prussia would win.)*

DIFFERENTIATING INSTRUCTION: ENGLISH LEARNERS

Understanding Italian and German Unification

Class Time 20 minutes

Task Creating flow charts

Purpose To develop understanding of the unification of Italy and Germany

Instructions To help students understand how Italy and Germany were unified, have them make flow charts for both Italy and Germany. Remind students that before they became single nations, both Italy and Germany were divided into smaller states and often had rulers who were outside of the area. Here is a chart for Italy.

Cavour gets the French to help drive Austria out of northern Italy.

↓

Garibaldi wins control of southern Italy.

↓

Cavour and Garibaldi agree to unite Italy under one king.

↓

Vatican City in Rome remains under control of the pope.

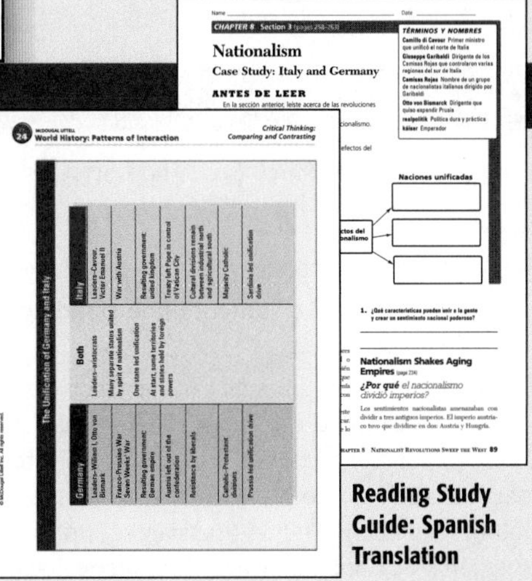

Critical Thinking Transparencies

Reading Study Guide: Spanish Translation

History Makers

Otto von Bismarck

How could Bismarck evoke such strong and different responses from people? *(He was single-minded and uncompromising.)*

For his unshakable determination and his "blood and iron" policies, Bismarck earned the title "the Iron Chancellor." One of Bismarck's acquaintances said, "He listens only to himself, and if once in a while he hears someone else it is only something that suits his purpose; then he picks up a phrase and drops everything else. This can all be attributed to the fundamental trait of his character: concentrated energy."

INTEGRATED TECHNOLOGY

Rubric The time line should
- list Bismark's actions to unite Germany
- be accurate and brief

In-Depth Resources: Unit 2
- Primary Source: Nationalist Speech, p. 84

More About . . .

The Seven Weeks' War

The Austrian troops outnumbered the Prussian troops, but the brilliant Prussian general Helmuth von Moltke made use of a new invention, the railroad, to move troops quickly and efficiently. He also used other new inventions such as the telegraph and the rapid-fire "needle gun" to win a quick and decisive victory.

History Makers

Otto von Bismarck
1815–1898

To some Germans, Bismarck was the greatest and noblest of Germany's statesmen. They say he almost single-handedly unified the nation and raised it to greatness. To others, he was nothing but a devious politician who abused his powers and led Germany into dictatorship.

His speeches, letters, and memoirs show him to be both crafty and deeply religious. At one moment, he could declare, "It is the destiny of the weak to be devoured by the strong." At another moment he might claim, "We Germans shall never wage aggressive war, ambitious war, a war of conquest."

INTEGRATED TECHNOLOGY

INTERNET ACTIVITY Create an interactive time line of Bismarck's actions to unite Germany. Go to **classzone.com** for your research.

German term means "the politics of reality." The term is used to describe tough power politics with no room for idealism. With realpolitik as his style, Bismarck would become one of the commanding figures of German history.

With the king's approval, Bismarck declared that he would rule without the consent of parliament and without a legal budget. Those actions were in direct violation of the constitution. In his first speech as prime minister, he defiantly told members of the Prussian parliament, "It is not by means of speeches and majority resolutions that the great issues of the day will be decided—that was the great mistake of 1848 and 1849—but by blood and iron." C

MAIN IDEA
Hypothesizing
C Bismarck ignored both the parliament and the constitution. How do you think this action would affect Prussian government?
C. Possible Answer The parliament and constitution would grow weaker. The king and prime minister would grow stronger.

Prussia Expands In 1864, Bismarck took the first step toward molding an empire. Prussia and Austria formed an alliance and went to war against Denmark to win two border provinces, Schleswig and Holstein.

A quick victory increased national pride among Prussians. It also won new respect from other Germans and lent support for Prussia as head of a unified Germany. After the victory, Prussia governed Schleswig, while Austria controlled Holstein.

Seven Weeks' War Bismarck purposely stirred up border conflicts with Austria over Schleswig and Holstein. The tensions provoked Austria into declaring war on Prussia in 1866. This conflict was known as the Seven Weeks' War. The Prussians used their superior training and equipment to win a devastating victory. They humiliated Austria. The Austrians lost the region of Venetia, which was given to Italy. They had to accept Prussian annexation of more German territory.

With its victory in the Seven Weeks' War, Prussia took control of northern Germany. For the first time, the eastern and western parts of the Prussian kingdom were joined. In 1867, the remaining states of the north joined the North German Confederation, which Prussia dominated completely.

The Franco-Prussian War By 1867, a few southern German states remained independent of Prussian control. The majority of southern Germans were Catholics. Many in the region resisted domination by a Protestant Prussia. However, Bismarck felt he could win the support of southerners if they faced a threat from outside. He reasoned that a war with France would rally the south.

Bismarck was an expert at manufacturing "incidents" to gain his ends. For example, he created the impression that the French ambassador had insulted the Prussian king. The French reacted to Bismarck's deception by declaring war on Prussia on July 19, 1870.

The Prussian army immediately poured into northern France. In September 1870, the Prussian army surrounded the main French force at Sedan. Among the 83,000 French prisoners taken was Napoleon III himself. Parisians withstood a German siege until hunger forced them to surrender.

The Franco-Prussian War was the final stage in German unification. Now the nationalistic fever also seized people in southern Germany. They finally accepted Prussian leadership. On January 18, 1871, at the captured French palace of

DIFFERENTIATING INSTRUCTION: STRUGGLING READERS

Images Related to Nationalism

Class Time 45 minutes

Task Preparing a collage

Purpose To improve student understanding of nationalism

Instructions Many images can be associated with the rise of nationalism and the fall of empires. Ask students to work in pairs and choose one of the main topics in the section, such as the breakup of the Ottoman Empire, the fall of Russia, the Franco-Prussian War, or a leader such as Bismarck or Garibaldi. Have students review the text and brainstorm a list of visual images. For example, the rise of Prussia evokes images of the distinctive Prussian military uniform; the stern portrait of Bismarck; Bismarck's idea of "blood and iron"; trains carrying Prussian troops; the siege of Paris and the suffering of the Parisians; and the crowning of King William I as emperor. Then have them find and photocopy pictures from books, print images from the Internet, or create their own images. Have students combine their images and create a collage on the subject. They should display their collages in class. For help in thinking about their subjects, give students the Guided Reading worksheet for Unit 2, p. 75.

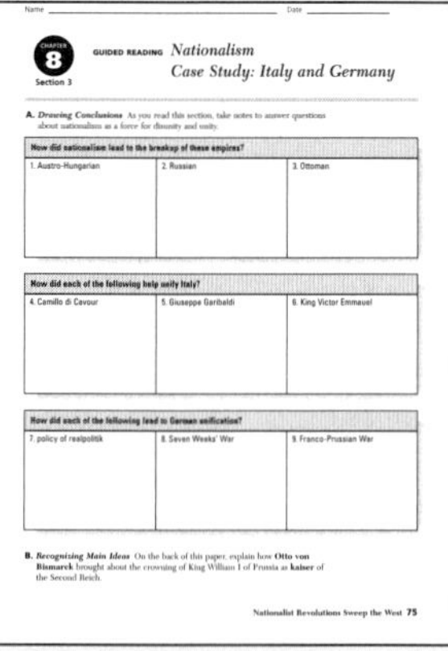

Name ______ Date ______

CHAPTER 8 Section 3 GUIDED READING *Nationalism*
Case Study: Italy and Germany

A. Drawing Conclusions As you read this section, take notes to answer questions about nationalism as a force for disunity and unity.

How did nationalism lead to the breakup of these empires?

1. Austro-Hungarian	2. Russian	3. Ottoman

How did each of the following help unify Italy?

4. Camillo di Cavour	5. Giuseppe Garibaldi	6. King Victor Emmanuel

How did each of the following lead to German unification?

7. policy of realpolitik	8. Seven Weeks' War	9. Franco-Prussian War

B. Recognizing Main Ideas On the back of this paper, explain how Otto von Bismarck brought about the crowning of King William I of Prussia as kaiser of the Second Reich.

Nationalist Revolutions Sweep the West 75

In-Depth Resources: Unit 2

Versailles, King Wilhelm I of Prussia was crowned **kaiser** (KY•zuhr), or emperor. Germans called their empire the Second Reich. (The Holy Roman Empire was the first.) Bismarck had achieved Prussian dominance over Germany and Europe "by blood and iron."

A Shift in Power

The 1815 Congress of Vienna had established five Great Powers in Europe—Britain, France, Austria, Prussia, and Russia. In 1815, the Great Powers were nearly equal in strength.The wars of the mid-1800s greatly strengthened one of the Great Powers, as Prussia joined with other German states to form Germany.

By 1871, Britain and Germany were clearly the most powerful, both militarily and economically. Austria and Russia lagged far behind. France struggled along somewhere in the middle. The European balance of power had broken down. This shift also found expression in the art of the period. In fact, during that century, artists, composers, and writers pointed to paths that they believed European society should follow.

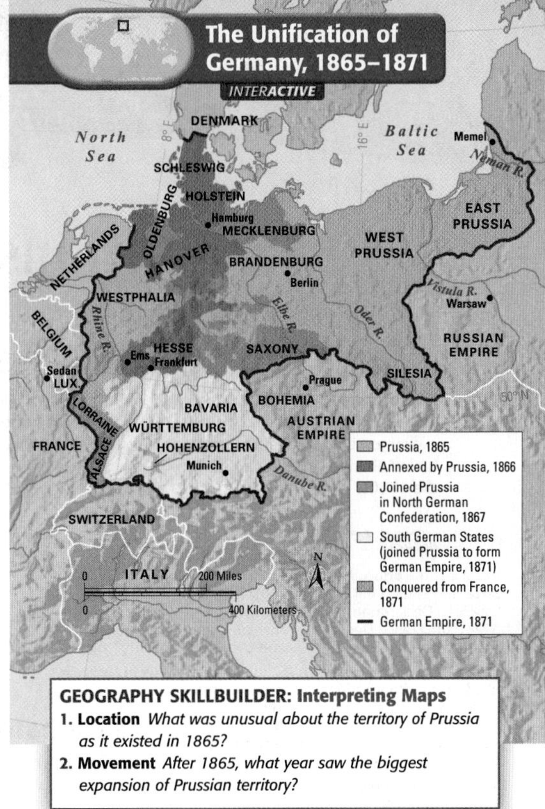

GEOGRAPHY SKILLBUILDER: Interpreting Maps

1. **Location** *What was unusual about the territory of Prussia as it existed in 1865?*
2. **Movement** *After 1865, what year saw the biggest expansion of Prussian territory?*

SECTION 3 ASSESSMENT

TERMS & NAMES 1. For each term or name, write a sentence explaining its significance.

• Russification • Camillo di Cavour • Giuseppe Garibaldi • Junker • Otto von Bismarck • realpolitik • kaiser

USING YOUR NOTES

2. Identify an event that made the unification of Italy or Germany possible. (10.2.5)

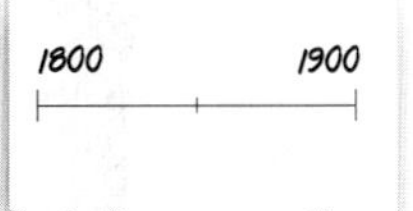

MAIN IDEAS

3. Which aging empires suffered from the forces of nationalism? (10.2.5)
4. What role did Garibaldi play in the unification of Italy? (10.2.5)
5. What advantages did Prussia have in leading the German states to unify? (10.2.5)

CRITICAL THINKING & WRITING

6. **CLARIFYING** How can nationalism be both a unifying and a disunifying force? (10.2.5)
7. **FORMING GENERALIZATIONS** Why did the Austrian, Russian, and Ottoman Empires face such great challenges to their control of land? (10.2.5)
8. **EVALUATING COURSES OF ACTION** Many liberals wanted government by elected parliaments. How was Bismarck's approach to achieving his goals different? (10.2.5)
9. **WRITING ACTIVITY** POWER AND AUTHORITY Write a one paragraph **biographical essay** on either Garibaldi or Cavour. (Writing 2.1.a)

CONNECT TO TODAY **CREATING A MAP AND DATABASE**

Study the chart on page 258. Research the names of nations that have emerged in the last ten years. Categorize each nation's nationalist movement using the chart. Then create a **database** and **map** showing the location of the new nations and the category into which each new nation falls. (CST 3)

History from Visuals

Interpreting the Map

Point out that the German Empire was built in just six years.

Extension Have students compare this map with a political map of Europe in the atlas. Ask, What territory was lost? *(East Prussia, most of West Prussia)*

SKILLBUILDER Answers

1. **Location** Hanover divided Westphalia from the rest of Prussia.
2. **Movement** 1871

A Shift in Power
10.2.5

Critical Thinking

- What effect might the shift in power have? *(Possible Answers: war between Germany and Britain; war to dominate lesser powers)*
- How did nationalism create the shift? *(Germany grew stronger through unification; Russia and Austria grew weaker through separation.)*

3 ASSESS

SECTION 3 ASSESSMENT

Have students work in pairs to answer the questions.

Formal Assessment

- Section Quiz, p. 138

4 RETEACH

Give students the Reteaching Activity for Section 3 to use in reviewing the section.

In-Depth Resources: Unit 2

- Reteaching Activity, p. 93

ANSWERS

1. Russification, p. 259 • Camillo di Cavour, p. 260 • Giuseppe Garibaldi, p. 260 • Junker, p. 261 • Otto von Bismarck, p. 261 • realpolitik, p. 261 • kaiser, p. 263
2. **Sample Answer:** Italy—1848 Cavour appointed prime minister; 1858 French help drive out Austria; 1860 Garibaldi gives up power to King Victor Emmanuel. Germany—1862 Bismarck appointed prime minister; 1866 Seven Weeks' War; 1870 Franco-Prussian War.
3. Austrian, Russian, and Ottoman Empires
4. His forces took control of Sicily and southern Italy.
5. It had a mainly German population and a powerful army. It was industrialized.
6. **Possible Answers:** unite people of the same ethnic group; unify different groups who have the same beliefs; separate people along ethnic lines; cause persecution of certain groups
7. **Possible Answers:** All had large ethnic groups who wished to be separate; all were controlled by conservatives who did not want to give up power.
8. He used military power to achieve goals and had little use for speeches and resolutions.
9. **Rubric** The biographical essay should
   - identify the individual and his role in history.
   - list significant events in the person's life.

CONNECT TO TODAY

Rubric The database and map should

- identify any new nations that have emerged in the last 10 years.
- categorize each nationalistic movement based on the chart.
- locate the new nations and their category.

LESSON PLAN

.7.OBJECTIVES

- Define romanticism and give examples of romantic literature and music.
- Explain the shift to realism and give examples of realistic art and literature.
- Explain why impressionists reacted against realism.

1 FOCUS & MOTIVATE

Ask students if they enjoy romantic or realistic books, art, and movies. Have students write their answers on a sheet of paper. Tell them to check their answers when they finish the section.

2 INSTRUCT

The Romantic Movement

10.3.7; 10.2.2; 10.2.5

Critical Thinking

- Which ideas of romanticism would encourage nationalism? *(Possible Answer: idealizing the past; glorifying heroes and their actions; cherishing folk traditions, music, and stories.)*

CALIFORNIA RESOURCES

California Reading Toolkit, p. L40
California Modified Lesson Plans for English Learners, p. 75
California Daily Standards Practice Transparencies, TT32
California Standards Enrichment Workbook, pp. 25–26, 31–32, 45–46
California Standards Planner and Lesson Plans, p. L71
California Online Test Practice
California Test Generator CD-ROM
California Easy Planner CD-ROM
California eEdition CD-ROM

Arc de Triomphe, Paris, France

Claude Monet, *Poppies*

4

Revolutions in the Arts

MAIN IDEA

CULTURAL INTERACTION Artistic and intellectual movements both reflected and fueled changes in Europe during the 1800s.

WHY IT MATTERS NOW

Romanticism and realism are still found in novels, dramas, and films produced today.

TERMS & NAMES

- romanticism
- realism
- impressionism

CALIFORNIA STANDARDS

10.2.2 List the principles of the Magna Carta, the English Bill of Rights (1689), the American Declaration of Independence (1776), the French Declaration of the Rights of Man and the Citizen (1789), and the U.S. Bill of Rights (1791).

10.2.5 Discuss how nationalism spread across Europe with Napoleon but was repressed for a generation under the Congress of Vienna and Concert of Europe until the Revolutions of 1848.

10.3.7 Describe the emergence of Romanticism in art and literature (e.g., the poetry of William Blake and William Wordsworth), social criticism (e.g., the novels of Charles Dickens), and the move away from Classicism in Europe.

REP 4 Students construct and test hypotheses; collect, evaluate, and employ information from multiple primary and secondary sources; and apply it in oral and written presentations.

HI 1 Students show the connections, causal and otherwise, between particular historical events and larger social, economic, and political trends and developments.

TAKING NOTES

Outlining Organize ideas and details about movements in the arts.

I. The Romantic Movement
A.
B.
II. The Shift to Realism in the Arts

SETTING THE STAGE During the early 1800s, artists focused on ideas of freedom, individual rights, and an idealistic view of history. After the great revolutions of 1848, political focus shifted to realpolitik. Similarly, intellectuals and artists expressed a "realistic" view of the world in which the rich pursued selfish interests while ordinary people struggled and suffered. Newly invented photography became both a way to detail this struggle and a tool for scientific investigation.

The Romantic Movement

At the end of the 18th century, the Enlightenment idea of reason gradually gave way to another major movement in art and ideas: **romanticism**. This movement reflected deep interest both in nature and in the thoughts and feelings of the individual. In many ways, romantic thinkers and writers reacted against the ideals of the Enlightenment. They turned from reason to emotion, from society to nature. Romantics rejected the rigidly ordered world of the middle class. Nationalism also fired the romantic imagination. For example, George Gordon, Lord Byron, one of the leading romantic poets of the time, fought for Greece's freedom.

The Ideas of Romanticism Emotion was a key element of romanticism. However, romanticism went beyond feelings. Romantics expressed a wide range of ideas and attitudes. In general, they shared these beliefs:

- emphasized inner feelings, emotions, and imagination
- focused on the mysterious, the supernatural, and the exotic, grotesque, or horrifying
- loved the beauties of untamed nature
- idealized the past as a simpler and nobler time
- glorified heroes and heroic actions
- cherished folk traditions, music, and stories
- valued the common people and the individual
- promoted radical change and democracy

Romanticism in Literature Poetry, music, and painting were best able to capture the emotion of romanticism. To romantics, poetry was the highest

▶ Romantic poet Lord Byron fought with Greek nationalists. He did not live to see their victory.

SECTION 4 PROGRAM RESOURCES

ALL STUDENTS

In-Depth Resources: Unit 2
- Guided Reading, p. 76
- History Makers: Beethoven, p. 89

Formal Assessment
- Section Quiz, p. 139

ENGLISH LEARNERS

In-Depth Resources in Spanish
- Guided Reading, p. 70

Reading Study Guide (Spanish), p. 91
Reading Study Guide Audio CD (Spanish)

STRUGGLING READERS

In-Depth Resources: Unit 2
- Guided Reading, p. 76
- Building Vocabulary, p. 77
- Reteaching Activity, p. 94

Reading Study Guide, p. 91
Reading Study Guide Audio CD

GIFTED AND TALENTED STUDENTS

Electronic Library of Primary Sources
- "Kubla Khan"
- from *Frankenstein*

INTEGRATED TECHNOLOGY

eEdition CD-ROM
Power Presentations CD-ROM
World Art and Cultures Transparencies
- AT53 *Couturiere*

Critical Thinking Transparencies
- CT60 Chapter 8 Visual Summary

Electronic Library of Primary Sources
- "Kubla Khan"
- from *Frankenstein*

classzone.com

form of expression. The British romantic poets William Wordsworth and Samuel Taylor Coleridge both honored nature as the source of truth and beauty. Later English romantic poets, such as Lord Byron, Percy Bysshe Shelley, and John Keats, wrote poems celebrating rebellious heroes, passionate love, and the mystery and beauty of nature. Like many romantics, many of these British poets lived stormy lives and died young. Byron, for example, died at the age of 36, while Shelley died at 29.

Germany produced one of the earliest and greatest romantic writers. In 1774, Johann Wolfgang von Goethe (YO•hahn VUHLF•gahng fuhn GER•tuh) published *The Sorrows of Young Werther*. Goethe's novel told of a sensitive young man whose hopeless love for a virtuous married woman drives him to suicide. Also in Germany, the brothers Jakob and Wilhelm Grimm collected German fairy tales and created a dictionary and grammar of the German language. Both the tales and the dictionary celebrated the German spirit.

Victor Hugo led the French romantics. His works also reflect the romantic fascination with history and the individual. His novels *Les Misérables* and *The Hunchback of Notre Dame* show the struggles of individuals against a hostile society.

The Gothic Novel Gothic horror stories became hugely popular. These novels often took place in medieval Gothic castles. They were filled with fearful, violent, sometimes supernatural events. Mary Shelley, wife of the poet Percy Bysshe Shelley, wrote one of the earliest and most successful Gothic horror novels, *Frankenstein*. The novel told the story of a monster created from the body parts of dead human beings.

Composers Emphasize Emotion Emotion dominated the music produced by romantic composers. These composers moved away from the tightly controlled, formal compositions of the Enlightenment period. Instead, they celebrated heroism and national pride with a new power of expression.

As music became part of middle-class life, musicians and composers became popular heroes. Composer and pianist Franz Liszt (lihst), for example, achieved earnings and popularity comparable to those of today's rock stars.

One of the composers leading the way into the Romantic period was also its greatest: Ludwig van Beethoven (LOOD•vihg vahn BAY•toh•vuhn). His work evolved from the classical music of the Enlightenment into romantic compositions. His Ninth Symphony soars, celebrating freedom, dignity, and the triumph of the human spirit.

Later romantic composers also appealed to the hearts and souls of their listeners. Robert Schumann's compositions sparkle with merriment. Like many romantic composers, Felix Mendelssohn drew on literature, such as Shakespeare's A *Midsummer Night's Dream*, as the inspiration for his music. Polish composer and concert pianist Frederic Chopin (SHOH•pan) used Polish dance rhythms in his music. Guiseppe Verdi and Richard Wagner brought European opera to a dramatic and theatrical high point. (A)

A. Possible Answers beauty, mystery, terror, heroism, passion, love, tragedy, isolation

MAIN IDEA

Summarizing

(A) What are some of the themes that are key to romantic literature and art?

History Makers

Ludwig van Beethoven
1770–1827

A genius of European music, Beethoven suffered the most tragic disability a composer can endure. At the age of 30, he began to go deaf. His deafness grew worse for 19 years. By 1819, it was total.

At first, Beethoven's handicap barely affected his career. By 1802, however, he knew that his hearing would only worsen. He suffered from bouts of depression. The depression would bring him to the brink of suicide. Nonetheless, he would rebound:

> *It seemed unthinkable for me to leave the world forever before I had produced all that I felt called upon to produce.*

INTEGRATED TECHNOLOGY

RESEARCH LINKS For more on Ludwig van Beethoven, go to **classzone.com**

More About . . .

Romanticism

Romanticism was based on emotional sensitivity and expression. The romantics' emotionalism often led to what many people considered scandalous behavior. The poet Percy Shelley ran away with Mary Godwin while he was still married to another woman. The poet Lord Byron, the writer Goethe, and the composer Liszt all had numerous love affairs. Despite Liszt's popularity, England's Queen Victoria and Prince Albert refused to attend his concert in London because of his scandalous reputation.

Electronic Library of Primary Sources
- "Kubla Khan"
- from *Frankenstein*

History Makers

Ludwig van Beethoven

How was it possible for Beethoven to compose music when he could no longer hear? *(He could hear it in his mind; he knew from the musical notation how notes fit together.)*

After 1819, Beethoven's friends could no longer communicate with him by speaking; they wrote messages to him in notebooks. Beethoven continued to compose, nonetheless. Although he wrote less in his last years, what he did produce was some of his greatest work.

In-Depth Resources: Unit 2
- History Makers: Beethoven, p. 89

DIFFERENTIATING INSTRUCTION: ENGLISH LEARNERS

Words Related to the Arts

Class Time 45 minutes

Task Identifying and explaining art terminology

Purpose To better understand text on the arts

Instructions Have students identify words used in the text that relate to the arts. List the terms on the chalkboard. Have students work in pairs, and assign four or five terms to each pair. Then draw a chart on the chalkboard like the one shown. Have students copy and complete the chart with information about their assigned terms. Have them use the text, a dictionary, an encyclopedia, or other references. Encourage students to use examples from the text or with which they are familiar.

Term	Meaning or characteristics	Example
fairy tale	fanciful story	"Cinderella"
Gothic story	story of horror, mystery, medieval castles	Frankenstein
symphony	long orchestral piece	Beethoven's Ninth Symphony
opera	theatrical piece set to music	The Flying Dutchman

The Shift to Realism in the Arts

10.3.7

Critical Thinking

- Why were novels particularly suitable for describing the realism of workers' lives? *(smallest details of workers' lives could be presented)*
- Who were the villains and the heroes of realist art? *(Villains—Upper class, businesspeople; Heroes—Working class)*

Analyzing Photographs

Motion Studies

Muybridge used a series of 12 to 24 cameras to take his motion pictures. Even then, some people criticized his pictures, arguing, for example, that a horse's legs could not be in such positions. Muybridge went on a lecture tour to explain animal locomotion. He used a zoopraxiscope to project his photographs in rapid succession. It was a predecessor of the movie camera.

SKILLBUILDER Answers

1. **Drawing Conclusions** There is a moment or two in which all four legs are off the ground.
2. **Developing Historical Perspective** *Possible Answers:* They would have seemed fantastic and unreal. They might be seen as scientific.

The Shift to Realism in the Arts

By the middle of the 19th century, rapid industrialization deeply affected everyday life in Europe. The growing class of industrial workers lived grim lives in dirty, crowded cities. Industrialization began to make the dreams of the romantics seem pointless. In literature and the visual arts, **realism** tried to show life as it was, not as it should be. Realist painting reflected the increasing political importance of the working class in the 1850s. Along with paintings, novels proved especially suitable for describing workers' suffering.

Photographers Capture Reality As realist painters and writers detailed the lives of actual people, photographers could record an instant in time with scientific precision. The first practical photographs were called daguerreotypes (duh•GEHR•uh•TYPS). They were named after their French inventor, Louis Daguerre. The images in his daguerreotypes were startlingly real and won him worldwide fame.

British inventor William Talbot invented a light-sensitive paper that he used to produce photographic negatives. The advantage of paper was that many prints could be made from one negative. The Talbot process also allowed photos to be reproduced in books and newspapers. Mass distribution gained a wide audience for the realism of photography. With its scientific, mechanical, and mass-produced features, photography was the art of the new industrial age.

Writers Study Society Realism in literature flourished in France with writers such as Honoré de Balzac and Émile Zola. Balzac wrote a massive series of almost 100 novels entitled *The Human Comedy*. They describe in detail the brutal struggle for wealth and power among all levels of French society. Zola's novels exposed the

Analyzing Photographs

Motion Studies

Eadweard Muybridge had a varied career as a photographer. He devoted part of his career to motion studies. These photographic studies froze the motion of an object at an instant in time. They allowed scientists to study motion and to better understand time. The equipment he built helped lead to the development of motion pictures.

This series of photographs taken in 1878, titled "The Horse in Motion," was designed to discover if all of a running horse's legs ever left the ground at the same time.

SKILLBUILDER: Interpreting Visual Sources

1. **Drawing Conclusions** *What do the series of photographs reveal about the question of whether all the legs of a horse ever left the ground at the same time?*
2. **Developing Historical Perspective** *What reaction do you think these pictures would have generated among the general public?*

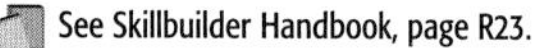

See Skillbuilder Handbook, page R23.

DIFFERENTIATING INSTRUCTION: STRUGGLING READERS

Understanding Art Movements

Class Time 45 minutes

Task Creating a piece of romantic, realistic, or impressionist art

Purpose To develop deeper understanding of the romantic, realistic, and impressionist movements

Instructions Tell students that the best way to understand any art movement is to create a piece of art that responds to the goals and incorporates the qualities of that movement.

- Have students choose one of the art movements featured in this section.
- Ask them to carefully review the description of the movement in the text and to take notes of the specific characteristics and goals of that movement. Have them use the Reading Study Guide, pp. 91–92.
- Have students create a work of art that fits the characteristics of that movement. Students might choose to write a brief story or poem, create a painting or drawing, or compose music.
- Allow students a few minutes to present their work to the class. Ask them to explain how their work follows the criteria for the movement they've chosen.

Reading Study Guide

MAIN IDEA

Forming Opinions

B Which do you think would be more effective in spurring reforms—photographs or a realist novel? Explain.

B. Possible Answers Answers will vary. Photograph—actual conditions could be seen; Novel—would allow for more details to be revealed.

miseries of French workers in small shops, factories, and coal mines. His revelations shocked readers and spurred reforms of labor laws and working conditions in France. The famous English realist novelist Charles Dickens created unforgettable characters and scenes of London's working poor. Many of the scenes were humorous, but others showed the despair of London's poor. In his book *Little Dorrit*, Dickens described the life of a working-class person as sheer monotony set in a gloomy neighborhood. B

Impressionists React Against Realism

Beginning in the 1860s, a group of painters in Paris reacted against the realist style. Instead of showing life "as it really was," they tried to show their impression of a subject or a moment in time. For this reason, their style of art came to be known as **impressionism**. Fascinated by light, impressionist artists used pure, shimmering colors to capture a moment seen at a glance.

Life in the Moment Unlike the realists, impressionists showed a more positive view of the new urban society in western Europe. Instead of abused workers, they showed shop clerks and dock workers enjoying themselves in dance halls and cafés. They painted performers in theaters and circuses. And they glorified the delights of the life of the rising middle class. Claude Monet (moh•NAY), Edgar Degas (duh•GAH), and Pierre-Auguste Renoir (ruhn•WHAR) were leaders in the movement that became very popular.

Composers also created impressions of mood and atmosphere. By using different combinations of instruments, tone patterns, and music structures, they were able to create mental pictures of such things as flashing lights, the feel of a warm summer day, or the sight of the sea. French composers Maurice Ravel and Claude Debussy are the most notable members of the impressionist music movement.

Changes in political, social, artistic, and intellectual movements during the 19th century signaled important changes in daily life. One of the most significant causes of change was industrialization, which you will learn about in Chapter 9.

SECTION 4 ASSESSMENT

TERMS & NAMES 1. For each term or name, write a sentence explaining its significance.

- romanticism
- realism
- impressionism

USING YOUR NOTES

2. What was the goal of realist writers? (10.3.7)

I. The Romantic Movement
A.
B.
II. The Shift to Realism in the Arts

MAIN IDEAS

3. What was the key element of romanticism? (10.3.7)
4. What characteristics did photography have that made it the art of the industrial age? (10.3.7)
5. What was the goal of impressionist painters? (10.3.7)

CRITICAL THINKING & WRITING

6. **COMPARING AND CONTRASTING** How are the movements of romanticism and realism alike and different? (10.3.7)
7. **ANALYZING CAUSES** How might a realist novel bring about changes in society? Describe the ways by which this might happen. (10.3.7)
8. **SUMMARIZING** How did nationalism influence the artistic movements you read about? (10.2.5)
9. **WRITING ACTIVITY** CULTURAL INTERACTION Listen to a piece of music by Beethoven, and then listen to a piece of contemporary music that you like. Write a **comparison-and-contrast essay** on the two pieces of music. (Writing 2.6.a)

CONNECT TO TODAY **Creating an Arts Chart**

Look at newspaper listings for films being shown today. Make a **chart** showing which of them might be categorized as romantic and which might be categorized as realistic. Present reasons why each film fell into the designated category. (REP 4)

Impressionists React Against Realism

10.3.7

Critical Thinking

- How is impressionism similar to and different from photography? *(Possible Answers: Similar—Captures moment in time; Different—More positive, colorful, fanciful)*
- Is impressionism more like realism or romanticism? Explain. *(Possible Answers: Romanticism—Gives a positive, optimistic view of life; Realism—Accurately captures a moment in life)*

3 ASSESS

SECTION 4 ASSESSMENT

Have students work in pairs to answer the questions.

Formal Assessment

- Section Quiz, p. 139

4 RETEACH

Review the section and chapter with students, using the Visual Summary.

Critical Thinking Transparencies

- CT60 Chapter 8 Visual Summary

In-Depth Resources: Unit 2

- Reteaching Activity, p. 94

ANSWERS

1. romanticism, p. 264 • realism, p. 266 • impressionism, p. 267
2. **Sample Answer:** I. A. The Ideas of Romanticism, B. Romanticism in Literature, C. The Gothic Novel, D. Composers Emphasize Emotion. II. A. Photographers Capture Reality, B. Writers Study Society. III. A. Life in the Moment. **Possible Answer:** give impression of moment in time
3. emotion
4. **Possible Answers:** scientific, mechanical, mass production of photos
5. to show a moment in time at a glance
6. Both occurred in painting, literature, and music. Romanticism saw ideal world; realism saw flawed world.
7. describes unhealthy conditions in factories, neighborhoods, the suffering of workers; these facts could affect news reporters, voters, and political scene
8. **Possible Answers:** provided themes for writers, composers, and artists; brought heroes and realistic situations to mind; encouraged dreams of better place
9. **Rubric** The comparison-and-contrast essay should
   - identify both pieces of music.
   - evaluate pieces using a set of standards.
   - draw conclusions about the pieces of music.

CONNECT TO TODAY

Rubric The chart should

- list at least 10 films.
- categorize all listed films.
- present reasons for each categorization.

History *through* Art

OBJECTIVES

1. Describe changes in art during the 19th century.
2. Appreciate the differences between romantic, realist, and impressionist paintings.

FOCUS & MOTIVATE

Ask students which of the three paintings seems the most modern? Why? *(Possible Answers: Romantic–Shows heroic action, occurs in the past like many movies; Realist–It's accurate, detailed, more like a photograph; Impressionist–It's brighter, more colorful like magazine art, not so dull as the other pictures)*

INSTRUCT

Critical Thinking

- What emotions are evoked by the romantic painting? *(Possible Answers: passion, determination, fear, anger)*
- How are society's values and ideas during a particular period of time expressed in the art produced? *(Artists are members of society and share society's values and ideas; these views are expressed in their paintings.)*

History *through* Art

Revolutions in Painting

European painting underwent revolutionary changes during the 1800s. In the early years, romanticism—which stressed emotion above all else—was the dominant style. As revolutions swept Europe in the 1840s, some artists rejected romanticism in favor of realism. They portrayed common people and everyday life in a realistic manner. Toward the end of the century, art underwent another revolution, influenced by scientific discoveries about vision. Impressionist painters experimented with light and color to capture their impressions of a passing moment.

CALIFORNIA STANDARDS

10.3.7 Describe the emergence of Romanticism in art and literature (e.g., the poetry of William Blake and William Wordsworth), social criticism (e.g., the novels of Charles Dickens), and the move away from Classicism in Europe.

HI 1 Students show the connections, causal and otherwise, between particular historical events and larger social, economic, and political trends and developments.

INTEGRATED TECHNOLOGY

RESEARCH LINKS For more on 19th-century painting go to **classzone.com**

▼ Romanticism

In their eagerness to explore emotion, romantic artists had certain favorite subjects: nature, love, religion, and nationalism. This painting, *The Lion Hunt* by Eugène Delacroix, shows that violence and exotic cultures were also popular themes. The swirling capes, snarling lions, and bold reds and yellows help convey the ferocity of the hunt.

RECOMMENDED RESOURCES

Books

Segalen, Victor. ***Essay on Exoticism: An Aesthetics of Diversity***. Trans. Yael Rachel Schlink. Durham, NC: Duke UP, 2002. Writing between 1904 and 1918, Segalen attempts to define "true Exoticism."

Vaughan, William. ***Romanticism and Art (The World of Art).*** London and New York: Thames and Hudson, 1994. A concise but thorough explanation of romanticism in painting. Also includes romantic writings.

Video

Art: A Question of Style. VHS and DVD. Films for the Humanities & Sciences, 1997. 800-257-5126.

The 19th Century: Romanticism and Realism. VHS and DVD. Films for the Humanities & Sciences, 2003. 800-257-5126. Respected authorities elaborate on the lives and works of the masters of romanticism and realism.

Software

Romanticism. CD-ROM. Society for Visual Education, 1994. 800-829-1900.

▲ **Realism**

The Stone Breakers by Gustave Courbet shows that realist artists tried to portray everyday life just as it was, without making it pretty or trying to tell a moralistic story. Notice how the workers' clothes are torn and shabby. The boy rests the heavy basket of stones on his knee to ease his burden, while the man bends to his task. The colors are dull and gritty, just as the job itself is.

▼ **Impressionism**

The impressionists wanted to record the perceptions of the human eye rather than physical reality. To do this, they tried to portray the effect of light on landscapes and buildings. They combined short strokes of many colors to create a shimmering effect. They also used brighter, lighter colors than the artists before them had used. As the painting *Ducal Palace, Venice* by Claude Monet shows, the impressionists often painted water because of its reflective nature.

Connect *to* Today

1. **Developing Historical Perspective** If you were a political revolutionary of the 1800s, which of these artistic styles would you use for your propaganda posters? Why?
   See Skillbuilder Handbook, page R12.
2. **Drawing Conclusions** Impressionism remains extremely popular more than a century after it was first developed. What do you think accounts for its popularity today?

More About . . .

Gustave Courbet

In the 1850s, Gustave Courbet helped establish the school of realism and became its undisputed leader. Many of Courbet's realist paintings portray rural society as he had seen it in his birthplace of Ornans in provincial France. Courbet tried to show the people and events of rural society realistically, rather than sentimentally or satirically. He showed peasants as possessing an inherent dignity and worth. In 1865, he painted a series of seascapes that made such an impression that they opened the way for the development of impressionism a few years later.

More About . . .

Impressionism

The term *impressionism* was coined in 1874 when Claude Monet exhibited a painting entitled *Impression: Sunrise.* A hostile art critic, unused to the unfinished, sketchy look of this new style of art, dismissed the entire art show as "impressionist." The term, which came to be applied to a whole group of artists, was intended as an insulting, derogatory name, but it soon became an expression of admiration.

World Art and Cultures Transparencies

- AT53 *Couturiere*

CONNECT TO TODAY: ANSWERS

1. Developing Historical Perspective

Possible Answer: realism, because it was best suited to portray the problems of common people for whom the revolutionaries were fighting

2. Drawing Conclusions

Possible Answers: Many people find the bright colors cheerful and pretty. Also, the subjects are usually not upsetting.

TERMS & NAMES

1. conservative, p. 253
2. liberal, p. 253
3. nationalism, p. 253
4. nation-state, p. 253
5. realpolitik, p. 261
6. romanticism, p. 264
7. realism, p. 266
8. impressionism, p. 267

MAIN IDEAS

Answers will vary

9. They resented the *peninsulares'* power; they were inspired by Enlightenment ideas and the American and French Revolutions; they felt no loyalty to the French-appointed king of Spain.
10. Iturbide initially opposed Mexican independence but eventually became its leader.
11. Dom Pedro was the ruler of Brazil and the son of the Portuguese king. He officially declared Brazilian independence in 1822.
12. Liberal—mostly middle-class merchants and business leaders; wanted more power for elected parliaments. Conservative—wealthy property owners and nobility; wanted traditional monarchies
13. The revolts were a failure. By 1849 the conservatives had regained control and Europe was back to its pre-1848 status.
14. tired of instability, wanted strong ruler to bring peace
15. Disunity—It broke up centuries-old empires into nation-states. Unity—It inspired people with the same history, culture, and language to form nation-states.
16. He used careful diplomacy, well-chosen alliances, and cunning.
17. He provoked Austria and France into separate wars, reasoning that the two wars would unite the German people behind Prussia.
18. emotions, mysterious or supernatural, untamed nature, simple times, heroes, folk traditions such as music and stories, common people, radical change, democracy
19. radical change, democracy, heroic actions, common people
20. Industrialization brought bad working and living conditions to many who lived in crowded and dirty cities.

Chapter 8 Assessment

TERMS & NAMES

Briefly explain the importance of each of the following to the revolutions in Latin America or Europe.

1. conservative
2. liberal
3. nationalism
4. nation-state
5. realpolitik
6. romanticism
7. realism
8. impressionism

MAIN IDEAS

Latin American Peoples Win Independence Section 1 (pages 247–252)

9. What caused the creoles in South America to rebel against Spain? (10.4.3)
10. What role did Agustín de Iturbide play in the independence of Mexico? (10.4.4)
11. Who was Dom Pedro, and what role did he play in Brazil's move to independence? (10.4.4)

Europe Faces Revolutions Section 2 (pages 253–257)

12. How is a liberal different from a conservative? (10.2.1)
13. How successful were the revolts of 1848? Explain. (10.2.5)
14. Why did the French accept Louis-Napoleon as an emperor? (10.2.4)

Case Study: Nationalism Section 3 (pages 258–263)

15. How did nationalism in the 1800s work as a force for both disunity and unity? (10.2.5)
16. What approaches did Camillo di Cavour use to acquire more territory for Piedmont-Sardinia? (10.2.5)
17. What strategy did Otto von Bismarck use to make Prussia the leader of a united Germany? (10.2.5)

Revolutions in the Arts Section 4 (pages 264–269)

18. What are five elements of romanticism? (10.3.7)
19. What are two ideas or attitudes of the romantic movement that reflect the ideals of nationalism? (10.3.7)
20. What new conditions caused a change in the arts from romanticism to realism? (10.3.7)

CRITICAL THINKING

1. USING YOUR NOTES
Using a chart, describe the nationalist movement in each of the countries listed and the results of each movement. (10.4.2)

Country	Nationalism and Its Results
Mexico	
Greece	
Italy	
Germany	

2. EVALUATING DECISIONS
POWER AND AUTHORITY Why do you think Giuseppe Garibaldi stepped aside to let Victor Emmanuel II rule areas that Garibaldi had conquered in southern Italy? (10.4.3)

3. ANALYZING MOTIVES
REVOLUTION How do you think nationalism might help revolutionaries overcome the disadvantages of old weapons and poor supplies to win a war for national independence? Explain. (10.2.5)

4. MAKING INFERENCES
Do you believe the Latin American revolutions would have occurred without a push from European events? Explain. (10.4.3)

5. SYNTHESIZING
CULTURAL INTERACTION How did artistic and intellectual movements reflect and fuel changes in Europe in the 1800s? (10.3.7)

VISUAL SUMMARY
Nationalist Revolutions Sweep the West
NATIONALISM
Latin America
• Enlightenment ideas
• Haiti: slave-led
• South America: creole-led, especially Bolívar and San Martín
• Brazil: royalty-led
1830 & 1848 Revolutions
• Reactions against conservatives
• A few reforms
• Most failed
Unification Movements
• Garibaldi begins in Italy.
• Prime Minister Cavour completes the task.
• Prime Minister Bismarck leads the way in Germany.
The Arts
• Romantics inspired by emotion
• Dedication to common people or the group
• Realists see flaws and set new goals for nation.
• Impressionists capture the moment.

CRITICAL THINKING

Answers will vary

1. **Possible Answers:** Mexico—Popular revolt against Spain; Greece—Revolt with international support for freedom from Ottoman Empire; Italy—Unified many territories into one country; Germany—Prussians unite the German states.
2. Garibaldi probably felt that King Victor Emmanuel had the experience and support to lead a united Italy.
3. Soldiers were inspired enough by nationalism to overcome disadvantages. Soldiers of the empires were uninspired to fight.
4. **Possible Answers:** Yes—Creoles were dissatisfied, inspired by Enlightenment ideas, wealthy enough to revolt. No—If the creoles had not opposed the French-appointed king, they would not have had reason to revolt.
5. The romantic movement reflected dreams of change. When changes did not occur, artists moved into realism, pushed to create a better world. Impressionists tried to capture a moment in time and ignore the reality of the time.

STANDARDS-BASED ASSESSMENT

Use the quotation and your knowledge of world history to answer questions 1 and 2.
Additional Test Practice, pp. S1–S33

PRIMARY SOURCE

When I say that we must strive continually to be ready for all emergencies, I advance the proposition that, on account of our geographical position, we must make greater efforts than other powers would be obliged to make in view of the same ends. We lie in the middle of Europe. We have at least three fronts on which we can be attacked. France has only an eastern boundary; Russia only its western, exposed to assault. . . . So we are spurred forward on both sides to endeavors which perhaps we would not make otherwise.

OTTO VON BISMARCK, *speech to the German parliament on February 6, 1888*

1. According to Bismarck, what key factor makes Germany a potential target for invasion? (10.2.5)
   A. dangerous neighbors
   B. three borders to protect
   C. location in the middle of Europe
   D. massive supplies of coal and iron

2. Based on his remarks above, what actions might Bismarck take? (10.2.5)
   A. form alliances with other nations in Europe
   B. make peace with France
   C. make peace with England
   D. expand industry

Use this 20th-century mural titled *Grito de Dolores* painted by Juan O'Gorman and your knowledge of world history to answer question 3.

3. Look at the people portrayed in the mural. What does the artist suggest about the Mexican revolt against the Spanish? (10.4.3)
   A. It was condemned by the Catholic Church.
   B. Only the poor fought against Spanish rule.
   C. People of all classes fought against Spanish rule.
   D. Only Indians fought Spanish rule.

INTEGRATED TECHNOLOGY
TEST PRACTICE Go to **classzone.com**
- Diagnostic tests
- Strategies
- Tutorials
- Additional practice

ALTERNATIVE ASSESSMENT

1. **Interact *with* History** (10.4.3)
   On page 246, you were asked to create a symbol for your newly independent country. Show your symbol to the class. Explain the elements of your design and what they are intended to express. With your classmates' comments in mind, what might you change in your design?

2. **WRITING ABOUT HISTORY** (Writing 2.4.a, b, c)
   Write a **speech** that might have been delivered somewhere in Europe at a rally for Greek independence. Urge the country's leaders to help the Greeks in their struggle for independence from the Ottoman Empire. Consider the following:
   - the connections of Greece to Europeans
   - reasons to support Greek revolutionaries
   - the cause of democracy

INTEGRATED TECHNOLOGY

Creating a Web Page (10.3.7, Writing 2.2.a)
Use the Internet, newspapers, magazines, and your own experience to make a list of movies that portray social and political conditions. Then create a Web page that classifies each portrayal as either romantic or realistic. Remember to focus on the meanings of the terms romantic and realistic as they apply to the two movements in art and literature. You may want to include on your Web page:
- descriptions of movie plots or character portrayals
- still shots from movies that support your conclusions
- romantic or realistic quotations from movies

STANDARDS-BASED ASSESSMENT

1. The correct answer is letter **B**. Letter **A** is not correct. Bismarck does not cite dangerous neighbors. Letter **C** is not correct. Bismarck mentions the location but does not cite it as a reason for invasion. Letter **D** is not correct. There is no mention of natural resources in the quotation.
2. The correct answer is letter **A**. Letter **B** is not correct. Making peace with France would only solve one border problem. Letter **C** is not correct. England has no borders with Germany. Letter **D** is not correct. The passage does not refer to economic ideas.
3. The correct answer is letter **C**. Eventually all classes fought against Spanish rule in Mexico. Letter **A** is not correct. Early on priests led the rebellion. Letter **B** is not correct. The mural shows people who clearly are not poor. Letter **D** is not correct. The mural shows people of many different classes.

Formal Assessment
- Chapter Test, Forms A, B, and C, pp. 140–154

California Test Generator CD-ROM
- Chapter Tests, Forms A, B, and C (English and Spanish)

ALTERNATIVE ASSESSMENT

1. Students may revise their symbols to reflect the comments they hear from the class. Ask students to display their designs in the classroom.
2. **Rubric** The speech should
   - identify reasons to support Greek revolutionaries.
   - explain what your country's leaders could do to support Greek revolutionaries.
   - encourage the listeners to get involved with the Greek cause.

INTEGRATED TECHNOLOGY

Rubric The Web site should
- clearly display examples of romantic and realist modern films.
- identify standards used to select the examples.
- be easy to navigate.

LESSON PLAN

OBJECTIVES

- Explain the stages of revolutions.
- Compare four revolutions.
- Compare the causes and effects of revolutions.

1 FOCUS & MOTIVATE

To help students review political revolutions, draw four columns on the chalkboard with one of the revolutions at the head of each column. Spend 5–10 minutes listing what students learned about each revolution in Unit 2.

2 INSTRUCT

Critical Thinking

- Analyze each revolution in terms of Stage 6 of the model. Which revolutions followed Stage 6? Which did not? *(Following Stage 6 were the English Civil War and Glorious Revolution and the French Revolution. The American Revolution and Latin American Revolutions did not follow Stage 6 because they did not reinstate their colonial rulers.)*
- What element of the Latin American revolutions made them different from the French Revolution and the English Civil War? *(In Latin America, people were fighting colonial rulers. In England and France, people revolted against their own rulers.)*

Revolutions Across Time

CALIFORNIA STANDARDS

10.2.3 Understand the unique character of the American Revolution, its spread to other parts of the world, and its continuing significance to other nations.

Revolution—which is a sudden or significant change in the old ways of doing things—can occur in many areas, such as government, technology, or art. In Unit 2, you studied political revolutions in Europe and the Americas, in which people rebelled against unjust rulers to gain more rights. Each revolution led to major changes in governmental, social, and economic structures. In these six pages, you will gain a better understanding of those revolutions by examining their similarities and differences.

English Civil War and Glorious Revolution ►
In 1642, civil war broke out between those who supported Parliament and those who supported the king. Parliament won and set up a commonwealth, led by Oliver Cromwell. In time, he became a dictator. After his death, the monarchy returned, but tensions built anew. In 1688, Parliament ousted King James II, shown at right, in the Glorious Revolution and invited William and Mary to rule.

1642 — 1776 — 1789

◄ American Revolution
After 1763, Americans began to resent British rule. Clashes such as the Boston Massacre, shown at left, took place. The colonies declared their independence **in 1776.** War ensued, and the United States won its freedom by defeating Britain.

▼ French Revolution
Beginning in 1789, the French people rose up to overthrow their king. The uprisings included the march by hungry women shown below. Differing goals soon split the revolutionaries. Several years of terror followed. Napoleon restored order and eventually made himself emperor of France.

DIFFERENTIATING INSTRUCTION: STRUGGLING READERS

Applying the Model of a Revolution

Class Time 30 minutes

Task Analyzing revolutions

Purpose To better understand the stages of revolution

Group students into teams of four to five. Make sure that each team has students at all reading levels. Have each team choose one of the revolutions. Students will then create a chart like the one that follows. They will write down the events of the revolution that fall into each stage of the model. After finishing their charts, students will share their ideas with the class. Refer students to chapters 5, 6, 7, and 8 in Unit 2 for help in creating their charts.

English Civil War

1 Fall of old order	2 Rule by moderates	3 Terror	4 Turn from radical rule	5 Military rule	6 Restoration
Cromwell defeats Charles I					

1791

▲ Latin American Revolutions
From 1791 to 1824, revolutions took place in Haiti, Mexico, and the huge Spanish empire that spread across Central and South America. By the end of that period, nearly all of Latin America had gained its independence from European control. One of South America's great liberators was José de San Martín, shown in the painting above.

Model of a Revolution

From his study of the French Revolution, historian Crane Brinton developed a model of the stages that revolutions often go through. The model below is based on his work. Compare it with the revolutions you learned about in this unit.

STAGE 1 **Fall of the Old Order**
Revolutions usually cannot occur until a ruler becomes weak. Often this weakness results in problems such as starvation and unfair taxes. Anger builds until the ruler is overthrown.

STAGE 2 **Rule by Moderates**
The people relax because they think they have achieved their goal. A moderate group rules. But simply overthrowing the old order rarely solves the problems that led to the revolution.

STAGE 3 **The Terror**
When people realize that the old problems still exist, they look for someone to blame. Radicals take control, push for more extreme changes, and execute "enemies of the revolution."

STAGE 4 **Turn from Radical Rule**
In time, the violence sickens people, and the use of terror ends. The former radicals adopt a more gradual plan for effecting change.

STAGE 5 **Military Rule**
The terror often kills most of a country's leaders. Then the turn from radicalism makes people doubt revolutionary ideals. A military leader steps into the gap and becomes dictator.

STAGE 6 **Restoration**
When the dictatorship ends, through death or overthrow, a power vacuum results. The order that existed before the revolution is restored.

Comparing & Contrasting

1. Which of the revolutions on the time line, besides the French Revolution, is most like the model? Explain.
2. Which revolution is least like the model? Explain.

273

More About . . .

Revolutions and Style

Revolutions have strong effects on styles. In England in the 1640s, people loyal to the king wore their hair long. Those loyal to Parliament had hair cut short over their ears. In China, followers of Mao Zedong wore plain "Mao suits." Russian Communists also wore very plain clothing. In France after 1789, everyone was addressed as "citizen." After the Russian Revolution, "comrade" took the place of "mister" and other titles.

More About . . .

Revolutionary Patterns

Friedrich Engels, a German thinker and supporter of Karl Marx, said, "People who boast that they have made a revolution always realize the next day that they did not know what they were doing, that the revolution they had made was quite different from the one they had intended to make."

Comparing & Contrasting

1. *Possible Answer:* Students may choose the English Civil War and Glorious Revolution because it follows most stages of the model and ends with restoration of the monarchy.
2. *Possible Answer:* Students may choose the American Revolution, which differed from the model in being a fight against colonial rule and resulting in a stable representative government.

RECOMMENDED RESOURCES

Books for the Teacher

Brinton, Crane, John B. Christopher, and Robert L. Wolf. ***Anatomy of Revolution.*** New York: Knopf, 1965.

Goodnough, David. ***Simón Bolívar: South American Liberator.*** Berkeley Heights, NJ: Enslow, 1998.

Callow, John. ***The Making of King James II.*** New York: Sutton, 2000.

Books for the Student

McDougal Littell Literature Connections. Azuela, Mariano. ***The Underdogs.*** 1997. An exciting story set during the aftermath of the Mexican Revolution of 1910.

Videos and Software

The French Revolution. CD-ROM. Clearvue 800-253-2788. Evaluates the causes, events, and significance of the French Revolution.

The Age of Revolutions: 1776-1848. Video. Social Studies School Service 800-421-4246. The ideals that inspired revolts against European monarchs crossed the Atlantic to North and South America.

The [American] Revolution. Video. Clearvue 800-253-2788.

Causes of the Revolutions

Critical Thinking

- How did the economic causes of revolution compare between North America and France? *(Colonial rulers in North America imposed taxes and controlled commerce. In France, the king oppressed the people who were poor and starving. The people in both places had no say in their government.)*
- In what ways do you think the English Civil War and Glorious Revolution might have influenced the other revolutions? *(showed that people can overthrow their rulers)*

More About . . .

Keeping Power

Aristotle said, "It is in the interests of a tyrant to make his subjects poor, so that . . . the people are so occupied with their daily tasks that they have no time for plotting. As an example of such measures . . . of keeping subjects perpetually at work and in poverty we may mention the pyramids of Egypt." It follows then that governments that try to improve the lives of their people may get into trouble. Alexis de Tocqueville noted, " . . . experience teaches us that, generally speaking, the most perilous moment for a bad government is one when it seeks to mend its ways."

SKILLBUILDER Answers

1. **Analyzing Causes** Two political causes appear most often: abuses by rulers and the desire of the people for rights and representation. The most frequent economic cause was high taxes. The most frequent social cause was the spread of Enlightenment ideas.
2. **Contrasting** The Latin American revolutions were partially triggered by news of Napoleon's conquest of Spain. Racial injustice was also a factor.

Causes of the Revolutions

CALIFORNIA STANDARDS

HI 2 Students recognize the complexity of historical causes and effects, including the limitations on determining cause and effect.

Each of the revolutions you studied in this unit had political, economic, and social causes, as shown in the chart below. Some of the causes mentioned on the chart are the subjects of the primary sources located on the next page. Use the chart and the primary sources together to understand the causes of revolution more fully.

	England	North America	France	Latin America
Political	• King claimed divine right. • King dissolved Parliament. • Parliament sought guarantee of freedoms.	• Colonists accused British leaders of tyranny. • Colonists demanded the same rights as English citizens.	• Third Estate wanted greater representation. • Louis XVI was a weak ruler; his wife was unpopular. • American Revolution inspired political ideas.	• French Revolution inspired political ideas. • Royal officials committed injustices and repression. • Napoleon's conquest of Spain triggered revolts.
Economic	• King wanted money for wars. • King levied taxes and fines without Parliament's approval.	• Britain imposed mercantilism. • Britain expected colonies to pay for defense. • Colonists opposed taxation without representation.	• Wars and royal extravagance created debt. • Inflation and famine caused problems. • Peasants made little money but paid high taxes.	• Peninsulares and creoles controlled wealth. • Lower classes toiled as peasants with little income or as slaves.
Social	• Early Stuart kings refused to make Puritan reforms. • Parliament feared James II would restore Catholicism.	• Colonists began to identify as Americans. • Colonists were used to some independence. • Enlightenment ideas of equality and liberty spread.	• Third Estate resented the First and Second estates' privileges. • Enlightenment ideas of equality and liberty spread.	• Only peninsulares and creoles had power. • Mestizos, mulattos, Africans, and Indians had little status. • Educated creoles spread Enlightenment ideas.

SKILLBUILDER: Interpreting Charts

1. **Analyzing Causes** *What was the most frequent political cause of revolution? economic cause? social cause?*
2. **Contrasting** *How did the causes of the revolutions in Latin America differ from those of the other three revolutions?*

◄ In the 1780s, many French peasants could not afford bread to feed their families. At the same time, Marie Antoinette spent so much money on clothes that her enemies called her Madame Deficit. The harsh contrast between starvation and luxury sparked the anger that led to the Revolution.

DIFFERENTIATING INSTRUCTION: GIFTED AND TALENTED STUDENTS

Examining Revolutions

Time 30 minutes

Task Analyzing other revolutions

Purpose To find patterns among revolutions

Have pairs of students use the library and the Internet to research revolutions in South Africa, Russia, China, Iran, Cambodia, the Philippines, and elsewhere. Each pair should choose one revolution. Students will create charts like the one on this page detailing the causes of the revolution.

Post the finished charts side by side and have a discussion comparing the various causes they listed. What patterns across the revolutions do they see?

One pattern they may discover is abuse of power by a country's leaders. In an extension activity, have each group name the leader who lost power in the revolution. They should also describe his or her background and examine the policies and behavior that contributed to the revolution.

PRIMARY SOURCE

Political Cartoon, 1789

This French political cartoon portrayed the way the privileges of the First and Second estates affected the Third Estate.

DOCUMENT-BASED QUESTION

Do you think a member of the First, Second, or Third Estate created this cartoon? Interpret the cartoon and explain who was most likely to hold the viewpoint conveyed.

PRIMARY SOURCE

INTERACTIVE

The English Bill of Rights, 1689

This excerpt from the English Bill of Rights attempted to justify the Glorious Revolution by describing the injustices King James II committed.

The late King James the Second, by the assistance of diverse evil counselors, judges and ministers employed by him, did endeavor to subvert and extirpate [destroy] the Protestant religion and the laws and liberties of this kingdom;

By assuming and exercising a power of dispensing with and suspending of laws and the execution of laws without consent of Parliament; . . .

By levying money for and to the use of the Crown by pretense of prerogative [privilege] for other time and in other manner than the same was granted by Parliament;

By raising and keeping a standing army within this kingdom in time of peace without consent of Parliament; . . .

By violating the freedom of election of members to serve in Parliament; . . .

And excessive bail hath been required of persons committed in criminal cases to elude the benefit of the laws made for the liberty of the subjects;

And excessive fines have been imposed;

And illegal and cruel punishments inflicted.

DOCUMENT-BASED QUESTION

According to this document, how did King James II take away power from Parliament? How did he violate the rights of citizens?

PRIMARY SOURCE

Political Cartoon, 1765

This political cartoon expressed an opinion about the Stamp Act. The act was a British law that required all legal and commercial documents in the American colonies to carry a stamp showing that a tax had been paid.

DOCUMENT-BASED QUESTION

What opinion does this cartoon express about the effect of the Stamp Act on the American economy?

Comparing & Contrasting

1. How are the opinions expressed by the three primary sources similar?
2. Reread the excerpt from the English Bill of Rights. Based on this document, what causes could you add to the chart on page 274?

275

More About . . .

King James II

When his brother Charles II became king in 1660, James, the Duke of York, became lord high admiral and greatly improved the navy's organization. He became interested in colonial activities and organized the seizure of New Amsterdam from the Dutch. In James's honor, the city was renamed New York.

PRIMARY SOURCE

Political Cartoon, 1789

Answer to Document-Based Question

Possible Answer: A member of the Third Estate probably created the cartoon because it shows how the First and Second Estates burdened and abused the Third Estate.

PRIMARY SOURCE

The English Bill of Rights

Answer to Document-Based Question

Possible Answer: King James II, without the approval of Parliament, suspended laws, levied taxes, kept a standing army, and interfered with the election of members of Parliament. He ignored laws made for the liberty of subjects, imposed excessive fines, and inflicted illegal and cruel punishments.

PRIMARY SOURCE

Political Cartoon, 1765

Answer to Document-Based Question

The cartoon indicates that the Stamp Act will kill the American economy.

Comparing & Contrasting

1. Each of the primary sources seeks to point out injustices. The two cartoons make visual statements. The English Bill of Rights provides a specific list of abuses.
2. The king kept a standing army, violated freedom of election, required excessive bail, and inflicted illegal and cruel punishments.

DIFFERENTIATING INSTRUCTION: ENGLISH LEARNERS

Analyzing Text

Class Time 30 minutes

Task Analyzing the English Bill of Rights

Purpose To understand some of the causes of the revolution in England

Have students work in small groups to figure out the meaning of each complaint against King James II. Students will slowly read through each point in the document and then write in their own words what they think the statement means.

For example, students might write

- *King James had evil people giving him advice.*
- *The king tried to destroy the Protestant religion.*
- *The king also tried to destroy the laws and freedoms of England.*
- *The king got rid of laws without getting an OK from Parliament.*

Have students continue to go through the document point by point. Remind students that the United States also has a Bill of Rights as part of the Constitution.

Effects of Revolutions

Critical Thinking

- What is wrong with representative government from the point of view of a monarch or a military leader? *(Power resides in the people, not in a single person, leaving no place for monarchs or dictators; voters often disagree, so clear decisions are difficult to achieve.)*
- How did the social effects of revolution in Latin America differ from those in North America and France? *(Latin America did not achieve social equality. North America and France did achieve greater social equality.)*

More About . . .

Thomas Paine

Nearly penniless and with only a letter of introduction from Benjamin Franklin, Paine arrived in America in 1774. He published *Common Sense* in 1776 to support independence. It quickly became a best seller of the time. It is one of the most influential and successful pamphlets in the history of political writing.

SKILLBUILDER Answers

1. **Contrasting** The revolutions in England and North America had positive effects in that they increased trade. The Revolution in France devastated the economy, and the Latin American revolutions allowed the upper classes to retain control of wealth.
2. **Recognizing Effects** They led to the end of colonial rule.

Effects of Revolutions

CALIFORNIA STANDARDS
10.2.1, CST 1, HI 1

The chart below shows political, economic, and social effects of the various revolutions. The primary sources on these two pages describe the political outcomes that three different revolutionaries expected to achieve. Use the chart and the primary sources together to understand the effects of revolution more fully.

	England	North America	France	Latin America
Political	• A constitutional monarchy was established. • The Bill of Rights increased Parliament's power and guaranteed certain rights. • The overthrow of a monarch helped inspire American revolutionaries.	• The United States gained independence. • The Constitution set up a republican government. • Revolutionary ideals continued to inspire groups seeking political equality. • The American Revolution inspired later revolutions.	• The Revolution led to a succession of governments: a republic, a dictatorship, a restored monarchy. • It created expectations for equality and freedom that sparked later uprisings in France. • It inspired later revolutions.	• Nearly all colonial rule in Latin America ended. • New countries were established. • Representative government was slow to develop. The military or the wealthy controlled much of the region until the late 1900s.
Economic	• Because it was answerable to taxpayers, Parliament encouraged trade.	• The removal of Britain's mercantilist policies allowed free enterprise to develop.	• The Revolution and ensuing wars with Europe devastated France's economy.	• Upper classes kept control of wealth. • Many places kept the plantation system.
Social	• England remained Protestant.	• The ideals of the Revolution continued to inspire groups seeking social equality.	• The French feudal system was abolished.	• Much of Latin America continued to have a strong class system.

SKILLBUILDER: Interpreting Charts
1. **Contrasting** *Which revolutions had positive economic effects, and which had negative? Explain.*
2. **Recognizing Effects** *What common political effect did the revolutions in North America and Latin America achieve?*

PRIMARY SOURCE

INTERACTIVE

Thomas Paine

In this excerpt from the pamphlet *Common Sense,* Thomas Paine described the ideal government he wanted to see set up after the American Revolution.

But where, say some, is the king of America? I'll tell you, friend, he reigns above, and doth not make havoc of mankind like the Royal Brute of Great Britain. . . . Let a day be solemnly set apart for proclaiming the charter [constitution]; let it be brought forth placed on the divine law, the Word of God; let a crown be placed thereon, by which the world may know, that so far as we approve of monarchy, that in America THE LAW IS KING. For as in absolute governments the king is law, so in free countries the law *ought* to BE king, and there ought to be no other.

DOCUMENT-BASED QUESTION
What did Paine believe should be the highest power in a new American government?

PRIMARY SOURCE
Thomas Paine

Answer to Document-Based Question
Paine believes that the law should be the highest power in the new American government.

CONNECTIONS ACROSS THE CURRICULUM

Language Arts

Class Time 30 minutes

Task Examining literature about the American Revolution

Purpose To examine the American Revolution through literature

Thomas Paine was one of many writers who inspired and influenced people during the time of the Revolution. Fiery speeches by Patrick Henry and letters written by Abigail Adams and Phillis Wheatley are all part of the story of the Revolution.

"No taxation without representation!" "Give me liberty or give me death!" "We hold these truths to be self-evident . . ." "We the people . . ." Many famous phrases have come from the writings of revolutionary leaders along with many of our favorite anecdotes—the Boston Tea Party, the "shot heard 'round the world," and George Washington at Valley Forge.

Have students use their literature textbooks, the library, and the Internet to compile a list of writings about the Revolution. Then have volunteers report to the class describing specific texts.

PRIMARY SOURCE

INTERACTIVE

Simón Bolívar

"The Jamaica Letter" is one of Simón Bolívar's most important political documents. In this excerpt, he discussed his political goals for South America after the revolution—and his fear that South Americans were not ready to achieve those goals.

The role of the inhabitants of the American hemisphere has for centuries been purely passive. Politically they were non-existent. . . . We have been harassed by a conduct which has not only deprived us of our rights but has kept us in a sort of permanent infancy with regard to public affairs. . . . Americans today, and perhaps to a greater extent than ever before, who live within the Spanish system occupy a position in society no better than that of serfs destined for labor. . . . Although I seek perfection for the government of my country, I cannot persuade myself that the New World can, at the moment, be organized as a great republic.

DOCUMENT-BASED QUESTION
Why did Bolívar believe that South Americans were not ready for a republican form of government?

PRIMARY SOURCE

INTERACTIVE

Maximilien Robespierre

In a speech given on February 5, 1794, Robespierre described his goals for the French Revolution. In this excerpt, he explained his reasons for using terror.

It is necessary to annihilate both the internal and external enemies of the republic or perish with its fall. Now, in this situation your first political maxim should be that one guides the people by reason, and the enemies of the people by terror.

If the driving force of popular government in peacetime is virtue, that of popular government during a revolution is both virtue and terror: virtue, without which terror is destructive; terror, without which virtue is impotent. Terror is only justice that is prompt, severe, and inflexible; it is thus an emanation of virtue; it is less a distinct principle than a consequence of the general principle of democracy applied to the most pressing needs of the patrie [nation].

DOCUMENT-BASED QUESTION
Why did Robespierre believe the use of terror against his enemies was necessary?

Comparing & Contrasting

1. Judging from the information on the chart, which revolutions resulted in the establishment of representative government, and which resulted in a return to tyrannical rule?
2. How do the political goals of the revolutionary leaders quoted here differ?
3. Compare the types of government set up in the United States, France, and Latin America after their revolutions. Did Paine, Robespierre, and Bolívar achieve the political goals quoted? Explain.

EXTENSION ACTIVITY
Revolutionary activity continued after the period covered by this unit. Two major 20th-century revolutions were the Russian Revolution (see Chapter 14) and the Chinese revolution and civil war (see Chapter 14 and Chapter 17). Read about one of these revolutions either in this textbook or in an encyclopedia. Then create a chart comparing that revolution with either the American Revolution or the French Revolution.

EXTENSION ACTIVITY

Rubric
Student charts should
- identify specific political, economic, and social causes and effects.
- clearly compare two revolutions.
- provide supporting evidence.

Here is one example of a possible chart.

INTEGRATED TECHNOLOGY

Interactive Several primary sources in this feature are available in an interactive format on the eEdition. Students can hear the sources read aloud and can get help with vocabulary and background information.

PRIMARY SOURCE
Simón Bolívar

Answer to Document-Based Question
He believed that South Americans were too conditioned to passively obey orders to take charge of their own governments.

PRIMARY SOURCE
Maximilien Robespierre

Answer to Document-Based Question
Robespierre believed without terror the gains of the Revolution would be lost.

More About . . .

Simón Bolívar
A brilliant general, Simón Bolívar led armies that eventually freed present-day Venezuela, Colombia, Ecuador, and Peru. Upper Peru eventually became the country of Bolivia, named after Bolívar.

More About . . .

Maximilien Robespierre
Assessments of Robespierre have been decidedly mixed over time. He fought passionately for liberty, but he was also deeply involved in the Reign of Terror. Eventually he was guillotined in front of a cheering mob.

Comparing & Contrasting

1. The revolutions in England and North America established representative government; the others did not.
2. Paine wanted the law to be the supreme power in American government. Bolívar did not plan to establish a republic because he believed Latin Americans were not ready for it. Robespierre intended to use terror as a tool to establish democracy.
3. Yes, for the most part, they did. Paine wanted law to be king, and the United States set up a constitutional government. As Bolívar expected, most of Latin America did not establish representative government for more than a century. Robespierre did use terror to control people, but it didn't enable him to bring about democracy.

Industrialism and the Race for Empire 1700–1914

Canton, China, about 1800

In this oil painting by a Chinese artist, the flags of Spain, the United States, Britain, and the Netherlands fly over the Chinese port at Canton.

Located about 80 miles up the Pearl River estuary, Canton (now called Guangzhou) was founded sometime between 1111 B.C. and 771 B.C. Until the mid-1800s, Canton was the only Chinese seat of commerce open to Westerners outside the Portuguese trading post at Macao. At Canton, Chinese officials confined foreign businesses, warehouses, and living quarters to a 1,100-foot-long stretch of waterfront and placed tight restrictions on the foreigners who lived and worked there.

In the mid-1800s, British and French forces fought and won two trade wars against China. As part of the peace settlement, five ports had to open their gates to Western business and trade. In response, secret societies in Canton joined local militias to rebel against the foreigners.

Previewing the Unit

This unit describes the effects of the Industrial Revolution on Western nations and the nations' race to divide Asia and Africa among themselves. Colonial rule brings more hardships than benefits to native peoples, who eventually rebel against Western rulers.

Revolution During the 1800s, Britain, the United States, and some European countries undergo great changes as a result of the Industrial Revolution. The widening gap between rich and poor prompts a series of social and political reforms.

Power and Authority With their superior technology and weapons, Western nations compete to acquire territory in Africa, Asia, and the South Pacific.

Economics Countries around the world react to Western influence. China falls under foreign domination, but Japan and Korea respond by modernizing their countries. Although Latin American nations free themselves from colonialism, they remain economically and politically unstable.

Although this painting shows Canton, China, the flags flying over the fenced-in areas near the shore are those of Spain, the United States, Great Britain, and the Netherlands. Canton was one of only two Chinese ports open to Westerners until 1842.

Comparing & Contrasting

Scientific and Technological Changes
In Unit 3, you will learn about scientific and technological changes that led to the Industrial Revolution and helped Western nations establish colonies around the world. At the end of the unit, you will have a chance to compare and contrast those changes. (See pages 396–401.)

Comparing & Contrasting

Tell students that the unit feature on pages 396–401 will help them appreciate the remarkable period of scientific and technological change that occurred between 1700 and 1914. Encourage students to use the images, time line, charts, and primary and secondary sources to enhance their understanding of Unit 3.

The Industrial Revolution, 1700–1900

CHAPTER RESOURCES	COPYMASTERS	ASSESSMENT
CHAPTER OVERVIEW The Industrial Revolution began in Britain, spread to other countries, and had a strong impact on economics, politics, and society.	**In-Depth Resources: Unit 3** • Building Vocabulary, p. 5 **Chapters in Brief** (in English and Spanish) **Block Schedule Pacing Guide**	**Chapter Assessment,** pp. 308–309 **Formal Assessment** • Chapter Tests, Forms A, B, and C, pp. 159–170 **Test Generator** **Integrated Assessment Book** **Online Test Practice**
SECTION 1 **The Beginnings of Industrialization** pp. 283–288 **OBJECTIVE** Describe the key inventions and improvements of the Industrial Revolution.	**In-Depth Resources: Unit 3** • Guided Reading, p. 1 • Primary Source: from "The Opening of the Liverpool to Manchester Railway," p. 9 • History Makers: James Watt, p. 16 • Reteaching Activity, p. 19 **Reading Study Guide,** p. 95	**Section 1 Assessment,** p. 288 **Formal Assessment** • Section Quiz, p. 155 **California Daily Standards Practice Transparencies,** TT93
SECTION 2 **Industrialization—Case Study: Manchester** pp. 289–294 **OBJECTIVE** Analyze the impact of industrialization on society.	**In-Depth Resources: Unit 3** • Guided Reading, p. 2 • Geography Application, p. 7 • Primary Source, p. 10 • Literature: from *Mary Barton,* p. 13 • Reteaching Activity, p. 20 **Reading Study Guide,** p. 97	**Section 2 Assessment,** p. 294 **Formal Assessment** • Section Quiz, p. 156 **California Daily Standards Practice Transparencies,** TT94
SECTION 3 **Industrialization Spreads** pp. 295–299 **OBJECTIVE** Trace the spread of industrialization through Europe and the United States.	**In-Depth Resources: Unit 3** • Guided Reading, p. 3 • Primary Source: "Life in a New England Factory," p. 11 • Reteaching Activity, p. 21 **Reading Study Guide,** p. 99	**Section 3 Assessment,** p. 299 **Formal Assessment** • Section Quiz, p. 157 **California Daily Standards Practice Transparencies,** TT95
SECTION 4 **Reforming the Industrial World** pp. 300–307 **OBJECTIVE** List the economic, social, and political reforms that arose from the Industrial Revolution.	**In-Depth Resources: Unit 3** • Guided Reading, p. 4 • Skillbuilder Practice, p. 6 • Primary Source, p. 12 • History Makers: de Saint-Simon, p. 17 • Connections Across Time/Cultures, p. 18 • Reteaching Activity, p. 22 **Reading Study Guide,** p. 101	**Section 4 Assessment,** p. 306 **Formal Assessment** • Section Quiz, p. 158 **California Daily Standards Practice Transparencies,** TT96

- eEdition Plus Online
- EasyPlanner Plus Online
- eTest Plus Online

Audio CDs
- Voices from the Past
- Reading Study Guides

Patterns of Interaction Video
- The Industrial and Electronic Revolutions

CD-ROMs
- eEdition
- Power Presentations
- EasyPlanner
- Electronic Library of Primary Sources
- Test Generator

---

eEdition CD-ROM

Patterns of Interaction Video Series

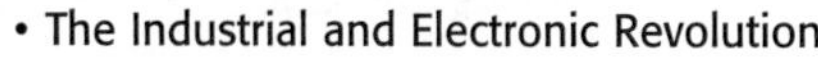

- The Industrial and Electronic Revolutions

classzone.com

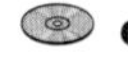

eEdition CD-ROM

Geography Transparencies
- GT25 The Industrial Revolution

World Art and Cultures Transparencies
- AT54 Arkwright's Cotton Mill

Electronic Library of Primary Sources
- from "Child Labor in the Mines"
- "The Sentencing of the Luddites"

classzone.com

eEdition CD-ROM

World Art and Cultures Transparencies

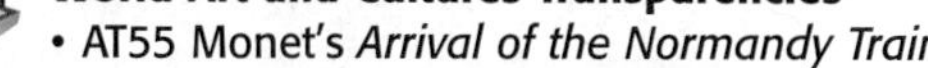

- AT55 Monet's *Arrival of the Normandy Train*

Electronic Library of Primary Sources
- from *A New England Girlhood*

classzone.com

eEdition CD-ROM

Critical Thinking Transparencies

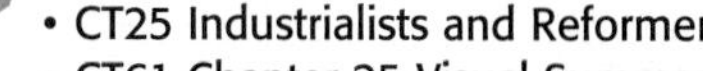

- CT25 Industrialists and Reformers
- CT61 Chapter 25 Visual Summary

Electronic Library of Primary Sources
- from *The Communist Manifesto*
- from "How I Served My Apprenticeship"

classzone.com

	Section 1	Section 2	Section 3	Section 4
California Reading Toolkit	p. L41	p. L42	p. L43	p. L44
California Modified Lesson Plans for English Learners	p. 77	p. 79	p. 81	p. 83
California Daily Standards Practice Transparencies	TT33	TT34	TT35	TT36
California Standards Enrichment Workbook	pp. 33–34, 35–36, 41–42	pp. 35–36, 37–38, 39–40	pp. 35–36, 37–38, 41–42, 47–48	pp. 35–36, 39–40, 41–42, 43–44
California Standards Planner and Lesson Plans	p. L73	p. L75	p. L77	p. L79
California Online Test Practice	classzone.com	classzone.com	classzone.com	classzone.com
California Test Generator CD-ROM	CD-ROM	CD-ROM	CD-ROM	CD-ROM
California Easy Planner CD-ROM	CD-ROM	CD-ROM	CD-ROM	CD-ROM
California eEdition CD-ROM	CD-ROM	CD-ROM	CD-ROM	CD-ROM

Chart Key:

Copymaster

Pupil's Edition

Audio Library

Teacher's Edition

CD-ROM

Overhead Transparency

Internet

Block Scheduling

Video

NO TIME?

If you do not have time to teach this chapter in full, assign the **Chapter in Brief** (also available in Spanish).

Previewing Resources for Differentiated Instruction

ENGLISH LEARNERS: Resources in Spanish

In-Depth Resources in Spanish

- Guided Reading (A)
- Skillbuilder Practice: Developing Historical Perspective (B)
- Geography Application: British Population Moves to the Cities

Chapters in Brief

Reading Study Guide (C)

Reading Study Guide Audio CD

Test Generator CD-ROM

- Chapter Test, Forms A, B, and C

Plus

Modified Lesson Plans for English Learners

Multi-Language Glossary of Social Studies Terms

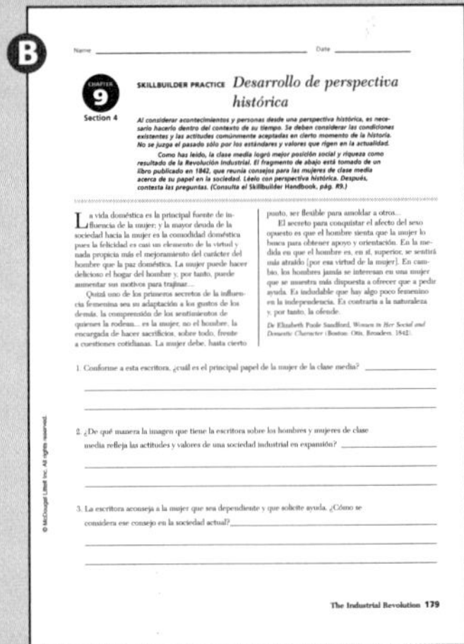

STRUGGLING READERS

In-Depth Resources: Unit 3

- Guided Reading (A)
- Building Vocabulary
- Skillbuilder Practice: Developing Historical Perspective
- Geography Application: British Population Moves to the Cities (B)
- Reteaching Activities

Chapters in Brief

Reading Study Guide

Reading Study Guide

Formal Assessment

- Chapter Test, Form A (C)

Plus

Reading Toolkit

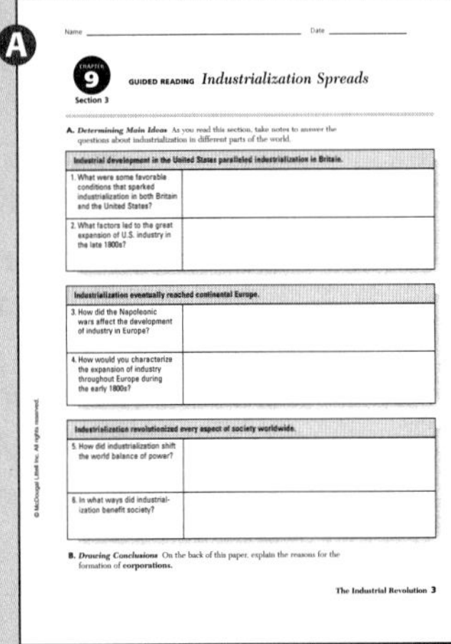

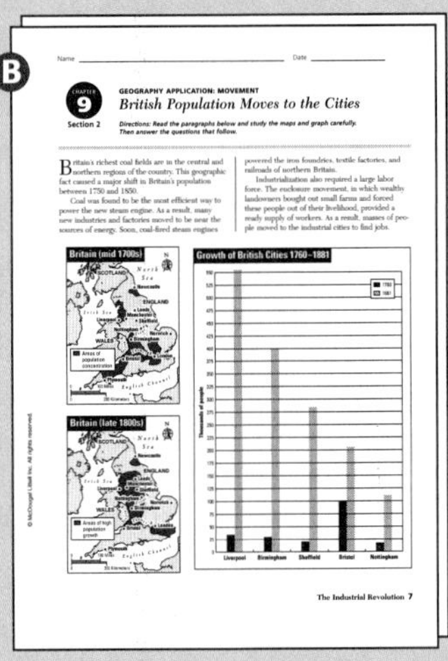

GIFTED AND TALENTED STUDENTS

In-Depth Resources: Unit 3

- Primary Source: from "The Opening of the Liverpool to Manchester Railway"; Testimony on Child Labor in Britain (A); "Life in a New England Factory"; from *The Wealth of Nations*
- Literature: from *Mary Barton*
- History Makers: James Watt; Henri de Saint-Simon
- Connections Across Time and Cultures: Enlightenment Ideals in an Industrial Age (B)

Electronic Library of Primary Sources

- from "Child Labor in the Mines"
- "The Sentencing of the Luddites"
- from *A New England Girlhood*
- from *The Communist Manifesto*
- from "How I Served My Apprenticeship"

Formal Assessment

- Chapter Test, Form C (C)

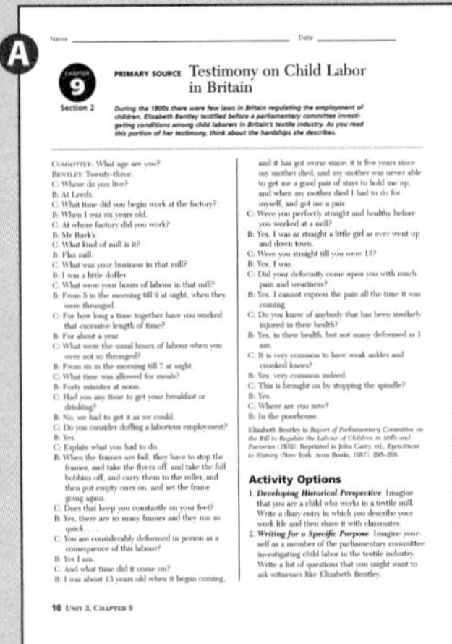

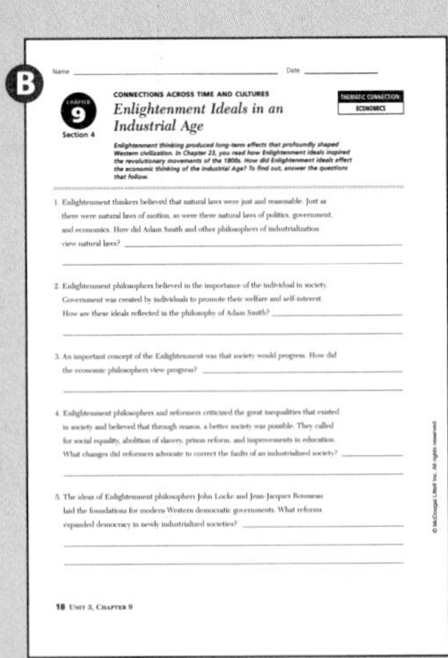

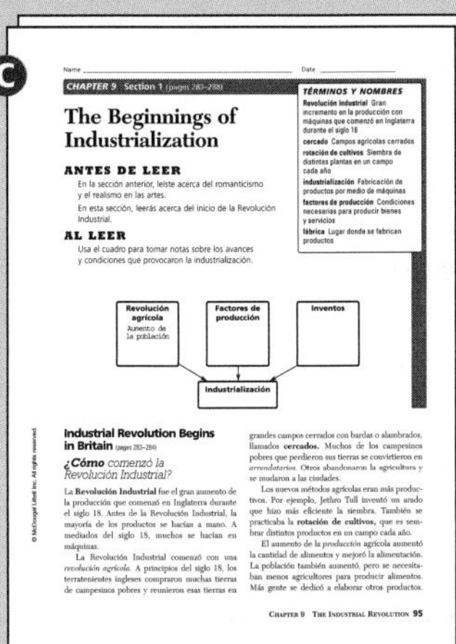

CHAPTER 9 Section 1

The Beginnings of Industrialization

ANTES DE LEER

AL LEER

Activities in the Teacher's Edition for English Learners

- Linking Causes and Effects, p. 287
- Understanding Workers and Factory Owners, p. 291
- Analyzing a Primary Source, p. 296
- Analyzing Key Terms, p. 303

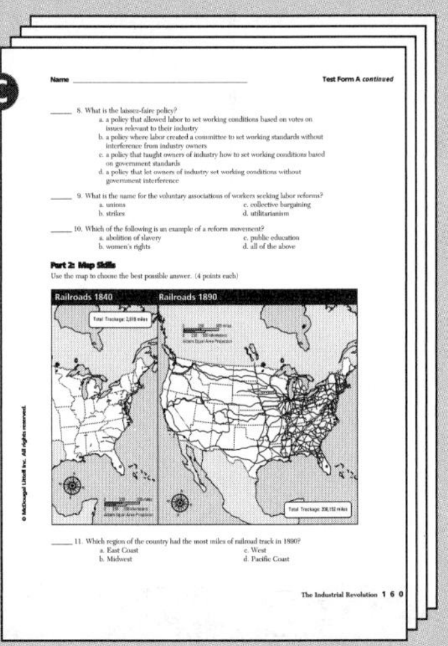

Part 2: Map Skills

Railroads 1840

Railroads 1890

Activities in the Teacher's Edition for Struggling Readers

- Understanding Technological Advances, p. 284
- Creating a Political Cartoon, p. 290
- Understanding Obstacles to Industrial Growth, p. 298

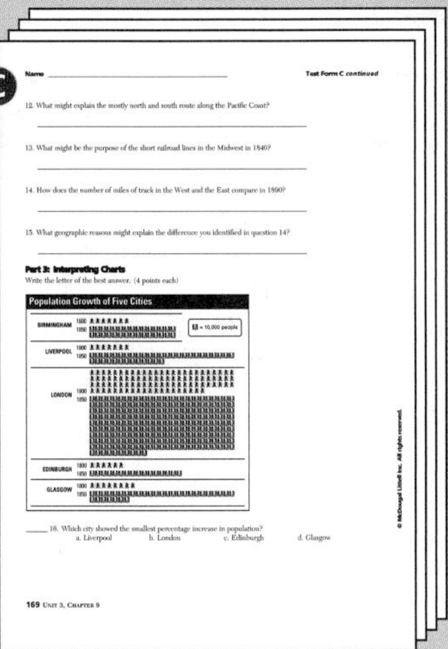

Part 3: Interpreting Charts

Population Growth of Five Cities

Activities in the Teacher's Edition for Gifted and Talented Students

- Connecting Inventions and Scientific Principles, p. 286
- Debating Effects of Industrialism, p. 292
- Planning an Industrial Fair, p. 297
- Researching Socialist, Marxist, and Utopian Societies, p. 301

INTEGRATED TECHNOLOGY

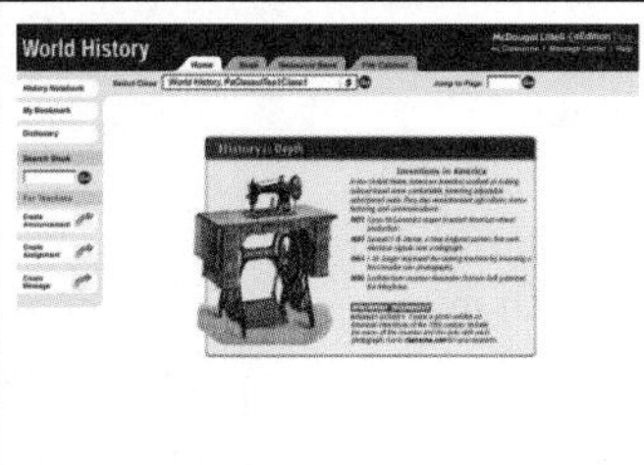

eEdition
- Interactive Visuals
- Interactive Maps
- Interactive Primary Sources

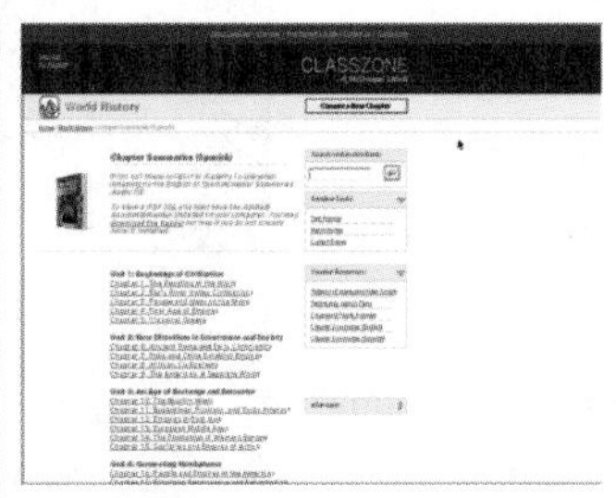

classzone.com
- Research Links
- Internet Activities
- Primary Sources
- Chapter Quiz
- Current Events

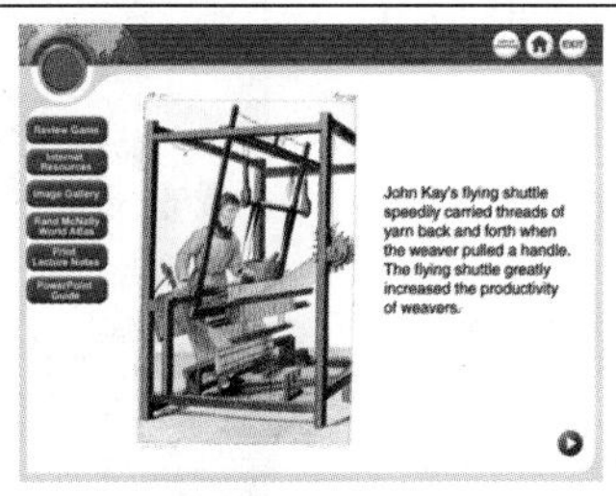

Power Presentations CD-ROM
- Lecture Notes
- Image Gallery
- Chapter Review Game

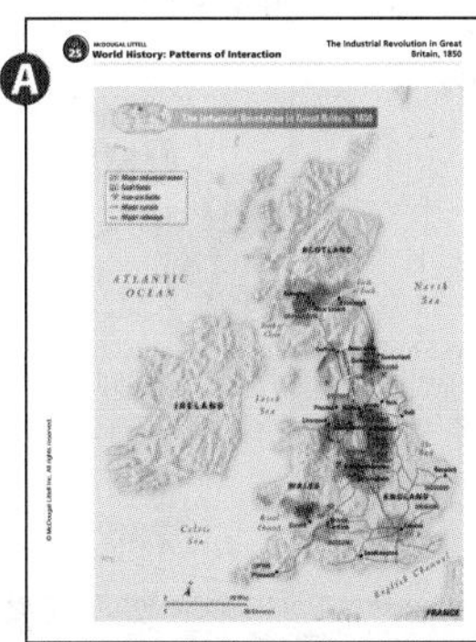

Critical Thinking Transparencies
- CT25 Industrialists and Reformers
- CT61 Chapter 25 Visual Summary

Geography Transparencies
- GT25 The Industrial Revolution in Great Britain, 1850 A

World Art and Cultures Transparencies
- AT54 Arkwright's Cotton Mill
- AT55 Monet's *Arrival of the Normandy Train*

Test Practice Transparencies TT93–TT96

Test Generator CD-ROM

EasyPlanner CD-ROM

Voices from the Past Audio CD

Online Test Practice

Electronic Library of Primary Sources

Patterns of Interaction Video Series

CHAPTER 9 • OBJECTIVE

Trace key events of the Industrial Revolution and analyze how these affected economics and politics.

Previewing Main Ideas

Ask students to recall the characteristics of revolution that they learned in their study of the American and French revolutions. Like these revolutions, the Industrial Revolution changed society on many levels. As students read, urge them to think about ways that the Industrial Revolution is similar to and different from those earlier revolutions.

Accessing Prior Knowledge

Ask students to speculate on what an Industrial Revolution might be. What do they know about industry? What do they know about railroads? Ask students if any of their family members have ever worked in a factory. Explain that during the Industrial Revolution, railroads and factories changed the way people lived, worked, and thought.

Geography *Answers*

SCIENCE AND TECHNOLOGY France, Belgium, and Germany had these industries.

EMPIRE BUILDING England appears to be the most industrialized.

ECONOMICS Access to waterways and natural resources could help industry develop in certain places.

CHAPTER 9

The Industrial Revolution, 1700–1900

Previewing Main Ideas

SCIENCE AND TECHNOLOGY From the spinning jenny to the locomotive train, there was an explosion of inventions and technological advances. These improvements paved the way for the Industrial Revolution.

Geography *What other European countries besides England had coal, iron, and textile industries in the 1800s?*

EMPIRE BUILDING The global power balance shifted after the Industrial Revolution. This shift occurred because industrialized nations dominated the rest of the world.

Geography *Study the map. Which country appears to be the most industrialized?*

ECONOMICS The Industrial Revolution transformed economic systems. In part, this was because nations dramatically changed the way they produced and distributed goods.

Geography *What geographic factors might have encouraged the development of industry in certain places?*

INTEGRATED TECHNOLOGY

eEdition
- Interactive Maps
- Interactive Visuals
- Interactive Primary Sources

VIDEO *Patterns of Interaction: The Industrial and Electronic Revolutions*

INTERNET RESOURCES

Go to **classzone.com** for:
- Research Links
- Internet Activities
- Primary Sources
- Chapter Quiz
- Maps
- Test Practice
- Current Events

EUROPE AND UNITED STATES

1701 Jethro Tull invents seed drill. ▶

1765 James Watt builds steam engine.

1700

1750

WORLD

1736 Qian-long begins his reign as emperor of China. (Imperial Palace compound at Beijing) ▶

280

TIME LINE DISCUSSION

Explain that the time line covers a period of industrial invention and progress. Inventions signaled the beginning of the industrial era.

1. Ask students to identify an important achievement in transportation. *(1765—steam engine)*
2. Which two achievements suggest progress in agriculture? When did they occur? *(seed drill—1701, cotton gin—1793)* How might better agricultural tools change everyday life? *(Possible Answer: might make lives easier)*
3. When did Marx and Engels publish their important work? *(1848)* What else was happening in the world around this time? *(Japanese modernization)*
4. What event occurred in Britain in 1875? *(Unions won the right to strike.)* How might this have changed workers' lives? *(Possible Answer: gave them some power)*
5. As Eli Whitney was changing the world with the cotton gin, how were Haitians changing their world? *(revolution)* What other revolutions can you recall from earlier units that also occurred around this time? *(U.S., French)*

History from Visuals

Interpreting the Map

Ask students to note the locations of major railroads constructed by 1870. *(widespread, but especially dense in England, Ireland, France, and Germany)* Ask students to think about how the development of new transportation might have improved the movement of people and products during the 1800s. How might this change the pace of life in the 19th century? *(people and products moving more quickly; pace of life faster)*

Extension Have students look at the map and at the graph of cotton consumption on page 285. Ask them how the spread of the British textile industry might be linked to the growth of cotton consumption. *(Textile industry uses cotton; the two grew together.)*

Point out that industrialization required taking large quantities of resources from the earth. In addition, both factories and transportation systems produced pollution. Ask students how this might have affected the environment. *(Possible Answer: problems for people and animals from polluted air and water, dwindling resources, land destruction)*

RECOMMENDED RESOURCES

Books for the Teacher

Smith, Adam. ***The Theory of Moral Sentiments.*** 1759. Amherst, NY: Prometheus Books, 2000. This lesser-known work of the great capitalist Adam Smith extols the virtues of being moral in a capitalist society. An examination of human feelings and values.

Stearns, Peter N., and John H. Hinshaw. ***The ABC-Clio World History Companion to the Industrial Revolution***. Santa Barbara, CA: ABC-Clio, 1996.

Books for the Student

Bland, Celia. ***The Mechanical Age: The Industrial Revolution in England.*** New York: Facts on File, 1995.

Hobsbawm, Eric J. ***Industry and Empire: The Birth of the Industrial Revolution.*** Updated ed. New York: New Press, 1999. Describes Britain's rise as the first industrial power, its eventual decline, and the effect of the Industrial Revolution on its citizens.

Macaulay, David. ***Mill***. Boston: Houghton Mifflin, 1989.

Videos and Software

The Luddites. VHS. Social Studies School Service, 1992. 800-421-4246. Strong resistance to new technology.

The Industrial Revolution. VHS. Library Video Company, 2000. 800-843-3620.

The Industrial Revolution. CD-ROM. Society for Visual Education, 1994. 800-829-1900.

Interact *with* History

Objectives

- Set the stage for studying the Industrial Revolution and analyzing its causes and effects.
- Connect the events and historical figures of the chapter with students' lives.

EXAMINING *the* ISSUES

Possible Answers

- Most students will say yes, as people today are encouraged to take action in their own interest. Some may hesitate to question authority.
- Some would run away: others would join a union; still others would choose school as a way out.

Discussion

Invite students to discuss today's preindustrial societies. What are some problems children face in these societies? *(hunger, malnutrition, lack of education, lack of clothing and basic health services)*

Interact *with* History

What are fair working conditions?

You are a 15-year-old living in England where the Industrial Revolution has spurred the growth of thousands of factories. Cheap labor is in great demand. Like millions of other teenagers, you do not go to school. Instead, you work in a factory 6 days a week, 14 hours a day. The small pay you receive is needed to help support your family. You trudge to work before dawn every day and work until after sundown. Inside the workplace the air is hot and foul, and after sunset it is so dark it is hard to see. Minding the machines is exhausting, dirty, and dangerous.

1 **Long hours:** The sun may be shining through the windows as this child's day begins, but it will have disappeared by the time his day ends.

2 **Dangerous machines:** Children usually worked in bare feet with no safety equipment among machines with many moving parts.

3 **Hot temperatures and dust-filled air:** Dust particles from thousands of bobbins cling to the clothing and hang in air heated by the machinery.

EXAMINING *the* ISSUES

- **Would you attempt to change your working conditions in the factory?**
- **Would you join a union, go to school, or run away?**

In small groups, discuss these questions. Share your conclusions with your class. In your discussions, think about how children lived in preindustrial and industrial societies all over the world. As you read about the changes caused by industrialization, note how reform movements eventually improved conditions for most laborers.

282 Chapter 9

WHY STUDY THE INDUSTRIAL REVOLUTION?

- All nations face problems of industrialization, such as air and water pollution, acid rain, and crowded cities.
- Today's global society depends on transportation and communication that can be traced to the Industrial Revolution.
- Industrialized nations such as those in western Europe continue to use low-wage labor from less-industrialized nations.
- Socialism and communism have increasingly given way to capitalism, causing major global upheavals in places such as Russia and eastern Europe.
- Tensions continue between the industrialized nations of Europe and North America and less-developed nations such as those in Africa.

Steam train on the Nancha Bank, China

Power plant in West Virginia, United States

1

The Beginnings of Industrialization

MAIN IDEA

SCIENCE AND TECHNOLOGY The Industrial Revolution started in England and soon spread to other countries.

WHY IT MATTERS NOW

The changes that began in Britain paved the way for modern industrial societies.

TERMS & NAMES

- Industrial Revolution
- enclosure
- crop rotation
- industrialization
- factors of production
- factory
- entrepreneur

SETTING THE STAGE In the United States, France, and Latin America, political revolutions brought in new governments. A different type of revolution now transformed the way people worked. The **Industrial Revolution** refers to the greatly increased output of machine-made goods that began in England in the middle 1700s. Before the Industrial Revolution, people wove textiles by hand. Then, machines began to do this and other jobs. Soon the Industrial Revolution spread from England to Continental Europe and North America.

Industrial Revolution Begins in Britain

In 1700, small farms covered England's landscape. Wealthy landowners, however, began buying up much of the land that village farmers had once worked. The large landowners dramatically improved farming methods. These innovations amounted to an agricultural revolution.

The Agricultural Revolution Paves the Way After buying up the land of village farmers, wealthy landowners enclosed their land with fences or hedges. The increase in their landholdings enabled them to cultivate larger fields. Within these larger fields, called **enclosures**, landowners experimented with more productive seeding and harvesting methods to boost crop yields. The enclosure movement had two important results. First, landowners tried new agricultural methods. Second, large landowners forced small farmers to become tenant farmers or to give up farming and move to the cities.

Jethro Tull was one of the first of these scientific farmers. He saw that the usual way of sowing seed by scattering it across the ground was wasteful. Many seeds failed to take root. He solved this problem with an invention called the seed drill in about 1701. It allowed farmers to sow seeds in well-spaced rows at specific depths. A larger share of the seeds took root, boosting crop yields.

Rotating Crops The process of **crop rotation** proved to be one of the best developments by the scientific farmers. The process improved upon older methods of crop rotation, such as the medieval three-field system. One year, for example, a farmer might plant a field with wheat, which exhausted soil nutrients. The next year he planted a root crop, such as turnips, to restore nutrients. This might be followed in turn by barley and then clover.

CALIFORNIA STANDARDS

10.3.1 Analyze why England was the first country to industrialize.

10.3.2 Examine how scientific and technological changes and new forms of energy brought about massive social, economic, and cultural change (e.g., the inventions and discoveries of James Watt, Eli Whitney, Henry Bessemer, Louis Pasteur, Thomas Edison).

10.3.5 Understand the connections among natural resources, entrepreneurship, labor, and capital in an industrial economy.

CST 1 Students compare the present with the past, evaluating the consequences of past events and decisions and determining the lessons that were learned.

HI 1 Students show the connections, causal and otherwise, between particular historical events and larger social, economic, and political trends and developments.

TAKING NOTES

Following Chronological Order On a time line, note important events in Britain's industrialization.

1700 — 1830

LESSON PLAN

OBJECTIVES

- Explain the beginnings of industrialization in Britain.
- Describe key inventions that furthered the Industrial Revolution.
- Identify transportation improvements.
- Trace the impact of railroads on British industry.

1 FOCUS & MOTIVATE

Note that the Industrial Revolution included key changes in the way people and goods could travel from one place to another. What are some ways that people and goods travel today? *(car, airplane, train, truck, ship)*

2 INSTRUCT

Industrial Revolution Begins in Britain

10.3.1

Critical Thinking

- Why might it be easier for large farmers to experiment than for family farmers? *(more resources)*

CALIFORNIA RESOURCES

California Reading Toolkit, p. L41
California Modified Lesson Plans for English Learners, p. 77
California Daily Standards Practice Transparencies, TT33
California Standards Enrichment Workbook, pp. 33–34, 35–36, 41–42
California Standards Planner and Lesson Plans, p. L73
California Online Test Practice
California Test Generator CD-ROM
California Easy Planner CD-ROM
California eEdition CD-ROM

SECTION 1 PROGRAM RESOURCES

ALL STUDENTS

In-Depth Resources: Unit 3
- Guided Reading, p. 1
- History Makers: James Watt, p. 16

Formal Assessment
- Section Quiz, p. 155

ENGLISH LEARNERS

In-Depth Resources in Spanish
- Guided Reading, p. 74

Reading Study Guide (Spanish), p. 95
Reading Study Guide Audio CD (Spanish)

STRUGGLING READERS

In-Depth Resources: Unit 3
- Guided Reading, p. 1
- Building Vocabulary, p. 5
- Reteaching Activity, p. 19

Reading Study Guide, p. 95
Reading Study Guide Audio CD

GIFTED AND TALENTED STUDENTS

In-Depth Resources: Unit 3
- Primary Source: from "The Opening of the Liverpool to Manchester Railway," p. 9

INTEGRATED TECHNOLOGY

eEdition CD-ROM
Voices from the Past Audio CD
Power Presentations CD-ROM
Patterns of Interaction Video Series
- *The Industrial and Electronic Revolutions*

classzone.com

More About . . .

The Business of War

Warfare in the early 1800s actually helped promote British business. Although British trade with Europe declined during the Napoleonic Wars, British victories gained new colonies and new markets. The British navy ruled the seas, making shipping safe for British merchants. In fact, French troops marched into Russia wearing English-made overcoats.

Tip for English Learners

List *land, labor,* and *capital* (wealth) on the board under the heading *factors of production*. Clarify what each factor means.

▸ An English farmer plants his fields in the early 1700s using a seed drill.

Livestock breeders improved their methods too. In the 1700s, for example, Robert Bakewell increased his mutton (sheep meat) output by allowing only his best sheep to breed. Other farmers followed Bakewell's lead. Between 1700 and 1786, the average weight for lambs climbed from 18 to 50 pounds. As food supplies increased and living conditions improved, England's population mushroomed. An increasing population boosted the demand for food and goods such as cloth. As farmers lost their land to large enclosed farms, many became factory workers. (A)

A. Answer It pushed farmers off the land, sent workers to the cities, and created a ready market for new goods.

MAIN IDEA

Recognizing Effects

(A) How did population growth spur the Industrial Revolution?

Why the Industrial Revolution Began in England In addition to a large population of workers, the small island country had extensive natural resources. **Industrialization**, which is the process of developing machine production of goods, required such resources. These natural resources included

- water power and coal to fuel the new machines
- iron ore to construct machines, tools, and buildings
- rivers for inland transportation
- harbors from which merchant ships set sail

In addition to its natural resources, Britain had an expanding economy to support industrialization. Businesspeople invested in the manufacture of new inventions. Britain's highly developed banking system also contributed to the country's industrialization. People were encouraged by the availability of bank loans to invest in new machinery and expand their operations. Growing overseas trade, economic prosperity, and a climate of progress led to the increased demand for goods.

Britain's political stability gave the country a tremendous advantage over its neighbors. Though Britain took part in many wars during the 1700s, none occurred on British soil. Their military successes gave the British a positive attitude. Parliament also passed laws to help encourage and protect business ventures. Other countries had some of these advantages. But Britain had all the **factors of production**, the resources needed to produce goods and services that the Industrial Revolution required. They included land, labor, and capital (or wealth).

Inventions Spur Industrialization

In an explosion of creativity, inventions now revolutionized industry. Britain's textile industry clothed the world in wool, linen, and cotton. This industry was the first to be transformed. Cloth merchants boosted their profits by speeding up the process by which spinners and weavers made cloth.

Changes in the Textile Industry As you will learn in the feature on textile technology on page 285, by 1800, several major inventions had modernized the cotton industry. One invention led to another. In 1733, a machinist named John Kay made a shuttle that sped back and forth on wheels. This flying shuttle, a boat-shaped piece

Inventions Spur Industrialization

10.3.5

Critical Thinking

- Why do you think one invention led to another? *(Possible Answer: observers get new ideas from seeing other inventors' work; new inventions make others possible; exciting atmosphere)*
- How were England's cotton industry and America's cotton growers linked? *(Possible Answer: interdependent, each needed the other equally)*

DIFFERENTIATING INSTRUCTION: STRUGGLING READERS

Understanding Technological Advances

Class Time 20 minutes

Task Identify machines powered by steam engines

Purpose To clarify the importance of the steam engine in the development of industrialization and transportation

Instructions Have students view the video, *The Industrial and Electronic Revolutions.* Provide them with additional information about technological advances from pages 287–288. Then have students work in groups. Ask them to use the video and text to brainstorm a list of some of the specific machines that were powered by steam engines.

Discuss the following questions:

- What else besides steam might be used to power factory machines?
- How else might boats be powered?
- How else might locomotives be powered?

If students need help with the text on pages 287–288, refer them to the Reading Study Guide for Section 1.

Patterns of Interaction Video Series: *The Industrial and Electronic Revolutions*

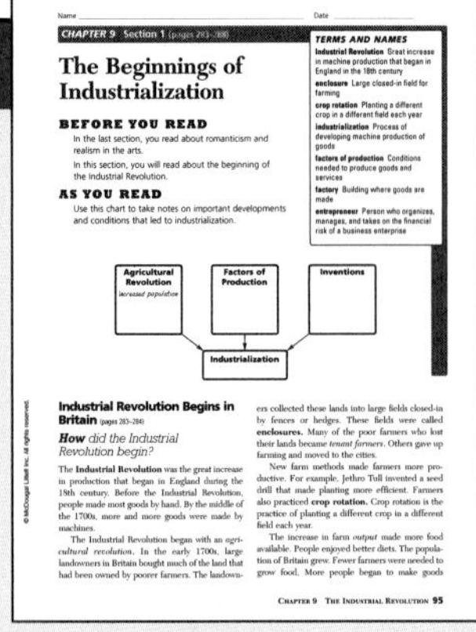

Name ______ Date ______

CHAPTER 9 Section 1 (pages 283–288)

The Beginnings of Industrialization

BEFORE YOU READ

In the last section, you read about romanticism and realism in the arts.

In this section, you will read about the beginning of the Industrial Revolution.

AS YOU READ

Use this chart to take notes on important developments and conditions that led to industrialization.

TERMS AND NAMES

Industrial Revolution Great increase in machine production that began in England in the 18th century

enclosure Large closed-in field for farming

crop rotation Planting a different crop in a different field each year

industrialization Process of developing machine production of goods

factors of production Conditions needed to produce goods and services

factory Building where goods are made

entrepreneur Person who organizes, manages, and takes on the financial risk of a business enterprise

Industrial Revolution Begins in Britain (pages 283–284)

***How** did the Industrial Revolution begin?*

The **Industrial Revolution** was the great increase in production that began in England during the 18th century. Before the Industrial Revolution, people made most goods by hand. By the middle of the 1700s, more and more goods were made by machines.

The Industrial Revolution began with an *agricultural revolution*. In the early 1700s, large landowners in Britain bought much of the land that had been owned by poorer farmers. The landowners collected these lands into large fields closed-in by fences or hedges. These fields were called **enclosures.** Many of the poor farmers who lost their lands became *tenant farmers*. Others gave up farming and moved to the cities.

New farm methods made farmers more productive. For example, Jethro Tull invented a seed drill that made planting more efficient. Farmers also practiced **crop rotation.** Crop rotation is the practice of planting a different crop in a different field each year.

The increase in farm *output* made more food available. People enjoyed better diets. The population of Britain grew. Fewer farmers were needed to grow food. More people began to make goods

CHAPTER 9 THE INDUSTRIAL REVOLUTION 95

Reading Study Guide

Textiles Industrialize First

The Industrial Revolution that began in Britain was spurred by a revolution in technology. It started in the textile industry, where inventions in the late 1700s transformed the manufacture of cloth. The demand for clothing in Britain had greatly increased as a result of the population boom caused by the agricultural revolution. These developments, in turn, had an impact worldwide. For example, the consumption of cotton rose dramatically in Britain (see graph at right). This cotton came from plantations in the American South, where cotton production skyrocketed from 1820 to 1860 in response to demand from English textile mills.

▶ John Kay's flying shuttle (below) speedily carried threads of yarn back and forth when the weaver pulled a handle on the loom. The flying shuttle greatly increased the productivity of weavers.

▲ Flying shuttle

CALIFORNIA STANDARDS

10.3.1 Analyze why England was the first country to industrialize.

HI 1 Students show the connections, causal and otherwise, between particular historical events and larger social, economic, and political trends and developments.

British Cotton Consumption, 1800–1900

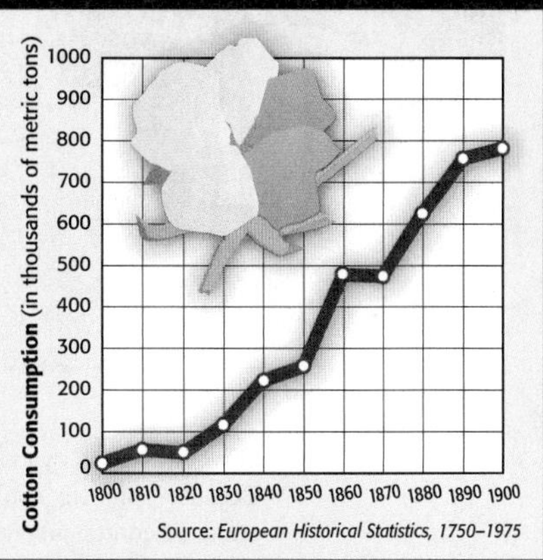

Source: *European Historical Statistics, 1750–1975*

Patterns of Interaction

Technology Transforms an Age: The Industrial and Electronic Revolutions

Inventions in the textile industry started in Britain and brought about the Industrial Revolution. This revolution soon spread to other countries. The process of industrialization is still spreading around the world, especially in developing countries. A similar technological revolution is occurring in electronics today, transforming the distribution of information around the world.

Connect *to* Today

1. **Synthesizing** How might the technological innovation and industrialization that took place in the textile industry during the Industrial Revolution have provided a model for other industries?
   See Skillbuilder Handbook, Page R21.
2. **Recognizing Effects** Research the textile industry today to learn how it has been affected by new technology, including computerization. Prepare a two-paragraph summary on the effects of the new technology.

Global Impact

OBJECTIVE

- Explore the global impact of inventions in the past and today.

INSTRUCT

Show the video. Point out that the first segment traces the origins of the Industrial Revolution and its effect on global relations. The second segment investigates how modern technology is creating opportunities for the worldwide exchange of information and ideas. Discuss how technology affects students' lives.

History from Visuals

Interpreting the Graph

Point out to students that the years increase by decades across the bottom of the chart. Also note that the scale on the left increases by 100,000 metric tons. Then ask students to identify the decade in which the steepest increase in British cotton consumption took place. *(1850–1860)*

Extension Have students suggest why cotton consumption might have fallen off between 1860 and 1870. *(Possible Answer: The American Civil War affected both cotton production and cotton consumption, as well as transportation.)*

CONNECT TO TODAY: ANSWERS

1. Synthesizing

Possible Answer: Many of the techniques of production and standardization were applicable to other industries as the Industrial Revolution developed. This can be seen, for example, in improvements in transportation when the steam engine was adapted to boats and railroads.

2. Recognizing Effects

Rubric Summaries should

- identify technology used in the textile industry.
- draw cause-and-effect links between technology and industry.
- reflect effective research and critical thinking.

History *in* Depth

Inventions in America

Have students research one of the inventions listed here. Then have them explain basic facts about the invention and the inventor's life.

INTEGRATED TECHNOLOGY

Rubric Successful photo exhibits should
- show a range of inventions.
- identify each invention and inventor.
- be visually appealing.

Tip for Struggling Readers

Help students make a chart like the one below and list major inventions or improvements in each category.

Textiles	Transport
Flying shuttle	Steam engine

More About . . .

The Cotton Gin

Eli Whitney's cotton gin made Southern planters rich, but not the inventor. The gin was easy to make and therefore easy to pirate. Whitney later pioneered the concept of interchangeable parts, building muskets from machine-made components.

History *in* Depth

Inventions in America

In the United States, American inventors worked at making railroad travel more comfortable, inventing adjustable upholstered seats. They also revolutionized agriculture, manufacturing, and communications:

1831 Cyrus McCormick's reaper boosted American wheat production.

1837 Samuel F. B. Morse, a New England painter, first sent electrical signals over a telegraph.

1851 I. M. Singer improved the sewing machine by inventing a foot treadle (see photograph).

1876 Scottish-born inventor Alexander Graham Bell patented the telephone.

INTEGRATED TECHNOLOGY

INTERNET ACTIVITY Create a photo exhibit on American inventions of the 19th century. Include the name of the inventor and the date with each photograph. Go to **classzone.com** for your research.

of wood to which yarn was attached, doubled the work a weaver could do in a day. Because spinners could not keep up with these speedy weavers, a cash prize attracted contestants to produce a better spinning machine. Around 1764, a textile worker named James Hargreaves invented a spinning wheel he named after his daughter. His spinning jenny allowed one spinner to work eight threads at a time.

At first, textile workers operated the flying shuttle and the spinning jenny by hand. Then, Richard Arkwright invented the water frame in 1769. This machine used the waterpower from rapid streams to drive spinning wheels. In 1779, Samuel Crompton combined features of the spinning jenny and the water frame to produce the spinning mule. The spinning mule made thread that was stronger, finer, and more consistent than earlier spinning machines. Run by waterpower, Edmund Cartwright's power loom sped up weaving after its invention in 1787. **B**

MAIN IDEA
Summarizing
B What inventions transformed the textile industry?
B. Answer flying shuttle; spinning jenny; water frame; spinning mule; power loom

The water frame, the spinning mule, and the power loom were bulky and expensive machines. They took the work of spinning and weaving out of the house. Wealthy textile merchants set up the machines in large buildings called **factories**. Factories needed waterpower, so the first ones were built near rivers and streams:

PRIMARY SOURCE

A great number of streams . . . furnish water-power adequate to turn many hundred mills: they afford the element of water, indispensable for scouring, bleaching, printing, dyeing, and other processes of manufacture: and when collected in their larger channels, or employed to feed canals, they supply a superior inland navigation, so important for the transit of raw materials and merchandise.

EDWARD BAINS, *The History of Cotton Manufacture in Great Britain* (1835)

England's cotton came from plantations in the American South in the 1790s. Removing seeds from the raw cotton by hand was hard work. In 1793, an American inventor named Eli Whitney invented a machine to speed the chore. His cotton gin multiplied the amount of cotton that could be cleaned. American cotton production skyrocketed from 1.5 million pounds in 1790 to 85 million pounds in 1810.

DIFFERENTIATING INSTRUCTION: GIFTED AND TALENTED STUDENTS

Connecting Inventions and Scientific Principles

Class Time 30 minutes

Task Researching inventions and their scientific principles

Purpose To understand the science behind the Industrial Revolution

Instructions Organize students in pairs or small groups. Challenge them with either of the following research tasks:
- Research James Watt's invention to determine the scientific principles on which it operated.
- Research Robert Fulton's steamboat, the *Clermont*. Students should find out how the boat used steam power to travel.

Students should draw a diagram to illustrate their findings, and then discuss their diagram and findings in class. The following resources might also be useful:

In-Depth Resources: Unit 3: "The Opening of the Liverpool-Manchester Railway," p. 9, and James Watt, p. 16.

In-Depth Resources: Unit 3

In-Depth Resources: Unit 3

Improvements in Transportation

Progress in the textile industry spurred other industrial improvements. The first such development, the steam engine, stemmed from the search for a cheap, convenient source of power. As early as 1705, coal miners were using steam-powered pumps to remove water from deep mine shafts. But this early model of a steam engine gobbled great quantities of fuel, making it expensive to run.

Watt's Steam Engine James Watt, a mathematical instrument maker at the University of Glasgow in Scotland, thought about the problem for two years. In 1765, Watt figured out a way to make the steam engine work faster and more efficiently while burning less fuel. In 1774, Watt joined with a businessman named Matthew Boulton. Boulton was an **entrepreneur** (AHN•truh•pruh•NUR), a person who organizes, manages, and takes on the risks of a business. He paid Watt a salary and encouraged him to build better engines.

Water Transportation Steam could also propel boats. An American inventor named Robert Fulton ordered a steam engine from Boulton and Watt. He built a steamboat called the *Clermont*, which made its first successful trip in 1807. The *Clermont* later ferried passengers up and down New York's Hudson River.

In England, water transportation improved with the creation of a network of canals, or human-made waterways. By the mid-1800s, 4,250 miles of inland channels slashed the cost of transporting both raw materials and finished goods.

Road Transportation British roads improved, too, thanks largely to the efforts of John McAdam, a Scottish engineer. Working in the early 1800s, McAdam equipped road beds with a layer of large stones for drainage. On top, he placed a carefully smoothed layer of crushed rock. Even in rainy weather heavy wagons could travel over the new "macadam" roads without sinking in mud.

Private investors formed companies that built roads and then operated them for profit. People called the new roads turnpikes because travelers had to stop at tollgates (turnstiles or turnpikes) to pay tolls before traveling farther.

The Railway Age Begins

Steam-driven machinery powered English factories in the late 1700s. A steam engine on wheels—the railroad locomotive—drove English industry after 1820.

Steam-Driven Locomotives In 1804, an English engineer named Richard Trevithick won a bet of several thousand dollars. He did this by hauling ten tons of iron over nearly ten miles of track in a steam-driven locomotive. Other British engineers soon built improved versions of Trevithick's locomotive. One of these early

▼ First-class passengers on the Liverpool-Manchester Railway in the 1830s rode in covered cars; all others, in open cars.

Improvements in Transportation
10.3.2

Critical Thinking

- Why did James Watt and Matthew Boulton need each other? *(Possible Answer: Inventors need both business and financial know-how.)*
- What might improved water and road transportation mean for families with workers at distant factories? *(Possible Answer: easier contact, travel in emergencies or for family events)*

In-Depth Resources: Unit 3

- Primary Source: "The Opening of the Liverpool to Manchester Railway," p. 9
- History Makers: James Watt, p. 16

More About . . .

Roads

In the late 1700s, British roads were worse than they had been 1,500 years earlier under Roman rule. Rain and mud often made roads impassable. Men were known to drown in potholes. In one region, an inland lighthouse was built to guide travelers over treacherous roads.

The Railway Age Begins
10.3.5

Critical Thinking

- Why did entrepreneurs want to link Liverpool and Manchester? *(Textile industry needed a port for its products.)*
- How do you think most Britains reacted to the railroad? *(Possible Answer: enthusiastically)*

DIFFERENTIATING INSTRUCTION: ENGLISH LEARNERS

Linking Causes and Effects

Class Time 10 minutes

Task Making a cause-effect diagram

Purpose To understand the causes and effects of the agricultural and Industrial revolutions

Instructions Review the section material with students. Then have small groups create diagrams that show the causes and effects of the agricultural and industrial revolutions. Provide the following list of causes and effects. Point out that some causes will have multiple effects.

Students who need help may use the Guided Reading worksheet in Spanish.

Causes	Effects
• enclosure movement	• small farmers move to factory jobs
• crop rotation	• higher crop yields • increased population
• inventions in textile machines	• increased textile production
• transportation improvements: steam engine, better roads • railroads expand	• helped people and goods move quickly • enlarged the market for industry

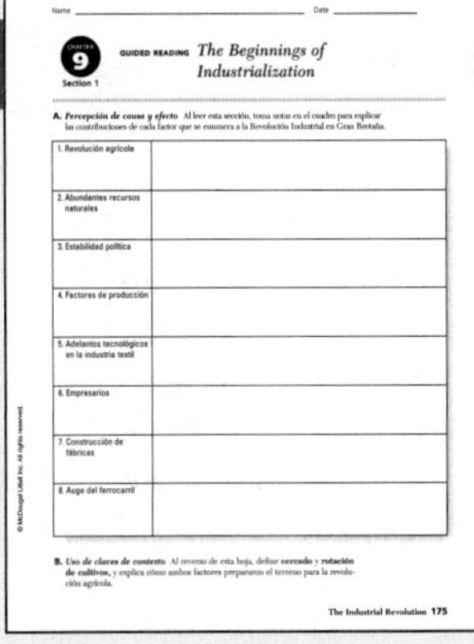

In-Depth Resources in Spanish

Tip for Gifted and Talented Students

Have students recall the factors that helped Britain establish itself as the world's first industrial power. Then tell students that, in 1997, Singapore topped the Geneva World Economic Forum's list of most competitive economies. Hong Kong came next, with the United States, Canada, New Zealand, Switzerland, and Great Britain following. Ask students how, if at all, the reasons for economic success might have changed since the 19th century.

③ ASSESS

SECTION 1 ASSESSMENT

After students complete the questions independently, invite volunteers to share the letters they wrote for item 9.

Formal Assessment
- Section Quiz, p. 155

④ RETEACH

Use the section subheads to reteach the information in the section. Have student pairs generate two key ideas for each subhead. List these on the board in an outline format.

In-Depth Resources: Unit 3
- Reteaching Activity, p. 19

▲ George Stephenson's *Rocket*

railroad engineers was George Stephenson. He had gained a solid reputation by building some 20 engines for mine operators in northern England. In 1821, Stephenson began work on the world's first railroad line. It was to run 27 miles from the Yorkshire coal fields to the port of Stockton on the North Sea. In 1825, the railroad opened. It used four locomotives that Stephenson had designed and built.

The Liverpool-Manchester Railroad News of this success quickly spread throughout Britain. The entrepreneurs of northern England wanted a railroad line to connect the port of Liverpool with the inland city of Manchester. The track was laid. In 1829, trials were held to choose the best locomotive for use on the new line. Five engines entered the competition. None could compare with the *Rocket*, designed by Stephenson and his son.

Smoke poured from the *Rocket*'s tall smokestack, and its two pistons pumped to and fro as they drove the front wheels. The locomotive hauled a 13-ton load at an unheard-of speed—more than 24 miles per hour. The Liverpool-Manchester Railway opened officially in 1830. It was an immediate success.

Railroads Revolutionize Life in Britain The invention and perfection of the locomotive had at least four major effects. First, railroads spurred industrial growth by giving manufacturers a cheap way to transport materials and finished products. Second, the railroad boom created hundreds of thousands of new jobs for both railroad workers and miners. These miners provided iron for the tracks and coal for the steam engines. Third, the railroads boosted England's agricultural and fishing industries, which could transport their products to distant cities.

Finally, by making travel easier, railroads encouraged country people to take distant city jobs. Also, railroads lured city dwellers to resorts in the countryside. Like a locomotive racing across the country, the Industrial Revolution brought rapid and unsettling changes to people's lives. Ⓒ

C. Answer Canals cut the cost of transporting materials; improved roads fostered the movement of heavy wagons; railroads linked manufacturing cities with raw materials.

MAIN IDEA
Synthesizing
Ⓒ How did improvements in transportation promote industrialization in Britain?

SECTION 1 ASSESSMENT

TERMS & NAMES 1. For each term or name, write a sentence explaining its significance.
- Industrial Revolution • enclosure • crop rotation • industrialization • factors of production • factory • entrepreneur

USING YOUR NOTES

2. Which of the events listed do you think was the most important? Explain. (10.3.5)

1700 — 1830

MAIN IDEAS

3. What were four factors that contributed to industrialization in Britain? (10.3.1)
4. How did rising population help the Industrial Revolution? (10.3.1)
5. What American invention aided the British textile industry? (10.3.1)

CRITICAL THINKING & WRITING

6. **EVALUATING** Was the revolution in agriculture necessary to the Industrial Revolution? Explain. (10.3.5)
7. **MAKING INFERENCES** What effect did entrepreneurs have upon the Industrial Revolution? (10.3.5)
8. **FORMING AND SUPPORTING OPINIONS** Do you agree with the statement that the steam engine was the greatest invention of the Industrial Revolution? Why? (10.3.2)
9. **WRITING ACTIVITY** SCIENCE AND TECHNOLOGY Write a **letter,** as a British government official during the Industrial Revolution, to an official in a nonindustrial nation explaining how the railroad has changed Britain. (Writing 2.5.b)

CONNECT TO TODAY CREATING AN ILLUSTRATED NEWS ARTICLE

Find information on a recent agricultural or technological invention or improvement. Write a two-paragraph **news article** about its economic effects and include an illustration, if possible. (10.3.5)

ANSWERS

1. Industrial Revolution, p. 283 • enclosure, p. 283 • crop rotation, p. 283 • industrialization, p. 284 • factors of production, p. 284 • factories, p. 286 • entrepreneur, p. 287
2. **Sample Answer:** Time lines should show events and inventions: seed drill, 1701; invention of flying shuttle, 1733; spinning jenny, 1764; steam engine, 1765; water frame, 1769; spinning mule, 1779; power loom, 1787; cotton gin, 1793; railroad opened, 1825. **Possible Answer:** the steam engine because it powered other inventions
3. large work force, expanding economy, natural resources, political stability
4. supplied extra workers, created demand
5. Eli Whitney's cotton gin
6. **Possible Answer:** Scientific farming was necessary to feed growing population, and also displaced small farmers into industrial labor force.
7. **Possible Answer:** They promoted it with willingness to risk capital on new inventions and ideas.
8. Opinions should be supported by facts.
9. **Rubric** Letters should
   - show how railroads changed Britain.
   - reflect a government official's view.

CONNECT TO TODAY

Rubric News articles should
- use journalistic style.
- describe the improvement clearly.
- include an illustration.

288 Chapter 9

Industrialization

Case Study: Manchester

MAIN IDEA

ECONOMICS The factory system changed the way people lived and worked, introducing a variety of problems.

WHY IT MATTERS NOW

Many less-developed countries are undergoing the difficult process of industrialization today.

TERMS & NAMES

- urbanization
- middle class

SETTING THE STAGE The Industrial Revolution affected every part of life in Great Britain, but proved to be a mixed blessing. Eventually, industrialization led to a better quality of life for most people. But the change to machine production initially caused human suffering. Rapid industrialization brought plentiful jobs, but it also caused unhealthy working conditions, air and water pollution, and the ills of child labor. It also led to rising class tensions, especially between the working class and the middle class.

Industrialization Changes Life

The pace of industrialization accelerated rapidly in Britain. By the 1800s, people could earn higher wages in factories than on farms. With this money, more people could afford to heat their homes with coal from Wales and dine on Scottish beef. They wore better clothing, too, woven on power looms in England's industrial cities. Cities swelled with waves of job seekers.

Industrial Cities Rise For centuries, most Europeans had lived in rural areas. After 1800, the balance shifted toward cities. This shift was caused by the growth of the factory system, where the manufacturing of goods was concentrated in a central location. Between 1800 and 1850, the number of European cities boasting more than 100,000 inhabitants rose from 22 to 47. Most of Europe's urban areas at least doubled in population; some even quadrupled. This period was one of **urbanization**—city building and the movement of people to cities.

▼ As cities grew, people crowded into tenements and row houses such as these in London.

CALIFORNIA STANDARDS

10.3.2 Examine how scientific and technological changes and new forms of energy brought about massive social, economic, and cultural change (e.g., the inventions and discoveries of James Watt, Eli Whitney, Henry Bessemer, Louis Pasteur, Thomas Edison).

10.3.3 Describe the growth of population, rural to urban migration, and growth of cities associated with the Industrial Revolution.

10.3.4 Trace the evolution of work and labor, including the demise of the slave trade and the effects of immigration, mining and manufacturing, division of labor, and the union movement.

CST 1 Students compare the present with the past, evaluating the consequences of past events and decisions and determining the lessons that were learned.

CST 3 Students use a variety of maps and documents to interpret human movement, including major patterns of domestic and international migration, changing environmental preferences and settlement patterns, the frictions that develop between population groups, and the diffusion of ideas, technological innovations, and goods.

TAKING NOTES

Outlining Organize main ideas and details.

I. Industrialization Changes Life
   A.
   B.
II. Class Tensions Grow

LESSON PLAN

OBJECTIVES

- Describe the social and economic effects of industrialization.
- Examine growing tensions between the middle and working classes.
- Identify positive effects of the Industrial Revolution.
- Describe Manchester as an industrial city.

1 FOCUS & MOTIVATE

Tell students that industrialization had positive and negative effects on people's lives in Manchester. Ask students to name positive and negative ways that industry affects their own lives. *(Possible Answer: consumer goods and jobs; health problems, pollution)*

2 INSTRUCT

Industrialization Changes Life
10.3.2; 10.3.3

Critical Thinking

- How do you think merchants viewed their workers? *(as property, as tools)*

CALIFORNIA RESOURCES

California Reading Toolkit, p. L42
California Modified Lesson Plans for English Learners, p. 79
California Daily Standards Practice Transparencies, TT34
California Standards Enrichment Workbook, pp. 35–36, 37–38, 39–40
California Standards Planner and Lesson Plans, p. L75
California Online Test Practice
California Test Generator CD-ROM
California Easy Planner CD-ROM
California eEdition CD-ROM

SECTION 2 PROGRAM RESOURCES

ALL STUDENTS

In-Depth Resources: Unit 3
- Guided Reading, p. 2
- Geography Application, p. 7

Formal Assessment
- Section Quiz, p. 156

ENGLISH LEARNERS

In-Depth Resources in Spanish
- Guided Reading, p. 75
- Geography Application, p. 79

Reading Study Guide, p. 97
Reading Study Guide Audio CD (Spanish)

STRUGGLING READERS

In-Depth Resources: Unit 3
- Guided Reading, p. 2
- Building Vocabulary, p. 5
- Reteaching Activity, p. 20

Reading Study Guide, p. 97
Reading Study Guide Audio CD

GIFTED AND TALENTED STUDENTS

In-Depth Resources: Unit 3
- Primary Source: Child Labor, p. 10
- Literature: from *Mary Barton,* p. 13

Electronic Library of Primary Sources

INTEGRATED TECHNOLOGY

eEdition CD-ROM
Power Presentations CD-ROM
Geography Transparencies
- GT25 The Industrial Revolution in Great Britain, 1850

World Art and Cultures Transparencies
- AT54 Arkwright's Cotton Mill at Cromford, Derbyshire, England

Electronic Library of Primary Sources
- from "Child Labor in the Mines"
- "The Sentencing of the Luddites"

classzone.com

History from Visuals

The Day of a Child Laborer

Have students study the visuals and imagine what it would be like to be William Cooper. Ask them if they think child labor exists in the world today.

In-Depth Resources: Unit 3

- Primary Source: Testimony on Child Labor in Britain, p. 10

More About . . .

Urban Growth

In the 1700s, Britain was primarily a rural country. By 1851, however, more of the British people lived in cities than in the countryside. In 1901, the ratio of urban to rural population was 3 to 1. The population of London in 1901 was 4.5 million.

In-Depth Resources: Unit 3

- Geography Application: British Population Moves to the Cities, p. 7

Geography Transparencies

- GT25 The Industrial Revolution in Great Britain, 1850

World Art and Cultures Transparencies

- AT54 Arkwright's Cotton Mill at Cromford, Derbyshire, England

The Day of a Child Laborer, William Cooper

William Cooper began working in a textile factory at the age of ten. He had a sister who worked upstairs in the same factory. In 1832, Cooper was called to testify before a parliamentary committee about the conditions among child laborers in the textile industry. The following sketch of his day is based upon his testimony.

5 A.M. The workday began. Cooper and his sister rose as early as 4:00 or 4:30 in order to get to the factory by 5:00. Children usually ate their breakfast on the run.

12 NOON The children were given a 40-minute break for lunch. This was the only break they received all day.

Factories developed in clusters because entrepreneurs built them near sources of energy, such as water and coal. Major new industrial centers sprang up between the coal-rich area of southern Wales and the Clyde River valley in Scotland. But the biggest of these centers developed in England. (See map on page 281.)

Britain's capital, London, was the country's most important city. It had a population of about one million people by 1800. During the 1800s, its population exploded, providing a vast labor pool and market for new industry. London became Europe's largest city, with twice as many people as its closest rival (Paris). Newer cities challenged London's industrial leadership. Birmingham and Sheffield became iron-smelting centers. Leeds and Manchester dominated textile manufacturing. Along with the port of Liverpool, Manchester formed the center of Britain's bustling cotton industry. During the 1800s, Manchester experienced rapid growth from around 45,000 in 1760 to 300,000 by 1850.

Living Conditions Because England's cities grew rapidly, they had no development plans, sanitary codes, or building codes. Moreover, they lacked adequate housing, education, and police protection for the people who poured in from the countryside to seek jobs. Most of the unpaved streets had no drains, and garbage collected in heaps on them. Workers lived in dark, dirty shelters, with whole families crowding into one bedroom. Sickness was widespread. Epidemics of the deadly disease cholera regularly swept through the slums of Great Britain's industrial cities. In 1842, a British government study showed an average life span to be 17 years for working-class people in one large city, compared with 38 years in a nearby rural area.

Elizabeth Gaskell's *Mary Barton* (1848) is a work of fiction. But it presents a startlingly accurate portrayal of urban life experienced by many at the time. Gaskell provides a realistic description of the dank cellar dwelling of one family in a Manchester slum:

A. Answer by describing their terrible living conditions

▼ Elizabeth Gaskell (1810–1865) was a British writer whose novels show a sympathy for the working class.

PRIMARY SOURCE (A)

You went down one step even from the foul area into the cellar in which a family of human beings lived. It was very dark inside. The window-panes many of them were broken and stuffed with rags . . . . the smell was so fetid [foul] as almost to knock the two men down. . . . they began to penetrate the thick darkness of the place, and to see three or four little children rolling on the damp, nay wet brick floor, through which the stagnant, filthy moisture of the street oozed up.

ELIZABETH GASKELL, *Mary Barton*

MAIN IDEA

Analyzing Primary Sources

(A) How does Gaskell indicate her sympathy for the working class in this passage?

But not everyone in urban areas lived miserably. Well-to-do merchants and factory owners often built luxurious homes in the suburbs.

DIFFERENTIATING INSTRUCTION: STRUGGLING READERS

Creating a Political Cartoon

Class Time 15 minutes

Task Cartooning to convey views

Purpose To understand problems of the Industrial Revolution

Instructions Review the primary source excerpt from this page, working with students to paraphrase its meaning in simple English. *(Life was very difficult for city residents. They lived in dark and crowded places. Children were cold. Buildings were polluted.)* Discuss other problems of industrialization. Then suggest that students create a political cartoon that highlights a condition or problem associated with the Industrial Revolution in Great Britain. Provide the following suggestions:

- air pollution
- conditions of rich people and poor people
- dangerous conditions in factories
- crowded conditions in tenements

Cartoons should combine drawings and text. Remind students that a political cartoon conveys a message in a humorous and thought-provoking way.

Provide the Section 2 Guided Reading as a resource.

In-Depth Resources: Unit 3

3 P.M. The children often became drowsy during the afternoon or evening hours. In order to keep them awake, adult overseers sometimes whipped the children.

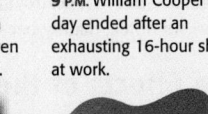

6 P.M. There was no break allowed for an evening meal. Children again ate on the run.

9 P.M. William Cooper's day ended after an exhausting 16-hour shift at work.

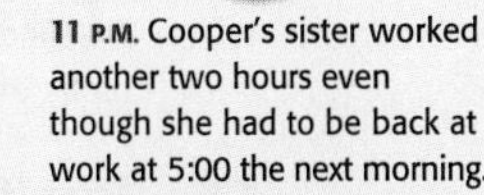

11 P.M. Cooper's sister worked another two hours even though she had to be back at work at 5:00 the next morning.

Working Conditions To increase production, factory owners wanted to keep their machines running as many hours as possible. As a result, the average worker spent 14 hours a day at the job, 6 days a week. Work did not change with the seasons, as it did on the farm. Instead, work remained the same week after week, year after year.

Industry also posed new dangers for workers. Factories were seldom well lit or clean. Machines injured workers. A boiler might explode or a drive belt might catch an arm. And there was no government program to provide aid in case of injury. The most dangerous conditions of all were found in coal mines. Frequent accidents, damp conditions, and the constant breathing of coal dust made the average miner's life span ten years shorter than that of other workers. Many women and children were employed in the mining industry because they were the cheapest source of labor.

Class Tensions Grow

Though poverty gripped Britain's working classes, the Industrial Revolution created enormous amounts of wealth in the nation. Most of this new money belonged to factory owners, shippers, and merchants. These people were part of a growing **middle class**, a social class made up of skilled workers, professionals, businesspeople, and wealthy farmers.

B. Answer upper class–landowners and aristocrats; upper middle class –managers, merchants, government employees, doctors, lawyers; lower middle class–factory overseers, skilled workers; a working class of unskilled laborers

The Middle Class The new middle class transformed the social structure of Great Britain. In the past, landowners and aristocrats had occupied the top position in British society. With most of the wealth, they wielded the social and political power. Now some factory owners, merchants, and bankers grew wealthier than the landowners and aristocrats. Yet important social distinctions divided the two wealthy classes. Landowners looked down on those who had made their fortunes in the "vulgar" business world. Not until late in the 1800s were rich entrepreneurs considered the social equals of the lords of the countryside.

Gradually, a larger middle class—neither rich nor poor—emerged. The upper middle class consisted of government employees, doctors, lawyers, and managers of factories, mines, and shops. The lower middle class included factory overseers and such skilled workers as toolmakers, mechanical drafters, and printers. These people enjoyed a comfortable standard of living. B

MAIN IDEA
Summarizing
B Describe the social classes in Britain.

The Working Class During the years 1800 to 1850, however, laborers, or the working class, saw little improvement in their living and working conditions. They watched their livelihoods disappear as machines replaced them. In frustration, some smashed the machines they thought were putting them out of work.

Tip for Gifted and Talented Students

Tell students that Elizabeth Gaskell's *Mary Barton* reflects the literary style called realism. Have students read and discuss the excerpt.

In-Depth Resources, Unit 3
- Literature: from *Mary Barton,* p. 13

Class Tensions Grow
10.3.4

Critical Thinking
- Why might the way merchants make money make landowners look down on them? *(Possible Answers: merchants work hard; work viewed as menial)*
- Was destroying machines a good solution to the problem? *(Possible Answers: not wise; new ones could be built; also could lead to factory closings)*

More About . . .
Luddites

The Luddites were angry not only about losing their jobs but also about the life changes forced on them by industrialization. Instead of working at home alongside their families, textile workers now faced dehumanizing factory conditions. People still sometimes use the term *Luddites* to refer to those opposed to modern technology.

Electronic Library of Primary Sources
- "The Sentencing of the Luddites"

DIFFERENTIATING INSTRUCTION: ENGLISH LEARNERS

Understanding Workers and Factory Owners

Class Time 15 minutes

Task Role-playing a meeting between workers and factory owners

Purpose To clarify the differences between industrialists and workers

Instructions Make sure that students have read and understood the subsections "Class Tensions Grow" and "Positive Effects of the Industrial Revolution." Show the art transparency to set the mood for the role-play. Ask them to suggest words that describe the pictured building. *(grim, dark, ugly, scary, unfriendly)* Then organize students in pairs. Have them create a short performance piece in which they role-play two main types of participants in the Industrial Revolution: factory owners and workers. Tell students that they should improvise a meeting between a worker and a factory owner in which the worker expresses his dissatisfaction with working conditions in the factory and the owner defends his practices on practical grounds.

Have students use the Reading Study Guide for Section 2, p. 97, to identify arguments for each side.

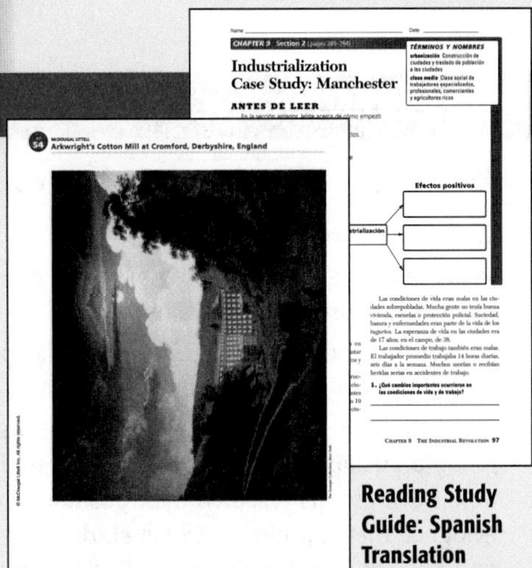

World Art and Culture Transparencies

Reading Study Guide: Spanish Translation

Positive Effects of the Industrial Revolution
10.3.2

Critical Thinking

- How did the Industrial Revolution provide hope of improvement? *(Possible Answer: Now status could be achieved by skill and work.)*
- How would joining together in groups help workers win better conditions and higher pay? *(Workers were needed; if enough took a stand, owners had to listen.)*

The Mills of Manchester
10.3.4

Critical Thinking

- How did geography play a role in Manchester's growth? *(Possible Answers: available resources and water access)*
- Why do you think young children continued to do heavy work in Manchester factories even after the Factory Act? What does this suggest about the relative power of industry compared to government? *(Possible Answer: Owners had no fear of the law, so they continued to use child labor. Industry was stronger than government.)*

One group of such workers was called the Luddites. They were named after Ned Ludd. Ludd, probably a mythical English laborer, was said to have destroyed weaving machinery around 1779. The Luddites attacked whole factories in northern England beginning in 1811, destroying laborsaving machinery. Outside the factories, mobs of workers rioted, mainly because of poor living and working conditions.

Positive Effects of the Industrial Revolution

Despite the problems that followed industrialization, the Industrial Revolution had a number of positive effects. It created jobs for workers. It contributed to the wealth of the nation. It fostered technological progress and invention. It greatly increased the production of goods and raised the standard of living. Perhaps most important, it provided the hope of improvement in people's lives.

The Industrial Revolution produced a number of other benefits as well. These included healthier diets, better housing, and cheaper, mass-produced clothing. Because the Industrial Revolution created a demand for engineers as well as clerical and professional workers, it expanded educational opportunities.

The middle and upper classes prospered immediately from the Industrial Revolution. For the workers it took longer, but their lives gradually improved during the 1800s. Laborers eventually won higher wages, shorter hours, and better working conditions after they joined together to form labor unions.

Long-Term Effects The long-term effects of the Industrial Revolution are still evident. Most people today in industrialized countries can afford consumer goods that would have been considered luxuries 50 or 60 years ago. In addition, their living and working conditions are much improved over those of workers in the 19th century. Also, profits derived from industrialization produced tax revenues. These funds have allowed local, state, and federal governments to invest in urban improvements and raise the standard of living of most city dwellers.

The economic successes of the Industrial Revolution, and also the problems created by it, were clearly evident in one of Britain's new industrial cities in the 1800s—Manchester.

CASE STUDY: Manchester

The Mills of Manchester

Manchester's unique advantages made it a leading example of the new industrial city. This northern English town had ready access to waterpower. It also had available labor from the nearby countryside and an outlet to the sea at Liverpool.

"From this filthy sewer pure gold flows," wrote Alexis de Tocqueville (ah•lehk•SEE duh TOHK•vihl), the French writer, after he visited Manchester in 1835. Indeed, the industrial giant showed the best and worst of the Industrial Revolution. Manchester's rapid, unplanned growth made it an unhealthy place for the poor people who lived and worked there. But wealth flowed from its factories. It went first to the mill owners and the new middle class. Eventually, although not immediately, the working class saw their standard of living rise as well.

Manchester's business owners took pride in mastering each detail of the manufacturing process. They worked many hours and risked their own money. For their efforts, they were rewarded with high profits. Many erected gracious homes on the outskirts of town.

To provide the mill owners with high profits, workers labored under terrible conditions. Children as young as six joined their parents in the factories. There, for six days a week, they toiled from 6 A.M. to 7 or 8 P.M., with only half an hour for

DIFFERENTIATING INSTRUCTION: GIFTED AND TALENTED STUDENTS

Debating Effects of Industrialism

Class Time 30 minutes

Task Preparing position statements and debating the merits of the Industrial Revolution

Purpose To consider the economic, social, political, and environmental effects of industrialization

Instructions Organize students in groups. Assign each group a position in favor of or opposed to industrialization. Have groups research their position and gather evidence that supports it. Direct students to the Testimony on Child Labor in Britain on p. 10 in In-Depth Resources: Unit 3 and to the information about the effects of industrialization on page 293. Students can then prepare position statements. Invite opposing groups to debate as you moderate. Remind students that their position statements should

- clearly state the issue being debated
- take a distinct position supported by facts and examples
- address opposing viewpoints directly and reasonably

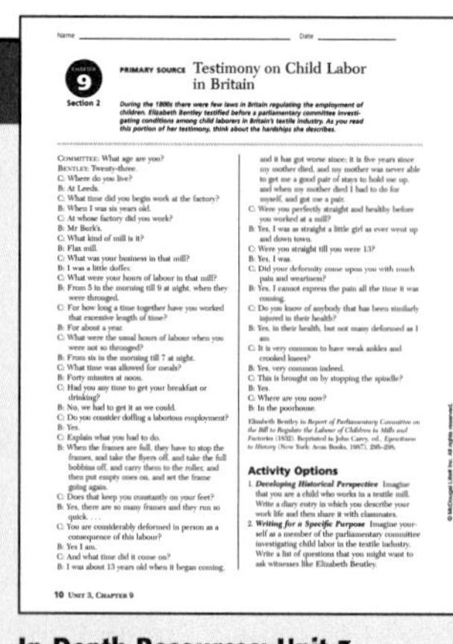

In-Depth Resources: Unit 3

> Analyzing Key Concepts

Industrialization

Industrialization is the process of developing industries that use machines to produce goods. This process not only revolutionizes a country's economy, it also transforms social conditions and class structures.

Effects of Industrialization

Industrialization

Working Conditions
- Industry created many new jobs.
- Factories were dirty, unsafe, and dangerous.
- Factory bosses exercised harsh discipline.
- ▶ **Long-Term Effect** Workers won higher wages, shorter hours, better conditions.

Social Classes
- Factory workers were overworked and underpaid.
- Overseers and skilled workers rose to lower middle class. Factory owners and merchants formed upper middle class.
- Upper class resented those in middle class who became wealthier than they were.
- ▶ **Long-Term Effect** Standard of living generally rose.

Size of Cities
- Factories brought job seekers to cities.
- Urban areas doubled, tripled, or quadrupled in size.
- Many cities specialized in certain industries.
- ▶ **Long-Term Effect** Suburbs grew as people fled crowded cities.

Living Conditions
- Cities lacked sanitary codes or building controls.
- Housing, water, and social services were scarce.
- Epidemics swept through the city.
- ▶ **Long-Term Effect** Housing, diet, and clothing improved.

CALIFORNIA STANDARDS

10.3.3 Describe the growth of population, rural to urban migration, and growth of cities associated with the Industrial Revolution.

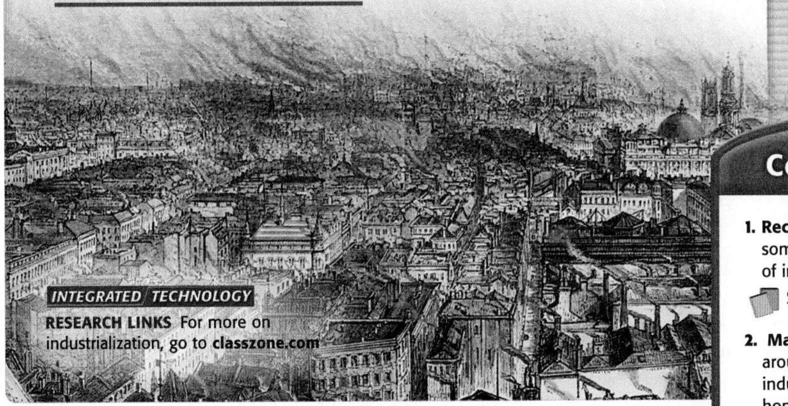

▼ This engraving shows urban growth and industrial pollution in Manchester.

INTEGRATED TECHNOLOGY

RESEARCH LINKS For more on industrialization, go to **classzone.com**

> DATA FILE

GROWTH OF CITIES

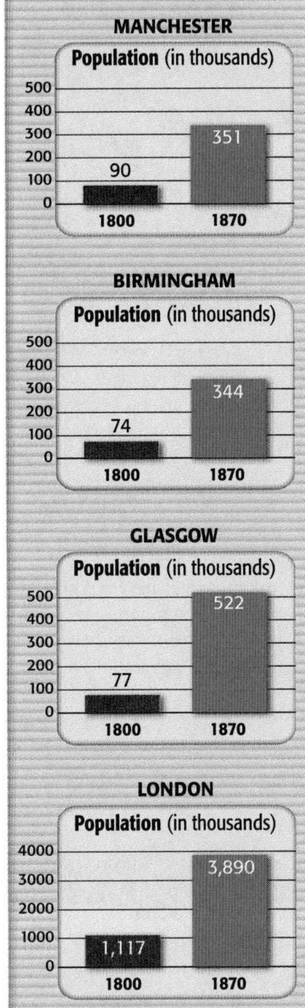

Population (in thousands)

City	1800	1870
MANCHESTER	90	351
BIRMINGHAM	74	344
GLASGOW	77	522
LONDON	1,117	3,890

Source: European Historical Statistics, 1750–1975

Connect *to* Today

1. **Recognizing Effects** What were some advantages and disadvantages of industrialization?

See Skillbuilder Handbook, page R6.

2. **Making Inferences** Many nations around the world today are trying to industrialize. What do you think they hope to gain from that process?

293

Analyzing Key Concepts

OBJECTIVE

- Trace the effects of industrialization on the people and cities of Britain.

INSTRUCT

Remind students that this period of history is called the Industrial Revolution. It was a revolution because industrialization changed nearly every aspect of people's lives, from their living and working conditions, to the structure of social classes and even the size of cities. As students study the chart, ask them to think of other categories that might be added.

History from Visuals

Interpreting the Chart

Ask students how many years each of the graphs covers. (70 years) Then ask how much the population of Manchester grew during this time period. (261,000) Have them repeat this calculation for the other cities. (Birmingham: 270,000; Glasgow: 445,000; London: 2,773,000) Which city grew the most? (London)

Extension Ask students which city's population in 1870 was the greatest number of times its population in 1800. *(Glasgow; 6.78 times its population in 1800.)*

CONNECT TO TODAY: ANSWERS

1. Recognizing Effects

Possible Answers: Advantages were the creation of a prosperous middle class, the creation of jobs and wealth, and improvements in diet and housing. Disadvantages were exploitation of workers and harsh working and living conditions.

2. Making Inferences

Possible Answer: They probably want to gain opportunity for their people, to experience economic growth, and to trade on the world market.

Connect *to* Today

Child Labor Today

Some studies estimate that over half the clothing sold in the United States is made in sweatshops where children work. Like the children of 19th-century Manchester, they labor to help support their families. Ask students to find out about overseas manufacturing operations that use child labor in such places as Haiti, Indonesia, and Honduras. Refer them to Web sites for CWFA and ILRF, as well as to the *Readers' Guide to Periodical Literature,* to locate current information. Have students share their findings, including steps being taken to correct the practice.

In-Depth Resources: Unit 3
- Primary Source: Testimony on Child Labor in Britain, p. 10

Electronic Library of Primary Sources
- from "Child Labor in the Mines"

3 ASSESS

SECTION 2 ASSESSMENT

Organize students in groups of four. After answering the questions independently, have students discuss answers as a group.

Formal Assessment
- Section Quiz, p. 156

4 RETEACH

Use the Reteaching Activity to help students review Section 2.

In-Depth Resources: Unit 3
- Reteaching Activity, p. 20

Connect *to* Today

Child Labor Today

To save on labor costs in the 1990s and 2000s, many corporations moved their manufacturing operations overseas to developing countries. There, in sweatshops, young children work long hours under wretched conditions. They are unprotected by child labor laws. For mere pennies per hour, children weave carpets, sort vegetables, or assemble expensive athletic shoes.

Several organizations are working to end child labor, including the Child Welfare League of America and the International Labor Rights Fund.

lunch and an hour for dinner. To keep the children awake, mill supervisors beat them. Tiny hands repaired broken threads in Manchester's spinning machines, replaced thread in the bobbins, or swept up cotton fluff. The dangerous machinery injured many children. The fluff filled their lungs and made them cough.

Until the first Factory Act passed in 1819, the British government exerted little control over child labor in Manchester and other factory cities. The act restricted working age and hours. For years after the act passed, young children still did heavy, dangerous work in Manchester's factories. C

MAIN IDEA

Drawing Conclusions

C Whose interests did child labor serve?

C. Possible Answer Factory owners profited by being able to pay children low wages; families also benefited from the wages children earned.

Putting so much industry into one place polluted the natural environment. The coal that powered factories and warmed houses blackened the air. Textile dyes and other wastes poisoned Manchester's Irwell River. An eyewitness observer wrote the following description of the river in 1862:

PRIMARY SOURCE

Steam boilers discharge into it their seething contents, and drains and sewers their fetid impurities; till at length it rolls on—here between tall dingy walls, there under precipices of red sandstone—considerably less a river than a flood of liquid manure.

HUGH MILLER, *"Old Red Sandstone"*

Like other new industrial cities of the 19th century, Manchester produced consumer goods and created wealth on a grand scale. Yet, it also stood as a reminder of the ills of rapid and unplanned industrialization.

As you will learn in Section 3, the industrialization that began in Great Britain spread to the United States and to continental Europe in the 1800s.

SECTION 2 ASSESSMENT

TERMS & NAMES 1. For each term or name, write a sentence explaining its significance.
- urbanization
- middle class

USING YOUR NOTES

2. Which change brought about by industrialization had the greatest impact? (10.3.4)

I. Industrialization Changes Life
A.
B.
II. Class Tensions Grow

MAIN IDEAS

3. Why did people flock to British cities and towns during the Industrial Revolution? (10.3.3)
4. What social class expanded as a result of industrialization? (10.3.3)
5. What were some of the negative effects of the rapid growth of Manchester? (10.3.2)

CRITICAL THINKING & WRITING

6. **SUMMARIZING** How did industrialization contribute to city growth? (10.3.3)
7. **EVALUATING** How were class tensions affected by the Industrial Revolution? (10.3.4)
8. **FORMING AND SUPPORTING OPINIONS** The Industrial Revolution has been described as a mixed blessing. Do you agree or disagree? Support your answer with text references. (10.3.4)
9. **WRITING ACTIVITY** ECONOMICS As a factory owner during the Industrial Revolution, write a **letter** to a newspaper justifying working conditions in your factory. (Writing 2.5.d)

CONNECT TO TODAY CREATING A COMPARISON CHART

Make a **comparison chart** listing information on child labor in three developing nations—one each from Asia, Africa, and Latin America—and compare with data from the United States. (10.3.4)

ANSWERS

1. urbanization, p. 289 • middle class, p. 291
2. **Sample Answer:** I. A. population growth, B. living and working conditions deteriorate. II. A. middle class prospers, B. working class protests. III. A. improved standard of living, B. increased hope for improvement. IV. A. great wealth for merchants, B. pollution, C. child labor. Students may say that an increased standard of living has the greatest impact.
3. to find jobs in factories
4. middle class
5. crowded housing, poor sanitation, pollution
6. **Possible Answer:** factory system led to manufacturing in central locations, creating jobs and economic opportunity
7. **Possible Answer:** upper classes looked down on new middle class; lower class rebelled against poor conditions
8. Answers will vary but should consider working conditions, living standards, family relations, and distribution of wealth.
9. **Rubric** Letters should
   - state and support the owner's position.
   - rebut other viewpoints.

CONNECT TO TODAY

Rubric Charts should
- list a country from each continent.
- clearly analyze data on child labor.
- compare three countries and the United States.

Steam train on the Nancha Bank, China

Power plant in West Virginia, United States

Industrialization Spreads

MAIN IDEA	WHY IT MATTERS NOW	TERMS & NAMES
EMPIRE BUILDING The industrialization that began in Great Britain spread to other parts of the world.	The Industrial Revolution set the stage for the growth of modern cities and a global economy.	• stock • corporation

SETTING THE STAGE Great Britain's favorable geography and its financial systems, political stability, and natural resources sparked industrialization. British merchants built the world's first factories. When these factories prospered, more laborsaving machines and factories were built. Eventually, the Industrial Revolution that had begun in Britain spread both to the United States and to continental Europe. Countries that had conditions similar to those in Britain were ripe for industrialization.

Industrial Development in the United States

The United States possessed the same resources that allowed Britain to mechanize its industries. America had fast-flowing rivers, rich deposits of coal and iron ore, and a supply of laborers made up of farm workers and immigrants. During the War of 1812, Britain blockaded the United States, trying to keep it from engaging in international trade. This blockade forced the young country to use its own resources to develop independent industries. Those industries would manufacture the goods the United States could no longer import.

Industrialization in the United States As in Britain, industrialization in the United States began in the textile industry. Eager to keep the secrets of industrialization to itself, Britain had forbidden engineers, mechanics, and toolmakers to leave the country. In 1789, however, a young British mill worker named Samuel Slater emigrated to the United States. There, Slater built a spinning machine from memory and a partial design. The following year, Moses Brown opened the first factory in the United States to house Slater's machines in Pawtucket, Rhode Island. But the Pawtucket factory mass-produced only one part of finished cloth, the thread.

In 1813, Francis Cabot Lowell of Boston and four other investors revolutionized the American textile industry. They mechanized every stage in the manufacture of cloth. Their weaving factory in Waltham, Massachusetts, earned them enough money to fund a larger

◂ Teenage mill girls at a Georgia cotton mill

CALIFORNIA STANDARDS

10.3.2 Examine how scientific and technological changes and new forms of energy brought about massive social, economic, and cultural change (e.g., the inventions and discoveries of James Watt, Eli Whitney, Henry Bessemer, Louis Pasteur, Thomas Edison).

10.3.3 Describe the growth of population, rural to urban migration, and growth of cities associated with the Industrial Revolution.

10.3.5 Understand the connections among natural resources, entrepreneurship, labor, and capital in an industrial economy.

10.4.1 Describe the rise of industrial economies and their link to imperialism and colonialism (e.g., the role played by national security and strategic advantage; moral issues raised by the search for national hegemony, Social Darwinism, and the missionary impulse; material issues such as land, resources, and technology).

TAKING NOTES

Comparing Use a Venn diagram to compare industrialization in the United States and in Europe.

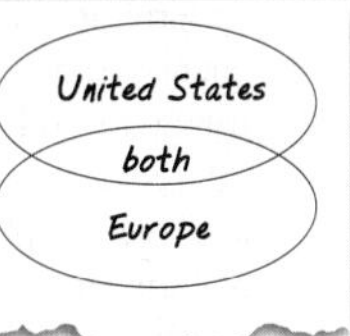

LESSON PLAN

OBJECTIVES

- Describe industrialization in the United States and Europe.
- Identify the effects of industrialization on the rest of the world.

1 FOCUS & MOTIVATE

Explain that industrialization spread unevenly to other parts of the world. Ask students to name countries they know of that are industrialized or are still developing. *(Possible Answers: Industrialized–U.S., any European nation, Canada, Australia. Still developing–Most African and Asian nations, many South American nations.)*

2 INSTRUCT

Industrial Development in the United States

10.3.5

Critical Thinking

- Why might railroads be even more important to U.S. industrialization than to that of Britain? *(Possible Answer: bigger country, more distance)*

CALIFORNIA RESOURCES

California Reading Toolkit, p. L43
California Modified Lesson Plans for English Learners, p. 81
California Daily Standards Practice Transparencies, TT35
California Standards Enrichment Workbook, pp. 35–36, 37–38, 41–42, 47–48
California Standards Planner and Lesson Plans, p. L77
California Online Test Practice
California Test Generator CD-ROM
California Easy Planner CD-ROM
California eEdition CD-ROM

SECTION 3 PROGRAM RESOURCES

ALL STUDENTS

In-Depth Resources: Unit 3
- Guided Reading, p. 3

Formal Assessment
- Section Quiz, p. 157

ENGLISH LEARNERS

In-Depth Resources in Spanish
- Guided Reading (Spanish), p. 76

Reading Study Guide (Spanish), p. 99
Reading Study Guide Audio CD (Spanish)

STRUGGLING READERS

In-Depth Resources: Unit 3
- Guided Reading, p. 3
- Building Vocabulary, p. 5
- Reteaching Activity, p. 21

Reading Study Guide, p. 99
Reading Study Guide Audio CD

GIFTED AND TALENTED STUDENTS

In-Depth Resources: Unit 3
- Primary Source: "Life in a New England Factory," p. 11

Electronic Library of Primary Sources
- from *A New England Girlhood*

INTEGRATED TECHNOLOGY

eEdition CD-ROM
Power Presentations CD-ROM
World Art and Cultures Transparencies
- AT55 Monet's *Arrival of the Normandy Train, Gare Saint-Lazare*

Electronic Library of Primary Sources
- from *A New England Girlhood*

classzone.com

History from Visuals

Interpreting the Map

Have students calculate the increase in trackage between 1840 and 1890.

Extension Ask students to name three states formed in the West between 1840 and 1890. *(Wyoming, California, Texas, New Mexico, Arizona, Oregon, Montana)*

SKILLBUILDER Answers

1. Region: East, Midwest

2. Movement: east to west

Tip for Gifted and Talented Students

Explain that Lucy Larcom was well educated and, while working in the Lowell mills, began a literary journal. She later became a teacher and journalist. Have students describe Lucy's attitude toward factory work. *(better than being a servant)*

Electronic Library of Primary Sources

• from *A New England Girlhood*

More About . . .

Early Railroads

Trains of the early 1800s were drawn by horses or even used sails to harness wind power. Passengers even had to get out and pull the train at times. Trains also had no lights, so they couldn't travel at night. With single tracks, trains often had to wait on sidings for hours to let other trains pass.

World Art and Cultures Transparencies

• AT55 Monet's *Arrival of the Normandy Train, Gare Saint-Lazare*

The Growth of Railroads in the United States

Railroad System, 1840

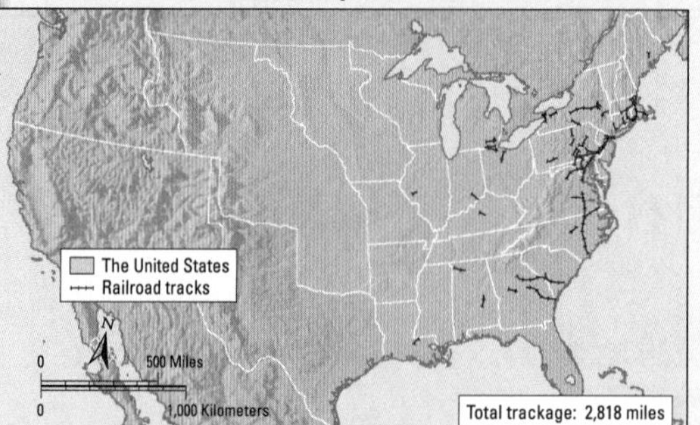

Railroad System, 1890

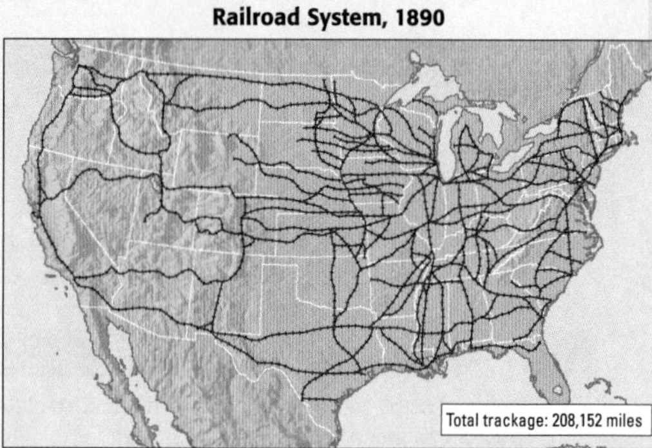

GEOGRAPHY SKILLBUILDER: Interpreting Maps

1. **Region** *In what part of the country were the first railroads built? By 1890, what other part of the country was densely covered by railroad tracks?*
2. **Movement** *In what direction did the railroads help people move across the country?*

operation in another Massachusetts town. When Lowell died, the remaining partners named the town after him. By the late 1820s, Lowell, Massachusetts, had become a booming manufacturing center and a model for other such towns.

Thousands of young single women flocked from their rural homes to work as mill girls in factory towns. There, they could make higher wages and have some independence. However, to ensure proper behavior, they were watched closely inside and outside the factory by their employers. The mill girls toiled more than 12 hours a day, 6 days a week, for decent wages. For some, the mill job was an alternative to being a servant and was often the only other job open to them:

PRIMARY SOURCE Ⓐ

Country girls were naturally independent, and the feeling that at this new work the few hours they had of everyday leisure were entirely their own was a satisfaction to them. They preferred it to going out as "hired help." It was like a young man's pleasure in entering upon business for himself. Girls had never tried that experiment before, and they liked it.

LUCY LARCOM, *A New England Girlhood*

MAIN IDEA

Analyzing Primary Sources

Ⓐ Why did Lucy Larcom think mill work benefited young women?

A. Answer Larcom believed that mill work offered women more free time and suited the independence of their country upbringing.

Textiles led the way, but clothing manufacture and shoemaking also underwent mechanization. Especially in the Northeast, skilled workers and farmers had formerly worked at home. Now they labored in factories in towns and cities such as Waltham, Lowell, and Lawrence, Massachusetts.

Later Expansion of U.S. Industry The Northeast experienced much industrial growth in the early 1800s. Nonetheless, the United States remained primarily agricultural until the Civil War ended in 1865. During the last third of the 1800s, the country experienced a technological boom. As in Britain, a number of causes contributed to this boom. These included a wealth of natural resources, among them oil, coal, and iron; a burst of inventions, such as the electric light bulb and the telephone; and a swelling urban population that consumed the new manufactured goods.

Also, as in Britain, railroads played a major role in America's industrialization. Cities like Chicago and Minneapolis expanded rapidly during the late 1800s. This

DIFFERENTIATING INSTRUCTION: ENGLISH LEARNERS

Analyzing a Primary Source

Class Time 20 minutes

Task Expressing Lucy Larcom's words in simpler language

Purpose To gain increased understanding of factory workers

Instructions Organize students in four groups and assign each group one sentence from the Lucy Larcom quotation. Ask students to discuss what their sentence means and to write it in simple language. Encourage students to use the following strategies as they paraphrase:

- break long sentences into parts, using commas when possible
- define unfamiliar words, using context or a dictionary
- paraphrase figures of speech
- reread paraphrase to check for sense

Write the following examples on the chalkboard as a guide:

hired help means "working as a servant for another family"

girl means "young woman"

entering upon business for himself means "starting a business"

When students have completed their paraphrases, have groups work together to construct the entire excerpt.

Farm girls liked to do things their own way. They liked factory work because they had freedom after work. They liked this better than working as a servant for another family. Men feel this way when they run their own business. Women hadn't been able to go into business, and now they had a chance to be on their own.

was due to their location along the nation's expanding railroad lines. Chicago's stockyards and Minneapolis's grain industries prospered by selling products to the rest of the country. Indeed, the railroads themselves proved to be a profitable business. By the end of the 1800s, a limited number of large, powerful companies controlled more than two-thirds of the nation's railroad tracks. Businesses of all kinds began to merge as the railroads had. Smaller companies joined together to form a larger one.

The Rise of Corporations Building large businesses like railroads required a great deal of money. To raise the money, entrepreneurs sold shares of **stock**, or certain rights of ownership. Thus people who bought stock became part owners of these businesses, which were called corporations. A **corporation** is a business owned by stockholders who share in its profits but are not personally responsible for its debts. Corporations were able to raise the large amounts of capital needed to invest in industrial equipment.

In the late 1800s, large corporations such as Standard Oil (founded by John D. Rockefeller) and the Carnegie Steel Company (founded by Andrew Carnegie) sprang up. They sought to control every aspect of their own industries in order to make big profits. Big business—the giant corporations that controlled entire industries—also made big profits by reducing the cost of producing goods. In the United States as elsewhere, workers earned low wages for laboring long hours, while stockholders earned high profits and corporate leaders made fortunes.

Continental Europe Industrializes

European businesses yearned to adopt the "British miracle," the result of Britain's profitable new methods of manufacturing goods. But the troubles sparked by the French Revolution and the Napoleonic wars between 1789 and 1815 had halted trade, interrupted communication, and caused inflation in some parts of the continent. European countries watched the gap widen between themselves and Britain. Even so, industrialization eventually reached continental Europe.

▼ Danish workers labor in a steel mill in this 1885 painting by Peter Severin Kroyer.

More About . . .

U.S. Railroads

Tell students that the number of miles of railroad track in the United States increased dramatically during the second half of the 1800s. Post the following years and figures: 1840–3,000 miles; 1865–35,000 miles; 1890–200,000 miles. Sketch a quick graph on the board to show the growth. Ask students to speculate about the impact of this growth on the nation. How might the railroads have helped unify the country? *(Possible Answer: through commerce, travel, exchange of ideas and information)*

Continental Europe Industrializes
10.3.2

Critical Thinking

- Why do you think Cockerill took secret plans to Belgium? *(to make money)*
- How did German industry help create political unity?. *(Possible Answer: railroads linked factories; the growing economy helped create political unity)*

DIFFERENTIATING INSTRUCTION: GIFTED AND TALENTED STUDENTS

Planning an Industrial Fair

Class Time 30 minutes

Task Planning an industrial fair that compares today's products with those displayed at London's 1851 Great Exhibition

Purpose To compare and contrast industrial technologies of the 1800s with those of the present

Instructions Tell students that London hosted the Great Exhibition in 1851 to showcase industry throughout the world. Have students research this exhibition. Then ask them to plan another exhibition that places modern products and technologies alongside those of the 1800s.

Invite students to write a description of the exhibits, with a sampling of images and text that show and describe major aspects of each exhibition. Tell students to include the following in their descriptions:

- reasons the featured technologies or products were chosen
- links between the Industrial Revolution and the industries of today

Have students post their exhibit samples and explain them to the class. When they have finished the activity, have students complete the Self-Assessment worksheet.

Integrated Assessment

Global Impact

Industrialization in Japan

Japan was one of the few countries outside Europe and the United States to attempt industrialization in the 1800s. Others included Mexico and Egypt, both in the late 1800s. Muhammad Ali, Egypt's ruler at the time, led his nation's progress. He reformed Egypt's government and improved communications. He also established cotton mills, a glass factory, and a sugar refinery. As with other industrialization processes, Egypt's often came at the expense of workers. For example, to develop commercial agriculture, landlords forced peasants to become tenant farmers and grow cash crops for sale to European markets.

More About . . .

German Unification

In the early 1800s, Germany was a confederation of 39 independent states. One man played a key role in changing that. Otto von Bismarck became prime minister of Prussia in 1862. Bismarck worked to establish Prussia's dominance and led several successful military campaigns to expand its influence. Victorious, Bismarck took lands for Prussia and restructured the German states into the North German Confederation. In 1871, Bismarck became chancellor and head of a united German nation.

Global Impact

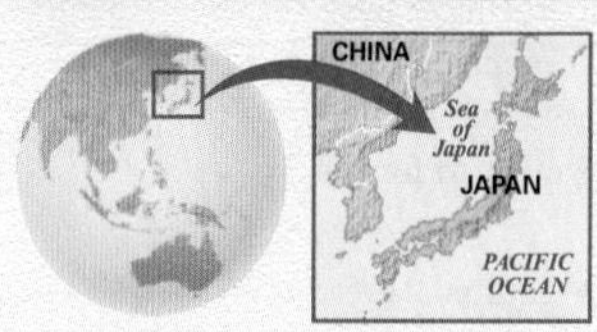

Industrialization in Japan

With the beginning of the Meiji era in Japan in 1868, the central government began an ambitious program to transform the country into an industrialized state. It financed textile mills, coal mines, shipyards, and cement and other factories. It also asked private companies to invest in industry.

Some companies had been in business since the 1600s. But new companies sprang up too. Among them was the Mitsubishi company, founded in 1870 and still in business.

The industrializing of Japan produced sustained economic growth for the country. But it also led to strengthening the military and to Japanese imperialism in Asia.

Beginnings in Belgium Belgium led Europe in adopting Britain's new technology. It had rich deposits of iron ore and coal as well as fine waterways for transportation. As in the United States, British skilled workers played a key role in industrializing Belgium.

Samuel Slater had smuggled the design of a spinning machine to the United States. Much like him, a Lancashire carpenter named William Cockerill illegally made his way to Belgium in 1799. He carried secret plans for building spinning machinery. His son John eventually built an enormous industrial enterprise in eastern Belgium. It produced a variety of mechanical equipment, including steam engines and railway locomotives. Carrying the latest British advances, more British workers came to work with Cockerill. Several then founded their own companies in Europe.

Germany Industrializes Germany was politically divided in the early 1800s. Economic isolation and scattered resources hampered countrywide industrialization. Instead, pockets of industrialization appeared, as in the coal-rich Ruhr Valley of west central Germany. Beginning around 1835, Germany began to copy the British model. Germany imported British equipment and engineers. German manufacturers also sent their children to England to learn industrial management. **B**

Most important, Germany built railroads that linked its growing manufacturing cities, such as Frankfurt, with the Ruhr Valley's coal and iron ore deposits. In 1858, a German economist wrote, "Railroads and machine shops, coal mines and iron foundries, spinneries and rolling mills seem to spring up out of the ground, and smokestacks sprout from the earth like mushrooms." Germany's economic strength spurred its ability to develop as a military power. By the late 1800s, a unified, imperial Germany had become both an industrial and a military giant.

MAIN IDEA
Analyzing Causes
B What factors slowed industrialization in Germany?
B. Answer Germany was politically divided, economically isolated, and its resources were scattered.

Expansion Elsewhere in Europe In the rest of Europe, as in Germany, industrialization during the early 1800s proceeded by region rather than by country. Even in countries where agriculture dominated, pockets of industrialization arose. For example, Bohemia developed a spinning industry. Spain's Catalonia processed more cotton than Belgium. Northern Italy mechanized its textile production, specializing in silk spinning. Serf labor ran factories in regions around Moscow and St. Petersburg.

In France, sustained industrial growth occurred after 1830. French industrialization was more measured and controlled than in other countries because the agricultural economy remained strong. As a result, France avoided the great social and economic problems caused by industrialization. A thriving national market for new French products was created after 1850, when the government began railroad construction.

For a variety of reasons, many European countries did not industrialize. In some nations, the social structure delayed the adoption of new methods of production. The accidents of geography held back others. In Austria-Hungary and Spain, transportation posed great obstacles. Austria-Hungary's mountains defeated railroad builders. Spain lacked both good roads and waterways for canals.

DIFFERENTIATING INSTRUCTION: STRUGGLING READERS

Understanding Obstacles to Industrial Growth

Class Time 15 minutes

Task Making a web graphic to show obstacles to industrial growth in Europe

Purpose To show why some European nations industrialized more quickly than others

Instructions Review the text under "Continental Europe Industrializes," using the Reading Study Guide pp. 99–100 to build understanding. For each nation discussed, ask students to list one or two factors that affected the rate of industrialization. Invite students to complete a web with factors that impeded the growth of industry in continental Europe. Tell students to consider the following:

- geography
- political stability
- war
- social structure

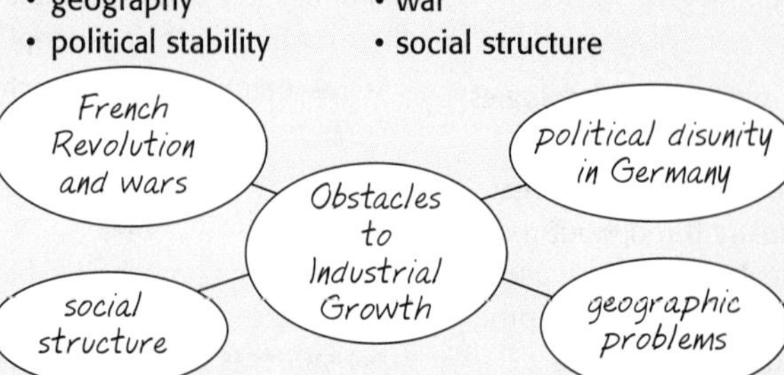

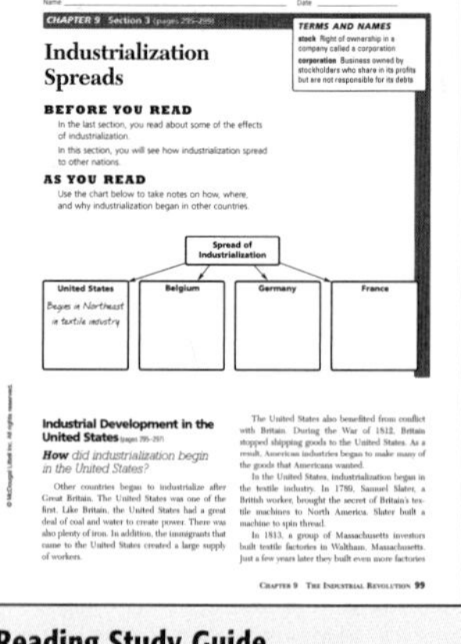

Reading Study Guide

The Impact of Industrialization

▲ The Crystal Palace Exposition in London in 1851 (shown above) celebrated the "works of industry of all nations."

The Industrial Revolution shifted the world balance of power. It increased competition between industrialized nations and poverty in less-developed nations.

Rise of Global Inequality Industrialization widened the wealth gap between industrialized and nonindustrialized countries, even while it strengthened their economic ties. To keep factories running and workers fed, industrialized countries required a steady supply of raw materials from less-developed lands. In turn, industrialized countries viewed poor countries as markets for their manufactured products.

Britain led in exploiting its overseas colonies for resources and markets. Soon other European countries, the United States, Russia, and Japan followed Britain's lead, seizing colonies for their economic resources. Imperialism, the policy of extending one country's rule over many other lands, gave even more power and wealth to these already wealthy nations. Imperialism was born out of the cycle of industrialization, the need for resources to supply the factories of Europe, and the development of new markets around the world. (See Chapter 11.) C

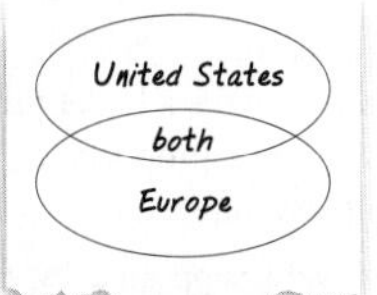

MAIN IDEA

Clarifying

C Why did imperialism grow out of industrialization?

C. Answer Industrialized countries seized colonies for raw materials and as markets.

Transformation of Society Between 1700 and 1900, revolutions in agriculture, production, transportation, and communication changed the lives of people in Western Europe and the United States. Industrialization gave Europe tremendous economic power. In contrast, the economies of Asia and Africa were still based on agriculture and small workshops. Industrialization revolutionized every aspect of society, from daily life to life expectancy. Despite the hardships early urban workers suffered, population, health, and wealth eventually rose dramatically in all industrialized countries. The development of a middle class created great opportunities for education and democratic participation. Greater democratic participation, in turn, fueled a powerful movement for social reform.

SECTION 3 ASSESSMENT

TERMS & NAMES 1. For each term or name, write a sentence explaining its significance.
- stock
- corporation

USING YOUR NOTES

2. Which development had the most impact in the United States? in continental Europe? (10.3.2)

United States / both / Europe

MAIN IDEAS

3. What early industries mechanized in the United States? (10.3.2)
4. Why did Belgium lead Europe in adopting industrialization? (10.3.5)
5. How did the Industrial Revolution shift the world balance of power? (10.3.2)

CRITICAL THINKING & WRITING

6. **RECOGNIZING BIAS** Go back to the quote from Lucy Larcom on page 296. Do you think her feelings about working in the mill are typical? Why or why not? (10.3.2)
7. **MAKING INFERENCES** Why was Britain unable to keep industrial secrets away from other nations? (10.3.5)
8. **FORMING AND SUPPORTING OPINIONS** What was the most significant effect of the Industrial Revolution? (10.3.3)
9. **WRITING ACTIVITY** EMPIRE BUILDING Draw a **political cartoon** that could have been used by the British government to show their sense of superiority over nonindustrialized nations they planned to colonize. (Writing 2.2.a)

INTEGRATED TECHNOLOGY **INTERNET ACTIVITY**

Use the Internet to research the economy of a less-developed nation in either Asia, Africa, or South America. Create a **database** of economic statistics for that country. (10.3.5)

INTERNET KEYWORD
country profiles

The Impact of Industrialization
10.3.3; 10.4.1

Critical Thinking
- What did less-developed countries get from industrialized nations? *(jobs, markets for their raw materials)*
- How do you think industrialized nations chose the areas they would colonize? *(Possible Answer: on the basis of their natural resources)*

3 ASSESS

SECTION 3 ASSESSMENT

Have pairs of students answer the questions, then trade partners with another pair. The new pairs can compare answers and exchange ideas before returning to their original partners to finalize answers.

Formal Assessment
- Section Quiz, p. 157

4 RETEACH

Have students complete the Reading Study Guide worksheet for Section 3, then review the diagrams students made for item 2 in the section assessment.

Reading Study Guide, p. 99

In-Depth Resources: Unit 3
- Reteaching Activity, p. 21

ANSWERS

1. stock, p. 297 • corporation, p. 297
2. **Sample Answer:** U.S.—Political unity, large distances. Both—Began in textiles, railroads important, resources important. Europe—Slowed by geography and social structure. Answers should show impact of industrialization on U.S. and on continental Europe.
3. textiles, clothing, shoemaking
4. rich deposits of iron and coal; good water transportation
5. promoted competition between industrialized nations and increased poverty in less-developed countries
6. **Possible Answer:** No, given her written record she may have been more independent than others of her time. Yes, she seems pleased with the experience and says others were also.
7. British workers wanted profits of making new industries in other nations.
8. **Possible Answers:** changes in society; greater gap between rich and poor; development of middle class; exploitation of colonies
9. **Rubric** Political cartoons should
   - show a British point of view.
   - reflect knowledge of industrialization.
   - include vivid details.

INTEGRATED TECHNOLOGY

Rubric Databases should
- explain the nation's economic structure.
- contain sufficient economic data.
- present information clearly.

LESSON PLAN

OBJECTIVES

- Identify thinkers and ideas that supported industrialization.
- Explain the origins and main concepts of socialism and Marxism.
- Examine unionization and legislative reform.
- Describe other reform movements of the 1800s.

1 FOCUS & MOTIVATE

Ask students how today's American government regulates industry and protects workers. *(Possible Answers: safety laws, taxes, workplace rules)*

2 INSTRUCT

The Philosophers of Industrialization

10.3.2; 10.3.5; 10.3.6

Critical Thinking

- How does laissez-faire economics reflect Enlightenment ideas of challenging power and authority? *(Possible Answer: minimizes government's role in economy)*

CALIFORNIA RESOURCES

California Reading Toolkit, p. L44
California Modified Lesson Plans for English Learners, p. 83
California Daily Standards Practice Transparencies, TT36
California Standards Enrichment Workbook, pp. 35–36, 39–40, 41–42, 43–44
California Standards Planner and Lesson Plans, p. L79
California Online Test Practice
California Test Generator CD-ROM
California Easy Planner CD-ROM
California eEdition CD-ROM

Steam train on the Nancha Bank, China

Power plant in West Virginia, United States

4

Reforming the Industrial World

MAIN IDEA	WHY IT MATTERS NOW	TERMS & NAMES
ECONOMICS The Industrial Revolution led to economic, social, and political reforms.	Many modern social welfare programs developed during this period of reform.	• laissez faire • Adam Smith • capitalism • utilitarianism • socialism • Karl Marx • communism • union • strike

CALIFORNIA STANDARDS

10.3.2 Examine how scientific and technological changes and new forms of energy brought about massive social, economic, and cultural change (e.g., the inventions and discoveries of James Watt, Eli Whitney, Henry Bessemer, Louis Pasteur, Thomas Edison).

10.3.4 Trace the evolution of work and labor, including the demise of the slave trade and the effects of immigration, mining and manufacturing, division of labor, and the union movement.

10.3.5 Understand the connections among natural resources, entrepreneurship, labor, and capital in an industrial economy.

10.3.6 Analyze the emergence of capitalism as a dominant economic pattern and the responses to it, including Utopianism, Social Democracy, Socialism, and Communism.

CST 4 Students relate current events to the physical and human characteristics of places and regions.

HI 6 Students conduct cost-benefit analyses and apply basic economic indicators to analyze the aggregate economic behavior of the U.S. economy.

SETTING THE STAGE In industrialized countries in the 19th century, the Industrial Revolution opened a wide gap between the rich and the poor. Business leaders believed that governments should stay out of business and economic affairs. Reformers, however, felt that governments needed to play an active role to improve conditions for the poor. Workers also demanded more rights and protection. They formed labor unions to increase their influence.

The Philosophers of Industrialization

The term **laissez faire** (LEHS•ay•FAIR) refers to the economic policy of letting owners of industry and business set working conditions without interference. This policy favors a free market unregulated by the government. The term is French for "let do," and by extension, "let people do as they please."

Laissez-faire Economics Laissez-faire economics stemmed from French economic philosophers of the Enlightenment. They criticized the idea that nations grow wealthy by placing heavy tariffs on foreign goods. In fact, they argued, government regulations only interfered with the production of wealth. These philosophers believed that if government allowed free trade—the flow of commerce in the world market without government regulation—the economy would prosper.

Adam Smith, a professor at the University of Glasgow, Scotland, defended the idea of a free economy, or free markets, in his 1776 book *The Wealth of Nations*. According to Smith, economic liberty guaranteed economic progress. As a result, government should not interfere. Smith's arguments rested on what he called the three natural laws of economics:

- the law of self-interest—People work for their own good.
- the law of competition—Competition forces people to make a better product.
- the law of supply and demand—Enough goods would be produced at the lowest possible price to meet demand in a market economy.

TAKING NOTES

Summarizing Use a chart to summarize the characteristics of capitalism and socialism.

Capitalism	Socialism
1.	1.
2.	2.
3.	3.

The Economists of Capitalism Smith's basic ideas were supported by British economists Thomas Malthus and David Ricardo. Like Smith, they believed that natural laws governed economic life. Their important ideas were the foundation of laissez-faire capitalism. **Capitalism** is an economic system in which the factors of production are privately owned and money is invested in business ventures to make a profit. These ideas also helped bring about the Industrial Revolution.

SECTION 4 PROGRAM RESOURCES

ALL STUDENTS

In-Depth Resources: Unit 3
- Guided Reading, p. 4
- History Makers: Henri de Saint-Simon, p. 17
- Skillbuilder Practice, p. 6

Formal Assessment
- Section Quiz, p. 158

ENGLISH LEARNERS

In-Depth Resources in Spanish
- Guided Reading, p. 77
- Skillbuilder Practice, p. 78

Reading Study Guide (Spanish), p. 101

Reading Study Guide Audio CD (Spanish)

STRUGGLING READERS

In-Depth Resources: Unit 3
- Guided Reading, p. 4
- Building Vocabulary, p. 5
- Reteaching Activity, p. 22

Reading Study Guide, p. 101

Reading Study Guide Audio CD

GIFTED AND TALENTED STUDENTS

In-Depth Resources: Unit 3
- Primary Source: from *The Wealth of Nations,* p. 12
- Connections Across Time and Cultures, p. 18

Electronic Library of Primary Sources
- from *The Communist Manifesto*
- from "How I Served My Apprenticeship"

INTEGRATED TECHNOLOGY

eEdition CD-ROM

Power Presentations CD-ROM

Critical Thinking Transparencies
- CT25 Industrialists and Reformers
- CT61 Chapter 25 Visual Summary

Electronic Library of Primary Sources

classzone.com

In *An Essay on the Principle of Population*, written in 1798, Thomas Malthus argued that population tended to increase more rapidly than the food supply. Without wars and epidemics to kill off the extra people, most were destined to be poor and miserable. The predictions of Malthus seemed to be coming true in the 1840s.

David Ricardo, a wealthy stockbroker, took Malthus's theory one step further in his book, *Principles of Political Economy and Taxation* (1817). Like Malthus, Ricardo believed that a permanent underclass would always be poor. In a market system, if there are many workers and abundant resources, then labor and resources are cheap. If there are few workers and scarce resources, then they are expensive. Ricardo believed that wages would be forced down as population increased.

Laissez-faire thinkers such as Smith, Malthus, and Ricardo opposed government efforts to help poor workers. They thought that creating minimum wage laws and better working conditions would upset the free market system, lower profits, and undermine the production of wealth in society. (A)

A. Answer Malthus said population growth could lead to starvation. Ricardo said it caused low wages.

MAIN IDEA
Summarizing
(A) What did Malthus and Ricardo say about the effects of population growth?

History Makers

Adam Smith
1723–1790

In his book *The Wealth of Nations*, Smith argued that if individuals freely followed their own self-interest, the world would be an orderly and progressive place. Social harmony would result without any government direction, "as if by an invisible hand."

Smith applied an invisible hand of his own. After his death, people discovered that he had secretly donated large sums of his income to charities.

INTEGRATED TECHNOLOGY
RESEARCH LINKS For more on Adam Smith, go to **classzone.com**

The Rise of Socialism

In contrast to laissez-faire philosophy, which advised governments to leave business alone, other theorists believed that governments should intervene. These thinkers believed that wealthy people or the government must take action to improve people's lives. The French writer Alexis de Tocqueville gave a warning:

PRIMARY SOURCE
Consider what is happening among the working classes. . . . Do you not see spreading among them, little by little, opinions and ideas that aim not to overturn such and such a ministry, or such laws, or such a government, but society itself, to shake it to the foundations upon which it now rests?

ALEXIS DE TOCQUEVILLE, 1848 speech

Utilitarianism English philosopher Jeremy Bentham modified the ideas of Adam Smith. In the late 1700s, Bentham introduced the philosoophy of **utilitarianism**. Bentham wrote his most influential works in the late 1700s. According to Bentham's theory, people should judge ideas, institutions, and actions on the basis of their utility, or usefulness. He argued that the government should try to promote the greatest good for the greatest number of people. A government policy was only useful if it promoted this goal. Bentham believed that in general the individual should be free to pursue his or her own advantage without interference from the state.

John Stuart Mill, a philosopher and economist, led the utilitarian movement in the 1800s. Mill came to question unregulated capitalism. He believed it was wrong that workers should lead deprived lives that sometimes bordered on starvation. Mill wished to help ordinary working people with policies that would lead to a more equal division of profits. He also favored a cooperative system of agriculture and women's rights, including the right to vote. Mill called for the government to do away with great differences in wealth. Utilitarians also pushed for reforms in the legal and prison systems and in education. (B)

B. Answer He wanted to equalize the distribution of wealth and give the poor a break; he favored a cooperative system of agriculture.

MAIN IDEA
Clarifying
(B) How did Mill want to change the economic system?

History Makers

Adam Smith

Ask students how they think buyers and sellers would act in the economy Adam Smith describes. *(buyers buy what they most want; sellers make or sell what buyers most want)* Tell students that Smith opposed government interference in business on principle. For example, he opposed the mercantilist policy of supporting industry through tariffs and other restrictions on competition. Discuss how trying to help business might be as harmful as trying to restrict it.

In-Depth Resources: Unit 3
- Primary Source: from *The Wealth of Nations*, p. 12
- Connections Across Time and Cultures: Enlightenment Ideals in an Industrial Age, p. 18

The Rise of Socialism
10.3.4; 10.3.6

Critical Thinking
- How does the utilitarian approach judge the worth of ideas? *(Possible Answer: Utilitarians ask if an idea helps enough people.)*
- Why do you think New Harmony lasted only three years? *(Possible Answer: perhaps people didn't really like living in a utopia)*

In-Depth Resources: Unit 3
- History Makers: Henri de Saint-Simon, p. 17

DIFFERENTIATING INSTRUCTION: GIFTED AND TALENTED STUDENTS

Researching Socialist, Marxist, and Utopian Societies

Class Time 45 minutes

Task Finding and sharing information about socialist, Marxist, and utopian societies

Purpose To examine how different economic approaches have been implemented around the world

Instructions Have students do research in response to one of the following prompts:

- Find out about countries that used socialist or Marxist forms of government, e.g. Scandinavia, Russia, China, Vietnam, Cuba, or the nations of eastern Europe. Learn how socialism was implemented and what happened as a result. Determine whether any countries today still practice socialism.
- Find out about utopian communities in Britain or the United States. Identify a particular community or group of communities and describe the principles that inspired them. Possible communities include New Harmony in Indiana or Brook Farm near Boston.

Invite students to share their research findings and materials orally, then respond to questions. Have students complete the Standards for Evaluating an Oral Presentation worksheet.

Standards for Evaluating an Oral Presentation

Integrated Assessment

Marxism: Radical Socialism
10.3.6

Critical Thinking

- How are the "haves" and the "have-nots" interdependent? *(Possible Answer: "Haves" need "have-nots" as workers; "have-nots" need "haves" to fund and run the means of producing goods.)*
- Do you think Marx agreed that people work for self-interest? Why or why not? *(Possible Answer: No, Marx believed they would work for the common good.)*

History Makers

Karl Marx

Ask students why Karl Marx might want to go to England. *(Possible Answer: It had a more open society than Germany at that time.)* Though a revolutionary, Marx disliked crowds and avoided demonstrations. He was said to be arrogant in debate and uncomfortable when he was in front of a mass audience. He remained poor almost on principle, yet accepted the financial aid of his friend Friedrich Engels.

Electronic Library of Primary Sources

- from *The Communist Manifesto*

Utopian Ideas Other reformers took an even more active approach. Shocked by the misery and poverty of the working class, a British factory owner named Robert Owen improved working conditions for his employees. Near his cotton mill in New Lanark, Scotland, Owen built houses, which he rented at low rates. He prohibited children under ten from working in the mills and provided free schooling.

Then, in 1824, he traveled to the United States. He founded a cooperative community called New Harmony in Indiana, in 1825. He intended this community to be a utopia, or perfect living place. New Harmony lasted only three years but inspired the founding of other communities.

Socialism French reformers such as Charles Fourier (FUR•ee•AY), Saint-Simon (san see•MOHN), and others sought to offset the ill effects of industrialization with a new economic system called socialism. In **socialism**, the factors of production are owned by the public and operate for the welfare of all.

Socialism grew out of an optimistic view of human nature, a belief in progress, and a concern for social justice. Socialists argued that the government should plan the economy rather than depend on free-market capitalism to do the job. They argued that government control of factories, mines, railroads, and other key industries would end poverty and promote equality. Public ownership, they believed, would help workers, who were at the mercy of their employers. Some socialists—such as Louis Blanc—advocated change through extension of the right to vote.

History Makers

Karl Marx
1818–1883

Karl Marx studied philosophy at the University of Berlin before he turned to journalism and economics. In 1849, Marx joined the flood of radicals who fled continental Europe for England. He had declared in *The Communist Manifesto* that "the working men have no country."

Marx's theories of socialism and the inevitable revolt of the working class made him little money. He earned a meager living as a journalist. His wealthy coauthor and fellow German, Friedrich Engels, gave Marx financial aid.

INTEGRATED TECHNOLOGY

RESEARCH LINKS For more on Karl Marx, go to **classzone.com**

Marxism: Radical Socialism

The writings of a German journalist named **Karl Marx** introduced the world to a radical type of socialism called Marxism. Marx and Friedrich Engels, a German whose father owned a textile mill in Manchester, outlined their ideas in a 23-page pamphlet called *The Communist Manifesto.*

The Communist Manifesto In their manifesto, Marx and Engels argued that human societies have always been divided into warring classes. In their own time, these were the middle class "haves" or employers, called the bourgeoisie (BUR•zhwah•ZEE), and the "have-nots" or workers, called the proletariat (PROH•lih•TAIR•ee•iht). While the wealthy controlled the means of producing goods, the poor performed backbreaking labor under terrible conditions. This situation resulted in conflict:

PRIMARY SOURCE

Freeman and slave, patrician and plebeian, lord and serf, guild-master and journeyman, in a word, oppressor and oppressed, stood in constant opposition to one another, carried on an uninterrupted, now hidden, now open fight, a fight that each time ended, either in a revolutionary reconstitution of society at large, or in the common ruin of the contending classes.

KARL MARX and **FRIEDRICH ENGELS**, *The Communist Manifesto* (1848)

According to Marx and Engels, the Industrial Revolution had enriched the wealthy and impoverished the poor. The two writers predicted that the workers would overthrow the owners: "The proletarians have nothing to lose but their chains. They have a world to win. Workingmen of all countries, unite." C

C. Possible Answer Marx and Engels believed the working class and the owners were natural enemies.

MAIN IDEA

Summarizing

C What were the ideas of Marx and Engels concerning relations between the owners and the working class?

SKILLBUILDER PRACTICE: DEVELOPING HISTORICAL PERSPECTIVE

Responding to Primary Sources

Class Time 15 minutes

Task Analyzing a primary source within its historical context

Purpose To practice the skill of developing historical perspective

Instructions Using historical perspective means evaluating a time in history based on the conditions that existed then rather than judging by current knowledge. For example, given Marxism's record of totalitarianism and economic failure in the 20th century, some students might wonder why people believed that Karl Marx's theories could improve their lives. However, knowing about the difficult conditions of workers can help students realize Marxism's appeal at the time. Ask students to reread the primary source on page 302 and answer these questions:

- What was the relationship between different social classes, according to Marx and Engels?
- What was the end result of this relationship?
- Do the terms *oppressor* and *oppressed* seem to adequately define all social relationships today?

Have students use the Skillbuilder Practice worksheet for more examples and practice.

In-Depth Resources: Unit 3

> Analyzing Key Concepts

Capitalism vs. Socialism

The economic system called capitalism developed gradually over centuries, beginning in the late Middle Ages. Because of the ways industrialization changed society, some people began to think that capitalism led to certain problems, such as the abuse of workers. They responded by developing a new system of economic ideas called socialism.

Capitalism	Socialism
• Individuals and businesses own property and the means of production.	• The community or the state should own property and the means of production.
• Progress results when individuals follow their own self-interest.	• Progress results when a community of producers cooperate for the good of all.
• Businesses follow their own self-interest by competing for the consumer's money. Each business tries to produce goods or services that are better and less expensive than those of competitors.	• Socialists believe that capitalist employers take advantage of workers. The community or state must act to protect workers.
• Consumers compete to buy the best goods at the lowest prices. This competition shapes the market by affecting what businesses are able to sell.	• Capitalism creates unequal distribution of wealth and material goods. A better system is to distribute goods according to each person's need.
• Government should not interfere in the economy because competition creates efficiency in business.	• An unequal distribution of wealth and material goods is unfair. A better system is to distribute goods according to each person's need.

SKILLBUILDER: Interpreting Charts

1. **Developing Historical Perspective** *Consider the following people from 19th-century Britain: factory worker, shop owner, factory owner, unemployed artisan. Which of them would be most likely to prefer capitalism and which would prefer socialism? Why?*
2. **Forming and Supporting Opinions** *Which system of economic ideas seems most widespread today? Support your opinion.*

The Future According to Marx Marx believed that the capitalist system, which produced the Industrial Revolution, would eventually destroy itself in the following way. Factories would drive small artisans out of business, leaving a small number of manufacturers to control all the wealth. The large proletariat would revolt, seize the factories and mills from the capitalists, and produce what society needed. Workers, sharing in the profits, would bring about economic equality for all people. The workers would control the government in a "dictatorship of the proletariat." After a period of cooperative living and education, the state or government would wither away as a classless society developed.

Marx called this final phase pure communism. Marx described **communism** as a form of complete socialism in which the means of production—all land, mines, factories, railroads, and businesses—would be owned by the people. Private property would in effect cease to exist. All goods and services would be shared equally.

Published in 1848, *The Communist Manifesto* produced few short-term results. Though widespread revolts shook Europe during 1848 and 1849, Europe's leaders eventually put down the uprisings. Only after the turn of the century did the fiery Marxist pamphlet produce explosive results. In the 1900s, Marxism inspired revolutionaries such as Russia's Lenin, China's Mao Zedong, and Cuba's Fidel Castro. These leaders adapted Marx's beliefs to their own specific situations and needs.

Analyzing Key Concepts

Capitalism vs. Socialism

Point out that the chart is a list of ideas that do not necessarily match up from one column to the other. Note that capitalism and Marxism differ in their ideas of progress. In capitalism, progress occurs when people pursue their self-interest. In Marxism, it occurs when the state is destroyed and a classless society emerges.

SKILLBUILDER Answers

1. **Developing Historical Perspective** The factory worker and unemployed artisan would prefer socialism because it sought to protect the working class. The shop owner and factory owner would prefer capitalism because it encouraged the acquisition of wealth.
2. **Forming and Supporting Opinions** Capitalism seems most widespread; many countries are moving more and more toward that system.

More About . . .

Revolutionary Upheaval

The most successful workers' revolt of the 1800s occurred in Paris in 1871. Calling for an end to unfair wages and working conditions, workers seized Paris and set up a people's government, called the Paris Commune. The Commune lasted just two months, then was crushed by French troops.

DIFFERENTIATING INSTRUCTION: ENGLISH LEARNERS

Analyzing Key Terms

Class Time 15 minutes

Task Defining key terms and examining their word parts to expand understanding

Purpose To broaden vocabulary and practice word analysis

Instructions Pair less-fluent English speakers with more-fluent speakers and have them work with the following terms from this section:

- laissez faire
- capitalism
- utilitarianism
- socialism
- communism
- union
- strike

Encourage students to quiz each other on the meaning of the terms. More fluent students might also explain the meaning of terms based on word parts. For example, *capitalism, utilitarianism, socialism*, and *communism* all combine root words with the suffix *-ism*. In this context, *-ism* is added to designate a doctrine, theory, or system of principles related to the root word. Thus, socialism means "the belief that the wealth of a country should be shared equally among all its citizens—or its entire *society*."

Students who need more help might use the Reading Study Guide in Spanish for Section 4.

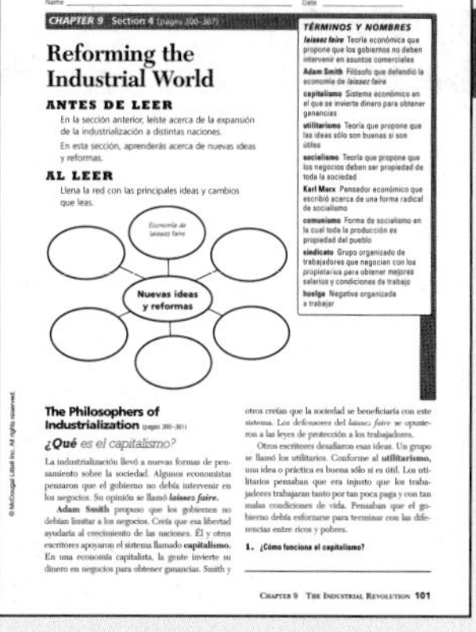

Reading Study Guide: Spanish Translation

Connect *to* Today

Communism Today

In the late 1980s, Soviet leaders decided that communism no longer served their people well. Instead, democratic and capitalist systems became the goal. In 1991, the Soviet Union disbanded, and Russia and 12 other nations became independent countries. China, on the other hand, continued to operate under communism, although the ideology has evolved. As a more open marketplace led to increased economic growth in the late 1980s, China moved away from the strict communist model. In fact, a 1999 People's Congress officially endorsed private enterprise.

Labor Unions and Reform Laws
10.3.4

Critical Thinking

- How did the growth of unions help workers? *(Possible Answer: More workers had more bargaining power.)*
- How do you think joining a union or supporting a reform law made workers feel? *(Possible Answer: less helpless and more hopeful)*

Connect *to* Today

Communism Today

Communism expanded to all parts of the world during the Cold War that followed the end of World War II. (See map on page 529.) At the peak of Communist expansion in the 1980s, about 20 nations were Communist-controlled, including two of the world's largest—China and the Soviet Union. However, dissatisfaction with the theories of Karl Marx had been developing.

Eventually, most Communist governments were replaced. Today, there are only five Communist countries—China, North Korea, Vietnam, and Laos in Asia and Cuba in the Caribbean. (See map above.)

In *The Communist Manifesto*, Marx and Engels stated their belief that economic forces alone dominated society. Time has shown, however, that religion, nationalism, ethnic loyalties, and a desire for democratic reforms may be as strong influences on history as economic forces. In addition, the gap between the rich and the poor within the industrialized countries failed to widen in the way that Marx and Engels predicted, mostly because of the various reforms enacted by governments.

Labor Unions and Reform Laws

Factory workers faced long hours, dirty and dangerous working conditions, and the threat of being laid off. By the 1800s, working people became more active in politics. To press for reforms, workers joined together in voluntary labor associations called **unions**.

Unionization A union spoke for all the workers in a particular trade. Unions engaged in collective bargaining, negotiations between workers and their employers. They bargained for better working conditions and higher pay. If factory owners refused these demands, union members could **strike**, or refuse to work.

Skilled workers led the way in forming unions because their special skills gave them extra bargaining power. Management would have trouble replacing such skilled workers as carpenters, printers, and spinners. Thus, the earliest unions helped the lower middle class more than they helped the poorest workers.

The union movement underwent slow, painful growth in both Great Britain and the United States. For years, the British government denied workers the right to form unions. The government saw unions as a threat to social order and stability. Indeed, the Combination Acts of 1799 and 1800 outlawed unions and strikes. Ignoring the threat of jail or job loss, factory workers joined unions anyway. Parliament finally repealed the Combination Acts in 1824. After 1825, the British government unhappily tolerated unions.

British unions had shared goals of raising wages for their members and improving working conditions. By 1875, British trade unions had won the right to strike and picket peacefully. They had also built up a membership of about 1 million people.

In the United States, skilled workers had belonged to unions since the early 1800s. In 1886, several unions joined together to form the organization that would become the American Federation of Labor (AFL). A series of successful strikes won AFL members higher wages and shorter hours.

Reform Laws Eventually, reformers and unions forced political leaders to look into the abuses caused by industrialization. In both Great Britain and the United States, new laws reformed some of the worst abuses of industrialization. In the 1820s and 1830s, for example, Parliament began investigating child labor and working conditions in factories and mines. As a result of its findings, Parliament passed the Factory Act of 1833. The new law made it illegal to hire children under 9 years old. Children from the ages of 9 to 12 could not work more than 8 hours a day. Young people from 13 to 17 could not work more than 12 hours. In 1842, the Mines Act prevented women and children from working underground.

COOPERATIVE ACTIVITY

Playing an Identity Game

Class Time 15 minutes

Task Playing a guessing game to identify historical figures

Purpose To reinforce students' knowledge of key thinkers from the early Industrial Age

Instructions Tell students that they are going to play a guessing game in which they try to identify important thinkers from the 1800s. Have pairs of students research the life and ideas of one of the people discussed in this section, such as:

- Adam Smith
- Thomas Malthus
- Karl Marx
- Robert Owen
- David Ricardo
- Jeremy Bentham
- Friedrich Engels
- Charles Fourier Saint-Simon

Then have students write a sentence or two describing the person without giving away his or her identity. To play the game, students should say their sentences to the class. The class can then ask up to five questions to determine the identity of the person being portrayed. Refer students to Critical Thinking Transparency CT25 for information.

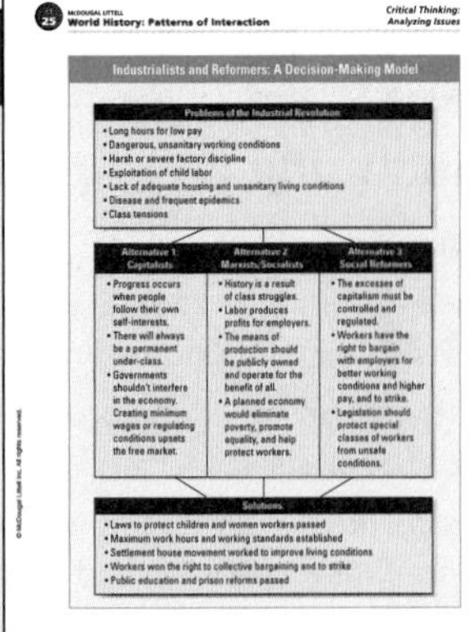

Critical Thinking Transparencies

MAIN IDEA

D Summarizing

What were some of the important reform bills passed in Britain during this period?

D. Answer Factory Act of 1833; Mines Act of 1842; Ten Hours Act of 1847

In 1847, the Parliament passed a bill that helped working women as well as their children. The Ten Hours Act of 1847 limited the workday to ten hours for women and children who worked in factories. D

Reformers in the United States also passed laws to protect child workers. In 1904, a group of progressive reformers organized the National Child Labor Committee to end child labor. Arguing that child labor lowered wages for all workers, union members joined the reformers. Together they pressured national and state politicians to ban child labor and set maximum working hours.

In 1919, the U.S. Supreme Court objected to a federal child labor law, ruling that it interfered with states' rights to regulate labor. However, individual states were allowed to limit the working hours of women and, later, of men.

▲ Hungarian workers meet to plan their strategy before a strike.

The Reform Movement Spreads

Almost from the beginning, reform movements rose in response to the negative impact of industrialization. These reforms included improving the workplace and extending the right to vote to working-class men. The same impulse toward reform, along with the ideals of the French Revolution, also helped to end slavery and promote new rights for women and children.

The Abolition of Slavery William Wilberforce, a highly religious man, was a member of Parliament who led the fight for abolition—the end of the slave trade and slavery in the British Empire. Parliament passed a bill to end the slave trade in the British West Indies in 1807. After he retired from Parliament in 1825, Wilberforce continued his fight to free the slaves. Britain finally abolished slavery in its empire in 1833.

British antislavery activists had mixed motives. Some, such as the abolitionist Wilberforce, were morally against slavery. Others viewed slave labor as an economic threat. Furthermore, a new class of industrialists developed who supported cheap labor rather than slave labor. They soon gained power in Parliament.

In the United States the movement to fulfill the promise of the Declaration of Independence by ending slavery grew in the early 1800s. The enslavement of African people finally ended in the United States when the Union won the Civil War in 1865. Then, enslavement persisted in the Americas only in Puerto Rico, Cuba, and Brazil. In Puerto Rico, slavery was ended in 1873. Spain finally abolished slavery in its Cuban colony in 1886. Not until 1888 did Brazil's huge enslaved population win freedom.

The Fight for Women's Rights The Industrial Revolution proved a mixed blessing for women. On the one hand, factory work offered higher wages than work done at home. Women spinners in Manchester, for example, earned much more money than women who stayed home to spin cotton thread. On the other hand, women factory workers usually made only one-third as much money as men did.

Women led reform movements to address this and other pressing social issues. During the mid-1800s, for example, women formed unions in the trades where they dominated. In Britain, some women served as safety inspectors in factories where other women worked. In the United States, college-educated women like Jane Addams ran settlement houses. These community centers served the poor residents of slum neighborhoods.

The Reform Movement Spreads

10.3.4

Critical Thinking

- How can slavery be an economic threat? *(Possible Answer: by providing unpaid labor that takes jobs from paid workers)*
- What do lower wages for women suggest about their place in industrial society? *(Possible Answer: less valued as workers)*

Tip for Struggling Readers

Help students identify connections between industrialization and reform movements. Post or provide the following chart and help students complete it.

Reform	Link to Industrialization
Abolition	
Women's rights	
Education	

CONNECTIONS ACROSS TIME AND CULTURES

Reform Through Art and Politics

Class Time 30 minutes

Task Researching ways people have sought reform through politics and the arts

Purpose To understand ongoing reactions to economic ideologies

Instructions Tell students that people have responded to the effects of industrialization in different ways since the 1800s. Many have protested industrialization; many have tried to reform its features in order to improve the lives of everyday people. Writers have conveyed their views through literature, actors and filmmakers through the visual medium, and politicians through their rhetoric. Ask students to research one of the following:

- the 1979 film *Norma Rae*
- the 1906 book *The Jungle* by Upton Sinclair
- Ross Perot, founder of the Reform Party
- John McCain, Arizona senator and former presidential candidate

Have students briefly summarize the person or work they researched and explain what particular reforms were sought.

History Makers

Jane Addams

Ask students what they think Jane Addams meant when she wrote that "women who had been given over too exclusively to study might...learn of life from life itself." *(Possible Answer: It would help women students to see how the rest of the world lived.)*

3 ASSESS

SECTION 4 ASSESSMENT

Have students answer the questions in pairs, then exchange papers with another pair to critique each other's answers.

Formal Assessment
- Section Quiz, p. 158

4 RETEACH

Present the Visual Summary as an overall review. Then have students work in groups to turn each head and subhead into a question. For example, the head "The Reform Movement Spreads" can become the question "How did the reform movement spread?" Invite groups to pose their questions to each other.

Critical Thinking Transparencies
- CT61 Chapter 25 Visual Summary

In-Depth Resources: Unit 3
- Reteaching Activity, p. 22

History Makers

Jane Addams
1860–1935

After graduating from college, Jane Addams wondered what to do with her life.

> *I gradually became convinced that it would be a good thing to rent a house in a part of the city where many primitive and actual needs are found, in which young women who had been given over too exclusively to study, might . . . learn of life from life itself.*

Addams and her friend Ellen Starr set up Hull House in a working-class district in Chicago. Eventually the facilities included a nursery, a gym, a kitchen, and a boarding house for working women. Hull House not only served the immigrant population of the neighborhood, it also trained social workers.

In both the United States and Britain, women who had rallied for the abolition of slavery began to wonder why their own rights should be denied on the basis of gender. The movement for women's rights began in the United States as early as 1848. Women activists around the world joined to found the International Council for Women in 1888. Delegates and observers from 27 countries attended the council's 1899 meeting. E

MAIN IDEA

E Making Inferences

Why might women abolitionists have headed the movement for women's rights?

E. Possible Answer Their work to gain rights for African Americans may have led them to try to gain equal rights for themselves.

Reforms Spread to Many Areas of Life In the United States and Western Europe, reformers tried to correct the problems troubling the newly industrialized nations. Public education and prison reform ranked high on the reformers' lists.

One of the most prominent U.S. reformers, Horace Mann of Massachusetts, favored free public education for all children. Mann, who spent his own childhood working at hard labor, warned, "If we do not prepare children to become good citizens . . . if we do not enrich their minds with knowledge, then our republic must go down to destruction." By the 1850s, many states were starting public school systems. In Western Europe, free public schooling became available in the late 1800s.

In 1831, French writer Alexis de Tocqueville had contrasted the brutal conditions in American prisons to the "extended liberty" of American society. Those who sought to reform prisons emphasized the goal of providing prisoners with the means to lead to useful lives upon release.

During the 1800s, democracy grew in industrialized countries even as foreign expansion increased. The industrialized democracies faced new challenges both at home and abroad. You will learn about these challenges in Chapter 10.

SECTION 4 ASSESSMENT

TERMS & NAMES 1. For each term or name, write a sentence explaining its significance.
• laissez faire • Adam Smith • capitalism • utilitarianism • socialism • Karl Marx • communism • union • strike

USING YOUR NOTES

2. What characteristics do capitalism and socialism share? (10.3.6)

Capitalism	Socialism
1.	1.
2.	2.
3.	3.

MAIN IDEAS

3. What were Adam Smith's three natural laws of economics? (10.3.6)
4. What kind of society did early socialists want? (10.3.6)
5. Why did workers join together in unions? (10.3.4)

CRITICAL THINKING & WRITING

6. **IDENTIFYING PROBLEMS** What were the main problems faced by the unions during the 1800s and how did they overcome them? (10.3.4)
7. **DRAWING CONCLUSIONS** Why do you think that Marx's "dictatorship of the proletariat" did not happen? (10.3.6)
8. **MAKING INFERENCES** Why did the labor reform movement spread to other areas of life? (10.3.4)
9. **WRITING ACTIVITY** ECONOMICS Write a two-paragraph **persuasive essay** on how important economic forces are in society. Support your opinion using evidence from this and previous chapters. (Writing 2.4.c)

CONNECT TO TODAY PREPARING AN ECONOMIC REPORT

Research a present-day corporation. Prepare an **economic report** that includes the corporation's structure, products or services, number of employees, and any other relevant economic information you are able to find. (10.3.5)

ANSWERS

1. laissez faire, p. 300 • Adam Smith, p. 300 • capitalism, p. 300 • utilitarianism, p. 301 • socialism, p. 302 • Karl Marx, p. 302 • communism, p. 303 • union, p. 304 • strike, p. 304

2. **Sample Answer:** Capitalism: 1. laws of competition, self-interest, supply and demand; 2. middle and worker classes; 3. private property and production ownership; 4. government doesn't interfere. Socialism: 1. community property and production ownership; 2. community protects workers; 3. classless society. Society is organized around economic ideas.
3. self-interest, competition, supply/demand
4. one with cooperation and economic planning where workers shared profits
5. to bargain together for better working conditions and higher wages
6. **Possible Answer:** denied right to organize or strike, unskilled workers lacked power; with strikes, by pushing Parliament to repeal Combination Acts
7. **Possible Answers:** Workers were not united or skilled enough to take over governments; democratic reforms helped protect workers.
8. **Possible Answer:** People saw that group effort could achieve reform.
9. **Rubric** Essays should
   - clearly state an opinion.
   - include supporting evidence.

CONNECT TO TODAY

Rubric Reports should
- clearly state the facts.
- explain the economics of the corporation.

INTERACTIVE

Industrialization

Industrialization eventually raised the standard of living for many people in Europe and North America in the 1800s. Yet the process also brought suffering to countless workers who crowded into filthy cities to toil for starvation wages. The following excerpts reveal a variety of perspectives on this major historical event.

CALIFORNIA STANDARDS

10.3.2 Examine how scientific and technological changes and new forms of energy brought about massive social, economic, and cultural change (e.g., the inventions and discoveries of James Watt, Eli Whitney, Henry Bessemer, Louis Pasteur, Thomas Edison).

HI 3 Students interpret past events and issues within the context in which an event unfolded rather than solely in terms of present-day norms and values.

A PRIMARY SOURCE

Mary Paul

Mary Paul worked in a textile factory in Lowell, Massachusetts. In an 1846 letter to her father in New Hampshire, the 16-year-old expressed her satisfaction with her situation at Lowell.

I am at work in a spinning room tending four sides of warp which is one girl's work. The overseer tells me that he never had a girl get along better than I do. . . . I have a very good boarding place, have enough to eat. . . . The girls are all kind and obliging. . . . I think that the factory is the best place for me and if any girl wants employment, I advise them to come to Lowell.

B PRIMARY SOURCE

Andrew Carnegie

In his autobiography, published in 1920, the multimillionaire industrialist views with optimism the growth of American industry.

One great advantage which America will have in competing in the markets of the world is that her manufacturers will have the best home market. Upon this they can depend for a return upon capital, and the surplus product can be exported with advantage, even when the prices received for it do no more than cover actual cost, provided the exports be charged with their proportion of all expenses. The nation that has the best home market, especially if products are standardized, as ours are, can soon outsell the foreign producer.

C PRIMARY SOURCE

Friedrich Engels

Friedrich Engels, who coauthored *The Communist Manifesto* and also managed a textile factory in Manchester, England, spent his nights wandering the city's slums.

Nobody troubles about the poor as they struggle helplessly in the whirlpool of modern industrial life. The working man may be lucky enough to find employment, if by his labor he can enrich some member of the middle classes. But his wages are so low that they hardly keep body and soul together. If he cannot find work, he can steal, unless he is afraid of the police; or he can go hungry and then the police will see to it that he will die of hunger in such a way as not to disturb the equanimity of the middle classes.

D PRIMARY SOURCE

Walter Crane

This political cartoon was published in *Cartoons for the Cause* in Britain in 1886. It shows the vampire bat of Capitalism attacking a laborer. Socialism is pictured as an angel who is coming to the rescue.

Document-Based QUESTIONS

1. Why would Andrew Carnegie (Source B) and Friedrich Engels (Source C) disagree about the effects of industrialization?
2. What might be reasons for 16-year-old Mary Paul's (Source A) satisfaction with her job and life in Lowell?
3. Why might the political cartoon by Walter Crane (Source D) be useful in getting workers to rally to the cause of socialism?

307

Different Perspectives

OBJECTIVE

- Understand that industrialization can be examined from several perspectives.

INSTRUCT

Help students understand the many points of view about the Industrial Revolution presented here. Mary Paul describes life as a Lowell mill worker. Andrew Carnegie offers the experience of a tycoon. Friedrich Engels outlines a communist view of industrialization, and Walter Crane offers a pro-socialism picture.

INTEGRATED TECHNOLOGY

Interactive This feature is available in an interactive format on the eEdition.

More About . . .

Effects of Industrialization

Have students consider ways that life today differs from life in the Industrial Revolution era.
- greater global interdependence
- mass production has raised standards of living, but crafts have declined
- nutrition has improved in many places, but many people still live with hunger
- cities have expanded
- many enjoy good jobs with good pay, but others still work at menial labor or in poor or dangerous conditions

Electronic Library of Primary Sources
- from "How I Served My Apprenticeship"

DOCUMENT-BASED QUESTIONS: ANSWERS

1. *Possible Answer*: Carnegie was an industrialist who made millions from his factories while Engels worked inside a factory, and saw conditions there.
2. *Possible Answer*: She was earning wages on her own and had some independence from her family.
3. *Possible Answer:* Workers who felt oppressed might see socialism as a way to improve their working and living conditions.

TERMS & NAMES

1. Industrial Revolution, p. 283
2. enclosure, p. 283
3. factory, p. 286
4. urbanization, p. 289
5. middle class, p. 291
6. corporation, p. 297
7. laissez faire, p. 300
8. socialism, p. 302
9. Karl Marx, p. 302
10. union, p. 304

MAIN IDEAS

Answers will vary.

11. water power and coal; iron ore; rivers; good harbors
12. forced small farmers to give up farming; caused forced migration to cities; some farmers became tenants
13. **Possible Answers:** steam engine, locomotive, factory, spinning jenny, flying shuttle; impact varies with invention
14. no sanitary codes; lack of adequate housing, education, police protection, running water, indoor plumbing; frequent epidemics
15. some industrialists became wealthier than landowners, threatening their power and spurring greater class division into upper class, upper-middle class, lower-middle class, working class
16. **Possible Answer:** dyes, wastes poisoned rivers; coal polluted air
17. The French Revolution caused political turmoil that interrupted communication, slowed trade, caused inflation.
18. Industrialized countries needed natural resources and customers from less-developed countries. These needs led to imperialism and colonization.
19. bourgeoisie ("haves," employers), proletariat ("have-nots," workers)
20. **Possible Answers:** formed unions, served as safety inspectors, rallied for abolition of slavery, founded the International Council for Women

Chapter 9 Assessment

VISUAL SUMMARY

The Industrial Revolution

Economic Effects

- New inventions and development of factories
- Rapidly growing industry in the 1800s
- Increased production and higher demand for raw materials
- Growth of worldwide trade
- Population explosion and expanding labor force
- Exploitation of mineral resources
- Highly developed banking and investment system
- Advances in transportation, agriculture, and communication

Social Effects

- Increase in population of cities
- Lack of city planning
- Loss of family stability
- Expansion of middle class
- Harsh conditions for laborers, including children
- Workers' progress versus laissez-faire economic attitudes
- Improved standard of living
- Creation of new jobs
- Encouragement of technological progress

Political Effects

- Child labor laws to end abuses
- Reformers urging equal distribution of wealth
- Trade unions formed
- Social reform movements, such as utilitarianism, utopianism, socialism, and Marxism
- Reform bills in Parliament and Congress

TERMS & NAMES

For each term or name below, briefly explain its connection to the Industrial Revolution.

1. Industrial Revolution
2. enclosure
3. factory
4. urbanization
5. middle class
6. corporation
7. laissez faire
8. socialism
9. Karl Marx
10. union

MAIN IDEAS

The Beginnings of Industrialization Section 1 (pages 283–288)

11. What were the four natural resources needed for British industrialization? (10.3.1)
12. How did the enclosure movement change agriculture in England? (10.3.2)
13. What were two important inventions created during the Industrial Revolution? Describe their impact. (10.3.5)

Case Study: Industrialization Section 2 (pages 289–294)

14. Describe living conditions in Britain during industrialization. (10.3.2)
15. How did the new middle class transform the social structure of Great Britain during industrialization? (10.3.4)
16. How did industrialization affect Manchester's natural environment? (10.3.3)

Industrialization Spreads Section 3 (pages 295–299)

17. Why were other European countries slower to industrialize than Britain? (10.3.5)
18. What might explain the rise of global inequality during the Industrial Revolution? (10.3.5)

Reforming the Industrial World Section 4 (pages 300–307)

19. What were the two warring classes that Marx and Engels outlined in *The Communist Manifesto*? (10.3.6)
20. How did women fight for change during the Industrial Revolution? (10.3.2)

CRITICAL THINKING

1. USING YOUR NOTES
In a chart, list some of the major technological advances and their effects on society. (10.3.2)

Technological Advance	Effect(s)

2. EVALUATING
SCIENCE AND TECHNOLOGY How significant were the changes that the Industrial Revolution brought to the world? Explain your conclusion. (10.3.2)

3. ANALYZING CAUSES AND RECOGNIZING EFFECTS
ECONOMICS How important were labor unions in increasing the power of workers? Give reasons for your opinion. (10.3.4)

4. DRAWING CONCLUSIONS
How did the Industrial Revolution help to increase Germany's military power? Support your answer with information from the chapter. (10.3.6)

5. DEVELOPING HISTORICAL PERSPECTIVE
EMPIRE BUILDING Would a nonindustrialized or an industrialized nation more likely be an empire builder? Why? (10.3.1)

CRITICAL THINKING

Answers will vary.

1. Advances: Kay's flying shuttle—helped speed up weaving; Arkwright's water frame—enabled more efficient weaving, created need for factories; cotton gin—sped up cleaning cotton; steam engine—provided power for factories.
2. **Possible Answers:** new social classes emerged; new political philosophies erupted; gap widened between industrialized nations and nonindustrialized nations; new inventions changed the way people and goods moved
3. **Possible Answer:** Labor unions helped workers gain bargaining power to raise wages and improve conditions.
4. **Possible Answer:** Germany's factories increased production of war material; massive economic strength fueled its growing military might.
5. **Possible Answer:** Industrialized nations have the economic capability to build overseas empires, the need for raw materials and new markets, and the power to control less-developed lands.

Use the quotation about industrialization and your knowledge of world history to answer questions 1 and 2. Additional Test Practice, pp. S1–S33

PRIMARY SOURCE

It was a town of red brick, or of brick that would have been red if the smoke and ashes had allowed it. . . . It was a town of machinery and tall chimneys, out of which interminable [endless] serpents of smoke trailed themselves for ever and ever. . . . It contained several large streets all very like one another, and many small streets still more like one another, inhabited by people equally like one another, who all went in and out at the same hours, with the same sound upon the same pavements, to do the same work, and to whom every day was the same as yesterday and tomorrow, and every year the counterpart of the last and the next.

CHARLES DICKENS, *Hard Times*

1. In this passage, the writer is trying to describe how (10.3.3)
   - **A.** people came from the countryside to the city to work in industry.
   - **B.** entrepreneurs built factories.
   - **C.** capitalism works.
   - **D.** difficult life is for workers in industrial cities.

2. What is Dickens's view of industrialization? (10.3.4)
   - **A.** that it is good for factory owners
   - **B.** that it brings progress to a nation
   - **C.** that it pollutes the air and exploits the workers
   - **D.** that it causes population growth

Use the graph below and your knowledge of world history to answer question 3.

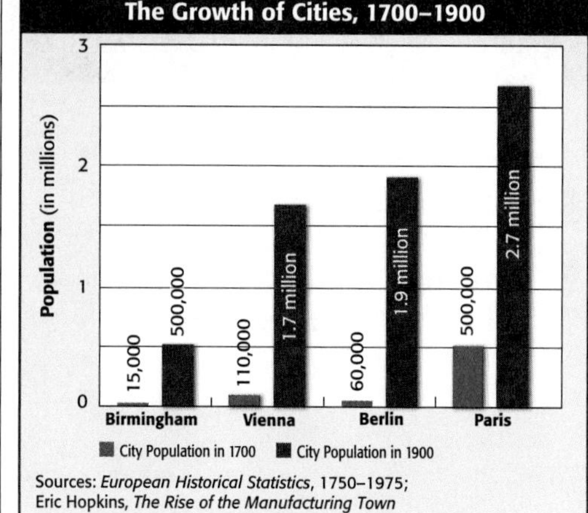

Sources: *European Historical Statistics*, 1750–1975; Eric Hopkins, *The Rise of the Manufacturing Town*

3. The graph above shows population growth in four European cities from 1700 to 1900, that is, before and after the Industrial Revolution. Which statement best describes the information in the chart? (CST 3)
   - **A.** All of the cities grew at the same rate.
   - **B.** The increase in population for each city was less than 2 million people.
   - **C.** Paris was the most populous city both before and after the Industrial Revolution.
   - **D.** Berlin's population in 1900 was four times its size in 1700.

INTEGRATED TECHNOLOGY

TEST PRACTICE Go to **classzone.com**
- Diagnostic tests
- Strategies
- Tutorials
- Additional practice

ALTERNATIVE ASSESSMENT

1. **Interact *with* History** (10.3.4)
   On page 282, you looked at working conditions in an English factory in the 19th century. Now that you have read the chapter about the Industrial Revolution, rethink your decision about what you would do to change your situation. What working conditions would you like to see change? What benefits might a union bring? What disadvantages might result if workers organize? Discuss your opinions with a small group.

2. **WRITING ABOUT HISTORY** (10.3.5, Writing 2.3.a)
   The Industrial Revolution's impact varied according to social class. Write a three-paragraph **expository essay** indicating how these people would view the changes in industry: an inventor, an entrepreneur, a skilled worker, and a hand weaver.

INTEGRATED TECHNOLOGY

Using Graphics Software (10.3.2, Writing 2.3.d)

Make a list of five major inventions or innovations of the Industrial Revolution. Research each to learn about the scientific, economic, and social changes that contributed to its development and the effects that it caused. Use the Internet, books, and other resources to conduct your research. Then use graphics software to create a chart, graph, or diagram depicting the relationship between the inventions and innovations, the changes, and the effects.

You may include some of the following:
- the plow
- the cotton gin
- the power loom
- the telegraph
- the sewing machine

STANDARD-BASED ASSESSMENT

1. The correct answer is letter **D**. Letter **A** is incorrect because the countryside is not mentioned. Letter **B** is incorrect because entrepreneurs are not discussed. Letter **C** is incorrect because the ills caused by capitalism are described.
2. The correct answer is letter **C**. Letter **A** is incorrect because Dickens does not refer to the role of factory owners. Letter **B** is incorrect because Dickens does not discuss the effect of industrialization on a nation. Letter **D** is incorrect because population growth is not discussed.
3. Letter **C** is correct. Letter **A** is incorrect because the cities grew at different rates. Letter **B** is incorrect because Paris grew by more than 2 million people. Letter **D** is incorrect because Berlin's population in 1900 was more than 30 times its size in 1700.

Formal Assessment
- Chapter Test, Forms A, B, and C, pp. 159–170

California Test Generator CD-ROM
- Chapter Tests, Forms A, B, and C (English and Spanish)

ALTERNATIVE ASSESSMENT

1. **Possible Answers:** changing conditions such as poor lighting and bad air in factories; bargaining power that a union could bring to bear upon the fight to improve working conditions; labor organization could lead to decline in individual productivity
2. **Rubric** Essays should
   - include a brief discussion of each of the four persons.
   - demonstrate an understanding of the economic role played by each.
   - be clearly written.

INTEGRATED TECHNOLOGY

Rubric Graphic organizers should
- include five inventions or innovations.
- show cause-and-effect relationships.
- be clearly presented.

CHAPTER 10 PLANNING GUIDE

An Age of Democracy and Progress, 1815–1914

CHAPTER RESOURCES	COPYMASTERS	ASSESSMENT
CHAPTER OVERVIEW Democratic ideals had a strong impact on Europe and its colonies, the United States expanded, and technology and science changed communication and daily life.	**In-Depth Resources: Unit 3** • Building Vocabulary, p. 27 **Chapters in Brief** (in English and Spanish) **Block Schedule Pacing Guide**	**Chapter Assessment,** pp. 334–335 **Formal Assessment** • Chapter Tests, Forms A, B, and C, pp. 175–189 **Test Generator** **Integrated Assessment Book** **Online Test Practice**
SECTION 1 **Democratic Reform and Activism** pp. 313–316 **OBJECTIVE** Describe democracy in Britain and France and development of the woman suffrage movement.	**In-Depth Resources: Unit 3** • Guided Reading, p. 23 • Primary Source, p. 31 • History Makers: Emmeline Pankhurst, p. 40 • Reteaching Activity, p. 43 **Reading Study Guide,** p. 105	**Section 1 Assessment,** p. 316 **Formal Assessment** • Section Quiz, p. 171 **California Daily Standards Practice Transparencies,** TT97
SECTION 2 **Self-Rule for British Colonies** pp. 317–323 **OBJECTIVE** Explain self-rule in Canada, Australia, and New Zealand and British domination of Ireland.	**In-Depth Resources: Unit 3** • Guided Reading, p. 24 • Geography Application, p. 29 • Primary Source, p. 32 • Literature: "Easter 1916," p. 35 • Reteaching Activity, p. 44 **Reading Study Guide,** p. 107	**Section 2 Assessment,** p. 321 **Formal Assessment** • Section Quiz, p. 172 **California Daily Standards Practice Transparencies,** TT98
SECTION 3 **War and Expansion in the United States** pp. 324–327 **OBJECTIVE** Trace U.S. expansion to the Pacific, the U.S. Civil War, and the postwar economy.	**In-Depth Resources: Unit 3** • Guided Reading, p. 25 • Primary Source: Railroad Poster, p. 33 • Reteaching Activity, p. 45 **Reading Study Guide,** p. 109	**Section 3 Assessment,** p. 327 **Formal Assessment** • Section Quiz, p. 173 **California Daily Standards Practice Transparencies,** TT99
SECTION 4 **Nineteenth-Century Progress** pp. 328–333 **OBJECTIVE** Summarize technological and scientific progress made in the late 1800s.	**In-Depth Resources: Unit 3** • Guided Reading, p. 26 • Skillbuilder Practice: Analyzing Issues, p. 28 • Primary Source, p. 34 • Literature: from *The Origin,* p. 37 • History Makers: Marie and Pierre Curie, p. 41 • Connections Across Time/Cultures, p. 42 • Reteaching Activity, p. 46 **Reading Study Guide,** p. 111	**Section 4 Assessment,** p. 333 **Formal Assessment** • Section Quiz, p. 174 **California Daily Standards Practice Transparencies,** TT100

INTEGRATED TECHNOLOGY

- eEdition Plus Online
- EasyPlanner Plus Online
- eTest Plus Online

Audio CDs
- Voices from the Past
- Reading Study Guides

Patterns of Interaction Video
- The Geography of Food

CD-ROMs
- eEdition
- Power Presentations
- EasyPlanner
- Electronic Library of Primary Sources
- Test Generator

---

eEdition CD-ROM

Electronic Library of Primary Sources
- from *Prisons and Prisoners*

classzone.com

---

eEdition CD-ROM

Geography Transparencies
- GT26 Canada: Growth of the Dominion

World Art and Cultures Transparencies
- AT57 Maori pigment container

Patterns of Interaction Video Series
- The Geography of Food

Electronic Library of Primary Sources
- "The Irish Potato Famine"

classzone.com

eEdition CD-ROM

Electronic Library of Primary Sources
- from A Message to Congress

classzone.com

---

eEdition CD-ROM

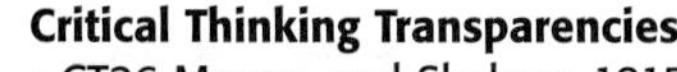
Critical Thinking Transparencies
- CT26 Movers and Shakers, 1815–1914
- CT62 Chapter 26 Visual Summary

Electronic Library of Primary Sources
- from *Journal of the Voyage of HMS Beagle*

classzone.com
- NetExplorations: Mass Entertainment

OVERVIEW OF CALIFORNIA RESOURCES

	Section 1	Section 2	Section 3	Section 4
California Reading Toolkit	p. L45	p. L46	p. L47	p. L48
California Modified Lesson Plans for English Learners	p. 85	p. 87	p. 89	p. 91
California Daily Standards Practice Transparencies	TT37	TT38	TT39	TT40
California Standards Enrichment Workbook	pp. 20–30, 39–40	pp. 49–50	pp. 37–38, 39–40	pp. 35–36, 47–48
California Standards Planner and Lesson Plans	p. L81	p. L83	p. L85	p. L87
California Online Test Practice	classzone.com	classzone.com	classzone.com	classzone.com
California Test Generator CD-ROM				
California Easy Planner CD-ROM				
California eEdition CD-ROM				

Chart Key:

Pupil's Edition

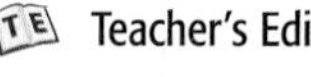
Teacher's Edition

Overhead Transparency

Block Scheduling

Copymaster

Audio Library

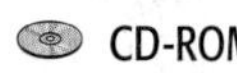
CD-ROM

Internet

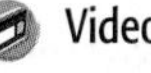
Video

NO TIME?

If you do not have time to teach this chapter in full, assign the **Chapter in Brief** (also available in Spanish).

Previewing Resources for Differentiated Instruction

ENGLISH LEARNERS: Resources in Spanish

In-Depth Resources in Spanish
- Guided Reading Ⓐ
- Skillbuilder Practice: Analyzing Issues Ⓑ
- Geography Application: The British Settle Australia and New Zealand

Chapters in Brief

Reading Study Guide Ⓒ

Reading Study Guide Audio CD

Test Generator CD-ROM
- Chapter Test, Forms A, B, and C

Plus

Modified Lesson Plans for English Learners

Multi-Language Glossary of Social Studies Terms

Ⓐ
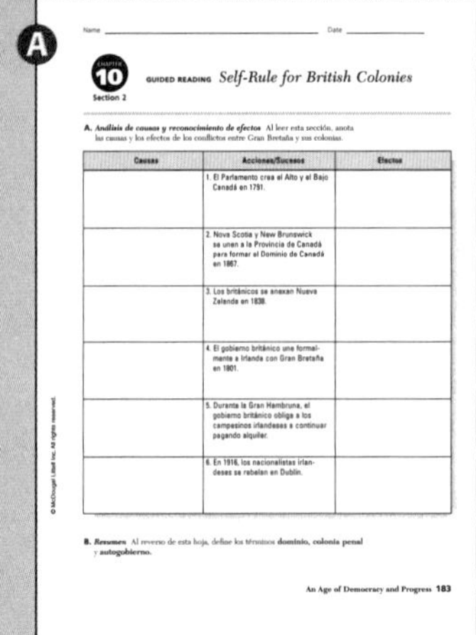
Self-Rule for British Colonies

Causas	Acciones/Sucesos	Efectos
	1. El Parlamento crea el Alto y el Bajo Canadá en 1791.	
	2. Nova Scotia y New Brunswick se unen a la Provincia de Canadá para formar el Dominio de Canadá en 1867.	
	3. Los británicos se anexan Nueva Zelanda en 1839.	
	4. El gobierno británico une formalmente a Irlanda con Gran Bretaña en 1801.	
	5. Durante la Gran Hambruna, el gobierno británico obliga a los campesinos irlandeses a continuar pagando alquiler.	
	6. En 1916, los nacionalistas irlandeses se rebelan en Dublín.	

Ⓑ
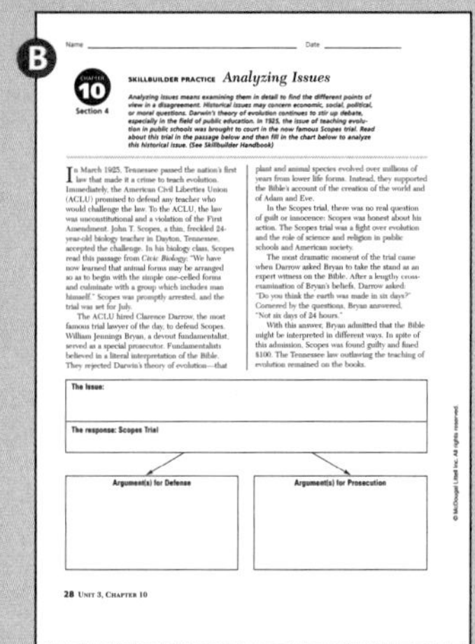
Analyzing Issues

STRUGGLING READERS

In-Depth Resources: Unit 3
- Guided Reading
- Building Vocabulary
- Skillbuilder Practice: Analyzing Issues
- Geography Application: The British Settle Australia and New Zealand Ⓐ
- Reteaching Activities

Chapters in Brief

Reading Study Guide Ⓑ

Reading Study Guide Audio CD

Formal Assessment
- Chapter Test, Form A Ⓒ

Plus

Reading Toolkit

Ⓐ
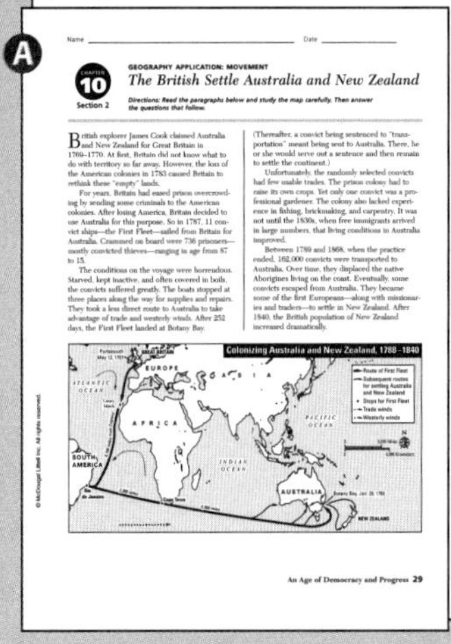
The British Settle Australia and New Zealand

Ⓑ
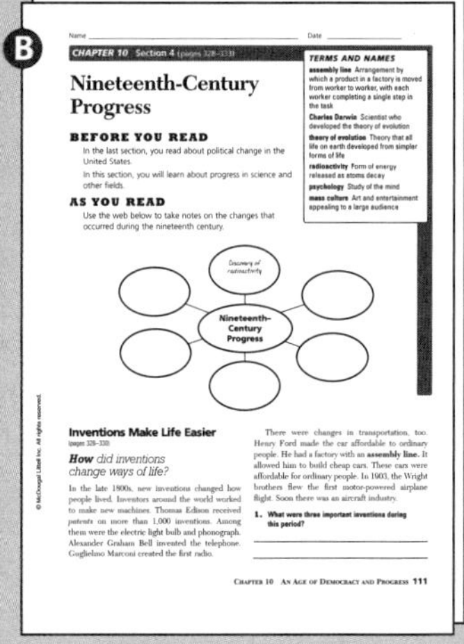
Nineteenth-Century Progress

GIFTED AND TALENTED STUDENTS

In-Depth Resources: Unit 3
- Primary Source: from *Five Years of My Life, 1894–1899;* Irish Petition to Emigrate Ⓐ; Railroad Poster Ⓑ; Orville Wright's Diary
- History Makers: Emmeline Pankhurst; Marie and Pierre Curie
- Literature: "Easter 1916" Ⓒ; from *The Origin: A Biographical Novel of Charles Darwin*
- Connections Across Time and Cultures: Breakthroughs in Science and Technology

Electronic Library of Primary Sources
- from *Prisons and Prisoners*
- "The Irish Potato Famine"
- from A Message to Congress on Indian Policy
- from *Journal of the Voyage of HMS Beagle*

Formal Assessment
- Chapter Test, Form C

Ⓐ

from Irish Petition to Emigrate, 1847

Ⓑ

Railroad Poster

Activities in the Teacher's Edition for English Learners

- The British Settle Australia and New Zealand, p. 319
- Comparing Casualty Rates of Different Wars, p. 326
- Understanding the Germ Theory of Disease, p. 330

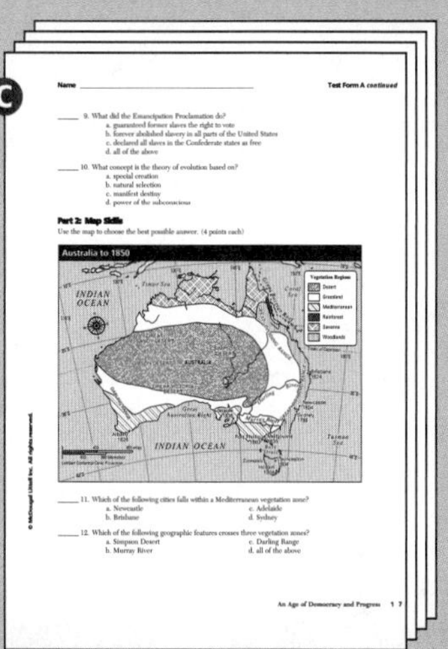

Activities in the Teacher's Edition for Struggling Readers

- Creating Campaign Materials, p. 314
- Causes and Effects of the Great Famine, p. 320
- The Chronology of the Civil War, p. 325

Activities in the Teacher's Edition for Gifted and Talented Students

- Analyzing Primary and Secondary Sources, p. 315
- Indigenous Peoples of Australia and New Zealand, p. 318
- Examining the Technology of Filmmaking, p. 332

INTEGRATED TECHNOLOGY

eEdition
- Interactive Visuals
- Interactive Maps
- Interactive Primary Sources

classzone.com
- Research Links
- Internet Activities
- Primary Sources
- Chapter Quiz
- Current Events
- NetExplorations: Mass Entertainment

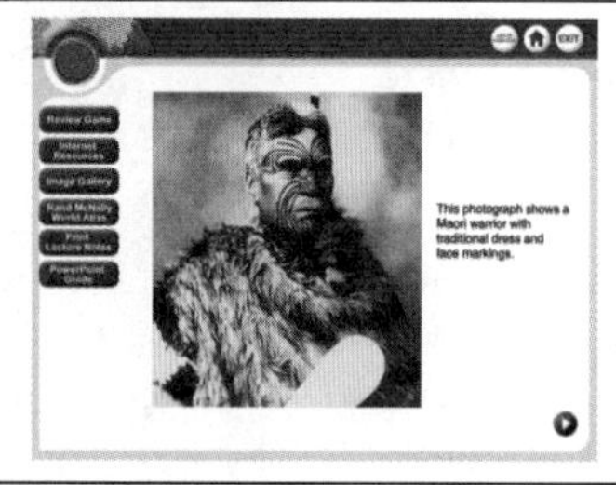

Power Presentations CD-ROM
- Lecture Notes
- Image Gallery
- Chapter Review Game

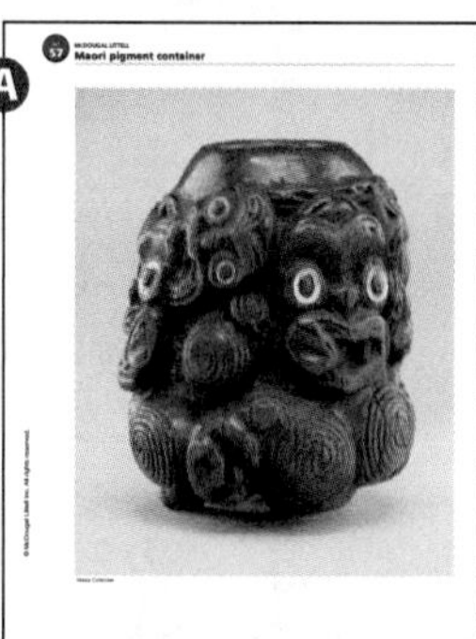

Critical Thinking Transparencies
- CT26 Movers and Shakers, 1815–1914
- CT62 Chapter 26 Visual Summary

Geography Transparencies
- GT26 Canada: Growth of the Dominion, 1867–Present

World Art and Cultures Transparencies
- AT57 Maori pigment container (A)

Test Practice Transparencies TT97–TT100

Test Generator CD-ROM

EasyPlanner CD-ROM

Voices from the Past Audio CD

Online Test Practice

Electronic Library of Primary Sources

Patterns of Interaction Video Series

CHAPTER 10 • OBJECTIVE

Trace the spread of democratic ideals and industrial and scientific progress in the 19th century.

Previewing Main Ideas

Point out that the three main ideas focus on changes in governmental structure. Britain's imperial control of some of its far-flung colonies decreased. At the same time, the United States expanded, aided by improved technology in transportation and communication.

Accessing Prior Knowledge

Ask students why democracy and progress might be connected. *(Possible Answers: Political freedom and self-expression encourage innovation in the arts and sciences. Democracy encourages economic freedom and competition, leading to new ideas.)*

Geography *Answers*

EMPIRE BUILDING The western democracies that existed in 1900 were Great Britain, France, the United States, and Canada.

POWER AND AUTHORITY It spanned a continent; it had extensive waterways, including rivers and lakes; by 1900, it had only two neighbors to contend with along largely friendly borders.

SCIENCE AND TECHNOLOGY The railroad united different regions of the country and enabled goods to reach markets more efficiently.

CHAPTER 10

An Age of Democracy and Progress, 1815–1914

Previewing Main Ideas

EMPIRE BUILDING During the 1800s, Great Britain gradually allowed three of its colonies—Canada, Australia, and New Zealand—greater self-rule. However, Britain maintained tight control over Ireland.

Geography *According to the map, what Western democracies existed in North America and Western Europe in 1900?*

POWER AND AUTHORITY The United States expanded across the continent during the 1800s and added new states to its territory to become a great power.

Geography *What geographical factors might have helped to make the United States a great power?*

SCIENCE AND TECHNOLOGY The transcontinental railroad helped to link the United States from the Atlantic Ocean to the Pacific Ocean. It was a triumph of 19th-century technology.

Geography *How might a technological achievement such as the transcontinental railroad have contributed to American prosperity?*

INTEGRATED TECHNOLOGY

eEdition
- Interactive Maps
- Interactive Visuals
- Interactive Primary Sources

INTERNET RESOURCES
Go to **classzone.com** for:
- Research Links
- Internet Activities
- Primary Sources
- Chapter Quiz
- Maps
- Test Practice
- Current Events

EUROPE

1837 ◀ Queen Victoria comes to power in Great Britain.

1845 Ireland is struck by famine.

1859 Darwin publishes theory of evolution.

1815

1850

WORLD

1821 Mexico wins independence from Spain.

1857 ◀ Sepoy Mutiny challenges British rule in India. (native troops in Britain's East India Company)

310

TIME LINE DISCUSSION

Point out to students that this time line reflects a century of rising optimism throughout the world.

1. Ask students to identify three events that show a change in relationship between colony and colonizer. *(1821—Mexican independence from Spain; 1857—Sepoy Mutiny in India; 1867—Dominion of Canada formed)* Which of these events did not occur in North America? *(1857—Sepoy Mutiny in India)*
2. What event ushered in the Victorian Age? *(1837—Queen Victoria comes to power in Great Britain)*
3. Ask students to identify three feats of engineering *(1869—Suez Canal opens; 1889—Eiffel Tower completed; 1914—Panama Canal opens)*
4. When and where did women first achieve the right to vote? *(1893—New Zealand)* What does this action indicate about the government of New Zealand compared to that of Great Britain, its former parent? *(New Zealand's government was more liberal.)*

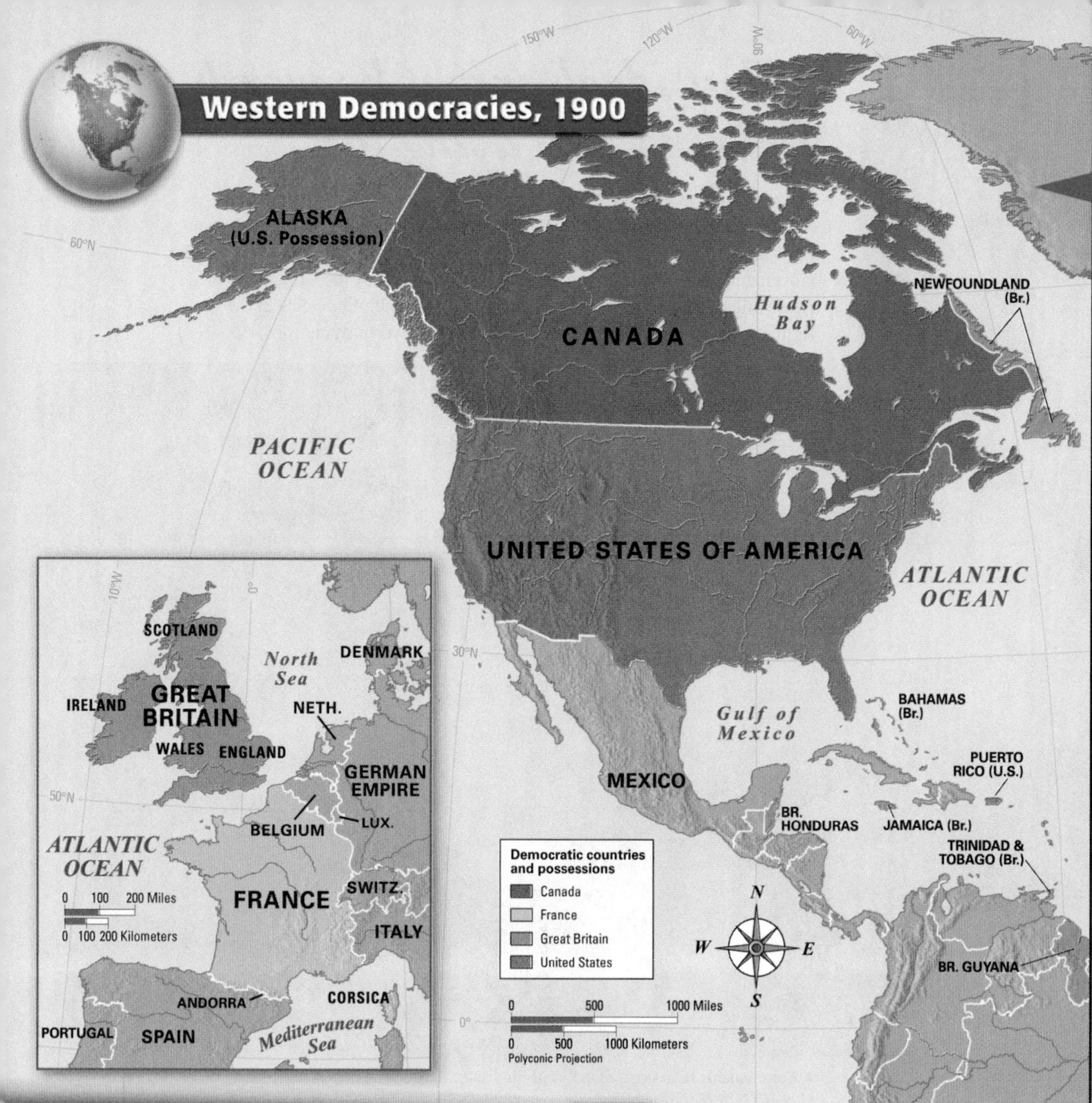

Western Democracies, 1900
150°W
120°W
90°W
60°W
60°N
30°N
0°
ALASKA
(U.S. Possession)
CANADA
Hudson
Bay
NEWFOUNDLAND
(Br.)
PACIFIC
OCEAN
UNITED STATES OF AMERICA
ATLANTIC
OCEAN
Gulf of
Mexico
BAHAMAS
(Br.)
PUERTO
RICO (U.S.)
MEXICO
BR.
HONDURAS
JAMAICA (Br.)
TRINIDAD &
TOBAGO (Br.)
BR. GUYANA
Democratic countries
and possessions
Canada
France
Great Britain
United States
N
S
E
W
0 500 1000 Miles
0 500 1000 Kilometers
Polyconic Projection
10°W
0°
50°N
SCOTLAND
North
Sea
DENMARK
IRELAND
GREAT
BRITAIN
NETH.
WALES
ENGLAND
GERMAN
EMPIRE
BELGIUM
LUX.
ATLANTIC
OCEAN
0 100 200 Miles
0 100 200 Kilometers
FRANCE
SWITZ.
ITALY
ANDORRA
CORSICA
PORTUGAL
SPAIN
Mediterranean
Sea

1871 Franco-Prussian War ends.

1889 Eiffel Tower is completed in Paris. ▶

1880

1915

1867 Dominion of Canada is formed.

1869 Suez Canal opens.

1893 New Zealand becomes first nation to allow women to vote.

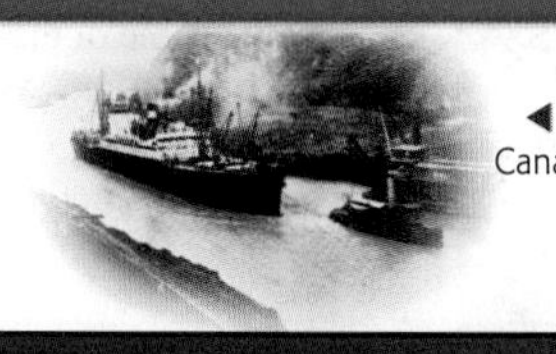

1914 ◀ Panama Canal opens.

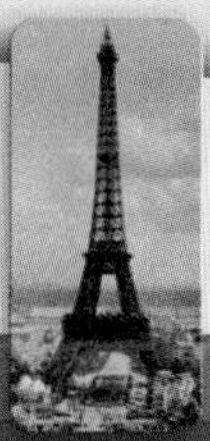

311

CHAPTER 10

History from Visuals

Interpreting the Map

Have students use the key to identify the location of democratic countries and possessions in 1900. Ask them what they have learned in previous chapters about similarities or connections among these countries. *(They shared similar values; they had been influenced by Enlightenment thinking; France and Britain had helped settle Canada and the United States; the American Revolution inspired the French Revolution.)* Why do they think so few Western nations were democratic in 1900? *(Possible Answer: Most had not had revolutions—rulers were too powerful or democratic traditions were too weak.)*

Extension Tell students that in this chapter, three major migrations are discussed: the movement of British convicts and others to Australia, the movement of settlers across the western United States, and the movement of thousands of Irish to the United States. Ask students if any of these movements affected their families or the families of anyone they know.

RECOMMENDED RESOURCES

Books for the Teacher

Holmquest, Harold J. ***Battle Maps of the Civil War.*** Las Cruces, NM: Yucca Tree Press, 2000. This atlas of battle sites identifies troop movements and describes battle strategies. The book is laid out in chronological order and includes a helpful index.

Schroeder, Paul W. ***The Transformation of European Politics, 1763–1848.*** New York: Oxford UP, 1994.

Books for the Student

McDougal Littell Literature Connections. Austen, Jane. ***Pride and Prejudice (with related readings).*** 1998. This story of courtship and marriage in 18th-century England is one of Jane Austen's best-loved novels.

Literature Connections
Pride and Prejudice
Jane Austen
and Related Readings

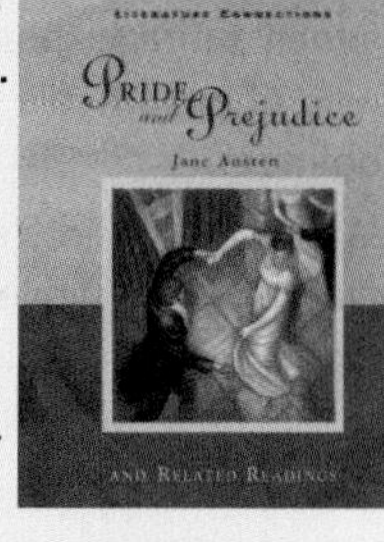

Erickson, Carolly. ***Her Little Majesty: The Life of Queen Victoria.*** New York, Simon & Schuster, 1997.

McDougal Littell Nextext. ***The Civil War.*** Presents key documents and memoirs from the period and offers literary perspectives on the times.

Videos and Software

The American Civil War: 1861–1865. CD-ROM. Films for the Humanities & Sciences. 800-257-5126.

Early Victorian London: 1837–1870. VHS and DVD. Films for the Humanities & Sciences. 800-257-5126.

Interact *with* History

Objectives

- Set the stage for studying the changes occurring during this period.
- Help students understand the issues involved in creating new forms of government.
- Help students connect with the people and events in this chapter.

EXAMINING *the* ISSUES

Possible Answers

- Some students might say that an unresponsive or corrupt government would move them to seek self-government.
- Some students may mention liberty, freedom, and justice as values worth fighting for.

Discussion

Ask students to discuss the ideals that inspired American and French revolutionaries. As they read this chapter, encourage them to think about whether the ideals that inspired people to action were similar or different.

Interact *with* History

What ideals might be worth fighting and dying for?

You are living in Paris in 1871. France is in a state of political upheaval following the Franco-Prussian War. When workers in Paris set up their own government, called the Paris Commune, French soldiers quickly stamp out the movement. Most of the Communards (the supporters of the Commune) are either killed or imprisoned. When your good friend Philippe dies in the fighting, you wonder whether self-government is worth dying for.

▲ Communards lie massacred in this painting titled *A Street in Paris in May 1871*, by Maximilien Luce.

EXAMINING *the* ISSUES

- **What might lead you to join a group seeking self-government?**
- **What ideals would you choose to help shape a new government?**

As a class, discuss these questions. During the discussion, think about some of the ideals that inspired American and French revolutionaries. As you read this chapter, consider the ideals that moved people to action. Also consider how people tried to change government to better reflect their ideals.

312 Chapter 10

WHY STUDY THE AGE OF DEMOCRACY AND PROGRESS?

- Britain and France are still important democracies.
- The woman suffrage movement was the beginning of a women's rights movement that continues.
- Canada, Australia, and New Zealand are strong democracies today, while Ireland is democratic but divided.
- Indigenous peoples of Australia and America have many contemporary issues in common.
- The civil-rights movements of African Americans and Hispanics are a legacy from this period.
- Many conveniences of modern life, including electric lights, telephones, and automobiles were invented during this period.

1

Activists for woman suffrage in London

Thomas Edison with phonograph

Democratic Reform and Activism

MAIN IDEA

POWER AND AUTHORITY Spurred by the demands of the people, Great Britain and France underwent democratic reforms.

WHY IT MATTERS NOW

During this period, Britain and France were transformed into the democracies they are today.

TERMS & NAMES

- suffrage
- Chartist movement
- Queen Victoria
- Third Republic
- Dreyfus affair
- anti-Semitism
- Zionism

SETTING THE STAGE Urbanization and industrialization brought sweeping changes to Western nations. People looking for solutions to the problems created by these developments began to demand reforms. They wanted to improve conditions for workers and the poor. Many people also began to call for political reforms. They demanded that more people be given a greater voice in government. Many different groups, including the middle class, workers, and women, argued that the right to vote be extended to groups that were excluded.

Britain Enacts Reforms

As Chapter 5 explained, Britain became a constitutional monarchy in the late 1600s. Under this system of government, the monarch serves as the head of state, but Parliament holds the real power. The British Parliament consists of a House of Lords and a House of Commons. Traditionally, members of the House of Lords either inherited their seats or were appointed. However, this changed in 1999, when legislation was passed that abolished the right of hereditary peers to inherit a seat in the House of Lords. Members of the House of Commons are elected by the British people.

In the early 1800s, the method of selecting the British government was not a true democracy. Only about five percent of the population had the right to elect the members of the House of Commons. Voting was limited to men who owned a substantial amount of land. Women could not vote at all. As a result, the upper classes ran the government.

The Reform Bill of 1832 The first group to demand a greater voice in politics was the wealthy middle class—factory owners, bankers, and merchants. Beginning in 1830, protests took place around England in favor of a bill in Parliament that would extend **suffrage**, or the right to vote. The Revolution of 1830 in France frightened parliamentary leaders. They feared that revolutionary violence would spread to Britain. Thus, Parliament passed the Reform Bill of 1832. This law eased the property requirements so that well-to-do men in the middle class could vote. The Reform Bill also modernized the districts for electing members of Parliament and gave the thriving new industrial cities more representation.

Chartist Movement Although the Reform Bill increased the number of British voters, only a small percentage of men were eligible to vote. A popular movement

CALIFORNIA STANDARDS

10.2.4 Explain how the ideology of the French Revolution led France to develop from constitutional monarchy to democratic despotism to the Napoleonic empire.

10.3.4 Trace the evolution of work and labor, including the demise of the slave trade and the effects of immigration, mining and manufacturing, division of labor, and the union movement.

CST 2 Students analyze how change happens at different rates at different times; understand that some aspects can change while others remain the same; and understand that change is complicated and affects not only technology and politics but also values and beliefs.

TAKING NOTES

Evaluating Courses of Action Use a chart to list and evaluate events in this section according to whether they expanded (+) or impeded (-) democracy.

Event	Evaluation

LESSON PLAN

OBJECTIVES

- Describe the evolution of British democracy.
- Explain the origin and goals of the woman suffrage movement.
- Trace the development of democratic institutions in France.

1 FOCUS & MOTIVATE

Ask students to name some groups in the United States that have fought for the right to vote. *(Possible Answers: women, African Americans, 18 year olds)*

2 INSTRUCT

Britain Enacts Reforms

10.3.4

Critical Thinking

- What was the major difference between the Reform Bill of 1832 and the Chartist movement? *(Reform Bill extended suffrage to wealthy middle class, Chartists wanted suffrage for all men)*

CALIFORNIA RESOURCES

California Reading Toolkit, p. L45
California Modified Lesson Plans for English Learners, p. 85
California Daily Standards Practice Transparencies, TT37
California Standards Enrichment Workbook, pp. 20–30, 39–40
California Standards Planner and Lesson Plans, p. L81
California Online Test Practice
California Test Generator CD-ROM
California Easy Planner CD-ROM
California eEdition CD-ROM

SECTION 1 PROGRAM RESOURCES

ALL STUDENTS

In-Depth Resources: Unit 3
- Guided Reading, p. 23
- History Makers: Emmeline Pankhurst, p. 40

Formal Assessment
- Section Quiz, p. 171

ENGLISH LEARNERS

In-Depth Resources in Spanish
- Guided Reading, p. 81

Reading Study Guide (Spanish), p. 105
Reading Study Guide Audio CD (Spanish)

STRUGGLING READERS

In-Depth Resources: Unit 3
- Guided Reading, p. 23
- Building Vocabulary, p. 27
- Reteaching Activity, p. 43

Reading Study Guide, p. 105
Reading Study Guide Audio CD

GIFTED AND TALENTED STUDENTS

In-Depth Resources: Unit 3
- Primary Source: from *Five Years of My Life, 1894–1899,* p. 31

Electronic Library of Primary Sources
- from *Prisons and Prisoners*

INTEGRATED TECHNOLOGY

eEdition CD-ROM
Voices from the Past Audio CD
Power Presentations CD-ROM
Electronic Library of Primary Sources
- from *Prisons and Prisoners*

classzone.com

History from Visuals

Interpreting Graphs

Point out that each reform bill added new groups to the voters' rolls. Which group was added in 1832? *(middle-class men)* 1867? *(working-class men)* 1884? *(rural men)*

Extension Ask students how a bill to raise working-class wages might have fared in Parliament—based on who was allowed to vote—if the bill had been introduced in 1832, 1867, or 1918. *(Probably would have been defeated in 1832, gotten more votes in 1867, and had a chance of passing in 1918.)*

SKILLBUILDER Answers

1. **Clarifying** 7 percent
2. **Comparing** 21 percent

History Makers

Queen Victoria and Prince Albert

Ask students how long Queen Victoria was in mourning for Prince Albert. *(about 40 years)* The image of Victoria as stern comes mainly from her later years. As a young queen, she was lively. Ask students to compare Queen Victoria to Elizabeth I and Elizabeth II, other important English queens.

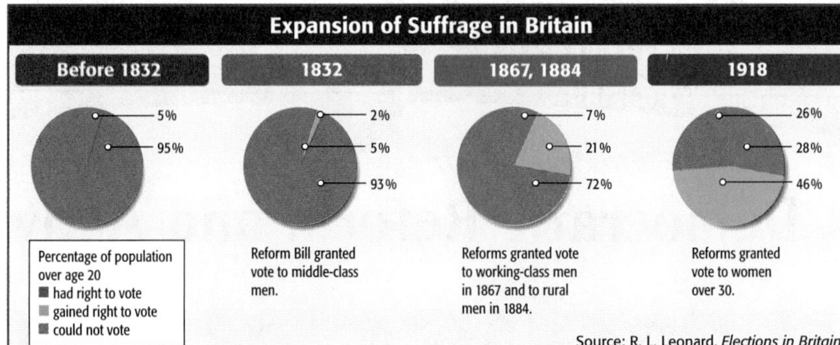

SKILLBUILDER: Interpreting Graphs

1. **Clarifying** *What percentage of the adults in Britain could vote in 1832?*
2. **Comparing** *By how much did the percentage of voters increase after the reforms of 1867 and 1884?*

arose among the workers and other groups who still could not vote to press for more rights. It was called the **Chartist movement** because the group first presented its demands to Parliament in a petition called The People's Charter of 1838.

The People's Charter called for suffrage for all men and annual Parliamentary elections. It also proposed to reform Parliament in other ways. In Britain at the time, eligible men voted openly. Since their vote was not secret, they could feel pressure to vote in a certain way. Members of Parliament had to own land and received no salary, so they needed to be wealthy. The Chartists wanted to make Parliament responsive to the lower classes. To do this, they demanded a secret ballot, an end to property requirements for serving in Parliament, and pay for members of Parliament.

Parliament rejected the Chartists' demands. However, their protests convinced many people that the workers had valid complaints. Over the years, workers continued to press for political reform, and Parliament responded. It gave the vote to working-class men in 1867 and to male rural workers in 1884. After 1884, most adult males in Britain had the right to vote. By the early 1900s, all the demands of the Chartists, except for annual elections, became law. (A)

The Victorian Age The figure who presided over all this historic change was **Queen Victoria**. Victoria came to the throne in 1837 at the age of 18. She was queen for nearly 64 years. During the Victorian Age, the British Empire reached the height of its wealth and power. Victoria was popular with her subjects, and she performed her duties capably. However, she was forced to accept a less powerful role for the monarchy.

The kings who preceded Victoria in the 1700s and 1800s had exercised great influence over Parliament. The spread of democracy in the 1800s shifted political power almost completely to Parliament, and especially to the elected House of Commons. Now the government was completely run by the prime minister and the cabinet.

History Makers

Queen Victoria and Prince Albert

About two years after her coronation, Queen Victoria (1819–1901) fell in love with her cousin Albert (1819–1861), a German prince. She proposed to him and they were married in 1840. Together they had nine children. Prince Albert established a tone of politeness and correct behavior at court, and the royal couple presented a picture of loving family life that became a British ideal.

After Albert died in 1861, the queen wore black silk for the rest of her life in mourning. She once said of Albert, "Without him everything loses its interest."

MAIN IDEA

Making Inferences

(A) Why do you think the Chartists demanded a secret ballot rather than public voting?

A. Possible Answers allowed people to vote their conscience, made voters less subject to intimidation, reduced power of bribery

DIFFERENTIATING INSTRUCTION: STRUGGLING READERS

Creating Campaign Materials

Class Time 40 minutes

Task Creating campaign materials for and against the Chartist movement

Purpose To clarify political issues in Great Britain in the 1800s; to improve persuasive writing and speaking skills

Instructions Divide students into small groups. Groups should work together to create posters, leaflets, and slogans for and against the principles of the Chartist movement.

Groups should represent the views of workers, the wealthy middle class, women, and the upper class. They may focus on individual issues such as expansion of suffrage, reform of Parliament, or secret balloting. Encourage students to reread the text under "Britain Enacts Reforms" and to use dictionaries or glossaries if needed. When groups are finished, each can display its materials and explain its viewpoint.

Students who need more help with the text should complete the Guided Reading activity for this section.

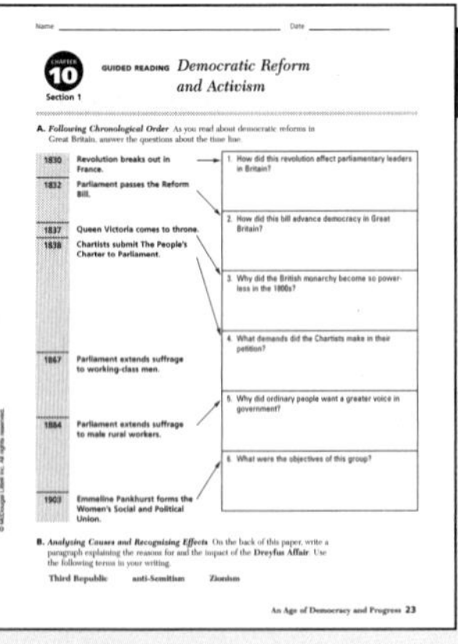

In-Depth Resources: Unit 3

Women Get the Vote

By 1890, several industrial countries had universal male suffrage (the right of all men to vote). No country, however, allowed women to vote. As more men gained suffrage, more women demanded the same.

Organization and Resistance During the 1800s, women in both Great Britain and the United States worked to gain the right to vote. British women organized reform societies and protested unfair laws and customs. As women became more vocal, however, resistance to their demands grew. Many people, both men and women, thought that woman suffrage was too radical a break with tradition. Some claimed that women lacked the ability to take part in politics.

Militant Protests After decades of peaceful efforts to win the right to vote, some women took more drastic steps. In Britain, Emmeline Pankhurst formed the Women's Social and Political Union (WSPU) in 1903. The WSPU became the most militant organization for women's rights. Its goal was to draw attention to the cause of woman suffrage. When asked about why her group chose militant means to gain women's rights, Pankhurst replied:

Global Impact

The Women's Movement

By the 1880s, women were working internationally to win more rights. In 1888, women activists from the United States, Canada, and Europe met in Washington, D.C., for the International Council of Women. In 1893, delegates and observers from many countries attended a large congress of women in Chicago. They came from lands as far apart as New Zealand, Argentina, Iceland, Persia, and China.

The first countries to grant suffrage to women were New Zealand (1893) and Australia (1902). Only in two European countries—Finland (1906, then part of the Russian Empire) and Norway (1913)—did women gain voting rights before World War I. In the United States, the territory of Wyoming allowed women to vote in 1869. Several other Western states followed suit.

PRIMARY SOURCE

I want to say here and now that the only justification for violence, the only justification for damage to property, the only justification for risk to the comfort of other human beings is the fact that you have tried all other available means and have failed to secure justice.

EMMELINE PANKHURST, *Why We Are Militant*

B. Answer The success of the militant group was not achieved until the end of World War I but it did call attention to their goals.

MAIN IDEA

Analyzing Motives

B Was the use of militant action effective in achieving the goal of woman suffrage? Explain.

Emmeline Pankhurst, her daughters Christabel and Sylvia, and other WSPU members were arrested and imprisoned many times. When they were jailed, the Pankhursts led hunger strikes to keep their cause in the public eye. British officials force-fed Sylvia and other activists to keep them alive.

Though the woman suffrage movement gained attention between 1880 and 1914, its successes were gradual. Women did not gain the right to vote in national elections in Great Britain and the United States until after World War I. B

France and Democracy

While Great Britain moved toward greater democracy in the late 1800s, democracy finally took hold in France.

The Third Republic In the aftermath of the Franco-Prussian War, France went through a series of crises. Between 1871 and 1914, France averaged a change of government almost yearly. A dozen political parties competed for power. Not until 1875 could the National Assembly agree on a new government. Eventually, the members voted to set up a republic. The **Third Republic** lasted over 60 years. However, France remained divided.

The Dreyfus Affair During the 1880s and 1890s, the Third Republic was threatened by monarchists, aristocrats, clergy, and army leaders. These groups wanted a monarchy or military rule. A controversy known as the **Dreyfus affair** became a battleground for these opposing forces. Widespread feelings of **anti-Semitism**, or prejudice against Jews, also played a role in this scandal.

Global Impact

The Women's Movement

American activist Lucretia Mott was one of those who thought that universal woman suffrage was too radical a demand. She argued against it in 1848, thinking it would discredit the fledgling women's rights movement and expose it to ridicule.

Electronic Library of Primary Sources

- from *Prisons and Prisoners*

Women Get the Vote

10.3.4

Critical Thinking

- Why did the idea of woman suffrage seem radical in the Victorian era? *(Possible Answer: Women's roles were seen as limited to home and family.)*
- How might militant tactics have hurt the cause of woman suffrage? *(Possible Answer: Violent protest might reinforce the idea that women lacked the ability to participate in politics.)*

France and Democracy

10.2.4

Critical Thinking

- How would you characterize the groups who opposed the Third Republic? *(Possible Answer: privileged classes who opposed democratic government)*
- Why was there an increase in immigration by Eastern European Jews to the United States in the late 19th century? *(They were persecuted in their home countries.)*

DIFFERENTIATING INSTRUCTION: GIFTED AND TALENTED STUDENTS

Analyzing Primary and Secondary Sources

Class Time 30 minutes

Task Reading primary and secondary source material and creating a display board

Purpose To deepen understanding of the woman suffrage movement in Britain

Instructions Have students complete the History Makers activity on Emmeline Pankhurst in the In-Depth Resources book, p. 40. Then have them use library sources or the Internet to find examples of Pankhurst's own writings or of other primary sources on the woman suffrage movement in Britain. Encourage students to research each side of the debate over woman suffrage. Sources might include contemporary news articles, pamphlets, letters, or speeches in Parliament.

Ask students to create a display board, including a brief synopsis of their research and quotations from their sources, along with photos or drawings as appropriate.

In-Depth Resources: Unit 3

More About . . .

The Dreyfus Affair

Even after the forgeries used to convict Dreyfus were exposed, the army refused to admit any error. Under pressure, it tried Dreyfus again, and again found him guilty. But this time the government pardoned Dreyfus for a crime he had never committed. Gifted students may want to read the primary source and summarize it for the class.

In-Depth Resources: Unit 3

- Primary Source: from *Five Years of My Life, 1894–1899,* p. 31

Tip for Struggling Readers

Explain that Zion is another name for Israel, the Jewish homeland.

▲ *Zola Under Attack,* painted in 1898 by Henry de Groux, shows Émile Zola surrounded by an anti-Semitic mob.

In 1894, Captain Alfred Dreyfus, one of the few Jewish officers in the French army, was accused of selling military secrets to Germany. A court found him guilty, based on false evidence, and sentenced him to life in prison. In a few years, new evidence showed that Dreyfus had been framed by other army officers.

Public opinion was sharply divided over the scandal. Many army leaders, nationalists, leaders in the clergy, and anti-Jewish groups refused to let the case be reopened. They feared sudden action would cast doubt on the honor of the army. Dreyfus's defenders insisted that justice was more important. In 1898, the writer Émile Zola published an open letter titled *J'accuse!* (I accuse) in a popular French newspaper. In the letter, Zola denounced the army for covering up a scandal. Zola was sentenced to a year in prison for his views, but his letter gave strength to Dreyfus's cause. Eventually, the French government declared his innocence.

The Rise of Zionism The Dreyfus case showed the strength of anti-Semitism in France and other parts of Western Europe. However, persecution of Jews was even more severe in Eastern Europe. Russian officials permitted pogroms (puh•GRAHMS), organized campaigns of violence against Jews. From the late 1880s on, thousands of Jews fled Eastern Europe. Many headed for the United States.

For many Jews, the long history of exile and persecution convinced them to work for a homeland in Palestine. In the 1890s, a movement known as **Zionism** developed to pursue this goal. Its leader was Theodor Herzl (HEHRT•suhl), a writer in Vienna. It took many years, however, before the state of Israel was established.

SECTION 1 ASSESSMENT

TERMS & NAMES 1. For each term or name, write a sentence explaining its significance.
• suffrage • Chartist movement • Queen Victoria • Third Republic • Dreyfus affair • anti-Semitism • Zionism

USING YOUR NOTES

2. Which of these events most expanded democracy, and why? (10.2.4)

Event	Evaluation

MAIN IDEAS

3. What were some effects of the Reform Bill of 1832? (10.3.4)
4. What was the goal of the WSPU in Britain? (10.3.4)
5. What was the Dreyfus affair? (10.2.4)

CRITICAL THINKING & WRITING

6. **COMPARING** Why was the road to democracy more difficult for France than for England? (10.2.4)
7. **SYNTHESIZING** Look again at the primary source on page 315. What is Pankhurst demanding? (CST 2)
8. **RECOGNIZING EFFECTS** What was the connection between anti-Semitism and Zionism? (CST 2)
9. **WRITING ACTIVITY** POWER AND AUTHORITY Among the Chartists' demands was pay for members of Parliament. Write a **letter to the editor** that supports or criticizes a pay raise for your legislators. (Writing 2.5.c)

CONNECT TO TODAY CREATING A POSTER

Find information on issues in today's world that involve a call for social justice. Then make a **poster** in which you illustrate what you regard as the most compelling example of a current social injustice. (10.3.4)

3 ASSESS

SECTION 1 ASSESSMENT

Have students work through the questions independently and then trade papers with a partner.

Formal Assessment

- Section Quiz, p. 171

4 RETEACH

Use the Reteaching Activity to review this section.

In-Depth Resources: Unit 3

- Reteaching Activity, p. 43

ANSWERS

1. suffrage, p. 313 • Chartist movement, p. 314 • Queen Victoria, p. 314 • Third Republic, p. 315 • Dreyfus affair, p. 315 • anti-Semitism, p. 315 • Zionism, p. 316
2. **Sample Answer:** Britain gradually extends suffrage to most adult males; important because government became more representative. Women in many countries demand the right to vote; greatest expansion of democracy because half the population of the planet is female. Dreyfus Affair in France; important because related to anti-Semitism and Zionism.
3. eased property requirements to vote; modernized electoral districts; gave industrial cities more representation
4. to draw attention to the cause of woman suffrage
5. Dreyfus was falsely accused and sentenced to prison for spying. It showed the strength of anti-Semitism in Europe.
6. France experienced a series of political and social crises that made a stable democracy difficult to achieve.
7. justice
8. Prejudice against Jews led to work for a Jewish homeland.
9. **Rubric** Letters should
   - support opinions with reasons.
   - use standard grammar and punctuation.

CONNECT TO TODAY

Rubric Posters should include
- at least one visual.
- slogans or captions.

Activists for woman suffrage in London

Thomas Edison with phonograph

Self-Rule for British Colonies

MAIN IDEA

EMPIRE BUILDING Britain allowed self-rule in Canada, Australia, and New Zealand but delayed it for Ireland.

WHY IT MATTERS NOW

Canada, Australia, and New Zealand are strong democracies today, while Ireland is divided.

TERMS & NAMES

- dominion
- Maori
- Aborigine
- penal colony
- home rule
- Irish Republican Army

SETTING THE STAGE By 1800, Great Britain had colonies around the world. These included outposts in Africa and Asia. In these areas, the British managed trade with the local peoples, but they had little influence over the population at large. In the colonies of Canada, Australia, and New Zealand, on the other hand, European colonists dominated the native populations. As Britain industrialized and prospered in the 1800s, so did these colonies. Some were becoming strong enough to stand on their own.

Canada Struggles for Self-Rule

Canada was originally home to many Native American peoples. The first European country to colonize Canada was France. The earliest French colonists, in the 1600s and 1700s, had included many fur trappers and missionaries. They tended to live among the Native Americans. Some French intermarried with Native Americans.

Great Britain took possession of the country in 1763 after it defeated France in the French and Indian War. The French who remained lived mostly in the lower St. Lawrence Valley. Many English-speaking colonists arrived in Canada after it came under British rule. Some came from Great Britain, and others were Americans who had stayed loyal to Britain after the American Revolution. They settled separately from the French along the Atlantic seaboard and the Great Lakes.

French and English Canada Religious and cultural differences between the mostly Roman Catholic French and the mainly Protestant English-speaking colonists caused conflict in Canada. Both groups pressed Britain for a greater voice in governing their own affairs. In 1791 the British Parliament tried to resolve both issues by creating two new Canadian provinces. Upper Canada (now Ontario) had an English-speaking majority. Lower Canada (now Quebec) had a French-speaking majority. Each province had its own elected assembly.

The Durham Report The division of Upper and Lower Canada temporarily eased tensions. In both colonies, the royal governor and a small group of wealthy British held most of the power. But during the early 1800s, middle-class professionals in both colonies began to demand political and economic reforms. In Lower Canada, these demands were also fueled by French resentment toward British rule. In the late 1830s, rebellions broke out in both Upper and Lower

CALIFORNIA STANDARDS

10.4.2 Discuss the locations of the colonial rule of such nations as England, France, Germany, Italy, Japan, the Netherlands, Russia, Spain, Portugal, and the United States.

CST 1 Students compare the present with the past, evaluating the consequences of past events and decisions and determining the lessons that were learned.

CST 4 Students relate current events to the physical and human characteristics of places and regions.

REP 2 Students identify bias and prejudice in historical interpretations.

REP 3 Students evaluate major debates among historians concerning alternative interpretations of the past, including an analysis of authors' use of evidence and the distinctions between sound generalizations and misleading oversimplifications.

TAKING NOTES

Comparing Use a chart to compare progress toward self-rule by recording significant events.

Country	Political Events
Canada	
Australia	
New Zealand	
Ireland	

LESSON PLAN

OBJECTIVES

- Describe how Canada achieved self-rule.
- Explain how Australia and New Zealand became democracies.
- Describe British domination of Ireland.

1 FOCUS & MOTIVATE

Ask students what they know about the relationship between Great Britain and Ireland today. *(Possible Answers: Northern Ireland is part of United Kingdom; Republic of Ireland is independent; all are part of the European Union.)*

2 INSTRUCT

Canada Struggles for Self-Rule

10.4.2

Critical Thinking

- How was Canada's relationship to Great Britain different from the U.S. relationship? *(United States not part of British Empire)*

CALIFORNIA RESOURCES

California Reading Toolkit, p. L46
California Modified Lesson Plans for English Learners, p. 87
California Daily Standards Practice Transparencies, TT38
California Standards Enrichment Workbook, pp. 49–50
California Standards Planner and Lesson Plans, p. L83
California Online Test Practice
California Test Generator CD-ROM
California Easy Planner CD-ROM
California eEdition CD-ROM

SECTION 2 PROGRAM RESOURCES

ALL STUDENTS

In-Depth Resources: Unit 3
- Guided Reading, p. 24
- Geography Application: The British Settle Australia and New Zealand, p. 29

Formal Assessment
- Section Quiz, p. 172

ENGLISH LEARNERS

In-Depth Resources in Spanish
- Guided Reading, p. 82
- Geography Application, p. 86

Reading Study Guide (Spanish), p. 107
Reading Study Guide Audio CD (Spanish)

STRUGGLING READERS

In-Depth Resources: Unit 3
- Guided Reading, p. 24
- Building Vocabulary, p. 27
- Reteaching Activity, p. 44

Reading Study Guide, p. 107
Reading Study Guide Audio CD

GIFTED AND TALENTED STUDENTS

In-Depth Resources: Unit 3
- Primary Source: Irish Petition to Emigrate, p. 32
- Literature: "Easter 1916," p. 35

Electronic Library of Primary Sources

INTEGRATED TECHNOLOGY

eEdition CD-ROM
Power Presentations CD-ROM
Geography Transparencies
- GT26 Canada: Growth of the Dominion

World Art and Cultures Transparencies
- AT57 Maori pigment container

Electronic Library of Primary Sources
Patterns of Interaction Video Series
- *The Geography of Food*

classzone.com

History *in* Depth

Acadians to Cajuns

The exile of the Acadians was described in Henry Wadsworth Longfellow's poem "Evangeline," published in 1847. The poem sparked renewed historical debate about the reasons behind the British expulsion of the Acadians. Like Evangeline, many Acadians wandered for years searching for friends and family throughout the British colonies.

Geography Transparencies

- GT26 Canada: Growth of the Dominion, 1867–Present

Australia and New Zealand

10.4.2

Critical Thinking

- How were the political reforms pioneered in Australia and New Zealand related to democratic reform in Great Britain? *(Secret ballot was a goal of the Chartist movement; woman suffrage occurred earlier in New Zealand than in Great Britain.)*
- How were the fates of Aborigines and Maori similar to that of indigenous peoples in the United States? *(All were conquered by European disease and weapons; lost land to white settlers.)*

More About . . .

Settlement of Australia

Every convict who got discharged in Australia for good behavior received 30 acres of land—50 acres if he was married, 10 more acres for each child. Descendants of some convicts ended up as major landowners.

History *in* Depth

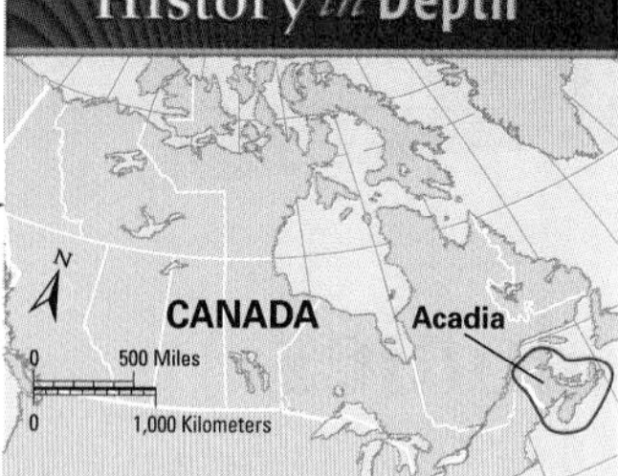

Acadians to Cajuns

Colonists from France founded the colony of Acadia on the eastern coast of what is now Canada in 1604. Tensions flared between these settlers and later arrivals from England and Scotland.

In 1713, the British gained control of Acadia and renamed it Nova Scotia (New Scotland). They expelled thousands of descendants of the original Acadians. Many eventually settled in southern Louisiana. Today, their culture still thrives in the Mississippi Delta area, where the people are called Cajuns (an alteration of Acadian).

Canada. The British Parliament sent a reform-minded statesman, Lord Durham, to investigate.

In 1839, Durham sent a report to Parliament that urged two major reforms. First, Upper and Lower Canada should be reunited as the Province of Canada, and British immigration should be encouraged. In this way, the French would slowly become part of the dominant English culture. Second, colonists in the provinces of Canada should be allowed to govern themselves in domestic matters. **A**

MAIN IDEA

Recognizing Effects

A How do you think Durham's report affected French-speaking Canadians?

A. Possible Answer They were subjected to greater influence of English-speaking majority, became smaller minority; all Canadians, including French, gained greater self-rule from Britain.

The Dominion of Canada By the mid-1800s, many Canadians believed that Canada needed a central government. A central government would be better able to protect the interests of Canadians against the United States, whose territory now extended from the Atlantic to the Pacific oceans. In 1867, Nova Scotia and New Brunswick joined the Province of Canada to form the Dominion of Canada. As a **dominion**, Canada was self-governing in domestic affairs but remained part of the British Empire.

Canada's Westward Expansion Canada's first prime minister, John MacDonald, expanded Canada westward by purchasing lands and persuading frontier territories to join the union. Canada stretched to the Pacific Ocean by 1871. MacDonald began the construction of a transcontinental railroad, completed in 1885.

Australia and New Zealand

The British sea captain James Cook claimed New Zealand in 1769 and part of Australia in 1770 for Great Britain. Both lands were already inhabited. In New Zealand, Cook was greeted by the **Maori**, a Polynesian people who had settled in New Zealand around A.D. 800. Maori culture was based on farming, hunting, and fishing.

When Cook reached Australia, he considered the land uninhabited. In fact, Australia was sparsely populated by **Aborigines**, as Europeans later called the native peoples. Aborigines are the longest ongoing culture in the world. These nomadic peoples fished, hunted, and gathered food.

Britain's Penal Colony Britain began colonizing Australia in 1788 with convicted criminals. The prisons in England were severely overcrowded. To solve this problem, the British government established a penal colony in Australia. A **penal colony** was a place where convicts were sent to serve their sentences. Many European nations used penal colonies as a way to prevent overcrowding of prisons. After their release, the newly freed prisoners could buy land and settle.

Free Settlers Arrive Free British settlers eventually joined the former convicts in both Australia and New Zealand. In the early 1800s, an Australian settler experimented with breeds of sheep until he found one that produced high quality wool and thrived in the country's warm, dry weather. Although sheep are not native to Australia, the raising and exporting of wool became its biggest business.

To encourage immigration, the government offered settlers cheap land. The population grew steadily in the early 1800s and then skyrocketed after a gold rush in 1851. The scattered settlements on Australia's east coast grew into separate colonies. Meanwhile, a few pioneers pushed westward across the vast dry interior and established outposts in western Australia.

DIFFERENTIATING INSTRUCTION: GIFTED AND TALENTED STUDENTS

Indigenous Peoples of Australia and New Zealand

Class Time 45 minutes

Task Researching and preparing an informal oral report

Purpose To appreciate the culture of Aborigines and Maori

Instructions Show transparency AT57 of the Maori pigment container. Explain to students that until the early 20th century, the Maori followed the age-old practice of tattooing their bodies. The pigments used for tattooing were kept in small containers such as this one, decorated with pieces of haliotis shell. Only seven Maori pigment containers are known to exist.

Encourage students to research the art, customs, and current situation of Aborigines and Maori in Australia and New Zealand. Students might search for articles in periodicals such as *National Geographic* or find books on the history and culture of these two groups. Students may be especially interested in the Aboriginal idea of the "Dream Time," Aboriginal dot art, and Maori woodwork. Ask them to try to see the world from an Aboriginal or Maori point of view. Students can prepare a brief, informal oral report for the class. Reports should focus on one aspect of Maori or Aboriginal culture and be well organized.

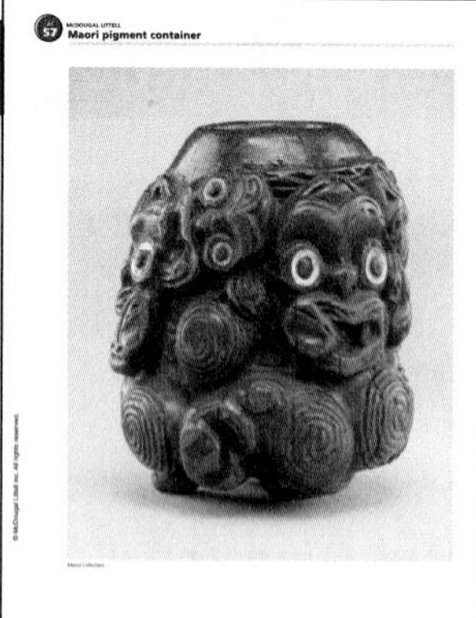

World Art and Cultures Transparencies

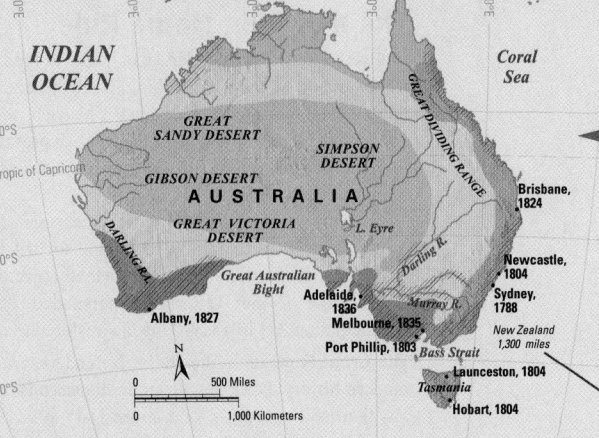

Australia and New Zealand to 1848

INTERACTIVE

Climate Regions
- Desert
- Grassland
- Mediterranean
- Rain forest
- Savanna
- Woodlands
- Densest Aborigine or Maori populations, around 1770
- • Date of European settlement

NEW ZEALAND: Tasman Sea; Russell, 1829; Auckland, 1840; New Plymouth, 1841; North I.; Nelson, 1841; Wellington, 1840; South I.; PACIFIC OCEAN; Dunedin, 1848; 0 200 Miles; 0 500 Kilometers; 170°E; 40°S

INDIAN OCEAN; Coral Sea; GREAT SANDY DESERT; SIMPSON DESERT; GIBSON DESERT; AUSTRALIA; GREAT VICTORIA DESERT; GREAT DIVIDING RANGE; DARLING RA.; L. Eyre; Darling R.; Murray R.; Great Australian Bight; Tropic of Capricorn; Brisbane, 1824; Newcastle, 1804; Sydney, 1788; Adelaide, 1836; Melbourne, 1835; Port Phillip, 1803; Albany, 1827; Bass Strait; Launceston, 1804; Tasmania; Hobart, 1804; New Zealand 1,300 miles; 0 500 Miles; 0 1,000 Kilometers; 110°E; 120°E; 130°E; 140°E; 150°E; 20°S; 30°S; 40°S

GEOGRAPHY SKILLBUILDER: Interpreting Maps
1. **Region** *What sort of climate region is found along the eastern coast of Australia?*
2. **Region** *What regions of Australia and New Zealand were most densely inhabited by native peoples?*

Settling New Zealand European settlement of New Zealand grew more slowly. This was because Britain did not claim ownership of New Zealand, as it did Australia. Rather, it recognized the land rights of the Maori. In 1814, missionary groups began arriving from Australia seeking to convert the Maori to Christianity.

The arrival of more foreigners stirred conflicts between the Maori and the European settlers over land. Responding to the settlers' pleas, the British decided to annex New Zealand in 1839 and appointed a governor to negotiate with the Maori. In a treaty signed in 1840, the Maori accepted British rule in exchange for recognition of their land rights.

Self-Government Like Canadians, the colonists of Australia and New Zealand wanted to rule themselves yet remain in the British Empire. During the 1850s, the colonies in both Australia and New Zealand became self-governing and created parliamentary forms of government. In 1901, the Australian colonies were united under a federal constitution as the Commonwealth of Australia. During the early 1900s, both Australia and New Zealand became dominions.

The people of Australia and New Zealand pioneered a number of political reforms. For example, the secret ballot, sometimes called the Australian ballot, was first used in Australia in the 1850s. In 1893, New Zealand became the first nation in the world to give full voting rights to women. However, only white women gained these rights.

▼ This photograph shows a Maori warrior with traditional dress and face markings.

Status of Native Peoples Native peoples and other non-Europeans were excluded from democracy and prosperity. Diseases brought by the Europeans killed Aborigines and Maori. As Australian settlement grew, the colonists displaced or killed many Aborigines.

In New Zealand, tensions between settlers and Maori continued to grow after it became a British colony. Between 1845 and 1872, the colonial government fought the Maori in a series of wars. Reduced by disease and outgunned by British weapons, the Maori were finally driven into a remote part of the country. (B)

B. Possible Answer Britain considered Australia uninhabited and claimed ownership, whereas it recognized land rights of Maoris.

MAIN IDEA
Contrasting
(B) How did the colonial settlement of Australia and New Zealand differ?

History from Visuals

Interpreting the Map

Ask students what the different colors on the map represent. *(climate zones)* In which climate zones did Europeans mainly settle? *(Mediterranean and woodlands)*

Extension Have students compare these maps to modern ones to see if the population patterns continued as shown here. Which is the most sparsely populated part of modern Australia? *(the central desert area)*

SKILLBUILDER Answers
1. **Region** woodlands
2. **Region** Australia—coastal regions of the northeast, northwest, southeast, and southwest; New Zealand—North Island

INTEGRATED TECHNOLOGY

Interactive An interactive version of this map is available on the eEdition.

More About . . .

The Australian Ballot

The secret ballot was just one of several political reforms introduced in the Australian provinces of Victoria and South Australia, where the cities of Melbourne and Adelaide are located. South Australia encouraged settlement by free Britons. It was known for religious toleration and formally separated church and state in the 1850s.

DIFFERENTIATING INSTRUCTION: ENGLISH LEARNERS

The British Settle Australia and New Zealand

Class Time 20 minutes

Task Reading, studying a map, and answering questions

Purpose To better understand British colonization in Australia and New Zealand

Instructions Use the Geography Application activity (also available in Spanish) to help students visually trace the route of British colonization and answer questions based on their reading and study of the map.

Combine the questions from the activity with these additional questions that require students to combine information on the ancillary with the map in the textbook.

1. What city is located where the First Fleet landed? *(Sydney)*
2. Where did the British settle later? *(Port Phillip, Newcastle, Albany, Melbourne, Adelaide)*
3. Which of these cities did free settlers colonize? *(Melbourne and Adelaide in the 1830s)*
4. How far did escaped convicts have to travel to reach New Zealand? *(1,300 miles)*

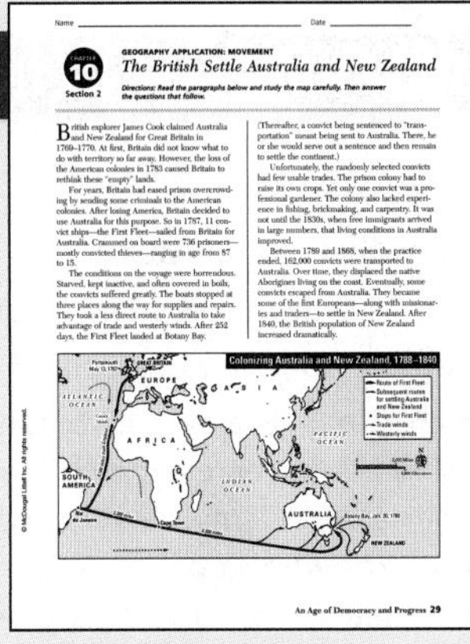

GEOGRAPHY APPLICATION: MOVEMENT
The British Settle Australia and New Zealand
Colonizing Australia and New Zealand, 1788–1840

In-Depth Resources: Unit 3

The Irish Win Home Rule
10.4.2

Critical Thinking

- Why did English laws for Ireland focus on religious differences in the 1500s and 1600s? *(After the Reformation, England became Protestant while Ireland remained Catholic.)*
- Why might Britain have been more reluctant to grant home rule to Ireland than to its other colonies? *(Possible Answer: because of Catholic majority and because it was closer to England)*

Analyzing Primary Sources

Starvation in Ireland

Ask students how the larger graph is related to the smaller one. *(Smaller graph gives a breakdown of the 18 percent who emigrated, showing where they went.)*

Answers to Document-Based Questions

1. **Determining Main Ideas** It resulted in mass starvation and disease.
2. **Clarifying** They decided to emigrate and seek a better life somewhere else.
3. **Comparing** United States

Electronic Library of Primary Sources

- "The Irish Potato Famine"

In-Depth Resources: Unit 3

- Primary Source: from Irish Petition to Emigrate, p. 32

The Irish Win Home Rule

English expansion into Ireland had begun in the 1100s, when the pope granted control of Ireland to the English king. English knights invaded Ireland, and many settled there to form a new aristocracy. The Irish, who had their own ancestry, culture, and language, bitterly resented the English presence. Laws imposed by the English in the 1500s and 1600s limited the rights of Catholics and favored the Protestant religion and the English language.

Over the years, the British government was determined to maintain its control over Ireland. It formally joined Ireland to Britain in 1801. Though a setback for Irish nationalism, this move gave Ireland representation in the British Parliament. Irish leader Daniel O'Connell persuaded Parliament to pass the Catholic Emancipation Act in 1829. This law restored many rights to Catholics.

The Great Famine In the 1840s, Ireland experienced one of the worst famines of modern history. For many years, Irish peasants had depended on potatoes as virtually their sole source of food. From 1845 to 1848, a plant fungus ruined nearly all of Ireland's potato crop. Out of a population of 8 million, about a million people died from starvation and disease over the next few years.

During the famine years, about a million and a half people fled from Ireland. Most went to the United States; others went to Britain, Canada, and Australia. At home, in Ireland, the British government enforced the demands of the English landowners that the Irish peasants pay their rent. Many Irish lost their land and fell hopelessly in debt, while large landowners profited from higher food prices.

Demands for Home Rule During the second half of the 1800s, opposition to British rule over Ireland took two forms. Some Irish wanted independence for Ireland. A greater number of Irish preferred **home rule**, local control over internal

Analyzing Primary Sources

Starvation in Ireland

A traveler described what he saw on a journey through Ireland in 1847:

PRIMARY SOURCE

> We entered a cabin. Stretched in one dark corner, scarcely visible, from the smoke and rags that covered them, were three children huddled together, lying there because they were too weak to rise, pale and ghastly, their little limbs—on removing a portion of the filthy covering—perfectly emaciated, eyes sunk, voice gone, and evidently in the last stage of actual starvation.
>
> **WILLIAM BENNETT,** quoted in *Narrative of a Recent Journey of Six Weeks in Ireland*

DOCUMENT-BASED QUESTIONS

1. **Determining Main Ideas** *What was the effect of the destruction of Ireland's potato crop on the population of Ireland?*
2. **Clarifying** *How did 18 percent of the population deal with the famine?*
3. **Comparing** *Which country received the most Irish emigrants?*

The Great Famine, 1845–1851

Fate of the Irish during the famine:

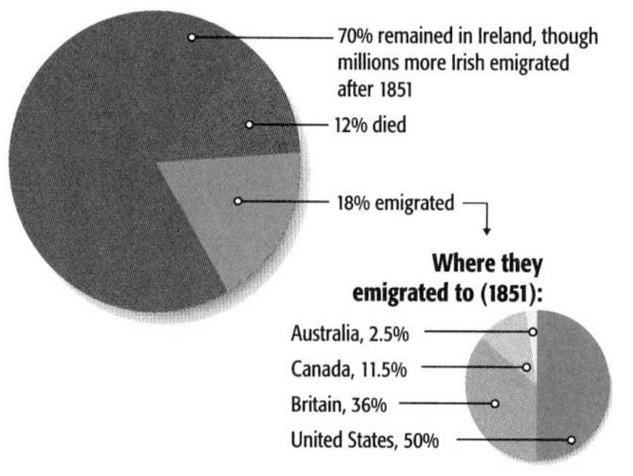

Sources: R. F. Foster, *Modern Ireland, 1600–1972;* D. Fitzpatrick, *Irish Emigration, 1804–1921*

DIFFERENTIATING INSTRUCTION: STRUGGLING READERS

Causes and Effects of the Great Famine

Class Time 20 minutes

Task Viewing a video and creating a chart

Purpose To better understand the Irish potato famine

Instructions Explain that before the famine the average Irish adult ate an estimated 9 to 14 pounds of potatoes a day. Have students view the video *The Geography of Food: The Impact of Potatoes and Sugar,* taking notes as they watch. Then ask small groups to create a cause-and-effect chart (using Critical Thinking Transparency CT75 as a model) showing the contributing factors that led to the famine and its effects on Irish and U.S. history.

Discuss how a single disaster such as the potato famine can have multiple causes and effects. How would Irish history have been different if the famine had been dealt with at the outset? *(Possible Answers: Population decline would have been minimized; relations between Irish and British might have been better.)* What would have been the effect on Irish emigration to the United States? *(Fewer people would have emigrated, affecting urbanization, labor force, politics, and the growth of Catholicism in the United States.)*

Patterns of Interaction Video Series

- *The Geography of Food*

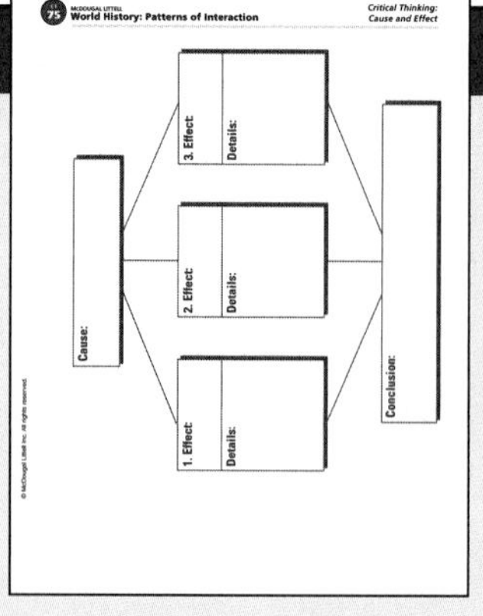

Critical Thinking Transparencies

matters only. The British, fearful of Irish moves toward independence, refused to consider either option.

One reason for Britain's opposition to home rule was concern for Ireland's Protestants. They feared being a minority in a country dominated by Catholics. Most Protestants lived in the northern part of Ireland, known as Ulster. Finally, in 1914, Parliament enacted a home rule bill for southern Ireland. Just one month before the plan was to take effect, World War I broke out in Europe. Irish home rule was put on hold.

Rebellion and Division Frustrated over the delay in gaining independence, a small group of Irish nationalists rebelled in Dublin during Easter week, 1916. British troops put down the Easter Rising and executed its leaders. Their fate, however, aroused wider popular support for the nationalist movement.

After World War I, the Irish nationalists won a victory in the elections for the British Parliament. To protest delays in home rule, the nationalist members decided not to attend Parliament. Instead, they formed an underground Irish government and declared themselves independent. The **Irish Republican Army** (IRA), an unofficial military force seeking independence for Ireland, staged a series of attacks against British officials in Ireland. The attacks sparked war between the nationalists and the British government.

In 1921, Britain divided Ireland and granted home rule to southern Ireland. Ulster, or Northern Ireland, remained a part of Great Britain. The south became a dominion called the Irish Free State. However, many Irish nationalists, led by Eamon De Valera, continued to seek total independence from Britain. In 1949, the Irish Free State declared itself the independent Republic of Ireland. C

C. Possible Answers Yes—it allowed the majority in each part to have its way. No—it has led to continuing violence and bloodshed.

MAIN IDEA

Evaluating Decisions

C Was Britain's policy in dividing Ireland successful? Why or why not?

Connect to Today

Northern Ireland Today

When Northern Ireland decided to stay united with Great Britain, many Catholics there refused to accept the partition, or division. In the late 1960s, Catholic groups began to demonstrate for more civil rights.

Their protests touched off fighting between Catholics and Protestants. Militant groups on both sides engaged in terrorism. This violent period, called the "troubles," continued into the 1990s.

In 1999, with a peace accord, Catholics and Protestants began sharing power in a new home-rule government. Nonetheless, tensions between the two sides remain.

INTEGRATED TECHNOLOGY

INTERNET ACTIVITY Design a Web page about the peace process in Northern Ireland today. Include Gerry Adams and David Trimble. Go to **classzone.com** for your research.

Connect to Today

Northern Ireland Today

The best-known militant group in Northern Ireland is the Irish Republican Army (IRA). Their roots go back to another underground army, The Irish Volunteers, and to the Fenians—a group founded after the potato famine to force the British out of Ireland.

INTEGRATED TECHNOLOGY

Rubric Web pages should
- show milestones of the peace process.
- identify Gerry Adams and David Trimble.
- include a mix of images and text.

In-Depth Resources: Unit 3
- Literature: "Easter 1916," p. 35

SECTION 2 ASSESSMENT

TERMS & NAMES 1. For each term or name, write a sentence explaining its significance.
- dominion
- Maori
- Aborigine
- penal colony
- home rule
- Irish Republican Army

USING YOUR NOTES

2. In what ways was Ireland different from the other three colonies? (10.4.2)

Country	Political Events
Canada	
Australia	
New Zealand	

MAIN IDEAS

3. What were the two major reforms urged by the Durham report? (10.4.2)
4. What was unusual about the first European settlers in Australia? (10.4.2)
5. What are the main countries to which the Irish emigrated during the famine? (10.4.2)

CRITICAL THINKING & WRITING

6. **COMPARING** How was Britain's policy toward Canada beginning in the late 1700s similar to its policy toward Ireland in the 1900s? (10.4.2)
7. **DRAWING CONCLUSIONS** What impact did the Great Famine have on the population of Ireland? (10.4.2)
8. **CLARIFYING** Why did Britain create Upper Canada and Lower Canada, and who lived in each colony? (10.4.2)
9. **WRITING ACTIVITY** EMPIRE BUILDING Britain encouraged emigration to each of the colonies covered in this section. What effects did this policy have on these areas? Write a **paragraph** to explain. (Writing 2.3.b)

INTEGRATED TECHNOLOGY **INTERNET ACTIVITY**

Use the Internet to find information on Irish emigration to the United States. Create a **bar graph** showing the years when the largest numbers of Irish came to the United States. (CST 1)

INTERNET KEYWORD
Irish immigration

3 ASSESS

SECTION 2 ASSESSMENT

Have small groups work together on the questions.

Formal Assessment
- Section Quiz, p. 172

4 RETEACH

Use the Reteaching Activity to review this section.

In-Depth Resources: Unit 3
- Reteaching Activity, p. 44

ANSWERS

1. dominion, p. 318 • Maori, p. 318 • Aborigine, p. 318 • penal colony, p. 318 • home rule, p. 320 • Irish Republican Army, p. 321

2. **Sample Answer**: Canada—Dominion 1867; Australia and New Zealand—Self-governing 1850s, dominions early 1900s; Ireland—Southern home rule 1921, Irish Free State becomes independent 1949, Ireland was closer to England, more subject to British control; gained home rule later; lost population, other three gained population.
3. Upper and Lower Canada should be reunited and self-governing; British immigration encouraged
4. They were convicted criminals.
5. United States, Britain, Canada, Australia
6. resolved conflicts with political divisions
7. About 1 million people died and another 1.5 million people emigrated.
8. to resolve conflicts between French Catholics (Lower Canada) and English Protestants (Upper Canada) and give each group voice in its own affairs
9. **Rubric** Paragraphs should
   - describe effect on native populations.
   - identify conflicts between French and English in Canada.
   - identify religious differences.

INTEGRATED TECHNOLOGY

Rubric Bar graphs should
- show emigration figures for several years.
- show years of peak Irish emigration.
- provide Web-based sources.

Social History

OBJECTIVES

- Describe life in early Australia.
- Compare it to life in Australia today.

FOCUS & MOTIVATE

Ask students to name some things they associate with Australia. *(Possible Answers: kangaroos, koala bears, boomerangs, 2000 Summer Olympics in Sydney)*

INSTRUCT

Critical Thinking

- How was settlement of Australia like settlement of the western United States? *(Possible Answers: gold rush around the same time, farming and ranching important, conflict between settlers and native peoples)*
- What can you infer about Australian settlement patterns compared to the United States, based on their population densities? *(Possible Answer: Larger parts of Australia are inhospitable to settlement.)*

Social History

Life in Early Australia

European explorers located Australia long after they had begun colonizing other lands. Dutch explorers were probably the first Europeans to reach Australia around 1605. Australia was not claimed by a European power, however, until the British did so in 1770.

Early Australia had many groups of people with diverse interests, including a native population that had lived on the island for at least 40,000 years. On these pages you will discover the occupations, motivations, and interests of some Australians in the 17th and 18th centuries.

INTEGRATED TECHNOLOGY

RESEARCH LINKS For more on early Australia, go to **classzone.com**

▼ Original Australians

Aboriginal society developed in close harmony with nature. There were between 200 and 300 Aboriginal languages, and most people were bilingual or multilingual. By 1900, half of Australia's original inhabitants had died fighting the British or from disease. The engraving below depicts an Aboriginal man with ceremonial face paint and scars. The other image below is an ancient Aboriginal rock painting.

▼ Gold Miners

In 1851, lured by the potential of striking it rich, thousands of people began prospecting for gold in Australia. Sometimes whole families moved to the gold fields, but life in the gold camps was hard and very few people struck it rich. Searching for gold was hard and dirty work, as this painting illustrates.

322

RECOMMENDED RESOURCES

Books

Davison, Graeme, John Hirst, and Stuart Macintyre eds. ***The Oxford Companion to Australian History***. Rev. ed. New York: Oxford UP, 2001. A comprehensive account of the key events and personalities that have shaped Australian history.

Sinclair, Karen. ***Maori Times, Maori Places.*** Lanham, MD: Rowman & Littlefield, 2003. An extensive study of the multifaceted Maori culture.

Vlietstra, Ronald E. ***Dutchman's Gold.*** Mt. Pleasant, Australia: Rio Bay, 2002. A firsthand account of life in colonial Australia from a young man who labored on farms and in goldfields.

Videos

Dreamtime of the Aborigines. VHS. Library Video Company, 1997. 800-843-3620. Leonard Nimoy hosts this investigation into the culture of the Aborigines.

History and Culture of Australia. CD-ROM. Social Studies School Service. 800-421-4246. Covers many aspects of Australian history, including Aboriginal history, early explorers, bushrangers, and "gold fever."

▲ **Farmers and Ranchers**
Free settlers made the journey to Australia willingly. Many went into farming and ranching. Farms provided much-needed food, and sheep ranching provided wool as a valuable export. Convicts were hired out to farmers and ranchers as cheap labor. Sheep ranching, shown in the picture above, remains an important part of Australia's economy.

▼ **Convicts**
Beginning in 1788, England sent both male and female prisoners to Australia—sometimes with their children. Convicts built public buildings, roads, and bridges. England stopped sending convicts to Australia in 1868. The prison ship shown here housed prisoners before they went to Australia.

CALIFORNIA STANDARDS

10.4.2 Discuss the locations of the colonial rule of such nations as England, France, Germany, Italy, Japan, the Netherlands, Russia, Spain, Portugal, and the United States.

> DATA FILE

Australia Today
- Australia still mines gold, but it also produces 95 percent of the world's precious opals and 99 percent of black opals.
- Australia has 24 million head of cattle and is the world's largest exporter of beef.
- Australians had 8.6 million cell phones in 2000.

Australia's Population
- In 2001, there was an average of 6.5 people per square mile in Australia. That same year in the United States there were 77.8 people per square mile.
- In Australia's 2001 census, 410,003 people identified themselves as being of indigenous origin.

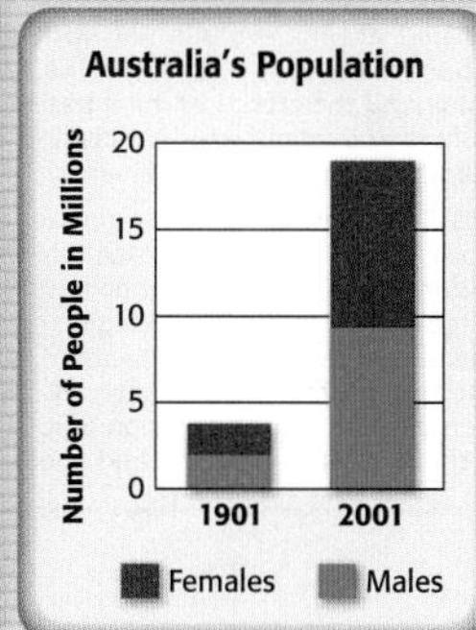

Connect *to* Today

1. **Forming and Supporting Opinions** Of the groups represented on this page, which do you believe had highest quality of living? Why?
   See Skillbuilder Handbook, page R20.
2. **Comparing and Contrasting** Use the Internet to research the issues that Australian Aborigines and Native Americans in the United States face today and compare them. How are they similar? How are they different?

323

More About . . .

Crime and Transportation

The Industrial Revolution in England displaced many rural and city people. Without work, many of these people were forced to steal for a living. In 1828, an estimated one out of every 822 residents of London was a professional criminal. Punishments were harsh to make up for the shortage of police officers (London had only 15). Over 160 offenses were punishable by death and many others by transportation. One criminal, for example, was sentenced to seven years in Australia for stealing two shoe buckles.

More About . . .

Original Australians

The word *aborigine* comes from the Latin *ab origine,* meaning *from the beginning.* Many descendants of the original Australians prefer to refer to themselves in terms from their own languages. Today, 44 percent of land in the Northwest Territory is Aboriginal land. By 1930, the population of Aboriginal people numbered only 75,000. Today the number is slightly higher than the estimated population at the time of European contact. Aboriginals became official citizens of Australia in 1967 and were given the right to vote in Federal elections and referendums.

CONNECT TO TODAY: ANSWERS

1. Forming and Supporting Opinions
Students should support their answers with specific examples. Some students may think farmers and ranchers had the best life because they were free settlers and had the greatest chance for success raising cattle or sheep to produce beef or wool for export.

2. Comparing and Contrasting
Possible Answers: Answers will vary based on research, but some topics that might come up are land and resource rights, legal jurisdiction, or tribal status.

LESSON PLAN

OBJECTIVES

- Trace U.S. expansion to the Pacific.
- Describe effects of the Civil War.
- Analyze postwar economic expansion.

1 FOCUS & MOTIVATE

Discuss how students' lives would be different if the United States were split in two. (*Possible Answers: different money; need a passport to travel between North and South; different laws*)

2 INSTRUCT

Americans Move West

10.3.4

Critical Thinking

- How was the effect of the Mexican-American War greater than its cause? *(It started over Texas, but the United States gained much more land.)*

Electronic Library of Primary Sources

- from a Message to Congress on Indian Policy

CALIFORNIA RESOURCES

California Reading Toolkit, p. L47
California Modified Lesson Plans for English Learners, p. 89
California Daily Standards Practice Transparencies, TT39
California Standards Enrichment Workbook, pp. 37–38, 39–40
California Standards Planner and Lesson Plans, p. L85
California Online Test Practice
California Test Generator CD-ROM
California Easy Planner CD-ROM
California eEdition CD-ROM

Activists for woman suffrage in London

Thomas Edison with phonograph

3

War and Expansion in the United States

MAIN IDEA

POWER AND AUTHORITY The United States expanded across North America and fought a civil war.

WHY IT MATTERS NOW

The 20th-century movements to ensure civil rights for African Americans and others are a legacy of this period.

TERMS & NAMES

- manifest destiny
- Abraham Lincoln
- secede
- U.S. Civil War
- Emancipation Proclamation
- segregation

CALIFORNIA STANDARDS

10.3.3 Describe the growth of population, rural to urban migration, and growth of cities associated with the Industrial Revolution.

10.3.4 Trace the evolution of work and labor, including the demise of the slave trade and the effects of immigration, mining and manufacturing, division of labor, and the union movement.

CST 3 Students use a variety of maps and documents to interpret human movement, including major patterns of domestic and international migration, changing environmental preferences and settlement patterns, the frictions that develop between population groups, and the diffusion of ideas, technological innovations, and goods.

SETTING THE STAGE The United States won its independence from Britain in 1783. At the end of the Revolutionary War, the Mississippi River marked the western boundary of the new republic. As the original United States filled with settlers, land-hungry newcomers pushed beyond the Mississippi. The government helped them by acquiring new territory for settlement. Meanwhile, tensions between northern and southern states over the issues of states' rights and slavery continued to grow and threatened to reach a boiling point.

Americans Move West

In 1803, President Thomas Jefferson bought the Louisiana Territory from France. The Louisiana Purchase doubled the size of the new republic and extended its boundary to the Rocky Mountains. In 1819, Spain gave up Florida to the United States. In 1846, a treaty with Great Britain gave the United States part of the Oregon Territory. The nation now stretched from the Atlantic to the Pacific oceans.

Manifest Destiny Many Americans believed in **manifest destiny**, the idea that the United States had the right and duty to rule North America from the Atlantic Ocean to the Pacific Ocean. Government leaders used manifest destiny to justify evicting Native Americans from their tribal lands.

The Indian Removal Act of 1830 made such actions official policy. This law enabled the federal government to force Native Americans living in the East to move to the West. Georgia's Cherokee tribe challenged the law before the Supreme Court. The Court, however, ruled that the suit was not valid. The Cherokees had to move. Most of them traveled 800 miles to Oklahoma, mainly on foot, on a journey later called the Trail of Tears. About a quarter of the Cherokees died on the trip. A survivor recalled how the journey began:

TAKING NOTES

Following Chronological Order Create a time line to record major events of the United States in the 19th century.

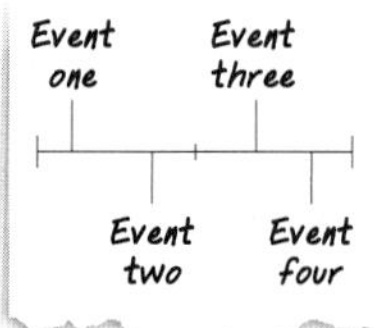

PRIMARY SOURCE

The day was bright and beautiful, but a gloomy thoughtfulness was depicted in the lineaments of every face. . . . At this very moment a low sound of distant thunder fell on my ear . . . and sent forth a murmur, I almost thought a voice of divine indignation for the wrong of my poor and unhappy countrymen, driven by brutal power from all they loved and cherished in the land of their fathers.

WILLIAM SHOREY COODEY, quoted in *The Trail of Tears*

SECTION 3 PROGRAM RESOURCES

ALL STUDENTS

In-Depth Resources: Unit 3
- Guided Reading, p. 25

Formal Assessment
- Section Quiz, p. 173

ENGLISH LEARNERS

In-Depth Resources in Spanish
- Guided Reading, p. 83

Reading Study Guide (Spanish), p. 109
Reading Study Guide Audio CD (Spanish)

STRUGGLING READERS

In-Depth Resources: Unit 3
- Guided Reading, p. 25
- Building Vocabulary, p. 27
- Reteaching Activity, p. 45

Reading Study Guide, p. 109
Reading Study Guide Audio CD

GIFTED AND TALENTED STUDENTS

In-Depth Resources: Unit 3
- Primary Source: Railroad Poster, p. 33

Electronic Library of Primary Sources
- from a Message to Congress on Indian Policy

INTEGRATED TECHNOLOGY

eEdition CD-ROM
Power Presentations CD-ROM
Electronic Library of Primary Sources
- from a Message to Congress on Indian Policy

classzone.com

When the Cherokees reached their destination, they ended up on land inferior to that which they had left. As white settlers moved west during the 19th century, the government continued to push Native Americans off their land.

Texas Joins the United States When Mexico had gained its independence from Spain in 1821, its territory included the lands west of the Louisiana Purchase. With Mexico's permission, American settlers moved into the Mexican territory of Texas. However, settlers were unhappy with Mexico's rule.

In 1836, Texans revolted against Mexican rule and won their independence. Then, in 1845, the United States annexed Texas. Since Mexico still claimed Texas, it viewed this annexation as an act of war.

War with Mexico Between May 1846 and February 1848, war raged between the two countries. Finally, Mexico surrendered. As part of the settlement of the Mexican-American War, Mexico ceded territory to the United States. The Mexican Cession included California and a huge area in the Southwest. In 1853, the Gadsden Purchase from Mexico brought the lower continental United States to its present boundaries.

U.S. Expansion, 1783–1853

INTERACTIVE

- U.S. in 1783
- Louisiana Purchase, 1803
- Florida Cession, 1819
- By treaty with Great Britain, 1818 and 1842
- Texas Annexation, 1845
- Oregon, 1846
- Mexican Cession, 1848
- Gadsden Purchase, 1853

CANADA · By treaty with Great Britain, 1818 · By treaty with Great Britain, 1842 · OREGON · MEXICAN CESSION · LOUISIANA PURCHASE · UNITED STATES in 1783 · TEXAS ANNEXATION · GADSDEN PURCHASE · FLORIDA CESSION · MEXICO · PACIFIC OCEAN · ATLANTIC OCEAN · Gulf of Mexico · Missouri R. · Colorado R. · Mississippi R. · Ohio R. · Rio Grande · Tropic of Cancer · 40°N · 20°N · 60°N · 40°W · 120°W · 0 500 Miles · 0 1,000 Kilometers

GEOGRAPHY SKILLBUILDER: Interpreting Maps

1. **Movement** *What was the first territory to be added to the United States after 1783?*
2. **Region** *What present-day states were part of the Mexican Cession?*

Civil War Tests Democracy

America's westward expansion raised questions about what laws and customs should be followed in the West. Since the nation's early days, the northern and southern parts of the United States had followed different ways of life. Each section wanted to extend its own way of life to the new territories and states in the West.

North and South The North had a diversified economy, with both farms and industry. For both its factories and farms, the North depended on free workers. The South's economy, on the other hand, was based on just a few cash crops, mainly cotton. Southern planters relied on slave labor. (A)

MAIN IDEA

Contrasting

(A) What were the main economic differences between the Northern and Southern states?

A. Answer North had diversified economy with farms and industry, depended on free workers; South's economy relied on few cash crops and slave labor.

The economic differences between the two regions led to a conflict over slavery. Many Northerners considered slavery morally wrong. They wanted to outlaw slavery in the new western states. Most white Southerners believed slavery was necessary for their economy. They wanted laws to protect slavery in the West so that they could continue to raise cotton on the fertile soil there.

The disagreement over slavery fueled a debate about the rights of the individual states against those of the federal government. Southern politicians argued that the states had freely joined the Union, and so they could freely leave. Most Northerners felt that the Constitution had established the Union once and for all.

Civil War Breaks Out Conflict between the North and South reached a climax in 1860, when **Abraham Lincoln** was elected president. Southerners fiercely

History from Visuals

Interpreting the Map

Ask students what each color on the map represents. *(a U.S. land acquisition)* By how much did the United States grow during this period? *(tripled in size)*

Extension Ask students whether any obvious cultural influences survive in the regions shown here. *(Areas of Texas Annexation and Mexican Cession have distinct Hispanic influences.)*

SKILLBUILDER Answers

1. **Movement** Louisiana Territory
2. **Region** California, Nevada, Utah, parts of Arizona, New Mexico, Colorado, and Wyoming

INTEGRATED TECHNOLOGY

Interactive An interactive version of this map is available on the eEdition.

Civil War Tests Democracy
10.3.3

Critical Thinking

- Why did Southerners feel threatened by Lincoln's pledge to stop the spread of slavery? *(feared Northern interests would dominate Congress and slavery would be outlawed)*
- Why did Reconstruction end, and what happened as a result? *(federal troops no longer present to enforce federal laws that protected African Americans; southern states passed laws that limited rights of African Americans and enforced segregation)*

DIFFERENTIATING INSTRUCTION: STRUGGLING READERS

The Chronology of the Civil War

Class Time 30 minutes

Task Creating a time line

Purpose To understand the importance of Civil War events

Instructions Pair a struggling reader with a more proficient reader. Have students reread the section titled "Civil War Tests Democracy" and create a time line of events in the Civil War. A sample time line is shown here. Students may illustrate the time line if they choose. Invite students to share their time lines with the class, explaining why each event included is significant.

Students who need more help may complete the Reading Study Guide activity for this section.

1860—Abraham Lincoln becomes president. Many Southern people are angry.

1861—Southern soldiers fire guns at a fort. War begins.

1863—Lincoln issues the Emancipation Proclamation, which frees slaves in Southern states.

1865—The South surrenders.

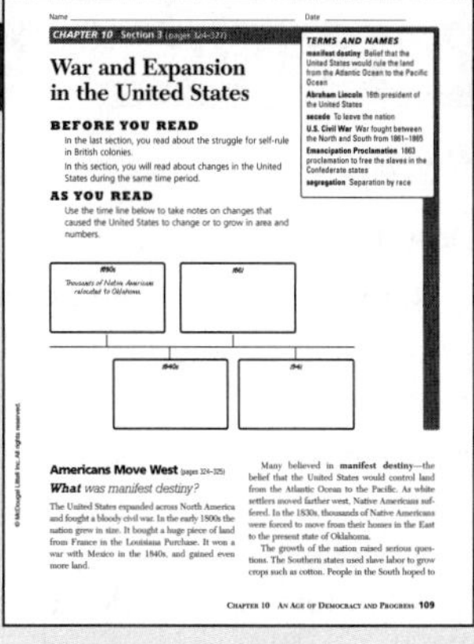
CHAPTER 10 Section 3

War and Expansion in the United States

TERMS AND NAMES

BEFORE YOU READ

AS YOU READ

Americans Move West

Reading Study Guide

History from Visuals

Interpreting the Map

After students have studied the map, point out the bar chart in the inset. Ask students how many total deaths there were in the war *(about 600,000)*. Which side had more deaths? *(the Union)*

Extension Have students discuss what problems the Union army would have encountered penetrating so deeply into the South. *(Possible Answers: setting up and protecting communication and supply lines; getting reinforcements and replacements; dealing with a hostile population)*

SKILLBUILDER Answers

1. **Movement** The Union strategy seemed to be to advance into the South and surround and confront Confederate forces.
2. **Human-Environment Interaction** the South, because most of the war was fought there; however, the North had the greater number of deaths

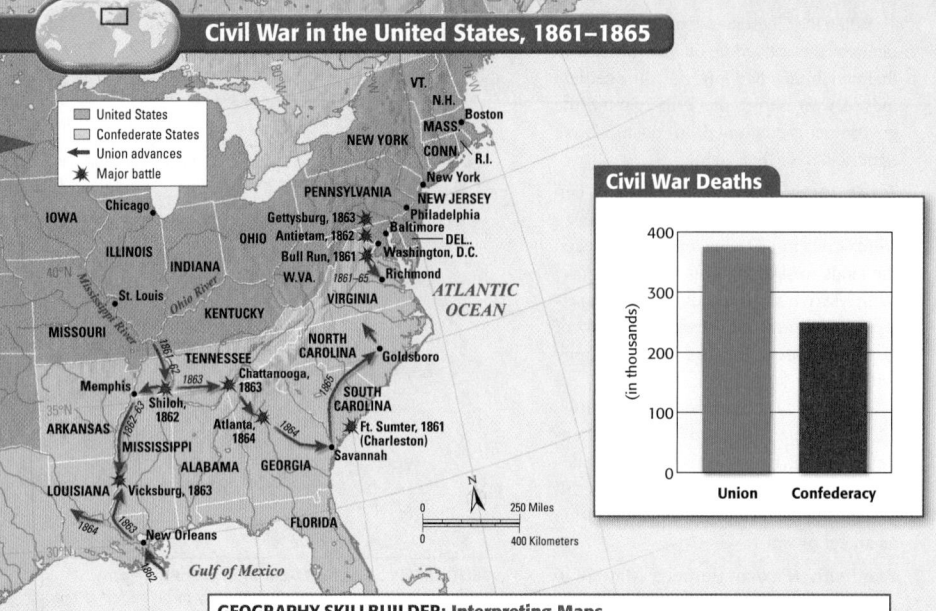

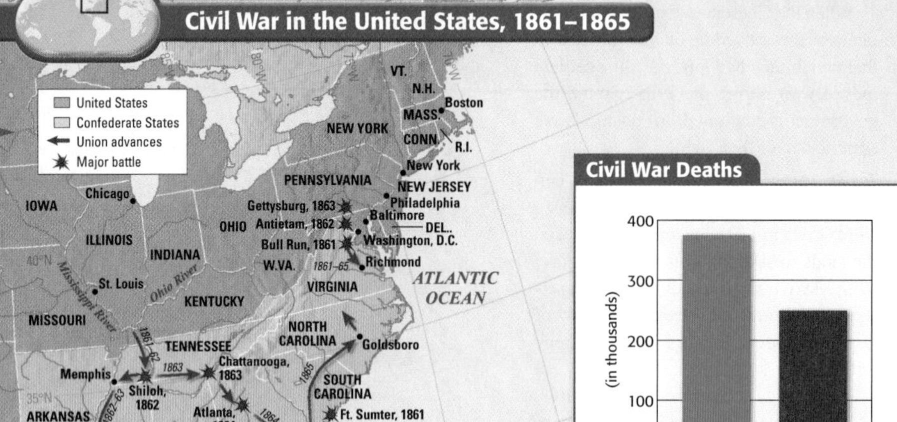

GEOGRAPHY SKILLBUILDER: Interpreting Maps

1. **Movement** *What can you tell about the strategy of the North to defeat the South?*
2. **Human-Environment Interaction** *Which side do you think suffered the most devastation? Why?*

opposed Lincoln, who had promised to stop the spread of slavery. One by one, Southern states began to **secede**, or withdraw, from the Union. These states came together as the Confederate States of America.

On April 12, 1861, Confederate forces fired on Fort Sumter, a federal fort in Charleston, South Carolina. Lincoln ordered the army to bring the rebel states back into the Union. The **U.S. Civil War** had begun. Four years of fighting followed, most of it in the South. Although the South had superior military leadership, the North had a larger population, better transportation, greater resources, and more factories. These advantages proved too much, and in April 1865, the South surrendered.

B. Answer No, he believed that ending slavery would help him achieve his primary goal—preserving the Union.

Abolition of Slavery Lincoln declared that the war was being fought to save the Union and not to end slavery. He eventually decided that ending slavery would help to save the Union. Early in 1863, he issued the **Emancipation Proclamation**, declaring that all slaves in the Confederate states were free. B

MAIN IDEA

Analyzing Issues

B Did the Emancipation Proclamation reflect a change in Lincoln's main goal for the war?

At first, the proclamation freed no slaves, because the Confederate states did not accept it as law. As Union armies advanced into the South, however, they freed slaves in the areas they conquered. The Emancipation Proclamation also showed European nations that the war was being fought against slavery. As a result, these nations did not send the money and supplies that the South had hoped they would.

In the aftermath of the war, the U.S. Congress passed the Thirteenth Amendment to the Constitution, which abolished slavery in the United States. The Fourteenth and Fifteenth Amendments extended the rights of citizenship to all Americans and guaranteed former slaves the right to vote.

Reconstruction From 1865 to 1877, Union troops occupied the South and enforced the constitutional protections. This period is called Reconstruction. After federal troops left the South, white Southerners passed laws that limited African

DIFFERENTIATING INSTRUCTION: ENGLISH LEARNERS

Comparing Casualty Rates of Different Wars

Class Time 40 minutes

Task Creating a bar graph of war casualties

Purpose To put the casualties of the Civil War in historic context by comparing them with those of other wars

Instructions Explain that the Civil War was one of the bloodiest wars in history. The use of heavy artillery in the field and the invention of the repeating rifle partly accounted for the high casualty rate. In fact, the Civil War remains the bloodiest war for the United States, except for World War II. Casualties (killed and wounded) were almost triple those for the Vietnam War and nearly exceeded U.S. casualties in all other wars combined, except for World War II.

Have students use the following information on war casualties to create a bar graph comparing different wars.

Civil War	646,392
World War I	320,710
World War II	1,079,162
Korea	140,200
Vietnam	211,556

Statistics from *World Almanac* 2003

Americans' rights and made it difficult for them to vote. Such laws also encouraged **segregation**, or separation, of blacks and whites in the South. African Americans continued to face discrimination in the North as well.

The Postwar Economy

The need for mass production and distribution of goods during the Civil War speeded industrialization. After the war, the United States experienced industrial expansion unmatched in history. By 1914, it was a leading industrial power.

C. Possible Answer drew people to the West, including many immigrants; by carrying raw materials to factories and finished goods to market, it boosted agriculture and industry; helped steel industry

Immigration Industrialization could not have occurred so rapidly without immigrants. During the 1870s, immigrants arrived at a rate of nearly 2,000 a day. By 1914, more than 20 million people had moved to the United States from Europe and Asia. Many settled in the cities of the Northeast and Midwest. Others settled in the open spaces of the West.

The Railroads As settlers moved west, so did the nation's rail system. In 1862, Congress had authorized money to build a transcontinental railroad. For seven years, immigrants and other workers dug tunnels, built bridges, and laid track. When the railroad was completed in 1869, railroads linked California with the eastern United States. C

MAIN IDEA
Recognizing Effects
C How did railroads affect the growth of the United States?

By 1900, nearly 200,000 miles of track crossed the nation. This system linked farm to city and boosted trade and industry. The railroads bought huge quantities of steel. Also, trains brought materials such as coal and iron ore to factories and moved the finished goods to market. They carried corn, wheat, and cattle from the Great Plains to processing plants in St. Louis, Chicago, and Minneapolis. These developments helped to make the United States a world leader.

History Makers

Abraham Lincoln
1809–1865

Lincoln passionately believed in preserving the Union. His upbringing might help explain why. The son of rural, illiterate parents, he educated himself. After working as rail splitter, boatman, storekeeper, and surveyor, he taught himself to be a lawyer. This career path led eventually to the White House.

In Europe, people stayed at the level of society into which they had been born. Yet the United States had been founded on the belief that all men were created equal. Small wonder that Lincoln fought to preserve the democracy he described as the "last best hope of earth."

SECTION 3 ASSESSMENT

TERMS & NAMES 1. For each term or name, write a sentence explaining its significance.
• manifest destiny • Abraham Lincoln • secede • U.S. Civil War • Emancipation Proclamation • segregation

USING YOUR NOTES

2. Which events contributed to U.S. expansion? (10.3.3)

Event one | Event three | Event two | Event four

MAIN IDEAS

3. What territory did the Mexican-American War open up to American settlers? (10.3.3)
4. What were some of the economic differences between the North and the South before the Civil War? (10.3.4)
5. How did the Civil War speed up America's industrialization? (10.3.3)

CRITICAL THINKING & WRITING

6. **DISTINGUISHING FACT FROM OPINION** Reread the quotation from William Shorey Coodey on page 324. What facts are conveyed in his statement? What opinions does he express about the Trail of Tears? (CST 3)
7. **COMPARING** What were the relative resources of the North and South in the U.S. Civil War? (10.3.4)
8. **MAKING INFERENCES** How might the Mexican Cession (see map, page 325) have consequences today? (CST 3)
9. **WRITING ACTIVITY** POWER AND AUTHORITY Imagine you are making the westward journey by wagon train. Write **journal entries** describing your experience. (Writing 2.1.c)

CONNECT TO TODAY MAKING A TABLE
Find information on countries today that are experiencing civil wars or conflicts. Make a **table** that includes the name of each country, the continent it is located on, and the dates of the conflict. (CST 3)

History Makers

Abraham Lincoln

How did Lincoln's life reflect the basis of American democracy? *(He rose from humble beginnings to become president.)* Abraham Lincoln was not a simple folk hero: he was shrewd, ambitious, and somewhat vain. At a time when most men made do with one suit in a lifetime, Lincoln bought two a year from the best tailor in town.

The Postwar Economy
10.3.3

Critical Thinking

- How might the Irish potato famine have affected U.S. industrialization? *(Famine caused many Irish to emigrate; these immigrants were part of rapid industrial growth.)*
- How did the railroad change the landscape of the West? *(increased settlement on the prairie, including towns, farms, and ranches)*

In-Depth Resources: Unit 3
- Primary Source: Railroad Poster, p. 33

3 ASSESS

SECTION 3 ASSESSMENT

Have students share their responses to question 5.

Formal Assessment
- Section Quiz, p. 173

4 RETEACH

Ask students to create a time line of the events in this section and discuss how each one relates to U.S. history.

ANSWERS

1. manifest destiny, p. 324 • Abraham Lincoln, p. 325 • secede, p. 326 • U.S. Civil War, p. 326 • Emancipation Proclamation, p. 326 • segregation, p. 327
2. **Sample Answer:** 1803—Louisiana Purchase; 1819—Florida Cession; 1845—Texas Annexation; 1846—British treaty; 1848—Mexican Cession; 1853—Gadsden Purchase; 1869—transcontinental railroad.
3. California and much of the Southwest
4. North had diversified economy and free workers; South was agricultural and had slaves.
5. It created a need for mass production and distribution of goods.
6. Facts—Elements of weather, people being evicted; Opinions—Thunder as "divine indignation," "my poor and unhappy countrymen," the "brutal power" of the whites.
7. North had more people, resources, and industry, better transportation; South had superior military leadership.
8. large Hispanic, bilingual population in the region with strong ties to Mexico; resentment of U.S. for taking Mexican territory
9. **Rubric** Journal entries should describe
   - the landscape.
   - traveling by wagon.
   - Native Americans.

CONNECT TO TODAY

Rubric Tables should
- mention contemporary civil conflicts.
- mention various continents: for example, Africa, Sierra Leone; South America, Venezuela; Asia, Kashmir.

LESSON PLAN

OBJECTIVES

- Describe inventions of the late 19th century and their impact on daily life.
- Trace advances in medicine and science.
- Describe the emergence of the social sciences.
- Explain the rise of mass culture.

❶ FOCUS & MOTIVATE

Ask students to discuss how electricity affects their lives today. *(Possible Answers: lights, heat, power to run appliances, television, computers, hybrid cars)*

❷ INSTRUCT

Inventions Make Life Easier

10.3.2

Critical Thinking

- How were the telephone and the radio superior to the telegraph? *(Telephone transmitted human voice rather than Morse Code; radio did not depend on wires.)*

CALIFORNIA RESOURCES

California Reading Toolkit, p. L48
California Modified Lesson Plans for English Learners, p. 91
California Daily Standards Practice Transparencies, TT40
California Standards Enrichment Workbook, pp. 35–36, 47–48
California Standards Planner and Lesson Plans, p. L87
California Online Test Practice
California Test Generator CD-ROM
California Easy Planner CD-ROM
California eEdition CD-ROM

Activists for woman suffrage in London

Thomas Edison with phonograph

4

Nineteenth-Century Progress

MAIN IDEA	WHY IT MATTERS NOW	TERMS & NAMES
SCIENCE AND TECHNOLOGY Breakthroughs in science and technology transformed daily life and entertainment.	Electric lights, telephones, cars, and many other conveniences of modern life were invented during this period.	• assembly line • Charles Darwin • theory of evolution • radioactivity • psychology • mass culture

CALIFORNIA STANDARDS

10.3.2 Examine how scientific and technological changes and new forms of energy brought about massive social, economic, and cultural change (e.g., the inventions and discoveries of James Watt, Eli Whitney, Henry Bessemer, Louis Pasteur, Thomas Edison).

10.4.1 Describe the rise of industrial economies and their link to imperialism and colonialism (e.g., the role played by national security and strategic advantage; moral issues raised by the search for national hegemony, Social Darwinism, and the missionary impulse; material issues such as land, resources, and technology).

CST 3 Students use a variety of maps and documents to interpret human movement, including major patterns of domestic and international migration, changing environmental preferences and settlement patterns, the frictions that develop between population groups, and the diffusion of ideas, technological innovations, and goods.

SETTING THE STAGE The Industrial Revolution happened because of inventions such as the spinning jenny and the steam engine. By the late 1800s, advances in both industry and technology were occurring faster than ever before. In turn, the demands of growing industries spurred even greater advances in technology. A surge of scientific discovery pushed the frontiers of knowledge forward. At the same time, in industrialized countries, economic growth produced many social changes.

Inventions Make Life Easier

In the early 1800s, coal and steam drove the machines of industry. By the late 1800s, new kinds of energy were coming into use. One was gasoline (made from oil), which powered the internal combustion engine. This engine would make the automobile possible. Another kind of energy was electricity. In the 1870s, the electric generator was developed, which produced a current that could power machines.

Edison the Inventor During his career, Thomas Edison patented more than 1,000 inventions, including the light bulb and the phonograph. Early in his career, Edison started a research laboratory in Menlo Park, New Jersey. Most of his important inventions were developed there, with help from the researchers he employed, such as Lewis H. Latimer, an African-American inventor. Indeed, the idea of a research laboratory may have been Edison's most important invention.

Bell and Marconi Revolutionize Communication Other inventors helped harness electricity to transmit sounds over great distances. Alexander Graham Bell was a teacher of deaf students who invented the telephone in his spare time. He displayed his device at the Philadelphia Centennial Exposition of 1876.

The Italian inventor Guglielmo Marconi used theoretical discoveries about electromagnetic waves to create the first radio in 1895. This device was important because it sent messages (using Morse Code) through the air, without the use of wires. Primitive radios soon became standard equipment for ships at sea.

TAKING NOTES

Summarizing Use a web diagram to connect people with their ideas and inventions.

Ford Sparks the Automobile Industry In the 1880s, German inventors used a gasoline engine to power a vehicle—the automobile. Automobile technology developed quickly, but since early cars were built by hand, they were expensive.

An American mechanic named Henry Ford decided to make cars that were affordable for most people. Ford used standardized, interchangeable parts. He

SECTION 4 PROGRAM RESOURCES

ALL STUDENTS

In-Depth Resources: Unit 3
- Guided Reading, p. 26
- Skillbuilder Practice: Analyzing Issues, p. 28
- History Makers: Marie and Pierre Curie, p. 41

Formal Assessment
- Section Quiz, p. 174

ENGLISH LEARNERS

In-Depth Resources in Spanish
- Guided Reading, p. 84
- Skillbuilder Practice: Analyzing Issues, p. 85

Reading Study Guide (Spanish), p. 111
Reading Study Guide Audio CD (Spanish)

STRUGGLING READERS

In-Depth Resources: Unit 3
- Guided Reading, p. 26
- Building Vocabulary, p. 27
- Skillbuilder Practice: Analyzing Issues, p. 28
- Reteaching Activity, p. 46

Reading Study Guide, p. 111
Reading Study Guide Audio CD

GIFTED AND TALENTED STUDENTS

In-Depth Resources: Unit 3
- Primary Source: from Orville Wright's Diary, p. 34
- Literature: from *The Origin,* p. 37
- Connections Across Time and Cultures, p. 42

Electronic Library of Primary Sources
- from *Journal of the Voyage of HMS* Beagle

INTEGRATED TECHNOLOGY

eEdition CD-ROM
Power Presentations CD-ROM
Electronic Library of Primary Sources
Critical Thinking Transparencies
- CT26 Movers and Shakers, 1815–1914
- CT62 Chapter 26 Visual Summary

classzone.com

Edison's Inventions

Thomas Alva Edison was one of the greatest inventors in history. He held thousands of patents for his inventions in over 30 countries. The United States Patent Office alone issued Edison 1,093 patents. Among his inventions was an electric light bulb, the phonograph, and motion pictures, all shown on this page.

Some scientists and historians, however, believe that Edison's greatest achievement was his development of the research laboratory. Edison worked with a team of different specialists to produce his creations. His precise manner is illustrated by his famous quote: "Genius is 1 percent inspiration and 99 percent perspiration."

INTEGRATED TECHNOLOGY

RESEARCH LINKS For more on Thomas Alva Edison, go to **classzone.com**

CALIFORNIA STANDARDS

10.3.5 Understand the connections among natural resources, entrepreneurship, labor, and capital in an industrial economy.

▲ Thomas Edison in his West Orange, New Jersey, laboratory, 1915

▼ **Motion pictures** The idea of "moving pictures" was not Edison's, but his "Kinetoscope," shown below, made movies practical.

THE MOVING PICTURE NEWS

THE EDISON KINETOSCOPE

WHY isn't your motion picture show making you the great big money you read about? How is it that the man in the next block can show the same pictures you do—and take the crowds away from you? We'll tell you. It's all in the machine—you need an

EDISON KINETOSCOPE

The Edison wins the crowd because it projects clear, flickerless pictures that don't tire the eyes and are a real pleasure to look at. There are no discouraging "intermissions for repairs". And the Edison Kinetoscope saves the extra money it makes, because it runs the longest time with the least upkeep expense. Get Posted. Send for Catalog 500 and a copy of the Edison Kinetogram.

Price, with Rheostat, 110 volts, 24-40 amperes - $225.00
Price, " 110 volt, 60 Cycle Transformer - - 245.00

THOMAS A. EDISON, Inc., 274 Lakeside Avenue, Orange, N. J.

▼ **Phonograph** Commonplace today, a device for recording sound did not exist until Thomas Edison invented it. He first demonstrated his phonograph in 1877.

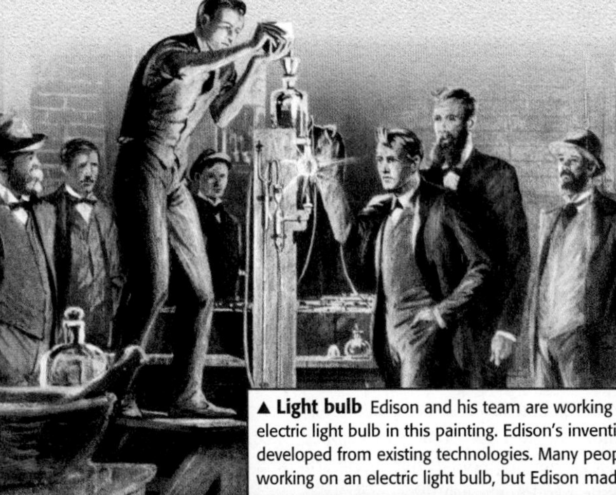

▲ **Light bulb** Edison and his team are working on an electric light bulb in this painting. Edison's inventions often developed from existing technologies. Many people were working on an electric light bulb, but Edison made it practical.

Connect *to* Today

1. **Clarifying** What did Edison mean when he said, "Genius is 1 percent inspiration and 99 percent perspiration"?

   See Skillbuilder Handbook, page R4.

2. **Forming and Supporting Opinions** Which of Edison's inventions shown on this page do you think has had the most influence?

329

Science & *Technology*

OBJECTIVE

- Explain the significance of Thomas Edison in the history of technology.

INSTRUCT

Introduce Edison as a key figure in the history of technology for his inventions and for his approach to solving problems. Discuss with students why his research laboratory might be considered his most significant achievement. *(Possible Answer: It established an approach to problem solving that has been followed for more than 100 years.)*

More About . . .

Thomas Edison

At age 24, Edison, a self-taught genius, invented a stock market ticker. He sold it for $40,000—a fortune at the time—and used the money to set up his research laboratory. Over the next few decades, inventions poured out of his laboratory at an astonishing rate. Edison has few peers in terms of the number and quality of inventions produced.

Tip for Gifted and Talented Students

The words *inspiration* and *perspiration* both contain the Latin root *spirare*, "to breathe."

CONNECT TO TODAY: ANSWERS

1. Clarifying

He meant that genius depends more on hard work than natural talent.

2. Forming and Supporting Opinions

Possible Answers: the light bulb, because it is a part of daily life for many people around the world; the phonograph, because its theories are still used in sound recording; the Kinetoscope, because it began the movie industry; the research laboratory, because it defined how systematic research is done today

More About . . .

The Wright Brothers

After their history-making flight in 1903, the Wright brothers worked for two years to develop a more practical airplane. By late 1905 they could fly for 39 minutes. In 1908, the U.S. Army contracted with them to make the first military plane, able to fly for an hour, averaging 40 miles per hour with a pilot and a passenger.

In-Depth Resources: Unit 3

- Primary Source: from Orville Wright's Diary, p. 34

New Ideas in Medicine
10.3.2

Critical Thinking

- Why was the germ theory an important breakthrough? *(provided a better understanding of how diseases were caused, suggested ways to prevent and treat many illnesses)*
- How were pasteurization and the use of antiseptics similar? *(Both were ways of killing germs.)*

More About . . .

Louis Pasteur

In 1885, Pasteur was working on a vaccine for rabies, one of the first vaccines ever developed. A mother rushed in with her boy who had just been bitten by a rabid dog. With the child facing nearly certain death, Pasteur had no choice but to try out his still highly experimental vaccine. The boy survived and a whole new category of medicine was born.

An Age of Inventions

▲ Telephone
Alexander Graham Bell demonstrated the first telephone in 1876. It quickly became an essential of modern life. By 1900, there were 1.4 million telephones in the United States. By 1912, there were 8.7 million.

▲ Airplane
Through trial and error, the Wright brothers designed wings that provided lift and balance in flight. Their design is based on principles that are still used in every aircraft.

◀ Automobile Assembly Line
Ford's major innovation was to improve efficiency in his factory. By introducing the assembly line, he reduced the time it took to build a car from 12.5 to 1.5 worker-hours.

also built them on an **assembly line**, a line of workers who each put a single piece on unfinished cars as they passed on a moving belt.

Assembly line workers could put together an entire Model T Ford in less than two hours. When Ford introduced this plain, black, reliable car in 1908, it sold for $850. As his production costs fell, Ford lowered the price. Eventually it dropped to less than $300. Other factories adopted Ford's ideas. By 1916, more than 3.5 million cars were traveling around on America's roads. (A)

MAIN IDEA
Making Inferences
(A) Why do you think Ford reduced the price of the Model T?
A. Answer so that more people could afford to buy a car and he could sell more

The Wright Brothers Fly Two bicycle mechanics from Dayton, Ohio, named Wilbur and Orville Wright, solved the age-old riddle of flight. On December 17, 1903, they flew a gasoline-powered flying machine at Kitty Hawk, North Carolina. The longest flight lasted only 59 seconds, but it started the aircraft industry.

New Ideas in Medicine

As you learned in Chapter 6, earlier centuries had established the scientific method. Now this method brought new insights into nature as well as practical results.

The Germ Theory of Disease An important breakthrough in the history of medicine was the germ theory of disease. It was developed by French chemist Louis Pasteur in the mid-1800s. While examining the fermentation process of alcohol, Pasteur discovered that it was caused by microscopic organisms he called bacteria. He also learned that heat killed bacteria. This led him to develop the process of pasteurization to kill germs in liquids such as milk. Soon, it became clear to Pasteur and others that bacteria also caused diseases.

Joseph Lister, a British surgeon, read about Pasteur's work. He thought germs might explain why half of surgical patients died of infections. In 1865, he ordered that his surgical wards be kept spotlessly clean. He insisted that wounds be washed in antiseptics, or germ-killing liquids. As a result, 85 percent of Lister's patients survived. Other hospitals adopted Lister's methods.

Public officials, too, began to understand that cleanliness helped prevent the spread of disease. Cities built plumbing and sewer systems and took other steps to improve public health. Meanwhile, medical researchers developed vaccines or cures for such deadly diseases as typhus, typhoid fever, diphtheria, and yellow fever. These advances helped people live longer, healthier lives.

DIFFERENTIATING INSTRUCTION: ENGLISH LEARNERS

Understanding the Germ Theory of Disease

Class Time 20 minutes

Task Reading, creating a chart, and writing a summary

Purpose To understand the germ theory of disease

Instructions Provide students with a K-W-L chart to fill in for "The Germ Theory of Disease."

Step 1: Work with students to activate their prior knowledge of the topic, then have them fill in what they know in the K (Know) column. Students may say that they know that germs are bad and that it's good to wash your hands when you have a cold.

Step 2: Help students formulate questions for reading. Ask them to write the questions in the W (Want to know) column. Questions might be: What is the relationship of germs and disease? Who discovered the existence of germs? How and when was the theory of germs created? How was the theory used?

Step 3: Have students read the three paragraphs. As they read, they can write down additional questions or fill in the answers to their questions in the L (Learned) column.

Step 4: Direct students to fill in the answers to their remaining questions.

Step 5: Help students use their K-W-L charts to draft a summary of what they have learned.

New Ideas in Science

No scientific idea of modern times aroused more controversy than the work of English naturalist **Charles Darwin**. The cause of the controversy was Darwin's answer to the question that faced biologists: How can we explain the tremendous variety of plants and animals on earth? A widely accepted answer in the 1800s was the idea of special creation—every kind of plant and animal had been created by God at the beginning of the world and had remained the same since then.

Darwin's Theory of Evolution Darwin challenged the idea of special creation. Based on his research as a naturalist on the voyage of the *H.M.S. Beagle,* he developed a theory that all forms of life, including human beings, evolved from earlier living forms that had existed millions of years ago.

In 1859, Darwin published his thinking in a book titled *On the Origin of Species by Means of Natural Selection.* According to the idea of natural selection, populations tend to grow faster than the food supply and so must compete for food. The members of a species that survive are those that are fittest, or best adapted to their environment. These surviving members of a species produce offspring that share their advantages. Gradually, over many generations, the species may change. In this way, new species evolve. Darwin's idea of change through natural selection came to be called the **theory of evolution**. B

MAIN IDEA

Clarifying

B According to Darwin, how does natural selection affect evolution?

B. Answer Because of competition for food, only the fittest members of a species survive to reproduce; these members pass their advantages on to their offspring, and gradually the species evolves.

Mendel and Genetics Although Darwin said that living things passed on their variations from one generation to the next, he did not know how they did so. In the 1850s and 1860s, an Austrian monk named Gregor Mendel discovered that there is a pattern to the way that certain traits are inherited. Although his work was not widely known until 1900, Mendel's work began the science of genetics.

Advances in Chemistry and Physics In 1803, the British chemist John Dalton theorized that all matter is made of tiny particles called atoms. Dalton showed that elements contain only one kind of atom, which has a specific weight. Compounds, on the other hand, contain more than one kind of atom.

In 1869, Dmitri Mendeleev (MEHN•duh•LAY•uhf), a Russian chemist, organized a chart on which all the known elements were arranged in order of weight, from lightest to heaviest. He left gaps where he predicted that new elements would be discovered. Later, his predictions proved correct. Mendeleev's chart, the Periodic Table, is still used today.

A husband and wife team working in Paris, Marie and Pierre Curie, discovered two of the missing elements, which they named radium and polonium. The elements were found in a mineral called pitchblende that released a powerful form of energy. In 1898, Marie Curie gave this energy the name **radioactivity**. In 1903, the Curies shared the Nobel Prize for physics for their work on radioactivity. In 1911, Marie Curie won the Nobel Prize for chemistry for the discovery of radium and polonium.

Physicists around 1900 continued to unravel the secrets of the atom. Earlier scientists believed that the atom was the smallest particle that existed. A British physicist named

History Makers

Marie Curie
1867–1934

Marie Curie's original name was Marya Sklodowska. Born in Warsaw, Poland, she emigrated to Paris to study, where she changed her name to Marie.

She achieved a number of firsts in her career. She was the first woman to teach in the Sorbonne, a world-famous college that was part of the University of Paris. She was the first woman to win a Nobel Prize—two, in fact.

In 1911, she won the Nobel prize for chemistry. In 1921, she made a journey to the U.S. In 1934, she died from leukemia caused by the radiation she had been exposed to in her work.

INTEGRATED TECHNOLOGY

RESEARCH LINKS For more on Marie Curie, go to **classzone.com.**

New Ideas in Science
10.3.2; 10.4.1

Critical Thinking
- Besides competing for food, what are some of the other conditions to which species must adapt? *(changes in geography, climate, disease, predators)*
- How would you describe the process by which advances in science take place? *(Possible Answer: Scientists build on the work of those who have gone before, asking and answering questions.)*

In-Depth Resources: Unit 3
- Connections Across Time and Cultures: Breakthroughs in Science and Technology, p. 42
- Literature: from *The Origin,* p. 37

Critical Thinking Transparencies
- CT26 Movers and Shakers, 1815–1914

Electronic Library of Primary Sources
- from *Journal of the Voyage of the HMS* Beagle

History Makers

Marie Curie

How did Marie Curie sacrifice herself for her work? *(She developed cancer from working with radium.)* As a young student in Paris, Marie Curie often worked in an unheated laboratory, subsisting on little more than bread and butter.

In-Depth Resources: Unit 3
- History Makers: Marie and Pierre Curie, p. 41

SKILLBUILDER LESSON: ANALYZING ISSUES

Studying Darwin's Theory of Evolution

Class Time 30 minutes

Task Analyzing text and creating a chart

Purpose To describe points of view regarding Darwin's theory

Instructions Explain that analyzing issues means examining them in detail to find and describe different points of view about them. Have students read the "Darwin's Theory of Evolution" subsection. Direct them to look for a central problem, and then read for facts that can help flesh out the discussion. A chart analyzing the issues connected with evolution is shown here.

Issue: *How can Earth's tremendous variety of plants and animals be explained?*

Facts: *Millions of different species exist; fossil records suggest changes over time.*

Biblical explanation	**Darwin's theory**
All species created by God at the same time in history	*Species populations compete for food; only fittest survive and pass on traits to offspring*

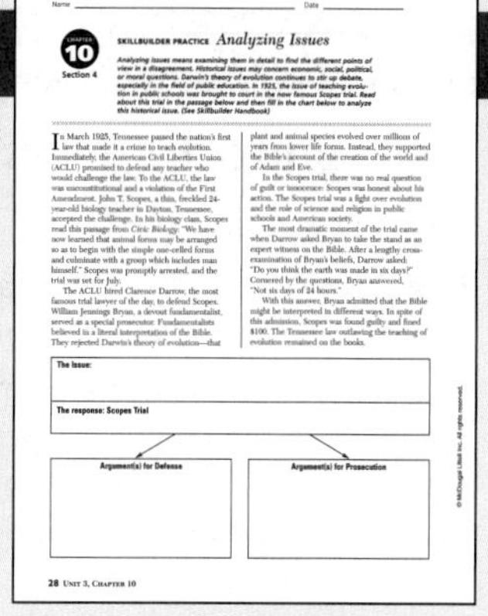

In-Depth Resources: Unit 3

Social Sciences Explore Behavior
10.4.1

Critical Thinking

- What was the inherent flaw in Social Darwinism? *(Ideas about the natural world do not necessarily apply in the same way to human society.)*
- How were Darwin and Freud similar? *(Both challenged previously held beliefs about human beings.)*

History *in* Depth

Social Darwinism

Spencer argued against governments helping the sick and infirm so that "natural selection" might eliminate these people and make society stronger. Ask students to debate Spencer's view.

The Rise of Mass Culture
10.3.2

Critical Thinking

- What was the long-term effect of movies on vaudeville? *(Movies ultimately put vaudeville out of business.)*
- Why did mass culture become big business? *(working class was a larger audience than wealthy; film technology created an international market; more profit)*

History *in* Depth

Social Darwinism

Charles Darwin (above) was a naturalist, but a number of 19th-century thinkers tried to apply his ideas to economics and politics. The leader in this movement was Herbert Spencer, an English philosopher.

Free economic competition, Spencer argued, was natural selection in action. The best companies make profits, while inefficient ones go bankrupt. Spencer applied the same rules to individuals. Those who were fittest for survival enjoyed wealth and success, while the poor remained poor because they were unfit. This idea became known as Social Darwinism. It also provided a rationalization for imperialism and colonialism.

Ernest Rutherford suggested that atoms were made up of yet smaller particles. Each atom, he said, had a nucleus surrounded by one or more particles called electrons. Soon other physicists such as Max Planck, Neils Bohr, and Albert Einstein were studying the structure and energy of atoms.

Social Sciences Explore Behavior

The scientific theories of the 1800s prompted scholars to study human society and behavior in a scientific way. Interest in these fields grew enormously during that century, as global expeditions produced a flood of new discoveries about ancient civilizations and world cultures. This led to the development of modern social sciences such as archaeology, anthropology, and sociology.

An important new social science was **psychology**, the study of the human mind and behavior. The Russian physiologist Ivan Pavlov believed that human actions were often unconscious reactions to experiences and could be changed by training.

Another pioneer in psychology, the Austrian doctor Sigmund Freud, also believed that the unconscious mind drives how people think and act. In Freud's view, unconscious forces such as suppressed memories, desires, and impulses shape behavior. He founded a type of therapy called psychoanalysis to deal with psychological conflicts created by these forces.

Freud's theories became very influential. However, his idea that the mind was beyond conscious control also shocked many people. The theories of Freud and Pavlov challenged the fundamental idea of the Enlightenment—that reason was supreme. The new ideas about psychology began to shake the 19th-century faith that humans could perfect themselves and society through reason. C

C. Possible Answer because it explored how a part of the mind that people were not aware of—the unconscious—influences people's thoughts and behavior

MAIN IDEA

Clarifying

C Why was the work of Pavlov and Freud groundbreaking?

The Rise of Mass Culture

In earlier periods, art, music, and theater were enjoyed by the wealthy. This group had the money, leisure time, and education to appreciate high culture. It was not until about 1900 that people could speak of **mass culture**—the appeal of art, writing, music, and other forms of entertainment to a larger audience.

Changes Produce Mass Culture There were several causes for the rise of mass culture. Their effects changed life in Europe and North America. Notice in the chart on the next page how working class people's lives were changed by mass culture. The demand for leisure activities resulted in a variety of new pursuits for people to enjoy. People went to music performances, movies, and sporting events.

Music Halls, Vaudeville, and Movies A popular leisure activity was a trip to the local music hall. On a typical evening, a music hall might offer a dozen or more different acts. It might feature singers, dancers, comedians, jugglers, magicians, and acrobats. In the United States, musical variety shows were called vaudeville. Vaudeville acts traveled from town to town, appearing at theaters.

During the 1880s, several inventors worked at trying to project moving images. One successful design came from France. Another came from Thomas Edison's laboratory. The earliest motion pictures were black and white and lasted less than a minute.

DIFFERENTIATING INSTRUCTION: GIFTED AND TALENTED STUDENTS

Examining the Technology of Filmmaking

Class Time 45 minutes

Task Researching and creating a multimedia presentation

Purpose To understand the impact of technology on movies

Instructions Encourage students to explore the ways that technology has advanced in different aspects of filmmaking. Students may find resources on the Internet or in the library. For their presentations, students may choose a particular film or give examples that illustrate the process in general. Encourage students to include text, graphics, visuals (still or video), and sound as appropriate to their presentations. Some possible approaches:

1. Create a multimedia timeline of major technological advances in moviemaking (such as sound, color, lighting, special effects, computerized animation, and digital cameras).
2. Illustrate technological advances by comparing movies that have been remade using new techniques (for example, *Ben Hur, King Kong, Superman*).
3. Describe how movie makeup artists create different types of characters, such as aliens, characters in horror films, and characters who age throughout a movie.
4. Explain the importance of music and sound effects and describe how sound editing occurs after a movie has been filmed.

Rise of Mass Culture		
Cause	**Effect/Cause**	**Effect**
• Public education	• Increase in literacy	• Mass market for books and newspapers
• Improvement in communications	• Publications cheaper and more accessible	• Mass market for books and newspapers
• Invention of phonograph and records	• More music directly in people's homes	• Greater demand for musical entertainment
• Shorter workday—10 hours shorter workweek—5-1/2 days	• More leisure time	• Greater demand for mass entertainment activities

SKILLBUILDER: Interpreting Charts
1. **Analyzing Causes** *What was the immediate cause for the increased demand for mass entertainment activities?*
2. **Recognizing Effects** *What was the ultimate effect of public education and improved communications?*

By the early 1900s, filmmakers were producing the first feature films. Movies quickly became big business. By 1910, five million Americans attended some 10,000 theaters each day. The European movie industry experienced similar growth.

Sports Entertain Millions With time at their disposal, more people began to enjoy sports and outdoor activities. Spectator sports now became entertainment. In the United States, football and baseball soared in popularity. In Europe, the first professional soccer clubs formed and drew big crowds. Favorite English sports such as cricket spread to the British colonies of Australia, India, and South Africa.

As a result of the growing interest in sports, the International Olympic Games began in 1896. They revived the ancient Greek tradition of holding an athletic competition every four years. Fittingly, the first modern Olympics took place in Athens, Greece, the country where the games had originated.

SECTION 4 ASSESSMENT

TERMS & NAMES 1. For each term or name, write a sentence explaining its significance.
• assembly line • Charles Darwin • theory of evolution • radioactivity • psychology • mass culture

USING YOUR NOTES
2. Which breakthrough helped most people? Why? (10.3.2)

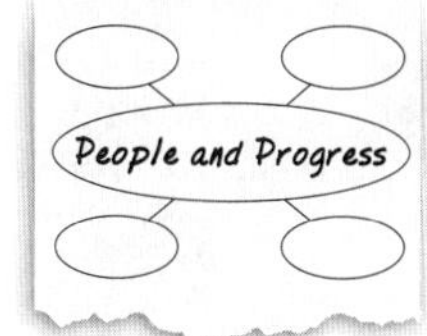

MAIN IDEAS
3. What effect did the assembly line have on production costs? (10.4.1)
4. How did Joseph Lister improve the survival rate of his patients? (10.3.2)
5. What effect did the spread of public education have on culture? (10.3.2)

CRITICAL THINKING & WRITING
6. **COMPARING AND CONTRASTING** How is the mass culture that rose at the end of the 19th century similar to mass culture today? How is it different? (10.3.2)
7. **RECOGNIZING EFFECTS** How did the germ theory change living conditions in Europe and the United States? (10.3.2)
8. **ANALYZING CAUSES** What changes led to the rise of mass culture around 1900? (10.3.2)
9. **WRITING ACTIVITY** SCIENCE AND TECHNOLOGY Write a two-paragraph **expository essay** in which you discuss whether advances in science and technology have had a largely positive or negative impact on society. (Writing 2.3.f)

CONNECT TO TODAY MAKING A POSTER
Find information on the current state of medicines such as antibiotics and problems with their use and overuse. Create a **poster** that shows examples of current antibiotics, their benefits, and their potential negative long-term impact. (10.3.2)

History from Visuals

Interpreting the Chart

Explain that the first column lists causes of the rise of mass culture. The second lists immediate effects, which are the causes of longer-term effects shown in the third column. An immediate cause is the one just before an event; the ultimate effects are those in the third column.

SKILLBUILDER Answers
1. **Analyzing Causes** increase in leisure time
2. **Recognizing Effects** produced a mass market for media

3 ASSESS

SECTION 4 ASSESSMENT

After students have completed the questions, engage the whole class in a discussion of question 6.

Formal Assessment
• Section Quiz, p. 174

4 RETEACH

Use the Visual Summary to review this section and chapter. Ask students to rank the inventions in order of importance.

Critical Thinking Transparencies
• CT62 Chapter 26 Visual Summary

In-Depth Resources: Unit 3
• Reteaching Activity, p. 46

ANSWERS

1. assembly line, p. 330 • Charles Darwin, p. 331 • theory of evolution, p. 331 • radioactivity, p. 331 • psychology, p. 332 • mass culture, p. 332

2. **Sample Answer:** Edison's electric light; Ford's assembly line; Pasteur's germ theory (most helpful because saved lives); Darwin's theory of evolution
3. It lowered production costs.
4. He used antiseptics—germ-killing liquids; ordered his surgical wards be kept clean.
5. increased literacy, bigger market for books and newspapers, greater demand for entertainment
6. Similarities—New technology and leisure still shape mass culture; movies and sports still popular. Differences—Internet has transformed sharing of culture; mass culture is now a global business.
7. Cities built plumbing and sewer systems to improve public health.
8. spread of education and literacy, new technologies, more leisure time
9. **Rubric** Expository essays should
• include positive and negative examples.
• show influences on today's society.
• support opinions with facts.

CONNECT TO TODAY
Rubric Posters should provide
• illustrations of antibiotics.
• data and statistics (both positive and negative) about using antibiotics.

TERMS & NAMES

1. suffrage, p. 313
2. anti-Semitism, p. 315
3. dominion, p. 318
4. home rule, p. 320
5. manifest destiny, p. 324
6. Emancipation Proclamation, p. 326
7. assembly line, p. 330
8. theory of evolution, p. 331

MAIN IDEAS

Answers will vary.

9. Reform Bill of 1832, expansion of suffrage in 1867 and 1884, secret ballot, members of Parliament received pay, end to property requirement for serving in Parliament
10. Decades of peaceful efforts to win the right to vote had been unsuccessful.
11. differences between English- and French-speaking Canadians
12. was not open to ordinary settlers but was used instead as a penal colony
13. Britain was concerned about the Protestants in Northern Ireland who wanted British protection.
14. Louisiana Purchase (from France), Florida Cession (from Spain), Texas Annexation, treaties with Britain, Mexican Cession, Gadsden Purchase (from Mexico)
15. The Southern economy depended on slavery. Many Northerners considered slavery to be morally wrong.
16. The members of a species that are best adapted to their environment survive.
17. The scientific theories of the 19th century motivated people to study society in a scientific way. The scientific method was applied to the study of human behavior.
18. contributed to the rise of mass culture by creating demand for mass entertainment activities

Chapter 10 Assessment

TERMS & NAMES

For each term or name below, briefly explain its connection to the reforms, crises, or advances of Western nations from 1815 to 1914.

1. suffrage
2. anti-Semitism
3. dominion
4. home rule
5. manifest destiny
6. Emancipation Proclamation
7. assembly line
8. theory of evolution

MAIN IDEAS

Democratic Reform and Activism Section 1 (pages 313–316)

9. What political reforms expanded democracy for men in Britain? (10.3.2)
10. Why did the woman suffrage movement in Great Britain become more militant? (10.3.2)

Self-Rule for British Colonies Section 2 (pages 317–323)

11. What cultural conflict caused problems for Canada? (10.4.2)
12. How did Australia's early history differ from that of other British colonies? (10.4.2)
13. Why did the British pass a home rule bill for southern Ireland only? (10.4.2)

War and Expansion in the United States Section 3 (pages 324–327)

14. In what ways did the United States gain territory in the 1800s? (10.4.2)
15. Why was the issue of slavery so divisive? (10.3.4)

Nineteenth-Century Progress Section 4 (pages 328–333)

16. What was Darwin's principle of natural selection? (10.4.1)
17. What prompted the growth of the social sciences? (10.3.2)
18. What were some of the effects of increased leisure time? (CST 2)

CRITICAL THINKING

1. **USING YOUR NOTES**
Create a web diagram of the major political, economic, social and cultural, and scientific and technological changes of the 1800s and early 1900s. (10.3.2)

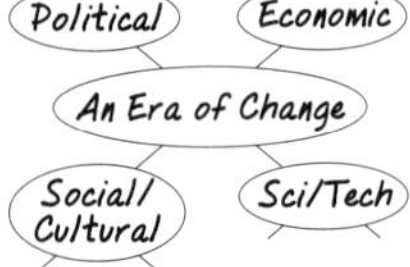

2. **RECOGNIZING EFFECTS**
SCIENCE AND TECHNOLOGY For a worker, what might be the advantages and disadvantages of an assembly line? (10.3.4)

3. **ANALYZING MOTIVES**
POWER AND AUTHORITY What effect did the call for home rule in British colonies have on Ireland's desire for independence? (10.4.2)

4. **HYPOTHESIZING**
Imagine that circumstances had forced the North to surrender to the South in the Civil War, causing two countries to share the region now occupied by the United States. What economic effects might this have had on the North? the South? the region as a whole? (10.3.2)

5. **DRAWING CONCLUSIONS**
How did manifest destiny help shape the U.S. government's policies of land acquisition? (10.4.2)

VISUAL SUMMARY

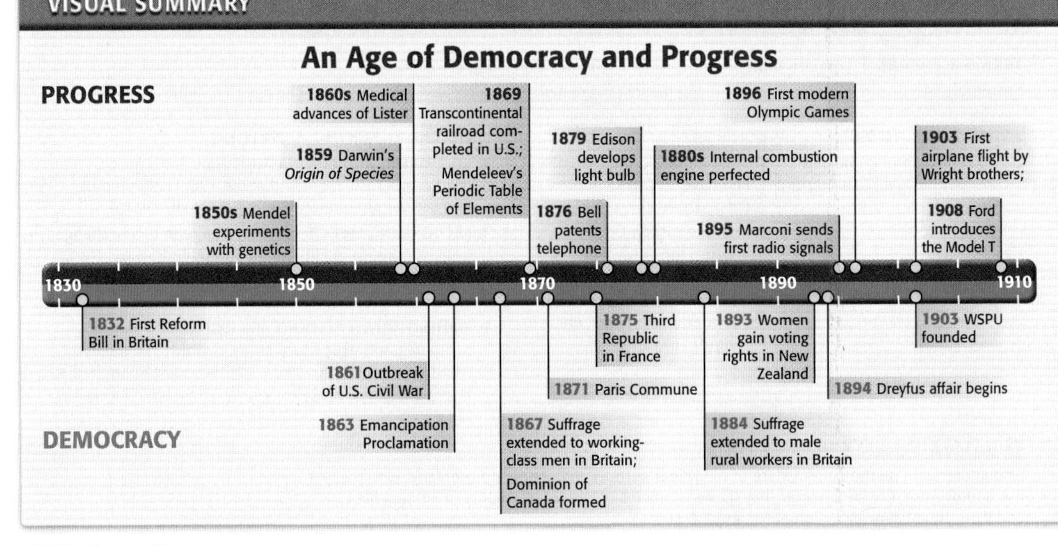

CRITICAL THINKING

Answers will vary.

1. Political—Extension of suffrage, self-rule, U.S. expansion, Civil War. Economic—U.S. abolishes slavery, industrialization, assembly line. Social/Cultural—Colonization of Australia/New Zealand, U.S. immigration, mass culture. Science/Technology—Electricity, telephone, automobile, germ theory, theory of evolution, atomic theory.
2. steady job, efficient use of time and energy, specialized, productive; repetition, impersonality
3. increased the demands of the Irish for independence from British rule
4. **Possible Answer:** If the North had surrendered, it probably wouldn't have developed as much industrially, slowing settlement of the West. The South would most likely have remained agricultural.
5. It was used to justify actions that gained new land for white settlers.

Use the declaration from the Seneca Falls convention (held in New York) and your knowledge of world history to answer questions 1 and 2.
Additional Test Practice, pp. S1–S33

PRIMARY SOURCE

The history of mankind is a history of repeated injuries and usurpations on the part of man toward woman, having in direct object the establishment of an absolute tyranny over her. To prove this, let facts be submitted to a candid world.

He has never permitted her to exercise her inalienable right to the elective franchise.

He has compelled her to submit to laws, in the formation of which she had no voice.

THE SENECA FALLS CONVENTION, *"Declaration of Sentiments"*

1. The purpose of the Seneca Falls convention was to (10.3.2)
   A. call for an end to slavery.
   B. call for the South to secede from the Union.
   C. call for women's rights.
   D. call for the release of Emmeline Pankhurst.

2. The style of this primary source is based on
   A. the U.S. Constitution.
   B. the U.S. Declaration of Independence.
   C. the Reform Bill of 1832.
   D. Émile Zola's *J'accuse!*

Use this cartoon (*A Court for King Cholera*) and your knowledge of world history to answer question 3.

3. Cholera is an infectious disease that has claimed many lives. What details does the artist show about what causes epidemic disease? (10.3.2)
   A. open windows and signs for travelers
   B. children playing with a rat and a woman digging in trash
   C. clothing hanging over the street
   D. crowded street scene

INTEGRATED TECHNOLOGY
TEST PRACTICE Go to **classzone.com**
- Diagnostic tests
- Strategies
- Tutorials
- Additional practice

STANDARDS-BASED ASSESSMENT

1. The correct answer is letter **C**. Letter **A** is incorrect because the main concern of the convention was women's rights. Letter **B** is incorrect because the convention was not primarily concerned with states' rights. Letter **D** is incorrect because Emmeline Pankhurst was a British suffragist, and the concern of the convention was primarily the American movement for women's rights.
2. The correct answer is letter **B**. Letter **A** is incorrect because the Constitution is a lengthy legal document. Letter **C** is incorrect because the Reform Bill was passed by the British Parliament. Letter **D** is incorrect because Zola's pamphlet was a defense of Dreyfus.
3. The correct answer is letter **B**. Letter **A** is incorrect because open windows do not cause disease. Letter **C** is incorrect because clothing hanging over the street might get dusty but not germ infested. Letter **D** is incorrect because a crowded street scene, in itself, would not cause disease.

Formal Assessment
- Chapter Test, Forms A, B, and C, pp. 175–189

California Test Generator CD-ROM
- Chapter Tests, Forms A, B, and C (English and Spanish)

ALTERNATIVE ASSESSMENT

1. **Interact *with* History** (10.2.4)
   On page 312, you considered what political ideals might be worth fighting and possibly even dying for. Now that you have read the chapter, reexamine your conclusions both in terms of the content of the chapter and your knowledge of events in the world today. Discuss your opinions with a small group. Consider:
   - political ideals
   - religious ideals
   - family values

2. **WRITING ABOUT HISTORY** (10.4.2, Writing 2.4.a–d)
   EMPIRE BUILDING Write an **editorial** that might have appeared in a newspaper in 19th-century New Zealand. In the editorial, address the issue of British settlers' taking land from the Maori, and the Maori response.
   Consider the following:
   - the original inhabitants of New Zealand
   - means for negotiating land disputes
   - balancing the rights of native peoples and new settlers

INTEGRATED TECHNOLOGY

Net Explorations: Mass Entertainment
(10.3.2; Writing 2.1.b, c, e)

Go to *NetExplorations* at **classzone.com** to learn more about the rise of mass culture and mass entertainment. Then use the Internet and the material at *NetExplorations* to research and write a newspaper article about spectators at one of the new forms of mass entertainment. Include in your article quotes from fictional visitors and their reactions to actual events and spectacles. You may want to mention one or more of the following:

- the Boston Pilgrims' victory over the Pittsburgh Pirates in baseball's first World Series
- the "Luna" ride at Coney Island
- a late 19th-century European appearance of Barnum & Bailey's circus
- a visit to the Palace of Electricity at the 1904 World's Fair in St. Louis

ALTERNATIVE ASSESSMENT

1. Some students might argue that democracy, freedom of speech, freedom of religion, and other basic liberties are worth fighting for. Others may argue that self-defense is the only legitimate reason to fight and possibly die. Accept all opinions that are well supported.
2. **Rubric** Editorials should
   - express a strong point of view supported by facts.
   - present the Maori side of the issue.
   - recommend a course of action.
   - be free of grammatical and spelling errors.
   - have a variety of sentence structures.

INTEGRATED TECHNOLOGY

Rubric Newspaper articles should
- include the who, what, where, when, why, and how of the story.
- include quotations from fictional spectators.
- cover one event in depth or several in the context of an overview of the topic.
- show evidence of having looked at several links on the site at **classzone.com**

CHAPTER 11 PLANNING GUIDE

The Age of Imperialism, 1850–1914

CHAPTER RESOURCES	COPYMASTERS	ASSESSMENT
CHAPTER OVERVIEW Western countries colonized large areas of Africa and Asia, leading to political and cultural changes.	**In-Depth Resources: Unit 3** • Building Vocabulary, p. 52 **Chapters in Brief** (in English and Spanish) **Block Schedule Pacing Guide**	**Chapter Assessment,** pp. 366–367 **Formal Assessment** • Chapter Tests, Forms A, B, and C, pp. 195–206 **Test Generator** **Online Test Practice**
Section 1 **The Scramble for Africa** pp. 339–344 **OBJECTIVE** Explain how and why most of Africa was divided among European powers.	**In-Depth Resources: Unit 3** • Guided Reading, p. 47 • Geography Application: Livingstone Explores Southern Africa, p. 54 • Primary Source: British Contract, p. 56 • Literature: "The Burial," p. 60 **Reading Study Guide,** p. 115	**Section 1 Assessment,** p. 344 **Formal Assessment** • Section Quiz, p. 190 **California Daily Standards Practice Transparencies,** TT101
Section 2 **Imperialism: Case Study—Nigeria** pp. 345–351 **OBJECTIVE** Analyze Britain's rule of Nigeria and contrast it with other types of imperialism.	**In-Depth Resources: Unit 3** • Guided Reading, p. 48 • Primary Source: Letter from Menelik II, p. 57 • Literature: from *Things Fall Apart,* p. 61 • History Makers: Menelik II, p. 63 • Connections Across Time and Cultures, p. 65 **Reading Study Guide,** p. 117	**Section 2 Assessment,** p. 350 **Formal Assessment** • Section Quiz, p. 191 **California Daily Standards Practice Transparencies,** TT102
Section 3 **Europeans Claim Muslim Lands** pp. 352–356 **OBJECTIVE** Trace the decline of the Ottoman Empire and the rise of geopolitics in Muslim lands.	**In-Depth Resources: Unit 3** • Guided Reading, p. 49 **Reading Study Guide,** p. 119	**Section 3 Assessment,** p. 356 **Formal Assessment** • Section Quiz, p. 192 **California Daily Standards Practice Transparencies,** TT103
Section 4 **British Imperialism in India** pp. 357–361 **OBJECTIVE** Summarize the impact of colonialism, rebellion, and the early nationalist movement in India.	**In-Depth Resources: Unit 3** • Guided Reading, p. 50 • Skillbuilder Practice: Analyzing Bias, p. 53 • Primary Source: Letter Opposing the English, p. 58 **Reading Study Guide,** p. 121 **Case Study 1:** India and Britain, p. 2	**Section 4 Assessment,** p. 361 **Formal Assessment** • Section Quiz, p. 193 **California Daily Standards Practice Transparencies,** TT104
Section 5 **Imperialism in Southeast Asia** pp. 362–365 **OBJECTIVE** Describe how imperialism affected Southeast Asia.	**In-Depth Resources: Unit 3** • Guided Reading, p. 51 • Primary Source: In Favor of Imperialism, p. 59 • History Makers: Mongkut, p. 64 **Reading Study Guide,** p. 123	**Section 5 Assessment,** p. 365 **Formal Assessment** • Section Quiz, p. 194 **California Daily Standards Practice Transparencies,** TT105

INTEGRATED TECHNOLOGY

- eEdition Plus Online
- EasyPlanner Plus Online
- eTest Plus Online

Audio CDs
- Voices from the Past
- Reading Study Guides

CD-ROMs
- eEdition
- Power Presentations
- EasyPlanner
- Electronic Library of Primary Sources
- Test Generator

eEdition CD-ROM

Electronic Library of Primary Sources
- "The Boer War: The Suffering of the Civilian Population"
- "Stanley Finds Livingstone"
- "Private Company Rule in the Congo"

classzone.com

eEdition CD-ROM

Electronic Library of Primary Sources
- from "Africa at the Center"

classzone.com

eEdition CD-ROM

World Art and Cultures Transparencies
- AT58 Reception at the Court of Sultan Selim II

classzone.com

eEdition CD-ROM

Geography Transparencies
- GT27 India Under British Rule, 1805–1886

World Art and Cultures Transparencies
- AT59 Raja Ram Singh in Procession

classzone.com

eEdition CD-ROM

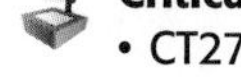

Critical Thinking Transparencies
- CT27 Comparing Imperialist Styles
- CT63 Chapter 27 Visual Summary

Electronic Library of Primary Sources
- from *Hawaii's Story by Hawaii's Queen*

classzone.com

OVERVIEW OF CALIFORNIA RESOURCES

	Section 1	Section 2	Section 3	Section 4	Section 5
California Reading Toolkit	p. L49	p. L50	p. L51	p. L52	p. L53
California Modified Lesson Plans for English Learners	p. 93	p. 95	p. 97	p. 99	p. 101
California Daily Standards Practice Transparencies	TT41	TT42	TT43	TT44	TT45
California Standards Enrichment Workbook	pp. 47–48, 49–50, 51–52	pp. 47–48, 49–50, 51–52	pp. 49–50, 51–52	pp. 47–48, 51–52, 53–54	pp. 47–48, 49–50, 51–52
California Standards Planner and Lesson Plans	p. L89	p. L91	p. L93	p. L95	p. L97
California Online Test Practice	classzone.com	classzone.com	classzone.com	classzone.com	classzone.com
California Test Generator CD-ROM					
California Easy Planner CD-ROM					
California eEdition CD-ROM					

Chart Key:

 Pupil's Edition

 Teacher's Edition

 Overhead Transparency

Block Scheduling

 Copymaster

 Audio Library

 CD-ROM

Internet

 Video

NO TIME?

If you do not have time to teach this chapter in full, assign the **Chapter in Brief** (also available in Spanish).

Previewing Resources for Differentiated Instruction

ENGLISH LEARNERS: Resources in Spanish

In-Depth Resources in Spanish
- Guided Reading Ⓐ
- Skillbuilder Practice: Analyzing Bias
- Geography Application: David Livingstone Explores Southern Africa Ⓑ

Chapters in Brief

Reading Study Guide Ⓒ

Reading Study Guide Audio CD

Test Generator CD-ROM
- Chapter Test, Forms A, B, and C

Plus

Modified Lesson Plans for English Learners

Multi-Language Glossary of Social Studies Terms

Ⓐ

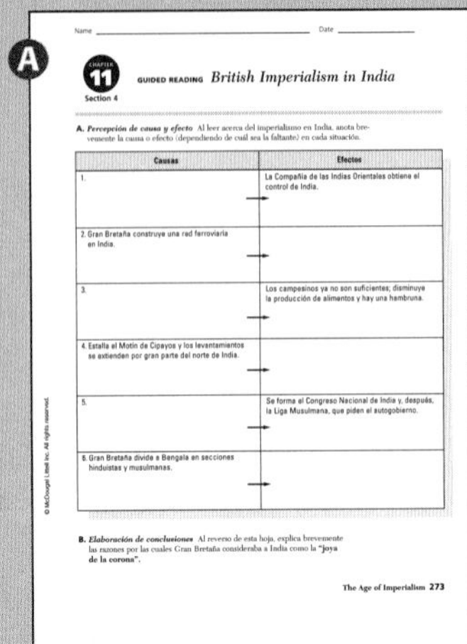

Chapter 11 Guided Reading: British Imperialism in India — Section 4

Ⓑ

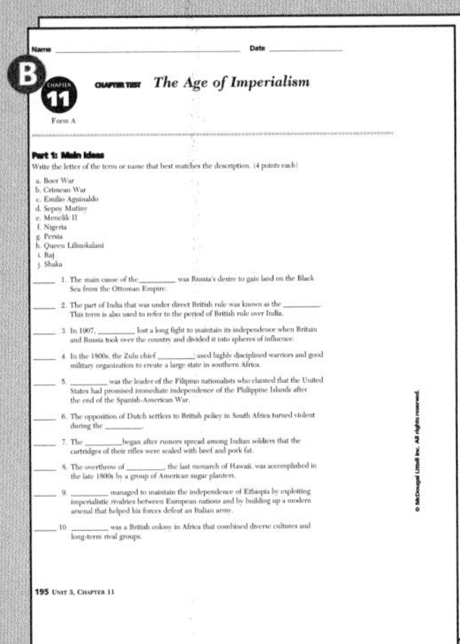

Chapter 11 Chapter Test: The Age of Imperialism — Form A

STRUGGLING READERS

In-Depth Resources: Unit 3
- Guided Reading
- Building Vocabulary Ⓐ
- Skillbuilder Practice: Analyzing Bias
- Geography Application: David Livingstone Explores Southern Africa
- Reteaching Activities Ⓑ

Chapters in Brief

Reading Study Guide

Reading Study Guide Audio CD

Formal Assessment
- Chapter Test, Form A Ⓒ

Plus

Reading Toolkit

Ⓐ

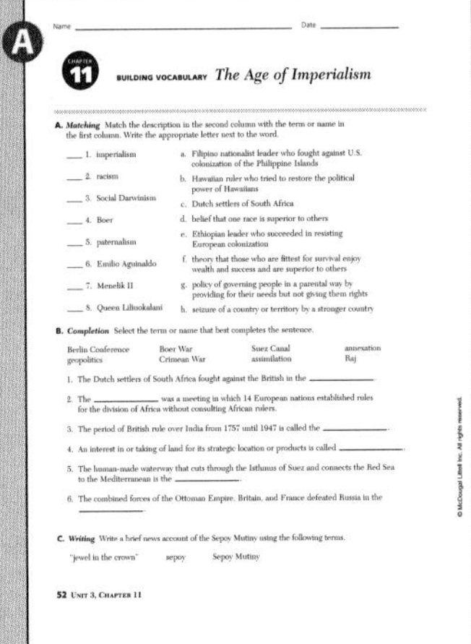

Chapter 11 Building Vocabulary: The Age of Imperialism

Ⓑ

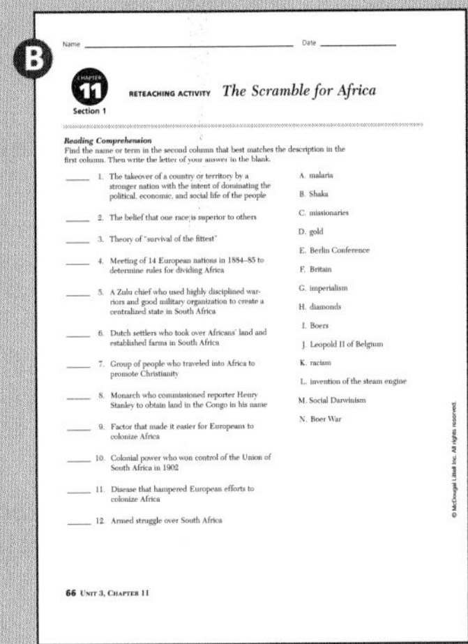

Chapter 11 Reteaching Activity: The Scramble for Africa — Section 1

GIFTED AND TALENTED STUDENTS

In-Depth Resources: Unit 3
- Primary Sources: British Contract with an African King; Letter from Menelik II; Letter Opposing the English; In Favor of Imperialism
- Literature: "The Burial" Ⓐ; from *Things Fall Apart* Ⓑ
- History Makers: Menelik II; Mongkut
- Connections Across Time and Cultures: Colonization and Imperialism Ⓒ

Electronic Library of Primary Sources
- "Stanley Finds Livingstone"
- from *Hawaii's Story by Hawaii's Queen*
- "The Boer War"
- from "Private Company Rule in the Congo"
- from "Africa at the Center"
- "The Rise of the Color Bar"

Formal Assessment
- Chapter Test, Form C

Ⓐ

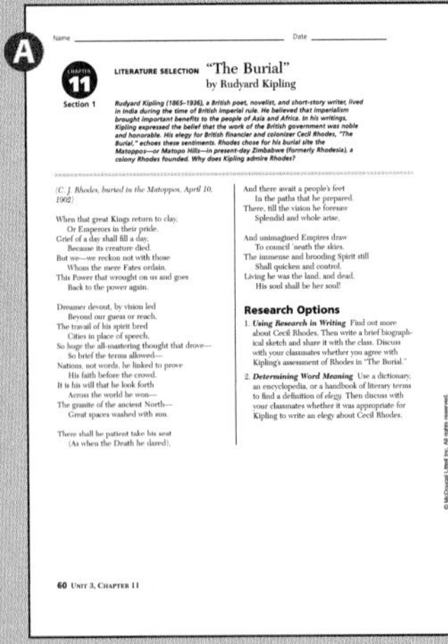

Chapter 11 Literature Selection: "The Burial" by Rudyard Kipling — Section 1

Ⓑ

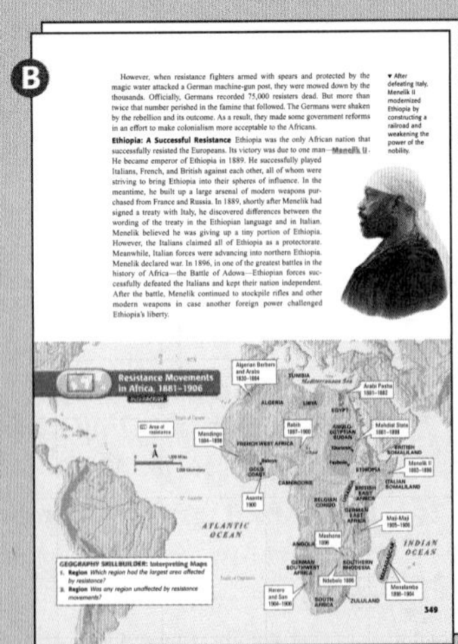

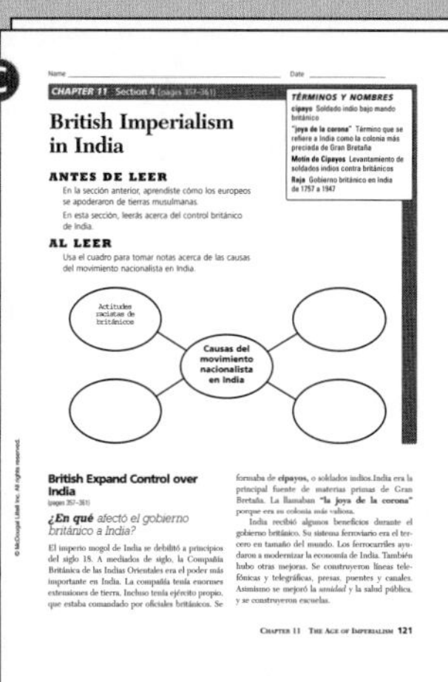

Name ______ Date ______

CHAPTER 11 Section 4 (pages 357–361)

British Imperialism in India

TÉRMINOS Y NOMBRES

cipayo Soldado indio bajo mando británico

"joya de la corona" Término que se refiere a India como la colonia más preciada de Gran Bretaña

Motín de Cipayos Levantamiento de soldados indios contra británicos

Raja Gobierno británico en India de 1757 a 1947

ANTES DE LEER

En la sección anterior, aprendiste cómo los europeos se apoderaron de tierras musulmanas.

En esta sección, leerás acerca del control británico de India.

AL LEER

Usa el cuadro para tomar notas acerca de las causas del movimiento nacionalista en India.

British Expand Control over India (pages 357–361)

***¿En qué** afectó el gobierno británico a India?*

El imperio mogol de India se debilitó a principios del siglo 18. A mediados de siglo, la Compañía Británica de las Indias Orientales era el poder más importante en India. La compañía tenía enormes extensiones de tierra. Incluso tenía ejército propio, que estaba comandado por oficiales británicos. Se formaba de **cipayos**, o soldados indios. India era la principal fuente de materias primas de Gran Bretaña. La llamaban **"la joya de la corona"** porque era su colonia más valiosa.

India recibió algunos beneficios durante el gobierno británico. Su sistema ferroviario era el tercero en tamaño del mundo. Los ferrocarriles ayudaron a modernizar la economía de India. También hubo otras mejoras. Se construyeron líneas telefónicas y telegráficas, presas, puentes y canales. Asimismo se mejoró la *sanidad* y la salud pública, y se construyeron escuelas.

CHAPTER 11 THE AGE OF IMPERIALISM 121

Activities in the Teacher's Edition for English Learners

- Imperialism, Racism, Social Darwinism, p. 341
- The Vocabulary of Imperialism, p. 347
- Understanding Reforms in Egypt, p. 355
- Causes and Effects of British Rule in India, p. 359

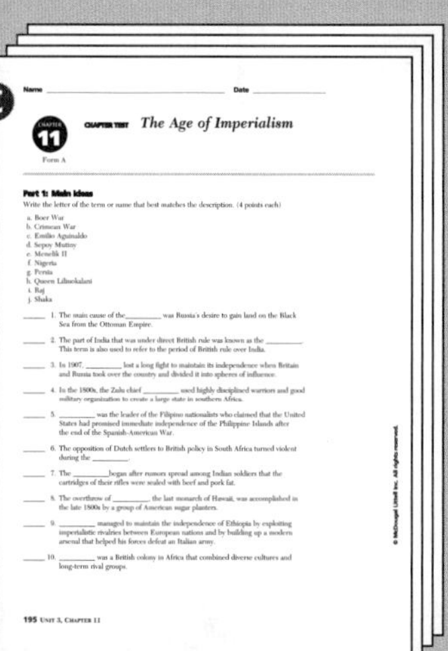

Name ______ Date ______

CHAPTER 11 CHAPTER TEST *The Age of Imperialism*

Form A

Part 1: Main Ideas

Write the letter of the term or name that best matches the description. (4 points each)

a. Boer War
b. Crimean War
c. Emilio Aguinaldo
d. Sepoy Mutiny
e. Menelik II
f. Nigeria
g. Persia
h. Queen Liliuokalani
i. Raj
j. Shaka

_____ 1. The main cause of the _____ was Russia's desire to gain land on the Black Sea from the Ottoman Empire.

_____ 2. The part of India that was under direct British rule was known as the _____. This term is also used to refer to the period of British rule over India.

_____ 3. In 1907, _____ lost a long fight to maintain its independence when Britain and Russia took over the country and divided it into spheres of influence.

_____ 4. In the 1800s, the Zulu chief _____ used highly disciplined warriors and good military organization to create a large state in southern Africa.

_____ 5. _____ was the leader of the Filipino nationalists who claimed that the United States had promised immediate independence of the Philippine Islands after the end of the Spanish-American War.

_____ 6. The opposition of Dutch settlers to British policy in South Africa turned violent during the _____.

_____ 7. The _____ began after rumors spread among Indian soldiers that the cartridges of their rifles were sealed with beef and pork fat.

_____ 8. The overthrow of _____, the last monarch of Hawaii, was accomplished in the late 1800s by a group of American sugar planters.

_____ 9. _____ managed to maintain the independence of Ethiopia by exploiting imperialistic rivalries between European nations and by building up a modern arsenal that helped his forces defeat an Italian army.

_____ 10. _____ was a British colony in Africa that combined diverse cultures and long-term rival groups.

195 UNIT 3, CHAPTER 11

Activities in the Teacher's Edition for Struggling Readers

- Events of the Boer War, p. 342
- African Resistance: Analyzing a Primary Source, p. 348
- Charting the Decline of the Ottoman Empire, p. 353
- Colonization in Southeast Asia, p. 363

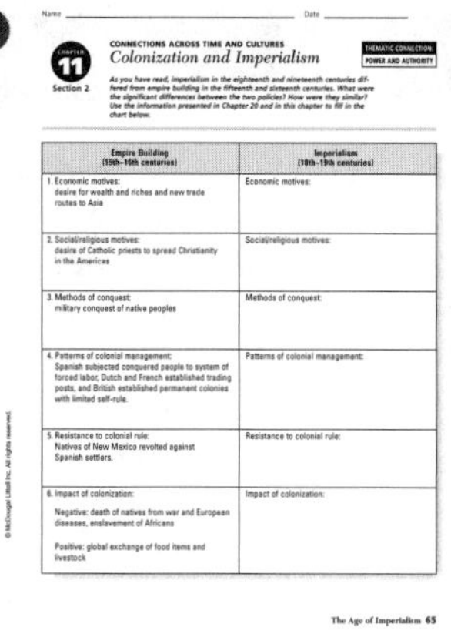

Name ______ Date ______

CHAPTER 11 Section 2

CONNECTIONS ACROSS TIME AND CULTURES

Colonization and Imperialism

THEMATIC CONNECTION: POWER AND AUTHORITY

As you have read, imperialism in the eighteenth and nineteenth centuries differed from empire building in the fifteenth and sixteenth centuries. What were the significant differences between the two policies? How were they similar? Use the information presented in Chapter 20 and in this chapter to fill in the chart below.

Empire Building (15th–16th centuries)	Imperialism (18th–19th centuries)
1. Economic motives: desire for wealth and riches and new trade routes to Asia	Economic motives:
2. Social/religious motives: desire of Catholic priests to spread Christianity in the Americas	Social/religious motives:
3. Methods of conquest: military conquest of native peoples	Methods of conquest:
4. Patterns of colonial management: Spanish subjected conquered people to system of forced labor, Dutch and French established trading posts, and British established permanent colonies with limited self-rule.	Patterns of colonial management:
5. Resistance to colonial rule: Natives of New Mexico revolted against Spanish settlers.	Resistance to colonial rule:
6. Impact of colonization: Negative: death of natives from war and European diseases, enslavement of Africans. Positive: global exchange of food items and livestock	Impact of colonization:

The Age of Imperialism 65

Activities in the Teacher's Edition for Gifted and Talented Students

- Tracing the Exploration of Southern Africa, p. 340
- Literature of Resistance, p. 349
- Debating Use of the Suez Canal, p. 354
- Colonialism in Literature, p. 358
- Analyzing a Speech, p. 364

INTEGRATED TECHNOLOGY

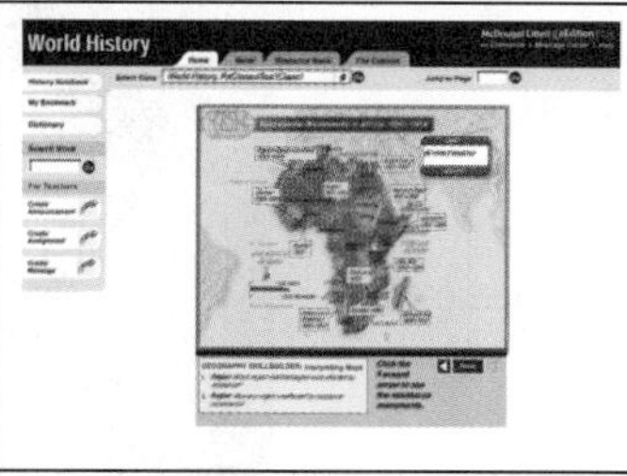

eEdition

- Interactive Visuals
- Interactive Maps
- Interactive Primary Sources

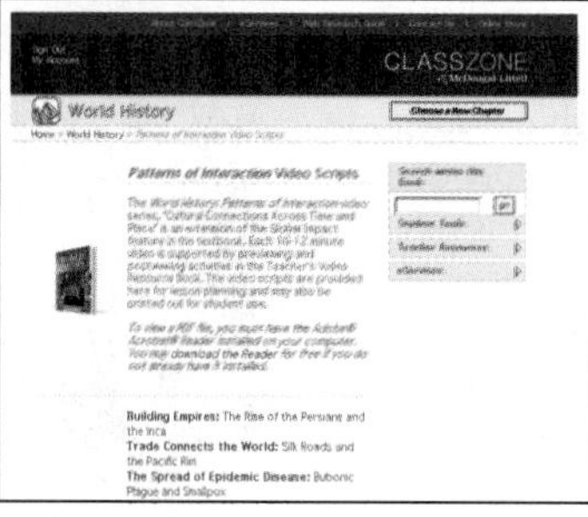

classzone.com

- Research Links
- Internet Activities
- Primary Sources
- Chapter Quiz
- Current Events

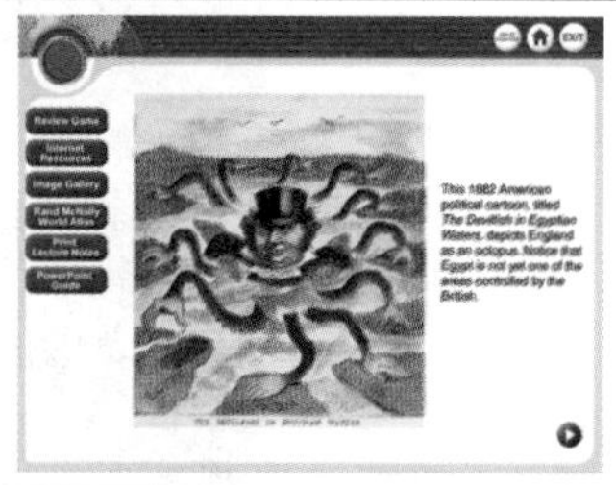

Power Presentations CD-ROM

- Lecture Notes
- Image Gallery
- Chapter Review Game

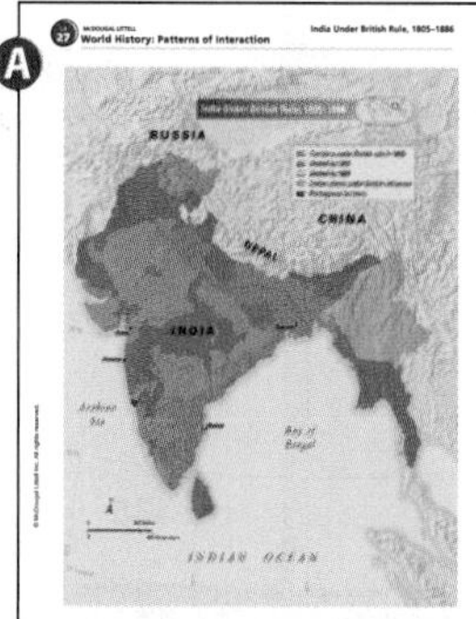

Critical Thinking Transparencies

- CT27 Comparing Imperialist Styles
- CT63 Chapter 27 Visual Summary

Geography Transparencies

- GT27 India Under British Rule, 1805–1886 (A)

World Art and Cultures Transparencies

- AT58 Reception at the Court of Sultan Selim III
- AT59 Rajah Ram Singh in Procession

Test Practice Transparencies TT101–TT105

Test Generator CD-ROM

EasyPlanner CD-ROM

Voices from the Past Audio CD

Online Test Practice

Electronic Library of Primary Sources

CHAPTER 11 • OBJECTIVE

Trace the spread of European influence through colonial expansion.

Previewing Main Ideas

The main ideas that characterize this period are among the driving forces of history. They continue to influence events in the modern world.

Accessing Prior Knowledge

Ask students what the words *imperialism* and *colonialism* mean to them. Explain that these terms describe expansion of one nation's power through occupation and domination of another. How do students think colonized nations might react? *(with resentment and, possibly, rebellion)* What effect might one nation's imperialism have on other powerful nations? *(They become imperialistic to maintain the balance of power.)*

Geography *Answers*

EMPIRE BUILDING Seven countries colonized Africa. Great Britain controlled India. The United States controlled the Philippines.

POWER AND AUTHORITY France and Great Britain claimed most of Africa.

ECONOMICS The colonial lands were much larger than the Western countries and included valuable natural resources.

CHAPTER 11

The Age of Imperialism, 1850–1914

Previewing Main Ideas

EMPIRE BUILDING During the 19th and early 20th centuries, Western powers divided Africa and colonized large areas of Asia.

Geography *Study the map and time line. How many countries colonized Africa? Which country controlled India? the Philippines?*

POWER AND AUTHORITY At the Berlin Conference in 1884–1885, European nations established rules for the division of Africa with little concern about how their actions would affect the African people.

Geography *Which two countries claimed most of Africa?*

ECONOMICS Industrialization increased the need for raw materials and new markets. Western imperialists were driven by this need as they looked for colonies to acquire.

Geography *Compare the size of the Western countries with the areas they colonized. Why were these Western powers interested in lands in Africa and Asia?*

INTEGRATED TECHNOLOGY

eEdition
- Interactive Maps
- Interactive Visuals
- Interactive Primary Sources

INTERNET RESOURCES

Go to **classzone.com** for:
- Research Links
- Internet Activities
- Primary Sources
- Chapter Quiz
- Maps
- Test Practice
- Current Events

AFRICA AND ASIA

1850
European trading with Africa becomes well established. (Asante brass sculpture) ▶

1869
Suez Canal opens.

1884–1885
Berlin Conference sets rules for African colonization.

1850 1875

WORLD

1852
Napoleon III proclaims himself emperor of France. ▶

1871
Bismarck completes unification of German Empire.

336

TIME LINE DISCUSSION

Point out that this period, which spans the end of the 19th and beginning of the 20th centuries, was marked by confrontation and upheaval, as well as territorial expansion, worldwide.

1. What was the political situation in Africa at the beginning of World War I? *(Most of it had come under European control.)*
2. How many years after the conclusion of the Berlin Conference did the Boer War begin? *(14)*
3. What evidence is there that the world was highly unstable and in conflict during this period? *(the occurrence of the Boer War, the Spanish-American War, the Mexican Revolution, and World War I)*
4. Around the turn of the century, what political and military actions was the United States involved in? *(acquisition of the Philippines, annexation of Hawaii, and victorious conclusion of the Spanish-American War)*
5. When did the trading relationship between Europe and Africa begin changing to one of colonization? *(between 1850 and 1884)*

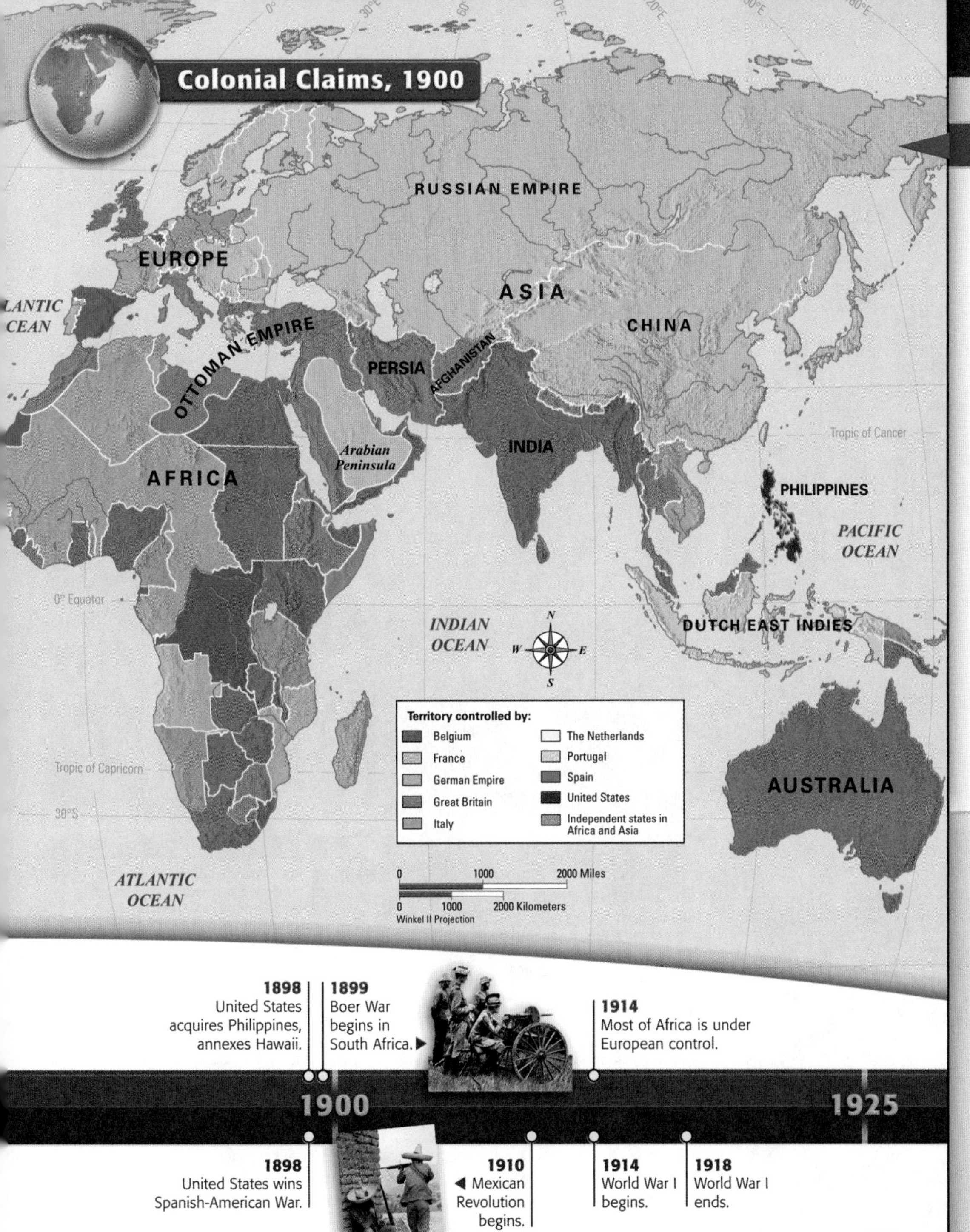

337

CHAPTER 11

History from Visuals

Interpreting the Map

Ask students to examine the map carefully. Which European power did not control territory in Africa in 1900? *(the Netherlands)* Which country was the greatest imperial power? *(Great Britain)* On which continents did Great Britain control territory? *(Africa, Asia, and Australia)* Have students discuss why they think Africa was so sought after. *(Possible Answer: It was a vast territory with no centralized power structure and many natural resources needed by Europeans.)*

Extension Ask students to compare the colonized areas of Africa and Asia with the modern maps in the Atlas. Have pairs of students research the modern nations using an almanac or other reference book and determine which, if any, are still colonized. *(None of the former colonies in Africa and Asia remain colonized today.)*

RECOMMENDED RESOURCES

Books for the Teacher

Copland, Ian., ed. ***The Burden of Empire***. Melbourne: Oxford UP, 1990. Study of imperialism and colonialism.

Hawkins, Mike. ***Social Darwinism in European and American Thought, 1860–1945: Nature as Model and Nature as Threat***. New York: Cambridge UP, 1997. Demonstrates the relevance of Social Darwinism through a study of European and American social and political thinkers.

Books for the Student

McDougal Littell Literature Connections. Achebe, Chinua. ***Things Fall Apart (with related readings).*** 1997. In this classic novel, the traditional ways of an Ibo village in Nigeria are challenged by new European ways.

Coetzee, J. M. ***Waiting for the Barbarians***. New York: Penguin, 1999. The story of a magistrate in an African settlement whose views about the native people change over time.

Videos and Software

Zulus at War. VHS. Ambrose Video, 1995. 800-526-4663. Depicts battles between Zulus and the British.

Imperialism. CD-ROM. Clearvue/EVA, 1994. 800-253-2788. Provides case studies, including the British in India and multiple powers in Africa.

Interact *with* History

Objectives

- Set the stage for the study of European colonization.
- Highlight some benefits and problems of imperialism.

EXAMINING *the* ISSUES

Possible Answers

- Advantages—New railways and roads, more jobs. Disadvantages—Less freedom, enforced labor, loss of family and culture.
- The photograph suggests that the colonizers were in charge of the African workers, reducing them to an inferior and displaced status in their own country.

Discussion

Ask students what they think happens to peoples who are conquered or colonized. *(They can be forced to adopt the culture of their conquerors; sometimes they have been allowed to retain some or all of their way of life; sometimes they resist and retain their sovereignty or are further subjugated.)*

Interact *with* History

How would you react to the colonizers?

You are a young South African living in the 1880s. Gold and diamonds have recently been discovered in your country. The European colonizers need laborers to work the mines, such as the one shown below in an 1888 photograph. Along with thousands of other South Africans, you've left your farm and rural village to work for the colonizers. Separated from your family and living in a city for the first time, you don't know what to expect.

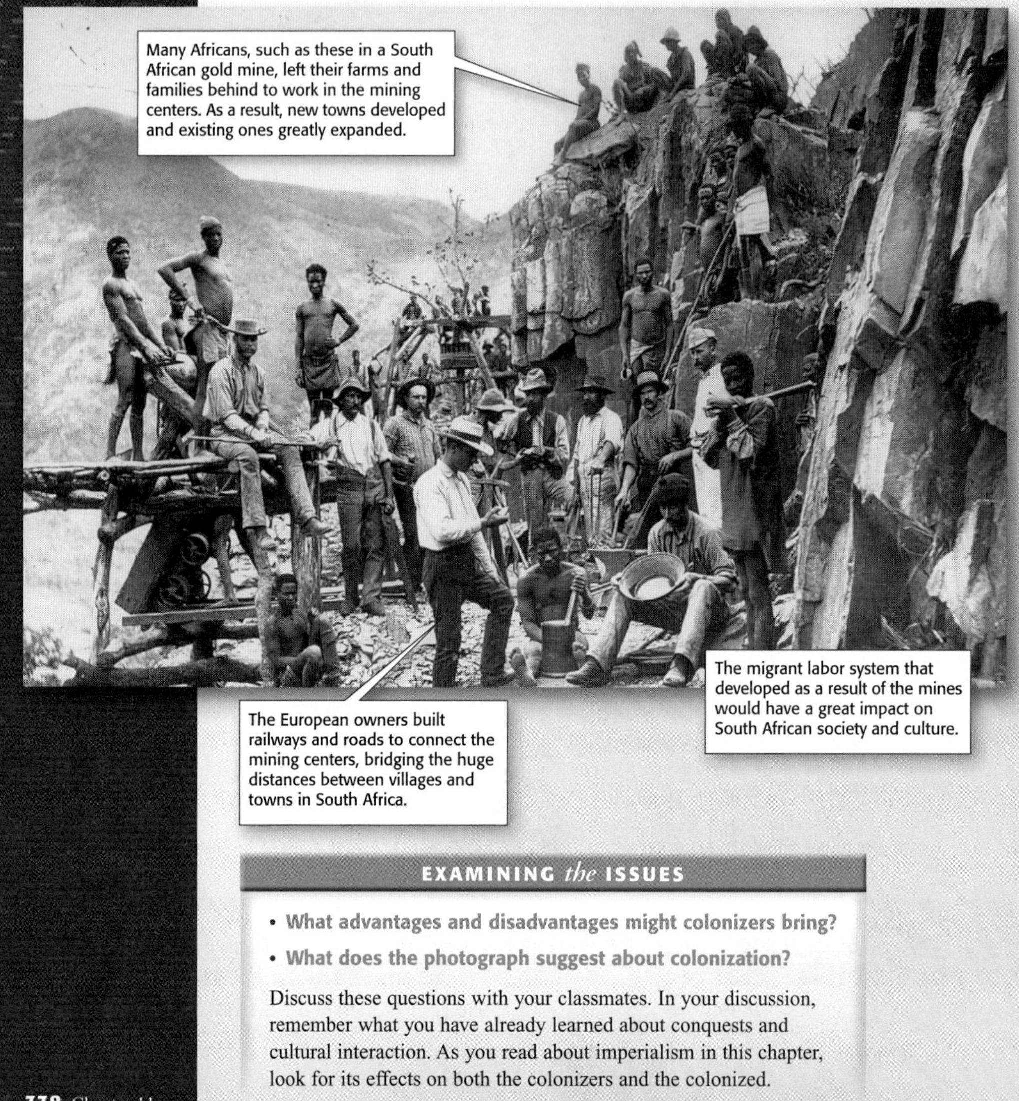

Many Africans, such as these in a South African gold mine, left their farms and families behind to work in the mining centers. As a result, new towns developed and existing ones greatly expanded.

The European owners built railways and roads to connect the mining centers, bridging the huge distances between villages and towns in South Africa.

The migrant labor system that developed as a result of the mines would have a great impact on South African society and culture.

EXAMINING *the* ISSUES

- **What advantages and disadvantages might colonizers bring?**
- **What does the photograph suggest about colonization?**

Discuss these questions with your classmates. In your discussion, remember what you have already learned about conquests and cultural interaction. As you read about imperialism in this chapter, look for its effects on both the colonizers and the colonized.

WHY STUDY THE AGE OF IMPERIALISM?

- Imperialism helped establish national powers that continue to influence world events.
- The roots of a global community were planted during this dynamic period of history.
- Many current conflicts have their roots in this colonial era, when longtime enemies were forced together by imperial nation building.
- The colonial influence in African and Asian countries persists today in language and in educational and other cultural systems and institutions.
- The uses and abuses of power that characterize this era offer lessons for modern nations with rapidly changing roles on an increasingly complex world stage.
- The struggles for independence in Southeast Asia have roots in imperialism.

Aboriginal bark painting from Milingimbi, Australia

Battle of Isandhlwana, 1879, Zululand (now in South Africa)

1

The Scramble for Africa

MAIN IDEA	WHY IT MATTERS NOW	TERMS & NAMES
EMPIRE BUILDING Ignoring the claims of African ethnic groups, kingdoms, and city-states, Europeans established colonies.	African nations continue to feel the effects of the colonial presence more than 100 years later.	• imperialism • racism • Social Darwinism • Berlin Conference • Shaka • Boer • Boer War

SETTING THE STAGE Industrialization stirred ambitions in many European nations. They wanted more resources to fuel their industrial production. They competed for new markets for their goods. Many nations looked to Africa as a source of raw materials and as a market for industrial products. As a result, colonial powers seized vast areas of Africa during the 19th and early 20th centuries. This seizure of a country or territory by a stronger country is called **imperialism**. As occurred throughout most of Africa, stronger countries dominated the political, economic, and social life of the weaker countries.

Africa Before European Domination

In the mid-1800s, on the eve of the European domination of Africa, African peoples were divided into hundreds of ethnic and linguistic groups. Most continued to follow traditional beliefs, while others converted to Islam or Christianity. These groups spoke more than 1,000 different languages. Politically, they ranged from large empires that united many ethnic groups to independent villages.

Europeans had established contacts with sub-Saharan Africans as early as the 1450s. However, powerful African armies were able to keep the Europeans out of most of Africa for 400 years. In fact, as late as 1880, Europeans controlled only 10 percent of the continent's land, mainly on the coast.

Furthermore, European travel into the interior on a large-scale basis was virtually impossible. Europeans could not navigate African rivers, which had many rapids, cataracts, and changing flows.The introduction of steam-powered riverboats in the early 1800s allowed Europeans to conduct major expeditions into the interior of Africa. Disease also discouraged European exploration.

Finally, Africans controlled their own trade networks and provided the trade items. These networks were specialized. The Chokwe, for example, devoted themselves to collecting ivory and beeswax in the Angolan highlands.

Nations Compete for Overseas Empires Those Europeans who did penetrate the interior of Africa were explorers, missionaries, or humanitarians who opposed the European and American slave trade. Europeans and Americans learned about Africa through travel books and newspapers. These publications competed for readers by hiring reporters to search the globe for stories of adventure, mystery, or excitement.

CALIFORNIA STANDARDS

10.4.1 Describe the rise of industrial economies and their link to imperialism and colonialism (e.g., the role played by national security and strategic advantage; moral issues raised by the search for national hegemony, Social Darwinism, and the missionary impulse; material issues such as land, resources, and technology).

10.4.2 Discuss the locations of the colonial rule of such nations as England, France, Germany, Italy, Japan, the Netherlands, Russia, Spain, Portugal, and the United States.

10.4.3 Explain imperialism from the perspective of the colonizers and the colonized and the varied immediate and long-term responses by the people under colonial rule.

HI 2 Students recognize the complexity of historical causes and effects, including the limitations on determining cause and effect.

TAKING NOTES

Outlining Use an outline to list the forces and events surrounding imperialism in Africa.

The Scramble for Africa
I. Africa Before European Domination
A.
B.
II. Forces Driving Imperialism

LESSON PLAN

OBJECTIVES

- Describe Africa before European domination.
- Summarize the motives of European colonizers and the factors that allowed them to control Africa.
- Identify three groups that clashed in South Africa.

1 FOCUS & MOTIVATE

Ask students to discuss times they may have tried to dominate someone younger, smaller, or weaker. How did they assert their power? *(Possible Answers: by force, coercion, or bribes)*

2 INSTRUCT

Africa Before European Domination

10.4.1; 10.4.2; 10.4.3

Critical Thinking

- Why did colonization of Africa begin in the Congo? *(Belgium supported Stanley's exploration of the Congo, which led to colonization.)*

CALIFORNIA RESOURCES
California Reading Toolkit, p. L49
California Modified Lesson Plans for English Learners, p. 93
California Daily Standards Practice Transparencies, TT41
California Standards Enrichment Workbook, pp. 47–48, 49–50, 51–52
California Standards Planner and Lesson Plans, p. L89
California Online Test Practice
California Test Generator CD-ROM
California Easy Planner CD-ROM
California eEdition CD-ROM

SECTION 1 PROGRAM RESOURCES

ALL STUDENTS

In-Depth Resources: Unit 3
- Guided Reading, p. 47
- Geography Application: Livingstone, p. 54

Formal Assessment
- Section Quiz, p. 191

ENGLISH LEARNERS

In-Depth Resources in Spanish
- Guided Reading, p. 88
- Geography Application, p. 94

Reading Study Guide (Spanish), p. 115
Reading Study Guide Audio CD (Spanish)

STRUGGLING READERS

In-Depth Resources: Unit 3
- Guided Reading, p. 47
- Building Vocabulary, p. 52
- Geography Application: Livingstone, p. 54
- Reteaching Activity, p. 66

Reading Study Guide, p. 115
Reading Study Guide Audio CD

GIFTED AND TALENTED STUDENTS

In-Depth Resources: Unit 3
- Primary Source: British Contract with an African King, p. 56
- Literature: "The Burial," p. 60

INTEGRATED TECHNOLOGY

eEdition CD-ROM
Voices from the Past Audio CD
Power Presentations CD-ROM
Electronic Library of Primary Sources
- "The Boer War"
- "Stanley Finds Livingstone"
- "Private Company Rule in the Congo"

classzone.com

More About . . .

Collecting Wild Rubber

Rubber production under Belgian rule was one of the worst exploitations of Africans in the history of African colonialism. Armed soldiers drove people into the forest to collect wild rubber. Those who refused were killed or mutilated. In some cases, a victim's hand was taken as a trophy to show the commissioner. The hands were then counted to determine that the soldiers had not wasted cartridges. European outrage over this practice forced the Belgians to discontinue it.

Forces Driving Imperialism
10.4.1

Critical Thinking

- How did the Industrial Revolution lead to European colonization? *(Factories in Europe needed more and more raw materials which could be gotten cheaply if the source was colonized.)*
- What basic assumption of Social Darwinism would Africans most likely disagree with? *(that fitness for survival is measured in scientific and technological development)*

In-Depth Resources: Unit 3

- Primary Source: British Contract with an African King, p. 56
- Literature: "The Burial," p. 60

Electronic Library of Primary Sources

- "Stanley Finds Livingstone"
- "Private Company Rule in the Congo"

▲ This stamp celebrates the centenary (100th) anniversary of Stanley and Livingstone's meeting in 1871.

The Congo Sparks Interest In the late 1860s, David Livingstone, a missionary from Scotland, traveled with a group of Africans deep into central Africa to promote Christianity. When several years passed with no word from him or his party, many people feared he was dead. An American newspaper hired reporter Henry Stanley to find Livingstone. In 1871, he found Dr. Livingstone on the shores of Lake Tanganyika. Stanley's famous greeting—"Dr. Livingstone, I presume?"—made headlines around the world.

Stanley set out to explore Africa himself and trace the course of the Congo River. His explorations sparked the interest of King Leopold II of Belgium, who commissioned Stanley to help him obtain land in the Congo. Between 1879 and 1882, Stanley signed treaties with local chiefs of the Congo River valley. The treaties gave King Leopold II of Belgium control of these lands.

Leopold claimed that his primary motive in establishing the colony was to abolish the slave trade and promote Christianity. However, he licensed companies that brutally exploited Africans by forcing them to collect sap from rubber plants. At least 10 million Congolese died due to the abuses inflicted during Leopold's rule. As a result of his cruelty, humanitarians around the world demanded changes. In 1908, the Belgian government took control of the colony away from Leopold. The Belgian Congo, as the colony later became known, was 80 times larger than Belgium. The Belgian government's seizure of the Congo alarmed France. Earlier, in 1882, the French had approved a treaty that gave France the north bank of the Congo River. Soon Britain, Germany, Italy, Portugal, and Spain were also claiming parts of Africa.

Forces Driving Imperialism

The motives that drove colonization in Africa were also at work in other lands. Similar economic, political, and social forces accelerated the drive to take over land in all parts of the globe. The Industrial Revolution in particular provided European countries with a reason to add lands to their control. As European nations industrialized, they searched for new markets and raw materials to improve their economies.

Belief in European Superiority The race for colonies also grew out of a strong sense of national pride. Europeans viewed an empire as a measure of national greatness. As the competition for colonies intensified, each country was determined to plant its flag on as much of the world as possible.

DIFFERENTIATING INSTRUCTION: GIFTED AND TALENTED STUDENTS

Tracing the Exploration of Southern Africa

Class Time 30 minutes

Task Studying a map of David Livingstone's travels

Purpose To appreciate the role of explorers in awakening European interest in Africa

Instructions Have students read the Geography Application worksheet on page 54 of In-Depth Resources: Unit 3. You might want to make a transparency of the map of Livingstone's travels on the bottom of that page. Ask students to work in pairs to study the map and discuss the material they have read. Then have them answer the questions on page 55 and discuss their answers with other pairs.

Ask students to compare the map of Livingstone's travels with the the map of Africa on page 343. Which European nations claimed the lands in the areas Livingstone explored? *(Belgium, Portugal, Great Britain, France, and Germany)* Do students think Livingstone would have approved or disapproved of the land grab? Why? *(Possible Answer: disapproved because he respected African culture and rejected the idea of European superiority)*

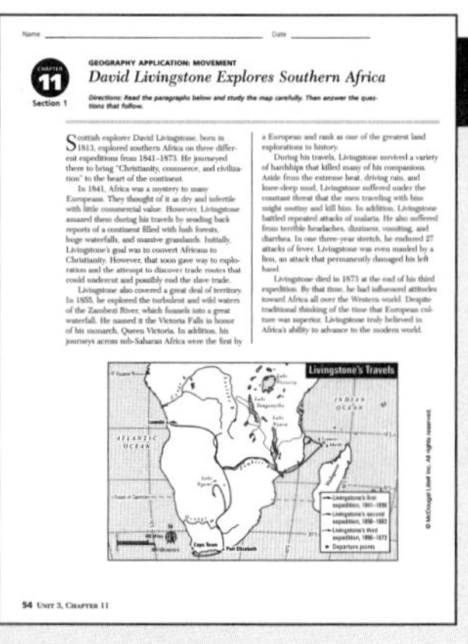
GEOGRAPHY APPLICATION: MOVEMENT

David Livingstone Explores Southern Africa

In-Depth Resources: Unit 3

Many Europeans believed that they were better than other peoples. The belief that one race is superior to others is called **racism**. The attitude was a reflection of **Social Darwinism**, a social theory of the time. In this theory, Charles Darwin's ideas about evolution and "survival of the fittest" were applied to human society. Those who were fittest for survival enjoyed wealth and success and were considered superior to others. According to the theory, non-Europeans were considered to be on a lower scale of cultural and physical development because they had not made the scientific and technological progress that Europeans had. Europeans believed that they had the right and the duty to bring the results of their progress to other countries. Cecil Rhodes, a successful businessman and a major supporter of British expansion, clearly stated this position:

MAIN IDEA
Analyzing Primary Sources
A What attitude about the British does Rhodes's statement display?
A. Answer British superiority to all other groups

PRIMARY SOURCE **A**
I contend that we [Britons] are the first race in the world, and the more of the world we inhabit, the better it is for the human race. . . . It is our duty to seize every opportunity of acquiring more territory and we should keep this one idea steadily before our eyes that more territory simply means more of the Anglo-Saxon race, more of the best, the most human, most honourable race the world possesses.

CECIL RHODES, *Confession of Faith,* 1877

▲ Rhodes's De Beers Consolidated Mines is the biggest diamond company in the world today.

The push for expansion also came from missionaries who worked to convert the peoples of Asia, Africa, and the Pacific Islands to Christianity. Many missionaries believed that European rule was the best way to end evil practices such as the slave trade. They also wanted to "civilize," that is, to "Westernize," the peoples of the foreign land.

Factors Promoting Imperialism in Africa Several factors contributed to the Europeans' conquest of Africa. One overwhelming advantage was the Europeans' technological superiority. The Maxim gun, invented in 1884, was the world's first automatic machine gun. European countries quickly acquired the Maxim, while the resisting Africans were forced to rely on outdated weapons.

European countries also had the means to control their empire. The invention of the steam engine allowed Europeans to easily travel on rivers to establish bases of control deep in the African continent. Railroads, cables, and steamships allowed close communications within a colony and between the colony and its controlling nation.

Even with superior arms and steam engines to transport them, another factor might have kept Europeans confined to the coast. They were highly susceptible to malaria, a disease carried by the dense swarms of mosquitoes in Africa's interior. The perfection of the drug quinine in 1829 eventually protected Europeans from becoming infected with this disease.

Factors within Africa also made the continent easier for Europeans to colonize. Africans' huge variety of languages and cultures discouraged unity among them. Wars fought between ethnic groups over land, water, and trade rights also prevented a unified stand. Europeans soon learned to play rival groups against each other.

The Division of Africa

Vocabulary
scramble: a frantic struggle to obtain something. The word is frequently used to describe the competition for African land.

The scramble for African territory had begun in earnest about 1880. At that time, the French began to expand from the West African coast toward western Sudan. The discoveries of diamonds in 1867 and gold in 1886 in South Africa increased European interest in colonizing the continent. No European power wanted to be left out of the race.

More About . . .

Cecil Rhodes

Cecil Rhodes first went to South Africa as a young man to improve his health. He became involved in the diamond business and amassed an immense fortune mining this plentiful natural resource of southern Africa. In his will, he left a portion of this fortune to Oxford University to establish scholarships for English-speaking students. Former President Clinton was among many illustrious Rhodes scholars.

More About . . .

Malaria

Malaria remains a deadly and widespread disease today, with over 40% of the world's population at risk. As many as 500 million cases and 1 million deaths occur each year.

The Division of Africa

10.4.2

Critical Thinking

- Why were no African rulers invited to attend the Berlin Conference? *(Europeans believed they had the right to decide Africa's fate.)*
- How did colonization change Africans' basic economy? *(Cash crops replaced families' food crops.)*

DIFFERENTIATING INSTRUCTION: ENGLISH LEARNERS

Imperialism, Racism, Social Darwinism

Class Time 25 minutes

Task Creating a chart of words ending in *-ism*

Purpose To learn a strategy for analyzing the *-ism* words

Instructions Point out to students that the three key terms on pages 339 and 341—*imperialism, racism*, and *Social Darwinism*—all end in the suffix *-ism*. Explain that this suffix is used to create nouns from other nouns, adjectives, or verbs and that it has several meanings, including "doctrine or theory" and "act or practice." Have students work in pairs or small groups to create a chart including the key term, the meaning of the suffix, and the meaning of the word. Ask them to brainstorm other *-ism* words and add them to their charts. Completed charts may look like this:

Word	Meaning of Suffix	Meaning of Word
imperialism	act	takeover of a country by a stronger one
racism	doctrine	belief in the superiority of one race
Social Darwinism	doctrine	ideas about "survival of the fittest" applied to humans
criticism	act	act of criticizing

Tip for English Learners

The word *Afrikaans* refers to the language spoken by the Dutch who settled South Africa. *Afrikaner* means an Afrikaans-speaking South African of European ancestry.

More About . . .

The Berlin Conference

King Leopold of Belgium had several motives for attending the Berlin Conference. He fancied himself a great statesman and wanted to build a kingdom in Africa that would extend from the Congo to the Nile. All he got, however, was the central Congo, primarily because France, Germany, and England wanted a buffer zone among their African holdings.

Three Groups Clash Over South Africa

10.4.2; 10.4.3

Critical Thinking

- What conclusion can you draw about the Zulus from their near-defeat of the British invaders? *(They were highly trained and motivated to fight for their land.)*
- How did the Boer War differ from other patterns of colonization in Africa? *(It was a war between European colonizers on African soil with minimal participation by native Africans.)*

Berlin Conference Divides Africa The competition was so fierce that European countries feared war among themselves. To prevent conflict, 14 European nations met at the **Berlin Conference** in 1884–85 to lay down rules for the division of Africa. They agreed that any European country could claim land in Africa by notifying other nations of its claims and showing it could control the area. The European nations divided the continent with little thought about how African ethnic or linguistic groups were distributed. No African ruler was invited to attend these meetings, yet the conference sealed Africa's fate. By 1914, only Liberia and Ethiopia remained free from European control. B

MAIN IDEA
Clarifying
B What was the purpose of the Berlin Conference?
B. Answer to lay down rules for the division of Africa

Demand for Raw Materials Shapes Colonies When European countries began colonizing, many believed that Africans would soon be buying European goods in great quantities. They were wrong; few Africans bought European goods. However, European businesses still needed raw materials from Africa. The major source of great wealth in Africa proved to be the continent's rich mineral resources. The Belgian Congo contained untold wealth in copper and tin. Even these riches seemed small compared with the gold and diamonds in South Africa.

Businesses eventually developed cash-crop plantations to grow peanuts, palm oil, cocoa, and rubber. These products displaced the food crops grown by farmers to feed their families.

Three Groups Clash over South Africa

South Africa demonstrated the impact that Europeans had on African peoples. The history of South Africa is a history of Africans, Dutch, and British clashing over land and resources. Although the African lands seemed empty to the Europeans, various ethnic groups had competing claims over huge areas. The local control of these lands, especially in the east, had been in dispute for about 100 years.

Zulus Fight the British From the late 1700s to the late 1800s, a series of local wars shook southern Africa. Around 1816, a Zulu chief, **Shaka**, used highly disciplined warriors and good military organization to create a large centralized state.

▼ Reinstated as ruler over part of his former nation, King Cetshwayo was soon driven away and died in exile in 1884.

Shaka's successors, however, were unable to keep the kingdom together against the superior arms of the British invaders. In 1879, after Zulu king Cetshwayo refused to dismiss his army and accept British rule, the British invaded the Zulu nation. Although the Zulus used spears and shields against British guns, they nearly defeated the great European army. In July 1879, however, the Zulus lost the Battle of Ulundi and their kingdom. The Zulu nation fell to British control in 1887.

Boers and British Settle in the Cape The first Europeans to settle in South Africa had been the Dutch. The Dutch came to the Cape of Good Hope in 1652 to establish a way station for their ships sailing between the Dutch East Indies and the Netherlands. Dutch settlers known as **Boers** (Dutch for "farmers") gradually took Africans' land and established large farms. (The Boers are also known as Afrikaners.) When the British took over the Cape Colony permanently in the early 1800s, they and the Boers clashed over British policy regarding land and slaves.

DIFFERENTIATING INSTRUCTION: STRUGGLING READERS

Events of the Boer War

Class Time 35 minutes

Task Charting the events in the Boer War

Purpose To clarify the causes and effects of the conflict

Instructions Have students work in pairs to reread the material about the Boer War. Ask them to think about the following questions:

- Who were the Boers? *(Settlers of Dutch descent)*
- Why did they clash with the British? *(The British claimed the South African colony and set up policies that the Boers didn't like.)*

Then hand out copies of Critical Thinking Transparency CT73 chronological order chart. Have students list the events in the Boer war in order.

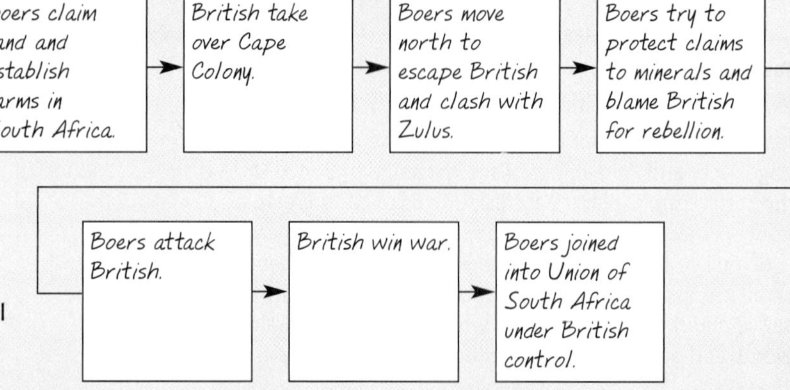

Boers claim land and establish farms in South Africa.
British take over Cape Colony.
Boers move north to escape British and clash with Zulus.
Boers try to protect claims to minerals and blame British for rebellion.
Boers attack British.
British win war.
Boers joined into Union of South Africa under British control.

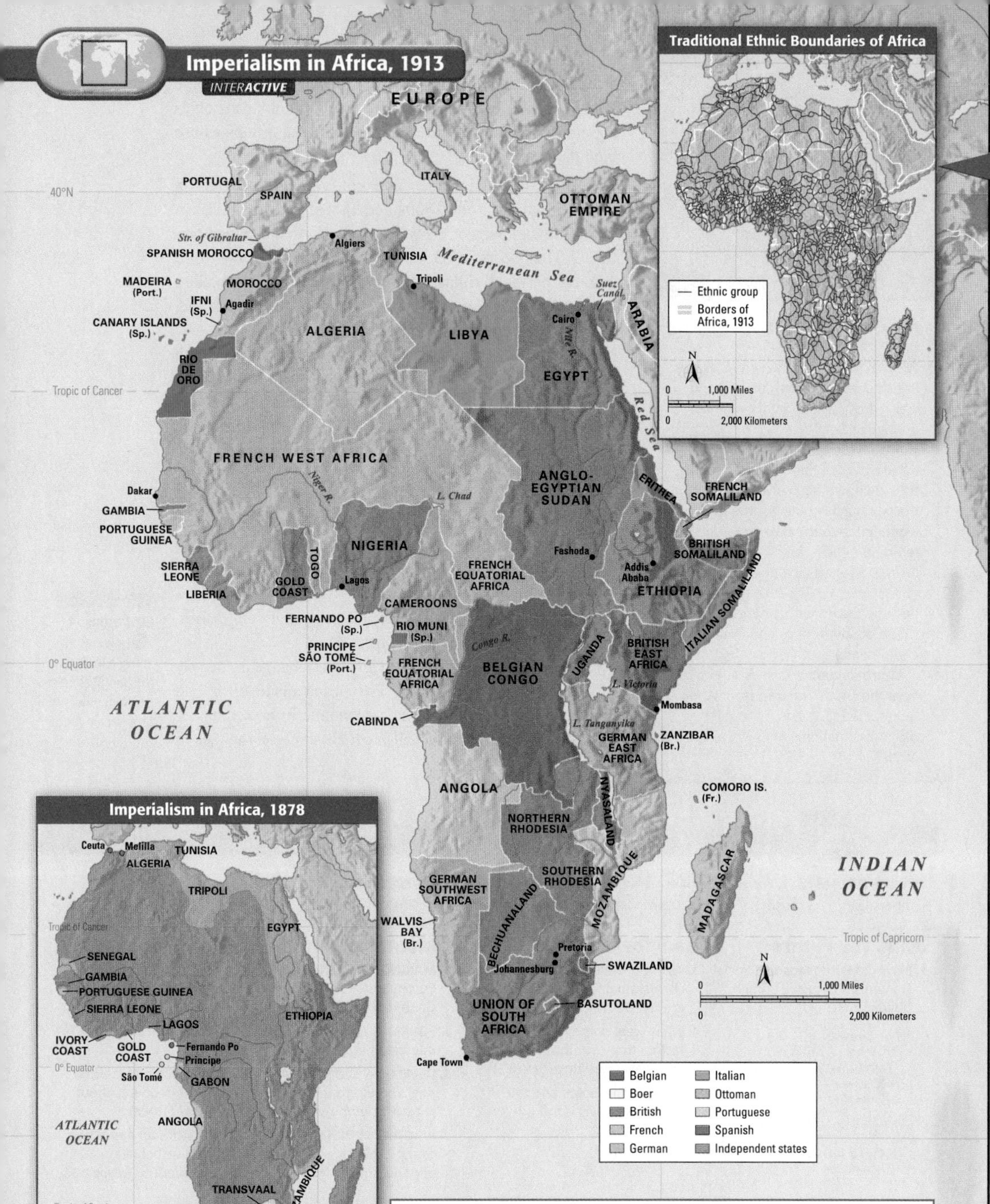

Imperialism in Africa, 1913

INTERACTIVE

Traditional Ethnic Boundaries of Africa

— Ethnic group
Borders of Africa, 1913

Imperialism in Africa, 1878

Belgian	Italian
Boer	Ottoman
British	Portuguese
French	Spanish
German	Independent states

GEOGRAPHY SKILLBUILDER: Interpreting Maps

1. **Region** *How does imperialism in Africa in 1878 compare with that in 1913?*
2. **Region** *What does the map of ethnic boundaries suggest about the number of ethnic groups in Africa in 1913?*

343

History from Visuals

Interpreting the Map

Ask students to examine the main map and the two inset maps. About what percentage of Africa was colonized by Europeans in 1878? *(10 percent)* In 1913? *(96 percent)* Which two imperial powers controlled the most African territory in 1913? *(France and Great Britain)* What was the largest single landholding at that time? *(French West Africa and Algeria)*

Extension Have students compare the main map and the map showing traditional ethnic boundaries. What do they notice? *(The borders of the colonies are drawn with no regard for ethnic boundaries.)* How might this fact have contributed to some of the problems that resulted from imperialism? *(Ethnic conflicts might have been incited or worsened by bringing hostile groups within colonial borders.)*

SKILLBUILDER Answers

1. **Region** Very little of the continent was colonized in 1878, while most of it had come under European control by 1913.
2. **Region** There were hundreds of different ethnic groups.

INTEGRATED TECHNOLOGY

Interactive This map is available in an interactive format on the eEdition, where students can view the African colonies of each imperial power separately.

COOPERATIVE LEARNING

Dramatizing South African History

Class Time 40 minutes

Task Creating and presenting skits dramatizing a central event in South African history

Purpose To understand history from different points of view

Instructions Divide students into three groups—Zulus, Boers, and British. Explain that each group will research, write, and perform a 5- to 10-minute skit dramatizing an event central to its role in the conflict over South Africa. Distribute "The Boer War: The Suffering of the Civilian Population" from the Electronic Library of Primary Sources. Instruct students to read for information that will help them portray the motives, feelings, and actions of their particular group. Then have the groups reread and discuss the material about the clash of cultures on pages 342–344 of the text. Ask them to choose an incident to portray that exemplifies their group's values and goals. Examples might include:

- Zulus—war council deciding whether or not to fight the British
- Boers—a day on the Great Trek
- British—the discovery of gold or diamonds in South Africa

Have students perform their skits for the class. You might suggest that other groups respond from their particular point of view.

Electronic Library of Primary Sources

- "The Boer War: The Suffering of the Civilian Population"

History *in* Depth

Winston Churchill and the Boer War

As a boy, Winston Churchill stuttered and was at the bottom of his class. His father, Lord Randolph Churchill, reportedly hated his son and wrote to the boy's grandmother that Winston lacked "cleverness, knowledge and any capacity for settled work." Churchill reacted by idolizing his father and trying to avenge his idol's failed political career with his own illustrious one. Winston succeeded not only in the political arena, but in the artistic one as well, winning the Nobel Prize for literature in 1953.

3 ASSESS

SECTION 1 ASSESSMENT

Have students work with a partner to answer the questions and discuss the answers.

Formal Assessment
- Section Quiz, p. 190

4 RETEACH

Have students read the Reading Study Guide and answer the questions to help them review the main ideas of the section.

Reading Study Guide, p. 115

In-Depth Resources: Unit 3
- Reteaching Activity, p. 66

History *in* Depth

Winston Churchill and the Boer War

Winston Churchill, who served as the British prime minister during World War II, first came to public attention during the Boer War.

A war correspondent, Churchill was traveling with British soldiers when their train was ambushed by the Boers. Churchill pulled some of the wounded men to safety. When he returned to help the others, however, he was arrested by a Boer soldier. (The soldier, Louis Botha, would later become the prime minister of the Union of South Africa and Churchill's close friend.)

Churchill managed to escape from the South African prison. When he returned to Britain, Churchill was hailed as a national hero at the age of 26.

In the 1830s, to escape the British, several thousand Boers began to move north. This movement has become known as the Great Trek. The Boers soon found themselves fighting fiercely with Zulu and other African groups whose land they were taking.

The Boer War Diamonds and gold were discovered in southern Africa in the 1860s and 1880s. Suddenly, adventurers from all parts of the world rushed in to make their fortunes. The Boers tried to keep these "outsiders" from gaining political rights. An attempt to start a rebellion against the Boers failed. The Boers blamed the British and, in 1899, took up arms against them.

In many ways, the **Boer War** (also known as the South African War) between the British and the Boers was the first modern "total" war. The Boers launched commando raids and used guerrilla tactics against the British. The British countered by burning Boer farms and imprisoning women and children in disease-ridden concentration camps.

Black South Africans were also involved in the war. Some fought; others served as scouts, guards, drivers, and workers. Many black South Africans were captured by the British and placed in concentration camps, where over 14,000 died.

Britain finally won the war. In 1910, the Boer republics were joined into a self-governing Union of South Africa, which was controlled by the British. C

The establishing of colonies signaled a change in the way of life of the Africans. The Europeans made efforts to change the political, social, and economic lives of the peoples they conquered. You will learn about these changes in Section 2.

C. Answer It was between two European nations, not between Europeans and Africans.

MAIN IDEA
Contrasting
C How was the struggle for land in the Boer War different from other takeovers in Africa?

SECTION  ASSESSMENT

TERMS & NAMES 1. For each term or name, write a sentence explaining its significance.
• imperialism • racism • Social Darwinism • Berlin Conference • Shaka • Boer • Boer War

USING YOUR NOTES

2. How did Europeans use Social Darwinism to justify empire building? (10.4.1)

The Scramble for Africa
I. Africa Before European Domination
A.
B.
II. Forces Driving Imperialism

MAIN IDEAS

3. Why did the Europeans control such a small portion of Africa in the 1800s? (10.4.2)
4. What were some of the internal factors that contributed to imperialism in Africa? (10.4.3)
5. Why did the Boers and the British fight over southern Africa? (10.4.3)

CRITICAL THINKING & WRITING

6. **MAKING INFERENCES** What can you infer about the Europeans' attitude toward Africans from the Berlin Conference? (10.4.3)
7. **FORMING OPINIONS** Why do you think Africans weren't interested in buying European products? (10.4.3)
8. **DEVELOPING HISTORICAL PERSPECTIVE** What problems might result from rearranging groups of people without regard for ethnic or linguistic traditions? (10.4.3)
9. **WRITING ACTIVITY** EMPIRE BUILDING Write an **expository essay** explaining which European motive behind imperialism in Africa was the most powerful. (Writing 2.3.b)

INTEGRATED TECHNOLOGY **INTERNET ACTIVITY**

Use the Internet to find out about the population and status of Afrikaners, or Boers, in South Africa today. Present your findings in an **oral report.** (10.4.3)

INTERNET KEYWORD
Afrikaners in South Africa

ANSWERS

1. imperialism, p. 339 • racism, p. 341 • Social Darwinism, p. 341 • Berlin Conference, p. 342 • Shaka, p. 342 • Boer, p. 342 • Boer War, p. 344

2. **Sample Answer:** I. A. diverse peoples, B. trading networks. II. A. racism, B. Social Darwinism, C. technological superiority, D. medical advances. Europeans believed they were superior people and had a duty and right to impose their culture on non-Europeans.
3. powerful African armies, impassable rivers, diseases
4. Africans' vast spectrum of languages and cultures, wars between ethnic groups, lack of weapons and technology
5. Both wanted access to gold and diamonds.
6. They thought Africans were inferior and had no right to decide the fate of their lands.
7. preferred their own products; had no use for European products
8. They might fight each other or try to return to their own people.
9. **Rubric** Expository essays should
   - indicate that economic competition was the strongest motivator.
   - include details from the chapter.

INTEGRATED TECHNOLOGY

Rubric Oral reports should
- discuss the number of Afrikaners living in South Africa today and their status.
- consider conflicts between Afrikaners and black South Africans.

Imperialism

Case Study: Nigeria

MAIN IDEA

POWER AND AUTHORITY Europeans embarked on a new phase of empire building that affected both Africa and the rest of the world.

WHY IT MATTERS NOW

Many former colonies have political problems that are the result of colonial rule.

TERMS & NAMES

- paternalism
- assimilation
- Menelik II

SETTING THE STAGE The Berlin Conference of 1884–85 was a European conference. And, although black South Africans participated in it, the Boer War was largely a European war. Europeans argued and fought among themselves over the lands of Africa. In carving up the continent, the European countries paid little or no attention to historical political divisions or to the many ethnic and language groupings in Africa. Uppermost in the minds of the Europeans was the ability to control Africa's land, its people, and its resources.

CALIFORNIA STANDARDS

10.4.1 Describe the rise of industrial economies and their link to imperialism and colonialism (e.g., the role played by national security and strategic advantage; moral issues raised by the search for national hegemony, Social Darwinism, and the missionary impulse; material issues such as land, resources, and technology).

10.4.2 Discuss the locations of the colonial rule of such nations as England, France, Germany, Italy, Japan, the Netherlands, Russia, Spain, Portugal, and the United States.

10.4.3 Explain imperialism from the perspective of the colonizers and the colonized and the varied immediate and long-term responses by the people under colonial rule.

A New Period of Imperialism

The imperialism of the 18th and 19th centuries was conducted differently from the explorations of the 15th and 16th centuries. In the earlier period, imperial powers often did not penetrate far into the conquered areas in Asia and Africa. Nor did they always have a substantial influence on the lives of the people. During this new period of imperialism, the Europeans demanded more influence over the economic, political, and social lives of the people. They were determined to shape the economies of the lands to benefit European economies. They also wanted the people to adopt European customs.

Forms of Control Each European nation had certain policies and goals for establishing colonies. To establish control of an area, Europeans used different techniques. Over time, four forms of colonial control emerged: colony, protectorate, sphere of influence, and economic imperialism. These terms are defined and discussed in the chart on page 346. In practice, gaining control of an area might involve the use of several of these forms.

Methods of Management European rulers also developed methods of day-to-day management of the colony. Two basic methods emerged. Britain and other nations—such as the United States in its Pacific Island colonies—preferred indirect control. France and most other European nations wielded a more direct control. Later, when colonies gained independence, the management method used had an influence on the type of government chosen in the new nation.

Indirect Control Indirect control relied on existing political rulers. In some areas, the British asked a local ruler to accept British authority to rule. These local officials handled much of the daily management of the colony. In addition,

TAKING NOTES

Summarizing Use a web to record the forms and methods of European imperialism in Africa, the resistance it met with, and its impact.

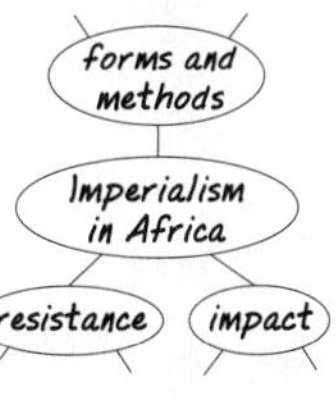

LESSON PLAN

OBJECTIVES

- Explain the different forms of colonial control.
- Trace British rule in Nigeria.
- Summarize African resistance movements.
- Analyze the impact of colonial rule in Africa.

1 FOCUS & MOTIVATE

Ask students what they already know about Nigeria. *(Possible Answers: English is the official language; authors Wole Soyinka and Chinua Achebe)* Explain that this country, the most populous in Africa, was a British colony until 1960.

2 INSTRUCT

A New Period of Imperialism

10.4.1; 10.4.2; 10.4.3

Critical Thinking

- How might assimilation be considered less harsh than paternalism? *(Possible Answer: Assimilation does not deny peoples' right to practice their own culture.)*

CALIFORNIA RESOURCES

California Reading Toolkit, p. L50
California Modified Lesson Plans for English Learners, p. 95
California Daily Standards Practice Transparencies, TT42
California Standards Enrichment Workbook, pp. 47–48, 49–50, 51–52
California Standards Planner and Lesson Plans, p. L91
California Online Test Practice
California Test Generator CD-ROM
California Easy Planner CD-ROM
California eEdition CD-ROM

SECTION 2 PROGRAM RESOURCES

ALL STUDENTS

In-Depth Resources: Unit 3
- Guided Reading, p. 48
- History Makers: Menelik II, p. 63

Formal Assessment
- Section Quiz, p. 191

ENGLISH LEARNERS

In-Depth Resources in Spanish
- Guided Reading, p. 89

Reading Study Guide (Spanish), p. 117
Reading Study Guide Audio CD (Spanish)

STRUGGLING READERS

In-Depth Resources: Unit 3
- Guided Reading, p. 48
- Building Vocabulary, p. 52
- Reteaching Activity, p. 67

Reading Study Guide, p. 117
Reading Study Guide Audio CD

GIFTED AND TALENTED STUDENTS

In-Depth Resources: Unit 3
- Primary Source: Letter from Menelik II, p. 57
- Literature: from *Things Fall Apart,* p. 61
- Connections Across Time and Cultures: Two Periods of Colonization and Imperialism, p. 65

Electronic Library of Primary Sources
- from "Africa at the Center"

INTEGRATED TECHNOLOGY

eEdition CD-ROM
Power Presentations CD-ROM
Electronic Library of Primary Sources
- from "Africa at the Center"

classzone.com

Analyzing Key Concepts

OBJECTIVE

- Compare the forms of imperialism and methods of management.

INSTRUCT

Point out to students that, although all imperialism involves subjugation of a weaker country by a stronger one, there are various forms of domination that grant different degrees of rights and participation to the dominated people. All of these forms of imperialism have been played out on the world stage.

More About . . .

Liberia

This country on the west coast of Africa was established by freed slaves from the United States and the West Indies. In fact, its name means "free land." The descendants of these African-American settlers, called Americo-Liberians, constitute only about 2.5 percent of Liberia's population but controlled the country until 1980. At that time, native Africans revolted and regained political power.

> Analyzing Key Concepts

Imperialism

Imperialism is a policy in which one country seeks to extend its authority by conquering other countries or by establishing economic and political dominance over other countries. The first chart below discusses the four forms of imperialist authority. The second chart shows the two management methods that can be used to control an area.

CALIFORNIA STANDARDS
10.4.1, REP 4

Forms of Imperialism

Form	Definition	Example
Colony	A country or a territory governed internally by a foreign power	Somaliland in East Africa was a French colony.
Protectorate	A country or a territory with its own internal government but under the control of an outside power	Britain established a protectorate over the Niger River delta.
Sphere of Influence	An area in which an outside power claims exclusive investment or trading privileges	Liberia was under the sphere of influence of the United States.
Economic Imperialism	An independent but less-developed country controlled by private business interests rather than other governments	The Dole Fruit company controlled pineapple trade in Hawaii.

Imperial Management Methods

Indirect Control	Direct Control
• Local government officials used • Limited self-rule • Goal: to develop future leaders • Government institutions are based on European styles but may have local rules.	• Foreign officials brought in to rule • No self-rule • Goal: assimilation • Government institutions are based only on European styles.
Examples: • British colonies such as Nigeria, India, Burma • U.S. colonies on Pacific Islands	Examples: • French colonies such as Somaliland, Vietnam • German colonies such as German East Africa • Portuguese colonies such as Angola

INTEGRATED TECHNOLOGY
RESEARCH LINKS For more on imperialism, go to **classzone.com**

> DATA FILE

In 1905, the British Empire
- was the largest and most powerful in the world's history.
- covered about 11 million square miles.
- had about 400 million inhabitants.

Today, the United Kingdom has 13 small dependent territories and is the head of a voluntary association of 54 independent states.

African Colonization and Independence
- In 1884, Western leaders met to divide Africa into colonial holdings.
- By 1914, nearly all of Africa had been distributed among European powers.
- European imperial powers set national borders in Africa without regard for local ethnic or political divisions. This continues to be a problem for African nations today.

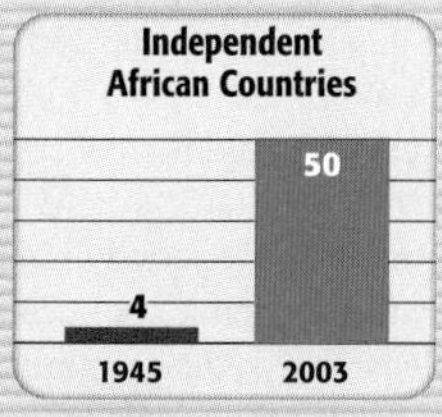

Connect *to* Today

1. **Forming and Supporting Opinions** Which form of managing imperial interests do you think would be most effective and why?
   See Skillbuilder Handbook, page R20.
2. **Recognizing Effects** Use the Internet or library resources to research the problems many African nations are facing today as a result of imperialism. Report your findings to the class.

CONNECT TO TODAY: ANSWERS

1. Forming and Supporting Opinions
Possible Answers: Indirect control—Because it involved local officials in government and was based on local laws, it would be more readily accepted by the colonized people and so, more effective. Direct control—Because it ignored local input, it would not be sidetracked by compromise and could effectively promote its programs.

2. Recognizing Effects
Possible Answers: Reports will vary based on research, but some topics that may be discussed are national borders dividing existing ethnic and political groups, reestablishing a food-crop agricultural system rather than a cash-crop system, and educating the population about African history—a topic suppressed under imperial rule.

each colony had a legislative council that included colonial officials as well as local merchants and professionals nominated by the colonial governor.

The assumption was that the councils would train local leaders in the British method of government and that a time would come when the local population would govern itself. This had happened earlier in the British colonies of Australia and Canada. In the 1890s, the United States began to colonize. It chose the indirect method of control for the Philippines.

Direct Control The French and other European powers preferred more direct control of their colonies. They viewed the Africans as unable to handle the complex business of running a country. Based on this attitude, the Europeans developed a policy called **paternalism**. Using that policy, Europeans governed people in a parental way by providing for their needs but not giving them rights. To accomplish this, the Europeans brought in their own bureaucrats and did not train local people in European methods of governing.

The French also supported a policy of **assimilation**. That policy was based on the idea that in time, the local populations would adopt French culture and become like the French. To aid in the transition, all local schools, courts, and businesses were patterned after French institutions. In practice, the French abandoned the ideal of assimilation for all but a few places and settled for a policy of "association," which was similar to indirect control. They recognized African institutions and culture but regarded them as inferior to French culture.

CASE STUDY: Nigeria

A British Colony

A close look at Britain's rule of Nigeria illustrates the forms of imperialism used by European powers to gain control of an area. It also shows management methods used to continue the control of the economic and political life of the area.

Gaining Control Britain gained control of southern Nigeria through both diplomatic and military means. Some local rulers agreed to sign treaties of protection with Britain and accepted British residents. However, others opposed the foreign intervention and rebelled against it. The British used force to put down and defeat these rebellions.

British conquest of northern Nigeria was accomplished by the Royal Niger Company. The company gained control of the palm-oil trade along the Niger River after the Berlin Conference gave Britain a protectorate over the Niger River delta. In 1914, the British claimed the entire area of Nigeria as a colony.

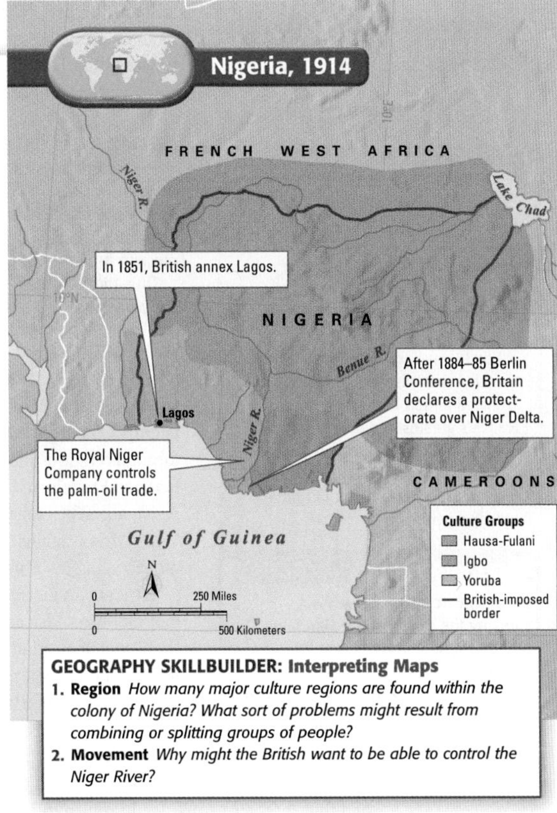

GEOGRAPHY SKILLBUILDER: Interpreting Maps

1. **Region** *How many major culture regions are found within the colony of Nigeria? What sort of problems might result from combining or splitting groups of people?*
2. **Movement** *Why might the British want to be able to control the Niger River?*

History from Visuals

Interpreting the Map

Make sure students understand that the colored areas represent traditional territories for the ethnic groups indigenous to Nigeria. Europeans generally disregarded such boundaries.

Extension Ask students to trace the map and to draw new borders that respect traditional ethnic territories. Does each ethnic group gain or lose land compared with the borders drawn by Europeans? *(Hausa-Fulani—gains; Igbo—remains the same; Yoruba—loses)*

SKILLBUILDER Answers

1. **Region** three; difficulty getting them to communicate and work together
2. **Movement** to gain control of trade on the river and access to all ethnic areas

A British Colony

10.4.2; 10.4.3

Critical Thinking

- Which of Nigeria's three main ethnic groups would have been most likely to unite? *(the Igbo and Yoruba, since they shared both religion and style of government)*
- Do you think direct rule would have worked better or worse than indirect rule with the Hausa-Fulani? Why? *(Possible Answer: Worse—Local officials probably would have resisted.)*

DIFFERENTIATING INSTRUCTION: ENGLISH LEARNERS

The Vocabulary of Imperialism

Class Time 20 minutes

Task Creating a chart showing the meanings of key terms and other words

Purpose To better understand imperialism

Instructions Have students create a chart in which they define in their own words the two key terms and other difficult vocabulary on this page. Suggest that they use the Reading Study Guide in Spanish for Section 2 on page 117 for help. They should also brainstorm related words and list them in their charts. Completed charts might look like this:

Word	Meaning	Related
legislative	having to do with the making of laws	legislator
nominated	named, appointed	nomination
paternalism	treating people as children	paternal
assimilation	adoption of a conqueror's culture by conquered	assimilate
diplomatic	done by discussion	diplomacy
bureaucrat	person who manages a government department	bureaucracy

Reading Study Guide: Spanish Translations

African Resistance
10.4.3

Critical Thinking
- Why do you think Africans resisted imperialism despite the superiority of European military technology? *(Possible Answer: They were fighting to retain their land and way of life.)*
- What strategy allowed Ethiopia to resist European dominance? *(pitting the European powers against each other)*

In-Depth Resources: Unit 3
- Primary Source: Letter from Menelik II, p. 57
- History Makers: Menelik II, p. 63

History Makers

Samori Touré

What character traits distinguished Samori Touré? *(nationalistic fervor, determination, and leadership)* When Touré was 20, his mother was taken as a slave, and Samori joined her captor's army to gain her release. This experience honed his military skills and determination to fight for his people.

INTEGRATED TECHNOLOGY

Rubric Maps should
- clearly indicate the borders of the Mandingo Empire.
- include the boundaries of modern African countries.

Managing the Colony In this new age of imperialism, it was necessary not only to claim a territory but also to govern the people living there. However, managing Nigeria would not prove to be easy. It was one of the most culturally diverse areas in Africa. (A)

About 250 different ethnic groups lived there. The three largest groups were the Hausa-Fulani in the north, the Yoruba in the southwest, and the Igbo in the southeast. These groups were different from one another in many ways, including language, culture, and religion. The Hausa-Fulani people were Muslim and had a strong central government. The Igbo and Yoruba peoples followed traditional religions and relied on local chiefs for control.

Britain did not have enough troops to govern such a complex area. As a result, the British turned to indirect rule of the land. Ruling indirectly through local officials worked well with the Hausa-Fulani. However, this management method did not work as well with the Igbo and Yoruba peoples. Their local chiefs resented having their power limited by the British.

MAIN IDEA

Summarizing

(A) Which forms of imperialistic control did Britain use in Nigeria?

A. Answers protectorate, colony, and economic imperialism (Royal Niger Company)

African Resistance

As in Nigeria, Africans across the continent resisted European attempts to colonize their lands. However, the contest between African states and European powers was never equal because of the Europeans' superior arms. Africans resisted the Europeans with whatever forces they could raise and often surprised the Europeans with their military ability. With the single exception of Ethiopia, though, all these attempts at resistance ultimately failed. Edward Morel, a British journalist who lived for a time in the Congo, made an observation about the Africans' dilemma:

PRIMARY SOURCE

Nor is violent physical opposition to abuse and injustice henceforth possible for the African in any part of Africa. His chances of effective resistance have been steadily dwindling with the increasing perfectibility in the killing power of modern armament.

Thus the African is really helpless against the material gods of the white man, as embodied in the trinity of imperialism, capitalistic exploitation, and militarism.

EDWARD MOREL, *The Black Man's Burden*

History Makers

Samori Touré
about 1830–1900

Samori Touré is a hero of the Mandingo people. His empire is often compared to the great Mali Empire of the 1300s.

Touré was a nationalist who built a powerful Mandingo kingdom by conquering neighboring states. His kingdom became the third largest empire in West Africa.

For 16 years, Touré opposed the French imperialists in West Africa. The well-armed Mandingo were France's greatest foe in West Africa, and the two armies clashed several times. The Mandingo Empire was finally brought down, not in battle, but by a famine.

INTEGRATED TECHNOLOGY

INTERNET ACTIVITY Draw a map showing the extent of the Mandingo Empire. Go to **classzone.com** for your research.

Unsuccessful Movements The unsuccessful resistance attempts included active military resistance and resistance through religious movements. Algeria's almost 50-year resistance to French rule was one outstanding example of active resistance. The resistance movement led by Samori Touré in West Africa against the French is another example. After modernizing his army, Touré fought the French for 16 years.

Africans in German East Africa put their faith in a spiritual defense. African villagers resisted the Germans' insistence that they plant cotton, a cash crop for export, rather than attend to their own food crops. In 1905, the belief suddenly arose that a magic water (*maji-maji*) sprinkled on their bodies would turn the Germans' bullets into water. The uprising became known as the Maji Maji rebellion. Over 20 different ethnic groups united to fight for their freedom. The fighters believed that their war had been ordained by God and that their ancestors would return to life and assist their struggle.

African Resistance: Analyzing a Primary Source

Class Time 25 minutes

Task Expressing Edward Morel's ideas in everyday language

Purpose To understand historical conditions

Instructions Have students work in small groups to reread the primary source quotation from Edward Morel on this page. Ask students to analyze the quotation sentence by sentence, and restate the ideas in their own words. Instruct them to discuss their restatements with their group and then record them to share with the whole class. Here are some examples:

It is impossible for Africans to fight against the wrongs done to them.

The white man's weapons are too powerful.

The white man has many things and large armies and a great desire to conquer land.

Ask students to discuss the following questions:

1. What kinds of weapons do you think the Africans had? *(Possible Answer: spears and sticks, some older guns)*
2. What "material goods of the white man" do you think Morel is referring to? *(Possible Answer: weapons but also road-building equipment, boats, machinery of various kinds)*

Tell students that the guns, equipment, and desire for raw materials made the imperialist powers successful conquerors.

However, when resistance fighters armed with spears and protected by the magic water attacked a German machine-gun post, they were mowed down by the thousands. Officially, Germans recorded 75,000 resisters dead. But more than twice that number perished in the famine that followed. The Germans were shaken by the rebellion and its outcome. As a result, they made some government reforms in an effort to make colonialism more acceptable to the Africans.

Ethiopia: A Successful Resistance Ethiopia was the only African nation that successfully resisted the Europeans. Its victory was due to one man—**Menelik II**. He became emperor of Ethiopia in 1889. He successfully played Italians, French, and British against each other, all of whom were striving to bring Ethiopia into their spheres of influence. In the meantime, he built up a large arsenal of modern weapons purchased from France and Russia. In 1889, shortly after Menelik had signed a treaty with Italy, he discovered differences between the wording of the treaty in the Ethiopian language and in Italian. Menelik believed he was giving up a tiny portion of Ethiopia. However, the Italians claimed all of Ethiopia as a protectorate. Meanwhile, Italian forces were advancing into northern Ethiopia. Menelik declared war. In 1896, in one of the greatest battles in the history of Africa—the Battle of Adowa—Ethiopian forces successfully defeated the Italians and kept their nation independent. After the battle, Menelik continued to stockpile rifles and other modern weapons in case another foreign power challenged Ethiopia's liberty.

▼ After defeating Italy, Menelik II modernized Ethiopia by constructing a railroad and weakening the power of the nobility.

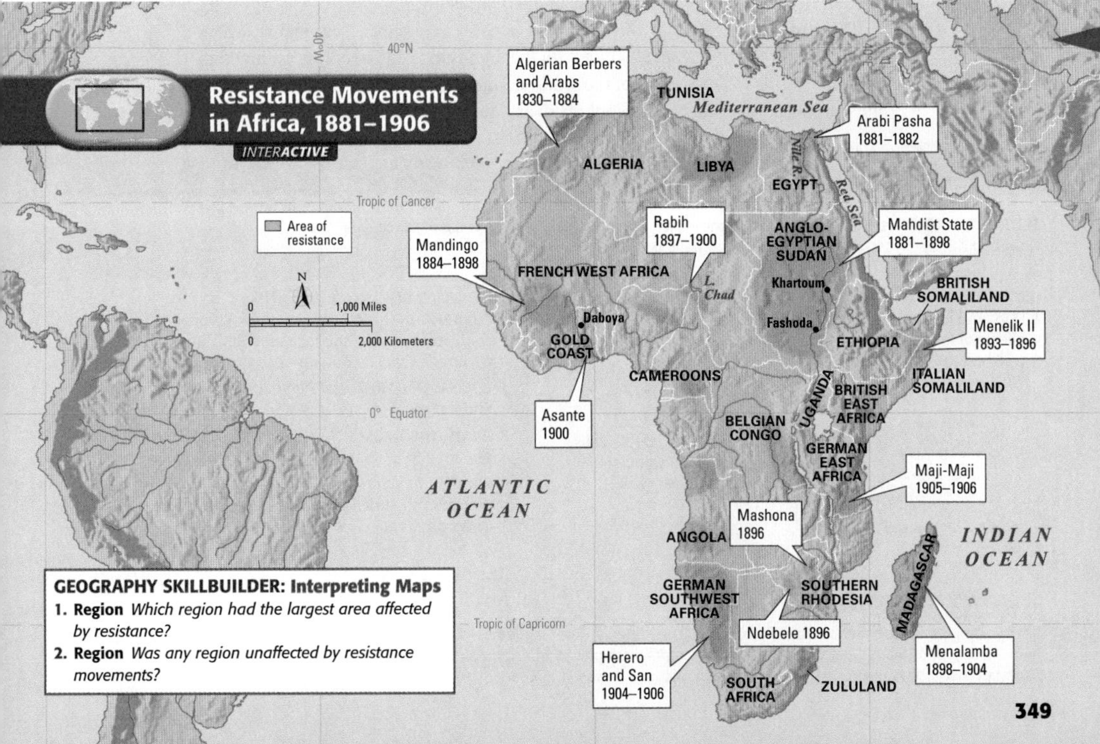

GEOGRAPHY SKILLBUILDER: Interpreting Maps
1. **Region** *Which region had the largest area affected by resistance?*
2. **Region** *Was any region unaffected by resistance movements?*

More About . . .

African Resistance

A fundamental cause of African resistance to imperialism was the completely alien nature of Western civilization, with its emphasis on science and technology. A member of the Herero, a people in southwestern Africa, observed: "The European is devoted to dead metals . . . [W]e get our joy out of living creatures."

History from Visuals

Interpreting the Map

Ask students which resistance movement occurred first. *(Algerian Berbers and Arabs)*

Extension Have students arrange the resistance movements along a time line. Make sure they notice that many of the movements overlap. Ask them to discuss possible reasons for this fact. *(Possible Answers: One movement could inspire others; trade routes among territories could spread word of resistance.)*

SKILLBUILDER Answers

1. **Region** Anglo-Egyptian Sudan
2. **Region** parts of northwest and central Africa

INTEGRATED TECHNOLOGY

Interactive An interactive version of this map on the eEdition allows students to focus on each resistance movement individually.

DIFFERENTIATING INSTRUCTION: GIFTED AND TALENTED STUDENTS

Literature of Resistance

Class Time 40 minutes

Task Reading and conducting a marketplace meeting based on Chinua Achebe's *Things Fall Apart*

Purpose To appreciate an African author's view of imperialism

Instructions Have students read the excerpt from Nigerian author Chinua Achebe's *Things Fall Apart* on pages 61–62 of In-Depth Resources: Unit 3. Have them discuss the views of imperialism the characters represent and relate them to what they have learned from their reading in this section of the text. Ask students to take the roles of the following characters in the village of Umuofia:

- Okonkwo
- Head messenger
- Obierika
- Okika

Then have them address a marketplace meeting about whether to go to war with the Europeans. Stress that they should explain and support their positions with facts and details from their reading.

LITERATURE SELECTION *from Things Fall Apart* by Chinua Achebe

The Age of Imperialism 61

In-Depth Resources: Unit 3

The Legacy of Colonial Rule
10.4.3

Critical Thinking

- Why might Africans have admired European culture, even though it was destroying their own? *(Possible Answer: It represented power and mastery of the environment.)*
- How did colonialism help reduce local warfare? *(Possible Answers: by controlling the actions of the people; by improving economic conditions and education)*

In-Depth Resources: Unit 3

- Connections Across Time and Cultures: Two Periods of Colonization and Imperialism, p. 65

3 ASSESS

SECTION 2 ASSESSMENT

Have students answer the questions individually and discuss their answers with a partner.

Formal Assessment

- Section Quiz, p. 191

4 RETEACH

Divide students into four groups and have each group fill out a cause-and-effect chart for one of the objectives listed at the beginning of the section.

Critical Thinking Transparencies

- CT75 Cause and Effect

In-Depth Resources: Unit 3

- Reteaching Activity, p. 67

The Legacy of Colonial Rule

European colonial rule forever altered Africans' lives. In some cases, the Europeans brought benefits, but for the most part, the effects were negative.

Negative Effects On the negative side, Africans lost control of their land and their independence. Many died of new diseases such as smallpox. They also lost thousands of their people in resisting the Europeans. Famines resulted from the change to cash crops in place of subsistence agriculture.

Africans also suffered from a breakdown of their traditional cultures. Traditional authority figures were replaced. Homes and property were transferred with little regard to their importance to the people. Men were forced to leave villages to find ways to support themselves and their families. Contempt for the traditional culture and admiration of European life undermined stable societies and caused identity problems for Africans.

The most harmful political legacy from the colonial period was the division of the African continent. Long-term rival chiefdoms were sometimes united, while at other times, kinship groups were split between colonies. The artificial boundaries combined or unnaturally divided groups, creating problems that plagued African colonies during European occupation. These boundaries continue to create problems for the nations that evolved from the former colonies.

Positive Effects On the positive side, colonialism reduced local warfare. Humanitarian efforts in some colonies improved sanitation and provided hospitals and schools. As a result, lifespans increased and literacy rates improved. Also positive was the economic expansion. African products came to be valued on the international market. To aid the economic growth, railroads, dams, and telephone and telegraph lines were built in African colonies. But for the most part, these benefited only European business interests, not Africans' lives.

The patterns of behavior of imperialist powers were similar, no matter where their colonies were located. Dealing with local traditions and peoples continued to cause problems in other areas of the world dominated by Europeans. Resistance to the European imperialists also continued, as you will see in Section 3. **B**

B. Possible Answer The European military would not be there to prevent rival groups from fighting.

MAIN IDEA

Drawing Conclusions

B Why might the problems caused by artificial boundaries continue after the Europeans left?

SECTION 2 ASSESSMENT

TERMS & NAMES 1. For each term or name, write a sentence explaining its significance.

- paternalism
- assimilation
- Menelik II

USING YOUR NOTES

2. Do you think the positive effects of imperialism outweighed the negative impact? Why or why not? (10.4.3)

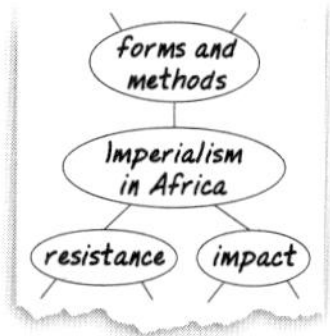

MAIN IDEAS

3. What idea is the policy of assimilation based on? (10.4.3)
4. Why were African resistance movements usually unsuccessful? (10.4.3)
5. How did colonial rule cause a breakdown in traditional African culture? (10.4.3)

CRITICAL THINKING & WRITING

6. **FORMING OPINIONS** Do you think Europeans could have conquered Africa if the Industrial Revolution had never occurred? Explain your answer. (10.4.1)
7. **COMPARING** How was the policy of paternalism like Social Darwinism? (10.4.1)
8. **ANALYZING CAUSES** Why would the French and Russians sell arms to Ethiopia? (10.4.2)
9. **WRITING ACTIVITY** POWER AND AUTHORITY Write a **speech** that you might deliver to colonial rulers, expressing your views on European imperialism in Africa. (Writing 2.6.b)

CONNECT TO TODAY **CREATING A POSTER**

After gaining its independence from Portugal in 1975, Angola was plagued by civil war for 27 years. Research to learn what role the legacy of colonialism played in Angola's conflict. Summarize your findings on a **poster** using text, pictures, maps, and charts. (10.4.3)

ANSWERS

1. paternalism, p. 347 • assimilation, p. 347 • Menelik II, p. 349
2. **Sample Answer:** Forms and methods—Colony, protectorate, sphere of influence, economic imperialism, direct control, indirect control; Resistance—Movements in all but Ethiopia failed; Impact—Societies and cultures devastated, traditional ethnic boundaries ignored. No—Africa still suffers from the colonial legacy.
3. the idea that local people would eventually be absorbed into the colonizers' culture
4. Europeans' superior weapons
5. traditional authorities replaced; men forced to leave their villages to find work; society undermined by contempt for traditional culture
6. **Possible Answer:** No—Technology provided access to the interior, rapid communication, superior weapons; these and treatment for malaria enabled Europeans to defeat all other armies.
7. Both saw Europeans as better able to run a colony than the local people.
8. **Possible Answer:** to prevent Britain or Italy from taking over Ethiopia
9. **Rubric** Speeches should
   - express a clear position.
   - be supported with facts and examples.
   - conclude with a summary of the position.

CONNECT TO TODAY

Rubric Posters should

- indicate the influence of artificial borders established by imperialists.
- mention recent stabilizing efforts.
- include visuals such as pictures, maps, charts, and time lines.

INTERACTIVE

Views of Imperialism

European imperialism extended to the continents beyond Africa. As imperialism spread, the colonizer and the colonized viewed the experience of imperialism in very different ways. Some Europeans were outspoken about the superiority they felt toward the peoples they conquered. Others thought imperialism was very wrong. Even the conquered had mixed feelings about their encounter with the Europeans.

CALIFORNIA STANDARDS

10.4.3 Explain imperialism from the perspective of the colonizers and the colonized and the varied immediate and long-term responses by the people under colonial rule.

A PRIMARY SOURCE

J. A. Hobson

Hobson's 1902 book, *Imperialism,* made a great impression on his fellow Britons.

For Europe to rule Asia by force for purposes of gain, and to justify that rule by the pretence that she is civilizing Asia and raising her to a higher level of spiritual life, will be adjudged by history, perhaps, to be the crowning wrong and folly of Imperialism. What Asia has to give, her priceless stores of wisdom garnered from her experience of ages, we refuse to take; the much or little which we could give we spoil by the brutal manner of our giving. This is what Imperialism has done, and is doing, for Asia.

B PRIMARY SOURCE

Dadabhai Naoroji

Dadabhai Naoroji was the first Indian elected to the British Parliament. In 1871, he delivered a speech about the impact of Great Britain on India.

To sum up the whole, the British rule has been—morally, a great blessing; politically peace and order on one hand, blunders on the other, materially, impoverishment. . . . The natives call the British system "Sakar ki Churi," the knife of sugar. That is to say there is no oppression, it is all smooth and sweet, but it is the knife, notwithstanding. I mention this that you should know these feelings. Our great misfortune is that you do not know our wants. When you will know our real wishes, I have not the least doubt that you would do justice. The genius and spirit of the British people is fair play and justice.

C PRIMARY SOURCE

Jules Ferry

The following is from a speech Ferry delivered before the French National Assembly on July 28,1883.

Nations are great in our times only by means of the activities which they develop; it is not simply 'by the peaceful shining forth of institutions . . .' that they are great at this hour. . . . Something else is needed for France: . . . that she must also be a great country exercising all of her rightful influence over the destiny of Europe, that she ought to propagate this influence throughout the world and carry everywhere that she can her language, her customs, her flag, her arms, and her genius.

D PRIMARY SOURCE

This 1882 American political cartoon, titled "The Devilfish in Egyptian Waters," depicts England as an octopus. Notice that Egypt is not yet one of the areas controlled by the British.

THE DEVILFISH IN EGYPTIAN WATERS.

Document-Based QUESTIONS

1. According to Hobson (Source A), what mistake did European imperialists make in Asia?
2. What position on imperialism does Jules Ferry take in Source C?
3. In Source D, what does the representation of England suggest about the cartoonist's view of British imperialism?
4. In what way does the view of imperialism in Source B contrast with that in Source D?

351

Different Perspectives

OBJECTIVE

- Compare and contrast four different views of imperialism.

INSTRUCT

People who wielded power in overseas colonies usually had dramatically different views of imperialism than those who spoke on behalf of the colonized. Speakers on both sides often expressed themselves in emotionally intense language, upholding their individual political opinions and moral beliefs.

INTEGRATED TECHNOLOGY

Interactive This feature is available in an interactive format on the eEdition. Students can hear readings of the sources, explanations, and background information.

Electronic Library of Primary Sources

- from "Africa at the Center"

Inclusion Tip

Visually impaired students may benefit from the enlarged version of the political cartoon on the eEdition.

DOCUMENT-BASED QUESTIONS: ANSWERS

1. They didn't take advantage of Asia's age-old wisdom.
2. He fully supports French imperialism, believing that colonized countries can only benefit from French influence.
3. The representation of England as a grasping octopus suggests a negative veiw of British imperialism. The cartoonist sees England as power-mad, voraciously seizing land around the world.
4. The writer of Source B believes that British imperialists are fundamentally fair and just. The author of Source D does not seem to see anything redeeming about British imperialism.

LESSON PLAN

OBJECTIVES

- Summarize the decline of the Ottoman Empire.
- Describe the Crimean War.
- Analyze Egypt's reforms.
- Evaluate Persia's response to foreign pressure.

1 FOCUS & MOTIVATE

Ask students what they know about the Ottoman Empire. *(Muslim faith, great expansion, social and cultural achievements, long-lived)* Explain that, in the late 19th century, this vast empire became a target for European imperialism.

2 INSTRUCT

Ottoman Empire Loses Power
10.4.3

Critical Thinking

- What part did internal corruption play in the decline of Ottoman power? *(It led to a weakened economy and technological stagnation.)*

CALIFORNIA RESOURCES

California Reading Toolkit, p. L51
California Modified Lesson Plans for English Learners, p. 97
California Daily Standards Practice Transparencies, TT43
California Standards Enrichment Workbook, pp. 49–50, 51–52
California Standards Planner and Lesson Plans, p. L93
California Online Test Practice
California Test Generator CD-ROM
California Easy Planner CD-ROM
California eEdition CD-ROM

Aboriginal bark painting from Milingimbi, Australia

Battle of Isandhlwana, 1879, Zululand (now in South Africa)

3

Europeans Claim Muslim Lands

MAIN IDEA

EMPIRE BUILDING European nations expanded their empires by seizing territories from Muslim states.

WHY IT MATTERS NOW

Political events in this vital resource area are still influenced by actions from the imperialistic period.

TERMS & NAMES

- geopolitics
- Crimean War
- Suez Canal

CALIFORNIA STANDARDS

10.4.2 Discuss the locations of the colonial rule of such nations as England, France, Germany, Italy, Japan, the Netherlands, Russia, Spain, Portugal, and the United States.

10.4.3 Explain imperialism from the perspective of the colonizers and the colonized and the varied immediate and long-term responses by the people under colonial rule.

CST 3 Students use a variety of maps and documents to interpret human movement, including major patterns of domestic and international migration, changing environmental preferences and settlement patterns, the frictions that develop between population groups, and the diffusion of ideas, technological innovations, and goods.

HI 5 Students analyze human modifications of landscapes and examine the resulting environmental policy issues.

SETTING THE STAGE The European powers who carved up Africa also looked elsewhere for other lands to control. The Muslim lands that rimmed the Mediterranean had largely been claimed as a result of Arab and Ottoman conquests. As you learned in Chapter 2, the Ottoman Empire at its peak stretched from Hungary in the north, around the Black Sea, and across Egypt all the way west to the borders of Morocco. (See map opposite.) But during the empire's last 300 years, it had steadily declined in power. Europeans competed with each other to gain control of this strategically important area.

Ottoman Empire Loses Power

The declining Ottoman Empire had difficulties trying to fit into the modern world. However, the Ottomans made attempts to change before they finally were unable to hold back the European imperialist powers.

Reforms Fail When Suleyman I, the last great Ottoman sultan, died in 1566, he was followed by a succession of weak sultans. The palace government broke up into a number of quarreling, often corrupt factions. Weakening power brought other problems. Corruption and theft had caused financial losses. Coinage was devalued, causing inflation. Once the Ottoman Empire had embraced modern technologies, but now it fell further and further behind Europe.

When Selim III came into power in 1789, he attempted to modernize the army. However, the older janissary corps resisted his efforts. Selim III was overthrown, and reform movements were temporarily abandoned. Meanwhile, nationalist feelings began to stir among the Ottomans' subject peoples. In 1830, Greece gained its independence, and Serbia gained self-rule. The Ottomans' weakness was becoming apparent to European powers, who were expanding their territories. They began to look for ways to take the lands away from the Ottomans.

TAKING NOTES

Determining Main Ideas Use a diagram to fill in three details that support the main idea.

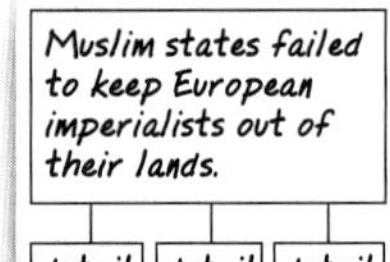

Muslim states failed to keep European imperialists out of their lands.
detail
detail
detail

Europeans Grab Territory

Geopolitics, an interest in or taking of land for its strategic location or products, played an important role in the fate of the Ottoman Empire. World powers were attracted to its strategic location. The Ottomans controlled access to the Mediterranean and the Atlantic sea trade. Merchants in landlocked countries

SECTION 3 PROGRAM RESOURCES

ALL STUDENTS

In-Depth Resources: Unit 3
- Guided Reading, p. 49

Formal Assessment
- Section Quiz, p. 192

ENGLISH LEARNERS

In-Depth Resources in Spanish
- Guided Reading, p. 90

Reading Study Guide (Spanish), p. 119
Reading Study Guide Audio CD (Spanish)

STRUGGLING READERS

In-Depth Resources: Unit 3
- Guided Reading, p. 49
- Building Vocabulary, p. 52
- Reteaching Activity, p. 68

Reading Study Guide, p. 119
Reading Study Guide Audio CD

INTEGRATED TECHNOLOGY

eEdition CD-ROM
Power Presentations CD-ROM
World Art and Cultures Transparencies
- AT58 Reception at the Court of Sultan Selim III

classzone.com

that lay beyond the Black Sea had to go through Ottoman lands. Russia, for example, desperately wanted passage for its grain exports across the Black Sea and into the Mediterranean Sea. This desire strongly influenced Russia's relations with the Ottoman Empire. Russia attempted to win Ottoman favor, formed alliances with Ottoman enemies, and finally waged war against the Ottomans. Discovery of oil in Persia around 1900 and in the Arabian Peninsula after World War I focused even more attention on the area.

Russia and the Crimean War Each generation of Russian czars launched a war on the Ottomans to try to gain land on the Black Sea. The purpose was to give Russia a warm-weather port. In 1853, war broke out between the Russians and the Ottomans. The war was called the **Crimean War**, after a peninsula in the Black Sea where most of the war was fought. Britain and France wanted to prevent the Russians from gaining control of additional Ottoman lands. So they entered the war on the side of the Ottoman Empire. The combined forces of the Ottoman Empire, Britain, and France defeated Russia. The Crimean War was the first war in which women, led by Florence Nightingale, established their position as army nurses. It was also the first war to be covered by newspaper correspondents.

A. Answer Even though the Ottomans were victorious, the war revealed their military weakness.

MAIN IDEA

Making Inferences

A How did the Crimean War help lead to the decline of the Ottoman Empire?

The Crimean War revealed the Ottoman Empire's military weakness. Despite the help of Britain and France, the Ottoman Empire continued to lose lands. The Russians came to the aid of Slavic people in the Balkans who rebelled against the Ottomans. The Ottomans lost control of Romania, Montenegro, Cyprus, Bosnia, Herzegovina, and an area that became Bulgaria. The Ottomans lost land in Africa too. By the beginning of World War I, the Ottoman Empire was reduced in size and in deep decline. A

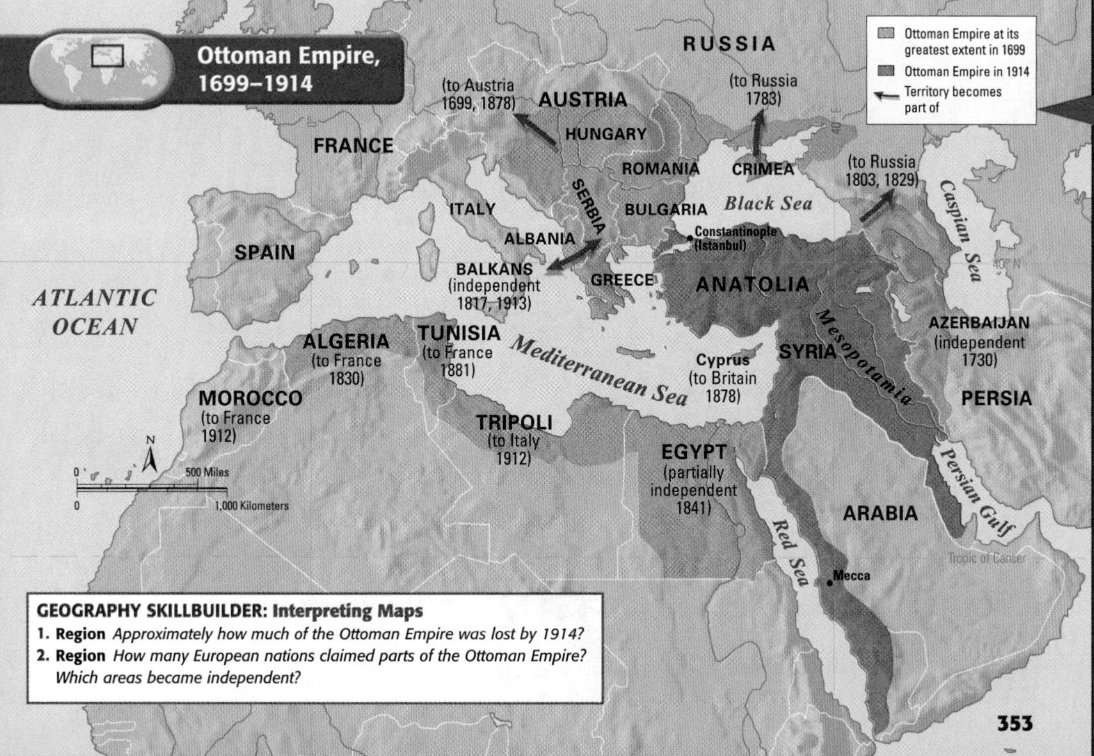

GEOGRAPHY SKILLBUILDER: Interpreting Maps
1. **Region** *Approximately how much of the Ottoman Empire was lost by 1914?*
2. **Region** *How many European nations claimed parts of the Ottoman Empire? Which areas became independent?*

353

Europeans Grab Territory
10.4.3

Critical Thinking
- Why did the discovery of oil in Persia increase the value of Ottoman territory? *(The oil had to pass through Ottoman land to Europe.)*
- In what way were Russian, British, and French motivations in the Crimean War similar? *(They all wanted to control Ottoman territory.)*

World Art and Cultures Transparencies
- AT58 Reception at the Court of Sultan Selim III

History from Visuals

Interpreting the Map
Which countries acquired land from the Ottomans? *(Austria, Russia, France, Italy, Britain, independent Azerbaijan, independent Balkans, and partially independent Egypt)*

Extension Ask students to compare this map with the one on page 343. Which parts of the African Ottoman Empire did European countries take over? *(Egypt and Suez–Britain; Libya/Tripoli–Italy; Algeria and Tunisia–France)*

SKILLBUILDER Answers
1. **Region** about two-thirds
2. **Region** five; Azerbaijan, Egypt, Balkans

DIFFERENTIATING INSTRUCTION: STRUGGLING READERS

Charting the Decline of the Ottoman Empire

Class Time 30 minutes

Task Making a cause-and-effect chart for the decline of the Ottoman Empire

Purpose To understand why Muslim states fell to Europeans

Instructions Have students read pages 119–120 of the Reading Study Guide and work with a partner to answer the questions. Have them discuss their answers with other pairs and reconcile any discrepancies. Then make copies of the cause-and-effect chart on page 49 of In-Depth Resources: Unit 3 and give a copy to each pair of students. Have them fill in the chart (ignoring the Suez Canal entry for the moment) and present their results to the class. A sample chart follows:

Death of Suleiman I	corruption, declining technological skills, internal quarrels
Rise of nationalism	further weakening of empire's internal control
Geopolitics	European interest in Ottoman land
Discovery of oil in Persia	increased motivation for seizing Ottoman territory

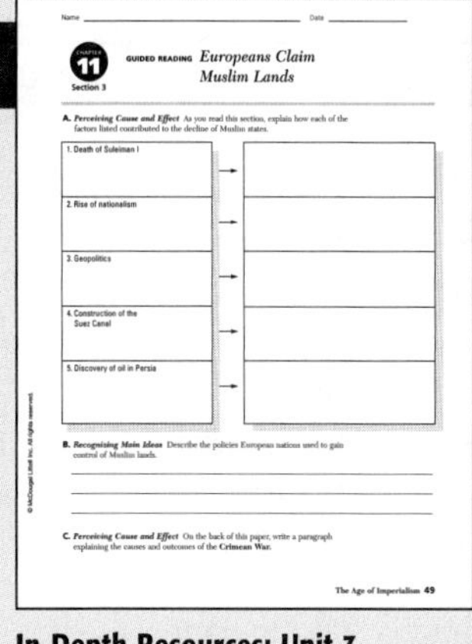

In-Depth Resources: Unit 3

More About . . .

The Khyber Pass

The 33-mile-long Khyber Pass winds through the Hindu Kush mountains, connecting the northern parts of Afghanistan and Pakistan. Alexander the Great's army entered India through the Khyber Pass in 326 B.C., and it has been a major trade and invasion route since that time. The British built a highway and railroad through the Pass during the 1920s.

Tip for Struggling Readers

When a country modernizes, it attempts to move away from traditional ways of doing such key things as farming. For farmers, that might mean planting new crops or using new types of farm machinery.

Egypt Initiates Reforms

10.4.2; 10.4.3

Critical Thinking

- How was Muhammad Ali's promotion of cotton production similar to European imperialists' actions in Africa? *(Both substituted production of cash crops for food crops.)*
- Why was the completion of the Suez Canal cause for international celebration? *(It greatly decreased the time needed to travel from Europe to East Africa and Asia.)*

The Great Game For much of the 19th century, Great Britain and Russia engaged in yet another geopolitical struggle, this time over Muslim lands in Central Asia. Known as the "Great Game," the war was waged over India, one of Britain's most profitable colonies. Russia sought to extend its empire and gain access to India's riches. Britain defended its colony and also attempted to spread its empire beyond India's borders. Afghanistan, which lay between the Russian and British empires, became the center of their struggle. (See the map on page 337.)

In the 1800s, Afghanistan was an independent Muslim kingdom. Its dry, mountainous terrain and determined people continually frustrated the invading imperial powers. After decades of fighting, Great Britain finally withdrew from Afghanistan in 1881. In 1921, Britain formally agreed that its empire would not extend beyond the Khyber Pass, which borders eastern Afghanistan. The newly formed Soviet Union, meanwhile, signed a nonaggression pact with Afghanistan. That agreement was honored until 1979, when the Soviet Union invaded Afghanistan.

Egypt Initiates Reforms

Observing the slow decline of the Ottoman Empire, some Muslim leaders decided that their countries would either have to adjust to the modern world or be consumed by it. Egypt initiated political and social reforms, in part to block European domination of its land.

▼ Muhammad Ali was a common soldier who rose to leadership as a result of his military skill and political shrewdness.

Military and Economic Reforms Modernization came to Egypt as a result of the interest in the area created by the French occupation. Egypt's strategic location at the head of the Red Sea appeared valuable to France and Britain. After Napoleon failed to win Egypt, a new leader emerged: Muhammad Ali. The Ottomans sent him as part of an expeditionary force to govern Egypt, but he soon broke away from Ottoman control. Beginning in 1831, he fought a series of battles in which he gained control of Syria and Arabia. Through the combined efforts of European powers, Muhammad Ali and his heirs were recognized as the hereditary rulers of Egypt.

Muhammad Ali began a series of reforms in the military and in the economy. Without foreign assistance, he personally directed a shift of Egyptian agriculture to a plantation cash crop—cotton. This brought Egypt into the international marketplace but at a cost to the peasants. They lost the use of lands they traditionally farmed and were forced to grow cash crops in place of food crops. B

B. Answer brought Egyptians into the international market, reduced production of food crops

MAIN IDEA

Recognizing Effects

B What two effects did raising cotton have on Egyptian agriculture?

The Suez Canal Muhammad Ali's efforts to modernize Egypt were continued by his grandson, Isma'il. Isma'il supported the construction of the **Suez Canal**. The canal was a human-made waterway that cut

DIFFERENTIATING INSTRUCTION: GIFTED AND TALENTED STUDENTS

Debating Use of the Suez Canal

Class Time 30 minutes

Task Debating about access to the Suez Canal

Purpose To broaden understanding of the Suez Canal by exploring different points of view

Instructions Divide students into two groups and explain that they will debate the proposition, "All countries should have equal access to strategic waterways such as the Suez Canal." Have each group appoint members to act as researchers, presenters, coaches, timekeepers, and producers of graphic aids. In their presentations, ask them to pay particular attention to the following issues:

- nations' access to vital waterways in the late 1850s
- the strategic importance of the canal
- the relationships among the nations that used the canal
- the rights of the nations that must oversee and maintain the canal

Have students stage a formal debate and ask the entire class to vote to determine the strongest argument. In addition to the debate, you might ask interested students to research access to the canal today. Who uses it? Who oversees it? Who does and does not have access to it?

History *in* Depth

Suez Canal

The Suez Canal was viewed as the "Lifeline of the Empire" because it allowed Britain quicker access to its colonies in Asia and Africa. In a speech to Parliament, Joseph Chamberlain explained that he believed Britain should continue its occupation of Egypt because of "the necessity for using every legitimate opportunity to extend our influence and control in that great African continent which is now being opened up to civilization and to commerce."

This painting represents the opening celebration of the canal on November 17, 1869.

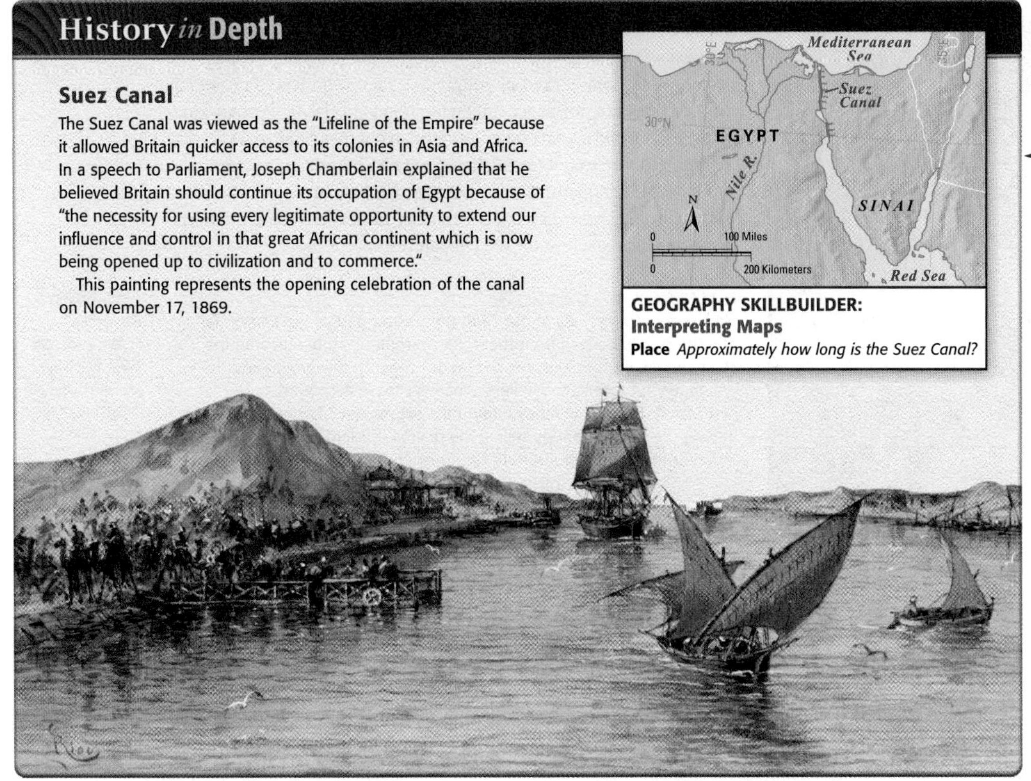

GEOGRAPHY SKILLBUILDER: Interpreting Maps
Place *Approximately how long is the Suez Canal?*

History *in* Depth

Interpreting the Map

In addition to connecting the Mediterranean Sea and Red Sea, what effect did the Suez Canal have on Egypt and Sinai? *(It created a barrier between them.)*

Extension Have students compare this map with the one on page 337. What route would Europeans have had to take to East Africa before the Suez Canal was built? *(through the Atlantic Ocean down the west coast, around the southern tip, and up the east coast of Africa)*

SKILLBUILDER Answer
Place about 100 miles

through the Isthmus of Suez. It connected the Red Sea to the Mediterranean. It was built mainly with French money from private interest groups, using Egyptian labor. The Suez Canal opened in 1869 with a huge international celebration. However, Isma'il's modernization efforts, such as irrigation projects and communication networks, were enormously expensive. Egypt soon found that it could not pay its European bankers even the interest on its $450 million debt. The British insisted on overseeing financial control of the canal, and in 1882 the British occupied Egypt.

Persia Pressured to Change

Elsewhere in southwest Asia, Russia and Britain competed to exploit Persia commercially and to bring that country under their own spheres of influence. (See map on page 353.) Russia was especially interested in gaining access to the Persian Gulf and the Indian Ocean. Twice Persia gave up territories to Russia, after military defeats in 1813 and 1828. Britain was interested in using Afghanistan as a buffer between India and Russia. In 1857, Persia resisted British demands but was forced to give up all claims to Afghanistan. Britain's interest in Persia increased greatly after the discovery of oil there in 1908.

Persia lacked the capital to develop its own resources. To raise money and to gain economic prestige, the Persian ruler began granting concessions to Western businesses. These concessions allowed businesses to buy the right to operate in a certain area or develop a certain product. For example, a British corporation, the Anglo-Persian Oil Company, began to develop Persia's rich oil fields in the early 1900s.

Persia Pressured to Change
10.4.2; 10.4.3

Critical Thinking

- What advantages did granting business concessions to Western countries offer Persia? *(income, development of their resources, and participation in world events)*
- How did Persia's granting of concessions eventually lead to its takeover by Britain and Russia? *(Concessions allowed Western countries to establish an economic foothold in Persia, which they exploited when the Persian government lost control of the country.)*

DIFFERENTIATING INSTRUCTION: ENGLISH LEARNERS

Understanding Reforms in Egypt

Class Time 25 minutes
Task Defining words and giving examples
Purpose To understand imperialism in Muslim lands
Instructions To help students understand what was happening in Egypt, Persia, and Russia, work with them on some of the vocabulary used on pages 354 and 355. Have pairs of students read the material under the headings "Egypt Initiates Reforms" and "Persia Pressured to Change." Have students identify words they find unfamiliar or difficult. Then work with them to develop definitions and examples for each word. Here are some examples:

Words	Definitions/Examples
modernization	Up-to-date, recent; Ex: modern weapons, new methods for farming, new communication systems
hereditary rulers	ruling power passed to family members; Ex: son who rules after his father
exploit	selfishly make use of; Ex: Asia, Russia, and Britain made use of Persia's resources without proper payment
buffer	a separation; Ex: Afghanistan separated India and Russia
economic prestige	wealth admired by others; Ex: Persia sold the right to develop oil fields to Western businesses to gain wealth and admiration.

More About . . .

Jamal al-Din al-Afghani

While in the British colony of India seeking an education in the mid-1850s, Jamal al-Din al-Afghani experienced firsthand the uprising of Muslims and Hindus against British imperial domination. He returned to Persia resolved to fight for his country's religious values and independence from foreign influence.

▲ Nasir al-Din was killed by one of al-Afghani's followers a few years after the boycott.

Battle over Tobacco Tension arose between the often corrupt rulers, who wanted to sell concessions to Europeans, and the people. The people were often backed by religious leaders who feared change or disliked Western influence in their nation. In 1890, Persian ruler Nasir al-Din sold a concession to a British company to export Persian tobacco. This action outraged Jamal al-Din al-Afghani, a leader who supported the modernization of Persia. He helped set up a tobacco boycott by the heavy-smoking Persians. In the following quote, he expresses his contempt for the Persian ruler:

PRIMARY SOURCE C

He has sold to the foes of our Faith the greater part of the Persian lands and the profits derived from them, for example . . . tobacco, with the chief centers of its cultivation, the lands on which it is grown and the warehouses, carriers, and sellers, wherever these are found. . . .

In short, this criminal has offered the provinces of Persia to auction among the Powers, and is selling the realms of Islam and the abodes of Muhammad and his household to foreigners.

JAMAL AL-DIN AL-AFGHANI, in a letter to Hasan Shirazi, April 1891

MAIN IDEA

Analyzing Primary Sources

C Why did al-Afghani condemn the actions of the Persian ruler?

C. Answer He sold the land and the profits from it to foreigners.

The tobacco boycott worked. Riots broke out, and the ruler was forced to cancel the concession. As unrest continued in Persia, however, the government was unable to control the situation. In 1906, a group of revolutionaries forced the ruler to establish a constitution. In 1907, Russia and Britain took over the country and divided it into spheres of influence. They exercised economic control over Persia.

In the Muslim lands, many European imperialists gained control by using economic imperialism and creating spheres of influence. Although some governments made attempts to modernize their nations, in most cases it was too little too late. In other areas of the globe, imperialists provided the modernization. India, for example, became a colony that experienced enormous change as a result of the occupation of the imperialist British. You will learn about India in Section 4.

3 ASSESS

SECTION 3 ASSESSMENT

Have students list the pages where answers to the questions can be found to help them review for the chapter assessment.

Formal Assessment
- Section Quiz, p. 192

4 RETEACH

Divide the class into six groups to portray the Ottoman Empire, Britain, France, Russia, Egypt, and Persia. Ask them to have a discussion in which the Asian and African countries explain why they came under European control and the European powers explain their reasons for seizing these lands.

In-Depth Resources: Unit 3
- Reteaching Activity, p. 68

SECTION 3 ASSESSMENT

TERMS & NAMES 1. For each term or name, write a sentence explaining its significance.
- geopolitics • Crimean War • Suez Canal

USING YOUR NOTES

2. What imperialistic forms of control did the Europeans use to govern these lands? (10.4.2)

Muslim states failed to keep European imperialists out of their lands.

detail | detail | detail

MAIN IDEAS

3. What is geopolitics? (10.4.2)
4. Why did Great Britain want to control the Suez Canal? (10.4.2)
5. Why did the Persian people oppose their ruler's policy of selling business concessions to Europeans? (10.4.3)

CRITICAL THINKING & WRITING

6. **COMPARING AND CONTRASTING** How were the reactions of African and Muslim rulers to imperialism similar? How were they different? (10.4.3)
7. **MAKING PREDICTIONS** What do you think happened as a result of Muhammad Ali's agriculture reform? (10.4.3)
8. **ANALYZING BIAS** What does the quotation in the History in Depth on page 355 suggest about Joseph Chamberlain's view of British imperialism in Africa? (10.4.3)
9. **WRITING ACTIVITY** EMPIRE BUILDING Write a **cause-and-effect paragraph** about reform efforts undertaken in Muslim lands. (Writing 2.2.a)

CONNECT TO TODAY **CREATING A TIME LINE**

Iran (formerly Persia) has undergone many changes since the late 1800s. Create a **time line** of important events in Iran's modern history. Include photographs that illustrate the events. (CST 3)

ANSWERS

1. geopolitics, p. 352 • Crimean War, p. 353 • Suez Canal, p. 354
2. **Sample Answer:** Details—Ottoman Empire tries to reform but fails; Egyptian leaders cannot complete modernization; Persia falls to economic imperialism. Europeans used spheres of influence and economic imperialism to govern the Muslim states.
3. an interest in or taking of land for its strategic location or products
4. for quicker access to its colonies in Africa and Asia
5. They disliked Western influence.
6. **Possible Answer:** Both resisted Europeans; Muslims tried to modernize to resist Western imperialism, but all the African rulers except Menelik II simply gave up their lands.
7. **Possible Answer:** food shortages and starvation
8. He believed that Africa would benefit from Britain's "civilizing" influence and from increased commerce.
9. **Rubric** Paragraphs should
   - list the reforms undertaken in Muslim lands.
   - describe the effects of these reforms.

CONNECT TO TODAY

Rubric Time lines should
- include events from 1979 to the present.
- be in chronological order.
- include photographs to illustrate events.

Aboriginal bark painting from Milingimbi, Australia

Battle of Isandhlwana, 1879, Zululand (now in South Africa)

4

British Imperialism in India

MAIN IDEA	WHY IT MATTERS NOW	TERMS & NAMES
EMPIRE BUILDING As the Mughal Empire declined, Britain seized Indian territory and soon controlled almost the whole subcontinent.	India, the second most populated nation in the world, has its political roots in this colony.	• sepoy • "jewel in the crown" • Sepoy Mutiny • Raj

SETTING THE STAGE British economic interest in India began in the 1600s, when the British East India Company set up trading posts at Bombay, Madras, and Calcutta. At first, India's ruling Mughal Dynasty kept European traders under control. By 1707, however, the Mughal Empire was collapsing. Dozens of small states, each headed by a ruler or maharajah, broke away from Mughal control. In 1757, Robert Clive led East India Company troops in a decisive victory over Indian forces allied with the French at the Battle of Plassey. From that time until 1858, the East India Company was the leading power in India.

CALIFORNIA STANDARDS

10.4.1 Describe the rise of industrial economies and their link to imperialism and colonialism (e.g., the role played by national security and strategic advantage; moral issues raised by the search for national hegemony, Social Darwinism, and the missionary impulse; material issues such as land, resources, and technology).

10.4.3 Explain imperialism from the perspective of the colonizers and the colonized and the varied immediate and long-term responses by the people under colonial rule.

10.4.4 Describe the independence struggles of the colonized regions of the world, including the roles of leaders, such as Sun Yat-sen in China, and the roles of ideology and religion.

British Expand Control over India

The area controlled by the East India Company grew over time. Eventually, it governed directly or indirectly an area that included modern Bangladesh, most of southern India, and nearly all the territory along the Ganges River in the north.

East India Company Dominates Officially, the British government regulated the East India Company's efforts both in London and in India. Until the beginning of the 19th century, the company ruled India with little interference from the British government. The company even had its own army, led by British officers and staffed by **sepoys**, or Indian soldiers. The governor of Bombay, Mountstuart Elphinstone, referred to the sepoy army as "a delicate and dangerous machine, which a little mismanagement may easily turn against us."

Britain's "Jewel in the Crown" At first, the British treasured India more for its potential than its actual profit. The Industrial Revolution had turned Britain into the world's workshop, and India was a major supplier of raw materials for that workshop. Its 300 million people were also a large potential market for British-made goods. It is not surprising, then, that the British considered India the brightest **"jewel in the crown,"** the most valuable of all of Britain's colonies.

The British set up restrictions that prevented the Indian economy from operating on its own. British policies called for India to produce raw materials for British manufacturing and to buy British goods. In addition, Indian competition with British goods was prohibited. For example, India's own handloom textile industry was almost put out of business by imported British textiles. Cheap cloth and ready-made clothes from England flooded the Indian market and drove out local producers.

TAKING NOTES

Recognizing Effects Use a diagram to identify the effects of the three causes listed.

Cause	Effect
1. Decline of the Mughal Empire	
2. Colonial policies	
3. Sepoy Mutiny	

LESSON PLAN

OBJECTIVES

- Describe the British takeover of India.
- Identify positive and negative aspects of British colonialism in India.
- Trace early nationalist movements in India.

1 FOCUS & MOTIVATE

Ask students if they have ever heard of the phrase *jewel in the crown*. What does it refer to? *(Britain's colony of India)* Explain that they will learn how this jewel did not passively accept being set on the head of a foreign monarch.

2 INSTRUCT

British Expand Control over India
10.4.1; 10.4.3

Critical Thinking

- Why did the governor of Bombay think the sepoys might turn against the British? *(The sepoys' primary allegiance was to their own country, not to Britain.)*

CALIFORNIA RESOURCES

California Reading Toolkit, p. L52
California Modified Lesson Plans for English Learners, p. 99
California Daily Standards Practice Transparencies, TT44
California Standards Enrichment Workbook, pp. 47–48, 51–52, 53–54
California Standards Planner and Lesson Plans, p. L95
California Online Test Practice
California Test Generator CD-ROM
California Easy Planner CD-ROM
California eEdition CD-ROM

SECTION 4 PROGRAM RESOURCES

ALL STUDENTS

In-Depth Resources: Unit 3
- Guided Reading, p. 50
- Skillbuilder Practice: Analyzing Bias, p. 53

Formal Assessment
- Section Quiz, p. 193

ENGLISH LEARNERS

In-Depth Resources in Spanish
- Guided Reading, p. 91
- Skillbuilder Practice, p. 93

Reading Study Guide (Spanish), p. 121
Reading Study Guide Audio CD (Spanish)

STRUGGLING READERS

In-Depth Resources: Unit 3
- Guided Reading, p. 50
- Skillbuilder Practice: Analyzing Bias, p. 53
- Reteaching Activity, p. 69

Reading Study Guide, p. 121
Reading Study Guide Audio CD

GIFTED AND TALENTED STUDENTS

In-Depth Resources: Unit 3
- Primary Source: Letter Opposing the English, p. 58

Electronic Library of Primary Sources
- "The Rise of the Color Bar"

INTEGRATED TECHNOLOGY

eEdition CD-ROM
Power Presentations CD-ROM
Geography Transparencies
- GT27 India Under British Rule, 1805–1886

World Art and Cultures Transparencies
- AT59 Raja Ram Singh in Procession

Electronic Library of Primary Sources
- "The Rise of the Color Bar"

classzone.com

More About . . .

British Economic Impact on Indian Society

British economic policies affected Indian classes unequally, although they were supposed to improve the lot of poor farmers. In fact, the only classes to benefit from British rule were the zamindars, or landowners, and the entrepreneurs of Calcutta. The farmers themselves remained as poor as ever throughout British rule.

British Transport Trade Goods India became increasingly valuable to the British after they established a railroad network there. Railroads transported raw products from the interior to the ports and manufactured goods back again. Most of the raw materials were agricultural products produced on plantations. Plantation crops included tea, indigo, coffee, cotton, and jute. Another crop was opium. The British shipped opium to China and exchanged it for tea, which they then sold in England.

Vocabulary
jute: a fiber used for sacks and cord

Trade in these crops was closely tied to international events. For example, the Crimean War in the 1850s cut off the supply of Russian jute to Scottish jute mills. This boosted the export of raw jute from Bengal, a province in India. Likewise, cotton production in India increased when the Civil War in the United States cut off supplies of cotton for British textile mills. **A**

MAIN IDEA
Summarizing
A On which continents were Indian goods being traded?
A. Answer Asia and Europe

Impact of Colonialism India both benefited from and was harmed by British colonialism. On the negative side, the British held much of the political and economic power. The British restricted Indian-owned industries such as cotton textiles. The emphasis on cash crops resulted in a loss of self-sufficiency for many villagers. The conversion to cash crops reduced food production, causing famines in the late 1800s. The British officially adopted a hands-off policy regarding Indian religious and social customs. Even so, the increased presence of missionaries and the racist attitude of most British officials threatened traditional Indian life.

On the positive side, the laying of the world's third largest railroad network was a major British achievement. When completed, the railroads enabled India to develop a modern economy and brought unity to the connected regions. Along with the railroads, a modern road network, telephone and telegraph lines, dams, bridges, and irrigation canals enabled India to modernize. Sanitation and public health improved. Schools and colleges were founded, and literacy increased. Also, British troops cleared central India of bandits and put an end to local warfare among competing local rulers.

History from Visuals

Interpreting the Map

Which countries in Asia were not under European domination in 1910? *(Arabia, Persia, Afghanistan, Nepal, Bhutan, Siam, China, Taiwan, Korea, Japan)*

Extension Ask students to identify the features indicated in the map that made India the "jewel in the crown" for Great Britain. Have them consider not only resources, but also India's strategic location. What problems would Britain have faced trying to trade in the Far East if it had not held India? *(a long and difficult journey by sea or overland through Europe and Asia)*

SKILLBUILDER Answers
1. **Region** Great Britain
2. **Location** It has access to Southeast Asia, East Asia, and Africa.

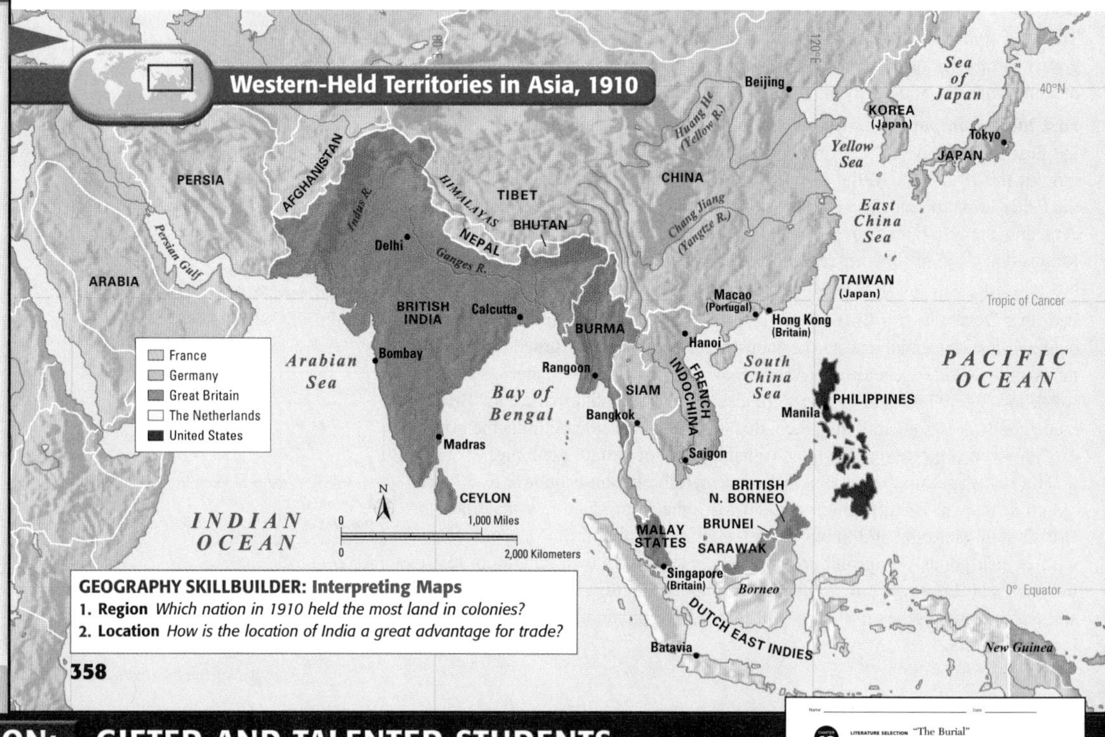

GEOGRAPHY SKILLBUILDER: Interpreting Maps
1. **Region** *Which nation in 1910 held the most land in colonies?*
2. **Location** *How is the location of India a great advantage for trade?*

358

DIFFERENTIATING INSTRUCTION: GIFTED AND TALENTED STUDENTS

Colonialism in Literature

Class Time 40 minutes

Task Reading and reporting on literary treatments of British colonialism in India

Purpose To learn more about life in British-ruled India

Instructions Have students read short stories and novels about the period of British rule in India. For a point of view sympathetic to the British, suggest that they read the fiction of Rudyard Kipling. They might start by reading Kipling's poem "The Burial" on page 60 of In-Depth Resources: Unit 3. For an Indian perspective, they might choose one of the following works:

- Prem Chand, *The Gift of a Cow*
- Rabindranath Tagore, *The Crescent Moon*
- Works by R. K. Narayan, such as *The Grandmother's Tale and Other Stories* and *A Tiger for Malgudi,* provide a contrast, depicting Indian village life relatively unchanged under British rule.

Have students report to the class on the point of view presented in their selection. Encourage them to critically evaluate the work and discuss how persuasive it is.

In-Depth Resources: Unit 3

Social History

Social Class in India

In the photograph at right, a British officer is waited on by Indian servants. This reflects the class system in India.

British Army

Social class determined the way of life for the British Army in India. Upper-class men served as officers. Lower-class British served at lesser rank and did not advance past the rank of sergeant. Only men with the rank of sergeant and above were allowed to bring their wives to India.

Each English officer's wife attempted to re-create England in the home setting. Like a general, she directed an army of 20 to 30 servants.

Indian Servants

Caste determined Indian occupations. Castes were divided into four broad categories called varna. Indian civil servants were of the third varna. House and personal servants were of the fourth varna.

Even within the varna, jobs were strictly regulated, which is why such large servant staffs were required. For example, in the picture here, both servants were of the same varna. However, the person washing the British officer's feet was of a different caste than the person doing the fanning.

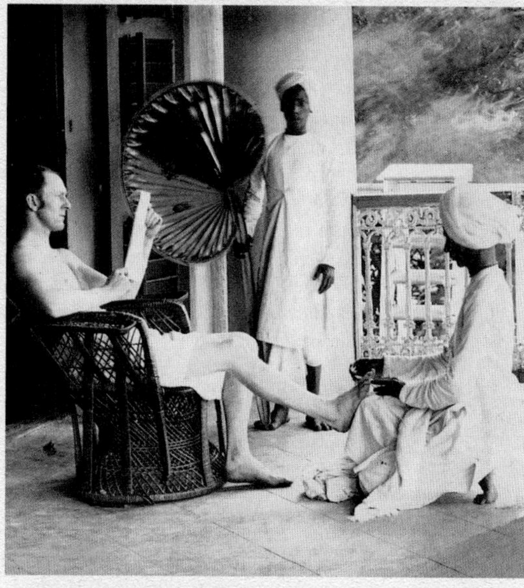

The Sepoy Mutiny

By 1850, the British controlled most of the Indian subcontinent. However, there were many pockets of discontent. Many Indians believed that in addition to controlling their land, the British were trying to convert them to Christianity. The Indian people also resented the constant racism that the British expressed toward them.

Indians Rebel As economic problems increased for Indians, so did their feelings of resentment and nationalism. In 1857, gossip spread among the sepoys, the Indian soldiers, that the cartridges of their new Enfield rifles were greased with beef and pork fat. To use the cartridges, soldiers had to bite off the ends. Both Hindus, who consider the cow sacred, and Muslims, who do not eat pork, were outraged by the news.

A garrison commander was shocked when 85 of the 90 sepoys refused to accept the cartridges. The British handled the crisis badly. The soldiers who had disobeyed were jailed. The next day, on May 10, 1857, the sepoys rebelled. They marched to Delhi, where they were joined by Indian soldiers stationed there. They captured the city of Delhi. From Delhi, the rebellion spread to northern and central India.

Some historians have called this outbreak the **Sepoy Mutiny**. The uprising spread over much of northern India. Fierce fighting took place. Both British and sepoys tried to slaughter each other's armies. The East India Company took more than a year to regain control of the country. The British government sent troops to help them. (B)

The Indians could not unite against the British due to weak leadership and serious splits between Hindus and Muslims. Hindus did not want the Muslim Mughal Empire restored. Indeed, many Hindus preferred British rule to Muslim rule. Most of the princes and maharajahs who had made alliances with the East India

B. Possible Answer Yes, he predicted problems with sepoy armies if they were not handled correctly. The mutiny was proof of this.

MAIN IDEA

Recognizing Effects

(B) Look back at Elphinstone's comment on page 357. Did the Sepoy Mutiny prove him correct?

Social History

Social Class in India

Make sure students understand that social class influenced the daily lives of both British army officers and their Indian servants. Ask students how the lives of these two groups differed. In what ways were they similar? *(Possible Answers: The dominant position of the British afforded them more leisure time than the Indians enjoyed. The groups were similar in that both socialized only with their own kind.)*

The Sepoy Mutiny

10.4.4

Critical Thinking

- What British action caused the sepoys' refusal of the cartridges to escalate? *(jailing of the rebellious soldiers)*
- How did the Sepoy Mutiny lead to increased British racism? *(Possible Answer: It built British resentment of the Indians' resistance and rebellion.)*

In-Depth Resources: Unit 3

- Primary Source: Letter Opposing the English, p. 58

Electronic Library of Primary Sources

- "The Rise of the Color Bar"

DIFFERENTIATING INSTRUCTION: ENGLISH LEARNERS

Causes and Effects of British Rule in India

Class Time 25 minutes

Task Creating a chart of causes and effects

Purpose To clarify important ideas about British imperialism in India

Instructions Divide students into small groups and have them read and discuss pages 357–361 of the text. Hand out copies of page 192 of In-Depth Resources in Spanish. Then have students work together to fill in the causes and effects missing from the chart. Instruct them to consult with other groups, if needed, to complete this task. Possible answers for the missing information might include:

1. Cause—Mughal Empire weakens and East India Company defeats Indian troops.
2. Effect—India becomes united and develops a modern economy.
3. Cause—British force India to produce cash crops.
4. Effect—British government takes direct command of India.
5. Cause—Nationalism grows in India.
6. Effect—Acts of terrorism take place.

Ask students to think about how history might have been different if any of the events listed as causes had not happened.

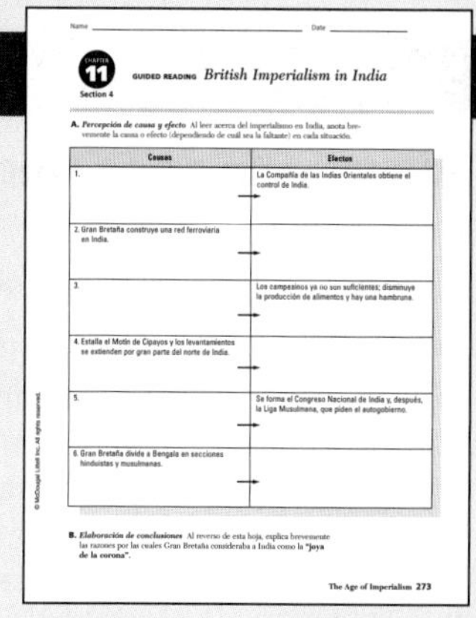

In-Depth Resources in Spanish

More About . . .

The British Raj

The term *raj* is a Hindi word meaning "rule" or "sovereignty." It has been used to refer both to British rule of India and to the viceroy of India, who was appointed by the British government for five or six years. By 1910, the Raj was one of the most powerful rulers in the world. He governed 300 million subjects and had one of the finest armies of the time.

Geography Transparencies

- GT27 India Under British Rule, 1805–1886

World Art and Cultures Transparencies

- AT59 Raja Ram Singh in Procession

Tip for English Learners

The "inherent superiority" statement by Lord Kitchener means he believes the English, from birth, were better than the Indians.

Company did not take part in the rebellion. The Sikhs, a religious group that had been hostile to the Mughals, also remained loyal to the British. Indeed, from then on, the bearded and turbaned Sikhs became the mainstay of Britain's army in India.

Turning Point The mutiny marked a turning point in Indian history. As a result of the mutiny, in 1858 the British government took direct command of India. The part of India that was under direct British rule was called the Raj. The term **Raj** referred to British rule over India from 1757 until 1947. A cabinet minister in London directed policy, and a British governor-general in India carried out the government's orders. After 1877, this official held the title of viceroy.

To reward the many princes who had remained loyal to Britain, the British promised to respect all treaties the East India Company had made with them. They also promised that the Indian states that were still free would remain independent. Unofficially, however, Britain won greater and greater control of those states.

The Sepoy Mutiny fueled the racist attitudes of the British. The British attitude is illustrated in the following quote by Lord Kitchener, British commander in chief of the army in India:

C. Possible Answers More of India was under British control; greater distrust between Indians and the British.

MAIN IDEA

Recognizing Effects

C In what ways did the Sepoy Mutiny change the political climate of India?

PRIMARY SOURCE

It is this consciousness of the inherent superiority of the European which has won for us India. However well educated and clever a native may be, and however brave he may prove himself, I believe that no rank we can bestow on him would cause him to be considered an equal of the British officer.

LORD KITCHENER, quoted in K. M. Panikkar, *Asia and Western Dominance*

The mutiny increased distrust between the British and the Indians. A political pamphlet suggested that both Hindus and Muslims "are being ruined under the tyranny and oppression of the . . . treacherous English." C

▼ This engraving shows sepoys attacking the British infantry at the Battle of Cawnpore in 1857.

SKILLBUILDER PRACTICE: ANALYZING BIAS

Identifying and Evaluating Biases

Class Time 25 minutes

Task Reading critically for biased material

Purpose To build skills in evaluating information

Instructions Explain to students that bias is a prejudiced point of view. Prejudiced views are typically formed without examining the facts and are unreasonable and negative. Biased historical accounts tend to be one-sided and to reflect the personal prejudices of the writer. Even though the account may be from a first-person primary source, it is important to examine the material to see if it is reasonable and based on thoughtful examination of facts. To help students detect biases, instruct them to look for language that conveys a strongly positive or negative slant on the subject.

Have students read "A Voice from the Past" on this page. Ask them to to analyze Kitchener's biases.

- Europeans are inherently superior.
- Natives can never be equal.
- Natives cannot be trusted with positions of authority, no matter how clever or well educated they are.
- Europeans must always remain in control.

In-Depth Resources: Unit 3

Nationalism Surfaces in India

In the early 1800s, some Indians began demanding more modernization and a greater role in governing themselves. Ram Mohun Roy, a modern-thinking, well-educated Indian, began a campaign to move India away from traditional practices and ideas. Sometimes called the "Father of Modern India," Ram Mohun Roy saw arranged child marriages and the rigid caste separation as parts of religious life that needed to be changed. He believed that if the practices were not changed, India would continue to be controlled by outsiders. Roy's writings inspired other Indian reformers to call for adoption of Western ways. Roy also founded a social reform movement that worked for change in India.

Besides modernization and Westernization, nationalist feelings started to surface in India. Indians hated a system that made them second-class citizens in their own country. They were barred from top posts in the Indian Civil Service. Those who managed to get middle-level jobs were paid less than Europeans. A British engineer on the East India Railway, for example, made nearly 20 times as much money as an Indian engineer.

D. Possible Answer Because these groups often were hostile to each other, it would make control of the areas easier.

MAIN IDEA

Analyzing Motives

D Why would the British think that dividing the Hindus and Muslims into separate sections would be good?

Nationalist Groups Form This growing nationalism led to the founding of two nationalist groups, the Indian National Congress in 1885 and the Muslim League in 1906. At first, such groups concentrated on specific concerns for Indians. By the early 1900s, however, they were calling for self-government.

The nationalists were further inflamed in 1905 by the partition of Bengal. The province was too large for administrative purposes, so the British divided it into a Hindu section and a Muslim section. As a result, acts of terrorism broke out. In 1911, yielding to pressure, the British took back the order and divided the province in a different way. D

Conflict over the control of India continued to develop between the Indians and the British in the following years. Elsewhere in Southeast Asia, the same struggles for control of land took place between local groups and the major European powers that dominated them. You will learn about them in Section 5.

SECTION 4 ASSESSMENT

TERMS & NAMES 1. For each term or name, write a sentence explaining its significance.
- sepoy
- "jewel in the crown"
- Sepoy Mutiny
- Raj

USING YOUR NOTES

2. Which of the effects you listed later became causes? (10.4.4)

Cause	Effect
1. Decline of the Mughal Empire	
2. Colonial policies	
3. Sepoy Mutiny	

MAIN IDEAS

3. Why did Britain consider India its "jewel in the crown"? (10.4.3)
4. Why didn't Indians unite against the British in the Sepoy Mutiny? (10.4.3)
5. What form did British rule take under the Raj? (10.4.3)

CRITICAL THINKING & WRITING

6. **MAKING INFERENCES** How did economic imperialism lead to India's becoming a British colony? (10.4.1)
7. **EVALUATING DECISIONS** What might the decision to grease the sepoys' cartridges with beef and pork fat reveal about the British attitude toward Indians? (10.4.3)
8. **SYNTHESIZING** How did imperialism contribute to unity and to the growth of nationalism in India? (10.4.4)
9. **WRITING ACTIVITY** EMPIRE BUILDING Write an **editorial** to an underground Indian newspaper, detailing grievances against the British and calling for self-government. (Writing 2.5.a)

CONNECT TO TODAY **CREATING A POLITICAL CARTOON**

In 1947, India was divided into two countries: mostly Hindu India and mostly Muslim Pakistan. However, the two countries maintain a tense relationship today. Research to learn about the cause of this tension and illustrate it in a **political cartoon.** (10.4.4)

Nationalism Surfaces in India
10.4.4

Critical Thinking
- How might child marriages and rigid caste separation have prevented India from becoming independent? *(Possible Answer: by keeping people's minds closed to modern ideas and approaches needed to operate independently in the modern world)*
- In what way were Indian nationalism and westernization compatible goals? *(Westernization provided Indians the ideas and technology to use in service of their own country.)*

3 ASSESS

SECTION 4 ASSESSMENT

Have students answer the questions without consulting the text, and then check their answers by locating the relevant information.

Formal Assessment
- Section Quiz, p. 193

4 RETEACH

Display the concept web graphic organizer. Ask students to work in groups to fill in the web, using this sentence as the main idea: "The Indian population never fully accepted British rule."

Critical Thinking Transparencies
- CT78 Concept Web

In-Depth Resources: Unit 3
- Reteaching Activity, p. 69

ANSWERS

1. sepoy, p. 357 • "jewel in the crown," p. 357 • Sepoy Mutiny, p. 359 • Raj, p. 360
2. **Sample Answer:** Effects–1. East India Company expanded its colonial territory; 2. Created resentment and nationalistic feelings among Indians; 3. Built support for nationalist groups. Each effect became the cause of the next effect.
3. because India was the most valuable British colony
4. weak leadership and conflicts between Hindus and Muslims
5. direct rule; India was divided into provinces and districts and ruled directly by British officials.
6. The British East India Company had its own army but was unable to regain control during the Sepoy Mutiny. This opened the way for Britain to step in, seize control, and claim India as a colony.
7. It revealed their insensitivity and indifference to Indians' religious customs.
8. Hindus and Muslims were united in hating British rule; all Indians resented job discrimination, lower pay, and condescension.
9. **Rubric** Editorials should
   - state the Indians' grievances against the British.
   - present supporting facts, reasons, and examples.
   - conclude with a call to action.

INTEGRATED TECHNOLOGY

Rubric Political cartoons should
- focus on a source of tension between India and Pakistan today.
- clearly identify each nation.
- exhibit originality.

LESSON PLAN

OBJECTIVES

- Summarize the acquisition of European colonies in Southeast Asia.
- Explain how Siam remained independent.
- Describe U.S. acquisition of the Philippines and Hawaii.

1 FOCUS & MOTIVATE

Ask students to explain what they know about countries such as Vietnam, Thailand, and the Philippines, all in the Pacific Rim. Explain that these countries have always had strategic value for imperialistic nations.

2 INSTRUCT

European Powers Invade the Pacific Rim

10.4.1; 10.4.2; 10.4.3

Critical Thinking

- What was the force above all others that drove imperialism in Southeast Asia? *(trade)*

CALIFORNIA RESOURCES

California Reading Toolkit, p. L53
California Modified Lesson Plans for English Learners, p. 101
California Daily Standards Practice Transparencies, TT45
California Standards Enrichment Workbook, pp. 47–48, 49–50, 51–52
California Standards Planner and Lesson Plans, p. L97
California Online Test Practice
California Test Generator CD-ROM
California Easy Planner CD-ROM
California eEdition CD-ROM

Aboriginal bark painting from Milingimbi, Australia

Battle of Isandhlwana, 1879, Zululand (now in South Africa)

5

Imperialism in Southeast Asia

MAIN IDEA	WHY IT MATTERS NOW	TERMS & NAMES
ECONOMICS Demand for Asian products drove Western imperialists to seek possession of Southeast Asian lands.	Southeast Asian independence struggles in the 20th century have their roots in this period of imperialism.	• Pacific Rim • King Mongkut • Emilio Aguinaldo • annexation • Queen Liliuokalani

CALIFORNIA STANDARDS

10.4.1 Describe the rise of industrial economies and their link to imperialism and colonialism (e.g., the role played by national security and strategic advantage; moral issues raised by the search for national hegemony, Social Darwinism, and the missionary impulse; material issues such as land, resources, and technology).

10.4.2 Discuss the locations of the colonial rule of such nations as England, France, Germany, Italy, Japan, the Netherlands, Russia, Spain, Portugal, and the United States.

10.4.3 Explain imperialism from the perspective of the colonizers and the colonized and the varied immediate and long-term responses by the people under colonial rule.

SETTING THE STAGE Just as the European powers rushed to divide Africa, they also competed to carve up the lands of Southeast Asia. These lands form part of the **Pacific Rim**, the countries that border the Pacific Ocean. Western nations desired the Pacific Rim lands for their strategic location along the sea route to China. Westerners also recognized the value of the Pacific colonies as sources of tropical agriculture, minerals, and oil. As the European powers began to appreciate the value of the area, they challenged each other for their own parts of the prize.

European Powers Invade the Pacific Rim

Early in the 18th century, the Dutch East India Company established control over most of the 3,000-mile-long chain of Indonesian islands. The British established a major trading port at Singapore. The French took over Indochina on the Southeast Asian mainland. The Germans claimed the Marshall Islands and parts of New Guinea and the Solomon islands.

The lands of Southeast Asia were perfect for plantation agriculture. The major focus was on sugar cane, coffee, cocoa, rubber, coconuts, bananas, and pineapple. As these products became more important in the world trade markets, European powers raced each other to claim lands.

TAKING NOTES

Clarifying Use a spider map to identify a Western power and the areas it controlled.

Dutch Expand Control The Dutch East India Company, chartered in 1602, actively sought lands in Southeast Asia. It seized Malacca from the Portuguese and fought the British and Javanese for control of Java. The discovery of oil and tin on the islands and the desire for more rubber plantations prompted the Dutch to gradually expand their control over Sumatra, part of Borneo, Celebes, the Moluccas, and Bali. Finally the Dutch ruled the whole island chain of Indonesia, then called the Dutch East Indies. (See map opposite.)

Management of plantations and trade brought a large Dutch population to the islands. In contrast to the British, who lived temporarily in India but retired in Britain, the Dutch thought of Indonesia as their home. They moved to Indonesia and created a rigid social class system there. The Dutch were on top, wealthy and educated Indonesians came next, and plantation workers were at the bottom. The Dutch also forced farmers to plant one-fifth of their land in specified export crops.

SECTION 5 PROGRAM RESOURCES

ALL STUDENTS

In-Depth Resources: Unit 3
- Guided Reading, p. 51
- History Makers: Mongkut, p. 64

Formal Assessment
- Section Quiz, p. 194

ENGLISH LEARNERS

In-Depth Resources in Spanish
- Guided Reading, p. 92

Reading Study Guide (Spanish), p. 123
Reading Study Guide Audio CD (Spanish)

STRUGGLING READERS

In-Depth Resources: Unit 3
- Guided Reading, p. 51
- Building Vocabulary, p. 52
- Reteaching Activity, p. 70

Reading Study Guide, p. 123
Reading Study Guide Audio CD

GIFTED AND TALENTED STUDENTS

In-Depth Resources: Unit 3
- Primary Source: In Favor of Imperialism, p. 59

Electronic Library of Primary Sources
- from *Hawaii's Story by Hawaii's Queen*

INTEGRATED TECHNOLOGY

eEdition CD-ROM
Power Presentations CD-ROM
Critical Thinking Transparencies
- CT27 Comparing Imperialist Styles
- CT63 Chapter 27 Visual Summary

Electronic Library of Primary Sources
- from *Hawaii's Story by Hawaii's Queen*

classzone.com

British Take the Malayan Peninsula To compete with the Dutch, the British sought a trading base that would serve as a stop for their ships that traveled the India-China sea routes. They found a large, sheltered harbor on Singapore, an island just off the tip of the Malay Peninsula. The opening of the Suez Canal and the increased demand for tin and rubber combined to make Singapore one of the world's busiest ports.

Britain also gained colonies in Malaysia and in Burma (modern Myanmar). Malaysia had large deposits of tin and became the world's leading rubber exporter. Needing workers to mine the tin and tap the rubber trees, Britain encouraged Chinese to immigrate to Malaysia. Chinese flocked to the area. As a result of such immigration, the Malays soon became a minority in their own country. Conflict between the resident Chinese and the native Malays remains unresolved today. (A)

A. Possible Answer They were searching for jobs.

MAIN IDEA

Analyzing Motives

(A) Why do you think so many Chinese moved to Malaysia?

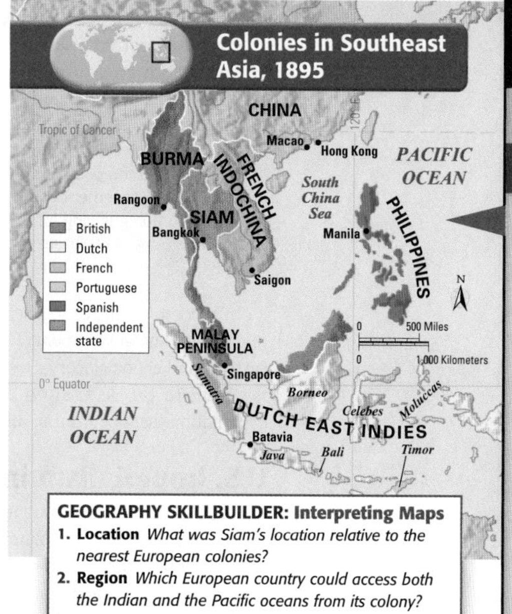

GEOGRAPHY SKILLBUILDER: Interpreting Maps
1. **Location** *What was Siam's location relative to the nearest European colonies?*
2. **Region** *Which European country could access both the Indian and the Pacific oceans from its colony?*

French Control Indochina The French had been active in Southeast Asia since the 17th century. They even helped the Nguyen (nuh•WIN) dynasty rise to power in Vietnam. In the 1840s, during the rule of an anti-Christian Vietnamese emperor, seven French missionaries were killed. Church leaders and capitalists who wanted a larger share of the overseas market demanded military intervention. Emperor Napoleon III ordered the French army to invade southern Vietnam. Later, the French added Laos, Cambodia, and northern Vietnam to the territory. The combined states would eventually be called French Indochina.

Using direct colonial management, the French themselves filled all important positions in the government bureaucracy. They did not encourage local industry. Four times as much land was devoted to rice production. However, the peasants' consumption of rice decreased because much of the rice was exported. Anger over this reduction set the stage for Vietnamese resistance against the French.

Colonial Impact In Southeast Asia, colonization brought mixed results. Economies grew based on cash crops or goods that could be sold on the world market. Roads, harbors, and rail systems improved communication and transportation but mostly benefited European business. However, education, health, and sanitation did improve.

Unlike other colonial areas, millions of people from other areas of Asia and the world migrated to work on plantations and in the mines in Southeast Asia. The region became a melting pot of Hindus, Muslims, Christians, and Buddhists. The resulting cultural changes often led to racial and religious clashes that are still seen today.

Siam Remains Independent

While its neighbors on all sides fell under the control of imperialists, Siam (present-day Thailand) maintained its independence throughout the colonial period. Siam lay between British-controlled Burma and French Indochina. (See map above.) France and Britain each aimed to prevent the other from gaining control of Siam. Knowing this, Siamese kings skillfully promoted Siam as a neutral zone between the two powers.

History from Visuals

Interpreting the Map

Ask students which colony covered the greatest expanse in the area. *(Dutch East Indies)* Which had the greatest land area? *(French Indochina)*

Extension Have students consult a reference book to determine the status of these former colonies today. *(None are now under foreign control.)*

SKILLBUILDER Answers

1. **Location** It was sandwiched between French Indochina and British Burma.
2. **Region** the Netherlands

Siam Remains Independent

10.4.3

Critical Thinking

- How did Siam's geographic location influence its political decisions? *(Its position between French and British colonies kept it neutral and resistant to foreign domination.)*
- What values motivated Mongkut and Chulalongkorn? *(respect for education, independence, and progress)*

In-Depth Resources: Unit 3

- History Makers: Mongkut, p. 64

Tip for Struggling Readers

After the invention of the automobile, there was a huge demand for rubber tires. Rubber was a driving force for imperialism in Southeast Asia.

DIFFERENTIATING INSTRUCTION: STRUGGLING READERS

Colonization in Southeast Asia

Class Time 25 minutes

Task Examining the events of imperialism in Southeast Asia

Purpose To understand how European powers colonized Southeast Asia

Instructions Have pairs of students read the Reading Study Guide for Section 5 and study the map on page 797. Remind students that they are probably already somewhat familiar with the present-day countries of Vietnam, Thailand, Cambodia, and the Philippines. Have students make a chart of how each imperial power impacted the lands they colonized.

Power	Lands Claimed	Major Trade Products
Dutch	Java, Sumatra, Borneo, Celebes, the Moluccas, Bali	Oil, tin, rubber
British	Malaysia, Burma	Tin, rubber
French	Vietnam, Laos, Cambodia	Rice
Americans	Philippines, Hawaii	Sugar, bananas, pineapples

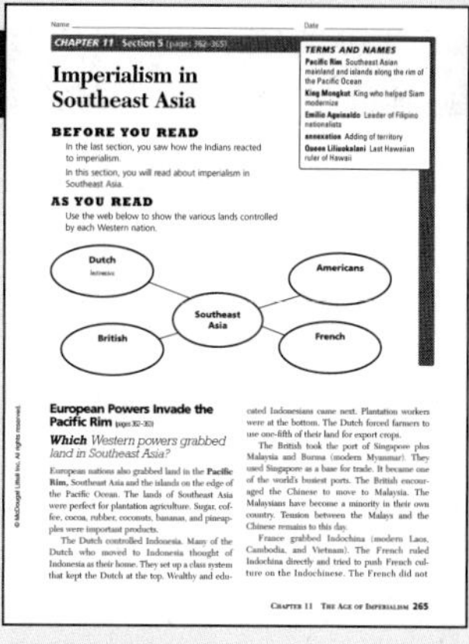

Reading Study Guide

U.S. Imperialism in the Pacific Islands
10.4.1; 10.4.2; 10.4.3

Critical Thinking

- Did President McKinley support or oppose imperialism? How do you know? *(support; His statement expresses typical imperialistic paternalism.)*
- What factors contributed to U.S. interest in Hawaii? *(its strategic location and sugar cane plantations)*

Critical Thinking Transparencies

- CT27 Comparing Imperialist Styles, 1850–1900

More About . . .

Emilio Aguinaldo

Emilio Aguinaldo's relationship with the United States fluctuated as he waged the ongoing battle to free his country from foreign influence. In 1898, he resisted Spanish occupation, fighting with the Americans when they attacked the Philippines during the Spanish-American War. Then, as head of the Filipino government, he fought U.S. occupation, a struggle he continued until he was captured in 1901 and swore allegiance to the United States. During World War II, he was again captured by American troops and held as a suspected collaborator with the Japanese occupiers.

Siam modernized itself under the guidance of **King Mongkut** and his son Chulalongkorn. In a royal proclamation, King Chulalongkorn showed his understanding of the importance of progress:

> **PRIMARY SOURCE**
> As the times and the course of things in our country have changed, it is essential to promote the advancement of all our academic and technical knowledge and to prevent it from succumbing [giving in] to competition from the outside. In order to achieve this, it is imperative to make haste in education so that knowledge and ability will increase.
>
> **KING CHULALONGKORN,** "Royal Proclamation in Education"

To accomplish the changes, Siam started schools, reformed the legal system, and reorganized the government. The government built its own railroads and telegraph systems and ended slavery. Because the changes came from their own government, the Siamese people escaped the social turmoil, racist treatment, and economic exploitation that occurred in other countries controlled by foreigners.

U.S. Imperialism in the Pacific Islands

Because Americans had fought for their independence from Britain, most of them disliked the idea of colonizing other nations. However, two groups of Americans were outspoken in their support of imperialism. One group of ambitious empire builders felt the United States should fulfill its destiny as a world power, colonizing like the Europeans. The other group, composed of business interests, welcomed the opening of new markets and trade possibilities.

The Philippines Change Hands The United States acquired the Philippine Islands, Puerto Rico, and Guam as a result of the Spanish-American War in 1898. Gaining the Philippines touched off a debate in the United States over imperialism. President McKinley's views swayed many to his side. He told a group of Methodist ministers his intention to "educate Filipinos, and uplift and Christianize them."

Vocabulary
Filipino: an inhabitant of the Philippine Islands

Filipino nationalists were not happy to trade one colonizer—the Spanish—for another, the Americans. **Emilio Aguinaldo** (eh•MEE•lyoh AH•gee•NAHL•doh), leader of the Filipino nationalists, claimed that the United States had promised immediate independence after the Spanish-American War ended. The nationalists declared independence and established the Philippine Republic.

▼ This photograph shows American soldiers fighting the Filipino nationalists in the early years of the war.

The United States plunged into a fierce struggle with the Filipino nationalists in 1899 and defeated them in 1902. The United States promised the Philippine people that it would prepare them for self-rule. To achieve this goal, the United States built roads, railroads, and hospitals, and set up school systems. However, as with other Southeast Asian areas, businessmen encouraged growing cash crops such as sugar at the expense of basic food crops. This led to food shortages for the Filipinos.

Hawaii Becomes a Republic U.S. interest in Hawaii began around the 1790s when Hawaii was a port on the way to China and East India. Beginning about the 1820s, sugar trade began to change the Hawaiian economy. Americans established sugar-cane plantations and became highly successful. By the mid-19th century, American sugar plantations accounted for 75 percent of Hawaii's wealth. At the same time, American sugar planters also gained great political power in Hawaii.

DIFFERENTIATING INSTRUCTION: GIFTED AND TALENTED STUDENTS

Analyzing a Speech

Class Time 20 minutes

Task Reading and discussing Albert Beveridge's speech to the U.S. Senate in 1898

Purpose To broaden understanding of views about U.S. imperialism

Instructions Hand out copies of the speech given by Albert Beveridge, a candidate for the U.S. Senate from Indiana in 1898, found on page 59 of In-Depth Resources: Unit 3. Ask volunteers to read sections of the speech aloud. Ask them to discuss the following questions:

- What did Beveridge want the U.S. to do? Why? *(bring the Philippines and Hawaii under U.S. control; provide new territories for U.S. citizens; bring progress and prosperity to the islands)*
- Based on the information in Chapter 11, which of his goals did the United States accomplish? *(acquiring the Philippines and Hawaii)*
- Which of Beveridge's arguments for expansion do you find most persuasive? Why? *(Possible Answer: establishing order, equity, and a government of law; these arguments reveal concern for the dominated people.)*

Name ______________________ Date __________

CHAPTER 11 Section 5

PRIMARY SOURCE **In Favor of Imperialism**
Speech by Albert Beveridge

While running for the Senate in 1898, Indiana's Albert Beveridge gave a campaign speech in which he explained why the United States should keep the Philippines. As you read this excerpt, consider his arguments in favor of U.S. imperialism.

It is a noble land that God has given us; a land that can feed and clothe the world; a land whose coastlines would enclose half the countries of Europe; a land set like a sentinel between the two imperial oceans of the globe, a greater England with a nobler destiny. It is a mighty people that He has planted on this soil; a people sprung from the most masterful blood of history; . . . a people imperial by virtue of their power, by right of their institutions, by authority of their heaven-directed purposes—the propagandists and not the misers of liberty.

It is a glorious history our God has bestowed upon His chosen people; a history whose keynote was struck by the Liberty Bell; a history heroic with faith in our mission and our future; a history of statesmen who flung the boundaries of the republic out into unexplored lands and savage wildernesses; a history of soldiers who carried the flag across the blazing deserts and through the ranks of hostile mountains, even to the gates of sunset; a history of a multiplying people who overran a continent in half a century. . . .

Therefore, in this campaign, the question is larger than a party question. It is an American question. It is a world question. Shall the American people continue in their restless march toward the commercial supremacy of the world? Shall free institutions broaden their blessed reign as the children of liberty wax in strength, until the empire of our principles is established over the hearts of all mankind? . . .

God bless the soldiers of 1898, children of the heroes of 1861, descendants of the heroes of 1776! In the halls of history they will stand side by side with those elder sons of glory, and the opposition to the government at Washington shall not deny them. No! They shall not be robbed of the honor due them, nor shall the republic be robbed of what they won for their country. . . .

Hawaii is ours; Puerto Rico is to be ours; at the prayer of the people, Cuba will finally be ours; . . . at the very least the flag of a liberal government is to float over the Philippines, and I pray God it may be the banner that Taylor unfurled in Texas and Frémont carried to the coast—the stars and stripes of glory.

The march of the flag! . . .

Think of the thousands of Americans who will pour into Hawaii and Puerto Rico when the republic's laws cover those islands with justice and safety! Think of the tens of thousands of Americans who will invade mine and field and forest in the Philippines when a liberal government . . . shall establish order and equity there! Think of the hundreds of thousands of Americans who will build a soap-and-water, common-school civilization of energy and industry in Cuba when a government of law replaced the double reign of anarchy and tyranny. Think of the prosperous millions that empress of islands will support when, obedient to the law of political gravitation, her people ask for the highest honor liberty can bestow, the sacred Order of the Stars and Stripes, the citizenship of the Great Republic!

from Thomas B. Reed, ed., *Modern Eloquence*, Vol. XI (Philadelphia, 1903), 224–243.

Discussion Questions

Clarifying

1. Whose hand did Beveridge see in America's destiny?
2. According to Beveridge, what would Hawaii, Puerto Rico, the Philippines, and Cuba gain from their association with the United States?
3. ***Drawing Conclusions*** Which arguments for the expansion of the American empire do you find most persuasive?

The Age of Imperialism **59**

In-Depth Resources: Unit 3

Then in 1890, the McKinley Tariff Act passed by the U.S. government set off a crisis in the islands. The act eliminated the tariffs on all sugar entering the United States. Now, sugar from Hawaii was no longer cheaper than sugar produced elsewhere. That change cut into the sugar producers' profits. Some U.S. business leaders pushed for **annexation** of Hawaii, or the adding of the territory to the United States. Making Hawaii a part of the United States meant that Hawaiian sugar could be sold for greater profits because American producers got an extra two cents a pound from the U.S. government.

About the same time, the new Hawaiian ruler, **Queen Liliuokalani** (luh•LEE•uh•oh•kuh•LAH•nee), took the throne. In 1893, she called for a new constitution that would increase her power. It would also restore the political power of Hawaiians at the expense of wealthy planters. To prevent this from happening, a group of American businessmen hatched a plot to overthrow the Hawaiian monarchy. In 1893, Queen Liliuokalani was removed from power.

In 1894, Sanford B. Dole, a wealthy plantation owner and politician, was named president of the new Republic of Hawaii. The president of the new republic asked the United States to annex it. At first, President Cleveland refused. In 1898, however, the Republic of Hawaii was annexed by the United States.

The period of imperialism was a time of great power and domination of others by mostly European powers. As the 19th century closed, the lands of the world were all claimed. The European powers now faced each other with competing claims. Their battles would become the focus of the 20th century.

History Makers

Queen Liliuokalani
1838–1917

Liliuokalani was Hawaii's only queen and the last monarch of Hawaii. She bitterly regretted her brother's loss of power to American planters and worked to regain power for the Hawaiian monarchy. As queen, she refused to renew a treaty signed by her brother that would have given commercial privileges to foreign businessmen. It was a decision that would cost her the crown.

INTEGRATED TECHNOLOGY

RESEARCH LINKS For more on Queen Liliuokalani, go to **classzone.com**

SECTION 5 ASSESSMENT

TERMS & NAMES 1. For each term or name, write a sentence explaining its significance.

• Pacific Rim • King Mongkut • Emilio Aguinaldo • annexation • Queen Liliuokalani

USING YOUR NOTES

2. Which Western power do you think had the most negative impact on its colonies? (10.4.1)

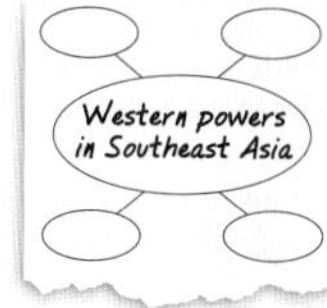

MAIN IDEAS

3. How were the Dutch East India Trading Company and the British East India Company similar? (10.4.2)
4. What changes took place in Southeast Asia as a result of colonial control? (10.4.3)
5. Why did some groups believe that the United States should colonize like the Europeans? (10.4.3)

CRITICAL THINKING & WRITING

6. **DRAWING CONCLUSIONS** How did the reforms of the Siamese kings help Siam remain independent? (10.4.3)
7. **ANALYZING BIAS** What does President McKinley's desire to "uplift and Christianize" the Filipinos suggest about his perception of the people? (10.4.3)
8. **ANALYZING MOTIVES** Why do you think Sanford Dole wanted the United States to annex Hawaii? (10.4.3)
9. **WRITING ACTIVITY** ECONOMICS Compose a **letter to the editor** expressing a Hawaiian's view on the U.S. businessmen who pushed for the annexation of Hawaii for economic gain. (Writing 2.5.d)

CONNECT TO TODAY **DRAWING A BAR GRAPH**

Research to find out about the economic situation of Southeast Asian countries today. Rank the economies and present your findings in a **bar graph.** (10.4.3)

History Makers

Queen Liliuokalani

How would you describe Queen Liliuokalani's politics? *(fiercely nationalistic)* Queen Liliuokalani received a modern education and toured the Western world before taking the throne of Hawaii. A talented musician, she is best known for her song "Aloha Oe," the national song of farewell in Hawaii.

Electronic Library of Pirmary Sources

• from *Hawaii's Story by Hawaii's Queen*

③ ASSESS

SECTION 5 ASSESSMENT

Have students complete the assessment and exchange papers with a partner to check their answers.

Formal Assessment

• Section Quiz, p. 194

④ RETEACH

Display the visual summary for Chapter 27 and divide the class into four groups. Have each group present the information about imperialism for the Dutch, British, French, or the United States.

Critical Thinking Transparencies

• CT63 Chapter 27 Visual Summary

In-Depth Resources: Unit 3

• Reteaching Activity, p. 70

ANSWERS

1. Pacific Rim, p. 362 • King Mongkut, p. 364 • Emilio Aguinaldo, p. 364 • annexation, p. 365 • Queen Liliuokalani, p. 365
2. **Sample Answer:** Dutch–Indonesia; British–Malay Peninsula; French–Indochina; U.S.–Philippines/Hawaii. Most negative impact–France, because it tried to completely subjugate the Indochinese by imposing its culture, government, industry, and agriculture
3. Both were trading companies that practiced economic imperialism.
4. economies grew; education and health improved; areas unified but lost local leaders; migration resulted in cultural change.
5. They believed the United States was destined to become a world power.
6. Siam modernized, making it competitive with Europeans.
7. **Possible Answer:** He saw them as primitive, irreligious, and inferior.
8. **Possible Answer:** He was a plantation owner and knew he would benefit from annexation.
9. **Rubric** Letters to the editor should
   • be written from the viewpoint of a Hawaiian.
   • express indignation at businessmen's desire to profit at Hawaii's expense.
   • call for an end to annexation.

CONNECT TO TODAY

Rubric Bar graphs should

• reveal information about Southeast Asian economies today.
• indicate which Southeast Asian countries have the healthiest economies.

TERMS & NAMES

1. imperialism, p. 339
2. racism, p. 341
3. Berlin Conference, p. 342
4. Menelik II, p. 349
5. geopolitics, p. 352
6. Suez Canal, p. 354
7. Raj, p. 360
8. Queen Liliuokalani, p. 365

MAIN IDEAS

Answers will vary.

9. nationalism, economic competition, racism, and missionary zeal
10. Many Africans lost their lives, had their crops destroyed, and had their lands burned. The survivors were placed under European rule.
11. colonies, protectorates, spheres of influence, and economic imperialism
12. Emperor Menelik II played the Italians, British, and French off against each other; bought a large arsenal of modern weapons from France and Russia; uncovered flaws in a treaty with Italy; and defeated Italian troops.
13. for their strategic location and natural resources
14. reforms, modernization, and resistance, though none of these methods worked
15. The British used India as a market for manufactured goods, driving native industries out of business; they also converted food crops to cash crops and exported India's natural resources to Great Britain.
16. outrage by the Indian soldiers that they were expected to bite off cartridges sealed with pork and beef fat, which was against both the Muslim and Hindu religions
17. The king made Siam a buffer zone between France and Britain; he and his descendants also made great efforts to modernize their country.
18. Some Americans wanted to join Europeans in imperialistic activities; others thought imperialism violated the ideals of democracy.

Chapter 11 Assessment

TERMS & NAMES

For each term or name below, briefly explain its connection to the imperialism of 1850–1914.

1. imperialism
2. racism
3. Berlin Conference
4. Menelik II
5. geopolitics
6. Suez Canal
7. Raj
8. Queen Liliuokalani

MAIN IDEAS

The Scramble for Africa Section 1 (pages 339–344)

9. What motivated the nations of Europe to engage in imperialist activities? (10.4.1)
10. What effect did the Boer War have on Africans? (10.4.3)

Case Study: Imperialism Section 2 (pages 345–351)

11. What are the forms of imperial rule? (10.4.1)
12. How did Ethiopia successfully resist European rule? (10.4.4)

Europeans Claim Muslim Lands Section 3 (pages 352–356)

13. Why were the European nations interested in controlling the Muslim lands? (10.4.2)
14. What methods did the Muslim leaders use to try to prevent European imperialism? (10.4.3)

British Imperialism in India Section 4 (pages 357–361)

15. How did the British transform India's economy? (10.4.1)
16. What caused the Sepoy Mutiny? (10.4.4)

Imperialism in Southeast Asia Section 5 (pages 362–365)

17. How did Siam manage to remain independent while other countries in the area were being colonized? (10.4.2)
18. Describe American attitudes toward colonizing other lands. (10.4.3)

CRITICAL THINKING

1. **USING YOUR NOTES**
In a chart, tell how the local people resisted the demands of the Europeans. (10.4.3)

Africa	Muslim lands	India	Southeast Asia

2. **RECOGNIZING EFFECTS**
ECONOMICS What effects did imperialism have on the economic life of the lands and people colonized by the European imperialists? (10.4.3)

3. **DRAWING CONCLUSIONS**
Why do you think the British viewed the Suez Canal as the lifeline of their empire? (10.4.1)

4. **SYNTHESIZING**
What positive and negative impact did inventions such as the railroad and the steamship have on the land and people conquered by the imperialists? (10.4.3)

5. **DEVELOPING HISTORICAL PERSPECTIVE**
EMPIRE BUILDING What economic, political, and social conditions encouraged the growth of imperialism in Africa and Asia? (10.4.1)

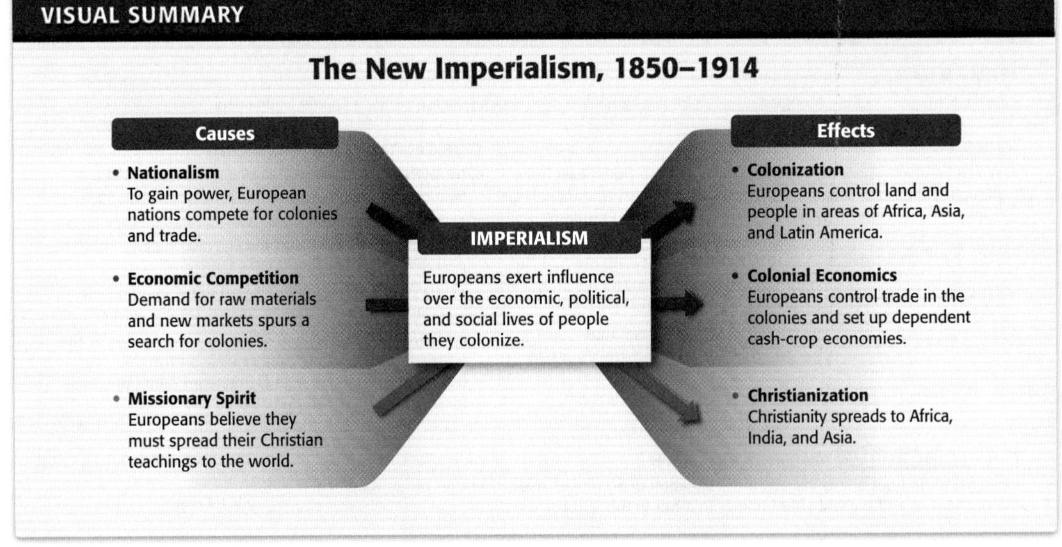

VISUAL SUMMARY
The New Imperialism, 1850–1914
Causes
• Nationalism
To gain power, European nations compete for colonies and trade.
• Economic Competition
Demand for raw materials and new markets spurs a search for colonies.
• Missionary Spirit
Europeans believe they must spread their Christian teachings to the world.
IMPERIALISM
Europeans exert influence over the economic, political, and social lives of people they colonize.
Effects
• Colonization
Europeans control land and people in areas of Africa, Asia, and Latin America.
• Colonial Economics
Europeans control trade in the colonies and set up dependent cash-crop economies.
• Christianization
Christianity spreads to Africa, India, and Asia.

CRITICAL THINKING

Answers will vary.

1. Africa—Armed resistance throughout the continent; Muslim lands—Attempts at modernization and reform; India—Armed rebellion and formation of nationalist parties; Southeast Asia—Armed resistance in some areas, modernization in others.
2. Agriculture changed from food crops to cash crops; colonies had to buy European finished goods, which reduced production of local goods; transportation and communication systems benefited Europeans, not the colonials.
3. Without the Suez Canal, the British would have had to travel around the west coast of Africa to reach many of their colonies.
4. Positive—New transportation systems for colonials. Negative—The means for colonizers to enter and establish control of lands in Africa and Asia.
5. The demands of industrialization led to the need for new sources of raw materials and new markets for manufactured goods; nations wanted to compete for the prestige and power imperialism brought; many felt the calling to Westernize and Christianize colonies.

Use the quotation from the king of the Asante people and your knowledge of world history to answer questions 1 and 2.
Additional Test Practice, pp. S1–S33

PRIMARY SOURCE

The suggestion that Ashanti [Asante] in its present state should come and enjoy the protection of Her Majesty the Queen and Empress of India, I may say this is a matter of serious consideration, and which I am happy to say we have arrived at the conclusion, that my kingdom of Ashanti will never commit itself to any such conclusion, that Ashanti must remain independent as of old, at the same time to remain friendly with all white men. I do not write this with a boastful spirit, but in the clear sense of its meaning. Ashanti is an independent kingdom.

KWAKU DUA III to Frederic M. Hodgson, December 27, 1889

1. What is Kwaku Dua III's answer to the queen? (10.4.3)
   - **A.** He would enjoy the protection of the queen.
   - **B.** He cannot commit himself at this time.
   - **C.** He is offended by her offer.
   - **D.** He refuses her offer.
2. Why do you think Kwaku Dua III responded that he wanted to remain friendly to white men? (10.4.3)
   - **A.** He wanted his country to be placed under the protection of white men.
   - **B.** He was trying to be diplomatic.
   - **C.** He wanted to adopt white men's culture.
   - **D.** He wanted the assistance of white men.

Use the map of the British Empire and your knowledge of world history to answer question 3.

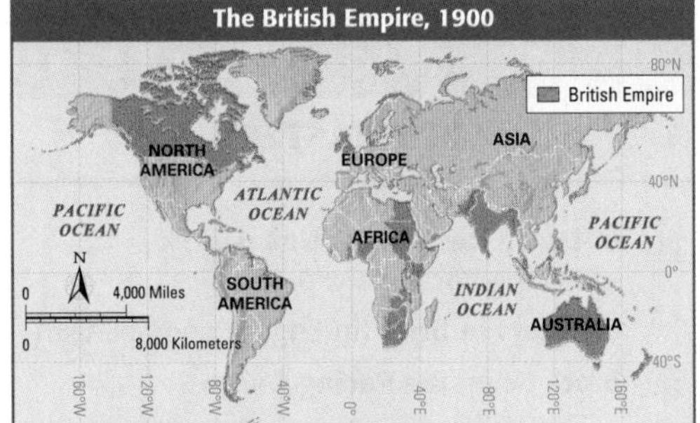

3. "The sun never sets on the British Empire" was a saying about the British Empire at the peak of its power. What do you think this saying meant? (10.4.2)
   - **A.** The British Empire had colonies in every part of the world.
   - **B.** The British felt that the sun revolved around them.
   - **C.** The British Empire represented sunlight and hope to the rest of the world.
   - **D.** The British were hard working and never slept.

INTEGRATED TECHNOLOGY
TEST PRACTICE Go to **classzone.com**
- Diagnostic tests
- Strategies
- Tutorials
- Additional practice

ALTERNATIVE ASSESSMENT

1. **Interact *with* History** (10.4.3)
   On page 338, you considered the advantages and disadvantages of colonialism. Now, make a chart showing the advantages and disadvantages to a local person living in a place that became a European colony. Next, make a similar chart for a European living in a foreign place. How do they compare? Discuss with members of your class a way to decide whether the advantages outweigh the disadvantages for each group.
2. **WRITING ABOUT HISTORY** (Writing 2.3.c)
   POWER AND AUTHORITY Write a **news article** about the effects of colonization. Be sure to address the following points:
   - Provide some background on the country you're writing about.
   - Tell where the colonizers have come from.
   - Describe how the colonizers treat the colonized people.
   - Include quotations from both the colonizers and the colonized.
   - Draw conclusions about each side's opinion of the other.

INTEGRATED TECHNOLOGY

Creating an Interactive Time Line (Writing 2.3.d)
Use the Internet and your textbook to create a time line of the events covered in Chapter 11. The time line on pages 336–337 can serve as a guide. Use graphics software to add maps and pictures that illustrate the events. Be sure to include the following on your time line:
- important events in the colonization of Africa and Asia
- efforts on the part of the colonies to resist the imperialist powers
- people who played important roles in the events
- places where key events occurred
- visuals that illustrate the events

STANDARDS-BASED ASSESSMENT

1. The correct answer is letter **D**. The king states that Ashanti (Asante) must remain independent. Letter **A** is not correct because the king does not say he would enjoy the queen's protection. Letter **B** is not correct because the king has made up his mind. Letter **C** is not correct because his language does not convey that he has taken offense.
2. The correct answer is letter **B**. The king probably feared offending the British because he knew he would not be able to resist them completely. Letter **A** is not correct because the king wanted Ashanti to remain independent. Letters **C** and **D** are not correct because he does not say he wants to adopt anyone's culture or accept anyone's assistance.
3. The correct answer is letter **A**. The sun would always be shining on one of Britain's colonies as the earth revolved.

Formal Assessment
- Chapter Tests, Forms A, B, and C, pp. 195–206

California Test Generator CD-ROM
- Chapter Tests, Forms A, B, and C (English and Spanish)

ALTERNATIVE ASSESSMENT

1. Local person: Advantages—Modern technology, education, and medical care, unified control of area. Disadvantages—Racism, economic imperialism, loss of freedom and control of land and culture.
   European: Advantages—New opportunities for wealth, travel, and advancement. Disadvantages—Distance from family, strange climate and people, new diseases, and potentially hostile population.
2. **Rubric** News articles should
   - identify the colonizers and country being colonized.
   - describe how the colonizers treat the colonized people.
   - include quotations from both the colonizers and the colonized.
   - draw conclusions about colonialism and its effects.

INTEGRATED TECHNOLOGY

Rubric Time lines should
- include the events listed in the time line on pages 336–337.
- include additional events drawn from the chapter.
- be presented in chronological order.
- include appropriate visuals.

CHAPTER 12 PLANNING GUIDE

Transformations Around the Globe, 1800–1914

CHAPTER RESOURCES	COPYMASTERS	ASSESSMENT
CHAPTER OVERVIEW China and Japan responded in different ways to the European powers. The United States influenced Latin America, and Mexico underwent a revolution.	**In-Depth Resources: Unit 3** • Building Vocabulary, p. 75 **Chapters in Brief** (in English and Spanish) **Block Schedule Pacing Guide**	**Chapter Assessment,** pp. 394–395 **Formal Assessment** • Chapter Tests, Forms A, B, and C, pp. 211–225 **Test Generator** **Integrated Assessment Book** **Online Test Practice**
SECTION 1 **China Resists Outside Influence** pp. 371–375 **OBJECTIVE** Summarize China's resistance to foreigners and its internal problems, and trace the growth of foreign influence and nationalism in China.	**In-Depth Resources: Unit 3** • Guided Reading, p. 71 • Geography Application: The Opium Wars, p. 77 • Primary Source: from Letter to Queen Victoria, p. 79 • History Makers: Cixi, p. 86 • Reteaching Activity, p. 90 **Reading Study Guide,** p. 127	**Section 1 Assessment,** p. 375 **Formal Assessment** • Section Quiz, p. 207 **California Daily Standards Practice Transparencies,** TT106
SECTION 2 **Modernization in Japan** pp. 376–381 **OBJECTIVE** Explain why Japan ended its isolation and developed imperialism.	**In-Depth Resources: Unit 3** • Guided Reading, p. 72 • Skillbuilder Practice: Analyzing Political Cartoons, p. 76 • Primary Source: from *The Autobiography of Yukichi Fukuzawa,* p. 80 • Reteaching Activity, p. 91 **Reading Study Guide,** p. 129	**Section 2 Assessment,** p. 379 **Formal Assessment** • Section Quiz, p. 208 **California Daily Standards Practice Transparencies,** TT107
SECTION 3 **U.S. Economic Imperialism** pp. 382–387 **OBJECTIVE** Describe Latin America after independence and explain how the United States put economic and political pressure on Latin America.	**In-Depth Resources: Unit 3** • Guided Reading, p. 73 • Primary Source: Panama Canal, p. 81 • Connections Across Time, p. 88 • Science & Technology, p. 89 • Reteaching Activity, p. 92 **Reading Study Guide,** p. 131	**Section 3 Assessment,** p. 387 **Formal Assessment** • Section Quiz, p. 209 **California Daily Standards Practice Transparencies,** TT108
SECTION 4 **Turmoil and Change in Mexico** pp. 388–393 **OBJECTIVE** Trace the political development of Mexico, from the Mexican War, through Juárez's reform movement, to the Mexican revolution.	**In-Depth Resources: Unit 3** • Guided Reading, p. 74 • Primary Source: from *The Plan of Ayala,* p. 82 • Literature: from *Tom Mix and Pancho Villa,* p. 83 • History Makers: Porfirio Díaz, p. 87 • Reteaching Activity, p. 93 **Reading Study Guide,** p. 133 **Case Study 9: Mexico and Japan,** p. 114	**Section 4 Assessment,** p. 393 **Formal Assessment** • Section Quiz, p. 210 **California Daily Standards Practice Transparencies,** TT109

INTEGRATED TECHNOLOGY

- eEdition Plus Online
- EasyPlanner Plus Online
- eTest Plus Online

Audio CDs
- Voices from the Past
- Reading Study Guides

CD-ROMs
- eEdition
- Power Presentations
- EasyPlanner
- Electronic Library of Primary Sources
- Test Generator

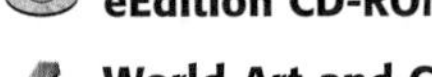

eEdition CD-ROM

World Art and Cultures Transparencies
- AT60 Sorting of Cocoons

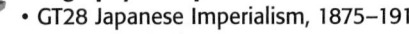

Electronic Library of Primary Sources
- from *Two Years in the Forbidden City*

classzone.com

eEdition CD-ROM

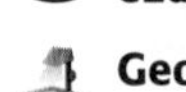

Geography Transparencies
- GT28 Japanese Imperialism, 1875–1910

World Art and Cultures Transparencies
- AT61 *Japanese Girl in Western Dress*

Electronic Library of Primary Sources
- from *Fifty Years of New Japan*

classzone.com

eEdition CD-ROM

Critical Thinking Transparencies
- CT28 Patterns of Resistance, 1830–1914

Electronic Library of Primary Sources
- from *The Rough Riders*

classzone.com

eEdition CD-ROM

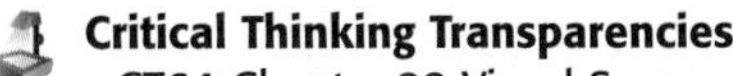

Critical Thinking Transparencies
- CT64 Chapter 28 Visual Summary

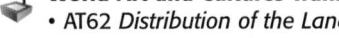

World Art and Cultures Transparencies
- AT62 *Distribution of the Land*

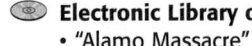

Electronic Library of Primary Sources
- "Alamo Massacre"

classzone.com

OVERVIEW OF CALIFORNIA RESOURCES

	Section 1	Section 2	Section 3	Section 4
California Reading Toolkit	p. L54	p. L55	p. L56	p. L57
California Modified Lesson Plans for English Learners	p. 103	p. 105	p. 107	p. 109
California Daily Standards Practice Transparencies	TT46	TT47	TT48	TT49
California Standards Enrichment Workbook	pp. 53–54	pp. 49–50	pp. 47–48	pp. 53–54
California Standards Planner and Lesson Plans	p. L99	p. L101	p. L103	p. L105
California Online Test Practice	classzone.com	classzone.com	classzone.com	classzone.com
California Test Generator CD-ROM				
California Easy Planner CD-ROM				
California eEdition CD-ROM				

Chart Key:

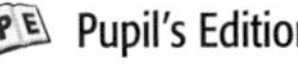
Pupil's Edition

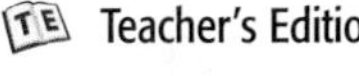
Teacher's Edition

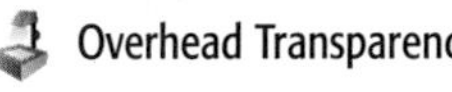
Overhead Transparency

Block Scheduling

Copymaster

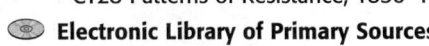

Audio Library

CD-ROM

Internet

Video

NO TIME?

If you do not have time to teach this chapter in full, assign the **Chapter in Brief** (also available in Spanish).

Previewing Resources for Differentiated Instruction

ENGLISH LEARNERS: Resources in Spanish

In-Depth Resources in Spanish

- Guided Reading (A)
- Skillbuilder Practice: Analyzing Political Cartoons
- Geography Application: The Opium Wars (B)

Chapters in Brief

Reading Study Guide (C)

Reading Study Guide Audio CD

Test Generator CD-ROM

- Chapter Test, Forms A, B, and C

Plus

Modified Lesson Plans for English Learners

Multi-Language Glossary of Social Studies Terms

(A)

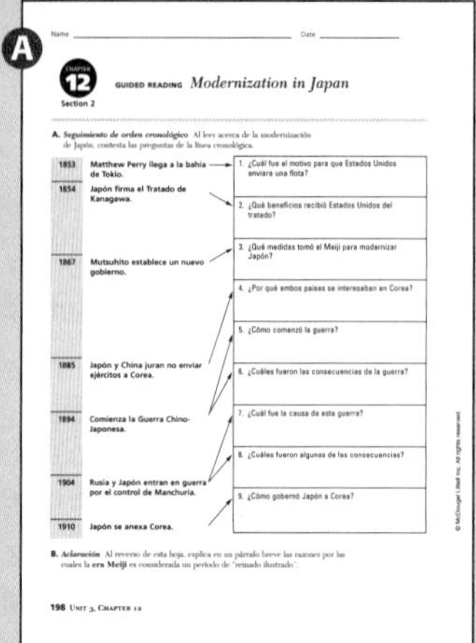

Chapter 12 Section 2 GUIDED READING *Modernization in Japan*

196 Unit 3, Chapter 12

(B)

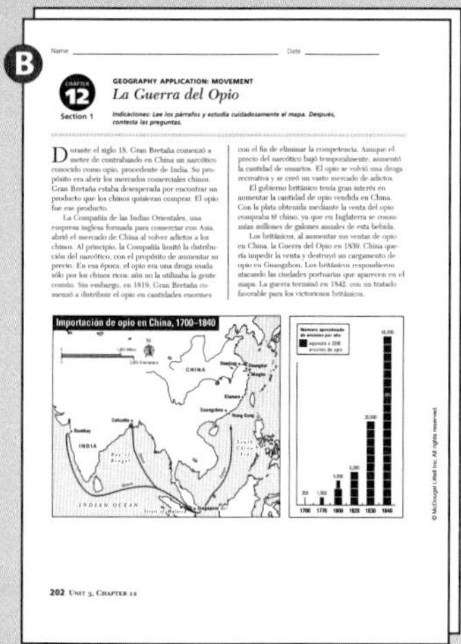

Chapter 12 Section 1 GEOGRAPHY APPLICATION: MOVEMENT *La Guerra del Opio*

Importación de opio en China, 1700–1840

202 Unit 3, Chapter 12

STRUGGLING READERS

In-Depth Resources: Unit 3

- Guided Reading (A)
- Building Vocabulary
- Skillbuilder Practice: Analyzing Political Cartoons
- Geography Application: The Opium Wars (B)
- Reteaching Activities

Chapters in Brief

Reading Study Guide (C)

Reading Study Guide Audio CD

Formal Assessment

- Chapter Test, Form A

Plus

Reading Toolkit

(A)

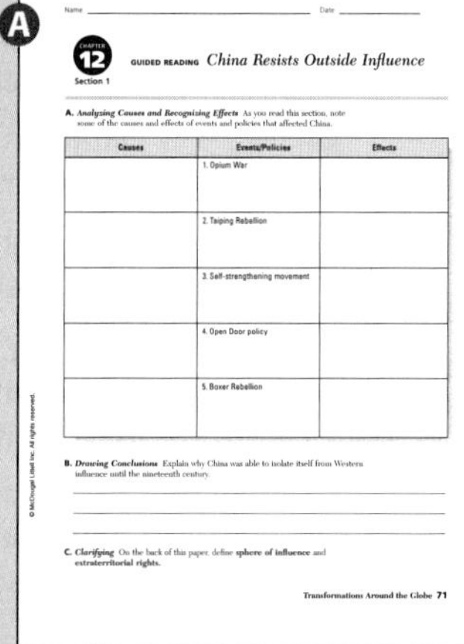

Chapter 12 Section 1 GUIDED READING *China Resists Outside Influence*

Causes	Events/Policies	Effects
	1. Opium War	
	2. Taiping Rebellion	
	3. Self-strengthening movement	
	4. Open Door policy	
	5. Boxer Rebellion	

Transformations Around the Globe 71

(B)

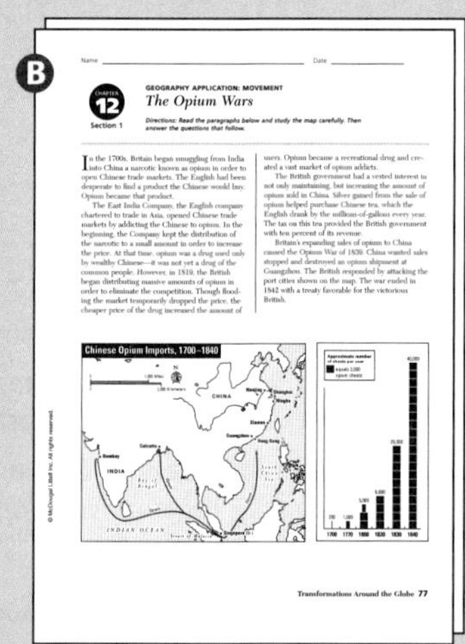

Chapter 12 Section 1 GEOGRAPHY APPLICATION: MOVEMENT *The Opium Wars*

Chinese Opium Imports, 1700–1840

Transformations Around the Globe 77

GIFTED AND TALENTED STUDENTS

In-Depth Resources: Unit 3

- Primary Sources: from Letter to Queen Victoria; from *The Autobiography of Yukichi Fukuzawa;* Building the Panama Canal; from *The Plan of Ayala*
- Literature: from *Tom Mix and Pancho Villa*
- History Makers: Cixi; Porfirio Díaz
- Connections Across Time and Cultures: Responses to Western Pressure (A)
- Science & Technology: Technology Revolutionizes Communications (B)

Electronic Library of Primary Sources

- from *Two Years in the Forbidden City*
- from *Fifty Years of New Japan*
- from *The Rough Riders*
- "Alamo Massacre"

Formal Assessment

- Chapter Test, Form C (C)

(A)

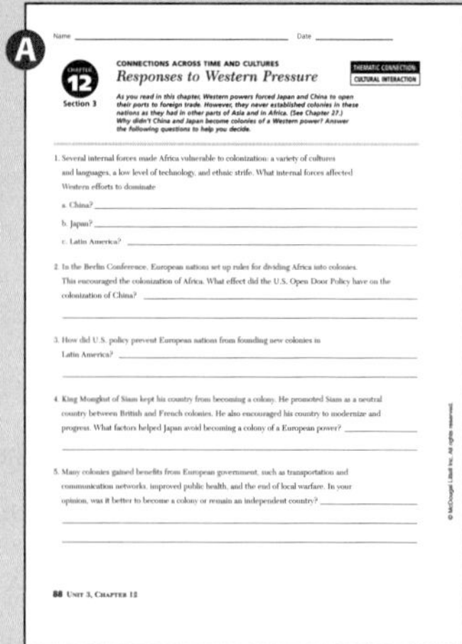

Chapter 12 Section 3 CONNECTIONS ACROSS TIME AND CULTURES *Responses to Western Pressure*

88 Unit 3, Chapter 12

(B)

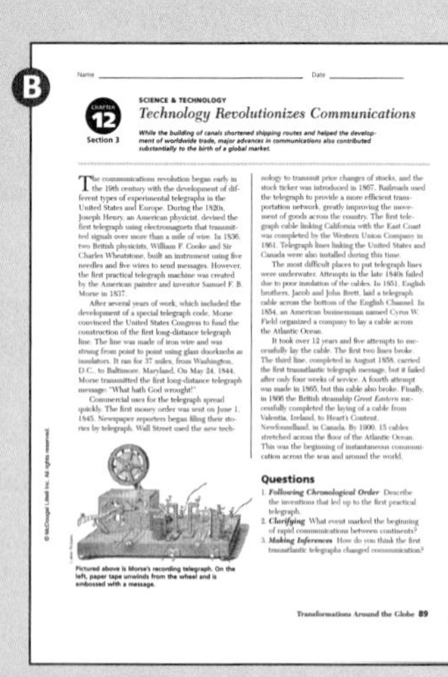

Chapter 12 Section 3 SCIENCE & TECHNOLOGY *Technology Revolutionizes Communications*

Transformations Around the Globe 89

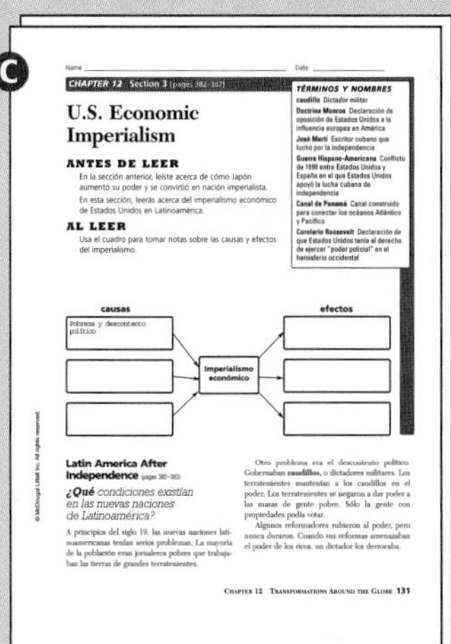

CHAPTER 12 Section 3

U.S. Economic Imperialism

ANTES DE LEER

AL LEER

TÉRMINOS Y NOMBRES

causas

efectos

Imperialismo económico

Latin America After Independence

¿Qué condiciones existían en las nuevas naciones de Latinoamérica?

CHAPTER 12 TRANSFORMATIONS AROUND THE GLOBE 131

Activities in the Teacher's Edition for English Learners

- Geography of the Opium Wars, p. 372
- Japan Adopts the Best of the West, p. 377
- Analyzing Quotations and Academic Vocabulary, p. 383
- Creating a Time Line of the Mexican Revolution, p. 389

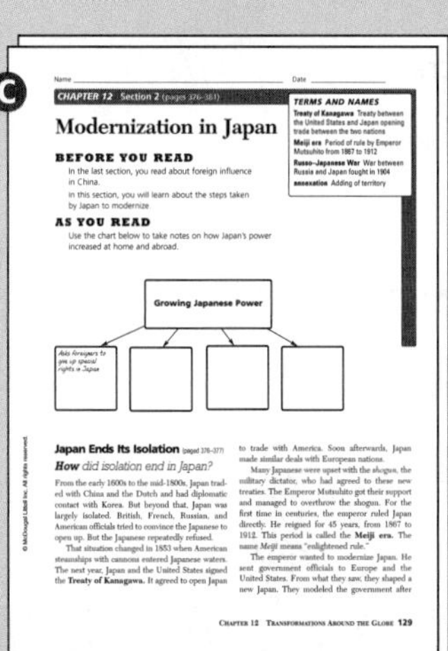

CHAPTER 12 Section 2

Modernization in Japan

BEFORE YOU READ

AS YOU READ

TERMS AND NAMES

Growing Japanese Power

Japan Ends Its Isolation

How did isolation end in Japan?

CHAPTER 12 TRANSFORMATIONS AROUND THE GLOBE 129

Activities in the Teacher's Edition for Struggling Readers

- Recognizing Causes and Effects, p. 374
- Chronology of Events in Latin America, p. 384
- Identifying Problems That Affected Mexico, p. 390

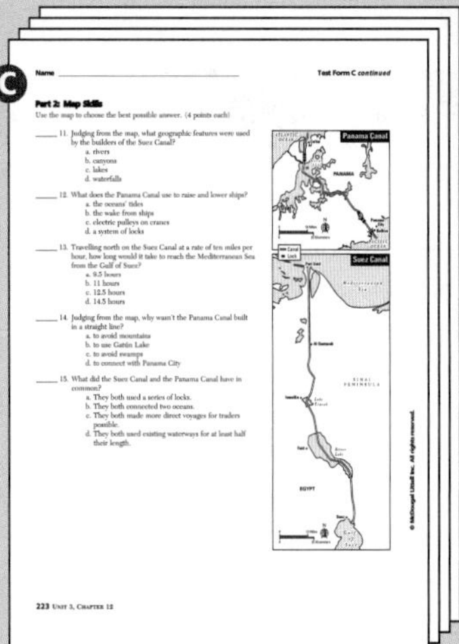

Test Form C continued

Part 2: Map Skills

Panama Canal

Suez Canal

Activities in the Teacher's Edition for Gifted and Talented Students

- Origins of the Taiping Rebellion, p. 373
- Analyzing Problems and Solutions in Imperialist Times, p. 385
- Performing as Villa and Zapata, p. 391

INTEGRATED TECHNOLOGY

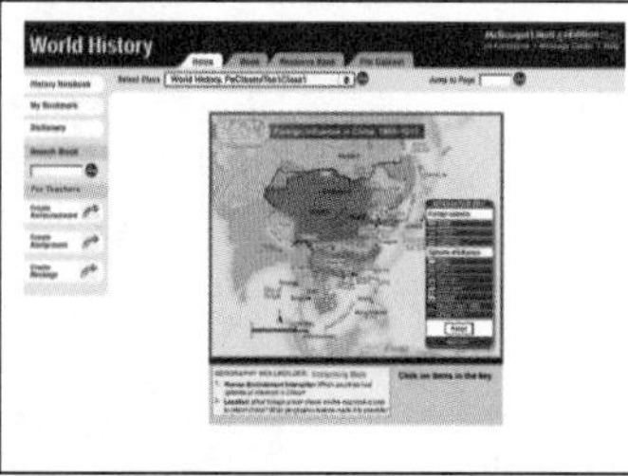

eEdition
- Interactive Visuals
- Interactive Maps
- Interactive Primary Sources

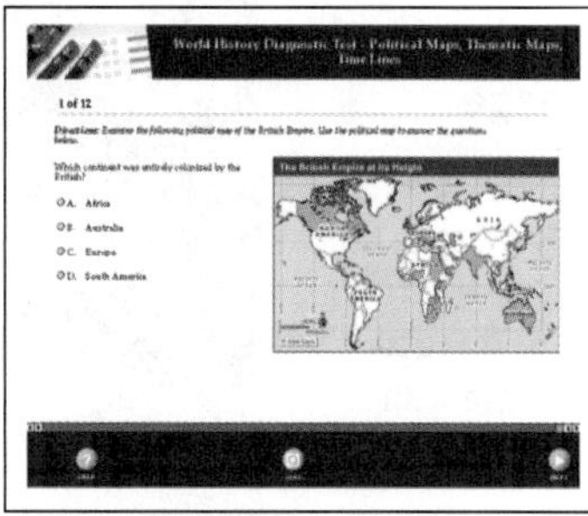

classzone.com
- Research Links
- Internet Activities
- Primary Sources
- Chapter Quiz
- Current Events

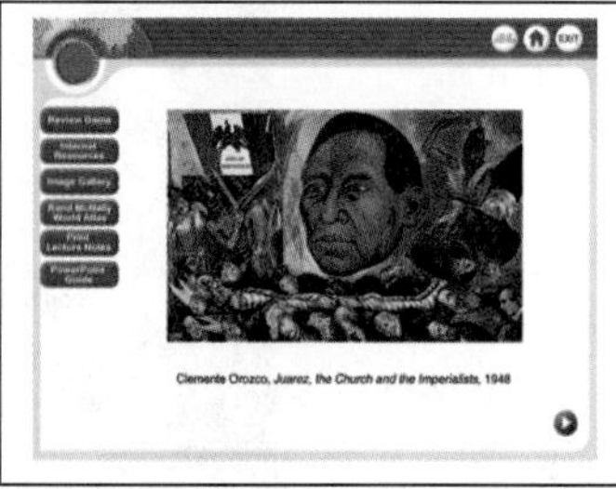

Clemente Orozco, Juarez, the Church and the Imperialists, 1948

Power Presentations CD-ROM
- Lecture Notes
- Image Gallery
- Chapter Review Game

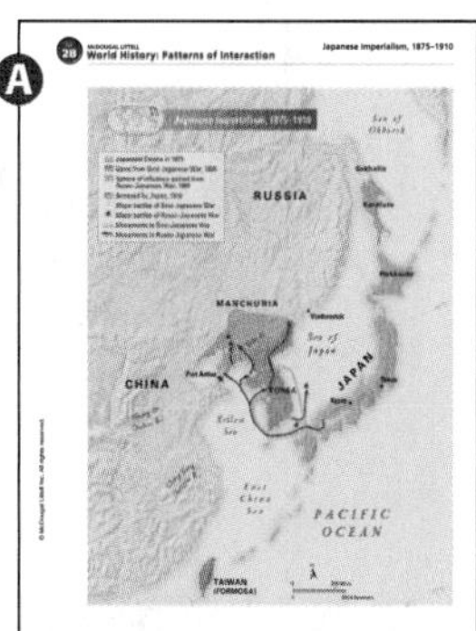

Critical Thinking Transparencies
- CT28 Patterns of Resistance, 1830–1914
- CT64 Chapter 28 Visual Summary

Geography Transparencies
- GT28 Japanese Imperialism, 1875–1910 Ⓐ

World Art and Cultures Transparencies
- AT60 Sorting of Cocoons
- AT61 *Japanese Girl in Western Dress*
- AT62 *Distribution of the Land*

Test Practice Transparencies TT106–TT109

Test Generator CD-ROM

EasyPlanner CD-ROM

Voices from the Past Audio CD

Online Test Practice

Electronic Library of Primary Sources

CHAPTER 12 • OBJECTIVE

Analyze the effects of imperialism, economic instability, and revolution on developing nations.

Previewing Main Ideas

Explain that during the 1800s, some nations sought to add to their empires by expanding into other countries with the use of force. The results of such imperialism were usually negative for poor countries. Fierce nationalism, civil unrest, and revolution were often the result.

Accessing Prior Knowledge

Ask students to recall what they have already learned about the history of China's and Japan's relationship with the outside world. Ask students to discuss what they know about Latin American countries' struggles for independence from colonial rule.

Geography *Answers*

EMPIRE BUILDING Britain, France, Germany, Japan, and Russia were involved in China.

CULTURAL INTERACTION These parts of China bordered areas that were occupied by, or under the control of, each power.

REVOLUTION *Possible Answer:* As an island nation, Japan needed a strong navy to protect itself against foreign nations, such as the United States and Britain, that were great sea powers.

CHAPTER 12

Transformations Around the Globe, 1800–1914

Previewing Main Ideas

EMPIRE BUILDING During the 19th and early 20th centuries, Great Britain, other European nations, the United States, and Japan sought political and economic influence over other countries.

Geography *What foreign powers were involved in China in the late 1800s?*

CULTURAL INTERACTION Imperialism brought new religions, philosophies, and technological innovations to East Asia and Latin America. People in these areas resisted some Western ideas and adopted or adapted others.

Geography *What geographic factors might explain why certain parts of China were under Japanese, Russian, and French influence?*

REVOLUTION Both China and Japan struggled to deal with foreign influence and to modernize. Mexico underwent a revolution that brought political and economic reforms.

Geography *Japan built up its navy as a step toward modernization. Why do you think Japan wanted a strong navy?*

INTEGRATED TECHNOLOGY

eEdition
- Interactive Maps
- Interactive Visuals
- Interactive Primary Sources

INTERNET RESOURCES
Go to **classzone.com** for:
- Research Links
- Internet Activities
- Primary Sources
- Chapter Quiz
- Maps
- Test Practice
- Current Events

EAST ASIA AND LATIN AMERICA

1823 Monroe Doctrine reflects special U.S. interest in Americas.

1839 China and Britain clash in Opium War.

1853 ◀ Commodore Perry enters Tokyo harbor.

1800 — 1825 — 1850

WORLD

1815 Congress of Vienna creates a new balance of power in Europe.

1858 Great Britain establishes direct control of India.

368

TIME LINE DISCUSSION

1. What two important canals, both having global impact, were constructed and opened between 1800 and 1925? *(Suez and Panama canals)*
2. Identify events showing the role the United States played in the Western Hemisphere. *(Possible Answers: 1823–Monroe Doctrine; 1898–Spanish-American War; 1914–Panama Canal)*
3. When did the United States first make official contact with Japan? *(1853–Commodore Perry enters Tokyo harbor.)*
4. Shortly after the United States made its desire for trade known in Tokyo harbor, Great Britain exerted power over what country? *(India)*
5. According to the map, which country had the greatest span of colonial possessions and spheres of influence combined? *(Britain)* Which country had the smallest span? *(Germany)*

Colonial Powers Carve Up China, 1850–1910

INTERACTIVE

RUSSIA
to Russia 1858
to Russia 1864
MONGOLIA autonomous 1912
MANCHURIA 1900–05 Russian, After 1905 Japanese
Sea of Okhotsk
Sakhalin
Vladivostok
Huang He
Beijing
KOREA to Japan 1910
Seoul
Pusan
Sea of Japan
JAPAN
Tokyo
Yokohama
Yellow Sea
CHINA
TIBET autonomous 1912
Nanjing
Shanghai
Chang Jiang
East China Sea
NEPAL
BHUTAN
Pescadores Islands
PACIFIC OCEAN
INDIA
Hong Kong (Br.)
Guangzhou
TAIWAN to Japan 1895
BURMA
Hainan
Bay of Bengal
SIAM
FRENCH INDOCHINA
Philippine Sea
PHILIPPINES to U.S. 1898
South China Sea
BRUNEI
INDIAN OCEAN
MALAYA
SARAWAK
SINGAPORE
BRITISH NORTH BORNEO

	Colonial possessions	Spheres of influence
British	■	■
French	■	■
German		■
Japanese	■	■
Russian	■	■

Qing Empire, 1850

0 300 600 Miles
0 300 600 Kilometers
Polyconic Projection

1869 Suez Canal opens.

1875

1898 ◀ United States wins Spanish-American War. (Teddy Roosevelt)

1900

1901 ◀ Australia becomes an independent nation. (British flag showing countries of the Empire)

1905 Russian soldiers open fire on protesting workers in St. Petersburg.

1910 Mexican Revolution begins.

1914 Panama Canal opens. ▶

1925

369

CHAPTER 12

History from Visuals

Interpreting the Map

Ask students to locate China, Mongolia, Manchuria, Korea, and Japan on the map. Point out that this region—sometimes called the Far East—had maintained very little contact with the West before the 1800s. Ask students why this might have been so. *(Possible Answers: distance; difficult travel; differences in language and culture)*

Explain that in contrast, Mexico and Latin America had close ties to Europe, despite their great distance from it. Encourage students to discuss similarities and differences between the Far East and Latin America. *(Possible Answer: Europeans colonized Latin American countries earlier.)*

Extension Ask students to use this map and the physical map of Asia in the textbook atlas to identify the main geographic features of China and Japan. Encourage them to consider resources, such as good ports, navigable rivers, and oceans.

INTEGRATED TECHNOLOGY

Interactive This feature is available in an interactive format on the eEdition. Students can examine foreign influences in East Asia country by country or all at once.

RECOMMENDED RESOURCES

Books for the Teacher

Burns, E. Bradford. ***Latin America: A Concise Interpretive History.*** Englewood Cliffs, NJ: Prentice, 1994.

Spence, Jonathan D. ***The Search for Modern China.*** New York: Norton, 1990.

Books for the Student

McDougal Littell Literature Connections. Azuela, Mariano. ***The Underdogs.*** 1997. Subtitled "A Novel of the Mexican Revolution," this is the story of Demetrio Macías, who witnesses the chaos and corruption of the revolutionary struggle.

Katz, Friedrich. ***The Life and Times of Poncho Villa.*** Stanford, CA: Stanford UP, 1998. Presents a detailed picture of Francisco Villa while separating fact from legend.

Videos and Software

The Battle of Tsushima–1905 A.D. VHS. Ambrose Video, 1995. 800-526-4663. Describes the Japanese victory over Russia and how it changed the balance of power in Asia.

History and Culture of Mexico. CD-ROM. Queue, 1997. 800-232-2224.

Interact *with* History

Objectives

- Set the stage for studying China's dealings with the West.
- Help students understand the issues that emerging nations face.
- Clarify reasons that nations become imperialistic.

EXAMINING *the* ISSUES

Answers

- *Possible Answers:* Positive—Previously unavailable items can now be bought; Chinese can learn about other cultures. Negative—Chinese may buy inexpensive foreign products, even if they are inferior.
- Invite pairs of students to role-play a situation in which one has an item the other wants. Have them negotiate a trade that is mutually satisfactory.

Discussion

Students might mention first encounters between European explorers such as Christopher Columbus and various Native American peoples. They might also mention the travels of Marco Polo or Zheng He.

Interact *with* History

Why might you seek out or resist foreign influence?

You are a local government official in 19th-century China. You are proud of your country, which produces everything that its people need. Like other Chinese officials, you discourage contact with foreigners. Nevertheless, people from the West are eager to trade with China.

Most foreign products are inferior to Chinese goods. However, a few foreign products are not available in China. You are curious about these items. At the same time, you wonder why foreigners are so eager to trade with China and what they hope to gain.

▲ Finely made lanterns were among the Chinese goods favored by Western merchants.

EXAMINING *the* ISSUES

- **How might foreign products affect the quality of life in China both positively and negatively?**
- **What demands might foreigners make on countries they trade with?**

As a class, discuss these questions. Recall what happened in other parts of the world when different cultures came into contact for the first time. As you read this chapter, compare the decisions various governments made about foreign trade and the reasons they made those decisions.

WHY STUDY TRANSFORMATIONS AROUND THE GLOBE?

- China remains an important member of the global community, with a huge population and growing political and economic power.
- Eastern beliefs, philosophies, and medicinal practices have gained interest and popularity in Western cultures.
- Japan studied Western business ideas and incorporated them with their own to become a globally competitive nation.
- Since World War II, Japan and the United States have overcome many past animosities. Mutual cultural awareness, beneficial trade relations, and time have worked toward mending the relationship between these nations.
- Mexico and the United States interact with each other constantly, sharing resources and trading goods and services.

Woodblock print of landscape by Katsushika Hokusai

Coffee (1935), Candido Portinari

China Resists Outside Influence

MAIN IDEA	WHY IT MATTERS NOW	TERMS & NAMES
CULTURAL INTERACTION Western economic pressure forced China to open to foreign trade and influence.	China has become an increasingly important member of the global community.	• Opium War • extraterritorial rights • Taiping Rebellion • sphere of influence • Open Door Policy • Boxer Rebellion

SETTING THE STAGE Out of pride in their ancient culture, the Chinese looked down on all foreigners. In 1793, however, the Qing emperor agreed to receive an ambassador from England. The Englishman brought gifts of the West's most advanced technology—clocks, globes, musical instruments, and even a hot-air balloon. The emperor was not impressed. In a letter to England's King George III, he stated that the Chinese already had everything they needed. They were not interested in the "strange objects" and gadgets that the West was offering them.

CALIFORNIA STANDARDS

10.4.4 Describe the independence struggles of the colonized regions of the world, including the roles of leaders, such as Sun Yat-sen in China, and the roles of ideology and religion.

CST 1 Students compare the present with the past, evaluating the consequences of past events and decisions and determining the lessons that were learned.

CST 4 Students relate current events to the physical and human characteristics of places and regions.

China and the West

China was able to reject these offers from the West because it was largely self-sufficient. The basis of this self-sufficiency was China's healthy agricultural economy. During the 11th century, China had acquired a quick-growing strain of rice from Southeast Asia. By the time of the Qing Dynasty, the rice was being grown throughout the southern part of the country. Around the same time, the 17th and 18th centuries, Spanish and Portuguese traders brought maize, sweet potatoes, and peanuts from the Americas. These crops helped China increase the productivity of its land and more effectively feed its huge population.

China also had extensive mining and manufacturing industries. Rich salt, tin, silver, and iron mines produced great quantities of ore. The mines provided work for tens of thousands of people. The Chinese also produced beautiful silks, high-quality cottons, and fine porcelain.

The Tea-Opium Connection Because of their self-sufficiency, the Chinese had little interest in trading with the West. For decades, the only place they would allow foreigners to do business was at the southern port of Guangzhou (gwahng•joh). And the balance of trade at Guangzhou was clearly in China's favor. This means that China earned much more for its exports than it spent on imports.

European merchants were determined to find a product the Chinese would buy in large quantities. Eventually they found one—opium. Opium is a habit-forming narcotic made from the poppy plant. Chinese doctors had been using it to relieve pain for hundreds of years. In the late 18th century, however, British merchants smuggled opium into China for nonmedical use. It took a few decades for opium smoking to catch on, but by 1835, as many as 12 million Chinese people were addicted to the drug.

TAKING NOTES

Identifying Problems Use a chart to identify the internal and external problems faced by China in the 1800s and early 1900s.

China's Problems	
Internal	External

LESSON PLAN

OBJECTIVES

- Explain China's resistance to foreigners.
- Describe rebellions that shook China.
- Summarize effects of China's reforms.
- Trace the growth of nationalism there.

1 FOCUS & MOTIVATE

Explain that this section describes the importance of foreign trade. Ask students to think of items associated with the United States that are the result of trade or influence from elsewhere. *(Possible Answers: pizza–Italy, Statue of Liberty–France)*

2 INSTRUCT

China and the West
10.4.4

Critical Thinking

- How did resistance to technology hurt China? *(China's outdated boats lost to British gunboats.)*
- How did the extraterritorial treaty help foreigners? *(not subject to law in certain ports)*

CALIFORNIA RESOURCES

California Reading Toolkit, p. L54
California Modified Lesson Plans for English Learners, p. 103
California Daily Standards Practice Transparencies, TT46
California Standards Enrichment Workbook, pp. 53–54
California Standards Planner and Lesson Plans, p. L99
California Online Test Practice
California Test Generator CD-ROM
California Easy Planner CD-ROM
California eEdition CD-ROM

SECTION 1 PROGRAM RESOURCES

ALL STUDENTS

In-Depth Resources: Unit 3
- Guided Reading, p. 71
- History Makers: Cixi, p. 86
- Geography Application: The Opium Wars, p. 77

Formal Assessment
- Section Quiz, p. 207

ENGLISH LEARNERS

In-Depth Resources in Spanish
- Guided Reading, p. 96
- Geography Application: The Opium Wars, p. 101

Reading Study Guide (Spanish), p. 127
Reading Study Guide Audio CD (Spanish)

STRUGGLING READERS

In-Depth Resources: Unit 3
- Guided Reading, p. 71
- Building Vocabulary, p. 75
- Geography Application: The Opium Wars, p. 77
- Reteaching Activity, p. 90

Reading Study Guide, p. 127
Reading Study Guide Audio CD

GIFTED AND TALENTED STUDENTS

In-Depth Resources: Unit 3
- Primary Source: from Letter to Queen Victoria, p. 79

Electronic Library of Primary Sources
- from *Two Years in the Forbidden City*

INTEGRATED TECHNOLOGY

eEdition CD-ROM
Voices from the Past Audio CD
Power Presentations CD-ROM
World Art and Cultures Transparencies
- AT60 Sorting of Cocoons

Electronic Library of Primary Sources
- from *Two Years in the Forbidden City*

classzone.com

More About . . .

China's Opium Addiction

In the 19th century, opium addiction spread rapidly among Chinese government employees and soldiers. Historians blame the drug for a decline in China's standard of living and for the deterioration of public services, which eventually led to massive peasant uprisings during the mid-1800s.

In-Depth Resources: Unit 3

- Primary Source: from Letter to Queen Victoria, p. 79

Growing Internal Problems

10.4.4

Critical Thinking

- What caused the increase in opium addiction in the mid-19th century? *(serious economic and social problems; opium was readily available)*
- How did Hong's withdrawal from everyday life contribute to the fall of the Taiping government? *(Leaders fought with one another, weakening the kingdom.)*
- What is ironic about the name Taiping, meaning "great peace"? *(The movement led to destruction and millions dead.)*

Connect *to* Today

Special Economic Zones

After the British defeated China in the Opium War of 1842, Shanghai became a major port of trade. Since then it has grown into one of the most crowded urban centers in the world.

War Breaks Out This growing supply of opium caused great problems for China. The Qing emperor was angry about the situation. In 1839, one of his highest advisers wrote a letter to England's Queen Victoria about the problem:

> **PRIMARY SOURCE**
> By what right do they [British merchants] . . . use the poisonous drug to injure the Chinese people? . . . I have heard that the smoking of opium is very strictly forbidden by your country; that is because the harm caused by opium is clearly understood. Since it is not permitted to do harm to your own country, then even less should you let it be passed on to the harm of other countries.
>
> **LIN ZEXU,** quoted in *China's Response to the West*

The pleas went unanswered, and Britain refused to stop trading opium. The result was an open clash between the British and the Chinese—the **Opium War** of 1839. The battles took place mostly at sea. China's outdated ships were no match for Britain's steam-powered gunboats. As a result, the Chinese suffered a humiliating defeat. In 1842, they signed a peace treaty, the Treaty of Nanjing. Ⓐ

This treaty gave Britain the island of Hong Kong. After signing another treaty in 1844, U.S. and other foreign citizens also gained **extraterritorial rights**. Under these rights, foreigners were not subject to Chinese law at Guangzhou and four other Chinese ports. Many Chinese greatly resented the foreigners and the bustling trade in opium they conducted.

MAIN IDEA

Analyzing Issues

Ⓐ What conflicting British and Chinese positions led to the Opium War?

A. Answer the British desire to trade with China and shift the balance of trade in its own favor; the Chinese resentment of the harm opium caused its citizens

Growing Internal Problems

Foreigners were not the greatest of China's problems in the mid-19th century, however. The country's own population provided an overwhelming challenge. The number of Chinese grew to 430 million by 1850, a 30 percent gain in only 60 years. Yet, in the same period of time, food production barely increased. As a result, hunger was widespread, even in good years. Many people became discouraged, and opium addiction rose steadily. As their problems mounted, the Chinese began to rebel against the Qing Dynasty.

Connect *to* Today

Special Economic Zones

Today, as in the late 1800s, the Chinese government limits foreign economic activity to particular areas of the country. Most of these areas, called special economic zones (SEZs), are located on the coast and waterways of southeastern China. Established in the late 1970s, the SEZs are designed to attract, but also control, foreign investment.

One of the most successful SEZs is Shanghai (pictured at right). By the late 1990s, dozens of foreign companies—including IBM of the United States, Hitachi of Japan, Siemens of Germany, and Unilever of Great Britain—had invested about $21 billion in the building and operating of factories, stores, and other businesses. This investment had a huge impact on the economy of Shanghai. Throughout the 1990s, it grew by more than 10 percent each year.

DIFFERENTIATING INSTRUCTION: ENGLISH LEARNERS

Geography of the Opium Wars

Class Time 40 minutes

Task Using a map, a graph, and text to answer comprehension questions

Purpose To practice reading maps and graphs; to improve understanding of important concepts in the chapter

Instructions When students have finished reading the "China and the West" section of the text, distribute the Geography Activity for this chapter (available in English and Spanish). Write difficult terms from the activity on the board along with their meanings. *(Possible Answers: "flooding the market" = making large amounts of a product available for sale, which lowers the price; "vested interest" = a personal reason for supporting something)* Have pairs of students work on reading the text, the map, and the chart and then answering the questions.

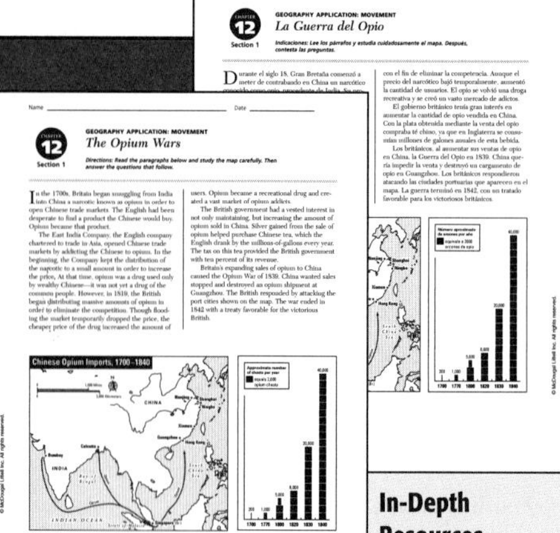
GEOGRAPHY APPLICATION: MOVEMENT
La Guerra del Opio

GEOGRAPHY APPLICATION: MOVEMENT
The Opium Wars

Chinese Opium Imports, 1700–1840

Transformations Around the Globe 77

In-Depth Resources in Spanish

In-Depth Resources: Unit 3

The Taiping Rebellion During the late 1830s, Hong Xiuquan (hung shee•oo•choo•ahn), a young man from Guangdong province in southern China, began recruiting followers to help him build a "Heavenly Kingdom of Great Peace." In this kingdom, all Chinese people would share China's vast wealth and no one would live in poverty. Hong's movement was called the **Taiping Rebellion**, from the Chinese word *taiping,* meaning "great peace."

By the 1850s, Hong had organized a massive peasant army of some one million people. Over time, the Taiping army took control of large areas of southeastern China. Then, in 1853, Hong captured the city of Nanjing and declared it his capital. Hong soon withdrew from everyday life and left family members and his trusted lieutenants in charge of the government of his kingdom.

B. Answer little change in the status of the people and massive death and destruction

MAIN IDEA

Recognizing Effects

B What were the results of the Taiping Rebellion?

The leaders of the Taiping government, however, constantly feuded among themselves. Also, Qing imperial troops and British and French forces all launched attacks against the Taiping. By 1864, this combination of internal fighting and outside assaults had brought down the Taiping government. But China paid a terrible price. At least 20 million—and possibly twice that many—people died in the rebellion. B

▲ A Taiping force surrounds and destroys an enemy village.

Foreign Influence Grows

The Taiping Rebellion and several other smaller uprisings put tremendous internal pressure on the Chinese government. And, despite the Treaty of Nanjing, external pressure from foreign powers was increasing. At the Qing court, stormy debates raged about how best to deal with these issues. Some government leaders called for reforms patterned on Western ways. Others, however, clung to traditional ways and accepted change very reluctantly.

Vocabulary
A *dowager* is a widow who holds a title or property from her deceased husband.

Resistance to Change During the last half of the 19th century, one person was in command at the Qing imperial palace. The Dowager Empress Cixi (tsoo•shee) held the reins of power in China from 1862 until 1908 with only one brief gap. Although she was committed to traditional values, the Dowager Empress did support certain reforms. In the 1860s, for example, she backed the self-strengthening movement. This program aimed to update China's educational system, diplomatic service, and military. Under this program, China set up factories to manufacture steam-powered gunboats, rifles, and ammunition. The self-strengthening movement had mixed results, however.

Other Nations Step In Other countries were well aware of China's continuing problems. Throughout the late 19th century, many foreign nations took advantage of the situation and attacked China. Treaty negotiations after each conflict gave these nations increasing control over China's economy. Many of Europe's major powers and Japan gained a strong foothold in China. This foothold, or **sphere of influence**, was an area in which the foreign nation controlled trade and investment. (See the map on page 374.)

The United States was a long-time trading partner with China. Americans worried that other nations would soon divide China into formal colonies and shut out American traders. To prevent this occurrence, in 1899 the United States declared

More About . . .

Hong Xiuquan

Hong Xiuquan had a dream in his early twenties that he believed ordered him to fight evil. From then on, he worked to overthrow the Qing dynasty. Hong had his own vision of Christianity, which forbade drugs, alcohol, and gambling. Under Hong, men and women were treated as equals. Women were allowed to fight for Hong's causes; however, the sexes were kept separate, even husbands and wives.

Foreign Influence Grows
10.4.4

Critical Thinking

- What is one indication that the self-strengthening movement was not entirely successful? *(China's military was still not strong enough to defeat its attackers.)*
- How did "sphere of influence" differ from the Open Door Policy? *(Sphere of influence–A specific country controlled trade in a certain area. Open Door Policy–All countries had equal trade opportunities.)*

Tip for English Learners

Explain that the word *sphere,* as part of the phrase "sphere of influence," means "area." A sphere is also a shape, such as a ball, a globe, or a planet.

DIFFERENTIATING INSTRUCTION: GIFTED AND TALENTED STUDENTS

Origins of the Taiping Rebellion

Class Time 45 minutes

Task Researching ideology behind the Taiping Rebellion

Purpose To share information with the class by creating an inventive presentation

Instructions Tell students that the ideas that fueled the Taiping Rebellion were a mix of ancient ideals and modern practical methods. For example, the rebels worked the land and shared resources collectively. Men and women also were treated as equals at home and in the workplace.

Encourage students to do additional research on the ideology behind this massive uprising, using encyclopedias and books such as Jean Chesneaux's *China from the Opium Wars to the 1911 Revolution.*

Have students present their information in a creative format, such as a mural, a Web site, or a skit. Students may choose to use a map in their presentations to orient the class to the areas in which the rebellion took place.

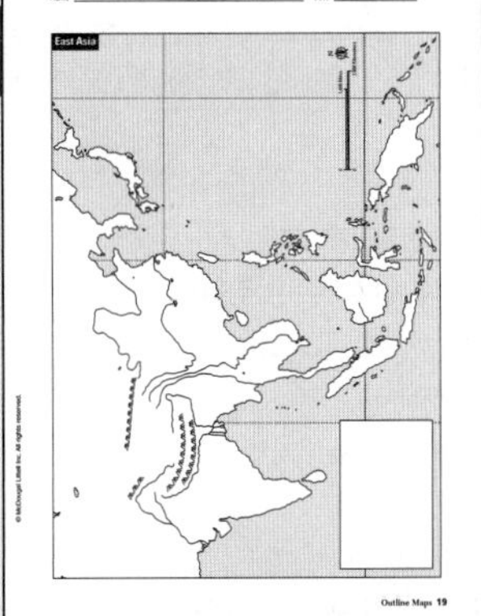

Geography Skills and Outline Maps

History from Visuals

Interpreting the Map

Ask students which nations had both colonies and spheres of influence in China. *(Great Britain, France, Japan)*

Extension The United States did not have a colony or a sphere of influence in China during this period. Have students research the history of U.S. dealings with China.

SKILLBUILDER Answers

1. **Human-Environment Interaction** Britain, France, Germany, Japan, Russia
2. **Location** Britain; the Chang Jiang

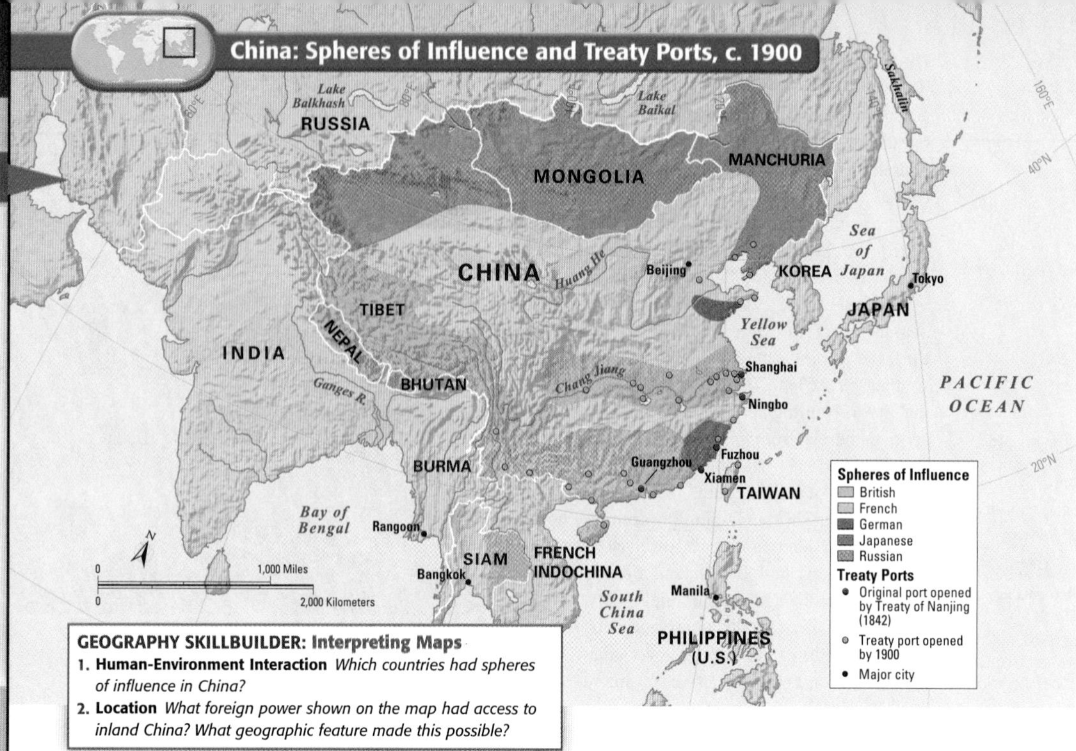

GEOGRAPHY SKILLBUILDER: Interpreting Maps

1. **Human-Environment Interaction** *Which countries had spheres of influence in China?*
2. **Location** *What foreign power shown on the map had access to inland China? What geographic feature made this possible?*

An Upsurge in Chinese Nationalism

10.4.4

Critical Thinking

- What act by the Dowager Empress helped cause the Boxer Rebellion? *(arresting Guangxu)*
- Why did Guangxu's arrest make the Chinese people unhappy? *(He was trying to make changes that would help them economically.)*

In-Depth Resources: Unit 3

- History Makers: Cixi, p. 86

Electronic Library of Primary Sources

- from *Two Years in the Forbidden City*

the **Open Door Policy**. This proposed that China's "doors" be open to merchants of all nations. Britain and the other European nations agreed. The policy thus protected both U.S. trading rights in China, and China's freedom from colonization. But the country was still at the mercy of foreign powers.

An Upsurge in Chinese Nationalism

Humiliated by their loss of power, many Chinese pressed for strong reforms. Among those demanding change was China's young emperor, Guangxu (gwahng•shoo). In June 1898, Guangxu introduced measures to modernize China. These measures called for reorganizing China's educational system, strengthening the economy, modernizing the military, and streamlining the government.

Most Qing officials saw these innovations as threats to their power. They reacted with alarm, calling the Dowager Empress back to the imperial court. On her return, she acted with great speed. She placed Guangxu under arrest and took control of the government. She then reversed his reforms. Guangxu's efforts brought about no change whatsoever. The Chinese people's frustration with their situation continued to grow.

The Boxer Rebellion This widespread frustration finally erupted into violence. Poor peasants and workers resented the special privileges granted to foreigners. They also resented Chinese Christians, who had adopted a foreign faith. To demonstrate their discontent, they formed a secret organization called the Society of Righteous and Harmonious Fists. They soon came to be known as the Boxers. Their campaign against the Dowager Empress's rule and foreigner privilege was called the **Boxer Rebellion**.

DIFFERENTIATING INSTRUCTION: STRUGGLING READERS

Recognizing Causes and Effects

Class Time 25 minutes

Task Creating a chart of causes and effects

Purpose To understand complex events in the struggle between China and Western powers

Instructions Explain that an event can have more than one effect. Divide students into small groups. Have them draw a chart like the one shown here and then work together to fill in the causes. Review students' charts as a class and discuss the different effects students listed.

Students who need more help may complete the Reading Study Guide for this lesson.

CAUSE	EFFECT	EFFECT
1. British bring opium to China.	Many Chinese become addicted.	Opium War
2. Hong Xiuquan starts Taiping Rebellion.	Rebels control south.	Millions die.
3. United States declares Open Door Policy.	China is safe from colonization.	China is still dominated by foreign powers.
4. Workers launch the Boxer Rebellion.	Chinese nationalism increases.	Major reforms are enacted.

Reading Study Guide

In the spring of 1900, the Boxers descended on Beijing. Shouting "Death to the foreign devils," the Boxers surrounded the European section of the city. They kept it under siege for several months. The Dowager Empress expressed support for the Boxers but did not back her words with military aid. In August, a multinational force of 19,000 troops marched on Beijing and quickly defeated the Boxers. C

MAIN IDEA
Analyzing Causes
C Why did the Boxer Rebellion fail?

C. Answer Dowager Empress Cixi expressed support but did not back up her words with actions. A multinational force overpowered the rebels.

Despite the failure of the Boxer Rebellion, a strong sense of nationalism had emerged in China. The Chinese people realized that their country must resist more foreign intervention. Even more important, they felt that the government must become responsive to their needs.

▲ A gang of Boxers attacks Chinese Christians.

The Beginnings of Reform At this point, even the Qing court realized that China needed to make profound changes to survive. In 1905, the Dowager Empress sent a select group of Chinese officials on a world tour to study the operation of different governments. The group traveled to Japan, the United States, Britain, France, Germany, Russia, and Italy. On their return in the spring of 1906, the officials recommended that China restructure its government. They based their suggestions on the constitutional monarchy of Japan. The empress accepted this recommendation and began making reforms. Although she convened a national assembly within a year, change was slow. In 1908, the court announced that it would establish a full constitutional government by 1917.

However, the turmoil in China did not end with these progressive steps. China experienced unrest for the next four decades as it continued to face internal and external threats. China's neighbor Japan also faced pressure from the West during this time. But it responded to this influence in a much different way.

More About . . .

Reform in China

In the early 1900s, women in China began questioning their traditional roles as wives and mothers. Exposed to Western fashions and Western ideas, many unwrapped the binding that crippled their feet and kept them close to home. Some pursued an education either in China or in Japan. These "nontraditional" women pledged loyalty to each other and gained support from men who promised to start a new social trend and marry women with the still-unfashionable "large" feet. Some women even joined the Revolutionary Alliance and worked along with men toward political reform in China.

SECTION 1 ASSESSMENT

TERMS & NAMES 1. For each term or name, write a sentence explaining its significance.
• Opium War • extraterritorial rights • Taiping Rebellion • sphere of influence • Open Door Policy • Boxer Rebellion

USING YOUR NOTES

2. Which created the most trouble for China, internal problems or external problems? Why? (10.4.4)

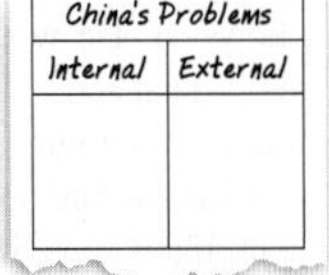

MAIN IDEAS

3. Why did the Chinese have little interest in trading with the West? (10.4.4)
4. What internal problems did China face prior to the Taiping Rebellion? (10.4.4)
5. Why did Emperor Guangxu's efforts at reform and modernization fail? (10.4.4)

CRITICAL THINKING & WRITING

6. **ANALYZING MOTIVES** Why do you think European powers established spheres of influence in China rather than colonies, as they did in Africa and other parts of Asia? (10.4.4)
7. **MAKING INFERENCES** What importance did spheres of influence have for China? (10.4.4)
8. **COMPARING AND CONTRASTING** What were the similarities and differences between the Taiping Rebellion and the Boxer Rebellion? (CST 1)
9. **WRITING ACTIVITY** CULTURAL INTERACTION Write a **dialogue** between two of Dowager Empress Cixi's advisers—one arguing for continued isolation, the other for openness to foreign influence and trade. (Writing 2.1.c)

INTEGRATED TECHNOLOGY **INTERNET ACTIVITY**

Use the Internet to find information on special economic zones in China. Use your findings to create an **annotated map** showing the location of these zones. (10.4.4)

INTERNET KEYWORDS
special economic zones, SEZs

3 ASSESS

SECTION 1 ASSESSMENT

Have students work individually to complete items 1 and 2 and work in small groups to complete the remaining items.

Formal Assessment
• Section Quiz, p. 207

4 RETEACH

Use the Guided Reading activity for Section 1 to review the main ideas for this section.

In-Depth Resources: Unit 3
• Guided Reading, p. 71
• Reteaching Activity, p. 90

ANSWERS

1. Opium War, p. 372 • extraterritorial rights, p. 372 • Taiping Rebellion, p. 373 • sphere of influence, p. 373 • Open Door Policy, p. 374 • Boxer Rebellion, p. 374

2. **Sample Answer:** Internal—Growing population, corrupt officials opposed to reform, inability to handle external problems. External—Influence of foreign powers, extraterritorial rights for foreigners, growing opium trade. Most troublesome—Internal, because resistance to reform led to more problems.
3. The Chinese were economically self-sufficient.
4. growing population, poor harvests, corruption, growing opium addiction
5. Qing officials felt threatened; Dowager Empress committed to tradition
6. **Possible Answer:** China's size and its centralized government made conquest difficult.
7. China had less control over trade and investment.
8. Taiping—Threatened Qing Dynasty. Boxer—Anger toward foreigners. Both failed, yet moved China toward reform.
9. **Rubric** Dialogues should
• include arguments for and against openness to outside influence.
• illustrate the turmoil the debate created.

INTEGRATED TECHNOLOGY

Rubric Annotated maps should
• identify locations of special economic zones in China.
• include interesting facts on these special economic zones.
• cite sources.

LESSON PLAN

OBJECTIVES

- Explain why Japan ended its isolation.
- Trace the growth of Japanese imperialism.

1 FOCUS & MOTIVATE

Discuss advantages and disadvantages of living in a modern society. *(Possible Answers: Technology makes life easier; rapid change can cause people to lose jobs.)*

2 INSTRUCT

Japan Ends Its Isolation
10.4.2

Critical Thinking

- What was one negative result of Japan isolating itself from the rest of the world? *(failure to modernize)*
- Why did Japan institute the Treaty of Kanagawa? *(to avoid threat of attack by Perry)*
- What other country that you have studied also looked to Europe and the United States as models for restructuring its society? *(China)*

CALIFORNIA RESOURCES
California Reading Toolkit, p. L55
California Modified Lesson Plans for English Learners, p. 105
California Daily Standards Practice Transparencies, TT47
California Standards Enrichment Workbook, pp. 49–50
California Standards Planner and Lesson Plans, p. L101
California Online Test Practice
California Test Generator CD-ROM
California Easy Planner CD-ROM
California eEdition CD-ROM

Woodblock print of landscape by Katsushika Hokusai

Coffee (1935), Candido Portinari

2

Modernization in Japan

MAIN IDEA	WHY IT MATTERS NOW	TERMS & NAMES
CULTURAL INTERACTION Japan followed the model of Western powers by industrializing and expanding its foreign influence.	Japan's continued development of its own way of life has made it a leading world power.	• Treaty of Kanagawa • Meiji era • Russo-Japanese War • annexation

CALIFORNIA STANDARDS

10.4.2 Discuss the locations of the colonial rule of such nations as England, France, Germany, Italy, Japan, the Netherlands, Russia, Spain, Portugal, and the United States.

CST 2 Students analyze how change happens at different rates at different times; understand that some aspects can change while others remain the same; and understand that change is complicated and affects not only technology and politics but also values and beliefs.

REP 4 Students construct and test hypotheses; collect, evaluate, and employ information from multiple primary and secondary sources; and apply it in oral and written presentations.

HI 1 Students show the connections, causal and otherwise, between particular historical events and larger social, economic, and political trends and developments.

TAKING NOTES
Analyzing Causes List the steps that Japan took toward modernization and the events that contributed to its growth as an imperialistic power.

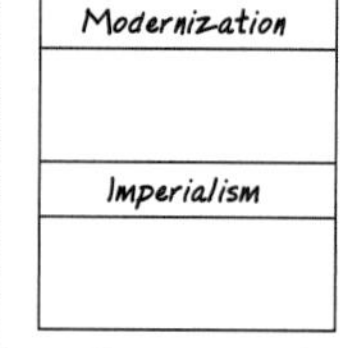

SETTING THE STAGE In the early 17th century, Japan had shut itself off from almost all contact with other nations. Under the rule of the Tokugawa shoguns, Japanese society was very tightly ordered. The shogun parceled out land to the daimyo, or lords. The peasants worked for and lived under the protection of their daimyo and his small army of samurai, or warriors. This rigid feudal system managed to keep the country free of civil war. Peace and relative prosperity reigned in Japan for two centuries.

Japan Ends Its Isolation

The Japanese had almost no contact with the industrialized world during this time of isolation. They continued, however, to trade with China and with Dutch merchants from Indonesia. They also had diplomatic contact with Korea. However, trade was growing in importance, both inside and outside Japan.

The Demand for Foreign Trade Beginning in the early 19th century, Westerners tried to convince the Japanese to open their ports to trade. British, French, Russian, and American officials occasionally anchored off the Japanese coast. Like China, however, Japan repeatedly refused to receive them. Then, in 1853, U.S. Commodore Matthew Perry took four ships into what is now Tokyo Harbor. These massive black wooden ships powered by steam astounded the Japanese. The ships' cannons also shocked them. The Tokugawa shogun realized he had no choice but to receive Perry and the letter Perry had brought from U.S. president Millard Fillmore.

Fillmore's letter politely asked the shogun to allow free trade between the United States and Japan. Perry delivered it with a threat, however. He would come back with a larger fleet in a year to receive Japan's reply. That reply was the **Treaty of Kanagawa** of 1854. Under its terms, Japan opened two ports at which U.S. ships could take on supplies. After the United States had pushed open the door, other Western powers soon followed. By 1860, Japan, like China, had granted foreigners permission to trade at several treaty ports. It had also extended extraterritorial rights to many foreign nations.

Meiji Reform and Modernization The Japanese were angry that the shogun had given in to the foreigners' demands. They turned to Japan's young emperor, Mutsuhito (moot•soo•HEE•toh), who seemed to symbolize the country's sense of

SECTION 2 PROGRAM RESOURCES

ALL STUDENTS
In-Depth Resources: Unit 3
- Guided Reading, p. 72

Formal Assessment
- Section Quiz, p. 208

ENGLISH LEARNERS
In-Depth Resources in Spanish
- Guided Reading, p. 97

Reading Study Guide (Spanish), p. 129
Reading Study Guide Audio CD (Spanish)

STRUGGLING READERS
In-Depth Resources: Unit 3
- Guided Reading, p. 72
- Building Vocabulary, p. 75
- Reteaching Activity, p. 91

Reading Study Guide, p. 129
Reading Study Guide Audio CD

GIFTED AND TALENTED STUDENTS
In-Depth Resources: Unit 3
- Primary Source: from *The Autobiography of Yukichi Fukuzawa,* p. 80

Electronic Library of Primary Sources

INTEGRATED TECHNOLOGY
eEdition CD-ROM
Power Presentations CD-ROM
Geography Transparencies
- GT28 Japanese Imperialism, 1875–1910

World Art and Cultures Transparencies
- AT61 *Japanese Girl in Western Dress*

Electronic Library of Primary Sources
- from *Fifty Years of New Japan*

classzone.com

pride and nationalism. In 1867, the Tokugawa shogun stepped down, ending the military dictatorships that had lasted since the 12th century. Mutsuhito took control of the government. He chose the name *Meiji* for his reign, which means "enlightened rule." Mutsuhito's reign, which lasted 45 years, is known as the **Meiji era**.

The Meiji emperor realized that the best way to counter Western influence was to modernize. He sent diplomats to Europe and North America to study Western ways. The Japanese then chose what they believed to be the best that Western civilization had to offer and adapted it to their own country. They admired Germany's strong centralized government, for example. And they used its constitution as a model for their own. The Japanese also admired the discipline of the German army and the skill of the British navy. They attempted to imitate these European powers as they modernized their military. Japan adopted the American system of universal public education and required that all Japanese children attend school. Their teachers often included foreign experts. Students could go abroad to study as well.

The emperor also energetically supported following the Western path of industrialization. By the early 20th century, the Japanese economy had become as modern as any in the world. The country built its first railroad line in 1872. The track connected Tokyo, the nation's capital, with the port of Yokohama, 20 miles to the south. By 1914, Japan had more than 7,000 miles of railroad. Coal production grew from half a million tons in 1875 to more than 21 million tons in 1913. Meanwhile, large, state-supported companies built thousands of factories. Traditional Japanese industries, such as tea processing and silk production, expanded to give the country unique products to trade. Developing modern industries, such as shipbuilding, made Japan competitive with the West.

Imperial Japan

Japan's race to modernize paid off. By 1890, the country had several dozen warships and 500,000 well-trained, well-armed soldiers. It had become the strongest military power in Asia.

Japan had gained military, political, and economic strength. It then sought to eliminate the extraterritorial rights of foreigners. The Japanese foreign minister assured foreigners that they could rely on fair treatment in Japan. This was because its constitution and legal codes were similar to those of European nations, he explained. His reasoning was convincing, and in 1894, foreign powers accepted the

China and Japan Confront the West

China	Both	Japan
• Remains committed to traditional values • Loses numerous territorial conflicts • Grants other nations spheres of influence within China • Finally accepts necessity for reform	• Have well-established traditional values • Initially resist change • Oppose Western imperialism	• Considers modernization to be necessary • Borrows and adapts Western ways • Strengthens its economic and military power • Becomes an empire builder

▲ The Dowager Empress Cixi (1862–1908)

▲ The Meiji Emperor Mutsuhito (1867–1912)

SKILLBUILDER: Interpreting Charts

1. **Contrasting** *According to the diagram, in what ways did China and Japan deal differently with Western influence?*
2. **Comparing** *What similar responses did each country share despite the different paths they followed?*

Imperial Japan
10.4.2

Critical Thinking

- What were the first steps toward imperialism for Japan? *(modernizing, increasing military power, ending extraterritorial rights)*
- How many wars did Japan engage in to control Korea? *(two—the Sino-Japanese and Russo-Japanese wars)*
- What country did Britain colonize in a manner similar to Japan's takeover of Korea? *(India)*

Geography Transparencies
- GT28 Japanese Imperialism, 1875–1910

Electronic Library of Primary Sources
- from *Fifty Years of New Japan*

History from Visuals

Interpreting the Chart

Ask students to summarize the information in the chart in their own words. *(Possible Answer: China and Japan both emerged from isolation. China took longer to reform and modernize than Japan did.)*

Extension Encourage interested students to find out more about China's military defeats in contrast to Japan's military victories. Suggest that they research the Second Opium War, the Russian takeover of Manchuria, and the Sino-French War.

SKILLBUILDER Answers

1. **Contrasting** China remained isolated from the West longer. Japan quickly adapted Western ways.
2. **Comparing** hatred of Western imperialism, initial resistance to change

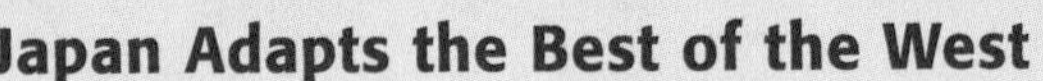

DIFFERENTIATING INSTRUCTION: ENGLISH LEARNERS

Japan Adapts the Best of the West

Class Time 15 minutes

Task Creating a graphic organizer

Purpose To understand what Japan adapted from other countries and what it means to adapt something

Instructions Tell students that, like China, Japan looked to the outside world when its leaders decided to make changes. Japan looked for countries that had the best ways of organizing government, the military, and education.

Have students work in pairs. Ask each pair to make a chart like the one pictured and then reread the text to find the information. Remind students that the word *adapt* means to change something to fit a new situation.

Nation	What Japan Adapted
Germany	government, constitution, army
Great Britain	navy
United States	educational system

More About . . .

Extraterritorial Rights

The Japanese showed how much they had learned about Western thinking when they convinced Western nations to give up their territorial rights in Japan. Realizing that a major reason that these nations fought for extraterritorial rights was that they didn't understand other nations' systems of justice, Japan assured them that its system was similar to their own and that they would receive fair treatment on Japanese soil.

Analyzing Political Cartoons

Warlike Japan

Have the class brainstorm adjectives that describe the animals' temperaments and activities in the cartoon. *(Possible Answer: Both animals are considered strong and fierce, but the bird of prey is dominating the bear.)*

Extension Suggest that interested students draw a cartoon that depicts the relationship between Japan and Korea during this era. Have students present their cartoons to the class and explain why they chose to portray these countries as they did.

SKILLBUILDER Answers

1. **Clarifying** Japan is pictured as a bird of prey and is wielding a bloodstained knife.
2. **Making Inferences** *Possible Answers:* the people of Manchuria; the people of Korea

abolition of extraterritorial rights for their citizens living in Japan. Japan's feeling of strength and equality with the Western nations rose.

As Japan's sense of power grew, the nation also became more imperialistic. As in Europe, national pride played a large part in Japan's imperial plans. The Japanese were determined to show the world that they were a powerful nation. (A)

MAIN IDEA
Making Inferences
(A) Why did Japan become imperialistic?
A. Possible Answer It had grown economically and militarily strong enough, and it wanted to show that it was a powerful nation.

Vocabulary
Sino: a prefix meaning "Chinese"

Japan Attacks China The Japanese first turned their sights to their neighbor, Korea. In 1876, Japan forced Korea to open three ports to Japanese trade. But China also considered Korea to be important both as a trading partner and a military outpost. Recognizing their similar interests in Korea, Japan and China signed a hands-off agreement. In 1885, both countries pledged that they would not send their armies into Korea.

In June 1894, however, China broke that agreement. Rebellions had broken out against Korea's king. He asked China for military help in putting them down. Chinese troops marched into Korea. Japan protested and sent its troops to Korea to fight the Chinese. This Sino-Japanese War lasted just a few months. In that time, Japan drove the Chinese out of Korea, destroyed the Chinese navy, and gained a foothold in Manchuria. In 1895, China and Japan signed a peace treaty. This treaty gave Japan its first colonies, Taiwan and the neighboring Pescadores Islands. (See the map on page 369.)

Russo-Japanese War Japan's victory over China changed the world's balance of power. Russia and Japan emerged as the major powers—and enemies—in East Asia. The two countries soon went to war over Manchuria. In 1903, Japan offered to recognize Russia's rights in Manchuria if the Russians would agree to stay out of Korea. But the Russians refused.

In February 1904, Japan launched a surprise attack on Russian ships anchored off the coast of Manchuria. In the resulting **Russo-Japanese War**, Japan drove

Analyzing Political Cartoons

Warlike Japan

Cartoonists often use symbols to identify the countries, individuals, or even ideas featured in their cartoons. Russia has long been symbolized as a bear by cartoonists. Here, the cartoonist uses a polar bear.

Prior to the Meiji era, cartoonists usually pictured Japan as a fierce samurai. Later, however, Japan often was symbolized by a caricature of Emperor Mutsuhito. Here, the cartoonist has exaggerated the emperor's physical features to make him look like a bird of prey.

SKILLBUILDER: Interpreting Political Cartoons

1. **Clarifying** *How does the cartoonist signify that Japan is warlike?*
2. **Making Inferences** *In their fight, Russia and Japan appear to be crushing someone. Who do you think this might be?*

SKILLBUILDER PRACTICE: ANALYZING POLITICAL CARTOONS

Understanding Political Cartoons

Class Time 30 minutes

Task Creating a chart

Purpose To learn how to analyze political cartoons

Instructions Explain that political cartoons use caricature and exaggeration to make a serious point. A caricature is a drawing that emphasizes a certain feature or characteristic of the subject.

Ask students to draw a chart like the one shown on this page. Have them identify the subject of the cartoon. *(Japan's defeat of Russia)* Next, ask students to identify important symbols and details. *(Japan looks angry and is holding a knife and a Russian soldier; Japan is digging claws into the polar bear, Russia; Russia is holding weapons but looks defeated; Russia is crushing what appears to be a man.)* Then have students interpret its message. *(Japan has defeated Russia; both Russia and Japan have crushed what we can assume is Korea.)* Ask students to collect two or three political cartoons and analyze them, recording their analysis in chart form. Students who need more practice with this skill should complete the Skillbuilder Practice activity for this chapter, which can be found in In-Depth Resources: Unit 3.

Identify subject	
Identify details and symbols	
Interpret message	

Russian troops out of Korea and captured most of Russia's Pacific fleet. It also destroyed Russia's Baltic fleet, which had sailed all the way around Africa to participate in the war.

In 1905, Japan and Russia began peace negotiations. U.S. president Theodore Roosevelt helped draft the treaty, which the two nations signed on a ship off Portsmouth, New Hampshire. This agreement, the Treaty of Portsmouth, gave Japan the captured territories. It also forced Russia to withdraw from Manchuria and to stay out of Korea.

Japanese Occupation of Korea After defeating Russia, Japan attacked Korea with a vengeance. In 1905, it made Korea a protectorate. Japan sent in "advisers," who grabbed more and more power from the Korean government. The Korean king was unable to rally international support for his regime. In 1907, he gave up control of the country. Within two years the Korean Imperial Army was disbanded. In 1910, Japan officially imposed **annexation** on Korea, or brought that country under Japan's control.

Vocabulary
protectorate: a country under the partial control and protection of another nation

The Japanese were harsh rulers. They shut down Korean newspapers and took over Korean schools. There they replaced the study of Korean language and history with Japanese subjects. They took land away from Korean farmers and gave it to Japanese settlers. They encouraged Japanese businessmen to start industries in Korea, but forbade Koreans from going into business. Resentment of Japan's repressive rule grew, helping to create a strong Korean nationalist movement. B

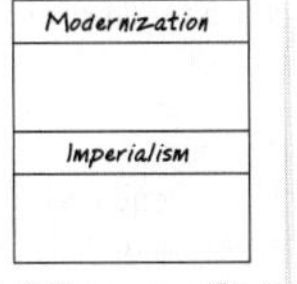

Clarifying
B How did Japan treat the Koreans after it annexed the country?
B. Answer harshly and brutally

The rest of the world clearly saw the brutal results of Japan's imperialism. Nevertheless, the United States and other European countries largely ignored what was happening in Korea. They were too busy with their own imperialistic aims, as you will learn in Section 3.

Global Impact

Western Views of the East

The Japanese victory over the Russians in 1905 exploded a strong Western myth. Many Westerners believed that white people were a superior race. The overwhelming success of European colonialism and imperialism in the Americas, Africa, and Asia had reinforced this belief. But the Japanese had shown Europeans that people of other races were their equals in modern warfare.

Unfortunately, Japan's military victory led to a different form of Western racism. Influenced by the ideas of Germany's Emperor Wilhelm II, the West imagined the Japanese uniting with the Chinese and conquering Europe. The resulting racist Western fear of what was called the *yellow peril* influenced world politics for many decades.

SECTION 2 ASSESSMENT

TERMS & NAMES 1. For each term or name, write a sentence explaining its significance.
- Treaty of Kanagawa
- Meiji era
- Russo-Japanese War
- annexation

USING YOUR NOTES

2. Do you think that Japan could have become an imperialist power if it had not modernized? Why or why not? (HI 1)

Modernization
Imperialism

MAIN IDEAS

3. How was the Treaty of Kanagawa similar to the treaties that China signed with various European powers? (10.4.2)
4. What steps did the Meiji emperor take to modernize Japan? (10.4.2)
5. How did Japan begin its quest to build an empire? (10.4.2)

CRITICAL THINKING & WRITING

6. **ANALYZING CAUSES** What influences were most important in motivating Japan to build its empire? (10.4.2)
7. **FORMING AND SUPPORTING OPINIONS** In your view, was Japan's aggressive imperialism justified? Support your answer with information from the text. (10.4.2)
8. **ANALYZING BIAS** How did Japan's victory in the Russo-Japanese War both explode and create stereotypes? (10.4.2)
9. **WRITING ACTIVITY** EMPIRE BUILDING In the role of a Japanese official, write a **letter** to the government of a Western power explaining why you think it is necessary for your country to build an empire. (Writing 2.5.a)

CONNECT TO TODAY CREATING A SYMBOL

Conduct research to discover the name that Akihito, the present emperor of Japan, chose for his reign. Then create a **symbol** that expresses the meaning of this name.

Global Impact

Western Views of the East

As students continue their study of world history, encourage them to look for examples of ongoing racism against the Japanese and against Japanese Americans, particularly during World War II. Also encourage further investigation of current relations between Japan and Korea. The Internet is a good resource.

Vocabulary Note: Academic Vocabulary

The terms *colony*, *protectorate*, and *annexed territory* have distinct meanings. A colony is controlled by a far-off country. A protectorate's government is partly controlled by another country. Annexed territory has been made part of another country.

3 ASSESS

SECTION 2 ASSESSMENT

Have students work in small groups to complete item 9 and the Connect to Today activity. Let groups share their final products with the class.

Formal Assessment
- Section Quiz, p. 208

4 RETEACH

Use the Reteaching Activity to review the main ideas of the section.

In-Depth Resources: Unit 3
- Reteaching Activity, p. 91

ANSWERS

1. Treaty of Kanagawa, p. 376 • Meiji era, p. 377 • Russo-Japanese War, p. 378 • annexation, p. 379
2. **Sample Answer:** Modernization—Military, government, and education. Imperialism—Defeat of China, Russia, Korean takeover. Modernization gave Japan the military strength to win wars.
3. granted trade permission to foreigners; extended extraterritorial rights
4. studied Western ways and moved toward industrialization
5. by gaining control of Korea
6. further intrusion by European trading nations into Japan and nearby lands; growing sense of power
7. Yes—Japan had to expand to compete against European powers. No—Harsh methods against other countries were not necessary for Japan's advancement.
8. The victory exploded the myth that European whites were superior in warfare. It created the myth of an Asian world takeover.
9. **Rubric** Letters should
   - explain Japan's reasons for wanting to build an empire.
   - express Japan's desire to be taken seriously as a major power.

CONNECT TO TODAY

Rubric Symbols should
- illustrate the meaning of the name.
- be drawn neatly.

History *through* Art

OBJECTIVES

- Understand the origin and process of woodblock printing.
- Appreciate the work of famous Japanese woodblock artists.

FOCUS & MOTIVATE

Woodblock printing requires intense concentration and steadiness of hand. Ask students to compare this art form with others they have studied, including painting and sculpting. Which art form would they, themselves, be most likely to enjoy, and why?

INSTRUCT

Critical Thinking

- What might the artist be revealing about Naniwaya Okita's character by portraying her gazing into a mirror? *(Possible Answers: concerned with beauty and appearance; vain or self-critical)*
- What is one possible theme of Katsushika Hokusai's *Under the Wave off Kanagawa? (Possible Answers: forces of nature; humans vs. nature)*

Tip for Gifted and Talented Students

Woodblock prints by different artists often have similar characteristics. Ask interested students to compare and contrast the work shown here by Utamaro with the fine art transparency *Japanese Girl in Western Dress,* by Yoshitoshi. Have them compare and contrast the expression, attire, and detail of the subjects, along with objects depicted.

World Art and Cultures Transparencies

- AT61 *Japanese Girl in Western Dress*

Japanese Woodblock Printing

CALIFORNIA STANDARDS
10.3.2, CST 4

Woodblock printing in Japan evolved from black-and-white prints created by Buddhists in the 700s. By the late 1700s, artists learned how to create multicolor prints.

Woodblock prints could be produced quickly and in large quantities, so they were cheaper than paintings. In the mid-1800s, a Japanese person could buy a woodblock print for about the same price as a bowl of noodles. As a result, woodblock prints like those shown here became a widespread art form. The most popular subjects included actors, beautiful women, urban life, and landscapes.

INTEGRATED TECHNOLOGY

RESEARCH LINKS For more on Japanese woodblock printing, go to **classzone.com**

▲ **Naniwaya Okita**

The artist Kitagawa Utamaro created many prints of attractive women. This print shows Naniwaya Okita, a famous beauty of the late 1700s. Her long face, elaborate hairstyle, and many-colored robes were all considered part of her beauty.

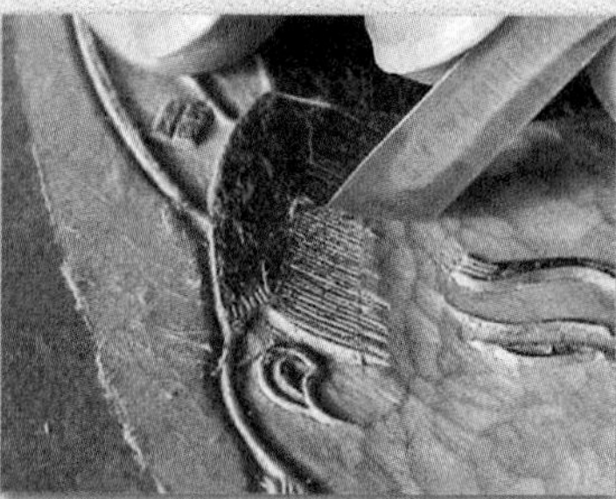

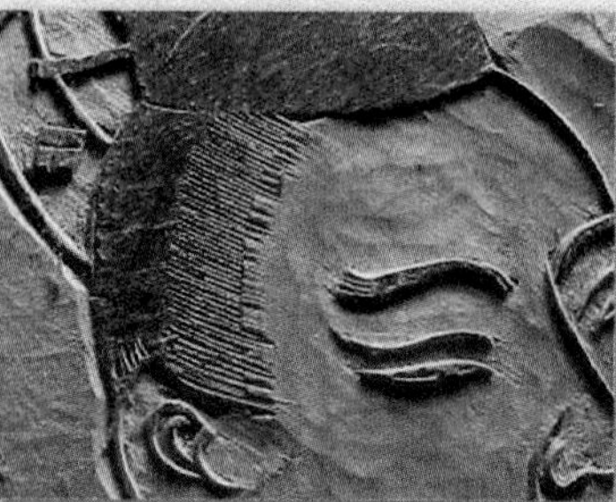

▲ **Carving the Block**

These photographs show a modern artist carving a block for the black ink. (The artist must carve a separate block for each color that will be in the final print.)

Carving the raised image requires precision and patience. For example, David Bull, the artist in the photographs, makes five cuts to create each strand of hair. One slip of the knife, and the block will be ruined.

RECOMMENDED RESOURCES

Books

Forrer, Matthi. ***Hokusai: Prints and Drawings.*** New York: Prestel USA, 2001. Includes 13 drawings and 151 woodblock prints by Hokusai.

Kobayashi, Tadashi. ***Ukiyo-E: An Introduction to Japanese Woodblock Prints***. New York: Kodansha International, 1997. Explores the world of Japanese woodcuts.

Nagata, Seiji. ***Hokusai: Genius of the Japanese Ukiyo-E.*** New York: Kodansha International, 2000.

Video

The Life & Works of Hokusai: The Art of Printmaking. VHS. Library Video Company, 2002. 800-843-3620.

380 Chapter 12

▲ **Under the Wave off Kanagawa**
Katsushika Hokusai was one of the most famous of all Japanese printmakers. This scene is taken from his well-known series *Thirty-Six Views of Mount Fuji.* Mount Fuji, which many Japanese considered sacred, is the small peak in the background of this scene.

▲ **Printing**
After the carved block is inked, the artist presses paper on it, printing a partial image. He or she repeats this stage for each new color. The artist must ensure that every color ends up in exactly the right place, so that no blocks of color extend beyond the outlines or fall short of them.

Connect *to* Today

1. **Making Inferences** What personal qualities and skills would an artist need to be good at making woodblock prints?
   See Skillbuilder Handbook, page R10.
2. **Forming and Supporting Opinions** Hokusai's print of the wave, shown above, remains very popular today. Why do you think this image appeals to modern people?

More About . . .

Kitagawa Utamaro

Utamaro is primarily known for his precise and masterful compositions of beautiful Japanese women. During the height of his success, he created prints of a famous military leader's wife and his concubines. For this act, he was arrested and handcuffed for 50 days, accused of insulting the leader's dignity. Utamaro did not fully recover from the experience emotionally; he did not paint again.

More About . . .

Katsushika Hokusai

Hokusai was a Japanese master artist and printmaker. Early in his career he helped develop the *ukiyo-e* tradition, or "pictures of the floating world." Enjoying his fame, Hokusai was sometimes known to paint in front of crowds, creating portraits of mythical figures up to 2,000 square feet. At the height of his popularity, he was summoned to paint before the ruler of Japan. Hokusai worked from age 18 to age 89, in his later years calling himself "the old man mad with painting."

CONNECT TO TODAY: ANSWERS

1. Making Inferences
Possible Answers: patience, precision, good drawing ability, a steady hand, the ability to organize a step-by-step process

2. Forming and Supporting Opinions
Possible Answers: the artistry, including the colors and the sweeping line of the waves; the print's portrayal of the beauty and danger in nature; the tension created by showing an enormous wave about to swamp a boat; the unusual perspective of an enormous wave and a tiny mountain

LESSON PLAN

OBJECTIVES

- Explain how Latin America's colonial legacy shaped its history.
- Document how foreign powers influenced Latin American economies.
- Trace effects of the Monroe Doctrine and the Roosevelt Corollary.

1 FOCUS & MOTIVATE

Discuss what benefits and problems independence can bring. *(Benefits—Don't have to obey anyone, responsible for own future. Problems—Help and advice may not be available.)*

2 INSTRUCT

Latin America After Independence
10.4.1

Critical Thinking

- What other country have you studied in this chapter in which the ruling class kept the working class from financial gain? *(Korea, during period of Japanese control)*

CALIFORNIA RESOURCES
California Reading Toolkit, p. L56
California Modified Lesson Plans for English Learners, p. 107
California Daily Standards Practice Transparencies, TT48
California Standards Enrichment Workbook, pp. 47–48
California Standards Planner and Lesson Plans, p. L103
California Online Test Practice
California Test Generator CD-ROM
California Easy Planner CD-ROM
California eEdition CD-ROM

3

Woodblock print of landscape by Katsushika Hokusai

Coffee (1935), Candido Portinari

U.S. Economic Imperialism

MAIN IDEA

EMPIRE BUILDING The United States put increasing economic and political pressure on Latin America during the 19th century.

WHY IT MATTERS NOW

This policy set the stage for 20th-century relations between Latin America and the United States.

TERMS & NAMES

- caudillo
- Monroe Doctrine
- José Martí
- Spanish-American War
- Panama Canal
- Roosevelt Corollary

CALIFORNIA STANDARDS

10.4.1 Describe the rise of industrial economies and their link to imperialism and colonialism (e.g., the role played by national security and strategic advantage; moral issues raised by the search for national hegemony, Social Darwinism, and the missionary impulse; material issues such as land, resources, and technology).

CST 3 Students use a variety of maps and documents to interpret human movement, including major patterns of domestic and international migration, changing environmental preferences and settlement patterns, the frictions that develop between population groups, and the diffusion of ideas, technological innovations, and goods.

HI 5 Students analyze human modifications of landscapes and examine the resulting environmental policy issues.

SETTING THE STAGE Latin America's long struggle to gain independence from colonial domination between the late 18th and the mid-19th centuries left the new nations in shambles. Farm fields had been neglected and were overrun with weeds. Buildings in many cities bore the scars of battle. Some cities had been left in ruins. The new nations of Latin America faced a struggle for economic and political recovery that was every bit as difficult as their struggle for independence had been.

Latin America After Independence

Political independence meant little for most citizens of the new Latin American nations. The majority remained poor laborers caught up in a cycle of poverty.

Colonial Legacy Both before and after independence, most Latin Americans worked for large landowners. The employers paid their workers with vouchers that could be used only at their own supply stores. Since wages were low and prices were high, workers went into debt. Their debt accumulated and passed from one generation to the next. In this system known as peonage, "free" workers were little better than slaves.

Landowners, on the other hand, only got wealthier after independence. Many new Latin American governments took over the lands owned by native peoples and by the Catholic Church. Then they put those lands up for sale. Wealthy landowners were the only people who could afford to buy them, and they snapped them up. But as one Argentinean newspaper reported, "Their greed for land does not equal their ability to use it intelligently." The unequal distribution of land and the landowners' inability to use it effectively combined to prevent social and economic development in Latin America.

TAKING NOTES
Following Chronological Order Use a time line to list the major events in U.S. involvement in Latin America.

1823 1898 1903 1914

Political Instability Political instability was another widespread problem in 19th-century Latin America. Many Latin American army leaders had gained fame and power during their long struggle for independence. They often continued to assert their power. They controlled the new nations as military dictators, or **caudillos** (kaw•DEEL•yohz). They were able to hold on to power because they were backed by the military. By the mid-1800s, nearly all the countries of Latin America were ruled by caudillos. One typical caudillo was Juan Vicente Gómez.

SECTION 3 PROGRAM RESOURCES

ALL STUDENTS
In-Depth Resources: Unit 3
- Guided Reading, p. 73

Formal Assessment
- Section Quiz, p. 209

ENGLISH LEARNERS
In-Depth Resources in Spanish
- Guided Reading, p. 98

Reading Study Guide (Spanish), p. 131
Reading Study Guide Audio CD (Spanish)

STRUGGLING READERS
In-Depth Resources: Unit 3
- Guided Reading, p. 73
- Building Vocabulary, p. 75
- Reteaching Activity, p. 92

Reading Study Guide, p. 131
Reading Study Guide Audio CD

GIFTED AND TALENTED STUDENTS
In-Depth Resources: Unit 3
- Primary Source: Building the Panama Canal, p. 81
- Connections Across Time and Cultures: Responses to Western Pressure, p. 88
- Science & Technology: Technology Revolutionizes Communications, p. 89

Electronic Library of Primary Sources
- from *The Rough Riders*

INTEGRATED TECHNOLOGY

eEdition CD-ROM
Power Presentations CD-ROM
Critical Thinking Transparencies
- CT28 Patterns of Resistance, 1830–1914

Electronic Library of Primary Sources
- from *The Rough Riders*

classzone.com

He was a ruthless man who ruled Venezuela for nearly 30 years after seizing power in 1908. "All Venezuela is my cattle ranch," he once boasted.

There were some exceptions, however. Reform-minded presidents, such as Argentina's Domingo Sarmiento, made strong commitments to improving education. During Sarmiento's presidency, between 1868 and 1874, the number of students in Argentina doubled. But such reformers usually did not stay in office long. More often than not, a caudillo, supported by the army, seized control of the government.

A. Answer poverty, lack of voice in government, lack of education

MAIN IDEA

Identifying Problems

A What difficulties did lower-class Latin Americans continue to face after independence?

The caudillos faced little opposition. The wealthy landowners usually supported them because they opposed giving power to the lower classes. In addition, Latin Americans had gained little experience with democracy under European colonial rule. So, the dictatorship of a caudillo did not seem unusual to them. But even when caudillos were not in power, most Latin Americans still lacked a voice in the government. Voting rights—and with them, political power—were restricted to the relatively few members of the upper and middle classes who owned property or could read. A

▲ Argentine reformer Domingo Sarmiento

Economies Grow Under Foreign Influence

When colonial rule ended in Latin America in the early 1800s, the new nations were no longer restricted to trading with colonial powers. Britain and, later, the United States became Latin America's main trading partners.

Old Products and New Markets Latin America's economies continued to depend on exports, no matter whom they were trading with. As during the colonial era, each country concentrated on one or two products. With advances in technology, however, Latin America's exports grew. The development of the steamship and the building of railroads in the 19th century, for example, greatly increased Latin American trade. Toward the end of the century, the invention of refrigeration helped increase Latin America's exports. The sale of beef, fruits and vegetables, and other perishable goods soared.

But foreign nations benefited far more from the increased trade than Latin America did. In exchange for their exports, Latin Americans imported European and North American manufactured goods. As a result, they had little reason to develop their own manufacturing industries. And as long as Latin America remained unindustrialized, it could not play a leading role on the world economic stage.

▼ Workers unload coffee beans at a plantation in Brazil. Until recently, Brazil's economy depended heavily on the export of coffee.

More About . . .

Caudillos

Caudillos ruled Latin America with a combination of bribery, patronage, and force. Although the constitutions of many Latin American nations were patterned after the U.S. Constitution, the documents were seldom upheld. As one of Latin America's greatest liberators, Simón Bolívar, put it, "Treaties are scraps of paper; constitutions, printed matter; elections, battles; freedom, anarchy; and life, a torment."

Economies Grow Under Foreign Influence

10.4.1

Critical Thinking

- How did the combination of railroads, steamships, and refrigeration help trade for Latin America? *(Refrigeration kept food from spoiling. Refrigerated compartments aboard ships and trains carried goods to distant markets.)*
- Why couldn't an unindustrialized country be a major world power? *(Possible Answers: depended too much on manufactured goods from other countries; poor weather could ruin the crops and the economy)*

DIFFERENTIATING INSTRUCTION: ENGLISH LEARNERS

Analyzing Quotations and Academic Vocabulary

Class Time 30 minutes

Task Understanding sophisticated terms and quotations

Purpose To improve comprehension

Instructions Have pairs of students find difficult words, phrases, or quotations in the subsections "Latin America After Independence" and "Economies Grow Under Foreign Influence." Ask each pair to create a chart like the one shown, with students working together to investigate meanings and contexts. Encourage students to use glossaries and dictionaries.

Term or Quotation	Clue	New Understanding
Colonial legacy, p. 382	Legacy means something left or handed down from the past.	The paragraph says "both before and after independence." "Colonial legacy" must mean what was left after colonial times.
"All Venezuela is my cattle ranch." p. 383	Restated: "I own everything, and I'll do what I want with it."	
unindustrialized, p. 383	Industrialized means a country has factories of its own.	

A Latin American Empire
10.4.1

Critical Thinking

- Why did U.S. security depend on Latin America? *(nearness—a hostile power could base operations in Latin America)*
- What caused Cubans to resent U.S. assistance in the Spanish-American War? *(After the war, the U.S. set up a military government in Cuba.)*
- What did the U.S. government do to secure its interest in Latin America? *(It established the Monroe Doctrine, issued the Roosevelt Corollary, and kept troops in Latin America.)*

Electronic Library of Primary Sources

- from *The Rough Riders*

History Makers

José Martí

José Martí was a much-admired poet and essayist as well as a revolutionary. One of Martí's poems was set to music in 1961, and the song "Guantanamera" was made famous by U.S. folksinger Pete Seeger. Play a recording of this song for the class and ask students who speak or have studied Spanish to translate it.

Inclusion Tip

For those students who are hearing impaired, locate the original poem "Guantanamera," and ask a student who is fluent in Spanish to translate it in writing.

Outside Investment and Interference Furthermore, Latin American countries used little of their export income to build roads, schools, or hospitals. Nor did they fund programs that would help them become self-sufficient. Instead, they often borrowed money at high interest rates to develop facilities for their export industries. Countries such as Britain, France, the United States, and Germany were willing lenders. The Latin American countries often were unable to pay back their loans, however. In response, foreign lenders sometimes threatened to collect the debt by force. At other times, they threatened to take over the facilities they had funded. In this way, foreign companies gained control of many Latin American industries. This began a new age of economic colonialism in Latin America.

History Makers

José Martí
1853–1895

José Martí was only 15 in 1868 when he first began speaking out for Cuban independence. In 1871, the Spanish colonial government punished Martí's open opposition with exile. Except for a brief return to his homeland in 1878, Martí remained in exile for about 20 years. For most of this time, he lived in New York City. There he continued his career as a writer and a revolutionary. "Life on earth is a hand-to-hand combat . . . between the law of love and the law of hate," he proclaimed.

While in New York, Martí helped raise an army to fight for Cuban independence. He died on the battlefield only a month after the war began. But Martí's cry for freedom echoes in his essays and poems and in folk songs about him that are still sung throughout the world.

INTEGRATED TECHNOLOGY

RESEARCH LINKS For more on José Martí, go to **classzone.com**

A Latin American Empire

Long before the United States had any economic interest in Latin American countries, it realized that it had strong links with its southern neighbors. Leaders of the United States were well aware that their country's security depended on the security of Latin America.

The Monroe Doctrine Most Latin American colonies had gained their independence by the early 1800s. But their position was not secure. Many Latin Americans feared that European countries would try to reconquer the new republics. The United States, a young nation itself, feared this too. So, in 1823, President James Monroe issued what came to be called the **Monroe Doctrine**. This document stated that "the American continents . . . are henceforth not to be considered as subjects for future colonization by any European powers." Until 1898, though, the United States did little to enforce the Monroe Doctrine. Cuba provided a real testing ground.

Cuba Declares Independence The Caribbean island of Cuba was one of Spain's last colonies in the Americas. In 1868, Cuba declared its independence and fought a ten-year war against Spain. In 1878, with the island in ruins, the Cubans gave up the fight. But some Cubans continued to seek independence from Spain. In 1895, **José Martí**, a writer who had been exiled from Cuba by the Spanish, returned to launch a second war for Cuban independence. Martí was killed early in the fighting, but the Cubans battled on.

By the mid-1890s, the United States had developed substantial business holdings in Cuba. Therefore it had an economic stake in the fate of the country. In addition, the Spanish had forced many Cuban civilians into concentration camps. Americans objected to the Spanish brutality. In 1898, the United States joined the Cuban war for independence. This conflict, which became known as the **Spanish-American War**, lasted about four months. U.S. forces launched their first attack not on Cuba but on the Philippine Islands, a Spanish colony thousands of miles away in the Pacific. Unprepared for a war on two fronts, the Spanish military quickly collapsed. (See the maps on the opposite page.) B

B. Answers to protect its economic interests in Cuba and to protest Spain's brutal treatment of Cuban civilians

MAIN IDEA

Analyzing Motives

B Why did the United States join the Cuban war for independence?

DIFFERENTIATING INSTRUCTION: STRUGGLING READERS

Chronology of Events in Latin America

Class Time 20 minutes

Task Creating a time line

Purpose To understand the chronological order and effects of Latin American historical events

Instructions Display Critical Thinking Transparency CT73. On the board, create a list of events like the one shown here. Ask students to work in small groups to create a chart like CT73 and fill it in using the events discussed under "A Latin American Empire." Students should locate the events in the text and place them in the chart in chronological order, providing the date and a brief explanation for each.

Panama Canal opens.
Monroe Doctrine issued.
Spanish-American War begins.
Roosevelt Corollary issued.
José Martí returns.

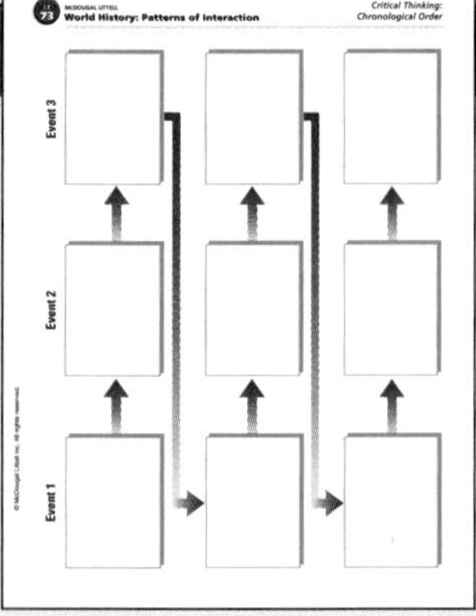

Critical Thinking Transparencies

The Spanish-American War, 1898: the Caribbean

The Spanish-American War, 1898: the Philippines

GEOGRAPHY SKILLBUILDER: Interpreting Maps

1. **Location** *Where is Cuba located in relation to the United States?*
2. **Location** *In the war, the United States launched its first attack against the Philippine Islands. Why might this have surprised the Spanish?*

In 1901, Cuba became an independent nation, at least in name. However, the United States installed a military government and continued to exert control over Cuban affairs. This caused tremendous resentment among many Cubans, who had assumed that the United States' aim in intervening was to help Cuba become truly independent. The split that developed between the United States and Cuba at this time continues to keep these close neighbors miles apart more than a century later.

After its defeat in the Spanish-American War, Spain turned over the last of its colonies. Puerto Rico, Guam, and the Philippines became U.S. territories. Having become the dominant imperial power in Latin America, the United States next set its sights on Panama.

Vocabulary
A *colossus* is a huge statue that towers over the surrounding area.

Connecting the Oceans Latin Americans were beginning to regard the United States as the political and economic "Colossus of the North." The United States was a colossus in geographic terms too. By the 1870s, the transcontinental railroad connected its east and west coasts. But land travel still was time-consuming and difficult. And sea travel between the coasts involved a trip of about 13,000 miles around the tip of South America. If a canal could be dug across a narrow section of Central America, however, the coast-to-coast journey would be cut in half.

The United States had been thinking about such a project since the early 19th century. In the 1880s, a French company tried—but failed—to build a canal across Panama. Despite this failure, Americans remained enthusiastic about the canal. And no one was more enthusiastic than President Theodore Roosevelt, who led the nation from 1901 to 1909. In 1903, Panama was a province of Colombia. Roosevelt offered that country $10 million plus a yearly payment for the right to build a canal. When the Colombian government demanded more money, the United States

History from Visuals

Interpreting the Map

Encourage students to study each map and determine where U.S. forces originated, landed, and attacked. *(Tampa–Santiago; Hong Kong–near Manila)*

Extension Ask interested students to check the textbook atlas and determine the distance between Florida and Hong Kong. Have students speculate on why the United States decided to launch two attacks against the Spanish in two separate regions of the world. *(difficult for Spanish to fight in two distant places)*

SKILLBUILDER Answers

1. **Location** Cuba is an island south of the United States.
2. **Location** The Spanish likely expected the first attack to be in Cuba.

More About . . .

Europe and Latin America

European powers interfered many times in Latin American affairs during the 19th century before the United States enforced the Monroe Doctrine: Britain–the Argentinean Falkland Islands (1833); France–Mexico and Uruguay (several times between the 1830s and the 1860s); and Spain–the Chincha Islands (1862–1866).

In-Depth Resources: Unit 3

- Connections Across Time and Cultures: Responses to Western Pressure, p. 88

DIFFERENTIATING INSTRUCTION: GIFTED AND TALENTED STUDENTS

Analyzing Problems and Solutions in Imperialist Times

Class Time 25 minutes

Task Creating a problem/solution chart

Purpose To analyze problems and solutions in imperialist history, 1830–1914

Instructions Display Critical Thinking Transparency CT28. Ask students to choose one of the three countries to analyze. Then display transparency CT77, a problem/solution graphic organizer. As students study the patterns of resistance in a country, have them create a similar chart with the appropriate information. Students may consult the text for additional information as they fill in the details.

When students have completed their charts, ask them to share their charts with the class. Discuss students' opinions of the outcome.

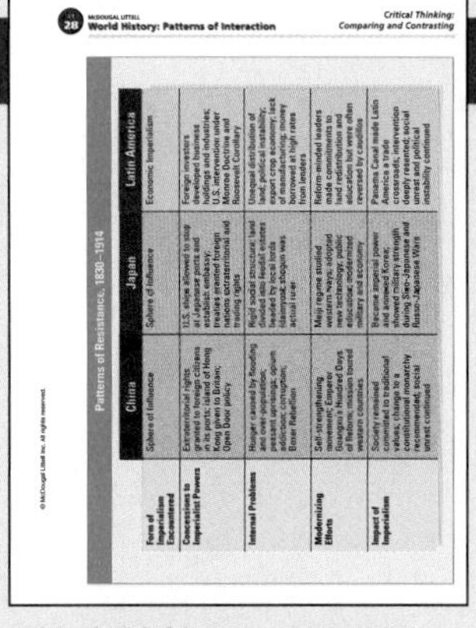

Critical Thinking Transparencies

Science & Technology

OBJECTIVE

- Understand the operation and significance of the Panama Canal.

INSTRUCT

Have interested students read Arthur Bullard's description of the creation of the Panama Canal.

In-Depth Resources: Unit 3

- Primary Source: Building the Panama Canal, p. 81
- Science & Technology: Technology Revolutionizes Communications, p. 89

INTEGRATED TECHNOLOGY

Interactive This image is available in an interactive format on the eEdition. Students can read explanations of how the locks operate.

More About . . .

Early Attempts at Canal Building

In 1878 the French obtained the right to build a canal across Panama. Their original plan was to build the canal at sea level, but problems quickly arose and plans were drawn up using locks, similar to today's. The effort ran into trouble, however, when politicians stole money from the canal company, eventually causing bankruptcy. Scientists were unable to stop epidemics of tropical diseases from killing numerous workers. These problems eventually halted the French effort.

Science & Technology

INTERACTIVE

Panama Canal

The Panama Canal is considered one of the world's greatest engineering accomplishments. Its completion changed the course of history by opening a worldwide trade route between the Atlantic and Pacific oceans. As shown in the diagram below, on entering the canal, ships are raised about 85 feet in a series of three locks. On leaving the canal, ships are lowered to sea level by another series of three locks.

The canal also had a lasting effect on other technologies. Since the early 1900s, ships have been built to dimensions that will allow them to pass through the canal's locks.

INTEGRATED TECHNOLOGY

RESEARCH LINKS For more on the Panama Canal, go to **classzone.com**

CALIFORNIA STANDARDS
10.4.1, HI 2

▲ Ships passing through the Pedro Miguel Locks

Panama Canal Cross-section

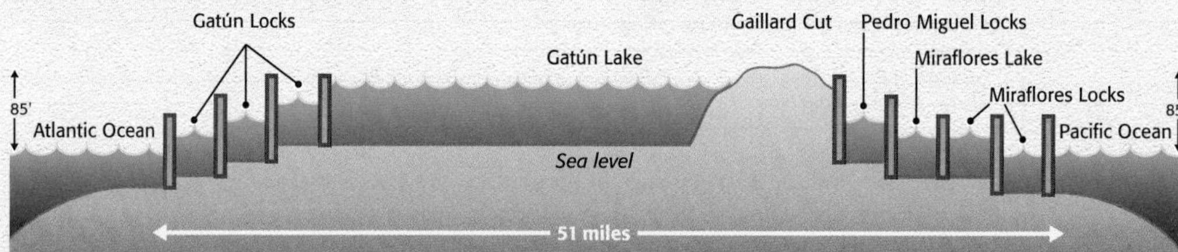

▲ This cross-section shows the different elevations and locks that a ship moves through on the trip through the canal.

Canal Facts

- The canal took ten years to build (1904–1914) and cost $380 million.
- During the construction of the canal, workers dug up more than 200 million cubic yards of earth.
- Thousands of workers died from diseases while building the canal.
- The trip from San Francisco to New York City via the Panama Canal is about 9,000 miles shorter than the trip around South America.
- The 51-mile trip through the canal takes 8 to 10 hours.
- The canal now handles more than 13,000 ships a year from around 70 nations carrying 192 million short tons of cargo.
- Panama took control of the canal on December 31, 1999.

Connect *to* Today

1. **Identifying Problems** What difficulties did workers face in constructing the canal?
See Skillbuilder Handbook, page R5.
2. **Evaluating Decisions** In the more than 90 years since it was built, do you think that the benefits of the Panama Canal to world trade have outweighed the costs in time, money, and human life? Explain your answer.

386

CONNECT TO TODAY: ANSWERS

1. Identifying Problems
Possible Answers: deadly diseases, unsafe working conditions, distance from family

2. Evaluating Decisions
Yes–World trade has benefited by saving time and money; the canal was an important step forward in engineering technology. No–Human life is more valuable than time or money; air travel and highways have made the canal less important.

responded by encouraging a revolution in Panama. The Panamanians had been trying to break away from Colombia for almost a century. In 1903, with help from the United States Navy, they won their country's independence. In gratitude, Panama gave the United States a ten-mile-wide zone in which to build a canal.

For the next decade, American engineers contended with floods and withering heat to build the massive waterway. However, their greatest challenge was the disease-carrying insects that infested the area. The United States began a campaign to destroy the mosquitoes that carried yellow fever and malaria, and the rats that carried bubonic plague. The effort to control these diseases was eventually successful. Even so, thousands of workers died during construction of the canal. The **Panama Canal** finally opened in 1914. Ships from around the world soon began to use it. Latin America had become a crossroads of world trade. And the United States controlled the tollgate. (C)

MAIN IDEA

Analyzing Motives

(C) Why was the United States so interested in building the Panama Canal?

C. Possible Answers because the canal would probvide a water route between the coasts of the United States and give the United States control over a direct trade link between the Atlantic and Pacific oceans

The Roosevelt Corollary The building of the Panama Canal was only one way that the United States expanded its influence in Latin America in the early 20th century. Its presence in Cuba and its large investments in many Central and South American countries strengthened its foothold. To protect those economic interests, in 1904, President Roosevelt issued a corollary, or extension, to the Monroe Doctrine. The **Roosevelt Corollary** gave the United States the right to be "an international police power" in the Western Hemisphere.

The United States used the Roosevelt Corollary many times in the following years to justify U.S. intervention in Latin America. U.S. troops occupied some countries for decades. Many Latin Americans protested this intervention, but they were powerless to stop their giant neighbor to the north. The U.S. government simply turned a deaf ear to their protests. It could not ignore the rumblings of revolution just over its border with Mexico, however. You will learn about this revolution in Section 4.

▼ This cartoon suggests that the Roosevelt Corollary turned the Caribbean into a U.S. wading pool.

More About . . .

The Roosevelt Corollary

The Roosevelt Corollary stated in part, "In the Western Hemisphere the adherence of the United States to the Monroe Doctrine may force the United States, however reluctantly, . . . to the exercise of an international police power." In the first half of the 20th century, the United States used this corollary to justify sending troops into Haiti, Nicaragua, the Dominican Republic, Mexico, Cuba, Honduras, Guatemala, and Costa Rica.

Electronic Library of Primary Sources

- from *The Rough Riders*

SECTION 3 ASSESSMENT

TERMS & NAMES 1. For each term or name, write a sentence explaining its significance.

- caudillo • Monroe Doctrine • José Martí • Spanish-American War • Panama Canal • Roosevelt Corollary

USING YOUR NOTES

2. Which event do you think was most beneficial to Latin America? Why? (10.4.1)

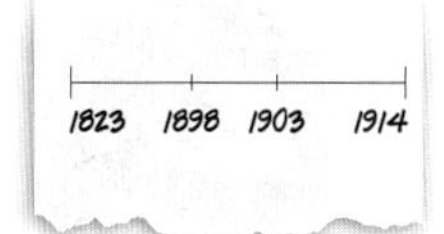

MAIN IDEAS

3. Why did the gap between rich and poor in Latin America grow after independence? (10.4.1)
4. What economic gains and setbacks did Latin American countries experience after independence? (10.4.1)
5. Why was the United States so interested in the security of Latin America? (10.4.1)

CRITICAL THINKING & WRITING

6. **ANALYZING MOTIVES** Why do you think upper-class Latin Americans favored governments run by caudillos? (10.4.1)
7. **FORMING OPINIONS** Do you think that U.S. imperialism was more beneficial or harmful to Latin American people? Explain. (10.4.1)
8. **CONTRASTING** How was the principle of the Roosevelt Corollary different from that of the Monroe Doctrine? (10.4.1)
9. **WRITING ACTIVITY** REVOLUTION Assume the role of a Cuban fighting for independence from Spain. Design a political **poster** that shows your feelings about the United States joining the struggle for independence. (Writing 2.2.b)

CONNECT TO TODAY **CREATING A DATAFILE**

Conduct research to find statistics on the ships and cargo that travel through the Panama Canal. Use your findings to create a **datafile** for usage of the canal in a recent year. (10.4.1)

3 ASSESS

SECTION 3 ASSESSMENT

Have students work in pairs to complete items 6 through 9 and Connect to Today. Students may also compare answers to items 1 through 5 with their partners.

Formal Assessment

- Section Quiz, p. 209

4 RETEACH

Use the Reading Study Guide to review the main ideas of the section.

Reading Study Guide, p. 131

In-Depth Resources: Unit 3

- Reteaching Activity, p. 92

ANSWERS

1. caudillo, p. 382 • Monroe Doctrine, p. 384 • José Martí, p. 384 • Spanish-American War, p. 384 • Panama Canal, p. 387 • Roosevelt Corollary, p. 387
2. **Sample Answer:** 1823–Monroe Doctrine; 1898–Spanish-American War; 1903–Panamanian rebellion; 1914–Panama Canal opened. Most beneficial–Opening of canal, because it changed trade
3. rich got wealthy through land purchases; increased debt for poor
4. Latin American trade greatly increased, but no industrialization
5. to ensure its own security
6. Caudillos protected upper-class privileges.
7. Beneficial–Jobs and exports helped farmers and workers. Harmful–No independence was gained.
8. The Monroe Doctrine was intended to discourage European intervention. The corollary authorized U.S. intervention regardless of European involvement.
9. **Rubric** Posters should
   - include text and visuals.
   - support or criticize U.S. intervention.

CONNECT TO TODAY

Rubric Datafiles should

- include the number of ships and the type and amount of cargo.
- use tables, charts, or graphs.

LESSON PLAN

OBJECTIVES

- Describe the role of Antonio López de Santa Anna in the history of Mexico.
- Trace Juárez's reform movement.
- Describe the rule of Porfirio Díaz.
- Explain the causes and results of the Mexican Revolution.

1 FOCUS & MOTIVATE

Ask students what they know about the current government of Mexico. As they read this section, ask them to contrast Mexico's government today with the turmoil of the past.

2 INSTRUCT

Santa Anna and the Mexican War
10.4.4

Critical Thinking

- What caused the battle between Texas and Mexico? *(Americans in Mexico-controlled Texas wanted self-rule.)*

Electronic Library of Primary Sources

- "Alamo Massacre"

CALIFORNIA RESOURCES
California Reading Toolkit, p. L57
California Modified Lesson Plans for English Learners, p. 109
California Daily Standards Practice Transparencies, TT49
California Standards Enrichment Workbook, pp. 53–54
California Standards Planner and Lesson Plans, p. L105
California Online Test Practice
California Test Generator CD-ROM
California Easy Planner CD-ROM
California eEdition CD-ROM

Woodblock print of landscape by Katsushika Hokusai

Coffee (1935), Candido Portinari

4

Turmoil and Change in Mexico

MAIN IDEA	WHY IT MATTERS NOW	TERMS & NAMES
REVOLUTION Political, economic, and social inequalities in Mexico triggered a period of revolution and reform.	Mexico has moved toward political democracy and is a strong economic force in the Americas.	• Antonio López de Santa Anna • Benito Juárez • *La Reforma* • Porfirio Díaz • Francisco Madero • "Pancho" Villa • Emiliano Zapata

CALIFORNIA STANDARDS

10.4.4 Describe the independence struggles of the colonized regions of the world, including the roles of leaders, such as Sun Yat-sen in China, and the roles of ideology and religion.

REP 4 Students construct and test hypotheses; collect, evaluate, and employ information from multiple primary and secondary sources; and apply it in oral and written presentations.

SETTING THE STAGE The legacy of Spanish colonialism and long-term political instability that plagued the newly emerging South American nations caused problems for Mexico as well. Mexico, however, had a further issue to contend with—a shared border with the United States. The "Colossus of the North," as the United States was known in Latin America, wanted to extend its territory all the way west to the Pacific Ocean. But most of the lands in the American Southwest belonged to Mexico.

Santa Anna and the Mexican War

During the early 19th century, no one dominated Mexican political life more than **Antonio López de Santa Anna**. Santa Anna played a leading role in Mexico's fight for independence from Spain in 1821. In 1829, he fought against Spain again as the European power tried to regain control of Mexico. Then, in 1833, Santa Anna became Mexico's president.

One of Latin America's most powerful caudillos, Santa Anna was a clever politician. He would support a measure one year and oppose it the next if he thought that would keep him in power. His policy seemed to work. Between 1833 and 1855, Santa Anna was Mexico's president four times. He gave up the presidency twice, however, to serve Mexico in a more urgent cause—leading the Mexican army in an effort to retain the territory of Texas.

TAKING NOTES
Comparing Use a chart to compare the major accomplishments of the Mexican leaders discussed in this section.

Leader	Major Accomplishment

The Texas Revolt In the 1820s, Mexico encouraged American citizens to move to the Mexican territory of Texas to help populate the country. Thousands of English-speaking colonists, or Anglos, answered the call. In return for inexpensive land, they pledged to follow the laws of Mexico. As the Anglo population grew, though, tensions developed between the colonists and Mexico over several issues, including slavery and religion. As a result, many Texas colonists wanted greater self-government. But when Mexico refused to grant this, Stephen Austin, a leading Anglo, encouraged a revolt against Mexico in 1835.

▶ Mexican leader Santa Anna

SECTION 4 PROGRAM RESOURCES

ALL STUDENTS
In-Depth Resources: Unit 3
- Guided Reading, p. 74
- History Makers: Porfirio Díaz, p. 87

Formal Assessment
- Section Quiz, p. 210

ENGLISH LEARNERS
In-Depth Resources in Spanish
- Guided Reading, p. 99

Reading Study Guide (Spanish), p. 133
Reading Study Guide Audio CD (Spanish)

STRUGGLING READERS
In-Depth Resources: Unit 3
- Guided Reading, p. 74
- Building Vocabulary, p. 75
- Reteaching Activity, p. 93

Reading Study Guide, p. 133
Reading Study Guide Audio CD

GIFTED AND TALENTED STUDENTS
In-Depth Resources: Unit 3
- Primary Source: from *The Plan of Ayala,* p. 82
- Literature: from *Tom Mix and Pancho Villa,* p. 83

Electronic Library of Primary Sources
- "Alamo Massacre"

INTEGRATED TECHNOLOGY
eEdition CD-ROM
Power Presentations CD-ROM
Critical Thinking Transparencies
- CT64 Chapter 28 Visual Summary

World Art and Cultures Transparencies
- AT62 *Distribution of the Land*

Electronic Library of Primary Sources
- "Alamo Massacre"

classzone.com

◀ Santa Anna's army met with strong resistance from the defenders of the Alamo.

Santa Anna led Mexican forces north to try to hold on to the rebellious territory. He won a few early battles, including a bitter fight at the Alamo, a mission in San Antonio. However, his fortunes changed at the Battle of San Jacinto. His troops were defeated and he was captured. Texan leader Sam Houston released Santa Anna after he promised to respect the independence of Texas. When Santa Anna returned to Mexico in 1836, he was quickly ousted from power.

War and the Fall of Santa Anna Santa Anna regained power, though, and fought against the United States again. In 1845, the United States annexed Texas. Outraged Mexicans considered this an act of aggression. In a dispute over the border, the United States invaded Mexico. Santa Anna's army fought valiantly, but U.S. troops defeated them after two years of war. In 1848, the two nations signed the Treaty of Guadalupe Hidalgo. The United States received the northern third of what was then Mexico, including California and the American Southwest. Santa Anna went into exile. He returned as dictator one final time, however, in 1853. After his final fall, in 1855, he remained in exile for almost 20 years. When he returned to Mexico in 1874, he was poor, blind, powerless, and essentially forgotten.

A. Answer Juárez was a poor Indian who worked for the powerless. Santa Anna was a well-to-do Creole concerned mainly with maintaining his own power.

Juárez and *La Reforma*

During the mid-19th century, as Santa Anna's power rose and fell, a liberal reformer, **Benito Juárez** (HWAHR•ehz), strongly influenced the politics of Mexico. Juárez was Santa Anna's complete opposite in background as well as in goals. Santa Anna came from a well-off Creole family. Juárez was a poor Zapotec Indian who was orphaned at the age of three. While Santa Anna put his own personal power first, Juárez worked primarily to serve his country. (A)

MAIN IDEA

Contrasting

(A) In what ways did Benito Juárez differ from Santa Anna?

Juárez Rises to Power Ancestry and racial background were important elements of political power and economic success in 19th-century Mexico. For that reason, the rise of Benito Juárez was clearly due to his personal leadership qualities. Juárez was raised on a small farm in the Mexican state of Oaxaca. When he was 12, he moved to the city of Oaxaca. He started going to school at age 15, and in 1829, he entered a newly opened state-run university. He received a law degree in 1831.

More About . . .

Antonio López de Santa Anna

Santa Anna was an opportunist who was true only to his own hunger for power, both inside and outside Mexico. In 1833, for example, he was elected as a liberal. When the country became more conservative, he too shifted to the right. Then, in 1845, U.S. president James Polk helped Santa Anna return from exile, with the understanding that Santa Anna would help mediate a peace agreement between the United States and Mexico over the status of Texas. Instead, Santa Anna led the Mexican army in battle against the United States.

Juárez and *La Reforma*

10.4.4

Critical Thinking

- How is the cycle of debt Mexicans experienced similar to peonage in Latin America? *(Rich landowners kept wages low and did not allow workers to buy land.)*
- What was one reason for Benito Juárez's rise to power and continued success? *(Possible Answers: He came from poverty, so people trusted him; he fought for years to help the people of Mexico get land and an education.)*

DIFFERENTIATING INSTRUCTION: ENGLISH LEARNERS

Creating a Time Line of the Mexican Revolution

Class Time 30 minutes

Task Creating a time line

Purpose To understand events and leaders of the Mexican Revolution

Instructions Have students keep track of the key terms and names in the section by placing them in a time line, like the one in the Reading Study Guide activity (also available in Spanish). Students can use the text and questions in the Reading Study Guide to determine whether any dates should be added to their time line. Encourage students to develop a color system, such as using a different color for each historical figure.

1861—Benito Juárez and his supporters win control of the government.

1862—France invades Mexico.

1872—Juárez dies of a heart attack.

1876—Porfirio Díaz takes over Mexico.

1911—Díaz gives up power.

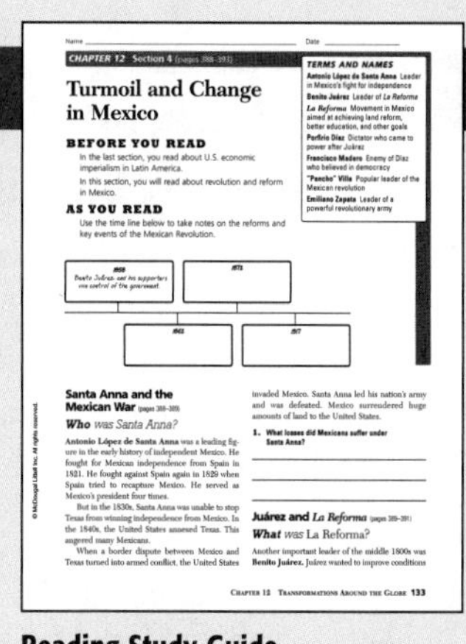

Reading Study Guide

Analyzing Art

Juárez: Symbol of Mexican Independence

José Clemente Orozco was a rare combination of philosopher and painter. He tried to present events realistically and to represent their true meaning. He said, "No artist has or ever has had political convictions of any sort. Those who profess them are not artists."

SKILLBUILDER Answers

1. **Contrasting** *Possible Answer:* The imperialists look old, small, and troubled by the burden of the emperor's body. The forces of independence look young, strong, and ready to fight.
2. **Drawing Conclusions** *Possible Answer:* Orozco looked on Juárez as a great hero and a symbol of Mexican independence.

More About . . .

Benito Juárez

Benito Juárez was a member of the Zapotec, a farming people known for their pottery and crafts. The Zapotec felt they could count on Juárez. When he was inaugurated governor of Oaxaca, a group of Zapotec gave him a petition that said, "You know what we need and you will give it to us, for you are good and will not forget that you are one of us."

Vocabulary Note: Pronunciation

Oaxaca is pronounced wuh•HAH•kah.

Analyzing Art

Juárez: Symbol of Mexican Independence

In 1948, more than 75 years after Benito Juárez's death, Mexican mural painter José Clemente Orozco celebrated him in the fresco *Juárez, the Church and the Imperialists.* A portrait of Juárez, which accentuates his Indian features, dominates the work. The supporters of Emperor Maximilian, carrying his body, are shown below Juárez. To either side of Juárez, the soldiers of Mexican independence prepare to attack these representatives of imperialism. By constructing the fresco in this way, Orozco seemed to suggest that Juárez was both a symbol of hope and a rallying cry for Mexican independence.

SKILLBUILDER: Interpreting Visual Sources

1. **Contrasting** *How is Orozco's portrayal of the imperialists different from his portrayal of the forces of independence?*
2. **Drawing Conclusions** *Based on this fresco, how do you think Orozco felt about Benito Juárez?*

He then returned to the city of Oaxaca, where he opened a law office. Most of his clients were poor people who could not otherwise have afforded legal assistance. Juárez gained a reputation for honesty, integrity, hard work, and good judgment. He was elected to the city legislature and then rose steadily in power. Beginning in 1847, he served as governor of the state of Oaxaca.

Juárez Works for Reform Throughout the late 1840s and early 1850s, Juárez worked to start a liberal reform movement. He called this movement ***La Reforma***. Its major goals were redistribution of land, separation of church and state, and increased educational opportunities for the poor. In 1853, however, Santa Anna sent Juárez and other leaders of *La Reforma* into exile.

Just two years later, a rebellion against Santa Anna brought down his government. Juárez and other exiled liberal leaders returned to Mexico to deal with their country's tremendous problems. As in other Latin American nations, rich landowners kept most other Mexicans in a cycle of debt and poverty. Liberal leader Ponciano Arriaga described how these circumstances led to great problems for both poor farmers and the government:

B. Answer the unequal distribution of land and extreme poverty of many Mexican peasants

MAIN IDEA

Analyzing Primary Sources

B What does Ponciano Arriaga think is Mexico's greatest problem?

PRIMARY SOURCE **B**

> There are Mexican landowners who occupy . . . an extent of land greater than the areas of some of our sovereign states, greater even than that of one of several European states. In this vast area, much of which lies idle, deserted, abandoned . . . live four or five million Mexicans who know no other industry than agriculture, yet are without land or the means to work it, and who cannot emigrate in the hope of bettering their fortunes. . . . How can a hungry, naked, miserable people practice popular government? How can we proclaim the equal rights of men and leave the majority of the nation in [this condition]?
>
> **PONCIANO ARRIAGA,** speech to the Constitutional Convention, 1856–1857

Not surprisingly, Arriaga's ideas and those of the other liberals in government threatened most conservative upper-class Mexicans. Many conservatives responded

DIFFERENTIATING INSTRUCTION: STRUGGLING READERS

Identifying Problems That Affected Mexico

Class Time 45 minutes

Task Charting problems and the people affected by them

Purpose To understand main ideas and conflicts in history

Instructions Explain that identifying problems in history means determining the difficulties faced by a group of people at a certain time. Ask pairs of students to identify one problem from each of the parts in this section. Students should name people who were affected by the problem or tried to solve it. While there may be several problems mentioned, encourage students to find and focus on main ideas. Encourage students to use headlines, images, and captions as guides to finding main ideas. Have students record their answers in a chart like this one.

Title of Part	Problem	People Involved
Santa Anna and the Mexican War	The United States took control of Texas.	Mexicans, Texans, Americans
Juárez and La Reforma	Juárez worked for reforms in government.	Peasants, Catholic Church, landowners
Porfirio Díaz and "Order and Progress"	Díaz became a dictator.	Peasants, landowners, businesspeople
The Revolution and Civil War	Leaders struggled for power.	Peasants, farmers, landowners

by launching a rebellion against the liberal government in 1858. They enjoyed some early successes in battle and seized control of Mexico City. The liberals kept up the fight from their headquarters in the city of Veracruz. Eventually the liberals gained the upper hand and, after three years of bitter civil war, they defeated the rebels. Juárez became president of the reunited country after his election in 1861.

The French Invade Mexico The end of the civil war did not bring an end to Mexico's troubles, though. Exiled conservatives plotted with some Europeans to reconquer Mexico. In 1862, French ruler Napoleon III responded by sending a large army to Mexico. Within 18 months, France had taken over the country. Napoleon appointed Austrian Archduke Maximilian to rule Mexico as emperor. Juárez and other Mexicans fought against French rule. After five years under siege, the French decided that the struggle was too costly. In 1867, Napoleon ordered the army to withdraw from Mexico. Maximilian was captured and executed.

Juárez was reelected president of Mexico in 1867. He returned to the reforms he had proposed more than ten years earlier. He began rebuilding the country, which had been shattered during years of war. He promoted trade with foreign countries, the opening of new roads, the building of railroads, and the establishment of a telegraph service. He set up a national education system separate from that run by the Catholic Church. In 1872, Juárez died of a heart attack. But after half a century of civil strife and chaos, he left his country a legacy of relative peace, progress, and reform.

Porfirio Díaz and "Order and Progress"

Juárez's era of reform did not last long, however. In the mid-1870s, a new caudillo, **Porfirio Díaz**, came to power. Like Juárez, Díaz was an Indian from Oaxaca. He rose through the army and became a noted general in the civil war and the fight against the French. Díaz expected to be rewarded with a government position for the part he played in the French defeat. Juárez refused his request, however. After this, Díaz opposed Juárez. In 1876, Díaz took control of Mexico by ousting the president. He had the support of the military, whose power had been reduced during and after the Juárez years. Indians and small landholders also supported him, because they thought he would work for more radical land reform.

During the Díaz years, elections became meaningless. Díaz offered land, power, or political favors to anyone who supported him. He terrorized many who refused to support him, ordering them to be beaten or put in jail. Using such strong-arm methods, Díaz managed to remain in power until 1911. Over the years, Díaz used a political slogan adapted from a rallying cry of the Juárez era. Juárez had called for "Liberty, Order, and Progress." Díaz, however, wanted merely "Order and Progress."

Díaz's use of dictatorial powers ensured that there was order in Mexico. But the country saw progress under Díaz too. Railroads expanded, banks were built, the currency stabilized, and foreign investment grew. Mexico seemed to be a stable, prospering country. Appearances were deceiving,

History Makers

Porfirio Díaz
1830–1915

To control all the various groups in Mexican society, Porfirio Díaz adopted an approach called *pan o palo*—"bread or the club." The "bread" he provided took many forms. To potential political opponents, he offered positions in his government. To business leaders, he gave huge subsidies or the chance to operate as monopolies in Mexico. And he won the support of the Church and wealthy landowners simply by promising not to meddle in their affairs. Those who turned down the offer of bread and continued to oppose Díaz soon felt the blow of the club. Thousands were killed, beaten, or thrown into jail.

His use of the club, Díaz admitted, was harsh and cruel—but also necessary if Mexico was to have peace. That peace, Díaz argued, enabled the country to progress economically. "If there was cruelty," he said, "results have justified it."

Porfirio Díaz and "Order and Progress"

10.4.4

Critical Thinking

- What is significant about Díaz's slogan "Order and Progress"? *(He omitted "Liberty," showing that he wasn't interested in freedom for all.)*
- After 41 years of rule, what evidence indicated that Díaz actually meant what his slogan said? *(Economic order and commerce had increased, but poor Mexicans remained poor and the rich had become richer.)*

History Makers

Porfirio Díaz

Díaz justified his use of violence against the Mexican people by claiming it was the only way to establish peace and order in Mexico. Over the course of his leadership, the condition of Mexico did improve. Railroads and banks were built and a new financial stability grew in the country. However, poor workers and farmers were still struggling to get by. Ask students if his *pan o palo* methods were successful, in their opinion. Ask them to back up their opinions with reasons.

In-Depth Resources, Unit 3

- History Makers: Porfirio Díaz, p. 87

DIFFERENTIATING INSTRUCTION: GIFTED AND TALENTED STUDENTS

Performing as Villa and Zapata

Class Time 45 minutes

Task Writing and performing dialogue

Purpose To better understand the Mexican revolutionaries' point of view

Instructions Distribute copies of the literature selection from *Tom Mix and Pancho Villa,* found in In-Depth Resources: Unit 3. Have students read the novel excerpt. Have small groups of students analyze the story and highlight the significant passages, including dialogue and description of setting and characters. From the highlighted portions, have students write a dialogue to be performed.

The dialogue should include the main ideas from the interaction between Zapata and Villa, as well as their points of view, and should include a beginning, middle, and end.

Students should assign roles among themselves. Students may want to include suggestions for costumes and a set for staging their dialogue.

Name ______________ Date ______________

CHAPTER 12 Section 4 LITERATURE SELECTION *from Tom Mix and Pancho Villa* by Clifford Irving

This novel is set during the Mexican Revolution. The fictional narrator is based on the real-life cowboy Tom Mix (1880–1940), a popular American silent and sound film actor who starred in Westerns. In the following excerpt, Mix describes the first face-to-face meeting between Francisco "Pancho" Villa and Emiliano Zapata. What are your impressions of the two revolutionary leaders?

The village of Xochimilco was a Zapatista stronghold near the floating flower gardens south of Mexico City. We rode on horseback, with a cloudless sky and the sun like a ripe tomato rising above the snowy peak of Popocatépetl. Trotting through cobbled streets that smelled of sizzling corn oil, Villa tilted his hat back and closed his eyes. Despite his troubles with Conchita del Hierro, his mouth drooped in a lazy smile: through the figurehead of Gutiérrez, he ruled Mexico. That wasn't what he wanted—he had always said so—but it didn't seem to displease him.

On the edge of Xochimilco we were met by Professor Otilio Montaño, the burly schoolteacher who had translated all of Zapata's thoughts into the Plan of Ayala. It was the best revolutionist document I had ever read, because it was the shortest. While the horses drank from goatskin buckets of water brought by Indian women, children ran out with wreaths of poppies and roses that they dumped in our path. The sun shone brightly on a breathlessly hot morning; the scent of the flowers was overpowering. Villa began to sneeze.

"My hay fever is coming back." He turned to me, groaning quietly. "I'll be dead by the time we get there."

The village band of Xochimilco, a few trumpets, a tuba and a bass drum, played "Las Mañanitas," and then the legendary leader from Morelos appeared, sauntering down the dusty main street with his retinue as we dismounted in front of the schoolhouse. I had seen pictures of Zapata, a former melon grower and army sergeant, but I still wasn't prepared for the man in the flesh.

Pancho Villa had come dressed in the clothes he had worn in the northern campaigns—his tan sweater with its frayed elbows, baggy khaki pants and riding boots, and the cool pith helmet that was now stained much the same color as his shirt. The rest of us, except for Rodolfo Fierro, wore our Texas scout hats and cartridge belts. Zapata looked as if the finest tailors in Mexico City had prepared him for the occasion and sewn his clothes around his body. . . . He wore a brilliant lavender shirt, a blue neckerchief and a short black silk jacket from whose pockets protruded two scarlet handkerchiefs. He was a short man, and his pointed Spanish boots sported four-inch-high heels. The gold-braided twenty-gallon sombrero made it dangerous to come within two feet of him without risking that the brim might cut your throat. His mustache extended beyond his cheeks; his dark eyes were large, liquid and mysterious. Candelario whispered to me, "He looks like the leader of a mariachi band."

But Villa, eyes leaking tears from the bouquets of flowers the children had pressed into his arms, ducked under the sombrero and gave Zapata the promised *embrazo*.

"Señor General, today I realize my dream. I meet the chief of the great revolution of the south."

In a languid voice, Zapata replied, "And I meet with honor the chief of the Northern Division."

Arm in arm they strolled into the schoolhouse where a large wooden table, scratched with the initials of children and lovers, had been placed in the center of a small classroom whose flaking walls were yellowed with age. Termites worked busily in the wooden beams overhead, so that peppery brown dust dropped steadily on our papers. Zapata had with him his brother Eufemio, Otilio Montaño, three generals and a journalist named Paulino Martinez. We all sat down, while the band gathered in the corridor and began to play. The big bass drum boomed in my ears, and it was hard to hear what the two chiefs were saying.

". . . a beautiful sombrero, Señor Zapata. It must keep you very cool in the hot weather."

"Very cool."

"I used to wear a sombrero, but in battle . . . hard to see the enemy if . . . what? A present from my wife in Chihuahua. Teddy Roosevelt . . . at San Juan."

Transformations Around the Globe 83

In-Depth Resources: Unit 3

Revolution and Civil War
10.4.4

Critical Thinking

- What event was responsible for Madero's calling for a revolution? *(his arrest and exile by Díaz)*
- What does "revolutionary" mean in reference to the Mexican Constitution? *(The constitution was a radical change from the past.)*

History Makers

Emiliano Zapata

Why do you think revolutionaries like Zapata were important to the Mexican Revolution? *(Possible Answer: Without strong, courageous people, real change may not occur.)*

Zapata spent much time working for reform in practical ways as well as on the battlefield. He established the country's first agricultural credit union, called the Rural Loan Bank, and tried to organize cooperatives for large sugar companies. When he met with a representative of President Wilson in 1915, he sought support from the U.S. government. Wilson had already recognized the Carranza government, and Zapata's request was denied.

In-Depth Resources: Unit 3
- from *The Plan of Ayala,* p. 82

INTEGRATED TECHNOLOGY

Rubric Biographical dictionaries should include
- all significant figures in the Revolution.
- specific achievements.
- important dates.

however. The wealthy acquired more and more land, which they did not put to good use. As a result, food costs rose steadily. Most Mexicans remained poor farmers and workers, and they continued to grow poorer. C

MAIN IDEA
Recognizing Effects
C What effects did Díaz's rule have on Mexico?
C. Answers political stability, some economic and industrial progress, but increasing poverty for most citizens

Revolution and Civil War

In the early 1900s, Mexicans from many walks of life began to protest Díaz's harsh rule. Idealistic liberals hungered for liberty. Farm laborers hungered for land. Workers hungered for fairer wages and better working conditions. Even some of Díaz's handpicked political allies spoke out for reform. A variety of political parties opposed to Díaz began to form. Among the most powerful was a party led by Francisco Madero.

History Makers

Emiliano Zapata 1879–1919

Shortly after Francisco Madero took office, he met with Emiliano Zapata, one of his leading supporters. Madero's reluctance to quickly enact real land reform angered Zapata. He left the meeting convinced that Madero was not the man to carry through the Mexican Revolution.

A few days later, Zapata issued the Plan of Ayala. This called for the removal of Madero and the appointment of a new president. The plan also demanded that the large landowners give up a third of their land for redistribution to the peasants. Zapata's rallying cry, "Land and Liberty," grew out of the Plan of Ayala.

When Venustiano Carranza ordered Zapata's assassination, he expected Zapata's revolutionary ideas on land reform to die with him. However, they lived on and were enacted by Alvaro Obregón, a follower of Zapata, who seized power from Carranza in 1920.

INTEGRATED TECHNOLOGY

INTERNET ACTIVITY Create a short biographical dictionary of leaders of the Mexican Revolution. Go to **classzone.com** for your research.

Madero Begins the Revolution Born into one of Mexico's ten richest families, **Francisco Madero** was educated in the United States and France. He believed in democracy and wanted to strengthen its hold in Mexico. Madero announced his candidacy for president of Mexico early in 1910. Soon afterward, Díaz had him arrested. From exile in the United States, Madero called for an armed revolution against Díaz.

The Mexican Revolution began slowly. Leaders arose in different parts of Mexico and gathered their own armies. In the north, Francisco **"Pancho" Villa** became immensely popular. He had a bold Robin Hood policy of taking money from the rich and giving it to the poor. South of Mexico City, another strong, popular leader, **Emiliano Zapata**, raised a powerful revolutionary army. Like Villa, Zapata came from a poor family. He was determined to see that land was returned to peasants and small farmers. He wanted the laws reformed to protect their rights. *"Tierra y Libertad"* ("Land and Liberty") was his battle cry. Villa, Zapata, and other armed revolutionaries won important victories against Díaz's army. By the spring of 1911, Díaz agreed to step down. He called for new elections.

Mexican Leaders Struggle for Power Madero was elected president in November 1911. However, his policies were seen as too liberal by some and not revolutionary enough by others. Some of those who had supported Madero, including Villa and Zapata, took up arms against him. In 1913, realizing that he could not hold on to power, Madero resigned. The military leader General Victoriano Huerta then took over the presidency. Shortly after, Madero was assassinated, probably on Huerta's orders.

Huerta was unpopular with many people, including Villa and Zapata. These revolutionary leaders allied themselves with Venustiano Carranza, another politician who wanted to overthrow Huerta. Their three armies advanced, seizing the Mexican countryside from Huerta's forces and approaching the capital, Mexico City. They overthrew Huerta only 15 months after he took power.

Carranza took control of the government and then turned his army on his former revolutionary allies. Both Villa and Zapata continued to fight. In 1919, however, Carranza lured

COOPERATIVE LEARNING

Creating a Historical Mural

Class Time 45 minutes

Task Creating poster-size murals

Purpose To help students understand Mexico's history

Instructions Divide students into small groups. Each group will create a poster-sized mural depicting an event in Mexican history and write explanatory paragraphs about that event.

Ask each group to choose an important event in Mexican history from this section for a mural subject. Group members should discuss their ideas and make preliminary sketches before they begin their mural. Supply groups with paper or posterboard and paints or markers.

Each group member should also write a paragraph describing the historic event, including his or her opinion about the outcome, and also how he or she contributed to the mural.

Encourage groups to present their murals to the class. Have each group elect a spokesperson to explain why they chose this event and to describe the mural and what it represents. Students may use creative symbols or images to depict attitudes, opinions, events, and outcomes.

Murals and graphics should display an understanding of the important events in Mexican history, show evidence of teamwork, and be clear and neat.

Land	Religion	Labor	Social Issues
• Breakup of large estates • Restrictions on foreign ownership of land • Government control of resources (oil)	• State takeover of land owned by the Church	• Minimum wage for workers • Right to strike • Institution of labor unions	• Equal pay for equal work • Limited legal rights for women (spending money and bringing lawsuits)

Reforms of Mexican Constitution of 1917

SKILLBUILDER: Interpreting Charts
1. **Making Inferences** *Which reforms do you think landowners resented?*
2. **Recognizing Effects** *Which reforms benefited workers?*

Zapata into a trap and murdered him. With Zapata's death, the civil war also came to an end. More than a million Mexicans had lost their lives.

The New Mexican Constitution Carranza began a revision of Mexico's constitution. It was adopted in 1917. A revolutionary document, that constitution is still in effect today. As shown in the chart above, it promoted education, land reforms, and workers' rights. Carranza did not support the final version of the constitution, however, and in 1920, he was overthrown by one of his generals, Alvaro Obregón.

D. Answer instituting constitutional reforms, stressing education, and promoting nationalism

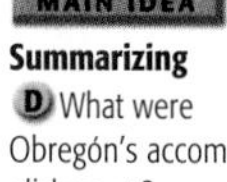

Summarizing
D What were Obregón's accomplishments?

Although Obregón seized power violently, he did not remain a dictator. Instead, he supported the reforms the constitution called for, particularly land reform. He also promoted public education. Mexican public schools taught a common language—Spanish—and stressed nationalism. In this way, his policies helped unite the various regions and peoples of the country. Nevertheless, Obregón was assassinated in 1928. D

The next year, a new political party, the Institutional Revolutionary Party (PRI), arose. Although the PRI did not tolerate opposition, it initiated an ongoing period of peace and political stability in Mexico. While Mexico was struggling toward peace, however, the rest of the world was on the brink of war.

SECTION 4 ASSESSMENT

TERMS & NAMES 1. For each term or name, write a sentence explaining its significance.
• Antonio López de Santa Anna • Benito Juárez • *La Reforma* • Porfirio Díaz • Francisco Madero • "Pancho" Villa • Emiliano Zapata

USING YOUR NOTES
2. Which leader do you think benefited Mexico most? Why? (10.4.4)

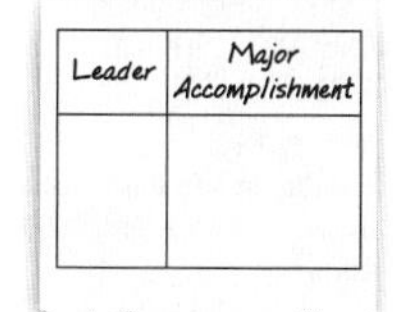

MAIN IDEAS
3. In what ways was Santa Anna a typical caudillo? (10.4.4)
4. How did Porfirio Díaz change the direction of government in Mexico? (10.4.4)
5. How were "Pancho" Villa and Emiliano Zapata different from other Mexican revolutionary leaders? (10.4.4)

CRITICAL THINKING & WRITING
6. **MAKING INFERENCES** Why might Benito Juárez's rise to power be considered surprising? (10.4.4)
7. **ANALYZING CAUSES** Why did Villa and Zapata turn against Madero? (10.4.4)
8. **SUPPORTING OPINIONS** The revision of Mexico's constitution is considered revolutionary. Do you agree with this characterization? Why or why not? (10.4.4)
9. **WRITING ACTIVITY** REVOLUTION Juárez's motto was "Liberty, Order, and Progress." Díaz's slogan was "Order and Progress." Write an **expository essay** explaining what this difference in goals meant for the people of Mexico. (Writing 2.3.b)

CONNECT TO TODAY **DESIGNING A CAMPAIGN POSTER**
Conduct research on the Institutional Revolutionary Party (PRI) today, particularly its political platform. Use your findings to design a **campaign poster** for the PRI in an upcoming election. (10.4.4)

History from Visuals

Interpreting the Chart
Before students read the chart, have them cover the text of the chart and just look at the column heads. What reforms do they think might have taken place? Then have them compare the actual reforms with their predictions.

Extension Suggest that interested students find out when Mexican women gained the right to vote and what other legal rights Mexican women have gained since 1917.

SKILLBUILDER Answers
1. **Making Inferences** breakup of large estates, restrictions on land ownership, nationalization of resources
2. **Recognizing Effects** minimum wage, right to strike, labor unions, equal pay for equal work

World Art and Cultures Transparencies
• AT62 *Distribution of the Land*

3 ASSESS

SECTION 3 ASSESSMENT

Have students work in pairs to complete item 2.

Formal Assessment
• Section Quiz, p. 210

4 RETEACH

Use the Visual Summary to review this section and chapter.

Critical Thinking Transparencies
• CT64 Chapter 28 Visual Summary

In-Depth Resources: Unit 3
• Reteaching Activity, p. 93

ANSWERS

1. Antonio López de Santa Anna, p. 388 • Benito Juárez, p. 389 • *La Reforma,* p. 390 • Porfirio Díaz, p. 391 • Francisco Madero, p. 392 • "Pancho" Villa, p. 392 • Emiliano Zapata, p. 392

2. **Sample Answer:** Juárez—Land, education reform. Madero—Revolution. Carranza—Revised constitution. Obregón—Land reform. Benefited Mexico most—Obregón, because reforms united various peoples of Mexico.
3. gained fame as a military leader; backed by military; aligned with upper classes; concerned with maintaining power
4. rejected reform, favored strict order
5. Both were poor peasants; other leaders were upper-class and well-educated or from the military
6. poor, Indian background; lawyer (other leaders from military)
7. They believed his policies were not revolutionary enough.
8. **Possible Answer:** Yes—It introduced reforms not addressed by former governments.
9. **Rubric** Expository essays should
• consider accomplishments of each.
• note loss of political freedom that resulted from Díaz's policies.

CONNECT TO TODAY
Rubric Campaign posters should
• convey the political goals of the PRI.
• use persuasive language and effective visuals.

TERMS & NAMES

1. Opium War, p. 372
2. Boxer Rebellion, p. 374
3. Meiji era, p. 377
4. Russo-Japanese War, p. 378
5. Monroe Doctrine, p. 384
6. Spanish-American War, p. 384
7. Benito Juárez, p. 389
8. Porfirio Díaz, p. 391

MAIN IDEAS

Answers will vary.

9. It had extensive natural resources and was essentially self-sufficient.
10. It helped trigger the Boxer Rebellion and led to a revived sense of Chinese nationalism.
11. Treaty of Kanagawa, granting permission to foreigners to trade at certain ports, granting of extraterritorial rights to foreigners. These actions led Japanese to believe they were losing control of their country, and they saw westernization as a way to regain control.
12. the Sino-Japanese War, which resulted in Japan gaining its first colonies; the Russo-Japanese War, which resulted in Japan's occupation of Korea
13. Colonialism left many Latin American countries politically and economically unstable and ripe for takeover by military strongmen. The army and the upper classes supported the caudillos, and the people were used to dictatorial rule.
14. ongoing imperialism, which kept most Latin American countries dependent and unable to develop politically or economically
15. Anglo colonists ignored Mexican laws and worked to gain independence from Mexico.
16. Both men were leaders in the revolution; they fought to aid and protect the poor.

Chapter 12 Assessment

TERMS & NAMES

For each term or name below, briefly explain its connection to the changes in global power between 1800 and 1914.

1. Opium War
2. Boxer Rebellion
3. Meiji era
4. Russo-Japanese War
5. Monroe Doctrine
6. Spanish-American War
7. Benito Juárez
8. Porfirio Díaz

MAIN IDEAS

China Resists Outside Influence Section 1 (pages 371–375)

9. Why was China traditionally not interested in trading with the West? (10.4.4)
10. Although Guangxu's effort at reform failed, what changes did it finally set in motion? (10.4.4)

Modernization in Japan Section 2 (pages 376–381)

11. What events caused Japan to end its isolation and begin to westernize? (10.4.1)
12. What were the results of Japan's growing imperialism at the end of the 19th century? (10.4.1)

U.S. Economic Imperialism Section 3 (pages 382–387)

13. How were Latin American caudillos able to achieve power and hold on to it? (10.4.4)
14. What effects did the Monroe Doctrine and the Roosevelt Corollary have on Latin America? (10.4.4)

Turmoil and Change in Mexico Section 4 (pages 388–393)

15. What were the major causes of tension between the Mexicans and the American colonists who settled in Texas? (10.4.4)
16. What roles did Francisco "Pancho" Villa and Emiliano Zapata play in the Mexican Revolution? (10.4.4)

CRITICAL THINKING

1. USING YOUR NOTES

On a time line, indicate the major events of Santa Anna's military and political career in Mexico. Why do you think he was able to remain in power for so long? (10.4.4)

Fights for independence from Spain

1820s

2. MAKING INFERENCES

Do you think that Emperor Guangxu would have been able to put his reforms into practice if the Dowager Empress Cixi had not intervened? Why or why not? (10.4.4)

3. COMPARING

CULTURAL INTERACTION How do Japan's efforts at westernization in the late 1800s compare with Japan's cultural borrowing of earlier times? (10.4.1)

4. EVALUATING COURSES OF ACTION

REVOLUTION Consider what you have learned in this and other chapters about Latin American colonial history and about how countries undergo change. What are the pros and cons of using both military strategies and peaceful political means to improve a country's economic, social, and political conditions? (HI 1)

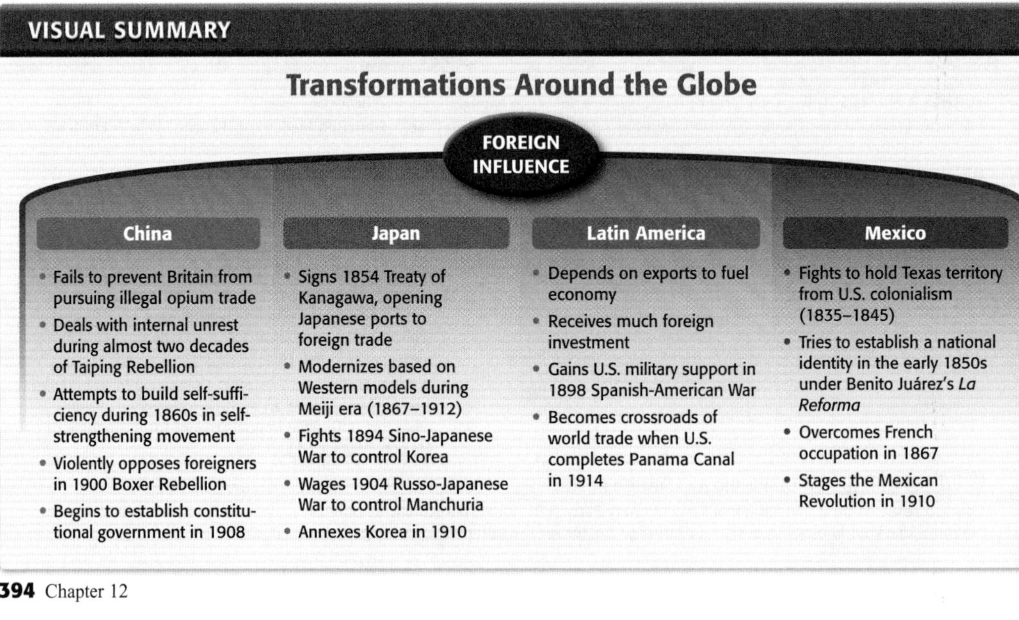

VISUAL SUMMARY
Transformations Around the Globe
FOREIGN INFLUENCE
China
• Fails to prevent Britain from pursuing illegal opium trade
• Deals with internal unrest during almost two decades of Taiping Rebellion
• Attempts to build self-sufficiency during 1860s in self-strengthening movement
• Violently opposes foreigners in 1900 Boxer Rebellion
• Begins to establish constitutional government in 1908
Japan
• Signs 1854 Treaty of Kanagawa, opening Japanese ports to foreign trade
• Modernizes based on Western models during Meiji era (1867–1912)
• Fights 1894 Sino-Japanese War to control Korea
• Wages 1904 Russo-Japanese War to control Manchuria
• Annexes Korea in 1910
Latin America
• Depends on exports to fuel economy
• Receives much foreign investment
• Gains U.S. military support in 1898 Spanish-American War
• Becomes crossroads of world trade when U.S. completes Panama Canal in 1914
Mexico
• Fights to hold Texas territory from U.S. colonialism (1835–1845)
• Tries to establish a national identity in the early 1850s under Benito Juárez's La Reforma
• Overcomes French occupation in 1867
• Stages the Mexican Revolution in 1910

CRITICAL THINKING

Answers will vary.

1. 1833—Becomes president of Mexico; 1835—Fights for Texas; 1836—Loses presidency; 1845—Loses Texas; 1853—Returns as dictator; 1855—Goes into exile. Santa Anna often changed his mind on policies if he thought it would keep him in power.
2. Yes—Guangxu gathered talented advisers and gained support from most reform-minded people. No—The Qing government was too strongly opposed to reform.
3. The Japanese borrowed what they considered the best elements of the culture and then adapted these elements to suit their traditions.
4. Military strategies let leaders control a country and enact policies but can cause great suffering. Peaceful political means take longer and are more difficult to achieve, but they usually allow the people a greater voice.

Use the excerpt—which deals with changes made during the Meiji era in Japan—and your knowledge of world history to answer questions 1 and 2.
Additional Test Practice, pp. S1–S33

PRIMARY SOURCE

In the second and third years of Meiji, the demand for foreign goods remarkably increased. Those who formerly looked upon them with contempt changed their minds and even dressed in foreign clothes. Our males adopted the European style. They put on fine tall hats instead of wearing large [queues] on their heads, and took to carrying sticks after discarding their swords. They dressed in coats of the English fashion and trousers of the American. They would only eat from tables and nothing would satisfy them but French cookery.

Tokyo Times, 1877

1. According to the excerpt, what happened in the second and third years of Meiji? (HI 1)
   - **A.** The Japanese ate only English food.
   - **B.** The Japanese wore only Japanese clothes.
   - **C.** The demand for foreign goods increased.
   - **D.** The demand for Japanese goods decreased.
2. Which statement best sums up the way the writer feels about the Japanese adoption of foreign ways? (REP 4)
   - **A.** The writer expresses no opinion of the matter.
   - **B.** The writer chooses to reserve judgment until a later date.
   - **C.** The writer feels that it is a good thing for Japan.
   - **D.** The writer feels that it is a bad thing for Japan.

Use the graph and your knowledge of world history to answer question 3.

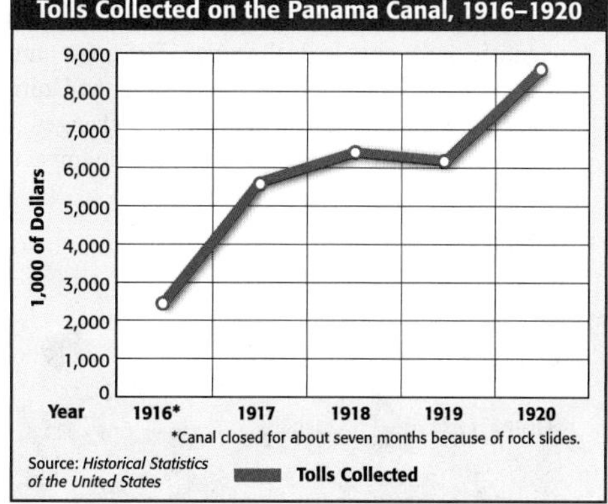

3. In which year did tolls collected on the Panama Canal first exceed $6 million? (10.4.2)
   - **A.** 1917
   - **B.** 1918
   - **C.** 1919
   - **D.** 1920

INTEGRATED TECHNOLOGY

TEST PRACTICE Go to **classzone.com**

- Diagnostic tests
- Tutorials
- Strategies
- Additional practice

ALTERNATIVE ASSESSMENT

1. **Interact *with* History** (CST 1)
   On page 370, you considered whether you would seek out or resist foreign influence. Now that you have learned how several countries dealt with foreign influence and what the results were, would you change your recommendation? Discuss your ideas in a small group.
2. **WRITING ABOUT HISTORY** (REP 4)
   EMPIRE BUILDING Write a **dialogue** that might have taken place between a conservative member of the Dowager Empress Cixi's court and an official in Emperor Mutsuhito's Meiji government. In the dialogue, have the characters discuss
   - the kinds of foreign intervention their countries faced
   - the actions their leaders took to deal with this foreign intervention

INTEGRATED TECHNOLOGY

Planning a Television News Special

(10.4.4; Writing 2.3.b, d, f)

On May 5, 1862, badly outnumbered Mexican forces defeated the French at the Battle of Puebla. Mexicans still celebrate their country's triumph on the holiday Cinco de Mayo. Working in a group with two other students, plan a television news special on how Cinco de Mayo is celebrated by Mexicans today. Focus on celebrations in Mexico or in Mexican communities in cities in the United States. Consider including

- information on the Battle of Puebla
- an explanation of how and why Cinco de Mayo became a national holiday
- images of any special activities or traditions that have become part of the celebration
- interviews with participants discussing how they feel about Cinco de Mayo

CHAPTER 12 ASSESSMENT

STANDARDS-BASED ASSESSMENT

1. The correct answer is letter **C**, as shown in the first sentence of the excerpt. Letter **A** is incorrect because the excerpt refers to some Japanese, not to all of them. Letter **B** is incorrect because the excerpt mentions men only. Letter **D** is incorrect because the excerpt does not state that demand for Japanese goods decreased; instead, it mentions an increase in demand for foreign goods and a dislike of certain Japanese clothes and foods.
2. The correct answer is letter **D**. Phrases such as "they would only eat from tables" and "nothing would satisfy them but" seem to suggest that the writer looks on these Western practices as absurd. Letters **A** and **B** are incorrect because the writer does have an opinion about the changes. Letter **C** is incorrect because the writer's tone is negative.
3. The correct answer is letter **B**. By following the 6 million grid line across, students will see that 1918 was the first year that tolls exceeded this number. Answers **A**, **C**, and **D** do not reflect the information on the graph.

Formal Assessment

- Chapter Test, Forms A, B, and C, pp. 211–225

California Test Generator CD-ROM

- Chapter Tests, Forms A, B, and C (English and Spanish)

ALTERNATIVE ASSESSMENT

1. Some students may answer that foreign influence is a necessary part of a modern industrialized state. Others may argue that foreign influence leads to domination and repression.
2. **Rubric** Dialogues should
   - include correct information about China and Japan in the late 1800s.
   - present persuasive arguments and counterarguments.
   - show an understanding of each government's point of view.

INTEGRATED TECHNOLOGY

Rubric TV news specials should

- show research on the Battle of Puebla.
- include information from several sources.
- provide in-depth information about the history of Cinco de Mayo.
- cite primary sources, such as the names of those interviewed.
- include photos or graphics of a celebration.
- show evidence of teamwork.

LESSON PLAN

OBJECTIVES

- Examine scientific and technological advances.
- Compare and contrast the economic, social, and cultural effects of science and technology on society.

1 FOCUS & MOTIVATE

To prepare students to learn about scientific and technological changes, ask the class to name what they think are the most important advances made in their lifetime. Spend a few minutes writing the students' ideas on the chalkboard.

2 INSTRUCT

Critical Thinking

- What are five categories into which the changes on the time line can be organized? *(manufacturing, transportation, communication, medicine, general science)*
- Which industries experienced the most advances during the period shown on the time line? *(Possible Answer: the textile industry, transportation, and communications)*

More About . . .

Automobiles

By 1916 more than 700,000 Model T's had been produced annually. The sticker price had dropped to $345. By 1927, fifteen million Model T's had been sold. Wide use of automobiles came to affect such things as dating, family connections, manufacturing patterns, and the national economy.

A Period of Change

The period from 1700 to 1914 was a time of tremendous scientific and technological change. The great number of discoveries and inventions in Europe and the United States promoted economic, social, and cultural changes. Use the information on these six pages to study the impact of scientific and technological changes.

CALIFORNIA STANDARDS
10.3.2, HI 1

▲ Steamboat
Robert Fulton held the first commercially successful steamboat run. One advantage of a steamboat was that it could travel against a river's current. These boats soon began to travel rivers around the world.

▲ Spinning Jenny
Using James Hargreaves's invention, a spinner could turn several spindles with one wheel and produce many threads. Machine-made thread was weak, so it was used only for the horizontal threads of fabric.

Theory of Atoms
John Dalton theorized that atoms are the basic parts of elements and that each type of atom has a specific weight. He was one of the founders of atomic chemistry.

1733 — 1764 — 1785 — 1803 — 1807 — 1830

Flying Shuttle
A shuttle is a holder that carries horizontal threads back and forth between the vertical threads in weaving. John Kay's mechanical flying shuttle enabled one weaver to do the work of two.

Power Loom
Edmund Cartwright created the first water-powered loom. Others later improved on the speed and efficiency of looms and the quality of the fabrics.

▼ Steam Locomotive
In 1830, the first steam locomotive was put into operation in the United States. Besides passengers, locomotives could rapidly transport tons of raw materials from mines to factories, and manufactured goods from factories to consumers and ports.

DIFFERENTIATING INSTRUCTION: GIFTED AND TALENTED STUDENTS

Tracking the Causes and Effects of Discoveries

Class Time 45 minutes

Task Researching inventions

Purpose To understand the cause-and-effect nature of scientific discovery

Instructions Have students choose one of these three inventions from the time line: the steamboat, the telephone, or the airplane. Using the library or the Internet, students should research the key discoveries that led up to the invention and the effect their invention had on future breakthroughs. Have students arrange their findings in a graphic.

Items listed before invention of the airplane would be gasoline engine and gliders. Items shown as effects would be jet planes, rockets, space shuttle.

Panama Canal
The Panama Canal shortened trips between the Atlantic and Pacific oceans by thousands of miles since ships no longer had to go around South America.

◄ Radioactivity
Marie Curie won the Nobel prize in chemistry for her (and her late husband's) discovery of the elements polonium and radium. Their work paved the way for later discoveries in nuclear physics and chemistry.

Antiseptics
Joseph Lister pioneered the use of carbolic acid to kill bacteria in operating rooms and later directly in wounds. The rate of death by infection after surgery dropped from about 50 to 15 percent.

Radio
Guglielmo Marconi's radio sent Morse code messages by electromagnetic waves that traveled through the air. It enabled rapid communication between distant places.

1865 1876 1879 1895 1903 1908 1911 1914

▼ Telephone
Alexander Graham Bell produced the first instrument that successfully carried the sounds of speech over electric wires. The telephone's design underwent a number of changes in its early years.

Airplane
The Wright brothers built the first machine-powered aircraft, which burned gasoline. The edge of the wing was adjusted during flight to steer.

Model T Ford
By using a moving assembly line, Henry Ford produced an automobile that working people could afford to buy.

Light Bulb
The light bulb that Thomas A. Edison and his staff made was first used in businesses and public buildings that installed small lighting plants. Cities slowly built the electrical systems needed to power lights.

Comparing & Contrasting

1. How were the steamboat and the locomotive similar in their impact?
2. How did the scientific theory of John Dalton differ from Joseph Lister's discovery in terms of its impact on daily life?

397

More About . . .

The Jacquard Loom and Computers

In 1801 French weaver Joseph-Marie Jacquard invented a method of programming a loom to create complex patterns, which earlier machines could not do. Jacquard used a long series of cards with holes punched in them that directed the loom's operation. Early computer designers noticed that these punched cards could represent the binary system of 0 and 1 that computers are based on. Herman Hollerith, an American inventor, used a similar punched card system to tabulate the 1890 United States census. Hollerith's machine was a huge success. In 1896 he started the Tabulating Machine Company, which by 1924 had become International Business Machines, or IBM.

Comparing & Contrasting

1. *Possible Answer:* Both could carry large loads. They both assisted industry in transporting raw materials and finished goods. They both also made passenger travel easier.
2. *Possible Answer:* Lister's discovery had the immediate practical effect of saving patients' lives. Dalton's theory paved the way for atomic science, rather than immediately benefiting daily life.

RECOMMENDED RESOURCES

Books for the Teacher

Hills, Richard L. ***Power from Steam: A History of the Stationary Steam Engine***. New York: Cambridge UP, 1993.

Smyth, A. L. ***John Dalton, 1766–1844: A Bibliography of Works by and About Him, With an Annotated List of His Surviving Apparatus and Personal Effects***. 2nd ed. Aldershot, Hampshire, UK: Ashgate, 1998.

Books for the Student

McDougal Littell *Nextext*. Charles Dickens, ***Great Expectations***. The classic story of a young orphan growing up in Victorian England during the Industrial Revolution.

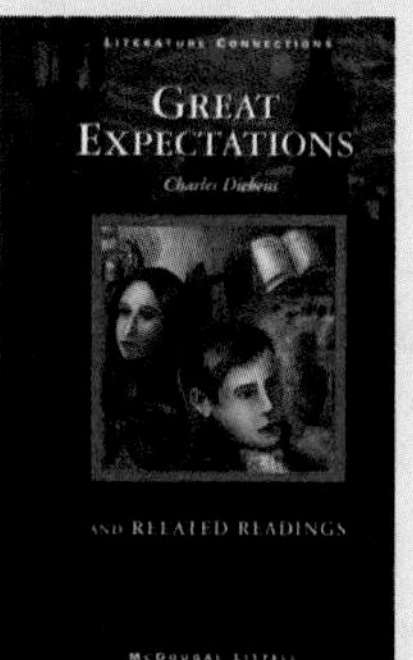

Videos and Software

Britain 1750–1900: Expansion, Trade, and Industry. CD-ROM. Films for the Humanities and Sciences. 800-257-5126. The effects of the Industrial Revolution in Britain.

Industrialization and Urbanization. VHS. The Library Video Company. 800-843-3620. The wide-ranging effects of the Industrial Revolution on American life.

Impact of Technological Change

Critical Thinking

- What negative effects did industrialization and technological change have on the workforce? *(Conditions for workers were very bad in factories, and children were exploited as cheap labor. Also, the assembly line put many people out of work as production became quicker and easier.)*
- How did workers benefit in the long run from industrialization? *(Poor working conditions led to the formation of unions and laws to protect workers' rights.)*
- How did the electric light and telephone help businesses? *(Possible Answer: The electric light allowed people to work longer hours because they could see into the nighttime. The telephone allowed instant, real-time communication between customers and other businesses.)*

SKILLBUILDER Answers

1. **Synthesizing** Children would have more time to go to school or to read popular publications.
2. **Analyzing Motives** Europeans built infrastructure in their colonies to get the raw materials to the ports and to enable colonial administrators to stay connected with areas of production.

Impact of Technological Change

Use the charts below, and the documents and photograph on the next page, to learn about some of the great changes technology produced.

CALIFORNIA STANDARDS

HI 2 Students recognize the complexity of historical causes and effects, including the limitations on determining cause and effect.

Technological Change

Industrialization

Economic Change

- Productivity increased, which led to an economic boom.
- Cheaper goods became available.
- A middle class emerged.
- Industries searched for overseas resources and markets, encouraging imperialism.
- Colonial economies were shaped to benefit Europe.

Social Change

- Cities grew at a rapid pace.
- Poor working and living conditions led to social unrest.
- Diseases spread in slums.
- Unions formed to protect workers.
- Laws were passed to improve working conditions.
- Immigration to North America increased.

Culture Change

- Businesses needed engineers, professionals, and clerical workers, so education was emphasized.
- The spread of public education increased literacy.
- The publishing industry grew; book and magazine sales boomed.
- Reform movements arose in response to unfair conditions.

Inventions/Progress

Economic Change

- Large machines led to the development of factories.
- Steamboats, canals, paved roads, and railroads opened travel to the interior of continents and reduced transportation costs.
- Investors formed corporations to undertake large projects.
- Superior arms and transport helped Europeans colonize.
- Inventions such as the telephone and electric light helped business grow.

Social Change

- Steamboats and railroads made travel cheaper and easier.
- The telegraph, telephone, and radio aided communication.
- Convenience products like canned food and ready-made clothes made daily life easier.
- The assembly line made products like cars affordable for many.
- Fewer workers were needed to produce the same amount of goods. Some workers lost jobs.

Culture Change

- People placed increasing emphasis on making homes more comfortable and convenient.
- Improvements in one aspect of agriculture and manufacturing promoted the creation of new inventions to improve other aspects.
- Mass culture grew through the availability of phonographs and movies, and an increase in leisure time.

SKILLBUILDER: Interpreting Charts

1. **Synthesizing** *How might limiting working hours for children promote literacy?*
2. **Analyzing Motives** *Why would Europeans build transportation and communication networks in their colonies?*

DIFFERENTIATING INSTRUCTION: STRUGGLING READERS

The Impact of Technological Change

Class Time 30 minutes

Task Reorganizing the chart

Purpose To better understand the effects of technological change

Instructions Divide the class into small groups, making sure that any struggling readers are in groups with more proficient readers. Ask the groups to read over the chart on this page, paying attention to what inventions are named specifically, such as the steamboat or the telephone. Have the groups place each invention into a new chart that is organized by invention.

Next to each invention in these new charts, the students should write in whatever economic, social, or cultural changes they think can be associated with the invention.

For the steamboat, for example, recorded changes might be lower transportation costs and easier travel.

By reorganizing information in this way, struggling readers may more easily make the connection between inventions and their effects on the world. Interested students may add recent inventions such as computers and cell phones to the chart.

PRIMARY SOURCE

Child Workers in Textile Factory

Many jobs did not require skilled workers, so children were hired to do them because they could be paid lower wages than adults. Some industries also hired children because their small fingers could fit between the machinery or handle fine parts more easily than adult fingers could.

DOCUMENT-BASED QUESTION
Judging by the children's appearance, how generous were the wages they received? Explain your answer.

PRIMARY SOURCE

INTERACTIVE

Impact of the Telephone

In this excerpt from "Thirty Years of the Telephone," published in September 1906, John Vaughn discussed how Bell's invention affected life in the United States.

Various industries, unknown thirty years ago, but now sources of employment to many thousands of workers, depend entirely on the telephone for support. . . . The Bell Companies employ over 87,000 persons, and it may be added, pay them well. . . . These figures may be supplemented by the number of telephones in use (5,698,000), by the number of miles of wire (6,043,000) in the Bell lines, and by the number of conversations (4,479,500,000) electrically conveyed in 1905. The network of wire connects more than 33,000 cities, towns, villages, and hamlets.

DOCUMENT-BASED QUESTION
What were some of the effects of the invention of the telephone?

SECONDARY SOURCE

INTERACTIVE

How Technology Aided Imperialism

In this excerpt from the book *Guns, Germs, and Steel,* Jared Diamond related an incident to show how technology helped Europeans conquer other lands.

In 1808 a British sailor named Charlie Savage equipped with muskets and excellent aim arrived in the Fiji Islands. [He] proceeded single-handedly to upset Fiji's balance of power. Among his many exploits, he paddled his canoe up a river to the Fijian village of Kasavu, halted less than a pistol shot's length from the village fence, and fired away at the undefended inhabitants. His victims were so numerous that . . . the stream beside the village was red with blood. Such examples of the power of guns against native peoples lacking guns could be multiplied indefinitely.

DOCUMENT-BASED QUESTION
How did guns give Europeans an advantage over native peoples?

Comparing & Contrasting

1. Reread the passage by John Vaughn and then compare it with the information on the chart. What could you add to the chart based on this passage?
2. Does the photograph of factory workers confirm or contradict the information on the chart? Explain.

399

PRIMARY SOURCE
Child Workers in Textile Factory

Answer to Document-Based Question
Possible Answer: The boys' pay must have been inadequate since their clothing looks worn and dirty, and the boy in front does not have shoes.

PRIMARY SOURCE
Impact of the Telephone

Answer to Document-Based Question
Possible Answer: It linked the country, provided many jobs in the telephone industry, and made other industries possible.

SECONDARY SOURCE
How Technology Aided Imperialism

Answer to Document-Based Question
Possible Answer: Guns enabled Europeans to overpower and kill from a distance large numbers of people who did not have comparable means of defending themselves.

INTEGRATED TECHNOLOGY

Interactive The primary and secondary sources in this feature are available in an interactive format on the eEdition. Students can listen to the sources, get help with vocabulary, and obtain background information.

Comparing & Contrasting

1. *Possible Answer:* Under "Inventions/Progress," an economic change could be added: To manufacture telephones and keep their networks working, new industries became necessary.
2. *Possible Answer:* The photo confirms the existence of poor working conditions that led to social unrest. The barefoot child could step on something and get injured.

DIFFERENTIATING INSTRUCTION: ENGLISH LEARNERS

Understanding Primary and Secondary Sources

Class Time 30 minutes

Task Rewording the Primary and Secondary Sources

Purpose To help students to understand the meaning of the sources

Instructions Pair English learners with more proficient English readers. Have the pairs of students read the Primary and Secondary Sources on this page out loud, line-by-line, asking for assistance with any words or ideas they do not understand. With the help of their partners, the English learners can then choose one of the sources and rewrite it, boiling the passage down to its main ideas.

For example, a student working with the Vaughn passage might write:

The invention of the telephone gave a lot of people new jobs. In 1905 there were more than 5 million telephones in use and over 6 million miles of telephone wire. The number of conversations was more than 4 billion. More than 33,000 cities, towns, villages, and crossroads were connected by telephone.

Impact of Scientific Change

Critical Thinking

- How is the development of scientific discoveries connected to the development of new inventions? *(Possible Answer: Inventions often spring from new scientific understanding. Conversely, an invention may lead to research on basic processes and thus to new understandings and inventions.)*

SKILLBUILDER Answers

1. **Drawing Conclusions** These services ensured the survival of more infants and allowed people to live longer and healthier lives.
2. **Analyzing Bias** The European colonizer would be more likely to accept Social Darwinism without question because it gave him or her the "right" to rule people who were less "fit" (according to the theory).

PRIMARY SOURCE
Chloroform Machine

Answer to Document-Based Question
Possible Answer: Practical inventions made some medical procedures possible for the first time. Those procedures led to new discoveries and better medical care.

Impact of Scientific Change

CALIFORNIA STANDARDS
10.3.2, HI 1, HI 3

Many scientific discoveries resulted in practical applications that affected daily life. Other discoveries increased our understanding of the way the universe works. Use the information on these two pages to explore the impact of scientific change.

Scientific Change

Economic Change	Social Change	Culture Change
• Discovery of quinine as a malaria treatment helped people colonize tropical areas. • Control of diseases like yellow fever and bubonic plague enabled the Panama Canal to be built. • More accurate clocks and new astronomical discoveries led to safer navigation, which improved shipping. • Study of electricity and magnetism led to the invention of the dynamo and motor, which aided industry.	• Vulcanized rubber was used for raincoats and car tires. • Discoveries about air, gases, and temperature resulted in better weather forecasting. • Vaccines and treatments were found for illnesses like diphtheria and heart disease; X-rays and other new medical techniques were developed. • Plumbing and sewers improved sanitation and public health. • Psychiatry improved the treatment of mental illness.	• Many scientific and technical schools were founded; governments began funding scientific research. • Psychological discoveries began to be applied to the social sciences, such as sociology and anthropology. • Some painters and writers created work that reflected the new psychological ideas. • Social Darwinism, the idea that some people were more "fit" than others, was used to justify racism.

SKILLBUILDER: Interpreting Charts

1. **Drawing Conclusions** *How do you think such advances in public health as vaccinations and sanitation services affected the lives of ordinary people?*
2. **Analyzing Bias** *Who would be more likely to accept the idea of social Darwinism–a European colonizer or an African in a colony? Why?*

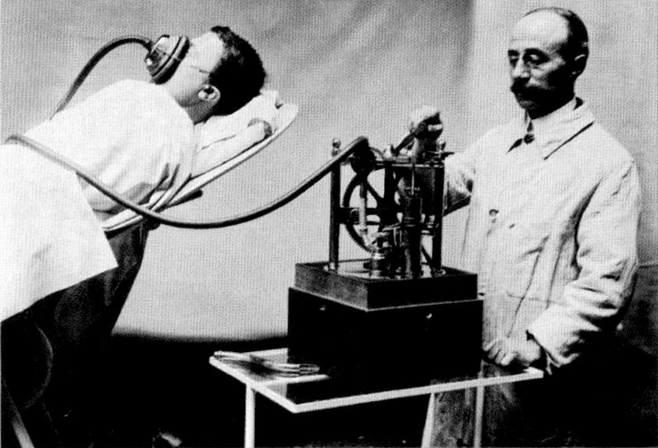

PRIMARY SOURCE

Chloroform Machine

The person with the mask is receiving the anesthetic chloroform. By removing pain, anesthetics enabled doctors to perform procedures—such as surgery—that would have been difficult for the patient to endure.

DOCUMENT-BASED QUESTION
How did practical inventions, like the chloroform machine, contribute to medicine and other sciences?

CONNECTIONS TO ECONOMICS

Economics

Class Time 30 minutes

Task Linking industries and inventions

Purpose To show how the automobile and aviation industries expanded the nation's economy

Instructions Divide the class into small groups. Have the groups use the library or the Internet to research industries that related to the automobile or to the airplane industry. Remind them to include parts, services, and changes in infrastructure such as roads. Have students create a poster to illustrate their ideas.

Here is a partial list of industries related to the automobile:

- road building
- gasoline stations
- repair shops
- public garages
- motels
- tourist camps
- auto parts stores
- automobile dealers
- auto-financing companies
- car washes

Have students estimate the impact of the automobile or the airplane on the national economy; then have them confirm their estimate through research.

PRIMARY SOURCE

Smallpox Vaccination

This newspaper engraving shows a Board of Health doctor administering the smallpox vaccine to poor people at a police station in New York City.

DOCUMENT-BASED QUESTION
Why would public health officials especially want to carry out vaccination programs in poor neighborhoods?

SECONDARY SOURCE

INTERACTIVE

Impact of Scientific Research

This passage from *The Birth of the Modern* by Paul Johnson discusses the far-reaching results of Michael Faraday's experiments with electromagnetism in the 1820s.

[By 1831, Faraday] had not only the first electric motor, but, in essence, the first dynamo: He could generate power. . . . What was remarkable about his work between 1820 and 1831 was that by showing exactly how mechanical could be transformed into electrical power, he made the jump between theoretical research and its practical application a comparatively narrow one. The electrical industry was the direct result of his work, and its first product, the electric telegraph, was soon in use. The idea of cause and effect was of great importance, for both industry and governments now began to appreciate the value of fundamental research and to finance it.

DOCUMENT-BASED QUESTION
How did Faraday's work affect society in the long term?

Comparing & Contrasting

1. In your opinion, was there more economic progress or social progress during the period 1700 to 1914? Use information from the charts on pages 398 and 400 to support your answer.
2. Consider the impact of medical advances and the idea of Social Darwinism on imperialism. How were their impacts alike?

EXTENSION ACTIVITY
Research a more recent scientific or technological change, such as the development of computer chips, plastics, the Internet, or space travel. Make a chart like the one shown on page 400 listing the economic, social, and cultural changes that have resulted.

401

PRIMARY SOURCE

Smallpox Vaccinations

Answer to Document-Based Question
Possible Answer: Contagious diseases are more likely to become epidemics where many people live in crowded conditions. The poor were the most likely to suffer and least likely to get good medical care on their own.

SECONDARY SOURCE

Impact of Scientific Research

Answer to Document-Based Question
Possible Answer: Faraday's work brought about the development of the electrical industry. It showed how pure science could have practical applications and made industry and government interested in funding science.

INTEGRATED TECHNOLOGY

Interactive The secondary source on this page is available in an interactive format on the eEdition. Students can listen to the excerpt and obtain background information.

Comparing & Contrasting

1. *Possible Answer:* Many students will feel it was a time of more economic progress because industry boomed. While there was some social progress, there was also an increase of problems, like the disparity between rich and poor and the racist policies of colonizers.
2. *Possible Answer:* Both medical advances and Social Darwinism had widespread impact on people of all classes.

EXTENSION ACTIVITY

Rubric Student charts should
- show the cultural, economic, and social effects of a recent scientific or technological change.
- display information in a way similar to the chart on page 400.

Here is an example of a possible chart.

Computer Chips

Economic Change	Social Change	Cultural Change
computer manufacturing and services industry	new communication net-works and styles	training for new skills, changes in publications

The World at War 1900–1945

***French Troops Cross the Yser River, 1917,* François Flameng (1856–1923)**

The first half of the 20th century was one of the most violent periods of world history. The first great carnage took place after an assassination in Sarajevo set off a chain reaction that drew nearly every nation in Europe into the bloody conflict of World War I. This watercolor painting shows French troops crossing pontoon bridges on Belgium's Yser River in August 1917.

Flameng's watercolor conveys some of the misery that soldiers endured on World War I's Western Front, which stretched from the North Sea to the Swiss border. It also shows the war's savage effects on the landscape.

The river depicted in the painting flows near the Ypres Salient, where some of the war's most horrifying slaughter took place. The Ypres Salient was a section of Allied-held Belgium projecting into German territory. It posed special dangers, exposing Allied soldiers to shellfire from three—and sometimes four—sides.

There, during the Passchendaele offensive of 1917, tens of thousands of men slogged, hid, fought, died, or disappeared in a landscape transformed by constant shelling and heavy rain. The offensive took its name from the village of Passchendaele, which Allied troops captured at the end of the campaign. Located about five miles east of the campaign's starting point, Passchendaele was won at a cost of at least half a million lives.

World War I was characterized by long, bloody battles. This painting by François Flameng shows one such engagement. French soldiers attempt to cross the River Yser in Belgium on pontoon bridges.

Comparing & Contrasting

The Changing Nature of Warfare
In Unit 4, you will learn about the changing nature of warfare in the 20th century. At the end of the unit, you will have a chance to compare and contrast different aspects of the wars you studied. (See pages 520–525.)

UNIT 4

Previewing the Unit

This unit covers a period of unprecedented violence and social upheaval.

Power and Authority Rivalries among European powers lead to a system of military alliances that, sparked by a political assassination, draws Europe and other regions into World War I. The victors dictate harsh peace terms, causing hard feelings that set the stage for World War II.

Revolution World War I helps ignite the Russian Revolution of 1917, which replaces czarist rule with the first Communist government.

After the fall of the Qing dynasty in China, nationalists and Communists vie for power. Nationalist movements rise in India and Southwest Asia.

New ideas in science, technology, and the arts emerge in the postwar period. The Great Depression of the 1930s brings new political crises. In response to aggression by Fascist Italy and Nazi Germany, Britain and France pursue a policy of appeasement, while the United States follows a path of isolationism.

The expansionism of Germany and Japan leads to World War II. After initial defeats in Europe and the Pacific, the Allies win the war.

Comparing & Contrasting

Tell students that the images, graph, and primary source documents presented in the unit feature on pages 520–525 will help them study the evolution of military technology. The feature will give students a deeper understanding of the conflicts they will read about in Unit 4.

CHAPTER 13 PLANNING GUIDE

The Great War, 1914–1918

CHAPTER RESOURCES	COPYMASTERS	ASSESSMENT
CHAPTER OVERVIEW Several factors led to World War I, a conflict that devastated Europe and had a major impact on the world.	**In-Depth Resources: Unit 4** • Building Vocabulary, p. 5 **Chapters in Brief** (in English and Spanish) **Block Schedule Pacing Guide**	**Chapter Assessment,** pp. 428–429 **Formal Assessment** • Chapter Tests, Forms A, B, and C, pp. 230–241 **Test Generator** **Integrated Assessment Book** **Online Test Practice**
SECTION 1 **Marching Toward War** pp. 407–410 **OBJECTIVE** List factors and events that led to World War I.	**In-Depth Resources: Unit 4** • Guided Reading, p. 1 • Skillbuilder Practice: Summarizing, p. 6 • Primary Source: The Murder of Archduke Franz Ferdinand, p. 9 • History Makers: Wilhelm II, p. 16 • Reteaching Activity, p. 20 **Reading Study Guide,** p. 137	**Section 1 Assessment,** p. 410 **Formal Assessment** • Section Quiz, p. 226 **California Daily Standards Practice Transparencies,** TT110
SECTION 2 **Europe Plunges into War** pp. 411–416 **OBJECTIVE** Describe military actions on the Western and Eastern fronts.	**In-Depth Resources: Unit 4** • Guided Reading, p. 2 • Geography Application: The Battle of the Somme, p. 7 • Primary Source: Poison Gas, p. 10 • Literature: from *All Quiet on the Western Front,* p. 13; "The Soldier" and "Dulce et Decorum Est," p. 15 • Science and Technology: Industrial Technology Creates Poison Gas, p. 19 • Reteaching Activity, p. 21 **Reading Study Guide,** p. 139	**Section 2 Assessment,** p. 415 **Formal Assessment** • Section Quiz, p. 227 **California Daily Standards Practice Transparencies,** TT111
SECTION 3 **A Global Conflict** pp. 417–423 **OBJECTIVE** Summarize the spread of the conflict, the Allies' push to victory, and the effects of the war.	**In-Depth Resources: Unit 4** • Guided Reading, p. 3 • Primary Source: The Zimmermann Note, p. 11 • Reteaching Activity, p. 22 **Reading Study Guide,** p. 141	**Section 3 Assessment,** p. 422 **Formal Assessment** • Section Quiz, p. 228 **California Daily Standards Practice Transparencies,** TT112
SECTION 4 **A Flawed Peace** pp. 424–427 **OBJECTIVE** Explain the Treaty of Versailles and its effects on European powers.	**In-Depth Resources: Unit 4** • Guided Reading, p. 4 • Primary Source: Signing the Treaty of Versailles, p. 12 • History Makers: Georges Clemenceau, p. 17 • Connections Across Time and Cultures: Vienna and Versailles, p. 18 • Reteaching Activity, p. 23 **Reading Study Guide,** p. 143	**Section 4 Assessment,** p. 427 **Formal Assessment** • Section Quiz, p. 229 **California Daily Standards Practice Transparencies,** TT113

INTEGRATED TECHNOLOGY

- eEdition Plus Online
- EasyPlanner Plus Online
- eTest Plus Online

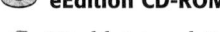

Audio CDs
- Voices from the Past
- Reading Study Guides

 **CD-ROMs**
- eEdition
- Power Presentations
- EasyPlanner
- Electronic Library of Primary Sources
- Test Generator

 **eEdition CD-ROM**

Electronic Library of Primary Sources
- "Death Comes to Sarajevo"

 **classzone.com**

 **eEdition CD-ROM**

 **World Art and Cultures Transparencies**
- AT63 *The Fate of the Animals*
- AT64 L'Assault

Electronic Library of Primary Sources
- "The German Army Marches Through Brussels"

 **classzone.com**

 **eEdition CD-ROM**

  **Critical Thinking Transparencies**
- CT29 The Human and Financial Costs of World War I

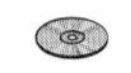  **Electronic Library of Primary Sources**
- "A Suffolk Farmhand at Gallipoli"

  **classzone.com**

 **eEdition CD-ROM**

 **Geography Transparencies**
- GT29 Danzig and the Polish Corridor

 **Critical Thinking Transparencies**
- CT65 Chapter 29 Visual Summary

 **Electronic Library of Primary Sources**
- The Fourteen Points

 **classzone.com**

OVERVIEW OF CALIFORNIA RESOURCES

	Section 1	Section 2	Section 3	Section 4
California Reading Toolkit	p. L58	p. L59	p. L60	p. L61
California Modified Lesson Plans for English Learners	p. 111	p. 113	p. 115	p. 117
California Daily Standards Practice Transparencies	TT50	TT51	TT52	TT53
California Standards Enrichment Workbook	pp. 55–56, 63–64	pp. 57–58	pp. 55–56, 59–60, 61–62, 67–68, 69–70	pp. 65–66, 67–68, 81–82
California Standards Planner and Lesson Plans	p. L107	p. L109	p. L111	p. L113
California Online Test Practice	classzone.com	classzone.com	classzone.com	classzone.com
California Test Generator CD-ROM				
California Easy Planner CD-ROM				
California eEdition CD-ROM				

Chart Key:

 Copymaster

 Pupil's Edition

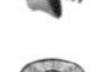 Audio Library

Teacher's Edition

 Overhead Transparency

 CD-ROM

Internet

 Block Scheduling

 Video

NO TIME?

If you do not have time to teach this chapter in full, assign the **Chapter in Brief** (also available in Spanish).

Previewing Resources for Differentiated Instruction

ENGLISH LEARNERS: Resources in Spanish

In-Depth Resources in Spanish
- Guided Reading Ⓐ
- Skillbuilder Practice: Summarizing Ⓑ
- Geography Application: The Battle of the Somme

Chapters in Brief

Reading Study Guide Ⓒ

Reading Study Guide Audio CD

Test Generator CD-ROM
- Chapter Test, Forms A, B, and C

Plus

Modified Lesson Plans for English Learners

Multi-Language Glossary of Social Studies Terms

Ⓐ
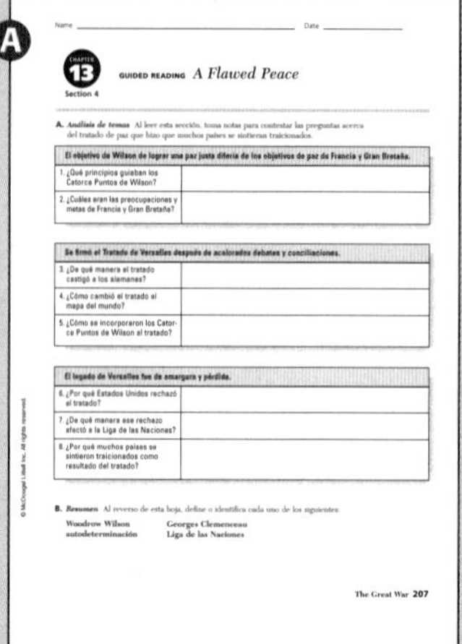

Ⓑ

STRUGGLING READERS

In-Depth Resources: Unit 4
- Guided Reading Ⓐ
- Building Vocabulary
- Skillbuilder Practice: Summarizing
- Geography Application: The Battle of the Somme Ⓑ
- Reteaching Activities

Chapters in Brief

Reading Study Guide

Reading Study Guide Audio CD

Formal Assessment
- Chapter Test, Form A Ⓒ

Plus

Reading Toolkit

Ⓐ
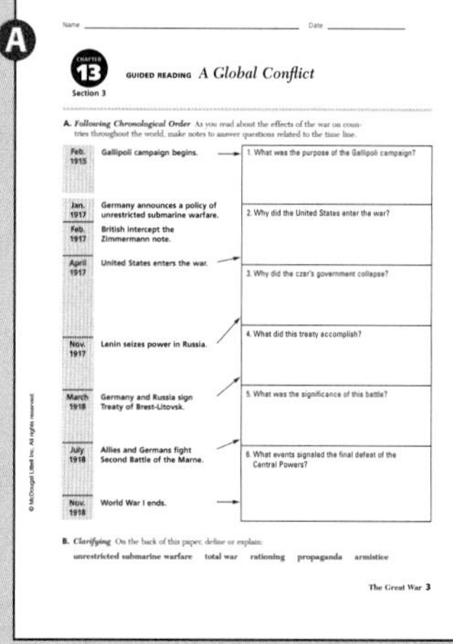

Ⓑ
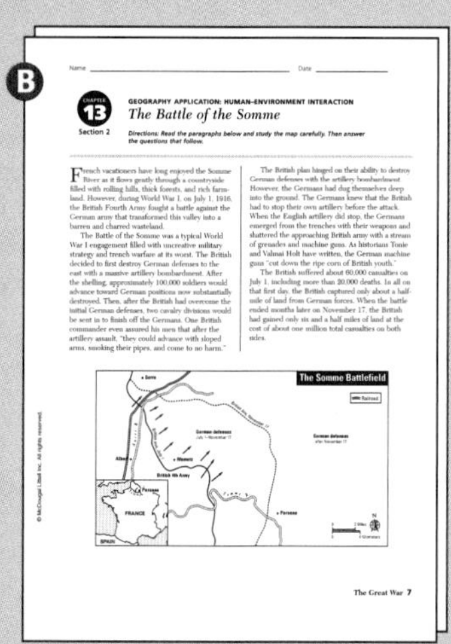

GIFTED AND TALENTED STUDENTS

In-Depth Resources: Unit 4
- Primary Source: The Murder of Archduke Franz Ferdinand; Poison Gas; The Zimmermann Note; Signing the Treaty of Versailles
- Literature: from *All Quiet on the Western Front;* "The Soldier" and "Dulce et Decorum Est" Ⓐ
- History Makers: Wilhelm II; Georges Clemenceau
- Connections Across Time and Cultures: Planning for Peace: Vienna and Versailles
- Science and Technology: Industrial Technology Creates Poison Gas Ⓑ

Electronic Library of Primary Sources
- "Death Comes to Sarajevo"
- "The German Army Marches Through Brussels"
- "A Suffolk Farmhand at Gallipoli"
- The Fourteen Points

Formal Assessment
- Chapter Test, Form C Ⓒ

Ⓐ

Ⓑ

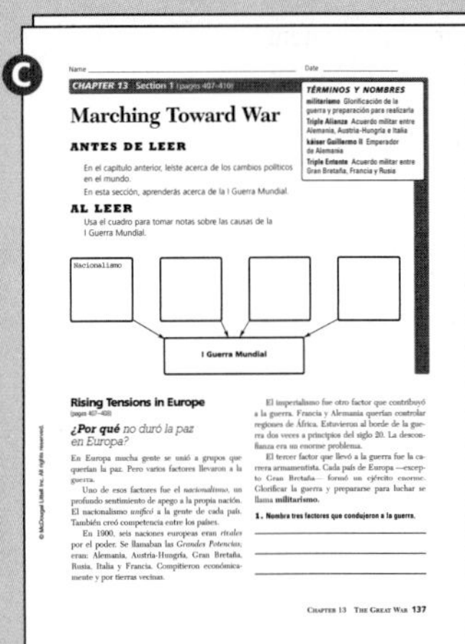

CHAPTER 13 Section 1

Marching Toward War

ANTES DE LEER

AL LEER

I Guerra Mundial

Rising Tensions in Europe

¿Por qué no duró la paz en Europa?

CAPÍTULO 13 THE GREAT WAR 137

Activities in the Teacher's Edition for English Learners

- Analyzing Compound Words, p. 412
- Learning the Vocabulary of War, p. 419

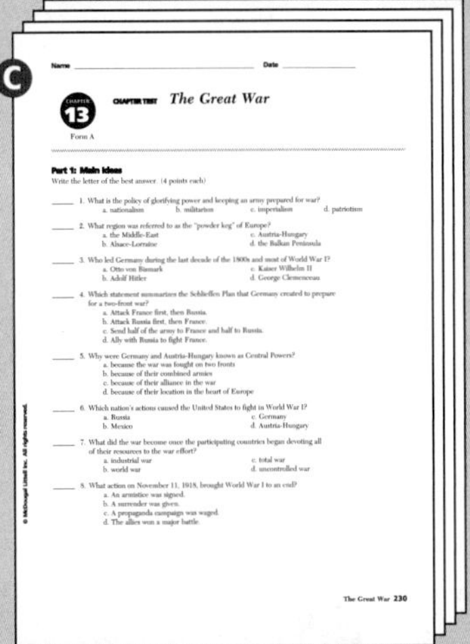

CHAPTER 13 CHAPTER TEST *The Great War*

Form A

Part 1: Main Ideas

The Great War 230

Activities in the Teacher's Edition for Struggling Readers

- Understanding Primary Sources, p. 408
- Analyzing the War on the Eastern Front, p. 414
- Explaining America's Entry into World War I, p. 418
- Understanding the Flawed Peace, p. 426

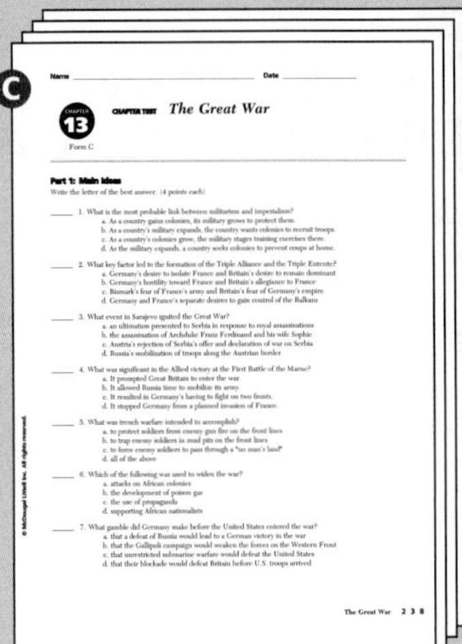

CHAPTER 13 CHAPTER TEST *The Great War*

Form C

Part 1: Main Ideas

The Great War 238

Activities in the Teacher's Edition for Gifted and Talented Students

- The Literature of War, p. 413
- Making a Propaganda Display, p. 420
- Debating the Provisions of the Versailles Treaty, p. 425

INTEGRATED TECHNOLOGY

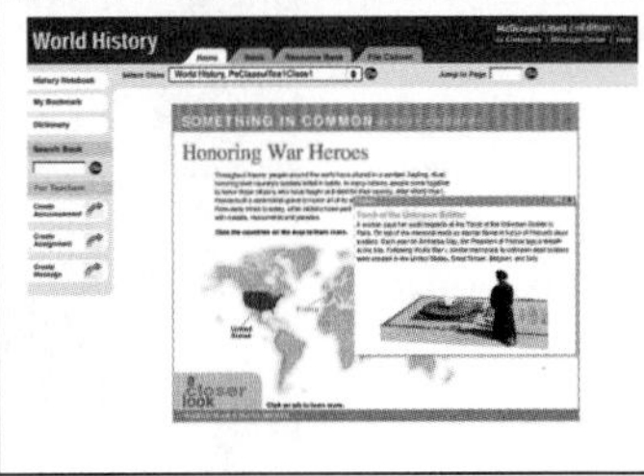

eEdition

- Interactive Visuals
- Interactive Maps
- Interactive Primary Sources

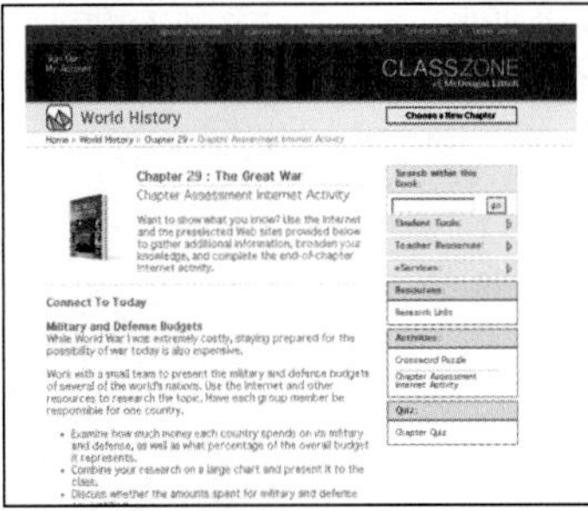

classzone.com

- Research Links
- Internet Activities
- Primary Sources
- Chapter Quiz
- Current Events

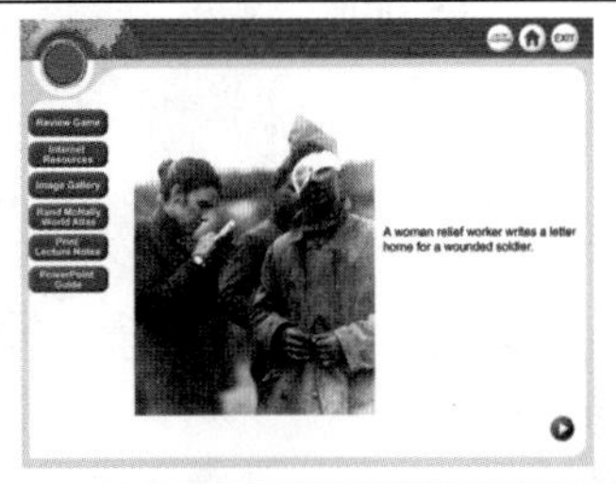

Power Presentations CD-ROM

- Lecture Notes
- Image Gallery
- Chapter Review Game

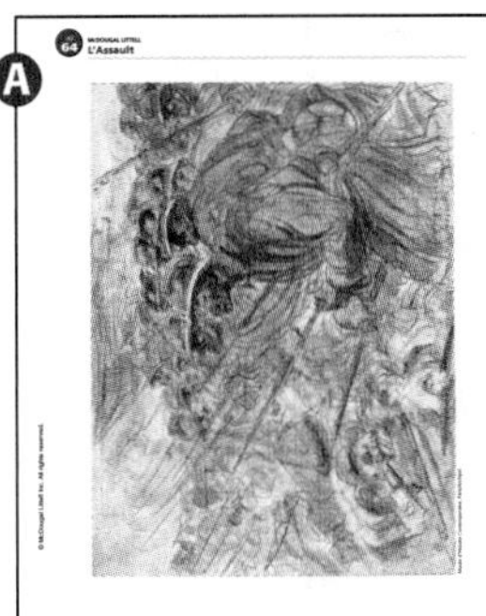

Critical Thinking Transparencies

- CT29 The Human and Financial Costs of World War I
- CT65 Chapter 29 Visual Summary

Geography Transparencies

- GT29 Danzig and the Polish Corridor

World Art and Cultures Transparencies

- AT63 *The Fate of the Animals*
- AT64 *L'Assault* (A)

Test Practice Transparencies TT110–TT113

Test Generator CD-ROM

EasyPlanner CD-ROM

Voices from the Past Audio CD

Online Test Practice

Electronic Library of Primary Sources

CHAPTER 13 • OBJECTIVE

Summarize the causes, events, and effects of World War I.

Previewing Main Ideas

The main ideas that are played out in the First World War continue to characterize the development of the modern world. Science and technology in particular exert an increasingly important influence.

Accessing Prior Knowledge

Ask students why they think World War I is called "The Great War". *(possibly because it was such a global conflict and because there could be no "World War I" until there had been a "World War II")* Have them ask family members to share stories of relatives who may have fought in this war.

Geography *Answers*

SCIENCE AND TECHNOLOGY The United Kingdom was the only nation that the Central Powers could invade only by airplane.

ECONOMICS Most of the land and sea routes to its allies were blocked by enemy positions.

POWER AND AUTHORITY The Central Powers may have had the greater challenge, since they were surrounded by enemies and were forced to divide their forces in a two-front war.

CHAPTER 13

The Great War, 1914–1918

Previewing Main Ideas

SCIENCE AND TECHNOLOGY Advances in weaponry, from improvements to the machine gun and airplane, to the invention of the tank, led to mass devastation during World War I.

Geography *Which Allied nation could the Central Powers invade only by airplane?*

ECONOMICS The war affected many European economies. Desperate for resources, the warring governments converted many industries to munitions factories. They also took greater control of the production of goods.

Geography *According to the map, why might Russia have struggled to obtain resources from its allies?*

POWER AND AUTHORITY The quest among European nations for greater power played a role in causing World War I. By the turn of the 20th century, relations among these countries had grown increasingly tense.

Geography *Which alliance may have had the greater challenge, given the geography of the conflict? Why?*

INTEGRATED TECHNOLOGY

eEdition
- Interactive Maps
- Interactive Visuals
- Interactive Primary Sources

INTERNET RESOURCES
Go to **classzone.com** for:
- Research Links
- Internet Activities
- Primary Sources
- Chapter Quiz
- Maps
- Test Practice
- Current Events

EUROPE

1914
World War I begins as Austria declares war on Serbia.

1915
◀ A World War I soldier readies for battle on the Western Front.

1914 1915

WORLD

1914
U.S.-built Panama Canal opens for operation.

May 1915
◀ German forces sink the British ship *Lusitania.*

404

TIME LINE DISCUSSION

Point out that World War I remained essentially a European conflict until 1917, when the United States joined the Allied Powers.

1. How might the sinking of the *Lusitania* by Germany have influenced the course of World War I? *(It might have intensified hostilities between Britain and Germany.)*
2. What domestic issues did Russia have to deal with in addition to its participation with the Allied Powers in World War I? *(the Russian Revolution and seizure of power by the communists)*
3. Who was president of the United States during World War I? *(Woodrow Wilson)*
4. What activity was the United States involved with in Central America when World War I broke out in Europe? *(completion of the Panama Canal)*
5. What events that occurred during this period added even more fatalities to those caused by a global war? *(the Russian Revolution and widespread outbreak of a deadly flu)*

Europe, 1914

Central Powers
Allied Powers
Nations neutral or not yet aligned

1916
French and Germans engage in battle at Verdun.

1917
U.S. war poster encourages enlistment as America enters war. ▶

1918
Armistice signed as Allies defeat Central Powers.

1916
U.S. President Woodrow Wilson wins reelection. ▶

1917
Communists seize power in Russian Revolution.

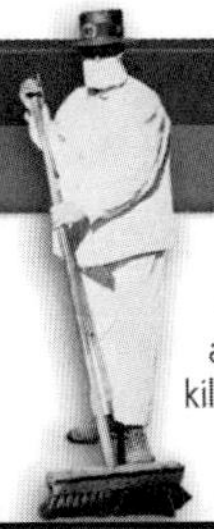

1918
◀ U.S. worker guards against deadly flu that kills millions worldwide.

History from Visuals

Interpreting the Map
Ask students to examine the map carefully. Point out that European countries joined to form two alliances. Based on the information on the map, which alliance controlled the most territory? *(the Allied Powers)* What factor do all the neutral countries except Switzerland and Luxembourg have in common? *(They are all coastal countries with access to major oceans or seas.)* From the French point of view, what was significant about the battle to defend the Marne River? *(Losing that battle would have allowed the Central Powers to penetrate more deeply into French territory.)*

Extension Have students turn to the modern map of Europe in the atlas and compare it with this map. Which countries no longer exist? *(Austria-Hungary, Serbia, Montenegro, Ottoman Empire)* Which new countries have been formed? *(Austria, Czech Republic, Slovakia, Poland, Hungary, Slovenia, Croatia, Macedonia, Lithuania, Latvia, Estonia, Belarus, Ukraine, Serbia and Montenegro, Moldova, Turkey, Finland)*

RECOMMENDED RESOURCES

Books for the Teacher

Dadrian, Vahakn N. ***The History of the Armenian Genocide***. Providence, RI: Berghahn, 1995.

Tuchman, Barbara. ***The Guns of August***. New York: Ballantine, 1994.

Books for the Student

Keegan, John. ***The First World War***. New York: Vintage, 2000. Leads the reader through the complex narrative of World War I.

McDougal Littell, Nextext. ***World War I.*** The story of the war by those who lived through it.

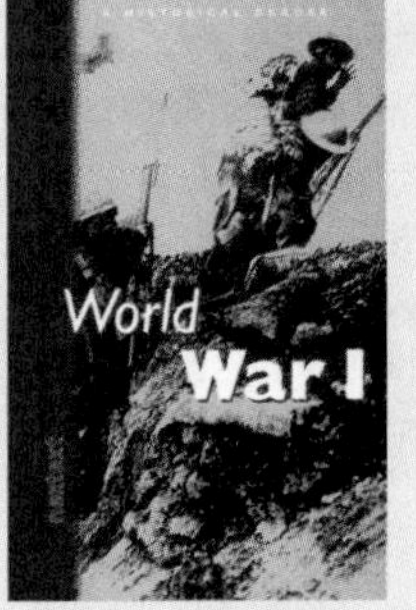

Videos and Software

1914–1919: Shell Shock. VHS and DVD. Films for the Humanities & Sciences, 1999. 800-257-5726. Peter Jennings hosts this look at the psychological impact of World War I.

The Causes of World War I. CD-ROM. Society for Visual Education, 1994. 800-829-1900. Political, economic, and social factors leading to the Great War.

The Shot that Started the Great War. VHS. Library Video Company, 1997. 800-843-3620. Examines the events surrounding the assassination of Archduke Ferdinand and his wife, Sophie.

Interact *with* History

Objectives

- Set the stage for investigation of World War I.
- Highlight some events and issues associated with the war.

EXAMINING *the* ISSUES

Possible Answers

- Yes—Friendship means supporting a friend, no matter what; No—Maintaining one's own beliefs and morals is more important than supporting a friend who acts against them.
- A nation or person might gain a reputation for disloyalty and lose the support of allies and friends in the future.

Discussion

Ask students what reasons for going to war might justify the death and destruction that inevitably result. *(Possible Answers: seizure of land, imprisonment or enslavement of one people by another, injustice or inhumanity of one country against its own or other people)*

Interact *with* History

Should you always support an ally?

World War I has begun. You are the leader of a European country and must decide what to do. Your nation is one of several that have agreed to support each other in the event of war. Some of your allies already have joined the fight. You oppose the thought of war and fear that joining will lead to even more lives lost. Yet, you believe in being loyal to your allies. You also worry that your rivals want to conquer all of Europe—and if you don't join the war now, your country may end up having to defend itself.

▲ A World War I poster urges nations to come to the aid of Serbia.

EXAMINING *the* ISSUES

- **Should you always support a friend, no matter what he or she does?**
- **What might be the long-term consequences of refusing to help an ally?**

As a class, discuss these questions. In your discussion, consider the various reasons countries go to war. As you read about World War I in this chapter, see what factors influenced the decisions of each nation.

WHY STUDY THE GREAT WAR?

- Territorial and political conflicts similar to those that led to World War I are still at work today.
- The interaction of World War I alliances offers lessons for a complex and fast-changing world.
- The development of new and destructive combat technology continues to drive conflicts—and keep them at a stalemate—creating a delicate balance in the 21st century.
- The long war with participation from around the globe opened the door for even greater and more global wars.
- Widely based wars such as World War I caused people to re-examine nationalism and national values.
- Bloody conflicts such as this one forced people to examine their values and beliefs with respect to aggression and use of deadly force.

American troops staging a gas attack to show ill effects of forgetting a gas mask, 1918

E. F. Skinner, *For King and Country* *(women in munitions factory)*

1

Marching Toward War

MAIN IDEA

POWER AND AUTHORITY In Europe, military buildup, nationalistic feelings, and rival alliances set the stage for a continental war.

WHY IT MATTERS NOW

Ethnic conflict in the Balkan region, which helped start the war, continued to erupt in that area in the 1990s.

TERMS & NAMES

- militarism
- Triple Alliance
- Kaiser Wilhelm II
- Triple Entente

SETTING THE STAGE At the turn of the 20th century, the nations of Europe had been largely at peace with one another for nearly 30 years. This was no accident. Efforts to outlaw war and achieve a permanent peace had been gaining momentum in Europe since the middle of the 19th century. By 1900, hundreds of peace organizations were active. In addition, peace congresses convened regularly between 1843 and 1907. Some Europeans believed that progress had made war a thing of the past. Yet in a little more than a decade, a massive war would engulf Europe and spread across the globe.

CALIFORNIA STANDARDS

10.5.1 Analyze the arguments for entering into war presented by leaders from all sides of the Great War and the role of political and economic rivalries, ethnic and ideological conflicts, domestic discontent and disorder, and propaganda and nationalism in mobilizing the civilian population in support of "total war."

10.5.5 Discuss human rights violations and genocide, including the Ottoman government's actions against Armenian citizens.

HI 1 Students show the connections, causal and otherwise, between particular historical events and larger social, economic, and political trends and developments.

Rising Tensions in Europe

While peace and harmony characterized much of Europe at the beginning of the 1900s, there were less visible—and darker—forces at work as well. Below the surface of peace and goodwill, Europe witnessed several gradual developments that would ultimately help propel the continent into war.

The Rise of Nationalism One such development was the growth of nationalism, or a deep devotion to one's nation. Nationalism can serve as a unifying force within a country. However, it also can cause intense competition among nations, with each seeking to overpower the other. By the turn of the 20th century, a fierce rivalry indeed had developed among Europe's Great Powers. Those nations were Germany, Austria-Hungary, Great Britain, Russia, Italy, and France.

This increasing rivalry among European nations stemmed from several sources. Competition for materials and markets was one. Territorial disputes were another. France, for example, had never gotten over the loss of Alsace-Lorraine to Germany in the Franco-Prussian War (1870). Austria-Hungary and Russia both tried to dominate in the Balkans, a region in southeast Europe. Within the Balkans, the intense nationalism of Serbs, Bulgarians, Romanians, and other ethnic groups led to demands for independence.

Imperialism and Militarism Another force that helped set the stage for war in Europe was imperialism. As Chapter 11 explained, the nations of Europe competed fiercely for colonies in Africa and Asia. The quest for colonies sometimes pushed European nations to the brink of war. As European countries continued to compete for overseas empires, their sense of rivalry and mistrust of one another deepened.

TAKING NOTES

Summarizing Create a time line of major events that led to the start of World War I.

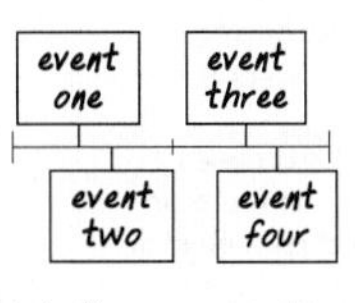

LESSON PLAN

OBJECTIVES

- Identify the political and military forces at work in Europe in the late 1800s.
- List the countries that made up the Triple Alliance and the Triple Entente.
- Summarize the events that set World War I in motion.

1 FOCUS & MOTIVATE

Ask students to discuss situations in which they formed alliances with others. How did they go about enlisting people in their cause? *(Possible Answers: convincing them of its rightness or of the consequences of remaining unallied)*

2 INSTRUCT

Rising Tensions in Europe

10.5.1

Critical Thinking

- How do imperialism and militarism work together to promote war? *(Militarism gives a nation the means to carry out its imperialistic aims of taking over other nations.)*

CALIFORNIA RESOURCES

California Reading Toolkit, p. L58
California Modified Lesson Plans for English Learners, p. 111
California Daily Standards Practice Transparencies, TT50
California Standards Enrichment Workbook, pp. 55–56, 63–64
California Standards Planner and Lesson Plans, p. L107
California Online Test Practice
California Test Generator CD-ROM
California Easy Planner CD-ROM
California eEdition CD-ROM

SECTION 1 PROGRAM RESOURCES

ALL STUDENTS

In-Depth Resources: Unit 4
- Guided Reading, p. 1
- Skillbuilder Practice: Summarizing, p. 6
- History Makers: Wilhelm II, p. 16

Formal Assessment
- Section Quiz, p. 226

ENGLISH LEARNERS

In-Depth Resources in Spanish
- Guided Reading, p. 103
- Skillbuilder Practice, p. 107

Reading Study Guide (Spanish), p. 137

Reading Study Guide Audio CD (Spanish)

STRUGGLING READERS

In-Depth Resources: Unit 4
- Guided Reading, p. 1
- Building Vocabulary, p. 5
- Skillbuilder Practice: Summarizing, p. 6
- Reteaching Activity, p. 20

Reading Study Guide, p. 137
Reading Study Guide Audio CD

GIFTED AND TALENTED STUDENTS

In-Depth Resources: Unit 4
- Primary Source: The Murder of Archduke Franz Ferdinand, p. 9

Electronic Library of Primary Sources
- "Death Comes to Sarajevo"

INTEGRATED TECHNOLOGY

eEdition CD-ROM
Voices from the Past Audio CD
Power Presentations CD-ROM
Electronic Library of Primary Sources
- "Death Comes to Sarajevo"

classzone.com

More About . . .

Militarism

By 1914, the standing armies of European nations included the following numbers of soldiers: Germany—4.5 million; Russia—5.9 million; France—4.2 million; Austria-Hungary—3 million. Britain had a navy nearly as large as the other navies combined.

Tangled Alliances

10.5.1

Critical Thinking

- What did Bismarck mean by calling Germany "a satisfied power"? *(that it had no further imperialistic aims)*
- How could a dispute between the Triple Alliance and the Triple Entente draw all of Europe into the conflict? *(by forcing the other countries to take sides in self-defense)*

History Makers

Kaiser Wilhelm II

What does Wilhelm II's deceitfulness say about his values? *(Possible Answer: Any means to power was justified.)* Wilhelm's extreme arrogance may have partly stemmed from his disability, a shriveled left arm.

In-Depth Resources: Unit 4

- History Makers: Wilhelm II, p. 16

Yet another troubling development throughout the early years of the 20th century was the rise of a dangerous European arms race. The nations of Europe believed that to be truly great, they needed to have a powerful military. By 1914, all the Great Powers except Britain had large standing armies. In addition, military experts stressed the importance of being able to quickly mobilize, or organize and move troops in case of a war. Generals in each country developed highly detailed plans for such a mobilization.

The policy of glorifying military power and keeping an army prepared for war was known as **militarism**. Having a large and strong standing army made citizens feel patriotic. However, it also frightened some people. As early as 1895, Frédéric Passy, a prominent peace activist, expressed a concern that many shared:

PRIMARY SOURCE

The entire able-bodied population are preparing to massacre one another; though no one, it is true, wants to attack, and everybody protests his love of peace and determination to maintain it, yet the whole world feels that it only requires some unforeseen incident, some unpreventable accident, for the spark to fall in a flash . . . and blow all Europe sky-high.

FRÉDÉRIC PASSY, quoted in *Nobel: The Man and His Prizes*

History Makers

Kaiser Wilhelm II
1859–1941

Wilhelm II was related to the leaders of two nations he eventually would engage in war. Wilhelm, George V of Great Britain, and Nicholas II of Russia were all cousins.

The kaiser thought a great deal of himself and his place in history. Once, when a doctor told him he had a small cold, Wilhelm reportedly responded, "No, it is a big cold. Everything about me must be big."

He also could be sly and deceitful. After forcing the popular Bismarck to resign, Wilhelm pretended to be upset. Most people, however, including Bismarck, were not fooled.

INTEGRATED TECHNOLOGY

RESEARCH LINKS For more on Wilhelm II, go to **classzone.com**

Tangled Alliances

Growing rivalries and mutual mistrust had led to the creation of several military alliances among the Great Powers as early as the 1870s. This alliance system had been designed to keep peace in Europe. But it would instead help push the continent into war.

Bismarck Forges Early Pacts Between 1864 and 1871, Prussia's blood-and-iron chancellor, Otto von Bismarck, freely used war to unify Germany. After 1871, however, Bismarck declared Germany to be a "satisfied power." He then turned his energies to maintaining peace in Europe.

Bismarck saw France as the greatest threat to peace. He believed that France still wanted revenge for its defeat in the Franco-Prussian War. Bismarck's first goal, therefore, was to isolate France. "As long as it is without allies," Bismarck stressed, "France poses no danger to us." In 1879, Bismarck formed the Dual Alliance between Germany and Austria-Hungary. Three years later, Italy joined the two countries, forming the **Triple Alliance**. In 1881, Bismarck took yet another possible ally away from France by making a treaty with Russia.

Shifting Alliances Threaten Peace In 1890, Germany's foreign policy changed dramatically. That year, **Kaiser Wilhelm II**—who two years earlier had become ruler of Germany—forced Bismarck to resign. A proud and stubborn man, Wilhelm II did not wish to share power with anyone. Besides wanting to assert his own power, the new kaiser was eager to show the world just how mighty Germany had become. The army was his greatest pride. "I and the army were born for one another," Wilhelm declared shortly after taking power.

DIFFERENTIATING INSTRUCTION: STRUGGLING READERS

Understanding Primary Sources

Class Time 20 minutes

Task Restating primary source material in everyday language

Purpose To grasp Frédéric Passy's ideas

Instructions Divide students into groups. Have a volunteer from each group read the Passy quotation aloud. Then have the group members discuss the main idea he is trying to get across. Instruct them to then return to the Primary Source quotation and restate the main idea of each phrase in their own words. After the groups are finished, have them share their restatements with the class and create a combined chart listing both Passy's original statements and their coordinated restatements. Completed charts may look like this:

Original Phrase	Restatement
1. The entire able-bodied population are preparing to massacre one another; though no one, it is true, wants to attack	1. People want to kill each other, but don't want to act first.
2. and everybody protests his love of peace and determination to maintain it	2. They say they want to keep peace.
3. yet the whole world feels that it only requires some unforeseen incident, some unpreventable accident, for the spark to fall in a flash and blow all Europe sky-high	3. They think that any small event could set off a war in Europe.

Wilhelm let his nation's treaty with Russia lapse in 1890. Russia responded by forming a defensive military alliance with France in 1892 and 1894. Such an alliance had been Bismarck's fear. War with either Russia or France would make Germany the enemy of both. Germany would then be forced to fight a two-front war, or a war on both its eastern and western borders.

Next, Wilhelm began a tremendous shipbuilding program in an effort to make the German navy equal to that of the mighty British fleet. Alarmed, Great Britain formed an entente, or alliance, with France. In 1907, Britain made another entente, this time with both France and Russia. The **Triple Entente**, as it was called, did not bind Britain to fight with France and Russia. However, it did almost certainly ensure that Britain would not fight against them.

By 1907, two rival camps existed in Europe. On one side was the Triple Alliance—Germany, Austria-Hungary, and Italy. On the other side was the Triple Entente—Great Britain, France, and Russia. A dispute between two rival powers could draw all the nations of Europe into war.

Crisis in the Balkans

Nowhere was that dispute more likely to occur than on the Balkan Peninsula. This mountainous peninsula in the southeastern corner of Europe was home to an assortment of ethnic groups. With a long history of nationalist uprisings and ethnic clashes, the Balkans was known as the "powder keg" of Europe.

A Restless Region By the early 1900s, the Ottoman Empire, which included the Balkan region, was in rapid decline. While some Balkan groups struggled to free themselves from the Ottoman Turks, others already had succeeded in breaking away from their Turkish rulers. These peoples had formed new nations, including Bulgaria, Greece, Montenegro, Romania, and Serbia.

Nationalism was a powerful force in these countries. Each group longed to extend its borders. Serbia, for example, had a large Slavic population. It hoped to absorb all the Slavs on the Balkan Peninsula. Russia, itself a mostly Slavic nation, supported Serbian nationalism. However, Serbia's powerful northern neighbor, Austria-Hungary, opposed such an effort. Austria feared that efforts to create a Slavic state would stir rebellion among its Slavic population.

In 1908, Austria annexed, or took over, Bosnia and Herzegovina. These were two Balkan areas with large Slavic populations. Serbian leaders, who had sought to rule these provinces, were outraged. In the years that followed, tensions between Serbia and Austria steadily rose. The Serbs continually vowed to take Bosnia and Herzegovina away from Austria. In response, Austria-Hungary vowed to crush any Serbian effort to undermine its authority in the Balkans. **A**

A. Answer Austria-Hungary feared that Serbia's growth would incite Slavic peoples within its own territory; Serbia resented Austria-Hungary's annexation of Bosnia and Herzegovina.

MAIN IDEA

Analyzing Issues

A What were the reasons for the hostility between Austria-Hungary and Serbia?

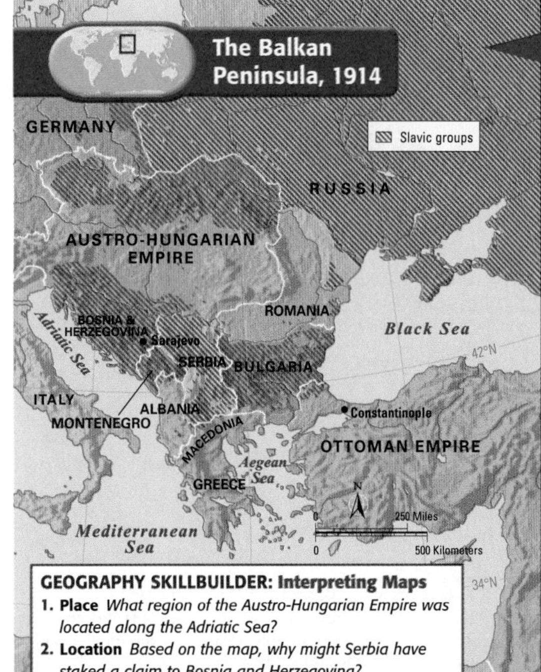

GEOGRAPHY SKILLBUILDER: Interpreting Maps

1. **Place** *What region of the Austro-Hungarian Empire was located along the Adriatic Sea?*
2. **Location** *Based on the map, why might Serbia have staked a claim to Bosnia and Herzegovina?*

Crisis in the Balkans

10.5.1

Critical Thinking

- How did nationalism contribute to the unrest in the Balkans? *(by motivating ethnic groups to fight for their territory)*
- What act by Austria-Hungary set the world on the path to war? *(annexation of Bosnia and Herzegovina)*

In-Depth Resources: Unit 4

- Primary Source: The Murder of Archduke Franz Ferdinand, p. 9

Electronic Library of Primary Sources

- "Death Comes to Sarajevo"

History from Visuals

Interpreting the Map

Have students study the map and examine the areas where Slavic groups lived.

Extension Ask students to discuss why Austria-Hungary wanted to annex Bosnia and Herzegovina. *(wanted to add areas of Slavic population to their territory)*

SKILLBUILDER Answers

1. **Place** Bosnia and Herzegovina
2. **Location** a common Slavic population

SKILLBUILDER PRACTICE: SUMMARIZING

Summarizing Main Ideas

Class Time 25 minutes

Task Identifying and restating the main ideas of a passage

Purpose To foster understanding and memory of ideas

Instructions Explain to students that summarizing is restating and condensing a passage by identifying the main ideas and putting them in different words. Stress that it is important for summaries to include words other than those of the original passage. A summary that used the same words as the original source without giving credit to that source would be seen as plagiarism. Inform students that summarizing material can help them clarify and remember it.

Then hand out copies of page 6 from In-Depth Resources: Unit 4. Ask students to work in pairs to summarize the passages provided. A sample summary follows:

Summary

Some Americans reacted against the war because of personal ties to European countries, because they saw it as a fight for economic power between Britain and Germany, because they hated war in general, or because they were reluctant to have their families involved. Supporters wanted to honor their cultural ties with Britain and maintain their trade relationship with Britain and France.

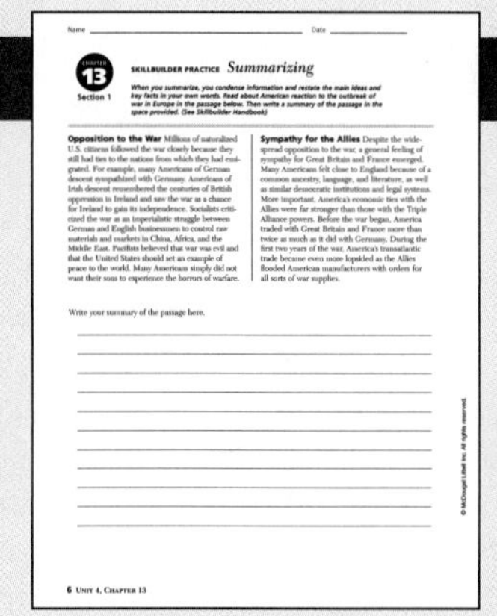
Name ______ Date ______

CHAPTER 13 Section 1

SKILLBUILDER PRACTICE *Summarizing*

When you summarize, you condense information and restate the main ideas and key facts in your own words. Read about American reaction to the outbreak of war in Europe in the passage below. Then write a summary of the passage in the space provided. (See Skillbuilder Handbook)

Opposition to the War Millions of naturalized U.S. citizens followed the war closely because they still had ties to the nations from which they had emigrated. For example, many Americans of German descent sympathized with Germany. Americans of Irish descent remembered the centuries of British oppression in Ireland and saw the war as a chance for Ireland to gain its independence. Socialists criticized the war as an imperialistic struggle between German and English businessmen to control raw materials and markets in China, Africa, and the Middle East. Pacifists believed that war was evil and that the United States should set an example of peace to the world. Many Americans simply did not want their sons to experience the horrors of warfare.

Sympathy for the Allies Despite the widespread opposition to the war, a general feeling of sympathy for Great Britain and France emerged. Many Americans felt close to England because of a common ancestry, language, and literature, as well as similar democratic institutions and legal systems. More important, America's economic ties with the Allies were far stronger than those with the Triple Alliance powers. Before the war began, America traded with Great Britain and France more than twice as much as it did with Germany. During the first two years of the war, America's transatlantic trade became even more lopsided as the Allies flooded American manufacturers with orders for all sorts of war supplies.

Write your summary of the passage here.

6 UNIT 4, CHAPTER 13

In-Depth Resources: Unit 4

History *in* Depth

The Armenian Massacre

Between 1915 and 1916, at least 600,000 Armenians died at the hands of the Turks. They were shot, tortured to death, or starved in concentration camps. Sometimes they were loaded onto barges and then thrown overboard. The Ottomans tried to justify this genocide by saying that the Armenians sided with Russia. Today, the government of Turkey claims that 300,000 died in deportation.

INTEGRATED TECHNOLOGY

Rubric Charts or graphics should

- identify the aspect of Armenian culture being described.
- include clear labels for each element.

3 ASSESS

SECTION 1 ASSESSMENT

Have students complete the assessment individually and exchange papers with a partner to check their answers.

Formal Assessment

- Section Quiz, p. 226

4 RETEACH

Have students share with the class the lead paragraphs they wrote in answer to item 2 in the Section Assessment.

In-Depth Resources: Unit 4

- Reteaching Activity, p. 20

History *in* Depth

The Armenian Massacre

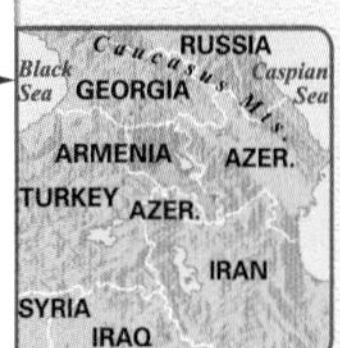

One group in southeastern Europe that suffered greatly for its independence efforts was the Armenians. By the 1880s, the roughly 2.5 million Armenians in the Ottoman Empire had begun to demand their freedom. As a result, relations between the group and its Turkish rulers grew strained.

Throughout the 1890s, Turkish troops killed tens of thousands of Armenians. When World War I erupted in 1914, the Armenians pledged their support to the Turks' enemies. In response, the Turkish government deported nearly 2 million Armenians. Along the way, more than 600,000 died of starvation or were killed by Turkish soldiers.

INTEGRATED TECHNOLOGY

INTERNET ACTIVITY Create a chart or graphic about any aspect of modern Armenian culture. Go to **classzone.com** for your research.

A Shot Rings Throughout Europe Into this poisoned atmosphere of mutual dislike and mistrust stepped the heir to the Austro-Hungarian throne, Archduke Franz Ferdinand, and his wife, Sophie. On June 28, 1914, the couple paid a state visit to Sarajevo, the capital of Bosnia. It would be their last. The royal pair was shot at point-blank range as they rode through the streets of Sarajevo in an open car. The killer was Gavrilo Princip, a 19-year-old Serbian and member of the Black Hand. The Black Hand was a secret society committed to ridding Bosnia of Austrian rule.

Because the assassin was a Serbian, Austria decided to use the murders as an excuse to punish Serbia. On July 23, Austria presented Serbia with an ultimatum containing numerous demands. Serbia knew that refusing the ultimatum would lead to war against the more powerful Austria. Therefore, Serbian leaders agreed to most of Austria's demands. They offered to have several others settled by an international conference.

Vocabulary
An *ultimatum* is a list of demands that, if not met, will lead to serious consequences.

Austria, however, was in no mood to negotiate. The nation's leaders, it seemed, had already settled on war. On July 28, Austria rejected Serbia's offer and declared war. That same day, Russia, an ally of Serbia with its largely Slavic population, took action. Russian leaders ordered the mobilization of troops toward the Austrian border.

Leaders all over Europe suddenly took notice. The fragile European stability seemed ready to collapse into armed conflict. The British foreign minister, the Italian government, and even Kaiser Wilhelm himself urged Austria and Russia to negotiate. But it was too late. The machinery of war had been set in motion.

SECTION 1 ASSESSMENT

TERMS & NAMES 1. For each term or name, write a sentence explaining its significance.
- militarism
- Triple Alliance
- Kaiser Wilhelm II
- Triple Entente

USING YOUR NOTES

2. Which event do you consider most significant? Why? (10.5.1)

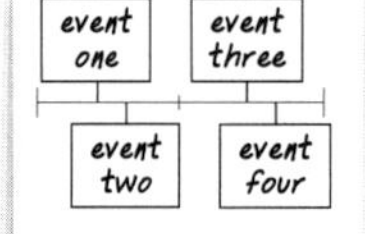

MAIN IDEAS

3. What were the three forces at work in Europe that helped set the stage for war? (10.5.1)
4. Who were the members of the Triple Alliance? the Triple Entente? (10.5.1)
5. What single event set in motion the start of World War I? (10.5.1)

CRITICAL THINKING & WRITING

6. **ANALYZING CAUSES** Which of the forces at work in Europe played the greatest role in helping to prompt the outbreak of war? (10.5.1)
7. **ANALYZING ISSUES** Was the description of the Balkans as the "powder keg" of Europe justified? Explain. (10.5.1)
8. **FORMING AND SUPPORTING OPINIONS** Do you think World War I was avoidable? Support your answer. (10.5.1)
9. **WRITING ACTIVITY** POWER AND AUTHORITY Write a brief **letter to the editor** of a European newspaper about what your views might have been on the coming war. (Writing 2.5.b)

CONNECT TO TODAY **CREATING A TIME LINE**

Working with a partner, use the library and other resources to create a **time line** of key events in the Balkans from 1914 until today. Limit your time line to the six to eight events you consider most significant. (Writing 2.2.d)

ANSWERS

1. militarism, p. 408 • Triple Alliance, p. 408 • Kaiser Wilhelm II, p. 408 • Triple Entente, p. 409
2. **Sample Answer:** Events—rise of European nationalism, imperialism, arms race, Bismarck's unification of Germany, formation of Triple Alliance, Wilhelm II's shipbuilding program, formation of Triple Entente, Austria-Hungary's annexation of Bosnia and Herzegovina, assassination of Archduke Franz Ferdinand. Archduke's assassination, because it ignited the smoldering embers of war
3. nationalism, imperialism, militarism
4. Triple Alliance—Germany, Austria-Hungary, Italy; Triple Entente—Great Britain, France, Russia
5. the assassination of Archduke Franz Ferdinand
6. Nationalism or imperialism—intensified the competition among nations; Militarism—led to arms buildup that made large-scale war possible
7. **Possible Answer:** justified because of the hostility and conflict among its many ethnic groups
8. No—too many powerful forces at work to stop the war; Yes—Nations could have heeded the call for negotiation and compromise.
9. **Rubric** Letters to the editor should
- clearly express the student's opinion.
- be supported by facts and details.
- be well written and organized.

CONNECT TO TODAY

Rubric Time lines should
- include key events in Balkan history.
- be well structured and easy to follow.

American troops staging a gas attack to show ill effects of forgetting a gas mask, 1918

E. F. Skinner, *For King and Country* *(women in munitions factory)*

2

Europe Plunges into War

MAIN IDEA

SCIENCE AND TECHNOLOGY One European nation after another was drawn into a large and industrialized war that resulted in many casualties.

WHY IT MATTERS NOW

Much of the technology of modern warfare, such as fighter planes and tanks, was introduced in World War I.

TERMS & NAMES

- Central Powers
- Allies
- Western Front
- Schlieffen Plan
- trench warfare
- Eastern Front

SETTING THE STAGE By 1914, Europe was divided into two rival camps. One alliance, the Triple Entente, included Great Britain, France, and Russia. The other, known as the Triple Alliance, included Germany, Austria-Hungary, and Italy. Austria-Hungary's declaration of war against Serbia set off a chain reaction within the alliance system. The countries of Europe followed through on their pledges to support one another. As a result, nearly all of Europe soon joined what would be the largest, most destructive war the world had yet seen.

The Great War Begins

In response to Austria's declaration of war, Russia, Serbia's ally, began moving its army toward the Russian-Austrian border. Expecting Germany to join Austria, Russia also mobilized along the German border. To Germany, Russia's mobilization amounted to a declaration of war. On August 1, the German government declared war on Russia.

Russia looked to its ally France for help. Germany, however, did not even wait for France to react. Two days after declaring war on Russia, Germany also declared war on France. Soon afterward, Great Britain declared war on Germany. Much of Europe was now locked in battle.

Nations Take Sides By mid-August 1914, the battle lines were clearly drawn. On one side were Germany and Austria-Hungary. They were known as the **Central Powers** because of their location in the heart of Europe. Bulgaria and the Ottoman Empire would later join the Central Powers in the hopes of regaining lost territories.

On the other side were Great Britain, France, and Russia. Together, they were known as the Allied Powers or the **Allies**. Japan joined the Allies within weeks. Italy joined later. Italy had been a member of the Triple Alliance with Germany and Austria-Hungary. However, the Italians joined the other side after accusing their former partners of unjustly starting the war.

In the late summer of 1914, millions of soldiers marched happily off to battle, convinced that the war would be short. Only a few people foresaw the horror ahead. One of them was Britain's foreign minister, Sir Edward Grey. Staring out over London at nightfall, Grey said sadly to a friend, "The lamps are going out all over Europe. We shall not see them lit again in our lifetime."

CALIFORNIA STANDARDS

10.5.2 Examine the principal theaters of battle, major turning points, and the importance of geographic factors in military decisions and outcomes (e.g., topography, waterways, distance, climate).

CST 2 Students analyze how change happens at different rates at different times; understand that some aspects can change while others remain the same; and understand that change is complicated and affects not only technology and politics but also values and beliefs.

CST 3 Students use a variety of maps and documents to interpret human movement, including major patterns of domestic and international migration, changing environmental preferences and settlement patterns, the frictions that develop between population groups, and the diffusion of ideas, technological innovations, and goods.

HI 4 Students understand the meaning, implication, and impact of historical events and recognize that events could have taken other directions.

TAKING NOTES

Outlining Use an outline to organize main ideas and details.

I. The Great War Begins
  A.
  B.
II. A Bloody Stalemate

LESSON PLAN

OBJECTIVES

- Describe the reaction to Austria's declaration of war.
- Summarize military events on the Western Front.
- Explain the development of the war on the Eastern Front.

1 FOCUS & MOTIVATE

Have students share any information they have from literature or movies about World War I. *(They may describe scenes from Erich Maria Remarque's* All Quiet on the Western Front.*)*

2 INSTRUCT

The Great War Begins
10.5.2

Critical Thinking

- Why did Germany declare war on France? *(It assumed France would align with Russia against the Central Powers.)*

Electronic Library of Primary Sources

- "The German Army Marches Through Brussels"

CALIFORNIA RESOURCES

California Reading Toolkit, p. L59
California Modified Lesson Plans for English Learners, p. 113
California Daily Standards Practice Transparencies, TT51
California Standards Enrichment Workbook, pp. 57–58
California Standards Planner and Lesson Plans, p. L109
California Online Test Practice
California Test Generator CD-ROM
California Easy Planner CD-ROM
California eEdition CD-ROM

SECTION 2 PROGRAM RESOURCES

ALL STUDENTS

In-Depth Resources: Unit 4
- Guided Reading, p. 2
- Geography Application: The Battle of the Somme, p. 7

Formal Assessment
- Section Quiz, p. 227

ENGLISH LEARNERS

In-Depth Resources in Spanish
- Guided Reading, p. 104
- Geography Application, p. 108

Reading Study Guide (Spanish), p. 139
Reading Study Guide Audio CD (Spanish)

STRUGGLING READERS

In-Depth Resources: Unit 4
- Guided Reading, p. 2
- Building Vocabulary, p. 5
- Reteaching Activity, p. 21

Reading Study Guide, p. 139
Reading Study Guide Audio CD

GIFTED AND TALENTED STUDENTS

In-Depth Resources: Unit 4
- Primary Source: Poison Gas, p. 10
- Literature: from *All Quiet on Western Front,* p. 13; "The Soldier" and "Dulce et Decorum Est," p. 15
- Science & Technology, p. 19

Electronic Library of Primary Sources
- "The German Army Marches Through Brussels"

INTEGRATED TECHNOLOGY

eEdition CD-ROM
Power Presentations CD-ROM
World Art and Cultures Transparencies
- AT63 *The Fate of the Animals*
- AT64 L'Assault

Electronic Library of Primary Sources
classzone.com

History from Visuals

Interpreting the Map

Have students examine the map and note the countries of northern Europe that remained neutral. *(Norway, Sweden, Denmark)*

Extension Ask students why they think Germany violated Belgium's neutrality but not that of the Netherlands or Switzerland. *(Possible Answer: The Netherlands does not border France, and the Germans planned to move west through France away from Switzerland.)*

SKILLBUILDER Answers

1. **Location** France
2. **Location** They were located between the Allies and had to split their forces between western and eastern fronts.

INTEGRATED TECHNOLOGY

Interactive Students can view this map in detail on the eEdition.

A Bloody Stalemate

10.5.2

Critical Thinking

- Why did Germany attack France first? *(It was better prepared for war than Russia was.)*
- Why were land gains so small? *(The sides were closely matched.)*

In-Depth Resources: Unit 4

- Geography Application: The Battle of the Somme, p. 7
- Primary Source: Poison Gas, p. 10

World Art and Cultures Transparencies

- AT63 *The Fate of the Animals*

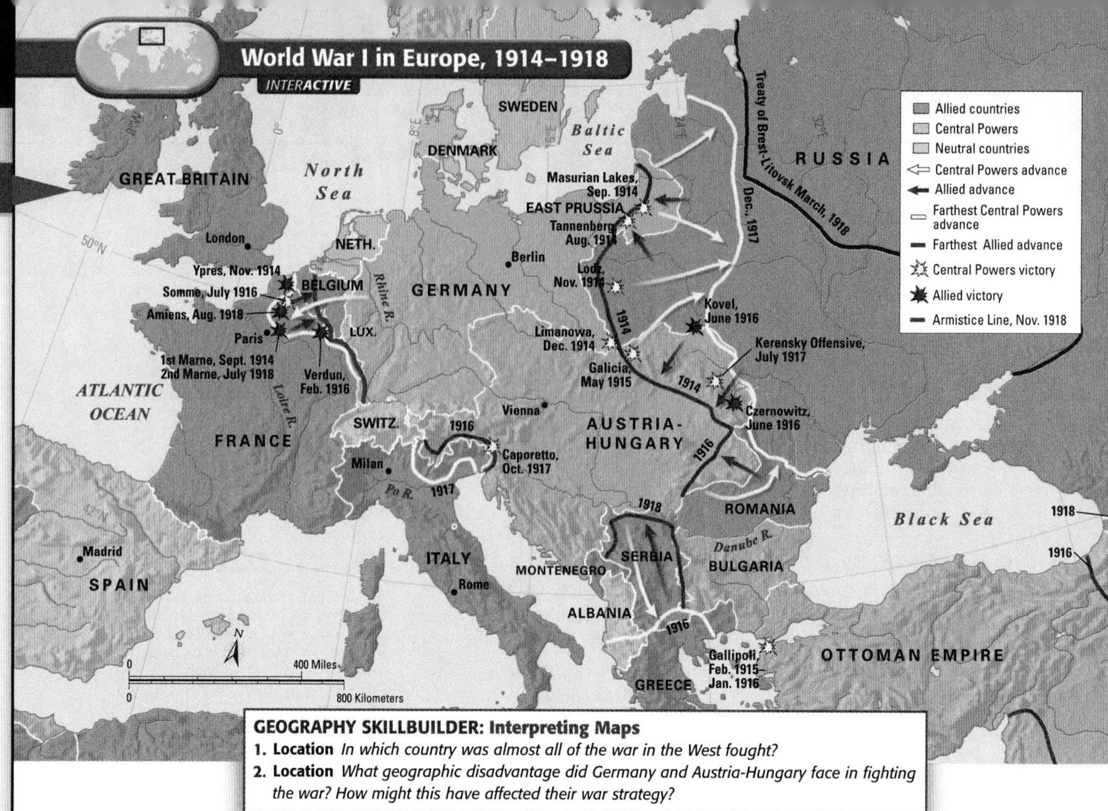

GEOGRAPHY SKILLBUILDER: Interpreting Maps

1. **Location** *In which country was almost all of the war in the West fought?*
2. **Location** *What geographic disadvantage did Germany and Austria-Hungary face in fighting the war? How might this have affected their war strategy?*

A Bloody Stalemate

It did not take long for Sir Edward Grey's prediction to ring true. As the summer of 1914 turned to fall, the war turned into a long and bloody stalemate, or deadlock, along the battlefields of France. This deadlocked region in northern France became known as the **Western Front**.

The Conflict Grinds Along Facing a war on two fronts, Germany had developed a battle strategy known as the **Schlieffen Plan**, named after its designer, General Alfred Graf von Schlieffen (SHLEE•fuhn). The plan called for attacking and defeating France in the west and then rushing east to fight Russia. The Germans felt they could carry out such a plan because Russia lagged behind the rest of Europe in its railroad system and thus would take longer to supply its front lines. Nonetheless, speed was vital to the Schlieffen Plan. German leaders knew they needed to win a quick victory over France.

Early on, it appeared that Germany would do just that. By early September, German forces had swept into France and reached the outskirts of Paris. A major German victory appeared just days away. On September 5, however, the Allies regrouped and attacked the Germans northeast of Paris, in the valley of the Marne River. Every available soldier was hurled into the struggle. When reinforcements were needed, more than 600 taxicabs rushed soldiers from Paris to the front. After four days of fighting, the German generals gave the order to retreat.

Although it was only the first major clash on the Western Front, the First Battle of the Marne was perhaps the single most important event of the war. The defeat

DIFFERENTIATING INSTRUCTION: ENGLISH LEARNERS

Analyzing Compound Words

Class Time 25 minutes

Task Creating a chart showing the meanings of compound vocabulary terms

Purpose To better understand the text

Instructions Explain to students that compound words are words made up of two other words. These word parts can be two nouns, as in *bookshelf,* or an adjective and a noun, as in *highway.* Have students work in small groups to create a chart on which they list compound words they find on this page along with the meaning of each word. Ask them to also brainstorm other compound words that use one of the component word parts (such as *bookend* for *bookshelf*) and add these to their charts.

A sample chart is shown below.

Compound Word	Meaning	Related Word
stalemate	state of inaction	checkmate
deadlock	standstill	deadbolt
battlefields	areas of conflict	cornfields
outskirts	perimeter	outlaw
northeast	north and east	southeast
taxicabs	hired cars	taxiway

of the Germans left the Schlieffen Plan in ruins. A quick victory in the west no longer seemed possible. In the east, Russian forces had already invaded Germany. Germany was going to have to fight a long war on two fronts. Realizing this, the German high command sent thousands of troops from France to aid its forces in the east. Meanwhile, the war on the Western Front settled into a stalemate. **A**

MAIN IDEA

Recognizing Effects

A Why was the Battle of the Marne so significant?

A. Possible Answer It meant the ruin of the Schlieffen Plan and the end to a quick victory for Germany.

War in the Trenches By early 1915, opposing armies on the Western Front had dug miles of parallel trenches to protect themselves from enemy fire. This set the stage for what became known as **trench warfare**. In this type of warfare, soldiers fought each other from trenches. And armies traded huge losses of human life for pitifully small land gains.

Life in the trenches was pure misery. "The men slept in mud, washed in mud, ate mud, and dreamed mud," wrote one soldier. The trenches swarmed with rats. Fresh food was nonexistent. Sleep was nearly impossible.

The space between the opposing trenches won the grim name "no man's land." When the officers ordered an attack, their men went over the top of their trenches into this bombed-out landscape. There, they usually met murderous rounds of machine-gun fire. Staying put, however, did not ensure one's safety. Artillery fire brought death right into the trenches. "Shells of all calibers kept raining on our sector," wrote one French soldier. "The trenches disappeared, filled with earth . . . the air was unbreathable. Our blinded, wounded, crawling, and shouting soldiers kept falling on top of us and died splashing us with blood. It was living hell."

The Western Front had become a "terrain of death." It stretched nearly 500 miles from the North Sea to the Swiss border. A British officer described it in a letter:

PRIMARY SOURCE

Imagine a broad belt, ten miles or so in width, stretching from the Channel to the German frontier near Basle, which is positively littered with the bodies of men and scarified with their rude graves; in which farms, villages and cottages are shapeless heaps of blackened masonry; in which fields, roads and trees are pitted and torn and twisted by shells and disfigured by dead horses, cattle, sheep and goats, scattered in every attitude of repulsive distortion and dismemberment.

VALENTINE FLEMING, quoted in *The First World War*

▼ Allied troops crawl through a trench along the Western Front.

413

More About . . .

Trench Warfare

At the Battle of the Somme in July, 1916, a soldier was expected to carry the following equipment: a rifle, a bayonet, grenades, 170 rounds of ammunition, a gas mask, a shovel and wire cutters, a full water bottle and food rations, extra clothing and medical supplies, and a portable cooking stove with fuel. Carrying about 66 pounds on his back, the soldier had to fight the enemy—assuming he lived while crossing "no man's land."

More About . . .

Valentine Fleming

Valentine Fleming was a member of Parliament and a major in the British army. His sons—Peter, a travel writer, and Ian, the author of the James Bond spy novels—were children during World War I. Fleming ended the letter this way: "It's going to be a *long* war in spite of the fact that on both sides every single man wants it stopped *at once*." He was killed in 1917, fighting on the Western Front.

DIFFERENTIATING INSTRUCTION: GIFTED AND TALENTED STUDENTS

The Literature of War

Class Time 40 minutes

Task Discussing literature of World War I

Purpose To better understand the personal experience and effects of the war

Instructions Have students read the literary selections on pages 13–15 of In-Depth Resources: Unit 4.

Explain that the authors of all three works experienced the horrors of World War I firsthand.

Ask students to work with a partner to complete the activities listed. Have them share their sensory-detail charts, letters, and biographical sketches with the class.

A chart of sensory details follows.

Sight	Sound	Feel
gleaming helmets	thunder of guns	torn
white mist	machine-gun rattle	hand
tapering rulers of searchlights	howls, pipings, hisses	cold
pale cradle of twilight	booming coalboxes	

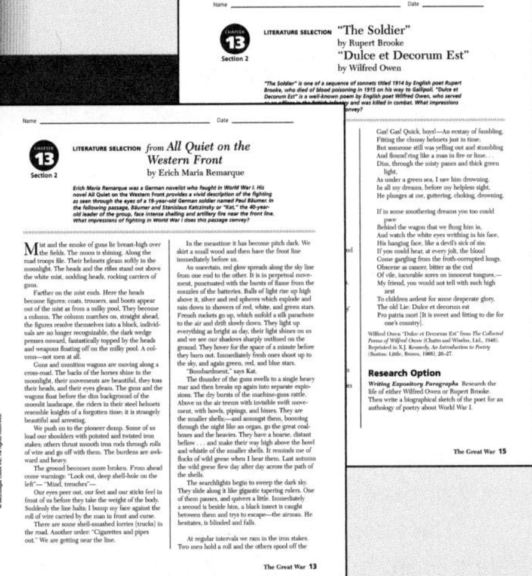

In-Depth Resources: Unit 4

History *in* Depth

The New Weapons of War

The first tanks were made in Great Britain and grew out of a design to put machine guns on motorcycles. When Britain shipped the first of the new vehicles to France, it labeled them "water tanks" to keep the weapon secret. The name stuck. The first tank drivers were from the upper class, because they were the only ones wealthy enough to have cars and know how to drive.

Vocabulary Note: Often-Confused Words

Make sure that students do not confuse the word *casualty* with the similar-looking word *causality*, which means "the relation between a cause and its effect."

The Battle on the Eastern Front

10.5.2

Critical Thinking

- Why might the war on the Eastern Front have been more mobile than that on the Western Front? *(Possible Answer: due to the extremely long border between Russia and Germany)*
- How did Russia's lack of industrialization affect its war efforts? *(It left Russian soldiers short of supplies and food, putting them at a disadvantage compared with the better-equipped Central Powers.)*

World Art and Cultures Transparencies

- AT64 *L'Assault*

History *in* Depth

The New Weapons of War

Poison Gas
Soldiers wore masks like those shown at left to protect themselves from poison gas. Gas was introduced by the Germans but used by both sides. Some gases caused blindness or severe blisters, others death by choking.

Machine Gun
The machine gun, which fires ammunition automatically, was much improved by the time of World War I. The gun, shown to the left, could wipe out waves of attackers and thus made it difficult for forces to advance.

Tank
The tank, shown to the left, was an armored combat vehicle that moved on chain tracks—and thus could cross many types of terrain. It was introduced by the British in 1916 at the Battle of the Somme.

Submarine
In 1914, the Germans introduced the submarine as an effective warship. The submarine's primary weapon against ships was the torpedo, an underwater missile.

Military strategists were at a loss. New tools of war—machine guns, poison gas, armored tanks, larger artillery—had not delivered the fast-moving war they had expected. All this new technology did was kill greater numbers of people more effectively.

The slaughter reached a peak in 1916. In February, the Germans launched a massive attack against the French near Verdun. Each side lost more than 300,000 men. In July, the British army tried to relieve the pressure on the French. British forces attacked the Germans northwest of Verdun, in the valley of the Somme River. In the first day of battle alone, more than 20,000 British soldiers were killed. By the time the Battle of the Somme ended in November, each side had suffered more than half a million casualties.

What did the warring sides gain? Near Verdun, the Germans advanced about four miles. In the Somme valley, the British gained about five miles.

Vocabulary
In war, a *casualty* is anyone killed, injured, captured, or considered missing in action.

The Battle on the Eastern Front

Even as the war on the Western Front claimed thousands of lives, both sides were sending millions more men to fight on the **Eastern Front**. This area was a stretch of battlefield along the German and Russian border. Here, Russians and Serbs battled Germans and Austro-Hungarians. The war in the east was a more mobile war than that in the west. Here too, however, slaughter and stalemate were common.

Early Fighting At the beginning of the war, Russian forces had launched an attack into both Austria and Germany. At the end of August, Germany counterattacked near the town of Tannenberg. During the four-day battle, the Germans crushed the

DIFFERENTIATING INSTRUCTION: STRUGGLING READERS

Analyzing the War on the Eastern Front

Class Time 25 minutes

Task Identifying Russia's weaknesses and strengths

Purpose To understand events on the Eastern Front

Instructions Divide students into small groups. Have them reread the material on pages 414–415 of the text and discuss it. Suggest that they write down any questions they have and note points that are unclear. Then hand out a copy of page 140 of the Reading Study Guide to each group. Have them read the summary of the war on the Eastern Front presented in the handout and discuss how it supports or differs from their understanding of the material in the text. Have them reconcile any disagreements in interpretation. Finally, have each group collaborate in answering question 3 on page 140. Ask a volunteer from each group to share his or her group's answer with the class. A sample answer follows.

Russia's weaknesses and strengths

Russia's main weakness was its lack of industries that could provide the supplies its troops needed.

Its major strength was its huge population that could fight the long war.

Reading Study Guide

invading Russian army and drove it into full retreat. More than 30,000 Russian soldiers were killed.

Russia fared somewhat better against the Austrians. Russian forces defeated the Austrians twice in September 1914, driving deep into their country. Not until December of that year did the Austrian army manage to turn the tide. Austria defeated the Russians and eventually pushed them out of Austria-Hungary.

Russia Struggles By 1916, Russia's war effort was near collapse. Unlike the nations of western Europe, Russia had yet to become industrialized. As a result, the Russian army was continually short on food, guns, ammunition, clothes, boots, and blankets. Moreover, the Allied supply shipments to Russia were sharply limited by German control of the Baltic Sea, combined with Germany's relentless submarine campaign in the North Sea and beyond. In the south, the Ottomans still controlled the straits leading from the Mediterranean to the Black Sea.

The Russian army had only one asset—its numbers. Throughout the war the Russian army suffered a staggering number of battlefield losses. Yet the army continually rebuilt its ranks from the country's enormous population. For more than three years, the battered Russian army managed to tie up hundreds of thousands of German troops in the east. As a result, Germany could not hurl its full fighting force at the west. B

Germany and her allies, however, were concerned with more than just the Eastern or Western Front. As the war raged on, fighting spread beyond Europe to Africa, as well as to Southwest and Southeast Asia. In the years after it began, the massive European conflict indeed became a world war.

B. Possible Answer Russia's huge army tied up German troops in the east and kept them from fighting in the west.

MAIN IDEA

Synthesizing

B Why was Russia's involvement in the war so important to the other Allies?

The Frozen Front

For soldiers on the Eastern Front, like those shown above, the overall misery of warfare was compounded by deadly winters. "Every day hundreds froze to death," noted one Austro-Hungarian officer during a particularly brutal spell.

Russian troops suffered too, mainly due to their lack of food and clothing. "I am at my post all the time—frozen [and] soaked . . . ," lamented one soldier. "We walk barefoot or in rope-soled shoes. It's incredible that soldiers of the Russian army are in rope-soled shoes!"

SECTION 2 ASSESSMENT

TERMS & NAMES 1. For each term or name, write a sentence explaining its significance.

• Central Powers • Allies • Western Front • Schlieffen Plan • trench warfare • Eastern Front

USING YOUR NOTES

2. What were some of the conditions that soldiers on the front lines had to face? (10.5.2)

I. The Great War Begins
A.
B.
II. A Bloody Stalemate

MAIN IDEAS

3. Which countries comprised the Central Powers? Which countries comprised the Allies? (10.5.2)
4. What were the characteristics of trench warfare? (10.5.2)
5. What factors contributed to Russia's war difficulties? (10.5.2)

CRITICAL THINKING & WRITING

6. **COMPARING AND CONTRASTING** How was war on the Western and Eastern Fronts different? How was it the same? (10.5.2)
7. **ANALYZING CAUSES** Why did the Schlieffen Plan ultimately collapse? Cite specific details from the text. (10.5.2)
8. **MAKING INFERENCES** Why might it be fair to say that no one won the battles of the Somme or Verdun? (10.5.2)
9. **WRITING ACTIVITY** SCIENCE AND TECHNOLOGY In an **explanatory essay,** describe the effects of the new technology on warfare. Use examples from your reading. (Writing 2.3.f)

CONNECT TO TODAY **PRESENTING AN ORAL REPORT**

Find an image of a World War I monument from any one of the combatant countries. In an **oral report**, present the image to the class and provide details about its origin and purpose. (Writing 2.6.c)

Social History

The Frozen Front

Germany drastically underestimated the Russians' determination and endurance when facing horrifying conditions. The Schlieffen Plan was based on the assumption that it would take Russia several months to mobilize. Instead, the Russian army was ready within ten days. It quickly defeated the Germans in one early battle and so threatened their army that German general Moltke took two corps from the Western Front and sent them east. The absence of these troops made it possible for the Allies to win the Battle of the Marne. Those relocated troops helped defeat the Russians at Tannenberg, however.

3 ASSESS

SECTION 2 ASSESSMENT

Have students share their outlines for question 2 with a partner and then keep them to refer to in studying for the chapter assessment.

Formal Assessment

• Section Quiz, p. 227

4 RETEACH

Have students use the Guided Reading activity for Section 2 to review the section.

In-Depth Resources: Unit 4

• Guided Reading, p. 2
• Reteaching Activity, p. 21

ANSWERS

1. Central Powers, p. 411 • Allies, p. 411 • Western Front, p. 412 • Schlieffen Plan, p. 412 • trench warfare, p. 413 • Eastern Front, p. 414

2. **Sample Answer**: I. Alliance System—Germany declares war on Russia and France, Great Britain declares war on Germany, Central Powers and Allies form; II. Bloody Stalemate—Germany pursues Schlieffen Plan, Allies win at Marne; III. Eastern Front—Germany and Austria push Russia back, Russia holds off Germany. fatigue, disease, hunger, rats, fear

3. Central Powers—Germany, Austria-Hungary, Bulgaria, Ottoman Empire; Allies—Great Britain, France, Russia, Japan, Italy

4. fighting from trenches and no man's land, huge losses for little territorial gain

5. lack of industrialization, shortages of food and supplies, German blockade of ports

6. Different—Western Front: Germany vs. Britain and France, Eastern Front: Russia and Serbia vs. Germany and Austria-Hungary, more mobile than Western Front; Same—huge numbers of soldiers killed, horrifying conditions, stalemate

7. It relied on Germany's winning a quick victory in France, which didn't happen.

8. Both sides lost many soldiers and gained little land.

9. **Rubric** Essays should
• be well structured with a thesis statement and supporting details.
• demonstrate knowledge of the subject.

CONNECT TO TODAY

Rubric Oral reports should
• address key details about the origins and purpose of the monument.
• be clearly presented.

Science & Technology

OBJECTIVE

- Analyze the contribution of aviation to the course of World War I.

INSTRUCT

Inform students that airplanes played a major role in the battles of World War I. Although the German air force ruled the skies at first, its dominance didn't last long. Both sides soon were engaged in a technological war to build more effective fighter planes.

In-Depth Resources: Unit 4

- Science and Technology: Industrial Technology Creates Poison Gas, p. 19

More About . . .

Aircraft Equipment

The parachute had been invented by the time World War I ended. German pilots carried parachutes, but American pilots did not. The U.S. War Department had a reason for banning them. The assumption was that pilots would be more likely to fly an injured plane to safety if they could not bail out when they were hit.

Science & *Technology*

Military Aviation

World War I introduced airplane warfare—and by doing so, ushered in an era of tremendous progress in the field of military aviation. Although the plane itself was relatively new and untested by 1914, the warring nations quickly recognized its potential as a powerful weapon. Throughout the conflict, countries on both sides built faster and stronger aircraft, and designed them to drop bombs and shoot at one another in the sky. Between the beginning and end of the war, the total number of planes in use by the major combatants soared from around 850 to nearly 10,000. After the war, countries continued to maintain a strong and advanced airforce, as they realized that supremacy of the air was a key to military victory.

▲ A World War I pilot shows off an early air-to-ground communication device.

INTEGRATED TECHNOLOGY

RESEARCH LINKS For more on military aviation go to **classzone.com**

CALIFORNIA STANDARDS

10.5.2, REP 4

1 Designers kept nearly all weight in the center, giving the planes tremendous maneuverability.

2 A timing device enabled machine guns to fire through the propeller.

3 Engines were continuously strengthened for greater speed and carrying capability.

Two Top Fighter Planes: A Comparison

	Fokker D VII (German)	Sopwith F1Camel (British)
Length	23 feet	18 feet 8 inches
Wingspan	29 feet 3 inches	28 feet
Maximum Speed	116 mph	122 mph
Maximum Height	22,900 feet	24,000 feet
Maximum Flight Time	1.5 hours	2.5 hours

416

Connect *to* Today

1. **Drawing Conclusions** Why would communication with someone outside the plane be important for pilots of World War I and today?

   See Skillbuilder Handbook, Page R11.

2. **Comparing** Using the Internet and other resources, find out more about a recent innovation with regard to fighter planes and explain its significance.

CONNECT TO TODAY: ANSWERS

1. Drawing Conclusions

Pilots need to be able to notify someone of their location in case they have to bail out; modern pilots rely on outside communication to locate enemy aircraft.

2. Comparing

Rubric Explanations should

- identify the recent fighter-plane innovation.
- clearly describe its significance.

American troops staging a gas attack to show ill effects of forgetting a gas mask, 1918

E. F. Skinner, *For King and Country* *(women in munitions factory)*

3

A Global Conflict

MAIN IDEA	WHY IT MATTERS NOW	TERMS & NAMES
ECONOMICS World War I spread to several continents and required the full resources of many governments.	The war propelled the United States to a new position of international power, which it holds today.	• unrestricted submarine warfare • total war • rationing • propaganda • armistice

SETTING THE STAGE World War I was much more than a European conflict. Australia and Japan, for example, entered the war on the Allies' side, while India supplied troops to fight alongside their British rulers. Meanwhile, the Ottoman Turks and later Bulgaria allied themselves with Germany and the Central Powers. As the war promised to be a grim, drawn-out affair, all the Great Powers looked for other allies around the globe to tip the balance. They also sought new war fronts on which to achieve victory.

CALIFORNIA STANDARDS

10.5.1 Analyze the arguments for entering into war presented by leaders from all sides of the Great War and the role of political and economic rivalries, ethnic and ideological conflicts, domestic discontent and disorder, and propaganda and nationalism in mobilizing the civilian population in support of "total war."

10.5.3 Explain how the Russian Revolution and the entry of the United States affected the course and outcome of the war.

10.5.4 Understand the nature of the war and its human costs (military and civilian) on all sides of the conflict, including how colonial peoples contributed to the war effort.

10.6.2 Describe the effects of the war and resulting peace treaties on population movement, the international economy, and shifts in the geographic and political borders of Europe and the Middle East.

10.6.3 Understand the widespread disillusionment with prewar institutions, authorities, and values that resulted in a void that was later filled by totalitarians.

War Affects the World

As the war dragged on, the main combatants looked beyond Europe for a way to end the stalemate. However, none of the alliances they formed or new battlefronts they opened did much to end the slow and grinding conflict.

The Gallipoli Campaign A promising strategy for the Allies seemed to be to attack a region in the Ottoman Empire known as the Dardanelles. This narrow sea strait was the gateway to the Ottoman capital, Constantinople. By securing the Dardanelles, the Allies believed that they could take Constantinople, defeat the Turks, and establish a supply line to Russia.

Gallipoli Campaign

Black Sea
Bosporus
Constantinople
Gallipoli Peninsula
Sea of Marmara
GREECE
OTTOMAN EMPIRE
Dardanelles
Aegean Sea
N
0 100 Miles
0 200 Kilometers

The effort to take the Dardanelles strait began in February 1915. It was known as the Gallipoli campaign. British, Australian, New Zealand, and French troops made repeated assaults on the Gallipoli Peninsula on the western side of the strait. Turkish troops, some commanded by German officers, vigorously defended the region. By May, Gallipoli had turned into another bloody stalemate. Both sides dug trenches, from which they battled for the rest of the year. In December, the Allies gave up the campaign and began to evacuate. They had suffered about 250,000 casualties.

Battles in Africa and Asia In various parts of Asia and Africa, Germany's colonial possessions came under assault. The Japanese quickly overran German outposts in

TAKING NOTES

Recognizing Effects Use a web diagram to show the effects of World War I.

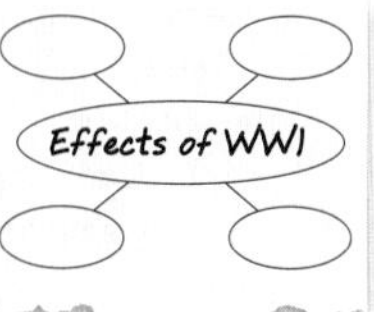

LESSON PLAN

OBJECTIVES

- Describe the spread of the conflict.
- Identify how governments established wartime economies.
- Summarize the Allies' push to victory.
- Explain the effects of the war.

1 FOCUS & MOTIVATE

Have students discuss conflicts they have been in that drew in more and more people. Explain that World War I spread globally in that way.

2 INSTRUCT

War Affects the World

10.5.4; 10.5.1

Critical Thinking

- Why did the Allies want to establish a supply line to Russia? *(to support their eastern ally)*
- How did the Zimmermann note draw America into the war? *(by threatening U.S. territory taken from Mexico)*

Electronic Library of Primary Sources

- "A Suffolk Farmhand at Gallipoli"

CALIFORNIA RESOURCES

California Reading Toolkit, p. L60
California Modified Lesson Plans for English Learners, p. 115
California Daily Standards Practice Transparencies, TT52
California Standards Enrichment Workbook, pp. 55–56, 59–60, 61–62, 67–68, 69–70
California Standards Planner and Lesson Plans, p. L111
California Online Test Practice
California Test Generator CD-ROM
California Easy Planner CD-ROM
California eEdition CD-ROM

SECTION 3 PROGRAM RESOURCES

ALL STUDENTS

In-Depth Resources: Unit 4
- Guided Reading, p. 3

Formal Assessment
- Section Quiz, p. 228

ENGLISH LEARNERS

In-Depth Resources in Spanish
- Guided Reading, p. 105

Reading Study Guide (Spanish), p. 141
Reading Study Guide Audio CD (Spanish)

STRUGGLING READERS

In-Depth Resources: Unit 4
- Guided Reading, p. 3
- Building Vocabulary, p. 5
- Reteaching Activity, p. 22

Reading Study Guide, p. 141
Reading Study Guide Audio CD

GIFTED AND TALENTED STUDENTS

In-Depth Resources: Unit 4
- Primary Source: The Zimmermann Note, p. 11

Electronic Library of Primary Sources
- "A Suffolk Farmhand at Gallipoli"

INTEGRATED TECHNOLOGY

eEdition CD-ROM
Power Presentations CD-ROM
Critical Thinking Transparencies
- CT29 The Human and Financial Costs of World War I

Electronic Library of Primary Sources
- "A Suffolk Farmhand at Gallipoli"

classzone.com

History from Visuals

Interpreting the Map

Have students examine the map and note that World War I involved people on all six inhabited continents. Ask them what difference there was between the involvement of the colonies of Africa and India. *(African colonials actually fought each other on African soil, whereas Indian soldiers fought alongside the British in Europe.)*

Extension Ask students to use the map to determine which participating countries did not experience fighting on their own soil. *(United States, Canada, Brazil, India, Australia, New Zealand, Japan)*

SKILLBUILDER Answers

1. **Region** Brazil, United States, Canada, India, Japan, Australia, New Zealand
2. **Location** Africa, Southwest Asia, Asia

INTEGRATED TECHNOLOGY

Interactive This map is available on the eEdition, where students can view its elements individually.

More About . . .

U-Boats

During 1917, German U-boats sank almost 3,000 ships carrying food, weapons, or troops to the war zones.

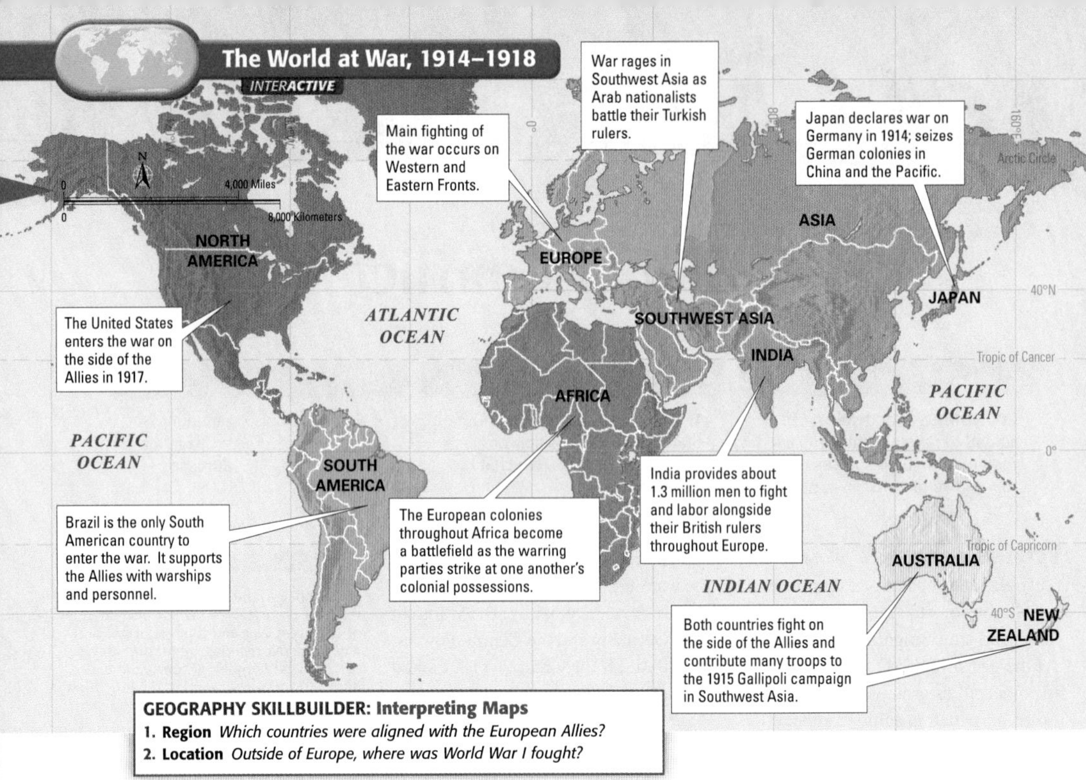

The World at War, 1914–1918
INTERACTIVE
0
4,000 Miles
0
8,000 Kilometers
NORTH AMERICA
ATLANTIC OCEAN
PACIFIC OCEAN
SOUTH AMERICA
EUROPE
AFRICA
SOUTHWEST ASIA
INDIA
ASIA
JAPAN
PACIFIC OCEAN
INDIAN OCEAN
AUSTRALIA
NEW ZEALAND
Arctic Circle
Tropic of Cancer
Tropic of Capricorn
40°N
40°S
0°
The United States enters the war on the side of the Allies in 1917.
Main fighting of the war occurs on Western and Eastern Fronts.
War rages in Southwest Asia as Arab nationalists battle their Turkish rulers.
Japan declares war on Germany in 1914; seizes German colonies in China and the Pacific.
Brazil is the only South American country to enter the war. It supports the Allies with warships and personnel.
The European colonies throughout Africa become a battlefield as the warring parties strike at one another's colonial possessions.
India provides about 1.3 million men to fight and labor alongside their British rulers throughout Europe.
Both countries fight on the side of the Allies and contribute many troops to the 1915 Gallipoli campaign in Southwest Asia.

GEOGRAPHY SKILLBUILDER: Interpreting Maps
1. **Region** *Which countries were aligned with the European Allies?*
2. **Location** *Outside of Europe, where was World War I fought?*

China. They also captured Germany's Pacific island colonies. English and French troops attacked Germany's four African possessions. They seized control of three.

Elsewhere in Asia and Africa, the British and French recruited subjects in their colonies for the struggle. Fighting troops as well as laborers came from India, South Africa, Senegal, Egypt, Algeria, and Indochina. Many fought and died on the battlefield. Others worked to keep the front lines supplied. To be sure, some colonial subjects wanted nothing to do with their European rulers' conflicts. Others volunteered in the hope that service would lead to their independence. This was the view of Indian political leader Mohandas Gandhi, who supported Indian participation in the war. "If we would improve our status through the help and cooperation of the British," he wrote, "it was our duty to win their help by standing by them in their hour of need."

America Joins the Fight In 1917, the focus of the war shifted to the high seas. That year, the Germans intensified the submarine warfare that had raged in the Atlantic Ocean since shortly after the war began. In January 1917, the Germans announced that their submarines would sink without warning any ship in the waters around Britain. This policy was called **unrestricted submarine warfare**.

The Germans had tried this policy before. On May 7, 1915, a German submarine, or U-boat, had sunk the British passenger ship *Lusitania.* The attack left 1,198 people dead, including 128 U.S. citizens. Germany claimed that the ship had been carrying ammunition, which turned out to be true. Nevertheless, the American public was outraged. President Woodrow Wilson sent a strong protest to Germany. After two further attacks, the Germans finally agreed to stop attacking neutral and passenger ships.

DIFFERENTIATING INSTRUCTION: STRUGGLING READERS

Explaining America's Entry into World War I

Class Time 20 minutes

Task Making a flowchart showing the events that led to America's entry into the war

Purpose To understand why the United States entered the war

Instructions Have students reread the material on pages 418–419 of the text. You might also suggest that they read page 141 of the Reading Study Guide and work with a partner to list the events that preceded the United States entering the war on the side of the Allies. Then have each pair of students create a flowchart like the one shown at right, indicating the events that pushed America into the conflict. You might want to hand out copies of the blank graphic provided in Critical Thinking Transparencies CT73 for students to fill in.

Germans use unrestricted submarine warfare.
↓
German U-boats sink three U.S. ships despite Wilson's warnings.
↓
Zimmermann note threatens U.S. territory gained from Mexico.
↓
U.S. feels duty to honor ties to Allies.

Desperate for an advantage over the Allies, however, the Germans returned to unrestricted submarine warfare in 1917. They knew it might lead to war with the United States. They gambled that their naval blockade would starve Britain into defeat before the United States could mobilize. Ignoring warnings by President Wilson, German U-boats sank three American ships.

In February 1917, another German action pushed the United States closer to war. Officials intercepted a telegram written by Germany's foreign secretary, Arthur Zimmermann, stating that Germany would help Mexico "reconquer" the land it had lost to the United States if Mexico would ally itself with Germany.

The Zimmermann note simply proved to be the last straw. A large part of the American population already favored the Allies. In particular, America felt a bond with England. The two nations shared a common ancestry and language, as well as similar democratic institutions and legal systems. More important, America's economic ties with the Allies were far stronger than those with the Central Powers. On April 2, 1917, President Wilson asked Congress to declare war on Germany. The United States entered the war on the side of the Allies.

War Affects the Home Front

By the time the United States joined the Allies, the war had been raging for nearly three years. In those three years, Europe had lost more men in battle than in all the wars of the previous three centuries. The war had claimed the lives of millions and had changed countless lives forever. The Great War, as the conflict came to be known, affected everyone. It touched not only the soldiers in the trenches, but civilians as well.

Governments Wage Total War World War I soon became a **total war**. This meant that countries devoted all their resources to the war effort. In Britain, Germany, Austria, Russia, and France, the entire force of government was dedicated to winning the conflict. In each country, the wartime government took control of the economy. Governments told factories what to produce and how much.

Global Impact

The Influenza Epidemic

In the spring of 1918, a powerful new enemy emerged, threatening nations on each side of World War I. This "enemy" was a deadly strain of influenza. The Spanish flu, as it was popularly known, hit England and India in May. By the fall, it had spread through Europe, Russia, Asia, and to the United States.

The influenza epidemic killed soldiers and civilians alike. In India, at least 12 million people died of influenza. In Berlin, on a single day in October, 1,500 people died. In the end, this global epidemic was more destructive than the war itself, killing 20 million people worldwide.

▶ City officials and street cleaners in Chicago guard against the Spanish flu.

War Affects the Home Front
10.5.4

Critical Thinking

- Why did wartime governments take control of their countries' economies? *(to ensure that all resources would be dedicated to winning the war)*
- How did total war lead to rationing? *(It meant devoting essential goods to the war effort, leaving less for those at home.)*

Global Impact

The Influenza Epidemic

Many epidemiologists now believe that the influenza epidemic started in army camps in the United States. Influenza was not a new disease in 1918, but it was targeting the young and healthy, including hundreds of thousands of soldiers in the trenches. To minimize the spread of infection, drinking fountains were blowtorched every hour, telephones were sterilized with alcohol, and people wore gauze masks. But the disease moved through the countryside and towns despite such precautions. Treatments that were suggested at the time included chewing snuff or tobacco, having tonsils or teeth removed, and sprinkling sulfur in shoes.

DIFFERENTIATING INSTRUCTION: ENGLISH LEARNERS

Learning the Vocabulary of War

Class Time 30 minutes

Task Identifying and finding the meanings of war-related words

Purpose To increase understanding of the text

Instructions Have students work with a partner to reread this page, looking for difficult vocabulary items relating to the war and its effects on the home front. Then ask them to do the following activities:

- Make a list of the vocabulary items.
- Look up each word in a dictionary.
- Write a definition using their own words.

Have students compile their information into a chart and share their charts with the class. Then have students collaborate to use each of the words in a sentence.

A sample chart follows.

Word	Meaning
munitions	guns and ammunition
rationing	limiting the supply of goods
censored	held back information
propaganda	one-sided information
morale	positive state of mind

More About . . .

Women During the War

War propaganda sought to glorify women's part in the war effort. In reality, however, women's work was dangerous and low paying. In Great Britain, for example, conditions in factories were so bad that the membership of women trade unionists increased 160 percent during the war. Women sometimes went on strike during the war in protest.

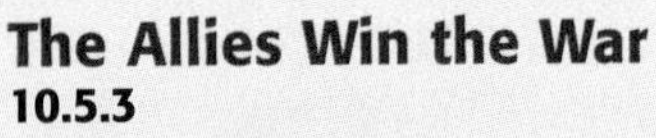

The Allies Win the War

10.5.3

Critical Thinking

- What effect did the Russian Revolution have on Russia's role in World War I? *(It brought Lenin to power, who withdrew Russia from the war and offered Germany a truce.)*
- How did the surrender of the Ottoman Empire and Bulgaria and the revolution in Austria-Hungary lead to the end of World War I? *(The collapse of Germany's allies left it with no support when the German government itself collapsed, resulting in the new German republic's signing an armistice with France.)*

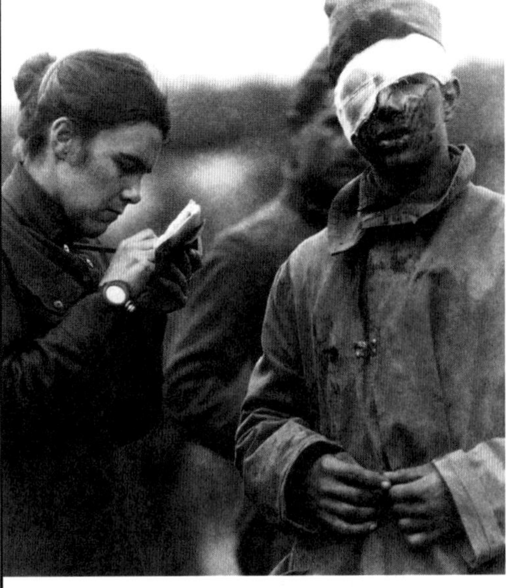

▲ A woman relief worker writes a letter home for a wounded soldier.

Numerous facilities were converted to munitions factories. Nearly every able-bodied civilian was put to work. Unemployment in many European countries all but disappeared.

So many goods were in short supply that governments turned to **rationing**. Under this system, people could buy only small amounts of those items that were also needed for the war effort. Eventually, rationing covered a wide range of goods, from butter to shoe leather.

Governments also suppressed antiwar activity, sometimes forcibly. In addition, they censored news about the war. Many leaders feared that honest reporting of the war would turn people against it. Governments also used **propaganda**, one-sided information designed to persuade, to keep up morale and support for the war. (A)

MAIN IDEA

Summarizing

(A) How did the governments of the warring nations fight a total war?

A. Possible Answer They took control of the economy, directed a rationing program, suppressed antiwar activity, censored news reports, and used propaganda.

Women and the War Total war meant that governments turned to help from women as never before. Thousands of women replaced men in factories, offices, and shops. Women built tanks and munitions, plowed fields, paved streets, and ran hospitals. They also kept troops supplied with food, clothing, and weapons. Although most women left the work force when the war ended, they changed many people's views of what women were capable of doing.

Women also saw the horrors of war firsthand, working on or near the front lines as nurses. Here, American nurse Shirley Millard describes her experience with a soldier who had lost both eyes and feet:

A PRIMARY SOURCE

He moaned through the bandages that his head was splitting with pain. I gave him morphine. Suddenly aware of the fact that he had [numerous] wounds, he asked: "Sa-ay! What's the matter with my legs?" Reaching down to feel his legs before I could stop him, he uttered a heartbreaking scream. I held his hands firmly until the drug I had given him took effect.

SHIRLEY MILLARD, *I Saw Them Die*

The Allies Win the War

With the United States finally in the war, the balance, it seemed, was about to tip in the Allies' favor. Before that happened, however, events in Russia gave Germany a victory on the Eastern Front, and new hope for winning the conflict.

Russia Withdraws In March 1917, civil unrest in Russia—due in large part to war-related shortages of food and fuel—forced Czar Nicholas to step down. In his place a provisional government was established. The new government pledged to continue fighting the war. However, by 1917, nearly 5.5 million Russian soldiers had been wounded, killed, or taken prisoner. As a result, the war-weary Russian army refused to fight any longer.

Eight months after the new government took over, a revolution shook Russia (see Chapter 14). In November 1917, Communist leader Vladimir Ilyich Lenin seized power. Lenin insisted on ending his country's involvement in the war. One of his first acts was to offer Germany a truce. In March 1918, Germany and Russia signed the Treaty of Brest-Litovsk, which ended the war between them.

DIFFERENTIATING INSTRUCTION: GIFTED AND TALENTED STUDENTS

Making a Propaganda Display

Class Time 35 minutes

Task Researching World War I propaganda and creating a display

Purpose To highlight the role of propaganda in maintaining morale and support for the war at home

Instructions Explain to students that during World War I, both the Central Powers and the Allies generated propaganda designed to create a negative view of the enemy and support for their own cause. Have students do research to find posters, flyers, and other graphics representing the enemy and enlisting support for the war effort at home. Ask them to collect the following information about each graphic:

- origin
- purpose
- intended audience
- method of distribution

Have students make copies of the graphics and mount them on a display board for presentation to the class. Each graphic should be accompanied by a caption explaining the information students have gathered about it.

Analyzing Primary Sources

Allied View of Armistice

News of the armistice affected the Allied and Central powers differently. Here, a U.S. soldier named Harry Truman, who would go on to become president, recalls the day the fighting stopped.

PRIMARY SOURCE

Every single one of them [the French soldiers] had to march by my bed and salute and yell, "Vive President Wilson, Vive le capitaine d'artillerie américaine!" No sleep all night. The infantry fired Very pistols, sent up all the flares they could lay their hands on, fired rifles, pistols, whatever else would make noise, all night long.

HARRY TRUMAN, quoted in *The First World War*

German Reaction to Armistice

On the other side of the fighting line, German officer Herbert Sulzbach struggled to inform his troops of the war's end.

PRIMARY SOURCE

"Hostilities will cease as from 12 noon today." This was the order which I had to read out to my men. The war is over. . . . How we looked forward to *this* moment; how we used to picture it as the most splendid event of our lives; and here we are now, humbled, our souls torn and bleeding, and know that we've surrendered. Germany has surrendered to the Entente!

HERBERT SULZBACH, *With the German Guns*

DOCUMENT-BASED QUESTIONS

1. **Summarizing** *What is the main difference between these two excerpts?*
2. **Drawing Conclusions** *How did Herbert Sulzbach's vision of the armistice differ from what actually occurred?*

The Central Powers Collapse Russia's withdrawal from the war at last allowed Germany to send nearly all its forces to the Western Front. In March 1918, the Germans mounted one final, massive attack on the Allies in France. As in the opening weeks of the war, the German forces crushed everything in their path. By late May 1918, the Germans had again reached the Marne River. Paris was less than 40 miles away. Victory seemed within reach.

By this time, however, the German military had weakened. The effort to reach the Marne had exhausted men and supplies alike. Sensing this weakness, the Allies—with the aid of nearly 140,000 fresh U.S. troops—launched a counterattack. In July 1918, the Allies and Germans clashed at the Second Battle of the Marne. Leading the Allied attack were some 350 tanks that rumbled slowly forward, smashing through the German lines. With the arrival of 2 million more American troops, the Allied forces began to advance steadily toward Germany. B

MAIN IDEA

Comparing

B How was the Second Battle of the Marne similar to the first?

B. Possible Answer Both times, the Allies defeated the Germans just as Germany seemed poised for victory.

Soon, the Central Powers began to crumble. First the Bulgarians and then the Ottoman Turks surrendered. In October, revolution swept through Austria-Hungary. In Germany, soldiers mutinied, and the public turned on the kaiser.

On November 9, 1918, Kaiser Wilhelm II stepped down. Germany declared itself a republic. A representative of the new German government met with French Commander Marshal Foch in a railway car near Paris. The two signed an **armistice**, or an agreement to stop fighting. On November 11, World War I came to an end.

The Legacy of the War

World War I was, in many ways, a new kind of war. It involved the use of new technologies. It ushered in the notion of war on a grand and global scale. It also left behind a landscape of death and destruction such as was never before seen.

Both sides in World War I paid a tremendous price in terms of human life. About 8.5 million soldiers died as a result of the war. Another 21 million were wounded. In addition, the war led to the death of countless civilians by way of

Analyzing Primary Sources

Before students read the Allied and German views of the armistice that ended World War I, have them predict what each will be. After reading the passages, ask students to discuss the accuracy of their predictions.

Answers to Document-Based Questions

1. **Summarizing** The Allied reaction is joyous; the German reaction is somber and shocked.
2. **Drawing Conclusions** Sulzbach believed that the armistice would follow a German victory, when, in fact, it came after Germany's surrender.

The Legacy of the War

10.6.2; 10.6.3

Critical Thinking

- What strategies new to World War I probably contributed to the destruction of homes, villages, and farms? *(trench and air warfare)*
- Why might Westerners have experienced disillusionment in the wake of World War I? *(Possible Answer: despair at the tremendous loss of life and economic devastation and at the uselessness of all the suffering)*

Critical Thinking Transparencies

- CT29 The Human and Financial Costs of World War I

CONNECTIONS ACROSS TIME AND CULTURES

Honoring War Heroes

Class Time 35 minutes

Task Investigating the various ways nations honor their war casualties

Purpose To appreciate how people keep alive the legacy of war

Instructions Tell students that throughout history, people around the world have shared in a somber, healing ritual: honoring soldiers killed in battle. In many nations, people come together to honor those citizens who fought and died for their country. After World War I, France built a ceremonial grave to honor all of its soldiers killed in the great conflict. Other nations have paid respects to their dead soldiers with medals, monuments, and parades.

Many nations, including France, the United States, Great Britain, Belgium, and Italy, have created memorials to unidentified war dead, often called the Tomb of the Unknown Soldier. Other memorials include statues, towers, such as Trajan's Column honoring the Roman emperor Trajan's victory over Dacia in A.D. 113, and other structures, such as the wall in Washington, D.C., honoring those who died or were missing in action during the Vietnam War. Have student volunteers describe war memorials they have seen.

History from Visuals

Interpreting the Graph

Have students examine the pie and line graphs. What information suggests a possible reason for the Allied victory? *(the much larger number of troops mobilized by the Allies)*

Extension Ask students to determine the number of battlefield deaths for the Allies and Central Powers based on the chart. Which side suffered greater losses? *(the Allies)*

SKILLBUILDER Answers

1. **Comparing** Russia
2. **Analyzing Issues** Germany, Russia, France, Austria-Hungary

❸ ASSESS

SECTION 3 ASSESSMENT

Have students work in small groups to answer the questions and check their answers.

Formal Assessment
- Section Quiz, p. 228

❹ RETEACH

Divide the class into two groups, one presenting the factors that brought the United States into the war, and the other describing the effects of the war on the home front.

In-Depth Resources: Unit 4
- Reteaching Activity, p. 22

World War I Statistics

Total Number of Troops Mobilized

- Allied Powers: 42 million
- Central Powers: 23 million

Battlefield Deaths of Major Combatants

- USA 116,000
- Ottoman Empire 325,000
- Germany 1.8 million
- Italy 650,000
- *British Empire 908,000
- Russia 1.7 million
- Austria-Hungary 1.2 million
- France 1.3 million

Source: *Encyclopaedia Britannica*

* Includes troops from Britain, Canada, Australia, New Zealand, India, and South Africa

SKILLBUILDER: Interpreting Graphs
1. **Comparing** *Which Allied nation suffered the greatest number of battlefield deaths?*
2. **Analyzing Issues** *Which four nations accounted for about 75 percent of all battlefield deaths?*

starvation, disease, and slaughter. Taken together, these figures spelled tragedy—an entire generation of Europeans wiped out.

The war also had a devastating economic impact on Europe. The great conflict drained the treasuries of European countries. One account put the total cost of the war at $338 billion, a staggering amount for that time. The war also destroyed acres of farmland, as well as homes, villages, and towns.

The enormous suffering that resulted from the Great War left a deep mark on Western society as well. A sense of disillusionment settled over the survivors. The insecurity and despair that many people experienced are reflected in the art and literature of the time.

Another significant legacy of the war lay in its peace agreement. As you will read in the next section, the treaties to end World War I were forged after great debate and compromise. And while they sought to bring a new sense of security and peace to the world, they prompted mainly anger and resentment.

SECTION 3 ASSESSMENT

TERMS & NAMES 1. For each term or name, write a sentence explaining its significance.
- unrestricted submarine warfare • total war • rationing • propaganda • armistice

USING YOUR NOTES

2. Which effect do you think was most significant? Why? (10.6.2)

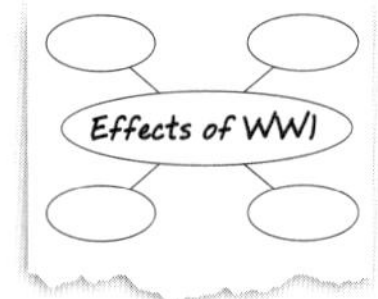

MAIN IDEAS

3. What factors helped prompt the United States to join the war for the Allies? (10.5.1)
4. What role did women play in the war? (10.5.1)
5. What was the significance of the Second Battle of the Marne? (10.5.4)

CRITICAL THINKING & WRITING

6. **ANALYZING ISSUES** In what ways was World War I truly a global conflict? (10.5.4)
7. **FORMING OPINIONS** Do you think governments are justified in censoring war news? Why or why not? (10.5.1)
8. **DRAWING CONCLUSIONS** Which of the non-European countries had the greatest impact on the war effort? Explain. (10.5.3)
9. **WRITING ACTIVITY** ECONOMICS Write a **paragraph** explaining how the concept of total war affected the warring nations' economies. (Writing 2.3.b)

CONNECT TO TODAY **CREATING A GRAPHIC**

Using the library and other resources, compare the role of women in combat today in any two countries. Display your comparison in a **chart** or other type of **graphic.** (Writing 2.3.d)

ANSWERS

1. unrestricted submarine warfare, p. 418 • total war, p. 419 • rationing, p. 420 • propaganda, p. 420 • armistice, p. 421
2. **Sample Answer**: Effects—millions dead, land destroyed, economies shattered, mass disillusionment. Most significant: the tremendous loss of life, because the dead were irreplaceable
3. Germany's unrestricted submarine warfare, Zimmermann note, U.S. ties with Britain and the Allies
4. They helped run factories, farms, and towns, and kept troops supplied with food, clothing, and weapons.
5. The Allies forced the Germans to retreat from France.
6. **Possible Answer**: The war was fought in many parts of the world by people from many nations.
7. **Possible Answers**: Justified—necessary to keep morale and loyalty high during war; Not justified—public has right to know the truth about the war
8. the United States, because it supplied the most troops and helped turn the tide in the Allies' favor
9. **Rubric** Paragraphs should
   - focus on the economic impact of total war.
   - be well organized with a strong thesis statement and good supporting details.

CONNECT TO TODAY

Rubric Graphics should
- be well researched and constructed.
- clearly depict the comparison of women's combat roles in the two countries.

INTERACTIVE

Views of War

When World War I broke out, Europe had not experienced a war involving all the major powers for nearly a century, since Napoleon's defeat in 1815. As a result, people had an unrealistic view of warfare. Many expected the war to be short and romantic. Many men enlisted in the army because of patriotism or out of a desire to defend certain institutions. What the soldiers experienced changed their view of war forever.

CALIFORNIA STANDARDS

10.5.4 Understand the nature of the war and its human costs (military and civilian) on all sides of the conflict, including how colonial peoples contributed to the war effort.

A PRIMARY SOURCE

Woodrow Wilson

On April 2, 1917, President Wilson asked Congress to declare war so that the United States could enter World War I. This excerpt from his speech gives some of his reasons.

The world must be made safe for democracy. Its peace must be planted upon the tested foundations of political liberty. We have no selfish ends to serve. We desire no conquest, no dominion. We seek no indemnities for ourselves, no material compensation for the sacrifice we shall freely make. We are but one of the champions of the rights of mankind. We shall be satisfied when those rights have been made as secure as the faith and the freedom of nations can make them.

B FICTION

Erich Maria Remarque

In the German novel *All Quiet on the Western Front*, Erich Maria Remarque draws upon his own wartime experience of trench warfare.

No one would believe that in this howling waste there could still be men; but steel helmets now appear on all sides of the trench, and fifty yards from us a machine-gun is already in position and barking.

The wire entanglements are torn to pieces. Yet they offer some obstacle. We see the storm-troops coming. Our artillery opens fire. . . .

I see [a French soldier], his face upturned, fall into a wire cradle. His body collapses, his hands remain suspended as though he were praying. Then his body drops clean away and only his hands with the stumps of his arms, shot off, now hang in the wire.

C POETRY

Wilfred Owen

The English poet Wilfred Owen was killed in the trenches just one week before World War I ended. This excerpt from his poem "Dulce et Decorum Est" describes a gas attack.

Gas! GAS! Quick, boys!—An ecstasy of fumbling,
Fitting the clumsy helmets just in time;
But someone still was yelling out and stumbling,
And flound'ring like a man in fire or lime . . .
Dim, through the misty panes and thick green light,
As under a green sea, I saw him drowning.

In all my dreams, before my helpless sight,
He plunges at me, guttering, choking, drowning.

D PRIMARY SOURCE

Maurice Neumont

France, 1918

This French poster is titled, "They Shall Not Pass, 1914–1918." Translated into English, the text at the bottom reads, "Twice I have stood fast and conquered on the Marne, my brother civilian. A deceptive 'peace offensive' will attack you in your turn; like me you must stand firm and conquer. Be strong and shrewd—beware of Boche [German] hypocrisy."

Document-Based QUESTIONS

1. What reasons does Woodrow Wilson (Source A) give for entering the war?
2. What emotions does the French poster (Source D) try to arouse?
3. Judging from Sources B and C, what was it like for the average soldier in the trenches? Explain how you think such experiences affected the average soldier's view of war.

Different Perspectives

OBJECTIVE

- Compare various views of World War I.

INSTRUCT

Tell students that these excerpts provide four different perspectives on war and its human toll. As they read each passage, have them imagine what it would have been like to be in the author's place.

More About . . .

Erich Maria Remarque

Born in Germany in 1898, Erich Maria Remarque joined the army when he was 18 and was wounded several times during the war. After it was over, he drove race cars and worked as a sportswriter while immortalizing his experiences in the novel *All Quiet on the Western Front*. The book was a global success and remains a classic description of the day-to-day experience of war in plain, unemotional terms.

INTEGRATED TECHNOLOGY

Interactive These excerpts and the poster are available in an interactive format on the eEdition. Students can get help with vocabulary, hear the excerpts read aloud, and obtain background information.

DOCUMENT-BASED QUESTIONS: ANSWERS

1. He says the United States entered the war to make the world safe for democracy and to protect the rights of humanity.
2. It arouses the emotions of patriotism, nationalistic fervor, and suspicion of, and anger toward, Germany.
3. The experience was gruesome, horrifying, and terrible. It may have made the soldiers hate warfare or made them feel they had passed a test of courage or endurance and been lucky to survive.

LESSON PLAN

OBJECTIVES

- Explain events that led to the Treaty of Versailles.
- Identify the effects of the treaty on European powers.

1 FOCUS & MOTIVATE

Ask students how they end arguments or conflicts they're involved in. *(Possible Answers: defeat of one side, with both sides letting the issue drop or agreeing to a compromise; a stalemate, with both sides agreeing to a compromise)*

2 INSTRUCT

The Allies Meet and Debate

10.6.1

Critical Thinking

- Why didn't Russia take part in the Big Four negotiations? *(It was involved in a civil war.)*

Geography Transparencies

- GT29 Danzig and the Polish Corridor

Electronic Library of Primary Sources

- The Fourteen Points

CALIFORNIA RESOURCES

California Reading Toolkit, p. L61
California Modified Lesson Plans for English Learners, p. 117
California Daily Standards Practice Transparencies, TT53
California Standards Enrichment Workbook, pp. 65–66, 67–68, 81–82
California Standards Planner and Lesson Plans, p. L113
California Online Test Practice
California Test Generator CD-ROM
California Easy Planner CD-ROM
California eEdition CD-ROM

American troops staging a gas attack to show ill effects of forgetting a gas mask, 1918

E. F. Skinner, *For King and Country (women in munitions factory)*

4

A Flawed Peace

MAIN IDEA

POWER AND AUTHORITY After winning the war, the Allies dictated a harsh peace settlement that left many nations feeling betrayed.

WHY IT MATTERS NOW

Hard feelings left by the peace settlement helped cause World War II.

TERMS & NAMES

- Woodrow Wilson
- Georges Clemenceau
- Fourteen Points
- self-determination
- Treaty of Versailles
- League of Nations

CALIFORNIA STANDARDS

10.6.1 Analyze the aims and negotiating roles of world leaders, the terms and influence of the Treaty of Versailles and Woodrow Wilson's Fourteen Points, and the causes and effects of the United States's rejection of the League of Nations on world politics.

10.6.2 Describe the effects of the war and resulting peace treaties on population movement, the international economy, and shifts in the geographic and political borders of Europe and the Middle East.

10.8.2 Understand the role of appeasement, nonintervention (isolationism), and the domestic distractions in Europe and the United States prior to the outbreak of World War II.

SETTING THE STAGE World War I was over. The killing had stopped. The terms of peace, however, still had to be worked out. On January 18, 1919, a conference to establish those terms began at the Palace of Versailles, outside Paris. Attending the talks, known as the Paris Peace Conference, were delegates representing 32 countries. For one year, this conference would be the scene of vigorous, often bitter debate. The Allied powers struggled to solve their conflicting aims in various peace treaties.

The Allies Meet and Debate

Despite representatives from numerous countries, the meeting's major decisions were hammered out by a group known as the Big Four: **Woodrow Wilson** of the United States, **Georges Clemenceau** of France, David Lloyd George of Great Britain, and Vittorio Orlando of Italy. Russia, in the grip of civil war, was not represented. Neither were Germany and its allies.

Wilson's Plan for Peace In January 1918, while the war was still raging, President Wilson had drawn up a series of peace proposals. Known as the **Fourteen Points**, they outlined a plan for achieving a just and lasting peace.

The first four points included an end to secret treaties, freedom of the seas, free trade, and reduced national armies and navies. The fifth goal was the adjustment of colonial claims with fairness toward colonial peoples. The sixth through thirteenth points were specific suggestions for changing borders and creating new nations. The guiding idea behind these points was **self-determination**. This meant allowing people to decide for themselves under what government they wished to live.

TAKING NOTES

Clarifying Use a chart to record the reaction by various groups to the Treaty of Versailles.

Reaction to Treaty	
Germany	
Africans & Asians	
Italy & Japan	

Finally, the fourteenth point proposed a "general association of nations" that would protect "great and small states alike." This reflected Wilson's hope for an organization that could peacefully negotiate solutions to world conflicts.

The Versailles Treaty As the Paris Peace Conference opened, Britain and France showed little sign of agreeing to Wilson's vision of peace. Both nations were concerned with national security. They also wanted to strip Germany of its war-making power.

The differences in French, British, and U.S. aims led to heated arguments among the nations' leaders. Finally a compromise was reached. The **Treaty of Versailles**

SECTION 4 PROGRAM RESOURCES

ALL STUDENTS

In-Depth Resources: Unit 4
- Guided Reading, p. 4
- History Makers: Georges Clemenceau, p. 17

Formal Assessment
- Section Quiz, p. 229

ENGLISH LEARNERS

In-Depth Resources in Spanish
- Guided Reading, p. 106

Reading Study Guide (Spanish), p. 143
Reading Study Guide Audio CD (Spanish)

STRUGGLING READERS

In-Depth Resources: Unit 4
- Guided Reading, p. 4
- Building Vocabulary, p. 5
- Reteaching Activity, p. 23

Reading Study Guide, p. 143
Reading Study Guide Audio CD

GIFTED AND TALENTED STUDENTS

In-Depth Resources: Unit 4
- Primary Source: Signing the Treaty of Versailles, p. 12
- Connections Across Time and Cultures: Planning for Peace: Vienna and Versailles, p. 18

Electronic Library of Primary Sources
- The Fourteen Points

INTEGRATED TECHNOLOGY

eEdition CD-ROM
Power Presentations CD-ROM
Geography Transparencies
- GT29 Danzig and the Polish Corridor

Critical Thinking Transparencies
- CT65 Chapter 13 Visual Summary

Electronic Library of Primary Sources
- The Fourteen Points

classzone.com

between Germany and the Allied powers was signed on June 28, 1919, five years to the day after Franz Ferdinand's assassination in Sarajevo. Adopting Wilson's fourteenth point, the treaty created a **League of Nations**. The league was to be an international association whose goal would be to keep peace among nations.

The treaty also punished Germany. The defeated nation lost substantial territory and had severe restrictions placed on its military operations. As tough as these provisions were, the harshest was Article 231. It was also known as the "war guilt" clause. It placed sole responsibility for the war on Germany's shoulders. As a result, Germany had to pay reparations to the Allies.

Vocabulary
Reparations is money paid by a defeated nation to compensate for damage or injury during a war.

All of Germany's territories in Africa and the Pacific were declared mandates, or territories to be administered by the League of Nations. Under the peace agreement, the Allies would govern the mandates until they were judged ready for independence.

A Troubled Treaty

The Versailles treaty was just one of five treaties negotiated by the Allies. In the end, these agreements created feelings of bitterness and betrayal—among the victors and the defeated.

The Creation of New Nations The Western powers signed separate peace treaties in 1919 and 1920 with each of the other defeated nations: Austria-Hungary, Bulgaria, and the Ottoman Empire. These treaties, too, led to huge land losses for the Central Powers. Several new countries were created out of the Austro-Hungarian Empire. Austria, Hungary, Czechoslovakia, and Yugoslavia were all recognized as independent nations.

The Ottoman Turks were forced to give up almost all of their former empire. They retained only the territory that is today the country of Turkey. The Allies carved up the lands that the Ottomans lost in Southwest Asia into mandates rather than independent nations. Palestine, Iraq, and Transjordan came under British control; Syria and Lebanon went to France.

Russia, which had left the war early, suffered land losses as well. Romania and Poland both gained Russian territory. Finland, Estonia, Latvia, and Lithuania, formerly part of Russia, became independent nations.

"A Peace Built on Quicksand" In the end, the Treaty of Versailles did little to build a lasting peace. For one thing, the United States—considered after the war to be the dominant nation in the world—ultimately rejected the treaty. Many Americans objected to the settlement and especially to President Wilson's League of Nations. Americans believed that the United States' best hope for peace was to stay out of European affairs. The United States worked out a separate treaty with Germany and its allies several years later.

History Makers

Woodrow Wilson
1856–1924

Wilson was tall and thin and often in poor health. He suffered from terrible indigestion and sometimes had to use a stomach pump on himself. A scholarly man, Wilson once served as president of Princeton University in New Jersey.

Passionate about international peace, he took on the U.S. Senate after it vowed to reject the Treaty of Versailles. During the political battle, he suffered a stroke that disabled him for the rest of his term.

Georges Clemenceau
1841–1929

The near opposite of Wilson, Clemenceau had a compact physique and a combative style that earned him the nickname "Tiger." He had worked as a physician and journalist before entering the political arena.

Determined to punish Germany, Clemenceau rarely agreed with Wilson and his larger quest for world peace. He once remarked of Wilson, "He thinks he is another Jesus Christ come upon earth to reform men."

INTEGRATED TECHNOLOGY

RESEARCH LINKS For more on Woodrow Wilson and Georges Clemenceau, go to **classzone.com**

History Makers

Woodrow Wilson and Georges Clemenceau

What problems might Woodrow Wilson and Georges Clemenceau have had in working together at Versailles? *(Possible Answer: Their completely different personalities might have made negotiation difficult.)* Georges Clemenceau's desire that Germany never again be able to threaten France was a primary motivation at Versailles. He even made this point symbolically at the signing of the document. He insisted that it take place in the Hall of Mirrors, where Wilhelm I had been made emperor of Germany in 1871.

In-Depth Resources: Unit 4
- History Makers: Georges Clemenceau, p. 17

A Troubled Treaty

10.6.2; 10.8.2

Critical Thinking
- How did the situation in African and Asian colonies compare before and after the mandate? *(It changed little, with no independence in sight.)*
- In what way was the Treaty of Versailles "a peace built on quicksand"? *(Its legacy of bitterness did not provide a solid basis for lasting peace.)*

DIFFERENTIATING INSTRUCTION: GIFTED AND TALENTED STUDENTS

Debating the Provisions of the Versailles Treaty

Class Time 40 minutes

Task Reading about the Versailles conference and enacting a debate

Purpose To appreciate the difficulty of negotiating a lasting peace

Instructions Have students research a variety of sources about the deliberations at Versailles. Suggest that they begin by reading the Primary Source document Signing the Treaty of Versailles by Harold Nicolson, found on page 12 of In-Depth Resources: Unit 4. Instruct them to use a dictionary of quotations, encyclopedia, biography, or account of the war to find at least one direct quote from each of the following major participants:

- Woodrow Wilson
- Georges Clemenceau
- David Lloyd George

Then have students break into pairs, with each pair representing one of the three major positions. The pairs may debate more than one opponent as well as different sides of the issue. At the end of each debate, have the class vote to determine the strongest argument.

Name ______ Date ______

CHAPTER 13 Section 4

PRIMARY SOURCE **Signing the Treaty of Versailles**
by Harold Nicolson

The Treaty of Versailles, a 200-page peace treaty between Germany and the Allied powers, was signed on June 28, 1919, in the Great Hall of Mirrors at the French palace of Versailles. Harold Nicolson (1886–1968), a British diplomat and writer, observed the proceedings. As you read this passage from Nicolson's eyewitness account, think about his impressions of the treaty signing.

We enter the Galerie des Glaces. . . . In the middle there is a horseshoe table for the plenipotentiaries [diplomatic agents]. In front of that, like a guillotine, is the table for the signatures. . . . There must be seats for over a thousand persons. This robs the ceremony of all privilege and therefore of all dignity. . . .

People step over the Aubusson benches and escabeaux [stools] to talk to friends. Meanwhile the delegates arrive in little bunches and push up the central aisle slowly. . . . The table is at last full. Clemenceau glances to right and left. . . . Clemenceau makes a sign to the ushers. They say 'Ssh! Ssh! Ssh!' . . . The officials of the Protocol of the Foreign Office move up the aisle and say, "Ssh! Ssh!" again. There is then an absolute hush, followed by a sharp military order. The Gardes Républicains at the doorway flash their swords into their scabbards with a loud click. 'Faites entrer les Allemands [Let the Germans come in],' says Clemenceau in the ensuing silence. His voice is distant but harshly penetrating. A hush follows.

Through the door at the end appear two huissiers [ushers] with silver chains. They march in single file. After them come four officers of France, Great Britain, America, and Italy. And then, isolated and pitiable, come the two German delegates. Dr Müller, Dr Bell. The silence is terrifying. Their feet upon a strip of parquet between the savonnerie carpets echo hollow and duplicate. They keep their eyes fixed away from those two thousand staring eyes, fixed upon the ceiling. They are deathly pale. They do not appear as representatives of a brutal militarism. . . .

They are conducted to their chairs. Clemenceau at once breaks the silence. 'Messieurs,' he rasps, 'la séance est ouverte [Gentlemen, the meeting is open].' He adds a few ill-chosen words. 'We are here to sign a Treaty of Peace.' . . . Then St. Quentin advances towards the Germans and with the utmost dignity leads them to the little table on which the Treaty is expanded. There is general tension. They sign. There is a general relaxation. Conversation hums again in an undertone. The delegates stand up one by one and pass onwards to the queue [line] which waits by the signature table. Meanwhile people buzz round the main table getting autographs. . . .

Suddenly from outside comes the crash of guns thundering a salute. It announces to Paris that the second Treaty of Versailles has been signed by Dr Müller and Dr Bell. . . .

We had been warned it [the signing] might last three hours. Yet almost at once it seemed that the queue was getting thin. . . . The huissiers began again their 'Ssh! Ssh!' cutting suddenly short the wide murmur which had again begun. There was a final hush. 'La séance est levée [The meeting is closed],' rasped Clemenceau. Not a word more or less.

We kept our seats while the Germans were conducted like prisoners from the dock, their eyes still fixed upon some distant point of the horizon.

from Harold Nicholson, *Peacemaking, 1919* (Constable, 1933). Reprinted in John Carey, ed., *Eyewitness to History* (New York: Avon, 1987), 490–492.

Discussion Questions

1. ***Clarifying*** Who opened and closed the meeting to sign the peace treaty?
2. ***Summarizing*** What words or phrases would you use to describe the mood at the signing according to Nicolson's account?
3. ***Using Visual Stimuli*** Compare Nicolson's written account with the visual representation in the painting on page 741 of your textbook. What are some of the similarities? What are some of the differences?

12 UNIT 4, CHAPTER 13

In-Depth Resources: Unit 4

History from Visuals

Interpreting the Maps

Have students examine the maps to determine the major changes that occurred between the beginning of the war and its end. Make sure they understand that color has no political meaning here, but merely distinguishes one country from another. Ask them what new nations were created from the former Austria-Hungary and northwestern portions of Russia. *(Austria, Czechoslovakia, Hungary, Yugoslavia, Poland, Lithuania, Latvia, Estonia, Finland)*

Extension What change had occurred in Great Britain after the war? *(Ireland had become a dominion of the British Commonwealth.)* Have students research when and how Ireland achieved its independence. *(home rule granted to southern Ireland in 1921; Independent Republic of Ireland declared in 1949)*

SKILLBUILDER Answers

1. **Region** Austria-Hungary
2. **Location** Russia

Europe Post-World War I

GEOGRAPHY SKILLBUILDER: Interpreting Maps

1. **Region** *Which Central Powers nation appears to have lost the most territory?*
2. **Location** *On which nation's former lands were most of the new countries created?*

DIFFERENTIATING INSTRUCTION: STRUGGLING READERS

Understanding the Flawed Peace

Class Time 25 minutes

Task Identifying main ideas about the Treaty of Versailles

Purpose To clarify the legacy of the war

Instructions Divide students into small groups and ask them to reread pages 424–427 of the text, looking for answers to the following questions about the Treaty of Versailles.

1. Which nations made most of the decisions about the terms of peace? *(United States, France, Great Britain, Italy)*
2. How did Great Britain and France feel about Germany? *(They wanted to punish Germany.)*
3. What was article 231? *(It made Germany pay back the losses it had caused.)*
4. What were mandated territories? *(former colonies that were placed under the control of one of the winners of the war)*
5. Why might the mandated territories feel resentful? *(Instead of being given their independence, they were placed under a different foreign control.)*

Students who need additional help can use the Guided Reading activity for Section 4.

In-Depth Resources: Unit 4

The Treaty of Versailles: Major Provisions

League of Nations	Territorial Losses	Military Restrictions	War Guilt
• International peace organization; enemy and neutral nations initially excluded • Germany and Russia excluded	• Germany returns Alsace-Lorraine to France; French border extended to west bank of Rhine River • Germany surrenders all of its overseas colonies in Africa and the Pacific	• Limits set on the size of the German army • Germany prohibited from importing or manufacturing weapons or war material • Germany forbidden to build or buy submarines or have an air force	• Sole responsibility for the war placed on Germany's shoulders • Germany forced to pay the Allies $33 billion in reparations over 30 years

SKILLBUILDER: Interpreting Charts
1. **Analyzing Issues** *In what ways did the treaty punish Germany?*
2. **Clarifying** *What two provinces were returned to France as a result of the treaty?*

A. Possible Answer They saw the mandate system as a continuation of European colonialism.

MAIN IDEA
Analyzing Issues
A What complaints did various mandated countries voice about the Treaty of Versailles?

In addition, the treaty with Germany, in particular the war-guilt clause, left a legacy of bitterness and hatred in the hearts of the German people. Other countries felt cheated and betrayed by the peace settlements as well. Throughout Africa and Asia, people in the mandated territories were angry at the way the Allies disregarded their desire for independence. The European powers, it seemed to them, merely talked about the principle of national self-determination. European colonialism, disguised as the mandate system, continued in Asia and Africa. A

Some Allied powers, too, were embittered by the outcome. Both Japan and Italy, which had entered the war to gain territory, had gained less than they wanted. Lacking the support of the United States, and later other world powers, the League of Nations was in no position to take action on these and other complaints. The settlements at Versailles represented, as one observer noted, "a peace built on quicksand." Indeed, that quicksand eventually would give way. In a little more than two decades, the treaties' legacy of bitterness would help plunge the world into another catastrophic war.

SECTION 4 ASSESSMENT

TERMS & NAMES 1. For each term or name, write a sentence explaining its significance.
• Woodrow Wilson • Georges Clemenceau • Fourteen Points • self-determination • Treaty of Versailles • League of Nations

USING YOUR NOTES
2. Which group was most justified in its reaction to the treaty? Why? (10.6.2)

Reaction to Treaty	
Germany	
Africans & Asians	
Italy & Japan	

MAIN IDEAS
3. What was the goal of Woodrow Wilson's Fourteen Points? (10.6.1)
4. What was the "war guilt" clause in the Treaty of Versailles? (10.6.1)
5. Why did the United States reject the Treaty of Versailles? (10.6.1)

CRITICAL THINKING & WRITING
6. **FORMING OPINIONS** Were the Versailles treaties fair? Consider all the nations affected. (10.6.1)
7. **ANALYZING MOTIVES** Why might the European Allies have been more interested in punishing Germany than in creating a lasting peace? (10.8.2)
8. **EVALUATING DECISIONS** Was the United States right to reject the Treaty of Versailles? Why or why not? (10.6.1)
9. **WRITING ACTIVITY** POWER AND AUTHORITY Create a list of five **interview questions** a reporter might ask Wilson or Clemenceau about the Paris Peace Conference. Then write the possible **answers** to those questions. (Writing 2.2.b)

INTEGRATED TECHNOLOGY **INTERNET ACTIVITY**
Use the Internet to explore a recent achievement or activity by the United Nations, the modern-day equivalent of the League of Nations. Present your findings in a brief **oral report** to the class. (Writing 2.3.b)

INTERNET KEYWORD
United Nations

History from Visuals

Interpreting the Chart
Have students examine the chart to identify how the provisions are grouped. Which column shows limitations on Germany's colonial power? *(Territorial Losses)* limitations on its military power? *(Military Restrictions)*

Extension Ask students to discuss how ordinary German citizens might have felt about the treaty. *(Possible Answers: cheated out of their territory, outraged at limitations on their military power, worried about the effects reparations would have on their economy)*

In-Depth Resources: Unit 4
• Connections Across Time and Cultures: Planning for Peace, p. 18

3 ASSESS

SECTION 4 ASSESSMENT

Have one student ask question 1 and the student who answers correctly ask question 2, and so on.

Formal Assessment
• Section Quiz, p. 229

4 RETEACH

Ask students to fill in a concept web detailing the provisions of the Treaty of Versailles.

In-Depth Resources: Unit 4
• Reteaching Activity, p. 23

Critical Thinking Transparencies
• CT65 Chapter 29 Visual Summary

ANSWERS

1. Woodrow Wilson, p. 424 • Georges Clemenceau, p. 424 • Fourteen Points, p. 424 • self-determination, p. 424 • Treaty of Versailles, p. 424 • League of Nations, p. 425

2. **Sample Answer**: Germany—bitterness and hatred at costs exacted; Africans and Asians—anger at lack of independence; Italy and Japan—disappointment at lack of territory gained. Germany, because it was punished most
3. to create a just and lasting peace throughout the world
4. provision that blamed Germany for the war and required reparations
5. desire to stay out of European affairs
6. **Possible Answers**: Fair—Germany was punished and new nations were established; Not fair—Germany was too harshly punished and colonies weren't granted independence.
7. They wanted to ensure Germany could not invade them again.
8. **Possible Answers**: Right—staying out of Europe the best way to avoid conflict; Wrong—ongoing cooperation with Europe the best way to ensure peace
9. **Rubric** Questions and answers should
   • follow a logical sequence.
   • show comprehension of the material.

INTEGRATED TECHNOLOGY
Rubric Oral reports should
• be informative and show evidence of solid research.
• demonstrate understanding of the UN.

TERMS & NAMES

1. Triple Alliance, p. 408
2. Triple Entente, p. 409
3. Central Powers, p. 411
4. Allies, p. 411
5. total war, p. 419
6. armistice, p. 421
7. Fourteen Points, p. 424
8. Treaty of Versailles, p. 424

MAIN IDEAS

Answers will vary.

9. Nationalism and imperialism intensified rivalry among nations, and militarism increased their fighting power.
10. It was home to many ethnic groups and had a history of ethnic clashes and nationalistic uprisings.
11. Germany's defeat there forced it to abandon the Schlieffen Plan and fight a two-front war.
12. Western Front—across France from North Sea to Swiss border; Eastern Front—along border between Russia and Germany and Austria-Hungary
13. military stalemate, huge losses on both sides, terrible conditions, little territorial gain
14. to conquer the Dardanelles and Constantinople and establish a supply line to Russia
15. unrestricted submarine warfare, Zimmermann note, common bond and sympathy with Allies
16. Governments devoted nearly all their resources—economic, manpower, and propaganda—to the war.
17. to keep peace among nations
18. Allies' governance of former colonies and territories, who wanted independence and viewed the mandate as continued colonialism

Chapter 13 Assessment

VISUAL SUMMARY

The Great War

Long-Term Causes

- Nationalism spurs competition among European nations.
- Imperialism deepens national rivalries.
- Militarism leads to large standing armies.
- The alliance system divides Europe into two rival camps.

Immediate Causes

- The assassination of Archduke Franz Ferdinand in June 1914 prompts Austria to declare war on Serbia.
- The alliance system requires nations to support their allies.

WORLD WAR I

Immediate Effects

- A generation of Europeans is killed or wounded.
- Dynasties fall in Germany, Austria-Hungary, and Russia.
- New countries are created.
- The League of Nations is established to help promote peace.

Long-Term Effects

- Many nations feel bitter and betrayed by the peace settlements.
- Forces that helped cause the war—nationalism, competition—remain.

TERMS & NAMES

For each term below, briefly explain its connection to World War I.

1. Triple Alliance
2. Triple Entente
3. Central Powers
4. Allies
5. total war
6. armistice
7. Fourteen Points
8. Treaty of Versailles

MAIN IDEAS

Marching Toward War Section 1 (pages 407–410)

9. How did nationalism, imperialism, and militarism help set the stage for World War I? (10.5.1)
10. Why was the Balkans known as "the powder keg of Europe"? (10.5.1)

Europe Plunges into War Section 2 (pages 411–416)

11. Why was the first Battle of the Marne considered so significant? (10.5.2)
12. Where was the Western Front? the Eastern Front? (10.5.2)
13. What were the characteristics of trench warfare? (10.5.2)

A Global Conflict Section 3 (pages 417–423)

14. What was the purpose of the Gallipoli campaign? (10.5.2)
15. What factors prompted the United States to enter the war? (10.5.3)
16. In what ways was World War I a total war? (10.5.1)

A Flawed Peace Section 4 (pages 424–427)

17. What was the purpose of the League of Nations? (10.6.1)
18. What was the mandate system, and why did it leave many groups feeling betrayed? (10.8.2)

CRITICAL THINKING

1. USING YOUR NOTES (10.5.1)

Trace the formation of the two major alliance systems that dominated Europe on the eve of World War I by providing the event that corresponds with each date on the chart.

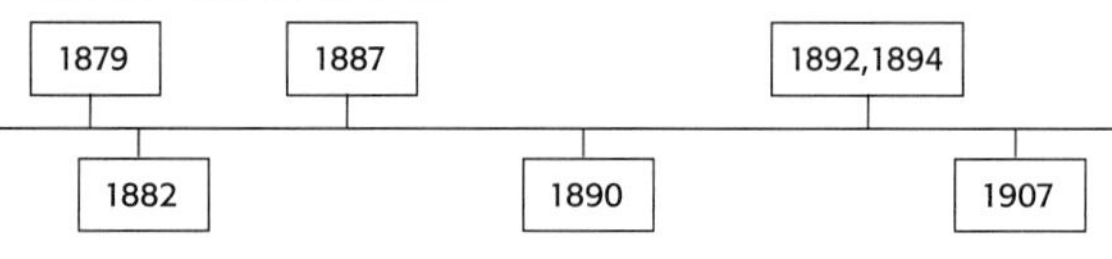

2. EVALUATING DECISIONS (10.6.1)

POWER AND AUTHORITY How did the Treaty of Versailles reflect the different personalities and agendas of the men in power at the end of World War I?

3. CLARIFYING (10.6.2)

ECONOMICS How did the war have both a positive and negative impact on the economies of Europe?

4. ANALYZING ISSUES (10.5.4)

One British official commented that the Allied victory in World War I had been "bought so dear [high in price] as to be indistinguishable from defeat." What did he mean by this statement? Use examples from the text to support your answer.

CRITICAL THINKING

Answers will vary.

1. 1879—Germany and Austria-Hungary form Dual Alliance; 1882—Italy joins Dual Alliance, forming Triple Alliance; 1881—Germany and Russia forge treaty; 1890—Germany lets treaty lapse; 1892, 1894—Russia and France form military alliance; 1907—Britain, Russia, and France form Triple Entente.
2. The harsh terms of the treaty reflected European leaders' desire to punish Germany; the League of Nations reflected Wilson's desire for lasting peace.
3. Positive—increased production and output, led to nearly full employment, provided work opportunities for women; Negative—destroyed farmland and towns, drained treasuries of many countries
4. Although the Allies won, victory came at a terrible price: a generation slaughtered, countries and economies in ruins, and survivors disillusioned and bitter.

Use the quotation about Germany's sinking of the British passenger ship *Lusitania* and your knowledge of world history to answer questions 1 and 2.
Additional Test Practice, pp. S1-S33.

PRIMARY SOURCE

The responsibility for the death of so many American citizens, which is deeply regretted by everyone in Germany, in a large measure falls upon the American government. It could not admit that Americans were being used as shields for English contraband [smuggled goods]. In this regard America had permitted herself to be misused in a disgraceful manner by England. And now, instead of calling England to account, she sends a note to the German government.

from *Vossische Zeitung,* May 18, 1915

1. Which of the following statements best describes the sentiments of the writer? (10.5.1)
   - **A.** The sinking of the *Lusitania* was a tragic mistake.
   - **B.** America was right to blame Germany for the attack.
   - **C.** The American government failed to protect its citizens.
   - **D.** England should keep its vessels off the Atlantic Ocean.
2. The sinking of the *Lusitania* ultimately played a role in prompting Germany to (10.5.1)
   - **A.** abandon the Schlieffen Plan.
   - **B.** halt unrestricted submarine warfare.
   - **C.** declare war on the United States.
   - **D.** begin a widespread rationing program.

Use this anti-German (Hun) World War I poster and your knowledge of world history to answer question 3.

HALT the HUN!
BUY U.S. GOVERNMENT BONDS
THIRD LIBERTY LOAN

3. Which of the following best describes the depiction of the German soldier in this poster? (10.5.1)
   - **A.** noble and courageous
   - **B.** weak and disorganized
   - **C.** cruel and barbaric
   - **D.** dangerous and cunning

INTEGRATED TECHNOLOGY

TEST PRACTICE Go to **classzone.com**
- Diagnostic tests
- Strategies
- Tutorials
- Additional practice

ALTERNATIVE ASSESSMENT

1. **Interact *with* History** (10.5.1)
   On page 406, you examined whether it is always right to support an ally or friend. Now that you have read the chapter, reevaluate your decision. If you chose to follow your ally into World War I, do you still feel it was the right thing to do? Why or why not? If you decided to stay out of war, what are your feelings now? Discuss your opinions with a small group.
2. **WRITING ABOUT HISTORY** (Writing 2.3.a, c, f)
   SCIENCE AND TECHNOLOGY Explain in several **paragraphs** which one of the new or enhanced weapons of World War I you think had the greatest impact on the war and why. Consider the following:
   - which weapon might have had the widest use
   - which weapon might have inflicted the greatest damage on the enemy

INTEGRATED TECHNOLOGY

Conducting Internet Research (Writing 2.3.a., d)

While World War I was extremely costly, staying prepared for the possibility of war today is also expensive. Work in groups of three or four to research the defense budgets of several of the world's nations. Have each group member be responsible for one country. Go to the *Web Research Guide* at **classzone.com** to learn about conducting research on the Internet. Use your research to
- examine how much money each country spends on defense, as well as what percentage of the overall budget such spending represents.
- create a large comparison chart of the countries' budgets.
- discuss with your classmates whether the amounts spent for military and defense are justified.

Present your research to the class. Include a list of your Web resources.

STANDARDS-BASED ASSESSMENT

1. The correct answer is letter **C**. The writer states that America did not take proper steps to keep its citizens safe. Letter **A** is incorrect because the writer insists Germany was justified in sinking the ship even though Americans died. Letter **B** is incorrect because the writer blames the American government, not Germany. Letter **D** is not correct because the writer does not express this view.
2. The correct answer is letter **B**. The sinking of the *Lusitania* so outraged America that Germany temporarily halted its unrestricted submarine warfare. Letter **A** is incorrect because the Schlieffen Plan dealt with the war on land, not at sea. Letter **C** is incorrect because the United States declared war on Germany almost two years after the *Lusitania* incident. Letter **D** is incorrect because the incident had no relation to rationing programs.
3. The correct answer is letter **C**. By showing the German soldier preparing to attack a woman and child, the poster depicts Germans as cruel and barbaric.

Formal Assessment
- Chapter Test, Forms A, B, and C, pp. 230–241

California Test Generator CD-ROM
- Chapter Tests, Forms A, B, and C (English and Spanish)

ALTERNATIVE ASSESSMENT

1. Enter war to support ally—Ties of common cause and shared history are strong and override other concerns; Stay out of war and don't support ally—Disagreement with ally's goals and methods of achieving them over-ride previous shared goals and alliances.
2. **Rubric** Paragraphs should
   - identify one weapon as having the greatest impact on the war.
   - support the choice with facts and reasons drawn from the text.
   - use standard grammatical conventions.

INTEGRATED TECHNOLOGY

Rubric Charts should
- show evidence of valid research.
- present comparisons in a clear, easy-to-follow format.

CHAPTER 14 PLANNING GUIDE

Revolution and Nationalism, 1900–1939

CHAPTER RESOURCES	COPYMASTERS	ASSESSMENT
CHAPTER OVERVIEW The political upheavals that swept through Russia, China, and India resulted in Russia forming a totalitarian state, China undergoing a civil war, and India gaining limited self-rule.	**In-Depth Resources: Unit 4** • Building Vocabulary, p. 28 **Chapters in Brief** (in English and Spanish) **Block Schedule Pacing Guide**	**Chapter Assessment,** pp. 458–459 **Formal Assessment** • Chapter Tests, Forms A, B, and C, pp. 246–260 **Test Generator** **Integrated Assessment Book** **Online Test Practice**
SECTION 1 **Revolutions in Russia** pp. 433–439 **OBJECTIVE** Describe the social unrest in Russia, the Bolshevik Revolution, and the resulting Communist government.	**In-Depth Resources: Unit 4** • Guided Reading, p. 24 • Skillbuilder Practice: Analyzing Causes and Recognizing Effects, p. 29 • Primary Source: from Bloody Sunday, p. 32 • History Makers: Vladimir Lenin, p. 40 • Reteaching Activity, p. 43 **Reading Study Guide,** p. 147	**Section 1 Assessment,** p. 439 **Formal Assessment** • Section Quiz, p. 242 **California Daily Standards Practice Transparencies,** TT114
SECTION 2 **Case Study: Totalitarianism—Stalinist Russia** pp. 440–447 **OBJECTIVE** Describe totalitarianism, the building of a totalitarian state in Russia, and the economic system under Stalin.	**In-Depth Resources: Unit 4** • Guided Reading, p. 25 • Primary Source: The Need for Progress, p. 33 • Literature: from *Darkness at Noon,* p. 36; from *1984,* p. 38 • Reteaching Activity, p. 44 **Reading Study Guide,** p. 149	**Section 2 Assessment,** p. 445 **Formal Assessment** • Section Quiz, p. 243 **California Daily Standards Practice Transparencies,** TT115
SECTION 3 **Imperial China Collapses** pp. 448–452 **OBJECTIVE** Summarize the collapse of Imperial China and the struggle between the Nationalists and Communists for control over China.	**In-Depth Resources: Unit 4** • Guided Reading, p. 26 • Geography Application: Nationalists Battle Warlords and Communists, p. 30 • Primary Source: from "The Peasants of Hunan," p. 34 • History Makers: Jiang Jieshi, p. 41 • Reteaching Activity, p. 45 **Reading Study Guide,** p. 151	**Section 3 Assessment,** p. 452 **Formal Assessment** • Section Quiz, p. 244 **California Daily Standards Practice Transparencies,** TT116
SECTION 4 **Nationalism in India and Southwest Asia** pp. 453–457 **OBJECTIVE** Trace the nationalist movement in India that resulted in limited self-rule and describe the independence movements in Southwest Asia.	**In-Depth Resources: Unit 4** • Guided Reading, p. 27 • Primary Source: from *Hind Swaraj,* p. 35 • Connections Across Time and Cultures: Nationalist Revolutions in Latin America and Asia, p. 42 • Reteaching Activity, p. 46 **Reading Study Guide,** p. 153 **Case Study 1: India and Britain,** p. 2	**Section 4 Assessment,** p. 457 **Formal Assessment** • Section Quiz, p. 245 **California Daily Standards Practice Transparencies,** TT117

INTEGRATED TECHNOLOGY

- eEdition Plus Online
- EasyPlanner Plus Online
- eTest Plus Online

Audio CDs
- Voices from the Past
- Reading Study Guides

CD-ROMs
- eEdition
- Power Presentations
- EasyPlanner
- Electronic Library of Primary Sources
- Test Generator

eEdition CD-ROM

World Art and Cultures Transparencies
- AT65 *Friendship of the People*

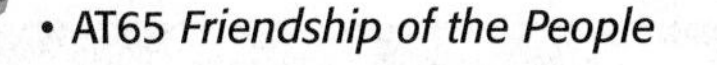

Electronic Library of Primary Sources
- from *Ten Days That Shook the World*

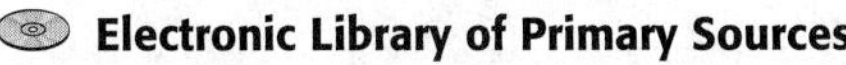

classzone.com

eEdition CD-ROM

Geography Transparencies
- GT30 European Totalitarianism by 1938

Electronic Library of Primary Sources
- from *1984*

classzone.com

eEdition CD-ROM

Electronic Library of Primary Sources
- from *Autobiography of a Chinese Girl*

classzone.com

eEdition CD-ROM

Critical Thinking Transparencies
- CT30 Time Machine: Revolution and Nationalism
- CT66 Chapter 30 Visual Summary

World Art and Cultures Transparencies
- AT66 Persian Musicians

Electronic Library of Primary Sources
- "Nonviolence"

classzone.com

OVERVIEW OF CALIFORNIA RESOURCES

	Section 1	Section 2	Section 3	Section 4
California Reading Toolkit	p. L62	p. L63	p. L64	p. L65
California Modified Lesson Plans for English Learners	p. 119	p. 121	p. 123	p. 125
California Daily Standards Practice Transparencies	TT54	TT55	TT56	TT57
California Standards Enrichment Workbook	pp. 43–44, 59–60, 69–70, 73–74, 75–76, 77–78	pp. 69–70, 73–74, 75–76, 77–78, 85–86	pp. 65–66, 79–80, 97–98	pp. 53–53
California Standards Planner and Lesson Plans	p. L115	p. L117	p. L119	p. L121
California Online Test Practice	classzone. com	classzone. com	classzone. com	classzone. com
California Test Generator CD-ROM				
California Easy Planner CD-ROM				
California eEdition CD-ROM				

Chart Key:

Copymaster

Pupil's Edition

Audio Library

Teacher's Edition

CD-ROM

Overhead Transparency

Internet

Block Scheduling

Video

NO TIME?

If you do not have time to teach this chapter in full, assign the **Chapter in Brief** (also available in Spanish).

Previewing Resources for Differentiated Instruction

ENGLISH LEARNERS: Resources in Spanish

In-Depth Resources in Spanish
- Guided Reading (A)
- Skillbuilder Practice: Analyzing Causes and Recognizing Effects
- Geography Application: Nationalists Battle Warlords and Communists (B)

Chapters in Brief

Reading Study Guide (C)

Reading Study Guide Audio CD

Test Generator CD-ROM
- Chapter Test, Forms A, B, and C

Plus

Modified Lesson Plans for English Learners

Multi-Language Glossary of Social Studies Terms

(A)

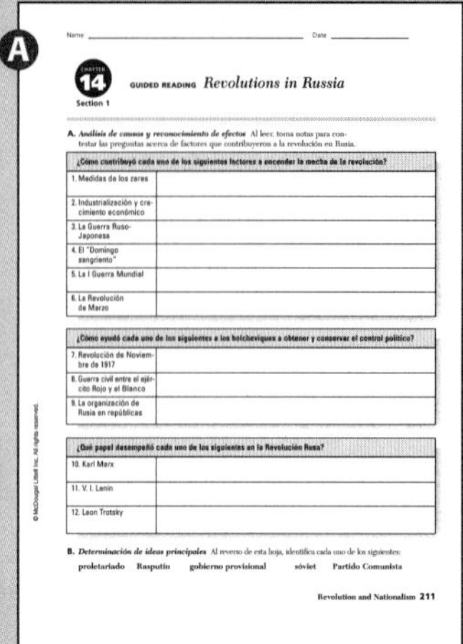

CHAPTER 14 Section 1 GUIDED READING *Revolutions in Russia*

A. *Análisis de causas y reconocimiento de efectos*

¿Cómo contribuyó cada uno de los siguientes factores a encender la mecha de la revolución?

1. Medidas de los zares	
2. Industrialización y crecimiento económico	
3. La Guerra Ruso-Japonesa	
4. El "Domingo sangriento"	
5. La I Guerra Mundial	
6. La Revolución de Marzo	

¿Cómo ayudó cada uno de los siguientes a los bolcheviques a obtener y conservar el control político?

7. Revolución de Noviembre de 1917	
8. Guerra civil entre el ejército Rojo y el Blanco	
9. La organización de Rusia en repúblicas	

¿Qué papel desempeñó cada uno de los siguientes en la Revolución Rusa?

10. Karl Marx	
11. V. I. Lenin	
12. León Trotsky	

B. *Determinación de ideas principales*

proletariado Rasputín gobierno provisional soviet Partido Comunista

Revolution and Nationalism 211

(B)

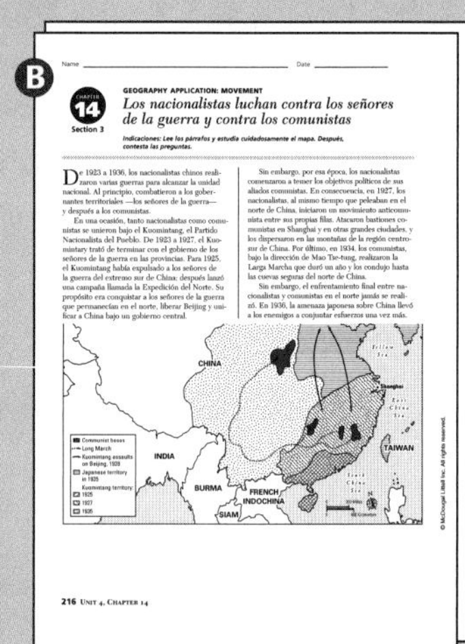

CHAPTER 14 Section 3 GEOGRAPHY APPLICATION: MOVEMENT

Los nacionalistas luchan contra los señores de la guerra y contra los comunistas

216 Unit 4, Chapter 14

STRUGGLING READERS

In-Depth Resources: Unit 4
- Guided Reading (A)
- Building Vocabulary
- Skillbuilder Practice: Analyzing Causes and Recognizing Effects (B)
- Geography Application: Nationalists Battle Warlords and Communists
- Reteaching Activities

Chapters in Brief

Reading Study Guide (C)

Reading Study Guide Audio CD

Formal Assessment
- Chapter Test, Form A

Plus

Reading Toolkit

(A)

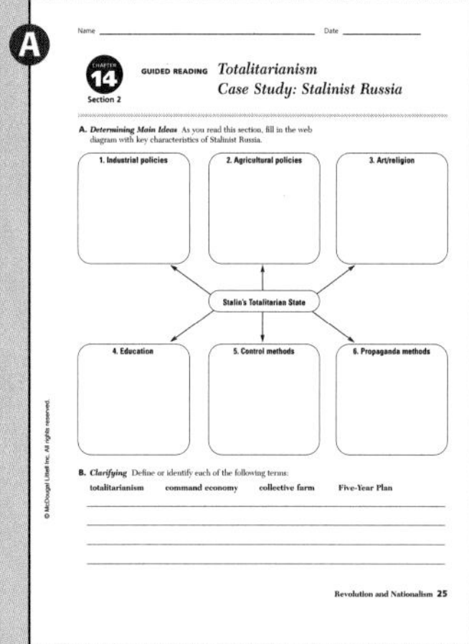

CHAPTER 14 Section 2 GUIDED READING *Totalitarianism Case Study: Stalinist Russia*

A. *Determining Main Ideas*

B. *Clarifying*

totalitarianism command economy collective farm Five-Year Plan

Revolution and Nationalism 25

(B)

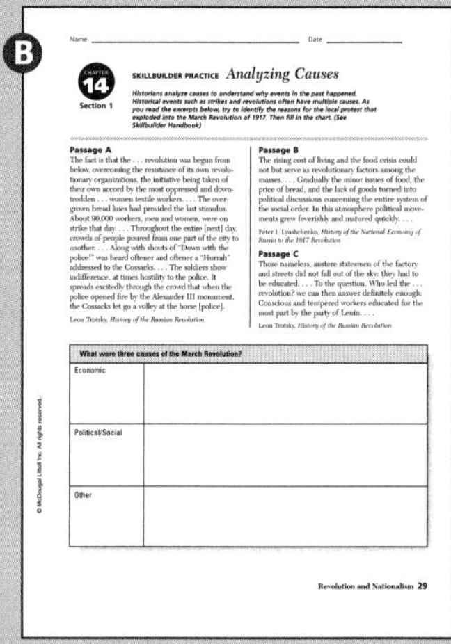

CHAPTER 14 Section 1 SKILLBUILDER PRACTICE *Analyzing Causes*

Passage A

Passage B

Passage C

What were three causes of the March Revolution?	
Economic	
Political/Social	
Other	

Revolution and Nationalism 29

GIFTED AND TALENTED STUDENTS

In-Depth Resources: Unit 4
- Primary Source: from Bloody Sunday; The Need for Progress; from "The Peasants of Hunan"; from *Hind Swaraj*
- History Makers: Vladimir Lenin; Jiang Jieshi
- Literature: from *Darkness at Noon* (A); from *1984*
- Connections Across Time and Cultures: Nationalist Revolutions in Latin America and Asia (B)

Electronic Library of Primary Sources
- from *Ten Days That Shook the World*
- from *1984*
- from *Autobiography of a Chinese Girl*
- "Nonviolence"

Formal Assessment
- Chapter Test, Form C (C)

(A)

CHAPTER 14 Section 2 LITERATURE SELECTION *from Darkness at Noon* by Arthur Koestler

Rubashov had the feeling that he was being watched through the spy-hole. Without looking, he knew that a pupil pressed to the hole was staring into the cell.

36 Unit 4, Chapter 14

(B)

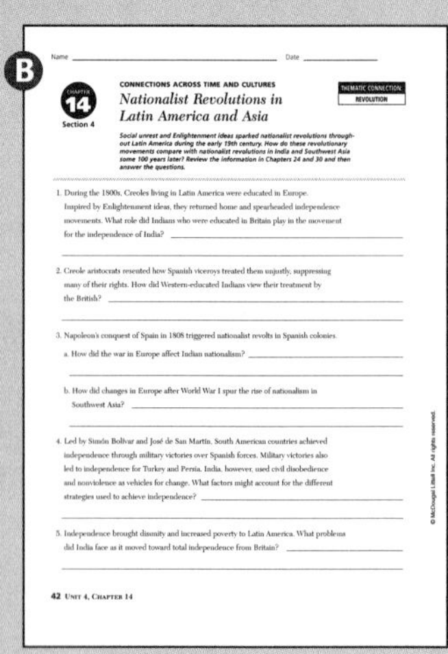

CHAPTER 14 Section 4 CONNECTIONS ACROSS TIME AND CULTURES *Nationalist Revolutions in Latin America and Asia*

42 Unit 4, Chapter 14

INTEGRATED TECHNOLOGY

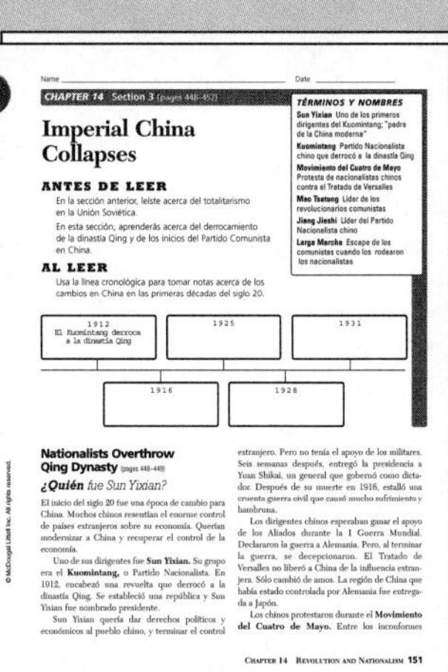

Activities in the Teacher's Edition for English Learners

- Clarifying Key Events, p. 435
- Key Terms of Totalitarianism, p. 444
- Describing the Long March, p. 451
- Indian Protests and British Responses, p. 455

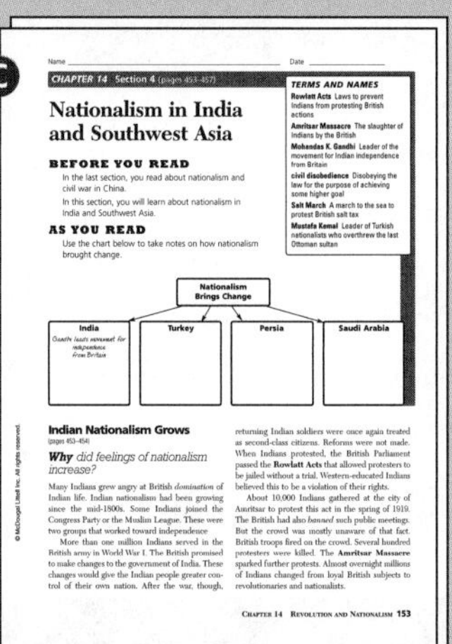

Activities in the Teacher's Edition for Struggling Readers

- Learning from Literature: *Doctor Zhivago,* p. 436
- Using Questions to Find Main Ideas, p. 443
- Chinese Geography and Politics, p. 450
- Using SQ3R, p. 456

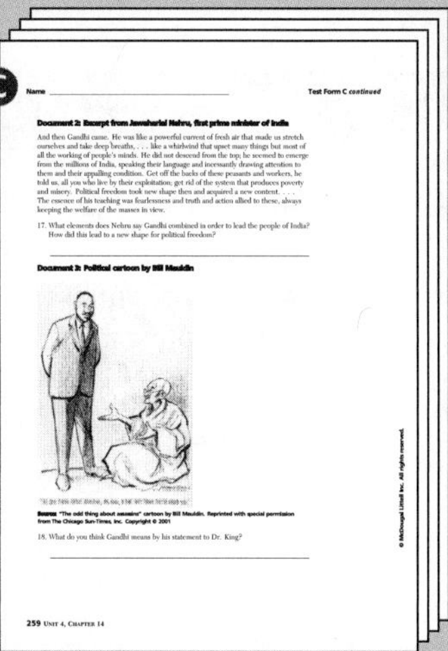

Activities in the Teacher's Edition for Gifted and Talented Students

- Researching the Origins of the Russian Revolution, p. 437
- Creating a Fictional Totalitarian State, p. 442
- The Writings of Mao Zedong, p. 449
- Investigating Examples of Civil Disobedience, p. 454

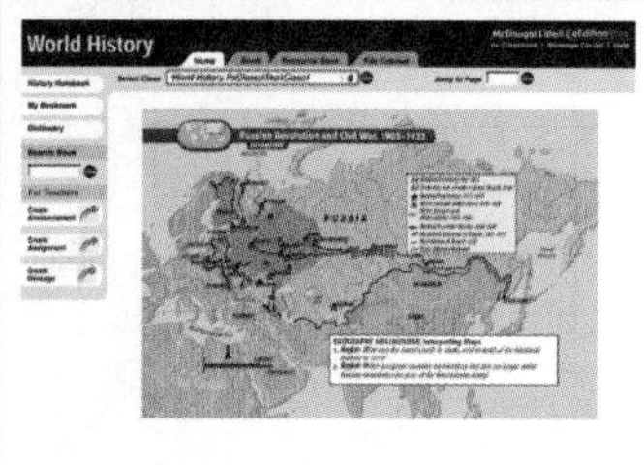

eEdition
- Interactive Visuals
- Interactive Maps
- Interactive Primary Sources

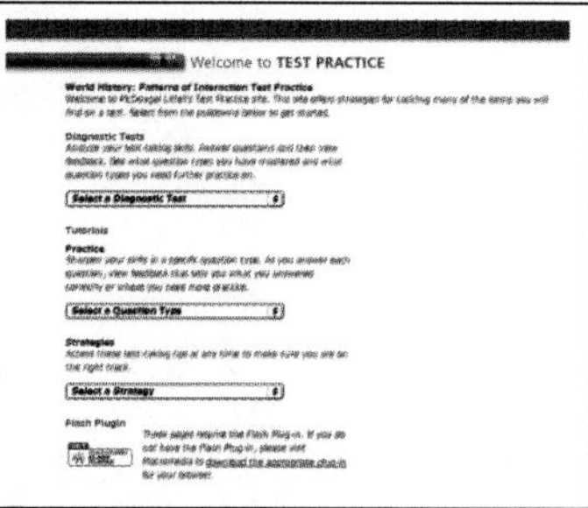

classzone.com
- Research Links
- Internet Activities
- Primary Sources
- Chapter Quiz
- Current Events

Power Presentations CD-ROM
- Lecture Notes
- Image Gallery
- Chapter Review Game

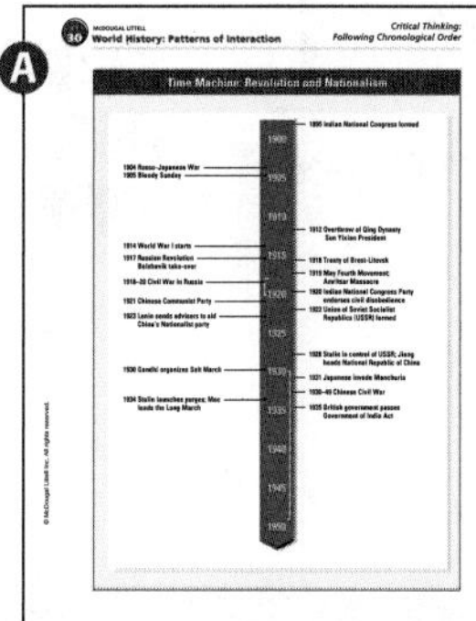

Critical Thinking Transparencies
- CT30 Time Machine: Revolution and Nationalism Ⓐ
- CT66 Chapter 30 Visual Summary

Geography Transparencies
- GT30 European Totalitarianism by 1938

World Art and Cultures Transparencies
- AT65 *Friendship of the People*
- AT66 Persian Musicians

Test Practice Transparencies TT114–TT117

Test Generator CD-ROM

EasyPlanner CD-ROM

Voices from the Past Audio CD

Online Test Practice

Electronic Library of Primary Sources

CHAPTER 14 • OBJECTIVE

Analyze the evolution of conflict between revolutionaries and nationalists before, during, and after World War I.

Previewing Main Ideas

During this time, the gap between rich and poor, especially in Russia and China, was enormous. Growing resentment of economic injustice became a major cause of revolutionary activity. After World War I, leaders in Russia, China, and Turkey launched new programs to modernize their countries. Advances in technology boosted industrial production. These countries were then able to resist foreign control and to compete in world affairs.

Accessing Prior Knowledge

Ask students to recall what they know about the roles Karl Marx, Vladimir Lenin, and Joseph Stalin played in the Russian Revolution and in the advent of Communism. In contrast, ask students to think of adjectives describing the nonviolent protests promoted by Gandhi. As students read this chapter, ask them to be aware of contrasts in the ways revolutionaries in Russia, China, and Southwest Asia achieved their political and leadership goals.

Geography *Answers*

REVOLUTION Revolutions took place in China in 1911 and in Russia in 1917.

POWER AND AUTHORITY New nations were Turkey and Saudi Arabia.

EMPIRE BUILDING France and Great Britain still control large areas of Southwest Asia.

CHAPTER 14

Revolution and Nationalism, 1900–1939

Previewing Main Ideas

REVOLUTION Widespread social unrest troubled China and Russia during the late 1800s and early 1900s. Eventually revolutions erupted.

Geography *Study the time line. In what years did revolutions take place in China and in Russia?*

POWER AND AUTHORITY New nations appeared during the 1920s and 1930s in the former Ottoman Empire in Southwest Asia. These nations adopted a variety of government styles—from a republic to a monarchy.

Geography *According to the map, which new nations in Southwest Asia emerged from the former Ottoman Empire?*

EMPIRE BUILDING Nationalist movements in Southwest Asia, India, and China successfully challenged the British, Ottoman, and Chinese Empires.

Geography *According to the map, which European nations still control large areas of Southwest Asia?*

INTEGRATED TECHNOLOGY

eEdition
- Interactive Maps
- Interactive Visuals
- Interactive Primary Sources

INTERNET RESOURCES

Go to **classzone.com** for:
- Research Links
- Internet Activities
- Primary Sources
- Chapter Quiz
- Maps
- Test Practice
- Current Events

EUROPE AND ASIA

1905 Russian workers protest for better conditions.

1911 ◀Chinese Nationalists oust the last Qing emperor. (Emperor P'u-i)

1917 Russian Bolsheviks rebel in October Revolution.

1900

1910

WORLD

1910 ◀ Mexican Revolution begins.

1914–1918 World War I

430

TIME LINE DISCUSSION

Point out that the years from 1900–1940 were a time of social unrest and great political changes, which resulted in the formation of new nations around the world.

1. Identify the leaders of the nationalist or revolutionary movements mentioned in the time line. *(Gandhi, Mustafa Kemal, Stalin, Mao Zedong, Mussolini, Hitler)*
2. What large events were taking place during this period that may have contributed to social unrest and revolution around the world? *(World War I and the stock market crash in the United States)*
3. In what year was the last emperor of China overthrown? *(1911)* Which emperor was it? *(Emperor P'u-i)*
4. What kind of leaders often take over after revolutions? *(dictators)*
5. Which dictator was taking over Italy during the time of Gandhi's peaceful protest in India? *(Mussolini)*
6. When did the Russian revolt begin? *(1917, Bolshevik October Revolution)*

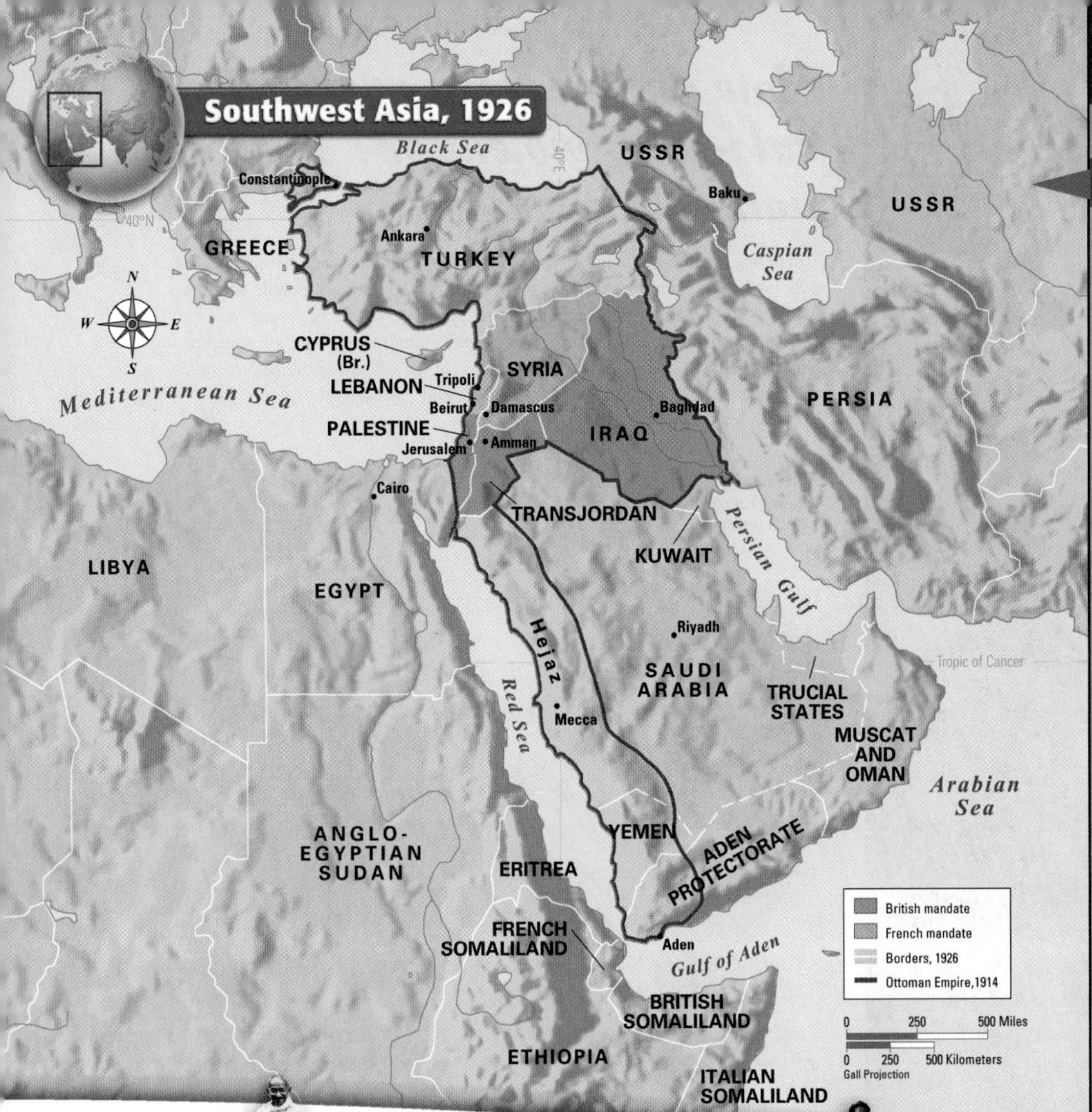

Southwest Asia, 1926
Black Sea
40°E
40°N
Constantinople
GREECE
Ankara
TURKEY
USSR
Baku
USSR
Caspian Sea
N
W
E
S
CYPRUS (Br.)
LEBANON
Tripoli
SYRIA
Mediterranean Sea
Beirut
Damascus
Baghdad
PERSIA
PALESTINE
Jerusalem
Amman
IRAQ
Cairo
TRANSJORDAN
Persian Gulf
KUWAIT
LIBYA
EGYPT
Hejaz
Riyadh
Tropic of Cancer
SAUDI ARABIA
TRUCIAL STATES
Red Sea
Mecca
MUSCAT AND OMAN
Arabian Sea
YEMEN
ADEN PROTECTORATE
ANGLO-EGYPTIAN SUDAN
ERITREA
British mandate
French mandate
Borders, 1926
Ottoman Empire,1914
FRENCH SOMALILAND
Aden
Gulf of Aden
BRITISH SOMALILAND
0 250 500 Miles
0 250 500 Kilometers
Gall Projection
ETHIOPIA
ITALIAN SOMALILAND

History from Visuals

Interpreting the Map

Ask students to locate Turkey, Iraq, Saudi Arabia, and Kuwait on the map and note the size of these countries in relation to one another. As they will learn in Section 4, the oil discovered in this area made these some of the richest countries in the world. Why would the discovery of oil make a country rich? *(Oil is needed to make petroleum, an essential fuel that commands a high price.)*

Extension Ask students to locate the Persian Gulf on the map. Interested students can research newspapers and magazines to find headlines involving the Persian Gulf over the last 20 years. Ask students to share their findings with the class. *(Headlines may involve U.S.-led Persian Gulf Wars of 1991 and 2003 and ongoing conflicts over oil.)*

1920 Gandhi leads ▶ Indian campaign of civil disobedience.

1923 Mustafa Kemal transforms Turkey into a republic.

1929 Stalin becomes dictator of Soviet Union.

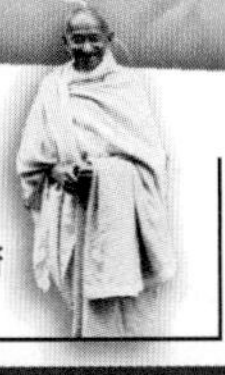

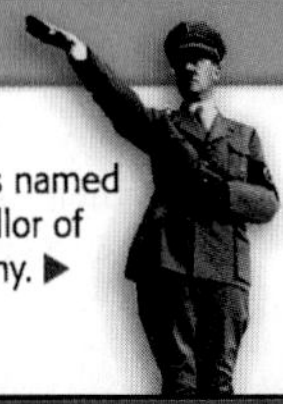

1934 Mao Zedong heads Long March. ▶

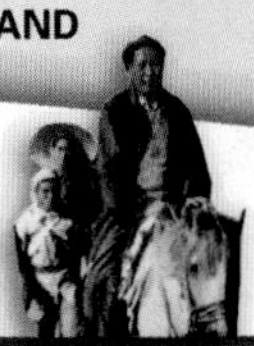

1920 — 1930 — 1940

1922 Mussolini comes to power in Italy.

1929 U.S. stock market crashes.

1933 Hitler is named chancellor of Germany. ▶

431

RECOMMENDED RESOURCES

Books for the Teacher

Pipes, Richard. ***A Concise History of the Russian Revolution.*** Ed. Peter Dimock. New York: Knopf, 1996.

Books for the Student

McDougal Littell Literature Connections. Orwell, George. ***Animal Farm* (with related readings).** 1997. A satirical look at the events of the Russian Revolution.

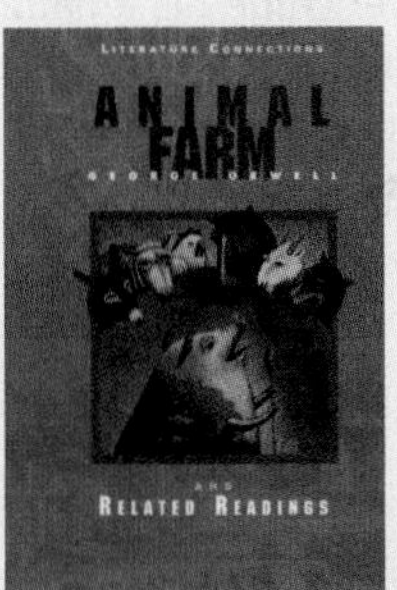

LITERATURE CONNECTIONS
ANIMAL FARM
RELATED READINGS

McDougal Littell Literature Connections. Orwell, George. ***1984* (with related readings).** 1997. A chilling vision of a future totalitarian society.

LITERATURE CONNECTIONS
1984
George Orwell
and Related Readings
McDOUGAL LITTELL

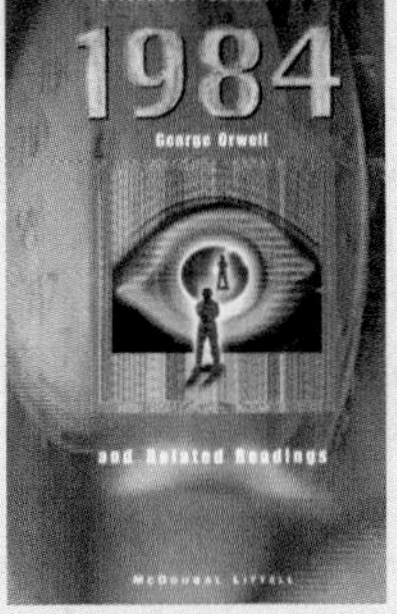

Videos

The Incredible March. VHS. Ambrose Video, 1997. 800-526-4663. The story of Mao Zedong and the birth of Chinese communism.

Power to the People. VHS. Films for the Humanities & Sciences, 1995. 800-257-5126. Examines the Russian Revolution and Gandhi's passive resistance to British rule in India.

The Russian Revolution. VHS. Library Video Company, 1995. 800-843-3620.

Doctor Zhivago. VHS and DVD. MGM/UA Home Videos, 1965.

Interact *with* History

Objectives

- Set the stage for studying revolutionary activity in Russia, China, and India.
- Help students understand revolutionary tactics and their impact.

EXAMINING *the* ISSUES

Possible Answers

- To help students think about this issue, have students discuss why nonviolent groups might be perceived as either weak or intimidating.
- Have students brainstorm possible outcomes resulting from the use of violence in revolutions. *(Possible Answers: rapid change, deaths and injuries, long-lasting bitterness)*

Discussion

Have students choose a revolution they have studied and discuss how the revolutionaries attempted to achieve their goals. They might discuss either the French or the American revolutions. Have students also note the nonviolent strategies of the civil rights movement in the United States and the protests against apartheid in South Africa.

Interact *with* History

How do you resist oppressive rule–with violent or nonviolent action?

You believe that the policies of your government are unjust and oppressive. The policies favor a small, wealthy class—but the vast majority of people are poor with few rights. The government has failed to tackle economic, social, and political problems. Many of your friends are joining revolutionary groups that plan to overthrow the government by force. Others support nonviolent methods of change, such as peaceful strikes, protests, and refusal to obey unjust laws. You wonder which course of action to choose.

▼ **Mao Zedong**, Communist leader, believed revolution would solve China's problems.

"Political power grows out of the barrel of a gun."

▼ **Mohandas K. Gandhi** became the leader of the independence movement to free India of British rule.

"Victory attained by violence is tantamount to a defeat, for it is momentary."

EXAMINING *the* ISSUES

- **How might armed and powerful opponents respond to groups committed to nonviolent action?**
- **Which strategy might prove more successful and bring more long-lasting consequences? Why?**

As a class, discuss these questions. In your discussion, consider what you have learned about the strategies revolutionaries use to accomplish change. As you read about the revolutions and independence movements, see which strategy was successful.

WHY STUDY REVOLUTION AND NATIONALISM?

- The Cold War clash between Communist and capitalist nations was one of the defining events of the 20th century.
- Communist Russia and the Bolshevik Revolution have been the subjects of great works of art and literature.
- The principles of communism became powerful forces in the world.
- The Communist movement begun by Mao Zedong had lasting impact on China and the world. In recent decades, China has rejoined the international community through trade and diplomatic relations.
- Many groups still implement the nonviolent principles of civil disobedience practiced in India in the 1920s.
- Southwest Asia has been the site of controversy over crude oil, a natural resource essential for industry and commerce all over the globe. The Persian Gulf remains a hotbed of international conflict.

1

Poster of Russian soldier with flag, by N. Tyrkurr

Temple of Heaven, Beijing, China

Revolutions in Russia

MAIN IDEA

REVOLUTION Long-term social unrest in Russia exploded in revolution, and ushered in the first Communist government.

WHY IT MATTERS NOW

The Communist Party controlled the Soviet Union until the country's breakup in 1991.

TERMS & NAMES

- proletariat
- Bolsheviks
- Lenin
- Rasputin
- provisional government
- soviet
- Communist Party
- Joseph Stalin

SETTING THE STAGE The Russian Revolution was like a firecracker with a very long fuse. The explosion came in 1917, yet the fuse had been burning for nearly a century. The cruel, oppressive rule of most 19th-century czars caused widespread social unrest for decades. Army officers revolted in 1825. Secret revolutionary groups plotted to overthrow the government. In 1881, revolutionaries angry over the slow pace of political change assassinated the reform-minded czar, Alexander II. Russia was heading toward a full-scale revolution.

Czars Resist Change

In 1881, Alexander III succeeded his father, Alexander II, and halted all reforms in Russia. Like his grandfather Nicholas I, Alexander III clung to the principles of autocracy, a form of government in which he had total power. Anyone who questioned the absolute authority of the czar, worshiped outside the Russian Orthodox Church, or spoke a language other than Russian was labeled dangerous.

Czars Continue Autocratic Rule To wipe out revolutionaries, Alexander III used harsh measures. He imposed strict censorship codes on published materials and written documents, including private letters. His secret police carefully watched both secondary schools and universities. Teachers had to send detailed reports on every student. Political prisoners were sent to Siberia, a remote region of eastern Russia.

To establish a uniform Russian culture, Alexander III oppressed other national groups within Russia. He made Russian the official language of the empire and forbade the use of minority languages, such as Polish, in schools. Alexander made Jews the target of persecution. A wave of pogroms—organized violence against Jews—broke out in many parts of Russia. Police and soldiers stood by and watched Russian citizens loot and destroy Jewish homes, stores, and synagogues.

When Nicholas II became czar in 1894, he continued the tradition of Russian autocracy. Unfortunately, it blinded him to the changing conditions of his times.

▶ Alexander III turned Russia into a police state, teeming with spies and informers.

CALIFORNIA STANDARDS

10.3.6 Analyze the emergence of capitalism as a dominant economic pattern and the responses to it, including Utopianism, Social Democracy, Socialism, and Communism.

10.5.3 Explain how the Russian Revolution and the entry of the United States affected the course and outcome of the war.

10.6.3 Understand the widespread disillusionment with prewar institutions, authorities, and values that resulted in a void that was later filled by totalitarians.

10.7.1 Understand the causes and consequences of the Russian Revolution, including Lenin's use of totalitarian means to seize and maintain control (e.g., the Gulag).

10.7.2 Trace Stalin's rise to power in the Soviet Union and the connection between economic policies, political policies, the absence of a free press, and systematic violations of human rights (e.g., the Terror Famine in Ukraine).

10.7.3 Analyze the rise, aggression, and human costs of totalitarian regimes (Fascist and Communist) in Germany, Italy, and the Soviet Union, noting especially their common and dissimilar traits.

TAKING NOTES

Following Chronological Order Create a time line to show major events in the changing of Russian government.

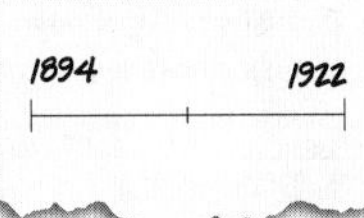

LESSON PLAN

OBJECTIVES

- Describe the autocratic methods of Alexander III and the economic changes under Nicholas II.
- Explain the crises that paved the way for the March Revolution and the end of czarist rule.
- Summarize the Bolshevik Revolution and its outcome.
- Explain Lenin's reforms and Stalin's rise.

1 FOCUS & MOTIVATE

Ask students what the terms *Red Army, Lenin,* and *communism* bring to mind, and ask them to describe in detail any relevant symbols and images.

2 INSTRUCT

Czars Resist Change

10.7.1

Critical Thinking

- Under Alexander III, what behavior would result in arrest as a political prisoner? *(questioning czar, practicing a foreign religion, not speaking Russian)*

CALIFORNIA RESOURCES

California Reading Toolkit, p. L62
California Modified Lesson Plans for English Learners, p. 119
California Daily Standards Practice Transparencies, TT54
California Standards Enrichment Workbook, pp. 43–44, 59–60, 69–70, 73–74, 75–76, 77–78
California Standards Planner and Lesson Plans, p. L115
California Online Test Practice
California Test Generator CD-ROM
California Easy Planner CD-ROM
California eEdition CD-ROM

SECTION 1 PROGRAM RESOURCES

ALL STUDENTS

In-Depth Resources: Unit 4
- Guided Reading, p. 24
- Skillbuilder Practice, p. 29
- History Makers: Vladimir Lenin, p. 40

Formal Assessment
- Section Quiz, p. 242

ENGLISH LEARNERS

In-Depth Resources in Spanish
- Guided Reading, p. 110
- Skillbuilder Practice, p. 114

Reading Study Guide (Spanish), p. 147

Reading Study Guide Audio CD (Spanish)

STRUGGLING READERS

In-Depth Resources: Unit 4
- Guided Reading, p. 24
- Building Vocabulary, p. 28
- Skillbuilder Practice, p. 29
- Reteaching Activity, p. 43

Reading Study Guide, p. 147

Reading Study Guide Audio CD

GIFTED AND TALENTED STUDENTS

In-Depth Resources: Unit 4
- Primary Source: from Bloody Sunday, p. 32

Electronic Library of Primary Sources
- from *Ten Days That Shook the World*

INTEGRATED TECHNOLOGY

eEdition CD-ROM
Voices from the Past Audio CD
Power Presentations CD-ROM
World Art and Cultures Transparencies
- AT65 *Friendship of the People*

Electronic Library of Primary Sources
- from *Ten Days That Shook the World*

classzone.com

Russia Industrializes

10.3.6; 10.6.3

Critical Thinking

- What similarities do you find between the revolutionary movement in Russia and the socioeconomic situations in Latin America, Mexico, and China? *(a harsh ruling class oppressing a lower class of workers and peasants)*
- What measures were taken to make Russia more competitive with Europe and the U.S.? *(taxes raised, investments by foreigners encouraged, railroad built, agricultural reforms)*

History Makers

Lenin

Before Lenin's triumphant return to Russia in 1917, he lived in Geneva, Switzerland, where he earned a meager income as a newspaper publisher and a journalist.

In-Depth Resources: Unit 4

- History Makers: Vladimir Lenin, p. 40

Crises at Home and Abroad

10.7.1; 10.5.3; 10.6.3

Critical Thinking

- What do you know about the outcome of the Russo-Japanese War? *(from Ch. 12–Russia's fleet destroyed; Russia forced out of Korea and Manchuria)*
- Why did entering World War I prove devastating for Nicholas? *(military failed; government fell)*

In-Depth Resources: Unit 4

- Primary Source: from Bloody Sunday, p. 32

Russia Industrializes

Rapid industrialization changed the face of the Russian economy. The number of factories more than doubled between 1863 and 1900. Still, Russia lagged behind the industrial nations of western Europe. In the 1890s, Nicholas's most capable minister launched a program to move the country forward. To finance the buildup of Russian industries, the government sought foreign investors and raised taxes. These steps boosted the growth of heavy industry, particularly steel. By around 1900, Russia had become the world's fourth-ranking producer of steel. Only the United States, Germany, and Great Britain produced more steel.

Vocabulary
minister: person in charge of an area of government, such as finance

With the help of British and French investors, work began on the world's longest continuous rail line—the Trans-Siberian Railway. Begun in 1891, the railway was not completed until 1916. It connected European Russia in the west with Russian ports on the Pacific Ocean in the east.

The Revolutionary Movement Grows Rapid industrialization stirred discontent among the people of Russia. The growth of factories brought new problems, such as grueling working conditions, miserably low wages, and child labor. The government outlawed trade unions. To try to improve their lives, workers unhappy with their low standard of living and lack of political power organized strikes. **A**

MAIN IDEA
Analyzing Causes
A Why did industrialization in Russia lead to unrest?
A. Possible Answer because factory workers felt exploited and resented their lack of political power

As a result of all of these factors, several revolutionary movements began to grow and compete for power. A group that followed the views of Karl Marx successfully established a following in Russia. The Marxist revolutionaries believed that the industrial class of workers would overthrow the czar. These workers would then form "a dictatorship of the proletariat." This meant that the **proletariat**—the workers—would rule the country.

In 1903, Russian Marxists split into two groups over revolutionary tactics. The more moderate Mensheviks (MEHN•shuh•vihks) wanted a broad base of popular support for the revolution. The more radical **Bolsheviks** (BOHL•shuh•vihks) supported a small number of committed revolutionaries willing to sacrifice everything for change.

The major leader of the Bolsheviks was Vladimir Ilyich Ulyanov (ool•YAH•nuhf). He adopted the name of **Lenin**. He had an engaging personality and was an excellent organizer. He was also ruthless. These traits would ultimately help him gain command of the Bolsheviks. In the early 1900s, Lenin fled to western Europe to avoid arrest by the czarist regime. From there he maintained contact with other Bolsheviks. Lenin then waited until he could safely return to Russia.

History Makers

V. I. Lenin
1870–1924

In 1887, when he was 17, Lenin's brother, Alexander, was hanged for plotting to kill the czar. Legend has it that this event turned Lenin into a revolutionary.

Though Alexander's execution influenced Lenin, he already harbored ill feelings against the government. By the early 1900s, he planned to overthrow the czar. After the revolution in 1917, Russians revered him as the "Father of the Revolution."

Following Lenin's death in 1924, the government placed his tomb in Red Square in Moscow. His preserved body, encased in a bulletproof, glass-topped coffin, is still on display. Many Russians today, though, favor moving Lenin's corpse away from public view.

INTEGRATED TECHNOLOGY

RESEARCH LINKS For more on V. I. Lenin, go to **classzone.com**

Crises at Home and Abroad

The revolutionaries would not have to wait long to realize their visions. Between 1904 and 1917, Russia faced a series of crises. These events showed the czar's weakness and paved the way for revolution.

The Russo-Japanese War In the late 1800s, Russia and Japan competed for control of Korea and Manchuria. The two nations signed a series of agreements over the territories,

SKILLBUILDER PRACTICE: ANALYZING CAUSES AND RECOGNIZING EFFECTS

Analyzing Causes of Unrest in Russia

Class Time 15 minutes

Task Analyzing causes of unrest in industrialized Russia

Purpose To clarify the political crises in Russia

Instructions Tell students that analyzing causes is the skill historians use to investigate *why* events in the past happened the way they did. Historical events often stem from multiple causes. Analyzing causes helps historians see how a series of events are related.

To answer the question, "Why did industrialization in Russia lead to unrest?" suggest that students reread the text on this page. Then have them create a multiple-causes chart like this one.

Causes	Effects
• Terrible working conditions in factories • Miserably low wages • Child labor • Huge gap between rich and poor	• Social unrest • Labor strikes • Revolutionary activity

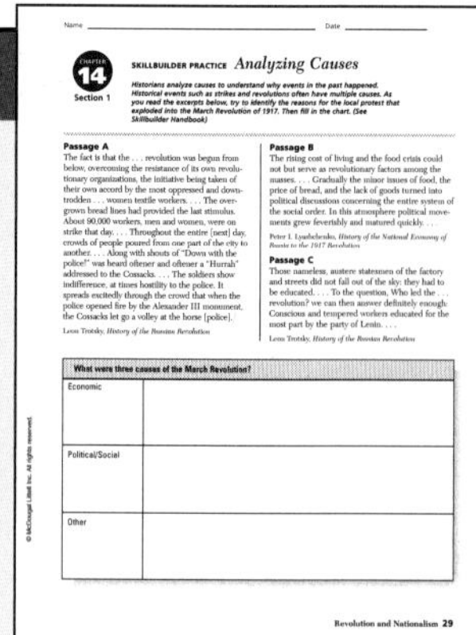
SKILLBUILDER PRACTICE *Analyzing Causes*

In-Depth Resources: Unit 4

but Russia broke them. Japan retaliated by attacking the Russians at Port Arthur, Manchuria, in February 1904. News of repeated Russian losses sparked unrest at home and led to a revolt in the midst of the war.

▲ Soldiers fired on unarmed workers demonstrating at the czar's Winter Palace on "Bloody Sunday."

Bloody Sunday: The Revolution of 1905 On January 22, 1905, about 200,000 workers and their families approached the czar's Winter Palace in St. Petersburg. They carried a petition asking for better working conditions, more personal freedom, and an elected national legislature. Nicholas II's generals ordered soldiers to fire on the crowd. More than 1,000 were wounded and several hundred were killed. Russians quickly named the event "Bloody Sunday."

Bloody Sunday provoked a wave of strikes and violence that spread across the country. In October 1905, Nicholas reluctantly promised more freedom. He approved the creation of the Duma (DOO•muh)—Russia's first parliament. The first Duma met in May 1906. Its leaders were moderates who wanted Russia to become a constitutional monarchy similar to Britain. But because he was hesitant to share his power, the czar dissolved the Duma after ten weeks.

Vocabulary
constitutional monarchy: a form of government in which a single ruler heads the state and shares authority with elected lawmakers

World War I: The Final Blow In 1914, Nicholas II made the fateful decision to drag Russia into World War I. Russia was unprepared to handle the military and economic costs. Its weak generals and poorly equipped troops were no match for the German army. German machine guns mowed down advancing Russians by the thousands. Defeat followed defeat. Before a year had passed, more than 4 million Russian soldiers had been killed, wounded, or taken prisoner. As in the Russo-Japanese War, Russia's involvement in World War I revealed the weaknesses of czarist rule and military leadership.

In 1915, Nicholas moved his headquarters to the war front. From there, he hoped to rally his discouraged troops to victory. His wife, Czarina Alexandra, ran the government while he was away. She ignored the czar's chief advisers. Instead, she fell under the influence of the mysterious **Rasputin** (ras•PYOO•tihn). A self-described "holy man," he claimed to have magical healing powers.

Nicholas and Alexandra's son, Alexis, suffered from hemophilia, a life-threatening disease. Rasputin seemed to ease the boy's symptoms. To show her gratitude, Alexandra allowed Rasputin to make key political decisions. He opposed reform measures and obtained powerful positions for his friends. In 1916, a group of nobles murdered Rasputin. They feared his increasing role in government affairs.

Meanwhile, on the war front Russian soldiers mutinied, deserted, or ignored orders. On the home front, food and fuel supplies were dwindling. Prices were wildly inflated. People from all classes were clamoring for change and an end to the war. Neither Nicholas nor Alexandra proved capable of tackling these enormous problems.

The March Revolution

In March 1917, women textile workers in Petrograd led a citywide strike. In the next five days, riots flared up over shortages of bread and fuel. Nearly 200,000 workers swarmed the streets shouting, "Down with the autocracy!" and "Down with the war!" At first the soldiers obeyed orders to shoot the rioters but later sided with them.

More About . . .

Rasputin

In December 1916, a small group of young aristocrats plotted Rasputin's assassination. They lured him to a mansion and fed him poisoned cakes. The poison apparently had no effect on Rasputin's extraordinary strength. The conspirators then shot him several times. Assuming he was finally dead, they threw him into the Neva River. When his body was discovered three days later, doctors confirmed the cause of his death was not poison or bullet wounds but drowning.

The March Revolution
10.7.1; 10.6.3

Critical Thinking

- How might the results of the March Revolution have been different if soldiers had not sided with the rioters? *(The general uprising leading to Nicholas's defeat may have been prevented.)*
- Why did the Germans help Lenin return to Russia? *(They believed Lenin's protests would weaken the Russian front and help Germany win.)*

DIFFERENTIATING INSTRUCTION: ENGLISH LEARNERS

Clarifying Key Events

Class Time 15 minutes

Task Creating newspaper headlines

Purpose To summarize key events

Instructions After students finish reading the section labeled "Crises at Home and Abroad," ask them to work in pairs to create newspaper headlines that summarize significant events. Encourage students to mimic the style and tone of newspaper headlines as much as possible. Ask students to read some sample headlines and note characteristics, such as brevity, shock value, and strong verbs.

Have pairs trade charts with each other and use the textbook to write two or three lines of detail about each headline. Then ask volunteers to read their headlines aloud.

Students might use this activity to sort out main ideas in passages where several events are discussed or chronology is difficult to follow, such as "The March Revolution."

Date	Headline
February 1904	Russians Fall to Japan at Port Arthur
January 22, 1905	Peaceful Protest Turns Deadly: 1,000 Dead
1914	Russia Enters the War
1916	Mystery Man Murdered
March 1917	Women of Petrograd Lead City in Strike

The Bolshevik Revolution

10.7.1; 10.7.3

Critical Thinking

- What were the results of the destruction of existing social and political structures in Russia? *(chaos, civil war)*
- What might have resulted from turning factories and farmland over to the workers? *(satisfaction because workers no longer oppressed; chaos because workers were disorganized)*

Electronic Library of Primary Sources

- from *Ten Days That Shook the World*

History from Visuals

Interpreting the Map

Have students point out each element of the map key on the map.

Extension Ask students to speculate why the civil war was fought mainly in western Russia. *(Possible Answer: That area contained many of the major cities and important military and administrative centers, along with the majority of Russia's population.)*

INTEGRATED TECHNOLOGY

Interactive This map is available in an interactive format on the eEdition.

SKILLBUILDER Answers

1. **Region** about 100 miles south of Barents Sea to the northern coast of the Caspian Sea (north to south); Yekaterinburg to the Latvian border (east to west)
2. **Region** Finland, Poland, Latvia, Estonia, Lithuania, and the Ukraine

The Czar Steps Down The local protest exploded into a general uprising—the March Revolution. It forced Czar Nicholas II to abdicate his throne. A year later revolutionaries executed Nicholas and his family. The three-century czarist rule of the Romanovs finally collapsed. The March Revolution succeeded in bringing down the czar. Yet it failed to set up a strong government to replace his regime.

Leaders of the Duma established a **provisional government**, or temporary government. Alexander Kerensky headed it. His decision to continue fighting in World War I cost him the support of both soldiers and civilians. As the war dragged on, conditions inside Russia worsened. Angry peasants demanded land. City workers grew more radical. Socialist revolutionaries, competing for power, formed soviets. **Soviets** were local councils consisting of workers, peasants, and soldiers. In many cities, the soviets had more influence than the provisional government. (B)

B. Answer Russians lost their faith in the provisional government and felt no better off than when they were under the czar.

MAIN IDEA

Making Inferences

(B) Why did Kerensky's decision to continue fighting the war cost him the support of the Russian people?

Lenin Returns to Russia The Germans believed that Lenin and his Bolshevik supporters would stir unrest in Russia and hurt the Russian war effort against Germany. They arranged Lenin's return to Russia after many years of exile. Traveling in a sealed railway boxcar, Lenin reached Petrograd in April 1917.

The Bolshevik Revolution

Lenin and the Bolsheviks soon gained control of the Petrograd soviet, as well as the soviets in other major Russian cities. By the fall of 1917, people in the cities were rallying to the call, "All power to the soviets." Lenin's slogan—"Peace, Land, and Bread"—gained widespread appeal. Lenin decided to take action.

The Provisional Government Topples In November 1917, without warning, armed factory workers stormed the Winter Palace in Petrograd. Calling themselves

GEOGRAPHY SKILLBUILDER: Interpreting Maps

1. **Region** *What was the extent (north to south, east to west) of the Bolshevik territory in 1919?*
2. **Region** *Which European countries had territory that was no longer within Russian boundaries because of the Brest-Litovsk treaty?*

DIFFERENTIATING INSTRUCTION: STRUGGLING READERS

Learning from Literature: *Doctor Zhivago*

Class Time 30 minutes

Task Reading and viewing excerpts from *Doctor Zhivago*

Purpose To understand the effects of the Bolshevik Revolution on the Russian people

Instructions Boris Pasternak's widely acclaimed novel, *Doctor Zhivago,* is the story of a wealthy family caught up in the civil war that followed the Bolshevik Revolution of 1917. In the opening pages of the novel, the title character reflects on the sweeping changes that have occurred. "He could remember a time in his early childhood when a large number of things were still known by his family name. There was a Zhivago factory, a Zhivago bank, Zhivago buildings, a Zhivago necktie pin, even a Zhivago cake. . . . And then suddenly all that was gone. They were poor."

Have students form small groups and read the three paragraphs under the head "Civil War Rages in Russia," page 437 of this textbook. Based on what they know about the effect of the civil war, ask students to discuss why they think the Zhivago family lost their wealth. You may wish to show excerpts from the film *Doctor Zhivago* to reinforce the turmoil of the revolution.

the Bolshevik Red Guards, they took over government offices and arrested the leaders of the provisional government. Kerensky and his colleagues disappeared almost as quickly as the czarist regime they had replaced.

Bolsheviks in Power Within days after the Bolshevik takeover, Lenin ordered that all farmland be distributed among the peasants. Lenin and the Bolsheviks gave control of factories to the workers. The Bolshevik government also signed a truce with Germany to stop all fighting and began peace talks.

In March 1918, Russia and Germany signed the Treaty of Brest-Litovsk. Russia surrendered a large part of its territory to Germany and its allies. The humiliating terms of this treaty triggered widespread anger among many Russians. They objected to the Bolsheviks and their policies and to the murder of the royal family.

▲ Red Army forces were victorious in the two-year civil war against the White Army.

Civil War Rages in Russia The Bolsheviks now faced a new challenge—stamping out their enemies at home. Their opponents formed the White Army. The White Army was made up of very different groups. There were those groups who supported the return to rule by the czar, others who wanted democratic government, and even socialists who opposed Lenin's style of socialism. Only the desire to defeat the Bolsheviks united the White Army. The groups barely cooperated with each other. At one point there were three White Armies fighting against the Bolsheviks' Red Army.

The revolutionary leader, Leon Trotsky, expertly commanded the Bolshevik Red Army. From 1918 to 1920, civil war raged in Russia. Several Western nations, including the United States, sent military aid and forces to Russia to help the White Army. However, they were of little help.

Causes and Effects of Two Russian Revolutions, 1917

Causes: Czarist Russia	**Effects/Causes:** March Revolution	**Effects:** Bolshevik Revolution
• Czar's leadership was weak.	• Czar abdicates.	• Provisional government is overthrown.
• Revolutionary agitation challenges the government.	• Provisional government takes over. • Lenin and soviets gain power.	• Bolsheviks take over.
• Widespread discontent found among all classes.	• Russia stays in World War I.	• Bolsheviks sign peace treaty with Germany and leave World War I. • Civil war begins in Russia.

SKILLBUILDER: Interpreting Charts
1. **Analyzing Causes** *What role did World War I play in the two revolutions?*
2. **Recognizing Effects** *Why were the effects of the March Revolution also causes of the Bolshevik Revolution?*

More About . . .

Leon Trotsky

Born Lev (or Leon) Davidovich Bronstein in 1879, Trotsky was converted to revolutionary socialism at a young age. After serving time in Siberia for revolutionary activity, he took the name Trotsky. Later he brought superb talent and organizational ability to the Bolshevik cause. Following the Bolshevik takeover in November 1917, Trotsky became commissar for foreign affairs.

History from Visuals

Interpreting the Chart

Point out that the causes begin with Czarist Russia in the left column, the effects of which are listed in the center column under "March Revolution." Those effects in turn become some of the causes of the Bolshevik Revolution.

Extension Ask students to choose one of the causes on the chart and write a paragraph explaining how it helped bring on the revolution.

SKILLBUILDER Answers

1. **Analyzing Causes** The widespread discontent about participation in the war forced out the czar and the provisional government and caused a civil war.
2. **Recognizing Effects** The problems of weak leadership and widespread discontent were not solved by the March Revolution.

DIFFERENTIATING INSTRUCTION: GIFTED AND TALENTED STUDENTS

Researching the Origins of the Russian Revolution

Class Time 45 minutes

Task Writing a short essay using original research

Purpose To analyze the origins of the Russian Communist movement

Instructions Ask students to consider the origins of the Bolshevik movement and to analyze the reaction of other countries, particularly the United States. Students should then write a one- to two-page essay about the origins of the Russian Revolution.

Offer these questions as consideration for research:

- How did the Bolshevik movement begin?
- What was the goal of the Red Army?
- What role did Marxism play in the revolution?
- What role did the soviets (local councils) play in the establishment of the USSR?
- Why did the United States support the White Army in 1918–1920, instead of siding with the Red Army?

For an in-depth look at the issues, have students read the material on Vladimir Lenin in In-Depth Resources: Unit 4.

Name ______ Date ______

CHAPTER 14 Section 1

HISTORYMAKERS Vladimir Lenin
Russian Revolutionary

"There is no other man who is absorbed by the revolution twenty-four hours a day, who has no other thoughts but the thought of revolution, and who even when he sleeps, dreams of nothing but revolution."—another Communist, speaking of Lenin

Vladimir Lenin was one of the century's most important leaders. Unhappy and disillusioned with the Russian monarchy, he led a group called the Bolsheviks in a revolution that gave him control of the largest nation in the world.

Born in 1870, Lenin was raised by two educated parents in a happy family. He showed intelligence and skill with classical languages. While in his teens, two shocks jolted his world. First, his father was threatened with losing his job by the government. Second, Lenin's older brother was hanged for conspiring against the czar. Within two years, Lenin had read the work of Karl Marx and believed that Russia needed a Communist revolution.

Lenin then began to write and to recruit new followers. He was arrested and served 15 months in prison followed by three years of exile in Siberia. When that ended in 1900, he traveled abroad, where he spent much of the next 17 years. During this time, he sharpened his ideas about Marxism.

Marxism said that industrial workers, called the proletariat, were in a struggle against capitalists, the people that owned businesses. Eventually, Marx said, the workers would overthrow the capitalists and form a new society called communism. However, Russia consisted mainly of peasants and only had a small number of industrial workers. Marxists wondered how a workers' revolution could occur.

Lenin saw the role of the party as essential, and his group became known as the Bolsheviks. The Bolsheviks, he said, would lead the people to the revolution they needed. However, many Marxists found it difficult to accept Lenin's iron rule. In 1912, he forced those who disagreed with him out of the party.

World War I brought another crisis. Communists all over Europe ignored class loyalty and chose to fight for their country instead. They joined their nations' armies to fight each other—not the capitalists. Lenin said that the war would help capitalists profit while workers suffered. He urged that Communists "transform the imperialist war into a civil war."

As the war continued, the Russian people suffered terribly. In March 1917, hungry, angry workers and soldiers overthrew the czar. Lenin and his supporters won permission from Germany to travel through German lands back to Russia.

Lenin accepted the new temporary government but said that it was not revolutionary enough. He urged that power go to the soviets, which were councils of workers set up in many cities. His position grew dangerous. He was branded a German agent and was forced to live in hiding in Finland. From that base, he issued a stream of writings urging immediate Russian withdrawal from the war and for the government to give land and bread to the people. These cries gained popularity. In late October, he returned to Russia, disguised for his safety. He persuaded the party's leaders that it was time to overthrow the provisional government but watched with alarm as no steps were taken. Finally, on November 7, 1917, the Bolsheviks overthrew the temporary government. The soviets chose the 47-year-old Lenin as their leader.

Lenin quickly made peace with Germany, giving up large chunks of Russian territory. A civil war, though, still raged in Russia between the Bolsheviks and their opponents. However, Lenin's leadership ensured that the new government would survive.

With peace came the question of how to rule the new state. The country was named the Union of Soviet Socialist Republics, and the Bolsheviks renamed themselves the Communist Party. In Lenin's last years, he struggled to prevent Stalin from gaining power. Lenin became ill and died in 1924.

Questions

1. ***Drawing Conclusions*** What is the danger of Lenin's idea of party leadership?
2. ***Making Inferences*** Why did the Germans allow Lenin and his associates to return to Russia?
3. ***Determining Main Ideas*** What obstacles did Lenin have to overcome to achieve his revolution?

40 UNIT 4, CHAPTER 14

In-Depth Resources: Unit 4

Lenin Restores Order

10.7.1

Critical Thinking

- Why was Lenin's NEP a surprising step, considering Russia's history? *(Russia's czars did not allow free trade.)*
- How did Lenin's Communist Party stray from Marx's original concept of communism? *(The Party became a dictatorship—one person in charge—instead of leadership by the people or proletariat.)*

Analyzing Key Concepts

Communism

Introduce communism to students as a key to understanding Russian history after 1917. Communism was based on achieving equality through uniform distribution of food and products, not on the potential of each citizen to compete and earn. These ideals quickly broke down. Those who championed this social system fell victim to the desire for control and absolute power themselves. In the end, the people who were to be helped by the system suffered under the oppression of dictatorial rule.

SKILLBUILDER Answer

Comparing and Contrasting Lenin included the peasants in the proletariat, used professional revolutionaries, and wanted a strong central government.

Russia's civil war proved far more deadly than the earlier revolutions. Around 14 million Russians died in the three-year struggle and in the famine that followed. The destruction and loss of life from fighting, hunger, and a worldwide flu epidemic left Russia in chaos. In the end, the Red Army crushed all opposition. The victory showed that the Bolsheviks were able both to seize power and to maintain it. C

MAIN IDEA

Identifying Problems

C What problems did Lenin and the Bolsheviks face after the revolution?

C. Answer Russia's involvement in World War I, social unrest, political opponents, civil war, famine

Comparing World Revolutions In its immediate and long-term effects, the Russian Revolution was more like the French Revolution than the American Revolution. The American Revolution expanded English political ideas into a constitutional government that built on many existing structures. In contrast, both the French and Russian revolutions attempted to destroy existing social and political structures. Revolutionaries in France and Russia used violence and terror to control people. France became a constitutional monarchy for a time, but the Russian Revolution established a state-controlled society that lasted for decades.

Lenin Restores Order

War and revolution destroyed the Russian economy. Trade was at a standstill. Industrial production dropped, and many skilled workers fled to other countries. Lenin turned to reviving the economy and restructuring the government.

New Economic Policy In March 1921, Lenin temporarily put aside his plan for a state-controlled economy. Instead, he resorted to a small-scale version of capitalism called the New Economic Policy (NEP). The reforms under the NEP allowed peasants to sell their surplus crops instead of turning them over to the government. The government kept control of major industries, banks, and means of communication, but it let some small factories, businesses, and farms operate under private ownership. The government also encouraged foreign investment.

Analyzing Key Concepts

Communism

Communism is a political and economic system of organization. In theory, property is owned by the community and all citizens share in the common wealth according to their need. In practice, this was difficult to achieve.

German philosopher Karl Marx saw communism as the end result of an essential historical process. Russian revolutionary Vladimir Lenin built on Marx's theories and sought ways of applying those theories. Ultimately, however, Lenin's communist state—the Union of Soviet Socialist Republics (USSR)—became a one-party, totalitarian system. This chart compares how Marx and Lenin viewed communism.

SKILLBUILDER: Interpreting Charts

Comparing and Contrasting *How did Lenin's ideas about communism differ from those of Marx?*

Evolution of Communist Thought

Marx	Lenin
• History was the story of class struggle.	• History was the story of class struggle.
• The struggle Marx saw was between capitalists and the proletariat, or the workers.	• The struggle Lenin saw was capitalists against the proletariat and the peasants.
• The proletariat's numbers would become so great and their condition so poor that a spontaneous revolution would occur.	• The proletariat and the peasants were not capable of leading a revolution and needed the guidance of professional revolutionaries.
• The revolution would end with a "dictatorship of the proletariat"—the communal ownership of wealth.	• After the revolution, the state needed to be run by a single party with disciplined, centrally directed administrators in order to ensure its goals. 

COOPERATIVE LEARNING

B

"Interviewing" Key Figures of Revolutionary Russia

Class Time 30 minutes

Task Role-playing and writing about key figures of the revolutionary period

Purpose To learn more about these historical personalities

Instructions Divide the class into pairs. Each pair will select a key figure from revolutionary Russia to investigate. Examples include Nicholas II, Alexandra, Rasputin, Lenin, Trotsky, or Kerensky.

One student will role-play the character while the other poses as a journalist/interviewer. Pairs of students should work together to conduct a believable interview and then write a newspaper story about the person.

When students have completed their news stories, pairs should read them aloud. Audience members will then conduct a question-and-answer session, such as would occur at a press conference. Encourage students to think of questions relevant to the particular figure's role in the Russian Revolution.

Collect all interviews and bind them into one journal for display in the classroom. Have students come up with an appropriate name for the journal, and ask a volunteer to create a cover page.

Thanks partly to the new policies and to the peace that followed the civil war, the country slowly recovered. By 1928, Russia's farms and factories were producing as much as they had before World War I.

Political Reforms Bolshevik leaders saw nationalism as a threat to unity and party loyalty. To keep nationalism in check, Lenin organized Russia into several self-governing republics under the central government. In 1922, the country was named the Union of Soviet Socialist Republics (USSR), in honor of the councils that helped launch the Bolshevik Revolution. D

MAIN IDEA
Summarizing
D How did the Communist government prevent nationalism from threatening the new state created by the revolution?
D. Possible Answer The Communists organized Russia under a central government; renamed the country after the Bolshevik councils.

The Bolsheviks renamed their party the **Communist Party**. The name came from the writings of Karl Marx. He used the word *communism* to describe the classless society that would exist after workers had seized power. In 1924, the Communists created a constitution based on socialist and democratic principles. In reality, the Communist Party held all the power. Lenin had established a dictatorship of the Communist Party, not "a dictatorship of the proletariat," as Marx had promoted.

Stalin Becomes Dictator

Lenin suffered a stroke in 1922. He survived, but the incident set in motion competition for heading up the Communist Party. Two of the most notable men were Leon Trotsky and **Joseph Stalin**. Stalin was cold, hard, and impersonal. During his early days as a Bolshevik, he changed his name to Stalin, which means "man of steel" in Russian. The name fit well.

Stalin began his ruthless climb to the head of the government between 1922 and 1927. In 1922, as general secretary of the Communist Party, he worked behind the scenes to move his supporters into positions of power. Lenin believed that Stalin was a dangerous man. Shortly before he died in 1924, Lenin wrote, "Comrade Stalin . . . has concentrated enormous power in his hands, and I am not sure that he always knows how to use that power with sufficient caution." By 1928, Stalin was in total command of the Communist Party. Trotsky, forced into exile in 1929, was no longer a threat. Stalin now stood poised to wield absolute power as a dictator.

SECTION 1 ASSESSMENT

TERMS & NAMES 1. For each term or name, write a sentence explaining its significance.
• proletariat • Bolsheviks • Lenin • Rasputin • provisional government • soviet • Communist Party • Joseph Stalin

USING YOUR NOTES

2. Which event on your time line caused the deaths of 14 million Russians? (10.7.2)

1894 — 1922

MAIN IDEAS

3. How did World War I help to bring about the Russian Revolution? (10.7.3)
4. What groups made up the Red Army and the White Army? (10.7.1)
5. Why did the Bolsheviks rename their party the Communist Party? (10.3.6)

CRITICAL THINKING & WRITING

6. **DRAWING CONCLUSIONS** How did the czar's autocratic policies toward the people lead to social unrest? (10.6.3)
7. **EVALUATING DECISIONS** What do you think were Czar Nicholas II's worst errors in judgment during his rule? (10.6.3)
8. **FORMING OPINIONS** Which of the events during the last phase of czarist rule do you think was most responsible for the fall of the czar? (10.6.3)
9. **WRITING ACTIVITY** REVOLUTION Write a paragraph **analysis** of Lenin's leadership in the success of the Bolshevik Revolution. (Writing 2.3.a)

INTEGRATED TECHNOLOGY **INTERNET ACTIVITY**
Use the Internet to visit Lenin's Tomb in Red Square in Moscow. Write an **evaluation** of the Web site. (Writing 2.3.c)

INTERNET KEYWORD
Lenin's mausoleum

Tip for Struggling Readers

Explain that "a dictatorship of the proletariat" is another way of saying that the proletariat–the people–take over the government and create a new society in which people are neither rich nor poor.

Stalin Becomes Dictator
10.7.2

Critical Thinking

- Why did Stalin force Trotsky into exile? *(Stalin saw him as a threat to taking total power.)*
- What was Lenin's main concern about Stalin? *(Lenin thought Stalin was power hungry and might abuse his power.)*

3 ASSESS

SECTION 1 ASSESSMENT

Have students work individually to answer the questions. Then have them compare and check their answers with a partner.

Formal Assessment
- Section Quiz, p. 242

4 RETEACH

Use the Guided Reading activity for Section 1 to review the main ideas for this section.

In-Depth Resources: Unit 4
- Guided Reading, p. 24
- Reteaching Activity, p. 43

ANSWERS

1. proletariat, p. 434 • Bolsheviks, p. 434 • Lenin, p. 434 • Rasputin, p. 435 • provisional government, p. 436 • soviet, p. 436 • Communist Party, p. 439 • Joseph Stalin, p. 439
2. **Sample Answer:** 1894—Nicholas II becomes czar; 1917—czarist rule ends; 1918–1920—Civil War; 1922—Union of Soviet Socialist Republics formed. Event—Russia's civil war cost 14 million lives.
3. troop morale low, fuel and food shortages at home
4. Red Army—the Bolsheviks; White Army—three factions of opposition to Red Army (czarists, democrats, anti-Lenin socialists)
5. Communisim was Karl Marx's name for a classless society and "dictatorship of the proletariat."
6. Czars ignored people's needs, ruled oppressively, failed to share power
7. **Possible Answers:** Russo-Japanese War, refusal to share power with the Duma, entry into World War I
8. **Possible Answers:** entry into World War I, hunger and discomfort at home
9. **Rubric** Analyses should
   - identify Lenin's leadership style.
   - present examples of Lenin's leadership.
   - evaluate Lenin's role in revolution.

INTEGRATED TECHNOLOGY

Rubric Evaluations should
- identify the site visited.
- list pros and cons based on criteria.
- clearly summarize the findings.

LESSON PLAN

OBJECTIVES

- Define totalitarianism.
- Describe Stalin's goal of transforming the Soviet Union into a totalitarian state.
- Summarize Stalin's state-controlled economic programs.
- Describe Soviet daily life.

1 FOCUS & MOTIVATE

Ask students to imagine what it would be like to not have the freedom to choose what they buy, where they work, what they eat, and what they say. What would they miss the most, and why?

2 INSTRUCT

A Government of Total Control
10.7.2

Critical Thinking

- Why does control of education help totalitarian regimes become successful? *(Children taught beliefs at an early age are less likely to question them later.)*

CALIFORNIA RESOURCES
California Reading Toolkit, p. L63
California Modified Lesson Plans for English Learners, p. 121
California Daily Standards Practice Transparencies, TT55
California Standards Enrichment Workbook, pp. 69–70, 73–74, 75–76, 77–78, 85–86
California Standards Planner and Lesson Plans, p. L117
California Online Test Practice
California Test Generator CD-ROM
California Easy Planner CD-ROM
California eEdition CD-ROM

2

Totalitarianism

CASE STUDY: Stalinist Russia

MAIN IDEA	WHY IT MATTERS NOW	TERMS & NAMES
POWER AND AUTHORITY After Lenin died, Stalin seized power and transformed the Soviet Union into a totalitarian state.	More recent dictators have used Stalin's tactics for seizing total control over individuals and the state.	• totalitarianism • Great Purge • command economy • Five-Year Plan • collective farm

CALIFORNIA STANDARDS

10.6.3 Understand the widespread disillusionment with prewar institutions, authorities, and values that resulted in a void that was later filled by totalitarians.

10.7.1 Understand the causes and consequences of the Russian Revolution, including Lenin's use of totalitarian means to seize and maintain control (e.g., the Gulag).

10.7.2 Trace Stalin's rise to power in the Soviet Union and the connection between economic policies, political policies, the absence of a free press, and systematic violations of human rights (e.g., the Terror Famine in Ukraine).

10.7.3 Analyze the rise, aggression, and human costs of totalitarian regimes (Fascist and Communist) in Germany, Italy, and the Soviet Union, noting especially their common and dissimilar traits.

10.8.4 Describe the political, diplomatic, and military leaders during the war (e.g., Winston Churchill, Franklin Delano Roosevelt, Emperor Hirohito, Adolf Hitler, Benito Mussolini, Joseph Stalin, Douglas MacArthur, Dwight Eisenhower).

TAKING NOTES
Categorizing Create a chart listing examples of methods of control used in the Soviet Union.

Methods of control	Example
1.	
2.	
3.	
4.	

SETTING THE STAGE Stalin, Lenin's successor, dramatically transformed the government of the Soviet Union. Stalin was determined that the Soviet Union should find its place both politically and economically among the most powerful of nations in the world. Using tactics designed to rid himself of opposition, Stalin worked to establish total control of all aspects of life in the Soviet Union. He controlled not only the government, but also the economy and many aspects of citizens' private lives.

A Government of Total Control

The term **totalitarianism** describes a government that takes total, centralized, state control over every aspect of public and private life. Totalitarian leaders appear to provide a sense of security and to give a direction for the future. In the 20th century, the widespread use of mass communication made it possible to reach into all aspects of citizens' lives.

A dynamic leader who can build support for his policies and justify his actions heads most totalitarian governments. Often the leader utilizes secret police to crush opposition and create a sense of fear among the people. No one is exempt from suspicion or accusations that he or she is an enemy of the state.

Totalitarianism challenges the highest values prized by Western democracies—reason, freedom, human dignity, and the worth of the individual. As the chart on the next page shows, all totalitarian states share basic characteristics.

To dominate an entire nation, totalitarian leaders devised methods of control and persuasion. These included the use of terror, indoctrination, propaganda, censorship, and religious or ethnic persecution.

Police Terror Dictators of totalitarian states use terror and violence to force obedience and to crush opposition. Normally, the police are expected to respond to criminal activity and protect the citizens. In a totalitarian state, the police serve to enforce the central government's policies. They may do this by spying on the citizens or by intimidating them. Sometimes they use brutal force and even murder to achieve their goals.

Indoctrination Totalitarian states rely on indoctrination—instruction in the government's beliefs—to mold people's minds. Control of education is absolutely essential to glorify the leader and his policies and to convince all citizens that their

SECTION 2 PROGRAM RESOURCES

ALL STUDENTS
In-Depth Resources: Unit 4
- Guided Reading, p. 25

Formal Assessment
- Section Quiz, p. 243

ENGLISH LEARNERS
In-Depth Resources in Spanish
- Guided Reading, p. 111

Reading Study Guide, p. 149
Reading Study Guide Audio CD (Spanish)

STRUGGLING READERS
In-Depth Resources: Unit 4
- Guided Reading, p. 25
- Building Vocabulary, p. 28
- Reteaching Activity, p. 44

Reading Study Guide, p. 149
Reading Study Guide Audio CD

GIFTED AND TALENTED STUDENTS
In-Depth Resources: Unit 4
- Primary Source: The Need for Progress, p. 33
- Literature: from *Darkness at Noon,* p. 36; from *1984,* p. 38

Electronic Library of Primary Sources
- from *1984*

INTEGRATED TECHNOLOGY

eEdition CD-ROM
Power Presentations CD-ROM
Geography Transparencies
- GT30 European Totalitarianism by 1938

Electronic Library of Primary Sources
- from *1984*

classzone.com

Analyzing Key Concepts

Totalitarianism

Totalitarianism is a form of government in which the national government takes control of all aspects of both public and private life. Thus, totalitarianism seeks to erase the line between government and society. It has an ideology, or set of beliefs, that all citizens are expected to approve. It is often led by a dynamic leader and a single political party.

Mass communication technology helps a totalitarian government spread its aims and support its policies. Also, surveillance technology makes it possible to keep track of the activities of many people. Finally, violence, such as police terror, discourages those who disagree with the goals of the government.

Key Traits of Totalitarianism

CALIFORNIA STANDARDS
10.7.3, REP 4

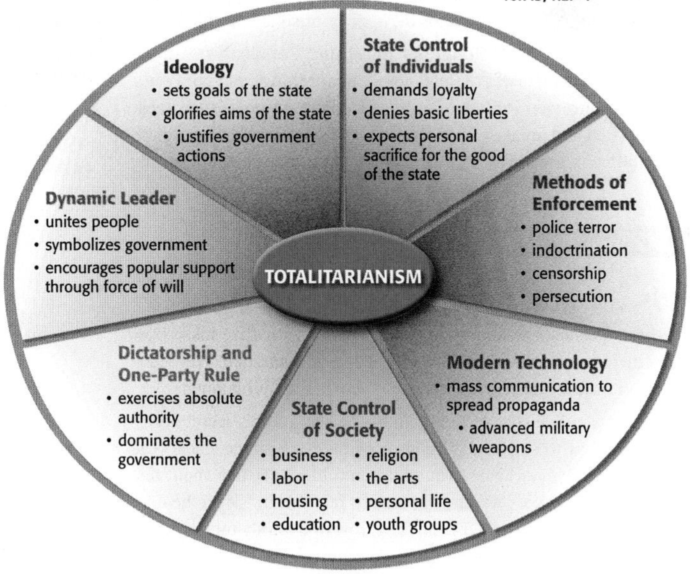

TOTALITARIANISM

Ideology
- sets goals of the state
- glorifies aims of the state
- justifies government actions

State Control of Individuals
- demands loyalty
- denies basic liberties
- expects personal sacrifice for the good of the state

Methods of Enforcement
- police terror
- indoctrination
- censorship
- persecution

Modern Technology
- mass communication to spread propaganda
- advanced military weapons

State Control of Society
- business
- labor
- housing
- education
- religion
- the arts
- personal life
- youth groups

Dictatorship and One-Party Rule
- exercises absolute authority
- dominates the government

Dynamic Leader
- unites people
- symbolizes government
- encourages popular support through force of will

Fear of Totalitarianism

George Orwell illustrated the horrors of a totalitarian government in his novel, *1984*. The novel depicts a world in which personal freedom and privacy have vanished. It is a world made possible through modern technology. Even citizens' homes have television cameras that constantly survey their behavior.

INTEGRATED TECHNOLOGY

RESEARCH LINKS For more on totalitarianism, go to **classzone.com**

DATA FILE

Totalitarian leaders in the 20th century

- Adolf Hitler (Germany) 1933–1945
- Benito Mussolini (Italy) 1925–1943
- Joseph Stalin (Soviet Union) 1929–1953
- Kim IL Sung (North Korea) 1948–1994
- Saddam Hussein (Iraq) 1979–2003

State Terror

- The two most infamous examples of state terror in the 20th century were in Nazi Germany and Stalinist Russia.
- An estimated12.5–20 million people were killed in Nazi Germany.
- An estimated 8–20 million people were killed in Stalinist Russia.

Totalitarianism Today

- There are many authoritarian regimes in the world, but there are very few actual totalitarian governments. In 2000, one monitoring agency identified five totalitarian regimes—Afghanistan, Cuba, North Korea, Laos, and Vietnam.

Connect *to* Today

1. **Synthesizing** How does a totalitarian state attempt to make citizens obey its rules?

See Skillbuilder Handbook, page R21.

2. **Hypothesizing** How would your life change if you lived in a totalitarian state?

441

Analyzing Key Concepts

OBJECTIVE

- Analyze the combination of traits used to create totalitarian governments.

INSTRUCT

Introduce totalitarianism to students as a key to understanding the Soviet Union in the mid-1900s and the current governments of Cuba, North Korea, Laos, and Vietnam. It is also key to understanding Germany, Italy, Afghanistan, and Iraq during parts of the 20th century.

Geography Transparencies
- GT30 European Totalitarianism by 1938

More About . . .

1984

George Orwell's novel depicts a frightening world where the sinister slogan "Big Brother Is Watching You" appears everywhere and citizens are constantly monitored. There is widespread use of propaganda. Even new words and phrases—called Newspeak—are adopted to serve the propaganda needs of the state.

Ask students to read the appendix to *1984*, which contains a description of Newspeak, and to explain some Newspeak to the class.

In-Depth Resources: Unit 4
- Literature: from *1984*, p. 38

Electronic Library of Primary Sources
- from *1984*

CONNECT TO TODAY: ANSWERS

1. Synthesizing

Possible Answer: The state attempts to make citizens obey its rules through indoctrination, propaganda, and censorship. Control of mass media and of education is essential. Totalitarian states may also use terror and violence to control citizens.

2. Hypothesizing

Possible Answers: Living in a totalitarian state means no individual freedoms, great personal sacrifice, and limited privacy. Personal choices such as where to live, what job to choose, and what beliefs to follow are all controlled by the state.

Tip For Struggling Readers

When information is *biased* it means the person or people giving the information have added their personal opinion, withheld some information, or distorted the facts. Bias is central to propaganda.

Stalin Builds a Totalitarian State

10.7.2; 10.8.4

Critical Thinking

- What is ironic about Stalin putting the Bolsheviks on trial for crimes against the state? *(The Bolshevik Revolution paved the way for Stalin's rise to power; Stalin was originally a Bolshevik.)*
- Why did children report their parents to the secret police? *(They were taught in school to trust educators and authorities above their own parents.)*

In-Depth Resources: Unit 4

- Primary Source: The Need for Progress, Speech by Joseph Stalin, p. 33
- Literature: from *Darkness at Noon,* p. 36

More About . . .

Artists, Writers, and Propaganda

Art and literature became tools of propaganda, as Stalin ordered intellectuals to become "engineers of human souls." Writers and artists who could successfully create works of propaganda were generously rewarded, often living better than the highest members of government.

▲ Members of a Russian youth group called Young Communists line up for a parade. Notice the picture of Stalin in the background.

unconditional loyalty and support are required. Indoctrination begins with very young children, is encouraged by youth groups, and is strongly enforced by schools.

Propaganda and Censorship Totalitarian states spread propaganda, biased or incomplete information used to sway people to accept certain beliefs or actions. Control of all mass media allows this to happen. No publication, film, art, or music is allowed to exist without the permission of the state. Citizens are surrounded with false information that appears to be true. Suggesting that the information is incorrect is considered an act of treason and severely punished. Individuals who dissent must retract their work or they are imprisoned or killed.

Religious or Ethnic Persecution Totalitarian leaders often create "enemies of the state" to blame for things that go wrong. Frequently these enemies are members of religious or ethnic groups. Often these groups are easily identified and are subjected to campaigns of terror and violence. They may be forced to live in certain areas or are subjected to rules that apply only to them. A

A. Possible Answer Indoctrination, because eventually those who oppose the regime will die and those who are indoctrinated will remain to support the ruler.

MAIN IDEA

Evaluating Courses of Action

A Of the weapons of totalitarianism, which allows the most long-term control?

CASE STUDY: Stalinist Russia

Stalin Builds a Totalitarian State

Stalin aimed to create a perfect Communist state in Russia. To realize his vision, Stalin planned to transform the Soviet Union into a totalitarian state. He began building his totalitarian state by destroying his enemies—real and imagined.

Police State Stalin built a police state to maintain his power. Stalin's secret police used tanks and armored cars to stop riots. They monitored telephone lines, read mail, and planted informers everywhere. Even children told authorities about disloyal remarks they heard at home. Every family came to fear the knock on the door in the early morning hours, which usually meant the arrest of a family member. The secret police arrested and executed millions of so-called traitors.

In 1934, Stalin turned against members of the Communist Party. In 1937, he launched the **Great Purge**, a campaign of terror directed at eliminating anyone who threatened his power. Thousands of old Bolsheviks who helped stage the Revolution in 1917 stood trial. They were executed or sent to labor camps for "crimes against the Soviet state." When the Great Purge ended in 1938, Stalin had gained total control of the Soviet government and the Communist Party. Historians estimate that during this time he was responsible for 8 million to 13 million deaths. B

MAIN IDEA

Recognizing Effects

B How would the actions of the Great Purge increase Stalin's power?

B. Answer He eliminated millions who opposed him.

Russian Propaganda and Censorship Stalin's government controlled all newspapers, motion pictures, radio, and other sources of information. Many Soviet writers, composers, and other artists also fell victim to official censorship. Stalin would not tolerate individual creativity that did not conform to the views of the state. Soviet newspapers and radio broadcasts glorified the achievements of communism, Stalin, and his economic programs.

Under Stalin, the arts also were used for propaganda. In 1930, an editorial in the Communist Party newspaper *Pravda* explained the purpose of art: "Literature, the

DIFFERENTIATING INSTRUCTION: GIFTED AND TALENTED STUDENTS

Creating a Fictional Totalitarian State

Class Time 45 minutes

Task Describing a fictional state

Purpose To investigate the differences between totalitarianism and a democratic system

Instructions Have small groups brainstorm examples for each key trait of totalitarianism identified in the chart on page 441. They will use these examples to help them create a fictional totalitarian state. They should invent a name for the state, identify its location, make up a name for the dictator, and list the effects of totalitarianism on individual lives. Each group should write a detailed description of the state and include how a leader or regime would go about changing life from a democratic, free country to one led by a dictator. Students might use a chart like the one in In-Depth Resources: Unit 4, page 25. Students may make their description into posters or graphics depicting their plan and/or effects of the plan once enacted.

Have groups present their fictional government to the class. Then start a discussion about the differences between life under totalitarianism and life in a democratic society. A leadoff question might be "What would a day in the classroom be like under this fictitious regime?"

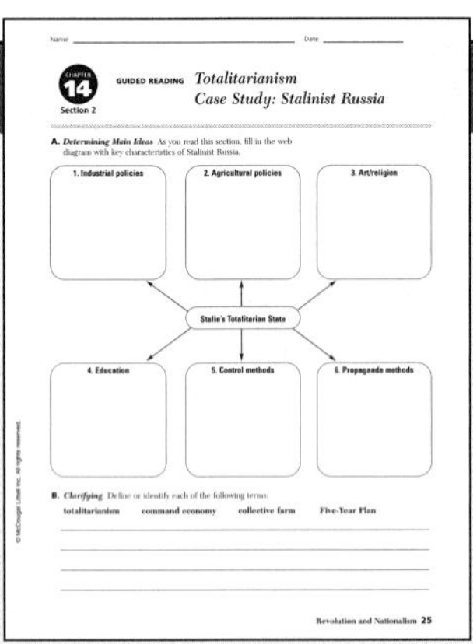

In-Depth Resources: Unit 4

cinema, the arts are levers in the hands of the proletariat which must be used to show the masses positive models of initiative and heroic labor."

Education and Indoctrination Under Stalin, the government controlled all education from nursery schools through the universities. Schoolchildren learned the virtues of the Communist Party. College professors and students who questioned the Communist Party's interpretations of history or science risked losing their jobs or faced imprisonment. Party leaders in the Soviet Union lectured workers and peasants on the ideals of communism. They also stressed the importance of sacrifice and hard work to build the Communist state. State-supported youth groups trained future party members.

Religious Persecution Communists aimed to replace religious teachings with the ideals of communism. Under Stalin, the government and the League of the Militant Godless, an officially sponsored group of atheists, spread propaganda attacking religion. "Museums of atheism" displayed exhibits to show that religious beliefs were mere superstitions. Yet many people in the Soviet Union still clung to their faiths.

Vocabulary
atheists: people who do not think there is a god

The Russian Orthodox Church was the main target of persecution. Other religious groups also suffered greatly. The police destroyed magnificent churches and synagogues, and many religious leaders were killed or sent to labor camps.

Achieving the perfect Communist state came at a tremendous cost to Soviet citizens. Stalin's total control of society eliminated personal rights and freedoms in favor of the power of the state.

History Makers

Joseph Stalin
1879–1953

Stalin was born in bitter poverty in Georgia, a region in southern Russia. Unlike the well-educated and cultured Lenin, Stalin was rough and crude.

Stalin tried to create a myth that he was the country's father and savior. Stalin glorified himself as the symbol of the nation. He encouraged people to think of him as "The Greatest Genius of All Times and Peoples."

Many towns, factories, and streets in the Soviet Union were named for Stalin. A new metal was called Stalinite. An orchid was named Stalinchid. Children standing before their desks every morning said, "Thank Comrade Stalin for this happy life."

INTEGRATED TECHNOLOGY

INTERNET ACTIVITY Create a Web page on Joseph Stalin. Include pictures and a time line of his rule in the USSR. Go to **classzone.com** for your research.

Stalin Seizes Control of the Economy

As Stalin began to gain complete control of society, he was setting plans in motion to overhaul the economy. He announced, "We are fifty or a hundred years behind the advanced countries. We must make good this distance in ten years." In 1928 Stalin's plans called for a **command economy**, a system in which the government made all economic decisions. Under this system, political leaders identify the country's economic needs and determine how to fulfill them.

An Industrial Revolution Stalin outlined the first of several **Five-Year Plans** for the development of the Soviet Union's economy. The Five-Year Plans set impossibly high quotas, or numerical goals, to increase the output of steel, coal, oil, and electricity. To reach these targets, the government limited production of consumer goods. As a result, people faced severe shortages of housing, food, clothing, and other necessary goods.

Stalin's tough methods produced impressive economic results. Although most of the targets of the first Five-Year Plan fell short, the Soviets made substantial gains. (See the graphs on page 444 for coal and steel production.) A second plan, launched in 1933, proved equally successful. From 1928 to 1937, industrial production of steel increased more than 25 percent.

History Makers

Joseph Stalin

Stalin was born in Russia in 1879. His father was a shoemaker who drank heavily and was reportedly physically abusive to his son. His mother was a poor peasant who worked to support the family. His father died when he was 14, and Stalin was sent to an Orthodox Russian seminary. He was later expelled for studying communism instead of theology. Stalin was married twice and had three children. Both wives died, as well as two sons. His surviving daughter, Svetlana, defected to the United States in 1967.

INTEGRATED TECHNOLOGY

Rubric Web pages should
- include highlights of Stalin's life as ruler of the Soviet Union.
- use pictures and/or photos.
- be accurate.

Stalin Seizes Control of the Economy
10.7.2; 10.7.3

Critical Thinking
- Why did Stalin limit the production of consumer goods? *(Money was put toward manufacturing steel, coal, oil, and electricity instead.)*
- Why wouldn't people want to live on a collective farm? *(no personal incentives, all labor was for the state)*

DIFFERENTIATING INSTRUCTION: STRUGGLING READERS

Using Questions to Find Main Ideas

Class Time 20 minutes

Task Turning headings into questions

Purpose To find and understand main ideas

Instructions Suggest that student pairs focus their reading by turning each heading into a question and then using the material below it and the subheadings to find the answer. Questions should begin with *why*, *how*, or *what.* Students should make a chart like the one shown and use it as they work through the section.

In addition to finding main ideas in the text, students can record new terms or difficult words as they encounter them in the third column. Once students have completed the section using their chart, ask volunteers which words were troublesome. As a group, use context and prior knowledge to understand the words and help unlock the meaning of the passages. For example, the headings on pages 440–441 could be turned into these questions:

Heading	Question	Answer	Difficult Words
A Government of Total Control	What is a government of total control?	State controls all parts of life	Indoctrination, propaganda
Totalitarianism	What is totalitarianism?	Total, centralized control	Ideology, surveillance

An Agricultural Revolution In 1928, the government began to seize over 25 million privately owned farms in the USSR. It combined them into large, government-owned farms, called **collective farms**. Hundreds of families worked on these farms, called collectives, producing food for the state. The government expected that the modern machinery on the collective farms would boost food production and reduce the number of workers. Resistance was especially strong among kulaks, a class of wealthy peasants. The Soviet government decided to eliminate them.

Peasants actively fought the government's attempt to take their land. Many killed livestock and destroyed crops in protest. Soviet secret police herded peasants onto collective farms at the point of a bayonet. Between 5 million and 10 million peasants died as a direct result of Stalin's agricultural revolution. By 1938, more than 90 percent of all peasants lived on collective farms. As you see in the charts below, agricultural production was on the upswing. That year the country produced almost twice the wheat than it had in 1928 before collective farming. C

C. Answer establishment of collective farms; use of terror and violence; destruction of the kulaks

MAIN IDEA

Clarifying

C What methods did Stalin use to bring agriculture under state control?

In areas where farming was more difficult, the government set up state farms. These state farms operated like factories. The workers received wages instead of a share of the profits. These farms were much larger than collectives and mostly produced wheat.

Daily Life Under Stalin

Stalin's totalitarian rule revolutionized Soviet society. Women's roles greatly expanded. People became better educated and mastered new technical skills. The dramatic changes in people's lives, came at great cost. Soviet citizens found their personal freedoms limited, consumer goods in short supply, and dissent prohibited.

Stalin's economic plans created a high demand for many skilled workers. University and technical training became the key to a better life. As one young man explained, "If a person does not want to become a collective farmer or just a cleaning woman, the only means you have to get something is through education."

Women Gain Rights The Bolshevik Revolution of 1917 declared men and women equal. Laws were passed to grant women equal rights. After Stalin became dictator, women helped the state-controlled economy prosper. Under his Five-Year

Daily Life Under Stalin

10.7.1; 10.7.3

Critical Thinking

- What was so revolutionary about education under Stalin? *(More people, including women, were given technical and professional educations.)*
- What were the expectations for women during this time? *(get an education, work full time, maintain a home, have and care for children)*

History from Visuals

Interpreting the Graphs

Emphasize that the bracketed years beneath the charts represent the first and second Five-Year Plans.

Extension Ask students to reread the text under the subheading "An Agricultural Revolution" and to explain the reasons for the sharp decline in livestock.

SKILLBUILDER Answers

1. **Clarifying** about 100,000 metric tons
2. **Drawing Conclusions** Industrial production increased greatly; production of livestock decreased, but wheat production increased.

The Buildup of the Soviet Economy, 1928–1938

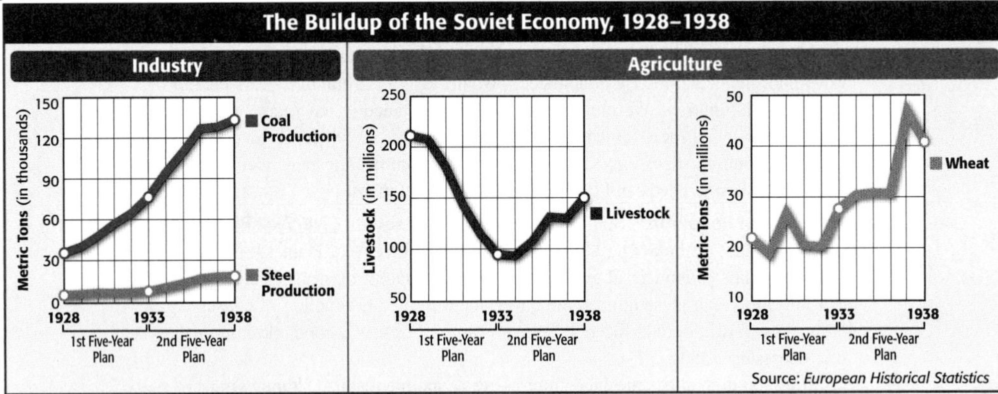

Source: *European Historical Statistics*

SKILLBUILDER: Interpreting Graphs

1. **Clarifying** *How many more metric tons of coal were produced in 1938 than in 1928?*
2. **Drawing Conclusions** *What do the graphs show about the contrast between the progress of industry and agriculture production under Stalin's first Five-Year Plan?*

DIFFERENTIATING INSTRUCTION: ENGLISH LEARNERS

Key Terms of Totalitarianism

Class Time 20 minutes

Task Recording word meanings and examples

Purpose To understand academic vocabulary

Instructions Have students work with some of the key terms that describe characteristics of totalitarianism. Examples are: *indoctrination, propaganda, censorship, religious persecution, ethnic persecution*, and *police state*.

Students will create charts defining each word using context, prior knowledge, and other sources such as dictionaries and glossaries. Then have them give an example of each of the terms. An example of *police state* might be "Police listen to telephone calls."

After students have shared their charts, lead a discussion on what life might be like under a totalitarian state.

Key Term	Meaning	Example
Indoctrination	Teaching the government's beliefs	All textbooks glorify Stalin's ideas.
Propaganda	Slanted and incomplete information	All books and movies present only the communist point of view.

Plans, they had no choice but to join the labor force. The state provided child care for all working mothers. Some young women performed the same jobs as men. Millions of women worked in factories and in construction. However, men continued to hold the best jobs.

Given new educational opportunities, women prepared for careers in engineering and science. Medicine, in particular, attracted many women. By 1950, they made up 75 percent of Soviet doctors.

Soviet women paid a heavy price for their rising status in society. Besides having full-time jobs, they were responsible for housework and child care. Motherhood is considered a patriotic duty in totalitarian regimes. Soviet women were expected to provide the state with future generations of loyal, obedient citizens. D

MAIN IDEA

Summarizing

D How did daily life under Stalin's rule change the lives of women in the Soviet Union?

D. Possible Answer Women had more educational and career opportunities, were forced to enter the work force, and were expected to bear children.

Total Control Achieved

By the mid-1930s, Stalin had forcibly transformed the Soviet Union into a totalitarian regime and an industrial and political power. He stood unopposed as dictator and maintained his authority over the Communist Party. Stalin would not tolerate individual creativity. He saw it as a threat to the conformity and obedience required of citizens in a totalitarian state. He ushered in a period of total social control and rule by terror, rather than constitutional government.

Like Russia, China would fall under the influence of Karl Marx's theories and Communist beliefs. The dynamic leader Mao Zedong would pave the way for transforming China into a totalitarian Communist state, as you will read in Section 3.

Social History

Ukrainian Kulaks

The kulaks in Ukraine (shown above) fiercely resisted collectivization. They murdered officials, torched the property of the collectives, and burned their own crops and grain in protest.

Recognizing the threat kulaks posed to his policies, Stalin declared that they should "liquidate kulaks as a class." The state took control of kulak land and equipment, and confiscated stores of food and grain. More than 3 million Ukrainians were shot, exiled, or imprisoned. Some 6 million people died in the government-engineered famine that resulted from the destruction of crops and animals. By 1935, the kulaks had been eliminated.

SECTION 2 ASSESSMENT

TERMS & NAMES 1. For each term or name, write a sentence explaining its significance.
• totalitarianism • Great Purge • command economy • Five-Year Plans • collective farm

USING YOUR NOTES

2. Which of the methods of control do you think was most influential in maintaining Stalin's power? Why? (10.7.1)

Methods of control	Example
1.	
2.	
3.	
4.	

MAIN IDEAS

3. What are the key traits of a totalitarian state? (10.7.3)
4. What are some ways totalitarian rulers keep their power? (10.7.3)
5. How did the Soviet economy change under the direction of Stalin? (10.7.2)

CRITICAL THINKING & WRITING

6. **CONTRASTING** How do totalitarian states and constitutional governments differ? (10.7.3)
7. **SUMMARIZING** Summarize Joseph Stalin's rise to power and how his control expanded. (10.8.4)
8. **EVALUATING COURSES OF ACTION** Were the Five-Year plans the best way to move the Soviet economy forward? Explain. (10.7.2)
9. **WRITING ACTIVITY** POWER AND AUTHORITY As an industrial worker, a female doctor, a Russian Orthodox priest, or a Communist Party member, write a **journal entry** about your life under Stalin. (Writing 2.1.c)

CONNECT TO TODAY **Graphing Russia's Economy**

Research Russia's industrial and agricultural production in the last 10 years. Create a series of **graphs** similar to those found on page 444. (Writing 2.3.d)

Social History

Ukrainian Kulaks

Before 1917, kulaks were central figures in peasant villages. They owned farms, livestock, and horses. They were wealthy enough to be able to hire laborers as farmhands and had enough land to be able to lease parts of it. The Soviet government regarded kulaks as capitalists because they made their own living and prospered financially. This was considered anticommunist and regarded as a threat.

Total Control Achieved

10.7.2

Critical Thinking

- Why did the people of Russia go along with Stalin's regime? *(belief it was for the good of the state; violent repression)*
- What is one primary way totalitarianism differs from democratic thinking? *(A totalitarian regime places ultimate value on itself, not on its citizens.)*

3 ASSESS

SECTION 2 ASSESSMENT

After students have responded to the questions independently, engage the whole class in a discussion of question 2.

Formal Assessment
- Section Quiz, p. 243

4 RETEACH

Use the Reteaching Activity to review the main ideas of the section.

In-Depth Resources: Unit 4
- Reteaching Activity, p. 44

ANSWERS

1. totalitarianism, p. 440 • Great Purge, p. 442 • command economy, p. 443 • Five-Year Plans, p. 443 • collective farm, 444

2. **Sample Answer:** 1. Police Terror–Great Purge, kulaks; 2. Propaganda–Government-controlled media; 3. Indoctrination–Education and training; 4. Persecution–Elimination of leadership. Most influential–Indoctrination, because it began in childhood.

3. dictatorship and one-party rule, dynamic leader, ideology, state control, modern technology, methods of enforcement

4. police terror, indoctrination, propaganda and censorship, persecution

5. Industry increased by more than 25 percent and production of wheat doubled. There were severe shortages of consumer goods.

6. **Possible Answers:** Totalitarian–Under one ruler; controlled society and people; use of force and propaganda. Democratic–Separation of powers; elected leaders; private ownership; military for defense.

7. general secretary of the Communist Party; eliminated competitors; controlled society, revamped economy

8. Yes–Soviet economy was failing, needed revamping. No–They cost millions of lives and sacrifices by consumers and workers.

9. **Rubric** Journal entries should
- refer to the person's role.
- identify hardships or advantages.

CONNECT TO TODAY

Rubric Graphs should
- present accurate statistics.
- be easy to read and interpret.
- cite sources.

History *through* Art

OBJECTIVES

- Recognize how propaganda was used in Stalinist Russia.
- Understand the tools used by a totalitarian leader to further a cause.

FOCUS & MOTIVATE

Propaganda is pervasive in our society today. It is used to sell products and to persuade people to join groups and organizations. Ask students how they recognize propaganda in daily life. Encourage them to bring examples for the class to examine and discuss.

INSTRUCT

Critical Thinking

- What message was Stalin sending through the posters? *(Working for the Communist cause was a good and worthy thing to do.)*
- How could these posters help achieve Stalin's goals for agriculture and industry? *(The propaganda on the posters influenced people to work harder to achieve economic goals.)*

More About . . .

Propaganda

The term *propaganda* is often used negatively to mean false or misleading types of persuasion. Propaganda may rely on a range of persuasive tactics—from factual evidence to outright lies. Soviet propagandists under Stalin made shrewd use of posters to create a new "reality"—an idealized vision of life in a totalitarian state.

Propaganda

You have read how a totalitarian government can use propaganda to support its goals. These pages show three examples of visual propaganda from the Soviet Union—low-cost posters, traditional painting, and altered photographs.

Posters were mass produced and placed in very visible areas. They were constant reminders of Communist policy and guides for proper thought. Artists were required to paint scenes that supported and glorified the Communist Party. Even photographs were altered if they contained individuals who had fallen out of favor with the party leadership.

CALIFORNIA STANDARDS

10.7.3 Analyze the rise, aggression, and human costs of totalitarian regimes (Fascist and Communist) in Germany, Italy, and the Soviet Union, noting especially their common and dissimilar traits.

CST 1 Students compare the present with the past, evaluating the consequences of past events and decisions and determining the lessons that were learned.

INTEGRATED TECHNOLOGY

RESEARCH LINKS For more on propaganda, go to **classzone.com**

◄ Factory Poster
"Help build the gigantic factories." This poster advertises a state loan for the building of large factories. Developing heavy industry was an important goal in the early days of the Soviet Union.

▼ Painting
In this painting the central figure, Communist leader Joseph Stalin, is greeted enthusiastically. The expressions of the diverse and happy crowd imply not only that Stalin has broad support, but that he is worshiped as well.

Woman Worker Poster ▲
A translation of this poster says, "What the October Revolution has given to working and peasant women." The woman is pointing to buildings such as a library, a worker's club, and a school for adults.

RECOMMENDED RESOURCES

Books

Jahn, Hubertus F. ***Patriotic Culture in Russia During World War I.*** Ithaca, NY: Cornell UP, 1995.

Taylor, Richard. ***Film Propaganda: Soviet Russia and Nazi Germany***. London and New York: I. B. Tauris, 1998.

Videos

Propaganda. VHS and DVD. Films for the Humanities & Sciences, 2000. 800-257-5126. Focuses on dictators and propagandists who shaped the perceptions of the masses in 20th-century Europe.

The October 1917 Revolution and After. VHS. Films for the Humanities & Sciences. 800-257-5126. Features Soviet propaganda films that dramatized events of the Revolution.

▼ Altered Photographs

Stalin attempted to enhance his legacy and erase his rivals from history by extensively altering photographs as this series shows.

1. The original photograph was taken in 1926 and showed, from left to right, Nikolai Antipov, Stalin, Sergei Kirov, and Nikolai Shvernik.
2. This altered image appeared in a 1949 biography of Stalin. Why Shvernik was removed is unclear—he was head of the Central Committee of the Communist Party until Stalin's death in 1954. Antipov, however, was arrested during Stalin's purge and executed in 1941.
3. This heroic oil painting by Isaak Brodsky is based on the original photograph, but only Stalin is left. Kirov was assassinated in 1934 by a student, but the official investigation report has never been released. Stalin did fear Kirov's popularity and considered him a threat to his leadership.

Connect *to* Today

1. **Forming and Supporting Opinions** Of the examples on this page, which do you think would have been most effective as propaganda? Why?
   See Skillbuilder Handbook, page R20.
2. **Comparing and Contrasting** What are the similarities and differences between propaganda and modern advertising campaigns? Support your answer with examples.

447

More About . . .

The Role of Propaganda

All governments, not only totalitarian regimes, use propaganda to generate public support for their policies, political parties, and candidates for office. Advertisers and various organizations also use propaganda techniques. Ask students why recognizing propaganda is important. *(Possible Answer: keeps people from being manipulated)*

More About . . .

The Lot of Soviet Workers

The idealism of building the world's first socialist state appealed to many Soviet citizens, especially in the 1930s when other nations were suffering from economic depression. Unlike the United States and Western Europe, no one was unemployed in Soviet society. And workers received benefits such as free education, free medical care, and pensions.

Inclusion Tip

Students who are visually impaired might benefit from an overhead transparency of a 1924 Soviet propaganda painting.

World Art and Cultures Transparencies

- AT65 Friendship of the People

CONNECT TO TODAY: ANSWERS

1. Forming and Supporting Opinions

Possible Answers: Posters—Easy to manufacture and could be placed where large numbers of people could see them; Paintings—A respected art form and all of the details of the image can be controlled; Altering photographs—Photographs appear to represent things as they are. If a photograph can be successfully manipulated, then it might maintain a claim to authenticity.

2. Comparing and Contrasting

Possible Answers: Similarities—Both promote a strong position, try to persuade citizens and consumers to believe in the ideas or product, can be colorful and appealing, and may tell only part of the truth. Differences—Propaganda often distorts and lies. Advertising can be selectively truthful, but consumer reactions can reduce outright lies. Propaganda is usually used to "sell" ideas or beliefs. Advertising is usually used to sell products or services.

LESSON PLAN

OBJECTIVES

- List problems the new Republic of China faced.
- Trace the rise of communism in China.
- Describe the civil war between Communists and Nationalists.

1 FOCUS & MOTIVATE

Students will learn about the Long March in this section. What periods of hardship have students studied in U.S. history? *(Possible Answer: Valley Forge)*

2 INSTRUCT

Nationalists Overthrow Qing Dynasty
10.9.4

Critical Thinking

- What event triggered civil war in China? *(the death of General Yuan Shikai)*
- What were the main weaknesses of the new republic? *(Possible Answers: weak central rule, lack of respect from other nations, country needed modernizing)*

CALIFORNIA RESOURCES
California Reading Toolkit, p. L64
California Modified Lesson Plans for English Learners, p. 123
California Daily Standards Practice Transparencies, TT56
California Standards Enrichment Workbook, pp. 65–66, 79–80, 97–98
California Standards Planner and Lesson Plans, p. L119
California Online Test Practice
California Test Generator CD-ROM
California Easy Planner CD-ROM
California eEdition CD-ROM

Poster of Russian soldier with flag, by N. Tyrkurr

3

Temple of Heaven, Beijing, China

Imperial China Collapses

MAIN IDEA

REVOLUTION After the fall of the Qing dynasty, nationalist and Communist movements struggled for power.

WHY IT MATTERS NOW

The seeds of China's late-20th-century political thought, communism, were planted at this time.

TERMS & NAMES

- Kuomintang
- Sun Yixian
- May Fourth Movement
- Mao Zedong
- Jiang Jieshi
- Long March

CALIFORNIA STANDARDS

10.6.1 Analyze the aims and negotiating roles of world leaders, the terms and influence of the Treaty of Versailles and Woodrow Wilson's Fourteen Points, and the causes and effects of the United States's rejection of the League of Nations on world politics.

10.8.1 Compare the German, Italian, and Japanese drives for empire in the 1930s, including the 1937 Rape of Nanking, other atrocities in China, and the Stalin-Hitler Pact of 1939.

10.9.4 Analyze the Chinese Civil War, the rise of Mao Tse-tung, and the subsequent political and economic upheavals in China (e.g., the Great Leap Forward, the Cultural Revolution, and the Tiananmen Square uprising).

SETTING THE STAGE In the early 1900s, China was ripe for revolution. China had faced years of humiliation at the hands of outsiders. Foreign countries controlled its trade and economic resources. Many Chinese believed that modernization and nationalism held the country's keys for survival. They wanted to build up the army and navy, to construct modern factories, and to reform education. Yet others feared change. They believed that China's greatness lay in its traditional ways.

TAKING NOTES

Comparing and Contrasting Make a chart to compare and contrast the actions of Jiang Jieshi and Mao Zedong in controlling China.

Jiang	Mao
1.	1.
2.	2.
3.	3.

Nationalists Overthrow Qing Dynasty

Among the groups pushing for modernization and nationalization was the **Kuomintang** (KWOH•mihn•TANG), or the Nationalist Party. Its first great leader was **Sun Yixian** (soon yee•shyahn). In 1911, the Revolutionary Alliance, a forerunner of the Kuomintang, succeeded in overthrowing the last emperor of the Qing dynasty. The Qing had ruled China since 1644.

Shaky Start for the New Republic In 1912, Sun became president of the new Republic of China. Sun hoped to establish a modern government based on the "Three Principles of the People": (1) nationalism—an end to foreign control, (2) people's rights—democracy, and (3) people's livelihood—economic security for all Chinese. Sun Yixian considered nationalism vital. He said, "The Chinese people . . . do not have national spirit. Therefore even though we have four hundred million people gathered together in one China, in reality, they are just a heap of loose sand." Despite his lasting influence as a revolutionary leader, Sun lacked the authority and military support to secure national unity.

Sun turned over the presidency to a powerful general, Yuan Shikai, who quickly betrayed the democratic ideals of the revolution. His actions sparked local revolts. After the general died in 1916, civil war broke out. Real authority fell into the hands of provincial warlords or powerful military leaders. They ruled territories as large as their armies could conquer.

▶ Sun Yixian led the overthrow of the last Chinese emperor.

SECTION 3 PROGRAM RESOURCES

ALL STUDENTS

In-Depth Resources: Unit 4
- Guided Reading, p. 26
- Geography Application, p. 30
- History Makers: Jiang Jieshi, p. 41

Formal Assessment
- Section Quiz, p. 244

ENGLISH LEARNERS

In-Depth Resources in Spanish
- Guided Reading, p. 112
- Geography Application, p. 115

Reading Study Guide (Spanish), p. 151
Reading Study Guide Audio CD (Spanish)

STRUGGLING READERS

In-Depth Resources: Unit 4
- Guided Reading, p. 26
- Building Vocabulary, p. 28
- Geography Application, p. 30
- Reteaching Activity, p. 45

Reading Study Guide, p. 151
Reading Study Guide Audio CD

GIFTED AND TALENTED STUDENTS

In-Depth Resources: Unit 4
- Primary Source: from "The Peasants of Hunan," p. 34

Electronic Library of Primary Sources
- from *Autobiography of a Chinese Girl*

INTEGRATED TECHNOLOGY

eEdition CD-ROM
Power Presentations CD-ROM
Electronic Library of Primary Sources
- from *Autobiography of a Chinese Girl*

classzone.com

World War I Spells More Problems In 1917, the government in Beijing, hoping for an Allied victory, declared war against Germany. Some leaders mistakenly believed that for China's participation the thankful Allies would return control of Chinese territories that had previously belonged to Germany. However, under the Treaty of Versailles, the Allied leaders gave Japan those territories.

When news of the Treaty of Versailles reached China, outrage swept the country. On May 4, 1919, over 3,000 angry students gathered in the center of Beijing. The demonstrations spread to other cities and exploded into a national movement. It was called the **May Fourth Movement**. Workers, shopkeepers, and professionals joined the cause. Though not officially a revolution, these demonstrations showed the Chinese people's commitment to the goal of establishing a strong, modern nation. Sun Yixian and members of the Kuomintang also shared the aims of the movement. But they could not strengthen central rule on their own. Many young Chinese intellectuals turned against Sun Yixian's belief in Western democracy in favor of Lenin's brand of Soviet communism. (A)

A. Answer weak leadership, civil war, terror of warlord armies, outcome of World War I, nationwide protests

MAIN IDEA

Identifying Problems

(A) What problems did the new Republic of China face?

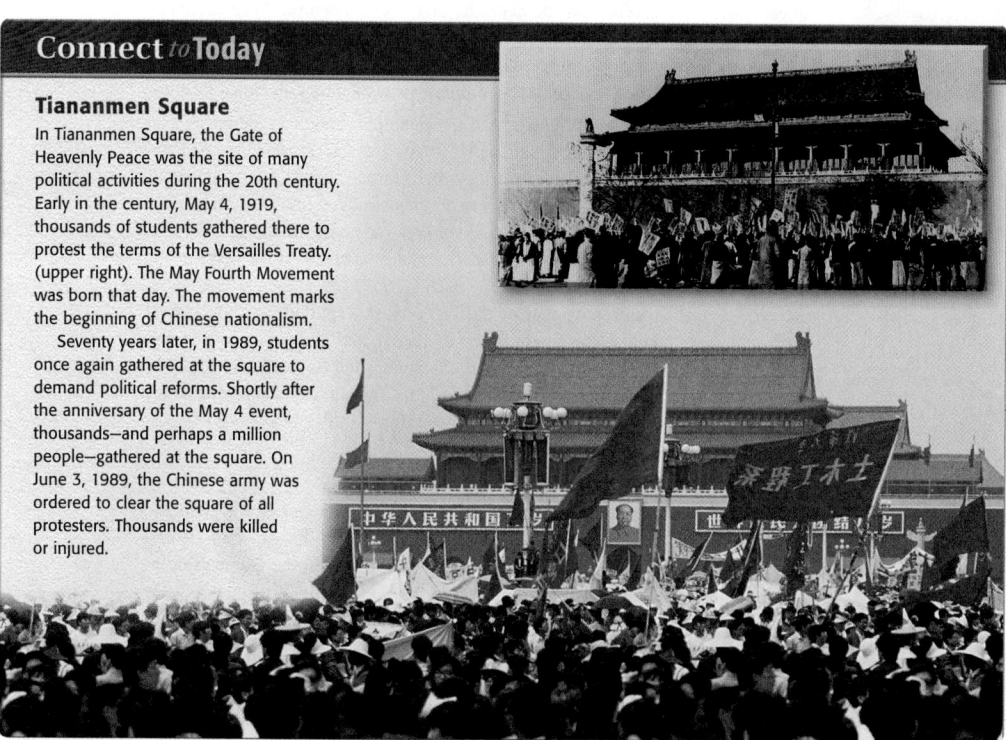

The Communist Party in China

In 1921, a group met in Shanghai to organize the Chinese Communist Party. **Mao Zedong** (MOW dzuh•dahng), an assistant librarian at Beijing University, was among its founders. Later he would become China's greatest revolutionary leader.

Mao Zedong had already begun to develop his own brand of communism. Lenin had based his Marxist revolution on his organization in Russia's cities. Mao envisioned a different setting. He believed he could bring revolution to a rural country

Connect *to* Today

Tiananmen Square

In Tiananmen Square, the Gate of Heavenly Peace was the site of many political activities during the 20th century. Early in the century, May 4, 1919, thousands of students gathered there to protest the terms of the Versailles Treaty. (upper right). The May Fourth Movement was born that day. The movement marks the beginning of Chinese nationalism.

Seventy years later, in 1989, students once again gathered at the square to demand political reforms. Shortly after the anniversary of the May 4 event, thousands—and perhaps a million people—gathered at the square. On June 3, 1989, the Chinese army was ordered to clear the square of all protesters. Thousands were killed or injured.

More About . . .

Sun Yixian

Sun traveled, organized, and plotted tirelessly to bring down the Qing dynasty. Qing officials tracked him to London. They kidnapped him, held him prisoner, and planned to ship him back to China for probable execution. Sun's British friends helped him escape his captors. The episode made him a world-famous leader. Sun Yixian is still known as the "father of modern China."

The Communist Party in China

10.9.4

Critical Thinking

- Why did Mao Zedong believe peasants would make true revolutionaries? *(Many were angry and determined.)*
- What did Mao do to strengthen the peasants loyal to his Communist Party? *(divided land among them)*
- In what way was the Nationalist government legitimized? *(Britain and the United States officially recognized it.)*

Connect *to* Today

Tiananmen Square

Though the 1989 protest was crushed, one Chinese student said, "Maybe we'll fail today. Maybe we'll fail tomorrow. But someday we'll succeed. It's a historical inevitability."

DIFFERENTIATING INSTRUCTION: GIFTED AND TALENTED STUDENTS

The Writings of Mao Zedong

Class Time 30 minutes

Task Reading and discussing a primary source

Purpose To formulate opinions about Mao's motives and results

Instructions Have students read the excerpt from Mao Zedong's "The Peasants of Hunan," found in In-Depth Resources: Unit 4. Use the discussion questions included on the sheet and these additional questions to spark a discussion.

- What does this excerpt reveal about Mao's character and personality? *(Possible Answers: forceful, determined, charismatic, uninterested in others' opinions)*
- Based on the excerpt, what conclusions can you draw about Mao's plans for revolution in China? *(Possible Answers: violent; will pit peasants against the rest of society)*
- According to Mao, who was the enemy in Chinese society? *("imperialists, warlords, corrupt officials, local bullies and bad gentry")* What did Mao promise would happen to them? *(They would stand before the peasantry, be judged, and possibly be killed.)*

PRIMARY SOURCE *from* The Peasants of Hunan
by Mao Zedong

Discussion Questions

In-Depth Resources: Unit 4

More About . . .

Joining the Chinese Army

In 1926, a teenage girl named Hsieh Ping-Ying joined the Chinese army to get over a broken heart and avoid a forced marriage. Encourage interested students to read the excerpt from her autobiography in the Electronic Library of Primary Sources.

Electronic Library of Primary Sources
- from *Autobiography of a Chinese Girl*

More About . . .

Mao's Guerrilla Tactics

From his mountain hideout, Mao waged guerrilla war against Jiang's armies. He outlined his strategy:

1. Retreat when the enemy advances.
2. Harass when the enemy encamps.
3. Attack when the enemy hesitates.
4. Pursue when the enemy retreats.

Such tactics were possible only with the support of local peasants.

Civil War Rages in China
10.9.4; 10.8.1

Critical Thinking
- What do you think is meant by the phrase "swimming in the peasant sea"? *(Possible Answer: being among the millions of peasants)*
- Did Jiang and Mao resolve their differences? *(There was no resolution; the Japanese invasion forced a truce between the sides.)*

where the peasants could be the true revolutionaries. He argued his point passionately in 1927:

PRIMARY SOURCE B
> The force of the peasantry is like that of the raging winds and driving rain. It is rapidly increasing in violence. No force can stand in its way. The peasantry will tear apart all nets which bind it and hasten along the road to liberation. They will bury beneath them all forces of imperialism, militarism, corrupt officialdom, village bosses and evil gentry.
>
> **MAO ZEDONG,** quoted in *Chinese Communism and the Rise of Mao*

MAIN IDEA
Analyzing Primary Sources
B What forces does Mao identify as those that the peasants will overcome?
B. Answer imperialism, militarism, corrupt officialdom, village bosses, and evil gentry

Lenin Befriends China While the Chinese Communist Party was forming, Sun Yixian and his Nationalist Party set up a government in south China. Like the Communists, Sun became disillusioned with the Western democracies that refused to support his struggling government. Sun decided to ally the Kuomintang with the newly formed Communist Party. He hoped to unite all the revolutionary groups for common action.

Lenin seized the opportunity to help China's Nationalist government. In 1923, he sent military advisers and equipment to the Nationalists in return for allowing the Chinese Communists to join the Kuomintang.

▲ Jiang Jieshi and the Nationalist forces united China under one government in 1928.

Peasants Align with the Communists After Sun Yixian died in 1925, **Jiang Jieshi** (jee•ahng jee•shee), formerly called Chiang Kai-shek, headed the Kuomintang. Jiang was the son of a middle-class merchant. Many of Jiang's followers were bankers and businesspeople. Like Jiang, they feared the Communists' goal of creating a socialist economy modeled after the Soviet Union's.

Jiang had promised democracy and political rights to all Chinese. Yet his government became steadily less democratic and more corrupt. Most peasants believed that Jiang was doing little to improve their lives. As a result, many peasants threw their support to the Chinese Communist Party. To enlist the support of the peasants, Mao divided land that the Communists won among the local farmers.

Nationalists and Communists Clash At first, Jiang put aside his differences with the Communists. Together Jiang's Nationalist forces and the Communists successfully fought the warlords. Soon afterward, though, he turned against the Communists.

In April 1927, Nationalist troops and armed gangs moved into Shanghai. They killed many Communist leaders and trade union members in the city streets. Similar killings took place in other cities. The Nationalists nearly wiped out the Chinese Communist Party.

In 1928, Jiang became president of the Nationalist Republic of China. Great Britain and the United States both formally recognized the new government. Because of the slaughter of Communists at Shanghai, the Soviet Union did not. Jiang's treachery also had long-term effects. The Communists' deep-seated rage over the massacre erupted in a civil war that would last until 1949.

Civil War Rages in China

By 1930, Nationalists and Communists were fighting a bloody civil war. Mao and other Communist leaders established themselves in the hills of south-central China. Mao referred to this tactic of taking his revolution to the countryside as "swimming in the peasant sea." He recruited the peasants to join his Red Army. He then trained them in guerrilla warfare. Nationalists attacked the Communists repeatedly but failed to drive them out.

The Long March In 1933, Jiang gathered an army of at least 700,000 men. Jiang's army then surrounded the Communists' mountain stronghold. Outnumbered, the

DIFFERENTIATING INSTRUCTION: STRUGGLING READERS

Chinese Geography and Politics

Class Time 35 minutes
Task Using text and a map to answer questions
Purpose To understand how geography affected Chinese politics in the 1920s and 1930s
Instructions Pair a struggling reader with a more proficient reader. Have each pair complete the Geography Application activity for this section, found in In-Depth Resources: Unit 4. Be sure that students understand how the map reflects three increases in Kuomintang territory. You may wish to list synonyms or definitions of difficult words on the board. Some examples are shown at right.

warlord	an independent local military leader; a territorial ruler
campaign	in this case, a military action
stronghold	a base of operations; a fortress
embarked on	started, began

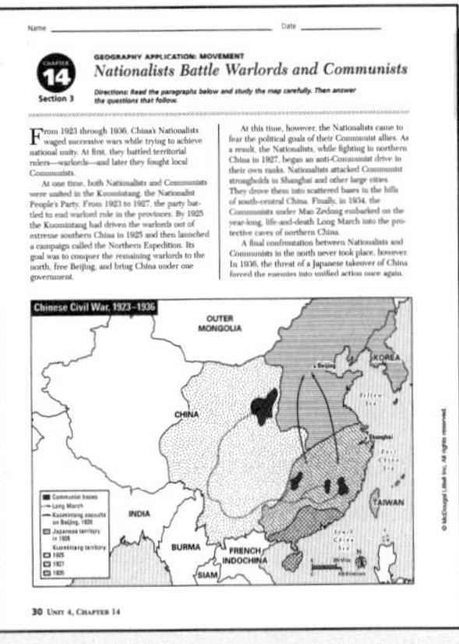

In-Depth Resources: Unit 4

History *in* Depth

The Long March

The Long March of the Chinese Communists from the south of China to the caves of Shaanxi [shahn•shee] in the north is a remarkable story. The march covered 6,000 miles, about the distance from New York to San Francisco and back again. They crossed miles of swampland. They slept sitting up, leaning back-to-back in pairs, to keep from sinking into the mud and drowning. In total, the Communists crossed 18 mountain ranges and 24 rivers in their yearlong flight from the Nationalist forces.

CALIFORNIA STANDARDS
10.9.4, CST 3

The Long March, 1934–1935

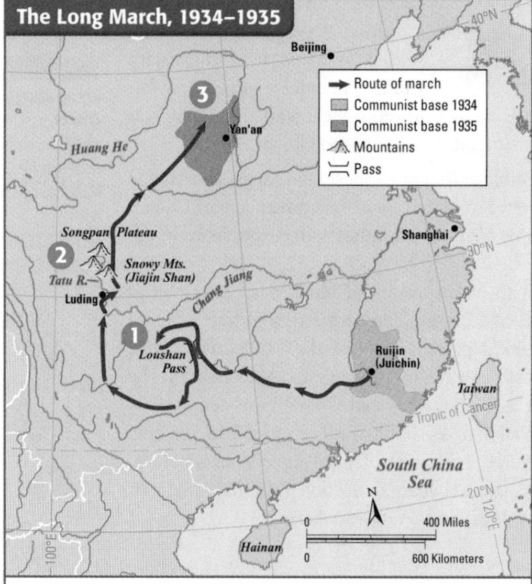

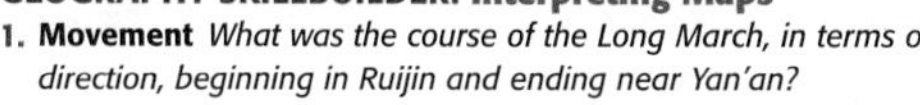

GEOGRAPHY SKILLBUILDER: Interpreting Maps
1. **Movement** *What was the course of the Long March, in terms of direction, beginning in Ruijin and ending near Yan'an?*
2. **Movement** *Why didn't Mao's forces move west or south?*

▼ In one of the more daring and difficult acts of the march, the Red Army crossed a bridge of iron chains whose planks had been removed.

▼ The Red Army had to cross the Snowy Mountains, some of the highest in the world. Every man carried enough food and fuel to last for ten days. They marched six to seven hours a day.

◀ After finally arriving at the caves in Shaanxi, Mao declared, "If we can survive all this, we can survive everything. This is but the first stage of our Long March. The final stage leads to Peking [Beijing]!"

History *in* Depth

The Long March

Ask students to use the map, photographs, and text to determine what obstacles the Red Army faced. *(hostile troops, mountains, swamps, rivers, living in caves, exhaustion, exposure to harsh weather)* Have students use library resources or the Internet to find more about the political effects of the Long March.

SKILLBUILDER Answers
1. **Movement** west, then north, then northeast
2. **Movement** geographic barriers such as mountains, lack of support in some areas

More About . . .

Effects of the Long March

By the time the Long March ended, Mao Zedong had been elected chairman of the Chinese Communist Party. The march had other long-term consequences as well: nearly all the Communist leaders who took power in 1949 had participated in it.

DIFFERENTIATING INSTRUCTION: ENGLISH LEARNERS

Describing the Long March

Class Time 35 minutes

Task Writing about or drawing scenes from the Long March

Purpose To describe the conditions faced in the Long March and commitment of the soldiers to their cause

Instructions Ask students to take turns reading aloud the text on this page. Then read aloud the passage entitled "The Long March" beginning on page 450. As you read, ask students to visualize the conditions of the journey, what the soldiers did to survive and to cross the rugged terrain, and the many obstacles they faced, including hunger, cold weather, and wounds from battling the Nationalist army.

After reading, ask students to write down two or three images that stuck with them. From those, ask students to choose one to work with. Students who are artistically inclined might reproduce the image in a sketch, mural, or painting. Others might personalize the image by creating a journal entry written from the perspective of a soldier who participated in a specific aspect of the Long March.

Ask volunteers to share their finished products with the class.

More About . . .

Three Principles of the People

Sun believed the principles could be broken down and achieved this way:

- Nationalism: initially opposition to the Qing dynasty, later referring to identity for minorities within China as well as for the country as a whole
- Democracy: also called "rights of the people"; Sun thought this could be achieved through a government run by election, initiative, and referendum
- Socialism: also called "people's livelihood"; thought to have meant equal land ownership through taxation

▲ A Japanese landing party approaches the Chinese mainland. The invasion forced Mao and Jiang to join forces to fight the Japanese.

Communist Party leaders realized that they faced defeat. In a daring move, 100,000 Communist forces fled. They began a hazardous, 6,000-mile-long journey called the **Long March**. Between 1934 and 1935, the Communists kept only a step ahead of Jiang's forces. Thousands died from hunger, cold, exposure, and battle wounds.

Finally, after a little more than a year, Mao and the seven or eight thousand Communist survivors settled in caves in northwestern China. There they gained new followers. Meanwhile, as civil war between Nationalists and Communists raged, Japan invaded China. C

MAIN IDEA
Recognizing Effects
C What were the results of the Long March?
C. Possible Answer Although at least two-thirds of the original marchers did not complete the journey, more Chinese people joined the Communists.

Civil War Suspended In 1931, as Chinese fought Chinese, the Japanese watched the power struggles with rising interest. Japanese forces took advantage of China's weakening situation. They invaded Manchuria, an industrialized province in the northeast part of China.

In 1937, the Japanese launched an all-out invasion of China. Massive bombings of villages and cities killed thousands of Chinese. The destruction of farms caused many more to die of starvation. By 1938, Japan held control of a large part of China.

The Japanese threat forced an uneasy truce between Jiang's and Mao's forces. The civil war gradually ground to a halt as Nationalists and Communists temporarily united to fight the Japanese. The National Assembly further agreed to promote changes outlined in Sun Yixian's "Three Principles of the People"—nationalism, democracy, and people's livelihood. As you will learn in Section 4, similar principles were also serving as a guiding force in India and Southwest Asia.

3 ASSESS

SECTION 3 ASSESSMENT

Assign pairs of students to discuss the questions and formulate joint responses.

Formal Assessment
- Section Quiz, p. 244

4 RETEACH

Use the Guided Reading activity for Section 3 to review the main ideas for this section.

In-Depth Resources: Unit 4
- Guided Reading, p. 26
- Reteaching Activity, p. 45

SECTION 3 ASSESSMENT

TERMS & NAMES 1. For each term or name, write a sentence explaining its significance.
• Kuomintang • Sun Yixian • May Fourth Movement • Mao Zedong • Jiang Jieshi • Long March

USING YOUR NOTES

2. Whose reforms had a greater appeal to the peasants? Why? (10.9.4)

Jiang	Mao
1.	1.
2.	2.
3.	3.

MAIN IDEAS

3. How did the Treaty of Versailles trigger the May Fourth Movement? (10.6.1)
4. How was Mao's vision of communism different from that of Lenin? (10.9.4)
5. What started the civil war in China? (10.9.4)

CRITICAL THINKING & WRITING

6. **RECOGNIZING EFFECTS** What influence did foreign nations have on China from 1912 to 1938? (10.6.1)
7. **ANALYZING CAUSES** What caused the Communist revolutionary movement in China to gain strength? (10.9.4)
8. **HYPOTHESIZING** If the Long March had failed, do you think the Nationalist party would have been successful in uniting the Chinese? Why or why not? (10.9.4)
9. **WRITING ACTIVITY** REVOLUTION Write a series of **interview questions** you would pose to Sun Yixian, Mao Zedong, and Jiang Jieshi. (Writing 2.5.b)

CONNECT TO TODAY REPORTING ON CURRENT EVENTS
Research the selection of the newest Communist Party leader of China. Write a brief **report** identifying that person and explaining how this new leader got into office. (Writing 2.1.a)

ANSWERS

1. Kuomintang, p. 448 • Sun Yixian, p. 448 • May Fourth Movement, p. 449 • Mao Zedong, p. 449 • Jiang Jieshi, p. 450 • Long March, p. 452

2. **Sample Answer:** Jiang—Head of Kuomintang, helped defeat warlords, forced the Long March; Mao—Won peasants by giving land, promised reform, survived Long March. Greater appeal—Mao's reforms, because he gave land to peasants.
3. When Japan received land China felt it deserved, a wave of protests occurred.
4. Mao—Peasants were basis of the revolution; Lenin—Urban workers were the base.
5. Nationalist attack on Communists in Shanghai
6. Treaty of Versailles led to May Fourth Movement; Soviet Union supported Sun's government; Britain and U.S. recognized Nationalist government; Japan's invasion of China united Jiang's and Mao's forces.
7. failures of the Kuomintang; corruption in Jiang's government; Soviet influence; poverty; Mao's leadership
8. Yes—Nationalists wanted to modernize and strengthen China. No—Jiang's government was weak, corrupt, and undemocratic.
9. **Rubric** Questions should
   - investigate goals of each participant.
   - reflect information from the chapter.

CONNECT TO TODAY

Rubric Reports should
- name the new leader.
- explain how the leader came to power.

4

Poster of Russian soldier with flag, by N. Tyrkurr

Temple of Heaven, Beijing, China

Nationalism in India and Southwest Asia

MAIN IDEA	WHY IT MATTERS NOW	TERMS & NAMES
EMPIRE BUILDING Nationalism triggered independence movements to overthrow colonial powers.	These independent nations—India, Turkey, Iran, and Saudi Arabia—are key players on the world stage today.	• Rowlatt Acts • Amritsar Massacre • Mohandas K. Gandhi • civil disobedience • Salt March • Mustafa Kemal

SETTING THE STAGE As you learned in Chapter 13, the end of World War I broke up the Ottoman Empire. The British Empire, which controlled India, began to show signs of cracking. The weakening of these empires stirred nationalist activity in India, Turkey, and some Southwest Asian countries. Indian nationalism had been growing since the mid-1800s. Many upper-class Indians who attended British schools learned European views of nationalism and democracy. They began to apply these political ideas to their own country.

CALIFORNIA STANDARDS

10.4.4 Describe the independence struggles of the colonized regions of the world, including the roles of leaders, such as Sun Yat-sen in China, and the roles of ideology and religion.

REP 3 Students evaluate major debates among historians concerning alternative interpretations of the past, including an analysis of authors' use of evidence and the distinctions between sound generalizations and misleading oversimplifications.

REP 4 Students construct and test hypotheses; collect, evaluate, and employ information from multiple primary and secondary sources; and apply it in oral and written presentations.

Indian Nationalism Grows

Two groups formed to rid India of foreign rule: the primarily Hindu Indian National Congress, or Congress Party, in 1885, and the Muslim League in 1906. Though deep divisions existed between Hindus and Muslims, they found common ground. They shared the heritage of British rule and an understanding of democratic ideals. These two groups both worked toward the goal of independence from the British.

World War I Increases Nationalist Activity Until World War I, the vast majority of Indians had little interest in nationalism. The situation changed as over a million Indians enlisted in the British army. In return for their service, the British government promised reforms that would eventually lead to self-government.

In 1918, Indian troops returned home from the war. They expected Britain to fulfill its promise. Instead, they were once again treated as second-class citizens. Radical nationalists carried out acts of violence to show their hatred of British rule. To curb dissent, in 1919 the British passed the **Rowlatt Acts**. These laws allowed the government to jail protesters without trial for as long as two years. To Western-educated Indians, denial of a trial by jury violated their individual rights.

Amritsar Massacre To protest the Rowlatt Acts, around 10,000 Hindus and Muslims flocked to Amritsar, a major city in the Punjab, in the spring of 1919. At a huge festival in an enclosed square, they intended to fast and pray and to listen to political

◂ Ali Jinnah, leader of the Muslim League of India, fought for Indian independence from Great Britain.

TAKING NOTES

Categorizing Create a web diagram identifying the styles of government adopted by nations in this section.

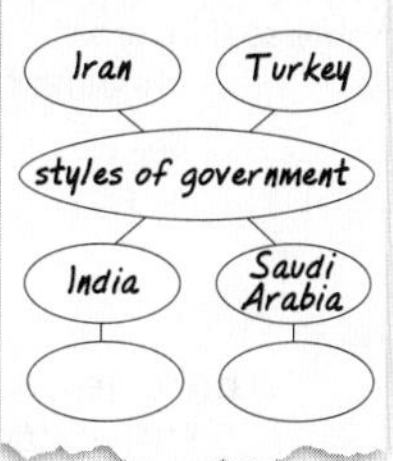

LESSON PLAN

OBJECTIVES

- Trace nationalist activity in India.
- Summarize Gandhi's nonviolent tactics.
- Explain how Indian self-rule heightened conflicts between Muslims and Hindus.
- Describe the rise of independence movements in Southwest Asia.

1 FOCUS & MOTIVATE

Ask students to think of specific times in their own lives when finding a peaceful way to get a need met has been more successful than making demands or beginning a conflict over the matter.

2 INSTRUCT

Indian Nationalism Grows

10.4.4

Critical Thinking

- The Amritsar Massacre is similar to what event in Russian history that also sparked a revolution? *(During Bloody Sunday, peaceful protesters were killed at St. Petersburg.)*

CALIFORNIA RESOURCES

California Reading Toolkit, p. L65
California Modified Lesson Plans for English Learners, p. 125
California Daily Standards Practice Transparencies, TT57
California Standards Enrichment Workbook, pp. 53–54
California Standards Planner and Lesson Plans, p. L121
California Online Test Practice
California Test Generator CD-ROM
California Easy Planner CD-ROM
California eEdition CD-ROM

SECTION 4 PROGRAM RESOURCES

ALL STUDENTS

In-Depth Resources: Unit 4
- Guided Reading, p. 27

Formal Assessment
- Section Quiz, p. 245

ENGLISH LEARNERS

In-Depth Resources in Spanish
- Guided Reading, p. 113

Reading Study Guide (Spanish), p. 153
Reading Study Guide Audio CD (Spanish)

STRUGGLING READERS

In-Depth Resources: Unit 4
- Guided Reading, p. 27
- Building Vocabulary, p. 28
- Reteaching Activity, p. 46

Reading Study Guide, p. 153
Reading Study Guide Audio CD

GIFTED AND TALENTED STUDENTS

In-Depth Resources: Unit 4
- Primary Source: from *Hind Swaraj,* p. 35
- Connections Across Time and Cultures: Nationalist Revolutions in Latin America and Asia, p. 42

Electronic Library of Primary Sources
- "Nonviolence"

INTEGRATED TECHNOLOGY

eEdition CD-ROM
Power Presentations CD-ROM
Critical Thinking Transparencies
- CT30 Time Machine: Revolution and Nationalism
- CT66 Chapter 30 Visual Summary

World Art and Cultures Transparencies
- AT66 Persian Musicians

Electronic Library of Primary Sources
- "Nonviolence"

classzone.com

Gandhi's Tactics of Nonviolence
10.4.4

Critical Thinking
- Why was civil disobedience a popular solution for Indians? *(They felt helpless to fight the British physically.)*
- How did the media influence the Indian independence movement? *(Support increased when newspapers worldwide reported the attack on peaceful Salt March protesters.)*

Analyzing Primary Sources

Satyagraha and Nonviolence
Ask students if it is likely that the use of body-force by the Indians would have been effective against the British government. *(Not likely–British were more prepared to fight than to counter the effects of civil disobedience.)*

Answers to Document-Based Questions
1. **Comparing** Body-force involves the use of violence, but not necessarily the sacrifice of self.
2. **Making Inferences** Gandhi believes that suffering must take place to achieve the goal. *Hind Swaraj* states: "Passive resistance is a method of securing rights by personal suffering." *The Origin of Nonviolence* states: "[T]here can only be one end to the struggle, and that is victory."

speeches. A small group of nationalists were also on the scene. The demonstration, especially the alliance of Hindus and Muslims, alarmed the British.

Most people at the gathering were unaware that the British government had banned public meetings. However, the British commander at Amritsar believed they were openly defying the ban. He ordered his troops to fire on the crowd without warning. The shooting continued for ten minutes. Unable to escape from the enclosed courtyard, nearly 400 Indians died and about 1,200 were wounded.

News of the slaughter, called the **Amritsar Massacre**, sparked an explosion of anger across India. Almost overnight, millions of Indians changed from loyal British subjects into nationalists. These Indians demanded independence. (A)

A. Answer Spirit of nationalism grew more intense; more Indians demanded independence.

MAIN IDEA
Recognizing Effects
(A) What changes resulted from the Amritsar massacre?

Gandhi's Tactics of Nonviolence
The massacre at Amritsar set the stage for **Mohandas K. Gandhi** (GAHN•dee) to emerge as the leader of the independence movement. Gandhi's strategy for battling injustice evolved from his deeply religious approach to political activity. His teachings blended ideas from all of the major world religions, including Hinduism, Islam, and Christianity. Gandhi attracted millions of followers. Soon they began calling him the Mahatma (muh•HAHT•muh), meaning "great soul."

Noncooperation When the British failed to punish the officers responsible for the Amritsar massacre, Gandhi urged the Indian National Congress to follow a policy of noncooperation with the British government. In 1920, the Congress Party endorsed **civil disobedience**, the deliberate and public refusal to obey an unjust law, and nonviolence as the means to achieve independence. Gandhi then launched his campaign

> Analyzing Primary Sources

Satyagraha
A central element of Gandhi's philosophy of nonviolence was called *satyagraha*, often translated as "soul-force" or "truth-force."

PRIMARY SOURCE

Passive resistance is a method of securing rights by personal suffering; it is the reverse of resistance by arms. When I refuse to do a thing that is repugnant to my conscience, I use soul-force. For instance, the government of the day has passed a law which is applicable to me: I do not like it, if, by using violence, I force the government to repeal the law, I am employing what may be termed body-force. If I do not obey the law and accept the penalty for its breach, I use soul-force. It involves sacrifice of self.

GANDHI Chapter XVII, *Hind Swaraj*

Nonviolence
In *The Origin of Nonviolence*, Gandhi offered a warning to those who were contemplating joining the struggle for independence.

PRIMARY SOURCE

[I]t is not at all impossible that we might have to endure every hardship that we can imagine, and wisdom lies in pledging ourselves on the understanding that we shall have to suffer all that and worse. If some one asks me when and how the struggle may end, I may say that if the entire community manfully stands the test, the end will be near. If many of us fall back under storm and stress, the struggle will be prolonged. But I can boldly declare, and with certainty, that so long as there is even a handful of men true to their pledge, there can only be one end to the struggle, and that is victory.

GANDHI *The Origin of Nonviolence*

DOCUMENT-BASED QUESTIONS
1. **Comparing** *How is soul-force different from body-force?*
2. **Making Inferences** *What do Gandhi's writings suggest about his view of suffering? Give examples from each document.*

DIFFERENTIATING INSTRUCTION: GIFTED AND TALENTED STUDENTS

Investigating Examples of Civil Disobedience
Class Time 30 minutes

Task Comparing strategies of nonviolent organizations

Purpose To learn more about the legacy of Gandhi's nonviolent tactics for battling injustice

Instructions Ask pairs of students to find an organization or movement that is dedicated to the principles of nonviolence as a strategy for effecting change. Examples include environmental, animal rights, and political activist movements. Students may also investigate Henry David Thoreau's essay "Civil Disobedience."

Students should focus on the goals of the organization or movement and the methods it uses to achieve those goals. Have students cite specific examples of nonviolent tactics, such as marches, demonstrations, boycotts, advertising campaigns, and acts of civil disobedience.

Each pair of students should then meet with another pair to exchange information and to draw comparisons among the movements or organizations they chose.

After the two sets of partners exchange information, the four students should make a Venn diagram comparing the goals and strategies of each organization or movement.

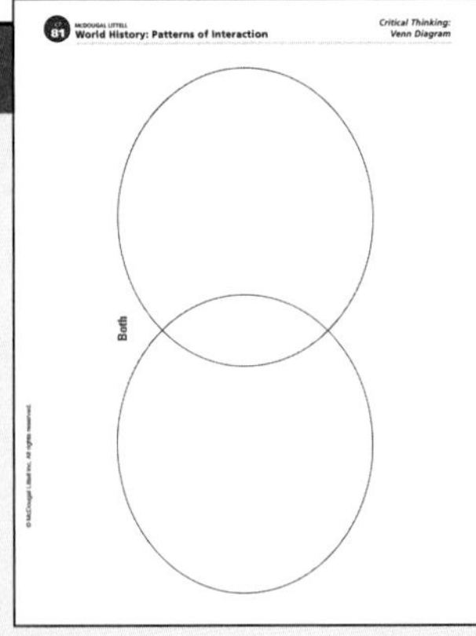

Critical Thinking Transparencies

of civil disobedience to weaken the British government's authority and economic power over India.

Boycotts Gandhi called on Indians to refuse to buy British goods, attend government schools, pay British taxes, or vote in elections. Gandhi staged a successful boycott of British cloth, a source of wealth for the British. He urged all Indians to weave their own cloth. Gandhi himself devoted two hours each day to spinning his own yarn on a simple handwheel. He wore only homespun cloth and encouraged Indians to follow his example. As a result of the boycott, the sale of British cloth in India dropped sharply.

Strikes and Demonstrations Gandhi's weapon of civil disobedience took an economic toll on the British. They struggled to keep trains running, factories operating, and overcrowded jails from bursting. Throughout 1920, the British arrested thousands of Indians who had participated in strikes and demonstrations. But despite Gandhi's pleas for nonviolence, protests often led to riots.

▲ Gandhi adopted the spinning wheel as a symbol of Indian resistance to British rule. The wheel was featured on the Indian National Congress flag, a forerunner of India's national flag.

The Salt March In 1930, Gandhi organized a demonstration to defy the hated Salt Acts. According to these British laws, Indians could buy salt from no other source but the government. They also had to pay sales tax on salt. To show their opposition, Gandhi and his followers walked about 240 miles to the seacoast. There they began to make their own salt by collecting seawater and letting it evaporate. This peaceful protest was called the **Salt March**.

Soon afterward, some demonstrators planned a march to a site where the British government processed salt. They intended to shut this saltworks down. Police officers with steel-tipped clubs attacked the demonstrators. An American journalist was an eyewitness to the event. He described the "sickening whacks of clubs on unprotected skulls" and people "writhing in pain with fractured skulls or broken shoulders." Still the people continued to march peacefully, refusing to defend themselves against their attackers. Newspapers across the globe carried the journalist's story, which won worldwide support for Gandhi's independence movement.

More demonstrations against the salt tax took place throughout India. Eventually, about 60,000 people, including Gandhi, were arrested. (B)

B. Answer
The protest against British rule was based on noncooperation and civil disobedience.

MAIN IDEA

Making Inferences
(B) How did the Salt March represent Gandhi's methods for change?

Britain Grants Limited Self-Rule

Gandhi and his followers gradually reaped the rewards of their civil disobedience campaigns and gained greater political power for the Indian people. In 1935, the British Parliament passed the Government of India Act. It provided local self-government and limited democratic elections, but not total independence.

However, the Government of India Act also fueled mounting tensions between Muslims and Hindus. These two groups had conflicting visions of India's future as an independent nation. Indian Muslims, outnumbered by Hindus, feared that Hindus would control India if it won independence. In Chapter 18, you will read about the outcome of India's bid for independence.

Tip for English Learners

Remind students that a boycott is a form of peaceful protest in which people decide as a group to refuse to buy certain products or goods in order to show disapproval of those who produce them.

More About . . .

Gandhi's Views

Gandhi's emphasis on the traditional values of village life and on handcrafted items made it clear to the majority of Indians that he understood and sympathized with their problems. Gandhi realized that any feeling of Indian nationalism had to begin with the village.

In-Depth Resources: Unit 4
- Primary Source: from *Hind Swaraj* (Indian Home Rule) by Gandhi

Electronic Library of Primary Sources
- "Nonviolence"

Britain Grants Limited Self-Rule

10.4.4

Critical Thinking
- In what ways was civil disobedience a more successful method than violence? *(Boycotts and noncooperation took away the British government's economic power and authority.)*
- What was the source of tension between Hindus and Muslims in India? *(different religious beliefs; Muslims feared the power of the more numerous Hindus.)*

DIFFERENTIATING INSTRUCTION: ENGLISH LEARNERS

Indian Protests and British Responses

Class Time 30 minutes

Task Creating a poster about the Indian independence movement

Purpose To explore the political tension between India and the British government during the independence movement

Instructions Have students create a poster protesting the way the Indians were treated by the British government.

To organize the information, have students draw two columns on paper. In the first column, have them list actions Gandhi and his followers took, including specific boycotts, strikes and demonstrations, and highlights of the Salt March. In the second column, ask students to list responses to those actions.

Using the information from their lists, students will create a poster that shows Indian protests and British responses. Students can use photographs, drawings, and captions to persuade others to join the independence movement. Students who need help can use the Reading Study Guide for Section 4.

Indian Actions	Response
Amritsar protest	British troops fire on unarmed crowd.
Boycotts	Sale of British products drops.
Salt March	Police officers club demonstrators.

History Makers

Mustafa Kemal

To reach his goal, Kemal even set rules for clothing: "A civilized, international dress is worthy and appropriate for our new nation, and we will wear it. Boots or shoes on our feet, trousers on our legs, shirt and tie, jacket and waistcoat—and, of course, to complete these, a . . . hat." In addition to changing clothing, in 1928, Kemal introduced the Latin alphabet, replacing the Arabic letters. He wanted people to forget their history under the Ottomans and to return to the roots of their ancient Turkish language.

Nationalism in Southwest Asia

10.4.4

Critical Thinking

- What did Kemal's reforms do for Turkey? *(gave Turkey a strong national identity by making legal, religious, and economic reforms)*
- In what major way did reforms in Iran and Saudi Arabia differ from those in Turkey? *(Iran and Saudi Arabia did not turn to democratic rule as Turkey did.)*

Critical Thinking Transparencies

- CT30 Time Machine: Revolution and Nationalism

World Art and Cultures Transparencies

- AT66 Persian Musicians

History Makers

Mustafa Kemal
1881–1938

As president of Turkey, Mustafa Kemal campaigned vigorously to mold the new republic into a modern nation. His models were the United States and other European countries.

Kemal believed that even the clothing of the Turks should be changed to reflect a civilized, international dress. To reach this goal, Kemal set rules for clothing. He required government workers to wear Western-style business suits and banned the fez, a brimless red felt hat that was part of traditional Turkish clothing.

Nationalism in Southwest Asia

The breakup of the Ottoman Empire and growing Western political and economic interest in Southwest Asia spurred the rise of nationalism in this region. Just as the people of India fought to have their own nation after World War I, the people of Southwest Asia also launched independence movements to rid themselves of imperial rulers.

Turkey Becomes a Republic At the end of World War I, the Ottoman Empire was forced to give up all its territories except Turkey. Turkish lands included the old Turkish homeland of Anatolia and a small strip of land around Istanbul.

In 1919, Greek soldiers invaded Turkey and threatened to conquer it. The Turkish sultan was powerless to stop the Greeks. However, in 1922, a brilliant commander, **Mustafa Kemal** (keh•MAHL), successfully led Turkish nationalists in fighting back the Greeks and their British backers. After winning a peace, the nationalists overthrew the last Ottoman sultan.

In 1923, Kemal became the president of the new Republic of Turkey, the first republic in Southwest Asia. To achieve his goal of transforming Turkey into a modern nation, he ushered in these sweeping reforms:

- separated the laws of Islam from the laws of the nation
- abolished religious courts and created a new legal system based on European law
- granted women the right to vote and to hold public office
- launched government-funded programs to industrialize Turkey and to spur economic growth

Kemal died in 1938. From his leadership, Turkey gained a new sense of its national identity. His influence was so strong that the Turkish people gave him the name Ataturk—"father of the Turks."

Persia Becomes Iran Before World War I, both Great Britain and Russia had established spheres of influence in the ancient country of Persia. After the war, when Russia was still reeling from the Bolshevik Revolution, the British tried to take over all of Persia. This maneuver triggered a nationalist revolt in Persia. In 1921, a Persian army officer seized power. In 1925 he deposed the ruling shah.

Persia's new leader, Reza Shah Pahlavi (PAL•uh•vee), like Kemal in Turkey, set out to modernize his country. He established public schools, built roads and railroads, promoted industrial growth, and extended women's rights. Unlike Kemal, Reza Shah Pahlavi kept all power in his own hands. In 1935, he changed the name of the country from the Greek name Persia to the traditional name Iran. C

C. Answer Both established policies and launched programs to modernize their countries.

MAIN IDEA

Comparing

C How were Kemal's leadership and Reza Shah Pahlavi's leadership similar?

Saudi Arabia Keeps Islamic Traditions While Turkey broke with many Islamic traditions, another new country held strictly to Islamic law. In 1902, Abd al-Aziz Ibn Saud (sah•OOD), a member of a once-powerful Arabian family, began a successful campaign to unify Arabia. In 1932, he renamed the new kingdom Saudi Arabia after his family.

Ibn Saud carried on Arab and Islamic traditions. Loyalty to the Saudi government was based on custom, religion, and family ties. Like Kemal and Reza Shah, Ibn Saud brought some modern technology, such as telephones and radios, to his

DIFFERENTIATING INSTRUCTION: STRUGGLING READERS

Using SQ3R

Class Time 20 minutes

Task Using the SQ3R strategy and recording answers in a chart

Purpose To clarify information about nationalism in Southwest Asia

Instructions Have students use the SQ3R study method to analyze events in Southwest Asia. Begin by writing the strategy on the board as follows: SQ3R = Survey; Question; Read; Recite or Record; Review.

1. Survey the pages by skimming for headings and topic sentences.
2. Jot down any questions about the text, such as what role nationalism played in Turkey, Iran, and Saudi Arabia.
3. Read the pages and look for answers to the questions.
4. Recite or record any answers that are found.
5. Review the information as a group, or with a partner, to answer any questions that remain.

1. Survey	2. Question	3. Read	4. Recite or Record	5. Review
Turkey Becomes a Republic	What is a republic?	Leaders and representatives elected	Voting, legal system	Turkey's government includes elections

country. However, modernization in Saudi Arabia was limited to religiously acceptable areas. There also were no efforts to begin to practice democracy.

Oil Drives Development While nationalism steadily emerged as a major force in Southwest Asia, the region's economy was also taking a new direction. The rising demand for petroleum products in industrialized countries brought new oil explorations to Southwest Asia. During the 1920s and 1930s, European and American companies discovered enormous oil deposits in Iran, Iraq, Saudi Arabia, and Kuwait. Foreign businesses invested huge sums of money to develop these oil fields. For example, the Anglo-Persian Oil Company, a British company, started developing the oil fields of Iran. Geologists later learned that the land around the Persian Gulf has nearly two-thirds of the world's known supply of oil.

This important resource led to rapid and dramatic economic changes and development. Because oil brought huge profits, Western nations tried to dominate this region. Meanwhile, these same Western nations were about to face a more immediate crisis as power-hungry leaders seized control in Italy and Germany.

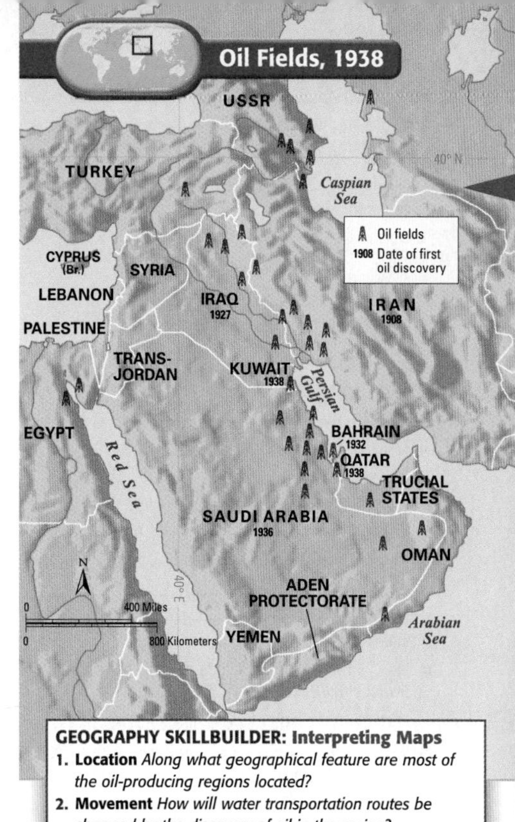

GEOGRAPHY SKILLBUILDER: Interpreting Maps
1. **Location** *Along what geographical feature are most of the oil-producing regions located?*
2. **Movement** *How will water transportation routes be changed by the discovery of oil in the region?*

SECTION 4 ASSESSMENT

TERMS & NAMES 1. For each term or name, write a sentence explaining its significance.
• Rowlatt Acts • Amritsar Massacre • Mohandas K. Gandhi • civil disobedience • Salt March • Mustafa Kemal

USING YOUR NOTES

2. Why do you think these nations adopted different styles of government? (10.4.4)

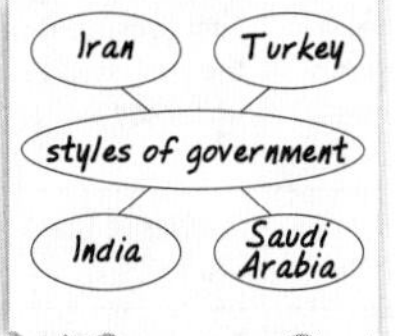

MAIN IDEAS

3. How did Gandhi's tactics of civil disobedience affect the British? (10.4.4)
4. How did Southwest Asia change as a result of nationalism? (10.4.4)
5. How did newly found petroleum supplies change the new nations in Southwest Asia? (10.4.4)

CRITICAL THINKING & WRITING

6. **HYPOTHESIZING** What do you think a nation might gain and lose by modernizing? (REP 4)
7. **RECOGNIZING EFFECTS** How did World War I create an atmosphere for political change in both India and Southwest Asia? (10.4.4)
8. **COMPARING AND CONTRASTING** Compare and contrast the different forms of government adopted by the four nations in this section. (10.4.4)
9. **WRITING ACTIVITY** POWER AND AUTHORITY Write a **persuasive essay** supporting the use of nonviolent resistance. (Writing 2.4.c)

CONNECT TO TODAY **GRAPHING OIL EXPORTS**
Do research to find out how many barrels of oil have been exported each year for the last ten years from Iran, Iraq, and Saudi Arabia. Create a **graph** showing your results. (Writing 2.3.d)

History from Visuals

Interpreting the Map

Ask students to note the progression of years in which oil was discovered in this region. Where was oil first discovered? *(Iran in 1908)*

Extension Ask interested students to research oil-related conflicts these countries have been involved in since the 1920s.

SKILLBUILDER Answers
1. **Location** Persian Gulf
2. **Movement** Routes into and out of the region will carry more traffic.

3 ASSESS
SECTION 4 ASSESSMENT

Divide questions among groups of students and ask them to present their answers orally.

Formal Assessment
• Section Quiz, p. 245

4 RETEACH

Use the Reteaching Activity and the Visual Summary to review this section and chapter.

Critical Thinking Transparencies
• CT66 Chapter 30 Visual Summary

In-Depth Resources: Unit 4
• Reteaching Activity, p. 46

ANSWERS

1. Rowlatt Acts, p. 453 • Amritsar Massacre, p. 454 • Mohandas K. Gandhi, p. 454 • civil disobedience, p. 454 • Salt March, p. 455 • Mustafa Kemal, p. 456
2. **Sample Answer:** Styles of government: Democratic self-rule—India; Republic—Turkey; Dictatorship—Iran; Monarchy—Saudi Arabia; **Possible Answer:** Each nation was led by a person with a different vision of how to govern.
3. reducing cloth sales, slowing transportation and production, filling jails to capacity
4. Three new nations emerged—Turkey, Persia/Iran, and Saudi Arabia.
5. dramatic economic changes; attempts by western nations to dominate region
6. **Possible Answers:** Gain—Freedom and democracy, improved status of women, better economic conditions. Lose—Sever links with traditions, cause unrest in society.
7. **Possible Answer:** issues of nationalism raised, new nations formed, Indians demanded self-rule promised before war.
8. India—Democratic elections; Turkey—Republic; Iran—Shah was dictator; Saudi Arabia—Ruling family, no democracy.
9. **Rubric** Persuasive essays should
• cite reasons supporting nonviolent resistance.
• refute opposing ideas.

CONNECT TO TODAY

Rubric Graphs should
• illustrate statistics clearly.
• show the differences among the nations.
• cite at least one source.

TERMS & NAMES

1. Bolsheviks, p. 434
2. Lenin, p. 434
3. soviet, p. 436
4. Joseph Stalin, p. 439
5. totalitarianism, p. 440
6. Mao Zedong, p. 449
7. Mohandas K. Gandhi, p. 454
8. civil disobedience, p. 454

MAIN IDEAS

Answers will vary.

9. recurring defeats in battle, death of many soldiers, low troop morale, food shortages led to strikes and riots
10. Its position on World War I led to discontent, and attacks by the Red Guards drove its leaders from power.
11. failure of the provisional government, growing power of the soviets; Treaty of Brest-Litovsk angered Russians; Bolsheviks tried to wipe out all enemies—Bolsheviks won
12. dictatorship, one-party rule; dynamic leader; rigid ideology; state control; dependence on modern technology; violence; enforcement through censorship and persecution
13. freedom of religion, speech, press, and expression, choice of job and home, artistic freedom
14. removed his enemy; police terror, propaganda, indoctrination; control of economy
15. Mao promoted land reform and better treatment for the peasants; Nationalists had done little for peasants.
16. to save the Communists who were being pursued by Nationalist forces
17. boycotts; strikes; refusal to pay British taxes, vote, or attend British schools; marches, demonstrations
18. set up legal system, rights extended to women, spurred economic growth by industrializing

Chapter 14 Assessment

TERMS & NAMES

Briefly explain the importance of each of the following in Russia, China, or India.

1. Bolsheviks
2. Lenin
3. soviet
4. Joseph Stalin
5. totalitarianism
6. Mao Zedong
7. Mohandas K. Gandhi
8. civil disobedience

MAIN IDEAS

Revolutions in Russia Section 1 (pages 433–439)

9. How did World War I lead to the downfall of Czar Nicholas II? (10.7.1)
10. Why did the provisional government fail? (10.7.1)
11. Explain the causes and outcome of Russia's civil war. (10.7.3)

Case Study: Totalitarianism Section 2 (pages 440–447)

12. What are the key traits of totalitarianism? (10.6.3)
13. What individual freedoms are denied in a totalitarian state? (10.7.2)
14. How did Joseph Stalin create a totalitarian state in the Soviet Union? (10.7.2)

Imperial China Collapses Section 3 (pages 448–452)

15. Why did the peasants align themselves with the Chinese Communists? (10.9.4)
16. Why did Mao Zedong undertake the Long March? (10.9.4)

Nationalism in India and Southwest Asia Section 4 (pages 453–457)

17. What are some examples of civil disobedience led by Mohandas Gandhi? (10.4.4)
18. What steps did Kemal take to modernize Turkey? (10.4.4)

CRITICAL THINKING

1. USING YOUR NOTES
In a diagram show the causes of changes in government in the countries listed. (10.6.3)

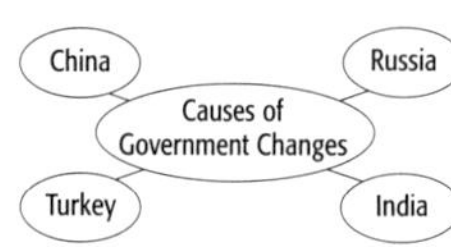

2. FORMING AND SUPPORTING OPINIONS
Which of the weapons of totalitarian governments do you think is most effective in maintaining control of a country? Explain. (10.6.3)

3. ANALYZING CAUSES
REVOLUTION What role did World War I play in the revolutions and nationalistic uprisings discussed in this chapter? (10.4.4)

4. HYPOTHESIZING
EMPIRE BUILDING Why were the empires discussed in this chapter unable to remain in control of all of their lands? (10.4.4)

5. RECOGNIZING EFFECTS
POWER AND AUTHORITY How did women's roles change under Stalin in Russia and Kemal in Turkey? (10.7.2)

VISUAL SUMMARY

Revolutionary Leaders: 1900–1939

	Lenin	Stalin	Sun Yixian	Mao Zedong	Gandhi	Kemal
Country	Russia	Russia	China	China	India	Turkey
Career	late 1890s–1924	early 1900s–1953	late 1890s–1925	early 1900s–1976	late 1800s–1948	early 1900s–1938
Key Role	Bolshevik revolutionary and first ruler of Communist Russia	Dictator	First president of the new Republic of China	Leader of the Chinese Communist Party	Leader of the Indian independence movement	First president of the new Republic of Turkey
Popular Name	"Father of the Revolution"	"Man of Steel"	"Father of Modern China"	"The Great Helmsman"	"Great Soul"	"Father of the Turks"
Goal	Promote a worldwide Communist revolution led by workers	Perfect a Communist state in Russia through totalitarian rule	Establish a modern government based on nationalism, democracy, and economic security	Stage a Communist revolution in China led by peasants	Achieve Indian self-rule through campaigns of civil disobedience	Transform Turkey into a modern nation

CRITICAL THINKING

Answers will vary.

1. Russia—World War I, food shortages, Bolsheviks; China—Imperial government failed; Turkey—Breakup of the Ottoman Empire; India—World War I, Amritsar Massacre, Gandhi's tactics.
2. **Possible Answer:** indoctrination, because it begins with children and pervades the society
3. **Possible Answers:** World War I broke up the Ottoman Empire, causing nationalists in its lands to press for independence. It also precipitated the fall of the Russian czar. Promises made to Indians before and during the war triggered demands for independence.
4. The old governments were too weak to respond to the demands of the population. Independence groups gained power, especially after World War I.
5. In both places, women's rights were expanded. More educational and work opportunities became available.

458 Chapter 14

Use the quotation and your knowledge of world history to answers questions 1 and 2
Additional Test Practice, pp. S1–S33

PRIMARY SOURCE

India does not need to be industrialized in the modern sense of the term. It has 7,500,000 villages scattered over a vast area 1,900 miles long, 1,500 broad. The people are rooted to the soil, and the vast majority are living a hand-to-mouth life. . . . Agriculture does not need revolutionary changes. The Indian peasant requires a supplementary industry. The most natural is the introduction of the spinning-wheel.

MOHANDAS K. GANDHI, Letter to Sir Daniel Hamilton

1. What picture does Gandhi present of India and its people? (10.4.4)
   - **A.** India is adequately industrialized.
   - **B.** India is dominated by the British.
   - **C.** India is primarily an agricultural nation.
   - **D.** Indians are well-off and do not need additional industries.
2. What did Gandhi believe about the spinning wheel? (10.4.4)
   - **A.** Gandhi believed that the spinning wheel would make Indians less dependent on the British economy.
   - **B.** Gandhi believed that the spinning wheel was a threat to the Indian economy.
   - **C.** Gandhi believed the main economic industry in India should be spinning cloth.
   - **D.** Gandhi believed the spinning wheel was not necessary to the Indian economy.

Use the graph and your knowledge of world history to answer question 3.

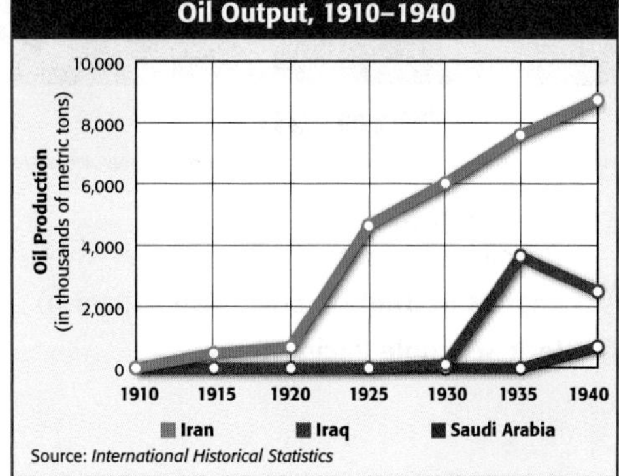

3. Between which years did Iran show a dramatic increase in oil production?
   - **A.** 1910–1920
   - **B.** 1920–1925
   - **C.** 1930–1935
   - **D.** 1935–1940

INTEGRATED TECHNOLOGY

TEST PRACTICE Go to **classzone.com**
- Diagnostic tests
- Tutorials
- Strategies
- Additional practice

ALTERNATIVE ASSESSMENT

1. **Interact *with* History** (10.4.4)

   On page 432, you played the role of a citizen whose country was brimming with revolutionary activity. You evaluated two tactics for change—violence and nonviolence. Now that you have read the chapter, how would you assess the pros and cons of Mao's and Gandhi's strategies? What role did violence play in the Russian and Chinese revolutions? How successful were Gandhi's nonviolent methods in India? Discuss your opinions in a small group.

2. **WRITING ABOUT HISTORY** (10.6.3; Writing 2.1.b, e)

   Write a **science fiction story** about a totalitarian state that uses modern technology to spread propaganda and control people. Refer to the case study on totalitarianism for ideas. Consider the following:
   - the need to control information
   - methods to control the actions of people
   - reasons people oppose totalitarian control of a country

INTEGRATED TECHNOLOGY

Writing a Documentary Film Script (Writing 2.3.b)

Write a documentary film script profiling a country where nationalistic revolutionary movements are currently active. Consider the following:
- What type of government is currently in power? (constitutional monarchy, single-party dictatorship, theocracy, republic) How long has it been in power?
- Who are the top political leaders, and how are they viewed inside and outside the country?
- Do citizens have complaints about their government? What are they?
- What nationalist revolutionary groups are active? What are their goals and strategies?

The script should also include narration, locations, sound, and visuals.

CHAPTER 14 ASSESSMENT

STANDARDS-BASED ASSESSMENT

1. The correct answer is letter **C**. Letter **A** is not correct because at the time of this letter India had not become industrialized. Letter **B** is not correct because the role of the British is not mentioned in the letter. Letter **D** is not correct because Gandhi mentions people living hand to mouth—India was not well off at the time of the letter.
2. The correct answer is letter **A**. Letter **B** is not correct—Gandhi recognizes the spinning wheel as helpful. Letter **C** is not correct—Gandhi calls for a supplementary industry, not a major one. Letter **D** is not correct—Gandhi suggests adding the spinning wheel to the Indian economy.
3. The correct answer is letter **B**. Production jumps by around 4,000 metric tons during the period. Letters **A**, **C**, and **D** are not correct because no increase in the years shown is as great as the period from 1920 to 1925.

Formal Assessment
- Chapter Test, Forms A, B, and C, pp. 246–260

California Test Generator CD-ROM
- Chapter Tests, Forms A, B, and C (English and Spanish)

ALTERNATIVE ASSESSMENT

1. **Possible Answers:** Students who originally advocated violent action may now side with Gandhi's strategy of noncooperation or nonviolent resistance, based on the success of his boycotts and demonstrations. However, they may note that India still had not achieved independence. Violence played a large part in the revolutions of both China and Russia. Using the aftermath of the Bolshevik Revolution as an example, students may also conclude that violence breeds violence.
2. **Rubric** Science fiction stories should
   - be set in a fictional time and location.
   - present reasons for a totalitarian state to control the people.
   - clearly illustrate the use of weapons of totalitarianism.

INTEGRATED TECHNOLOGY

Rubric Documentary film scripts should
- identify the country, its leaders, and its revolutionary groups.
- outline the grievances the people have against the current regime.
- identify the goals and strategies of revolutionary groups.
- include a list of locations, sound, and visuals to be used.

CHAPTER 15 PLANNING GUIDE

Years of Crisis, 1919–1939

CHAPTER RESOURCES	COPYMASTERS	ASSESSMENT
CHAPTER OVERVIEW Societies underwent political, economic, social, and scientific changes that brought them to the brink of another world war.	**In-Depth Resources: Unit 4** • Building Vocabulary, p. 51 **Chapters in Brief** (in English and Spanish) **Block Schedule Pacing Guide**	**Chapter Assessment,** pp. 486–487 **Formal Assessment** • Chapter Tests, Forms A, B, and C, pp. 265–276 **Test Generator** **Integrated Assessment Book** **Online Test Practice**
SECTION 1 **Postwar Uncertainty** pp. 463–469 **OBJECTIVE** Identify the scientific, artistic, social, and technological changes that took place during the 1920s and the impact they had on the world.	**In-Depth Resources: Unit 4** • Guided Reading, p. 47 • Primary Source: from An Interview with Charles A. Lindbergh, p. 55 • Literature: from *This Side of Paradise,* p. 59 • History Makers: Sigmund Freud, p. 62 • Reteaching Activity, p. 65 **Reading Study Guide,** p. 157	**Section 1 Assessment,** p. 467 **Formal Assessment** • Section Quiz, p. 261 **California Daily Standards Practice Transparencies,** TT118
SECTION 2 **A Worldwide Depression** pp. 470–475 **OBJECTIVE** Describe postwar Europe, the Weimar Republic, and the causes and effects of the Great Depression.	**In-Depth Resources: Unit 4** • Guided Reading, p. 48 • Skillbuilder Practice: Identifying Problems and Solutions, p. 52 • Primary Source: German Inflation, p. 56 • Reteaching Activity, p. 66 **Reading Study Guide,** p. 159	**Section 2 Assessment,** p. 475 **Formal Assessment** • Section Quiz, p. 262 **California Daily Standards Practice Transparencies,** TT119
SECTION 3 **Fascism Rises in Europe** pp. 476–480 **OBJECTIVE** Trace the rise of fascism in Italy and Germany and describe its impact.	**In-Depth Resources: Unit 4** • Guided Reading, p. 49 • Primary Source: Kristallnacht, p. 57 • Literature: Poems by Bertolt Brecht, p. 60 • Connections Across Time and Cultures: Absolutism and Fascism, p. 64 • Reteaching Activity, p. 67 **Reading Study Guide,** p. 161	**Section 3 Assessment,** p. 480 **Formal Assessment** • Section Quiz, p. 263 **California Daily Standards Practice Transparencies,** TT120
SECTION 4 **Aggressors Invade Nations** pp. 481–485 **OBJECTIVE** Compare the attempts by fascist nations to gain power with the efforts of democratic nations to preserve peace.	**In-Depth Resources: Unit 4** • Guided Reading, p. 50 • Geography Application: Spain During the 1930s, p. 53 • Primary Source: The Bombing of Guernica, p. 58 • History Makers: Francisco Franco, p. 63 • Reteaching Activity, p. 68 **Reading Study Guide,** p. 163	**Section 4 Assessment,** p. 485 **Formal Assessment** • Section Quiz, p. 264 **California Daily Standards Practice Transparencies,** TT121

INTEGRATED TECHNOLOGY

- eEdition Plus Online
- EasyPlanner Plus Online
- eTest Plus Online

Audio CDs
- Voices from the Past
- Reading Study Guides

CD-ROMs
- eEdition
- Power Presentations
- EasyPlanner
- Electronic Library of Primary Sources
- Test Generator

eEdition CD-ROM

World Art and Cultures Transparencies
- AT67 *The Twittering Machine*
- AT68 *Electric Prisms*

Electronic Library of Primary Sources
- "The Death of God"

classzone.com
- NetExplorations: Life in the 1920s

eEdition CD-ROM

Electronic Library of Primary Sources
- "Famine in Russia"

classzone.com

eEdition CD-ROM

World Art and Cultures Transparencies
- AT69 Pillars of Society

Critical Thinking Transparencies
- CT31 Economic Crisis: Between Two Fires

Electronic Library of Primary Sources
- from Memos on the Aims of Germany and Japan

classzone.com

eEdition CD-ROM

Geography Transparencies
- GT31 Expansion of Nazi Germany

Critical Thinking Transparencies
- CT67 Chapter 31 Visual Summary

Electronic Library of Primary Sources
- from Speech in the House of Commons

classzone.com

OVERVIEW OF CALIFORNIA RESOURCES

	Section 1	Section 2	Section 3	Section 4
California Reading Toolkit	p. L66	p. L67	p. L68	p. L69
California Modified Lesson Plans for English Learners	p. 127	p. 129	p. 131	p. 133
California Daily Standards Practice Transparencies	TT58	TT59	TT60	TT61
California Standards Enrichment Workbook	pp. 71–72	pp. 67–68, 69–70, 81–82, 85–86	pp. 77–78, 79–80, 87–88	pp. 71–72, 77–78, 81–82, 85–86
California Standards Planner and Lesson Plans	p. L123	p. L125	p. L127	p. L129
California Online Test Practice	classzone.com	classzone.com	classzone.com	classzone.com
California Test Generator CD-ROM	CD-ROM	CD-ROM	CD-ROM	CD-ROM
California Easy Planner CD-ROM	CD-ROM	CD-ROM	CD-ROM	CD-ROM
California eEdition CD-ROM	CD-ROM	CD-ROM	CD-ROM	CD-ROM

Chart Key:

Copymaster

Pupil's Edition

Audio Library

Teacher's Edition

CD-ROM

Overhead Transparency

Internet

Block Scheduling

Video

NO TIME?

If you do not have time to teach this chapter in full, assign the **Chapter in Brief** (also available in Spanish).

Previewing Resources for Differentiated Instruction

ENGLISH LEARNERS: Resources in Spanish

In-Depth Resources in Spanish
- Guided Reading Ⓐ
- Skillbuilder Practice: Identifying Problems and Solutions Ⓑ
- Geography Application: Spain During the 1930s

Chapters in Brief

Reading Study Guide Ⓒ

Reading Study Guide Audio CD

Test Generator CD-ROM
- Chapter Test, Forms A, B, and C

Plus

Modified Lesson Plans for English Learners

Multi-Language Glossary of Social Studies Terms

Ⓐ
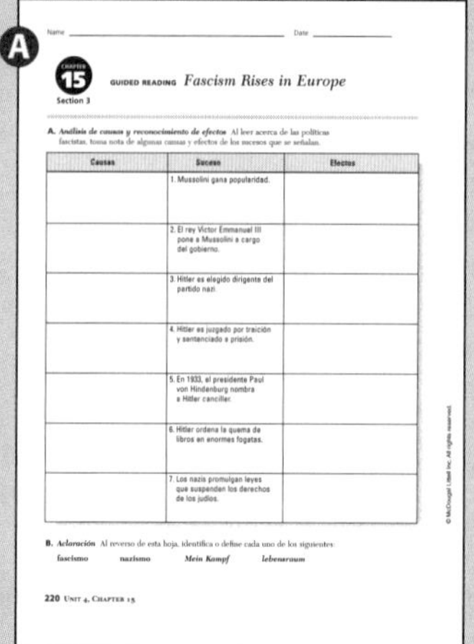
CHAPTER 15 Section 3 GUIDED READING *Fascism Rises in Europe*

A. *Análisis de causas y reconocimiento de efectos*

Causas	Sucesos	Efectos
	1. Mussolini gana popularidad.	
	2. El rey Víctor Emmanuel III pone a Mussolini a cargo del gobierno.	
	3. Hitler es elegido dirigente del partido nazi.	
	4. Hitler es juzgado por traición y sentenciado a prisión.	
	5. En 1932, el presidente Paul von Hindenburg nombra a Hitler canciller.	
	6. Hitler ordena la quema de libros en enormes fogatas.	
	7. Los nazis promulgan leyes que suspenden los derechos de los judíos.	

220 Unit 4, Chapter 15

Ⓑ

CHAPTER 15 Section 2 SKILLBUILDER PRACTICE *Identificación de problemas*

222 Unit 4, Chapter 15

STRUGGLING READERS

In-Depth Resources: Unit 4
- Guided Reading Ⓐ
- Building Vocabulary
- Skillbuilder Practice: Identifying Problems and Solutions
- Geography Application: Spain During the 1930s Ⓑ
- Reteaching Activities

Chapters in Brief

Reading Study Guide

Reading Study Guide Audio CD

Formal Assessment
- Chapter Test, Form A Ⓒ

Plus

Reading Toolkit

Ⓐ
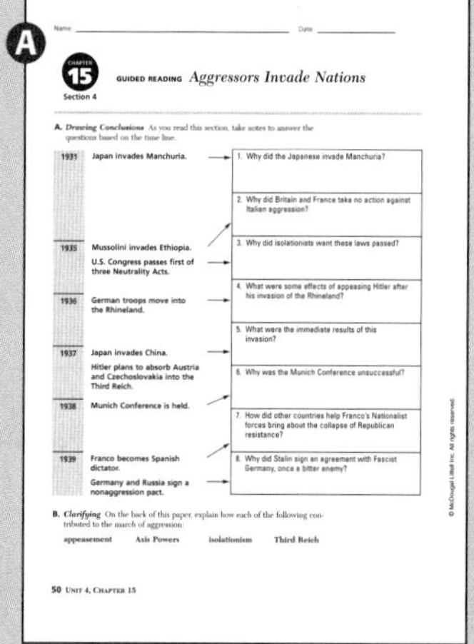
CHAPTER 15 Section 4 GUIDED READING *Aggressors Invade Nations*

A. *Drawing Conclusions* As you read this section, take notes to answer the questions based on the time line.

1931 Japan invades Manchuria.
1. Why did the Japanese invade Manchuria?
2. Why did Britain and France take no action against Italian aggression?
1935 Mussolini invades Ethiopia. U.S. Congress passes first of three Neutrality Acts.
3. Why did isolationists want these laws passed?
1936 German troops move into the Rhineland.
4. What were some effects of appeasing Hitler after his invasion of the Rhineland?
5. What were the immediate results of this invasion?
1937 Japan invades China. Hitler plans to absorb Austria and Czechoslovakia into the Third Reich.
1938 Munich Conference is held.
6. Why was the Munich Conference unsuccessful?
7. How did other countries help Franco's Nationalist forces bring about the collapse of Republican resistance?
1939 Franco becomes Spanish dictator. Germany and Russia sign a nonaggression pact.
8. Why did Stalin sign an agreement with Fascist Germany, once a bitter enemy?

B. *Clarifying* On the back of this paper, explain how each of the following contributed to the march of aggression.

appeasement Axis Powers isolationism Third Reich

50 Unit 4, Chapter 15

Ⓑ
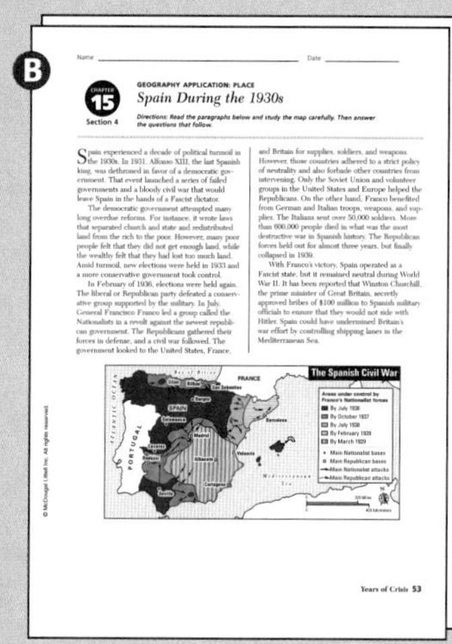
CHAPTER 15 Section 4 GEOGRAPHY APPLICATION: PLACE *Spain During the 1930s*

Directions: Read the paragraphs below and study the map carefully. Then answer the questions that follow.

Years of Crisis 53

GIFTED AND TALENTED STUDENTS

In-Depth Resources: Unit 4
- Primary Source: from An Interview with Charles A. Lindbergh; German Inflation; *Kristallnacht;* The Bombing of Guernica
- Literature: from *This Side of Paradise;* Poems by Bertolt Brecht
- History Makers: Sigmund Freud; Francisco Franco Ⓐ
- Connections Across Time and Cultures: Absolutism and Fascism

Electronic Library of Primary Sources
- "The Death of God"
- "Famine in Russia"
- from Memos on the Aims of Germany and Japan
- from Speech in the House of Commons Ⓑ

Formal Assessment
- Chapter Test, Form C Ⓒ

Ⓐ

CHAPTER 15 Section 4 HISTORYMAKERS Francisco Franco
Cautious Dictator

Questions

Years of Crisis 63

Ⓑ
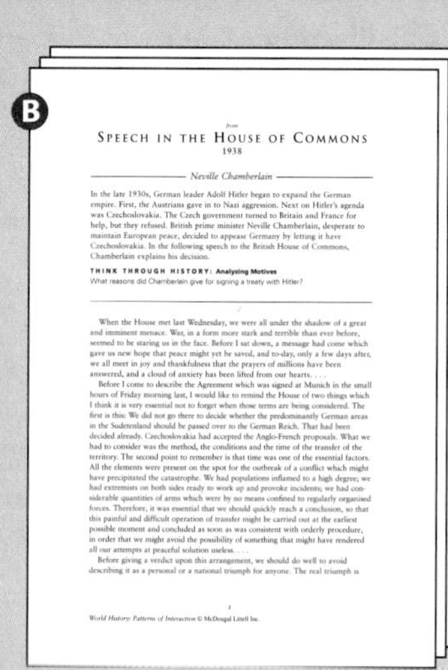
SPEECH IN THE HOUSE OF COMMONS
1938
— Neville Chamberlain —

THINK THROUGH HISTORY: Analyzing Motives

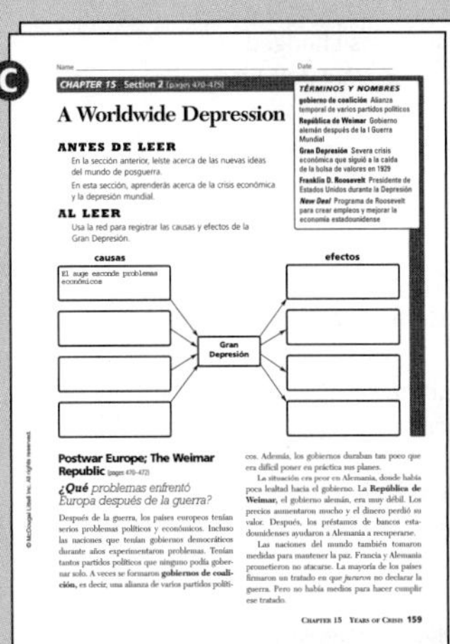

Activities in the Teacher's Edition for English Learners

- Understanding Key Terms, p. 465
- Understanding Inflation, p. 471
- Analyzing a Primary Source, p. 478
- Analyzing Churchill's Speech, p. 484

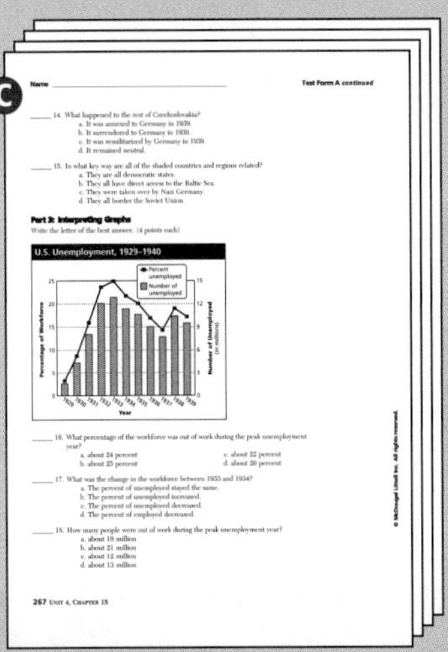

Activities in the Teacher's Edition for Struggling Readers

- Charting the Effects of Technology, p. 466
- Comparing Global Responses to the Great Depression, p. 474
- Identifying Causes and Effects, p. 479
- Headlining the News, p. 482

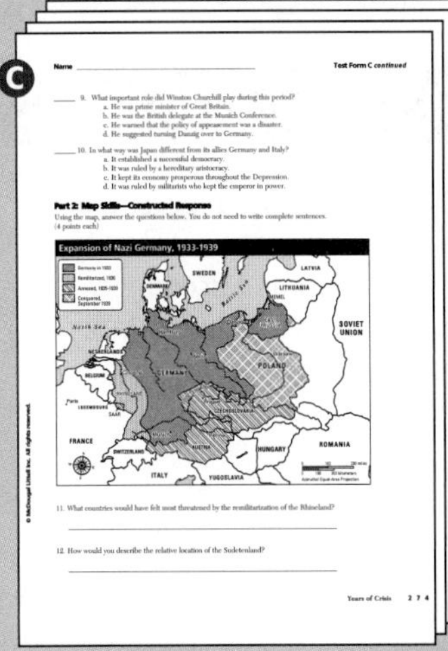

Activities in the Teacher's Edition for Gifted and Talented Students

- Exploring the Literature of the 1920s, p. 464
- Creating a Political Cartoon, p. 473
- Comparing Fascism and 17th-Century Absolutism, p. 477
- Contrasting Literary Responses to the Spanish Civil War, p. 483

INTEGRATED TECHNOLOGY

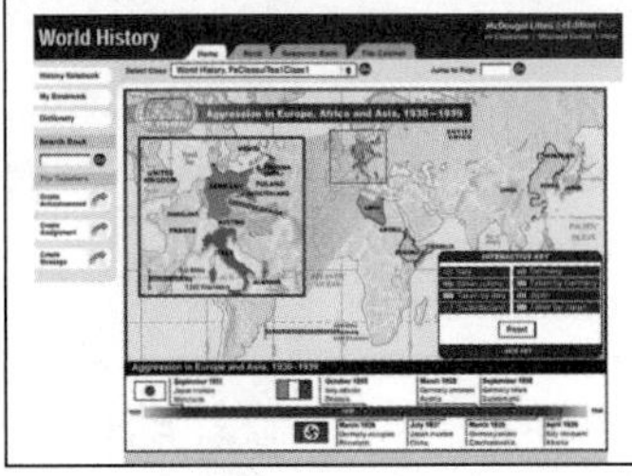

eEdition

- Interactive Visuals
- Interactive Maps
- Interactive Primary Sources

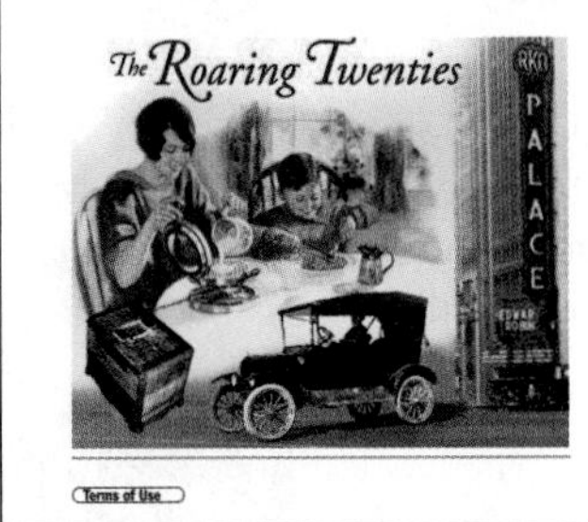

classzone.com

- Research Links
- Internet Activities
- Primary Sources
- Chapter Quiz
- NetExplorations: Life in the 1920s
- Current Events

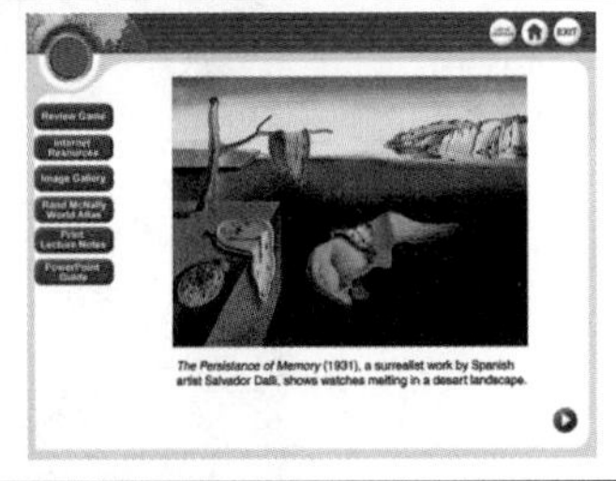

Power Presentations CD-ROM

- Lecture Notes
- Image Gallery
- Chapter Review Game

Critical Thinking Transparencies

- CT31 Economic Crisis: Between Two Fires
- CT67 Chapter 31 Visual Summary

Geography Transparencies

- GT31 Expansion of Nazi Germany, 1933–1939

World Art and Cultures Transparencies

- AT67 *The Twittering Machine*
- AT68 *Electric Prisms*
- AT69 Pillars of Society (A)

Test Practice Transparencies TT118–TT121

Test Generator CD-ROM

EasyPlanner CD-ROM

Voices from the Past Audio CD

Online Test Practice

Electronic Library of Primary Sources

CHAPTER 15 • OBJECTIVE

Analyze the economic, political, social, and scientific changes that brought the world to the brink of a second world war.

Previewing Main Ideas

The main ideas that are identified here delineate the important factors that combined to create a world in crisis. For more information about these main ideas, see pages xxvi–xxvii.

Accessing Prior Knowledge

Ask students to share stories they might have heard about the Great Depression in their families. Explain that this devastating economic situation was only one of many developments in a rapidly changing and unstable world.

Geography *Answers*

SCIENCE AND TECHNOLOGY Lindbergh flew from North America to Europe.

ECONOMICS The expansion of Italy, Germany, and Japan changed the balance of world power.

POWER AND AUTHORITY In 1939, Germany invaded Poland.

CHAPTER 15

Years of Crisis, 1919–1939

Previewing Main Ideas

SCIENCE AND TECHNOLOGY In the 1920s, new scientific ideas changed the way people looked at the world. New inventions improved transportation and communication.

Geography *Innovations in transportation allowed pilot Charles Lindbergh to fly solo from North America across the Atlantic Ocean. Toward what continent did Lindbergh fly?*

ECONOMICS The collapse of the American economy in 1929 triggered a depression that threatened the economic and political systems of countries throughout the world.

Geography *Study the map and time line. What events occurred after the economic crisis that changed the balance of world power?*

POWER AND AUTHORITY In the 1930s, several countries—including Japan, Germany, and Italy—adopted aggressive, militaristic policies.

Geography *What land did Germany invade in 1939?*

INTEGRATED TECHNOLOGY

eEdition
- Interactive Maps
- Interactive Visuals
- Interactive Primary Sources

INTERNET RESOURCES

Go to classzone.com for:
- Research Links
- Internet Activities
- Primary Sources
- Chapter Quiz
- Maps
- Test Practice
- Current Events

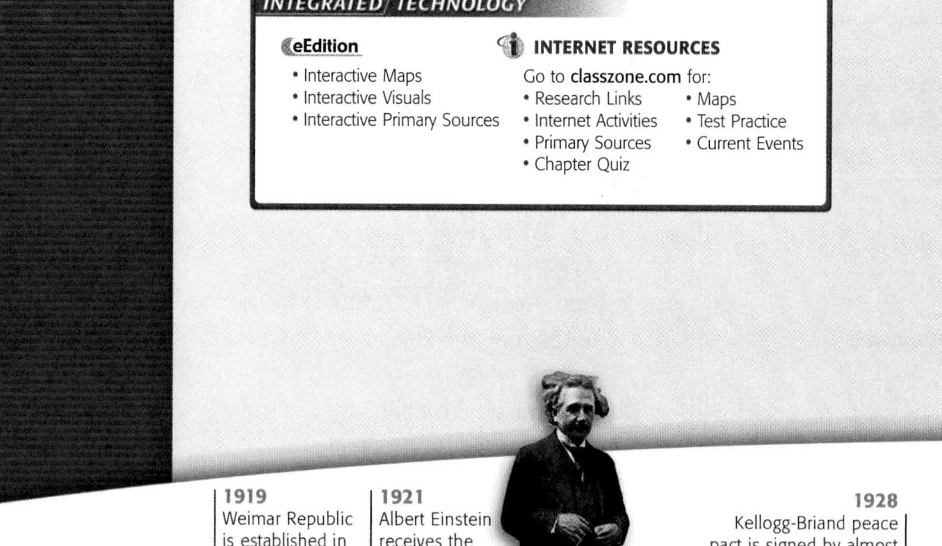

EUROPE

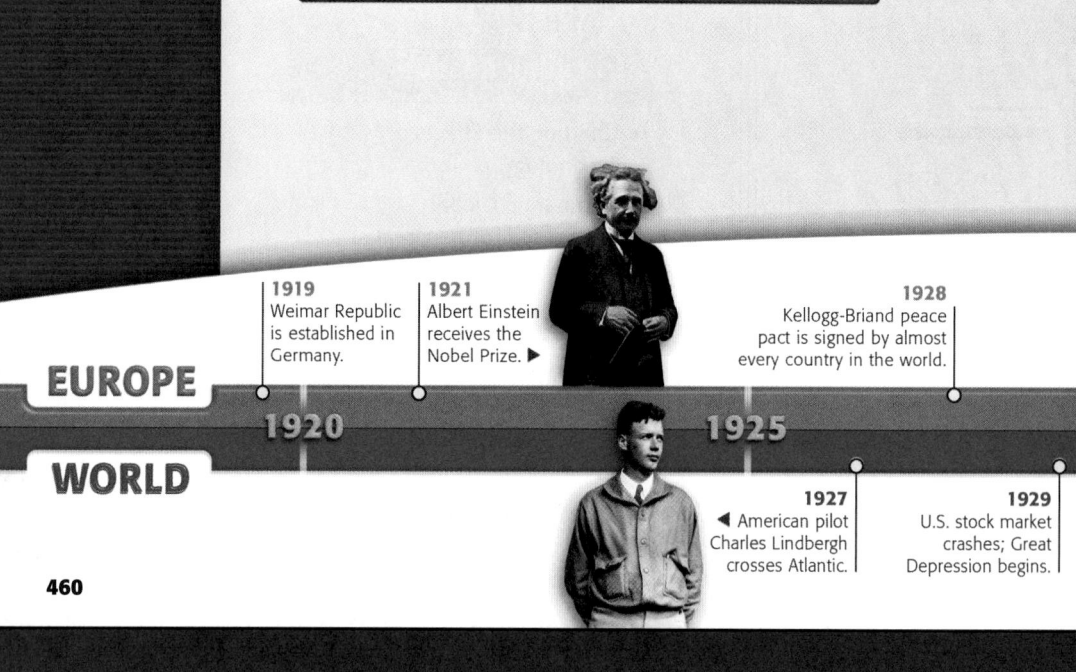

1919 Weimar Republic is established in Germany.

1921 Albert Einstein receives the Nobel Prize. ▶

1928 Kellogg-Briand peace pact is signed by almost every country in the world.

1920 1925

WORLD

1927 ◀ American pilot Charles Lindbergh crosses Atlantic.

1929 U.S. stock market crashes; Great Depression begins.

TIME LINE DISCUSSION

Make sure students understand that this time line essentially spans the era between the end of World War I and the beginning of World War II. It identifies scientific, technological, economic, social, and political events that contributed to another major conflict.

1. Based on the entries in the time line, do you think the Kellogg-Briand peace pact was effective? Why or why not? *(It wasn't effective because both Japan and Italy attacked other countries after it was signed.)*
2. How many years after the Weimar Republic was established in Germany was Hitler named chancellor? *(14 years)*
3. What political situation was Italy involved in when the Spanish Civil War began? *(invasion of Ethiopia)*
4. In which year does Japanese aggression begin? *(1931 invasion of Manchuria)*
5. Which entries on the time line suggest that this was a time of great scientific and technological, as well as political and economic, change? *(Einstein receives the Nobel Prize and Charles Lindbergh crosses the Atlantic.)*

CHAPTER 15

History from Visuals

Interpreting the Map

Ask students to examine the location of the countries on the map. What countries other than Poland were particularly vulnerable to attack by Germany? *(Czechoslovakia, Austria, Denmark, the Netherlands, Belgium, Luxembourg, Switzerland, and France)* What did Germany gain by invading Poland? *(union with East Prussia, which had been cut off from Germany by a strip of Poland; Poland's land and resources.)*

Extension Have students turn to the modern map of Europe in the atlas and compare it with this map. Did Germany have more or less territory in the 1930s than it has today? *(more territory)* Based on the map on this page, what prediction would students make about the territory Germany would control in the years following 1939? *(It would expand even further.)*

RECOMMENDED RESOURCES

Books for the Teacher

Guérin, Daniel. ***The Brown Plague: Travels in Late Weimar and Early Nazi Germany.*** Trans. Robert Schwartzwald. Durham, NC: Duke UP, 1994. First-person account of the rise of Hitler and the Nazis.

Mih, Walter C., and Bernard Einstein. ***The Fascinating Life and Theory of Albert Einstein***. Huntington, NY: Nova Science Publishers, 2000. Having formulated the theory of relativity, Einstein helped reshape people's view of the cosmos. This book discusses his life while focusing on his theories and ideas.

Books for the Student

Burg, David F. ***The Great Depression: An Eyewitness History***. New York: Facts On File, 1996.

Terkel, Studs. ***Hard Times: An Oral History of the Great Depression.*** New York: New Press, 2000. This oral history is by the men and women who lived during the Great Depression. It features the jobless, hoboes, employed people, and even the rich.

Videos and Software

Heil Hitler: Confessions of a Hitler Youth. VHS. Ambrose Video, 1991. 800-526-4663. The Third Reich, as viewed by a man who joined Hitler's cause at age ten.

1929–1936: Stormy Weather. VHS and DVD. Films for the Humanities & Sciences, 1999. 800-257-5126. Peter Jennings hosts this look at the Great Depression.

The Causes of World War II. CD-ROM. Society for Visual Education, 1994. 800-829-1900.

Interact *with* History

Objectives

- Set the stage for studying the years of crisis, 1919–1939.
- Identify some of the issues confronting nations, their leaders, and their citizens during this time.

EXAMINING *the* ISSUES

Possible Answers

- The first candidate appeals to German patriotism and bitterness over the Treaty of Versailles and calls for strong national unity to solve problems. The second candidate's strategy involves working with other nations toward a slower resolution of problems.
- The first candidate makes a stronger appeal to the listeners' emotions.

Discussion

Ask students why people may have lost faith in democratic governments in the 1920s and 1930s. *(Possible Answer: the collapse of the stock market and Great Depression in the world's foremost democratic society)*

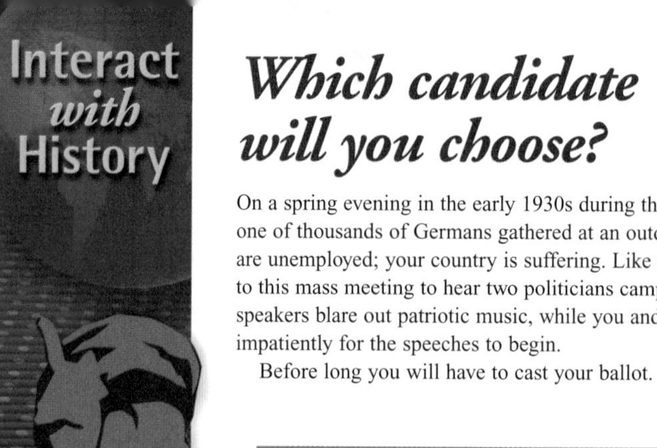

Which candidate will you choose?

On a spring evening in the early 1930s during the Great Depression, you are one of thousands of Germans gathered at an outdoor stadium in Munich. You are unemployed; your country is suffering. Like everyone else, you have come to this mass meeting to hear two politicians campaigning for office. Huge speakers blare out patriotic music, while you and the rest of the crowd wait impatiently for the speeches to begin.

Before long you will have to cast your ballot.

First candidate's platform	Second candidate's platform
• Remember Germany's long and glorious past • Replace our present indecisive leadership with a strong, effective leader • Rebuild the army to protect against enemies • Regain the lands taken unfairly from us • Make sacrifices to return to economic health • Put the welfare of the state above all, and our country will be a great power again	• Realize that there are no simple or quick solutions to problems • Put people back to work, but economic recovery will be slow • Provide for the poor, elderly, and sick • Avoid reckless military spending • Act responsibly to safeguard democracy • Be a good neighbor country; honor our debts and treaty commitments

EXAMINING *the* ISSUES

- **What strategy does each candidate have for solving the nation's problems?**
- **Which candidate makes the stronger appeal to the listener's emotions?**

As a class, discuss these questions. In your discussion, remember what you have read about the defeated nations' bitterness toward the Versailles Treaty following World War I. As you read this chapter, notice that dictators were voted into power as people lost faith in democratic government in the 1920s and 1930s.

462

WHY STUDY YEARS OF CRISIS, 1919–1939?

- The political and economic events that took place during this period led the world into a second, devastating, global conflict.
- The Great Depression and its effect on economies around the world shook people's faith and led governments to institute extensive economic changes and safeguards.
- The rapid development of communication and transportation technology during this era forever changed the way we view our planet and interact with its people.
- Scientific discoveries and developments by people such as Albert Einstein and Sigmund Freud ushered in a drastically new way of thinking about ourselves and our world.
- The atmosphere of crisis and unrest in this period spawned enduring artistic and literary responses that still speak to an unsettled world.
- Evaluating the events of these years with the knowledge of what followed can help nations work together to prevent their happening again.

People waiting for a free lunch for the unemployed, 1930

Magazine cover, 1926

Postwar Uncertainty

MAIN IDEA

SCIENCE AND TECHNOLOGY The postwar period was one of loss and uncertainty but also one of invention, creativity, and new ideas.

WHY IT MATTERS NOW

Postwar trends in physics, psychiatry, art, literature, communication, music, and transportation still affect our lives.

TERMS & NAMES

- Albert Einstein
- theory of relativity
- Sigmund Freud
- existentialism
- Friedrich Nietzsche
- surrealism
- jazz
- Charles Lindbergh

SETTING THE STAGE The horrors of World War I shattered the Enlightenment belief that progress would continue and reason would prevail. In the postwar period, people began questioning traditional beliefs. Some found answers in new scientific developments, which challenged the way people looked at the world. Many enjoyed the convenience of technological improvements in transportation and communication. As society became more open, women demanded more rights, and young people adopted new values. Meanwhile, unconventional styles and ideas in literature, philosophy, and music reflected the uncertain times.

A New Revolution in Science

The ideas of Albert Einstein and Sigmund Freud had an enormous impact on the 20th century. These thinkers were part of a scientific revolution as important as that brought about centuries earlier by Copernicus and Galileo.

Impact of Einstein's Theory of Relativity German-born physicist **Albert Einstein** offered startling new ideas on space, time, energy, and matter. Scientists had found that light travels at exactly the same speed no matter what direction it moves in relation to earth. In 1905, Einstein theorized that while the speed of light is constant, other things that seem constant, such as space and time, are not. Space and time can change when measured relative to an object moving near the speed of light—about 186,000 miles per second. Since relative motion is the key to Einstein's idea, it is called the **theory of relativity**. Einstein's ideas had implications not only for science but also for how people viewed the world. Now uncertainty and relativity replaced Isaac Newton's comforting belief of a world operating according to absolute laws of motion and gravity.

Influence of Freudian Psychology The ideas of Austrian physician **Sigmund Freud** were as revolutionary as Einstein's. Freud treated patients with psychological problems. From his experiences, he constructed a theory about the human mind. He believed that much of human behavior is irrational, or beyond reason. He called the irrational part of the mind the unconscious. In the unconscious, a number of drives existed, especially pleasure-seeking drives, of which the conscious mind was unaware. Freud's ideas weakened faith in reason. Even so, by the 1920s, Freud's theories had developed widespread influence.

CALIFORNIA STANDARDS

10.6.4 Discuss the influence of World War I on literature, art, and intellectual life in the West (e.g., Pablo Picasso, the "lost generation" of Gertrude Stein, Ernest Hemingway).

CST 2 Students analyze how change happens at different rates at different times; understand that some aspects can change while others remain the same; and understand that change is complicated and affects not only technology and politics but also values and beliefs.

REP 1 Students distinguish valid arguments from fallacious arguments in historical interpretations.

REP 4 Students construct and test hypotheses; collect, evaluate, and employ information from multiple primary and secondary sources; and apply it in oral and written presentations.

TAKING NOTES

Summarizing Use a chart to identify two people who contributed to each field.

Field	Contributors
science	
literature and philosophy	
art and music	
technology	

LESSON PLAN

OBJECTIVES

- Explain how new scientific theories challenged old beliefs.
- Describe how the brutality of war prompted philosophers and writers to explore new ideas.
- Summarize new styles in art, architecture, and music.
- Identify the changing roles of women.
- Trace new technological advances.

1 FOCUS & MOTIVATE

Ask students how they respond after going through a disturbing event such as a quarrel with friends or major illness. *(Possible Answers: questioning and seeking change)*

2 INSTRUCT

A New Revolution in Science

10.6.4

Critical Thinking

- In what way were Freud's ideas as revolutionary as Einstein's? *(They replaced the deeply held belief in human rationality.)*

CALIFORNIA RESOURCES

California Reading Toolkit, p. L66
California Modified Lesson Plans for English Learners, p. 127
California Daily Standards Practice Transparencies, TT58
California Standards Enrichment Workbook, pp. 71–72
California Standards Planner and Lesson Plans, p. L123
California Online Test Practice
California Test Generator CD-ROM
California Easy Planner CD-ROM
California eEdition CD-ROM

SECTION 1 PROGRAM RESOURCES

ALL STUDENTS

In-Depth Resources: Unit 4
- Guided Reading, p. 47
- History Makers: Sigmund Freud, p. 62

Formal Assessment
- Section Quiz, p. 261

ENGLISH LEARNERS

In-Depth Resources in Spanish
- Guided Reading, p. 117

Reading Study Guide (Spanish), p. 157
Reading Study Guide Audio CD (Spanish)

STRUGGLING READERS

In-Depth Resources: Unit 4
- Guided Reading, p. 47
- Building Vocabulary, p. 51
- Reteaching Activity, p. 65

Reading Study Guide, p. 157
Reading Study Guide Audio CD

GIFTED AND TALENTED STUDENTS

In-Depth Resources: Unit 4
- Primary Source: from An Interview with Charles A. Lindbergh, p. 55
- Literature: from *This Side of Paradise,* p. 59

Electronic Library of Primary Sources
- "The Death of God"

INTEGRATED TECHNOLOGY

eEdition CD-ROM
Voices from the Past Audio CD
Power Presentations CD-ROM
World Art and Cultures Transparencies
- AT67 *The Twittering Machine*
- AT68 *Electric Prisms*

classzone.com
- NetExplorations: Life in the 1920s

Literature in the 1920s
10.6.4

Critical Thinking

- Why did writers' visions of the present and future change? *(The brutality of World War I caused them to think the present and future would be changed by this experience.)*
- How might Nietzsche's ideas have influenced politicians? *(by providing philosophical support for the actions of powerful dictators)*

In-Depth Resources: Unit 4
- History Makers: Sigmund Freud, p. 62

Electronic Library of Primary Sources
- "The Death of God"

classzone.com
- NetExplorations: Life in the 1920s

Literature in the 1920s

The brutality of World War I caused philosophers and writers to question accepted ideas about reason and progress. Disillusioned by the war, many people also feared the future and expressed doubts about traditional religious beliefs. Some writers and thinkers expressed their anxieties by creating disturbing visions of the present and the future.

In 1922, T. S. Eliot, an American poet living in England, wrote that Western society had lost its spiritual values. He described the postwar world as a barren "wasteland," drained of hope and faith. In 1921, the Irish poet William Butler Yeats conveyed a sense of dark times ahead in the poem "The Second Coming": "Things fall apart; the centre cannot hold; / Mere anarchy is loosed upon the world."

Writers Reflect Society's Concerns The horror of war made a deep impression on many writers. The Czech-born author Franz Kafka wrote eerie novels such as *The Trial* (1925) and *The Castle* (1926). His books feature people caught in threatening situations they can neither understand nor escape. The books struck a chord among readers in the uneasy postwar years.

Many novels showed the influence of Freud's theories on the unconscious. The Irish-born author James Joyce gained widespread attention with his stream-of-consciousness novel *Ulysses* (1922). This book focuses on a single day in the lives of three people in Dublin, Ireland. Joyce broke with normal sentence structure and vocabulary in a bold attempt to mirror the workings of the human mind.

Vocabulary
stream of consciousness: a literary technique used to present a character's thoughts and feelings as they develop

Thinkers React to Uncertainties In their search for meaning in an uncertain world, some thinkers turned to the philosophy known as **existentialism**. A major leader of this movement was the philosopher Jean Paul Sartre (SAHR•truh) of France. Existentialists believed that there is no universal meaning to life. Each person creates his or her own meaning in life through choices made and actions taken.

Analyzing Primary Sources

Writers of the "Lost Generation"

F. Scott Fitzgerald was only 23 years old when *This Side of Paradise*, his novel of the "Lost Generation," was published. Ask students to research the lives of Fitzgerald and his wife, Zelda, and consider how they represent both the desperation and the frantic gaiety of expatriate artists.

Answers to Document-Based Questions

1. **Making Inferences** The future is elusive and unreachable, and full of promises that can never be fulfilled.
2. **Drawing Conclusions** sad, depressing, hopeless, defeated

In-Depth Resources: Unit 4
- Literature: from *This Side of Paradise,* p. 59

Analyzing Primary Sources

Writers of the "Lost Generation"

During the 1920s, many American writers, musicians, and painters left the United States to live in Europe. These expatriates, people who left their native country to live elsewhere, often settled in Paris. American writer Gertrude Stein called them the "Lost Generation." They moved frantically from one European city to another, trying to find meaning in life. Life empty of meaning is the theme of F. Scott Fitzgerald's *The Great Gatsby* (1925).

PRIMARY SOURCE

And as I sat there brooding on the old, unknown world, I thought of Gatsby's wonder when he first picked out the green light at the end of Daisy's dock. He had come a long way to this blue lawn, and his dream must have seemed so close that he could hardly fail to grasp it. He did not know that it was already behind him, somewhere back in that vast obscurity beyond the city, where the dark fields of the republic rolled on under the night.

Gatsby believed in the green light, the . . . future that year by year recedes before us. It eluded us then, but that's no matter—tomorrow we will run faster, stretch out our arms farther. . . . And one fine morning—

So we beat on, boats against the current, borne back ceaselessly into the past.

F. SCOTT FITZGERALD, *The Great Gatsby*

A 1920s photo of F. Scott Fitzgerald

DOCUMENT-BASED QUESTIONS

1. **Making Inferences** *What seems to be the narrator's attitude toward the future?*
2. **Drawing Conclusions** *How would you describe the overall mood of the excerpt?*

DIFFERENTIATING INSTRUCTION: GIFTED AND TALENTED STUDENTS

Exploring the Literature of the 1920s

Class Time 35 minutes

Task Analyzing literature from the "Lost Generation"

Purpose To identify ways in which literature reflected society's concerns

Instructions Have students work with a partner to reread the excerpt from F. Scott Fitzgerald's *The Great Gatsby* on this page and the selection from *This Side of Paradise* on page 59 of In-Depth Resources: Unit 4. Ask the pairs of students to do the following activities:

- Read the selections silently and aloud.
- Discuss the ideas presented and how they relate to the historical period.
- Think about the questions that follow the selection.

Then have the groups summarize what they have learned from each selection and discuss how the ideas presented are alike and different. *(Possible Answers: Both selections express disillusionment and lack of hope for the future in response to the mass destruction and political and economic unrest following World War I.* This Side of Paradise *is more cynical, focusing on loss of individuality and of heroes, while* The Great Gatsby *expresses a more generalized and deeper despair.)*

LITERATURE SELECTION *from This Side of Paradise* by F. Scott Fitzgerald

In-Depth Resources: Unit 4

The existentialists were influenced by the German philosopher **Friedrich Nietzsche** (NEE•chuh). In the 1880s, Nietzsche wrote that Western ideas such as reason, democracy, and progress had stifled people's creativity and actions. Nietzsche urged a return to the ancient heroic values of pride, assertiveness, and strength. His ideas attracted growing attention in the 20th century and had a great impact on politics in Italy and Germany in the 1920s and 1930s.

Revolution in the Arts

Although many of the new directions in painting and music began in the prewar period, they evolved after the war.

Artists Rebel Against Tradition Artists rebelled against earlier realistic styles of painting. They wanted to depict the inner world of emotion and imagination rather than show realistic representations of objects. Expressionist painters like Paul Klee and Wassily Kandinsky used bold colors and distorted or exaggerated forms.

Inspired by traditional African art, Georges Braque of France and Pablo Picasso of Spain founded Cubism in 1907. Cubism transformed natural shapes into geometric forms. Objects were broken down into different parts with sharp angles and edges. Often several views were depicted at the same time.

Surrealism, an art movement that sought to link the world of dreams with real life, was inspired by Freud's ideas. The term *surreal* means "beyond or above reality." Surrealists tried to call on the unconscious part of their minds. Many of their paintings have an eerie, dreamlike quality and depict objects in unrealistic ways. (A)

MAIN IDEA
Making Inferences
(A) What was the major trend in postwar art?
A. Answer Artists broke away from realism; some tried to draw on the unconscious part of their mind.

Composers Try New Styles In both classical and popular music, composers moved away from traditional styles. In his ballet masterpiece, *The Rite of Spring,* the Russian composer Igor Stravinsky used irregular rhythms and dissonances, or harsh combinations of sound. The Austrian composer Arnold Schoenberg rejected traditional harmonies and musical scales.

A new popular musical style called **jazz** emerged in the United States. It was developed by musicians, mainly African Americans, in New Orleans, Memphis, and Chicago. It swept the United States and Europe. The lively, loose beat of jazz seemed to capture the new freedom of the age.

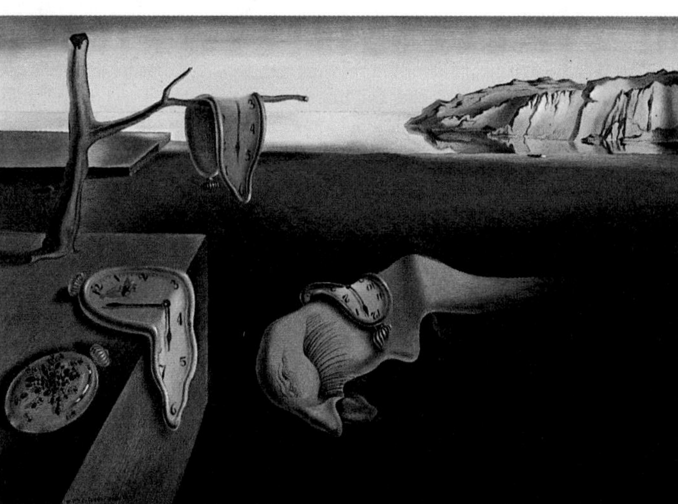

◄ *The Persistence of Memory* (1931), a surrealist work by Spanish artist Salvador Dali, shows watches melting in a desert.

Revolution in the Arts
10.6.4

Critical Thinking

- How was surrealism connected with Freud's ideas? *(By depicting dream images, it accepted and validated the reality of Freud's concept of the unconsciousness.)*
- What aspects of earlier music did new composers rebel against? *(its tonality, harmony, and strict rhythms)*

World Art and Cultures Transparencies

- AT67 *The Twittering Machine*
- AT68 *Electric Prisms*

More About . . .

The Persistence of Memory

Salvador Dali called his *The Persistence of Memory* "a hand-painted dream photograph." The work mixes realism with absurd images like the soft watches. Some critics have suggested that these watches imply the disintegration of normal time. Insects feeding on the watches seem to reinforce this idea of a world in the grip of destruction.

More About . . .

Jazz

Jazz musicians are known for *improvisation,* or creating variations of the music as they play it. Often the music is *syncopated,* with irregular rhythmic patterns and accents falling in unexpected places. These elements give jazz its characteristic energy and excitement.

DIFFERENTIATING INSTRUCTION: ENGLISH LEARNERS

Understanding Key Terms

Class Time 25 minutes

Task Creating a chart of three key terms

Purpose To clarify the sense and meaning of three key terms used in this chapter

Instructions Explain to students that the concepts presented on this page are difficult ones, so they shouldn't be discouraged if they have problems understanding them in one reading. Suggest that students work together in pairs to read the Spanish translation of the Guided Reading material provided on page 117 of In-Depth Resources in Spanish. Instruct them to pay particular attention to the key terms *existentialism, surrealism*, and *jazz*. Have them discuss this material and then reread the English text on this page. Then have students create charts like the one here.

Key Term	Meaning	How It Reflects the Time
existentialism	belief that people make their own meaning	shows reaction to uncertain world
surrealism	art form based on images from the unconscious	uses new images and forms
jazz	loose, free style of music	breaks with order and discipline

Society Challenges Convention
10.6.4

Critical Thinking

- How did the changes in women's clothes reflect their changing roles? *(The new styles gave them greater freedom.)*
- What goals were women seeking in the 1920s? *(greater participation in society, expanded career options, and control over their bodies)*

Technological Advances Improve Life
10.6.4

Critical Thinking

- Which technological advance do you think had the greatest effect on society? *(Possible Answers: transportation–gave people more mobility and options for work and pleasure; communication–gave people access to more information)*
- How might World War I have spurred developments in the radio? *(It was needed for battlefront communication.)*

More About . . .

Flappers

In the 1920s, stylish women were called flappers. The term referred to the loose unrestricted styles worn by young women. It also refected the attitudes of the young women. They were breaking away from old ideas and expectations like a fledging breaking (flapping) out of the nest. Flappers became a symbol for the era's rebellious youth.

▲ Women like these marching in a 1912 suffrage parade in New York City helped gain American women's right to vote in 1920.

Society Challenges Convention

World War I had disrupted traditional social patterns. New ideas and ways of life led to a new kind of individual freedom during the 1920s. Young people especially were willing to break with the past and experiment with modern values.

Women's Roles Change The independent spirit of the times showed clearly in the changes women were making in their lives. The war had allowed women to take on new roles. Their work in the war effort was decisive in helping them win the right to vote. After the war, women's suffrage became law in many countries, including the United States, Britain, Germany, Sweden, and Austria.

Women abandoned restrictive clothing and hairstyles. They wore shorter, looser garments and had their hair "bobbed," or cut short. They also wore makeup, drove cars, and drank and smoked in public. Although most women still followed traditional paths of marriage and family, a growing number spoke out for greater freedom in their lives. Margaret Sanger and Emma Goldman risked arrest by speaking in favor of birth control. As women sought new careers, the numbers of women in medicine, education, journalism, and other professions increased. B

B. Answer Women won the right to vote, changed style of dress, sought new careers.

MAIN IDEA

Summarizing

B How did the changes of the postwar years affect women?

Technological Advances Improve Life

During World War I, scientists developed new drugs and medical treatments that helped millions of people in the postwar years. The war's technological advances were put to use to improve transportation and communication after the war.

The Automobile Alters Society The automobile benefited from a host of wartime innovations and improvements—electric starters, air-filled tires, and more powerful engines. Cars were now sleek and brightly polished, complete with headlights and chrome-plated bumpers. In prewar Britain, autos were owned exclusively by the rich. British factories produced 34,000 autos in 1913. After the war, prices dropped, and the middle class could afford cars. By 1937, the British were producing 511,000 autos a year.

DIFFERENTIATING INSTRUCTION: STRUGGLING READERS

Charting the Effects of Technology

Class Time 20 minutes

Task Creating a chart showing the ways technological advances in transportation and communications changed life in the 1920s and 1930s

Purpose To clarify information in the text

Instructions Have students reread the material from the bottom of page 466 through page 467. Also suggest that they read the last section of page 158 of the Reading Study Guide. Then divide students into four groups with each group focusing on either the automobile, the airplane, radio, or movies.

Have each group discuss the way its technology changed people's lives and fill in their section of the class chart. You might want to copy and enlarge the vertical chart in Critical Thinking Transparencies CT80 for students to use.

A sample chart follows:

Automobiles	Airplanes	Radio	Movies
People traveled for pleasure; New businesses developed to serve travelers; Workers moved to suburbs and drove to city jobs.	Major passenger airlines were established; International travel became a possibility; Pioneering pilots broke records.	Commercial radio stations flourished; People had ready access to news, entertainment, and other information.	They provided a new form of entertainment; With the addition of sound, movies gained wider appeal and impact.

Increased auto use by the average family led to lifestyle changes. More people traveled for pleasure. In Europe and the United States, new businesses opened to serve the mobile tourist. The auto also affected where people lived and worked. People moved to suburbs and commuted to work in the cities.

Airplanes Transform Travel International air travel became an objective after the war. In 1919, two British pilots made the first successful flight across the Atlantic, from Newfoundland to Ireland. In 1927, an American pilot named **Charles Lindbergh** captured world attention with a 33-hour solo flight from New York to Paris. Most of the world's major passenger airlines were established during the 1920s. At first only the rich were able to afford air travel. Still, everyone enjoyed the exploits of the aviation pioneers, including those of Amelia Earhart. She was an American who, in 1932, became the first woman to fly solo across the Atlantic.

C. Possible Answers Autos were improved; airlines carried passengers; most families owned a radio.

MAIN IDEA
Recognizing Effects
C What were the results of the peacetime adaptations of the technology of war?

Radio and Movies Dominate Popular Entertainment Guglielmo Marconi conducted his first successful experiments with radio in 1895. However, the real push for radio development came during World War I.

In 1920, the world's first commercial radio station—KDKA in Pittsburgh, Pennsylvania—began broadcasting. Almost overnight, radio mania swept the United States. Every major city had stations broadcasting news, plays, and even live sporting events. Soon most families owned a radio. C

Motion pictures were also a major industry in the 1920s. Many countries, from Cuba to Japan, produced movies. In Europe, film was a serious art form. However, in the Hollywood district of Los Angeles, where 90 percent of all films were made, movies were entertainment.

The king of Hollywood's silent screen was the English-born Charlie Chaplin, a comic genius best known for his portrayal of the lonely little tramp bewildered by life. In the late 1920s, the addition of sound transformed movies.

The advances in transportation and communication that followed the war had brought the world in closer touch. Global prosperity came to depend on the economic well-being of all major nations, especially the United States.

▲ Dressed in a ragged suit and oversize shoes, Charlie Chaplin's little tramp used gentle humor to get himself out of difficult situations.

More About . . .

Charles Lindbergh

Nicknamed, "Lucky Lindy" and "Lone Eagle" by the press, Lindbergh won international fame and became the object of hero worship following his solo, nonstop flight across the Atlantic. He had been a stunt flyer at county fairs and an airmail pilot before competing for the $25,000 prize offered for the first nonstop New York–Paris flight. Several pilots had been killed or injured seeking the prize, which had been offered since 1919.

In-Depth Resources: Unit 4
- Primary Source: from "An Interview with Charles Lindbergh," p. 55

SECTION 1 ASSESSMENT

TERMS & NAMES 1. For each term or name, write a sentence explaining its significance.
• Albert Einstein • theory of relativity • Sigmund Freud • existentialism • Friedrich Nietzsche • surrealism • jazz • Charles Lindbergh

USING YOUR NOTES
2. In your opinion, whose contribution has had the most lasting impact? (10.6.4)

Field	Contributors
science	
literature and philosophy	

MAIN IDEAS
3. Why were the ideas of Einstein and Freud revolutionary? (10.6.4)
4. How did literature in the 1920s reflect the uncertainty of the period? (10.6.4)
5. What impact did the increased use of the automobile have on average people? (10.6.4)

CRITICAL THINKING & WRITING
6. **HYPOTHESIZING** Why do you think writers and artists began exploring the unconscious? (10.6.4)
7. **DEVELOPING HISTORICAL PERSPECTIVE** Why did some women begin demanding more political and social freedom? (10.6.4)
8. **MAKING INFERENCES** Why were new medical treatments and inventions developed during World War I? (10.6.4)
9. **WRITING ACTIVITY** SCIENCE AND TECHNOLOGY Write an **advertisement** that might have appeared in a 1920s newspaper or magazine for one of the technological innovations discussed in this section. (Writing 2.4.b)

CONNECT TO TODAY **PREPARING AN ORAL REPORT**
Movies in the 1920s reflected the era. What do films made today say about our age? Review some recent, representative films and present your ideas in an **oral report.** (Writing 2.2.a)

3 ASSESS

SECTION 1 ASSESSMENT

Have students work with a partner to complete the questions and check their answers.

Formal Assessment
- Section Quiz, p. 261

4 RETEACH

Use the Guided Reading worksheet for Section 1 to review the main ideas of the section.

In-Depth Resources: Unit 4
- Guided Reading, p. 47
- Reteaching Activity, p. 65

ANSWERS

1. Albert Einstein, p. 463 • theory of relativity, p. 463 • Sigmund Freud, p. 463 • existentialism, p. 464 • Friedrich Nietzsche, p. 465 • surrealism, p. 465 • jazz, p. 465 • Charles Lindbergh, p. 467
2. **Sample Answer:** Science–Albert Einstein, Sigmund Freud, Literature–Friedrich Nietzsche, James Joyce; Arts–Pablo Picasso, Arnold Schoenberg; Technology–Charles Lindbergh, Guglielmo Marconi. **Possible Answer**: Einstein's because his theories are still transforming science and mathematics
3. They weakened faith in reason and changed people's view of the world.
4. It focused on the meaninglessness of life.
5. It allowed them to drive for pleasure and commute to work.
6. **Possible Answers**: Real life was too brutal; the unconscious offered escape.
7. **Possible Answer**: They had gained freedom during World War I and didn't want to give it up.
8. **Possible Answers**: to help war casualties and improve the technology of warfare
9. **Rubric** Advertisements should
   - be written for a 1920s audience.
   - celebrate the product's original features.
   - include slogans or catchy phrases.
   - incorporate pictures or drawings.

CONNECT TO TODAY
Rubric Oral reports should
- summarize themes from recent films.
- be supported by details from movies.
- compare the 1920s and the present.

Social History

OBJECTIVES

- Identify the changes that made the use of electrical appliances more practical.
- Describe the effects of the new labor-saving devices on people's lives.

FOCUS & MOTIVATE

Ask students to discuss both the positive and negative effects of technology on their lives. *(Possible Answers: Positive–makes communication, travel, and awareness of global events fast and easy; Negative–isolates people from personal interaction)*

INSTRUCT

Critical Thinking

- How might owning a refrigerator have made housewives feel more isolated? *(They wouldn't have the social outlet of shopping frequently.)*
- Why might twice as many Ford employees have had irons as washing machines? *(Irons were less expensive.)*

More About . . .

Electric Appliances

Another revolutionary appliance, the gas or electric stove, was actually among the first labor-saving devices introduced into postwar kitchens. This technological advance replaced stoves fueled by coal or wood and relieved people of the physically taxing burden of hauling these fuels for cooking. By the 1920s, many homes also included electric refrigerators.

Social History

Labor-Saving Devices in the United States

Several changes that took place during the 1920s made the use of electrical household appliances more widespread.

- Wiring for electricity became common. In 1917, only 24 percent of U.S. homes had electricity; by 1930, that figure was almost 70 percent.
- Merchants offered the installment plan, which allowed buyers to make payments over time. That way, people could purchase appliances even if they didn't have the whole price.
- The use of advertising grew. Ads praised appliances, claiming that they would shorten tasks and give women more free time.

Ironically, the new labor-saving devices generally did not decrease the amount of time women spent doing housework. Because the tasks became less physically difficult, many families stopped hiring servants to do the work and relied on the wife to do all the jobs herself.

INTEGRATED TECHNOLOGY

RESEARCH LINKS For more on daily life in the 1920s, go to **classzone.com**

CALIFORNIA STANDARDS

10.3.5 Understand the connections among natural resources, entrepreneurship, labor, and capital in an industrial economy.

▼ Refrigerator

People used to keep perishable food in iceboxes cooled by large chunks of ice that gradually melted and had to be replaced. Electric refrigerators, like the one in this 1929 advertisement, kept the food at a fairly constant temperature, which reduced spoilage. Because food kept longer, housewives could shop less frequently.

▼ Washing Machine

To do laundry manually, women had to carry and heat about 50 gallons of water for each load. They rubbed the clothes on ridged washboards, rinsed them in tubs, and wrung them out by hand.

This early electric washing machine, photographed in 1933, made the job less strenuous. The casters on the legs made it easier to move tubs of water. The two rollers at the top of the machine squeezed water from clothes. That innovation alone saved women's wrists from constant strain.

RECOMMENDED RESOURCES

Books

Petroski, Henry. ***The Evolution of Useful Things***. Reprint ed. New York: Vintage Books, 1994.

Williams, Trevor I., ed. ***A History of Invention: From Stone Axes to Silicon Chips***. Rev. ed. New York: Checkmark Books, 2000. Includes information on the invention of the telephone, the refrigerator, and the vacuum cleaner.

Videos

Inventions. VHS. Films for the Humanities & Sciences, 1995. 800-257-5126. Explores the impact of many inventions, with a close look at the radio and mass communications.

Radio History. VHS and DVD. Films for the Humanities & Sciences, 1997. 800-257-5126.

Telephone: Quest for Instant Communication. VHS. Library Video Company, 1994. 800-843-3620.

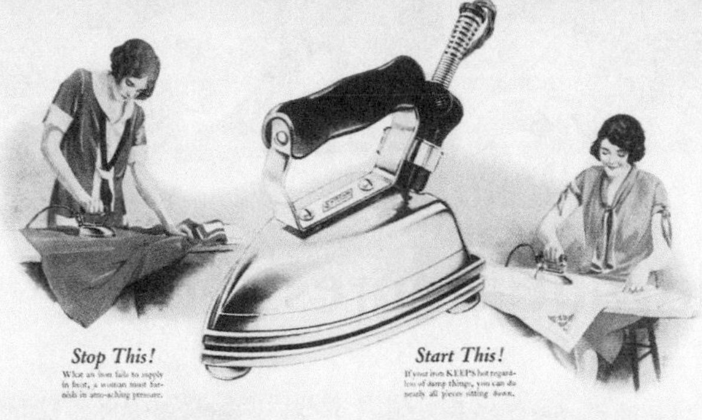

Stop This!
Start This!
Five women's magazine editors agree that women would sit to iron if they could

▲ Iron

Before electrical appliances, women heated irons on a stove. The irons cooled quickly, and as they did so, women had to push down harder to press out wrinkles. Early electric irons also had inconsistent heat. This 1926 ad offered an electric iron that stayed evenly hot, so women didn't have to put so much force into their ironing. Therefore, they could iron sitting down.

Coffee Pot ►

The electric coffee pot shown in this 1933 photograph was a vacuum pot. The water in the bottom chamber would come to a boil and bubble up into the top chamber, where the grounds were. The resulting vacuum in the lower chamber pulled the liquid back through the grounds and into the lower chamber.

Twice the cleaning...
twice the leisure!
Premier Duplex

◄ Vacuum Cleaner

This 1920 ad promised "Twice as many rooms cleaned. . . . twice as much leisure left for you to enjoy." However, women rarely experienced that benefit. Because the new appliances made housework easier, people began to expect homes to be cleaner. As a result, many women vacuumed more often and generally used their newfound "leisure" time to do even more household chores than before.

> DATA FILE

APPLIANCES IN THE HOME

- In 1929, a survey of 100 Ford employees showed that 98 of them had electric irons in their homes.
- The same survey showed that 49 of the 100 had washing machines at home.

Source: *Historical Statistics of the United States*

Source: *Historical Statistics of the United States*

Connect *to* Today

1. **Analyzing Issues** What benefits did advertisers promise that the new electrical appliances would provide for women? Explain whether women actually received those benefits.
See Skillbuilder Handbook, page R17.
2. **Comparing and Contrasting** Ask two or three adults about the way that technology has affected their work life and whether modern technologies are "labor-saving devices." How do your findings compare to the effect of electrical appliances in the 1920s?

469

More About . . .

Vacuum Cleaners

The first motorized vacuum cleaner, powered by gasoline, was invented and patented by John Thurman in 1899. Two years later, a British patent for a vacuum cleaner was awarded to Herbert Booth. This was quickly followed by American variations including a machine that sucked dust into a wet sponge and a massive device set up in the cellar of a house and connected to every room with a series of pipes. This contraption was moved from house to house by an army of men. Not to be outdone, in 1903, John Thurman began offering home vacuuming services to St. Louis housewives for $4.

CONNECT TO TODAY: ANSWERS

1. Analyzing Issues

The advertisers promised that the appliances were more efficient and that they would give women more time for other activities. The appliances did make work less strenuous, but most women just ended up doing more chores.

2. Comparing and Contrasting

Many adults will report that modern technology has increased their workload; for example e-mail and wireless phones have created the expectation that workers will stay in touch with the office even on their days off. This is similar to what happened in the 1920s when new appliances actually caused women to do more household chores.

LESSON PLAN

OBJECTIVES

- Describe the impact of World War I on postwar Europe.
- Identify the problems faced by the Weimar Republic.
- Trace the events that led to the financial collapse of the U.S. economy.
- Analyze the worldwide effects of the Great Depression.

1 FOCUS & MOTIVATE

Have students share what they have heard about the Great Depression. Note the devastating effect this event had on the world economy.

2 INSTRUCT

Postwar Europe

10.6.2; 10.6.3

Critical Thinking

- Why were democratic governments often unstable? *(little experience, too many political parties)*

Electronic Library of Primary Sources

- "Famine in Russia"

CALIFORNIA RESOURCES

California Reading Toolkit, p. L67
California Modified Lesson Plans for English Learners, p. 129
California Daily Standards Practice Transparencies, TT59
California Standards Enrichment Workbook, pp. 67–68, 69–70, 81–82, 85–86
California Standards Planner and Lesson Plans, p. L125
California Online Test Practice
California Test Generator CD-ROM
California Easy Planner CD-ROM
California eEdition CD-ROM

People waiting for a free lunch for the unemployed, 1930

Magazine cover, 1926

2

A Worldwide Depression

MAIN IDEA

ECONOMICS An economic depression in the United States spread throughout the world and lasted for a decade.

WHY IT MATTERS NOW

Many social and economic programs introduced worldwide to combat the Great Depression are still operating.

TERMS & NAMES

- coalition government
- Weimar Republic
- Great Depression
- Franklin D. Roosevelt
- New Deal

CALIFORNIA STANDARDS

10.6.2 Describe the effects of the war and resulting peace treaties on population movement, the international economy, and shifts in the geographic and political borders of Europe and the Middle East.

10.6.3 Understand the widespread disillusionment with prewar institutions, authorities, and values that resulted in a void that was later filled by totalitarians.

10.8.2 Understand the role of appeasement, nonintervention (isolationism), and the domestic distractions in Europe and the United States prior to the outbreak of World War II.

10.8.4 Describe the political, diplomatic, and military leaders during the war (e.g., Winston Churchill, Franklin Delano Roosevelt, Emperor Hirohito, Adolf Hitler, Benito Mussolini, Joseph Stalin, Douglas MacArthur, Dwight Eisenhower).

SETTING THE STAGE By the late 1920s, European nations were rebuilding war-torn economies. They were aided by loans from the more prosperous United States. Only the United States and Japan came out of the war in better financial shape than before. In the United States, Americans seemed confident that the country would continue on the road to even greater economic prosperity. One sign of this was the booming stock market. Yet the American economy had serious weaknesses that were soon to bring about the most severe economic downturn the world had yet known.

Postwar Europe

In both human suffering and economic terms, the cost of World War I was immense. The Great War left every major European country nearly bankrupt. In addition, Europe's domination in world affairs declined after the war.

Unstable New Democracies War's end saw the sudden rise of new democracies. From 1914 to 1918, Europe's last absolute rulers had been overthrown. The first of the new governments was formed in Russia in 1917. The Provisional Government, as it was called, hoped to establish constitutional and democratic rule. However, within months it had fallen to a Communist dictatorship. Even so, for the first time, most European nations had democratic governments.

Many citizens of the new democracies had little experience with representative government. For generations, kings and emperors had ruled Germany and the new nations formed from Austria-Hungary. Even in France and Italy, whose parliaments had existed before World War I, the large number of political parties made effective government difficult. Some countries had a dozen or more political groups. In these countries, it was almost impossible for one party to win enough support to govern effectively. When no single party won a majority, a **coalition government**, or temporary alliance of several parties, was needed to form a parliamentary majority. Because the parties disagreed on so many policies, coalitions seldom lasted very long.

Frequent changes in government made it hard for democratic countries to develop strong leadership and move toward long-term goals. The weaknesses of a coalition government became a major problem in times of crisis. Voters in several countries were then willing to sacrifice democratic government for strong, authoritarian leadership.

TAKING NOTES

Recognizing Effects Use a diagram to show the effects of the Great Depression in the United States.

SECTION 2 PROGRAM RESOURCES

ALL STUDENTS

In-Depth Resources: Unit 4
- Guided Reading, p. 48
- Skillbuilder Practice: Identifying Problems and Solutions, p. 52

Formal Assessment
- Section Quiz, p. 262

ENGLISH LEARNERS

In-Depth Resources in Spanish
- Guided Reading, p. 118
- Skillbuilder Practice, p. 121

Reading Study Guide (Spanish), p. 159

Reading Study Guide Audio CD (Spanish)

STRUGGLING READERS

In-Depth Resources: Unit 4
- Guided Reading, p. 48
- Building Vocabulary, p. 51
- Skillbuilder Practice: Identifying Problems and Solutions, p. 52
- Reteaching Activity, p. 66

Reading Study Guide, p. 159

Reading Study Guide Audio CD

GIFTED AND TALENTED STUDENTS

In-Depth Resources: Unit 4
- Primary Source: German Inflation, p. 56

Electronic Library of Primary Sources
- "Famine in Russia"

INTEGRATED TECHNOLOGY

eEdition CD-ROM

Power Presentations CD-ROM

Electronic Library of Primary Sources CD-ROM
- "Famine in Russia"

classzone.com

The Weimar Republic

Germany's new democratic government was set up in 1919. Known as the **Weimar** (WY•MAHR) **Republic**, it was named after the city where the national assembly met. The Weimar Republic had serious weaknesses from the start. First, Germany lacked a strong democratic tradition. Furthermore, postwar Germany had several major political parties and many minor ones. Worst of all, millions of Germans blamed the Weimar government, not their wartime leaders, for the country's defeat and postwar humiliation caused by the Versailles Treaty. (A)

MAIN IDEA
Identifying Problems
(A) What political problems did the Weimar Republic face?
A. Answers lack of democratic tradition, too many political parties, blamed for country's defeat

Inflation Causes Crisis in Germany Germany also faced enormous economic problems that had begun during the war. Unlike Britain and France, Germany had not greatly increased its wartime taxes. To pay the expenses of the war, the Germans had simply printed money. After Germany's defeat, this paper money steadily lost its value. Burdened with heavy reparations payments to the Allies and with other economic problems, Germany printed even more money. As a result, the value of the mark, as Germany's currency was called, fell sharply. Severe inflation set in. Germans needed more and more money to buy even the most basic goods. For example, in Berlin a loaf of bread cost less than a mark in 1918, more than 160 marks in 1922, and some 200 billion marks by late 1923. People took wheelbarrows full of money to buy food. As a result, many Germans questioned the value of their new democratic government.

▼ German children use stacks of money as building blocks during the 1923 inflation.

Attempts at Economic Stability Germany recovered from the 1923 inflation thanks largely to the work of an international committee. The committee was headed by Charles Dawes, an American banker. The Dawes Plan provided for a $200 million loan from American banks to stabilize German currency and strengthen its economy. The plan also set a more realistic schedule for Germany's reparations payments.

Put into effect in 1924, the Dawes Plan helped slow inflation. As the German economy began to recover, it attracted more loans and investments from the United States. By 1929, German factories were producing as much as they had before the war.

Efforts at a Lasting Peace As prosperity returned, Germany's foreign minister, Gustav Stresemann (STRAY•zuh•MAHN), and France's foreign minister, Aristide Briand (bree•AHND), tried to improve relations between their countries. In 1925, the two ministers met in Locarno, Switzerland, with officials from Belgium, Italy, and Britain. They signed a treaty promising that France and Germany would never

The Weimar Republic
10.6.2; 10.6.3

Critical Thinking

- How did Germany's postwar economic problems begin during the war? *(Germany had not raised taxes during the war, so it printed new money, which caused runaway inflation.)*
- What was a major weakness of the Kellogg-Briand Treaty? *(no means of enforcing its provisions)*

More About . . .

The Weimar Republic

At the time they signed the Versailles Treaty, the men who became the leaders of the Weimar government recognized that the agreement would cause grave problems for Germany. Yet they felt they had no option but to sign it. The German people never forgave them.

More About . . .

Germany's Money Problems

Economists typically define severe inflation as an annual inflation rate of 10 percent or higher. The German government's printing of large amounts of currency to keep it afloat after the war caused prices in Germany to rise more than 1 trillion percent from August 1922 to November 1923. In 1923, $1 in U.S. currency was worth over 4 trillion German marks.

In-Depth Resources: Unit 4
- Primary Source: German Inflation, p. 56

DIFFERENTIATING INSTRUCTION: ENGLISH LEARNERS

Understanding Inflation

Class Time 20 minutes

Task Making a flow chart about inflation

Purpose To clarify Germany's economic problems

Instructions Explain that inflation is an economic situation that comes about when the amount of money in circulation increases. This happened in Germany because the government had spent more during World War I than it collected in taxes and other payments. To raise more money, the German government just printed more of its money, the mark. By 1923, it was printing 400 quadrillion (400,000,000,000,000,000) marks a day! With so much money in circulation, its value goes down. As its value goes down, prices rise. This forces the government to print even more money to pay its bills. Ask students to work in small groups to create flow charts that trace these steps in Germany's inflation.

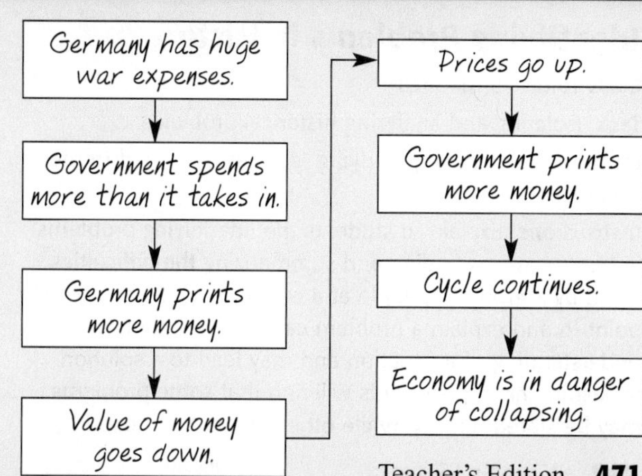
Germany has huge war expenses.
Government spends more than it takes in.
Germany prints more money.
Value of money goes down.
Prices go up.
Government prints more money.
Cycle continues.
Economy is in danger of collapsing.

Financial Collapse
10.6.2

Critical Thinking

- Why might Americans have been buying less in the years preceding the stock market crash? *(More than half of American families were too poor to afford manufactured goods.)*
- How did margin buying contribute to the stock market crash? *(It created a false prosperity that could not sustain a huge change in stock prices)*

History *in* Depth

Investing in Stocks

In the 1920s, the United States, in response to surging demand for cars, radios, entertainment, and a share in the growing aviation industry, led investors into the stock market in search of fast profits. The number of shares bought and sold on the New York Stock Exchange rose between 1925 and 1929 from 113 million to more than a billion. Small investors were lured into the market by stories of ordinary people becoming instant millionaires by buying and selling stocks. The graph shows how dramatically stock prices dropped after the market crash in 1929.

again make war against each other. Germany also agreed to respect the existing borders of France and Belgium. It then was admitted to the League of Nations.

In 1928, the hopes raised by the "spirit of Locarno" led to the Kellogg-Briand peace pact. Frank Kellogg, the U.S. Secretary of State, arranged this agreement with France's Briand. Almost every country in the world, including the Soviet Union, signed. They pledged "to renounce war as an instrument of national policy."

Unfortunately, the treaty had no means to enforce its provisions. The League of Nations, the obvious choice as enforcer, had no armed forces. The refusal of the United States to join the League also weakened it. Nonetheless, the peace agreements seemed a good start.

Financial Collapse

In the late 1920s, American economic prosperity largely sustained the world economy. If the U.S. economy weakened, the whole world's economic system might collapse. In 1929, it did.

A Flawed U.S. Economy Despite prosperity, several weaknesses in the U.S. economy caused serious problems. These included uneven distribution of wealth, overproduction by business and agriculture, and the fact that many Americans were buying less.

By 1929, American factories were turning out nearly half of the world's industrial goods. The rising productivity led to enormous profits. However, this new wealth was not evenly distributed. The richest 5 percent of the population received 33 percent of all personal income in 1929. Yet 60 percent of all American families earned less than $2,000 a year. Thus, most families were too poor to buy the goods being produced. Unable to sell all their goods, store owners eventually cut back their orders from factories. Factories in turn reduced production and laid off workers. A downward economic spiral began. As more workers lost their jobs, families bought even fewer goods. In turn, factories made further cuts in production and laid off more workers.

During the 1920s, overproduction affected American farmers as well. Scientific farming methods and new farm machinery had dramatically increased crop yields. American farmers were producing more food. Meanwhile, they faced new competition from farmers in Australia, Latin America, and Europe. As a result, a worldwide surplus of agricultural products drove prices and profits down.

Unable to sell their crops at a profit, many farmers could not pay off the bank loans that kept them in business. Their unpaid debts weakened banks and forced some to close. The danger signs of overproduction by factories and farms should have warned people against gambling on the stock market. Yet no one heeded the warning. 

The Stock Market Crashes In 1929, New York City's Wall Street was the financial capital of the world. Banks and investment companies lined its sidewalks. At Wall Street's New York Stock Exchange, optimism about the booming U.S. economy showed in soaring prices for stocks. To get in on the boom, many middle-income people began buying

History *in* Depth

Investing in Stocks

Stocks are shares of ownership in a company. Businesses get money to operate by selling "shares" of stock to investors, or buyers. Companies pay interest on the invested money in the form of dividends to the shareholders. Dividends rise or fall depending on a company's profits.

Investors do not buy stocks directly from the company; instead, stockbrokers transact the business of buying and selling.

Investors hope to make more money on stocks than if they put their money elsewhere, such as in a savings account with a fixed rate of interest. However, if the stock price goes down, investors lose money when they sell their stock at a lower price than when they bought it.

Stock Prices, 1925–1933

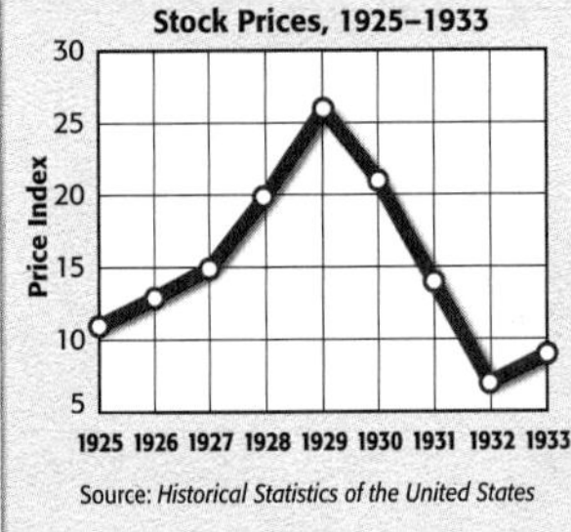

Source: *Historical Statistics of the United States*

B. Answers uneven distribution of wealth, overproduction by business, lessening demand for consumer goods, dropping farm profits

MAIN IDEA

Identifying Problems

B What major weaknesses had appeared in the American economy by 1929?

SKILLBUILDER PRACTICE: IDENTIFYING PROBLEMS AND SOLUTIONS

Identifying Problems in History

Class Time 35 minutes

Task Isolating and analyzing historical problems

Purpose To identify underlying problems that led to the Great Depression

Instructions Explain to students that identifying problems in history means finding and summarizing the difficulties faced by a group of people at a certain time. Being able to point to and explain a problem can lead to a thorough understanding of a situation and may lead to a solution. In reading history, students will find that some problems may be stated directly, while others might be implied by the ways people act. For example, workers being laid off indicates that there are problems in an economic system that prevent it from providing full employment.

Ask students to identify the problems in the U.S. economy that led to the Great Depression. *(uneven distribution of wealth, business overproduction, lessening demand for consumer goods, and decreasing farm profits)* Ask whether these problems were stated directly in the text or implied by people's actions. *(Most were stated directly.)* Then have students suggest problems that led to others. *(Reduction in overproduction led to layoffs and unemployment.)*

In-Depth Resources: Unit 4

Social History

Life in the Depression

During the Great Depression of 1929 to 1939, millions of people worldwide lost their jobs or their farms. At first the unemployed had to depend on the charity of others for food, clothing, and shelter. Many, like the men in this photo taken in New York City, made their home in makeshift shacks. Local governments and charities opened soup kitchens to provide free food. There were long lines of applicants for what work was available, and these jobs usually paid low wages.

INTEGRATED TECHNOLOGY

INTERNET ACTIVITY Create a photo-essay on the Great Depression in the United States. Go to **classzone.com** for your research.

stocks on margin. This meant that they paid a small percentage of a stock's price as a down payment and borrowed the rest from a stockbroker. The system worked well as long as stock prices were rising. However, if they fell, investors had no money to pay off the loan.

In September 1929, some investors began to think that stock prices were unnaturally high. They started selling their stocks, believing the prices would soon go down. By Thursday, October 24, the gradual lowering of stock prices had become an all-out slide downward. A panic resulted. Everyone wanted to sell stocks, and no one wanted to buy. Prices plunged to a new low on Tuesday, October 29. A record 16 million stocks were sold. Then the market collapsed.

The Great Depression

People could not pay the money they owed on margin purchases. Stocks they had bought at high prices were now worthless. Within months of the crash, unemployment rates began to rise as industrial production, prices, and wages declined. A long business slump, which would come to be called the **Great Depression**, followed. The stock market crash alone did not cause the Great Depression, but it quickened the collapse of the economy and made the Depression more difficult. By 1932, factory production had been cut in half. Thousands of businesses failed, and banks closed. Around 9 million people lost the money in their savings accounts when banks had no money to pay them. Many farmers lost their lands when they could not make mortgage payments. By 1933, one-fourth of all American workers had no jobs.

A Global Depression The collapse of the American economy sent shock waves around the world. Worried American bankers demanded repayment of their overseas loans, and American investors withdrew their money from Europe. The American market for European goods dropped sharply as the U.S. Congress placed high tariffs on imported goods so that American dollars would stay in the United States and pay for American goods. This policy backfired. Conditions worsened for the United

Vocabulary
tariffs: taxes charged by a government on imported or exported goods

Social History

Life in the Depression

From 1931 through 1933, the depression in the United States deepened. In 1932 alone, more than 32,000 businesses folded. By August of that year, 5,000 banks had closed. Unable to pay teachers, state governments let them go, cut terms, or shut schools down entirely. The businesses that survived did so by cutting production and wages. In 1929, manufacturing workers earned an average of $25 a week; by 1933, their pay had dropped to $16.73. And they were the lucky ones—they still had jobs.

INTEGRATED TECHNOLOGY

Rubric Photojournalism essays should
- show the effects of the Great Depression on different types of people.
- include captions that explain the depression's toll.

The Great Depression
10.6.2

Critical Thinking
- How did the raising of U.S. tariffs expand the worldwide depression? *(other nations retaliated and world trade became even worse)*
- Why might the depression have affected countries such as Asia and Latin America? *(because they were trading partners of the United States)*

DIFFERENTIATING INSTRUCTION: GIFTED AND TALENTED STUDENTS

Creating a Political Cartoon

Class Time 35 minutes

Task Creating a political cartoon about the Great Depression

Purpose To clarify the effects of this global crisis

Instructions Divide students into two groups. Have one group research the impact of the Great Depression on the United States and the other group research its effects on Western European countries. When the groups have compiled their research have them do the following activities:
- Discuss how the Great Depression spread from the United States to the rest of the Western world.
- Brainstorm ways they can express this spread or indicate the effects on a particular country in a political cartoon.

You might suggest, for example, that they show how raising tariffs hurt world trade and deepened the depression. Stress to students that their political cartoons should express one idea or opinion, clearly show a specific effect or response, and include an appropriate caption. Have students display their political cartoons in the classroom.

History from Visuals

Interpreting the Graphs

Have students read the graph key to identify which color line represents each nation. Ask students which nation responded most effectively to the depression based solely on the unemployment data shown. *(Germany)*

Extension Ask students to study both charts. Have them observe how the unemployment rate is related to world imports and exports. *(As unemployment goes up the imports and exports go down)* Next, have the students predict how the world trade export and import bars would look in the years between 1934–1938. *(Trade will go down in 1934, pick up a bit until 1938, when it will be down again.)*

SKILLBUILDER Answers

1. **Comparing** Germany; 30 percent
2. **Clarifying** about $25 billion; about $22 billion

The World Confronts the Crisis

10.8.2; 10.8.4

Critical Thinking

- Was Britain's or France's response to the economic crisis more effective? Why? *(Possible Answer: Britain's because it cut unemployment and achieved slow, steady recovery)*
- How were the responses of the Scandinavian countries and the United States similar? *(Both created jobs through public works projects and provided welfare services for their citizens.)*

Sources: *European Historical Statistics: 1750–1970; Historical Statistics of the United States: Colonial Times to 1970.*

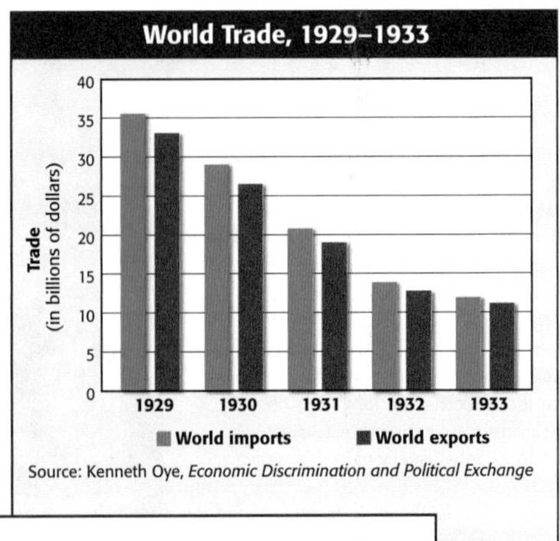

Source: Kenneth Oye, *Economic Discrimination and Political Exchange*

SKILLBUILDER: Interpreting Graphs

1. **Comparing** *What nation had the highest rate of unemployment? How high did it reach?*
2. **Clarifying** *Between 1929 and 1933, how much did world exports drop? What about world imports?*

States. Many countries that depended on exporting goods to the United States also suffered. Moreover, when the United States raised tariffs, it set off a chain reaction. Other nations imposed their own higher tariffs. World trade dropped by 65 percent. This contributed further to the economic downturn. Unemployment rates soared.

Effects Throughout the World Because of war debts and dependence on American loans and investments, Germany and Austria were particularly hard hit. In 1931, Austria's largest bank failed. In Asia, both farmers and urban workers suffered as the value of exports fell by half between 1929 and 1931. The crash was felt heavily in Latin America as well. As European and U.S. demand for such Latin American products as sugar, beef, and copper dropped, prices collapsed.

The World Confronts the Crisis

The Depression confronted democracies with a serious challenge to their economic and political systems. Each country met the crisis in its own way.

Britain Takes Steps to Improve Its Economy The Depression hit Britain severely. To meet the emergency, British voters elected a multiparty coalition known as the National Government. It passed high protective tariffs, increased taxes, and regulated the currency. It also lowered interest rates to encourage industrial growth. These measures brought about a slow but steady recovery. By 1937, unemployment had been cut in half, and production had risen above 1929 levels. Britain avoided political extremes and preserved democracy.

France Responds to Economic Crisis Unlike Britain, France had a more self-sufficient economy. In 1930, it was still heavily agricultural and less dependent on foreign trade. Nevertheless, by 1935, one million French workers were unemployed.

The economic crisis contributed to political instability. In 1933, five coalition governments formed and fell. Many political leaders were frightened by the growth of antidemocratic forces both in France and in other parts of Europe. So in 1936, moderates, Socialists, and Communists formed a coalition. The Popular Front, as it was called, passed a series of reforms to help the workers. Unfortunately, price increases quickly offset wage gains. Unemployment remained high. Yet France also preserved democratic government.

DIFFERENTIATING INSTRUCTION: STRUGGLING READERS

Comparing Global Responses to the Great Depression

Class Time 30 minutes

Task Creating a chart comparing international responses to the depression

Purpose To identify international responses to the worldwide depression

Instructions Have students reread "The World Confronts the Crisis" on pages 474–475 of the text. Divide students into four groups and assign each group to be responsible for one of the following global areas:

- Britain
- France
- Scandinavia
- United States

Then have groups fill in a chart indicating their area's response to the Great Depression and how effective it was.

Country	Response	Effectiveness
Britain	political coalition, tariffs, taxes	slow recovery, democracy preserved
France	political instability, worker reforms	high unemployment, democracy preserved
Scandinavia	public works projects, welfare, taxes	economic health, democracy preserved
United States	public works projects, welfare, economic reform	slow recovery, democracy preserved

Socialist Governments Find Solutions The Socialist governments in the Scandinavian countries of Denmark, Sweden, and Norway also met the challenge of economic crisis successfully. They built their recovery programs on an existing tradition of cooperative community action. In Sweden, the government sponsored massive public works projects that kept people employed and producing. All the Scandinavian countries raised pensions for the elderly and increased unemployment insurance, subsidies for housing, and other welfare benefits. To pay for these benefits, the governments taxed all citizens. Democracy remained intact.

Recovery in the United States In 1932, in the first presidential election after the Depression had begun, U.S. voters elected **Franklin D. Roosevelt**. His confident manner appealed to millions of Americans who felt bewildered by the Depression. On March 4, 1933, the new president sought to restore Americans' faith in their nation.

Analyzing Primary Sources

C What effect do you think Roosevelt's speech had on the American people?

C. Answer The speech calmed them, prepared them to take action that could help them deal with the Depression.

PRIMARY SOURCE C

This great Nation will endure as it has endured, will revive and will prosper. . . . let me assert my firm belief that the only thing we have to fear is fear itself—nameless, unreasoning, unjustified terror which paralyzes needed efforts to convert retreat into advance.

FRANKLIN ROOSEVELT, First Inaugural Address

▲ Stricken with polio in 1921, Roosevelt vowed he would not allow bodily disability to defeat his will.

Roosevelt immediately began a program of government reform that he called the **New Deal**. Large public works projects helped to provide jobs for the unemployed. New government agencies gave financial help to businesses and farms. Large amounts of public money were spent on welfare and relief programs. Roosevelt and his advisers believed that government spending would create jobs and start a recovery. Regulations were imposed to reform the stock market and the banking system.

The New Deal did eventually reform the American economic system. Roosevelt's leadership preserved the country's faith in its democratic political system. It also established him as a leader of democracy in a world threatened by ruthless dictators, as you will read about in Section 3.

More About . . .

The New Deal

By the late 1930s, the U.S. government had spent $10 billion on the construction of 122,000 public buildings, 664,000 miles of roads, 77,000 bridges, and 285 airports in Roosevelt's New Deal program. Although the New Deal improved economic conditions, full recovery did not occur until after the United States entered World War II in 1942. At that time, production of war materials led to almost full employment for Americans.

SECTION 2 ASSESSMENT

TERMS & NAMES 1. For each term or name, write a sentence explaining its significance.
• coalition government • Weimar Republic • Great Depression • Franklin D. Roosevelt • New Deal

USING YOUR NOTES

2. What did President Roosevelt do to try to counter the effects of the Great Depression? (10.8.4)

MAIN IDEAS

3. How did World War I change the balance of economic power in the world? (10.8.2)
4. What problems did the collapse of the American economy cause in other countries? (10.6.2)
5. How did Europe respond to the economic crisis? (10.6.3)

CRITICAL THINKING & WRITING

6. **MAKING PREDICTIONS** What did the weakness of the League of Nations in 1928 suggest about its future effectiveness? (10.8.2)
7. **ANALYZING CAUSES** List one cause for each of the following effects: American market for European goods dropped; unemployment rates soared; European banks and businesses closed. (10.8.2)
8. **EVALUATING COURSES OF ACTION** Why do you think Roosevelt immediately established the New Deal? (10.8.4)
9. **WRITING ACTIVITY** ECONOMICS Write **headlines** on the stock market crash and the world's response to it. (Writing 2.1.a)

INTEGRATED TECHNOLOGY **INTERNET ACTIVITY**

Use the Internet to follow the ups and downs of the stock market for a week. Chart the stock market's course in a **line graph.** (Writing 2.3.d)

INTERNET KEYWORD
stock market

3 ASSESS

SECTION 2 ASSESSMENT

Have students present and discuss with the class the concept webs they created for question 2 in the section assessment.

Formal Assessment
• Section Quiz, p. 262

4 RETEACH

Have students work in small groups to fill in the charts in the Guided Reading activity on page 48 of In-Depth Resources: Unit 4.

In-Depth Resources: Unit 4
• Guided Reading, p. 48
• Reteaching Activity, p. 66

ANSWERS

1. coalition government, p. 470 • Weimar Republic, p. 471 • Great Depression, p. 473 • Franklin D. Roosevelt, p. 475 • New Deal, p. 475
2. **Sample Answer:** Effects—failed businesses, closed banks, lost savings, foreclosed farms, rising unemployment. He instituted an economic reform program called the New Deal.
3. **Possible Answer**: Europe's resources had been drained by the war; Japan and the U.S. were economically strong.
4. slumping economies, diminishing trade, soaring unemployment, financial panic
5. Britain—tariffs, increased taxes, currency regulation; France—worker reforms; Scandinavia—public works projects, welfare packages
6. **Possible Answer:** It would be too weak to be effective in a crisis.
7. **Possible Answers:** high U.S. tariffs; drop in world trade; demand for repayment of U.S. loans and investment withdrawal
8. **Possible Answer:** He knew the program would give people hope, create many jobs, and begin economic recovery.
9. **Rubric** Headlines should
• report the stock market crash and the world's response.
• convey each idea in a few strong words.
• grab the reader's attention.

INTEGRATED TECHNOLOGY

Rubric The line graph should
• show the course of the stock market for a week.
• indicate whether the market has gone up, down, or remained steady.
• provide clues about the state of the U.S. economy today.

LESSON PLAN

OBJECTIVES

- Describe Mussolini's creation of a Fascist state in Italy.
- Discuss the rise of Hitler, the Nazis, and extension of Hitler's power.
- Trace the shift from democratic governments to dictatorships in Eastern Europe.

1 FOCUS & MOTIVATE

Ask students to discuss what they know about Adolf Hitler and Nazism. *(Possible Answers: Holocaust and drive for world dominion)* Explain that Hitler was not the only brutal dictator to come to power at this time.

2 INSTRUCT

Fascism's Rise in Italy

10.7.3

Critical Thinking

- Does fascism or communism seem to be more concerned with the welfare of the people? *(communism; Fascism is more concerned with the state.)*

CALIFORNIA RESOURCES

California Reading Toolkit, p. L68
California Modified Lesson Plans for English Learners, p. 131
California Daily Standards Practice Transparencies, TT60
California Standards Enrichment Workbook, pp. 77–78, 79–80, 87–88
California Standards Planner and Lesson Plans, p. L127
California Online Test Practice
California Test Generator CD-ROM
California Easy Planner CD-ROM
California eEdition CD-ROM

People waiting for a free lunch for the unemployed, 1930

3

Magazine cover, 1926

Fascism Rises in Europe

MAIN IDEA	WHY IT MATTERS NOW	TERMS & NAMES
POWER AND AUTHORITY In response to political turmoil and economic crises, Italy and Germany turned to totalitarian dictators.	These dictators changed the course of history, and the world is still recovering from their abuse of power.	• fascism • Benito Mussolini • Adolf Hitler • Nazism • *Mein Kampf* • *lebensraum*

CALIFORNIA STANDARDS

10.7.3 Analyze the rise, aggression, and human costs of totalitarian regimes (Fascist and Communist) in Germany, Italy, and the Soviet Union, noting especially their common and dissimilar traits.

10.8.1 Compare the German, Italian, and Japanese drives for empire in the 1930s, including the 1937 Rape of Nanking, other atrocities in China, and the Stalin-Hitler Pact of 1939.

10.8.5 Analyze the Nazi policy of pursuing racial purity, especially against the European Jews; its transformation into the Final Solution; and the Holocaust that resulted in the murder of six million Jewish civilians.

SETTING THE STAGE Many democracies, including the United States, Britain, and France, remained strong despite the economic crisis caused by the Great Depression. However, millions of people lost faith in democratic government. In response, they turned to an extreme system of government called fascism. Fascists promised to revive the economy, punish those responsible for hard times, and restore order and national pride. Their message attracted many people who felt frustrated and angered by the peace treaties that followed World War I and by the Great Depression.

Fascism's Rise in Italy

Fascism (FASH•IHZ•uhm) was a new, militant political movement that emphasized loyalty to the state and obedience to its leader. Unlike communism, fascism had no clearly defined theory or program. Nevertheless, most Fascists shared several ideas. They preached an extreme form of nationalism, or loyalty to one's country. Fascists believed that nations must struggle—peaceful states were doomed to be conquered. They pledged loyalty to an authoritarian leader who guided and brought order to the state. In each nation, Fascists wore uniforms of a certain color, used special salutes, and held mass rallies.

In some ways, fascism was similar to communism. Both systems were ruled by dictators who allowed only their own political party (one-party rule). Both denied individual rights. In both, the state was supreme. Neither practiced any kind of democracy. However, unlike Communists, Fascists did not seek a classless society. Rather, they believed that each class had its place and function. In most cases, Fascist parties were made up of aristocrats and industrialists, war veterans, and the lower middle class. Also, Fascists were nationalists, and Communists were internationalists, hoping to unite workers worldwide.

TAKING NOTES

Comparing and Contrasting Use a chart to compare Mussolini's rise to power and his goals with Hitler's.

Hitler	Mussolini
Rise:	Rise:
Goals:	Goals:

Mussolini Takes Control Fascism's rise in Italy was fueled by bitter disappointment over the failure to win large territorial gains at the 1919 Paris Peace Conference. Rising inflation and unemployment also contributed to widespread social unrest. To growing numbers of Italians, their democratic government seemed helpless to deal with the country's problems. They wanted a leader who would take action.

SECTION 3 PROGRAM RESOURCES

ALL STUDENTS

In-Depth Resources: Unit 4
- Guided Reading, p. 49

Formal Assessment
- Section Quiz, p. 263

ENGLISH LEARNERS

In-Depth Resources in Spanish
- Guided Reading, p. 119

Reading Study Guide (Spanish), p. 161
Reading Study Guide Audio CD (Spanish)

STRUGGLING READERS

In-Depth Resources: Unit 4
- Guided Reading, p. 49
- Building Vocabulary, p. 51
- Reteaching Activity, p. 67

Reading Study Guide, p. 161
Reading Study Guide Audio CD

GIFTED AND TALENTED STUDENTS

In-Depth Resources: Unit 4
- Primary Source: Kristallnacht, p. 57
- Literature: Poems by Brecht, p. 60
- Connections Across Time and Cultures, p. 64

Electronic Library of Primary Sources
- from Memos on the Aims of Germany and Japan

INTEGRATED TECHNOLOGY

eEdition CD-ROM
Power Presentations CD-ROM
World Art and Cultures Transparencies
- AT69 Pillars of Society

Critical Thinking Transparencies
- CT31 Economic Crisis: Between Two Fires

Electronic Library of Primary Sources
- from Memos on the Aims of Germany and Japan

classzone.com

Analyzing Key Concepts

Fascism

Fascism is a political movement that promotes an extreme form of nationalism and militarism. It also includes a denial of individual rights and dictatorial one-party rule. Nazism was the Fascist movement that developed in Germany in the 1920s and the 1930s; it included a belief in the racial superiority of the German people. The Fascists in Italy were led by Benito Mussolini, shown in the chart at right.

SKILLBUILDER: Interpreting Charts

1. **Synthesizing** *Which political, cultural, and economic characteristics helped make fascism an authoritarian system?*
2. **Making Inferences** *What characteristics of fascism might make it attractive to people during times of crisis such as the Great Depression?*

A newspaper editor and politician named **Benito Mussolini** boldly promised to rescue Italy by reviving its economy and rebuilding its armed forces. He vowed to give Italy strong leadership. Mussolini had founded the Fascist Party in 1919. As economic conditions worsened, his popularity rapidly increased. Finally, Mussolini publicly criticized Italy's government. Groups of Fascists wearing black shirts attacked Communists and Socialists on the streets. Because Mussolini played on the fear of a workers' revolt, he began to win support from the middle classes, the aristocracy, and industrial leaders.

In October 1922, about 30,000 Fascists marched on Rome. They demanded that King Victor Emmanuel III put Mussolini in charge of the government. The king decided that Mussolini was the best hope for his dynasty to survive. After widespread violence and a threatened uprising, Mussolini took power "legally." (A)

MAIN IDEA
Clarifying
(A) What promises did Mussolini make to the Italian people?
A. Answer He promised to revive their economy, rebuild the armed forces, and provide strong leadership.

Il Duce's Leadership Mussolini was now Il Duce (ihl DOO•chay), or the leader. He abolished democracy and outlawed all political parties except the Fascists. Secret police jailed his opponents. Government censors forced radio stations and publications to broadcast or publish only Fascist doctrines. Mussolini outlawed strikes. He sought to control the economy by allying the Fascists with the industrialists and large landowners. However, Mussolini never had the total control achieved by Joseph Stalin in the Soviet Union or Adolf Hitler in Germany.

Hitler Rises to Power in Germany

When Mussolini became dictator of Italy in the mid-1920s, **Adolf Hitler** was a little-known political leader whose early life had been marked by disappointment. When World War I broke out, Hitler found a new beginning. He volunteered for the German army and was twice awarded the Iron Cross, a medal for bravery.

Analyzing Key Concepts

Fascism

The term *fascism* comes from the Latin word *fascis*, a bundle of wooden rods tied around an ax handle that was the symbol of authority in ancient Rome. Based on the information in the graphic, how was this authority wielded in fascist states? *(Possible Answer: harshly, without regard for individuals' rights and with total control by a ruthless dictator)*

SKILLBUILDER Answers

1. **Synthesizing** one-party rule, censorship, secret police, and state control of property
2. **Making Inferences** Charismatic leadership and the focus on action might appeal to people who want their problems solved in a time of crisis.

Critical Thinking Transparencies

- CT31 Economic Crisis: Between Two Fires

Hitler Rises to Power in Germany
10.8.1

Critical Thinking

- What personal characteristics helped Hitler gain success as a leader? *(He was an organizer, a good speaker, persistent and driven to reach his goal.)*
- What did Hitler believe were the rights and duties of the German "master race"? *(Possible Answer: elimination of "inferior races" and world dominion)*

DIFFERENTIATING INSTRUCTION: GIFTED AND TALENTED STUDENTS

Comparing Fascism and 17th-Century Absolutism

Class Time 30 minutes

Task Comparing and contrasting the characteristics of Fascist dictators and absolute monarchs

Purpose To to clarify the meaning of fascism

Instructions Have students review the material on fascism. Have them discuss with a partner the characteristics of fascism and its dictators and note any questions they have. Then give a copy of Connections Across Time and Cultures, p. 64 of In-Depth Resources: Unit 4 to each pair. Instruct students to work together to answer the questions and then share their answers with the class. Sample answers follow:

1. The economic and political devastation following World War I led to the rise of Fascism.
2. Fascist leaders increased their power by instituting one-party rule under a supreme leader.
3. Controlling property, outlawing strikes, and allying with industrialists and landowners were the steps Fascist leaders took to control their economies.
4. Fascist leaders controlled the lives of citizens by using censorship and indoctrination.
5. Nationalist and, in the case of the Nazis, racist beliefs were the basis of Fascist leaders' unlimited power.

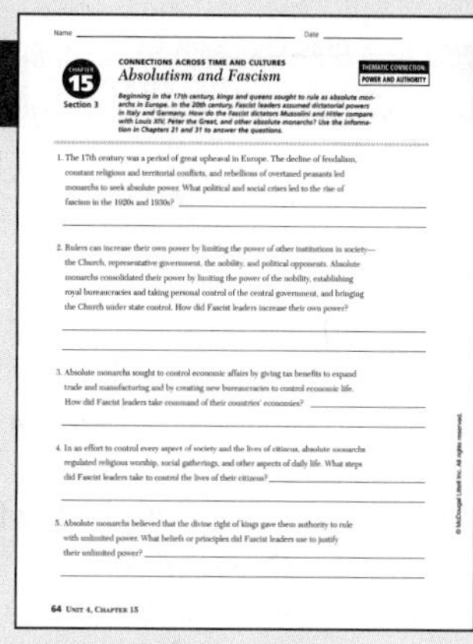

In-Depth Resources: Unit 4

History Makers

Benito Mussolini and Adolf Hitler

In what ways were Mussolini's and Hitler's speaking styles similar? *(Both were charismatic, theatrical speakers who used emotional appeal to rouse audiences.)*

Tip for English Learners

Point out the similarity of the German key terms and their English equivalents: *mein*–"my;" *lebens*–"living;" *raum*–"room" or "space."

Hitler Becomes Chancellor

10.7.3; 10.8.1; 10.8.5

Critical Thinking

- Why might Germans have put their faith in Hitler? *(Possible Answer: He put people to work and revived the economy.)*
- What does Kristallnacht demonstrate about the power of the Nazis? *(Their control over the people was very strong.)*

In-Depth Resources: Unit 4

- Primary Source: Kristallnacht, p. 57
- Literature: Poems by Bertold Brecht, p. 60

History Makers

Benito Mussolini
1883–1945

Because Mussolini was of modest height, he usually chose a location for his speeches where he towered above the crowds—often a balcony high above a public square. He then roused audiences with his emotional speeches and theatrical gestures and body movements.

Vowing to lead Italy "back to her ways of ancient greatness," Mussolini peppered his speeches with aggressive words such as *war* and *power.*

Adolf Hitler
1889–1945

Like Mussolini, Hitler could manipulate huge audiences with his fiery oratory. Making speeches was crucial to Hitler. He believed: "All great world-shaking events have been brought about . . . by the spoken word!"

Because he appeared awkward and unimposing, Hitler rehearsed his speeches. Usually he began a speech in a normal voice. Suddenly, he spoke louder as his anger grew. His voice rose to a screech, and his hands flailed the air. Then he would stop, smooth his hair, and look quite calm.

INTEGRATED TECHNOLOGY

RESEARCH LINKS For more on Benito Mussolini and Adolf Hitler, go to **classzone.com**

The Rise of the Nazis At the end of the war, Hitler settled in Munich. In 1919, he joined a tiny right-wing political group. This group shared his belief that Germany had to overturn the Treaty of Versailles and combat communism. The group later named itself the National Socialist German Workers' Party, called Nazi for short. Its policies formed the German brand of fascism known as **Nazism**. The party adopted the swastika, or hooked cross, as its symbol. The Nazis also set up a private militia called the storm troopers or Brown Shirts.

Within a short time, Hitler's success as an organizer and speaker led him to be chosen *der Führer* (duhr FYUR•uhr), or the leader, of the Nazi party. Inspired by Mussolini's march on Rome, Hitler and the Nazis plotted to seize power in Munich in 1923. The attempt failed, and Hitler was arrested. He was tried for treason but was sentenced to only five years in prison. He served less than nine months.

While in jail, Hitler wrote ***Mein Kampf*** (*My Struggle*). This book set forth his beliefs and his goals for Germany. Hitler asserted that the Germans, whom he incorrectly called "Aryans," were a "master race." He declared that non-Aryan "races," such as Jews, Slavs, and Gypsies, were inferior. He called the Versailles Treaty an outrage and vowed to regain German lands. Hitler also declared that Germany was overcrowded and needed more ***lebensraum***, or living space. He promised to get that space by conquering eastern Europe and Russia.

After leaving prison in 1924, Hitler revived the Nazi Party. Most Germans ignored him and his angry message until the Great Depression ended the nation's brief postwar recovery. When American loans stopped, the German economy collapsed. Civil unrest broke out. Frightened and confused, Germans now turned to Hitler, hoping for security and firm leadership.

Hitler Becomes Chancellor

The Nazis had become the largest political party by 1932. Conservative leaders mistakenly believed they could control Hitler and use him for their purposes. In January 1933, they advised President Paul von Hindenburg to name Hitler chancellor. Thus Hitler came to power legally. Soon after, General Erich Ludendorff, a former Hitler ally, wrote to Hindenburg:

Vocabulary
chancellor: the prime minister or president in certain countries

PRIMARY SOURCE

By naming Hitler as Reichschancellor, you have delivered up our holy Fatherland to one of the greatest [rabblerousers] of all time. I solemnly [predict] that this accursed man will plunge our Reich into the abyss and bring our nation into inconceivable misery.

ERICH LUDENDORFF, letter to President Hindenburg, February 1, 1933

DIFFERENTIATING INSTRUCTION: ENGLISH LEARNERS

Analyzing a Primary Source

Class Time 15 minutes

Task Looking up difficult words and restating the primary source quotation

Purpose To increase vocabulary and understanding of the text

Instructions Have students work in pairs to reread the primary source quotation on this page. Have one student read the passage aloud while the other follows along in the text and marks difficult or unfamiliar vocabulary words. Then ask students to use a dictionary to find the meaning of each word and create a chart restating the meanings in their own terms. Finally, have the pairs collaborate in creating a simple, original restatement of Ludendorff's ideas. Sample charts and restatement follow:

Word	Meaning
delivered up	turned over
rabblerousers	troublemakers
predict	foretell, say in advance
accursed	hateful, under a curse
abyss	deep or bottomless pit
inconceivable	unthinkable, not to be believed

Restatement
You have just turned Germany over to a terrible troublemaker. He will destroy the country.

Once in office, Hitler called for new elections, hoping to win a parliamentary majority. Six days before the election, a fire destroyed the Reichstag building, where the parliament met. The Nazis blamed the Communists. By stirring up fear of the Communists, the Nazis and their allies won by a slim majority.

B. Answer because he restored pride in Germany, cut unemployment, repudiated the hated Versailles Treaty, and promised to regain lost German lands

Hitler used his new power to turn Germany into a totalitarian state. He banned all other political parties and had opponents arrested. Meanwhile, an elite, black-uniformed unit called the SS (*Schutzstaffel,* or protection squad) was created. It was loyal only to Hitler. In 1934, the SS arrested and murdered hundreds of Hitler's enemies. This brutal action and the terror applied by the Gestapo, the Nazi secret police, shocked most Germans into total obedience.

The Nazis quickly took command of the economy. New laws banned strikes, dissolved independent labor unions, and gave the government authority over business and labor. Hitler put millions of Germans to work. They constructed factories, built highways, manufactured weapons, and served in the military. As a result, the number of unemployed dropped from about 6 million to 1.5 million in 1936. B

MAIN IDEA

Making Inferences

B Why did Germans at first support Hitler?

The Führer Is Supreme Hitler wanted more than just economic and political power—he wanted control over every aspect of German life. To shape public opinion and to win praise for his leadership, Hitler turned the press, radio, literature, painting, and film into propaganda tools. Books that did not conform to Nazi beliefs were burned in huge bonfires. Churches were forbidden to criticize the Nazis or the government. Schoolchildren had to join the Hitler Youth (for boys) or the League of German Girls. Hitler believed that continuous struggle brought victory to the strong. He twisted the philosophy of Friedrich Nietzsche to support his use of brute force.

Hitler Makes War on the Jews Hatred of Jews, or anti-Semitism, was a key part of Nazi ideology. Although Jews were less than 1 percent of the population, the Nazis used them as scapegoats for all Germany's troubles since the war. This led to a wave of anti-Semitism across Germany. Beginning in 1933, the Nazis passed laws depriving Jews of most of their rights. Violence against Jews mounted. On the

▼ At a 1933 rally in Nuremberg, Germany, storm troopers carried flags bearing the swastika.

More About . . .

Support for Hitler

During the 1920s, Hitler's Nazi party attracted few supporters outside of fanatical anti-Semites, ultra-nationalists, and disgruntled war veterans. However, the 1929 depression swelled the Nazi ranks.

World Art and Cultures Transparencies

- AT69 Pillars of Society

More About . . .

The SS

The *Schutzstaffel*, or SS, was originally formed in 1923 as the personal bodyguard for Hitler. Under Heinrich Himmler, the SS became the elite of the Nazi empire. The two requirements for wearing the SS's black shirts with the death's head insignia were unconditional loyalty to Hitler and "racial purity."

More About . . .

The Swastika

The Nazis did not invent the swastika, but merely adopted a symbol that had been used by many civilizations throughout history. It has been found on Greek coins and Celtic monuments in Europe, Byzantine buildings and Buddhist inscriptions in Asia, and Indian artifacts in North and South America.

DIFFERENTIATING INSTRUCTION: STRUGGLING READERS

B

Identifying Causes and Effects

Class Time 35 minutes

Task Charting causes and effects of main events

Purpose To identify the causes and effects leading to the rise of power of Hitler and the Nazi Party.

Instructions Make copies of the Guided Reading activity, p. 49 of In-Depth Resources: Unit 4. Then divide the class into small groups and give a copy of the chart to each group. Instruct students to focus on events 3–7. They should reread the text to identify a cause and effect for each. Then have them work together to fill in the chart. Make sure they notice that these events form a cause-and-effect chain, with each effect leading to the cause of the next event. Finally, have students share their charts with the class. Sample answers follow:

3. Cause—his success as a politician; Effect—plots to seize power
4. Cause—plot to seize power fails; Effect—is released after only nine months
5. Cause—promises strong leadership; Effect—takes total control of Germany
6. Cause—mistrusts non-Nazi ideas; Effect—extends his control and power
7. Cause—Nazi hatred of Jews; Effect—begins total elimination of Jews

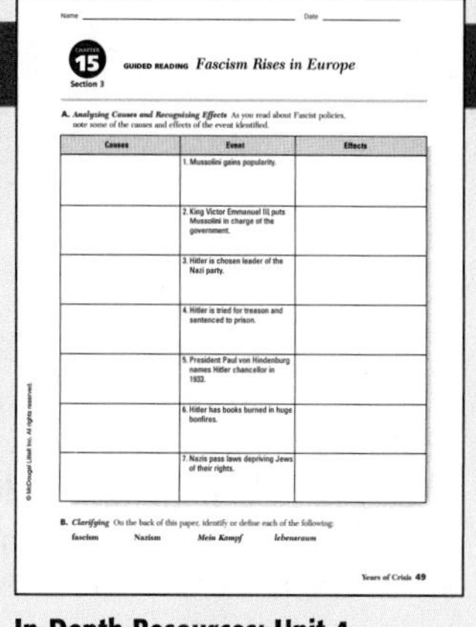

Name ____________ Date ______

CHAPTER 15 Section 3 GUIDED READING *Fascism Rises in Europe*

A. ***Analyzing Causes and Recognizing Effects*** As you read about Fascist policies, note some of the causes and effects of the event identified.

Causes	Event	Effects
	1. Mussolini gains popularity.	
	2. King Victor Emmanuel III puts Mussolini in charge of the government.	
	3. Hitler is chosen leader of the Nazi party.	
	4. Hitler is tried for treason and sentenced to prison.	
	5. President Paul von Hindenburg names Hitler chancellor in 1933.	
	6. Hitler has books burned in huge bonfires.	
	7. Nazis pass laws depriving Jews of their rights.	

B. ***Clarifying*** On the back of this paper, identify or define each of the following:

fascism **Nazism** ***Mein Kampf*** ***lebensraum***

Years of Crisis 49

In-Depth Resources: Unit 4

Global Impact

Fascism in Argentina

Ask interested students to research the life of Juan Perón. Suggest that they compare and contrast his leadership style with that of the European dictators he admired.

Other Countries Fall to Dictators

10.7.1

Critical Thinking

- Why were dictators so successful in gaining power in Eastern Europe? *(They had the support of military forces and wealthy landowners)*
- What do totalitarian states gain by restricting civil rights? *(control of their citizens)*

Electronic Library of Primary Sources

- from Memos on the Aims of Germany and Japan

3 ASSESS

SECTION 3 ASSESSMENT

Have students work in small groups, dividing the questions up among themselves and discussing the answers together.

Formal Assessment

- Section Quiz, p. 263

4 RETEACH

Assign students the roles of Italian or German citizens. Have them present their views of Mussolini and Hitler to the class.

In-Depth Resources: Unit 4

- Reteaching Activity, p. 67

Global Impact

Fascism in Argentina

Juan Perón served as Argentina's president from 1946 to 1955 and again in 1973 and 1974. The two years he spent in Europe before World War II greatly influenced his strong-man rule.

A career army officer, Perón went to Italy in 1939 for military training. He then served at the Argentine embassy in Rome. A visit to Berlin gave Perón a chance to see Nazi Germany. The ability of Hitler and Mussolini to manipulate their citizens impressed Perón.

When Perón himself gained power, he patterned his military dictatorship on that of the European Fascists.

night of November 9, 1938, Nazi mobs attacked Jews in their homes and on the streets and destroyed thousands of Jewish-owned buildings. This rampage, called *Kristallnacht* (Night of the Broken Glass), signaled the real start of the process of eliminating the Jews from German life. You'll learn more about this in Chapter 16.

Other Countries Fall to Dictators

While Fascists took power in Italy and Germany, the nations formed in eastern Europe after World War I also were falling to dictators. In Hungary in 1919, after a brief Communist regime, military forces and wealthy landowners joined to make Admiral Miklós Horthy the first European postwar dictator. In Poland, Marshal Jozef Pilsudski (pihl•SOOT•skee) seized power in 1926. In Yugoslavia, Albania, Bulgaria, and Romania, kings turned to strong-man rule. They suspended constitutions and silenced foes. In 1935, only one democracy, Czechoslovakia, remained in eastern Europe.

Only in European nations with strong democratic traditions—Britain, France, and the Scandinavian countries—did democracy survive. With no democratic experience and severe economic problems, many Europeans saw dictatorship as the only way to prevent instability.

By the mid-1930s, the powerful nations of the world were split into two antagonistic camps—democratic and totalitarian. And to gain their ends, the Fascist dictatorships had indicated a willingness to use military aggression. Although all of these dictatorships restricted civil rights, none asserted control with the brutality of the Russian Communists or the Nazis.

SECTION 3 ASSESSMENT

TERMS & NAMES 1. For each term or name, write a sentence explaining its significance.

- fascism • Benito Mussolini • Adolf Hitler • Nazism • *Mein Kampf* • *lebensraum*

USING YOUR NOTES

2. Do you think Hitler and Mussolini were more alike or different? Explain why. (10.7.3)

Hitler	Mussolini
Rise:	Rise:
Goals:	Goals:

MAIN IDEAS

3. What factors led to the rise of fascism in Italy? (10.7.3)
4. How did Hitler maintain power? (10.8.5)
5. Why did the leadership of many eastern European nations fall to dictators? (10.7.3)

CRITICAL THINKING & WRITING

6. **DRAWING CONCLUSIONS** Why did a movement like fascism and leaders like Mussolini and Hitler come to power during a period of crisis? (10.7.3)
7. **ANALYZING MOTIVES** Why do you think Hitler had German children join Nazi organizations? (10.8.5)
8. **SYNTHESIZING** What emotions did both Hitler and Mussolini stir in their followers? (10.7.3)
9. **WRITING ACTIVITY** POWER AND AUTHORITY Reread the History Makers on Mussolini and Hitler on page 478. Then write a **description** of the techniques the two leaders used to appear powerful to their listeners. (Writing 2.2.c)

CONNECT TO TODAY **PRESENTING AN ORAL REPORT**

Some modern rulers have invaded other countries for political and economic gain. Research to learn about a recent invasion and discuss your findings in an **oral report.** (Writing 2.1.a)

ANSWERS

1. fascism, p. 476 • Benito Mussolini, p. 477 • Adolf Hitler, p. 477 • Nazism, p. 478 • *Mein Kampf*, p. 478 • *lebensraum*, p. 478
2. **Sample Answer:** Hitler–Rise: appointed chancellor, became dictator, revived economy; Goals: regain lost land and take over more; purge country of non-German people. Mussolini–Rise: appointed leader, became dictator, took over economy; Goals: return Italy to ancient greatness. More alike because their rise and goals were similar
3. betrayal perceived at Paris Peace Conference, rising inflation/unemployment, social unrest
4. had enemies murdered by the SS, used media and arts for propaganda, made children join Nazi organizations
5. Without democratic traditions, they saw dictators as a means to stability.
6. **Possible Answer:** They blamed others for the country's problems and offered simple solutions.
7. **Possible Answer**: He used their impressionability to create a new generation of followers.
8. **Possible Answers:** fear of outsiders, pride, loyalty, and patriotism
9. **Rubric** Descriptions should
   - discuss Hitler's and Mussolini's speech techniques.
   - point out that both used emotional appeals and theatrical gestures.

CONNECT TO TODAY

Rubric Oral reports should

- identify and describe the ruler's goals and methods.
- discuss an invasion led by a modern ruler.
- summarize the outcome of the invasion.

People waiting for a free lunch for the unemployed, 1930

Magazine cover, 1926

Aggressors Invade Nations

MAIN IDEA

POWER AND AUTHORITY As Germany, Italy, and Japan conquered other countries, the rest of the world did nothing to stop them.

WHY IT MATTERS NOW

Many nations today take a more active and collective role in world affairs, as in the United Nations.

TERMS & NAMES

- appeasement
- Axis Powers
- Francisco Franco
- isolationism
- Third Reich
- Munich Conference

SETTING THE STAGE By the mid-1930s, Germany and Italy seemed bent on military conquest. The major democracies—Britain, France, and the United States—were distracted by economic problems at home and longed to remain at peace. With the world moving toward war, many nations pinned their hopes for peace on the League of Nations. As fascism spread in Europe, however, a powerful nation in Asia moved toward a similar system. Following a period of reform and progress in the 1920s, Japan fell under military rule.

CALIFORNIA STANDARDS

10.6.4 Discuss the influence of World War I on literature, art, and intellectual life in the West (e.g., Pablo Picasso, the "lost generation" of Gertrude Stein, Ernest Hemingway).

10.7.3 Analyze the rise, aggression, and human costs of totalitarian regimes (Fascist and Communist) in Germany, Italy, and the Soviet Union, noting especially their common and dissimilar traits.

10.8.2 Understand the role of appeasement, nonintervention (isolationism), and the domestic distractions in Europe and the United States prior to the outbreak of World War II.

10.8.4 Describe the political, diplomatic, and military leaders during the war (e.g., Winston Churchill, Franklin Delano Roosevelt, Emperor Hirohito, Adolf Hitler, Benito Mussolini, Joseph Stalin, Douglas MacArthur, Dwight Eisenhower).

Japan Seeks an Empire

During the 1920s, the Japanese government became more democratic. In 1922, Japan signed an international treaty agreeing to respect China's borders. In 1928, it signed the Kellogg-Briand Pact renouncing war. Japan's parliamentary system had several weaknesses, however. Its constitution put strict limits on the powers of the prime minister and the cabinet. Most importantly, civilian leaders had little control over the armed forces. Military leaders reported only to the emperor.

Militarists Take Control of Japan As long as Japan remained prosperous, the civilian government kept power. But when the Great Depression struck in 1929, many Japanese blamed the government. Military leaders gained support and soon won control of the country. Unlike the Fascists in Europe, the militarists did not try to establish a new system of government. They wanted to restore traditional control of the government to the military. Instead of a forceful leader like Mussolini or Hitler, the militarists made the emperor the symbol of state power.

Keeping Emperor Hirohito as head of state won popular support for the army leaders who ruled in his name. Like Hitler and Mussolini, Japan's militarists were extreme nationalists. They wanted to solve the country's economic problems through foreign expansion. They planned a Pacific empire that included a conquered China. The empire would provide Japan with raw materials and markets for its goods. It would also give Japan room for its rising population.

Japan Invades Manchuria Japanese businesses had invested heavily in China's northeast province, Manchuria. It was an area rich in iron and coal. In 1931, the Japanese army seized Manchuria, despite objections from the Japanese parliament. The army then set up a puppet government. Japanese engineers and technicians began arriving in large numbers to build mines and factories.

TAKING NOTES

Following Chronological Order Use a time line to trace the movement of Japan from democratic reform to military aggression.

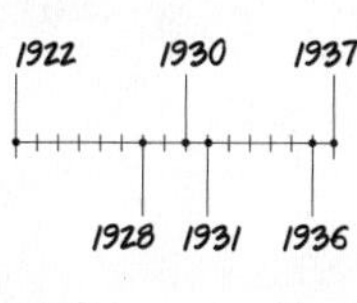

LESSON PLAN

OBJECTIVES

- Describe Japan's attempts to build an empire.
- Trace the moves of European Fascists in seeking world power.
- Summarize why British and French appeasement and American isolationism failed to stop Fascist aggression.

1 FOCUS & MOTIVATE

Ask students what they would do if they saw someone being attacked by an older or stronger person. *(Possible Answers: refuse to get involved, try to reason with the aggressor, help defend the victim)*

2 INSTRUCT

Japan Seeks an Empire
10.8.4

Critical Thinking

- How did the Japanese invasion of Manchuria illustrate the weakness of the League of Nations? *(The League was unable to control Japanese activities.)*

CALIFORNIA RESOURCES

California Reading Toolkit, p. L69
California Modified Lesson Plans for English Learners, p. 133
California Daily Standards Practice Transparencies, TT61
California Standards Enrichment Workbook, pp. 71–72, 77–78, 81–82, 85–86
California Standards Planner and Lesson Plans, p. L129
California Online Test Practice
California Test Generator CD-ROM
California Easy Planner CD-ROM
California eEdition CD-ROM

SECTION 4 PROGRAM RESOURCES

ALL STUDENTS

In-Depth Resources: Unit 4
- Guided Reading, p. 50
- Geography Application: Spain During the 1930s, p. 53
- History Makers: Francisco Franco, p. 63

Formal Assessment
- Section Quiz, p. 264

ENGLISH LEARNERS

In-Depth Resources in Spanish
- Guided Reading, p. 120
- Geography Application, p. 122

Reading Study Guide (Spanish), p. 163

Reading Study Guide Audio CD (Spanish)

STRUGGLING READERS

In-Depth Resources: Unit 4
- Guided Reading, p. 50
- Building Vocabulary, p.51
- Geography Application, p. 54
- Reteaching Activity, p. 68

Reading Study Guide, p. 163
Reading Study Guide Audio CD

GIFTED AND TALENTED STUDENTS

In-Depth Resources: Unit 4
- Primary Source: The Bombing of Guernica, p. 58

Electronic Library of Primary Sources
- from Speech in the House of Commons

INTEGRATED TECHNOLOGY

eEdition CD-ROM
Power Presentations CD-ROM
Geography Transparencies
- GT31 Expansion of Nazi Germany

Critical Thinking Transparencies
- CT67 Chapter 31 Visual Summary

Electronic Library of Primary Sources
- from Speech in the House of Commons

classzone.com

European Aggressors on the March
10.8.4; 10.7.3

Critical Thinking
- What role did the League of Nations play in the successful takeover of Ethiopia? *(None; its weakness allowed Italy to control Ethiopia.)*
- Why did European democracies fail to help Spain? *(Possible Answer: their already-established policy of appeasement)*

More About . . .

Ethiopia and the League of Nations
After Italy attacked Ethiopia, the League of Nations called for an embargo restricting loans to and exports from Italy. Britain and France feared angering Mussolini, however, and refused to place an embargo on oil. Britain also refused to stop Italian troops and arms from moving through the Suez Canal, fatally weakening the League.

History from Visuals

Interpreting the Time Line
Have students identify the three aggressor nations shown on the time line. *(Japan, Italy and Germany)* Which nation's aggression began the earliest? *(Japan)* Which nation attacked the most countries? *(Germany)*

Extension Have students add to the time line as they read about subsequent events in the chapter.

The Japanese attack on Manchuria was the first direct challenge to the League of Nations. In the early 1930s, the League's members included all major democracies except the United States. The League also included the three countries that posed the greatest threat to peace—Germany, Japan, and Italy. When Japan seized Manchuria, many League members vigorously protested. Japan ignored the protests and withdrew from the League in 1933. **A**

> **MAIN IDEA**
> **Making Inferences**
> **A** What was the major weakness of the League of Nations?
> A. Answer The League had no enforcement power—it could not make nations follow its decrees.

Japan Invades China Four years later, a border incident touched off a full-scale war between Japan and China. Japanese forces swept into northern China. Despite having a million soldiers, China's army led by Jiang Jieshi was no match for the better equipped and trained Japanese.

Beijing and other northern cities as well as the capital, Nanjing, fell to the Japanese in 1937. Japanese troops killed tens of thousands of captured soldiers and civilians in Nanjing. Forced to retreat westward, Jiang Jieshi set up a new capital at Chongqing. At the same time, Chinese guerrillas led by China's Communist leader, Mao Zedong, continued to fight the Japanese in the conquered area.

European Aggressors on the March
The League's failure to stop the Japanese encouraged European Fascists to plan aggression of their own. The Italian leader Mussolini dreamed of building a colonial empire in Africa like those of Britain and France.

Mussolini Attacks Ethiopia Ethiopia was one of Africa's three independent nations. The Ethiopians had successfully resisted an Italian attempt at conquest during the 1890s. To avenge that defeat, Mussolini ordered a massive invasion of Ethiopia in October 1935. The spears and swords of the Ethiopians were no match for Italian airplanes, tanks, guns, and poison gas.

The Ethiopian emperor, Haile Selassie, urgently appealed to the League for help. Although the League condemned the attack, its members did nothing. Britain continued to let Italian troops and supplies pass through the British-controlled Suez Canal on their way to Ethiopia. By giving in to Mussolini in Africa, Britain and France hoped to keep peace in Europe.

Hitler Defies Versailles Treaty Hitler had long pledged to undo the Versailles Treaty. Among its provisions, the treaty limited the size of Germany's army. In March 1935, the Führer announced that Germany would not obey these restrictions. The League issued only a mild condemnation.

The League's failure to stop Germany from rearming convinced Hitler to take even greater risks. The treaty had forbidden German troops to enter a 30-mile-wide zone on either side of the Rhine River. Known as the Rhineland, the zone formed

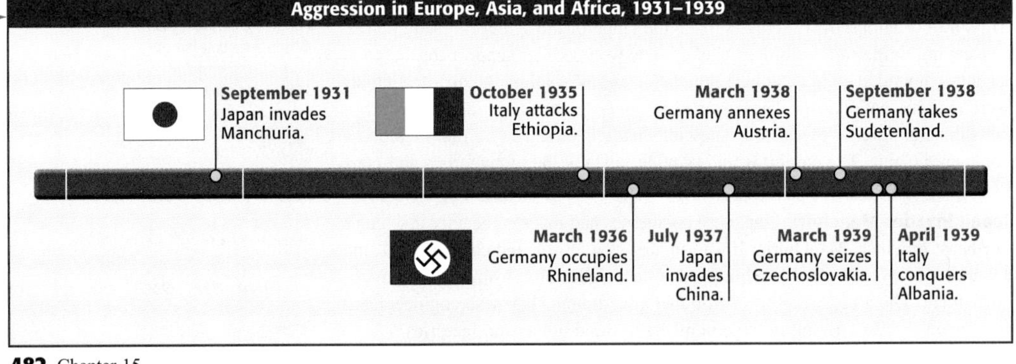

Aggression in Europe, Asia, and Africa, 1931–1939
September 1931 Japan invades Manchuria.
October 1935 Italy attacks Ethiopia.
March 1938 Germany annexes Austria.
September 1938 Germany takes Sudetenland.
March 1936 Germany occupies Rhineland.
July 1937 Japan invades China.
March 1939 Germany seizes Czechoslovakia.
April 1939 Italy conquers Albania.

DIFFERENTIATING INSTRUCTION: STRUGGLING READERS

Headlining the News
Class Time 25 minutes

Task Writing news headlines covering military actions

Purpose To identify and remember main ideas

Instructions Have students review the text on pages 481-483. Also, give them page 163 of the Reading Study Guide. Then divide students into three groups. Explain that they will be acting as journalists covering military moves made by Japan, Italy, and Germany.

Instruct each group to write two headlines describing their particular country's actions. Remind them that their headlines do not need to be full sentences. Headlines should be short and should capture the main idea of the event using strong nouns and verbs. Have them share their news flashes with the class. Here are some examples.

Japan	Manchuria Falls to Japan; Japanese Slaughter Chinese at Nanjing
Italy	Italy Overpowers Ethiopia; League of Nations Looks Away
Germany	Hitler Ignores Treaty; Germany Sweeps into Rhineland

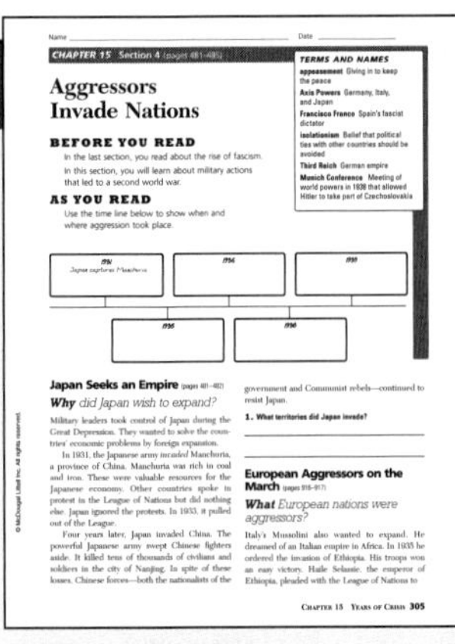
CHAPTER 15 Section 4
Aggressors Invade Nations
BEFORE YOU READ
AS YOU READ
Japan Seeks an Empire
European Aggressors on the March

Reading Study Guide

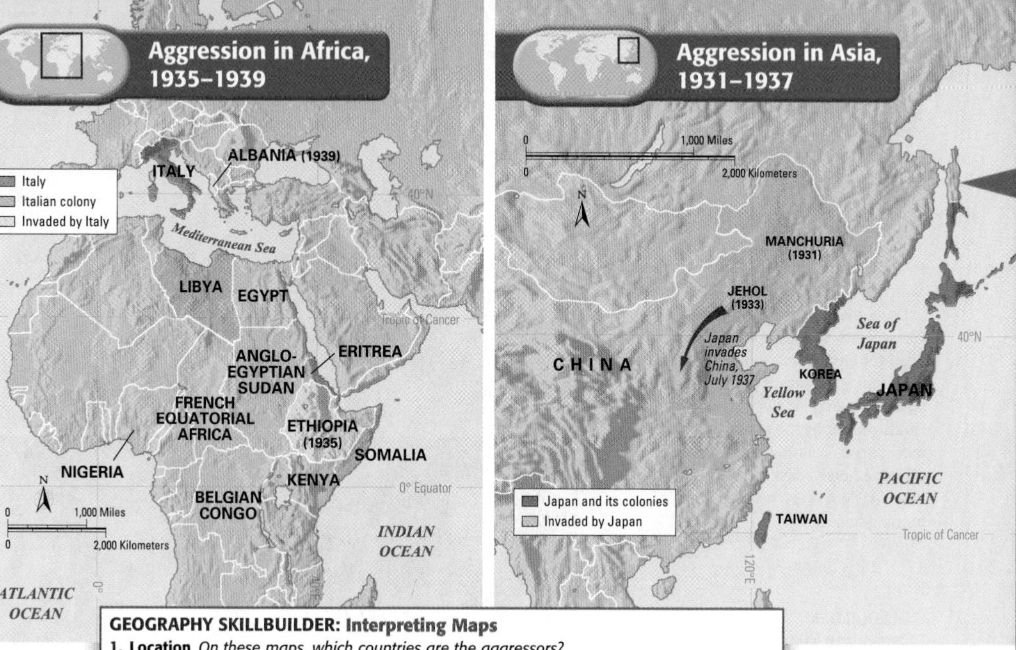

GEOGRAPHY SKILLBUILDER: Interpreting Maps
1. **Location** *On these maps, which countries are the aggressors?*
2. **Movement** *On what two continents did the aggression occur?*

a buffer between Germany and France. It was also an important industrial area. On March 7, 1936, German troops moved into the Rhineland. Stunned, the French were unwilling to risk war. The British urged **appeasement**, giving in to an aggressor to keep peace.

Hitler later admitted that he would have backed down if the French and British had challenged him. The German reoccupation of the Rhineland marked a turning point in the march toward war. First, it strengthened Hitler's power and prestige within Germany. Second, the balance of power changed in Germany's favor. France and Belgium were now open to attack from German troops. Finally, the weak response by France and Britain encouraged Hitler to speed up his expansion.

Hitler's growing strength convinced Mussolini that he should seek an alliance with Germany. In October 1936, the two dictators reached an agreement that became known as the Rome-Berlin Axis. A month later, Germany also made an agreement with Japan. Germany, Italy, and Japan came to be called the **Axis Powers**.

Vocabulary
axis: a straight line around which an object rotates. Hitler and Mussolini expected their alliance to become the axis around which Europe would rotate.

Civil War Erupts in Spain Hitler and Mussolini again tested the will of the democracies of Europe in the Spanish Civil War. Spain had been a monarchy until 1931, when a republic was declared. The government, run by liberals and Socialists, held office amid many crises. In July 1936, army leaders, favoring a Fascist-style government, joined General **Francisco Franco** in a revolt. Thus began a civil war that dragged on for three years.

Hitler and Mussolini sent troops, tanks, and airplanes to help Franco's forces, which were called the Nationalists. The armed forces of the Republicans, as supporters of Spain's elected government were known, received little help from abroad. The Western democracies remained neutral. Only the Soviet Union sent equipment and advisers. An international brigade of volunteers fought on the Republican side. Early in 1939, Republican resistance collapsed. Franco became Spain's Fascist dictator.

History from Visuals

Interpreting the Map

Ask students what the light purple and light pink areas represent. *(lands attacked or claimed by Italy and Japan)*

Extension Ask students to study the two maps. Ask why Italy looked to Africa for colonies and not to Europe. *(Germany was in control of most areas north of Italy.)* Then ask what is the most likely direction Japan will move to extend its empire. *(south)*

SKILLBUILDER Answers
1. **Location** Italy and Japan
2. **Movement** Africa and Asia

More About . . .

Francisco Franco

After the Nationalist victory in the Spanish Civil War, General Franco declared himself military chief. He ruled Spain until his death in 1975. Initially, his reign was quite harsh, including the execution of 200,000 Spaniards between 1939 and 1943. He sympathized with the Axis countries but did not enter World War II.

In-Depth Resources: Unit 4
- History Makers: Francisco Franco, p. 63
- Geography Application: Spain During the 1930s, p. 54

DIFFERENTIATING INSTRUCTION: GIFTED AND TALENTED STUDENTS

Contrasting Literary Responses to the Spanish Civil War

Class Time 40 minutes

Task Reading literary works about the Spanish Civil War and discussing their differences

Purpose To gain an insider's perspective on the war

Instructions American author Ernest Hemingway and British writer George Orwell wrote books that offer an insider's perspective on the Spanish Civil War. Hemingway's novel *For Whom the Bell Tolls*, written in 1940, fictionalizes the impressions he formed of the conflict as a war correspondent. In 1938, Orwell, best known for his novels *1984* and *Animal Farm*, wrote *Homage to Catalonia,* a nonfiction work about his experiences and disillusionment as a soldier fighting for the Republicans. Have students read one of these works, taking notes about its perspective on the reasons for, reactions to, and outcome of the Spanish Civil War.

Then have students stage a "From Where I Stand" discussion in which they assume their author's point of view and explain it to the class.

After comparing and contrasting the idealism of Hemingway's hero and Orwell's more cynical outlook, have students discuss which point of view they support.

Analyzing Art

Interpreting the Visuals

Inform students that the air attacks on Guernica killed a thousand people, one out of every eight residents. Picasso's depiction of the event is huge—11 feet high and 25 feet long.

Extension Ask students how Picasso's use of images and color captures the horrors of the war. *(Possible Answers: Mutilated images and a black-and-gray palette suggest stark suffering.)*

SKILLBUILDER Answers

1. **Analyzing Motives** *Possible Answers:* informing about the war and swaying opinion against Franco
2. **Hypothesizing** *Possible Answers:* anger, horror, hatred of the Franco regime

In-Depth Resources: Unit 4

- Primary Source: The Bombing of Guernica, p. 58

Democratic Nations Try to Preserve Peace

10.6.4; 10.8.2

Critical Thinking

- How did World War I affect U.S. policy? *(U.S. became isolationist; desire for Europeans to handle their own problems)*
- What message did Hitler take from appeasement? *(that France and Britain would not become involved)*

Geography Transparencies

- GT31 Expansion of Nazi Germany

Electronic Library of Primary Sources

- from Speech in the House of Commons

> Analyzing Art

Guernica

On April 26, 1937, Franco's German allies bombed the ancient Basque city of Guernica in Spain. The photograph (above) shows the city reduced to rubble by the bombing. However, Spanish artist Pablo Picasso's painting, called *Guernica* (below), captures the human horror of the event.

Using the geometric forms of Cubism, Picasso shows a city and people that have been torn to pieces. Unnatural angles and overlapping images of people, severed limbs, and animals reflect the suffering and chaos caused by the attack. At left, a mother cries over her dead child. In the center, a horse screams and a soldier lies dead. At right, a woman falls from a burning house.

SKILLBUILDER: Interpreting Visual Sources

1. **Analyzing Motives** *What were Picasso's probable motives for painting* Guernica?
2. **Hypothesizing** *What feelings do you think* Guernica *stirred in the public in the late 1930s?*

Democratic Nations Try to Preserve Peace

Instead of taking a stand against Fascist aggression in the 1930s, Britain and France repeatedly made concessions, hoping to keep peace. Both nations were dealing with serious economic problems as a result of the Great Depression. In addition, the horrors of World War I had created a deep desire to avoid war.

United States Follows an Isolationist Policy Many Americans supported **isolationism**, the belief that political ties to other countries should be avoided. Isolationists argued that entry into World War I had been a costly error. Beginning in 1935, Congress passed three Neutrality Acts. These laws banned loans and the sale of arms to nations at war.

The German Reich Expands On November 5, 1937, Hitler announced to his advisers his plans to absorb Austria and Czechoslovakia into the **Third Reich** (ryk), or German Empire. The Treaty of Versailles prohibited *Anschluss* (AHN•SHLUS), or a union between Austria and Germany. However, many Austrians supported unity with Germany. In March 1938, Hitler sent his army into Austria and annexed it. France and Britain ignored their pledge to protect Austrian independence.

Hitler next turned to Czechoslovakia. About three million German-speaking people lived in the western border regions of Czechoslovakia called the Sudetenland. (See map, page 461.) This heavily fortified area formed the Czechs' main defense against Germany. The Anschluss raised pro-Nazi feelings among Sudeten Germans. In September 1938, Hitler demanded that the Sudetenland be given to Germany. The Czechs refused and asked France for help.

DIFFERENTIATING INSTRUCTION: ENGLISH LEARNERS

Analyzing Churchill's Speech

Class Time 20 minutes

Task Restating the main ideas of Winston Churchill's speech

Purpose To understand Winston Churchill's point of view

Instructions Divide the class into seven groups and assign each group one of the following phrases of Winston Churchill's statement on page 485:

- We are in the presence of a disaster of the first magnitude
- we have sustained a defeat without a war
- And do not suppose that this is the end
- This is only the first sip, the first foretaste of a bitter cup
- which will be proffered to us year by year
- unless, by a supreme recovery of moral health and martial vigor
- we arise again and take our stand for freedom as in the olden time

Ask each group to read its phrase aloud, look up any difficult words, and restate it in everyday language. Have them compile their phrases into a complete restatement such as this:

Restatement

This is a terrible time . . . we have lost a war we didn't fight . . . The struggle is not over yet . . . this is only the beginning of a painful lesson we will be taught again and again unless we make our values and our army stronger and fight for freedom like we used to.

Britain and France Again Choose Appeasement France and Britain were preparing for war when Mussolini proposed a meeting of Germany, France, Britain, and Italy in Munich, Germany. The **Munich Conference** was held on September 29, 1938. The Czechs were not invited. British prime minister Neville Chamberlain believed that he could preserve peace by giving in to Hitler's demand. Britain and France agreed that Hitler could take the Sudetenland. In exchange, Hitler pledged to respect Czechoslovakia's new borders.

When Chamberlain returned to London, he told cheering crowds, "I believe it is peace for our time." Winston Churchill, then a member of the British Parliament, strongly disagreed. He opposed the appeasement policy and gloomily warned of its consequences:

▲ Chamberlain waves the statement he read following the Munich Conference.

B. Possible Answer He believed that appeasing the Fascists was tantamount to surrendering to them.

MAIN IDEA

Analyzing Primary Sources

B Why did Churchill believe that Chamberlain's policy of appeasement was a defeat for the British?

PRIMARY SOURCE B

We are in the presence of a disaster of the first magnitude. . . . we have sustained a defeat without a war. . . . And do not suppose that this is the end. . . . This is only the first sip, the first foretaste of a bitter cup which will be proffered to us year by year unless, by a supreme recovery of moral health and martial vigor, we arise again and take our stand for freedom as in the olden time.

WINSTON CHURCHILL, speech before the House of Commons, October 5, 1938

Less than six months after the Munich meeting, Hitler took Czechoslovakia. Soon after, Mussolini seized Albania. Then Hitler demanded that Poland return the former German port of Danzig. The Poles refused and turned to Britain and France for aid. But appeasement had convinced Hitler that neither nation would risk war.

Nazis and Soviets Sign Nonaggression Pact Britain and France asked the Soviet Union to join them in stopping Hitler's aggression. As Stalin talked with Britain and France, he also bargained with Hitler. The two dictators reached an agreement. Once bitter enemies, Fascist Germany and Communist Russia now publicly pledged never to attack one another. On August 23, 1939, their leaders signed a nonaggression pact. As the Axis Powers moved unchecked at the end of the decade, war appeared inevitable.

SECTION 4 ASSESSMENT

TERMS & NAMES 1. For each term or name, write a sentence explaining its significance.

• appeasement • Axis Powers • Francisco Franco • isolationism • Third Reich • Munich Conference

USING YOUR NOTES

2. What event was the most significant? Why? (10.8.2)

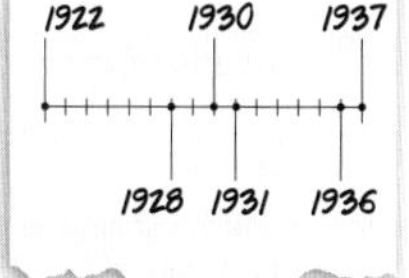

MAIN IDEAS

3. Compare the militarists in Japan with the European Fascists. (10.7.3)
4. Which countries formed the Axis Powers? (10.7.3)
5. What were the effects of isolationism and appeasement? (10.8.2)

CRITICAL THINKING & WRITING

6. **SYNTHESIZING** What similar goals did Hitler, Mussolini, and Hirohito share? (10.8.4)
7. **FORMING OPINIONS** Do you think the Fascist nations of the Axis Powers could have been stopped? Explain. (10.7.3)
8. **EVALUATING DECISIONS** Why weren't the Czechs invited to take part in the Munich Conference? (10.8.2)
9. **WRITING ACTIVITY** POWER AND AUTHORITY Write a **letter to the editor** in which you voice your opinion about the U.S. policy of isolationism during the 1930s. (Writing 2.4.c)

CONNECT TO TODAY STAGING A DEBATE

Established in 1945, the United Nations was intended to be an improvement on the League of Nations. Research to learn about the recent successes and failures of the UN. Then hold a **debate** in which you argue whether the institution should be preserved. (Writing 2.5.a)

More About . . .

Winston Churchill

Early in his political career, Winston Churchill's independent mindset often caused him problems. However, this trait made him willing to speak out against the Nazi threat when few others in Britain would do so. Churchill was Britain's foremost critic of appeasement, seeing clearly that this policy would only increase Hitler's belief that he would not be stopped in his grab for power and territory.

3 ASSESS

SECTION 4 ASSESSMENT

Have students work independently to answer the questions with open books.

Formal Assessment
• Section Quiz, p. 264

4 RETEACH

Have students review the short- and long-term causes and effects of the Great Depression and how it led to the outbreak of World War II, using the visual summary on page CT67 of Critical Thinking Transparencies as a guide.

Critical Thinking Transparencies
• CT67 Chapter 31 Visual Summary

In-Depth Resources: Unit 4
• Reteaching Activity, p. 68

ANSWERS

1. appeasement, p. 483 • Axis Powers, p. 483 • Francisco Franco, p. 483 • isolationism, p. 484 • Third Reich, p. 484 • Munich Conference, p. 485

2. **Sample Answer:** 1922—agrees to respect China's borders; 1928—signs Kellogg-Briand Pact; 1930—military gains control; 1931—invades Manchuria; 1936—allies with Germany; 1937—invades China. **Possible Answer:** allying with Germany, because this strengthened Germany and helped draw the world into war
3. Both were very nationalistic and wanted to expand; Europeans wanted new governments; Japan wanted military control.
4. Germany, Italy, and Japan
5. Aggressor nations continued their aggression unchecked.
6. **Possible Answers:** to extend their power and rule an empire
7. **Possible Answer:** possibly if the League of Nations had more authority or Western democracies had opposed them
8. **Possible Answer:** They probably would have pressed for war, which France and Britain wanted to avoid at all costs.
9. **Rubric** Letters to the editor should
• take a stand on U.S. isolationism.
• support opinions with details and examples.
• end with a call for action.

CONNECT TO TODAY

Rubric Debates should
• clearly state the issue to be debated.
• identify and support major points on each side.
• include specific incidents to support opinions.

TERMS & NAMES

1. Albert Einstein, p. 463
2. Sigmund Freud, p. 463
3. Weimar Republic, p. 471
4. New Deal, p. 475
5. fascism, p. 476
6. Benito Mussolini, p. 477
7. Adolf Hitler, p. 477
8. appeasement, p. 483
9. Francisco Franco, p. 483
10. Munich Conference, p. 485

MAIN IDEAS

Answers will vary.

11. They created a revolution in science and the study of human behavior, disturbing many people and leading them to question their own beliefs.
12. passenger airlines, improved autos, widespread radio broadcasting, movies
13. lacked democratic tradition and strong ruling party, blamed for Versailles Treaty and loss in WWI
14. investors buying on margin and selling, hoping to reinvest at lower rates; panic selling due to falling prices; stocks losing value
15. dissatisfaction with Paris Peace Conference, unemployment, fear of communist revolution, democratic government unable to solve problems
16. Germans a master race and other "races" inferior; Treaty of Versailles intolerable and Hitler to reclaim territory; takeover of territory to provide *lebensraum*
17. foreign expansion, gaining raw materials from China, increasing living space
18. The military was convinced Hitler could succeed; the balance of power favored Germany, with France and Belgium open to attack; Hitler continued to pursue military and territorial expansion.

Chapter 15 Assessment

VISUAL SUMMARY

The Great Depression

Long-Term Causes

- World economies are connected.
- Some countries have huge war debts from World War I.
- Europe relies on American loans and investments.
- Prosperity is built on borrowed money.
- Wealth is unequally distributed.

Immediate Causes

- U.S. stock market crashes.
- Banks demand repayment of loans.
- Farms fail and factories close.
- Americans reduce foreign trade to protect economy.
- Americans stop loans to foreign countries.
- American banking system collapses.

WORLDWIDE ECONOMIC DEPRESSION

Immediate Effects

- Millions become unemployed worldwide.
- Businesses go bankrupt.
- Governments take emergency measures to protect economies.
- Citizens lose faith in capitalism and democracy.
- Nations turn toward authoritarian leaders.

Long-Term Effects

- Nazis take control in Germany.
- Fascists come to power in other countries.
- Democracies try social welfare programs.
- Japan expands in East Asia.
- World War II breaks out.

TERMS & NAMES

For each term or name below, briefly explain its connection to world history from 1919 to 1939.

1. Albert Einstein
2. Sigmund Freud
3. Weimar Republic
4. New Deal
5. fascism
6. Benito Mussolini
7. Adolf Hitler
8. appeasement
9. Francisco Franco
10. Munich Conference

MAIN IDEAS

Postwar Uncertainty Section 1 (pages 463–469)

11. What effect did Einstein's theory of relativity and Freud's theory of the unconscious have on the public? (10.6.4)
12. What advances were made in transportation and communication in the 1920s and 1930s? (10.6.4)

A Worldwide Depression Section 2 (pages 470–475)

13. Why was the Weimar Republic considered weak? (10.8.2)
14. What caused the stock market crash of 1929? (10.8.2)

Fascism Rises in Europe Section 3 (pages 476–480)

15. For what political and economic reasons did the Italians turn to Mussolini? (10.7.3)
16. What beliefs and goals did Hitler express in *Mein Kampf*? (10.7.3)

Aggressors Invade Nations Section 4 (pages 481–485)

17. How did Japan plan to solve its economic problems? (10.8.1)
18. Why was Germany's reoccupation of the Rhineland a significant turning point toward war? (10.8.1)

CRITICAL THINKING

1. **USING YOUR NOTES**
ECONOMICS Use a sequence graphic to identify the events that led to the stock market collapse. (10.6.2)

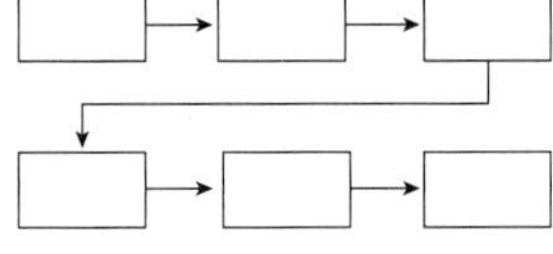

2. **MAKING INFERENCES**
POWER AND AUTHORITY What were the advantages and disadvantages of being under Fascist rule? (10.7.3)
3. **DRAWING CONCLUSIONS**
What weaknesses made the League of Nations an ineffective force for peace in the 1920s and 1930s? (10.8.2)
4. **SYNTHESIZING**
SCIENCE AND TECHNOLOGY How did the scientific and technological revolutions of the 1920s help set the stage for transportation in the United States today? (CST 2)
5. **HYPOTHESIZING**
What might have been the outcome if Great Britain, France, and other European nations had not chosen to appease German, Italian, and Japanese aggression? (10.8.2)

CRITICAL THINKING

Answers will vary.

1. stock prices high; investors sell stocks; prices fall; panic develops; prices plunge further; stock market crashes
2. Advantages—strong leadership, end to social unrest, government put people back to work; Disadvantages—only one political party, no democracy, rights limited, censorship, complete loss of civil rights for certain groups
3. no armed forces to stop aggression, weakened by lack of U.S. membership, did not represent all the world's powers
4. Car and plane travel are routine, allowing people to commute to work, relocate, and travel for pleasure.
5. War might have been avoided.

Use the quotation from a live radio report during the Munich Conference and your knowledge of world history to answer questions 1 and 2.
Additional Test Practice, pp. S1–S33

PRIMARY SOURCE

It took the Big Four [France, Britain, Italy, and Germany] just five hours and twenty-five minutes here in Munich today to dispel the clouds of war and come to an agreement over the partition of Czechoslovakia. There is to be no European war. . . the price of that peace is, roughly, the ceding by Czechoslovakia of the Sudeten territory to Herr Hitler's Germany. The German Führer gets what he wanted, only he has to wait a little longer for it.

WILLIAM SHIRER, quoted in *The Strenuous Decade*

1. Why did France, Britain, and Italy agree to give the Sudeten territory to Germany? (10.8.2)
   A. to provoke war
   B. to avoid war
   C. to make Czechoslovakia happy
   D. to make Czechoslovakia unhappy

2. How were the expectations expressed in the radio report overturned by reality? (10.8.2)
   A. Czechoslovakia refused to give the Sudeten territory to Hitler.
   B. Hitler did not get what he wanted.
   C. The Big Four didn't come to an agreement over Czechoslovakia.
   D. Europe was not saved from war.

Use the photograph of Adolf Hitler and your knowledge of world history to answer question 3.

3. Why do you think Hitler had his photograph taken with this little girl? (10.8.4)
   A. to demonstrate his power
   B. to frighten his enemies
   C. to make him appear more human
   D. to demonstrate his hatred of Jews

INTEGRATED TECHNOLOGY

TEST PRACTICE Go to **classzone.com**
- Diagnostic tests
- Strategies
- Tutorials
- Additional practice

ALTERNATIVE ASSESSMENT

1. **Interact *with* History** (10.8.4)
   On page 462, you chose a candidate to support in German elections in the early 1930s. Now that you have read the chapter, did what you read confirm your decision? Why or why not? Would the candidate you selected have a good or bad effect on the rest of the world? Discuss your opinions with a small group.

2.  **WRITING ABOUT HISTORY** (Writing 2.4.b)
   Write a **radio script** for a report on a speech given by Hitler or Mussolini. Imagine that you have just seen the dictator deliver the speech and you want to share your impressions with the public in your broadcast. Be sure to
   - summarize the main ideas of the speech.
   - describe the speaker's gestures and facial expressions.
   - provide phrases that demonstrate the emotional power of the speech.
   - convey the public's response to the speech.
   - offer your opinion of the speech and speaker.

INTEGRATED TECHNOLOGY

NetExplorations: Life in the 1920s (10.6.4)
Go to *NetExplorations* at **classzone.com** to learn more about life in the 1920s. Use your research to create a Web page on films from that era. Consider including
- reviews of the films, including a positive or negative recommendation.
- background information about silent films.
- biographical information about the stars and directors of the films.
- stills and clips from the films.
- a comparison between films of the 1920s and modern films.

STANDARDS-BASED ASSESSMENT

1. The correct answer is letter **B**. Europeans hoped to avoid war by giving Hitler what he wanted. Letter **A** is incorrect because Europeans did not want to go to war. Letters **C** and **D** are incorrect because the other European powers were not concerned with Czechoslovakia's reaction.
2. The correct answer is letter **D**. The unchecked aggression of the Axis Powers drew Europe into World War II. Letter **A** is incorrect because Czechoslovakia was powerless against Germany. Letter **B** is incorrect because Hitler did get what he wanted. Letter **C** is incorrect because the Big Four did come to an agreement about Czechoslovakia.
3. The correct answer is letter **C**. The photograph suggests that Hitler loves children and they love him.

Formal Assessment
- Chapter Tests, Forms A, B, and C, pp. 265–276

California Test Generator CD-ROM
- Chapter Tests, Forms A, B, and C (English and Spanish)

ALTERNATIVE ASSESSMENT

1. Supported first candidate—may withdraw support based on totalitarian rule and great suffering it meant for Germans and their enemies; Supported second candidate—may choose to support first candidate based on Hitler's rebuilding German economy and uniting the country
2. **Rubric** Radio scripts should
   - summarize the speech.
   - explain its emotional appeal.
   - describe the speaker's style.
   - describe the audience's response.
   - comment on the speaker's message.

INTEGRATED TECHNOLOGY

Rubric Web sites should
- present reviews of several movies from the 1920s.
- include stills and clips from the films.
- provide information about each film's director and stars.
- compare these films with modern ones.

CHAPTER 16 PLANNING GUIDE

World War II, 1939–1945

CHAPTER RESOURCES	COPYMASTERS	ASSESSMENT
CHAPTER OVERVIEW During World War II, the Allied forces defeated the Axis powers, the Jewish people suffered through the Holocaust, and Europe and Japan were left physically and economically devastated by the war.	**In-Depth Resources: Unit 4** • Building Vocabulary, p. 74 **Chapters in Brief** (in English and Spanish) **Block Schedule Pacing Guide**	**Chapter Assessment,** pp. 518–519 **Formal Assessment** • Chapter Tests, Forms A, B, and C, pp. 282–293 **Test Generator** **Integrated Assessment Book** **Online Test Practice**
SECTION 1 **Hitler's Lightning War** pp. 491–496 **OBJECTIVE** Describe how Germany overran much of Europe and North Africa.	**In-Depth Resources: Unit 4** • Guided Reading, p. 69 • Primary Source: from *Berlin Diary,* p. 78 • History Makers: Charles de Gaulle, p. 85; Winston Churchill, p. 86 • Reteaching Activity, p. 88 **Reading Study Guide,** p. 167	**Section 1 Assessment,** p. 496 **Formal Assessment** • Section Quiz, p. 277 **California Daily Standards Practice Transparencies,** TT122
SECTION 2 **Japan's Pacific Campaign** pp. 497–501 **OBJECTIVE** Explain how the Japanese expanded their power in the Pacific.	**In-Depth Resources: Unit 4** • Guided Reading, p. 70 • Geography Application: The Fall of Singapore, p. 76 • Reteaching Activity, p. 89 **Reading Study Guide,** p. 169	**Section 2 Assessment,** p. 501 **Formal Assessment** • Section Quiz, p. 278 **California Daily Standards Practice Transparencies,** TT123
SECTION 3 **The Holocaust** pp. 502–505 **OBJECTIVE** Describe the results of the "Final Solution."	**In-Depth Resources: Unit 4** • Guided Reading, p. 71 • Primary Source: from *Diary,* p. 80 • Literature: from *Night,* p. 82 • Reteaching Activity, p. 90 **Reading Study Guide,** p. 171	**Section 3 Assessment,** p. 505 **Formal Assessment** • Section Quiz, p. 279 **California Daily Standards Practice Transparencies,** TT124
SECTION 4 **The Allied Victory** pp. 506–513 **OBJECTIVE** Summarize the Allied campaigns and the events that led to surrender.	**In-Depth Resources: Unit 4** • Guided Reading, p. 72 • Skillbuilder Practice, p. 75 • Primary Sources: from *Farewell to Manzanar,* p. 79; from *Hiroshima,* p. 81 • Reteaching Activity, p. 91 **Reading Study Guide,** p. 173	**Section 4 Assessment,** p. 513 **Formal Assessment** • Section Quiz, p. 280 **California Daily Standards Practice Transparencies,** TT125
SECTION 5 **Europe and Japan in Ruins** pp. 514–517 **OBJECTIVE** Compare postwar governments in Europe and Japan.	**In-Depth Resources: Unit 4** • Guided Reading, p. 73 • Connections Across Time, p. 87 • Reteaching Activity, p. 92 **Reading Study Guide,** p. 175 **Case Study 9: Mexico and Japan,** p. 114	**Section 5 Assessment,** p. 517 **Formal Assessment** • Section Quiz, p. 281 **California Daily Standards Practice Transparencies,** TT126

INTEGRATED TECHNOLOGY

- eEdition Plus Online
- EasyPlanner Plus Online
- eTest Plus Online

 **Audio CDs**
- Voices from the Past
- Reading Study Guides

CD-ROMs
- eEdition
- Power Presentations
- EasyPlanner
- Electronic Library of Primary Sources
- Test Generator

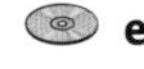 **eEdition CD-ROM**

 **Geography Transparencies**
- GT32 The Battle of Britain, 1940–1941

 **Electronic Library of Primary Sources**
- from "Blood, Toil, Tears, and Sweat"

 **classzone.com**

 **eEdition CD-ROM**

Electronic Library of Primary Sources
- from "Japanese Attack Sinks HMS *Repulse*"

 **classzone.com**

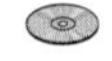 **eEdition CD-ROM**

 **World Art And Cultures Transparencies**
- AT70 German and American propaganda posters

 **classzone.com**

 **eEdition CD-ROM**

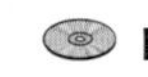 **Electronic Library of Primary Sources**
- from Testimony on Atomic Energy

 **Patterns of Interaction Video Series**
- Modern and Medieval Weapons

  **classzone.com**

 **Critical Thinking Transparencies**
- CT32 Causes and Effects of World War II
- CT68 Chapter 32 Visual Summary

 **World Art And Cultures Transparencies**
- AT71 *Liberation*

Electronic Library of Primary Sources
- from Affidavit Given at Nuremberg, 1946

OVERVIEW OF CALIFORNIA RESOURCES

	Section 1	Section 2	Section 3	Section 4	Section 5
California Reading Toolkit	p. L70	p. L71	p. L72	p. L73	p. L74
California Modified Lesson Plans for English Learners	p. 135	p. 137	p. 139	p. 141	p. 143
California Daily Standards Practice Transparencies	TT62	TT63	TT64	TT65	TT66
California Standards Enrichment Workbook	pp. 77–78, 83–84, 85–86, 89–90	pp. 83–84, 85–86, 89–90	pp. 85–86, 87–88, 89–90	pp. 83–84, 85–86, 91–92	pp. 85–86, 89–90
California Standards Planner and Lesson Plans	p. L131	p. L133	p. L135	p. L137	p. L139
California Online Test Practice	classzone. com	classzone. com	classzone. com	classzone. com	classzone. com
California Test Generator CD-ROM					
California Easy Planner CD-ROM					
California eEdition CD-ROM					

Chart Key:

 Pupil's Edition
 Teacher's Edition
Overhead Transparency
 Block Scheduling
 Copymaster
 Audio Library
 CD-ROM
Internet
 Video

NO TIME?

If you do not have time to teach this chapter in full, assign the **Chapter in Brief** (also available in Spanish).

Previewing Resources for Differentiated Instruction

ENGLISH LEARNERS: Resources in Spanish

In-Depth Resources in Spanish
- Guided Reading Ⓐ
- Skillbuilder Practice: Following Chronological Order Ⓑ
- Geography Application: The Fall of Singapore

Chapters in Brief

Reading Study Guide Ⓒ

Reading Study Guide Audio CD

Test Generator CD-ROM
- Chapter Test, Forms A, B, and C

Plus

Modified Lesson Plans for English Learners

Multi-Language Glossary of Social Studies Terms

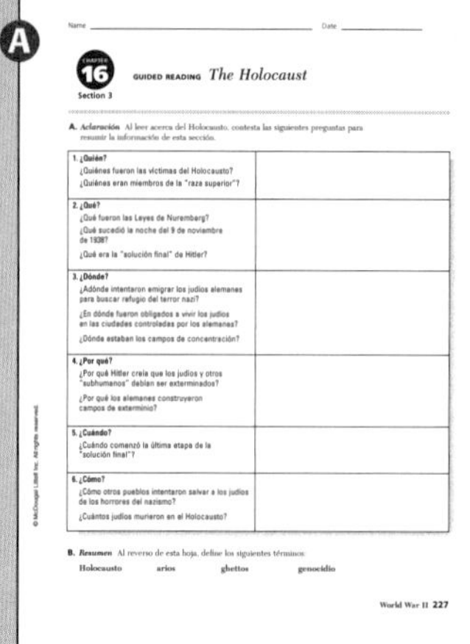
CHAPTER 16 Section 3 GUIDED READING *The Holocaust*

World War II 227

CHAPTER 16 Section 4 SKILLBUILDER PRACTICE *Seguimiento de orden cronológico*

230 Unit 4, Chapter 16

STRUGGLING READERS

In-Depth Resources: Unit 4
- Guided Reading Ⓐ
- Building Vocabulary
- Skillbuilder Practice: Following Chronological Order
- Geography Application: The Fall of Singapore Ⓑ
- Reteaching Activities

Chapters in Brief

Reading Study Guide Ⓒ

Reading Study Guide Audio CD

Formal Assessment
- Chapter Test, Form A

Plus

Reading Toolkit

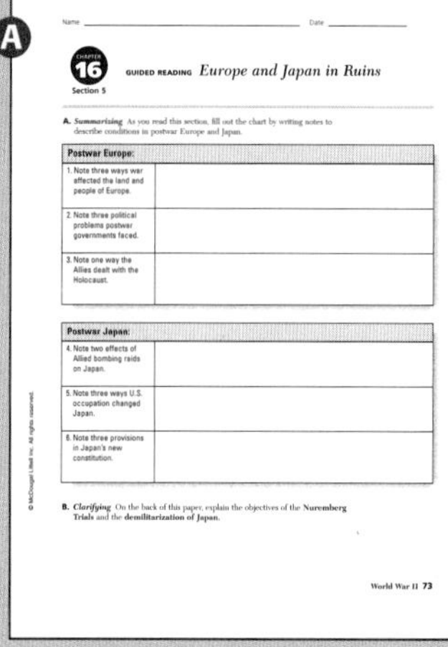
CHAPTER 16 Section 5 GUIDED READING *Europe and Japan in Ruins*

World War II 73

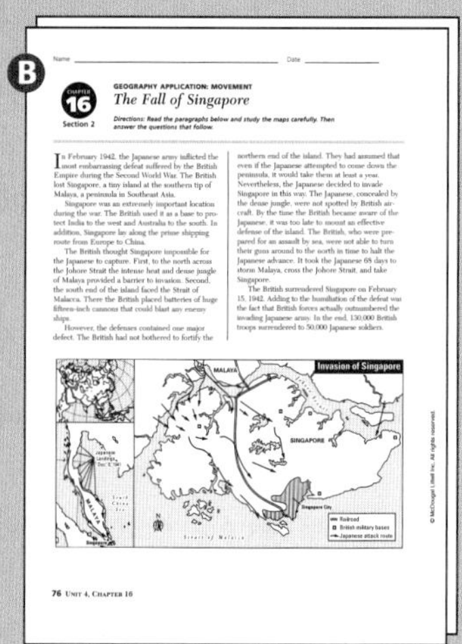
CHAPTER 16 Section 2 GEOGRAPHY APPLICATION: MOVEMENT *The Fall of Singapore*

76 Unit 4, Chapter 16

GIFTED AND TALENTED STUDENTS

In-Depth Resources: Unit 4
- Primary Sources: from *Berlin Diary;* from *The Diary of a Young Girl* Ⓐ; from *Farewell to Manzanar;* from *Hiroshima*
- History Makers: Charles de Gaulle; Winston Churchill
- Literature: from *Night*
- Connections Across Time and Cultures: Two World Wars Ⓑ

Electronic Library of Primary Sources
- from "Blood, Toil, Tears, and Sweat"
- from "Japanese Attack Sinks HMS *Repulse*"
- from Testimony Before the Special Senate Committee on Atomic Energy
- from Affidavit Given at Nuremberg, 1946

Formal Assessment
- Chapter Test, Form C Ⓒ

CHAPTER 16 Section 3 PRIMARY SOURCE from *The Diary of a Young Girl* by Anne Frank

80 Unit 4, Chapter 16

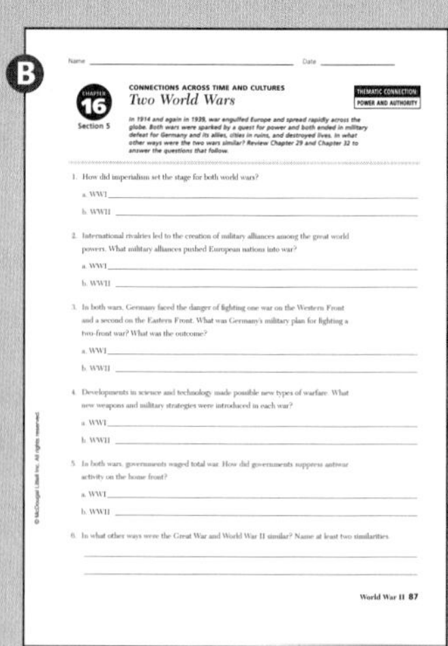
CHAPTER 16 Section 5 CONNECTIONS ACROSS TIME AND CULTURES *Two World Wars*

World War II 87

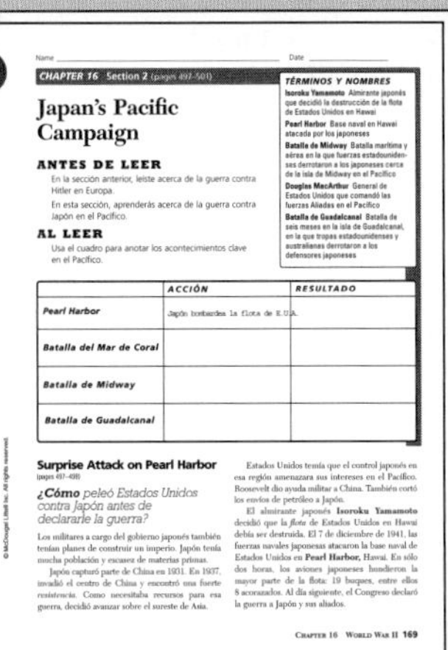

Activities in the Teacher's Edition for English Learners

- Rescue at Dunkirk, p. 493
- Understanding Key Events, p. 500
- Analyzing German and American Propaganda, p. 503
- Report from Stalingrad, p. 507
- Persuading Americans to Help Displaced Persons, p. 515

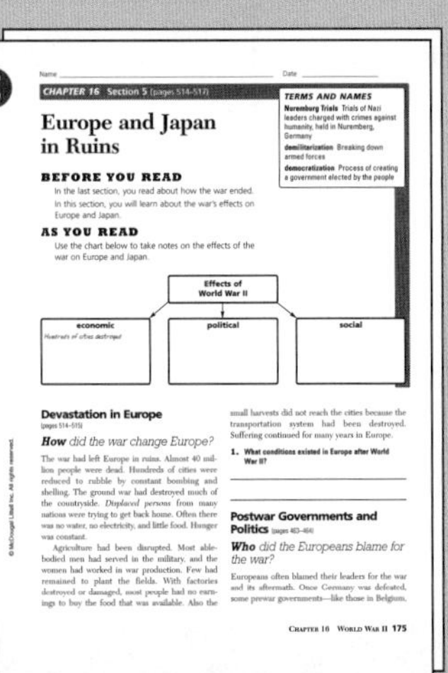

Activities in the Teacher's Edition for Struggling Readers

- Charting the War on the Eastern Front, p. 494
- Understanding Geography in the Battle for Singapore, p. 499
- A Chronology of the Holocaust, p. 504
- Creating Posters for the Home Front, p. 508

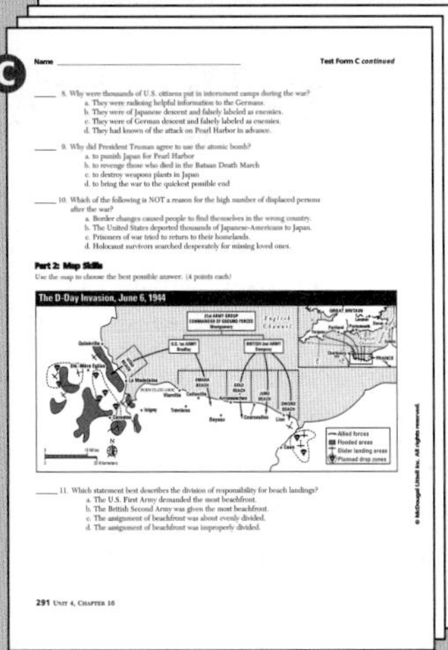

Activities in the Teacher's Edition for Gifted and Talented Students

- Recognizing the Value of War Technology, p. 492
- Comparing Reactions to Japanese Expansion, p. 498
- Debating Reparations for Internees, p. 509
- Comparing the World Wars, p. 516

INTEGRATED TECHNOLOGY

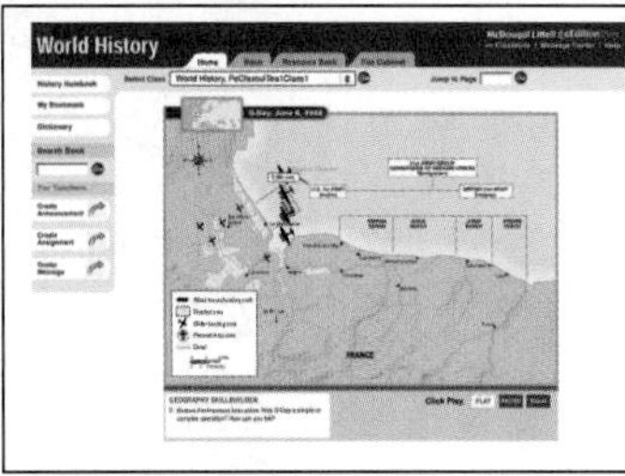

eEdition
- Interactive Visuals
- Interactive Maps
- Interactive Primary Sources

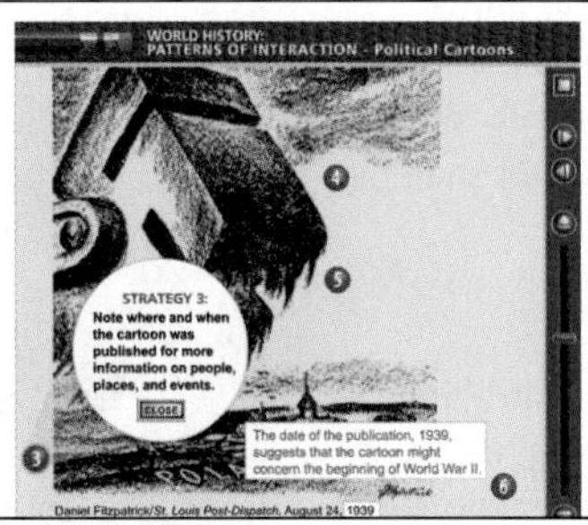

classzone.com
- Research Links
- Internet Activities
- Primary Sources
- Chapter Quiz
- Current Events

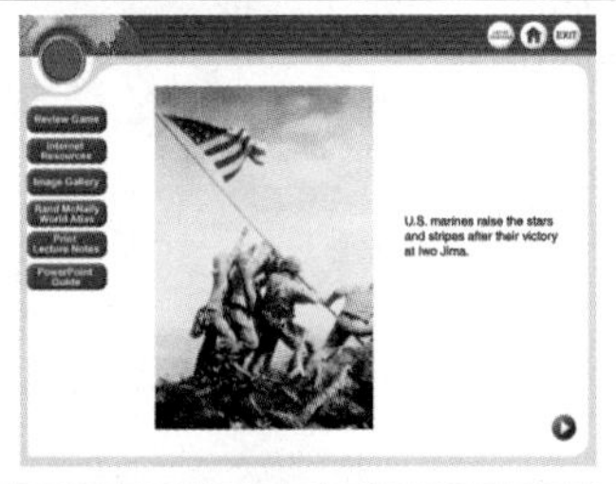

Power Presentations CD-ROM
- Lecture Notes
- Image Gallery
- Chapter Review Game

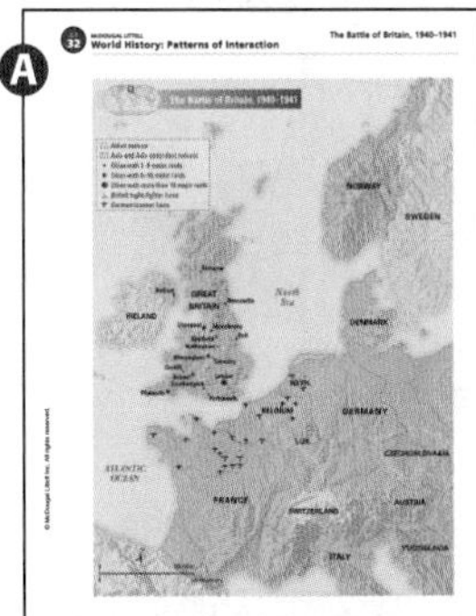

Critical Thinking Transparencies
- CT32 Causes and Effects of World War II
- CT68 Chapter 32 Visual Summary

Geography Transparencies
- GT32 The Battle of Britain, 1940–1941 (A)

World Art and Cultures Transparencies
- AT70 German and American propaganda posters
- AT71 *Liberation*

Test Practice Transparencies TT122–TT126

Test Generator CD-ROM

EasyPlanner CD-ROM

Voices from the Past Audio CD

Online Test Practice

Electronic Library of Primary Sources

Patterns of Interaction Video Series

CHAPTER 16 • OBJECTIVE

Analyze the causes and results of World War II.

Previewing Main Ideas

Discuss the roles of aggressive ideology, powerful weapons, and an educated workforce in determining the military power of a country. These traits influenced the outcome of World War II and continue to shape politics today.

Accessing Prior Knowledge

Ask students what they know about World War II and how they learned it. Discuss the importance of family stories, movies, and television shows in shaping views of the past.

Geography *Answers*

EMPIRE BUILDING They controlled all or part of France, Luxembourg, Belgium, the Netherlands, Germany, Liechtenstein, Austria, Italy, Denmark, Norway, Finland, Estonia, Latvia, Lithuania, Poland, Czechoslovakia, Hungary, Yugoslavia, Albania, Romania, Bulgaria, Greece, Tunisia, Morocco, Libya, Egypt, and the Soviet Union. (They also controlled other countries not shown on this map—Japan, Korea, Manchuria, Burma, Thailand, French Indochina, Malaya, the Dutch East Indies, and New Guinea.)

SCIENCE AND TECHNOLOGY Great Britain is an island, so it relied on shipping of troops and supplies, and submarines threatened its ships.

ECONOMICS The United States was located far from the fighting, so its factories and transportation routes were not under constant threat of bombing as European factories were.

CHAPTER 16

World War II, 1939–1945

Previewing Main Ideas

EMPIRE BUILDING Germany, Italy, and Japan tried to build empires. They began their expansion by conquering other nations and dominating them politically and economically.

Geography *What areas did the Axis powers control at the height of their power?*

SCIENCE AND TECHNOLOGY Far-reaching developments in science and technology changed the course of World War II. Improvements in aircraft, tanks, and submarines and the development of radar and the atomic bomb drastically altered the way wars were fought.

Geography *Why might submarines have been a key weapon for the Axis powers in their fight against Great Britain?*

ECONOMICS Fighting the Axis terror weakened the economies of Great Britain, the Soviet Union, and other European countries. In contrast, when the United States entered the war, its economy grew sharply. The strength of the American economy bolstered the Allied war effort.

Geography *In terms of location, why was the American economy able to function at a high level while the European economies struggled?*

INTEGRATED TECHNOLOGY

eEdition
- Interactive Maps
- Interactive Visuals
- Interactive Primary Sources

VIDEO *Patterns of Interaction: Modern and Medieval Weapons*

INTERNET RESOURCES
Go to classzone.com for:
- Research Links
- Internet Activities
- Primary Sources
- Chapter Quiz
- Maps
- Test Practice
- Current Events

EUROPE AND THE MEDITERRANEAN

Sept. 1939 Germany invades Poland; France and Great Britain declare war on Germany. (political cartoon) ▼

June 1940 France surrenders to Germany; Battle of Britain begins.

June 1941 Germans invade Soviet Union.

1939 1940 1941

PACIFIC

Dec. 1941 ◄ Japan attacks Pearl Harbor.

488

TIME LINE DISCUSSION

Explain that World War II was the most devastating and influential conflict in Western history. The two coalitions in the war were the Axis Powers (Germany, Italy, and Japan) and the Allies (Great Britain, France, the United States, and the Soviet Union).

1. How long did World War II last in Europe? *(six years)*
2. How long after France declared war on Germany did France surrender? *(about nine months)*
3. The United States and the Soviet Union joined the Allies in 1941. What happened to each of these countries in that year? *(Each was attacked by a member of the Axis.)*
4. On the Pacific time line, how is the event for December 1941 unlike the other four events? *(It is the only one that is not a defeat for Japan.)*
5. Which event on the Europe and the Mediterranean time line indicates that the Allies had begun to go on the offensive? *(The Allies invade North Africa in November 1942)*
6. How long after Japan attacked Pearl Harbor did it surrender? *(four years)*
7. Why was February 1943 a bad month for the Axis powers? *(The Germans and the Japanese each suffered a major defeat.)*

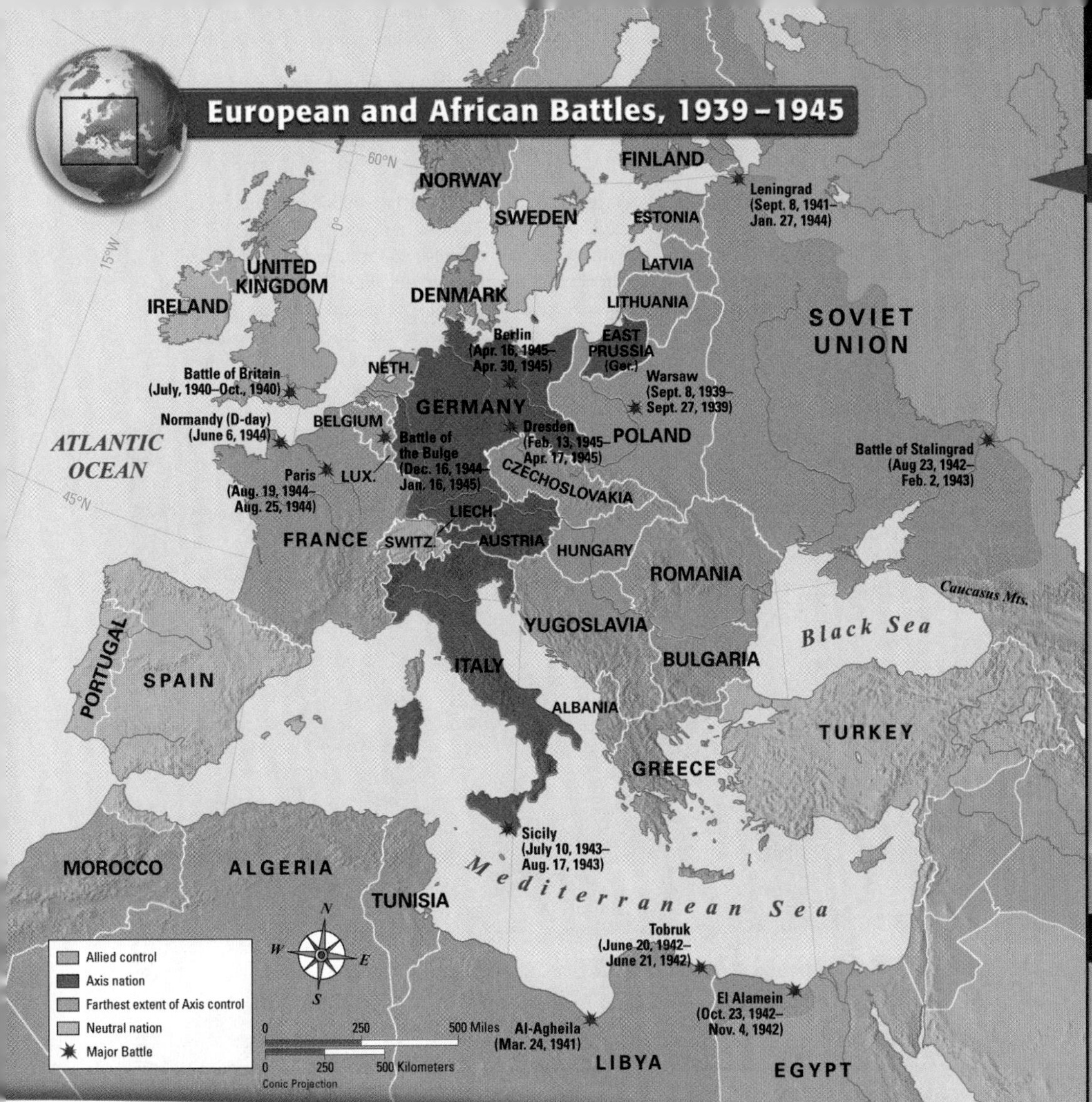

European and African Battles, 1939–1945
60°N
15°W
0°
45°N
NORWAY
FINLAND
SWEDEN
ESTONIA
LATVIA
LITHUANIA
Leningrad (Sept. 8, 1941–Jan. 27, 1944)
UNITED KINGDOM
IRELAND
DENMARK
SOVIET UNION
Berlin (Apr. 16, 1945–Apr. 30, 1945)
EAST PRUSSIA (Ger.)
Warsaw (Sept. 8, 1939–Sept. 27, 1939)
NETH.
Battle of Britain (July, 1940–Oct., 1940)
Normandy (D-day) (June 6, 1944)
BELGIUM
GERMANY
Dresden (Feb. 13, 1945–Apr. 17, 1945)
POLAND
ATLANTIC OCEAN
Battle of the Bulge (Dec. 16, 1944–Jan. 16, 1945)
Paris (Aug. 19, 1944–Aug. 25, 1944)
LUX.
CZECHOSLOVAKIA
Battle of Stalingrad (Aug 23, 1942–Feb. 2, 1943)
LIECH.
FRANCE
SWITZ.
AUSTRIA
HUNGARY
ROMANIA
Caucasus Mts.
Black Sea
PORTUGAL
SPAIN
YUGOSLAVIA
ITALY
BULGARIA
ALBANIA
TURKEY
GREECE
Sicily (July 10, 1943–Aug. 17, 1943)
MOROCCO
ALGERIA
TUNISIA
Mediterranean Sea
Tobruk (June 20, 1942–June 21, 1942)
El Alamein (Oct. 23, 1942–Nov. 4, 1942)
Al-Agheila (Mar. 24, 1941)
LIBYA
EGYPT
N
S
E
W
Allied control
Axis nation
Farthest extent of Axis control
Neutral nation
Major Battle
0 250 500 Miles
0 250 500 Kilometers
Conic Projection

Nov. 1942
Allies invade North Africa.

Feb. 1943
Germans surrender at Stalingrad.

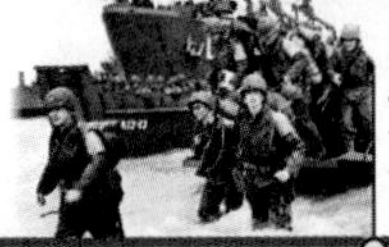

June 1944
◀ D-Day invasion takes place.

May 1945
Germany surrenders.

1942 1943 1944 1945

June 1942
Allies defeat Japan at Battle of Midway.

Feb. 1943
Allies defeat Japan at Guadalcanal.

Oct. 1944
Japanese suffer devastating defeat at the Battle of Leyte Gulf.

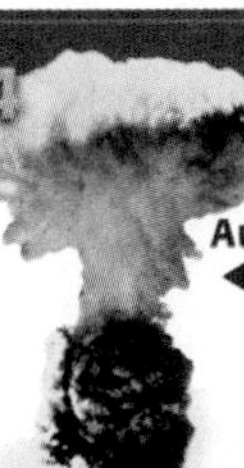

Aug.–Sept. 1945
◀ Allies use atomic bombs; Japan surrenders.

History from Visuals

Interpreting the Map

Ask students to note the major European and African battles of World War II. Where did most major battles occur? *(Possible Answers: Most occurred close to water, either on a major river or near the Mediterranean Sea or the Atlantic Ocean. Most occurred in a strip of northern Europe between southern Britain and Poland. Most were fought in large cities.)* Which of these generalizations is most significant? Why? *(Possible Answer: Fighting in cities suggests that civilians were important in the war.)*

Extension Compare this map with a climate map. How do the climates of Leningrad, Stalingrad, and El Alamein differ? *(Leningrad and Stalingrad are colder; El Alamein is more moderate but much drier.)*

More About . . .

The Geography of Battles

The spatial distribution of battles in the two world wars varied greatly. In World War I, most battles occurred on the Eastern Front or the Western Front. In World War II, troops were more mobile, so the battles were more spread out and more destructive.

RECOMMENDED RESOURCES

Books for the Teacher

Cohen, Daniel. ***The Manhattan Project.*** Brookfield, CT: Millbrook, 1999.

Miller, Nathan. ***War at Sea: A Naval History of World War II.*** New York: Scribner, 1995.

Books for the Student

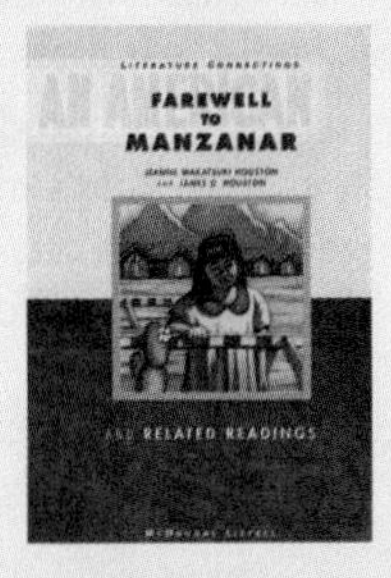

LITERATURE CONNECTIONS
FAREWELL TO MANZANAR
AND RELATED READINGS

McDougal Littell Literature Connections. Houston, Jeanne Wakatsuki and James D. Houston. ***Farewell to Manzanar (with related readings).*** 1998.

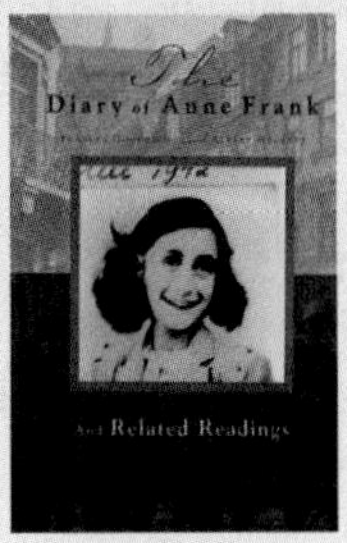

The Diary of Anne Frank
and Related Readings

McDougal Littell Literature Connections. Goodrich, Frances, and Albert Hackett. ***The Diary of Anne Frank (with related readings).*** 1997. Pulitzer Prize–winning play based on the famous diary.

McDougal Littell Nextext. ***World War II.*** Features the major people and events of this devastating conflict.

Videos and Software

The Atomic Bomb VHS. Ambrose Video, 1995. 800-526-4663.

Stories from the Warsaw Ghetto. CD-ROM. Library Video Company, 1997.

Interact *with* History

Objectives
- Set the stage for studying World War II.
- Help students recognize the hard decisions facing people as World War II began.

EXAMINING *the* ISSUES

Possible Answers
- Students may say that they would support participation in a war if their country had been directly attacked or oppose participation if they believed the cause was not just.
- Civilians provide the weapons, food, and other supplies that soldiers need.

Discussion
Tell students that attitudes about the causes and results of World War I made many people reluctant to participate in another war. Discuss whether people had learned the lessons of history accurately. *(Yes—It made sense to try to avoid another world war. No—It would be a mistake to ignore attacks on an ally.)*

Interact *with* History

Under what circumstances is war justified?

Every day your newspaper carries stories of the latest bombing raids on London and other British cities. The photographs of the devastation are shocking. As you read the stories and view the photographs, you wonder what the United States should do to help Great Britain, its longtime ally. The editorial pages of the newspapers ask the same question. Should the United States stand aside and let the European nations settle the issues themselves? Should it offer help to Great Britain in the form of arms and other supplies? Or should the United States join Britain in its struggle against the Axis powers?

▲ A German bombing raid on London during the Battle of Britain

EXAMINING *the* ISSUES

- **What circumstances would lead you to support or oppose your country's participation in a war?**
- **How are civilians sometimes as much a part of a war effort as soldiers?**

As a class, discuss these questions. In your discussion, weigh the arguments for and against fighting. As you read about World War II, think about the role that civilians play in a situation of total war. Think also about the hard moral choices that people often face in times of war.

490 Chapter 16

WHY STUDY WORLD WAR II?

- Principles that united the Allies, such as democracy and international cooperation, are widely supported today.
- Japan still lives under the constitution imposed on it after World War II—including its limits on the military.
- The Jewish state of Israel was created shortly after the war.
- The war caused Europeans to build multinational institutions to promote security. These institutions have made Europe more peaceful and prosperous.
- The use of nuclear weapons on Hiroshima and Nagasaki opened a new age in warfare and unleashed a fear that continues to exist.
- The war left the United States and the Soviet Union as the world's most powerful countries, a change in the balance of power that affected world politics for the following 50 years.

Adolf Hitler on his 50th birthday, April 20, 1939

Poster encouraging Americans to buy war bonds

1 Hitler's Lightning War

MAIN IDEA	WHY IT MATTERS NOW	TERMS & NAMES
EMPIRE BUILDING Using the sudden mass attack called the blitzkrieg, Germany overran much of Europe and North Africa.	Hitler's actions set off World War II. The results of the war still affect the politics and economics of today's world.	• nonaggression pact • blitzkrieg • Charles de Gaulle • Winston Churchill • Battle of Britain • Erwin Rommel • Atlantic Charter

SETTING THE STAGE During the 1930s, Hitler played on the hopes and fears of the Western democracies. Each time the Nazi dictator grabbed new territory, he would declare an end to his demands. Peace seemed guaranteed—until Hitler moved again. After his moves into the Rhineland, Austria, and Czechoslovakia, Hitler turned his eyes to Poland. After World War I, the Allies had cut out the Polish Corridor from German territory to give Poland access to the sea. In 1939, Hitler demanded that the Polish Corridor be returned to Germany.

Germany Sparks a New War in Europe

At this point, as you recall from Chapter 15, Soviet dictator Joseph Stalin signed a ten-year **nonaggression pact** with Hitler. After being excluded from the Munich Conference, Stalin was not eager to join with the West. Also, Hitler had promised him territory. In a secret part of the pact, Germany and the Soviet Union agreed to divide Poland between them. They also agreed that the USSR could take over Finland and the Baltic countries of Lithuania, Latvia, and Estonia.

Germany's Lightning Attack After signing this nonaggression pact, Hitler quickly moved ahead with plans to conquer Poland. His surprise attack took place at dawn on September 1, 1939. German tanks and troop trucks rumbled across the Polish border. At the same time, German aircraft and artillery began a merciless bombing of Poland's capital, Warsaw.

France and Great Britain declared war on Germany on September 3. But Poland fell some time before those nations could make any military response. After his victory, Hitler annexed the western half of Poland. That region had a large German population.

The German invasion of Poland was the first test of Germany's newest military strategy—the **blitzkrieg** (BLIHTS•kreeg), or "lightning war." It involved using fast-moving airplanes and tanks, followed by massive infantry forces, to take enemy defenders by surprise and quickly overwhelm them. In the case of Poland, the strategy worked.

The Soviets Make Their Move On September 17, Stalin sent Soviet troops to occupy the eastern half of Poland. Stalin then moved to annex countries to the north of Poland. Lithuania, Latvia, and Estonia fell without a struggle, but Finland resisted. In November, Stalin sent nearly one million Soviet troops into

CALIFORNIA STANDARDS

10.7.3 Analyze the rise, aggression, and human costs of totalitarian regimes (Fascist and Communist) in Germany, Italy, and the Soviet Union, noting especially their common and dissimilar traits.

10.8.3 Identify and locate the Allied and Axis powers on a map and discuss the major turning points of the war, the principal theaters of conflict, key strategic decisions, and the resulting war conferences and political resolutions, with emphasis on the importance of geographic factors.

10.8.4 Describe the political, diplomatic, and military leaders during the war (e.g., Winston Churchill, Franklin Delano Roosevelt, Emperor Hirohito, Adolf Hitler, Benito Mussolini, Joseph Stalin, Douglas MacArthur, Dwight Eisenhower).

10.8.6 Discuss the human costs of the war, with particular attention to the civilian and military losses in Russia, Germany, Britain, the United States, China, and Japan.

TAKING NOTES

Recognizing Effects Use a chart to identify the effects of some of the early events of World War II.

Cause	Effect
First blitzkrieg	
Allies stranded at Dunkirk	
Lend-Lease Act	

LESSON PLAN

OBJECTIVES

- Summarize the events that led to war.
- Describe the fall of France and the Battle of Britain.
- Explain the conflicts in the Mediterranean and on the Eastern Front.
- Describe U.S. aid to the Allies.

1 FOCUS & MOTIVATE

The Nazis attacked rapidly with massive force. Discuss whether recent wars have involved the use of this technique. *(Possible Answer: Air assaults early in the second Gulf War were designed to produce "shock and awe" in the Iraqi ranks.)*

2 INSTRUCT

Germany Sparks a New War in Europe

10.7.3; 10.8.3; 10.8.4

Critical Thinking

- What suggested that the West would not aid the Soviets? *(The West had abandoned an ally, the Czechs, and the Soviets were communists.)*

CALIFORNIA RESOURCES

California Reading Toolkit, p. L70
California Modified Lesson Plans for English Learners, p. 135
California Daily Standards Practice Transparencies, TT62
California Standards Enrichment Workbook, pp. 77–78, 83–84, 85–86, 89–90
California Standards Planner and Lesson Plans, p. L131
California Online Test Practice
California Test Generator CD-ROM
California Easy Planner CD-ROM
California eEdition CD-ROM

SECTION 1 PROGRAM RESOURCES

ALL STUDENTS

In-Depth Resources: Unit 4
- Guided Reading, p. 69
- History Makers: Charles de Gaulle, p. 85; Winston Churchill, p. 86

Formal Assessment
- Section Quiz, p. 277

ENGLISH LEARNERS

In-Depth Resources in Spanish
- Guided Reading, p. 124

Reading Study Guide (Spanish), p. 167
Reading Study Guide Audio CD (Spanish)

STRUGGLING READERS

In-Depth Resources: Unit 4
- Guided Reading, p. 69
- Building Vocabulary, p. 74
- Reteaching Activity, p. 88

Reading Study Guide, p. 167
Reading Study Guide Audio CD

GIFTED AND TALENTED STUDENTS

In-Depth Resources: Unit 4
- Primary Source: from *Berlin Diary,* p. 78

Electronic Library of Primary Sources
- from "Blood, Toil, Tears, and Sweat"

INTEGRATED TECHNOLOGY

eEdition CD-ROM
Voices from the Past Audio CD
Power Presentations CD-ROM
Geography Transparencies
- GT32 The Battle of Britain, 1940–1941

Electronic Library of Primary Sources
- from "Blood, Toil, Tears, and Sweat"

classzone.com

The Fall of France

10.8.3; 10.8.4; 10.8.6

Critical Thinking

- How did the retreat at Dunkirk affect Britain's ability to fight Hitler? *(saved troops to fight later)*
- Do you think that de Gaulle's speech applied to the British who had evacuated at Dunkirk? *(Yes—He resented any refusal to fight Hitler. No—He was speaking only to the French.)*

History from Visuals

Interpreting the Map

Which countries did Germany have to cross water to seize? *(Norway, Finland, Algeria, Tunisia)*

Extension Use the political map of Europe in the textbook atlas to measure Germany's expansion. About how far is Berlin from Leningrad? *(1,000 miles)* from the Spanish border? *(950 miles)* from the Greek coast? *(1,000 miles)*

SKILLBUILDER Answers

1. **Region** France, Belgium, the Netherlands, Denmark, Norway, Czechoslovakia, Austria, Hungary, Yugoslavia, Albania, Greece, Bulgaria, Romania, Poland, Lithuania, Latvia, Estonia, Finland, the Soviet Union
2. **Location** It was centrally located in Europe and could attack in all directions.

INTEGRATED TECHNOLOGY

Interactive This image is available in an interactive format on the eEdition.

Finland. The Soviets expected to win a quick victory, so they were not prepared for winter fighting. This was a crucial mistake.

The Finns were outnumbered and outgunned, but they fiercely defended their country. In the freezing winter weather, soldiers on skis swiftly attacked Soviet positions. In contrast, the Soviets struggled to make progress through the deep snow. The Soviets suffered heavy losses, but they finally won through sheer force of numbers. By March 1940, Stalin had forced the Finns to accept his surrender terms. (A)

MAIN IDEA

Analyzing Motives

(A) What were Stalin's goals in Europe at the beginning of World War II?

A. Possible Answer Stalin aimed at expanding the Soviet Union's territory and power, while keeping his country out of the war.

The Phony War After they declared war on Germany, the French and British had mobilized their armies. They stationed their troops along the Maginot (MAZH•uh•NOH) Line, a system of fortifications along France's border with Germany. There they waited for the Germans to attack—but nothing happened. With little to do, the bored Allied soldiers stared eastward toward the enemy. Equally bored, German soldiers stared back from their Siegfried Line a few miles away. Germans jokingly called it the *sitzkrieg,* or "sitting war." Some newspapers referred to it simply as "the phony war."

Suddenly, on April 9, 1940, the calm ended. Hitler launched a surprise invasion of Denmark and Norway. In just four hours after the attack, Denmark fell. Two months later, Norway surrendered as well. The Germans then began to build bases along the Norwegian and Danish coasts from which they could launch strikes on Great Britain.

The Fall of France

In May of 1940, Hitler began a dramatic sweep through the Netherlands, Belgium, and Luxembourg. This was part of a strategy to strike at France. Keeping the Allies' attention on those countries, Hitler then sent an even larger force of tanks

SKILLBUILDER: Interpreting Maps

1. **Region** *Which countries did Germany invade?*
2. **Location** *In what way was Germany's geographic location an advantage when it was on the offensive in the war?*

DIFFERENTIATING INSTRUCTION: GIFTED AND TALENTED STUDENTS

Recognizing the Value of War Technology

Class Time 30 minutes

Task Researching and reporting on military technology developed during World War II

Purpose To understand how war stimulates technological advances

Instructions Discuss historical examples of new technology that gave a country a military advantage over its rivals. For example, in the 800s B.C., the Assyrians had better iron weapons than their rivals, in the 1300s the Ottoman Turks started using cannon, and in the early 1900s the British pioneered the use of the tank.

Divide students into four groups to research one of the following technologies:

- radar
- decoding devices
- jet propulsion
- rockets

Groups should trace the development, use, and effectiveness of each technology, and then present reports to the class. Discuss whether each technology had an impact on the outcome of a war and whether it affected the ethics of war.

and troops to slice through the Ardennes (ahr•DEHN). This was a heavily wooded area in northern France, Luxembourg, and Belgium. Moving through the forest, the Germans "squeezed between" the Maginot Line. From there, they moved across France and reached the country's northern coast in ten days.

Rescue at Dunkirk After reaching the French coast, the German forces swung north again and joined with German troops in Belgium. By the end of May 1940, the Germans had trapped the Allied forces around the northern French city of Lille (leel). Outnumbered, outgunned, and pounded from the air, the Allies retreated to the beaches of Dunkirk, a French port city near the Belgian border. They were trapped with their backs to the sea.

In one of the most heroic acts of the war, Great Britain set out to rescue the army. It sent a fleet of about 850 ships across the English Channel to Dunkirk. Along with Royal Navy ships, civilian craft—yachts, lifeboats, motorboats, paddle steamers, and fishing boats—joined the rescue effort. From May 26 to June 4, this amateur armada, under heavy fire from German bombers, sailed back and forth from Britain to Dunkirk. The boats carried some 338,000 battle-weary soldiers to safety.

France Falls Following Dunkirk, resistance in France began to crumble. By June 14, the Germans had taken Paris. Accepting the inevitable, French leaders surrendered on June 22, 1940. The Germans took control of the northern part of the country. They left the southern part to a puppet government headed by Marshal Philippe Pétain (pay•TAN), a French hero from World War I. The headquarters of this government was in the city of Vichy (VEESH•ee).

After France fell, **Charles de Gaulle** (duh GOHL), a French general, set up a government-in-exile in London. He committed all his energy to reconquering France. In a radio broadcast from England, de Gaulle called on the people of France to join him in resisting the Germans:

> **PRIMARY SOURCE**
> It is the bounden [obligatory] duty of all Frenchmen who still bear arms to continue the struggle. For them to lay down their arms, to evacuate any position of military importance, or agree to hand over any part of French territory, however small, to enemy control would be a crime against our country.
>
> **GENERAL CHARLES DE GAULLE,** quoted in *Charles de Gaulle: A Biography*

De Gaulle went on to organize the Free French military forces that battled the Nazis until France was liberated in 1944.

The Battle of Britain

With the fall of France, Great Britain stood alone against the Nazis. **Winston Churchill**, the new British prime minister, had already declared that his nation would never give in. In a rousing speech, he proclaimed, "We shall fight on the beaches, we shall fight on the landing grounds, we shall fight in the fields and in the streets . . . we shall never surrender."

Hitler now turned his mind to an invasion of Great Britain. His plan was first to knock out the Royal Air Force (RAF) and then to land more than 250,000 soldiers on England's shores.

History Makers

Winston Churchill
1874–1965

Possibly the most powerful weapon the British had as they stood alone against Hitler's Germany was the nation's prime minister—Winston Churchill. "Big Winnie," Londoners boasted, "was the lad for us."

Although Churchill had a speech defect as a youngster, he grew to become one of the greatest orators of all time. He used all his gifts as a speaker to rally the people behind the effort to crush Germany. In one famous speech he promised that Britain would

> *. . . wage war, by sea, land and air, with all our might and with all the strength that God can give us . . . against a monstrous tyranny.*

INTEGRATED TECHNOLOGY

RESEARCH LINKS For more on Winston Churchill, go to **classzone.com**

More About . . .

Charles de Gaulle

At 6 feet 4 inches, de Gaulle was an imposing figure, and his manner was often arrogant. "I am France," he declared. De Gaulle's arrogance irritated Allied leaders. But he prevailed, and when France was liberated, his resistance movement was recognized as the legitimate government of France.

In-Depth Resources: Unit 4
- History Makers: Charles de Gaulle, p. 85

History Makers

Winston Churchill

When Buckingham Palace was bombed in September 1940, some officials wanted to keep the news quiet. "Stupid fools," Churchill barked. "Spread the news at once! Let the humble people of London know . . . that the King and Queen are sharing their perils with them!"

Electronic Library of Primary Sources
- from "Blood, Toil, Tears, and Sweat"

The Battle of Britain

10.8.3; 10.8.4; 10.8.6

Critical Thinking
- What advantage did the Luftwaffe have over the RAF? *(more planes)*
- How might the German attacks on Britain have strengthened Britain's resistance? *(Attacks on cities inspired the British to fight.)*

Geography Transparencies
- GT32 The Battle of Britain, 1940–1941

DIFFERENTIATING INSTRUCTION: ENGLISH LEARNERS

Reporting on the Rescue at Dunkirk

Class Time 40 minutes

Task Writing a radio or newspaper report about events at Dunkirk

Purpose To improve writing skills and understanding of text

Instructions Divide students into small groups. Have each group reread the subsection entitled "Rescue at Dunkirk." Write definitions or synonyms for difficult words on the board. *(outnumbered = having too many enemies; civilian = not part of an army, navy, or air force; armada = a large group of warships)*

Then have groups write a short radio or newspaper report that describes the events at Dunkirk. Encourage students to use strong verbs and vivid, descriptive language.

Groups should select one member to read the report aloud to the class. Discuss why Dunkirk is considered an example of bravery. *(People who weren't soldiers risked death to rescue threatened troops.)*

Students who need more help should complete the Reading Study Guide activity for this section (also available in Spanish).

CHAPTER 16 Section 1
Hitler's Lightning War
ANTES DE LEER
AL LEER
TÉRMINOS Y NOMBRES

Reading Study Guide: Spanish Translation

Tip for Struggling Readers

"Enigma," the name of the German code, means a statement, situation, or person that is baffling, like a puzzle or a mystery.

More About . . .

The Battle of Britain

During the bombings, a police officer reported on a group he found in an old railway tunnel: "The first thing I heard was a great hollow hubbub, a sort of soughing [sighing] and wailing, as if there were animals down there moaning and crying. And then this terrible stench hit me. It was worse than dead bodies. . . . I stopped. Ahead of me I could see faces peering towards me lit by candles and lanterns. It was like a painting of hell."

The Mediterranean and the Eastern Front

10.8.3

Critical Thinking

- How long had the German-Soviet pact existed when Hitler began planning to invade his ally? *(less than one year)*
- Compare the losses of the Germans and the Soviets at Leningrad and Moscow. *(The Soviets lost more people, especially civilians, but Germany could afford its losses less.)*

▲ A London bus is submerged in a bomb crater after a German air raid.

In the summer of 1940, the Luftwaffe (LOOFT•VAHF•uh), Germany's air force, began bombing Great Britain. At first, the Germans targeted British airfields and aircraft factories. Then, on September 7, 1940, they began focusing on the cities, especially London, to break British morale. Despite the destruction and loss of life, the British did not waver.

Vocabulary *Luftwaffe* is the German word for "air weapon."

The RAF, although badly outnumbered, began to hit back hard. Two technological devices helped turn the tide in the RAF's favor. One was an electronic tracking system known as radar. Developed in the late 1930s, radar could tell the number, speed, and direction of incoming warplanes. The other device was a German code-making machine named Enigma. A complete Enigma machine had been smuggled into Great Britain in the late 1930s. Enigma enabled the British to decode German secret messages. With information gathered by these devices, RAF fliers could quickly launch attacks on the enemy.

To avoid the RAF's attacks, the Germans gave up daylight raids in October 1940 in favor of night bombing. At sunset, the wail of sirens filled the air as Londoners flocked to the subways, which served as air-raid shelters. Some rode out the bombing raids at home in smaller air-raid shelters or basements. This **Battle of Britain** continued until May 10, 1941. Stunned by British resistance, Hitler decided to call off his attacks. Instead, he focused on the Mediterranean and Eastern Europe. The Battle of Britain taught the Allies a crucial lesson. Hitler's attacks could be blocked. **B**

MAIN IDEA
Recognizing Effects
B Why was the outcome of the Battle of Britain important for the Allies?
B. Answer because it taught them that Hitler's attacks could be stopped and turned back

The Mediterranean and the Eastern Front

The stubborn resistance of the British in the Battle of Britain caused a shift in Hitler's strategy in Europe. He decided to deal with Great Britain later. He then turned his attention east to the Mediterranean area and the Balkans—and to the ultimate prize, the Soviet Union.

Axis Forces Attack North Africa Germany's first objective in the Mediterranean region was North Africa, mainly because of Hitler's partner, Mussolini. Despite its alliance with Germany, Italy had remained neutral at the beginning of the war. With Hitler's conquest of France, however, Mussolini knew he had to take action. After declaring war on France and Great Britain, Mussolini moved into France.

Mussolini took his next step in North Africa in September 1940. While the Battle of Britain was raging, he ordered his army to attack British-controlled Egypt. Egypt's Suez Canal was key to reaching the oil fields of the Middle East. Within a week, Italian troops had pushed 60 miles inside Egypt, forcing British units back. Then both sides dug in and waited.

Vocabulary The *Middle East* includes the countries of Southwest Asia and northeast Africa.

Britain Strikes Back Finally, in December, the British struck back. The result was a disaster for the Italians. By February 1941, the British had swept 500 miles across North Africa and had taken 130,000 Italian prisoners. Hitler had to step in to save his Axis partner. To reinforce the Italians, Hitler sent a crack German tank force, the Afrika Korps, under the command of General **Erwin Rommel**. In late March 1941, Rommel's Afrika Korps attacked. Caught by surprise, British forces retreated east to Tobruk, Libya. (See the map on page 489.)

DIFFERENTIATING INSTRUCTION: STRUGGLING READERS

Charting the War on the Eastern Front

Class Time 30 minutes

Task Creating a chart of events leading to the siege of Moscow

Purpose To understand the relationships among key events in the war

Instructions Divide students into pairs. Each pair should create a flow chart tracing events in the Mediterranean and on the Eastern Front leading to the siege of Moscow. Have students display their charts in the classroom. Discuss how students approached the assignment differently. A sample chart is shown here.

Italy attacks Egypt, which is under British control.
↓ British strike back, capturing 130,000 Italian soldiers.
↓ Germany sends General Rommel and tanks to attack British soldiers.
↓
↓

After fierce fighting for Tobruk, the British began to drive Rommel back. By mid-January 1942, Rommel had retreated to where he had started. By June 1942, the tide of battle turned again. Rommel regrouped, pushed the British back across the desert, and seized Tobruk—a shattering loss for the Allies. Rommel's successes in North Africa earned him the nickname "Desert Fox."

The War in the Balkans While Rommel campaigned in North Africa, other German generals were active in the Balkans. Hitler had begun planning to attack his ally, the USSR, as early as the summer of 1940. The Balkan countries of southeastern Europe were key to Hitler's invasion plan. Hitler wanted to build bases in southeastern Europe for the attack on the Soviet Union. He also wanted to make sure that the British did not interfere.

To prepare for his invasion, Hitler moved to expand his influence in the Balkans. By early 1941, through the threat of force, he had persuaded Bulgaria, Romania, and Hungary to join the Axis powers. Yugoslavia and Greece, which had pro-British governments, resisted. In early April 1941, Hitler invaded both countries. Yugoslavia fell in 11 days. Greece surrendered in 17. In Athens, the Nazis celebrated their victory by raising swastikas on the Acropolis.

Hitler Invades the Soviet Union With the Balkans firmly in control, Hitler could move ahead with Operation Barbarossa, his plan to invade the Soviet Union. Early in the morning of June 22, 1941, the roar of German tanks and aircraft announced the beginning of the invasion. The Soviet Union was not prepared for this attack. Although it had the largest army in the world, its troops were neither well equipped nor well trained.

The invasion rolled on week after week until the Germans had pushed 500 miles inside the Soviet Union. As the Soviet troops retreated, they burned and destroyed everything in the enemy's path. The Russians had used this scorched-earth strategy against Napoleon.

On September 8, German forces put Leningrad under siege. By early November, the city was completely cut off from the rest of the Soviet Union. To force a surrender, Hitler was ready to starve the city's more than 2.5 million inhabitants. German bombs destroyed warehouses where food was stored. Desperately hungry, people began eating cattle and horse feed, as well as cats and dogs and, finally, crows and rats. Nearly one million people died in Leningrad during the winter of 1941–1942. Yet the city refused to fall.

▼ Russian soldiers prepare to attack German lines outside Leningrad.

More About . . .

The Siege of Leningrad

During the siege, as composer Dmitri Shostakovich worked on his Seventh, or "Leningrad," Symphony, he also broadcast appeals to the people to resist the invaders. "When I walk through the city," he said, "a feeling of deep conviction grows within me that Leningrad will always stand, grand and beautiful, on the banks of the Neva . . ." Authorities moved Shostakovich to a safer city, where he finished the symphony. The score was put on microfilm and flown out of the Soviet Union to the West. Years later, the composer wrote that the work was not about the German siege of the city but about the suffering of Leningrad under the terrible Stalinist purges of the 1930s.

COOPERATIVE LEARNING

Comparing and Contrasting Two Leaders

Class Time 45 minutes

Task Reading about Charles de Gaulle and Winston Churchill and creating a chart

Purpose To understand how individual leaders have affected history

Instructions Divide the class into small groups. Have each group read the History Makers activities on Charles de Gaulle and Winston Churchill from the In-Depth Resources book. Then display Critical Thinking transparency CT74, the Compare and Contrast chart. Ask groups to create similar charts comparing and contrasting the two leaders and drawing conclusions about them. Encourage students to consider these factors when creating their charts:

- de Gaulle's and Churchill's family backgrounds
- their successes or failures as students
- their military and political careers
- their personality and character

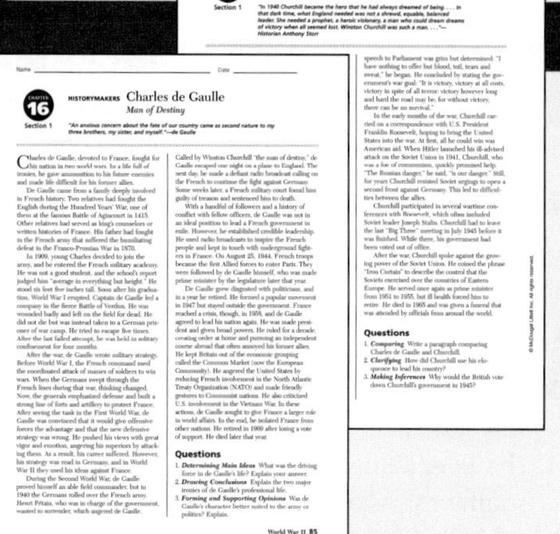
HISTORYMAKERS Winston Churchill
English Bulldog

HISTORYMAKERS Charles de Gaulle
Man of Destiny

In-Depth Resources: Unit 4

The United States Aids Its Allies
10.8.3; 10.8.4

Critical Thinking

- Under what conditions do you think the United States should remain neutral when other countries are fighting? *(Possible Answer: when the conflict does not threaten the United States)*
- Do you think Germany was justified in attacking cargo ships? *(Yes—The ships carried arms for killing Germans. No—The United States was neutral.)*
- The Atlantic Charter upheld the right of people to choose their own government. What wars occurred when people tried to do this? *(Possible Answers: American Revolution, American Civil War, Nigerian Civil War, ongoing conflict in Chechnya)*

3 ASSESS

SECTION 1 ASSESSMENT

Have students work in pairs to answer the questions. Then have them exchange answers and compare their responses.

Formal Assessment
- Section Quiz, p. 277

4 RETEACH

Have students work in small groups to create a time line of major events from 1939 through 1941. Have students compare their time lines and discuss the differences.

In-Depth Resources: Unit 4
- Reteaching Activity, p. 88

Impatient with the progress in Leningrad, Hitler looked to Moscow, the capital and heart of the Soviet Union. A Nazi drive on the capital began on October 2, 1941. By December, the Germans had advanced to the outskirts of Moscow. Soviet General Georgi Zhukov (ZHOO•kuhf) counterattacked. As temperatures fell, the Germans, in summer uniforms, retreated. Ignoring Napoleon's winter defeat 130 years before, Hitler sent his generals a stunning order: "No retreat!" German troops dug in about 125 miles west of Moscow. They held the line against the Soviets until March 1943. Hitler's advance on the Soviet Union gained nothing but cost the Germans 500,000 lives. C

MAIN IDEA

Making Inferences

C What does the fact that German armies were not prepared for the Russian winter indicate about Hitler's expectations for the Soviet campaign?

C. Possible Answer Hitler expected a quick victory in the Soviet Union and did not think that his army would still be in combat by the time winter set in.

The United States Aids Its Allies

Most Americans felt that the United States should not get involved in the war. Between 1935 and 1937, Congress passed a series of Neutrality Acts. The laws made it illegal to sell arms or lend money to nations at war. But President Roosevelt knew that if the Allies fell, the United States would be drawn into the war. In September 1939, he asked Congress to allow the Allies to buy American arms. The Allies would pay cash and then carry the goods on their own ships.

Under the Lend-Lease Act, passed in March 1941, the president could lend or lease arms and other supplies to any country vital to the United States. By the summer of 1941, the U.S. Navy was escorting British ships carrying U.S. arms. In response, Hitler ordered his submarines to sink any cargo ships they met.

Although the United States had not yet entered the war, Roosevelt and Churchill met secretly and issued a joint declaration called the **Atlantic Charter**. It upheld free trade among nations and the right of people to choose their own government. The charter later served as the Allies' peace plan at the end of World War II.

On September 4, a German U-boat fired on a U.S. destroyer in the Atlantic. In response, Roosevelt ordered navy commanders to shoot German submarines on sight. The United States was now involved in an undeclared naval war with Hitler. To almost everyone's surprise, however, the attack that actually drew the United States into the war did not come from Germany. It came from Japan.

SECTION 1 ASSESSMENT

TERMS & NAMES 1. For each term or name, write a sentence explaining its significance.
- nonaggression pact • blitzkrieg • Charles de Gaulle • Winston Churchill • Battle of Britain • Erwin Rommel • Atlantic Charter

USING YOUR NOTES

2. Which of the listed events might be considered a turning point for the Allies? Why? (10.8.3)

Cause	Effect
First blitzkrieg	
Allies stranded at Dunkirk	
Lend-Lease Act	

MAIN IDEAS

3. Why were the early months of World War II referred to as the "phony war"? (10.8.3)
4. Why was Egypt of strategic importance in World War II? (10.8.3)
5. Why did President Franklin Roosevelt want to offer help to the Allies? (10.8.4)

CRITICAL THINKING & WRITING

6. **CLARIFYING** What do you think is meant by the statement that Winston Churchill possibly was Britain's most powerful weapon against Hitler's Germany? (10.8.4)
7. **MAKING INFERENCES** What factors do you think a country's leaders consider when deciding whether to surrender or fight? (10.8.3)
8. **COMPARING** How were Napoleon's invasion of Russia and Hitler's invasion of the Soviet Union similar? (10.8.6)
9. **WRITING ACTIVITY** EMPIRE BUILDING Write a **magazine article** on German conquests in Europe through 1942. (Writing 2.3.b)

CONNECT TO TODAY **PREPARING AN ORAL REPORT**

Conduct research into "stealth" technology, which is designed to evade radar. Use your findings to prepare a brief **oral report** titled "How Stealth Technology Works." (Writing 2.2.f)

ANSWERS

1. nonaggression pact, p. 491 • blitzkrieg, p. 491 • Charles de Gaulle, p. 493 • Winston Churchill, p. 493 • Battle of Britain, p. 494 • Erwin Rommel, p. 494 • Atlantic Charter, p. 496

2. **Sample Answer:** Blitzkrieg—Fall of Poland. Dunkirk—338,000 soldiers saved. Lend-Lease—War goods to Allies. Turning point—Battle of Britain showed that Hitler could be halted.
3. Both sides made preparations for war, but very little action took place.
4. The Suez Canal was the route to the oil of southwest Asia.
5. He feared an Allied defeat would pull the United States into the war.
6. His powerful speeches boosted the morale of the British people.
7. **Possible Answers:** the country's ability to fight, its willingness to accept casualties, the costs of foreign control
8. underestimated the defending army, the problems created by a scorched-earth policy, and the dangers of a Russian winter; ended in disaster
9. **Rubric** Magazine articles should
   - describe early German advances.
   - analyze reasons for Germany's success.
   - be written in a journalistic style.

CONNECT TO TODAY

Rubric Oral reports should
- explain how stealth technology is used to evade radar.
- be clear and succinct.

Adolf Hitler on his 50th birthday, April 20, 1939

Poster encouraging Americans to buy war bonds

Japan's Pacific Campaign

MAIN IDEA

EMPIRE BUILDING Japan attacked Pearl Harbor in Hawaii and brought the United States into World War II.

WHY IT MATTERS NOW

World War II established the United States as a leading player in international affairs.

TERMS & NAMES

- Isoroku Yamamoto
- Pearl Harbor
- Battle of Midway
- Douglas MacArthur
- Battle of Guadalcanal

SETTING THE STAGE Like Hitler, Japan's military leaders also had dreams of empire. Japan's expansion had begun in 1931. That year, Japanese troops took over Manchuria in northeastern China. Six years later, Japanese armies swept into the heartland of China. They expected quick victory. Chinese resistance, however, caused the war to drag on. This placed a strain on Japan's economy. To increase their resources, Japanese leaders looked toward the rich European colonies of Southeast Asia.

Surprise Attack on Pearl Harbor

By October 1940, Americans had cracked one of the codes that the Japanese used in sending secret messages. Therefore, they were well aware of Japanese plans for Southeast Asia. If Japan conquered European colonies there, it could also threaten the American-controlled Philippine Islands and Guam. To stop the Japanese advance, the U.S. government sent aid to strengthen Chinese resistance. And when the Japanese overran French Indochina—Vietnam, Cambodia, and Laos—in July 1941, Roosevelt cut off oil shipments to Japan.

Despite an oil shortage, the Japanese continued their conquests. They hoped to catch the European colonial powers and the United States by surprise. So they planned massive attacks on British and Dutch colonies in Southeast Asia and on American outposts in the Pacific—at the same time. Admiral **Isoroku Yamamoto** (ih•soh•ROO•koo YAH•muh•MOH•toh), Japan's greatest naval strategist, also called for an attack on the U.S. fleet in Hawaii. It was, he said, "a dagger pointed at [Japan's] throat" and must be destroyed.

Day of Infamy Early in the morning of December 7, 1941, American sailors at **Pearl Harbor** in Hawaii awoke to the roar of explosives. A Japanese attack was underway! U.S. military leaders had known from a coded Japanese message that an attack might come. But they did not know when or where it would occur. Within two hours, the Japanese had sunk or damaged 19 ships, including 8 battleships, moored in Pearl Harbor. More than 2,300 Americans were killed—with over 1,100 wounded. News of the attack stunned the American people. The next day, President Roosevelt addressed Congress. December 7, 1941, he declared, was "a date which will live in infamy." Congress quickly accepted his request for a declaration of war on Japan and its allies.

CALIFORNIA STANDARDS

10.8.3 Identify and locate the Allied and Axis powers on a map and discuss the major turning points of the war, the principal theaters of conflict, key strategic decisions, and the resulting war conferences and political resolutions, with emphasis on the importance of geographic factors.

10.8.4 Describe the political, diplomatic, and military leaders during the war (e.g., Winston Churchill, Franklin Delano Roosevelt, Emperor Hirohito, Adolf Hitler, Benito Mussolini, Joseph Stalin, Douglas MacArthur, Dwight Eisenhower).

10.8.6 Discuss the human costs of the war, with particular attention to the civilian and military losses in Russia, Germany, Britain, the United States, China, and Japan.

TAKING NOTES

Recognizing Effects Use a chart to identify the effects of four major events of the war in the Pacific between 1941 and 1943.

Event	Effect

LESSON PLAN

OBJECTIVES

- Explain how Japanese expansionism led to war with the Allies in Asia.
- Describe Japan's early battle successes.
- Explain how the Allies were able to stop Japanese expansion.
- Summarize Allied battle strategy.

1 FOCUS & MOTIVATE

Discuss how countries justify starting wars. Consider whether surprise attacks are ever completely unforeseen.

2 INSTRUCT

Surprise Attack on Pearl Harbor
10.8.3; 10.8.4; 10.8.6

Critical Thinking

- How did Yamamoto justify a preemptive strike on the United States? How might American actions have justified his concern? *(He argued that the United States had threatened Japan. Roosevelt had cut off oil shipments.)*

CALIFORNIA RESOURCES

California Reading Toolkit, p. L71
California Modified Lesson Plans for English Learners, p. 137
California Daily Standards Practice Transparencies, TT63
California Standards Enrichment Workbook, pp. 83–84, 85–86, 89–90
California Standards Planner and Lesson Plans, p. L133
California Online Test Practice
California Test Generator CD-ROM
California Easy Planner CD-ROM
California eEdition CD-ROM

SECTION 2 PROGRAM RESOURCES

ALL STUDENTS

In-Depth Resources: Unit 4
- Guided Reading, p. 70
- Geography Application: The Fall of Singapore, p. 76

Formal Assessment
- Section Quiz, p. 278

ENGLISH LEARNERS

In-Depth Resources in Spanish
- Guided Reading, p. 125
- Geography Application: The Fall of Singapore, p. 130

Reading Study Guide (Spanish), p. 169
Reading Study Guide Audio CD (Spanish)

STRUGGLING READERS

In-Depth Resources: Unit 4
- Guided Reading, p. 70
- Geography Application: The Fall of Singapore, p. 76
- Building Vocabulary, p. 74
- Reteaching Activity, p. 89

Reading Study Guide, p. 169
Reading Study Guide Audio CD

GIFTED AND TALENTED STUDENTS

Electronic Library of Primary Sources
- from "Japanese Attack Sinks HMS *Repulse*"

INTEGRATED TECHNOLOGY

eEdition CD-ROM
Power Presentations CD-ROM
Electronic Library of Primary Sources
- from "Japanese Attack Sinks HMS *Repulse*"

classzone.com

Japanese Victories
10.8.6

Critical Thinking

- What can you infer about the attitude of many Asians toward colonization from the effort by the Japanese to win their support? *(European and American colonial rulers were unpopular.)*
- Summarize the fighting in the Pacific between December 1941 and April 1942. *(Possible Answer: Japan had a series of victories, some easy and some hard-fought.)*

Electronic Library of Primary Sources

- from "Japanese Attack Sinks HMS *Repulse*"

More About . . .

Corregidor

Known as The Rock, the island fortress of Corregidor in Manila Bay was the last U.S. position in the Philippines to surrender. For a month after the fall of Bataan, 13,000 American and Filipino troops held out in a concrete cave called Malinta Tunnel. Bombarded night and day by Japanese guns and suffering from hunger and exhaustion, the defenders finally surrendered on May 6 when Japanese troops swarmed over the rock. The last message sent from Corregidor said: "Everyone is bawling like a baby. They are piling dead and wounded in our tunnel . . . The jig is up." The commander, Lieutenant General Jonathan Wainwright, and other survivors joined the Bataan Death March.

▲ The *U.S.S. West Virginia* is engulfed by flames after taking a direct hit during the Japanese attack on Pearl Harbor.

Almost at the same time of the Pearl Harbor attack, the Japanese launched bombing raids on the British colony of Hong Kong and American-controlled Guam and Wake Island. (See the map on the opposite page.) They also landed an invasion force in Thailand. The Japanese drive for a Pacific empire was under way.

Japanese Victories

Lightly defended, Guam and Wake Island quickly fell to Japanese forces. The Japanese then turned their attention to the Philippines. In January 1942, they marched into the Philippine capital of Manila. American and Filipino forces took up a defensive position on the Bataan (buh•TAN) Peninsula on the northwestern edge of Manila Bay. At the same time, the Philippine government moved to the island of Corregidor just to the south of Bataan. After about three months of tough fighting, the Japanese took the Bataan Peninsula in April. Corregidor fell the following month.

The Japanese also continued their strikes against British possessions in Asia. After seizing Hong Kong, they invaded Malaya from the sea and overland from Thailand. By February 1942, the Japanese had reached Singapore, strategically located at the southern tip of the Malay Peninsula. After a fierce pounding, the colony surrendered. Within a month, the Japanese had conquered the resource-rich Dutch East Indies (now Indonesia), including the islands of Java, Sumatra, Borneo, and Celebes (SEHL•uh•BEEZ). The Japanese also moved westward, taking Burma. From there, they planned to launch a strike against India, the largest of Great Britain's colonies.

By the time Burma fell, Japan had taken control of more than 1 million square miles of Asian land. About 150 million people lived in this vast area. Before these conquests, the Japanese had tried to win the support of Asians with the anticolonialist idea of "East Asia for the Asiatics." After victory, however, the Japanese quickly made it clear that they had come as conquerors. They often treated the people of their new colonies with extreme cruelty.

However, the Japanese reserved the most brutal treatment for Allied prisoners of war. The Japanese considered it dishonorable to surrender, and they had contempt for the prisoners of war in their charge. On the Bataan Death March—a forced march of more than 50 miles up the peninsula—the Japanese subjected their captives to terrible cruelties. One Allied prisoner of war reported:

PRIMARY SOURCE

I was questioned by a Japanese officer, who found out that I had been in a Philippine Scout Battalion. The [Japanese] hated the Scouts. . . . Anyway, they took me outside and I was forced to watch as they buried six of my Scouts alive. They made the men dig their own graves, and then had them kneel down in a pit. The guards hit them over the head with shovels to stun them and piled earth on top.

LIEUTENANT JOHN SPAINHOWER, quoted in *War Diary 1939–1945*

Of the approximately 70,000 prisoners who started the Bataan Death March, only 54,000 survived.

DIFFERENTIATING INSTRUCTION: GIFTED AND TALENTED STUDENTS

Comparing Reactions to Japanese Expansion

Class Time 15 minutes

Task Researching how other countries responded to news of Japanese imperialism in eastern Asia

Purpose To place Japanese expansion in a global context by understanding how other countries viewed it

Instructions Divide students into five groups. Have each pair research the response of one country to the spread of the Japanese empire in 1941 and 1942. For sources, students could use books and Web sites on the general history of World War II and on the history of individual countries.

Each group of students should focus on the reaction to Japan among countries or territories in one category:

- territories conquered by Japan before 1941, such as Korea and Manchuria
- territories conquered by Japan in 1941 and 1942, such as Burma, Thailand, French Indochina, and the Philippines
- countries threatened by Japan, such as India and Australia
- countries supportive of Japan's expansion, such as Germany and Italy
- countries opposed to Japan's expansion, such as Great Britain and the Soviet Union

Have students report to the class what they have learned.

World War II in Asia and the Pacific, 1941–1945

INTERACTIVE

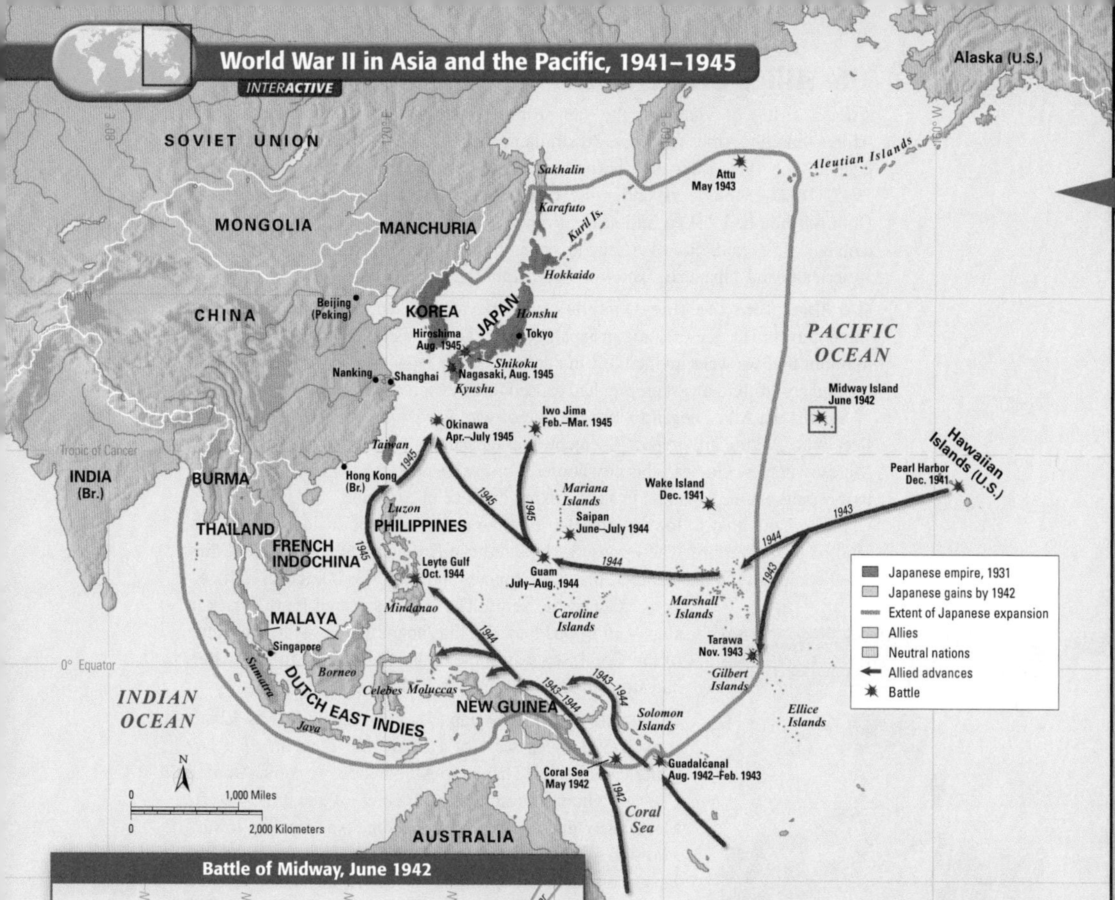

SOVIET UNION
MONGOLIA
MANCHURIA
CHINA
KOREA
JAPAN
INDIA (Br.)
BURMA
THAILAND
FRENCH INDOCHINA
PHILIPPINES
MALAYA
DUTCH EAST INDIES
NEW GUINEA
AUSTRALIA
PACIFIC OCEAN
INDIAN OCEAN
Alaska (U.S.)
Aleutian Islands
Attu May 1943
Sakhalin
Karafuto
Kuril Is.
Hokkaido
Honshu
Tokyo
Beijing (Peking)
Hiroshima Aug. 1945
Shikoku
Nagasaki, Aug. 1945
Kyushu
Nanking
Shanghai
Okinawa Apr.–July 1945
Iwo Jima Feb.–Mar. 1945
Midway Island June 1942
Hawaiian Islands (U.S.)
Pearl Harbor Dec. 1941
Taiwan
Hong Kong (Br.)
Luzon
Mariana Islands
Saipan June–July 1944
Wake Island Dec. 1941
Guam July–Aug. 1944
Leyte Gulf Oct. 1944
Mindanao
Caroline Islands
Marshall Islands
Tarawa Nov. 1943
Gilbert Islands
Ellice Islands
Singapore
Sumatra
Borneo
Celebes
Moluccas
Java
Solomon Islands
Guadalcanal Aug. 1942–Feb. 1943
Coral Sea May 1942
Coral Sea
Tropic of Cancer
0° Equator

Japanese empire, 1931
Japanese gains by 1942
Extent of Japanese expansion
Allies
Neutral nations
Allied advances
Battle

0 1,000 Miles
0 2,000 Kilometers

Battle of Midway, June 1942

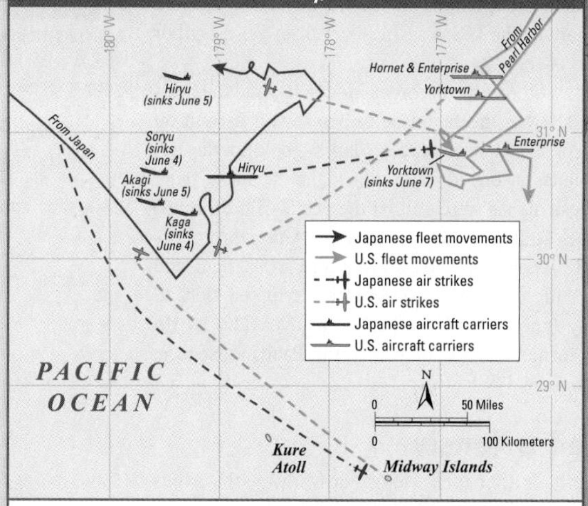

Hiryu (sinks June 5)
Soryu (sinks June 4)
Akagi (sinks June 5)
Kaga (sinks June 4)
From Japan
Hornet & Enterprise
Yorktown
From Pearl Harbor
Enterprise
Yorktown (sinks June 7)
PACIFIC OCEAN
Kure Atoll
Midway Islands
31° N
30° N
29° N

Japanese fleet movements
U.S. fleet movements
Japanese air strikes
U.S. air strikes
Japanese aircraft carriers
U.S. aircraft carriers

0 50 Miles
0 100 Kilometers

Some Japanese search aircraft were late getting into the air. As a result, the Japanese were completely unaware that U.S. ships were nearby.

The Japanese warship *Mikuma* lists and begins to sink after being struck by bombs from American aircraft during the Battle of Midway.

GEOGRAPHY SKILLBUILDER: Interpreting Maps

1. **Location** *Which battle was fought in the most northern region?*
2. **Movement** *From what two general directions did Allied forces move in on Japan?*

History from Visuals

Interpreting the Map

From the location of battles, what was the Allied strategy in the Pacific? *(to move closer to Japan until they reached it)*

Extension Compare this map with the political map of Asia in the textbook atlas. Which islands are now a U.S. territory? *(the Marianas)*

SKILLBUILDER Answers

1. **Location** Attu Island in May 1943
2. **Movement** east and south

INTEGRATED TECHNOLOGY

Interactive This image is available in an interactive format on the eEdition. Students can examine parts of the map in detail.

In-Depth Resources: Unit 4

- Geography Application: The Fall of Singapore, p. 76

More About . . .

Admiral Yamamoto

From serving as a naval attaché in Washington, D.C., Yamamoto recognized America's industrial might. In 1940 he said that Japan could not defeat the United States. Later, he supported—with some concerns—the strike on Pearl Harbor: "In the first six to twelve months of a war with the United States and Britain, I will run wild and win victory after victory. After that, I have no expectation of success."

DIFFERENTIATING INSTRUCTION: STRUGGLING READERS

Understanding Geography in the Battle for Singapore

Class Time 40 minutes

Task Analyzing Japan's conquest of Singapore and other battles

Purpose To understand the roles of geography and surprise in military attacks

Instructions Distribute the Geography Application activity found in In-Depth Resources: Unit 4 (also available in Spanish). Pair a struggling reader with a more adept reader. Have each pair read the text and take notes on it. Some sample notes are shown at right. After students have completed the activity, discuss other examples of where geography contributed to an effective surprise attack. *(Possible Answer: Japan against the United States in December 1941)*

Feb. 1942—Japan took Singapore from Britain

Singapore important because of location—defense and trading

British protected south end of island but not north end

Japanese surprised British, attacked from north

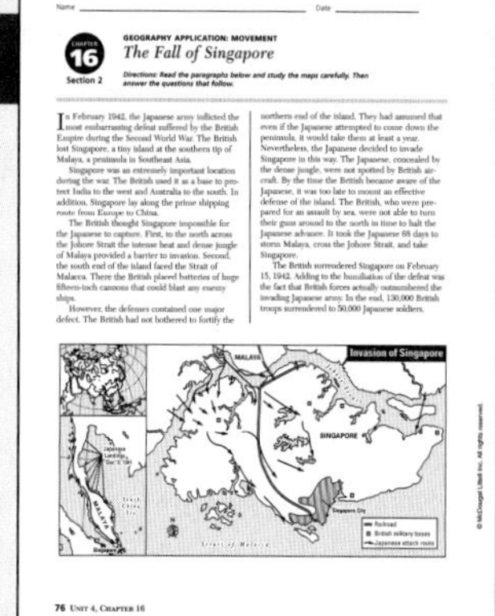
GEOGRAPHY APPLICATION: MOVEMENT
The Fall of Singapore

In-Depth Resources: Unit 4

The Allies Strike Back
10.8.3; 10.8.4

Critical Thinking

- What did the Battle of the Coral Sea imply about the importance of air power in the Pacific? *(It was important: it even determined naval battles.)*
- How did Midway show the value of military intelligence? *(Breaking a Japanese code aided the victory.)*

History Makers
Douglas MacArthur

What makes MacArthur's declaration "I shall return" memorable? *(It is short, personal, and confident.)* Flamboyant and self-assured, MacArthur skillfully publicized himself, which is partly why Generals George Marshall and Dwight Eisenhower did not like him. Have interested students research and identify qualities that gained MacArthur loyal supporters and fierce critics.

An Allied Offensive
10.8.3

Critical Thinking

- What were potential disadvantages of the "island-hop" plan? *(Possible Answer: difficult to supply faraway troops)*
- Do you think the Allies progressed quickly against the Japanese? *(Yes—The Allies covered vast distances and hundreds of islands. No—Success took years of bloodshed.)*

The Allies Strike Back

After a string of victories, the Japanese seemed unbeatable. Nonetheless, the Allies—mainly Americans and Australians—were anxious to strike back in the Pacific. The United States in particular wanted revenge for Pearl Harbor. In April 1942, 16 B-25 bombers under the command of Lieutenant Colonel James H. Doolittle bombed Tokyo and several other Japanese cities. The bombs did little damage. The raid, however, made an important psychological point to both Americans and Japanese: Japan was vulnerable to attack.

The Allies Turn the Tide Doolittle's raid on Japan raised American morale and shook the confidence of some in Japan. As one Japanese citizen noted, "We started to doubt that we were invincible." In addition, some Japanese worried that defending and controlling a vast empire had caused them to spread their resources too thin.

Vocabulary
invincible: unconquerable

Slowly, the Allies began to turn the tide of war. Early in May 1942, an American fleet with Australian support intercepted a Japanese strike force headed for Port Moresby in New Guinea. This city housed a critical Allied air base. Control of the air base would put the Japanese in easy striking distance of Australia.

In the battle that followed—the Battle of the Coral Sea—both sides used a new kind of naval warfare. The opposing ships did not fire a single shot. In fact, they often could not see one another. Instead, airplanes taking off from huge aircraft carriers attacked the ships. The Allies suffered more losses in ships and troops than did the Japanese. However, the Battle of the Coral Sea was something of a victory, for the Allies had stopped Japan's southward advance.

History Makers

General Douglas MacArthur 1880–1964

Douglas MacArthur's qualities as a leader and a fighting soldier emerged in France during World War I. Showing incredible dash and courage on the battlefield, he received several decorations for bravery. And he won promotion from the rank of major to brigadier general.

After serving in several positions in the United States, MacArthur received a posting to the Philippines in 1935. He remained there until shortly before the islands fell in 1941. But he left very reluctantly. In a message to the troops who remained behind, he vowed, "I shall return." As you will read later in the chapter, MacArthur kept his promise.

The Battle of Midway Japan next targeted Midway Island, some 1,500 miles west of Hawaii, the location of a key American airfield. Thanks to Allied code breakers, Admiral Chester Nimitz, commander in chief of the U.S. Pacific Fleet, knew that a huge Japanese force was heading toward Midway. Admiral Yamamoto himself was in command of the Japanese fleet. He hoped that the attack on Midway would draw the whole of the U.S. Pacific Fleet from Pearl Harbor to defend the island. (A)

On June 4, with American forces hidden beyond the horizon, Nimitz allowed the Japanese to begin their assault on the island. As the first Japanese planes got into the air, American planes swooped in to attack the Japanese fleet. Many Japanese planes were still on the decks of the aircraft carriers. The strategy was a success. American pilots destroyed 332 Japanese planes, all four aircraft carriers, and one support ship. Yamamoto ordered his crippled fleet to withdraw. By June 7, 1942, the battle was over. The **Battle of Midway** turned the tide of war in the Pacific. (See the inset map on page 499.)

MAIN IDEA
Analyzing Motives
(A) Why might the Americans send their entire Pacific Fleet to defend Midway Island?
A. Possible Answer Midway was located just west of Hawaii, so the Americans would want to keep the Japanese away from this important American territory.

An Allied Offensive

With morale high after their victory at Midway, the Allies took the offensive. The war in the Pacific involved vast distances. Japanese troops had dug in on hundreds of islands across the ocean. General **Douglas MacArthur**, the commander of the Allied land forces in the Pacific, developed a plan to handle this problem.

DIFFERENTIATING INSTRUCTION: ENGLISH LEARNERS

Understanding Key Events

Class Time 40 minutes

Task Completing a chart

Purpose To understand the significance of key events in the section

Instructions Divide students into pairs. Distribute copies of the Guided Reading activity for this section. Have each pair search the chapter and write in their own words what happened at each event and why it was important to world history.

Explain that this section contains some sophisticated military and political terms that may be a challenge for students. Encourage students to use the textbook glossary or a dictionary to look up difficult words. You may wish to list the following terms on the board to help students' comprehension.

infamy = being evil or terrible

strike = military attack

anticolonialism = being against colonial powers, such as Britain and France

turn the tide = to make a change

Guided Reading: Japan's Pacific Campaign

In-Depth Resources: Unit 4

MAIN IDEA

Identifying Problems

B If the vast distances of the Pacific caused problems for the Allies, how might they have also caused problems for the Japanese?

B. Possible Answer Supplying their outposts and keeping the Allies out of thousands of square miles of ocean would be problems for the Japanese.

MacArthur believed that storming each island would be a long, costly effort. Instead, he wanted to "island-hop" past Japanese strongholds. He would then seize islands that were not well defended but were closer to Japan. B

MacArthur's first target soon presented itself. U.S. military leaders had learned that the Japanese were building a huge air base on the island of Guadalcanal in the Solomon Islands. The Allies had to strike fast before the base was completed and became another Japanese stronghold. At dawn on August 7, 1942, several thousand U.S. Marines, with Australian support, landed on Guadalcanal and the neighboring island of Tulagi.

The marines had little trouble seizing Guadalcanal's airfield. But the battle for control of the island turned into a savage struggle as both sides poured in fresh troops. In February 1943, after six months of fighting on land and at sea, the **Battle of Guadalcanal** finally ended. After losing more than 24,000 of a force of 36,000 soldiers, the Japanese abandoned what they came to call "the Island of Death."

To American war correspondent Ralph Martin and the U.S. soldiers who fought there, Guadalcanal was simply "hell":

▲ U.S. Marines storm ashore at Guadalcanal.

PRIMARY SOURCE

Hell was red furry spiders as big as your fist, . . . enormous rats and bats everywhere, and rivers with waiting crocodiles. Hell was the sour, foul smell of the squishy jungle, humidity that rotted a body within hours. . . . Hell was an enemy . . . so fanatic that it used its own dead as booby traps.

RALPH G. MARTIN, *The GI War*

As Japan worked to establish a new order in Southeast Asia and the Pacific, the Nazis moved ahead with Hitler's design for a new order in Europe. This design included plans for dealing with those Hitler considered unfit for the Third Reich. You will learn about these plans in Section 3.

SECTION 2 ASSESSMENT

TERMS & NAMES 1. For each term or name, write a sentence explaining its significance.
• Isoroku Yamamoto • Pearl Harbor • Battle of Midway • Douglas MacArthur • Battle of Guadalcanal

USING YOUR NOTES

2. Which event was most important in turning the tide of the war in the Pacific against the Japanese? Why? (10.8.3)

Event	Effect

MAIN IDEAS

3. How did the Japanese plan to catch the European colonial powers and the United States by surprise? (10.8.3)
4. In what way was the Battle of the Coral Sea a new kind of naval warfare? (10.8.3)
5. What was General Douglas MacArthur's island-hopping strategy? (10.8.4)

CRITICAL THINKING & WRITING

6. **EVALUATING DECISIONS** Did Admiral Yamamoto make a wise decision in bombing Pearl Harbor? Explain. (10.8.6)
7. **ANALYZING MOTIVES** Why do you think the Japanese changed their approach from trying to win the support of the colonized peoples to acting as conquerors? (10.8.3)
8. **IDENTIFYING PROBLEMS** What problems did Japan face in building an empire in the Pacific? (10.8.3)
9. **WRITING ACTIVITY** EMPIRE BUILDING Imagine you are a foreign diplomat living in Asia during World War II. Write **journal entries** describing the Japanese advance across Asia and the Pacific during 1941 and 1942. (Writing 2.1.e)

INTEGRATED TECHNOLOGY **INTERNET ACTIVITY**

Use the Internet to research the Pearl Harbor Memorial in Hawaii. Create a **Web page** that describes the memorial and provides background information on the attack. (Writing 2.3.b)

INTERNET KEYWORD
Pearl Harbor

Inclusion Tip

Students who have difficulty focusing on written material may better understand the island-hopping strategy by using a model. Have students make a model of a string of islands using a chess set. They should place the pieces of one color across the board, with the powerful pieces spread out. Discuss how MacArthur planned to leave the strong pieces in place and attack the weaker ones at first.

3 ASSESS

SECTION 2 ASSESSMENT

As a class, discuss answers to question 2.

Formal Assessment
• Section Quiz, p. 278

4 RETEACH

Have two students play the roles of Yamamoto and Nimitz and stage a conversation between the two as they explain their goals and strategy at the Battle of Midway. Have the other students in the class act as newspaper reporters and ask questions.

In-Depth Resources: Unit 4
• Reteaching Activity, p. 89

ANSWERS

1. Isoroku Yamamoto, p. 497 • Pearl Harbor, p. 497 • Battle of Midway, p. 500 • Douglas MacArthur, p. 500 • Battle of Guadalcanal, p. 501
2. **Sample Answer:** Attack on Pearl Harbor—U.S. enters the war. Attack on Tokyo—Japan shows vulnerability. Battle of Midway—Strong Allied victory. Battle of Guadalcanal—Long and bloody struggle. Turning point—Midway severely damaged the Japanese navy.
3. attacking several places at once
4. Planes from aircraft carriers dominated.
5. seize weakly held islands first
6. Unwise—It drew Americans away from Europe. Wise—It weakened a likely foe.
7. **Possible Answer:** no longer needed local support after conquest
8. **Possible Answers:** controlling a vast empire, opposition from colonial interests, fear of vulnerability at home
9. **Rubric** Journal entries should
   • list Japanese conquests.
   • include precise and relevant details.
   • state opinions and feelings.

INTEGRATED TECHNOLOGY

Rubric Web pages should
• offer information on the memorial.
• include relevant visuals.
• be well organized and accurate.

LESSON PLAN

OBJECTIVES

- Trace the course of the persecution of Jews by the Nazis.
- Describe the results of the "Final Solution."

1 FOCUS & MOTIVATE

Ask students what they know about the Holocaust. Note that the Nazis focused on Jews but viewed many groups as inferior.

2 INSTRUCT

The Holocaust Begins

10.8.4; 10.8.5; 10.8.6

Critical Thinking

- What were the immediate and the underlying causes of *Kristallnacht*? *(Immediate—A Jew shot a German. Underlying—Many Europeans blamed Jews for social and political problems.)*
- How did anti-Semitism outside of Germany contribute to the problems of Jews in Germany? *(Countries refused to accept Jewish refugees.)*

CALIFORNIA RESOURCES

California Reading Toolkit, p. L72
California Modified Lesson Plans for English Learners, p. 139
California Daily Standards Practice Transparencies, TT64
California Standards Enrichment Workbook, pp. 85–86, 87–88, 89–90
California Standards Planner and Lesson Plans, p. L135
California Online Test Practice
California Test Generator CD-ROM
California Easy Planner CD-ROM
California eEdition CD-ROM

3

Adolf Hitler on his 50th birthday, April 20, 1939

Poster encouraging Americans to buy war bonds

The Holocaust

MAIN IDEA	WHY IT MATTERS NOW	TERMS & NAMES
EMPIRE BUILDING During the Holocaust, Hitler's Nazis killed six million Jews and five million other "non-Aryans."	The violence against Jews during the Holocaust led to the founding of Israel after World War II.	• Aryan • Holocaust • *Kristallnacht* • ghetto • "Final Solution" • genocide

CALIFORNIA STANDARDS

10.8.4 Describe the political, diplomatic, and military leaders during the war (e.g., Winston Churchill, Franklin Delano Roosevelt, Emperor Hirohito, Adolf Hitler, Benito Mussolini, Joseph Stalin, Douglas MacArthur, Dwight Eisenhower).

10.8.5 Analyze the Nazi policy of pursuing racial purity, especially against the European Jews; its transformation into the Final Solution; and the Holocaust that resulted in the murder of six million Jewish civilians.

10.8.6 Discuss the human costs of the war, with particular attention to the civilian and military losses in Russia, Germany, Britain, the United States, China, and Japan.

HI 4 Students understand the meaning, implication, and impact of historical events and recognize that events could have taken other directions.

SETTING THE STAGE As part of their vision for Europe, the Nazis proposed a new racial order. They proclaimed that the Germanic peoples, or **Aryans**, were a "master race." (This was a misuse of the term *Aryan.* The term actually refers to the Indo-European peoples who began to migrate into the Indian subcontinent around 1500 B.C.) The Nazis claimed that all non-Aryan peoples, particularly Jewish people, were inferior. This racist message would eventually lead to the **Holocaust**, the systematic mass slaughter of Jews and other groups judged inferior by the Nazis.

The Holocaust Begins

To gain support for his racist ideas, Hitler knowingly tapped into a hatred for Jews that had deep roots in European history. For generations, many Germans, along with other Europeans, had targeted Jews as the cause of their failures. Some Germans even blamed Jews for their country's defeat in World War I and for its economic problems after that war.

In time, the Nazis made the targeting of Jews a government policy. The Nuremberg Laws, passed in 1935, deprived Jews of their rights to German citizenship and forbade marriages between Jews and non-Jews. Laws passed later also limited the kinds of work that Jews could do.

"Night of Broken Glass" Worse was yet to come. Early in November 1938, 17-year-old Herschel Grynszpan (GRIHN•shpahn), a Jewish youth from Germany, was visiting an uncle in Paris. While Grynszpan was there, he received a postcard. It said that after living in Germany for 27 years, his father had been deported to Poland. On November 7, wishing to avenge his father's deportation, Grynszpan shot a German diplomat living in Paris.

TAKING NOTES

Analyzing Bias Use a web diagram to identify examples of Nazi persecution.

When Nazi leaders heard the news, they launched a violent attack on the Jewish community. On November 9, Nazi storm troopers attacked Jewish homes, businesses, and synagogues across Germany and murdered close to 100 Jews. An American in Leipzig wrote, "Jewish shop windows by the hundreds were systematically . . . smashed. . . . The main streets of the city were a positive litter of shattered plate glass." It is for this reason that the night of November 9 became known as ***Kristallnacht*** (krih•STAHL•NAHKT), or "Night of Broken Glass." A 14-year-old boy described his memory of that awful night:

SECTION 3 PROGRAM RESOURCES

ALL STUDENTS

In-Depth Resources: Unit 4
- Guided Reading, p. 71

Formal Assessment
- Section Quiz, p. 279

ENGLISH LEARNERS

In-Depth Resources in Spanish
- Guided Reading (Spanish), p. 126

Reading Study Guide (Spanish), p. 171
Reading Study Guide Audio CD (Spanish)

STRUGGLING READERS

In-Depth Resources: Unit 4
- Guided Reading, p. 71
- Building Vocabulary, p. 74
- Reteaching Activity, p. 90

Reading Study Guide, p. 171
Reading Study Guide Audio CD

GIFTED AND TALENTED STUDENTS

In-Depth Resources: Unit 4
- Primary Source: from *The Diary of a Young Girl,* p. 80
- Literature: from *Night,* p. 82

INTEGRATED TECHNOLOGY

eEdition CD-ROM
Power Presentations CD-ROM
World Art and Cultures Transparencies
- AT70 German and American propaganda posters

classzone.com

PRIMARY SOURCE

All the things for which my parents had worked for eighteen long years were destroyed in less than ten minutes. Piles of valuable glasses, expensive furniture, linens—in short, everything was destroyed. . . . The Nazis left us, yelling, "Don't try to leave this house! We'll soon be back again and take you to a concentration camp to be shot."

M. I. LIBAU, quoted in *Never to Forget: The Jews of the Holocaust*

Kristallnacht marked a major step-up in the Nazi policy of Jewish persecution. The future for Jews in Germany looked truly grim.

A Flood of Refugees After *Kristallnacht*, some Jews realized that violence against them was bound to increase. By the end of 1939, a number of German Jews had fled to other countries. Many however, remained in Germany. Later, Hitler conquered territories in which millions more Jews lived.

At first, Hitler favored emigration as a solution to what he called "the Jewish problem." Getting other countries to continue admitting Germany's Jews became an issue, however. After admitting tens of thousands of Jewish refugees, such countries as France, Britain, and the United States abruptly closed their doors to further immigration. Germany's foreign minister observed, "We all want to get rid of our Jews. The difficulty is that no country wishes to receive them."

Isolating the Jews When Hitler found that he could not get rid of Jews through emigration, he put another plan into effect. He ordered Jews in all countries under his control to be moved to designated cities. In those cities, the Nazis herded the Jews into dismal, overcrowded **ghettos**, or segregated Jewish areas. The Nazis then sealed off the ghettos with barbed wire and stone walls. They hoped that the Jews inside would starve to death or die from disease. (A)

MAIN IDEA

Recognizing Effects

(A) What steps did Hitler take to rid Germany of Jews?

A. Answer He tried to force them to emigrate. When this plan failed, he ordered all Jews moved into ghettos, where he hoped they would die of starvation or disease.

Even under these horrible conditions, the Jews hung on. Some formed resistance organizations within the ghettos. They also struggled to keep their traditions. Ghetto theaters produced plays and concerts. Teachers taught lessons in secret schools. Scholars kept records so that one day people would find out the truth.

▲ After 1941, all Jews in German-controlled areas had to wear a yellow Star of David patch.

The "Final Solution"

Hitler soon grew impatient waiting for Jews to die from starvation or disease. He decided to take more direct action. His plan was called the "**Final Solution**." It was actually a program of **genocide**, the systematic killing of an entire people.

▼ German soldiers round up Jews in the Warsaw ghetto.

More About . . .

Jews in France

The Vichy government helped the Nazis persecute French Jews. When Marshal Henri Pétain was questioned about persecutions, he replied, "As for free-masons, I hate them, as for communists I am afraid of them, as for the Jews it is not my fault." Most Jews detained in Vichy France were housed in windowless barracks surrounded by barbed wire. In 1941, one reporter wrote: "These people have been detained for reasons they, in many instances, do not understand and . . . they are without the slightest information about what is to be their future." After 1942, Nazis began transporting Jews to work or be killed in camps in Eastern Europe.

The "Final Solution"

10.8.5

Critical Thinking

- Why did Hitler begin mass killings of Jews? *(Starvation and disease were not killing them fast enough.)*
- What was the difference between a concentration camp and an extermination camp? *(Concentration camps were slave-labor prisons. Extermination camps were for mass murder.)*
- What is the theme of the quotation from Elie Wiesel on page 505? *(He will never forget those who died in the Holocaust.)*

DIFFERENTIATING INSTRUCTION: ENGLISH LEARNERS

Analyzing German and American Propaganda

Class Time 20 minutes

Task Comparing propaganda posters

Purpose To understand propaganda

Instructions Explain that propaganda is information that is spread to make a cause more popular or to damage the cause of an enemy. Display Transparency AT70. (Note that information and discussion questions on the transparency are at the back of the transparency book.)

Tell students that the text on the first poster is French for "Abandoned People, Have Faith in the German Soldier." Ask:

- Why are these posters examples of propaganda? *(Possible Answer: They are designed to provoke intense feelings about a political matter.)*
- For what audience was the first poster created? *(French people; poster is in French)*
- How are Nazis portrayed in the first poster? *(Possible Answers: handsome, gentle, noble, caring, cheerful)* in the second poster? *(Possible Answer: as cold-eyed murderers)*

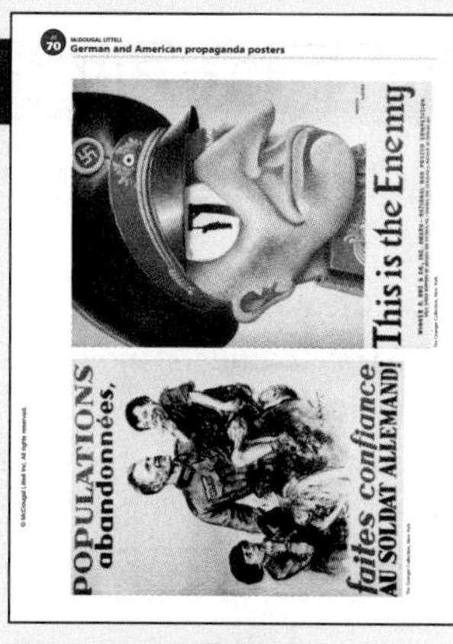

World Art and Cultures Transparencies

More About . . .

The "Final Solution"

Reinhard Heydrich, head of the SS intelligence service, spelled out the "Final Solution" in January 1942 at a conference of Nazi leaders. "The Reichführer SS has forbidden any further emigration of Jews. The Jews remaining in the Reich and all European Jews in our present and future spheres of influence will be evacuated to the East for the final solution."

In-Depth Resources: Unit 4

- Primary Source: from *The Diary of a Young Girl,* p. 80
- Literature: from *Night,* p. 82

History *in* Depth

Jewish Resistance

In the ghetto of Kovno in Lithuania, Jews took an oath to resist Nazis. "I promise to fight with all my powers against the Nazi occupation; to endanger their encampments; disrupt their transport; burn and blow up bridges; destroy railroads; organize and help carry through acts of sabotage at every opportunity and under all circumstances, without sparing myself—and when necessary, to offer up my life." Ask students to research how Jews in ghettos and camps conducted sabotage.

Hitler believed that his plan of conquest depended on the purity of the Aryan race. To protect racial purity, the Nazis had to eliminate other races, nationalities, or groups they viewed as inferior—as "subhumans." They included Roma (gypsies), Poles, Russians, homosexuals, the insane, the disabled, and the incurably ill. But the Nazis focused especially on the Jews. B

MAIN IDEA

Analyzing Bias

B How was the "Final Solution" a natural outcome of Nazi racial theory?

B. Possible Answer To remain a super race, the Aryans had to remain pure. Therefore, all the inferior races, especially the Jews, had to be eliminated.

The Killings Begin As Nazi troops swept across Eastern Europe and the Soviet Union, the killings began. Units from the SS (Hitler's elite security force) moved from town to town to hunt down Jews. The SS and their collaborators rounded up men, women, children, and even babies and took them to isolated spots. They then shot their prisoners in pits that became the prisoners' graves.

Jews in communities not reached by the killing squads were rounded up and taken to concentration camps, or slave-labor prisons. These camps were located mainly in Germany and Poland. Hitler hoped that the horrible conditions in the camps would speed the total elimination of the Jews.

The prisoners worked seven days a week as slaves for the SS or for German businesses. Guards severely beat or killed their prisoners for not working fast enough. With meals of thin soup, a scrap of bread, and potato peelings, most prisoners lost 50 pounds in the first few months. Hunger was so intense, recalled one survivor, "that if a bit of soup spilled over, prisoners would . . . dig their spoons into the mud and stuff the mess in their mouths."

The Final Stage The "Final Solution" reached its last stage in 1942. At that time, the Nazis built extermination camps equipped with huge gas chambers that could kill as many as 6,000 human beings in a day. (See the map on page 519.)

When prisoners arrived at Auschwitz (OUSH•vihts), the largest of the extermination camps, they paraded before a committee of SS doctors. With a wave of the hand, these doctors separated the strong—mostly men—from the weak—mostly women, young children, the elderly, and the sick. Those labeled as weak would die that day. They were told to undress for a shower and then led into a chamber with

History *in* Depth

Jewish Resistance

Even in the extermination camps, Jews rose up and fought against the Nazis. At Treblinka in August 1943, and at Sobibor in October 1943, small groups of Jews revolted. They killed guards, stormed the camp armories and stole guns and grenades, and then broke out. In both uprisings, about 300 prisoners escaped. Most were killed soon after. Of those who survived, many joined up with partisan groups and continued to fight until the end of the war.

Late in 1944, prisoners at Auschwitz revolted, too. Like the escapees at Treblinka and Sobibor, most were caught and killed. Young women like Ella Gartner and Roza Robota made the Auschwitz uprising possible. Gartner smuggled gunpowder into the camp from the munitions factory where she worked. Robota helped organize resistance in the camp. Gartner and Robota were executed on January 6, 1945. Less than a month later, Auschwitz was liberated.

▲ Ella Gartner

▶ Roza Robota

DIFFERENTIATING INSTRUCTION: STRUGGLING READERS

A Chronology of the Holocaust

Class Time 20 minutes

Task Creating a time line

Purpose To understand the different events that made up the Holocaust

Instructions Explain that creating a time line can be an effective way of taking notes. Pair a struggling reader with a more proficient reader. Have pairs review the content of this section and create a time line that summarizes major events in students' own words. A sample time line is shown here. Encourage students to use their time lines to help them review the material before a quiz or test.

- *Nov. 1938—Kristallnacht—Nazi soldiers murder Jews.*
- *1939—Other countries stop letting Jews in.*
- *Early 1940s—Nazis first isolate Jews in ghettos, then send them to prisons or labor camps.*
- *Early 1942—Nazis build death camps.*

Students who need more help with the text should complete the Reading Study Guide activity for this section.

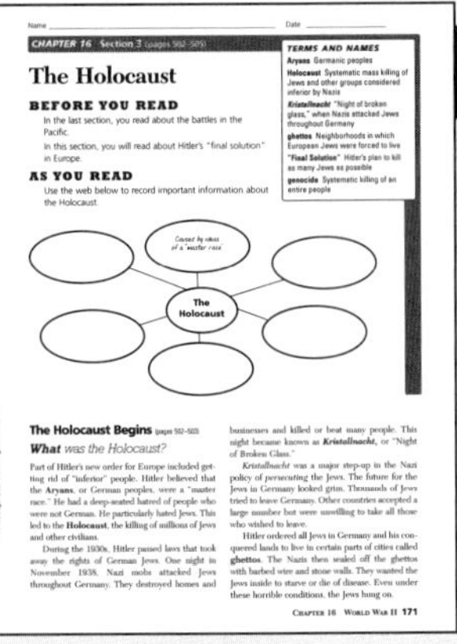

CHAPTER 16 Section 3

The Holocaust

BEFORE YOU READ

AS YOU READ

TERMS AND NAMES

Reading Study Guide

Jews Killed Under Nazi Rule*			
	Original Jewish Population	Jews Killed	Percent Surviving
Poland	3,300,000	2,800,000	15%
Soviet Union (area occupied by Germans)	2,100,000	1,500,000	29%
Hungary	404,000	200,000	49%
Romania	850,000	425,000	50%
Germany/Austria	270,000	210,000	22%

*Estimates Source: Hannah Vogt, *The Burden of Guilt*

fake showerheads. After the doors were closed, cyanide gas poured from the showerheads. All inside were killed in a matter of minutes. Later, the Nazis installed crematoriums, or ovens, to burn the bodies.

The Survivors Some six million European Jews died in these death camps and in Nazi massacres. Fewer than four million survived. Some escaped the horrors of the death camps with help from non-Jewish people. These rescuers, at great risk to their own lives, hid Jews in their homes or helped them escape to neutral countries.

Those who survived the camps were changed forever by what they had experienced. As Elie Wiesel, nearly 15 years old when he entered Auschwitz, noted:

PRIMARY SOURCE

Never shall I forget the little faces of the children, whose bodies I saw turned into wreaths of smoke beneath a silent blue sky. Never shall I forget those flames which consumed my faith forever. . . . Never shall I forget those moments which murdered my God and my soul and turned my dreams to dust. . . . Never.

ELIE WIESEL, quoted in *Night*

SECTION 3 ASSESSMENT

TERMS & NAMES 1. For each term or name, write a sentence explaining its significance.

• Aryan • Holocaust • *Kristallnacht* • ghetto • "Final Solution" • genocide

USING YOUR NOTES

2. What Nazi actions were part of the "Final Solution"? (10.8.5)

Nazi persecution

MAIN IDEAS

3. What was the new racial order proposed by the Nazis? (10.8.5)
4. What Nazi action marked the final stage of the "Final Solution"? (10.8.5)
5. How did some non-Jews oppose Hitler's "Final Solution"? (10.8.6)

CRITICAL THINKING & WRITING

6. **ANALYZING MOTIVES** Why might people want to blame a minority group for most of their country's problems? (10.8.5)
7. **MAKING INFERENCES** Why do you think the German people went along with the Nazi policy of persecution of the Jews? (10.8.5)
8. **RECOGNIZING EFFECTS** What impact did the Holocaust have on the Jewish population of Europe? (10.8.6)
9. **WRITING ACTIVITY** SCIENCE AND TECHNOLOGY Write a **persuasive essay** discussing how German scientists, engineers, and doctors asked to participate in the Holocaust might have opposed Hitler's policy. (Writing 2.4.a)

CONNECT TO TODAY CREATING A MAP

Find information on instances of genocide and ethnic cleansing in the last 20 years. Use the information to create an **annotated map** titled "Genocide in the Late 20th Century." (Writing 2.3.d)

More About . . .

Nazi Medicine

German doctors used Jews for medical experiments that often resulted in great suffering or death. For example, doctors infected prisoners with typhus and other diseases to see how long they could survive. To practice surgery, student doctors would operate on prisoners without anesthesia. Many of these experiments had no medical value.

3 ASSESS

SECTION 3 ASSESSMENT

Divide the questions among student groups and have them present their responses orally to the class.

Formal Assessment

• Section Quiz, p. 279

4 RETEACH

As a class, create a chart on the board listing the acts against Jews by Nazis and the impact of each.

In-Depth Resources: Unit 4

• Reteaching Activity, p. 90

ANSWERS

1. Aryan, p. 502 • Holocaust, p. 502 • *Kristallnacht,* p. 502 • ghetto, p. 503 • "Final Solution," p. 503 • genocide, p. 503

2. **Sample Answer:** Nuremberg Laws, *Kristallnacht,* ghettos, concentration camps. "Final Solution"—program designed to kill Jews by starving, shooting, or gassing them, or by working them to death.
3. The Aryans were a "master race" and all others were inferior.
4. extermination camps
5. They hid Jews in their homes or helped them escape Germany.
6. **Possible Answer:** Blaming a minority takes responsibility away from a country and its leaders.
7. **Possible Answers:** out of fear or out of agreement
8. It reduced the Jewish population by about two-thirds and left the survivors devastated.
9. **Rubric** Persuasive essays should
   - appeal to moral values.
   - identify options for opposing the Nazis.
   - consider consequences of various actions.

CONNECT TO TODAY

Rubric Annotated maps should
- identify countries where genocide or ethnic cleansing has occurred.
- include explanatory captions.
- cite sources.

LESSON PLAN

OBJECTIVES

- Describe the Allied strategy in Europe.
- List efforts made on the home front.
- Summarize events that led to the surrender of Germany and of Japan.

1 FOCUS & MOTIVATE

Discuss what students already know about World War II battles. *(Students may mention films such as* Saving Private Ryan *or television series such as* Band of Brothers.)

2 INSTRUCT

The Tide Turns on Two Fronts

10.8.3; 10.8.4

Critical Thinking

- What did the debate about a second front imply about relationships among the Allies? *(Britain and the United States were closer to each other than to the Soviet Union.)*
- How would you compare Midway and Stalingrad? *(Both halted expansion, but Stalingrad was longer, bloodier, and on land.)*

CALIFORNIA RESOURCES

California Reading Toolkit, p. L73
California Modified Lesson Plans for English Learners, p. 141
California Daily Standards Practice Transparencies, TT65
California Standards Enrichment Workbook, pp. 83–84, 85–86, 91–92
California Standards Planner and Lesson Plans, p. L137
California Online Test Practice
California Test Generator CD-ROM
California Easy Planner CD-ROM
California eEdition CD-ROM

Adolf Hitler on his 50th birthday, April 20, 1939

4

Poster encouraging Americans to buy war bonds

The Allied Victory

MAIN IDEA

EMPIRE BUILDING Led by the United States, Great Britain, and the Soviet Union, the Allies scored key victories and won the war.

WHY IT MATTERS NOW

The Allies' victory in World War II set up conditions for both the Cold War and today's post-Cold War world.

TERMS & NAMES

- Dwight D. Eisenhower
- Battle of Stalingrad
- D-Day
- Battle of the Bulge
- kamikaze

CALIFORNIA STANDARDS

10.8.3 Identify and locate the Allied and Axis powers on a map and discuss the major turning points of the war, the principal theaters of conflict, key strategic decisions, and the resulting war conferences and political resolutions, with emphasis on the importance of geographic factors.

10.8.4 Describe the political, diplomatic, and military leaders during the war (e.g., Winston Churchill, Franklin Delano Roosevelt, Emperor Hirohito, Adolf Hitler, Benito Mussolini, Joseph Stalin, Douglas MacArthur, Dwight Eisenhower).

10.9.1 Compare the economic and military power shifts caused by the war, including the Yalta Pact, the development of nuclear weapons, Soviet control over Eastern European nations, and the economic recoveries of Germany and Japan.

HI 2 Students recognize the complexity of historical causes and effects, including the limitations on determining cause and effect.

TAKING NOTES

Recognizing Effects Use a chart to identify the outcomes of several major World War II battles.

Battle	Outcome
Battle of El Alamein	
Battle of Stalingrad	
D-Day Invasion	

SETTING THE STAGE On December 22, 1941, just after Pearl Harbor, Winston Churchill and President Roosevelt met at the White House to develop a joint war policy. Stalin had asked his allies to relieve German pressure on his armies in the east. He wanted them to open a second front in the west. This would split the Germans' strength by forcing them to fight major battles in two regions instead of one. Churchill agreed with Stalin's strategy. The Allies would weaken Germany on two fronts before dealing a deathblow. At first, Roosevelt was torn, but ultimately he agreed.

The Tide Turns on Two Fronts

Churchill wanted Britain and the United States to strike first at North Africa and southern Europe. The strategy angered Stalin. He wanted the Allies to open the second front in France. The Soviet Union, therefore, had to hold out on its own against the Germans. All Britain and the United States could offer in the way of help was supplies. Nevertheless, late in 1942, the Allies began to turn the tide of war both in the Mediterranean and on the Eastern Front.

The North African Campaign As you recall from Section 1, General Erwin Rommel took the key Libyan port city of Tobruk in June 1942. With Tobruk's fall, London sent General Bernard Montgomery—"Monty" to his troops—to take control of British forces in North Africa. By the time Montgomery arrived, however, the Germans had advanced to an Egyptian village called El Alamein (AL•uh•MAYN), west of Alexandria. (See the map on page 508.) They were dug in so well that British forces could not go around them. The only way to dislodge them, Montgomery decided, was with a massive frontal attack. The Battle of El Alamein began on the night of October 23. The roar of about 1,000 British guns took the Axis soldiers totally by surprise. They fought back fiercely and held their ground for several days. By November 4, however, Rommel's army had been beaten. He and his forces fell back.

As Rommel retreated west, the Allies launched Operation Torch. On November 8, an Allied force of more than 100,000 troops—mostly Americans—landed in Morocco and Algeria. American general **Dwight D. Eisenhower** led this force. Caught between Montgomery's and Eisenhower's armies, Rommel's Afrika Korps was finally crushed in May 1943.

SECTION 4 PROGRAM RESOURCES

ALL STUDENTS

In-Depth Resources: Unit 4
- Guided Reading, p. 72
- Skillbuilder Practice, p. 75

Formal Assessment
- Section Quiz, p. 280

ENGLISH LEARNERS

In-Depth Resources in Spanish
- Guided Reading, p. 127
- Skillbuilder Practice, p. 129

Reading Study Guide (Spanish), p. 173

Reading Study Guide Audio CD (Spanish)

STRUGGLING READERS

In-Depth Resources: Unit 4
- Guided Reading, p. 72
- Building Vocabulary, p. 74
- Skillbuilder Practice, p. 75
- Reteaching Activity, p. 91

Reading Study Guide, p. 173

Reading Study Guide Audio CD

GIFTED AND TALENTED STUDENTS

In-Depth Resources: Unit 4
- Primary Sources: from *Farewell to Manzanar,* p. 79; from *Hiroshima,* p. 81

Electronic Library of Primary Sources
- from Testimony Before the Special Senate Committee on Atomic Energy

INTEGRATED TECHNOLOGY

eEdition CD-ROM
Power Presentations CD-ROM
Patterns of Interaction Video Series
- Arming for War: Modern and Medieval Weapons

classzone.com

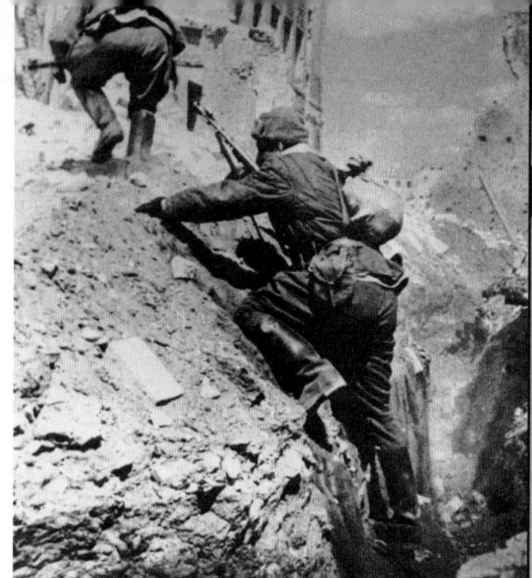

▲ Soviet troops launch an attack during the battle for Stalingrad.

The Battle for Stalingrad As Rommel suffered defeats in North Africa, German armies also met their match in the Soviet Union. The German advance had stalled at Leningrad and Moscow late in 1941. And the bitter winter made the situation worse. When the summer of 1942 arrived, however, Hitler sent his Sixth Army, under the command of General Friedrich Paulus, to seize the oil fields in the Caucasus Mountains. The army was also to capture Stalingrad (now Volgograd), a major industrial center on the Volga River. (See the map on page 508.)

The **Battle of Stalingrad** began on August 23, 1942. The Luftwaffe went on nightly bombing raids that set much of the city ablaze and reduced the rest to rubble. The situation looked desperate. Nonetheless, Stalin had already told his commanders to defend the city named after him to the death.

By early November 1942, Germans controlled 90 percent of the ruined city. Then another Russian winter set in. On November 19, Soviet troops outside the city launched a counterattack. Closing in around Stalingrad, they trapped the Germans inside and cut off their supplies. General Paulus begged Hitler to order a retreat. But Hitler refused, saying the city was "to be held at all costs." (A)

MAIN IDEA
Making Inferences
(A) What advantages might a weaker army fighting on its home soil have over a stronger invading army?
A. Possible Answers would know the territory better than the invading army; would have the support of the local population; would have the additional passion that comes with defending one's own home

On February 2, 1943, some 90,000 frostbitten, half-starved German troops surrendered to the Soviets. These pitiful survivors were all that remained of an army of 330,000. Stalingrad's defense had cost the Soviets over one million soldiers. The city was 99 percent destroyed. However, the Germans were now on the defensive, with the Soviets pushing them steadily westward.

The Invasion of Italy As the Battle of Stalingrad raged, Stalin continued to urge the British and Americans to invade France. However, Roosevelt and Churchill decided to attack Italy first. On July 10, 1943, Allied forces landed on Sicily and captured it from Italian and German troops about a month later.

The conquest of Sicily toppled Mussolini from power. On July 25, King Victor Emmanuel III had the dictator arrested. On September 3, Italy surrendered. But the Germans seized control of northern Italy and put Mussolini back in charge. Finally, the Germans retreated northward, and the victorious Allies entered Rome on June 4, 1944. Fighting in Italy, however, continued until Germany fell in May 1945. On April 27, 1945, Italian resistance fighters ambushed some German trucks near the northern Italian city of Milan. Inside one of the trucks, they found Mussolini disguised as a German soldier. They shot him the next day and later hung his body in downtown Milan for all to see.

The Allied Home Fronts

Wherever Allied forces fought, people on the home fronts rallied to support them. In war-torn countries like the Soviet Union and Great Britain, civilians endured extreme hardships. Many lost their lives. Except for a few of its territories, such as Hawaii, the United States did not suffer invasion or bombing. Nonetheless, Americans at home made a crucial contribution to the Allied war effort. Americans produced the weapons and equipment that would help win the war.

More About . . .

The Battle of Stalingrad

With most of the city in rubble from bombing and shelling, the Soviets defended Stalingrad street by street and house by house in one of the fiercest of all battles of the war. As German soldiers advanced, the Soviets moved back, setting mines and booby traps everywhere they could. In one instance, a sailor armed with only a Molotov cocktail died throwing himself under an advancing tank, which exploded. In another instance, a Soviet soldier died beside a German tank upon which he had written a message in his own blood: "I will die, but my country and the Party will win."

The Allied Home Fronts
10.8.6

Critical Thinking

- How would you summarize the difference between the home fronts of the United States and its major allies? *(Possible Answer: Life was harder for Soviet and British civilians than for Americans.)*
- Why were so many women needed to work in war industries? *(Millions of men were serving as soldiers.)*
- How would you contrast the way Japanese Americans were treated with how they acted during World War II? *(The government treated them as security risks, but many volunteered for the military.)*

DIFFERENTIATING INSTRUCTION: ENGLISH LEARNERS

News Report from Stalingrad

Class Time 35 minutes

Task Writing a "you are there" newscast about the Battle of Stalingrad

Purpose To understand what happened at Stalingrad and why it was important; to improve writing skills

Instructions Divide students into small groups. Have each group reread the information on this page about the Battle of Stalingrad. Encourage groups to use glossaries or dictionaries to help them understand challenging words. Then have each group write a radio news broadcast from the point of view of an American reporter witnessing the battle. News reports should be from 30 to 90 seconds long and may include notations of sound effects. Reports should explain who is fighting, why the battle is important, and what the outcome of the battle could mean. Encourage students to include facts, details, and quotations from the textbook and to use vivid, descriptive language. Have each group elect a member to perform the report for the class.

Students who need more help may complete the Reading Study Guide activity for this lesson (also available in Spanish).

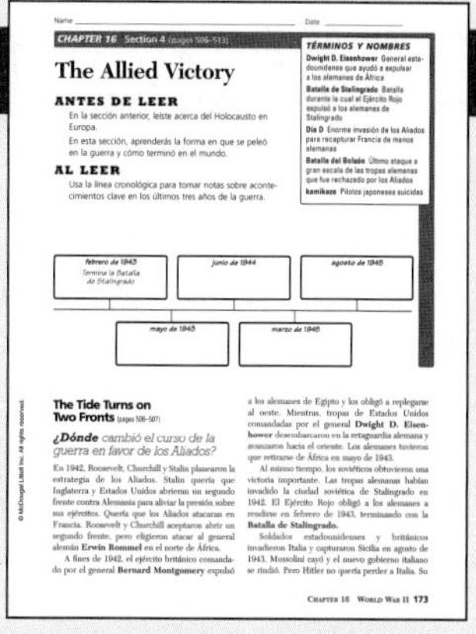

Name ______ Date ______

CHAPTER 16 Section 4 (pages 506–513)

The Allied Victory

ANTES DE LEER

En la sección anterior, leíste acerca del Holocausto en Europa.

En esta sección, aprenderás la forma en que se peleó en la guerra y cómo terminó en el mundo.

AL LEER

Usa la línea cronológica para tomar notas sobre acontecimientos clave en los últimos tres años de la guerra.

TÉRMINOS Y NOMBRES

Dwight D. Eisenhower General estadounidense que ayudó a expulsar a los alemanes de África

Batalla de Stalingrado Batalla durante la cual el Ejército Rojo expulsó a los alemanes de Stalingrado

Día D Enorme invasión de los Aliados para recapturar Francia de manos alemanas

Batalla del Bolsón Último ataque a gran escala de las tropas alemanas que fue rechazado por los Aliados

kamikaze Pilotos japoneses suicidas

febrero de 1943 — *Termina la Batalla de Stalingrado*
mayo de 1943
junio de 1944
marzo de 1945
agosto de 1945

The Tide Turns on Two Fronts (pages 506–507)

***¿Dónde** cambió el curso de la guerra en favor de los Aliados?*

En 1942, Roosevelt, Churchill y Stalin planearon la estrategia de los Aliados. Stalin quería que Inglaterra y Estados Unidos abrieran un segundo frente contra Alemania para aliviar la presión sobre sus ejércitos. Quería que los Aliados atacaran en Francia. Roosevelt y Churchill aceptaron abrir un segundo frente, pero eligieron atacar al general alemán **Erwin Rommel** en el norte de África.

A fines de 1942, el ejército británico comandado por el general **Bernard Montgomery** expulsó a los alemanes de Egipto y los obligó a replegarse al oeste. Mientras, tropas de Estados Unidos comandadas por el general **Dwight D. Eisenhower** desembarcaron en la retaguardia alemana y avanzaron hacia el oriente. Los alemanes tuvieron que retirarse de África en mayo de 1943.

Al mismo tiempo, los soviéticos obtuvieron una victoria importante. Las tropas alemanas habían invadido la ciudad soviética de Stalingrado en 1942. El Ejército Rojo obligó a los alemanes a rendirse en febrero de 1943, terminando con la **Batalla de Stalingrado.**

Soldados estadounidenses y británicos invadieron Italia y capturaron Sicilia en agosto de 1943. Mussolini cayó y el nuevo gobierno italiano se rindió. Pero Hitler no quería perder a Italia. Su

CHAPTER 16 WORLD WAR II 173

Reading Study Guide: Spanish Translation

History from Visuals

Interpreting the Map

Study the map key. Why do you think the cartographer selected the colors used on this map? *(Axis and Axis-controlled are related colors, with the controlled nations lighter to indicate they are not the core of the alliance. The color for the Allies contrasts with these colors. Neutral nations are a neutral color, gray.)*

SKILLBUILDER Answers

1. **Region** Ireland, Spain, Portugal, Sweden, Switzerland
2. **Movement** Germany

INTEGRATED TECHNOLOGY

Interactive This image is available in an interactive format on the eEdition. Students can examine parts of the map in detail.

More About . . .

Attack on Dresden

On February 13, 1945, Allied bombers launched a massive attack on Dresden, a city southeast of Berlin with little military value. The assault created raging firestorms that killed up to 135,000 people, mostly civilians. One author described the city as a "furnace fueled by people." Dresden is now a symbol of "total war": massive attacks to break a country's fighting spirit.

DIFFERENTIATING INSTRUCTION: STRUGGLING READERS

Creating Posters for the Home Front

Class Time 40 minutes

Task Creating posters about war-related themes

Purpose To understand one method governments used to increase public support for World War II

Instructions Tell students that posters were one of the ways that governments encouraged people to rally around the war effort. Point out the poster on page 509, which was designed to appeal to children and teenagers.

Pair a struggling reader with a more proficient reader. Have pairs reread "The Allied Home Fronts" subsection. Then have the pairs use information from this subsection to create a poster of their own. Posters might have one or more of these themes:

- encouraging civilians to specific efforts, such as recycling, working in a munitions factory, or buying war stamps and bonds
- describing hardships faced in other Allied nations
- calling for support of government leaders, soldiers, or the war effort

If time permits, have students use library resources or the Internet to research World War II posters. Show these posters in class and compare them with the posters students made. Discuss whether the World War II–era posters would be effective today.

Mobilizing for War Defeating the Axis powers required mobilizing for total war. In the United States, factories converted their peacetime operations to wartime production and made everything from machine guns to boots. Automobile factories produced tanks. A typewriter company made armor-piercing shells. By 1944, between 17 and 18 million U.S. workers—many of them women—had jobs in war industries.

With factories turning out products for the war, a shortage of consumer goods hit the United States. From meat and sugar to tires and gasoline, from nylon stockings to laundry soap, the American government rationed scarce items. Setting the speed limit at 35 miles per hour also helped to save gasoline and rubber. In European countries directly affected by the war, rationing was even more drastic.

Vocabulary
rationed: distributed in limited amounts

To inspire their people to greater efforts, Allied governments conducted highly effective propaganda campaigns. In the Soviet Union, a Moscow youngster collected enough scrap metal to produce 14,000 artillery shells. And a Russian family used its life savings to buy a tank for the Red Army. In the United States, youngsters saved their pennies and bought government war stamps and bonds to help finance the war.

▲ American schoolchildren helped the war effort by recycling scrap metal and rubber and by buying war bonds.

War Limits Civil Rights Government propaganda also had a negative effect. After Pearl Harbor, a wave of prejudice arose in the United States against Japanese Americans. Most lived in Hawaii and on the West Coast. The bombing of Pearl Harbor frightened Americans. This fear, encouraged by government propaganda, was turned against Japanese Americans. They were suddenly seen as "the enemy." On February 19, 1942, President Roosevelt issued an executive order calling for the internment of Japanese Americans because they were considered a threat to the country. B

MAIN IDEA
Analyzing Motives
B Why did U.S. government propaganda try to portray the Japanese as sinister?

B. Possible Answer It would be easier to get Americans' support to fight the Japanese if they believed they were opposing evil.

In March, the military began rounding up "aliens" and shipping them to relocation camps. The camps were restricted military areas located far away from the coast. Such locations, it was thought, would prevent these "enemy aliens" from assisting a Japanese invasion. However, two-thirds of those interned were Nisei, native-born American citizens whose parents were Japanese. Many of them volunteered for military service and fought bravely for the United States, even though their families remained in the camps.

Victory in Europe

While the Allies were dealing with issues on the home front, they also were preparing to push toward victory in Europe. In 1943, the Allies began secretly building an invasion force in Great Britain. Their plan was to launch an attack on German-held France across the English Channel.

The D-Day Invasion By May 1944, the invasion force was ready. Thousands of planes, ships, tanks, and landing craft and more than three million troops awaited the order to attack. General Dwight D. Eisenhower, the commander of this enormous force, planned to strike on the coast of Normandy, in northwestern France. The Germans knew that an attack was coming. But they did not know where it would be launched. To keep Hitler guessing, the Allies set up a huge dummy army with its own headquarters and equipment. This make-believe army appeared to be preparing to attack the French seaport of Calais (ka•LAY).

More About . . .

The Home Front

While many people in Britain were collecting pots and pans for scrap metal, in the United States war bond rallies were held across the nation. Movie stars and other celebrities often appeared at these rallies and were very effective in helping raise billions of dollars in bonds sales.

Victory in Europe

10.8.3; 10.8.4

Critical Thinking

- How quickly after D-Day did the Allies liberate Paris? *(within three months)* What does this indicate about the relative strength of the Allies and the Axis forces? *(The Allies were stronger.)*
- What caused Germany to surrender? *(Allied and Soviet troops were preparing to take Berlin; Hitler had committed suicide.)*

DIFFERENTIATING INSTRUCTION: GIFTED AND TALENTED STUDENTS

Debating Reparations for Internees

Class Time 30 minutes

Task Holding a debate on the issue of reparations for Japanese Americans who were interned

Purpose To understand the issue of reparations

Instructions Explain that in 1988, the United States government admitted that the country had been wrong to incarcerate Japanese Americans during World War II and authorized payments of $20,000 to survivors of the camps.

Divide the class into pairs. Each pair should prepare a debate on providing reparations payments to Japanese Americans. One student should support the action and the other should oppose it. Some of the issues that students might address in their debate include:

- why the internment of Japanese Americans was unjust
- the payment of reparations to other groups, such as to African Americans for slavery or to Native Americans for the loss of their land
- possible alternatives to reparations

For background information, students should consult their textbook, library resources, the Internet, or the primary source excerpt from *Farewell to Manzanar,* found in the In-Depth Resources book.

PRIMARY SOURCE *from Farewell to Manzanar*
by Jeanne Wakatsuki Houston

In-Depth Resources: Unit 4

History from Visuals

Interpreting the Map

How wide was the Allied invasion front? *(around 45 miles)* Discuss the impact of invading along such a broad front. *(It spread the defense but required extensive coordination.)*

SKILLBUILDER Answers

1. **Human-Environment Interaction** flooding
2. **Movement** to move quickly into the interior

INTEGRATED TECHNOLOGY

Interactive This image is available in an interactive format on the eEdition.

History Makers

General Dwight D. Eisenhower

Discuss the traits of Eisenhower that inspired loyalty. *(Possible Answers: intelligence, ability to work closely with others)* Eisenhower once said, "When they [soldiers] called me Uncle Ike or . . . just plain Ike, I knew everything was going well."

INTEGRATED TECHNOLOGY

Rubric Illustrated reports should
- identify landmarks in Eisenhower's career.
- describe his personality and character.
- use visuals to emphasize key points.

The D-Day Invasion, June 6, 1944

INTERACTIVE

English Channel

21st ARMY GROUP COMMANDER OF GROUND FORCES Montgomery

U.S. 1st ARMY Bradley

BRITISH 2nd ARMY Dempsey

Quinéville, Ste.-Mère Eglise, UTAH BEACH, POINTE-DU-HOC, OMAHA BEACH, GOLD BEACH, JUNO BEACH, SWORD BEACH, La Madeleine, Vierville, Colleville, Arromanches, Courseulles, Isigny, Trévières, Bayeux, Lion, Carentan, to St.-Lô, Caen

London, UNITED KINGDOM, Dover, Portsmouth, Torquay, Portland, Calais, Straits of Dover, English Channel, Cherbourg, FRANCE, 50° N, 48° N, 2° E

Allied forces
Flooded areas
Glider landing areas
Planned drop zones

GEOGRAPHY SKILLBUILDER: Interpreting Maps

1. **Human-Environment Interaction** *What environmental problem might have been encountered by 1st Army soldiers landing at Utah Beach?*
2. **Movement** *Looking at the map, what might have been the Allied strategy behind parachuting troops into France?*

History Makers

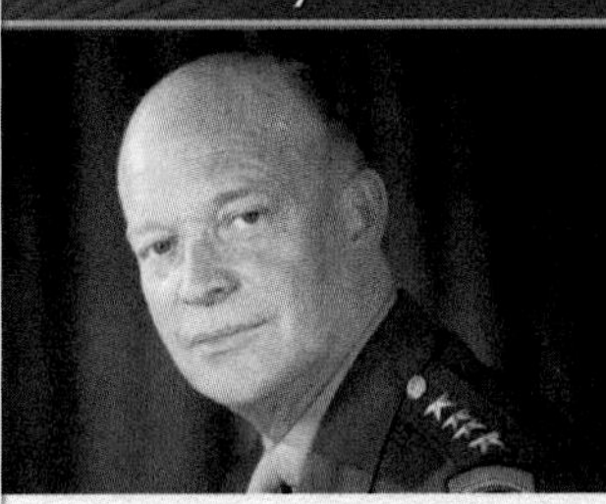

General Dwight D. Eisenhower
1890–1969

In his career, U.S. General Dwight Eisenhower had shown an uncommon ability to work with all kinds of people—even competitive Allies. His chief of staff said of Eisenhower, "The sun rises and sets on him for me." He was also wildly popular with the troops, who affectionately called him "Uncle Ike."

So it was not a surprise when, in December 1943, U.S. Army Chief of Staff George Marshall named Eisenhower as supreme commander of the Allied forces in Europe. The new commander's "people skills" enabled him to join American and British forces together to put a permanent end to Nazi aggression.

INTEGRATED TECHNOLOGY

INTERNET ACTIVITY Create an illustrated report on Eisenhower's military career. Go to **classzone.com** for your research.

Code-named Operation Overlord, the invasion of Normandy was the largest land and sea attack in history. The invasion began on June 6, 1944—known as **D-Day**. At dawn on that day, British, American, French, and Canadian troops fought their way onto a 60-mile stretch of beach in Normandy. (See the map on this page.) The Germans had dug in with machine guns, rocket launchers, and cannons. They sheltered behind concrete walls three feet thick. Not surprisingly, the Allies took heavy casualties. Among the American forces alone, more than 2,700 men died on the beaches that day.

Despite heavy losses, the Allies held the beachheads. Within a month of D-Day, more than one million additional troops had landed. Then, on July 25, the Allies punched a hole in the German defenses near Saint-Lô (san•LOH), and the United States Third Army, led by General George Patton, broke out. A month later, the Allies marched triumphantly into Paris. By September, they had liberated France, Belgium, and Luxembourg. They then set their sights on Germany.

Vocabulary
beachheads: enemy shoreline captured just before invading forces move inland

The Battle of the Bulge As Allied forces moved toward Germany from the west, the Soviet army was advancing toward Germany from the east. Hitler now faced a war on two fronts. In a desperate gamble, he decided to counterattack in the west. Hitler hoped a victory would split American and British forces and break up Allied supply lines. Explaining the reasoning behind his plan, Hitler said, "This battle is to decide whether we shall live or die. . . . All resistance must be broken in a wave of terror."

On December 16, German tanks broke through weak American defenses along a 75-mile front in the Ardennes. The push into Allied lines gave the campaign its name—the **Battle of the Bulge**. Although caught off guard, the Allies eventually pushed the Germans back. The Germans had little choice but to retreat, since there were no reinforcements available.

SKILLBUILDER PRACTICE: FOLLOWING CHRONOLOGICAL ORDER

Putting Events in Sequence

Class Time 35 minutes

Task Ordering events in the sequence in which they occurred

Purpose To develop skill at using chronological order

Instructions Explain that chronological thinking is an important part of our lives. Putting events in the order they occurred is often a key to understanding relationships between events, particularly between causes and effects and between problems and solutions. Dates in a text and words such as *after, next,* and *as* often provide clues to the order of events.

Divide students into small groups. Have each group work together to put the events described under the head "Victory in Europe" (pages 509–511) in chronological order.

For more practice following chronological order, have students complete the Skillbuilder Practice activity for this lesson.

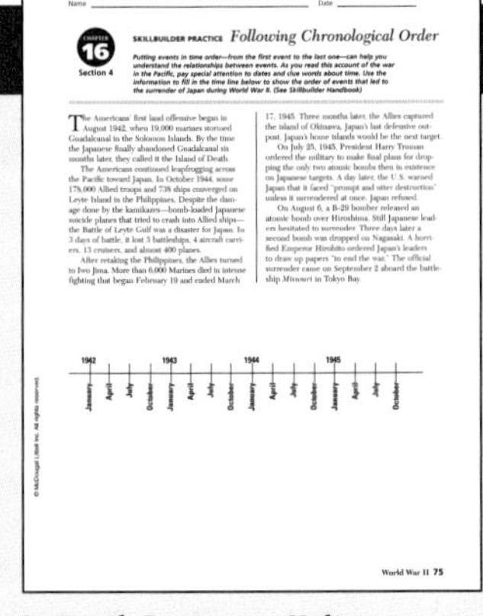

In-Depth Resources: Unit 4

510 Chapter 16

Germany's Unconditional Surrender After the Battle of the Bulge, the war in Europe rapidly drew to a close. In late March 1945, the Allies rolled across the Rhine River into Germany. By the middle of April, a noose was closing around Berlin. About three million Allied soldiers approached Berlin from the southwest. Another six million Soviet troops approached from the east. By April 25, 1945, the Soviets had surrounded the capital and were pounding the city with artillery fire.

While Soviet shells burst over Berlin, Hitler prepared for his end in an underground headquarters beneath the crumbling city. On April 29, he married his longtime companion, Eva Braun. The next day, Hitler and Eva Braun committed suicide. Their bodies were then carried outside and burned.

On May 7, 1945, General Eisenhower accepted the unconditional surrender of the Third Reich from the German military. President Roosevelt, however, did not live to witness the long-awaited victory. He had died suddenly on April 12, as Allied armies were advancing toward Berlin. Roosevelt's successor, Harry Truman, received the news of the Nazi surrender. On May 9, the surrender was officially signed in Berlin. The United States and other Allied powers celebrated V-E Day—Victory in Europe Day. After nearly six years of fighting, the war in Europe had ended.

Victory in the Pacific

Although the war in Europe was over, the Allies were still fighting the Japanese in the Pacific. With the Allied victory at Guadalcanal, however, the Japanese advances in the Pacific had been stopped. For the rest of the war, the Japanese retreated before the counterattack of the Allied powers.

The Japanese in Retreat By the fall of 1944, the Allies were moving in on Japan. In October, Allied forces landed on the island of Leyte (LAY•tee) in the Philippines. General Douglas MacArthur, who had been ordered to leave the islands before their surrender in May 1942, waded ashore at Leyte with his troops. On reaching the beach, he declared, "People of the Philippines, I have returned."

▼ U.S. marines raise the Stars and Stripes after their victory at Iwo Jima.

Actually, the takeover would not be quite that easy. The Japanese had devised a bold plan to halt the Allied advance. They would destroy the American fleet, thus preventing the Allies from resupplying their ground troops. This plan, however, required risking almost the entire Japanese fleet. They took this gamble on October 23, in the Battle of Leyte Gulf. Within four days, the Japanese navy had lost disastrously—eliminating it as a fighting force in the war. Now, only the Japanese army and the feared kamikaze stood between the Allies and Japan. The **kamikazes** were Japanese suicide pilots. They would sink Allied ships by crash-diving their bomb-filled planes into them.

Vocabulary
These pilots took their name from the *kamikaze,* or "divine wind," that saved Japan from a Mongol invasion in 1281.

In March 1945, after a month of bitter fighting and heavy losses, American Marines took Iwo Jima (EE•wuh JEE•muh), an island 760 miles from Tokyo. On April 1, U.S. troops moved onto the island of Okinawa, only about 350 miles from southern Japan. The Japanese put up a desperate fight. Nevertheless, on June 21, one of the bloodiest land battles of the war ended. The Japanese lost over 100,000 troops, and the Americans 12,000.

Victory in the Pacific
10.8.4; 10.9.1

Critical Thinking

- How was the Battle of Leyte Gulf similar to the Battle of the Bulge? *(Both were last, desperate efforts that failed.)*
- What does the use of kamikazes indicate about the strength of the Japanese navy? *(It was so weak they had to hope that suicidal missions would halt the American advance.)*
- What alternatives did the United States have to making a full-scale invasion of Japan or to using atomic bombs there? *(Possible Answers: using conventional weapons, seizing selected targets, blockading Japan, supporting leaders who saw defeat coming, negotiating a treaty)*

More About . . .

The Kamikaze

The word *kamikaze* means "divine wind." It refers to a typhoon that in 1281 saved Japan by destroying the Mongol navy. The Japanese hoped that the kamikaze pilots would be able to save Japan from an Allied invasion.

CONNECTIONS ACROSS TIME AND CULTURES

Modern and Medieval Weapons

Class Time 45 minutes

Task Watching and responding to a video

Purpose To understand how new weapons affected battles in medieval times, during World War II, and in recent years

Instructions Show students the video *Arming for War: Modern and Medieval Weapons.* When students have watched the video, use the following questions to begin a discussion.

- What pattern do you see repeating in this video? *(New developments in weapons can change the outcomes of wars and cause arms races.)*
- What are advantages and disadvantages of developing new weapons? *(Advantages–Opponents lack similar weapons; may end conflicts sooner. Disadvantages–Expensive, destructive, leads to arms races.)*
- What recent developments have there been in weapons technology? *(Possible Answers: Stealth bombers, night-vision goggles, "smart bombs")*

To explore this issue further, have students complete the political cartoons activity in the Teacher's Resource Book.

Name ______ Date ______

VIDEO **Political Cartoons**
The Atomic Bomb: Good or Bad?

Examine each cartoon and answer the questions.

On August 6, 1945, the United States dropped an atomic bomb on the Japanese city of Hiroshima, killing about 70,000 people instantly. Three days later a second atomic bomb was dropped on the city of Nagasaki, prompting the Japanese surrender that ended World War II. World reaction to the use of this weapon was mixed. Many people accepted the U.S. government's argument that by making an invasion of Japan unnecessary, the dropping of the bombs saved many lives. Others, however, worried that a terrifying new force had been unleashed upon a world unprepared to control it. These two sentiments are reflected in the following cartoons, which appeared shortly after the bombings.

"But for the Grace of God—"

Memphis Commercial Appeal, August 1945

INTERPRETING TEXT AND VISUALS

1. In this cartoon, what is the meaning of the ghostly soldier labeled "avoided costs"?
2. What do you think is the cartoonist's attitude toward the dropping of atomic bombs on Japan?

"Baby Play with Nice Ball?"

Sir David Low, *The London Standard,* August 1945

INTERPRETING TEXT AND VISUALS

3. In this cartoon, whom does the adult in the white jacket represent? What is the "nice ball" he is offering?
4. What concerns about the use of atomic power is the cartoonist expressing?

Arming for War: Modern and Medieval Weapons 69

Patterns of Interaction Teacher's Resource Book

Global Impact

OBJECTIVE

- Understand key events in the development and use of the first atomic bomb.

INSTRUCT

Point out that the first atomic bombs, though incredibly powerful for 1945, are small by today's standards. Ask students how confident they are in humans' ability to control such potent weapons. *(Possible Answers: confident, because nobody wants to risk world destruction; not confident, because several countries have access to such weapons)*

Show *Arming for War: Modern and Medieval Weapons* to demonstrate that arms races have existed throughout history.

- The first segment of the video chronicles nations' quests for new weapons during World War I and World War II.
- The second segment shows students that arms races took place in medieval times as well, when the longbow and other weapons changed military history.

Patterns of Interaction

- *Arming for War: Modern and Medieval Weapons*

Electronic Library of Primary Sources

- from Testimony Before the Special Senate Committee on Atomic Energy

Global Impact: Arming for War

The Atomic Bomb

On the eve of World War II, scientists in Germany succeeded in splitting the nucleus of a uranium atom, releasing a huge amount of energy. Albert Einstein wrote to President Franklin Roosevelt and warned him that Nazi Germany might be working to develop atomic weapons. Roosevelt responded by giving his approval for an American program, later code-named the Manhattan Project, to develop an atomic bomb. Roosevelt's decision set off a race to ensure that the United States would be the first to develop the bomb.

CALIFORNIA STANDARDS
10.8.6, HI 3

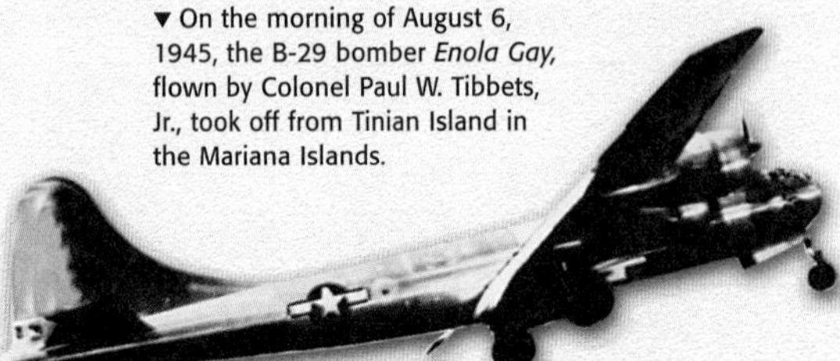

▼ On the morning of August 6, 1945, the B-29 bomber *Enola Gay*, flown by Colonel Paul W. Tibbets, Jr., took off from Tinian Island in the Mariana Islands.

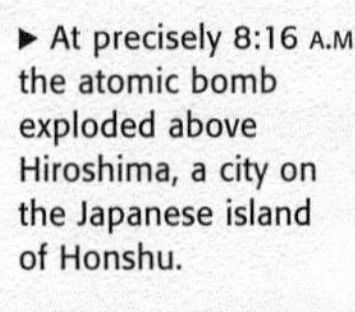

► At precisely 8:16 A.M., the atomic bomb exploded above Hiroshima, a city on the Japanese island of Honshu.

Patterns of Interaction
Arming for War: Modern and Medieval Weapons

Just as in World War I, the conflicts of World War II spurred the development of ever more powerful weapons. Mightier tanks, more elusive submarines, faster fighter planes—all emerged from this period. From ancient times to the present day, the pattern remains the same: Every new weapon causes other countries to develop weapons of similar or greater force. This pattern results in a deadly race for an ultimate weapon: for example, the atomic bomb.

Hiroshima: Day of Fire

Impact of the Bombing	
Ground temperatures	7,000°F
Hurricane force winds	980 miles per hour
Energy released	20,000 tons of TNT
Buildings destroyed	62,000 buildings
Killed immediately	70,000 people
Dead by the end of 1945	140,000 people
Total deaths related to A-bomb	210,000 people

The overwhelming destructive power of the Hiroshima bomb, and of the bomb dropped on Nagasaki three days later, changed the nature of war forever. Nuclear destruction also led to questions about the ethics of scientists and politicians who chose to develop and use the bomb.

▼ Nagasaki citizens trudge through the still smoldering ruins of their city in this photograph by Yosuke Yamahata.

512

Connect *to* Today

1. **Making Inferences** What advantages did the United States have over Germany in the race to develop the atomic bomb?
   See Skillbuilder Handbook, page R10.
2. **Comparing and Contrasting** If you were to design a memorial to the victims of the Hiroshima and Nagasaki bombings, what symbol would you use? Make a sketch of your memorial.

CONNECT TO TODAY: ANSWERS

1. Making Inferences

Possible Answer: The U.S. mainland was insulated from the war. Scientists and technicians were able to pursue their research with less disruption than the Germans had. Also, scientists such as Albert Einstein had fled Germany to work in the United States.

2. Comparing and Contrasting

Possible Answers: A diagram of an atom splitting would highlight the source of the power. A peace symbol might emphasize the hope that such a terrible weapon would never be used again. A mushroom cloud would focus attention on the explosion. A Japanese flag with an American flag would remind viewers of the nations that participated in the conflict.

The Japanese Surrender After Okinawa, the next stop for the Allies had to be Japan. President Truman's advisers had informed him that an invasion of the Japanese homeland might cost the Allies half a million lives. Truman had to make a decision whether to use a powerful new weapon called the atomic bomb, or A-bomb. Most of his advisers felt that using it would bring the war to the quickest possible end. The bomb had been developed by the top-secret Manhattan Project, headed by General Leslie Groves and chief scientist J. Robert Oppenheimer. Truman first learned of the new bomb's existence when he became president.

The first atomic bomb was exploded in a desert in New Mexico on July 16, 1945. President Truman then warned the Japanese. He told them that unless they surrendered, they could expect a "rain of ruin from the air." The Japanese did not reply. So, on August 6, 1945, the United States dropped an atomic bomb on Hiroshima, a Japanese city of nearly 350,000 people. Between 70,000 and 80,000 people died in the attack. Three days later, on August 9, a second bomb was dropped on Nagasaki, a city of 270,000. More than 70,000 people were killed immediately. Radiation fallout from the two explosions killed many more.

The Japanese finally surrendered to General Douglas MacArthur on September 2. The ceremony took place aboard the United States battleship *Missouri* in Tokyo Bay. With Japan's surrender, the war had ended. Now, countries faced the task of rebuilding a war-torn world.

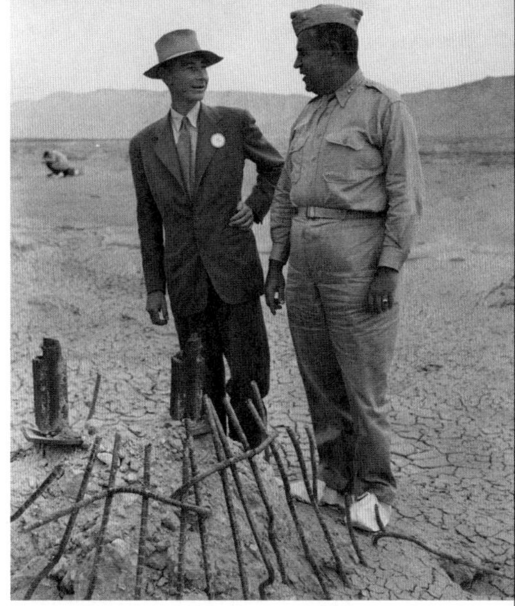

▲ J. Robert Oppenheimer (left) and General Leslie Groves inspect the site of the first atomic bomb test near Alamogordo, New Mexico.

More About . . .

Colonel Tibbets

The plane that dropped the atom bomb on Hiroshima was called the *Enola Gay* and was piloted by Colonel Paul W. Tibbets, Jr. He described what he saw after releasing the bomb: "Down below the thing [the mushroom cloud] reminded me more of a boiling pot of tar than any other description I can give it. It was black and boiling underneath with a steam haze on top of it . . . We had seen the city when we went in, and there was nothing to see when we came back. It was covered by this boiling, black-looking mass."

In-Depth Resources: Unit 4

• Primary Source: from *Hiroshima,* p. 81

SECTION  4 ASSESSMENT

TERMS & NAMES 1. For each term or name, write a sentence explaining its significance.

• Dwight D. Eisenhower • Battle of Stalingrad • D-Day • Battle of the Bulge • kamikaze

USING YOUR NOTES

2. Which battle do you think was most important in turning the war in favor of the Allies? Why? (10.8.3)

Battle	Outcome
Battle of El Alamein	
Battle of Stalingrad	
D-Day Invasion	

MAIN IDEAS

3. Why did Stalin want the United States and Britain to launch a second front in the west? (10.8.4)
4. How did the Allies try to conceal the true location for the D-Day landings? (10.8.3)
5. What brought about the Japanese surrender? (10.8.3)

CRITICAL THINKING & WRITING

6. **CLARIFYING** How do governments gather support for a war effort on the home front? (10.8.3)
7. **ANALYZING ISSUES** Should governments have the power to limit the rights of their citizens during wartime? Explain your answer. (10.8.3)
8. **FORMING AND SUPPORTING OPINIONS** Did President Truman make the correct decision in using the atomic bomb? Why or why not? (10.9.1)
9. **WRITING ACTIVITY** SCIENCE AND TECHNOLOGY Write a **research report** on the work of the Manhattan Project in developing the atomic bomb. (Writing 2.3.b)

CONNECT TO TODAY **CREATING A POSTER**

During World War II, the U.S. government used propaganda posters to encourage citizens to support the war effort. Create a similar kind of **poster** to encourage support for a war on litter in your neighborhood. (Writing 2.4.b)

❸ ASSESS

SECTION 4 ASSESSMENT

As a class, discuss students' answers to question 7.

Formal Assessment

• Section Quiz, p. 280

❹ RETEACH

Use the Reteaching Activity to review this section.

In-Depth Resources: Unit 4

• Reteaching Activity, p. 91

ANSWERS

1. Dwight D. Eisenhower, p. 506 • Battle of Stalingrad, p. 507 • D-Day, p. 510 • Battle of the Bulge, p. 510 • kamikaze, p. 511
2. **Sample Answer:** El Alamein—Rommel defeated. Stalingrad—Victory on the eastern front. D-Day—The recapture of Western Europe began. Most important—Stalingrad, because it put Hitler on the defensive.
3. to relieve pressure on the Soviets
4. prepared a dummy army to attack Calais
5. the use of atomic weapons
6. **Possible Answers:** rationing materials that are essential to the war effort; raising money; using propaganda
7. No—Rights must still be protected. Yes—Short-term restrictions may provide long-term protection.
8. Yes—It ended the war quickly. No—It killed many innocent people.
9. **Rubric** Research reports should
   • identify leading scientists involved in the Manhattan Project.
   • describe the goal of the project.
   • cite sources.

CONNECT TO TODAY

Rubric Posters should

• clearly illustrate the goal.
• explain the problems with litter.
• employ propaganda techniques.

LESSON PLAN

OBJECTIVES

- Describe conditions in Europe in 1945.
- Identify the political consequences of the Allied victory in postwar Europe.
- Summarize how defeat and occupation affected political and civic life in Japan.
- Describe Japan's postwar constitution.

1 FOCUS & MOTIVATE

Discuss whether military aggression achieves goals. *(Possible Answer: did not for Germany and Japan in World War II)*

2 INSTRUCT

Devastation in Europe
10.8.6

Critical Thinking

- Compare the devastation in Europe after World War I and World War II. *(World War II resulted in far more deaths and dislocated many more people.)*

World Art and Cultures Transparencies
- AT71 *Liberation*

CALIFORNIA RESOURCES
California Reading Toolkit, p. L74
California Modified Lesson Plans for English Learners, p. 143
California Daily Standards Practice Transparencies, TT66
California Standards Enrichment Workbook, pp. 85–86, 89–90
California Standards Planner and Lesson Plans, p. L139
California Online Test Practice
California Test Generator CD-ROM
California Easy Planner CD-ROM
California eEdition CD-ROM

Adolf Hitler on his 50th birthday, April 20, 1939

5

Poster encouraging Americans to buy war bonds

Europe and Japan in Ruins

MAIN IDEA	WHY IT MATTERS NOW	TERMS & NAMES
ECONOMICS World War II cost millions of human lives and billions of dollars in damages. It left Europe and Japan in ruins.	The United States survived World War II undamaged, allowing it to become a world leader.	• Nuremberg Trials • demilitarization • democratization

CALIFORNIA STANDARDS

10.8.4 Describe the political, diplomatic, and military leaders during the war (e.g., Winston Churchill, Franklin Delano Roosevelt, Emperor Hirohito, Adolf Hitler, Benito Mussolini, Joseph Stalin, Douglas MacArthur, Dwight Eisenhower).

10.8.6 Discuss the human costs of the war, with particular attention to the civilian and military losses in Russia, Germany, Britain, the United States, China, and Japan.

CST 1 Students compare the present with the past, evaluating the consequences of past events and decisions and determining the lessons that were learned.

CST 4 Students relate current events to the physical and human characteristics of places and regions.

SETTING THE STAGE After six long years of war, the Allies finally were victorious. However, their victory had been achieved at a very high price. World War II had caused more death and destruction than any other conflict in history. It left 60 million dead. About one-third of these deaths occurred in one country, the Soviet Union. Another 50 million people had been uprooted from their homes and wandered the countryside in search of somewhere to live. Property damage ran into billions of U.S. dollars.

Devastation in Europe

By the end of World War II, Europe lay in ruins. Close to 40 million Europeans had died, two-thirds of them civilians. Constant bombing and shelling had reduced hundreds of cities to rubble. The ground war had destroyed much of the countryside. Displaced persons from many nations were left homeless.

A Harvest of Destruction A few of the great cities of Europe—Paris, Rome, and Brussels—remained largely undamaged by war. Many, however, had suffered terrible destruction. The Battle of Britain left huge areas of London little more than blackened ruins. Warsaw, the capital of Poland, was almost completely destroyed. In 1939, Warsaw had a population of nearly 1.3 million. When Soviet soldiers entered the city in January 1945, only 153,000 people remained. Thousands of tons of Allied bombs had demolished 95 percent of the central area of Berlin. One U.S. officer stationed in the German capital reported, "Wherever we looked we saw desolation. It was like a city of the dead."

TAKING NOTES
Comparing and Contrasting Use a Venn diagram to compare and contrast the aftermath of World War II in Europe and Japan.

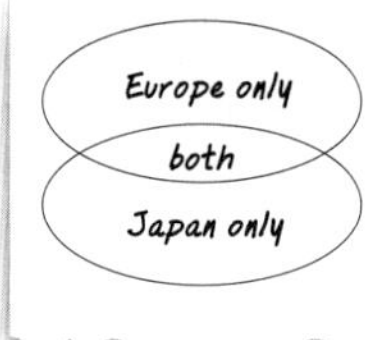

After the bombings, many civilians stayed where they were and tried to get on with their lives. Some lived in partially destroyed homes or apartments. Others huddled in cellars or caves made from rubble. They had no water, no electricity, and very little food.

A large number of people did not stay where they were. Rather, they took to the roads. These displaced persons included the survivors of concentration camps, prisoners of war, and refugees who found themselves in the wrong country when postwar treaties changed national borders. They wandered across Europe, hoping to find their families or to find a safe place to live.

Simon Weisenthal, a prisoner at Auschwitz, described the search made by Holocaust survivors:

SECTION 5 PROGRAM RESOURCES

ALL STUDENTS
In-Depth Resources: Unit 4
- Guided Reading, p. 73

Formal Assessment
- Section Quiz, p. 281

ENGLISH LEARNERS
In-Depth Resources in Spanish
- Guided Reading, p. 128

Reading Study Guide (Spanish), p. 175
Reading Study Guide Audio CD (Spanish)

STRUGGLING READERS
In-Depth Resources: Unit 4
- Guided Reading, p. 73
- Building Vocabulary, p. 74
- Reteaching Activity, p. 92

Reading Study Guide, p. 175
Reading Study Guide Audio CD

GIFTED AND TALENTED STUDENTS
In-Depth Resources: Unit 4
- Connections Across Time and Cultures, p. 87

INTEGRATED TECHNOLOGY
eEdition CD-ROM
Power Presentations CD-ROM
Critical Thinking Transparencies
- CT32 Causes and Effects of World War II
- CT68 Chapter 32 Visual Summary

World Art and Cultures Transparencies
- AT71 *Liberation*

Electric Library of Primary Sources
- from Affidavit Given at Nuremberg, 1946.

classzone.com

Costs of World War II: Allies and Axis			
	Direct War Costs	Military Killed/Missing	Civilians Killed
United States	$288.0 billion*	292,131**	–
Great Britain	$117.0 billion	272,311	60,595
France	$111.3 billion	205,707***	173,260†
USSR	$93.0 billion	13,600,000	7,720,000
Germany	$212.3 billion	3,300,000	2,893,000††
Japan	$41.3 billion	1,140,429	953,000

* In 1994 dollars.
** An additional 115,187 servicemen died from non-battle causes.
*** Before surrender to Nazis.
† Includes 65,000 murdered Jews.
†† Includes about 170,000 murdered Jews and 56,000 foreign civilians in Germany.

SKILLBUILDER: Interpreting Charts
1. **Drawing Conclusions** *Which of the nations listed in the chart suffered the greatest human costs?*
2. **Comparing** *How does U.S. spending on the war compare with the spending of Germany and Japan?*

History from Visuals

Interpreting the Chart

Discuss why the figures for the military combine killed and missing. *(Those missing were probably dead.)*

SKILLBUILDER Answers
1. **Drawing Conclusions** the USSR and Germany
2. **Comparing** The United States spent more than Germany and Japan combined.

PRIMARY SOURCE

Across Europe a wild tide of frantic survivors was flowing. . . . Many of them didn't really know where to go. . . . And yet the survivors continued their pilgrimage of despair. . . . "Perhaps someone is still alive. . . ." Someone might tell where to find a wife, a mother, children, a brother—or whether they were dead. . . . The desire to find one's people was stronger than hunger, thirst, fatigue.

SIMON WEISENTHAL, quoted in *Never to Forget: The Jews of the Holocaust*

Misery Continues After the War The misery in Europe continued for years after the war. The fighting had ravaged Europe's countryside, and agriculture had been completely disrupted. Most able-bodied men had served in the military, and the women had worked in war production. Few remained to plant the fields. With the transportation system destroyed, the meager harvests often did not reach the cities. Thousands died as famine and disease spread through the bombed-out cities. The first postwar winter brought more suffering as people went without shoes and coats.

A. Possible Answer Since Germany's entire leadership had been Nazi for 12 years, no real democratic leadership had been allowed to develop.

Postwar Governments and Politics

Despairing Europeans often blamed their leaders for the war and its aftermath. Once the Germans had lost, some prewar governments—like those in Belgium, Holland, Denmark, and Norway—returned quickly. In countries like Germany, Italy, and France, however, a return to the old leadership was not desirable. Hitler's Nazi government had brought Germany to ruins. Mussolini had led Italy to defeat. The Vichy government had collaborated with the Nazis. Much of the old leadership was in disgrace. Also, in Italy and France, many resistance fighters were communists. A

MAIN IDEA
Identifying Problems
A Why might it have been difficult to find democratic government leaders in post-Nazi Germany?

After the war, the Communist Party promised change, and millions were ready to listen. In both France and Italy, Communist Party membership skyrocketed. The communists made huge gains in the first postwar elections. Anxious to speed up a political takeover, the communists staged a series of violent strikes. Alarmed French and Italians reacted by voting for anticommunist parties. Communist Party membership and influence began to decline. And they declined even more as the economies of France and Italy began to recover.

More About . . .

Displaced Persons

To help them cross European borders on their way to Palestine, Jews donned uniforms with the insignia CAJR and carried papers stamped with an authentic-looking seal. Few questioned the insignia, which stood for Committee for Assistance to Jewish Refugees.

Postwar Governments and Politics

10.8.4; 10.8.6

Critical Thinking
- What evidence indicates that the people of Belgium, Holland, Denmark, and Norway did not blame their leaders for the war's aftermath? *(Prewar governments returned to power.)*
- Under what conditions should leaders be charged with waging a war of aggression? *(Possible Answer: when world opinion is strongly united)*

DIFFERENTIATING INSTRUCTION: ENGLISH LEARNERS

Persuading Americans to Help Displaced Persons

Class Time 35 minutes
Task Creating a brochure
Purpose To explain the effects of World War II on soldiers and civilians in Europe; to practice persuasive writing skills
Instructions Divide students into small groups. Have each group create a brochure that urges Americans to help displaced persons in Europe. Group members should reread the "Devastation in Europe" subsection, searching for information useful to the brochures, such as

- facts and statistics about the number of refugees
- who the refugees are and why they are homeless
- what their living conditions are like
- what or whom they are seeking

Encourage students to use descriptive, persuasive language. Students may illustrate the brochures with drawings or designs.

If students need more help with this section, assign the Reading Study Guide activity (available in English and Spanish).

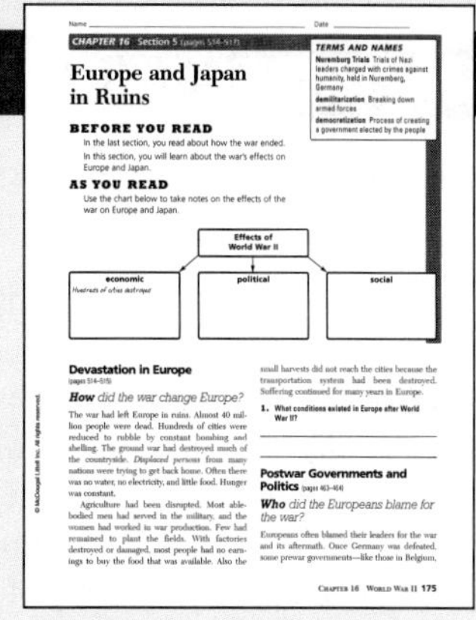
Reading Study Guide

Connect *to* Today

A New War Crimes Tribunal

Have students start a file on the progress of investigations into genocide, war crimes, or other acts prosecuted by international tribunals.

Electronic Library of Primary Sources

- from Affidavit Given at Nuremberg, 1946.

Postwar Japan

10.8.6

Critical Thinking

- Japan continues to have a small military. How might this help its economy? *(A larger military would absorb more money that could be used for other investments.)*
- How were labor unions to help Japan? *(Possible Answers: by aiding democracy and prosperity; by giving Japanese workers rights they had not had previously; by breaking down the old social order)*

Tip for English Learners

Explain that the prefix *de-*, as in *demilitarization* or *decode*, often means to undo an action.

More About . . .

Demilitarization

MacArthur dismissed all Japanese senior military officials actively involved in promoting aggression since 1931. In Japan, just under 0.5 percent of the population were barred from public office. In Germany, 2.5 percent were.

Connect *to* Today

A New War Crimes Tribunal

In 1993, the UN established the International Criminal Tribunal for the Former Yugoslavia (ICTY) to prosecute war crimes committed in the Balkan conflicts of the 1990s. (See Chapter 19.) This was the first international war crimes court since those held in Nuremberg and Tokyo after World War II.

The ICTY issued its first indictment in 1994 and began trial proceedings in 1996. By mid-2003, more than 30 defendants had been tried and found guilty. They received sentences of 5 to 48 years in jail. Another 25 were on trial or awaiting trial. The most prominent of these defendants was Slobadan Milosevic, the former president of Yugoslavia. He was charged with 66 counts of genocide, crimes against humanity, and other war crimes.

The Nuremberg Trials While nations were struggling to recover politically and economically, they also tried to deal with the issue of war crimes. During 1945 and 1946, an International Military Tribunal representing 23 nations put Nazi war criminals on trial in Nuremberg, Germany. In the first of these **Nuremberg Trials**, 22 Nazi leaders were charged with waging a war of aggression. They were also accused of committing "crimes against humanity"—the murder of 11 million people.

Adolf Hitler, SS chief Heinrich Himmler, and Minister of Propaganda Joseph Goebbels had committed suicide long before the trials began. However, Hermann Göring, the commander of the Luftwaffe; Rudolf Hess, Hitler's former deputy; and other high-ranking Nazi leaders remained to face the charges.

Hess was found guilty and was sentenced to life in prison. Göring received a death sentence, but cheated the executioner by committing suicide. Ten other Nazi leaders were hanged on October 16, 1946. Hans Frank, the "Slayer of Poles," was the only convicted Nazi to express remorse: "A thousand years will pass," he said, "and still this guilt of Germany will not have been erased." The bodies of those executed were burned at the concentration camp of Dachau (DAHK•ow). They were cremated in the same ovens that had burned so many of their victims.

Postwar Japan

The defeat suffered by Japan in World War II left the country in ruins. Two million lives had been lost. The country's major cities, including the capital, Tokyo, had been largely destroyed by bombing raids. The atomic bomb had turned Hiroshima and Nagasaki into blackened wastelands. The Allies had stripped Japan of its colonial empire.

Occupied Japan General Douglas MacArthur, who had accepted the Japanese surrender, took charge of the U.S. occupation of Japan. MacArthur was determined to be fair and not to plant the seeds of a future war. Nevertheless, to ensure that peace would prevail, he began a process of **demilitarization**, or disbanding the Japanese armed forces. He achieved this quickly, leaving the Japanese with only a small police force. MacArthur also began bringing war criminals to trial. Out of 25 surviving defendants, former Premier Hideki Tojo and six others were condemned to hang.

MacArthur then turned his attention to **democratization**, the process of creating a government elected by the people. In February 1946, he and his American political advisers drew up a new constitution. It changed the empire into a constitutional monarchy like that of Great Britain. The Japanese accepted the constitution. It went into effect on May 3, 1947.

MacArthur was not told to revive the Japanese economy. However, he was instructed to broaden land ownership and increase the participation of workers and farmers in the new democracy. To this end, MacArthur put forward a plan that required absentee landlords with huge estates to sell land to the government. The government then sold the land to tenant farmers at reasonable prices. Other reforms pushed by MacArthur gave workers the right to create independent labor unions. B

B. Possible Answer The reduced influence of military leaders and increased economic power of the Japanese people might result in a wider sharing of power in Japan.

MAIN IDEA

Making Inferences

B How would demilitarization and a revived economy help Japan achieve democracy?

DIFFERENTIATING INSTRUCTION: GIFTED AND TALENTED STUDENTS

Comparing the World Wars

Class Time 45 minutes

Task Comparing and contrasting World War I and World War II

Purpose To understand patterns in history

Instructions Pair students. Distribute the Connections Across Time and Cultures activity for this section, which can be found in In-Depth Resources: Unit 4. Have students work together to complete the questions that compare and contrast the two world wars. Remind students to review Chapter 13 as well as Chapter 16 as they work on the items.

You may wish to use the following Critical Thinking Transparencies to help students complete the activity: CT13, The Human and Financial Costs of World War I; and CT16, Causes and Effects of World War II.

Ask students to make a generalization about how the two wars were similar and how they differed. *(Possible Answers: Similarities—Massive loss of life, new technologies invented, effects lasted for generations. Differences—Conscious attempt after World War II not to plant the seeds of a future war; World War II led to the creation of atomic and nuclear weapons)*

In-Depth Resources: Unit 4

C. Possible Answer The Japanese wanted to keep their emperor—a monarch. The American system had no place for monarchs.

MAIN IDEA
Analyzing Causes
C Why did the Americans choose the British system of government for the Japanese, instead of the American system?

Occupation Brings Deep Changes

The new constitution was the most important achievement of the occupation. It brought deep changes to Japanese society. A long Japanese tradition had viewed the emperor as divine. He was also an absolute ruler whose will was law. The emperor now had to declare that he was not divine. That admission was as shocking to the Japanese as defeat. His power was also dramatically reduced. Like the ruler of Great Britain, the emperor became largely a figurehead—a symbol of Japan. C

The new constitution guaranteed that real political power in Japan rested with the people. The people elected a two-house parliament, called the Diet. All citizens over the age of 20, including women, had the right to vote. The government was led by a prime minister chosen by a majority of the Diet. A constitutional bill of rights protected basic freedoms. One more key provision of the constitution—Article 9—stated that the Japanese could no longer make war. They could fight only if attacked.

In September 1951, the United States and 47 other nations signed a formal peace treaty with Japan. The treaty officially ended the war. Some six months later, the U.S. occupation of Japan was over. However, with no armed forces, the Japanese agreed to a continuing U.S. military presence to protect their country. The United States and Japan, once bitter enemies, were now allies.

In the postwar world, enemies not only became allies. Sometimes, allies became enemies. World War II had changed the political landscape of Europe. The Soviet Union and the United States emerged from the war as the world's two major powers. They also ended the war as allies. However, it soon became clear that their postwar goals were very different. This difference stirred up conflicts that would shape the modern world for decades.

▲ Emperor Hirohito and U.S. General Douglas MacArthur look distant and uncomfortable as they pose here.

SECTION 5 ASSESSMENT

TERMS & NAMES 1. For each term or name, write a sentence explaining its significance.
• Nuremberg Trials • demilitarization • democratization

USING YOUR NOTES

2. How did the aftermath of the war in Europe differ from the aftermath of the war in Japan? (10.8.6)

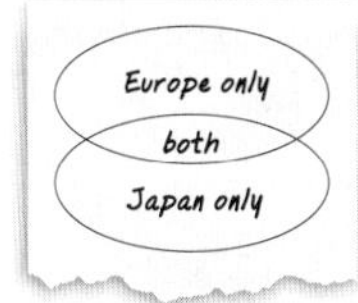

MAIN IDEAS

3. Why did so many Europeans take to the roads and wander the countryside after the war? (10.8.6)
4. How did the Allies deal with the issue of war crimes in Europe? (10.8.6)
5. What three programs did General Douglas MacArthur introduce during the U.S. occupation of Japan? (10.8.4)

CRITICAL THINKING & WRITING

6. **ANALYZING CAUSES** Why do you think that many Europeans favored communism after World War II? (10.8.6)
7. **FORMING AND SUPPORTING OPINIONS** Do you think it was right for the Allies to try only Nazi and Japanese leaders for war crimes? Why or why not? (10.8.6)
8. **MAKING INFERENCES** Why was demilitarization such an important part of the postwar program for Japan? (10.8.6)
9. **WRITING ACTIVITY** ECONOMICS As an observer for the U.S. government, write a **report** on the economic situation in Europe after World War II. Illustrate your report with charts and graphs. (Writing 2.3.d)

CONNECT TO TODAY **CREATING A RADIO NEWS REPORT**
Conduct research on a recent trial at the International War Crimes Tribunal in The Hague. Use your findings to create a two-minute radio **news report** on the trial. (Writing 2.1.a)

Occupation Brings Deep Changes
10.8.4; 10.8.6

Critical Thinking

- How did Japan's postwar constitution compare to the U.S. Constitution? *(Both had an elected legislature, voting rights for men and women, and a bill of rights. Japan's had a prime minister and lacked power to make war.)*
- How did changes in the emperor's postwar role symbolize the changes in Japan? *(It marked the end of some of the traditions that had led Japan into war and the beginning of a new and more democratic era.)*

3 ASSESS

SECTION 5 ASSESSMENT

Have students answer the questions individually and then meet in small groups to discuss their answers.

Formal Assessment
• Section Quiz, p. 281

4 RETEACH

Use the Visual Summary to review this section and chapter.

Critical Thinking Transparencies
• CT68 Chapter 32 Visual Summary

In-Depth Resources: Unit 4
• Reteaching Activity, p. 92

ANSWERS

1. Nuremberg Trials, p. 516 • demilitarization, p. 516 • democratization, p. 516
2. **Sample Answer:** Europe—More displaced persons, famine, communism. Japan—New constitution, radiation from atomic weapons. Both—Death and destruction.
3. People were looking for family members and trying to return home.
4. established International Military Tribunal to try Nazi leaders
5. demilitarization, democratization, economic recovery
6. **Possible Answers:** People lost faith in leaders of the past who had started or conducted the war; communism promised change for people who were suffering.
7. Yes—The acts were horrendous and people deserved punishment. No—Bloodshed and destruction are always a part of war.
8. **Possible Answer:** Militarism had fueled Japanese aggression in World War II and could do so again.
9. **Rubric** Reports should
   • explain Europe's economic difficulties.
   • use visuals effectively.
   • present information fairly.

CONNECT TO TODAY
Rubric News reports should
• explain how the tribunal works.
• identify the defendant and the charges.
• explain the verdict.

TERMS & NAMES

1. blitzkrieg, p. 491
2. Atlantic Charter, p. 496
3. Battle of Midway, p. 500
4. Holocaust, p. 502
5. genocide, p. 503
6. D-Day, p. 510
7. Nuremberg Trials, p. 516
8. demilitarization, p. 516

MAIN IDEAS

Answers will vary.

9. the German attack on Poland in September 1939
10. It was the key for access to the oil fields of Southwest Asia.
11. to destroy the United States Fleet
12. by appealing to their hatred for the colonial powers and by pushing the idea of "Asia for the Asiatics"
13. forced emigration, relocation to ghettos, work in concentration camps
14. death camps
15. Governments needed to supply their armies with materials. Many industries switched to producing war-related goods, causing a shortage of consumer goods.
16. the name used by Allied military leaders for the invasion of Europe in June 1944
17. Many cities were in ruins, so people went in search of a place to live; prisoners of war and Holocaust survivors looked for their families; postwar treaties forced some people to move.
18. demilitarization and democratization

Chapter 16 Assessment

TERMS & NAMES

For each term or name below, briefly explain its connection to World War II.

1. blitzkrieg
2. Atlantic Charter
3. Battle of Midway
4. Holocaust
5. genocide
6. D-Day
7. Nuremberg Trials
8. demilitarization

MAIN IDEAS

Hitler's Lightning War Section 1 (pages 491–496)

9. What event finally unleashed World War II? (10.8.3)
10. Why was capturing Egypt's Suez Canal so important to the Axis powers? (10.8.3)

Japan's Pacific Campaign Section 2 (pages 497–501)

11. What was Yamamoto's objective at Pearl Harbor? (10.8.3)
12. How did Japan try to win support from other Asian countries? (10.8.3)

The Holocaust Section 3 (pages 502–505)

13. Name two tactics that Hitler used to rid Germany of Jews before creating his "Final Solution." (10.8.5)
14. What tactics did Hitler use in his "Final Solution"? (10.8.5)

The Allied Victory Section 4 (pages 506–513)

15. Why were consumer goods rationed during the war? (10.9.1)
16. What was Operation Overlord? (10.8.3)

Europe and Japan in Ruins Section 5 (pages 514–517)

17. Why did Europeans leave their homes after the war? (10.8.6)
18. What were two of the most important steps that MacArthur took in Japan following the war? (10.8.6)

CRITICAL THINKING

1. USING YOUR NOTES

Copy the chart into your notebook and specify for each listed battle or conflict whether the Axis powers or the Allied powers gained an advantage. (HI 3)

Battle/Conflict	Allied or Axis Powers?
Battle of Britain	
War in the Balkans	
Pearl Harbor	
Battle of the Coral Sea	
Battle of Midway	

2. DRAWING CONCLUSIONS

Consider the personalities, tactics, and policies of Hitler, Rommel, MacArthur, and Churchill. What qualities make a good war leader? (10.8.4)

3. COMPARING AND CONTRASTING

EMPIRE BUILDING Compare and contrast Japan's and Germany's goals in World War II. (10.8.4)

4. EVALUATING COURSES OF ACTION

ECONOMICS Why do you think the governments of the United States and other countries encouraged people on the home front to organize programs for such activities as scrap collection and Victory gardens? (10.8.3)

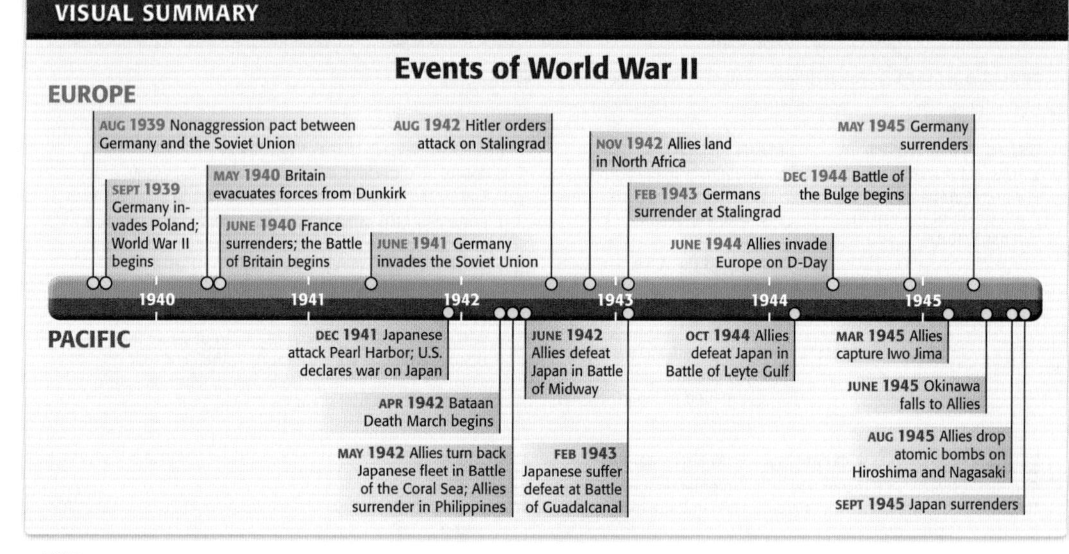
VISUAL SUMMARY
Events of World War II
EUROPE
AUG 1939 Nonaggression pact between Germany and the Soviet Union
SEPT 1939 Germany invades Poland; World War II begins
MAY 1940 Britain evacuates forces from Dunkirk
JUNE 1940 France surrenders; the Battle of Britain begins
JUNE 1941 Germany invades the Soviet Union
AUG 1942 Hitler orders attack on Stalingrad
NOV 1942 Allies land in North Africa
FEB 1943 Germans surrender at Stalingrad
JUNE 1944 Allies invade Europe on D-Day
DEC 1944 Battle of the Bulge begins
MAY 1945 Germany surrenders
1940
1941
1942
1943
1944
1945
PACIFIC
DEC 1941 Japanese attack Pearl Harbor; U.S. declares war on Japan
APR 1942 Bataan Death March begins
MAY 1942 Allies turn back Japanese fleet in Battle of the Coral Sea; Allies surrender in Philippines
JUNE 1942 Allies defeat Japan in Battle of Midway
FEB 1943 Japanese suffer defeat at Battle of Guadalcanal
OCT 1944 Allies defeat Japan in Battle of Leyte Gulf
MAR 1945 Allies capture Iwo Jima
JUNE 1945 Okinawa falls to Allies
AUG 1945 Allies drop atomic bombs on Hiroshima and Nagasaki
SEPT 1945 Japan surrenders

CRITICAL THINKING

Answers will vary.

1. Battle of Britain—Allies. War in the Balkans—Axis. Pearl Harbor—Axis. Battle of the Coral Sea—Allies. Battle of Midway—Allies. Battle of Stalingrad—Allies.
2. ability to unite people behind a common cause; ability to persuade people that the cause the leader represents is noble; powerful personality
3. Japan wanted European colonial powers and the United States out of Asia. Germany wanted Germans to be ethnically pure and also wanted to make up for losses suffered after World War I. Both wanted to expand their territory, resources, and wealth.
4. These programs made a positive contribution to the war effort by providing scrap metal for use in making weapons and ammunition and by freeing up foodstuffs for use elsewhere. These programs also got the people on the home front involved and gave them the feeling that they were a part of the war effort.

Use the excerpt and your knowledge of world history to answer question 1.
Additional Test Practice, pp. S1–S33

PRIMARY SOURCE

But there was no military advantage in hurling the bomb upon Japan without warning. The least we might have done was to announce to our foe that we possessed the atomic bomb; that its destructive power was beyond anything known in warfare; and that its terrible effectiveness had been experimentally demonstrated in this country. . . . If [Japan] doubted the good faith of our representations, it would have been a simple matter to select a demonstration target in the enemy's own country at a place where the loss of human life would be at a minimum. If, despite such warning, Japan had still held out, we would have been in a far less questionable position had we then dropped the bombs on Hiroshima and Nagasaki.

The Christian Century, August 29, 1945

1. According to the writer, what is the least the Allies might have done with regard to using the atomic bomb? (CST 2)

A. tell Japan that they possessed the atomic bomb, a weapon with incredible destructive power
B. demonstrate it on a selected target in the United States where loss of life would be limited
C. invite Japanese leaders to a demonstration explosion of the bomb in the United States
D. drop the bomb on cities in Germany as well as on Japanese cities

Use the map and your knowledge of world history to answer question 2.

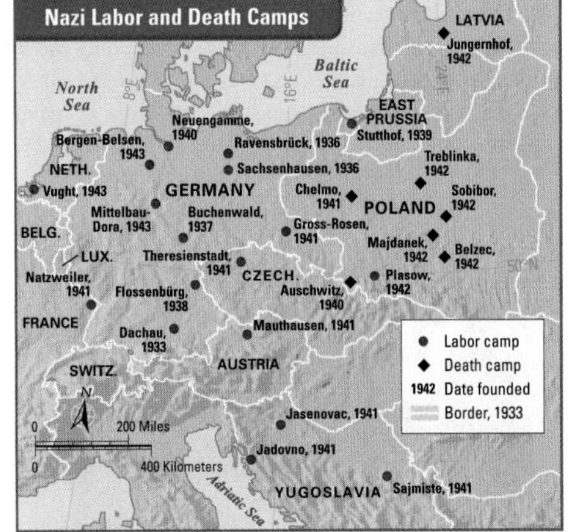

2. In which country were most death camps located? (10.8.5)

A. Austria
B. Germany
C. Poland
D. Yugoslavia

INTEGRATED TECHNOLOGY
TEST PRACTICE Go to **classzone.com**
• Diagnostic tests
• Tutorials
• Strategies
• Additional practice

ALTERNATIVE ASSESSMENT

1. Interact *with* History (10.8.3)
On page 490, you had to decide under what circumstances war is justified. Now that you have read the chapter, do you think that Germany and Japan were justified in waging war? Were the Allies justified in declaring war on Germany and Japan? As you think about these questions, consider the moral issues that confront world leaders when they contemplate war as an option.

2. WRITING ABOUT HISTORY (Writing 2.3.b, d)
SCIENCE AND TECHNOLOGY Conduct research on the scientific and technological developments used in the Allied war effort. Use your findings to create several **information cards** for a card series titled "Science and Technology During World War II." Organize the information on your cards in the following categories:
• name of invention or development
• country
• year
• use in the war
• use today

INTEGRATED TECHNOLOGY

Writing an Internet-Based Research Paper
(Writing 2.3.b)

During World War II, many consumer-goods manufacturers switched to the production of military goods. Many of these companies still exist. Working with a partner, use the Internet to research one such company. Find out what products the company made before and during the war, and how the company's wartime role affected its reputation. Go to the *Web Research Guide* at **classzone.com** to learn about conducting research on the Internet.

Present the results of your research in a well-organized paper. Be sure to
• apply a search strategy when using directories and search engines to locate Web resources
• judge the usefulness and reliability of each Web site
• correctly cite your Web sources
• edit for organization and correct use of language

STANDARDS-BASED ASSESSMENT

1. Letter **A** is the correct answer. The writer states that the least that could have been done was to "announce to our foe that we possessed the atomic bomb." Letter **B** is incorrect because the writer suggests this course of action only if the Japanese doubted Allied claims to possess such a powerful weapon. Letters **C** and **D** are incorrect because the writer does not offer these alternative courses of action.
2. Letter **C** is the correct answer, because all the death camps were located in Poland. Letters **A**, **B**, and **D** are incorrect because only labor camps were located in these countries.

Formal Assessment
• Chapter Test, Forms A, B, and C, pp. 282–293

California Test Generator CD-ROM
• Chapter Tests, Forms A, B, and C (English and Spanish)

ALTERNATIVE ASSESSMENT

1. Students may cite some of these issues: the importance of stopping dangerous leaders before they become powerful; the value of cooperation among countries for their mutual defense; the dangers of isolationism; the need to defend moral values with military force; the goal of finding a way to solve international conflicts using a judicial process instead of a military one; the role an international organization can play in coordinating opposition to aggression.
2. **Rubric** Information cards should
• record information accurately.
• present information clearly and succinctly.
• include graphic representations of information where appropriate.

INTEGRATED TECHNOLOGY

Rubric Papers should
• report facts accurately.
• present information clearly.
• use details and examples to support main ideas.
• cite at least three Internet-based sources.

LESSON PLAN

OBJECTIVES

- Examine the development of warfare technology.
- Examine the growing effects of war on civilians.
- Compare the events and effects of World War I and World War II.

1 FOCUS & MOTIVATE

To help students review the changing nature of warfare, make two columns on the chalkboard. Label one column World War I and the other World War II. Have students list what they remember about each war, how it was fought, and how the war impacted the lives of the people whose countries were involved.

2 INSTRUCT

Critical Thinking

- Which of the weapons shown on these two pages are still available in the 21st century? *(They are all still available, although an atomic bomb has not been used since World War II and the possession or use of poisonous gas has been prohibited by the UN since 1972.)*
- Why was poison gas a particularly dangerous weapon to use? (*Possible Answer: Like any gas, poison gas must have been hard to control. Once it was released into the air, it could be carried by the wind to unintended targets.*)

Technology of War

In Unit 4, you studied the economic and political upheavals that led to two world wars. For the first time, war involved not only the interested countries, but also their allies near and far and their colonies in far-flung places. In the next six pages, you will analyze the widespread use of machines and other technologies as tools for fighting and the increasingly involved role of civilians in war.

CALIFORNIA STANDARDS

HI 1 Students show the connections, causal and otherwise, between particular historical events and larger social, economic, and political trends and developments.

Maxim Machine Gun ▲
Hiram Maxim (above) invented the first portable, automatic machine gun. Machine guns fired hundreds of rounds per minute and were used by all the combatants in World War I.

Tanks ▲
Tanks, like the early British model shown above, enabled armies to travel over uneven ground and barbed wire. Although too slow to be used to full advantage at first, they were devastating against soldiers in trenches.

1884 — 1909 — 1915 — 1916

▼ First Military Plane
The earliest military planes were used for reconnaissance of enemy positions. A passenger could drop bombs (below) and, in later World War I models, operate a machine gun.

Poison Gas ▼
Poison gases were introduced to help break the stalemate of trench warfare. They caused suffocation, blistered skin, or blindness (below) to those exposed.

DIFFERENTIATING INSTRUCTION: GIFTED AND TALENTED STUDENTS

Photo Essays

Class Time 45 minutes

Task Creating a photo essay

Purpose To understand the effects of war technology

Have students use the Internet or the library to find more photographs like the ones on pages 520 and 521. Ask them to choose one of the technologies from the time line and find 10 to 15 photographs showing the technology in use, or its effects. Once they have collected enough images, have the students arrange their pictures in a book or on a poster for classroom display. Students should write a brief caption for each photograph explaining the image and putting it in context.

For example, a photo essay on blitzkrieg could have pictures of several of the specific elements that made up a blitzkrieg—such as tanks, planes, and artillery—along with captions describing these elements. They could be followed by images of a blitzkrieg in action, with captions explaining anything that might be unclear in the photographs. Finally, the essay could show the aftereffects of a blitzkrieg, such as ruined towns or cities.

Blitzkrieg ▲
The Germans used blitzkrieg or "lightning war" to invade Poland. They employed air strikes, fast tanks, and artillery, followed by soldiers sped into battle on trucks (shown above). They swiftly overwhelmed Poland and disrupted its command and communications.

Atomic Bomb ►
The United States dropped two atomic bombs on Japan and became the first nation to use nuclear weapons. An atomic bomb (right) creates an explosion that causes massive damage. The radioactive particles released are carried by winds for weeks.

1939 1944 1945

▼German Me 262
Military jet planes were first used by the Germans in 1944. These planes added speed to fire power. The Me 262 (below) was the only jet to be used extensively in World War II.

Comparing & Contrasting

1. How did technology change the nature of war in the 20th century?
2. Compared with earlier guns, what made machine guns so effective?
3. How did airplanes change the way war was carried out?

More About . . .

The Atomic Bomb

In 1942, in an effort to build the first atomic bomb before Germany did, the U.S. government created the Manhattan Project. The bomb was built in the desert laboratory of Los Alamos, New Mexico, directed by J. Robert Oppenheimer. On July 16, 1945, Oppenheimer and his team detonated the first atomic bomb. "We knew the world would not be the same," said Oppenheimer. Less than a month later, the United States dropped atomic bombs on Hiroshima and Nagasaki in Japan, causing Japan to surrender. After the war, Oppenheimer openly opposed the development of a hydrogen bomb, and in his later life, he spent much of his time writing about the problems of intellectual ethics and morality.

Comparing & Contrasting

1. Weapons became more powerful and deadly. Armored vehicles allowed soldiers to get farther, faster. Planes enabled attacks on enemies from above.
2. A machine gun could fire hundreds of rounds per minute.
3. For the first time, combatants could spy on the enemy from a relatively safe distance and gain a good idea of his position. Planes also provided a new method of attack—from the air.

RECOMMENDED RESOURCES

Books for the Teacher

Powaski, Ronald E. ***Lightning War: Blitzkrieg in the West, 1940.*** New York: Wiley, 2002.

Weglyn, Michi Nishiura. ***Years of Infamy: The Untold Story of America's Concentration Camps.*** Updated ed. Seattle: U of Washington P, 1995. A history of the internment of Japanese-Americans during World War II.

Books for the Student

Hersey, John. ***Hiroshima.*** Reprint edition. New York: Vintage Books, 1989. This journalistic masterpiece tells, through their own accounts, the stories of survivors of the atomic bomb dropped on Hiroshima.

McDougal Littell Nextext. ***The Atomic Bomb.*** Includes 25 source documents and 29 photographs offering various perspectives on the United States' development and use of the atomic bomb during World War II.

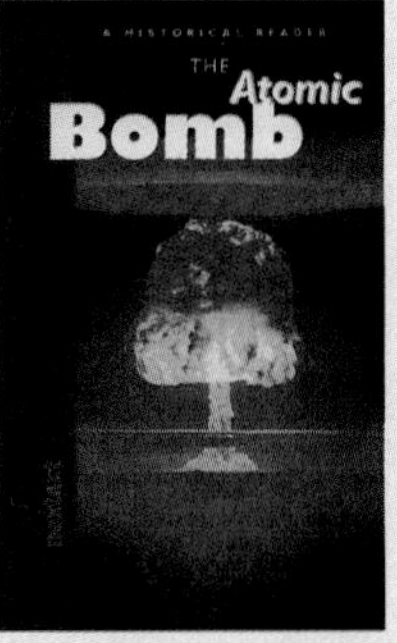

Videos

The Changing Face of War. VHS. Films for the Humanities & Sciences. 800-257-5126. A look at the changing technology and practices of war in the 20th century.

Facing Hate. VHS and DVD. Films for the Humanities & Sciences. 800-257-5126. Bill Moyers interviews Elie Wiesel about his childhood experiences at Auschwitz.

Last Voyage of the Lusitania. VHS. Library Video Company. 800-843-3620. Examines why the *Lusitania* was torpedoed and shows an expedition to photograph the sunken wreckage.

Expansion of Warfare

Critical Thinking

- How might British reaction to the bombing of London compare with the reaction of Americans to the September 11th attacks? (*Possible Answer: The reactions would be very similar. In both cases, civilians were shocked and horrified to witness the destruction of war for the first time, and in their own "back yards."*)
- How was Darwin's theory of evolution used to support some nations' genocide campaigns? (*Perpetrators of genocide had their own interpretation of "survival of the fittest." They believed they were superior to other races and therefore had the natural right to overthrow and destroy them.*)

London

Answer to Document-Based Question

Possible Answer: The kind of destruction shown could well be demoralizing to civilians and could possibly encourage antiwar feelings by the victims of the attacks.

Lusitania

Answer to Document-Based Question

Possible Answer: They would probably elicit anti-German feelings. The large number of civilian dead mentioned would be upsetting.

Expansion of Warfare

World War I and World War II both began as localized wars. As the allies of the opposing combatants became involved in the wars, combat spread to distant parts of the world. Countries attacked each other's colonies, attempted to gain territory for themselves, dedicated massive amounts of physical and human resources, and sometimes sought to kill entire populations.

Total War

A feature of warfare in the 20th century was how entire national economies were directed toward the war effort. As a result, civilians were not only potential victims of combat, but they also became actual targets themselves. Civilians also became active participants, producing arms, food, vehicles, and other goods needed for war. Many factories stopped producing consumer goods and began making products needed by the military.

London ►
The photograph shows a section of London destroyed by bombs in the Battle of Britain during World War II.

DOCUMENT-BASED QUESTION
What effect do you think the kind of destruction shown in the photograph had on the residents of London?

CALIFORNIA STANDARDS

10.8.5 Analyze the Nazi policy of pursuing racial purity, especially against the European Jews; its transformation into the Final Solution; and the Holocaust that resulted in the murder of six million Jewish civilians.

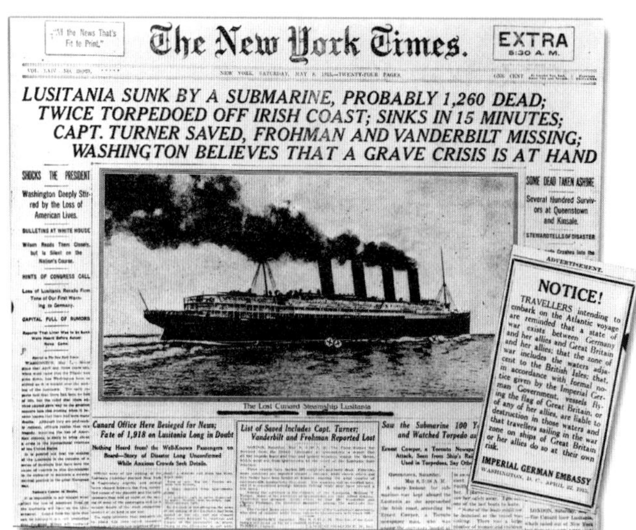

"All the News That's Fit to Print."

The New York Times. EXTRA 5:30 A.M.

LUSITANIA SUNK BY A SUBMARINE, PROBABLY 1,260 DEAD;
TWICE TORPEDOED OFF IRISH COAST; SINKS IN 15 MINUTES;
CAPT. TURNER SAVED, FROHMAN AND VANDERBILT MISSING;
WASHINGTON BELIEVES THAT A GRAVE CRISIS IS AT HAND

SHOCKS THE PRESIDENT

Washington Deeply Stirred by the Loss of American Lives.

SOME DEAD TAKEN ASHORE

Several Hundred Survivors at Queenstown and Kinsale.

The Lost Cunard Steamship Lusitania

Cunard Office Here Besieged for News; Fate of 1,918 on Lusitania Long in Doubt

List of Saved Includes Capt. Turner; Vanderbilt and Frohman Reported Lost

Saw the Submarine 100 Yards Off and Watched Torpedo

NOTICE!

IMPERIAL GERMAN EMBASSY

◄ *Lusitania*
This newspaper shows the headline and various articles about the sinking of the British passenger ship *Lusitania* during World War I. Note also the announcement from the German embassy warning civilians not to travel to Great Britain because Germany considered it a war zone.

DOCUMENT-BASED QUESTION
What effect would the headline and photograph have on the American public?

CONNECTIONS ACROSS TIME AND CULTURES

News of the Day

Class Time 30 minutes

Task Finding headlines from past wars

Purpose To compare and contrast different approaches to news coverage

Have students use the library or the Internet to find newspaper headlines and articles from past world conflicts. Have them look not only at American news sources, but at foreign news sources as well. Once the students have collected about half a dozen articles, ask them to evaluate the articles with the following questions:

- How does the reporting of a nation involved in a conflict differ from the reporting of an outside country?
- How is shock value used?
- What reaction is the reporter trying to elicit from the reader?
- How are headlines chosen to convey the greatest impact with the fewest words?

Have students address these questions in a brief report, which they can then display along with the headlines and articles.

Genocide

Genocide is the calculated and methodical destruction of a national, religious, ethnic, or racial group. The perpetrators consider their victims inferior or wish to take over their lands and property, or both. The mass killing of Armenians by Ottoman Turks beginning in 1915 is considered the first genocide of the 20th century. During the Holocaust, the Nazis killed more than 6 million people. As a result, in 1948 the United Nations approved an international convention to prevent and punish genocide.

PRIMARY SOURCE

INTERACTIVE

Genocide in WWI

The following excerpts are from telegrams sent to the secretary of state by the U.S. embassy in the Ottoman Empire. They concern the situation of Armenians in Turkey. The first passage was written by the American Consul General at Beirut and describes the deportation of villagers from the Zeitoon region, and the second calls attention to the killing of people in eastern Turkey.

July 20, 1915:
Whole villages were deported at an hours notice, with no opportunity to prepare for the journey, not even in some cases to gather together the scattered members of the family, so that little children were left behind. . . .

In many cases the men were (those of military age were nearly all in the army) bound tightly together with ropes or chains. Women with little children in their arms, or in the last days of pregnancy were driven along under the whip like cattle. Three different cases came under my knowledge where the woman was delivered on the road, and because her brutal driver hurried her along she died. . . .

These people are being scattered in small units, three or four families in a place, among a population of different race and religion, and speaking a different language. I speak of them as being composed of families, but four fifths of them are women and children.

July 31, 1915:
[The president of a charitable organization] has information from [a] reliable source that Armenians, mostly women and children, deported from the Erzerum district, have been massacred near Kemakh. . . . Similar reports comes from other sources showing that but few of these unfortunate people will ever reach their stated destination.

DOCUMENT-BASED QUESTION
What would be the result of scattering Armenian villagers in unfamiliar places under such terrible conditions?

PRIMARY SOURCE

INTERACTIVE

Genocide in WWII

Primo Levi describes how prisoners at the Nazi concentration camp of Auschwitz were selected for death.

Each one of us, as he comes naked out of the Tagesraum [common room] into the cold October air, has to run the few steps between the two doors, give the card to the SS man [the Nazi guard] and enter the dormitory door. The SS man, in the fraction of a second between two successive crossings, with a glance at one's back and front, judges everyone's fate, and in turn gives the card to the man on his right or his left, and this is the life or death of each of us. In three or four minutes a hut of 200 men is 'done', as is the whole camp of twelve thousand men in the course of the afternoon.

Jammed in the charnel-house [a place of great suffering] of the Tagesraum, I gradually felt the human pressure around me slacken, and in a short time it was my turn. Like everyone, I passed by with a brisk and elastic step, trying to hold my head high, my chest forward and my muscles contracted and conspicuous. With the corner of my eye I tried to look behind my shoulders, and my card seemed to end on the right.

DOCUMENT-BASED QUESTION
What was the Nazis' attitude toward selecting prisoners to be killed?

Comparing & Contrasting

1. Judging from the examples on these two pages, in what ways did warfare expand to include civilians?
2. If civilians manufacture materials for the war effort, should they be military targets? Why or why not?
3. How did modern weaponry contribute to both the sinking of the *Lusitania* and the bombing of London?

523

PRIMARY SOURCE
Genocide in WWI

Answer to Document-Based Question
Possible Answer: Many would die along the way from the terrible conditions. Those who survived would be destitute in unfamiliar places with no means of making a living. Many probably lost their ethnic identity. By deporting as well as killing a large number of Armenians, the Turks succeeded in greatly reducing a national group.

PRIMARY SOURCE
Genocide in WWII

Answer to Document-Based Question
Possible Answer: Prisoners were chosen in a mechanical, businesslike way. They were not treated like human beings.

Comparing & Contrasting

1. *Possible Answer:* Civilians were the specific victims of campaigns that had no military value in London, Turkey, and eastern Europe. They were the only casualties in the sinking of the *Lusitania*.
2. *Possible Answer:* Yes—because they are actively participating in the war effort. No—because often the only jobs available are in factories making war materials, so they have not chosen to support the war in the same way that a soldier does.
3. *Possible Answer:* A submarine sank the *Lusitania,* and bombs dropped from airplanes destroyed London—both examples of modern weapons.

DIFFERENTIATING INSTRUCTION: STRUGGLING READERS

Reading About Genocide

Class Time 30 minutes

Task Deconstruct primary sources

Purpose To understand examples of genocide

Pair struggling readers with more proficient readers and have them read aloud the primary sources on this page. The pairs should discuss the meaning of each paragraph, or every line, so that the meaning of the source is clear. After discussing each source in detail, the struggling readers should rewrite each paragraph, drawing out all the main ideas and images.

For instance, one main idea from the Primo Levi excerpt could be written as follows:

Nazi guards take only a fraction of a second to choose life or death for each prisoner.

Make sure that struggling readers understand any new vocabulary, such as:

- **SS,** Hitler's elite Schutzstaffel guards, who were responsible for the mass killings in the concentration camps
- **Deported,** to be sent out of a country

The Human Cost of War

Critical Thinking

- What was the purpose of interning thousands of Japanese Americans? (*The government was afraid that some Japanese-American citizens might sympathize with their homeland and spy for the Japanese.*)
- Do you think this treatment was justified? Why or why not? (*Possible Answer: It is understandable for the government to worry about internal security. However, these were American citizens. They could have been treated with more trust and respect.*)

PRIMARY SOURCE
Trench Warfare

Answer to Document-Based Question
He sounds very businesslike, but cares about the men under his command.

PRIMARY SOURCE
Iwo Jima

Answer to Document-Based Question
Possible Answer: The soldiers probably had to harden themselves emotionally against the enemy and be prepared to die themselves.

SKILLBUILDER Answer
Possible Answer: More powerful weapons and the greater geographical area covered in combat contributed to the greater number of deaths in World War II.

INTEGRATED TECHNOLOGY

Interactive The primary sources on pages 523-525 are available in an interactive format on the eEdition. Students can hear the primary sources read aloud and can obtain background information.

The Human Cost of War

CALIFORNIA STANDARDS
10.5.4, HI 2

The global nature of World Wars I and II wreaked a level of destruction unknown before. National economies were exhausted; farmland, towns, and villages were destroyed. More soldiers died in World War I than in all the conflicts of the previous three centuries, and millions more died in World War II. Civilians died by the millions as a result of military operations, concentration camps, the bombing of towns and cities, and starvation and disease.

Military Cost

Both sides in the two world wars suffered tremendous military casualties, including dead, wounded, and missing in action. About 8.5 million soldiers died in World War I and 19.4 million in World War II. The excerpts show how weapons and tactics contributed to the large number of casualties.

PRIMARY SOURCE

INTERACTIVE

Trench Warfare

British sergeant major Ernest Shephard remembers the first day of the Battle of the Somme in his diary.

A lovely day, intensely hot. Lots of casualties in my trench. The enemy are enfilading us with heavy shell, dropping straight on us. A complete trench mortar battery of men killed by one shell, scores of dead and badly wounded in trench . . . Every move we make brings intense fire, as trenches so badly battered the enemy can see all our movements. Lot of wounded [from the front] . . . several were hit again and killed in trench. We put as many wounded as possible in best spots in trench and I sent a lot down, but I had so many of my own men killed and wounded that after a time I could not do this. . . .

[L]iterally we were blown from place to place. Men very badly shaken. As far as possible we cleared trenches of debris and dead. These we piled in heaps, enemy shells pitching on them made matters worse.

DOCUMENT-BASED QUESTION
Judging from the quotation, what was Shephard's attitude toward the battle?

PRIMARY SOURCE

INTERACTIVE

Iwo Jima

Japan lost 21,000 soldiers and the United States 6,800 in the Battle of Iwo Jima. A U.S. Marines correspondent described part of the fighting below.

Behind a rolling artillery barrage and with fixed bayonets, the unit leaped forward in . . . [a] charge and advanced to the very mouths of the fixed [Japanese] defenses. . . . [T]he men flung themselves at the tiny flaming holes, throwing grenades and jabbing with bayonets. Comrades went past, hurdled the defenses and rushed across Airfield no. 2. . . . Men died at every step. That was how we broke their line. . . .

Across the field we attacked a ridge. The enemy rose up out of holes to hurl our assault back. The squads re-formed and went up again. At the crest they plunged on the [Japanese] with bayonets. . . . The [Japanese] on the ridge were annihilated.

DOCUMENT-BASED QUESTION
What attitude do you think the soldiers on both sides had to adopt to fight in such a bloody conflict as this?

Military Casualties, World War I and World War II

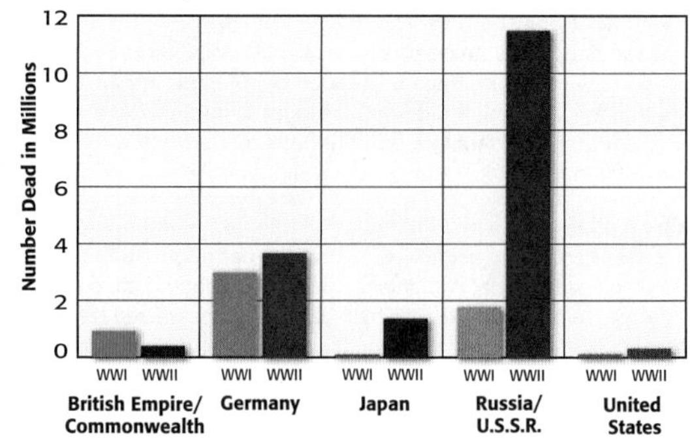

Source: Encyclopaedia Britannica

SKILLBUILDER: Interpreting Graphs
What factors may have contributed to the increased number of deaths in World War II over World War I?

DIFFERENTIATING INSTRUCTION: ENGLISH LEARNERS

Descriptions of War

Class Time 30 minutes

Task Reviewing primary sources

Purpose To fully understand firsthand accounts of battle

The two primary sources on this page are written in abbreviated styles that may cause difficulty for English learners. Pair students who are learning English with more proficient readers and have them carefully review the two primary sources on this page. Proficient readers should explain that the description of trench warfare drops some verbs and articles for the sake of brevity. Have the pairs rewrite some of these sentence fragments into complete sentences.

For instance:

"Men very badly shaken" could be rewritten as "The men are very badly shaken."

The following vocabulary should be explained also:

Enfilading means to rake with gunfire.

Annihilated means completely destroyed.

A *barrage* is artillery fire used to screen and protect friendly troops.

Civilian Cost

Civilians suffered not only as the direct victims of war, but also from the loss of their homes, the workplaces that gave them an income and produced useful goods, and the farms that supplied food. They also experienced the unsanitary conditions that resulted from bombing.

PRIMARY SOURCE

INTERACTIVE

Displaced Persons

Laura de Gozdawa Turczynowicz, an American married to a Polish nobleman, described fleeing the advance of the German army into Suwalki, Poland.

At the [Vilno] station were crowds of Suwalki people. One man of our acquaintance had brought with him only his walking stick! Another man had become separated from his young son, fourteen, and daughter, sixteen, . . . and the poor father was on the verge of losing his reason. . . .

Such a lot of people came for help that my money melted like snow in the sunshine. I took just as many as could be packed in our [hotel] rooms. . . .

The next day dragged wearily along, everybody waiting, living only to hear better news. The city was rapidly filling with refugees. In one place, an old convent, they were given a roof to sleep under, and hot tea.

DOCUMENT-BASED QUESTION
Under what conditions did the Polish refugees flee from the Germans?

PRIMARY SOURCE

Internment Camps

After Pearl Harbor, thousands of Japanese Americans were sent to internment camps mainly located in the western United States.

DOCUMENT-BASED QUESTION
Judging from the photograph, what was the government's attitude toward Japanese Americans?

PRIMARY SOURCE

INTERACTIVE

Atomic Bomb

In this excerpt, Dr. Tatsuichiro Akizuki describes the people who began arriving at his hospital in Nagasaki the day the bomb was dropped.

It was all he could do to keep standing. Yet it didn't occur to me that he had been seriously injured. . . .

As time passed, more and more people in a similar plight came up to the hospital . . . All were of the same appearance, sounded the same. "I'm hurt, *hurt!* I'm burning! Water!" They all moaned the same lament. . . .[T]hey walked with strange, slow steps, groaning from deep inside themselves as if they had travelled from the depths of hell. They looked whitish; their faces were like masks.

DOCUMENT-BASED QUESTION
Why did the doctor not recognize his patients' symptoms?

Comparing & Contrasting

1. Given the conditions described during trench warfare and on Iwo Jima, why would soldiers continue to fight?
2. How were the human costs of war, military and civilian, similar to each other? How were they different?
3. Given what you have read on these pages, if another world war broke out, would you prefer to be in the military or to be a civilian? Why?

EXTENSION ACTIVITY
Look up the numbers of civilian casualties suffered in different countries during World War II in an encyclopedia or other reference source. Use the graph on page 524 as a model. Be sure to include the countries with the most significant figures in different parts of the world. Write a paragraph explaining why these countries had the greatest number of casualties.

525

PRIMARY SOURCE
Displaced Persons

Answer to Document-Based Question
Possible Answer: People left hurriedly with no plans for the journey or for a place to stay.

PRIMARY SOURCE
Internment Camps

Answer to Document-Based Question
Possible Answer: The large number of soldiers guarding them suggests that the government considered them dangerous.

PRIMARY SOURCE
Atomic Bomb

Answer to Document-Based Question
The patients had radiation sickness, which the doctor had never encountered before.

Comparing & Contrasting

1. *Possible Answer:* patriotism, orders, or survival instinct
2. *Possible Answer:* They are similar because death, whether military or civilian, is still death. They are different because soldiers know that they may die in the line of duty, but civilians do not make that assumption.
3. *Possible Answer:* Some students may say that they would prefer to be in the military in order to defend their country. Others may say that civilians can also contribute greatly to a war effort and that it is not necessary to be in the military to make a contribution.

EXTENSION ACTIVITY

Instructions You may wish to give students the following list of resources to help them find the numbers of civilian casualties.

- *Encyclopaedia Britannica,* 2003, Table 7: World War II Casualties
- *World War II: A Statistical Survey.* Facts on File, 1993
- John Keegan, ed. *Times Atlas of the Second World War.* Crescent, 1994
- Micheal Clodfelter. *Warfare and Armed Conflicts: A Statistical Reference to Casualty and Other Figures, 1500–2000.* 2nd ed, Jefferson, NC, McFarland, 2002

Rubric Student graphs should
- resemble the graph on page 524.
- identify countries with significant civilian casualty rates.
- include countries from around the world.
- explain in a paragraph the reasons these countries had the greatest numbers of casualties.

Perspectives On the Present 1945–present

The Berlin Wall November 10, 1989

Right on the border between East and West Berlin, at the Pariser Platz, the Brandenburg Gate (pictured at right) was once the symbol of a divided Berlin. After the fall of the Berlin Wall in 1989, the gate became the symbol of German reunification.

At the end of World War II, the Allied powers divided Germany and its capital, Berlin, into zones of occupation. Eventually, the zones were consolidated. West Germany and West Berlin came to be associated with western Europe and the United States; East Germany and East Berlin were connected with the Soviet Union.

Between 1949 and 1961, about two and a half million East Germans fled to West Germany. To help stem the tide of emigration, East Germany decided to build a wall around West Berlin and prevent access to West Berlin and West Germany.

Begun in August 1961, the wall would ultimately stretch 28 miles across Berlin and 75 miles around West Berlin. The Berlin Wall quickly became one of the most notorious symbols of the Cold War.

This divide was in place until the 1980s, when reform movements swept through the Soviet Union and Eastern Europe. The pressure for reform was eventually brought to bear on East German authorities, who finally agreed to open the nation's borders on November 9, 1989.

The photograph at right, taken the day after the borders were opened, shows a group of people standing on top of the Berlin Wall, just to the west of the Brandenburg Gate.

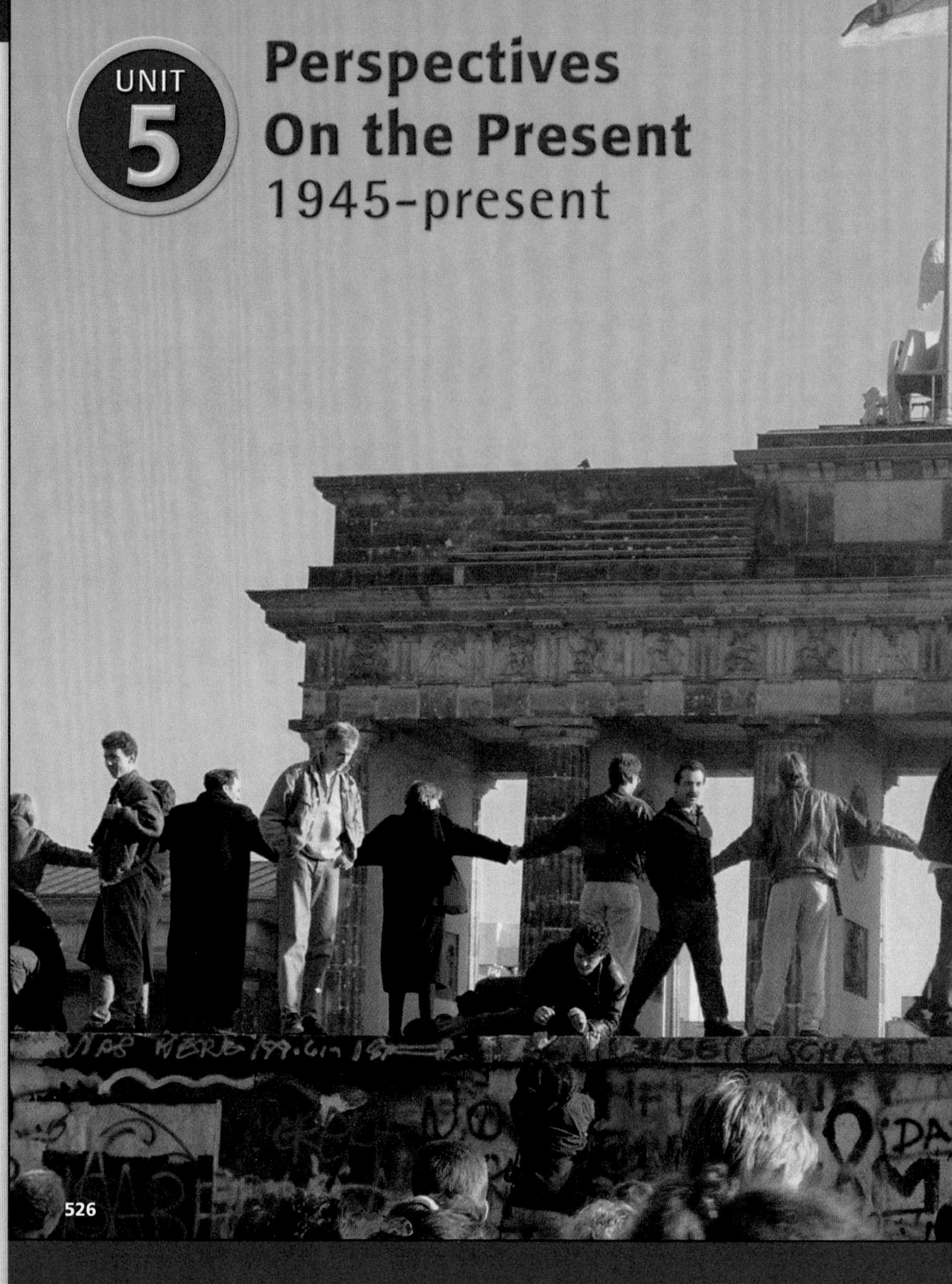

On November 10, 1989, all borders between East and West Germany were opened. Here, people celebrate in front of the Brandenburg Gate, one of the former border crossings between East and West.

Comparing & Contrasting

Nation Building
In Unit 5, you will learn about the emergence or growth of several different nations. At the end of the unit, you will have a chance to compare and contrast the nations you have studied. (See pages 666–671.)

527

Previewing the Unit

This unit describes the momentous political, social, and economic changes occurring around the globe after World War II.

Power and Authority With much of Europe and parts of Asia in ruins after World War II, the United States and the Soviet Union emerge as rival superpowers. Their political and military confrontations dominate world affairs for the next 40 years.

Revolution The end of World War II also heralds the end of colonialism, as native peoples in Africa, Asia, and the South Pacific demand independence. Although some European nations try to hold onto their colonies, others help native populations prepare for independent rule.

The 1980s and 1990s witness a dramatic shift toward democracy in many areas around the world. The Soviet Union dissolves into 15 separate republics, while military dictatorships fall in Latin America. Nigeria and South Africa pursue democratic goals, and China reforms its economy.

Science and Technology Advances in science, communications, and technology improve life for many people and help create a global economy. Nations around the world must adjust to new patterns of work, ensure the rights of their diverse populations, protect their environments, and achieve peaceful relations with their neighbors.

Comparing & Contrasting

The unit feature on pages 666–671 uses charts, images, time lines, and primary source documents to compare five developing nations. Explain to students that these resources will help them to understand how the nations in Unit 5 are attempting to organize and govern themselves.

CHAPTER 17 PLANNING GUIDE

Restructuring the Postwar World, 1945–Present

CHAPTER RESOURCES	COPYMASTERS	ASSESSMENT
CHAPTER OVERVIEW The United States and the Soviet Union competed for economic and military superiority and both countries extended their control over other nations.	**In-Depth Resources: Unit 5** • Building Vocabulary, p. 21 **Chapters in Brief** (in English and Spanish) **Block Schedule Pacing Guide**	**Chapter Assessment,** pp. 558–559 **Formal Assessment** • Chapter Tests, Forms A, B, and C, pp. 299–313 **Test Generator** **Integrated Assessment Book** **Online Test Practice**
SECTION 1 **The Cold War: Superpowers Face Off** pp. 531–537 **OBJECTIVE** Analyze the global competition between the United States and the Soviet Union.	**In-Depth Resources: Unit 5** • Guided Reading, p. 1 • Literature: from *The Nuclear Age,* p. 14 • Connections Across Time/Cultures, p. 19 • Science and Technology, p. 20 • Reteaching Activity, p. 21 **Reading Study Guide,** p. 179 **Case Study 2,** p. 16	**Section 1 Assessment,** p. 536 **Formal Assessment** • Section Quiz, p. 294 **California Daily Standards Practice Transparencies,** TT127
SECTION 2 **Communists Take Power in China** pp. 538–541 **OBJECTIVE** Explain how the Communists took control of China.	**In-Depth Resources: Unit 5** • Guided Reading, p. 2 • Skillbuilder Practice, p. 7 • Primary Source, p. 10 • Reteaching Activity, p. 22 **Reading Study Guide,** p. 181 **Case Study 2,** p. 16	**Section 2 Assessment,** p. 541 **Formal Assessment** • Section Quiz, p. 295 **California Daily Standards Practice Transparencies,** TT128
SECTION 3 **Wars in Korea and Vietnam** pp. 542–547 **OBJECTIVE** Describe the Korean and Vietnam Wars.	**In-Depth Resources: Unit 5** • Guided Reading, p. 3 • Primary Source, p 11 • History Makers: Ho Chi Minh, p. 17 • Reteaching Activity, p. 23 **Reading Study Guide,** p. 183	**Section 3 Assessment,** p. 547 **Formal Assessment** • Section Quiz, p. 296 **California Daily Standards Practice Transparencies,** TT129
SECTION 4 **The Cold War Divides the World** pp. 548–553 **OBJECTIVE** Describe how the Cold War affected nations.	**In-Depth Resources: Unit 5** • Guided Reading, p. 4 • Geography Application, p. 8 • Primary Source, p. 12 • History Makers: Ruholla Khomeini, p. 18 • Reteaching Activity, p. 24 **Reading Study Guide,** p. 185	**Section 4 Assessment,** p. 553 **Formal Assessment** • Section Quiz, p. 297 **California Daily Standards Practice Transparencies,** TT130
SECTION 5 **The Cold War Thaws** pp. 554–557 **OBJECTIVE** Trace the development of the Cold War.	**In-Depth Resources: Unit 5** • Guided Reading, p. 5 • Primary Source: Political Cartoon, p. 13 • Reteaching Activity, p. 25 **Reading Study Guide,** p. 187	**Section 5 Assessment,** p. 557 **Formal Assessment** • Section Quiz, p. 298 **California Daily Standards Practice Transparencies,** TT131

INTEGRATED TECHNOLOGY

- eEdition Plus Online
- EasyPlanner Plus Online
- eTest Plus Online

 **Audio CDs**

- Voices from the Past
- Reading Study Guides

CD-ROMs

- eEdition
- Power Presentations
- EasyPlanner
- Electronic Library of Primary Sources
- Test Generator

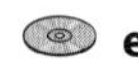 **eEdition CD-ROM**

 **Geography Transparencies**

- GT33 The Berlin Airlift, 1948–1949

 **classzone.com**

 **eEdition CD-ROM**

 **World Art and Cultures Transparencies**

- AT72 *Spring Walk to the Chi-Ch'ang Park*

 **classzone.com**

 **eEdition CD-ROM**

 **World Art and Cultures Transparencies**

- AT73 *Laying a Road*

 **Electronic Library of Primary Sources**

- from "Peace Without Conquest"

 **classzone.com**

 **eEdition CD-ROM**

 **Critical Thinking Transparencies**

- CT33 Global Superpowers Face Off

 **Electronic Library of Primary Sources**

- from *444 Days: The Hostages Remember*

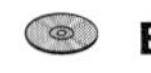

 **classzone.com**

 **eEdition CD-ROM**

 **Critical Thinking Transparencies**

- CT69 Chapter 33 Visual Summary

 **Electronic Library of Primary Sources**

- Speech on Stalin by Nikita Khrushchev
- from *A Student's Diary*

OVERVIEW OF CALIFORNIA RESOURCES

	Section 1	Section 2	Section 3	Section 4	Section 5
California Reading Toolkit	p. L75	p. L76	p. L77	p. L78	p. L79
California Modified Lesson Plans for English Learners	p. 145	p. 147	p. 149	p. 151	p. 153
California Daily Standards Practice Transparencies	TT67	TT68	TT69	TT70	TT71
California Standards Enrichment Workbook	pp. 95–96	pp. 93–94, 97–98	pp. 53–54	pp. 93–94, 95–96, 99–100	pp. 91–92, 93–94, 99–100, 103–104
California Standards Planner and Lesson Plans	p. L141	p. L143	p. L145	p. L147	p. L149
California Online Test Practice	classzone.com	classzone.com	classzone.com	classzone.com	classzone.com
California Test Generator CD-ROM					
California Easy Planner CD-ROM					
California eEdition CD-ROM					

Chart Key:

 Copymaster

 Pupil's Edition

 Audio Library

 Teacher's Edition

 CD-ROM

Overhead Transparency

 Block Scheduling

Internet

 Video

NO TIME?

If you do not have time to teach this chapter in full, assign the **Chapter in Brief** (also available in Spanish).

Previewing Resources for Differentiated Instruction

ENGLISH LEARNERS: Resources in Spanish

In-Depth Resources in Spanish

- Guided Reading Ⓐ
- Skillbuilder Practice: Interpreting Charts Ⓑ
- Geography Application: The Cuban Missile Crisis

Chapters in Brief

Reading Study Guide Ⓒ

Reading Study Guide Audio CD

Test Generator CD-ROM

- Chapter Test, Forms A, B, and C

Plus

Modified Lesson Plans for English Learners

Multi-Language Glossary of Social Studies Terms

Ⓐ

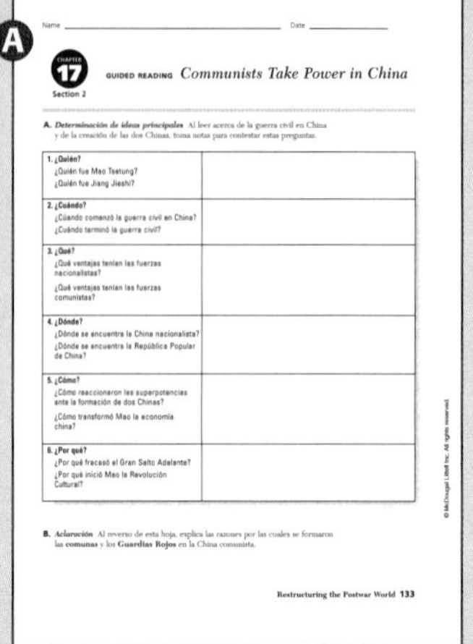

Ⓑ

STRUGGLING READERS

In-Depth Resources: Unit 5

- Guided Reading Ⓐ
- Building Vocabulary
- Skillbuilder Practice: Interpreting Charts
- Geography Application: The Cuban Missile Crisis Ⓑ
- Reteaching Activities

Chapters in Brief

Reading Study Guide Ⓒ

Reading Study Guide Audio CD

Formal Assessment

- Chapter Test, Form A

Plus

Reading Toolkit

Ⓐ

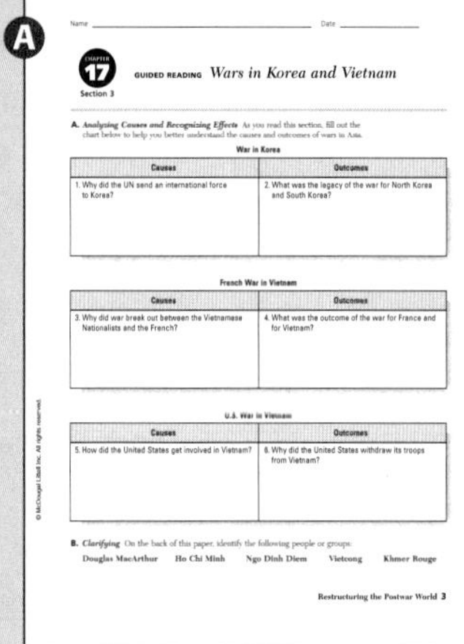

Ⓑ

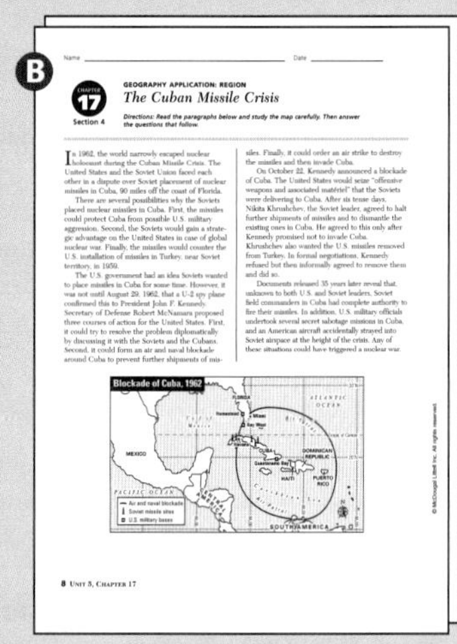

GIFTED AND TALENTED STUDENTS

In-Depth Resources: Unit 5

- Primary Source: from *No Tears for Mao;* from *When Heaven and Earth Changed Places;* The Cuban Missile Crisis (Speech by John F. Kennedy); Political Cartoon Ⓐ
- Literature: from *The Nuclear Age*
- History Makers: Ho Chi Minh; Ruholla Khomeini
- Connections Across Time and Cultures: Restoring the Peace
- Science and Technology: Super Spy Plane Ⓑ

Electronic Library of Primary Sources

- from "Peace Without Conquest"
- from *444 Days: The Hostages Remember*
- Speech on Stalin by Nikita Khrushchev
- from *A Student's Diary*

Formal Assessment

- Chapter Test, Form C Ⓒ

Ⓐ

Ⓑ

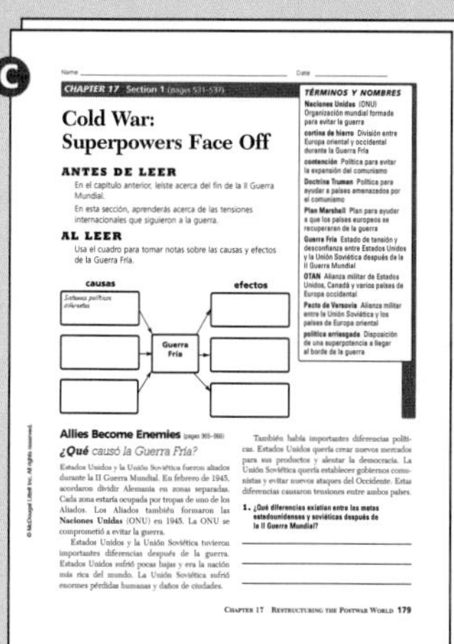

CHAPTER 17 Section 1

Cold War:
Superpowers Face Off

ANTES DE LEER

AL LEER

causas

efectos

Guerra Fría

TÉRMINOS Y NOMBRES

Allies Become Enemies

¿Qué causó la Guerra Fría?

CHAPTER 17 RESTRUCTURING THE POSTWAR WORLD 179

Activities in the Teacher's Edition for English Learners

- Understanding the Cold War, p. 533
- The Chronology of the Korean War, p. 543
- U.S. and Cuba, p. 550
- Summarizing and Sequencing Events, p. 556

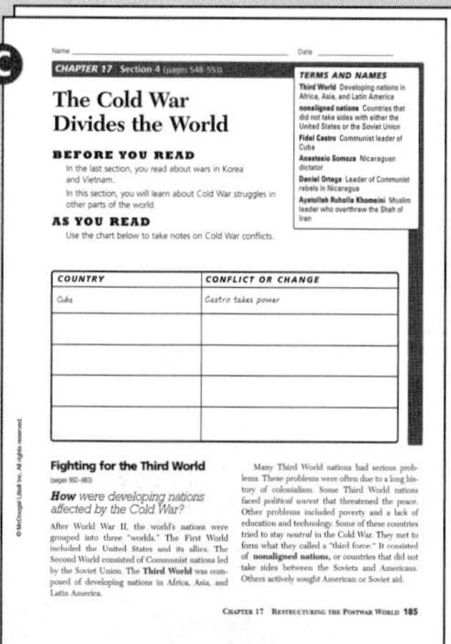

CHAPTER 17 Section 4

The Cold War
Divides the World

BEFORE YOU READ

AS YOU READ

TERMS AND NAMES

COUNTRY	CONFLICT OR CHANGE
Cuba	Castro takes power

Fighting for the Third World

How were developing nations affected by the Cold War?

CHAPTER 17 RESTRUCTURING THE POSTWAR WORLD 185

Activities in the Teacher's Edition for Struggling Readers

- The Berlin Airlift, p. 534
- Understanding Communist China, p. 540
- Vietnam War Posters, p. 546
- Time Line for the Cold War, p. 552
- Honoring Cold War Heroes, p. 555

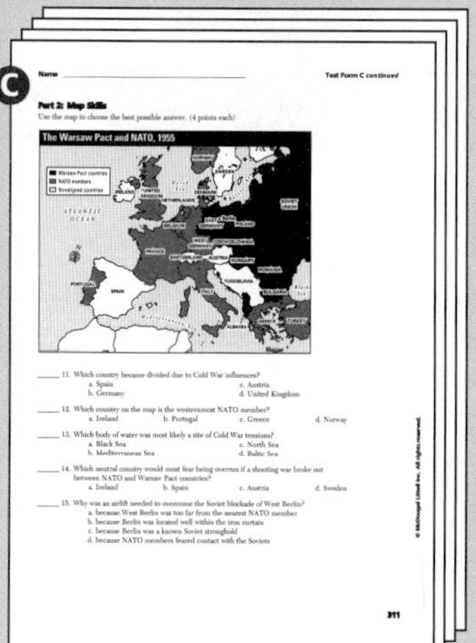

Test Form C continued

Part 2: Map Skills

The Warsaw Pact and NATO, 1955

Activities in the Teacher's Edition for Gifted and Talented Students

- Literature of the Cold War, p. 535
- Art and War, p. 545
- Cuban Missile Crisis, p. 551

INTEGRATED TECHNOLOGY

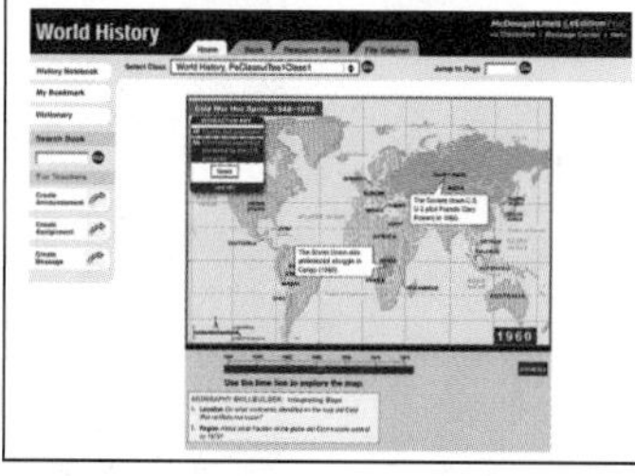

World History

eEdition

- Interactive Visuals
- Interactive Maps
- Interactive Primary Sources

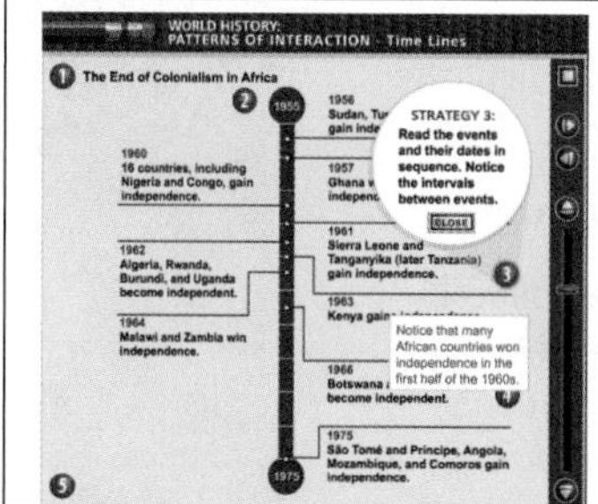

WORLD HISTORY: PATTERNS OF INTERACTION · Time Lines
The End of Colonialism in Africa
STRATEGY 3: Read the events and their dates in sequence. Notice the intervals between events.
CLOSE
1960 16 countries, including Nigeria and Congo, gain independence.
1962 Algeria, Rwanda, Burundi, and Uganda become independent.
1964 Malawi and Zambia win independence.
1957 Ghana
1961 Sierra Leone and Tanganyika (later Tanzania) gain independence.
1963 Kenya
Notice that many African countries won independence in the first half of the 1960s.
1966 Botswana
become independent.
1975 São Tomé and Príncipe, Angola, Mozambique, and Comoros gain independence.

classzone.com

- Research Links
- Internet Activities
- Primary Sources
- Chapter Quiz
- Current Events

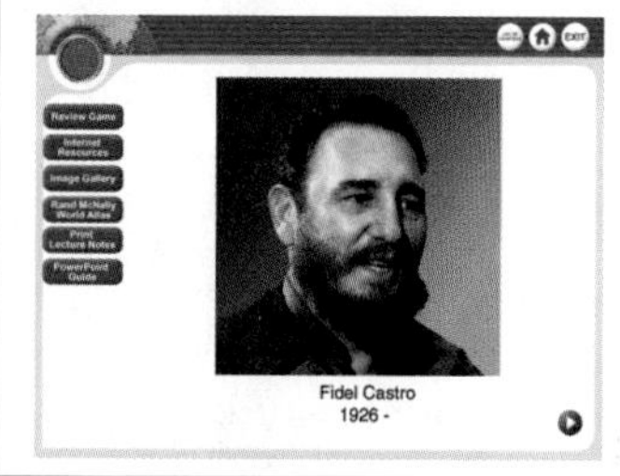

Fidel Castro
1926 -

Power Presentations CD-ROM

- Lecture Notes
- Image Gallery
- Chapter Review Game

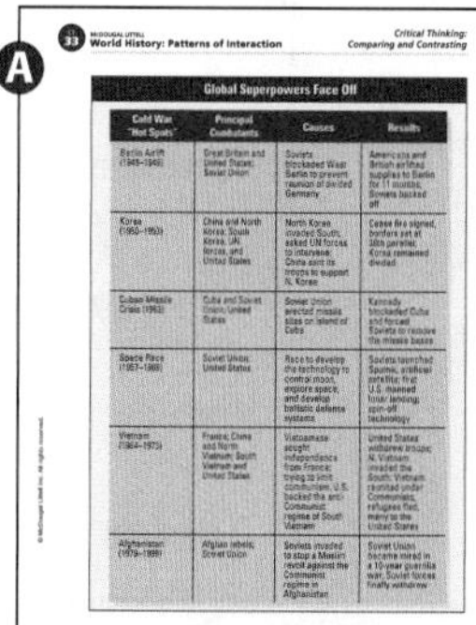

World History: Patterns of Interaction

Critical Thinking: Comparing and Contrasting

Global Superpowers Face Off

Critical Thinking Transparencies

- CT33 Global Superpowers Face Off (A)
- CT69 Chapter 33 Visual Summary

Geography Transparencies

- GT33 The Berlin Airlift, 1948–1949

World Art and Cultures Transparencies

- AT72 *Spring Walk to the Chi-Ch'ang Park*
- AT73 *Laying a Road*

Test Practice Transparencies TT127–TT131

Test Generator CD-ROM

EasyPlanner CD-ROM

Voices from the Past Audio CD

Online Test Practice

Electronic Library of Primary Sources

CHAPTER 17 • OBJECTIVE

Analyze the conflicts between competing economic systems and the restructuring of alliances from 1945 to the present.

Previewing Main Ideas

Explain that the repressive governments and conflicts students will read about in this chapter were nothing new to the world. What set this period apart was the global scale of the conflict as two superpowers competed for dominance. The competition reached to all parts of the world and repeatedly brought the nations to the brink of nuclear war.

Accessing Prior Knowledge

Point out that many of the political events of this period were driven by two political philosophies students have already studied, communism and realpolitik. Guide a review of these two views. Then have students evaluate current events and decide if these views still matter, or if some new philosophy has taken hold.

Geography *Answers*

ECONOMICS *Possible Answer:*
In 1949 the world was divided into two opposing groups—Communist and non-Communist countries.

REVOLUTION The Americas were not under Communism in 1949.

EMPIRE BUILDING *Possible Answer:*
The division on the map lumps many different countries and cultures together under broad categories.

CHAPTER 17

Restructuring the Postwar World,

1945–Present

Previewing Main Ideas

ECONOMICS Two conflicting economic systems, capitalism and communism, competed for influence and power after World War II. The superpowers in this struggle were the United States and the Soviet Union.
Geography *Study the map and the key. What does the map show about the state of the world in 1949?*

REVOLUTION In Asia, the Americas, and Eastern Europe, people revolted against repressive governments or rule by foreign powers. These revolutions often became the areas for conflict between the two superpowers.
Geography *Look at the map. Which of the three areas mentioned was not Communist in 1949?*

EMPIRE BUILDING The United States and the Soviet Union used military, economic, and humanitarian aid to extend their control over other countries. Each also tried to prevent the other superpower from gaining influence.
Geography *Why might the clear-cut division shown on this map be misleading?*

INTEGRATED TECHNOLOGY

eEdition
- Interactive Maps
- Interactive Visuals
- Interactive Primary Sources

INTERNET RESOURCES
Go to **classzone.com** for:
- Research Links
- Internet Activities
- Primary Sources
- Chapter Quiz
- Maps
- Test Practice
- Current Events

WORLD 1945 – 1965

1945 ◀ United Nations formed.

1947 Independent India partitioned into India and Pakistan.

1949 Communists take control of China.

1957 Soviets launch *Sputnik.*

1957 Ghana achieves independence from Great Britain. ▶

1959 Cuba becomes Communist. (Fidel Castro) ▶

528

TIME LINE DISCUSSION

Explain that the conflicts and disagreements as well as the new alliances that emerged immediately after World War II continue to drive many of the world's events today.

1. Point out that the United Nations is the most important international organization in history. In what year was the United Nations formed? What events has the UN been involved with in recent years? *(1945; Possible Answers: weapons search in Iraq, war against terrorism, peace keeping)*
2. Explain that a race into space was one aspect of the competition between the United States and the Soviet Union. The Soviets achieved the first success with the launching of Sputnik. How many years passed from the time the Soviet Union launched Sputnik until U.S. astronauts landed on the moon? *(12 years)*
3. What happened in South Africa in 1994? *(first all-race election was held)*
4. During what ten-year period did communism experience the most successes? What were they? *(1949–1959; Communists gained control of China and Cuba and launched Sputnik.)*
5. After the Berlin Wall was knocked down, what other defeat for the Communists is shown on the time line? *(Communists voted out of power in Nicaragua)*

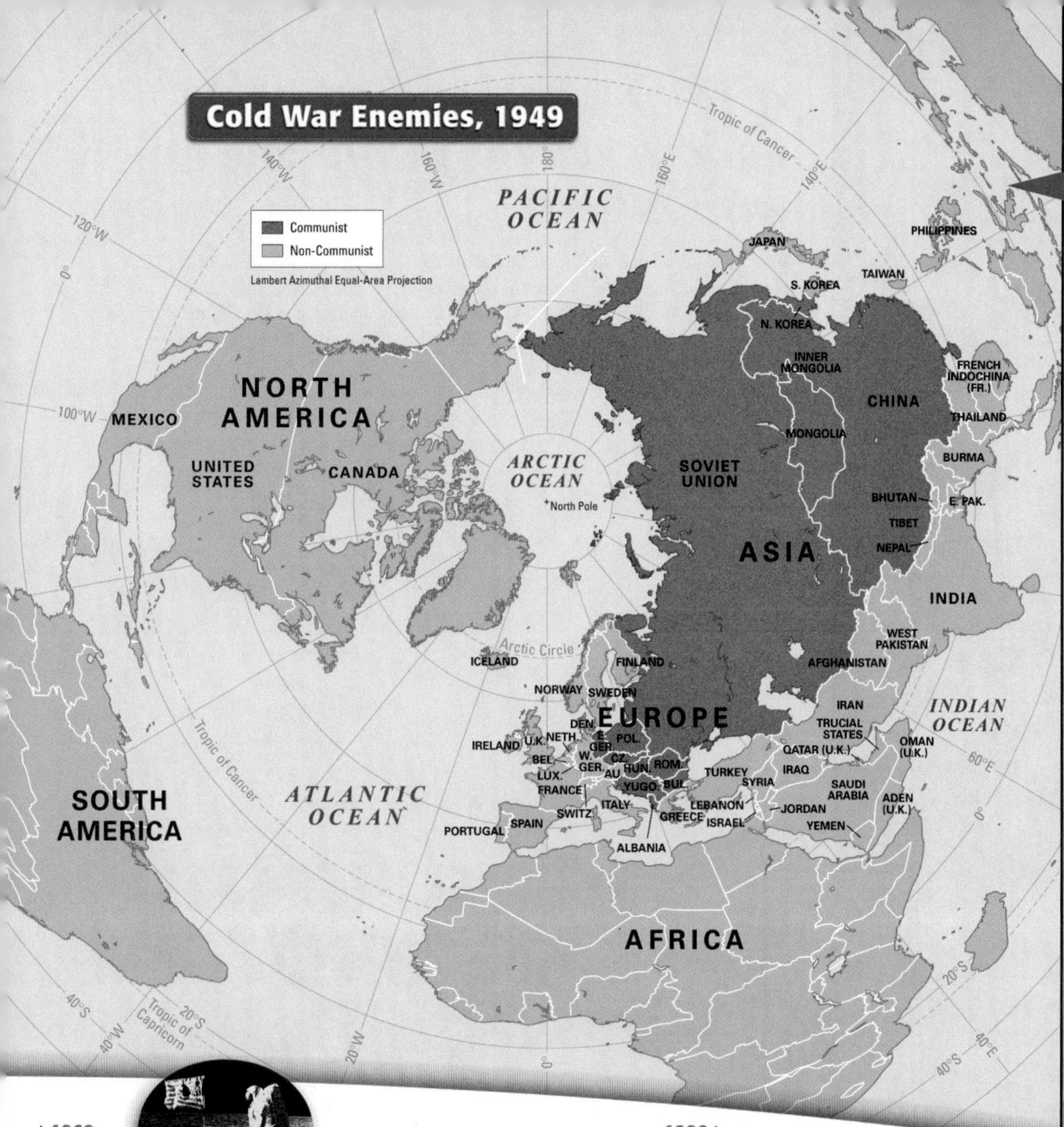

Cold War Enemies, 1949

Communist
Non-Communist
Lambert Azimuthal Equal-Area Projection

1969 U.S. lands astronauts on the moon. ▶

1975 Vietnam War ends.

1990 Communists voted out of power in Nicaragua.

2000 South Korea and North Korea meet to improve relations.

1985

2003

1973 Arab forces attack Israel in the Yom Kippur War.

1989 ◀ Berlin Wall is knocked down in Germany.

1994 First all-race election in South Africa is held. (Nelson Mandela) ▶

History from Visuals

Interpreting the Map

Tell students that geography played an important role in the development of U.S. and Soviet Cold War strategies. Point out the huge landmass of the Soviet Union and the two oceans that surround the United States. Ask students how these factors may have influenced the countries' policies. *(The oceans offered the United States natural defense and motivated its leaders to build air and sea power. In contrast, the Soviet Union was vulnerable to land invasion, which led Soviet leaders to build massive armies.)*

Extension With the class, brainstorm a list of questions regarding the relationship between the United States and the Soviet Union. For example: What was the capital of the Soviet Union? How far is it from the U.S. capital? How far apart were the Soviet Union and the United States at their closest point? Where is that? Divide the questions among students and have them find the answers using classroom resources. Have students share their answers in class discussion. *(Moscow, about 4,900 miles; about 55 miles, northwest Alaska and northeast Soviet Union at the Bering Strait)*

RECOMMENDED RESOURCES

Books for the Teacher

Kutler, Stanley, ed. ***Encyclopedia of the Vietnam War***. New York: Scribner's, 1996.

Cohen, Daniel. ***Joseph McCarthy: The Misuse of Political Power.*** Brookfield, CT: Millbrook, 1996.

Books for the Student

McDougal Littell Literature Connections. Myers, Walter Dean. ***Fallen Angels (with related readings).*** 1997. In this novel a small group of men come of age during the Vietnam War.

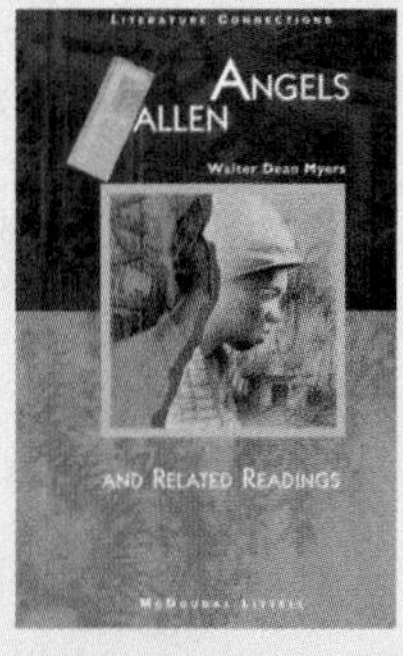

McDougal Littell Literature Connections. Kawashimav Watkins, Yoko. ***So Far from the Bamboo Grove (with related readings).*** 1997. This memoir describes the odyssey of a Japanese family from Korea to Japan at the end of World War II.

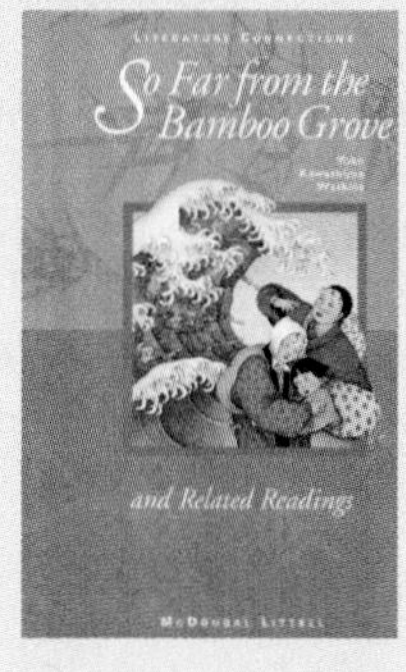

Videos and Software

From the Bay of Pigs to the Brink. VHS. Films for the Humanities & Sciences, 1993. 800-257-5126.

The War at Home. VHS. Library Video Company, 1998. 800-843-3620. Examines the effects of the Vietnam War on the American home front.

Decisions, Decisions Series: The Cold War. CD-ROM. Tom Snyder Productions, 1997. 800-342-0236.

Interact *with* History

Objectives

- Set the stage for studying the Cold War.
- Help students recognize how the Cold War affected nations throughout the world.

EXAMINING *the* ISSUES

Possible Answers

- increased taxes, political unrest at home and in other country, other superpower might try to exert its power, increased risk of war, stronger position in world affairs
- Students may say that such countries might have to sacrifice their ideals or their political and economic security.

Discussion

Ask students to identify ways in which the United States has sought to influence other countries. *(Possible Answers: threat of invasion or isolation, economic sanctions or rewards, financial or military aid, political support for leaders, opposition to policies in UN)*

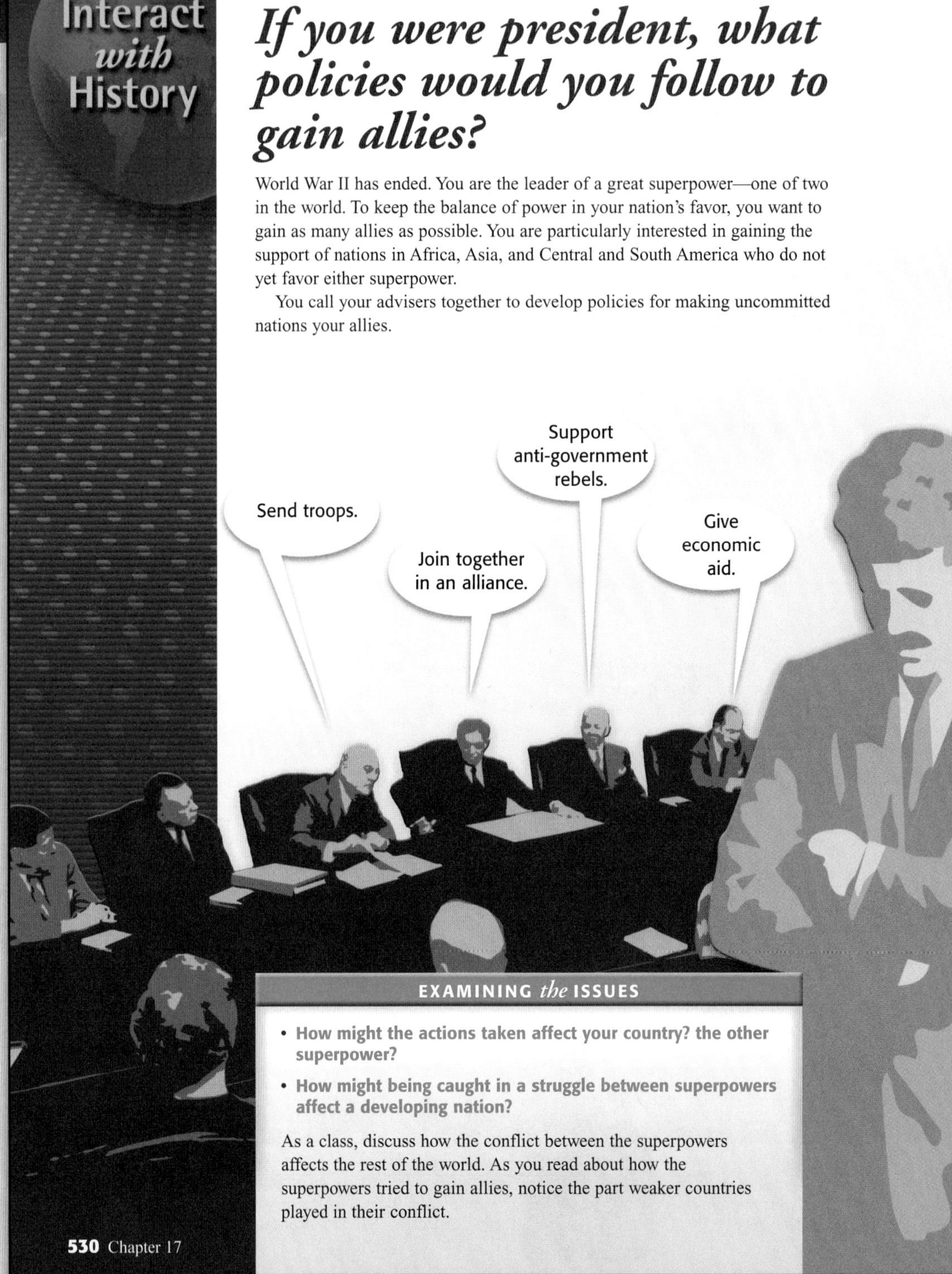

Interact *with* History

If you were president, what policies would you follow to gain allies?

World War II has ended. You are the leader of a great superpower—one of two in the world. To keep the balance of power in your nation's favor, you want to gain as many allies as possible. You are particularly interested in gaining the support of nations in Africa, Asia, and Central and South America who do not yet favor either superpower.

You call your advisers together to develop policies for making uncommitted nations your allies.

Send troops.
Join together in an alliance.
Support anti-government rebels.
Give economic aid.

EXAMINING *the* ISSUES

- **How might the actions taken affect your country? the other superpower?**
- **How might being caught in a struggle between superpowers affect a developing nation?**

As a class, discuss how the conflict between the superpowers affects the rest of the world. As you read about how the superpowers tried to gain allies, notice the part weaker countries played in their conflict.

WHY STUDY THE RESTRUCTURING OF THE POSTWAR WORLD?

- Russia remains a world power even after the breakup of the Soviet Union. Relations and agreements between the Soviet Union and the United States continue to affect U.S.–Russia relations today.
- Alliances built through NATO during the Cold War remain a cornerstone of U.S. foreign relations. Commitments to the organization continue to affect political, economic, and military decisions.
- The United Nations was formed to promote peace and stabilize relations among the world's nations. It continues to be an important resource for resolving issues among nations.
- China is an emerging economic and military power. Relations that developed between China and the United States, as well as with Russia, can have vast significance now and in the future.

Military parade in Red Square, Moscow, USSR, 1987

Buzz Aldrin and the U.S. flag on the moon, 1969

Cold War: Superpowers Face Off

MAIN IDEA

ECONOMICS The opposing economic and political philosophies of the United States and the Soviet Union led to global competition.

WHY IT MATTERS NOW

The conflicts between the United States and the Soviet Union played a major role in reshaping the modern world.

TERMS & NAMES

- United Nations
- iron curtain
- containment
- Truman Doctrine
- Marshall Plan
- Cold War
- NATO
- Warsaw Pact
- brinkmanship

SETTING THE STAGE During World War II, the United States and the Soviet Union had joined forces to fight against the Germans. The Soviet army marched west; the Americans marched east. When the Allied soldiers met at the Elbe River in Germany in 1945, they embraced each other warmly because they had defeated the Nazis. Their leaders, however, regarded each other much more coolly. This animosity caused by competing political philosophies would lead to a nearly half-century of conflict called the Cold War.

CALIFORNIA STANDARDS

10.9.3 Understand the importance of the Truman Doctrine and the Marshall Plan, which established the pattern for America's postwar policy of supplying economic and military aid to prevent the spread of Communism and the resulting economic and political competition in arenas such as Southeast Asia (i.e., the Korean War, Vietnam War), Cuba, and Africa.

Allies Become Enemies

Even before World War II ended, the U.S. alliance with the Soviet Union had begun to unravel. The United States was upset that Joseph Stalin, the Soviet leader, had signed a nonaggression pact with Germany in 1939. Later, Stalin blamed the Allies for not invading German-occupied Europe earlier than 1944. Driven by these and other disagreements, the two allies began to pursue opposing goals.

Yalta Conference: A Postwar Plan The war was not yet over in February 1945. But the leaders of the United States, Britain, and the Soviet Union met at the Soviet Black Sea resort of Yalta. There, they agreed to divide Germany into zones of occupation controlled by the Allied military forces. Germany also would have

TAKING NOTES

Following Chronological Order Organize important early Cold War events in a time line.

1945 — 1960

Yalta conference — U-2 incident

▶ Winston Churchill, Franklin D. Roosevelt, and Joseph Stalin meet at Yalta in 1945.

LESSON PLAN

OBJECTIVES

- Analyze the U.S.-Soviet postwar split.
- Explain how Soviet domination of Eastern Europe developed.
- Describe U.S. containment of Communist expansion.
- Define the Cold War.

1 FOCUS & MOTIVATE

Ask students to name the world's superpowers. Ask, have there been other superpowers in the past? *(Superpower: United States; Possible Answers: past superpowers: Soviet Union, United Kingdom)*

2 INSTRUCT

Allies Become Enemies
10.9.3

Critical Thinking

- What made 1945 an especially good time to found the United Nations? *(Possible Answers: Superpowers still on good terms. With war fresh on their minds, most people supported the effort to promote peace.)*

CALIFORNIA RESOURCES

California Reading Toolkit, p. L75
California Modified Lesson Plans for English Learners, p. 145
California Daily Standards Practice Transparencies, TT67
California Standards Enrichment Workbook, pp. 95–96
California Standards Planner and Lesson Plans, p. L141
California Online Test Practice
California Test Generator CD-ROM
California Easy Planner CD-ROM
California eEdition CD-ROM

SECTION 1 PROGRAM RESOURCES

ALL STUDENTS

In-Depth Resources: Unit 5
- Guided Reading, p. 1

Formal Assessment
- Section Quiz, p. 294

ENGLISH LEARNERS

In-Depth Resources in Spanish
- Guided Reading, p. 132

Reading Study Guide (Spanish), p. 179
Reading Study Guide Audio CD (Spanish)

STRUGGLING READERS

In-Depth Resources: Unit 5
- Guided Reading, p. 1
- Building Vocabulary, p. 6
- Reteaching Activity, p. 21

Reading Study Guide, p. 179
Reading Study Guide Audio CD

GIFTED AND TALENTED STUDENTS

In-Depth Resources: Unit 5
- Literature: from *The Nuclear Age,* p. 14
- Connections Across Time and Cultures: Restoring the Peace, p. 19
- Science and Technology: Super Spy Plane, p. 20

INTEGRATED TECHNOLOGY

eEdition CD-ROM
Voices from the Past Audio CD
Power Presentations CD-ROM
Geography Transparencies
- GT33 The Berlin Airlift, 1948–1949

classzone.com

More About . . .

The Security Council

In 1965, the membership in The Security Council was increased to 15. Nonpermanent members are elected by the UN General Assembly and serve two years. Members are chosen for regional balance. Five members come from Africa or Asia, one from eastern Europe, two from Latin America, and two from Western Europe.

History from Visuals

Interpreting the Map

Ask students to name the Communist countries shown on the map. *(Soviet Union, East Germany, Poland, Czechoslovakia, Hungary, Romania, Yugoslavia, Bulgaria, Albania)*

Extension Have students stage a debate between U.S. and Soviet spokespeople defending their postwar goals.

SKILLBUILDER Answers

1. **Drawing Conclusions** Poland, Czechoslovakia, Hungary, Romania, Yugoslavia, Bulgaria, Albania, East Germany
2. **Comparing** encourage democracy (U.S.), encourage communism (Soviet), reunite Germany (U.S.), keep Germany divided (Soviet)

INTEGRATED TECHNOLOGY

Interactive This map is available in an interactive format on the eEdition.

to pay the Soviet Union to compensate for its loss of life and property. Stalin agreed to join the war against Japan. He also promised that Eastern Europeans would have free elections. A skeptical Winston Churchill predicted that Stalin would keep his pledge only if the Eastern Europeans followed "a policy friendly to Russia."

Creation of the United Nations In June 1945, the United States and the Soviet Union temporarily set aside their differences. They joined 48 other countries in forming the **United Nations** (UN). This international organization was intended to protect the members against aggression. It was to be based in New York.

The charter for the new peacekeeping organization established a large body called the General Assembly. There, each UN member nation could cast its vote on a broad range of issues. An 11-member body called the Security Council had the real power to investigate and settle disputes, though. Its five permanent members were Britain, China, France, the United States, and the Soviet Union. Each could veto any Security Council action. This provision was intended to prevent any members of the Council from voting as a bloc to override the others.

Differing U.S. and Soviet Goals Despite agreement at Yalta and their presence on the Security Council, the United States and the Soviet Union split sharply after the war. The war had affected them very differently. The United States, the world's richest and most powerful country, suffered 400,000 deaths. But its cities and factories remained intact. The Soviet Union had at least 50 times as many fatalities. One in four Soviets was wounded or killed. Also, many Soviet cities were demolished. These contrasting situations, as well as political and economic differences, affected the two countries' postwar goals. (See chart below.) **A**

A. Answer Their aims were in conflict: the U.S. wanted to promote the economic recovery and growth of Western Europe; the Soviet Union wanted to protect itself and spread communism.

MAIN IDEA

Summarizing

A Why did the United States and the Soviet Union split after the war?

Superpower Aims in Europe

INTERACTIVE

United States

- Encourage democracy in other countries to help prevent the rise of Communist governments
- Gain access to raw materials and markets to fuel booming industries
- Rebuild European governments to promote stability and create new markets for U.S. goods
- Reunite Germany to stabilize it and increase the security of Europe

Soviet Union

- Encourage communism in other countries as part of a worldwide workers' revolution
- Rebuild its war-ravaged economy using Eastern Europe's industrial equipment and raw materials
- Control Eastern Europe to protect Soviet borders and balance the U.S. influence in Western Europe
- Keep Germany divided to prevent its waging war again

SKILLBUILDER: Interpreting Maps and Charts

1. **Drawing Conclusions** *Which countries separated the Soviet Union from Western Europe?*
2. **Comparing** *Which U.S. and Soviet aims in Europe conflicted?*

CONNECTIONS ACROSS TIME AND CULTURES

Peacekeeping Institutions

Class Time 20 minutes

Task Comparing and contrasting the League of Nations and the UN

Purpose To analyze the League of Nations and the UN

Instructions Project Critical Thinking Transparency CT74 and complete it with the headings shown. Then give students copies of the worksheet for Connections Across Time and Cultures: Restoring the Peace. Have students work in pairs. Tell them to copy the chart and use it to compare and contrast the UN with the League of Nations, which they studied in chapters 13 and 15. Ask them to consider why the League failed and the UN has endured and been somewhat successful in promoting world peace.

	League of Nations	United Nations
Purpose	international peacekeeping	international peacekeeping
Established		
Disbanded		
Member nations		
Accomplishments		

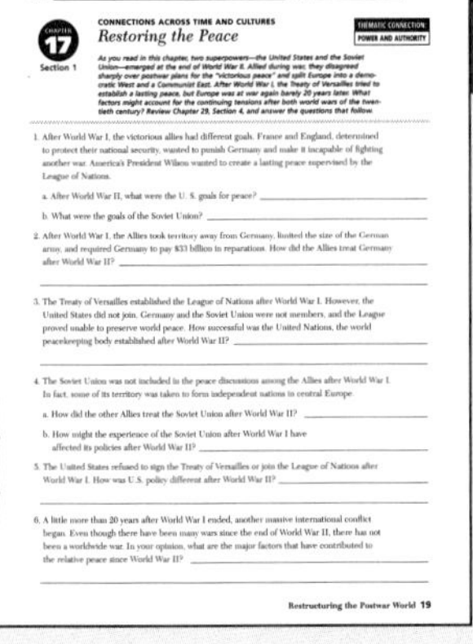

In-Depth Resources: Unit 5

Eastern Europe's Iron Curtain

A major goal of the Soviet Union was to shield itself from another invasion from the west. Centuries of history had taught the Soviets to fear invasion. Because it lacked natural western borders, Russia fell victim to each of its neighbors in turn. In the 17th century, the Poles captured the Kremlin. During the next century, the Swedes attacked. Napoleon overran Moscow in 1812. The Germans invaded Russia during World Wars I and II.

Soviets Build a Buffer As World War II drew to a close, the Soviet troops pushed the Nazis back across Eastern Europe. At war's end, these troops occupied a strip of countries along the Soviet Union's own western border. Stalin regarded these countries as a necessary buffer, or wall of protection. He ignored the Yalta agreement and installed or secured Communist governments in Albania, Bulgaria, Hungary, Czechoslovakia, Romania, Poland, and Yugoslavia.

▲ The Iron Curtain is shown dropping on Czechoslovakia in this 1948 political cartoon.

The Soviet leader's American partner at Yalta, Franklin D. Roosevelt, had died on April 12, 1945. To Roosevelt's successor, Harry S. Truman, Stalin's reluctance to allow free elections in Eastern European nations was a clear violation of those countries' rights. Truman, Stalin, and Churchill met at Potsdam, Germany, in July 1945. There, Truman pressed Stalin to permit free elections in Eastern Europe. The Soviet leader refused. In a speech in early 1946, Stalin declared that communism and capitalism could not exist in the same world.

B. Possible Answer because the West would be unable to penetrate Eastern Europe now that it was under Soviet control

An Iron Curtain Divides East and West Europe now lay divided between East and West. Germany had been split into two sections. The Soviets controlled the eastern part, including half of the capital, Berlin. Under a Communist government, East Germany was named the German Democratic Republic. The western zones became the Federal Republic of Germany in 1949. Winston Churchill described the division of Europe:

MAIN IDEA

Analyzing Primary Sources
B Why might Winston Churchill use "iron curtain" to refer to the division between Western and Eastern Europe?

PRIMARY SOURCE B

From Stettin in the Baltic to Trieste in the Adriatic, an iron curtain has descended across the continent. Behind that line lie all the capitals of the ancient states of Central and Eastern Europe. . . . All these famous cities and the populations around them lie in the Soviet sphere and all are subject in one form or another, not only to Soviet influence but to a very high and increasing measure of control from Moscow.

WINSTON CHURCHILL, "Iron Curtain" speech, March 5, 1946

Churchill's phrase "**iron curtain**" came to represent Europe's division into mostly democratic Western Europe and Communist Eastern Europe.

United States Tries to Contain Soviets

U.S.-Soviet relations continued to worsen in 1946 and 1947. An increasingly worried United States tried to offset the growing Soviet threat to Eastern Europe. President Truman adopted a foreign policy called **containment**. It was a policy directed at blocking Soviet influence and stopping the expansion of communism. Containment policies included forming alliances and helping weak countries resist Soviet advances.

Eastern Europe's Iron Curtain
10.9.3

Critical Thinking

- Why did Stalin refuse to allow free elections in eastern Europe? *(He wanted eastern Europe under Communist control as a buffer against invasion.)*
- How is "iron curtain" an apt term for the division between democratic and Communist Europe? *(Iron is visually and physically impenetrable and cuts off contact between each side.)*

Tip for Struggling Readers

Winston Churchill's language may give some students difficulty. Explain that *Stettin* and *Trieste* are cities in Europe; the *Baltic* and *Adriatic* are seas. The "*Soviet sphere*" refers to the circle or area of influence. Help students paraphrase the quotation for greater understanding.

United States Tries to Contain Soviets
10.9.3

Critical Thinking

- How were the Truman Doctrine and the Marshall Plan alike? *(Both provided economic assistance to countries opposed to Communisim.)*
- Why didn't Russia want the occupied zones of Germany to be reunited? *(feared Germany would again become a military threat)*

DIFFERENTIATING INSTRUCTION: ENGLISH LEARNERS

Understanding the Cold War

Class Time 45 minutes

Task Creating political cartoons

Purpose To use political cartoons as a means of understanding the cold war

Instructions Call students' attention to the political cartoon at the top of the page. Discuss the symbols with students: the iron wall represents the iron curtain; the hammer and sickle represents the Soviet Union or Communism; the arm represents the people of Czechoslovakia; the torch represents liberty. Discuss the meaning of the cartoon: The iron curtain has come down on the people of Czechoslovakia, squelching their attempt to achieve liberty. Explain that political cartoons typically use strong symbolism to communicate an opinion about events.

Have students work in four groups and assign each of the parts of this section to a different group. Tell each group to read and discuss their section. Have them evaluate and discuss their ideas and thoughts about the events. Then have them brainstorm ideas for expressing an opinion in a political cartoon about one or more of the events. Allow them to work individually or as a group to create a cartoon. Have students post their cartoons on the wall and use them as basis for a class review of the main ideas.

More About . . .

The Truman Doctrine

When Stalin broke his promise to hold free elections in Europe, Truman saw a repetition of Hitler's broken promises to Britain and France before World War II. He was determined not to mimic the British and French indecision that led to such a disaster in the war. He therefore took a tough line with Stalin. "A totalitarian state is no different whether you call it Nazi, Fascist, Communist, or Franco's Spain," he wrote in a letter to his daughter. "I went to Potsdam [the final wartime conference of The Big Three in 1945] with the kindliest feeling toward Russia—in a year and a half they cured me of it."

History from Visuals

Interpreting the Chart

Ask students how much aid Iceland received. How many countries received more than $1 billion in aid? *($29 million; 4)*

Extension Have students use an almanac or statistical abstract to find out which countries listed in the chart currently rank among the top 10 U.S. trading partners. *(Germany, Great Britain, France)*

SKILLBUILDER Answers

1. **Drawing Conclusions** Great Britain
2. **Making Inferences** *Possible Answer:* They were the principal U.S. allies during World War II.

The Truman Doctrine In a speech asking Congress for foreign aid for Turkey and Greece, Truman contrasted democracy with communism:

> **PRIMARY SOURCE**
> One way of life is based upon the will of the majority, and is distinguished by free institutions . . . free elections . . . and freedom from political oppression. The second way of life is based upon the will of a minority forcibly imposed upon the majority. It relies upon terror and oppression . . . fixed elections, and the suppression of personal freedoms. I believe it must be the policy of the United States to support free people . . . resisting attempted subjugation [control] by armed minorities or by outside pressures.
> **PRESIDENT HARRY S. TRUMAN,** speech to Congress, March 12, 1947

Truman's support for countries that rejected communism was called the **Truman Doctrine**. It caused great controversy. Some opponents objected to American interference in other nations' affairs. Others argued that the United States could not afford to carry on a global crusade against communism. Congress, however, immediately authorized more than $400 million in aid to Turkey and Greece.

C. Answer help European countries rebuild and become strong enough to resist Communist expansion

MAIN IDEA

Making Inferences

C What was Truman's major reason for offering aid to other countries?

The Marshall Plan Much of Western Europe lay in ruins after the war. There was also economic turmoil—a scarcity of jobs and food. In 1947, U.S. Secretary of State George Marshall proposed that the United States give aid to needy European countries. This assistance program, called the **Marshall Plan**, would provide food, machinery, and other materials to rebuild Western Europe. (See chart.) As Congress debated the $12.5 billion program in 1948, the Communists seized power in Czechoslovakia. Congress immediately voted approval. The plan was a spectacular success. Even Communist Yugoslavia received aid after it broke away from Soviet domination. **C**

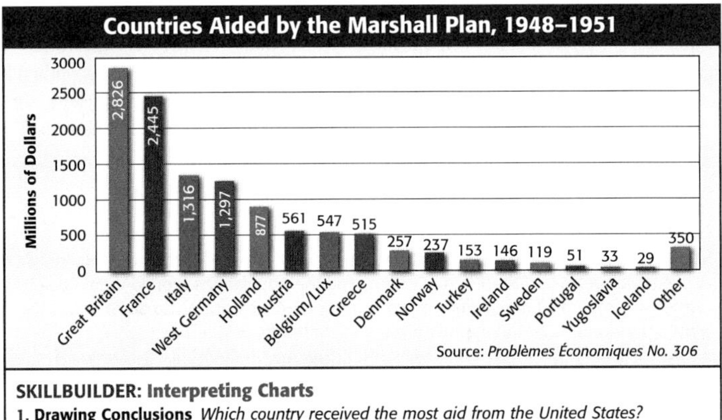

SKILLBUILDER: Interpreting Charts

1. **Drawing Conclusions** *Which country received the most aid from the United States?*
2. **Making Inferences** *Why do you think Great Britain and France received so much aid?*

The Berlin Airlift While Europe began rebuilding, the United States and its allies clashed with the Soviet Union over Germany. The Soviets wanted to keep their former enemy weak and divided. But in 1948, France, Britain, and the United States decided to withdraw their forces from Germany and allow their occupation zones to form one nation. The Soviet Union responded by holding West Berlin hostage.

Although Berlin lay well within the Soviet occupation zone of Germany, it too had been divided into four zones. (See map on next page.) The Soviet Union cut off highway, water, and rail traffic into Berlin's western zones. The city faced starvation. Stalin gambled that the Allies would surrender West Berlin or give up

DIFFERENTIATING INSTRUCTION: STRUGGLING READERS

The Berlin Airlift

Class Time 20 minutes

Task Answering questions about the Berlin Airlift

Purpose To better understand the conflict between the U.S. and its allies and the Soviet Union

Instructions Show Geography Transparency GT33, The Berlin Airlift. Remind students that allied planes made 278,000 flights over 11 months to keep West Berlin out of the hands of the Soviet Union. Have pairs of students work together to answer the following questions:

1. Why did the Soviet Union set up a blockade around West Berlin? *(To force the Allies to either give up their parts of the city or give up the idea of allowing Germany to become one nation.)*
2. Why was the Soviet Union so afraid of allowing Germany to become a single nation? *(Russia is close to Germany. The Russians had been invaded by the German army. Russia wanted to keep Germany weak and divided.)*
3. Why did the Allies fly food and supplies into Berlin? *(They didn't want to give in to Stalin because they disliked and distrusted him. They were opposed to communism.)*

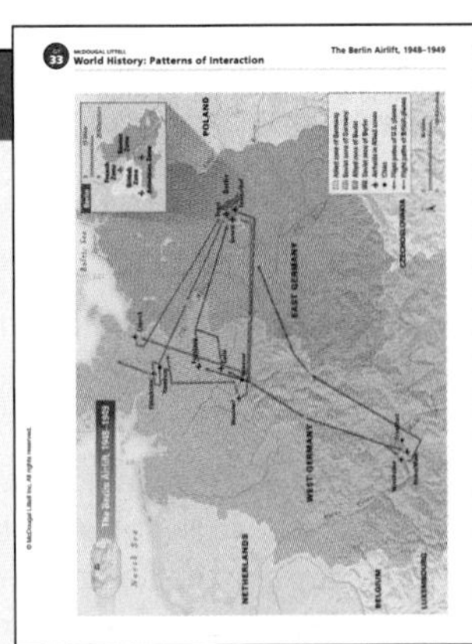

Geography Transparencies

History *in* Depth

The Berlin Airlift

From June 1948 to May 1949, Allied planes took off and landed every three minutes in West Berlin. On 278,000 flights, pilots brought in 2.3 million tons of food, fuel, medicine, and even Christmas gifts to West Berliners.

Divided Germany, 1948–1949

Occupation zones: British, French, Soviet, U.S.; Air corridor; Airport

History *in* Depth

The Berlin Airlift

The Soviets believed the blockade would force the allies to give up Berlin. In fact, the allies were able to turn the tables on the Soviet Union. First, the airlift operated in two directions, both supplying the Berliners with needed goods and also keeping Berlin's economy alive by allowing industry to continue exporting goods. Second, the allies placed an embargo on exports from the Communist nations, bringing about economic hardships that helped force the Soviet Union to release its grip on Berlin.

Geography Transparencies

- GT33 The Berlin Airlift, 1948–1949

MAIN IDEA

Summarizing

D What Soviet actions led to the Berlin airlift?

D. Answer the Soviet blockade of West Berlin

their idea of reunifying Germany. But American and British officials flew food and supplies into West Berlin for nearly 11 months. In May 1949, the Soviet Union admitted defeat and lifted the blockade. **D**

The Cold War Divides the World

These conflicts marked the start of the **Cold War** between the United States and the Soviet Union. A cold war is a struggle over political differences carried on by means short of military action or war. Beginning in 1949, the superpowers used spying, propaganda, diplomacy, and secret operations in their dealings with each other. Much of the world allied with one side or the other. In fact, until the Soviet Union finally broke up in 1991, the Cold War dictated not only U.S. and Soviet foreign policy, but influenced world alliances as well.

Superpowers Form Rival Alliances The Berlin blockade heightened Western Europe's fears of Soviet aggression. As a result, in 1949, ten western European nations joined with the United States and Canada to form a defensive military alliance. It was called the North Atlantic Treaty Organization (**NATO**). An attack on any NATO member would be met with armed force by all member nations.

The Soviet Union saw NATO as a threat and formed it's own alliance in 1955. It was called the **Warsaw Pact** and included the Soviet Union, East Germany, Czechoslovakia, Poland, Hungary, Romania, Bulgaria, and Albania. In 1961, the East Germans built a wall to separate East and West Berlin. The Berlin Wall symbolized a world divided into rival camps. However, not every country joined the new alliances. Some, like India, chose not to align with either side. And China, the largest Communist country, came to distrust the Soviet Union. It remained nonaligned.

The Threat of Nuclear War As these alliances were forming, the Cold War threatened to heat up enough to destroy the world. The United States already had atomic bombs. In 1949, the Soviet Union exploded its own atomic weapon. President Truman was determined to develop a more deadly weapon before the Soviets did. He authorized work on a thermonuclear weapon in 1950.

The Cold War Divides the World

10.9.3

Critical Thinking

- How did the arms race help prevent war between the superpowers? *(weapons were so devastating neither side was willing to risk war)*
- How did a Soviet dominance in space pose a threat to the United States? *(Space could be used against the U.S. for surveillance and military purposes; technology developed for space would give the Soviets an advantage in all kinds of military technology.)*

DIFFERENTIATING INSTRUCTION: GIFTED AND TALENTED STUDENTS

Literature of the Cold War

Class Time 45 minutes

Task Analyzing the literature of the Cold War

Purpose To understand the effects of the Cold War on literature and society

Instructions The Cold War affected not only politics, but literature as well. Fiction took on new dimensions as writers reflected on the realities of life during the Cold War and the possibilities that the war opened up. Spy novels such as John le Carre's *The Spy Who Came in from the Cold,* for example, include agents with double agendas and sophisticated technology. Science fiction works such as Ray Bradbury's *The Martian Chronicles* and Jack Finney's *The Body Snatchers* explore what the world might be like if Cold War trends in nuclear weapons and pervasive fear continued. Tim O'Brien's *The Nuclear Age* provides a realistic view of what it was like living during the Cold War. Have students read one of these books and write a report that analyzes how realistic it seems in today's world. Alternatively, have students read the excerpt from O'Brien's *The Nuclear Age* in In-Depth Resources for Unit 5, pages 14–16.

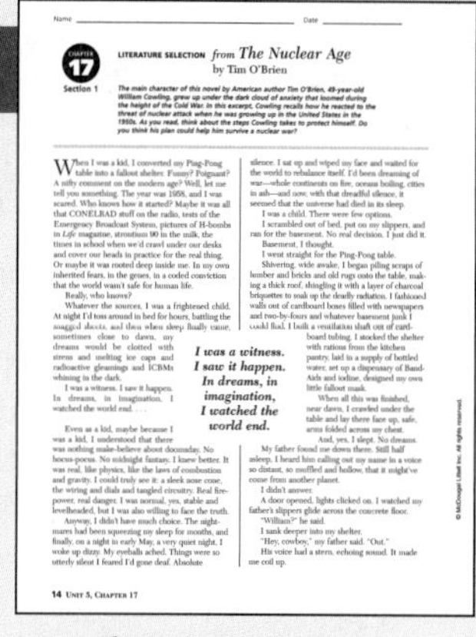

LITERATURE SELECTION *from The Nuclear Age* by Tim O'Brien

I was a witness. I saw it happen. In dreams, in imagination, I watched the world end.

In-Depth Resources: Unit 5

More About . . .

U-2

The U-2 was first flown in 1955 and became central to U.S. strategic surveillance during the 1960s. It flew at 494 miles per hour and cruised at about 70,000 feet. In addition to its use over the Soviet Union, it was used to observe the Soviet missile buildup in Cuba in 1962. The U-2 was in service only until the mid-1960s when it was replaced by a new, much faster surveillance plane, the SR-71 Blackbird.

In-Depth Resources: Unit 5
- Science & Technology: Super Spy Plane, p. 20

The hydrogen or H-bomb would be thousands of times more powerful than the A-bomb. Its power came from the fusion, or joining together, of atoms, rather than the splitting of atoms, as in the A-bomb. In 1952, the United States tested the first H-bomb. The Soviets exploded their own in 1953.

Dwight D. Eisenhower became the U.S. president in 1953. He appointed the firmly anti-Communist John Foster Dulles as his secretary of state. If the Soviet Union or its supporters attacked U.S. interests, Dulles threatened, the United States would "retaliate instantly, by means and at places of our own choosing." This willingness to go to the brink, or edge, of war became known as **brinkmanship**. Brinkmanship required a reliable source of nuclear weapons and airplanes to deliver them. So, the United States strengthened its air force and began producing stockpiles of nuclear weapons. The Soviet Union responded with its own military buildup, beginning an arms race that would go on for four decades. **E**

E. Answer The U.S. and the Soviet Union began a contest to see who could amass the greater number of nuclear weapons more quickly.

MAIN IDEA
Recognizing Effects
E How did the U.S. policy of brinkmanship contribute to the arms race?

The Cold War in the Skies The Cold War also affected the science and education programs of the two countries. In August 1957, the Soviets announced the development of a rocket that could travel great distances—an intercontinental ballistic missile, or ICBM. On October 4, the Soviets used an ICBM to push *Sputnik,* the first unmanned satellite, above the earth's atmosphere. Americans felt they had fallen behind in science and technology, and the government poured money into science education. In 1958, the United States launched its own satellite.

In 1960, the skies again provided the arena for a superpower conflict. Five years earlier, Eisenhower had proposed that the United States and the Soviet Union be able to fly over each other's territory to guard against surprise nuclear attacks. The Soviet Union said no. In response, the U.S. Central Intelligence Agency (CIA) started secret high-altitude spy flights over Soviet territory in planes called U-2s. In May 1960, the Soviets shot down a U-2 plane, and its pilot, Francis Gary Powers, was captured. This U-2 incident heightened Cold War tensions.

While Soviet Communists were squaring off against the United States, Communists in China were fighting a civil war for control of that country.

3 ASSESS

SECTION 1 ASSESSMENT

Have students work in pairs to answer the questions. Have volunteers share their charts for Item 2 with the class.

Formal Assessment
- Section Quiz, p. 294

4 RETEACH

Have students use the Reading Study Guide for Section 1 for reviewing the main ideas of the section.

Reading Study Guide, pp. 179–180 (also in Spanish)

In-Depth Resources: Unit 5
- Reteaching Activity, p. 21

SECTION 1 ASSESSMENT

TERMS & NAMES 1. For each term or name, write a sentence explaining its significance.
• United Nations • iron curtain • containment • Truman Doctrine • Marshall Plan • Cold War • NATO • Warsaw Pact • brinkmanship

USING YOUR NOTES

2. Which effect of the Cold War was the most significant? Explain. (10.9.3)

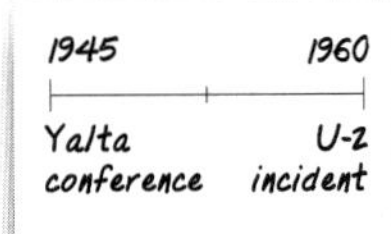

MAIN IDEAS

3. What was the purpose in forming the United Nations? (10.9.3)
4. What was the goal of the Marshall Plan? (10.9.3)
5. What were the goals of NATO and the Warsaw Pact? (10.9.3)

CRITICAL THINKING & WRITING

6. **COMPARING AND CONTRASTING** What factors help to explain why the United States and the Soviet Union became rivals instead of allies? (10.9.3)
7. **ANALYZING MOTIVES** What were Stalin's objectives in supporting Communist governments in Eastern Europe? (10.9.3)
8. **ANALYZING ISSUES** Why might Berlin be a likely spot for trouble to develop during the Cold War? (10.9.3)
9. **WRITING ACTIVITY** ECONOMICS Draw a **political cartoon** that shows either capitalism from the Soviet point of view or communism from the U.S. point of view. (Writing 2.4.b)

INTEGRATED TECHNOLOGY **INTERNET ACTIVITY**

Use the Internet to research NATO today. Prepare a **chart** listing members today and the date they joined. Then compare it with a list of the founding members. (Writing 2.3.d)

INTERNET KEYWORD
North Atlantic Treaty Organization

ANSWERS

1. United Nations, p. 532 • iron curtain, p. 533 • containment, p. 533 • Truman Doctrine, p. 534 • Marshall Plan, p. 534 • Cold War, p. 535 • NATO, p. 535 • Warsaw Pact, p. 535 • brinkmanship, p. 536

2. **Sample Answer:** 1945—Yalta Conference; 1945—United Nations; 1946—Iron Curtain; 1947—Truman Doctrine; 1947—Marshall Plan; 1948—Berlin Airlift; 1949—NATO; 1955—Warsaw Pact; 1960—U2 incident. Students may say the Marshall Plan was most significant because it rebuilt Europe.
3. to protect members against aggression
4. to provide aid to European countries damaged by World War II
5. **Possible Answer:** Both military alliances had been formed to contain its enemies with force, if necessary.
6. **Possible Answer:** competition for leadership, different goals, conflicting ideologies
7. **Possible Answers:** to protect borders; to counteract U.S. influence; to have access to raw materials; to keep Germany from rebuilding and threatening Russia
8. **Possible Answer:** The West wanted to keep Berlin free even though it was inside Communist East Germany.
9. **Rubric** The political cartoon should
   - have either a Soviet or American viewpoint.
   - be understandable to the viewer.
   - exhibit creativity.

INTEGRATED TECHNOLOGY

Rubric The chart should
- be clearly labeled.
- contain date, membership, and purpose for each alliance.
- present data in an understandable style.

The Space Race

Beginning in the late 1950s, the United States and the Soviet Union competed for influence not only among the nations of the world, but in the skies as well. Once the superpowers had ICBMs (intercontinental ballistic missiles) to deliver nuclear warheads and aircraft for spying missions, they both began to develop technology that could be used to explore—and ultimately control—space. However, after nearly two decades of costly competition, the two superpowers began to cooperate in space exploration.

INTEGRATED TECHNOLOGY

RESEARCH LINKS For more on the space race, go to **classzone.com**

CALIFORNIA STANDARDS

10.9.2 Analyze the causes of the Cold War, with the free world on one side and Soviet client states on the other, including competition for influence in such places as Egypt, the Congo, Vietnam, and Chile.

▲ In a major technological triumph, the United States put human beings on the moon on July 20, 1969. Astronaut Buzz Aldrin is shown on the lunar surface with the lunar lander spacecraft.

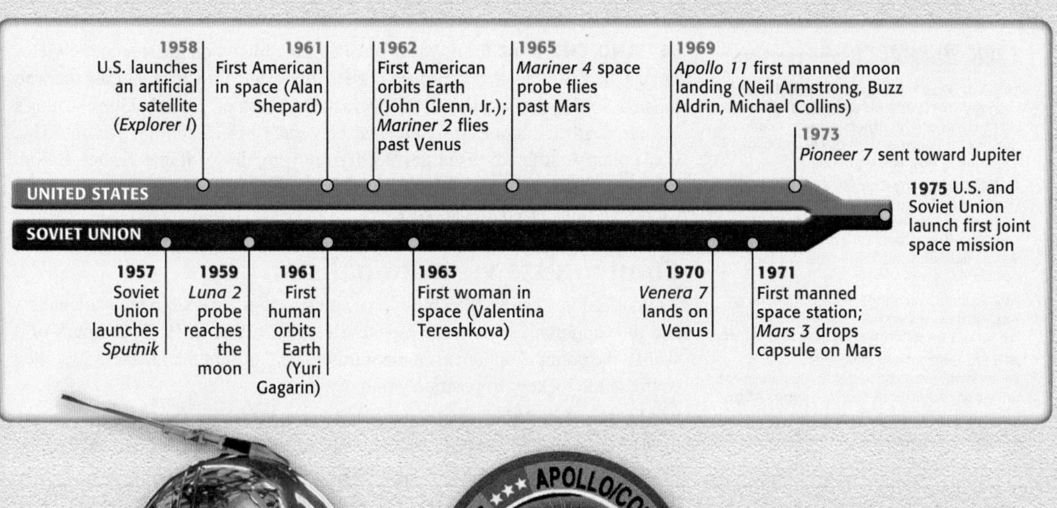

UNITED STATES
1958 U.S. launches an artificial satellite (*Explorer I*)
1961 First American in space (Alan Shepard)
1962 First American orbits Earth (John Glenn, Jr.); *Mariner 2* flies past Venus
1965 *Mariner 4* space probe flies past Mars
1969 *Apollo 11* first manned moon landing (Neil Armstrong, Buzz Aldrin, Michael Collins)
1973 *Pioneer 7* sent toward Jupiter
1975 U.S. and Soviet Union launch first joint space mission
SOVIET UNION
1957 Soviet Union launches *Sputnik*
1959 *Luna 2* probe reaches the moon
1961 First human orbits Earth (Yuri Gagarin)
1963 First woman in space (Valentina Tereshkova)
1970 *Venera 7* lands on Venus
1971 First manned space station; *Mars 3* drops capsule on Mars

◄ The joint *Apollo* and *Soyuz* mission ushered in an era of U.S.-Soviet cooperation in space.

▲ The Soviet Union launched *Sputnik*, the first successful artificial space satellite, on October 4, 1957. As it circled the earth every 96 minutes, Premier Nikita Khrushchev boasted that his country would soon be "turning out long-range missiles like sausages." The United States accelerated its space program. After early failures, a U.S. satellite was launched in 1958.

Connect *to* Today

1. **Comparing** Which destinations in space did both the United States and the Soviet Union explore?
   See Skillbuilder Handbook, page R7.
2. **Making Inferences** What role might space continue to play in achieving world peace?

537

Science & Technology

OBJECTIVE

- Describe important milestones in the history of space exploration.

INSTRUCT

Emphasize that although the space program developed as a direct result of the arms race, it has become primarily a scientific endeavor. Along the way, it has given the United States and the Soviet Union (now Russia) the opportunity to cooperate in exploring space. Point out that the patch for the Apollo/Soyuz mission demonstrates how far the collaboration has gone—all the way to combined U.S.-Soviet flights.

More About . . .

Current Space Exploration

The exploration of space goes forward with many projects. First among them is the International Space Station, which is the largest and most sophisticated space craft ever built. It has been continuously occupied since November 2, 2000. The United States' MER mission will land two robot rovers to explore the surface of Mars in 2004. The Hubble Space Telescope continues to provide scientists with detailed views of deep space that were never possible from Earth. The United States has many other projects underway and planned. Some projects are in cooperation with other nations.

CONNECT TO TODAY: ANSWERS

1. Comparing

The United States and the Soviet Union both explored Venus, Mars, and the moon.

2. Making Inferences

Possible Answers: Joint space explorations may build trust and cooperation among participating nations. The sharing of science and technology may prevent one nation from gaining an advantage over other nations that might lead to new weapons used to control others.

LESSON PLAN

OBJECTIVES

- Analyze the civil war between the Nationalists and the Communists.
- Explain how China split into two nations.
- Describe how Mao's Marxist regime transformed China.

1 FOCUS & MOTIVATE

Have students list the qualities that can make someone a great leader. Then explain that when China underwent a civil war, each side was led by a charismatic leader. Tell students to evaluate these leaders as they read and decide which shares more of the qualities they've listed.

2 INSTRUCT

Communists vs. Nationalists
10.9.4

Critical Thinking

- How did Mao's use of money compare to Jiang's? *(Mao spent money on the peasants; Jiang allowed money to be taken by corrupt officers.)*

CALIFORNIA RESOURCES
California Reading Toolkit, p. L76
California Modified Lesson Plans for English Learners, p. 147
California Daily Standards Practice Transparencies, TT68
California Standards Enrichment Workbook, pp. 93–94, 97–98
California Standards Planner and Lesson Plans, p. L143
California Online Test Practice
California Test Generator CD-ROM
California Easy Planner CD-ROM
California eEdition CD-ROM

2

Military parade in Red Square, Moscow, USSR, 1987

Buzz Aldrin and the U.S. flag on the moon, 1969

Communists Take Power in China

MAIN IDEA	WHY IT MATTERS NOW	TERMS & NAMES
REVOLUTION After World War II, Chinese Communists defeated Nationalist forces and two separate Chinas emerged.	China remains a Communist country and a major power in the world.	• Mao Zedong • Jiang Jieshi • commune • Red Guards • Cultural Revolution

CALIFORNIA STANDARDS

10.9.2 Analyze the causes of the Cold War, with the free world on one side and Soviet client states on the other, including competition for influence in such places as Egypt, the Congo, Vietnam, and Chile.

10.9.4 Analyze the Chinese Civil War, the rise of Mao Tse-tung, and the subsequent political and economic upheavals in China (e.g., the Great Leap Forward, the Cultural Revolution, and the Tiananmen Square uprising).

HI 2 Students recognize the complexity of historical causes and effects, including the limitations on determining cause and effect.

HI 3 Students interpret past events and issues within the context in which an event unfolded rather than solely in terms of present-day norms and values.

SETTING THE STAGE In World War II, China fought on the side of the victorious Allies. But the victory proved to be a hollow one for China. During the war, Japan's armies had occupied and devastated most of China's cities. China's civilian death toll alone was estimated between 10 to 22 million persons. This vast country suffered casualties second only to those of the Soviet Union. However, conflict did not end with the defeat of the Japanese. In 1945, opposing Chinese armies faced one another.

TAKING NOTES
Recognizing Effects Use a chart to identify the causes and effects of the Communist Revolution in China.

Cause	Effect
1.	1.
2.	2.
3.	3.

Communists vs. Nationalists

As you read in Chapter 14, a bitter civil war was raging between the Nationalists and the Communists when the Japanese invaded China in 1937. During World War II, the political opponents temporarily united to fight the Japanese. But they continued to jockey for position within China.

World War II in China Under their leader, **Mao Zedong** (MOW dzuh•dahng), the Communists had a stronghold in northwestern China. From there, they mobilized peasants for guerrilla war against the Japanese in the northeast. Thanks to their efforts to promote literacy and improve food production, the Communists won the peasants' loyalty. By 1945, they controlled much of northern China.

Meanwhile, the Nationalist forces under **Jiang Jieshi** (jee•ahng jee•shee) dominated southwestern China. Protected from the Japanese by rugged mountain ranges, Jiang gathered an army of 2.5 million men. From 1942 to 1945, the United States sent the Nationalists at least $1.5 billion in aid to fight the Japanese. Instead of benefiting the army, however, these supplies and money often ended up in the hands of a few corrupt officers. Jiang's army actually fought few battles against the Japanese. Instead, the Nationalist army saved its strength for the coming battle against Mao's Red Army. After Japan surrendered, the Nationalists and Communists resumed fighting.

Civil War Resumes The renewed civil war lasted from 1946 to 1949. At first, the Nationalists had the advantage. Their army outnumbered the Communists' army by as much as three to one. And the United States continued its support by providing nearly $2 billion in aid. The Nationalist forces, however, did little to win popular support. With China's economy collapsing, thousands of Nationalist soldiers deserted to the Communists. In spring 1949, China's major cities fell to

SECTION 2 PROGRAM RESOURCES

ALL STUDENTS

In-Depth Resources: Unit 5
- Guided Reading, p. 2
- Skillbuilder Practice: Interpreting Charts, p. 7

Formal Assessment
- Section Quiz, p. 295

ENGLISH LEARNERS

In-Depth Resources in Spanish
- Guided Reading, p. 133
- Skillbuilder Practice: Interpreting Charts, p. 137

Reading Study Guide (Spanish), p. 181

Reading Study Guide Audio CD (Spanish)

STRUGGLING READERS

In-Depth Resources: Unit 5
- Guided Reading, p. 2
- Building Vocabulary, p. 6
- Skillbuilder Practice: Interpreting Charts, p. 7
- Reteaching Activity, p. 22

Reading Study Guide, p. 181
Reading Study Guide Audio CD

GIFTED AND TALENTED STUDENTS

In-Depth Resources: Unit 5
- Primary Source: from *No Tears for Mao,* p. 10

INTEGRATED TECHNOLOGY

eEdition CD-ROM
Power Presentations CD-ROM
World Art and Cultures Transparencies
- AT72 Spring Walk to the Chi-Ch'ang Park

classzone.com

Nationalists		Communists
Jiang Jieshi	**Leader**	Mao Zedong
Southern China	**Area Ruled**	Northern China
United States	**Foreign Support**	Soviet Union
Defeat of Communists	**Domestic Policy**	National liberation
Weak due to inflation and failing economy	**Public Support**	Strong due to promised land reform for peasants
Ineffective, corrupt leadership and poor morale	**Military Organization**	Experienced, motivated guerrilla army

Chinese Political Opponents, 1945

SKILLBUILDER: Interpreting Charts
1. **Drawing Conclusions** *Which party's domestic policy might appeal more to Chinese peasants?*
2. **Forming and Supporting Opinions** *Which aspect of the Communist approach do you think was most responsible for Mao's victory? Explain.*

A. Possible Answer The victory of the Chinese Communists reinforced U.S. belief that the Communists would take over the world.

MAIN IDEA
Recognizing Effects
A How did the outcome of the Chinese civil war contribute to Cold War tensions?

the well-trained Red forces. Mao's troops were also enthusiastic about his promise to return land to the peasants. The remnants of Jiang's shattered army fled south. In October 1949, Mao Zedong gained control of the country. He proclaimed it the People's Republic of China. Jiang and other Nationalist leaders retreated to the island of Taiwan, which Westerners called Formosa.

Mao Zedong's victory fueled U.S. anti-Communist feelings. Those feelings only grew after the Chinese and Soviets signed a treaty of friendship in 1950. Many people in the United States viewed the takeover of China as another step in a Communist campaign to conquer the world. A

The Two Chinas Affect the Cold War

China had split into two nations. One was the island of Taiwan, or Nationalist China, with an area of 13,000 square miles. The mainland, or People's Republic of China, had an area of more than 3.5 million square miles. The existence of two Chinas, and the conflicting international loyalties they inspired, intensified the Cold War.

The Superpowers React After Jiang Jieshi fled to Taiwan, the United States helped him set up a Nationalist government on that small island. It was called the Republic of China. The Soviets gave financial, military, and technical aid to Communist China. In addition, the Chinese and the Soviets pledged to come to each other's defense if either was attacked. The United States tried to halt Soviet expansion in Asia. For example, when Soviet forces occupied the northern half of Korea after World War II and set up a Communist government, the United States supported a separate state in the south.

China Expands under the Communists In the early years of Mao's reign, Chinese troops expanded into Tibet, India, and southern, or Inner, Mongolia. Northern, or Outer, Mongolia, which bordered the Soviet Union, remained in the Soviet sphere.

In a brutal assault in 1950 and 1951, China took control of Tibet. The Chinese promised autonomy to Tibetans, who followed their religious leader, the Dalai Lama. When China's control over Tibet tightened in the late 1950s, the Dalai Lama fled to India. India welcomed many Tibetan refugees after a failed revolt in Tibet in

History from Visuals

Interpreting the Chart

Make sure that students understand that the middle column identifies the topic of each row. Ask which rows help explain why the Nationalists lost to the Communists. *(the last three)*

Extension Have students examine a map and contrast the topography, cities, and resources of northern and southern China. Which area seems to be better developed and more economically important? *(southern China)* Ask students to discuss how Mao triumphed over Jiang despite his weaker geographic position.

SKILLBUILDER Answers
1. **Drawing Conclusions** Communists
2. **Forming and Supporting Opinions** *Possible Answers:* military organization and public support.

The Two Chinas Affect the Cold War
10.9.2

Critical Thinking

- How did the Cold War contribute to Jiang's survival? *(It ensured aid and protection from the U.S., which wanted to maintain some influence in China.)*
- How did Chinese promises to the Tibetan people resemble the Soviet Union's promises to the countries of eastern Europe? *(Both promised autonomy but later took control away.)*

SKILLBUILDER PRACTICE: INTERPRETING CHARTS

Understanding Nationalists and Communists

Class Time 20 minutes
Task Interpreting a chart
Purpose To practice skills in using charts
Instructions Explain that charts provide a visual presentation of information that clarifies the relationships among ideas and makes them easier to grasp. In a chart, information is grouped into categories. Reading down the columns and across the rows of a chart offers a quick summary of the information in a category. It also makes the comparison and contrast between entries clear.
Ask students the following questions:

1. Based on the chart, which characteristics did the Nationalists and Communists share? *(none)*
2. Which category indicates that the conflict in China was part of the Cold War? *(foreign support)*
3. Which category indicates that the Nationalists and the Communists were directly opposed? *(domestic policy)*

For students who need additional help, use the Skillbuilder Practice worksheet for Unit 5, p. 7

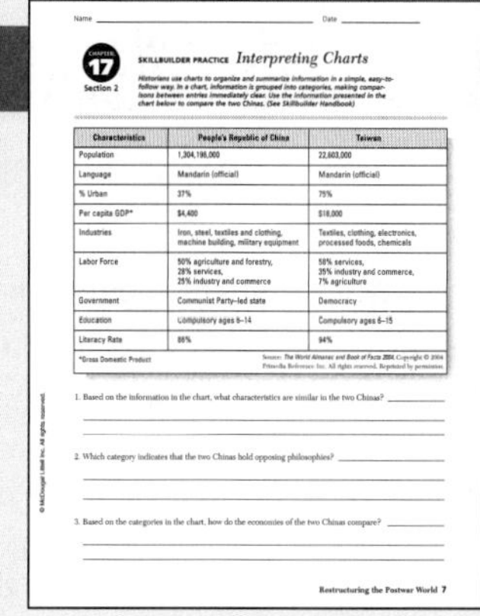

In-Depth Resources: Unit 5

History Makers

Mao Zedong

Ask students what qualities made Mao a strong leader. *(recognized the power of the peasants, their need for economic opportunity)*

In 1972, when President Nixon told Mao Zedong that his teachings had transformed China and affected the whole world, Mao replied, "All I have done is change Beijing and a few of its suburbs." Considering the size of China's population (a quarter of the world's total), however, Mao may have been the most influential leader of the 20th century.

The Communists Transform China

10.9.4

Critical Thinking

- What was the significance of Mao's role as head of both the Communist party and the national government? *(nation was united behind single leader, had clear goals and political philosophy)*
- How did nationalizing industry further the Communist goal of social equality? *(eliminated private ownership and with it the wealth of some compared to moderate or low income of others)*
- Why were intellectuals targeted in the Cultural Revolution? *(They were the elite, not consistent with social equality.)*

History Makers

Mao Zedong
1893–1976

Born into a peasant family, Mao embraced Marxist socialism as a young man. Though he began as an urban labor organizer, Mao quickly realized the revolutionary potential of China's peasants. In 1927, Mao predicted:

> *The force of the peasantry is like that of the raging winds and driving rain. . . . They will bury beneath them all forces of imperialism, militarism, corrupt officialdom, village bosses and evil gentry.*

Mao's first attempt to lead the peasants in revolt failed in 1927. But during the Japanese occupation, Mao and his followers won widespread peasant support by reducing rents and promising to redistribute land.

INTEGRATED TECHNOLOGY

RESEARCH LINKS For more on Mao Zedong, go to **classzone.com**

1959. As a result, resentment between India and China grew. In 1962, they clashed briefly over the two countries' unclear border. The fighting stopped but resentment continued.

The Communists Transform China

For decades, China had been in turmoil, engaged in civil war or fighting with Japan. So, when the Communists took power, they moved rapidly to strengthen their rule over China's 550 million people. They also aimed to restore China as a powerful nation.

Communists Claim a New "Mandate of Heaven" After taking control of China, the Communists began to tighten their hold. The party's 4.5 million members made up just 1 percent of the population. But they were a disciplined group. Like the Soviets, the Chinese Communists set up two parallel organizations, the Communist party and the national government. Mao headed both until 1959.

Mao's Brand of Marxist Socialism Mao was determined to reshape China's economy based on Marxist socialism. Eighty percent of the people lived in rural areas, but most owned no land. Instead, 10 percent of the rural population controlled 70 percent of the farmland. Under the Agrarian Reform Law of 1950, Mao seized the holdings of these landlords. His forces killed more than a million landlords who resisted. He then divided the land among the peasants. Later, to further Mao's socialist principles, the government forced peasants to join collective farms. Each of these farms was comprised of 200 to 300 households.

Mao's changes also transformed industry and business. Gradually, private companies were nationalized, or brought under government ownership. In 1953, Mao launched a five-year plan that set high production goals for industry. By 1957, China's output of coal, cement, steel, and electricity had increased dramatically. B

MAIN IDEA

Analyzing Issues

B What aspects of Marxist socialism did Mao try to bring to China?

B. Answer collective ownership of land, communal living, government control of industry

"The Great Leap Forward" To expand the success of the first Five-Year Plan, Mao proclaimed the "Great Leap Forward" in early 1958. This plan called for still larger collective farms, or **communes**. By the end of 1958, about 26,000 communes had been created. The average commune sprawled over 15,000 acres and supported over 25,000 people. In the strictly controlled life of the communes, peasants worked the land together. They ate in communal dining rooms, slept in communal dormitories, and raised children in communal nurseries. And they owned nothing. The peasants had no incentive to work hard when only the state profited from their labor.

The Great Leap Forward was a giant step backward. Poor planning and inefficient "backyard," or home, industries hampered growth. The program was ended in 1961 after crop failures caused a famine that killed about 20 million people.

New Policies and Mao's Response China was facing external problems as well as internal ones in the late 1950s. The spirit of cooperation that had bound the Soviet Union and China began to fade. Each sought to lead the worldwide Communist movement. As they also shared the longest border in the world, they faced numerous territorial disputes.

DIFFERENTIATING INSTRUCTION: STRUGGLING READERS

Understanding Communist China

Class Time 30 minutes

Task Writing letters about China

Purpose To master information about Communist China

Instructions Tell students to choose a date during the 1930s through 1960s. Then have them imagine that they are living at this time. Remind them that important events were occurring in China throughout this period, including the Chinese civil war between the Communists and the Nationalists, the invasion of Tibet, the establishment of the Communes, the Cold War, and the Cultural Revolution. Explain to students that they have a friend who lives in China. Ask them to write a letter to their friend in which they ask questions about life and events in China at that time. They should limit their questions to information that can be found or inferred from details in the text. You may wish to review the format of a friendly letter with students before they begin to write.

When students have finished writing, have them exchange letters and write a response. When they've finished these letters, tell them to meet with their partner to review their letters and check the accuracy of their answers. For help, have students use the Reading Study Guide for the section.

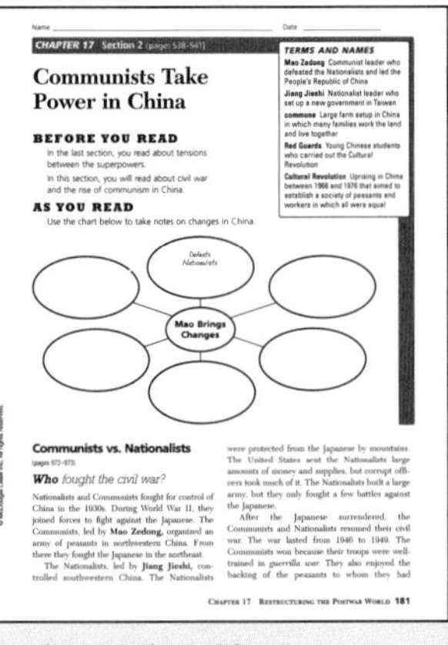

CHAPTER 17 Section 2

Communists Take Power in China

BEFORE YOU READ

AS YOU READ

TERMS AND NAMES

Communists vs. Nationalists

Who fought the civil war?

Reading Study Guide

After the failure of the Great Leap Forward and the split with the Soviet Union, Mao reduced his role in government. Other leaders moved away from Mao's strict socialist ideas. For example, farm families could live in their own homes and could sell crops they grew on small private plots. Factory workers could compete for wage increases and promotions.

Mao thought China's new economic policies weakened the Communist goal of social equality. He was determined to revive the revolution. In 1966, he urged China's young people to "learn revolution by making revolution." Millions of high school and college students responded. They left their classrooms and formed militia units called **Red Guards**.

The Cultural Revolution The Red Guards led a major uprising known as the **Cultural Revolution**. Its goal was to establish a society of peasants and workers in which all were equal. The new hero was the peasant who worked with his hands. The life of the mind—intellectual and artistic activity—was considered useless and dangerous. To stamp out this threat, the Red Guards shut down colleges and schools. They targeted anyone who resisted the regime. Intellectuals had to "purify" themselves by doing hard labor in remote villages. Thousands were executed or imprisoned.

Chaos threatened farm production and closed down factories. Civil war seemed possible. By 1968, even Mao admitted that the Cultural Revolution had to stop. The army was ordered to put down the Red Guards. Zhou Enlai (joh ehn•leye), Chinese Communist party founder and premier since 1949, began to restore order. While China was struggling to become stable, the Cold War continued to rage. Two full-scale wars were fought—in Korea and in Vietnam. C

C. Possible Answer The social upheaval it caused brought about economic chaos and threatened civil war.

MAIN IDEA
Drawing Conclusions
C Why did the Cultural Revolution fail?

History *in* Depth

The Red Guards

The Red Guards were students, mainly teenagers. They pledged their devotion to Chairman Mao and the Cultural Revolution. From 1966 to 1968, 20 to 30 million Red Guards roamed China's cities and countryside causing widespread chaos. To smash the old, non-Maoist way of life, they destroyed buildings and beat and even killed Mao's alleged enemies. They lashed out at professors, government officials, factory managers, and even parents.

Eventually, even Mao turned on them. Most were exiled to the countryside. Others were arrested and some executed.

History *in* Depth

The Red Guards

The Cultural Revolution gave rise to a new class system in China from which the Red Guard arose. At the new bottom was the "Black Five" class. It was made up of people unacceptable to the revolutionaries—landlords, rich peasants, and others labeled "counter-revolutionaries," or "Bad People." The "Red Five" class included the heroes of the revolution—poor peasants, workers, and revolutionary soldiers. Only youth in the Red Five class were allowed to join Mao's Red Guards.

In-Depth Resources: Unit 5
- Primary Source: from *No Tears for Mao,* p. 9

SECTION 2 ASSESSMENT

TERMS & NAMES 1. For each term or name, write a sentence explaining its significance.
- Mao Zedong • Jiang Jieshi • commune • Red Guards • Cultural Revolution

USING YOUR NOTES

2. Which effect of the Communist Revolution in China do you think had the most permanent impact? Explain. (10.9.4)

Cause	Effect
1.	1.
2.	2.
3.	3.

MAIN IDEAS

3. How did the Chinese Communists increase their power during World War II? (10.9.4)
4. What actions did the Nationalists take during World War II? (10.9.4)
5. What was the goal of the Cultural Revolution? (10.9.4)

CRITICAL THINKING & WRITING

6. **MAKING INFERENCES** Why did the United States support the Nationalists in the civil war in China? (10.9.4)
7. **ANALYZING ISSUES** What policies or actions enabled the Communists to defeat the Nationalists in their long civil war? (10.9.4)
8. **IDENTIFYING PROBLEMS** What circumstances prevented Mao's Great Leap Forward from bringing economic prosperity to China? (10.9.4)
9. **WRITING ACTIVITY** REVOLUTION Write **summaries** of the reforms Mao Zedong proposed for China that could be placed on a propaganda poster. (Writing 2.3.b)

CONNECT TO TODAY **CREATING A COMPARISON CHART**
Find political, economic, and demographic information on the People's Republic of China and Taiwan, and make a **comparison chart.** (Writing 2.3.d)

3 ASSESS

SECTION 2 ASSESSMENT

Direct students to work in small groups to answer the questions. Have them check their answers in the text.

Formal Assessment
- Section Quiz, p. 295

4 RETEACH

Use the Reteaching Activity for Section 2 to review the main ideas of the section.

In-Depth Resources, Unit 5
- Reteaching Activity, p. 22

ANSWERS

1. Mao Zedong, p. 538 • Jiang Jieshi, p. 538 • commune, p. 540 • Red Guards, p. 541 • Cultural Revolution, p. 541

2. **Sample Answer:** cause—civil war; effect—two Chinas; cause—superpowers reacted; effect—Soviets supported Communists; U.S. supported Taiwan; cause—Communists controlled mainland; effect—China expanded; cause—Mandate of Heaven; effect—reshaped economy; cause—Great Leap Forward; effect—failure of economy; cause—Cultural Revolution; effect—destruction of intellectual, artistic base. **Possible Answers:** land distribution remade the economy; cultural revolution caused chaos.

3. mobilized peasants for war, promoted literacy, and improved food production
4. fought occasional battles against the Japanese, took aid from United States
5. to establish a society of peasants and workers in which all were equal
6. **Possible Answer:** U.S. did not want Communists to control another country.
7. **Possible Answer:** won peasants' loyalty; trained troops in guerrilla techniques; promised land reform
8. **Possible Answer:** lack of privacy and personal life, lack of incentives for working hard, poor planning, crop failure
9. **Rubric** The summaries should
- identify key reforms.
- be understandable to the viewer.
- be written in brief phrases.

CONNECT TO TODAY
Rubric The chart should
- include information for both China and Taiwan.
- show evidence of thorough research.
- present data in a style that will aid in understanding the information.

LESSON PLAN

OBJECTIVES

- Trace the course and consequences of the Korean War.
- Summarize the causes of the Vietnam War and describe its aftermath.
- Describe conditions in Cambodia and Vietnam after the Vietnam War.

1 FOCUS & MOTIVATE

Ask students to recall the problems faced the divided Germany. Korea and Vietnam were also divided. What problems do they think these countries faced? *(Possible Answers: Cold War pressures from the United States and Russia; internal pressure to reunite the countries)*

2 INSTRUCT

War in Korea

10.4.4

Critical Thinking

- Why would the Soviet Union boycott the Security Council, thereby allowing the UN to enter the Korean war? *(Possible Answer: They didn't think the UN would go to war.)*

CALIFORNIA RESOURCES

California Reading Toolkit, p. L77
California Modified Lesson Plans for English Learners, p. 149
California Daily Standards Practice Transparencies, TT69
California Standards Enrichment Workbook, pp. 53–54
California Standards Planner and Lesson Plans, p. L145
California Online Test Practice
California Test Generator CD-ROM
California Easy Planner CD-ROM
California eEdition CD-ROM

Military parade in Red Square, Moscow, USSR, 1987

Buzz Aldrin and the U.S. flag on the moon, 1969

3

Wars in Korea and Vietnam

MAIN IDEA

REVOLUTION In Asia, the Cold War flared into actual wars supported mainly by the superpowers.

WHY IT MATTERS NOW

Today, Vietnam is a Communist country, and Korea is split into Communist and non-Communist nations.

TERMS & NAMES

- 38th parallel
- Douglas MacArthur
- Ho Chi Minh
- domino theory
- Ngo Dinh Diem
- Vietcong
- Vietnamization
- Khmer Rouge

CALIFORNIA STANDARDS

10.4.4 Describe the independence struggles of the colonized regions of the world, including the roles of leaders, such as Sun Yat-sen in China, and the roles of ideology and religion.

SETTING THE STAGE When World War II ended, Korea became a divided nation. North of the **38th parallel**, a line that crosses Korea at 38 degrees north latitude, Japanese troops surrendered to Soviet forces. South of this line, the Japanese surrendered to American troops. As in Germany, two nations developed. (See map on next page.) One was the Communist industrial north, whose government had been set up by the Soviets. The other was the non-Communist rural south, supported by the Western powers.

War in Korea

By 1949, both the United States and the Soviet Union had withdrawn most of their troops from Korea. The Soviets gambled that the United States would not defend South Korea. So they supplied North Korea with tanks, airplanes, and money in an attempt to take over the peninsula.

TAKING NOTES

Comparing and Contrasting Use a diagram to compare and contrast the Korean and Vietnam Wars.

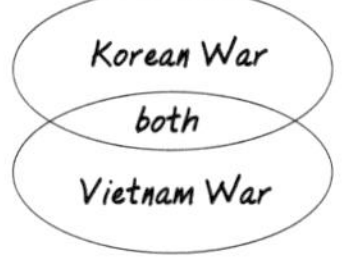

Standoff at the 38th Parallel On June 25, 1950, North Koreans swept across the 38th parallel in a surprise attack on South Korea. Within days, North Korean troops had penetrated deep into the south. President Truman was convinced that the North Korean aggressors were repeating what Hitler, Mussolini, and the Japanese had done in the 1930s. Truman's policy of containment was being put to the test. And Truman resolved to help South Korea resist communism.

South Korea also asked the United Nations to intervene. When the matter came to a vote in the Security Council, the Soviets were absent. They had refused to take part in the Council to protest admission of Nationalist China (Taiwan), rather than

▶ UN forces landing at Inchon in South Korea in 1950

SECTION 3 PROGRAM RESOURCES

ALL STUDENTS

In-Depth Resources: Unit 5
- Guided Reading, p. 3
- History Makers: Ho Chi Minh, p. 17

Formal Assessment
- Section Quiz, p. 296

ENGLISH LEARNERS

In-Depth Resources in Spanish
- Guided Reading, p. 134

Reading Study Guide (Spanish), p. 183
Reading Study Guide Audio CD (Spanish)

STRUGGLING READERS

In-Depth Resources: Unit 5
- Guided Reading, p. 3
- Building Vocabulary, p. 6
- Reteaching Activity, p. 23

Reading Study Guide, p. 183
Reading Study Guide Audio CD

GIFTED AND TALENTED STUDENTS

In-Depth Resources: Unit 5
- Primary Source: from *When Heaven and Earth Changed Places,* p. 11

Electronic Library of Primary Sources
- from "Peace Without Conquest"

INTEGRATED TECHNOLOGY

eEdition CD-ROM
Power Presentations CD-ROM
World Art and Cultures Transparencies
- AT73 *Laying a Road*

Electronic Library of Primary Sources
- from "Peace Without Conquest"

classzone.com

Communist China, into the UN. As a result, the Soviet Union could not veto the UN's plan to send an international force to Korea to stop the invasion. A total of 15 nations, including the United States and Britain, participated under the command of General **Douglas MacArthur**.

Meanwhile, the North Koreans continued to advance. By September 1950, they controlled the entire Korean peninsula except for a tiny area around Pusan in the far southeast. That month, however, MacArthur launched a surprise attack. Troops moving north from Pusan met with forces that had made an amphibious landing at Inchon. Caught in this "pincer action," about half of the North Koreans surrendered. The rest retreated.

The Fighting Continues The UN troops pursued the retreating North Koreans across the 38th parallel into North Korea. They pushed them almost to the Yalu River at the Chinese border. The UN forces were mostly from the United States. The Chinese felt threatened by these troops and by an American fleet off their coast. In October 1950, they sent 300,000 troops into North Korea.

War in Korea, 1950–1953

INTERACTIVE

- Farthest North Korean advance, September 1950
- Farthest UN advance, November 1950
- Farthest Chinese and North Korean advance, January 1951
- Armistice line, 1953

GEOGRAPHY SKILLBUILDER: Interpreting Maps

1. **Movement** *What was the northernmost Korean city UN troops had reached by November 1950?*
2. **Movement** *Did North or South Korean forces advance farther into the other's territory?*

The Chinese greatly outnumbered the UN forces. By January 1951, they had pushed UN and South Korean troops out of North Korea. The Chinese then moved into South Korea and captured the capital of Seoul. "We face an entirely new war," declared MacArthur. He called for a nuclear attack against China. Truman viewed MacArthur's proposals as reckless. "We are trying to prevent a world war, not start one," he said. MacArthur tried to go over the President's head by taking his case to Congress and the press. In response, Truman removed him.

Over the next two years, UN forces fought to drive the Chinese and North Koreans back. By 1952, UN troops had regained control of South Korea. Finally, in July 1953, the UN forces and North Korea signed a cease-fire agreement. The border between the two Koreas was set near the 38th parallel, almost where it had been before the war. In the meantime, 4 million soldiers and civilians had died. (A)

A. Answer About 4 million Koreans and soldiers died and neither North nor South Korea had gained any territory.

MAIN IDEA

Recognizing Effects

(A) What effects did the Korean war have on the Korean people and nation?

Aftermath of the War After the war, Korea remained divided. A demilitarized zone, which still exists, separated the two countries. In North Korea, the Communist dictator Kim Il Sung established collective farms, developed heavy industry, and built up the military. At Kim's death in 1994, his son Kim Jong Il took power. Under his rule, Communist North Korea developed nuclear weapons but had serious economic problems. On the other hand, South Korea prospered, thanks partly to massive aid from the United States and other countries. In the 1960s, South

History from Visuals

Interpreting the Map

Make sure students understand that this map traces the course of the Korean War over time. Ask, Which color line marks the extent of the first North Korean surge? *(red)* From which direction did Chinese troops attack in 1950? *(northwest).*

Extension Have students create a time line that shows the advances and retreats of troops in the Korean War. Have them use the information on this map to create the framework for their time line and use classroom or Internet resources to add more detailed information.

INTEGRATED TECHNOLOGY

Interactive This map is available in an interactive format on the eEdition. Students can view the step-by-step progress of the war.

SKILLBUILDER Answers

1. **Movement** Chosan
2. **Movement** Both occupied nearly all of the enemy's territory at some point.

Vocabulary Note: Words in Context

Point out the word *amphibious*. Tell students that it means that the soldiers invaded Korea from the water and then came ashore. Explain that this word comes from the same base word as *amphibian*, a class of animals that live in the water part of their lives and on land part of their lives. Examples include frogs and salamanders.

DIFFERENTIATING INSTRUCTION: ENGLISH LEARNERS

The Chronology of the Korean War

Class Time 20 minutes

Task Creating a chronology of the Korean War

Purpose To clarify the sequence of events leading up to and through the Korean War

Instructions Ask students to review the text on pages 542–543 that discusses the War in Korea. Then project transparency CT73 and guide students in creating a chronology of the war. Lead the discussion by asking questions such as the following:

- When was Korea divided into two nations?
- On what date did North Korea invade South Korea?
- What had happened by September 1950?
- What happened immediately after North Korea had almost overrun the entire peninsula?
- When did the Chinese invade the Korean peninsula?
- What had happened by the end of November 1950?
- What was the situation in Korea in January 1951?
- When was a cease-fire finally signed?

Complete the chart with students' answers, encouraging additional questions and discussion. Then urge students to copy the chart for their notes.

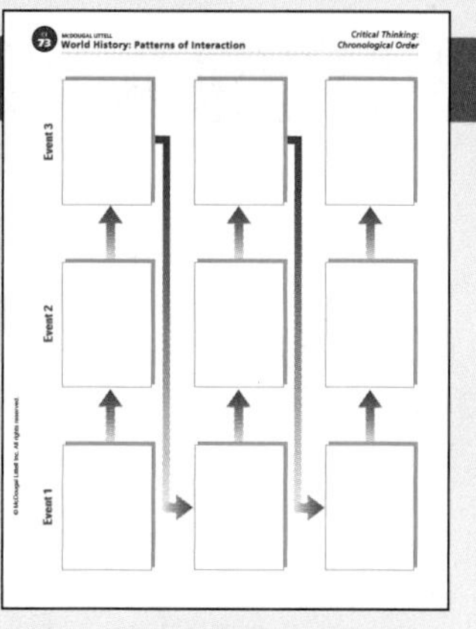

Critical Thinking Transparencies

War Breaks Out in Vietnam
10.4.4

Critical Thinking

- How were the Vietnamese Nationalists and Communists different from the Nationalists and Communists in China after World War II? *(China—Nationalists and Communists fought each other; Vietnam—they fought together against the French.)*
- How did the Cold War influence the international peace conference's decision to divide Vietnam? *(It responded to the pressures of Soviet Union and United States.)*

History Makers

Ho Chi Minh

Ask students if it was consistent for Ho Chi Minh to remain a Communist and still believe that "all men are created equal"? Have them explain. *(Yes, because as a Communist, he wanted all people to share economic equality.)*

In 1945, Ho sent two telegrams to President Truman seeking a seat on a British-American-Russian-Chinese Advisory Commission on the Far East that would decide the fate of Indochina. Truman ignored him. Have students discuss why they think the United States refused to deal with Ho.

In-Depth Resources: Unit 5

- History Makers: Ho Chi Minh, p. 17

Korea concentrated on developing its industry and expanding foreign trade. A succession of dictatorships ruled the rapidly developing country. With the 1987 adoption of a democratic constitution, however, South Korea established free elections. During the 1980s and 1990s, South Korea had one of the highest economic growth rates in the world.

Political differences have kept the two Koreas apart, despite periodic discussions of reuniting the country. North Korea's possession of nuclear weapons is a major obstacle. The United States still keeps troops in South Korea.

War Breaks Out in Vietnam

Much like its involvement in the Korean War, the involvement of the United States in Vietnam stemmed from its Cold War containment policy. After World War II, stopping the spread of communism was the principal goal of U.S. foreign policy.

The Road to War In the early 1900s, France controlled most of resource-rich Southeast Asia. (French Indochina included what are now Vietnam, Laos, and Cambodia.) But nationalist independence movements had begun to develop. A young Vietnamese nationalist, **Ho Chi Minh**, turned to the Communists for help in his struggle. During the 1930s, Ho's Indochinese Communist party led revolts and strikes against the French.

The French responded by jailing Vietnamese protesters. They also sentenced Ho to death. He fled into exile, but returned to Vietnam in 1941, a year after the Japanese seized control of his country during World War II. Ho and other nationalists founded the Vietminh (Independence) League. The Japanese were forced out of Vietnam after their defeat in 1945. Ho Chi Minh believed that independence would follow, but France intended to regain its colony.

History Makers

Ho Chi Minh
1890–1969

When he was young, the poor Vietnamese Nguyen That (uhng•wihn thaht) Thanh worked as a cook on a French steamship. In visiting U.S. cities where the boat docked, he learned about American culture and ideals. He later took a new name—Ho Chi Minh, meaning "He who enlightens." Though a Communist, in proclaiming Vietnam's independence from France in 1945, he declared, "All men are created equal."

His people revered him, calling him Uncle Ho. However, Ho Chi Minh did not put his democratic ideals into practice. He ruled North Vietnam by crushing all opposition.

The Fighting Begins Vietnamese Nationalists and Communists joined to fight the French armies. The French held most major cities, but the Vietminh had widespread support in the countryside. The Vietminh used hit-and-run tactics to confine the French to the cities. In France the people began to doubt that their colony was worth the lives and money the struggle cost. In 1954, the French suffered a major military defeat at Dien Bien Phu. They surrendered to Ho.

The United States had supported France in Vietnam. With the defeat of the French, the United States saw a rising threat to the rest of Asia. President Eisenhower described this threat in terms of the **domino theory**. The Southeast Asian nations were like a row of dominos, he said. The fall of one to communism would lead to the fall of its neighbors. This theory became a major justification for U.S. foreign policy during the Cold War era. (B)

B. Possible Answer intervention in any situation that might otherwise result in gains of territory or power by the Communists

MAIN IDEA

Making Inferences

(B) What actions might the United States have justified by the domino theory?

Vietnam—A Divided Country After France's defeat, an international peace conference met in Geneva to discuss the future of Indochina. Based on these talks, Vietnam was divided at 17° north latitude. North of that line, Ho Chi Minh's Communist forces governed. To the south, the United States and France set up an anti-Communist government under the leadership of **Ngo Dinh Diem** (NOH dihn D'YEM).

COOPERATIVE LEARNING

Vietnam War Movie

Class Time 45 minutes

Task Scripting scenes for a Vietnam War movie

Purpose To develop an understanding of the political and personal realities of the Vietnam War.

Instructions Have students work in small groups to brainstorm a scene for a movie about the Vietnam War. They may choose any perspective: that of U.S. soldiers, Vietcong, or South Vietnamese civilians, for example. Emphasize that they should focus on a single dramatic situation and several well-defined characters. Tell them that the setting and plot of their scene should be as realistic as possible. Encourage them to consider the following:

- Where does the scene take place? What does it look like?
- What is the weather like? Is it hot or cold? Is it raining or clear?
- What time is it? What season?
- What events have led up to the scene they are describing?
- Who are their characters? What do they think of their situation?

Have students work together to write the scene. Remind them that their scripts should include descriptive passages, stage directions, and realistic dialogue. Have students meet with other groups and share their ideas and read their dialogue.

War in Vietnam, 1957–1973

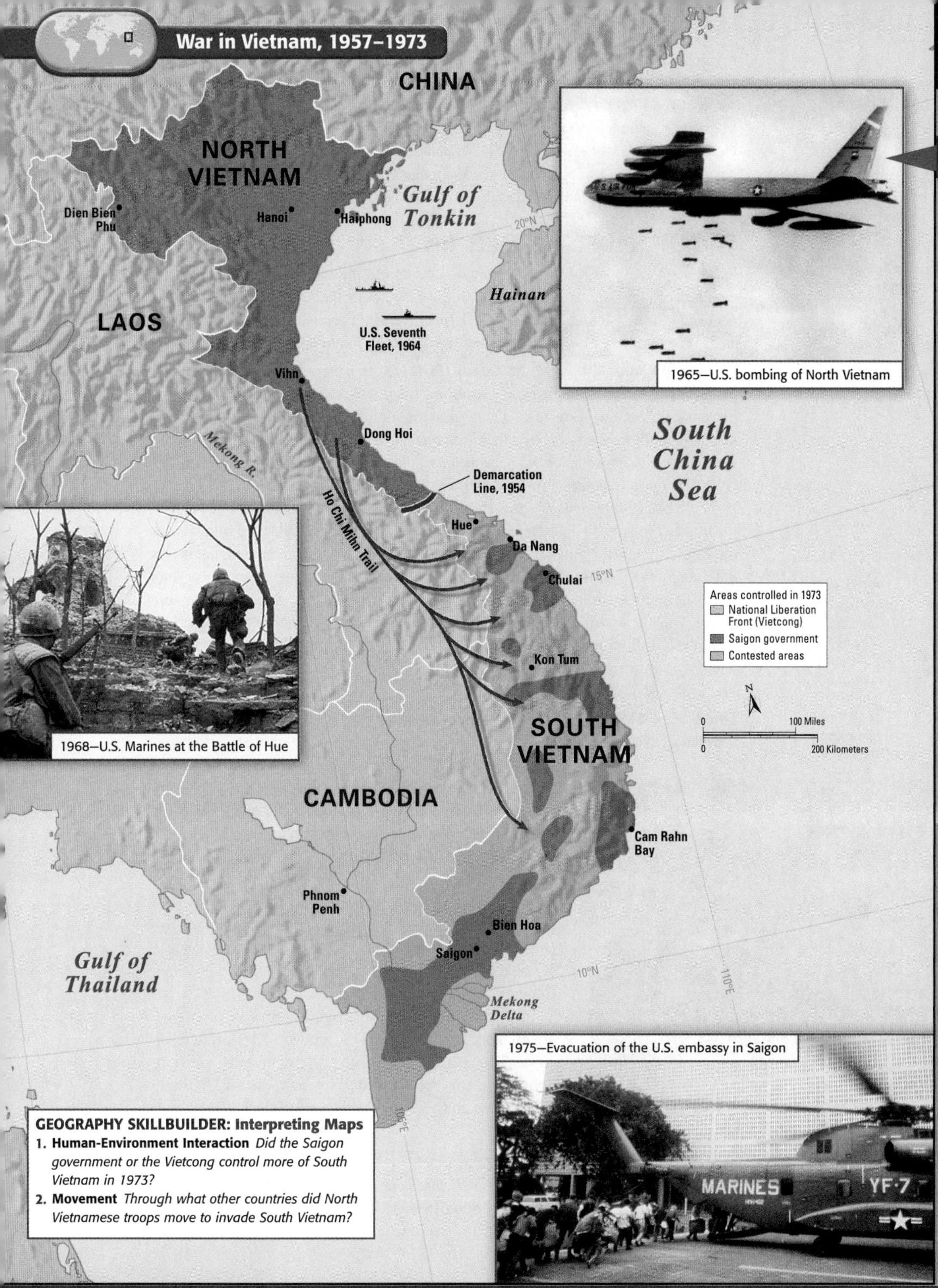

CHINA
NORTH VIETNAM
Dien Bien Phu
Hanoi
Haiphong
Gulf of Tonkin
20°N
Hainan
LAOS
U.S. Seventh Fleet, 1964
Vihn
Dong Hoi
Mekong R.
Demarcation Line, 1954
Ho Chi Minh Trail
Hue
Da Nang
Chulai
15°N
Kon Tum
South China Sea
SOUTH VIETNAM
CAMBODIA
Cam Rahn Bay
Phnom Penh
Bien Hoa
Saigon
10°N
110°E
105°E
Gulf of Thailand
Mekong Delta

Areas controlled in 1973
- National Liberation Front (Vietcong)
- Saigon government
- Contested areas

N
0 — 100 Miles
0 — 200 Kilometers

1965—U.S. bombing of North Vietnam

1968—U.S. Marines at the Battle of Hue

1975—Evacuation of the U.S. embassy in Saigon

GEOGRAPHY SKILLBUILDER: Interpreting Maps

1. **Human-Environment Interaction** *Did the Saigon government or the Vietcong control more of South Vietnam in 1973?*
2. **Movement** *Through what other countries did North Vietnamese troops move to invade South Vietnam?*

History from Visuals

Interpreting the Map

Have students study the map key and then contrast the colors shown in South Vietnam with those shown in North Vietnam. Ask, In which country were several armies battling for territory? *(South Vietnam)*

Extension Have students compare this map to one that shows Vietnam's terrain and vegetation. What problems might those geographic features create for armies conducting a ground war? *(Swampy coastal plains and densely jungled mountains would make troop movement difficult.)*

SKILLBUILDER Answers

1. **Human-Environment Interaction** Vietcong
2. **Movement** Laos, Cambodia

In-Depth Resources: Unit 5

- Primary Source: from *When Heaven and Earth Changed Places,* p. 11

DIFFERENTIATING INSTRUCTION: GIFTED AND TALENTED STUDENTS

Art and War

Class Time 30 minutes

Task Analyzing Vietnamese war art

Purpose To learn about the art and society of Vietnam during the Vietnam War

Instructions Project transparency AT73 from World Art and Cultures Transparencies. Explain to students that a Vietnamese artist produced this painting during the time of the Vietnam War. It depicts soldiers building a road through a forest. Ask students to find details in the image that identify the workers as soldiers. Point out that these are guerrilla fighters: they lack uniforms, although they wear helmets. Discuss the role of women in supporting the troops. Invite students to share other responses to the picture. Then ask them to do Internet research to learn more about art produced during the long war and to view more examples. Have them find one painting or other art object to examine in detail. Have them make a copy and present it to the group. As a group, ask them to talk about the dominant themes of Vietnamese war art. Ask, What attitude toward war does this art project?

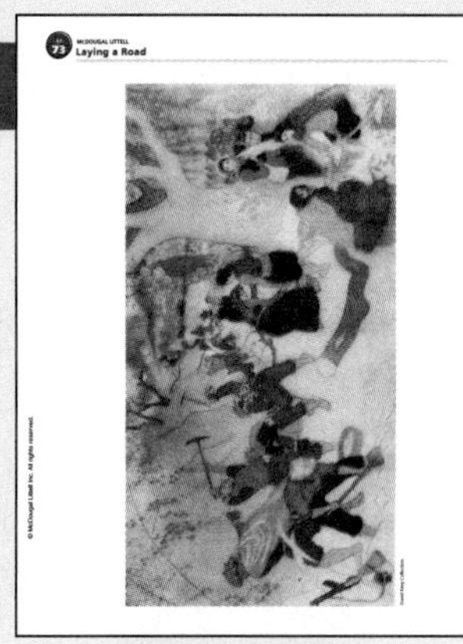

World Art and Cultures Transparencies

Tip for English Learners

Explain that a coup is a sudden, illegal overthrow of a government. It is an abbreviated form of the French phrase *coup d'etat,* which means "blow at state." In other words, it is a "strike at the state."

The United States Gets Involved

10.4.4

Critical Thinking

- Why did the attack on the U.S. destroyers provide a basis for sending in troops? *(direct attack on United States)*
- How were the South Vietnamese and American people alike? Why? *(Both opposed the war because of the many casualties.)*

More About . . .

The Gulf of Tonkin Incident

The Gulf of Tonkin incident took place at night during a storm. The two U.S. destroyers picked up the images of 22 torpedoes on their tracking systems. No one saw the Vietnamese attackers, however, and the next morning Captain Herrick, who commanded the ships, decided his radar might have mistaken "freak weather effects" for an attack. To this day, no one knows whether the attacks used to justify American escalation of the Vietnam War ever really took place.

Electronic Library of Primary Sources

- from "Peace Without Conquest" by Lyndon B. Johnson

Diem ruled the south as a dictator. Opposition to his government grew. Communist guerrillas, called **Vietcong**, began to gain strength in the south. While some of the Vietcong were trained soldiers from North Vietnam, most were South Vietnamese who hated Diem. Gradually, the Vietcong won control of large areas of the countryside. In 1963, a group of South Vietnamese generals had Diem assassinated. But the new leaders were no more popular than he had been. It appeared that a takeover by the Communist Vietcong, backed by North Vietnam, was inevitable.

The United States Gets Involved

Faced with the possibility of a Communist victory, the United States decided to escalate, or increase, its involvement. Some U.S. troops had been serving as advisers to the South Vietnamese since the late 1950s. But their numbers steadily grew, as did the numbers of planes and other military equipment sent to South Vietnam.

U.S. Troops Enter the Fight In August 1964, U.S. President Lyndon Johnson told Congress that North Vietnamese patrol boats had attacked two U.S. destroyers in the Gulf of Tonkin. As a result, Congress authorized the president to send U.S. troops to fight in Vietnam. By late 1965, more than 185,000 U.S. soldiers were in combat on Vietnamese soil. U.S. planes had also begun to bomb North Vietnam. By 1968, more than half a million U.S. soldiers were in combat there.

The United States had the best-equipped, most advanced army in the world. Yet it faced two major difficulties. First, U.S. soldiers were fighting a guerrilla war in unfamiliar jungle terrain. Second, the South Vietnamese government that they were defending was becoming more unpopular. At the same time, support for the Vietcong grew, with help and supplies from Ho Chi Minh, the Soviet Union, and China. Unable to win a decisive victory on the ground, the United States turned to air power. U.S. forces bombed millions of acres of farmland and forest in an attempt to destroy enemy hideouts. This bombing strengthened peasants' opposition to the South Vietnamese government.

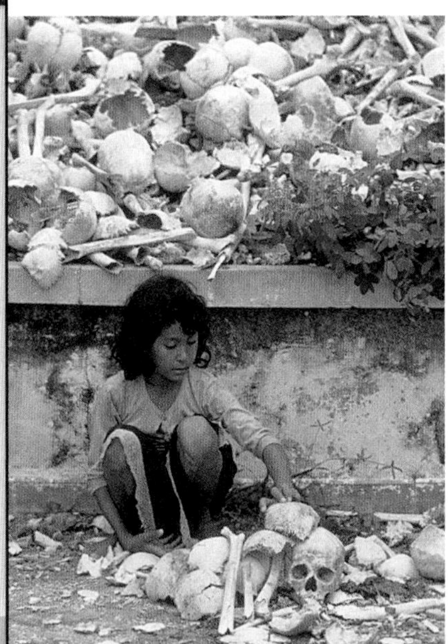

▼ The skulls and bones of Cambodian citizens form a haunting memorial to the brutality of its Communist government in the 1970s.

The United States Withdraws During the late 1960s, the war grew increasingly unpopular in the United States. Dissatisfied young people began to protest the tremendous loss of life in a conflict on the other side of the world. Bowing to intense public pressure, President Richard Nixon began withdrawing U.S. troops from Vietnam in 1969.

Nixon had a plan called **Vietnamization**. It allowed for U.S. troops to gradually pull out, while the South Vietnamese increased their combat role. To pursue Vietnamization while preserving the South Vietnamese government, Nixon authorized a massive bombing campaign against North Vietnamese bases and supply routes. He also authorized bombings in neighboring Laos and Cambodia to destroy Vietcong hiding places.

In response to protests and political pressure at home, Nixon kept withdrawing U.S. troops. The last left in 1973. Two years later, the North Vietnamese overran South Vietnam. The war ended, but more than 1.5 million Vietnamese and 58,000 Americans lost their lives.

Postwar Southeast Asia

War's end did not bring an immediate halt to bloodshed and chaos in Southeast Asia. Cambodia (also known as Kampuchea) was under siege by Communist rebels.

DIFFERENTIATING INSTRUCTION: STRUGGLING READERS

Vietnam War Posters

Class Time 25 minutes

Task Creating a war poster to protest or support the Vietnam War

Purpose To analyze support or opposition to the Vietnam War

Instructions Guide a discussion of why the United States entered the Vietnam War. Point out that many Americans opposed the war and explain that thousands of people demonstrated against it. Create a pro-and-con chart on the board to summarize the positions. Tell students to consider the arguments and decide whether they are for continuing the war or for pulling out of Vietnam. If students need more help, have them use the Reading Study Guide, pages 183–184. Then ask them to create a poster stating their position.

Pros	Cons
stop the spread of communism	thousands of U.S. soldiers are dying
support the legitimate South Vietnam government	thousands of Vietnamese are dying
	the country is being destroyed

During the war, it had suffered U.S. bombing when it was used as a sanctuary by North Vietnamese and Vietcong troops.

Cambodia in Turmoil In 1975, Communist rebels known as the **Khmer Rouge** set up a brutal Communist government under the leadership of Pol Pot. In a ruthless attempt to transform Cambodia into a Communist society, Pol Pot's followers slaughtered 2 million people. This was almost one quarter of the nation's population. The Vietnamese invaded in 1978. They overthrew the Khmer Rouge and installed a less repressive government. But fighting continued. The Vietnamese withdrew in 1989. In 1993, under the supervision of UN peacekeepers, Cambodia adopted a democratic constitution and held free elections. C

C. Possible Answer His followers killed nearly 2 million people.

MAIN IDEA

Recognizing Effects

C What was one of the effects of Pol Pot's efforts to turn Cambodia into a rural society?

Vietnam after the War After 1975, the victorious North Vietnamese imposed tight controls over the South. Officials sent thousands of people to "reeducation camps" for training in Communist thought. They nationalized industries and strictly controlled businesses. They also renamed Saigon, the South's former capital, Ho Chi Minh City. Communist oppression caused 1.5 million people to flee Vietnam. Most escaped in dangerously overcrowded ships. More than 200,000 "boat people" died at sea. The survivors often spent months in refugee camps in Southeast Asia. About 70,000 eventually settled in the United States or Canada. Although Communists still govern Vietnam, the country now welcomes foreign investment. The United States normalized relations with Vietnam in 1995.

While the superpowers were struggling for advantage during the Korean and Vietnam wars, they also were seeking influence in other parts of the world.

Connect *to* Today

Vietnam Today

Vietnam remains a Communist country. But, like China, it has introduced elements of capitalism into its economy. In 1997, a travel magazine claimed that Hanoi, the capital of Vietnam, "jumps with vitality, its streets and shops jammed with locals and handfuls of Western tourists and businesspeople." Above, two executives tour the city.

Along Hanoi's shaded boulevards, billboards advertise U.S. and Japanese copiers, motorcycles, video recorders, and soft drinks. On the streets, enterprising Vietnamese businesspeople offer more traditional services. These include bicycle repair, a haircut, a shave, or a tasty snack.

SECTION 3 ASSESSMENT

TERMS & NAMES 1. For each term or name, write a sentence explaining its significance.

• 38th parallel • Douglas MacArthur • Ho Chi Minh • domino theory • Ngo Dinh Diem • Vietcong • Vietnamization • Khmer Rouge

USING YOUR NOTES

2. In what ways were the causes and effects of the wars in Korea and Vietnam similar? (10.4.4)

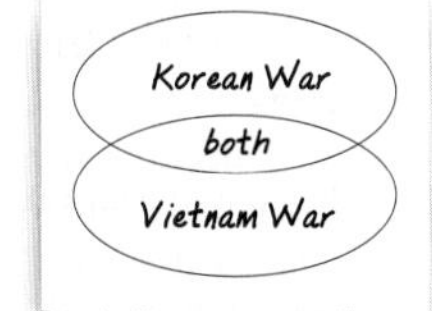

MAIN IDEAS

3. What role did the United Nations play in the Korean War? (10.4.4)
4. How did Vietnam become divided? (10.4.4)
5. What was the Khmer Rouge's plan for Cambodia? (10.4.4)

CRITICAL THINKING & WRITING

6. **ANALYZING MOTIVES** What role did the policy of containment play in the involvement of the United States in wars in Korea and Vietnam? (10.4.4)
7. **IDENTIFYING CAUSES** How might imperialism be one of the causes of the Vietnam War? (10.4.4)
8. **FORMING OPINIONS** Do you think U.S. involvement in Vietnam was justified? Why or why not? (10.4.4)
9. **WRITING ACTIVITY** EMPIRE BUILDING Write a two-paragraph **expository essay** for either the United States or the Soviet Union supporting its involvement in Asia. (Writing 2.3.a)

CONNECT TO TODAY **WRITING A BIOGRAPHY**

Research the present-day leader of one of the countries discussed in this section. Then write a three-paragraph **biography**. (Writing 2.1.a)

Postwar Southeast Asia

10.4.4

Critical Thinking

- How accurately did the domino theory explain events in Southeast Asia? *(Not very; Cambodia is democratic.)*
- How has Vietnam changed since the first years after the war? *(fewer economic restrictions, strong economy)*

Connect *to* Today

Vietnam Today

In seeking economic growth through foreign investment, Vietnam is following the example of China, South Korea, and other east Asia countries. One victim of this growth has been the environment. The number of elephants in Vietnam, for example, has dropped from 2,000 to 300.

3 ASSESS

SECTION 3 ASSESSMENT

Have students work in pairs to answer the questions.

Formal Assessment

- Section Quiz, p. 296

4 RETEACH

Assign the Reading Study Guide for Section 3 for reviewing main ideas.

Reading Study Guide, pp. 183–184 (also in Spanish)

In-Depth Resources: Unit 5

- Reteaching Activity, p. 23

ANSWERS

1. 38th parallel, p. 542 • Douglas MacArthur, p. 543 • Ho Chi Minh, p. 544 • domino theory, p. 544 • Ngo Dinh Diem, p. 544 • Vietcong, p. 546 • Vietnamization, p. 546 • Khmer Rouge, p. 547
2. **Sample Answer:** Korean War—neither side gained an advantage; Vietnam War—Soviet-supported North Vietnamese won; Both—U.S. and Soviet involvement stemmed from Cold War; land was destroyed; millions of people died. **Possible Answer:** Similar because of intervention by the U.S.; many deaths.
3. The UN sent an international force to Korea to stop the North Korean invasion of South Korea.
4. peace settlement after French defeat
5. to turn Cambodia into a communist society
6. **Possible Answer:** U.S. trying to prevent Korea and Vietnam from becoming communist.
7. The struggle against French colonialism began the fighting in Vietnam.
8. **Possible Answers:** Yes—important to stop communism. No—nations should decide for themselves.
9. **Rubric** The expository essay should
   - demonstrate an understanding of the issues involved.
   - clearly state a position.
   - present supporting reasons.

CONNECT TO TODAY

Rubric The biography should

- convey accurate information about the subject's life.
- be logically organized.
- be written in an interesting style.

LESSON PLAN

OBJECTIVES

- Explain how the Cold War affected developing nations.
- Describe superpower confrontations in Latin America after World War II.
- Identify Cold War conflicts in the Middle East.

1 FOCUS & MOTIVATE

When businesses compete for customers, they may advertise, give extra service, have sales, and give prizes away. Ask what superpowers might do to win the loyalty of poor nations. *(Possible Answers: foreign aid, espionage, propaganda)*

2 INSTRUCT

Fighting for the Third World

10.9.2; 10.9.3

Critical Thinking

- Should the U.S. sometimes engage in assassination? *(Possible Answers: Yes—it may save lives by ending despotic governments; No—U.S. should never condone murder.)*

CALIFORNIA RESOURCES

California Reading Toolkit, p. L78
California Modified Lesson Plans for English Learners, p. 151
California Daily Standards Practice Transparencies, TT70
California Standards Enrichment Workbook, pp. 93–94, 95–96, 99–100
California Standards Planner and Lesson Plans, p. L147
California Online Test Practice
California Test Generator CD-ROM
California Easy Planner CD-ROM
California eEdition CD-ROM

4

Military parade in Red Square, Moscow, USSR, 1987

Buzz Aldrin and the U.S. flag on the moon, 1969

The Cold War Divides the World

MAIN IDEA	WHY IT MATTERS NOW	TERMS & NAMES
REVOLUTION The superpowers supported opposing sides in Latin American and Middle Eastern conflicts.	Many of these areas today are troubled by political, economic, and military conflict and crisis.	• Third World • nonaligned nations • Fidel Castro • Anastasio Somoza • Daniel Ortega • Ayatollah Ruhollah Khomeini

CALIFORNIA STANDARDS

10.9.2 Analyze the causes of the Cold War, with the free world on one side and Soviet client states on the other, including competition for influence in such places as Egypt, the Congo, Vietnam, and Chile.

10.9.3 Understand the importance of the Truman Doctrine and the Marshall Plan, which established the pattern for America's postwar policy of supplying economic and military aid to prevent the spread of Communism and the resulting economic and political competition in arenas such as Southeast Asia (i.e., the Korean War, Vietnam War), Cuba, and Africa.

10.9.5 Describe the uprisings in Poland (1952), Hungary (1956), and Czechoslovakia (1968) and those countries' resurgence in the 1970s and 1980s as people in Soviet satellites sought freedom from Soviet control.

CST 1 Students compare the present with the past, evaluating the consequences of past events and decisions and determining the lessons that were learned.

HI 2 Students recognize the complexity of historical causes and effects, including the limitations on determining cause and effect.

TAKING NOTES

Determining Main Ideas Use a chart to list main points about Third World confrontations.

Country	Conflict
Cuba	
Nicaragua	
Iran	

SETTING THE STAGE Following World War II, the world's nations were grouped politically into three "worlds." The first was the industrialized capitalist nations, including the United States and its allies. The second was the Communist nations led by the Soviet Union. The **Third World** consisted of developing nations, often newly independent, who were not aligned with either superpower. These nonaligned countries provided yet another arena for competition between the Cold War superpowers.

Fighting for the Third World

The Third World nations were located in Latin America, Asia, and Africa. They were economically poor and politically unstable. This was largely due to a long history of colonialism. They also suffered from ethnic conflicts and lack of technology and education. Each needed a political and economic system around which to build its society. Soviet-style communism and U.S.-style free-market democracy were the main choices.

Cold War Strategies The United States, the Soviet Union, and, in some cases, China, used a variety of techniques to gain influence in the Third World. (See feature on next page.) They backed wars of revolution, liberation, or counterrevolution. The U.S. and Soviet intelligence agencies—the CIA and the KGB—engaged in various covert, or secret, activities, ranging from spying to assassination attempts. The United States also gave military aid, built schools, set up programs to combat poverty, and sent volunteer workers to many developing nations. The Soviets offered military and technical assistance, mainly to India and Egypt.

Association of Nonaligned Nations Other developing nations also needed assistance. They became important players in the Cold War competition between the United States, the Soviet Union, and later, China. But not all Third World countries wished to play a role in the Cold War. As mentioned earlier India vowed to remain neutral. Indonesia, a populous island nation in Southeast Asia, also struggled to stay uninvolved. In 1955, it hosted many leaders from Asia and Africa at the Bandung Conference. They met to form what they called a "third force" of independent countries, or **nonaligned nations**. Some nations, such as India and Indonesia, were able to maintain their neutrality. But others took sides with the superpowers or played competing sides against each other.

SECTION 4 PROGRAM RESOURCES

ALL STUDENTS

In-Depth Resources: Unit 5
- Guided Reading, p. 4
- Geography Application: The Cuban Missile Crisis, p. 8
- History Makers: Ruhollah Khomeini, p. 18

Formal Assessment
- Section Quiz, p. 297

ENGLISH LEARNERS

In-Depth Resources in Spanish
- Guided Reading, p. 135
- Geography Application, p. 138

Reading Study Guide (Spanish), p. 185
Reading Study Guide Audio CD (Spanish)

STRUGGLING READERS

In-Depth Resources: Unit 5
- Guided Reading, p. 4
- Building Vocabulary, p. 6
- Geography Application, p. 8
- Reteaching Activity, p. 24

Reading Study Guide, p. 185
Reading Study Guide Audio CD

GIFTED AND TALENTED STUDENTS

In-Depth Resources: Unit 5
- Primary Source: The Cuban Missile Crisis, p. 12

Electronic Library of Primary Sources
- from *444 Days: The Hostages Remember*

INTEGRATED TECHNOLOGY

eEdition CD-ROM
Power Presentations CD-ROM
Critical Thinking Transparencies
- CT33 Global Superpowers Face Off

Electronic Library of Primary Sources
- from *444 Days: The Hostages Remember*

classzone.com

History *in* Depth

How the Cold War Was Fought

During the Cold War, the United States and the Soviet Union both believed that they needed to stop the other side from extending its power. What differentiated the Cold War from other 20th century conflicts was that the two enemies did not engage in a shooting war. Instead, they pursued their rivalry by using the strategies shown below.

Egypt built the Aswan Dam with Soviet aid.

NATO, 1955
Warsaw Pact, 1955
Non-aligned, 1955

Major Strategies of the Cold War

Foreign Aid	Espionage	Multinational Alliances
The two superpowers tried to win allies by giving financial aid to other nations. For instance, Egypt took aid from the Soviet Union to build the Aswan High Dam (see photograph above).	Fearing the enemy might be gaining the advantage, each side spied on the other. One famous incident was the Soviet downing of a U.S. U-2 spy plane in 1960.	To gain the support of other nations, both the Soviet Union and the United States entered into alliances. Two examples of this were NATO and the Warsaw Pact (shown on map above).
Propaganda	**Brinkmanship**	**Surrogate Wars**
Both superpowers used propaganda to try to win support overseas. For example, Radio Free Europe broadcast radio programs about the rest of the world into Eastern Europe.	The policy of brinkmanship meant going to the brink of war to make the other side back down. One example was the Cuban Missile Crisis.	The word surrogate means substitute. Although the United States and the Soviet Union did not fight each other directly, they fought indirectly by backing opposing sides in many smaller conflicts.

SKILLBUILDER: Interpreting Visuals

1. **Generalizing** *Judging from the map, how would you describe the effect on Europe of multinational alliances?*
2. **Analyzing Motives** *What motive did the two superpowers have for fighting surrogate wars?*

CALIFORNIA STANDARDS

10.9.2 Analyze the causes of the Cold War, with the free world on one side and Soviet client states on the other, including competition for influence in such places as Egypt, the Congo, Vietnam, and Chile.

History *in* Depth

How the Cold War Was Fought

The Cold War can be dated from 1946 when Winston Churchill defined the iron curtain and asserted the will of the West to halt communist expansion. In 1947, Bernard Baruch, a financier and presidential advisor, first used the term "Cold War." During a congressional debate he declared: "Let us not be deceived—we are today in the midst of a cold war." A year later, he added the phrase, "which is getting warmer." He was, in fact, reporting on the rise in world tensions as the United States and the Soviet Union intensified their competition. This war reached its peak between 1948 and 1953.

SKILLBUILDER Answers

1. **Generalizing** Europe was pretty much split down the middle in its allegiance to the two superpowers.
2. **Analyzing Motives** *Possible Answer:* to stop the other superpower from gaining control of the country where the surrogate war was taking place

COOPERATIVE LEARNING

Cold War Thermometer

Class Time 30 minutes

Task Making a Cold War temperature chart

Purpose To explore the fluctuations in tensions over the course of the Cold War.

Instructions Explain to students that the levels of tension between the United States and Soviet Union varied over time. Some confrontations, such as the Cuban Missile Crisis, raised tension to especially high levels; it could easily have erupted in war. Other individual events weren't nearly so hot, but during the late 1940s and early 1950s, a lot of events happened during a short period. The frequency of events increased the overall tensions.

Have students work in groups and brainstorm ways of tracking the rise and fall of Cold War tensions on a temperature scale. You might suggest, for example, that they consider a scale such as degrees C—degrees of crisis—and assign a number to each confrontation or avoidance of confrontation between the superpowers. Then have small groups each choose a Cold War incident, write a short description of their incident, and assign it a rating on the crisis scale. Have the groups meet and plot their individual incidents on a crisis temperature chart. As a group, they might assign a higher temperature to a period when events were frequent.

History from Visuals

Interpreting the Map

Point out that the U.S. containment policy was only partly successful. Ask students which Communist countries were not on the same continent as the Soviet Union and China. *(Angola, Congo, Mozambique, Cuba)*

Extension Have students do research to determine the outcome of interventions by the United States and the Soviets in various countries around the world.

INTEGRATED TECHNOLOGY

Interactive This map is available in an interactive format on the eEdition. It includes an interactive timeline that allows students to view the development of events over time.

SKILLBUILDER Answers

1. **Location** Australia
2. **Region** about one-third

Cold War Hot Spots, 1948–1975

INTERACTIVE

1. The United States helps Greece defeat Communist-led rebels (1946–1949) and gives economic and military aid to Turkey (1947–1950).
2. Communists retain or gain control after bloody wars in Korea (1950–1953) and Vietnam (1957–1975).
3. The Soviets down U.S. U-2 pilot Francis Gary Powers in 1960.
4. The United States and the Soviet Union bring the world to the brink of nuclear war during the Cuban missile crisis in 1962.
5. The Soviet Union aids anticolonial struggles in Congo (1960), Mozambique (1971), and Angola (1974).
6. Britain helps Indonesia repress a Communist uprising in 1965.
7. The United States intervenes in the governments of Guatemala (1954), Bolivia (1956), and Chile (1973).

Communist expansion
Communist expansion prevented by U.S. and allies

NORTH AMERICA, UNITED STATES, CUBA, GUATEMALA, SOUTH AMERICA, BOLIVIA, CHILE, EUROPE, GERMANY, GREECE, TURKEY, EGYPT, IRAN, AFRICA, CONGO, ANGOLA, MOZAMBIQUE, SOVIET UNION, ASIA, CHINA, NORTH KOREA, SOUTH KOREA, VIETNAM, MALAYSIA, INDONESIA, AUSTRALIA, PACIFIC OCEAN, ATLANTIC OCEAN, INDIAN OCEAN, Arctic Circle, Tropic of Cancer, Equator, Tropic of Capricorn, 0, 3,000 Miles, 0, 5,000 Kilometers

GEOGRAPHY SKILLBUILDER: Interpreting Maps

1. **Location** *On what continents identified on the map did Cold War conflicts not occur?*
2. **Region** *About what fraction of the globe did Communists control by 1975?*

Confrontations in Latin America

After World War II, rapid industrialization, population growth, and a lingering gap between the rich and the poor led Latin American nations to seek aid from both superpowers. At the same time, many of these countries alternated between short-lived democracy and harsh military rule. As described in Chapter 12, U.S. involvement in Latin America began long before World War II. American businesses backed leaders who protected U.S. interests but who also often oppressed their people. After the war, communism and nationalistic feelings inspired revolutionary movements. These found enthusiastic Soviet support. In response, the United States provided military and economic assistance to anti-Communist dictators.

Fidel Castro and the Cuban Revolution In the 1950s, Cuba was ruled by an unpopular dictator, Fulgencio Batista, who had U.S. support. Cuban resentment led to a popular revolution, which overthrew Batista in January 1959. A young lawyer named **Fidel Castro** led that revolution. At first, many people praised Castro for bringing social reforms to Cuba and improving the economy. Yet Castro was a harsh dictator. He suspended elections, jailed or executed his opponents, and tightly controlled the press.

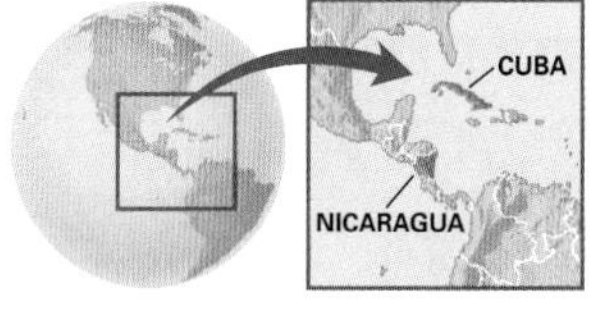

When Castro nationalized the Cuban economy, he took over U.S.-owned sugar mills and refineries. In response, Eisenhower ordered an embargo on all trade with Cuba. Castro then turned to the Soviets for economic and military aid.

Confrontations in Latin America

10.9.2; 10.9.3

Critical Thinking

- How did the U.S. policy toward Cuba backfire? *(By supporting Batista, and then opposing Castro, the U.S. drove Cuba into the Soviet sphere.)*
- What did the Cuban Missile Crisis reveal about the policy of the United States? *(demonstrated U.S. would stand firm against Communist expansion)*

DIFFERENTIATING INSTRUCTION: ENGLISH LEARNERS

U.S. and Cuba

Class Time 45 minutes

Task Preparing a collage on the history of Cuba since 1950

Purpose To gain a better understanding of people and events involving Cuba

Instructions Because Cuba is so near to the United States, it has always been an object of America's attention. Ask students to investigate this relationship over the past fifty years. Tell students to use the Internet and library resources to find photographs, headlines, quotations, and other artifacts concerning Cuba during the Cold War. They might use the following key words as starting points for a search:

- Fulgencio Batista
- Fidel Castro
- embargo
- Bay of Pigs invasion
- Cuban Missile Crisis
- Communism in Cuba

Have students make copies of the images they find or use colored markers to copy quotations and newspaper headlines. Then have them work together to assemble a collage about Cuba and events of the Cold War. Have them use the Reading Study Guide for Section 4 as an additional resource.

The Cold War Divides the World

Reading Study Guide

In 1960, the CIA began to train anti-Castro Cuban exiles. In April 1961, they invaded Cuba, landing at the Bay of Pigs. However, the United States did not provide the hoped for air support. Castro's forces easily defeated the invaders, humiliating the United States.

Nuclear Face-off: the Cuban Missile Crisis The failed Bay of Pigs invasion convinced Soviet leader Nikita Khrushchev that the United States would not resist Soviet expansion in Latin America. So, in July 1962, Khrushchev secretly began to build 42 missile sites in Cuba. In October, an American spy plane discovered the sites. President John F. Kennedy declared that missiles so close to the U.S. mainland were a threat. He demanded their removal and also announced a naval blockade of Cuba to prevent the Soviets from installing more missiles.

Castro protested his country's being used as a pawn in the Cold War:

PRIMARY SOURCE

Cuba did not and does not intend to be in the middle of a conflict between the East and the West. Our problem is above all one of national sovereignty. Cuba does not mean to get involved in the Cold War.

FIDEL CASTRO, quoted in an interview October 27, 1962

But Castro and Cuba were deeply involved. Kennedy's demand for the removal of Soviet missiles put the United States and the Soviet Union on a collision course. People around the world feared nuclear war. Fortunately, Khrushchev agreed to remove the missiles in return for a U.S. promise not to invade Cuba. **A**

The resolution of the Cuban Missile Crisis left Castro completely dependent on Soviet support. In exchange for this support, Castro backed Communist revolutions in Latin America and Africa. Soviet aid to Cuba, however, ended abruptly with the breakup of the Soviet Union in 1991. This loss dealt a crippling blow to the Cuban economy. But the aging Castro refused to adopt economic reforms or to give up power.

A. Answer U.S.–desire to protect itself and prevent the spread of communism; Soviet–desire to support its Communist ally

MAIN IDEA

Contrasting

A What differing U.S. and Soviet aims led to the Cuban missile crisis?

Civil War in Nicaragua Just as the United States had supported Batista in Cuba, it had funded the Nicaraguan dictatorship of **Anastasio Somoza** and his family since 1933. In 1979, Communist Sandinista rebels toppled Somoza's son. Both the United States and the Soviet Union initially gave aid to the Sandinistas and their leader, **Daniel Ortega** (awr•TAY•guh). The Sandinistas, however, gave assistance to other Marxist rebels in nearby El Salvador. To help the El Salvadoran government fight those rebels, the United States supported Nicaraguan anti-Communist forces called the Contras or *contrarevolucionarios*. **B**

The civil war in Nicaragua lasted more than a decade and seriously weakened the country's economy. In 1990, President Ortega agreed to hold free elections, the first in the nation's history. Violeta Chamorro, a reform candidate, defeated him. The Sandinistas were also defeated in elections in 1996 and 2001.

B. Answer because the Sandinistas were supporting socialist rebels in El Salvador

MAIN IDEA

Analyzing Motives

B Why did the U.S. switch its support from the Sandinistas to the Contras?

History Makers

Fidel Castro
1926–

The son of a wealthy Spanish-Cuban farmer, Fidel Castro became involved in politics at the University of Havana. He first tried to overthrow the Cuban dictator, Batista, in 1953. He was imprisoned, but vowed to continue the struggle for independence:

> *Personally, I am not interested in power nor do I envisage assuming it at any time. All that I will do is to make sure that the sacrifices of so many compatriots should not be in vain.*

Despite this declaration, Castro has ruled Cuba as a dictator for more than 40 years.

INTEGRATED TECHNOLOGY

INTERNET ACTIVITY Create a time line of the important events in Castro's rule of Cuba. Go to **classzone.com** for your research.

History Makers

Fidel Castro

How do you account for Castro's change from a modest leader seeking his people's freedom into a dictator? *(corrupted by power)*

Since 1959, when he overthrew the Batista regime, Castro has withstood numerous attempts to topple his regime through assassination, invasion, and economic pressure. He is the world's longest-surviving Communist ruler.

INTEGRATED TECHNOLOGY

Rubric Time lines should
- include a list of significant events.
- be accurate and brief.

More About . . .

The Sandinistas

The Sandinista National Liberation Front was formed in 1961. It drew its support from students, workers, and peasants. The Sandinista government included non-Communists as well as Communists, although during the long civil war, many non-Communists dropped out of the party, allowing it to drift more into the Soviet camp. Even so, the Sandinistas never adopted the Soviet economic plan. Small and medium-sized farms and businesses remained private. Some political opposition was also tolerated, which ultimately allowed Nicaraguans to vote the Sandinistas out of power. Today, they remain as an opposition party.

DIFFERENTIATING INSTRUCTION: GIFTED AND TALENTED STUDENTS

Cuban Missile Crisis

Class Time 25 minutes

Task Preparing a news broadcast reporting the Cuban Missile Crisis

Purpose To gain a better understanding of events and tensions during the Cuban Missile Crisis

Instructions Explain to students that the Cuban Missile Crisis developed quickly and took the public by complete surprise. Have them work in a group as a news team to duplicate the urgency and drama of a live broadcast of the time. Students should prepare by mastering details of the event as presented in their text as well as in the Geography Application and in the Speech by John F. Kennedy in In-Depth Resources for Unit 5. You might also ask them to do additional research to find more in-depth details.

Then have students divide up roles. These might include the news anchors and reporters, key figures involved in the event, such as President Kennedy and Secretary McNamara, and citizens of the time who might give their reactions to events. Students should write a brief script outline and then present their broadcast to the class.

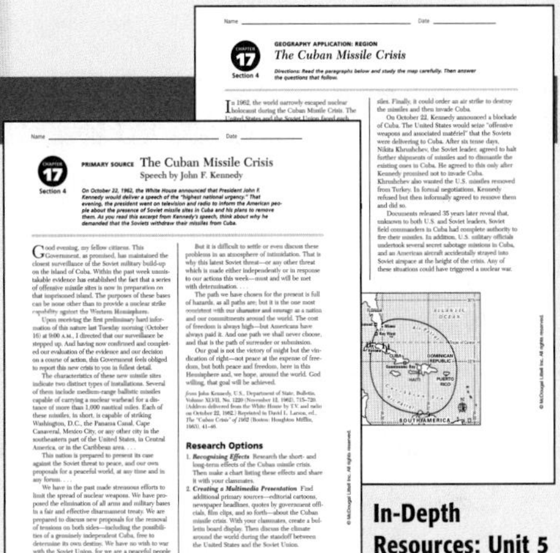

GEOGRAPHY APPLICATION: REGION
The Cuban Missile Crisis

PRIMARY SOURCE The Cuban Missile Crisis
Speech by John F. Kennedy

In-Depth Resources: Unit 5

In-Depth Resources: Unit 5

Confrontations in the Middle East

10.9.2; 10.9.5

Critical Thinking

- Was Communism the cause of the ouster of Shah Pahlavi from Iran? Explain. *(No. Nationalism and protecting traditional Islamic values were)*
- Could the United States have gained Khomeini's support by withdrawing aid to the shah? *(No. He opposed the threat of Western influence and values on Islamic values.)*

More About . . .

American Hostages in Iran

Taking diplomats hostage was so unprecedented that no one dreamed how long the Iranian crisis would endure. One of the hostages recalled that he refused to take off his jacket or tie after he was blindfolded and strapped to a chair on the first day because he was due at a dinner party that night. At the same time, his most pressing worry was notifying his "very chic Iranian hostess" that he was not going to be able to attend her party.

In-Depth Resources: Unit 5

- History Makers: Ruholla Khomeini, p. 18

Electronic Library of Primary Sources

- from *444 Days: The Hostages Remember*

Confrontations in the Middle East

As the map on page 550 shows, Cold War confrontations continued to erupt around the globe. The oil-rich Middle East attracted both superpowers.

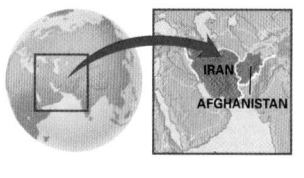

Religious and Secular Values Clash in Iran Throughout the Middle East, oil industry wealth fueled a growing clash between traditional Islamic values and modern Western materialism. In no country was this cultural conflict more dramatically shown than in Iran (Persia before 1935). After World War II, Iran's leader, Shah Mohammed Reza Pahlavi (pah•luh•vee), embraced Western governments and wealthy Western oil companies. Iranian nationalists resented these foreign alliances and united under Prime Minister Muhammed Mossadeq (moh•sah•DEHK). They nationalized a British-owned oil company and, in 1953, forced the shah to flee. Fearing Iran might turn to the Soviets for support, the United States helped restore the shah to power. C

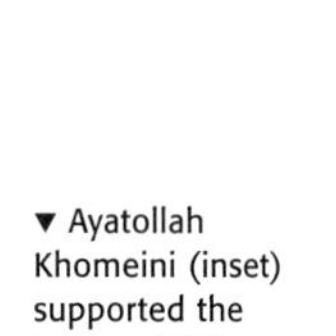

MAIN IDEA

Analyzing Motives

C Why did the United States support the shah of Iran?

C. Answer to maintain the shah's alliance with the West and prevent the Soviets from gaining influence in Iranas

The United States Supports Secular Rule With U.S. support, the shah westernized his country. By the end of the 1950s, Iran's capital, Tehran, featured gleaming skyscrapers, foreign banks, and modern factories. Millions of Iranians, however, still lived in extreme poverty. The shah tried to weaken the political influence of Iran's conservative Muslim leaders, known as ayatollahs (eye•uh• TOH•luhz), who opposed Western influences. The leader of this religious opposition, **Ayatollah Ruholla Khomeini** (koh• MAY•nee), was living in exile. Spurred by his tape-recorded messages, Iranians rioted in every major city in late 1978. Faced with overwhelming opposition, the shah fled Iran in 1979. A triumphant Khomeini returned to establish an Islamic state and to export Iran's militant form of Islam.

Khomeini's Anti-U.S. Policies Strict adherence to Islam ruled Khomeini's domestic policies. But hatred of the United States, because of U.S. support for the shah, was at the heart of his foreign policy. In 1979, with the ayatollah's blessing, young Islamic revolutionaries seized the U.S. embassy in Tehran. They took more than 60 Americans hostage and demanded the United States force the shah to face trial. Most hostages remained prisoners for 444 days before being released in 1981.

Khomeini encouraged Muslim radicals elsewhere to overthrow their secular governments. Intended to unify Muslims, this policy heightened tensions between Iran and its neighbor and territorial rival, Iraq. A military leader, Saddam Hussein (hoo•SAYN), governed Iraq as a secular state.

▼ Ayatollah Khomeini (inset) supported the taking of U.S. hostages by Islamic militants in Tehran in 1979.

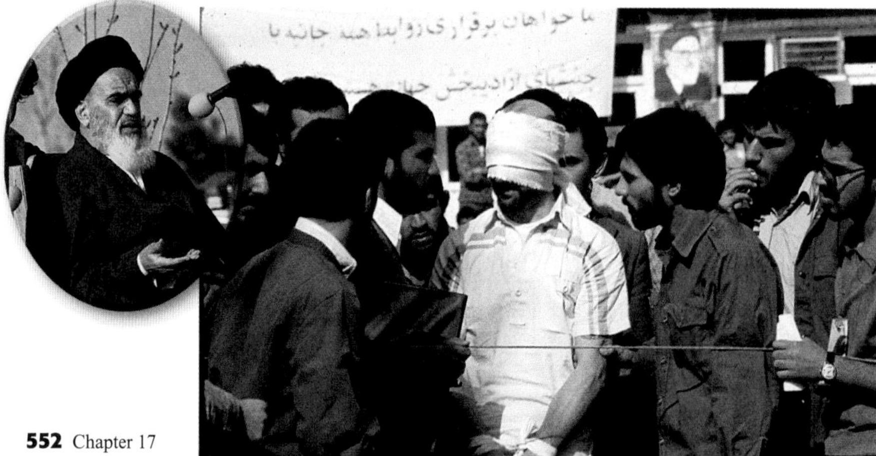

DIFFERENTIATING INSTRUCTION: STRUGGLING READERS

Time Line for the Cold War

Class Time 20 minutes

Task Completing a time line of major events during the Cold War

Purpose To identify and develop understanding of the sequence of events during the Cold War

Instructions Draw the following time line on the chalkboard. Then have students work as a group at the board to write at least one event for either Latin America or the Middle East for each date shown on the time line. Alternatively, break students into smaller groups and have them copy the time line onto a piece of paper and complete it. Have them use their texts to find the information. If they need additional help, provide them with the Guided Reading worksheet for Section 4.

Latin America

1953 1959 1961 1962 1978 1979 1981 1988 1989 1990 1996

Middle East

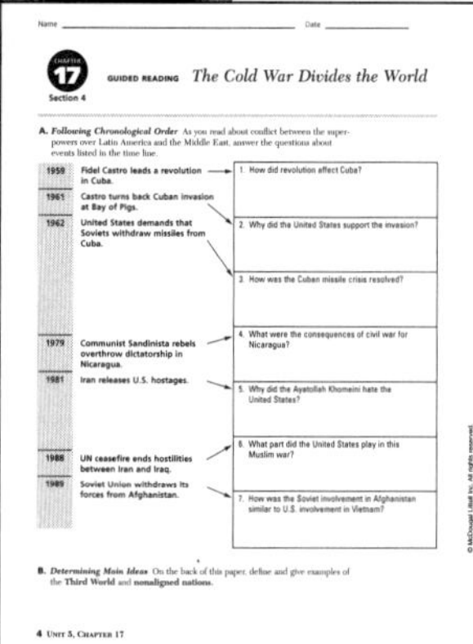

Name ______ Date ______

CHAPTER 17 Section 4 GUIDED READING *The Cold War Divides the World*

A. ***Following Chronological Order*** As you read about conflict between the superpowers over Latin America and the Middle East, answer the questions about events listed in the time line.

1959	Fidel Castro leads a revolution in Cuba.	1. How did revolution affect Cuba?
1961	Castro turns back Cuban invasion at Bay of Pigs.	2. Why did the United States support the invasion?
1962	United States demands that Soviets withdraw missiles from Cuba.	3. How was the Cuban missile crisis resolved?
1979	Communist Sandinista rebels overthrow dictatorship in Nicaragua.	4. What were the consequences of civil war for Nicaragua?
1981	Iran releases U.S. hostages.	5. Why did the Ayatollah Khomeini hate the United States?
1988	UN ceasefire ends hostilities between Iran and Iraq.	6. What part did the United States play in this Muslim war?
1989	Soviet Union withdraws its forces from Afghanistan.	7. How was the Soviet involvement in Afghanistan similar to U.S. involvement in Vietnam?

B. ***Determining Main Ideas*** On the back of this paper, define and give examples of the **Third World** and **nonaligned nations**.

4 Unit 5, Chapter 17

In-Depth Resources: Unit 5

War broke out between Iran and Iraq in 1980. The United States secretly gave aid to both sides because it did not want the balance of power in the region to change. The Soviet Union, on the other hand, had long been a supporter of Iraq. A million Iranians and Iraqis died in the war before the UN negotiated a ceasefire in 1988.

The Superpowers Face Off in Afghanistan For several years following World War II, Afghanistan maintained its independence from both the neighboring Soviet Union and the United States. In the 1950s, however, Soviet influence in the country began to increase. In the late 1970s, a Muslim revolt threatened to topple Afghanistan's Communist regime. This revolt led to a Soviet invasion in 1979.

D. Answer Both superpowers became mired in long, bloody struggles with guerrilla forces who ultimately defeated them.

MAIN IDEA

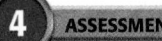

Comparing

D In what ways were U.S. involvement in Vietnam and Soviet involvement in Afghanistan similar?

The Soviets expected to prop up the Afghan Communists and quickly withdraw. Instead, just like the United States in Vietnam, the Soviets found themselves stuck. And like the Vietcong in Vietnam, rebel forces outmaneuvered a military superpower. Supplied with American weapons, the Afgan rebels, called mujahideen, or holy warriors, fought on. D

The United States had armed the rebels because they considered the Soviet invasion a threat to Middle Eastern oil supplies. President Jimmy Carter warned the Soviets against any attempt to gain control of the Persian Gulf. To protest the invasion, he stopped U.S. grain shipments to the Soviet Union and ordered a U.S. boycott of the 1980 Moscow Olympics. In the 1980s, a new Soviet president, Mikhail Gorbachev, acknowledged the war's devastating costs. He withdrew all Soviet troops by 1989. By then, internal unrest and economic problems were tearing apart the Soviet Union itself.

Connect *to* Today

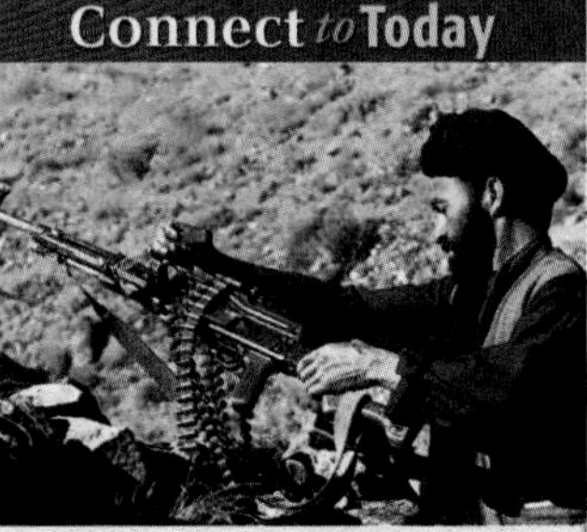

The Taliban

Islamic religious students, or taliban, were among the *mujahideen* rebels who fought the Soviet occupation of Afghanistan. Various groups of students loosely organized themselves during a civil war among *mujahideen* factions that followed the Soviet withdrawal in 1989.

In 1996, one of these groups, called the Taliban, seized power and established an Islamic government. At first, they were popular among many Afghans. But they imposed a repressive rule especially harsh on women, and failed to improve the lives of the people. They also gave sanctuary to international Islamic terrorists. In 2001, an anti-terrorist coalition led by the United States drove them from power.

Connect *to* Today

The Taliban

The Taliban had little support outside of Afghanistan. Most countries opposed their policy toward women, their severe criminal punishments, and their destruction of non-Islamic art relics. One of the worst crimes against non-Islamic art was the destruction of two giant Buddhas, one more than 175 feet high, that dated from the 4th and 5th centuries.

SECTION 4 ASSESSMENT

TERMS & NAMES 1. For each term or name, write a sentence explaining its significance.
• Third World • nonaligned nations • Fidel Castro • Anastasio Somoza • Daniel Ortega • Ayatollah Ruholla Khomeini

USING YOUR NOTES

2. Which confrontation had the most lasting significance? (10.9.3)

Country	Conflict
Cuba	
Nicaragua	
Iran	

MAIN IDEAS

3. How was the Cuban Missile Crisis resolved? (10.9.2)
4. What was significant about the 1990 elections in Nicaragua? (10.9.2)
5. Why did the Soviet Union invade Afghanistan? (10.9.5)

CRITICAL THINKING & WRITING

6. **MAKING INFERENCES** What advantages and disadvantages might being nonaligned have offered a developing nation during the Cold War? (10.9.2)
7. **COMPARING** What similarities do you see among U.S. actions in Nicaragua, Cuba, and Iran? (10.9.3)
8. **ANALYZING CAUSES** What were the reasons that Islamic fundamentalists took control of Iran? (10.9.5)
9. **WRITING ACTIVITY** REVOLUTION For either Cuba, Nicaragua, or Iran, write an annotated **time line** of events discussed in this section. (Writing 2.3.d)

CONNECT TO TODAY **WRITING AN OPINION PAPER**

Research the effects of the U.S. trade embargo on Cuba. Write a two-paragraph **opinion paper** on whether it would be in the best interests of the United States to lift that embargo. (Writing 2.4.a)

3 ASSESS

SECTION 4 ASSESSMENT

Have students answer the questions individually. Then have them meet in small groups to discuss and check their work.

Formal Assessment
• Section Quiz, p. 297

4 RETEACH

Instruct students to use the Reteaching Activity to review the main ideas of the section.

In-Depth Resources: Unit 5
• Reteaching Activity, p. 24

ANSWERS

1. Third World, p. 548 • nonaligned nations, p. 548 • Fidel Castro, p. 550 • Anastasio Somoza, p. 551 • Daniel Ortega, p. 551 • Ayatollah Ruholla Khomeini, p. 552
2. **Sample Answer:** Cuba—dictator to Communist, later resisted U.S. invasion; Nicaragua—dictator to Communist, then democratic; Iran—dictator to Islamic fundamentalist. **Possible Answer:** students may choose Cuba because of proximity to the U.S. and the duration.
3. Soviet Union withdrew missiles; U.S. pledged not to invade Cuba.
4. first free elections in Nicaragua's history
5. to support the Communist regime
6. **Possible Answer:** Advantages—control over own politics and economies; ability to accept help from either side; Disadvantages—lack of economic and military support from superpowers
7. **Possible Answer:** U.S. supported dictators who were overthrown by popular uprisings. It intervened in all three countries to protect its interests—a takeover by Communist Sandinistas in Nicaragua and by Castro in Cuba, and loss of vital oil supplies from Iran.
8. **Possible Answers:** wanted to return to traditional values; they were opposed to Western influences.
9. **Rubric** The time line should
• be organized chronologically.
• contain all major events described for either Cuba, Nicaragua, or Iran.

CONNECT TO TODAY

Rubric The opinion paper should
• clearly state a position about the issue.
• present supporting reasons.
• rebut the other point of view.

LESSON PLAN

OBJECTIVES

- Analyze Soviet domination of Eastern Europe and the Soviet Union-China split.
- Trace the origins of détente and its effects on the Cold War.
- Describe the renewal of Cold War tensions in the 1980s.

1 FOCUS & MOTIVATE

Ask students if Stalin's name belongs on a list of famous bullies. Point out that real-life bullies can be punished, although not always in their lifetime.

2 INSTRUCT

Soviet Policy in Eastern Europe and China

10.9.1; 10.9.2; 10.9.5

Critical Thinking

- Why was the Soviet Union determined to keep Hungary as a satellite? *(to keep it as a buffer zone; to prevent other East European nations from rebelling)*

CALIFORNIA RESOURCES

California Reading Toolkit, p. L79
California Modified Lesson Plans for English Learners, p. 153
California Daily Standards Practice Transparencies, TT71
California Standards Enrichment Workbook, pp. 91–92, 93–94, 99–100, 103–104
California Standards Planner and Lesson Plans, p. L149
California Online Test Practice
California Test Generator CD-ROM
California Easy Planner CD-ROM
California eEdition CD-ROM

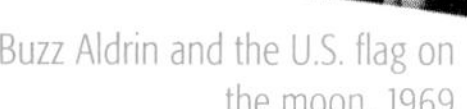

Military parade in Red Square, Moscow, USSR, 1987

Buzz Aldrin and the U.S. flag on the moon, 1969

5

The Cold War Thaws

MAIN IDEA	WHY IT MATTERS NOW	TERMS & NAMES
EMPIRE BUILDING The Cold War began to thaw as the superpowers entered an era of uneasy diplomacy.	The United States and the countries of the former Soviet Union continue to cooperate and maintain a cautious peace.	• Nikita Khrushchev • Leonid Brezhnev • John F. Kennedy • Lyndon Johnson • détente • Richard M. Nixon • SALT • Ronald Reagan

CALIFORNIA STANDARDS

10.9.1 Compare the economic and military power shifts caused by the war, including the Yalta Pact, the development of nuclear weapons, Soviet control over Eastern European nations, and the economic recoveries of Germany and Japan.

10.9.2 Analyze the causes of the Cold War, with the free world on one side and Soviet client states on the other, including competition for influence in such places as Egypt, the Congo, Vietnam, and Chile.

10.9.5 Describe the uprisings in Poland (1952), Hungary (1956), and Czechoslovakia (1968) and those countries' resurgence in the 1970s and 1980s as people in Soviet satellites sought freedom from Soviet control.

10.9.7 Analyze the reasons for the collapse of the Soviet Union, including the weakness of the command economy, burdens of military commitments, and growing resistance to Soviet rule by dissidents in satellite states and the non-Russian Soviet republics.

SETTING THE STAGE In the postwar years, the Soviet Union kept a firm grip on its satellite countries in Eastern Europe. These countries were Poland, Czechoslovakia, Hungary, Romania, Bulgaria, Albania, and East Germany. (Yugoslavia had broken away from Soviet control in 1948, although it remained Communist.) The Soviet Union did not allow them to direct and develop their own economies. Instead, it insisted that they develop industries to meet Soviet needs. These policies greatly hampered Eastern Europe's economic recovery.

Soviet Policy in Eastern Europe and China

More moderate Soviet leaders came to power after Stalin's death. They allowed satellite countries somewhat more independence, as long as they remained allied with the Soviet Union. During the 1950s and 1960s, however, growing protest movements in Eastern Europe threatened the Soviet grip on the region. Increasing tensions with China also diverted Soviet attention and forces.

Destalinization and Rumblings of Protest After Stalin died in 1953, **Nikita Khrushchev** became the dominant Soviet leader. In 1956, the shrewd, tough Khrushchev denounced Stalin for jailing and killing loyal Soviet citizens. His speech signaled the start of a policy called destalinization, or purging the country of Stalin's memory. Workers destroyed monuments of the former dictator. Khrushchev called for "peaceful competition" with capitalist states.

But this new Soviet outlook did not change life in satellite countries. Their resentment at times turned to active protest. In October 1956, for example, the Hungarian army joined protesters to overthrow Hungary's Soviet-controlled government. Storming through the capital, Budapest, mobs waved Hungarian flags with the Communist hammer-and-sickle emblem cut out. "From the youngest child to the oldest man," one protester declared, "no one wants communism."

A popular and liberal Hungarian Communist leader named Imre Nagy (IHM•ray nahj) formed a new government. Nagy promised free elections and demanded Soviet troops leave. In response, Soviet tanks and infantry entered Budapest in November. Thousands of Hungarian freedom fighters armed themselves with pistols and bottles, but were overwhelmed. A pro-Soviet government was installed, and Nagy was eventually executed.

TAKING NOTES

Outlining Organize main ideas and details about the Cold War thaw.

I. Soviet Policy in Eastern Europe and China
  A.
  B.
II. From Brinkmanship to Détente

SECTION 5 PROGRAM RESOURCES

ALL STUDENTS

In-Depth Resources: Unit 5
- Guided Reading, p. 5

Formal Assessment
- Section Quiz, p. 298

ENGLISH LEARNERS

In-Depth Resources in Spanish
- Guided Reading, p. 136

Reading Study Guide (Spanish), p. 187
Reading Study Guide Audio CD (Spanish)

STRUGGLING READERS

In-Depth Resources: Unit 5
- Guided Reading, p. 5
- Building Vocabulary, p. 6
- Reteaching Activity, p. 25

Reading Study Guide, p. 187
Reading Study Guide Audio CD

GIFTED AND TALENTED STUDENTS

In-Depth Resources: Unit 5
- Primary Source: Political Cartoon, p. 13

Electronic Library of Primary Sources
- Speech on Stalin by Nikita Khrushchev
- from *A Student's Diary*

INTEGRATED TECHNOLOGY

eEdition CD-ROM
Power Presentations CD-ROM
Critical Thinking Transparencies
- CT69 Chapter 33 Visual Summary

Electronic Library of Primary Sources
- Speech on Stalin by Nikita Khrushchev
- from *A Student's Diary*

classzone.com

History Makers

Imre Nagy (1896–1958)

Imre Nagy was born into a peasant family in Hungary. During World War I, he was captured by the Soviets and recruited into their army. He then became a Communist.

Nagy held several posts in his country's Communist government, but his loyalty remained with the peasants. Because of his independent approach, he fell in and out of favor with the Soviet Union. In October 1956, he led an anti-Soviet revolt. After the Soviets forcefully put down the uprising, they tried and executed him.

In 1989, after Communists lost control of Hungary's government, Nagy was reburied with official honors.

▲ Czech demonstrators fight Soviet tanks in 1968.

Alexander Dubček (1921–1992)

Alexander Dubček was the son of a Czech Communist Party member. He moved rapidly up through its ranks, becoming party leader in 1968.

Responding to the spirit of change in the 1960s, Dubček instituted broad reforms during the so-called Prague Spring of 1968. The Soviet Union reacted by sending tanks into Prague to suppress a feared revolt. The Soviets expelled Dubček from the party. He regained political prominence in 1989, when the Communists agreed to share power in a coalition government. When Czechoslovakia split into two nations in 1992, Dubček became head of the Social Democratic Party in Slovakia.

The Revolt in Czechoslovakia Despite the show of force in Hungary, Khrushchev lost prestige in his country as a result of the Cuban Missile Crisis in 1962. In 1964, party leaders voted to remove him from power. His replacement, **Leonid Brezhnev**, quickly adopted repressive domestic policies. The party enforced laws to limit such basic human rights as freedom of speech and worship. Government censors controlled what writers could publish. Brezhnev clamped down on those who dared to protest his policies. For example, the secret police arrested many dissidents, including Aleksandr Solzhenitsyn, winner of the 1970 Nobel Prize for literature. They then expelled him from the Soviet Union. (A)

> **MAIN IDEA**
> **Analyzing Issues**
> (A) Why was Nikita Khruschev removed from power in 1964?
> A. Possible Answer because he lost face during the Cuban Missile Crisis of 1962

Brezhnev made clear that he would not tolerate dissent in Eastern Europe either. His policy was put to the test in early 1968. At that time, Czech Communist leader Alexander Dubček (DOOB•chehk) loosened controls on censorship to offer his country socialism with "a human face." This period of reform, when Czechoslovakia's capital bloomed with new ideas, became known as Prague Spring. However, it did not survive the summer. On August 20, armed forces from the Warsaw Pact nations invaded Czechoslovakia. Brezhnev justified this invasion by claiming the Soviet Union had the right to prevent its satellites from rejecting communism, a policy known as the Brezhnev Doctrine.

The Soviet-Chinese Split While many satellite countries resisted Communist rule, China was committed to communism. In fact, to cement the ties between Communist powers, Mao and Stalin had signed a 30-year treaty of friendship in 1950. Their spirit of cooperation, however, ran out before the treaty did.

The Soviets assumed the Chinese would follow Soviet leadership in world affairs. As the Chinese grew more confident, however, they resented being in Moscow's shadow. They began to spread their own brand of communism in Africa and other

History Makers

Imre Nagy and Alexander Dubček

Why was Dubček able to survive the Soviets whereas Nagy could not?
(Nagy led an actual revolt; Dubček led a reform movement, not a revolt.)

Imre Nagy and Alexander Dubček were unlikely heroes. Nagy seemed to be more of an idealistic bookworm than a man of action. Nevertheless, he not only agreed to lead the Hungarian uprising, but also defended his country's bid for independence with his life. A Hungarian supporter said, "If his life was a question mark, his death was an answer."

In contrast, Dubček played by Communist rules and rose steadily through the ranks. He revealed his reformist colors, however, in 1967 when he won the support of political and economic reformers. He granted greater freedom of expression to the press and in 1968 proposed a full-blown reform program designed to democratize the country.

More About . . .

The Brezhnev Doctrine

Leonid Brezhnev's claim that the Soviet Union had a right to prevent its satellite countries from rejecting Communism came to be known as the Brezhnev Doctrine. This policy was invoked as late as 1979 to justify the Soviet invasion of Afghanistan.

DIFFERENTIATING INSTRUCTION: STRUGGLING READERS

Honoring Cold War Heroes

Class Time 30 minutes

Task Writing statements and staging a ceremony to honor heroes of the Cold War

Purpose To evaluate Cold War issues and personalities

Instructions Have students work in small groups and choose a Cold War hero, such as Imre Nagy or John F. Kennedy. Then tell them to write a testimonial honoring that person's contributions to history. The testimonial statements should:

- identify the hero.
- describe the person's actions during the Cold War that earned recognition.
- describe the challenges, dangers, or other obstacles the person faced.
- convey the person's personality.
- provide biographical information.

You might also ask groups to create visual materials, such as posters and collages to accompany their statements. The materials should depict the hero's actions or the events that surrounded him. Then provide time for an awards ceremony. Have each group select one member to represent the group and make the presentation. Use the Guided Reading worksheet for additional help with the section.

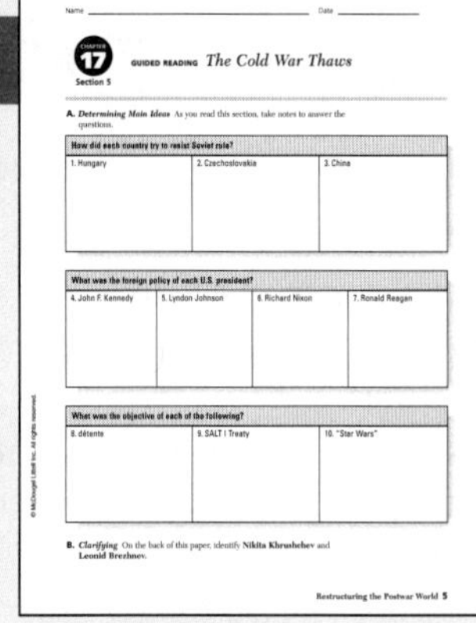

Name ______ Date ______

CHAPTER 17 Section 5 GUIDED READING *The Cold War Thaws*

A. *Determining Main Ideas* As you read this section, take notes to answer the questions.

How did each country try to resist Soviet rule?		
1. Hungary	2. Czechoslovakia	3. China

What was the foreign policy of each U.S. president?			
4. John F. Kennedy	5. Lyndon Johnson	6. Richard Nixon	7. Ronald Reagan

What was the objective of each of the following?		
8. détente	9. SALT I Treaty	10. "Star Wars"

B. *Clarifying* On the back of this paper, identify **Nikita Khrushchev** and **Leonid Brezhnev**.

Restructuring the Postwar World 5

In-Depth Resources: Unit 5

From Brinkmanship to Détente

10.9.2

Critical Thinking

- Who was the Soviet leader who blinked? What happened to him? *(Krushchev; removed from power)*
- How was the SALT I Treaty an example of realpolitik? *(practical, flexible solution to arms race)*

Electronic Library of Primary Sources

- Speech on Stalin by Nikita Khrushchev
- from *A Student's Diary*

Tip for English Learners

Read Secretary Rusk's statement and call attention to the metaphor "eyeball to eyeball . . . just blinked." Tell students that when two people confront each other, it's sometimes said they're standing eyeball to eyeball, or staring at each other. If one blinks, it's because that person has lost courage and given up.

parts of Asia. In 1959, Khrushchev punished the Chinese by refusing to share nuclear secrets. The following year, the Soviets ended technical economic aid. The Soviet-Chinese split grew so wide that fighting broke out along their common border. After repeated incidents, the two neighbors maintained a fragile peace.

From Brinkmanship to Détente

In the 1970s, the United States and the Soviet Union finally backed away from the aggressive policies of brinkmanship that they had followed during the early postwar years. The superpowers slowly moved to lower tensions.

Brinkmanship Breaks Down The brinkmanship policy followed during the presidencies of Eisenhower, Kennedy, and Johnson led to one terrifying crisis after another. Though these crises erupted all over the world, they were united by a common fear. Nuclear war seemed possible.

In 1960, the U-2 incident prevented a meeting between the United States and the Soviet Union to discuss the buildup of arms on both sides. Then, during the administration of **John F. Kennedy** in the early 1960s, the Cuban Missile Crisis made the superpowers' use of nuclear weapons a real possibility. (See page 551.) The crisis ended when Soviet ships turned back to avoid a confrontation at sea. "We're eyeball to eyeball," the relieved U.S. Secretary of State Dean Rusk said, "and I think the other fellow just blinked." But Kennedy's secretary of defense, Robert McNamara, admitted how close the world had come to disaster:

B. Possible Answers Yes, because the Soviets had installed missiles in Cuba with the intent to use them against the United States. No, because the Soviets intended their missiles only to be a threat and not used.

PRIMARY SOURCE B

In the face of an air attack [on Cuba] and in the face of the probability of a ground attack, it was certainly possible, and I would say probable, that a Cuban sergeant or Soviet officer in a missile silo, without authority from Moscow, would have launched one or more of those intermediate-range missiles, equipped with a nuclear warhead, against one or more of the cities on the East Coast of the United States.

ROBERT MCNAMARA, quoted in *Inside the Cold War*

MAIN IDEA

Analyzing Primary Sources

B Do you think that Robert McNamara's view of the Soviet threat in Cuba was justified? Explain.

Tensions remained high. After the assassination of Kennedy in 1963, **Lyndon Johnson** assumed the presidency. Committed to stopping the spread of communism, President Johnson escalated U.S. involvement in the war in Vietnam.

The United States Turns to Détente Widespread popular protests wracked the United States during the Vietnam War. And the turmoil did not end with U.S. withdrawal. As it tried to heal its internal wounds, the United States backed away from its policy of direct confrontation with the Soviet Union. **Détente**, a policy of lessening Cold War tensions, replaced brinkmanship under **Richard M. Nixon**.

Vocabulary
Détente is a French word meaning "a loosening."

▼ U.S. president Nixon visits China in 1972, accompanied by Chinese premier Zhou Enlai (left).

President Nixon's move toward détente grew out of a philosophy known as realpolitik. This term comes from the German word meaning "realistic politics." In practice, realpolitik meant dealing with other nations in a practical and flexible manner. While the United States continued to try to contain the spread of communism, the two superpowers agreed to pursue détente and to reduce tensions.

Nixon Visits Communist Powers Nixon's new policy represented a personal reversal as well as a political shift for the country. His rise in politics in the 1950s was largely due to his strong anti-Communist position. Twenty years later, he became the first U.S. president to visit Communist China. The visit made sense in a world in which three, not just two,

DIFFERENTIATING INSTRUCTION: ENGLISH LEARNERS

Summarizing and Sequencing Events

Class Time 15 minutes

Task Identifying and using key vocabulary

Purpose To clarify understanding of events of the Cold War

Instructions Divide the class into six groups. Have each group create a poster about a key Cold War event. Possible events include the following:

- 1956 Hungarian uprising
- Prague Spring
- Cuban missile crisis
- expansion of the war in Vietnam
- President Nixon's visit to China
- Soviet invasion of Afghanistan
- signing of the Salt I Treaty

Have students provide a heading, slogan, or very brief caption for their posters. The posters can be a straightforward representation of the events, or they can present an editorial comment on the events. Have students share responsibilities for presenting their posters to the class. For help, provide students with the Reading Study Guide in Spanish for Section 5.

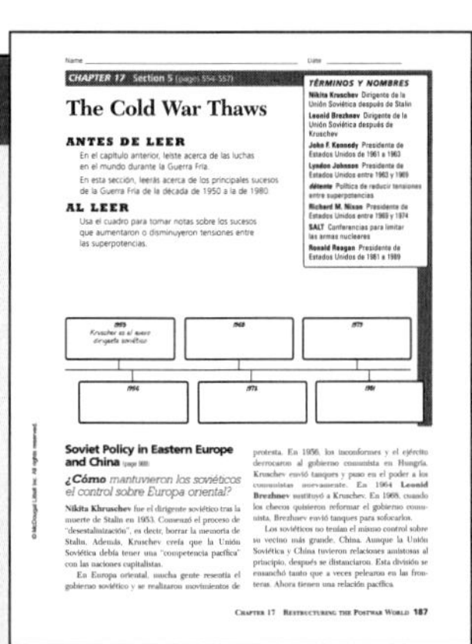

Reading Study Guide: Spanish Translation

superpowers eyed each other suspiciously. "We want the Chinese with us when we sit down and negotiate with the Russians," Nixon explained.

Three months after visiting Beijing in February 1972, Nixon visited the Soviet Union. After a series of meetings called the Strategic Arms Limitation Talks (**SALT**), Nixon and Brezhnev signed the SALT I Treaty. This five-year agreement, limited to 1972 levels the number of intercontinental ballistic and submarine-launched missiles each country could have. In 1975, 33 nations joined the United States and the Soviet Union in signing a commitment to détente and cooperation, the Helsinki Accords.

REAGAN
FOR PRESIDENT
Let's make America great again.

▲ Ronald Reagan's 1980 political poster highlights the strong patriotic theme of his campaign.

The Collapse of Détente

Under presidents Nixon and Gerald Ford, the United States improved relations with China and the Soviet Union. In the late 1970s, however, President Jimmy Carter was concerned over harsh treatment of protesters in the Soviet Union. This threatened to prevent a second round of SALT negotiations. In 1979, Carter and Brezhnev finally signed the SALT II agreement. When the Soviets invaded Afghanistan later that year, however, the U.S. Congress refused to ratify SALT II. Concerns mounted as more nations, including China and India, began building nuclear arsenals.

C. Answer Nixon pursued a policy of détente, or easing of tensions. Reagan brought tensions to a new height.

MAIN IDEA

Contrasting

C In what ways did Nixon's and Reagan's policies toward the Soviet Union differ?

Reagan Takes an Anti-Communist Stance A fiercely anti-Communist U.S. president, **Ronald Reagan**, took office in 1981. He continued to move away from détente. He increased defense spending, putting both economic and military pressure on the Soviets. In 1983, Reagan also announced the Strategic Defense Initiative (SDI), a program to protect against enemy missiles. It was not put into effect but remained a symbol of U.S. anti-Communist sentiment. C

Tensions increased as U.S. activities such as arming Nicaragua's Contras pushed the United States and Soviet Union further from détente. However, a change in Soviet leadership in 1985 brought a new policy toward the United States and the beginnings of a final thaw in the Cold War. Meanwhile, as you will learn in the next chapter, developing countries continued their own struggles for independence.

SECTION 5 ASSESSMENT

TERMS & NAMES 1. For each term or name, write a sentence explaining its significance.
• Nikita Khrushchev • Leonid Brezhnev • John F. Kennedy • Lyndon Johnson • détente • Richard M. Nixon • SALT • Ronald Reagan

USING YOUR NOTES

2. What do you consider the most significant reason for the collapse of détente? (10.9.7)

I. Soviet Policy in Eastern Europe and China
A.
B.
II. From Brinkmanship to Détente

MAIN IDEAS

3. What effects did destalinization have on Soviet satellite countries? (10.9.5)
4. What changes did Alexander Dubček seek to make in Czechoslovakia in 1968, and what happened? (10.9.5)
5. Why was the policy of brinkmanship replaced? (10.9.7)

CRITICAL THINKING & WRITING

6. **DEVELOPING HISTORICAL PERSPECTIVE** In view of Soviet postwar era policies toward Eastern Europe, what reasons did people in Eastern Europe have for resistance? (10.9.1)
7. **EVALUATING DECISIONS** Do you think it was a wise political move for Nixon to visit Communist China and the Soviet Union? Why or why not? (10.9.7)
8. **RECOGNIZING EFFECTS** What was the result of Reagan's move away from détente? (10.9.7)
9. **WRITING ACTIVITY** REVOLUTION Write a short **poem** or **song lyrics** expressing protest against Communist rule by a citizen of a country behind the Iron Curtain. (Writing 2.1.e)

CONNECT TO TODAY **WRITING A SUMMARY**

Look through a major newspaper or newsmagazine for articles on Eastern European countries. Then, write a brief **summary** of recent developments there. (Writing 2.3.b)

The Collapse of Détente
10.9.7

Critical Thinking

- What would have been two effects of Congress's refusal to ratify SALT II? *(Possible Answers: expansion of nuclear arsenals; greater risk of nuclear war)*
- How did SDI increase world tensions? *(threatened détente and started new arms race)*

3 ASSESS

SECTION 5 ASSESSMENT

Have students work in pairs to answer the questions.

Formal Assessment
- Section Quiz, p. 298

4 RETEACH

Have students use the Reading Study Guide for Section 5 and the Visual Summary to review the main ideas of the section.

Reading Study Guide, pp. 387–388 (also in Spanish)

Critical Thinking Transparencies
- CT69 Chapter 33 Visual Summary

In-Depth Resources: Unit 5
- Reteaching Activity, p. 25

ANSWERS

1. Nika Krushchev, p. 554 • Leonid Brezhnev, p. 555 • John F. Kennedy, p. 556 • Lyndon Johnson, p. 556 • détente, p. 556 • Richard M. Nixon, p. 556 • SALT, p. 557 • Ronald Reagan, p. 557

2. **Sample Answer:** I. A. destalinization; B. revolt in Hungary, C. revolt in Czechoslovakia; D. Soviet-Chinese split; II. A. U-2 incident, B. Cuban missile crisis, C. escalation of Vietnam War, D. end to Vietnam war, E. Nixon's China trip; F. SALT I treaty; III. A. non-ratification of SALT II, B. SDI
Possible Answers: Détente collapsed because of refusal to ratify SALT II, Soviet invasion of Afghanistan, SDI.
3. **Possible Answer:** None; their resentment and protest against Soviet rule continued
4. **Possible Answer:** Dubček attempted to moderate socialism; Soviets invaded.
5. **Possible Answer:** U.S. decided to reduce tensions.
6. absence of freedom, subordination to Communist control and Soviet interests
7. **Possible Answers:** Wise—Nuclear war threatened world. China could not be ignored. Unwise—Visit hurt efforts to contain communism
8. **Possible Answer:** Tensions increased between the superpowers.
9. **Rubric** The poem or song lyrics should
   - give an idea of life under communism.
   - give reasons to revolt.
   - use rhythm and repetition.

CONNECT TO TODAY

Rubric The summary should
- show an understanding of the articles.
- convey the information accurately.

TERMS & NAMES

1. containment, p. 533
2. Cold War, p. 535
3. Mao Zedong, p. 538
4. Cultural Revolution, p. 541
5. 38th parallel, p. 542
6. Vietnamization, p. 546
7. Fidel Castro, p. 550
8. Nikita Khrushchev, p. 554
9. détente, p. 556
10. SALT, p. 557

MAIN IDEAS

Answers will vary.

11. They believed the United States should not interfere with other nations' affairs, that it lacked resources to carry out a worldwide war on communism, and that economic aid might support dictators.
12. It proved that it would go to the brink itself by building up a nuclear arsenal and competing aggressively in the arms race.
13. The United States supported the Nationalists. The Soviet Union supported the Communists.
14. Both programs failed to create the powerful socialist nation Mao envisioned and actually weakened it.
15. Four million people died, and North and South Korea remained divided at the 38th parallel, as before the war.
16. unfamiliar jungle terrain, guerrilla warfare, and lack of popular support for the South Vietnamese government they were bolstering
17. They needed financial aid and investment to help them industrialize as well as a political and economic system on which to model their governments.
18. It secretly built 42 missile sites in Cuba.
19. It did not allow the East Europeans to run their own economies or give them enough money to repair war damages. It also promoted industries necessary to the Soviets, not to the satellite countries.
20. Dealing with nations in a realistic manner, which meant giving up long-held fear and hatred of communism. Pursuit of this policy helped ease Cold War tensions

Chapter 17 Assessment

TERMS & NAMES

For each term or name below, briefly explain its connection to the restructuring of the postwar world since 1945.

1. containment
2. Cold War
3. Mao Zedong
4. Cultural Revolution
5. 38th parallel
6. Vietnamization
7. Fidel Castro
8. Nikita Khrushchev
9. détente
10. SALT

MAIN IDEAS

Cold War: Superpowers Face Off Section 1 (pages 531–537)

11. Why did some Americans oppose the Truman Doctrine? (10.9.3)
12. How did the Soviet Union respond to the U.S. policy of brinkmanship? (10.9.2)

Communists Take Power in China Section 2 (pages 538–541)

13. Who did the superpowers support in the Chinese civil war? (10.9.4)
14. What were the results of Mao Zedong's Great Leap Forward and Cultural Revolution? (10.9.4)

Wars in Korea and Vietnam Section 3 (pages 542–547)

15. What effects did the Korean War have on Korea's land and it's people? (10.4.4)
16. What difficulties did the U.S. Army face fighting the war in Vietnam? (10.9.2)

The Cold War Divides the World Section 4 (pages 548–553)

17. Why did developing nations often align themselves with one or the other superpower? (10.9.2)
18. How did the Soviet Union respond to the Bay of Pigs? (10.9.2)

The Cold War Thaws Section 5 (pages 554–557)

19. In what ways did Soviet actions hamper Eastern Europe's economic recovery after World War II? (10.9.5)
20. What policies characterized realpolitik? (10.9.7)

CRITICAL THINKING

1. USING YOUR NOTES
Use a diagram to show superpower Cold War tactics. (10.9.2)

2. COMPARING
EMPIRE BUILDING In what ways were the United States and the Soviet Union more similar than different? (10.9.2)

3. HYPOTHESIZING
ECONOMICS How might the Cold War have proceeded if the United States had been economically and physically damaged in World War II? (10.9.3)

4. DRAWING CONCLUSIONS
REVOLUTION Which two Cold War events had the greatest impact on the U.S. decision to pursue détente? (10.9.2)

5. MAKING INFERENCES
Why do you think the United States and the Soviet Union chose cooperation in space after years of competition? (10.9.2)

VISUAL SUMMARY

Cold War, 1946–1980

United States

- 1946 Institutes containment policy
- 1948 Begins Marshall Plan
- 1948 U.S. and Britain fly airlift to break Soviet blockade of Berlin
- 1950 Communist North Korea attacks South Korea
- 1952 Tests first H-bomb
- 1953 Adopts brinkmanship policy
- 1960 U-2 incident reignites superpower tension
- 1962 U.S. blockades Cuba in response to buildup of Soviet missiles
- 1965 Sends troops to Vietnam
- 1972 Nixon and Brezhnev sign SALT I treaty
- 1980 U.S. boycotts Moscow Olympics to protest Soviet invasion of Afghanistan

Soviet Union

- 1950 Signs friendship treaty with China
- 1953 Tests first H-bomb
- 1956 Puts down Hungarian revolt
- 1957 Launches *Sputnik*, starting space race
- 1968 Sends tanks into Prague
- 1979 Invades Afghanistan

CRITICAL THINKING

Possible Answers

1. backing wars or revolutions; spying; increasing military forces and nuclear arsenals; providing military and economic aid; setting up schools
2. Both the United States and Soviet Union wanted to be the dominant world power. Both became involved in conflicts to achieve that end. Both felt their political and economic systems were best.
3. The Cold War might not have developed, because the Soviet Union might not have felt it necessary to build a wall of satellite nations to protect itself; the United States might not have had the resources to offer aid such as the Marshall Plan.
4. Students may say that the Vietnam War was the most significant event to change U.S. policy because the war failed to stop the spread of communism in Vietnam, and it was opposed at home.
5. The costs of the space race to each country and the fact that the United States and the Soviet Union wanted to step back from brinkmanship led to cooperation.

Use the quotation and your knowledge of world history to answer questions 1 and 2.
Additional Test Practice, pp. S1-S33

The following poem by Ho Chi Minh was broadcast over Hanoi Radio on January 1, 1968.

PRIMARY SOURCE

This Spring far outshines the previous Springs,
Of victories throughout the land come happy tidings.
South and North, rushing heroically together, shall
smite the American invaders!
Go Forward!
Total victory shall be ours.

HO CHI MINH, quoted in *America and Vietnam*

1. In Ho's opinion, who was the enemy in the Vietnam War? (10.9.2)
   - **A.** the South Vietnamese
   - **B.** the changing seasons
   - **C.** the United States
   - **D.** the French

2. What purpose might the North Vietnamese have had in broadcasting this poem? (10.9.2)
   - **A.** to show that their political leader was also a poet
   - **B.** to warn the United States that it would be defeated
   - **C.** to single out the North Vietnamese people for special attention
   - **D.** to be used as propaganda to show that North and South were fighting together

Use the chart and your knowledge of world history to answer question 3.

U.S.–Soviet Military Power, 1986–1987

U.S.		Soviet
1,010	Intercontinental ballistic missiles	1,398
640	Submarine-launched missiles	983
260	Long-range bombers	160
24,700	Nuclear warheads	36,800
0	Antiballistic missile launchers	100
14	Aircraft carriers	5
2,143,955	Armed forces personnel	5,130,000

Sources: The Military Balance 1986–1987; Nuclear Weapons Databook, Vol. IV, Soviet Nuclear Weapons

3. The chart clearly shows that (10.9.2)
   - **A.** the United States had more troops than the Soviet Union.
   - **B.** the Soviet Union had clear superiority in the number of ballistic missiles.
   - **C.** the United States and the Soviet Union were equal in nuclear warheads.
   - **D.** the Soviet Union had more aircraft carriers.

INTEGRATED TECHNOLOGY

TEST PRACTICE Go to **classzone.com**
- Diagnostic tests
- Strategies
- Tutorials
- Additional practice

ALTERNATIVE ASSESSMENT

1. **Interact *with* History** (10.9.2)
   On page 530, you considered what policies a nation might follow to gain allies. Now that you have learned more about the Cold War, would your decision change? Discuss your ideas with a small group.

2. **WRITING ABOUT HISTORY** (Writing 2.4.c)
   Study the information in the infographic on how the Cold War was fought on page 549. Write a two-paragraph **persuasive essay** on which means was the most successful for the United States and which was most successful for the Soviet Union.

   Consider the following:
   - who received foreign aid
   - whether propaganda was successful
   - how strong the military alliances were
   - what was gained in surrogate wars

INTEGRATED TECHNOLOGY

Creating an Interactive Time Line (10.9.2)

In October 1962, President John F. Kennedy and his advisers had to defuse a potentially devastating nuclear standoff with the Soviet Union. Using books, the Internet, and other resources, create an interactive time line of the crisis. Use graphics software to add maps and photographs. In addition to noting key dates, use the time line to address some of the following:
- Who were members of Kennedy's inner circle during the crisis?
- What did Kennedy say about the events in his first public address to the nation?
- How did Soviet premier Nikita Krushchev approach the crisis in Cuba?
- What details did Americans learn only after the crisis had been resolved?

STANDARDS-BASED ASSESSMENT

1. Letter **C** is the correct answer. Letter **A** is not correct because Ho wanted the South to join with the North. Letter **B** is not correct because the seasons are just given passing mention. Letter **D** is not correct because the French are not referred to in the poem.
2. Letter **D** is the correct answer. Letter **A** is not correct because it was not important that their political leader also wrote poems. Letter **B** is not correct because it was only partly a warning to the United States. Letter **C** is not correct because it was aimed at both the South Vietnamese and the North Vietnamese.
3. Letter **B** is the correct answer. Letter **A** is not correct because the Soviet Union had more troops. Letter **C** is not correct because they did not have an equal number of nuclear warheads; the Soviet Union had more. Letter **D** is not correct because the United States had more.

Formal Assessment
- Chapter Test, Forms A, B, and C, pp. 299–313

California Test Generator CD-ROM
- Chapter Tests, Forms A, B, and C (English and Spanish)

ALTERNATIVE ASSESSMENT

1. Students should consider the consequences of their answers. Effects on the economy, on political support, on the military, and the society should be reviewed.
2. **Rubric** The persuasive essay should
   - reflect the student's understanding of the basic concepts of the Cold War.
   - clearly state the selection for the United States and for the Soviet Union.
   - present supporting reasons for the selections.

INTEGRATED TECHNOLOGY

Rubric Interactive time lines should
- identify the key players.
- explain the events.
- give statements by Kennedy and Krushchev.
- discuss the problems faced.
- explain the resolution.

CHAPTER 18 PLANNING GUIDE

The Colonies Become New Nations, 1945–Present

CHAPTER RESOURCES	COPYMASTERS	ASSESSMENT
CHAPTER OVERVIEW After World War II, independence movements swept through many colonies in Africa and Asia and, as a result, new nations were formed.	**In-Depth Resources: Unit 5** • Building Vocabulary, p. 31 **Chapters in Brief** (in English and Spanish) **Block Schedule Pacing Guide**	**Chapter Assessment,** pp. 594–595 **Formal Assessment** • Chapter Tests, Forms A, B, and C, pp. 319–330 **Test Generator** **Online Test Practice**
SECTION 1 **The Indian Subcontinent Achieves Freedom** pp. 563–569 **OBJECTIVE** Trace the struggles for freedom on the Indian subcontinent.	**In-Depth Resources: Unit 5** • Guided Reading, p. 26 • Primary Source, p. 35 **Reading Study Guide,** p. 191 **Case Study 1: India and Britain,** p. 2	**Section 1 Assessment,** p. 569 **Formal Assessment** • Section Quiz, p. 314 **California Daily Standards Practice Transparencies,** TT132
SECTION 2 **Southeast Asian Nations Gain Independence** pp. 570–577 **OBJECTIVE** Trace the independence movements in the Philippines, Burma, Malaysia, Singapore, and Indonesia.	**In-Depth Resources: Unit 5** • Guided Reading, p. 27 • Primary Source, p. 36 • Literature, p. 39 **Reading Study Guide,** p. 193 **Case Study 4,** p. 44	**Section 2 Assessment,** p. 575 **Formal Assessment** • Section Quiz, p. 315 **California Daily Standards Practice Transparencies,** TT133
SECTION 3 **New Nations in Africa** pp. 578–582 **OBJECTIVE** Explain the independence movements and struggles in Ghana, Kenya, Congo, and Angola.	**In-Depth Resources: Unit 5** • Guided Reading, p. 28 • Skillbuilder Practice, p. 32 • Geography Application, p. 33 • Primary Source, p. 37 • Literature: Négritude poems, p. 40 • History Makers: Jomo Kenyatta, p. 42 • Connections Across Time/Cultures, p. 44 **Reading Study Guide,** p. 195 **Case Study 4,** p. 44	**Section 3 Assessment,** p. 582 **Formal Assessment** • Section Quiz, p. 316 **California Daily Standards Practice Transparencies,** TT134
SECTION 4 **Conflicts in the Middle East** pp. 583–589 **OBJECTIVE** Describe the formation of Israel and the conflicts in the Middle East.	**In-Depth Resources: Unit 5** • Guided Reading, p. 29 • Primary Source, p. 38 • History Makers: Golda Meir, p. 43 **Reading Study Guide,** p. 197 **Case Study 5: Syria and Israel,** p. 58	**Section 4 Assessment,** p. 589 **Formal Assessment** • Section Quiz, p. 317 **California Daily Standards Practice Transparencies,** TT135
SECTION 5 **Central Asia Struggles** pp. 590–593 **OBJECTIVE** Summarize the struggles for independence in Central Asia.	**In-Depth Resources: Unit 5** • Guided Reading, p. 30 **Reading Study Guide,** p. 199 **Case Study 10,** p. 128	**Section 5 Assessment,** p. 593 **Formal Assessment** • Section Quiz, p. 318 **California Daily Standards Practice Transparencies,** TT135.5

INTEGRATED TECHNOLOGY

- eEdition Plus Online
- EasyPlanner Plus Online
- eTest Plus Online

 **Audio CDs**
- Voices from the Past
- Reading Study Guides

CD-ROMs
- eEdition
- Power Presentations
- EasyPlanner
- Electronic Library of Primary Sources
- Test Generator

 **eEdition CD-ROM**

 **World Art and Cultures Transparencies**

- AT74 *Veni, Vidi, Vici*

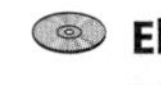 **Electronic Library of Primary Sources**
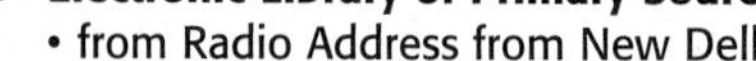
- from Radio Address from New Delhi

 **classzone.com**

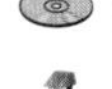 **eEdition CD-ROM**

 **Geography Transparencies**
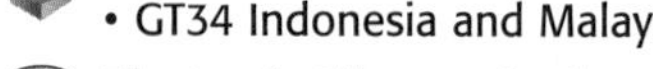
- GT34 Indonesia and Malaysia

 **Electronic Library of Primary Sources**
- "The Fall of President Marcos"

 **classzone.com**

 **eEdition CD-ROM**

 **classzone.com**

 **eEdition CD-ROM**

 **World Art and Cultures Transparencies**
- AT75 *After the Storm*

 **Critical Thinking Transparencies**
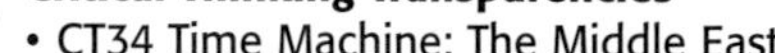
- CT34 Time Machine: The Middle East

 **Electronic Library of Primary Sources**
- "Enough of Blood and Tears"

 **eEdition CD-ROM**

 **Critical Thinking Transparencies**
- CT70 Chapter 34 Visual Summary

 **classzone.com**

OVERVIEW OF CALIFORNIA RESOURCES

	Section 1	Section 2	Section 3	Section 4	Section 5
California Reading Toolkit	p. L80	p. L81	p. L82	p. L83	p. L84
California Modified Lesson Plans for English Learners	p. 155	p. 157	p. 159	p. 161	p. 163
California Daily Standards Practice Transparencies	TT72	TT73	TT74	TT75	TT76
California Standards Enrichment Workbook	pp. 53–54	pp. 53–54	pp. 53–54, 93–94	pp. 101–102	pp. 103–104
California Standards Planner and Lesson Plans	p. L151	p. L153	p. L155	p. L157	p. L159
California Online Test Practice	classzone.com	classzone.com	classzone.com	classzone.com	classzone.com
California Test Generator CD-ROM					
California Easy Planner CD-ROM					
California eEdition CD-ROM					

Chart Key:

 Copymaster
 Pupil's Edition
Audio Library
Teacher's Edition
 CD-ROM
 Overhead Transparency
 Internet
 Block Scheduling
 Video

NO TIME?

If you do not have time to teach this chapter in full, assign the **Chapter in Brief** (also available in Spanish).

Previewing Resources for Differentiated Instruction

ENGLISH LEARNERS: Resources in Spanish

In-Depth Resources in Spanish

- Guided Reading Ⓐ
- Skillbuilder Practice: Evaluating Decisions and Courses of Action
- Geography Application: The Congo Gains Independence Ⓑ

Chapters in Brief

Reading Study Guide Ⓒ

Reading Study Guide Audio CD

Test Generator CD-ROM

- Chapter Test, Forms A, B, and C

Plus

Modified Lesson Plans for English Learners

Multi-Language Glossary of Social Studies Terms

Ⓐ

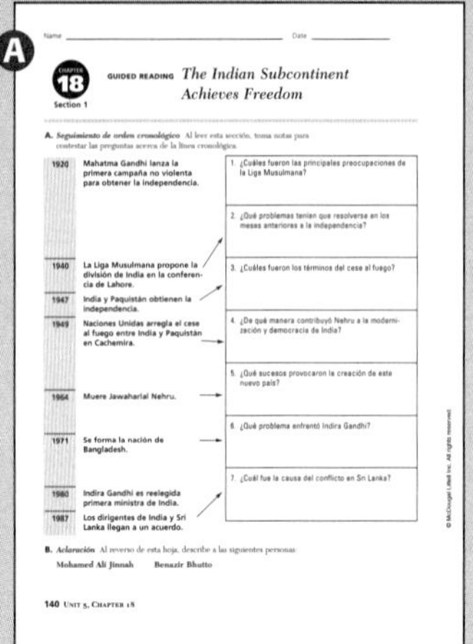

Chapter 18 Section 1 GUIDED READING *The Indian Subcontinent Achieves Freedom*

Ⓑ

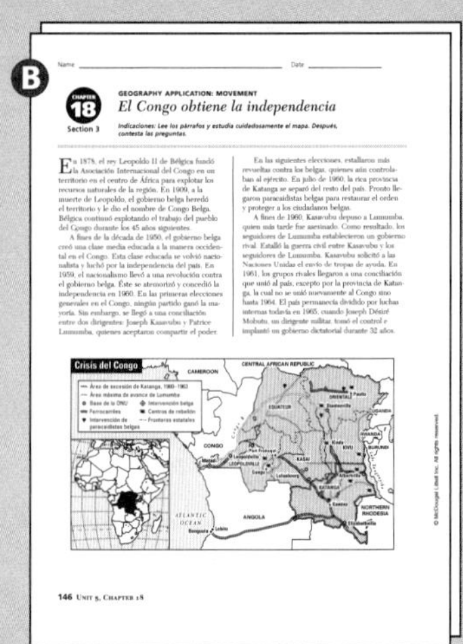

Chapter 18 Section 3 GEOGRAPHY APPLICATION: MOVEMENT *El Congo obtiene la independencia*

STRUGGLING READERS

In-Depth Resources: Unit 5

- Guided Reading Ⓐ
- Building Vocabulary
- Skillbuilder Practice: Evaluating Decisions and Courses of Action Ⓑ
- Geography Application: The Congo Gains Independence
- Reteaching Activities

Chapters in Brief

Reading Study Guide Ⓒ

Reading Study Guide Audio CD

Formal Assessment

- Chapter Test, Form A

Plus

Reading Toolkit

Ⓐ

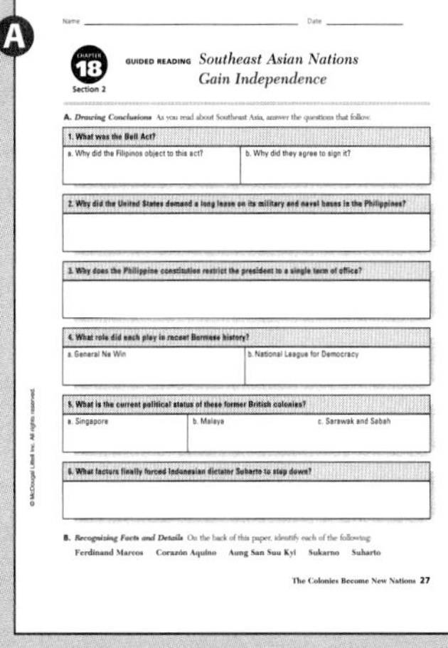

Chapter 18 Section 2 GUIDED READING *Southeast Asian Nations Gain Independence*

Ⓑ

Chapter 18 Section 3 SKILLBUILDER PRACTICE *Evaluating Decisions*

GIFTED AND TALENTED STUDENTS

In-Depth Resources: Unit 5

- Primary Source: from "First Servant of the Indian People;" from *The Snap Revolution*; Farewell Without Tears; The Balfour Declaration Ⓐ
- Literature: from *The Year of Living Dangerously*; Négritude poems Ⓑ
- History Makers: Jomo Kenyatta; Golda Meir
- Connections Across Time and Cultures: Becoming a New Nation Ⓒ

Electronic Library of Primary Sources

- from Radio Address from New Delhi
- "The Fall of President Marcos"
- "Enough of Blood and Tears"

Formal Assessment

- Chapter Test, Form C

Ⓐ

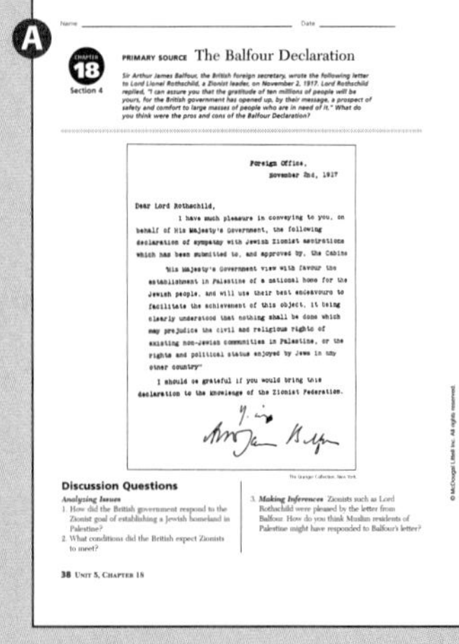

Chapter 18 Section 4 PRIMARY SOURCE The Balfour Declaration

Ⓑ

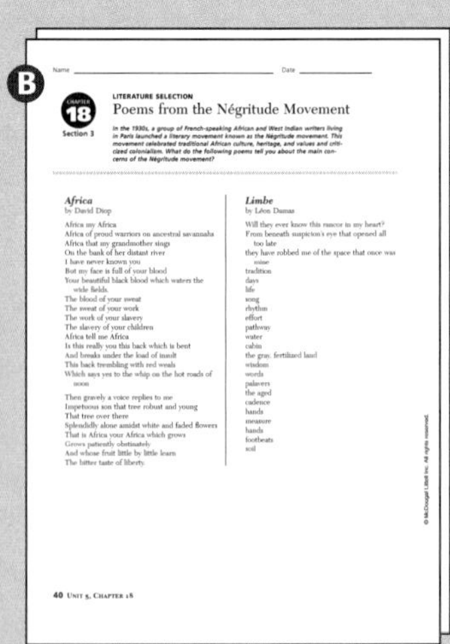

Chapter 18 Section 3 LITERATURE SELECTION Poems from the Négritude Movement

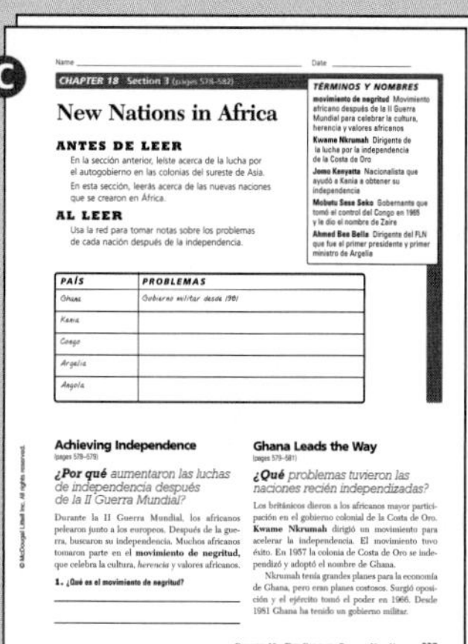
CHAPTER 18 Section 3

New Nations in Africa

ANTES DE LEER

AL LEER

PAÍS	PROBLEMAS
Ghana	
Kenia	
Congo	
Argelia	
Angola	

Achieving Independence

¿Por qué aumentaron las luchas de independencia después de la II Guerra Mundial?

Ghana Leads the Way

¿Qué problemas tuvieron las naciones recién independizadas?

CHAPTER 18 THE COLONIES BECOME NEW NATIONS 337

Activities in the Teacher's Edition for English Learners

- Tracking Independence Movements, p. 567
- Clarifying Sequence, p. 574
- Analyzing the Congo Crisis, p. 580
- Organizing Events, p. 587
- Defining Difficult Language, p. 592

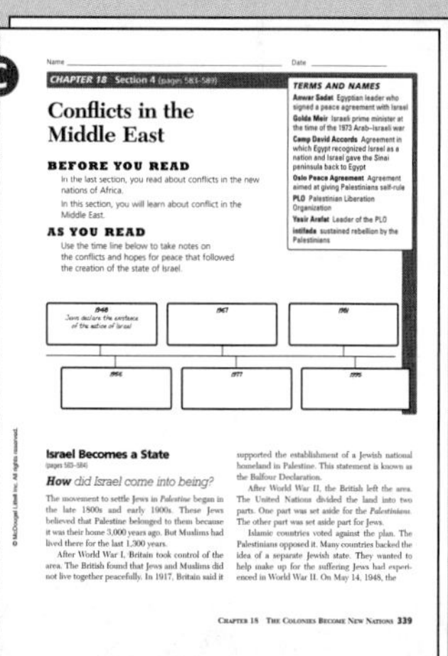
CHAPTER 18 Section 4

Conflicts in the Middle East

BEFORE YOU READ

AS YOU READ

TERMS AND NAMES

Israel Becomes a State

How did Israel come into being?

CHAPTER 18 THE COLONIES BECOME NEW NATIONS 339

Activities in the Teacher's Edition for Struggling Readers

- Outlining Major Ideas, p. 565
- Analyzing Geographic Impact, p. 572
- Leadership Styles, p. 581
- Determining Main Ideas, p. 588
- Identifying Central Asian Nations, p. 591

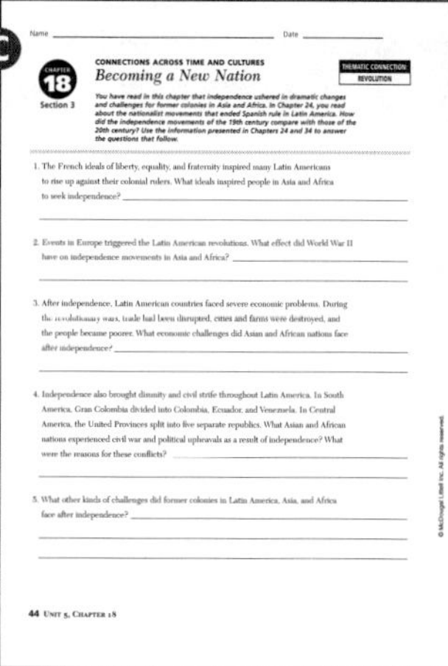
CHAPTER 18 Section 3

CONNECTIONS ACROSS TIME AND CULTURES

Becoming a New Nation

44 UNIT 5, CHAPTER 18

Activities in the Teacher's Edition for Gifted and Talented Students

- Writing Indian Political Statements, p. 564
- The Story of Aquino's Victory, p. 571
- Exploring the Balfour Declaration, p. 584

INTEGRATED TECHNOLOGY

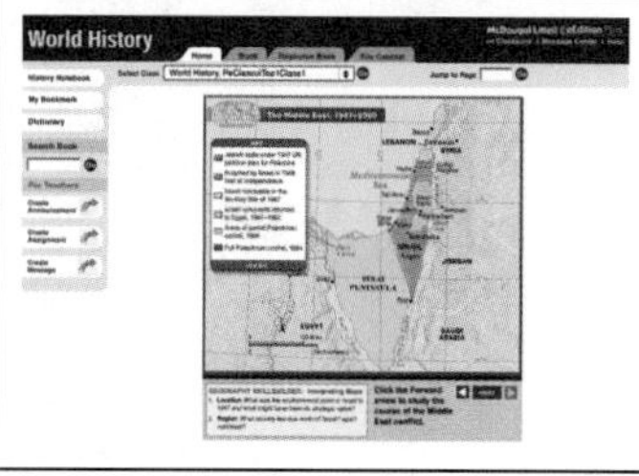
World History

eEdition

- Interactive Visuals
- Interactive Maps
- Interactive Primary Sources

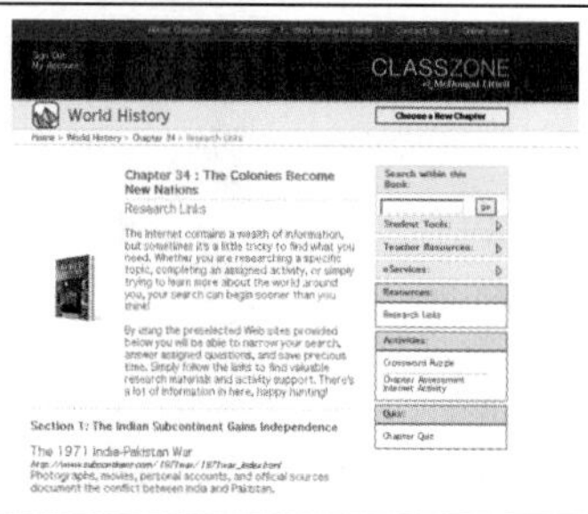
CLASSZONE
World History
Chapter 34 : The Colonies Become New Nations

classzone.com

- Research Links
- Internet Activities
- Primary Sources
- Chapter Quiz
- Current Events

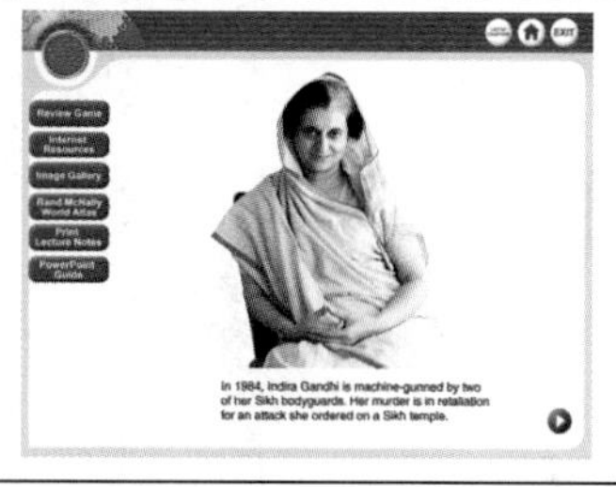
In 1984, Indira Gandhi is machine-gunned by two of her Sikh bodyguards. Her murder is in retaliation for an attack she ordered on a Sikh temple.

Power Presentations CD-ROM

- Lecture Notes
- Image Gallery
- Chapter Review Game

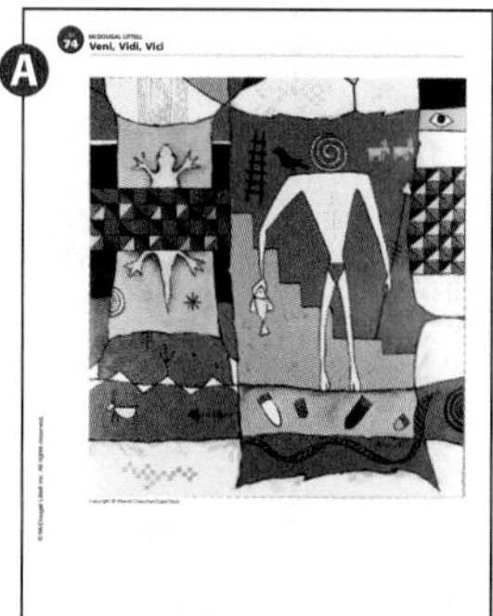
Veni, Vidi, Vici

Critical Thinking Transparencies

- CT34 Time Machine: The Middle East Conflict
- CT70 Chapter 34 Visual Summary

Geography Transparencies

- GT34 Indonesia and Malaysia, 1945–1976

World Art and Cultures Transparencies

- AT74 *Veni, Vidi, Vici* Ⓐ
- AT75 *After the Storm*

Test Practice Transparencies TT132–TT135.5

Test Generator CD-ROM

EasyPlanner CD-ROM

Voices from the Past Audio CD

Online Test Practice

Electronic Library of Primary Sources

CHAPTER 18 • OBJECTIVE

Trace independence movements and political conflicts in Africa and Asia as colonialism gave way after World War II.

Previewing Main Ideas

Recall with students the ideas and emotions that motivated America's founders to seek independence. Discuss how people everywhere share a desire for self-determination and note that independence movements surged after World War II. Ask students what conditions might motivate people to fight for their independence.

Accessing Prior Knowledge

Tell students that whenever nations or colonies become independent, they create their own national flag. Ask students what they think the American flag represents. How do they feel when they see it? How do others respond to it? Extend the discussion to new nations: What might creating a flag mean for a new nation and what might it symbolize to its people, to a nation's former rulers, and to the rest of the world?

Geography *Answers*

REVOLUTION Africa saw the most countries gain independence.

POWER AND AUTHORITY The Philippines dealt with dictatorship in the years following independence.

ECONOMICS Britain enjoyed resources from the greatest number of regions.

CHAPTER 18

The Colonies Become New Nations, 1945–Present

Previewing Main Ideas

REVOLUTION Independence movements swept Africa and Asia as World War II ended. Through both nonviolent and violent means, revolutionaries overthrew existing political systems to create their own nations.

Geography *Which continent witnessed the greatest number of its countries gain independence?*

POWER AND AUTHORITY Systems of government shifted for one billion people when colonies in Africa and Asia gained their freedom. New nations struggled to unify their diverse populations. In many cases, authoritarian rule and military dictatorships emerged.

Geography *According to the time line, which southeast Asian country dealt with dictatorship in the years following independence?*

ECONOMICS The emergence of new nations from European- and U.S.-ruled colonies brought a change in ownership of vital resources. In many cases, however, new nations struggled to create thriving economies.

Geography *Which colonial power had enjoyed the resources from the greatest number of regions of the world?*

INTEGRATED TECHNOLOGY

eEdition
- Interactive Maps
- Interactive Visuals
- Interactive Primary Sources

INTERNET RESOURCES
Go to **classzone.com** for:
- Research Links
- Internet Activities
- Primary Sources
- Chapter Quiz
- Maps
- Test Practice
- Current Events

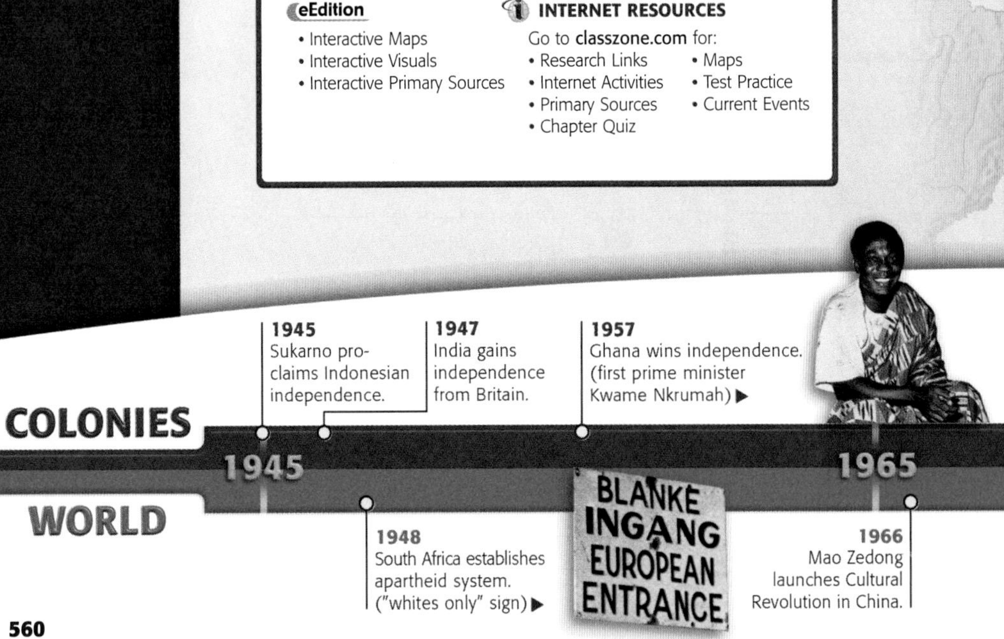

COLONIES
WORLD
1945
1965
1945 Sukarno proclaims Indonesian independence.
1947 India gains independence from Britain.
1957 Ghana wins independence. (first prime minister Kwame Nkrumah) ▶
1948 South Africa establishes apartheid system. ("whites only" sign) ▶
BLANKE INGANG EUROPEAN ENTRANCE
1966 Mao Zedong launches Cultural Revolution in China.
560

TIME LINE DISCUSSION

Tell students that one of the effects of World War II was to awaken a desire for independence in colonial countries in Asia, Africa, and the Middle East. This time line reflects some major movements to overthrow European rule and to achieve independence.

1. What countries in Africa and Asia shown on the time line fought to become independent nations? In what years? *(Indonesia—1945; India—1947; Ghana—1957.)*
2. How many years passed between Indonesia's proclamation of independence and Ghanaian independence? How do you think independence movements affect other nations? *(12 years; They affect other nations who are struggling for independence.)*
3. In which countries were internal changes taking place? *(South Africa and China)*
4. What occurred in the Philippines in 1986? in Zaire in 1997? How are the two events similar? *(In both places a dictatorship failed.)*
5. What happened in the Soviet Union in 1991? How does this event reflect the general pattern of the time line? *(Soviet Union broke up, shows general tendency to move away from old governing patterns.)*

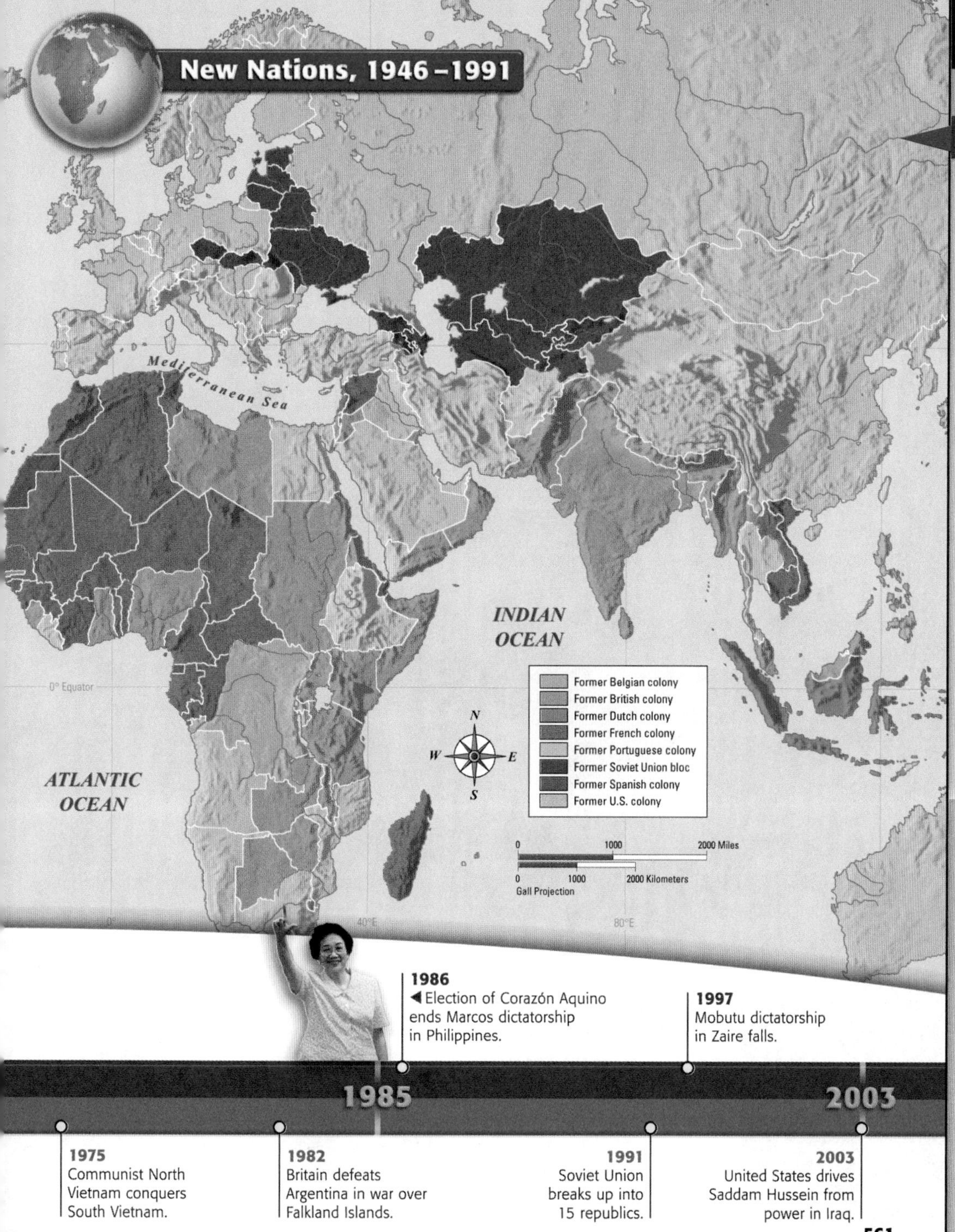

561

CHAPTER 18

History from Visuals

Interpreting the Map

Tell students that many of the new nations shown on this map had diverse populations, thrown together by arbitrary boundaries established by their colonizers. These diverse groups had to unite to establish their new governments. But mistakes were made, and old ethnic hostilities sometimes persisted. Have students identify which two countries had the most colonies in Africa. *(France and Britain)*

Extension Tell students that the natural resources and geography of a colony significantly affected how willing the colonizers were to give up the land. In Kenya, Algeria, and Indonesia, colonizers who had lived there for generations were reluctant to leave. Ask students to recall what resources in Indonesia were especially important to the Europeans. *(rubber, sugar cane, coffee, cocoa, coconuts, banana, pineapple, oil, tin)*

RECOMMENDED RESOURCES

Books for the Teacher

Malik, Muhammad Aslam. **The Making of the Pakistan Resolution**. Karachi, Pakistan: Oxford UP, 2001.

Murray, Jocelyn, ed. ***Cultural Atlas of Africa.*** New York: Checkmark Books, 1998. Covering the whole continent, this book looks at everything from religion to art, along with the various tribes and languages in each country. Excellent illustrations and photographs.

Books for the Student

Frank, Katherine. ***Indira: The Life of Indira Nehru Gandhi.*** Boston: Houghton Mifflin, 2002.

Stewart, Whitney. ***Aung San Suu Kyi: Fearless Voice of Burma.*** Minneapolis: Lerner, 1997. Based on personal interviews, this book lays out the history of Burmese politics and the Nobel Prize-winner's struggle to democratize her native country.

Videos and Software

Israel: A Nation Is Born Collection. VHS. Library Video Company, 1992. 800-843-3620. This documentary is hosted by Abba Eban, former Israeli ambassador to the U.S..

The Suez Crisis: 1956. VHS and DVD. Films for the Humanities and Sciences. 800-257-5126. A look at the African side of the 1956 Arab-Israeli conflict.

Encarta: Africana. CD-ROM. Library Video Company, 1999. 800-843-3620.

Interact *with* History

Objectives

- Set the stage for studying independence movements in colonies after World War II.
- Connect the events and historical figures of the chapter with students' lives.

EXAMINING *the* ISSUES

Possible Answers

- establish order, earn people's trust by sharing honest assessment of problems, create plan to reach realistic initial goals, organize government and plan long-term goals
- religions and ethnic differences and animosities

Discussion

Ask students to discuss the U.S. movement for independence that culminated in the outbreak of the Revolution in 1776. How did its leaders work to unify diverse groups within the new nation? *(They created a government that balanced both national and state goals and interests.)*

Interact *with* History

How would you build a new nation?

As a political leader of a former colony, you watch with pride as your country becomes independent. However, you know that difficult days lay ahead. You want peace and prosperity for your nation. To accomplish this, however, you need to create a sound government and a strong economy. In addition, food and adequate health care are scarce and many people receive little education. These and other challenges await your immediate attention.

▼ Agriculture

▼ Health Care

▲ Education

▲ Employment

▲ Voting Rights

EXAMINING *the* ISSUES

- **What are the first steps you would take? Why?**
- **What might be the most difficult challenge to overcome?**

As a class, discuss these questions. Remember what you have learned about what makes a stable and unified nation. As you read about the emergence of new nations around the world, note what setbacks and achievements they make in their effort to build a promising future.

WHY STUDY HOW COLONIES BECOME NEW NATIONS?

- Understanding the desire for independence and freedom held by peoples around the world helps put the various struggles into context.
- Some emerging democracies in Africa and Asia used the United States as a model.
- The power and influence of the Pacific Rim nations are likely to expand over time.
- Religious and ethnic strife in countries such as Pakistan and India creates violence that impacts the United States politically and economically.
- The conflict in the Middle East continues to threaten the stability of the world.
- Security issues in central Asian nations pose a threat to world peace and security.

Temple decoration, Chiang Mai, Thailand

Floating market, Bangkok, Thailand

1 The Indian Subcontinent Achieves Freedom

MAIN IDEA

POWER AND AUTHORITY New nations emerged from the British colony of India.

WHY IT MATTERS NOW

India today is the largest democracy in the world.

TERMS & NAMES

- Congress Party
- Muslim League
- Muhammad Ali Jinnah
- partition
- Jawaharlal Nehru
- Indira Gandhi
- Benazir Bhutto

SETTING THE STAGE After World War II, dramatic political changes began to take place across the world. This was especially the case with regard to the policy of colonialism. Countries that held colonies began to question the practice. After the world struggle against dictatorship, many leaders argued that no country should control another nation. Others questioned the high cost and commitment of holding colonies. Meanwhile, the people of colonized regions continued to press even harder for their freedom. All of this led to independence for one of the largest and most populous colonies in the world: British-held India.

CALIFORNIA STANDARDS

10.4.4 Describe the independence struggles of the colonized regions of the world, including the roles of leaders, such as Sun Yat-sen in China, and the roles of ideology and religion.

CST 1 Students compare the present with the past, evaluating the consequences of past events and decisions and determining the lessons that were learned.

CST 4 Students relate current events to the physical and human characteristics of places and regions.

A Movement Toward Independence

The British had ruled India for almost two centuries. Indian resistance to Britain, which had existed from the beginning, intensified in 1939, when Britain committed India's armed forces to World War II without first consulting the colony's elected representatives. The move left Indian nationalists stunned and humiliated. Indian leader Mohandas Gandhi launched a nonviolent campaign of noncooperation with the British. Officials imprisoned numerous nationalists for this action. In 1942, the British tried to gain the support of the nationalists by promising governmental changes after the war. But the offer did not include Indian independence.

As they intensified their struggle against the British, Indians also struggled with each other. India has long been home to two main religious groups. In the 1940s, India had approximately 350 million Hindus and about 100 million Muslims. The Indian National Congress, or the **Congress Party**, was India's national political party. Most members of the Congress Party were Hindus, but the party at times had many Muslim members.

In competition with the Congress Party was the **Muslim League**, an organization founded in 1906 in India to protect Muslim interests. Members of the league felt that the mainly Hindu Congress Party looked out primarily for Hindu interests. The leader of the Muslim League, **Muhammad Ali Jinnah** (mu•HAM•ihd ah•LEE JINH•uh), insisted that all Muslims resign from the Congress Party. The Muslim League stated that it would never accept Indian independence if it meant rule by the Hindu-dominated Congress Party. Jinnah stated, "The only thing the Muslim has in common with the Hindu is his slavery to the British."

TAKING NOTES

Following Chronological Order Create a time line of prominent Indian prime ministers from independence through the current day.

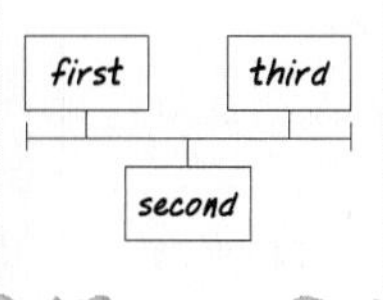

LESSON PLAN

OBJECTIVES

- Describe the partition of India.
- Summarize the leadership of Nehru.
- Explain the division of Pakistan.
- Summarize independence struggles in Bangladesh and Sri Lanka.

1 FOCUS & MOTIVATE

Note that many independence movements in Asia faced challenges from ethnic division and conflict. How do ethnic groups in U.S. communities get along? *(Possible Answers: mostly stay separate, sometimes argue with other groups, mingle freely)*

2 INSTRUCT

A Movement Toward Independence

10.4.4

Critical Thinking

- How did British policy toward Indians spur the independence movement? *(British actions against Indian representatives raised strong feelings of Indian nationalism.)*

CALIFORNIA RESOURCES

California Reading Toolkit, p. L80
California Modified Lesson Plans for English Learners, p. 155
California Daily Standards Practice Transparencies, TT72
California Standards Enrichment Workbook, pp. 53–54
California Standards Planner and Lesson Plans, p. L151
California Online Test Practice
California Test Generator CD-ROM
California Easy Planner CD-ROM
California eEdition CD-ROM

SECTION 1 PROGRAM RESOURCES

ALL STUDENTS

In-Depth Resources: Unit 5
- Guided Reading, p. 26

Formal Assessment
- Section Quiz, p. 314

ENGLISH LEARNERS

In-Depth Resources in Spanish
- Guided Reading, p. 140

Reading Study Guide (Spanish), p. 191
Reading Study Guide Audio CD (Spanish)

STRUGGLING READERS

In-Depth Resources: Unit 5
- Guided Reading, p. 26
- Building Vocabulary, p. 31
- Reteaching Activity, p. 45

Reading Study Guide, p. 191
Reading Study Guide Audio CD

GIFTED AND TALENTED STUDENTS

In-Depth Resources: Unit 5
- Primary Source: from "First Servant of the Indian People," p. 35

Electronic Library of Primary Sources
- from Radio Address from New Delhi

INTEGRATED TECHNOLOGY

eEdition CD-ROM
Voices from the Past Audio CD
Power Presentations CD-ROM
World Art and Cultures Transparencies
- AT74 *Veni, Vidi, Vici*

Electronic Library of Primary Sources
- from Radio Address from New Delhi

classzone.com

Freedom Brings Turmoil

When World War II ended, Britain found itself faced with enormous war debts. As a result, British leaders began to rethink the expense of maintaining and governing distant colonies. With India continuing to push for independence, the stage was set for the British to hand over power. However, a key problem emerged: Who should receive the power—Hindus or Muslims?

Partition and Bloodshed Muslims resisted attempts to include them in an Indian government dominated by Hindus. Rioting between the two groups broke out in several Indian cities. In August 1946, four days of clashes in Calcutta left more than 5,000 people dead and more than 15,000 hurt.

British officials soon became convinced that partition, an idea first proposed by India's Muslims, would be the only way to ensure a safe and secure region. **Partition** was the term given to the division of India into separate Hindu and Muslim nations. The northwest and eastern regions of India, where most Muslims lived, would become the new nation of Pakistan. (Pakistan, as the map shows, comprised two separate states in 1947: West Pakistan and East Pakistan.)

The British House of Commons passed an act on July 16, 1947, that granted two nations, India and Pakistan, independence in one month's time. In that short period, more than 500 independent native princes had to decide which nation they would join. The administration of the courts, the military, the railways, and the police—the whole of the civil service—had to be divided down to the last paper clip. Most difficult of all, millions of Indian citizens—Hindus, Muslims, and yet another significant religious group, the Sikhs—had to decide where to go.

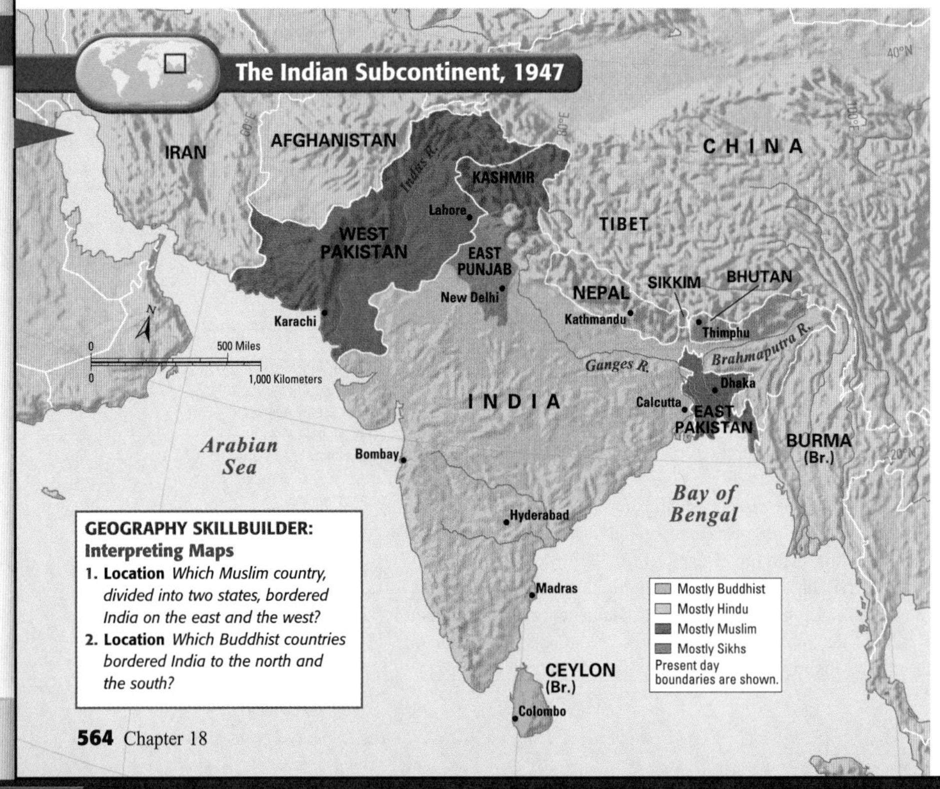

Freedom Brings Turmoil
10.4.4

Critical Thinking

- Why do you think the British moved so quickly after World War II to grant independence to India? *(Possible Answer: wanted to be free of costs and problems)*
- How might people's attachments to their communities, traditional lands, or religion add to the violence of relocation? *(Possible Answer: People may be protective of their communities or lands, or they may dislike others of different ethnicity or religion, which can create tension.)*

History from Visuals

Interpreting the Map

Tell students that although India has a large Muslim population, Muslims are not a majority in most of India's states. Have students identify areas where potential conflicts over religion might erupt. *(Border areas between two different religions could possibly be locations where conflicts arise.)*

Extension Have students compare this map with a current political map. What mostly non-Hindu areas are part of India? *(East Punjab, Sikkim)* What mostly Hindu area is not part of India? *(Nepal)*

SKILLBUILDER Answers

1. **Location** Pakistan
2. **Location** Bhutan to the north; Ceylon (Sri Lanka) to the south

DIFFERENTIATING INSTRUCTION: GIFTED AND TALENTED STUDENTS

Writing Indian Political Statements

Class Time 45 minutes

Task Writing political statements representing different views on the partition of India

Purpose To understand different perspectives on an issue

Instructions Organize students into four groups. Groups will represent the following factions:

- Indian National Congress
- Muslim League
- British government
- Gandhi's followers

Have each group research and write political statements on the partition of India. Statements should be consistent with what a leader or significant member of the faction represented would say. Tell students that their statements should

- accurately outline the opinions of the faction represented.
- use specific details to back up a point of view.

Have the groups share their statements and allow a question-and-answer period in which each group answers questions about the position they represent.

During the summer of 1947, 10 million people were on the move in the Indian subcontinent. As people scrambled to relocate, violence among the different religious groups erupted. Muslims killed Sikhs who were moving into India. Hindus and Sikhs killed Muslims who were headed into Pakistan. A Muslim woman and doctor, Zahida Amjad Ali, recalled her ordeal of fleeing from Delhi to Pakistan by train:

PRIMARY SOURCE

All passengers were forced into compartments like sheep and goats. Because of which the heat and suffocating atmosphere was intensified and it was very hard to breathe. In the ladies compartment women and children were in a terrible condition. Women tried in vain to calm down and comfort their children. If you looked out the window you could see dead bodies lying in the distance. At many places you could see corpses piled on top of each other and no one seemed to have any concern. . . . These were the scenes that made your heart bleed and everybody loudly repented their sins and recited verses asking God's forgiveness. Every moment seemed to be the most terrifying and agonizing.

ZAHIDA AMJAD ALI, quoted in *Freedom, Trauma, Continuities*

In all, an estimated 1 million died. "What is there to celebrate?" Gandhi mourned. "I see nothing but rivers of blood." Gandhi personally went to the Indian capital of Delhi to plead for fair treatment of Muslim refugees. While there, he himself became a victim of the nation's violence. A Hindu extremist who thought Gandhi too protective of Muslims shot and killed him on January 30, 1948.

The Battle for Kashmir As if partition itself didn't result in enough bloodshed between India's Muslims and Hindus, the two groups quickly squared off over the small region of Kashmir. Kashmir lay at the northern point of India next to Pakistan. Although its ruler was Hindu, Kashmir had a majority Muslim population. Shortly after independence, India and Pakistan began battling each other for control of the region. The fighting continued until the United Nations arranged a cease-fire in 1949. The cease-fire left a third of Kashmir under Pakistani control and the rest under Indian control. The two countries continue to fight over the region today. (A)

A. Answer Kashmir had a large Muslim population but was ruled by a Hindu. Since it bordered both India and Pakistan, both groups staked a claim to it.

MAIN IDEA

Analyzing Causes

(A) What was the cause of the conflict between India and Pakistan over Kashmir?

Connect *to* Today

The Coldest War

No part of Kashmir is beyond a fight for India and Pakistan—including the giant Siachen glacier high above the region. The dividing line established by the 1949 cease-fire did not extend to the glacier because officials figured neither side would try to occupy such a barren and frigid strip of land.

They figured wrong. In 1984, both sides sent troops to take the glacier, and they have been dug in ever since. At altitudes nearing 21,000 feet, Indian and Pakistani soldiers shoot at each other from trenches in temperatures that reach 70 degrees below zero. While it is believed that more soldiers have died from the cold than from enemy bullets, neither side will budge.

Modern India

With the granting of its independence on August 15, 1947, India became the world's largest democracy. As the long-awaited hour of India's freedom approached, **Jawaharlal Nehru**, the independent nation's first prime minister, addressed the country's political leaders:

PRIMARY SOURCE

Long years ago, we made a tryst [appointment] with destiny, and now the time comes when we shall redeem our pledge, not wholly or in full measure, but very substantially. At the stroke of the midnight hour, when the world sleeps, India will wake to life and freedom.

JAWAHARLAL NEHRU, speech before the Constituent Assembly, August 14, 1947

Connect *to* Today

The Coldest War

The battle for Kashmir is a complex situation involving not only religion and ethnicity, but also environment, specifically water resources.

The melting waters of the Siachen Glacier flow into the Indus River. The river is a source of water for both India and Pakistan. The Indus River flows through India toward Kashmir and Pakistan. If the waters flowing through Kashmir were cut off, Pakistan would face dire consequences. In Pakistan, the waters of the Indus allow for an immense irrigated area—bigger than the area of England. So, control of the glacier and the water flowing from it is a major political issue affecting the economies of both nations.

Modern India

10.4.4

Critical Thinking

- Why do you think Nehru wanted to organize states by language? Explain. *(Possible Answer: provides common ground and method of communication)*
- Why is nuclear war between India and Pakistan more worrisome than traditional war? *(Possible Answer: Nuclear weapons create more far-reaching damage than conventional weapons; the region is home to more than a billion people.)*

DIFFERENTIATING INSTRUCTION: STRUGGLING READERS

Outlining Major Ideas

Class Time 15 minutes

Task Outlining key points in the text

Purpose To identify main ideas and clarify connections between key points

Instructions Review the section material with students. First, post the sample outline for pages 563–567, as it appears here. Explain that each capital letter represents a major subsection (red in the text), roman numerals represent the black sub-subheads, and lowercase letters represent supporting details. Students should fill in two or three supporting details under each numbered subhead. If students need additional help, help them reshape each subhead into a question. For example, "The Battle for Kashmir" becomes "Why was there a battle over Kashmir?" Answering this question will help students identify key supporting details.

Divide students in small groups. Have groups create an outline of the section, using the headings in the text.

A. A Movement Toward Independence
B. Freedom Brings Turmoil
    I. Partition and Bloodshed
        a.
        b.
    II. The Battle for Kashmir
        a.
        b.
C. Modern India
    I. Nehru Leads India
    II. Troubled Times
    III. Twenty-first Century Challenges

History Makers

Jawaharlal Nehru

How might Nehru's experiences in England have influenced his views on India's poor? *(Possible Answer: saw great contrast between Indian poverty and British prosperity)* Explain that Nehru was jailed several times after his return from England, each time for a role in the independence movement. Discuss how Nehru's nine jailings might have increased his support for independence.

In-Depth Resources: Unit 5

- Primary Source: from "First Servant of the Indian People", p. 35

World Art and Cultures Transparencies

- AT74 *Veni, Vidi, Vici*

Electronic Library of Primary Sources

- from Radio Address from New Delhi

More About . . .

Sikh Separatists

Even before the partition of the Indian subcontinent, Sikhs were agitating for a separate state. Their hopes were not realized and eventually they made the choice to join India rather than Pakistan.

History Makers

Jawaharlal Nehru
1889–1964

Nehru's father was an influential attorney, and so the first prime minister of India grew up amid great wealth. As a young man, he lived and studied in England. "In my likes and dislikes I was perhaps more an Englishman than an Indian," he once remarked.

Upon returning to India, however, he became moved by the horrible state in which many of his fellow Indians lived. "A new picture of India seemed to rise before me," he recalled, "naked, starving, crushed, and utterly miserable." From then on, he devoted his life to improving conditions in his country.

INTEGRATED TECHNOLOGY
RESEARCH LINKS For more on Jawaharlal Nehru, go to **classzone.com**

Nehru Leads India Nehru served as India's leader for its first 17 years of independence. He had been one of Gandhi's most devoted followers. Educated in Britain, Nehru won popularity among all groups in India. He emphasized democracy, unity, and economic modernization.

Nehru used his leadership to move India forward. He led other newly independent nations of the world in forming an alliance of countries that were neutral in the Cold War conflicts between the United States and the Soviet Union. On the home front, Nehru called for a reorganization of the states by language. He also pushed for industrialization and sponsored social reforms. He tried to elevate the status of the lower castes, or those at the bottom of society, and expand the rights of women.

Troubled Times Nehru died in 1964. His death left the Congress Party with no leader strong enough to hold together the many political factions that had emerged with India's independence. Then, in 1966, Nehru's daughter, **Indira Gandhi**, was chosen prime minister. After a short spell out of office, she was reelected in 1980.

Although she ruled capably, Gandhi faced many challenges, including the growing threat from Sikh extremists who themselves wanted an independent state. The Golden Temple at Amritsar stood as the religious center for the Sikhs. From there, Sikh nationalists ventured out to attack symbols of Indian authority. In June 1984, Indian army troops overran the Golden Temple. They killed about 500 Sikhs and destroyed sacred property. In retaliation, Sikh bodyguards assigned to Indira Gandhi gunned her down. This violent act set off another murderous frenzy, causing the deaths of thousands of Sikhs.

In the wake of the murder of Indira Gandhi, her son, Rajiv (rah•JEEV) Gandhi, took over as prime minister. His party, however, lost its power in 1989 because of accusations of widespread corruption. In 1991, while campaigning again for prime minister near the town of Madras, Rajiv was killed by a bomb. Members of a group opposed to his policies claimed responsibility.

Twenty-First Century Challenges Since winning election as prime minister in 1998, Atal Bihari Vajpayee, leader of the Hindu nationalist party, has ruled over a vibrant but often unstable nation. He faces challenges brought on by an increasing population that is expected to push India past China as the world's most populous nation by 2035. In addition, the country is racked with social inequality and constantly threatened by religious strife.

Even more troubling are India's tense relations with its neighbor Pakistan, and the fact that both have become nuclear powers. In 1974, India exploded a "peaceful" nuclear device. For the next 24 years, the nation quietly worked on building up its nuclear capability. In 1998, Indian officials conducted five underground nuclear tests. Meanwhile, the Pakistanis had been building their own nuclear program. Shortly after India conducted its nuclear tests, Pakistan demonstrated that it, too, had nuclear weapons. The presence of these weapons in the hands of such bitter

CONNECTIONS ACROSS TIME AND CULTURES

Nuclear Weapons in India and Pakistan

Class Time 30 minutes

Task Creating a time line showing the development of nuclear weapons in India and Pakistan

Purpose To analyze causes and recognize effects of the nuclear race between India and Pakistan

Instructions Have students reread the second paragraph under the heading, "Twenty-First Century Challenges". Help them understand that the nuclear race between the two nations escalated during the Cold War. Each nation received help from one of the sides in that war. Both nations responded to the actions of the other by increasing nuclear capability.

Have students search online to trace the nuclear history of India and Pakistan and create time lines showing events that led to escalation. When the time lines are finished conduct a class discussion to identify the cause-and-effect relationships shown on the time lines.

enemies and neighbors has become a matter of great international concern, especially in light of their continuing struggle over Kashmir:

PRIMARY SOURCE

Now that India and Pakistan have tested nuclear weapons, the dispute over their border region of lush valleys and jagged Himalayan peaks has become a matter of urgent concern. . . . [There is] fear that a remote but savage ethnic and religious conflict could deteriorate into a nuclear exchange with global consequences. India and Pakistan must learn to talk to each other and move toward a more trusting relationship.

The *New York Times,* June 28, 1998

Pakistan Copes with Freedom

The history of Pakistan since independence has been no less turbulent than that of India. Pakistan actually began as two separate and divided states, East Pakistan and West Pakistan. East Pakistan lay to the east of India, West Pakistan to the northwest. These regions were separated by more than 1,000 miles of Indian territory. In culture, language, history, geography, economics, and ethnic background, the two regions were very different. Only the Islamic religion united them.

Civil War From the beginning, the two regions of Pakistan experienced strained relations. While East Pakistan had the larger population, it was often ignored by West Pakistan, home to the central government. In 1970, a giant cyclone and tidal wave struck East Pakistan and killed an estimated 266,000 residents. While international aid poured into Pakistan, the government in West Pakistan did not quickly transfer that aid to East Pakistan. Demonstrations broke out in East Pakistan, and protesters called for an end to all ties with West Pakistan.

On March 26, 1971, East Pakistan declared itself an independent nation called Bangladesh. A civil war followed between Bangladesh and Pakistan. Eventually,

A Turbulent History

Pakistan
1977
Ali Bhutto
Prime Minister Ali Bhutto of Pakistan is deposed in a coup led by General Zia. Bhutto is later hanged for having ordered the assassination of a political opponent.
1988
General Zia
General Zia, president of Pakistan, dies in a mysterious plane crash.
1950
1960
1970
1980
1990
India
1948
Mohandas Gandhi
Gandhi is shot to death by a Hindu extremist. The assassin opposes Gandhi's efforts to achieve equal treatment for all Indians, including Muslims.
1984
Indira Gandhi
Indira Gandhi is gunned down by two of her Sikh bodyguards. Her murder is in retaliation for an attack she ordered on a Sikh temple.
1991
Rajiv Gandhi
Rajiv Gandhi is killed by a bomb while campaigning. The bomb is carried by a woman opposed to Gandhi's policies.

Pakistan Copes with Freedom

10.4.4

Critical Thinking

- How did geography play a role in Pakistan's problems? *(Possible Answer: division into two distinct areas led to disunity; exposed coastal location led to storm damage)*
- Why do you think India intervened in the Pakistani civil war? What might its concern have been? *(Possible Answer: to ensure stability in region; spread of war to India, refugees into India)*

Inclusion Tip

For students with dyslexia, clarify the directions of east and west. Explain that these terms are used here as part of nation names. Refer students back to the map on p. 564 to gain a fuller understanding of Pakistan's divided geography. Have students find and identify East Pakistan and West Pakistan on the map.

History from Visuals

Interpreting the Time Line

Ask students how many politically related deaths are referenced in the time line. *(five, including the assassination that Bhutto was charged with ordering and the mysterious death of General Zia)*

Extension Have students write a paragraph giving their conclusions about the events on the time line and their relationship to British colonial policies.

DIFFERENTIATING INSTRUCTION: ENGLISH LEARNERS

Tracking Independence Movements

Class Time 20 minutes

Task Making a chart of the independence histories of South Asian nations

Purpose To clarify students' understanding of independence movements in South Asia and to help them highlight key players in these movements

Instructions Use the Guided Reading worksheet and Reading Study Guide for section 1 to review the section material with students. Then work with students to create a chart listing the following:

- countries of South Asia
- former colonizer
- major events
- their date of independence
- prominent leaders

Create and post a sample chart like the one shown here. Help students complete the section on India. Tell them to complete the remaining sections as they read the section.

	India	Pakistan	Bangladesh	Sri Lanka
Date	1947			
Colonizer	Great Britain			
Leaders	Indira Gandhi, Jawaharlal Nehru			
Events	partition			

Indian forces stepped in and sided with Bangladesh. About two weeks after the arrival of Indian troops, Pakistan forces surrendered. More than 1 million people died in the war. Pakistan lost about one-seventh of its area and about one-half of its population to Bangladesh. (B)

A Pattern of Instability Pakistan, however, could ill afford to dwell on its lost territory, for there were many problems at home. Muhammad Ali Jinnah, the first governor-general of Pakistan, died shortly after independence. This left the nation without strong leadership. As a result, Pakistan went through a series of military coups, the first in 1958. Ali Bhutto took control of the country following the civil war. A military coup in 1977 led by General Zia removed Bhutto, who was later executed for crimes allegedly committed while in office.

After Zia's death, Bhutto's daughter, **Benazir Bhutto**, was twice elected prime minister. After months of disorder, she was removed from office in 1996. Nawaz Sharif became prime minister after the 1997 elections. In 1999, army leaders ousted Sharif in yet another coup and imposed military rule over Pakistan. The nation continues to struggle with challenges from Muslim militants and ongoing disputes with India, especially over the territory of Kashmir.

MAIN IDEA

Comparing

(B) How does the history of Pakistan in 1971 parallel the history of India in 1947?

B. Answer As India was partitioned into India and Pakistan, Pakistan was divided into Pakistan and Bangladesh.

Bangladesh and Sri Lanka Struggle

Meanwhile, the newly created nations of Bangladesh and Sri Lanka struggled with enormous problems of their own in the decades following independence.

Bangladesh Faces Many Problems The war with Pakistan had ruined the economy of Bangladesh and fractured its communications system. Rebuilding the shattered country seemed like an overwhelming task. Sheik Mujibur Rahman became the nation's first prime minister. He appeared more interested in strengthening his own power than in rebuilding his nation. He soon took over all authority and declared Bangladesh a one-party state. In August 1975, military leaders assassinated him.

Over the years Bangladesh has attempted with great difficulty to create a more democratic form of government. Charges of election fraud and government corruption are common. In recent years, however, the government has become more stable. The latest elections were held in October of 2001, and Begum Khaleda Zia took over as the nation's prime minister.

In the years following its independence, Bangladesh also has had to cope with crippling natural disasters. Bangladesh is a low-lying nation that is subject to many cyclones and tidal waves. Massive storms regularly flood the land, ruin crops and

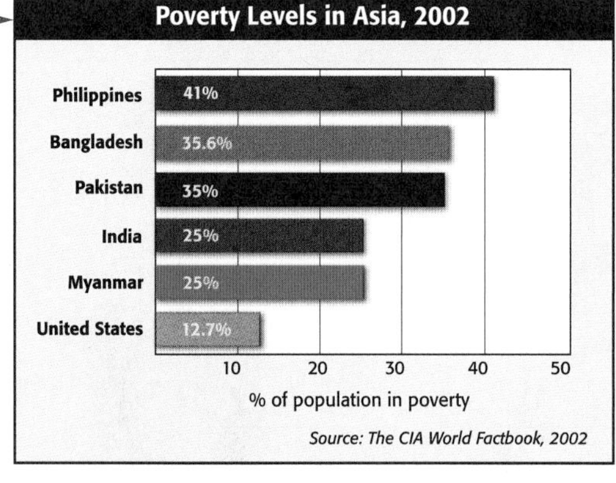

▼ Overcrowded and poor villages are a common sight throughout Bangladesh.

Bangladesh and Sri Lanka Struggle

10.4.4

Critical Thinking

- How might the future of Bangladesh have been different if Pakistan's civil war had taken place on West Pakistan's soil? *(Possible Answer: Bangladesh less damaged, more able to recover)*
- What reasons do you think people have for wanting self-determination? *(Possible Answers: want to control their own affairs; feel mistreated by the controlling government)*

History from Visuals

Interpreting a Graph

Ask students how the poverty of Bangladesh compares to that of the United States. *(It is about three times as great.)* Then ask how Bangladesh compares to other nations in Asia. *(It is in about the middle of the nations shown in the graph.)*

Extension Ask students to research the poverty levels of Sri Lanka and compare it with the other nations in South Asia.

CONNECTIONS TO GEOGRAPHY

Geography in Bangladesh

Class Time 20 minutes

Task Identifying problems and solutions to geographic challenges

Purpose To show how geographic elements can challenge a nation's very survival

Instructions Tell students that the nation of Bangladesh suffers from the extremes of nature. In 1988, floods killed 2,000 people and left 30 million homeless. In 1991, a ferocious cyclone killed 130,000. That storm prompted the government to spend millions of dollars to build defenses against natural disasters. As a result, when a similar cyclone struck in 1994, the death toll was limited to a little more than 200.

Ask students to choose one of the following problems:

- expensive disaster cleanup
- rebuilding infrastructure such as roads and railways
- the cost of large-scale homelessness
- the threat of epidemics due to disruption of clean water supplies

Then using a chart similar to the one found in the Skillbuilder Handbook page R5, chart the problem and brainstorm solutions Bangladesh might use to deal with the problem.

homes, and take lives. A particularly powerful cyclone hit in 1991 and killed approximately 139,000 people. Such catastrophes, along with a rapidly growing population, have put much stress on the country's economy. Bangladesh is one of the poorest nations in the world. The per capita income there is about $360 per year.

Civil Strife Grips Sri Lanka Another newly freed and deeply troubled country on the Indian subcontinent is Sri Lanka, a small, teardrop-shaped island nation just off the southeast coast of India. Formerly known as Ceylon, Sri Lanka gained its independence from Britain in February of 1948. Two main ethnic groups dominate the nation. Three-quarters of the population are Sinhalese, who are Buddhists. A fifth are Tamils, a Hindu people of southern India and northern Sri Lanka.

Sri Lanka's recent history has also been one of turmoil. A militant group of Tamils has long fought an armed struggle for a separate Tamil nation. Since 1981, thousands of lives have been lost. In an effort to end the violence, Rajiv Gandhi and the Sri Lankan president tried to reach an accord in 1987. The agreement called for Indian troops to enter Sri Lanka and help disarm Tamil rebels. This effort was not successful, and the Indian troops left in 1990. A civil war between Tamils and other Sri Lankans continues today.

As difficult as post-independence has been for the countries of the Indian subcontinent, the same can be said for former colonies elsewhere. As you will read in the next section, a number of formerly held territories in Southeast Asia faced challenges as they became independent nations.

▲ This emblem of the separatist group Liberation Tigers of Tamil Eelam represents the struggle for independence of the Tamils.

History from Visuals

Interpreting the Image

Invite students to describe the various images found on the poster and discuss their meaning. Point out, for example, the ring of bullets and the bayonets.

Extension Ask students to find out the meaning of the letters surrounding the bullets. Suggest an Internet language translation site as a likely information source.

SECTION 1 ASSESSMENT

TERMS & NAMES 1. For each term or name, write a sentence explaining its significance.
• Congress Party • Muslim League • Muhammad Ali Jinnah • partition • Jawaharlal Nehru • Indira Gandhi • Benazir Bhutto

USING YOUR NOTES

2. What tragic connection did many of the leaders share? (10.4.4)

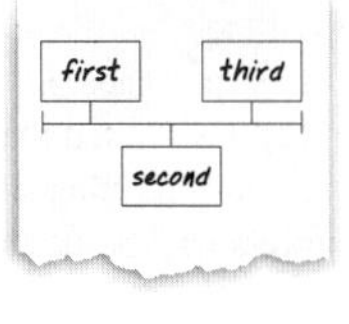

MAIN IDEAS

3. Why did British officials partition India into India and Pakistan? (10.4.4)
4. In what way did Pakistan also undergo a partition? (10.4.4)
5. What is the main cause today of civil strife in Sri Lanka? (10.4.4)

CRITICAL THINKING & WRITING

6. **SYNTHESIZING** Why might India's political and economic success be so crucial to the future of democracy in Asia? (10.4.4)
7. **ANALYZING ISSUES** How did religious and cultural differences create problems for newly emerging nations? (10.4.4)
8. **DRAWING CONCLUSIONS** Why has the conflict between India and Pakistan over Kashmir become such a concern to the world today? (10.4.4)
9. **WRITING ACTIVITY** POWER AND AUTHORITY Write several **paragraphs** detailing the problems shared by leaders of India and Pakistan. (Writing 2.3.b)

CONNECT TO TODAY **CREATING A GRAPHIC**

Research the current percentages of religions in India, Pakistan, Bangladesh, or Sri Lanka. Create a **graphic** of your choosing to illustrate your findings. (Writing 2.3.d)

③ ASSESS

SECTION 1 ASSESSMENT

Organize students into groups. Have students take turns reading the section assessment questions and leading a discussion about the answers. Invite groups to present their answers orally to the whole class.

Formal Assessment
• Section Quiz, p. 314

④ RETEACH

Review the main ideas of the section, subhead by subhead. Use the Guided Reading worksheet as a teaching aid.

In-Depth Resources, Unit 5
• Guided Reading, p. 26
• Reteaching Activity, p. 45

ANSWERS

1. Congress Party, p. 563 • Muslim League, p. 563 • Muhammad Ali Jinnah, p. 563 • partition, p. 564 • Jawaharlal Nehru, p. 565 • Indira Gandhi, p. 566 • Benazir Bhutto, p. 568
2. **Sample Answer:** Jawaharlal Nehru, Indira Gandhi, Rajiv Gandhi, Atal Bihari Vajpayee; They were killed or faced violence.
3. to create separate nations for Muslims and Hindus, who struggled to get along
4. East Pakistan became Bangladesh.
5. fight with Tamil separatists
6. **Possible Answer:** very populous country and world's largest democracy; has great influence in area
7. led to partition of India, battle for Kashmir, civil strife in Sri Lanka
8. Both nations have nuclear weapons.
9. **Rubric** Paragraphs should
• note problems of minority populations.
• recognize struggle for democracy.
• list problems of poverty and economic development.

CONNECT TO TODAY

Rubric Graphics should
• show percentage data clearly.
• identify the nation and groups.
• be visually appealing.

LESSON PLAN

OBJECTIVES

- Summarize the Philippine' independence movement.
- Identify problems facing Burma, Malaysia, and Singapore.
- Trace Indonesia's fight for independence.

1 FOCUS & MOTIVATE

Have students discuss the pros and cons of children or spouses taking over on a leader's death or retirement. *(Possible Answers: Pros—Familiarity, similar goals; Cons—No ability to lead, interested only in power or profit.)*

2 INSTRUCT

The Philippines Achieves Independence

10.4.4

Critical Thinking

- Why was the location of the Philippines a factor in the U.S. desire to have a presence there? *(It is near the USSR and China.)*

CALIFORNIA RESOURCES

California Reading Toolkit, p. L81
California Modified Lesson Plans for English Learners, p. 157
California Daily Standards Practice Transparencies, TT73
California Standards Enrichment Workbook, pp. 53–54
California Standards Planner and Lesson Plans, p. L153
California Online Test Practice
California Test Generator CD-ROM
California Easy Planner CD-ROM
California eEdition CD-ROM

Temple decoration, Chiang Mai, Thailand

Floating market, Bangkok, Thailand

2

Southeast Asian Nations Gain Independence

MAIN IDEA	WHY IT MATTERS NOW	TERMS & NAMES
ECONOMICS Former colonies in Southeast Asia worked to build new governments and economies.	The power and influence of the Pacific Rim nations are likely to expand during the next century.	• Ferdinand Marcos • Corazón Aquino • Aung San Suu Kyi • Sukarno • Suharto

CALIFORNIA STANDARDS

10.4.4 Describe the independence struggles of the colonized regions of the world, including the roles of leaders, such as Sun Yat-sen in China, and the roles of ideology and religion.

CST 2 Students analyze how change happens at different rates at different times; understand that some aspects can change while others remain the same; and understand that change is complicated and affects not only technology and politics but also values and beliefs.

SETTING THE STAGE World War II had a significant impact on the colonized groups of Southeast Asia. During the war, the Japanese seized much of Southeast Asia from the European nations that had controlled the region for many years. The Japanese conquest helped the people of Southeast Asia see that the Europeans were far from invincible. When the war ended, and the Japanese themselves had been forced out, many Southeast Asians refused to live again under European rule. They called for and won their independence, and a series of new nations emerged.

TAKING NOTES

Summarizing Use a chart to summarize the major challenges that Southeast Asian countries faced after independence.

Nation	Challenges Following Independence
The Philippines	
Burma	
Indonesia	

The Philippines Achieves Independence

The Philippines became the first of the world's colonies to achieve independence following World War II. The United States granted the Philippines independence in 1946, on the anniversary of its own Declaration of Independence, the Fourth of July.

The United States and the Philippines The Filipinos' immediate goals were to rebuild the economy and to restore the capital of Manila. The city had been badly damaged in World War II. The United States had promised the Philippines $620 million in war damages. However, the U.S. government insisted that Filipinos approve the Bell Act in order to get the money. This act would establish free trade between the United States and the Philippines for eight years, to be followed by gradually increasing tariffs. Filipinos were worried that American businesses would exploit the resources and environment of the Philippines. In spite of this concern, Filipinos approved the Bell Act and received their money.

The United States also wanted to maintain its military presence in the Philippines. With the onset of the Cold War (see Chapter 17), the United States needed to protect its interests in Asia. Both China and the Soviet Union were rivals of the United States at the time. Both were Pacific powers with bases close to allies of the United States and to resources vital to U.S. interests. Therefore, the United States demanded a 99-year lease on its military and naval bases in the Philippines. The bases, Clark Air Force Base and Subic Bay Naval Base near Manila, proved to be critical to the United States later in the staging of the Korean and Vietnam wars.

SECTION 2 PROGRAM RESOURCES

ALL STUDENTS

In-Depth Resources: Unit 5
- Guided Reading, p. 27

Formal Assessment
- Section Quiz, p. 315

ENGLISH LEARNERS

In-Depth Resources in Spanish
- Guided Reading, p. 141

Reading Study Guide (Spanish), p. 193
Reading Study Guide Audio CD (Spanish)

STRUGGLING READERS

In-Depth Resources: Unit 5
- Guided Reading, p. 27
- Building Vocabulary, p. 31
- Reteaching Activity, p. 46

Reading Study Guide, p. 193
Reading Study Guide Audio CD

GIFTED AND TALENTED STUDENTS

In-Depth Resources: Unit 5
- Primary Source: from *The Snap Revolution,* p. 36
- Literature: from *The Year of Living Dangerously,* p. 39

Electronic Library of Primary Sources
- "The Fall of President Marcos"

INTEGRATED TECHNOLOGY

eEdition CD-ROM
Power Presentations CD-ROM
Geography Transparencies
- GT34 Indonesia and Malaysia, 1945–1976

Electronic Library of Primary Sources
- "The Fall of President Marcos"

classzone.com

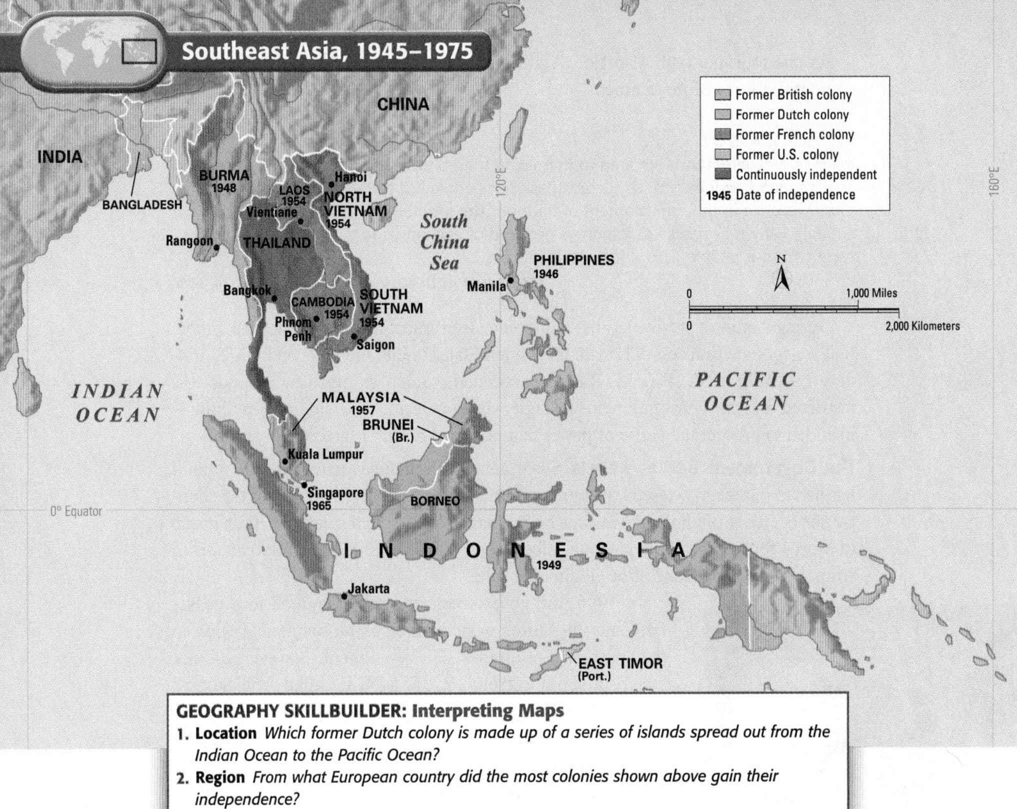

GEOGRAPHY SKILLBUILDER: Interpreting Maps

1. **Location** *Which former Dutch colony is made up of a series of islands spread out from the Indian Ocean to the Pacific Ocean?*
2. **Region** *From what European country did the most colonies shown above gain their independence?*

These military bases also became the single greatest source of conflict between the United States and the Philippines. Many Filipinos regarded the bases as proof of American imperialism. Later agreements shortened the terms of the lease, and the United States gave up both bases in 1992. (A)

MAIN IDEA
Making Inferences
(A) Why might the United States have been interested in maintaining military bases in the Philippines?
A. Possible Answer To protect its economic and political interests. The Philippines were located within striking distance of many potential hot spots in the region.

After World War II, the Philippine government was still almost completely dependent on the United States economically and politically. The Philippine government looked for ways to lessen this dependency. It welcomed Japanese investments. It also broadened its contacts with Southeast Asian neighbors and with nonaligned nations.

From Marcos to Ramos Ferdinand Marcos was elected president of the Philippines in 1965. The country suffered under his rule from 1966 to 1986. Marcos imposed an authoritarian regime and stole millions of dollars from the public treasury. Although the constitution limited Marcos to eight years in office, he got around this restriction by imposing martial law from 1972 to 1981. Two years later, his chief opponent, Benigno Aquino, Jr., was assassinated as he returned from the United States to the Philippines, lured by the promise of coming elections.

In the elections of 1986, Aquino's widow, **Corazón Aquino**, challenged Marcos. Aquino won decisively, but Marcos refused to acknowledge her victory. When he declared himself the official winner, a public outcry resulted. He was forced into exile in Hawaii, where he later died. In 1995, the Philippines succeeded in recovering $475 million Marcos had stolen from his country and deposited in Swiss banks.

History from Visuals

Interpreting the Map

Ask students to find the first and last nation to achieve independence. *(The Philippines, Singapore)* Which nation remained free? *(Thailand)*

Extension Have students look up, in an almanac or the *Statesman's Yearbook*, the trading partners of these nations. Ask students which nations continue to trade heavily with their former colonizers.

SKILLBUILDER Answers
1. **Location** Indonesia
2. **Region** France

Geography Transparencies
- GT34 Indonesia and Malaysia, 1945–1976

More About . . .

Benigno Aquino

The assassination of the popular Benigno Aquino was the catalyst for the downfall of Ferdinand Marcos. Aquino was gunned down moments after he landed in Manila on August 21, 1983. The public was outraged at the act and blamed Marcos for the murder. Huge demonstrations were staged, calling for new presidential elections. Aquino's widow Corazón ran on the ticket and won. Marcos refused to step down and eventually was driven out of the country.

Electronic Library of Primary Sources
- "The Fall of President Marcos"

DIFFERENTIATING INSTRUCTION: GIFTED AND TALENTED STUDENTS

The Story of Aquino's Victory

Class Time 45 minutes

Task Writing newspaper stories about the election of Corazón Aquino

Purpose To develop a historical perspective on a watershed event

Instructions Tell students that the 1986 Philippine presidential election was dramatic. Both Marcos and Aquino declared victory; international observers charged Marcos with voting fraud; supporters changed sides; and the public forced Marcos into exile. Huge rallies made news around the world. Ask students to imagine they are foreign correspondents covering the election. Have them write a story, or series of stories, for U.S. newspapers. In addition to using the primary source found in the In-Depth Resources, page 36, they may want to consult 1986 issues of newspapers and magazines for additional details. After students complete their stories, have them share the stories in discussion groups.

Name ____ Date ____

18 Section 2

PRIMARY SOURCE *from* The Snap Revolution
by James Fenton

Activity Options

36 Unit 5, Chapter 18

In-Depth Resources: Unit 5

British Colonies Gain Independence
10.4.4

Critical Thinking

- Why might military governments such as Burma's dislike democratic ideals? *(Possible Answer: military works by authority, rather than by consensus)*
- Why do you think ethnic groups in Malaya resisted British efforts to unite them? How is this similar to uniting people of different religions? *(Possible Answer: want separate identities; both problems require getting people to tolerate differences)*

History Makers

Aung San Suu Kyi

The military government in Burma offered Aung San Suu Kyi the chance for freedom if she would leave the country. Why did she not take the government's offer to free her? *(Possible Answer: She felt it would weaken her cause, especially after she'd gained the power of the Nobel Prize.)* Explain that she refused to leave until a civilian government was restored to Burma and all political prisoners were freed.

As she took the oath of office, Aquino promised to usher in a more open and democratic form of government.

PRIMARY SOURCE

I pledge a government dedicated to upholding truth and justice, morality and decency in government, freedom and democracy. I ask our people not to relax, but to maintain more vigilance in this, our moment of triumph. The Motherland can't thank them enough, yet we all realize that more is required of each of us to achieve a truly just society for our people. This is just the beginning.

CORAZÓN AQUINO, inaugural speech, Feb. 24, 1986

During Aquino's presidency, the Philippine government ratified a new constitution. It also negotiated successfully with the United States to end the lease on the U.S. military bases. In 1992, Fidel V. Ramos succeeded Aquino as president. Ramos was restricted by the constitution to a single six-year term. The single-term limit is intended to prevent the abuse of power that occurred during Marcos's 20-year rule.

The Government Battles Rebels Since gaining its independence, the Philippines has had to battle its own separatist group. For centuries, the southern part of the country has been a stronghold of Muslims known as the Moros. In the early 1970s, a group of Moros formed the Moro National Liberation Front (MNLF). They began an armed struggle for independence from Philippine rule.

In 1996, the government and rebels agreed to a cease-fire, and the Moros were granted an autonomous region in the southern Philippines. The agreement, however, did not satisfy a splinter group of the MNLF called Abu Sayyaf. These rebels have continued fighting the government, often using terror tactics to try to achieve their goals. In 2000, they kidnapped 21 people including foreign tourists. While the group eventually was freed, subsequent kidnappings by Abu Sayyaf have resulted in the death of several hostages. The current Philippines president, Gloria Macapagal Arroyo, has launched an all-out military response to this group. The United States has provided military assistance to the government's efforts.

History Makers

Aung San Suu Kyi
1945–

Aung San Suu Kyi won the Nobel Peace Prize in 1991 for her efforts to establish democracy in Myanmar. She could not accept the award in person, however, because she was still under house arrest.

The Nobel Prize committee said that in awarding her the peace prize, it intended:

> *to show its support for the many people throughout the world who are striving to attain democracy, human rights, and ethnic conciliation by peaceful means. Suu Kyi's struggle is one of the most extraordinary examples of civil courage in Asia in recent decades.*

British Colonies Gain Independence

Britain's timetable for granting independence to its Southeast Asian colonies depended on local circumstances. Burma had been pressing for independence from Britain for decades. It became a sovereign republic in 1948. In 1989, Burma was officially named Myanmar (myahn•MAH), its name in the Burmese language.

Burma Experiences Turmoil After gaining freedom, Burma suffered one political upheaval after another. Its people struggled between repressive military governments and pro-democracy forces. Conflict among Communists and ethnic minorities also disrupted the nation. In 1962, General Ne Win set up a military government, with the goal of making Burma a socialist state. Although Ne Win stepped down in 1988, the military continued to rule repressively.

In 1988, **Aung San Suu Kyi** (owng sahn soo chee) returned to Burma after many years abroad. She is the

DIFFERENTIATING INSTRUCTION: STRUGGLING READERS

Analyzing Geographic Impact

Class Time 15 minutes

Task Analyzing maps of Southeast Asia

Purpose To clarify the importance of geography to political and military strategies

Instructions Have students look at the map on page 571 and the map of Southeast Asia in the atlas at the front of this book. Explain that U.S. business has strong interests in Hong Kong, Singapore, and Indonesia. Have students note how close the Philippines is to these areas. Discuss why having military bases in the area would support the strategic and economic interests of the United States. If necessary, explain that the presence of these bases might discourage others in the region from interfering with U.S. interests. Ask students what international changes might have supported the United States' giving up the bases. Recall the end of the Cold War and discuss how it changed U.S. concerns about the area. Give students the outline map of the Pacific Region and ask them to circle and name the various countries in the region. Make sure they note the location of Hawaii and the West Coast of the United States.

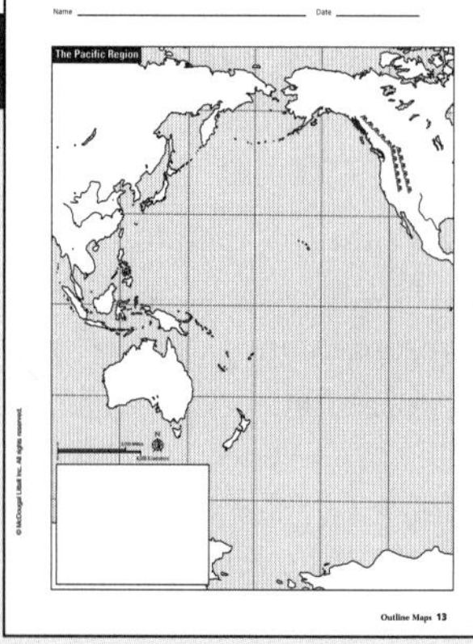

Geography Skills and Outline Maps

daughter of Aung San, a leader of the Burmese nationalists' army killed years before by political rivals. Aung San Suu Kyi became active in the newly formed National League for Democracy. For her pro-democracy activities, she was placed under house arrest for six years by the government. In the 1990 election—the country's first multiparty election in 30 years—the National League for Democracy won 80 percent of the seats. The military government refused to recognize the election, and it kept Aung San Suu Kyi under house arrest. She was finally released in 1995, only to be placed under house arrest again in 2000. Freed in 2002, she was detained again in 2003, leaving many residents to doubt whether Burma will embrace democracy anytime soon.

Vocabulary
House arrest is confinement to one's quarters, or house, rather than to prison.

Malaysia and Singapore During World War II, the Japanese conquered the Malay Peninsula, formerly ruled by the British. The British returned to the peninsula after the Japanese defeat in 1945. They tried, unsuccessfully, to organize the different peoples of Malaya into one state. They also struggled to put down a Communist uprising. Ethnic groups resisted British efforts to unite their colonies on the peninsula and in the northern part of the island of Borneo. Malays were a slight majority on the peninsula, while Chinese were the largest group on the southern tip, the island of Singapore.

In 1957, officials created the Federation of Malaya from Singapore, Malaya, Sarawak, and Sabah. The two regions—on the Malay Peninsula and on northern Borneo—were separated by 400 miles of ocean. In 1965, Singapore separated from the federation and became an independent city-state. The federation, consisting of Malaya, Sarawak, and Sabah, became known as Malaysia. A coalition of many ethnic groups maintained steady economic progress in Malaysia.

Singapore, which has one of the busiest ports in the world, has become an extremely prosperous nation. Lee Kuan Yew ruled Singapore as prime minister from 1959 to 1990. Under his guidance, Singapore emerged as a banking center as well as a center of trade. It had a standard of living far higher than any of its Southeast Asian neighbors. In 1997, the Geneva World Economic Forum listed the world's strongest economies. Singapore topped the list. It was followed, in order, by Hong Kong, the United States, Canada, New Zealand, Switzerland, and Great Britain. (B)

B. Possible Answer
They are capitalist economies.

MAIN IDEA
Making Inferences
(B) What do the top economies listed by the Geneva World Economic Forum have in common?

▼ A glittering skyline rises above the bustling harbor of Singapore.

Vocabulary Note
Explain that in this context, the term *house arrest* refers to confinement at home.

More About . . .

New Economies
Gross domestic product (GDP) is one way that economists measure prosperity in a nation. They measure the dollar value of the goods and services a nation produces. To find the GDP per capita, economists divide the GDP by the number of workers in a nation. In 1965, soon after independence, Singapore had a GDP per capita under $1,000. By 1991, this tiny nation had a GDP per capita of about $13,000. In 2001 the figure was $20,544. The Philippines' GDP per capita was under $1,000 in 1965 and changed very little in the years to 1991. By 2001 that number was $1,240. Ask students how they think Singapore's busy port may have helped it build prosperity. *(through shipping trade)*

COOPERATIVE LEARNING

Creating a Brochure
Class Time 45 minutes

Task Creating a brochure promoting Singapore

Purpose To study one Southeast Asian nation in depth.

Instructions Organize students in groups of four. Ask each group to research a different aspect of Singapore. Possibilities are:

- standard of living
- cultural life
- business opportunities
- government

After students complete their research, have groups create a section of a brochure promoting the city-state. Before beginning, the class should decide on the intended audience. Each group should name a researcher, a writer-editor, a designer-illustrator, and a producer, who will meet with like members from the other groups to coordinate their efforts. Remind students that their brochures should

- be tailored to the intended audience.
- show evidence of careful research.
- be written clearly and concisely.
- convey visual information clearly.

Indonesia Gains Independence from the Dutch
10.4.4

Critical Thinking

- Why do you think the U.S. and UN supported Indonesia's independence? *(Possible Answer: believed Indonesia deserved self-determination)*
- What are the possible challenges to uniting Indonesia? *(Possible Answer: geography, ethnic tensions, language barriers, religious hatreds)*

In-Depth Resources: Unit 5

- Literature: from *The Year of Living Dangerously,* p. 39

Tip for English Learners

Review and explain colloquial language from the page, for example: *bloodbath, police state, rules of the game,* and *main pillars of democracy.*

More About . . .

Megawati Sukarnoputri

Like Aun San Suu Kyi, Megawati Sukarnoputri is the daughter of a national hero. Her father Sukarno led Indonesia to independence. In 2001 she was appointed president of Indonesia, after her term as vice president. She came to power after President Wahid was driven from power on charges of corruption. Megawati has strong grass-roots support and is viewed as a corruption-free individual.

Indonesia Gains Independence from the Dutch

Like members of other European nations, the Dutch, who ruled the area of Southeast Asia known as Indonesia, saw their colonial empire crumble with the onset of World War II. The Japanese conquered the region and destroyed the Dutch colonial order. When the war ended and the defeated Japanese were forced to leave, the people of Indonesia moved to establish a free nation.

Sukarno Leads the Independence Movement Leading the effort to establish an independent Indonesia was **Sukarno** (soo•KAHR•noh), known only by his one name. In August 1945, two days after the Japanese surrendered, Sukarno proclaimed Indonesia's independence and named himself president. A guerrilla army backed him. The Dutch, supported initially by Britain and the United States, attempted to regain control of Indonesia. But after losing the support of the United Nations and the United States, the Dutch agreed to grant Indonesia its independence in 1949.

The new Indonesia became the world's fourth most populous nation. It consisted of more than 13,600 islands, with 300 different ethnic groups, 250 languages, and most of the world's major religions. It contained the world's largest Islamic population. Sukarno, who took the official title of "life-time president," attempted to guide this diverse nation in a parliamentary democracy.

Instability and Turmoil Sukarno's efforts to build a stable democratic nation were unsuccessful. He was not able to manage Indonesia's economy, and the country slid downhill rapidly. Foreign banks refused to lend money to Indonesia and inflation occasionally soared as high as one thousand percent. In 1965, a group of junior army officers attempted a coup. A general named **Suharto** (suh•HAHR•toh) put down the rebellion. He then seized power for himself and began a bloodbath in which 500,000 to 1 million Indonesians were killed.

Vocabulary
A *coup* is the sudden overthrow of a government by a small group of people.

Suharto, officially named president in 1967, turned Indonesia into a police state and imposed frequent periods of martial law. Outside observers heavily criticized him for his annexation of nearby East Timor in 1976 and for human rights violations there. (See the map on page 571.) Suharto's government also showed little tolerance for religious freedoms.

Bribery and corruption became commonplace. The economy improved under Suharto for a while but from 1997 through 1998 the nation suffered one of the worst financial crises in its history. Growing unrest over both government repression and a crippling economic crisis prompted Suharto to step down in 1998. While turmoil continued to grip the country, it moved slowly toward democracy. The daughter of Sukarno, Megawati Sukarnoputri, was elected to the presidency in 2001.

Upon taking office, the new president hailed the virtues of democracy and urged her fellow Indonesians to do what they could to maintain such a form of government:

C. Answer respect for the people's voice and respect for the rule of law

PRIMARY SOURCE C

Democracy requires sincerity and respect for the rules of the game. Beginning my duty, I urge all groups to sincerely and openly accept the outcome of the democratic process . . . . In my opinion, respect for the people's voice, sincerity in accepting it, and respect for the rules of game are the main pillars of democracy which we will further develop. I urge all Indonesians to look forward to the future and unite to improve the life and our dignity as a nation.

MEGAWATI SUKARNOPUTRI, July 23, 2001

MAIN IDEA

Analyzing Primary Sources

C What are the cornerstones of democracy, according to Sukarnoputri?

DIFFERENTIATING INSTRUCTION: ENGLISH LEARNERS

Clarifying Sequence

Class Time 20 minutes

Task Arranging events in sequential order

Purpose To trace the sequence in which Southeast Asian nations achieved independence and to highlight related challenges

Instructions Review the section material with students, using the Spanish editions of the Guided Reading worksheet and Reading Study Guide. Then organize students in groups of six.

Have groups list the nations discussed in this chapter:

- the Philippines
- Malaysia
- East Timor
- Singapore
- Burma/Myanmar
- Indonesia

Tell group members to arrange themselves in the order in which these six nations achieved independence. Then ask each student to make a statement telling when, how, and from whom his or her country achieved independence.

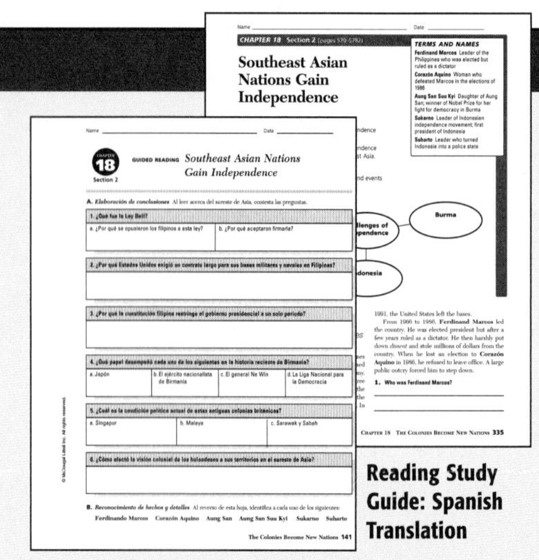
Southeast Asian Nations Gain Independence

Southeast Asian Nations Gain Independence

Reading Study Guide: Spanish Translation

In-Depth Resources in Spanish

Sukarnoputri faces enormous challenges, including a still-fragile economy, ethnic strife, security problems, and a government still hobbled by corruption.

East Timor Wins Independence As Indonesia worked to overcome its numerous obstacles, it lost control of East Timor. Indonesian forces had ruled the land with brutal force since Suharto seized it in the 1970s. The East Timorese, however, never stopped pushing to regain their freedom. Jose Ramos Horta, an East Timorese independence campaigner, won the 1996 Nobel Peace Prize (along with East Timor's Roman Catholic bishop) for his efforts to gain independence for the region without violence.

In a United Nations-sponsored referendum held in August 1999, the East Timorese voted overwhelmingly for independence. The election angered pro-Indonesian forces in the region. They ignored the referendum results and went on a bloody rampage. They killed hundreds and forced thousands into refugee camps in West Timor, which is a part of Indonesia. UN intervention forces eventually brought peace to the area. In 2002 East Timor celebrated independence.

As on the Indian subcontinent, violence and struggle were part of the transition in Southeast Asia from colonies to free nations. The same would be true in Africa, where numerous former colonies shed European rule and created independent countries in the wake of World War II.

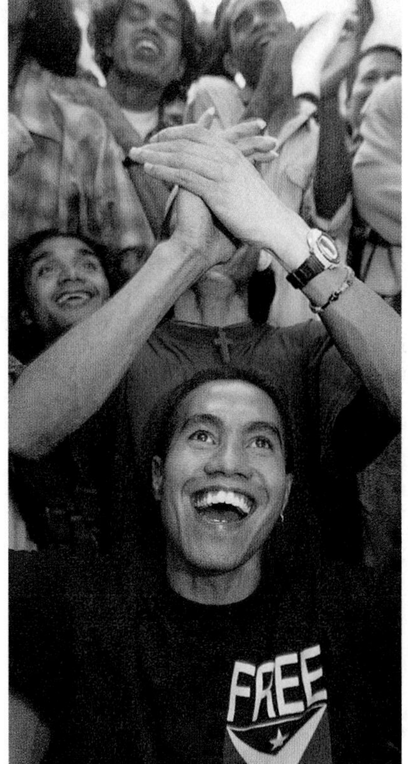

▲ East Timorese celebrate their overwhelming vote for independence in 1999.

SECTION 2 ASSESSMENT

TERMS & NAMES 1. For each term or name, write a sentence explaining its significance.
• Ferdinand Marcos • Corazón Aquino • Aung San Suu Kyi • Sukarno • Suharto

USING YOUR NOTES

2. Which nation faced the greatest challenges? Why? (10.4.4)

Nation	Challenges Following Independence
The Philippines	
Burma	
Indonesia	

MAIN IDEAS

3. Why did the retention of U.S. military bases in the Philippines so anger Filipinos? (10.4.4)
4. What was the outcome of the 1990 Myanmar election? How did the government respond? (10.4.4)
5. How did Suharto come to power in Indonesia? (10.4.4)

CRITICAL THINKING & WRITING

6. **CLARIFYING** How did World War II play a role in the eventual decolonization of Southeast Asia? (10.4.4)
7. **MAKING INFERENCES** Why do you think that the United States demanded a 99-year lease on military and naval bases in the Philippines? (10.4.4)
8. **COMPARING AND CONTRASTING** What was similar and different about the elections that brought defeat to the ruling governments in the Philippines and in Burma? (10.4.4)
9. **WRITING ACTIVITY** ECONOMICS Write a two-paragraph **expository essay** contrasting Singapore's economy with others in Southeast Asia. (Writing 2.3.a)

CONNECT TO TODAY CREATING A TELEVISION NEWS SCRIPT

Locate several of the most recent news articles about one of the countries discussed in this section. Combine the stories into a brief television **news script** and present it to the class. (Writing 2.3.b)

More About . . .

East Timor

Before Indonesia took control of East Timor, the island had seen other colonizers. The Portuguese arrived in the early 1500s, followed soon after by the Spanish. Britain also had a short period of control over Timor. However, apart from Japanese occupation during World War II, the Portuguese mostly retained control of East Timor. Indonesian forces then invaded in 1976 and absorbed East Timor as a province. Unlike Indonesia, where religious differences abound, most East Timorese are Christian.

3 ASSESS

SECTION 2 ASSESSMENT

Have students work in pairs. One partner can read the section assessment questions aloud as the other partner lists pages from the section where the answers can be found.

Formal Assessment
• Section Quiz, p. 315

4 RETEACH

Have students exchange the charts they made for item 2 in the assessment. Together, review the charts to help students understand the challenges of newly independent countries.

In-Depth Resources: Unit 5
• Reteaching Activity, p. 46

ANSWERS

1. Ferdinand Marcos, p. 571 • Corazón Aquino, p. 571 • Aung San Suu Kyi, p. 572 • Sukarno, p. 574 • Suharto, p. 574
2. **Sample Answer:** Philippines—Election corruption, power abuse, rebel groups; Burma—Repressive military; Malaysia—Ethnic differences, Communist uprising; Indonesia—Many islands, ethnic groups, languages, religions; East Timor—Conflict over independence. **Possible Answer**: Indonesia, due to size and diversity
3. many saw bases as imperialistic
4. National League for Democracy gained majority, but military refused to honor results and arrested NLD leader.
5. seized power after foiling a coup attempt
6. Japanese occupied area and ejected previous colonial powers.
7. to protect U.S. economic and political interests; to remind surrounding nations of U.S. military force
8. both governments ignored results; Philippine government finally stepped down, Myanmar retained power.
9. **Rubric** Expository essays should
• clearly convey contrasts.
• reflect full understanding of topic.

CONNECT TO TODAY

Rubric Scripts should
• be well organized and easy to follow.
• stress main points of each event.
• support main points with details.

Social History

OBJECTIVES

- Explain how the past and present coexist in Southeast Asia.
- Summarize population and economic information about Southeast Asia.

FOCUS & MOTIVATE

Ask students which of the photographs on these pages show Southeast Asia the way they envision it. Which photographs are the most surprising? Why?

INSTRUCT

Critical Thinking

- What problems might face rural Thais when they visit cities such as Bangkok? *(Possible Answer: unfamiliarity with traffic, noise, and crowding)*
- What characteristics of Indonesian housing indicate a gap between rich and poor? *(Possible Answer: high-rise, modern tower next to decrepit shacks)*

Changing Times in Southeast Asia

As you have read, many countries in Southeast Asia have undergone revolutionary changes in their political and social organization. The region continues to struggle with its past and to face new challenges, but democratic reforms are becoming more common.

The past and present exist side by side throughout much of Southeast Asia. For an increasing number of Southeast Asians, housing, transportation, even purchasing food are a mixture of old and new. These images explore the differences between traditional and modern, rich and poor, past and present.

INTEGRATED TECHNOLOGY

RESEARCH LINKS For more on life in Southeast Asia, go to **classzone.com**

CALIFORNIA STANDARDS
10.11, CST 4

▲▼ Transportation
The water buffalo-drawn cart (shown above) is a common sight in rural Thailand. It is a mode of transport that reaches deep into the past.

In Bangkok, Thailand (shown below)—with its cars, motorcycles, and public buses—transportation is a very different thing. These distinctly past and present modes of transportation symbolize the changes many Southeast Asian countries are facing.

◄ Housing
The luxury apartment building (background) in Jakarta, Indonesia, towers over the shabby and polluted slum of Muarabaru (foreground). Indonesia declared its independence in 1945, but was not recognized by the United Nations until 1950. Since independence, Indonesians have enjoyed relative economic prosperity, but bridging the gap between rich and poor is an issue that faces Indonesia and much of Southeast Asia.

RECOMMENDED RESOURCES

Books

Dick, H. W., and Peter J. Rimmer. ***Cities, Transport and Communications: The Integration of Southeast Asia Since 1850.*** New York: Macmillan, 2003. A study of the impact of globalization on the cities of Southeast Asia.

Fahn, James David. ***A Land on Fire: The Environmental Consequences of the Southeast Asian Boom.*** Boulder, CO: Westview, 2003. Southeast Asia's fight to protect the environment.

Litvack, Jennie I., and Denis A. Rondinelli. ***Market Reform in Vietnam.*** Westport, CT: Quorum, 1999.

Videos

Bangkok. VHS. Library Video Company, 1994. 800-843-3620. The many contrasts of Bangkok, from its Buddhist temples to its business districts and open-air markets.

Indonesia: Urban Development in Jakarta. VHS and DVD. Films for the Humanities and Sciences, 1996. 800-257-5126. Follows a day in the life of a 12-year-old boy.

Living in Vietnam. VHS. Library Video Company, 2001. 800-843-3620.

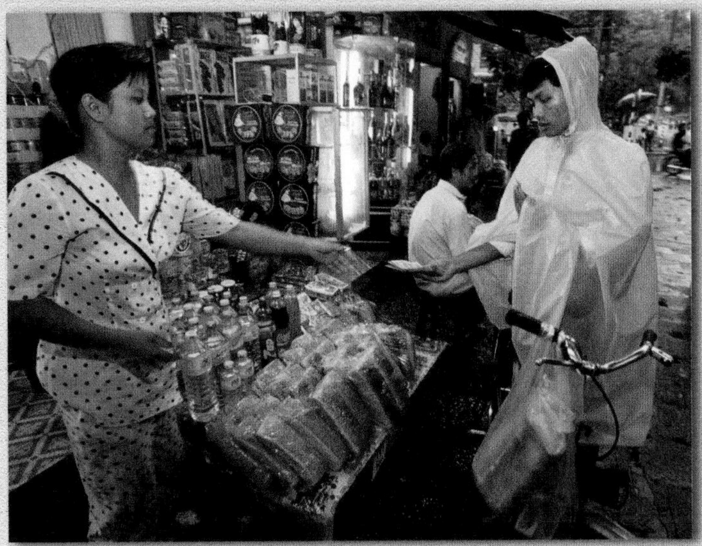

▲▼ Markets

As the post-colonial economies of Southeast Asia grow, traditional markets, like the floating market in Thailand (shown below), give way to the modern convenience of stores with prepackaged foods, like this street-side store (above) in Vietnam.

> DATA FILE

SOUTHEAST ASIA

Geography

- Eleven countries are generally referred to as Southeast Asia: Brunei, Cambodia, East Timor, Indonesia, Laos, Malaysia, Myanmar, the Philippines, Singapore, Thailand, and Vietnam.

Population

- About 8 percent of the world's population lives in Southeast Asia.
- Indonesia is the world's fourth most populous country, behind China, India, and the United States.

Economics

- Ten Southeast Asian nations—Indonesia, Malaysia, the Philippines, Singapore, Brunei, Cambodia, Laos, Vietnam, Myanmar, and Thailand—make up a trading alliance known as the Association of South-East Asian Nations (ASEAN)

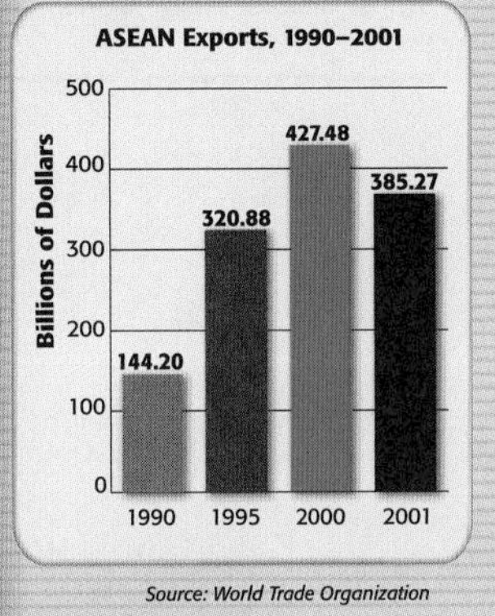

Source: World Trade Organization

Connect *to* Today

1. **Drawing Conclusions** Why might some countries in Southeast Asia have more successful economies than others?
   See Skillbuilder Handbook, page R10.
2. **Forming and Supporting Opinions** Are the issues facing Southeast Asians discussed here also a concern for Americans? Why or why not?

More About . . .

Transportation in Thailand

Thailand's waterways offer a method of transportation that bridges the past and present. The Thai people have used the rivers of the Chao Phraya delta since ancient times. Today, they've added man-made canals to expand water transportation. This is important because, while the road system is growing, Thailand's rainy climate often floods the roadways. Helicopters and airplanes also offer access to very mountainous areas.

More About . . .

ASEAN

In addition to the five founding members, ASEAN also includes Vietnam, Laos, Myanmar, Cambodia, and Brunei. Together these nations represent 500 million people and gross domestic products of $737 billion. The member nations' total trade is worth $720 billion. ASEAN works hard to secure unity amongst member nations. Unity helps the organization gain strong economic bargaining power around the world. In addition, after joining the organization, the member nations have avoided military confrontation among themselves.

CONNECT TO TODAY: ANSWERS

1. Drawing Conclusions

Possible Answer: The countries of the Association of South-East Asian Nations (ASEAN) might be more prosperous because they are part of a trading alliance.

2. Forming and Supporting Opinions

Possible Answer: Bridging the gap between rich and poor is a problem facing Americans, though perhaps less dramatically. U.S. transportation systems are fairly modern throughout the nation, but modern markets are displacing farmer's markets and family-owned stores in some places. In other places, farmer's markets have made a comeback as Americans seek fresh or organic produce.

LESSON PLAN

OBJECTIVES

- Identify factors affecting the success of African independence efforts.
- Describe the independence of Ghana and Kenya.
- Explain civil wars and independence struggles in Congo and Angola.

1 FOCUS & MOTIVATE

Tell students that many newly independent African nations struggled under rulers who would not share power. How does the U.S. government create shared power? *(Possible Answer: Constitution mandates three branches and shared power with states.)*

2 INSTRUCT

Achieving Independence
10.9.4

Critical Thinking

- How were the struggles of newly independent nations in Africa and Southeast Asia similar? *(Both began after World War II and both had ethnic divisions.)*

CALIFORNIA RESOURCES
California Reading Toolkit, p. L82
California Modified Lesson Plans for English Learners, p. 159
California Daily Standards Practice Transparencies, TT74
California Standards Enrichment Workbook, pp. 53–54, 93–94
California Standards Planner and Lesson Plans, p. L155
California Online Test Practice
California Test Generator CD-ROM
California Easy Planner CD-ROM
California eEdition CD-ROM

Temple decoration, Chiang Mai, Thailand

3

Floating market, Bangkok, Thailand

New Nations in Africa

MAIN IDEA	WHY IT MATTERS NOW	TERMS & NAMES
REVOLUTION After World War II, African leaders threw off colonial rule and created independent countries.	Today, many of those independent countries are engaged in building political and economic stability.	• Negritude movement • Kwame Nkrumah • Jomo Kenyatta • Ahmed Ben Bella • Mobutu Sese Seko

CALIFORNIA STANDARDS

10.4.4 Describe the independence struggles of the colonized regions of the world, including the roles of leaders, such as Sun Yat-sen in China, and the roles of ideology and religion.

10.9.2 Analyze the causes of the Cold War, with the free world on one side and Soviet client states on the other, including competition for influence in such places as Egypt, the Congo, Vietnam, and Chile.

SETTING THE STAGE Throughout the first half of the 20th century, Africa resembled little more than a European outpost. As you recall, the nations of Europe had marched in during the late 1800s and colonized much of the continent. Like the diverse groups living in Asia, however, the many different peoples of Africa were unwilling to return to colonial domination after World War II. And so, in the decades following the great global conflict, they, too, won their independence from foreign rule and went to work building new nations.

Achieving Independence

The African push for independence actually began in the decades before World War II. French-speaking Africans and West Indians began to express their growing sense of black consciousness and pride in traditional Africa. They formed the **Negritude movement**, a movement to celebrate African culture, heritage, and values.

When World War II erupted, African soldiers fought alongside Europeans to "defend freedom." This experience made them unwilling to accept colonial domination when they returned home. The war had changed the thinking of Europeans too. Many began to question the cost, as well as the morality, of maintaining colonies abroad. These and other factors helped African colonies gain their freedom throughout the 1950s and 1960s.

TAKING NOTES
Clarifying Use a chart to list an idea, an event, or a leader important to that country's history.

Ghana	
Kenya	
Zaire	
Algeria	
Angola	

The ways in which African nations achieved independence, however, differed across the continent. In Chapter 11, you learned that European nations employed two basic styles of government in colonial Africa—direct and indirect. Under indirect rule, local officials did much of the governing and colonists enjoyed limited self-rule. As a result, these colonies generally experienced an easier transition to independence. For colonies under direct rule, in which foreigners governed at all levels and no self-rule existed, independence came with more difficulty. Some colonies even had to fight wars of liberation, as European settlers refused to surrender power to African nationalist groups.

No matter how they gained their freedom, however, most new African nations found the road to a strong and stable nation to be difficult. They had to deal with everything from creating a new government to establishing a postcolonial economy. Many new countries were also plagued by great ethnic strife. In colonizing Africa, the Europeans had created artificial borders that had little to

SECTION 3 PROGRAM RESOURCES

ALL STUDENTS

In-Depth Resources: Unit 5
- Guided Reading, p. 28
- Skillbuilder Practice, p. 32
- Geography Application, p. 33
- History Makers: Jomo Kenyatta, p. 42

Formal Assessment
- Section Quiz, p. 316

ENGLISH LEARNERS

In-Depth Resources in Spanish
- Guided Reading, p. 142
- Skillbuilder Practice, p. 144
- Geography Application, p. 145

Reading Study Guide (Spanish), p. 195
Reading Study Guide Audio CD (Spanish)

STRUGGLING READERS

In-Depth Resources: Unit 5
- Guided Reading, p. 28
- Building Vocabulary, p. 31
- Skillbuilder Practice, p. 32
- Geography Application, p. 33
- Reteaching Activity, p. 47

Reading Study Guide, p. 195
Reading Study Guide Audio CD

GIFTED AND TALENTED STUDENTS

In-Depth Resources: Unit 5
- Primary Source: Farewell Without Tears, p. 37
- Literature: Négritude poems, p. 40
- Connections Across Time and Cultures: Becoming a New Nation, p. 44

INTEGRATED TECHNOLOGY

eEdition CD-ROM
Power Presentations CD-ROM
classzone.com

do with the areas where ethnic groups actually lived. While national borders separated people with similar cultures, they also enclosed traditional enemies who began fighting each other soon after the Europeans left. For many African nations, all of this led to instability, violence, and an overall struggle to deal with their newly gained independence.

Ghana Leads the Way

The British colony of the Gold Coast became the first African colony south of the Sahara to achieve independence. Following World War II, the British in the Gold Coast began making preparations. For example, they allowed more Africans to be nominated to the Legislative Council. However, the Africans wanted full freedom. The leader of their largely nonviolent movement was **Kwame Nkrumah** (KWAH•mee uhn•KROO•muh). Starting in 1947, he worked to liberate the Gold Coast from the British. Nkrumah organized strikes and boycotts and was often imprisoned by the British government. Ultimately, his efforts were successful.

On receiving its independence in 1957, the Gold Coast took the name Ghana. This name honored a famous West African kingdom of the past. Nkrumah became Ghana's first prime minister and later its president-for-life. Nkrumah pushed through new roads, new schools, and expanded health facilities. These costly projects soon crippled the country. His programs for industrialization, health and welfare, and expanded educational facilities showed good intentions. However, the expense of the programs undermined the economy and strengthened his opposition.

Vocabulary
Pan-African refers to a vision of strengthening all of Africa, not just a single country.

In addition, Nkrumah was often criticized for spending too much time on Pan-African efforts and neglecting economic problems in his own country. He dreamed of a "United States of Africa." In 1966, while Nkrumah was in China, the army and police in Ghana seized power. Since then, the country has shifted back and forth between civilian and military rule and has struggled for economic stability. In 2000, Ghana held its first open elections.

History Makers

Jomo Kenyatta
1891–1978

A man willing to spend years in jail for his beliefs, Kenyatta viewed independence as the only option for Africans.

> *The African can only advance to a "higher level" if he is free to express himself, to organize economically, politically and socially, and to take part in the government of his own country.*

On the official day that freedom finally came to Kenya, December 12, 1963, Kenyatta recalls watching with overwhelming delight as the British flag came down and the new flag of Kenya rose up. He called it "the greatest day in Kenya's history and the happiest day in my life."

INTEGRATED TECHNOLOGY

RESEARCH LINKS For more on Jomo Kenyatta, go to **classzone.com**

Fighting for Freedom

In contrast to Ghana, nations such as Kenya and Algeria had to take up arms against their European rulers in order to ultimately win their freedom.

A. Answer The British granted Ghana its independence peacefully, while British settlers in Kenya fought to remain in control.

MAIN IDEA
Contrasting
A How did the granting of independence to the British colonies of Ghana and Kenya differ?

Kenya Claims Independence The British ruled Kenya, and many British settlers resisted Kenyan independence—especially those who had taken over prize farmland in the northern highlands of the country. They were forced to accept African self-government as a result of two developments. One was the strong leadership of Kenyan nationalist **Jomo Kenyatta**. The second was the rise of a group known as the Mau Mau (MOW mow). This was a secret society made up mostly of native Kenyan farmers forced out of the highlands by the British. **A**

Using guerrilla war tactics, the Mau Mau sought to push the white farmers into leaving the highlands. Kenyatta claimed to have no connection to the Mau Mau. However, he refused to condemn the organization. As a result, the

Ghana Leads the Way
10.4.4

Critical Thinking

- What might be the advantages to having a president for life? *(Possible Answer: able to follow through on agenda or major changes)*
- What might be the advantages of a United States of Africa? *(Possible Answer: global bargaining power in economic and political matters)*

History Makers

Jomo Kenyatta

Ask what students think Kenyatta meant by the quote. *(that Africans could achieve more if they were allowed the freedoms other people had)*

Kenyatta's policies and approach were quite successful—Kenya's economy grew dramatically in the 20 years after independence.

In-Depth Resources: Unit 5

- History Makers: Jomo Kenyatta, p. 42
- Connections Across Time and Cultures, p. 44

Fighting for Freedom
10.4.4

Critical Thinking

- Why were the British willing to let Ghana go, but not Kenya? *(British colonists living there opposed it.)*
- How might unemployment in Algeria lead to the rise of Islamic fundamentalism? *(Possible Answer: It may have offered answers or solutions to their dissatisfaction.)*

SKILLBUILDER PRACTICE: EVALUATING DECISIONS AND COURSES OF ACTION

Analyzing Historical Decisions

Class Time 20 minutes

Task Developing opinions in response to decisions made by a historical leader

Purpose To practice the skill of evaluating decisions and courses of action

Instructions Historians look at decisions made in the past and evaluate both their short-term and long-term consequences. For example, historians still debate President Truman's decision to use the atomic bomb to end the war with Japan. Ask students to read the paragraphs under "Ghana Leads the Way." Then ask them the following questions:

1. For what sorts of programs in Ghana was Nkrumah criticized? *(roads, schools, health facilities)* Do you think the criticism was justified? *(Answers will vary.)*
2. What were other criticisms of Nkrumah? *(spending too much time on Pan-African efforts and neglecting economic problems in Ghana)*
3. What are alternative ways Nkrumah might have handled the economy? *(Possible Answer: He might have put emphasis on strengthening the economy rather than on expensive development plans and projects.)*

Have students use the Skillbuilder Practice worksheet for more examples and practice.

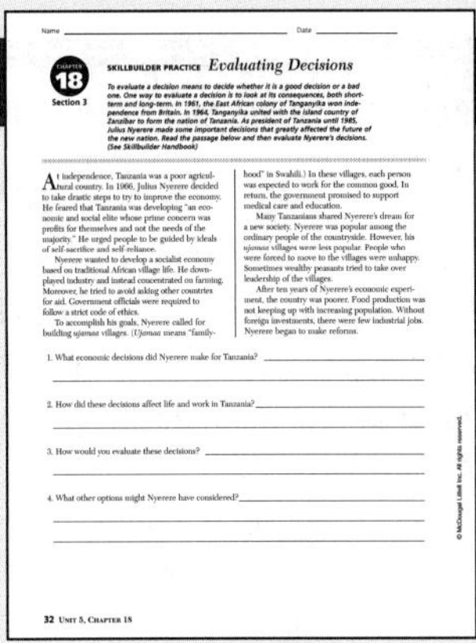

In-Depth Resources: Unit 5

History from Visuals

Interpreting the Maps

Ask students to identify the countries that were created out of 1955 French West Africa. *(Senegal, Mauritania, Mali, Niger, Upper Volta, Guinea, Ivory Coast)*

Extension Have students use an almanac or other reference tool to determine the present status of the colonies shown on the 1975 map.

SKILLBUILDER Answers

1. **Place** Libya, Egypt, Ethiopia, South Africa, Liberia
2. **Location** 1960s

INTEGRATED TECHNOLOGY

Interactive These images are available in an interactive format on the eEdition.

Tip for Struggling Readers

Some students may benefit from viewing the map information in list format. Have them set up a three-column chart with headings "Independent Nation," "Original Colony," and "Date of Independence." Students can then complete the chart with information from the two maps.

Independent Nation	Original Colony	Date of Independence
Chad	French Equatorial Africa	1960

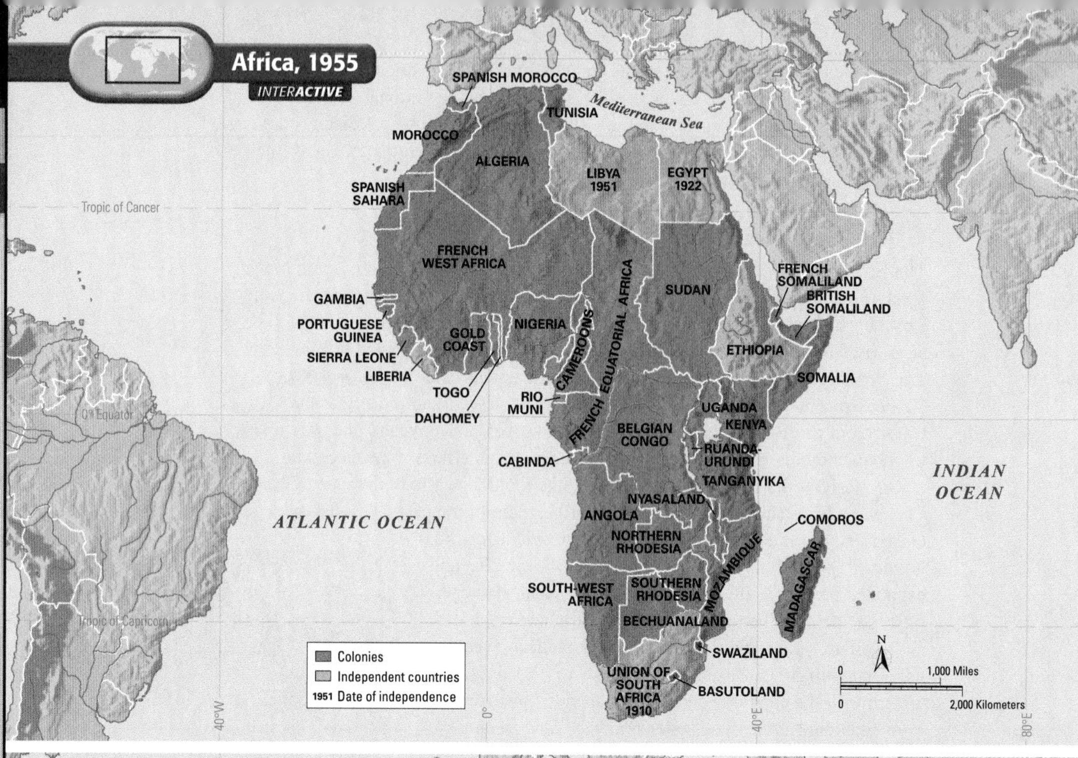

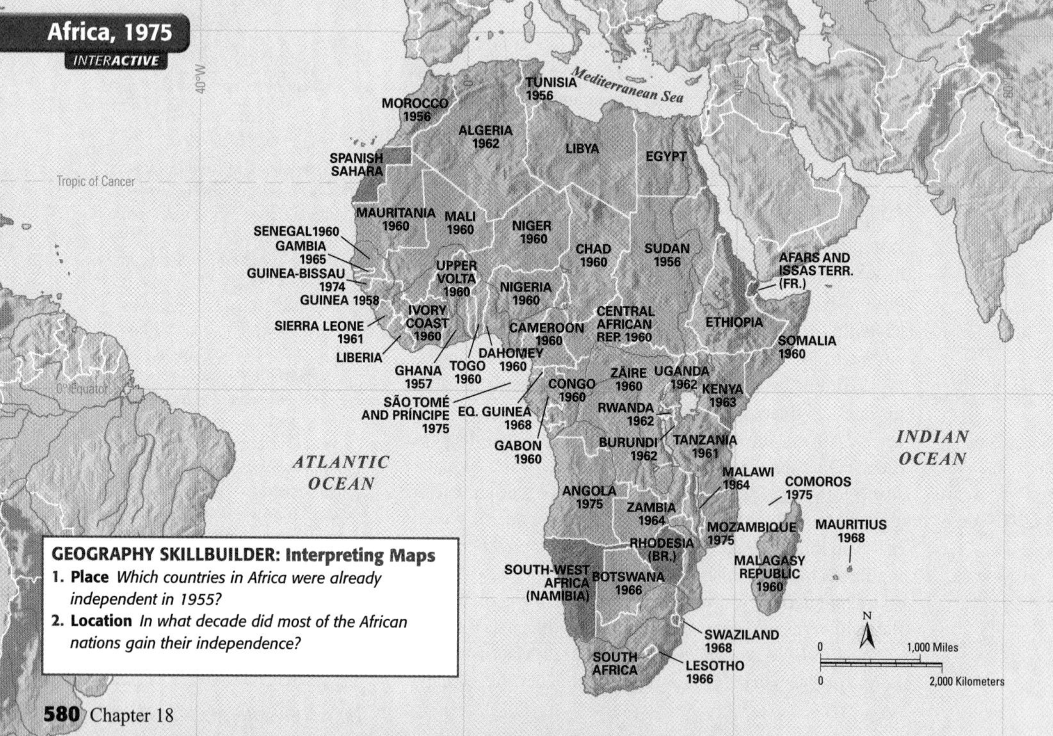

GEOGRAPHY SKILLBUILDER: Interpreting Maps

1. **Place** *Which countries in Africa were already independent in 1955?*
2. **Location** *In what decade did most of the African nations gain their independence?*

DIFFERENTIATING INSTRUCTION: ENGLISH LEARNERS

Analyzing the Congo Crisis

Class Time 20 minutes

Task Examining a map to explore the movement of various groups in the Congo crisis from 1960 to 1965

Purpose To use maps as a vehicle to describe activities in the Congo crisis

Instructions Make copies or transparencies of the Chapter 34 Geography Application map. Then have students help you make a list of the participants in the Congo crisis and of the movement of troops during the rebellions of 1960–1965. If you are using a transparency, have individual students point out:

- various points of the rebel advance.
- railways.
- centers of rebellion.
- UN troop bases.
- sites of intervention by Belgian paratroopers.

Ask students to comment on the political situation in the Congo at this time. Why were so many different groups involved in the fighting?

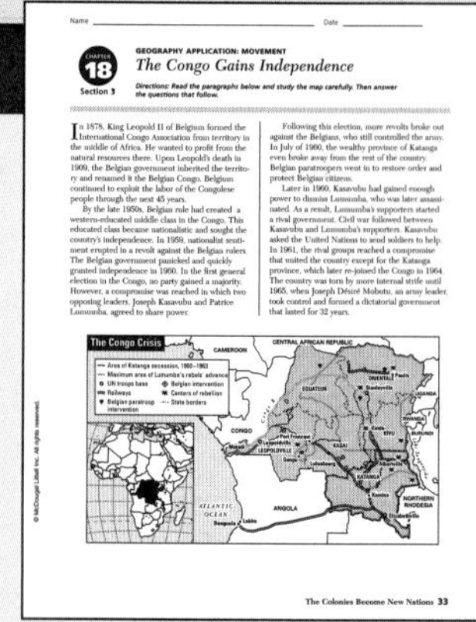

In-Depth Resources: Unit 5

British imprisoned him for nearly a decade. By the time the British granted Kenya independence in 1963, more than 10,000 Africans and 100 settlers had been killed.

Kenyatta became president of the new nation. He worked hard to unite the country's various ethnic and language groups. Kenyatta died in 1978. His successor, Daniel arap Moi, was less successful in governing the country. Moi faced increasing opposition to his one-party rule. Adding to the nation's woes were corruption in Moi's government and ethnic conflicts that killed hundreds and left thousands homeless. Moi stepped down in 2002, and a new party gained power through free elections.

Algeria Struggles with Independence France's principal overseas colony, Algeria, had a population of one million French colonists and nine million Arabs and Berber Muslims. After World War II, the French colonists refused to share political power with the native Algerians. In 1954, the Algerian National Liberation Front, or FLN, announced its intention to fight for independence. The French sent about half a million troops into Algeria to fight the FLN. Both sides committed atrocities. The FLN prevailed, and Algeria gained its independence in July 1962.

The leader of the FLN, **Ahmed Ben Bella**, became first president of the newly independent Algeria. He attempted to make Algeria a socialist state, but was overthrown in 1965 by his army commander. From 1965 until 1988, Algerians tried unsuccessfully to modernize and industrialize the nation. Unemployment and dissatisfaction with the government contributed to the rise of religious fundamentalists who wanted to make Algeria an Islamic state. The chief Islamic party, the Islamic Salvation Front (FIS), won local and parliamentary elections in 1990 and 1991. However, the ruling government and army refused to accept the election results. As a result, a civil war broke out between Islamic militants and the government. The war continues, on and off, to this day.

Civil War in Congo and Angola

Civil war also plagued the new nations of Congo and Angola. Congo's problems lay in its corrupt dictatorship and hostile ethnic groups. Meanwhile, Angola's difficulties stemmed from intense political differences.

B. Answer The Belgians left it with a ruined economy and no social services, and provided no preparation for independence.

MAIN IDEA

Recognizing Effects

B Why was the Congo vulnerable to turmoil after independence?

Freedom and Turmoil for Congo Of all the European possessions in Africa, one of the most exploited was the Belgian Congo. Belgium had ruthlessly plundered the colony's rich resources of rubber and copper. In addition, Belgian officials ruled with a harsh hand and provided the population with no social services. They also had made no attempt to prepare the people for independence. Not surprisingly, Belgium's granting of independence in 1960 to the Congo (known as Zaire from 1971 to 1997) resulted in upheaval. B

After years of civil war, an army officer, Colonel Joseph Mobutu, later known as **Mobutu Sese Seko** (moh•BOO•too SAY•say SAY•koh), seized power in 1965. For 32 years, Mobutu ruled the country that he renamed Zaire. He maintained control though a combination of force, one-party rule, and gifts to supporters. Mobutu successfully withstood several armed rebellions. He was finally overthrown in 1997 by rebel leader Laurent Kabila after months of civil war. Shortly thereafter, the country was renamed the Democratic Republic of the Congo.

▲ Mobuto Sese Seko

On becoming president, Kabila promised a transition to democracy and free elections by April 1999. Such elections never came. By 2000 the nation endured another round of civil war, as three separate rebel groups sought to overthrow Kabila's autocratic rule. In January 2001, a bodyguard assassinated Kabila.

Civil War in Congo and Angola
10.9.2

Critical Thinking

- How was Kabila's rule similar to that of other leaders in newly independent nations? *(Possible Answer: He promised democracy but seized autocratic rule once in power.)*
- How did interference by outside forces impact the war in Angola? *(Possible Answer: Aid from outside forces kept the war going and reduced the chance of a peaceful end to the war.)*

In-Depth Resources: Unit 5

- Primary Source: Farewell Without Tears, letter from Patrice Lumumba, p. 37

More About . . .

Overthrowing Mobutu

Congo rebels, led by Laurent Kabila, overthrew Mobutu in just seven months. They encountered little opposition as they moved across the country. The *New York Times* called the Zaire government "a house that had been eaten by termites. The rebels came along and pushed it over." That is, the corruption of Mobutu's rule had undermined his support among the people.

DIFFERENTIATING INSTRUCTION: STRUGGLING READERS

Exploring Leadership Styles

Class Time 20 minutes

Task Discussing leadership styles of African leaders

Purpose To clarify the methods of leadership in newly independent African nations.

Instructions Use the Guided Reading worksheet and Reading Study Guide for Section 3 to review the section material with students. Then assign groups of students the roles of various leaders they have read about in this section:

- Kwame Nkrumah
- Jomo Kenyatta
- Mobutu Sese Seko
- Ahmed Ben Bella

Have students discuss their leader's methods of ruling the country. They should discuss the success or failure of the leader's style of governing. Have each group give a brief report describing the leadership style and its success or failure.

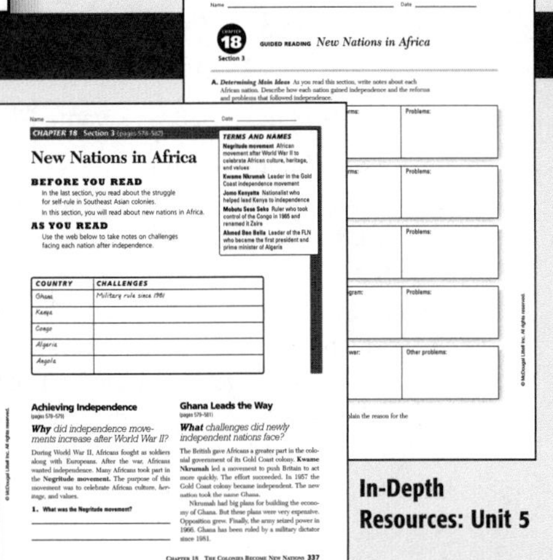

In-Depth Resources: Unit 5

Reading Study Guide

History *in* Depth

Genocide in Rwanda

Rwandan ethnic violence spilled into the Congo as well. Within days after Laurent Kabila took over, rumors began to surface about massacres in the Congo of Hutu refugees from Rwanda. Kabila's army included large numbers of Tutsis. The refugees were ethnic Hutus who fled Rwanda in 1994 after a Tutsi-led government came to power.

More About . . .

Cuban Troops in Angola

Cuban troops went to Angola as a part of Fidel Castro's program of "Cuban internationalism." In addition to military troops, Cuba sent teachers, doctors, and laborers. There were so many Cubans in medical service that in the 1980s Spanish was the preferred language of the Angolan medical community.

3 ASSESS

SECTION 3 ASSESSMENT

Pair students to respond to the assessment questions together.

Formal Assessment
- Section Quiz, p. 316

4 RETEACH

Direct students to the maps on page 1014. Use the two maps to review the main ideas of the section.

In-Depth Resources: Unit 5
- Reteaching Activity, p. 47

History *in* Depth

Genocide in Rwanda

Of all the African nations that have struggled with ethnic violence, perhaps none has seen more blood spilled than Rwanda. The tiny nation in East Africa gained its independence in 1962. Over the next 30 years, its main ethnic groups, Hutus and Tutsis, often clashed.

In the spring of 1994, the Rwandan president, a Hutu, died in a suspicious plane crash. In the months that followed, Hutus slaughtered about 1 million Tutsis before Tutsi rebels put an end to the killings. The United Nations set up a tribunal to punish those responsible for the worst acts of genocide.

His son, Joseph Kabila, took power and began a quest for peace. In July of 2002, some of the rebel forces agreed to a cease-fire, offering hope that a larger peace might one day become a reality.

War Tears at Angola To the southwest of Congo lies Angola, a country that not only had to fight to gain its freedom but to hold itself together after independence. The Portuguese had long ruled Angola and had no desire to stop. When an independence movement broke out in the colony, Portugal sent in 50,000 troops. The cost of the conflict amounted to almost half of Portugal's national budget. The heavy cost of fighting, as well as growing opposition at home to the war, prompted the Portuguese to withdraw from Angola in 1975.

Almost immediately, the Communist-leaning MPLA (Popular Movement for the Liberation of Angola) declared itself the new nation's rightful government. This led to a prolonged civil war, as various rebel groups fought the government and each other for power. Each group received help from outside sources. The MPLA was assisted by some 50,000 Cuban troops and by the Soviet Union. The major opposition to the MPLA was UNITA (National Union for the Total Independence of Angola), to which South Africa and the United States lent support. For decades, the two sides agreed to and then abandoned various cease-fire agreements. In 2002, the warring sides agreed to a peace accord, and the long civil war came to an end.

As the colonies of Africa worked to become stable nations, the new nation of Israel was emerging in the Middle East. Its growth, as you will read in the next section, upset many in the surrounding Arab world and prompted one of the longest-running conflicts in modern history.

SECTION 3 ASSESSMENT

TERMS & NAMES 1. For each term or name, write a sentence explaining its significance.
- Negritude movement
- Kwame Nkrumah
- Jomo Kenyatta
- Ahmed Ben Bella
- Mobutu Sese Seko

USING YOUR NOTES

2. Which item had the greatest impact on its country? Why? (10.4.4)

Ghana	
Kenya	
Zaire	
Algeria	
Angola	

MAIN IDEAS

3. Who were the Mau Mau of Kenya? What was their goal? (10.4.4)
4. What sparked the present-day civil struggle in Algeria? (10.4.4)
5. What prompted Portugal to eventually grant Angola its freedom? (10.4.4)

CRITICAL THINKING & WRITING

6. **DRAWING CONCLUSIONS** How did the way in which European colonialists carved up Africa in the 1800s lead to civil strife in many new African nations? (10.4.4)
7. **ANALYZING MOTIVES** Why did the United States and the Soviet Union participate in Angola's civil war? (10.9.2)
8. **ANALYZING ISSUES** Why do you think revolution swept so many African nations following their independence from European rule? (10.4.4)
9. **WRITING ACTIVITY** REVOLUTION Imagine you are a reporter covering a revolution in one of the African nations. Write a **headline** and **article** describing it. (Writing 2.3.b)

INTEGRATED TECHNOLOGY **INTERNET ACTIVITY**

Use the Internet to examine the current status of two countries discussed in this section. Choose from various economic, governmental, and social statistics and display your information in a **comparison chart.** (Writing 2.3.d)

INTERNET KEYWORD
country profiles

ANSWERS

1. Negritude movement, p. 578 • Kwame Nkrumah, p. 579 • Jomo Kenyatta, p. 579 • Ahmed Ben Bella, p. 581 • Mobutu Sese Seko, p. 581

2. **Sample answer:** Ghana—Nkrumah damaged economy through costly projects; Kenya—Kenyatta fought against British; Zaire—Mobutu overthrown; Algeria—French colonists fought independence; long civil war; Angola—Portuguese fought to keep country but gave up; long civil war. **Possible Answers:** Jomo Kenyatta's leadership in Kenya—without his efforts Kenya may have struggled longer to gain freedom; civil war in Angola—it lasted for two decades.

3. resistance group of Kenyan farmers; force British farmers from the land
4. government's refusal to accept recent election victories of Islamic party
5. high cost of fighting for control; opposition at home to colonialism
6. **Possible Answer:** Europeans created artificial borders dividing ethnic groups and enclosing those at odds. Groups fought after Europeans left.
7. Soviets wanted to support Communist government; U.S. wanted to stop this.
8. desire for freedom had been building; colonial departure left instability
9. **Rubric** Articles should
- include a strong and catchy headline.
- explain the revolution and its causes.
- be clearly organized and well written.

INTEGRATED TECHNOLOGY

Rubric Charts should
- identify the two nations.
- provide similar types of statistics.
- clearly compare the two nations.

Temple decoration, Chiang Mai, Thailand

Floating market, Bangkok, Thailand

4

Conflicts in the Middle East

MAIN IDEA	WHY IT MATTERS NOW	TERMS & NAMES
POWER AND AUTHORITY Division of Palestine after World War II made the Middle East a hotbed of competing nationalist movements.	The conflict in the Middle East threatens the stability of the world today.	• Anwar Sadat • Golda Meir • PLO • Yasir Arafat • Camp David Accords • intifada • Oslo Peace Accords

SETTING THE STAGE In the years following World War II, the Jewish people won what for so long had eluded them: their own state. The gaining of their homeland along the eastern coast of the Mediterranean Sea, however, came at a heavy price. A Jewish state was unwelcome in this mostly Arab region, and the resulting hostility led to a series of wars. Perhaps no Arab people, however, have been more opposed to a Jewish state than the Palestinians, who claim that much of the Jewish land belongs to them. These two groups have waged a bloody battle that goes on today.

Israel Becomes a State

The land called Palestine now consists of Israel, the West Bank, and the Gaza Strip. To Jews, their claim to the land dates back 3,000 years, when Jewish kings ruled the region from Jerusalem. To Palestinians (both Muslim and Christian), the land has belonged to them since the Jews were driven out around A.D. 135. To Arabs, the land has belonged to them since their conquest of the area in the 7th century.

After being forced out of Palestine during the second century, the Jewish people were not able to establish their own state and lived in different countries throughout the world. The global dispersal of the Jews is known as the Diaspora. During the late 19th and early 20th centuries, a group of Jews began returning to the region their ancestors had fled so long ago. They were known as Zionists, people who favored a Jewish national homeland in Palestine. At this time, Palestine was still part of the Ottoman Empire, ruled by Islamic Turks. After the defeat of the Ottomans in World War I, the League of Nations asked Britain to oversee Palestine until it was ready for independence.

By this time, the Jews had become a growing presence in Palestine, and were already pressing for their own nation in the territory. The Palestinians living in the region strongly opposed such a move. In a 1917 letter to Zionist leaders, British Foreign Secretary Sir Arthur Balfour promoted the idea of creating a Jewish homeland in Palestine while protecting the "rights of existing non-Jewish communities." Despite the Balfour Declaration, however, efforts to create a Jewish state failed—and hostility between Palestinians and Jews continued to grow.

CALIFORNIA STANDARDS

10.9.6 Understand how the forces of nationalism developed in the Middle East, how the Holocaust affected world opinion regarding the need for a Jewish state, and the significance and effects of the location and establishment of Israel on world affairs.

REP 1 Students distinguish valid arguments from fallacious arguments in historical interpretations.

REP 4 Students construct and test hypotheses; collect, evaluate, and employ information from multiple primary and secondary sources; and apply it in oral and written presentations.

HI 4 Students understand the meaning, implication, and impact of historical events and recognize that events could have taken other directions.

TAKING NOTES

Following Chronological Order Use a graphic to fill in some important political and military events that occurred following the Suez Crisis.

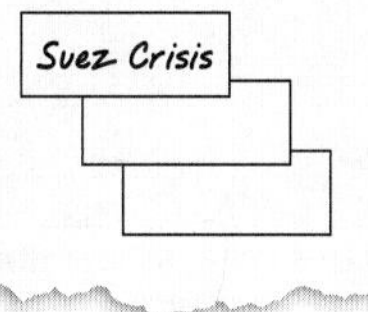

LESSON PLAN

OBJECTIVES

- Describe the formation of Israel.
- Trace the conflicts between Israel and Arab states.
- Describe the Palestinian struggle for independence.
- Explain Arab-Israeli peace efforts.

1 FOCUS & MOTIVATE

Explain that Israelis and Palestinians live daily with heightened security measures. What security measures do students face in their schools or communities? *(Possible Answers: metal detectors in schools or airports, police presence)*

2 INSTRUCT

Israel Becomes a State
10.9.6

Critical Thinking

- How could the claims to land in Palestine be true for Jews, Palestinians, and Arabs? *(All three groups claimed lands based on previous residence.)*

CALIFORNIA RESOURCES

California Reading Toolkit, p. L83
California Modified Lesson Plans for English Learners, p. 161
California Daily Standards Practice Transparencies, TT75
California Standards Enrichment Workbook, pp. 101–102
California Standards Planner and Lesson Plans, p. L157
California Online Test Practice
California Test Generator CD-ROM
California Easy Planner CD-ROM
California eEdition CD-ROM

SECTION 4 PROGRAM RESOURCES

ALL STUDENTS

In-Depth Resources: Unit 5
- Guided Reading, p. 29
- History Makers: Golda Meir, p. 43

Formal Assessment
- Section Quiz, p. 317

ENGLISH LEARNERS

In-Depth Resources in Spanish
- Guided Reading, p. 143

Reading Study Guide (Spanish), p. 197
Reading Study Guide Audio CD (Spanish)

STRUGGLING READERS

In-Depth Resources: Unit 5
- Guided Reading, p. 29
- Building Vocabulary, p. 31
- Reteaching Activity, p. 48

Reading Study Guide, p. 197
Reading Study Guide Audio CD

GIFTED AND TALENTED STUDENTS

In-Depth Resources: Unit 5
- Primary Source: The Balfour Declaration, p. 38

Electronic Library of Primary Sources
- "Enough of Blood and Tears"

INTEGRATED TECHNOLOGY

eEdition CD-ROM
Power Presentations CD-ROM
World Art and Cultures Transparencies
- AT75 *After the Storm*

Critical Thinking Transparencies
- CT34 Time Machine: The Middle East Conflict

Electronic Library of Primary Sources
- "Enough of Blood and Tears"

classzone.com

Israel and Arab States in Conflict

10.9.6

Critical Thinking

- How did fighting prevent the establishment of the Palestinian state? *(Possible Answer: Israel took some of the land; chaos of war made it difficult.)*
- How did Israel triumph so quickly in the Six-Day War? *(Possible Answer: by moving preemptively; highly motivated and better equipped)*

History from Visuals

Interpreting the Map

Ask students to identify the access Israelis and Palestinians have to the Mediterranean and Red Seas. *(Israelis have seaports on the Mediterranean; Palestinians have access from the Gaza Strip. Israelis can reach the Red Sea through the Gulf of Aqaba; Palestinians have no access.)*

Extension Have students make a list of the nations which surround Israel. Then have students write a brief observation about Israel's relations with her neighbors.

SKILLBUILDER Answers

1. **Location** Elat; It gave Israel access, by way of the Gulf of Aqaba, to the Red Sea.
2. **Region** Lebanon; Jordan; Syria

INTEGRATED TECHNOLOGY

Interactive This feature is available in an interactive format on the eEdition.

At the end of World War II, the United Nations took up the matter. In 1947, the UN General Assembly voted for a partition of Palestine into a Palestinian state and a Jewish state. Jerusalem was to be an international city owned by neither side. The terms of the partition gave Jews 55 percent of the area even though they made up only 34 percent of the population. In the wake of the war and the Holocaust, the United States and many European nations felt great sympathy for the Jews.

All of the Islamic countries voted against partition, and the Palestinians rejected it outright. They argued that the UN did not have the right to partition a country without considering the wishes of the majority of its people. Finally, the date was set for the formation of Israel, May 14, 1948. On that date, David Ben Gurion, long-time leader of the Jews residing in Palestine, announced the creation of an independent Israel. **A**

A. Answer The UN recommended the partition of Palestine into a Palestinian state and a Jewish state, with Jerusalem as an international city.

MAIN IDEA

Summarizing

A What recommendations did the UN make for Palestine?

Israel and Arab States in Conflict

The new nation of Israel got a hostile greeting from its neighbors. The day after it proclaimed itself a state, six Islamic states—Egypt, Iraq, Jordan, Lebanon, Saudi Arabia, and Syria—invaded Israel. The first of many Arab-Israeli wars, this one ended within months in a victory for Israel. Full-scale war broke out again in 1956, 1967, and 1973.

Largely as a result of this fighting, the state that the UN had set aside for Palestinians never came into being. Israel seized half the land in the 1948–1949 fighting. While the fighting raged, at least 600,000 Palestinians fled, migrating from the areas under Israeli control. They settled in UN-sponsored refugee camps that ringed the borders of their former homeland. Meanwhile, various Arab nations seized other Palestinian lands. Egypt took control of the Gaza Strip, while Jordan annexed the West Bank of the Jordan River. (See the map at left.)

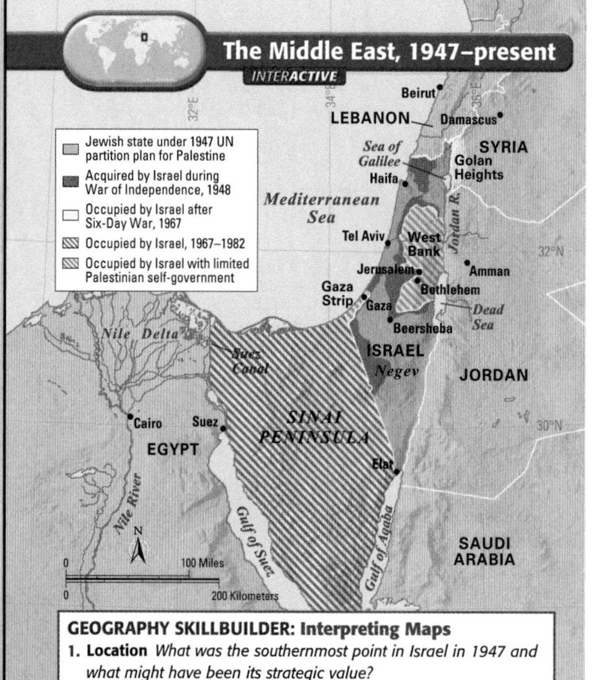

GEOGRAPHY SKILLBUILDER: Interpreting Maps

1. **Location** *What was the southernmost point in Israel in 1947 and what might have been its strategic value?*
2. **Region** *What country lies due north of Israel? east? northeast?*

The 1956 Suez Crisis The second Arab-Israeli war followed in 1956. That year, Egypt seized control of the Suez Canal, which ran along Egypt's eastern border between the Gulf of Suez and the Mediterranean Sea. Egyptian president Gamal Abdel Nasser sent in troops to take the canal, which was controlled by British interests. The military action was prompted in large part by Nasser's anger over the loss of U.S. and British financial support for the building of Egypt's Aswan Dam.

Outraged, the British made an agreement with France and Israel to retake the canal. With air support provided by their European allies, the Israelis marched on the Suez Canal and quickly defeated the Egyptians. However, pressure from

DIFFERENTIATING INSTRUCTION: GIFTED AND TALENTED STUDENTS

Exploring the Balfour Declaration

Class Time 30 minutes

Task Analyzing the impact of the Balfour Declaration

Purpose To identify the effects of the Balfour Declaration on the conflict between Israel and the Arab states

Instructions Have students read and discuss the Balfour Declaration on p. 38, In-Depth Resources: Unit 5. Then ask students if they think that Jews and non-Jews living in Palestine might have understood the Balfour Declaration differently. Use these questions to guide the discussion:

- How might the Jews have interpreted it?
- How might Muslims and Christians already living there have understood the document?
- Could the declaration have been worded differently and still have achieved its purpose of appeasing both sides?

Finally, have the students draft a series of questions to pose to Sir Balfour and to Lord Rothschild regarding the declaration.

Name ______ Date ______

CHAPTER 18 Section 4

PRIMARY SOURCE The Balfour Declaration

Sir Arthur James Balfour, the British foreign secretary, wrote the following letter to Lord Lionel Rothschild, a Zionist leader, on November 2, 1917. Lord Rothschild replied, "I can assure you that the gratitude of ten millions of people will be yours, for the British government has opened up, by their message, a prospect of safety and comfort to large masses of people who are in need of it." What do you think were the pros and cons of the Balfour Declaration?

Foreign Office,
November 2nd, 1917

Dear Lord Rothschild,

I have much pleasure in conveying to you, on behalf of His Majesty's Government, the following declaration of sympathy with Jewish Zionist aspirations which has been submitted to, and approved by, the Cabinet.

"His Majesty's Government view with favour the establishment in Palestine of a national home for the Jewish people, and will use their best endeavours to facilitate the achievement of this object, it being clearly understood that nothing shall be done which may prejudice the civil and religious rights of existing non-Jewish communities in Palestine, or the rights and political status enjoyed by Jews in any other country"

I should be grateful if you would bring this declaration to the knowledge of the Zionist Federation.

Discussion Questions

Analyzing Issues

1. How did the British government respond to the Zionist goal of establishing a Jewish homeland in Palestine?
2. What conditions did the British expect Zionists to meet?
3. *Making Inferences* Zionists such as Lord Rothschild were pleased by the letter from Balfour. How do you think Muslim residents of Palestine might have responded to Balfour's letter?

38 Unit 5, Chapter 18

In-Depth Resources: Unit 5

the world community, including the United States and the Soviet Union, forced Israel and the Europeans to withdraw from Egypt. This left Egypt in charge of the canal and thus ended the Suez Crisis.

Arab-Israeli Wars Continue Tensions between Israel and the Arab states began to build again in the years following the resolution of the Suez Crisis. By early 1967, Nasser and his Arab allies, equipped with Soviet tanks and aircraft, felt ready to confront Israel. "We are eager for battle in order to force the enemy to awake from his dreams," Nasser announced, "and meet Arab reality face to face." He moved to close off the Gulf of Aqaba, Israel's outlet to the Red Sea.

Convinced that the Arabs were about to attack, the Israelis struck airfields in Egypt, Iran, Jordan, and Syria. Safe from air attack, Israeli ground forces struck like lightning on three fronts. Israel defeated the Arab states in what became known as the Six-Day War, because it was over in six days. Israel lost 800 troops in the fighting, while Arab losses exceeded 15,000.

As a consequence of the Six-Day War, Israel gained control of the old city of Jerusalem, the Sinai Peninsula, the Golan Heights, and the West Bank. Israelis saw these new holdings along their southern, eastern, and western borders as a key buffer zone against further Arab attacks. Palestinians who lived in Jerusalem were given the choice of Israeli or Jordanian citizenship. Most chose the latter. Palestinians who lived in the other areas were not offered Israeli citizenship and simply came under Jewish control.

B. Answer Some territory changed hands; hostilities continued; instability threatened the region.

MAIN IDEA

Recognizing Effects

B What were some of the effects of the Arab-Israeli conflicts?

A fourth Arab-Israeli conflict erupted in October 1973. Nasser's successor, Egyptian president **Anwar Sadat** (AHN•wahr suh•DAT), planned a joint Arab attack on the date of Yom Kippur, the holiest of Jewish holidays. This time the Israelis were caught by surprise. Arab forces inflicted heavy casualties and recaptured some of the territory lost in 1967. The Israelis, under their prime minister, **Golda Meir** (MY•uhr), launched a counterattack and regained most of the lost territory. Both sides agreed to a truce after several weeks of fighting, and the Yom Kippur war came to an end. B

History Makers

Golda Meir
1898–1978

Meir was born in Kiev, Russia, but grew up in the American Heartland. Although a skilled carpenter, Meir's father could not find enough work in Kiev. So he sold his tools and other belongings and moved his family to Milwaukee, Wisconsin. Meir would spend more than a decade in the United States before moving to Palestine.

The future Israeli prime minister exhibited strong leadership qualities early on. When she learned that many of her fellow fourth grade classmates could not afford textbooks, she created the American Young Sisters Society, an organization that succeeded in raising the necessary funds.

The Palestine Liberation Organization As Israel and its Arab neighbors battled each other, the Palestinians struggled for recognition. While the United Nations had granted the Palestinians their own homeland, the Israelis had seized much of that land, including the West Bank and Gaza Strip, during its various wars. Israel insisted that such a move was vital to its national security.

In 1964, Palestinian officials formed the Palestine Liberation Organization (**PLO**) to push for the formation of a Palestinian state. Originally, the PLO was an umbrella organization made up of different groups—laborers, teachers, lawyers, and guerrilla fighters. Soon, guerrilla groups came to dominate the organization and insisted that the only way to achieve their goal was through armed struggle. In 1969 **Yasir Arafat** (YAH•sur AR•uh•FAT) became chairman of the PLO. Throughout the 1960s and 1970s the group carried out numerous attacks against Israel. Some of Israel's Arab neighbors supported the organization's goals by allowing the PLO to operate from their lands.

History Makers

Golda Meir

Explain that Meir served Israel as ambassador to the Soviet Union, minister of labor, and foreign minister before becoming prime minister. Have students compare Golda Meir's achievements with those of similarly qualified women of her generation in the United States. Ask how they would explain the differences. *(Possible Answers: Reform movements have traditionally held progressive views of women. The small, young nation of Israel needed the kind of leadership she could offer.)*

In-Depth Resources: Unit 5

• History Makers: Golda Meir, p. 43

More About . . .

Anwar Sadat

The failure of the Yom Kippur war changed the attitude of Anwar Sadat toward the Israelis. In 1977, he stunned the Egyptian parliament when he said that he would go to Israel to speak to its legislature about peace negotiations. He believed that peace with Israel would create what he called a "peace dividend" for both Egypt and Israel.

His actions began the peace process that ended with the Camp David Accords (see next page) and won Sadat and Israeli Prime Minister Menachem Begin the Nobel Prize for peace.

COOPERATIVE LEARNING

B

Researching West Bank Settlements

Class Time 30 minutes

Task Researching various positions on the issue of Israeli settlements on the West Bank

Purpose To identify the points of view regarding the West Bank

Instructions Ask students to form groups of three or four. Have them do research, using the Internet, newspapers, and current magazines, on the issue of Israeli settlements on the West Bank and their effect on the Palestinian and Jewish populations and the prospects for peace in the region. Have each group research the various positions on the issue and list the arguments for each position. Tell students that their lists should:

- clearly convey various sides of the issue.
- list an equal number of arguments for all sides.
- be fair and impartial.

After students present their lists, hold a class discussion on recommendations for solving the West Bank problem. Then have students complete the Standards for Evaluating a Cooperative Activity worksheet.

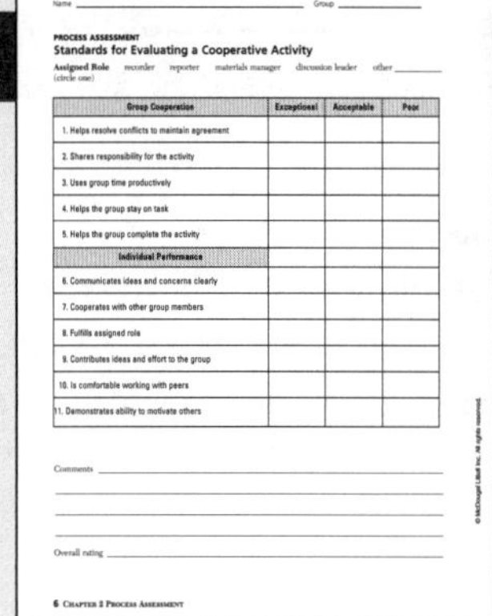

Name ______ Group ______

PROCESS ASSESSMENT

Standards for Evaluating a Cooperative Activity

Assigned Role (circle one) recorder reporter materials manager discussion leader other ______

Group Cooperation	Exceptional	Acceptable	Poor
1. Helps resolve conflicts to maintain agreement			
2. Shares responsibility for the activity			
3. Uses group time productively			
4. Helps the group stay on task			
5. Helps the group complete the activity			
Individual Performance			
6. Communicates ideas and concerns clearly			
7. Cooperates with other group members			
8. Fulfills assigned role			
9. Contributes ideas and effort to the group			
10. Is comfortable working with peers			
11. Demonstrates ability to motivate others			

Comments ______

Overall rating ______

6 CHAPTER 2 PROCESS ASSESSMENT

Integrated Assessment

Analyzing Primary Sources

Ask students to read both primary sources. Then ask them from what perspective each is written, military or personal? How, if at all, does this change students' response to the views stated? *(Palestinian view–personal; Israeli view–military; Possible Answer: Personal view is more accessible and more likely to create sympathy.)*

Critical Thinking Transparencies

- CT34 Time Machine: The Middle East Conflict

World Art and Cultures Transparencies

- AT75 *After the Storm*

Answers to Document-Based Questions

1. **Analyzing Issues** *Possible Answer:* He believes the Israelis have acted like a colonial power–seizing land for their own gain.
2. **Drawing Conclusions** *Possible Answer:* to give up all hostilities toward Israel and show a commitment to creating a lasting peace.

Efforts at Peace

10.9.6

Critical Thinking

- Why do you think Sadat's peace initiative enraged Arabs? *(Possible Answer: It offered to recognize Israel.)*
- How are Yitzhak Rabin and Anwar Sadat similar? *(Possible Answer: Both were courageous leaders who were killed for their willingness to compromise in the interest of peace.)*

> Analyzing Primary Sources

The Palestinian View

Writer Fawaz Turki articulates the view held by many of his fellow Palestinians—that the Israelis are illegal occupiers of Palestinian land.

PRIMARY SOURCE

These people have walked off with our home and homeland, with our movable and immovable property, with our land, our farms, our shops, our public buildings, our paved roads, our cars, our theaters, our clubs, our parks, our furniture, our tricycles. They hounded us out of ancestral patrimony [land] and shoved us in refugee camps. . . . Now they were astride the whole of historic Palestine and then some, jubilant at the new role as latter day colonial overlords.

FAWAZ TURKI, quoted in *The Arab-Israeli Conflict*

The Israeli View

Many Israelis, including former Israeli General Abraham Tamir, feel that controlling Palestinian lands is vital to their security.

PRIMARY SOURCE

Since the establishment of the State of Israel, its national security policy has been designed to defend its existence, integrity and security, and not for expansionist territorial aspirations. Hence, if Arab confrontation states did not initiate wars against Israel or pose threats to its existence, then Israel would not start a war . . . to extend its territories . . . Our national security policy created from its very beginning the linkage between Israel's political willingness for peace and Israel's military capability to repel aggression of any kind and scale.

ABRAHAM TAMIR, quoted in *From War to Peace*

DOCUMENT-BASED QUESTIONS

1. **Analyzing Issues** *Why does Fawaz Turki refer to the Israelis as colonizers?*
2. **Drawing Conclusions** *What might be the best way for the Palestinians to regain control of their land, according to Abraham Tamir?*

Efforts at Peace

In November 1977, just four years after the Yom Kippur war, Anwar Sadat stunned the world by extending a hand to Israel. No Arab country up to this point had recognized Israel's right to exist. In a dramatic gesture, Sadat went before the Knesset, the Israeli parliament, and invited his one-time enemies to join him in a quest for peace.

PRIMARY SOURCE

Today, through my visit to you, I ask you why don't we stretch our hands with faith and sincerity and so that together we might . . . remove all suspicion of fear, betrayal, and bad intention? Why don't we stand together with the courage of men and the boldness of heroes who dedicate themselves to a sublime [supreme] aim? Why don't we stand together with the same courage and daring to erect a huge edifice [building] of peace? An edifice that . . . serves as a beacon for generations to come with the human message for construction, development, and the dignity of man.

ANWAR SADAT, Knesset speech, November 20, 1977

Sadat emphasized that in exchange for peace Israel would have to recognize the rights of Palestinians. Furthermore, it would have to withdraw from territory seized in 1967 from Egypt, Jordan, and Syria.

U.S. president Jimmy Carter recognized that Sadat had created a historic opportunity for peace. In 1978, Carter invited Sadat and Israeli prime minister Menachem Begin (mehn•AHK•hehm BAY•gihn) to Camp David, the presidential retreat in rural Maryland. Isolated from the press and from domestic political pressures, Sadat and Begin worked to reach an agreement. After 13 days of negotiations, Carter triumphantly announced that Egypt recognized Israel as a legitimate state. In exchange, Israel agreed to return the Sinai Peninsula to Egypt. Signed in 1979, the **Camp David Accords** ended 30 years of hostilities between Egypt and Israel and became the first signed agreement between Israel and an Arab country.

CONNECTIONS ACROSS TIME AND CULTURES

Efforts at Peace

Class Time 30 minutes

Task Investigating negotiations at Camp David

Purpose To identify factors affecting the ongoing Arab-Israeli conflict

Instructions Tell students that over time two U.S. presidents have invited Arab and Jewish leaders to Camp David to work out a path to peace. In the first meeting in 1978, President Carter invited Anwar Sadat of Egypt and Menachem Begin of Israel in a meeting that resulted in the Camp David Accords. In 2000 President Clinton invited Ehud Barak of Israel and Yasir Arafat of Palestine. That meeting ended in failure to reach a compromise.

Have small groups of students research one of the meetings at Camp David. Ask them to focus on the following:

- list the participants in each meeting
- describe the major participants in terms of their personalities and personal histories
- identify the major issues under negotiation
- characterize the tone and quality of the meeting
- describe the outcome of the meeting

After students have completed their research, have them share their findings with the class.

MAIN IDEA

Clarifying

C What was the significance of the Camp David Accords?

C. Answer It was the first signed agreement between Israel and an Arab country.

While world leaders praised Sadat, his peace initiative enraged many Arab countries. In 1981, a group of Muslim extremists assassinated him. However, Egypt's new leader, Hosni Mubarak (HAHS•nee moo•BAHR•uhk), has worked to maintain peace with Israel. C

Israeli-Palestinian Tensions Increase One Arab group that continued to clash with the Israelis was the Palestinians, a large number of whom lived in the West Bank and Gaza Strip—lands occupied by Israel. During the 1970s and 1980s, the military wing of the PLO intensified its armed struggle against Israel. Israel responded forcefully, bombing suspected rebel bases in Palestinian towns. In 1982, the Israeli army went as far as invading the neighboring country of Lebanon in an attempt to destroy Palestinian strongholds. The Israelis soon became involved in Lebanon's civil war and were forced to withdraw.

In 1987, Palestinians began to express their frustrations in a widespread campaign of civil disobedience called the **intifada**, or "uprising." The intifada took the form of boycotts, demonstrations, attacks on Israeli soldiers, and rock throwing by unarmed teenagers. The intifada continued into the 1990s, with little progress made toward a solution. However, the civil disobedience affected world opinion, which, in turn, put pressure on Israel to seek negotiations with the Palestinians. Finally, in October 1991, Israeli and Palestinian delegates met for a series of peace talks.

The Oslo Peace Accords Negotiations between the two sides made little progress, as the status of the Palestinian territories occupied by Israel proved to be a bitterly divisive issue. In 1993, however, secret talks held in Oslo, Norway, produced a surprise agreement: a document called the Declaration of Principles, also known as the **Oslo Peace Accords**. Israel, under the leadership of Prime Minister Yitzhak Rabin (YIHTS•hahk rah•BEEN), agreed to grant the Palestinians self-rule in the Gaza Strip and the West Bank, beginning with the town of Jericho. Rabin and Arafat signed the agreement on September 13, 1993.

The difficulty of making the agreement work was demonstrated by the assassination of Rabin in 1995. He was killed by a right-wing Jewish extremist who opposed concessions to the Palestinians. Rabin was succeeded as prime minister by Benjamin Netanyahu (neh•tan•YAH•hoo), who had opposed the Oslo Accords. Still, Netanyahu made efforts to keep to the agreement. In January 1997, Netanyahu met with Arafat to work out plans for a partial Israeli withdrawal from the West Bank.

The Israeli–Palestinian Struggle

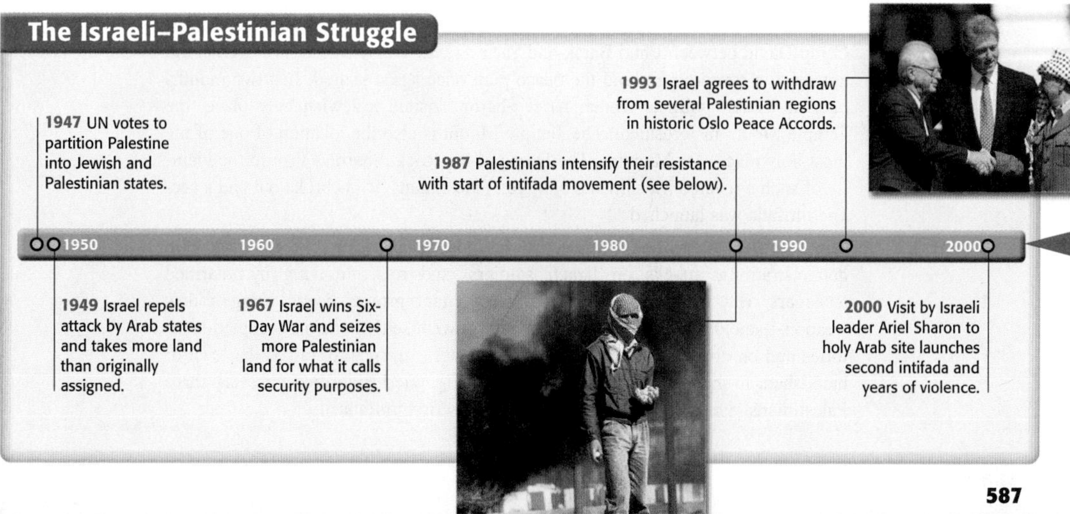

1947 UN votes to partition Palestine into Jewish and Palestinian states.
1949 Israel repels attack by Arab states and takes more land than originally assigned.
1967 Israel wins Six-Day War and seizes more Palestinian land for what it calls security purposes.
1987 Palestinians intensify their resistance with start of intifada movement (see below).
1993 Israel agrees to withdraw from several Palestinian regions in historic Oslo Peace Accords.
2000 Visit by Israeli leader Ariel Sharon to holy Arab site launches second intifada and years of violence.
1950
1960
1970
1980
1990
2000

587

More About . . .

Lebanon's Civil War

Conflicts between Lebanese Christians and Muslims supported by the PLO erupted into a civil war in 1975. In 1982 Israel occupied Lebanon in an effort to drive out PLO troops and leaders. By 1985, Israel had withdrawn its troops except for a security zone at the Lebanese-Israeli border.

More About . . .

Oslo Peace Agreement

The achievements of PLO chairman Yasir Arafat, Israeli prime minister Yitzhak Rabin, and Israeli foreign minister Shimon Peres were recognized in 1994 when the Nobel Peace Prize was awarded jointly to the three of them. Have students compare the Camp David Accords with the Oslo Peace Agreement.

Electronic Library of Primary Sources

- "Enough of Blood and Tears" by Yitzhak Rabin

History from Visuals

Interpreting the Time Line

Using the dates on the time line, how long has the Israeli-Palestinian struggle gone on? *(51 years)*

Extension Ask students which major Arab-Israeli conflict is not shown on the time line. *(Yom Kippur war)* Have students write an entry to add the Yom Kippur war to the time line.

DIFFERENTIATING INSTRUCTION: ENGLISH LEARNERS

Organizing Events Chronologically

Class Time 15 minutes

Task Making a time line of events

Purpose To trace the sequence of events in the Arab-Israeli conflict

Instructions Review the section material with students taking turns reading aloud. Whenever a reader encounters a date, ask students what occurred on that date. Have them write down the date and the event. Lists should include the following events:

- birth of new state of Israel
- Suez Crisis
- Six-Day War
- PLO formed
- Sadat assassinated
- Sadat offers peace
- first intifada
- Camp David Accords
- Rabin assassinated
- Oslo Peace Accords
- second intifada
- Sharon visits the Temple Mount
- Yom Kippur war
- "road map" to peace

Then have students compare their lists with each other and with the time line on page 587. Students may also check their lists against the transparency. After correcting any errors, have students create a large-size time line for the class beginning with the birth of the new state of Israel.

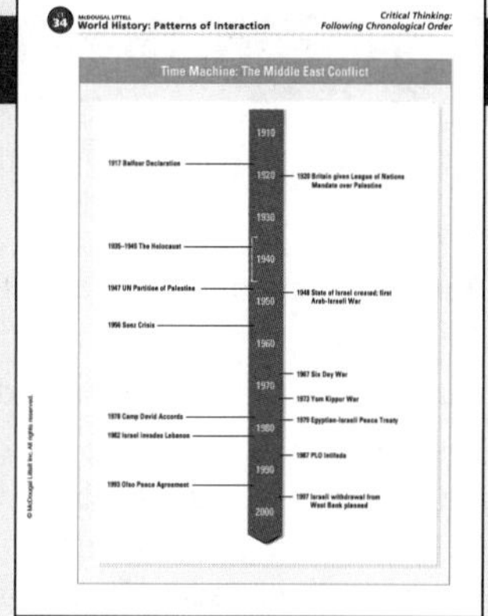

Critical Thinking Transparencies

History *in* Depth

Signs of Hope

Seeds of Peace founder, John Wallach, found that the most difficult task for campers was to break out of old habits and attitudes. Particularly difficult was living in the same building with someone you considered the enemy.

Wallach told of an Israeli who was found walking outside his bunkhouse one night about 2 A.M. When asked why he wasn't sleeping, the Israeli replied, "I can't fall asleep because I am afraid the Palestinian kid in my bunk is gonna knife me."

Peace Slips Away

10.9.6

Critical Thinking

- Why do you think Sharon's visit to the Temple Mount so angered Palestinians? *(Possible Answer: His presence suggested that it belonged to Israel or the Jews.)*
- What do you think are the main obstacles to peace between Israel and the Arab states? How has each side caused problems? *(Possible Answers: mistrust, extremists on both sides; with continued aggression and violence)*

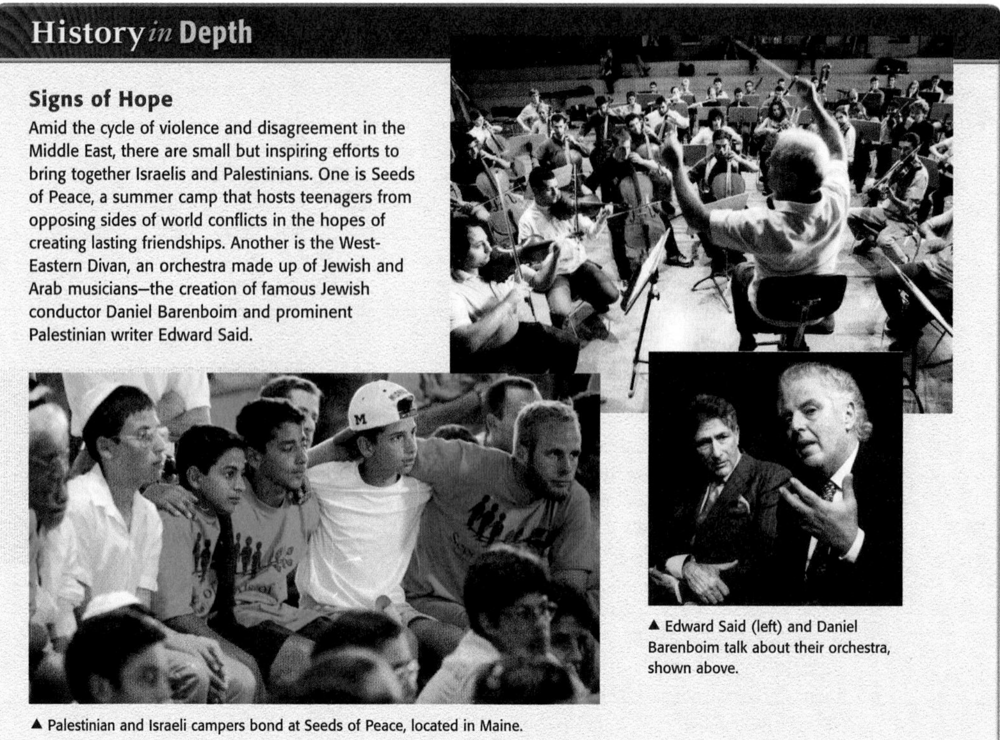

History *in* Depth

Signs of Hope

Amid the cycle of violence and disagreement in the Middle East, there are small but inspiring efforts to bring together Israelis and Palestinians. One is Seeds of Peace, a summer camp that hosts teenagers from opposing sides of world conflicts in the hopes of creating lasting friendships. Another is the West-Eastern Divan, an orchestra made up of Jewish and Arab musicians—the creation of famous Jewish conductor Daniel Barenboim and prominent Palestinian writer Edward Said.

▲ Edward Said (left) and Daniel Barenboim talk about their orchestra, shown above.

▲ Palestinian and Israeli campers bond at Seeds of Peace, located in Maine.

Peace Slips Away

In 1999, the slow and difficult peace negotiations between Israel and the Palestinians seemed to get a boost. Ehud Barak won election as Israeli prime minister. Many observers viewed him as a much stronger supporter of the peace plan than Netanyahu had been. The world community, led by the United States, was determined to take advantage of such a development.

In July of 2000, U.S. president Bill Clinton hosted a 15-day summit meeting at Camp David between Ehud Barak and Yasir Arafat. The two men, however, could not reach a compromise, and the peace plan once again stalled. Just two months later an Israeli political leader, Ariel Sharon, visited a Jewish holy place, the Temple Mount in Jerusalem. The Temple Mount is also the location of one of the most holy places for Muslims, The Dome of the Rock. Sharon's visit to the vicinity of such a revered Muslim site outraged Palestinians. Riots broke out and a second intifada was launched.

The Conflict Intensifies The second intifada began much like the first with demonstrations, attacks on Israeli soldiers, and rock throwing by unarmed teenagers. But this time the Palestinian militant groups began using a new weapon—suicide bombers. Their attacks on Jewish settlements in occupied territories and on civilian locations throughout Israel significantly raised the level of bloodshed. In the first 17 months of the uprising, one Israeli died for every three Palestinians, a rate much higher than during the first intifada.

DIFFERENTIATING INSTRUCTION: STRUGGLING READERS

Determining Main Ideas

Class Time 25 minutes

Task Creating questions about the conflicts in the Middle East

Purpose To determine main ideas and supporting details

Instructions Have pairs of students use the Reading Study Guide and the textbook to review section material. Start by turning heads and subheads into questions. For example, the heading "Israel and Arab States in Conflict" might become the question: When and why were Israel and the Arab states in conflict? After the questions have been written, the pair trades questions with another pair and writes out answers for each question. The pair writing the questions should check the answers for accuracy.

Make sure students understand the chronology of the conflict beginning with the creation of the state of Israel in 1948. Review the events of the Holocaust and discuss how those events influenced the United Nations in the partition of Palestine.

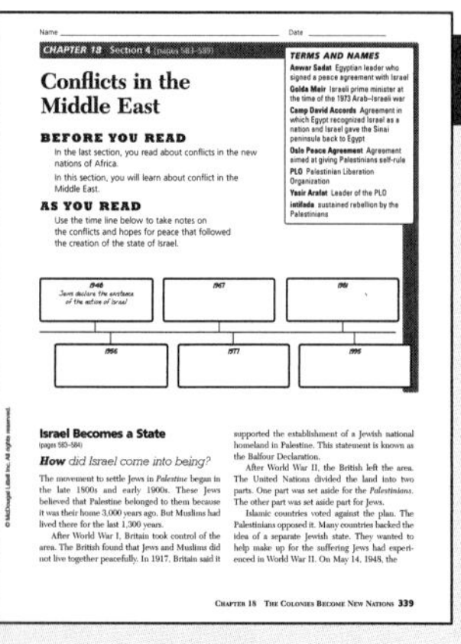

Reading Study Guide

In response to the uprising, Israeli forces moved into Palestinian refugee camps and clamped down on militants. Troops destroyed buildings in which they suspected extremists were hiding and bulldozed entire areas of Palestinian towns and camps. The Israeli army even bombed Arafat's headquarters, trapping him inside his compound for many days.

In recent years, peace between these two bitter enemies has seemed farther away than ever. In 2001, Ariel Sharon was elected Israeli prime minister. A former military leader, Sharon refused to negotiate with the Palestinians until attacks on Israelis stopped. Meanwhile, relations between Yasir Arafat and Israeli leaders grew so strained that Israeli officials declared they no longer would meet with the long-time leader of the PLO.

Working Toward a Solution Despite all this, peace efforts continue. Under intense pressure from the world community, Arafat agreed to take a less prominent role in peace talks with Israel. In early 2003, Palestinian leaders appointed their first-ever prime minister, high-ranking PLO official, Mahmoud Abbas. In his new position, Abbas became the main negotiator for the Palestinian side. Shortly afterward, U.S. president George W. Bush brought together Sharon and Abbas to begin working on a new peace plan known as the "road map."

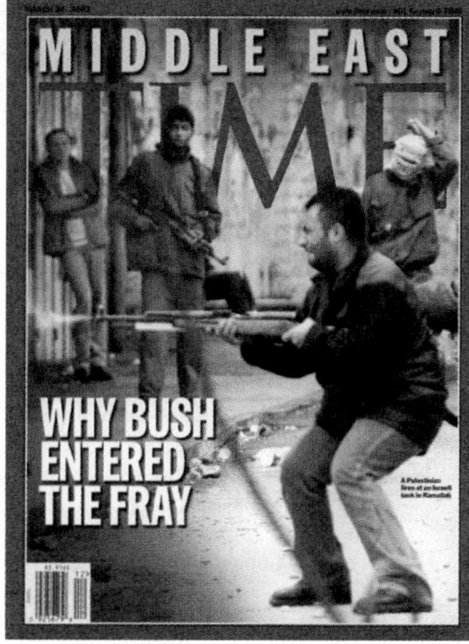

▲ A U.S. magazine cover highlights America's involvement in the Middle East crisis.

The two men appeared committed to reaching an agreement. Abbas declared, "Our goal is two states, Israel and Palestine, living side by side in peace and security." Meanwhile, Sharon expressed his desire to see Palestinians "govern themselves in their own state." To be sure, many divisive issues remain between the two groups. With leaders from both sides willing to work together, however, hope remains that harmony will one day come to this region.

SECTION 4 ASSESSMENT

TERMS & NAMES 1. For each term or name, write a sentence explaining its significance.

• Anwar Sadat • Golda Meir • PLO • Yasir Arafat • Camp David Accords • intifada • Oslo Peace Accords

USING NOTES

2. Which event was most important? Why? (10.9.6)

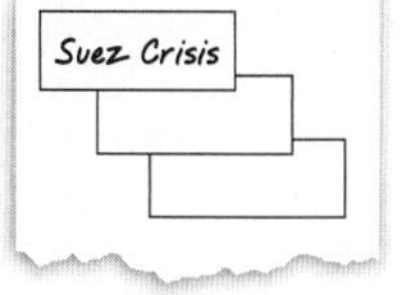

MAIN IDEAS

3. What historic claim do both Palestinians and Jews make to the land of Palestine? (10.9.6)
4. What land did Israel gain from the wars against its Arab neighbors? (10.9.6)
5. What were the terms of the Oslo Accords? (10.9.6)

CRITICAL THINKING & WRITING

6. **COMPARING** How was the creation of Israel similar to the establishment of an independent India? (10.9.6)
7. **DRAWING CONCLUSIONS** Why do you think all the Israeli-Palestinian accords ultimately have failed? (10.9.6)
8. **ANALYZING ISSUES** Some have said that the Palestinian-Israeli conflict represents the struggle of right against right. Explain why you agree or disagree. (10.9.6)
9. **WRITING ACTIVITY** POWER AND AUTHORITY In groups, create a list of ten **interview questions** for Gamal Abdel Nasser, Anwar Sadat, Yasir Arafat, Yitzhak Rabin, or a current leader of either Israel or Palestine. (Writing 2.5.b)

CONNECT TO TODAY

DRAWING A POLITICAL CARTOON

Draw a **political cartoon** or other type of image that conveys your thoughts about the stalled peace effort today between Palestinians and Israelis. (Writing 2.4.b)

More About . . .

Mahmoud Abbas

Abbas and Yasir Arafat worked together after co-founding the organization Fatah, which is part of the PLO. Abbas was born in 1935 in British Mandate Palestine, in an area now claimed by Israel. Known also as Abu Mazen, Abbas is highly educated and brought that education to bear as a fundraiser and then negotiator. Many credit him with the main ideas of the Oslo Accords. In September of 2003 Abbas resigned as prime minister after the peace plan known as "the road map" came apart as violence escalated once again. After Arafat's death on November 11, 2004, Abbas was selected by the PLO executive committee to lead the PLO.

3 ASSESS

SECTION 4 ASSESSMENT

Have students work in pairs. As one partner reads an assessment item aloud, the other partner jots down key points to include in the answer. Partners then trade places to repeat.

Formal Assessment

• Section Quiz, p. 317

4 RETEACH

Use the Reteaching Activity for Section 4 to review the main ideas of the section.

In-Depth Resources: Unit 5

• Reteaching Activity, p. 48

ANSWERS

1. Anwar Sadat, p. 585 • Golda Meir, p. 585 • PLO, p. 585 • Yasir Arafat, p. 585 • Camp David Accords, p. 586 • intifada, p. 587 • Oslo Peace Accords, p. 587

2. Suez Crisis; Six-Day War; Yom Kippur war; PLO formed; Camp David Accords; Sadat killed; first intifada; Oslo Peace Accords; Rabin killed; second intifada; **Possible Answer:** Six-Day War. It is the war in which Israel seized much of the now-disputed land.
3. Jews say their kings ruled region 3,000 years ago; Palestinians say land was theirs since Jews driven out in A.D. 135
4. old city of Jerusalem, Sinai Peninsula, Golan Heights, West Bank
5. Palestinian self-rule in West Bank and Gaza Strip
6. both involved partitioning a region
7. **Possible Answer:** Both sides feel too strongly about the issue of land and thus cannot compromise.
8. **Possible Answer:** Both sides have legitimate claims to the land and have reasonable arguments to make.
9. **Rubric** Questions should
   • present a range of issues.
   • show grasp of Middle East issues.
   • show evidence of teamwork.

CONNECT TO TODAY

Rubric Cartoons should
• clearly convey their main point.
• show grasp of the chosen issue.
• be visually appealing.

LESSON PLAN

OBJECTIVES

- Identify challenges facing the nations of the former Soviet Union.
- Describe Afghanistan's struggle for independence and possible role in global terrorism.

1 FOCUS & MOTIVATE

Ask students what challenges a nation faces after becoming independent. *(keeping the economy going, protecting its citizens, solving issues of education and social concern)*

2 INSTRUCT

Freedom Brings New Challenges

10.9.7

Critical Thinking

- How is the problem of ethnic hostility in the former Soviet republics similar to that of post-colonial Africa? *(Possible Answer: Outside authority kept control of ethnic hostility; without that control, hostilities flared.)*

CALIFORNIA RESOURCES

California Reading Toolkit, p. L84
California Modified Lesson Plans for English Learners, p. 163
California Daily Standards Practice Transparencies, TT76
California Standards Enrichment Workbook, pp. 103–104
California Standards Planner and Lesson Plans, p. L159
California Online Test Practice
California Test Generator CD-ROM
California Easy Planner CD-ROM
California eEdition CD-ROM

Temple decoration, Chiang Mai, Thailand

5

Floating market, Bangkok, Thailand

Central Asia Struggles

MAIN IDEA	WHY IT MATTERS NOW	TERMS & NAMES
POWER AND AUTHORITY Lands controlled or influenced by the Soviet Union struggle with the challenges of establishing new nations.	The security issues in these nations pose a threat to world peace and security.	• Transcaucasian Republics • Central Asian Republics • mujahideen • Taliban

CALIFORNIA STANDARDS

10.9.7 Analyze the reasons for the collapse of the Soviet Union, including the weakness of the command economy, burdens of military commitments, and growing resistance to Soviet rule by dissidents in satellite states and the non-Russian Soviet republics.

HI 2 Students recognize the complexity of historical causes and effects, including the limitations on determining cause and effect.

HI 3 Students interpret past events and issues within the context in which an event unfolded rather than solely in terms of present-day norms and values.

SETTING THE STAGE For thousands of years, the different peoples of Central Asia suffered invasions and domination by powerful groups such as the Mongols, Byzantines, Ottomans, and finally the Communist rulers of the Soviet Union. While such occupation brought many changes to this region, its various ethnic groups worked to keep alive much of their culture. They also longed to create nations of their own, a dream they realized in the early 1990s with the collapse of the Soviet Union. In the decade since then, however, these groups have come to know the challenges of building strong and stable independent nations.

Freedom Brings New Challenges

In 1991 the Soviet Union collapsed, and the republics that it had conquered emerged as 15 independent nations. Among them were those that had made up the Soviet empire's southern borders. Geographers often group these new nations into two geographic areas.

Armenia, Azerbaijan, and Georgia make up the **Transcaucasian Republics**. These three nations lie in the Caucasus Mountains between the Black and Caspian seas. East of the Caspian Sea and extending to the Tian Shan and Pamir mountains lie the five nations known as the **Central Asian Republics**. They are Uzbekistan, Turkmenistan, Tajikistan, Kazakhstan, and Kyrgyzstan.

TAKING NOTES

Outlining Use an outline to organize main ideas and details.

Freedom Brings New Challenges
A.
B.
Afghanistan and the World
A.
B.

Economic Struggles Since gaining independence, these nations have struggled economically and are today some of the poorest countries in the world. Much of the problem stems from their heavy reliance on the Soviet Union for economic help. As a result, they have had a difficult time standing on their own. Economic practices during the Soviet era have created additional problems. The Soviets, for example, converted much of the available farmland in the Central Asian Republics to grow "white gold"—cotton. Dependence on a single crop has hurt the development of a balanced economy in these nations.

Azerbaijan, which is located among the oil fields of the Caspian Sea, has the best chance to build a solid economy based on the income from oil and oil products. Meanwhile, Kazakhstan and Turkmenistan are working hard to tap their large reserves of oil and natural gas.

Ethnic and Religious Strife Fighting among various ethnic and religious groups has created another obstacle to stability for many of the newly independent

SECTION 5 PROGRAM RESOURCES

ALL STUDENTS

In-Depth Resources: Unit 5
- Guided Reading, p. 30

Formal Assessment
- Section Quiz, p. 318

ENGLISH LEARNERS

In-Depth Resources in Spanish
- Guided Reading, p. 144

Reading Study Guide (Spanish), p. 199
Reading Study Guide Audio CD (Spanish)

STRUGGLING READERS

In-Depth Resources: Unit 5
- Guided Reading, p. 30
- Building Vocabulary, p. 31
- Reteaching Activity, p. 49

Reading Study Guide, p. 199
Reading Study Guide Audio CD

INTEGRATED TECHNOLOGY

eEdition CD-ROM
Power Presentations CD-ROM
Critical Thinking Transparencies
- CT70 Chapter 34 Visual Summary

classzone.com

A. Answer The Soviets kept a lid on all such hostilities through repressive rule.

MAIN IDEA

Clarifying

Ⓐ Why was there little ethnic or religious strife in Central Asia during Soviet rule?

countries of Central Asia. The region is home to a number of different peoples, including some with long histories of hostility toward each other. With their iron-fisted rule, the Soviets kept a lid on these hostilities and largely prevented any serious ethnic clashes. After the breakup of the Soviet Union, however, long-simmering ethnic rivalries erupted into fighting. Some even became small regional wars.

Such was the case in Azerbaijan. Within this mostly Muslim country lies Nagorno-Karabakh, a small region of mainly Armenian Christians. In the wake of the Soviet Union's collapse, the people of this area declared their independence. Azerbaijan had no intention of letting go of this land, and fighting quickly broke out. Neighboring Armenia rushed to aid the Armenian people in the district. The war raged from 1991 through 1994, when the two sides agreed to a cease-fire. The status of Nagorno-Karabakh remains unresolved. Ⓐ

Afghanistan and the World

Just to the south of the Central Asian Republics lies one of the region's more prominent nations. Afghanistan is a small nation with both mountainous and desert terrain. It is one of the least-developed countries in the world, as most of its inhabitants are farmers or herders. And yet, over the past several decades, this mostly Muslim nation has grabbed the world's attention with two high-profile wars—one against the Soviet Union and the other against the United States.

Struggle for Freedom Afghanistan has endured a long history of struggle. During the 1800s, both Russia and Britain competed for control of its land. Russia wanted access to the Indian Ocean through Afghanistan, while Britain wanted control of the land in order to protect the northern borders of its Indian Empire. Britain fought three separate wars with the Afghanis before eventually leaving in 1919.

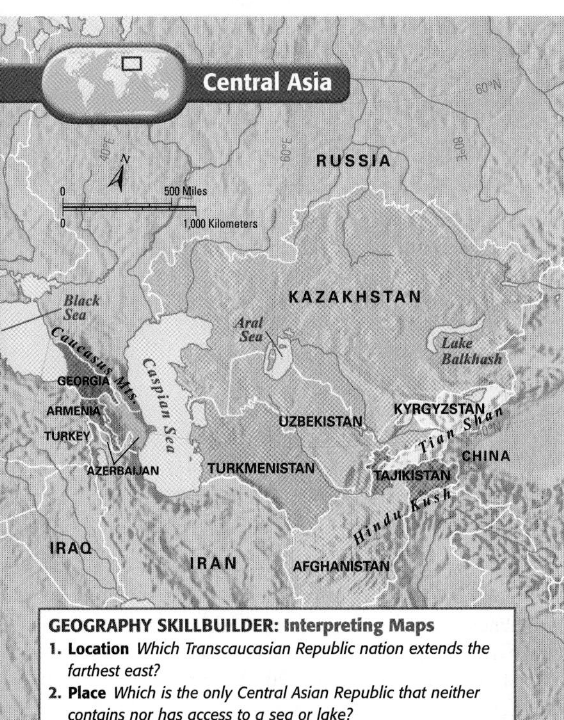

GEOGRAPHY SKILLBUILDER: Interpreting Maps

1. **Location** *Which Transcaucasian Republic nation extends the farthest east?*
2. **Place** *Which is the only Central Asian Republic that neither contains nor has access to a sea or lake?*

▼ The terrain of Central Asia varies widely, from mountains to plains.

Afghanistan and the World
10.9.7

Critical Thinking

- Why might access to the Indian Ocean be important to Russia? *(Possible Answer: eased trade from that part of a vast nation)*
- Why might people accept a lack of freedom, such as the Taliban created? *(Possible Answer: They may think the order and security that such an authority creates is worth the loss of freedom.)*

History from Visuals

Interpreting the Map

Ask students to identify a nation that has divided territory. *(Azerbaijan)* How might this contribute to tensions with Armenia? *(Armenian territory is the divider.)*

Extension Have students use an atlas or other reference to compare this map with maps showing the area's relief. Discuss ways that tall mountains challenge area nations.

SKILLBUILDER Answers

1. **Location** Kazakhstan
2. **Place** Tajikistan

DIFFERENTIATING INSTRUCTION: STRUGGLING READERS

Identifying Central Asian Nations

Class Time 15 minutes

Task Creating and charting names

Purpose To understand Central Asian terminology better

Instructions Highlight the names of the 15 former Soviet republics. Ask volunteers to attempt pronunciation. Then demonstrate correct pronunciation yourself, using this list:

- Armenia: ahr•MEE•nee•uh
- Georgia: JAWR•juh
- Turkmenistan: TURK•mehn•ih•STAN
- Kazakhstan: KAH•zahk•STAHN
- Azerbaijan: AZ•uhr•by•JAHN
- Uzbekistan: uz•BEHK•ih•STAN
- Tajikistan: tah•JIHK•ih•STAN
- Kyrgyzstan: KEER•gee•STAHN

Work with students to create a two-column chart with headings "Proper Noun" and "Proper Adjective." Clarify how to turn each proper noun type into a proper adjective in order to describe a person from that nation.

Proper Noun	Proper Adjective
Armenia	Armenian
Azerbaijan	Azerbaijani
Georgia	Georgian
Uzbekistan	Uzbek
Turkmenistan	Turkmen

More About . . .

Soviet-Afghani War

The war between the Soviet Union and Afghanistan has been compared to the United States war in Vietnam. In both cases, a large powerful nation eventually withdrew from an area when the costs of fighting guerillas became prohibitive.

Soviet forces entered Afghanistan in 1979 and did not leave until 1989. The Soviets were successful in occupying cities but were unable to secure the countryside. Only by using bomb and chemical attacks were they able to gain control of the rural areas.

Opposition to involvement by Soviet troops steadily grew stronger at home in the Soviet Union. By the time the Soviets left in 1989, 14,453 soldiers had died fighting against the mujahideen.

History *in* Depth

Destroying the Past

Ask students to create a list of rules that they think should govern treatment of world cultural sites such as the one shown. Students might consider how art would be protected in times of conflict or under extremist governments.

INTEGRATED TECHNOLOGY

Rubric Successful research should

- list country names.
- identify artifacts correctly.
- include only key artifacts.

That year, Afghanistan declared itself an independent nation and established a monarchy. The government implemented various reforms and tried to modernize the country. In 1964, the country devised a constitution that sought to establish a more democratic style of government. However, officials could not agree on a reform program and most people showed little interest in the effort to transform the government. As a result, a democratic system failed to develop.

Pushing Back the Soviets Nonetheless, Afghanistan had grown stable enough to establish good relations with many Western European nations and to hold its own on the world stage. When the Cold War conflict between the United States and Soviet Union broke out, Afghanistan chose to remain neutral. However, over the years, it received aid from both of the opposing superpowers.

Situated so close to the Soviet Union, however, Afghanistan could not hold out against the force of communism forever. In 1973, military leaders overthrew the government. Five years later, in 1978, a rival group with strong ties to the Soviet Union seized control of the country. Much of the population opposed the group and its strong association with communism. Many Afghanis felt that Communist policies conflicted with the teachings of Islam.

The opposition forces banded together to form a group known as the **mujahideen** (moo•JAH•heh•DEEN), or holy warriors. These rebels took up arms and fought fiercely against the Soviet-supported government. The rebellion soon prompted the Soviet Union to step in. In 1979 and 1980, Soviet troops rolled into Afghanistan to conquer the country and add it to their Communist empire.

With the Soviets' superior military force and advanced weaponry, the war had all the makings of a quick and lopsided affair. But the Afghan rebels used the land and guerrilla tactics to their advantage. In addition, the United States provided financial and military assistance. After nearly 10 years of bloody and fruitless fighting, the Soviet Union withdrew its troops. The Afghanis had taken on the world's Communist superpower and won. **B**

MAIN IDEA
Drawing Conclusions
B Why do you think the Soviets finally decided to leave Afghanistan?
B. Possible Answer They no longer had the will or desire to continue fighting against the Afghanis and their guerrilla tactics.

Rise and Fall of the Taliban With the Soviets gone, various Afghan rebel groups began battling each other for control of the country. A conservative Islamic group known as the **Taliban** emerged as the victor. By 1998, it controlled 90 percent of the country. Another rebel group, the Northern Alliance, held the northwest corner of the country. Observers initially viewed the Taliban as a positive force, as it brought order to the war-torn nation, rooted out corruption, and promoted the growth of business.

However, the group followed an extreme interpretation of Islamic law and applied it to nearly every aspect of Afghan society. Taliban leaders restricted women's lives by forbidding them to go to school or hold jobs. They banned everything from television and movies to modern music. Punishment for violating the rules included severe beatings, amputation, and even execution.

Even more troubling to the world community was the Taliban's role in the growing problem of world terrorism, which you will read more about in Chapter 20. Western

History *in* Depth

Destroying the Past

Among the Taliban's extreme policies that stemmed from their interpretation of Islam, one in particular shocked and angered historians around the world. In the years after gaining power, Taliban leaders destroyed some of Afghanistan's most prized artifacts—two centuries-old Buddhas carved out of cliffs.

The Taliban deemed the giant statues offensive to Islam. Ignoring pleas from scholars and museums, they demolished the ancient figures with dynamite and bombs. One of the two statues was thought to have dated back to the third century A.D.

INTEGRATED TECHNOLOGY

INTERNET ACTIVITY Choose a country and highlight its top archaeological treasures. Go to **classzone.com** for your research.

DIFFERENTIATING INSTRUCTION: ENGLISH LEARNERS

Defining Difficult Language

Class Time 15 minutes

Task Defining figurative or colloquial language

Purpose To clarify the general meaning of the text

Instructions Explain that the text on page 592 contains many examples of figurative or colloquial language. Clarify that such language has a meaning different from its literal dictionary definition, and that context is a useful clue to meaning. Have students find the language listed below and take turns reading the appropriate sentence aloud. Discuss what students think each phrase means.

- hold its own on the world stage
- banded together
- with strong ties
- troops rolled in
- guerrilla tactics
- superpowers
- lopsided affair
- war-torn
- took up arms
- had all the makings
- taken on
- rooted out

Then have students create a list in which they define the language in their own words. Here is an example:

took up arms = began to fight against

For help, have students use the Reading Study Guide in Spanish for Section 1.

leaders accused the Taliban of allowing terrorist groups to train in Afghanistan. The Taliban also provided refuge for terrorist leaders, including Osama bin Laden, whose al-Qaeda organization is thought to be responsible for numerous attacks on the West—including the attacks on the World Trade Center in New York and the Pentagon in Washington, D.C., on September 11, 2001.

In the wake of the September 11 attacks, the U.S. government demanded that the Taliban turn over bin Laden. After its leaders refused, the United States took military action. In October 2001, U.S. forces began bombing Taliban air defense, airfields, and command centers, as well as al-Qaeda training camps. On the ground, the United States provided assistance to anti-Taliban forces, such as the Northern Alliance. By December, the United States had driven the Taliban from power.

▲ Captured Taliban fighters look out from a jail cell near the Afghani capital of Kabul.

Challenges Ahead With the Taliban defeated, Afghan officials selected a new government under the leadership of Hamid Karzai. His government faces the enormous task of rebuilding a country that has endured more than two decades of warfare. What's more, Afghanistan remains a country of roughly a dozen ethnic groups with distinct language and cultural patterns, all of which makes the job of creating a unified nation a difficult one.

The challenge before Afghanistan, however, is neither unique nor new. As you will read in the next chapter, over the past 50 years countries around the world have attempted to shed their old and often repressive forms of rule and implement a more democratic style of government.

More About . . .

Hamid Karzai

Hamid Karzai was selected to rule the country by the Loya Jerga, a traditional assembly of tribal representatives. Mr. Karzai comes from a prominent family whose members have been leaders in Afghanstan for centuries. His father, a parliamentary deputy, was assassinated in 1999, probably by the Taliban.

SECTION 5 ASSESSMENT

TERMS & NAMES 1. For each term or name, write a sentence explaining its significance.
• Transcaucasian Republics • Central Asian Republics • mujahideen • Taliban

USING YOUR NOTES

2. Which challenge for the Central Asian nations is most difficult to overcome? (10.9.7)

Freedom Brings New Challenges
A.
B.
Afghanistan and the World
A.
B.

MAIN IDEA

3. What countries make up the Transcaucasian Republics? the Central Asian Republics? (10.9.7)
4. Why did Afghanis oppose the notion of Communist rule? (10.9.7)
5. Why did the United States take military action against the Taliban? (10.9.7)

CRITICAL THINKING & WRITING

6. **MAKING INFERENCES** Some historians call the Soviet-Afghan war the Soviet Union's "Vietnam." What do they mean by this reference? Do you agree with it? (10.9.7)
7. **DRAWING CONCLUSIONS** Why might Afghanis have been willing to accept Taliban rule by 1998? (10.9.7)
8. **IDENTIFYING PROBLEMS** Why did the new nations of Central Asia experience such economic difficulties? (10.9.7)
9. **WRITING ACTIVITY** POWER AND AUTHORITY Imagine you are a speechwriter for Hamid Karzai. Write what you feel would be an appropriate **first paragraph** for his initial speech upon taking power. (Writing 2.4.b)

CONNECT TO TODAY CREATING A TIME LINE
Choose one of the countries discussed in this section and create a **time line** of the eight to ten most significant events in its history over the last 50 years. (Writing 2.3.d)

③ ASSESS

SECTION 5 ASSESSMENT

Have students answer the questions independently, then review their answers with a small group.

Formal Assessment
• Section Quiz, p. 318

④ RETEACH

Use the Reteaching Activity for Section 5 and the Visual Summary to review this section and chapter.

Critical Thinking Transparencies
• CT70 Chapter 34 Visual Summary

In-Depth Resources: Unit 5
• Reteaching Activity, p. 49

ANSWERS

1. Transcaucasian Republics, p. 590 • Central Asian Republics, p. 590 • mujahideen, p. 592 • Taliban, p. 592

2. I. A. economic struggles, B. ethnic/religious strife. II. A. fight for independence, B. Taliban brings Islamic fundamentalism. C. support for terrorism. **Possible Answer:** ethnic diversity and tension
3. Transcaucasian—Armenia, Azerbaijan, Georgia; Central Asia—Uzbekistan, Turkmenistan, Tajikistan, Kazakhstan, Kyrgyzstan
4. felt communism conflicted with Islam
5. The Taliban refused to hand over bin Laden.
6. **Possible Answer:** Both were long drawn-out wars, in which a strong nation failed to defeat a seemingly weaker enemy. Most will agree, as U.S. also retreated without victory.
7. **Possible Answer:** Afghanis might be worn out from war and chaos enough to choose order and security offered by the Taliban.
8. **Possible Answer:** too much dependence on single crop, economic development unnecessary under Soviets
9. **Rubric** Paragraphs should
• present a clear thesis with details.
• focus on challenges for Karzai as leader.

CONNECT TO TODAY
Rubric Time line should
• highlight key events.
• follow a logical sequence.

TERMS & NAMES

1. partition, p. 564
2. Jawaharlal Nehru, p. 565
3. Indira Gandhi, p. 566
4. Corazón Aquino, p. 571
5. Jomo Kenyatta, p. 579
6. Anwar Sadat, p. 585
7. PLO, p. 585
8. mujahideen, p. 592

MAIN IDEAS

Answers will vary.

9. India and Pakistan
10. Some Tamils, a Hindu people, want to establish a separate nation. The Buddhist majority opposes this.
11. U.S. got free trading rights; Filipinos feared exploitation of natural resources and environment.
12. leader of the Indonesian independence movement; nation's first president
13. for spending too much money on programs nation couldn't afford; too much time on Pan-African affairs
14. unprepared for governing freely
15. Egypt seized canal in 1956; Israelis, with British/French support, invaded to recapture, withdrew under world pressure
16. Israeli-Egyptian agreement: Egypt would recognize Israel as nation and Israel would return the Sinai Peninsula
17. Armenia, Azerbaijan, Georgia
18. group that controlled Afghanistan in mid-1990s, imposed strict Islamic laws on nation and its people

Chapter 18 Assessment

VISUAL SUMMARY

The Struggle for Independence

The time line shows the dates on which various countries in Asia and Africa achieved their independence after World War II. It also shows (in parentheses) the countries from which they achieved independence.

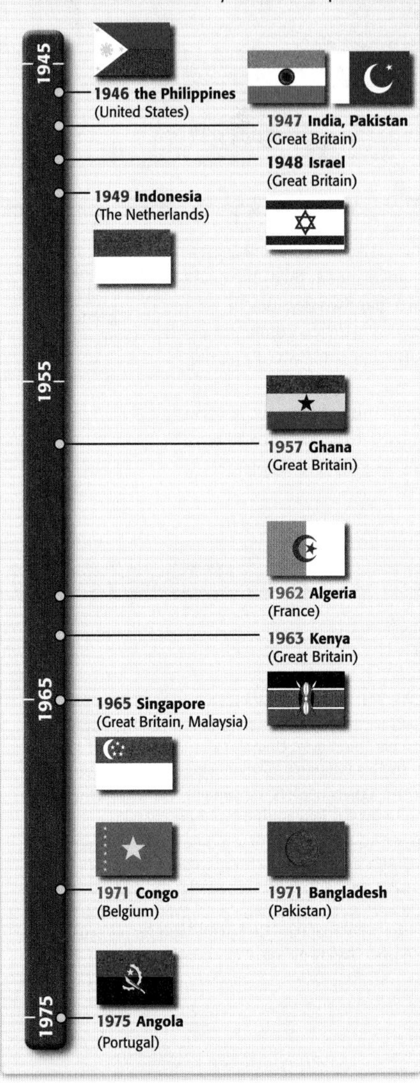

TERMS & NAMES

For each term or name below, briefly explain its connection to colonial independence around the world after World War II.

1. partition
2. Jawaharlal Nehru
3. Indira Gandhi
4. Corazón Aquino
5. Jomo Kenyatta
6. Anwar Sadat
7. PLO
8. mujahideen

MAIN IDEAS

The Indian Subcontinent Achieves Freedom Section 1 (pages 563–569)

9. What two nations emerged from the British colony of India in 1947? (10.4.4)
10. Briefly explain the reason for the civil disorder in Sri Lanka. (10.4.4)

Southeast Asian Nations Gain Independence Section 2 (pages 570–577)

11. What concerns did the Filipinos have regarding the Bell Act? (10.4.4)
12. Who was Sukarno? (10.4.4)

New Nations in Africa Section 3 (pages 578–582)

13. Why were Kwame Nkrumah's politics criticized? (10.4.4)
14. Why did Zaire face such difficulty upon gaining independence? (10.4.4)

Conflicts in the Middle East Section 4 (pages 583–589)

15. What was the Suez Crisis? (10.9.6)
16. What were the Camp David Accords? (10.9.6)

Central Asia Struggles Section 5 (pages 590–593)

17. Which nations comprise the Transcaucasian Republics? (10.9.7)
18. What was the Taliban? (10.9.7)

CRITICAL THINKING

1. USING YOUR NOTES

Use a web diagram to show some of the challenges that newly independent nations have faced. (10.4.4)

2. FORMING AND SUPPORTING OPINIONS

REVOLUTION Do you think there should be a limit to the methods revolutionaries use? Explain your opinion. (HI 4)

3. ANALYZING ISSUES

ECONOMICS Why have so many of the new nations that emerged over the past half-century struggled economically? (10.4.4)

4. DRAWING CONCLUSIONS

In your view, was religion a unifying or destructive force as colonies around the world became new nations? Support your answer with specific examples from the text. (10.4.4)

CRITICAL THINKING

Answers will vary.

1. **Possible Answers:** constant threat of revolution, former colonizers' continued meddling, developing a viable economy and government, civil war, random boundaries
2. **Possible Answers:** Yes—The ends do not justify the means; No—Sometimes all possible force is necessary.
3. **Possible Answer:** many were dependent on former colonizer, war and corruption after independence also hurt economies
4. **Possible Answer:** It has mostly been destructive. Hindu and Muslim tension led to death of nearly 1 million Indians and a partitioned nation. Religious differences have led to violence and instability in Sri Lanka, the Middle East, and Africa.

Use the following excerpt from the Balfour Declaration and your knowledge of world history to answer questions 1 and 2.
Additional Test Practice, pp. S1–S33

PRIMARY SOURCE

His Majesty's Government view with favour the establishment in Palestine of a national home for the Jewish people, and will use their best endeavours to facilitate the achievement of this object, it being clearly understood that nothing shall be done which may prejudice the civil and religious rights of existing non-Jewish communities in Palestine, or the rights and political status enjoyed by Jews in any other country.

ARTHUR JAMES BALFOUR, in a letter to Lord Rothschild, November 2, 1917

1. The intent of the British government was to (10.9.6)
   - **A.** give all of Palestine to the Jewish people.
   - **B.** leave Palestine in the hands of the Arabs.
   - **C.** divide Palestine between Jews and Arabs.
   - **D.** ensure justice for Jews around the world.

2. The group most likely to have opposed the Balfour Declaration was the (10.9.6)
   - **A.** Arabs.
   - **B.** Jews.
   - **C.** French.
   - **D.** Americans.

Use the political cartoon about Corazón Aquino's election victory and your knowledge of world history to answer question 3.

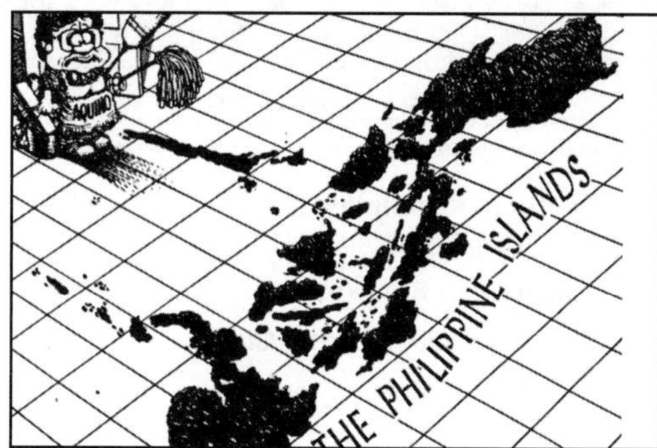

3. Aquino was expected by many to "clean up" the Philippines by ending years of (10.4.4)
   - **A.** slavery.
   - **B.** dictatorship.
   - **C.** business corruption.
   - **D.** unchecked pollution.

INTEGRATED TECHNOLOGY

TEST PRACTICE Go to **classzone.com**
- Diagnostic tests
- Strategies
- Tutorials
- Additional practice

ALTERNATIVE ASSESSMENT

1. **Interact *with* History** (10.4.4)
   On page 562, you discussed the most important areas to address in building a new nation. Now that you have read about the efforts by so many former colonies to forge new countries, do you think that you focused on the right areas? Work as a class to identify the main factors that determine whether a new nation struggles or thrives. Be sure to cite specific examples from the text.

2. 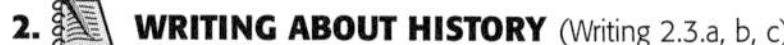 **WRITING ABOUT HISTORY** (Writing 2.3.a, b, c)
   POWER AND AUTHORITY Select one of the leaders discussed in this chapter. Review the decisions the leader made while in power. Write an evaluation of the leader's decisions and his or her impact on the country. Consider the following
   - the leader's views on government and democracy
   - the leader's handling of the economy
   - the leader's accomplishments and failures

INTEGRATED TECHNOLOGY

Creating a Database (10.4.4)

Use the Internet, library, and other reference materials to create a database showing the economic growth of any four countries discussed in this chapter. Create one table for each country, with column headings for each measure of economic growth you chose to record and row headings for each 10-year period. Then insert the most current data you can find. Consider the following questions to get started.
- What statistics will be most useful in making comparisons between nations?
- Which nations have capitalist economies? What other types of economies did you discover?
- Which nations have "one crop" economies?

STANDARDS-BASED ASSESSMENT

1. The correct answer is letter **C**. Letter **A** is incorrect because the letter favors protecting non-Jewish communities. Letter **B** is incorrect because the letter favors a Jewish state. Letter **D** is incorrect because the letter discusses rights for Jews in Palestine.
2. Letter **A** is correct. Letter **B** is incorrect because the letter advances Jewish interests. Letters **C** and **D** are incorrect because the letter does not discuss French or American interests.
3. The correct answer is letter **B**. Letter **A** is incorrect because slavery did not exist in the Philippines at this time. Letter **C** is incorrect because Aquino was elected to get rid of a dictator, not deal with business corruption. Letter **D** is incorrect because pollution was not an issue at this time.

Formal Assessment
- Chapter Tests, Forms A, B, and C, pp. 319–330

California Test Generator CD-ROM
- Chapter Tests, Forms A, B, and C (English and Spanish)

ALTERNATIVE ASSESSMENT

1. **Possible Answers:** Include diverse ethnicities in government, avoid corruption at all costs; Earning people's trust is most important as it will help limit civil strife.
2. **Rubric** The evaluation should
   - identify the leader and key decisions.
   - clearly state impact of the decisions.
   - include a well-supported opinion.

INTEGRATED TECHNOLOGY

Rubric Databases should
- convey information clearly.
- provide a full and comprehensive economic picture of each nation.
- identify the sources of information used in the database.

CHAPTER 19 PLANNING GUIDE

Struggles for Democracy, 1945–Present

CHAPTER RESOURCES	COPYMASTERS	ASSESSMENT
CHAPTER OVERVIEW China and nations in Latin America, Africa, and the former Soviet bloc struggled for democracy.	**In-Depth Resources: Unit 5** • Building Vocabulary, p. 55 **Chapters in Brief** (in English and Spanish) **Block Schedule Pacing Guide**	**Chapter Assessment,** pp. 632–633 **Formal Assessment** • Chapter Tests, Forms A, B, and C, pp. 336–347 **Test Generator** **Online Test Practice**
SECTION 1 **Democracy—Case Study: Latin American Democracies** pp. 599–605 **OBJECTIVE** Summarize Brazil's, Mexico's, and Argentina's efforts to build democracy.	**In-Depth Resources: Unit 5** • Guided Reading, p. 50 • Geography Application, p. 57 • Literature: from *Brazil,* p. 63 • History Makers: Juan and Eva Perón, p. 66 • Reteaching Activity, p. 69 **Case Studies 7 and 8,** pp. 86 and 100	**Section 1 Assessment,** p. 605 **Formal Assessment** • Section Quiz, p. 331 **California Daily Standards Practice Transparencies,** TT136
SECTION 2 **The Challenge of Democracy in Africa** pp. 606–611 **OBJECTIVE** Describe the struggles to establish democracies in Africa.	**In-Depth Resources: Unit 5** • Guided Reading, p. 51 • Primary Sources, pp. 59, 60 • History Makers: Nelson Mandela, p. 67 • Reteaching Activity, p. 70 **Case Studies 4 and 8,** pp. 44 and 100	**Section 2 Assessment,** p. 611 **Formal Assessment** • Section Quiz, p. 332 **California Daily Standards Practice Transparencies,** TT137
SECTION 3 **The Collapse of the Soviet Union** pp. 612–617 **OBJECTIVE** Explain the breakup of the Soviet Union.	**In-Depth Resources: Unit 5** • Guided Reading, p. 52 • Primary Source: Political Cartoon, p. 61 • Reteaching Activity, p. 71 **Case Studies 2 and 3,** pp. 16 and 30	**Section 3 Assessment,** p. 617 **Formal Assessment** • Section Quiz, p. 333 **California Daily Standards Practice Transparencies,** TT138
SECTION 4 **Changes in Central and Eastern Europe** pp. 618–624 **OBJECTIVE** Summarize the reforms and changes in Europe.	**In-Depth Resources: Unit 5** • Guided Reading, p. 53 • Primary Source: The Road to Marjača, p. 62 • Connections Across Time/Cultures, p. 68 • Reteaching Activity, p. 72 **Case Study 3,** p. 30	**Section 4 Assessment,** p. 624 **Formal Assessment** • Section Quiz, p. 334 **California Daily Standards Practice Transparencies,** TT139
SECTION 5 **China: Reform and Reaction** pp. 625–631 **OBJECTIVE** Analyze China's policies toward capitalism and democracy.	**In-Depth Resources: Unit 5** • Guided Reading, p. 54 • Skillbuilder Practice, p. 56 • Reteaching Activity, p. 73 **Reading Study Guide,** p. 209	**Section 5 Assessment,** p. 629 **Formal Assessment** • Section Quiz, p. 335 **California Daily Standards Practice Transparencies,** TT140

INTEGRATED TECHNOLOGY

- eEdition Plus Online
- EasyPlanner Plus Online
- eTest Plus Online

Audio CDs
- Voices from the Past
- Reading Study Guides

CD-ROMs
- eEdition
- Power Presentations
- EasyPlanner
- Electronic Library of Primary Sources
- Test Generator

eEdition CD-ROM

World Art and Cultures Transparencies

- AT76 *The Family*

classzone.com

eEdition CD-ROM

World Art and Cultures Transparencies

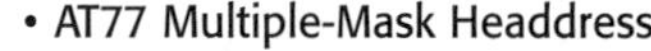

- AT77 Multiple-Mask Headdress

Electronic Library of Primary Sources
- from "Masakhane–Let Us Build Together"

Patterns of Interaction Video Series
- Revolutions in Latin America and South Africa

eEdition CD-ROM

Electronic Library of Primary Sources

classzone.com

eEdition CD-ROM

Geography Transparencies

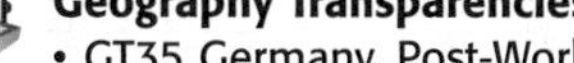

- GT35 Germany, Post-World War I–Present

World Art and Cultures Transparencies

- AT78 *Burning Rods*

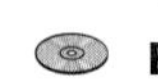

Electronic Library of Primary Sources
- Destruction of the Berlin Wall
- "Will I Ever Go Home Again?"

eEdition CD-ROM

Critical Thinking Transparencies
- CT35 Democratic Struggles
- CT71 Chapter 35 Visual Summary

Electronic Library of Primary Sources
- "The Massacre in Tiananmen Square"

classzone.com

OVERVIEW OF CALIFORNIA RESOURCES

	Section 1	Section 2	Section 3	Section 4	Section 5
California Reading Toolkit	p. L85	p. L86	p. L87	p. L88	p. L89
California Modified Lesson Plans for English Learners	p. 165	p. 167	p. 169	p. 171	p. 173
California Daily Standards Practice Transparencies	TT77	TT78	TT79	TT80	TT81
California Standards Enrichment Workbook	pp. 107–108, 109–110, 111–112	pp. 107–108, 109–110, 111–112	pp. 103–104	pp. 91–92, 99–100, 103–104	pp. 97–98, 107–108, 109–110, 111–112
California Standards Planner and Lesson Plans	p. L161	p. L163	p. L165	p. L167	p. L169
California Online Test Practice	classzone.com	classzone.com	classzone.com	classzone.com	classzone.com
California Test Generator CD-ROM	CD-ROM	CD-ROM	CD-ROM	CD-ROM	CD-ROM
California Easy Planner CD-ROM	CD-ROM	CD-ROM	CD-ROM	CD-ROM	CD-ROM
California eEdition CD-ROM	CD-ROM	CD-ROM	CD-ROM	CD-ROM	CD-ROM

Chart Key:

 Pupil's Edition

 Teacher's Edition

 Overhead Transparency

Block Scheduling

 Copymaster

 Audio Library

 CD-ROM

 Internet

Video

NO TIME?

If you do not have time to teach this chapter in full, assign the **Chapter in Brief** (also available in Spanish).

Previewing Resources for Differentiated Instruction

ENGLISH LEARNERS: Resources in Spanish

In-Depth Resources in Spanish

- Guided Reading (A)
- Skillbuilder Practice: Analyzing Primary and Secondary Sources
- Geography Application: Democracy in Central and South America (B)

Chapters in Brief

Reading Study Guide (C)

Reading Study Guide Audio CD

Test Generator CD-ROM

- Chapter Test, Forms A, B, and C

Plus

Modified Lesson Plans for English Learners

Multi-Language Glossary of Social Studies Terms

(A)

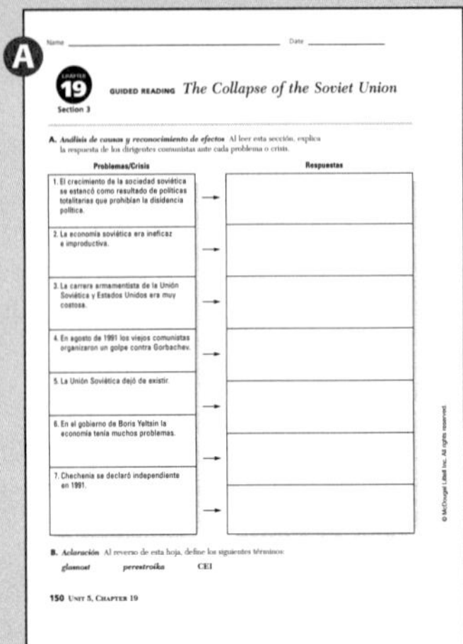

Chapter 19, Section 3 — GUIDED READING *The Collapse of the Soviet Union*

(B)

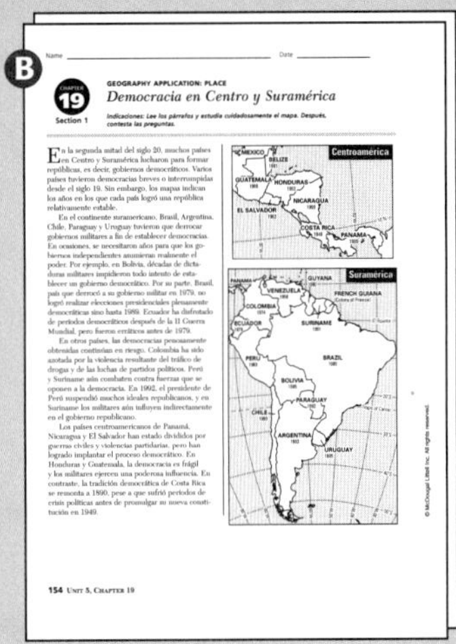

Chapter 19, Section 1 — GEOGRAPHY APPLICATION: PLACE *Democracia en Centro y Suramérica*

STRUGGLING READERS

In-Depth Resources: Unit 5

- Guided Reading (A)
- Building Vocabulary
- Skillbuilder Practice: Analyzing Primary and Secondary Sources (B)
- Geography Application: Democracy in Central and South America
- Reteaching Activities

Chapters in Brief

Reading Study Guide (C)

Reading Study Guide Audio CD

Formal Assessment

- Chapter Test, Form A

Plus

Reading Toolkit

(A)

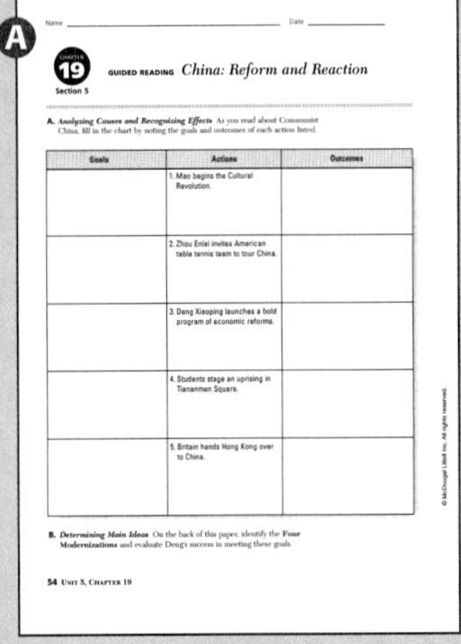

Chapter 19, Section 5 — GUIDED READING *China: Reform and Reaction*

(B)

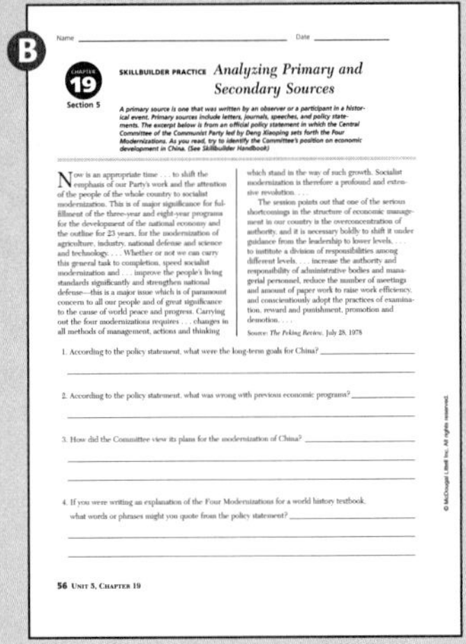

Chapter 19, Section 5 — SKILLBUILDER PRACTICE *Analyzing Primary and Secondary Sources*

GIFTED AND TALENTED STUDENTS

In-Depth Resources: Unit 5

- Primary Source: from *Kaffir Boy*; Mandela's Inaugural Address; Political Cartoon (A); The Road to Marjača
- Literature: from *Brazil* (B)
- History Makers: Juan and Eva Perón; Nelson Mandela
- Connections Across Time and Cultures: The Breakup of Two Empires (C)

Electronic Library of Primary Sources

- from "Masakhane–Let Us Build Together"
- Destruction of the Berlin Wall
- "Will I Ever Go Home Again?"
- "The Massacre in Tiananmen Square"

Formal Assessment

- Chapter Test, Form C

(A)

Chapter 19, Section 3 — PRIMARY SOURCE Political Cartoon

Activity Options

(B)

Chapter 19, Section 1 — LITERATURE SELECTION *from Brazil* by John Updike

The mill was a single vast room where giant looms kept up a clatter which pressed on Tristão's ears with a million small concussions.

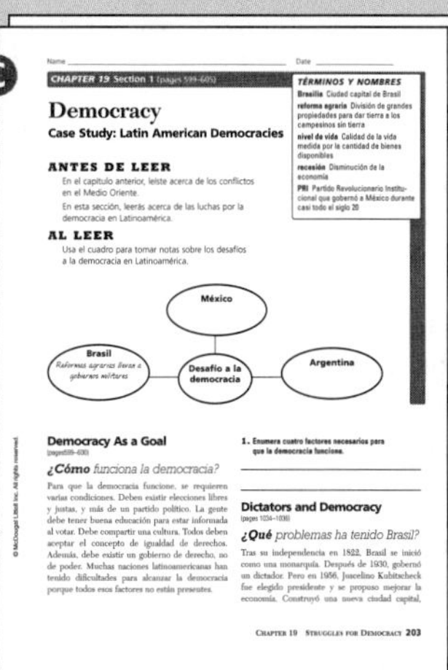

CHAPTER 19 Section 1

Democracy

Case Study: Latin American Democracies

ANTES DE LEER

AL LEER

TÉRMINOS Y NOMBRES

México

Brasil

Desafío a la democracia

Argentina

Democracy As a Goal

¿Cómo funciona la democracia?

Dictators and Democracy

¿Qué problemas ha tenido Brasil?

CHAPTER 19 STRUGGLES FOR DEMOCRACY 203

Activities in the Teacher's Edition for English Learners

- Obstacles to Democracy, p. 600
- Creating a South Africa Glossary, p. 609
- Charting Gorbachev's Reforms, p. 613
- Writing Mini-Biographies, p. 619

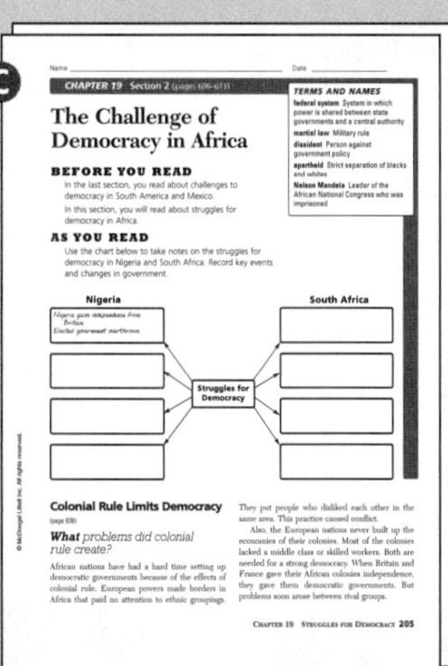

CHAPTER 19 Section 2

The Challenge of Democracy in Africa

BEFORE YOU READ

AS YOU READ

TERMS AND NAMES

Nigeria

South Africa

Struggles for Democracy

Colonial Rule Limits Democracy

What problems did colonial rule create?

CHAPTER 19 STRUGGLES FOR DEMOCRACY 205

Activities in the Teacher's Edition for Struggling Readers

- Change in Mexico, p. 604
- South African Leaders, p. 610
- Russia Under Boris Yeltsin, p.616
- Analyzing a Political Cartoon, p. 620
- Causes and Effects of Chinese Reforms, p. 626

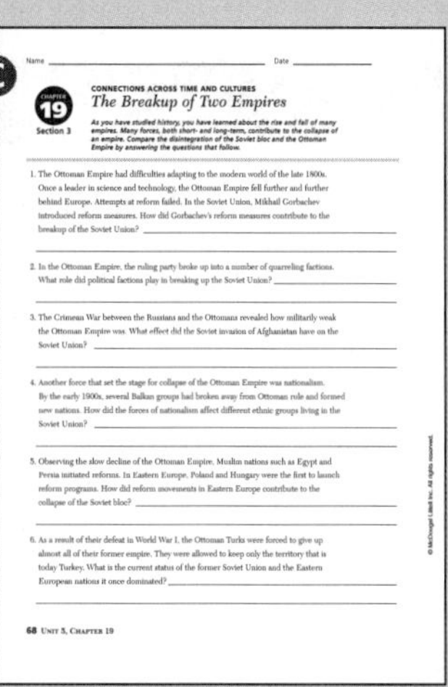

CONNECTIONS ACROSS TIME AND CULTURES

The Breakup of Two Empires

68 UNIT 5, CHAPTER 19

Activities in the Teacher's Edition for Gifted and Talented Students

- Writing About Episodes in Mexico's History, p. 603
- Politics in Nigeria, p. 608
- Creating a Biography of Boris Yeltsin, p. 615
- International Criminal Tribunal, p. 622
- Writing a Poem, p. 628

INTEGRATED TECHNOLOGY

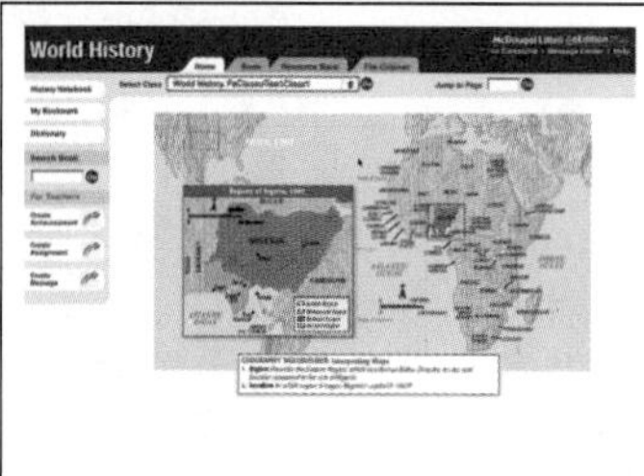

eEdition

- Interactive Visuals
- Interactive Maps
- Interactive Primary Sources

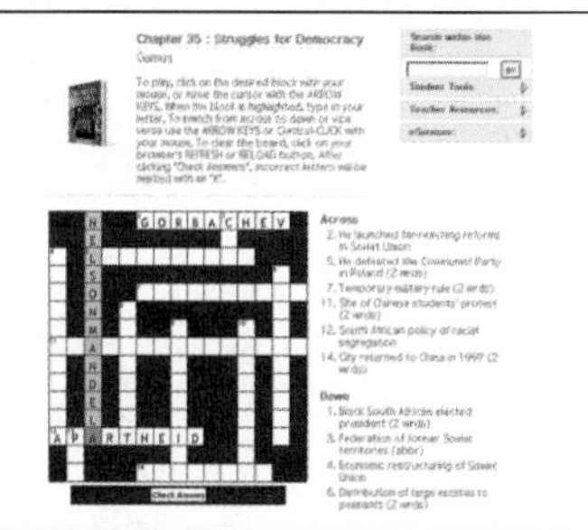

classzone.com

- Research Links
- Internet Activities
- Primary Sources
- Chapter Quiz
- Current Events

Power Presentations CD-ROM

- Lecture Notes
- Image Gallery
- Chapter Review Game

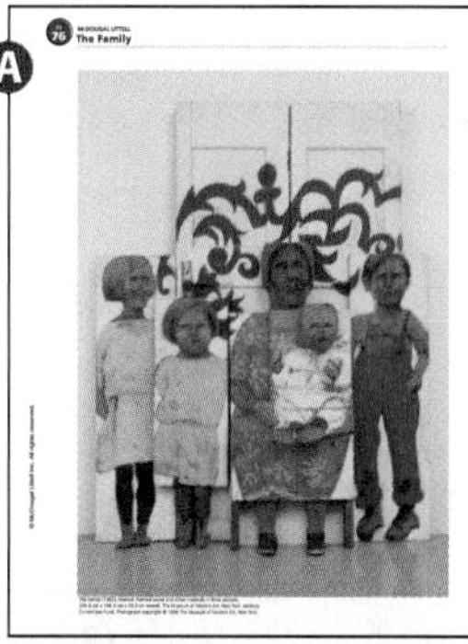

Critical Thinking Transparencies

- CT35 Democratic Struggles Around the Globe
- CT71 Chapter 35 Visual Summary

Geography Transparencies

- GT35 Germany, Post-World War I–Present

World Art and Cultures Transparencies

- AT76 *The Family* Ⓐ
- AT77 Multiple-Mask Headdress, AT78 *Burning Rods*

Test Practice Transparencies TT136–TT140

Test Generator CD-ROM

EasyPlanner CD-ROM

Voices from the Past Audio CD

Online Test Practice

Electronic Library of Primary Sources

Patterns of Interaction Video Series

CHAPTER 19 • OBJECTIVE

Understand struggles for change in Latin America, Africa, the former Soviet bloc, and China.

Previewing Main Ideas

Tell students to begin thinking about what defines a democracy. Then ask them to consider ways in which countries with authoritarian governments might transform themselves into democracies. *(Possible Answers: allow multiple political parties, hold free elections)* Ask them to examine the implications of both incremental and revolutionary change. *(Possible Answer: Revolutionary change comes quickly but can include violence.)*

Accessing Prior Knowledge

Have students think about the involvement of the United States in conflicts in Southwest Asia. Ask students how successful the United States has been in establishing democratic governments and institutions in Afghanistan and Iraq. What obstacles have impeded U.S. efforts? *(Possible Answers: cultural and religious differences, damage to infrastructures and economies)*

Geography *Answers*

ECONOMICS Republics and federal republics seem to predominate.

REVOLUTION China and North Korea remain Communist.

CULTURAL INTERACTION Parliamentary democracy predominates in the labeled countries of Europe.

CHAPTER 19

Struggles for Democracy, 1945–Present

Previewing Main Ideas

ECONOMICS Many nations, such as Brazil, Poland, Russia, and China, discovered that economic stability is important for democratic progress.
Geography *Which type of government seems to predominate in the Western Hemisphere?*

REVOLUTION In 1989, revolutions overthrew Communist governments in the Soviet Union and Central and Eastern Europe. In China, the Communist government and the army put down a student protest calling for democracy.
Geography *Which two countries in the Eastern Hemisphere are still Communist?*

CULTURAL INTERACTION Chinese students imported democratic ideas from the West. Democratic reforms spread across Central and Eastern Europe, causing Communist governments to fall.
Geography *Which type of government predominates in the labeled countries of Europe?*

INTEGRATED TECHNOLOGY

eEdition
- Interactive Maps
- Interactive Visuals
- Interactive Primary Sources

INTERNET RESOURCES
Go to **classzone.com** for:
- Research Links
- Internet Activities
- Primary Sources
- Chapter Quiz
- Maps
- Test Practice
- Current Events

WORLD

1948 South Africa imposes apartheid policy of racial discrimination.

1959 ◀ Fidel Castro seizes power in Cuba.

1967 Nigerian civil war begins.

1945 — 1965

USA

1948 Harry Truman wins second term as president. ▶

1964 Congress authorizes President Johnson to send troops to Vietnam.

1969 Neil Armstrong on the moon i lunar landing.

596

TIME LINE DISCUSSION

Point out to students that the time line covers a period of unprecedented change in Europe and South Africa. For the first time, many nations had the opportunity to elect their own officials and choose their own economic systems.

1. How many years did the policy of apartheid last before it was revoked? *(46 years—from 1948 to 1994)*
2. Who was the U.S. president when South Africa established apartheid? *(Harry Truman)* Who was U.S. president when the policy was dismantled? *(Bill Clinton)*
3. Why is 1959 a significant year in the history of Cuba? *(That is the year in which Fidel Castro seized power.)*
4. When did Chinese leader Deng Xiaoping initiate economic reforms? *(1978)*
5. During the 1960s, what conflict was the United States involved in? *(the war in Vietnam)*

Types of Government, 2003

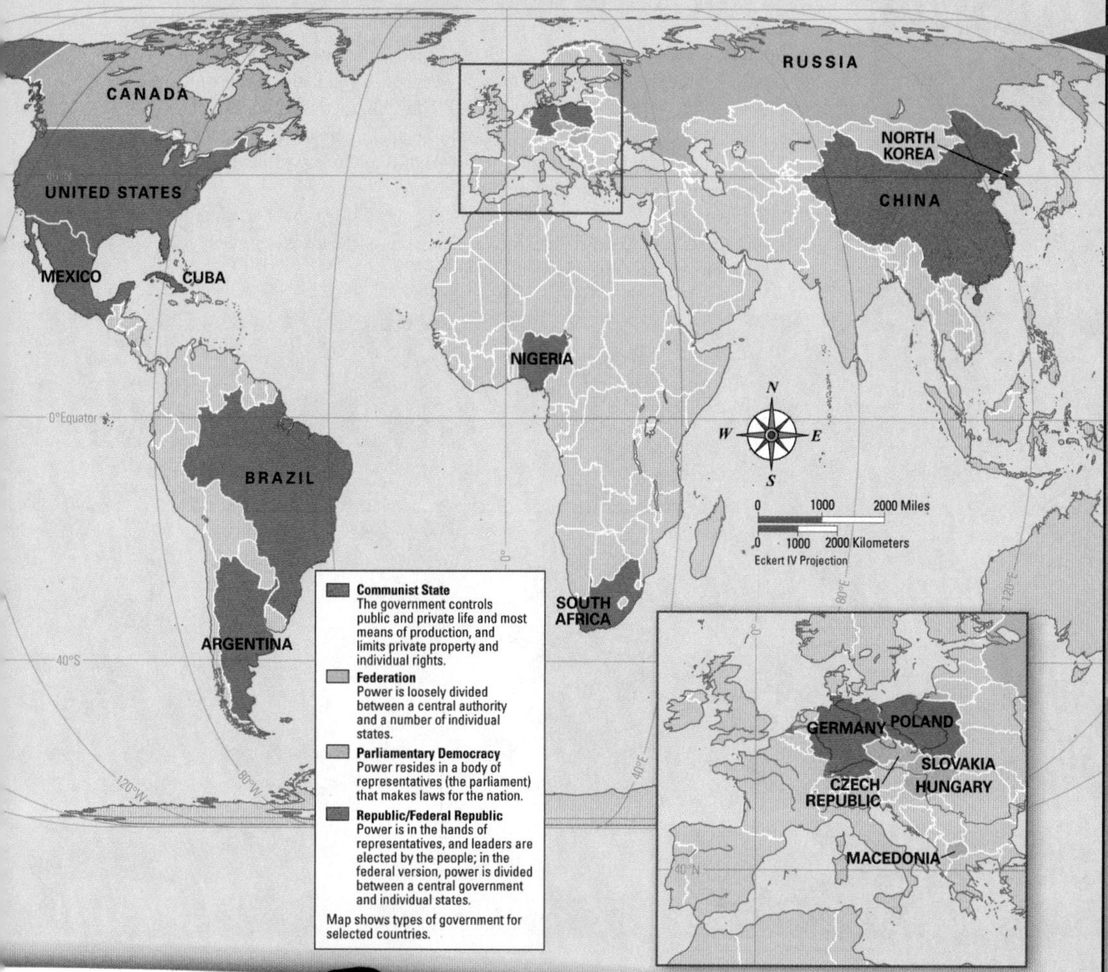

CANADA
UNITED STATES
MEXICO
CUBA
BRAZIL
ARGENTINA
NIGERIA
SOUTH AFRICA
RUSSIA
NORTH KOREA
CHINA
GERMANY
POLAND
SLOVAKIA
HUNGARY
CZECH REPUBLIC
MACEDONIA

0°Equator
40°S
120°W
80°W
40°E
80°E
120°E
N S E W
0 1000 2000 Miles
0 1000 2000 Kilometers
Eckert IV Projection

Communist State The government controls public and private life and most means of production, and limits private property and individual rights.

Federation Power is loosely divided between a central authority and a number of individual states.

Parliamentary Democracy Power resides in a body of representatives (the parliament) that makes laws for the nation.

Republic/Federal Republic Power is in the hands of representatives, and leaders are elected by the people; in the federal version, power is divided between a central government and individual states.

Map shows types of government for selected countries.

1978 Deng Xiaoping begins economic reforms in China. ▶

1989 Berlin Wall comes down.

1994 South Africa holds its first multiracial election.

1985

2005

1980 ◀ Ronald Reagan elected president.

1988 George Bush elected president.

1992 Bill Clinton elected president.

2000 George W. Bush elected president.

597

History from Visuals

Interpreting the Map

Tell students that, as they study Chapter 19, they will learn more about many of the countries highlighted on the map. Then explain that the colors of the countries correspond to the different types of governments defined in the key. Ask students which countries highlighted on the map are communist states. *(Cuba, China, North Korea)* Which types of government prevail in the United States and Canada? *(United States–Federal republic; Canada–Parliamentary democracy)*

Extension Ask students to locate and examine a map that shows the different administrative divisions in the Russian Federation. Have them make a list of the different types of divisions and the number of territories within each type.

RECOMMENDED RESOURCES

Books for the Teacher

Berry, Ian. ***Living Apart: South Africa Under Apartheid.*** London: Phaidon, 1996.

Winn, Peter. ***Americas: The Changing Face of Latin America and the Caribbean.*** Berkeley: U of California P, 1999.

Books for the Student

McDougal Littell Literature Connections. Head, Bessie. ***When Rain Clouds Gather (with related readings).*** 1997. In this novel, Makhaya flees South Africa for Botswana in the mid-1960s.

McDougal Littell Literature Connections. Mathabane, Mark. ***Kaffir Boy (with related readings).*** 1998. In this powerful memoir, Mathabane shows how the human spirit endures even in the face of apartheid.

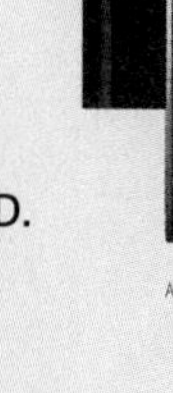

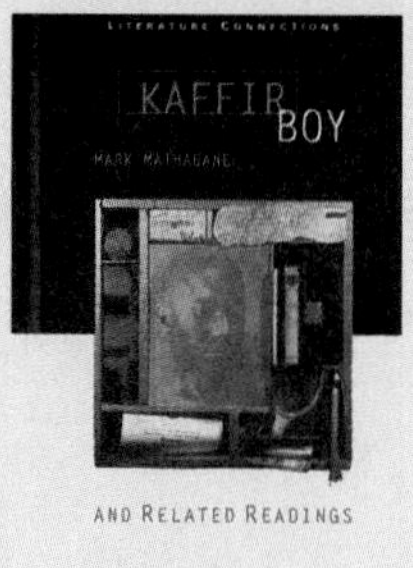

Videos and Software

Conversations with Gorbachev. VHS and DVD. Films for the Humanities & Sciences, 1994. 800-257-5126.

The Last Days of Apartheid. CD-ROM. Society for Visual Education, 1996. 800-829-1900.

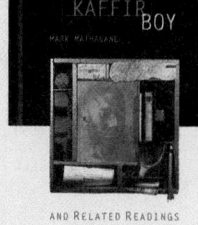

Interact *with* History

Objectives

- Consider reasons for the popularity of democratic forms of government.
- Describe the institutions, rights, and practices that define a democracy.

EXAMINING *the* ISSUES

Possible Answers

- Students might consider the rights guaranteed to American citizens in the U.S. Constitution, particularly in the Bill of Rights.
- Students may mention voting, running for office, and volunteering for political campaigns. Government classes in schools and public-service announcements in the media may encourage participation.

Discussion

Ask students to think about what they learned when they studied ancient Greece. How was the democracy of ancient Greece different from most modern democracies? *(Ancient Greece had a direct democracy. In other words, citizens ruled directly rather than through elected representatives. However, the democracy of ancient Greece excluded many people, including women and enslaved persons.)*

Interact *with* History

Why do so many people want democracy?

Your grandparents came to the United States because they wanted to live in a democracy. Although that was more than 50 years ago, you know that people in many parts of the world still seek democracy today. On the news, you watch stories about protesters, such as those in Venezuela, who are demanding more democracy and freedom. Their demonstrations are often led by students and sometimes help to bring about democratic reform.

One evening you and a friend are watching a news story about a leader who has promised his people greater democracy. What might you answer when your friend asks why so many people want democracy?

Protesters march in Caracas, Venezuela, in opposition to the policies of President Hugo Chávez.

EXAMINING *the* ISSUES

- **What rights and institutions are necessary for a government to be democratic?**
- **How do citizens participate in a democracy? How can participation be encouraged?**

Discuss these questions in class and list important points on the board. For your discussion, consider what you know about democracy in ancient Greece and in the United States. As you read this chapter, think about the challenges many countries face in trying to develop democratic systems.

598 Chapter 19

WHY STUDY STRUGGLES FOR DEMOCRACY?

- Democracies are more likely than many other forms of government to take an active role in protecting the environment. Anyone interested in environmental issues is likely to be concerned with democratic stability in nations, such as Brazil, that are home to invaluable ecosystems.
- The United States makes economic contributions to many nations, both directly and indirectly—through the International Monetary Fund, for example. The benefits of such aid are likely to be much greater when administered by democratic institutions.
- Democratic movements in Africa should interest anyone who hopes to see an end to the tremendous human suffering caused by warfare and disease on that continent.
- The prospects for democratic reform in the former Soviet republics will be significant to anyone worried about the nuclear and biological weapons that remain in that region.
- Those interested in political change will be curious to see how U.S. leaders' decision to engage rather than isolate communist China will affect the speed and scope of political reform there.

Democracy

Case Study: Latin American Democracies

MAIN IDEA	WHY IT MATTERS NOW	TERMS & NAMES
ECONOMICS In Latin America, economic problems and authoritarian rule delayed democracy.	By the mid-1990s, almost all Latin American nations had democratic governments.	• Brasília • land reform • standard of living • recession • PRI

SETTING THE STAGE By definition, democracy is government by the people. Direct democracy, in which all citizens meet to pass laws, is not practical for nations. Therefore, democratic nations developed indirect democracies, or republics, in which citizens elect representatives to make laws for them. For example, the United States is a republic. But democracy is more than a form of government. It is also a way of life and an ideal goal. A democratic way of life includes practices such as free and open elections.

CALIFORNIA STANDARDS

10.10.1 Understand the challenges in the regions, including their geopolitical, cultural, military, and economic significance and the international relationships in which they are involved.

10.10.2 Describe the recent history of the regions, including political divisions and systems, key leaders, religious issues, natural features, resources, and population patterns.

10.10.3 Discuss the important trends in the regions today and whether they appear to serve the cause of individual freedom and democracy.

CST 3 Students use a variety of maps and documents to interpret human movement, including major patterns of domestic and international migration, changing environmental preferences and settlement patterns, the frictions that develop between population groups, and the diffusion of ideas, technological innovations, and goods.

Democracy As a Goal

The chart below lists four practices in a democracy, together with conditions that help these democratic practices succeed. Many nations follow these practices to a large degree. However, establishing democracy is a process that takes years.

Even in the United States, the establishment of democracy has taken time. Although the principle of equality is part of the Constitution, many Americans have struggled for equal rights. To cite one example, women did not receive the right to vote until 1920. Democracy is always a "work in progress."

Making Democracy Work

Common Practices	Conditions That Foster Those Practices
• Free elections	• Having more than one political party • Universal suffrage—all adult citizens can vote
• Citizen participation	• High levels of education and literacy • Economic security • Freedoms of speech, press, and assembly
• Majority rule, minority rights	• All citizens equal before the law • Shared national identity • Protection of such individual rights as freedom of religion • Representatives elected by citizens to carry out their will
• Constitutional government	• Clear body of traditions and laws on which government is based • Widespread education about how government works • National acceptance of majority decisions • Shared belief that no one is above the law

TAKING NOTES

Summarizing Use a chart to sum up the steps Brazil, Mexico, and Argentina have taken toward democracy.

Nation	Steps toward democracy
Brazil	
Mexico	
Argentina	

LESSON PLAN

OBJECTIVES

- Identify key features of democracy.
- Describe Brazil's and Mexico's efforts to build democracy.
- Describe key events in postwar Argentina.

1 FOCUS & MOTIVATE

In what ways is U.S. democracy a "work in progress"? *(Possible Answers: concerns over civil liberties, the influence of lobbyists, campaign funding, and affirmative action)*

2 INSTRUCT

Democracy As a Goal
10.10.3

Critical Thinking

- Can one nation *force* another to become a democracy? *(No—Democratization is an organic process. Yes—With enough financial and human resources, it would be possible.)*

CALIFORNIA RESOURCES

California Reading Toolkit, p. L85
California Modified Lesson Plans for English Learners, p. 165
California Daily Standards Practice Transparencies, TT77
California Standards Enrichment Workbook, pp. 107–108, 109–110, 111–112
California Standards Planner and Lesson Plans, p. L161
California Online Test Practice
California Test Generator CD-ROM
California Easy Planner CD-ROM
California eEdition CD-ROM

SECTION 1 PROGRAM RESOURCES

ALL STUDENTS

In-Depth Resources: Unit 5
- Guided Reading, p. 50
- Geography Application: Democracy in Central and South America, p. 57
- History Makers: Juan and Eva Perón, p. 66

Formal Assessment
- Section Quiz, p. 330

ENGLISH LEARNERS

In-Depth Resources in Spanish
- Guided Reading, p. 147
- Geography Application: Democracy in Central and South America, p. 153

Reading Study Guide (Spanish), p. 201
Reading Study Guide Audio CD (Spanish)

STRUGGLING READERS

In-Depth Resources: Unit 5
- Guided Reading, p. 50
- Building Vocabulary, p. 55
- Geography Application: Democracy in Central and South America, p. 57
- Reteaching Activity, p. 69

Reading Study Guide, p. 201
Reading Study Guide Audio CD

GIFTED AND TALENTED STUDENTS

In-Depth Resources: Unit 5
- Literature: from *Brazil,* p. 63

INTEGRATED TECHNOLOGY

eEdition CD-ROM
Voices from the Past Audio CD
Power Presentations CD-ROM
World Art and Cultures Transparencies
- AT76 *The Family*

classzone.com

Tip for Gifted and Talented Students

Tell students that Thomas Jefferson once remarked that "Eternal vigilance is the price of liberty." Ask them to explain what Jefferson meant by this remark. *(Possible Answer: People must pay attention to what government does so that freedoms are not taken away.)*

Dictators and Democracy

10.10.1; 10.10.2; 10.10.3

Critical Thinking

- What are the potential benefits and drawbacks of the foreign investment encouraged by Kubitschek and his successors? *(Benefit–It would allow Brazil to pursue projects it could not finance itself. Drawback–Brazil might have to surrender some control over its domestic affairs to foreign investors.)*
- What factors would you consider before introducing land reform? *(Possible Answers: fairness, how to persuade landowners, how to ensure cooperation of the military and police)*
- Why is it significant that Cardoso, a promoter of free markets, was trained as a Marxist scholar? *(Possible Answer: Marxists see markets as a way for capitalists to take advantage of their wealth.)*

World Art and Cultures Transparencies

- AT76 *The Family*

Democratic institutions may not ensure stable, civilian government if other conditions are not present. The participation of a nation's citizens in government is essential to democracy. Education and literacy—the ability to read and write—give citizens the tools they need to make political decisions. Also, a stable economy with a strong middle class and opportunities for advancement helps democracy. It does so by giving citizens a stake in the future of their nation. (A)

MAIN IDEA
Making Inferences
(A) Why would democracy suffer if citizens didn't participate?
A. Possible Answer If a low percentage of the citizens voted, then a minority would end up making decisions, which contradicts majority rule.

Other conditions advance democracy. First, a firm belief in the rights of the individual promotes the fair and equal treatment of citizens. Second, rule by law helps prevent leaders from abusing power without fear of punishment. Third, a sense of national identity helps encourage citizens to work together for the good of the nation.

The struggle to establish democracy continued into the 21st century as many nations abandoned authoritarian rule for democratic institutions. However, a United Nations study released in July 2002 warned that the spread of democracy around the world could be derailed if free elections in poor countries are not followed by economic growth. The UN Development Program's annual report warned particularly about Latin America.

CASE STUDY: Brazil

Dictators and Democracy

Many Latin American nations won their independence from Spain and Portugal in the early 1800s. However, three centuries of colonial rule left many problems. These included powerful militaries, economies that were too dependent on a single crop, and large gaps between rich and poor. These patterns persisted in the modern era.

After gaining independence from Portugal in 1822, Brazil became a monarchy. This lasted until 1889, when Brazilians established a republican government, which a wealthy elite controlled. Then, in the 1930s, Getulio Vargas became dictator. Vargas suppressed political opposition. At the same time, however, he promoted economic growth and helped turn Brazil into a modern industrial nation.

Kubitschek's Ambitious Program After Vargas, three popularly elected presidents tried to steer Brazil toward democracy. Juscelino Kubitschek (zhoo•suh•LEE•nuh KOO•bih•chehk), who governed from 1956 to 1961, continued to develop Brazil's economy. Kubitschek encouraged foreign investment to help pay for development projects. He built a new capital city, **Brasília** (bruh•ZIHL•yuh), in the country's interior. Kubitschek's dream proved expensive. The nation's foreign debt soared and inflation shot up.

Kubitschek's successors proposed reforms to ease economic and social problems. Conservatives resisted this strongly. They especially opposed the plan for **land reform**—breaking up large estates and distributing that land to peasants. In 1964, with the blessing of wealthy Brazilians, the army seized power in a military coup. (B)

MAIN IDEA
Analyzing Motives
(B) Why might the wealthy have preferred military rule to land reform?
B. Possible Answer They feared that land reform would take away their property and believed the army would protect their property rights.

Military Dictators For two decades military dictators ruled Brazil. Emphasizing economic growth, the generals fostered foreign investment. They began huge development projects in the Amazon jungle. The economy boomed.

The boom had a downside, though. The government froze wages and cut back on social programs. This caused a decline in the **standard of living**, or level of material comfort, which is judged by the amount of goods people have. When Brazilians protested, the government imposed censorship. It also jailed, tortured, and sometimes killed government critics. Nevertheless, opposition to military rule continued to grow.

The Road to Democracy By the early 1980s, a **recession**, or slowdown in the economy, gripped Brazil. At that point, the generals decided to open up the political system. They allowed direct elections of local, state, and national officials.

DIFFERENTIATING INSTRUCTION: ENGLISH LEARNERS

Obstacles to Democracy

Class Time 20 minutes

Task Rewording a chart

Purpose To have students review information in a chart

Instructions Divide students into small groups. Tell students to read "Democracy As a Goal" on pages 599–600. Then ask them to redraw the chart on page 599. Have groups replace the second column heading with "Conditions That *Stop* Those Practices" and rewrite the entries to reflect the new heading. Point out that simply changing words to their opposite will not always result in a logical entry. Examples from rows two and three follow.

Citizen participation

- Few people can read or go to school.
- People don't know if they will have money in the future.
- People are not allowed to say what they think to others, in newspapers or magazines, on television or radio, or in public places.

Majority rule, minority rights

- Some citizens have few or no rights.
- People don't think of themselves as one nation.
- Individual rights, such as freedom of religion, are not respected.
- Citizens have few or no elected representatives in the government.

Latin America, 2003

GEOGRAPHY SKILLBUILDER: Interpreting Maps

1. **Location** *Which country—Argentina, Brazil, or Mexico—spans the equator?*
2. **Region** *Which one of the three countries has a coast on the Caribbean Sea?*

History from Visuals

Interpreting the Map

Point out that Latin America is made up of South America, Mexico, Central America, and the West Indies. Ask students to list the countries of Central America. *(Guatemala, El Salvador, Honduras, Nicaragua, Costa Rica, Panama, Belize)*

Extension Ask students to review their textbook or use other resources to find out which colonial powers are associated with the following countries: Mexico, Belize, Haiti, Suriname, and Brazil. *(Mexico—Spain; Belize—Britain; Haiti—France; Suriname—Netherlands; Brazil—Portugal)*

SKILLBUILDER Answers

1. **Location** Brazil
2. **Region** Mexico

More About . . .

Latin American Languages

In 1989, several prominent publications attributed this remark to Vice President Dan Quayle: "I was recently on a tour of Latin America, and the only regret I have was that I didn't study Latin harder in school so I could converse with those people." The quotation turned out to be a fabrication, but many people believed it because of the vice president's reputation as a poor public speaker. Of course, the people of Latin America do not speak Latin, but rather languages derived from Latin—Romance languages such as Spanish, Portuguese, and French.

COOPERATIVE LEARNING

Designing an Interactive Map of Latin America

Class Time 40 minutes

Task Creating a design for an interactive map

Purpose To increase students' knowledge about the nations of Latin America

Instructions Divide the class into heterogeneous groups. Explain to students that they are going to create a design for an interactive map based on the map on this page. Have them use the textbook to find information about some of the countries on the map.

After students have compiled their data, have them create a design that describes how their maps will look and how users will interact with the map. Encourage students to be creative with their designs. Students might want to tailor the visual aspects of their maps to the types of information they have chosen. For example, if they feature economic information, they could incorporate clickable icons shaped like coins. Also, to access the data they have collected, students could have users click on a country's name, answer a multiple-choice question from a pull-down menu, or drag items from a data list to the country with which the data corresponds.

History from Visuals

Interpreting the Graphs

Tell students that line graphs show changes in quantities over time. Ask them to look at the debt/inflation figures for each year listed. In what five-year period did the debt go up and the inflation rate go down? *(1965–1970)*

Extension Ask students what political event corresponds to the most precipitous drop in Brazil's rate of inflation. *(the election of Fernando Henrique Cardoso in 1994)*

SKILLBUILDER Answers

1. **Clarifying** about $230 billion
2. **Comparing** 1990

One-Party Rule

10.10.1; 10.10.2; 10.10.3

Critical Thinking

- What benefits and drawbacks might Cárdenas have considered before nationalizing Mexico's oil industry? *(Possible Answers: Benefit–More revenue for Mexican government. Drawback–Animosity and potential military action of foreign powers divested of property.)*
- Why would President Fox concern himself with the legal status of Mexican immigrants in the United States? *(Possible Answer: The money that immigrants send to their families may contribute to the economic well-being of Mexico.)*

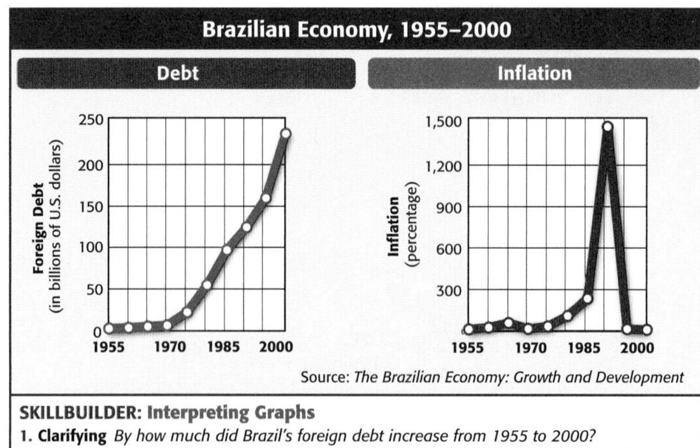

SKILLBUILDER: Interpreting Graphs

1. **Clarifying** *By how much did Brazil's foreign debt increase from 1955 to 2000?*
2. **Comparing** *Of the years shown on the line graph, which was the worst year for inflation?*

In 1985, a new civilian president, José Sarney (zhoh•ZAY SAHR•nay), took office. Sarney inherited a country in crisis because of foreign debt and inflation. He proved unable to solve the country's problems and lost support. The next elected president fared even worse. He resigned because of corruption charges. C

In 1994 and again in 1998, Brazilians elected Fernando Henrique Cardoso, who achieved some success in tackling the nation's economic and political problems. Although trained as a Marxist scholar, Cardoso became a strong advocate of free markets. One of his main concerns was the widening income gap in Brazil. He embarked on a program to promote economic reform.

MAIN IDEA

Analyzing Issues

C In your opinion, which of the problems faced by Sarney was worse? Explain.

C. Possible Answers the foreign debt, because it put Brazil under the power of other nations; inflation, because no one could get ahead

The 2002 Presidential Election In the presidential election of October 2002, Cardoso's handpicked successor to lead his centrist coalition was José Serra. Serra faced two candidates who proposed a sharp break with Cardoso's pro-business policies. These candidates included Luiz Inácio Lula da Silva, a candidate of the leftist Workers Party.

An economic crisis hit many countries in South America, including Brazil, in 2002. Because of stalled economic growth, rising unemployment, and poverty, there was a backlash against free-market economic policies. This made the election of 2002 a close contest. Da Silva, the leftist candidate, won the hotly disputed election, defeating the ruling party candidate, Serra. Da Silva has proved a more moderate president than his supporters and opponents had expected. Although Brazil faces many challenges, it continues on the path of democracy.

CASE STUDY: Mexico

One-Party Rule

Unlike Brazil, Mexico enjoyed relative political stability for most of the 20th century. Following the Mexican Revolution, the government passed the Constitution of 1917. The new constitution outlined a democracy and promised reforms.

Beginnings of One-Party Domination From 1920 to 1934, Mexico elected several generals as president. However, these men did not rule as military dictators. They did create a ruling party—the National Revolutionary Party, which dominated Mexico under various names for the rest of the 20th century.

CONNECTIONS TO LITERATURE

Discussing John Updike's *Brazil*

Class Time 40 minutes

Task Exchanging notes or e-mails

Purpose To explore John Updike's *Brazil*

Instructions Divide students into pairs and have them read the selection from *Brazil* in In-Depth Resources: Unit 5. Explain to students that they will be exchanging short notes or e-mails in which they will discuss Updike's work paragraph by paragraph. Tell students that their notes should be informal and just a few sentences in length. The notes should contain observations, criticisms, explanations, questions, or anything else that reflects students' engagement with the text. The student's partner would then respond before the pair moved on to the next paragraph. After they have exchanged notes on each paragraph in the passage, discuss the selection as a class. Ask, How is Brazil changing during the time covered in the excerpt? *(Possible Answer: It is becoming more democratic.)*

Name ______ Date ______

CHAPTER 19 Section 1

LITERATURE SELECTION *from Brazil*
by John Updike

In this novel, American author John Updike traces the political, economic, and social changes that took place in Brazil from the mid-1960s to the mid-1980s through the eyes of Tristão Reposo, a child of the Rio slums, and his wife Isabel Leme, who grew up in the upper class. What does this excerpt reveal about Brazil's economic and political development?

Yes, they lived happily then, in São Paulo, first in an apartment in Higienopolis, and then in a house in the Jardim América district, off the Rua Groenlândia, for a dozen years in all. The Leme brothers succeeded in obtaining for Tristão a position in middle management, not at the *fusca* plant where he had tightened engine-mounting bolts opposite gap-toothed Oscar—for *fuscas* were no longer made—but at a textile mill in São Bernardo, one of the so-called ABCD cities, industrial satellites of São Paulo.

The mill was a single vast room where giant looms kept up a clatter which pressed on Tristão's ears with a million small concussions; each noise was smaller than the clashes of metal on metal in the fusca factory, but there were many more of them. At first, he tried to understand the intricacies—the warp, the weft, the batten and its beating-in, the ways in which twill differed from plain weave, or tabby, and how variations in lifting the threads of the warp with the heddles produced satin and damask, warp-pile velvet and weft-pile corduroy, and the truly dizzying operation whereby many spinning cones of thread, drawn by a mechanical drawboy controlled by punched cards, could be woven to make elaborately figured fabrics.

The mill was a single vast room where giant looms kept up a clatter which pressed on Tristão's ears with a million small concussions.

The shuttle, that carried the weft threads back and forth under the lifted warps that formed the shed, was the basic awkwardness, he perceived, for at the heart of the weaving there must be this moment of suspension when the shuttle flies, or its flying is imitated by rapiers, by dummy-shuttles, and even by jets of air or water that propel the thread from one edge, called a selvage, of the cloth to the other, making a "pick." Just so, at the heart of our lives lies a supernatural leap, an oscillating unlikelihood. Miraculously, the looms clanked and clattered, repeating the shedding, the picking, and the beating-in with a merciless speed that yet did not snap threads: there was no resistance in the material universe to an inhuman acceleration. The human attendants of the machines, indeed, looked grotesquely lackadaisical and soft, like wet clay dropped here and there, idle spectators who would suddenly spring into action at the depletion of a bright-colored cone or glistening heavy shuttle. The workers, mostly women, wore kerchiefs to keep their long hair from becoming entangled with the machines, which in a flicker of mindless operation would pull their scalps loose from their skulls. Some of these women had Indian blood; others had come with the Japanese immigration, or the Italian before it, or among those varied Middle Eastern peoples lumped as turcos, Turks.

And then there was another giant room of the factory, in which the altogether different operation of knitting was carried on by machines built on quite different principles, needles being the fundamental unit, ingeniously bent needles of two types: spring beard and latch, the latch having a tiny pivot closing the needle's loop and permitting the stitch to be cast off. The needles in a variety of gauges ranging from the size of a pencil to that of a mouse whisker were arrayed in bars or circles, cylinders or plates, controlled by moving cams that imitated the motion of knitting over and over and over, gnashing like piranhas, producing sheets or tubes of knitted fabric as coarse as ski sweaters or as seductively filmy as pantyhose. Tristão's attempt at understanding the details of manufacture gave him terrible, million-toothed dreams and lasted but a few weeks; then he perceived that his role was to understand merely his relation to the men above him in the management chain, and those below him, and to fit

Struggles for Democracy 63

In-Depth Resources: Unit 5

From 1934 to 1940, President Lázaro Cárdenas (KAHR•day•nahs) tried to improve life for peasants and workers. He carried out land reform and promoted labor rights. He nationalized the Mexican oil industry, kicking out foreign oil companies and creating a state-run oil industry. After Cárdenas, however, a series of more conservative presidents turned away from reform.

The Party Becomes the PRI In 1946, the main political party changed its name to the Institutional Revolutionary Party, or **PRI**. In the half-century that followed, the PRI became the main force for political stability in Mexico.

Although stable, the government was an imperfect democracy. The PRI controlled the congress and won every presidential election. The government allowed opposition parties to compete, but fraud and corruption tainted the elections.

Even as the Mexican economy rapidly developed, Mexico continued to suffer severe economic problems. Lacking land and jobs, millions of Mexicans struggled for survival. In addition, a huge foreign debt forced the government to spend money on interest payments. Two episodes highlighted Mexico's growing difficulties. In the late 1960s, students and workers began calling for economic and political change. On October 2, 1968, protesters gathered at the site of an ancient Aztec market in Mexico City. Soldiers hidden in the ruins opened fire on the protesters. The massacre claimed several hundred lives.

D. Answer If prices for that product drop, the economy is severely damaged.

MAIN IDEA

Recognizing Effects

D Why does over-reliance on one product weaken an economy?

A second critical episode occurred during the early 1980s. By that time, huge new oil and natural gas reserves had been discovered in Mexico. The economy had become dependent on oil and gas exports. In 1981, world oil prices fell, cutting Mexico's oil and gas revenues in half. Mexico went into an economic decline. D

Economic and Political Crises The 1980s and 1990s saw Mexico facing various crises. In 1988, opposition parties challenged the PRI in national elections. The PRI candidate, Carlos Salinas, won the presidency. Even so, opposition parties won seats in the congress and began to force a gradual opening of the political system.

Analyzing Political Cartoons

Military Rule and Democracy

Throughout the 20th century, many Latin American countries were ruled by military dictators or political bosses. Most typically, the dictator's support came from the wealthy and the military. But sometimes the dictator's support came from the people.

SKILLBUILDER: Interpreting Visual Sources

1. **Drawing Conclusions** *Do dictators typically take into account the opinions of the people they rule?*
2. **Making Inferences** *What does this cartoon suggest about the dictator's attitude toward the opinion of the people he rules?*

"My goodness, if I'd known how badly you wanted democracy I'd have given it to you ages ago."

More About . . .

Massacre at Tlatelolco

The protest at the ancient Aztec market of Tlatelolco took place at a time of worldwide student protests. It also occurred on the eve of the Mexico City Olympics, when Mexico was eager to present a positive image to the world. But the events at Tlatelolco were not the only manifestation of unrest at the 1968 Olympics. As the U.S. flag rose at a medal ceremony for the winners of the 200-meter race, African-American sprinters Tommie Smith and John Carlos stood on the medal podium with heads bowed and fists raised in a controversial protest against racism in the United States.

Analyzing Political Cartoons

Military Rule and Democracy

Ask what visual clues the cartoonist used to show that the speaker is a dictator. *(Possible Answers: in an elaborate military uniform, standing on a balcony above a crowd)*

SKILLBUILDER Answers

1. **Drawing Conclusions** Dictators typically do not concern themselves with the opinions of their subjects.
2. **Making Inferences** It suggests that he is ruled by the wishes of the people, which is one source of the cartoon's humor.

DIFFERENTIATING INSTRUCTION: GIFTED AND TALENTED STUDENTS

Writing About Episodes in Mexico's History

Class Time 40 minutes

Task Writing a magazine article

Purpose To learn more about 20th-century Mexico

Instructions Have students read "One-Party Rule" on pages 602–604. After they have finished reading, tell students to use facts and details from the text to write a magazine article about an event described in the passage—for example, nationalization of the Mexican oil industry or the massacre at the Aztec ruins. Tell them to pick an event and to choose a magazine for which they wish to write. Before they begin their essay, students should identify the magazine's readership. Are readers younger or older, more or less educated, progressive or conservative, wealthy or less well off? Tell students to keep this audience in mind as they write their articles. After they have completed their articles, have students add a paragraph at the head of their article that describes the readership. At the end of the article, ask them to write a paragraph that describes how their essay was tailored or not tailored to this readership. (Students might opt to challenge the magazine's readers—at least to an extent allowed by the magazine's editors.)

History from Visuals

Interpreting the Graph

Ask students which of the nations represented is not a South American country. *(Mexico)*

SKILLBUILDER Answers

1. **Comparing** Argentina, Chile, Uruguay
2. **Comparing** Bolivia, Ecuador, Colombia

Political and Economic Disorder

10.10.1; 10.10.2; 10.10.3

Critical Thinking

- How might the Catholic Church have become an enemy of President Juan Perón? *(Possible Answer: Perón may have initiated policies that offended Church officials or harmed Church interests.)*
- Why might the Argentine military have attacked the Falkland Islands? *(Possible Answers: They may have believed that the United Kingdom would be unwilling to defend such a distant and relatively insignificant territory. Undertaking such a campaign may have been perceived as a way to unite Argentines behind their military rulers.)*

In-Depth Resources: Unit 5

- Geography Application: Democracy in Central and South America, p. 57

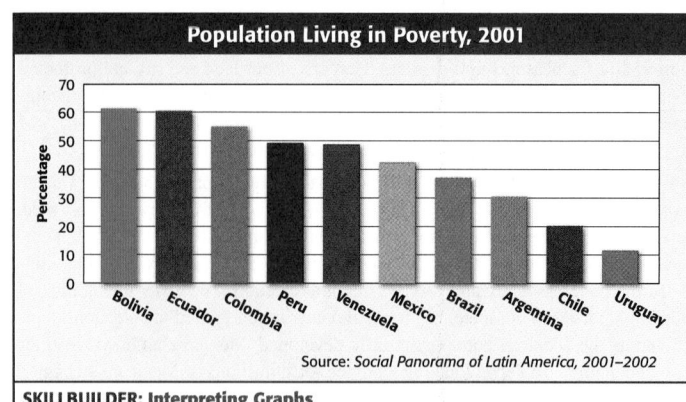

Population Living in Poverty, 2001

Percentage (0–70): Bolivia, Ecuador, Colombia, Peru, Venezuela, Mexico, Brazil, Argentina, Chile, Uruguay

Source: *Social Panorama of Latin America, 2001–2002*

SKILLBUILDER: Interpreting Graphs

1. **Comparing** *In which three countries of Latin America is the percentage of people living in poverty the lowest?*
2. **Comparing** *In which three countries is the poverty rate highest?*

During his presidency, Salinas signed NAFTA, the North American Free Trade Agreement. NAFTA removed trade barriers between Mexico, the United States, and Canada. In early 1994, peasant rebels in the southern Mexican state of Chiapas (chee•AH•pahs) staged a major uprising. Shortly afterward, a gunman assassinated Luis Donaldo Colosio, the PRI presidential candidate for the upcoming election.

The PRI Loses Control After these events, Mexicans grew increasingly concerned about the prospects for democratic stability. Nevertheless, the elections of 1994 went ahead. The new PRI candidate, Ernesto Zedillo (zuh•DEE•yoh), won. Opposition parties continued to challenge the PRI.

In 1997, two opposition parties each won a large number of congressional seats, denying the PRI control of congress. Then, in 2000, Mexican voters ended 71 years of PRI rule by electing center-right candidate Vicente Fox as president.

New Policies and Programs Fox's agenda was very ambitious. He advocated reforming the police, rooting out political corruption, ending the rebellion in Chiapas, and opening up Mexico's economy to free-market forces.

Fox also argued that the United States should legalize the status of millions of illegal Mexican immigrant workers. Fox hoped that a negotiated agreement between the United States and Mexico would provide amnesty for these undocumented Mexican workers in the United States. In the wake of the terrorist attacks of September 11, 2001, any such agreement appeared remote. However, in 2002, Fox created a cabinet-level agency to lobby for the interests of Mexico's 22 million citizens who lived abroad, a great many of whom lived in the United States. In the meantime, Mexico's democracy continued to strengthen.

▲ President Vicente Fox of Mexico

CASE STUDY: Argentina

Political and Economic Disorder

Mexico and Brazil were not the only Latin American countries where democracy had made progress. By the late 1990s, most of Latin America was under democratic rule.

Perón Rules Argentina Argentina had struggled to establish democracy. It was a major exporter of grain and beef. It was also an industrial nation with a large working class. In 1946, Argentine workers supported an army officer, Juan Perón, who won the presidency and then established a dictatorship.

DIFFERENTIATING INSTRUCTION: STRUGGLING READERS

Tracing Change in Mexico

Class Time 30 minutes

Task Creating a time line

Purpose To use a visual aid to help students understand the order of recent political history of Mexico

Instructions Pair students. Explain that creating a time line can improve students' understanding of the material and can be helpful to review before a test. Ask pairs to review "One-Party Rule" on pages 602–604 and write down significant events and dates. Then have students order the events on a time line. A sample time line is shown.

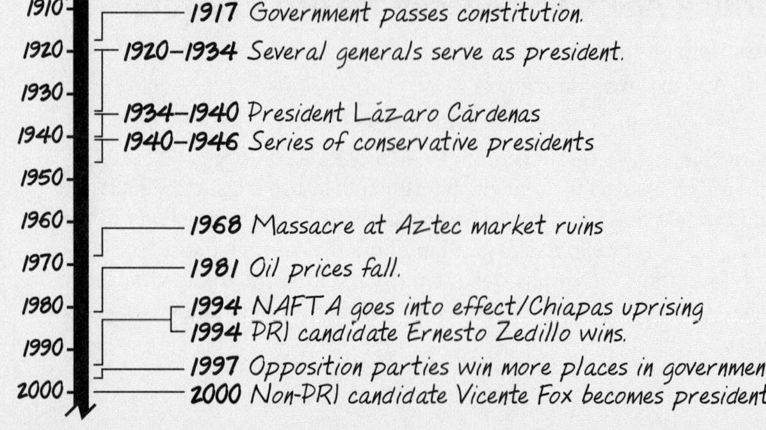

Perón did not rule alone. He received critical support from his wife, Eva—known as Evita to the millions of Argentines who idolized her. Together, the Peróns created a welfare state. The state offered social programs with broad popular appeal but limited freedoms. After Eva's death in 1952, Perón's popularity declined and his enemies—the military and the Catholic Church—moved against him. In 1955, the military ousted Perón and drove him into exile.

Vocabulary
welfare state: a government that tries to provide for all its citizens' needs—including health, education, and employment

▲ Eva Perón

Repression in Argentina For many years, the military essentially controlled Argentine politics. Perón returned to power once more, in 1973, but ruled for only a year before dying in office. By the mid-1970s, Argentina was in chaos.

In 1976, the generals seized power again. They established a brutal dictatorship and hunted down political opponents. For several years, torture and murder were everyday events. By the early 1980s, several thousand Argentines had simply disappeared, kidnapped by their own government.

E. Answer The military government lost a humiliating war and had to turn the government over to civilians.

Democracy and the Economy In 1982, the military government went to war with Britain over the nearby Falkland Islands and suffered a defeat. Disgraced, the generals agreed to step down. In 1983, Argentines elected Raúl Alfonsín (ahl•fohn•SEEN) president in the country's first free election in 37 years. E

MAIN IDEA
Analyzing Causes
E What finally caused military rule to end in Argentina?

During the 1980s, Alfonsín worked to rebuild democracy and the economy. Carlos Menem gained the presidency in 1989 and continued the process. He attempted to stabilize the currency and privatize industry. By the late 1990s, however, economic problems intensified as the country lived beyond its means.

A Growing Crisis In December 2001, the International Monetary Fund (IMF) refused to provide financial aid to Argentina. Then President Fernando de la Rua resigned in the face of protests over the economy. He was succeeded by Eduardo Duhalde, who tried to deal with the economic and social crisis. In 2002, Argentina had an unemployment rate of about 24 percent. The country defaulted on $132 billion in debt, the largest debt default in history, and devalued its currency. In 2003, Argentina struggled to regain its political and economic footing. In elections that year, Nestor Kirchner became the new president of Argentina.

SECTION 1 ASSESSMENT

TERMS & NAMES 1. For each term or name, write a sentence explaining its significance.
• Brasília • land reform • standard of living • recession • PRI

USING YOUR NOTES
2. Which country do you think has made the most progress? Explain. (10.10.3)

Nation	Steps toward democracy
Brazil	
Mexico	
Argentina	

MAIN IDEAS
3. What role did the military play in shaping the economy of Brazil? (10.10.2)
4. What were some of the positive benefits of one-party rule in Mexico? (10.10.2)
5. What effect did the Falklands war have on the military government in Argentina? (10.10.2)

CRITICAL THINKING & WRITING
6. **COMPARING AND CONTRASTING** Compare and contrast the roles of the military in the governments of Brazil, Mexico, and Argentina. (10.10.2)
7. **SYNTHESIZING** What have been some of the obstacles to democracy in Latin America? (10.10.1)
8. **DEVELOPING HISTORICAL PERSPECTIVE** What are some of the attributes of democracy? (10.10.3)
9. **WRITING ACTIVITY** ECONOMICS What might be the effect of a welfare state (such as that created in Argentina by the Peróns) on a nation's economy? Support your opinions in a two-paragraph **essay.** (Writing 2.4.c)

CONNECT TO TODAY MAKING A GRAPH
Research the economies of Mexico, Brazil, and Argentina to determine which is doing the best. Present your findings in a **graph.** (Writing 2.3.d)

Vocabulary Note: Academic Vocabulary
Some students may misunderstand the term *welfare state* because of the negative connotations associated with the term *welfare*. Help students understand the broader meaning of *welfare state* by explaining more about its historical background, such as public provision of basic education.

More About . . .

Eva Perón
British composer Andrew Lloyd Webber and lyricist Tim Rice based their hit Broadway musical *Evita* (1978) on the life of Eva Perón. In 1996, the musical was made into a movie starring Madonna and Antonio Banderas.

In-Depth Resources: Unit 5
• History Makers: Juan and Eva Perón, p. 66

3 ASSESS

SECTION 1 ASSESSMENT
Have students work in pairs to answer the questions and then share their answers with other pairs.

Formal Assessment
• Section Quiz, p. 330

4 RETEACH
Have students write at least three statements about each country's quest for democracy.

In-Depth Resources: Unit 5
• Guided Reading, p. 50
• Reteaching Activity, p. 69

ANSWERS

1. Brasília, p. 600 • land reform, p. 600 • standard of living, p. 600 • recession, p. 600 • PRI, p. 603
2. **Sample Answer:** Brazil—Direct elections; Mexico—Democratic constitution; Argentina—Civilian government. Most progress—Mexico, because of economy and multiple parties.
3. It emphasized economic growth and opened Brazil to foreign investment.
4. political stability, civilian rule
5. It led to the end of military rule.
6. In Brazil and Argentina, the military overthrew civilian governments but were eventually forced to yield power and allow free elections. In Mexico, the military has never directly controlled the government.
7. **Possible Answers:** powerful militaries; rule of law weak
8. **Possible Answers:** free elections; citizen participation
9. **Rubric** Essays should discuss
• the reasons for social programs.
• the strain on a weak or developing economy of social programs.

CONNECT TO TODAY
Rubric Graphs should
• use a standard economic indicator, such as GDP.
• cite sources.

LESSON PLAN

OBJECTIVES

- Explain Africa's legacy of colonialism.
- Describe Nigeria's civil war and events in Nigeria since 1970.
- Trace the history of white rule in South Africa and the change to democracy.

1 FOCUS & MOTIVATE

Ask students when legal segregation ended in the United States. *(Some students will cite the passage of the 1964 Civil Rights Act.)*

2 INSTRUCT

Colonial Rule Limits Democracy

10.10.1; 10.10.2

Critical Thinking

- Do you think colonial powers deliberately ignored ethnic and cultural divisions when they established boundaries? *(No–Competition with rival powers determined such decisions. Yes–Such divisions made colonies easier to manage.)*

CALIFORNIA RESOURCES

California Reading Toolkit, p. L86
California Modified Lesson Plans for English Learners, p. 167
California Daily Standards Practice Transparencies, TT78
California Standards Enrichment Workbook, pp. 107–108, 109–110, 111–112
California Standards Planner and Lesson Plans, p. L163
California Online Test Practice
California Test Generator CD-ROM
California Easy Planner CD-ROM
California eEdition CD-ROM

A man chisels a piece of the Berlin Wall for a souvenir just after the fall of communism in East Germany

Soldiers of the Chinese People's Liberation Army in Hong Kong, 1998

2 The Challenge of Democracy in Africa

MAIN IDEA

REVOLUTION As the recent histories of Nigeria and South Africa show, ethnic and racial conflicts can hinder democracy.

WHY IT MATTERS NOW

In 1996, as Nigeria struggled with democracy, South Africa adopted a bill of rights that promotes racial equality.

TERMS & NAMES

- federal system
- martial law
- dissident
- apartheid
- Nelson Mandela

CALIFORNIA STANDARDS

10.10.1 Understand the challenges in the regions, including their geopolitical, cultural, military, and economic significance and the international relationships in which they are involved.

10.10.2 Describe the recent history of the regions, including political divisions and systems, key leaders, religious issues, natural features, resources, and population patterns.

10.10.3 Discuss the important trends in the regions today and whether they appear to serve the cause of individual freedom and democracy.

REP 3 Students evaluate major debates among historians concerning alternative interpretations of the past, including an analysis of authors' use of evidence and the distinctions between sound generalizations and misleading oversimplifications.

REP 4 Students construct and test hypotheses; collect, evaluate, and employ information from multiple primary and secondary sources; and apply it in oral and written presentations.

TAKING NOTES

Comparing Use a Venn diagram to compare political events in Nigeria and South Africa.

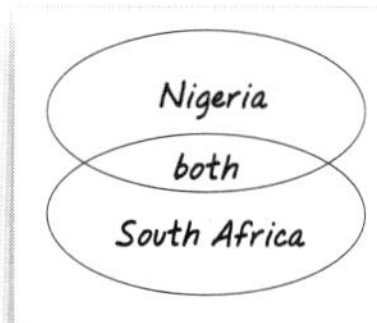

SETTING THE STAGE Beginning in the late 1950s, dozens of European colonies in Africa gained their independence and became nations. As in Latin America, the establishment of democracy in Africa proved difficult. In many cases, the newly independent nations faced a host of problems that slowed their progress toward democracy. The main reason for Africa's difficulties was the negative impact of colonial rule. European powers had done little to prepare their African colonies for independence.

Colonial Rule Limits Democracy

The lingering effects of colonialism undermined efforts to build stable, democratic economies and states. This can be seen throughout Africa.

European Policies Cause Problems When the Europeans established colonial boundaries, they ignored existing ethnic or cultural divisions. New borders divided peoples of the same background or threw different—often rival—groups together. Because of this, a sense of national identity was difficult to develop. After independence, the old colonial boundaries became the borders of the newly independent states. As a result, ethnic and cultural conflicts remained.

Other problems had an economic basis. European powers had viewed colonies as sources of wealth for the home country. The colonial powers encouraged the export of one or two cash crops, such as coffee or rubber, rather than the production of a range of products to serve local needs. Europeans developed plantations and mines but few factories. Manufactured goods were imported from European countries. These policies left new African nations with unbalanced economies and a small middle class. Such economic problems lessened their chances to create democratic stability.

European rule also disrupted African family and community life. In some cases, colonial powers moved Africans far from their families and villages to work in mines or on plantations. In addition, most newly independent nations still lacked a skilled, literate work force that could take on the task of building a new nation.

Short-Lived Democracies When Britain and France gave up their colonies, they left fragile democratic governments in place. Soon problems threatened those governments. Rival ethnic groups often fought for power. Strong militaries became tools for ambitious leaders. In many cases, a military dictatorship replaced democracy.

SECTION 2 PROGRAM RESOURCES

ALL STUDENTS

In-Depth Resources: Unit 5
- Guided Reading, p. 51
- History Makers: Nelson Mandela, p. 67

Formal Assessment
- Section Quiz, p. 331

ENGLISH LEARNERS

In-Depth Resources in Spanish
- Guided Reading, p. 148

Reading Study Guide (Spanish), p. 203
Reading Study Guide Audio CD (Spanish)

STRUGGLING READERS

In-Depth Resources: Unit 5
- Guided Reading, p. 51
- Building Vocabulary, p. 55
- Reteaching Activity, p. 70

Reading Study Guide, p. 203
Reading Study Guide Audio CD

GIFTED AND TALENTED STUDENTS

In-Depth Resources: Unit 5
- Primary Sources: from *Kaffir Boy,* p. 59; Mandela's Inaugural Address, p. 60

Electronic Library of Primary Sources
- from "Masakhane–Let Us Build Together"

INTEGRATED TECHNOLOGY

eEdition CD-ROM
Power Presentations CD-ROM
World Art and Cultures Transparencies
- AT77 Multiple-Mask Headdress

Electronic Library of Primary Sources
- from "Masakhane–Let Us Build Together"

Patterns of Interaction Video
- Struggling Toward Democracy: Revolutions in Latin America and South Africa

classzone.com

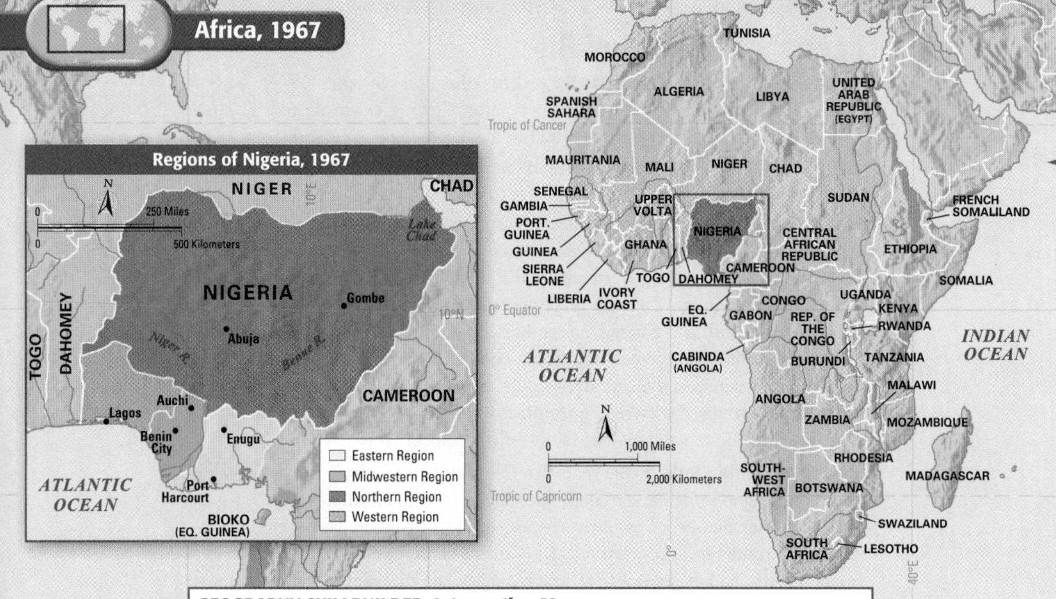

GEOGRAPHY SKILLBUILDER: Interpreting Maps
1. **Region** *Describe the Eastern Region, which seceded as Biafra. Describe its size and location compared to the rest of Nigeria.*
2. **Location** *In which region is Lagos, Nigeria's capital in 1967?*

Civil War in Nigeria

Nigeria, a former British colony, won its independence peacefully in 1960. Nigeria is Africa's most populous country and one of its richest. However, the country was ethnically divided. This soon created problems that led to war.

A Land of Many Peoples Three major ethnic groups live within Nigeria's borders. In the north are the Hausa-Fulani, who are mostly Muslim. In the south are the Yoruba and the Igbo (also called Ibo), who are mostly Christians, Muslims, or animists, who believe that spirits are present in animals, plants, and natural objects. The Yoruba, a farming people with a tradition of kings, live to the west. The Igbo, a farming people who have a democratic tradition, live to the east.

After independence, Nigeria adopted a **federal system**. In a federal system, power is shared between state governments and a central authority. The Nigerians set up three states, one for each region and ethnic group, with a political party in each.

War with Biafra Although one group dominated each state, the states also had ethnic minorities. In the Western Region, non-Yoruba minorities began to resent Yoruba control. In 1963, they tried to break away and form their own region. This led to fighting. In January 1966, a group of army officers, most of them Igbo, seized power in the capital city of Lagos. These officers abolished the regional governments and declared **martial law**, or temporary military rule.

The Hausa-Fulani, who did not trust the Igbo, launched an attack from the north. They persecuted and killed many Igbo. The survivors fled east. In 1967, the Eastern Region seceded from Nigeria, declaring itself the new nation of Biafra (bee•AF•ruh).

The Nigerian government then went to war to reunite the country. The Igbo were badly outnumbered and outgunned. In 1970, Biafra surrendered. Nigeria was reunited, but perhaps more than a million Igbo died, most from starvation. (A)

A. Answer They were forced to rejoin Nigeria; a million died.

MAIN IDEA

Recognizing Effects

(A) What was the effect of the war on the Igbo?

History from Visuals

Interpreting the Map

Have students identify Nigeria and its major cities. Point out the inset map and help students understand how it relates to the larger map.

Extension Have students compare this map with the political and physical maps of Africa in the textbook atlas. How do Nigeria's geography and size make it one of the more important nations in Africa? *(It is one of the larger countries and has access to the sea.)*

SKILLBUILDER Answers
1. **Region** Biafra is in the southeastern part of Nigeria and is small, though comparable in size to the Western Region.
2. **Location** the Western Region

Civil War in Nigeria
10.10.1; 10.10.2

Critical Thinking
- Why might ethnic identity in Nigeria be more important than national identity? *(Possible Answer: The nation is based on artificial colonial borders.)*
- Based on the events in Biafra, how significant was Igbo representation in the federal government? *(Possible Answer: It was probably weak. If the Igbo had been well-represented at the federal level, they might have sought a political resolution to their dispute with the Yoruba.)*

World Art and Cultures Transparencies
- AT77 Multiple-Mask Headdress

COOPERATIVE LEARNING

B

Ethnic Groups in Nigeria

Class Time 15 minutes

Task Creating a chart of Nigeria's ethnic groups

Purpose To familiarize students with characteristics of Nigeria's major ethnic groups

Instructions Divide students into small groups. Ask each group to create a table with four columns. Then have students read "Civil War in Nigeria" on this page. Ask them to fill in their tables as they read the passage. An example follows. Discuss what conflicts are likely to occur between such groups. *(Possible Answer: differences over religion and preferred type of government)*

Ethnic Group	Location	Culture
Hausa-Fulani	north	mostly Muslim
Yoruba	south	Christian, Muslim, and animist; farming people with tradition of kings
Igbo/Ibo	south	Christian, Muslim, and animist; farming people with democratic traditions

Nigeria's Nation-Building
10.10.1; 10.10.2; 10.10.3

Critical Thinking

- Why do you think the Nigerian government paid to rebuild the rebellious Igbo region? *(Possible Answer: wanted to reunite the country rather than punish rebellion)*
- Is canceling debts incurred by nations such as Nigeria a good idea? *(Good—It would allow governments to devote more resources to public health and education. Bad—It would hurt lenders and send the message to borrowers that there are no repercussions for financial mismanagement.)*

Analyzing Primary Sources

Ken Saro-Wiwa

Ask students to read the primary source from Ken Saro-Wiwa. Then lead students in a discussion focused on determining which tactic is more difficult for people who are resisting an oppressive regime—nonviolence or violence.

Extension Ask students to use the library or the Internet to find out where Nigeria's Ogoni people live. *(in the south, in the Niger River delta area)*

Answers to Document-Based Questions

1. **Drawing Conclusions** government was ruthless and murderous
2. **Making Inferences** He seems contemptuous of their power; though they have the power to execute him, they are fools.

Nigeria's Nation-Building

After the war, Nigerians returned to the process of nation-building. "When the war ended," noted one officer, "it was like a referee blowing a whistle in a football game. People just put down their guns and went back to the business of living." The Nigerian government did not punish the Igbo. It used federal money to rebuild the Igbo region.

Federal Government Restored The military governed Nigeria for most of the 1970s. During this time, Nigerian leaders tried to create a more stable federal system, with a strong central government and a number of regional units. The government also tried to build a more modern economy, based on oil income.

In 1979, the military handed power back to civilian rulers. Nigerians were cheered by the return to democracy. Some people, however, remained concerned about ethnic divisions in the nation. Nigerian democracy was short-lived. In 1983, the military overthrew the civilian government, charging it with corruption. A new military regime, dominated by the Hausa-Fulani, took charge.

A Return to Civilian Rule In the years that followed, the military governed Nigeria, while promising to bring back civilian rule. The army held elections in 1993, which resulted in the victory of popular leader Moshood Abiola. However, officers declared the results invalid, and a dictator, General Sani Abacha, took control.

General Abacha banned political activity and jailed **dissidents**, or government opponents. Upon Abacha's death in 1998, General Abdulsalami Abubakar seized power and promised to end military rule. He kept his word. In 1999, Nigerians elected their first civilian president, Olusegun Obasanjo, in nearly 20 years. In 2003, Obasanjo was reelected.

> Analyzing Primary Sources

Ken Saro-Wiwa

On November 10, 1995, Nigeria hanged nine political prisoners—all critics of the military government. Many around the world believed the nine were convicted on false charges to silence them. One of the nine was Ken Saro-Wiwa, a noted writer and activist. Shortly before his death, Saro-Wiwa smuggled several manuscripts out of prison.

DOCUMENT-BASED QUESTIONS

1. **Drawing Conclusions** *What do Saro-Wiwa's imprisonment and execution suggest about the government of the military dictator, General Sani Abacha?*
2. **Making Inferences** *What seems to be Saro-Wiwa's attitude toward his persecutors?*

PRIMARY SOURCE

Injustice stalks the land like a tiger on the prowl. To be at the mercy of buffoons [fools] is the ultimate insult. To find the instruments of state power reducing you to dust is the injury. . . .

It is also very important that we have chosen the path of non-violent struggle. Our opponents are given to violence and we cannot meet them on their turf, even if we wanted to. Non-violent struggle offers weak people the strength which they otherwise would not have. The spirit becomes important, and no gun can silence that. I am aware, though, that non-violent struggle occasions more death than armed struggle. And that remains a cause for worry at all times. Whether the Ogoni people will be able to withstand the rigors of the struggle is yet to be seen. Again, their ability to do so will point the way of peaceful struggle to other peoples on the African continent. It is therefore not to be underrated.

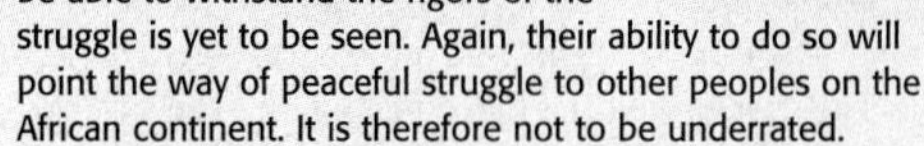

KEN SARO-WIWA, *A Month and a Day: A Detention Diary*

DIFFERENTIATING INSTRUCTION: GIFTED AND TALENTED STUDENTS

Politics and Oil in Nigeria

Class Time 30 minutes

Task Delivering a television news report

Purpose To learn about current events in Nigeria

Instructions After students have read "Civil War in Nigeria" and "Nigeria's Nation-Building" on pages 607–608, have them use the Internet or the library to search for information about Nigeria's oil industry. Tell students to focus on the oil industry's impact on Nigeria's economy and politics.

After they have finished their research, ask students to use their findings to create and deliver a brief news report. Tell students they will be reporting for a major news network and that their story will target viewers who know little or nothing about Nigeria. Explain that, because they are reporting for a major network, they will be expected to be objective. After they complete the project, have students discuss how they made their reports objective and what they might have added if they had been allowed to express a subjective point of view.

President Obasanjo Obasanjo was an ethnic Yoruba from southwest Nigeria. As a critic of Nigerian military regimes, he had spent three years in jail (1995–1998) under Sani Abacha. As a former general, Obasanjo had the support of the military.

Obasanjo worked for a strong, unified Nigeria. He made some progress in his battle against corruption. He also attempted to draw the attention of the world to the need for debt relief for Nigeria. In May 2001, he called on President George W. Bush to support the canceling of Nigeria's $30 billion debt to the international community. Obasanjo saw debt relief as essential to the relief of hunger and the future of democracy in Nigeria and the rest of Africa.

Despite Obasanjo's efforts, Nigeria was still beset by a variety of problems. These included war, violence, corruption, poverty, and hunger. Nonetheless, Nigeria was increasing its oil exports and experiencing economic growth.

South Africa Under Apartheid

In South Africa, racial conflict was the result of colonial rule. From its beginnings under Dutch and British control, South Africa was racially divided. A small white minority ruled a large black majority. In 1910, South Africa gained self-rule as a dominion of the British Empire. In 1931, it became an independent member of the British Commonwealth. Although South Africa had a constitutional government, the constitution gave whites power and denied the black majority its rights.

Apartheid Segregates Society In 1948, the National Party came to power in South Africa. This party promoted Afrikaner, or Dutch South African, nationalism. It also instituted a policy of **apartheid**, complete separation of the races. The minority government banned social contacts between whites and blacks. It established segregated schools, hospitals, and neighborhoods.

In 1959, the minority government set up reserves, called homelands, for the country's major black groups. Blacks were forbidden to live in white areas unless they worked as servants or laborers for whites. The homelands policy was totally unbalanced. Although blacks made up about 75 percent of the population, the government set aside only 13 percent of the land for them. Whites kept the best land. (B)

MAIN IDEA

Making Inferences

(B) How did the policy of apartheid strengthen whites' hold on power?

B. Possible Answers It kept the races separate; forced blacks to use segregated, inferior facilities; and gave whites the best land.

Blacks Protest The blacks of South Africa resisted the controls imposed by the white minority. In 1912, they formed the African National Congress (ANC) to fight for their rights. The ANC organized strikes and boycotts to protest racist policies. The government banned the ANC and imprisoned many of its members. One was ANC leader **Nelson Mandela** (man•DEHL•uh).

The troubles continued. In 1976, riots over school policies broke out in the black township of Soweto, leaving about 600 students dead. In 1977, police beat popular protest leader Stephen Biko to death while he was in custody. As protests mounted, the government declared a nationwide state of emergency in 1986.

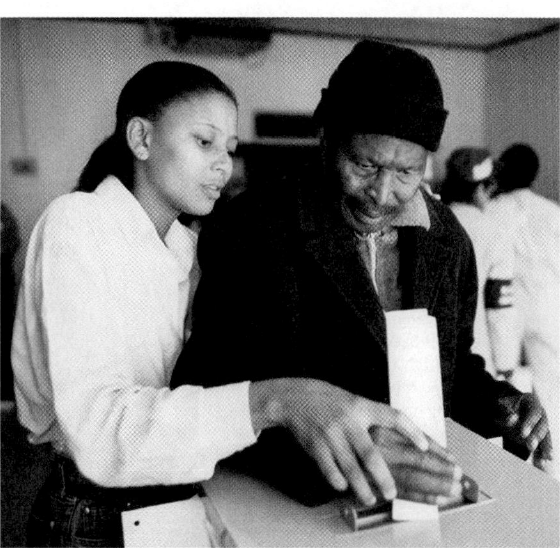

▼ A young South African poll worker helps an elderly man to vote in the first election open to citizens of all races.

South Africa Under Apartheid
10.10.1; 10.10.2

Critical Thinking

- Why didn't South Africa's black majority use its greater numbers to overpower the white minority? *(Possible Answers: Whites had greater military strength. Poverty may have made it difficult to organize resistance.)*
- Ask students if the United States had anything comparable to South Africa's "homelands." *(Possible Answers: Some students might argue that reservations for Native Americans are similar. Others may note that discriminatory policies, such as "redlining"—refusing to offer home mortgages or home insurance to certain areas because of the race or income of the residents—contributed to the formation of ghettos.)*

In-Depth Resources: Unit 5

- Primary Source: from *Kaffir Boy*, p. 59

Tip for Gifted and Talented Students

As the former colonies of the British Empire gained independence, they decided to join Britain in a free, voluntary association called the British Commonwealth. The members have no legal or formal obligation to one another, but rather are held together by shared traditions and institutions, as well as by economic self-interest. Today, there are more than 50 members in the Commonwealth. (In 1946, the word *British* was dropped from the organization's title.)

DIFFERENTIATING INSTRUCTION: ENGLISH LEARNERS

Creating a South Africa Glossary

Class Time 20 minutes

Task Creating a glossary

Purpose To familiarize students with difficult words

Instructions Have students read "South Africa Under Apartheid" on this page. Then have them use the text and a dictionary to create a glossary of challenging words in the passage. Tell students that words should be in alphabetical order and that students should note the number of the paragraph in which the word appears. A sample glossary follows.

African National Congress organization that wanted to end apartheid (4)

Afrikaner a Dutch South African (2)

apartheid complete separation of races (2)

homelands poor-quality land set aside for South Africa's major black groups (3)

Nelson Mandela African National Congress leader (4)

Stephen Biko popular protest leader killed by police (5)

Struggle for Democracy
10.10.1; 10.10.2; 10.10.3

Critical Thinking

- Do you think economic sanctions can help eliminate racism? *(No—Sanctions do not change the way people think. Yes—Sanctions gradually contribute to a shift in people's beliefs.)*
- Why would the *New York Times* assert that Mbeki's views on AIDS might undermine "all his good work"? *(Possible Answer: believed that Mbeki's statements called into question his suitability for public office)*

Electronic Library of Primary Sources

- from "Masakhane—Let Us Build Together"

History Makers

Nelson Mandela and F. W. de Klerk

Ask students why legal training might be useful to political leaders such as Nelson Mandela and F. W. de Klerk. *(Possible Answer: would be indispensable to leaders seeking to end discrimination)*

Both Mandela and de Klerk were called traitors by some members of their own parties. Some whites believed that black rule would destroy South Africa, while some members of the ANC wanted to rid South Africa of all whites. Moderate voices won out, and both races are working together.

In-Depth Resources: Unit 5

- Primary Source: Mandela's Inaugural Address, p. 60
- History Makers: Nelson Mandela, p. 67

Patterns of Interaction Video Series

- Revolutions in Latin America and South Africa

Struggle for Democracy

By the late 1980s, South Africa was under great pressure to change. For years, a black South African bishop, Desmond Tutu, had led an economic campaign against apartheid. He asked foreign nations not to do business with South Africa. In response, many nations imposed trade restrictions. They also isolated South Africa in other ways, for example, by banning South Africa from the Olympic Games. (In 1984, Tutu won the Nobel Peace Prize for his nonviolent methods.) C

MAIN IDEA

Recognizing Effects

C How did Desmond Tutu help force South Africa to end apartheid?

C. Answer He convinced the world to bring economic pressure on South Africa.

The First Steps In 1989, white South Africans elected a new president, F. W. de Klerk. His goal was to transform South Africa and end its isolation. In February 1990, he legalized the ANC and also released Nelson Mandela from prison.

These dramatic actions marked the beginning of a new era in South Africa. Over the next 18 months, the South African parliament repealed apartheid laws that had segregated public facilities and restricted land ownership by blacks. World leaders welcomed these changes and began to ease restrictions on South Africa.

Although some legal barriers had fallen, others would remain until a new constitution was in place. First, the country needed to form a multiracial government. After lengthy negotiations, President de Klerk agreed to hold South Africa's first universal elections, in which people of all races could vote, in April 1994.

Majority Rule Among the candidates for president were F. W. de Klerk and Nelson Mandela. During the campaign, the Inkatha Freedom Party—a rival party to the ANC—threatened to disrupt the process. Nevertheless, the vote went smoothly. South Africans of all races peacefully waited at the polls in long lines. To no one's surprise, the ANC won 63 percent of the vote. They won 252 of 400 seats in the National Assembly (the larger of the two houses in Parliament). Mandela was elected president. Mandela stepped down in 1999, but the nation's democratic government continued.

A New Constitution In 1996, after much debate, South African lawmakers passed a new, more democratic constitution. It guaranteed equal rights for all citizens. The constitution included a bill of rights modeled on the U.S. Bill of Rights. The political changes that South Africa had achieved gave other peoples around the world great hope for the future of democracy.

South Africa Today In 1999, ANC official Thabo Mbeki won election as president in a peaceful transition of power. As Mbeki assumed office, he faced a number of serious challenges. These included high crime rates—South Africa's

History Makers

Nelson Mandela
1918–

Nelson Mandela has said that he first grew interested in politics when he heard elders in his village describe how freely his people lived before whites came. Inspired to help his people regain that freedom, Mandela trained as a lawyer and became a top official in the ANC. Convinced that apartheid would never end peacefully, he joined the armed struggle against white rule. For this, he was imprisoned for 27 years.

After his presidential victory, Mandela continued to work to heal his country.

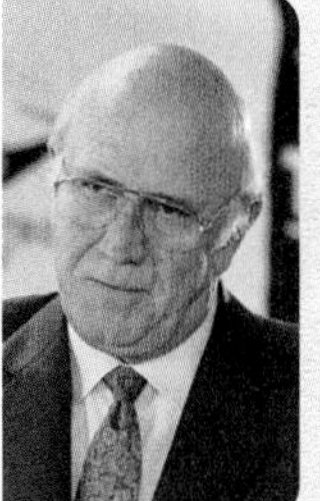

F. W. de Klerk
1936–

Like Mandela, Frederik W. de Klerk also trained as a lawyer. Born to an Afrikaner family with close links to the National Party, de Klerk was elected to Parliament in 1972.

A firm party loyalist, de Klerk backed apartheid but was also open to reform. Friends say that his flexibility on racial issues stemmed from his relatively liberal religious background.

In 1993, de Klerk and Mandela were jointly awarded the Nobel Peace Prize for their efforts to bring democracy to South Africa.

INTEGRATED TECHNOLOGY

RESEARCH LINKS For more on Nelson Mandela and F. W. de Klerk, go to **classzone.com**

DIFFERENTIATING INSTRUCTION: STRUGGLING READERS

South African Leaders

Class Time 15 minutes

Task Creating a Venn diagram

Purpose To help students learn about the backgrounds of Nelson Mandela and F. W. de Klerk

Instructions Ask students to draw a Venn diagram in their notebooks. Then ask them to read the History Makers feature on this page and fill in the diagram. An example follows.

Nelson Mandela	Both	F. W. de Klerk
born in 1918; black; inspired by elders' stories of former freedoms; top official in ANC; joined violent struggle against apartheid; imprisoned 27 years	trained as lawyers; presidents of South Africa; sought to bring democracy to South Africa; won Nobel Peace Prize	born in 1936; white Afrikaner; served in Parliament; backed apartheid but open to reform; liberal religious background

South Africa, 1948–2000

- 1948 National Party comes to power, passes apartheid laws
- 1959 Black homelands established
- 1960 Sharpeville Massacre, 69 protesters killed
- 1962 Nelson Mandela jailed
- 1976 600 black students killed during Soweto protest
- 1977 Stephen Biko killed in police custody
- 1989 F. W. de Klerk elected president
- 1990 ANC legalized and Mandela released
- 1994 ANC wins 63% of the vote; Mandela elected president
- 1996 New constitution adopted
- 1999 ANC candidate Thabo Mbeki elected president

▲ This was South Africa's flag from 1927 to 1994.

rape and murder rates were among the highest in the world. Unemployment stood at about 40 percent among South Africa's blacks, and about 60 percent lived below the poverty level. In addition, an economic downturn discouraged foreign investment.

Mbeki promoted a free-market economic policy to repair South Africa's infrastructure and to encourage foreign investors. In 2002, South Africa was engaged in negotiations to establish free-trade agreements with a number of countries around the world, including those of the European Union as well as Japan, Canada, and the United States. This was an attempt at opening the South African economy to foreign competition and investment, and promoting growth and employment.

One of the biggest problems facing South Africa was the AIDS epidemic. Some estimates concluded that 6 million South Africans were likely to die of AIDS by 2010. Mbeki disputed that AIDS was caused by HIV (human immunodeficiency virus). His opinion put South Africa at odds with the scientific consensus throughout the world. The *New York Times* stated that Mbeki was in danger of undermining "all his good work with his stance on AIDS."

In Section 3, you will read how democratic ideas changed another part of the world, the Communist Soviet Union.

▲ South Africa adopted this flag in 1994.

More About . . .

Thabo Mbeki

South African President Thabo Mbeki's controversial statements have not been restricted to AIDS. About the 2003 war in Iraq, Mbeki remarked that "The prospect facing the people of Iraq should serve as sufficient warning that in [the] future we too might have others descend on us, guns in hand to force-feed us [with their democracy]." Mbeki insisted that democracy had to be homegrown and practiced within a country's social context, not imported.

SECTION 2 ASSESSMENT

TERMS & NAMES 1. For each term or name, write a sentence explaining its significance.

• federal system • martial law • dissident • apartheid • Nelson Mandela

USING YOUR NOTES

2. Which country is more democratic? Explain. (10.10.3)

Nigeria / both / South Africa

MAIN IDEAS

3. What effect did old colonial boundaries have on newly independent African states? (10.10.2)
4. What was the outcome of the war between Nigeria and Biafra? (10.10.2)
5. What were the homelands in South Africa? (10.10.2)

CRITICAL THINKING & WRITING

6. **IDENTIFYING PROBLEMS** What do you think is the main problem that Nigeria must overcome before it can establish a democratic government? (10.10.1)
7. **ANALYZING ISSUES** What are some of the important issues facing South Africa today? (10.10.1)
8. **RECOGNIZING EFFECTS** What were the main negative effects of the European colonizers' economic policies? (10.10.2)
9. **WRITING ACTIVITY** REVOLUTION Working in small teams, write **biographies** of South African leaders who were instrumental in the revolutionary overturn of apartheid. Include pictures if possible. (Writing 2.1.a)

CONNECT TO TODAY MAKING AN ORAL REPORT

Do research on the current policy of Thabo Mbeki and the South African government on HIV and AIDS in South Africa. Report your findings in an **oral report** to the class. (Writing 2.3.a)

❸ ASSESS

SECTION 2 ASSESSMENT

Have students answer the questions and then discuss their answers to items 6 and 7 in class.

Formal Assessment
• Section Quiz, p. 331

❹ RETEACH

Have students make a time line (similar to the one on this page) showing important events in Nigeria's struggle for democracy. Discuss why Nigeria has had a difficult time achieving self-government.

In-Depth Resources: Unit 5
• Guided Reading, p. 51 (also in Spanish)
• Reteaching Activity, p. 70

ANSWERS

1. federal system, p. 607 • martial law, p. 607 • dissident, p. 608 • apartheid, p. 609 • Nelson Mandela, p. 609

2. **Sample Answer:** Nigeria—Civil war when Biafra seceded; South Africa—Passage of apartheid; Both—Former British colonies. South Africa's institutions make it more democratic.
3. dividing people of similar backgrounds or throwing rival groups together
4. Nigeria defeated and reabsorbed Biafra.
5. reserves set up by the minority white government for major black groups
6. **Possible Answer:** Leaders must end corruption and see that Nigeria's people benefit from its resource wealth.
7. high crime rates, unemployment, economic downturn, AIDS epidemic
8. **Possible Answers:** border issues; economic dependence on one or two products
9. **Rubric** Biographies should
   • describe important events in a person's life.
   • explain how the person helped overturn apartheid.

CONNECT TO TODAY

Rubric Oral reports should
• explain the government's policy.
• be well researched and clearly presented.

LESSON PLAN

OBJECTIVES

- Discuss Mikhail Gorbachev and his reforms.
- Identify events leading to the breakup of the Soviet Union.
- Describe Russia under Boris Yeltsin.
- Describe Russia under Vladimir Putin.

1 FOCUS & MOTIVATE

Ask students to describe what happens when a government collapses. *(Possible Answers: confusion, violence, economic disruption)*

2 INSTRUCT

Gorbachev Moves Toward Democracy
10.9.7

Critical Thinking

- Why did it take so long for Soviet leaders to reform their system? *(Possible Answers: They were blinded by political ideology; they were interested in their own power and wealth, not the state's.)*

CALIFORNIA RESOURCES
California Reading Toolkit, p. L87
California Modified Lesson Plans for English Learners, p. 169
California Daily Standards Practice Transparencies, TT79
California Standards Enrichment Workbook, pp. 103–104
California Standards Planner and Lesson Plans, p. L165
California Online Test Practice
California Test Generator CD-ROM
California Easy Planner CD-ROM
California eEdition CD-ROM

A man chisels a piece of the Berlin Wall for a souvenir just after the fall of communism in East Germany

Soldiers of the Chinese People's Liberation Army in Hong Kong, 1998

3

The Collapse of the Soviet Union

MAIN IDEA	WHY IT MATTERS NOW	TERMS & NAMES
REVOLUTION Democratic reforms brought important changes to the Soviet Union.	Russia continues to struggle to establish democracy.	• Politburo • Mikhail Gorbachev • glasnost • perestroika • Boris Yeltsin • CIS • "shock therapy"

CALIFORNIA STANDARDS

10.9.7 Analyze the reasons for the collapse of the Soviet Union, including the weakness of the command economy, burdens of military commitments, and growing resistance to Soviet rule by dissidents in satellite states and the non-Russian Soviet republics.

CST 3 Students use a variety of maps and documents to interpret human movement, including major patterns of domestic and international migration, changing environmental preferences and settlement patterns, the frictions that develop between population groups, and the diffusion of ideas, technological innovations, and goods.

REP 4 Students construct and test hypotheses; collect, evaluate, and employ information from multiple primary and secondary sources; and apply it in oral and written presentations.

SETTING THE STAGE After World War II, the Soviet Union and the United States engaged in a Cold War, which you read about in Chapter 17. Each tried to increase its worldwide influence. The Soviet Union extended its power over much of Eastern Europe. By the 1960s, it appeared that communism was permanently established in the region. During the 1960s and 1970s, the Soviet Union's Communist leadership kept tight control over the Soviet people. But big changes, including democratic reforms, were on the horizon.

Gorbachev Moves Toward Democracy

Soviet premier Leonid Brezhnev and the **Politburo**—the ruling committee of the Communist Party—crushed all political disagreement. Censors decided what writers could publish. The Communist Party also restricted freedom of speech and worship. After Brezhnev's death in 1982, the aging leadership of the Soviet Union tried to hold on to power. However, each of Brezhnev's two successors died after only about a year in office. Who would succeed them?

A Younger Leader To answer that question, the Politburo debated between two men. One was **Mikhail Gorbachev** (mih•KYL GAWR•buh•chawf). Gorbachev's supporters praised his youth, energy, and political skills. With their backing, Gorbachev became the party's new general secretary. In choosing him, Politburo members did not realize they were unleashing another Russian Revolution.

The Soviet people welcomed Gorbachev's election. At 54, he was the youngest Soviet leader since Stalin. Gorbachev was only a child during Stalin's ruthless purge of independent-minded party members. Unlike other Soviet leaders, Gorbachev decided to pursue new ideas.

TAKING NOTES
Following Chronological Order Use a time line to record significant events in the Soviet Union and Russia.

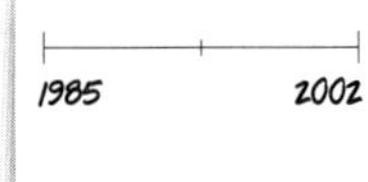

Glasnost Promotes Openness Past Soviet leaders had created a totalitarian state. It rewarded silence and discouraged individuals from acting on their own. As a result, Soviet society rarely changed, and the Soviet economy stagnated. Gorbachev realized that economic and social reforms could not occur without a free flow of ideas and information. In 1985, he announced a policy known as **glasnost** (GLAHS•nuhst), or openness.

Glasnost brought remarkable changes. The government allowed churches to open. It released dissidents from prison and allowed the publication of books by previously banned authors. Reporters investigated problems and criticized officials.

SECTION 3 PROGRAM RESOURCES

ALL STUDENTS
In Depth Resources: Unit 5
- Guided Reading, p. 52

Formal Assessment
- Section Quiz, p. 332

ENGLISH LEARNERS
In Depth Resources in Spanish
- Guided Reading, p. 149

Reading Study Guide (Spanish), p. 205
Reading Study Guide Audio CD (Spanish)

STRUGGLING READERS
In Depth Resources: Unit 5
- Guided Reading, p. 52
- Building Vocabulary, p. 55
- Reteaching Activity, p. 71

Reading Study Guide, p. 205
Reading Study Guide Audio CD

GIFTED AND TALENTED STUDENTS
In Depth Resources: Unit 5
- Primary Source: Political Cartoon, p. 61

INTEGRATED TECHNOLOGY
eEdition CD-ROM
Power Presentations CD-ROM
classzone.com

> **Analyzing Political Cartoons**

Glasnost

Mikhail Gorbachev's policies of glasnost and perestroika shook up the traditional way of doing things in the Soviet economy and in the society at large.

JEFF STAHLER
Courtesy Cincinnati Post

SKILLBUILDER:
Interpreting Visual Sources

1. **Making Inferences** *One arrow points down the road toward stagnation. Where is the other arrow, pointing in the opposite direction, likely to lead?*
2. **Drawing Conclusions** *Why might the Soviet Union look different to the figure in the cartoon?*

Reforming the Economy and Politics

The new openness allowed Soviet citizens to complain about economic problems. Consumers protested that they had to stand in lines to buy food and other basics.

Economic Restructuring Gorbachev blamed these problems on the Soviet Union's inefficient system of central planning. Under central planning, party officials told farm and factory managers how much to produce. They also told them what wages to pay and what prices to charge. Because individuals could not increase their pay by producing more, they had little motive to improve efficiency. (A)

> **MAIN IDEA**
> **Making Inferences**
> (A) Why would it be inefficient for the central government to decide what should be produced all over the country?
> A. Possible Answer because the central government would not understand local conditions, needs, or problems

In 1985, Gorbachev introduced the idea of **perestroika** (PEHR•ih•STROY•kuh), or economic restructuring. In 1986, he made changes to revive the Soviet economy. Local managers gained greater authority over their farms and factories, and people were allowed to open small private businesses. Gorbachev's goal was not to throw out communism, but to make the economic system more efficient and productive.

Democratization Opens the Political System Gorbachev also knew that for the economy to improve, the Communist Party would have to loosen its grip on Soviet society and politics. In 1987, he unveiled a third new policy, called democratization. This would be a gradual opening of the political system.

The plan called for the election of a new legislative body. In the past, voters had merely approved candidates who were handpicked by the Communist Party. Now, voters could choose from a list of candidates for each office. The election produced many surprises. In several places, voters chose lesser-known candidates and reformers over powerful party bosses.

Foreign Policy Soviet foreign policy also changed. To compete militarily with the Soviet Union, President Ronald Reagan had begun the most expensive military buildup in peacetime history, costing more than $2 trillion. Under pressure from U.S. military spending, Gorbachev realized that the Soviet economy could not afford the costly arms race. Arms control became one of Gorbachev's top priorities. In December 1987, he and Reagan signed the Intermediate-Range Nuclear Forces (INF) Treaty. This treaty banned nuclear missiles with ranges of 300 to 3,400 miles.

Analyzing Political Cartoons

Glasnost

Ask students if they are familiar with the reference to "Toto" in the cartoon bubble. *(a play on the famous line in the movie* The Wizard of Oz, *in which Dorothy says to her dog, "Toto, I've a feeling we're not in Kansas anymore.")*

Extension Ask students if they can think of any Russian words that have entered English as loanwords. *(Possible Answers: beluga, mammoth, steppe, babushka)*

SKILLBUILDER Answers

1. **Making Inferences** away from stagnation to a dynamic new society and economy
2. **Drawing Conclusions** because Gorbachev's policies were so different

Reforming the Economy and Politics
10.9.7

Critical Thinking

- Why might Gorbachev have chosen to allow private businesses only on a small scale? *(Possible Answer: He believed that broader reforms would have harmed the interests of powerful people to whom he was politically vulnerable.)*
- Why might people have voted for powerful party bosses rather than for candidates who advocated change? *(Possible Answer: They may not have dared to risk the anger of the powerful bosses.)*

DIFFERENTIATING INSTRUCTION: ENGLISH LEARNERS

Charting Gorbachev's Reforms

Class Time 20 minutes

Task Creating a table

Purpose To familiarize students with Gorbachev's three major reform policies

Instructions Have students read pages 612–613 and create a three-column list like the one shown. Students who need more help should complete the Reading Study Guide activity for this lesson (also available in Spanish).

glasnost	perestroika	democratization
• = "openness" • Churches opened • Political prisoners released • Banned authors allowed to publish books • Okay for reporters to criticize officials	• = "economic restructuring" • Managers of farms and factories could make more decisions on their own • People could open small private businesses • Tried to preserve communism	• Gradual opening of the political system • Election of a new group of lawmakers • Communist Party no longer chose all candidates

The Soviet Union Faces Turmoil
10.9.7

Critical Thinking

- Based on Gorbachev's use of force in Lithuania in 1991, what were his views on the future of the Soviet Union at that time? *(Possible Answer: He probably had faith in the survival of the Union, otherwise he would not have ordered the attack on unarmed civilians.)*
- Why might Soviet military leaders have ignored orders to attack the parliament? *(Possible Answer: probably believed that the military would fare better under reformers)*
- Why might the August coup have accelerated the breakup of the Soviet Union? *(central authority too weak to prevent secessions)*

In Depth Resources: Unit 5

- Primary Source: Political Cartoon, p. 61

History Makers

Mikhail Gorbachev and Boris Yeltsin

Ask students to describe the differences between the characters of Gorbachev and Yeltsin. *(Possible Answer: Gorbachev seems more deliberative and diplomatic, while Yeltsin appears impulsive.)*

Gorbachev brought a new sense of energy and style to official life in the Soviet Union. He even walked through crowds, shaking hands like an American politician, a custom unheard of in Soviet politics.

The Soviet Union Faces Turmoil

Gorbachev's new thinking led him to support movements for change in both the economic and political systems within the Soviet Union. Powerful forces for democracy were building in the country, and Gorbachev decided not to oppose reform. Glasnost, perestroika, and democratization were all means to reform the system. However, the move to reform the Soviet Union ultimately led to its breakup.

Various nationalities in the Soviet Union began to call for their freedom. More than 100 ethnic groups lived in the Soviet Union. Russians were the largest, most powerful group. However, non-Russians formed a majority in the 14 Soviet republics other than Russia.

Ethnic tensions brewed beneath the surface of Soviet society. As reforms loosened central controls, unrest spread across the country. Nationalist groups in Georgia, Ukraine, and Moldavia (now Moldova) demanded self-rule. The Muslim peoples of Soviet Central Asia called for religious freedom.

Lithuania Defies Gorbachev The first challenge came from the Baltic nations of Lithuania, Estonia, and Latvia. These republics had been independent states between the two world wars, until the Soviets annexed them in 1940. Fifty years later, in March 1990, Lithuania declared its independence. To try to force it back into the Soviet Union, Gorbachev ordered an economic blockade of the republic.

Although Gorbachev was reluctant to use stronger measures, he feared that Lithuania's example might encourage other republics to secede. In January 1991, Soviet troops attacked unarmed civilians in Lithuania's capital. The army killed 14 and wounded hundreds.

Yeltsin Denounces Gorbachev The assault in Lithuania and the lack of economic progress damaged Gorbachev's popularity. People looked for leadership to **Boris Yeltsin**. He was a member of parliament and former mayor of Moscow. Yeltsin criticized the crackdown in Lithuania and the slow pace of reforms. In June 1991, voters chose Yeltsin to become the Russian Federation's first directly elected president.

In spite of their rivalry, Yeltsin and Gorbachev faced a common enemy in the old guard of Communist officials. Hard-liners—conservatives who opposed reform—were furious that Gorbachev had given up the Soviet Union's role as the dominant force in Eastern Europe. They also feared losing their power and privileges. These officials vowed to overthrow Gorbachev and undo his reforms.

History Makers

Mikhail Gorbachev
1931–

Mikhail Gorbachev's background shaped the role he would play in history. Both of his grandfathers were arrested during Stalin's purges. Both were eventually freed. However, Gorbachev never forgot his grandfathers' stories.

After working on a state farm, Gorbachev studied law in Moscow and joined the Communist Party. As an official in a farming region, Gorbachev learned much about the Soviet system and its problems.

He advanced quickly in the party. When he became general secretary in 1985, he was the youngest Politburo member and a man who wanted to bring change. He succeeded. Although he pursued reform to save the Soviet Union, ultimately he triggered its breakup.

Boris Yeltsin
1931–

Boris Yeltsin was raised in poverty. For 10 years, his family lived in a single room.

As a youth, Yeltsin earned good grades but behaved badly. Mikhail Gorbachev named him party boss and mayor of Moscow in 1985. Yeltsin's outspokenness got him into trouble. At one meeting, he launched into a bitter speech criticizing conservatives for working against perestroika. Gorbachev fired him for the sake of party unity.

Yeltsin made a dramatic comeback and won a seat in parliament in 1989. Parliament elected him president of Russia in 1990, and voters reelected him in 1991. Due at least in part to his failing health (heart problems), Yeltsin resigned in 1999.

COOPERATIVE LEARNING

Creating a Travel Guide

Class Time 35 minutes

Task Creating a travel brochure

Purpose To familiarize students with a former Soviet republic

Instructions Divide students into pairs and tell them that they will be assembling a travel guide booklet for Lithuania. Explain that they are to use the library or the Internet to gather information. Tell each group that they will need to allocate responsibility for each section of their booklet before they begin their research. Each booklet should include a short historical essay; details about geography and climate; concise outlines of Lithuania's government, economy, and people; and brief descriptions of its languages and religions. Students can also choose to include additional information, such as the current average cost of airfare; an outline of the country's arts; maps and other visuals; and details about Lithuania's currency, major newspapers and magazines, places to stay and eat, and the best spots to shop or be entertained. Encourage students to think carefully about how to order their information and to be creative in designing their guides.

GEOGRAPHY SKILLBUILDER: Interpreting Maps
1. **Place** *What are the 15 republics of the former Soviet Union?*
2. **Region** *Which republic received the largest percentage of the former Soviet Union's territory?*

The August Coup On August 18, 1991, the hardliners detained Gorbachev at his vacation home on the Black Sea. They demanded his resignation as Soviet president. Early the next day, hundreds of tanks and armored vehicles rolled into Moscow. However, the Soviet people had lost their fear of the party. They were willing to defend their freedoms. Protesters gathered at the Russian parliament building, where Yeltsin had his office.

Around midday, Yeltsin emerged and climbed atop one of the tanks. As his supporters cheered, Yeltsin declared, "We proclaim all decisions and decrees of this committee to be illegal. . . . We appeal to the citizens of Russia to . . . demand a return of the country to normal constitutional developments."

On August 20, the hardliners ordered troops to attack the parliament building, but they refused. Their refusal turned the tide. On August 21, the military withdrew its forces from Moscow. That night, Gorbachev returned to Moscow. **B**

MAIN IDEA
Analyzing Motives
B Why do you think the Soviet troops refused the order to attack the parliament building?
B. Possible Answers They were inspired by Yeltsin's courage, they were sick of Communist rule, or they were unwilling to gun down civilians.

End of the Soviet Union The coup attempt sparked anger against the Communist Party. Gorbachev resigned as general secretary of the party. The Soviet parliament voted to stop all party activities. Having first seized power in 1917 in a coup that succeeded, the Communist Party now collapsed because of a coup that failed.

The coup also played a decisive role in accelerating the breakup of the Soviet Union. Estonia and Latvia quickly declared their independence. Other republics soon followed. Although Gorbachev pleaded for unity, no one was listening. By early December, all 15 republics had declared independence.

Yeltsin met with the leaders of other republics to chart a new course. They agreed to form the Commonwealth of Independent States, or **CIS**, a loose federation of former Soviet territories. Only the Baltic republics and Georgia declined to

History from Visuals

Interpreting the Map

List the former Soviet republics that do not share a border with Russia. *(Moldova, Armenia, Turkmenistan, Uzbekistan, Tajikistan, and Kyrgyzstan)*

Extension Which of the former Soviet republics do you think have the best prospects for economic and political success? *(Possible Answer: Estonia, Latvia, and Lithuania, because of their proximity to Europe and access to the Baltic Sea)*

SKILLBUILDER Answers
1. **Place** Russia, Kazakhstan, Ukraine, Turkmenistan, Uzbekistan, Belarus, Kyrgyzstan, Tajikistan, Azerbaijan, Georgia, Lithuania, Latvia, Estonia, Moldova, Armenia
2. **Region** Russia

More About . . .

The August Coup

The coup attempt hurt Gorbachev politically by making it appear that he lacked control. Yeltsin, on the other hand, emerged as a triumphant figure. To many Soviets, Gorbachev seemed to represent the past, and Yeltsin symbolized the future.

Vocabulary Note: Word Origins
The U.S. state of Georgia is named for England's King George II. The name for the Republic of Georgia is said to derive from *gurj*—a Persian name for the region's inhabitants.

DIFFERENTIATING INSTRUCTION: GIFTED AND TALENTED STUDENTS

Creating a Biography of Boris Yeltsin

Class Time 40 minutes
Task Writing a biography of Boris Yeltsin
Purpose To learn more about a Soviet leader
Instructions Tell students that they will be writing a biography about Boris Yeltsin for young readers. Explain that readers will be about ten years old, so the books need to be written at a level that such an audience can understand. Before students begin their research, ask them to create a preliminary design for their books. Have them decide on a number of chapters or sections. These might include chapters about Yeltsin's childhood and education, his work experience and involvement with the Communist Party, his family life, Yeltsin's presidency, and his retirement. Suggest to students that they include a glossary at the end of their books so that readers can look up difficult terms, such as *Communist Party.* Ask students to think hard about how to enliven the text for young readers. Encourage them to think of ways to connect the information to readers' lives and to incorporate lots of interesting pictures and other visuals—maps and illustrated time lines, for example.

Russia Under Boris Yeltsin
10.9.7

Critical Thinking

- What consequences might result from 800-percent inflation? *(Possible Answers: development of a black market; widespread poverty; increase in crime)*
- How might Yeltsin's response to Chechnya's declaration of independence parallel Gorbachev's reaction to Lithuania's? *(Possible Answer: Yeltsin may have felt that using force in Chechnya would discourage other regions of the Russian Republic from seceding.)*

More About . . .

Boris Yeltsin's Retirement

Yeltsin announced his retirement on New Year's Eve of 2000. During his speech to the Russian people, he expressed remorse for the hardship his policies had caused, saying, "I want to ask you for forgiveness, because many of our hopes have not come true, because what we thought would be easy turned out to be painfully difficult. I ask [you] to forgive me for not fulfilling some hopes of those people who believed that we would be able to jump from the grey, stagnating, totalitarian past into a bright, rich and civilized future in one go. I myself believed in this. But it could not be done in one fell swoop. In some respects I was too naive. Some of the problems were too complex."

join. The formation of the CIS meant the death of the Soviet Union. On Christmas Day 1991, Gorbachev announced his resignation as president of the Soviet Union, a country that ceased to exist.

Russia Under Boris Yeltsin

As president of the large Russian Federation, Boris Yeltsin was now the most powerful figure in the CIS. He would face many problems, including an ailing economy, tough political opposition, and an unpopular war.

Yeltsin Faces Problems One of Yeltsin's goals was to reform the Russian economy. He adopted a bold plan known as **"shock therapy,"** an abrupt shift to free-market economics. Yeltsin lowered trade barriers, removed price controls, and ended subsidies to state-owned industries.

Vocabulary
subsidies: government funds given in support of industries

Initially, the plan produced more shock than therapy. Prices soared; from 1992 to 1994, the inflation rate averaged 800 percent. Many factories dependent on government money had to cut production or shut down entirely. This forced thousands of people out of work. By 1993, most Russians were suffering economic hardship:

PRIMARY SOURCE

A visitor to Moscow cannot escape the feeling of a society in collapse. Child beggars accost foreigners on the street. . . . Children ask why they should stay in school when educated professionals do not make enough money to survive. . . . A garment worker complains that now her wages do not cover even the food bills, while fear of growing crime makes her dread leaving home.

DAVID M. KOTZ, "The Cure That Could Kill"

Economic problems fueled a political crisis. In October 1993, legislators opposed to Yeltsin's policies shut themselves inside the parliament building. Yeltsin ordered troops to bombard the building, forcing hundreds of rebel legislators to surrender. Many were killed. Opponents accused Yeltsin of acting like a dictator. C

MAIN IDEA
Evaluating Decisions
C Compare Yeltsin's action here to his actions during the August Coup. Which were more supportive of democracy?

C. Possible Answer
He was more supportive of democracy during the August Coup, because he defied a military takeover. Here he used the military to stay in power.

Chechnya Rebels Yeltsin's troubles included war in Chechnya (CHEHCH•nee•uh), a largely Muslim area in southwestern Russia. In 1991, Chechnya declared its independence, but Yeltsin denied the region's right to secede. In 1994, he ordered 40,000 Russian troops into the breakaway republic. Russian forces reduced the capital city of Grozny (GROHZ•nee) to rubble. News of the death and destruction sparked anger throughout Russia.

With an election coming, Yeltsin sought to end the war. In August 1996, the two sides signed a cease-fire. That year, Yeltsin won reelection. War soon broke out again between Russia and Chechnya, however. In 1999, as the fighting raged, Yeltsin resigned and named Vladimir Putin as acting president.

▼ A Russian soldier throws away a spent shell case near the Chechnyan capital of Grozny.

DIFFERENTIATING INSTRUCTION: STRUGGLING READERS

Russia Under Boris Yeltsin

Class Time 25 minutes

Task Rewriting passages in students' own words

Purpose To help students understand the text by having them rephrase passages

Instructions Tell students to pick two paragraphs from "Russia Under Boris Yeltsin" and paraphrase them. Make the activity more enjoyable for students by encouraging them to use informal language. A sample paragraph follows.

Students who need more help should complete the Guided Reading activity for this section.

Yeltsin Has a Rough Time

One thing Yeltsin wanted to do was to bring free markets to Russia. He didn't want to take his time about it, so he just plowed right ahead with his plans. He made it easier for other nations to trade with Russia by charging them less. He told the government to stop deciding what prices people had to sell stuff for. And he stopped giving money to industries that were owned by the government.

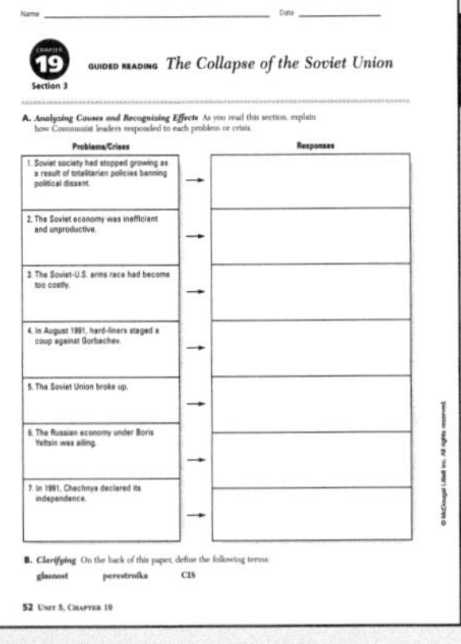
Name ______________ Date ______

19 Section 3 GUIDED READING *The Collapse of the Soviet Union*

A. ***Analyzing Causes and Recognizing Effects*** As you read this section, explain how Communist leaders responded to each problem or crisis.

Problems/Crises		Responses
1. Soviet society had stopped growing as a result of totalitarian policies banning political dissent.	→	
2. The Soviet economy was inefficient and unproductive.	→	
3. The Soviet-U.S. arms race had become too costly.	→	
4. In August 1991, hard-liners staged a coup against Gorbachev.	→	
5. The Soviet Union broke up.	→	
6. The Russian economy under Boris Yeltsin was ailing.	→	
7. In 1991, Chechnya declared its independence.	→	

B. ***Clarifying*** On the back of this paper, define the following terms:
glasnost **perestroika** **CIS**

52 Unit 5, Chapter 19

In Depth Resources: Unit 5

Russia Under Vladimir Putin

Putin forcefully dealt with the rebellion in Chechnya—a popular move that helped him win the presidential election in 2000. Nonetheless, the fighting in the region dragged on for years.

Troubles Continue in Chechnya In 2002, Russia said that the war in Chechnya was nearing an end. In July 2002, the Kremlin said it would begin pulling some of its 80,000 troops out of Chechnya, but Russia had made and broken such a promise before. Then, in October 2002, Chechen rebels seized a theater in Moscow, and more than 150 people died in the rescue attempt by Russian forces.

Economic, Political, and Social Problems The nation's economic problems continued, and some observers wondered whether Russian democracy could survive. A decade of change and reform between 1992 and 2002 caused enormous social upheaval in Russia. Experts estimated that there were between 30,000 and 50,000 homeless children on the streets of Moscow. About half of these children were younger than 13. Other indications of a society experiencing severe stress included high rates of domestic violence and unemployment, a steep population decline, and declines in the standard of living and the average life expectancy.

Nonetheless, there were some signs of improvement under Putin. He stated that he favored a market economy, but one adapted to Russia's special circumstances. Unrest in the Soviet Union had an enormous impact on Central and Eastern Europe, as you will read in the next section.

History Makers

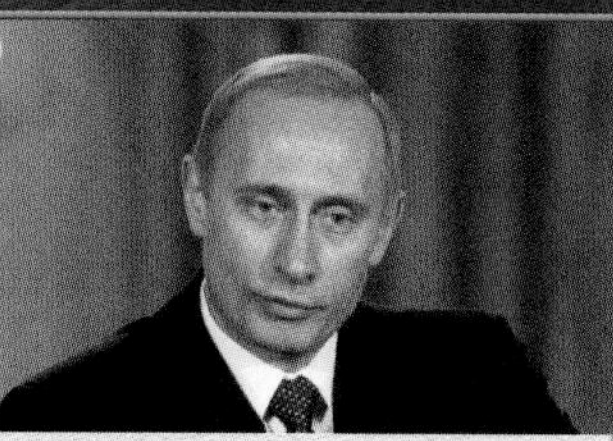

Vladimir Putin
1952–

Vladimir Putin worked for 15 years as an intelligence officer in the KGB (Committee for State Security). Six of those years were spent in East Germany. In 1990, at the age of 38, he retired from the KGB with the rank of lieutenant colonel.

Putin became first deputy mayor of Leningrad. In 1996, he moved to Moscow, where he joined the presidential staff. Eventually, Boris Yeltsin appointed Putin prime minister. When Yeltsin resigned at the end of 1999, he appointed Putin acting president. In March 2000, Putin won election as president.

INTEGRATED TECHNOLOGY

RESEARCH LINKS For more on Vladimir Putin, go to **classzone.com**

SECTION 3 ASSESSMENT

TERMS & NAMES 1. For each term or name, write a sentence explaining its significance.

• Politburo • Mikhail Gorbachev • glasnost • perestroika • Boris Yeltsin • CIS • "shock therapy"

USING YOUR NOTES

2. In what year did the Soviet Union break apart? (10.9.7)

1985 — 2002

MAIN IDEAS

3. What are some of the changes that Gorbachev made to the Soviet economy? (10.9.7)
4. After the breakup of the Soviet Union, what problems did Yeltsin face as the president of the Russian Federation? (10.9.7)
5. How did Putin deal with Chechnya? (10.9.7)

CRITICAL THINKING & WRITING

6. **SYNTHESIZING** How did Gorbachev's reforms help to move the Soviet Union toward democracy? (10.9.7)
7. **ANALYZING ISSUES** What are some of the problems that faced President Vladimir Putin in Russia? (10.9.7)
8. **COMPARING** In what ways were the policies of Gorbachev, Yeltsin, and Putin similar? (10.9.7)
9. **WRITING ACTIVITY** REVOLUTION It has been said that Gorbachev's reforms led to another Russian Revolution. In your opinion, what did this revolution overthrow? Support your opinion in a two-paragraph **essay.** (Writing 2.3.a)

INTEGRATED TECHNOLOGY **INTERNET ACTIVITY**

Use the Internet to research the situation in Chechnya today. Make a **poster** that includes a time line of the conflict, the leaders of the two sides, and war images. (CST 3)

INTERNET KEYWORD
Chechnya

Russia Under Vladimir Putin
10.9.7

Critical Thinking

- How might Russians have felt about Yeltsin appointing Putin instead of calling an early election? *(Possible Answers: Some may have seen the move as a setback for democratic reform. Others may have seen the appointment as a wise move that would help maintain stability.)*
- Ask students what they think will happen to the Russian Republic if the current economic trend continues. *(Possible Answers: regional secession movements, a military coup)*

History Makers

Vladimir Putin

Why might Yeltsin have chosen Putin as his successor? *(Possible Answer: Yeltsin felt he could trust Putin to carry out the reforms he had initiated.)*

3 ASSESS

SECTION 3 ASSESSMENT

Have students work in small groups to discuss the questions.

Formal Assessment

• Section Quiz, p. 332

4 RETEACH

Have students use the Guided Reading activity to review main ideas.

In Depth Resources: Unit 5

• Guided Reading, p. 52 (also in Spanish)
• Reteaching Activity, p. 71

ANSWERS

1. Politburo, p. 612 • Mikhail Gorbachev, p. 612 • glasnost, p. 612 • perestroika, p. 613 • Boris Yeltsin, p. 614 • CIS, p. 615 • "shock therapy," p. 616
2. **Sample Answer:** 1985 to 1987—Gorbachev introduces glasnost; 1991—coup attempt; 1992—Yeltsin's "shock therapy" begins; 1994—Russian forces destroy Chechen capital; 2000—Putin elected president. The Soviet Union collapsed in 1991.
3. gave local managers more authority, encouraged establishment of small businesses
4. economic reform, political opposition, rebellion in Chechnya
5. He took a hard line, gaining popularity with Russian voters.
6. by initiating glasnost and perestroika, which promoted civic and economic liberalization
7. rebellion in Chechnya, economic problems, social upheaval
8. All supported glasnost and perestroika; all favored economic reform; all favored greater democratization.
9. **Rubric** Essays should mention
   - the breakup of the Soviet Union.
   - that authoritarian rule was replaced by more democratic practices.
   - that conservative Communists lost power.

INTEGRATED TECHNOLOGY

Rubric Posters should
- reflect current information on the conflict.
- use appropriate visuals.

LESSON PLAN

OBJECTIVES

- Explain reforms in Poland and Hungary.
- Summarize changes in Germany.
- Describe democratic change in Czechoslovakia and Romania.
- Explain the conflict in the former Yugoslavia.

1 FOCUS & MOTIVATE

Ask students how living in a communist country might change their lives. *(Possible Answers: limits on speech and worship, fewer consumer goods available)*

2 INSTRUCT

Poland and Hungary Reform

10.9.1; 10.9.5

Critical Thinking

- Why might Hungary's Communist Party have voted itself out of existence? *(Possible Answer: Communism had a bad reputation, so party members may have wished to regroup under a different name.)*

CALIFORNIA RESOURCES

California Reading Toolkit, p. L88
California Modified Lesson Plans for English Learners, p. 171
California Daily Standards Practice Transparencies, TT80
California Standards Enrichment Workbook, pp. 91–92, 99–100, 103–104
California Standards Planner and Lesson Plans, p. L167
California Online Test Practice
California Test Generator CD-ROM
California Easy Planner CD-ROM
California eEdition CD-ROM

A man chisels a piece of the Berlin Wall for a souvenir just after the fall of communism in East Germany

4

Changes in Central and Eastern Europe

Soldiers of the Chinese People's Liberation Army in Hong Kong, 1998

MAIN IDEA	WHY IT MATTERS NOW	TERMS & NAMES
CULTURAL INTERACTION Changes in the Soviet Union led to changes throughout Central and Eastern Europe.	Many Eastern European nations that overthrew Communist governments are still struggling with reform.	• Solidarity • Lech Walesa • reunification • ethnic cleansing

CALIFORNIA STANDARDS

10.9.1 Compare the economic and military power shifts caused by the war, including the Yalta Pact, the development of nuclear weapons, Soviet control over Eastern European nations, and the economic recoveries of Germany and Japan.

10.9.5 Describe the uprisings in Poland (1952), Hungary (1956), and Czechoslovakia (1968) and those countries' resurgence in the 1970s and 1980s as people in Soviet satellites sought freedom from Soviet control.

10.9.7 Analyze the reasons for the collapse of the Soviet Union, including the weakness of the command economy, burdens of military commitments, and growing resistance to Soviet rule by dissidents in satellite states and the non-Russian Soviet republics.

TAKING NOTES

Analyzing Causes Use a chart to record reasons that nations in Central and Eastern Europe broke apart.

Former nations	Reasons for breakup
Yugoslavia	
Czecho-slovakia	

SETTING THE STAGE The Soviet reforms of the late 1980s brought high hopes to the people of Central and Eastern Europe. For the first time in decades, they were free to make choices about the economic and political systems governing their lives. However, they soon discovered that increased freedom sometimes challenges the social order. Mikhail Gorbachev's new thinking in the Soviet Union led him to urge Central and Eastern European leaders to open up their economic and political systems.

Poland and Hungary Reform

The aging Communist rulers of Europe resisted reform. However, powerful forces for democracy were building in their countries. In the past, the threat of Soviet intervention had kept such forces in check. Now, Gorbachev was saying that the Soviet Union would not oppose reform.

Poland and Hungary were among the first countries in Eastern Europe to embrace the spirit of change. In 1980, Polish workers at the Gdansk shipyard went on strike, demanding government recognition of their union, **Solidarity**. When millions of Poles supported the action, the government gave in to the union's demands. Union leader **Lech Walesa** (lehk vah•WEHN•sah) became a national hero.

Solidarity Defeats Communists The next year, however, the Polish government banned Solidarity again and declared martial law. The Communist Party discovered that military rule could not revive Poland's failing economy. In the 1980s, industrial production declined, while foreign debt rose to more than $40 billion.

Public discontent deepened as the economic crisis worsened. In August 1988, defiant workers walked off their jobs. They demanded raises and the legalization of Solidarity. The military leader, General Jaruzelski (YAH•roo•ZEHL•skee), agreed to hold talks with Solidarity leaders. In April 1989, Jaruzelski legalized Solidarity and agreed to hold Poland's first free election since the Communists took power.

In elections during 1989 and 1990, Polish voters voted against Communists and overwhelmingly chose Solidarity candidates. They elected Lech Walesa president.

Poland Votes Out Walesa After becoming president in 1990, Lech Walesa tried to revive Poland's bankrupt economy. Like Boris Yeltsin, he adopted a strategy of shock therapy to move Poland toward a free-market economy. As in Russia, inflation and unemployment shot up. By the mid-1990s, the economy was improving.

SECTION 4 PROGRAM RESOURCES

ALL STUDENTS

In-Depth Resources: Unit 5
- Guided Reading, p. 53

Formal Assessment
- Section Quiz, p. 333

ENGLISH LEARNERS

In-Depth Resources in Spanish
- Guided Reading, p. 150

Reading Study Guide (Spanish), p. 207
Reading Study Guide Audio CD (Spanish)

STRUGGLING READERS

In-Depth Resources: Unit 5
- Guided Reading, p. 53
- Building Vocabulary, p. 55
- Reteaching Activity, p. 72

Reading Study Guide, p. 207
Reading Study Guide Audio CD

GIFTED AND TALENTED STUDENTS

In-Depth Resources: Unit 5
- Primary Source: from The Road to Manjača, p. 62
- Connections Across Time and Cultures, p. 68

Electronic Library of Primary Sources

INTEGRATED TECHNOLOGY

eEdition CD-ROM
Power Presentations CD-ROM
Geography Transparencies
- GT35 Germany, Post World War I–Present

World Art and Cultures Transparencies
- AT78 *Burning Rods*

Electronic Library of Primary Sources
- "Destruction of the Berlin Wall"
- "Will I Ever Go Home Again?"

classzone.com

Nevertheless, many Poles remained unhappy with the pace of economic progress. In the elections of 1995, they turned Walesa out of office in favor of a former Communist, Aleksander Kwasniewski (kfahs•N'YEHF•skee).

Poland Under Kwasniewski President Kwasniewski led Poland in its drive to become part of a broader European community. In 1999, Poland became a full member of NATO. As a NATO member, Poland provided strong support in the war against terrorism after the attack on the World Trade Center in New York on September 11, 2001. In appreciation of Poland's support, President Bush invited Kwasniewski to Washington for a formal state visit in July 2002.

Kwasniewski continued the efforts of previous leaders to establish a strong market economy in Poland. Although unemployment and poverty continued to be deep-rooted problems, Kwasniewski pushed for democracy and free markets.

Hungarian Communists Disband Inspired by the changes in Poland, Hungarian leaders launched a sweeping reform program. To stimulate economic growth, reformers encouraged private enterprise and allowed a small stock market to operate. A new constitution permitted a multiparty system with free elections.

Vocabulary
deposed: removed from power

The pace of change grew faster when radical reformers took over a Communist Party congress in October 1989. The radicals deposed the party's leaders and then dissolved the party itself. Here was another first: a European Communist Party had voted itself out of existence. A year later, in national elections, the nation's voters put a non-Communist government in power.

In 1994, a socialist party—largely made up of former Communists—won a majority of seats in Hungary's parliament. The socialist party and a democratic party formed a coalition, or alliance, to rule.

In parliamentary elections in 1998, a liberal party won the most seats in the National Assembly. In 1999, Hungary joined the North Atlantic Treaty Organization as a full member. In the year 2001, there was a general economic downtown in Hungary. This was due to weak exports, decline in foreign investment, and excessive spending on state pensions and increased minimum wages.

Germany Reunifies

While Poland and Hungary were moving toward reform, East Germany's 77-year-old party boss, Erich Honecker, dismissed reforms as unnecessary. Then, in 1989, Hungary allowed vacationing East German tourists to cross the border into Austria. From there they could travel to West Germany. Thousands of East Germans took this new escape route to the west. (A)

A. Answer The government of Hungary gave East Germans access to Hungary as an escape route to Austria and West Germany.

MAIN IDEA
Analyzing Causes
(A) How did the fall of communism in Hungary contribute to turmoil in East Germany?

Fall of the Berlin Wall In response, the East German government closed its borders entirely. By October 1989, huge demonstrations had broken out

▼ The fall of the Berlin Wall, November 10, 1989

More About . . .

Lech Walesa

When Lech Walesa was 18 months old, his father died. Before dying, he predicted that his wife would be proud of Lech someday.

At 24, Walesa began to work at the shipyard in Gdansk, Poland. He took up the struggle for free trade unions after seeing police shoot protesters. During the 1980 strike, Walesa and others locked themselves inside the shipyard. This attracted the attention of the world to their demands for a legally recognized union and the right to strike.

The government granted these demands but later outlawed Solidarity and jailed Walesa and other leaders. After his release, Walesa won both the Nobel Prize and his country's presidency.

Germany Reunifies
10.9.7

Critical Thinking

- Why did Hungary and Austria allow East Germans to cross their borders? *(to pressure East German leaders into initiating reforms)*
- How might West Germans' views about reunification have changed over time? *(Possible Answer: At first, they were overjoyed to be reunited. Later, they worried about economic sacrifices.)*

Electronic Library of Primary Sources

- "Destruction of the Berlin Wall"

Geography Transparencies

- GT35 Germany, Post World War I–Present

DIFFERENTIATING INSTRUCTION: ENGLISH LEARNERS

Writing Mini-Biographies

Class Time 15 minutes

Task Writing short biographies

Purpose To familiarize students with important individuals from the recent history of Poland

Instructions Ask students to read "Poland and Hungary Reform" on pages 618–619, listing the people mentioned in the text as they read. Then have students write down information next to each individual's name that describes why they are relevant to the passage.

Students who need more help should complete the Reading Study Guide activity for this section (also available in Spanish).

Mikhail Gorbachev *Soviet reformer who encouraged Central and Eastern Europe to change economic and political systems*

Lech Walesa *A leader of Poland's Solidarity union who became president of Poland in 1990*

General Jaruzelski *Poland's military leader who agreed to hold free elections*

Boris Yeltsin *Russian president who introduced economic "shock therapy"*

Aleksander Kwasniewski *Former communist who became president of Poland in 1995*

in cities across East Germany. The protesters demanded the right to travel freely, and later added the demand for free elections. Honecker lost his authority with the party and resigned on October 18.

In June 1987, President Reagan had stood before the Berlin Wall and demanded: "Mr. Gorbachev, tear down this wall!" Two years later, the wall was indeed about to come down. The new East German leader, Egon Krenz, boldly gambled that he could restore stability by allowing people to leave East Germany. On November 9, 1989, he opened the Berlin Wall. The long-divided city of Berlin erupted in joyous celebration. Krenz's dramatic gamble to save communism did not work. By the end of 1989, the East German Communist Party had ceased to exist.

Reunification With the fall of Communism in East Germany, many Germans began to speak of **reunification**—the merging of the two Germanys. However, the movement for reunification worried many people, who feared a united Germany.

The West German chancellor, Helmut Kohl, assured world leaders that Germans had learned from the past. They were now committed to democracy and human rights. Kohl's assurances helped persuade other European nations to accept German reunification. Germany was officially reunited on October 3, 1990. B

MAIN IDEA

Clarifying

B Why would Europeans fear the reunification of Germany?

B. Possible Answer A reunified Germany would be larger and stronger than the two separate Germanys—and could once again be a military threat as Nazi Germany had been.

Germany's Challenges The newly united Germany faced serious problems. More than 40 years of Communist rule had left eastern Germany in ruins. Its railroads, highways, and telephone system had not been modernized since World War II. East German industries produced goods that could not compete in the global market.

Rebuilding eastern Germany's bankrupt economy was going to be a difficult, costly process. To pay these costs, Kohl raised taxes. As taxpayers tightened their belts, workers in eastern Germany faced a second problem—unemployment. Inefficient factories closed, depriving millions of workers of their jobs.

A New Chancellor In 1998, voters turned Kohl out of office and elected a new chancellor, Gerhard Schroeder, of the Socialist Democratic Party. Schroeder started out as a market reformer, but the slow growth of the German economy made the task of reform difficult. Although Germany had the world's third largest economy, it was the slowest-growing economy in Europe in the early years of the 21st century. Germany's unemployment rate was among the highest in Europe, and rising inflation was also a continuing problem. Nonetheless, Schroeder won re-election in 2002.

Reunification forced Germany to rethink its role in international affairs. As Central Europe's largest country, Germany gained global responsibilities. Schroeder and his foreign minister took an active role in European affairs.

GEOGRAPHY SKILLBUILDER: Interpreting Maps
1. **Location** *What is the relative location of business centers? Give possible reasons.*
2. **Movement** *Why might Hamburg and Kiel be shipbuilding centers, and what does this suggest about the movement of goods?*

More About . . .

Germany's Challenges

After communism fell, refugees flooded into Germany from the poorer countries of Eastern Europe. This angered many Germans, who accused foreigners of stealing jobs by working for cheap wages. Thousands of angry young people joined neo-Nazi groups, which began to carry out violent actions against foreigners. In May 1993, five Turkish immigrants died when their house was set on fire. Attacks such as this revived the ugly memories of Nazi violence in the 1930s. By the 1990s, however, Germany had deep democratic roots, and millions of Germans spoke out against racism and antiforeign violence.

History from Visuals

Interpreting the Map

Have students look over the major German industries listed in the key. Ask if they know of any products from these industries that are exported to the United States. *(Possible Answer: Mercedes-Benz cars)*

SKILLBUILDER Answers

1. **Location** They are near borders and ports, which makes international trade easier.
2. **Movement** They are near rivers and the sea, which provide a way to ship goods around the world.

DIFFERENTIATING INSTRUCTION: STRUGGLING READERS

Analyzing a Political Cartoon

Class Time 25 minutes

Task Analyzing a political cartoon

Purpose To have students think more about the events that shook communist Europe in October 1989

Instructions Have students study the political cartoon in In-Depth Resources: Unit 5. If students are having difficulty understanding the cartoon, encourage them to review "The Soviet Union Faces Turmoil" (pp. 614–616), "Poland and Hungary Reform" (pp. 618–619), and "Germany Reunifies" (pp. 619–620).

After they have studied the cartoon, ask students what has taken the place of trick or treat. *(reform, freedom)* What does USSR stand for, and what is the symbol on the bear's apron? *(Union of Soviet Socialist Republics; hammer and sickle–which represented the alliance of Soviet workers and peasants)* Why is the USSR represented as a bear? *(The bear is a national symbol of Russia.)* After students have answered these questions, have them complete the activity options.

In-Depth Resources: Unit 5

Democracy Spreads in Czechoslovakia

Changes in East Germany affected other European countries, including Czechoslovakia and Romania.

Czechoslovakia Reforms While huge crowds were demanding democracy in East Germany, neighboring Czechoslovakia remained quiet. A conservative government led by Milos Jakes resisted all change. In 1989, the police arrested several dissidents. Among these was the Czech playwright Václav Havel (VAH•tslahv HAH•vehl), a popular critic of the government.

On October 28, 1989, about 10,000 people gathered in Wenceslas Square in the center of Prague. They demanded democracy and freedom. Hundreds were arrested. Three weeks later, about 25,000 students inspired by the fall of the Berlin Wall gathered in Prague to demand reform. Following orders from the government, the police brutally attacked the demonstrators and injured hundreds.

The government crackdown angered the Czech people. Huge crowds gathered in Wenceslas Square. They demanded an end to Communist rule. On November 25, about 500,000 protesters crowded into downtown Prague. Within hours, Milos Jakes and his entire Politburo resigned. One month later, a new parliament elected Václav Havel president of Czechoslovakia.

Czechoslovakia Breaks Up In Czechoslovakia, reformers also launched an economic program based on "shock therapy." The program caused a sharp rise in unemployment. It especially hurt Slovakia, the republic occupying the eastern third of Czechoslovakia.

Unable to agree on economic policy, the country's two parts—Slovakia and the Czech Republic—drifted apart. In spite of President Václav Havel's pleas for unity, a movement to split the nation gained support among the people. Havel resigned because of this. Czechoslovakia split into two countries on January 1, 1993.

Havel was elected president of the Czech Republic. He won reelection in 1998. Then, in 2003, Havel stepped down as president, in part because of ill health. The Czech parliament chose Václav Klaus, a right-wing economist and former prime minister, to succeed him. The economy of the Czech Republic slowly improved in the face of some serious problems. The Czech Republic pushed to become a full member of the European Union (EU) by 2004.

Slovakia, too, proceeded on a reformist, pro-Western path. It experienced one of the highest economic growth rates in the region in 2002. It hoped to join both NATO and the EU in the near future.

Overthrow in Romania

By late 1989, only Romania seemed unmoved by the calls for reform. Romania's ruthless Communist dictator Nicolae Ceausescu (chow•SHES•koo) maintained a firm grip on power. His secret police enforced his orders brutally. Nevertheless, Romanians were aware of the reforms in other countries. They began a protest movement of their own.

A Popular Uprising In December, Ceausescu ordered the army to fire on demonstrators in the city of Timisoara

Social History

The Romanian Language

The Romanians are the only people in Eastern Europe whose ancestry and language go back to the ancient Romans. Romanian is the only Eastern European language that developed from Latin. For this reason, Romanian is very different from the other languages spoken in the region.

Today's Romanians are descended from the Dacians (the original people in the region), the Romans, and tribes that arrived later, such as the Goths, Huns, and Slavs.

Romanian remains the official language today. Minority groups within Romania (such as Hungarians, Germans, Gypsies, Jews, Turks, and Ukrainians) sometimes speak their own ethnic languages among themselves. Nonetheless, almost all the people speak Romanian as well.

INTEGRATED TECHNOLOGY

INTERNET ACTIVITY Create a poster on all the Romance languages, which developed from Latin. Go to **classzone.com** for your research.

Democracy Spreads in Czechoslovakia
10.9.5

Critical Thinking

- Why is the fall of communism in Czechoslovakia sometimes called the "Velvet Revolution"? *(Possible Answer: happened relatively smoothly)*
- What, in addition to economic differences, may have led to the division of Czechoslovakia? *(Possible Answer: ethnic differences)*

Overthrow in Romania
10.9.5; 10.9.7

Critical Thinking

- How could Ceausescu have been shocked by the sudden collapse of his power? *(Possible Answer: He may have mistaken fear of his power for loyalty.)*
- What factors might predispose some post-Communist states to corruption? *(Possible Answers: antiquated infrastructures; greater distance from democratic countries)*

Social History

The Romanian Language

Isolation of Romanian from other Romance tongues and close contact with Slavic languages and Hungarian caused Romanian phonology and grammar to develop differently.

INTEGRATED TECHNOLOGY

Rubric Posters should
- identify the different languages.
- use appropriate visuals.

COOPERATIVE LEARNING

Debating the Merits of Economic "Shock Therapy"

Class Time 45 minutes

Task Preparing for and holding a debate

Purpose To improve understanding of historical events and hone persuasive speaking skills

Instructions Divide students into small groups. Remind students that they learned in Section 3 that Boris Yeltsin's plan of economic "shock therapy" initially produced more shock than therapy. Have groups review Sections 3 and 4 so that they are able to describe the following in their own words:

- what economic "shock therapy" is
- which governments have tried it
- what the results have been

Have half the groups gather information that shows positive results of this type of economic change. The other groups should look for negative results. As a class, discuss whether the positive results of economic shock therapy are worth the disruption it causes.

The Breakup of Yugoslavia
10.9.1; 10.9.5; 10.9.7

Critical Thinking

- Why might it have been easier for Slovenia and Croatia to win independence than Bosnia and Herzegovina? *(Possible Answers: stronger militarily; ethnically more homogeneous)*
- Why might Muslims make up a large percentage of Bosnia and Herzegovina's and Kosovo's populations? *(These regions were once part of the Muslim Ottoman Empire.)*
- Why was Milosevic extradited instead of being tried in Serbia? *(Possible Answer: Many Serbians continued to support him.)*

More About . . .

Ethnic Differences

Most Serbs are Orthodox Christians, unlike Croats, who are primarily Roman Catholic, and Muslims, who follow Islam. In the past, Croats and Muslims have dominated Serbs. Muslim Turks ruled Serbia for 400 years. During World War II, Croats joined forces with the Nazis in persecuting Serbs.

Tip for English Learners

Explain to students that a *broker* is somebody who acts as an intermediary, or go-between. A broker negotiates agreements between different people or groups.

(tee•mee•SHWAH•rah). The army killed and wounded hundreds of people. The massacre in Timisoara ignited a popular uprising against Ceausescu. Within days, the army joined the people. Shocked by the collapse of his power, Ceausescu and his wife attempted to flee. They were captured, however, and then tried and executed on Christmas Day, 1989. Romania held general elections in 1990, 1992, and 1996. In the 2000 elections, Ion Iliescu was elected to a third term as president. C

MAIN IDEA

Contrasting

C Contrast the democratic revolutions in Czechoslovakia and Romania.

C. Answer In Czechoslovakia, the Communist government resigned without violence. In Romania, the government used violence, and the victorious protesters executed Ceausescu.

The Romanian Economy Throughout the 1990s, Romania struggled with corruption and crime as it tried to salvage its economy. In 2001, overall production was still only 75 percent of what it had been in 1989, the year of Ceausescu's overthrow. In the first years of the 21st century, two-thirds of the economy was still state owned.

However, the government made economic reforms to introduce elements of capitalism. The government also began to reduce the layers of bureaucracy in order to encourage foreign investors. Furthermore, in order to achieve membership in the European Union, the Romanian government began to move away from a state-controlled economy.

The Breakup of Yugoslavia

Ethnic conflict plagued Yugoslavia. This country, formed after World War I, had eight major ethnic groups—Serbs, Croats, Muslims, Slovenes, Macedonians, Albanians, Hungarians, and Montenegrins. Ethnic and religious differences dating back centuries caused these groups to view one another with suspicion. After World War II, Yugoslavia became a federation of six republics. Each republic had a mixed population.

A Bloody Breakup Josip Tito, who led Yugoslavia from 1945 to 1980, held the country together. After Tito's death, ethnic resentments boiled over. Serbian leader Slobodan Milosevic (mee•LOH•sheh•vihch) asserted leadership over Yugoslavia. Many Serbs opposed Milosevic and his policies and fled the country.

Two republics, Slovenia and Croatia, declared independence. In June 1991, the Serbian-led Yugoslav army invaded both republics. After months of bloody fighting, both republics freed themselves from Serbian rule. Early in 1992, Bosnia-Herzegovina joined Slovenia and Croatia in declaring independence. (In April, Serbia and Montenegro formed a new Yugoslavia.) Bosnia's population included Muslims (44 percent), Serbs (31 percent), and Croats (17 percent). While Bosnia's Muslims and Croats backed independence, Bosnian Serbs strongly opposed it. Supported by Serbia, the Bosnian Serbs launched a war in March 1992.

▼ A view of downtown Sarajevo through a bullet-shattered window

During the war, Serbian military forces used violence and forced emigration against Bosnian Muslims living in Serb-held lands. Called **ethnic cleansing**, this policy was intended to rid Bosnia of its Muslim population. By 1995, the Serbian military controlled 70 percent of Bosnia. In December of that year, leaders of the three factions involved in the war signed a UN- and U.S.-brokered peace treaty. In September 1996, Bosnians elected a three-person presidency, one leader from each ethnic group. By 2001, Bosnia and

DIFFERENTIATING INSTRUCTION: GIFTED AND TALENTED STUDENTS

International Criminal Tribunal for the Former Yugoslavia

Class Time 20 minutes

Task Delivering a speech summarizing the work of the International Criminal Tribunal for the Former Yugoslavia

Purpose To familiarize students with efforts to bring war criminals to justice

Instructions Ask students to use the library or the Internet to learn about the work of the International Criminal Tribunal for the Former Yugoslavia (ICTFY). Explain that the ICTFY was established by a May 1993 UN Security Council resolution for the prosecution of war crimes committed in the former Yugoslavia. Tell students that they will be using their research to prepare an oral report summarizing the work of the tribunal, which they will deliver to the class. Encourage students to include information about the location and structure of the tribunal; important indictments, trials, and appeals (such as the trial of former Yugoslav president Slobodan Milosevic); and efforts to arrest top fugitives, such as Radovan Karadzic and Ratko Mladic. Students may use the primary source activity from In-Depth Resources: Unit 5 for background information.

PRIMARY SOURCE *from* The Road to Manjača
by Orhan Bosnević

In-Depth Resources: Unit 5

Ethnic Groups in the Former Yugoslavia

Many ethnic and religious groups lived within Yugoslavia, which was a federation of six republics. The map shows how the ethnic groups were distributed. Some of those groups held ancient grudges against one another. The chart summarizes some of the cultural differences among the groups.

CALIFORNIA STANDARDS

10.9.7 Analyze the reasons for the collapse of the Soviet Union, including the weakness of the command economy, burdens of military commitments, and growing resistance to Soviet rule by dissidents in satellite states and the non-Russian Soviet republics.

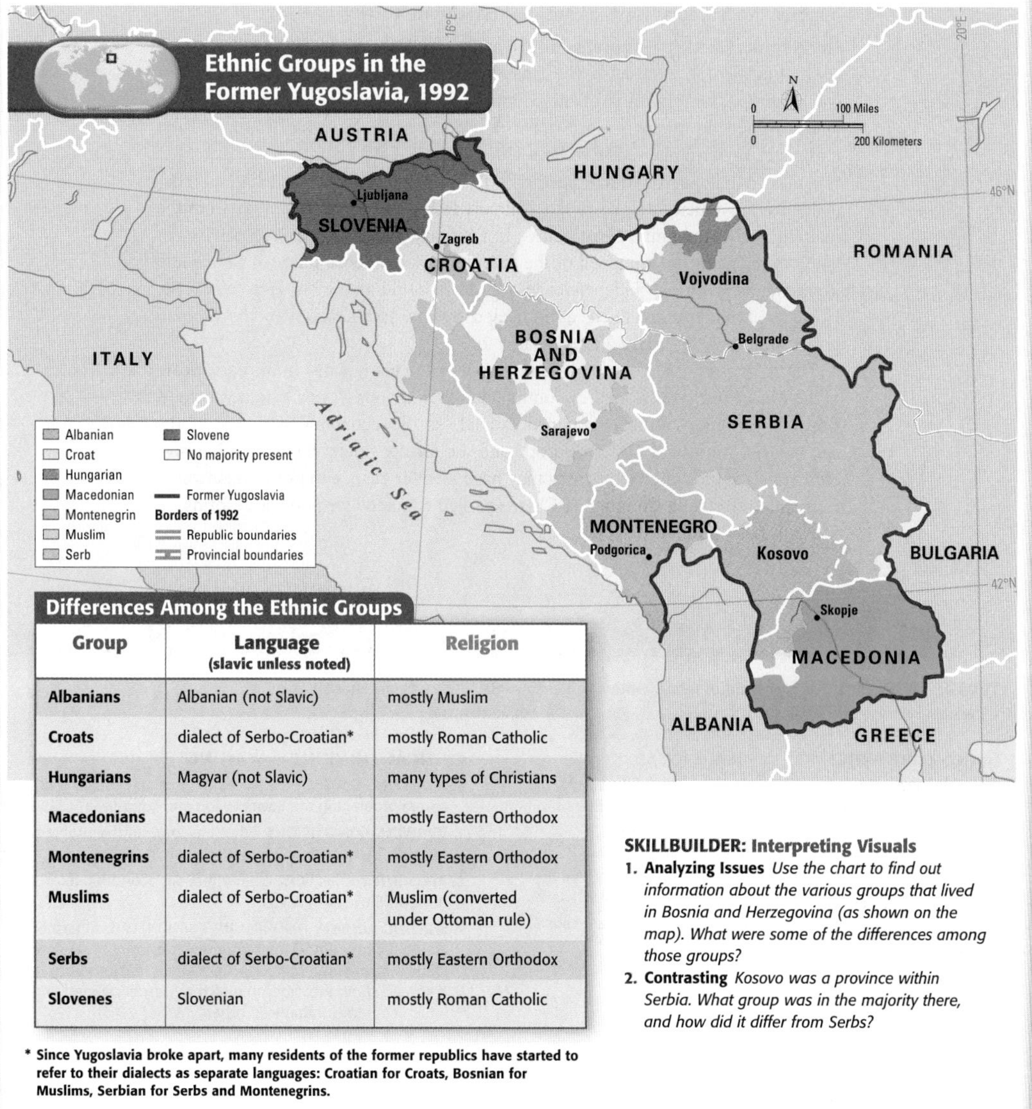

Differences Among the Ethnic Groups

Group	Language (slavic unless noted)	Religion
Albanians	Albanian (not Slavic)	mostly Muslim
Croats	dialect of Serbo-Croatian*	mostly Roman Catholic
Hungarians	Magyar (not Slavic)	many types of Christians
Macedonians	Macedonian	mostly Eastern Orthodox
Montenegrins	dialect of Serbo-Croatian*	mostly Eastern Orthodox
Muslims	dialect of Serbo-Croatian*	Muslim (converted under Ottoman rule)
Serbs	dialect of Serbo-Croatian*	mostly Eastern Orthodox
Slovenes	Slovenian	mostly Roman Catholic

*** Since Yugoslavia broke apart, many residents of the former republics have started to refer to their dialects as separate languages: Croatian for Croats, Bosnian for Muslims, Serbian for Serbs and Montenegrins.**

SKILLBUILDER: Interpreting Visuals

1. **Analyzing Issues** *Use the chart to find out information about the various groups that lived in Bosnia and Herzegovina (as shown on the map). What were some of the differences among those groups?*
2. **Contrasting** *Kosovo was a province within Serbia. What group was in the majority there, and how did it differ from Serbs?*

History *in* Depth

OBJECTIVE

- Identify linguistic, ethnic, and religious differences in the former Yugoslavia.

INSTRUCT

Explain that the map shows ethnic groups in the former Yugoslavia and the chart identifies linguistic and religious differences. Point out that the distinction between ethnic and religious identity is complex and that the two sometimes overlap. Have students identify evidence of this overlap in the feature. *(Muslim is listed as an ethnic group in the map key.)*

In-Depth Resources: Unit 5

- Primary Source: from The Road to Manjača, p. 62

Electronic Library of Primary Sources

- "Will I Ever Go Home Again?"

More About . . .

Serbo-Croatian

Vocabulary and pronunciation differences exist among the Croatian, Bosnian, and Serbian dialects, but these differences are no real obstacle to verbal communication. The Croats and Bosnians use the Roman, or Latin, alphabet. The Serbs and Montenegrins use the Cyrillic alphabet.

SKILLBUILDER: ANSWERS

1. Analyzing Issues

There were three major religions practiced there (Catholicism, Orthodox Christianity, and Islam); three different dialects were spoken.

2. Contrasting

The Albanians were the majority; they were not Slavic, and they were Muslim, not Christian.

More About . . .

Macedonia

Macedonia escaped much of the ethnic violence that plagued Yugoslavia after it began to disintegrate in the early 1990s. Even so, it came close to civil war a decade after declaring independence. In early 2001, ethnic Albanian rebels staged an uprising. After months of skirmishes, the EU and NATO were able to broker a peace deal under which Albanian fighters laid down their arms in return for greater recognition of their rights. In late 2001, this agreement was formalized in a new constitution.

Herzegovina began to stand on its own without as much need for supervision by the international community. D

Rebellion in Kosovo The Balkan region descended into violence and bloodshed again in 1998, this time in Kosovo, a province in southern Serbia made up almost entirely of ethnic Albanians. As an independence movement in Kosovo grew increasingly violent, Serbian military forces invaded the province and fought back with a harsh hand. In response to growing reports of atrocities—and the failure of diplomacy to bring peace—NATO began a bombing campaign against Yugoslavia in the spring of 1999. After enduring more than two months of sustained bombing, Yugoslav leaders finally withdrew their troops from Kosovo.

The Region Faces Its Problems In the early years of the 21st century, there were conflicting signs in Yugoslavia. Slobodan Milosevic was extradited to stand trial for war crimes. A large portion of the country's foreign debt was erased. Despite an independence movement in Kosovo, parliamentary elections under UN supervision took place in November 2001 without violence.

And in Montenegro (which together with Serbia made up Yugoslavia), an independence movement seemed to lack support from the people as well as from the international community. Nonetheless, in February 2003, Yugoslavia's parliament voted to replace what remained of the federation with a loose union of Serbia and Montenegro. Outright independence for each could come as early as 2006. However, problems remained, as indicated by the assassination of the Serbian prime minister, Zoran Djindjic, in March 2003.

The nations of Central and Eastern Europe made many gains in the early years of the 21st century. Even so, they continued to face serious obstacles to democracy. Resolving ethnic conflicts remained crucial, as did economic progress. If the nations of Central and Eastern Europe and the former Soviet Union can improve their standard of living, democracy may have a better chance to grow. Meanwhile, economic reforms in Communist China sparked demands for political reforms, as you will read in the next section.

MAIN IDEA

Identifying Problems

D Why did Bosnia's mixed population cause a problem after Bosnia declared independence?

D. Answer Bosnia's Serbs did not want to lose their ties to Serbia, while Croats and Muslims did.

3 ASSESS

SECTION 4 ASSESSMENT

As a class, discuss the answer to question 2.

Formal Assessment
- Section Quiz, p. 333

4 RETEACH

Arrange small groups of students in the classroom to mimic the geographic locations of the countries discussed in this section. Tell each group which country they represent and have them explain who they are, who the prominent people in their country are, and what is currently going on in their country.

In-Depth Resources: Unit 5
- Guided Reading, p. 53 (also in Spanish)
- Reteaching Activity, p. 72

SECTION 4 ASSESSMENT

TERMS & NAMES 1. For each term or name, write a sentence explaining its significance.
- Solidarity
- Lech Walesa
- reunification
- ethnic cleansing

USING YOUR NOTES

2. Which nation seems to have done best since the breakup? Explain. (10.9.5)

Former nations	Reasons for breakup
Yugoslavia	
Czecho-slovakia	

MAIN IDEAS

3. How did Solidarity affect Communist rule in Poland? (10.9.7)
4. What effect did reunification have on Germany's international role? (10.9.1)
5. What was the main cause of the breakup of Czechoslovakia? (10.9.5)

CRITICAL THINKING & WRITING

6. **ANALYZING CAUSES** Why did ethnic tension become such a severe problem in the Soviet Union and Yugoslavia? (10.9.5)
7. **DRAWING CONCLUSIONS** What are some of the problems faced in 21st century Central and Eastern Europe? (10.9.7)
8. **RECOGNIZING EFFECTS** What effect did economic reform have on Slovakia? (10.9.7)
9. **WRITING ACTIVITY** CULTURAL INTERACTION With a partner, create a **cause-and-effect diagram** to show how democratic reform spread through Central and Eastern Europe. It should show the order in which reform happened and which countries influenced others. (Writing 2.3.d)

CONNECT TO TODAY MAKING A PIE GRAPH

Research the size of the populations of Central and Eastern Europe countries mentioned in this section. Construct a **pie graph** showing the comparative sizes of the populations. (Writing 2.3.d)

ANSWERS

1. Solidarity, p. 618 • Lech Walesa, p. 618 • reunification, p. 620 • ethnic cleansing, p. 622
2. **Sample Answer:** Yugoslavia–Ethnic tensions, loss of Tito's authority, Serbian aggression. Czechoslovakia–Economic problems. Best–Slovakia had one of the best economic growth rates in the area.
3. It undermined Communist rule.
4. It made Germany the largest country in Central Europe, and with that came new international responsibilities.
5. disagreements over economic policy
6. In the past, Communist leaders had suppressed nationalism. With the spread of democratic reforms, many ethnic groups demanded self-rule.
7. ethnic conflict, economic slowdown, and the need for political reform
8. Economic reform caused a sharp rise in unemployment in Slovakia, which undermined Czechoslovakian unity.
9. **Rubric** Diagrams should
   - include only important events.
   - show how each event led to the next.
   - show how various nations influenced one another.

CONNECT TO TODAY

Rubric Pie graphs should show that
- Germany and Poland are the most populous.
- the countries created by the breakup of Yugoslavia are among the least populous.

5

A man chisels a piece of the Berlin Wall for a souvenir just after the fall of communism in East Germany

Soldiers of the Chinese People's Liberation Army in Hong Kong, 1998

China: Reform and Reaction

MAIN IDEA

CULTURAL INTERACTION In response to contact with the West, China's government has experimented with capitalism but has rejected calls for democracy.

WHY IT MATTERS NOW

After the 1997 death of Chinese leader Deng Xiaoping, President Jiang Zemin seemed to be continuing Deng's policies.

TERMS & NAMES

- Zhou Enlai
- Deng Xiaoping
- Four Modernizations
- Tiananmen Square
- Hong Kong

SETTING THE STAGE The trend toward democracy around the world also affected China to a limited degree. A political reform movement arose in the late 1980s. It built on economic reforms begun earlier in the decade. However, although the leadership of the Communist Party in China generally supported economic reform, it opposed political reform. China's Communist government clamped down on the political reformers. At the same time, it maintained a firm grip on power in the country.

CALIFORNIA STANDARDS

10.9.4 Analyze the Chinese Civil War, the rise of Mao Tse-tung, and the subsequent political and economic upheavals in China (e.g., the Great Leap Forward, the Cultural Revolution, and the Tiananmen Square uprising).

10.10.1 Understand the challenges in the regions, including their geopolitical, cultural, military, and economic significance and the international relationships in which they are involved.

10.10.2 Describe the recent history of the regions, including political divisions and systems, key leaders, religious issues, natural features, resources, and population patterns.

10.10.3 Discuss the important trends in the regions today and whether they appear to serve the cause of individual freedom and democracy.

The Legacy of Mao

After the Communists came to power in China in 1949, Mao Zedong set out to transform China. Mao believed that peasant equality, revolutionary spirit, and hard work were all that was needed to improve the Chinese economy.

However, lack of modern technology damaged Chinese efforts to increase agricultural and industrial output. In addition, Mao's policies stifled economic growth. He eliminated incentives for higher production. He tried to replace family life with life in the communes. These policies took away the peasants' motive to work for the good of themselves and their families.

Facing economic disaster, some Chinese Communists talked of modernizing the economy. Accusing them of "taking the capitalist road," Mao began the Cultural Revolution in 1966 to cleanse China of antirevolutionary influences.

Mao's Attempts to Change China

Mao's Programs	Program Results
First Five-Year Plan 1953–1957	• Industry grew 15 percent a year. • Agricultural output grew very slowly.
Great Leap Forward 1958–1961	• China suffered economic disaster—industrial declines and food shortages. • Mao lost influence.
Cultural Revolution 1966–1976	• Mao regained influence by backing radicals. • Purges and conflicts among leaders created economic, social, and political chaos.

TAKING NOTES

Following Chronological Order Use a diagram to show events leading up to the demonstration in Tiananmen Square.

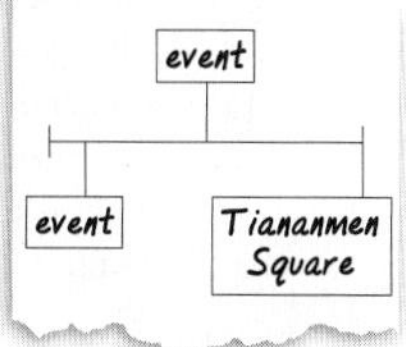

LESSON PLAN

OBJECTIVES

- Summarize Mao Zedong's rule.
- Explain changes under Deng Xiaoping.
- Describe China's democracy movement.
- Discuss the relationship between economic and political change in China.

1 FOCUS & MOTIVATE

In this section, students will read about the Tiananmen Square massacre. Ask students if they can think of a similar crackdown in U.S. history. *(Some students might mention the Boston Massacre.)*

2 INSTRUCT

The Legacy of Mao
10.9.4

Critical Thinking

- Do you think Chinese peasants favored a Communist takeover of China? *(Yes—Communism promised equality. No—Mao's policies were unfavorable to family life and made work less rewarding.)*

CALIFORNIA RESOURCES

California Reading Toolkit, p. L89
California Modified Lesson Plans for English Learners, p. 173
California Daily Standards Practice Transparencies, TT81
California Standards Enrichment Workbook, pp. 97–98, 107–108, 109–110, 111–112
California Standards Planner and Lesson Plans, p. L169
California Online Test Practice
California Test Generator CD-ROM
California Easy Planner CD-ROM
California eEdition CD-ROM

SECTION 5 PROGRAM RESOURCES

ALL STUDENTS

In-Depth Resources: Unit 5
- Guided Reading, p. 54
- Skillbuilder Practice, p. 56

Formal Assessment
- Section Quiz, p. 334

ENGLISH LEARNERS

In-Depth Resources in Spanish
- Guided Reading, p. 151
- Skillbuilder Practice, p. 152

Reading Study Guide (Spanish), p. 209
Reading Study Guide Audio CD (Spanish)

STRUGGLING READERS

In-Depth Resources: Unit 5
- Guided Reading, p. 54
- Building Vocabulary, p. 55
- Skillbuilder Practice, p. 56
- Reteaching Activity, p. 73

Reading Study Guide, p. 209
Reading Study Guide Audio CD

GIFTED AND TALENTED STUDENTS

Electronic Library of Primary Sources
- "The Massacre in Tiananmen Square"

INTEGRATED TECHNOLOGY

eEdition CD-ROM
Power Presentations CD-ROM
Critical Thinking Transparencies
- CT35 Democratic Struggles Around the Globe
- CT71 Chapter 35 Visual Summary

Electronic Library of Primary Sources
- "The Massacre in Tiananmen Square"

classzone.com

China and the West
10.9.4; 10.10.1; 10.10.2

Critical Thinking

- Why might Zhou have chosen to invite a U.S. table-tennis team to China? *(Possible Answer: politically neutral way to open relations with the West)*
- Ask students if Deng's Four Modernizations are consistent with communism. *(Possible Answer: No—Motivation by profit and private enterprise are practices that communism was supposed to eliminate.)*

More About . . .

Deng Xiaoping

Deng Xiaoping embraced economic pragmatism—he was interested in results, not communist theory. He summed up his views by saying, "It doesn't matter whether a cat is black or white, so long as it catches mice." A key figure in world history, Deng is remembered for opening up China's economy while maintaining strict communist rule.

Tip for Gifted and Talented Students

Students may be mystified about what exactly defines communism. Explain that their confusion is warranted. In fact, not long before his death in 1883, Karl Marx, author of *The Communist Manifesto*, remarked to his son-in-law, "One thing I am certain of; that is that I myself am not a Marxist."

▲ Zhou Enlai, a translator, Mao Zedong, President Nixon, and Henry Kissinger meet in Beijing in 1972.

Instead of saving radical communism, however, the Cultural Revolution turned many people against it. In the early 1970s, China entered another moderate period under **Zhou Enlai** (joh ehn•ly). Zhou had been premier since 1949. During the Cultural Revolution, he had tried to restrain the radicals. **A**

MAIN IDEA

Recognizing Effects

A What was the ultimate result of Mao's radical Communist policies?

A. Answer The destructiveness of the Cultural Revolution turned many Chinese people away from radical communism.

China and the West

Throughout the Cultural Revolution, China played almost no role in world affairs. In the early 1960s, China had split with the Soviet Union over the leadership of world communism. In addition, China displayed hostility toward the United States because of U.S. support for the government on Taiwan.

China Opened Its Doors China's isolation worried Zhou. He began to send out signals that he was willing to form ties to the West. In 1971, Zhou startled the world by inviting an American table-tennis team to tour China. It was the first visit by an American group to China since 1949.

The visit began a new era in Chinese-American relations. In 1971, the United States reversed its policy and endorsed UN membership for the People's Republic of China. The next year, President Nixon made a state visit to China. He met with Mao and Zhou. The three leaders agreed to begin cultural exchanges and a limited amount of trade. In 1979, the United States and China established diplomatic relations.

Economic Reform Both Mao and Zhou died in 1976. Shortly afterward, moderates took control of the Communist Party. They jailed several of the radicals who had led the Cultural Revolution. By 1980, **Deng Xiaoping** (duhng show•pihng) had emerged as the most powerful leader in China. He was the last of the "old revolutionaries" who had ruled China since 1949.

Although a lifelong Communist, Deng boldly supported moderate economic policies. Unlike Mao, he was willing to use capitalist ideas to help China's economy. He embraced a set of goals known as the **Four Modernizations**. These called for progress in agriculture, industry, defense, and science and technology. Deng launched an ambitious program of economic reforms.

First, Deng eliminated Mao's communes and leased the land to individual farmers. The farmers paid rent by delivering a fixed quota of food to the government. They could then grow crops and sell them for a profit. Under this system, food production increased by 50 percent in the years 1978 to 1984.

Deng extended his program to industry. The government permitted private businesses to operate. It gave the managers of state-owned industries more freedom to set production goals. Deng also welcomed foreign technology and investment.

Deng's economic policies produced striking changes in Chinese life. As incomes increased, people began to buy appliances and televisions. Chinese youths now wore stylish clothes and listened to Western music. Gleaming hotels filled with foreign tourists symbolized China's new policy of openness.

DIFFERENTIATING INSTRUCTION: STRUGGLING READERS

Causes and Effects of Chinese Reforms

Class Time 30 minutes

Task Making a diagram

Purpose To help readers understand Deng Xiaoping's "Four Modernizations"

Instructions After students have read the material on pages 626–627, have them create a simple cause-effect chart about Deng Xiaoping's Four Modernizations. A sample chart is shown. Point out that an effect (such as incomes increasing) can in turn become a cause.

Students who need more help should complete the Guided Reading activity for this section.

Reform	Effect
Farmers given more control	Food production went up.
Private businesses and foreign investment allowed, industry managers given more control.	Incomes increased.
Incomes increased.	Gap between rich and poor got wider.
Students demanded political reforms.	Deng Xiaoping sent in soldiers.

In-Depth Resources: Unit 5

Massacre in Tiananmen Square

Deng's economic reforms produced a number of unexpected problems. As living standards improved, the gap between the rich and poor widened. Increasingly, the public believed that party officials profited from their positions.

Furthermore, the new policies admitted not only Western investments and tourists but also Western political ideas. Increasing numbers of Chinese students studied abroad and learned about the West. In Deng's view, the benefits of opening the economy exceeded the risks. Nevertheless, as Chinese students learned more about democracy, they began to question China's lack of political freedom. B

MAIN IDEA

Analyzing Causes

B How did economic reform introduce new political ideas to China?

B. Answer Western businesses and tourists brought Western ideas into the country, and students went to school overseas for economic reasons but learned about democracy.

Students Demand Democracy In 1989, students sparked a popular uprising that stunned China's leaders. Beginning in April of that year, more than 100,000 students occupied **Tiananmen** (tyahn•ahn•mehn) **Square**, a huge public space in the heart of Beijing. The students mounted a protest for democracy. (See photograph on page 630.)

The student protest won widespread popular support. When thousands of students began a hunger strike to highlight their cause, people poured into Tiananmen Square to support them. Many students called for Deng Xiaoping to resign.

Deng Orders a Crackdown Instead of considering political reform, Deng declared martial law. He ordered about 100,000 troops to surround Beijing. Although many students left the square after martial law was declared, about 5,000 chose to remain and continue their protest. The students revived their spirits by defiantly erecting a 33-foot statue that they named the "Goddess of Democracy."

On June 4, 1989, the standoff came to an end. Thousands of heavily armed soldiers stormed Tiananmen Square. Tanks smashed through barricades and crushed the Goddess of Democracy. Soldiers sprayed gunfire into crowds of frightened students. They also attacked protesters elsewhere in Beijing. The assault killed hundreds and wounded thousands.

Analyzing Primary Sources

Training the Chinese Army

After the massacre in Tiananmen Square, Xiao Ye (a former Chinese soldier living in the United States) explained how Chinese soldiers are trained to obey orders without complaint.

PRIMARY SOURCE

We usually developed bleeding blisters on our feet after a few days of . . . hiking. Our feet were a mass of soggy peeling flesh and blood, and the pain was almost unbearable. . . . We considered the physical challenge a means of tempering [hardening] ourselves for the sake of the Party. . . . No one wanted to look bad. . . .

And during the days in Tiananmen, once again the soldiers did not complain. They obediently drove forward, aimed, and opened fire on command. In light of their training, how could it have been otherwise?

XIAO YE, "Tiananmen Square: A Soldier's Story"

DOCUMENT-BASED QUESTIONS

1. **Making Inferences** *For whom did the soldiers seem to believe they were making their physical sacrifices?*
2. **Drawing Conclusions** *What attitude toward obeying orders did their training seem to encourage in the soldiers?*

Massacre in Tiananmen Square

10.9.4; 10.10.1; 10.10.2

Critical Thinking

- Why might Deng have been successful in crushing dissent when so many Eastern European leaders had failed? *(Possible Answers: He controlled the media. He had made efforts to reform Chinese communism.)*
- Why are students so often involved in protest movements? *(Possible Answers: youthful idealism; they have the time to protest)*

Electronic Library of Primary Sources

- "The Massacre in Tiananmen Square"

Analyzing Primary Sources

Training the Chinese Army

Ask students how the training and attitude of U.S. soldiers might be different from Xiao Ye's. *(Some students might argue that the training is similar, but that most U.S. soldiers would be unlikely to fire on peaceful protesters, even if they were ordered to do so.)*

Extension Ask interested students to find out if any formal rules exist regarding when a U.S. soldier should disobey the direct orders of a superior officer. Students might begin with the *Uniform Code of Military Justice.*

Answers to Document-Based Questions

1. **Making Inferences** the Communist Party
2. **Drawing Conclusions** to follow orders blindly

SKILLBUILDER PRACTICE: ANALYZING PRIMARY AND SECONDARY SOURCES

Analyzing Primary and Secondary Sources

Class Time 20 minutes

Task Comparing primary and secondary sources

Purpose To help students understand the difference between the two types of sources

Instructions Explain that primary sources provide firsthand evidence of historical events. They can include manuscripts, photographs, maps, artifacts, audio and video recordings, oral histories, postcards, and posters. Secondary sources are materials, such as textbooks, that synthesize and interpret primary materials.

Have students read "Massacre in Tiananmen Square" and the "Analyzing Primary Sources" feature on this page. Lead a class discussion that focuses on how reading the primary source—the excerpt from Xiao Ye's "Tiananmen Square: A Soldier's Story"—changes, or does not change, the impression of the massacre that they received from the secondary source (the textbook).

For more practice, have students complete the Skillbuilder activity for this chapter.

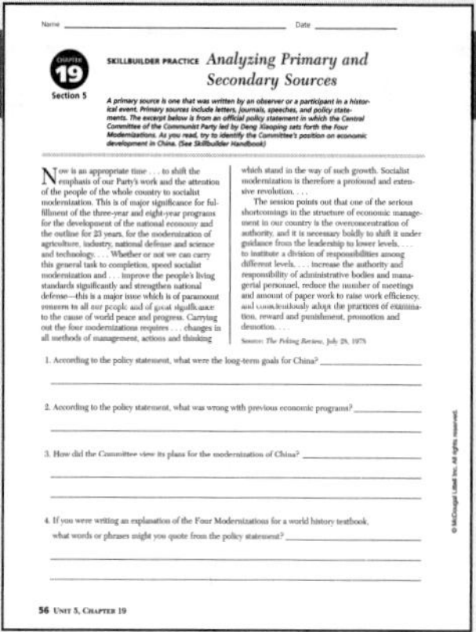

In-Depth Resources: Unit 5

China Enters the New Millennium

10.10.1; 10.10.2; 10.10.3

Critical Thinking

- Why might U.S. leaders pressure China to improve its human rights record? *(Possible Answers: concern about the way the Chinese government treats its citizens; human rights record might interfere with the economic relationship between the United States and China)*
- Why might China have promised to respect Hong Kong's economic system and political liberties for 50 years? *(Possible Answer: It saw Hong Kong as a potential revenue stream. China neither wanted to disturb the economic system nor to cause the emigration of the people who managed and sustained it.)*

History Makers

Jiang Zemin

Ask students why Jiang Zemin might have been chosen to succeed Deng Xiaoping as president. *(Communist Party officials may have seen his administrative competence and industrial background as useful skills in a time of economic transition.)*

In an October 1995 speech at the UN, Jiang Zemin asserted that "Certain big powers, often under the cover of 'freedom,' 'democracy,' and 'human rights,' set out to encroach upon the sovereignty of other countries."

The attack on Tiananmen Square marked the beginning of a massive government campaign to stamp out protest. Police arrested thousands of people. The state used the media to announce that reports of a massacre were untrue. Officials claimed that a small group of criminals had plotted against the government. Television news, however, had already broadcast the truth to the world.

China Enters the New Millennium

The brutal repression of the prodemocracy movement left Deng firmly in control of China. During the final years of his life, Deng continued his program of economic reforms.

Although Deng moved out of the limelight in 1995, he remained China's leader. In February 1997, after a long illness, Deng died. Communist Party General Secretary Jiang Zemin (jee•ahng zeh•meen) assumed the presidency.

China Under Jiang Many questions arose after Deng's death. What kind of leader would Jiang be? Would he be able to hold on to power and ensure political stability? A highly intelligent and educated man, Jiang had served as mayor of Shanghai. He was considered skilled, flexible, and practical. However, he had no military experience. Therefore, Jiang had few allies among the generals. He also faced challenges from rivals, including hard-line officials who favored a shift away from Deng's economic policies.

History Makers

Jiang Zemin
1926–

Jiang Zemin was trained as an engineer. After working as an engineer, heading several technological institutes, and serving as minister of the electronics industry, he moved up in politics.

In 1982, he joined the Central Committee of the Communist Party in China. He became mayor of Shanghai in 1985, in which post he proved to be an effective administrator. In 1989, he became general secretary of the Chinese Communist Party. This promotion was largely due to his support for the government's putdown of the prodemocracy demonstrations in that year. In 1993, he became president. In 2003, he stepped down and was replaced by Hu Jintao; however, Jiang retained power behind the scenes.

Other questions following Deng's death had to do with China's poor human rights record, its occupation of Tibet, and relations with the United States. During the 1990s, the United States pressured China to release political prisoners and ensure basic rights for political opponents. China remained hostile to such pressure. Its government continued to repress the prodemocracy movement. Nevertheless, the desire for freedom still ran through Chinese society. If China remained economically open but politically closed, tensions seemed bound to surface.

In late 1997, Jiang paid a state visit to the United States. During his visit, U.S. protesters demanded more democracy in China. Jiang admitted that China had made some mistakes but refused to promise that China's policies would change.

President Jiang Zemin and Premier Zhu Rongji announced their retirement in late 2002. Jiang's successor was Hu Jintao. However, Jiang was expected to wield influence over his successor behind the scenes. Hu became president of the country and general secretary of the Communist Party. Jiang remained political leader of the military. Both supported China's move to a market economy.

Transfer of Hong Kong Another major issue for China was the status of **Hong Kong**. Hong Kong was a thriving business center and British colony on the southeastern coast of China. On July 1, 1997, Great Britain handed Hong Kong over to China, ending 155 years of colonial rule. As part of the transfer, China promised to respect Hong Kong's economic system and political liberties for 50 years.

Many of Hong Kong's citizens worried about Chinese rule and feared the loss of their freedoms. Others, however, saw the transfer as a way to reconnect with their Chinese

DIFFERENTIATING INSTRUCTION: GIFTED AND TALENTED STUDENTS

Writing a Poem About Human Rights

Class Time 20 minutes

Task Writing a poem

Purpose To encourage students to think deeply about human rights issues

Instructions Tell students to read "China Enters the New Millennium" and "China Beyond 2000" on pages 628–629. Ask them to pay close attention to the passages that address human rights issues and to think carefully about the statement that "Supporters of [the normalization of trade with China] argue that the best way to prompt political change in China is through greater engagement rather than isolation." Tell students to use these passages as a springboard for creating a poem about human rights issues in today's global society.

Encourage volunteers to read their poems in front of the class.

heritage. In the first four or five years after the transfer, the control of mainland China over Hong Kong tightened.

China Beyond 2000

The case of China demonstrates that the creation of democracy can be a slow, fitful, and incomplete process. Liberal reforms in one area, such as the economy, may not lead immediately to political reforms.

Economics and Politics In China, there has been a dramatic reduction in poverty. Some experts argue that China managed to reform its economy and reduce poverty because it adopted a gradual approach to selling off state industries and privatizing the economy rather than a more abrupt approach. At any rate, as the global economy slowed in the early years of the 21st century, China managed to maintain economic growth.

▲ People celebrate in Tiananmen Square after Beijing won the bid for the 2008 Olympic Games.

People in China and around the world have a desire for more political freedom. As economic and social conditions improve—for example, as the middle class expands and educational opportunities grow—the prospects for democracy also may improve. In addition, as countries are increasingly linked through technology and trade, they will have more opportunity to influence each other politically. In 2000, for example, the U.S. Congress voted to normalize trade with China. Supporters of such a move argue that the best way to prompt political change in China is through greater engagement rather than isolation. Another sign of China's increasing engagement with the world is its successful campaign to host the 2008 Summer Olympics in Beijing.

SECTION 5 ASSESSMENT

TERMS & NAMES 1. For each term or name, write a sentence explaining its significance.
• Zhou Enlai • Deng Xiaoping • Four Modernizations • Tiananmen Square • Hong Kong

USING YOUR NOTES

2. Other than the demonstration in Tiananmen Square, which of these events was most important? Explain. (10.9.4)

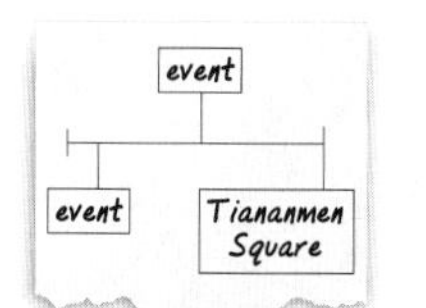

MAIN IDEAS

3. What effect did Mao's policies have on economic growth? (10.9.4)
4. What were some of Deng Xiaoping's economic reforms? (10.10.2)
5. How would you describe China's record on human rights? (10.10.2)

CRITICAL THINKING & WRITING

6. **SUPPORTING OPINIONS** Based on what you have read about the Chinese government, do you think Hong Kong will keep its freedoms under Chinese rule? Explain. (10.10.3)
7. **FOLLOWING CHRONOLOGICAL ORDER** What were some of the events that followed the demonstration in Tiananmen Square? (10.9.4)
8. **COMPARING AND CONTRASTING** Has there been greater progress in political or economic reform in China? (10.10.2)
9. **WRITING ACTIVITY** CULTURAL INTERACTION Imagine that you are a Chinese student visiting the West. Write a **letter** home in which you explain what you have seen. (Writing 2.1.c)

CONNECT TO TODAY **MAKING A POSTER**
China will be hosting the 2008 Summer Olympics in Beijing. Research the efforts that China is making to prepare the city for the festivities and present your findings in a **poster.** (Writing 2.3.d)

China Beyond 2000
10.10.3

Critical Thinking

- What might have happened if China's leaders had adopted a "shock therapy" economic policy? *(Possible Answer: It might have caused economic upheaval and widespread popular discontent, perhaps even leading to overthrow of the regime.)*
- Do you think the best way to prompt political change in China is through greater engagement, not isolation? *(Yes—The United States is unlikely to change the human rights situation in China through a boycott. China would simply seek economic and political relationships with other nations. No—Abuse of human rights should not be tolerated.)*

③ ASSESS

SECTION 5 ASSESSMENT

Divide questions among groups. Have them present answers orally.

Formal Assessment
- Section Quiz, p. 334

④ RETEACH

Use CT35 and the Visual Summary to review this section and chapter.

Critical Thinking Transparencies
- CT35 Democratic Struggles Around the Globe
- CT71 Chapter 35 Visual Summary

In-Depth Resources: Unit 5
- Reteaching Activity, p. 73

ANSWERS

1. Zhou Enlai, p. 626 • Deng Xiaoping, p. 626 • Four Modernizations, p. 626 • Tiananmen Square, p. 627 • Hong Kong, p. 628
2. **Sample Answer:** 1971—Zhou opens China to West. 1980s—Four Modernizations (most important because changed economy).
3. They undermined economic growth.
4. limited sales for profit; privatization of some businesses
5. relatively poor
6. It is difficult to predict, but so far Hong Kong has been given some freedom.
7. Chinese government massacred protesters and repressed the pro-democracy movement.
8. economic reform
9. **Rubric** Letters should
   - mention characteristics of Western democracy such as free elections, majority rule, minority rights, and citizen participation.
   - use standard grammar and punctuation.

CONNECT TO TODAY

Rubric Posters should include
- information about new sports and visitor facilities.
- effective visuals.

History *through* Art

OBJECTIVES

- Describe the relationship between photography and journalism.
- Explain how the work of photojournalists could be used politically.

FOCUS & MOTIVATE

Make a list on the board of the most powerful photojournalistic images students have seen in the last 12 months. Then have students vote for the most powerful image of those listed. Students should explain which elements of the image make it the most powerful.

INSTRUCT

Critical Thinking

- How might journalism have been different before the advent of photography? *(Possible Answer: Journalists may have had to use much more descriptive language to give readers a picture of an event or person.)*
- Can photojournalism be biased? *(Yes—Photographers can influence the perception of an event by what they choose to photograph and the way in which they photograph it. Editors, by choosing which photographs to include with a story, can also influence the way in which readers perceive a story. No—Pictures do not lie.)*

Photojournalism

From the earliest days of photography, magazines and newspapers have used photographs to convey the news. Photojournalists must respond quickly to recognize a history-making moment and to record that moment before it passes. As the photographs on this page demonstrate, photojournalists have captured many of the democratic struggles that have occurred in the last few decades. In some cases, news photographs have helped protesters or oppressed people gain the support of the world.

CALIFORNIA STANDARDS

10.10.1 Understand the challenges in the regions, including their geopolitical, cultural, military, and economic significance and the international relationships in which they are involved.

HI 1 Students show the connections, causal and otherwise, between particular historical events and larger social, economic, and political trends and developments.

INTEGRATED TECHNOLOGY

RESEARCH LINKS For more on photojournalism, go to **classzone.com**

Flight from Srebrenica ►
During the conflicts in Bosnia and Herzegovina, the United Nations declared the city of Srebrenica a safe area. Even so, the Bosnian Serb army invaded in July 1995 and expelled more than 20,000 Muslims—nearly all of them women, children, or elderly people. In addition, the soldiers held more than 7,000 men and boys prisoner and over a five-day period massacred them.

▼ Man Defying Tanks
A single Chinese man blocked tanks on their way to crush prodemocracy protests in Tiananmen Square in June 1989. No one knows for sure what happened to the man afterward—or even who he was. Even so, this image has become one of the enduring photographs of the 20th century; it has come to stand for one man's courage in defying tyranny.

RECOMMENDED RESOURCES

Books

Agence France-Presse and Mathew Giles, eds. ***Facing the World: Great Moments in Photojournalism.*** New York: Harry N. Abrams, 2001.

Horton, Brian. ***Associated Press Guide to Photojournalism.*** New York: McGraw-Hill/Contemporary Books, 2000. An analysis of what constitutes a successful news photo, supported by more than 100 photos from the AP archives.

Video

Photography: Making Art and Recording Life. VHS and DVD. Films for the Humanities & Sciences, 2001. Describes a number of genres in photographic art, including photojournalism.

Abuelas de Plaza de Mayo ▲
From 1976 to 1983, the military government of Argentina tortured and killed thousands of political dissidents and sometimes stole their children. In this demonstration in December 1979, the *Abuelas de Plaza de Mayo* (Grandmothers of the Plaza de Mayo) demanded to know the fate of their relatives. The banner they carried reads "Disappeared Children."

Fall of the Wall ▼
When the East German government opened the Berlin Wall in November 1989, a huge celebration broke out. Some people began to use pickaxes to demolish the wall entirely. Others danced on top of the wall. (See also the image on page 619.)

Voting Line
When South Africa held its first all-race election in April 1994, people were so eager to vote that they stood in lines that sometimes stretched nearly a kilometer (0.62 mile).

Connect *to* Today

1. **Forming and Supporting Opinions** Which of these photographs do you think has the greatest impact on the viewer? Explain why.
   See Skillbuilder Handbook, page R20.
2. **Forming and Supporting Opinions** Using Internet or library resources, find a news photograph that you think effectively shows a recent historic event. Bring a copy of the photograph to class, and explain orally or in writing what it conveys about the event.

631

More About . . .

Srebrenica

In August 2001, the International Criminal Tribunal for the former Yugoslavia sentenced Radislav Krstic to 46 years in prison for his actions at Srebrenica. Krstic, 53, was found guilty of genocide, extermination, murder, persecution, and forced transfer of civilians. General Krstic is the highest-ranking Bosnian Serb to be tried by the tribunal and the first to be found guilty of genocide. "In July 1995 General Krstic, individually you agreed to evil. And this is why today this trial chamber convicts you and sentences you to 46 years in prison," said Judge Almiro Rodrigues.

More About . . .

Argentine Military Government

In July 2003, a Spanish judge issued international arrest warrants against 46 former members of the Argentine armed forces. They were accused of the genocide and torture of Spanish nationals between 1976 and 1983. Backers of the judge are hopeful that the Argentine government will annul a law that shields former military officers from extradition for alleged human rights violations. As many as 30,000 people were "disappeared" in the Argentine military's campaign against political dissidents.

CONNECT TO TODAY: ANSWERS

1. Forming and Supporting Opinions
Some students may choose the photo of the grandmothers of the Plaza de Mayo because it effectively shows the anger and outrage of the women.

2. Forming and Supporting Opinions
Students should choose news photos of significant historic events, such as recent terrorist attacks or wars. Their explanation should describe what aspect of the historic event the photograph conveys.

TERMS & NAMES

1. PRI, p. 603
2. apartheid, p. 609
3. Nelson Mandela, p. 609
4. Mikhail Gorbachev, p. 612
5. glasnost, p. 612
6. Lech Walesa, p. 618
7. Deng Xiaoping, p. 626
8. Tiananmen Square, p. 627

MAIN IDEAS

Answers will vary.

9. free elections, citizen participation, majority rule, constitutional government
10. the military
11. Ethnic conflict between the Igbo on one side and the Hausa-Fulani and Yoruba on the other led the Igbo region to secede. The government went to war to reunify the country.
12. legalization of the ANC, holding of all-race (universal) elections, writing of a new constitution and bill of rights
13. glasnost, perestroika, democratization
14. an attempt in 1991 by hardline Communists to force Gorbachev to resign and to undo his reforms; failed because the people would not go along with it
15. Poland, Hungary, East Germany, Czechoslovakia, and Romania
16. The loss of Tito's leadership allowed ethnic conflicts to rise to the surface; when Serbia tried to dominate the other republics, several of them declared independence.
17. Zhou Enlai made overtures to the United States, and Deng Xiaoping initiated economic reforms.
18. It massacred demonstrators in Tiananmen Square, publicly lied about what had happened, and continued to repress the pro-democracy movement.

Chapter 19 Assessment

TERMS & NAMES

For each term or name below, briefly explain its connection to the democratic movements that took place from 1945 to the present.

1. PRI
2. apartheid
3. Nelson Mandela
4. Mikhail Gorbachev
5. glasnost
6. Lech Walesa
7. Deng Xiaoping
8. Tiananmen Square

MAIN IDEAS

Case Study: Latin American Democracies Section 1 (pages 599–605)

9. What are four common democratic practices? (10.10.3)
10. What group held up democratic progress in both Brazil and Argentina until the 1980s? (10.10.3)

The Challenge of Democracy in Africa Section 2 (pages 606–611)

11. What brought about the civil war in Nigeria? (10.10.2)
12. What were three significant steps toward democracy taken by South Africa in the 1990s? (10.10.2)

The Collapse of the Soviet Union Section 3 (pages 612–617)

13. What were the main reforms promoted by Soviet leader Mikhail Gorbachev? (10.9.7)
14. What was the August Coup and how did it end? (10.9.7)

Changes in Central and Eastern Europe Section 4 (pages 618–624)

15. Which nations overthrew Communist governments in 1989? (10.9.5)
16. What led to the breakup of Yugoslavia? (10.9.5)

China: Reform and Reaction Section 5 (pages 625–631)

17. What changes took place in China during the 1970s? (10.9.4)
18. How did the Chinese government react to demands for democratic reform? (10.9.4)

CRITICAL THINKING

1. **USING YOUR NOTES**
List several leaders who helped their nations make democratic progress. Cite one positive action. (10.10.3)

Leader	Nation	Positive Action

2. **ANALYZING ISSUES**
CULTURAL INTERACTION What are some examples from this chapter in which the negative impact of one culture on another blocked democratic progress? (10.10.1)

3. **SYNTHESIZING**
Consider what conditions helped democratic movements succeed and what conditions caused difficulties for them. What do you think were their hardest challenges? (10.10.1)

4. **DRAWING CONCLUSIONS**
ECONOMICS How does a nation's economy affect its democratic progress? (10.10.3)

5. **SUMMARIZING**
What were Deng Xiaoping's economic reforms for China? (10.9.4)

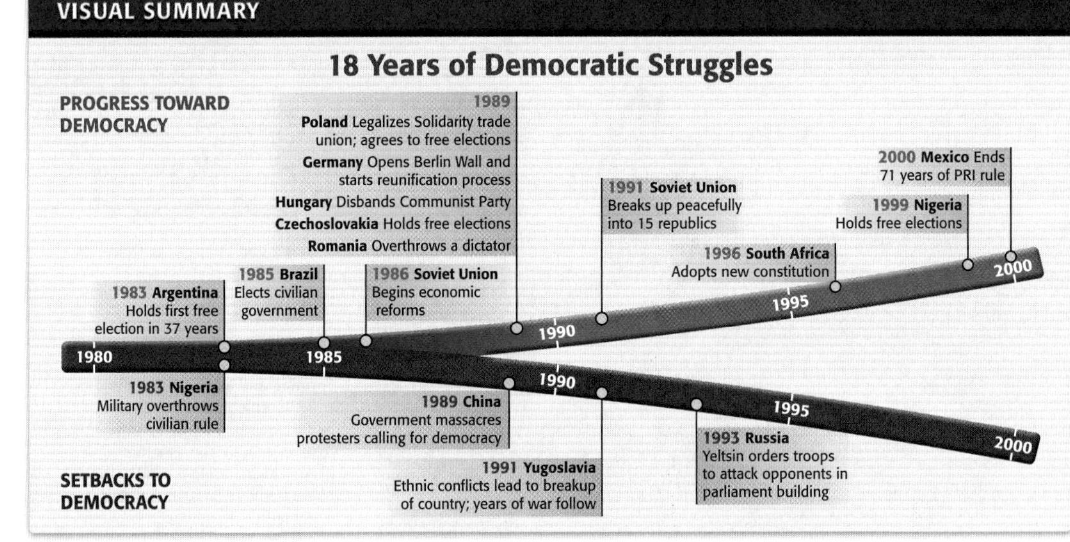

VISUAL SUMMARY
18 Years of Democratic Struggles
PROGRESS TOWARD DEMOCRACY
1983 Argentina Holds first free election in 37 years
1985 Brazil Elects civilian government
1986 Soviet Union Begins economic reforms
1989 Poland Legalizes Solidarity trade union; agrees to free elections
Germany Opens Berlin Wall and starts reunification process
Hungary Disbands Communist Party
Czechoslovakia Holds free elections
Romania Overthrows a dictator
1991 Soviet Union Breaks up peacefully into 15 republics
1996 South Africa Adopts new constitution
1999 Nigeria Holds free elections
2000 Mexico Ends 71 years of PRI rule
1980
1985
1990
1995
2000
1983 Nigeria Military overthrows civilian rule
1989 China Government massacres protesters calling for democracy
1991 Yugoslavia Ethnic conflicts lead to breakup of country; years of war follow
1993 Russia Yeltsin orders troops to attack opponents in parliament building
SETBACKS TO DEMOCRACY

CRITICAL THINKING

Answers will vary.

1. Raúl Alfonsín—Reformed democracy and economy; Nelson Mandela—Protested apartheid and called for economic reform and reconciliation; Mikhail Gorbachev—Initiated reforms.
2. The legacy of colonialism hindered democratic progress in Africa; ethnic clashes in Eastern Europe led to civil war.
3. Advantages—Increasing literacy rates and quality of life; worldwide media. Difficulties—Colonial legacy, ethnic and racial conflicts, oppressive governments, centrally controlled economies. Most challenging—Ethnic and racial conflicts.
4. A floundering economy can make political reform difficult. Likewise, political chaos can make it difficult to achieve economic reform.
5. Deng initiated economic reforms, including the lease of land to individual farmers, encouragement of small business and foreign investment, and a partial return to the profit motive.

Use the quotation and your knowledge of world history to answer questions 1 and 2.
Additional Test Practice, pp. S1–S33

PRIMARY SOURCE

Whatever else you can say about the new Hong Kong, it will be more Chinese. Liu Heung-shing, the editor of the new Hong Kong magazine *The Chinese,* says that "for any meaningful art and culture to take off here, Hong Kong must find somewhere to anchor itself. To find that anchor, people will have to go north [to mainland China]." . . . Increasing numbers of Hong Kong's Cantonese speakers are studying mainland Mandarin. . . . At the same time that [Hong Kong] must resist China to retain Britain's legacy of rule of law, it knows that the most logical place for it to turn for commerce and culture is China.

ORVILLE SCHELL, "The Coming of Mao Zedong Chic"

1. What is the main change that is taking place in Hong Kong's culture? (10.10.3)
   - **A.** China is looking to Hong Kong for cultural inspiration.
   - **B.** Hong Kong is turning to China for cultural inspiration.
   - **C.** Hong Kong is turning to the West for cultural inspiration.
   - **D.** Hong Kong is turning inward.

2. What point of view might a Hong Kong politician have about this change? (10.10.3)
   - **A.** may fear China will restrict the city's freedoms
   - **B.** may welcome tighter controls from China
   - **C.** may threaten military action against China
   - **D.** may vow never to cooperate with mainland China

Use this political cartoon and your knowledge of world history to answer question 3.

3. What is the cartoon saying about the state of communism in Poland, China, and the Soviet Union? (10.9.7)
   - **A.** Communism is thriving.
   - **B.** Communism is helping nations gain economic health.
   - **C.** Communism is failing around the world.
   - **D.** Communism is sick but will recover.

INTEGRATED TECHNOLOGY

TEST PRACTICE Go to **classzone.com**
- Diagnostic tests
- Strategies
- Tutorials
- Additional practice

ALTERNATIVE ASSESSMENT

1. **Interact *with* History** (10.10.3)
   REVOLUTION On page 598, you considered why so many people want democracy. Now that you've read the chapter, have your explanations changed? Would you add anything to what you said before? Would you change anything you said before?

2.  **WRITING ABOUT HISTORY** (Writing 2.6.a–d)
   A government official has asked you for suggestions on how to move a Communist economy to a free-market economy. Go through the chapter and compile a "Things to Do" **report** based on actions that other governments have taken. Consider the following issues:
   - unemployment
   - inflation
   - political effects
   - social upheaval

INTEGRATED TECHNOLOGY

Creating a Virtual Field Trip (10.10.4)

With two other classmates, plan a two-week virtual field trip to explore the sights in China, including the Forbidden City and the sites of the 2008 Summer Olympics. After selecting and researching the sites you'd like to visit, use maps to determine your itinerary. Consider visiting these places and enjoying these excursions:
- Sites of the 2008 Summer Olympic games
- Sites around Beijing
- Great Wall
- A cruise along the Chang Jiang or Huang He rivers
- Three Gorges Dam
- Shanghai

For each place or excursion, give one reason why it is an important destination on a field trip to China. Include pictures and sound in your presentation.

STANDARDS-BASED ASSESSMENT

1. The correct answer is letter **B**. Letter **A** is incorrect because it is Hong Kong rather than China that is seeking a new cultural inspiration after Britain returned it to the control of China. Letter **C** is incorrect because Hong Kong needs to replace the Western influence of Britain, Europe, and America with the nearby Chinese culture. Letter **D** is incorrect because as an island community, Hong Kong is dependent upon others for its livelihood and vitality.
2. Letter **A** is the correct answer. Letter **B** is incorrect because people who have experienced relative freedom and independence would be unlikely to favor tighter controls. Letter **C** is incorrect because Hong Kong is a small island with no military. Letter **D** is incorrect because it is in Hong Kong's interests as an island business-oriented community to get along with its neighbors.
3. Letter **C** is the correct answer. Letter **A** is incorrect because communism is failing around the world. Letter **B** is incorrect because Communist economies are being replaced around the world by market economies. Letter **D** is incorrect because democratic governments and free-market economies are replacing Communist governments and economies around the world.

Formal Assessment
- Chapter Test, Forms A, B, and C, pp. 335–346

California Test Generator CD-ROM
- Chapter Tests, Forms A, B, and C (English and Spanish)

ALTERNATIVE ASSESSMENT

1. Ask students to list the explanations they would add, delete, or change. Most will probably note that everyone wants those rights and privileges that democracy supports, such as freedom of speech and worship and the right to pursue economic opportunity.
2. **Rubric** Reports should mention
   - granting individual farmers ownership of the land they work.
   - restoring the profit motive to the economy.
   - allowing foreign investment.
   - making state-owned industries more efficient, or perhaps privatizing them.
   - gradually allowing greater freedoms.

INTEGRATED TECHNOLOGY

Rubric Virtual field trips should
- list a number of interesting sites to visit.
- provide informative details about each site.
- give persuasive reasons for visiting each destination.
- include relevant pictures and sound.

CHAPTER 20 PLANNING GUIDE

Global Interdependence, 1960–Present

CHAPTER RESOURCES	COPYMASTERS	ASSESSMENT
CHAPTER OVERVIEW Through advances in science and technology, the world became globally interdependent and, as a result, faced new challenges.	**In-Depth Resources: Unit 5** • Building Vocabulary, p. 79 **Chapters in Brief** (in English and Spanish) **Block Schedule Pacing Guide**	**Chapter Assessment,** pp. 664–665 **Formal Assessment** • Chapter Tests, Forms A, B, and C, pp. 353–364 **Test Generator** **Online Test Practice**
SECTION 1 **The Impact of Science and Technology** pp. 637–640 **OBJECTIVE** Identify recent advances and their effects.	**In-Depth Resources: Unit 5** • Guided Reading, p. 74 • Primary Source: from "Down to Earth," p. 83 • Reteaching Activity, p. 93 **Reading Study Guide,** p. 215	**Section 1 Assessment,** p. 640 **Formal Assessment** • Section Quiz, p. 348 **California Daily Standards Practice Transparencies,** TT141
SECTION 2 **Global Economic Development** pp. 641–647 **OBJECTIVE** Describe the development of the global economy and its effects.	**In-Depth Resources: Unit 5** • Guided Reading, p. 75 • Skillbuilder Practice, p. 80 • Geography Application, p. 81 • Primary Source: Recycling Symbol, p. 84 • Literature: "Paper," p. 87 • Reteaching Activity, 94 **Case Study 7,** p. 86	**Section 2 Assessment,** p. 646 **Formal Assessment** • Section Quiz, p. 349 **California Daily Standards Practice Transparencies,** TT142
SECTION 3 **Global Security Issues** pp. 648–652 **OBJECTIVE** Summarize security, human rights, and health issues.	**In-Depth Resources: Unit 5** • Guided Reading, p. 76 • Primary Source: Declaration, p. 85 • History Makers: Kofi Annan, p. 91 • Reteaching Activity, p. 95 **Case Studies 5 and 6,** pp. 58 and 72	**Section 3 Assessment,** p. 652 **Formal Assessment** • Section Quiz, p. 350 **California Daily Standards Practice Transparencies,** TT143
SECTION 4 **Terrorism Case Study: September 11, 2001** pp. 653–658 **OBJECTIVE** Describe the September 11 attacks and the U.S. response.	**In-Depth Resources: Unit 5** • Guided Reading, p. 77 • Reteaching Activity, p. 96 **Reading Study Guide,** p. 221	**Section 4 Assessment,** p. 658 **Formal Assessment** • Section Quiz, p. 351 **California Daily Standards Practice Transparencies,** TT143.5
SECTION 5 **Cultures Blend in a Global Age** pp. 659–663 **OBJECTIVE** Analyze the increase in worldwide cultural interaction.	**In-Depth Resources: Unit 5** • Guided Reading, p. 78 • Primary Source: "Cupid," p. 86 • Connections Across Time, p. 92 • Reteaching Activity, p. 97 **Reading Study Guide,** p. 223	**Section 5 Assessment,** p. 663 **Formal Assessment** • Section Quiz, p. 352 **California Daily Standards Practice Transparencies,** TT144

INTEGRATED TECHNOLOGY

- eEdition Plus Online
- EasyPlanner Plus Online
- eTest Plus Online

Audio CDs
- Voices from the Past
- Reading Study Guides

CD-ROMs
- eEdition
- Power Presentations
- EasyPlanner
- Electronic Library of Primary Sources
- Test Generator

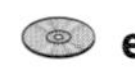 **eEdition CD-ROM**

  **Patterns of Interaction Video Series**
- The Industrial and Electronic Revolutions

 **classzone.com**

 **Geography Transparencies**
- GT36 World Per Capita Income

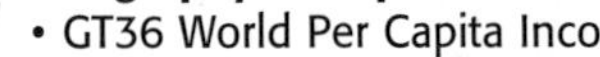

 **World Art and Cultures Transparencies**

 **Electronic Library of Primary Sources**

 **Patterns of Interaction Video Series**
- Trade Connects the World

 **classzone.com**
- NetExplorations: The Environment

 **eEdition CD-ROM**

  **Critical Thinking Transparencies**
- CT36 Patterns of Refugee Movement

 **classzone.com**

 **eEdition CD-ROM**

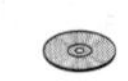 **Electronic Library of Primary Sources**
- "The Making of a Terrorist"

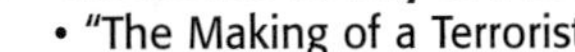

 **classzone.com**

 **World Art and Cultures Transparencies**

 **Critical Thinking Transparencies**
- CT72 Chapter 36 Visual Summary

 **Electronic Library of Primary Sources**
- "Un-American Ugly Americans"
- "Television Is Defying Borders"

 **Patterns of Interaction Video Series**
- The United States and the World

 **classzone.com**

OVERVIEW OF CALIFORNIA RESOURCES

	Section 1	Section 2	Section 3	Section 4	Section 5
California Reading Toolkit	p. L90	p. L91	p. L92	p. L93	p. L94
California Modified Lesson Plans for English Learners	p. 175	p. 177	p. 179	p. 181	p. 183
California Daily Standards Practice Transparencies	TT82	TT83	TT84	TT85	TT86
California Standards Enrichment Workbook	pp. 113–114	pp. 107–108, 111–112, 113–114	pp. 91–92, 105–106, 109–110, 111–112, 113–114	pp. 111–112	pp. 107–108, 113–114
California Standards Planner and Lesson Plans	p. L171	p. L173	p. L175	p. L177	p. L179
California Online Test Practice	classzone.com	classzone.com	classzone.com	classzone.com	classzone.com
California Test Generator CD-ROM					
California Easy Planner CD-ROM					
California eEdition CD-ROM					

Chart Key:

 Copymaster

Pupil's Edition

 Teacher's Edition

Audio Library

 CD-ROM

 Overhead Transparency

 Internet

 Block Scheduling

 Video

NO TIME?

If you do not have time to teach this chapter in full, assign the **Chapter in Brief** (also available in Spanish).

ENGLISH LEARNERS: Resources in Spanish

In-Depth Resources in Spanish

- Guided Reading Ⓐ
- Skillbuilder Practice: Analyzing Motives Ⓑ
- Geography Application: Deforestation in Brazil

Chapters in Brief

Reading Study Guide Ⓒ

Reading Study Guide Audio CD

Test Generator CD-ROM

- Chapter Test, Forms A, B, and C

Plus

Modified Lesson Plans for English Learners

Multi-Language Glossary of Social Studies Terms

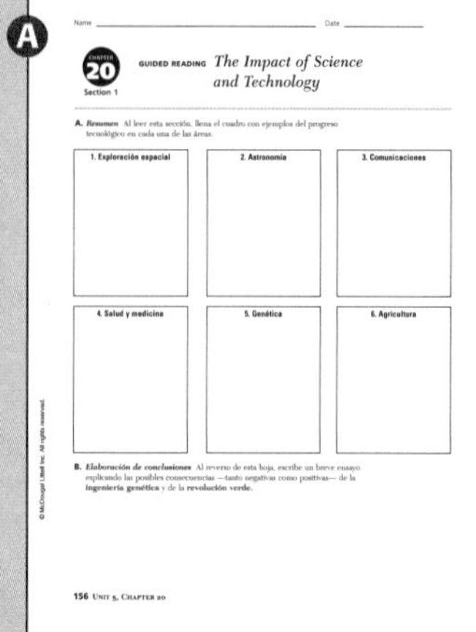

CHAPTER 20 Section 1 GUIDED READING The Impact of Science and Technology

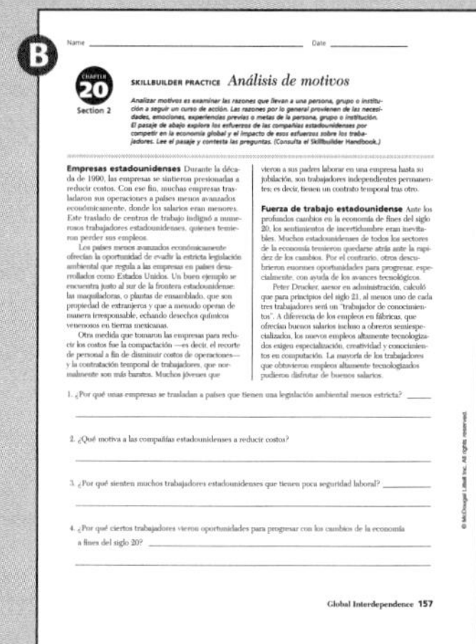

CHAPTER 20 Section 2 SKILLBUILDER PRACTICE Análisis de motivos

STRUGGLING READERS

In-Depth Resources: Unit 5

- Guided Reading Ⓐ
- Building Vocabulary
- Skillbuilder Practice: Analyzing Motives
- Geography Application: Deforestation in Brazil Ⓑ
- Reteaching Activities

Chapters in Brief

Reading Study Guide Ⓒ

Reading Study Guide Audio CD

Formal Assessment

- Chapter Test, Form A

Plus

Reading Toolkit

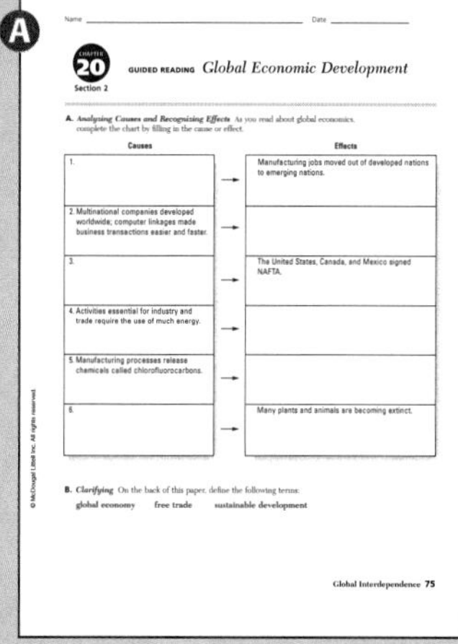

CHAPTER 20 Section 2 GUIDED READING Global Economic Development

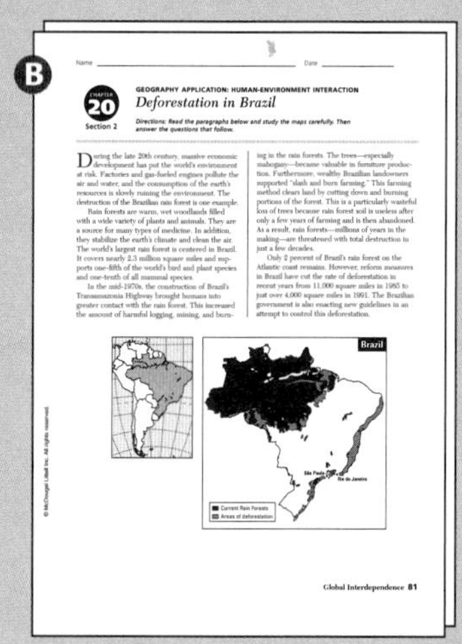

CHAPTER 20 Section 2 GEOGRAPHY APPLICATION: HUMAN-ENVIRONMENT INTERACTION Deforestation in Brazil

GIFTED AND TALENTED STUDENTS

In-Depth Resources: Unit 5

- Primary Sources: from "Down to Earth"; Recycling Symbol Ⓐ; The Universal Declaration of Human Rights; "Cupid's a Korean Computer, Making Wise Matches"
- Literature: "Paper" Ⓑ
- History Makers: Kofi Annan
- Connections Across Time and Cultures: Progress and Change Ⓒ

Electronic Library of Primary Sources

- "Tackling the Menace of Space Junk"
- "The Making of a Terrorist"
- "Un-American Ugly Americans"
- "Television Is Defying Borders"

Formal Assessment

- Chapter Test, Form C

CHAPTER 20 Section 2 PRIMARY SOURCE Recycling Symbol

CHAPTER 20 Section 2 LITERATURE SELECTION "Paper" by Catherine Lim

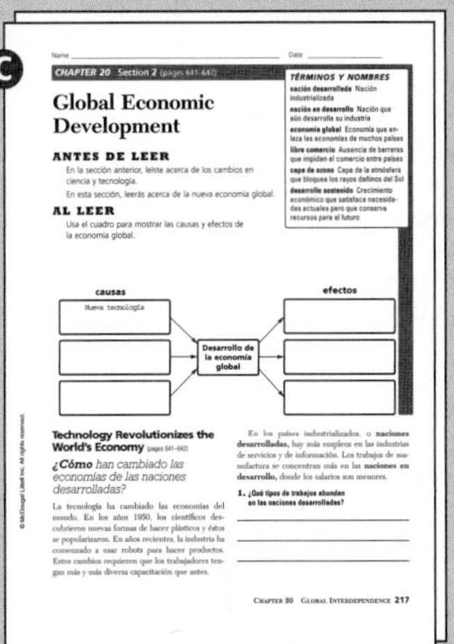

Name ______ Date ______

CHAPTER 20 Section 2 (pages 641–647)

Global Economic Development

TÉRMINOS Y NOMBRES

nación desarrollada Nación industrializada

nación en desarrollo Nación que aún desarrolla su industria

economía global Economía que enlaza las economías de muchos países

libre comercio Ausencia de barreras que impidan el comercio entre países

capa de ozono Capa de la atmósfera que bloquea los rayos dañinos del Sol

desarrollo sostenido Crecimiento económico que satisface necesidades actuales pero que conserva recursos para el futuro

ANTES DE LEER

En la sección anterior, leíste acerca de los cambios en ciencia y tecnología.

En esta sección, leerás acerca de la nueva economía global.

AL LEER

Usa el cuadro para mostrar las causas y efectos de la economía global.

causas: Nueva tecnología → Desarrollo de la economía global → efectos

Technology Revolutionizes the World's Economy (pages 641–642)

¿Cómo han cambiado las economías de las naciones desarrolladas?

La tecnología ha cambiado las economías del mundo. En los años 1950, los científicos descubrieron nuevas formas de hacer plásticos y éstos se popularizaron. En años recientes, la industria ha comenzado a usar robots para hacer productos. Estos cambios requieren que los trabajadores tengan más y más diversa capacitación que antes.

En los países industrializados, o **naciones desarrolladas,** hay más empleos en las industrias de servicios y de información. Los trabajos de manufactura se concentran más en las **naciones en desarrollo,** donde los salarios son menores.

1. **¿Qué tipos de trabajos abundan en las naciones desarrolladas?**

CHAPTER 20 GLOBAL INTERDEPENDENCE 217

© McDougal Littell Inc. All rights reserved.

Activities in the Teacher's Edition for English Learners

- Understanding Medical Vocabulary, p. 651
- Understanding Words in Context, p. 654
- Creating Cultural Self-Portraits, p. 661

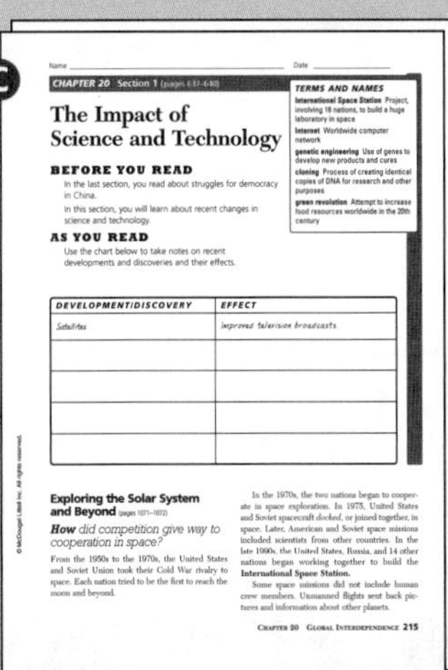

Name ______ Date ______

CHAPTER 20 Section 1 (pages 637–640)

The Impact of Science and Technology

TERMS AND NAMES

International Space Station Project, involving 16 nations, to build a huge laboratory in space

Internet Worldwide computer network

genetic engineering Use of genes to develop new products and cures

cloning Process of creating identical copies of DNA for research and other purposes

green revolution Attempt to increase food resources worldwide in the 20th century

BEFORE YOU READ

In the last section, you read about struggles for democracy in China.

In this section, you will learn about recent changes in science and technology.

AS YOU READ

Use the chart below to take notes on recent developments and discoveries and their effects.

DEVELOPMENT/DISCOVERY	EFFECT
Satellites	Improved television broadcasts

Exploring the Solar System and Beyond (pages 1071–1072)

***How** did competition give way to cooperation in space?*

From the 1950s to the 1970s, the United States and Soviet Union took their Cold War rivalry to space. Each nation tried to be the first to reach the moon and beyond.

In the 1970s, the two nations began to cooperate in space exploration. In 1975, United States and Soviet spacecraft *docked*, or joined together, in space. Later, American and Soviet space missions included scientists from other countries. In the late 1990s, the United States, Russia, and 14 other nations began working together to build the **International Space Station.**

Some space missions did not include human crew members. Unmanned flights sent back pictures and information about other planets.

CHAPTER 20 GLOBAL INTERDEPENDENCE 215

© McDougal Littell Inc. All rights reserved.

Activities in the Teacher's Edition for Struggling Readers

- Dramatizing Space Travel, p. 638
- Effects of Oil, p. 645
- Summarizing Progress for Women, p. 650
- Mapping Terrorism, p. 655
- Using a Spider Map to Summarize Text, p. 660

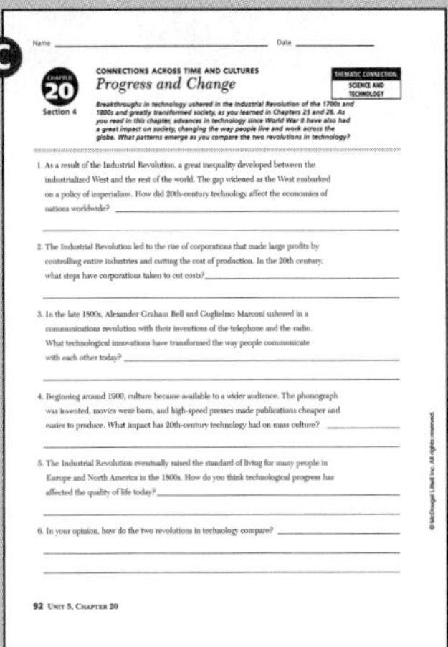

Name ______ Date ______

CHAPTER 20 Section 4

CONNECTIONS ACROSS TIME AND CULTURES

Progress and Change

THEMATIC CONNECTION: SCIENCE AND TECHNOLOGY

Breakthroughs in technology ushered in the Industrial Revolution of the 1700s and 1800s and greatly transformed society, as you learned in Chapters 25 and 26. As you read in this chapter, advances in technology since World War II have also had a great impact on society, changing the way people live and work across the globe. What patterns emerge as you compare the two revolutions in technology?

1. As a result of the Industrial Revolution, a great inequality developed between the industrialized West and the rest of the world. The gap widened as the West embarked on a policy of imperialism. How did 20th-century technology affect the economies of nations worldwide?
2. The Industrial Revolution led to the rise of corporations that made large profits by controlling entire industries and cutting the cost of production. In the 20th century, what steps have corporations taken to cut costs?
3. In the late 1800s, Alexander Graham Bell and Guglielmo Marconi ushered in a communications revolution with their inventions of the telephone and the radio. What technological innovations have transformed the way people communicate with each other today?
4. Beginning around 1900, culture became available to a wider audience. The phonograph was invented, movies were born, and high-speed presses made publications cheaper and easier to produce. What impact has 20th-century technology had on mass culture?
5. The Industrial Revolution eventually raised the standard of living for many people in Europe and North America in the 1800s. How do you think technological progress has affected the quality of life today?
6. In your opinion, how do the two revolutions in technology compare?

92 UNIT 5, CHAPTER 20

© McDougal Littell Inc. All rights reserved.

Activities in the Teacher's Edition for Gifted and Talented Students

- Advances in Modern Medicine, p. 639
- Evaluating NAFTA, p. 643
- Ethnic Conflicts, p. 649
- Analyzing the Damage After September 11, p. 656
- Staging an International Literature Fair, p. 662

INTEGRATED TECHNOLOGY

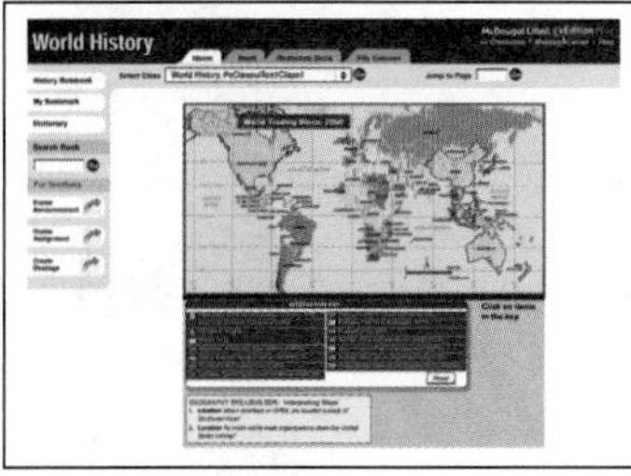

eEdition

- Interactive Visuals
- Interactive Maps
- Interactive Primary Sources

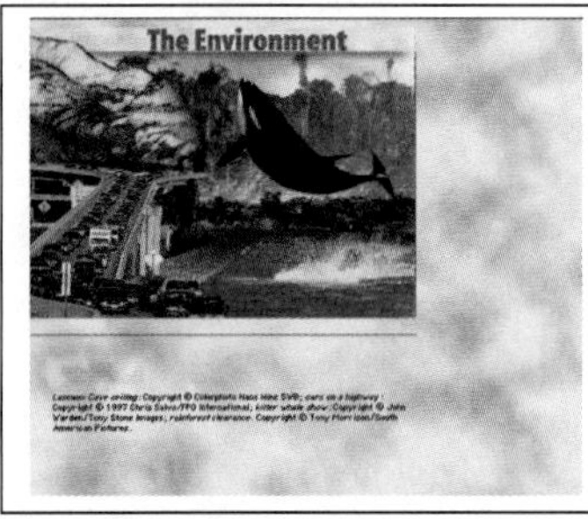

classzone.com

- Research Links
- Internet Activities
- Primary Sources
- Chapter Quiz
- NetExplorations: The Environment
- Current Events

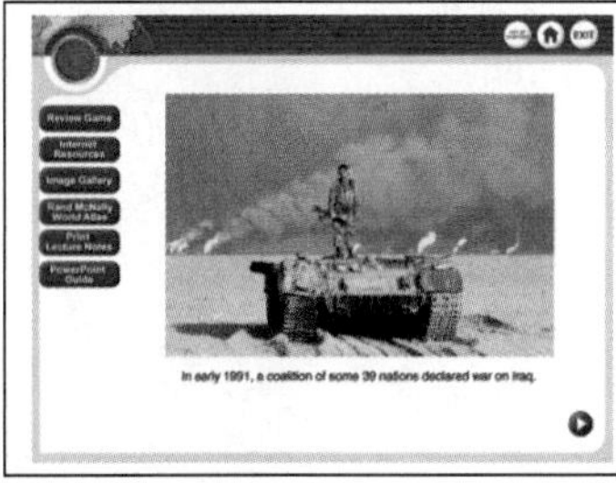

Power Presentations CD-ROM

- Lecture Notes
- Image Gallery
- Chapter Review Game

Critical Thinking Transparencies

- CT36 Patterns of Refugee Movement
- CT72 Chapter 36 Visual Summary

Geography Transparencies

- GT36 World Per Capita Income

World Art and Cultures Transparencies

- AT79 *Time Goes By*
- AT80 *Technology* (Korean video sculpture) A

Test Practice Transparencies TT141–TT144

Test Generator CD-ROM

EasyPlanner CD-ROM

Voices from the Past Audio CD

Online Test Practice

Electronic Library of Primary Sources

Patterns of Interaction Video Series

CHAPTER 20 • OBJECTIVE

Explain the variety of ways in which global interdependence affects people's lives.

Previewing Main Ideas

Point out that the main ideas on this page describe different ways in which people around the world are connected. Technology has been a major factor in increasing global interdependence.

Accessing Prior Knowledge

Ask students what comes to mind when they hear the phrase *global interdependence.* What does it imply about the peoples, languages, cultures, economies, and politics of the world? (*Possible Answer: people around the world needing one another and sharing many aspects of their lives*)

Geography *Answers*

SCIENCE AND TECHNOLOGY The map illustrates migration around the world, showing that people from different countries are coming in contact with one another.

CULTURAL INTERACTION Canada and the United States are major destinations for immigrants.

ECONOMICS Most countries with the highest net migration rate are economically developed countries.

POWER AND AUTHORITY Most countries with the highest net migration rate have democratic forms of government.

CHAPTER 20

Global Interdependence, 1960–Present

Previewing Main Ideas

SCIENCE AND TECHNOLOGY Advances in science and technology have changed the lives of people around the globe. Improved communications and transportation have allowed goods, services, and ideas to move rapidly.

Geography *How does this map illustrate the idea of global interdependence?*

CULTURAL INTERACTION Inventions and innovations have brought the nations of the world closer and exposed people to other cultures. Cultures are now blending ideas and customs much faster than before.

Geography *Which countries in the Western Hemisphere are major destinations for immigrants?*

ECONOMICS Since World War II, nations have worked to expand trade and commerce in world markets. Changes in technology have blurred national boundaries and created a global market.

Geography *What do most countries with a net migration rate above 3.0 have in common economically?*

POWER AND AUTHORITY Since the end of World War II, nations have adopted collective efforts to ensure their security. One of the greatest challenges in maintaining global security is international terrorism.

Geography *What do most countries with a net migration rate above 3 have in common politically?*

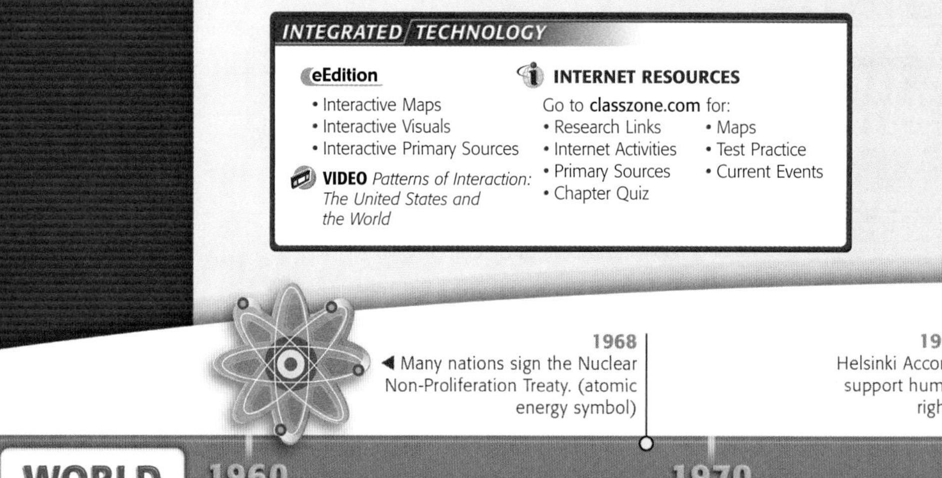

INTEGRATED TECHNOLOGY

eEdition
- Interactive Maps
- Interactive Visuals
- Interactive Primary Sources

VIDEO *Patterns of Interaction: The United States and the World*

INTERNET RESOURCES

Go to **classzone.com** for:
- Research Links
- Internet Activities
- Primary Sources
- Chapter Quiz
- Maps
- Test Practice
- Current Events

WORLD 1960 1970

1968 ◀ Many nations sign the Nuclear Non-Proliferation Treaty. (atomic energy symbol)

1972 U.S. and Soviet Union agree to joint space venture. Terrorists carry out attack at the Summer Olympic games in Munich. (masked terrorist in Munich) ▶

1975 Helsinki Accords support human rights.

634

TIME LINE DISCUSSION

Point out to students that this time line highlights some key events that demonstrate the growth of global interdependence. Ask them to look for both positive and negative events that link people.

1. Ask students to name an event that marks a major step toward a global economy. *(Possible Answer: 1995–World Trade Organization is set up.)*
2. Identify an agreement that was meant to increase security or to protect individual freedoms in the world. *(Possible Answers: 1968–Nuclear Non-Proliferation Treaty; 1975–Helsinki Accords)*
3. Ask students to identify an event that had a negative impact on the environment. *(1986–accident at Soviet nuclear power plant in Chernobyl)*
4. How many years elapsed between the isolation of the AIDS virus and the completion of the Human Genome Project? *(20)* How might these events be related? *(Possible Answer: Genetic research may hold the key to medical advances such as the development of a vaccine for AIDS.)*

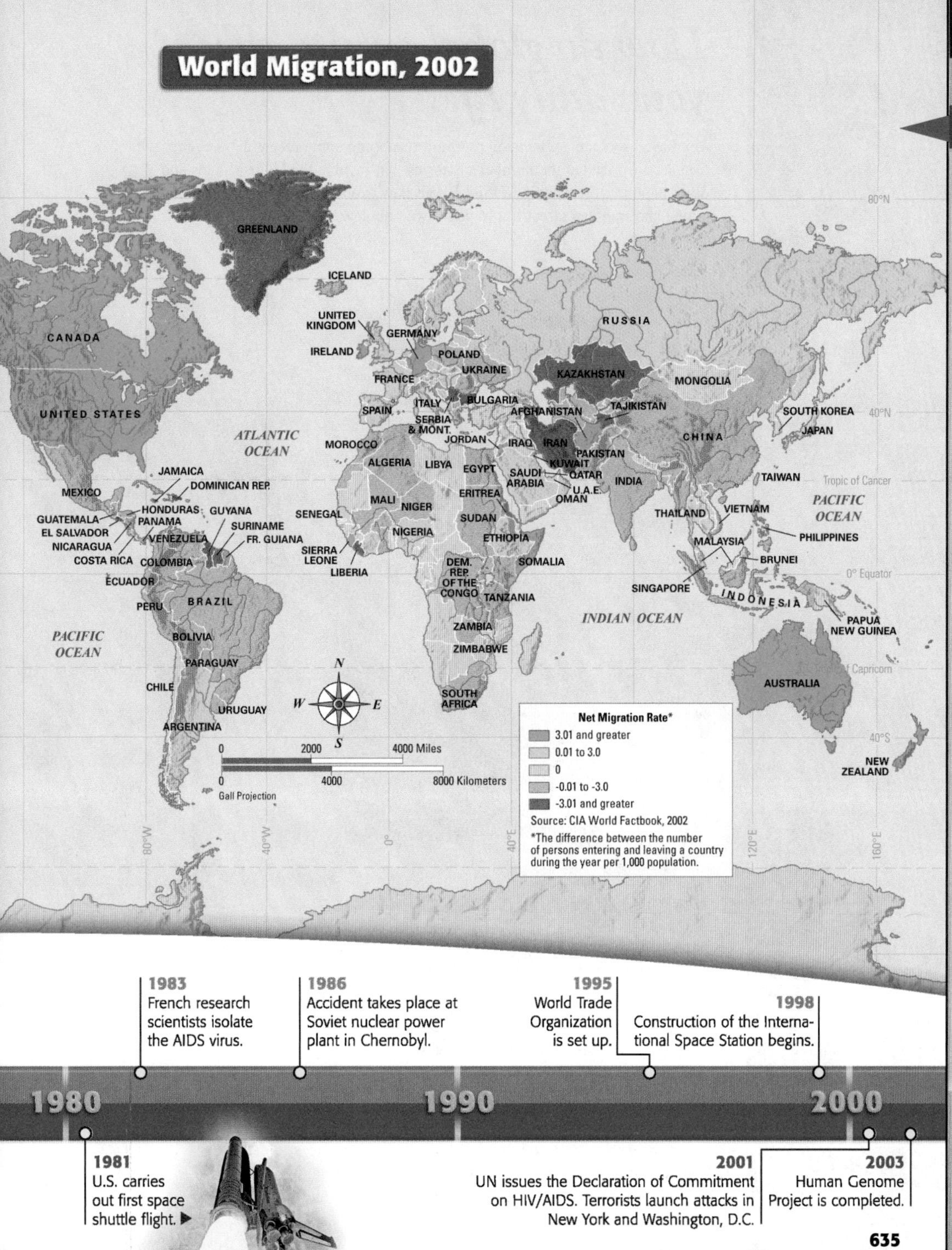

CHAPTER 20

History from Visuals

Interpreting the Map

Have students use the key to identify some of the countries that have the highest net migration—in other words, more people arriving than leaving. *(Canada, United States, Australia, New Zealand, Germany, Ireland, French Guiana, Sierra Leone, Somalia, Eritrea, Afghanistan, Jordan)* What are some countries with the lowest net migration? *(Greenland, Kazakhstan, Iran, Bulgaria, El Salvador)* Ask students to discuss some of the reasons people might choose to go to another country. *(Possible Answers: leave because of poor climate, unstable political situation, lack of economic opportunity; go to a country that offers more opportunities in jobs and education, political or religious freedom, hope of a better future)*

Extension Point out to students that air travel now allows for the rapid exchange of people, goods, and ideas, allowing a greater mixing of cultures than ever before. Have students discuss some of the benefits and drawbacks of this exchange. What might be some of the drawbacks? *(Possible Answers: terrorism, infectious diseases, transport of harmful plants and insects)* What might be some advantages of such free exchange? *(Possible Answers: cultural enrichment, greater understanding of other people and countries)*

RECOMMENDED RESOURCES

Books for the Teacher

Friedman, Thomas L. ***Longitudes and Attitudes: Exploring the World After September 11.*** New York: Farrar, 2002. A compilation of Friedman's Pulitzer Prize–winning articles.

Rawlins, Gregory J. E. ***Moths to the Flame: The Seductions of Computer Technology.*** Cambridge, MA: MIT P, 1996.

Books for the Student

Goldfarb, Theodore D. ***Taking Sides: Clashing Views of Controversial Environmental Issues.*** New York: McGraw Hill Higher Education, 2000. Introduces students to controversies in environmental policy and science.

Videos and Software

Cappuccino Trail: The Global Economy in a Cup. VHS and DVD. Films for the Humanities & Sciences, 2001. 800-257-5126.

Nerds 2.0.1: A Brief History of the Internet. VHS. PBS Home Video, 1998. 877-727-7467. Features interviews with such key figures as Microsoft founder Bill Gates and World Wide Web inventor Tim Berners-Lee.

Space Exploration. CD-ROM. Library Video Company, 1999. 800-843-3620. A hands-on exploration of spaceships, telescopes, and rocketry.

Interact *with* History

Objectives

- Introduce students to the concept of a global community.
- Give students a broad perspective on world events.
- Help students appreciate the many ways in which the world's nations are interdependent.

EXAMINING *the* ISSUES

Possible Answers

- The war in Iraq and the Homeland Security Alert are both related to international terrorism.
- Violence, contagious diseases, and scientific breakthroughs are important to people all over the world.

Discussion

Ask students to discuss these questions. Encourage students to keep in mind what they have learned about how the world has changed since World War II. Ask them how the Cold War, the movement for colonial independence, and the growth of democracy made nations increasingly dependent on one another. *(Possible Answers: During the Cold War, nations depended on the balance of power between the United States and the Soviet Union. Independent, democratic countries are linked by the free exchange of people, goods, and ideas.)*

Interact *with* History

How do global events affect your daily life?

You have just seen a television program recapping some recent news events. You are surprised at the number of stories that involve the United States and other countries. You begin to think about how events in such distant places as China and Iraq can affect life in your own country.

▼ War in Iraq, 2003

▼ Mapping the Human Genome

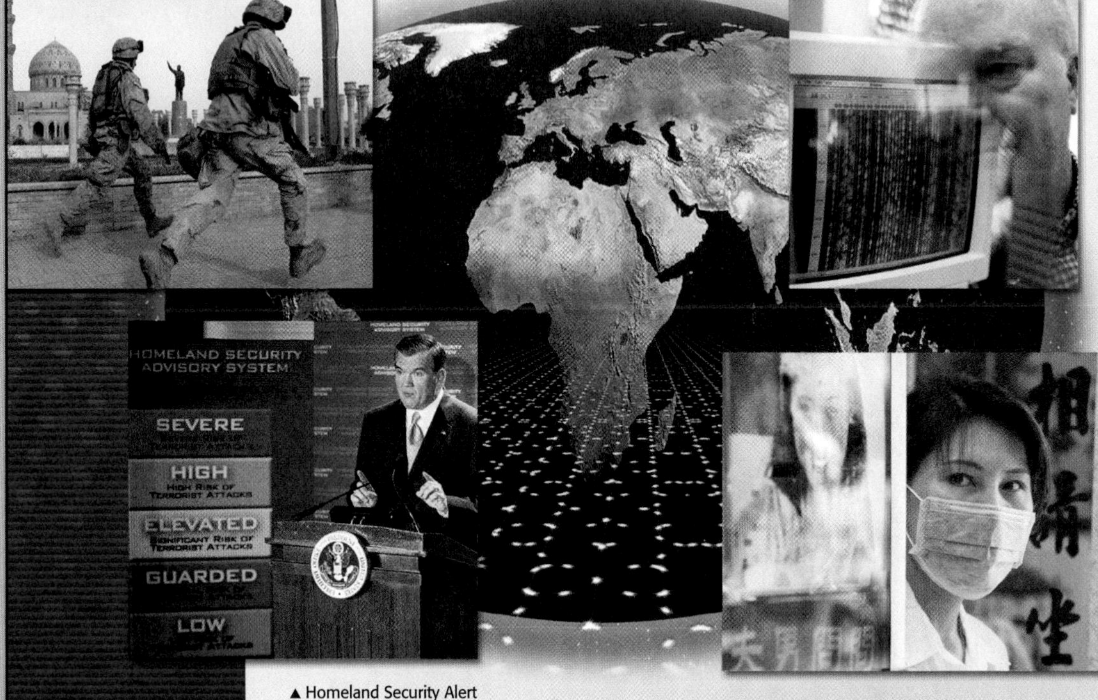

▲ Homeland Security Alert

▲ Severe Acute Respiratory Syndrome in China

EXAMINING *the* ISSUES

- **How do the events shown in the photographs illustrate the political interdependence of different nations?**
- **What do these events tell you about scientific and cultural interdependence among nations?**

As a class, discuss these questions. Remember what you have learned about the recent history of nations in different regions of the world. Try to think of reasons that nations are becoming increasingly dependent on one another. As you read this chapter, look for examples of economic, political, and cultural interdependence among the nations of the world.

WHY STUDY GLOBAL INTERDEPENDENCE?

- Advances in science and technology, such as the growth of the Internet, affect the lives of people around the world.
- Globalization will have long-term consequences for local economies and cultures (see the Analyzing Key Concepts feature on page 644).
- The need to find sustainable methods of economic growth is crucial to the environmental health of the planet.
- To ensure personal security, it is essential to understand how security within and between nations can be improved.
- Human rights and world health are issues that affect all individuals.
- People and nations can work together against the dangers posed by terrorism.
- Globalization of culture affects everything from sports and the arts to music and fashion (see the Global Impact feature on pages 660–661).

1

The Impact of Science and Technology

MAIN IDEA	WHY IT MATTERS NOW	TERMS & NAMES
SCIENCE AND TECHNOLOGY Advances in technology after World War II led to increased global interaction and improved quality of life.	Advances in science and technology affect the lives of people around the world.	• International Space Station • Internet • genetic engineering • cloning • green revolution

SETTING THE STAGE Beginning in the late 1950s, the United States and the Soviet Union competed in the exploration of space. The Soviets launched Earth's first artificial satellite and put the first human in orbit around the planet. By the late 1960s, however, the United States had surpassed the Soviets. U.S. astronauts landed on the moon in 1969. The heavy emphasis on science and technology that the space race required led to the development of products that changed life for people across the globe.

Exploring the Solar System and Beyond

In its early years, competition between the United States and the Soviet Union in the space race was intense. Eventually, however, space exploration became one of the world's first and most successful arenas for cooperation between U.S. and Soviet scientists.

Cooperation in Space In 1972, years before the end of the Cold War, the United States and Soviet space programs began work on a cooperative project—the docking of U.S. and Soviet spacecraft in orbit. This goal was achieved on July 17, 1975, when spacecraft from the two countries docked some 140 miles above Earth. Television viewers across the globe watched as the hatch between the space vehicles opened and crews from Earth's fiercest rival countries greeted each other.

This first cooperative venture in space between the United States and the Soviet Union was an isolated event. People from different countries, however, continued to work together to explore space. The Soviets were the first to send an international crew into space. The crew of *Soyuz 28,* which orbited Earth in 1978, included a Czech cosmonaut. Since the mid-1980s, crews on United States space shuttle flights have included astronauts from Saudi Arabia, France, Germany, Canada, Italy, Japan, Israel, and Mexico. (Space shuttles are larger than other spacecraft and are reusable.) Shuttle missions put crews in orbit around Earth to accomplish a variety of scientific and technological tasks.

The space shuttle is being used in the most ambitious cooperative space venture. The project, sponsored by the United States, Russia, and 14 other nations, involves the building of the **International Space Station** (ISS). Since 1998, U.S. shuttles and Russian spacecraft have transported sections of the ISS to be assembled in space. By the time it is completed, the ISS will cover an area the size

CALIFORNIA STANDARDS

10.11 Students analyze the integration of countries into the world economy and the information, technological, and communications revolutions (e.g., television, satellites, computers).

CST 3 Students use a variety of maps and documents to interpret human movement, including major patterns of domestic and international migration, changing environmental preferences and settlement patterns, the frictions that develop between population groups, and the diffusion of ideas, technological innovations, and goods.

TAKING NOTES

Recognizing Effects Use a chart to list the effects of scientific and technological developments.

Developments	Effects
Communications	
Health and Medicine	
Green Revolution	

LESSON PLAN

OBJECTIVES

- Trace the exploration of outer space.
- Identify effects of expanding global communications.
- Evaluate effects of advances in health care, medicine, and agriculture.

1 FOCUS & MOTIVATE

Discuss ways that advances in technology have changed the ways students communicate. *(Possible Answers: voice mail, e-mail, cell phones, fax machines)*

2 INSTRUCT

Exploring the Solar System and Beyond

10.11

Critical Thinking

- Why did the crash of the shuttle *Columbia* adversely affect the International Space Station? *(Possible Answers: Safety questions put the shuttle program on hold; the shuttle transports people and supplies to the ISS.)*

CALIFORNIA RESOURCES

California Reading Toolkit, p. L90
California Modified Lesson Plans for English Learners, p. 175
California Daily Standards Practice Transparencies, TT82
California Standards Enrichment Workbook, pp. 113–114
California Standards Planner and Lesson Plans, p. L171
California Online Test Practice
California Test Generator CD-ROM
California Easy Planner CD-ROM
California eEdition CD-ROM

SECTION 1 PROGRAM RESOURCES

ALL STUDENTS

In-Depth Resources: Unit 5
- Guided Reading, p. 74

Formal Assessment
- Section Quiz, p. 348

ENGLISH LEARNERS

In-Depth Resources in Spanish
- Guided Reading, p. 155

Reading Study Guide (Spanish), p. 215
Reading Study Guide Audio CD (Spanish)

STRUGGLING READERS

In-Depth Resources: Unit 5
- Guided Reading, p. 74
- Building Vocabulary, p. 79
- Reteaching Activity, p. 93

Reading Study Guide, p. 215
Reading Study Guide Audio CD

GIFTED AND TALENTED STUDENTS

In-Depth Resources: Unit 5
- Primary Source: from "Down to Earth," p. 83

INTEGRATED TECHNOLOGY

eEdition CD-ROM
Voices from the Past Audio CD
Power Presentations CD-ROM
Patterns of Interaction Video Series
- The Industrial and Electronic Revolutions

classzone.com

Expanding Global Communications
10.11

Critical Thinking

- Why does the phrase *global village* describe the results of satellite communication? *(Possible Answer: Events all over the world can be experienced with the immediacy of events in one's neighborhood.)*
- What power have individuals gained from the miniaturization of computers? *(Possible Answer: Knowledge once available only to computer experts is available to ordinary people.)*

More About . . .

Computer Chips

Silicon is used for computer chips because it can be made to conduct electricity at room temperature. The chips that tell computers and other electronic devices what to do are microprocessors. They were first used in desktop calculators in 1971.

More About . . .

Changes in Communication

The video "The Industrial and Electronic Revolutions" analyzes how advances in technology have caused a global communications revolution.

Patterns of Interaction Video Series

- The Industrial and Electronic Revolutions

▲ This view of the ISS was taken from the space shuttle *Endeavor.*

of a football field and house a crew of six. Since October 2000, smaller crews have been working aboard the ISS. By early 2003, they had conducted more than 100 experiments. However, the suspension of the shuttle program after the crash of the shuttle *Columbia* in February 2003 put the future of the ISS in question.

Exploring the Universe Unmanned space probes have been used to study the farther reaches of the solar system. The Soviet *Venera* spacecraft in the 1970s and the U.S. probe *Magellan* in 1990 provided in-depth information about Venus. On a 12-year journey that began in 1977, the U.S. *Voyager 2* sent dazzling pictures of Jupiter, Saturn, Uranus, and Neptune back to Earth. Both the United States and the Soviet Union have shown particular interest in the planet Mars. The United States probe *Pathfinder,* which landed on Mars in 1997, provided spectacular results.

In 1990, the U.S. space agency, NASA, and the European space agency, ESA, worked together to develop and launch the Hubble Space Telescope. This orbiting telescope continues to observe and send back images of objects in the most remote regions of the universe. (A)

MAIN IDEA

Hypothesizing

(A) Why might rival nations cooperate in space activities but not on Earth?

A. Possible Answer The great expense can be shared. Scientists, not politicians, plan the activities.

Expanding Global Communications

Since the 1960s, artificial satellites launched into orbit around Earth have aided worldwide communications. With satellite communication, the world has been gradually transformed into a global village. Today, political and cultural events occurring in one part of the world often are witnessed live by people thousands of miles away. This linking of the globe through worldwide communications is made possible by the miniaturization of the computer.

Smaller, More Powerful Computers In the 1940s, when computers first came into use, they took up a huge room. The computer required fans or an elaborate air-conditioning system to cool the vacuum tubes that powered its operations. In the years since then, however, the circuitry that runs the computer has been miniaturized and made more powerful. This change is due, in part, to the space program, for which equipment had to be downsized to fit into tiny space capsules. Silicon chips replaced the bulky vacuum tubes used earlier. Smaller than contact lenses, silicon chips hold millions of microscopic circuits.

Following this development, industries began to use computers and silicon chips to run assembly lines. Today a variety of consumer products such as microwave ovens, telephones, keyboard instruments, and cars use computers and chips. Computers have become essential in most offices, and millions of people around the globe have computers in their homes.

▼ Some computers are so small that they can be held in the hand.

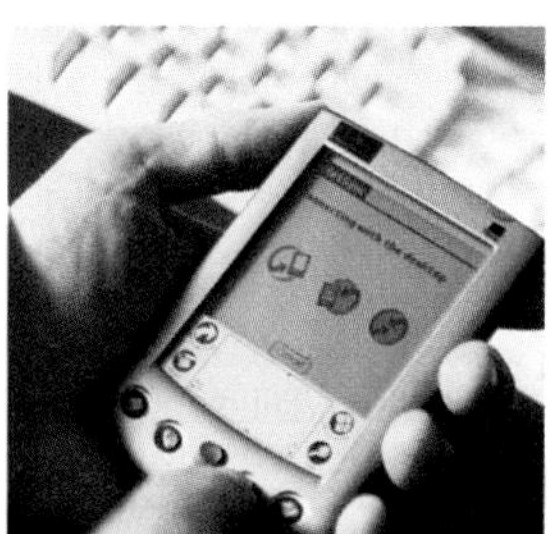

DIFFERENTIATING INSTRUCTION: STRUGGLING READERS

Dramatizing Space Travel

Class Time 45 minutes

Task Researching and putting together a class presentation

Purpose To help students experience and express the drama and challenges of space exploration

Instructions To achieve broad coverage of various events, divide the class into four groups. Each will research a particular period: 1950–1967, 1968–1978, 1979–1989, and 1990–present. Mix students of varying reading abilities in each group. Have students use library and Internet resources to gather firsthand and eyewitness reports of events such as the first walk on the moon in 1969 and the explosion of the space shuttle *Challenger* in 1986.

After each group collects two or three accounts, have the groups meet as a class. Select one account from each group and decide in which order to present the accounts. Then ask each group to prepare its own skit or dramatic reading and present it to the class.

Students who need more help with this section should use the Reading Study Guide, available in English and Spanish.

Reading Study Guide

Access to the Internet, 2002

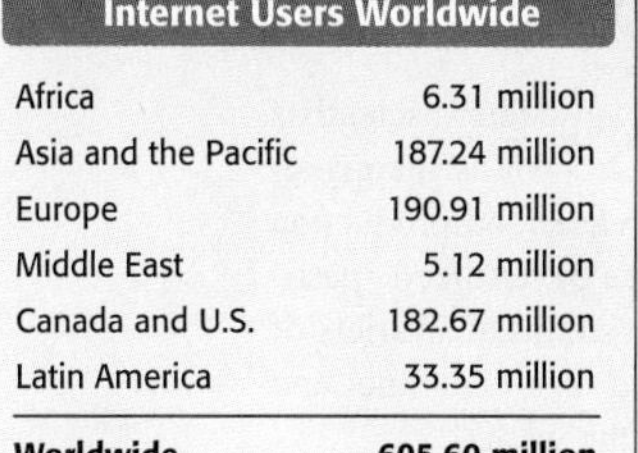

Internet Users Worldwide

Africa	6.31 million
Asia and the Pacific	187.24 million
Europe	190.91 million
Middle East	5.12 million
Canada and U.S.	182.67 million
Latin America	33.35 million
Worldwide	**605.60 million**

Source: Nua Internet Surveys

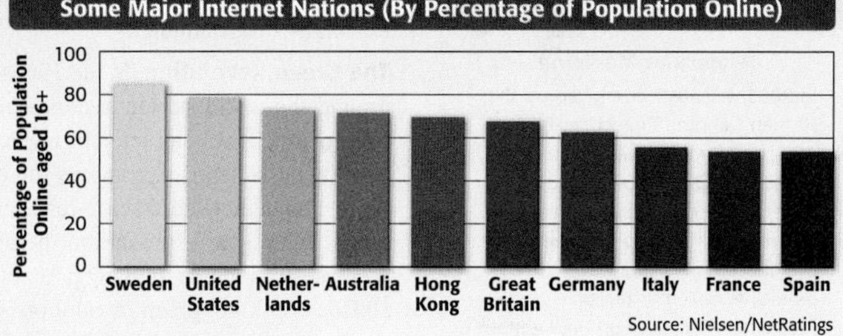

Source: Nielsen/NetRatings

SKILLBUILDER: Interpreting Charts and Graphs
1. **Comparing** *In which world region do most Internet users live?*
2. **Drawing Conclusions** *How would you describe most of the nations with large percentages of their populations online?*

Communications Networks Starting in the 1990s, businesses and individuals began using the **Internet**. The Internet is the voluntary linkage of computer networks around the world. It began in the late 1960s as a method of linking scientists so they could exchange information about research. Through telephone-line links, business and personal computers can be hooked up with computer networks. These networks allow users to communicate with people across the nation and around the world. Between 1995 and late 2002, the number of worldwide Internet users soared from 26 million to more than 600 million.

B. Answer computers, Internet, fax machines

MAIN IDEA
Summarizing
B What types of technology have recently changed the workplace?

Conducting business on the Internet has become a way of life for many. The Internet, along with fax machines, transmits information electronically to remote locations. Both paved the way for home offices and telecommuting—working at home using a computer connected to a business network. Once again, as it has many times in the past, technology has changed how and where people work. B

Transforming Human Life

Advances with computers and communications networks have transformed not only the ways people work but lifestyles as well. Technological progress in the sciences, medicine, and agriculture has improved the quality of the lives of millions of people.

Health and Medicine Before World War II, surgeons seldom performed operations on sensitive areas such as the eye or the brain. However, in the 1960s and 1970s, new technologies, such as more powerful microscopes, the laser, and ultrasound, were developed. Many of these technologies advanced surgical techniques.

Advances in medical imaging also helped to improve health care. Using data provided by CAT scans and MRI techniques, doctors can build three-dimensional images of different organs or regions of the body. Doctors use these images to diagnose injuries, detect tumors, or collect other medical information.

In the 1980s, genetics, the study of heredity through research on genes, became a fast-growing field of science. Found in the cells of all organisms, genes are hereditary units that cause specific traits, such as eye color, in every living organism. Technology allowed scientists to isolate and examine individual genes that are responsible for different traits. Through **genetic engineering**, scientists were able to introduce new genes into an organism to give that organism new traits.

Another aspect of genetic engineering is **cloning**. This is the creation of identical copies of DNA, the chemical chains of genes that determine heredity. Cloning actually allows scientists to reproduce both plants and animals that are identical to

History from Visuals

Interpreting the Chart

Point out that the table shows the breakdown of Internet users by world regions. The bar graph shows the percentage of online usage in some major nations. Which nation that has high Internet usage is not shown on the bar graph? *(Canada)*

Extension Ask students which countries on the bar graph are from the region with highest Internet usage. *(Sweden, Netherlands, Great Britain, Germany, Italy, France, Spain)*

SKILLBUILDER Answers
1. **Comparing** Europe
2. **Drawing Conclusions** developed nations

Tip for English Learners

Explain that the word *telecommute* contains the prefix *tele-*, which means "distance" or "far off." What other words have this prefix? *(Possible Answers: telephone, television)*

Transforming Human Life
10.11

Critical Thinking

- How do new medical imaging techniques relate to the need for surgery? *(Possible Answer: Doctors are able to see inside the body without having to do as much exploratory surgery.)*
- In what way was the green revolution not green? *(Possible Answer: Pesticides and fertilizers are not generally environmentally friendly.)*

DIFFERENTIATING INSTRUCTION: GIFTED AND TALENTED STUDENTS

Advances in Modern Medicine

Class Time 45 minutes

Task Researching and preparing a news special

Purpose To expand knowledge about scientific advances in medicine

Instructions Encourage interested students to do additional research on the Internet or in scientific or medical journals concerning advances in modern medicine. Some possible topics to research include:

- imaging techniques such as MRI and CAT scans
- surgical methods such as the use of lasers
- gene therapy
- organ transplantation
- the ongoing search for plants with naturally occurring medicinal properties

Suggest that students prepare their information in the form of a television or radio news special that they can share with the class. News specials should include a description of a particular medical advance, examples of practical applications, and a conclusion about the significance of the advance.

Social History

Molecular Medicine

Genetic diseases are not just hereditary. Genes affected by viruses or environmental toxins may also contribute to illness. As researchers gain more understanding of the molecular nature of disease, they expect more accurate testing and diagnoses and medications that cause fewer side effects. A major risk involved for those undergoing genetic testing is the question of how the knowledge of their genetic makeup may be used by insurers or employers.

Social History

Molecular Medicine

In 2003, scientists employed on the Human Genome Project completed work on a map of the thousands of genes contained in DNA—human genetic material. The information provided by this map has helped in the development of a new field of medicine. Called "molecular medicine," it focuses on how genetic diseases develop and progress.

Researchers in molecular medicine are working to identify the genes that cause various diseases. This will help in detecting diseases in their early stages of development. Another area of interest to researchers is gene therapy. This involves replacing a patient's diseased genes with normal ones. The ultimate aim of workers in this field is to create "designer drugs" based on a person's genetic makeup.

existing plants and animals. The application of genetics research to everyday life has led to many breakthroughs, especially in agriculture.

The Green Revolution In the 1960s, agricultural scientists around the world started a campaign known as the **green revolution**. It was an attempt to increase food production worldwide. Scientists promoted the use of fertilizers, pesticides, and high-yield, disease-resistant strains of a variety of crops. The green revolution helped avert famine and increase crop yields in many parts of the world.

However, the green revolution had its negative side. Fertilizers and pesticides often contain dangerous chemicals that may cause cancer and pollute the environment. Also, the cost of the chemicals and the equipment to harvest more crops was far too expensive for an average peasant farmer. Consequently, owners of small farms received little benefit from the advances in agriculture. In some cases, farmers were forced off the land by larger agricultural businesses.

Advances in genetics research seem to be helping to fulfill some of the goals of the green revolution. In this new "gene revolution," resistance to pests is bred into plant strains, reducing the need for pesticides. Plants being bred to tolerate poor soil conditions also reduce the need for fertilizers. The gene revolution involves some risks, including the accidental creation of disease-causing organisms. However, the revolution holds great promise for increasing food production in a world with an expanding population. C

Science and technology have changed the lives of millions of people. What people produce and even their jobs have changed. These changes have altered the economies of nations. Not only have nations become linked through communications networks but they are also linked in a global economic network, as you will see in Section 2.

C. Possible Answers Positive—more food available, reduced need for fertilizer; negative—accidental creation of disease-causing organisms

MAIN IDEA

Recognizing Effects

C What are some of the positive and negative effects of genetic engineering?

③ ASSESS

SECTION 1 ASSESSMENT

Have students complete questions 1–5 individually. Then divide the class into three groups and have each group do one of questions 6, 7, and 8.

Formal Assessment

- Section Quiz, p. 348

④ RETEACH

Have the class complete a two-column pro-and-con chart on the various applications of technology covered in this section.

In-Depth Resources: Unit 5

- Reteaching Activity, p. 93

SECTION 1 ASSESSMENT

TERMS & NAMES 1. For each term or name, write a sentence explaining its significance.
- International Space Station
- Internet
- genetic engineering
- cloning
- green revolution

USING YOUR NOTES

2. Which of the three developments do you think has had the greatest global effect? Why? (10.11)

Developments	Effects
Communications	
Health and Medicine	
Green Revolution	

MAIN IDEAS

3. How does the development of the International Space Station show that space exploration has become a cooperative endeavor? (10.11)
4. How has the development of the computer and Internet changed people work? (10.11)
5. What areas of medicine have benefited from scientific and technological developments? (10.11)

CRITICAL THINKING & WRITING

6. **MAKING INFERENCES** Why do you think that space exploration became an arena for cooperation between the Soviet Union and the United States? (10.11)
7. **HYPOTHESIZING** How do you think the Internet will affect the world of work in the future? (10.11)
8. **FORMING AND SUPPORTING OPINIONS** Is there a limit to how far cloning should go? Why or why not? (10.11)
9. **WRITING ACTIVITY** SCIENCE AND TECHNOLOGY Use encyclopedia yearbooks and science magazines to identify a technological advance made in the last year. Write a brief **report** on its impact on daily life. (Writing 2.3.b)

CONNECT TO TODAY CREATING A GRAPH

Conduct research into how people use the Internet. Use your findings to construct a **graph** showing the most common Internet activities. (Writing 2.3.d)

ANSWERS

1. International Space Station, p. 637 • Internet, p. 639 • genetic engineering, p. 639 • cloning, p. 639 • green revolution, p. 640
2. **Sample Answer:** Communications—Worldwide television, home offices and telecommuting; Health and Medicine—Improved diagnoses and surgery, genetic engineering; Green Revolution—Increased crop yields, decreased use of pesticides. Greatest global effect—Green Revolution, because food production affects everyone.
3. It is sponsored by 16 nations.
4. Many people now have home offices and telecommute by using a home computer connected to a network.
5. diagnoses, surgical procedures
6. **Possible Answer:** Both nations saw the advantages of sharing costs and information, pooling resources, and increasing goodwill.
7. **Possible Answer:** More telecommuting will decrease office size and reduce the need for business travel.
8. **Possible Answer:** Cloning humans for medical research or cloning plants to create biological weapons goes too far.
9. **Rubric** Reports should
   - describe the advance and its impact.
   - cite sources.

CONNECT TO TODAY

Rubric Graphs should
- indicate the most common Internet activities cited in surveys.
- be clearly labeled.

Global Economic Development

MAIN IDEA

ECONOMICS The economies of the world's nations are so tightly linked that the actions of one nation affect others.

WHY IT MATTERS NOW

Every individual is affected by the global economy and the environment.

TERMS & NAMES

- developed nation
- emerging nation
- global economy
- free trade
- ozone layer
- sustainable growth

SETTING THE STAGE At the end of World War II, much of Europe and Asia lay in ruins, with many of the major cities leveled by bombing. The devastation of the war was immense. However, with aid from the United States, the economies of Western European nations and Japan began expanding rapidly within a decade. Their growth continued for half a century, long after the United States ceased supplying aid. Advances in science and technology contributed significantly to this ongoing economic growth.

Technology Revolutionizes the World's Economy

In both Asia and the Western world, an explosion in scientific knowledge prompted great progress that quickly led to new industries. A prime example was plastics. In the 1950s, a process to develop plastics from petroleum at low pressures and low temperatures was perfected. Within a few years, industries made a host of products easily and cheaply out of plastics. Other technological advances have also changed industrial processes, lowered costs, and increased the quality or the speed of production. For example, robotic arms on automobile assembly lines made possible the fast and safe manufacture of high-quality cars.

Information Industries Change Economies Technological advances in manufacturing reduced the need for factory workers. But in other areas of the economy, new demands were emerging. Computerization and communications advances changed the processing of information. By the 1980s, people could transmit information quickly and cheaply. Information industries such as financial services, insurance, market research, and communications services boomed. Those industries depended on "knowledge workers," or people whose jobs focus on working with information.

The Effects of New Economies In the postwar era, the expansion of the world's economies led to an increase in the production of goods and services so that many nations benefited. The economic base of some nations shifted. Manufacturing jobs began to move out of **developed nations**, those nations with the industrialization, transportation, and business facilities for advanced production of manufactured goods. The jobs moved to **emerging nations**, those in the process of becoming industrialized. Emerging nations became prime locations for new manufacturing operations. Some economists believe these areas were chosen because

CALIFORNIA STANDARDS

10.10.1 Understand the challenges in the regions, including their geopolitical, cultural, military, and economic significance and the international relationships in which they are involved.

10.10.3 Discuss the important trends in the regions today and whether they appear to serve the cause of individual freedom and democracy.

10.11 Students analyze the integration of countries into the world economy and the information, technological, and communications revolutions (e.g., television, satellites, computers).

HI 1 Students show the connections, causal and otherwise, between particular historical events and larger social, economic, and political trends and developments.

HI 5 Students analyze human modifications of landscapes and examine the resulting environmental policy issues.

TAKING NOTES

Categorizing Use a web diagram to identify the forces that have shaped the global economy.

LESSON PLAN

OBJECTIVES

- Discuss the effects of technology on the world economy.
- Define the global economy.
- Describe the environmental impact of global development.

1 FOCUS & MOTIVATE

Ask students if they or their families have recently bought something made in another country. *(Possible Answers: clothing, shoes, consumer electronics, cars)*

2 INSTRUCT

Technology Revolutionizes the World's Economy

10.11

Critical Thinking

- How has the new economy affected the lives of factory workers in the United States? *(Jobs have decreased because of technology and movement of manufacturing to emerging nations.)*

CALIFORNIA RESOURCES

California Reading Toolkit, p. L91
California Modified Lesson Plans for English Learners, p. 177
California Daily Standards Practice Transparencies, TT83
California Standards Enrichment Workbook, pp. 107–108, 111–112, 113–114
California Standards Planner and Lesson Plans, p. L173
California Online Test Practice
California Test Generator CD-ROM
California Easy Planner CD-ROM
California eEdition CD-ROM

SECTION 2 PROGRAM RESOURCES

ALL STUDENTS

In-Depth Resources: Unit 5
- Guided Reading, p. 75
- Skillbuilder Practice: Analyzing Motives, p. 80
- Geography Application, p. 81

Formal Assessment
- Section Quiz, p. 349

ENGLISH LEARNERS

In-Depth Resources in Spanish
- Guided Reading, p. 156
- Skillbuilder Practice: Analyzing Motives, p. 159
- Geography Application, p. 160

Reading Study Guide (Spanish), p. 217
Reading Study Guide Audio CD (Spanish)

STRUGGLING READERS

In-Depth Resources: Unit 5
- Guided Reading, p. 75
- Skillbuilder Practice: Analyzing Motives, p. 80
- Geography Application, p. 81

Reading Study Guide, p. 217
Reading Study Guide Audio CD

GIFTED AND TALENTED STUDENTS

In-Depth Resources: Unit 5
- Primary Source: Recycling Symbol, p. 84
- Literature: "Paper", p. 87

Electronic Library of Primary Sources
- "Tackling the Menace of Space Junk"

INTEGRATED TECHNOLOGY

eEdition CD-ROM
Power Presentations CD-ROM
Geography Transparencies
- GT36 World Per Capita Income

World Art and Cultures Transparencies
Patterns of Interaction Video Series
- Trade Connects the World

Economic Globalization
10.10.1; 10.10.3; 10.11

Critical Thinking

- Why is improved technology important to multinational corporations? *(Possible Answer: Some technologies allow use of fewer or less-educated workers.)*
- Why might developed countries benefit most from globalization? *(Possible Answer: higher-paying jobs available; less manufacturing-related pollution)*

More About . . .

Multinational Corporations

The global economy includes about 37,000 multinational corporations, which control one-third of the world's wealth (excluding governmental assets). Because these corporations carry such weight in the global economy, some policymakers are pushing the World Trade Organization (WTO) to adopt guidelines to regulate them.

History from Visuals

Interpreting the Graph

Remind students that GDP stands for gross domestic product–the total value of all services and goods produced within a country's borders within a certain period.

Extension What two industries are represented by most of the multinationals shown? *(automotive, oil/petroleum)*

SKILLBUILDER Answers
1. **Comparing** Poland
2. **Clarifying** Mitsubishi and Mitsui

they had many eager workers whose skills fit manufacturing-type jobs. Also, these workers would work for less money than those in developed nations. On the other hand, information industries that required better-educated workers multiplied in the economies of developed nations. Thus the changes brought by technology then changed the workplace of both developed and emerging nations.

Economic Globalization

Economies in different parts of the world have been linked for centuries through trade and through national policies, such as colonialism. However, a true global economy did not begin to take shape until well into the second half of the 1800s. The **global economy** includes all the financial interactions—among people, businesses, and governments—that cross international borders. In recent decades, several factors hastened the process of globalization. Huge cargo ships could inexpensively carry enormous supplies of fuels and other goods from one part of the world to another. Telephone and computer linkages made global financial transactions quick and easy. In addition, multinational corporations developed around the world. Ⓐ

MAIN IDEA
Analyzing Causes
Ⓐ What elements helped to accelerate the process of globalization?
A. Answer better communication and transportation systems and the development of multinational companies

Multinational Corporations, 2002

Based on a comparison of revenues with GDP, some of the top multinationals have economies bigger than those of several countries.

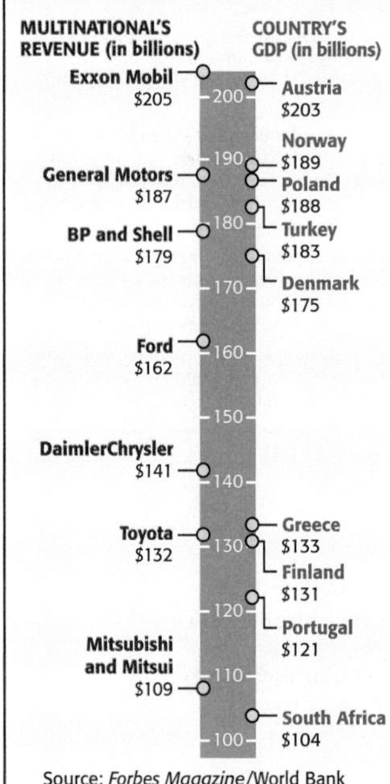

Source: *Forbes Magazine*/World Bank

SKILLBUILDER: Interpreting Graphs
1. **Comparing** *Which has the larger economy, Poland or Ford?*
2. **Clarifying** *Which multinationals have an economy greater than that of South Africa but smaller than that of Portugal?*

Multinational Corporations Companies that operate in a number of different countries are called multinational or transnational corporations. U.S. companies such as Exxon Mobil, General Motors, and Ford; European companies such as BP, DaimlerChrysler, and Royal Dutch/Shell; and Japanese companies such as Toyota, Mitsubishi, and Mitsui all became multinational giants.

All of these companies have established manufacturing plants, offices, or stores in many countries. For their manufacturing plants, they select spots where the raw materials or labor are cheapest. This enables them to produce components of their products on different continents. They ship the various components to another location to be assembled. This level of economic integration allows such companies to view the whole world as the market for their goods. Goods or services are distributed throughout the world as if there were no national boundaries.

Expanding Free Trade Opening up the world's markets to trade is a key aspect of globalization. In fact, a major goal of globalization is **free trade**, or the elimination of trade barriers, such as tariffs, among nations. This movement toward free trade is not new. As early as 1947, nations began discussing ways to open trade. The result of these discussions was the General Agreement on Tariffs and Trade (GATT). Over the years, several meetings among the nations that signed the GATT have brought about a general lowering of protective tariffs and considerable expansion of free trade. Since 1995, the World Trade Organization (WTO) has overseen the GATT to ensure that trade among nations flows as smoothly and freely as possible.

Vocabulary
tariff: a tax on goods imported from another country

Regional Trade Blocs A European organization set up in 1951 promoted tariff-free trade among member countries. This experiment in economic cooperation was so successful that six years later, a new organization, the European Economic Community (EEC), was formed. Over time,

SKILLBUILDER PRACTICE: ANALYZING MOTIVES

Analyzing Motives of Multinational Corporations

Class Time 20 minutes

Task Analyzing and discussing information

Purpose To understand the motives behind the establishment of multinational corporations

Instructions Explain that people and governments make decisions and take actions based on many factors, which may be complex and confusing even to the people involved. Among these factors are the motives, or reasons, for why people act as they do. Examining the needs, emotions, prior experiences, and goals of a person or government can help historians understand the motives that lie behind historical decisions.

Ask students to examine the text and the graph on this page and think about the reasons multinational corporations are established. Have them consider these questions:

1. What needs or goals might motivate corporations? *(Possible Answers: profit, longevity, desire to be successful)*
2. What do corporations gain from operating worldwide? *(Possible Answers: more flexibility, greater profits)*
3. What do consumers gain from buying products made by multinational corporations? *(Possible Answer: lower prices)*

For more help with this skill, see the Skillbuilder Handbook and the Skillbuilder Practice activity for this lesson, found in In-Depth Resources: Unit 5.

World Trading Blocs, 2003

INTERACTIVE

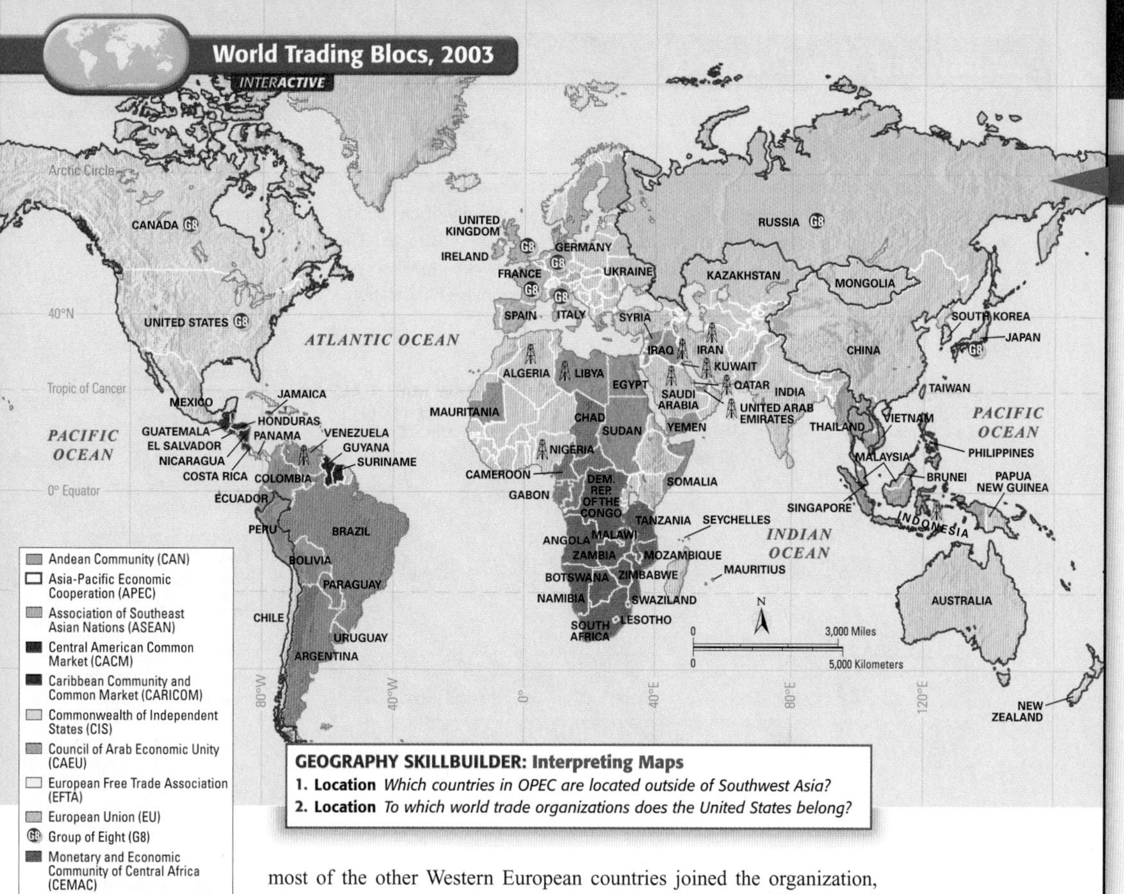

- Andean Community (CAN)
- Asia-Pacific Economic Cooperation (APEC)
- Association of Southeast Asian Nations (ASEAN)
- Central American Common Market (CACM)
- Caribbean Community and Common Market (CARICOM)
- Commonwealth of Independent States (CIS)
- Council of Arab Economic Unity (CAEU)
- European Free Trade Association (EFTA)
- European Union (EU)
- G8 Group of Eight (G8)
- Monetary and Economic Community of Central Africa (CEMAC)
- North American Free Trade Agreement (NAFTA)
- Organization of the Petroleum Exporting Countries (OPEC)
- Southern Common Market (MERCOSUR)
- Southern African Development Community (SADC)

GEOGRAPHY SKILLBUILDER: Interpreting Maps

1. **Location** *Which countries in OPEC are located outside of Southwest Asia?*
2. **Location** *To which world trade organizations does the United States belong?*

most of the other Western European countries joined the organization, which has been known as the European Union (EU) since 1992. Several of the former Communist nations of Eastern Europe also have applied to become EU members.

Through this economic unification, Europe began to exert a major force in the world economy. The economic success of the EU inspired countries in other regions to make trade agreements with each other. The North American Free Trade Agreement (NAFTA), put into effect in 1994, called for the gradual elimination of tariffs and trade restrictions among Canada, the United States, and Mexico. Organizations in Asia, Africa, Latin America, and the South Pacific have also created regional trade policies.

Globalization—For and Against In recent years, there has been considerable debate on the impact of globalization. Supporters suggest that open, competitive markets and the free flow of goods, services, technology, and investments benefit all nations. Globalization, they argue, has resulted in a dramatic increase in the standard of living across the world. Even some opponents agree that practically all nations have seen some benefit from globalization. However, they note that the developed nations have benefited the most. Other opponents charge that globalization has been a disaster for the poorest countries. They suggest that many poor countries are worse off today than they were in the past. They argue that investment practices, trade agreements, and aid packages must be designed to protect the interests of the poorest nations.

History from Visuals

Interpreting the Map

Which countries are members of the Group of Eight? *(United States, Canada, United Kingdom, Germany, France, Italy, Russia, Japan)*

Extension Ask students to name the trading groups located partly or entirely in Africa. *(OPEC, CAEU, CEMAC, SADC)*

SKILLBUILDER Answers

1. **Location** Venezuela, Nigeria, Algeria, Libya, Indonesia
2. **Location** NAFTA, Group of Eight, APEC

INTEGRATED TECHNOLOGY

Interactive An interactive version of this map is available on the eEdition. Students can view members of each trading group separately or in successive combinations.

More About . . .

NAFTA

The assumptions underlying the formation of NAFTA are the same as those underlying the European Union: lowering or eliminating tariffs and other trade barriers should cause regional trade and economic growth to increase significantly. Some U.S. and Canadian citizens opposed the agreement, fearing that their countries would lose jobs to Mexico, where wages tend to be lower.

DIFFERENTIATING INSTRUCTION: GIFTED AND TALENTED STUDENTS

Evaluating NAFTA

Class Time 45 minutes

Task Researching and debating an issue

Purpose To help students understand the North American economy; to improve persuasive-speaking skills

Instructions NAFTA has been controversial since its enactment in 1994. Proponents touted its advantages for the region and for the U.S. economy. Critics warned of dire consequences in the areas of balance of trade, labor, and the environment. Ask students to research what current thoughts are about the success or failure of the agreement. After preliminary research on the Internet or in newspapers or magazines, have each student choose a particular aspect to follow up in depth. Possible topics to research include:

- how the balance of trade has changed in the region
- how NAFTA has affected the labor market
- what impact NAFTA has had on the environment
- who the key proponents and opponents are
- how current reality compares to predictions

Make sure students also check the background of their sources.

When students have completed their research, have them present a panel discussion to the class.

Analyzing Key Concepts

OBJECTIVES

- Explain globalization.
- Summarize opposing points of view on globalization.

INSTRUCT

Introduce globalization as a key phenomenon of world history since the 1990s. Point out that the global corporation shown has manufacturing and production centers located in a number of developed countries and produces a variety of products sold throughout the world. Have students discuss the ways globalization has affected the goods and services they purchase. Ask students to think about the pros and cons of globalization.

Patterns of Interaction Video Series
- Trade Connects the World

Geography Transparencies
- GT36 World Per Capita Income

More About . . .

The World Trade Organization

The Internet and use of e-mail had a major impact on the organizing of large-scale protests against the World Trade Organization (WTO) at its 1999 conference in Seattle, Washington. More than 50,000 people voiced their concerns about the impact of globalization and multinational corporations on the environment and labor markets. Critics of the organization come from both developed and developing countries.

> Analyzing Key Concepts

Globalization

CALIFORNIA STANDARDS 10.11, CST 2

Globalization can be described in broad terms as a process that makes something worldwide in its reach or operation. Currently, globalization is most often used in reference to the spread and diffusion of economic or cultural influences. The graphics below focus on economic globalization. The first shows a global corporation. The second lists some arguments for and against economic globalization.

Global Corporation

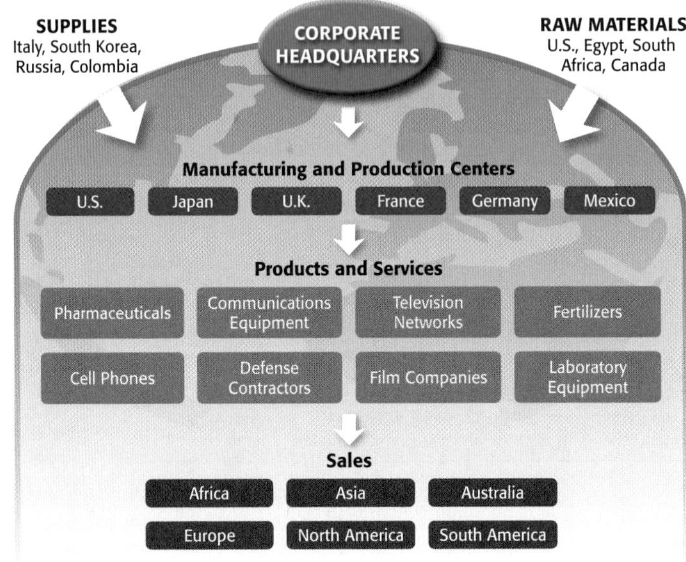

Arguments for and Against Economic Globalization

For	Against
• promotes peace through trade	• creates conflict because of an inherently unfair system
• raises the standard of living around the world	• benefits developed nations disproportionately
• creates jobs in emerging countries	• takes jobs from high-paid laborers in developed countries
• promotes investment in less developed countries	• benefits those who already have money
• creates a sense of world community	• erodes local cultures

INTEGRATED TECHNOLOGY

RESEARCH LINKS For more on globalization, go to **classzone.com**

> DATA FILE

INTERNATIONAL REGULATION

Many countries have joined international organizations to help regulate and stimulate the global economy. Such groups face the same criticisms against globalization in general.

World Trade Organization (WTO)
- Stated goal: "Help trade flow smoothly, freely, fairly, and predictably"
- 146 member nations; around 30 nations negotiating for admission (193 countries in the world)
- WTO members account for over 97 percent of world trade.

International Monetary Fund (IMF)
- Stated goal: "Promote international monetary cooperation; to foster economic growth and high levels of employment; and to provide temporary financial assistance to countries"
- 184 member countries
- In March 2003, IMF total resources were around $300 billion.

The World Bank Group
- Stated goal: "A world free of poverty"
- 184 member countries
- In 2002, this group provided $19.5 billion to emerging countries.

Connect *to* Today

1. **Making Inferences** How are money and culture related to each other when discussing globalization?
See Skillbuilder Handbook, page R10.
2. **Making Predictions** Will globalization continue or will another process replace it? Why or why not?

CONNECT TO TODAY: ANSWERS

1. Making Inferences

Possible Answer: Wealthy, developed countries that are able to play a larger role in the global economy are more likely to spread their culture around the world.

2. Making Predictions

In support of globalization continuing, students might cite the growing number of countries involved in the WTO, IMF, and World Bank and the lack of limitations on the power of multinational corporations. Other students might say that there are growing grassroots movements dedicated to encouraging the strengthening of local cultures and economies.

Impact of Global Development

The development of the global economy has had a notable impact on the use of energy and other resources. Worldwide demand for these resources has led to both political and environmental problems.

Political Impacts Manufacturing requires the processing of raw materials. Trade requires the transport of finished goods. These activities, essential for development, require the use of much energy. For the past 50 years, one of the main sources of energy used by developed and emerging nations has been oil. For nations with little of this resource available in their own land, disruption of the distribution of oil causes economic and political problems.

On the other hand, nations possessing oil reserves have the power to affect economic and political situations in countries all over the world. For example, in the 1970s the Organization of Petroleum Exporting Countries (OPEC) declared an oil embargo—a restriction of trade. This contributed to a significant economic decline in many developed nations during that decade.

In 1990, Iraq invaded Kuwait and seized the Kuwaiti oil fields. Fears began to mount that Iraq would also invade Saudi Arabia, another major source of oil. This would have put most of the world's petroleum supplies under Iraqi control. Economic sanctions imposed by the UN failed to persuade Iraq to withdraw from Kuwait. Then, in early 1991, a coalition of some 39 nations declared war on Iraq. After several weeks of fighting, the Iraqis left Kuwait and accepted a cease-fire. This Persian Gulf War showed the extent to which the economies of nations are globally linked.

Environmental Impacts Economic development has had a major impact on the environment. The burning of coal and oil as an energy source releases carbon dioxide into the atmosphere, causing health-damaging air pollution and acid rain. Some scientists believe that the buildup of carbon dioxide in the atmosphere also has contributed to global warming.

The release of chemicals called chlorofluorocarbons (CFCs), used in refrigerators, air conditioners, and manufacturing processes, has destroyed ozone in Earth's upper atmosphere. The **ozone layer** is our main protection against the Sun's damaging ultraviolet rays. With the increase in ultraviolet radiation reaching Earth's surface, the incidence of skin cancer continues to rise in many parts of the world. Increased ultraviolet radiation also may result in damage to populations of plants and plankton at the bases of the food chains, which sustain all life on Earth.

▼ During the 1991 Persian Gulf War, the Iraqis set hundreds of Kuwaiti oil wells ablaze. Smoke from these fires clouded the skies more than 250 miles away.

645

Impact of Global Development
10.10.1; 10.10.3

Critical Thinking

- What was the impact of the 1991 Persian Gulf War on the environment? *(Possible Answer: Burning oil fields polluted the atmosphere.)*
- How does United States' dependence on foreign oil make its economy vulnerable? *(Possible Answer: Oil is needed to keep offices, factories, and transportation systems running. The price of oil affects the price of other goods.)*

In-Depth Resources: Unit 5

- Geography Application: Deforestation in Brazil, p. 81
- Primary Source: Recycling Symbol, p. 84

Electronic Library of Primary Sources

- "Tackling the Menace of Space Junk"

More About . . .

The 1991 Persian Gulf War

The first Gulf War showed how nations depend on one another. Southwest Asia contains 65 percent of all known oil resources. When Iraq threatened to cut off supplies of oil from the region, nations around the world worked together to stop that threat. The war resulted in great environmental damage. More than 465 million gallons of oil were dumped into the Persian Gulf.

INTEGRATED TECHNOLOGY

An interactive feature on the 1991 Persian Gulf War is on the eEdition.

DIFFERENTIATING INSTRUCTION: STRUGGLING READERS

Evaluating the Effects of Oil

Class Time 20 minutes

Task Creating a concept web

Purpose To improve understanding of the text

Instructions Ask students to reread the text on this page, looking for references to oil and petroleum. Then display Critical Thinking Transparency CT78. As a class, create a concept web that shows the effects oil has on the economy and the environment. A partly completed web is at right.

Oil affects the economy and the environment.

- Source of energy
- Not all countries have oil.
- OPEC restricted oil supply in 1970s
- Persian Gulf War
- Causes pollution
- May affect global warming

History from Visuals

Interpreting the Photographs

Point out the key at the bottom of the image that shows the colors used to indicate various levels of ozone. Ask students what general conclusion they can draw by comparing the two images. *(Possible Answer: There was much less ozone in the Southern Hemisphere in 2000.)* Explain that scientists have discovered a hole in the ozone layer in an area above the continent of Antarctica. Every spring, ozone in this location decreases. The hole gets bigger each year and has dropped to 33 percent of the 1975 amount.

Extension Ask students to use a dictionary to find out how far from the earth the ozone layer is located. *(6–30 miles)*

Ozone Levels

A large area of the ozone layer has become much thinner in recent years.

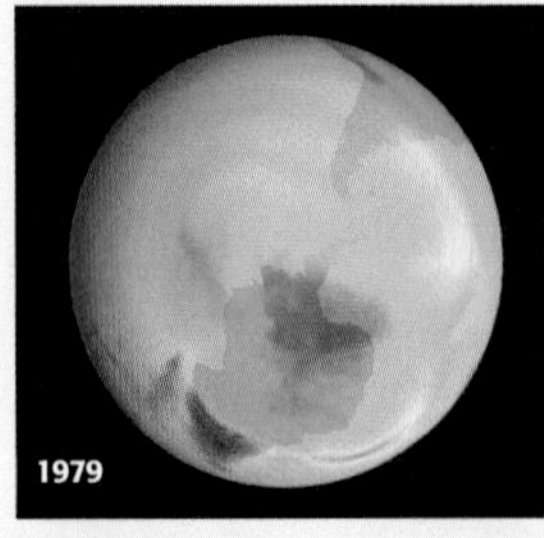

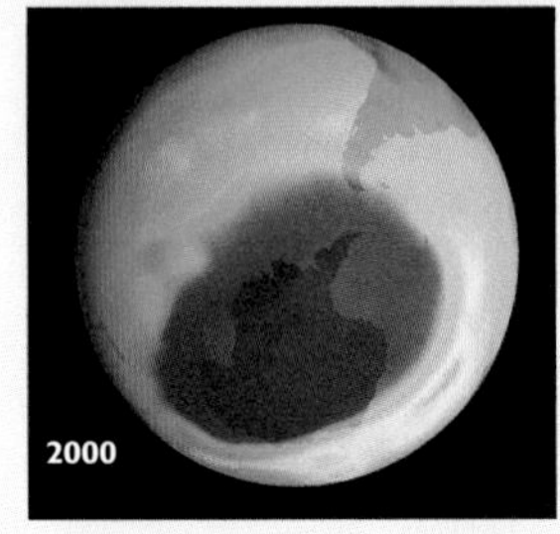

less ozone more ozone

Economic development has also led to problems with the land. Large-scale soil erosion is a worldwide problem due to damaging farming techniques. The habitat destruction that comes from land development has also led to shrinking numbers of wildlife around the world. At present, the extinction rate of plants and animals is about a thousand times greater than it would naturally be, and appears to be increasing. This high extinction rate means that certain species can no longer serve as an economic resource. The resulting loss of wildlife could endanger complex and life-sustaining processes that keep Earth in balance.

"Sustainable Growth" Working together, economists and scientists are looking for ways to reduce the negative effect that development has on the environment. Their goal is to manage development so that growth can occur, but without destroying air, water, and land resources. The concept is sometimes called "green growth." Many people feel that the negative impact of economic growth on the environment will not be completely removed.

But "greener growth," also known as **sustainable growth**, is possible. This involves two goals: meeting current economic needs, while ensuring the preservation of the environment and the conservation of resources for future generations. Making such plans and putting them into practice have proved to be difficult. But many scientists believe that meeting both goals is essential for the health of the planet in the future. Because the economies of nations are tied to their political climates, such development plans will depend on the efforts of nations in both economic and political areas. B

B. Answer Sustainable growth involves meeting current economic needs without endangering the environment or depleting resources.

MAIN IDEA
Clarifying
B What is meant by the term *sustainable growth*?

SECTION 2 ASSESSMENT

TERMS & NAMES 1. For each term or name, write a sentence explaining its significance.
• developed nation • emerging nation • global economy • free trade • ozone layer • sustainable growth

USING YOUR NOTES

2. Which of these forces do you think has had the greatest impact on the development of a global economy? (10.11)

MAIN IDEAS

3. Why are "knowledge workers" becoming more important in the developed nations? (10.10.3)
4. What impact did the economic success of the EU have on other regions of the world? (10.10.3)
5. How has global economic development affected the environment? (10.10.1)

CRITICAL THINKING & WRITING

6. **RECOGNIZING EFFECTS** In what ways has technology changed the workplace of people across the world? (10.11)
7. **ANALYZING MOTIVES** Why might some nations favor imposing tariffs on the imports of certain products? (10.10.1)
8. **SUPPORTING OPINIONS** Do you think that sustainable growth is possible? Why or why not? (10.10.1)
9. **WRITING ACTIVITY** ECONOMICS Make a survey of the labels on class members' clothing and shoes. List the countries in which these items were produced. Write a short **explanation** of how the list illustrates the global economy. (Writing 2.3.a)

CONNECT TO TODAY CREATING A POSTER

Recycling is an important aspect of sustainable growth. Create a **poster** encouraging local businesses to recycle cans, paper products, and plastics. (Writing 2.4.c)

3 ASSESS

SECTION 2 ASSESSMENT

Have students work as a class to complete a concept web for question 2 on the chalkboard.

Formal Assessment
• Section Quiz, p. 349

4 RETEACH

Use the map on page 643 and the graphics on page 644 to review the main ideas in the section.

In-Depth Resources: Unit 5
• Reteaching Activity, p. 94

ANSWERS

1. developed nation, p. 641 • emerging nation, p. 641 • global economy, p. 642 • free trade, p. 642 • ozone layer, p. 645 • sustainable growth, p. 646
2. **Sample Answer:** Advances in communication and transportation; development of multinational corporations; expanded free trade; regional trading agreements. Greatest impact—Free trade, because it has removed many economic barriers.
3. number of information industries has increased in developed nations
4. It inspired other countries to make regional trade agreements.
5. pollution, damage to the ozone layer, deterioration of farmland
6. **Possible Answer:** Developed nations—More people work in information industries, some people telecommute; Emerging nations—More people work in manufacturing.
7. to protect their own industries from competing products
8. **Possible Answers:** Yes—Industrial practices can be adjusted to limit adverse impact on environment. No—The negative impact of economic growth can never be completely removed.
9. **Rubric** Explanations should
• note the array of countries on the list.
• point out that recognizable American brand names may be produced elsewhere.

CONNECT TO TODAY

Rubric Posters should
• illustrate the goal—recycling.
• explain why businesses should support that goal.

INTERACTIVE

Economics and the Environment

Economists, politicians, and environmentalists came up with the concept of "sustainable growth"—both economic development and environmental protection are considered when producing a development plan for a nation. Some people see the relationship between economics and the environment as strained and getting worse. Others view policies protecting the environment as harmful to economies and ultimately harmful to the environment. The selections below examine these different perspectives.

CALIFORNIA STANDARDS

10.10.1 Understand the challenges in the regions, including their geopolitical, cultural, military, and economic significance and the international relationships in which they are involved.

A PRIMARY SOURCE

Lester R. Brown

Lester R. Brown is president of the Earth Policy Institute, which researches how to attain an environmentally sustainable economy and assesses current economic programs around the world.

Most decisions taken in economic policy are made by economic advisors. You can see this in the World Bank's annual development reports where they see the environment as a sub-sector of the economy. However, if you look at it as a natural scientist or ecologist, you have to conclude that the economy is a subset of the earth's ecosystem. . . .

Many of the problems that we face are the result of the incompatibility of the economy with the ecosystem. The relationship between the global economy, which has expanded sixfold over the last half century, and the earth's ecosystem is a very stressed one. The manifestations of this stress are collapsing fisheries, falling water tables, shrinking forests, expanding deserts, rising carbon dioxide levels, rising temperatures, melting ice, dying coral reefs, and so forth. Not only is this a stressed relationship but a deteriorating one.

B PRIMARY SOURCE

The Liberty Institute

The Liberty Institute is based in India and seeks to strengthen individual rights, rule of law, limited government, and free markets.

The market is the natural ally of the environment. Environmental resources, like other economic resources can be most efficiently allocated if these are brought under the discipline of the marketplace. It is ironic . . . [that] rather than creating a market for environmental resources, new restrictions are being imposed on the economy in the name of protecting the environment.

Environmental quality is like a value-added product that becomes economically affordable and technologically viable with economic growth. It is no paradox therefore that the environment is much cleaner and safer in industrially developed countries that adopted a more market-friendly approach. . . .

The market allows the consumer to register his price preference for a particular quality of product, including environmental quality.

C POLITICAL CARTOON

Chris Madden

Educating through humor, cartoonist Chris Madden illustrates the close connection between the environment and economics. A "ship of fools" is a metaphor for human weakness.

The ship of fools and the rocks of short-term economic planning

Document-Based QUESTIONS

1. Compare Sources A and B. Which perspective do you support? Why?
2. In your own words, describe the meaning of the cartoon in Source C.
3. Research an environmental issue facing your community and how economics is a part of the debate. Present your findings to the class.

647

Different Perspectives

OBJECTIVE

- Compare different points of view on the question of sustainable development.

INSTRUCT

Ask students to consider whether sustainable development is possible. Suggest that they find articles or editorials that address these questions:

- What is the best way to help the economies of developing nations grow?
- How much does a nation's economy need to grow for its people to prosper?
- Who has the right to a nation's resources?
- Who is responsible for protecting and repairing damage to the environment?

Make sure students understand that the search for answers to these complex questions shapes the continuing debate on this topic.

classzone.com

- NetExplorations: The Environment

INTEGRATED TECHNOLOGY

Interactive This feature is available in an expanded interactive format on the eEdition. An enlarged version of the political cartoon is available, as are links to more information about the sources.

Inclusion Tip

Students who have difficulty reading primary sources may benefit from the audio versions, available on the eEdition.

DOCUMENT-BASED QUESTIONS: ANSWERS

1. *Possible Answers:* A, because natural resources are difficult or impossible to restore once they have been damaged; B, because consumers can demand that manufacturers produce environmentally friendly products.
2. The cartoonist is making the point that the blissful ignorance many people enjoy with regard to the environment will come to a sudden halt when poor economic planning leads to a deteriorating environment.
3. Answers will vary based on research, but encourage students to use newspapers, magazines, and interviews with local officials or environmental groups.

LESSON PLAN

OBJECTIVES

- Identify ways that nations deal with issues of war and peace.
- Give examples of human rights issues and world health issues.
- Explain the increase in migration and discuss its worldwide effects.

1 FOCUS & MOTIVATE

Ask students what kind of world events might threaten their personal security. *(Possible Answers: violence, including terrorism or war; ethnic, religious, or gender prejudice; infectious disease)*

2 INSTRUCT

Issues of War and Peace

10.9.1; 10.9.8

Critical Thinking

- Why might UN peacekeepers be more effective than one nation's forces? *(Possible Answer: UN forces are from different countries, so they are less likely to take sides.)*

CALIFORNIA RESOURCES
California Reading Toolkit, p. L92
California Modified Lesson Plans for English Learners, p. 179
California Daily Standards Practice Transparencies, TT84
California Standards Enrichment Workbook, pp. 91–92, 105–106, 109–110, 111–112, 113–114
California Standards Planner and Lesson Plans, p. L175
California Online Test Practice
California Test Generator CD-ROM
California Easy Planner CD-ROM
California eEdition CD-ROM

Integrated circuit

3

International Space Station

Global Security Issues

MAIN IDEA

POWER AND AUTHORITY Since 1945, nations have used collective security efforts to solve problems.

WHY IT MATTERS NOW

Personal security of the people of the world is tied to security within and between nations.

TERMS & NAMES

- proliferation
- Universal Declaration of Human Rights
- political dissent
- gender inequality
- AIDS
- refugee

CALIFORNIA STANDARDS

10.9.1 Compare the economic and military power shifts caused by the war, including the Yalta Pact, the development of nuclear weapons, Soviet control over Eastern European nations, and the economic recoveries of Germany and Japan.

10.9.8 Discuss the establishment and work of the United Nations and the purposes and functions of the Warsaw Pact, SEATO, NATO, and the Organization of American States.

10.10.2 Describe the recent history of the regions, including political divisions and systems, key leaders, religious issues, natural features, resources, and population patterns.

10.10.3 Discuss the important trends in the regions today and whether they appear to serve the cause of individual freedom and democracy.

10.11 Students analyze the integration of countries into the world economy and the information, technological, and communications revolutions (e.g., television, satellites, computers).

TAKING NOTES

Categorizing Use a chart to list collective methods employed by the world's nations to increase global security.

Method	Examples
Form military alliances	NATO, SEATO, Warsaw Pact

SETTING THE STAGE World War II was one of history's most devastating conflicts. More than 55 million people died as a result of bombings, the Holocaust, combat, starvation, and disease. Near the end of the war, one of humankind's most destructive weapons, the atomic bomb, killed more than 100,000 people in Hiroshima and Nagasaki in a matter of minutes. Perhaps because of these horrors, world leaders look for ways to make the earth a safer, more secure place to live.

Issues of War and Peace

In the years after the end of World War II, the Cold War created new divisions and tensions among the world's nations. This uneasy situation potentially threatened the economic, environmental, and personal security of people across the world. So, nations began to work together to pursue collective security.

Nations Unite and Take Action Many nations consider that having a strong military is important to their security. After World War II, nations banded together to create military alliances. They formed the North Atlantic Treaty Organization (NATO), the Southeast Asia Treaty Organization (SEATO), the Warsaw Pact, and others. The member nations of each of these alliances generally pledged military aid for their common defense.

In addition to military alliances to increase their security, world leaders also took steps to reduce the threat of war. The United Nations (UN) works in a variety of ways toward increasing collective global security.

Peacekeeping Activities One of the major aims of the UN is to promote world peace. The UN provides a public forum, private meeting places, and skilled mediators to help nations try to resolve conflicts at any stage of their development. At the invitation of the warring parties, the UN also provides peacekeeping forces. These forces are made up of soldiers from different nations. They work to carry out peace agreements, monitor cease-fires, or put an end to fighting to allow peace negotiations to go forward.

As of the end of 2002, the UN had close to 40,000 soldiers and police in 13 peacekeeping forces around the world. Some forces, such as those in India and Pakistan, have been in place for decades. Others, such as those in East Timor, achieved their goals in only a few months.

SECTION 3 PROGRAM RESOURCES

ALL STUDENTS

In-Depth Resources: Unit 5
- Guided Reading, p. 76
- History Makers: Kofi Annan, p. 91

Formal Assessment
- Section Quiz, p. 350

ENGLISH LEARNERS

In-Depth Resources in Spanish
- Guided Reading, p. 157

Reading Study Guide (Spanish), p. 219
Reading Study Guide Audio CD (Spanish)

STRUGGLING READERS

In-Depth Resources: Unit 5
- Guided Reading, p. 76
- Building Vocabulary, p. 79
- Reteaching Activity, p. 95

Reading Study Guide, p. 219
Reading Study Guide Audio CD

GIFTED AND TALENTED STUDENTS

In-Depth Resources: Unit 5
- Primary Source: from The Universal Declaration of Human Rights, p. 85

INTEGRATED TECHNOLOGY

eEdition CD-ROM
Power Presentations CD-ROM
Critical Thinking Transparencies
- CT36 Patterns of Refugee Movement

classzone.com

Weapons of Mass Destruction Nations have not only worked to prevent and contain conflicts, they also have forged treaties to limit the manufacturing, testing, and trade of weapons. The weapons of most concern are those that cause mass destruction. These include nuclear, chemical, and biological weapons that can kill thousands, even millions of people.

▲ In central Baghdad, a U.S. Marine watches as a statue of Saddam Hussein is pulled down.

In 1968, many nations signed a Nuclear Non-Proliferation Treaty to help prevent the **proliferation**, or spread, of nuclear weapons to other nations. In the 1970s, the United States and the Soviet Union signed the Strategic Arms Limitation Treaties. In the 1980s, both countries talked about deactivating some of their nuclear weapons. Many nations also signed treaties promising not to produce biological or chemical weapons.

Disarming Iraq Other nations, however, have tried to develop weapons of mass destruction. Iraq, for example, used chemical weapons in conflicts during the 1980s. Many people suspected that the Iraqi leader, Saddam Hussein, had plans to develop biological and nuclear weapons too. As part of the cease-fire arrangements in the Persian Gulf War, Iraq agreed to destroy its weapons of mass destruction. UN inspectors were sent to monitor this disarmament process. However, in 1998, the Iraqis ordered the inspectors to leave.

In 2002, Saddam Hussein again was suspected of developing weapons of mass destruction. The UN Security Council issued a resolution threatening Iraq with "severe consequences" unless weapons inspectors were allowed to return. Iraq complied, but when some UN members suspected that the Iraqis were not fully cooperating, a coalition led by the United States and Great Britain sent troops to disarm Iraq by force in March 2003. Saddam Hussein's government fell after four weeks of fighting. Hussein was later captured December 13, 2003. By November 2004, no weapons of mass destruction had been found.

Ethnic and Religious Conflicts Conflicts among people of different racial, national, religious, linguistic, or cultural groups are not new. The roots of some struggles are decades—even centuries—old. Such conflicts include those between Protestants and Catholics in Ireland, between Palestinians and Israelis in the Middle East, and among Serbs, Bosnians, and Croats in the former Yugoslavia.

Ethnic and religious conflicts have often led to terrible violence. People caught in these conflicts sometimes suffered torture, or massacres of their whole towns or villages. The Kurds of southwest Asia have been the victims of such violence. For decades, Kurds have wanted their own separate country. But their traditional lands cross the borders of three nations—Turkey, Iran, and Iraq. In the past, the Turks responded to Kurdish nationalism by forbidding Kurds to speak their native language. The Iranians also persecuted the Kurds, attacking them over religious issues. In the late 1980s, the Iraqis dropped poison gas on the Kurds, killing 5,000. Several international organizations, including the UN, are working to end the human rights abuses inflicted upon the Kurds.

More About . . .

Nuclear Weapons

The United States, Russia, Great Britain, France, China, Pakistan, and India have nuclear weapons, and it is likely that Israel does. North Korea, Iran, and some countries of the former Soviet Union may also have the ability to produce nuclear weapons.

Tip for Gifted and Talented Students

The word *proliferation* comes from Latin meaning "bearing offspring."

More About . . .

The Kurds

The Kurds, a nomadic people, follow their herds through the mountains and high plateaus of eastern Turkey, western Iran, and northern Iraq. Recently, many have begun to settle in urban areas, where they have adopted the customs and occupations of non-Kurds.

DIFFERENTIATING INSTRUCTION: GIFTED AND TALENTED STUDENTS

Understanding Ethnic Conflicts

Class Time 45 minutes

Task Researching and creating a short documentary

Purpose To deepen students' understanding of the effect of ethnic conflicts on children and teenagers

Instructions Ask students to choose an example of ethnic conflict to research. Encourage them to choose different countries in order to present a diversity of experiences. Have students use the Internet, books, newspapers, or magazines to research how the particular ethnic conflict affects families, especially the lives of children and teenagers. Ask them to include personal stories whenever possible. A pair of students might work together to present stories from both sides–for example, a story of Israeli and Palestinian children. Stories might involve young people as victims, combatants, or peacemakers.

Have students prepare short documentaries to share the stories they have researched with the class. Use the documentaries as the basis for a class discussion. Ask the class to notice similarities and differences among the experiences of people in different conflicts.

Human Rights Issues
10.9.8; 10.10.2; 10.10.3

Critical Thinking

- Why does publicizing human rights violations lead to reform? *(Possible Answers: The force of public opinion can make governments change. The worst violations often occur in secret.)*
- Why is political dissent important in ending human rights abuses? *(Possible Answer: People must be free to criticize the government in order to gain support for change.)*

In-Depth Resources: Unit 5

- Primary Source: from the Universal Declaration of Human Rights, p. 85

History Makers

Mother Teresa

Ask students what caused Mother Teresa to establish the Order of the Missionaries of Charity. *(her vow to help the poor of India)* This order was eventually recognized as under the jurisdiction of Rome. Members take vows of poverty, chastity, obedience, and service to the poor. Suggest that students do further research on the activities of the order today.

Human Rights Issues

In 1948, the UN issued the **Universal Declaration of Human Rights**, which set human rights standards for all nations. It stated that "All human beings are born free and equal in dignity and rights. . . . Everyone has the right to life, liberty, and security of person." The declaration further listed specific rights that all human beings should have. Later, in the Helsinki Accords of 1975, the UN addressed the issues of freedom of movement and freedom to publish and exchange information.

Both the declaration and the accords are nonbinding. However, the sentiments in these documents inspired many people around the world. They made a commitment to ensuring that basic human rights are respected. The UN and other international agencies, such as Amnesty International, identify and publicize human rights violations. They also encourage people to work toward a world in which liberty and justice are guaranteed for all.

Vocabulary
A *nonbinding* agreement means that a nation does not suffer a penalty if it does not meet the terms of the declaration.

Continuing Rights Violations Despite the best efforts of various human rights organizations, protecting human rights remains an uphill battle. Serious violations of fundamental rights continue to occur around the world.

One type of violation occurs when governments try to stamp out **political dissent**, or the difference of opinion over political issues. In many countries around the world, from Cuba to Iran to Myanmar, individuals and groups have been persecuted for holding political views that differ from those of the people in power. In some countries, ethnic or racial hatreds lead to human rights abuses. In Rwanda, for example, fighting between Hutus and Tutsis—the two main ethnic groups—led to horrendous rights violations. In 1994, Hutus massacred about 500,000 Tutsis in one of the worst cases of genocide. (A)

MAIN IDEA
Analyzing Issues
(A) What responsibilities do nations have for protecting human rights in other countries?
A. Possible Answers Nations should do all they can to end human rights violations wherever they take place.

History Makers

Mother Teresa 1910–1997

Mother Teresa was one of the great champions of human rights for all people. Born Agnes Gonxha Bojaxhiu in what today is Macedonia, Mother Teresa joined a convent in Ireland at the age of 18. A short time later, she headed to India to teach at a girls' school. Over time, she noticed many sick and homeless people in the streets. She soon vowed to devote her life to helping India's poor.

In 1948, she established the Order of the Missionaries of Charity in Calcutta, which committed itself to serving the sick, needy, and unfortunate. In recognition of her commitment to the downtrodden, Mother Teresa received the Nobel Peace Prize in 1979.

INTEGRATED TECHNOLOGY
RESEARCH LINKS For more on Mother Teresa, go to **classzone.com**

Women's Status Improves In the past, when women in Western nations entered the work force, they often faced discrimination in employment and salary. In non-Western countries, many women not only faced discrimination in jobs, they were denied access to education. In regions torn by war or ethnic conflict, they were often victims of violence and abuse. As women suffered, so too did their family members, especially children.

However, in the 1970s, a heightened awareness of human rights encouraged women in many countries to work to improve their lives. They pushed for new laws and government policies that gave them greater equality. In 1975, the UN held the first of several international conferences on women's status in the world. The fourth conference was held in Beijing, China, in 1995. It addressed such issues as preventing violence against women and empowering women to take leadership roles in politics and in business.

In 2000, the UN reviewed the status of women. Its report, titled *Progress of the World's Women 2000,* found that women had made notable gains during the 1990s, especially in the areas of education and work. Even so, the report concluded that **gender inequality**—the difference between men and women in terms of wealth and status—still very much existed.

DIFFERENTIATING INSTRUCTION: STRUGGLING READERS

Summarizing Progress for Women

Class Time 30 minutes

Task Reading, creating a concept web, and writing a summary

Purpose To help students understand the causes that led to an improvement in the status of women

Instructions Pair a struggling reader with a more proficient reader. Suggest that students make a concept web similar to Critical Thinking Transparency CT78 to help them understand in what ways the status of women improved between 1970 and 2000.

Have students read the paragraphs on this page about women's status. Suggest that they summarize the information in each paragraph and enter it in their web. They should include information on the challenges that women have faced in different parts of the world. Have students share their web diagrams so they learn different ways of organizing information.

Students who need more help may complete the Reading Study Guide activity for this section.

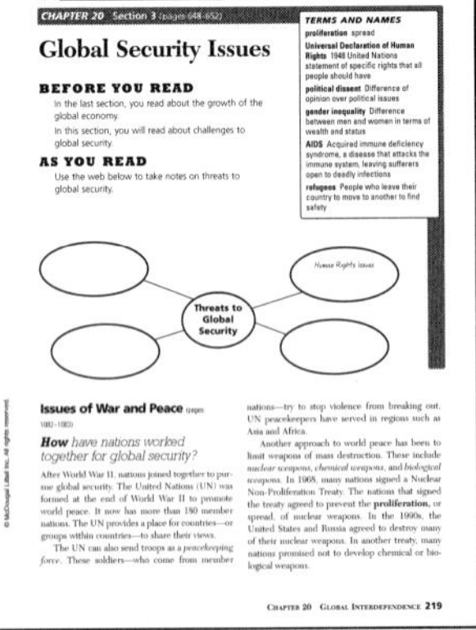

Name ______ Date ______

CHAPTER 20 Section 3 (pages 648–652)

Global Security Issues

BEFORE YOU READ
In the last section, you read about the growth of the global economy.
In this section, you will read about challenges to global security.

AS YOU READ
Use the web below to take notes on threats to global security.

TERMS AND NAMES
proliferation spread
Universal Declaration of Human Rights 1948 United Nations statement of specific rights that all people should have
political dissent Difference of opinion over political issues
gender inequality Difference between men and women in terms of wealth and status
AIDS Acquired immune deficiency syndrome, a disease that attacks the immune system, leaving sufferers open to deadly infections
refugees People who leave their country to move to another to find safety

Issues of War and Peace (pages 1082–1083)

How have nations worked together for global security?

After World War II, nations joined together to pursue global security. The United Nations (UN) was formed at the end of World War II to promote world peace. It now has more than 180 member nations. The UN provides a place for countries—or groups within countries—to share their views.

The UN can also send troops as a *peacekeeping force*. These soldiers—who come from member nations—try to stop violence from breaking out. UN peacekeepers have served in regions such as Asia and Africa.

Another approach to world peace has been to limit weapons of mass destruction. These include *nuclear weapons, chemical weapons,* and *biological weapons*. In 1968, many nations signed a Nuclear Non-Proliferation Treaty. The nations that signed the treaty agreed to prevent the **proliferation**, or spread, of nuclear weapons. In the 1990s, the United States and Russia agreed to destroy many of their nuclear weapons. In another treaty, many nations promised not to develop chemical or biological weapons.

CHAPTER 20 GLOBAL INTERDEPENDENCE 219

Reading Study Guide

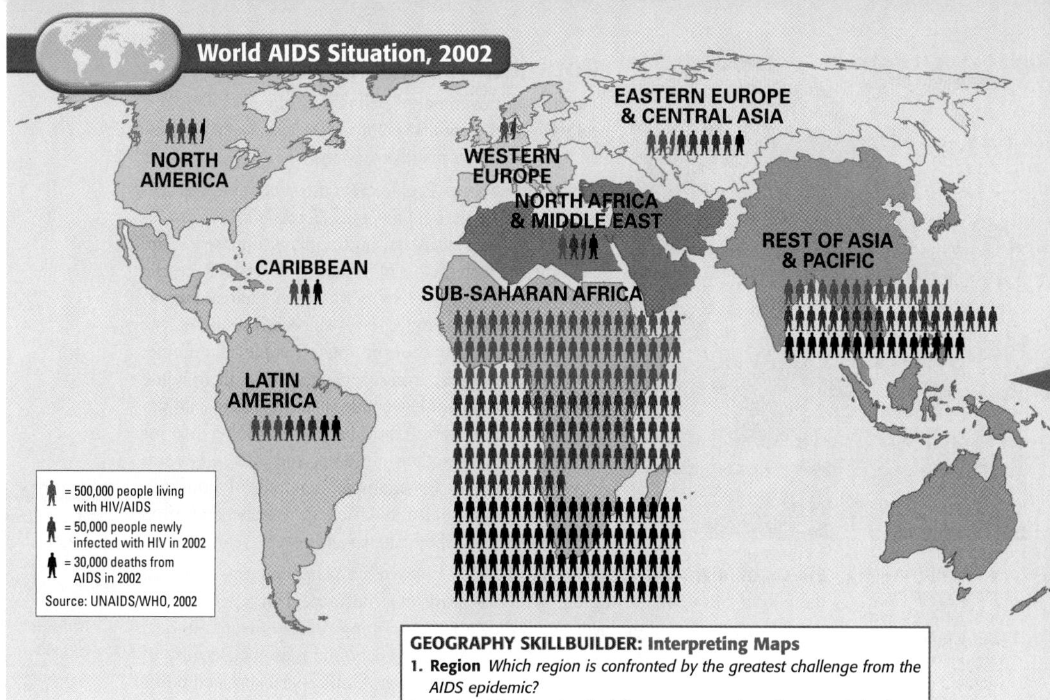

GEOGRAPHY SKILLBUILDER: Interpreting Maps

1. **Region** *Which region is confronted by the greatest challenge from the AIDS epidemic?*
2. **Region** *Which region had the greatest number of new HIV infections in 2002, Latin America or Eastern Europe and Central Asia?*

Health Issues

In recent decades, the enjoyment of a decent standard of health has become recognized as a basic human right. However, for many people across the world, poor health is still the norm. World health faced a major threat in 2003, with the outbreak of severe acute respiratory syndrome (SARS). This pneumonia-like disease emerged in China and rapidly spread to other Asian countries, Europe, and North America. Afraid of infection, many people canceled travel to Asia. The resulting loss of business hurt the economies of several Asian countries.

The AIDS Epidemic Perhaps the greatest global health issue is a disease known as **AIDS**, or acquired immune deficiency syndrome. It attacks the immune system, leaving sufferers open to deadly infections. The disease was first detected in the early 1980s. Since that time, AIDS has claimed the lives of nearly 25 million people worldwide. By the end of 2002, there were 42 million people across the world living with HIV (the virus that causes AIDS) or AIDS. And in 2002, 5 million people were newly infected with HIV.

While AIDS is a worldwide problem, Sub-Saharan Africa has suffered most from the epidemic. About 70 percent of the world's HIV and AIDS sufferers live in this region. And in 2002, on average more than 6,500 people died of AIDS each day. Most of the people dying are between the ages of 15 and 49—the years when people are at their most productive economically. AIDS, therefore, is reducing the number of people available as workers, managers, and entrepreneurs. As a result, economic growth is slowing in many countries in the region.

In response to the devastating impact of the disease, the UN issued the Declaration of Commitment on HIV/AIDS in 2001. This document set targets for halting the spread of AIDS and provided guidelines on how countries could pool their efforts.

Tip for Struggling Readers

Sub-Saharan Africa refers to the part of the continent that is below, or south of, the Sahara Desert.

History from Visuals

Interpreting the Map

How would the relative difference in the rate of infection between Sub-Saharan Africa and North America be stated as a ratio? *(70 to 1)* Where is AIDS having the least impact? *(Western Europe)*

Extension Ask students to use the political map of Africa in the textbook atlas to locate the countries of Botswana, Lesotho, Namibia, South Africa, Swaziland, Zambia, and Zimbabwe. The HIV infection rate in these countries is estimated to be one in five persons aged 15 to 49.

SKILLBUILDER Answers

1. **Region** Sub-Saharan Africa
2. **Region** Eastern Europe and Central Asia

Health Issues

10.9.8; 10.10.2; 10.10.3

Critical Thinking

- What do SARS and AIDS have in common? *(both infectious diseases)*
- Why is AIDS particularly a problem in poorer countries? *(Possible Answer: lower standard of living and poorer health-care facilities there)*

DIFFERENTIATING INSTRUCTION: ENGLISH LEARNERS

Understanding Medical Vocabulary

Class Time 20 minutes

Task Looking up words in a dictionary and making a chart

Purpose To break down complex phrases into smaller parts

Instructions Explain that a good strategy to use while reading is to break down long phrases into parts. Have students analyze the meaning of *severe acute respiratory syndrome (SARS)* and *acquired immune deficiency syndrome (AIDS)*. Point out that the first letter of each word is used to create the acronym that is a shorthand word for the disease. Students should create a two-column chart. Have students define the words, using English or Spanish dictionaries as needed.

Ask students to notice what word both diseases have in common *(syndrome)*. Ask them to identify the key word or words in each name that describes how and where the disease affects the body. *(SARS–respiratory; AIDS–immune deficiency)*

Severe	serious, damaging, dangerous
Acute	a medical term that means "happens suddenly or rapidly"
Respiratory	affecting breathing, related to lungs
Syndrome	group of symptoms (signs or indications of a disease) that together define an illness

Population Movement
10.10.2; 10.10.3; 10.11

Critical Thinking
- Why do refugees have a more difficult time than other immigrants? *(Possible Answer: often forced to flee without having anyplace to go)*
- How does a country's labor market affect its attitude toward immigrants? *(Possible Answer: If unemployment is high, a country may not want immigrants who will compete with citizens for jobs.)*

Critical Thinking Transparencies
- CT36 Patterns of Refugee Movement

3 ASSESS
SECTION 3 ASSESSMENT
Have students work in pairs to answer question 1. Then have groups of four work together to answer question 2. Ask students to complete questions 3–8 as a class.

Formal Assessment
- Section Quiz, p. 350

4 RETEACH
List the phrases *international peace, human rights, world health,* and *global migration* on the board. Divide the class into four groups. Have each group present the main ideas about one of these issues to the class. Then ask students to discuss how the four issues relate to global security.

In-Depth Resources: Unit 5
- Reteaching Activity, p. 95

▲ Two Afghan girls quietly wait for food at a refugee camp on the Afghanistan-Iran border.

Population Movement
The global movement of people has increased dramatically in recent years. This migration has taken place for both negative and positive reasons.

Push-Pull Factors People often move because they feel pushed out of their homelands. Lack of food due to drought, natural disasters, and political oppression are examples of push factors of migration. In 2001 alone, the number of **refugees**—people who leave their country to move to another to find safety—stood at 12 million.

Not only negative events push people to migrate. Most people have strong connections to their home countries and do not leave unless strong positive attractions pull them away. They hope for a better life for themselves and for their children, and thus migrate to developed nations. For example, hundreds of thousands of people migrate from Africa to Europe and from Latin America to the United States every year. B

MAIN IDEA
Analyzing Causes
B What push and pull factors cause people to migrate?
B. Answer Push: natural disasters, political problems, lack of food. Pull: hope for a better life

Effects of Migration Everyone has the right to leave his or her country. However, the country to which a migrant wants to move may not accept that person. The receiving country might have one policy about accepting refugees from political situations, and another about migrants coming for economic reasons. Because of the huge volume of people migrating from war-torn, famine-stricken, and politically unstable regions, millions of immigrants have no place to go. Crowded into refugee camps, often under squalid conditions, these migrants face a very uncertain future.

On the positive side, immigrants often are a valuable addition to their new country. They help offset labor shortages in a variety of industries. They bring experiences and knowledge that can spur the economy. In addition, they contribute to the sharing, shaping, and blending of a newly enriched culture.

SECTION 3 ASSESSMENT

TERMS & NAMES 1. For each term or name, write a sentence explaining its significance.
• proliferation • Universal Declaration of Human Rights • political dissent • gender inequality • AIDS • refugee

USING YOUR NOTES

2. What methods have resulted in the greatest contribution to global security? Why? (10.9.1)

Method	Examples
Form military alliances	NATO, SEATO, Warsaw Pact

MAIN IDEAS

3. What steps have nations taken to control the proliferation of weapons of mass destruction? (10.10.2)
4. How has AIDS affected the economy of Sub-Saharan Africa? (10.10.2)
5. What positive effects does immigration have? (10.10.2)

CRITICAL THINKING & WRITING

6. **MAKING INFERENCES** Why might nations want to retain or develop an arsenal of nuclear, biological, and chemical weapons? (10.10.3)
7. **IDENTIFYING PROBLEMS** How are ethnic and religious conflicts related to problems of global security? (10.10.2)
8. **RECOGNIZING EFFECTS** How can individuals affect social conditions around the world? Consider the example of Mother Teresa when writing your answer. (CST 2)
9. **WRITING ACTIVITY** SCIENCE AND TECHNOLOGY Write a **paragraph** explaining how advances in science and technology have increased global security threats. (Writing 2.3.b)

CONNECT TO TODAY **CREATING A DATABASE**
Locate recent information on refugees around the world. Use your findings to create a **database** of charts and graphs titled "The Global Refugee Situation." (Writing 2.3.d)

ANSWERS
1. proliferation, p. 649 • Universal Declaration of Human Rights, p. 650 • political dissent, p. 650 • gender inequality, p. 650 • AIDS, p. 651 • refugee, p. 652
2. **Sample Answer:** Formation of the UN–Reduced threat of conflict, promoted peace; Arms-control agreements–Reduced number of weapons of mass destruction. Most important–Arms control, because it lessens the threat of mass destruction.
3. nuclear nonproliferation treaties, treaties limiting biological and chemical weapons
4. The region has lost many of its most economically productive people, leading to slower economic growth.
5. Immigrants can offset labor shorages, bring experience and knowledge, and contribute elements of their culture.
6. as a deterrent
7. **Possible Answer:** Conflicts can destabilize the countries involved. Refugees may also create security problems.
8. by bringing problems to the attention of the world community
9. **Rubric** Paragraphs should
   - note how biological and chemical weapons are a threat to security.
   - describe how improved transportation has made the movement of such weapons easier.

CONNECT TO TODAY
Rubric Databases should
- give details of the world refugee situation.
- include a variety of charts and graphs.

Integrated circuit

International Space Station

Terrorism

CASE STUDY: September 11, 2001

MAIN IDEA

POWER AND AUTHORITY
Terrorism threatens the safety of people all over the world.

WHY IT MATTERS NOW

People and nations must work together against the dangers posed by terrorism.

TERMS & NAMES

- terrorism
- cyberterrorism
- Department of Homeland Security
- USA Patriot Act

SETTING THE STAGE Wars are not the only threat to international peace and security. **Terrorism**, the use of violence against people or property to force changes in societies or governments, strikes fear in the hearts of people everywhere. Recently, terrorist incidents have increased dramatically around the world. Because terrorists often cross national borders to commit their acts or to escape to countries friendly to their cause, most people consider terrorism an international problem.

CALIFORNIA STANDARDS

10.10.3 Discuss the important trends in the regions today and whether they appear to serve the cause of individual freedom and democracy.

What Is Terrorism?

Terrorism is not new. Throughout history, individuals, small groups, and governments have used terror tactics to try to achieve political or social goals, whether to bring down a government, eliminate opponents, or promote a cause. In recent times, however, terrorism has changed.

Modern Terrorism Since the late 1960s, more than 14,000 terrorist attacks have occurred worldwide. International terrorist groups have carried out increasingly destructive, high-profile attacks to call attention to their goals and to gain major media coverage. Many countries also face domestic terrorists who oppose their governments' policies or have special interests to promote.

The reasons for modern terrorism are many. The traditional motives, such as gaining independence, expelling foreigners, or changing society, still drive various terrorist groups. These groups use violence to force concessions from their enemies, usually the governments in power. But other kinds of terrorists, driven by radical religious and cultural motives, began to emerge in the late 20th century.

The goal of these terrorists is the destruction of what they consider the forces of evil. This evil might be located in their own countries or in other parts of the world. These terrorists are ready to use any kind of weapon to kill their enemies. They are even willing to die to ensure the success of their attacks.

Terrorist Methods Terrorist acts involve violence. The weapons most frequently used by terrorists are the bomb and the bullet. The targets of terrorist attacks often are crowded places where people normally feel safe—subway stations, bus stops, restaurants, or shopping malls, for example. Or terrorists might target something that symbolizes what they are against, such as a government building

TAKING NOTES

Categorizing Use a chart to note information about the September 11 terrorist attacks and other terrorist incidents around the world.

World Terrorist Incidents
September 11 Attacks

LESSON PLAN

OBJECTIVES

- Define modern terrorism and give examples from around the world.
- Describe the September 11, 2001, terrorist attacks on the United States.
- Summarize U.S. response to this attack.

1 FOCUS & MOTIVATE

Ask students to discuss what their personal experiences were in connection with the September 11, 2001, terrorist attacks.

2 INSTRUCT

What Is Terrorism?

10.10.3

Critical Thinking

- How might globalization be a factor in the growth of terrorism? *(Possible Answer: Some terrorists may believe globalization undermines local or religious values.)*

Electronic Library of Primary Sources

- "The Making of a Terrorist"

CALIFORNIA RESOURCES

California Reading Toolkit, p. L93
California Modified Lesson Plans for English Learners, p. 181
California Daily Standards Practice Transparencies, TT85
California Standards Enrichment Workbook, pp. 111–112
California Standards Planner and Lesson Plans, p. L177
California Online Test Practice
California Test Generator CD-ROM
California Easy Planner CD-ROM
California eEdition CD-ROM

SECTION 4 PROGRAM RESOURCES

ALL STUDENTS

In-Depth Resources: Unit 5
- Guided Reading, p. 77

Formal Assessment
- Section Quiz, p. 351

ENGLISH LEARNERS

In-Depth Resources in Spanish
- Guided Reading, p. 158

Reading Study Guide (Spanish), p. 221
Reading Study Guide Audio CD (Spanish)

STRUGGLING READERS

In-Depth Resources: Unit 5
- Guided Reading, p. 77
- Building Vocabulary, p. 79
- Reteaching Activity, p. 96

Reading Study Guide, p. 221
Reading Study Guide Audio CD

GIFTED AND TALENTED STUDENTS

Electronic Library of Primary Sources
- "The Making of a Terrorist"

INTEGRATED TECHNOLOGY

eEdition CD-ROM
Power Presentations CD-ROM
Electronic Library of Primary Sources
- "The Making of a Terrorist"

classzone.com

More About . . .

Internet Security

The U.S. government significantly increased spending on computer security after the attacks of September 11, 2001. Carnegie Mellon University received a multimillion dollar, five-year grant to study cyberterrorism. One aspect of the research focused on ways to identify hackers or terrorists in the act of attempting to disrupt computer systems. Researchers are also exploring methods of making computers shut down automatically when attacked.

Tip for English Learners

Point out that the affixes *-ism* (action, process or practice of) and *-ist* (one who performs an action) are added to the word *terror* (intense fear) to create new words. What *-ism* words do students recall from earlier chapters? *(communism, imperialism, Social Darwinism)*

Terrorism Around the World

10.10.3

Critical Thinking

- How would you compare terrorism in the Middle East to terrorism in Northern Ireland? *(Both involve opposing groups fighting over control of territory.)*
- Why was the attack on the Tokyo subway system significant? *(It focused attention on the use of chemical weapons by terrorists.)*

▲ The sarin gas attack in the Tokyo subway in 1995 is the most notorious act of biochemical terrorism.

or a religious site. Such targets are carefully chosen in order to gain the most attention and to achieve the highest level of intimidation. (A)

Recently, some terrorist groups have used biological and chemical agents in their attacks. These actions involved the release of bacteria or poisonous gases into the atmosphere. While both biological and chemical attacks can inflict terrible casualties, they are equally powerful in generating great fear among the public. This development in terrorism is particularly worrisome, because biochemical agents are relatively easy to acquire. Laboratories all over the world use bacteria and viruses in the development of new drugs. And the raw materials needed to make some deadly chemical agents can be purchased in many stores.

Cyberterrorism is another recent development. This involves politically motivated attacks on information systems, such as hacking into computer networks or spreading computer viruses. Experts suggest that as more governments and businesses switch to computers to store data and run operations, the threat of cyberterrorism will increase.

MAIN IDEA

Analyzing Motives

(A) Of what value would gaining public attention be to a terrorist group?

A. Possible Answer It allows them to tell thousands what their positions are on issues that concern them.

Responding to Terrorism Governments take various steps to stamp out terrorism. Most adopt a very aggressive approach in tracking down and punishing terrorist groups. This approach includes infiltrating the groups to gather information on membership and future plans. It also includes striking back harshly after a terrorist attack, even to the point of assassinating known terrorist leaders.

Another approach governments use is to make it more difficult for terrorists to act. This involves eliminating extremists' sources of funds and persuading governments not to protect or support terrorist groups. It also involves tightening security measures so as to reduce the targets vulnerable to attack.

Terrorism Around the World

The problem of modern international terrorism first came to world attention in a shocking way during the 1972 Summer Olympic Games in Munich, Germany (then West Germany). Members of a Palestinian terrorist group killed two Israeli athletes and took nine others hostage. Five of the terrorists, all the hostages, and a police officer were later killed in a bloody gun battle. Since then, few regions of the world have been spared from terrorist attacks.

The Middle East Many terrorist organizations have roots in the Israeli-Palestinian conflict over land in the Middle East. Groups such as the Palestine Islamic Jihad, Hamas, and Hizballah have sought to prevent a peace settlement between Israel and the Palestinians. They want a homeland for the Palestinians on their own terms, with the most extreme among them denying Israel's right to exist. In a continual cycle of violence, the Israelis retaliate after most terrorist attacks, and the terrorists strike again. Moderates in the region believe that the only long-term solution is a compromise between Israel and the Palestinians over the issue of land. However, the violence has continued with only an occasional break.

DIFFERENTIATING INSTRUCTION: ENGLISH LEARNERS

Understanding Words in Context

Class Time 20 minutes

Task Reading, defining unfamiliar terms, and paraphrasing

Purpose To understand various forms of terrorism

Instructions Read aloud the two paragraphs at the top of the page that describe different forms of terrorism. As you read each sentence, write down difficult or unfamiliar words or phrases on the chalkboard. Ask students to look for clues as they read—such as synonyms or examples—to help them understand these terms. As students discover the clue words, write them down opposite the words in your list. After you have defined all the unfamiliar terms, ask the students to summarize the paragraphs in their own words. Your list might include:

biological agents	living substances (point out that agents here are not people)
biochemical	biological + chemical
cyberterrorism	cyber (having to do with computers) + terrorism
information systems	computer networks
hacking	breaking into computer systems illegally
computer virus	secret computer program that spreads through a computer and causes it to break down (the way a biological virus can cause disease)

Europe Many countries in Europe have been targets of domestic terrorists who oppose government policies. For example, for decades the mostly Catholic Irish Republican Army (IRA) engaged in terrorist attacks against Britain because it opposed British control of Northern Ireland. Since 1998, however, the British, the IRA, and representatives of Northern Ireland's Protestants have been negotiating a peaceful solution to the situation.

Asia Afghanistan, in Southwest Asia, became a haven for international terrorists after the Taliban came to power in 1996. (See Chapter 18.) In that year, Osama bin Laden, a Saudi Arabian millionaire involved in terrorist activities, moved to Afghanistan. There he began using mountain hideouts as a base of operations for his global network of Muslim terrorists known as al-Qaeda.

Terrorist groups have arisen in East Asia, as well. One, known as Aum Shinrikyo ("Supreme Truth"), is a religious cult that wants to control Japan. In 1995, cult members released sarin, a deadly nerve gas, in subway stations in Tokyo. Twelve people were killed and more than 5,700 injured. This attack brought global attention to the threat of biological and chemical agents as terrorist weapons.

Africa Civil unrest and regional wars were the root causes of most terrorist activity in Africa at the end of the 20th century. But al-Qaeda cells operated in many African countries, and several major attacks against U.S. personnel and facilities in Africa were linked to al-Qaeda. In 1998, for example, bombings at the U.S. embassies in Kenya and Tanzania left over 200 dead and more than 5,000 people injured. The United States responded to these attacks with missile strikes on suspected terrorist facilities in Afghanistan and in Sudan, where bin Laden was based from 1991 to 1996.

Latin America Narcoterrorism, or terrorism linked to drug trafficking, is a major problem in Latin America, particularly in Colombia. The powerful groups that control that country's narcotics trade have frequently turned to violence. The Revolutionary Armed Forces of Colombia (FARC) is a left-wing guerrilla group that has links with these drug traffickers. The FARC has attacked Colombian political, military, and economic targets, as well as those with American ties. **B**

B. Possible Answers conflict over territory, government control, religious beliefs, civil unrest, narcotics trafficking

MAIN IDEA

Analyzing Causes

B What are some reasons for terrorism in various regions of the world?

International Terrorist Attacks

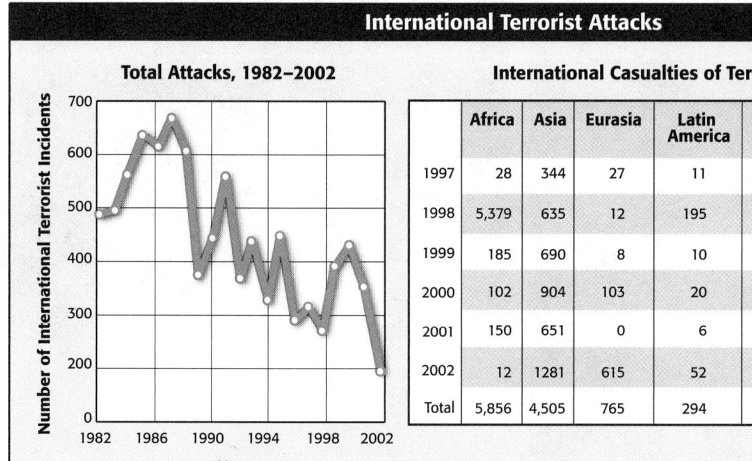

International Casualties of Terrorism, 1997–2002

	Africa	Asia	Eurasia	Latin America	Middle East	North America	Western Europe
1997	28	344	27	11	480	7	17
1998	5,379	635	12	195	68	0	405
1999	185	690	8	10	31	0	16
2000	102	904	103	20	78	0	4
2001	150	651	0	6	513	4,091	20
2002	12	1281	615	52	772	0	6
Total	5,856	4,505	765	294	1,942	4,098	468

Source: U.S. Department of State

SKILLBUILDER: Interpreting Charts and Graphs

1. **Comparing** *Which three areas suffered the greatest numbers of casualties of terrorism?*
2. **Drawing Conclusions** *How would you describe the overall trend in worldwide terrorist attacks since the mid-1980s?*

More About . . .

Al-Qaeda

Al-Qaeda was established in the late 1980s to support Muslims fighting against the Soviet Union in Afghanistan. The organization trained thousands in paramilitary skills and has groups located in 100 countries. Since the September 11, 2001, attacks on the United States, more than 3,000 suspects have been arrested throughout the world. Yet al-Qaeda has been involved in ongoing terrorist attacks, including the bombing of a Bali nightclub in 2002.

Tip for Struggling Readers

The word *narcoterrorism* comes from combining *narcotics* (another word for drugs) and *terrorism*.

History from Visuals

Interpreting the Chart

Explain to students that the line graph shows the total number of terrorist attacks each year for a 20-year period. Line graphs are used to show trends. The chart shows the total number of casualties each year over a five-year period in different regions of the world. Point out that there is not necessarily a correlation between the number of attacks and the number of casualties.

SKILLBUILDER Answers

1. **Comparing** Africa, Asia, and North America
2. **Drawing Conclusions** decreasing

DIFFERENTIATING INSTRUCTION: STRUGGLING READERS

Mapping Terrorism Around the World

Class Time 30 minutes

Task Reading and creating a map

Purpose To visualize the location of terrorist activity

Instructions Pair a struggling reader with a more proficient reader. Ask students to read the section on Terrorism Around the World, making note of every place name that is mentioned. *(Munich, Germany; land claimed by both Israelis and Palestinians; Britain and Northern Ireland; Afghanistan; Saudi Arabia; Tokyo, Japan; Kenya; Tanzania; Sudan; Colombia)*

Have students use the textbook atlas or a globe to help them find each of the places mentioned. Then have students use a blank world map from the Geography Skills and Outline Maps book to show each location and label it to identify its significance. Ask students how this activity affected their comprehension of the material. Encourage students to refer to an atlas whenever they are reading text that includes place names.

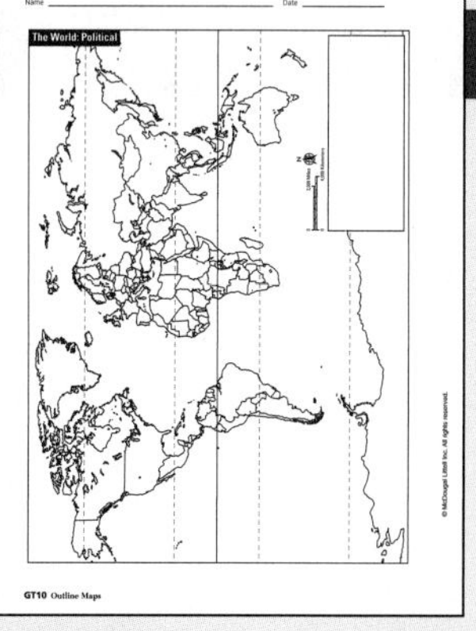

Geography Skills and Outline Maps

Attack on the United States
10.10.3

Critical Thinking

- Why were Americans so shocked by the attack of September 11, 2001? *(Possible Answer: Americans had thought that terrorism was confined to other parts of the world.)*
- How would you contrast the anthrax attacks with the attack of September 11? *(Possible Answer: little loss of life compared to September 11, but widespread feeling of vulnerability)*

More About . . .

Anthrax

Anthrax is a very old disease, mentioned in the Bible and by ancient Greek and Roman writers. It mostly infects animals such as cows and sheep. The form of anthrax that affects the lungs was called woolsorter's disease. Humans contracted it by inhaling spores from the wool of infected animals. Louis Pasteur developed a vaccine in 1881.

History from Visuals

Interpreting the Photographs

Point out that the photographs were taken from different perspectives. Ask students to describe differences between them. *(Possible Answer: New York–taken from the ground up at the time of the event; Pentagon–aerial view after the attack.)*

Extension Ask students to describe the different feelings they have looking at the two photos.

CASE STUDY: September 11, 2001

Attack on the United States

On the morning of September 11, 2001, 19 Arab terrorists hijacked four airliners heading from East Coast airports to California. In a series of coordinated strikes, the hijackers crashed two of the jets into the twin towers of the World Trade Center in New York City and a third into the Pentagon outside Washington, D.C. The fourth plane crashed in an empty field in Pennsylvania. C

MAIN IDEA
Making Inferences
C Why were the specific targets of the September 11 attacks selected by the terrorists?
C. Possible Answers They were symbols of American power. Also, many people would be killed in the World Trade Center, heightening the level of intimidation.

The Destruction The planes, loaded with fuel, became destructive missiles when they crashed into the World Trade Center and the Pentagon. The explosions and fires so weakened the damaged skyscrapers that they crumbled to the ground less than two hours after impact. The fire and raining debris caused nearby buildings to collapse as well. The damage at the Pentagon, though extensive, was confined to one section of the building.

The toll in human lives was great. About 3,000 people died in the attacks. All passengers on the four planes were killed, as well as workers and visitors in the World Trade Center and the Pentagon. The dead included more than 340 New York City firefighters and 60 police officers who rushed to the scene to help and were buried in the rubble when the skyscrapers collapsed.

The Impact of the Attack September 11 had a devastating impact on the way Americans looked at life. Many reported feeling that everything had changed—that life would never be the same. Before, Americans had viewed terrorism as something that happened in other countries. Now they felt vulnerable and afraid.

This sense of vulnerability was underscored just a few days after September 11, when terrorism struck the United States again. Letters containing spores of a bacterium that causes the disease anthrax were sent to people in the news media and to members of Congress in Washington, D.C. Anthrax bacteria, when inhaled, can

Destruction in New York City and the Pentagon

▲ The strike on the Pentagon left a charred, gaping hole in the southwest side of the building.

◀ Stunned bystanders look on as smoke billows from the twin towers of the World Trade Center.

656 Chapter 20

DIFFERENTIATING INSTRUCTION: GIFTED AND TALENTED STUDENTS

Analyzing the Damage After September 11

Class Time 45 minutes

Task Researching and creating a visual presentation

Purpose To understand the scope of the damage caused by the terrorist attacks on the World Trade Center and the Pentagon

Instructions Encourage students to explore the types of damage caused by the terrorist attacks and to analyze the causes. Students may find resources on the Internet or in the library from newspaper or magazine articles. After students have researched a topic, ask them to present their findings in the form of a display board, model, diagram, or photo essay. Some possible approaches:

1. Why did the airplanes cause so much damage when they crashed into the World Trade Center?
2. How did the design of the World Trade Center lead to the collapse of the towers and nearby buildings?
3. Given what happened, was the loss of life greater or less than might have been expected? Why?
4. What kind of environmental damage did the attacks cause?
5. What confined the damage in the Pentagon to one area?
6. How was the Pentagon designed to withstand attack?

Have students share their findings with the class.

▲ A hazardous materials team prepares to enter a congressional building during the anthrax scare.

damage the lungs and cause death. Five people who came in contact with spores from the tainted letters died of inhalation anthrax. Two were postal workers.

Investigators did not find a link between the September 11 attacks and the anthrax letters. Some of them believed that the letters might be the work of a lone terrorist rather than an organized group. Regardless of who was responsible for the anthrax scare, it caused incredible psychological damage. Many Americans were now fearful of an everyday part of life—the mail.

The United States Responds

Immediately after September 11, the United States called for an international effort to combat terrorist groups. President George W. Bush declared, "This battle will take time and resolve. But make no mistake about it: we will win."

As a first step in this battle, the U.S. government organized a massive effort to identify those responsible for the attacks. Officials concluded that Osama bin Laden directed the terrorists. The effort to bring him to justice led the United States to begin military action against Afghanistan in October, as you read in Chapter 18.

Antiterrorism Measures The federal government warned Americans that additional terrorist attacks were likely. It then took action to prevent such attacks. The **Department of Homeland Security** was created in 2002 to coordinate national efforts against terrorism. Antiterrorism measures included a search for terrorists in the United States and the passage of antiterrorism laws.

The al-Qaeda network was able to carry out its terrorist attacks partly through the use of "sleepers." These are agents who move to a country, blend into a community, and then, when directed, secretly prepare for and carry out terrorist acts. A search to find any al-Qaeda terrorists who remained in the United States was begun. Officials began detaining and questioning Arabs and other Muslims whose behavior was considered suspicious or who had violated immigration regulations.

Some critics charged that detaining these men was unfair to the innocent and violated their civil rights. However, the government held that the actions were justified because the hijackers had been Arabs. The government further argued that it was not unusual to curtail civil liberties during wartime in order to protect national security. This argument was also used to justify a proposal to try some terrorist suspects in military tribunals rather than in criminal courts. On October 26, 2001,

The United States Responds
10.10.3

Critical Thinking

- Why did the USA Patriot Act order banks to investigate large foreign accounts? *(Possible Answer: to find possible sources of money used to fund terrorist organizations)*
- What was the psychological impact of using sky marshals and National Guard troops for aviation security? *(Possible Answer: made people feel it was safe to fly)*

More About . . .

Homeland Security Alert System

Shortly after its establishment in 2002, the Department of Homeland Security created a five-level, color-coded alert system to keep Americans informed about the likelihood of imminent terrorist attack. (See the photograph on page 636.) The system ranged from green at the low end to red at the high end, signaling a severe risk of attack. For the first year the level was generally set at yellow, *elevated*. In February 2003, prior to the beginning of the war in Iraq, the alert level was raised to orange, *high*. Critics of the effectiveness of the system included many U.S. mayors whose cities were forced to invest extra money in emergency personnel whenever the code level was raised.

CONNECTIONS ACROSS TIME AND CULTURES

Balancing Civil Liberties and National Security

Class Time 40 minutes

Task Researching and creating a chart

Purpose To compare the limiting of civil liberties in the interest of national security at different times of crisis

Instructions Divide the class into small groups. Ask each group to choose an earlier time when civil liberties were restricted to protect national security. Students may learn about the topic by doing research on the Internet, in encyclopedias, or in books. Have students compare the earlier time with antiterrorism measures enacted by the United States in response to the September 11 attacks, especially the USA Patriot Act. Students may use copies of Critical Thinking Transparency CT74 to help them compare and contrast the two examples and draw some conclusions. After groups have shared their charts with the class, conduct a general class discussion about the restricting of civil liberties in the interest of national security. Some possible topics include:

1. The Alien and Sedition Act of 1798
2. The American Civil War
3. World War I
4. The Red Scare of the 1920s
5. World War II
6. Cold War anticommunism/McCarthyism

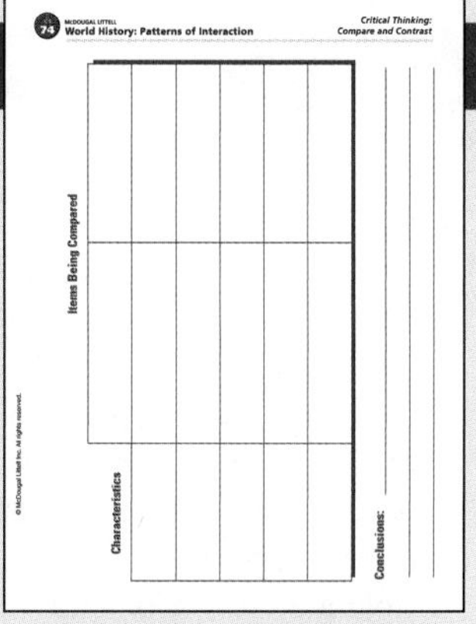

Critical Thinking Transparencies

More About . . .

Aviation Security

In less than two years following the September 11, 2001, terrorist attack, the new Transportation Security Administration spent more than $9 billion on improvements in aviation security. The number of federal airport screeners hired topped 55,000. In spite of these efforts, areas of concern still existed. While passenger baggage was routinely being screened for explosives, the other cargo carried by planes was not being screened. With the large number of ground workers with access to aircraft–including caterers, mechanics, and baggage handlers–thorough background checks of all airport personnel was critical.

3 ASSESS

SECTION 4 ASSESSMENT

Have students answer questions 1–6 individually. Discuss questions 7 and 8 as a class.

Formal Assessment
- Section Quiz, p. 351

4 RETEACH

Use the Reteaching Activity to review this section.

In-Depth Resources: Unit 5
- Reteaching Activity, p. 96

▲ Passengers wait to go through a security check at La Guardia Airport in New York.

President Bush signed an antiterrorism bill into law. The law, known as the **USA Patriot Act**, allowed the government to
- detain foreigners suspected of terrorism for seven days without charging them with a crime
- tap all phones used by suspects and monitor their e-mail and Internet use
- make search warrants valid across states
- order U.S. banks to investigate sources of large foreign accounts
- prosecute terrorist crimes without any time restrictions or limitations.

Again, critics warned that these measures allowed the government to infringe on people's civil rights.

Aviation Security The federal government also increased its involvement in aviation security. The Federal Aviation Administration (FAA) ordered airlines to install bars on cockpit doors to prevent passengers from gaining control of planes, as the hijackers had done. Sky marshals—trained security officers—were assigned to fly on planes, and National Guard troops began patrolling airports.

The Aviation and Transportation Security Act, which became law in November 2001, made airport security the responsibility of the federal government. Previously, individual airports had been responsible. The law provided for a federal security force that would inspect passengers and carry-on bags. It also required the screening of checked baggage.

Airline and government officials debated these and other measures for making air travel more secure. Major concerns were long delays at airports and respect for passengers' privacy. It has also become clear that public debate over security measures will continue as long as the United States fights terrorism and tries to balance national security with civil rights.

SECTION 4 ASSESSMENT

TERMS & NAMES 1. For each term or name, write a sentence explaining its significance.
• terrorism • cyberterrorism • Department of Homeland Security • USA Patriot Act

USING YOUR NOTES

2. How were the September 11 terrorist attacks unique? How were they similar to other terrorist incidents? (10.10.3)

MAIN IDEAS

3. How has terrorism changed in recent years? (10.10.3)
4. What methods do terrorists use? (10.10.3)
5. What steps did the United States take in response to the terrorist attacks of September 11, 2001? (10.10.3)

CRITICAL THINKING & WRITING

6. **ANALYZING MOTIVES** What might cause individuals to use terror tactics to bring about change? (10.10.3)
7. **FORMING AND SUPPORTING OPINIONS** Is it important for the U.S. government to respect peoples' civil rights as it wages a war against terrorism? Why or why not? (10.10.3)
8. **DRAWING CONCLUSIONS** What do you think has been the greatest impact of terrorism on American life? (10.10.3)
9. **WRITING ACTIVITY** SCIENCE AND TECHNOLOGY Conduct research on how science and technology are used to combat terrorism. Then write an **illustrated report** titled "Science and Counterterrorism." (Writing 2.3.d)

INTEGRATED TECHNOLOGY **INTERNET ACTIVITY**

Use the Internet to research terrorist incidents since the end of 2001. Use your findings to create a **time line** titled "Recent Major Terrorist Attacks." (Writing 2.3.d)

INTERNET KEYWORD
terrorism

ANSWERS

1. terrorism, p. 653 • cyberterrorism, p. 654 • Department of Homeland Security, p. 657 • USA Patriot Act, p. 658
2. **Sample Answer:** World Incidents–Munich Olympics, 1972; Tokyo subway attacks, 1995; bombings in U.S. embassies, 1998. Unique–In scale; Similar–Designed to cause death and destruction and gain worldwide attention.
3. now is usually driven by religious and cultural motives
4. violent attacks, biological or chemical attacks, cyberterrorism
5. removed Taliban government from Afghanistan, established Department of Homeland Security, passed antiterrorism law, improved aviation security
6. **Possible Answer:** feel regular political activity won't cause change
7. **Possible Answers:** Yes–Limiting freedoms means terrorists win. No–We must defeat terrorists, whatever the costs.
8. **Possible Answers:** continued fear, limits on civil rights, the economic cost of fighting terrorism
9. **Rubric** Illustrated reports should
   - show how science helps fight terrorism.
   - include appropriate visual materials.

INTEGRATED TECHNOLOGY

Rubric Time lines should
- include major worldwide terrorist incidents since the end of 2001.
- clearly calibrate time measurements.

5

Integrated circuit

International Space Station

Cultures Blend in a Global Age

MAIN IDEA	WHY IT MATTERS NOW	TERMS & NAMES
CULTURAL INTERACTION Technology has increased contact among the world's people, changing their cultures.	Globalization of culture has changed the ways people live, their perceptions, and their interactions.	• popular culture • materialism

SETTING THE STAGE Since the beginnings of civilization, people have blended ideas and ways of doing things from other cultures into their own culture. The same kind of cultural sharing and blending continues today. But, because of advances in technology, it occurs at a much more rapid pace and over much greater distances. Twenty-first-century technologies allow people from all over the world to have increasing interaction with one another. Such contacts promote widespread sharing of cultures.

CALIFORNIA STANDARDS

10.10.1 Understand the challenges in the regions, including their geopolitical, cultural, military, and economic significance and the international relationships in which they are involved.

10.11 Students analyze the integration of countries into the world economy and the information, technological, and communications revolutions (e.g., television, satellites, computers).

CST 3 Students use a variety of maps and documents to interpret human movement, including major patterns of domestic and international migration, changing environmental preferences and settlement patterns, the frictions that develop between population groups, and the diffusion of ideas, technological innovations, and goods.

Cultural Exchange Accelerates

Cultural elements that reflect a group's common background and changing interests are called **popular culture**. Popular culture involves music, sports, movies, clothing fashions, foods, and hobbies or leisure activities. Popular culture around the world incorporates features from many different lands. Of all the technologies that contribute to such cultural sharing, television, movies, and other mass media have been the most powerful.

Mass Media More people in the United States have televisions than telephones. In fact, 98 percent of American households have at least one television set. Eighty-six percent of the homes have videocassette recorders (VCRs). In Western Europe, too, most households have one or more televisions. Access to television is not so widespread in the emerging nations, but it is growing. Recent estimates suggest that about half the population of the emerging world—some 2.5 billion people—have regular access to a television set.

Television provides a window to the world through daily newscasts and documentaries. The speed at which television can present information helps create an up-to-the-minute shared experience of global events. For example, in 2003, millions of television viewers across the world watched the war in Iraq. Wars, natural disasters, and political drama in faraway places have become a part of everyday life.

Television and other mass media, including radio and movies, are among the world's most popular forms of entertainment. Popular programs not only entertain but also show how people in other parts of the world live and what they value. Mass media is the major way popular culture spreads to all parts of the globe.

International Elements of Popular Culture The entertainment field, especially television, has a massive influence on popular culture. People from around

TAKING NOTES

Categorizing Use a web diagram to identify areas of popular culture that have become international in scope.

LESSON PLAN

OBJECTIVES

- Trace the increase in worldwide cultural interaction.
- Describe influences on world culture.
- Explain cultural bias and explore possibilities for cultural understanding.

1 FOCUS & MOTIVATE

Discuss how international culture affects students' lives. *(Possible Answers: music, food, films)*

2 INSTRUCT

Cultural Exchange Accelerates

10.10.1; 10.11

Critical Thinking

- What are some conclusions about American life that people of other countries might draw from American television? *(Possible Answers: high standard of living; violence)*

CALIFORNIA RESOURCES

California Reading Toolkit, p. L94
California Modified Lesson Plans for English Learners, p. 183
California Daily Standards Practice Transparencies, TT86
California Standards Enrichment Workbook, pp. 107–108, 113–114
California Standards Planner and Lesson Plans, p. L179
California Online Test Practice
California Test Generator CD-ROM
California Easy Planner CD-ROM
California eEdition CD-ROM

SECTION 5 PROGRAM RESOURCES

ALL STUDENTS

In-Depth Resources: Unit 5
- Guided Reading, p. 78

Formal Assessment
- Section Quiz, p. 352

ENGLISH LEARNERS

In-Depth Resources in Spanish
- Guided Reading, p. 159

Reading Study Guide (Spanish), p. 223
Reading Study Guide Audio CD (Spanish)

STRUGGLING READERS

In-Depth Resources: Unit 5
- Guided Reading, p. 78
- Building Vocabulary, p. 79
- Reteaching Activity, p. 97

Reading Study Guide, p. 223
Reading Study Guide Audio CD

GIFTED AND TALENTED STUDENTS

In-Depth Resources: Unit 5
- Primary Source: "Cupid's a Computer," p. 86
- Connections Across Time and Cultures, p. 92

Electronic Library of Primary Sources
- "Un-American Ugly Americans"
- "Television Is Defying Borders"

INTEGRATED TECHNOLOGY

eEdition CD-ROM
Power Presentations CD-ROM
World Art and Cultures Transparencies
- AT80 *Technology* (Korean video sculpture)

Critical Thinking Transparencies
- CT72 Chapter 36 Visual Summary

Patterns of Interaction Video Series
- Cultural Crossroads: The United States and the World

classzone.com

Global Patterns

International Baseball

Baseball gained popularity in Japan in the 1930s when American professional teams toured there. Men who learned baseball in the United States taught the sport to local populations in Latin America. Little League baseball began in the 1930s and expanded rapidly after World War II. Youngsters in the United States and approximately 30 other nations play the sport. Baseball caps are worn by millions around the globe.

INTEGRATED TECHNOLOGY

Rubric Scrapbooks should include
- players from several countries.
- photographs and captions.

Global Patterns

International Baseball

The sport of baseball is an example of global popular culture. When American missionaries and teachers arrived in Japan in the 1870s, they introduced the game of baseball. Over the years the game gained popularity there. Today, some Major League teams have Japanese players and several American players play in the Japanese league.

Baseball spread to Mexico, Cuba, Puerto Rico, Panama, and the Dominican Republic in the late 19th and early 20th centuries. Today baseball is a popular game in these and other Latin American countries. And more than 25 percent of the players in Major League Baseball come from Latin America.

INTEGRATED TECHNOLOGY

INTERNET ACTIVITY Create a scrapbook of foreign players in Major League Baseball. Go to **classzone.com** for your research.

the world are avid viewers of American TV programs. For example, in Bhutan, a tiny country high in the Himalaya, ESPN, HBO, Cartoon Network, and CNN are among the most-watched channels. CNN truly is a global channel, since it reaches more than 200 million households in over 200 countries.

Television broadcasts of sporting events provide a front-row seat for sports fans all over the globe. Basketball and soccer are among the most popular televised sports. National Basketball Association (NBA) games are televised in over 200 countries. In China, for example, broadcasts of NBA games of the week regularly attract an audience in the millions. One of the most-watched international sporting events is the soccer World Cup. Nearly 63 million viewers worldwide watched the 2002 World Cup Final.

Music is another aspect of popular culture that has become international. As the equipment for listening to music has become more portable, there are only a few places in the world that do not have access to music from other cultures. People from around the world dance to reggae bands from the Caribbean, chant rap lyrics from the United States, play air guitar to rowdy European bands, and enjoy the fast drumming of Afropop tunes. And the performers who create this music often gain international fame. (A)

A. Answer They have made certain sports, music, and entertainment programs popular internationally.

MAIN IDEA

Recognizing Effects

(A) What effects have television and mass media had on popular culture?

Global Impact

Rock 'n' Roll

Rock 'n' roll combines influences reflecting the diversity of America's population. The importance of African-American music to the history of rock 'n' roll is acknowledged by all music and social historians. Interpreting the meaning of that influence is more challenging. Few people can even agree on a good definition of rock, except to stay that it has a strong beat.

Global Impact: Cultural Crossroads

Rock 'n' Roll

In the middle of the 1950s, a new style of music emerged on the American scene. It was called rock 'n' roll. The music explored social and political themes. Rock music, which seemed to adults to reflect a youth rebellion, soon became the dominant popular music for young people across the world. As the influence of rock music spread, international artists added their own traditions, instruments, and musical styles to the mix called rock.

"The King" ►

"Rock and roll music, if you like it and you feel it, you just can't help but move to it. That's what happens to me, I can't help it."—Elvis Presley, called the "King of rock 'n' roll" by many.

U2 ►

U2, led by singer Bono (right), is one of the world's most popular and influential rock bands. Over a career spanning more than 20 years, this Irish band has kept its music vibrant and fresh by absorbing and reworking all manner of musical styles. The band has drawn on the blues, gospel, 1950s rock 'n' roll, 1960s protest songs, and hip-hop to create a very distinctive kind of music.

660 Chapter 20

DIFFERENTIATING INSTRUCTION: STRUGGLING READERS

Using a Spider Map to Summarize Text

Class Time 20 minutes

Task Creating a spider map

Purpose To understand how information is organized

Instructions Have pairs of students read the text under "Cultural Exchange Accelerates" on pages 659 and 660. Display Critical Thinking Transparency CT79. Explain that using a spider map can help students take accurate notes and remember how different facts and details relate to one another. As a class, fill out the spider web with main ideas and details from the text.

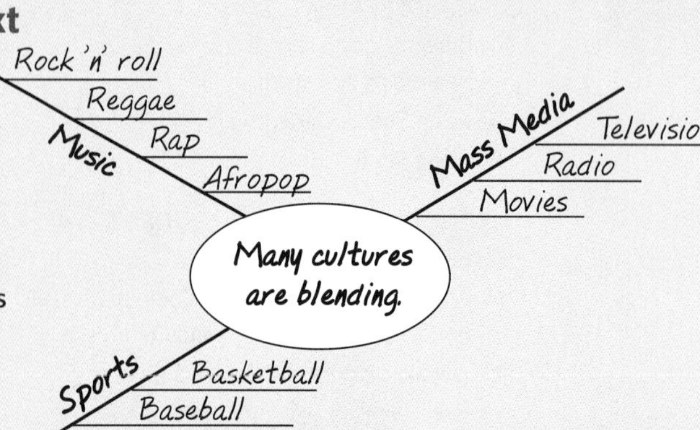

Critical Thinking Transparencies

World Culture Blends Many Influences

Greater access to the ideas and customs of different cultures often results in cultural blending. As cultural ideas move with people among cultures, some beliefs and habits seem to have a greater effect than others. In the 20th century, ideas from the West have been very dominant in shaping cultures in many parts of the globe.

Westernizing Influences on Different Cultures Western domination of the worldwide mass media helps explain the huge influence the West has on many different cultures today. However, heavy Western influence on the rest of the world's cultures is actually rooted in the 19th century. Western domination of areas all over the globe left behind a legacy of Western customs and ideas. Western languages are spoken throughout the world, mainly because of Europe's history of colonization in the Americas, Asia, and Africa.

Over the past 50 years, English has emerged as the premier international language. English is spoken by about 500 million people as their first or second language. Although more people speak Mandarin Chinese than English, English speakers are more widely distributed. English is the most common language used on the Internet and at international conferences. The language is used by scientists, diplomats, doctors, and businesspeople around the world. The widespread use of English is responsible, in part, for the emergence of a dynamic global culture.

Western influence can be seen in other aspects of popular culture. For example, blue jeans are the clothes of choice of most of the world's youth. Western business suits are standard uniforms among many people. American-style hamburgers and soft drinks can be purchased in many countries of the world. Mickey Mouse and other Disney characters are almost universally recognized. Western influence also has an effect on ways of thinking in other parts of the world. For example, people

▲ **"World Pop"**
Youssou N'Dour, a singer from the West African country of Senegal, blends traditional African styles with American rock to create a new form that has been called "world-pop fusion."

Patterns of Interaction
Cultural Crossroads: The United States and the World

The spread of American culture, including sports, fashion, and fast food, has created an international culture recognizable in all corners of the globe. In some cases American culture is simply a powerful influence, as other societies blend American culture with local customs. Cultural blending is evident even in America's past. Symbols of American culture like baseball and hot dogs are themselves the result of cross-cultural influences.

Connect *to* Today

1. **Making Inferences** How have improvements in technology and global communications aided in the blending of musical styles?
   See Skillbuilder Handbook, page R10.
2. **Creating Oral Presentations** Find out the global origins of such aspects of American culture as rock 'n' roll and baseball. Report your findings to the class in an oral presentation.

World Culture Blends Many Influences
10.10.3; 10.11

Critical Thinking

- How do the mass media promote materialism? *(Possible Answers: portray certain lifestyles, create desires for consumer goods)*
- How does the Internet promote world culture? *(Possible Answers: access to international media, museums, and music; e-mail allows less expensive global communication)*

In-Depth Resources: Unit 5

- Primary Source: from "Cupid's a Korean Computer . . .", p. 86

Electronic Library of Primary Sources

- "Un-American Ugly Americans"

INTEGRATED TECHNOLOGY

Show "Cultural Crossroads: The United States and the World" to demonstrate how interaction among peoples can affect culture and everyday life.

Patterns of Interaction Video Series

- "Cultural Crossroads: The United States and the World"

CONNECT TO TODAY Answers

1. **Making Inferences** Electronic equipment gives musicians more versatility. Modern communications technology provides easy access to music worldwide.
2. **Creating Oral Presentations**
   Rubric Oral presentations should
   - focus on one aspect of American culture.
   - discuss how culture spreads.

DIFFERENTIATING INSTRUCTION: ENGLISH LEARNERS

Creating Cultural Self-Portraits

Class Time 30 minutes

Task Creating a self-portrait

Purpose To help students examine and express their cultural heritage

Instructions Have students create self-portraits that depict both the influence of other cultures on them and the influence of their cultural heritage on American society. Ask students to think about the culture they have inherited from their ancestors as well as the ways they are shaped by the current culture of the United States and other countries. Then ask them to think of examples of how their cultural heritage is part of the United States today.

Have them first make life-size outline drawings of themselves. They can either produce their own realistic or impressionistic images or ask a partner to trace their outline on a sheet of butcher paper. Have them fill in their outlines with drawings, words, or objects that express the cultural interactions that make them who they are.

Create a class display of students' self-portraits. Use the self-portraits as the basis for a class discussion about how cultural influences can blend and affect personal style and character.

More About . . .

Fast Food and Popular Culture

Although most countries still favor their own regional cuisines, fast food is now part of world popular culture. Fast food has also expanded far beyond McDonald's hamburgers. Asian stir-fry, Mexican tacos, Indian samosas, and French croissants are now part of many international fast-food menus.

More About . . .

The Nobel Prize

The award is named for Swedish industrialist Alfred Nobel, who endowed prizes for physics, chemistry, physiology or medicine, literature, and peace in his will in 1895. Thousands of people are involved in selecting a winner from the 100 to 250 nominees per category. Prizes include grants of money.

Future Challenges and Hopes

10.10.3; 10.11

Critical Thinking

- Why is preservation of different languages important? *(Possible Answer: Language is a cornerstone of culture.)*
- How do environmental issues bring countries together? *(Possible Answers: Actions have impact beyond national borders. We all have an interest in protecting Earth's resources.)*

▲ Kenzaburo Oe of Japan was awarded the Nobel literature prize in 1994. Oe studied Western literature in college, and he has used Western literary styles to tell stories about his personal life and the myths and history of his country.

▲ South African writer Nadine Gordimer won the Nobel Prize for Literature in 1991. Many of her novels and stories published prior to 1991 focused on the evils of the apartheid system. As a result, much of her work was censored or banned by the South African government.

from many different cultures have adopted **materialism**, the Western mindset of placing a high value on acquiring material possessions.

Non-Western Influences Cultural ideas are not confined to moving only from the West to other lands. Non-Western cultures also influence people in Europe and the United States. From music and clothing styles to ideas about art and architecture, to religious and ethical systems, non-Western ideas are incorporated into Western life. And cultural blending of Western and non-Western elements opens communications channels for the further exchange of ideas throughout the globe.

The Arts Become International Modern art, like popular culture, has become increasingly international. Advances in transportation and technology have facilitated the sharing of ideas about art and the sharing of actual works of art. Shows and museums throughout the world exhibit art of different styles and from different places. It became possible to see art from other cultures that had not previously been available to the public.

Literature, too, has become internationally appreciated. Well-known writers routinely have their works translated into dozens of languages, resulting in truly international audiences. The list of Nobel Prize winners in literature over the last 20 years reflects a broad variety of nationalities, including Nigerian, Egyptian, Mexican, South African, West Indian, Japanese, Polish, Chinese, and Hungarian. B

MAIN IDEA

Summarizing

B Name three advances that allow a greater sharing of the arts.

B. Answer technology, improved transportation, and widespread translations

Future Challenges and Hopes

Many people view with alarm the development of a global popular culture heavily influenced by Western, and particularly American, ways of life. They fear that this will result in the loss of their unique identity as a people or nation. As a result, many countries have adopted policies that reserve television broadcast time for national programming. For example, France requires that 40 percent of broadcast time be set aside for French-produced programs. And in South Korea, the government limits foreign programming to just 20 percent of broadcast time.

DIFFERENTIATING INSTRUCTION: GIFTED AND TALENTED STUDENTS

Staging an International Literature Fair

Class Time 45 minutes

Task Choosing a piece of literature and presenting an oral response

Purpose To help students appreciate the international character and universal themes of literature

Instructions Have students survey world literature textbooks or library and Internet sources and choose a work that interests them. They might choose a novel, short story, or poem. English learners might want to read a work in their native language. Make sure that a variety of cultures and literary genres are represented. Have students write a summary and personal response to their work and present it orally in the class literature fair.

Students may wish to choose a Literature Selection from one of the In-Depth Resources books, such as "Paper" by Catherine Lim, shown at right.

Name ______ Date ______

CHAPTER 20 Section 2 LITERATURE SELECTION "Paper" by Catherine Lim

Malaysian author Catherine Lim set this short story in Singapore, an island nation that became known as one of the Four Tigers of Asia—the name given to Asian countries that experienced dramatic economic growth beginning in the 1970s. What price does Tay Soon, the story's main character, pay for his dreams of success?

What's so grand about marble flooring and a swimming pool?

In-Depth Resources: Unit 5

Some countries take a different approach to protecting cultural diversity in the media. Television programmers take American shows and rework them according to their own culture and traditions. As an Indian media researcher noted, "We really want to see things our own way." Other countries take more drastic steps to protect their cultural identity. They strictly censor the mass media to keep unwanted ideas from entering their nation.

C. Possible Answer Some people may try harder to stay unique by holding on to parts of their culture such as language and customs.

MAIN IDEA

Recognizing Effects

C How do people react against greater global interdependence?

Sometimes people respond to perceived threats to their culture by trying to return to traditional ways. Cultural practices and rites of passage may receive even more emphasis as a group tries to preserve its identity. In some countries, native groups take an active role in preserving the traditional ways of life. For example, the Maori in New Zealand have revived ancestral customs rather than face cultural extinction. Many Maori cultural activities are conducted in a way that preserves Maori ways of thinking and behaving. In 1987, the New Zealand government recognized the importance of this trend by making the Maori language one of the country's official languages. C

Global Interdependence Despite the fear and uncertainty accompanying global interdependence, economic, political, and environmental issues do bring all nations closer together. Nations have begun to recognize that they are dependent on other nations and deeply affected by the actions of others far away. As elements of everyday life and expressions of culture become more international in scope, people across the world gain a sense of connectedness with people in other areas of the world. For example, the response to the events of September 11, 2001, was international in scope. People from around the world expressed their concern and support for the United States. It was as if this act of terrorism had struck their own countries.

Throughout history, human beings have faced challenges to survive and to live better. In the 21st century, these challenges will be faced by people who are in increasing contact with one another. They have a greater stake in learning to live in harmony together and with the physical planet. As Martin Luther King, Jr., stated, "Our loyalties must transcend our race, our tribe, our class, and our nation; and this means we must develop a world perspective."

More About . . .

Television and the Preservation of Culture

Television can be a means of promoting traditional, local culture. In Thailand, for example, a form of comedy called *likay*, which has been performed for centuries at provincial fairs, has now been adapted for TV. Someday, these traditional comedies may be exported and become part of global popular culture.

World Art and Cultures Transparencies
- AT80 *Technology* (Korean video sculpture)

Electronic Library of Primary Sources
- "Television Is Defying Borders"

SECTION 5 ASSESSMENT

TERMS & NAMES 1. For each term or name, write a sentence explaining its significance.
- popular culture
- materialism

USING YOUR NOTES

2. Which of the international popular culture aspects has the greatest effect on your life? Why? (10.11)

MAIN IDEAS

3. How do the mass media spread popular culture across the world? (10.11)
4. Why do Western cultures tend to dominate other cultures? (10.11)
5. What steps have governments and people taken to protect cultural diversity? (10.10.1)

CRITICAL THINKING & WRITING

6. **CLARIFYING** Why are the mass media such an effective means of transmitting culture? (10.11)
7. **RECOGNIZING EFFECTS** Do you think that limiting the amount of foreign television programming is an effective way to protect cultural diversity? Why or why not? (10.11)
8. **FORMING AND SUPPORTING OPINIONS** "Ethnocentrism—the belief in the superiority of one's own ethnic group—has taken hold in the world." Do you agree or disagree? Explain. (10.10.1)
9. **WRITING ACTIVITY** CULTURAL INTERACTION Write a **letter** to a friend in another country describing the elements of American popular culture they might appreciate. (Writing 2.1.e)

CONNECT TO TODAY CREATING A SCRAPBOOK

Study current newspapers and magazines to find pictures that show cultural blending. Create a **scrapbook** of these pictures. Write captions explaining how each picture illustrates cultural blending. (Writing 2.3.d)

3 ASSESS

SECTION 5 ASSESSMENT

Divide students into groups. Assign each group two of the first eight questions to answer. Then form new groups, consisting of one student from each of the original groups. These groups should share and discuss their answers.

Formal Assessment
- Section Quiz, p. 352

4 RETEACH

Use the Visual Summary to review this section and chapter.

Critical Thinking Transparencies
- CT72 Chapter 36 Visual Summary

In-Depth Resources: Unit 5
- Reteaching Activity, p. 97

ANSWERS

1. popular culture, p. 659 • materialism, p. 662
2. **Sample Answer:** Television, movies, food, sports, music, art, clothing fashions. Greatest effect—Television, because of amount of time spent watching it.
3. through popular entertainment
4. **Possible Answer:** Western cultures dominate the worldwide mass media, thereby influencing other cultures. Western influence on other cultures is also rooted in 19th-century colonialism.
5. limiting amount of foreign TV, adapting foreign programs to reflect local culture, censoring mass media, returning to traditional ways
6. **Possible Answer:** because they are worldwide
7. **Possible Answers:** Yes—A mix of foreign and national programs supports cultural diversity. No—Limiting other cultures limits diversity.
8. **Possible Answers:** Yes—More people are returning to traditional ways of life. No—More people are valuing diversity.
9. **Rubric** Letters should explain
   - elements of American popular culture.
   - why these cultural elements matter.

CONNECT TO TODAY

Rubric Scrapbooks should
- include a variety of examples.
- explain how the pictures represent cultural blending.

TERMS & NAMES

1. Internet, p. 639
2. genetic engineering, p. 639
3. global economy, p. 642
4. free trade, p. 642
5. political dissent, p. 650
6. refugee, p. 652
7. terrorism, p. 653
8. USA Patriot Act, p. 658
9. popular culture, p. 659
10. materialism, p. 662

MAIN IDEAS

Answers will vary.

11. Satellites and computers link the globe in a communications network; how and where people work have changed; diagnoses and treatment of diseases have improved; increased crop yields make more food available.
12. to increase food production worldwide
13. A developed nation has all the necessary facilities to manufacture goods; an emerging nation is in the process of becoming industrialized.
14. to ensure that trade among nations flows as freely and smoothly as possible
15. military alliances, United Nations, arms agreements
16. UN Universal Declaration of Human Rights; Helsinki Accords; continued work by UN agencies and international organizations such as Amnesty International to make people aware of human rights violations
17. violent attacks, biological or chemical attacks, cyberterrorism
18. used military force against the Taliban government in Afghanistan, established Department of Homeland Security to coordinate efforts against terrorism, passed antiterrorism laws, improved aviation security
19. television, movies, radio, and other mass media
20. Western colonization in the 19th century had lasting effects; English serves as an international language; Western popular culture has been widely accepted.

Chapter 20 Assessment

TERMS & NAMES

For each term or name below, briefly explain its connection to global interdependence from 1960 to the present.

1. Internet
2. genetic engineering
3. global economy
4. free trade
5. political dissent
6. refugee
7. terrorism
8. USA Patriot Act
9. popular culture
10. materialism

MAIN IDEAS

The Impact of Science and Technology Section 1 (pages 637–640)

11. In what ways have science and technology changed the lives of people today? (10.11)
12. What was the goal of the green revolution? (10.10.2)

Global Economic Development Section 2 (pages 641–647)

13. How are a developed nation and an emerging nation different? (10.10.1)
14. What is the World Trade Organization's function? (10.11)

Global Security Issues Section 3 (pages 648–652)

15. What methods has the world community used to resolve conflicts since World War II? (10.10.3)
16. What efforts have been made to guarantee basic human rights? (10.9.8)

Case Study: Terrorism Section 4 (pages 653–658)

17. What methods do terrorists employ? (10.10.3)
18. How did the United States respond to the terrorist attacks of September 11, 2001? (10.10.3)

Cultures Blend in a Global Age Section 5 (pages 659–663)

19. Which technologies have had the most powerful impact on cultural sharing? (10.11)
20. Why have Western influences had a major impact all over the world? (10.11)

CRITICAL THINKING

1. USING YOUR NOTES

SCIENCE AND TECHNOLOGY Use the diagram to show how advances in science and technology have changed lifestyles. (10.11)

Cause	Effect
Miniaturization of computer parts →	
Expanded global communication →	
Genetic research →	

2. EVALUATING COURSES OF ACTION

POWER AND AUTHORITY How is the UN working to address the unresolved problems of the world? (10.9.8)

3. IDENTIFYING SOLUTIONS

CULTURAL INTERACTION Imagine you are the culture minister of a small country. What steps would you take to ensure that your country's cultural identity is protected? Explain why you think these steps would be effective. (10.10.1)

4. RECOGNIZING EFFECTS

ECONOMICS How are individuals affected by the global economy? (10.11)

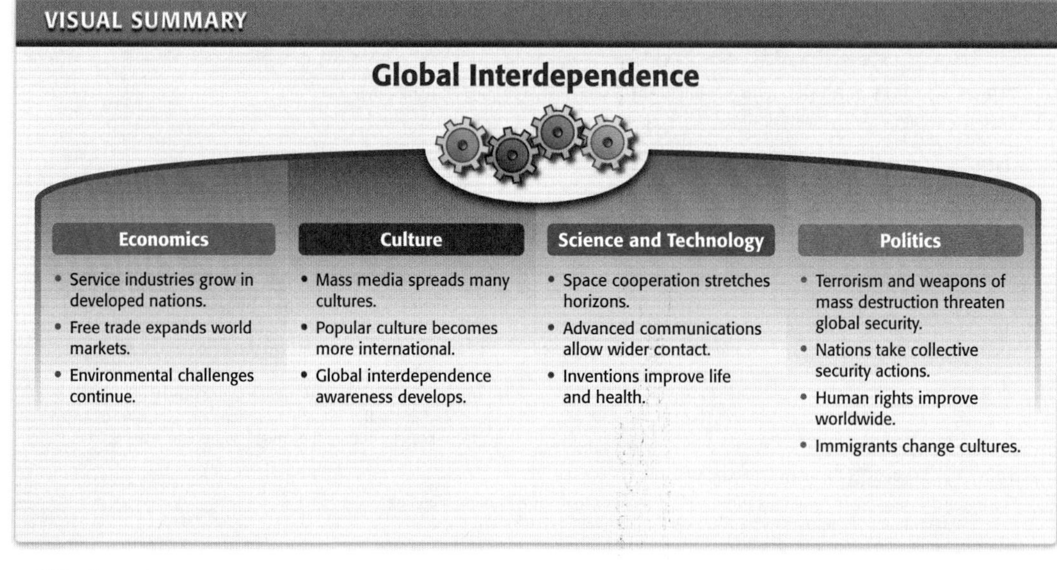

VISUAL SUMMARY
Global Interdependence
Economics
• Service industries grow in developed nations.
• Free trade expands world markets.
• Environmental challenges continue.
Culture
• Mass media spreads many cultures.
• Popular culture becomes more international.
• Global interdependence awareness develops.
Science and Technology
• Space cooperation stretches horizons.
• Advanced communications allow wider contact.
• Inventions improve life and health.
Politics
• Terrorism and weapons of mass destruction threaten global security.
• Nations take collective security actions.
• Human rights improve worldwide.
• Immigrants change cultures.

CRITICAL THINKING

Answers will vary.

1. Miniaturization of computer parts—Information revolution in industry and personal computers; Expanded global communication—Internationalization of culture; Genetic research—Green revolution, genetic engineering, molecular medicine.
2. The UN sends peacekeepers to resolve conflicts around the world; it defends human rights; it makes efforts to ensure that all people have healthy lives.
3. Work to limit the influence of Western popular culture by limiting the number of foreign programs broadcast on television; rework popular foreign television programs to reflect local culture; encourage citizens to practice traditional ways of life.
4. The global economy affects the nature of work—who does it, as well as how and where it gets done. Also, freer trade should lead to cheaper goods and services and, therefore, a lower cost of living.

Use the passage, which was written by a German journalist, and your knowledge of world history to answer questions 1 and 2.
Additional Test Practice, pp. S1–S33

PRIMARY SOURCE

Imagine a roomful of 14-year-olds—from Germany, Japan, Israel, Russia and Argentina. Obviously, they would all be wearing Levi's and baseball caps. But how would they relate to one another? They would communicate in English, though haltingly and with heavy accents. About what? . . . They would debate the merits of Nike versus Converse, of Chameleon versus Netscape. Sure, they would not discuss Herman Melville or George Gershwin, but neither would they compare notes on Dante or Thomas Mann. The point is that they would talk about icons and images "made in the U.S.A."

JOSEF JOFFE, from "America the Inescapable"

1. Which statement best describes the passage's main idea? (10.11)
   - **A.** Many teenagers have little understanding of world literature.
   - **B.** American popular culture plays a major role in teenagers' lives.
   - **C.** All teenagers communicate in English.
   - **D.** Most teenagers wear American-made clothes.

2. Which is the most likely way that teenagers in other countries learn about American popular culture? (10.11)
   - **A.** through the mass media
   - **B.** through discussions with their parents
   - **C.** through school textbooks
   - **D.** through Internet bulletin boards

Use the graph and your knowledge of world history to answer question 3.

Number of Refugees, 1992–2002

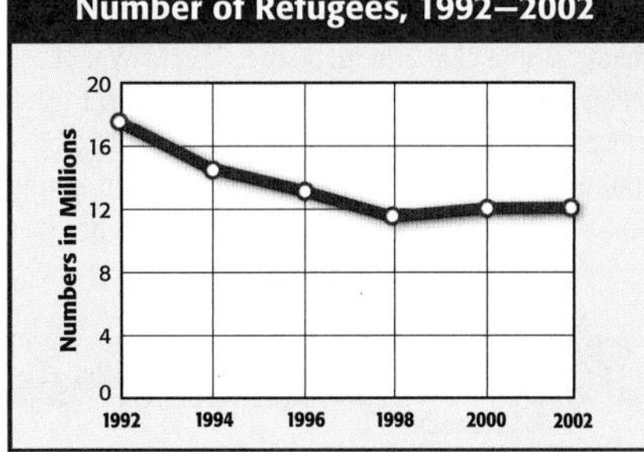

3. Which statement best describes the overall trend shown in this graph? (CST 3)
   - **A.** There has been a steady rise in the number of refugees.
   - **B.** The number of refugees has risen dramatically.
   - **C.** There has been a steady fall in the number of refugees.
   - **D.** The number of refugees has fallen dramatically.

INTEGRATED TECHNOLOGY

TEST PRACTICE Go to **classzone.com**
- Diagnostic tests
- Tutorials
- Strategies
- Additional practice

ALTERNATIVE ASSESSMENT

1. **Interact *with* History** (10.11)
   After reading Chapter 20, do you believe events in other nations affect your life? Which kinds of events are more likely to affect you in a very personal way? Create a survey about global interdependence to ask students in your class or school. Consider organizing your questions in four broad categories: science and technology, economics, security, and culture.

2.  **WRITING ABOUT HISTORY** (Writing 2.3.b)
   Use the Internet and library resources to find information on SARS. Use your findings to write a brief **report.** Your report should cover the following topics:
   - where and when the disease emerged.
   - possible causes and methods of prevention.
   - statistics on the disease.

INTEGRATED TECHNOLOGY

NetExplorations: The Environment (Writing 2.1.c)

Go to *NetExplorations* at **classzone.com** to learn more about the environment and the dangers it faces. Working in a team with three other students, find information on a recent discovery concerning changes in the environment. Use your findings to create the script for a 10-minute television news segment on the discovery and its implications for everyday life. The script should include

- a description and explanation of the discovery
- interviews on the subject with scientists, government officials, and representatives of non-governmental organizations
- references to locations, sound, and visuals
- a concluding statement on the overall significance of the discovery and what, if anything, needs to be done about it

STANDARDS-BASED ASSESSMENT

1. Letter **B** is correct, since the last line of the excerpt states that the teenagers' main topic of conversation would be "icons and images *made in the U.S.A.*" Letters **A** and **D** are incorrect because even though both could be inferred from the excerpt, neither is the main point. Letter **C** is incorrect because this point is not made in the excerpt.
2. Letter **A** is correct because mass media is the major way in which popular culture is transmitted across the globe. Letters **B**, **C**, and **D** are incorrect. Even though they are possible ways in which students might learn about American popular culture, they are not the most likely ways.
3. Letter **C** is correct because the overall trend shown in the graph is a steady fall in the number of refugees. Letter **D** is incorrect because the overall trend is not a dramatic fall. Letters **A** and **B** are incorrect because they both state that the trend is on the rise.

Formal Assessment
- Chapter Test, Forms A, B, and C, pp. 353–364

California Test Generator CD-ROM
- Chapter Tests, Forms A, B, and C (English and Spanish)

ALTERNATIVE ASSESSMENT

1. **Possible Answers**: Most students will agree that international events affect their lives. Some may say that aspects of world culture such as mass media and music affect them most personally. Others may mention worries about the effects of terrorism, war, contagious disease, or environmental damage.

2. **Rubric** Reports should
   - provide information about the origin of SARS.
   - outline possible causes and steps taken to prevent future outbreaks.
   - provide important statistics.
   - include sources.
   - be free of grammatical and spelling errors.

INTEGRATED TECHNOLOGY

Rubric Scripts should
- include a description and explanation of a recent discovery about the environment.
- include material from interviews.
- analyze the significance of the discovery and recommend follow-up actions.
- describe locations, sounds, and visuals.
- show evidence of material from several links on the site at **classzone.com**

LESSON PLAN

OBJECTIVES

- Examine the development of five nations.
- Compare and contrast the characteristics of five developing nations.
- Understand problems facing developing nations.

1 FOCUS & MOTIVATE

To prepare students for a discussion of developing nations, write on the board the names of the five nations covered in this unit. Ask the class to name any distinctive elements of the nations that they are aware of, either from the unit or from their own experience, and spend five to ten minutes writing these elements next to the names of the countries.

2 INSTRUCT

Critical Thinking

Could the United States be considered a developing nation? Why or why not? (*Possible Answer: While the United States is continually adjusting and growing, it is not considered a developing nation. It has a constitution that has lasted more than 200 years. It has a stable economy and a stable government and has laws to protect basic human rights.*)

Five Developing Nations

CALIFORNIA STANDARDS

10.4.4 Describe the independence struggles of the colonized regions of the world, including the roles of leaders, such as Sun Yat-sen in China, and the roles of ideology and religion.

Nation building is the creation of a state with a national identity. In Unit 5, you studied many nations that emerged since World War II. Forming a politically and economically stable country that safeguards basic human rights is a formidable task, especially in places where the people have different ethnic or religious backgrounds and different traditions and goals. To succeed, a new nation must forge a national identity. In the next six pages, you will see how five countries are working to become developed nations.

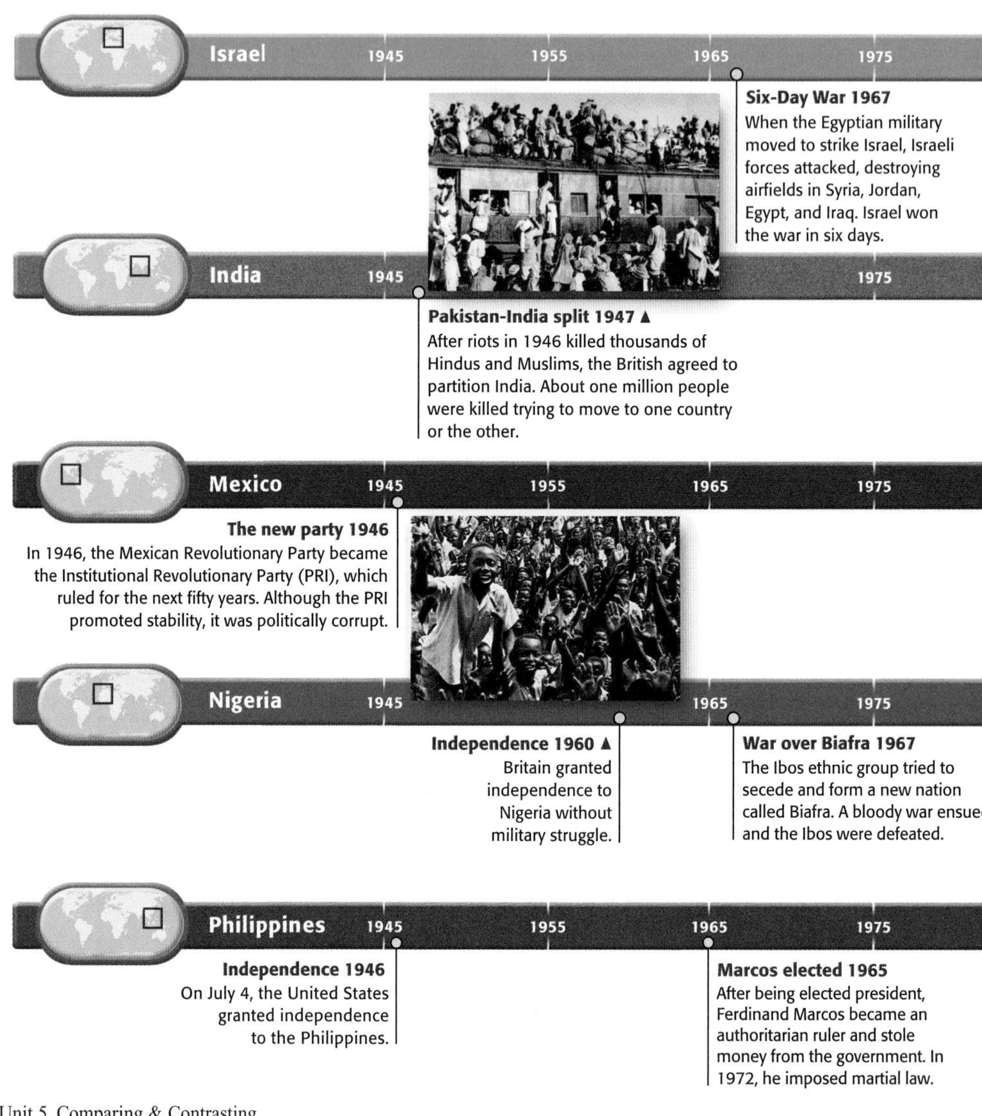

Israel 1945 1955 1965 1975
Six-Day War 1967
When the Egyptian military moved to strike Israel, Israeli forces attacked, destroying airfields in Syria, Jordan, Egypt, and Iraq. Israel won the war in six days.
India 1945 1975
Pakistan-India split 1947 ▲
After riots in 1946 killed thousands of Hindus and Muslims, the British agreed to partition India. About one million people were killed trying to move to one country or the other.
Mexico 1945 1955 1965 1975
The new party 1946
In 1946, the Mexican Revolutionary Party became the Institutional Revolutionary Party (PRI), which ruled for the next fifty years. Although the PRI promoted stability, it was politically corrupt.
Nigeria 1945 1965 1975
Independence 1960 ▲
Britain granted independence to Nigeria without military struggle.
War over Biafra 1967
The Ibos ethnic group tried to secede and form a new nation called Biafra. A bloody war ensued and the Ibos were defeated.
Philippines 1945 1955 1965 1975
Independence 1946
On July 4, the United States granted independence to the Philippines.
Marcos elected 1965
After being elected president, Ferdinand Marcos became an authoritarian ruler and stole money from the government. In 1972, he imposed martial law.

DIFFERENTIATING INSTRUCTION: GIFTED AND TALENTED STUDENTS

Front Page News

Class Time 45 minutes

Task Writing a newspaper article

Purpose To better understand a key moment in a developing nation's history

Have students use the Internet and the library to research one of the events on the time lines. They should concentrate their research on the facts of the event itself, finding pictures of the event, if possible. When they have gathered enough information, have the students write a front page newspaper article about the event. The article should have a headline and should be written as if the event had just happened and was a breaking news story.

For example, an article about Nigeria's first free election could begin as follows:

FREE ELECTION

ABUJA, Nigeria – After almost 20 years of military dictatorship, Nigeria held its first free election today . . .

Using headlines, pictures, and captions, students can format their articles to look like actual newspapers. They should display their front page stories in the classroom.

1985 1995 present

Camp David Accords 1979
Egypt and Israel signed the first treaty between Arabs and Israelis.

First intifada 1987 ►
The intifada was a widespread campaign of civil disobedience. Palestinians all over Israel participated in boycotts, demonstrations, rock throwing, and attacks on Israeli soldiers.

1985 1995 present

Indira Gandhi killed 1984
In October, prime minister Indira Gandhi was shot by two of her Sikh bodyguards in retaliation for an attack on a Sikh temple where terrorists were hiding.

Leadership changes 1998
The Congress Party had been in power in India since the country's creation in 1947, but in 1998 the Hindu nationalist party gained control.

1985 1995 present

Political opening 1988
In 1988, opposition parties were able to seriously challenge the ruling party for the first time.

Zapatista Uprising 1994 ►
Rebels seized control of several towns in the state of Chiapas, demanding more democracy and a better life for the native people.

1985 1995 present

Free election 1999
Nigeria held its first free election after almost 20 years of military dictators.

1985 1995 present

Fall of Marcos rule 1986 ▲
Marcos was forced into exile when he attempted to falsify the results of the 1986 election. Corazón Aquino became president.

Comparing & Contrasting

1. What are some problems that can arise in developing nations as a result of ethnic, religious, and economic problems?
2. How do Israel's religious problems differ from those of the other countries on the time line?

667

More About . . .

The Second Intifada

Though there were a series of peace treaties between Israel and its neighbors throughout the 1990s, tensions between Israel and Palestine grew. In 2000, as the two sides became deadlocked over the status of Jerusalem, a second intifada (the Arab word for *uprising* or *shaking off*) was begun by Palestine. Palestine's militia and suicide bombers killed hundreds of Israelis, and Israeli forces responded with bombings that killed thousands of Palestinians. In 2002, Israel reclaimed almost all of the West Bank, which had been divided up with Palestine in a 1995 treaty.

Comparing & Contrasting

1. *Possible Answer:* Ethnic and religious differences or economic problems such as uneven distribution of wealth can lead to rebellion and a lack of national unity.
2. Israel's major problems are with its Muslim neighbors, not among Israelis themselves.

RECOMMENDED RESOURCES

Books for the Teacher

Carey, Roane. ***The New Intifada: Resisting Israel's Apartheid***. New York: Verso, 2001.

Celoza, Albert F. ***Ferdinand Marcos and the Philippines***. Westport, CT: Praeger, 1997.

Sherman, John. ***War Stories: A Memoir of Nigeria and Biafra***. Indianapolis: Mesa Verde, 2002.

Books for the Student

Marcos, Subcomandante. ***Questions and Swords: Folktales of the Zapatista Revolution***. El Paso, TX: Cinco Puntos, 2001.

Oren, Michael B. ***Six Days of War: June 1967 and the Making of the Modern Middle East***. New York: Oxford UP, 2002.

Videos

Israel: The First Forty Years. VHS. Films for the Humanities & Sciences. 800-257-5126.

India After Independence. VHS. Films for the Humanities & Sciences. 800-257-5126.

Mexico: Its History, People & Government. VHS. The Library Video Company. 800-843-3620.

National Characteristics

Critical Thinking

- In which country might the issue of language be the least problematic? Why? (*Possible Answer: While more than 200 languages are spoken in India, the most common language, Hindi, is the official language. Also, many people probably share English as a common language because of the colonial heritage and because it is used in education.*)
- What reaction might Israel's Muslim and Christian populations have to Israel's flag? Why? (*Possible Answer: Israel's flag features the Star of David, a Jewish symbol. Israel's Muslim and Christian citizens may feel discounted or displaced by their own flag.*)

National Characteristics

Many developing nations are trying to bring together a patchwork of ethnic groups that historically competed or were hostile to each other. To complicate matters more, the groups often speak different languages. Choosing one group's language as the official language could earn government leaders the ill-will of the other groups. Moreover, the traditions of one group might be objectionable to another for moral or religious reasons. The chart below describes the current situation in the five sample countries.

	Political		Cultural	
	Government	**Flag**	**Language**	**Religion**
Israel	• Parliamentary democracy • Unicameral Knesset (parliament) • President elected for seven-year term by Knesset • Prime minister heads the largest party in the Knesset • Supreme Court appointed for life by president		• Hebrew (official) • Arabic (official for minority Arabs) • English (used commonly)	• Jewish, 80.1% • Muslim, 14.6% • Christian, 2.1%
India	• Federal Republic • Bicameral legislature elected by people and state assemblies • President chosen by electoral college; five-year term • Prime minister chosen by ruling party • Supreme Court appointed by president to serve until age 65		• Hindi (official and most common) • Over 200 languages spoken • English (used in education and government)	• Hindu, 81.3% • Muslim, 12% • Christian, 2.3% • Sikh, 1.9% • Buddhist, Jain, Parsi in small numbers
Mexico	• Federal Republic • Bicameral legislature, elected by popular vote or by party vote • President elected by popular vote for six-year term • Supreme Court appointed by president with consent of the Senate		• Spanish • Mayan, Nahuatl and other indigenous languages	• Roman Catholic, 89% • Protestant, 6%
Nigeria	• Republic • Bicameral legislature elected by popular vote • President elected by popular vote for one or two four-year terms • Supreme Court appointed by president		• English (official) • Hausa, Yoruba, Igbo, Fulani	• Muslim, 50% • Christian, 40% • Indigenous faiths, 10%
Philippines	• Republic • Bicameral legislature elected by popular vote • President elected by popular vote for six-year term • Supreme Court appointed by president to serve until age 70		• Filipino (official) • English (official) • Eight major dialects	• Roman Catholic, 83% • Protestant, 9% • Muslim, 5%

DIFFERENTIATING INSTRUCTION: STRUGGLING READERS

Organizing Information

Class Time 30 minutes

Task Reorganizing information from the chart

Purpose To understand how the chart displays information

Divide the class into small groups, making sure that any struggling readers are grouped with more proficient readers. Have each group examine the chart on this page and decide on a different piece of information to emphasize. For instance, if the group wanted to make a chart organized by religions, it might look like this:

	Israel	India	Mexico	Nigeria	Philippines
Muslim	14.6%	12%		50%	5%
Christian	2.1%	2.3%		40%	
Protestant			6%		9%
Catholic			89%		83%
Jewish	80.1%				
Hindu		81.3%			

By reorganizing the chart in this way, struggling readers can extract the information they want and display it in a way that is clearer to them.

CALIFORNIA STANDARDS

CST 3 Students use a variety of maps and documents to interpret human movement, including major patterns of domestic and international migration, changing environmental preferences and settlement patterns, the frictions that develop between population groups, and the diffusion of ideas, technological innovations, and goods.

Economic	
Trading	**Main Export**
• Imports: crude oil, grains, military equipment, raw materials • Exports: fruits, vegetables, cut diamonds, high-technology equipment.	• cut diamonds
• Imports: crude oil, machinery, fertilizer, chemicals, gems • Exports: software services, engineering products, gems, jewelry, textiles, chemicals, leather goods	• textiles and clothing 
• Imports: metalworking and agricultural machinery, electrical equipment, car parts for assembly and repair • Exports: petroleum products, silver, manufactured goods, cotton, coffee, fruits, and vegetables	• manufactured goods 
• Imports: machinery, chemicals, manufactured goods, food • Exports: petroleum and petroleum products, cocoa, rubber	• petroleum 
• Imports: fuels, consumer goods, raw materials, capital goods • Exports: coconut products, clothing, electronic products, machinery, and transport equipment	• electronics 

"How can [a people] think of themselves as a national people if they don't even have a single language unifying them? Language is one of the most important instruments of nation-building, a potentially powerful unifying force."

David Lamb, from *The Africans*

Comparing & Contrasting

1. What similarities are there among the governments of the countries listed on the chart?
2. Why does David Lamb think language is such an important part of nation building?

Comparing & Contrasting

1. *Possible Answer:* All of the developing nations on the chart are democracies and have a three-branch government with a president or prime minister in the executive branch. They all have supreme courts appointed by the president.
2. *Possible Answer:* India, Mexico, and Nigeria are trying to unite different ethnic, religious, and cultural groups. Developing a common identity would help them all arrive at common goals and strategies for solving the broader problems the nations face.

CONNECTIONS ACROSS TIME AND CULTURES

National Exports

Class Time 45 minutes

Task Researching national exports

Purpose To learn how countries choose what to export

Have students choose one of the countries from the chart and use the library and the Internet to gather information on that country's exports. Tell students their main goal is to try to discover why these goods or materials are exported by the country they are researching. Ask them to consider these questions as they conduct their research:

- Does the country have a surplus of a certain material?
- Are the country's people particularly skilled at a certain trade? If so, why?
- Who does the country export its products to?
- Why would other countries go to this country for this product?

Have students write a brief report that answers the questions and makes clear why some countries are well suited to export certain products.

Important Trends

Critical Thinking

Which of these leaders seems to have the clearest plan for dealing with his or her nation's issues? (*Possible Answer: Prime Minister Sharon speaks in relatively specific terms about what he feels must happen for the good of his nation.*)

PRIMARY SOURCE

Israel

Answer to Document-Based Question

Sharon believes that Israel's objectives should be to promote the welfare of the Jewish people as well as Jewish values by absorbing Jewish immigrants, keeping in touch with Jews overseas, and providing Zionist education at home.

PRIMARY SOURCE

India

Answer to Document-Based Question

For Kalam, the government has to remain neutral to bring together people from all the different religious traditions.

PRIMARY SOURCE

Mexico

Answer to Document-Based Question

Fox thinks Mexico needs to provide people with education and jobs and develop rural areas.

Important Trends

CALIFORNIA STANDARDS
10.4.4, 10.10.2, HI 1, HI 3

In their inaugural speeches, the following leaders outlined the principal problems they wished to address during their terms in office. Below are some highlights of what they said. Note that the problems they discuss are shared by many of the developing nations you studied in Unit 5.

PRIMARY SOURCE

INTERACTIVE

Israel

Prime Minister Ariel Sharon discusses the Israeli national identity.

I believe wholeheartedly that the State of Israel has no greater resource than themselves, the Jewish people. We shall strengthen the bond and connection with the Jews of the Diaspora and the Zionist education of our education system. We will work towards bringing masses of Jewish immigrants to Israel and their absorption in the country. We must educate our children towards values: to respect for others, to equality between people, to national pride and love of country.

DOCUMENT-BASED QUESTION

In Sharon's view, what should be the continuing objectives of Israel?

PRIMARY SOURCE

INTERACTIVE

India

President Abdul Kalam stresses the importance of keeping religion separate from government.

I wish to emphasize my unflinching commitment to the principle of secularism, which is the cornerstone of our nationhood and which is the key feature of our civilization strength. During the last one year I met a number of spiritual leaders of all religions. They all echoed one message, that is, unity of minds and hearts of our people will happen and we will see the golden age of our country, very soon. I would like to endeavor to work for bringing about unity of minds among the divergent traditions of our country.

DOCUMENT-BASED QUESTION

Why does Kalam think India needs a secular government?

PRIMARY SOURCE

INTERACTIVE

Mexico

Equal rights and economic opportunities are what the poor need in the view of President Vicente Fox.

I emphatically maintain that social justice is part of an efficient economy, not its adversary. It is time we recognized that everything cannot be solved by the State, nor can everything be solved by the market. I believe that the vote for democracy is inseparable from the vote for social equity.

Quality education, employment and regional development are the levers to remove, once and for all, the signs of poverty, which are inequity, injustice, discrimination and exclusion.

DOCUMENT-BASED QUESTION

According to Fox, what does Mexico have to provide its poor so they can obtain social equity?

DIFFERENTIATING INSTRUCTION: ENGLISH LEARNERS

Understanding National Issues

Class Time 30 minutes

Task Rephrasing text

Purpose To better understand the issues that face developing nations

Pair English learners with students who are proficient in English. Have the pairs of students carefully review the primary sources, paying particular attention to any words or phrases that are unfamiliar. For instance, make sure that students understand the following vocabulary:

- the Diaspora: scattered colonies of exiled Jews who have settled outside of Palestine
- Zionist: relating to the movement for the establishment of a Jewish community in Palestine
- secularism: indifference to or rejection of religious considerations

Have students rewrite the main idea of each excerpt in their own words.

Here is an example for the Kalam excerpt:

I believe keeping government separate from religion will help us achieve unity.

PRIMARY SOURCE

Nigeria

President Olusegun Obasanjo explains his plan to curb the military.

The incursion of the military into government has been a disaster for our country and for the military over the last thirty years. . . . [P]rofessionalism has been lost. Youths go into the military not to pursue a noble career but with the sole intention of taking part in coups and to be appointed as military administrators of states and chairmen of task forces. . . . A great deal of reorientation has to be undertaken and a re-definition of roles, re-training and re-education will have to be done to ensure that the military submits to civil authority and regains its pride, professionalism and traditions. We shall restore military cooperation and exchanges with our traditional friends.

DOCUMENT-BASED QUESTION

How does President Obasanjo propose to change the military culture in Nigeria?

PRIMARY SOURCE

INTERACTIVE

Philippines

President Gloria Macapagal Arroyo discusses the importance of the rule of law.

Politics and political power as traditionally practiced and used in the Philippines are among the roots of the social and economic inequities that characterize our national problems. Thus, to achieve true reforms, we need to outgrow our traditional brand of politics based on patronage and personality. Traditional politics is the politics of the status quo. It is a structural part of our problem.

We need to promote a new politics of true party programs and platforms, of an institutional process of dialogue with our citizenry. This new politics is the politics of genuine reform. It is a structural part of the solution.

DOCUMENT-BASED QUESTION

According to Macapagal Arroyo, how does traditional politics promote poverty and how does party politics promote social equity?

Comparing & Contrasting

1. How does Kalam's view of religion in national self-identity and government contrast with Sharon's?
2. How might party politics as described by Macapagal Arroyo help to achieve the solutions Fox considers essential?

EXTENSION ACTIVITY

Choose one of the countries studied in Unit 5 that became independent after World War II. Research on the Internet how that country has fared in recent times. Use the Web sites of major newspapers, magazines, and other news organizations to find information on how ethnic, religious, economic, and other relevant concerns are being handled. Organize this information into an oral presentation to explain how the country is or is not changing.

671

PRIMARY SOURCE

Nigeria

Answer to Document-Based Question

Obasanjo thinks that three things are necessary: "re-definition of roles, re-training," and exchanges with other countries to ensure civilian authority over the military.

PRIMARY SOURCE

Philippines

Answer to Document-Based Question

Macapagal Arroyo points out that traditional politics encourages politicians to help friends, not to solve national problems. Party politics would force politicians to think about the nation's problems, design solutions, and present these to the people.

Comparing & Contrasting

1. *Possible Answer:* For Sharon, Judaism is at the heart of Israel's identity, and the government's job is to provide a safe home for all Jews and promote Jewish values. Other religions are to be respected. In India, where religious differences encourage rivalry among groups, Kalam supports unity amid diverse traditions and would like to see religious differences played down.
2. *Possible Answer:* Political parties could propose and adopt plans to increase the number of schools, promote business and employment opportunities, and provide needed assistance to agricultural areas and rural towns.

EXTENSION ACTIVITY

Instructions Chapters 18 and 19 in Unit 5 cover countries that became independent after World War II. For this activity, students can choose any of the following countries:

India	Pakistan	Bangladesh
Sri Lanka	Philippines	Myanmar (Burma)
Indonesia	Ghana	Kenya
Algeria	Congo	Angola
Israel	Afghanistan	Nigeria

After choosing a country, students should look for recent information about the government, the economy, and any ongoing political problems.

Rubric Student presentations should
- address relevant concerns of a developing nation from Unit 5.
- be based on Internet research.
- clearly explain how the country is or is not changing.

EPILOGUE • OBJECTIVE

Examine issues facing the world community, including technological and environmental change, distribution of resources, and global security.

Previewing Main Ideas

Ask students to begin thinking about contemporary global problems in light of the different historical themes—especially economic themes—that they have used throughout this book to examine world history. Encourage students to think about who controls the world's wealth and resources and about how those resources are used to satisfy the world's needs and wants.

Accessing Prior Knowledge

Have students come up with a list of unresolved global problems. Then ask them to create a corresponding list that names people and organizations that they have heard or read about who are working to solve the problems.

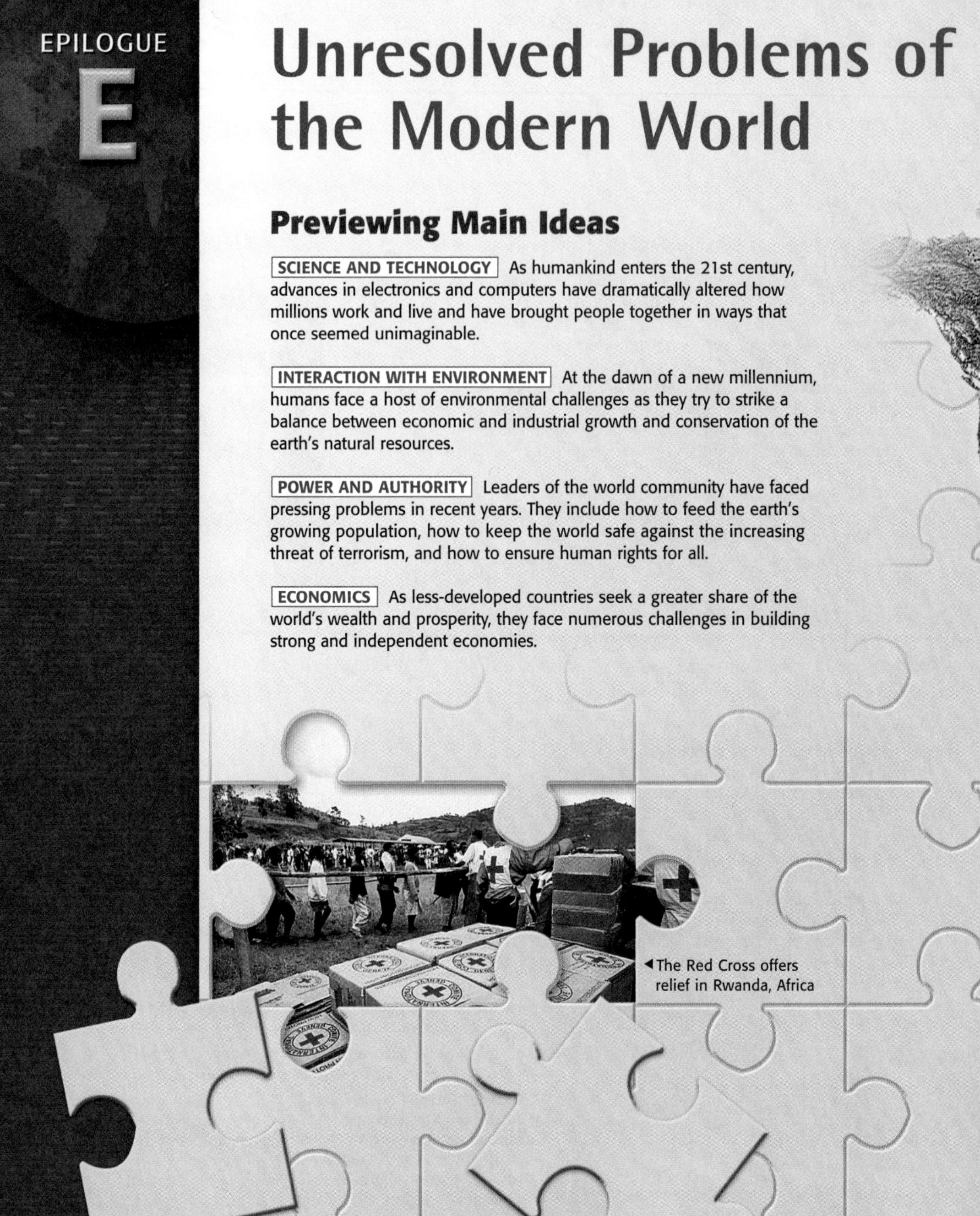

EPILOGUE E

Unresolved Problems of the Modern World

Previewing Main Ideas

SCIENCE AND TECHNOLOGY As humankind enters the 21st century, advances in electronics and computers have dramatically altered how millions work and live and have brought people together in ways that once seemed unimaginable.

INTERACTION WITH ENVIRONMENT At the dawn of a new millennium, humans face a host of environmental challenges as they try to strike a balance between economic and industrial growth and conservation of the earth's natural resources.

POWER AND AUTHORITY Leaders of the world community have faced pressing problems in recent years. They include how to feed the earth's growing population, how to keep the world safe against the increasing threat of terrorism, and how to ensure human rights for all.

ECONOMICS As less-developed countries seek a greater share of the world's wealth and prosperity, they face numerous challenges in building strong and independent economies.

◄ The Red Cross offers relief in Rwanda, Africa

672

◄Coalition troops battle in Iraq

◄Burning of the Brazilian Amazon Rain Forest

ilies of the missing in march for justice

►Victims of the Khumer Rouge regime in Cambodia

History from Visuals

Interpreting the Visual

The images on these two pages suggest that many problems of the modern world have not been solved. In the image on the far left, Red Cross relief workers distribute food in war-torn Rwanda. At bottom center, the protesters are members of the "Families of Detained and Disappeared" group demonstrating against General Pinochet in Chile. At top, a U.S. soldier returns fire in Basra, Iraq. At the bottom of the page, a rain forest burns in Brazil and human skulls from victims of the Khmer Rouge are displayed in a grim reminder of the "killing fields" of Cambodia.

Extension Have students discuss other world problems they know about. Ask them to share any solutions they can imagine for any of these problems.

RECOMMENDED RESOURCES

Books

Donnelly, Jack. ***Universal Human Rights in Theory and Practice.*** Ithaca: Cornell UP, 2002.

Forsythe, David P. ***Human Rights in International Relations.*** Cambridge: Cambridge UP, 2000.

Friedman, Thomas L. ***Longitudes and Attitudes: Exploring the World After September 11.*** New York: Farrar, 2002.

Heymann, Jody, ed. ***Global Inequalities at Work: Work's Impact on the Health of Individuals, Families, and Societies.*** Oxford: Oxford UP, 2003.

Klare, Michael T. ***Resource Wars: The New Landscape of Global Conflict.*** New York: Holt, 2002.

Sen, Amartya. ***Development as Freedom.*** New York: Knopf, 1999.

Shiklomanov, I. A. and John C. Rodda, eds. ***World Water Resources at the Beginning of the Twenty-First Century.*** Cambridge: Cambridge UP, 2003.

Videos

Commanding Heights: The Battle for the World Economy. VHS and DVD. Social Studies School Service, 2002. 800-421-4246.

Emerging Powers. VHS. Social Studies School Service, 1996. 800-421-4246.

Interact *with* History

Objectives

- Consider how the mass media have made it easier for people to stay informed about local, regional, and world issues.
- Describe ways citizens can make a difference in their part of the world.

EXAMINING *the* ISSUES

Answers

- Among the problems students might mention are pollution, poverty, homelessness, hunger, public health issues, racism, and violence.
- Students might discuss performing volunteer work, writing letters, organizing fundraisers, donating money, or joining protests.

Discussion

As students ponder why they should get involved in their community, ask them to think about the "veil of ignorance" discussed by the American political philosopher John Rawls (1921–2002). Rawls argued that as people begin to decide what principles society should be based on, they should make these decisions as if they were ignorant of their own racial, social, religious, and economic position within society. Principles established in this way would ensure that the least well-off person was treated justly.

Interact *with* History

What can you do to make a difference?

In this age of multimedia—from radio and magazines to television and the Internet—it is easier than ever to become informed about today's major issues and challenges. As you learn about these challenges, you wonder what you can do in your community to address them. Although you are not yet a voter or in the working world, you are interested in joining a local organization or activity to help make a difference in your part of the world.

▲ College students build a home for an underprivileged family in Mississippi.

EXAMINING *the* ISSUES

- What are some environmental, economic, and social concerns of your country or community?
- What things might you do locally to address these concerns?

As a class, discuss these questions. As you consider how to address the major challenges facing your country and community, talk about why you think it is important to get involved.

674 Epilogue

WHY STUDY UNRESOLVED PROBLEMS OF THE MODERN WORLD?

- Pollution affects everyone to some degree, and use of polluting substances in the United States affects relations with other nations. For example, the United States is the world's leading emitter of carbon dioxide. In March 2001, President George W. Bush announced that the United States would not sign the Kyoto Protocol. If ratified, the treaty would commit industrialized nations to reducing emissions of greenhouse gases such as carbon dioxide.
- Poverty affects citizens of the United States. Child poverty rates in the United States are substantially higher than in most other Western industrialized nations. About 16 percent of U.S. children—almost 12 million—lived in poverty in 2001. Seven percent, about 5 million, lived in extreme poverty.
- Poverty causes hunger. According to the U.S. Department of Agriculture, in 2001 more than 10 percent of all U.S. households, representing 20 million adults and 13 million children, were "food insecure."
- Like other nations, the United States is vulnerable to biological attacks. In October 2001, anthrax spores were sent through the U.S. mail to two media corporations and two U.S. senators. Five people died in the attacks, and about a dozen more became seriously ill.

Trees stunted by acid rain, Mount Mitchell, North Carolina

Grand Central Station, August 15, 2003

1 Technology Transforms Life

MAIN IDEA	WHY IT MATTERS NOW	TERMS & NAMES
SCIENCE AND TECHNOLOGY The rapid emergence of new technologies holds promises as well as challenges for people around the world.	New technology touches nearly every aspect of life for many people.	• mass media

SETTING THE STAGE For centuries, people have used science to find new ways to do things. But the pace of technological change has increased dramatically since the second half of the 20th century. The development of the silicon chip and other electronic circuits has paved the way for revolutions in electronics and computers. These technological revolutions have dramatically impacted numerous aspects of daily life, from how people live and work to the ways in which they communicate.

CALIFORNIA STANDARDS

10.10.3 Discuss the important trends in the regions today and whether they appear to serve the cause of individual freedom and democracy.

10.11 Students analyze the integration of countries into the world economy and the information, technological, and communications revolutions (e.g., television, satellites, computers).

CST 4 Students relate current events to the physical and human characteristics of places and regions.

A Revolution in Electronics

New forms of electronic circuits have made possible the production of powerful new machines, such as computers. Computers, along with advances in telecommunications, have greatly changed the way people handle information. They have done so by vastly increasing the speed at which information can be carried.

The Influence of Computers The earliest and most basic use of computers was computing—figuring out complex math problems. As electronic circuits have grown faster, computers have been able to solve problems even more quickly. Powerful computers can make billions of computations every second.

The ability to compute quickly makes computers very helpful. They are used to guide rockets and satellites into space. Air traffic controllers use them to track airline traffic. Many automobiles use computers to control fuel gauges, engines, and even brakes. Banks and other businesses use computers to keep track of accounts and inventory. In 1997, an IBM-built computer named Deep Blue defeated world chess champion Garry Kasparov in a six-game chess match. Some people feared that computers might some day control humans. David Gelernter, a Yale University computer science professor, offered a different opinion:

PRIMARY SOURCE

Deep Blue is just a machine. It doesn't have a mind any more than a flowerpot has a mind. . . . Machines will continue to make life easier, healthier, richer, and more puzzling. And humans will continue to care . . . about the same things they always have: about themselves, about one another and, many of them, about God. On those terms, machines have never made a difference. And they never will.

DAVID GELERNTER, *Time*

TAKING NOTES

Summarizing Use a chart to list various technological innovations and what effect each has had on daily life.

Innovation	Effect

LESSON PLAN

OBJECTIVES

- Describe how computers have spurred advances in many fields and allowed people to communicate more quickly.
- List ways that recent technologies have influenced workplaces and cultures around the world.

1 FOCUS & MOTIVATE

Ask students if they can think of specific ways in which technological changes during their lifetime have affected them. *(Possible Answers: impact of cell phones, instant messaging, innovations in the way music is reproduced and distributed)*

2 INSTRUCT

A Revolution in Electronics
10.11

Critical Thinking

- What might a society's increasing reliance on computer technology imply about that society's values? *(Possible Answer: Speed is very important.)*
- Do new technologies emerge and transform culture, or do cultural needs and desires give rise to new technologies? *(Possible Answer: Technologies are created to fill needs or desires, but they can also cause new needs or desires.)*

DIFFERENTIATING INSTRUCTION: STRUGGLING READERS

Summarizing the Effects of New Technologies

Class Time 25 minutes

Task Creating a concept web about technology

Purpose To help students understand the widespread effects of technological change

Instructions Have pairs of students read "A Revolution in Electronics" on pages 675 and 677, helping each other with difficult words and concepts. When students have finished, draw a concept web on the board. As a class, complete the web so that it summarizes the information in the text. Explain that a concept web can be a useful way to take notes.

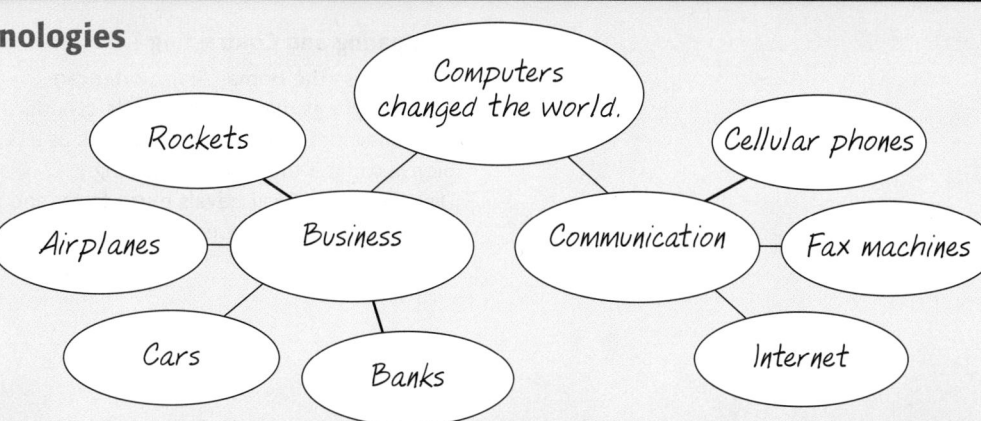

Computers changed the world.
Business: Rockets, Airplanes, Cars, Banks
Communication: Cellular phones, Fax machines, Internet

History *in* Depth

OBJECTIVE

- Discuss the impact of rapidly changing technologies.

INSTRUCT

Tell students that technology has changed so rapidly that some industries are struggling to keep pace. For example, MP3 technology, used to compress audio files, has made it much easier to transfer music electronically. To discourage the practice of illegally sharing copyrighted music online, the Recording Industry Association of America started legal proceedings against hundreds of people in September 2003. People found guilty could face fines of up to $150,000 for each illegally downloaded song.

More About . . .

Biometric Identification

Biometric identification systems translate patterns in a person's irises, fingerprints, face, voice, or other characteristics into mathematical algorithms. The algorithms are then stored on a computer chip or a machine-readable strip. When a person's features are scanned by a biometric device, a computer compares those patterns with the patterns detected when the person was originally scanned.

Recently, the United States passed legislation that will require all non–U.S. citizens to carry visas or passports with biometric identifiers.

History *in* Depth

A Continuous Revolution

CALIFORNIA STANDARDS
10.11, REP 4

Electronic and computer technologies, it seems, are advancing at a breakneck pace. Every day, people are working to improve the latest equipment and devices or to create something entirely new. The result is an ongoing revolution in the way we do everything from travel to communicate. Perhaps nowhere is the pace of change faster than in the fields of computers and electronics—where what was once considered science fiction has become a reality.

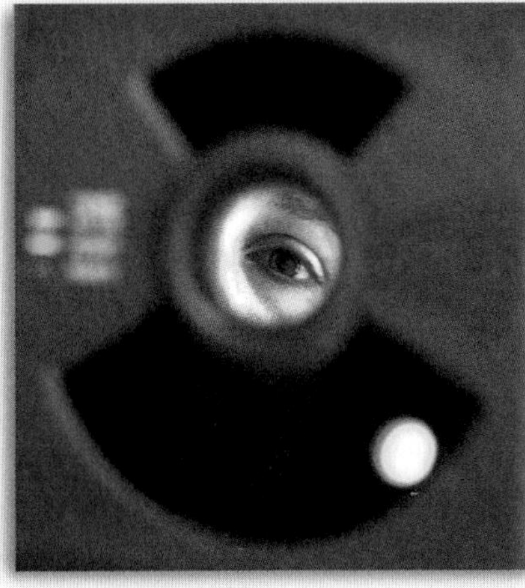

▲ Iris Identification
A woman looks through the Iris Access system, which scans the iris, or colored ring around the eye's pupil. Like fingerprints, the iris is unique to each person.

▲ Human Transporter
A police officer travels his beat on the Segway Human Transporter, an electric-powered machine that one drives simply by leaning forward. The Segway travels at a top speed of about 12 miles per hour.

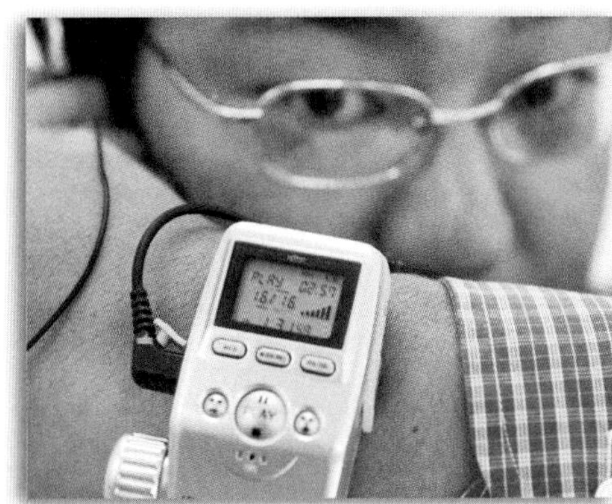

◄ Miniature Music Player
A music lover shows off his MP3 music player-wristwatch, which enables him to download and listen to his favorite songs from pay-for-use Internet sites.

DOCUMENT-BASED QUESTIONS

1. **Comparing and Contrasting** *What advantages and disadvantages does the Human Transporter have to a bicycle or automobile?*
2. **Forming and Supporting Opinions** *Which of these inventions do you consider to be the most important? Why?*

CONNECT TO TODAY: ANSWERS

1. Comparing and Contrasting
Advantages—The Human Transporter can go many places that an automobile cannot; the transporter can go as many places as a bicycle without the work of pedaling. Disadvantages—A car travels much faster and is more suitable for bad weather; bikes need no recharging.

2. Forming and Supporting Opinions
Most students will choose the iris indentification device, for it can be used to improve safety and security, while other inventions enhance leisure and recreation activities.

Information Spreads in New Ways Electronic technology also has had a great impact on how people communicate. People are increasing their use of cellular phones, fax machines, and computers—including the Internet—to move information instantly across the planet. As a result, people can very easily conduct business, or just chat from great distances. These technologies have helped draw the world closer together.

The Internet has become one of the most exciting ways for people to communicate. People can use the Internet to find ever-increasing amounts of information. More and more businesses advertise and sell their goods on the Internet. Governments use the Internet to provide their citizens with more information than ever before. In addition, people around the world can use chat rooms and electronic mail, or e-mail, to send messages to one another. (A)

MAIN IDEA

Hypothesizing

(A) How do you think the Internet will affect businesses in the 21st century?

A. Possible Answer Students may say that the Internet will continue to change the way people buy and sell goods. Some might even suggest that the Internet could put many stores out of business.

Global Impact

"Chat Room Savior" Sean Redden

On the afternoon of April 14, 1997, Sean Redden, a seventh-grader in Denton, Texas, received a startling message through the Internet: "Help me. I'm having trouble breathing." At first, Sean thought the message was a joke. When the pleas continued, though, Sean realized that the emergency was real.

In fact, the writer—Tarja Laitinen, a 20-year-old student in Finland, 7,000 miles away—was having a seizure. Sean's mother phoned 911, and after a series of phone calls, Finnish rescue workers found Tarja and rushed her to the hospital. Thanks to Sean and the Internet, Tarja's life was saved.

A Connected World

The Internet and other new technologies have made the world a much smaller place, as these advances have enabled the flow of information, ideas, and entertainment across cities and nations, and across the globe.

A Changing Workforce Rapid communications and data transmission have helped to transform workplaces around the world. Many white-collar workers now "telecommute," or do their jobs by computer from home. Investors can conduct business in any market in the world, from almost anywhere, by using telephones, fax machines, and computers. Television, radio, and the Internet can instantly give investors the news and information they need to conduct business. As a result, some professionals no longer need to live near business offices. In addition, modern telecommunications allow trading, banking, and financial transactions to be done electronically.

As you read in Chapter 20, technological changes such as these have had both positive and negative effects on businesses and workers. In manufacturing, robots perform more and more jobs that were once done by people. As a result, many companies have cut their workforces. In more technologically advanced economies, employment is shifting from blue-collar industries to high-tech industries. Many workers are being forced to improve their skills in order to keep their jobs because high-tech industries need workers with more technical skills.

Furthermore, high-tech workplaces are found mainly in industrialized countries, such as the United States, Japan, and the countries of western Europe. This technological imbalance has given rise to a new kind of economic imperialism in which the industrialized nations dominate less-developed countries.

Cultures Converge The **mass media**—which include television, radio, movies, the music industry, and the popular press—are expanding their influence with the growth of technology. Television has spread to the extent that billions of people around the planet now watch sporting events such as the Olympics and the World Cup soccer championships. In addition, some 2 billion people worldwide viewed the funeral of Princess Diana of England on live television in 1997.

Global Impact

"Chat Room Savior" Sean Redden

The last message Sean Redden received from Tarja Laitinen explained that she could hear paramedics in the hallway. None of the people involved in Texas knew what had become of her until Interpol, an international crime prevention organization, contacted Texas police to report that that the incident was not a hoax and that "Ms. Laitinen got the medical attention she badly needed that night and is now doing well."

A Connected World

10.10.3

Critical Thinking

- How might rapid advances in communications technology affect how communities are built? *(Possible Answer: Since people can buy things and do business through computers, homes may not need to be as close to commercial or business areas.)*
- Is cultural globalization a positive or negative phenomenon? *(Positive—A new, richer culture will emerge by combining what is best from dominant and local cultures. Negative—Many nations do not have the resources to protect local cultures from the overwhelming influence of Western culture.)*

DIFFERENTIATING INSTRUCTION: GIFTED AND TALENTED STUDENTS

Debating the Pros and Cons of Technology

Class Time 40 minutes

Task Developing arguments in favor of or against a statement

Purpose To sharpen understanding of complex issues

Instructions Divide students into groups of four. Have each group choose one of the statements listed at right. Two members of each group should work together to develop arguments in favor of the statement. The other two members should develop arguments against it. Arguments should be based on the text and on students' knowledge or research. When groups have finished, have them debate their question. Poll the class about which side was more effective.

- New technologies lead to new problems.
- Someday computers will control humans.
- New methods of identification will lead to a "police state" where the government monitors everything and everyone.
- Internet-based communities are not as worthwhile as more traditional communities.
- People who oppose technology are just afraid of what they don't yet understand.
- Technology and mass media have led to a new and better global culture.
- Technology and traditional ways of life can coexist peacefully.

More About . . .

Globalization

Media critic Neil Postman was asked whether globalization would make the world more homogeneous. He responded: "We seem to be experiencing the opposite. . . . all over the world, we see a kind of reversion to tribalism. People are going back to their tribal roots in order to find a sense of identity. . . . we see it in Russia, in Yugoslavia, in Canada, in the United States. . . . Why is [it] that every group now not only is more aware of its own grievances but seems to want its own education? You know, we want an Afro-centric curriculum and a Korean-centric curriculum, and a Greek-centered curriculum. What is it about all this globalization of communication that is making people return to more—to smaller units of identity? It's a puzzlement."

3 ASSESS

SECTION 1 ASSESSMENT

Ask students to work in small groups to answer the questions. Then discuss as a class the responses to question 7.

4 RETEACH

Ask volunteers to use the headers to summarize the main content of this section for the class.

▲ A traveler talks by cell phone in rural Israel.

Because the media now reach around the world, they are able to spread images, ideas, and fashions from one country to another. Many of these ideas or trends travel from the developed world outward. But the mass media also bring cultural offerings from Africa, Asia, and Latin America to wealthier nations. The increased familiarity in Europe and the United States with African music, Asian philosophy, and Latin American literature demonstrates the power of the mass media to promote a greater awareness of and mixing of different cultures. For instance, the English translation of *Como Agua Para Chocolate* (Like Water for Chocolate), the popular novel by Laura Esquivel, sold over two million copies in the United States. **B**

MAIN IDEA

Recognizing Effects

B How have new technologies affected your own life?

B. Possible Answer Students may mention items such as cable and satellite television, beepers, cell phones, CDs, computer games, the Internet and give examples of how they use these items.

Old Ways Abandoned As mass media spread new images and ideas, however, they may cause deep changes in traditional cultures. Old ways may be lost. In some cases, people experience a loss of identity and culture. Or they may find themselves in conflict over competing values. In addition, some observers, such as author and columnist Thomas Friedman, worry that so much technology is weakening the old and more personal ways of interacting:

PRIMARY SOURCE

Yes, globalization and the Internet can bring people together who have never connected before—like my mom and her French Internet bridge partners. But rather than creating new kinds of communities, this technology often creates a false sense of connection and intimacy. It's like two beepers communicating with each other. Can we really connect with each other through E-mail or Internet bridge or chat rooms? Or is all this standardizing technology just empowering us to reach farther into the world while exempting us from the real work required to build relationships and community with the folks next door?

THOMAS FRIEDMAN, *The Lexus and the Olive Tree*

Sometimes the challenge posed by new ideas and technology can stimulate the desire to preserve traditions. Technology may even play a positive role in this process. In the Amazon region of Brazil, for example, some native Brazilians are using video cameras to document and preserve traditional ways of life.

SECTION 1 ASSESSMENT

TERMS & NAMES 1. For the following term, write a sentence explaining its significance.

- mass media

USING YOUR NOTES

2. Which innovation has had the greatest impact? Why? (10.10.3)

Innovation	Effect

MAIN IDEAS

3. What are three modern communications devices? (10.11)
4. How has technology led to the emergence of telecommuting? (10.11)
5. What has been the main effect of the growth of mass media? (10.11)

CRITICAL THINKING & WRITING

6. **IDENTIFYING PROBLEMS** What challenges has technology created for some in the workforce? (10.11)
7. **RECOGNIZING EFFECTS** What are the benefits and drawbacks of the spread of mass media? (10.10.3)
8. **ANALYZING ISSUES** What problems, if any, do you see arising from the growth of the Internet? (10.11)
9. **WRITING ACTIVITY** SCIENCE AND TECHNOLOGY With a partner, use the library or the Internet to review the past year's issues of a leading science journal. Write a **report** on an important technological advance that was made during the year. (Writing 2.3.c)

CONNECT TO TODAY **CREATING A CHART**

Create a two-column **chart** that lists the top three or four technological devices you use and briefly explains the benefits of using each one. (Writing 2.3.d)

ANSWERS

1. mass media, p. 677
2. **Sample Answer:** Computers—New ways to travel, do business, and communicate; the Internet—New types of communities; Mass media—Global culture. Greatest impact—Computers, because they made the other innovations possible.
3. cellular phones, e-mail, and the Internet
4. The Internet and other communications devices enable some workers to interact with their office from home.
5. the spread of different cultures throughout the world
6. Many workers have been replaced by machines, while others have had to learn new skills to stay employed.
7. Benefits—Countries are able to experience and appreciate many cultures. Drawbacks—Some cultures risk losing their identity and traditions.
8. **Possible Answers:** spread of hateful and obscene materials; illegal downloading of copyrighted material
9. **Rubric** Reports should
   - be well organized and clearly written.
   - demonstrate knowledge of the subject.
   - cite at least one source.

CONNECT TO TODAY

Rubric Charts should

- be well organized and easy to follow.
- clearly convey the reasons students use the devices.

Trees stunted by acid rain, Mount Mitchell, North Carolina

Grand Central Station, August 15, 2003

Environmental Challenges

MAIN IDEA

INTERACTION WITH ENVIRONMENT Technology and industrialization have created environmental challenges that affect the entire world.

WHY IT MATTERS NOW

Failure to solve environmental problems will threaten the health of the planet.

TERMS & NAMES

- greenhouse effect
- sustainable development

SETTING THE STAGE Technology and industrialization have helped to raise standards of living for many people. But they have also affected the global environment. For two centuries, industrialization has increased the demands for energy and natural resources. In addition, industry and technology have increased the amount of pollution on the planet. Pollution and the potential shortage of natural resources have prompted everyone from world leaders to ordinary citizens to look for ways to better protect our natural surroundings.

CALIFORNIA STANDARDS

10.10.3 Discuss the important trends in the regions today and whether they appear to serve the cause of individual freedom and democracy.

CST 4 Students relate current events to the physical and human characteristics of places and regions.

World Concern over the Environment

Two major areas of concern are the effects of industrial pollution on the earth's atmosphere and on its climate. As you read in Chapter 20, environmentalists are especially concerned that various human-made chemicals are destroying the ozone layer, which protects earth from the sun's damaging rays. Scientists also are worried about global warming, also known as the **greenhouse effect**.

The Greenhouse Effect Scientists use the term *greenhouse effect* to describe problems caused by industrial pollution. Much of this pollution comes in the form of gases, such as carbon dioxide. These gases—sometimes called greenhouse gases—are the exhaust from factories and automobiles. The gases create a kind of ceiling, like the roof of a greenhouse, that traps heat near the earth's surface. This buildup of heat near the earth's surface causes a gradual warming of the earth's atmosphere.

Not all scientists agree with the theory of the greenhouse effect. But tests do indicate that the earth's climate is slowly warming. If this trend continues, deserts will expand and crops will fail. The polar icecaps will melt and oceans will rise.

To combat this problem, the industrialized nations have called for limits on the release of greenhouse gases. In the past, developed nations were the worst polluters. But future limits would have the greatest effect on those countries that are trying to industrialize. So far, developing countries have resisted strict limits. They argue that they are being asked to carry too much of the burden for reducing greenhouse gases.

Air Pollution Varies In addition to its possible warming effects, air pollution can be a serious health hazard. In recent years, many cities in Europe and the United States have taken steps to clean up the air. But air pollution is still severe

TAKING NOTES

Determining Main Ideas Use a web chart to take notes on the environmental problems that the world faces.

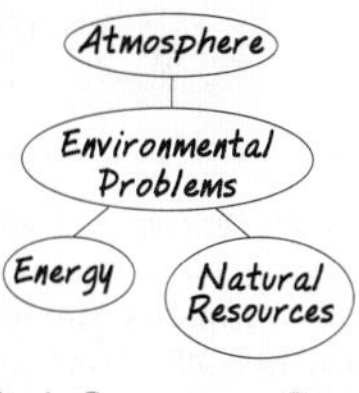

LESSON PLAN

OBJECTIVES

- Discuss concerns about effects of pollution, including the greenhouse effect and destruction of the ozone layer.
- Describe depletion of natural resources, including rain forests and water.
- Explore issues raised by energy usage.

1 FOCUS & MOTIVATE

Ask students what the U.S. government has done to protect the environment. *(Students might mention the creation of the Environmental Protection Agency in 1970 or the passage of the Clean Water Act in 1972.)*

2 INSTRUCT

World Concern over the Environment

10.10.3

Critical Thinking

- How might economic interests affect scientific research on the greenhouse effect? *(Possible Answer: Industries that produce greenhouse gases might support research that questions the greenhouse effect.)*
- Why might many Asian nations have been slow to pass environmental protection legislation? *(Possible Answer: to give industries time to develop without the encumbrance of environmental regulations)*

DIFFERENTIATING INSTRUCTION: GIFTED AND TALENTED STUDENTS

The Greenhouse Effect and the Ozone Layer

Class Time 45 minutes

Task Delivering an oral report on environmental problems

Purpose To help students understand the difference between the greenhouse effect and the depletion of the ozone layer

Instructions Divide students into groups. After groups have read the passage on this page about the greenhouse effect, have them carry out further research on the phenomenon at the library or on the Internet. In addition to researching the greenhouse effect, ask students to gather information on the depletion of the ozone layer. Explain that they will be using this information to put together an oral report. Reports should be 10 to 15 minutes and should include a slide show or other visuals, including diagrams, images, and time lines. Among the topics students might include are the composition of the earth's atmosphere, the different greenhouse gases, ozone, chlorofluorocarbons (CFCs), ultraviolet radiation, and the Montreal and Kyoto Protocols. Have students prepare a brief fact sheet to hand out after their presentation. The fact sheet should include brief explanations and contact information, such as phone numbers or Web addresses for environmental agencies, that people can use to learn more about the two phenomena.

Depletion of Natural Resources

10.10.3

Critical Thinking

- How can governments promote the use of renewable resources? *(by providing subsidies to industries developing such resources, by regulating nonrenewable resources)*
- Can you think of other pollution issues not mentioned in the text? *(Possible Answers: nuclear waste, noise pollution)*

History from Visuals

Interpreting the Graph

Ask students how many square miles of the Amazon rain forest were cut down between 1978 and 1997. *(about 248,000)* Have students determine the annual rate of deforestation based on this figure. *(about 13,000 square miles per year)*

Extension Have students use the library or the Internet to find out whether the depletion of the Amazon rain forest has continued.

SKILLBUILDER Answer

1. Clarifying about 341,000 square miles

in many parts of the world, especially Asia. The World Health Organization has pointed out that 13 of the world's 15 most-polluted cities are in Asia.

Meanwhile, South Korea, China, and Japan have begun talks to reduce the effects of pollution caused by China's rapid industrialization. And some Chinese cities are trying to reduce air pollution locally. For example, Shanghai has reportedly banned leaded gasoline and diesel fuel, which cause heavy pollution.

Depletion of Natural Resources

While air pollution and global warming are indeed a growing concern, so too is the growing strain on natural resources. Due largely to industrialization and increasing population, vital resources such as clean water, forests, and energy supplies all run the risk of becoming scarce.

Scarcity of Clean Water In the developing world, water pollution and scarcity of clean water are serious problems. One-fourth of the world's population has no access to clean water. Eighty percent of all illnesses in developing nations can be traced to inadequate supplies of fresh water.

In some parts of the world, nations share the water supplies in lakes and rivers. In southwest Asia, for example, Israel and Jordan share the Jordan River—an essential source of water for farming. Any nation that pollutes shared water or stops water from flowing into a neighboring country runs the risk of starting an international conflict. Many nations try to cooperate to make sure water supplies remain clean.

In the United States, California has complex water issues. The state's large population and agricultural industry have put severe pressure on water resources. The problems worsened during a drought that lasted from 1987 to 1992. However, the state limited the negative effects of the drought by developing new ways to conserve and use water.

Destruction of Rain Forests Another critical resource issue is the destruction of tropical rain forests in such countries as Malaysia and Brazil. By 1990, the world

Depletion of the Brazilian Amazon Rain Forest

Extent of Deforestation, 1997

13%

■ Total area: 1.6 million square miles

Source: *The Brazilian Amazon Rain Forest; World Forests from Deforestation to Transition?*

SKILLBUILDER: Interpreting Graphs

Clarifying *About how many square miles of the Brazilian Amazon rain forest were deforested by 1997?*

DIFFERENTIATING INSTRUCTION: STRUGGLING READERS

Evaluating Arguments about the Environment

Class Time 30 minutes

Task Summarizing and detecting bias in primary sources

Purpose To understand conflicting points of view

Instructions Pair students and ask them to read the Analyzing Primary Sources feature on the opposite page. Encourage pairs to use dictionaries or glossaries for help with difficult words. Then have one member of each pair write a summary of the first primary source and the other summarize the second. Summaries should be in students' own words and should be no longer than a sentence or two. *(Possible Answer: Keye–Some people don't want any trees cut down, even though they grow back. That means that people in the lumber business are suffering. Wilson–Forests are complicated, and they make the clean air and water we need. They belong to all the people, so they shouldn't be cut down.)*

Ask volunteers to read their summaries. Discuss what evidence of bias students can detect in each primary source. *(Possible Answer: Keye is the leader of a logging group, so he is naturally interested in what will benefit members of his group. Wilson is a researcher at a university, so he is likely to focus more on environmental arguments and less on economic ones.)*

Analyzing Primary Sources

Economics

Deforestation is an issue that often pits economic and environmental interests against one another. Here, William Wade Keye, chairman of the Northern California Society of American Foresters, criticizes the efforts of environmentalists.

PRIMARY SOURCE

It used to be about protecting spotted owls, saving old-growth forests or putting an end to clear-cutting. That was 1990. . . . Now the demand is for absolute purity. To many environmentalists in 2001, nothing less than "zero-cut" is acceptable—no commercial timber harvesting from America's vast network of publicly owned national forests. Not one stick. . . . In a region blessed with some of the planet's most fertile and sustainable temperate forest ecosystems, struggling sawmill communities are subsisting on raw logs imported from hundreds—sometimes even thousands—of miles away.

WILLIAM WADE KEYE, from *Southern Loggin' Times*

Environmentalism

Edward O. Wilson, a research professor emeritus at Harvard University, makes it clear that environmental concerns should outweigh all else when considering America's forests.

PRIMARY SOURCE

If we have learned anything from the scientific studies of forests, it is that each such environment is a unique combination of thousands of kinds of plants, animals, and microorganisms. . . . It is this biological diversity that creates a healthy ecosystem—a self-assembled powerhouse generating clean water, productive soil and fresh air, all without human intervention and completely free of charge. . . . America's national forests are the common property of its citizens. They are a public trust of incalculable value. They should be freed from commercial logging altogether and cut only very locally and in extreme cases.

EDWARD O. WILSON, from *The Washington Post*

DOCUMENT-BASED QUESTIONS

1. **Recognizing Effects** *What effect have environmental regulations had on the logging industry, according to Keye?*
2. **Analyzing Issues** *What reason does Wilson give for arguing that forests should be maintained and protected?*

had lost more than half its rain forests to logging or farming operations. Experts estimated that another 20 percent had been lost by the year 2000.

This loss could affect all people on the planet. The rain forests help to maintain water quality, recycle rainfall and oxygen into the atmosphere, and protect the soil. These forests also are home to as many as half of the world's species of plants and animals.

In recent years, nations like Brazil have made efforts to slow the destruction of the rain forests. Success has been limited, however, by Brazil's desire to develop economically. As one American diplomat put it, "Environmental concerns are a luxury of the rich, and this is not a rich country. Brazilians are not going to just preserve the Amazon. They are going to develop it. The question is, how."

Many other developing nations face the same problem as Brazil. They need to achieve **sustainable development**, the process of creating economic growth while preserving the environment.

A Growing Appetite for Energy

Sustainable development depends on using energy sources wisely. All sources of energy can be defined as renewable or nonrenewable. Renewable energy sources, such as wind, water, and solar power, can be replenished. Nonrenewable energy sources, such as oil and coal, cannot. Although nonrenewable sources are generally cheaper to use, supplies are limited. Also, their use can cause environmental damage.

Energy Use and its Challenges Eighty percent of the earth's energy supply now comes from nonrenewable sources. Developed countries consume most of this

Analyzing Primary Sources

Economics and Environmentalism

Ask students if they think that William Wade Keye makes a legitimate argument. *(Yes—Environmentalists have no right to rob a community of its livelihood to save a few trees that will grow back anyway. No—The environment cannot be sacrificed to save a small number of jobs.)*

Answers to Document-Based Questions

1. **Recognizing Effects** They have caused many sawmill communities to struggle economically.
2. **Analyzing Issues** *Possible Answers:* Forests play a key role in creating a healthy ecosystem; national forests belong to all citizens.

A Growing Appetite for Energy

10.10.3

Critical Thinking

- Why might leading users of energy be reluctant to curb their consumption? *(Possible Answer: Cutting back is likely to be difficult and expensive.)*
- Why might it be difficult to hold large energy companies responsible for their actions? *(Possible Answer: They have enormous financial and legal resources at their disposal.)*

DIFFERENTIATING INSTRUCTION: ENGLISH LEARNERS

Renewable and Nonrenewable Energy Sources

Class Time 40 minutes

Task Compiling an image booklet of energy resources

Purpose To help students improve their vocabulary

Instructions Ask pairs of students to make a two-column list and to label one side "Renewable Energy Sources" and the other "Nonrenewable Energy Sources." As they read "A Growing Appetite for Energy," have pairs list different energy sources in the appropriate column. *(Renewable—Wind, water, solar. Nonrenewable—Oil, coal, wood, nuclear fuel.)* After they have compiled their lists, have pairs design a booklet that features these energy sources. Booklets must include a cover design, a table of contents, and a short introduction and conclusion. Booklets should feature images of the different energy sources accompanied by written explanations. The text might include information about environmental effects, economic costs, or how much of the energy consumed in the United States is produced by a specific source. Students can draw the images or gather pictures from magazines or other media. Encourage students to be creative and to express an opinion about an appropriate energy policy in their conclusions.

Connect *to* Today

Alternative Fuel Cars

The success of hydrogen-powered automobiles in limiting the use of nonrenewable sources of energy will depend on how the hydrogen is produced. *The National Hydrogen Energy Roadmap* indicates that "up to 90 percent of all hydrogen will be refined from oil, natural gas, and other fossil fuels—in a process using energy generated by burning oil, coal, and natural gas. The remaining 10 percent will be [taken] from water using nuclear energy." Therefore, scientists are trying to develop renewable energy sources, such as wastewater, wind, and sunlight.

More About . . .

The Valdez Disaster

In December 2002, a federal judge in Alaska reduced to $4 billion the punitive damages imposed on Exxon for the Valdez disaster. The oil company said it planned to appeal the decision.

3 ASSESS

SECTION 2 ASSESSMENT

After students respond to the items, have them form pairs to evaluate each other's responses.

4 RETEACH

Discuss question 6 as a class. Ask students to cite information from the section to support their answers. Have the class formulate a group answer to the question.

Connect *to* Today

Alternative Fuel Cars

Automobiles, which run on oil-based gasoline, use a great deal of the world's nonrenewable energy. But perhaps not for long. Automakers have begun creating cars fueled by alternative power, such as hydrogen—one of the most abundant natural elements on earth.

While it may be a while before such cars catch on, the trend toward environmentally safer vehicles is growing. California, for example, recently required the production of millions of low-emission vehicles—which use a combination of gas and electric power—over the next two decades.

energy. Although these nations account for just 25 percent of the world's population, they use 75 percent of the energy consumed worldwide.

Using nonrenewable energy has many environmental effects. The burning of coal emits greenhouse gases. Cutting down trees leads to soil erosion and the expansion of deserts in some areas. Nuclear power plants produce radioactive wastes that can remain hazardous for many years. (A)

MAIN IDEA
Identifying Problems
(A) What are some problems associated with the use of nonrenewable energy?
A. Answer Its supply is limited and it can pose a threat to the environment.

The Exxon Valdez Oil Spill Oil spills are another example of energy-related pollution. Every year, several serious oil spills take place around the world. They foul water and shorelines and kill sea life. Although oil companies take precautions to prevent spills, spills appear to be an inevitable result of oil use.

The largest oil spill in U.S. history occurred in March 1989. The giant oil tanker Exxon Valdez hit a reef in Prince William Sound, off the coast of Alaska. The ship spilled 11 million gallons of crude oil into the sea. The environmental consequences were horrendous. But the federal government responded forcefully. It ordered a cleanup and forced Exxon to pay more than $5 billion in damages.

Solutions for the 21st Century Government action and stronger regulations may provide solutions to the world's environmental problems in the 21st century. In the long run, however, improved technology might stand as the best hope for a cleaner environment. More inexpensive ways to use renewable energy sources, such as wind and solar power, may reduce air pollution and the greenhouse effect. In any event, the nations of the world will need to agree on how to achieve sustainable development in this new millennium.

SECTION 2 ASSESSMENT

TERMS & NAMES 1. For each term, write a sentence explaining its significance.
• greenhouse effect • sustainable development

USING YOUR NOTES

2. Which set of problems do you consider to be the most serious? Why? (10.10.3)

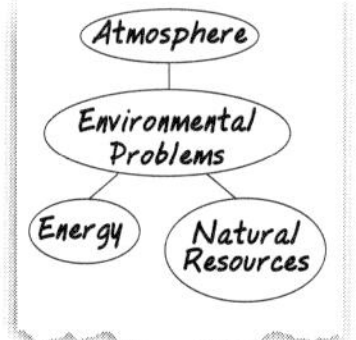

MAIN IDEAS

3. What are the main greenhouse gases? (10.10.3)
4. What natural resources does the world community fear are becoming scarce? (10.10.3)
5. What is the difference between renewable and nonrenewable energy? (10.10.3)

CRITICAL THINKING & WRITING

6. **HYPOTHESIZING** Why do you think the environmental problems of the earth have become more dangerous? (10.10.3)
7. **FORMING AND SUPPORTING OPINIONS** Should developing nations have to meet the same environmental standards as developed nations? Why or why not? (10.10.3)
8. **ANALYZING ISSUES** Should developed nations take any responsibility for preventing the destruction of the rain forests? Explain. (10.10.3)
9. **WRITING ACTIVITY** INTERACTION WITH ENVIRONMENT Write one or two **slogans** that might encourage your community to better protect the environment. (Writing 2.4.b)

CONNECT TO TODAY **CREATING A VISUAL**

Examine your local newspaper to determine an environmental problem in your community. Then create a **poster, cartoon,** or other **graphic** that depicts that problem. (Writing 2.3.d)

ANSWERS

1. greenhouse effect, p. 679 • sustainable development, p. 681
2. **Sample Answer:** Atmosphere—Greenhouse effect, air pollution; Natural Resources—Water scarcity, destruction of rain forests; Energy—Nonrenewable resources, nuclear waste, oil spills. Most serious—Atmosphere, because it affects the climate of the entire planet.
3. exhaust from factories and automobiles
4. clean water, forests, energy
5. Renewable energy can be replenished or reused; nonrenewable cannot.
6. **Possible Answers:** Population increases put greater strains on resources; technological change has led to more industry and more pollution.
7. Yes—It is important to protect the environment. No—Developing nations deserve the same opportunity to make their economies grow as developed nations have had.
8. Yes—Developed nations should protect the rain forests to preserve water quality and reduce the greenhouse effect. No—Rain forests belong to the countries where they exist.
9. **Rubric** Slogans should
   • convey a clear and strong message.
   • be persuasive and easy to comprehend.

CONNECT TO TODAY

Rubric Visuals should
• relate to a local environmental problem.
• be easy to understand.

Trees stunted by acid rain, Mount Mitchell, North Carolina

Grand Central Station, August 15, 2003

3

Feeding a Growing Population

MAIN IDEA	WHY IT MATTERS NOW	TERMS & NAMES
POWER AND AUTHORITY Population growth has put great pressure on the earth's resources, including the food supply.	Nations must find ways to support their growing human populations or else face famines.	• overpopulation • biorevolution

SETTING THE STAGE As humanity moves further into the 21st century, another issue of growing concern is world hunger. Potential causes of famine are overpopulation, forces of nature, and war. **Overpopulation** occurs when there are too many people for the natural resources of an area to support. In some cases, it is war or natural catastrophes that push groups into starvation. Across the globe, nations are working to implement both temporary and more long lasting measures aimed at reducing starvation and hunger.

CALIFORNIA STANDARDS

10.10.3 Discuss the important trends in the regions today and whether they appear to serve the cause of individual freedom and democracy.

CST 4 Students relate current events to the physical and human characteristics of places and regions.

Causes of World Hunger

Since 1950, the world's population has more than doubled, to about 6 billion people. More growth is predicted. According to researchers, the world's population will increase to nearly 10 billion by 2050. Rapid population growth directly affects the quality of life on the planet. As more people try to live on a limited supply of natural resources, poverty rates rise—and so too does the risk of widespread hunger.

The Role of Nature In some areas of the world, changes in the climate have played a major role in creating famine. In Africa, for example, rainfall was plentiful during the 1950s and 1960s. The rain helped produce good crops and steady economic growth for many African nations. In 1968, however, drought began to weaken African agriculture. In the 1970s and 1980s, rainfall returned to typically low levels. In many areas, food supplies ran short. Ethiopia, for example, confronted severe famines in the 1980s and 1990s because of drought. Tens of thousands of Ethiopians died. Many others suffered malnutrition and disease.

The situation is just as grim in other African nations. Traveling through Zimbabwe in late 2002, U.S. government official Tony P. Hall recalled witnessing the devastating effects of hunger:

PRIMARY SOURCE

I . . . met children in school, some of whom had not eaten at all that day. Others had a cup of tea for breakfast and nothing for lunch. Some were showing clear signs of malnutrition—with their hair turning orange and their limbs like twigs. The headmaster said that about 40 percent of the kids have dropped out of school. A few kids had their eyes glazed over and showed little ability to learn the lessons in front of them.

TONY P. HALL, statement in Harare, Zimbabwe, October 11, 2002

TAKING NOTES

Comparing and Contrasting Use a chart to compare and contrast the advantages and disadvantages of the green revolution and the biorevolution.

Green Revolution	Bio-revolution

LESSON PLAN

OBJECTIVES

- List the natural and human-made causes of world hunger.
- Describe advances and difficulties in food production.
- Discuss solutions to population problems, including improving economies, limiting population growth, and improving the status of women.

1 FOCUS & MOTIVATE

Ask students if they know the approximate population of the United States. *(over 292 million)*

2 INSTRUCT

Causes of World Hunger

10.10.3

Critical Thinking

- Why might Africa be especially vulnerable to famine? *(Possible Answers: climate, high birth rates, wars)*
- What is meant by "government-produced famine"? *(War, severe economic problems, or an unstable government can limit how much food a country can produce and prevent outside agencies such as the Red Cross from delivering food and medical aid.)*

DIFFERENTIATING INSTRUCTION: ENGLISH LEARNERS

Frequently Asked Questions about World Hunger

Class Time 30 minutes

Task Answering questions about world hunger

Purpose To improve understanding of causes and effects

Instructions Pair students. Have them read the material under "Causes of World Hunger." Encourage them to consult a dictionary or glossary for help with difficult terms. Then assign each group one of the questions at right. Pairs should use information from the text to write a complete and thoughtful answer in their own words. Ask volunteers to read their answers aloud. Then collect the information in a notebook or binder for classroom reference.

- How does population affect hunger? *(More people have to live on a limited supply of water, food, and land.)*
- How does climate affect hunger? *(Lack of rain can limit food supplies.)*
- How do governments affect hunger? *(Well-organized governments can get food to places where it is needed. Governments that are poorly organized or at war can prevent food from being farmed or from reaching people who need it.)*

History from Visuals

Interpreting the Graph

According to the forecast, what will the world population be in 2015? *(about 7.4 billion)*

Extension Encourage students who have Internet access to visit the U.S. Census Bureau Web site. There they can find population clocks that show up-to-the-second national and world population estimates.

SKILLBUILDER Answers

1. **Comparing** Asia and Oceania
2. **Analyzing Issues** Africa will have the highest percentage growth; Asia and Oceania will have the highest total growth.

Revolutions in Food Production
10.10.3

Critical Thinking

- How might efforts to increase food production worsen the very problem they attempt to solve? *(Increasing the food supply might enable further population growth, which, eventually, would make food supplies inadequate.)*
- Why might the biorevolution be proceeding despite the troubling issues it raises? *(Possible Answers: World hunger is a serious problem that must be addressed, even if solutions are not perfect; companies that own patents to bioengineered crops may make enormous profits.)*

Forecast for World Population

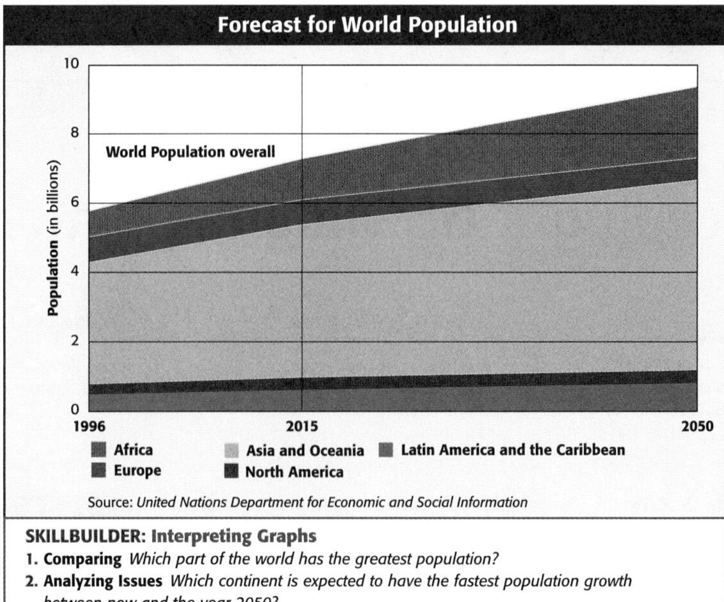

Source: *United Nations Department for Economic and Social Information*

SKILLBUILDER: Interpreting Graphs
1. **Comparing** *Which part of the world has the greatest population?*
2. **Analyzing Issues** *Which continent is expected to have the fastest population growth between now and the year 2050?*

Government-Produced Famine In addition to droughts, wars have contributed to famine. The drought that hit Ethiopia in the early 1990s hit Somalia as well. But Somalia was also engaged in a civil war that disrupted food production and delivery by outside relief agencies. As a result, thousands of Somalis died of starvation, and more than a million refugees fled the nation.

The reduction in food supply caused by drought and war created deep problems for many African nations. While agriculture declined, the prices for major African exports also fell. High African birth rates made these problems even worse. Food supplies were getting smaller while populations were getting larger. (A)

MAIN IDEA
Recognizing Effects
(A) How have droughts and wars affected African food supplies?
A. Answer Droughts have reduced the amount of food that African farmers can grow. Wars have disrupted food production and distribution.

Revolutions in Food Production

One response to the problem of rapid population growth, and the potential for hunger and starvation it brings, has been to boost food production. As you read in Chapter 20, agricultural scientists around the world embarked on what became known as the green revolution—a successful effort to increase food production through the use of fertilizers, pesticides and high-yield strains of crops.

Unfortunately, the techniques of the green revolution often call for much irrigation, or watering, of crops. Because many African nations have limited water supplies, they have not been able to make full use of the new seeds. This severely limits the usefulness of these methods in much of Africa, where there is little water.

Moreover, the new hybrid varieties of plants require chemicals, such as fertilizers, herbicides, and pesticides, to help them grow. This requirement has caused a number of problems. First, the chemicals are expensive. Peasant farmers usually cannot afford them. Second, the use of such chemicals often clashes with age-old methods of farming. Third, these chemicals pose a threat to the environment.

Vocabulary
A *pesticide* is a chemical used to kill insects; a *herbicide* is one used to destroy plants, especially weeds.

In addition to the methods of the green revolution, genetic research has played a growing role in agricultural science in recent years. In this approach, scientists

DIFFERENTIATING INSTRUCTION: GIFTED AND TALENTED STUDENTS

Debating the Use of Genetically Modified Foods

Class Time 40 minutes

Task Conducting research and holding an informal debate

Purpose To learn more about a complex issue that affects the food we eat every day

Instructions Have individual students read the material about genetically altered foods on page 685. Then have pairs of students do further research on the topic at the library or on the Internet. Helpful keywords include the following:

- genetically modified
- genetically altered
- GMO
- Flavr Savr tomato
- Frankenfood

Ask pairs to educate themselves on the basic issues surrounding genetically modified foods. Then have them decide which student will choose to argue in favor of such foods and which will argue against them.

When students have finished their research, stage an informal debate in the classroom. Have the class vote on which side presented the best arguments.

alter plant genes to produce new plants that are more productive and more resistant to pests and disease.

This **biorevolution**, or gene revolution, has led to some important developments. For example, one U.S. company has developed a genetically altered tomato that ripens more slowly than other tomatoes. This means that the altered tomatoes keep much of their flavor and freshness longer. Similar tests are being conducted with other kinds of produce. B

MAIN IDEA
Clarifying
B How has the biorevolution helped increase food production?
B. Answer by producing new plants that are more productive and more resistant to pests and disease

But the biorevolution has raised some troubling issues. Critics fear that altering genes may accidentally create new disease-causing organisms. Another fear is that plants produced by altering genes may become diseased more easily. As with the green revolution, science offers great opportunities in the search for more food, but the results may also have negative consequences.

Other Solutions to Population Problems

Various approaches to curbing overpopulation have been proposed over the years. Three main strategies are to improve the economies of less-developed countries, to limit population growth, and to improve the status of women.

Improving Economies Many experts believe that the best way to tackle overpopulation is through economic development. When a country's economy improves, birth rates fall. They do so for two reasons. First, women become pregnant less frequently because more newborn children survive. More children survive because stronger economies provide better health care, nutrition, and child-care education for mothers. Second, when economies are strong, families do not need as many children to work to support the family and parents in their old age. The result is slower population growth and less risk of widespread hunger.

Limiting Population Growth A second major strategy is to lower the rate at which the population is growing. In 1994, in Cairo, Egypt, the International Conference on Population and Development met for the third time. Delegates

History *in* Depth

Red Cross and UNICEF

Two organizations that have played a crucial role in supplying food and other forms of aid to needy populations are UNICEF and the Red Cross. UNICEF, the United Nations Children's Fund, was founded in 1946 to help children in Europe after World War II. Now, it provides food, medicine, and education funds to children in developing countries.

The Red Cross was first established in the 1800s to help war victims. Later it branched into peacetime service, including emergency food relief. The work of both of these organizations has been instrumental in helping to combat starvation, disease, and hardship in many lands.

▲ Red Cross workers hand out food in war-torn Rwanda, Africa.

A UNICEF official vaccinates an Afghan woman against the tetanus disease. ▶

Other Solutions to Population Problems
10.10.3

Critical Thinking

- What conflicts exist within the issue of limiting population growth? *(Possible Answers: between public health and personal freedom; between government organizations and religious organizations)*
- How might improving economies and improving the status of women be related? *(Without improved economic conditions, women will have difficulty finding alternatives to traditional child-rearing roles.)*

History *in* Depth

Red Cross and UNICEF

Students may be familiar with the Red Cross because this international organization sponsors first-aid classes and swimming classes in many communities. They also may have heard of UNICEF, which provides special emergency missions to help children caught in war, famine, or environmental disasters.

DIFFERENTIATING INSTRUCTION: STRUGGLING READERS

Overpopulation: Problems and Solutions

Class Time 15 minutes

Task Creating a problem-solution chart

Purpose To understand concepts and relationships in the text

Instructions Ask individual students to reread "Revolutions in Food Production" and "Other Solutions to Population Problems" on pages 684–686. As a class, complete a chart like the one at right.

Overpopulation	
Definition: Too many people, not enough food, water, or land	
Problem	**Solution**
Not enough food	Green revolution = use fertilizers, weed killers, and bug killers (but can be expensive and hurt environment) Biorevolution = use seeds that scientists have experimented on (better plants, but may cause diseases if not properly tested)
Economy is weak	
Population is growing too fast	
Women have little chance for an education or a good job	

More About . . .

Dr. Nafis Sadik

Dr. Nafis Sadik studied medicine in Pakistan and the United States. She began her career practicing obstetrics and gynecology in rural Pakistan. In 1970, she was named director-general of Pakistan's Central Family Planning Council, but she left a year later to join the United Nations Population Fund. By 1987, she had become that agency's executive director. She retired in December 2000 but remained active, serving as special adviser to the secretary-general, who in June 2002 appointed Sadik as Special Envoy for HIV/AIDS in Asia.

agreed on a plan to keep population growth to a minimum through the year 2050. It called for greater use of family planning, reductions in child mortality, and increased women's rights. Some delegates did not support the entire plan, but it passed nonetheless.

Some critics have pointed out problems in limiting population growth when it is carried out in extreme ways. A strict policy may reduce birth rates at the expense of personal freedom, or it may target specific groups that cannot defend their rights. For example, church leaders and some politicians in Peru have charged that a government program has forced poor Indian women to undergo sterilization, making them unable to have children. The critics have said that poor, uneducated women are lured into having the sterilization procedure by health workers who promise gifts for the families.

▲ Dr. Nafis Sadik stands outside United Nations headquarters in New York City.

Improving Women's Status Most experts believe that protecting the rights of women is essential to reducing birth rates. For example, the birth rate for uneducated Peruvian women in recent years was 6.2. By contrast, the rate for Peruvian women with some college education was only 1.7. According to population experts like Dr. Nafis Sadik of the United Nations Population Fund, there is a close link between women's status in society and population growth. The greater the status of women, the lower the birth rates.

Improving conditions for women will be a crucial part of any effort to solve the world's population problem. However, other actions will also need to be taken to reduce the threat of famine and food shortages. New technologies may provide a key to increasing food supplies. In addition, creating and protecting political stability around the world can help to ensure that people have access to food. The best way to conquer starvation, however, may be to improve the economies of developing nations.

③ ASSESS

SECTION 3 ASSESSMENT

Have students answer the questions individually and then meet in small groups to discuss their answers.

④ RETEACH

Ask groups of students to write a brief summary of the content under each headline. Have groups exchange their summaries with other groups.

SECTION 3 ASSESSMENT

TERMS & NAMES 1. For each term, write a sentence explaining its significance.
- overpopulation
- biorevolution

USING YOUR NOTES

2. Which of these campaigns combats hunger more effectively? Why? (10.10.3)

Green Revolution	Bio-revolution

MAIN IDEAS

3. What are the main causes of famine in the world? (10.10.3)
4. Why have some countries been unable to benefit from the green revolution? (10.10.3)
5. What are the three main strategies for controlling overpopulation? (10.10.3)

CRITICAL THINKING & WRITING

6. **MAKING INFERENCES** How will improving women's rights have an impact on population problems? (10.10.3)
7. **ANALYZING ISSUES** Do the benefits of new agricultural techniques outweigh the drawbacks? Explain. (10.10.3)
8. **FORMING AND SUPPORTING OPINIONS** Should governments establish policies to reduce population growth? Why or why not? (10.10.3)
9. **WRITING ACTIVITY** POWER AND AUTHORITY Write an **expository essay** identifying and explaining the different positions governments have taken on the issue of population growth. (Writing 2.3.b)

CONNECT TO TODAY CREATING A CHART

Choose a country and track its population figures over the past century on a **chart**. Display your chart to the class and discuss possible reasons for the trends you found. (Writing 2.3.d)

ANSWERS

1. overpopulation, p. 683 • biorevolution, p. 685
2. **Sample Answer:** Green Revolution—Can increase food production, but requires much water and expensive, harmful chemicals. Biorevolution—Can produce bigger and more disease-resistant plants, but may cause diseases. More effective—The biorevolution, because it does not require irrigation techniques.
3. overpopulation, drought or other forces of nature, war
4. because of the need for substantial amounts of irrigation
5. improving economies, limiting population growth, improving the status of women
6. Studies show that as women's social status improves, birth rates decline.
7. Yes—It is important to increase food production. No—New technologies will jeopardize the environment.
8. Yes—Overpopulation will be a serious problem in the next century. No—Governments should not be so deeply involved in personal matters.
9. **Rubric** Expository essays should
- explain positions on the issue.
- include a thesis and supporting details.

CONNECT TO TODAY

Rubric Charts should
- be clear and neat.
- cite at least one source.

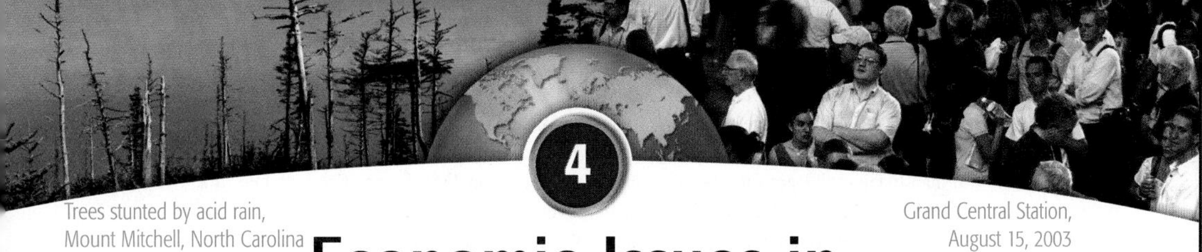

Trees stunted by acid rain, Mount Mitchell, North Carolina

Grand Central Station, August 15, 2003

4

Economic Issues in the Developing World

MAIN IDEA

ECONOMICS Developing nations face a set of economic challenges that must be resolved.

WHY IT MATTERS NOW

Sustainable economic development enables more people to lead productive lives and makes the world more stable.

TERMS & NAMES

- less-developed countries (LDCs)
- investment capital
- World Bank
- International Monetary Fund (IMF)
- grassroots development

SETTING THE STAGE The economies of the industrialized nations grew rapidly after World War II. Such has not been the case, however, for many **less-developed countries (LDCs)**, or countries not fully industrialized. Among other things, the LDCs have lacked financial resources and a strong infrastructure—roads, airports, plumbing, and electrical systems—necessary for economic growth. Nevertheless, the industrialized nations have remained interested in the LDCs as sources of raw materials and as potential markets for goods. Indeed, the industrialized nations would like the economies of the LDCs to become strong and stable.

CALIFORNIA STANDARDS

10.10.3 Discuss the important trends in the regions today and whether they appear to serve the cause of individual freedom and democracy.

CST 4 Students relate current events to the physical and human characteristics of places and regions.

Providing International Aid

Most economists cite the following factors as necessary for economic development:

- **investment capital**, funds to pay for the construction of industries and infrastructure, such as roads and bridges
- technology to help companies and workers be as productive as possible
- healthy and well-trained workers to help reduce waste and inefficiency
- qualified managers to make sure that workers and materials are used efficiently

Roots of the Difficulties A serious problem that LDCs face is how to acquire these factors. Many people believe that imperialism and colonialism are the reasons that the LDCs have not industrialized. The imperial nations limited the economic growth of their colonies. In addition, the colonial governments robbed the colonized people of the chance to govern themselves. When most colonized regions gained their independence after World War II, they had underdeveloped economies and weak political traditions. These problems made it difficult for the LDCs to achieve stable economic growth. In recent years, however, more and more LDCs have been developing stable democratic governments and making greater strides toward a stronger economy.

Industrialized nations have tried to work with the LDCs by providing aid through international organizations, such as the **World Bank** and the **International Monetary Fund (IMF)**. The World Bank provides loans for large-scale development projects, such as dams. The IMF offers emergency loans to countries in financial crisis.

TAKING NOTES

Identifying Solutions Create a web diagram showing the various solutions to creating economic growth.

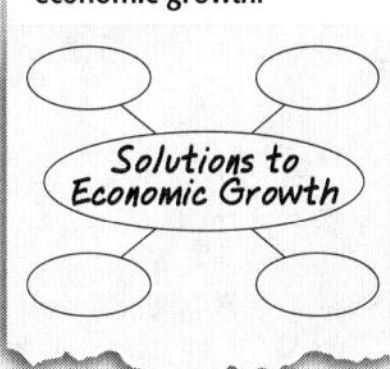

LESSON PLAN

OBJECTIVES

- List the factors that aid economic growth in less-developed countries (LDCs).
- Discuss ways to promote economic growth in LDCs and compare the effects of free trade and protectionism on economic growth.

1 FOCUS & MOTIVATE

In this section, students will read about economic issues in the developing world. Ask students why the U.S. government might take an interest in such issues. *(Possible Answers: out of concern for the economically less fortunate; out of interest in new markets and sources of raw materials)*

2 INSTRUCT

Providing International Aid

10.10.3

Critical Thinking

- How might an abundance of natural resources or raw materials be a potential hindrance to economic development in an LDC? *(Possible Answer: Because of its weaker economic position, an LDC may be compelled to lease, sell, or otherwise dispose of its resources in a way not in its own best economic interest.)*
- How might the membership of international agencies such as the World Bank and International Monetary Fund influence their policies toward LDCs? *(Possible Answer: The policies of the WB and IMF will likely be influenced by the interests of industrialized countries, which are the agencies' largest shareholders.)*

DIFFERENTIATING INSTRUCTION: ENGLISH LEARNERS

Understanding Economic Development

Class Time 20 minutes

Task Understanding main ideas

Purpose To help English learners review main ideas

Instructions After students have read "Providing International Aid" on pages 687–688, have them return to the bulleted list on page 687. On the list are the things that must happen before a country can have a strong economy. Ask students to examine the list and elaborate on the factors that are listed there. Have pairs of students work together to write one or two statements about each point in the bulleted list. They can rewrite the information in their own words, ask questions, or draw pictures to review the information. Examples of rewritten statements follow.

- "Investment capital to pay for the construction of industries and infrastructure, such as roads and bridges." Tell students that the word *infrastructure* means a base or foundation. *(Countries need money to pay for building large projects such as roads or bridges.)*
- "Technology to help companies and workers be as productive as possible." *(A country needs modern factories to make products such as cars and computers.)*
- "Healthy and well-trained workers to help reduce waste and inefficiency." *(Workers need to be well fed and to have good medical care. They also need to be trained.)*

Tip for Gifted and Talented Students

Explain that voting power in the IMF is determined by member nations' quotas, or fees. Quotas are based broadly on members' size in the world economy. Each IMF member has 250 basic votes plus one additional vote for each 100,000 of quota. The United States has 371,743 votes, just over 17 percent of the total.

Different Economic Approaches

10.10.3

Critical Thinking

- What does the development of microcredit programs imply about local lending institutions? *(Possible Answer: Where such programs are established, no lending institutions exist, or if they do exist, they are not accessible to many people.)*
- Why might protectionists fear international competition? *(Possible Answer: Competition could force businesses to reduce what they charge for products or services, potentially reducing revenues or causing businesses to fail.)*

Tense Relations International agencies can play an important role in development, but they also have drawbacks. The World Bank, for example, might fund a project that it considers worthy, such as a large dam. But the project may do little to help the people of a country. The IMF, as well, has been criticized for setting harsh financial conditions upon countries receiving IMF loans. For instance, the IMF might require a country to cut its government spending drastically.

Latin American nations have had troubled relationships with international lenders. For instance, Brazil repeatedly clashed with the IMF since the 1980s over economic policy and repayment schedules. By 1997, Brazil had worked out a repayment plan, but its debt level remained very high—$200 billion by the middle of 1999.

Different Economic Approaches

Today, many LDCs use two main approaches to spur economic growth—investment by multinational corporations and smaller, more localized efforts known collectively as grassroots development.

Multinational Corporations As you learned in Chapter 20, multinational corporations are companies that do business in many countries. These giant companies build factories in countries where the costs of labor and materials are low in order to increase their profits. Multinational companies often bring jobs, investment capital, and technology to nations that need them. Yet some of these companies have been criticized for exploiting workers and harming the environment in their host countries.

▼ Residents of Ho Chi Minh City, Vietnam, travel beneath advertisements for various international companies.

Most LDCs want multinational companies to invest in them because the multinationals do create jobs. Some LDCs offer multinational corporations favorable tax rates and work regulations. For instance, Nicaragua offers a package of benefits to multinational clothing firms that operate *maquilas,* or factories, in Nicaragua. The package exempts the companies from having to pay income taxes for ten years and allows them to pay a minimum wage of 41 cents an hour.

On the whole, Nicaraguan *maquilas* are a mixed blessing for the country. The unemployment rate is high, and the *maquilas* provide jobs. But maquilas do little to contribute technology, capital, or infrastructure to the country.

Grassroots Development Another approach to economic development is **grassroots development**. Grassroots development calls for small-scale, community-based projects to help poor people lift themselves from poverty. Grassroots programs usually focus on helping individuals and communities to improve their lives. Grassroots development responds to community needs and can help raise standards of living while preserving local customs.

DIFFERENTIATING INSTRUCTION: GIFTED AND TALENTED STUDENTS

Biography of Dr. Muhammed Yunus

Class Time 30 minutes

Task Writing a biography of Dr. Muhammed Yunus

Purpose To learn more about the history of microcredit

Instructions After students have read the passages on the practice of microcredit on page 689, ask them to use the library or the Internet to find out more about the practice. Tell them to focus their research on Dr. Muhammed Yunus, a founder of the Grameen Bank of Bangladesh, one of the world's best known microcredit institutions. Explain to students that they will be writing a short biography of Dr. Yunus to be featured in a magazine of their own choosing. As they conduct their research and write their biographies, have them answer the following questions:

- How did Dr. Yunus get involved with making small loans to poor individuals with no credit?
- What are the people like who get the small loans?
- What percentage of the borrowers actually pay back the loans?
- In what ways has this program benefited people in Bangladesh?

After they have completed their biographies, have students add a paragraph at the end that discusses how the ideas of Dr. Yunus have been used in other places around the world.

An example of a grassroots development program is microcredit. Microcredit programs give small loans—often less than $100—to individuals as seed money to enable them to begin small-scale businesses and lift themselves from poverty. Many organizations, including the World Bank and multinational corporations, run microcredit programs.

Julia Sairitupac, a single mother living in Sarita Colonia, Peru, was one person who benefitted from the microcredit program. She received between $100 and $200 for kitchen tools and other equipment to help her struggling business selling fruit juice and *salchipapas* (hot dogs and french fries.) "I feel like I have begun, for the first time, to leave poverty," she said. "Although my work requires many sacrifices, I want to continue progressing and install my business in my own home, which, with the help of my children, we are already building bit by bit."

No matter what approach is used, however, the development process is slow. And the gap between rich and poor nations remains large. Although the economic output of Asia and Africa grew during the 1980s, these regions still lag far behind the richer, more productive nations.

A. Possible Answer
Some students may support free trade because they want unrestricted trading. Others might support protectionism as a way for countries to protect their workers and industries.

Free Trade or Protectionism Another key issue that developing countries face is whether to follow policies of protectionism or free trade. Free trade, as you learned in Chapter 20, is the reduction of trade barriers among nations. This includes eliminating tariffs, or taxes on imported goods. Supporters of free trade believe that doing away with tariffs stimulates commerce by increasing trade among nations. Protectionists are those who oppose free trade. They support tariffs as a way to protect local products and industries from international competition.

Since the 1980s, many LDCs have embraced free trade under the terms established by the General Agreement on Tariffs and Trade (GATT) and the North American Free Trade Agreement (NAFTA), both of which were detailed in Chapter 20. Regional trading blocs are now forming in Latin America, Africa, and Asia. These blocs may provide many LDCs with the support they need to strengthen their economies. The success of these trading blocs appears to be crucial to the economic growth and long-term stability of developing countries. (A)

MAIN IDEA
Forming and Supporting Opinions
(A) Do you support free trade or protectionism? Why?

SECTION 4 ASSESSMENT

TERMS & NAMES 1. For each term or name, write a sentence explaining its significance.
• less-developed countries (LDCs) • investment capital • World Bank • International Monetary Fund (IMF) • grassroots development

USING YOUR NOTES

2. Which solution do you think most LDCs will choose? (10.10.3)

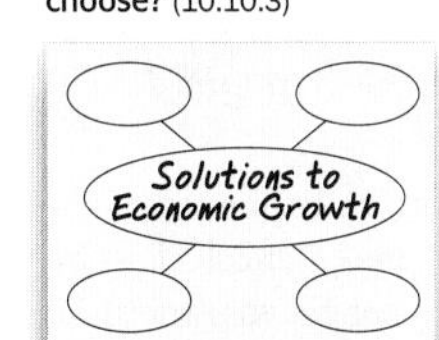

MAIN IDEAS

3. What are the main factors needed for economic development? (10.10.3)
4. What are the two main approaches to economic development in LDCs? (10.10.3)
5. How do supporters of free trade and protectionism differ in their view of tariffs? (10.10.3)

CRITICAL THINKING & WRITING

6. **ANALYZING ISSUES** What are the advantages and disadvantages to grassroots development? (10.10.3)
7. **CLARIFYING** What factors must LDCs consider in making plans to develop their economies? (10.10.3)
8. **FORMING AND SUPPORTING OPINIONS** Do organizations providing economic aid have the right to place restrictions on their aid? Why or why not? (10.10.3)
9. **WRITING ACTIVITY** ECONOMICS Imagine you are an editorial writer for a newspaper in a developing nation. Write a brief **editorial** expressing your view on free trade versus protectionism. (Writing 2.4.a)

CONNECT TO TODAY CREATE A TIME LINE
Choose a developing country in Latin America, Africa, or Asia and create a **time line** of significant economic events in its history over the past 50 years. (Writing 2.3.d)

More About . . .

Free Trade

Some observers have suggested that policymakers' praise of free trade is somewhat disingenuous. For example, economist Dean Baker has described how many U.S. trade agreements reduce trade barriers to manufactured goods and thereby place U.S. manufacturing workers in direct competition with lower-paid overseas workers. However, few trade agreements reduce trade barriers (primarily professional and licensing restrictions) to highly paid professions, such as medicine and law. In these professions, where such barriers remain, it is difficult for foreign professionals to qualify as professionals in the United States.

Case Study 7, Mexico and Brazil: Two Developing Nations, p. 86

3 ASSESS

SECTION 4 ASSESSMENT

Have students work in small groups to complete a web diagram like the one in question 2. Hold a class discussion to share concept webs and discuss which solution students think most LDCs would choose.

4 RETEACH

Have students define all the terms in question 1 and relate each term to economic issues in the develoing world.

ANSWERS

1. less-developed countries (LDCs), p. 687 • investment capital, p. 687 • World Bank, p. 687 • International Monetary Fund (IMF), p. 687 • grassroots development, p. 688
2. **Sample Answer:** 1. Loans by the World Bank and the IMF. 2. Investment by multinational companies. 3. Grassroots development. 4. Microcredit. **Possible Answer:** Most LDCs may choose investment by multinational corporations because of the quick creation of jobs.
3. investment capital, technology, well-trained workforce, qualified managers
4. investment by multinational corporations, grassroots development
5. Free trade supporters oppose tariffs as a barrier to greater trade and commerce among nations. Protectionists favor tariffs as a way to protect local industry.
6. Advantages include the development of businesses that meet community needs. Disadvantages include the small scale of projects.
7. needs of citizens, development of infrastructure, education of workers, availability of resources
8. Yes—The money belongs to the nations that provide the aid. No—Rich nations have no right to tell other nations what to do.
9. **Rubric** Editorials should
   - be well organized with a clear thesis statement and supporting details.
   - demonstrate a clear understanding of the subject matter.

CONNECT TO TODAY
Rubric Time lines should
- include significant events that had an impact on the country's history.
- be well organized and easy to follow.

LESSON PLAN

OBJECTIVES

- Analyze reasons for the worldwide arms trade and explain how people are trying to restrict it.
- List weapons of mass destruction and identify the threats they pose to peace, security, and human survival.
- Explain the reasons for the U.S. involvement in Iraq.

1 FOCUS & MOTIVATE

In this section, students will read about global security issues. Ask students what they believe is the greatest threat to national security. *(Possible Answer: international terrorism)*

2 INSTRUCT

Worldwide Arms Trade

10.9.1

Critical Thinking

- Why might the U.S. government have been so heavily involved in the arms trade during the Cold War? *(Possible Answer: in order to arm its Cold War allies)*
- Why might an explosion in the illegal arms trade have occurred after the end of the Cold War? *(Possible Answer: The disintegration of the Soviet Union may have flooded the black market with weapons from former republics and allies.)*

5

Trees stunted by acid rain, Mount Mitchell, North Carolina

Grand Central Station, August 15, 2003

Seeking Global Security

MAIN IDEA	WHY IT MATTERS NOW	TERMS & NAMES
POWER AND AUTHORITY War, terrorism, and weapons of mass destruction threaten the safety of people all over the world.	People can work against the dangers posed by war, terrorism, and weapons of mass destruction.	• conventional arms • bioweapons

CALIFORNIA STANDARDS

10.9.1 Compare the economic and military power shifts caused by the war, including the Yalta Pact, the development of nuclear weapons, Soviet control over Eastern European nations, and the economic recoveries of Germany and Japan.

10.9.8 Discuss the establishment and work of the United Nations and the purposes and functions of the Warsaw Pact, SEATO, NATO, and the Organization of American States.

CST 4 Students relate current events to the physical and human characteristics of places and regions.

SETTING THE STAGE Among the most pressing issues facing the world community today are warfare and terrorism. So long as nations continue to use the threat of military force as a tool of foreign policy, armed conflicts will erupt. In addition, the threat of terrorism—the use of violence against people or property to force changes in societies or governments—strikes fear in the hearts of many people. Nevertheless, many nations and organizations have been working together to reduce the threats of such violence and bloodshed.

Worldwide Arms Trade

Many people hoped that the end of the Cold War would reduce the risk of armed conflict around the world. However, developments following the Cold War have introduced new threats. First, the collapse of the Soviet empire led to political instability and violence in parts of the world the Soviets once controlled. Second, a bustling international arms trade has emerged to ensure that few conflicts around the world suffer from a shortage of weapons.

The Market for Weapons During the Cold War, the main suppliers of **conventional arms**—tanks, planes, rifles, and all other non-nuclear weapons—were the United States, Western Europe, and the Soviet Union. These nations sold most of their weapons to developing nations. This government-sponsored trade has declined considerably since the mid-1980s, but it has not ceased.

What has grown, however, is the illegal market for weapons. Many of the weapons bought on the illegal market find their way to trouble spots around the world. These illegal weapons have frequently contributed to armed conflict in regions with political, ethnic, or religious tensions.

TAKING NOTES

Summarizing Create a diagram to illustrate the sources of threats to international peace and security.

Threats to International Peace and Security

Protests against Weapons Sales Some people are beginning to take action against international arms dealers. In Belgium, the Flemish Forum voor Vredesaktie (Forum for Peace Action) has organized nonviolent protests against the Armed Forces Communication and Electronics Association (AFCEA), which held its annual arms fair in Brussels, Belgium, in 1997. Protesters convinced Belgian customs officers to seize all of the military equipment at the fair that year because the equipment was not properly licensed.

DIFFERENTIATING INSTRUCTION: STRUGGLING READERS

Worldwide Arms Trade

Class Time 25 minutes

Task Making an outline

Purpose To help students study the text

Instructions Explain to students that condensing information may help them to better understand the text. Have students read "Worldwide Arms Trade" on pages 690–691. After they have read the text, have them outline the material. For each subsection, ask students to write one sentence that expresses that subsection's most important points. An example follows.

Worldwide Arms Trade

Introduction

- After the end of the Cold War, areas once controlled by the Soviet Union experienced violence and instability.

The Market for Weapons

- Since the end of the Cold War, the sale of arms by the United States, Western Europe, and places in the old Soviet Union has dropped off, but the illegal market for weapons has grown.

Protests against Weapon Sales

- Protesters try to take action against international arms dealers. Some protests have been successful, but the arms trade continues to be strong.

Demonstrations such as those in Belgium have a long way to go before they stop international arms deals. But opponents of the arms trade are determined not to abandon their fight.

Weapons of Mass Destruction

Weapons of mass destruction, which you read about in Chapter 20, pose a different kind of threat to peace. Such weapons, which include nuclear armaments and biological and chemical weapons, have the potential to kill or injure large numbers of people at one time. Many of these tools of war are the products of sophisticated technologies. Even so, some are frighteningly easy to make and use.

The Threat of Nuclear Weapons The existence of nuclear weapons poses a significant threat to world peace—and even to human survival. In the years since World War II, a number of nations have developed nuclear weapons while other countries continue working toward that goal. Opponents of nuclear weapons have tried to prevent the proliferation, or spread, of such weapons.

A major step toward stopping nuclear proliferation was the Treaty on the Non-Proliferation of Nuclear Weapons (NPT). This treaty was passed by the United Nations General Assembly in 1968. It went into force in 1970 for 25 years. In 1995, 170 nations signed on to renew the NPT forever. Only India and Pakistan have continued to test nuclear arms. However, there is growing concern that hostile nations, such as North Korea, are on the verge of developing nuclear weapons. Such a dilemma highlights the continuing threat of nuclear war.

Biological and Chemical Weapons The possible proliferation of biological and chemical weapons is also a growing concern to many nations. These weapons are

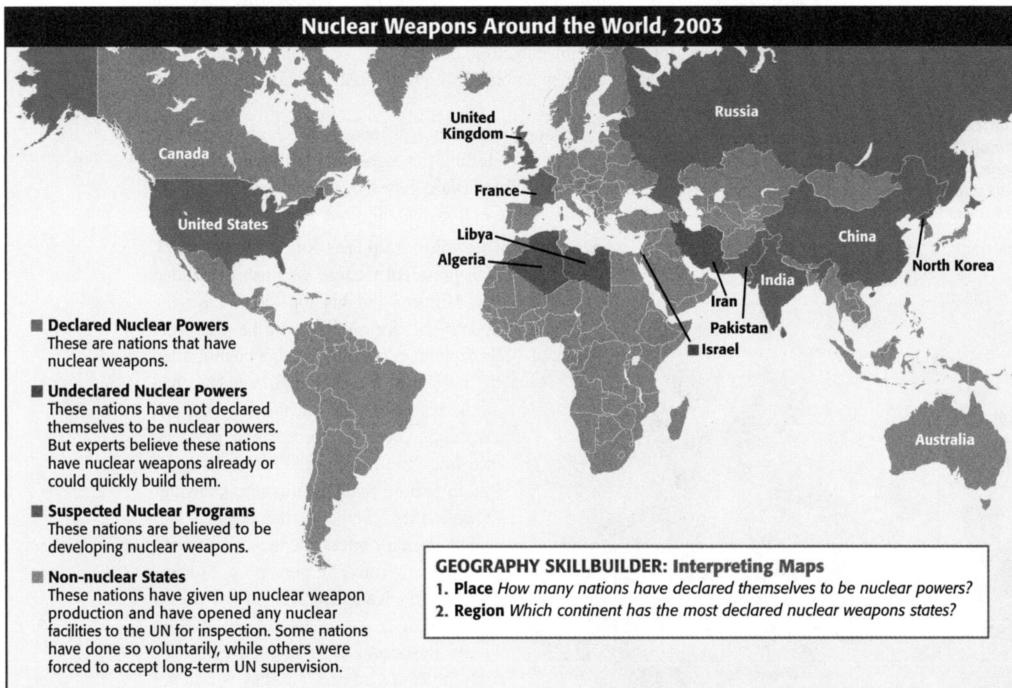

Nuclear Weapons Around the World, 2003
Russia
United Kingdom
Canada
France
United States
Libya
Algeria
China
North Korea
India
Iran
Pakistan
Israel
Australia
Declared Nuclear Powers
These are nations that have nuclear weapons.
Undeclared Nuclear Powers
These nations have not declared themselves to be nuclear powers. But experts believe these nations have nuclear weapons already or could quickly build them.
Suspected Nuclear Programs
These nations are believed to be developing nuclear weapons.
Non-nuclear States
These nations have given up nuclear weapon production and have opened any nuclear facilities to the UN for inspection. Some nations have done so voluntarily, while others were forced to accept long-term UN supervision.

GEOGRAPHY SKILLBUILDER: Interpreting Maps

1. **Place** *How many nations have declared themselves to be nuclear powers?*
2. **Region** *Which continent has the most declared nuclear weapons states?*

Weapons of Mass Destruction

10.9.8

Critical Thinking

- Ask students what U.S. policy should be toward nations that have not signed or that are in violation of the NPT. *(Possible Answers: aggressive diplomacy to convince countries to sign the treaty or to comply with the treaty; close monitoring; economic sanctions; military action)*
- What steps might governments take to protect their people against chemical and biological attacks? *(focus foreign intelligence activities on finding and eradicating supplies; put domestic detection systems into place; develop antidotes, antibiotics, and vaccines; create emergency plans in case of attack)*

Tip for Struggling Readers

Proliferation means to increase in number, so *nuclear proliferation* refers to an increase in the number of nuclear weapons.

History from Visuals

Interpreting the Map

Ask students which countries are among those suspected of having nuclear programs. *(Algeria, Libya, Iran, and North Korea)*

Extension Which country is an undeclared nuclear power? *(Israel)*

SKILLBUILDER Answers

1. **Place** seven
2. **Region** Asia

DIFFERENTIATING INSTRUCTION: GIFTED AND TALENTED STUDENTS

North Korea's Nuclear Threat

Class Time 40 minutes

Task Planning a documentary about the nuclear threat posed by North Korea

Purpose To familiarize students with issues related to nuclear weapons

Instructions After they have read "Weapons of Mass Destruction" on pages 691 and 692, divide students into small groups and explain that they will plan a 10-minute documentary on the nuclear threat posed by North Korea. Tell students that, in order to put together an outline for their documentaries, they should begin by carrying out preliminary research at the library or on the Internet. Students may find the chapter on North Korea—"North Korea: Endgame of the Cold War"—in Chalmers Johnson's *Blowback* a useful starting point. Tell students that their documentaries should primarily be visual productions, with a narrative read in the background. After putting together a skeleton outline, students should do in-depth research to flesh out their documentary. Encourage students to divide work among group members. Some students might focus on composing the narrative, while others concentrate on finding audiovisual material. As students wrap up their research, have them write a script that carefully coordinates the visual and narrative elements of their documentary.

The War in Iraq
10.9.8

Critical Thinking

- Why might the United States and Britain have disagreed with European countries about letting UN weapons inspections continue? *(Possible Answer: They may have believed that they risked great destruction and loss of life if they did not act quickly.)*
- Why didn't U.S. troops simply withdraw after defeating Saddam Hussein's regime? *(Possible Answer: The United States wanted to take part in the formation of a new government to ensure that such a regime did not reemerge in Iraq.)*

More About . . .

Coalition Forces
President George W. Bush had great difficulty convincing other world leaders to join the United States and Britain in the military campaign against Iraq. Among the countries included in a March 2003 list of the "Coalition of the Willing" were Afghanistan, Albania, Australia, Azerbaijan, Bulgaria, Colombia, the Czech Republic, Denmark, El Salvador, Eritrea, Estonia, Ethiopia, Georgia, Hungary, Italy, Japan, Latvia, Lithuania, Macedonia, the Netherlands, Nicaragua, the Philippines, Poland, Romania, Slovakia, South Korea, Spain, Turkey, the United Kingdom and Uzbekistan.

relatively easy to produce and distribute, making them much more available than nuclear weapons to terrorists and less-developed countries. Author Richard Preston feels that biological weapons, or **bioweapons**, can be the most deadly:

PRIMARY SOURCE Ⓐ

Bioweapons are microorganisms, bacteria or viruses, that invade the body, multiply inside it, and destroy it. Bioweapons can be used as strategic weapons. That is, they are incredibly powerful and dangerous. They can kill huge numbers of people if they are used properly, and their effects are not limited to one place or a small target. Chemical weapons, on the other hand, can be used only tactically. It is virtually impossible to put enough of a chemical in the air in a high enough concentration to wipe out a large number of people over a large territory. And chemicals aren't alive and can't spread through an infectious process.

RICHARD PRESTON, "The Bioweaponeers," *The New Yorker*

MAIN IDEA

Analyzing Primary Sources

Ⓐ Why are biological weapons more destructive than chemical weapons?

A. Answer Biological weapons are potentially more destructive because they can use infectious microorganisms to kill people.

The War in Iraq

In the spring of 2003, amid growing worries about terrorism and the development of deadly weapons that resulted from the terrorist attacks of September 11, 2001, the United States confronted the leader of Iraq, Saddam Hussein. The longtime dictator had concerned the world community for years. During the 1980s, Hussein had used chemical weapons to put down a rebellion in Iraq. In 1990, he had invaded Kuwait, only to be pushed back by a U.S.-led military effort. In light of such history, many viewed Hussein as a threat to peace and stability in the world. As a result, the United States led an effort to remove the Iraqi leader from power.

The Path to War Throughout much of 2002, the United States and other nations accused Hussein of developing weapons of mass destruction. Bowing to world pressure, Hussein allowed inspectors from the United Nations to search Iraq for such outlawed weapons. Some investigators, however, insisted that the Iraqis were not fully cooperating with the inspections. U.S. and British officials soon threatened to use force to disarm Iraq.

The UN Security Council debated what action to take next. Some countries, such as France and Germany, called for letting the inspectors continue searching for weapons. British prime minister Tony Blair, however, accused the Iraqis of "deception and evasion" and insisted inspections would never work.

▼ With war reporters looking on, coalition troops battle enemy soldiers outside the town of Basra in Iraq.

Operation Iraqi Freedom In March 2003, U.S. president George W. Bush demanded that Hussein and his top aides leave the country or face a military strike. The Iraqi leader refused. Within days, a coalition led by the United States and Britain launched air strikes in and around the Iraqi capital, Baghdad. Coalition forces then marched into Iraq through Kuwait. The invasion of Iraq to remove Saddam Hussein, known as Operation Iraqi Freedom, had begun.

The military operation met with strong opposition from numerous countries. Some world leaders criticized the policy of attacking a nation to prevent it from future misdeeds. U.S. and British officials, however, argued that they would not wait for Hussein to strike first.

DIFFERENTIATING INSTRUCTION: ENGLISH LEARNERS

Understanding the War with Iraq

Class Time 20 minutes

Task Creating a time line

Purpose To use a visual aid to help students understand the order of events in Iraq

Instructions Ask students to review "The War in Iraq" on pages 692–693 and write down significant events and dates. Then have student order the events on a time line. Time lines might include the following events:

1980s: Saddam Hussein uses chemicals to put down a rebellion in Iraq.

1990: Iraq invades Kuwait but is pushed back by U.S.-led military effort.

2002: Weapons inspectors search Iraq for weapons of mass destruction (WMD).

March 2003: U.S. demands that Hussein and top aides leave the country. After Hussein's refusal, the U.S. and Britain invade Iraq—an action opposed by many other countries.

April 2003: Baghdad falls, signaling the end of Saddam's regime.

Encourage students to use the library or the Internet to add more events and dates to their time lines.

As coalition forces marched north to Baghdad, troops parachuted into northern Iraq and began moving south toward the capital city. By early April, Baghdad had fallen and the regime of Saddam Hussein had collapsed. After less than four weeks of fighting, the coalition had won the war.

The Struggle Continues Despite the coalition victory, much work remained in Iraq. With the help of U.S. officials, Iraqis began rebuilding their nation. They established an interim government several months after the war. The new governing body went to work creating a constitution and planning democratic elections.

B. Answer rebuilding the nation; creating a new government; maintaining order; locating weapons of mass destruction

Meanwhile, numerous U.S. troops had to remain behind to help maintain order in Iraq and battle pockets of fighters loyal to Hussein. The defeated Iraqi dictator disappeared toward the end of the war but was later captured on December 13, 2003. Finally, the United States and Britain came under increasing fire for failing to find any weapons of mass destruction in the months after the conflict ended. U.S. and British officials insisted that it would be only a matter of time before they found Hussein's deadly arsenal. As of late November 2004, no weapons of mass destruction had been found. B

▲ President George W. Bush (right) and Prime Minister Tony Blair stood together throughout the war.

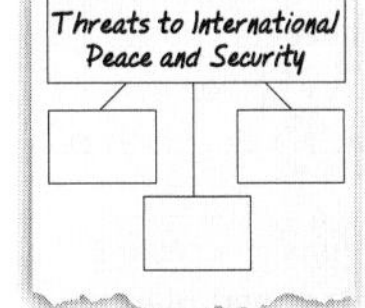

MAIN IDEA

Identifying Problems

B What challenges remained in Iraq after the conflict ended?

Despite the unresolved issues, coalition leaders declared the defeat of Saddam Hussein to be a victory for global security. "The war on terror is not over, yet it is not endless," declared President Bush shortly after the fighting. "We do not know the day of final victory, but we have seen the turning of the tide. No act of the terrorists will change our purpose, or weaken our resolve, or alter their fate. Their cause is lost. Free nations will press on to victory."

SECTION 5 ASSESSMENT

TERMS & NAMES 1. For each term, write a sentence explaining its significance.
• conventional arms • bioweapons

USING YOUR NOTES

2. Which of the threats to peace and security is the most dangerous? Why? (10.9.1)

Threats to International Peace and Security

MAIN IDEAS

3. Why is the growth of the illegal arms market a threat to world peace? (10.9.1)
4. What are the types of weapons of mass destruction? (10.9.1)
5. What was the result of Operation Iraqi Freedom? (10.9.1)

CRITICAL THINKING & WRITING

6. **SUMMARIZING** List ways in which people and nations of the world have attempted to control threats to the world's peace and security. (10.9.8)
7. **ANALYZING ISSUES** What reasons might nations have to retain or maintain a nuclear or bioweapons arsenal? (10.9.1)
8. **EVALUATING DECISIONS** Do you think the United States was justified in invading Iraq? Why or why not? (10.9.8)
9. **WRITING ACTIVITY** POWER AND AUTHORITY Imagine you are a speechwriter for President Bush. Write the introductory **paragraph** of a speech to coalition forces after their victory in Iraq. (Writing 2.4.c)

INTEGRATED TECHNOLOGY **INTERNET ACTIVITY**

Use the Internet to research an armed conflict somewhere in the world. Use your findings to deliver a brief **oral report** about the origins and impact of the conflict. (Writing 2.3.a)

INTERNET KEYWORD
global conflict

More About . . .

The Continuing Struggle

The Bush administration declared the end of major combat in Iraq on May 1, 2003. Between May 1 and October 15, 2003, according to the U.S. Central Command, 163 U.S. service personnel were killed in Iraq. Most of the victims were killed in combat, usually in ambushes involving rocket-propelled grenades (RPG) and sniper attacks. By early November of 2004, there were over 1,100 American troop casualties, 27 of them women.

3 ASSESS

SECTION 5 ASSESSMENT

Ask students to summarize in their own words the threats that weapons and terrorism pose to world peace and to describe ways people are dealing with these threats.

4 RETEACH

Ask students to work in small groups to answer question 6. Have students discuss which method of controlling conflict is most likely to be successful.

ANSWERS

1. conventional arms, p. 690 • bioweapons, p. 692
2. **Sample Answer:** 1. Conventional weapons. 2. Nuclear weapons. 3. Biological and chemical weapons. 4. Terrorism. **Possible Answer:** Some students might say weapons of mass destruction because of their potential to kill so many people.
3. It fuels and prolongs conflicts.
4. nuclear, chemical, and biological weapons
5. Saddam Hussein was ousted from power.
6. **Possible Answer:** UN peacekeeping forces have been deployed to help nations end fighting and to carry out negotiations for peace.
7. Nations may want to keep such weapons for security. They could be used as a deterrent against an attack by another country or terrorists.
8. Yes—The invasion was justified in order to get rid of the regime of Saddam Hussein and its threat to global security. No—Attacking Iraq preemptively was unjustified.
9. **Rubric** Paragraphs should
   • be written in a clear and organized manner.
   • contain the overriding theme of the larger speech.

INTEGRATED TECHNOLOGY

Rubric Oral reports should
• be delivered in a clear and engaging manner.
• show evidence of good research and a clear understanding of the subject.

LESSON PLAN

OBJECTIVES

- Describe the Universal Declaration of Human Rights and cite human rights violations from around the world.
- Explain why children are among the most vulnerable of the world's citizens.
- List successes in human rights, such as women's rights.

1 FOCUS & MOTIVATE

In this section, students will read about human rights issues. Ask students if they can think of any high-profile cases of human rights abuses. *(Some students might mention the detention of Burmese activist Aung San Suu Kyi, the long jail term of Nelson Mandela, or other cases.)*

2 INSTRUCT

The Struggle for Human Rights

10.9.8

Critical Thinking

- Why might a Universal Declaration of Human Rights have been signed in 1948? *(Some students may know that the declaration was adopted by the newly formed United Nations not long after the horrific human rights catastrophes of World War II.)*
- Can you think of any human rights violations from U.S. history? *(Possible Answers: slavery, internment of Japanese-American citizens during World War II, forced relocation and extermination of Native Americans)*

Trees stunted by acid rain, Mount Mitchell, North Carolina

Grand Central Station, August 15, 2003

6

Defending Human Rights and Freedoms

MAIN IDEA	WHY IT MATTERS NOW	TERMS & NAMES
POWER AND AUTHORITY Human rights and freedoms have become a major international concern.	Protecting fundamental rights for all people is an important way to improve life in the 21st century.	• Universal Declaration of Human Rights

CALIFORNIA STANDARDS

10.9.8 Discuss the establishment and work of the United Nations and the purposes and functions of the Warsaw Pact, SEATO, NATO, and the Organization of American States.

10.10.1 Understand the challenges in the regions, including their geopolitical, cultural, military, and economic significance and the international relationships in which they are involved.

CST 4 Students relate current events to the physical and human characteristics of places and regions.

SETTING THE STAGE Since the end of World War II, the international community, working through the United Nations and other organizations, has made human rights a primary concern in international affairs. Human rights are the basic rights and freedoms that all people are entitled to enjoy. The UN has passed several declarations setting standards for such rights and freedoms. Around the world, however, repressive governments continue to deny people these rights. Thus, numerous political and organization leaders remain committed to bringing human rights to all people who inhabit the earth.

The Struggle for Human Rights

The **Universal Declaration of Human Rights** was adopted by the United Nations in 1948. This declaration defines human rights goals for the world community. The preamble of the declaration lists several reasons why the declaration is necessary, including the need to promote friendly relations between nations.

Article 1 of the declaration states, "All human beings are born free and equal in dignity and rights. They are endowed with reason and conscience and should act towards one another in a spirit of brotherhood." The declaration goes on to spell out the rights that all nations should seek to guarantee for their citizens.

With regard to people's basic rights, the declaration states, "The will of the people shall be the basis of the authority of government" and that "everyone has the right to take part in the government of his country." The declaration also calls for free and fair elections. Finally, it calls for basic civil liberties such as freedom of speech and religion as well as freedom from political terror.

Various organizations, including UN agencies and independent groups such as Amnesty International and Americas Watch, observe whether countries are meeting human rights standards. These groups perform a valuable service by helping to improve conditions and even save lives.

Despite the best efforts of human rights organizations, protecting human rights remains an uphill battle. Serious violations of fundamental rights continue to occur around the world. The violations result from a number of causes, including political dissent, racial or ethnic hatreds, and religious differences.

Political Dissent Opposition to political dissent—the difference of opinion over political issues—is one of the most common causes of human rights violations.

TAKING NOTES

Clarifying Use a chart to list the steps being taken to improve human rights for particular groups.

Group	Improvements
Children	
Women	

DIFFERENTIATING INSTRUCTION: STRUGGLING READERS

Causes of Human Rights Violations

Class Time 20 minutes

Task Creating a chart showing the major causes of human rights violations

Purpose To familiarize students with different types of human rights violations

Instructions Ask students to create a table with four columns and three rows in their notebooks. Have them label the table "Causes of Human Rights Violations." The first row should be labeled "Cause," the second row, "Description," and the third row, "Example." After they have drawn their tables, have students read "The Struggle for Human Rights" on pages 694 and 695. Ask them to fill in their tables as they read the text. An example follows.

Causes of Human Rights Violations

Cause	Political Dissent	Ethnic and Racial Conflicts	Religious Persecution
Description	Persecution of individuals and groups for holding political views that differ from those in power	Persecution of individuals and groups for belonging to a different ethnic or racial group	Persecution of individuals and groups for belonging to a different religious group
Example	Sani Abacha's imprisoning of Moshood Abiola in Nigeria	Hutu massacre of Tutsi in Rwanda	Chinese persecution of Tibetans

In many countries around the world, from El Salvador to Iran to the former Soviet Union, individuals and groups have been persecuted for holding political views that differ from those of the people in power.

There are many examples of political rights violations in the world. One nation that has been criticized for abuses is Nigeria. General Sani Abacha of Nigeria earned a reputation as a ruthless military dictator. Despite repeated statements that he intended to open up the Nigerian government and hold free elections, Abacha imprisoned his political opponents. Abacha took power in 1993 during the chaos that erupted after results of the presidential election held that year were wiped out. Abacha refused to make public the results of that election. Among his prisoners was Moshood Abiola, a wealthy businessman who many believe won the 1993 election. Abacha died in June 1998. In a hopeful sign for the future, his successor has instituted democratic civilian rule. (A)

MAIN IDEA

Making Inferences

(A) Why do you think some government leaders try to repress political dissent?

A. Possible Answer They are afraid that such dissent might weaken their rule and cause them to lose power.

Ethnic and Racial Conflicts In some countries, ethnic or racial hatreds lead to human rights abuses. For example, human rights groups have charged the fundamentalist Muslim military regime in Sudan of committing genocide against the Nuba, an agricultural people in southern Sudan. In addition, Christian groups have accused the Sudanese regime of persecuting Christians, many of whom live in the southern region of Sudan.

In Rwanda, fighting between Hutus and Tutsis—the two main ethnic groups—has led to horrendous rights violations. In 1994, Hutus massacred up to 500,000 Tutsis in the worst case of genocide since the 1970s Khmer Rouge reign of terror in Cambodia.

Religious Persecution Human rights violations based on religious differences have also occurred. Such violations often have ethnic and political overtones. For example, Tibetans—under Chinese rule since 1950—have been persecuted by the Chinese for their Buddhist religion, their traditional culture, and their desire for political independence. [Many Tibetan leaders were imprisoned in China in the 1990s.] And the Dalai Lama, the most important Tibetan religious leader, remained in exile.

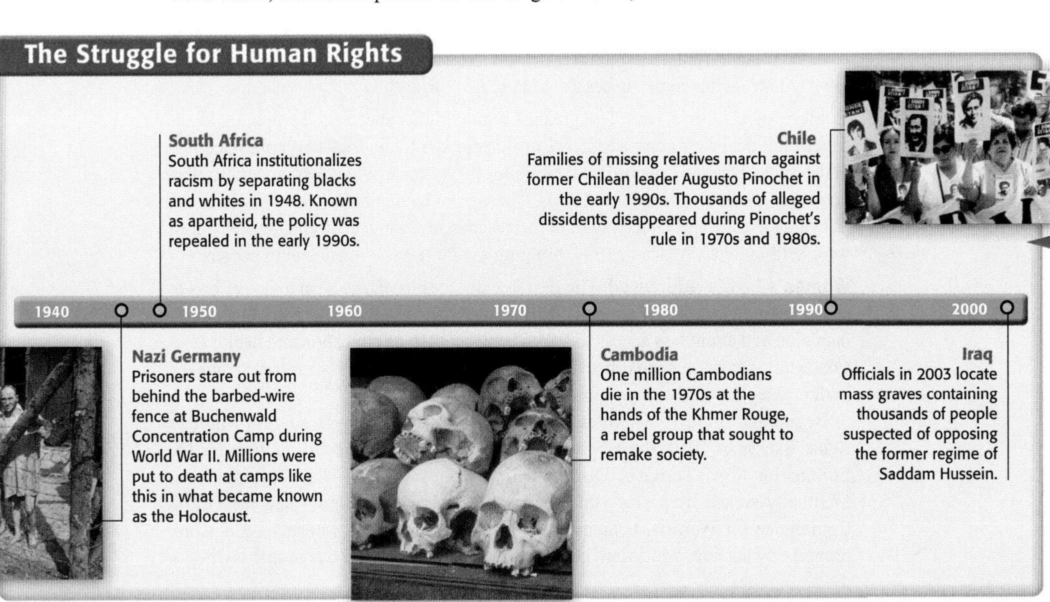

The Struggle for Human Rights
1940
1950
1960
1970
1980
1990
2000
South Africa
South Africa institutionalizes racism by separating blacks and whites in 1948. Known as apartheid, the policy was repealed in the early 1990s.
Chile
Families of missing relatives march against former Chilean leader Augusto Pinochet in the early 1990s. Thousands of alleged dissidents disappeared during Pinochet's rule in 1970s and 1980s.
Nazi Germany
Prisoners stare out from behind the barbed-wire fence at Buchenwald Concentration Camp during World War II. Millions were put to death at camps like this in what became known as the Holocaust.
Cambodia
One million Cambodians die in the 1970s at the hands of the Khmer Rouge, a rebel group that sought to remake society.
Iraq
Officials in 2003 locate mass graves containing thousands of people suspected of opposing the former regime of Saddam Hussein.

More About . . .

Tibetan Protests

Nine Tibetan women with scarves wrapped around their mouths staged a silent protest at the Forum on Women in Huairou, China, in 1995. This forum is commonly called the Beijing Women's Conference. The women did not gain official entry into the conference. So they held their own gathering to draw attention to the plight of Tibetans, especially women, under Chinese rule.

The women also stressed their opposition to Chinese policies to limit population. The protesters claimed that Tibet has no population problem and that China has forced Chinese family limitation policies on Tibetan women as a form of social and political control.

History from Visuals

Interpreting the Time Line

In what year did South Africa institutionalize racism by separating blacks and whites? How long after the Holocaust did this occur? *(1948; about 3 years)*

Extension How many Cambodians were killed by the Khmer Rouge during the 1970s? *(approximately 1 million)*

DIFFERENTIATING INSTRUCTION: GIFTED AND TALENTED STUDENTS

Learning More about Human Rights

Class Time 20 minutes

Task Learning about ways to support the cause of human rights

Purpose To learn about human rights violations and ways to prevent them

Instructions Explain to students that there are a number of organizations, including United Nations agencies and independent groups, such as Human Rights Watch, Amnesty International, and Americas Watch, that investigate and expose human rights violations and hold abusers to account.

These groups also provide the public with a number of ways to support the cause of human rights, including letter writing. Divide students into three or four groups, and ask them to visit the Web site of one of the human rights organizations listed at left. Ask them to review some of the letter-writing campaigns and other activities that the organization has coordinated. Students can collect their information into a human rights booklet. Interested students may choose to participate in one of the letter-writing campaigns or possibly in other activities. Have anyone who has participated lead a class discussion on the different campaigns in which they took part.

Children at Risk
10.9.8; 10.10.1

Critical Thinking

- Why have so many nations failed to pass labor laws to protect children? *(Possible Answer: They may believe that their economies require the economic contributions of children.)*
- Why might the Magna Carta be an appropriate analogy for the Convention on the Rights of the Child? *(Possible Answer: Like the Magna Carta, it enumerates rights that future generations will be responsible for extending and putting into practice.)*

Signs of Hope
10.9.8; 10.10.1

Critical Thinking

- Why might international organizations have begun to address women's rights issues in the 1970s? *(Possible Answer: The women's rights movement in Western nations during the 1960s may have led to greater participation by women in international organizations and their demand that such issues be addressed at the international level.)*
- Why might many of the former Soviet republics and former members of the Soviet bloc have been successful in making the transition to democratic forms of government? *(Possible Answer: Many of the countries are located close to existing European democracies, from which they can seek political and economic support.)*

▲ Former child laborer Iqbal Masih became an outspoken critic of the practice.

Children at Risk

Children are the most vulnerable of the world's citizens. They are among those who run the highest risk of suffering human rights abuses. The abuses children suffer are mainly social and economic, and they occur primarily in less-developed countries. A lack of food, education, and health care is foremost among these abuses.

In addition, children in many parts of the world are forced to work long hours, often in dangerous conditions, for little or no pay. During the early 1990s Iqbal Masih, a child activist from Pakistan, helped bring attention to the plight of child labor. To help pay off a debt owed by his family, Masih was forced at age four to work for a local carpet maker. He often worked 12-hour days, and frequently was chained to his work station. At age 10, he escaped and worked with various international organizations to highlight the problem of child workers and free thousands of children from forced labor. In 1995, he was shot and killed shortly after returning to Pakistan.

Meanwhile, the United Nations has played a leading role in trying to improve conditions for children around the world. In 1989, the UN adopted a document called the Convention on the Rights of the Child. Known as the Magna Carta for Children, this document established a framework for children's rights. It covers basic rights, such as health care and education, and calls for protection against the exploitation, abuse, and neglect of children. Similar goals were advanced in 1990 at the World Summit for Children, where world leaders adopted a 25-point program in favor of children's welfare.

Signs of Hope

The work of the international community is a positive sign in the struggle to advance human rights. Despite great obstacles, efforts to make human rights a priority are achieving some successes around the world.

Human Rights Successes The greatest human rights successes have come in the area of political rights and freedoms. In Europe, most countries that were once part of the Soviet bloc have opened up their political systems to allow for democratic elections and the free expression of ideas. There have been similar successes in South Africa, where the apartheid system of racial separation came to an end. Free elections were held in South Africa in 1994, bringing a multiracial government to power.

Women's Rights Addressed The past few decades have also seen major efforts to advance human rights for women. Throughout the world, women tend to be poorer than men and attain less access to social benefits such as education and health care. Conditions for women are especially poor in the less-developed countries. But even in the richer nations, women often have second-class status.

Beginning in the 1970s, international organizations began to address women's rights issues. In 1979, the UN adopted a measure called the Convention for the Elimination of All Forms of Discrimination Against Women. The convention was eventually signed by nearly 100 nations. In 1995, the UN sponsored the Fourth Conference on Women, held in Beijing, China. Issues of women's leadership, property ownership, education, health, and population control were top priorities at the conference.

DIFFERENTIATING INSTRUCTION: ENGLISH LEARNERS

Practice with Difficult Words

Class Time 20 minutes

Task Identifying and reviewing difficult vocabulary

Purpose To help students build their vocabularies

Instructions As students read the section "Children at Risk" on this page, ask them to write down words that they find difficult. When they have finished reading the text, ask them to look up the words in a dictionary, write down the definition next to the word, and then write one or two new sentences in their own words that restate the meaning of the original sentence. Teachers should help students choose the definition that corresponds to the word's meaning in the passage. Encourage students to be creative in formulating their own sentences. Examples follow.

vulnerable: capable of being physically or emotionally wounded *(Children are the most easily hurt of all people.)*

abuse: physical maltreatment *(Children are hurt by being forced to work long hours.)*

plight: an unfortunate, difficult, or precarious situation *(Child labor is a very bad situation for children.)*

adopted: to accept formally and put into effect (*The UN accepted a document called the Convention on the Rights of the Child.)*

exploitation: using for a selfish purpose *(The UN works to protect children against being used to make money for others.)*

Human Rights in the 21st Century Progress in all areas of human rights is encouraging—but it is only a beginning. Much work must still be done before people in all countries of the world have the democratic rights and freedoms set forth in the Universal Declaration of Human Rights.

However, important trends in the world provide reasons to hope for continued progress on human rights. Rising levels of education are providing people with the skills to exercise their political rights and improve their lives. Modern communications networks are helping human rights organizations like Amnesty International to investigate and report on human rights abuses. In addition, today's mass media can make people instantly aware of abuses in the world.

But perhaps the greatest reason for optimism regarding human rights arises from world history since 1989. In early 1989, millions of people in the Soviet Union, Eastern Europe, and South Africa lived under repressive governments that denied basic political rights, such as the right to vote in a multi-party election. Then, beginning with Poland later in 1989, one country after another threw off its old regime and turned to a democratic form of government. The Soviet Union came to an end in 1991. In that same year, the republic of Russia had its first free presidential election. And in 1994, South Africa held its first universal elections, in which people of all races could vote.

These historic events transformed the world by extending human rights and democratic institutions to millions of people. They continue to inspire optimism that millions more can win their human and political rights while the new century is still young. (B)

B. Possible Answer Some students might say that nations should do everything they can to protect human rights. Others might say that nations should not interfere with the internal affairs of other countries.

MAIN IDEA

Forming and Supporting Opinions

(B) What responsibilities do nations have for protecting human rights in foreign countries?

Connect *to* Today

Sweatshop Protests

In recent years, one human rights issue—the plight of sweatshop workers—has stirred protests by young people in the United States. Students at many universities have reacted angrily to reports that much of the college apparel sold on campus is produced by overseas laborers who work long hours for little pay.

Students, like those shown here, have staged sit-ins and marches to demand an end to this practice. Their efforts have made an impact, as various schools have refused to buy clothing made in such conditions.

INTEGRATED TECHNOLOGY

INTERNET ACTIVITY Write a brief report on any campus protest. Go to **classzone.com** for your research.

Connect *to* Today

Sweatshop Protests

Economists differ on the usefulness of the protests. One group, the Academic Consortium on International Trade, accuses protesters of oversimplifying a complex subject and says the protests could make life harder for workers in developing countries. They point out that factories making clothing for U.S. markets often pay their workers more than local businesses.

Other scholars, including economist Robert Pollin, say that salaries for Mexican workers could be as much as doubled without affecting sales or corporate profits and with only a 1 to 3 percent rise in retail prices.

INTEGRATED TECHNOLOGY

Rubric Reports should
- identify a specific campus protest.
- describe the events.
- explain the results of the protest.

SECTION 6 ASSESSMENT

TERMS & NAMES 1. For the following term, write a sentence explaining its significance.
- Universal Declaration of Human Rights

USING YOUR NOTES

2. Which group do you think has made the greatest progress? Explain. (10.10.1)

Group	Improvements
Children	
Women	

MAIN IDEAS

3. What are two examples of human rights? (10.9.8)
4. What are the three main causes of human rights violations? (10.9.8)
5. What trends have raised hopes that progress will be made in protecting human rights? (10.9.8)

CRITICAL THINKING & WRITING

6. **MAKING INFERENCES** What role can the mass media play in helping people understand human rights problems? (10.9.8)
7. **IDENTIFYING PROBLEMS** What problems might arise when a government takes an official role in protecting human rights at home and abroad? (10.10.1)
8. **ANALYZING ISSUES** Which group in society do you think needs the most help in obtaining human rights? Why? (10.10.1)
9. **WRITING ACTIVITY** POWER AND AUTHORITY Write an **expository paragraph** explaining which human right you consider the most important and why. (Writing 2.3.a)

CONNECT TO TODAY **DELIVERING AN ORAL REPORT**

Choose a country and investigate its record with regard to human rights. Present your findings in an **oral report** to the class. (Writing 2.3.a)

3 ASSESS

SECTION 6 ASSESSMENT

Ask students to work in small groups to complete question 2. Then let them discuss their answers with the rest of the class.

4 RETEACH

Have students work in pairs and use the headings to review the main content of the section.

ANSWERS

1. Universal Declaration of Human Rights, p. 694
2. **Sample Answer:** Children—Convention on the Rights of the Child; UN efforts to improve conditions for children. Women—UN sponsored women's conferences; UN efforts to end discrimination against women. **Possible Answers:** Children because of greater media attention; women because of the women's movement.
3. the right to take part in government process, freedom of speech and religion
4. political dissent, racial or ethnic hatred, religious differences
5. increased education and modern communications
6. Mass media can quickly inform many people about human rights violations.
7. They might run into opposition from other governments, who may resent other nations telling them how to run their country.
8. Some students might say children, because they have very little political voice. Others might say political dissenters, for they are battling their government, which is often the most powerful entity in a country.
9. **Rubric** Expository paragraphs should
   - contain an identifiable topic sentence.
   - support the topic sentence with appropriate details.

CONNECT TO TODAY

Rubric Oral reports should
- show evidence of thorough research and clear knowledge of the subject.
- be well organized and easy to understand.

TERMS & NAMES

1. mass media, p. 677
2. greenhouse effect, p. 679
3. sustainable development, p. 681
4. overpopulation, p. 683
5. less-developed countries, p. 687
6. investment capital, p. 687
7. World Bank, p. 687
8. grassroots development, p. 688
9. bioweapons, p. 692
10. Universal Declaration of Human Rights, p. 694

MAIN IDEAS

Answers will vary.

11. computers, automobiles, air and space travel, air traffic control, business accounts and inventory, telecommunications, the Internet, security
12. A number of workers "telecommute," or conduct their jobs from home; in more developed economies, employment is shifting from blue-collar manufacturing industries to high-tech industries.
13. It contributes to the greenhouse effect, destroys the ozone layer, and can cause deserts to expand and crops to fail.
14. Rain forests maintain water quality, recycle rainfall and oxygen into the atmosphere, and protect the soil.
15. drought and war
16. international agencies that lend money to nations to help economies grow and prevent financial crisis
17. Microcredit programs give small loans to people, usually in developing regions, so they can start businesses to lift them out of poverty.
18. maintaining peace and order, locating Saddam Hussein, finding weapons of mass destruction
19. Terrorist acts can happen almost anywhere, and terrorists are using more destructive weapons.
20. The UN adopted the Convention on the Rights of the Child. The UN also held a World Summit for Children in 1990 to adopt a plan for children's welfare.

Epilogue Assessment

TERMS & NAMES

Briefly explain the importance of each of the following terms and names to the unresolved problems the world faces in the 21st century.

1. mass media
2. greenhouse effect
3. sustainable development
4. overpopulation
5. less-developed countries
6. investment capital
7. World Bank
8. grassroots development
9. bioweapons
10. Universal Declaration of Human Rights

MAIN IDEAS

Technology Transforms Life Section 1 (pages 675–678)

11. Describe two ways in which the revolution in electronics has changed the world. (10.11)
12. Name two ways in which technology has transformed the workplace. (10.11)

Environmental Challenges Section 2 (pages 679–682)

13. Discuss three environmental effects of air pollution. (CST 4)
14. How do rain forests benefit the environment? (CST 4)

Feeding a Growing Population Section 3 (pages 683–686)

15. What factors have contributed to famine in Africa? (CST 4)

Economic Issues in the Developing World Section 4 (pages 687–689)

16. What are the IMF and the World Bank? (10.10.3)
17. What is microcredit? (10.10.3)

Seeking Global Security Section 5 (pages 690–693)

18. What challenges remained in Iraq after Operation Iraqi Freedom? (CST 4)
19. Why does terrorism frighten so many people? (CST 4)

Defending Human Rights and Freedoms Section 6 (pages 694–697)

20. How has the UN attempted to protect the rights of children? (10.9.8)

CRITICAL THINKING

1. USING YOUR NOTES

SCIENCE AND TECHNOLOGY Use a problem-solution chart to show how technology can help solve two of the unresolved problems of the modern world. (10.11)

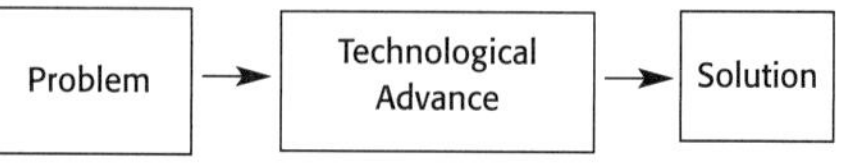

2. ANALYZING ISSUES

Which unresolved problem of the modern world do you think poses the most serious threat to humanity? Explain. (CST 4)

3. FORMING AND SUPPORTING OPINIONS

ECONOMICS Which of the four factors necessary for economic development discussed on page 687 do you consider to be the most vital? Explain. (10.10.3)

VISUAL SUMMARY

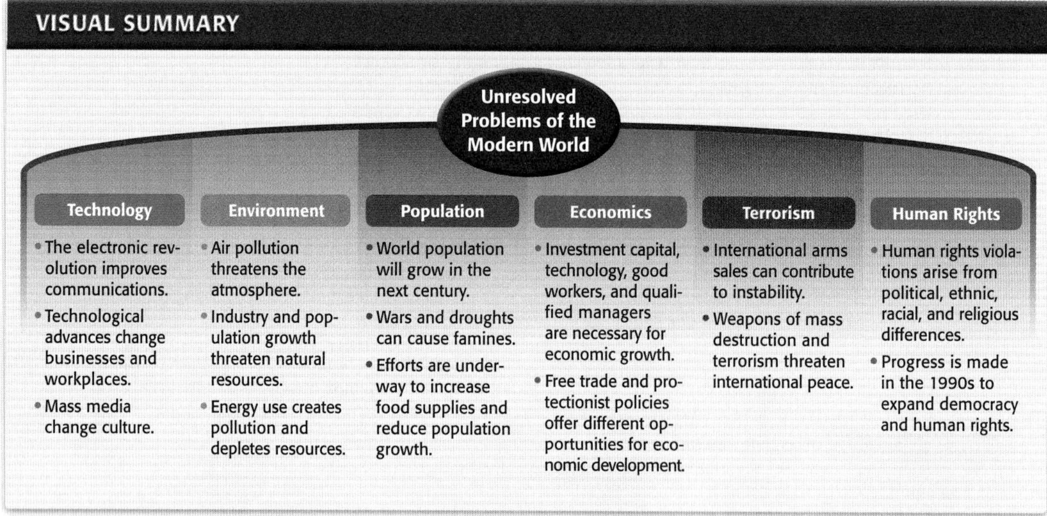

Unresolved Problems of the Modern World
Technology
• The electronic revolution improves communications.
• Technological advances change businesses and workplaces.
• Mass media change culture.
Environment
• Air pollution threatens the atmosphere.
• Industry and population growth threaten natural resources.
• Energy use creates pollution and depletes resources.
Population
• World population will grow in the next century.
• Wars and droughts can cause famines.
• Efforts are underway to increase food supplies and reduce population growth.
Economics
• Investment capital, technology, good workers, and qualified managers are necessary for economic growth.
• Free trade and protectionist policies offer different opportunities for economic development.
Terrorism
• International arms sales can contribute to instability.
• Weapons of mass destruction and terrorism threaten international peace.
Human Rights
• Human rights violations arise from political, ethnic, racial, and religious differences.
• Progress is made in the 1990s to expand democracy and human rights.

CRITICAL THINKING

Answers will vary.

1. Problem—Greenhouse effect; Technological advance—Development of renewable, nonpolluting sources of energy; Solution—Ability to use wind or solar power will reduce air pollution.
2. Some students might say protecting the environment, because pollution threatens the planet. Others might say weapons of mass destruction, because they can threaten lives.
3. Some students might say investment capital because it is difficult to build a business without seed money; others might say highly trained workers or managers because they are crucial to running an industry. Others may cite technology as the most vital because it allows businesses to be so much more productive.

> STANDARDS-BASED ASSESSMENT

Use the chart and your knowledge of world history to answer questions 1 and 2.
Additional Test Practice, pp. S1-S33

Country	Infant Mortality Rate, 2002 (per 1,000 live births)	Life Expectancy at Birth, 2002 (years)	Per Capita GDP, 2000 (U.S. Dollars)
India	62	63 (male) 64 (female)	2,200
Ethiopia	99	43 (male) 45 (female)	600
France	4	75 (male) 83 (female)	24,400
United States	7	75 (male) 80 (female)	36,200

Source: *The World Almanac, and Book of Facts 2003*

1. In which nation does a newborn have the best chance of surviving?

A. India
B. Ethiopia
C. France
D. United States

2. Which of the following can be said about prosperous nations?

A. They have a largely illiterate population.
B. They have a low infant mortality rate.
C. Their residents have a short life expectancy.
D. They have a population that is mostly female.

Use this passage about concerns over North Korea and its possible nuclear capabilities to answer question 3.

PRIMARY SOURCE

It is hard to exaggerate the danger in North Korea's finger-on-trigger taunts to America and the world that it already has a few nuclear bombs, is busily producing the stuff to build more, and will make use of them in whatever way it chooses... More weapons means enough spares to be able, say, to test one to intimidate the neighbors; or to auction one off to the highest bidder (an Iran, a Libya, or perhaps even [terrorist leader] Osama bin Laden).

THE ECONOMIST, May 3, 2003

3. A major concern expressed by the authors is that North Korea could supply nuclear weapons to (10.10.1)

A. terrorists.
B. corporations.
C. its neighbors.
D. the United States.

INTEGRATED TECHNOLOGY

TEST PRACTICE Go to **classzone.com**

- Diagnostic tests
- Tutorials
- Strategies
- Additional practice

ALTERNATIVE ASSESSMENT

1. Interact *with* History (CST 3)

On page 674, you considered various social, economic, and environmental problems that exist in your country and community and discussed ways to address these problems. Now that you have read the chapter, what do you think are the most pressing challenges the world faces today? Do you agree with all the actions being taken to meet these challenges? What are some ways that you and others might address these challenges on a local level? Discuss your ideas in small groups.

2. WRITING ABOUT HISTORY (Writing 2.5.a–d)

POWER AND AUTHORITY Using the library or the Internet, research a problem that exists in your community. After you have collected your information, write a letter to your congressional representative about what might be done to solve the problem you have chosen.

Consider the following:

- How did the problem start?
- What effect does it have on the community?
- What is the best way to address the problem?

INTEGRATED TECHNOLOGY

Create a Multimedia Presentation (CST 3)

All of the unresolved problems discussed in the Epilogue have long histories. With a group of students, choose one of the six problems and create a multimedia presentation that explains the history of the problem you have chosen. Use the Internet, periodicals, and other library sources to research your presentation.

- Find historical, literary, musical, and visual materials that relate to your topic and collect them for a class presentation.
- Give your presentation to the rest of the class. Explain the history of the problem you chose, ending with the current situation.

STANDARDS-BASED ASSESSMENT

1. The correct answer is letter **C.** Of the nations shown on the chart, France has the lowest infant mortality rate. Letter **A** is incorrect because India has the second-highest rate shown on the chart. Letter **B** is incorrect because Ethiopia has the highest rate shown on the chart. Letter **D** is incorrect because the infant mortality rate in the United States is not as low as it is in France.
2. The correct answer is letter **B.** The countries with the highest per capita GDP also have the lowest infant mortality rates. Letter **A** is incorrect because nowhere on the chart are literacy rates discussed. Letter **C** is incorrect because the countries with the highest per capita GDP have the longest life expectancies. Letter **D** is incorrect. The chart does not examine the size of male and female populations.
3. The correct answer is letter **A.** The authors fear that North Korea could provide nuclear weapons to the terrorist leader Osama bin Laden as well as to a number of hostile countries. Letter **B** is incorrect because the passage makes no mention of corporations. Letter **C** is incorrect because the concern of the writers is not that North Korea could provide nuclear weapons to its neighbors but that it could try to intimidate them by conducting nuclear tests. Letter **D** is incorrect because the United States is a nation that North Korea would "taunt," not provide with weapons, according to the writers.

ALTERNATIVE ASSESSMENT

1. After examining the major challenges facing the world today, students might say that it is important to get involved in grassroots and community activities to try to improve life for people at the local level. They might add that the more people who get involved locally, the greater the chance of solving a problem on a global scale.
2. **Rubric** Letters to Congress should be
   - written in a respectful manner.
   - well organized and clear, explaining the problem and a possible solution.

INTEGRATED TECHNOLOGY

Rubric Presentations should

- provide a sound and thorough examination of the problem.
- offer a balance of elements from different media.
- communicate visually and verbally.
- use information from at least three sources.

A GLOBAL VIEW

Teaching Strategies

A Global View presents an overview of the world's five major religions and an ethical system. As seen in a contemporary context, religion continues to be an enduring and vital part of our modern world. For historical information related to each religion and system, see the Chapter Connection references throughout.

These pages may be usefully presented at the beginning of a course to give students a sense of the contemporary practice of the religions and systems before they study their historical development. Or the pages for each may be presented as it is introduced in the text. World Religions and Ethical Systems can also be presented as a contemporary overview after Islam, the last major faith to develop, is treated (Chapter 10).

To students who wonder why Confucianism is distinguished from the "five major religions," you might explain that because of its strong emphasis on providing guidance for personal behavior, Confucianism is considered by many to be an ethical system rather than a religion.

The Study of Religions

Encourage students to examine each religion on its own terms and not to judge it by the standards of other religions. You might explain to students that this approach may involve trying to deal in a non-biased fashion with concepts that run counter to their own beliefs.

A Global View

Religion is defined as an organized system of beliefs, ceremonies, practices, and worship that centers on one or more gods. As many chapters in this book explain, religion has had a significant impact on world history. Throughout the centuries, religion has guided the beliefs and actions of millions around the globe. It has brought people together. But it has also torn them apart.

Religion continues to be a dominant force throughout the world, affecting everything from what people wear to how they behave. There are thousands of religions in the world. The following pages concentrate on five major religions and on Confucianism, an ethical system. They examine some of the characteristics and rituals that make these religions and systems similar as well as unique. They also present some of each religion's sects and denominations.

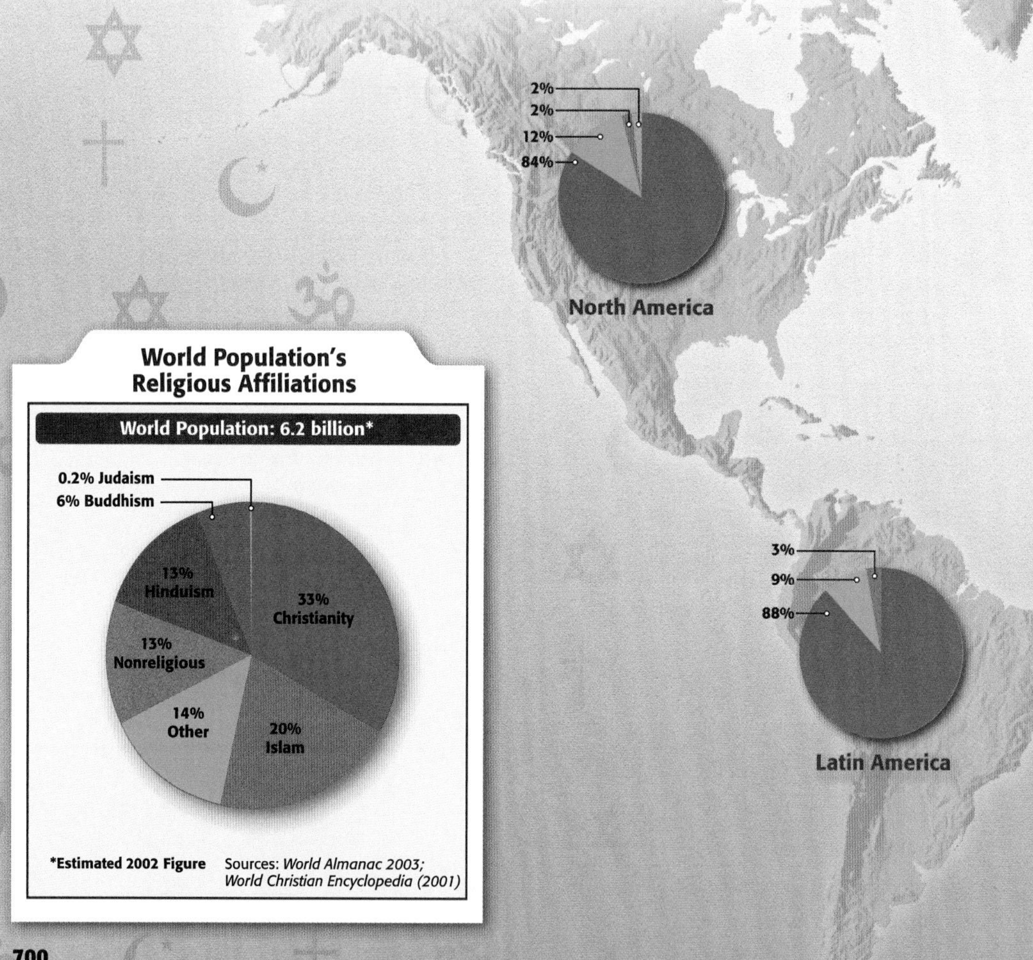

RECOMMENDED RESOURCES

Books

Bowker, John. ***World Religions: The Great Faiths Explored and Explained.*** New York: DK Publishing, 1997. An amply illustrated overview of world religions, including ancient and native religions.

Clarke, Peter B., ed. ***The World's Religions: Understanding the Living Faiths.*** Pleasantville: Reader's Digest, 1993. Religions from historical and contemporary perspectives.

Osborne, Mary Pope. ***One World, Many Religions: The Ways We Worship.*** New York: Random House, 1996. A discussion of world religions, with bibliography.

Videos and Software

Beliefs and Believers. RMI Media Productions, 1992. 800-745-5480. Twenty-four one-hour videos dealing with myth, doctrine, ritual, and ethics in world religions.

Faith and Belief: Five Major World Religions. Knowledge Unlimited, 1992. 800-356-2303. Origins and beliefs of Hinduism, Buddhism, Judaism, Christianity, and Islam.

Religions of the World. CD-ROM. SVE & Churchill Media. 800-829-1900. Explores the diverse beliefs and practices of four of the world's major religions: Islam, Hinduism, Judaism, and Buddhism.

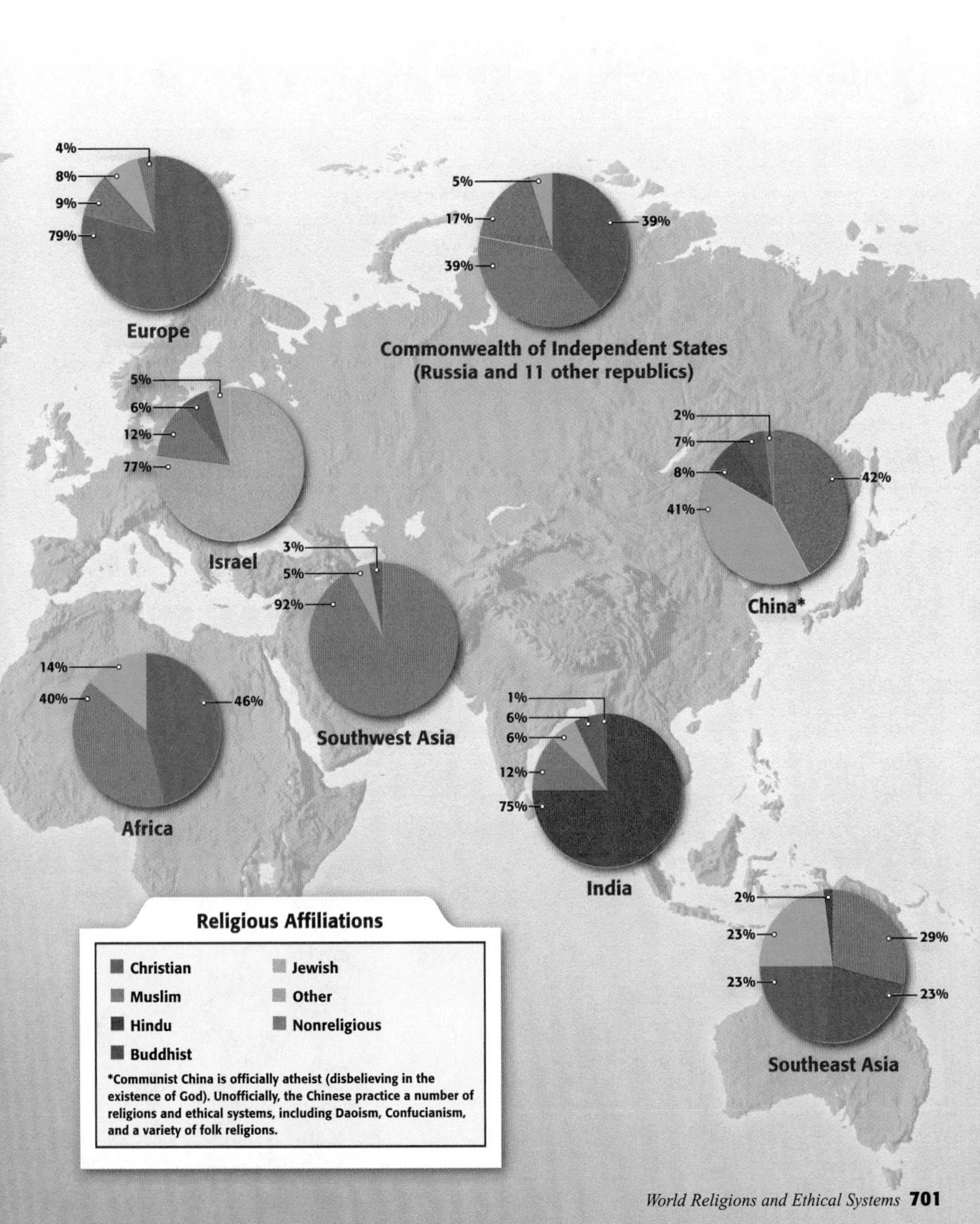

Religious Affiliation

You may wish to stress to your students that the percentages presented here are based on estimates of the numbers of people affiliated with the religions. The percentages are derived from official census figures, which may contain some inaccuracies because of flawed sampling methods and the political agendas of the reporting countries. The figures do, however, give a reasonable picture of the religious beliefs of the world's people, based on the best data available.

"Nonreligious"

In certain countries, such as Communist China and those that belong to the Commonwealth of Independent States, the governments are or have been officially anti-religious. As a result, the official counting of religious and nonreligious citizens may be biased in favor of the nonreligious, in an effort to demonstrate popular support for the government policy.

In addition, social pressures against religious observance in such countries often lead people to hide their true beliefs. Thus, the category "Nonreligious" should be regarded skeptically in some cases.

CONNECTIONS TO MATHEMATICS

Creating Bar Graphs

Class Time 45 minutes

Task Creating bar graphs showing religious affiliations in different areas of the world

Purpose To present and compare information presented in different visual formats

Instructions Have student pairs work together to create bar graphs showing the data presented in the pie charts on these pages. Tell them that the vertical axis of each graph should display percentages from 0% to 100%, and the bars should represent the major religions. You may want to draw a sample graph on the board to demonstrate. Encourage students to plot the graphs manually on graph paper, or by one of the many available computer-graphing programs.

After student pairs have created their bar graphs, have them compare the pie charts with the bar graphs. Ask students, which format allows them to compare religious affiliations within a country or region more easily? Which allows them to compare religious affiliations throughout the world more easily? Challenge students to describe what they think are the strong points of each format.

BUDDHISM

Worship Practices

The most common form of Buddhist worship is meditation (deep thought or reflection) before sacred images of the Buddha. Believers may meditate before shrines in their homes or in temples. They may offer gifts of food, flowers, or candles out of respect for or worship of the Buddha. (Some Buddhists consider the Buddha a god, though he himself did not.) Both in temples and at home, worshipers burn incense and light candles before images of the Buddha. The light of the candles recalls the light of Buddha's wisdom.

Ritual

One of the most important symbols in Buddhist ritual and art is the lotus flower, which has acquired deep religious meaning over the centuries. The lotus flower takes root in mud but blossoms on the surface of tranquil water. Through the lotus, Buddhists are reminded that the spiritual life of a believer can blossom in enlightenment even though it is rooted in the impurity of the world and the heart.

References to the lotus occur in early Buddhist scriptures. As a result of the long tradition about the lotus, worshipers often offer lotus flowers at shrines and temples. Festival days, such as the Buddha's birthday, provide special occasions for offering the lotus.

Buddhism

Buddhism has influenced Asian religion, society, and culture for over 2,500 years. Today, most Buddhists live in Sri Lanka, East and Southeast Asia, and Japan. Buddhism consists of several different sects. A religious sect is a group within a religion that distinguishes itself by one or more unique beliefs.

Buddhists are united in their belief in the Buddha's teachings, known as the dharma. Because the Buddha is said to have "set in motion the wheel of the dharma" during his first sermon, his teaching is often symbolized by a wheel, as shown above. The Buddha taught that the key to happiness was detachment from all worldly goods and desires. This was achieved by following the Noble Eightfold Path, or the Middle Way, a life between earthly desires and extreme forms of self-denial.

INTEGRATED TECHNOLOGY

RESEARCH LINKS For more on Buddhism, go to **classzone.com**

Ritual ►
Women in Rangoon, Myanmar, sweep the ground so that monks can avoid stepping on and killing any insects. Many Buddhists believe in rebirth, the idea that living beings, after death, are reborn and continue to exist. Buddhists believe that all living beings possess the potential for spiritual growth—and the possibility of rebirth as humans.

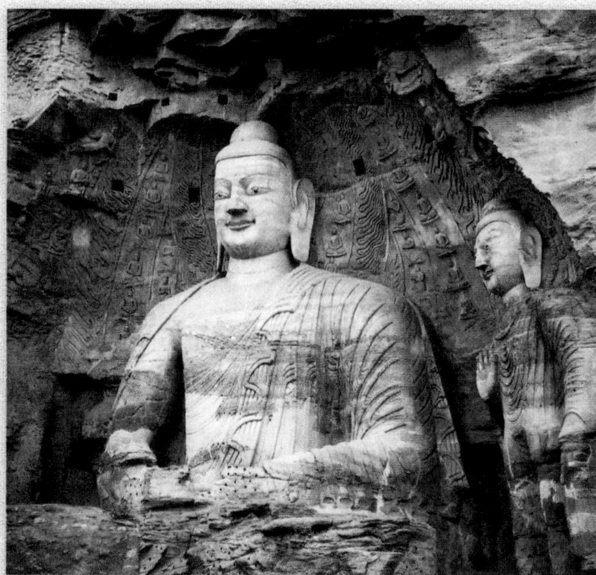

▲ Worship Practices
Statues of the Buddha, such as this one in China, appear in shrines throughout Asia. Buddhists strive to follow the Buddha's teachings through meditation, a form of religious contemplation. They also make offerings at shrines, temples, and monasteries.

▼ Leadership
Those who dedicate their entire life to the teachings of the Buddha are known as Buddhist monks and nuns. In many Buddhist sects, monks are expected to lead a life of poverty, meditation, and study. Here, Buddhist monks file past shrines in Thailand. To learn humility, monks must beg for food and money.

DIFFERENTIATING INSTRUCTION: ENGLISH LEARNERS

Creating a Glossary of Key Words

Class Time 30 minutes

Task Creating a chart to show the meaning of key words

Purpose To understand Buddhism better

Instructions Have students create a chart in which they define key words that describe Buddhist beliefs and practices. Tell them to list each word and its meaning and to describe its importance to Buddhism briefly. An example is at right.

Encourage students to create similar charts for each religion and ethical system presented in this section.

Key Word	Meaning	Description
dharma	Buddha's teachings	Buddha taught that the key to happiness was detachment from worldly desires
rebirth	The idea that living beings, after death, are reborn	Rebirth allows people the possibility for spiritual growth
meditation	A form of religious contemplation	Buddhists use meditation to help them follow the Buddha's teachings

Learn More About Buddhism

Major Buddhist Sects

Buddhism → Theravada, Mahayana, Mantrayana

The Three Cardinal Faults

This image depicts what Buddhists consider the three cardinal faults of humanity: greed (the pig); hatred (the snake); and delusion (the rooster).

Dhammapada

THE DHAMMAPADA
TRANSLATED FOR THE MODERN READER BY EKNATH EASWARAN

PRIMARY SOURCE

One of the most well-known Buddhist scriptures is the *Dhammapada*, or *Verses of Righteousness.* The book is a collection of sayings on Buddhist practices. In this verse, Buddhists are instructed to avoid envying others:

> *Let him not despise what he has received, nor should he live envying the gains of others. The disciple who envies the gains of others does not attain concentration.*
>
> *Dhammapada* 365

Sects

Buddhists are united in their respect for the Buddha and in their search for nirvana (enlightenment and liberation from suffering). But various groups understand the Buddha's message in somewhat different ways.

Theravada Buddhism is marked by an effort to stay as close as possible to the Buddha's recorded teachings. The Theravada ideal is the arhat, a saint who reaches nirvana alone. The arhat's pursuit of nirvana is carried out in a monastery, away from the world.

Mahayana Buddhism is more accepting of change and of the world. It considers reaching nirvana as an effort of all believers working together. The Mahayana ideal is the bodhisattva, a human who delays personal nirvana and returns to the world by rebirth to help others attain nirvana.

Leadership

There are significant religious and social differences in the leadership styles of Theravada and Mahayana Buddhism.

Theravada Buddhists try to follow the Buddha's own ideas on what an ideal society should be like. In his view, the king, the monks, and the laity (ordinary people) had important responsibilities to one another. For example, monks guided the spiritual development and schooling of the community as well as gave advice and resolved conflict. Laypeople, in return, had to provide support to the monks in the form of money and food.

Mahayana Buddhists tend to downplay Buddhism as a social force and concentrate more on its spiritual features.

DIFFERENTIATING INSTRUCTION: STRUGGLING READERS

Analyzing a Primary Source

Class Time 30 minutes

Task Expressing the ideas of Buddhist scripture in everyday language

Purpose To understand a primary source better

Instructions Have students get together with a partner and read the excerpt from the *Dhammapada.* Ask them to rewrite the excerpt in their own words. Explain that the pronouns *him* and *he* in the excerpt refer to a Buddhist follower. The excerpt might be rewritten as follows:

A Buddhist follower should be happy with his or her own belongings and not be jealous of what others have. The follower who is jealous of others will not be able to meditate and achieve happiness.

Have students discuss the ideas expressed in the excerpt with their partner. Have they ever envied another's belongings? How did envying that person make them feel? *(Students will probably say that they felt dissatisfied and unhappy.)* How does the excerpt support what they learned about the Buddhist belief in the key to happiness? *(The Buddha taught that the key to happiness was to let go of possessions.)*

CHRISTIANITY

Ritual

The Christian calendar contains important days (sometimes called feast days or holy days) that give a religious dimension to the year and recall important events in Christian history. In many traditions, the most important of these days are Christmas, Easter, and Pentecost (marking the descent of the Holy Spirit to inspire Jesus' closest followers, called the Apostles). Many Christians also observe religious seasons. For example, Advent and Lent are seasons of reflection and self-denial.

Worship Practices

Holy Communion is perhaps the most important rite of worship in Christianity. This rite recalls Jesus' actions and words during his Last Supper with his disciples, when he identified bread and wine with his body and blood.

Christian denominations differ in their ideas about the meaning of Communion. In Eastern Orthodoxy, Roman Catholicism, and some Protestant denominations, the rite of Communion is viewed as an actual reenactment of Christ's sacrifice of his life for the human race. The bread and wine are sanctified to become Christ's actual body and blood.

Many Protestants, however, look upon Communion as symbols of Christ's body and blood. Protestants differ in their beliefs about the nature of the bread and wine.

Christianity

Christianity is the largest religion in the world, with about 2 billion followers. It is based on the life and teachings of Jesus Christ. Most Christians are members of one of three major groups: Roman Catholic, Protestant, or Eastern Orthodox. Christianity teaches the existence of only one God. Christians regard Jesus as the son of God. They believe that Jesus entered the world and died to save humanity from sin. The cross shown above, a symbol of the crucifixion of Jesus Christ, represents Jesus' love for humanity by dying for its sins. Christians believe that they reach salvation by following the teachings of Jesus Christ.

INTEGRATED TECHNOLOGY

RESEARCH LINKS For more on Christianity, go to **classzone.com**

Ritual ►
Each year, hundreds of thousands of Christians from all over the world visit the Basilica of Guadalupe in northern Mexico City. The church is considered the holiest in Mexico. It is near the site where the Virgin Mary, the mother of Jesus Christ, is said to have appeared twice in 1531. Out of deep respect for Mary, some pilgrims approach the holy cathedral on their knees.

Worship Practices ►
Worshiping as a group is an important part of Christian life. Most Protestant services include praying, singing, and a sermon. Some services include baptism and communion, in which bread and wine are consumed in remembrance of Jesus' death.

Communion celebrates the last meal Jesus took with his disciples, as illustrated here in the *Last Supper* by Leonardo da Vinci.

704

DIFFERENTIATING INSTRUCTION: GIFTED AND TALENTED STUDENTS

Last Supper by Leonardo da Vinci

Class Time 45 minutes

Task Analyzing a work of art

Purpose To deepen understanding of the relationship between art and religion

Instructions Tell students that the painting on this page, *Last Supper,* shows Jesus with his 12 disciples. In the painting, Jesus has just made an announcement and the disciples are reacting to it. Challenge students to use the Internet and other research tools to learn more about the painting and its meaning. Have students answer the following questions:

- How does the artist make Jesus the focus of his painting? *(He places Jesus in the center.)*
- What does Jesus tell his disciples? *(One of them is about to betray him.)*
- Which one of the disciples will betray Jesus? Which figure represents him in the painting? *(Judas Iscariot; He is placed just to Christ's right clutching a money bag.)*
- What action does this representation foreshadow? *(It foreshadows the actual betrayal, when Judas points out Christ to the men who have come to arrest him.)*

World Art and Cultures Transparencies
- AT36 *Last Supper*

Learn More About Christianity

Major Christian Sects

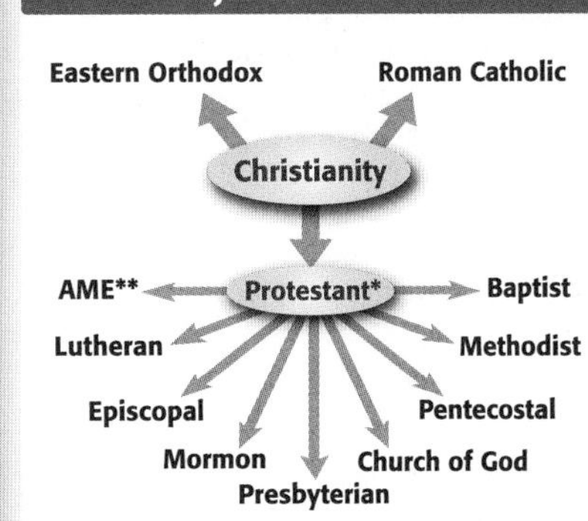

*In the United States alone, there are 30 Protestant denominations with over 400,000 members in each.
**African Methodist Episcopal

Fish Symbol

The fish is an early symbol of Christianity. There are many theories about the origin of the symbol, but some Christians believe that it derives from the fact that Jesus called his disciples, or followers, "fishers of men."

The Bible

PRIMARY SOURCE

The Bible is the most sacred book of the Christian religion. It is divided into two major parts: the Old Testament, which focuses on Jewish history, and the New Testament, which describes the teachings of Jesus Christ. The following verse from the New Testament reveals the fundamental teaching of Jesus:

> *"Men, what must I do to be saved?" And they said, "Believe in the Lord Jesus, and you will be saved, you and your household."*
>
> Acts 16:30–31

▲ Leadership
In some Christian churches, the person who performs services in the local church is known as a priest. Shown here is a priest of the Ethiopian Orthodox Church. These priests, like the ministers and clergy in other Christian sects, conduct worship services and preside over marriages and funerals. Monks and nuns also provide leadership and guidance in the Christian church.

Sects

There are many more Protestant groups that could have been mentioned on this page. Others include Congregationalist churches, the United Church of Christ, the Mennonites, the Quakers, the Seventh Day Adventists, the Christian Scientists, the Jehovah's Witnesses, and more. Each of the Christian sects has its own teachings, history, and organization.

Some Christians look sadly on the divisions in their religion, since such divisions contradict Jesus' wish "that they [Jesus' followers] may all be one." More recently, there has been a tendency to accept diversity in organizations such as the National Council of Churches, for example.

Leadership

In most Christian churches, a group of clergy looks after the spiritual welfare of believers. They preside at worship services, baptize people, perform marriages, and preside at funerals.

Leaders of local Orthodox, Roman Catholic, and Anglican churches are called priests. In many Protestant groups, leaders of local churches are called ministers. A minister's calling and education give him or her the right to preside at worship. Nonetheless, Protestants tend to stress the equality of Christians, so the differences in the roles of the clergy and the people are less important than in other Christian groups. In fact, some Protestants—like the Quakers—usually have no ministers.

CONNECTIONS ACROSS TIME AND CULTURES

Modern Christian Missionaries

Class Time 45 minutes

Task Researching the work of modern Christian missionaries

Purpose To understand modern connections to traditional religious practices

Instructions Tell students that over the centuries, Christians have converted people throughout the world. Motivation for Christians' missionary work came from Jesus himself, who asked his followers to carry the faith to the whole world.

Besides religion, missionaries also impacted various cultures through education and Western ways of living. Some of these impacts were positive; some were not.

Have small groups of students research to learn about the work of modern Christian missionaries. What are some of the modern missionaries' goals? What methods do they use to obtain their goals? Do you agree or disagree with the missionaries' approaches? Ask students to name some Christian missionaries of the 20th and 21st centuries. *(Albert Schweitzer; Mother Teresa; priests and nuns working in foreign countries)*

HINDUISM

Ritual

Hindus worship in both temples and at home—as individuals and families, not as congregations. A temple normally contains a principal shrine dedicated to an important god or goddess.

A temple usually contains numerous other shrines, each devoted to a particular god. Individuals devoted to particular divinities perform their worship at those gods' altars. Hindus do not feel that they are worshiping the images of the gods; they believe that the gods themselves inhabit the images. Temples are also the scene of annual festivals celebrating high points in the lives of the gods.

At home, worship or puja takes place around a family shrine. The shrine is dedicated to a god or goddess that is part of the family tradition.

Leadership

Spiritual leadership in the Hindu community is the responsibility of the Brahmin class. Because of good works performed in previous lives, Brahmins have earned a karma that entitles them to be born in the highest social class, or caste.

Brahmins take on the roles of priests, philosophers, artists, and teachers in Hindu society. They are responsible for performing sacrifices in temples and for the care of the shrines of the gods. Some of the priestly sacrifices can be traced back 3,000 years.

Hinduism

Hinduism, one of the world's oldest surviving religions, is the major religion of India. It also has followers in Indonesia, as well as in parts of Africa, Europe, and the Western Hemisphere. Hinduism is a collection of religious beliefs that developed over thousands of years. Hindus worship several gods, which represent different forms of Brahman. Brahman is the most divine spirit in the Hindu religion. Hinduism, like Buddhism, stresses that persons reach true enlightenment and happiness only after they free themselves from their earthly desires. Followers of Hinduism achieve this goal through worship, the attainment of knowledge, and a lifetime of virtuous acts. The sound "Om," or "Aum," shown above, is the most sacred syllable for Hindus. It often is used in prayers.

INTEGRATED TECHNOLOGY

RESEARCH LINKS For more on Hinduism, go to **classzone.com**

▼ Ritual

Each year, thousands of Hindus make a pilgrimage to India's Ganges River. The Ganges is considered a sacred site in the Hindu religion. Most Hindus come to bathe in the water, an act they believe will cleanse and purify them. The sick and disabled come in the belief that the holy water might cure their ailments.

COOPERATIVE LEARNING

Water Symbolism in Religion

Class Time 30 minutes

Task Comparing the role and symbolism of water in different religions

Purpose To learn about religious symbols

Instructions Tell students that water plays an important role in many religions. For example, water is essential to the Christian rite of baptism. Point out that water also has a symbolic meaning in many religions.

Divide students into groups of three or four and have them do research about the role and symbolic meaning of water in Christianity and Hinduism. Have them organize their findings in a chart like the one shown here.

	Christianity	Hinduism
Role of Water	used in baptism and cleansing rituals	water of the Ganges River used for ritual bathing
Symbolic Meaning	symbolizes the washing away of sin and a birth into a new life	symbolizes a cleansing act; Hindus believe the water will purify and cure them

▲ **Leadership**
Gurus, or spiritual teachers, play a major role in spreading Hindu beliefs. These holy men are believed to have had the gods' words revealed to them. Brahmin priests, like the one shown here, are also religious leaders. They take care of the divine images in the temples and read from the sacred books.

▲ **Celebration**
Each spring, Hindus in India celebrate the festival of Holi. Originally a harvest festival, Holi also symbolizes the triumph of good over evil. The festival recalls the story of Prince Prahlada, who faced death rather than cease worshiping Vishnu. During this joyous celebration, people dance in the streets and shower each other with colored powder and dyed water.

Learn More About Hinduism

Major Hindu Sects

Hinduism
Shaktism
Reform Hinduism
Vaishnavites
Shaivites

Three Main Gods

This statue represents Brahma, creator of the universe. Brahma, Vishnu, and Shiva are the three main gods of Hinduism. Vishnu is the preserver of the universe, while Shiva is its destroyer.

Rig Veda

PRIMARY SOURCE

The Vedas are the oldest Hindu scriptures—and they are older than the sacred writings of any other major religion. The following is a verse from the Rig Veda, the oldest of the four Vedas:

> *He who gives liberally goes straight to the gods; on the high ridge of heaven he stands exalted.*
>
> Rig Veda 1.125.5

Sects

Followers of Shaktism worship the supreme goddess of Hinduism, Shakti ("energy" or "force"). She may take on merciful aspects—such as Lakshmi, the partner of Vishnu—or destructive forms, such as Kali the Destroyer.

Hindus who follow Vaishnavism pay special devotion to Vishnu the Preserver. Followers of Shaivism are devoted to the worship of Shiva the Destroyer. They seek to rid their souls of earthly bonds to attain "the nature of Shiva."

Reform Hinduism arose in the 19th century as a response to contact with Islam and the West. Reformers advocated strict monotheism, denounced statues and the caste system, and supported rights for women and Western forms of education.

Celebration

Another joyous Hindu festival is Diwali, which marks the beginning of the Hindu new year. When it gets dark, believers light many small lamps. The lights serve to frighten away demons and welcome back the god Rama, who, tradition says, was driven out of his kingdom.

A celebration focused more on the family is the ceremony of the sacred thread. It is a coming-of-age ceremony for boys in the three highest of the five castes. Sometimes, it is celebrated the day before a boy marries. The boy's father drapes a sacred thread over his son's left shoulder and under his right arm. From that moment on, the boy will wear the thread as a symbol that he is "twice born," having been born first into the world and then into the religious life.

DIFFERENTIATING INSTRUCTION: ENGLISH LEARNERS

Clarifying Hindu Terms

Class Time 20 minutes

Task Distinguishing among similar Hindu terms

Purpose To clarify the meaning of religious terms

Instructions Students may be confused by the similar Hindu terms *Brahma, Brahman,* and *Brahmin.* Point out that the terms all have their root in the Sanskrit word *brahma,* meaning "prayer."

To help students distinguish among the terms, ask them to list the words and their meanings in a chart like the one here. Encourage students to refer to the chart as they read the pages on Hinduism.

Term	Meaning
Brahma	one of the three main Hindu gods; Brahma is the creator of the universe
Brahman	the most divine spirit in the Hindu religion; Hindu gods represent different forms of Brahman
Brahmin	the highest Hindu social class; Brahmins often serve as priests and religious leaders

ISLAM

Ritual

Muslims may eat all foods except those *haram,* or specifically forbidden, by the Qur'an. Foods that are *haram* include pork, blood, and the meat of animals found dead, animals of prey, and animals slaughtered in the name of any god but Allah. When slaughtering meat, a Muslim butcher pronounces the name of Allah. This tradition arose to recognize God's generosity and his work as the Creator, and meat so blessed is said to be *halal.* Since both Jews and Christians worship the same God as Muslims, many Muslims believe Islamic law allows them to eat meat slaughtered by Jews or Christians.

Celebration

The end of Ramadan fasting is celebrated by a major Islamic holiday called Id al-Fitr. The celebration begins with a worship service that may be held in a mosque or a public place.

Later, the site of the celebration moves to the home. There, many festive foods that were not eaten during Ramadan, including sweets, are shared with family members and friends.

The other great Islamic religious holiday, called Eid al-Adha, takes place in the last month of the Islamic calendar. Eid al-Adha commemorates the faithfulness of the prophet Abraham, who was willing to sacrifice his own son to obey God's command.

Islam

Islam is a religion based on the teachings of the prophet Muhammad. Followers of Islam, known as Muslims, believe that God revealed these teachings to Muhammad through the angel Gabriel. Muslims are concentrated from southwest to central Asia and parts of Africa. Islam also has many followers in Southeast Asia. Sunni Muslims believe that their leaders should follow Muhammad's example. Shi'a Muslims believe that their leaders should be Muhammad's descendants.

Islam teaches the existence of only one God, called Allah in the Arabic language. Muslims believe in all prophets of Judaism and Christianity. They show their devotion by performing lifelong acts of worship known as the Five Pillars of Islam. These include faith, prayer, almsgiving (charity), fasting, and a pilgrimage to Mecca. The crescent moon (shown above) has become a familiar symbol for Islam. It may be related to the new moon that begins each month in the Islamic lunar calendar, which orders religious life for Muslims. The five points of the star may represent the Five Pillars of Islam.

INTEGRATED TECHNOLOGY

RESEARCH LINKS For more on Islam, go to **classzone.com**

▼ Ritual

At least once in their lifetime, all Muslims who are physically and financially able go on hajj, or pilgrimage, to the holy city of Mecca in Saudi Arabia. There, pilgrims perform several rites, or acts of worship. One rite, shown here, is walking seven times around the Ka'aba—the house of worship that Muslims face in prayer.

708

CONNECTIONS TO SCIENCE

The Muslim Calendar

Class Time 30 minutes

Task Applying the Muslim calendar to U.S. dates

Purpose To understand the differences between the Gregorian and the Muslim calendar

Instructions Tell students that unlike the Gregorian, or solar calendar used in the West, the Muslim calendar is lunar—that is, based on the phases of the moon. The lunar year is about 11 days shorter than the solar year. As a result, Muslim dates move backward 11 days each year to correspond with the dates of the Gregorian calendar. Thus, during a period of 32.5 solar years, a Muslim date moves through all four seasons.

Have pairs of students apply Muslim calendar dates to U.S. holidays. Pairs will need this year's Gregorian calendar to answer the following questions:

- On what day would New Year's Day be celebrated according to the Muslim calendar? *(December 21)*
- On what day would the Fourth of July be celebrated? *(June 23)*

Have students discuss what would happen if U.S. holidays moved through the seasons. How might celebrations of a holiday like the Fourth of July be different in different seasons?

▲ **Celebration**
During the sacred month known as Ramadan, Muslims fast, or abstain from food and drink, from dawn to sunset. The family shown here is ending their fast. The most important night of Ramadan is called the Night of Power. This is believed to be the night the angel Gabriel first spoke to Muhammad.

▲ **Worship Practices**
Five times a day Muslims throughout the world face Mecca and pray to Allah. Pictured here are Muslims praying at a mosque in Turkey.

There are no priests or other clergy in Islam. However, a Muslim community leader known as the imam conducts the prayers in a mosque. Islam also has a scholar class called the ulama, which includes religious teachers.

Learn More About Islam

Major Islamic Sects

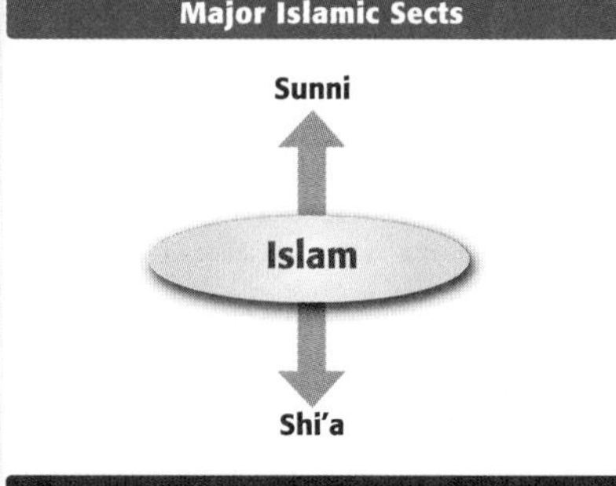

Prayer Rug

Muslims often pray by kneeling on a rug. The design of the rug includes a pointed or arch-shaped pattern. The rug must be placed so that the arch points toward Mecca.

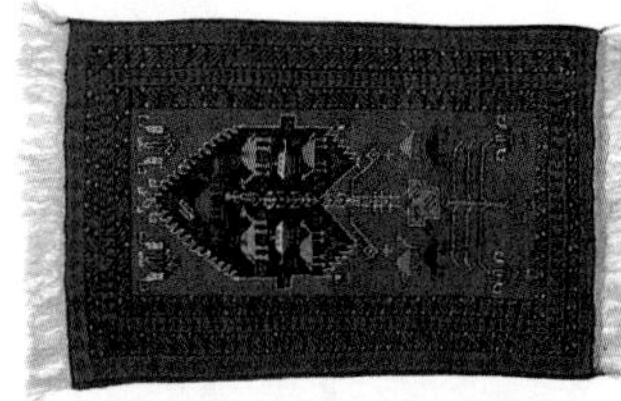

The Qur'an

PRIMARY SOURCE

The Qur'an, the sacred book of Muslims, consists of verses grouped into 114 chapters, or suras. The book is the spiritual guide on matters of Muslim faith. It also contains teachings for Muslim daily life. In the following verse, Muslims are instructed to appreciate the world's physical and spiritual riches:

> *Do you not see that God has subjected to your use all things in the heavens and on earth, and has made His bounties flow to you in exceeding measure, both seen and unseen?*
>
> Qur'an, sura 31:20

Sects

The split between Sunni and Shi'a Muslims arose from a dispute over who should succeed Muhammad as political leader of the Muslim community. Two theories emerged as to who should lead Muslims. The Sunni sect believed that any religious leader who had demonstrated a deep understanding of Muslim tradition had earned the right to leadership. In contrast, the Shi'a sect believed that only those directly related to the Prophet through Ali, Muhammad's son-in-law, could legitimately rule. Today, the Shi'a tradition is concentrated mainly in Iran and Iraq, while Sunni Islam predominates in the rest of the Islamic world.

Worship Practices

A basic part of formal Islamic worship is called *salah,* a ritual prayer. In areas that have a large enough Muslim population, the *salah* takes place in a mosque. Instead of containing chairs or pews, the worship space in a mosque is a large, often carpeted area that faces toward the Ka'aba in Mecca.

Muslim men and boys are required to participate in congregational worship on Friday at noon. Because of household duties, women and girls are exempt from this responsibility. Near the beginning of a formal worship service, Muslims raise their hands up to their ears and declare, "Allahu Akbar" ("Allah is greatest").

At each stage of the ceremony, worshipers stand, bow, and touch their foreheads to the ground twice. Verses from the Qur'an are read and prayers are said in Arabic.

DIFFERENTIATING INSTRUCTION: STRUGGLING READERS

Paraphrasing a Primary Source

Class Time 30 minutes

Task Rephrasing and explaining a primary source

Purpose To improve student understanding of the primary source

Instructions Students may have difficulty understanding the long, one-sentence excerpt from the Qur'an. Tell students that it may help to break the sentence up into several phrases and to restate their meaning. For example, "Do you not see that God has subjected to your use . . ." could be rewritten as "Don't you see that God has given you . . ."

Divide students into groups of three or four. Assign each group part of the primary source excerpt and ask them to paraphrase it. When groups are finished, combine their work into a chart like the one here.

Phrase	Paraphrase
all things in the heavens and on earth	everything the physical and spiritual world has to offer
and has made His bounties flow to you	and has given all of this to you
in exceeding measure	generously
both seen and unseen	in ways that you can both see and feel spiritually

Finally, invite students to put the phrases together and paraphrase the entire excerpt.

JUDAISM

Worship Practices

A synagogue (often *temple* in the Reform and Conservative traditions) is usually built so that the congregation faces toward Jerusalem during worship. An ark, or cabinet, at the front of the synagogue contains the scroll of the Torah, the most sacred books of the Hebrew Bible. A lamp called the eternal light hangs before the ark, symbolizing the eternal presence of God. A rabbi ("teacher") leads prayers and reads passages of the Hebrew Bible or Torah during the service. He or she also delivers the sermon. During worship, the rabbi is assisted by a cantor (or musical leader) who chants prayers.

Ritual

Some Jews follow strict dietary laws based on passages from the Hebrew Bible. These laws have established what is kosher, or acceptable, for Jews to eat. Kosher laws forbid the eating of animals considered unclean. These animals include pigs and shellfish.

The preparation of food is a significant part of kosher law. Animals must be killed in a certain way—a single cut across the neck made with a knife absent of nicks. This is intended to kill the animal as quickly and painlessly as possible. Before the meat is cooked, it must be drained of its blood.

Additional kosher laws determine everything from the preparation of food to what foods may not be eaten together.

Judaism

Judaism is the religion of the more than 14 million Jews throughout the world. Judaism was the first major religion to teach the existence of only one god. The basic laws and teachings of Judaism come from the Torah, the first five books of the Hebrew Bible. Judaism teaches that a person serves God by studying the Torah and living by its teachings. Orthodox Jews obey the Torah without question. Conservative and Reform Jews interpret the Torah to make its teachings relevant to today's world. The Star of David (shown above), also called the Shield of David, is the universal symbol of Judaism. The emblem refers to King David, who ruled the kingdom of Israel from about 1000–962 B.C.

INTEGRATED TECHNOLOGY

RESEARCH LINKS For more on Judaism, go to **classzone.com**

Ritual ►
Major events in a Jew's life are marked by special rites and ceremonies. When Jewish children reach the age of 13, for example, they enter the adult religious community. The event is marked in the synagogue with a ceremony called a bar mitzvah for a boy and a bat mitzvah for a girl, shown here.

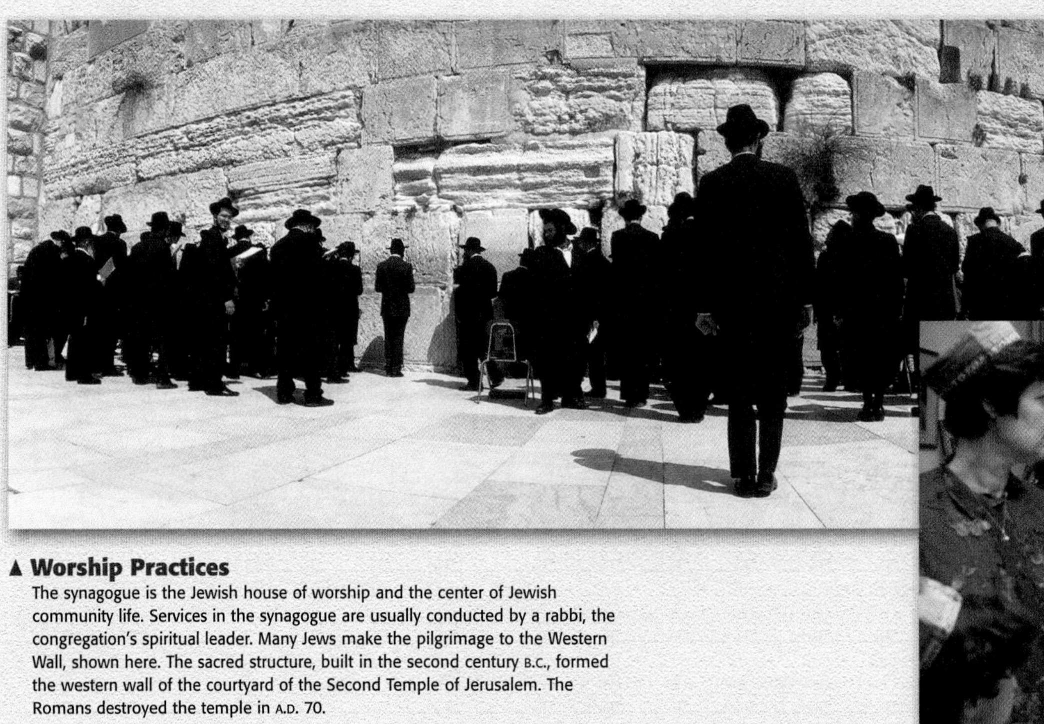

▲ Worship Practices
The synagogue is the Jewish house of worship and the center of Jewish community life. Services in the synagogue are usually conducted by a rabbi, the congregation's spiritual leader. Many Jews make the pilgrimage to the Western Wall, shown here. The sacred structure, built in the second century B.C., formed the western wall of the courtyard of the Second Temple of Jerusalem. The Romans destroyed the temple in A.D. 70.

710

DIFFERENTIATING INSTRUCTION: ENGLISH LEARNERS

Using an Outline to Take Notes

Class Time 30 minutes

Task Creating an outline to organize difficult information

Purpose To use an outline to record information on Judaism

Instructions Some students may have trouble keeping track of the information presented on these pages. Have these students use an outline to record the information. Tell them to organize their outline using the paragraphs and headings on these pages: Introduction, Ritual, Worship Practices, Celebration. Under each heading, students should record the paragraph's main ideas and details. A partial example is at right.

I. Introduction
  A. Torah
    1. first five books of Hebrew Bible
    2. contain basic laws and teachings of Judaism
II. Ritual
  A. Bar and Bat Mitzvah
III. Worship Practices
  A. synagogue
IV. Celebration
  A. Purim

▼ **Celebration**

Jews celebrate a number of holidays that honor their history as well as their God. Pictured here are Jews celebrating the holiday of Purim. Purim is a festival honoring the survival of the Jews who, in the fifth century B.C., were marked for death by their Persian rulers.

Jews celebrate Purim by sending food and gifts. They also dress in costumes and hold carnivals and dances.

Learn More About Judaism

Major Jewish Sects

Reform — Judaism — Orthodox

Conservative

Yarmulke

Out of respect for God, Jewish men are not supposed to leave their head uncovered. Therefore, many Orthodox and Conservative Jews wear a skullcap known as a yarmulke, or kippah.

The Torah

PRIMARY SOURCE

During a synagogue service, the Torah scroll is lifted, while the congregation declares: "This is the Law which Moses set before the children of Israel." The following verse from the Torah makes clear Moses' law regarding belief in one God:

> *Hear O Israel: the Lord our God, the Lord is One.*
>
> Deuteronomy 6:4

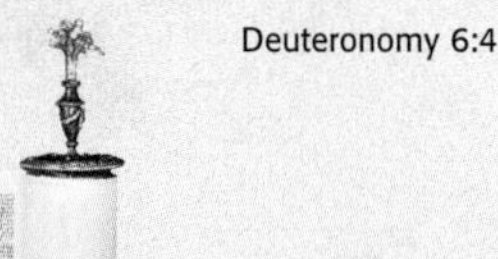

Sects

In the 19th century, Jews divided into three groups. The divisions were based on how closely believers followed the traditions recorded in the Torah and in commentaries on the Torah (the Talmud).

In Orthodox Judaism, believers follow traditional dietary (kosher) laws. During worship, Orthodox Jews pray in Hebrew—with men and women sitting apart. Orthodox men always cover their heads out of respect for God. Married women cover their heads with hats, scarves, or wigs.

Reform Judaism arose from efforts to adapt Judaism to life in the West. Reform Jews have changed some traditional practices.

Conservative Judaism represents an attempt to strike a balance between Orthodox and Reform Judaism. Conservatives balance tradition with the needs of modern practitioners.

Celebration

The Jewish year is marked by a series of holy days that remind Jews of their beliefs, history, and traditions. Rosh Hashanah is a one- or two-day festival that marks the beginning of the new year in the Jewish calendar. Passover, or Pesach, lasts for seven or eight days and recalls the departure of the Jews from Egypt, where they had been enslaved.

COOPERATIVE LEARNING

Jewish History

Class Time 45 minutes

Task Learning about events and people in Jewish history

Purpose To increase understanding of a religion's heritage

Instructions Divide students into groups of three or four and have them use the Internet and other research tools to learn about important events in Jewish history. Suggest that students present their findings using the following methods:

- a time line of important events and people
- pictures—original artwork or photocopies of reproductions—illustrating the events
- biographies—similar to the History Makers found in this book—of important figures, including David and Solomon
- newspaper reports of events, written as if students were witnessing the incidents
- a Web page with links to biographies, articles, and visuals

Have student groups share their findings with the class. You might encourage interested students to create similar presentations of the other religions discussed in this section.

CONFUCIANISM

Celebration

Respect for Confucius has not been limited to Asians. Jesuit missionaries who arrived in China in the late 1500s came to believe that many of Confucius' teachings were in accord with Christianity. Some missionaries even wrestled with the question of whether Chinese converts to Christianity could continue to participate in Confucian ancestor worship. The missionaries admired Confucius so much that they wrote letters home which provided materials for books about Confucius.

Some Jesuits compared Confucius to Aristotle (whom they called the Philosopher) by calling him the Philosopher of the Chinese. His high moral standards and humanistic view of the world reminded them of the ideas of the Greek philosopher and the humanistic ideals of the Renaissance.

Leadership

Confucius was born about 551 B.C. in northeastern China. His impoverished mother instilled a love of learning in him, and he eventually became a successful teacher.

One way Confucius tried to spread his ethical views in China was by holding government office. China's leaders, however, found his honesty and frankness to be impractical, even dangerous.

Despite his political setbacks, Confucius's reputation as a man of conscience and thought attracted many followers. Since then, his ideas have influenced millions.

Confucianism

With no clergy and with no gods to worship, Confucianism is not a religion in the traditional sense. Rather, it is an ethical system that provides direction for personal behavior and good government. However, this ancient philosophy guides the actions and beliefs of millions of Chinese and other peoples of the East. Thus, many view it as a religion.

Confucianism is a way of life based on the teachings of the Chinese scholar Confucius. It stresses social and civic responsibility. Over the centuries, however, Confucianism has greatly influenced people's spiritual beliefs as well. While East Asians declare themselves to follow any one of a number of religions, many also claim to be Confucian. The yin and yang symbol shown above represents opposite forces in the world working together. It symbolizes the social order and harmony that Confucianism stresses.

INTEGRATED TECHNOLOGY

RESEARCH LINKS For more on Confucianism, go to **classzone.com**

▼ Celebration

While scholars remain uncertain of Confucius's date of birth, people throughout East Asia celebrate it on September 28. In Taiwan, it is an official holiday, known as Teachers' Day. The holiday also pays tribute to teachers. Confucius himself was a teacher, and he believed that education was an important part of a fulfilled life. Here, dancers take part in a ceremony honoring Confucius.

CONNECTIONS ACROSS THE CURRICULUM: ART

Confucian Influence on Art

Class Time 30 minutes

Task Identifying Confucian ideals in a work of art

Purpose To understand the influence of Confucianism better

Instructions Tell students that many traditional Chinese paintings reflect Confucius's ideals of harmony and serenity, both in human interaction and in nature. These works stress the calm order of the universe. Pair students and have them study World Art and Cultures Transparency AT60 (Sorting of Cocoons). Challenge students to answer the following questions about the painting:

- How would you describe the mood of the painting? *(Possible Answers: calm, tranquil, harmonious)*
- What elements in the painting help convey this mood? *(Possible Answers: soft colors, the expressions on the figures' faces, the flowing river)*
- How does the painting present family life? *(Possible Answers: as serene, harmonious, with children watching parents work)*
- What does the painting suggest about the ideal relationship between people and nature? *(Possible Answer: People should live in harmony with nature.)*

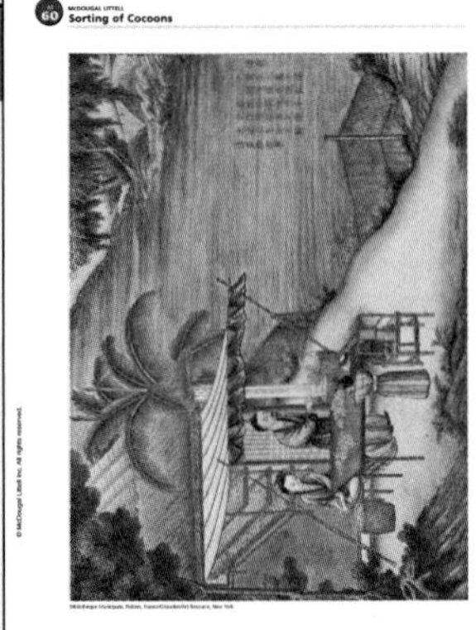

World Art and Cultures Transparency AT60

Leadership ►
Confucius was born at a time of crisis and violence in China. He hoped his ideas and teachings would restore the order of earlier times to his society. But although he was active in politics, he never had enough political power to put his ideas into practice. Nonetheless, his ideas would become the foundation of Chinese thought for more than 2,000 years.

▲ Ritual
A key aspect of Confucianism is filial piety, the respect children owe their parents. Traditionally, filial piety meant complete obedience to one's parents during their lifetime. It also required the performance of certain rituals after their death. In this 12th-century Chinese painting, a sage instructs a pupil on the virtue of filial piety.

Learn More About Confucianism

The Five Relationships

Confucius believed society should be organized around five basic relationships between the following:

1. ruler ⟷ subject
2. father ⟷ son
3. husband ⟷ wife
4. older brother ⟷ younger brother
5. friend ⟷ friend

Confucius's Golden Rule

"Do not do unto others what you would not want others to do unto you."

The *Analects*

PRIMARY SOURCE

The earliest and most authentic record of Confucius's ideas was collected by his students. Around 400 B.C., they compiled Confucius's thoughts in a book called the *Analects*. In the following selection from the *Analects*, Confucius (the Master) advises people to avoid judging others:

> *The Master said: "Don't worry if people don't recognize your merits; worry that you may not recognize theirs."*
>
> *Analects* 1.16

Confucius's Golden Rule

Several religious thinkers and philosophers have formulated rules of conduct similar to Confucius's Golden Rule. Well known to the Christian world is Jesus' statement in the Gospel of Matthew: "In everything, do to others what you would have them do to you." The rule may be framed positively (Jesus' "Do to others . . .") or negatively (Confucius's "Do not do unto others . . ."). The moral content of the rule, however, remains essentially the same. It urges us to see other people as similar to ourselves—a moral breakthrough in the ancient world.

Ritual

Confucius's ethics emphasized earthly rather than heavenly matters. Nevertheless, Confucius approved of the rituals of traditional Chinese religion. These included sacrifices to the gods and to ancestors.

While he did not express precise teachings about the supernatural, Confucius did believe in a heavenly force for good. He taught that the first requirement for living a fully human life was respect for the will of heaven. He is quoted as having said, "Heaven appointed me to teach my doctrines." A phrase often quoted from his writings is "He who offends against heaven has no one to whom he can pray."

DIFFERENTIATING INSTRUCTION: GIFTED AND TALENTED STUDENTS

Researching Daoism

Class Time 45 minutes

Task Learning about another Chinese philosophy

Purpose To expand knowledge and understanding of Chinese philosophies

Instructions Have students research to learn about Daoism, another Chinese philosophy that many people, particularly in Asia, consider to be a religion. Point out that, like Confucianism, Daoism has a great influence on Chinese society, art, and literature. Have students record their findings in a chart, like the one shown here.

After students have filled in their charts, have them compare Daoism with Confucianism. Ask them how are the two philosophies similar? How do they differ?

Founder	Laozi
Philosophical Book	Dao De Jing
Symbol	yin and yang
Basic Beliefs	• Nature is more important than the social order. • People should live a simple life close to nature. • A universal force, called the Dao, guides all things.

Teaching Strategies

The chart summarizes information concerning the five world religions and Confucianism presented in the World Religions and Ethical Systems feature of the Pupil's Edition. Presented in an accessible format, it provides essential information that can be supplemented by information in the textbook, by further reading, or by your knowledge or that of your students.

Stress that the digest of beliefs and values presented in the comparison chart is just a starting point and that each belief system can be the subject of in-depth research and study.

One important source for religious teachings is the holy book(s) of each faith. These books are listed in the chart, and they represent each religion's deepest expression of its teachings.

Stress that all these texts are to be treated with respect and that truly appreciating them may involve going beyond the views and opinions of one's own culture.

A Comparison

	Buddhism	Christianity	Hinduism	Islam	Judaism	Confucianism
Followers Worldwide (estimated 2001 figures)	362 million	2 billion	820 million	1.2 billion	14.5 million	6.3 million
Name of Deity	The Buddha did not teach a personal deity.	God	Three main gods: Brahma, Vishnu, Shiva	God (Allah)	God (Yahweh)	Confucius (viewed by many as a god)
Founder	The Buddha	Jesus Christ	No one founder	Muhammad	Abraham	Confucius
Holy Book	No one book—sacred texts, including the *Dhammapada*	Bible	No one book—sacred texts, including the Vedas, the Puranas	Qur'an	Hebrew Bible, including the Torah	the *Analects*, the Five Classics
Leadership	Buddhist monks and nuns	Priests, ministers, monks, and nuns	Guru, holy man, Brahmin priest	No clergy but a scholar class called the ulama and the imam, who may lead prayers	Rabbis	No clergy
Basic Beliefs	• Persons achieve complete peace and happiness (nirvana) by eliminating their attachment to worldly things. • Nirvana is reached by following the Noble Eightfold Path: Right views; Right resolve; Right speech; Right conduct; Right livelihood; Right effort; Right mindfulness; Right concentration.	• There is only one God, who watches over and cares for his people. • Jesus Christ was the son of God. He died to save humanity from sin. His death and resurrection made eternal life possible for others.	• The soul never dies, but is continually reborn. • Persons achieve happiness and enlightenment after they free themselves from their earthly desires. • Freedom from earthly desires comes from a lifetime of worship, knowledge, and virtuous acts.	• Persons achieve salvation by following the Five Pillars of Islam and living a just life. These pillars are: faith; prayer; almsgiving, or charity to the poor; fasting, which Muslims perform during Ramadan; pilgrimage to Mecca.	• There is only one God, who watches over and cares for his people. • God loves and protects his people, but also holds people accountable for their sins and shortcomings. • Persons serve God by studying the Torah and living by its teachings.	• Social order, harmony, and good government should be based on strong family relationships. • Respect for parents and elders is important to a well-ordered society. • Education is important both to the welfare of the individual and to society.

714

ANSWERS

MAIN IDEAS

1. by detaching one's self from all worldly goods and desires—achieved by following the Noble Eightfold Path, or the Middle Way
2. Buddhists believe that all living beings possess the potential for spiritual growth and the possibility of rebirth as humans.
3. Christians believe Christ to be the Son of God. They also believe that he died to save humanity from sin, and that humans reach salvation by following Christ's teachings.
4. They hope to reach salvation.
5. sacred site—Hindus believe that it has healing powers
6. Brahma, Vishnu, and Shiva
7. the Night of Power, because it is believed to be the night the angel Gabriel first spoke to Muhammad
8. faith, prayer, almsgiving, fasting, and pilgrimage to Mecca
9. sacred because it is all that remains of the Second Temple of Jerusalem, destroyed around A.D. 70
10. congregation's spiritual leader; conducts services in the synagogue
11. ruler and subject, father and son, husband and wife, older brother and younger brother, friend and friend
12. It requires complete obedience to parents during their lifetime and the performance of rituals after their death.

Assessment

MAIN IDEAS

Buddhism (pages 702–703)

1. According to the Buddha, how does one achieve happiness and fulfillment?
2. Why do Buddhists take special care to avoid killing any living being?

Christianity (pages 704–705)

3. Why is Jesus Christ central to the Christian religion?
4. What do Christians hope to achieve by following the teachings of Jesus Christ?

Hinduism (pages 706–707)

5. What is the importance of the Ganges River in Hinduism?
6. Who are the three main gods of Hinduism?

Islam (pages 708–709)

7. What is the most important night of Ramadan? Why?
8. What are the Five Pillars of Islam?

Judaism (pages 710–711)

9. Why do Jews consider the Western Wall to be sacred?
10. What is the role of the rabbi in the Jewish tradition?

Confucianism (pages 712–713)

11. Around what five relationships did Confucius believe society should be organized?
12. According to tradition, what does filial piety require of children?

CRITICAL THINKING

1. **COMPARING AND CONTRASTING** Using information from the text and chart at left, choose two religions and identify their similarities and differences in a Venn diagram.

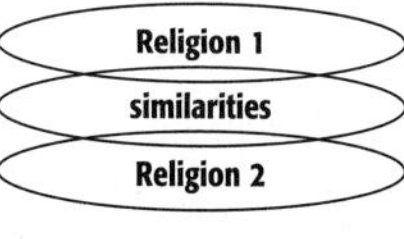

2. **SYNTHESIZING** What basic principles do all of the religions have in common?
3. **DRAWING CONCLUSIONS** What role does religion play in people's everyday lives?
4. **MAKING INFERENCES** Why do you think ritual and celebrations are an important part of all religions?
5. **FORMING OPINIONS** What do you think people hope to gain from their religion?

STANDARDS-BASED ASSESSMENT

Use the quotation and your knowledge of world history to answer questions 1 and 2.
Additional Test Practice, pp. S1–S33

PRIMARY SOURCE

Human beings are spiritual animals. Indeed, there is a case for arguing that *Homo sapiens* is also *Homo religiosus*. Men and women started to worship gods as soon as they became recognizably human; they created religions at the same time they created works of art. . . . These early faiths expressed the wonder and mystery that seem always to have been an essential component of the human experience of this beautiful yet terrifying world. Like art, religion has been an attempt to find meaning and value in life, despite the suffering that flesh is heir to.

KAREN ARMSTRONG, *History of God*

1. With which of the following opinions would Armstrong probably agree?
   - **A.** People are naturally religious.
   - **B.** People have no need of religion.
   - **C.** People only believe in what they can see.
   - **D.** People created religion out of fear.
2. According to Armstrong, what is the main similarity between art and religion?
   - **A.** They both express the suffering human beings must endure.
   - **B.** They first appeared at around the same time.
   - **C.** They both place value on beauty.
   - **D.** They are both used to find life's meaning.

INTEGRATED TECHNOLOGY

TEST PRACTICE Go to **classzone.com**

- Diagnostic tests
- Strategies
- Tutorials
- Additional practice

ALTERNATIVE ASSESSMENT

1. **Interact *with* History**
   Imagine that you could meet one of the founders listed in the chart on page 714. What questions would you ask about his life and beliefs? What views of your own would you share? Take turns role-playing your conversation with a partner.
2. **WRITING ABOUT HISTORY**
   Research to learn more about one of the celebrations you read about in this section. Then write a three-paragraph **essay** about its origins. Discuss the celebration's history, symbolism, and meaning.

ASSESSMENT

STANDARDS-BASED ASSESSMENT

1. The correct answer is letter **A.** Armstrong points out that people started to worship gods as soon as they became recognizably human. Letter **B** is not correct because Armstrong believes people turned to religion to make sense of the world. Letter **C** is not correct because Armstrong believes people are spiritual. Letter **D** is not correct because Armstrong believes people recognized the beauty, wonder, and mystery of the world.
2. The correct answer is letter **D.** Armstrong states that both art and religion have been used to find meaning and value in life. Letters **A, B,** and **C** are not correct. Although Armstrong discusses human suffering, the facts that art and religion appeared at around the same time, and the value both place on beauty, don't provide the main similarities.

CRITICAL THINKING

Answers will vary.

1. **Possible Answer:** Buddhism and Hinduism: Similarities—Both stress key to happiness is detachment from earthly goods and desires; both preach a type of reincarnation; neither has one Holy Book. Differences—Buddhism has a founder (Buddha), while Hinduism has no one founder; Buddhists reject the notion of a deity, while Hindus worship several gods.
2. doing good; respecting all life; participating in one's community; honoring one's elders; maintaining peace and harmony in the world
3. provides guidance on daily behavior and on relationships with family, friends, and others
4. Rituals and celebrations enable worshipers of a single faith to come together, thus reinforcing their sense of community. They also teach worshipers about the history, symbolism, and meaning of their religion.
5. a sense of peace, belonging, fulfillment; a sense that life has purpose and meaning

ALTERNATIVE ASSESSMENT

1. Encourage students to brainstorm their question before they begin. Each partner should reread the appropriate pages about the chosen founder.
2. **Rubric** The essay should
   - discuss the origins and meaning of the celebration.
   - describe the customs and symbolism.

McDougal Littell

MODERN WORLD HISTORY

PATTERNS OF INTERACTION

Skillbuilder Handbook

Refer to the Skillbuilder Handbook when you need help in answering Main Idea questions or questions in Section Assessments and Chapter Assessments. In addition, the handbook will help you answer questions about maps, charts, and graphs.

R1

1.1 Determining Main Ideas

The **MAIN IDEA** is a statement that sums up the most important point of a paragraph, a passage, an article, or a speech. Determining the main idea will increase your understanding as you read about historic events, people, and places. Main ideas are supported by details and examples.

Understanding the Skill

STRATEGY: IDENTIFY THE TOPIC. To find the main idea of a passage, first identify the topic. Then, as you read, define the central idea about the topic that the many details explain or support. The following passage contains information about the Renaissance. The diagram organizes the information to help you determine the main idea.

1. **Identify the topic by first looking at the title or subtitle.** This title suggests a quick way to identify the topic by looking for the name of the Renaissance woman, Isabella d'Este.
2. **Look at the beginning and ending sentences of each paragraph for possible clues to the main idea.**
3. **Read the entire passage.** Look for details about the topic. What central idea do they explain or support?

1 A Renaissance Woman

Isabella d'Este was a woman who lived during the Renaissance. This historic period produced the ideal, or "universal," man—one who excelled in many fields. The concept of universal excellence applied almost exclusively to men. 2 Yet a few women managed to succeed in exercising power.

2 Isabella d'Este was one such woman. Born into the ruling family of the city-state of Ferrara, she married the ruler of Mantua, another city-state. Isabella brought many Renaissance artists to her court and acquired an art collection that was famous throughout Europe. She was also skilled in politics. When her husband was taken captive in war, Isabella defended Mantua and won his release. 3

STRATEGY: MAKE A DIAGRAM. State the topic and list the supporting details in a chart. Use the information you record to help you state the main idea.

Think how each detail supports the main idea.

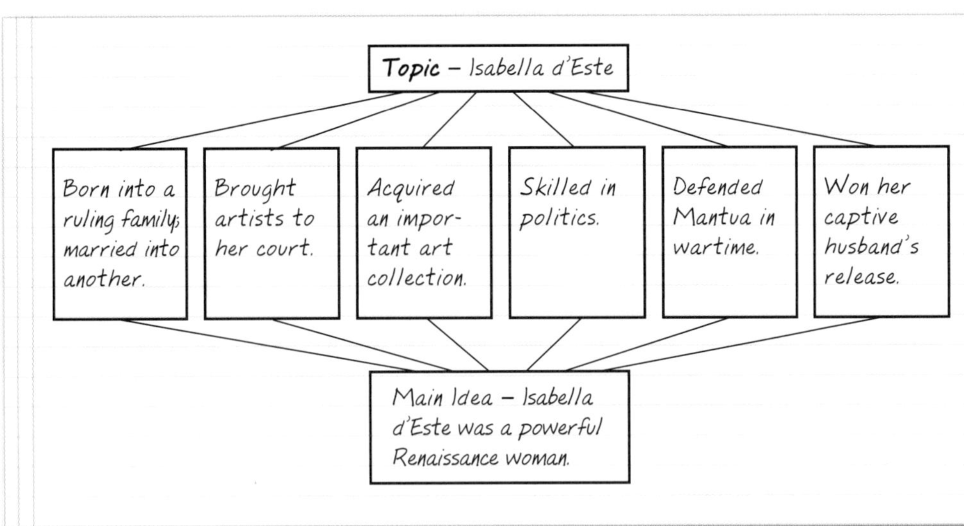
Topic – Isabella d'Este
Born into a ruling family; married into another.
Brought artists to her court.
Acquired an important art collection.
Skilled in politics.
Defended Mantua in wartime.
Won her captive husband's release.
Main Idea – Isabella d'Este was a powerful Renaissance woman.

Applying the Skill

MAKE YOUR OWN DIAGRAM. Turn to Chapter 3, page 96. Read "Technology Makes Exploration Possible." Make a diagram, like the one above, to identify the topic, the most important details, and the main idea of the passage.

1.2 Following Chronological Order

CHRONOLOGICAL ORDER is the order in which events happen in time. Historians need to figure out the order in which things happened to get an accurate sense of the relationships among events. As you read history, figure out the sequence, or time order, of events.

Understanding the Skill

STRATEGY: LOOK FOR TIME CLUES. The following paragraph is about the rulers of England after the death of Henry VIII. Notice how the time line that follows puts the events in chronological order.

1. **Look for clue words about time.** These are words like *first, initial, next, then, before, after, followed, finally,* and *by that time.*
2. **Use specific dates provided in the text.**
3. **Watch for references to previous historical events that are included in the background.**

Henry's Children Rule England

(1) After the death of Henry VIII in (2) 1547, each of his three children eventually ruled. This created religious turmoil. Edward VI became king at age nine and ruled only six years. During his reign, the Protestants gained power. Edward's half-sister Mary (1) followed him to the throne. She was a Catholic who returned the English Church to the rule of the pope. Mary had many Protestants killed. England's (1) next ruler was Anne Boleyn's daughter, Elizabeth. After inheriting the throne in 1558, Elizabeth I returned her kingdom to Protestantism. In (2) 1559 Parliament followed Elizabeth's (3) request and set up a national church much like the one under Henry VIII.

STRATEGY: MAKE A TIME LINE.

If the events are complex, make a time line of them. Write the dates below the line and the events above the line.

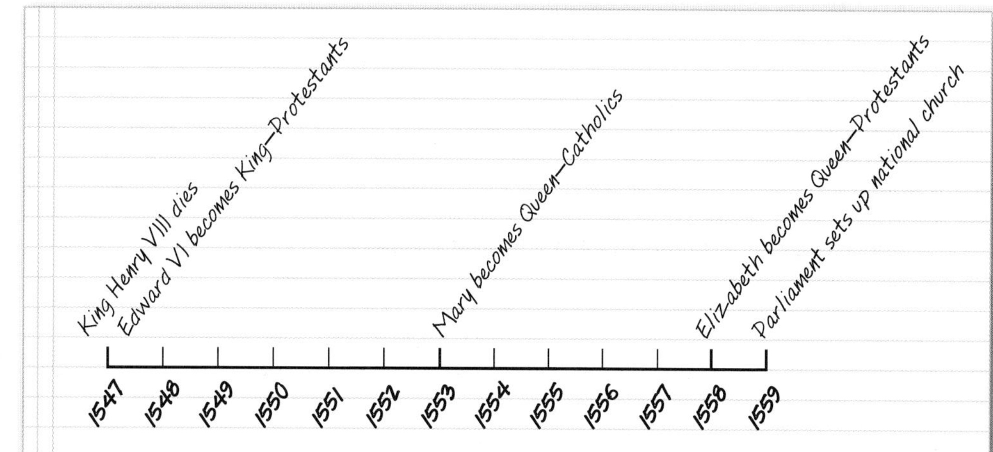

Applying the Skill

MAKE YOUR OWN TIME LINE. Skim Chapter 19, Section 4, "Changes in Central and Eastern Europe," to find out about the spread of democracy in parts of Europe controlled by the former Soviet Union. List the important dates and events. Start with the demonstrations in East Germany in October 1989, include events in Czechoslovakia and Romania, and end with reunification of Germany in October of 1990. Decide on a scale for your time line. Show the important dates below the line and write what happened on each date above the line.

1.3 Clarifying; Summarizing

CLARIFYING means making clear and fully understanding what you read. One way to do this is by asking yourself questions about the material. In your answers, restate in your own words what you have read.

SUMMARIZING means condensing what you read into fewer words. You state only the main ideas and the most important details. In your own words, reduce the paragraph or section into a brief report of its general ideas.

Understanding the Skill

STRATEGY: UNDERSTAND AND CONDENSE THE TEXT. The passage below tells about trade in West Africa between 300 and 1600. Following the description is a summary that condenses and also clarifies the key information.

1. **Summarize: Look for topic sentences stating the main idea.** These are often at the beginning of a section or paragraph. Restate each main idea briefly.
2. **Clarify: Look up words or concepts you don't know.**
3. **Summarize: Include key facts and statistics.** Watch for numbers, dates, quantities, percentages, and facts.
4. **Clarify: Make sure you understand.** Ask yourself questions and answer them. For example, who's carrying what?

West African Trade

(1) The wealth of the savanna empires was based on trade in two precious commodities, gold and salt. The gold came from a forest region south of the (2) savanna between the Niger and Senegal rivers. Working in utmost secrecy, miners dug gold from shafts as much as 100 feet deep or sifted it from fast-moving streams. (3) Until about 1350, at least two thirds of the world's supply of gold came from West Africa.

Although rich in gold, the savanna and forest areas lacked salt, a material essential to human life. In contrast, the (3) Sahara contained abundant deposits of salt. Arab traders, eager to obtain West African gold, carried salt across the Sahara by camel caravan. After a long journey, they reached the market towns of the savanna. (4) Meanwhile, the other traders brought gold north from the forest region. The two sets of merchants met in trading centers such as Timbuktu. Royal officials made sure that all traders weighed goods fairly and did business according to law.

STRATEGY: FIND AND CLEARLY RESTATE THE MAIN IDEA.

MAIN IDEA
Gold and salt were traded in West Africa.

STRATEGY: WRITE A SUMMARY.

Clarify and Summarize: Write a summary to clarify your understanding of the main ideas.

Summary
Trade in West Africa was based on gold from the south and salt from the north. Gold was mined in the forest regions. Two thirds of all the world's gold supply came from West Africa. Salt came from the desert. Arab traders met with African traders at trade centers such as Timbuktu.

Applying the Skill

CLARIFY AND WRITE YOUR OWN SUMMARY. Turn to Chapter 14, pages 440–442, and read "A Government of Total Control." Note the main ideas. Look up any words you don't recognize. Then write a summary of the section. Condense the section in your own words.

1.4 Identifying Problems and Solutions

IDENTIFYING PROBLEMS means finding and understanding the difficulties faced by a particular group of people at a certain time. Noticing how the people solved their problems is **IDENTIFYING SOLUTIONS.** Checking further to see how well those solutions worked is identifying outcomes.

Understanding the Skill

STRATEGY: LOOK FOR PROBLEMS AND SOLUTIONS. The passage below summarizes some economic problems facing Latin American nations during the early 20th century.

1. **Look for implied problems.** Problems may be suggested indirectly. This sentence suggests that a serious problem in Latin America was the uneven division of wealth.
2. **Look for problems people face.**
3. **Look for solutions people tried to deal with each problem.**
4. **Check outcomes to the solutions.** See how well the solutions worked. Sometimes the solution to one problem caused another problem.

Land Reform In Latin America

In Latin America, concentration of productive land in the hands of a (1) few created extremes of wealth and poverty. Poor peasants had no choice but to work large estates owned by a few wealthy families. Landlords had no reason to invest in expensive farm machinery when labor was so cheap. (2) Farming methods were inefficient and economic development was slow.

As Latin American nations began to modernize in the 20th century, land ownership became a political issue. In response, a handful of countries began land reform programs. These programs (3) divided large estates into smaller plots. Small plots of land were in turn distributed to farm families or granted to villages for communal farming. However, just turning over the land to the landless was not enough. (4) Peasant farmers needed instruction, seeds, equipment, and credit. If the land and the people were to be productive, governments would have to provide assistance to the peasants.

STRATEGY: MAKE A CHART.

Summarize the problems and solutions in a chart. Identify the problem or problems and the steps taken to solve them. Look for the short- and long-term effects of the solutions.

Problems	Solutions	Outcomes
A few wealthy people owned most of the land. Inefficient farming resulted in slow economic development.	Land reform programs divided large estates into smaller plots.	Peasants were given land, and communal farms were set up.
Peasants lacked equipment, resources, skills.	Governments would have to assist with loans and instruction.	Not stated.

Applying the Skill

MAKE YOUR OWN CHART. Turn to Chapter 15 and read "Postwar Europe" on page 470. Make a chart that lists the problems Germany faced after World War I. List the solutions that were tried and whatever outcomes are mentioned.

R5

1.5 Analyzing Causes and Recognizing Effects

CAUSES are the events, conditions, and other reasons that lead to an event. Causes happen before the event in time; they explain why it happened. **EFFECTS** are the results or consequences of the event. One effect often becomes the cause of other effects, resulting in a chain of events. Causes and effects can be both short-term and long-term. Examining **CAUSE-AND-EFFECT RELATIONSHIPS** helps historians see how events are related and why they took place.

Understanding the Skill

STRATEGY: KEEP TRACK OF CAUSES AND EFFECTS AS YOU READ. The passage below describes events leading to the rise of feudalism in Japan. The diagram that follows summarizes the chain of causes and effects.

❶ **Causes: Look for clue words that show cause.** These include *because, due to, since,* and *therefore.*

❷ **Look for multiple causes and multiple effects.** The weakness of the central government caused the three effects (a,b,c) shown here.

❸ **Effects: Look for results or consequences.** Sometimes these are indicated by clue words such as *brought about, led to, as a result,* and *consequently.*

❹ **Notice that an effect may be the cause of another event.** This begins a chain of causes and effects.

Feudalism Comes to Japan

For most of the Heian period, the rich Fujiwara family held the real power in Japan. Members of this family held many influential posts. By about the middle of the 11th century, the power of the central government and the Fujiwaras began to slip. This was ❶ due in part to court families' greater interest in luxury and artistic pursuits than in governing.

❷ Since the central government was weak, **(a)** large landowners living away from the capital set up private armies. ❸ As a result, **(b)** the countryside became lawless and dangerous. Armed soldiers on horseback preyed on farmers and travelers, while pirates took control of the seas. **(c)** For safety, farmers and small landowners traded parts of their land to strong warlords in exchange for protection. ❹ Because the lords had more land, the lords gained more power. This marked the beginning of a feudal system of localized rule like that of ancient China and medieval Europe.

STRATEGY: MAKE A CAUSE-AND-EFFECT DIAGRAM.

Summarize cause-and-effect relationships in a diagram. Starting with the first cause in a series, fill in the boxes until you reach the end result.

Cause →	Effect/Cause →	Effect/Cause →	Effect
Ruling families had little interest in governing.	Weak central government was unable to control the land.	• Landowners set up private armies. • Countryside became dangerous. • Farmers traded land for safety under warlords.	Feudalism was established in Japan.

Applying the Skill

MAKE YOUR OWN CAUSE-AND-EFFECT DIAGRAM. Turn to Chapter 12, pages 389–391. Read "Juárez and *La Reforma*" and make notes about the causes and effects of Juárez's reform movement in Mexico. Make a diagram, like the one shown above, to summarize the information you find.

1.6 Comparing and Contrasting

Historians compare and contrast events, personalities, ideas, behaviors, beliefs, and institutions in order to understand them thoroughly. **COMPARING** involves finding both similarities and differences between two or more things. **CONTRASTING** means examining only the differences between them.

Understanding the Skill

STRATEGY: LOOK FOR SIMILARITIES AND DIFFERENCES. The following passage describes life in the ancient Greek city-states of Sparta and Athens. The Venn diagram below shows some of the similarities and differences between the two city-states.

1. **Compare: Look for features that two subjects have in common.** Here you learn that both Athens and Sparta started out as farming communities.
2. **Compare: Look for clue words indicating that two things are alike.** Clue words include *all, both, like, as, likewise,* and *similarly.*
3. **Contrast: Look for clue words that show how two things differ.** Clue words include *unlike, by contrast, however, except, different,* and *on the other hand.*

Sparta and Athens

The Greek city-states developed separately but shared certain characteristics, (1) including language and religion. Economically, all began as farming economies, and all except Sparta eventually moved to trade. Politically, (2) all city-states, except for Sparta, evolved into early forms of democracies.

The leader in the movement to democracy was Athens. After a series of reforms, every Athenian citizen was considered equal before the law. However, as in the other Greek city-states, only about one fifth of the population were citizens. Slaves did much of the work, so Athenian citizens were free to create works of art, architecture, and literature, including drama.

(3) By contrast, Sparta lived in constant fear of revolts by *helots,* people who were held in slave-like conditions to work the land. The city was set up as a military dictatorship, and Spartan men dedicated their lives to the military. (4) In Sparta, duty, strength, and discipline were valued over beauty, individuality, and creativity. As a result, Spartans created little art, architecture, or literature.

4. **Contrast: Look for ways in which two things are different.** Here you learn that Athens and Sparta had different values.

STRATEGY: MAKE A VENN DIAGRAM.

Compare and Contrast: Summarize similarities and differences in a Venn diagram. In the overlapping area, list characteristics shared by both subjects. Then, in one oval list the characteristics of one subject not shared by the other. In the other oval, list unshared characteristics of the second subject.

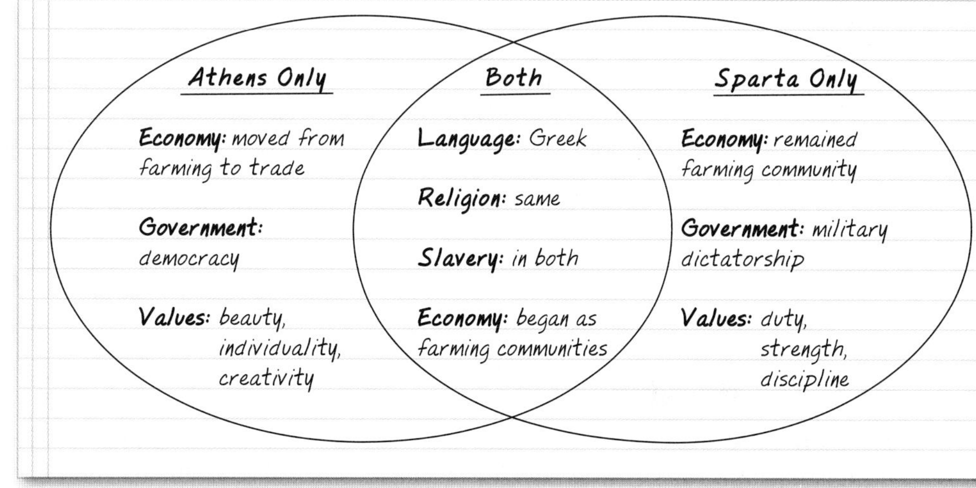

Athens Only
Economy: moved from farming to trade
Government: democracy
Values: beauty, individuality, creativity
Both
Language: Greek
Religion: same
Slavery: in both
Economy: began as farming communities
Sparta Only
Economy: remained farming community
Government: military dictatorship
Values: duty, strength, discipline

Applying the Skill

MAKE YOUR OWN VENN DIAGRAM. Turn to Chapter 4, pages 130–131, and read the section called "Native Americans Respond." Make a Venn diagram comparing and contrasting Dutch and English colonists' relations with Native Americans.

R7

1.7 Distinguishing Fact from Opinion

FACTS are events, dates, statistics, or statements that can be proved to be true. Facts can be checked for accuracy. **OPINIONS** are judgments, beliefs, and feelings of the writer or speaker.

Understanding the Skill

STRATEGY: FIND CLUES IN THE TEXT. The following excerpt tells about the uprising of Jews in the Warsaw ghetto in 1943. The chart summarizes the facts and opinions.

1. **Facts: Look for specific names, dates, statistics, and statements that can be proved.** The first two paragraphs provide a factual account of the event.
2. **Opinion: Look for assertions, claims, hypotheses, and judgments.** Here Goebbels expresses his opinion of the uprising and of the Jews.
3. **Opinion: Look for judgment words that the writer uses to describe the people and events.** Judgment words are often adjectives that are used to arouse a reader's emotions.

The Warsaw Ghetto Uprising

With orders from Himmler to crush the Jews, (1) the Nazis attacked on April 19, 1943, at the start of the holiday of Passover. (1) Two thousand armed SS troops entered the ghetto, marching with tanks, rifles, machine guns, and trailers full of ammunition. The Jewish fighters were in position—in bunkers, in windows, on rooftops. (1) They had rifles and handguns, hand grenades and bombs that they had made. And they let fly. . . .

Unbelievably, the Jews won the battle that day. The Germans were forced to retreat. . . . (1) The Germans brought in more troops, and the fighting intensified. German pilots dropped bombs on the ghetto. . . .

(2) On May 1, Goebbels [Nazi propaganda minister] wrote in his diary: "Of course this jest will probably not last long." He added a complaint. "But it shows what one can expect of the Jews if they have guns."

Goebbels' tone was mocking. But his forecast was inevitable—and correct. . . . Goebbels did not record in his diary, when the uprising was over, that the (3) starving Jews of the ghetto, with their (3) pathetic supply of arms, had held out against the German army for forty days, longer than Poland or France had held out.

Source: *A Nightmare in History*, by Miriam Chaikin. (New York: Clarion Books, 1987) pp. 77–78

STRATEGY: MAKE A CHART.

Divide facts and opinions in a chart. Summarize and separate the facts from the opinions expressed in a passage.

FACTS	OPINIONS
On April 19, 1943, 2,000 armed SS troops attacked the Warsaw ghetto. Jewish fighters held out for 40 days.	***Goebbels:*** *The uprising was a jest, but showed the danger of letting Jews get hold of guns.* ***Author:*** *It is difficult to believe that Warsaw Jews with their pathetic supply of arms were able to defeat the powerful Nazis.*

Applying the Skill

MAKE YOUR OWN CHART. Turn to Chapter 10, page 335. Find the Primary Source from the Seneca Falls Convention. Make a chart in which you summarize the facts in your own words, and list the opinions and judgments stated. Look carefully at the language used in order to separate one from the other.

2.1 Categorizing

CATEGORIZING means organizing similar kinds of information into groups. Historians categorize information to help them identify and understand historical patterns.

Understanding the Skill

STRATEGY: DECIDE WHAT INFORMATION NEEDS TO BE CATEGORIZED. The following passage describes India's Taj Mahal, a memorial built by a Mughal ruler. As you read, look for facts and details that are closely related. Then choose appropriate categories.

1 **Look at topic sentences for clues to defining categories.**

2 **Look at the type of information each paragraph contains.** A paragraph often contains similar kinds of information.

Building the Taj Mahal

1 Some 20,000 workers labored for 22 years to build the famous tomb. It is made of white marble brought from 250 miles away. The minaret towers are about 130 feet high. The building itself is 186 feet square.

1 The design of the building is a blend of Hindu and Muslim styles. The pointed 2 arches are of Muslim design, and the perforated marble 2 windows and 2 doors are typical of a style found in Hindu temples.

The inside of the building is a glittering garden of 2 thousands of carved marble flowers inlaid with tiny precious stones. One tiny flower, one inch square, had 60 different inlays.

STRATEGY: MAKE A CHART.

3 **Add a title.**

4 **Sort information into the categories you have chosen.**

5 **Make one column for each category.**

3 THE TAJ MAHAL

4 Labor	Dimensions	Design features
• 20,000 workers • 22 years to complete	• Minaret towers: 130 feet high • Building: 186 feet	• Made of white marble • Pointed arches (Muslim influence) • Perforated marble windows and doors (Hindu influence) • Interior: thousands of carved marble flowers inlaid with precious stones
5	5	5

Applying the Skill

MAKE YOUR OWN CHART. Turn to Chapter 6, page 203. Read "New Artistic Styles." Decide what categories you will use to organize the information. Then make a chart, like the one above, that organizes the information in the passage into the categories you have chosen.

2.2 Making Inferences

Inferences are ideas and meanings not stated in the material. **MAKING INFERENCES** means reading between the lines to extend the information provided. Your inferences are based on careful study of what is stated in the passage as well as your own common sense and previous knowledge.

Understanding the Skill

STRATEGY: DEVELOP INFERENCES FROM THE FACTS. This passage describes the Nok culture of West Africa. Following the passage is a diagram that organizes the facts and ideas that lead to inferences.

1. **Read the stated facts and ideas.**
2. **Use your knowledge, logic, and common sense to draw conclusions.** You could infer from these statements that the Nok were a settled people with advanced technology and a rich culture.
3. **Consider what you already know that could apply.** Your knowledge of history might lead you to infer the kinds of improvements in life brought about by better farming tools.
4. **Recognize inferences that are already made.** Phrases like "the evidence suggests" or "historians believe" indicate inferences and conclusions experts have made from historical records.

The Nok Culture

(1) The earliest known culture of West Africa was that of the Nok people. They lived in what is now Nigeria between 900 B.C. and A.D. 200. Their name came from the village where the first artifacts from their culture were discovered by archaeologists. The (2) Nok were farmers. They were also (2) the first West African people known to smelt iron. The Nok began making iron around 500 B.C., using it to make tools for farming and weapons for hunting. (3) These iron implements lasted longer than wood or stone and vastly improved the lives of the Nok.

Nok artifacts have been found in an area stretching for 300 miles between the Niger and Benue rivers. (2) Many are sculptures made of terra cotta, a reddish-brown clay. Carved in great artistic detail, some depict the heads of animals such as elephants and others depict human heads. The features of some of the heads reveal a great deal about their history. One of the human heads, for example, shows an elaborate hairdo arranged in six buns, a style that is still worn by some people in Nigeria today. (4) This similarity suggests that the Nok may have been the ancestors of modern-day Africans.

STRATEGY: MAKE A CHART.

Summarize the facts and inferences you make in a chart.

Stated Facts and Ideas	*Inferences*
• *iron farming tools* • *iron harder than wood* • *tools improved life*	*iron tools improved agriculture and contributed to cultural development*
• *Nok artifacts found in 300-mile radius*	*Nok culture spread across this area*
• *heads carved in great artistic detail*	*Nok were skilled potters and sculptors*
• *sculptures included elephant heads*	*elephants played a role in people's lives*

Applying the Skill

MAKE YOUR OWN CHART. Read the poem by Vittoria Colonna in Chapter 1, page 43. Using a chart like the one above, make inferences from the poem about its author, its subject, and the culture it comes from.

R10

2.3 Drawing Conclusions

DRAWING CONCLUSIONS means analyzing what you have read and forming an opinion about its meaning. To draw conclusions, you look closely at the facts, combine them with inferences you make, and then use your own common sense and experience to decide what the facts mean.

Understanding the Skill

STRATEGY: COMBINE INFORMATION TO DRAW CONCLUSIONS. The passage below presents information about the reunification of East and West Germany in 1990. The diagram that follows shows how to organize the information to draw conclusions.

1. **Read carefully to understand all the facts.** Fact: Reunification brought social and political freedoms to East Germans.
2. **Read between the lines to make inferences.** Inference: After a market economy was introduced, many industries in eastern Germany failed, which put people out of work.
3. **Use the facts to make an inference.** Inference: Reunification put a strain on government resources.
4. **Ask questions of the material.** What are the long-term economic prospects for eastern Germany? Conclusion: Although it faced challenges, it seemed to have a greater chance for success than other former Communist countries.

Germany is Reunified

On October 3, 1990, Germany once again became a single nation. (1) After more than 40 years of Communist rule, most East Germans celebrated their new political freedoms. Families that had been separated for years could now visit whenever they chose.

Economically, the newly united Germany faced serious problems. More than 40 years of Communist rule had left East Germany in ruins. Its transportation and telephone systems had not been modernized since World War II. State-run industries in East Germany had to be turned over to private control and operate under free-market rules. (2) However, many produced shoddy goods that could not compete in the global market.

Rebuilding eastern Germany's bankrupt economy was going to be a difficult, costly process. (3) Some experts estimated the price tag for reunification could reach $200 billion. In the short-term, the government had to provide (2) unemployment benefits to some 1.4 million workers from the east who found themselves out of work.

(4) In spite of these problems, Germans had reasons to be optimistic. Unlike other Eastern European countries, who had to transform their Communist economies by their own means, East Germany had the help of a strong West Germany. Many Germans may have shared the outlook expressed by one worker: "Maybe things won't be rosy at first, but the future will be better."

STRATEGY: MAKE A DIAGRAM.

Summarize the facts, inferences, and your conclusion in a diagram.

Facts →	Inferences →	Conclusion About Passage
East Germans gained freedoms.	East Germans welcomed the end of Communist rule.	Although eastern Germany was in bad shape at the time of reunification, it had the advantage of the strength of western Germany as it made the transition to democracy and capitalism.
Transportation and telephone systems were outmoded.	Rebuilding took time.	
State-run industries produced shoddy goods.	Industries couldn't compete in free-market economy.	
Unemployment skyrocketed.	Reunification put a great financial burden on Germany.	
Cost for reunification could be $200 billion.		

Applying the Skill

MAKE A DIAGRAM. Look at Chapter 5, Section 1, pages 158–159, on the decline of the Spanish empire. As you read, draw conclusions based on the facts. Use the diagram above as a model for organizing facts, inferences, and conclusions about the passage.

R11

2.4 Developing Historical Perspective

DEVELOPING HISTORICAL PERSPECTIVE means understanding events and people in the context of their times. It means not judging the past by current values, but by taking into account the beliefs of the time.

Understanding the Skill

STRATEGY: LOOK FOR VALUES OF THE PAST. The following passage was written by Bartolomé de Las Casas, a Spanish missionary who defended the rights of Native Americans. It challenges an argument presented by a scholar named Sepúlveda, who held that the Spaniards had the right to enslave the Native Americans. Following the passage is a chart that summarizes the information from a historical perspective.

1 **Identify the historical figure, the occasion, and the date.**

2 **Look for clues to the attitudes, customs, and values of people living at the time.** As a Spanish missionary, Las Casas assumes that Europeans are more civilized than Native Americans and that Native Americans need to be converted to Catholicism.

3 **Explain how people's actions and words reflected the attitudes, values, and passions of the era.** Las Casas challenges prejudices about Native Americans that were widely held in Europe. His language emphasizes a favorable comparison between Native American and European societies.

4 **Notice words, phrases, and settings that reflect the period.** Las Casas speaks from a time when Europeans looked to classical Greece as a benchmark for civilization.

1 In Defense of the Indians (1550)
Bartolomé de Las Casas

Now if we shall have shown that among our Indians of the western and southern shores 2 (granting that we call them barbarians and that they are barbarians) there are important kingdoms, large numbers of people who live settled lives in a society, great cities, kings, judges and laws, persons who engage in commerce, buying, selling, lending, and the other contracts of the law of nations, will it not stand proved that the Reverend Doctor Sepúlveda has spoken wrongly and viciously against peoples like these?. . . From the fact that the Indians are barbarians it does not necessarily follow that they are incapable of government and have to be ruled by others, 2 except to be taught about the Catholic faith and to be admitted to the holy sacraments. 3 They are not ignorant, inhuman, or bestial. Rather, long before they had heard the word Spaniard they had 3 properly organized states, wisely ordered by excellent laws, religion, and custom. They cultivated friendship and, bound together in common fellowship, lived in populous cities in which they wisely administered the affairs of both peace and war justly and equitably, truly governed by laws that at very many points surpass ours, and could have won 4 the admiration of the sages of Athens. . . .

STRATEGY: WRITE A SUMMARY.

Use historical perspective to understand Las Casas's attitudes. In a chart, list key words, phrases, and details from the passage. In a short paragraph, summarize the basic values and attitudes of Las Casas.

Key Phrases	*Las Casas's In Defense of the Indians*
• *barbarians* • *Catholic faith* • *not inhuman, ignorant, or bestial* • *properly organized states, wisely ordered* • *sages of Athens*	*Las Casas argues that Native Americans are not inhuman and do not deserve cruelty and slavery. Rather, they are fully capable of "coming up" to the level of Spanish civilization. Although he makes the statement that Native Americans are barbarians, his language and comparisons seem to suggest that he believes them to be highly civilized in many respects. At the same time, he believes in the importance of converting them to Catholicism.*

Applying the Skill

WRITE YOUR OWN SUMMARY. Turn to Chapter 2, page 75, and read the excerpt from the *Life of Mehmed the Conqueror.* Read the passage using historical perspective. Then summarize your ideas in a chart like the one above.

2.5 Formulating Historical Questions

FORMULATING HISTORICAL QUESTIONS is important as you examine primary sources—firsthand accounts, documents, letters, and other records of the past. As you analyze a source, ask questions about what it means and why it is significant. Then, when you are doing research, write questions that you want your research to answer. This step will help to guide your research and organize the information you collect.

Understanding the Skill

STRATEGY: QUESTION WHAT YOU READ. The Muslim scholar Ibn Battuta published an account of his journeys in Asia and Africa in the 1300s. The following passage is part of his description of China. After the passage is a web diagram that organizes historical questions about it.

1. **Ask about the historical record itself.** Who produced it? When was it produced?
2. **Ask about the facts presented.** Who were the main people? What did they do? What were they like?
3. **Ask about the person who created the record.** What judgments or opinions does the author express?
4. **Ask about the significance of the record.** How would you interpret the information presented? How does it fit in with the history of this time and place? What more do you need to know to answer these questions?

(1) Ibn Battuta in China, Around 1345

(2) The Chinese themselves are infidels, who worship idols and burn their dead like the Hindus. . . . In every Chinese city there is a quarter for Muslims in which they live by themselves, and in which they have mosques both for the Friday services and for other religious purposes. The Muslims are honored and respected. (3) The Chinese infidels eat the flesh of swine and dogs, and sell it in their markets. (2) They are wealthy folk and well-to-do, but they make no display either in their food or their clothes. You will see one of their principal merchants, a man so rich that his wealth cannot be counted, wearing a coarse cotton tunic. But there is one thing that the Chinese take a pride in, that is gold and silver plate. Every one of them carries a stick, on which they lean in walking, and which they call "the third leg." (4) Silk is very plentiful among them, because the silk-worm attaches itself to fruits and feeds on them without requiring much care. For that reason, it is so common as to be worn by even the very poorest there. Were it not for the merchants it would have no value at all, for a single piece of cotton cloth is sold in their country for the price of many pieces of silk.

STRATEGY: MAKE A WEB DIAGRAM.

Investigate a topic in more depth by asking questions. Ask a large question and then ask smaller questions that explore and develop from the larger question.

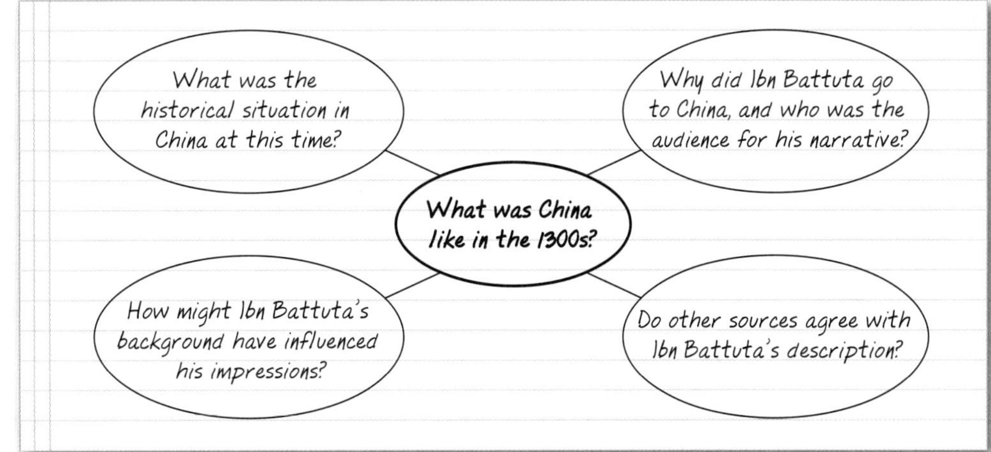
What was the historical situation in China at this time?
Why did Ibn Battuta go to China, and who was the audience for his narrative?
What was China like in the 1300s?
How might Ibn Battuta's background have influenced his impressions?
Do other sources agree with Ibn Battuta's description?

Applying the Skill

MAKE YOUR OWN WEB DIAGRAM. Turn to the quotation by Olaudah Equiano in Chapter 4, page 135. Use a web diagram to write historical questions about the passage.

R13

2.6 Making Predictions

MAKING PREDICTIONS means projecting the outcome of a situation that leaders or groups face or have faced in the past. Historians use their knowledge of past events and the decisions that led up to them to predict the outcome of current situations. Examining decisions and their alternatives will help you understand how events in the past shaped the future.

Understanding the Skill

STRATEGY: IDENTIFY DECISIONS. The following passage describes relations between Cuba and the United States following Fidel Castro's successful attempt to overthrow former Cuban dictator Fulgencio Batista. The chart lists decisions that affected U.S./Cuban relations, along with alternative decisions and predictions of their possible outcomes.

1 To help you identify decisions, look for words such as *decide, decision,* and *chose.*

2 Notice how one political decision often leads to another.

3 Notice both positive and negative decisions.

U.S./Cuban Relations under Castro

During the 1950s, Cuban dictator Fidel Castro 1 chose to nationalize the Cuban economy, which resulted in the takeover of U.S.-owned sugar mills and refineries. 2 U.S. President Eisenhower responded by ordering an embargo on all trade with Cuba. As relations between the two countries deteriorated, Cuba became more dependent on the USSR for economic and military aid. In 1960, the CIA trained anti-Castro Cuban exiles to invade Cuba. 3 Although they landed at Cuba's Bay of Pigs, the United States 1 decided not to provide them with air support. Castro's forces defeated the exiles, which humiliated the United States.

STRATEGY: MAKE A CHART.

4 Use a chart to record decisions.

5 Suggest alternative decisions.

6 Predict a possible outcome for each alternative decision.

4 Decisions	5 Alternative Decisions	6 Prediction of Outcome
Castro nationalized Cuban economy.	Castro did not nationalize Cuban economy.	There was no United States embargo of trade with Cuba.
The United States placed an embargo on trade with Cuba.	The United States continued to trade with Cuba.	Cuba continued to depend on the United States economically.
CIA trained Cuban exiles, who invaded Cuba.	The CIA did not train exiles to invade Cuba.	There was no invasion of Cuba.
The United States did not provide air support for the invasion.	The United States provided air support to the invaders.	The United States successfully invaded Cuba.

APPLYING THE SKILL

MAKE A CHART like the one above. Turn to Chapter 5, page 181, and read the first four paragraphs of the section "English Civil War." Identify three decisions of England's King Charles I. Record them on your chart, along with an alternative decision for each. Then predict a possible outcome for each alternative decision.

2.7 Hypothesizing

HYPOTHESIZING means developing a possible explanation for historical events. A hypothesis is an educated guess about what happened in the past or a prediction about what might happen in the future. A hypothesis takes available information, links it to previous experience and knowledge, and comes up with a possible explanation, conclusion, or prediction.

Understanding the Skill

STRATEGY: FIND CLUES IN THE READING. In studying the Indus Valley civilization, historians do not yet know exactly what caused that culture to decline. They have, however, developed hypotheses about what happened to it. Read this passage and look at the steps that are shown for building a hypothesis. Following the passage is a chart that organizes the information.

1. **Identify the event, pattern, or trend you want to explain.**
2. **Determine the facts you have about the situation.** These facts support various hypotheses about what happened to the Indus Valley civilization.
3. **Develop a hypothesis that might explain the event.** Historians hypothesize that a combination of ecological change and sudden catastrophe caused the Indus Valley civilization to collapse.
4. **Determine what additional information you need to test the hypothesis.** You might refer to a book about India, for example, to learn more about the impact of the Aryan invasions.

1 Mysterious End to Indus Valley Culture

2 Around 1750 B.C., the quality of building in the Indus Valley cities declined. Gradually, the great cities fell into decay. What happened? Some historians think that the Indus River changed course, as it tended to do, so that its floods no longer fertilized the fields near the cities. Other scholars suggest that people wore out the valley's land. They overgrazed it, overfarmed it, and overcut its trees, brush, and grass.

As the Indus Valley civilization neared its end, around 1500 B.C., a sudden catastrophe may have had a hand in the cities' downfall. 2 Archaeologists have found a half-dozen groups of skeletons in the ruins of Mohenjo-Daro, seemingly never buried. 3 Their presence suggests that the city, already weakened by its slow decline, may have been abandoned after a natural disaster or a devastating attack from human enemies. The Aryans, a nomadic people from north of the Hindu Kush mountains, swept into the Indus Valley at about this time. 4 Whether they caused the collapse of the Indus Valley civilization or followed in its wake is not known.

STRATEGY: MAKE A CHART.

Use a chart to summarize your hypothesis about events. Write down your hypothesis and the facts that support it. Then you can see what additional information you need to help prove or disprove it.

Hypothesis	*Facts that support the hypothesis*	*Additional information needed*
A combination of ecological change and sudden catastrophe caused the Indus Valley civilization to collapse	• *Building quality declined* • *Indus River tended to change course* • *Unburied skeletons were found at Mohenjo-Daro* • *Aryan invasions occurred around same time*	• *What was Indus Valley culture like?* • *What were the geographical characteristics of the region?* • *How did overfarming tend to affect the environment?* • *What factors affected the decline of other ancient civilizations?*

Applying the Skill

MAKE YOUR OWN CHART. Turn to Chapter 3, page 111, and read the Primary Source. Predict what impact the introduction of firearms might have had on Japan. Then read the surrounding text material. List facts that support your hypothesis and what additional information you might gather to help prove or disprove it.

Skillbuilder Handbook

2.8 Analyzing Motives

ANALYZING MOTIVES means examining the reasons why a person, group, or government takes a particular action. To understand those reasons, consider the needs, emotions, prior experiences, and goals of the person or group.

Understanding the Skill

STRATEGY: LOOK FOR REASONS WHY. On June 28, 1914, Serb terrorists assassinated Austria-Hungary's Archduke Franz Ferdinand and his wife when they visited Sarajevo, the capital of Bosnia. In the following passage, Borijove Jevtic, a Serb terrorist, explains why the assassination occurred. Before this passage, he explains that the terrorists had received a telegram stating that the Archduke would be visiting Sarajevo on June 28. The diagram that follows summarizes the motives of the terrorists for murdering the Archduke.

1. **Look for motives based on basic needs and human emotions.** Needs include food, shelter, safety, freedom. Emotions include fear, anger, pride, desire for revenge, and patriotism, for example.
2. **Look for motives based on past events or inspiring individuals.**
3. **Notice both positive and negative motives.**

The Assassination of the Archduke

How dared Franz Ferdinand, not only the representative of the oppressor but in his own person an (1) arrogant tyrant, enter Sarajevo on that day? Such an entry was a (1) studied insult.

(2) 28 June is a date engraved deeply in the heart of every Serb, so that the day has a name of its own. It is called the vidovnan. It is the day on which the old Serbian kingdom was conquered by the Turks at the battle of Amselfelde in 1389. It is also the day on which in the second Balkan War the Serbian arms took glorious revenge on the Turk for his old victory and for the years of enslavement.

(3) That was no day for Franz Ferdinand, the new oppressor, to venture to the very doors of Serbia for a display of the force of arms which kept us beneath his heel.

Our decision was taken almost immediately. Death to the tyrant!

STRATEGY: MAKE A DIAGRAM.

Make a diagram that summarizes motives and actions. List the important action in the middle of the diagram. Then list motives in different categories around the action.

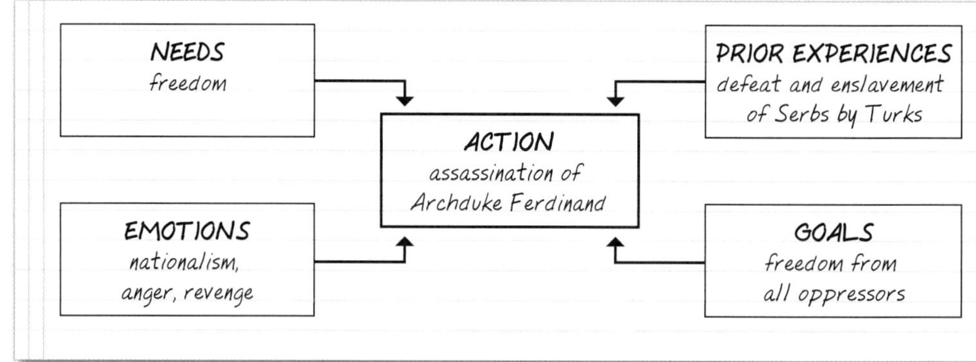

Applying the Skill

MAKE YOUR OWN DIAGRAM. Turn to Chapter 11, Section 1, "The Scramble for Africa." Read the section and look for motives of European nations in acquiring lands in other parts of the world. Make a diagram, like the one above, showing the European nations' motives for taking the land.

R16

2.9 Analyzing Issues

An issue is a matter of public concern or debate. Issues in history are usually economic, social, political, or moral. Historical issues are often more complicated than they first appear. **ANALYZING AN ISSUE** means taking a controversy apart to find and describe the different points of view about the issue.

Understanding the Skill

STRATEGY: LOOK FOR DIFFERENT SIDES OF THE ISSUE. The following passage describes working conditions in English factories in the early 1800s. The cluster diagram that follows the passage helps you to analyze the issue of child labor.

1. **Look for a central problem with its causes and effects.**
2. **Look for facts and statistics.** Factual information helps you understand the issue and evaluate the different sides or arguments.
3. **Look for different sides to the issue.** You need to consider all sides of an issue before deciding your position.

Children at Work

❶ Child labor was one of the most serious problems of the early Industrial Revolution. Children as young as 6 years worked exhausting jobs in factories and mines. Because wages were very low, many families in cities could not survive unless all their members, including children, worked.

❷ In most factories, regular work hours were 6 in the morning to 6 in the evening, often with two "over-hours" until 8. It was common for 40 or more children to work together in one room—a room with little light or air. Those who lagged behind in their work were often beaten. Because safety was a low concern for many factory owners, accidents were common.

In 1831, Parliament set up a committee to investigate abuses of child labor. ❷ Medical experts reported that long hours of factory work caused young children to become crippled or stunted in their growth. They recommended that children younger than age 14 should work no more than 8 hours. ❸ Factory owners responded that they needed children to work longer hours in order to be profitable. As one owner testified, reduced working hours for children would "much reduce the value of my mill and machinery, and consequently of . . . my manufacture." As a result of the committee's findings, Parliament passed the Factory Act of 1833. The act made it illegal to hire children under 9 years old, and it limited the working hours of older children.

STRATEGY: MAKE A CLUSTER DIAGRAM.

If an issue is complex, make a cluster diagram. A cluster diagram can help you analyze an issue.

Issue: Should Parliament restrict child labor?
Facts: • Children as young as 6 years worked.
• Working hours were typically 12 hours a day, often with 2 hours overtime.
• Working conditions were dangerous, unhealthy, and inhumane.
• Factory work caused deformities in young children.
In favor of child labor:
Who: factory owners, some parents
Reasons: Shorter hours would reduce profits. Children's income essential for families.
Against child labor:
Who: medical examiners
Reasons: Children working in factories suffered permanent deformities.

Applying the Skill

MAKE YOUR OWN CLUSTER DIAGRAM. Chapter 18, page 564, describes the partition of India. Make a cluster diagram to analyze the issue and the positions of the people involved.

R17

2.10 Analyzing Bias

BIAS is a prejudiced point of view. Historical accounts that are biased tend to be one-sided and reflect the personal prejudices of the historian.

Understanding the Skill

STRATEGY: THINK ABOUT THE WRITER AS YOU READ. The European explorer Amerigo Vespucci reached the coast of Brazil in 1502, on his second voyage to the Americas. Below are his impressions of the people he met.

1. **Identify the author and information about him or her.** Does the author belong to a special-interest group, social class, political party, or movement that might promote a one-sided or slanted viewpoint on the subject?
2. **Search for clues.** Are there words, phrases, statements, or images that might convey a positive or negative slant? What might these clues reveal about the author's bias?
3. **Examine the evidence.** Is the information that the author presents consistent with other accounts? Is the behavior described consistent with human nature as you have observed it?

(1) Amerigo Vespucci Reports on the People of Brazil

For twenty-seven days I ate and slept among them, and what I learned about them is as follows.

Having no laws and no religious faith, they live according to nature. (2) They understand nothing of the immortality of the soul. There is no possession of private property among them, for everything is in common. They have no boundaries of kingdom or province. They have no king, nor do they obey anyone. Each one is his own master. (3) There is no administration of justice, which is unnecessary to them, because in their code no one rules…

They are also (2) a warlike people and very cruel to their own kind… That which made me… astonished at their wars and cruelty was that I could not understand from them why they made war upon each other, considering that they held no private property or sovereignty of empire and kingdoms and (3) did not know any such thing as lust for possession, that is pillaging or a desire to rule, which appear to me to be the causes of wars and every disorderly act. When we requested them to state the cause, they did not know how to give any other cause than that this curse upon them began in ancient times and they sought to avenge the deaths of their forefathers.

STRATEGY: MAKE A CHART.

Make a chart of your analysis. For each of the heads listed on the left side of the chart, summarize information presented in the passage.

Vespucci's impressions of the native peoples of Brazil

author, date	Amerigo Vespucci, 1502
occasion	exploration of coast of Brazil on second voyage to Americas
tone	judging, negative, superior
bias	Since the native people do not live in organized states and have no private property, they have no system of authority, laws, or moral principles. They have no apparent religious beliefs. They are warlike and cruel and seem to make war on one another for no reason. The author's comments about the soul seem to show a bias towards his own religious beliefs. He also reveals a prejudice that European customs and practices are superior to all others.

Applying the Skill

MAKE YOUR OWN CHART. Look at the quotation by the Qing emperor Kangxi in the Primary Source in Chapter 3, page 115. Summarize the underlying assumptions and biases using a chart like the one shown.

R18

2.11 Evaluating Decisions and Courses of Action

EVALUATING DECISIONS means making judgments about the decisions that historical figures made. Historians evaluate decisions on the basis of their moral implications and their costs and benefits from different points of view.

EVALUATING VARIOUS COURSES OF ACTION means carefully judging the choices that historical figures had to make. By doing this, you can better understand why they made some of the decisions they did.

Understanding the Skill

STRATEGY: LOOK FOR CHOICES AND REASONS. The following passage describes the decisions U.S. President John Kennedy had to make when he learned of Soviet missile bases in Cuba. As you read it, think of the alternative responses he could have made at each turn of events. Following the passage is a chart that organizes information about the Cuban missile crisis.

1. **Look at decisions made by individuals or by groups.** Notice the decisions Kennedy made in response to Soviet actions.
2. **Look at the outcome of the decisions.**
3. **Analyze a decision in terms of the choices that were possible.** Both Kennedy and Khrushchev faced the same choice. Either could carry out the threat, or either could back down quietly and negotiate.

The Cuban Missile Crisis

During the summer of 1962, the flow of Soviet weapons into Cuba—including nuclear missiles—greatly increased. (1) President Kennedy responded cautiously at first, issuing a warning that the United States would not tolerate the presence of offensive nuclear weapons in Cuba. Then, on October 16, photographs taken by American U-2 planes showed the president that the Soviets were secretly building missile bases on Cuba. Some of the missiles, armed and ready to fire, could reach U.S. cities in minutes.

(1) On the evening of October 22, the president made public the evidence of missiles and stated his ultimatum: any missile attack from Cuba would trigger an all-out attack on the Soviet Union. Soviet ships continued to head toward the island, while the U.S. navy prepared to stop them and U.S. invasion troops massed in Florida. To avoid confrontation, the Soviet ships suddenly halted. (2) Soviet Premier Nikita Khrushchev offered to remove the missiles from Cuba in exchange for a pledge not to invade the island. Kennedy agreed, and the crisis ended.

(3) Some people criticized Kennedy for practicing brinkmanship, when private talks might have resolved the crisis without the threat of nuclear war. Others believed he had been too soft and had passed up a chance to invade Cuba and oust its Communist leader, Fidel Castro.

STRATEGY: MAKE A CHART.

Make a simple chart of your analysis. The problem was that Soviet nuclear missiles were being shipped to Cuba. The decision to be made was how the United States should respond.

Kennedy's Choices	*Pros*	*Cons*	*My Evaluation*
Publicly confront Khrushchev with navy and prepare for war.	*Show Khrushchev and world the power and strong will of the U.S.; force him to back off.*	*Nuclear war could occur.*	*In your opinion, which was the better choice? Why?*
Say nothing to U.S. public and negotiate quietly.	*Avoid frightening U.S. citizens and avoid threat of nuclear war.*	*The U.S. would look weak publicly; Khrushchev could carry out plan.*	

Applying the Skill

MAKE A CHART. Chapter 15, page 485, describes the decisions British and French leaders made when Hitler took over the Sudetenland in Czechoslovakia just before World War II. Make a chart, like the one shown, to summarize the pros and cons of their choice of appeasement and evaluate their decision yourself.

2.12 Forming and Supporting Opinions

Historians do more than reconstruct facts about the past. They also **FORM OPINIONS** about the information they encounter. Historians form opinions as they interpret the past and judge the significance of historical events and people. They **SUPPORT THEIR OPINIONS** with logical thinking, facts, examples, quotes, and references to events.

Understanding the Skill

STRATEGY: FIND ARGUMENTS TO SUPPORT YOUR OPINION. In the following passage, journalist Paul Gray summarizes differing opinions about the significance and impact of Columbus's voyages. As you read, develop your own opinion about the issue.

1. **Decide what you think about a subject after reading all the information available to you.** After reading this passage, you might decide that Columbus's legacy was primarily one of genocide, cruelty, and slavery. On the other hand, you might believe that, despite the negatives, his voyages produced many long-term benefits.
2. **Consider the opinions and interpretations of historians and other experts.** Weigh their arguments as you form your own opinion.
3. **Support your opinion with facts, quotes, and examples, including references to similar events from other historical eras.**

How Should History View the Legacy of Columbus?

In one version of the story, Columbus and the Europeans who followed him (1) brought civilization to two immense, sparsely populated continents, in the process fundamentally enriching and altering the Old World from which they had themselves come.

Among other things, Columbus' journey was the first step in a long process that eventually produced the United States of America, (2) a daring experiment in democracy that in turn became a symbol and a haven of individual liberty for people throughout the world. But the revolution that began with his voyages was far greater than that. It altered science, geography, philosophy, agriculture, law, religion, ethics, government—the sum, in other words, of what passed at the time as Western culture.

Increasingly, however, there is a counterchorus, an opposing rendition of the same events that deems Columbus' first footfall in the New World to be fatal to the world he invaded, and even to the rest of the globe. The indigenous peoples and their cultures were doomed by European (3) arrogance, (3) brutality, and (3) infectious diseases. Columbus' gift was (3) slavery to those who greeted him; (1) his arrival set in motion the ruthless destruction, continuing at this very moment, of the natural world he entered. Genocide, ecocide, exploitation… are deemed to be a form of Eurocentric theft of history from [the Native Americans].

STRATEGY: MAKE A CHART.

Summarize your opinion and supporting information in a chart. Write an opinion and then list facts, examples, interpretations, or other information that support it.

Opinion: *Voyages of Columbus brought more bad than good to the Americas*

Facts:	***Historical interpretations:***
• *Europeans replaced existing cultures with their own.* • *European diseases killed many Native Americans.* • *Columbus enslaved Native Americans.*	• *Europeans were arrogant and brutal.* • *Columbus's arrival set in motion ruthless destruction of environment.* • *Through conquest and exploitation, Europeans "stole" Native Americans' history and culture.*

Applying the Skill

MAKE YOUR OWN CHART. Look at the Different Perspectives on Economics and the Environment in Chapter 20, page 647. Read the selections and form your own opinion about the concept of sustainable development. Summarize your supporting data in a chart like the one shown above.

Skillbuilder Handbook

2.13 Synthesizing

SYNTHESIZING is the skill historians use in developing interpretations of the past. Like detective work, synthesizing involves putting together clues, information, and ideas to form an overall picture of a historical event. A synthesis is often stated as a generalization, or broad summary statement.

Understanding the Skill

STRATEGY: BUILD AN INTERPRETATION AS YOU READ. The passage below describes the first settlement of the Americas. The highlighting indicates the different kinds of information that lead to a synthesis—an overall picture of Native American life.

1. **Read carefully to understand the facts.** Facts such as these enable you to base your interpretations on physical evidence.
2. **Look for explanations that link the facts together.** This statement is based on the evidence provided by baskets, bows and arrows, and nets, which are mentioned in the sentences that follow.
3. **Consider what you already know that could apply.** Your general knowledge will probably lead you to accept this statement as reasonable.
4. **Bring together the information you have about a subject.** This interpretation brings together different kinds of information to arrive at a new understanding of the subject.

The First Americans

(1) From the discovery of chiseled arrowheads and charred bones at ancient sites, it appears that the earliest Americans lived as big game hunters. The woolly mammoth, their largest prey, provided them with food, clothing, and bones for constructing tools and shelters. (2) People gradually shifted to hunting small game and gathering available plants. They created baskets to collect nuts, wild rice, chokeberries, gooseberries, and currants. Later they invented bows and arrows to hunt small game such as jackrabbits and deer. They wove nets to fish the streams and lakes.

Between 10,000 and 15,000 years ago, a revolution took place in what is now central Mexico. People began to raise plants as food. Maize may have been the first domesticated plant, with pumpkins, peppers, beans, and potatoes following. Agriculture spread to other regions.

(3) The rise of agriculture brought about tremendous changes to the Americas. Agriculture made it possible for people to remain in one place. It also enabled them to accumulate and store surplus food. As their surplus increased, people had the time to develop skills and more complex ideas about the world. (4) From this agricultural base rose larger, more stable societies and increasingly complex societies.

STRATEGY: MAKE A CLUSTER DIAGRAM.

Summarize your synthesis in a cluster diagram. Use a cluster diagram to organize the facts, opinions, examples, and interpretations that you have brought together to form a synthesis.

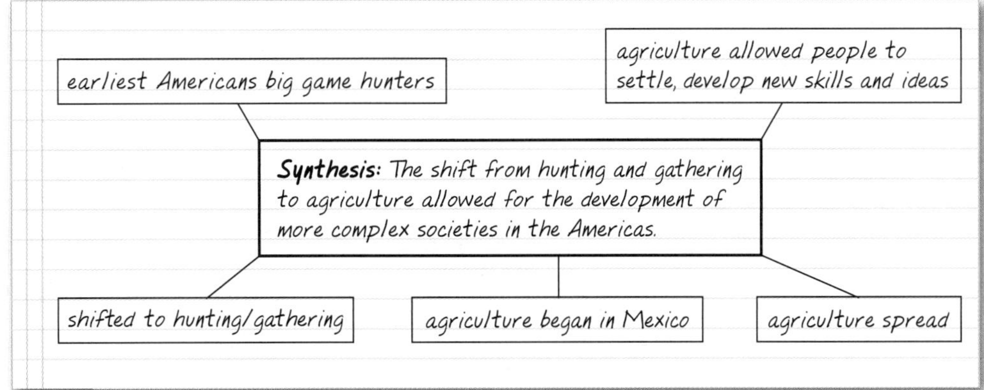
earliest Americans big game hunters
agriculture allowed people to settle, develop new skills and ideas
Synthesis: The shift from hunting and gathering to agriculture allowed for the development of more complex societies in the Americas.
shifted to hunting/gathering
agriculture began in Mexico
agriculture spread

Applying the Skill

MAKE YOUR OWN CLUSTER DIAGRAM. In Chapter 1 on pages 54–55, the beginnings of the Protestant Reformation are discussed. Read the passage and look for information to support a synthesis about its fundamental causes. Summarize your synthesis in a cluster diagram.

3.1 Analyzing Primary and Secondary Sources

PRIMARY SOURCES are written or created by people who lived during a historical event. The writers might have been participants or observers. Primary sources include letters, diaries, journals, speeches, newspaper articles, magazine articles, eyewitness accounts, and autobiographies.

SECONDARY SOURCES are derived from primary sources by people who were not present at the original event. They are written after the event. They often combine information from a number of different accounts. Secondary sources include history books, historical essays, and biographies.

Understanding the Skill

STRATEGY: EVALUATE THE INFORMATION IN EACH TYPE OF SOURCE. This passage describes political reforms made by Pericles, who led Athens from 461 to 429 B.C. It is mainly a secondary source, but it includes a primary source in the form of a speech.

1. **Secondary Source: Look for information collected from several sources.** Here the writer presents an overall picture of the reforms made by Pericles and the reasons for them.
2. **Secondary Source: Look for analysis and interpretation.** A secondary source provides details and perspective that are missing in a primary source. It also provides context for the primary source.
3. **Primary Source: Identify the author and evaluate his or her credentials.** How is the speaker connected to the event? Here, this speaker is Pericles himself.
4. **Primary Source: Analyze the source using historical perspective.** Read the source for factual information while also noting the speaker's opinions, biases, assumptions, and point of view.

Stronger Democracy in Athens

(1) To strengthen democracy, Pericles increased the number of public officials who were paid salaries. Before, only wealthier citizens could afford to hold public office because most positions were unpaid. Now even the poorest could serve if elected or chosen by lot. (2) This reform made Athens one of the most democratic governments in history. However, political rights were still limited to those with citizenship status—a minority of Athens' total population.

The introduction of direct democracy was an important legacy of Periclean Athens. Few other city-states practiced this style of government. In Athens, male citizens who served in the assembly established all the important policies that affected the polis. In a famous "Funeral Oration" for soldiers killed in the Peloponnesian War, (3) Pericles expressed his great pride in Athenian democracy:

> (4) *Our constitution is called a democracy because power is in the hands not of a minority but of the whole people. When it is a question of settling private disputes, everyone is equal before the law; when it is a question of putting one person before another in positions of public responsibility, what counts is not membership of a particular class, but the actual ability which the man possesses. No one, as long as he has it in him to be of service to the state, is kept in political obscurity because of poverty.*

STRATEGY: MAKE A CHART.

Summarize information from primary and secondary sources on a chart.

Primary Source	Secondary Source
Author: Pericles **Qualifications:** main figure in the events described **Information:** describes his view of Athenian democracy—power in the hands of "the whole people"	**Author:** world history textbook **Qualifications:** had access to multiple accounts of event **Information:** puts events in historical perspective—Athens one of most democratic governments in history but limited rights to citizens

Applying the Skill

MAKE YOUR OWN CHART. Read the passage "Mehmed II Conquers Constantinople" in Chapter 2, pages 74–75, which includes a quote from the Greek historian Kritovoulos. Make a chart in which you summarize information from the primary and secondary sources.

3.2 Visual, Audio, and Multimedia Sources

In addition to written accounts, historians use many kinds of **VISUAL SOURCES.** These include paintings, photographs, political cartoons, and advertisements. Visual sources are rich with historical details and sometimes reflect the mood and trends of an era better than words can.

Spoken language has always been a primary means of passing on human history. **AUDIO SOURCES,** such as recorded speeches, interviews, press conferences, and radio programs, continue the oral tradition today.

Movies, CD-ROMs, television, and computer software are the newest kind of historical sources, called **MULTIMEDIA SOURCES.**

Understanding the Skill

STRATEGY: EXAMINE THE SOURCE CAREFULLY. Below are two portraits from the late 1700s, one of Marie Antoinette, the queen of France, and one of a woman who sells vegetables at the market. The chart that follows summarizes historical information gained from interpreting and comparing the two paintings.

1. **Identify the subject and source.**
2. **Identify important visual details.** Look at the faces, poses, clothing, hairstyles, and other elements.
3. **Make inferences from the visual details.** Marie Antoinette's rich clothing and her hand on the globe symbolize her wealth and power. The contrast between the common woman's ordinary clothing and her defiant pose suggests a different attitude about power.

Use comparisons, information from other sources, and your own knowledge to give support to your interpretation. Royalty usually had their portraits painted in heroic poses. Ordinary people were not usually the subjects of such portraits. David's choice of subject and pose suggests that he sees the common people as the true heroes of France.

A Woman of the Revolution [La maraîchère] (1795), Jacques Louis David 1

Marie Antoinette, Jacques Gautier d'Agoty 1

STRATEGY: MAKE A CHART.

Summarize your interpretation in a simple chart.

Subject	Visual Details	Inferences	Message
Common woman	Face is worn and clothing is plain, but her head is held high and she wears the red scarf of revolution	Has worked hard for little in life, but strong, proud, and defiant	Although the details are strikingly different, the two paintings convey similar characteristics about their subjects.
Marie Antoinette	Richly dressed and made up; strikes an imperial pose	Lives life of comfort and power; proud, strong, and defiant	

Applying the Skill

MAKE YOUR OWN CHART. Turn to the painting *School of Athens* by Raphael in Chapter 1, page 45. Use a chart, like the one above, to analyze and interpret the painting.

3.3 Using the Internet

The **INTERNET** is a network of computers associated with universities, libraries, news organizations, government agencies, businesses, and private individuals worldwide. Each location on the Internet has a **HOME PAGE** with its own address, or **URL.**

With a computer connected to the Internet, you can reach the home pages of many organizations and services. You might view your library's home page to find the call number of a book or visit an online magazine to read an article. On some sites you can view documents, photographs, and even moving pictures with sound.

The international collection of home pages, known as the **WORLD WIDE WEB,** is a good source of up-to-the-minute information about current events as well as in-depth research on historical subjects. This textbook contains many suggestions for navigating the World Wide Web. Begin by entering **CLASSZONE.COM** to access the home page for McDougal Littell World History.

Understanding the Skill

STRATEGY: EXPLORE THE ELEMENTS ON THE SCREEN. The computer screen below shows the home page of the history area at PBS, the national public television service based in Washington, D.C.

1. **Go directly to a Web page.** If you know the address of a particular Web page, type the address in the box at the top of the screen and press ENTER (or RETURN). After a few seconds, the Web page will appear on your screen.
2. **Explore the links.** Click on any one of the images or topics to find out more about a specific subject. These links take you to another page at this Web site. Some pages include links to related information that can be found at other places on the Internet.
3. **Learn more about the page.** Scan the page to learn the types of information contained at this site. This site has information about PBS history programs as well as other historical information and special features.
4. **Explore the features of the page.** This page has a feature that lets you compare life today with life in the 1700s.

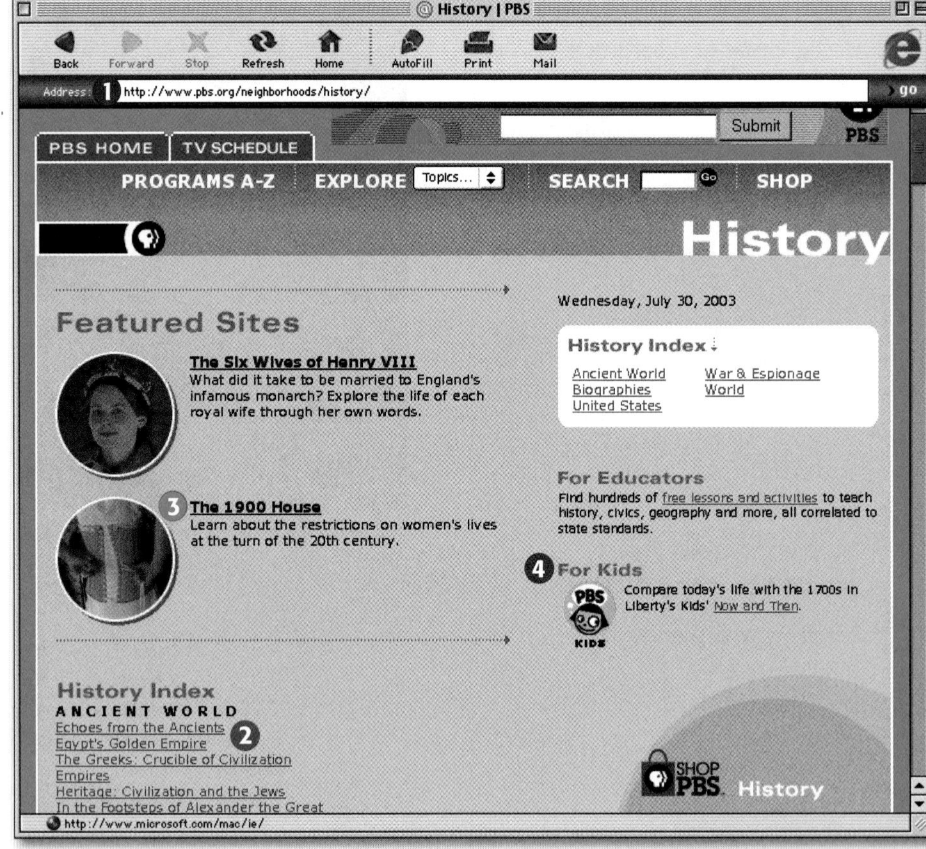

PBS History screen shot courtesy of PBS ONLINE®.

Applying the Skill

DO YOUR OWN INTERNET RESEARCH. Explore the web sites for Chapter 18 located at classzone.com. **PATH: CLASSZONE.COM** ➔ Social Studies ➔ World History ➔ Chapter 18 ➔ Research Links.

3.4 Interpreting Maps

MAPS are representations of features on the earth's surface. Historians use maps to locate historical events, to show how geography has influenced history, and to illustrate human interaction with the environment.

Different kinds of maps are used for specific purposes.

POLITICAL MAPS show political units, from countries, states, and provinces, to counties, districts, and towns. Each area is shaded a different color.

PHYSICAL MAPS show mountains, hills, plains, rivers, lakes, and oceans. They may use contour lines to indicate elevations on land and depths under water.

HISTORICAL MAPS illustrate such things as economic activity, political alliances, land claims, battles, population density, and changes over time.

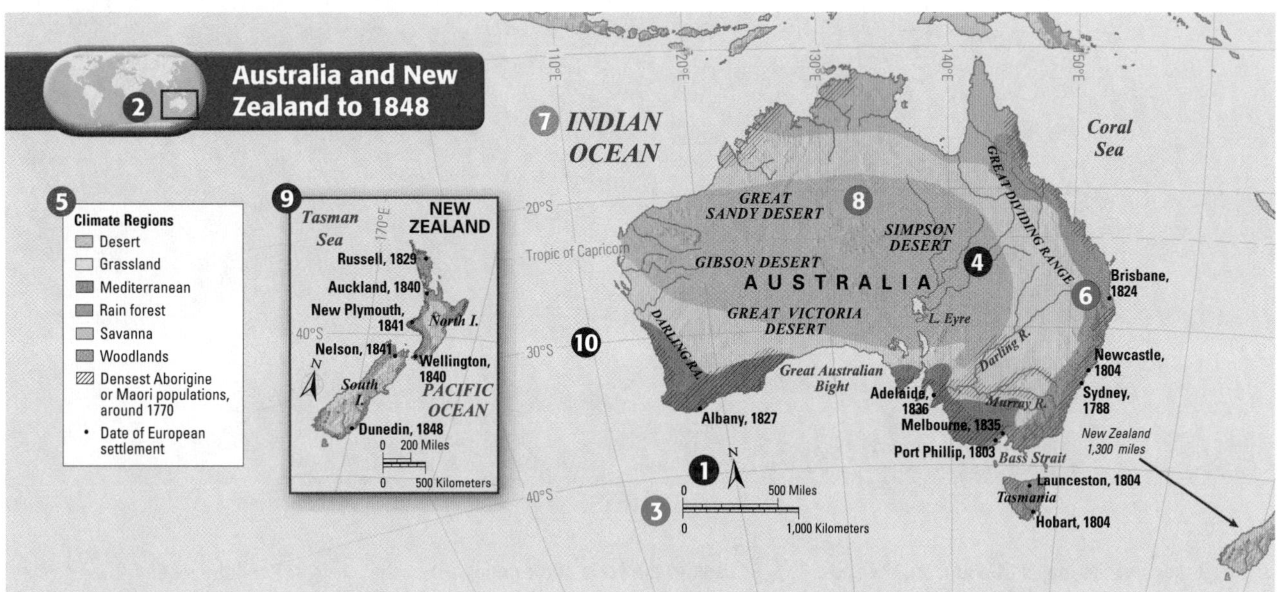

1. **Compass Rose** The compass rose is a feature indicating the map's orientation on the globe. It may show all four cardinal directions (N, S, E, W) or just indicate north.

2. **Locator** A locator map shows which part of the world the map subject area covers.

3. **Scale** The scale shows the ratio between a unit of length on the map and a unit of distance on the earth. The maps in this book usually show the scale in miles and kilometers.

4. **Lines** Lines indicate rivers and other waterways, political boundaries, roads, and routes of exploration or migration.

5. **Legend or Key** The legend or key explains the symbols, lines, and special colors that appear on the map.

6. **Symbols** Locations of cities and towns often appear as dots. A capital city is often shown as a star or as a dot with a circle around it. Picture symbols might be used to indicate an area's products, resources, and special features.

7. **Labels** Key places such as cities, bodies of water, and landforms are labeled. Key dates, such as those for the founding of cities, may also be labeled.

8. **Colors** Maps use colors and shading for various purposes. On physical maps, color may be used to indicate different physical regions or altitudes. On political maps, color can distinguish different political units. On specialty maps, color can show variable features such as population density, languages, or cultural areas.

9. **Inset** An inset is a small map that appears within a larger map. It often shows an area of the larger map in greater detail. Inset maps may also show a different area that is in some way related to the area shown on the larger map.

10. **Lines of Latitude and Longitude** Lines of latitude and longitude appear on maps to indicate the absolute location of the area shown.
    - Lines of latitude show distance measured in degrees north or south of the equator.
    - Lines of longitude show distance measured in degrees east or west of the prime meridian, which runs through Greenwich, England.

R25

3.4 *(Continued)*

Understanding the Skill

STRATEGY: READ ALL THE ELEMENTS OF THE MAP. The historical maps below show European landholdings in North America in 1754 and after 1763. Together they show changes over time.

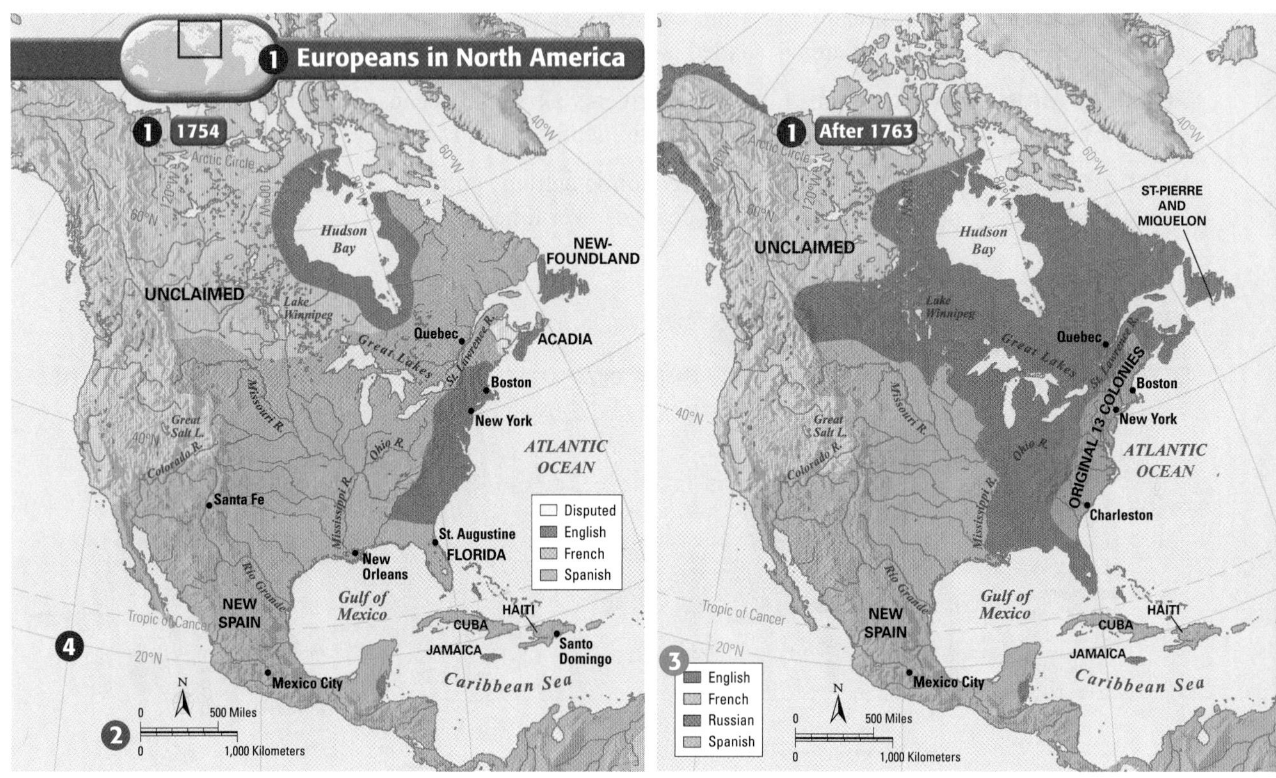

1 Look at the map's title to learn the subject and purpose of the map. What area does the map cover? What does the map tell you about the area? Here the maps show North America in 1754 and after 1763 with the purpose of comparing European claims at two different times.

2 Look at the scale and compass. The scale shows you how many miles or kilometers are represented. Here the scale is 500 actual miles to approximately 5/8 inch on the map. The compass shows you which direction on the map is north.

3 Read the legend. The legend tells you what the symbols and colors on the map mean.

4 Find where the map area is located on the earth. These maps show a large area from the Arctic Circle to below latitude 20°N and 40° to 140°W.

STRATEGY: MAKE A CHART. Study the maps and pose questions about how the geographic patterns and distributions changed. Use the answers to create a chart.

Relate the map to the five geography themes by making a chart. The five themes are described on pages xxxii–xxxiii. Ask questions about the themes and record your answers on the chart.

What Was the Location? *Large area from Arctic Circle to below 20° N, and 40° to 140° W*

What Was the Place? *North American continent*

What Was the Region? *Western Hemisphere*

Was There Any Movement? *Between 1754 and 1763, land claimed by France was taken over by the other two colonial powers. Spain expanded its territories northward, while Britain expanded westward.*

How Did Humans Interact with the Environment? *Europeans carved out political units in the continent, which already had inhabitants. They claimed vast areas, with waterways and large mountain ranges to cross.*

Applying the Skill

MAKE YOUR OWN CHART. Turn to Chapter 3, page 100, and study the map titled "Europeans in the East, 1487–1700." Make a chart, like the one shown above, in which you summarize what the map tells you according to the five geography themes.

3.5 Interpreting Charts

CHARTS are visual presentations of materials. Historians use charts to organize, simplify, and summarize information in a way that makes it more meaningful or easier to remember. Several kinds of charts are commonly used.

SIMPLE CHARTS are used to summarize information or to make comparisons.

TABLES are used to organize statistics and other types of information into columns and rows for easy reference.

DIAGRAMS provide visual clues to the meaning of the information they contain. Venn diagrams are used for comparisons. Web diagrams are used to organize supporting information around a central topic. Illustrated diagrams or diagrams that combine different levels of information are sometimes called **INFOGRAPHICS.**

Understanding the Skill

STRATEGY: STUDY ALL THE ELEMENTS OF THE CHART. The infographic below conveys a great deal of information about the three estates, or classes, that existed in 18th-century France. The infographic visually combines a political cartoon, a bulleted chart, a pie graph, and a bar graph.

Read the title.

Identify the symbols and colors and what they represent. Here, three colors are used consistently in the infographic to represent the three estates.

Study each of the elements of the infographic. The political cartoon visually represents the power of the First and Second Estates over the Third Estate. The bulleted chart gives details about the estates. The two graphs give statistics.

Look for the main idea. Make connections among the types of information presented. What was the relationship among the three estates?

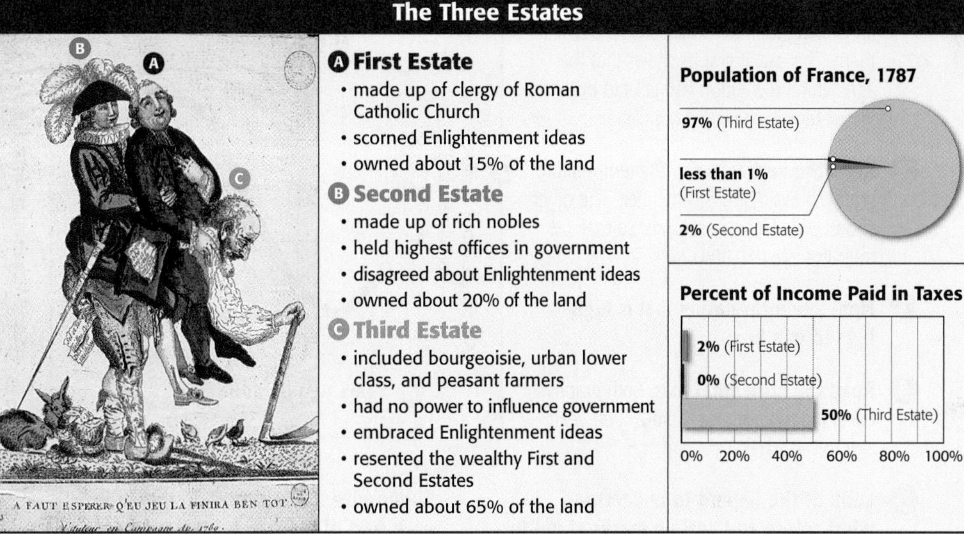

The Three Estates
B
A
C
A FAUT ESPERER Q'EU JEU LA FINIRA BEN TOT
A First Estate
• made up of clergy of Roman Catholic Church
• scorned Enlightenment ideas
• owned about 15% of the land
B Second Estate
• made up of rich nobles
• held highest offices in government
• disagreed about Enlightenment ideas
• owned about 20% of the land
C Third Estate
• included bourgeoisie, urban lower class, and peasant farmers
• had no power to influence government
• embraced Enlightenment ideas
• resented the wealthy First and Second Estates
• owned about 65% of the land
Population of France, 1787
97% (Third Estate)
less than 1% (First Estate)
2% (Second Estate)
Percent of Income Paid in Taxes
2% (First Estate)
0% (Second Estate)
50% (Third Estate)
0% 20% 40% 60% 80% 100%

Look for geographic patterns and distributions. Pose questions about the way land is distributed among the three estates. Include your answers in your summary paragraph.

STRATEGY: WRITE A SUMMARY.

Write a paragraph to summarize what you learned from the chart.

In 1787, French society was unevenly divided into three estates. Ninety-seven percent of the people belonged to the Third Estate. They had no political power, paid high taxes, and owned only 65 percent of the land. The First Estate, made up of the clergy, and the Second Estate, made up of rich nobles, held the power, the wealth, and more than their share of the land. Both opposed change and took advantage of the Third Estate.

Applying the Skill

WRITE YOUR OWN SUMMARY. Turn to Chapter 9, page 293, and look at the chart titled "Industrialization." Study the chart and write a paragraph in which you summarize what you learn from it.

R27

3.6 Interpreting Graphs

GRAPHS show statistical information in a visual manner. Historians use graphs to show comparative amounts, ratios, economic trends, and changes over time.

LINE GRAPHS can show changes over time, or trends. Usually, the horizontal axis shows a unit of time, such as years, and the vertical axis shows quantities.

PIE GRAPHS are useful for showing relative proportions. The circle represents the whole, such as the entire population, and the slices represent the different groups that make up the whole.

BAR GRAPHS compare numbers or sets of numbers. The length of each bar indicates a quantity. With bar graphs, it is easy to see at a glance how different categories compare.

Understanding the Skill

STRATEGY: STUDY ALL THE ELEMENTS OF THE GRAPH. The line graphs below show average global temperatures and world population figures over a period of 25,000 years. Pose questions about geographic patterns and distributions shown on this graph; for example, when did worldwide temperature start to rise?

1. **Read the title to identify the main idea of the graph.** When two subjects are shown, look for a relationship between them. This set of graphs shows that the agricultural revolution had links to both global temperature and population.
2. **Read the vertical axis.** The temperature graph shows degrees Fahrenheit. The other shows population in millions, so that 125 indicates 125,000,000.
3. **Note any information that is highlighted in a box.**
4. **Read the horizontal axis.** Both graphs cover a period of time from 25,000 years ago to 0 (today).
5. **Look at the legend to understand what colors and certain marks stand for.**

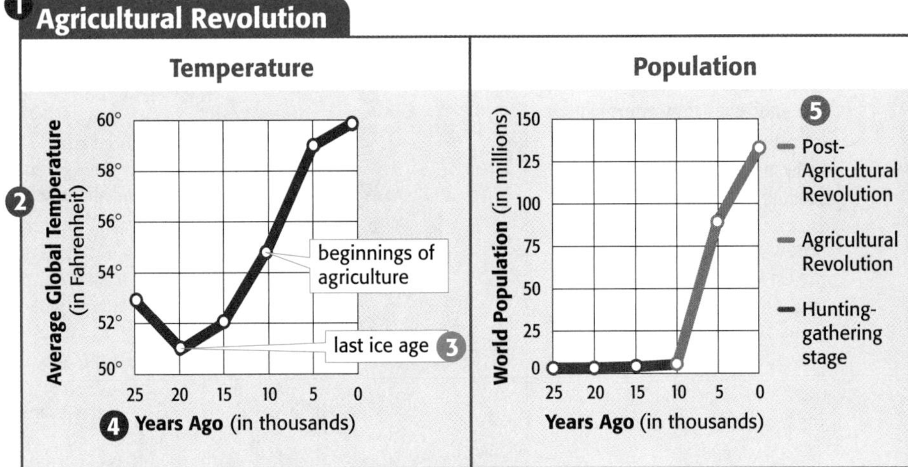

Summarize the information shown in each part of the graph. What trends or changes are shown in each line graph?

STRATEGY: WRITE A SUMMARY.

Use the answers to your questions about geographic patterns and distributions to write your summary paragraph.

Write a paragraph to summarize what you learned from the graphs.

Some 20,000 years ago, after the last Ice Age, temperatures started to rise worldwide. This steady rise in average temperature from 51° to 55° made possible the beginnings of agriculture. As a result of the agricultural revolution, world population grew from about 2 million to about 130 million over a period of 10,000 years.

Applying the Skill

WRITE YOUR OWN SUMMARY. Turn to Chapter 15, page 474, and look at the graph "World Trade, 1929–1933." Study the graph and write a paragraph in which you summarize what you learn from it.

3.7 Analyzing Political Cartoons

POLITICAL CARTOONS are drawings that express the artist's point of view about a local, national, or international situation or event. They may criticize, show approval, or draw attention to a particular issue, and may be either serious or humorous. Political cartoonists often use symbols as well as other visual clues to communicate their message.

Understanding the Skill

STRATEGY: EXAMINE THE CARTOON CAREFULLY. The cartoon below was drawn during the period of détente—a lessening of Cold War tensions between the United States and the Soviet Union.

1. **Look at the cartoon as a whole to determine the subject.**
2. **Look for symbols, which are especially effective in communicating ideas visually.** In this cartoon, Szabo uses symbols that stand for two nations. The stars and stripes stand for the United States. The hammer and sickle stand for the Soviet Union.
3. **Analyze the visual details, which help express the artist's point of view.** The lit fuse suggests that the world is in immediate danger. The United States and the Soviet Union are cooperating to reduce the danger by cutting the fuse.

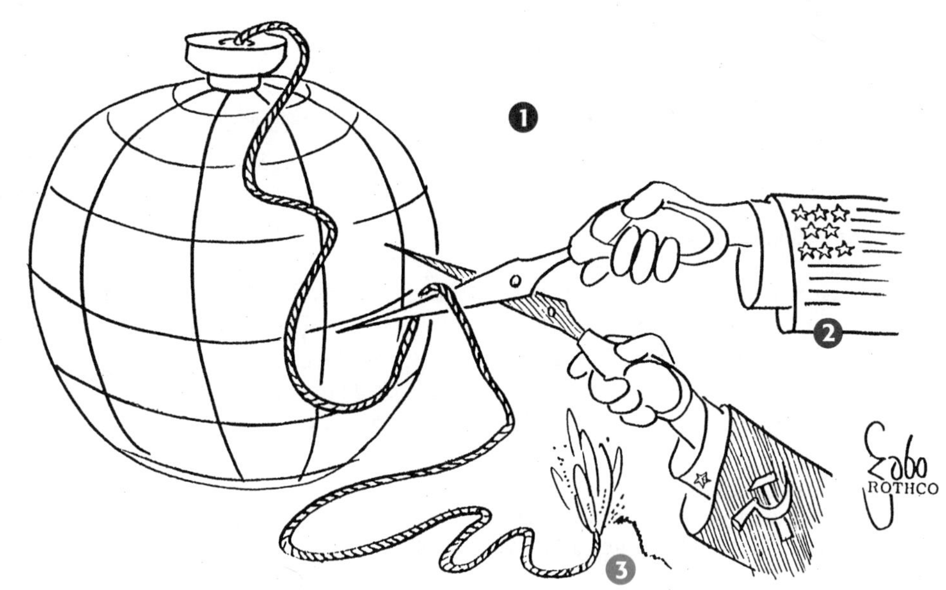

STRATEGY: MAKE A CHART.

Summarize your analysis in a chart. Look for details and analyze their significance. Then decide on the message of the cartoon.

Symbols and Visual Details	*Significance*	*Message*
• *Stars and stripes* • *Hammer and sickle* • *Lit fuse* • *Both nations hold the scissors*	• *United States* • *Soviet Union* • *Danger* • *Cooperation*	*The United States and the Soviet Union are trying to prevent their differences from destroying the world.*

Applying the Skill

MAKE YOUR OWN CHART. Turn to the political cartoon in Chapter 7, page 218. Read the information provided in the chart and graphs to help you understand the basis for the cartoon. Note the clothing and apparent attitudes of the figures in the drawing, as well as how they relate to one another. Then make a chart like the one above.

R29

4.1 Writing for Social Studies

WRITING FOR SOCIAL STUDIES requires you to describe an idea, a situation, or an event. Often, you will be asked to take a stand on a particular issue or to make a specific point. To successfully describe an event or make a point, your writing needs to be clear, concise, and accurate. When you write reports or term papers, you will also need to create a bibliography of your sources; and you need to evaluate how reliable those sources are.

Understanding the Skill

STRATEGY: ORGANIZE INFORMATION AND WRITE CLEARLY. The following passage describes the rise and fall of Napoleon Bonaparte. Notice how the strategies below helped the writer explain the historical importance of Napoleon's power.

❶ **Focus on your topic.** Be sure that you clearly state the main idea of your piece so that your readers know what you intend to say.

❷ **Collect and organize your facts.** Collect accurate information about your topic to support the main idea you are trying to make. Use your information to build a logical case to prove your point

To express your ideas clearly, use standard grammar, spelling, sentence structure, and punctuation when writing for social studies. Proofread your work to make sure it is well organized and grammatically correct.

❶ The Rise and Fall of Napoleon, 1799–1814

The power that Napoleon used to bring order to France after the Revolution ultimately proved to be his undoing. Under his command, the troops drove out members of the legislature in 1799 and helped Napoleon seize control of France. ❷ As emperor of France, he stabilized the country's economy. He even created a code of laws. However, Napoleon wanted to control all of Europe. But he made mistakes that cost him his empire. He established a blockade in 1806 to prevent trade between Great Britain and other Europeans nations. But smugglers, aided by the British, managed to get cargo through. He angered Spain by replacing the country's king with his own brother. In 1812, Napoleon also invaded Russia by using many troops who were not French and who felt little loyalty to him. Eventually, all the main powers of Europe joined forces and defeated Napoleon in the spring of 1814.

STRATEGY: USE STANDARD FORMATS WHEN MAKING CITATIONS. Use standard formats when citing books, magazines, newspapers, electronic media, and other sources. The following examples will help you to interpret and create bibliographies.

❸ **Video**

❹ **Newspaper**

❺ **Magazine**

❻ **Online database**

❼ **Book**

❸ Fire and Ice. Prod. HistoryAlive Videocassette. BBC Video, 1998.

❹ Gutierrez, Andrew R. "Memorial for Scott at Antarctic." Los Angeles Times 8 January 2001: 14A.

❺ Hansen, Ron. "The Race for the South Pole." Smithsonian Institute 28 June 1999: 112.

❻ "Scott's Run for the South Pole." Facts on File. Online. Internet. 28 February 2000.

❼ Solomon, Susan. The Coldest March: Scott's Fatal Antarctic Expedition. New Haven, CT: Yale UP, 2001.

Applying the Skill

WRITE YOUR OWN RESPONSE. Turn to Chapter 7, Section 4, "Napoleon's Empire Collapses." Read the section and use the strategies above to write your answer to question 6 on page 237.

Find three or four different sources on the Internet or in the library relating to Napoleon's fall. Create a short bibliography and use standard formats for each type of source. Be sure to interpret, or evaluate, how reliable your sources are.

4.2 Creating a Map

CREATING A MAP can help you understand routes, regions, landforms, political boundaries, or other geographical information.

Understanding the Skill

STRATEGY: CREATE A MAP to clarify information and help you visualize what you read. Creating a map is similar to taking notes, except that you draw much of the information. After reading the passage below, a student sketched the map shown.

> **The French Explore North America**
>
> A number of Frenchmen were among the early explorers of North America. In 1534, Jacques Cartier sailed up a broad river that he named the St. Lawrence. When he came to a large island dominated by a mountain, he called the island Mont Real, which eventually became known as Montreal. In 1608, another French explorer, Samuel de Champlain, sailed further up the St. Lawrence and laid claim to a region he called Quebec. In 1673, Jacques Marquette and Louis Joliet explored the Great Lakes and the upper Mississippi River. Nearly 10 years later, Sieur de La Salle explored the lower Mississippi and claimed the entire river valley for France.

1. **Create a title that shows the purpose of the map.**
2. **Consider the purpose of the map as you decide which features to include.** Because the main purpose of this sketch map is to show the routes of early explorers, it includes a scale of distance.
3. **Find one or more maps to use as a guide.** For this sketch map, the student consulted a historical map and a physical map.
4. **Create a legend to explain any colors or symbols used.**

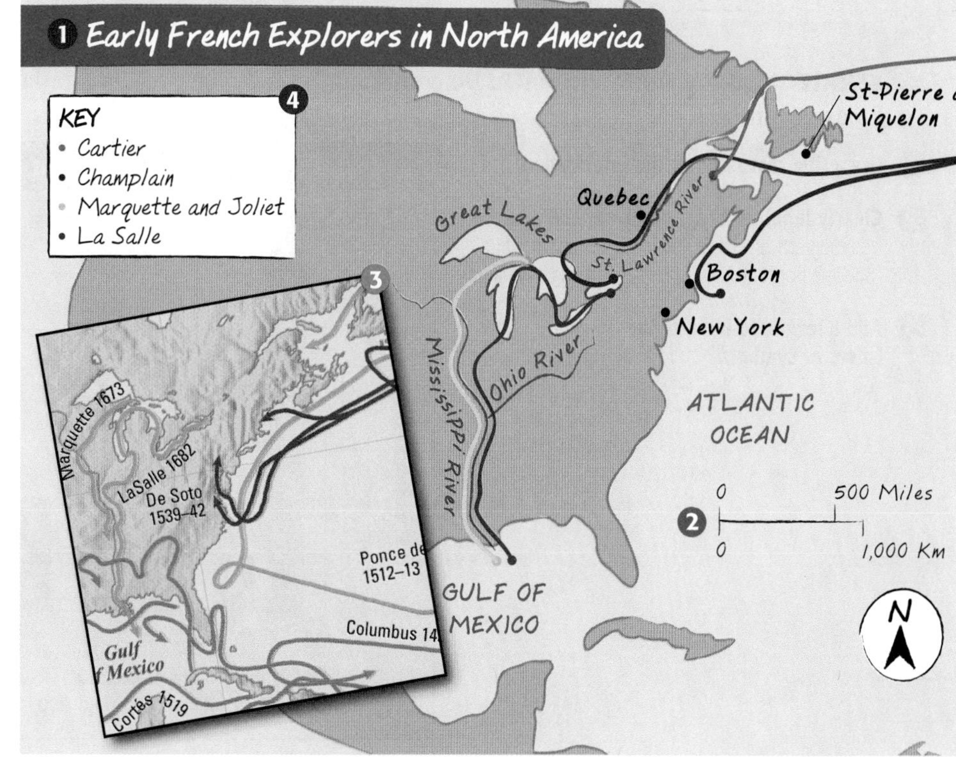

Applying the Skill

MAKE YOUR OWN SKETCH MAP. Turn to Chapter 4, page 122, and read the first three paragraphs of the section "Spanish Conquests in Peru." Create a sketch map showing the cities where Pizarro conquered the Inca. Use either a modern map of Peru or an historic map of the Incan Empire as a guide. (The conquered cities of the empire also belong to the modern nation of Peru.) Include a scale of miles to show the distance traveled by the Spanish to make their conquests. Add a legend to indicate which conquest involved a battle and which did not.

R31

4.3 Creating Charts and Graphs

CHARTS and **GRAPHS** are visual representations of information. (See Skillbuilders 3.5, Interpreting Charts, and 3.6, Interpreting Graphs.) Three types of graphs are **BAR GRAPHS, LINE GRAPHS,** and **PIE GRAPHS.** Use a line graph to show changes over time, or trends. Use a pie graph to show relative proportions. Use a bar graph to display and compare information about quantities. Use a **CHART** to organize, simplify, and summarize information.

Understanding the Skill

STRATEGY: CREATE A BAR GRAPH. Choose the information that you wish to compare. After reading the following paragraph, a student created the bar graph below to compare population shifts in three European cities.

Population Shifts

The decline of the Roman Empire led to major population shifts. As Roman centers of trade and government collapsed, nobles retreated to the rural areas. Roman cities were left without strong leadership. The population of Rome dropped from 350,000 in A.D. 100 to 50,000 in A.D. 900. During the same period, other cities in the empire experienced similar declines. For example, the population of Trier, Germany, dropped from 100,000 to around 13,000. The population of Lyon, France, experienced an even greater decline, dropping from 100,000 to approximately 12,000.

STRATEGY: ORGANIZE THE DATA. Be consistent in how you present similar kinds of information.

1. **Use a title that sums up the information.**
2. **Clearly label vertical and horizontal axes.** Use the vertical axis to show increasing quantities. Label the horizontal axis with what is being compared.
3. **Add a legend to indicate the meaning of any colors or symbols.**

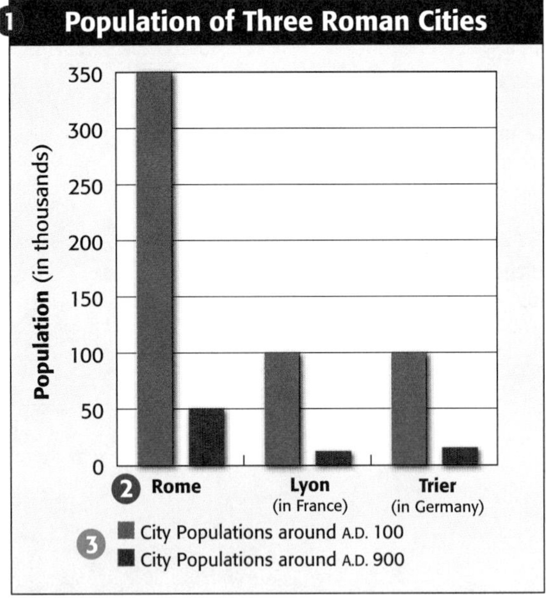

Applying the Skill

CREATE A BAR GRAPH. Turn to Chapter 7, page 236. Study the map "Napoleon's Russian Campaign, 1812." Use the information to create a bar graph showing the number of soldiers in Napoleon's army from June 1812 to December 6, 1812. Label the vertical axis Soldiers (in thousands) and show the grid in increments of 100, beginning with 0 and ending with 500. Provide a bar for each of the following dates: June 1812, September 7, 1812, November 1812, and December 6, 1812. Label each bar with the number of soldiers. Add a title. Be sure to read carefully the information in the boxes on the chart for each date you include in your graph.

4.4 Creating and Using a Database

A **DATABASE** is a collection of data, or information, that is organized so that you can find and retrieve information on a specific topic quickly and easily. Once a computerized database is set up, you can search it to find specific information without going through the entire database. The database will provide a list of all information in the database related to your topic. Learning how to use a database will help you learn how to create one.

Understanding the Skill

STRATEGY: CREATE THE DATABASE. First, identify the topic of the database. Both words in this title, "Five Empires," are important. These words were used to begin the research for this database.

1 Determine the order of presentation of information. For example, will you list items from largest to smallest? from oldest to newest? The five empires are listed in order of date, from earliest empire to latest.

2 Identify the entries included under each heading. Here, five empires from the text were chosen as topics for research.

3 Ask yourself what kind of data to include. For example, what geographic patterns and distributions will be shown? Your choice of data will provide the column headings. The key words *Dates, Greatest Territory,* and *Greatest Population* were chosen to focus the research.

Five Empires

	1 Dates	Greatest Territory*	3 Greatest Population**
2 **Persian**	550 B.C.–330 B.C.	2.0	14.0
Roman	27 B.C.–A.D. 476	3.4	54.8
Byzantine	A.D. 395–A.D. 1453	1.4	30.0
Mongol	A.D. 1206–A.D. 1380	11.7	125.0
Aztec	A.D. 1325–A.D. 1521	0.2	6.0

4 * Estimated in millions of square miles
** Estimated in millions of people

4 Add labels or footnotes as necessary to clarify the nature of the data presented. Are the figures shown in thousands? hundred of thousands? millions? Users of the database need to know what the figures represent.

STRATEGY: USE THE DATABASE. Use the database to help you find information quickly. For example, in this database you could search for "empires with populations of more than 10 million" and compile a list including the Persian, Roman, Byzantine, and Mongol empires.

Applying the Skill

CREATE A DATABASE for World War II that shows the dates and locations of important battles, estimated casualty figures, and the significance of the outcome for each battle. Use information presented in Chapter 16 to find the data. Follow a chart format similar to the one above for your database. Then use the database to list the three battles that resulted in the highest number of casualties.

R33

4.5 Creating a Model

WHEN YOU CREATE A MODEL, you use information and ideas to show an event or a situation in a visual way. A model might be a poster or a diagram drawn to explain how something happened. Or, it might be a three-dimensional model, such as a diorama, that depicts an important scene or situation.

Understanding the Skill

STRATEGY: CREATE A MODEL. The poster below shows the hardships and dangers that children faced while working in the textile factories in the early 1800s. Use the strategies listed below to help you create your own model.

1. **Gather the information you need to understand the situation or event.** In this case, you need to be able to show the hardships and dangers of child labor.
2. **Visualize and sketch an idea for your model.** Once you have created a picture in your mind, make an actual sketch to plan how it might look.
3. **Think of symbols you may want to use.** Since the model should give information in a visual way, think about ways you can use color, pictures, or other visuals to tell the story.

Gather the supplies you will need and create the model. For example, you may need crayons and markers.

Child Labor in Britain in the Early 1800s

INDUSTRY COMES TO MANCHESTER, ENGLAND!

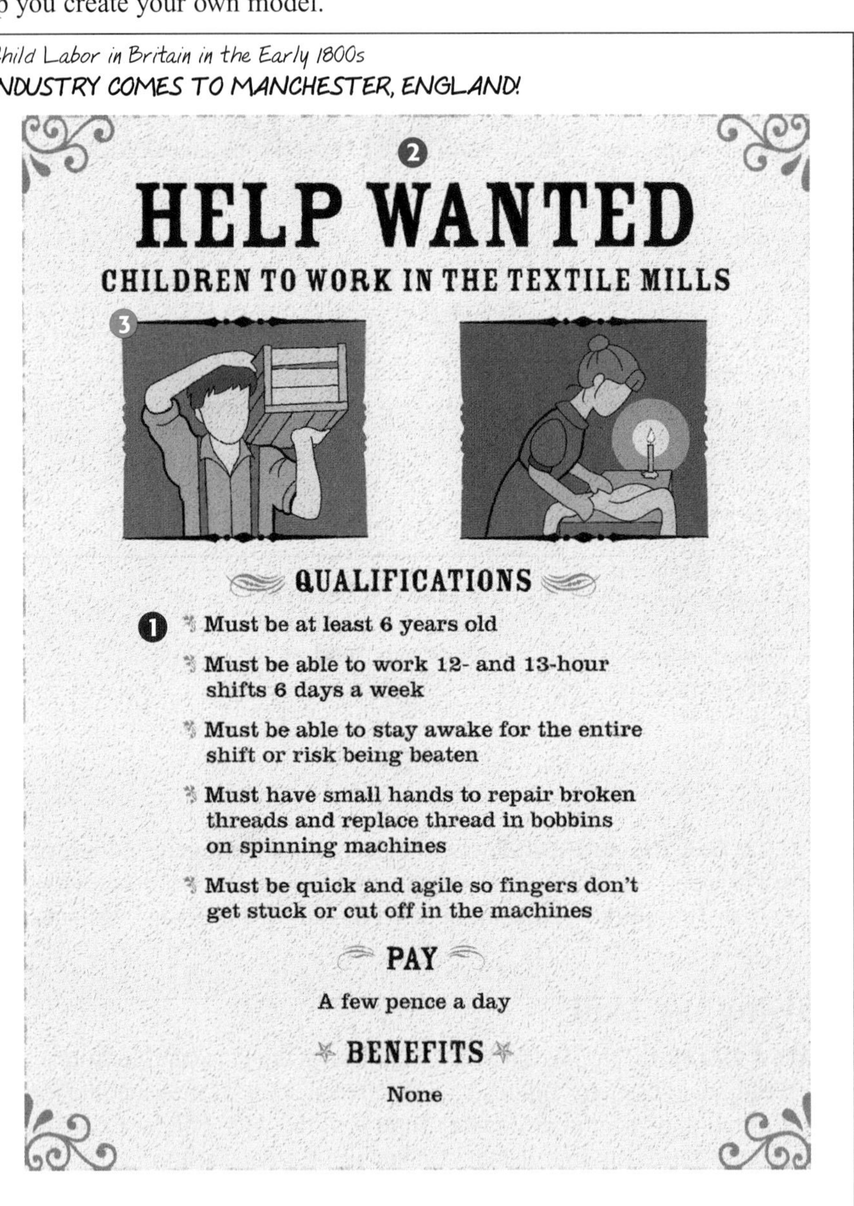

2
HELP WANTED
CHILDREN TO WORK IN THE TEXTILE MILLS
3
QUALIFICATIONS
1
Must be at least 6 years old
Must be able to work 12- and 13-hour shifts 6 days a week
Must be able to stay awake for the entire shift or risk being beaten
Must have small hands to repair broken threads and replace thread in bobbins on spinning machines
Must be quick and agile so fingers don't get stuck or cut off in the machines
PAY
A few pence a day
BENEFITS
None

Applying the Skill

CREATE YOUR OWN MODEL. Read the Interact with History feature on page 282. Create a poster that shows how working conditions might be made more fair in England during the Industrial Revolution.

4.6 Creating/Interpreting a Research Outline

When you **CREATE A RESEARCH OUTLINE,** you arrange information you have gathered into an organized format. When you **INTERPRET A RESEARCH OUTLINE,** you use the outline's structure to guide you in writing a research report or paper that is clear and focused.

Understanding the Skill

STRATEGY: DECIDE HOW IDEAS ARE CONNECTED, THEN CREATE AN OUTLINE. As you research a topic, you are likely to gather names, dates, facts, and ideas. All of this information needs to be organized to show how the ideas connect to one another. To decide how the ideas connect, think about your purpose for writing the research report.

For example, suppose you are writing a report about Napoleon's retreat from Moscow. You might choose to create an outline using the sequence of events or using the causes and effects that led to the destruction of the Grand Army. Your outline would reflect your purpose.

1 An outline begins with a statement of purpose.

2 An outline is divided into two or more major sections, introduced by Roman numerals (I, II).

3 Each major section is divided into two or more subsections introduced by capital letters (A, B).

4 The subsections may be divided into sub-subsections introduced by Arabic numerals (1, 2).

Chronological outline

(1) Purpose: Describe the events that led to Napoleon's defeat in Russia.

(2) I. Napoleon's defeat in Russia
- A. June 1812
  - 1. march into Russia
  - 2. scorched-earth policy
- B. September 7, 1812
  - 1. Battle of Borodino
  - 2. narrow victory for the French
- C. September 14, 1812
  - 1. arrival in Moscow
  - 2. city in flames

(2) II. Napoleon's defeat in Russia
- A. mid-October 1812
  - 1. waiting for offer of peace
  - 2. too late to advance
  - 3. begins retreat from Moscow
- B. early November 1812
  - 1. retreat in snow storm
  - 2. attack by Russians

Cause-and-effect outline

Purpose: Describe the reasons for Napoleon's defeat in Russia.

I. Napoleon's mistakes
- (3) A. troops not loyal to Napoleon
- B. waited too long to retreat
  - (4) 1. starvation
  - 2. winter snows

II. Russian tactics
- A. scorched-earth policy
- B. no offer of peace from the czar
- C. attacks on the retreating army

STRATEGY: INTERPRET THE OUTLINE TO WRITE A RESEARCH REPORT.

Use the organization of the outline to choose signal words that match your purpose for writing.

Signal words to show time-order	*Signal words to show cause and effect*
dates: September 14, 1812	*because*
time frames: for five weeks	*so*
order: first, next, then, last	*as a result*

Applying the Skill

CREATE YOUR OWN OUTLINE. Read Chapter 13, "The Great War, 1914–1918." Create an outline that shows a sequence of events leading up to World War I or that shows the series of causes and effects that resulted in the war. Choose appropriate signal words to write a rough draft from your outline.

R35

4.7 Creating Oral Presentations

When you **CREATE AN ORAL PRESENTATION,** you prepare a speech or a talk to give before an audience. The object of an oral presentation is to provide information about a particular topic or to persuade an audience to think or act in a particular way.

Understanding the Skill

STRATEGY: CHOOSE A TOPIC. The following is an excerpt from a student's speech in support of recycling.

❶ **State your theme or point of view.**

❷ **Include facts or arguments to support your theme.**

❸ **Choose words and images that reflect the theme.** The comparison to Disneyland is a visual image that helps to communicate the amount of waste in the Fresh Kills Landfill.

❶ To help preserve the earth's dwindling natural resources, Americans need to get serious about recycling. At the moment, our track record is not very good. ❷ Although people in the United States account for less than 5% of the world's population, they use 40% of the world's resources, and generate a huge amount of waste. The Fresh Kills Landfill, which serves New York City, is a prime example. It contains so much garbage that Fresh Kills Landfill is ❸ four times the size of Disneyland. And that's just New York's garbage.

With so many people throwing so much away, is there any point in trying to change things? The answer is yes! Recyling one glass bottle saves enough energy to light a 100-watt light bulb for four hours. Twenty-five million trees could be saved every year by recycling just 10% of our newspapers. Making new aluminum products from recycled aluminum, rather than from bauxite, uses 95% less energy. By increasing the recycling of our bottles, jars, cans, and paper, we could dramatically reduce our demand for trees, fossil fuels, and other precious resources.

STRATEGY: USE THESE TIPS FOR SUCCESSFUL ORAL PRESENTATIONS.

- Maintain eye contact with your audience.
- Use gestures and body language to emphasize main points.
- Pace yourself. Speak slowly and distinctly.
- Vary your tone to help bring out the message you wish to make.

STRATEGY: PRACTICE THE PRESENTATION in front of a mirror or ask a friend or family member to listen to your presentation and give you feedback.

Applying the Skill

CREATE YOUR OWN ORAL PRESENTATION. Turn to Chapter 6. Choose a topic from the "New" section of one of the "Changing Idea" boxes on pages 192, 195, 204, or 208. Create an oral presentation in which you explain how the idea was new and why it was important. Use information from the chapter to support your chosen idea.

4.8 Creating Written Presentations

CREATING A WRITTEN PRESENTATION means writing an in-depth report on a topic in history. Your objective may be to inform or to support a particular point of view. To succeed, your writing must be clear and well organized. For additional information on creating a historical research paper, see Skillbuilder 4.1, Writing for Social Studies.

Understanding the Skill

STRATEGY: CREATE AN OUTLINE such as the one below. Use it as a guide to write your presentation.

1 **State the main idea.**

2 **Organize the information by category.**

3 **Add supporting facts and details.**

1 *The Incan Empire*

I. The Inca created a large and highly developed empire.

2 A. A Theocracy
1. Members of only 11 families could rule
2. Rulers believed to be descendants of the sun god
3. Religion supported the state; worship of the sun god, Inti, amounted to worship of the king

B. Expansion
1. Rulers conquered new territories to acquire wealth
2. Pachacuti created the largest empire in the Americas
3. Size by 1500: 2,500 miles along western coast, 16 million people

C. Unifying strategies
3 1. Rulers practiced diplomacy
2. Rulers imposed a single official language, Quechua
3. Schools taught conquered peoples the Incan ways
4. Extensive system of roads led to Cuzco, the capital

D. Early socialism
1. Supported aged and disabled
2. Rewarded citizens' labor with food and beer

E. Culturally advanced
1. Elaborate calendar system
2. Artisans created works in gold and silver
3. Exception: no writing system, but oral tradition

R37

4.8 (Continued)

STRATEGY: EDIT AND REVISE YOUR PRESENTATION.

1. **Use punctuation marks for their correct purposes.** A comma follows a prepositional phrase at the beginning of a sentence.
2. **Capitalize all proper nouns.** Three lines under a letter means to capitalize.
3. **Check spelling with both an electronic spell checker and a dictionary.**
4. **Use consistent verb tense.** Use past tense for events in the past.
5. **Check for common agreement errors.** Subjects and verbs must agree in person and number.
6. **Use correct sentence structure.** Every sentence must have a subject and a verb.

The Incan Empire

The Inca created the largest empire ever seen in the Americas. Despite its size **1** *, the Incan Empire was highly unified. Its government was diplomatic, bureaucratic, and socialist in nature, and its ruler was believed to be a god-king.*

The Incan ruler was selected from one of 11 noble families, who were believed to have descended from **2** *inti, the sun god. Religion therefore supported the state, for worship of the sun god amounted to worship of the king. Thus, the empire was a theocracy, which is a state believed to be ruled directly by divine guidance.*

The empire's expansion was largely the result of an important tradition: dead rulers retained the wealth they **3** *ac^c^umulated during their lives. To acquire wealth of their own, succeeding rulers often attempted to conquer new territories. One such ruler, Pachacuti, conquered all of Peru and many neighboring lands as well. By 1500, the Incan Empire extended 2,500 miles along the coast of western South America and included an estimated 16 million people.*

Incan rulers used a number of strategies to achieve unification. They practiced diplomacy by allowing conquered peoples to retain their own customs as long as they were loyal to the state. The Inca imposed a single official language, Quechua, to be used throughout the empire. They founded schools to teach Incan ways. They **4** *~~build~~ built 14,000 miles of roads and bridges, which connected cities in conquered areas with Cuzco, the Incan capital.*

The government's concern for the welfare of its citizens suggests an early form of socialism. Citizens worked for the state and, in turn, were taken care of. At public feasts, food and beer **5** *~~was~~ were distributed as a reward for labor. In addition, the aged and disabled often received state support.*

Among the many cultural achievements of the Inca were the development of an elaborate calendar system and the creation of beautiful works in gold and silver. Surprisingly, **6** *the Inca had no system of writing. They preserved their history and literature by means of an oral tradition.*

Applying the Skill

CREATE A TWO-PAGE WRITTEN PRESENTATION on a topic of historical importance that interests you.

Skillbuilder Handbook

R38

Primary Source Handbook

CONTENTS

R39

More About . . .

The Rig Veda

The Rig Veda contains some complex riddles. These riddles have presented problems for Western scholars translating the Rig Veda. One scholar notes that the riddles are just as puzzling in the original Sanskrit as they are in English. It seems that puzzlement may have been one of the goals of the Rig Veda's creators. Most of the riddles are deliberately constructed to be unsolvable, thus emphasizing to the reader just how much is unknowable in the universe. Here is an example of a riddle from another hymn:

> Two birds, friends joined together,
> clutch the same tree. One of
> them eats the sweet fruit; the
> other looks on without eating.

The birds may represent humans, while the tree is knowledge and eternal life. The point of the riddle is that some people will be rewarded with these things while others will not.

Vocabulary Note
immortality: not subject to death

from the Rig Veda

SETTING THE STAGE The Rig Veda is one of the sacred scriptures of the Aryans, who invaded India around 1500 B.C. The oldest of four Vedas, or books of wisdom, it contains 1,028 hymns to Aryan gods. The "Creation Hymn" speculates about how the world was created.

PRIMARY SOURCE

There was neither non-existence nor existence then; there was neither the realm of space nor the sky which is beyond. What stirred? Where? In whose protection? Was there water, bottomlessly deep?

There was neither death nor immortality then. There was no distinguishing sign of night nor of day. That one breathed, windless, by its own impulse. Other than that there was nothing beyond.

Darkness was hidden by darkness in the beginning; with no distinguishing sign, all this was water. The life force that was covered with emptiness, that one arose through the power of heat.

Desire came upon that one in the beginning; that was the first seed of mind. Poets seeking in their heart with wisdom found the bond of existence in non-existence.

Their cord was extended across. Was there below? Was there above? There were seed-placers; there were powers. There was impulse beneath; there was giving-forth above.

Who really knows? Who will here proclaim it? Whence was it produced? Whence is this creation? The gods came afterwards, with the creation of this universe. Who then knows whence it has arisen?

Whence this creation has arisen—perhaps it formed itself, or perhaps it did not—the one who looks down on it, in the highest heaven, only he knows—or perhaps he does not know.

▲ Indra, the Aryan god of war, seated on an elephant

DOCUMENT-BASED QUESTIONS

1. *What is the basic two-part structure of the "Creation Hymn"?*
2. *Who knows how the universe was created, according to the "Creation Hymn"?*
3. *What questions does the hymn raise about how the universe was created? What answers does it give?*
4. *What are you told about "that one" who is mentioned in the hymn?*
5. *What might the following words mean: "The gods came afterwards, with the creation of this universe"?*

ANSWERS TO DOCUMENT-BASED QUESTIONS

1. First it speculates about what existed before the world was created; then, it asks questions about how the world was created.
2. Only he who looks down on it knows, or perhaps no one at all knows.
3. The poem asks what there was before creation, what started creation, and who really knows how the universe was created. It suggests that before creation, there was only darkness, water, and a life force that began creation. The poem answers that no one really knows how the universe was created, except perhaps the one who looks down on it.
4. Readers are told that "that one" caused itself to breathe, that it arose through the power of heat, and that desire created a life force that then could create the world.
5. These words suggest that in Aryan thought the gods are not the source of creation.

from the King James Bible, Psalm 23

SETTING THE STAGE The Book of Psalms is the hymnal of ancient Israel. Most of the psalms were written to be used during worship in the temple. Many have been traditionally attributed to King David, who ruled over Israel around 1000 B.C. The Book of Psalms contains 150 songs on a variety of topics. Psalm 23 focuses on the relationship between God and the individual.

PRIMARY SOURCE

The Lord is my shepherd;
I shall not want.
He maketh me to lie down in green pastures;
he leadeth me beside the still waters;

he restoreth my soul.
He leadeth me in the paths of righteousness
for his name's sake.

Yea, though I walk through the valley
of the shadow of death,

I will fear no evil: for thou art with me;
thy rod and thy staff they comfort me.

Thou preparest a table before me
in the presence of mine enemies:

Thou anointest my head with oil; my cup runneth over.

Surely goodness and mercy shall follow me
all the days of my life,

and I will dwell in the house of the Lord forever.

▲ David, the young shepherd, plays his pipe and a bell.

DOCUMENT-BASED QUESTIONS

1. *The rod and the staff are two tools of the shepherd. What does this suggest about the role of the Lord, "my shepherd"?*
2. *What kind of relationship does the person speaking have with the Lord?*
3. *In this psalm, the Lord is also presented as a generous host. What are some examples of this?*
4. *Why does the speaker expect goodness and mercy to follow him all the days of his life?*

Primary Source Handbook

More About . . .

Psalm 23

Psalm 23 is probably the most familiar of all the psalms. It is sometimes associated with funerals and death. It has also made its way into popular music for hundreds of years. It has appeared in everything from classical compositions of the 18th century to contemporary rap, reggae, and gospel.

More About . . .

King David

Psalm 23 is one of several attributed to King David. According to the Bible, when David was young, he invented musical instruments and was a talented lyre player (a lyre is a type of harp). He also gained recognition for his singing ability. A Jewish legend tells of how David came to compose the psalms. When he went to sleep, David hung his lyre over his bed. During the night, the four winds would pluck the strings of his lyre, and David would awaken and sing along. These songs, led by the winds, eventually became the psalms. While there is much debate over how many psalms David actually wrote, he remains strongly associated with them.

Vocabulary Note

anointest: to apply oil to the body for grooming

psalm: a sacred song or hymn

ANSWERS TO DOCUMENT-BASED QUESTIONS

1. The Lord guides and protects the speaker of the psalm as a shepherd protects his flock.
2. The speaker has a close personal relationship with the Lord, from whom he receives special protection and care.
3. The Lord offers his guest food, oil for grooming, and an overflowing cup.
4. *Possible Answers:* because the Lord has always taken care of him in the past; because he trusts the Lord and the strength of their relationship.

More About . . .

The Analects

The *Analects* were not written down by Confucius himself but by his disciples. The process of writing down the vast amount of Confucian wisdom may have taken centuries. The *Analects* were meant to be studied and meditated upon over the course of a lifetime, and many of the passages became sayings because people memorized the entire work.

More About . . .

Confucian Philosophy

The *Analects* emphasizes two virtues: humanity and justice. Confucius believed that societies should be based on humanity, or *jen*. While several of his sayings involve humaneness, he never gives a clear definition of it, except for implying that to be humane is to love one another. Confucius' virtue of justice is synonymous with "duty" and "principle." He was very critical of political leaders who did things solely for their own advantage, and he lived his life in accordance with his beliefs. Confucius became a teacher in order to share his wisdom instead of using it for political gain.

Vocabulary Note
prudence: good judgment
reciprocity: a relationship consisting of mutual giving and taking
zealous: very committed

from the Analects of Confucius

SETTING THE STAGE The *Analects (analect* means "a selection") is a short collection of about 500 sayings, dialogues, and brief stories, that was put together over a period of many years following Confucius' death. The *Analects* presents Confucius' teachings on how people should live to create an orderly and just society. Over time, Confucian thought became the basis for the Chinese system of government and remained a part of Chinese life into the 20th century.

PRIMARY SOURCE

The Master [Confucius] said: "Don't worry if people don't recognize your merits; worry that you may not recognize theirs." (1.16)

The Master said: "To study without thinking is futile [useless]. To think without studying is dangerous." (2.15)

Lord Ji Kang asked: "What should I do in order to make the people respectful, loyal, and zealous?" The Master said: "Approach them with dignity and they will be respectful. Be yourself a good son and a kind father, and they will be loyal. Raise the good and train the incompetent, and they will be zealous." (2.20)

The Master said: "Authority without generosity, ceremony without reverence, mourning without grief—these, I cannot bear to contemplate." (3.26)

The Master said: "Don't worry if you are without a position; worry lest you do not deserve a position. Do not worry if you are not famous; worry lest you do not deserve to be famous." (4.14)

The Master said: "Without ritual, courtesy is tiresome; without ritual, prudence is timid; without ritual, bravery is quarrelsome; without ritual, frankness is hurtful. When gentlemen treat their kin generously, common people are attracted to goodness; when old ties are not forgotten, common people are not fickle." (8.2)

Zingong asked: "Is there any single word that could guide one's entire life?" The master said: "Should it not be *reciprocity?* What you do not wish for yourself, do not do to others." (15.24)

▲ Confucius

DOCUMENT-BASED QUESTIONS

1. *What kinds of behavior does Confucius talk about in the* Analects?
2. *Do you think Confucius views human nature in an optimistic or a pessimistic way? Explain your opinion.*
3. *What does Confucius mean by* reciprocity?
4. *What kind of person does Confucius seem to be?*
5. *Are the teachings in the* Analects *surprising in any way? Explain.*
6. *Does Confucius seem more concerned with individual behavior or with behavior toward others?*

ANSWERS TO DOCUMENT-BASED QUESTIONS

1. He talks about how a person should view his or her own worth and how a person should relate to others. He emphasizes courtesy, respect, kindness, and courage.
2. Students who think Confucius' view is optimistic might say that he offers his teachings with the expectation that people can learn from them and will change their behavior. Those who think he is pessimistic might point out his description of negative behavior in 2.15, 3.26, and 8.2.
3. Reciprocity means treating others as you would like them to treat you.
4. Confucius' aim is to live a moral and virtuous life and to teach others to live such a life. He looks for the most ethical, courteous, and generous way to respond to every situation. He is humble, but he is also firm in stating his views and ideas.
5. *Possible Answer:* Students may express surprise that some of the ideas are so similar to those found in the teachings of other cultures and religions, especially the similarity of 15.24 to the golden rule.
6. Most students will say that Confucius seems most concerned with behavior toward others. The teachings in 2.15 and 4.14 are directly concerned with individual behavior; the rest of the teachings are concerned with behavior toward others or virtuous behavior in general.

from History of the Peloponnesian War

by Thucydides

SETTING THE STAGE Thucydides was a Greek historian who wrote about the bitter 27-year-long Peloponnesian War between Athens and Sparta. As one of the ten military leaders of Athens, Thucydides was probably in attendance when Pericles, the greatest Athenian statesman of his time, gave a funeral oration. This speech honored the Athenian warriors who had been killed during the first year of the war. In the following excerpt, Pericles speaks of the distinctive qualities of Athens.

PRIMARY SOURCE

Our love of what is beautiful does not lead to extravagance; our love of the mind does not make us soft. We regard wealth as something to be properly used, rather than as something to boast about. As for poverty, no one need be ashamed to admit it: the real shame is in not taking practical measures to escape from it. Here each individual is interested not only in his own affairs but in the affairs of state as well: even those who are mostly occupied with their own business are extremely well-informed on general politics—this is a peculiarity of ours: we do not say that a man who takes no interest in politics is a man who minds his own business; we say that he has no business here at all. We Athenians, in our own persons, take our decisions on policy or submit them to proper discussions: for we do not think that there is an incompatibility between words and deeds; the worst thing is to rush into action before the consequences have been properly debated. And this is another point where we differ from other people. We are capable at the same time of taking risks and of estimating them beforehand. Others are brave out of ignorance; and, when they stop to think, they begin to fear. But the man who can most truly be accounted brave is he who best knows the meaning of what is sweet in life and of what is terrible, and then goes out undeterred to meet what is to come.

▲ Bust of Pericles; Roman copy of the Greek original

More About . . .

Pericles' Funeral Oration

Thucydides includes an account of what a public funeral would have involved. Two days before the ceremony, the bones of the dead were put in a tent where people gave offerings. On the day of the ceremony, a funeral procession began, with wagons bearing coffins. There was a coffin for the remains of members of each tribe. One wagon was empty; it represented those missing in battle. Everyone, including foreigners, was allowed to take part in the ceremony. The procession stopped just outside the city walls at a spot designated for public burial, and this is where Pericles gave his oration.

More About . . .

Pericles

At the time Pericles delivered his funeral oration, it was unclear if Athens was going to win the war. Part of Pericles' strategy was to bring Athenians into walled cities for their protection, but this led to terrible outbreaks of bubonic plague. Pericles himself died of the disease in 429 B.C.

Vocabulary Note
incompatibility: not in harmony
undeterred: not prevented

DOCUMENT-BASED QUESTIONS

1. *Why is it important to Pericles that all citizens participate in public life?*
2. *What seems to be the Athenians' attitude toward politics?*
3. *Why do the Athenians view public discussion as useful before taking action?*
4. *In what ways do Athenians lead a balanced life, according to Pericles?*
5. *What is Pericles's definition of courage?*
6. *According to Pericles, who has political power in Athens?*

ANSWERS TO DOCUMENT-BASED QUESTIONS

1. According to Pericles, all citizens need to take an active interest in public life. In a democracy, power is in the hands of the whole people, which requires that all citizens stay involved. Also, for the Athenians the well-being of the community is everyone's business.
2. The Athenians believed that every individual should take an active interest in politics.
3. The Athenians discuss possible risks before they take action, so they know what they are getting into.
4. Their interests in artistic and intellectual matters do not make them shrink from the responsibilities of politics and war.
5. Courage means accurately assessing the risks of a particular course of action and then still going ahead if duty requires it.
6. All Athenian citizens have power, not just a single person or small group.

More About . . .

The Trial of Socrates

Throughout the *Apology*, Socrates claims that most Athenians are biased against him. He tells the jury "…I have already been accused in your hearing by a great many people for a great many years, though without a word of truth…"

Socrates was very concerned that the biases of the jury would affect the outcome of his trial, and in fact they did. People were biased against him for several reasons. Many Athenians were upset following the end of the Peloponnesian War. Athens had become chaotic and politically unstable as various ruling factions overthrew each other, and Socrates was seen as an instigator.

He publicly criticized the democracy and was characterized as anti-democratic, although he had been equally critical of the oligarchy when it was in power. His physical appearance also turned people against him. Socrates lived in a state of self-imposed poverty, always walking barefoot and sometimes wearing the same old clothes for weeks. The Athenians saw this as a deliberate rejection of their sumptuous lifestyle.

Vocabulary Note

acquittal: finding someone to be not guilty
impudence: offensively bold behavior
oligarchy: government by a few

from the Apology

by Plato

SETTING THE STAGE Socrates and Plato were two of the most important philosophers in history. Plato studied under Socrates in Athens. Though Socrates was popular with the young, some Athenians viewed him as a threat to Athenian traditions and ideals. In 399 B.C., a group of citizens came together to prosecute him, charging him with neglecting the gods of Athens and corrupting its youth. Socrates was brought to trial. A jury of 500 citizens heard the charges against him; then Socrates presented his own defense. By a majority of votes, Socrates was sentenced to death. Plato attended Socrates' trial and later based the *Apology* on his memory of what he had heard. In the following excerpt, Socrates addresses the jury.

PRIMARY SOURCE

Well, gentlemen, for the sake of a very small gain in time you are going to earn the reputation—and the blame from those who wish to disparage [belittle] our city—of having put Socrates to death, "that wise man"—because they will say I am wise even if I am not, these people who want to find fault with you. If you had waited just a little while, you would have had your way in the course of nature. You can see that I am well on in life and near to death. . . .

No doubt you think, gentlemen, that I have been condemned for lack of the arguments which I could have used if I had thought it right to leave nothing unsaid or undone to secure my acquittal. But that is very far from the truth. It is not a lack of arguments that has caused my condemnation, but a lack of effrontery [rude boldness] and impudence, and the fact that I have refused to address you in the way which would give you most pleasure. You would have liked to hear me weep and wail, doing and saying all sorts of things which I regard as unworthy of myself, but which you are used to hearing from other people. But I did not think then that I ought to stoop to servility [disgracefully humble behavior] because I was in danger, and I do not regret now the way in which I pleaded my case. I would much rather die as the result of this defense than live as the result of the other sort. In a court of law, just as in warfare, neither I nor any other ought to use his wits to escape death by any means. In battle it is often obvious that you could escape being killed by giving up your arms and throwing yourself upon the mercy of your pursuers, and in every kind of danger there are plenty of devices for avoiding death if you are unscrupulous enough to stick at nothing. But I suggest, gentlemen, that the difficulty is not so much to escape death; the real difficulty is to escape from doing wrong, which is far more fleet of foot.

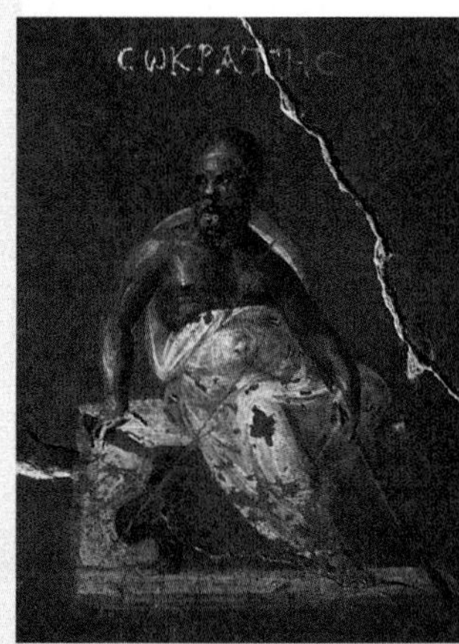

▲ Roman fresco painting of Socrates

DOCUMENT-BASED QUESTIONS

1. *Socrates says that if his accusers would have waited, they could have had what they wanted. What do they want?*
2. *Socrates insists that he would rather die than have to defend himself in a different way. What would be so wrong if Socrates had defended himself in a different way?*
3. *What does Socrates mean when he says that evil is more of a threat to people than death?*
4. *Why doesn't Socrates tell the jury what it wants to hear?*
5. *What values do you think are most important to Socrates?*

ANSWERS TO DOCUMENT-BASED QUESTIONS

1. They want him dead.
2. He would be violating his own moral principles. Socrates does not believe that he has done anything wrong; he is not going to beg for mercy or humiliate himself.
3. Everyone will eventually die, but death is not an evil by itself. Evil is more of a threat than death, perhaps because we have to choose constantly between good and evil in our lives.
4. He thought that telling the jury what it wanted to hear would compromise his principles.
5. Socrates has devoted his life to virtue. It is more important for him to do right than to save his own life. He feels that moral principles should not be compromised even at the risk of death.

from the Annals

by Tacitus

SETTING THE STAGE Tacitus was one of the greatest historians of ancient Rome. He lived in troubled times (A.D. 56–120) when plague and fire frequently ravaged Rome. The *Annals* deals with events from the death of Augustus in A.D. 14 to the death of Nero in A.D. 68. In the following excerpt, Tacitus tells about a terrible fire that swept through Rome in A.D. 64. The fire began near the Circus Maximus, an arena in which chariot races were held, and raged out of control for several days. At the time, Nero was emperor. Many Romans believed that Nero himself had set fire to the city in order to rebuild it according to his own designs.

PRIMARY SOURCE

Now started the most terrible and destructive fire which Rome had ever experienced. It began in the Circus, where it adjoins the . . . hills. Breaking out in shops selling inflammable goods, and fanned by the wind, the conflagration [large fire] instantly grew and swept the whole length of the Circus. There were no walled mansions or temples, or any other obstructions which could arrest it. First, the fire swept violently over the level spaces. Then it climbed the hills—but returned to ravage the lower ground again. It outstripped every countermeasure. The ancient city's narrow winding streets and irregular blocks encouraged its progress.

Terrified, shrieking women, helpless old and young, people intent on their own safety, people unselfishly supporting invalids or waiting for them, fugitives and lingerers alike—all heightened the confusion. When people looked back, menacing flames sprang up before them or outflanked them. When they escaped to a neighboring quarter, the fire followed—even districts believed remote proved to be involved. Finally, with no idea where or what to flee, they crowded on to the country roads, or lay in the fields. Some who had lost everything—even their food for the day—could have escaped, but preferred to die. So did others, who had failed to rescue their loved ones. Nobody dared fight the flames. Attempts to do so were prevented by menacing gangs. Torches, too, were openly thrown in, by men crying that they acted under orders. Perhaps they had received orders. Or they may just have wanted to plunder unhampered.

Nero was at Antium. He only returned to the city when the fire was approaching the mansion he had built to link the Gardens of Maecenas to the Palatine. The flames could not be prevented from overwhelming the whole of the Palatine, including his palace. Nevertheless, for the relief of the homeless, fugitive masses he threw open the Field of Mars, including Agrippa's public buildings, and even his own gardens. Nero also constructed emergency accommodation for the destitute [poor] multitude. Food was brought from Ostia and neighboring towns, and the price of corn was cut. . . . Yet these measures, for all their popular character, earned no gratitude. For a rumor had spread that, while the city was burning, Nero had gone to his private stage and, comparing modern calamities with ancient, had sung of the destruction of Troy. . . .

[P]eople believed that Nero was ambitious to found a new city to be called after himself.

DOCUMENT-BASED QUESTIONS

1. *Who might have ordered the menacing gangs to keep the fire burning?*
2. *What might have been Nero's motive if he indeed caused the fire to be started?*
3. *What actions of Nero suggest that he may not have ordered the burning of Rome?*
4. *What effect might a public calamity such as a fire or an earthquake have on political stability?*
5. *What different interpretations might the people of the time have given to such an event?*
6. *What might you have done to save yourself in the burning of Rome?*

Primary Source Handbook

More About . . .

The Annals

Tacitus and his fellow Romans approached history differently from the way in which we do today. In Book 4 of the *Annals*, Tacitus writes:

> Descriptions of countries, the vicissitudes of battles, commanders dying on the field of honour, such are the episodes that arrest and renew the interest of the reader. . .

For the Romans, written history was entertainment. Tacitus also wrote the *Annals* to instill patriotism and to glorify Rome for members of the upperclass—usually the only ones able to read. Roman historians were seen as artists, and they attempted to present history using oratorical skills. Historical events were sometimes depicted in the form of speeches, using archaic Latin words to indicate the historical setting.

As time passed and people began to rely on historians for less biased accounts, the accuracy of Tacitus' work was questioned. The *Annals* were at one point considered a forgery, but this has been disproven. Today, many scholars believe that most of Tacitus' work is accurate.

Vocabulary Note

annals: a history or chronological sequence of events

Palatine: one of the seven hills of ancient Rome; the location of many imperial palaces

ANSWERS TO DOCUMENT-BASED QUESTIONS

1. Possibly Nero, who might have wished the fire to consume Rome.
2. The fire afforded him the opportunity to rebuild the city according to his own designs.
3. Nero responded promptly and even generously to the victims of the fire, opening his own gardens, building temporary housing, and importing food.
4. In a political capital such as Rome, such an event might result in political turmoil and chaos that would threaten the stability of the state.
5. Some probably saw it as a political plot on the part of the emperor to solidify his power and remake Rome in his own image; others probably saw it as a sign of displeasure on the part of the gods with Rome's moral failings.
6. Some students might suggest fleeing to the Tiber and following the river out of Rome. Others might suggest hiding underground in basements, caves, and dungeons.

More About . . .

The Qur'an

Oral recitation of the Qur'an is extremely important to Muslims. Some professional Qur'anic reciters are famous throughout the Islamic world, and their recordings sell many copies. These recordings are played throughout the day in public places.

More About . . .

Muhammad and His Wife

When Muhammad was 25 years old, he married a woman named Khadija. She was 15 years older than he and quite wealthy. They came to know each other through business dealings, and Khadija eventually proposed to Muhammad because she admired his character and honesty.

Because he was poor, Muhammad was reluctant to marry her at first, but he finally accepted. Later, when Muhammad received the first revelation from the archangel Gabriel, he doubted himself. He rushed back to his wife and told her that he was either going insane or becoming a poet. Khadija brought Muhammad to visit her cousin, a Christian, who confirmed that Muhammad had been chosen as a prophet. He also told Muhammad that, like other prophets, he would be ostracized when he spoke to the world about his revelations.

Vocabulary Note

alms: money or goods given as charity to the poor

sovereign: one that exercises supreme authority

from the Qur'an

SETTING THE STAGE In about A.D. 610, when the prophet Muhammad was 40 years old, he is said to have received his first visit from the archangel Gabriel. According to tradition, during this visit Gabriel revealed the Word of God to Muhammad. This revelation, or act of revealing, was the first of many experienced by Muhammad throughout his life. Together, these revelations formed the basis of the faith called Islam, which literally means "surrender to the will of Allah" (God). At first Muhammad reported God's revelations orally, and his followers memorized them and recited them in ritual prayers. Later the revelations were written down in a book called the Qur'an, which means "recitation."

PRIMARY SOURCE

The Exordium

In the Name of God, the Compassionate, the Merciful
Praise be to God, Lord of the Universe,
The Compassionate, the Merciful,
Sovereign of the Day of Judgment!
You alone we worship, and to You alone we turn for help.
Guide us to the straight path,
The path of those whom You have favored,
Not of those who have incurred Your wrath,
Nor of those who have gone astray.

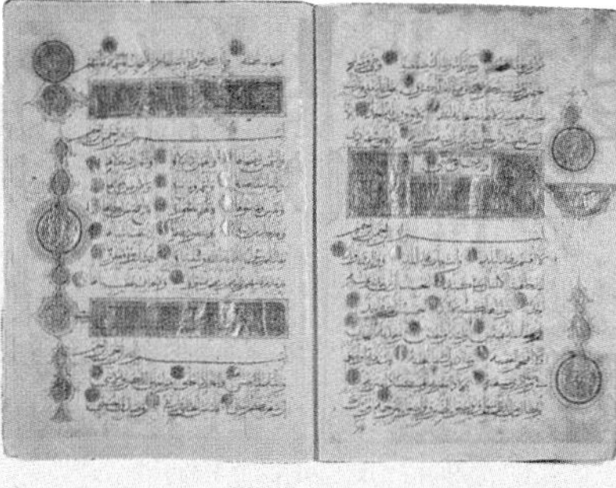

▲ Qur'an with colored inscriptions and decorative medallions from the 12th or 13th century

Faith in God

In the Name of God, the Compassionate, the Merciful
All that is in the heavens and the earth gives glory to God. He is the Mighty, the Wise One.

It is He that has sovereignty over the heavens and the earth. He ordains life and death, and has power over all things.

He is the First and the Last, the Visible and the Unseen. He has knowledge of all things.

It was He who created the heavens and the earth in six days, and then mounted the throne. He knows all that goes into the earth and all that emerges from it, all that comes down from heaven and all that ascends to it. He is with you wherever you are. God is cognizant [aware] of all your actions.

He has sovereignty over the heavens and the earth. To God shall all things return. He causes the night to pass into the day, and causes the day to pass into the night. He has knowledge of the inmost thoughts of men.

Have faith in God and His Apostle and give in alms of that which He has made your inheritance; for whoever of you believes and gives in alms shall be richly rewarded.

And what cause have you not to believe in God, when the Apostle calls on you to have faith in your Lord, who has made a covenant [agreement] with you, if you are true believers?

DOCUMENT-BASED QUESTIONS

1. Exordium *means a beginning or introduction. What qualities of God are emphasized in "The Exordium"?*
2. *What might be the purpose of the first five paragraphs in "Faith in God"?*
3. *What are some of the qualities and actions that make a person righteous?*
4. *How do these excerpts support the idea of "God, the Compassionate, the Merciful"?*
5. *How might the words of the Qur'an be applied to governments or social groups?*
6. *What kind of rules or guidelines for behavior do you think a person should follow in life? How do these compare with those in the Qur'an?*

ANSWERS TO DOCUMENT-BASED QUESTIONS

1. God is praised as compassionate, merciful, and sovereign over all the universe.
2. The first five paragraphs in this section give reasons why a person should have faith in God.
3. Believing in God, being mindful of what God has done for people, practicing charity and goodness, trusting in God, and proclaiming God's goodness all make a person righteous.
4. God has created the world for people to live in; God is aware of everyone's actions; God encourages people to live a virtuous life.
5. Countries might practice charity toward poorer or less fortunate nations; governments might incorporate principles of religion into their laws; businesses might care more about practicing charity and kindness than making profits.
6. Answers will vary. Encourage students to be specific in describing their rules or guidelines for behavior and to base their comparisons and contrasts on specific passages in the Qur'an.

from The Pillow Book

by Sei Shōnagon

SETTING THE STAGE Sei Shōnagon served as a lady in waiting to Empress Sadako during the last decade of the 900s. During this period, Shōnagon kept a diary recording many aspects of court life. This diary was published as *The Pillow Book,* a collection of character sketches, lists, anecdotes, and poems that provides a vivid glimpse into the lives of the Japanese nobility during the Heian period (794–1185). During this period, the capital was moved to Heian, the present-day city of Kyoto, and a highly refined court society arose among the upper class. The book reveals Shōnagon as an intelligent woman who enjoyed conversing and matching wits with men as equals. Scholar and translator Arthur Waley has called the collection of observations and anecdotes of Heian court life "the most important document of the period that we possess."

PRIMARY SOURCE

from "Hateful Things"

One is in a hurry to leave, but one's visitor keeps chattering away. If it is someone of no importance, one can get rid of him by saying, "You must tell me all about it next time"; but, should it be the sort of visitor whose presence commands one's best behavior, the situation is hateful indeed. . . .

A man who has nothing in particular to recommend him discusses all sorts of subjects at random as though he knew everything. . . .

To envy others and to complain about one's own lot; to speak badly about people; to be inquisitive about the most trivial matters and to resent and abuse people for not telling one, or, if one does manage to worm out some facts, to inform everyone in the most detailed fashion as if one had known all from the beginning—oh, how hateful!

One is just about to be told some interesting piece of news when a baby starts crying.

A flight of crows circle about with loud caws.

An admirer has come on a clandestine [secret] visit, but a dog catches sight of him and starts barking. One feels like killing the beast. . . .

One has gone to bed and is about to doze off when a mosquito appears, announcing himself in a reedy voice. One can actually feel the wind made by his wings and, slight though it is, one finds it hateful in the extreme.

A carriage passes with a nasty, creaking noise. Annoying to think that the passengers may not even be aware of this! If I am traveling in someone's carriage and I hear it creaking, I dislike not only the noise but also the owner of the carriage.

One is in the middle of a story when someone butts in and tries to show that he is the only clever person in the room. Such a person is hateful, and so, indeed, is anyone, child or adult, who tries to push himself forward.

One is telling a story about old times when someone breaks in with a little detail that he happens to know, implying that one's own version is inaccurate—disgusting behavior! . . .

A newcomer pushes ahead of the other members in a group; with a knowing look, this person starts laying down the law and forcing advice upon everyone—most hateful.

DOCUMENT-BASED QUESTIONS

1. *What sort of listing does this excerpt provide?*
2. *How would you describe the author, based on the things she finds hateful?*
3. *Murasaki Shikibu, a contemporary, described Shōnagon as self-satisfied. Do you agree or disagree?*
4. *What might Shōnagon's list of hateful things suggest about Heian court life?*
5. *Which item in Shōnagon's list do you find most hateful?*

More About . . .

The Pillow Book

One section of *The Pillow Book*, dated to A.D. 994, tells of how Shōnagon obtained the paper for her book. The brother of Empress Sadako had brought some old notebooks to the palace. These were intended to be used for a history book, but Shōnagon asked if she could have them to make "a pillow." The term *pillow* was used to refer to diaries of this time period. They may have gotten their name because they were often kept in the drawer of the wooden pillows used for sleeping. People kept diaries in their pillows so that they could write down things that occurred to them during the night.

More About . . .

Sei Shōnagon

It is unclear if Sei Shōnagon intended her pillow book to be read by others. It is very disorganized and contains several lists of names that held meaning only for Shōnagon herself. About A.D. 996, a gentleman came to visit Shōnagon and accidentally discovered the book, which he took with him. It was passed around the court and eventually became very popular.

Vocabulary Note

anecdote: a short account of an interesting or humorous incident

ANSWERS TO DOCUMENT-BASED QUESTIONS

1. The writer lists a whole series of things that she finds hateful.
2. Students might describe Shōnagon as proud, arrogant, sensitive.
3. Most students will probably agree, citing Shōnagon's evident appreciation of her own tastes and talents and her contempt for those she considers beneath her. On the other hand, she does not think it is good to be envious or to complain. She criticizes people who are rude or are know-it-alls.
4. It was very refined, with great attention paid to subtle details. This implies a great deal of leisure time for those who participated in court life. These were probably people who did not have to worry about providing for the necessities of life, such as food and shelter.
5. Answers will vary. Accept all reasonable responses.

More About . . .

The Magna Carta

After being signed by King John in 1215, the Magna Carta was revised three times, and the final version of 1225 became law. Hundreds of years later, it remains a part of modern law.

The constitutions of England and Australia are directly descended from it, and the Constitution of the United States is also based on many of the same concepts. For example, the fifth amendment of the Bill of Rights states "No person shall...be deprived of life, liberty, or property, without due process of law," and the sixth states "...the accused shall enjoy the right to a speedy and public trial, by an impartial jury." The rights defined in these amendments are very similar to those of articles 39 and 40 of the Magna Carta.

In England, some of the articles continue to exist as laws. Until 1970, for example, a law of the Magna Carta prohibited the use of fish weirs (a very old type of trap) in rivers to keep them clear for boats. Other laws remain in effect, relatively unchanged. In general, the Magna Carta is the basis for balanced governmental power and protection of certain rights in several countries.

Vocabulary Note

aforesaid: said before

allegation: a statement asserting something without proof

levied: collected

from the Magna Carta

SETTING THE STAGE King John ruled England from 1199 to 1216. When he raised taxes to finance his wars, his nobles revolted. On June 15, 1215, they forced King John to agree to the Magna Carta (Great Charter). This document, drawn up by English nobles and reluctantly approved by the king, guaranteed certain basic political rights.

PRIMARY SOURCE

1. In the first place [I, John,] have granted to God and by this for our present Charter have confirmed, for us and our heirs . . . , that the English church shall be free, and shall have its rights undiminished and its liberties unimpaired. . . . We have also granted to all the free men of our realm for ourselves and our heirs for ever, all the liberties written below, to have and hold, them and their heirs from us and our heirs. . . .

12. No scutage [tax] or aid is to be levied in our realm except by the common counsel of our realm, unless it is for the ransom of our person, the knighting of our eldest son or the first marriage of our eldest daughter; and for these only a reasonable aid is to be levied. Aids from the city of London are to be treated likewise.

13. And the city of London is to have all its ancient liberties and free customs both by land and water. Furthermore, we will and grant that all other cities, boroughs, towns and ports shall have all their liberties and free customs.

20. A free man shall not be amerced [fined] for a trivial offense; and for a serious offense he shall be amerced according to its gravity, saving his livelihood; and a merchant likewise, saving his merchandise; in the same way a villein [serf] shall be amerced saving his wainage [farming tools]; if they fall into our mercy. And none of the aforesaid amercements shall be imposed except by the testimony of reputable men of the neighborhood.

▲ King John signs the Magna Carta.

21. Earls and barons shall not be amerced [fined] except by their peers and only in accordance with the nature of the offense. . . .

38. Henceforth no bailiff shall put anyone on trial by his own unsupported allegation, without bringing credible witnesses to the charge.

39. No free man shall be taken or imprisoned or disseised [dispossessed] or outlawed or exiled or in any way ruined, nor will we go or send against him, except by the lawful judgment of his peers or by the law of the land.

40. To no one will we sell, to no one will we deny or delay right or justice.

DOCUMENT-BASED QUESTIONS

1. *According to Article 1, to whom does the king grant the rights enumerated in the Magna Carta?*
2. *What are some of the liberties granted by the king to his subjects?*
3. *What do Articles 38 and 39 suggest about the fairness of arrests and trials in King John's England?*
4. *What does Article 40 suggest about the king's use of power?*
5. *What impact might the Magna Carta have had on developing ideas of representative government?*

ANSWERS TO DOCUMENT-BASED QUESTIONS

1. To "all the free men of our realm and our heirs forever."
2. Taxes will not be imposed without the consent of a council; no one shall be imprisoned without due process and trial by jury.
3. They suggest that people were often unfairly accused, arrested, and tried and that there needed to be restrictions placed on the king and his agents in this respect.
4. It suggests that abuse of power was common and needed to be restricted.
5. The ways in which the Magna Carta restricted and limited the powers of the king might have served as an example to the colonists of the importance of limiting the power of any central government so that it would not become too powerful.

from the Popol Vuh

SETTING THE STAGE The selection you are about to read is an excerpt from an important Maya work—the *Popol Vuh.* The *Popol Vuh,* or "Book of the Community," contains the Maya story of the creation of the world. It was written not long after the Spanish conquest by an anonymous Maya noble, who may have been trying to keep the work from becoming lost as a result of his people's defeat.

PRIMARY SOURCE

This is the beginning of the Ancient Word, here in this place called Quiché. Here we shall inscribe, we shall implant the Ancient Word, the potential and source for everything done in the citadel of Quiché, in the nation of Quiché people. . . .

This is the account, here it is:
Now it still ripples, now it still murmurs, ripples, it still sighs, still hums, and it is empty under the sky.

Here follow the first words, the first eloquence:

There is not yet one person, one animal, bird, fish, crab, tree, rock, hollow, canyon, meadow, forest. Only the sky alone is there; the face of the earth is not clear. Only the sea alone is pooled under all the sky; there is nothing whatever gathered together. It is at rest; not a single thing stirs. It is held back, kept at rest under the sky.

Whatever there is that might be is simply not there: only the pooled water, only the calm sea, only it alone is pooled.

Whatever might be is simply not there: only murmurs, ripples, in the dark, in the night. Only the Maker, Modeler alone, Sovereign Plumed Serpent, the Bearers, Begetters are in the water, a glittering light. They are there, they are enclosed in quetzal feathers, in blue-green.

Thus the name, "Plumed Serpent." They are great knowers, great thinkers in their very being.

And of course there is the sky, and there is also the Heart of Sky. This is the name of the god, as it is spoken.

And then came his word, he came here to the Sovereign Plumed Serpent, here in the blackness, in the early dawn. He spoke with the Sovereign Plumed Serpent, and they talked, then they thought, then they worried. They agreed with each other, they joined their words, their thoughts. Then it was clear, then they reached accord in the light, and then humanity was clear, when they conceived the growth, the generation of trees, of bushes, and the growth of life, of humankind, in the blackness, in the early dawn, all because of the Heart of Sky, named Hurricane. Thunderbolt Hurricane comes first, the second is Newborn Thunderbolt, and the third is Sudden Thunderbolt. So there were three of them, as Heart of Sky, who came to the Sovereign Plumed Serpent, when the dawn of life was conceived: "How should the sowing be, and the dawning? Who is to be the provider, nurturer?"

"Let it be this way, think about this: this water should be removed, emptied out for the formation of the earth's own plate and platform, then should come the sowing, the dawning of the sky-earth. But there will be no high days and no bright praise for our work, our design, until the rise of the human work, the human design," they said.

DOCUMENT-BASED QUESTIONS

1. *What are some of the names of the gods in this excerpt?*
2. *What are the gods thinking and talking about in this excerpt?*
3. *How do the gods seem to feel about their creation?*
4. *Why do the gods seem to think that humans are necessary to their creation?*
5. *What does this seem to imply about the relationship between gods and humans?*
6. *What surprised you most as you read this excerpt from the* Popol Vuh*?*

More About . . .

The *Popol Vuh*

The Quiché controlled the highlands of Guatemala. At the apex of their power in the late 15th century they ruled 26,000 square miles of territory containing approximately one million inhabitants. In 1524, the Quiché capital of Utatlán was conquered by the Spanish. Most of the nobles were burned at the stake, but a few of the lords managed to escape to a place called Chichicastenango. The *Popol Vuh* was discovered there in 1701. It had been transcribed into Quiché using Latin letters by an unknown transcriber.

More About . . .

Maya Writing

The Maya wrote innumerable texts, ranging from myths like the *Popol Vuh* to history and astronomy books. The Maya writing system consisted of *glyphs*, or symbols that represented words and sounds. The Spanish considered the Maya writing system "pagan" and tried to eliminate it. Most important texts were written on a bark that was covered with plaster to make it white. Nearly all of these were destroyed by the Spanish. The Spanish did teach Maya scribes to write in European script, so certain texts were translated from Maya languages and preserved.

Vocabulary Note
citadel: a stronghold
eloquence: persuasive, powerful speech
quetzal: a brilliant bronze-green and red bird

ANSWERS TO DOCUMENT-BASED QUESTIONS

1. Some of the names are Sovereign Plumed Serpent, Heart of Sky, Thunderbolt Hurricane, Newborn Thunderbolt, and Sudden Thunderbolt.
2. The gods are thinking and talking about the very beginning of the world, their creation.
3. They seem hopeful that humans will praise their work; pleased; optimistic that their design will turn out well; worried about completing their work.
4. To praise the work of the gods and to observe the high days, the days of the sacred calendar.
5. It seems to imply that humans help to define the gods, who can only achieve full consciousness with the cooperation of humans to praise them and their creation.
6. Responses will vary. Ask students why they found a particular aspect of the selection surprising or what they had been expecting instead.

More About . . .

Niccolò Machiavelli

"Machiavellian" means "characterized by self-interest, deceit, and cunning." Machiavelli is seen widely as being unethical, but many scholars argue that this view is not completely accurate. His political theory is often summarized as "the ends justify the means," which, according to popular belief, implies that even the most evil acts are justifiable in order to get what one wants.

The popular misconception of the phrase seems to be the result of mistranslation. A more accurate translation is "in the actions of all men, and especially of princes, where there is no impartial arbiter, one must consider the final result." Machiavelli seems to have believed that ethics had a role in decisions. One of his goals in *The Prince* was to evaluate successful and unsuccessful rulers. He claims that successful rulers keep the public interest in mind instead of personal interest.

Machiavelli did justify violence in politics but saw it as a tool princes could decide to use for the benefit of the public. Unfortunately, he fell victim to political violence himself. In the early 16th century, he was suspected of being involved in a plot against the Medici family, and he was tortured.

Vocabulary Note

consonant: in agreement
patrimony: inheritance
rapine: forcible seizure of another's property

from The Prince

by Niccolò Machiavelli

SETTING THE STAGE Niccolò Machiavelli wrote a political guidebook for Renaissance rulers titled *The Prince* (1513). Machiavelli wrote the book to encourage Lorenzo de' Medici to expand his power in Florence. The book argues for a practical, realistic view of human nature and politics.

PRIMARY SOURCE

A prince should make himself feared in such a way that if he does not gain love, he at any rate avoids hatred; for fear and the absence of hatred may well go together, and will be always attained by one who abstains from interfering with the property of his citizens and subjects or with their women. And when he is obliged to take the life of any one, let him do so when there is a proper justification and manifest reason for it; but above all he must abstain from taking the property of others, for men forget more easily the death of their father than the loss of their patrimony. Then also pretexts for seizing property are never wanting, and one who begins to live by rapine will always find some reason for taking the goods of others, whereas causes for taking life are rarer and more fleeting.

But when the prince is with his army and has a large number of soldiers under his control, then it is extremely necessary that he should not mind being thought cruel; for without this reputation he could not keep an army united or disposed to any duty. Among the noteworthy actions of Hannibal is numbered this, that although he had an enormous army, composed of men of all nations and fighting in foreign countries, there never arose any dissension [disagreement] either among them or against the prince, either in good fortune or in bad. This could not be due to anything but his inhuman cruelty, which together with his infinite other virtues, made him always venerated and terrible in the sight of his soldiers, and without it his other virtues would not have sufficed to produce that effect. Thoughtless writers admire on the one hand his actions, and on the other blame the principal cause of them.

And that it is true that his other virtues would not have sufficed may be seen from the case of Scipio [a famous Roman general and opponent of Hannibal] . . . , whose armies rebelled against him in Spain, which arose from nothing but his excessive kindness, which allowed more license to the soldiers than was consonant with military discipline.

▲ Niccolò Machiavelli

DOCUMENT-BASED QUESTIONS

1. *What does Machiavelli believe is the relationship for a ruler and his people between fear on the one hand and love and hatred on the other?*
2. *Why does Machiavelli say that a ruler must show himself to be capable of cruelty to his army?*
3. *What does Machiavelli cite Hannibal as an example of? Explain.*
4. *How was the Roman general Scipio different from Hannibal?*
5. *Why does Machiavelli consider cruelty a virtue in a leader?*
6. *Are Machiavelli's thoughts on rulers still relevant today? Why or why not?*

ANSWERS TO DOCUMENT-BASED QUESTIONS

1. Machiavelli argues that a prince can be feared without necessarily being either loved or hated by his people.
2. Without demonstrating his capacity for cruelty, a ruler would not be able to maintain the necessary discipline in his army.
3. For Machiavelli, Hannibal is an example of a good ruler because he was not afraid to display cruelty when necessary. This allowed him to maintain discipline in his army through many difficult situations.
4. Scipio's army rebelled against him because he was too kind and gentle with them.
5. Because cruelty enables the ruler to be respected and feared and thus maintain order. This social order allows the ruler to display other virtues that without cruelty he would not be able to exercise.
6. Accept all reasonable responses. In democratic nations, a ruler is no longer all powerful and unrestricted in his exercise of power. The leader must appeal to the people to support his actions. However, in states that are not democratic, Machiavelli's observations still seem to have great authority.

from Utopia

by Sir Thomas More

SETTING THE STAGE Sir Thomas More's *Utopia* is a work of fiction devoted to the exploration of ideas. In 1516, when *Utopia* was published, English society was marked by great extremes in wealth, education, and status. In his book, More criticizes the evils of poverty and wealth that he sees in England. More describes a faraway land called Utopia that does not have the inequalities and injustices of England. Utopian society is governed according to principles of reason. As a result, everyone has work and everyone is educated. Since private property has been abolished there, the citizens have no need for money. Instead, all that is produced is shared equally.

PRIMARY SOURCE

Agriculture is the one pursuit which is common to all, both men and women, without exception. They are all instructed in it from childhood, partly by principles taught in school, partly by field trips to the farms closer to the city as if for recreation. Here they do not merely look on, but, as opportunity arises for bodily exercise, they do the actual work.

Besides agriculture (which is, as I said, common to all), each is taught one particular craft as his own. This is generally either wool-working or linen-making or masonry or metal-working or carpentry. There is no other pursuit which occupies any number worth mentioning. As for clothes, these are of one and the same pattern throughout the island and down the centuries, though there is a distinction between the sexes and between the single and the married. The garments are comely [pleasing] to the eye, convenient for bodily movement, and fit for wear in heat and cold. Each family, I say, does its own tailoring.

Of the other crafts, one is learned by each person, and not the men only, but the women too. The latter as the [women] have the lighter occupations and generally work wool and flax. To the men are committed the remaining more laborious crafts. For the most part, each is brought up in his father's craft, for which most have a natural inclination. But if anyone is attracted to another occupation, he is transferred by adoption to a family pursuing that craft for which he has a liking. Care is taken not only by his father but by the authorities, too, that he will be assigned to a [serious] and honorable householder. Moreover, if anyone after being thoroughly taught one craft desires another also, the same permission is given. Having acquired both, he practices his choice unless the city has more need of the one than of the other.

▲ Title page of a French edition of *Utopia*

DOCUMENT-BASED QUESTIONS

1. *How many occupations does each Utopian have? What are they?*
2. *Why might Utopians all wear clothes cut from the same pattern?*
3. *Most Utopian men learn their father's craft, and most workers follow the same schedules. What are the benefits and drawbacks of such a system?*
4. *What might be some of the advantages of living in Utopia?*
5. *What might be some of the disadvantages of living in Utopia?*
6. *What present-day societies do you think are most like Utopia? Explain.*

More About . . .

Utopia

Thomas More had conflicting views on many of the issues discussed in *Utopia*. He recognized serious problems in Europe at the time but was unsure how to solve them. He decided to write the book following a tradition called *serio ludere*—"to play seriously." The *serio ludere* style appealed to More because he was divided on so many issues. He realized that there were no clear answers to certain questions and therefore resisted making decisions. By "playing seriously" he was able to present an alternative to European society in a playful way.

It is hard to tell how More intended *Utopia* to be received. His dividedness of mind appears in the name of the book itself and in that of its central character. The word "Utopia" is a combination of the Greek words *ou* ("not") and *topos* ("place") with a Latin ending. Together it means "No place." The title of the book is a pun on the Greek word *eutopos*, meaning "good place." More chose the name Hythloday for the adventurer who tells the tale of Utopia. His name means "expert in nonsense." By having an "expert in nonsense" tell the tale of a happy "no place," More downplayed the seriousness of his work.

Vocabulary Note

flax: a plant that yields oil and fiber for textiles

ANSWERS TO DOCUMENT-BASED QUESTIONS

1. Two—each Utopian practices agriculture; in addition, each person practices one other occupation, such as wool-working, linen-making, masonry, metal-working, or carpentry.
2. It is more practical for them to wear the same clothes; the uniform clothing emphasizes that they are all equal; a similar practice is the requirement of wearing school uniforms.
3. Possible benefits—everyone has a place in society; no one is overworked. Possible drawbacks—takes away incentive for people to work hard; discourages innovation; people might lack the freedom to develop their talents.
4. There would probably be a great emphasis on rational schemes, order, and equality. No one would starve or be homeless.
5. Disadvantages might be too much state control, not enough privacy, not enough opportunity for developing individual talents and interests.
6. Answers will vary. Accept all reasonable responses.

More About . . .

The Federalist

It was vital to the formation of the fledgling United States that New York ratify the Constitution, so the Federalists began writing letters to counter attacks by Anti-Federalists. Alexander Hamilton enlisted his friends John Jay and James Madison to help write letters to the New York City press. A year later, Thomas Jefferson called their writings "the best commentary on the principles of government ever written."

More About . . .

Publius

Madison, Jay, and Hamilton wrote under the name "Publius." They chose the name because Publius was a Roman hero responsible for establishing a stable republic in Rome. New Yorkers would not have been surprised to read editorials by classical Romans. At the time, classical Rome and Greece were very popular. The Founding Fathers were often painted as if they were Roman senators, and towns in upstate New York were named Rome, Syracuse, and Romulus.

Vocabulary Note
judicious: exhibiting sound judgment
practicable: possible

from The Federalist, "Number 51"

by James Madison

SETTING THE STAGE James Madison wrote 29 of the essays in *The Federalist* papers to argue in favor of ratifying the Constitution of the United States. In *The Federalist,* "Number 51," Madison explains how the government set up by the Constitution will protect the rights of the people by weakening the power of any interest, or group, to dominate the government.

PRIMARY SOURCE

It is of great importance in a republic not only to guard against the oppression of its rulers, but to guard one part of the society against the injustice of the other part. Different interests necessarily exist in different classes of citizens. If a majority be united by a common interest, the rights of the minority will be insecure. There are but two methods of providing against this evil: the one by creating a will in the community independent of the majority—that is, of the society itself; the other, by comprehending in the society so many separate descriptions of citizens as will render an unjust combination of a majority of the whole very improbable, if not impracticable. . . .

Whilst all authority in it will be derived from and dependent on the society, the society itself will be broken into so many parts, interests and classes of citizens, that the rights of individuals, or of the minority, will be in little danger from interested combinations of the majority. In a free government the security for civil rights must be the same as that for religious rights. It consists in the one case in the multiplicity of interests, and in the other in the multiplicity of sects. . . .

In the extended republic of the United States, and among the great variety of interests, parties, and sects which it embraces, a coalition of a majority of the whole society could seldom take place on any other principles than those of justice and the general good. . . .

It is no less certain that it is important . . . that the larger the society, provided it lie within a practicable sphere, the more duly capable it will be of self-government. And happily for the republican cause, the practicable sphere may be carried to a very great extent by a judicious modification and mixture of the *federal principle.*

▲ James Madison

DOCUMENT-BASED QUESTIONS

1. *Madison argues that society must be protected from abuses by rulers and by whom else?*
2. *What two methods does Madison suggest a society can use to protect minority rights?*
3. *Does Madison regard special interests in a society as a good thing or a bad? Explain.*
4. *Why does Madison believe that a large republic is likely to protect justice?*
5. *Why does Madison believe that a society broken into many parts will not endanger minority rights?*
6. *Does Madison think most people work for the common good or their own interests? Explain.*

ANSWERS TO DOCUMENT-BASED QUESTIONS

1. One part of society must be protected from the other, and the minority must be protected from the majority.
2. By creating a will in the community that is not dependent on the majority, and by creating so many different types of citizens to make it impossible for any to create a majority.
3. Madison regards special interests as fulfilling a useful function of providing balance and preventing any one group in society from oppressing others.
4. Because there are so many sects, none will be able to gain too much power.
5. Because no group will be strong enough to oppress the others.
6. Most people work for their own interests, but he thought different groups with different interests would balance each other and thereby guarantee the rights of all.

from A Vindication of the Rights of Woman

by Mary Wollstonecraft

SETTING THE STAGE Although a number of 18th-century British writers discussed the role of women in society, none became as celebrated for her feminist views as Mary Wollstonecraft (1759–1797). Early in her life, Wollstonecraft learned the value of independence and became openly critical of a society that treated females as inferior creatures who were socially, financially, and legally dependent on men. In 1792, Wollstonecraft published *A Vindication of the Rights of Woman,* in which she called for an end to the prevailing injustices against females. Although her opinions on women's rights may seem conservative by modern standards, they were radical in 18th-century Britain.

PRIMARY SOURCE

My own sex, I hope, will excuse me if I treat them like rational creatures, instead of flattering their *fascinating* graces, and viewing them as if they were in a state of perpetual childhood, unable to stand alone. I earnestly wish to point out in what true dignity and human happiness consists—I wish to persuade women to endeavor to acquire strength, both of mind and body, and to convince them that the soft phrases, susceptibility of heart, delicacy of sentiment, and refinement of taste, are almost synonymous with epithets [terms] of weakness, and that those beings who are only the objects of pity and that kind of love, which has been termed its sister, will soon become objects of contempt. . . .

The education of women has, of late, been more attended to than formerly; yet they are still reckoned a frivolous sex, and ridiculed or pitied by the writers who endeavor by satire or instruction to improve them. It is acknowledged that they spend many of the first years of their lives in acquiring a smattering of accomplishments; meanwhile strength of body and mind are sacrificed to libertine [indecent] notions of beauty, to the desire of establishing themselves—the only way women can rise in the world—by marriage. And this desire making mere animals of them, when they marry they act as such children may be expected to act: they dress, they paint, and nickname God's creatures. Surely these weak beings are only fit for a seraglio [harem]! Can they be expected to govern a family with judgment, or take care of the poor babes whom they bring into the world?

▲ Mary Wollstonecraft

DOCUMENT-BASED QUESTIONS

1. *What is the subject and purpose of Wollstonecraft's essay?*
2. *According to Wollstonecraft, why isn't the system of marriage beneficial to women?*
3. *Would you like to hear Wollstonecraft speak on women's rights? Why or why not?*
4. *How does a woman's lack of education affect her husband and children?*
5. *Do you think that Wollstonecraft believes in the complete equality of men and women?*
6. *In your opinion, what social issues would concern Wollstonecraft today? Would she still feel a need to defend women's rights?*

More About . . .

A Vindication of the Rights of Woman

At the time Mary Wollstonecraft published *A Vindication of the Rights of Woman,* few women had the courage or the ability to assert that they were equal to men. Wollstonecraft's book caused an uproar, and it was met with everything from enthusiasm to hatred. One of Wollstonecraft's contemporaries called her "a hyena in petticoats."

More About . . .

Mary Wollstonecraft

Mary Wollstonecraft lived an adventurous, dramatic, and dangerous life. In 1795, an American businessman sent her on a mission to Sweden. One of his trading ships filled with silver had mysteriously disappeared there, and he decided Wollstonecraft would make a good diplomat. At the time, the British knew very little about Scandinavia, and it was a long, treacherous journey between England and Sweden. Wollstonecraft stubbornly made her way to and from Sweden accompanied by her daughter and nanny. The trio had many adventures along the way.

Vocabulary Note

frivolous: unworthy of serious attention
vindication: providing support for

ANSWERS TO DOCUMENT-BASED QUESTIONS

1. Her subject is the place of women in society. Her purpose seems to be to persuade her readers that the education of women must change for the better.
2. Wollstonecraft thinks that women focus on improving their superficial attributes, such as physical beauty, so they can marry but that they are then dependent on their husbands. Such dependence makes them no better than animals or children and renders them incapable of raising and educating children of their own.
3. Some students would undoubtedly like to hear Wollstonecraft speak and others would not. Ask students to provide reasons for their likes and dislikes.
4. She may be a weak wife and a mother with little judgment in raising her children.
5. Most students will probably think that Wollstonecraft is arguing for as much equality as was conceivable in her time.
6. *Possible Answers:* inequality in the workplace, unequal access to education, conflicts faced by women who want both to work outside the home and to raise a family.

More About . . .

Élisabeth Vigée-Lebrun

Élisabeth Vigée-Lebrun had a long and successful career as a portrait painter, painting at least 622 portraits. In her *Memoirs* she recalls being interested in portraits from an early age:

> I was sent to boarding-school at the age of six, and remained there until I was eleven. During that time I scrawled on everything at all seasons; my copy-books, and even my schoomates', I decorated with marginal drawings . . .

One of the keys to her success was the relationship she developed with her subjects. She regarded portrait painting as a conversation between herself and the "sitter" and managed to make her subjects appear comfortable and life-like. Vigée-Lebrun's talent gained her world-wide recognition, and she enjoyed the company of everyone from Catherine the Great of Russia to Benjamin Franklin. When she went to the theater, the audience gave her a round of applause. Although surrounded by some of the most famous people in the world, she treated all of them equally. When the French Revolution began, her popularity and savoir-faire saved her.

Vocabulary Note
incessantly: continually
stringing up: hanging

from the Memoirs of Madame Vigée-Lebrun

by Élisabeth Vigée-Lebrun

SETTING THE STAGE Élisabeth Vigée-Lebrun was a gifted artist who painted portraits of the French nobility. In her memoirs she recalls events of her own life amidst the turmoil of the French Revolution, which began in 1789. She frequently painted Marie Antoinette, queen of France. Vigée-Lebrun became frightened by the increasingly aggressive harassment of the nobility by the revolutionaries and resolved to leave France. She and her daughter escaped at night by stagecoach.

PRIMARY SOURCE

I had my carriage loaded, and my passport ready, so that I might leave next day with my daughter and her governess, when a crowd of national guardsmen burst into my room with their muskets. Most of them were drunk and shabby, and had terrible faces. A few of them came up to me and told me in the coarsest language that I must not go, but that I must remain. I answered that since everybody had been called upon to enjoy his liberty, I intended to make use of mine. They would barely listen to me, and kept on repeating, "You will not go, citizeness; you will not go!" Finally they went away. I was plunged into a state of cruel anxiety when I saw two of them return. But they did not frighten me, although they belonged to the gang, so quickly did I recognize that they wished me no harm. "Madame," said one of them, "we are your neighbors, and we have come to advise you to leave, and as soon as possible. You cannot live here; you are changed so much that we feel sorry for you. But do not go in your carriage: go in the stage-coach; it is much safer." . . .

Opposite me in the coach was a very filthy man, who stunk like the plague, and told me quite simply that he had stolen watches and other things. . . . Not satisfied with relating his fine exploits to us, the thief talked incessantly of stringing up such and such people on lamp-posts, naming a number of my own acquaintances. My daughter thought this man very wicked. He frightened her, and this gave me the courage to say, "I beg you, sir, not to talk of killing before this child."

▲ *Self-Portrait in a Straw Hat* by Élisabeth Vigée-Lebrun

DOCUMENT-BASED QUESTIONS

1. *What does Vigée-Lebrun do to escape the Reign of Terror in France?*
2. *What details does Vigée-Lebrun use to create a vivid picture of the national guardsmen? What impression of them does the author convey?*
3. *What concerns does Vigée-Lebrun reveal in her account of her escape from Paris?*
4. *As you read, how did you feel about the situation Vigée-Lebrun finds herself in?*
5. *What seem to be Vigée-Lebrun's feelings about the French Revolution?*
6. *Do you find Vigée-Lebrun a sympathetic person? Why or why not?*

ANSWERS TO DOCUMENT-BASED QUESTIONS

1. She fled France in a stagecoach.
2. She describes them as drunk and shabby, with terrible faces and coarse language. They appear as rough, cruel, and scarcely in control of themselves.
3. She reveals her concern for her daughter; she is frightened but courageous in protecting her child from the rough language of one of the passengers in the coach.
4. Students will probably empathize with her situation as a woman in peril in a chaotic society. You might ask students if they know of countries or societies that have experienced similar turmoil.
5. She is frightened by the Revolution, which threatens her livelihood, the lives of her friends, and her own safety. She shows concern for her rich acquaintances and reveals little concern for the poor.
6. Some students will find her sympathetic because they find her courage or personality appealing; others will find her support of an oppressive aristocracy unsympathetic.

from the Report on Child Labor

by the Sadler Committee

SETTING THE STAGE In 1831 a parliamentary committee headed by Michael Thomas Sadler investigated child labor in British factories. The following testimony by Elizabeth Bentley, who worked as a child in a textile mill, is drawn from the records of the Sadler Committee. Michael Thomas Sadler is asking the questions.

PRIMARY SOURCE

What age are you?—Twenty-three. . . .

What time did you begin to work at a factory?—When I was six years old. . . .

What kind of mill is it?—Flax mill. . . .

What was your business in that mill?—I was a little doffer [cleaner of textile machines].

What were your hours of labor in that mill?—From 5 in the morning till 9 at night, when they were thronged [busy].

For how long a time together have you worked that excessive length of time?—For about half a year.

What were your usual hours of labor when you were not so thronged?—From 6 in the morning till 7 at night.

What time was allowed for your meals?—Forty minutes at noon.

Had you any time to get your breakfast or drinking?—No, we got it as we could.

And when your work was bad, you had hardly any time to eat it at all?—No; we were obliged to leave it or take it home, and when we did not take it, the overlooker [foreman] took it, and gave it to his pigs.

Do you consider doffing a laborious employment?—Yes.

Explain what it is you had to do.—When the frames are full, they have to stop the frames, and take the flyers off, and take the full bobbins off, and carry them to the roller; and then put empty ones on, and set the frames on again.

Does that keep you constantly on your feet?—Yes, there are so many frames and they run so quick.

Your labor is very excessive?—Yes; you have not time for any thing.

Suppose you flagged a little, or were too late, what would they do?—Strap [beat] us.

Are they in the habit of strapping those who are last in doffing?—Yes.

Constantly?—Yes.

Girls as well as boys?—Yes.

Have you ever been strapped?—Yes.

Severely?—Yes.

Could you eat your food well in that factory?—No, indeed, I had not much to eat, and the little I had I could not eat it, my appetite was so poor, and being covered with dust; and it was no use to take it home, I could not eat it, and the overlooker took it, and gave it to the pigs. . .

DOCUMENT-BASED QUESTIONS

1. *From the employers' and parents' point of view, what might have been some of the reasons for child labor?*
2. *What were some of the difficult working conditions faced by children in the factories?*
3. *How many hours per day did Elizabeth Bentley work when the factory was really busy, and when it was not so busy?*
4. *Do children work this hard today in factories in this country? What about in other parts of the world?*

More About . . .

The Sadler Committee

Michael Sadler was a member of Parliament and headed the Sadler Committee in an attempt to get a labor bill passed. He believed that some parents were forcing their children to work and support the entire family. The *Report on Child Labor* provoked so much outrage that Parliament passed the Factory Act of 1833. The Act applied only to textile mills and did not prohibit child labor, but it did prevent children under the age of 9 from working in the mills. It also limited the number of hours children could work.

More About . . .

Child Labor

In 1831, working conditions in Britain's factories, mills, and mines were terrible. Thousands of children worked long hours every day. Children as young as 6 and 7 were sent down narrow mine shafts to dig coal. The mines often caught on fire. Children also worked around unprotected machinery in factories and mills. Because of their small size, they were forced into tight spaces to clean the machines. A German visitor to an English industrial city wrote that being there was like "living in the midst of the army just returned from a campaign" because so many people were missing arms and legs.

Vocabulary Note

flagged: declined in energy

ANSWERS TO DOCUMENT-BASED QUESTIONS

1. Employers probably found children more agile around the textile machinery and easier to control and discipline; parents may have needed the extra money to help put food on the table.
2. Exhausting work, long hours, insufficient food, physical punishment.
3. She worked a 16-hour day when the factory was really busy and a 13-hour day when it was less busy.
4. Child labor laws restrict the conditions, places, and hours of child labor in this country. However, in other countries child labor involving poor working conditions and excessive hours is still a sad fact of life.

More About . . .

Lincoln's Second Inaugural Address

March 4, 1865, was a cold, wet day in Washington D.C. It had been raining for several days, and there was nearly a foot of mud in some parts of the city. Thousands of people had come to see Lincoln's second inauguration. They overwhelmed the hotels and ended up sleeping in hallways and ballrooms.

At 11:30 AM, the mile-long inaugural parade entered the city. For the first time in U.S. history, black soldiers marched in the parade and received a warm welcome from the crowd. When Lincoln began reading his speech, sunlight finally appeared through the clouds. This was perceived as a good omen, and Lincoln said, "It made my heart jump."

The improvement in the weather probably came as a relief after an embarrassing morning. Prior to the inauguration of the president, the vice-president, Andrew Johnson, was privately sworn in at the Senate's chambers. Johnson had been afflicted by typhoid fever just before the ceremony and consumed a large amount of whiskey to settle his nerves. He gave a long, rambling speech that lasted over an hour and at one point grabbed a Bible and began kissing it. After Johnson's speech, Lincoln told the leader of the inaugural parade, "Don't let [Johnson] speak outside."

Vocabulary Note

interest: cause or principle
malice: a desire to harm others
scourge: a source of widespread devastation

from the Second Inaugural Address

by Abraham Lincoln

SETTING THE STAGE President Lincoln delivered his Second Inaugural Address on March 4, 1865, just before the end of the American Civil War. In this excerpt, he recalls the major cause of the war and vows to fight for the restoration of peace and unity.

PRIMARY SOURCE

One-eighth of the whole population were colored slaves. . . . These slaves constituted a peculiar and powerful interest. All knew that this interest was somehow the cause of the war. To strengthen, perpetuate, and extend this interest was the object for which the insurgents [rebels] would rend the Union even by war, while the Government claimed no right to do more than to restrict the territorial enlargement of it. Neither party expected for the war the magnitude or the duration which it has already attained. Neither anticipated that the cause of the conflict might cease with or even before the conflict itself should cease. Each looked for an easier triumph, and a result less fundamental and astounding. Both read the same Bible and pray to the same God, and each invokes His aid against the other. . . . Fondly do we hope, fervently do we pray, that this mighty scourge of war may speedily pass away. Yet, if God wills that it continue until all the wealth piled by the bondsman's [slave's] two hundred and fifty years of unrequited [unpaid for] toil shall be sunk, and until every drop of blood drawn with the lash shall be paid by another drawn with the sword, as was said three thousand years ago, so still it must be said "the judgments of the Lord are true and righteous altogether."

With malice toward none, with charity for all, with firmness in the right as God gives us to see the right, let us strive on to finish the work we are in, to bind up the nation's wounds, to care for him who shall have borne the battle and for his widow and his orphan, to do all which may achieve and cherish a just and lasting peace among ourselves and with all nations.

▲ Abraham Lincoln

DOCUMENT-BASED QUESTIONS

1. *According to Lincoln's Second Inaugural Address, why did the Confederacy go to war?*
2. *Why might Southerners have feared that prohibiting slavery in new territories would threaten slavery where it already existed?*
3. *Why do you think Lincoln believes it would be wiser for Americans not to blame one another?*
4. *In 1865, if the South had asked to rejoin the Union without ending slavery, do you think Lincoln would have agreed?*
5. *Reread the last sentence of Lincoln's speech. Do you think Americans are still working to reach the goals set by Lincoln?*

ANSWERS TO DOCUMENT-BASED QUESTIONS

1. To strengthen, perpetuate, and extend slavery against the wishes of the federal government to restrict its territorial enlargement.
2. Slave states would have proportionally less representation in the federal government.
3. Lincoln knew that the task of rebuilding the nation after the war would be less difficult if Americans were able to work together.
4. Lincoln would probably not have accepted the offer. He saw slavery as the cause of the war. Even if the South had returned to the Union, its system of slavery would have caused the same problems and conflicts again.
5. Answers will vary. Accept all reasonable responses.

from The Natural Rights of Civilized Women

by Elizabeth Cady Stanton

SETTING THE STAGE Elizabeth Cady Stanton (1815–1902) led the fight for women's equality. Her first memory was the birth of a sister when she was four. So many people said, "What a pity it is she's a girl!" that Stanton felt sorry for the new baby. She later wrote, "I did not understand at that time that girls were considered an inferior order of beings." Stanton was determined to prove that girls were just as important as boys. The following excerpt comes from an address that Stanton gave to the New York state legislature in 1860 on a bill for woman suffrage that was before the state senate.

PRIMARY SOURCE

Now do not think, gentlemen, we wish you to do a great many troublesome things for us. We do not ask our legislators to spend a whole session in fixing up a code of laws to satisfy a class of most unreasonable women. We ask no more than the poor devils in the Scripture asked, "Let us alone." In mercy, let us take care of ourselves, our property, our children, and our homes. True, we are not so strong, so wise, so crafty as you are, but if any kind friend leaves us a little money, or we can by great industry earn fifty cents a day, we would rather buy bread and clothes for our children than cigars and champagne for our legal protectors.

There has been a great deal written and said about protection. We as a class are tired of one kind of protection, that which leaves us everything to do, to dare, and to suffer, and strips us of all means for its accomplishment. We would not tax man to take care of us. No, the Great Father has endowed all His creatures with necessary powers for self-support, self-defense, and protection. We do not ask man to represent us, it is hard enough in times like these to represent himself. So long as the mass of men spend most of their time on the fence, not knowing which way to jump, they are surely in no condition to tell us where we had better stand. In pity for man, we would no longer hang like a millstone round his neck. Undo what man did for us in the Dark Ages and strike out all special legislation for us; strike the words "white male" from all your constitutions and then, with fair sailing, let us sink or swim, live or die, survive or perish together.

▲ Elizabeth Cady Stanton

DOCUMENT-BASED QUESTIONS

1. *What basic right is Stanton asking for?*
2. *What sorts of special considerations and laws does Stanton think women are entitled to?*
3. *What group does Stanton think benefits unfairly from current laws and legislation?*
4. *According to Stanton, do women want special protection under the law? Explain.*
5. *What does Stanton mean by the "Dark Ages"?*
6. *What social issues do you think Stanton would address in today's world?*

More About . . .

Elizabeth Cady Stanton

As a young woman, Elizabeth Cady Stanton had direct contact with the reform movements of the time. She met several fugitive slaves seeking refuge in her cousin's home, which was also where she met her future husband, abolitionist Henry Stanton. When Elizabeth Cady married Henry Stanton, she demanded that the word "obey" be removed from the ceremony.

The couple went to the World's Anti-Slavery Convention in London for their honeymoon. At the convention, women were not allowed to be seated, and Cady Stanton was infuriated. She decided that women needed a convention of their own to assert their rights. Shortly thereafter she and her husband moved to the town of Seneca Falls in upstate New York. There she began raising a family that would eventually include seven children. At the age of 32, she wrote that she felt like a "caged lioness."

She brought together other outraged women and, in July 1848, held the first Women's Rights Convention. Three hundred men and women, including abolitionist Frederick Douglass, attended the convention, and Cady Stanton established herself as a leading figure in the fight for women's rights.

Vocabulary Note
legislators: law-makers
suffrage: the right or privilege of voting

ANSWERS TO DOCUMENT-BASED QUESTIONS

1. The right of women to equality.
2. None—she simply wants women to gain the right to vote and then be left alone to pursue their own interests and development.
3. White males benefit unfairly. Cady Stanton thinks that if that group's special privileges are ended, then there will be greater equality in society.
4. No—women want equality under the law, not special protection.
5. The "Dark Ages" were when women were regarded as requiring special protection under the law.
6. Answers will vary. Some students may think that women's rights would still be her priority; others may cite other issues.

More About . . .

The Fourteen Points

Woodrow Wilson delivered the Fourteen Points with several goals in mind. He hoped to raise the morale of Americans and outline the reasons for going to war. His goal for the governments of France and Britain was to get them to be more generous and straightforward in the treaties they made.

Points one and fourteen were key to fulfilling these goals. Point one, calling for open agreements, was devised in response to secret treaties made by Germany's opponents earlier in the war. These treaties divided up land for colonies and sought revenge against Germany. Point fourteen promoted the League of Nations, which eventually became the United Nations.

Wilson had mixed success in achieving his goals. The U.S. Senate did not approve of the country becoming a League of Nations member. In 1918, Germany was forced by France and Britain to accept a harsh peace settlement. The spirit of the Fourteen Points survives, however, in the United Nations.

Vocabulary Note
impartial: fair
integrity: the quality of being undivided

The Fourteen Points

by Woodrow Wilson

SETTING THE STAGE Nine months after the United States entered World War I, President Wilson delivered to Congress a statement of war aims. This statement became known as the "Fourteen Points." In the speech, Wilson set forth 14 proposals for reducing the risk of war in the future. Numbers have been inserted to help identify the main points, as well as those omitted.

PRIMARY SOURCE

All the peoples of the world are in effect partners . . . , and for our own part we see very clearly that unless justice be done to others it will not be done to us. The program of the world's peace, therefore, is our program; and that program, . . . as we see it, is this:
[1] Open covenants [agreements] of peace, openly arrived at, after which there shall be no private international understandings of any kind but diplomacy shall proceed frankly and in the public view.
[2] Absolute freedom of navigation upon the seas . . . in peace and war. . . .
[3] The removal, so far as possible, of all economic barriers and the establishment of an equality of trade conditions among all the nations. . . .
[4] Adequate guarantees given and taken that national armaments [weapons and war supplies] will be reduced. . . .
[5] A free, open-minded, and absolutely impartial adjustment of all colonial claims, based upon . . . the principle that . . . the interests of the populations concerned must have equal weight with the . . . claims of the government whose title is to be determined.
[6–13: These eight points deal with specific boundary changes.]
[14] A general association of nations must be formed under specific covenants for the purpose of affording mutual guarantees of political independence and territorial integrity to great and small states alike.

▲ British Prime Minister David Lloyd George, French Premier Georges Clemenceau, and President Woodrow Wilson walk in Paris during negotiations for the Treaty of Versailles.

DOCUMENT-BASED QUESTIONS

1. *Why should diplomacy avoid private dealings and proceed in public view?*
2. *How might agreements arrived at in public prevent another world war?*
3. *How might equality of trade be important to keeping the peace?*
4. *What must nations join together to guarantee?*
5. *What might be unusual about a leader such as Wilson calling for an impartial adjustment of colonial claims?*
6. *How successful do you think Wilson's ideas have been in the 20th and 21st centuries?*

ANSWERS TO DOCUMENT-BASED QUESTIONS

1. So that nations will be aware of the consequences of their actions.
2. The alliance system before World War I pulled one country after another into the war. Not every country knew all the conditions of various treaties, which made the situation more unstable. A public agreement would mean other countries would know the terms and help to hold the agreement together.
3. If nations trade under equal terms, they are less likely to have economic disputes, which could turn into military disputes.
4. That they can remain politically independent and not have their territory taken.
5. Usually leaders of powerful nations argue for their country's narrow interests. Wilson seems willing to consider the claims of others—specifically the colonial populations.
6. Students may think that Wilson's ideas have not been very successful because after World War I, nations continued to engage in secret dealings, military buildups, and repression of other nations. Others may think that Wilson's ideas gained more success later with the United Nations and its peacekeeping efforts, arms reduction treaties, and successful movements for national independence.

from Night

by Elie Wiesel

SETTING THE STAGE Elie Wiesel (EHL•ee vee•ZEHL) was a Jewish boy from Romania. In 1944, when Wiesel was just 15, the Nazis sent the Jews of his town to Auschwitz in Poland. Wiesel's mother and one of his sisters died there. Wiesel and his father were sent to the Buchenwald concentration camp, where Wiesel's father died just a few months before the camp was liberated. In this excerpt from *Night,* Wiesel describes the terror he experienced on his way to Auschwitz.

PRIMARY SOURCE

The train stopped at Kaschau, a little town on the Czechoslovak frontier. We realized then that we were not going to stay in Hungary. Our eyes were opened, but too late.

The door of the car slid open. A German officer, accompanied by a Hungarian lieutenant-interpreter, came up and introduced himself.

"From this moment, you come under the authority of the German army. Those of you who still have gold, silver, or watches in your possession must give them up now. Anyone who is later found to have kept anything will be shot on the spot. Secondly, anyone who feels ill may go to the hospital car. That's all."

The Hungarian lieutenant went among us with a basket and collected the last possessions from those who no longer wished to taste the bitterness of terror. "There are eighty of you in this wagon," added the German officer. "If anyone is missing, you'll all be shot, like dogs. . . ."

They disappeared. The doors were closed. We were caught in a trap, right up to our necks. The doors were nailed up; the way back was finally cut off. The world was a cattle wagon hermetically [completely] sealed.

▲ Elie Wiesel

DOCUMENT-BASED QUESTIONS

1. *What does the narrator mean when he says, "Our eyes were opened, but too late"?*
2. *What might be the effect on people of uprooting them from their homes?*
3. *What does the narrator mean when he describes "those who no longer wished to taste the bitterness of terror"?*
4. *What might be the effect of sealing people up in railway cars?*
5. *This excerpt is from a book called* Night. *What might be the meaning of the title?*
6. *What elements in this excerpt show the Germans treating the Jews as less than human?*

Primary Source Handbook

More About . . .

Auschwitz

In the spring of 1944, two prisoners escaped from Auschwitz. They wrote a detailed account of their experiences at the camp, and the information eventually reached the Allies. In the summer of 1944, the complex's role as a death camp was confirmed. Pleas were made for the United States to bomb the 44 railroad lines that brought prisoners into the camp, but the proposal was rejected. The operation was called "impracticable" because it would divert resources from other bombing missions. Another request was made to the Allies, asking that they bomb Auschwitz itself. While some prisoners would have died if this had occurred, many more lives would have been saved if Auschwitz had been destroyed. The Allies rejected this proposal as well. They did bomb the factories at Auschwitz, as Wiesel recalls:

> We were not afraid...if a bomb had fallen on the blocks, it alone would have killed hundreds on the spot. But we were no longer afraid of death...Every bomb that exploded filled us with joy, and gave us new confidence in life.

Vocabulary Note

Auschwitz: Nazi Germany's largest concentration and extermination camp

ANSWERS TO DOCUMENT-BASED QUESTIONS

1. They realized they were being taken to a concentration camp or they realized that now there was no escape.
2. It might make them sad and weak, unable to fight back. It might also allow the Nazis to control their land more easily.
3. Those who have retained any of their possessions will be shot, so it is better to give up the possessions immediately rather than risk death if they are later discovered.
4. People would be likely to feel cut off from any hope of aid or assistance from the outside world.
5. It might refer to the dark times faced by Wiesel and other victims of the Holocaust.
6. The Nazis took away the people's possessions and threatened them with death, to shoot them "like dogs."

More About . . .

Japanese-Americans

In 1869, the first Japanese settlement was established near Sacramento, California, and a stream of immigrants followed. In 1880, the U.S. census counted 148 Japanese. Sixty years later, there were 275,000, all of them concentrated in California, Oregon, Washington, and Hawaii.

Because most Japanese came between 1885 and 1924, three distinct generations were recognized: the Issei (first generation), Nisei (second generation), and Sansei (third generation). The Issei and Nisei generations were sent to the internment camps. In all, more than 120,000 Japanese-Americans were detained. They faced poor living conditions and dislocation of family members.

The Sansei (third generation) came of age in the 1960s as the civil rights movement gained momentum. They brought the injustices of the camps to light and sought reparations for members of the earlier generations.

Vocabulary Note
internment: to be confined, especially in wartime
Sierras: a mountain range in eastern California

from Farewell to Manzanar

by Jeanne Wakatsuki Houston and James D. Houston

SETTING THE STAGE When Japan's attack on Pearl Harbor drew the United States into World War II, people on the west coast of the United States began to fear that those of Japanese descent living in their communities might secretly aid Japan. Despite the fact that there was no evidence of Japanese-American espionage or sabotage, President Franklin D. Roosevelt signed an order that cleared the way for the removal of Japanese people from their homes. Jeanne Wakatsuki was seven years old when her family was relocated. As this excerpt from her memoir opens, her family is living in Los Angeles after having been forced to move twice by the government, and is about to be moved a third time to Manzanar.

PRIMARY SOURCE

The American Friends Service helped us find a small house in Boyle Heights, another minority ghetto, in downtown Los Angeles, now inhabited briefly by a few hundred Terminal Island refugees. Executive Order 9066 had been signed by President Roosevelt, giving the War Department authority to define military areas in the western states and to exclude from them anyone who might threaten the war effort. There was a lot of talk about internment, or moving inland, or something like that in store for all Japanese Americans. I remember my brothers sitting around the table talking very intently about what we were going to do, how we would keep the family together. They had seen how quickly Papa was removed, and they knew now that he would not be back for quite a while. Just before leaving Terminal Island, Mama had received her first letter, from Bismarck, North Dakota. He had been imprisoned at Fort Lincoln, in an all-male camp for enemy aliens. . . .

The name Manzanar meant nothing to us when we left Boyle Heights. We didn't know where it was or what it was. We went because the government ordered us to. And in the case of my older brothers and sisters, we went with a certain amount of relief. They had all heard stories of Japanese homes being attacked, of beatings in the streets of California towns. . . .

The simple truth is the camp was no more ready for us when we got there than we were ready for it. We had only the dimmest ideas of what to expect. Most of the families, like us, had moved out from southern California with as much luggage as each person could carry. Some old men left Los Angeles wearing Hawaiian shirts and Panama hats and stepped off the bus at an altitude of 4,000 feet, with nothing available but sagebrush and tarpaper to stop the April winds pouring down off the back side of the Sierras.

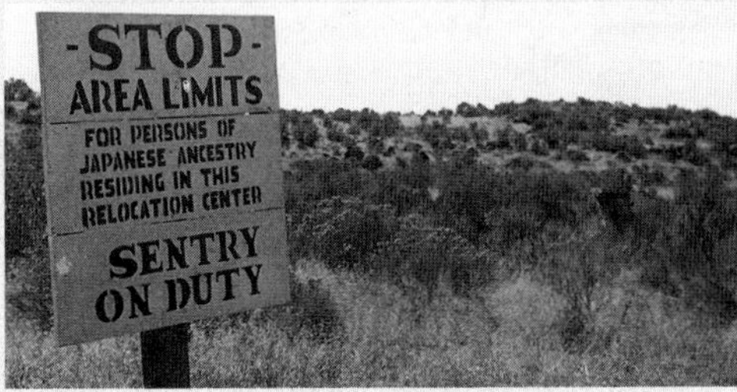

▲ Camp boundary sign in California, 1943

DOCUMENT-BASED QUESTIONS

1. *In the foreword to* Farewell to Manzanar, *Jeanne Wakatsuki Houston says, "It has taken me 25 years to reach the point where I could talk openly about Manzanar." Why do you think it took so long for her to be able to talk about her experience?*
2. *Do you think that a forced internment, like that experienced by the Wakatsuki family, could happen in America today? Why or why not?*
3. *What is your impression of the Wakatsuki family?*
4. *How do you think you would have reacted if you had been brought to Manzanar?*

ANSWERS TO DOCUMENT-BASED QUESTIONS

1. When it was over, she may have wanted to move on with her life and not think about Manzanar anymore. She may have been too hurt and horrified to discuss it.
2. Some students may say that the civil rights laws passed in the 1960s would prevent such an occurrence in the United States or that our society today is more accepting and less suspicious of other cultures and would not consider such an action. Others might believe that forced internment is quite possible, even today.
3. Many students may say that the family is brave and resourceful.
4. Some students may say that they would not have reacted as bravely as the Wakatsukis. Other students may say that they would have been able to endure the conditions at Manzanar.

from the Inaugural Address

by Nelson Mandela

SETTING THE STAGE The son of a tribal chief, Nelson Mandela became a leader in the African National Congress (ANC), a political party that called for racial equality. In 1964, Mandela, who had advocated acts of sabotage against the government, was sentenced to life in prison, where he became an international symbol of South Africa's struggle against apartheid. After his release, Mandela agreed to work peacefully for racial justice. In 1993, Mandela was awarded a Nobel Prize, and the next year he became president of South Africa. The selection below comes from a speech he gave in 1994 when he was inaugurated as president of South Africa.

PRIMARY SOURCE

We are both humbled and elevated by the honor and privilege that you, the people of South Africa, have bestowed on us, as the first President of a united, democratic, nonracial, and nonsexist South Africa, to lead our country out of the valley of darkness.

We understand it still that there is no easy road to freedom.

We know it well that none of us acting alone can achieve success.

We must therefore act together as a united people, for national reconciliation, for nation building, for the birth of a new world.

Let there be justice for all.

Let there be peace for all.

Let there be work, bread, water and salt for all.

Let each know that for each the body, the mind, and the soul have been freed to fulfill themselves.

Never, never and never again shall it be that this beautiful land will again experience the oppression of one by another and suffer the indignity of being the skunk of the world.

Let freedom reign.

The sun shall never set on so glorious a human achievement!

God bless Africa!

▲ Nelson Mandela

DOCUMENT-BASED QUESTIONS

1. *What challenges do you think Mandela expects as the first black president of South Africa?*
2. *Do you think Mandela was speaking only to the audience gathered before him? Explain.*
3. *What does Mandela mean when he says that South Africa must never again be thought of as the "skunk of the world"?*
4. *What are some examples of Mandela's use of repetition in his speech?*

More About . . .

President Mandela

Nelson Mandela faced serious challenges when he became president. South Africa had been dominated by whites for years, and the major institutions like the security forces, businesses, media sources, and the stock exchange all served white interests.

In 1994, the United Nations ranked the quality of life in South Africa and found that if white South Africa were ranked as a separate country, its quality of life would have put it 24th in the world, just below Spain. If black South Africa were ranked alone, it would be 123rd in the world, below Vietnam and in the ranks of the world's poorest countries. On average, white South Africans' salaries were eight times higher than those of blacks. Half the population lacked adequate sanitation, and one-third were illiterate.

When Mandela's presidency ended five years later, in 1999, South Africa faced high crime and unemployment rates. Overall, however, the dismantling of the apartheid system was much more peaceful than people had expected. In his final speech as president, Mandela said, "The long walk continues."

Vocabulary Note

reconciliation: reestablishing a close relationship between parties; to resolve differences

ANSWERS TO DOCUMENT-BASED QUESTIONS

1. Possibly eliminating poverty, establishing social justice, bringing about national reconciliation, and being recognized as a legitimate leader are the great challenges.
2. Most students will probably think that Mandela was speaking to the world and not just the audience before him. He needed to let the world know that South Africa was changing.
3. In slang, a skunk is a despicable person. Mandela means that South Africa's policy of apartheid made it despised, and this must never happen again.
4. The first four paragraphs begin with the word "we," by which Mandela implies the unity of all South Africans. Paragraphs 5–8 all begin with the word "let." These repeated words and phrases help to give structure to his speech and make it memorable and eloquent.

More About . . .

I Have a Dream

Martin Luther King did not deliver his speech until the late afternoon of August 28, 1963. He gave the speech as a sermon and considered the audience his congregation. He developed a call-and-response rhythm with them, gaining momentum with every word. One marcher recalls that everyone listening to King's speech that day felt that he was speaking to them individually. King's widow, Coretta Scott King, remembers, "At that moment, it seemed as if the Kingdom of God appeared. But it only lasted for a moment."

More About . . .

The March on Washington

Those who had marched with Martin Luther King before had experienced violent confrontations at the hands of the police. The march leaders met with the police chief of the District of Columbia prior to the march. Concerned about police brutality and rioting, one of the march leaders asked the chief what he should tell the marchers to expect on that hot summer day. The chief replied, "Tell them not to put any mayonnaise on their sandwiches." The chief's response was a relief to the march leaders, and the spirit of the march was good-natured, much like an enormous picnic.

Vocabulary Note

creed: a system of principles

Gentile: a Christian

from I Have a Dream

by Martin Luther King, Jr.

SETTING THE STAGE On August 28, 1963, Martin Luther King, Jr., gave his most famous speech at the March on Washington. In it, he shared his dream of equality for all.

PRIMARY SOURCE

I say to you today, my friends, that even though we face the difficulties of today and tomorrow, I still have a dream. It is a dream deeply rooted in the American dream.

I have a dream that one day this nation will rise up and live out the true meaning of its creed—we hold these truths to be self-evident that all men are created equal.

I have a dream that my four little children will one day live in a nation where they will not be judged by the color of their skin but by the content of their character.

I have a dream today!

This is our hope. This is the faith that I will go back to the South with. . . . With this faith we will be able to work together, to pray together, to struggle together, to go to jail together, to stand up for freedom together, knowing that we will be free one day. This will be the day, this will be the day when all of God's children will be able to sing with new meaning "My country 'tis of thee, sweet land of liberty, of thee I sing. Land where my fathers died, land of the Pilgrim's pride, from every mountainside, let freedom ring!" And if America is to be a great nation, this must become true.

And when this happens, when we allow freedom to ring, when we let it ring from every tenement and every hamlet, from every state and every city, we will be able to speed up that day when all of God's children, black men and white men, Jews and Gentiles, Protestants and Catholics, will be able to join hands and sing in the words of the old Negro spiritual, "Free at last, free at last. Thank God Almighty, we are free at last."

▲ Martin Luther King, Jr., Washington, D.C., August 28, 1963

DOCUMENT-BASED QUESTIONS

1. *How do civil rights fit into the American dream?*
2. *Why do you think civil rights workers were willing to go to jail?*
3. *Why does King declare that the United States is not living up to its creed?*
4. *What does King say must happen before America can be considered a truly great nation?*

ANSWERS TO DOCUMENT-BASED QUESTIONS

1. People can only live the American dream if they have civil rights. The American dream and promise is that all Americans have civil rights.
2. To show their respect for the law while standing up for what they believed.
3. Although the Declaration of Independence claimed that "all men are created equal," many Americans still faced discrimination and inequality because of the color of their skin.
4. All Americans, including African Americans, must enjoy the same freedoms.

An Open Letter

by Cesar Chavez

SETTING THE STAGE In 1969, Cesar Chavez wrote a letter in which he denied accusations that he had used violence to win decent wages and better benefits for farm workers.

PRIMARY SOURCE

Today . . . we remember the life and sacrifice of Martin Luther King, Jr., who gave himself totally to the nonviolent struggle for peace and justice. In his letter from Birmingham jail, Dr. King describes better than I could our hopes for the strike and boycott: "Injustice must be exposed, with all the tension its exposure creates, to the light of human conscience and the air of public opinion before it can be cured." For our part, I admit that we have seized upon every tactic and strategy consistent with the morality of our cause to expose that injustice and thus to heighten the sensitivity of the American conscience so that farmworkers will have without bloodshed their own union and the dignity of bargaining with the agribusiness [large-scale farming] employers. . . .

Our strikers here in Delano and those who represent us throughout the world are well trained for this struggle. . . . They have been taught not to lie down and die or to flee in shame, but to resist with every ounce of human endurance and spirit. To resist not with retaliation in kind but to overcome with love and compassion, with ingenuity and creativity, with hard work and longer hours, with stamina and patient tenacity, with truth and public appeal, with friends and allies, with mobility and discipline, with politics and law, and with prayer and fasting. They were not trained in a month or even a year; after all, this new harvest season will mark our fourth full year of strike and even now we continue to plan and prepare for the years to come. . . .

We shall overcome and change if not by retaliation or bloodshed but by a determined nonviolent struggle carried on by those masses of farmworkers who intend to be free and human.

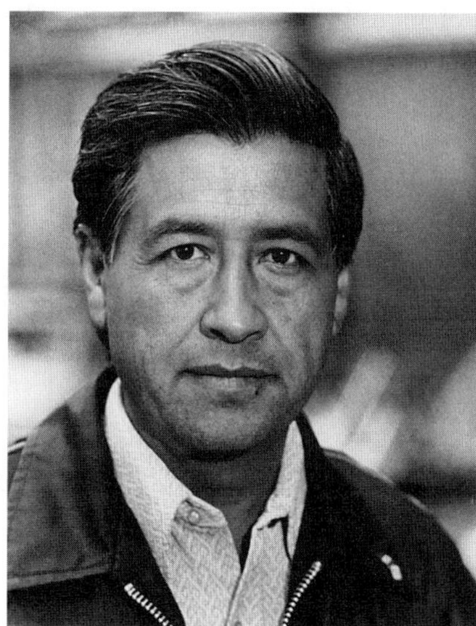

▲ Cesar Chavez, 1974

DOCUMENT-BASED QUESTIONS

1. *Why do you think farm workers wanted to organize a union?*
2. *Why might it be necessary to train for nonviolent protest?*
3. *Why do you think Chavez refers to Martin Luther King, Jr., in his speech?*
4. *In what ways were the problems faced by King and Chavez similar and different?*

Primary Source Handbook

More About . . .

Cesar Chavez

When Cesar Chavez was ten years old, his family lost their farm in Arizona.

In 1939, Chavez and his family joined thousands of others who had migrated to California to work as migrant farm laborers. Many of the 250,000 migrant workers already in California had come during the Depression. Their struggles were the basis for John Steinbeck's powerful novel *The Grapes of Wrath.*

Mexican-American workers faced the same hardships as those who had come earlier, but they also experienced fierce racism. White migrant workers feared for their own jobs and resisted the Mexican-American workers. Chavez observed the miserable conditions of migrant farm labor firsthand and was eventually drawn to union organizing.

In 1962, Chavez convened the first meeting of the National Farm Worker's Association, or FWA. The FWA became the United Farm Workers of America (UFW) in 1971 and worked to promote better conditions for migrant workers. Chavez made a commitment to non-violence, even going on a hunger strike in 1988. He died in 1993.

Vocabulary Note

ingenuity: cleverness

tenacity: holding to something strongly

ANSWERS TO DOCUMENT-BASED QUESTIONS

1. Without a union, farm workers would have a hard time bargaining with the large businesses that employed them.
2. Protesters need to learn how to avoid the urge to fight back, to avoid injury, and how to help those who might be injured during protests.
3. Chavez wants to point out that the farm workers also followed nonviolence as King did.
4. Chavez was primarily trying to solve economic problems, while King's focus was on political and legal problems. Both leaders expressed their hopes that all people would be free.

NOTE: *Boldfaced words are terms that appear in this handbook.*

BOYCOTT

A refusal to have economic dealings with a person, a business, an organization, or a country.

The purpose of a boycott is to show disapproval of particular actions or to force changes in those actions. A boycott often involves an economic act, such as refusing to buy a company's goods or services.

Civil rights campaigners in the United States used boycotts to great effect during the 1950s and 1960s. For example, African Americans in Montgomery, Alabama, organized a bus boycott in 1955 to fight segregation on city buses. The boycotters kept many buses nearly empty for 381 days. The boycott ended when the Supreme Court outlawed bus segregation.

During the 1960s, groups in many countries launched boycotts against South African businesses to protest the policy of apartheid, or complete separation of the races. In the picture above, demonstrators march to protest a tour of Great Britain by the South African rugby team in 1969. Worldwide boycotts helped to bring about the end of apartheid in the 1990s. For information on the dismantling of the apartheid system, read page 610.

In many countries, labor unions have used boycotts to win concessions for their members. Consumer groups, too, have organized boycotts to win changes in business practices.

BUSINESS CYCLE

A pattern of increases and decreases in economic activity.

A business cycle generally consists of four distinct phases—expansion, peak, contraction, and trough—as shown in the graph in the next column. An expansion is marked by increased business activity. The **unemployment rate** falls, businesses produce more, and consumers buy more goods and services. A peak is a transition period in which expansion slows. A contraction, or **recession,** occurs when business activity decreases. The unemployment rate rises, while both production and consumer spending fall. A deep and long-lasting contraction is called a **depression.** Business activity reaches its lowest point during a trough. After time, business activity starts to increase and a new cycle begins.

The Business Cycle

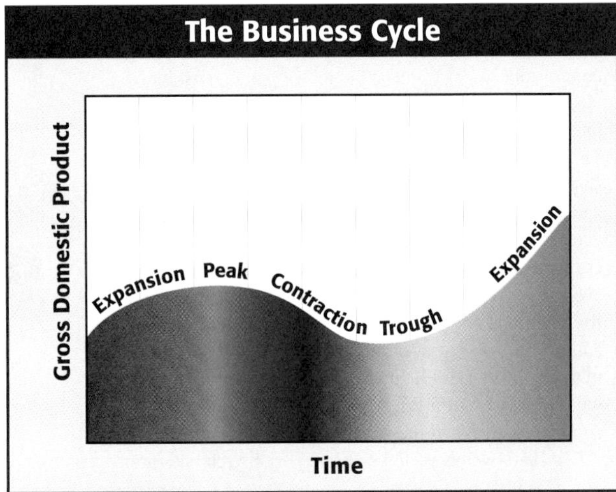

CAPITALISM

An economic system in which there is private ownership of natural resources and capital goods.

The basic idea of capitalism is that producers are driven by the desire to make a profit, the money left over after costs have been subtracted from revenues. This desire for profit motivates producers to provide consumers with the goods and services they desire. Prices and wages are determined by **supply and demand.**

Along with the opportunity to earn a profit there is a risk. Businesses tend to fail if they do not produce goods people want at prices they are willing to pay. Because anyone is free to start a business or enterprise, a capitalist system is also known as a **free enterprise** system.

Capitalism contrasts with **socialism,** an economic system in which the government owns and controls capital and sets prices and production levels. Critics of the capitalist system argue that it allows decisions that ought to be made democratically to be made instead by powerful business owners and that it allows too-great disparities in wealth and well-being between the poor and the rich. For a comparison of capitalism and socialism, read the Analyzing Key Concepts on page 303.

COMMUNISM

An economic system based on one-party rule, government ownership of the means of production, and decision making by centralized authorities.

Under communism there is little or no private ownership of property and little or no political freedom. Government planners make economic decisions, such as which and how many goods and services should be produced. Individuals have little say in a communist economy. Such a system, Communists believe, would end inequality. For more information on the ideas on which communism is based, read Chapter 9, Section 4.

During the 20th century, most communist economies failed to achieve their goals. Economic decisions frequently were made to benefit only Communist Party officials. Also, government economic planning was inefficient, often creating shortages of goods. Those goods that were available were often of poor quality.

People became discontented with the lack of prosperity and political freedom and began to call for change. These demands led in the late 1980s and early 1990s to the collapse of communist governments in the Soviet Union and Eastern Europe.

Even governments that clung to communism—China, for example—have introduced elements of **free enterprise.** The picture above shows people lining up at automated teller machines (ATMs) in Shanghai, one of China's largest free-enterprise zones. (For information on free enterprise in Shanghai, read the Connect to Today on page 372.) While China has allowed greater economic freedom for its citizens, it has not given them more political freedom.

CONSUMER PRICE INDEX (CPI)

A measure of the change in cost of the goods and services most commonly bought by consumers. In some countries, the CPI is called the retail price index.

The CPI is calculated by surveying the prices of a "basket" of goods and services bought by typical consumers. In Germany, the CPI follows the prices of more than 750 goods and services bought by average consumers on a regular basis. Items on which consumers spend a good deal of their income, such as food, are given more weight in the CPI than items on which consumers spend less.

Price changes are calculated by comparing current prices with prices at a set time in the past. In 2003, for example, the German CPI used the year 2000 as this base. Prices for this year are given a base value of 100. The prices for subsequent years are expressed as percentages of the base. Therefore, a CPI of 103 means that prices have risen by 3 percent since 2000. The graph below illustrates changes in the German CPI from 1992 to 2002.

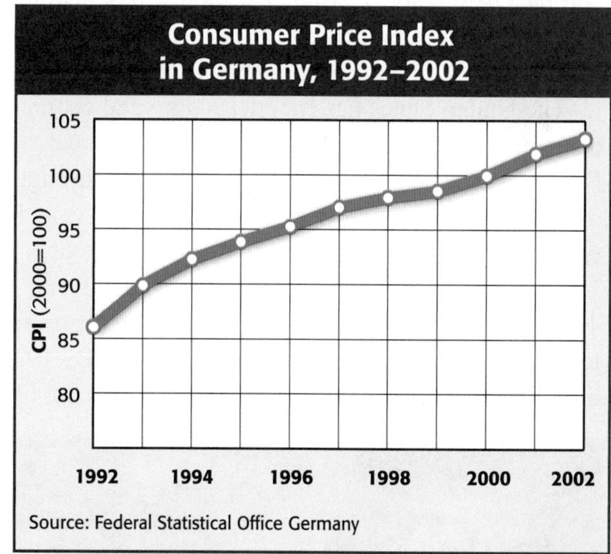

CORPORATION

A company owned by stockholders who have ownership rights to the company's profits.

Stockholders are issued stock, or shares of ownership in the corporation. A corporation sells stock to raise money to do business. Stockholders buy stock in the hope that the corporation will turn a profit. When a corporation does make a profit, stockholders often receive a dividend, a share of the corporation's income after taxes.

R65

The corporation is a legal entity in itself and, therefore, is separate from its owners. As a result, business losses and debts are the responsibility of the corporation alone. Creditors cannot seek payment from the owners, whose liability is limited to the value of the stock they own.

DEFICIT SPENDING

A situation in which a government spends more money than it receives in revenues.

For the most part, the government engages in deficit spending when the economy is in a contraction phase of the **business cycle.** The government borrows or issues money to finance deficit spending.

In theory, the extra funds should stimulate business activity, pushing the economy into an expansion phase. As the economy recovers, revenues should increase, providing the government with a budget surplus. The government then can use the surplus to pay back the money it borrowed.

DEPRESSION

A very severe and prolonged contraction in economic activity.

During a depression, consumer spending, production levels, wages, prices, and profits fall sharply. Many businesses fail, and many workers lose their jobs.

The United States has experienced several economic depressions in its history. The worst was the Great Depression, which started in 1929 and lasted throughout the 1930s. Between 1929 and 1932, business activity in the United States decreased by an average of 10 percent each year. During the same period, some 40 percent of the country's banks failed, and prices for farm products dropped more than 50 percent. By 1933, the worst year of the Great Depression, 25 percent of American workers were unemployed. Americans in the thousands took to the roads and rail in search of gainful employment. The best job some could find was selling apples on street corners.

The situation in other countries was equally bad. In Great Britain, the unemployment rate averaged 14 percent throughout the Great Depression and hit a peak of 25 percent in early 1931. Unemployment was particularly problematic in such traditional industries as coal mining, shipbuilding, and textiles. The picture at the bottom of the previous column shows unemployed miners' families at a soup kitchen. For information about the global impact of the Great Depression and how the world responded to this economic crisis, read pages 473–475.

DEVELOPED NATION

A nation that has achieved industrialization, a market economy, widespread ownership of private property, and a relatively high standard of living.

Developed nations include the United States, Canada, most European countries, Japan, South Korea, Australia, and New Zealand. Although developed nations account for only one-quarter of the world's population, they produce more than three-quarters of the world's **gross domestic product (GDP).** Economists frequently use per capita GDP (GDP divided by the population) to establish a nation's level of economic development. Most developed nations have per capita GDPs in excess of $20,000.

E-COMMERCE

All forms of buying and selling goods and services electronically.

Short for "electronic commerce," e-commerce refers to business activity on the Internet and on private computer networks. There are two main types of e-commerce: business-to-consumer and business-to-business.

Consumer-related e-commerce includes sales to the public over the computer, usually through a seller's Web site. Many business transactions can be completed wholly electronically, such as sales of computer software, which can be paid for with a credit card number and delivered over the Internet directly to the buyer's computer. A growing proportion of financial transactions are also moving online, such as electronic banking and **stock market** trading, or e-trading. The convenience of online shopping has turned it into a booming enterprise. Between 1998 and 2002, for instance, U.S. consumer spending online grew from about $7.7 billion to more than $45 billion.

R66

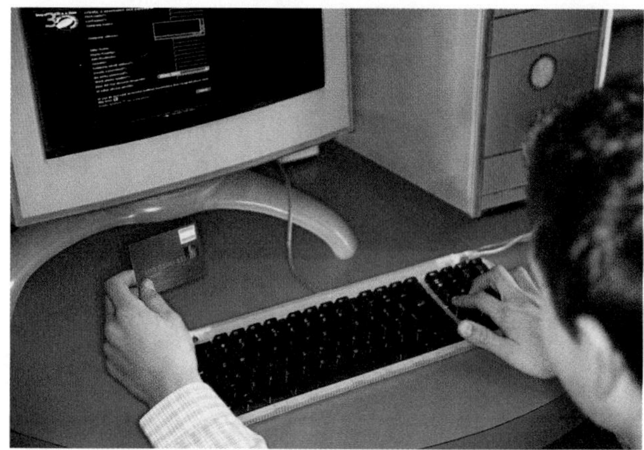

Business-to-business e-commerce is growing at an even greater rate, reaching around $700 billion in 2002. Much of that business includes Web-site design and servicing and online advertising. Businesses also use networked computers to purchase supplies and merchandise and to access information from subscription services.

For many businesses, e-commerce is not only convenient but also cost-effective. On average, corporations spend $100 on paperwork alone each time they make a purchase. Moving those transactions online could save companies millions of dollars annually.

EMBARGO

A government ban on trade with another nation, sometimes backed by military force.

In a civil embargo, the nation imposing an embargo prevents exports to or imports from the country against which it has declared the embargo. A hostile embargo involves seizing the goods of another nation.

The major purpose of an embargo is to show disapproval of a nation's actions. For example, in 1980 the United States imposed a civil embargo on grain sales to the Soviet Union to protest the December 1979 Soviet invasion of Afghanistan.

EMERGING NATION

A nation that has lower levels of agricultural and industrial production, lower savings and investment, fewer resources, and lower per capita ***gross domestic product (GDP)*** *than* ***developed nations.***

Emerging nations are sometimes called *developing nations* or *less-developed countries (LDCs).* Most countries in Africa, Asia, and Latin America and the Caribbean are considered emerging nations. Some three-quarters of the world's population lives in emerging nations, yet these nations produce less than one-quarter of the world's GDP. Therefore, emerging nations have low per capita GDPs; many have a per capita GDP of less than $1,000.

FREE ENTERPRISE

An economic system based on the private ownership of the means of production, free markets, and the right of individuals to make most economic decisions.

The free enterprise system is also called the free market system or **capitalism.** The United States has a free enterprise economic system. The diagram below illustrates how a free enterprise economy works.

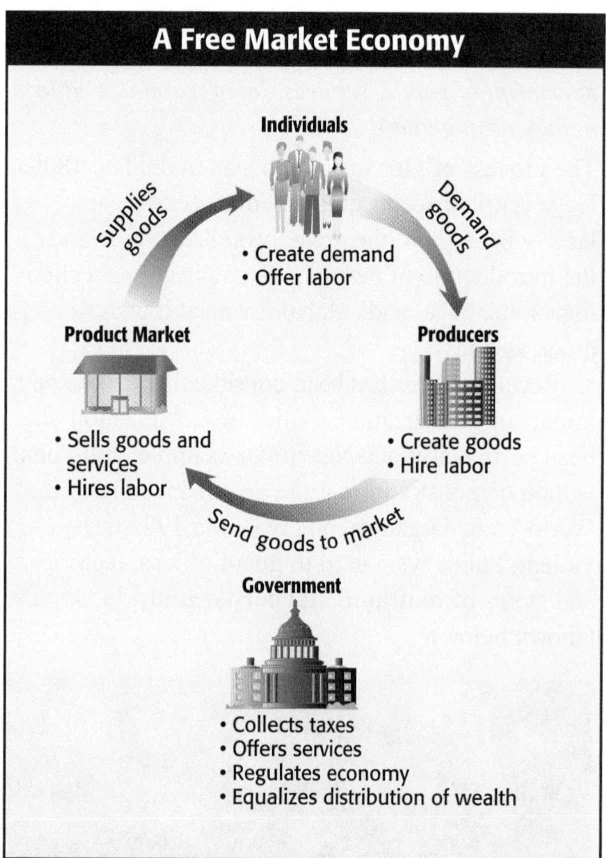

In a free enterprise system, producers and consumers are motivated by self-interest. To maximize their profits, producers try to make goods and services that consumers want. Producers also engage in competition through lowering prices, advertising their products, and improving product quality, to encourage consumers to buy their goods. Consumers serve their self-interest by purchasing the best goods and services for the lowest price.

Government plays a limited, but important, role in most free enterprise economies:

- It regulates economic activity to ensure there is fair competition, such as by preventing and prosecuting fraud and barring **monopolies.**

R67

- It produces certain necessary goods and services that private producers consider unprofitable, such as roadways.
- It protects the public health and safety, such as through building codes, environmental protection laws, and labor laws.
- It provides economic stability, such as by regulating banks, coining money, and supervising unemployment insurance programs.

GLOBALIZATION

The process of rapid economic integration among countries. This integration involves the increased movement of goods, services, labor, capital, and technology throughout the world.

The process of globalization began in the late 1800s. However, its pace has increased in recent years largely because of the drive toward free trade and the introduction of new telecommunications technologies that have made global financial transactions quick and easy.

Recently, there has been considerable debate on the impact of globalization. Critics of globalization have been particularly outspoken. For example, antiglobalization demonstrations at the Seattle meeting of the World Trade Organization (WTO) in 1999 turned violent. Police were used to guard offices, factories, and stores of **multinational corporations** in the city (shown below).

For a review of the arguments for and against globalization, read the Analyzing Key Concepts on page 644.

GOLD STANDARD

A monetary system in which a country's basic unit of currency is valued at, and can be exchanged for, a fixed amount of gold.

The gold standard tends to curb **inflation,** since a government cannot put more currency into circulation than it can back with its gold supplies. This gives people confidence in the currency.

This advantage is also a weakness of the gold standard. During times of **recession,** a government may want to increase the amount of money in circulation to encourage economic growth. Economic disruption during the Great Depression of the 1930s caused most nations to abandon the gold standard. The United States moved to a modified gold standard in 1934 and abandoned the gold standard completely in 1971.

GROSS DOMESTIC PRODUCT (GDP)

The market value of all the goods and services produced in a nation within a specific time period, such as a quarter (three months) or a year.

Gross domestic product is the standard measure of how a nation's economy is performing. If GDP is growing, the economy is probably in an expansion phase. If GDP is not increasing or is declining, the economy is probably in a contraction phase.

GDP is calculated by adding four components: spending by individual consumers on goods and services; investment in such items as new factories, new factory machinery, and houses; government spending on goods and services; and net exports—the value of exports less the value of imports. (See the diagram below.) GDP figures are presented in two ways. Nominal GDP is reported in current dollars. Real GDP is reported in constant dollars, or dollars adjusted for **inflation.**

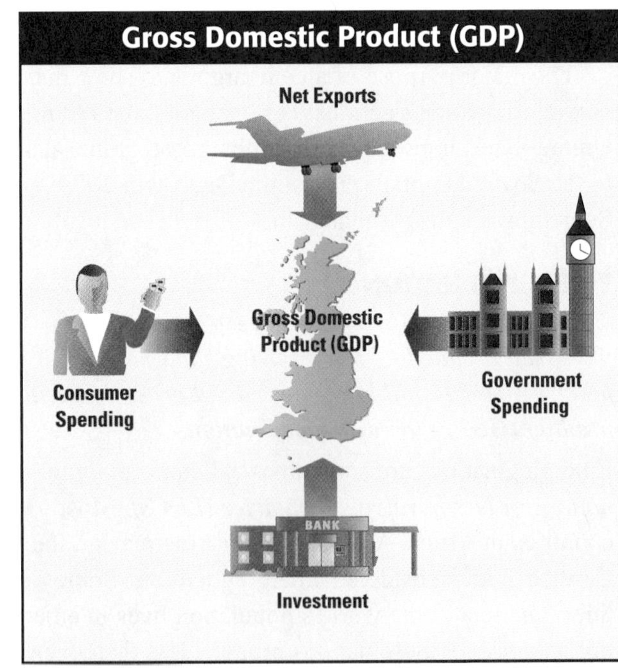

R68

INFLATION

A sustained rise in the average level of prices.

Since more money is required to make purchases when prices rise, inflation is sometimes defined as a decrease in the purchasing value of money. Economists measure price changes with various price indexes. The most widely used index in the United States is the **consumer price index (CPI).**

Inflation may result if the demand for goods increases without an increase in the production of goods. Inflation may also take place if the cost of producing goods increases. Producers pass on increased costs, such as higher wages and more expensive raw materials, by charging consumers higher prices.

INTEREST RATE

The cost of borrowing money.

Interest is calculated as a yearly percentage, or rate, of the money borrowed. A 10 percent interest rate, therefore, would require a borrower to pay $10 per year for every $100 borrowed.

When interest rates are low, people will borrow more, because the cost of borrowing is lower. However, they will save and invest less, because the return on their savings or investment is lower. With high interest rates, people save and invest more but borrow less. Because interest rates affect the economy, governments take steps to control them. The United States government does this through the Federal Reserve System, the nation's central banking system. The graph below shows the relationship between the rate of **inflation** and interest rates in the American economy over time.

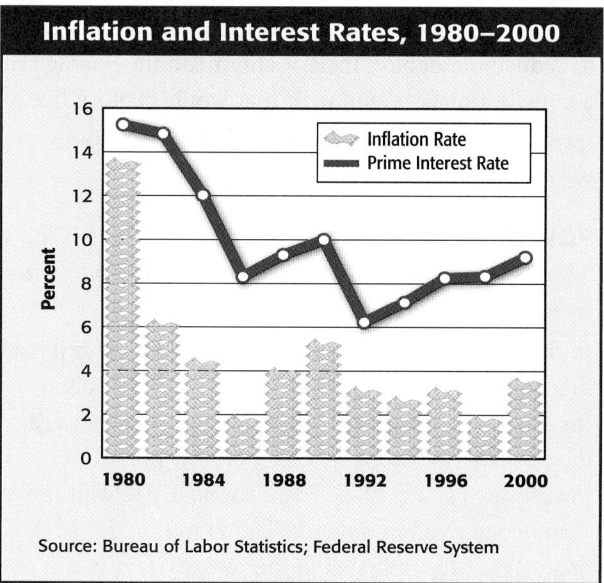

KEYNESIAN ECONOMICS

The use of government spending to encourage economic activity by increasing the demand for goods.

This economic approach is based on the ideas of British economist John Maynard Keynes (shown below). In a 1936 study, Keynes pointed out that during economic downturns, more people are unemployed and have less income to spend. As a result, businesses cut production and lay off more workers.

Keynes's answer to this problem was for government to increase spending and reduce taxes. This would stimulate demand for goods and services by replacing the decline in consumer demand. Government would want goods and services for its new programs. More people would be working and earning an income and, therefore, would want to buy more goods and services. Businesses would increase production to meet this new demand. As a result, the economy would soon recover.

Critics maintain, however, that Keynesian economics has led to the growth of government and to high taxes, inflation, high unemployment, and greatly reduced economic growth.

MINIMUM WAGE

The minimum amount of money that employers may legally pay their employees for a set period of time worked.

Legislation sets the minimum wage at a fixed hourly, weekly, or monthly rate. In some countries, the minimum wage applies to all workers. In others, it applies only to workers in particular industries. Also, some countries set a different minimum wage for men, women, and young workers. The first country to pass minimum wage laws was New Zealand in 1894. Since that time, most industrialized countries have adopted such legislation. The graph on the next page shows estimates of minimum monthly wage rates in selected countries.

The first federal minimum wage law in the United States, the Fair Labor Standards Act of 1938, set the base wage at 25 cents an hour. Since then, amendments to the act have raised this hourly rate to $5.15, effective in 1997. The Fair Labor Standards Act applies to workers in most businesses involved in interstate commerce.

R69

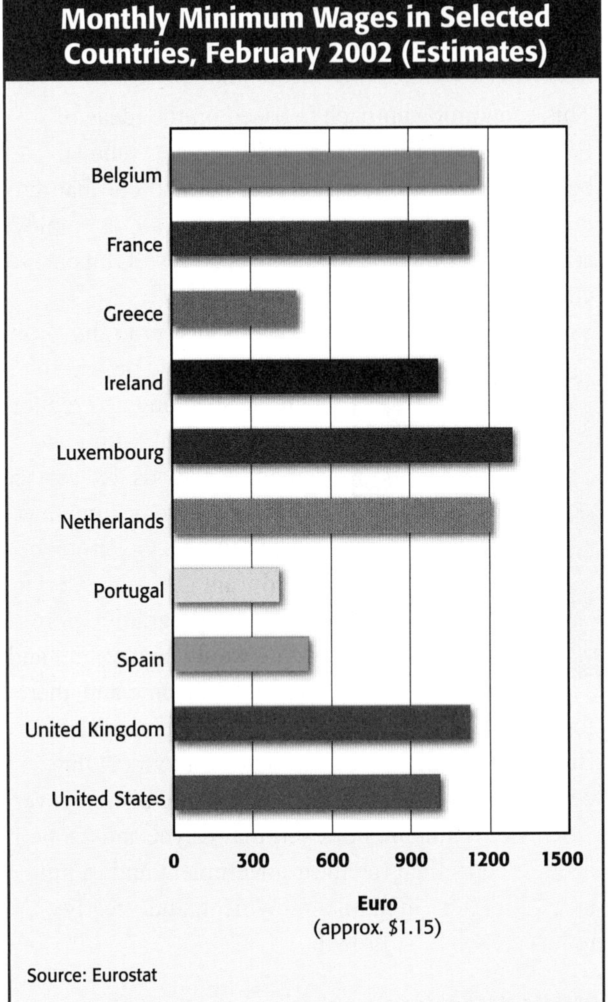

The original intent of minimum wage laws was to ensure that all workers earned enough to survive. However, some economists maintain that these laws may have reduced the chances for unskilled workers to get jobs. They argue that the minimum wage raises the **unemployment rate** because it increases labor costs for business.

MONOPOLY

A situation in which only one seller controls the production, supply, or pricing of a product for which there are no close substitutes.

In the United States, basic public services such as electrical power distributors and cable television suppliers operate as local monopolies. This way of providing utilities is economically more efficient than having several competing companies running electricity or cable lines in the same area.

Monopolies, however, can be harmful to the economy. Since it has no competition, a monopoly does not need to respond to the wants of consumers by improving product quality or by charging fair prices. The government counters the threat of monopoly either by breaking up or regulating the monopoly.

MULTINATIONAL CORPORATION

*A **corporation** that operates in more than one country.*

ExxonMobil (United States), DaimlerChrysler (Germany), Royal Dutch/Shell (Netherlands), BP (Great Britain), and Toyota (Japan) are examples of multinational corporations. A multinational corporation's foreign operations, including factories, offices, and stores, are usually wholly owned subsidiaries run by managers from the home country. Some multinationals, however, enter foreign markets by establishing joint ventures with foreign businesses. Others gain access to foreign markets by buying large amounts of stock in foreign companies.

Such tactics have allowed some multinationals to grow into economic giants with a truly global reach. For more information on the size of some top multinationals, see the graph on page 642.

NATIONAL DEBT

The money owed by a national government.

During wartime, economic recession, or at other times, the government may employ **deficit spending.** However, the government may not pay back all the money it has borrowed to fund this policy. Each year's government budget deficit adds to the country's national debt. By August 2003, the national debt of the United States stood at $6.74 trillion, or about $23,000 for each citizen.

The rapid growth of the U.S. national debt since 1980 has prompted many Americans to call for changes in government economic policies. Some suggest that the government raise taxes and cut spending to reduce the debt. Others recommend the passage of a constitutional amendment that would require the government to have a balanced budget, spending only as much as it takes in.

POVERTY

*The lack of adequate income to maintain a minimum **standard of living.***

In the United States, this adequate income is referred to as the poverty threshold. The poverty threshold for a family of four in 2001 was $18,104. That year, the poverty rate stood at 11.7 percent, one of the lowest rates since 1979. Even so, nearly 33 million Americans lived in poverty. The graph on the next page shows the changes in the poverty rate in the United States since 1981.

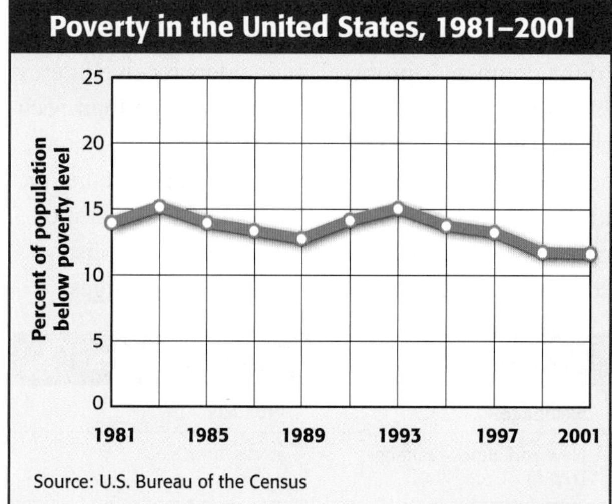

Because the factors used to determine poverty vary so much from country to country, world poverty figures are difficult to calculate. As a result, such international organizations as the World Bank and the United Nations view poverty differently. These organizations track extreme poverty, the threshold for which is less than $1 a day. In 1999, more than one billion people worldwide lived below this level. And according to World Bank estimates, another 1.5 billion lived on less than $2 a day.

PRODUCTIVITY

The relationship between the output of goods and services and the input of resources.

Productivity is the amount of goods or services that a person can produce at a given time. It is closely linked to economic growth, which is defined as an increase in a nation's real **gross domestic product (GDP)** from one year to the next. A substantial rise in productivity means the average worker is producing more, a key factor in spurring economic expansion. Between 1995 and the early 2000s, for example, worker productivity in the United States increased about 2.5 percent each year. This increase, along with other economic factors, helped the nation's real GDP grow an average of about 3.5 percent during those years.

A number of elements affect productivity, including available supplies of labor and raw materials, education and training, attitudes toward work, and technological innovations. Computer technology, for instance, is believed to have played a significant role in bolstering productivity during the 1990s by allowing workers to do their jobs more quickly and efficiently. Computer-operated robot arms (above, right) have greatly increased production in the automobile industry.

Conversely, a lack of adequate training and fewer technological innovations were thought to be behind the meager productivity growth rates of the 1970s and 1980s—when productivity rose at an annual rate of less than 1 percent.

RECESSION

A period of declining economic activity.

In economic terms, a recession takes place when the **gross domestic product (GDP)** falls for two quarters, or six months, in a row. The United States has experienced several of these **business-cycle** contractions in its history. On average, they have lasted about a year. If a recession persists and economic activity plunges, it is called a **depression.**

SOCIALISM

An economic system in which the government owns most of the means of production and distribution.

Like **communism,** the goal of socialism is to use the power of government to reduce inequality and meet people's needs. Under socialism, however, the government usually owns only major industries, such as coal, steel, and transportation. Other industries are privately owned but regulated by the government. Government and individuals, therefore, share economic decision-making. Also, under socialism, the government may provide such services as reasonably priced health care. The diagram on the next page shows the level of government involvement in various types of economic systems.

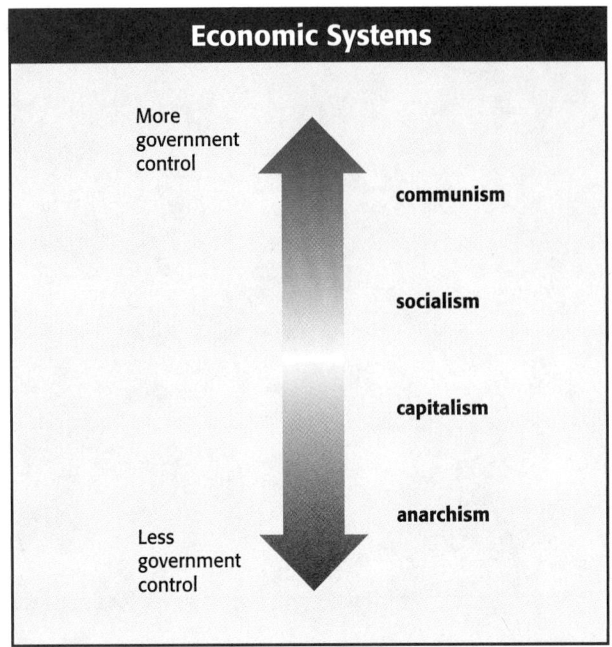

Some countries, such as Sweden, are called democratic socialist countries. In these nations there is less government ownership of property than in communist nations. These nations also have democratically elected governments.

Critics of socialism maintain that this system leads to less efficiency and higher taxes than does the **capitalist,** or **free enterprise,** system. For a comparison of socialism and capitalism, read the Analyzing Key Concepts on page 303.

STANDARD OF LIVING

The overall economic situation in which people live.

Economists differ on how best to measure the standard of living. Some suggest average personal income, while others propose per capita **gross domestic product**—the GDP divided by the population. Another possible measure is the value of the goods and services bought by consumers during a year. In general terms, the nation's standard of living rises as these measures rise. Some people argue that measuring the quality of life also requires consideration of noneconomic factors such as pollution, health, work hours, and even political freedom.

STOCK MARKET *or* STOCK EXCHANGE

A place where stocks and bonds are bought and sold.

Large companies often need extra money to fund expansion and to help cover operating costs. To raise money, they sell stocks, or shares of ownership, in their companies. They also may borrow by issuing bonds, or certificates of debt, promising to repay the money borrowed, plus interest.

Individuals invest in stocks and bonds to make a profit. Most stockholders receive dividends, or a share of the company's profits. Bondholders receive interest. Investors may also make a profit by selling their securities. This sale of stocks and bonds takes place on stock exchanges. Since stocks and bonds together are known as securities, a stock exchange is sometimes called a securities exchange. The table below lists some of the world's most active stock exchanges.

Selected World Stock Exchanges

Exchange	Products
New York Stock Exchange (NYSE)	stocks, bonds
American Stock Exchange (AMEX) (New York)	stocks, bonds, options
National Association of Securities Dealers Automated Quotations (NASDAQ)	over-the-counter stocks
London Stock Exchange	stocks
Tokyo Stock Exchange	stocks, bonds, futures, options
Hong Kong Exchanges	stocks, bonds, futures, options
German Stock Exchange (Frankfurt) (pictured below)	stocks

The largest and most important exchange in the United States is the New York Stock Exchange. Activity on this and other exchanges often signals how well the economy is doing. A bull market, when stock prices rise, usually indicates economic expansion. A bear market, when stock prices fall, usually indicates economic contraction.

Economics Handbook

A rapid fall in stock prices is called a crash. The worst stock market crash in the United States came in October 1929. To help protect against another drastic stock market crash, the federal government set up the Securities and Exchange Commission (SEC), which regulates the trading of securities. For more information on stocks and the stock market, read the History in Depth on page 472.

STRIKE

A work stoppage by employees to gain higher wages, better working conditions, or other benefits.

Strikes are also sometimes used as political protests. A strike is usually preceded by a failure in collective bargaining—the negotiation of contracts between labor unions and employers. Union members may decide to call a strike if they believe negotiations with the employer are deadlocked. In the United States, collective bargaining and strikes are regulated by the NLRA, or Wagner Act, of 1935, which is administered by the National Labor Relations Board (NLRB). There are also wildcat strikes, which are not authorized by unions.

Strikes often have a huge impact on everyday life, as the picture below illustrates. Commuters jam the platform of a subway station in Paris, France, during a one-day strike by transport workers in 2003. The strike, over pay and working conditions, shut down about half of the Paris subway network and severely disrupted traffic on the rest.

When strikes do occur, union representatives and employers try to negotiate a settlement. An outside party is sometimes asked to help work out an agreement.

SUPPLY AND DEMAND

The forces that determine prices of goods and services in a market economy.

Supply is the amount of a good or service that producers are willing and able to produce at a given price. Demand is the amount of a good or service consumers are willing and able to buy at a given price. In general, producers are willing to produce more of a good or service when prices are high; conversely, consumers are willing to buy more of a good or service when prices are low.

The table and graph below show supply and demand for a certain product. The line *S* shows the amount of the good that producers would be willing to make at various prices. The line *D* shows the amount that consumers would be willing to buy at various prices. Point *E*, where the two lines intersect, is called the equilibrium price. It is the price at which the amount produced and the amount demanded would be the same.

When the equilibrium price is the market price, the market operates efficiently. At prices above the equilibrium price, consumers will demand less than producers supply. Producers, therefore, will have to lower their prices to sell the surplus, or excess, products. At prices below equilibrium, consumers will demand more. Producers will be able to raise their prices because the product is scarce, or in short supply.

Supply and Demand

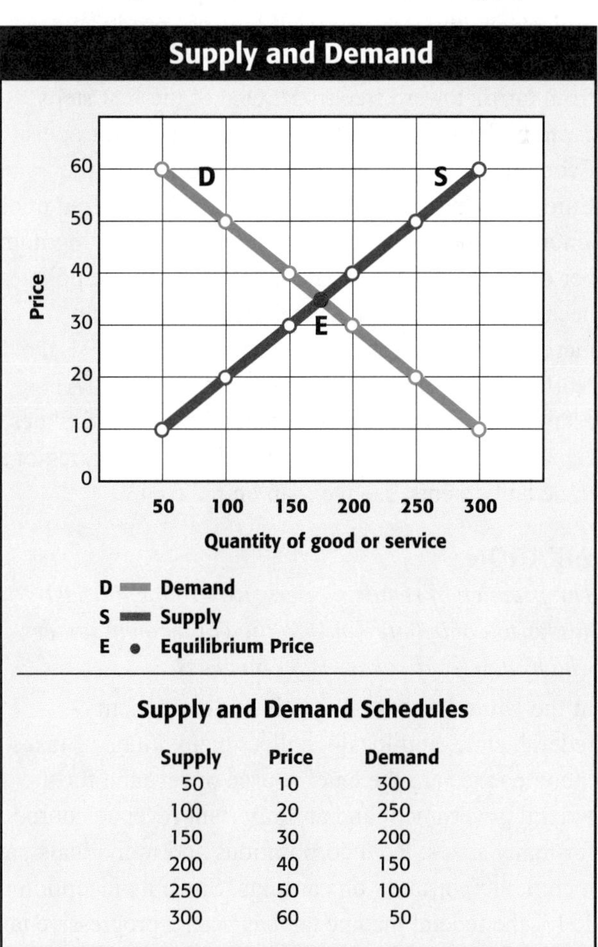

Supply and Demand Schedules

Supply	Price	Demand
50	10	300
100	20	250
150	30	200
200	40	150
250	50	100
300	60	50

R73

SUPPLY-SIDE ECONOMICS

Government policies designed to stimulate the production of goods and services, or the supply side of the economy.

Supply-side economists developed these policies in opposition to **Keynesian economics.** Supply-side policies call for low tax rates particularly in income from investments. Lower taxes mean that people keep more of what they earn. Therefore, supply-side economists argue, people will work harder in order to earn more. They will then use their extra income to save and invest. This investment will fund the development of new businesses and, as a result, create more jobs.

TARIFF

A fee charged for goods brought into a state or country from another state or country.

Governments have collected tariffs since ancient times. Initially, tariffs were used to raise revenue. As time went on, however, governments used them as a way to control imports. In the United States, for example, Congress created tariffs in 1789 to raise revenue and to protect American products from foreign competition. Soon, however, special interest groups used tariffs to protect specific industries and increase profits.

After World War II, many governments moved away from tariffs toward free trade. One of the first steps came in the 1950s, with the creation of the European Economic Community (EEC), now known as the European Union. The EEC encouraged tariff-free trade among its members. In recent decades, a growing number of U.S. economists have favored free trade policies because they believe that such policies will help increase U.S. exports to other countries. In 1994, the North American Free Trade Agreement (NAFTA) established a free-trade zone among the United States, Canada, and Mexico. For more information on regional trade agreements, see the map on page 643.

TAXATION

The practice of requiring persons, groups, or businesses to contribute funds to the government under which they reside or transact business.

In the United States, all levels of government—federal, state, and local—collect many kinds of taxes. Income taxes are the chief source of revenue for the federal government and an important revenue source for many states. Both corporations and individuals pay income tax, or taxes on earnings. Since its inception in 1913, the federal income tax has been a progressive tax, one that is graduated, or scaled, such that those with greater incomes are taxed at a greater rate. Sales taxes are another important source of income for state governments.

Property taxes are the main source of funds for local governments. Property tax is calculated as a percentage of the assessed value of real estate—land and improvements such as buildings.

TRADE

The exchange of goods and services between countries.

Almost all nations produce goods that other countries need, and they sell (export) those goods to buyers in other countries. At the same time, they buy (import) goods from other countries as well. For example, Americans sell goods such as wheat to people in Japan and buy Japanese goods such as automobiles in return.

The relationship between the value of a country's imports and the value of its exports is called the *balance of trade.* If a country exports more than it imports, it has a trade surplus. However, if the value of a country's imports exceeds the value of its exports, the country has a trade deficit. As the graph below shows, Japan maintained a trade surplus throughout the 1990s.

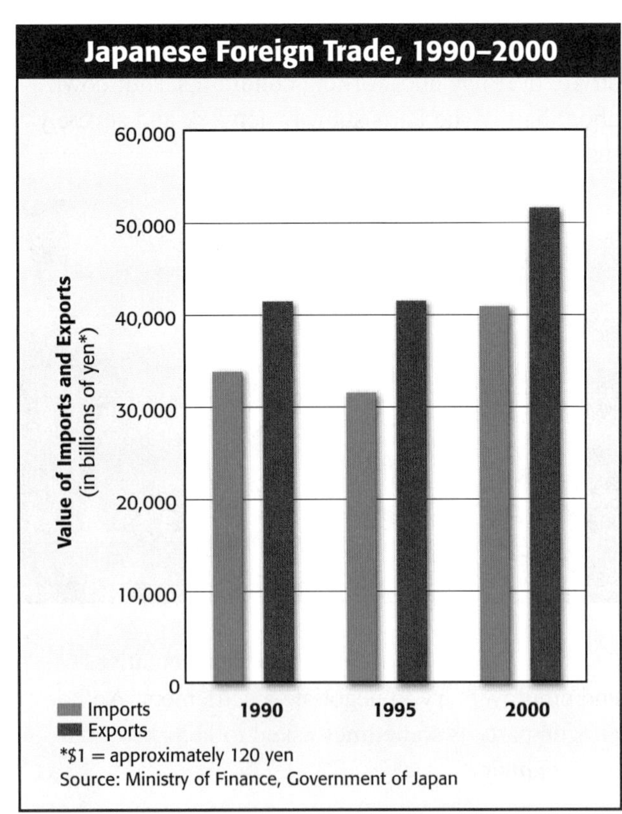

Economics Handbook

Nations that trade with one another often become dependent on one another's products. Sometimes this brings nations closer together, as it did the United States, Great Britain, and France before World War I. At other times it causes tension among nations, such as that between the United States and Arab oil-producing countries in the 1970s. For an example of how trade influences foreign policy, see page 645.

UNEMPLOYMENT RATE

The percentage of the labor force that is unemployed but actively looking for work.

The labor force consists of all civilians of working age, normally 15 to 16 years of age and older, who are employed or who are unemployed but actively looking and available for work. In the United States, the size of the labor force and the unemployment rate are determined by surveys conducted by the U.S. Bureau of the Census.

The unemployment rate provides an indicator of economic health. Rising unemployment rates signal a contraction in the economy, while falling rates indicate an economic expansion. The graphs below show two different methods of portraying unemployment in Canada.

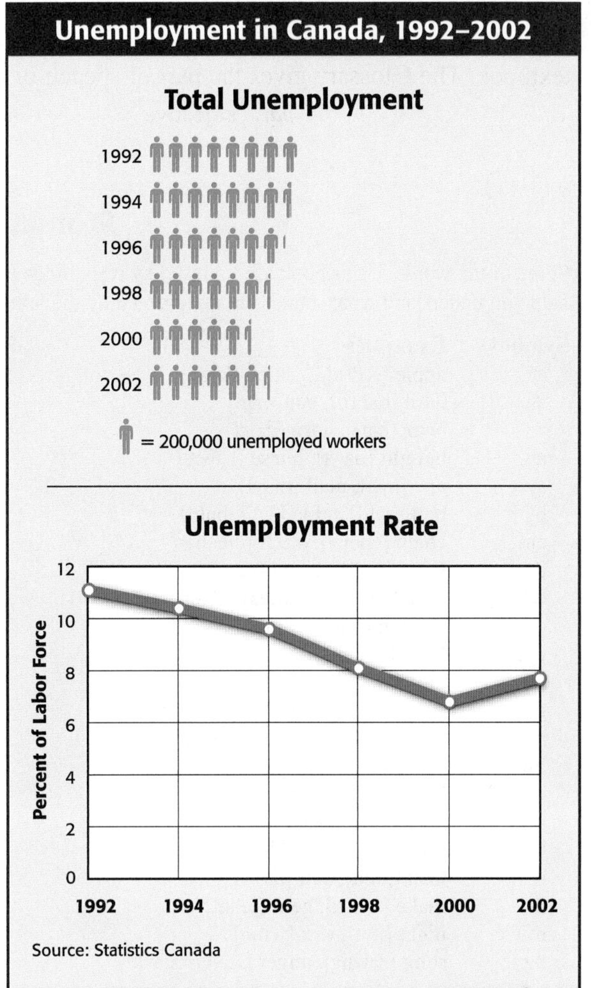

Economics Handbook

Glossary

The Glossary is an alphabetical listing of many of the key terms from the chapters, along with their meanings. The definitions listed in the Glossary are the ones that apply to the way the words are used in this textbook. The Glossary gives the part of speech of each word. The following abbreviations are used:

adj. **adjective** ***n.*** **noun** ***v.*** **verb**

Pronunciation Key

Some of the words in this book are followed by respellings that show how the words are pronounced. The following key will help you understand what sounds are represented by the letters used in the respellings.

Symbol	Examples	Symbol	Examples
a	**a**pple [AP•uhl], c**a**tch [kach]	oh	r**oa**d, [rohd], kn**ow** [noh]
ah	b**a**rn [bahrn], p**o**t [paht]	oo	sch**oo**l [skool], gl**ue** [gloo]
air	b**ear** [bair], d**are** [dair]	ow	**ou**t [owt], c**ow** [kow]
aw	b**ough**t [bawt], h**or**se [hawrs]	oy	c**oi**n [koyn], b**oy**s [boyz]
ay	**a**pe [ayp], m**ai**l [mayl]	p	**p**ig [pihg], to**p** [tahp]
b	**b**ell [behl], ta**b**le [TAY•buhl]	r	**r**ose [rohz], sta**r** [stahr]
ch	**ch**ain [chayn], di**tch** [dihch]	s	**s**oap [sohp], i**c**y [EYE•see]
d	**d**og [dawg], rain**ed** [raynd]	sh	**sh**are [shair], na**ti**on [NAY•shuhn]
ee	**e**ven [EE•vuhn], m**ea**l [meel]	t	**t**ired [tyrd], boa**t** [boht]
eh	**e**gg [ehg], t**e**n [tehn]	th	**th**in [thihn], mo**th**er [MUH•thuhr]
eye	**i**ron [EYE•uhrn]	u	p**u**ll [pul], l**oo**k [luk]
f	**f**all [fawl], lau**gh** [laf]	uh	b**u**mp [buhmp], **a**wake [uh•WAYK],
g	**g**old [gohld], bi**g** [bihg]		happ**e**n [HAP•uhn], penc**i**l [PEHN•suhl],
h	**h**ot [haht], ex**h**ale [ehks•HAYL]		pil**o**t [PY•luht]
hw	**wh**ite [hwyt]	ur	**ear**th [urth], b**ir**d [burd], w**or**m [wurm]
ih	**i**nto [IHN•too], s**i**ck [sihk]	v	**v**ase [vays], lo**ve** [luhv]
j	**j**ar [jahr], ba**dge** [baj]	w	**w**eb [wehb], t**w**in [twihn]
k	**c**at [kat], lu**ck** [luhk]	y	As a consonant: **y**ard [yahrd], m**u**le [myool]
l	**l**oad [lohd], ba**ll** [bawl]		As a vowel: **i**ce [ys], tr**ie**d [tryd], s**igh** [sy]
m	**m**ake [mayk], ge**m** [jehm]	z	**z**one [zohn], rea**s**on [REE•zuhn]
n	**n**ight [nyt], wi**n** [wihn]	zh	trea**s**ure [TREHZH•uhr], gara**ge** [guh•RAHZH]
ng	so**ng** [sawng], a**n**ger [ANG•guhr]		

Syllables that are stressed when the words are spoken appear in CAPITAL LETTERS in the respellings. For example, the respelling of *patterns* (PAT•uhrnz) shows that the first syllable of the word is stressed.

Syllables that appear in SMALL CAPITAL LETTERS are also stressed, but not as strongly as those that appear in capital letters. For example, the respelling of *interaction* (IHN•tuhr•AK•shuhn) shows that the third syllable receives the main stress and the first syllable receives a secondary stress.

A

Aborigine [AB•uh•RIHJ•uh•nee] *n.* a member of any of the native peoples of Australia. (p. 318)

absolute monarch [MAHN•uhrk] *n.* a king or queen who has unlimited power and seeks to control all aspects of society. (p. 160)

Allies [uh•LYZ] *n.* in World War I, the nations of Great Britain, France, and Russia, along with the other nations that fought on their side; also, the group of nations—including Great Britain, the Soviet Union, and the United States—that opposed the Axis Powers in World War II. (p. 411)

Amritsar Massacre *n.* killing by British troops of nearly 400 Indians gathered at Amritsar to protest the Rowlatt Acts. (p. 454)

Anabaptist [AN•uh•BAP•tihst] *n.* in the Reformation, a member of a Protestant group that believed in baptizing only those persons who were old enough to decide to be Christian and believed in the separation of church and state. (p. 62)

Anglican [ANG•glih•kuhn] *adj.* relating to the Church of England. (p. 60)

annexation [AN•ihk•SAY•shuhn] *n.* the adding of a region to the territory of an existing political unit. (pp. 365, 379)

annul [uh•NUHL] *v.* to cancel or set aside. (p. 58)

anti-Semitism [AN•tee•SEHM•ih•TIHZ•uhm] *n.* prejudice against Jews. (p. 315)

R76

Glossary

apartheid [uh•PAHRT•HYT] *n.* a South African policy of complete legal separation of the races, including the banning of all social contacts between blacks and whites. (p. 609)

appeasement *n.* the making of concessions to an aggressor in order to avoid war. (p. 483)

armistice [AHR•mih•stihs] *n.* an agreement to stop fighting. (p. 421)

Aryans [AIR•ee•uhnz] *n.* to the Nazis, the Germanic peoples who formed a "master race." (p. 502)

assembly line *n.* in a factory, an arrangement in which a product is moved from worker to worker, with each person performing a single task in its manufacture. (p. 330)

assimilation [uh•SIHM•uh•LAY•shuhn] *n.* a policy in which a nation forces or encourages a subject people to adopt its institutions and customs. (p. 347)

Atlantic Charter *n.* a declaration of principles issued in August 1941 by British prime minister Winston Churchill and U.S. president Franklin Roosevelt, on which the Allied peace plan at the end of World War II was based. (p. 496)

Atlantic slave trade *n.* the buying, transporting, and selling of Africans for work in the Americas. (p. 133)

Axis Powers *n.* in World War II, the nations of Germany, Italy, and Japan, which had formed an alliance in 1936. (p. 483)

B

balance of power *n.* a political situation in which no one nation is powerful enough to pose a threat to others. (p. 238)

The Balkans [BAWL•kuhnz] *n.* the region of southeastern Europe now occupied by Greece, Albania, Bulgaria, Romania, the European part of Turkey, and the former republics of Yugoslavia. (p. 255)

baroque [buh•ROHK] *adj.* relating to a grand, ornate style that characterized European painting, music, and architecture in the 1600s and early 1700s. (p. 203)

Battle of Britain *n.* a series of battles between German and British air forces, fought over Britain in 1940–1941. (p. 494)

Battle of Guadalcanal [GWAHD•uhl•kuh•NAL] *n.* a 1942–1943 battle of World War II, in which Allied troops drove Japanese forces from the Pacific island of Guadalcanal. (p. 501)

Battle of Midway *n.* a 1942 sea and air battle of World War II, in which American forces defeated Japanese forces in the central Pacific. (p. 500)

Battle of Stalingrad [STAH•lihn•GRAD] *n.* a 1942–1943 battle of World War II, in which German forces were defeated in their attempt to capture the city of Stalingrad in the Soviet Union. (p. 507)

Battle of the Bulge *n.* a 1944–1945 battle in which Allied forces turned back the last major German offensive of World War II. (p. 510)

Battle of Trafalgar [truh•FAL•guhr] *n.* an 1805 naval battle in which Napoleon's forces were defeated by a British fleet under the command of Horatio Nelson. (p. 233)

Berlin Conference *n.* a meeting (1884–1885) at which representatives of European nations agreed upon rules for the European colonization of Africa. (p. 342)

Bill of Rights *n.* the first ten amendments to the U.S. Constitution, which protect citizens' basic rights and freedoms. (p. 211)

blitzkrieg [BLIHTS•KREEG] *n.* "lightning war"—a form of warfare in which surprise attacks with fast-moving airplanes are followed by massive attacks with infantry forces. (p. 491)

blockade [blah•KAYD] *n.* the use of troops or ships to prevent commercial traffic from entering or leaving a city or region. (p. 234)

Boer [bohr] *n.* a Dutch colonist in South Africa. (p. 342)

Boer War *n.* a conflict, lasting from 1899 to 1902, in which the Boers and the British fought for control of territory in South Africa. (p. 344)

Bolsheviks [BOHL•shuh•VIHKS] *n.* a group of revolutionary Russian Marxists who took control of Russia's government in November 1917. (p. 434)

Boxer Rebellion *n.* a 1900 revolt in China, aimed at ending foreign influence in the country. (p. 374)

boyar [boh•YAHR] *n.* a landowning noble of Russia. (p. 174)

brinkmanship *n.* a policy of threatening to go to war in response to any enemy aggression. (p. 536)

C

cabinet *n.* a group of advisers or ministers chosen by the head of a country to help make government decisions. (p. 183)

Calvinism [KAL•vih•NIHZ•uhm] *n.* a body of religious teachings based on the ideas of the reformer John Calvin. (p. 61)

Camp David Accords *n.* the first signed agreement between Israel and an Arab country, in which Egyptian president Anwar Sadat recognized Israel as a legitimate state and Israeli prime minister Menachem Begin agreed to return the Sinai Peninsula to Egypt. (p. 586)

capitalism *n.* an economic system based on private ownership and on the investment of money in business ventures in order to make a profit. (pp. 139, 300)

Catholic Reformation [REHF•uhr•MAY•shuhn] *n.* a 16th-century movement in which the Roman Catholic Church sought to make changes in response to the Protestant Reformation. (p. 64)

R77

caudillos [kaw•DEEL•yoh] *n.* a military dictator of a Latin American country. (p. 382)

Central Powers *n.* in World War I, the nations of Germany and Austria-Hungary, along with the other nations that fought on their side. (p. 411)

Chartist movement *n.* in 19th-century Britain, members of the working class demanded reforms in Parliament and in elections, including suffrage for all men. (p. 314)

checks and balances *n.* measures designed to prevent any one branch of government from dominating the others. (p. 211)

CIS *n.* the Commonwealth of Independent States—a loose association of former Soviet republics that was formed after the breakup of the Soviet Union. (p. 615)

civil disobedience *n.* a deliberate and public refusal to obey a law considered unjust. (p. 454)

cloning [KLOH•nihng] *n.* the creation of plants or animals that are genetically identical to an existing plant or animal. (p. 639)

coalition [KOH•uh•LIHSH•uhn] **government** *n.* a government controlled by a temporary alliance of several political parties. (p. 470)

Cold War *n.* the state of diplomatic hostility between the United States and the Soviet Union in the decades following World War II. (p. 535)

collective farm *n.* a large government-controlled farm formed by combining many small farms. (p. 444)

colony *n.* a land controlled by another nation. (p. 120)

Columbian Exchange *n.* the global transfer of plants, animals, and diseases that occurred during the European colonization of the Americas. (p. 137)

command economy *n.* an economic system in which the government makes all economic decisions. (p. 443)

commune [KAHM•YOON] *n.* in Communist China, a collective farm on which a great number of people work and live together. (p. 540)

Communist Party *n.* a political party practicing the ideas of Karl Marx and V.I. Lenin; originally the Russian Bolshevik Party. (p. 439)

communism *n.* an economic system in which all means of production—land, mines, factories, railroads, and businesses—are owned by the people, private property does not exist, and all goods and services are shared equally. (p. 303)

Concert [KAHN•SURT] **of Europe** *n.* a series of alliances among European nations in the 19th century, devised by Prince Klemens von Metternich to prevent the outbreak of revolutions. (p. 240)

concordat [kuhn•KAWR•DAT] *n.* a formal agreement—especially one between the pope and a government, dealing with the control of Church affairs. (p. 230)

Congress of Vienna [vee•EHN•uh] *n.* a series of meetings in 1814–1815, during which the European leaders sought to establish long-lasting peace and security after the defeat of Napoleon. (p. 238)

Congress Party *n.* a major national political party in India—also known as the Indian National Congress. (p. 563)

conquistadors [kahng•KEE•stuh•DAWRZ] *n.* the Spanish soldiers, explorers, and fortune hunters who took part in the conquest of the Americas in the 16th century. (p. 120)

conservative *n.* in the first half of the 19th century, a European—mainly wealthy landowners and nobles—who wanted to preserve the traditional monarchies of Europe. (p. 253)

constitutional monarchy [MAHN•uhr•kee] *n.* a system of governing in which the ruler's power is limited by law. (p. 183)

containment *n.* a U.S. foreign policy adopted by President Harry Truman in the late 1940s, in which the United States tried to stop the spread of communism by creating alliances and helping weak countries to resist Soviet advances. (p. 533)

Continental System *n.* Napoleon's policy of preventing trade between Great Britain and continental Europe, intended to destroy Great Britain's economy. (p. 234)

corporation *n.* a business owned by stockholders who share in its profits but are not personally responsible for its debts. (p. 297)

Council of Trent *n.* a meeting of Roman Catholic leaders, called by Pope Paul III to rule on doctrines criticized by the Protestant reformers. (p. 65)

coup d'état [KOO day•TAH] *n.* a sudden seizure of political power in a nation. (p. 230)

creole [KREE•OHL] *n.* in Spanish colonial society, a colonist who was born in Latin America to Spanish parents. (p. 247)

Crimean [kry•MEE•uhn] **War** *n.* a conflict, lasting from 1853 to 1856, in which the Ottoman Empire, with the aid of Britain and France, halted Russian expansion in the region of the Black Sea. (p. 353)

crop rotation *n.* the system of growing a different crop in a field each year to preserve the fertility of the land. (p. 283)

Cultural Revolution *n.* a 1966–1976 uprising in China led by the Red Guards, with the goal of establishing a society of peasants and workers in which all were equal. (p. 541)

cyberterrorism *n.* politically motivated attacks on information systems. (p. 654)

D

daimyo [DY•mee•OH] *n.* a Japanese feudal lord who commanded a private army of samurai. (p. 108)

D-Day *n.* June 6, 1944—the day on which the Allies began their invasion of the European mainland during World War II. (p. 510)

Declaration of Independence *n.* a statement of the reasons for the American colonies' break with Britain, approved by the Second Continental Congress in 1776. (p. 207)

demilitarization [dee•MIHL•ih•tuhr•ih•ZAY•shuhn] *n.* a reduction in a country's ability to wage war, achieved by disbanding its armed forces and prohibiting it from acquiring weapons. (p. 516)

democratization *n.* the process of creating a government elected by the people. (p. 516)

Department of Homeland Security *n.* U.S. federal agency created in 2002 to coordinate national efforts against terrorism. (p. 657)

détente [day•TAHNT] *n.* a policy of reducing Cold War tensions that was adopted by the United States during the presidency of Richard Nixon. (p. 556)

developed nation *n.* a nation with all the facilities needed for the advanced production of manufactured goods. (p. 641)

devshirme [dehv•SHEER•meh] *n.* in the Ottoman Empire, the policy of taking boys from conquered Christian peoples to be trained as Muslim soldiers. (p. 76)

dissident [DIHS•ih•duhnt] *n.* an opponent of a government's policies or actions. (p. 608)

divine right *n.* the idea that monarchs are God's representatives on earth and are therefore answerable only to God. (p. 160)

dominion *n.* in the British Empire, a nation (such as Canada) allowed to govern its own domestic affairs. (p. 318)

domino theory *n.* the idea that if a nation falls under Communist control, nearby nations will also fall under Communist control. (p. 544)

Dreyfus [DRY•fuhs] **affair** *n.* a controversy in France in the 1890s, centering on the trial and imprisonment of a Jewish army officer, Captain Alfred Dreyfus, who had been falsely accused of selling military secrets to Germany. (p. 315)

Dutch East India Company *n.* a company founded by the Dutch in the early 17th century to establish and direct trade throughout Asia. (p. 100)

E

Eastern Front *n.* in World War I, the region along the German-Russian border where Russians and Serbs battled Germans, Austrians, and Turks. (p. 414)

Edict of Nantes [EE•DIHKT uhv NAHNT] *n.* a 1598 declaration in which the French king Henry IV promised that Protestants could live in peace in France and could set up houses of worship in some French cities. (p. 162)

Emancipation Proclamation [ih•MAN•suh•PAY•shuhn PRAHK•luh•MAY•shuhn] *n.* a declaration issued by U.S. president Abraham Lincoln in 1863, stating that all slaves in the Confederate states were free. (p. 326)

emerging nation *n.* a nation in which the process of industrialization is not yet complete. (p. 641)

émigré [EHM•ih•GRAY] *n.* a person who leaves his native country for political reasons, like the nobles and others who fled France during the peasant uprisings of the French Revolution. (p. 224)

enclosure *n.* one of the fenced-in or hedged-in fields created by wealthy British landowners on land that was formerly worked by village farmers. (p. 283)

encomienda [ehng•kaw•MYEHN•dah] *n.* a grant of land made by Spain to a settler in the Americas, including the right to use Native Americans as laborers on it. (p. 123)

English Civil War *n.* a conflict, lasting from 1642 to 1649, in which Puritan supporters of Parliament battled supporters of England's monarchy. (p. 181)

enlightened despot [DEHS•puht] *n.* one of the 18th-century European monarchs who was inspired by Enlightenment ideas to rule justly and respect the rights of subjects. (p. 204)

Enlightenment *n.* an 18th-century European movement in which thinkers attempted to apply the principles of reason and the scientific method to all aspects of society. (p. 195)

entrepreneur [AHN•truh•pruh•NUR] *n.* a person who organizes, manages, and takes on the risks of a business. (p. 287)

estate [ih•STAYT] n. one of the three social classes in France before the French Revolution—the First Estate consisting of the clergy; the Second Estate, of the nobility; and the Third Estate, of the rest of the population. (p. 217)

Estates-General [ih•STAYTS•JEHN•uhr•uhl] *n.* an assembly of representatives from all three of the estates, or social classes, in France. (p. 219)

ethnic cleansing *n.* a policy of murder and other acts of brutality by which Serbs hoped to eliminate Bosnia's Muslim population after the breakup of Yugoslavia. (p. 622)

existentialism [EHG•zih•STEHN•shuh•LIHZ•uhm] *n.* a philosophy based on the idea that people give meaning to their lives through their choices and actions. (p. 464)

extraterritorial [EHK•struh•TEHR•ih•TAWR•ee•uhl] **rights** *n.* an exemption of foreign residents from the laws of a country. (p. 372)

F

factors of production *n.* the resources—including land, labor, and capital—that are needed to produce goods and services. (p. 284)

Glossary

R79

factory *n.* a large building in which machinery is used to manufacture goods. (p. 286)

fascism [FASH•IHZ•uhm] *n.* a political movement that promotes an extreme form of nationalism, a denial of individual rights, and a dictatorial one-party rule. (p. 476)

favorable balance of trade *n.* an economic situation in which a country sells more goods abroad than it buys from abroad. (p. 141)

federal system *n.* a system of government in which power is divided between a central authority and a number of individual states. (pp. 211, 607)

"Final Solution" *n.* Hitler's program of systematically killing the entire Jewish people. (p. 503)

Five-Year Plans *n.* plans outlined by Joseph Stalin in 1928 for the development of the Soviet Union's economy. (p. 443)

Four Modernizations *n.* a set of goals adopted by the Chinese leader Deng Xiaoping in the late 20th century, involving progress in agriculture, industry, defense, and science and technology. (p. 626)

Fourteen Points *n.* a series of proposals in which U.S. president Woodrow Wilson outlined a plan for achieving a lasting peace after World War I. (p. 424)

free trade *n.* commerce between nations without economic restrictions or barriers (such as tariffs). (p. 642)

French and Indian War *n.* a conflict between Britain and France for control of territory in North America, lasting from 1754 to 1763. (p. 130)

G

gender inequality *n.* the difference between men and women in terms of wealth and status. (p. 650)

genetic [juh•NEHT•ihk] **engineering** *n.* the transferring of genes from one living thing to another in order to produce an organism with new traits. (p. 639)

genocide [JEHN•uh•SYD] *n.* the systematic killing of an entire people. (p. 503)

geocentric theory *n.* in the Middle Ages, the earth-centered view of the universe in which scholars believed that the earth was an immovable object located at the center of the universe. (p. 189)

geopolitics [JEE•oh•PAHL•ih•tihks] *n.* a foreign policy based on a consideration of the strategic locations or products of other lands. (p. 352)

ghazi [GAH•zee] *n.* a warrior for Islam. (p. 73)

ghettos [GEHT•ohz] *n.* city neighborhoods in which European Jews were forced to live. (p. 503)

glasnost [GLAHS•nuhst] *n.* a Soviet policy of openness to the free flow of ideas and information, introduced in 1985 by Mikhail Gorbachev. (p. 612)

global economy *n.* all the financial interactions—involving people, businesses, and governments—that cross international boundaries. (p. 642)

Glorious Revolution *n.* the bloodless overthrow of the English king James II and his replacement by William and Mary. (p. 182)

Great Depression *n.* the severe economic slump that followed the collapse of the U.S. stock market in 1929. (p. 473)

Great Fear *n.* a wave of senseless panic that spread through the French countryside after the storming of the Bastille in 1789. (p. 221)

Great Purge *n.* a campaign of terror in the Soviet Union during the 1930s, in which Joseph Stalin sought to eliminate all Communist Party members and other citizens who threatened his power. (p. 442)

green revolution *n.* a 20th-century attempt to increase food resources worldwide, involving the use of fertilizers and pesticides and the development of disease-resistant crops. (p. 640)

guerrilla [guh•RIHL•uh] *n.* a member of a loosely organized fighting force that makes surprise attacks on enemy troops occupying his or her country. (p. 235)

guillotine [GIHL•uh•TEEN] *n.* a machine for beheading people, used as a means of execution during the French Revolution. (p. 226)

H

habeas corpus [HAY•bee•uhs KAWR•puhs] *n.* a document requiring that a prisoner be brought before a court or judge so that it can be decided whether his or her imprisonment is legal. (p. 182)

haiku [HY•koo] *n.* a Japanese form of poetry, consisting of three unrhymed lines of five, seven, and five syllables. (p. 110)

heliocentric [HEE•lee•oh•SEHN•trihk] **theory** *n.* the idea that the earth and the other planets revolve around the sun. (p. 190)

Holocaust [HAHL•uh•KAWST] *n.* a mass slaughter of Jews and other civilians, carried out by the Nazi government of Germany before and during World War II. (p. 502)

Holy Alliance *n.* a league of European nations formed by the leaders of Russia, Austria, and Prussia after the Congress of Vienna. (p. 240)

home rule *n.* a control over internal matters granted to the residents of a region by a ruling government. (p. 320)

humanism [HYOO•muh•NIHZ•uhm] *n.* a Renaissance intellectual movement in which thinkers studied classical texts and focused on human potential and achievements. (p. 38)

Hundred Days *n.* the brief period during 1815 when Napoleon made his last bid for power, deposing the French king and again becoming emperor of France. (p. 237)

I

imperialism [ihm•PEER•ee•uh•LIHZ•uhm] *n.* a policy in which a strong nation seeks to dominate other countries politically, economically, or socially. (p. 339)

impressionism [ihm•PREHSH•uh•NIHZ•uhm] *n.* a movement in 19th-century painting, in which artists reacted against realism by seeking to convey their impressions of subjects or moments in time. (p. 267)

indulgence [ihn•DUHL•juhns] *n.* a pardon releasing a person from punishments due for a sin. (p. 55)

industrialization [ihn•DUHS•tree•uh•lih•ZAY•shuhn] *n.* the development of industries for the machine production of goods. (p. 284)

Industrial Revolution *n.* the shift, beginning in England during the 18th century, from making goods by hand to making them by machine. (p. 283)

intendant [ihn•TEHN•duhnt] *n.* a French government official appointed by the monarch to collect taxes and administer justice. (p. 164)

International Space Station *n.* cooperative venture sponsored by the United States, Russia, and 14 other nations to establish and maintain a working laboratory for scientific experimentation in space. (p. 637)

Internet *n.* a linkage of computer networks that enables people around the world to exchange information and communicate with one another. (p. 639)

intifada *n.* Palestinian campaign of civil disobedience against Israeli occupation of the West Bank and Gaza Strip, which continued into the 1990s. (p. 587)

Irish Republican Army (IRA) *n.* an unofficial nationalist military force seeking independence for Ireland from Great Britain. (p. 321)

iron curtain *n.* during the Cold War, the boundary separating the Communist nations of Eastern Europe from the mostly democratic nations of Western Europe. (p. 533)

isolationism *n.* a policy of avoiding political or military involvement with other countries. (p. 484)

J

janissary [JAN•ih•SEHR•ee] *n.* a member of an elite force of soldiers in the Ottoman Empire. (p. 76)

jazz *n.* a 20th-century style of popular music developed mainly by African-American musicians. (p. 465)

Jesuits [JEHZH•oo•ihts] *n.* members of the Society of Jesus, a Roman Catholic religious order founded by Ignatius of Loyola. (p. 65)

"jewel in the crown" *n.* the British colony of India—so called because of its importance in the British Empire, both as a supplier of raw materials and as a market for British trade goods. (p. 357)

joint-stock company *n.* a business in which investors pool their wealth for a common purpose, then share the profits. (p. 139)

K

kabuki [kuh•BOO•kee] *n.* a type of Japanese drama in which music, dance, and mime are used to present stories. (p. 110)

kaiser [KY•zuhr] *n.* a German emperor (from the Roman title *Caesar*). (p. 263)

kamikaze [KAH•mih•KAH•zee] *n.* during World War II, Japanese suicide pilots trained to sink Allied ships by crashing bomb-filled planes into them. (p. 511)

Khmer Rouge [roozh] *n.* a group of Communist rebels who seized power in Cambodia in 1975. (p. 547)

Kristallnacht [krih•STAHL•NAHKT] *n.* "Night of Broken Glass"—the night of November 9, 1938, on which Nazi storm troopers attacked Jewish homes, businesses, and synagogues throughout Germany. (p. 502)

Kuomintang [KWOH•mihn•TANG] *n.* the Chinese Nationalist Party, formed after the fall of the Qing Dynasty in 1912. (p. 448)

L

laissez faire [LEHS•ay FAIR] *n.* the idea that government should not interfere with or regulate industries and businesses. (p. 300)

land reform *n.* a redistribution of farmland by breaking up large estates and giving the resulting smaller farms to peasants. (p. 600)

La Reforma [lah reh•FAWR•mah] *n.* a liberal reform movement in 19th-century Mexico, led by Benito Juárez. (p. 390)

League of Nations *n.* an international association formed after World War I with the goal of keeping peace among nations. (p. 425)

lebensraum [LAY•buhns•ROWM] *n.* "living space"—the additional territory that, according to Adolf Hitler, Germany needed because it was overcrowded. (p. 478)

Legislative [LEHJ•ih•SLAY•tihv] **Assembly** *n.* a French congress with the power to create laws and approve declarations of war, established by the Constitution of 1791. (p. 223)

legitimacy [luh•JIHT•uh•muh•see] *n.* the hereditary right of a monarch to rule. (p. 239)

liberal *n.* in the first half of the 19th century, a European—mainly middle-class business leaders and merchants—who wanted to give more political power to elected parliaments. (p. 253)

Long March *n.* a 6,000-mile journey made in 1934–1935 by Chinese Communists fleeing from Jiang Jieshi's Nationalist forces. (p. 452)

Lutheran [LOO•thuhr•uhn] *n.* a member of a Protestant church founded on the teachings of Martin Luther. (p. 56)

lycée [lee•SAY] *n.* a government-run public school in France. (p. 230)

M

Manchus [MAN•chooz] *n.* a people, native to Manchuria, who ruled China during the Qing Dynasty (1644–1912). (p. 105)

R81

manifest destiny *n.* the idea, popular among mid-19th-century Americans, that it was the right and the duty of the United States to rule North America from the Atlantic Ocean to the Pacific Ocean. (p. 324)

Maori [MOW•ree] *n.* a member of a Polynesian people who settled in New Zealand around A.D. 800. (p. 318)

Marshall Plan *n.* a U.S. program of economic aid to European countries to help them rebuild after World War II. (p. 534)

martial [MAHR•shuhl] **law** *n.* a temporary rule by military authorities over a civilian population, usually imposed in times of war or civil unrest. (p. 607)

mass culture *n.* the production of works of art and entertainment designed to appeal to a large audience. (p. 332)

materialism *n.* a placing of high value on acquiring material possessions. (p. 662)

May Fourth Movement *n.* a national protest in China in 1919, in which people demonstrated against the Treaty of Versailles and foreign interference. (p. 449)

Meiji [MAY•JEE] **era** *n.* the period of Japanese history from 1867 to 1912, during which the country was ruled by Emperor Mutsuhito. (p. 377)

Mein Kampf [MYN KAHMPF] *n.* "My Struggle"—a book written by Adolf Hitler during his imprisonment in 1923–1924, in which he set forth his beliefs and his goals for Germany. (p. 478)

mercantilism [MUR•kuhn•tee•LIHZ•uhm] *n.* an economic policy under which nations sought to increase their wealth and power by obtaining large amounts of gold and silver and by selling more goods than they bought. (p. 140)

mestizo [mehs•TEE•zoh] *n.* a person of mixed Spanish and Native American ancestry. (p. 123)

middle class *n.* a social class made up of skilled workers, professionals, businesspeople, and wealthy farmers. (p. 291)

middle passage *n.* the voyage that brought captured Africans to the West Indies, and later to North and South America, to be sold as slaves—so called because it was considered the middle leg of the triangular trade. (p. 135)

militarism [MIHL•ih•tuh•RIHZ•uhm] *n.* a policy of glorifying military power and keeping a standing army always prepared for war. (p. 408)

Ming Dynasty *n.* a Chinese dynasty that ruled from 1368 to 1644. (p. 102)

Monroe Doctrine *n.* a U.S. policy of opposition to European interference in Latin America, announced by President James Monroe in 1823. (p. 384)

Mughal [MOO•guhl] *n.* one of the nomads who invaded the Indian subcontinent in the 16th century and established a powerful empire there. (p. 82)

mujahideen [moo•JAH•heh•DEEN] *n.* in Afghanistan, holy warriors who banded together to fight the Soviet-supported government in the late 1970s. (p. 592)

mulattos [mu•LAT•ohz] *n.* persons of mixed European and African ancestry. (p. 248)

Munich [MYOO•nihk] **Conference** *n.* a 1938 meeting of representatives from Britain, France, Italy, and Germany, at which Britain and France agreed to allow Nazi Germany to annex part of Czechoslovakia in return for Adolf Hitler's pledge to respect Czechoslovakia's new borders. (p. 485)

Muslim League *n.* an organization formed in 1906 to protect the interests of India's Muslims, which later proposed that India be divided into separate Muslim and Hindu nations. (p. 563)

N

Napoleonic [nuh•POH•lee•AHN•ihk] **Code** *n.* a comprehensive and uniform system of laws established for France by Napoleon. (p. 230)

National Assembly *n.* a French congress established by representatives of the Third Estate on June 17, 1789, to enact laws and reforms in the name of the French people. (p. 220)

nationalism *n.* the belief that people should be loyal mainly to their nation—that is, to the people with whom they share a culture and history—rather than to a king or empire. (p. 253)

nation-state *n.* an independent geopolitical unit of people having a common culture and identity. (p. 253)

NATO [NAY•toh] *n.* the North Atlantic Treaty Organization—a defensive military alliance formed in 1949 by ten Western European nations, the United States, and Canada. (p. 535)

Nazism [NAHT•SIHZ•uhm] *n.* the fascist policies of the National Socialist German Workers' party, based on totalitarianism, a belief in racial superiority, and state control of industry. (p. 478)

Negritude [NEE•grih•TOOD] **movement** *n.* a movement in which French-speaking Africans and West Indians celebrated their heritage of traditional African culture and values. (p. 578)

neoclassical [NEE•oh•KLAS•ih•kuhl] *adj.* relating to a simple, elegant style (based on ideas and themes from ancient Greece and Rome) that characterized the arts in Europe during the late 1700s. (p. 203)

New Deal *n.* U.S. president Franklin Roosevelt's economic reform program designed to solve the problems created by the Great Depression. (p. 475)

nonaggression [NAHN•uh•GRESHS•uhn] **pact** *n.* an agreement in which nations promise not to attack one another. (p. 491)

nonaligned nations *n.* the independent countries that remained neutral in the Cold War competition between the United States and the Soviet Union. (p. 548)

R82

Nuremberg [NUR•uhm•BURG] **Trials** *n.* a series of court proceedings held in Nuremberg, Germany, after World War II, in which Nazi leaders were tried for aggression, violations of the rules of war, and crimes against humanity. (p. 516)

O

Old Regime [ray•ZHEEM] *n.* the political and social system that existed in France before the French Revolution. (p. 217)

Open Door Policy *n.* a policy, proposed by the United States in 1899, under which all nations would have equal opportunities to trade in China. (p. 374)

Opium War *n.* a conflict between Britain and China, lasting from 1839 to 1842, over Britain's opium trade in China. (p. 372)

Oslo Peace Accords *n.* an agreement in 1993 in which Israeli prime minister Rabin granted Palestinian self-rule in the Gaza Strip and the West Bank. (p. 587)

ozone layer *n.* a layer of Earth's upper atmosphere, which protects living things from the sun's damaging ultraviolet rays. (p. 645)

P

Pacific Rim *n.* the lands surrounding the Pacific Ocean—especially those in Asia. (p. 362)

Panama Canal *n.* a human-made waterway connecting the Atlantic and Pacific oceans, built in Panama by the United States and opened in 1914. (p. 387)

partition *n.* a division into parts, like the 1947 division of the British colony of India into the two nations of India and Pakistan. (p. 564)

paternalism [puh•TUR•nuh•LIHZ•uhm] *n.* a policy of treating subject people as if they were children, providing for their needs but not giving them rights. (p. 347)

patron [PAY•truhn] *n.* a person who supports artists, especially financially. (p. 38)

Peace of Augsburg [AWGZ•BURG] *n.* a 1555 agreement declaring that the religion of each German state would be decided by its ruler. (p. 58)

penal [PEE•nuhl] **colony** *n.* a colony to which convicts are sent as an alternative to prison. (p. 318)

peninsulares [peh•neen•soo•LAH•rehs] *n.* in Spanish colonial society, colonists who were born in Spain. (p. 247)

Peninsular [puh•NIHN•syuh•luhr] **War** *n.* a conflict, lasting from 1808 to 1813, in which Spanish rebels, with the aid of British forces, fought to drive Napoleon's French troops out of Spain. (p. 235)

perestroika [PEHR•ih•STROY•kuh] *n.* a restructuring of the Soviet economy to permit more local decision making, begun by Mikhail Gorbachev in 1985. (p. 613)

perspective [puhr•SPEHK•tihv] *n.* an artistic technique that creates the appearance of three dimensions on a flat surface. (p. 40)

philosophe [FIHL•uh•SAHF] *n.* one of a group of social thinkers in France during the Enlightenment. (p. 196)

Pilgrims *n.* a group of people who, in 1620, founded the colony of Plymouth in Massachusetts to escape religious persecution in England. (p. 128)

plebiscite [PLEHB•ih•SYT] *n.* a direct vote in which a country's people have the opportunity to approve or reject a proposal. (p. 230)

PLO *n.* the Palestine Liberation Organization—an organization dedicated to the establishment of an independent state for Palestinians in the Middle East. (p. 585)

Politburo [PAHL•iht•BYOOR•oh] *n.* the ruling committee of the Communist Party in the Soviet Union. (p. 612)

political dissent *n.* the difference of opinion over political issues. (p. 650)

popular culture *n.* the cultural elements—sports, music, movies, clothing, and so forth—that reflect a group's common background and changing interests. (p. 659)

predestination [pree•DEHS•tuh•NAY•shuhn] *n.* the doctrine that God has decided all things beforehand, including which people will be eternally saved. (p. 61)

Presbyterian [PREHZ•bih•TEER•ee•uhn] *n.* a member of a Protestant church governed by presbyters (elders) and founded on the teachings of John Knox. (p. 62)

PRI *n.* the Institutional Revolutionary Party—the main political party of Mexico. (p. 603)

proletariat [PROH•lih•TAIR•ee•iht] *n.* in Marxist theory, the group of workers who would overthrow the czar and come to rule Russia. (p. 434)

proliferation [pruh•LIHF•uh•RAY•shuhn] *n.* a growth or spread—especially the spread of nuclear weapons to nations that do not currently have them. (p. 649)

propaganda [PRAHP•uh•GAN•duh] *n.* information or material spread to advance a cause or to damage an opponent's cause. (p. 420)

Protestant [PRAHT•ih•stuhnt] *n.* a member of a Christian church founded on the principles of the Reformation. (p. 56)

provisional government *n.* a temporary government. (p. 436)

psychology [sy•KAHL•uh•jee] *n.* the study of the human mind and human behavior. (p. 332)

Puritans *n.* a group of people who sought freedom from religious persecution in England by founding a colony at Massachusetts Bay in the early 1600s. (p. 128)

Q

Qing [chihng] **Dynasty** *n.* China's last dynasty, which ruled from 1644 to 1912. (p. 105)

R

racism [RAY•SIHZ•uhm] *n.* the belief that one race is superior to others. (p. 341)

Glossary

radical *n.* in the first half of the 19th century, a European who favored drastic change to extend democracy to all people. (p. 253)

radioactivity *n.* a form of energy released as atoms decay. (p. 331)

Raj [rahj] *n.* the British-controlled portions of India in the years 1757–1947. (p. 360)

rationing [RASH•uh•nihng] *n.* the limiting of the amounts of goods people can buy—often imposed by governments during wartime, when goods are in short supply. (p. 420)

realism *n.* a 19th-century artistic movement in which writers and painters sought to show life as it is rather than life as it should be. (p. 266)

realpolitik [ray•AHL•POH•lih•TEEK] *n.* "the politics of reality"—the practice of tough power politics without room for idealism. (p. 261)

recession *n.* a slowdown in a nation's economy. (p. 600)

Red Guards *n.* militia units formed by young Chinese people in 1966 in response to Mao Zedong's call for a social and cultural revolution. (p. 541)

Reformation [REHF•uhr•MAY•shuhn] *n.* a 16th-century movement for religious reform, leading to the founding of Christian churches that rejected the pope's authority. (p. 55)

refugee *n.* a person who leaves his or her country to move to another to find safety. (p. 652)

Reign [rayn] **of Terror** *n.* the period, from mid-1793 to mid-1794, when Maximilien Robespierre ruled France nearly as a dictator and thousands of political figures and ordinary citizens were executed. (p. 226)

Renaissance [REHN•ih•SAHNS] *n.* a period of European history, lasting from about 1300 to 1600, during which renewed interest in classical culture led to far-reaching changes in art, learning, and views of the world. (p. 37)

Restoration [REHS•tuh•RAY•shuhn] *n.* the period of Charles II's rule over England, after the collapse of Oliver Cromwell's government. (p. 182)

reunification [ree•YOO•nuh•fih•KAY•shuhn] *n.* a bringing together again of things that have been separated, like the reuniting of East Germany and West Germany in 1990. (p. 620)

romanticism [roh•MAN•tih•SIHZ•uhm] *n.* an early-19th-century movement in art and thought, which focused on emotion and nature rather than reason and society. (p. 264)

Roosevelt Corollary [ROH•zuh•VEHLT KAWR•uh•lehr•ee] *n.* President Theodore Roosevelt's 1904 extension of the Monroe Doctrine, in which he declared that the United States had the right to exercise "police power" throughout the Western Hemisphere. (p. 387)

Rowlatt Acts *n.* laws passed in 1919 that allowed the British government in India to jail anti-British protesters without trial for as long as two years. (p. 453)

Russification [RUHS•uh•fih•KAY•shuhn] *n.* the process of forcing Russian culture on all ethnic groups in the Russian Empire. (p. 259)

Russo-Japanese War *n.* a 1904–1905 conflict between Russia and Japan, sparked by the two countries' efforts to dominate Manchuria and Korea. (p. 378)

S

Safavid [suh•FAH•VIHD] *n.* a member of a Shi'a Muslim dynasty that built an empire in Persia in the 16th–18th centuries. (p. 78)

salon [suh•LAHN] *n.* a social gathering of intellectuals and artists, like those held in the homes of wealthy women in Paris and other European cities during the Enlightenment. (p. 202)

SALT *n.* the Strategic Arms Limitation Talks—a series of meetings in the 1970s, in which leaders of the United States and the Soviet Union agreed to limit their nations' stocks of nuclear weapons. (p. 557)

Salt March *n.* a peaceful protest against the Salt Acts in 1930 in India in which Mohandas Gandhi led his followers on a 240-mile walk to the sea, where they made their own salt from evaporated seawater. (p. 455)

sans-culottes [SANS•kyoo•LAHTS] *n.* in the French Revolution, a radical group made up of Parisian wage-earners and small shopkeepers who wanted a greater voice in government, lower prices, and an end to food shortages. (p. 224)

Schlieffen [SHLEE•fuhn] **Plan** *n.* Germany's military plan at the outbreak of World War I, according to which German troops would rapidly defeat France and then move east to attack Russia. (p. 412)

scientific method *n.* a logical procedure for gathering information about the natural world, in which experimentation and observation are used to test hypotheses. (p. 191)

Scientific Revolution *n.* a major change in European thought, starting in the mid-1500s, in which the study of the natural world began to be characterized by careful observation and the questioning of accepted beliefs. (p. 189)

scorched-earth policy *n.* the practice of burning crops and killing livestock during wartime so that the enemy cannot live off the land. (p. 235)

secede [sih•SEED] *v.* to withdraw formally from an association or alliance. (p. 326)

secular [SEHK•yuh•luhr] *adj.* concerned with worldly rather than spiritual matters. (p. 38)

segregation [SEHG•rih•GAY•shuhn] *n.* the legal or social separation of people of different races. (p. 327)

self-determination [SEHLF•dih•TUR•muh•NAY•shuhn] *n.* the freedom of a people to decide under what form of government they wish to live. (p. 424)

sepoy [SEE•POY] *n.* an Indian soldier serving under British command. (p. 357)

Sepoy Mutiny [MYOOT•uh•nee] *n.* an 1857 rebellion of Hindu and Muslim soldiers against the British in India. (p. 359)

Seven Years' War *n.* a conflict in Europe, North America, and India, lasting from 1756 to 1763, in which the forces of Britain and Prussia battled those of Austria, France, Russia, and other countries. (p. 173)

shah [shah] *n.* hereditary monarch of Iran. (p. 80)

"shock therapy" *n.* an economic program implemented in Russia by Boris Yeltsin in the 1990s, involving an abrupt shift from a command economy to a free-market economy. (p. 616)

Sikh [seek] *n.* a member of a nonviolent religious group whose beliefs blend elements of Buddhism, Hinduism, and Sufism. (p. 85)

skepticism [SKEHP•tih•SIHZ•uhm] *n.* a philosophy based on the idea that nothing can be known for certain. (p. 163)

social contract *n.* the agreement by which people define and limit their individual rights, thus creating an organized society or government. (p. 195)

Social Darwinism [DAHR•wih•NIHZ•uhm] *n.* the application of Charles Darwin's ideas about evolution and "survival of the fittest" to human societies—particularly as justification for imperialist expansion. (p. 341)

socialism *n.* an economic system in which the factors of production are owned by the public and operate for the welfare of all. (p. 302)

Solidarity [SAHL•ih•DAR•ih•tee] *n.* a Polish labor union that during the 1980s became the main force of opposition to Communist rule in Poland. (p. 618)

soviet [SOH•vee•EHT] *n.* one of the local representative councils formed in Russia after the downfall of Czar Nicholas II. (p. 436)

Spanish-American War *n.* an 1898 conflict between the United States and Spain, in which the United States supported Cubans' fight for independence. (p. 384)

sphere of influence *n.* a foreign region in which a nation has control over trade and other economic activities. (p. 373)

standard of living *n.* the quality of life of a person or a population, as indicated by the goods, services, and luxuries available to the person or people. (p. 600)

strike *v.* to refuse to work in order to force an employer to meet certain demands. (p. 304)

Suez [soo•EHZ] **Canal** *n.* a human-made waterway, which was opened in 1869, connecting the Red Sea and the Mediterranean Sea. (p. 354)

suffrage [SUHF•rihj] *n.* the right to vote. (p. 313)

sultan *n.* "overlord," or "one with power"; title for Ottoman rulers during the rise of the Ottoman Empire. (p. 73)

surrealism [suh•REE•uh•LIHZ•uhm] *n.* a 20th-century artistic movement that focuses on the workings of the unconscious mind. (p. 465)

sustainable growth *n.* economic development that meets people's needs but preserves the environment and conserves resources for future generations. (p. 646)

T

Taiping [ty•pihng] **Rebellion** *n.* a mid-19th century rebellion against the Qing Dynasty in China, led by Hong Xiuquan. (p. 373)

Taj Mahal [TAHZH muh•HAHL] *n.* a beautiful tomb in Agra, India, built by the Mughal emperor Shah Jahan for his wife Mumtaz Mahal. (p. 85)

Taliban *n.* conservative Islamic group that took control of Afghanistan after the Soviet Union withdrew its troops; driven from power by U.S. forces in December, 2001, because of its harboring of suspected terrorists. (p. 592)

Tennis Court Oath *n.* a pledge made by the members of France's National Assembly in 1789, in which they vowed to continue meeting until they had drawn up a new constitution. (p. 220)

terrorism *n.* the use of force or threats to frighten people or governments to change their policies. (p. 653)

theocracy [thee•AHK•ruh•see] *n.* a government controlled by religious leaders. (p. 62)

theory of evolution *n.* the idea, proposed by Charles Darwin in 1859, that species of plants and animals arise by means of a process of natural selection. (p. 331)

theory of relativity [REHL•uh•TIHV•ih•tee] *n.* Albert Einstein's ideas about the interrelationships between time and space and between energy and matter. (p. 463)

Third Reich [ryk] *n.* the Third German Empire, established by Adolf Hitler in the 1930s. (p. 484)

Third Republic *n.* the republic that was established in France after the downfall of Napoleon III and ended with the German occupation of France during World War II. (p. 315)

Third World *n.* during the Cold War, the developing nations not allied with either the United States or the Soviet Union. (p. 548)

Thirty Years' War *n.* a European conflict over religion and territory and for power among ruling families, lasting from 1618 to 1648. (p. 169)

Tiananmen [tyahn•ahn•mehn] **Square** *n.* a huge public space in Beijing, China; in 1989, the site of a student uprising in support of democratic reforms. (p. 627)

Tokugawa Shogunate [TOH•koo•GAH•wah SHOH•guh•niht] *n.* a dynasty of shoguns that ruled a unified Japan from 1603 to 1867. (p. 110)

totalitarianism [toh•TAL•ih•TAIR•ee•uh•NIHZ•uhm] *n.* government control over every aspect of public and private life. (p. 440)

total war *n.* a conflict in which the participating countries devote all their resources to the war effort. (p. 419)

Treaty of Kanagawa [kah•NAH•gah•wah] *n.* an 1854 agreement between the United States and Japan, which opened two Japanese ports to U.S. ships and allowed the United States to set up an embassy in Japan. (p. 376)

Treaty of Tordesillas [TAWR•day•SEEL•yahs] *n.* a 1494 agreement between Portugal and Spain, declaring that newly discovered lands to the west of an imaginary line in the Atlantic Ocean would belong to Spain and newly discovered lands to the east of the line would belong to Portugal. (p. 99)

Treaty of Versailles [vuhr•SY] *n.* the peace treaty signed by Germany and the Allied powers after World War I. (p. 424)

trench warfare *n.* a form of warfare in which opposing armies fight each other from trenches dug in the battlefield. (p. 413)

triangular trade *n.* the transatlantic trading network along which slaves and other goods were carried between Africa, England, Europe, the West Indies, and the colonies in the Americas. (p. 134)

Triple Alliance *n.* a military alliance between Germany, Austria-Hungary, and Italy in the years preceding World War I. (p. 408)

Triple Entente [ahn•TAHNT] *n.* a military alliance between Great Britain, France, and Russia in the years preceding World War I. (p. 409)

Truman Doctrine *n.* announced by President Harry Truman in 1947, a U.S. policy of giving economic and military aid to free nations threatened by internal or external opponents. (p. 534)

UV

union *n.* an association of workers, formed to bargain for better working conditions and higher wages. (p. 304)

United Nations *n.* an international peacekeeping organization founded in 1945 to provide security to the nations of the world. (p. 532)

Universal Declaration of Human Rights *n.* a 1948 statement in which the United Nations declared that all human beings have rights to life, liberty, and security. (p. 650)

unrestricted submarine warfare *n.* the use of submarines to sink without warning any ship (including neutral ships and unarmed passenger liners) found in an enemy's waters. (p. 418)

urbanization [UR•buh•nih•ZAY•shuhn] *n.* the growth of cities and the migration of people into them. (p. 289)

U.S.A. Patriot Act *n.* an antiterrorism bill of 2001 that strengthened governmental rights to detain foreigners suspected of terrorism and prosecute terrorist crimes. (p. 658)

U.S. Civil War *n.* a conflict between Northern and Southern states of the United States over the issue of slavery, lasting from 1861 to 1865. (p. 326)

utilitarianism [yoo•TIHL•ih•TAIR•ee•uh•NIHZ•uhm] *n.* the theory, proposed by Jeremy Bentham in the late 1700s, that government actions are useful only if they promote the greatest good for the greatest number of people. (p. 301)

utopia [yoo•TOH•pee•uh] *n.* an imaginary land described by Thomas More in his book *Utopia*—hence, an ideal place. (p. 48)

vernacular [vuhr•NAK•yuh•luhr] *n.* the everyday language of people in a region or country. (p. 41)

Vietcong [vee•EHT•KAHNG] *n.* a group of Communist guerrillas who, with the help of North Vietnam, fought against the South Vietnamese government in the Vietnam War. (p. 546)

Vietnamization [vee•EHT•nuh•mih•ZAY•shuhn] *n.* President Richard Nixon's strategy for ending U.S. involvement in the Vietnam War, involving a gradual withdrawal of American troops and replacement of them with South Vietnamese forces. (p. 546)

W

War of the Spanish Succession *n.* a conflict, lasting from 1701 to 1713, in which a number of European states fought to prevent the Bourbon family from controlling Spain as well as France. (p. 167)

Warsaw Pact *n.* a military alliance formed in 1955 by the Soviet Union and seven Eastern European countries. (p. 535)

Weimar [WY•MAHR] **Republic** *n.* the republic that was established in Germany in 1919 and ended in 1933. (p. 471)

Western Front *n.* in World War I, the region of northern France where the forces of the Allies and the Central Powers battled each other. (p. 412)

westernization *n.* an adoption of the social, political, or economic institutions of Western—especially European or American—countries. (p. 176)

XYZ

Zionism [ZY•uh•NIHZ•uhm] *n.* a movement founded in the 1890s to promote the establishment of a Jewish homeland in Palestine. (p. 316)

Spanish Glossary

A

Aborigine [aborigen] *s.* miembro de cualquiera de los pueblos nativos de Australia. (pág. 318)

absolute monarch [monarca absoluto] *s.* rey o reina que tiene poder ilimitado y que procura controlar todos los aspectos de la sociedad. (pág. 160)

Allies [Aliados] *s.* durante la I Guerra Mundial, las naciones de Gran Bretaña, Francia y Rusia, junto con otras que lucharon a su lado; también, el grupo de naciones —entre ellas Gran Bretaña, la Unión Soviética y Estados Unidos— opuestas a las Potencias del Eje en la II Guerra Mundial. (pág. 411)

Amritsar Massacre [Masacre de Amritsar] *s.* matanza por tropas británicas de casi 400 indios, reunidos en Amritsar para protestar contra las Leyes Rowlatt. (pág. 454)

Anabaptist [anabaptista] *s.* en la Reforma, miembro de un grupo protestante que enseñaba que sólo los adultos podían ser bautizados, y que la Iglesia y el Estado debían estar separados. (pág. 62)

Anglican [anglicano] *adj.* relacionado con la Iglesia de Inglaterra. (pág. 60)

annexation [anexión] *s.* añadir una región al territorio de una unidad política existente. (págs. 365, 379)

annul [anular] *v.* cancelar o suspender. (pág. 58)

anti-Semitism [antisemitismo] *s.*prejuicio contra los judíos. (pág. 315)

apartheid *s.* política de Sudáfrica de separación total y legalizada de las razas; prohibía todo contacto social entre negros y blancos. (pág. 609)

appeasement [apaciguamiento] *s.* otorgar concesiones a un agresor a fin de evitar la guerra. (pág. 483)

armistice [armisticio] *s.* acuerdo de suspender combates. (pág. 421)

Aryans [arios] *s.* para los nazis, los pueblos germanos que formaban una "raza maestra". (pág. 502)

assembly line [línea de montaje] *s.* en una fábrica, correa que lleva un producto de un trabajador a otro, cada uno de los cuales desempeña una sola tarea. (pág. 330)

assimilation [asimilación] *s.* política de una nación de obligar o alentar a un pueblo subyugado a adoptar sus instituciones y costumbres. (pág. 347)

Atlantic Charter [Carta del Atlántico] *s.* declaración de principios emitida en agosto de 1941 por el primer ministro británico Winston Churchill y el presidente de E.U.A. Franklin Roosevelt, en la cual se basó el plan de paz de los Aliados al final de la II Guerra Mundial. (pág. 496)

Atlantic slave trade [trata de esclavos del Atlántico] *s.* compra, transporte y venta de africanos para trabajar en las Américas. (pág. 133)

Axis Powers [Potencias del Eje] *s.* en la II Guerra Mundial, las naciones de Alemania, Italia y Japón, que formaron una alianza en 1936. (pág. 483)

B

balance of power [equilibrio de poder] *s.* situación política en que ninguna nación tiene suficiente poder para ser una amenaza para las demás. (pág. 238)

The Balkans [Balcanes] *s.* región del sureste de Europa ocupada actualmente por Grecia, Albania, Bulgaria, Rumania, la parte eureopea de Turquía y las antiguas repúblicas de Yugoslavia. (pág. 255)

baroque [barroco] *s.* estilo grandioso y ornamentado del arte, la música y la arquitectura a fines del siglo 17 y principios del 18. (pág. 203)

Battle of Britain [Batalla Británica] *s.* batallas entre las fuerzas aéreas de Alemania y Gran Bretaña que se libraron sobre el territorio británico entre 1940–1941. (pág. 494)

Battle of Guadalcanal [Batalla de Guadalcanal] *s.* batalla de la II Guerra Mundial ocurrida en 1942–1943 en que las fuerzas aliadas expulsaron a las fuerzas japonesas de la isla de Guadalcanal en el Pacífico. (pág. 501)

Battle of Midway [Batalla del Midway] *s.* batalla aérea y naval de la II Guerra Mundial librada en 1941 en que las fuerzas estadounidenses derrotaron a las japonesas en el Pacífico central. (pág. 500)

Battle of Stalingrad [Batalla de Stalingrado] *s.* batalla de la II Guerra Mundial ocurrida en 1942–1943 en que las fuerzas alemanas perdieron y no lograron capturar la ciudad de Stalingrado en la Unión Soviética. (pág. 507)

Battle of the Bulge [Batalla del Bolsón] *s.* batalla de 1944–45 en que las fuerzas aliadas repulsaron la última ofensiva alemana de envergadura en la II Guerra Mundial. (pág. 510)

Battle of Trafalgar [Batalla de Trafalgar] *s.* batalla naval de 1805 en que las fuerzas de Napoleón fueron derrotadas por una flota inglesa al mando de Horacio Nelson. (pág. 233)

Berlin Conference [Conferencia de Berlín] de 1884–1885 *s.* reunión en la cual representantes de las naciones europeas acordaron reglas para la colonización europea de África. (pág. 342)

Bill of Rights [Carta de Derechos] *s.* primeras diez enmiendas a la Constitución de E.U.A., que protegen los derechos y libertades básicos de los ciudadanos. (pág. 211)

blitzkrieg *s.* "guerra relámpago"; táctica bélica de ataque sorpresa con aviones rápidos, seguidos de numerosas fuerzas de infantería. (pág. 491)

blockade [bloqueo] *s.* desplazamiento de tropas o barcos para impedir para evitar la entrada o salida de todo tráfico comercial a una ciudad o región. (pág. 234)

Boer [bóer] *s.* colono holandés que se estableció en Sudáfrica. (pág. 342)

Boer War [Guerra de los Bóers] *s.* conflicto de 1899 a 1902 entre los bóers y los británicos por el control de territorio en Sudáfrica. (pág. 344)

Bolsheviks [bolcheviques] *s.* grupo de marxistas revolucionarios rusos que tomó el control del gobierno ruso en noviembre de 1917. (pág. 434)

R87

Boxer Rebellion [Rebelión de los Bóxers] *s.* rebelión de 1900 en China contra la influencia extranjera en el país. (pág. 374)

boyar [boyardos] *s.* el noble terrateniente de Rusia. (pág. 174)

brinkmanship [política arriesgada] *s.* política de amenazar con lanzarse a la guerra en respuesta a una agresión enemiga. (pág. 536)

C

cabinet [gabinete] *s.* grupo de asesores o ministros escogidos por el jefe de gobierno de un país para que participen en la toma de decisiones del gobierno. (pág. 183)

Calvinism [calvinismo] *s.* conjunto de enseñanzas religiosas basadas en las ideas del reformador Juan Calvino. (pág. 61)

Camp David Accords [Acuerdos de Camp David] *s.* primer tratado firmado entre Israel y un país árabe, en que el presidente Anwar Sadat de Egipto reconoció el derecho a existir de Israel y el primer ministro israelí Menachem Begin acordó devolver la península del Sinaí a Egipto. (pág. 586)

capitalism [capitalismo] *s.* sistema económico basado en la propiedad privada y en la inversión de dinero en empresas comerciales con el objetivo de obtener ganancias. (págs. 573, 734)

Catholic Reformation [Contrarreforma] *s.* movimiento del siglo 16 en el que la Iglesia Católica intentó reformarse en respuesta a la Reforma protestante. (pág. 64)

caudillos *s.* dictador militar de un país latinoamericano. (pág. 382)

Central Powers [Potencias Centrales] *s.* en la I Guerra Mundial, las naciones de Alemania y Austro-Hungría, y las demás que lucharon a su lado. (pág. 411)

Chartist movement [movimiento cartista] *s.* movimiento de reforma inglés del siglo 19 en que miembros de la clase trabajadora pidieron reformas en el Parlamento y en las elecciones, como el voto para todos los hombres. (pág. 314)

checks and balances [control y compensación de poderes] *s.* medidas para evitar que una rama del gobierno domine sobre las otras. (pág. 211)

CIS [CEI] *s.* Comunidad de Estados Independientes: asociación de los antiguos territorios soviéticos formada cuando la Unión Soviética se desmembró. (pág. 615)

civil disobedience [desobediencia civil] *s.* negativa pública y deliberada a obedecer una ley considerada injusta. (pág. 454)

cloning [clonación] *s.* creación de plantas o animales genéticamente idénticos a plantas o animales existentes. (pág. 639)

coalition government [gobierno de coalición] *s.* gobierno controlado por una alianza temporal de varios partidos políticos. (pág. 470)

Cold War [Guerra Fría] *s.* estado de hostilidad diplomática entre Estados Unidos y la Unión Soviética en las décadas siguientes a la II Guerra Mundial. (pág. 535)

collective farm [granja colectiva] *s.* granja controlada por el gobierno, formada mediante la unión de muchas pequeñas granjas. (pág. 444)

colony [colonia] *s.* tierra controlada por una nación distante. (pág. 120)

Columbian Exchange [trasferencia colombina] *s.* transferencia mundial de plantas, animales y enfermedades durante la colonización europea de América. (pág. 137)

command economy [economía de mando] *s.*sistema económico en el que el gobierno toma todas las decisiones económicas. (pág. 443)

commune [comuna] *s.* en la China comunista, granja colectiva en la que mucha gente trabaja y vive junta. (pág. 540)

communism [comunismo] *s.* sistema económico en el que todos los medios de producción —tierras, minas, fábricas, ferrocarriles y negocios— son propiedad del pueblo, en que no existe la propiedad privada, y en que todos los productos y servicios se comparten por igual. (pág. 303)

Communist Party [Partido Comunista] *s.* partido político basado en las ideas de Karl Marx y V. I. Lenin; originalmente el Partido Bolchevique ruso. (pág. 439)

Concert of Europe [Concierto de Europa] *s.* serie de alianzas entre naciones europeas en el siglo 19, ideadas por el príncipe Klemens von Metternich para impedir revoluciones. (pág. 240)

concordat [concordato] *s.* acuerdo firmado entre Napoleón y el Papa para establecer una nueva relación entre la Iglesia y el Estado. (pág. 230)

Congress of Vienna [Congreso de Viena] *s.* serie de reuniones en 1814 y 1815 en las cuales los dirigentes europeos trataron de establecer una paz y seguridad duraderas tras la derrota de Napoleón. (pág. 238)

Congress Party [Partido del Congreso] *s.* importante partido político nacional de India; también se llama Congreso Nacional de India. (pág. 563)

conquistadors [conquistadores] *s.* soldados, exploradores y aventureros españoles que participaron en la conquista de América en el siglo 16. (pág. 120)

conservative [conservadore] *s.* en la primera mitad del siglo 19, el europeo —principalmente los terratenientes y nobles acaudalados— que quería preservar las monarquías tradicionales. (pág. 253)

constitutional monarchy [monarquía constitucional] *s.* monarquía en que el poder del gobernante está limitado por la ley. (pág. 183)

containment [contención] *s.* política exterior estadounidense adoptada por el presidente Harry Truman a fines de la década de 1940 para impedir la expansión del comunismo creando alianzas con países débiles y ayudándolos a contener los avances soviéticos. (pág. 533)

Continental System [Sistema Continental] *s.* política de Napoleón de impedir el comercio de Gran Bretaña con la Europa continental para destruir la economía británica. (pág. 234)

corporation [corporación] *s.* empresa de accionistas que comparten las ganancias pero que no son personalmente responsables de sus deudas. (pág. 297)

Council of Trent [Concilio de Trento] *s.* reunión de líderes de la Iglesia Católica Romana, convocada por el papa Pablo III, para fallar sobre varias doctrinas criticadas por los reformadores protestantes. (pág. 65)

coup d'etat [golpe de Estado] *s.* toma repentina del poder político de una nación. (pág. 230)

creole [criollo] *s.* en la sociedad española colonial, el colono nacido en Latinoamérica de padres españoles. (pág. 247)

Crimean War [Guerra de Crimea] *s.* conflicto de 1853 a 1856, en el cual el imperio otomano, con ayuda de Gran Bretaña y Francia, frenó la expansión rusa en la región del mar Negro. (pág. 353)

crop rotation [rotación de cultivos] *s.* sistema que cultiva distintos productos en un campo cada año para conservar la fertilidad de la tierra. (pág. 283)

Cultural Revolution [Revolución Cultural] *s.* levantamiento de 1966–1976 en China, encabezado por los Guardias Rojos de Mao Tsetung, con el propósito de establecer una sociedad de campesinos y trabajadores donde todos fue-ran iguales. (pág. 541)

cyberterrorism [terrorismo cibernético] *s.* ataques por motivos políticos contra sistemas de tecnología informática. (pág. 654)

D

daimyo *s.* señor feudal de Japón que comandaba un ejército privado de samurais. (pág. 108)

D-Day [Día D] *s.* 6 de junio de 1944; día elegido para la invasión aliada de Europa continental durante la II Guerra Mundial. (pág. 510)

Declaration of Independence [Declaración de Independencia] *s.* declaración de las razones de la ruptura de las colonias americanas con Gran Bretaña, aprobada por el Segundo Congreso Continental. (pág. 207)

demilitarization [desmilitarización] *s.* reducción de la capacidad bélica de un país que se logra desbandando sus fuerzas armadas y prohibiéndole que adquiera armas. (pág. 516)

democratization [democratización] *s.* proceso de crear un gobierno elegido por el pueblo. (pág. 516)

Department of Homeland Security [Departamento de la Seguridad del Territorio Nacional] *s.* agencia federal estadounidense creada en 2002 para coordinar una estrategia nacional integral contra el terrorismo. (pág. 657)

détente *s.* política de reducir las tensiones de la Guerra Fría, adoptada por Estados Unidos durante la presidencia de Richard Nixon. (pág. 556)

developed nation [país desarrollado] *s.* nación con las instalaciones necesarias para la producción avanzada de productos manufacturados. (pág. 641)

devshirme *s.* en el imperio otomano, política de llevarse a los niños de los pueblos cristianos conquistados para entrenarlos como soldados musulmanes. (pág. 76)

dissident [disidente] *s.* opositor a la política oficial de un gobierno. (pág. 608)

divine right [derecho divino] *s.* noción de que los monarcas son representantes de Dios en la Tierra y, por lo tanto, sólo le deben responder a él. (pág. 160)

dominion [dominio] *s.* en el imperio británico, una nación (como Canadá) a la que se permitía gobernar sus asuntos internos. (pág. 318)

domino theory [teoría del dominó] *s.* noción de que si una nación cae bajo control comunista, los países vecinos también lo harán. (pág. 544)

Dreyfus affair [caso Dreyfus] *s.* controversia surgida en Francia en la década de 1890 por el juicio y encarcelamiento del capitán Alfred Dreyfus, oficial judío falsamente acusado de vender secretos militares a Alemania. (pág. 315)

Dutch East India Company [Compañía Holandesa de las Indias Orientales] *s.* empresa fundada por holandeses a principios del siglo 17 para establecer y dirigir comercio por todo Asia. (pág. 100)

E

Eastern Front [Frente Oriental] *s.* en la I Guerra Mundial, región a lo largo de la frontera ruso-alemana donde rusos y servios pelearon contra alemanes, austriacos y turcos. (pág. 414)

Edict of Nantes [Edicto de Nantes] *s.* declaración en que el rey francés Enrique IV prometió que los protestantes podían vivir en paz en Francia y tener centros de veneración en algunas ciudades. (pág. 162)

Emancipation Proclamation [Proclama de Emancipación] *s.* declaración emitida por el presidente Abraham Lincoln en 1862, asentando la libertad de todos los esclavos de los estados confederados. (pág. 326)

emerging nation [nación emergente] *s.* nación en proceso de industrialización cuyo desarrollo no ha terminado todavía. (pág. 641)

émigré *s.* quien abandona su país de origen por razones políticas, como los nobles y otros que huyeron de Francia durante los levantamientos campesinos de la Revolución Francesa. (pág. 224)

enclosure [cercado] *s.* uno de los campos rodeados de cercas o de arbustos que crearon terratenientes británicos ricos en tierras que antes trabajaban los campesinos. (pág. 283)

encomienda *s.* tierras otorgadas por España a un colonizador de América, con el derecho de hacer trabajar a los amerindios que vivían en ellas. (pág. 123)

English Civil War [Guerra Civil Inglesa] *s.* conflicto de 1642 a 1649 en que los seguidores puritanos del Parlamento lucharon contra los defensores de la monarquía de Inglaterra. (pág. 181)

enlightened despot [déspota ilustrado] *s.* uno de los monarcas europeos del siglo 18 inspirados por las ideas de la Ilustración a gobernar con justicia y respeto a los derechos de sus súbditos. (pág. 204)

Enlightenment [Ilustración] *s.* movimiento del siglo 18 en Europa que trató de aplicar los principios de la razón y el método científico a todos los aspectos de la sociedad. (pág. 195)

entrepreneur [empresario] *s.* persona que organiza, administra y asume los riesgos de un negocio. (pág. 287)

R89

estate [estado] *s.* una de las tres clases sociales existentes en Francia antes de la Revolución Francesa; el primer estado era el de la clerecía; el segundo era el de la nobleza; y el tercero era del resto de la población. (pág. 217)

Estates-General [Estados Generales] *s.* asamblea de representantes de los tres estados, o clases sociales, de Francia. (pág. 219)

ethnic cleansing [limpia étnica] *s.* política de asesinatos y otros actos de brutalidad con que los servios quisieron eliminar la población musulmana de Bosnia después de la división de Yugoslavia. (pág. 622)

existentialism [existencialismo] *s.* filosofía basada en la idea de que el ser humano da significado a su vida con sus decisiones y acciones. (pág. 464)

extraterritorial rights [derechos extraterritoriales] *s.* exención a los extranjeros de las leyes de un país. (pág. 372)

F

factors of production [factores de producción] *s.* recursos —como tierra, mano de obra y capital— necesarios para producir bienes y servicios. (pág. 284)

factory [fábrica] *s.* construcción amplia en que se manufacturan productos con maquinaria. (pág. 286)

fascism [fascismo] *s.* movimiento político que postula una forma extrema de nacionalismo, la supresión de los derechos individuales y un régimen dictatorial de un solo partido. (pág. 476)

favorable balance of trade [balanza comercial favorable] *s.* situación económica en la cual un país exporta más de lo que importa, es decir, que vende más productos de los que compra en el extranjero. (pág. 141)

federal system [sistema federal] *s.* sistema de gobierno en el que el poder se divide entre una autoridad central y varios estados. (págs. 211, 607)

"Final Solution" [solución final] *s.* programa de Hitler de asesinar sistemáticamente a todo el pueblo judío. (pág. 503)

Five-Year Plans [Planes de Cinco Años] *s.* planes delineados por José Stalin en 1928 para desarrollar la economía de la Unión Soviética. (pág. 443)

Four Modernizations [cuatro modernizaciones] *s.* serie de objetivos adoptados por el líder chino Deng Xiaoping a finales del siglo 20 con miras al progreso en agricultura, industria, defensa, y ciencia y tecnología. (pág. 626)

Fourteen Points [los catorce puntos] *s.* serie de propuestas en que el presidente estadounidense Woodrow Wilson esbozó un plan para alcanzar una paz duradera después de la I Guerra Mundial. (pág. 424)

free trade [libre comercio] *s.* comercio entre naciones sin restricciones o barreras económicas (tales como aranceles). (pág. 642)

French and Indian War [Guerra contra Franceses e Indígenas] *s.* conflicto entre Gran Bretaña y Francia por control de territorio en Norteamérica, de 1754 a 1763. (pág. 130)

G

gender inequality [desigualdad de género] *s.* diferencia entre hombres y mujeres con respecto a riqueza y posición social. (pág. 650)

genetic engineering [ingeniería genética] *s.* transferencia de genes de un organismo a otro para producir un organismo con nuevos rasgos. (pág. 639)

genocide [genocidio] *s* .matanza sistemática de todo un pueblo. (pág. 503)

geocentric theory [teoría geocéntrica] *s.* teoría de la Edad Media en la que los eruditos creían que la Tierra era objeto fijo, localizado en el centro del universo. (pág. 189)

geopolitics [geopolítica] *s* .política exterior basada en una consideración de la ubicación estratégica o de los productos de otras tierras. (pág. 352)

ghazi *s.* guerrero del islam. (pág. 73)

ghettos *s.* barrios en que tenían que vivir los judíos europeos. (pág. 503)

glasnost *s.* política soviética de "apertura" a la libre circulación de ideas e información introducida en 1985 por Mijail Gorbachev. (pág 1046)

global economy [economía global] *s.* todas las interacciones financieras —entre individuos, empresas y gobiernos— que rebasan fronteras internacionales. (pág. 642)

Glorious Revolution [Revolución Gloriosa] *s.* derrocamiento incruento del rey Jacobo II de Inglaterra, quien fue reemplazado por Guillermo y María. (pág. 182)

Great Depression [Gran Depresión] *s.* crisis económica aguda que siguió a la caída del mercado de valores en 1929. (pág. 473)

Great Fear [Gran Miedo] *s.* ola de temor insensato que se extendió por las provincias francesas después de la toma de la Bastilla en 1789. (pág. 221)

Great Purge [Gran Purga] *s.* campaña de terror en la Unión Soviética durante la década de 1930, en la cual José Stalin trató de eliminar a todos los miembros del Partido Comunista y ciudadanos que amenazaban su poder. (pág. 442)

green revolution [revolución verde] *s.* esfuerzo en el siglo 20 de aumentar los alimentos en el mundo entero, a través del uso de fertilizantes y pesticidas, y de la creación de cultivos resistentes a enfermedades. (pág. 640)

guerrilla [guerrillero] *s.* miembro de una unidad de combate informal que ataca por sorpresa las tropas enemigas que ocupan su país. (pág. 235)

guillotine [guillotina] *s.* máquina para decapitar con que se hicieron ejecuciones durante la Revolución Francesa. (pág. 226)

H

habeas corpus *s.* documento que requiere que un detenido comparezca ante un tribunal o juez para que se determine si su detención es legal. (pág. 182)

haiku *s.* poema japonés que tiene tres versos no rimados de cinco, siete y cinco sílabas. (pág. 110)

heliocentric theory [teoría heliocéntrica] *s.* idea de que la Tierra y los otros planetas giran en torno al Sol. (pág. 190)

Holocaust [Holocausto] *s.* matanza en masa de judíos y otros civiles, ejecutada por el gobierno de la Alemania nazi, antes y durante la II Guerra Mundial. (pág. 502)

Holy Alliance [Alianza Sagrada] *s.* liga de naciones europeas formada por los dirigentes de Rusia, Austria y Prusia después del Congreso de Viena. (pág. 240)

home rule [autogobierno] *s.* control sobre asuntos internos que da el gobierno a los residentes de una región. (pág. 320)

humanism [humanismo] *s.* movimiento intelectual del Renacimiento que estudió los textos clásicos y se enfocó en el potencial y los logros humanos. (pág. 38)

Hundred Days [Cien Días] *s.* corto período de 1815 en que Napoleón hizo su último intento de recuperar el poder, depuso al rey francés y de nuevo se proclamó emperador de Francia. (pág. 237)

I

imperialism [imperialismo] *s.* política en que una nación fuerte buscar dominar la vida política, económica y social de otros países. (pág. 339)

impressionism [impresionismo] *s.* movimiento de la pintura del siglo 19 en reacción al realismo, que buscaba dar impresiones personales de sujetos o momentos. (pág. 267)

indulgence [indulgencia] *s.* perdón que libera al pecador de la penitencia por un pecado. (pág. 55)

industrialization [industrialización] *s.* desarrollo de industrias para la producción con máquinas. (pág. 284)

Industrial Revolution [Revolución Industrial] *s.* cambio, que comenzó en Inglaterra durante el siglo 18, de la producción manual a la producción con máquinas. (pág. 283)

intendant [intendente] *s.* funcionario del gobierno francés nombrado por el monarca para recaudar impuestos e impartir justicia. (pág. 164)

International Space Station [Estación Espacial Internacional] *s.* colaboración patrocinada por Estados Unidos, Rusia y otras 14 naciones para establecer y mantener un laboratorio activo para realizar experimentos científicos en el espacio. (pág. 637)

Internet *s.* vinculación de redes de computadora que permite a gente de todo el mundo comunicarse e intercambiar información. (pág. 639)

intifada [intifada] *s.* campaña palestina de desobediencia civil contra la ocupación israelí de Cisjordania y la Franja de Gaza, que continuó en la década de 1990. (pág. 587)

Irish Republican Army (IRA) [Ejército Republicano Irlandés (el IRA)] *s.* fuerza paramilitar nacionalista que lucha porque Gran Bretaña dé la independencia la Irlanda del Norte. (pág. 321)

iron curtain [cortina de hierro] *s.* durante la Guerra Fría, división que separaba las naciones comunistas de Europa oriental de las naciones democráticas de Europa occidental. (pág. 533)

isolationism [aislacionismo] *s.* política de evitar lazos políticos o militares con otros países. (pág. 484)

J

janissary [janísero] *s.* miembro de una fuerza élite de soldados del imperio otomano. (pág. 76)

jazz *s.* estilo de música popular del siglo 20 concebido principalmente por músicos afroamericanos. (pág. 465)

Jesuits [jesuitas] *s.* miembros de la Sociedad de Jesús, orden católica romana fundada por Ignacio de Loyola. (pág. 65)

"jewel in the crown" ["joya de la corona"] *s.* colonia británica de India, así llamada por su importancia para el imperio británico, tanto como proveedor de materia prima como mercado para sus productos. (pág. 357)

joint-stock company [sociedad de capitales] *s.* negocio en el que los inversionistas reúnen capital para un propósito común y después comparten las ganancias. (pág. 139)

K

kabuki *s.* forma de teatro japonés en que se representa una historia con música, danza y mímica. (pág. 110)

kaiser *s.* emperador alemán (del título romano Caesar). (pág. 263)

kamikaze *s.* durante la II Guerra Mundial, pilotos suicidas japoneses entrenados para hundir barcos de los Aliados lanzándose sobre ellos con aviones llenos de bombas. (pág. 511)

Khmer Rouge *s.* grupo de rebeldes comunistas que tomaron el poder en Camboya en 1975. (pág. 547)

Kristallnacht *s.* "Noche de cristales rotos": noche del 9 de noviembre de 1938, en que milicianos nazis atacaron hogares, negocios y sinagogas judíos en toda Alemania. (pág. 502)

Kuomintang *s.* Partido Nacionalista de China, formado después de la caída de la dinastía Qing en 1912. (pág. 448)

L

laissez faire *s.* idea de que el gobierno no debe regular ni interferir en las industrias y empresas. (pág. 300)

land reform [reforma agraria] *s.* redistribución de tierras agrícolas con división de grandes latifundios y reparto de fincas a campesinos. (pág. 600)

La Reforma *s.* movimiento de reforma liberal en el siglo 19 en México fundado por Benito Juárez. (pág. 390)

League of Nations [Liga de las Naciones] *s.* organización internacional formada después de la I Guerra Mundial cuyo propósito era mantener la paz entre las naciones. (pág. 425)

lebensraum *s.* "espacio vital": territorio adicional que, según Adolfo Hitler, Alemania necesitaba porque estaba sobrepoblada. (pág. 478)

Legislative Assembly [Asamblea Legislativa] *s.* congreso creado por la Constitución francesa de 1791, con poder para emitir leyes y aprobar declaraciones de guerra. (pág. 223)

legitimacy [legitimidad] *s.* derecho hereditario de un monarca a gobernar. (pág. 239)

R91

liberal [liberale] *s.* en la primera mitad del siglo 19, el europeo —principalmente empresarios y comerciantes de clase media— que deseaba darle más poder político a los parlamentos elegidos. (pág. 253)

Long March [Larga Marcha] *s.* viaje de 6,000 millas que realizaron en 1934–35 las fuerzas comunistas de China para escapar de las fuerzas nacionalistas de Jiang Jieshi. (pág. 452)

Lutheran [luterano] *s.* miembro de una iglesia protestante basada en las enseñanzas de Martín Lutero. (pág. 56)

lycée [liceo] *s.* escuela pública en Francia. (pág. 230)

M

Manchus [manchú] *s.* pueblo originario de Manchuria que gobernó en China durante la dinastía Qing (1644–1912). (pág. 105)

manifest destiny [destino manifiesto] *s.* idea popular en el siglo 19 en Estados Unidos de que era su derecho y obligación regir Norteamérica, desde el océano Atlántico hasta el Pacífico. (pág. 324)

Maori [maorí] *s.* miembro de un pueblo polinesio establecido en Nueva Zelanda hacia 800 d.C. (pág. 318)

Marshall Plan [Plan Marshall] programa estadounidense de ayuda económica a países europeos para su reconstrucción después de la II Guerra Mundial. (pág. 534)

martial law [ley marcial] *s.* gobierno militar temporal impuesto a la población civil, normalmente en época de guerra o de trastornos civiles. (pág. 607)

mass culture [cultura de masas] *s.* producción de obras de arte y diversión concebidas con el fin de atraer a un amplio público. (pág. 332)

materialism [materialismo] *s.* alto interés en la adquisición de posesiones materiales. (pág. 662)

May Fourth Movement [Movimiento del 4 de Mayo] *s.* protesta nacional china en 1919 con manifestaciones contra el Tratado de Versalles y la interferencia extranjera. (pág. 449)

Meiji era [era Meiji] *s.* período de la historia japonesa entre 1867 y 1912, cuando gobernó el emperador Mutshito. (pág. 377)

Mein Kampf *[Mi lucha]* *s.* libro escrito por Adolfo Hitler en prisión (1923–1924), en el cual expone sus creencias y sus ideales para Alemania. (pág. 478)

mercantilism [mercantilismo] *s.* política económica de aumentar la riqueza y poder de una nación obteniendo grandes cantidades de oro y plata, y vendiendo más bienes de los que se compran. (pág. 140)

mestizo *s.* mezcla de español y amerindio. (pág. 123)

middle class [clase media] *s.* clase social formada por trabajadores especializados, profesionales, comerciantes y granjeros acaudalados. (pág. 291)

middle passage [travesía intermedia] *s.* viaje que trajo a africanos capturados al Caribe y, posteriormente, a América del Norte y del Sur, para venderlos como esclavos; recibió este nombre porque era considerada la porción media del triángulo comercial trasatlántico. (pág. 135)

militarism [militarismo] *s.* política de glorificar el poder militar y de mantener un ejército permanente, siempre preparado para luchar. (pág. 408)

Ming Dynasty [dinastía Ming] *s.* dinastía que reinó en China desde 1368 hasta 1644. (pág. 102)

Monroe Doctrine [doctrina Monroe] *s.* política estadounidense de oposición a la interferencia europea en Latinoamérica, anunciada por el presidente James Monroe en 1823. (pág. 384)

Mughal [mogol] *s.* uno de los nómadas que invadieron el subcontinente de India en el siglo 16 y establecieron un poderoso imperio. (pág. 82)

mujahideen [muyahidin] *s.* guerreros religiosos afganos que se unieron para luchar contra el gobierno apoyado por los soviéticos a fines de la década de 1970. (pág. 592)

mulattos [mulatos] *s.* personas de ascendencia europea y africana. (pág. 248)

Munich Conference [Conferencia de Munich] *s.* reunión en 1938 de Inglaterra, Francia, Italia y Alemania, en la cual Gran Bretaña y Francia aceptaron que la Alemania nazi anexara parte de Checoslovaquia, a cambio de la promesa de Adolfo Hitler de respetar las nuevas fronteras checas. (pág. 485)

Muslim League [Liga Musulmana] *s.* organización formada en 1906 para proteger los intereses de los musulmanes de India; después propuso la división del país en dos naciones: una musulmana y una hindú. (pág. 563)

N

Napoleonic Code [código napoleónico] *s.* sistema extenso y uniforme de leyes establecido para Francia por Napoleón. (pág. 230)

National Assembly [Asamblea Nacional] *s.* congreso francés establecido el 17 de junio de 1789 por representantes del Tercer Estado para promulgar leyes y reformas en nombre del pueblo. (pág. 220)

nationalism [nacionalismo] *s.* creencia de que la principal lealtad del pueblo debe ser a su nación —es decir, a la gente con quien comparte historia y cultura— y no al rey o al imperio. (pág. 253)

nation-state [nación Estado] *s.* nación independiente de gente que tiene una cultura e identidad común. (pág. 253)

NATO [OTAN] *s.* Organización del Tratado del Atlántico Norte: alianza militar defensiva formada en 1949 por diez naciones de Europa occidental, Estados Unidos y Canadá. (pág. 535)

Nazism [nazismo] *s.* políticas fascistas del Partido Nacional socialista de los Trabajadores de Alemania, basadas en el totalitarismo, la creencia en superioridad racial y el control estatal de la industria. (pág. 478)

Negritude movement [movimiento de negritud] *s.* movimiento de africanos de lengua francesa que celebra el legado de la cultura tradicional africana y sus valores. (pág. 578)

neoclassical [neoclásico] *adj.* relacionado con un estilo sencillo y elegante (inspirado en ideas y temas de la antigua Grecia y Roma) que caracterizó las artes en Europa a fines del siglo 18. (pág. 203)

New Deal *s.* programa de reformas económicas del presidente Franklin D. Roosevelt ideado para solucionar los problemas creados por la Gran Depresión. (pág. 475)

nonaggression pact [pacto de no agresión] *s.* acuerdo en que dos o más naciones prometen no atacarse. (pág. 491)

nonaligned nations [países no alineados] *s.* naciones independientes que permanecieron neutrales durante la Guerra Fría entre Estados Unidos y la Unión Soviética. (pág. 548)

Nuremberg Trials [juicios de Nuremberg] *s.* serie de juicios realizados en Nuremberg, Alemania, tras la II Guerra Mundial a líderes nazis por agresión, violación a las leyes de guerra y crímenes contra la humanidad. (pág. 516)

O

Old Regime [antiguo régimen] *s.* sistema político y social que existía en Francia antes de la Revolución Francesa. (pág. 217)

Open Door Policy [política de puertas abiertas] *s.* política propuesta por E.U.A. en 1899, que postulaba que todas las naciones tuvieran las mismas oportunidades de comerciar con China. (pág. 374)

Opium War [Guerra del Opio] *s.* conflicto entre Inglaterra y China, de 1839 a 1842, por el comercio inglés de opio en China. (pág. 372)

Oslo Peace Accords [Acuerdos de Paz de Oslo] *s.* acuerdos de 1993 cuando el primer ministro israelí, Rabin, otorgó autonomía a Palestina en la Franja de Gaza y Cisjordania. (pág. 587)

ozone layer [capa de ozono] *s.* capa de la atmósfera superior de la Tierra que protege a los seres vivos de los rayos ultravioleta de la luz solar. (pág. 645)

P

Pacific Rim [Cuenca del Pacífico] *s.* tierras que bordean el océano Pacífico, especialmente las de Asia. (pág. 362)

Panama Canal [canal de Panamá] *s.* vía marítima que une al océano Atlántico con el Pacífico, construida en Panamá por Estados Unidos y terminada en 1914. (pág. 387)

partition [partición] *s.* división en partes, como la división en 1947 de la colonia británica de India en dos naciones: India y Paquistán. (pág. 564)

paternalism [paternalismo] *s.* política de tratar a los gobernados como si fueran niños, atendiendo a sus necesidades pero sin darles derechos. (pág. 347)

patron [mecenas] *s.* persona que apoya a los artistas, especialmente, en el aspecto financiero. (pág. 38)

Peace of Augsburg [Paz de Augsburgo] *s.* acuerdo realizado en 1555 que declaró que la religión de cada Estado alemán sería decidida por su gobernante. (pág. 58)

penal colony [colonia penal] *s.* colonia a donde se mandan convictos como alternativa a una prisión. (pág. 318)

peninsulares *s.* en la sociedad española colonial, colonos nacidos en España. (pág. 247)

Peninsular War [Guerra Peninsular] *s.* conflicto de 1808–1813 en que los rebeldes españoles lucharon con la ayuda de Gran Bretaña para expulsar de España las tropas de Napoleón. (pág. 235)

perestroika *s.* reestructuración de la economía soviética para permitir mayor poder de decisión local, iniciada por Mijail Gorbachev en 1985. (pág. 613)

perspective [perspectiva] *s.* técnica artística que crea la apariencia de tres dimensiones en una superficie plana. (pág. 40)

philosophe *s.* miembro de un grupo de pensadores sociales de la Ilustración en Francia. (pág. 196)

Pilgrims [peregrinos] *s.* grupo que en 1620 fundó la colonia de Plymouth en Massachusetts para escapar de persecución religiosa en Inglaterra. (pág. 128)

plebiscite [plebiscito] *s.* voto directo mediante el cual la población de un país tiene la oportunidad de aceptar o rechazar una propuesta. (pág. 230)

PLO [OLP] *s.* Organización de Liberación Palestina: organización dedicada a establecer un Estado independiente para los palestinos en el Medio Oriente. (pág. 585)

Politburo [Politburó] *s.* comité dirigente del Partido Comunista en la Unión Soviética. (pág. 612)

political dissent [disidencia política] *s.* diferencia de opiniones sobre asuntos políticos. (pág. 650)

popular culture [cultura popular] *s.* elementos culturales—deportes, música, cine, ropa, etc.—que muestran los antecedentes comunes de un grupo y sus intereses cambiantes. (pág. 659)

predestination [predestinación] *s.* doctrina que postula que Dios ha decidido todo de antemano, incluso quiénes obtendrán la salvación eterna. (pág. 61)

Presbyterian [presbiteriano] *s.* miembro de una iglesia protestante gobernada por presbíteros conforme a las enseñanzas de John Knox. (pág. 62)

PRI *s.* Partido Revolucionario Institucional: principal partido político en México. (pág. 603)

proletariat [proletariado] *s.* según la teoría marxista, el grupo de trabajadores que derrocaría al zar y gobernaría a Rusia. (pág. 434)

proliferation [proliferación] *s.* crecimiento o expansión, especialmente la expansión de armas nucleares a naciones que actualmente no las tienen. (pág. 649)

propaganda *s.* información o material distribuido para apoyar una causa o socavar una causa opuesta. (pág. 420)

Protestant [protestante] *s.* miembro de una iglesia cristiana fundada de acuerdo a los principios de la Reforma. (pág. 56)

provisional government [gobierno provisional] *s.* gobierno temporal. (pág. 436)

psychology [psicología] *s.* estudio de la mente y la conducta humanas. (pág. 332)

Puritans [puritanos] *s.* grupo que, para liberarse de la persecución religiosa en Inglaterra, fundó una colonia en la bahía de Massachusetts a principios del siglo 17. (pág. 128)

R93

Q

Qing Dynasty [dinastía Qing] *s.* última dinastía china; reinó de 1644 a 1912. (pág. 105)

R

racism [racismo] *s.* creencia de que una raza es superior a otras. (pág. 341)

radical [radicale] *s.* en la primera mitad del siglo 19, el europeo a favor de cambios drásticos para extender la democracia a toda la población. (pág. 253)

radioactivity [radioactividad] *s.* forma de energía liberada mediante la descomposición de átomos. (pág. 331)

Raj *s.* porciones de India controladas por Gran Bretaña de 1757 a 1947. (pág. 360)

rationing [racionamiento] *s.* limitación de la cantidad de bienes que la población puede comprar, generalmente impuesta por un gobierno durante una guerra debido a escasez. (pág. 420)

realism [realismo] *s.* movimiento artístico del siglo 19 en que los escritores y pintores trataron de mostrar la vida como es, no como debiera ser. (pág. 266)

realpolitik *s.* "política de la realidad"; posición política dura que no da lugar al idealismo. (pág. 261)

recession [recesión] *s.* descenso de la economía de una nación. (pág. 600)

Red Guards [Guardias Rojos] *s.* unidades de milicianos formadas por jóvenes chinos en 1966 en respuesta al llamado de Mao Zedong a llevar a cabo una revolución social y cultural. (pág. 541)

Reformation [Reforma] *s.* movimiento del siglo 16 para realizar cambios religiosos que llevó a la fundación de iglesias cristianas que rechazaron la autoridad del Papa. (pág. 55)

refugee [refugiado] *s.* persona que sale de su país a otro país para buscar seguridad. (pág. 652)

Reign of Terror [Régimen del Terror] *s.* período entre 1793–1794 en que Maximilien Robespierre gobernó a Francia casi como dictador, durante el cual fueron ejecutados miles de personajes políticos y de ciudadanos comunes. (pág. 226)

Renaissance [Renacimiento] *s.* período de la historia europea de aproximadamente 1300 a 1600, durante el cual renació un interés en la cultura clásica que generó importantes cambios en el arte, la educación y la visión del mundo. (pág. 37)

Restoration [Restauración] *s.* en Inglaterra, período del reinado de Carlos II, después del colapso del gobierno de Oliver Cromwell. (pág. 182)

reunification [reunificación] *s.* proceso de unir dos elementos que estaban separados, como la reunificación de Alemania oriental y Alemania occidental en 1990. (pág. 620)

romanticism [romanticismo] *s.* movimiento de principios del siglo 19 en el arte y las ideas que recalca la emoción y la naturaleza, más que la razón y la sociedad. (pág. 264)

Roosevelt Corollary [corolario Roosevelt] *s.* ampliación de la doctrina Monroe, emitida por el presidente Theodore Roosevelt en 1904, en que declaró que Estados Unidos tenía el derecho de ejercer "poderes policiales" en el hemisferio occidental. (pág. 387)

Rowlatt Acts [Leyes Rowlatt] *s.* leyes, ratificadas en 1919, que los permitían al gobierno británico en India encarcelar a manifestantes por dos años sin juicio. (pág. 453)

Russification [rusificación] *s.* proceso que obliga a todos los grupos étnicos a adoptar la cultura rusa en el imperio ruso. (pág. 259)

Russo-Japanese War [Guerra Ruso-Japonesa] *s.* conflicto de 1904–1905 entre Rusia y Japón, causada por el interés de los dos países de dominar Manchuria y Corea. (pág. 378)

S

Safavid [safávido] *s.* miembro de una dinastía musulmana shi'a que construyó un imperio en Persia del siglo 16 al 18. (pág. 78)

salon [salón] *s.* reunión social de intelectuales y artistas, como las que celebraban en sus hogares señoras acaudaladas de París y otras ciudades europeas durante la Ilustración. (pág. 202)

SALT *s.* Conversaciones para la Limitación de Armas Estratégicas: serie de reuniones durante la década de 1970 en que líderes de Estados Unidos y la Unión Soviética acordaron limitar el número de armas nucleares de sus países. (pág. 557)

Salt March [Marcha de la Sal] *s.* manifestación pacífica en 1930 en India ocasionada por las Leyes de la Sal; Mohandas Gandhi condujo a sus seguidores, caminando 240 millas al mar, donde hicieron su propia sal del agua de mar evaporada. (pág. 455)

sans-culottes *s.* en la Revolución Francesa, grupo político radical de parisienses asalariados y pequeños comerciantes que anhelaban más voz en el gobierno, bajas de precios y fin a la escasez de alimentos. (pág. 224)

Schlieffen Plan [Plan Schlieffen] *s.* plan militar alemán al comienzo de la I Guerra Mundial, que preveía que Alemania derrotaría rápidamente a Francia y después atacaría a Rusia en el este. (pág. 412)

scientific method [método científico] *s.* procedimiento lógico para reunir información sobre el mundo natural, en que se usa experimentación y observación para poner a prueba hipótesis. (pág. 191)

Scientific Revolution [Revolución Científica] *s.* profundo cambio en el pensamiento europeo que comenzó a mediados del siglo 16, en que el estudio del mundo natural se caracterizó por cuidadosa observación y cuestionamiento de teorías aceptadas. (pág. 189)

scorched-earth policy [política de arrasamiento de campos] *s.* práctica de quemar campos de cultivo y de matar ganado durante la guerra para que el enemigo no pueda vivir de las tierras. (pág. 235)

secede [seceder] *v.* retirarse formalmente de una asociación o alianza. (pág. 326)

secular *adj.* relacionado con lo mundano más que con los asuntos espirituales. (pág. 38)

segregation [segregación] *s.* separación legal o social de gente de diferentes razas. (pág. 327)

self-determination [autodeterminación] *s.* libertad de un pueblo para decidir libremente la forma de gobierno que desea. (pág. 424)

sepoy [cipayo] *s.* soldado hindú bajo el mando británico. (pág. 357)

Sepoy Mutiny [Motín de Cipayos] *s.* rebelión de 1857 de soldados hindúes y musulmanes contra los británicos en India. (pág. 359)

Seven Years' War [Guerra de los Siete Años] *s.* conflicto en Europa, Norteamérica e India de 1756 a 1763, en que las fuerzas de Inglaterra y Prusia lucharon con las de Austria, Francia, Rusia y otros países. (pág. 173)

shah [sha] *s.* monarca hereditario de Irán. (pág. 80)

"shock therapy" [terapia de shock] *s.* programa económico implementado en Rusia por Boris Yeltsin en la década de 1990, que implicó un cambio abrupto de una economía de mando a una economía de mercado libre. (pág. 616)

Sikh [sikh] *s.* miembro de un grupo religioso no violento cuyas creencias combinaban elementos del budismo, el hinduismo y el sufismo. (pág. 85)

skepticism [escepticismo] *s.* filosofía basada en la noción de que nada puede saberse con certeza. (pág. 163)

social contract [contrato social] *s.* acuerdo mediante el cual el pueblo define y limita sus derechos individuales, creando así una sociedad o gobierno organizados. (pág. 195)

Social Darwinism [darvinismo social] *s.* aplicación de las teorías de Charles Darwin sobre la evolución y la "sobrevivencia del más apto" a las sociedades humanas, particularmente como justificación para la expansión imperialista. (pág. 341)

socialism [socialismo] *s.* sistema económico en el cual los factores de producción son propiedad del pueblo y se administran para el bienestar de todos. (pág. 302)

Solidarity [Solidaridad] *s.* sindicato polaco de trabajadores que presentó la principal fuerza de oposición al gobierno comunista en Polonia en la década de 1980. (pág. 618)

soviet *s.* consejo local de representantes formado en Rusia después de la caída del zar Nicolás II. (pág. 436)

Spanish-American War [Guerra Hispano-Americana] *s.* conflicto de 1898 entre Estados Unidos y España, en que Estados Unidos apoyó la lucha de independencia cubana. (pág. 384)

sphere of influence [esfera de influencia] *s.* región extranjera en que una nación controla el comercio y otras actividades económicas. (pág. 373)

standard of living [nivel de vida] *s.* calidad de la vida de una persona o población que se mide conforme a los bienes, servicios y lujos que tiene a su disposición. (pág. 600)

strike [huelga] *s.* paro de trabajo para obligar al patrón a acceder a ciertas demandas. (pág. 304)

Suez Canal [canal de Suez] *s.* canal marítimo que une al mar Rojo y al golfo de Suez con el mar Mediterráneo, cuya construcción terminó en 1869. (pág. 354)

suffrage [sufragio] *s.* derecho al voto. (pág. 313)

sultan [sultán] *s.* "jefe supremo" o "el que tiene poder"; título de los gobernantes otomanos durante el auge del imperio otomano. (pág. 73)

surrealism [surrealismo] *s.* movimiento artístico del siglo 20 que se concentra en el inconsciente. (pág. 465)

sustainable growth [crecimiento sostenido] *s.* desarrollo económico que satisface las necesidades de la población pero preserva el entorno y conserva recursos para futuras generaciones. (pág. 646)

T

Taiping Rebellion [Rebelión Taiping] *s.* rebelión a mediados del siglo 19 contra la dinastía Qing en China, encabezada por Hong Xiuquan. (pág. 373)

Taj Mahal *s.* bella tumba en Agra, India, construida por el emperador mogol Shah Jahan para su esposa Mumtaz Mahal. (pág. 85)

Taliban [Talibán] *s.* grupo musulmán conservador que tomó el poder en Afganistán después de que la Unión Soviética retiró sus tropas; expulsado por el ejército estadounidense en diciembre de 2001 por darles amparo a sospechosos de terrorismo. (pág. 592)

Tennis Court Oath [Juramento de la Cancha de Tenis] *s.* promesa hecha por los miembros de la Asamblea Nacional de Francia en 1789 de permanecer reunidos hasta que elaboraran una nueva constitución. (pág. 220)

terrorism [terrorismo] *s.* uso de la fuerza o de amenazas para presionar a personas o gobiernos a que cambien sus políticas. (pág. 653)

theocracy [teocracia] *s.* gobierno controlado por líderes religiosos. (pág. 62)

theory of evolution [teoría de la evolución] *s.* concepto propuesto por Charles Darwin en 1859 de que las especies de plantas y animales surgen debido a un proceso de selección natural. (pág. 331)

theory of relativity [teoría de la relatividad] *s.* ideas de Albert Einstein acerca de la interrelación entre el tiempo y el espacio, y entre la energía y la materia. (pág. 463)

Third Reich [Tercer Reich] *s.* Tercer Imperio Alemán establecido por Adolfo Hitler en la década de 1930. (pág. 484)

Third Republic [Tercera República] *s.* república establecida en Francia después de la caída de Napoleón III; acabó con la ocupación alemana de Francia durante la II Guerra Mundial. (pág. 315)

Third World [Tercer Mundo] *s.* durante la Guerra Fría, naciones que no se aliaron ni con Estados Unidos ni con la Unión Soviética. (pág. 548).

Thirty Years' War [Guerra de los Treinta Años] *s.* conflicto europeo de 1618 a 1648 por cuestiones religiosas, territoriales y de poder entre familias reinantes. (pág. 169)

Tiananmen Square [Plaza Tiananmen] *s.* plaza pública en Beijing, China; sede en 1989 de un enorme levantamiento estudiantil en favor de reformas democráticas. (pág. 627)

R95

Tokugawa Shogunate [shogunato Tokugawa] *s.* dinastía de shogúns que gobernó un Japón unificado de 1603 a 1867. (pág. 110)

totalitarianism [totalitarismo] *s.* gobierno que controla todo aspecto de la vida pública y privada. (pág. 440)

total war [guerra total] *s.* conflicto en el que los países participantes dedican todos sus recursos a la guerra. (pág. 419)

Treaty of Kanagawa [Tratado de Kanagawa] *s.* acuerdo de 1854 entre Estados Unidos y Japón, que abrió dos puertos japoneses a los barcos de Estados Unidos y le permitió abrir una embajada en Japón. (pág. 376)

Treaty of Tordesillas [Tratado de Tordesillas] *s.* acuerdo de 1494 entre Portugal y España que estableció que las tierras descubiertas al oeste de una línea imaginaria en el océano Atlántico pertenecerían a España y las tierras al este pertenecerían a Portugal. (pág. 99)

Treaty of Versailles [Tratado de Versalles] *s.* acuerdo de paz firmado por Alemania y los Aliados después de la I Guerra Mundial. (pág. 424)

trench warfare [guerra de trincheras] *s.* forma de guerra en la que dos ejércitos contrincantes luchan detrás de trincheras cavadas en el campo de batalla. (pág. 413)

triangular trade [triángulo comercial] *s.* red comercial trasatlántica que transportaba esclavos y productos entre África, Inglaterra, Europa continental, el Caribe y las colonias de Norteamérica. (pág. 134)

Triple Alliance [Triple Alianza] *s.* alianza militar establecida entre Alemania, Austro-Hungría e Italia antes de la I Guerra Mundial. (pág. 408)

Triple Entente [Triple Entente] *s.* alianza militar entre Gran Bretaña, Francia y Rusia establecida antes de la I Guerra Mundial. (pág. 409)

Truman Doctrine [Doctrina Truman] *s.* política estadounidense de dar ayuda económica y militar a las naciones libres amenazadas por oponentes internos o externos, anunciada por el presidente Harry Truman en 1947. (pág. 534)

UV

union [sindicato] *s.* asociación de trabajadores formada para negociar mejores salarios y condiciones de trabajo. (pág. 304)

United Nations [Organización de las Naciones Unidas (ONU)] *s.* organización internacional fundada en 1945 con el propósito de ofrecer seguridad a las naciones del mundo. (pág. 532)

Universal Declaration of Human Rights [Declaración Universal de Derechos Humanos] *s.* declaración en que la ONU proclamó en 1948 que todos los seres humanos tienen derecho a la vida, la libertad y la seguridad. (pág. 650)

unrestricted submarine warfare [guerra submarina irrestricta] *s.* uso de submarinos para hundir sin alerta previa cualquier barco (incluso barcos neutrales y de pasajeros sin armamento) que se encuentre en aguas enemigas. (pág. 418)

urbanization [urbanización] *s.* crecimiento de ciudades y migración hacia ellas. (pág. 289)

U.S.A. Patriot Act [Ley Patriota de E.U.A.] *s.* proyecto de ley antiterrorista de 2001 que hizo más fuerte los derechos gubernamentales para detener a extranjeros sospechosos de terrorismo y para procesar crímenes terroristas. (pág. 658)

U.S. Civil War [Guerra Civil de E.U.A.] *s.* conflicto entre los estados del Norte y el Sur de Estados Unidos desde 1861 a 1865, sobre el asunto de la esclavitud. (pág. 326)

utilitarianism [utilitarismo] *s.* teoría, propuesta por Jeremy Bentham a fines del siglo 18, de que las acciones del gobierno sólo son útiles si promueven el mayor bien para el mayor número de personas. (pág. 301)

utopia [Utopía] *s.* tierra imaginaria descrita por Tomás Moro en su libro del mismo nombre; lugar ideal. (pág. 48)

vernacular *s.* lenguaje común y corriente de la gente de una región o país. (pág. 41)

Vietcong *s.* grupo de guerrilleros comunistas que, con la ayuda de Vietnam del Norte, pelearon contra el gobierno de Vietnam del Sur durante la Guerra de Vietnam. (pág. 546)

Vietnamization [vietnamización] *s.* estrategia del presidente de E.U.A. Richard Nixon para terminar con la participación en la Guerra de Vietnam, mediante el retiro gradual de tropas estadounidenses y su reemplazo con fuerzas survietnamitas. (pág. 546)

W

War of the Spanish Succession [Guerra de Sucesión Española] *s.* conflicto de 1701 a 1713 en que varios Estados europeos lucharon para impedir que la familia Borbón controlara a España, como a Francia. (pág. 167)

Warsaw Pact [Pacto de Varsovia] *s.* alianza militar formada en 1955 por la Unión Soviética y siete países de Europa oriental. (pág. 535)

Weimar Republic [República de Weimar] *s.* república establecida en Alemania en 1919 que acabó en 1933. (pág. 471)

Western Front [Frente Occidental] *s.* en la I Guerra Mundial, región del norte de Francia donde peleaban las fuerzas de los Aliados y de las Potencias Centrales. (pág. 412)

westernization [occidentalización] *s.* adopción de las instituciones sociales, políticas o económicas del Occidente, especialmente de Europa o Estados Unidos. (pág. 176)

XYZ

Zionism [sionismo] *s.* movimiento fundado en la década de 1890 para promover el establecimiento de una patria judía en Palestina. (pág. 316)

Index

An *i* preceding an italic page reference indicates that there is an illustration, and usually text information as well, on that page. An *m* or a *c* preceding an italic page reference indicates a map or chart, as well as text information on that page.

A

B

Index

C

R99

Index

Index

Index

F

G

R103

R104

Index

Index

Index

R107

O

P

R109

Index

R111

T

Index

R113

U

R115

Y

Z

Acknowledgments

Text Acknowledgments

Chapter 2, page 75: Excerpt from *The Islamic World* by William H. McNeill and M.R. Waldham. Copyright © 1973 by The University of Chicago Press. Reprinted by permission of The University of Chicago Press.

Chapter 3, page 110: Haiku poem, from *Matsuo Basho,* translated by Makoto Veda. By permission of Makoto Veda.

Chapter 4, page 126: Excerpt from "I Won't Be Celebrating Columbus Day," by Suzan Shown Harjo. Copyright © 1991 by Suzan Shown Harjo. Reprinted by permission of Suzan Shown Harjo.

Chapter 13, page 423: Excerpt from *All Quiet on the Western Front* by Erich Maria Remarque. Copyright 1929, 1930 by Little, Brown and Company. Copyright renewed © 1957, 1958 by Erich Maria Remarque. "Im Westen Nichts Neues" by Erich Maria Remarque. Copyright 1928 by Ullstein A. G. Copyright renewed © 1956 by Erich Maria Remarque. All rights reserved. Used by permission of Pryor, Cashman, Sherman & Flynn on behalf of the Estate of Erich Maria Remarque.

Excerpt from "Dulce et Decorum Est," from *The Collected Poems of Wilfred Owen* by Wilfred Owen. Copyright © 1963 by Chatto & Windus, Ltd. Used by permission of New Directions Publishing Corp.

Chapter 14, page 454: Excerpt from *The Origin of Nonviolence* by M. K. Gandhi. Published by Cambridge University Press. Reprinted with the permission of Cambridge University Press.

Chapter 15, page 464: Excerpt from *The Great Gatsby* by F. Scott Fitzgerald. Copyright © 1925 by Charles Scribner's Sons. Copyright renewed 1953 by Frances Scott Fitzgerald Lanahan. Used by permission of Scribner, an imprint of Simon & Schuster Adult Publishing Group.

Chapter 19, page 627: Excerpt from "Tienanmen Square: A Soldier's Story," by Xiao Ye from *Teenage Soldiers, Adult Wars.* Reprinted by permission of the Rosen Publishing Group.

page 1067: Excerpts from "The Coming of Mao Zedong Chic," from *Newsweek,* May 19, 1997, Newsweek, Inc. All rights reserved. Reprinted by permission.

Chapter 20, page 647: Excerpt from "The Market is Green," by the Liberty Institute, New Delhi. Copyright © May 1999. Reprinted by permission of the Liberty Institute, New Delhi, India.

Excerpt from "Eco-Economy: Building an Economy for the Earth," by Lester Brown. Speech, Colloquium on Global Partnerships for Sustainable Development: Harnessing Action for the 21st Century; 24 March 2002 <http://www.earth-policy.org/Transcripts/TERI-4-02.htm>. Reprinted by permission of the Earth Policy Institute.

COMPARING & CONTRASTING FEATURES

Unit 2, Page 276: Excerpt from *The French Revolution,* edited by Paul H. Beik. Copyright © 1971 by Paul H. Beik. Reprinted by permission of HarperCollins Publishers Inc.

Unit 3, Page 401: Excerpt from *The Birth of the Modern: World Society 1815–1830* by Paul Johnson. Copyright © 1991 by Paul Johnson. Reprinted by permission of HarperCollins Publishers Inc.

Unit 4, Page 523: Excerpt from *If This is a Man (Survival in Auschwitz)* by Primo Levi, translated by Stuart Woolf. Copyright © 1960 by Orion Press, Inc. Copyright © 1958 by Giulio Einaudi editore S.P.A. Reprinted by permission of Penguin Putnam, Inc., a division of Penguin Group (USA) Inc.

PRIMARY SOURCE HANDBOOK

Page R40: "Creation Hymn," from *The Rig Veda,* translated by Wendy Doniger O'Flaherty (Penguin Classics, 1981). Copyright © 1981 by Wendy Doniger O'Flaherty. Reproduced by permission of Penguin Books Ltd.

Page R42: Excerpt from *The Analects of Confucius,* translated by Simon Leys. Copyright © 1997 by Pierre Ryckmans. Reprinted by permission of W. W. Norton & Company, Inc.

Page R43: Excerpt from "Pericles' Funeral Oration," from *History of the Peloponnesian War* by Thucydides, translated by Rex Warner (Penguin Classics, 1954). Copyright © 1954 by Rex Warner. Reproduced by permission of Penguin Books Ltd.

Page R44: Excerpt from the *Apology* by Plato, translated by Hugh Tredennick, from *The Collected Dialogues of Plato,* edited by Edith Hamilton and Huntington Cairns. Copyright © 1961 by Princeton University Press. Reprinted by permission of Princeton University Press.

Page R45: Excerpt from "The Burning of Rome," from *The Annals of Imperial Rome* by Tacitus, translated by Michael Grant (Penguin Classics, 1956; sixth revised edition, 1989). Copyright © 1956, 1959, 1971, 1973, 1975, 1977, 1989, 1996 by Michael Grant Publications. Reprinted by permission of Penguin Books Ltd.

Page R46: Excerpt from *The Koran,* translated by N. J. Dawood (Penguin Classics, 1956; fifth revised edition, 1990). Copyright © 1956, 1959, 1966, 1968, 1974, 1990, 1995 by N. J. Dawood. Reprinted by permission of Penguin Books Ltd.

Page R47: Excerpt from *The Pillow Book of Sei Shōnagon,* translated and edited by Ivan Morris. Copyright © 1967 by Ivan Morris. Reprinted by permission of Columbia University Press.

Page R48: Excerpt from the *Magna Carta* by J. C. Holt. Copyright © 1965 by Cambridge University Press. Reprinted with permission of Cambridge University Press.

Page R49: Excerpt from *Popol Vuh: The Definitive Edition of the Mayan Book of The Dawn of Life and The Glories of Gods and Kings,* translated by Dennis Tedlock. Copyright © 1985 by Dennis Tedlock, 1996 (revised and additional material) by Dennis Tedlock. Reprinted with the permission of Simon & Schuster Adult Publishing Group.

Page R51: Excerpt from *Utopia* by St. Thomas More, edited by Edward Surtz, S.J. Copyright © 1964 by Yale University. Reproduced by permission of Yale University Press.

Page R59: Excerpt from *Night* by Elie Wiesel, translated by Stella Rodway. Copyright © 1960 by MacGibbon & Kee. Copyright renewed 1988 by the Collins Publishing Group. Reprinted by permission of Hill and Wang, a division of Farrar, Straus & Giroux, Inc.

R117

Page R60: Excerpt from *Farewell to Manzanar* by James D. Houston and Jeanne Wakatsuki Houston. Copyright © 1973 by James D. Houston. Reprinted by permission of Houghton Mifflin Company. All rights reserved.

Page R61: Excerpt from "Glory and Hope" by Nelson Mandela, from *Vital Speeches of the Day,* Vol. LX, No. 16 (1 June 1994), page 486. Reprinted by permission of City News Publishing Company, Inc.

Page R62: Excerpt from "I Have A Dream" by Dr. Martin Luther King Jr. Copyright © 1963 by Dr. Martin Luther King Jr., copyright renewed 1991 by Coretta Scott King. Reprinted by arrangement with the Estate of Martin Luther King Jr., c/o Writers House as agent for the proprietor, New York, N.Y.

Page R63: Excerpt from "An Open Letter" by Cesar Chavez. Copyright © Cesar E. Chavez Foundation. Reprinted by permission of the Cesar E. Chavez Foundation.

McDougal Littell Inc. has made every effort to locate the copyright holders for selections used in this book and to make full acknowledgment for their use. Omissions brought to our attention will be corrected in a subsequent edition.

Art and Photography Credits

Maps supplied by Mapping Specialists

COVER

Sydney Opera House © Jerry Driend/Getty Images; sky © Rob Matheson/Corbis; Napoleon © Bettmann/Corbis; Queen Victoria (late 19th century). Victoria and Albert Museum, London. Photo © Victoria and Albert Museum, London/Art Resource, New York; *Simon Bolivar* (pre-20th century), unknown artist. Archives Charmet, Paris. Photo © The Bridgeman Art Library; Aung San Suu Kyi © Tom Wagner/Corbis SABA; Ghandi © Getty Images.

FRONT MATTER

Sydney Opera House © Jerry Driend/Getty Images; sky © Rob Matheson/Corbis; Napoleon © Bettmann/Corbis; Queen Victoria (late 19th century). Victoria and Albert Museum, London. Photo © Victoria and Albert Museum, London/Art Resource, New York; *Simon Bolivar* (pre-20th century), unknown artist. Archives Charmet, Paris. Photo © The Bridgeman Art Library; Aung San Suu Kyi © Tom Wagner/Corbis SABA; Ghandi © Getty Images.

Introduction

viii *top left* Greek engraving from red-figure vase. Bibliothèque des Arts Décoratifs, Paris. Photo © Dagli Orti/The Art Archive; *top right* © Corbis; *center left* Page from the Koran (ninth century), Islamic School. Bibliothèque Nationale, Tunis, Tunisia. Photo © Lauros/Giraudon/Bridgeman Art Library ; *center* Athena (A.D. 490). Kunsthistorisches Museum, Vienna, Austria. Photo © Erich Lessing/Art Resource, New York; *bottom, The Signing of the Constitution.* Howard Chandler Christy. Private Collection. Photo © Art Resource, New York ; **ix** *left* © Explorer, Paris/SuperStock; *right (top to bottom)* © Tim Hursley/SuperStock; Elizabeth l (1588), George Gower. Courtesy of The National Portrait Gallery, London; Shah Tahmasp I receiving the Moghul Emperor Humayun. Period of Abbas II. Photo © Giraudon/Art Resource, New York; Globe by Martin Behaim (about 1492). Bibliothèque Nationale, Paris. Photo © Giraudon/Art Resource, New York; **x** *left (top to bottom)* Detail of *Marriage of Louis XIV, King of France and Marie Therese of Austria* (17th century), unknown artist. Musée de Tesse, Le Mans, France. Photo © Dagli Orti/The Art Archive; *Louis XIV, King of France* (1701), Hyacinthe Rigaud. Louvre, Paris. Photo © Erich Lessing/Art Resource, New York; Isaac Newton's reflecting telescope (1672). Photo by Eileen Tweedy/Royal Society/The Art Archive; *Combat Before the Hotel de Ville, July 28th, 1830,* Victor Schnetz. Musée du Petit Palais, Paris. Photo by Bulloz © Réunion des Musées Nationaux/Art Resource, New York; *right* © Todd A. Gipstein/Corbis; **xi** *left* Aboriginal bark painting of abstract picture of body, Lipunja. Milingibi, Australia. Photo © Dagli Orti/Musée des Arts Africains et Oceaniens/The Art Archive; *right (top to bottom) The Battle of Isandhlwana* (1879), Charles Fripp. National Army Museum, London. Photo © The Art Archive; © Bettmann/Corbis; The Granger Collection, New York; The Granger Collection, New York; **xii** *left (top to bottom)* © Getty Images; Popperfoto; © Bettmann/Corbis; © UPI/Bettmann/Corbis; *right* © KJ Historical/Corbis; **xiii** *left* © Steve Vidler/SuperStock; *right (top to bottom)* © SuperStock; Imperial War Museum. Photo © The Art Archive; © David Turnley/Corbis; © Corbis Sygma; **xiv** *top left* © Will & Deni McIntyre/Corbis; *top right* © Mario Tama/Getty Images; *bottom left* © Reuters NewMedia Inc./Corbis; *bottom right* © Reuters New Media Inc./Corbis; **xxx** *top left, Alexander the Great,* Relief by Landolin Ohnmacht. Photo by AKG London; *bottom right Combat Before the Hotel de Ville, July 28th 1830,* Victor Schnetz. Musée du Petit Palais, Paris. Photo by Bulloz © Réunion des Musées Nationaux/Art Resource, New York; **xxxi** *top* © Chad Ehlers/Getty Images; *bottom* © Bettmann/Corbis; **xxxii–xxxiii** © Pacific Stock/Orion Press; **xxxiii** Travel Pix; **xxxvi** Stephen Alvarez/National Geographic Image Collection; **xxxvii** *top* © Kenneth Garrett; *center* Flying man, Leonardo da Vinci. Sketch from *Codex Atlanticus.* Biblioteca Ambrosiana, Milan, Italy/Art Resource, New York; *bottom* © Warren Morgan/Corbis.

Prologue

0–1 © Reuters NewMedia Inc./Corbis; **0** © AFP/Corbis; **2** *left* © David Lees/Corbis; *right* © Scala/Art Resource, New York; **3** *top* © Bettmann/Corbis; *bottom* National Archives; **4** © AFP/Corbis; **5** *top left* Young girl winning chariot race, Greek engraving from red-figure vase. Bibliothèque des Arts Décoratifs, Paris. Photo © Dagli Orti/The Art Archive; *top right* © Corbis; **7** Bust of Solon (630–560 A.D.). Greek. Photo © Scala/Art Resource, New York; **9** *top right, bottom left, bottom right* American School of Classical Studies at Athens, Agora Excavations; *center* Goddess Athena, (A.D. 490). Kunsthistorisches Museum, Vienna, Austria. Photo © Erich Lessing/Art Resource, New York; **10** Emperor Justinian (ninth century A.D.). Byzantine Mosaic. Musée de Chartres, France. Photo © SuperStock; **11** Bibliotheque Nationale de France; **12** *top left* © Richard T. Nowitz/Corbis; *top right* Detail of zodiac mosaic (fourth century). Tiberias, Israel. Photo © Garo Nalbandian/Israelimages.com; **13** © Bettmann/Corbis; **15** Page from the Koran (ninth century), Islamic School. Bibliothèque Nationale, Tunis, Tunisia. Photo © Lauros/Giraudon/Bridgeman Art Library; **16** © Bettmann/Corbis; **17** The Granger

Art and Photography Credits (Cont.)

Collection; **18** *top left* © Corbis; *top right* © Archivo Iconografico, S.A./Corbis; *bottom* The Granger Collection; **19** National Archives; **20** *The House of Commons in Session* (1710), Peter Tillemans. Houses of Parliament, Westminster, London. Photo © Bridgeman Art Library; **21** © Christie's Images/Corbis; **23** *top right King William II* (18th century), English school. Photo © National Trust Photographic Library/Derrick E. Witty/ Bridgeman Art Library; *top left Queen Mary II* (18th century) English school. Photo © National Trust Photographic Library/Derrick E. Witty/Bridgeman Art Library ; **24** *top left* Copernican Solar System (1661). From *Harmonia Macronici.* Andreae Cellarius. Page 30. Victoria and Albert Museum, London. Photo © Art Resource, New York; *top right* © Bettmann/Corbis; **25** © Archivo Iconografico, S.A./Corbis; **26** *The Signing of the Constitution* Howard Chandler Christy. Private Collection. Photo © Art Resource, New York; **27** *James Madison* Gilbert Stuart. Photo © SuperStock; **28** The Granger Collection;

UNIT ONE

32–33 *La Salle's Louisiana expedition in 1684,* J. A. Theodore Gudin. Photo © Réunion des Musées Nationaux/Art Resource, New York.

Chapter 1

34 *top* Bust of Lorenzo de Medici (15th or 16th century). Museo di Andrea del Castagno, Uffizi, Florence, Italy. Photo © Scala/Art Resource, New York; *bottom* Jar with dragon (1425–1435), Ming dynasty, reign of Xuande. Porcelain painted in underglaze blue. 19" high (48.3 cm). Gift of Robert E. Tod, 1937, The Metropolitan Museum of Art, New York. Photo © 2003 The Metropolitan Museum of Art; **35** *left* Gutenberg Bible (about 1455). Volume II, f. 45v-46. PML 818 ch1 ff1. The Pierpont Morgan Library, New York. Photo © The Pierpont Morgan Library/Art Resource, New York; *right* Detail of nobles entertained in garden by musicians and dancers (about 1590), Mughal. Photo © British Library/The Art Archive; **36** *The Madonna of Chancellor Rolin* (about 1434), Jan van Eyck. Louvre, Paris. Photo © Scala/Art Resource, New York; **37** *top left* © Photodisc/Getty Images; *top right* © Ulf E. Wallin/Getty Images; **38** Detail of *Lorenzo de Medici and the Arts in Florence* (about 1634–1636), Giovanni da Sangiovanni. Palazzo Pitti, Florence, Italy. Photo © Dagli Orti/The Art Archive; **39** *left Portrait of Baldassare Castilione* (date unknown), Raphael. Louvre, Paris. © Scala/Art Resource, New York; *right* The Granger Collection, New York; **40** *Marriage of the Virgin* (1504), Raphael. Brera, Milan, Italy. Photo © Scala/Art Resource, New York; **41** *top* © Stephano Bianchetti/Corbis; *bottom* The Granger Collection, New York; **42** *Portrait of Niccolo Machiavelli,* Santi di Tito. Palazzo Vecchio, Florence, Italy. Photo © Scala/Art Resource, New York; **43** The Granger Collection, New York; **44–45** © SuperStock, Inc.; **44** *Mona Lisa* (1503–1506), Leonardo da Vinci. Louvre, Paris. Photo by R.G. Ojeda © Réunion des Musées Nationaux/Art Resource, New York; **45** *The School of Athens* (15th century), Raphael. Stanza della Segnatura, Vatican Palace, Vatican State. Photo © Scala/Art Resource, New York; *bottom* © Bettmann/Corbis; **46** *top left* © Photodisc/Getty Images; *top right* © Ulf E. Wallin/Getty Images; **47** *Peasant Wedding* (1568), Peter Brueghel the Elder. Kunsthistorisches Museum, Vienna, Austria. Photo © Saskia Ltd./Art Resource, New York; **48** *left* Christine de Pizan teaches her son (about 1430). Harley MS 4431, f. 26 ff. The British Library, London. Photo by AKG London/British Library; *right Thomas More, Lord Chancellor* (late 15th century) Private Collection. Photo © The Stapleton Collection/The Bridgeman Art Library; **49** *left, Othello* movie still. Castle Rock/Dakota Films/The Kobal Collection; *center, 10 Things I Hate About You* movie still. Touchstone/The Kobal Collection; *top right, Romeo & Juliet* movie still. Merrick Morton/20th Century Fox/The Kobal Collection; *bottom right, Ran* movie still. Herald Ace/Nippon Herald/Greenwich/The Kobal Collection; **50** Illustration by Peter Dennis/Linda Rogers Associates; **52–53** MS Sloane 2596, f. **52.** British Library. Photo by AKG London/British Library; **52** *top* Koninklijk Museum voor Schone Kunsten, Antwerpen, Belgium; *center left* By permission of the Folger Shakespeare Library, Washington, D.C.; *center* Musée de la parfumerie Fragonard, Paris. Photo © Dagli Orti/The Art Archive; **53** The Shakespeare Birthplace Trust; **54** *top left* © Photodisc/Getty Images; *top right* © Ulf E. Wallin/Getty Images; **55** *Portrait of Martin Luther* (1529), Lucas Cranach the Elder. Museo Poldi Pezzoli, Milan, Italy. Photo © The Bridgeman Art Library; **58** *left Portrait of Henry VIII, King of England* (1540), Hans Holbein the Younger. Galleria Nazionale d'Arte Antica, Rome. Photo © Scala/Art Resource, New York; *right* Courtesy of the National Portrait Gallery, London; **59** *top left* © Stapleton Collection/Corbis; *bottom left Mary I Tudor, Queen of England* (1554), Antonis Moro or Mor. Museo del Prado Madrid. Photo © Dagli Orti/The Art Archive; *right Elizabeth I, Queen of England,* Federico Zuccari. Pinacoteca Nazionale di Siena. Photo © Dagli Orti/The Art Archive; **60** *s*(1588), George Gower. Courtesy of the National Portrait Gallery, London; **61** *left* © Photodisc/Getty Images; *right* © Ulf E. Wallin/Getty Images; **62** *John Calvin as a Young Man.* Flemish School. Bibliothèque Publique et Universitaire, Geneva, Switzerland. Photo © Erich Lessing/Art Resource, New York; **64** *Marguerite d'Angouleme, Queen of Navarre* (16th century). Musée Condé, Chantilly, France. Photo © Bridgeman-Giraudon/Art Resource, New York; **65** *Pope Paul III Farnese at the Council of Trent* (1560–1566), Taddeo and Federico Zuccari. Farnese Palace Caprarola. Photo © Dagli Orti/The Art Archive; **66** © Richard T. Nowitz/Corbis; **67** Martin Luther, German priest and Protestant reformer, caricature as seven-headed monster. The British Library. Photo © British Library/The Art Archive; **68** *top to bottom* © SuperStock, Inc.; Illustration by Peter Dennis/Linda Rogers Associates; *Portrait of Martin Luther* (1529) Lucas Cranach the Elder. Museo Poldi Pezzoli, Milan, Italy. Photo © The Bridgeman Art Library; Detail of *Pope Paul III Farnese at the Council of Trent* (1560–1566), Taddeo and Federico Zuccari. Farnese Palace Caprarola. Photo © Dagli Orti/The Art Archive; **69** © Bettmann/Corbis.

Chapter 2

70 *top* Topkapi Palace Museum, Istanbul, Turkey. Photo © Laura Lushington/Sonia Halliday Photographs; *bottom left* Pectoral ornament in the form of a double-headed serpent. Aztec. The British Museum, London. Photo © Werner Forman/Art Resource, New York; *bottom right* By permission of the British Library; **71** © Burstein Collection/Corbis; **72** Shah Tahmasp I receiving the Moghul Emperor Humayun (1660s). Period of Abbas II. Chihil Sutun, Isfahan, Iran. Photo © Giraudon/Art Resource, New York; **73** *top left* James L. Stanfield/National Geographic Image Collection; *top right* © SuperStock, Inc.; **75** Taking of Constantinople by the Turks, MS Fr. 9087 f. 207. Voyage d'Outremer de Bertrand de la Broquiere, Bibliothèque Nationale, Paris. Photo © Sonia Halliday Photographs; **76** *Suleiman the Magnificent.* Galleria degli Uffizi, Florence, Italy. Photo © Dagli Orti/The Art Archive; **77** Sonia Halliday Photographs; **79** Chihil Sutun, Isfahan, Iran. Photo © SEF/Art Resource, New York; **81** Dome of south Iwan (1611–1638). Safavid dynasty. Majid-i Shah, Isfahan, Iran. Photo © SEF/Art Resource, New York; **83** *top left* James L. Stanfield/National Geographic Image Collection; *top right* © SuperStock, Inc.;

84 *Portrait of Akbar andPrince Salim* (19th century). India, Mughal. Gift of Sally Sample Aal, 1997. The Newark Museum, Newark, New Jersey. Photo © The Newark Museum/Art Resource, New York; **85** *left* © Bettmann/Corbis; *left center* © Wally McNamee/Corbis; *right center, right* AP/Wide World Photos ; **86** © Brian A. Vikander/Corbis; **88** *top* Dagger handle in the form of a horse's head. Mughal. India. Victoria and Albert Museum, London. Photo © Victoria and Albert Museum, London/The Bridgeman Art Library; bottom © Abbie Enock/Travel Ink/Corbis; **89** *top* Tent hanging (early 18th century). Mughal dynasty. Victoria and Albert Museum, London. Photo © Victoria and Albert Museum, London/Art Resource, New York; *left* Akbar on the elephant Hawai pursuing the elephant rau Bagha (about 1590). Double page miniature from the Akbarnama. Mughal. Victoria and Albert Museum, London. Photo © Victoria and Albert Museum, London/Art Resource, New York.

Chapter 3

92 *left* Helmet (about 1500), Turkish. Victoria and Albert Museum, London. Photo © Victoria and Albert Museum, London/Art Resource, New York; *right* Detail of St. Vincent Polyptych (15th century), Nuno Goncalves. Museu Nacional de Arte Antiga, Lisbon, Portugal. Photo © Scala/Art Resource, New York; **93** *left* © The Flag Institute; *right Washington Crossing the Delaware,* Eastman Johnson. Copy after the Emmanuel Leutze painting in the Metropolitan Museum of Art, New York. Private Collection. Photo © Art Resource, New York; **94** India Orientalis (1606), Gerard Mercator and Jodocus Hondius. Atlas sive cosmographicae Meditationes. Courtesy Sotheby's, London; **95** *top left* © Culver Pictures, Inc./SuperStock, Inc.; *top right* K'ossu (about 1600), Late Ming dynasty. China. Victoria and Albert Museum, London. Photo © Sally Chappell/The Art Archive; *bottom* Globe by Martin Behaim (about 1492). Bibliothèque Nationale, Paris. Photo © Giraudon/Art Resource, New York; **96** Detail of St. Vincent Polyptych (15th century), Nuno Goncalves. Museu Nacional de Arte Antiga, Lisbon, Portugal. Photo © Scala/Art Resource, New York; **97** *background* © Bettmann/Corbis; *top right* Courtesy of Bibliothèque Nationale, Paris; *bottom left* Compass with sextant and dial (1617), Elias Allen. Victoria and Albert Museum, London. Photo © Victoria and Albert Museum, London/Art Resource, New York; *bottom center* © Dorling Kindersley; **98** © Bettmann/Corbis; **99** © Stapleton Collection/Corbis; **101** Corbis; **102** *top left* © Culver Pictures, Inc./SuperStock, Inc.; *top right* K'ossu (about 1600) Late Ming dynasty. China. Victoria and Albert Museum, London, UK. Photo © Sally Chappell/The Art Archive; *bottom right* Ming vase. Chinese School. Musée des Arts Asiatiques-Guimet, Paris. Photo © The Bridgeman Art Library; **104** *top right* © John T. Young/Corbis; *center right* © Brian A. Vikander/Corbis; *bottom right* © Harvey Lloyd/Getty Images; **105** Palace Museum, Beijing, China; **106** Marriage ceremony (19th century). China.Victoria and Albert Museum, London. Photo by Eileen Tweedy/The Art Archive; **107** The Granger Collection, New York; **108** *top left* © Culver Pictures, Inc./SuperStock, Inc.; *top right* K'ossu (about 1600), Late Ming dynasty. China. Victoria and Albert Museum, London, UK. Photo © Sally Chappell/The Art Archive; *bottom* Rijksmuseum, Amsterdam, The Netherlands; **109** © B.S.P.I./Corbis; **110** © Asian Art & Archeology/Corbis **111** © Asian Art & Archaeology/Corbis; *inset* © Michael S. Yamashita/Corbis; **112** © 1995 Christie's Images, Ltd; **113** Monk Tokiyori. Musée des Arts Asiatiques-Guimet, Paris. Photo by Richard Lambert © Réunion des Musées Nationaux/Art Resource, New York; **114** Dutch Merchant ship plate (1756), Qing dynasty. China. Musée des Arts Asiatiques-Guimet, Paris. Photo © Réunion des Musées Nationaux/Art Resource, New York; **115** The Granger Collection, New York.

Chapter 4

116 *top* © Archivo Iconografico, S.A./Corbis; bottom *Portrait of Tokugawa Ieyasu* (17th century). Japanese. Private Collection. Photo © The Bridgeman Art Library; **117** *left* The Granger Collection, New York; *right The Taking of the Bastille, 14 July 1789* (18th century), French School. Musée de la Ville de Paris, Musée Carnevalet, Paris. Photo © The Bridgeman Art Library; **118** Battle for Tenochtitlan between Cortés and Spaniards and Aztecs (16th century). Antochiw Collection, Mexico. Photo © Mireille Vautier/The Art Archive; **119** *top left* © Bettmann/Corbis; *top right* Detail of letter from Christopher Columbus to his son Diego (5 February 1505). General Archive of the Indies, Seville, Spain. Photo © Dagli Orti/The Art Archive; **120** *Christopher Columbus* (15th century), Sebastiano del Piombo. Metropolitan Museum of Art, New York. Photo © The Bridgeman Art Library; **123** *left* The Granger Collection, New York; **right** South American Pictures; **124** The Granger Collection, New York; **126** The Granger Collection, New York; **127** *top left* Detail of letter from Christopher Columbus to his son Diego (5 February 1505). General Archive of the Indies, Seville, Spain. Photo © Dagli Orti/The Art Archive; *top right* © Bettmann/Corbis; **128** The Granger Collection, New York; **129** North Carolina Collection, University of North Carolina, Chapel Hill; **132** *top left* © Bettmann/Corbis; *top right* Detail of letter from Christopher Columbus to his son Diego (5 February 1505). General Archive of the Indies, Seville, Spain. Photo © Dagli Orti/The Art Archive; **133** The Granger Collection, New York; **135** *center* The Granger Collection, New York; *right* The Newberry Library, Chicago; **137** *top left* Detail of letter from Christopher Columbus to his son Diego (5 February 1505). General Archive of the Indies, Seville, Spain. Photo © Dagli Orti/The Art Archive; *top right* © Bettmann/Corbis; **139** The Granger Collection, New York; **143** The Granger Collection, New York; **144** Portrait of the last Inca Chief, Atahualpa. Private Collection. Photo © The Bridgeman Art Library; **145** *top left Cosimo de'Medici, the Elder,* Agnolo Bronzino. Museo Mediceo, Florence, Italy. Photo © Scala/Art Resource, New York; *top right* © Sakamoto Photo Research Laboratory/Corbis; *bottom* © Bettmann/Corbis; **147** *top* © Araldo de Luca/Corbis; *bottom left* Nautilus pitcher (about 1570). Francesco de Medici Collection. Museo degli Argenti, Florence, Italy. Photo © Erich Lessing/Art Resource, New York; *bottom right* John Bigelow Taylor/American Museum of Natural History, No. 4959(2); **148** *top* © Yann Arthus-Bertrand/Corbis; *bottom* © Steve Vidler/SuperStock, Inc.; **149** © Archivo Iconografico, S.A./Corbis.

UNIT TWO

150–151 The Taking of the Bastille, July 14, 1789, unknown artist. Musée National du Chateau, Versailles, France. Photo © Erich Lessing/Art Resource, New York.

Chapter 5

152 *top Philip II, King of Spain and Portugal* (16th century), Alonso Sanchez Coello. Museo del Prado, Madrid, Spain. Photo © Erich Lessing/Art Resource, New York; *bottom Francisco Pizarro* (1835), Amable-Paul Coutan. Chateaux de Versailles et de Trianon, Versailles, France. Photo by Franck Raux © Réunion des Musées Nationaux/Art Resource, New York; **153** *top* The Granger Collection, New York; *bottom* © Pallava Bagla/Corbis; **154** *Louis XIV, King of France* (1701), Hyacinthe Rigaud. Louvre, Paris. Photo © Erich Lessing/Art Resource, New York; **155** *top left* Detail of *Marriage of Louis XIV, King of*

Art and Photography Credits (Cont.)

France and Marie Therese of Austria (17th century), unknown artist. Musée de Tesse, Le Mans, France. Photo © Dagli Orti/The Art Archive; *top right* © Todd A. Gipstein/Corbis; **156** The Granger Collection, New York; **157** *Las Meninas or The Family of Philip IV*, (about 1656), Diego Rodriguez de Silva y Velasquez. Prado, Madrid, Spain. Photo © The Bridgeman Art Library; **158** Tulipa gesaeriana no. 1908 (late 16th–early 17th century), Jacopo Ligozzi. Gabinetto dei Disegni e delle Stampe. Ufizzi, Florence, Italy. Photo © Scala/Art Resource, New York; **159** The Granger Collection, New York; **162** *top left* Detail of *Marriage of Louis XIV, King of France and Marie Therese of Austria* (17th century), unknown artist. Musée de Tesse, Le Mans, France. Photo © Dagli Orti/The Art Archive; *top right* © Todd A. Gipstein/Corbis; **163** *Cardinal Richelieu* (1636), Phillippe de Champaigne. Musée Condé, Chantilly, France. Photo © Giraudon/Art Resource, New York; **164** Detail of *Colbert Presenting Louis XIV the Members of the Royal Academy of Sciences in 1667,* Henri Tetstelin. Photo © Gerard Blot/Réunion Musées Nationaux; **165** *Louis de Rouvroy, Duke of Saint-Simon* (1887), Viger du Vigneau. Chateaux de Versailles et de Trianon, Versailles, France. Photo © Réunion des Musées Nationaux/Art Resource, New York; **166** © Archivo Iconografico, S.A./Corbis; *left inset* © Archivo Iconografico, S.A./Corbis; *center inset* © Adam Woolfitt/Corbis; *right inset* © Ben Mangor/SuperStock, Inc.; **167** *Battle of Denain, 24th July 1712* (1839), Jean Alaux. Chateau de Versailles et de Trianon, France. Photo © Giraudon/The Bridgeman Art Library; **169** *top left* Detail of *Marriage of Louis XIV, King of France and Marie Therese of Austria* (17th century), unknown artist. Musée de Tesse, Le Mans, France. Photo © Dagli Orti/The Art Archive; *top right* © Todd A. Gipstein/Corbis; **171** Flag of the Imperial Hapsburg dynasty (about 1700). Heeresgeschichtliches Museum, Vienna, Austria. © The Bridgeman Art Library; **172** *top* Detail of *Empress Maria Theresa of Austria.* Museum der Stadt Wien. Photo © Dagli Orti/The Art Archive; *center* Schloss Charlottenburg, Berlin/Bildarchiv Preussischer Kulturbesitz, Berlin; **174** *top left* Detail of *Marriage of Louis XIV, King of France and Marie Therese of Austria* (17th century), unknown artist. Musée de Tesse, Le Mans, France. Photo © Dagli Orti/The Art Archive; *top right* © Todd A. Gipstein/Corbis; **175** The Granger Collection, New York; **178** *top right* © Dorling Kindersley; *center left* Costumes of Crimean tribes (1888), A. Racinet. From Historical Costumes vol, V. Musée des Arts Décoratifs, Paris. Photo © Dagli Orti/The Art Archive; *bottom* © Historical Picture Archive/Corbis; **179** *top Shrovetide* (1919), Boris Kustidiev. The I. Brodsky Museum, St. Petersburg, Russia. Photo courtesy of the Smithsonian Institution Traveling Exhibition Service; *bottom* © Scheufler Collection/Corbis; **180** *top left* Detail of *Marriage of Louis XIV, King of France and Marie Therese of Austria* (17th century), unknown artist. Musée de Tesse, Le Mans, France. Photo © Dagli Orti/The Art Archive; *top right* © Todd A. Gipstein/Corbis; **181** The Granger Collection, New York.

Chapter 6

186 *left Portrait of a Princess Holding a Wine Cup* (17th–18th century). Mughal. India. The Newark Museum, Newark, New Jersey. Photo © The Newark Museum/Art Resource, New York; *right* Isaac Newton's reflecting telescope (1672), Royal Society. Photo by Eileen Tweedy/The Art Archive; **187** *left* Statuette of a Lohan. Ching dynasty. Musée des Arts Asiatiques-Guimet, Paris. Photo © Giraudon/Art Resource, New York; *right* © Leif Skoogfors/Corbis; **188** *A Philosopher Gives a Lecture on the Orrery* (1766), Joseph Wright. Canvas. Derby Museum and Art Gallery, Derby, Great Britain. Photo © Erich Lessing/Art Resource, New York; **189** *top left* Copernican Solar System (1661). From Harmonia Macronici, Andreae Cellarius. Page 30. Photo © Victoria and Albert Museum, London/Art Resource, New York; *top right* © Bettmann/Corbis; **191** *Galileo Before the Holy Office of the Vatican,* John Nicolas Robert-Fleury. Oil on canvas. Louvre, Paris. Photo by Gerard Blot © Réunion des Musées Nationaux /Art Resource, New York; **192** *left* © Bettmann/Corbis; *right* Isaac Newton's reflecting telescope (1672). Royal Society. Photo by Eileen Tweed/The Art Archive; **193** © Bettmann/Corbis; **194** *The Anatomy Lesson of Dr. Tulp,* Rembrandt van Rijn. Mauritshuis, The Hague, The Netherlands. Photo © Scala/Art Resource, New York; **195** *top left* Copernican Solar System (1661). From Harmonia Macronici, Andreae Cellarius. Page 30. Photo © Victoria and Albert Museum, London/Art Resource, New York; *top right* © Bettmann/Corbis; **196** The Granger Collection; **197** *left* The Granger Collection, New York; *right* The Granger Collection, New York; **199** Mary Evans Picture Library; **201** The Granger Collection, New York; **202** *top left* Copernican Solar System (1661). From Harmonia Macronici, Andreae Cellarius. Page 30. Photo © Victoria and Albert Museum, London/Art Resource, New York; *top right* © Bettmann/Corbis; **203** © Kevin Fleming/Corbis; **204** *Joseph II, Emperor of Austria and of the Holy Roman Empire, King of Hungary and Bohemia* (18th century). Musée du Château de Versailles. Photo © Dagli Orti/The Art Archive; **205** © Anatoly Sapronenkov/Tomsk Regional Arts Museum/SuperStock, Inc.; **206** *top left* Copernican Solar System (1661). From Harmonia Macronici, Andreae Cellarius. Page 30. Photo © Victoria and Albert Museum, London/Art Resource, New York; *top right* © Bettmann/Corbis; *bottom* Snuff box. French.The Metropolitan Museum of Art, gift of William H. Huntington, 1883 (83.2.228); **207** Detail of *Thomas Jefferson* (about 1805), Rembrandt Peale. Oil on canvas. Photo © Collection of the New-York Historical Society; **210** © Corbis; **211** © Jon Feingersh/Stock Boston, Inc./PictureQuest **213** *El sueño de la razón produce monstruos* [The sleep of reason produces monsters] from *Los Caprichos* (1799), Francisco José de Goya y Lucientes. Etching and burnished aquatint, 21.5cm. x 15 cm. Bequest of William P. Babcock. Courtesy of Museum of Fine Arts, Boston.

Chapter 7

214 *right* Reduced model of a guillotine. Musée de la Ville de Paris, Musée Carnavalet, Paris. Photo © Giraudon/Art Resource, New York; *left George Washington,* George Healy. Musée du Château de Versailles. Photo © Dagli Orti/The Art Archive; **215** *top* Detail of *Napoleon Bonaparte, Emperor of France.* Musée du Château de Versailles. Photo © Dagli Orti/The Art Archive; *bottom* The Granger Collection, New York; **216** *The Conquerors of the Bastille Before the Hotel de Ville* (1839), Paul Delaroche. Musée du Petit Palais, Paris. Photo © Erich Lessing/Art Resource, New York; **217** *top left* © SuperStock, Inc.; *top right* © Christie's Images/Corbis; **218** *Detail of Caricature of the three estates: Il faut esperer que le jeu finira bientôt.* Color engraving, 18th century. Musée de la Ville de Paris, Musée Carnavalet, Paris. Photo by Bulloz © Réunion des Musées Nationaux /Art Resource, New York; **219** *left Louis XVI, King of France.* Musée de Château de Versailles. Photo © Dagli Orti/The Art Archive; *right Marie Antoinette, Queen of France.* Replica of work painted in 1778. Musée du Château de Versailles. Photo © Dagli Orti/The Art Archive; **220** *The Storming of the Bastille, Paris, France, July 14, 1789.* Gouache. Musée Carnavalet, Paris. Photo © Dagli Orti/The Art Archive; **222** *left* © SuperStock, Inc.; *right* © Christie's Images/Corbis; **223** *Arrest of Louis XVI, King of France and his family attempting to flee the country at Varennes, France June 21–22, 1791.* Musée Carnavalet, Paris. Photo © Dagli Orti/The Art Archive; **224** Musées Royaux des Beaux-Arts, Brussels, Belgium. Photo © Giraudon/Art Resource, New York; **225** Illustration by Patrick Whelan; **226** *Portrait of*

R121

Robespierre, Louis L. Boilly. Musée des Beaux-Arts, Lille, France. Photo R.G. Ojeda © Réunion des Musées Nationaux/Art Resource, New York; **227** *Portrait of Danton* (18th century) Musée de la Ville de Paris, Musée Carnavalet, Paris. Photo © Giraudon/Art Resource, New York; **228** © Bettmann/Corbis; **229** *top left* © SuperStock, Inc.; *top right* © Christie's Images/Corbis; *230 Portrait of Bonaparte, premier consul* (1803), Francois Gerard. Oil on canvas. Musée Condé, Chantilly, France. Photo by Harry Brejat © Réunion des Musées Nationaux/Art Resource, New York; **231** *Napoleon Bonaparte,* Jacques-Louis David. Chateau de Malmaison, Rueil-Malmaison, France. Photo © Giraudon/Art Resource, New York; **234** *top left* © SuperStock, Inc.; *top right* © Christie's Images/Corbis; *bottom* Fotomas Index; **235** © Archivo Iconografico, S.A./Corbis; **237** © Public Record Office/Topham-HIP/The Image Works; **238** *top left* © SuperStock, Inc.; *top right* © Christie's Images/Corbis; **239** © Christel Gerstenberg/Corbis; **242** *left Parisian sans culotte* (18th century), unknown artist. Musée de la Ville de Paris, Musée Carnavalet, Paris. Photo © Giraudon/Art Resource, New York; *right* Reduced model of a guillotine. Musée de la Ville de Paris, Musée Carnavalet, Paris. Photo © Giraudon/Art Resource, New York.

Chapter 8

244 *left Napoleon in His Study at the Tuileries* (1812). Jacques-Louis David. Collection of Prince and Princess Napoleon, Paris. Photo © Giraudon/Art Resource, New York; *right Miguel Hidalgo y Costilla* (1895). From Mexican publication Patria e Independencia, folleto illustrado. Antiochiw Collection, Mexico. Photo © Mireille Vautier/The Art Archive; **245** *left* © Hulton-Deutsch Collection/Corbis; right © Francis G. Mayer/Corbis; 246 Courtesy of the Flag Institute; 247 left © Michael S. Lewis/Corbis; *right* © Archivo Iconografico, S.A./Corbis; **248** *Portrait of Francois-Dominique Toussaint, known as Toussaint L'Ouverture,* unknown artist. Musée des Arts d'Oceanie, Paris. Photo J.G. Berizzi © Réunion des Musées Nationaux/Art Resource, New York; **249** *left* © Christie's Images/Corbis; *right* The Granger Collection, New York; **250** © Bettmann/Corbis; **253** *top left* © Michael S. Lewis/Corbis; *top right* © Archivo Iconografico, S.A./Corbis; *bottom Klemens Metternich, Austrian prince and statesman.* Museo Glauco, Lombardi, Parma, Italy. Photo © Dagli Orti/The Art Archive; **255** © Archivo Iconografico, S.A./Corbis; **256** *Combat Before the Hotel de Ville, July 28th, 1830,* Victor Schnetz. Musée du Petit Palais, Paris. Photo by Bulloz © Réunion des Musées Nationaux/Art Resource, New York; **257** © Corbis; **261** The Granger Collection, New York; **262** © Bettmann/Corbis; **264** *top left* © Michael S. Lewis/Corbis; *top right* © Archivo Iconografico, S.A./Corbis; *bottom* © Bettmann/Corbis; **265** *Portrait of Ludwig von Beethoven,* unknown artist. Beethoven House, Bonn, Germany. Photo © Snark/Art Resource, New York; **266** © Hulton-Deutsch Collection/Corbis; **268** *Lion Hunt* (about 1860), Eugène Delacroix, French 1798–1863. Potter Palmer Collection, 1922.404, Reproduction. The Art Institute of Chicago, Chicago, Illinois; **269** *top The Stone Breakers* (1849), Gustave Courbet. Gemäldegalerie, Dresden, Germany. Photo © The Bridgeman Art Library; *bottom* © Francis G. Mayer/Corbis; **271** The Granger Collection, New York; **272–273** *bottom* The Granger Collection, New York; **272** *left* The Bloody Massacre perpetrated in...Boston on March 5th, 1770. Paul Revere. Colored engraving. The Gilder Lehrman Collection on deposit at The Pierpont Morgan Library. GLC 1868. Photo by Joseph Zehavi © The Pierpont Morgan Library/Art Resource, New York; *right Portrait of James II* (about 1685), Benedetto Gennari the Younger. Historical Portraits Ltd, London. Photo © The Bridgeman Art Library; **273** The Granger Collection, New York; **274** *left* Detail of *Marie-Antoinette Standing in her Court Robe with a Rose in her Hand (*1779), Louise Elizabeth Vigée-LeBrun. Châteaux de Versailles et de Trianon, Versailles, France. Photo © Réunion des Musées Nationaux/Art Resource, New York; *bottom right* © Photodisc/Getty Images; **275** *top Il faut esperer que le jeu finira bientot* [Peasant carrying a nobleman and a cleric] (1789). Musée de la Ville de Paris, Musée Carnavalet, Paris. Photo © Giraudon/Art Resource, New York; *bottom* The Granger Collection, New York; **276** The Granger Collection, New York; **277** *top* The Granger Collection, New York; *center Maximilien Robespierre.* Musée Carnavalet, Paris. Photo © Dagli Orti/The Art Archive.

UNIT THREE

278–279 Martyn Gregory Gallery, London.

Chapter 9

280 *top* The Granger Collection, New York; *bottom* © Brian A. Vikander/Corbis; **281** *left* © Bettmann/Corbis; *right* Cover of *The Communist Manifesto* by Karl Marx and Friedrich Engels, edited by Martin Malia, © 1998 by Martin Malia. Used by permission of Signet, an imprint of Penguin Group USA; **282** © Corbis; **283** *top left* © Collin Garratt/Milepost 92 1/2/Corbis; *top right* © H. David Seawell/Corbis; **284** © Getty Images; **285** *center* Blind man using a loom (1817), Dr. Sebastien Guillie. Plate 17 from Essai su l'Instruction des Aveugles. Colored engraving. Bibliothèque de l'Institut d'Ophtalmologie, Paris/Archives Charmet. Photo © The Bridgeman Art Library. *left* © Michael St. Maur Sheil/Corbis; *bottom* Sheffield Galleries & Museum Trust; **286** © Bettmann/Corbis; **287** Liverpool and Manchester passenger train (about 1830). National Railway Museum, York, North Yorkshire, UK. Photo © The Bridgeman Art Library; **288** © Getty Images; **289** The Granger Collection, New York; **293** The Granger Collection, New York; **294** © Steve Raymer/Corbis; **295** *top left* © Collin Garratt/Milepost 92 1/2/Corbis; *top right* © H. David Seawell/Corbis; *bottom* © Corbis; **297** *The Steel Workers at Biermeister and Wain* (1885), Peter Severin Kroyer. Statens Museum for Kunst, Copenhagen, Denmark. Photo © Snark/Art Resource, New York; **299** Mary Evans Picture Library; **300** *top left* © Collin Garratt/Milepost 92 1/2/Corbis; *top right* © H. David Seawell/Corbis; **301** © Bettmann/Corbis; **302** © Archivo Iconografico, S.A./Corbis; **305** *Strike* (1895), Mihaly Munkacsy. Magyar Nemzeti Galeria, Budapest, Hungary. Photo © The Bridgeman Art Library; **306** Jane Addams (about 1920), George de Forest Brush. National Portrait Gallery, Smithsonian Institution, Washington, D.C. Photo © National Portrait Gallery, Smithsonian Institution/Art Resource, New York; **307** Woodcut, from Cartoons for the Cause (1886), Walter Crane.

Chapter 10

310 *top* Queen Victoria (late 19th century). Victoria and Albert Museum, London. Photo © Victoria and Albert Museum, London/Art Resource, New York; *bottom* © The Stapleton Collection/Bridgeman Art Library; **311** *top* The Granger Collection, New York; *bottom* © Corbis; **312** *Une rue de Paris en mai 1871, ou La Commune* [A Paris street in May 1871, or The commune] (1903–1905), Maximilien Luce. Oil on canvas. Musée D'Orsay, Paris. Photo © Erich Lessing/Art Resource, New York; **313** *top left* © Hulton-Deutsch Collection/Corbis; *top right* © Bettmann/Corbis; **314** © Bettmann/Corbis; **316**

Art and Photography Credits (Cont.)

Zola Under Attack (1898), Henry de Groux. Photo by Musée Emile Zola, Médan, France; **317** *top left* © Hulton-Deutsch Collection/Corbis; *top right* © Bettmann/Corbis; **319** © Sean Sexton Collection/Corbis; **322** *center* Nouvelle-Hollande. Cour-Rou-Bari-Gal., Plate XVIII from Atlas historique: du Voyage de decouvertes aux terres australes, by Charles Alexandre Leseur and Nicolas-Martin Petit. State Library of South Australia; *center right* © Charles & Josette Lenars/Corbis; *bottom Australian Gold Diggings* (about 1855), Edwin Stocqueler. National Library of Australia, Canberra; **323** *top* © Graham Monro/photolibrary/PictureQuest; *bottom* The Granger Collection, New York; **324** *top left* © Hulton-Deutsch Collection/Corbis; *top right* © Bettmann/Corbis; **327** Library of Congress; **328** *top left* © Hulton-Deutsch Collection/Corbis; *top right* © Bettmann/Corbis; **329** *top right* The Granger Collection, New York; *center left* Institute of Experimental Physics/University of Innsbruck, Austria; *center right* Library of Congress; *bottom* The Granger Collection, New York; **330** *left* © Bettmann/Corbis; *center* © Bettmann/Corbis; *right* The Granger Collection, New York; **331** The Granger Collection, New York; **332** © Bettmann/Corbis; **335** By permission of the British Library.

Chapter 11

336 *top* © Werner Forman/Art Resource, New York; *bottom* The Bowes Museum, County Durham, Great Britain; **337** *top* © Bettmann/Corbis; *bottom* © Bettmann/Corbis; **338** © Getty Images; **339** *top left* Aboriginal Bark painting of abstract picture of body (19th–20th century), Lipunja. Musée des Arts Africains et Océaniens. Photo © Dagli Orti/The Art Archive; *top right The Battle of Isandhlwana* (19th century), Charles Fripp. National Army Museum, London. Photo © The Art Archive; **340** The Granger Collection, New York; **341** The Granger Collection, New York; **342** *Cetshwayo, King of the Zulus,* Carl Rudolph Sohn. The Royal Collection (England). Photo © 2003 Her Majesty Queen Elizabeth II; **344** © Hulton-Deutsch Collection/Corbis; **349** © Culver Pictures; **351** The Granger Collection, New York; **352** *top left* Aboriginal Bark painting of abstract picture of body, Lipunja. Musée des Arts Africains et Océaniens. Photo © Dagli Orti/The Art Archive; *top right The Battle of Isandhlwana* (19th century), Charles Fripp. National Army Museum, London. Photo © The Art Archive; **354** *Mehemet Ali, Viceroy of Egypt* (19th century), Louis Charles Auguste Couder. Chateau de Versailles, France. Photo © Lauros-Giraudon/The Bridgeman Art Library; **355** *Shipping on the Suez Canal* (1869), Edouard Riou. Chateau de Compiègne, Oise, France. Photo © Lauros-Giraudon/The Bridgeman Art Library; **356** *Portrait of Nasir Al-Din Shah* (19th century), unknown artist. Louvre, Paris. Photo © Réunion des Musées Nationaux/Art Resource, New York; **357** *top left* Aboriginal Bark painting of abstract picture of body, Lipunja. Musée des Arts Africains et Océaniens. Photo © Dagli Orti/The Art Archive; *top right The Battle of Isandhlwana* (19th century), Charles Fripp. National Army Museum, London. Photo © The Art Archive; *bottom A Sepoy (an Indian Soldier in the French Battalion) at Pondicherry* (19th century), Racinet. Photo © The Stapleton Collection/The Bridgeman Art Library; **359** © Getty Images; **360** The Granger Collection, New York; **362** *top left* Aboriginal Bark painting of abstract picture of body, Lipunja. Milingibi, Australia. Musée des Arts Africains et Oceaniens. Photo © Dagli Orti/The Art Archive; *top right The Battle of Isandhlwana (*19th century), Charles Fripp. National Army Museum, London. Photo © The Art Archive; **364** © Corbis; **365** The Granger Collection, New York.

Chapter 12

368 © Bettmann/Corbis; **369** *top left* © Corbis; *bottom left* Union Flag with portrait of Queen Victoria and British Colonies. The Bodleian Library, Oxford, England, John Johnson Collection (Printed Fabrics 1). Photo © The Bodleian Library/The Art Archive; *top right* © Corbis; **370** © Historical Picture Archive/Corbis; **371** *top left View of Landscape* (18th–19th century), Katsushika Hokusai. Oriental Art Museum, Genoa, Italy. Photo © Dagli Orti/The Art Archive; *top right* © Archivo Iconografico, S.A./Corbis; **372** © David Lawrence/Corbis; **373** The Granger Collection, New York; **375** © SuperStock, Inc.; **376** *top left View of Landscape* (18th–19th century), Katsushika Hokusai. Oriental Art Museum, Genoa, Italy. Photo © Dagli Orti/The Art Archive; *top right* © Archivo Iconografico, S.A./Corbis; **377** *left* The Granger Collection, New York; *right* © Bettmann/Corbis; **378** Mary Evans Picture Library; **380** *left* © Sakamoto Photo Research Laboratory/Corbis; *top right* Photo by Fumi Bull. Courtesy David Bull; *center right* Photo by Fumi Bull. Courtesy David Bull; *bottom right* Photo by Fumi Bull. Courtesy David Bull; **381** *top* © Historical Picture Archive/Corbis; *bottom* Photo by Fumi Bull. Courtesy David Bull; **382** *top left View of Landscape* (18th–19th century), Katsushika Hokusai. Oriental Art Museum, Genoa, Italy. Photo © Dagli Orti/The Art Archive; *top right* © Archivo Iconografico, S.A./Corbis; **383** top © Bettmann/Corbis; **bottom** © Underwood & Underwood/Corbis; **384** The Granger Collection, New York; **386** © Danny Lehman/Corbis; **387** The Granger Collection, New York; **388** *top left View of Landscape* (18th–19th century), Katsushika Hokusai. Oriental Art Museum, Genoa, Italy. Photo © Dagli Orti/The Art Archive; *top right* © Archivo Iconografico, S.A./Corbis; *bottom right* The Granger Collection, New York; **389** © Bettmann/Corbis; **390** The Granger Collection, New York; **391** *Portrait of Porfirio Diaz.* Antochiw Collection, Mexico. Photo © Mireille Vautier/The Art Archive; **392** *Emiliano Zapata* (19th–20th century), unknown artist. National History Museum, Mexico City. Photo © Dagli Orti/The Art Archive; **396** *top left, right* The Granger Collection, New York; *bottom* © Bettmann/Corbis; **397** *top, bottom* © Bettmann/Corbis; **399** © Corbis; **400** © Bettmann/Corbis; **401** The Granger Collection, New York.

UNIT FOUR

402–403 French troops crossing over pontoon bridges on the River Yser, Belgium, August, 1917. Musée de L'Armée, Paris. Photo © Dagli Orti/Art Archive.

Chapter 13

404 *top* © The Image Bank/Getty Images; **bottom** © Bettmann/Corbis; **405** *left* Mary Evans Picture Library; *center* © Bettmann/Corbis; *right* © Bettmann/Corbis; **406** Library of Congress; **407** *top left* © Bettmann/Corbis; *top right For King and Country* (20th century), E. F. Skinner. Royal Collection, United Kingdom. Photo by Eileen Tweedy/The Art Archive; **408** Mary Evans/Weimar Archive; **411** *top left* © Bettmann/Corbis; *top right For King and Country* (20th century), E. F. Skinner. Royal Collection, United Kingdom. Photo by Eileen Tweedy/The Art Archive; **413** © Corbis; **414** *top* © Popperfoto; *bottom* © Getty Images; **415** © Hulton-Deutsch Collection/Corbis; **416** *top* © Hulton-Deutsch Collection/Corbis; *bottom* © Fraser May; **417** *top left* © Bettmann/Corbis; *top right For King and Country* (20th century), E. F. Skinner. Royal Collection,

R123

United Kingdom. Photo by Eileen Tweedy/The Art Archive; **419** © Bettmann/Corbis; **420** © Corbis; **423** Library of Congress; **424** *top left* © Bettmann/Corbis; *top right For King and Country* (20th century), E. F. Skinner. Royal Collection, United Kingdom. Photo by Eileen Tweedy/The Art Archive; **425** *top Thomas Woodrow Wilson* (1921), Edmund Charles Tarbell. National Portrait Gallery, Smithsonian Institution. Photo © National Portrait Gallery, Smithsonian Institution/Art Resource, New York; *bottom Portrait of George Clemenceau* (1879–1880), Edouard Manet. Musée d'Orsay, Paris. Photo © Erich Lessing/Art Resource, New York; **429** Library of Congress.

Chapter 14

430 *top* © Bettmann/Corbis; **bottom** © The Flag Institute; **431** *left* © Elliott & Fry/Getty Images; center © Getty Images; *right* © AFP/Corbis; **432** *left* © Getty Images; *right* © Bettmann/Corbis; **433** *bottom* © Archivo Iconografico, S.A./Corbis; **434** © Bettmann/Corbis; **435** © 2003 Tass/Sovfoto; **436** Mapping Specialists; **437** Itar-Tass/Sovfoto; **438** *left* © Archivo Iconografico, S.A./Corbis; *right* © Bettmann/Corbis; **440** *top left* © Swim Ink/Corbis; *top right* © Patrick Field/Eye Ubiquitous/Corbis; **442** © Bettmann/Corbis; **443** David King Collection, London; **445** Itar-Tass/Sovfoto; **446** *top left, top right* Collection of the International Institute of Social History, Amsterdam, Netherlands; *bottom* CTK/Eastfoto; **441** David King Collection, London; **448** *top left* © Swim Ink/Corbis; *top right* © Patrick Field/Eye Ubiquitous/Corbis; *bottom* © Getty Images; **449** *inset* Photo by Sidney D. Gamble; *bottom* © Peter Turnley/Corbis; **450** © Corbis; **451** *top right* From Chinese Communist Sketches and Autobiographies of the Old Guard: Red Dust by Nym Wales. June 1972. Greenwood Publishing Group; *bottom left* AP/Wide World Photos; *bottom right* © Rene Burri/Magnum Photos; **452** © Getty Images; **453** *top left* © Swim Ink/Corbis; *top left* © Patrick Field/Eye Ubiquitous/Corbis; *bottom* © Bettmann/Corbis; **455** *top* Photo by Margaret Bourke-White ©Time Life Pictures/Getty Images; *inset* © The Flag Institute; **456** © Hulton-Deutsch Collection/Corbis; **458** *left to right* © Bettmann/Corbis; David King Collection, London; © Getty Images; © Getty Images; © Bettmann/Corbis; © Hulton-Deutsch Collection/Corbis.

Chapter 15

460 *top* © Getty Images; *bottom* Library of Congress; **461** *left* Roger-Viollet; **right** © Hulton-Deutsch Collection/Corbis; **462** © 1995 Chicago Historical Society; **463** *top left* Chicago Historical Society; *top right* Life cover (July 1, 1926) Fred Cooper; **464** AP/Wide World Photos; **465** *The Persistence of Memory* (1931), Salvador Dali. Oil on canvas, 9 1/2" x 13" (162.1934). The Museum of Modern Art, New York. Given anonymously. © 2003 Salvador Dali, Gala-Salvador Dali Foundation/Artists Rights Society (ARS), New York. Digital Image © The Museum of Modern Art/Licensed by Scala/Art Resource, New York; **466** The Granger Collection, New York; **467** © Bettmann/Corbis; **468** *left* The Granger Collection, New York; *right* © Schenectady Museum/Hall of Electrical History Foundation/Corbis; **469** *top* The Granger Collection, New York; *center* © Schenectady Museum/Hall of Electrical History Foundation/Corbis; **bottom** The Granger Collection, New York; **470** *top left* Chicago Historical Society; *top right* Life cover (July 1, 1926) Fred Cooper; **471** © Getty Images; **473** © Museum of the City of New York; **475** The Granger Collection, New York; **476** *top left* Chicago Historical Society; **top right** Life cover (July 1, 1926) Fred Cooper; **477** © Getty Images; **478** *top* © Getty Images; *bottom* © Getty Images; **479** © Getty Images; **480** © Bettmann/Corbis; **481** *top left* Chicago Historical Society; *top right* Life cover (July 1, 1926) Fred Cooper; **484** *top* © Corbis; *bottom* The Granger Collection, New York; **485** © Getty Images; **487** © Bettmann/Corbis.

Chapter 16

488 *left* The Granger Collection, New York; *right* © Museum of Flight/Corbis; **489** *top* © Bettmann/Corbis; *bottom* U.S. Air Force; **490** German planes bombing London, England (1940), La Domenica del Corriere. Photo © Dagli Orti/Art Archive; **491** *top left* © Getty Images; *top right* © KJ Historical/Corbis; **493** The Granger Collection, New York; **494** © William Vandivert/Getty Images; **495** Photo © The Art Archive; **497** *top left* © Getty Images; *top right* © KJ Historical/Corbis; **498** © UPI/Bettmann/Corbis; **499** The Granger Collection, New York; **500** © Bettmann/Corbis; **501** AP/Wide World Photos; **502** *top left* © Getty Images; *top right* © KJ Historical/Corbis; **503** *top* Courtesy of the Spertus Museum, Chicago; *bottom* © Hulton-Deutsch Collection/Corbis; **504** Courtesy of the United States Holocaust Memorial Museum Photo Archives; **506** *top left* © Getty Images; *top right* © KJ Historical/Corbis; **507** © Getty Images; **509** The Advertising Archive Ltd; **510** © Bettmann/Corbis; **511** © Getty Images; **512** *top left* © UPI/Bettmann/Corbis; *top right* U.S. Air Force; *bottom* Photo of aftermath of bombing of Nagasaki, August 10, 1945, by Yosuke Yamahata. Photo restoration by TX Unlimited, San Francisco; **513** © Bettmann/Corbis; **514** *top left* © Getty Images; *right* © KJ Historical/Corbis; **516** © AFP/Corbis; **517** AP/Wide World Photos. **520** *top left* © Bettmann/Corbis; *top right, bottom right* © Getty Images; *bottom left* © Corbis; **521** *top* © Corbis; *bottom* National Air and Space Museum/Smithsonian Institution; **522** *top* © William Vandivert/Getty News Images; *bottom* ©Bettmann/Corbis; **525** © Hulton-Deutsch Collection/Corbis.

UNIT FIVE

526–527 © Jacques Langevin/Corbis Sygma.

Chapter 17

528 *top* © Wally McNamee/Corbis; *bottom* © The Flag Institute; **529** *left* NASA; *center* © Peter Turnley/Corbis; *right* © David Turnley/Corbis; **530** *left* © Bettmann/Corbis; *right* © Geoffrey Clements/Corbis; **531** *top left* © Peter Turnley/Corbis; *top right* NASA; *bottom* Imperial War Museum. Photo © Art Archive; **533** Tom Little/Nashville Tennessean; **535** © UPI/Bettmann/Corbis; **537** *top, bottom center* NASA; *bottom left* Tass/Sovfoto; **538** *top left* © Peter Turnley/Corbis; *top right* NASA **539** *left* © Corbis; *right* © Roman Soumar/Corbis; **540** © Getty Images; **541** © Bettmann/Corbis; **542** *top left* © Peter Turnley/Corbis; *top right* NASA; *bottom* © Getty Images; **544** © Getty Images; **545** *top* USAF/TRH Pictures; *center* © Bettmann/Corbis; *bottom* © Nik Wheeler/Black Star; **546** © Les Stone/Corbis Sygma; **547** © Catherine Karnow/Corbis; **548** *top left* © Peter Turnley/Corbis; *top right* NASA; **549** © Bettmann/Corbis; **551** © Wally McNamee/Corbis; **552** *right, left* © Alain Mingam/Getty News Services; **553** AP/Wide World Photos; **554** *top left* © Peter Turnley/Corbis; *top right* NASA; **555** *left* © 1994 Sovfoto/PictureQuest; *center* AP/Wide World Photos; *right* © Peter Turnley/Corbis; **556** © Wally McNamee/Corbis; **557** Collection of David J. and Janice L. Frent.